Collins
Spanish
Dictionary

HarperCollins Publishers
Westerhill Road
Bishopbriggs
Glasgow
G64 2QT
Great Britain

Third Edition 2004

Latest Reprint 2004

© HarperCollins Publishers 1997, 2000, 2004

ISBN 0–00–719630-x

Collins® and Bank of English® are registered trademarks of HarperCollins Publishers Limited

www.collins.co.uk

A catalogue record for this book is available from the British Library

HarperCollins Publishers, Inc.
10 East 53rd Street, New York, NY 10022

ISBN 0–06–057578-6

Library of Congress Cataloging-in-Publication Data has been applied for

www.harpercollins.com

First HarperCollins edition published 1998

HarperCollins books may be purchased for educational, business, or sales promotional use. For information, please write to: Special Markets Department, HarperCollins Publishers Inc., 10 East 53rd Street, New York, NY 10022

Dictionary text typeset by Morton Word Processing Ltd, Scarborough

Grammar text typeset by Wordcraft, Glasgow

Printed in Italy by Legoprint S.P.A.

Acknowledgements
We would like to thank those authors and publishers who kindly gave permission for copyright material to be used in the Collins Word Web. We would also like to thank Times Newspapers Ltd for providing valuable data.

Jeremy Butterfield, Mike Gonzalez, Gerry Breslin
Teresa Alvarez García, Brian Steel
Ana Cristina Llompart, José Miguel Galván Déniz

editorial staff

Megan Thomson, Val McNulty, Irene Lakhani, Sharon Hunter
Tracy Lomas, Claire Evans, Jane Horwood, Linda Chestnutt
Enrique González Sandinero, Caitlin McMahon

series editor
Lorna Sinclair

editorial management
Vivian Marr

INTRODUCTION

You may be starting Spanish for the first time, or you may wish to extend your knowledge of the language. Perhaps you want to read and study Spanish books, newspapers and magazines, or perhaps simply have a conversation with Spanish speakers. Whatever the reason, whether you're a student, a tourist or want to use Spanish for business, this is the ideal book to help you understand and communicate. This modern, user-friendly dictionary gives priority to everyday vocabulary and the language of current affairs, business, computing and tourism, and, as in all Collins dictionaries, the emphasis is firmly placed on contemporary language and expressions.

HOW TO USE THE DICTIONARY

Below you will find an outline of how information is presented in your dictionary. Our aim is to give you the maximum amount of detail in the clearest and most helpful way.

Entries

A typical entry in your dictionary will be made up of the following elements:

Phonetic transcription

Phonetics appear in square brackets immediately after the headword. They are shown using the International Phonetic Alphabet (IPA), and a complete list of the symbols used in this system can be found on page xiv. The pronunciation given is for Castilian Spanish except where a word is solely used in Latin America, when we give the Latin American pronunciation. A further guide to the differences in types of Spanish pronunciation is given on page xiv.

Grammatical information

All words belong to one of the following parts of speech: noun, verb, adjective, adverb, pronoun, article, conjunction, preposition, abbreviation. Nouns can be singular or plural and, in Spanish, masculine or feminine. Verbs can be transitive, intransitive, reflexive or impersonal. Parts of speech appear in *italics* immediately after the phonetic spelling of the headword. The gender of the translation also appears in *italics* immediately following the key element of the translation, except where this is a regular masculine singular noun ending in "o", or a regular feminine singular noun ending in "a".

Often a word can have more than one part of speech. Just as the English word **chemical** can be an adjective or a noun, the Spanish word **conocido** can be an adjective ("(well-)known") or a noun ("acquaintance"). In the same way the verb **to walk** is sometimes transitive, ie it takes an object ("to walk the dog") and sometimes intransitive, ie it doesn't take an object ("to walk to school"). To help you find the meaning you are looking for quickly and for clarity of presentation, the different part of speech categories are separated by a black lozenge ◆.

Meaning divisions

Most words have more than one meaning. Take, for example, **punch** which can be, amongst other things, a blow with the fist or an object used for making holes. Other words are translated differently depending on the context in which they are used. The transitive verb **to put on**, for example, can be translated by "ponerse", "encender" etc depending on *what* it is you are putting on. To help you select the most appropriate translation in every context, entries are divided according to meaning. Each different meaning is introduced by an "indicator" in *italics* and in brackets. Thus, the examples given above will be shown as follows:

> **punch** *n* (*blow*) golpe *m*, puñetazo; (*tool*) punzón *m*

> **put on** *vt* (*clothes, lipstick etc*) ponerse; (*light etc*) encender

Likewise, some words can have a different meaning when used to talk about a specific subject area or field. For example **bishop**, which in a religious context means a high-ranking clergyman, is also the name of a chess piece. To show English speakers which translation to use, we have added "subject field labels" in capitals and in brackets, in this case (*CHESS*):

> **bishop** *n* obispo; (*CHESS*) alfil *m*

Field labels are often shortened to save space. You will find a complete list of abbreviations used in the dictionary on page xii.

Translations

Most English words have a direct translation in Spanish and vice versa, as shown in the examples given above. Sometimes, however, no exact equivalent exists in the target language. In such cases we have given an approximate equivalent, indicated by the sign ≈. An example is **British Rail**, the Spanish equivalent of which is "RENFE". There is no exact equivalent since the bodies in the two countries are quite different:

> **British Rail (BR)** *n* ≈ RENFE *f* (*SP*)

On occasion it is impossible to find even an approximate equivalent. This may be the case, for example, with the names of types of food:

> **fabada** *nf bean and sausage stew*

Here the translation (which doesn't exist) is replaced by an explanation. For increased clarity the explanation, or "gloss", is shown in *italics*.

It is often the case that a word, or a particular meaning of a word, cannot be translated in isolation. The translation of **Dutch**, for example, is "holandés/esa". However, the phrase **to go Dutch** is rendered by "pagar cada uno lo suyo". Even an expression as simple as **washing powder** needs a separate translation since it translates as "detergente (en polvo)", not "polvo para lavar". This is where your dictionary will prove to be particularly informative and useful since it contains an abundance of compounds, phrases and idiomatic expressions.

Levels of formality and familiarity

In English you instinctively know when to say **I'm broke** or **I'm a bit short of cash** and when to say **I don't have any money**. When you are trying to understand someone who is speaking Spanish, however, or when you yourself try to speak Spanish, it is important to know what is polite and what is less so, and what you can say in a relaxed situation but not in a formal context. To help you with this, on the Spanish-English side we have added the label (*fam*) to show that a Spanish meaning or expression is colloquial, while those meanings or expressions which are vulgar are given an exclamation mark (*fam!*), warning you they can cause serious offence. Note also that on the English-Spanish side, translations which are vulgar are followed by an exclamation mark in brackets.

Keywords

Words labelled in the text as KEYWORDs, such as **have** and **do** or their Spanish equivalents **tener** and **hacer**, have been given special treatment because they form the basic elements of the language. This extra help will ensure that you know how to use these complex words with confidence.

Cultural information

Entries which appear separated from the main text by a line above and below them explain aspects of culture in Spanish and English-speaking countries. Subject areas covered include politics, education, media and national festivals.

Spanish alphabetical order

In 1994 the **Real Academia Española** and the Spanish American language academies jointly decided to stop treating CH and LL as separate letters in Spanish, thereby bringing it into line with European spelling norms. This means that **chapa** and **lluvia** will be filed in letters C and L respectively. Of course, it should also be remembered that words like **cancha** and **callar**, with **ch** and **ll** in the middle of the words, will also have changed places alphabetically, now being found after **cáncer** and **cáliz** respectively. Spanish however still has one more letter than English with Ñ treated separately, between N and O.

abreviatura	**ab(b)r**	abbreviation
adjetivo, locución adjetiva	**adj**	adjective, adjectival phrase
administración, lengua administrativa	**ADMIN**	administration
adverbio, locución adverbial	**adv**	adverb, adverbial phrase
agricultura	**AGR**	agriculture
alguien	**algn**	
América Latina	**AM**	Latin America
anatomía	**ANAT**	anatomy
arquitectura	**ARQ, ARCH**	architecture
astrología, astronomía	**ASTRO**	astrology, astronomy
el automóvil	**AUT(O)**	the motor car and motoring
aviación, viajes aéreos	**AVIAT**	flying, air travel
biología	**BIO(L)**	biology
botánica, flores	**BOT**	botany
inglés británico	**BRIT**	British English
química	**CHEM**	chemistry
	CINE	cinema
lengua familiar (! vulgar)	**col (!)**	colloquial usage (! particularly offensive)
comercio, finanzas, banca	**COM(M)**	commerce, finance, banking
informática	**COMPUT**	computing
conjunción	**conj**	conjunction
construcción	**CONSTR**	building
compuesto	**cpd**	compound element
cocina	**CULIN**	cookery
economía	**ECON**	economics
electricidad, electrónica	**ELEC**	electricity, electronics
enseñanza, sistema escolar	**ESCOL**	schooling, schools
España	**ESP**	Spain
especialmente	**esp**	especially
exclamación, interjección	**excl**	exclamation, interjection
femenino	**f**	feminine
lengua familiar (! vulgar)	**fam (!)**	colloquial usage (! particularly offensive)
ferrocarril	**FERRO**	railways
uso figurado	**fig**	figurative use
fotografía	**FOTO**	photography
(verbo inglés) del cual la partícula es inseparable	**fus**	(phrasal verb) where the particle is inseparable
generalmente	**gen**	generally
geografía, geología	**GEO**	geography, geology
geometría	**GEOM**	geometry
informática	**INFORM**	computing
invariable	**inv**	invariable
irregular	**irreg**	irregular
lo jurídico	**JUR**	law
América Latina	**LAM**	Latin America
gramática, lingüística	**LING**	grammar, linguistics
literatura	**LIT**	literature
masculino	**m**	masculine
matemáticas	**MAT(H)**	mathematics
medicina	**MED**	medical term, medicine
masculino/femenino	**m/f**	masculine/feminine

lo militar, ejército	**MIL**	military matters
música	**MUS**	music
sustantivo, nombre	**n**	noun
navegación, náutica	**NAUT**	sailing, navigation
sustantivo no empleado en el plural	**no pl**	collective (uncountable) noun, not used in plural
sustantivo numérico	**num**	numeral noun
complemento	**obj**	(grammatical) object
	o.s.	oneself
peyorativo	**pey, pej**	derogatory, pejorative
fotografía	**PHOT**	photography
fisiología	**PHYSIOL**	physiology
plural	**pl**	plural
política	**POL**	politics
participio de pasado	**pp**	past participle
prefijo	**pref**	prefix
preposición	**prep**	preposition
pronombre	**pron**	pronoun
psicología, psiquiatría	**PSICO, PSYCH**	psychology, psychiatry
tiempo pasado	**pt**	past tense
ferrocarril	**RAIL**	railways
religión, lo eclesiástico	**REL**	religion, church service
	sb	somebody
enseñanza, sistema escolar	**SCOL**	schooling, schools
singular	**sg**	singular
España	**SP**	Spain
	sth	something
subjuntivo	**subjun**	subjunctive
sujeto	**su(b)j**	(grammatical) subject
sufijo	**suff**	suffix
tauromaquia	**TAUR**	bullfighting
también	**tb**	also
teatro	**TEAT**	
técnica, tecnología	**TEC(H)**	technical term, technology
telecomunicaciones	**TELEC, TEL**	telecommunications
	THEAT	theatre
imprenta, tipografía	**TIP, TYP**	typography, printing
televisión	**TV**	television
sistema universitario	**UNIV**	universities
inglés norteamericano	**US**	American English
verbo	**vb**	verb
verbo intransitivo	**vi**	intransitive verb
verbo pronominal	**vr**	reflexive verb
verbo transitivo	**vt**	transitive verb
zoología, animales	**ZOOL**	zoology
marca registrada	**®**	registered trademark
indica un equivalente cultural	**≈**	introduces a cultural equivalent

SPANISH PRONUNCIATION

Consonants

b	[b]	<u>b</u>om<u>b</u>a	see notes on *v* below
	[ß]	la<u>b</u>or	
c	[k]	<u>c</u>aja	*c* before *a, o* or *u* is pronounced as in *cat*
ce, ci	[θe, θi]	<u>c</u>ero	*c* before *e* or *i* is pronounced as in *thin*
		<u>c</u>ielo	and as *s* in *sin* in Latin America and parts
	[se, si][1]	vo<u>c</u>ero	of Spain
		noti<u>c</u>iero	
ch	[tʃ]	<u>ch</u>iste	*ch* is pronounced as *ch* in *chair*
d	[d]	<u>d</u>anés	at the beginning of a word or after *l* or *n*,
	[ð]	ciu<u>dad</u>	*d* is pronounced as in English. In any other position it is like *th* in *the*
g	[g]	<u>g</u>afas	*g* before *a, o* or *u* is pronounced as in *gap*,
		<u>g</u>uerra	if at the beginning of a word or after *n*. In
	[ɣ]	pa<u>g</u>a	other positions the sound is softened
ge, gi	[xe, xi]	<u>g</u>ente	*g* before *e* or *i* is pronounced similar to *ch*
		<u>g</u>irar	in Scottish lo*ch*
h		<u>h</u>aber	*h* is always silent in Spanish
j	[x]	<u>j</u>ugar	*j* is pronounced like *ch* in Scottish lo*ch*
ll	[ʎ]	ta<u>ll</u>e	*ll* is pronounced like the *lli* in mi*lli*on
ñ	[ɲ]	ni<u>ñ</u>o	*ñ* is pronounced like the *ni* in o*ni*on
q	[k]	<u>q</u>ue	*q* is pronounced as *k* in *king*
r, rr	[r]	quita<u>r</u>	*r* is always pronounced in Spanish, unlike
	[rr]	ga<u>rr</u>a	the silent *r* in dance*r*. *rr* and *r* at the beginning of a word are trilled, like a Scottish *r*
s	[s]	quizá<u>s</u>	*s* is usually pronounced as in pa*ss*, but
		i<u>s</u>la	before *b, d, g, l, m* or *n* it is pronounced as in ro*s*e
v	[b]	<u>v</u>ía	*v* is pronounced something like *b*. At the
	[ß]	di<u>v</u>idir	beginning of a word or after *m* or *n* it is pronounced as *b* in *boy*. In any other position it is pronounce with the lips in position to pronounce *b* of *boy*, but not meeting
w	[b]	<u>w</u>áter	pronounced either like Spanish *b*, or like
	[w]	<u>wh</u>iskey	English *w*
z	[θ]	tena<u>z</u>	*z* is pronounced as *thin* *thin* and as *s* in
	[s][1]	i<u>z</u>ada	*sin* in Latin America and parts of Spain
	[ks]	tó<u>x</u>ico	*x* is pronounced as in to*x*in except in
	[s]	<u>x</u>enofobia	informal Spanish or at the beginning of a word

f, k, l, m, n, p and t are pronounced as in English.

[1]Only shown in Latin American entries.

Vowels

a	[a]	p**a**ta	not as long as *a* in f**a**r. When followed by a consonant in the same syllable (i.e. in a closed syllable), as in am**a**nte, the *a* is short, as in b**a**t
e	[e]	m**e**	like *e* in th**e**y. In a closed syllable, as in g**e**nte, the *e* is short as in p**e**t
i	[i]	p**i**no	as in m**ea**n or mach**i**ne
o	[o]	l**o**	as in l**o**cal. In a closed syllable, as in c**o**ntrol, the *o* is short as in c**o**t
u	[u]	l**u**nes	as in r**u**le. It is silent after *q*, and in *gue, gui*, unless marked *güe, güi* e.g. antig**ü**edad, when it is pronounced like *w* in w**o**lf

Semivowels

| i, y | [j] | b**i**en h**i**elo **y**unta | pronounced like *y* in **y**es |
| u | [w] | h**u**evo f**u**ente antig**ü**edad | unstressed *u* between consonant and vowel is pronounced like *w* in w**e**ll. See also notes on *u* above |

Dipthongs

ai, ay	[ai]	b**ai**le	as *i* in r**i**de
au	[au]	**au**to	as *ou* in sh**ou**t
ei, ey	[ei]	bu**ey**	as *ey* in gr**ey**
eu	[eu]	d**eu**da	both elements pronounced independently [e] + [u]
oi, oy	[oi]	h**oy**	as *oy* in t**oy**

Stress

The rules of stress in Spanish are as follows:

(a) when a word ends in a vowel or in *n* or *s*, the second last syllable is stressed: pat**a**ta, pat**a**tas, c**o**me, c**o**men

(b) when a word ends in a consonant other than *n* or *s*, the stress falls on the last syllable: par**e**d, habl**a**r

(c) when the rules set out in a and b are not applied, an acute accent appears over the stressed vowel: com**ú**n, geograf**í**a, ingl**é**s

In the phonetic transcription, the symbol ['] precedes the syllable on which the stress falls.

In general, we give the pronunciation of each entry in square brackets after the word in question.

xi

SPANISH VERB FORMS

1 Gerund *2* Imperative *3* Present *4* Preterite *5* Future *6* Present subjunctive *7* Imperfect subjunctive *8* Past participle *9* Imperfect

acertar *2* acierta *3* acierto, aciertas, acierta, aciertan *6* acierte, aciertes, acierte, acierten

acordar *2* acuerda *3* acuerdo, acuerdas, acuerda, acuerdan *6* acuerde, acuerdes, acuerde, acuerden

advertir *1* advirtiendo *2* advierte *3* advierto, adviertes, advierte, advierten *4* advirtió, advirtieron *6* advierta, adviertas, advierta, advirtamos, advirtáis, adviertan *7* advirtiera *etc*

agradecer *3* agradezco *6* agradezca *etc*

aparecer *3* aparezco *6* aparezca *etc*

aprobar *2* aprueba *3* apruebo, apruebas, aprueba, aprueban *6* apruebe, apruebes, apruebe, aprueben

atravesar *2* atraviesa *3* atravieso, atraviesas, atraviesa, atraviesan *6* atraviese, atravieses, atraviese, atraviesen

caber *3* quepo *4* cupe, cupiste, cupo, cupimos, cupisteis, cupieron *5* cabré *etc* *6* quepa *etc* *7* cupiera *etc*

caer *1* cayendo *3* caigo *4* cayó, cayeron *6* caiga *etc* *7* cayera *etc*

calentar *2* calienta *3* caliento, calientas, calienta, calientan *6* caliente, calientes, caliente, calienten

cerrar *2* cierra *3* cierro, cierras, cierra, cierran *6* cierre, cierres, cierre, cierren

COMER *1* comiendo *2* come, comed *3* como, comes, come, comemos, coméis, comen *4* comí, comiste, comió, comimos, comisteis, comieron *5* comeré, comerás, comerá, comeremos, comeréis, comerán *6* coma, comas, coma, comamos, comáis, coman *7* comiera, comieras, comiera, comiéramos, comierais, comieran *8* comido *9* comía, comías, comía, comíamos, comíais, comían

conocer *3* conozco *6* conozca *etc*

contar *2* cuenta *3* cuento, cuentas, cuenta, cuentan *6* cuente, cuentes, cuente, cuenten

costar *2* cuesta *3* cuesto, cuestas, cuesta, cuestan *6* cueste, cuestes, cueste, cuesten

dar *3* doy *4* di, diste, dio, dimos, disteis, dieron *7* diera *etc*

decir *2* di *3* digo *4* dije, dijiste, dijo, dijimos, dijisteis, dijeron *5* diré *etc* *6* diga *etc* *7* dijera *etc* *8* dicho

despertar *2* despierta *3* despierto, despiertas, despierta, despiertan *6* despierte, despiertes, despierte, despierten

divertir *1* divirtiendo *2* divierte *3* divierto, diviertes, divierte, divierten *4* divirtió, divirtieron *6* divierta, diviertas, divierta, divirtamos, divirtáis, diviertan *7* divirtiera *etc*

dormir *1* durmiendo *2* duerme *3* duermo, duermes, duerme, duermen *4* durmió, durmieron *6* duerma, duermas, duerma, durmamos, durmáis, duerman *7* durmiera *etc*

empezar *2* empieza *3* empiezo, empiezas, empieza, empiezan *4* empecé *6* empiece, empieces, empiece, empecemos, empecéis, empiecen

entender *2* entiende *3* entiendo, entiendes, entiende, entienden *6* entienda, entiendas, entienda, entiendan

ESTAR *2* está *3* estoy, estás, está, están *4* estuve, estuviste, estuvo, estuvimos, estuvisteis, estuvieron *6* esté, estés, esté, estén *7* estuviera *etc*

HABER *3* he, has, ha, hemos, han *4* hube, hubiste, hubo, hubimos, hubisteis, hubieron *5* habré *etc* *6* haya *etc* *7* hubiera *etc*

HABLAR *1* hablando *2* habla, hablad *3* hablo, hablas, habla, hablamos, habláis, hablan *4* hablé, hablaste, habló, hablamos, hablasteis, hablaron *5* hablaré, hablarás, hablará, hablaremos, hablaréis, hablarán *6* hable, hables, hable, hablemos, habléis, hablen *7* hablara, hablaras, hablara, habláramos, hablarais, hablaran *8* hablado *9* hablaba, hablabas, hablaba, hablábamos, hablabais, hablaban

hacer *2* haz *3* hago *4* hice, hiciste, hizo, hicimos, hicisteis, hicieron *5* haré *etc* *6* haga *etc* *7* hiciera *etc* *8* hecho

instruir *1* instruyendo *2* instruye *3* instruyo, instruyes, instruye, instruyen *4* instruyó, instruyeron *6* instruya *etc* *7* instruyera *etc*

ir *1* yendo *2* ve *3* voy, vas, va, vamos, vais, van *4* fui, fuiste, fue, fuimos, fuisteis, fueron *6* vaya, vayas, vaya, vayamos, vayáis, vayan 7 fuera *etc* 8 iba, ibas, iba, íbamos, ibais, iban

jugar 2 juega 3 juego, juegas, juega, juegan 4 jugué 6 juegue *etc*

leer 1 leyendo 4 leyó, leyeron 7 leyera *etc*

morir 1 muriendo 2 muere 3 muero, mueres, muere, mueren 4 murió, murieron 6 muera, mueras, muera, muramos, muráis, mueran 7 muriera *etc* 8 muerto

mostrar 2 muestra 3 muestro, muestras, muestra, muestran 6 muestre, muestres, muestre, muestren

mover 2 mueve 3 muevo, mueves, mueve, mueven 6 mueva, muevas, mueva, muevan

negar 2 niega 3 niego, niegas, niega, niegan 4 negué 6 niegue, niegues, niegue, neguemos, neguéis, nieguen

ofrecer 3 ofrezco 6 ofrezca *etc*

oír 1 oyendo 2 oye 3 oigo, oyes, oye, oyen 4 oyó, oyeron 6 oiga *etc* 7 oyera *etc*

oler 2 huele 3 huelo, hueles, huele, huelen 6 huela, huelas, huela, huelan

parecer 3 parezco 6 parezca *etc*

pedir 1 pidiendo 2 pide 3 pido, pides, pide, piden 4 pidió, pidieron 6 pida *etc* 7 pidiera *etc*

pensar 2 piensa 3 pienso, piensas, piensa, piensan 6 piense, pienses, piense, piensen

perder 2 pierde 3 pierdo, pierdes, pierde, pierden 6 pierda, pierdas, pierda, pierdan

poder 1 pudiendo 2 puede 3 puedo, puedes, puede, pueden 4 pude, pudiste, pudo, pudimos, pudisteis, pudieron 5 podré *etc* 6 pueda, puedas, pueda, puedan 7 pudiera *etc*

poner 2 pon 3 pongo 4 puse, pusiste, puso, pusimos, pusisteis, pusieron 5 pondré *etc* 6 ponga *etc* 7 pusiera *etc* 8 puesto

preferir 1 prefiriendo 2 prefiere 3 prefiero, prefieres, prefiere, prefieren 4 prefirió, prefirieron 6 prefiera, prefieras, prefiera, prefiramos, prefiráis, prefieran 7 prefiriera *etc*

querer 2 quiere 3 quiero, quieres, quiere, quieren 4 quise, quisiste, quiso, quisimos, quisisteis, quisieron 5 querré *etc* 6 quiera, quieras, quiera, quieran 7 quisiera *etc*

reír 2 ríe 3 río, ríes, ríe, ríen 4 rio, rieron 6 ría, rías, ría, riamos, riáis, rían 7 riera *etc*

repetir 1 repitiendo 2 repite 3 repito,

repites, repite, repiten 4 repitió, repitieron 6 repita *etc* 7 repitiera *etc*

rogar 2 ruega 3 ruego, ruegas, ruega, ruegan 4 rogué 6 ruegue, ruegues, ruegue, roguemos, roguéis, rueguen

saber 3 sé 4 supe, supiste, supo, supimos, supisteis, supieron 5 sabré *etc* 6 sepa *etc* 7 supiera *etc*

salir 2 sal 3 salgo 5 saldré *etc* 6 salga *etc*

seguir 1 siguiendo 2 sigue 3 sigo, sigues, sigue, siguen 4 siguió, siguieron 6 siga *etc* 7 siguiera *etc*

sentar 2 sienta 3 siento, sientas, sienta, sientan 6 siente, sientes, siente, sienten

sentir 1 sintiendo 2 siente 3 siento, sientes, siente, sienten 4 sintió, sintieron 6 sienta, sientas, sienta, sintamos, sintáis, sientan 7 sintiera *etc*

SER 2 sé 3 soy, eres, es, somos, sois, son 4 fui, fuiste, fue, fuimos, fuisteis, fueron 6 sea *etc* 7 fuera *etc* 9 era, eras, era, éramos, erais, eran

servir 1 sirviendo 2 sirve 3 sirvo, sirves, sirve, sirven 4 sirvió, sirvieron 6 sirva *etc* 7 sirviera *etc*

soñar 2 sueña 3 sueño, sueñas, sueña, sueñan 6 sueñe, sueñes, sueñe, sueñen

tener 2 ten 3 tengo, tienes, tiene, tienen 4 tuve, tuviste, tuvo, tuvimos, tuvisteis, tuvieron 5 tendré *etc* 6 tenga *etc* 7 tuviera *etc*

traer 1 trayendo 3 traigo 4 traje, trajiste, trajo, trajimos, trajisteis, trajeron 6 traiga *etc* 7 trajera *etc*

valer 2 val 3 valgo 5 valdré *etc* 6 valga *etc*

venir 2 ven 3 vengo, vienes, viene, vienen 4 vine, viniste, vino, vinimos, vinisteis, vinieron 5 vendré *etc* 6 venga *etc* 7 viniera *etc*

ver 3 veo 6 vea *etc* 8 visto 9 veía *etc*

vestir 1 vistiendo 2 viste 3 visto, vistes, viste, visten 4 vistió, vistieron 6 vista *etc* 7 vistiera *etc*

VIVIR 1 viviendo 2 vive 3 vivo, vives, vive, vivimos, vivís, viven 4 viví, viviste, vivió, vivimos, vivisteis, vivieron 5 viviré, vivirás, vivirá, viviremos, viviréis, vivirán 6 viva, vivas, viva, vivamos, viváis, vivan 7 viviera, vivieras, viviera, viviéramos, vivierais, vivieran 8 vivido 9 vivía, vivías, vivía, vivíamos, vivías, vivían

volver 2 vuelve 3 vuelvo, vuelves, vuelve, vuelven 6 vuelva, vuelvas, vuelva, vuelvan 8 vuelto

For additional information on Spanish verb formation, see pp 6-162 of Grammar section

NÚMEROS

NUMBERS

uno (un, una)*	1	one
dos	2	two
tres	3	three
cuatro	4	four
cinco	5	five
seis	6	six
siete	7	seven
ocho	8	eight
nueve	9	nine
diez	10	ten
once	11	eleven
doce	12	twelve
trece	13	thirteen
catorce	14	fourteen
quince	15	fifteen
dieciséis	16	sixteen
diecisiete	17	seventeen
dieciocho	18	eighteen
diecinueve	19	nineteen
veinte	20	twenty
veintiuno(-un, -una)*	21	twenty-one
veintidós	22	twenty-two
treinta	30	thirty
treinta y uno(un, una)*	31	thirty-one
treinta y dos	32	thirty-two
cuarenta	40	forty
cincuenta	50	fifty
sesenta	60	sixty
setenta	70	seventy
ochenta	80	eighty
noventa	90	ninety
cien(ciento)**	100	a hundred, one hundred
ciento uno(un, una)*	101	a hundred and one
ciento dos	102	a hundred and two
ciento cincuenta y seis	156	a hundred and fifty-six
doscientos(as)	200	two hundred
trescientos(as)	300	three hundred
quinientos(as)	500	five hundred
mil	1,000	a thousand
mil tres	1,003	a thousand and three
dos mil	2,000	two thousand
un millón	1,000,000	a million

* 'uno' (+ 'veintiuno' etc) agrees in gender (but not number) with its noun: treinta y una personas; the masculine form is shortened to 'un' unless it stands alone: veintiún caballos, veintiuno.

** 'ciento' is used in compound numbers, except when it multiplies: ciento diez, but cien mil. 'Cien' is used before nouns: cien hombres, cien casas.

NÚMEROS

NUMBERS

primero(primer, primera), 1º, 1er/1a, 1era	first, 1st
segundo(a), 2º/2a	second, 2nd
tercero(tercer, tercera), 3º, 3er/3a, 3era	third, 3rd
cuarto(a), 4º/4a	fourth, 4th
quinto(a)	fifth, 5th
sexto(a)	sixth, 6th
séptimo(a)	seventh
octavo(a)	eighth
noveno(a); nono(a)	ninth
décimo(a)	tenth
undécimo(a)	eleventh
duodécimo(a)	twelfth
decimotercio(a)	thirteenth
decimocuarto(a)	fourteenth
decimoquinto(a)	fifteenth
decimosexto(a)	sixteenth
decimoséptimo(a)	seventeenth
decimoctavo(a)	eighteenth
decimonono(a)	nineteenth
vigésimo(a)	twentieth
vigésimo primero(a)	twenty-first
vigésimo segundo(a)	twenty-second
trigésimo(a)	thirtieth
trigésimo primero(a)	thirty-first
trigésimo segundo(a)	thirty-second
cuadragésimo(a)	fortieth
quincuagésimo(a)	fiftieth
sexagésimo(a)	sixtieth
septuagésimo(a)	seventieth
octogésimo(a)	eightieth
nonagésimo(a)	ninetieth
centésimo(a)	hundredth
centésimo primero(a)	hundred-and-first
milésimo(a)	thousandth

LA HORA

THE TIME

¿qué hora es?

what time is it?

es la una
son las cuatro
medianoche, las doce de la noche
la una (de la madrugada)

it's one o'clock
it's four o'clock
midnight
one o'clock (in the morning), one
  (a.m.)

la una y cinco
la una y diez
la una y cuarto *or* quince
la una y veinticinco

five past one
ten past one
a quarter past one, one fifteen
twenty-five past one, one twenty-
  five

la una y media *or* treinta
las dos menos veinticinco, la una
  treinta y cinco
las dos menos veinte, la una
  cuarenta
las dos menos cuarto, la una
  cuarenta y cinco
las dos menos diez, la una
  cincuenta
mediodía, las doce (de la mañana)
las dos (de la tarde)

las siete (de la tarde)

half-past one, one thirty
twenty-five to two, one thirty-five

twenty to two, one forty

a quarter to two, one forty-five

ten to two, one fifty

twelve o'clock, midday, noon
two o'clock (in the afternoon), two
  (p.m.)
seven o'clock (in the evening),
  seven (p.m.)

¿a qué hora?

at what time?

a medianoche
a las siete
a las una

at midnight
at seven o'clock
at one o'clock

en veinte minutos
hace diez minutos

in twenty minutes
ten minutes ago

LA FECHA

THE DATE

hoy
mañana
pasado mañana
ayer
antes de ayer, anteayer
la víspera
el día siguiente

today
tomorrow
the day after tomorrow
yesterday
the day before yesterday
the day before, the previous day
the next *or* following day

la mañana	morning
la tarde	evening
esta mañana	this morning
esta tarde	this evening
esta tarde	this afternoon
ayer por la mañana	yesterday morning
ayer por la tarde	yesterday evening
mañana por la mañana	tomorrow morning
mañana por la tarde	tomorrow evening
en la noche del sábado al domingo	during Saturday night, during the night of Saturday to Sunday
vendrá el sábado	he's coming on Saturday
los sábados	on Saturdays
todos los sábados	every Saturday
el sábado pasado	last Saturday
el sábado que viene, el próximo sábado	next Saturday
del sábado en ocho días	a week on Saturday
del sábado en quince días	a fortnight or two weeks on Saturday
de lunes a sábado	from Monday to Saturday
todos los días	every day
una vez a la semana	once a week
una vez ala mes	once a month
dos veces a la semana	twice a week
hace una semana o ocho días	a week ago
hace quince días	a fortnight or two weeks ago
el año pasado	last year
dentro de dos días	in two days
dentro de ocho días o una semana	in a week
dentro de quince días	in a fortnight or two weeks
el mes que viene, el próximo mes	next month
el año que viene, el próximo año	next year

¿a qué o a cuántos estamos?	*what day is it?*
el 1/24 octubre de 1996	the 1st/24th of October 1996, October 1st/24th 1996
en 1996	in 1996
mil novecientos noventa y cinco	nineteen ninety-five
44 a. de J.C.	44 BC
14 d. de J.C.	14 AD
en el (siglo) XIX	in the nineteenth century
en los años treinta	in the thirties
érase una vez ...	once upon a time ...

Español-Inglés
Spanish-English

advocate.

abogar [aβo'ɣar] *vi*: ~ **por** to plead for; (*fig*) to advocate.

abogue [a'βoɣe] *etc vb V* **abogar.**

abolengo [aβo'lengo] *nm* ancestry, lineage.

abolición [aβoli'θjon] *nf* abolition.

abolir [aβo'lir] *vt* to abolish; (*cancelar*) to cancel.

abolladura [aβoʎa'ðura] *nf* dent.

abollar [aβo'ʎar] *vt* to dent.

abominable [aβomi'naβle] *adj* abominable.

abominación [aβomina'θjon] *nf* abomination.

abonado, a [aβo'naðo, a] *adj* (*deuda*) paid(-up) ♦ *nm/f* subscriber.

abonar [aβo'nar] *vt* to pay;(*deuda*) to settle; (*terreno*) to fertilize; (*idea*) to endorse; ~**se** *vr* to subscribe; ~ **dinero en una cuenta** to pay money into an account, credit money to an account.

abono [a'βono] *nm* payment; fertilizer; subscription.

abordable [aβor'ðaβle] *adj* (*persona*) approachable.

abordar [aβor'ðar] *vt* (*barco*) to board; (*asunto*) to broach; (*individuo*) to approach.

aborigen [aβo'rixen] *nm/f* aborigine.

aborrecer [aβorre'θer] *vt* to hate, loathe.

aborrezca [aβo'rreθka] *etc vb V* **aborrecer.**

abortar [aβor'tar] *vi* (*malparir*) to have a miscarriage; (*deliberadamente*) to have an abortion.

aborto [a'βorto] *nm* miscarriage; abortion.

abotagado, a [aβota'ɣaðo, a] *adj* swollen.

abotonar [aβoto'nar] *vt* to button (up), do up.

abovedado, a [aβoβe'ðaðo, a] *adj* vaulted, domed.

abr. *abr* (= *abril*) Apr.

abrace [a'βraθe] *etc vb V* **abrazar.**

abrasar [aβra'sar] *vt* to burn (up); (*AGR*) to dry up, parch.

abrazadera [aβraθa'ðera] *nf* bracket.

abrazar [aβra'θar] *vt* to embrace, hug; ~**se** *vr* to embrace, hug each other.

abrazo [a'βraθo] *nm* embrace, hug; **un** ~ (*en carta*) with best wishes.

abrebotellas [aβreβo'teʎas] *nm inv* bottle opener.

abrecartas [aβre'kartas] *nm inv* letter opener.

abrelatas [aβre'latas] *nm inv* tin (*BRIT*) o can (*US*) opener.

abrevadero [aβreβa'ðero] *nm* watering place.

abreviar [aβre'βjar] *vt* to abbreviate;

(*texto*) to abridge; (*plazo*) to reduce ♦
bueno, para ~ well, to cut a long story short.

abreviatura [aβreβja'tura] *nf* abbreviation.

abridor [aβri'ðor] *nm* (*de botellas*) bottle opener; (*de latas*) tin (*BRIT*) o can (*US*) opener.

abrigar [aβri'ɣar] *vt* (*proteger*) to shelter; (*suj: ropa*) to keep warm; (*fig*) to cherish; ~**se** *vr* to take shelter, protect o.s (*de* from); (*con ropa*) to cover (o.s.) up; **¡abrígate bien!** wrap up well!

abrigo [a'βriɣo] *nm* (*prenda*) coat, overcoat; (*lugar protegido*) shelter; **al** ~ **de** in the shelter of.

abrigue [a'βriɣe] *etc vb V* **abrigar.**

abril [a'βril] *nm* April.

abrillantar [aβriʎan'tar] *vt* (*pulir*) to polish; (*fig*) to enhance.

abrir [a'βrir] *vt* to open (up); (*camino etc*) to open up; (*apetito*) to whet; (*lista*) to head ♦ *vi* to open; ~**se** *vr* to open (up); (*extenderse*) to open out; (*cielo*) to clear; ~ **un negocio** to start up a business; **en un** ~ **y cerrar de ojos** in the twinkling of an eye; ~**se paso** to find o force a way through.

abrochar [aβro'tʃar] *vt* (*con botones*) to button (up); (*zapato, con broche*) to do up; ~**se** *vr*: ~**se los zapatos** to tie one's shoelaces.

abrogación [aβroɣa'θjon] *nf* repeal.

abrogar [aβro'ɣar] *vt* to repeal.

abrumador, a [aβruma'ðor, a] *adj* (*mayoría*) overwhelming.

abrumar [aβru'mar] *vt* to overwhelm; (*sobrecargar*) to weigh down.

abrupto, a [a'βrupto, a] *adj* abrupt; (*empinado*) steep.

absceso [aβs'θeso] *nm* abscess.

absentismo [aβsen'tismo] *nm* (*de obreros*) absenteeism.

absolución [aβsolu'θjon] *nf* (*REL*) absolution; (*JUR*) acquittal.

absoluto, a [aβso'luto, a] *adj* absolute; (*total*) utter, complete; **en** ~ *adv* not at all.

absolver [aβsol'βer] *vt* to absolve; (*JUR*) to pardon; (: *acusado*) to acquit.

absorbente [aβsor'βente] *adj* absorbent; (*interesante*) absorbing, interesting; (*exigente*) demanding.

absorber [aβsor'βer] *vt* to absorb; (*embeber*) to soak up; ~**se** *vr* to become absorbed.

absorción [aβsor'θjon] *nf* absorption; (*COM*) takeover.

absorto, a [aβ'sorto, a] *pp de* **absorber** ♦ *adj*

engrossed.

..., a [aßs'temjo, a] adj teetotal.

...ión [aßsten'θjon] nf abstention.

...dré [aßsten'dre] etc vb V **abstenerse**.

...enerse [aßste'nerse] vr: ~ **(de)** to
...ostain o refrain (from).

abstenga [aßs'tenga] etc vb V **abstenerse**.

abstinencia [aßsti'nenθja] nf abstinence;
(*ayuno*) fasting.

abstracción [aßstrak'θjon] nf abstraction.

abstracto, a [aß'strakto, a] adj abstract; **en**
~ in the abstract.

abstraer [aßstra'er] vt to abstract; ~**se** vr to
be o become absorbed.

abstraído, a [aßstra'iðo, a] adj absent-
minded.

abstraiga [aßs'traiɣa] etc, **abstraje**
[aßs'traxe] etc, **abstrayendo**
[aßstra'jendo] etc vb V **abstraer**.

abstuve [aßs'tuße] etc vb V **abstenerse**.

absuelto [aß'swelto] pp de **absolver**.

absurdo, a [aß'surðo, a] adj absurd; **lo** ~
es que ... the ridiculous thing is that ...
♦ nm absurdity.

abuchear [aßutʃe'ar] vt to boo.

abucheo [aßu'tʃeo] nm booing; **ganarse un**
~ (*TEAT*) to be booed.

abuela [a'ßwela] nf grandmother;
¡cuéntaselo a tu ~! (*fam!*) do you think I
was born yesterday? (*fam*); **no tener/**
necesitar ~ (*fam*) to be full of o.s./blow
one's own trumpet.

abuelita [aßwe'lita] nf granny.

abuelo [a'ßwelo] nm grandfather;
(*antepasado*) ancestor; ~**s** nmpl
grandparents.

abulense [aßu'lense] adj of Ávila ♦ nm/f
native o inhabitant of Ávila.

abulia [a'ßulja] nf lethargy.

abúlico, a [a'ßuliko, a] adj lethargic.

abultado, a [aßul'taðo, a] adj bulky.

abultar [aßul'tar] vt to enlarge; (*aumentar*)
to increase; (*fig*) to exaggerate ♦ vi to be
bulky.

abundancia [aßun'danθja] nf: **una** ~ **de**
plenty of; **en** ~ in abundance.

abundante [aßun'dante] adj abundant,
plentiful.

abundar [aßun'dar] vi to abound, be
plentiful; ~ **en una opinión** to share an
opinion.

aburguesarse [aßurɣe'sarse] vr to become
middle-class.

aburrido, a [aßu'rriðo, a] adj (*hastiado*)
bored; (*que aburre*) boring.

aburrimiento [aßurri'mjento] nm boredom,
tedium.

aburrir [aßu'rrir] vt to bore; ~**se** vr to be

bored, get bored; ~**se como una almeja**
u **ostra** to be bored stiff.

abusar [aßu'sar] vi to go too far; ~ **de** to
abuse.

abusivo, a [aßu'sißo, a] adj (*precio*)
exorbitant.

abuso [a'ßuso] nm abuse; ~ **de confianza**
betrayal of trust.

abyecto, a [aß'jekto, a] adj wretched,
abject.

A.C. abr (= *Año de Cristo*) A.D.

a/c abr (= *al cuidado de*) c/o; (= *a cuenta*)
on account.

acá [a'ka] adv (*lugar*) here; **pasearse de** ~
para allá to walk up and down; **¡vente**
para ~! come over here!; **¿de cuándo** ~?
since when?

acabado, a [aka'ßaðo, a] adj finished,
complete; (*perfecto*) perfect; (*agotado*)
worn out; (*fig*) masterly ♦ nm finish.

acabar [aka'ßar] vt (*llevar a su fin*) to finish,
complete; (*consumir*) to use up; (*rematar*)
to finish off ♦ vi to finish, end; (*morir*) to
die; ~**se** vr to finish, stop; (*terminarse*) to
be over; (*agotarse*) to run out; ~ **con** to
put an end to; ~ **mal** to come to a sticky
end; **esto acabará conmigo** this will be
the end of me; ~ **de llegar** to have just
arrived; **acababa de hacerlo** I had just
done it; ~ **haciendo** o **por hacer algo** to
end up (by) doing sth; **¡se acabó!**
(*¡basta!*) that's enough!; (*se terminó*) it's
all over!; **se me acabó el tabaco** I ran
out of cigarettes.

acabóse [aka'ßose] nm: **esto es el** ~ this is
the limit.

acacia [a'kaθja] nf acacia.

academia [aka'ðemja] nf academy; (*ESCOL*)
private school; V tb **colegio**.

académico, a [aka'ðemiko, a] adj
academic.

acaecer [akae'θer] vi to happen, occur.

acaezca [aka'eθka] etc vb V **acaecer**.

acallar [aka'ʎar] vt (*silenciar*) to silence;
(*calmar*) to pacify.

acalorado, a [akalo'raðo, a] adj (*discusión*)
heated.

acalorarse [akalo'rarse] vr (*fig*) to get
heated.

acampada [akam'paða] nf: **ir de** ~ to go
camping.

acampanado, a [akampa'naðo, a] adj
flared.

acampar [akam'par] vi to camp.

acanalado, a [akana'laðo, a] adj (*hierro*)
corrugated.

acanalar [akana'lar] vt to groove; (*ondular*)
to corrugate.

acantilado [akanti'laðo] *nm* cliff.
acaparador, a [akapara'ðor, a] *nm/f* monopolizer.
acaparar [akapa'rar] *vt* to monopolize; (*acumular*) to hoard.
acápite [a'kapite] *nm* (*AM*) paragraph; **punto ~** full stop, new paragraph.
acaramelado, a [akarame'laðo, a] *adj* (*CULIN*) toffee-coated; (*fig*) sugary.
acariciar [akari'θjar] *vt* to caress; (*esperanza*) to cherish.
acarrear [akarre'ar] *vt* to transport; (*fig*) to cause, result in; **le acarreó muchos disgustos** it brought him lots of problems.
acaso [a'kaso] *adv* perhaps, maybe ♦ *nm* chance; **¿~ es mi culpa?** (*AM fam*) what makes you think it's my fault?; **(por) si ~** (just) in case.
acatamiento [akata'mjento] *nm* respect; (*de la ley*) observance.
acatar [aka'tar] *vt* to respect; (*ley*) to obey, observe.
acatarrarse [akata'rrarse] *vr* to catch a cold.
acaudalado, a [akauða'laðo, a] *adj* well-off.
acaudillar [akauði'ʎar] *vt* to lead, command.
acceder [akθe'ðer] *vi* to accede, agree; **~ a** (*INFORM*) to access.
accesible [akθe'siβle] *adj* accessible; **~ a** open to.
accésit, *pl* **accésits** [ak'θesit, ak'θesits] *nm* consolation prize.
acceso [ak'θeso] *nm* access, entry; (*camino*) access road; (*MED*) attack, fit; (*de cólera*) fit; (*POL*) accession; (*INFORM*) access; **~ aleatorio/directo/secuencial o en serie** (*INFORM*) random/direct/sequential o serial access; **de ~ múltiple** multi-access.
accesorio, a [akθe'sorjo, a] *adj* accessory ♦ *nm* accessory; **~s** *nmpl* (*AUTO*) accessories, extras; (*TEAT*) props.
accidentado, a [akθiðen'taðo, a] *adj* uneven; (*montañoso*) hilly; (*azaroso*) eventful ♦ *nm/f* accident victim.
accidental [akθiðen'tal] *adj* accidental; (*empleo*) temporary.
accidentarse [akθiðen'tarse] *vr* to have an accident.
accidente [akθi'ðente] *nm* accident; **por ~** by chance; **~s** *nmpl* unevenness *sg*, roughness *sg*.
acción [ak'θjon] *nf* action; (*acto*) action, act; (*TEAT*) plot; (*COM*) share; (*JUR*) action, lawsuit; **capital en acciones** share

capital; **~ liberada/ordinaria/preferente** fully-paid/ordinary/preference share.
accionamiento [akθjona'mjento] *nm* (*de máquina*) operation.
accionar [akθjo'nar] *vt* to work, operate; (*INFORM*) to drive.
accionista [akθjo'nista] *nm/f* shareholder.
acebo [a'θeβo] *nm* holly; (*árbol*) holly tree.
acechanza [aθe'tʃanθa] *nf* = **acecho**.
acechar [aθe'tʃar] *vt* to spy on; (*aguardar*) to lie in wait for.
acecho [a'θetʃo] *nm*: **estar al ~ (de)** to lie in wait (for).
acedera [aθe'ðera] *nf* sorrel.
aceitar [aθei'tar] *vt* to oil, lubricate.
aceite [a'θeite] *nm* oil; (*de oliva*) olive oil; **~ de hígado de bacalao** cod-liver oil.
aceitera [aθei'tera] *nf* oilcan.
aceitoso, a [aθei'toso, a] *adj* oily.
aceituna [aθei'tuna] *nf* olive.
aceitunado, a [aθeitu'naðo, a] *adj* olive *cpd*; **de tez aceitunada** olive-skinned.
acelerador [aθelera'ðor] *nm* accelerator.
acelerar [aθele'rar] *vt* to accelerate; **~se** *vr* to hurry.
acelga [a'θelɣa] *nf* chard, beet.
acendrado, a [aθen'draðo, a] *adj*: **de ~ carácter español** typically Spanish.
acendrar [aθen'drar] *vt* to purify.
acento [a'θento] *nm* accent; (*acentuación*) stress; **~ cerrado** strong o thick accent.
acentuar [aθen'twar] *vt* to accent; to stress; (*fig*) to accentuate; (*INFORM*) to highlight.
acepción [aθep'θjon] *nf* meaning.
aceptación [aθepta'θjon] *nf* acceptance; (*aprobación*) approval.
aceptar [aθep'tar] *vt* to accept; to approve.
acequia [a'θekja] *nf* irrigation ditch.
acera [a'θera] *nf* pavement (*BRIT*), sidewalk (*US*).
acerado, a [aθe'raðo, a] *adj* steel; (*afilado*) sharp; (*fig: duro*) steely; (: *mordaz*) biting.
acerbo, a [a'θerβo, a] *adj* bitter; (*fig*) harsh.
acerca [a'θerka]: **~ de** *prep* about, concerning.
acercar [aθer'kar] *vt* to bring o move nearer; **~se** *vr* to approach, come near.
acerico [aθe'riko] *nm* pincushion.
acero [a'θero] *nm* steel; **~ inoxidable** stainless steel.
acerque [a'θerke] *etc vb V* **acercar**.
acérrimo, a [a'θerrimo, a] *adj* (*partidario*) staunch; (*enemigo*) bitter.
acertado, a [aθer'taðo, a] *adj* correct; (*apropiado*) apt; (*sensato*) sensible.
acertar [aθer'tar] *vt* (*blanco*) to hit; (*solución*) to get right; (*adivinar*) to guess

♦ *vi* to get it right, be right; ~ **a** to manage to; ~ **con** to happen *o* hit on.

acertijo [aθer'tixo] *nm* riddle, puzzle.

acervo [a'θerßo] *nm* heap; ~ **común** undivided estate.

achacar [atʃa'kar] *vt* to attribute.

achacoso, a [atʃa'koso, a] *adj* sickly.

achantar [atʃan'tar] *vt* (*fam*) to scare, frighten; ~**se** *vr* to back down.

achaque [a'tʃake] *etc vb* V **achacar** ♦ *nm* ailment.

achatar [atʃa'tar] *vt* to flatten.

achicar [atʃi'kar] *vt* to reduce; (*humillar*) to humiliate; (*NAUT*) to bale out; ~**se** (*ropa*) to shrink; (*fig*) to humble o.s.

achicharrar [atʃitʃa'rrar] *vt* to scorch, burn.

achicoria [atʃi'korja] *nf* chicory.

achinado, a [atʃi'naðo, a] *adj* (*ojos*) slanting; (*AM*) half-caste.

achique [a'tʃike] *etc vb* V **achicar**.

acholado, a [atʃo'laðo, a] *adj* (*AM*) half-caste.

achuchar [atʃu'tʃar] *vt* to crush.

achuchón [atʃu'tʃon] *nm* shove; **tener un** ~ (*MED*) to be poorly.

achuras [a'tʃuras] *nf* (*AM CULIN*) offal.

aciago, a [a'θjaɣo, a] *adj* ill-fated, fateful.

acicalar [aθika'lar] *vt* to polish; (*adornar*) to bedeck; ~**se** *vr* to get dressed up.

acicate [aθi'kate] *nm* spur; (*fig*) incentive.

acidez [aθi'ðeθ] *nf* acidity.

ácido, a ['aθiðo, a] *adj* sour, acid ♦ *nm* acid; (*fam: droga*) LSD.

acierto [a'θjerto] *etc vb* V **acertar** ♦ *nm* success; (*buen paso*) wise move; (*solución*) solution; (*habilidad*) skill, ability; (*al adivinar*) good guess; **fue un** ~ **suyo** it was a sensible choice on his part.

aclamación [aklama'θjon] *nf* acclamation; (*aplausos*) applause.

aclamar [akla'mar] *vt* to acclaim; to applaud.

aclaración [aklara'θjon] *nf* clarification, explanation.

aclarar [akla'rar] *vt* to clarify, explain; (*ropa*) to rinse ♦ *vi* to clear up; ~**se** *vr* (*suj: persona*: *explicarse*) to understand; (*fig*: *asunto*) to become clear; ~**se la garganta** to clear one's throat.

aclaratorio, a [aklara'torjo, a] *adj* explanatory.

aclimatación [aklimata'θjon] *nf* acclimatization.

aclimatar [aklima'tar] *vt* to acclimatize; ~**se** *vr* to become *o* get acclimatized; ~**se a algo** to get used to sth.

acné [ak'ne] *nm* acne.

acobardar [akoßar'ðar] *vt* to daunt, intimidate; ~**se** *vr* (*atemorizarse*) to be intimidated; (*echarse atrás*): ~**se (ante)** to shrink back (from).

acodarse [ako'ðarse] *vr*: ~ **en** to lean on.

acogedor, a [akoxe'ðor, a] *adj* welcoming; (*hospitalario*) hospitable.

acoger [ako'xer] *vt* to welcome; (*abrigar*) to shelter; ~**se** *vr* to take refuge; ~**se a** (*pretexto*) to take refuge in; (*ley*) to resort to.

acogida [ako'xiða] *nf* reception; refuge.

acoja [a'koxa] *etc vb* V **acoger**.

acojonante [akoxo'nante] *adj* (*ESP fam*) tremendous.

acolchar [akol'tʃar] *vt* to pad; (*fig*) to cushion.

acólito [a'kolito] *nm* (*REL*) acolyte; (*fig*) minion.

acometer [akome'ter] *vt* to attack; (*emprender*) to undertake.

acometida [akome'tiða] *nf* attack, assault.

acomodado, a [akomo'ðaðo, a] *adj* (*persona*) well-to-do.

acomodador, a [akomoða'ðor, a] *nm/f* usher(ette).

acomodar [akomo'ðar] *vt* to adjust; (*alojar*) to accommodate; ~**se** *vr* to conform; (*instalarse*) to install o.s.; (*adaptarse*) to adapt o.s.; ¡**acomódese a su gusto!** make yourself comfortable!

acomodaticio, a [akomoða'tiθjo, a] *adj* (*pey*) accommodating, obliging; (*manejable*) pliable.

acompañamiento [akompaɲa'mjento] *nm* (*MUS*) accompaniment.

acompañante, a [akompa'ɲante, a] *nm/f* companion.

acompañar [akompa'ɲar] *vt* to accompany, go with; (*documentos*) to enclose; ¿**quieres que te acompañe?** do you want me to come with you?; ~ **a algn a la puerta** to see sb to the door *o* out; **le acompaño en el sentimiento** please accept my condolences.

acompasar [akompa'sar] *vt* (*MUS*) to mark the rhythm of.

acomplejado, a [akomple'xaðo, a] *adj* neurotic.

acomplejar [akomple'xar] *vt* to give a complex to; ~**se** *vr*: ~**se (con)** to get a complex (about).

acondicionado, a [akondiθjo'naðo, a] *adj* (*TEC*) in good condition.

acondicionador [akondiθjona'ðor] *nm* conditioner.

acondicionar [akondiθjo'nar] *vt* to get

ready, prepare; (*pelo*) to condition.
acongojar [akongo'xar] *vt* to distress, grieve.
aconsejable [akonse'xaßle] *adj* advisable.
aconsejar [akonse'xar] *vt* to advise, counsel; **~se** *vr*: **~se con** *o* **de** to consult.
acontecer [akonte'θer] *vi* to happen, occur.
acontecimiento [akonteθi'mjento] *nm* event.
acontezca [akon'teθka] *etc vb* V **acontecer.**
acopiar [ako'pjar] *vt* (*recoger*) to gather; (*COM*) to buy up.
acopio [a'kopjo] *nm* store, stock.
acoplador [akopla'ðor] *nm*: **~ acústico** (*INFORM*) acoustic coupler.
acoplamiento [akopla'mjento] *nm* coupling, joint.
acoplar [ako'plar] *vt* to fit; (*ELEC*) to connect; (*vagones*) to couple.
acoquinar [akoki'nar] *vt* to scare; **~se** *vr* to get scared.
acorazado, a [akora'θaðo, a] *adj* armour-plated, armoured ♦ *nm* battleship.
acordar [akor'ðar] *vt* (*resolver*) to agree, resolve; (*recordar*) to remind; **~se** *vr* to agree; **~se (de algo)** to remember (sth).
acorde [a'korðe] *adj* (*MUS*) harmonious; **~ con** (*medidas etc*) in keeping with ♦ *nm* chord.
acordeón [akorðe'on] *nm* accordion.
acordonado, a [akorðo'naðo, a] *adj* (*calle*) cordoned-off.
acorralar [akorra'lar] *vt* to round up, corral; (*fig*) to intimidate.
acortar [akor'tar] *vt* to shorten; (*duración*) to cut short; (*cantidad*) to reduce; **~se** *vr* to become shorter.
acosar [ako'sar] *vt* to pursue relentlessly; (*fig*) to hound, pester; **~ a algn a preguntas** to pester sb with questions.
acoso [a'koso] *nm* relentless pursuit; (*fig*) hounding; **~ sexual** sexual harassment.
acostar [akos'tar] *vt* (*en cama*) to put to bed; (*en suelo*) to lay down; (*barco*) to bring alongside; **~se** *vr* to go to bed; to lie down.
acostumbrado, a [akostum'braðo, a] *adj* (*habitual*) usual; **estar ~ a (hacer) algo** to be used to (doing) sth.
acostumbrar [akostum'brar] *vt*: **~ a algn a algo** to get sb used to sth ♦ *vi*: **~ (a hacer algo)** to be in the habit (of doing sth); **~se** *vr*: **~se a** to get used to.
acotación [akota'θjon] *nf* (*apunte*) marginal note; (*GEO*) elevation mark; (*de límite*) boundary mark; (*TEAT*) stage direction.

acotar [ako'tar] *vt* (*terreno*) to mark out; (*fig*) to limit; (*caza*) to protect.
acotejar [akote'xar] *vt* (*AM*) to put in order, arrange.
ácrata ['akrata] *adj, nm/f* anarchist.
acre ['akre] *adj* (*sabor*) sharp, bitter; (*olor*) acrid; (*fig*) biting ♦ *nm* acre.
acrecentar [akreθen'tar] *vt* to increase, augment.
acreciente [akre'θjente] *etc vb* V **acrecentar.**
acreditado, a [akreði'taðo, a] *adj* (*POL*) accredited; (*COM*): **una casa acreditada** a reputable firm.
acreditar [akreði'tar] *vt* (*garantizar*) to vouch for, guarantee; (*autorizar*) to authorize; (*dar prueba de*) to prove; (*COM: abonar*) to credit; (*embajador*) to accredit; **~se** *vr* to become famous; (*demostrar valía*) to prove one's worth; **~se de** to get a reputation for.
acreedor, a [akree'ðor, a] *adj*: **~ a** worthy of ♦ *nm/f* creditor; **~ común/diferido/con garantía** (*COM*) unsecured/deferred/secured creditor.
acribillar [akrißi'ʎar] *vt*: **~ a balazos** to riddle with bullets.
acrimonia [akri'monja], **acritud** [akri'tuð] *nf* acrimony.
acrobacia [akro'ßaθja] *nf* acrobatics; **~ aérea** aerobatics.
acróbata [a'kroßata] *nm/f* acrobat.
acta ['akta] *nf* certificate; (*de comisión*) minutes *pl*, record; **~ de nacimiento/de matrimonio** birth/marriage certificate; **~ notarial** affidavit; **levantar ~** (*JUR*) to make a formal statement *o* deposition.
actitud [akti'tuð] *nf* attitude; (*postura*) posture; **adoptar una ~ firme** to take a firm stand.
activar [akti'ßar] *vt* to activate; (*acelerar*) to speed up.
actividad [aktißi'ðað] *nf* activity; **estar en plena ~** to be in full swing.
activo, a [ak'tißo, a] *adj* active; (*vivo*) lively ♦ *nm* (*COM*) assets *pl*; **~ y pasivo** assets and liabilities; **~ circulante/fijo/inmaterial/invisible** (*COM*) current/fixed/intangible/invisible assets; **~ realizable** liquid assets; **~s congelados** *o* **bloqueados** frozen assets; **estar en ~** (*MIL*) to be on active service.
acto ['akto] *nm* act, action; (*ceremonia*) ceremony; (*TEAT*) act; **en el ~** immediately; **hacer ~ de presencia** (*asistir*) to attend (formally).
actor [ak'tor] *nm* actor; (*JUR*) plaintiff.
actora [ak'tora] *adj*: **parte ~** prosecution;

(*demandante*) plaintiff.

actriz [ak'triθ] *nf* actress.

actuación [aktwa'θjon] *nf* action; (*comportamiento*) conduct, behaviour; (*JUR*) proceedings *pl*; (*desempeño*) performance.

actual [ak'twal] *adj* present(-day), current; **el 6 del** ~ the 6th of this month.

actualice [aktwa'liθe] *etc vb V* **actualizar**.

actualidad [aktwali'ðað] *nf* present; ~**es** *nfpl* news *sg*; **en la** ~ nowadays, at present; **ser de gran** ~ to be current.

actualización [aktwaliθa'θjon] *nf* updating, modernization.

actualizar [aktwali'θar] *vt* to update, modernize.

actualmente [aktwal'mente] *adv* at present; (*hoy día*) nowadays.

actuar [ak'twar] *vi* (*obrar*) to work, operate; (*actor*) to act, perform ♦ *vt* to work, operate; ~ **de** to act as.

actuario, a [ak'twarjo] *nm/f* clerk; (*COM*) actuary.

acuarela [akwa'rela] *nf* watercolour.

acuario [a'kwarjo] *nm* aquarium; **A**~ (*ASTRO*) Aquarius.

acuartelar [akwarte'lar] *vt* (*MIL: alojar*) to quarter.

acuático, a [a'kwatiko, a] *adj* aquatic.

acuchillar [akutʃi'ʎar] *vt* (*TEC*) to plane (down), smooth.

acuciar [aku'θjar] *vt* to urge on.

acuclillarse [akukli'ʎarse] *vr* to crouch down.

ACUDE [a'kuðe] *nf abr* = *Asociación de Consumidores y Usuarios de España.*

acudir [aku'ðir] *vi* to attend, turn up; ~ **a** to turn to; ~ **en ayuda de** to go to the aid of; ~ **a una cita** to keep an appointment; ~ **a una llamada** to answer a call; **no tener a quién** ~ to have nobody to turn to.

acuerdo [a'kwerðo] *etc vb V* **acordar** ♦ *nm* agreement; (*POL*) resolution; ~ **de pago respectivo** (*COM*) knock-for-knock agreement; **A**~ **general sobre aranceles aduaneros y comercio** (*COM*) General Agreement on Tariffs and Trade; **tomar un** ~ to pass a resolution; **¡de** ~!, agreed!; **de** ~ **con** (*persona*) in agreement with; (*acción, documento*) in accordance with; **de común** ~ by common consent; **estar de** ~ (*persona*) to agree; **llegar a un** ~ to come to an understanding.

acueste [a'kweste] *etc vb V* **acostar**.

acullá [aku'ʎa] *adv* over there.

acumular [akumu'lar] *vt* to accumulate, collect.

acunar [aku'nar] *vt* to rock (to sleep).

acuñar [aku'ɲar] *vt* (*moneda*) to mint; (*frase*) to coin.

acuoso, a [a'kwoso, a] *adj* watery.

acupuntura [akupun'tura] *nf* acupuncture.

acurrucarse [akurru'karse] *vr* to crouch; (*ovillarse*) to curl up.

acurruque [aku'rruke] *etc vb V* **acurrucarse**.

acusación [akusa'θjon] *nf* accusation.

acusado, a [aku'saðo, a] *adj* (*JUR*) accused; (*marcado*) marked; (*acento*) strong.

acusar [aku'sar] *vt* to accuse; (*revelar*) to reveal; (*denunciar*) to denounce; (*emoción*) to show; ~ **recibo** to acknowledge receipt; **su rostro acusó extrañeza** his face registered surprise; ~**se** *vr*: ~**se (de)** to confess (to).

acuse [a'kuse] *nm*: ~ **de recibo** acknowledgement of receipt.

acústico, a [a'kustiko, a] *adj* acoustic ♦ *nf* (*de una sala etc*) acoustics *pl*; (*ciencia*) acoustics *sg*.

ADA ['aða] *nf abr* (*ESP*: = *Ayuda del Automovilista*) ≈ AA, RAC (*BRIT*), AAA (*US*).

adagio [a'ðaxjo] *nm* adage; (*MUS*) adagio.

adalid [aða'lið] *nm* leader, champion.

adaptación [aðapta'θjon] *nf* adaptation.

adaptador [aðapta'ðor] *nm* (*ELEC*) adapter; ~ **universal** universal adapter.

adaptar [aðap'tar] *vt* to adapt; (*acomodar*) to fit; (*convertir*): ~ **(para)** to convert (to).

adecentar [aðeθen'tar] *vt* to tidy up.

adecuado, a [aðe'kwaðo, a] *adj* (*apto*) suitable; (*oportuno*) appropriate; **el hombre** ~ **para el puesto** the right man for the job.

adecuar [aðe'kwar] *vt* (*adaptar*) to adapt; (*hacer apto*) to make suitable.

adefesio [aðe'fesjo] *nm* (*fam*): **estaba hecha un** ~ she looked a sight.

a. de J.C. *abr* (= *antes de Jesucristo*) B.C.

adelantado, a [aðelan'taðo, a] *adj* advanced; (*reloj*) fast; **pagar por** ~ to pay in advance.

adelantamiento [aðelanta'mjento] *nm* advance, advancement; (*AUTO*) overtaking.

adelantar [aðelan'tar] *vt* to move forward; (*avanzar*) to advance; (*acelerar*) to speed up; (*AUTO*) to overtake ♦ *vi* (*ir delante*) to go ahead; (*progresar*) to improve; (*tb*: ~**se**) *vr*: *tomar la delantera*) to go forward, advance; ~**se a algn** to get ahead of sb; ~**se a los deseos de algn** to anticipate sb's wishes.

adelante [aðe'lante] *adv* forward(s),

onward(s), ahead ◊ *excl* come in!; **de hoy en** ~ from now on; **más** ~ later on; (*más allá*) further on.

adelanto [aðe'lanto] *nm* advance; (*mejora*) improvement; (*progreso*) progress; (*dinero*) advance; **los ~s de la ciencia** the advances of science.

adelgace [aðel'ɣaθe] *etc vb V* **adelgazar**.

adelgazar [aðelɣa'θar] *vt* to thin (down); (*afilar*) to taper ◊ *vi* to get thin; (*con régimen*) to slim down, lose weight.

ademán [aðe'man] *nm* gesture; **ademanes** *nmpl* manners; **en ~ de** as if to.

además [aðe'mas] *adv* besides; (*por otra parte*) moreover; (*también*) also; ~ **de** besides, in addition to.

ADENA [a'ðena] *nf abr* (*ESP*: = *Asociación para la Defensa de la Naturaleza*) organization for nature conservation.

adentrarse [aðen'trarse] *vr*: ~ **en** to go into, get inside; (*penetrar*) to penetrate (into).

adentro [a'ðentro] *adv* inside, in; **mar ~** out at sea; **tierra ~** inland ◊ *nm*: **dijo para sus ~s** he said to himself.

adepto, a [a'ðepto, a] *nm/f* supporter.

aderece [aðe'reθe] *etc vb V* **aderezar**.

aderezar [aðere'θar] *vt* (*ensalada*) to dress; (*comida*) to season.

aderezo [aðe'reθo] *nm* dressing; seasoning.

adeudar [aðeu'ðar] *vt* to owe; ~**se** *vr* to run into debt; ~ **una suma en una cuenta** to debit an account with a sum.

a.D.g. *abr* (= *a Dios gracias*) D.G. (= *Deo gratias*: thanks be to God).

adherirse [aðe'rirse] *vr*: ~ **a** to adhere to; (*fig*) to follow.

adhesión [aðe'sjon] *nf* adhesion; (*fig*) adherence.

adhesivo, a [aðe'siβo, a] *adj* adhesive ◊ *nm* sticker.

adhiera [a'ðjera] *etc*, **adhiriendo** [aði'rjendo] *etc vb V* **adherirse**.

adicción [aðik'θion] *nf* addiction.

adición [aði'θjon] *nf* addition.

adicional [aðiθjo'nal] *adj* additional; (*INFORM*) add-on.

adicionar [aðiθjo'nar] *vt* to add.

adicto, a [a'ðikto, a] *adj*: ~ **a** (*droga etc*) addicted to; (*dedicado*) devoted to ◊ *nm/f* supporter, follower; (*toxicómano etc*) addict.

adiestrar [aðjes'trar] *vt* to train, teach; (*conducir*) to guide, lead; ~**se** *vr* to practise; (*enseñarse*) to train o.s.

adinerado, a [aðine'raðo, a] *adj* wealthy.

adiós [a'ðjos] *excl* (*para despedirse*)

goodbye!, cheerio!; (*al pasar*) hello!

aditivo [aði'tiβo] *nm* additive.

adivinanza [aðiβi'nanθa] *nf* riddle.

adivinar [aðiβi'nar] *vt* (*profetizar*) to prophesy; (*conjeturar*) to guess.

adivino, a [aði'βino, a] *nm/f* fortune-teller.

adj *abr* (= *adjunto*) encl.

adjetivo [aðxe'tiβo] *nm* adjective.

adjudicación [aðxuðika'θjon] *nf* award; (*COM*) adjudication.

adjudicar [aðxuði'kar] *vt* to award; ~**se** *vr*: ~**se algo** to appropriate sth.

adjudique [aðxu'ðike] *etc vb V* **adjudicar**.

adjuntar [aðxun'tar] *vt* to attach, enclose.

adjunto, a [að'xunto, a] *adj* attached, enclosed ◊ *nm/f* assistant.

adminículo [aðmi'nikulo] *nm* gadget.

administración [aðministra'θjon] *nf* administration; (*dirección*) management; ~ **pública** civil service; **A~ de Correos** General Post Office.

administrador, a [aðministra'ðor, a] *nm/f* administrator; manager(ess).

administrar [aðminis'trar] *vt* to administer.

administrativo, a [aðministra'tiβo, a] *adj* administrative.

admirable [aðmi'raβle] *adj* admirable.

admiración [aðmira'θjon] *nf* admiration; (*asombro*) wonder; (*LING*) exclamation mark.

admirar [aðmi'rar] *vt* to admire; (*extrañar*) to surprise; ~**se** *vr* to be surprised; **se admiró de saberlo** he was amazed to hear it; **no es de ~ que ...** it's not surprising that ...

admisible [aðmi'siβle] *adj* admissible.

admisión [aðmi'sjon] *nf* admission; (*reconocimiento*) acceptance.

admitir [aðmi'tir] *vt* to admit; (*aceptar*) to accept; (*dudas*) to leave room for; **esto no admite demora** this must be dealt with immediately.

admón. *abr* (= *administración*) admin.

admonición [aðmoni'θjon] *nf* warning.

ADN *nm abr* (= *acido desoxirribonucleico*) DNA.

adobar [aðo'βar] *vt* (*preparar*) to prepare; (*cocinar*) to season.

adobe [a'ðoβe] *nm* adobe, sun-dried brick.

adocenado, a [aðoθe'naðo, a] *adj* (*fam*) mediocre.

adoctrinar [aðoktri'nar] *vt* to indoctrinate.

adolecer [aðole'θer] *vi*: ~ **de** to suffer from.

adolescente [aðoles'θente] *nm/f* adolescent, teenager ◊ *adj* adolescent, teenage.

adolezca [aðo'leθka] *etc vb V* **adolecer**.
adonde [a'ðonde] *adv* (to) where.
adónde [a'ðonde] *adv* = **dónde**.
adondequiera [aðonde'kjera] *adv* wherever.
adopción [aðop'θjon] *nf* adoption.
adoptar [aðop'tar] *vt* to adopt.
adoptivo, a [aðop'tißo, a] *adj* (*padres*) adoptive; (*hijo*) adopted.
adoquín [aðo'kin] *nm* paving stone.
adorar [aðo'rar] *vt* to adore.
adormecer [aðorme'θer] *vt* to put to sleep; **~se** *vr* to become sleepy; (*dormirse*) to fall asleep.
adormezca [aðor'meθka] *etc vb V* **adormecer**.
adormilarse [aðormi'larse] *vr* to doze.
adornar [aðor'nar] *vt* to adorn.
adorno [a'ðorno] *nm* adornment; (*decoración*) decoration.
adosado, a [aðo'saðo, a] *adj* (*casa*) semidetached.
adquiera [að'kjera] *etc vb V* **adquirir**.
adquirir [aðki'rir] *vt* to acquire, obtain.
adquisición [aðkisi'θjon] *nf* acquisition; (*compra*) purchase.
adrede [a'ðreðe] *adv* on purpose.
Adriático [að'rjatiko] *nm*: **el (Mar)** ~ the Adriatic (Sea).
adscribir [aðskri'ßir] *vt* to appoint; **estuvo adscrito al servicio de ...** he was attached to ...
adscrito [að'skrito] *pp de* **adscribir**.
aduana [a'ðwana] *nf* customs *pl*; (*impuesto*) (customs) duty.
aduanero, a [aðwa'nero, a] *adj* customs *cpd* ♦ *nm/f* customs officer.
aducir [aðu'θir] *vt* to adduce; (*dar como prueba*) to offer as proof.
adueñarse [aðwe'narse] *vr*: ~ **de** to take possession of.
adulación [aðula'θjon] *nf* flattery.
adular [aðu'lar] *vt* to flatter.
adulterar [aðulte'rar] *vt* to adulterate ♦ *vi* to commit adultery.
adulterio [aðul'terjo] *nm* adultery.
adúltero, a [a'ðultero, a] *adj* adulterous ♦ *nm/f* adulterer/adulteress.
adulto, a [a'ðulto, a] *adj, nm/f* adult.
adusto, a [a'ðusto, a] *adj* stern; (*austero*) austere.
aduzca [a'ðuθka] *etc vb V* **aducir**.
advenedizo, a [aðβene'ðiθo, a] *nm/f* upstart.
advenimiento [aðβeni'mjento] *nm* arrival; (*al trono*) accession.
adverbio [að'βerßjo] *nm* adverb.
adversario, a [aðβer'sarjo, a] *nm/f* adversary.

adversidad [aðβersi'ðað] *nf* adversity; (*contratiempo*) setback.
adverso, a [að'βerso, a] *adj* adverse; (*suerte*) bad.
advertencia [aðβer'tenθja] *nf* warning; (*prefacio*) preface, foreword.
advertir [aðβer'tir] *vt* (*observar*) to notice; (*avisar*): ~ **a algn de** to warn sb about *o* of.
Adviento [að'ßjento] *nm* Advent.
advierta [að'ßjerta] *etc*, **advirtiendo** [aðßir't jendo] *etc vb V* **advertir**.
adyacente [aðja'θente] *adj* adjacent.
aéreo, a [a'ereo, a] *adj* aerial; (*tráfico*) air *cpd*.
aerobic [ae'roßik] *nm* aerobics *sg*.
aerodeslizador [aeroðesliða'ðor] *nm* hovercraft.
aerodinámico, a [aeroði'namiko, a] *adj* aerodynamic.
aeródromo [ae'roðromo] *nm* aerodrome.
aerograma [aero'ɣrama] *nm* airmail letter.
aeromodelismo [aeromoðe'lismo] *nm* model aircraft making, aeromodelling.
aeromozo, a [aero'moso, a] *nm/f* (*AM*) flight attendant, air steward(ess).
aeronáutica, a [aero'nautiko, a] *adj* aeronautical.
aeronave [aero'naße] *nm* spaceship.
aeroplano [aero'plano] *nm* aeroplane.
aeropuerto [aero'pwerto] *nm* airport.
aerosol [aero'sol] *nm* aerosol, spray.
a/f *abr* (= *a favor*) in favour.
afabilidad [afaßili'ðað] *nf* affability, pleasantness.
afable [a'faßle] *adj* affable, pleasant.
afamado, a [afa'maðo, a] *adj* famous.
afán [a'fan] *nm* hard work; (*deseo*) desire; **con** ~ keenly.
afanar [afa'nar] *vt* to harass; (*fam*) to pinch; **~se** *vr*: **~se por** to strive to.
afanoso, a [afa'noso, a] *adj* (*trabajo*) hard; (*trabajador*) industrious.
AFE ['afe] *nf abr* (= *Asociación de Futbolistas Españoles*) ≈ F.A.
afear [afe'ar] *vt* to disfigure.
afección [afek'θjon] *nf* affection; (*MED*) disease.
afectación [afekta'θjon] *nf* affectation.
afectado, a [afek'taðo, a] *adj* affected.
afectar [afek'tar] *vt* to affect, have an effect on; (*AM*: *dañar*) to hurt; **por lo que afecta a esto** as far as this is concerned.
afectísimo , a [afek'tisimo, a] *adj* affectionate; **suyo** ~ yours truly.
afectivo, a [afek'tißo, a] *adj* affective.
afecto, a [a'fekto, a] *adj*: ~ **a** fond of; (*JUR*)

subject to ♦ *nm* affection; **tenerle ~ a algn** to be fond of sb.

afectuoso, a [afek'twoso, a] *adj* affectionate.

afeitar [afei'tar] *vt* to shave; **~se** *vr* to shave.

afeminado, a [afemi'naðo, a] *adj* effeminate.

aferrar [afe'rrar] *vt* to moor; (*fig*) to grasp ♦ *vi* to moor; **~se** *vr* (*agarrarse*) to cling on; **~se a un principio** to stick to a principle; **~se a una esperanza** to cling to a hope.

Afganistán [afɣanis'tan] *nm* Afghanistan.

afgano, a [af'ɣano, a] *adj*, *nm/f* Afghan.

afiance [a'fjanθe] *etc vb V* **afianzar**.

afianzamiento [afjanθa'mjento] *nm* strengthening; security.

afianzar [afjan'θar] *vt* to strengthen, secure; **~se** *vr* to steady o.s.; (*establecerse*) to become established.

afiche [a'fitʃe] *nm* (*AM*) poster.

afición [afi'θjon] *nf*: **~ a** fondness *o* liking for; **la ~** the fans *pl*; **pinto por ~** I paint as a hobby.

aficionado, a [afiθjo'naðo, a] *adj* keen, enthusiastic; (*no profesional*) amateur ♦ *nm/f* enthusiast, fan; amateur.

aficionar [afiθjo'nar] *vt*: **~ a algn a algo** to make sb like sth; **~se** *vr*: **~se a algo** to grow fond of sth.

afilado, a [afi'laðo, a] *adj* sharp.

afilador [afila'ðor] *nm* knife grinder.

afilalápices [afila'lapiθes] *nm inv* pencil sharpener.

afilar [afi'lar] *vt* to sharpen; **~se** *vr* (*cara*) to grow thin.

afiliación [afilja'θjon] *nf* (*de sindicatos*) membership.

afiliado, a [afi'ljaðo, a] *adj* subsidiary ♦ *nm/f* affiliate.

afiliarse [afi'ljarse] *vr* to affiliate.

afín [a'fin] *adj* (*parecido*) similar; (*conexo*) related.

afinar [afi'nar] *vt* (*TEC*) to refine; (*MUS*) to tune ♦ *vi* to play/sing in tune.

afincarse [afin'karse] *vr* to settle.

afinidad [afini'ðað] *nf* affinity; (*parentesco*) relationship; **por ~** by marriage.

afirmación [afirma'θjon] *nf* affirmation.

afirmar [afir'mar] *vt* to affirm, state; (*sostener*) to strengthen; **~se** *vr* (*recuperar el equilibrio*) to steady o.s.; **~se en lo dicho** to stand by what one has said.

afirmativo, a [afirma'tiβo, a] *adj* affirmative.

aflicción [aflik'θjon] *nf* affliction; (*dolor*) grief.

afligir [afli'xir] *vt* to afflict; (*apenar*) to

distress; **~se** *vr*: **~se (por** *o* **con** *o* **de)** to grieve (about *o* at); **no te aflijas tanto** you must not let it affect you like this.

aflija [a'flixa] *etc vb V* **afligir**.

aflojar [aflo'xar] *vt* to slacken; (*desatar*) to loosen, undo; (*relajar*) to relax ♦ *vi* (*amainar*) to drop; (*bajar*) to go down; **~se** *vr* to relax.

aflorar [aflo'rar] *vi* (*GEO*, *fig*) to come to the surface, emerge.

afluencia [aflu'enθja] *nf* flow.

afluente [aflu'ente] *adj* flowing ♦ *nm* (*GEO*) tributary.

afluir [aflu'ir] *vi* to flow.

afluya [a'fluja] *etc*, **afluyendo** [aflu'jendo] *etc vb V* **afluir**.

afmo., a. *abr* (= *afectísimo, a suyo, a*) Yours.

afónico, a [a'foniko, a] *adj*: **estar ~** to have a sore throat; to have lost one's voice.

aforar [afo'rar] *vt* (*TEC*) to gauge; (*fig*) to value.

aforo [a'foro] *nm* (*TEC*) gauging; (*de teatro etc*) capacity; **el teatro tiene un ~ de 2,000** the theatre can seat 2,000.

afortunado, a [afortu'naðo, a] *adj* fortunate, lucky.

afrancesado, a [afranθe'saðo, a] *adj* francophile; (*pey*) Frenchified.

afrenta [a'frenta] *nf* affront, insult; (*deshonra*) dishonour (*BRIT*), dishonor (*US*), shame.

afrentoso, a [afren'toso, a] *adj* insulting; shameful.

África ['afrika] *nf* Africa; **~ del Sur** South Africa.

africano, a [afri'kano, a] *adj*, *nm/f* African.

afrontar [afron'tar] *vt* to confront; (*poner cara a cara*) to bring face to face.

after ['after] *nm*, **afterhours** [after'auars] *nm inv* after-hours club.

afuera [a'fwera] *adv* out, outside; **por ~** on the outside; **~s** *nfpl* outskirts.

ag. *abr* (= *agosto*) Aug.

agachar [aɣa'tʃar] *vt* to bend, bow; **~se** *vr* to stoop, bend.

agalla [a'ɣaʎa] *nf* (*ZOOL*) gill; **~s** *nfpl* (*MED*) tonsillitis *sg*; (*ANAT*) tonsils; **tener ~s** (*fam*) to have guts.

agarradera [aɣarra'ðera] *nf* (*AM*), **agarradero** [aɣarra'ðero] *nm* handle; **~s** *nfpl* pull *sg*, influence *sg*.

agarrado, a [aɣa'rraðo, a] *adj* mean, stingy.

agarrar [aɣa'rrar] *vt* to grasp, grab; (*AM*) to take, catch ♦ *vi* (*planta*) to take root; **~se** *vr* to hold on (tightly); (*meterse uno con otro*) to grapple (with each other);

agarrársela con algn (*AM*) to pick on sb;
agarró y se fue (*esp AM fam*) he upped
and went.

agarrotar [aɣarro'tar] *vt* (*lío*) to tie tightly;
(*persona*) to squeeze tightly; (*reo*) to
garrotte; ~**se** *vr* (*motor*) to seize up;
(*MED*) to stiffen.

agasajar [aɣasa'xar] *vt* to treat well, fête.

agave [a'ɣaβe] *nf* agave.

agazapar [aɣaθa'par] *vt* (*coger*) to grab
hold of; ~**se** *vr* (*agacharse*) to crouch
down.

agencia [a'xenθja] *nf* agency; ~ **de
créditos/publicidad/viajes** credit/
advertising/travel agency; ~
inmobiliaria estate agent's (office) (*BRIT*),
real estate office (*US*); ~ **matrimonial**
marriage bureau.

agenciar [axen'θjar] *vt* to bring about; ~**se**
vr to look after o.s.; ~**se algo** to get hold
of sth.

agenda [a'xenda] *nf* diary; ~ **electrónica**
PDA; ~ **telefónica** telephone directory.

agente [a'xente] *nm* agent; (*de policía*)
policeman; ~ **femenino** policewoman; ~
de bolsa stockbroker; ~ **inmobiliario**
estate agent (*BRIT*), realtor (*US*); ~ **de
negocios** (*COM*) business agent; ~ **de
seguros** insurance broker; ~ **de viajes**
travel agent; ~**s sociales** social
partners.

ágil ['axil] *adj* agile, nimble.

agilidad [axili'ðað] *nf* agility, nimbleness.

agilizar [axili'θar] *vt* to speed up.

agitación [axita'θjon] *nf* (*de mano etc*)
shaking, waving; (*de líquido etc*) stirring;
agitation.

agitar [axi'tar] *vt* to wave, shake; (*líquido*)
to stir; (*fig*) to stir up, excite; ~**se** *vr* to
get excited; (*inquietarse*) to get worried
o upset.

aglomeración [axlomera'θjon] *nf*: ~ **de
tráfico/gente** traffic jam/mass of people.

aglomerar [axlome'rar] *vt*, ~**se** *vr* to crowd
together.

agnóstico, a [ax'nostiko, a] *adj, nm/f*
agnostic.

ag.º *abr* = **ag.**

agobiante [aɣo'βjante] *adj* (*calor*)
oppressive.

agobiar [aɣo'βjar] *vt* to weigh down;
(*oprimir*) to oppress; (*cargar*) to burden;
sentirse agobiado por to be
overwhelmed by.

agobio [a'ɣoβjo] *nm* (*peso*) burden; (*fig*)
oppressiveness.

agolpamiento [aɣolpa'mjento] *nm* crush.

agolparse [aɣol'parse] *vr* to crowd

together.

agonía [aɣo'nia] *nf* death throes *pl*; (*fig*)
agony, anguish.

agonice [aɣo'niθe] *etc vb V* **agonizar**.

agonizante [aɣoni'θante] *adj* dying.

agonizar [aɣoni'θar] *vi* (*tb:* **estar
agonizando**) to be dying.

agorero, a [aɣo'rero, a] *adj* ominous ♦ *nm/f*
soothsayer; **ave agorera** bird of ill omen.

agostar [aɣos'tar] *vt* (*quemar*) to parch;
(*fig*) to wither.

agosto [a'ɣosto] *nm* August; (*fig*) harvest;
hacer su ~ to make one's pile.

agotado, a [aɣo'taðo, a] *adj* (*persona*)
exhausted; (*acabado*) finished; (*COM*)
sold out; (: *libros*) out of print; (*pila*) flat.

agotador, a [aɣota'ðor, a] *adj* exhausting.

agotamiento [aɣota'mjento] *nm*
exhaustion.

agotar [aɣo'tar] *vt* to exhaust; (*consumir*)
to drain; (*recursos*) to use up, deplete;
~**se** *vr* to be exhausted; (*acabarse*) to run
out; (*libro*) to go out of print.

agraciado, a [aɣra'θjaðo, a] *adj* (*atractivo*)
attractive; (*en sorteo etc*) lucky.

agraciar [aɣra'θjar] *vt* (*JUR*) to pardon;
(*con premio*) to reward; (*hacer más
atractivo*) to make more attractive.

agradable [aɣra'ðaβle] *adj* pleasant, nice.

agradar [aɣra'ðar] *vt, vi* to please; ~**se** *vr* to
like each other.

agradecer [aɣraðe'θer] *vt* to thank; (*favor
etc*) to be grateful for; **le agradecería me
enviara ...** I would be grateful if you
would send me ...; ~**se** *vr*: **¡se agradece!**
much obliged!

agradecido, a [aɣraðe'θiðo, a] *adj* grateful;
¡muy ~! thanks a lot!

agradecimiento [aɣraðeθi'mjento] *nm*
thanks *pl*; gratitude.

agradezca [aɣra'ðeθka] *etc vb V* **agradecer**.

agrado [a'ɣraðo] *nm*: **ser de tu** *etc* ~ to be
to your *etc* liking.

agrandar [aɣran'dar] *vt* to enlarge; (*fig*) to
exaggerate; ~**se** *vr* to get bigger.

agrario, a [a'ɣrarjo, a] *adj* agrarian, land
cpd; (*política*) agricultural, farming
cpd.

agravante [aɣra'βante] *adj* aggravating
♦ *nf* complication; **con la** ~ **de que ...**
with the further difficulty that ...

agravar [aɣra'βar] *vt* (*pesar sobre*) to make
heavier; (*irritar*) to aggravate; ~**se** *vr* to
worsen, get worse.

agraviar [aɣra'βjar] *vt* to offend; (*ser
injusto con*) to wrong; ~**se** *vr* to take
offence.

agravio [a'ɣraβjo] *nm* offence; wrong;

(*JUR*) grievance.

agraz [a'ɣraθ] *nm* (*uva*) sour grape; **en** ~ (*fig*) immature.

agredir [aɣre'ðir] *vt* to attack.

agregado [aɣre'ɣaðo] *nm* aggregate; (*persona*) attaché; (*profesor*) assistant professor.

agregar [aɣre'ɣar] *vt* to gather; (*añadir*) to add; (*persona*) to appoint.

agregue [a'ɣreɣe] *etc vb V* **agregar**.

agresión [aɣre'sjon] *nf* aggression; (*ataque*) attack.

agresivo, a [aɣre'siβo, a] *adj* aggressive.

agreste [a'ɣreste] *adj* (*rural*) rural; (*fig*) rough.

agriar [a'ɣrjar] *vt* (*fig*) to (turn) sour; **~se** *vr* to turn sour.

agrícola [a'ɣrikola] *adj* farming *cpd*, agricultural.

agricultor, a [aɣrikul'tor, a] *nm/f* farmer.

agricultura [aɣrikul'tura] *nf* agriculture, farming.

agridulce [aɣri'ðulθe] *adj* bittersweet; (*CULIN*) sweet and sour.

agrietarse [aɣrje'tarse] *vr* to crack; (*la piel*) to chap.

agrimensor, a [aɣrimen'sor, a] *nm/f* surveyor.

agringado, a [aɣrin'gaðo, a] *adj* gringolike.

agrio, a ['aɣrjo, a] *adj* bitter.

agronomía [aɣrono'mia] *nf* agronomy, agriculture.

agrónomo, a [a'ɣronomo, a] *nm/f* agronomist, agricultural expert.

agropecuario, a [aɣrope'kwarjo, a] *adj* farming *cpd*, agricultural.

agrupación [aɣrupa'θjon] *nf* group; (*acto*) grouping.

agrupar [aɣru'par] *vt* to group; (*INFORM*) to block; **~se** *vr* (*POL*) to form a group; (*juntarse*) to gather.

agua ['aɣwa] *nf* water; (*NAUT*) wake; (*ARQ*) slope of a roof; **~s** *nfpl* (*de joya*) water *sg*, sparkle *sg*; (*MED*) water *sg*, urine *sg*; (*NAUT*) waters; **~s abajo/arriba** downstream/upstream; ~ **bendita/ destilada/potable** holy/distilled/drinking water; ~ **caliente** hot water; ~ **corriente** running water; ~ **de colonia** eau de cologne; ~ **mineral (con/sin gas)** (fizzy/ non-fizzy) mineral water; **~s jurisdiccionales** territorial waters; **~s mayores** excrement *sg*; ~ **pasada no mueve molino** it's no use crying over spilt milk; **estar con el** ~ **al cuello** to be up to one's neck; **venir como** ~ **de mayo** to be a godsend.

aguacate [aɣwa'kate] *nm* avocado (pear).

aguacero [aɣwa'θero] *nm* (heavy) shower, downpour.

aguachirle [aɣwa'tʃirle] *nm* (*bebida*) slops *pl*.

aguado, a [a'ɣwaðo, a] *adj* watery, watered down ♦ *nf* (*AGR*) watering place; (*NAUT*) water supply; (*ARTE*) watercolour.

aguafiestas [aɣwa'fjestas] *nm/f inv* spoilsport.

aguafuerte [aɣwa'fwerte] *nf* etching.

aguaitar [aɣwai'tar] *vt* (*AM*) to watch.

aguanieve [aɣwa'njeβe] *nf* sleet.

aguantable [aɣwan'taβle] *adj* bearable, tolerable.

aguantar [aɣwan'tar] *vt* to bear, put up with; (*sostener*) to hold up ♦ *vi* to last; **~se** *vr* to restrain o.s.; **no sé cómo aguanta** I don't know how he can take it.

aguante [a'ɣwante] *nm* (*paciencia*) patience; (*resistencia*) endurance; (*DEPORTE*) stamina.

aguar [a'ɣwar] *vt* to water down; (*fig*): ~ **la fiesta a algn** to spoil sb's fun.

aguardar [aɣwar'ðar] *vt* to wait for.

aguardentoso, a [aɣwarðen'toso, a] *adj* (*pey: voz*) husky, gruff.

aguardiente [aɣwar'ðjente] *nm* brandy, liquor.

aguarrás [aɣwa'rras] *nm* turpentine.

aguce [a'ɣuθe] *etc vb V* **aguzar**.

agudeza [aɣu'ðeθa] *nf* sharpness; (*ingenio*) wit.

agudice [aɣu'ðiθe] *etc vb V* **agudizar**.

agudizar [aɣuði'θar] *vt* to sharpen; (*crisis*) to make worse; **~se** *vr* to worsen, deteriorate.

agudo, a [a'ɣuðo, a] *adj* sharp; (*voz*) high-pitched, piercing; (*dolor, enfermedad*) acute.

agüe ['aɣwe] *etc vb V* **aguar**.

agüero [a'ɣwero] *nm*: **buen/mal** ~ good/ bad omen; **ser de buen** ~ to augur well; **pájaro de mal** ~ bird of ill omen.

aguerrido, a [aɣe'rriðo, a] *adj* hardened; (*fig*) experienced.

aguijar [aɣi'xar] *vt* to goad; (*incitar*) to urge on ♦ *vi* to hurry along.

aguijón [aɣi'xon] *nm* sting; (*fig*) spur.

aguijonear [aɣixone'ar] *vt* = **aguijar**.

águila ['aɣila] *nf* eagle; (*fig*) genius.

aguileño, a [aɣi'leɲo, a] *adj* (*nariz*) aquiline; (*rostro*) sharp-featured.

aguinaldo [aɣi'naldo] *nm* Christmas box.

aguja [a'ɣuxa] *nf* needle; (*de reloj*) hand; (*ARQ*) spire; (*TEC*) firing-pin; **~s** *nfpl* (*ZOOL*) ribs; (*FERRO*) points.

...ar [aɣuxere'ar] *vt* to make holes in; *(entrar)* to pierce.

...ero [aɣu'xero] *nm* hole; *(COM)* deficit.

...ujetas [aɣu'xetas] *nfpl* stitch *sg*; *(rigidez)* stiffness *sg*.

aguzar [aɣu'θar] *vt* to sharpen; *(fig)* to incite; **~ el oído** to prick up one's ears.

aherrumbrarse [aerrum'brarse] *vr* to get rusty.

ahí [a'i] *adv* there; *(allá)* over there; **de ~ que** so that, with the result that; **~ llega** here he comes; **por ~** *(dirección)* that way; **¡hasta ~ hemos llegado!** so it has come to this!; **¡~ va!** *(objeto)* here it comes!; *(individuo)* there he goes!; **~ donde le ve** as sure as he's standing there.

ahijado, a [ai'xaðo, a] *nm/f* godson/daughter.

ahijar [ai'xar] *vt*: **~ algo a algn** *(fig)* to attribute sth to sb.

ahínco [a'inko] *nm* earnestness; **con ~** eagerly.

ahíto, a [a'ito, a] *adj*: **estoy ~** I'm full up.

ahogado, a [ao'ɣaðo, a] *adj (en agua)* drowned; *(emoción)* pent-up; *(grito)* muffled.

ahogar [ao'ɣar] *vt (en agua)* to drown; *(asfixiar)* to suffocate, smother; *(fuego)* to put out; **~se** *vr (en agua)* to drown; *(por asfixia)* to suffocate.

ahogo [a'oɣo] *nm (MED)* breathlessness; *(fig)* distress; *(problema económico)* financial difficulty.

ahogue [a'oɣe] *etc vb V* **ahogar**.

ahondar [aon'dar] *vt* to deepen, make deeper; *(fig)* to go deeply into ♦ *vi*: **~ en** to go deeply into.

ahora [a'ora] *adv* now; *(hace poco)* a moment ago, just now; *(dentro de poco)* in a moment; **~ voy** I'm coming; **~ mismo** right now; **~ bien** now then; **por ~** for the present.

ahorcado, a [aor'kaðo, a] *nm/f* hanged person.

ahorcar [aor'kar] *vt* to hang; **~se** *vr* to hang o.s.

ahorita [ao'rita], **ahoritita** [aori'tita] *adv* *(esp AM: fam)* right now.

ahorque [a'orke] *etc vb V* **ahorcar**.

ahorrar [ao'rrar] *vt (dinero)* to save; *(esfuerzos)* to save, avoid; **~se** *vr*: **~se molestias** to save o.s. trouble.

ahorrativo, a [aorra'tißo, a] *adj* thrifty.

ahorro [a'orro] *nm (acto)* saving; *(frugalidad)* thrift; **~s** *nmpl* savings.

ahuecar [awe'kar] *vt* to hollow (out); *(voz)* to deepen ♦ *vi*: **¡ahueca!** *(fam)* beat it!

(fam); **~se** *vr* to give o.s. airs.

ahueque [a'weke] *etc vb V* **ahuecar**.

ahumar [au'mar] *vt* to smoke, cure; *(llenar de humo)* to fill with smoke ♦ *vi* to smoke; **~se** *vr* to fill with smoke.

ahuyentar [aujen'tar] *vt* to drive off, frighten off; *(fig)* to dispel.

AI *nf abr* (= *Amnistía Internacional*) AI.

aimara [ai'mara], **aimará** [aima'ra] *adj, nm/f* Aymara.

aindiado, a [aindi'aðo, a] *adj (AM)* Indian-like.

airado, a [ai'raðo, a] *adj* angry.

airar [ai'rar] *vt* to anger; **~se** *vr* to get angry.

aire ['aire] *nm* air; *(viento)* wind; *(corriente)* draught; *(MUS)* tune; **~s** *nmpl*: **darse ~s** to give o.s. airs; **al ~ libre** in the open air; **~ acondicionado** air conditioning; **tener ~ de** to look like; **estar de buen/mal ~** to be in a good/bad mood; **estar en el ~** *(RADIO)* to be on the air; *(fig)* to be up in the air.

airear [aire'ar] *vt* to ventilate; *(fig: asunto)* to air; **~se** *vr* to take the air.

airoso, a [ai'roso, a] *adj* windy; draughty; *(fig)* graceful.

aislado, a [ais'laðo, a] *adj (remoto)* isolated; *(incomunicado)* cut off; *(ELEC)* insulated.

aislante [ais'lante] *nm (ELEC)* insulator.

aislar [ais'lar] *vt* to isolate; *(ELEC)* to insulate; **~se** *vr* to cut o.s. off.

ajar [a'xar] *vt* to spoil; *(fig)* to abuse; **~se** *vr* to get crumpled; *(fig: piel)* to get wrinkled.

ajardinado, a [axarði'naðo, a] *adj* landscaped.

ajedrez [axe'ðreθ] *nm* chess.

ajenjo [a'xenxo] *nm (bebida)* absinth(e).

ajeno, a [a'xeno, a] *adj (que pertenece a otro)* somebody else's; **~ a** foreign to; **~ de** free from, devoid of; **por razones ajenas a nuestra voluntad** for reasons beyond our control.

ajetreado, a [axetre'aðo, a] *adj* busy.

ajetrearse [axetre'arse] *vr (atarearse)* to bustle about; *(fatigarse)* to tire o.s. out.

ajetreo [axe'treo] *nm* bustle.

ají [a'xi] *nm* chil(l)i, red pepper; *(salsa)* chil(l)i sauce.

ajiaco [axi'ako] *nm (AM)* potato and chil(l)i stew.

ajilimoje [axili'moxe] *nm* sauce of garlic and pepper; **~s** *nmpl (fam)* odds and ends.

ajo ['axo] *nm* garlic; **~ porro** *o* **puerro** leek; **(tieso) como un ~** *(fam)* snobbish; **estar**

en el ~ to be mixed up in it.

ajorca [a'xorka] nf bracelet.

ajuar [a'xwar] nm household furnishings pl; (de novia) trousseau; (de niño) layette.

ajustado, a [axus'taðo, a] adj (tornillo) tight; (cálculo) right; (ropa) tight(-fitting); (DEPORTE: resultado) close.

ajustar [axus'tar] vt (adaptar) to adjust; (encajar) to fit; (TEC) to engage; (TIP) to make up; (apretar) to tighten; (concertar) to agree (on); (reconciliar) to reconcile; (cuenta) to settle ♦ vi to fit.

ajuste [a'xuste] nm adjustment; (COSTURA) fitting; (acuerdo) compromise; (de cuenta) settlement; (INFORM) patch.

al [al] = a + el; V a.

ala ['ala] nf wing; (de sombrero) brim; (futbolista) winger; ~ **delta** hang-glider; **andar con el ~ caída** to be downcast; **cortar las ~s a algn** to clip sb's wings; **dar ~s a algn** to encourage sb.

alabanza [ala'βanθa] nf praise.

alabar [ala'βar] vt to praise.

alacena [ala'θena] nf cupboard (BRIT), closet (US).

alacrán [ala'kran] nm scorpion.

ALADI [a'laði] nf abr = Asociación Latinoamericana de Integración.

alado, a [a'laðo, a] adj winged.

ALALC [a'lalk] nf abr (= Asociación Latinoamericana de Libre Comercio) LAFTA.

alambicado, a [alambi'kaðo, a] adj distilled; (fig) affected.

alambicar [alambi'kar] vt to distil.

alambique [alam'bike] etc vb V alambicar ♦ nm still.

alambrada [alam'braða] nf, **alambrado** [alam'braðo] nm wire fence; (red) wire netting.

alambre [a'lambre] nm wire; ~ **de púas** barbed wire.

alambrista [alam'brista] nm/f tightrope walker.

alameda [ala'meða] nf (plantío) poplar grove; (lugar de paseo) avenue, boulevard.

álamo ['alamo] nm poplar; ~ **temblón** aspen.

alano [a'lano] nm mastiff.

alarde [a'larðe] nm show, display; **hacer ~ de** to boast of.

alardear [alarðe'ar] vi to boast.

alargador [alarɣa'ðor] nm extension cable o lead.

alargar [alar'ɣar] vt to lengthen, extend; (paso) to hasten; (brazo) to stretch out; (cuerda) to pay out; (conversación) to spin out; ~**se** vr to get longer.

alargue [a'larɣe] etc vb V alargar.

alarido [ala'riðo] nm shriek.

alarma [a'larma] nf alarm; **voz de ~** warning note; **dar la ~** to raise the alarm.

alarmante [alar'mante] adj alarming.

alarmar [alar'mar] vt to alarm; ~**se** vr to get alarmed.

alavés, esa [ala'βes, esa] adj of Álava ♦ nm/f native o inhabitant of Álava.

alazán [ala'θan] nm sorrel.

alba ['alβa] nf dawn.

albacea [alβa'θea] nm/f executor/executrix.

albaceteño, a [alβaθe'teɲo, a] adj of Albacete ♦ nm/f native o inhabitant of Albacete.

albahaca [al'βaka] nf (BOT) basil.

Albania [al'βanja] nf Albania.

albañal [alβa'ɲal] nm drain, sewer.

albañil [alβa'ɲil] nm bricklayer; (cantero) mason.

albarán [alβa'ran] nm (COM) invoice.

albarda [al'βarða] nf packsaddle.

albaricoque [alβari'koke] nm apricot.

albedrío [alβe'ðrio] nm: **libre ~** free will.

alberca [al'βerka] nf reservoir; (AM) swimming pool.

albergar [alβer'ɣar] vt to shelter; (esperanza) to cherish; ~**se** vr (refugiarse) to shelter; (alojarse) to lodge.

albergue [al'βerɣe] etc vb V albergar ♦ nm shelter, refuge; ~ **de juventud** youth hostel.

albis ['alβis] adv: **quedarse en ~** not to have a clue.

albóndiga [al'βondiɣa] nf meatball.

albor [al'βor] nm whiteness; (amanecer) dawn.

alborada [alβo'raða] nf dawn; (diana) reveille.

alborear [alβore'ar] vi to dawn.

albornoz [alβor'noθ] nm (de los árabes) burnous; (para el baño) bathrobe.

alboroce [alβo'roθe] etc vb V alborozar.

alborotar [alβoro'tar] vi to make a row ♦ vt to agitate, stir up; ~**se** vr to get excited; (mar) to get rough.

alboroto [alβo'roto] nm row, uproar.

alborozar [alβoro'θar] vt to gladden; ~**se** vr to rejoice, be overjoyed.

alborozo [alβo'roθo] nm joy.

albricias [al'βriθjas] nfpl: ¡~! good news!

álbum, pl **álbums** o **álbumes** ['alβum] nm album.

albumen [al'βumen] nm egg white, albumen.

alcabala [alka'βala] nf (AM) roadblock.

alcachofa [alka't∫ofa] *nf* (globe) artichoke; (*TIP*) golf ball; (de ducha) shower head.

alcahueta [alka'weta] *nf* procuress.

alcahuete [alka'wete] *nm* pimp.

alcalde, esa [al'kalde, alkal'desa] *nm/f* mayor(ess).

alcaldía [alkal'dia] *nf* mayoralty; (*lugar*) mayor's office.

álcali ['alkali] *nm* (*QUÍMICA*) alkali.

alcance [al'kanθe] *etc vb V* **alcanzar** ♦ *nm* (*MIL, RADIO*) range; (*fig*) scope; (*COM*) adverse balance, deficit; **estar al/fuera del ~ de algn** to be within/beyond one's reach; (*fig*) to be within one's powers/ over one's head; **de gran ~** (*MIL*) long-range; (*fig*) far-reaching.

alcancía [alkan'θia] *nf* money box.

alcanfor [alkan'for] *nm* camphor.

alcantarilla [alkanta'riʎa] *nf* (de aguas cloacales) sewer; (en la calle) gutter.

alcanzar [alkan'θar] *vt* (algo: con la mano, el pie) to reach; (alguien: en el camino etc) to catch up (with); (autobús) to catch; (suj: bala) to hit, strike ♦ *vi* (ser suficiente) to be enough; **~ algo a algn** to hand sth to sb; **alcánzame la sal, por favor** pass the salt please; **~ a hacer** to manage to do.

alcaparra [alka'parra] *nf* (*BOT*) caper.

alcatraz [alka'traθ] *nm* gannet.

alcayata [alka'jata] *nf* hook.

alcázar [al'kaθar] *nm* fortress; (*NAUT*) quarter-deck.

alce ['alθe] *etc vb V* **alzar**.

alcista [al'θista] *adj* (*COM, ECON*): **mercado ~** bull market; **la tendencia ~** the upward trend ♦ *nm* speculator.

alcoba [al'koßa] *nf* bedroom.

alcohol [al'kol] *nm* alcohol; **no bebe ~** he doesn't drink (alcohol).

alcoholemia [alkoo'lemia] *nf* blood alcohol level; **prueba de la ~** breath test.

alcoholice [alko'liθe] *etc vb V* **alcoholizarse**.

alcohólico, a [al'koliko, a] *adj, nm/f* alcoholic.

alcoholímetro [alko'limetro] *nm* Breathalyser ®, drunkometer (*US*).

alcoholismo [alko'lismo] *nm* alcoholism.

alcoholizarse [alkoli'θarse] *vr* to become an alcoholic.

alcornoque [alkor'noke] *nm* cork tree; (*fam*) idiot.

alcotana [alko'tana] *nf* pickaxe; (*DEPORTE*) ice-axe.

alcurnia [al'kurnja] *nf* lineage.

alcuza [al'kusa] *nf* (*AM*) cruet.

aldaba [al'daßa] *nf* (door) knocker.

aldea [al'dea] *nf* village.

aldeano, a [alde'ano, a] *adj* village *cpd* ♦ *nm/f* villager.

ale ['ale] *excl* come on!, let's go!

aleación [alea'θjon] *nf* alloy.

aleatorio, a [alea'torjo, a] *adj* random, contingent; **acceso ~** (*INFORM*) random access.

aleccionador, a [alekθjona'ðor, a] *adj* instructive.

aleccionar [alekθjo'nar] *vt* to instruct; (adiestrar) to train.

aledaño, a [ale'ðaɲo, a] *adj*: **~ a** bordering on ♦ *nmpl*: **~s** outskirts.

alegación [aleɣa'θjon] *nf* allegation.

alegar [ale'ɣar] *vt* (dificultad etc) to plead; (*JUR*) to allege ♦ *vi* (*AM*) to argue; **~ que ...** to give as an excuse that ...

alegato [ale'ɣato] *nm* (*JUR*) allegation; (escrito) indictment; (declaración) statement; (*AM*) argument.

alegoría [aleɣo'ria] *nf* allegory.

alegrar [ale'ɣrar] *vt* (causar alegría) to cheer (up); (fuego) to poke; (fiesta) to liven up; **~se** *vr* (*fam*) to get merry o tight; **~se de** to be glad about.

alegre [a'leɣre] *adj* happy, cheerful; (*fam*) merry, tight; (licencioso) risqué, blue.

alegría [ale'ɣria] *nf* happiness; merriment; **~ vital** joie de vivre.

alegrón [ale'ɣron] *nm* (*fig*) sudden joy.

alegue [a'leɣe] *etc vb V* **alegar**.

alejamiento [alexa'mjento] *nm* removal; (distancia) remoteness.

alejar [ale'xar] *vt* to move away, remove; (*fig*) to estrange; **~se** *vr* to move away.

alelado, a [ale'laðo, a] *adj* (bobo) foolish.

alelar [ale'lar] *vt* to bewilder.

aleluya [ale'luja] *nm* (canto) hallelujah.

alemán, ana [ale'man, ana] *adj, nm/f* German ♦ *nm* (lengua) German.

Alemania [ale'manja] *nf* Germany; **~ Occidental/Oriental** West/East Germany.

alentador, a [alenta'ðor, a] *adj* encouraging.

alentar [alen'tar] *vt* to encourage.

alergia [a'lerxja] *nf* allergy.

alero [a'lero] *nm* (de tejado) eaves *pl*; (de foca, *DEPORTE*) flipper; (*AUTO*) mudguard.

alerta [a'lerta] *adj inv, nm* alert.

aleta [a'leta] *nf* (de pez) fin; (de ave) wing; (de coche) mudguard.

aletargar [aletar'ɣar] *vt* to make drowsy; (entumecer) to make numb; **~se** *vr* to grow drowsy; to become numb.

aletargue [ale'tarɣe] *etc vb V* **aletargar**.

aletear [alete'ar] *vi* to flutter; (ave) to flap its wings; (individuo) to wave one's arms.

alevín [ale'ßin] *nm* fry, young fish.

alevosía [aleßo'sia] *nf* treachery.

alfabetización [alfaßetiθa'θjon] *nf*: **campaña de** ~ literacy campaign.

alfabeto [alfa'ßeto] *nm* alphabet.

alfajor [alfa'xor] *nm* (*ESP: polvorón*) *cake eaten at Christmas time.*

alfalfa [al'falfa] *nf* alfalfa, lucerne.

alfaque [al'fake] *nm* (*NAUT*) bar, sandbank.

alfar [al'far] *nm* (*taller*) potter's workshop; (*arcilla*) clay.

alfarería [alfare'ria] *nf* pottery; (*tienda*) pottery shop.

alfarero [alfa'rero] *nm* potter.

alféizar [al'feiθar] *nm* window-sill.

alférez [al'fereθ] *nm* (*MIL*) second lieutenant; (*NAUT*) ensign.

alfil [al'fil] *nm* (*AJEDREZ*) bishop.

alfiler [alfi'ler] *nm* pin; (*broche*) clip; (*pinza*) clothes peg (*BRIT*) *o* pin (*US*); ~ **de gancho** (*AM*) safety pin; **prendido con** ~**es** shaky.

alfiletero [alfile'tero] *nm* needle case.

alfombra [al'fombra] *nf* carpet; (*más pequeña*) rug. ♦ **alfombrar** [alfom'brar] *vt* to carpet.

alfombrilla [alfom'briʎa] *nf* rug, mat; (*INFORM*) mouse mat *o* pad.

alforja [al'forxa] *nf* saddlebag.

alforza [al'forθa] *nf* pleat.

algarabía [alɣara'ßia] *nf* (*fam*) gibberish; (*griterío*) hullabaloo.

algarada [alɣa'raða] *nf* outcry; **hacer** *o* **levantar una** ~ to kick up a tremendous fuss.

Algarbe [al'xarße] *nm*: **el** ~ the Algarve.

algarroba [alɣa'rroßa] *nf* carob.

algarrobo [alɣa'rroßo] *nm* carob tree.

algas ['alɣas] *nfpl* seaweed *sg*.

algazara [alɣa'θara] *nf* din, uproar.

álgebra ['alxeßra] *nf* algebra.

álgido, a ['alxiðo, a] *adj* icy; (*momento etc*) crucial, decisive.

algo ['alɣo] *pron* something; (*en frases interrogativas*) anything ♦ *adv* somewhat, rather; **por** ~ **será** there must be some reason for it; **es** ~ **difícil** it's a bit awkward.

algodón [alɣo'ðon] *nm* cotton; (*planta*) cotton plant; ~ **de azúcar** candy floss (*BRIT*), cotton candy (*US*); ~ **hidrófilo** cotton wool (*BRIT*), absorbent cotton (*US*).

algodonero, a [alɣoðo'nero, a] *adj* cotton *cpd* ♦ *nm/f* cotton grower ♦ *nm* cotton plant.

algoritmo [alɣo'ritmo] *nm* algorithm.

alguacil [alɣwa'θil] *nm* bailiff; (*TAUR*) mounted official.

alguien ['alɣjen] *pron* someone, somebody; (*en frases interrogativas*) anybody.

alguno, a [al'ɣuno, a] *adj* (*delante de nm*: **algún**) some; (*después de n*): **no tiene talento alguno** he has no talent, he hasn't any talent ♦ *pron* (*alguien*) someone, somebody; **algún que otro libro** some book or other; **algún día iré** I'll go one *o* some day; **sin interés alguno** without the slightest interest; **alguno que otro** an occasional one; **algunos piensan** some (people) think; **alguno de ellos** one of them.

alhaja [a'laxa] *nf* jewel; (*tesoro*) precious object, treasure.

alhelí [ale'li] *nm* wallflower, stock.

aliado, a [a'ljaðo, a] *adj* allied.

alianza [a'ljanθa] *nf* (*POL etc*) alliance; (*anillo*) wedding ring.

aliar [a'ljar] *vt* to ally; ~**se** *vr* to form an alliance.

alias ['aljas] *adv* alias.

alicaído, a [alika'iðo, a] *adj* (*MED*) weak; (*fig*) depressed.

alicantino, a [alikan'tino, a] *adj* of Alicante ♦ *nm/f* native *o* inhabitant of Alicante.

alicatar [alika'tar] *vt* to tile.

alicate(s) [ali'kate(s)] *nm(pl)* pliers *pl*; ~ **de uñas** nail clippers.

aliciente [ali'θjente] *nm* incentive; (*atracción*) attraction.

alienación [aljena'θjon] *nf* alienation.

aliento [a'ljento] *etc vb V* **alentar** ♦ *nm* breath; (*respiración*) breathing; **sin** ~ breathless; **de un** ~ in one breath; (*fig*) in one go.

aligerar [alixe'rar] *vt* to lighten; (*reducir*) to shorten; (*aliviar*) to alleviate; (*mitigar*) to ease.

alijo [a'lixo] *nm* (*NAUT*) unloading; (*contrabando*) smuggled goods.

alimaña [ali'maɲa] *nf* pest.

alimentación [alimenta'θjon] *nf* (*comida*) food; (*acción*) feeding; (*tienda*) grocer's (shop); ~ **continua** (*en fotocopiadora etc*) stream feed.

alimentador [alimenta'ðor] *nm*: ~ **de papel** sheet-feeder.

alimentar [alimen'tar] *vt* to feed; (*nutrir*) to nourish; ~**se** *vr*: ~**se (de)** to feed (on).

alimenticio, a [alimen'tiθjo, a] *adj* food *cpd*; (*nutritivo*) nourishing, nutritious.

alimento [ali'mento] *nm* food; (*nutrición*) nourishment; ~**s** *nmpl* (*JUR*) alimony *sg*.

alimón [ali'mon]: **al** ~ *adv* jointly, together.

alineación [alinea'θjon] *nf* alignment; (*DEPORTE*) line-up.

alineado, a [aline'aðo, a] *adj* (*TIP*): **(no)** ~ **(un)**justified; ~ **a la izquierda/derecha** ranged left/right.

alinear [aline'ar] *vt* to align; (*TIP*) to justify; ~**se** *vr* to line up; ~**se en** to fall in with.

aliñar [ali'ɲar] *vt* (*CULIN*) to dress.

aliño [a'liɲo] *nm* (*CULIN*) dressing.

alisar [ali'sar] *vt* to smooth.

aliso [a'liso] *nm* alder.

alistamiento [alista'mjento] *nm* recruitment.

alistar [ali'star] *vt* to recruit; ~**se** *vr* to enlist; (*inscribirse*) to enrol; (*AM*: *prepararse*) to get ready.

aliviar [ali'βjar] *vt* (*carga*) to lighten; (*persona*) to relieve; (*dolor*) to relieve, alleviate.

alivio [a'liβjo] *nm* alleviation, relief; ~ **de luto** half-mourning.

aljibe [al'xiβe] *nm* cistern.

allá [a'ʎa] *adv* (*lugar*) there; (*por ahí*) over there; (*tiempo*) then; ~ **abajo** down there; **más** ~ further on; **más** ~ **de** beyond; ¡~ **tú!** that's your problem!

allanamiento [aʎana'mjento] *nm* (*AM POLICÍA*) raid, search; ~ **de morada** housebreaking.

allanar [aʎa'nar] *vt* to flatten, level (out); (*igualar*) to smooth (out); (*fig*) to subdue; (*JUR*) to burgle, break into; (*AM POLICÍA*) to raid, search; ~**se** *vr* to fall down; ~**se a** to submit to, accept.

allegado, a [aʎe'ɣaðo, a] *adj* near, close ♦ *nm/f* relation.

allende [a'ʎende] *adv* on the other side ♦ *prep*: ~ **los mares** beyond the seas.

allí [a'ʎi] *adv* there; ~ **mismo** right there; **por** ~ over there; (*por ese camino*) that way.

alma ['alma] *nf* soul; (*persona*) person; (*TEC*) core; **se le cayó el** ~ **a los pies** he became very disheartened; **entregar el** ~ to pass away; **estar con el** ~ **en la boca** to be scared to death; **lo siento en el** ~ I am truly sorry; **tener el** ~ **en un hilo** to have one's heart in one's mouth; **estar como** ~ **en pena** to suffer; **ir como** ~ **que lleva el diablo** to go at breakneck speed.

almacén [alma'θen] *nm* (*depósito*) warehouse, store; (*MIL*) magazine; (*AM*) grocer's shop, foodstore, grocery store (*US*); **(grandes) almacenes** *nmpl* department store *sg*; ~ **depositario** (*COM*) depository.

almacenaje [almaθe'naxe] *nm* storage; ~ **secundario** (*INFORM*) backing storage.

almacenamiento [almaθena'mjento] *nm*

(*INFORM*) storage; ~ **temporal en disco** disk spooling.

almacenar [almaθe'nar] *vt* to store, put in storage; (*INFORM*) to store; (*proveerse*) to stock up with.

almacenero [almaθe'nero] *nm* warehouseman; (*AM*) grocer, shopkeeper.

almanaque [alma'nake] *nm* almanac.

almeja [al'mexa] *nf* clam.

almenas [al'menas] *nfpl* battlements.

almendra [al'mendra] *nf* almond.

almendro [al'mendro] *nm* almond tree.

almeriense [alme'rjense] *adj* of Almería ♦ *nm/f* native *o* inhabitant of Almería.

almiar [al'mjar] *nm* haystack.

almíbar [al'miβar] *nm* syrup.

almidón [almi'ðon] *nm* starch.

almidonado, a [almiðo'naðo, a] *adj* starched.

almidonar [almiðo'nar] *vt* to starch.

almirantazgo [almiran'taθɣo] *nm* admiralty.

almirante [almi'rante] *nm* admiral.

almirez [almi'reθ] *nm* mortar.

almizcle [al'miθkle] *nm* musk.

almizclero [almiθ'klero] *nm* musk deer.

almohada [almo'aða] *nf* pillow; (*funda*) pillowcase.

almohadilla [almoa'ðiʎa] *nf* cushion; (*TEC*) pad; (*AM*) pincushion.

almohadillado, a [almoaðiʎ'ʎaðo, a] *adj* (*acolchado*) padded.

almohadón [almoa'ðon] *nm* large pillow.

almorcé [almor'θe], **almorcemos** [almor'θemos] *etc vb V* **almorzar**.

almorranas [almo'rranas] *nfpl* piles, haemorrhoids (*BRIT*), hemorrhoids (*US*).

almorzar [almor'θar] *vt*: ~ **una tortilla** to have an omelette for lunch ♦ *vi* to (have) lunch.

almuerce [al'mwerθe] *etc vb V* **almorzar**.

almuerzo [al'mwerθo] *etc vb V* **almorzar** ♦ *nm* lunch.

aló [a'lo] *excl* (*esp AM TELEC*) hello!

alocado, a [alo'kaðo, a] *adj* crazy.

alojamiento [aloxa'mjento] *nm* lodging(s) (*pl*); (*viviendas*) housing.

alojar [alo'xar] *vt* to lodge; ~**se** *vr*: ~**se en** to stay at; (*bala*) to lodge in.

alondra [a'londra] *nf* lark, skylark.

alpaca [al'paka] *nf* alpaca.

alpargata [alpar'ɣata] *nf* espadrille.

Alpes ['alpes] *nmpl*: **los** ~ the Alps.

alpinismo [alpi'nismo] *nm* mountaineering, climbing.

alpinista [alpi'nista] *nm/f* mountaineer, climber.

alpino, a [al'pino, a] *adj* alpine.

alpiste [al'piste] *nm* (*semillas*) birdseed; (*AM fam: dinero*) dough; (*fam: alcohol*) booze.

alquería [alke'ria] *nf* farmhouse.

alquilar [alki'lar] *vt* (*suj: propietario: inmuebles*) to let, rent (out); (: *coche*) to hire out; (: *TV*) to rent (out); (*suj: alquilador: inmuebles, TV*) to rent; (: *coche*) to hire; **"se alquila casa"** "house to let (*BRIT*) o to rent (*US*)"

alquiler [alki'ler] *nm* renting, letting; hiring; (*arriendo*) rent; hire charge; **de ~** for hire; **~ de automóviles** car hire.

alquimia [al'kimja] *nf* alchemy.

alquitrán [alki'tran] *nm* tar.

alrededor [alreðe'ðor] *adv* around, about; **~es** *nmpl* surroundings; **~ de** *prep* around, about; **mirar a su ~** to look (round) about one.

Alsacia [al'saθja] *nf* Alsace.

alta ['alta] *nf* (*certificate of*) discharge; **dar a algn de ~** to discharge sb; **darse de ~** (*MIL*) to join, enrol; (*DEPORTE*) to declare o.s. fit.

altanería [altane'ria] *nf* haughtiness, arrogance.

altanero, a [alta'nero, a] *adj* haughty, arrogant.

altar [al'tar] *nm* altar.

altavoz [alta'βoθ] *nm* loudspeaker; (*amplificador*) amplifier.

alteración [altera'θjon] *nf* alteration; (*alboroto*) disturbance; **~ del orden público** breach of the peace.

alterar [alte'rar] *vt* to alter; to disturb; **~se** *vr* (*persona*) to get upset.

altercado [alter'kaðo] *nm* argument.

alternar [alter'nar] *vt* to alternate ♦ *vi*, **~se** *vr* to alternate; (*turnar*) to take turns; **~ con** to mix with.

alternativo, a [alterna'tiβo, a] *adj* alternative; (*alterno*) alternating ♦ *nf* alternative; (*elección*) choice; **alternativas** *nfpl* ups and downs; **tomar la alternativa** (*TAUR*) to become a fully-qualified bullfighter.

alterno, a [al'terno, a] *adj* (*BOT, MAT*) alternate; (*ELEC*) alternating.

alteza [al'teθa] *nf* (*tratamiento*) highness.

altibajos [alti'βaxos] *nmpl* ups and downs.

altillo [al'tiʎo] *nm* (*GEO*) small hill; (*AM*) attic.

altiplanicie [altipla'niθje] *nf*, **altiplano** [alti'plano] *nm* high plateau.

altisonante [altiso'nante] *adj* high-flown, high-sounding.

altitud [alti'tuð] *nf* altitude, height; **a una**

~ de at a height of.

altivez [alti'βeθ] *nf* haughtiness, arrogance.

altivo, a [al'tiβo, a] *adj* haughty, arrogant.

alto, a ['alto, a] *adj* high; (*persona*) tall; (*sonido*) high, sharp; (*noble*) high, lofty; (*GEO, clase*) upper ♦ *nm* halt; (*MUS*) alto; (*GEO*) hill; (*AM*) pile ♦ *adv* (*estar*) high; (*hablar*) loud, loudly ♦ *excl* halt!; **la pared tiene 2 metros de ~** the wall is 2 metres high; **en alta mar** on the high seas; **en voz alta** in a loud voice; **las altas horas de la noche** the small (*BRIT*) o wee (*US*) hours; **en lo ~ de** at the top of; **pasar por ~** to overlook; **~s y bajos** ups and downs; **poner la radio más ~** to turn the radio up; **¡más ~, por favor!** louder, please!

altoparlante [altopar'lante] *nm* (*AM*) loudspeaker.

altramuz [altra'muθ] *nm* lupin.

altruismo [al'truismo] *nm* altruism.

altura [al'tura] *nf* height; (*NAUT*) depth; (*GEO*) latitude; **la pared tiene 1.80 de ~** the wall is 1 metre 80 (cm) high; **a esta ~ del año** at this time of the year; **estar a la ~ de las circunstancias** to rise to the occasion; **ha sido un partido de gran ~** it has been a terrific match.

alubia [a'luβja] *nf* French bean, kidney bean.

alucinación [aluθina'θjon] *nf* hallucination.

alucinante [aluθi'nante] *adj* (*fam: estupendo*) great, super.

alucinar [aluθi'nar] *vi* to hallucinate ♦ *vt* to deceive; (*fascinar*) to fascinate.

alud [a'luð] *nm* avalanche; (*fig*) flood.

aludir [alu'ðir] *vi*: **~ a** to allude to; **darse por aludido** to take the hint; **no te des por aludido** don't take it personally.

alumbrado [alum'braðo] *nm* lighting.

alumbramiento [alumbra'mjento] *nm* lighting; (*MED*) childbirth, delivery.

alumbrar [alum'brar] *vt* to light (up) ♦ *vi* (*iluminar*) to give light; (*MED*) to give birth.

aluminio [alu'minjo] *nm* aluminium (*BRIT*), aluminum (*US*).

alumnado [alum'naðo] *nm* (*UNIV*) student body; (*ESCOL*) pupils *pl*.

alumno, a [a'lumno, a] *nm/f* pupil, student.

alunice [alu'niθe] *etc vb V* **alunizar**.

alunizar [aluni'θar] *vi* to land on the moon.

alusión [alu'sjon] *nf* allusion.

alusivo, a [alu'siβo, a] *adj* allusive.

aluvión [alu'βjon] *nm* (*GEO*) alluvium; (*fig*) flood; **~ de improperios** torrent of abuse.

alvéolo [al'βeolo] *nm* (*ANAT*) alveolus; (*fig*)

network.

alza ['alθa] *nf* rise; (*MIL*) sight; ~**s fijas/ graduables** fixed/adjustable sights; **al** *o* **en** ~ (*precio*) rising; **jugar al** ~ to speculate on a rising *o* bull market; **cotizarse** *o* **estar en** ~ to be rising.

alzado, a [al'θaðo, a] *adj* (*gen*) raised; (*COM: precio*) fixed; (: *quiebra*) fradulent; **por un tanto** ~ for a lump sum ♦ *nf* (*de caballos*) height; (*JUR*) appeal.

alzamiento [alθa'mjento] *nm* (*aumento*) rise, increase; (*acción*) lifting, raising; (*mejor postura*) higher bid; (*rebelión*) rising; (*COM*) fraudulent bankruptcy.

alzar [al'θar] *vt* to lift (up); (*precio, muro*) to raise; (*cuello de abrigo*) to turn up; (*AGR*) to gather in; (*TIP*) to gather; ~**se** *vr* to get up, rise; (*rebelarse*) to revolt; (*COM*) to go fraudulently bankrupt; (*JUR*) to appeal; ~**se con el premio** to carry off the prize.

a.m. *abr* (*AM*: = *ante meridiem*) a.m.

ama ['ama] *nf* lady of the house; (*dueña*) owner; (*institutriz*) governess; (*madre adoptiva*) foster mother; ~ **de casa** housewife; ~ **de cría** *o* **de leche** wet-nurse; ~ **de llaves** housekeeper.

amabilidad [amaβili'ðað] *nf* kindness; (*simpatía*) niceness.

amabilísimo, a [amaβi'lisimo, a] *adj superlativo de* **amable**.

amable [a'maβle] *adj* kind; nice.

amaestrado, a [amaes'traðo, a] *adj* (*animal*) trained; (: *en circo etc*) performing.

amaestrar [amaes'trar] *vt* to train.

amagar [ama'ɣar] *vt, vi* to threaten.

amago [a'maɣo] *nm* threat; (*gesto*) threatening gesture; (*MED*) symptom.

amague [a'maɣe] *etc vb V* **amagar**.

amainar [amai'nar] *vt* (*NAUT*) to lower, take in; (*fig*) to calm ♦ *vi*, ~**se** *vr* to drop, die down; **el viento amaina** the wind is dropping.

amalgama [amal'ɣama] *nf* amalgam.

amalgamar [amalɣa'mar] *vt* to amalgamate; (*combinar*) to combine, mix.

amamantar [amaman'tar] *vt* to suckle, nurse.

amancebarse [amanθe'βarse] *vr* (*pareja*) to live together.

amanecer [amane'θer] *vi* to dawn; (*fig*) to appear, begin to show ♦ *nm* dawn; **el niño amaneció afiebrado** the child woke up with a fever.

amanerado, a [amane'raðo, a] *adj* affected.

amanezca [ama'neθka] *etc vb V* **amanecer**.

amansar [aman'sar] *vt* to tame; (*persona*) to subdue; ~**se** *vr* (*persona*) to calm down.

amante [a'mante] *adj*: ~ **de** fond of ♦ *nm/f* lover.

amanuense [ama'nwense] *nm* (*escribiente*) scribe; (*copista*) copyist; (*POL*) secretary.

amañar [ama'ɲar] *vt* (*gen*) to do skilfully; (*pey: resultado*) to alter.

amaño [a'maɲo] *nm* (*habilidad*) skill; ~**s** *nmpl* (*TEC*) tools; (*fig*) tricks.

amapola [ama'pola] *nf* poppy.

amar [a'mar] *vt* to love.

amargado, a [amar'ɣaðo, a] *adj* bitter; embittered.

amargar [amar'ɣar] *vt* to make bitter; (*fig*) to embitter; ~**se** *vr* to become embittered.

amargo, a [a'marɣo, a] *adj* bitter.

amargor [amar'ɣor] *nm* (*sabor*) bitterness; (*fig*) grief.

amargue [a'marɣe] *etc vb V* **amargar**.

amargura [amar'ɣura] *nf* = **amargor**.

amarillento, a [amari'ʎento, a] *adj* yellowish; (*tez*) sallow.

amarillismo [amari'ʎismo] *nm* (*de prensa*) sensationalist journalism.

amarillo, a [ama'riʎo, a] *adj, nm* yellow.

amarra [a'marra] *nf* (*NAUT*) mooring line; ~**s** *nfpl* (*fig*) protection *sg*; **tener buenas** ~**s** to have good connections; **soltar** ~**s** to set off.

amarrar [ama'rrar] *vt* to moor; (*sujetar*) to tie up.

amartillar [amarti'ʎar] *vt* (*fusil*) to cock.

amasar [ama'sar] *vt* to knead; (*mezclar*) to mix, prepare; (*confeccionar*) to concoct.

amasijo [ama'sixo] *nm* kneading; mixing; (*fig*) hotchpotch.

amateur ['amatur] *nm/f* amateur.

amatista [ama'tista] *nf* amethyst.

amazacotado, a [amaθako'taðo, a] *adj* (*terreno, arroz etc*) lumpy.

amazona [ama'θona] *nf* horsewoman.

Amazonas [ama'θonas] *nm*: **el (Río)** ~ the Amazon.

ambages [am'baxes] *nmpl*: **sin** ~ in plain language.

ámbar ['ambar] *nm* amber.

Amberes [am'beres] *nm* Antwerp.

ambición [ambi'θjon] *nf* ambition.

ambicionar [ambiθjo'nar] *vt* to aspire to.

ambicioso, a [ambi'θjoso, a] *adj* ambitious.

ambidextro, a [ambi'ðekstro, a] *adj* ambidextrous.

ambientación [ambjenta'θjon] *nf* (*CINE, LIT etc*) setting; (*RADIO etc*) sound effects *pl*.

ambientador – amortización

ambientador [ambjenta'ðor] *nm* air freshener.

ambientar [ambjen'tar] *vt* (*gen*) to give an atmosphere to; (*LIT etc*) to set.

ambiente [am'bjente] *nm* (*tb fig*) atmosphere; (*medio*) environment; (*AM*) room.

ambigüedad [ambiɣwe'ðað] *nf* ambiguity.

ambiguo, a [am'biɣwo, a] *adj* ambiguous.

ámbito ['ambito] *nm* (*campo*) field; (*fig*) scope.

ambos, as ['ambos, as] *adj pl*, *pron pl* both.

ambulancia [ambu'lanθja] *nf* ambulance.

ambulante [ambu'lante] *adj* travelling, itinerant; (*biblioteca*) mobile.

ambulatorio [ambula'torio] *nm* state health-service clinic.

ameba [a'meβa] *nf* amoeba.

amedrentar [ameðren'tar] *vt* to scare.

amén [a'men] *excl* amen; ~ **de** *prep* besides, in addition to; **en un decir** ~ in the twinkling of an eye; **decir** ~ **a todo** to have no mind of one's own.

amenace [ame'naθe] *etc vb V* **amenazar**.

amenaza [ame'naθa] *nf* threat.

amenazar [amena'θar] *vt* to threaten ♦ *vi*: ~ **con hacer** to threaten to do.

amenidad [ameni'ðað] *nf* pleasantness.

ameno, a [a'meno, a] *adj* pleasant.

América [a'merika] *nf* (*continente*) America, the Americas; (*EEUU*) America; (*Hispanoa~*) Latin *o* South America; ~ **del Norte/del Sur** North/South America; ~ **Central/Latina** Central/Latin America.

americanismo [amerika'nismo] *nm* Americanism.

americano, a [ameri'kano, a] *adj*, *nm/f* (*V* **América**) American; Latin *o* South American ♦ *nf* coat, jacket.

americe [ame'riθe] *etc vb V* **amerizar**.

amerindio, a [ame'rindjo, a] *adj*, *nm/f* Amerindian, American Indian

amerizaje [ameri'θaxe] *nm* (*AVIAT*) landing (on the sea).

amerizar [ameri'θar] *vi* (*AVIAT*) to land (on the sea).

ametralladora [ametraʎa'ðora] *nf* machine gun.

amianto [a'mjanto] *nm* asbestos.

amigable [ami'ɣaβle] *adj* friendly.

amígdala [a'miɣðala] *nf* tonsil.

amigdalitis [amiɣða'litis] *nf* tonsillitis.

amigo, a [a'miɣo, a] *adj* friendly ♦ *nm/f* friend; (*amante*) lover; ~ **de lo ajeno** thief; ~ **corresponsal** penfriend; **hacerse** ~**s** to become friends; **ser** ~ **de** to like, be fond of; **ser muy** ~**s** to be close friends.

amigote [ami'ɣote] *nm* mate (*BRIT*), buddy.

amilanar [amila'nar] *vt* to scare; ~**se** *vr* to get scared.

aminorar [amino'rar] *vt* to diminish; (*reducir*) to reduce; ~ **la marcha** to slow down.

amistad [amis'tað] *nf* friendship; ~**es** *nfpl* friends.

amistoso, a [amis'toso, a] *adj* friendly.

amnesia [am'nesja] *nf* amnesia.

amnistía [amnis'tia] *nf* amnesty.

amnistiar [amnis'tjar] *vt* to amnesty, grant an amnesty to.

amo ['amo] *nm* owner; (*jefe*) boss.

amodorrarse [amoðo'rrarse] *vr* to get sleepy.

amolar [amo'lar] *vt* to annoy.

amoldar [amol'dar] *vt* to mould; (*adaptar*) to adapt.

amonestación [amonesta'θjon] *nf* warning; **amonestaciones** *nfpl* marriage banns.

amonestar [amones'tar] *vt* to warn; to publish the banns of.

amoniaco [amo'njako] *nm* ammonia.

amontonar [amonto'nar] *vt* to collect, pile up; ~**se** *vr* (*gente*) to crowd together; (*acumularse*) to pile up; (*datos*) to accumulate; (*desastres*) to come one on top of another.

amor [a'mor] *nm* love; (*amante*) lover; **hacer el** ~ to make love; ~ **interesado** cupboard love; ~ **propio** self-respect; **por (el)** ~ **de Dios** for God's sake; **estar al** ~ **de la lumbre** to be close to the fire.

amoratado, a [amora'taðo, a] *adj* purple, blue with cold; (*con cardenales*) bruised.

amordace [amor'ðaθe] *etc vb V* **amordazar**.

amordazar [amorða'θar] *vt* to muzzle; (*fig*) to gag.

amorfo, a [a'morfo, a] *adj* amorphous, shapeless.

amorío [amo'rio] *nm* (*fam*) love affair.

amoroso, a [amo'roso, a] *adj* affectionate, loving.

amortajar [amorta'xar] *vt* (*fig*) to shroud.

amortice [amor'tiθe] *etc vb V* **amortizar**.

amortiguador [amortiɣwa'ðor] *nm* shock absorber; (*parachoques*) bumper; (*silenciador*) silencer; ~**es** *nmpl* (*AUTO*) suspension *sg*.

amortiguar [amorti'ɣwar] *vt* to deaden; (*ruido*) to muffle; (*color*) to soften.

amortigüe [amor'tiɣwe] *etc vb V* **amortiguar**.

amortización [amortiθa'θjon] *nf* redemption; repayment; (*COM*) capital allowance.

amortizar [amorti'θar] *vt* (*ECON: bono*) to redeem; (: *capital*) to write off; (: *préstamo*) to pay off.

amoscarse [amos'karse] *vr* to get cross.

amosque [a'moske] *etc vb* V **amoscarse**.

amotinar [amoti'nar] *vt* to stir up, incite (to riot); **~se** *vr* to mutiny.

amparar [ampa'rar] *vt* to protect; **~se** *vr* to seek protection; (*de la lluvia etc*) to shelter.

amparo [am'paro] *nm* help, protection; **al ~ de** under the protection of.

amperímetro [ampe'rimetro] *nm* ammeter.

amperio [am'perjo] *nm* ampère, amp.

ampliable [am'pljaßle] *adj* (*INFORM*) expandable.

ampliación [amplja'θjon] *nf* enlargement; (*extensión*) extension.

ampliar [am'pljar] *vt* to enlarge; to extend.

amplificación [amplifika'θjon] *nf* enlargement.

amplificador [amplifika'ðor] *nm* amplifier.

amplificar [amplifi'kar] *vt* to amplify.

amplifique [ampli'fike] *etc vb* V **amplificar**.

amplio, a ['ampljo, a] *adj* spacious; (*falda etc*) full; (*extenso*) extensive; (*ancho*) wide.

amplitud [ampli'tuð] *nf* spaciousness; extent; (*fig*) amplitude; **~ de miras** broadmindedness; **de gran ~** far-reaching.

ampolla [am'poʎa] *nf* blister; (*MED*) ampoule.

ampolleta [ampo'ʎeta] *nf* (*AM*) (light) bulb.

ampuloso, a [ampu'loso, a] *adj* bombastic, pompous.

amputar [ampu'tar] *vt* to cut off, amputate.

amueblar [amwe'ßlar] *vt* to furnish.

amuleto [amu'leto] *nm* (lucky) charm.

amurallar [amura'ʎar] *vt* to wall up *o* in.

anacarado, a [anaka'raðo, a] *adj* mother-of-pearl *cpd*.

anacardo [ana'karðo] *nm* cashew (nut).

anaconda [ana'konda] *nf* anaconda.

anacronismo [anakro'nismo] *nm* anachronism.

ánade ['anaðe] *nm* duck.

anagrama [ana'ɣrama] *nm* anagram.

anales [a'nales] *nmpl* annals.

analfabetismo [analfaße'tismo] *nm* illiteracy.

analfabeto, a [analfa'ßeto, a] *adj, nm/f* illiterate.

analgésico [anal'xesiko] *nm* painkiller, analgesic.

analice [ana'liθe] *etc vb* V **analizar**.

análisis [a'nalisis] *nm inv* analysis; **~ de costos-beneficios** cost-benefit analysis; **~ de mercados** market research; **~ de sangre** blood test.

analista [ana'lista] *nm/f* (*gen*) analyst; (*POL, HISTORIA*) chronicler; **~ de sistemas** (*INFORM*) systems analyst.

analizar [anali'θar] *vt* to analyse.

analogía [analo'xia] *nf* analogy; **por ~ con** on the analogy of.

analógico, a [ana'loxiko, a] *adj* analogue.

análogo, a [a'naloɣo, a] *adj* analogous, similar.

ananá(s) [ana'na(s)] *nm* pineapple.

anaquel [ana'kel] *nm* shelf.

anaranjado, a [anaran'xaðo, a] *adj* orange (-coloured).

anarquía [anar'kia] *nf* anarchy.

anarquismo [anar'kismo] *nm* anarchism.

anarquista [anar'kista] *nm/f* anarchist.

anatematizar [anatemati'θar] *vt* (*REL*) to anathematize; (*fig*) to curse.

anatemice [anate'miθe] *etc vb* V **anatemizar**.

anatomía [anato'mia] *nf* anatomy.

anca ['anka] *nf* rump, haunch; **~s** *nfpl* (*fam*) behind *sg*; **llevar a algn en ~s** to carry sb behind one.

ancestral [anθes'tral] *adj* (*costumbre*) age-old.

ancho, a ['antʃo, a] *adj* wide; (*falda*) full; (*fig*) liberal ♦ *nm* width; (*FERRO*) gauge; **le viene muy ~ el cargo** (*fig*) the job is too much for him; **ponerse ~** to get conceited; **quedarse tan ~** to go on as if nothing had happened; **estar a sus anchas** to be at one's ease.

anchoa [an'tʃoa] *nf* anchovy.

anchura [an'tʃura] *nf* width; (*extensión*) wideness.

anchuroso, a [antʃu'roso, a] *adj* wide.

anciano, a [an'θjano, a] *adj* old, aged ♦ *nm/f* old man/woman ♦ *nm* elder.

ancla ['ankla] *nf* anchor; **levar ~s** to weigh anchor.

ancladero [ankla'ðero] *nm* anchorage.

anclar [an'klar] *vi* to (drop) anchor.

andadas [an'daðas] *nfpl* (*aventuras*) adventures; **volver a las ~** to backslide.

andaderas [anda'ðeras] *nfpl* baby-walker *sg*.

andadura [anda'ðura] *nf* gait; (*de caballo*) pace.

Andalucía [andalu'θia] *nf* Andalusia.

andaluz, a [anda'luθ, a] *adj, nm/f* Andalusian.

andamio [an'damjo] *nm*, **andamiaje** [anda'mjaxe] *nm* scaffold(ing).

andanada [anda'naða] nf (fig) reprimand;
soltarle a algn una ~ to give sb a rocket.

andante [an'dante] adj: **caballero** ~ knight
errant.

andar [an'dar] vt to go, cover, travel ♦ vi to
go, walk, travel; (funcionar) to go, work;
(estar) to be ♦ nm walk, gait, pace; ~**se** vr
(irse) to go away o off; ~ **a pie/a
caballo/en bicicleta** to go on foot/on
horseback/by bicycle; **¡anda!** (sorpresa)
go on!; **anda en** o **por los 40** he's about
40; **¿en qué andas?** what are you up to?;
andamos mal de dinero/tiempo we're
badly off for money/we're short of time;
~**se por las ramas** to beat about the
bush; **no** ~**se con rodeos** to call a spade
a spade (fam); **todo se andará** all in good
time; **anda por aquí** it's round here
somewhere; ~ **haciendo algo** to be doing
sth.

andariego, a [anda'rjeɣo, a] adj fond of
travelling.

andas ['andas] nfpl stretcher sg.

andén [an'den] nm (FERRO) platform;
(NAUT) quayside; (AM: acera) pavement
(BRIT), sidewalk (US).

Andes ['andes] nmpl: **los** ~ the Andes.

andinismo [andin'ismo] nm (AM)
mountaineering, climbing.

andino, a [an'dino, a] adj Andean, of the
Andes.

Andorra [an'dorra] nf Andorra.

andrajo [an'draxo] nm rag.

andrajoso, a [andra'xoso, a] adj ragged.

andurriales [andu'rrjales] nmpl out-of-the-
way place sg, the sticks; **en esos** ~ in
that godforsaken spot.

anduve [an'duße], **anduviera** [andu'ßjera]
etc vb V andar.

anécdota [a'nekðota] nf anecdote, story.

anegar [ane'ɣar] vt to flood; (ahogar) to
drown; ~**se** vr to drown; (hundirse) to
sink.

anegue [a'neɣe] etc vb V anegar.

anejo, a [a'nexo, a] adj attached ♦ nm (ARQ)
annexe.

anemia [a'nemja] nf anaemia.

anestesia [anes'tesja] nf anaesthetic; ~
general/local general/local anaesthetic.

anestesiar [aneste'sjar] vt to anaesthetize
(BRIT), anesthetize (US).

anestésico [anes'tesiko] nm anaesthetic.

anexar [anek'sar] vt to annex; (documento)
to attach; (INFORM) to append.

anexión [anek'sjon] nf, **anexionamiento**
[aneksjona'mjento] nm annexation.

anexionar [aneksjo'nar] vt to annex; ~**se**
vr: ~ **un país** to annex a country.

anexo, a [a'nekso, a] adj attached ♦ nm
annexe.

anfetamina [anfeta'mina] nf
amphetamine.

anfibio, a [an'fißjo, a] adj amphibious ♦ nm
amphibian.

anfiteatro [anfite'atro] nm amphitheatre;
(TEAT) dress circle.

anfitrión, ona [anfi'trjon, ona] nm/f
host(ess).

ángel ['anxel] nm angel; ~ **de la guarda**
guardian angel; **tener** ~ to have charm.

Ángeles ['anxeles] nmpl: **los** ~ Los
Angeles.

angélico, a [an'xeliko, a], **angelical**
[anxeli'kal] adj angelic(al).

angina [an'xina] nf (MED): ~ **de pecho**
angina; **tener** ~**s** to have a sore throat o
throat infection.

anglicano, a [angli'kano, a] adj, nm/f
Anglican.

anglicismo [angli'θismo] nm anglicism.

anglosajón, ona [anglosa'xon, 'xona] adj,
nm/f Anglo-Saxon.

Angola [an'gola] nf Angola.

angoleño, a [ango'leɲo, a] adj, nm/f
Angolan.

angosto, a [an'gosto, a] adj narrow.

anguila [an'gila] nf eel; ~**s** nfpl slipway sg.

angula [an'gula] nf elver, baby eel.

ángulo ['angulo] nm angle; (esquina)
corner; (curva) bend.

angustia [an'gustja] nf anguish.

angustiar [angus'tjar] vt to distress,
grieve; ~**se** vr to be distressed (por at, on
account of).

anhelante [ane'lante] adj eager; (deseoso)
longing.

anhelar [ane'lar] vt to be eager for; to long
for, desire ♦ vi to pant, gasp.

anhelo [a'nelo] nm eagerness; desire.

anhídrido [a'niðriðo] nm: ~ **carbónico**
carbon dioxide.

anidar [ani'ðar] vt (acoger) to take in,
shelter ♦ vi to nest; (fig) to make one's
home.

anilina [ani'lina] nf aniline.

anilla [a'niʎa] nf ring; (las) ~**s** (DEPORTE)
the rings.

anillo [a'niʎo] nm ring; ~ **de boda** wedding
ring; ~ **de compromiso** engagement
ring; **venir como** ~ **al dedo** to suit to a
tee.

ánima ['anima] nf soul; **las** ~**s** the Angelus
(bell) sg.

animación [anima'θjon] nf liveliness;
(vitalidad) life; (actividad) bustle.

animado, a [ani'maðo, a] adj (vivo) lively;

(*vivaz*) animated; (*concurrido*) bustling; (*alegre*) in high spirits; **dibujos ~s** cartoon *sg*.

animador, a [anima'ðor, a] *nm/f* (*TV*) host(ess) ♦ *nf* (*DEPORTE*) cheerleader.

animadversión [animaðßer'sjon] *nf* ill-will, antagonism.

animal [ani'mal] *adj* animal; (*fig*) stupid ♦ *nm* animal; (*fig*) fool; (*bestia*) brute.

animalada [anima'laða] *nf* (*gen*) silly thing (to do *o* say); (*ultraje*) disgrace.

animar [ani'mar] *vt* (*BIO*) to animate, give life to; (*fig*) to liven up, brighten up, cheer up; (*estimular*) to stimulate; **~se** *vr* to cheer up, feel encouraged; (*decidirse*) to make up one's mind.

ánimo ['animo] *nm* soul, mind; (*valentía*) courage ♦ *excl* cheer up!; **cobrar ~** to take heart; **dar ~(s) a** to encourage.

animoso, a [ani'moso, a] *adj* brave; (*vivo*) lively.

aniñado, a [ani'ɲaðo, a] *adj* (*facción*) childlike; (*carácter*) childish.

aniquilar [aniki'lar] *vt* to annihilate, destroy.

anís [a'nis] *nm* (*grano*) aniseed; (*licor*) anisette.

aniversario [anißer'sarjo] *nm* anniversary.

Ankara [an'kara] *nf* Ankara.

ano ['ano] *nm* anus.

anoche [a'notʃe] *adv* last night; **antes de ~** the night before last.

anochecer [anotʃe'θer] *vi* to get dark ♦ *nm* nightfall, dark; **al ~** at nightfall.

anochezca [ano'tʃeθka] *etc vb V* **anochecer**.

anodino, a [ano'ðino, a] *adj* dull, anodyne.

anomalía [anoma'lia] *nf* anomaly.

anonadado, a [anona'ðaðo, a] *adj* stunned.

anonimato [anoni'mato] *nm* anonymity.

anónimo, a [a'nonimo, a] *adj* anonymous; (*COM*) limited ♦ *nm* (*carta*) anonymous letter; (: *maliciosa*) poison-pen letter.

anorak [ano'rak], *pl* **anoraks** *nm* anorak.

anorexia [ano'reksja] *nf* anorexia.

anormal [anor'mal] *adj* abnormal.

anotación [anota'θjon] *nf* note; annotation.

anotar [ano'tar] *vt* to note down; (*comentar*) to annotate.

anquilosado, a [ankilo'saðo, a] *adj* (*fig*) stale, out of date.

anquilosamiento [ankilosa'mjento] *nm* (*fig*) paralysis, stagnation.

ansia ['ansja] *nf* anxiety; (*añoranza*) yearning.

ansiar [an'sjar] *vt* to long for.

ansiedad [ansje'ðað] *nf* anxiety.

ansioso, a [an'sjoso, a] *adj* anxious;

(*anhelante*) eager; **~ de** *o* **por algo** greedy for sth.

antagónico, a [anta'ɣoniko, a] *adj* antagonistic; (*opuesto*) contrasting.

antagonista [antaɣo'nista] *nm/f* antagonist.

antaño [an'taɲo] *adv* long ago.

Antártico [an'tartiko] *nm*: **el (océano) ~** the Antarctic (Ocean).

Antártida [an'tartiða] *nf* Antarctica.

ante ['ante] *prep* before, in the presence of; (*encarado con*) faced with ♦ *nm* suede; **~ todo** above all.

anteanoche [antea'notʃe] *adv* the night before last.

anteayer [antea'jer] *adv* the day before yesterday.

antebrazo [ante'ßraθo] *nm* forearm.

antecámara [ante'kamara] *nf* (*ARQ*) anteroom; (*antesala*) waiting room; (*POL*) lobby.

antecedente [anteθe'ðente] *adj* previous ♦ *nm*: **~s** *nmpl* (*profesionales*) background *sg*; **~s penales** criminal record; **no tener ~s** to have a clean record; **estar en ~s** to be well-informed; **poner a algn en ~s** to put sb in the picture.

anteceder [anteθe'ðer] *vt* to precede, go before.

antecesor, a [anteθe'sor, a] *nm/f* predecessor.

antedicho, a [ante'ðitʃo, a] *adj* aforementioned.

antelación [antela'θjon] *nf*: **con ~** in advance.

antemano [ante'mano]: **de ~** *adv* beforehand, in advance.

antena [an'tena] *nf* antenna; (*de televisión etc*) aerial.

anteojeras [anteo'xeras] *nfpl* blinkers (*BRIT*), blinders (*US*).

anteojo [ante'oxo] *nm* eyeglass; **~s** *nmpl* (*esp AM*) glasses, spectacles.

antepasados [antepa'saðos] *nmpl* ancestors.

antepecho [ante'petʃo] *nm* guardrail, parapet; (*repisa*) ledge, sill.

antepondré [antepon'dre] *etc vb V* **anteponer**.

anteponer [antepo'ner] *vt* to place in front; (*fig*) to prefer.

anteponga [ante'ponɣa] *etc vb V* **anteponer**.

anteproyecto [antepro'jekto] *nm* preliminary sketch; (*fig*) blueprint; (*POL*): **~ de ley** draft bill.

antepuesto, a [ante'pwesto, a] *pp de* **anteponer**.

antepuse [ante'puse] *etc vb V* **anteponer**.

anterior [ante'rjor] *adj* preceding, previous.

anterioridad [anterjori'ðað] *nf*: **con ~ a** prior to, before.

anteriormente [anterjor'mente] *adv* previously, before.

antes ['antes] *adv* sooner; (*primero*) first; (*con prioridad*) before; (*hace tiempo*) previously, once; (*más bien*) rather ♦ *prep*: ~ **de** before ♦ *conj*: ~ **(de) que** before; ~ **bien** (but) rather; **dos días** ~ two days before *o* previously; **mucho/poco** ~ long/shortly before; ~ **muerto que esclavo** better dead than enslaved; **tomo el avión** ~ **que el barco** I take the plane rather than the boat; **cuanto** ~, **lo** ~ **posible** as soon as possible; **cuanto** ~ **mejor** the sooner the better.

antesala [ante'sala] *nf* anteroom.

antiadherente [antiaðe'rente] *adj* non-stick.

antiaéreo, a [antia'ereo, a] *adj* anti-aircraft.

antialcohólico, a [antial'koliko, a] *adj*: **centro** ~ (*MED*) detoxification unit.

antibalas [anti'ßalas] *adj inv*: **chaleco** ~ bulletproof jacket.

antibiótico [anti'ßjotiko] *nm* antibiotic.

anticiclón [antiθi'klon] *nm* anti-cyclone.

anticipación [antiθipa'θjon] *nf* anticipation; **con 10 minutos de** ~ 10 minutes early.

anticipado, a [antiθi'paðo, a] *adj* (in) advance; **por** ~ in advance.

anticipar [antiθi'par] *vt* to anticipate; (*adelantar*) to bring forward; (*COM*) to advance; ~**se** *vr*: ~**se a su época** to be ahead of one's time.

anticipo [anti'θipo] *nm* (*COM*) advance; *V tb* **anticipación**.

anticonceptivo, a [antikonθep'tißo, a] *adj, nm* contraceptive; **métodos** ~**s** methods of birth control.

anticongelante [antikonxe'lante] *nm* antifreeze.

anticonstitucional [antikonstituθjo'nal] *adj* unconstitutional.

anticuado, a [anti'kwaðo, a] *adj* out-of-date, old-fashioned; (*desusado*) obsolete.

anticuario [anti'kwarjo] *nm* antique dealer.

anticuerpo [anti'kwerpo] *nm* antibody.

antidemocrático, a [antiðemo'kratiko, a] *adj* undemocratic.

antideportivo, a [antiðepor'tißo, a] *adj* unsporting.

antidepresivo [antiðepre'sißo] *nm* antidepressant.

antideslumbrante [antiðeslum'brante] *adj* (*INFORM*) anti-dazzle.

antidoping [anti'ðopin] *adj inv* anti-drug.

antídoto [an'tiðoto] *nm* antidote.

antidroga [anti'ðroɣa] *adj inv* anti-drug; **brigada** ~ drug squad.

antiestético, a [anties'tetiko, a] *adj* unsightly.

antifaz [anti'faθ] *nm* mask; (*velo*) veil.

antiglobalización [antiglobaliθa'θjon] anti-globalization; **manifestantes** ~ anti-globalization protesters.

antigualla [anti'ɣwaʎa] *nf* antique; (*reliquia*) relic; ~**s** *nfpl* old things.

antiguamente [antiɣwa'mente] *adv* formerly; (*hace mucho tiempo*) long ago.

antigüedad [antiɣwe'ðað] *nf* antiquity; (*artículo*) antique; (*rango*) seniority.

antiguo, a [an'tiɣwo, a] *adj* old, ancient; (*que fue*) former; **a la antigua** in the old-fashioned way.

antihigiénico, a [anti'xjeniko, a] *adj* unhygienic.

antihistamínico, a [antista'miniko, a] *adj*, *nm* antihistamine.

antiinflacionista [antinflaθjo'nista] *adj* anti-inflationary, counter-inflationary.

antillano, a [anti'ʎano, a] *adj, nm/f* West Indian.

Antillas [an'tiʎas] *nfpl*: **las** ~ the West Indies, the Antilles; **el mar de las** ~ the Caribbean Sea.

antílope [an'tilope] *nm* antelope.

antimonopolios [antimono'poljos] *adj inv*: **ley** ~ anti-trust law.

antinatural [antinatu'ral] *adj* unnatural.

antiparras [anti'parras] *nfpl* (*fam*) specs.

antipatía [antipa'tia] *nf* antipathy, dislike.

antipático, a [anti'patiko, a] *adj* disagreeable, unpleasant.

Antípodas [an'tipoðas] *nfpl*: **las** ~ the Antipodes.

antiquísimo, a [anti'kisimo, a] *adj* ancient.

antirreglamentario, a [antirreɣlamen'tarjo, a] *adj* (*gen*) unlawful; (*POL etc*) unconstitutional.

antirrobo [anti'rroßo] *nm* (*tb* **dispositivo** ~) (*para casas etc*) burglar alarm; (*para coches*) car alarm.

antisemita [antise'mita] *adj* anti-Semitic ♦ *nm/f* anti-Semite.

antiséptico, a [anti'septiko, a] *adj, nm* antiseptic.

antiterrorista [antiterro'rista] *adj* antiterrorist; **la lucha** ~ the fight against terrorism.

antítesis [an'titesis] *nf inv* antithesis.

antojadizo, a [antoxa'ðiθo, a] *adj*

capricious.

antojarse [anto'xarse] *vr* (*desear*): **se me antoja comprarlo** I have a mind to buy it; (*pensar*): **se me antoja que** I have a feeling that.

antojo [an'toxo] *nm* caprice, whim; (*rosa*) birthmark; (*lunar*) mole; **hacer a su ~** to do as one pleases.

antología [antolo'xia] *nf* anthology.

antonomasia [antono'masja] *nf*: **por ~** par excellence.

antorcha [an'tortʃa] *nf* torch.

antro ['antro] *nm* cavern; **~ de corrupción** (*fig*) den of iniquity.

antropófago, a [antro'pofaɣo, a] *adj, nm/f* cannibal.

antropología [antropolo'xia] *nf* anthropology.

antropólogo, a [antro'poloɣo, a] *nm/f* anthropologist.

anual [a'nwal] *adj* annual.

anualidad [anwali'ðað] *nf* annuity, annual payment; **~ vitalicia** life annuity.

anuario [a'nwarjo] *nm* yearbook.

anudar [anu'ðar] *vt* to knot, tie; (*unir*) to join; **~se** *vr* to get tied up; **se me anudó la voz** I got a lump in my throat.

anulación [anula'θjon] *nf* annulment; cancellation; repeal.

anular [anu'lar] *vt* to annul, cancel; (*suscripción*) to cancel; (*ley*) to repeal ♦ *nm* ring finger.

anunciación [anunθja'θjon] *nf* announcement; **A~** (*REL*) Annunciation.

anunciante [anun'θjante] *nm/f* (*COM*) advertiser.

anunciar [anun'θjar] *vt* to announce; (*proclamar*) to proclaim; (*COM*) to advertise.

anuncio [a'nunθjo] *nm* announcement; (*señal*) sign; (*COM*) advertisement; (*cartel*) poster; (*TEAT*) bill; **~s por palabras** classified ads.

anverso [am'berso] *nm* obverse.

anzuelo [an'θwelo] *nm* hook; (*para pescar*) fish hook; **tragar el ~** to swallow the bait.

añadido [aɲa'ðiðo] *nm* addition.

añadidura [aɲaði'ðura] *nf* addition, extra; **por ~** besides, in addition.

añadir [aɲa'ðir] *vt* to add.

añejo, a [a'ɲexo, a] *adj* old; (*vino*) vintage; (*jamón*) well-cured.

añicos [a'ɲikos] *nmpl*: **hacer ~** to smash, shatter; **hacerse ~** to smash, shatter.

añil [a'ɲil] *nm* (*BOT, color*) indigo.

año ['aɲo] *nm* year; **¡Feliz A~ Nuevo!** Happy New Year!; **tener 15 ~s** to be 15

(years old); **los ~s 80** the eighties; **~ bisiesto/escolar** leap/school year; **~ fiscal** fiscal *o* tax year; **estar de buen ~** to be in good shape; **en el ~ de la nana** in the year dot; **el ~ que viene** next year.

añoranza [aɲo'ranθa] *nf* nostalgia; (*anhelo*) longing.

añorar [aɲo'rar] *vt* to long for.

añoso, a [a'ɲoso, a] *adj* ancient, old.

aovado, a [ao'βaðo, a] *adj* oval.

aovar [ao'βar] *vi* to lay eggs.

apabullar [apaβu'ʎar] *vt* (*lit, fig*) to crush.

apacentar [apaθen'tar] *vt* to pasture, graze.

apacible [apa'θiβle] *adj* gentle, mild.

apaciente [apa'θjente] *etc vb V* **apacentar.**

apaciguar [apaθi'ɣwar] *vt* to pacify, calm (down).

apacigüe [apa'θiɣwe] *etc vb V* **apaciguar.**

apadrinar [apaðri'nar] *vt* to sponsor, support; (*REL*) to act as godfather to.

apagado, a [apa'ɣaðo, a] *adj* (*volcán*) extinct; (*color*) dull; (*voz*) quiet; (*sonido*) muted, muffled; (*persona*) apático; listless; **estar ~** (*fuego, luz*) to be out; (*radio, TV etc*) to be off.

apagar [apa'ɣar] *vt* to put out; (*color*) to tone down; (*sonido*) to silence, muffle; (*sed*) to quench; (*INFORM*) to toggle off; **~se** *vr* (*luz, fuego*) to go out; (*sonido*) to die away; (*pasión*) to wither; **~ el sistema** (*INFORM*) to close *o* shut down.

apagón [apa'ɣon] *nm* blackout, power cut.

apague [a'paɣe] *etc vb V* **apagar.**

apaisado, a [apai'saðo, a] *adj* (*papel*) landscape *cpd*.

apalabrar [apala'βrar] *vt* to agree to; (*obrero*) to engage.

Apalaches [apa'latʃes] *nmpl*: **(Montes) ~** Appalachians.

apalear [apale'ar] *vt* to beat, thrash; (*AGR*) to winnow.

apañado, a [apa'ɲaðo, a] *adj* (*mañoso*) resourceful; (*arreglado*) tidy; (*útil*) handy.

apañar [apa'ɲar] *vt* to pick up; (*asir*) to take hold of, grasp; (*reparar*) to mend, patch up; **~se** *vr* to manage, get along; **apañárselas por su cuenta** to look after number one (*fam*).

apaño [a'paɲo] *nm* (*COSTURA*) patch; (*maña*) skill; **esto no tiene ~** there's no answer to this one.

aparador [apara'ðor] *nm* sideboard; (*escaparate*) shop window.

aparato [apa'rato] *nm* apparatus; (*máquina*) machine; (*doméstico*) appliance; (*boato*) ostentation; (*INFORM*)

device; ~ **de facsímil** facsimile
(machine), fax; ~ **respiratorio**
respiratory system; ~s **de mando** (AVIAT
etc) controls.

aparatoso, a [apara'toso, a] adj showy,
ostentatious.

aparcamiento [aparka'mjento] nm car
park (BRIT), parking lot (US).

aparcar [apar'kar] vt, vi to park.

aparear [apare'ar] vt (objetos) to pair,
match; (animales) to mate; ~**se** vr to form
a pair; to mate.

aparecer [apare'θer] vi, ~**se** vr to appear;
apareció borracho he turned up drunk.

aparejado, a [apare'xaðo, a] adj fit,
suitable; **ir** ~ **con** to go hand in hand
with; **llevar** o **traer** ~ to involve.

aparejador, a [aparexa'ðor, a] nm/f (ARQ)
quantity surveyor.

aparejar [apare'xar] vt to prepare; (caballo)
to saddle, harness; (NAUT) to fit out, rig
out.

aparejo [apa'rexo] nm preparation; (de
caballo) harness; (NAUT) rigging; (de
poleas) block and tackle.

aparentar [aparen'tar] vt (edad) to look;
(fingir): ~ **tristeza** to pretend to be sad.

aparente [apa'rente] adj apparent;
(adecuado) suitable.

aparezca [apa'reθka] etc vb V **aparecer**.

aparición [apari'θjon] nf appearance; (de
libro) publication; (fantasma) spectre.

apariencia [apa'rjenθja] nf (outward)
appearance; **en** ~ outwardly, seemingly.

aparque [a'parke] etc vb V **aparcar**.

apartado, a [apar'taðo, a] adj separate;
(lejano) remote ♦ nm (tipográfico) paragraph; ~ **(de correos)** post office box.

apartamento [aparta'mento] nm
apartment, flat (BRIT).

apartamiento [aparta'mjento] nm
separation; (aislamiento) remoteness;
(AM) apartment, flat (BRIT).

apartar [apar'tar] vt to separate; (quitar) to
remove; (MINERALOGÍA) to extract; ~**se** vr
(separarse) to separate, part; (irse) to move
away; (mantenerse aparte) to keep away.

aparte [a'parte] adv (separadamente)
separately; (además) besides ♦ prep: ~ **de**
apart from ♦ nm (TEAT) aside;
(tipográfico) new paragraph; "**punto y** ~"
"new paragraph".

apasionado, a [apasjo'naðo, a] adj
passionate; (pey) biassed, prejudiced
♦ nm/f admirer.

apasionante [apasjo'nante] adj exciting.

apasionar [apasjo'nar] vt to arouse passion in; ~**se** vr to get excited; **le apasiona**

el fútbol she's crazy about football.

apatía [apa'tia] nf apathy.

apático, a [a'patiko, a] adj apathetic.

apátrida [a'patriða] adj stateless.

Apdo. nm abr (= Apartado (de Correos))
P.O. Box.

apeadero [apea'ðero] nm halt, stopping
place.

apearse [ape'arse] vr (jinete) to dismount;
(bajarse) to get down o out; (de coche) to
get out, alight; **no** ~ **del burro** to refuse
to climb down.

apechugar [apetʃu'ɣar] vi: ~ **con algo** to
face up to sth.

apechugue [ape'tʃuɣe] etc vb V **apechugar**.

apedrear [apeðre'ar] vt to stone.

apegarse [ape'ɣarse] vr: ~ **a** to become
attached to.

apego [a'peɣo] nm attachment, devotion.

apegue [a'peɣe] etc vb V **apegarse**.

apelación [apela'θjon] nf appeal.

apelar [ape'lar] vi to appeal; ~ **a** (fig) to
resort to.

apelativo [apela'tiβo] nm (LING)
appellative; (AM) surname.

apellidar [apeʎi'ðar] vt to call, name; ~**se**
vr: **se apellida Pérez** her (sur)name's
Pérez.

apellido [ape'ʎiðo] nm surname; see boxed
note.

APELLIDO

In the Spanish-speaking world most
people use two surnames, or **apellidos**;
the first is their father's first family name,
and the second their mother's first family
name. For example, if Juan García López
married Carmen Pérez Rodríguez, their
children's surname would be García Pérez.
Married women retain their own
surname(s) and sometimes add their
husband's first surname to theirs: Carmen
Pérez de García. This woman could also be
referred to as (la) Señora de García. In
Latin America the second surname is
usually shortened to an initial in
correspondence: Juan García L.

---

apelmazado, a [apelma'θaðo, a] adj
compact, solid.

apelotonar [apeloto'nar] vt to roll into a
ball; ~**se** vr (gente) to crowd together.

apenar [ape'nar] vt to grieve, trouble; (AM:
avergonzar) to embarrass; ~**se** vr to
grieve; (AM) to be embarrassed.

apenas [a'penas] adv scarcely, hardly
♦ conj as soon as, no sooner.

apéndice [a'pendiθe] *nm* appendix.
apendicitis [apendi'θitis] *nf* appendicitis.
Apeninos [ape'ninos] *nmpl* Apennines.
apercibimiento [aperθiβi'mjento] *nm* (*aviso*) warning.
apercibir [aperθi'βir] *vt* to prepare; (*avisar*) to warn; (*JUR*) to summon; (*AM*) to notice, see; ~**se** *vr* to get ready; ~**se de** to notice.
aperitivo [aperi'tiβo] *nm* (*bebida*) aperitif; (*comida*) appetizer.
apero [a'pero] *nm* (*AGR*) implement; ~**s** *nmpl* farm equipment *sg*.
apertura [aper'tura] *nf* (*gen*) opening; (*POL*) openness, liberalization; (*TEAT etc*) beginning; ~ **de un juicio hipotecario** (*COM*) foreclosure.
aperturismo [apertu'rismo] *nm* (*POL*) (policy of) liberalization.
apesadumbrar [apesaðum'brar] *vt* to grieve, sadden; ~**se** *vr* to distress o.s.
apestar [apes'tar] *vt* to infect ♦ *vi*: ~ (**a**) to stink (of).
apestoso, a [apes'toso, a] *adj* (*hediondo*) stinking; (*asqueroso*) sickening.
apetecer [apete'θer] *vt*: **¿te apetece una tortilla?** do you fancy an omelette?
apetecible [apete'θiβle] *adj* desirable; (*comida*) tempting.
apetezca [ape'teθka] *etc vb V* **apetecer**.
apetito [ape'tito] *nm* appetite.
apetitoso, a [apeti'toso, a] *adj* (*gustoso*) appetizing; (*fig*) tempting.
apiadarse [apja'ðarse] *vr*: ~ **de** to take pity on.
ápice ['apiθe] *nm* apex; (*fig*) whit, iota; **ni un** ~ not a whit; **no ceder un** ~ not to budge an inch.
apicultor, a [apikul'tor, a] *nm/f* beekeeper, apiarist.
apicultura [apikul'tura] *nf* beekeeping.
apiladora [apila'ðora] *nf* (*para máquina impresora*) stacker.
apilar [api'lar] *vt* to pile o heap up; ~**se** *vr* to pile up.
apiñado, a [api'ɲaðo, a] *adj* (*apretado*) packed.
apiñar [api'ɲar] *vt* to crowd; ~**se** *vr* to crowd o press together.
apio ['apjo] *nm* celery.
apisonadora [apisona'ðora] *nf* (*máquina*) steamroller.
aplacar [apla'kar] *vt* to placate; ~**se** *vr* to calm down.
aplace [a'plaθe] *etc vb V* **aplazar**.
aplanamiento [aplana'mjento] *nm* smoothing, levelling.
aplanar [apla'nar] *vt* to smooth, level;

(*allanar*) to roll flat, flatten; ~**se** *vr* (*edificio*) to collapse; (*persona*) to get discouraged.
aplaque [a'plake] *etc vb V* **aplacar**.
aplastar [aplas'tar] *vt* to squash (flat); (*fig*) to crush.
aplatanarse [aplata'narse] *vr* to get lethargic.
aplaudir [aplau'ðir] *vt* to applaud.
aplauso [a'plauso] *nm* applause; (*fig*) approval, acclaim.
aplazamiento [aplaθa'mjento] *nm* postponement.
aplazar [apla'θar] *vt* to postpone, defer.
aplicación [aplika'θjon] *nf* application; (*esfuerzo*) effort; **aplicaciones de gestión** business applications.
aplicado, a [apli'kaðo, a] *adj* diligent, hard-working.
aplicar [apli'kar] *vt* (*gen*) to apply; (*poner en vigor*) to put into effect; (*esfuerzos*) to devote; ~**se** *vr* to apply o.s.
aplique [a'plike] *etc vb V* **aplicar** ♦ *nm* wall light o lamp.
aplomo [a'plomo] *nm* aplomb, self-assurance.
apocado, a [apo'kaðo, a] *adj* timid.
apocamiento [apoka'mjento] *nm* timidity; (*depresión*) depression.
apocarse [apo'karse] *vr* to feel small o humiliated.
apocopar [apoko'par] *vt* (*LING*) to shorten.
apócope [a'pokope] *nf* apocopation; **gran es** ~ **de grande** "gran" is the shortened form of "grande".
apócrifo, a [a'pokrifo, a] *adj* apocryphal.
apodar [apo'ðar] *vt* to nickname.
apoderado [apoðe'raðo] *nm* agent, representative.
apoderar [apoðe'rar] *vt* to authorize, empower; (*JUR*) to grant (a) power of attorney to; ~**se** *vr*: ~**se de** to take possession of.
apodo [a'poðo] *nm* nickname.
apogeo [apo'xeo] *nm* peak, summit.
apolillado, a [apoli'ʎaðo, a] *adj* moth-eaten.
apolillarse [apoli'ʎarse] *vr* to get moth-eaten.
apología [apolo'xia] *nf* eulogy; (*defensa*) defence.
apoltronarse [apoltro'narse] *vr* to get lazy.
apoplejía [apople'xia] *nf* apoplexy, stroke.
apoque [a'poke] *etc vb V* **apocar**.
apoquinar [apoki'nar] *vt* (*fam*) to cough up, fork out.
aporrear [aporre'ar] *vt* to beat (up).
aportación [aporta'θjon] *nf* contribution.

aportar [apor'tar] *vt* to contribute ♦ *vi* to reach port.
aposentar [aposen'tar] *vt* to lodge, put up.
aposento [apo'sento] *nm* lodging; (*habitación*) room.
apósito [a'posito] *nm* (*MED*) dressing.
apostar [apos'tar] *vt* to bet, stake; (*tropas etc*) to station, post ♦ *vi* to bet.
aposta(s) [a'posta(s)] *adv* on purpose.
apostatar [aposta'tar] *vi* (*REL*) to apostatize; (*fig*) to change sides.
a posteriori [aposte'rjori] *adv* at a later date *o* stage; (*LÓGICA*) a posteriori.
apostilla [apos'tiʎa] *nf* note, comment.
apóstol [a'postol] *nm* apostle.
apóstrofo [a'postrofo] *nm* apostrophe.
apostura [apos'tura] *nf* neatness, elegance.
apoteósico, a [apote'osiko, a] *adj* tremendous.
apoyar [apo'jar] *vt* to lean, rest; (*fig*) to support, back; ~**se** *vr*: ~**se en** to lean on.
apoyo [a'pojo] *nm* support, backing.
apreciable [apre'θjaßle] *adj* considerable; (*fig*) esteemed.
apreciación [apreθja'θjon] *nf* appreciation; (*COM*) valuation.
apreciar [apre'θjar] *vt* to evaluate, assess; (*COM*) to appreciate, value ♦ *vi* (*ECON*) to appreciate.
aprecio [a'preθjo] *nm* valuation, estimate; (*fig*) appreciation.
aprehender [apreen'der] *vt* to apprehend, detain; (*ver*) to see, observe.
aprehensión [apreen'sjon] *nf* detention, capture.
apremiante [apre'mjante] *adj* urgent, pressing.
apremiar [apre'mjar] *vt* to compel, force ♦ *vi* to be urgent, press.
apremio [a'premjo] *nm* urgency; ~ **de pago** demand note.
aprender [apren'der] *vt, vi* to learn; ~ **a conducir** to learn to drive; ~**se** *vr*: ~**se algo** to learn sth (off) by heart.
aprendiz, a [apren'diθ, a] *nm/f* apprentice; (*principiante*) learner, trainee; ~ **de comercio** business trainee.
aprendizaje [aprendi'θaxe] *nm* apprenticeship.
aprensión [apren'sjon] *nm* apprehension, fear.
aprensivo, a [apren'sißo, a] *adj* apprehensive.
apresar [apre'sar] *vt* to seize; (*capturar*) to capture.
aprestar [apres'tar] *vt* to prepare, get ready; (*TEC*) to prime, size; ~**se** *vr* to get

ready.
apresto [a'presto] *nm* (*gen*) preparation; (*sustancia*) size.
apresurado, a [apresu'raðo, a] *adj* hurried, hasty.
apresuramiento [apresura'mjento] *nm* hurry, haste.
apresurar [apresu'rar] *vt* to hurry, accelerate; ~**se** *vr* to hurry, make haste; **me apresuré a sugerir que** ... I hastily suggested that ...
apretado, a [apre'taðo, a] *adj* tight; (*escritura*) cramped.
apretar [apre'tar] *vt* to squeeze, press; (*mano*) to clasp; (*dientes*) to grit; (*TEC*) to tighten; (*presionar*) to press together, pack ♦ *vi* to be too tight; ~**se** *vr* to crowd together; ~ **la mano a algn** to shake sb's hand; ~ **el paso** to quicken one's step.
apretón [apre'ton] *nm* squeeze; ~ **de manos** handshake.
aprieto [a'prjeto] *etc vb V* **apretar** ♦ *nm* squeeze; (*dificultad*) difficulty, jam; **estar en un** ~ to be in a jam; **ayudar a algn a salir de un** ~ to help sb out of trouble.
a priori [apri'ori] *adv* beforehand; (*LÓGICA*) a priori.
aprisa [a'prisa] *adv* quickly, hurriedly.
aprisionar [aprisjo'nar] *vt* to imprison.
aprobación [aproßa'θjon] *nf* approval.
aprobado [apro'ßaðo] *nm* (*nota*) pass mark.
aprobar [apro'ßar] *vt* to approve (of); (*examen, materia*) to pass ♦ *vi* to pass.
apropiación [apropja'θjon] *nf* appropriation.
apropiado, a [apro'pjaðo, a] *adj* appropriate.
apropiarse [apro'pjarse] *vr*: ~ **de** to appropriate.
aprovechado, a [aproße'tʃaðo, a] *adj* industrious, hardworking; (*económico*) thrifty; (*pey*) unscrupulous.
aprovechamiento [aproßetʃa'mjento] *nm* use, exploitation.
aprovechar [aproße'tʃar] *vt* to use; (*explotar*) to exploit; (*experiencia*) to profit from; (*oferta, oportunidad*) to take advantage of ♦ *vi* to progress, improve; ~**se** *vr*: ~**se de** to make use of; (*pey*) to take advantage of; **¡que aproveche!** enjoy your meal!
aprovisionar [aproßisjo'nar] *vt* to supply.
aproximación [aproksima'θjon] *nf* approximation; (*de lotería*) consolation prize.
aproximadamente [aproksimaða'mente] *adv* approximately.

aproximado, a [aproksi'maðo, a] *adj* approximate.

aproximar [aproksi'mar] *vt* to bring nearer; ~**se** *vr* to come near, approach.

apruebe [a'prweβe] *etc vb V* **aprobar**.

aptitud [apti'tuð] *nf* aptitude; (*capacidad*) ability; ~ **para los negocios** business sense.

apto, a ['apto, a] *adj* (*apropiado*) fit, suitable (*para* for, to); (*hábil*) capable; ~/**no** ~ **para menores** (*CINE*) suitable/unsuitable for children.

apuesto, a [a'pwesto, a] *etc vb V* **apostar** ♦ *adj* neat, elegant ♦ *nf* bet, wager.

apuntador [apunta'ðor] *nm* prompter.

apuntalar [apunta'lar] *vt* to prop up.

apuntar [apun'tar] *vt* (*con arma*) to aim at; (*con dedo*) to point at *o* to; (*anotar*) to note (down); (*datos*) to record; (*TEAT*) to prompt; ~**se** *vr* (*DEPORTE: tanto, victoria*) to score; (*ESCOL*) to enrol; ~ **una cantidad en la cuenta de algn** to charge a sum to sb's account; ~**se en un curso** to enrol on a course; ¡**yo me apunto**! count me in!.

apunte [a'punte] *nm* note; (*TEAT: voz*) prompt; (: *texto*) prompt book.

apuñalar [apuɲa'lar] *vt* to stab.

apurado, a [apu'raðo, a] *adj* needy; (*difícil*) difficult; (*peligroso*) dangerous; (*AM*) hurried, rushed; **estar en una situación apurada** to be in a tight spot; **estar ~** to be in a hurry.

apurar [apu'rar] *vt* (*agotar*) to drain; (*recursos*) to use up; (*molestar*) to annoy; ~**se** *vr* (*preocuparse*) to worry; (*esp AM*: *darse prisa*) to hurry.

apuro [a'puro] *nm* (*aprieto*) fix, jam; (*escasez*) want, hardship; (*vergüenza*) embarrassment; (*AM*) haste, urgency.

aquejado, a [ake'xaðo, a] *adj*: ~ **de** (*MED*) afflicted by.

aquejar [ake'xar] *vt* (*afligir*) to distress; **le aqueja una grave enfermedad** he suffers from a serious disease.

aquel, aquella, aquellos, as [a'kel, a'keʎa, a'keʎos, as] *adj* that; (*pl*) those.

aquél, aquélla, aquéllos, as [a'kel, a'keʎa, a'keʎos, as] *pron* that (one); (*pl*) those (ones).

aquello [a'keʎo] *pron* that, that business.

aquí [a'ki] *adv* (*lugar*) here; (*tiempo*) now; ~ **arriba** up here; ~ **mismo** right here; ~ **yace** here lies; **de** ~ **a siete días** a week from now.

aquietar [akje'tar] *vt* to quieten (down), calm (down).

Aquisgrán [akis'ɣran] *nm* Aachen, Aix-la-Chapelle.

A.R. *abr* (= *Alteza Real*) R.H.

ara ['ara] *nf* (*altar*) altar; **en** ~**s de** for the sake of.

árabe ['araβe] *adj* Arab, Arabian, Arabic ♦ *nm/f* Arab ♦ *nm* (*LING*) Arabic.

Arabia [a'raβja] *nf* Arabia; ~ **Saudí** *o* **Saudita** Saudi Arabia.

arábigo, a [a'raβiɣo, a] *adj* Arab, Arabian, Arabic.

arácnido [a'rakniðo] *nm* arachnid.

arado [a'raðo] *nm* plough.

aragonés, esa [araɣo'nes, esa] *adj*, *nm/f* Aragonese ♦ *nm* (*LING*) Aragonese.

arancel [aran'θel] *nm* tariff, duty; ~ **de aduanas** (customs) duty.

arandela [aran'dela] *nf* (*TEC*) washer; (*chorrera*) frill.

araña [a'raɲa] *nf* (*ZOOL*) spider; (*lámpara*) chandelier.

arañar [ara'ɲar] *vt* to scratch.

arañazo [ara'ɲaθo] *nm* scratch.

arar [a'rar] *vt* to plough, till.

araucano, a [arau'kano, a] *adj*, *nm/f* Araucanian.

arbitraje [arβi'traxe] *nm* arbitration.

arbitrar [arβi'trar] *vt* to arbitrate in; (*recursos*) to bring together; (*DEPORTE*) to referee ♦ *vi* to arbitrate.

arbitrariedad [arβitrarje'ðað] *nf* arbitrariness; (*acto*) arbitrary act.

arbitrario, a [arβi'trarjo] *adj* arbitrary.

arbitrio [ar'βitrjo] *nm* free will; (*JUR*) adjudication, decision; **dejar al** ~ **de algn** to leave to sb's discretion.

árbitro ['arβitro] *nm* arbitrator; (*DEPORTE*) referee; (*TENIS*) umpire.

árbol ['arβol] *nm* (*BOT*) tree; (*NAUT*) mast; (*TEC*) axle, shaft.

arbolado, a [arβo'laðo, a] *adj* wooded; (*camino*) tree-lined ♦ *nm* woodland.

arboladura [arβola'ðura] *nf* rigging.

arbolar [arβo'lar] *vt* to hoist, raise.

arboleda [arβo'leða] *nf* grove, plantation.

arbusto [ar'βusto] *nm* bush, shrub.

arca ['arka] *nf* chest, box; **A~ de la Alianza** Ark of the Covenant; **A~ de Noé** Noah's Ark.

arcada [ar'kaða] *nf* arcade; (*de puente*) arch, span; ~**s** *nfpl* retching *sg*.

arcaico, a [ar'kaiko, a] *adj* archaic.

arce ['arθe] *nm* maple tree.

arcén [ar'θen] *nm* (*de autopista*) hard shoulder; (*de carretera*) verge.

archiconocido, a [artʃikono'θiðo, a] *adj* extremely well-known.

archipiélago [artʃi'pjelaɣo] *nm*

archipelago.

archisabido, a [artʃisa'βiðo, a] *adj* extremely well-known.

archivador [artʃißa'ðor] *nm* filing cabinet; ~ **colgante** suspension file.

archivar [artʃi'βar] *vt* to file (away); (*INFORM*) to archive.

archivo [ar't ʃißo] *nm* archive(s) (*pl*); (*INFORM*) file; **A~ Nacional** Public Record Office; **~s policíacos** police files; **nombre de** ~ (*INFORM*) filename; ~ **adjunto** (*INFORM*) attachment; ~ **de seguridad** (*INFORM*) backup file.

arcilla [ar'θiʎa] *nf* clay.

arco ['arko] *nm* arch; (*MAT*) arc; (*MIL*, *MUS*) bow; (*AM DEPORTE*) goal; ~ **iris** rainbow.

arcón [ar'kon] *nm* large chest.

arder [ar'ðer] *vt* to burn; ~ **sin llama** to smoulder; **estar que arde** (*persona*) to fume.

ardid [ar'ðið] *nm* ruse.

ardiente [ar'ðjente] *adj* ardent.

ardilla [ar'ðiʎa] *nf* squirrel.

ardor [ar'ðor] *nm* (*calor*) heat, warmth; (*fig*) ardour; ~ **de estómago** heartburn.

ardoroso, a [arðo'roso, a] *adj* passionate.

arduo, a ['arðwo, a] *adj* arduous.

área ['area] *nf* area; (*DEPORTE*) penalty area.

ARENA [a'rena] *nf abr* (*El Salvador: POL*) = Alianza Republicana Nacionalista.

arena [a'rena] *nf* sand; (*de una lucha*) arena.

arenal [are'nal] *nm* (*arena movediza*) quicksand.

arenga [a'renga] *nf* (*fam*) sermon.

arengar [aren'gar] *vt* to harangue.

arengue [a'renge] *etc vb V* **arengar**.

arenillas [are'niʎas] *nfpl* (*MED*) stones.

arenisca [are'niska] *nf* sandstone; (*cascajo*) grit.

arenoso, a [are'noso, a] *adj* sandy.

arenque [a'renke] *nm* herring.

arepa [a'repa] *nf* (*AM*) corn pancake.

arete [a'rete] *nm* earring.

argamasa [arɣa'masa] *nf* mortar, plaster.

Argel [ar'xel] *n* Algiers.

Argelia [ar'xelja] *nf* Algeria.

argelino, a [arxe'lino, a] *adj, nm/f* Algerian.

Argentina [arxen'tina] *nf*: **(la)** ~ **the** Argentine, Argentina.

argentino, a [arxen'tino, a] *adj* Argentinian; (*de plata*) silvery ♦ *nm/f* Argentinian.

argolla [ar'ɣoʎa] *nf* (*large*) ring; (*AM: de matrimonio*) wedding ring.

argot [ar'ɣo] *nm, pl* **argots** [ar'ɣo, ar'ɣos] slang.

argucia [ar'ɣuθja] *nf* subtlety, sophistry.

argüir [ar'ɣwir] *vt* to deduce; (*discutir*) to argue; (*indicar*) to indicate, imply; (*censurar*) to reproach ♦ *vi* to argue.

argumentación [arɣumenta'θjon] *nf* (line of) argument.

argumentar [arɣumen'tar] *vt, vi* to argue.

argumento [arɣu'mento] *nm* argument; (*razonamiento*) reasoning; (*de novela etc*) plot; (*CINE, TV*) storyline.

arguyendo [arɣu'jendo] *etc vb V* **argüir**.

aria ['arja] *nf* aria.

aridez [ari'ðeθ] *nf* aridity, dryness.

árido, a ['ariðo, a] *adj* arid, dry; **~s** *nmpl* dry goods.

Aries ['arjes] *nm* Aries.

ariete [a'rjete] *nm* battering ram.

ario, a ['arjo, a] *adj* Aryan.

arisco, a [a'risko, a] *adj* surly; (*insociable*) unsociable.

aristocracia [aristo'kraθja] *nf* aristocracy.

aristócrata [aris'tokrata] *nm/f* aristocrat.

aristocrático, a [aristo'kratiko, a] *adj* aristocratic.

aritmética [arit'metika] *nf* arithmetic.

aritmético, a [arit'metiko, a] *adj* arithmetic(al) ♦ *nm/f* arithmetician.

arma ['arma] *nf* arm; **~s** *nfpl* arms; ~ **blanca** blade, knife; (*espada*) sword; ~ **de fuego** firearm; **~s cortas** small arms; **~s de destrucción masiva** weapons of mass destruction; **rendir las ~s** to lay down one's arms; **ser de ~s tomar** to be somebody to be reckoned with.

armada [ar'maða] *nf* armada; (*flota*) fleet; *V tb* **armado**.

armadillo [arma'ðiʎo] *nm* armadillo.

armado, a [ar'maðo, a] *adj* armed; (*TEC*) reinforced.

armador [arma'ðor] *nm* (*NAUT*) shipowner.

armadura [arma'ðura] *nf* (*MIL*) armour; (*TEC*) framework; (*ZOOL*) skeleton; (*FÍSICA*) armature.

armamentista [armamen'tista], **armamentístico, a** [armamen'tistiko, a] *adj* arms *cpd*.

armamento [arma'mento] *nm* armament; (*NAUT*) fitting-out.

armar [ar'mar] *vt* (*soldado*) to arm; (*máquina*) to assemble; (*navío*) to fit out; **~la, ~ un lío** to start a row; **~se** *vr*: **~se de valor** to summon up one's courage.

armario [ar'marjo] *nm* wardrobe; **salir del** ~ to come out (of the closet).

armatoste [arma'toste] *nm* (*mueble*) monstrosity; (*máquina*) contraption.

armazón [arma'θon] *nf o m* body, chassis; (*de mueble etc*) frame; (*ARQ*) skeleton.

Armenia [ar'menja] *nf* Armenia.

armería [arme'ria] _nf_ (_museo_) military museum; (_tienda_) gunsmith's.

armiño [ar'miɲo] _nm_ stoat; (_piel_) ermine.

armisticio [armis'tiθjo] _nm_ armistice.

armonía [armo'nia] _nf_ harmony.

armónica [ar'monika] _nf_ harmonica; _V tb_ **armónico**.

armonice [armo'niθe] _etc vb V_ **armonizar**.

armónico, a [ar'moniko, a] _adj_ harmonic.

armonioso, a [armo'njoso, a] _adj_ harmonious.

armonizar [armoni'θar] _vt_ to harmonize; (_diferencias_) to reconcile ♦ _vi_ to harmonize; ~ **con** (_fig_) to be in keeping with; (_colores_) to tone in with.

arnés [ar'nes] _nm_ armour; **arneses** _nmpl_ harness _sg_.

aro ['aro] _nm_ ring; (_tejo_) quoit; (_AM: pendiente_) earring; **entrar por el** ~ to give in.

aroma [a'roma] _nm_ aroma.

aromaterapia [aromate'rapja] _nf_ aromatherapy.

aromático, a [aro'matiko, a] _adj_ aromatic.

arpa ['arpa] _nf_ harp.

arpegio [ar'pexjo] _nm_ (_MUS_) arpeggio.

arpía [ar'pia] _nf_ (_fig_) shrew.

arpillera [arpi'ʎera] _nf_ sacking, sackcloth.

arpón [ar'pon] _nm_ harpoon.

arquear [arke'ar] _vt_ to arch, bend; ~**se** _vr_ to arch, bend.

arqueo [ar'keo] _nm_ (_gen_) arching; (_NAUT_) tonnage.

arqueología [arkeolo'xia] _nf_ archaeology.

arqueológico, a [arkeo'loxiko, a] _adj_ archaeological.

arqueólogo, a [arke'oloɣo, a] _nm/f_ archaeologist.

arquero [ar'kero] _nm_ archer, bowman; (_AM DEPORTE_) goalkeeper.

arquetipo [arke'tipo] _nm_ archetype.

arquitecto, a [arki'tekto, a] _nm/f_ architect; ~ **paisajista** _o_ **de jardines** landscape gardener.

arquitectónico, a [arkitek'toniko, a] _adj_ architectural.

arquitectura [arkitek'tura] _nf_ architecture.

arrabal [arra'βal] _nm_ suburb; ~**es** _nmpl_ outskirts.

arrabalero, a [arraβa'lero, a] _adj_ (_fig_) common, coarse.

arracimarse [arraθi'marse] _vr_ to cluster together.

arraigado, a [arrai'ɣaðo, a] _adj_ deep-rooted; (_fig_) established.

arraigar [arrai'ɣar] _vt_ to establish ♦ _vi_, ~**se** _vr_ to take root; (_persona_) to settle.

arraigo [a'rraiɣo] _nm_ (_raíces_) roots _pl_; (_bienes_) property; (_influencia_) hold; **hombre de** ~ man of property.

arraigue [a'rraiɣe] _etc vb V_ **arraigar**.

arrancada [arran'kaða] _nf_ (_arranque_) sudden start.

arrancar [arran'kar] _vt_ (_sacar_) to extract, pull out; (_arrebatar_) to snatch (away); (_pedazo_) to tear off; (_página_) to rip out; (_suspiro_) to heave; (_AUTO_) to start; (_INFORM_) to boot; (_fig_) to extract ♦ _vi_ (_AUTO, máquina_) to start; (_ponerse en marcha_) to get going; ~ **información a algn** to extract information from sb; ~ **de** to stem from.

arranque [a'rranke] _etc vb V_ **arrancar** ♦ _nm_ sudden start; (_AUTO_) start; (_fig_) fit, outburst.

arras ['arras] _nfpl_ pledge _sg_, security _sg_.

arrasar [arra'sar] _vt_ (_aplanar_) to level, flatten; (_destruir_) to demolish.

arrastrado, a [arras'traðo, a] _adj_ poor, wretched.

arrastrador [arrastra'ðor] _nm_ (_en máquina impresora_) tractor.

arrastrar [arras'trar] _vt_ to drag (along); (_fig_) to drag down, degrade; (_suj: agua, viento_) to carry away ♦ _vi_ to drag, trail on the ground; ~**se** _vr_ to crawl; (_fig_) to grovel; **llevar algo arrastrado** to drag sth along.

arrastre [a'rrastre] _nm_ drag, dragging; (_DEPORTE_) crawl; **estar para el** ~ (_fig_) to have had it.

array [a'rrai] _nm_ (_INFORM_) array; ~ **empaquetado** (_INFORM_) packed array.

arrayán [arra'jan] _nm_ myrtle.

arre ['arre] _excl_ gee up!

arrear [arre'ar] _vt_ to drive on, urge on ♦ _vi_ to hurry along.

arrebañar [arreβa'ɲar] _vt_ (_juntar_) to scrape together.

arrebatado, a [arreβa'taðo, a] _adj_ rash, impetuous; (_repentino_) sudden, hasty.

arrebatar [arreβa'tar] _vt_ to snatch (away), seize; (_fig_) to captivate; ~**se** _vr_ to get carried away, get excited.

arrebato [arre'βato] _nm_ fit of rage, fury; (_éxtasis_) rapture; **en un** ~ **de cólera** in an outburst of anger.

arrebolar [arreβo'lar] _vt_ to redden; ~**se** _vr_ (_enrojecer_) to blush.

arrebujar [arreβu'xar] _vt_ (_objetos_) to jumble together; ~**se** _vr_ to wrap o.s. up.

arrechar [arre'tʃar] (_AM_) _vt_ to arouse, excite; ~**se** _vr_ to become aroused.

arrechucho [arre'tʃutʃo] _nm_ (_MED_) turn.

arreciar [arre'θjar] _vi_ to get worse; (_viento_) to get stronger.

arrecife [arre'θife] nm reef.
arredrar [arre'ðrar] vt (hacer retirarse) to
drive back; ~**se** vr (apartarse) to draw
back; ~**se ante algo** to shrink away
from sth.
arreglado, a [arre'ɣlaðo, a] adj (ordenado)
neat, orderly; (moderado) moderate,
reasonable.
arreglar [arre'ɣlar] vt (poner orden) to tidy
up; (algo roto) to fix, repair; (problema) to
solve; ~**se** vr to reach an understanding;
arreglárselas (fam) to get by, manage.
arreglo [a'rreɣlo] nm settlement; (orden)
order; (acuerdo) agreement; (MUS)
arrangement, setting; (INFORM) array;
con ~ a in accordance with; **llegar a un**
~ to reach a compromise.
arrellanarse [arreʎa'narse] vr to sprawl; ~
en el asiento to lie back in one's chair.
arremangar [arreman'gar] vt to roll up,
turn up; ~**se** vr to roll up one's sleeves.
arremangue [arre'mange] etc vb V
arremangar.
arremeter [arreme'ter] vt to attack,
assault; ~ **contra algn** to attack sb.
arremetida [arreme'tiða] nf assault.
arremolinarse [arremoli'narse] vr to crowd
around, mill around; (corriente) to swirl,
eddy.
arrendador, a [arrenda'ðor, a] nm/f
landlord/lady.
arrendamiento [arrenda'mjento] nm
letting; (el alquilar) hiring; (contrato)
lease; (alquiler) rent.
arrendar [arren'dar] vt to let; to hire; to
lease; to rent.
arrendatario, a [arrenda'tarjo, a] nm/f
tenant.
arreos [a'rreos] nmpl harness sg, trappings.
arrepentido, a [arrepen'tiðo, a] nm/f (POL)
reformed terrorist.
arrepentimiento [arrepenti'mjento] nm
regret, repentance.
arrepentirse [arrepen'tirse] vr to repent; ~
de (haber hecho) algo to regret (doing)
sth.
arrepienta [arre'pjenta] etc,
arrepintiendo [arrepin'tjendo] etc vb V
arrepentirse.
arrestar [arres'tar] vt to arrest; (encarcelar)
to imprison.
arresto [a'rresto] nm arrest; (MIL)
detention; (audacia) boldness, daring; ~
domiciliario house arrest.
arriar [a'rrjar] vt (velas) to haul down;
(bandera) to lower, strike; (un cable) to
pay out.
arriate [a'rrjate] nm (BOT) bed; (camino)

road.

arriba [a'rriβa] adv **1** (posición) above;
desde ~ from above; ~ **del todo** at the
very top, right on top; **Juan está** ~ Juan
is upstairs; **lo** ~ **mencionado** the
aforementioned; **aquí/allí** ~ up here/
there; **está hasta** ~ **de trabajo** (fam) he's
up to his eyes in work (fam)
2 (dirección) up, upwards; **más** ~ higher
o further up; **calle** ~ up the street
3: de ~ **abajo** from top to bottom; **mirar**
a algn de ~ **abajo** to look sb up and
down
4: para ~: **de 50 euros para** ~ from 50
euros up(wards); **de la cintura (para)** ~
from the waist up
♦ adj: **de** ~: **el piso de** ~ the upstairs flat
(BRIT) o apartment; **la parte de** ~ the top
o upper part
♦ prep: ~ **de** (AM) above; ~ **de 200 dólares**
more than 200 dollars
♦ excl: ¡~! up!; ¡**manos** ~! hands up!; ¡~
España! long live Spain!

arribar [arri'βar] vi to put into port; (esp
AM: llegar) to arrive.
arribista [arri'βista] nm/f parvenu(e),
upstart.
arribo [a'rriβo] nm (esp AM) arrival.
arriendo [a'rrjendo] etc vb V **arrendar** ♦ nm
= **arrendamiento.**
arriero [a'rrjero] nm muleteer.
arriesgado, a [arrjes'ɣaðo, a] adj
(peligroso) risky; (audaz) bold, daring.
arriesgar [arrjes'ɣar] vt to risk; (poner en
peligro) to endanger; ~**se** vr to take a risk.
arriesgue [a'rrjesɣe] etc vb V **arriesgar.**
arrimar [arri'mar] vt (acercar) to bring
close; (poner de lado) to set aside; ~**se** vr
to come close o closer; ~**se a** to lean on;
(fig) to keep company with; (buscar
ayuda) to seek the protection of;
arrímate a mí cuddle up to me.
arrinconado, a [arrinko'naðo, a] adj
forgotten, neglected.
arrinconar [arrinko'nar] vt to put in a
corner; (fig) to put on one side;
(abandonar) to push aside.
arriscado, a [arris'kaðo, a] adj (GEO)
craggy; (fig) bold, resolute.
arroba [a'rroβa] nf (peso) 25 pounds;
(INFORM: en dirección electrónica) at; **tiene**
talento por ~**s** he has loads o bags of
talent.
arrobado, a [arro'βaðo, a] adj entranced,
enchanted.

arrobamiento [arroßa'mjento] *nm* ecstasy.
arrobar [arro'ßar] *vt* to enchant; ~**se** *vr* to be enraptured; (*místico*) to go into a trance.
arrodillarse [arroði'ʎarse] *vr* to kneel (down).
arrogancia [arro'ɣanθja] *nf* arrogance.
arrogante [arro'ɣante] *adj* arrogant.
arrojar [arro'xar] *vt* to throw, hurl; (*humo*) to emit, give out; (*COM*) to yield, produce; ~**se** *vr* to throw o hurl o.s.
arrojo [a'rroxo] *nm* daring.
arrollador, a [arroʎa'ðor, a] *adj* crushing, overwhelming.
arrollar [arro'ʎar] *vt* (*enrollar*) to roll up; (*suj: inundación*) to wash away; (*AUTO*) to run over; (*DEPORTE*) to crush.
arropar [arro'par] *vt* to cover (up), wrap up; ~**se** *vr* to wrap o.s. up.
arrostrar [arros'trar] *vt* to face (up to); ~**se** *vr*: ~**se con algn** to face up to sb.
arroyo [a'rrojo] *nm* stream; (*de la calle*) gutter; **poner a algn en el** ~ to turn sb onto the streets.
arroz [a'rroθ] *nm* rice; ~ **con leche** rice pudding.
arrozal [arro'θal] *nm* paddy field.
arruga [a'rruɣa] *nf* fold; (*de cara*) wrinkle; (*de vestido*) crease.
arrugar [arru'ɣar] *vt* to fold; to wrinkle; to crease; ~**se** *vr* to get wrinkled; to get creased.
arrugue [a'rruɣe] *etc vb V* **arrugar**.
arruinar [arrwi'nar] *vt* to ruin, wreck; ~**se** *vr* to be ruined.
arrullar [arru'ʎar] *vi* to coo ♦ *vt* to lull to sleep.
arrumaco [arru'mako] *nm* (*caricia*) caress; (*halago*) piece of flattery.
arrumbar [arrum'bar] *vt* (*objeto*) to discard; (*individuo*) to silence.
arrurruz [arru'rruθ] nm arrowroot.
arsenal [arse'nal] *nm* naval dockyard; (*MIL*) arsenal.
arsénico [ar'seniko] *nm* arsenic.
arte ['arte] *nm* (*gen m en sg y siempre f en pl*) art; (*maña*) skill, guile; **por** ~ **de magia** (as if) by magic; **no tener** ~ **ni parte en algo** to have nothing whatsoever to do with sth; ~**s** *nfpl* arts; **Bellas A**~**s** Fine Art *sg*; ~**s y oficios** arts and crafts.
artefacto [arte'fakto] *nm* appliance; (*ARQUEOLOGÍA*) artefact.
arteria [ar'terja] *nf* artery.
arterial [arte'rjal] *adj* arterial; (*presión*) blood *cpd*.
arterio(e)sclerosis [arterjo(e)skle'rosis] *nf inv* hardening of the arteries,

arteriosclerosis.
artesa [ar'tesa] *nf* trough.
artesanía [artesa'nia] *nf* craftsmanship; (*artículos*) handicrafts *pl*.
artesano, a [arte'sano, a] *nm/f* artisan, craftsman/woman.
ártico, a ['artiko, a] *adj* Arctic ♦ *nm*: **el** (**océano**) **Á**~ the Arctic (Ocean).
articulación [artikula'θjon] *nf* articulation; (*MED, TEC*) joint.
articulado, a [artiku'laðo, a] *adj* articulated; jointed.
articular [artiku'lar] *vt* to articulate; to join together.
articulista [artiku'lista] *nm/f* columnist, contributor (to a newspaper).
artículo [ar'tikulo] *nm* article; (*cosa*) thing, article; (*TV*) feature, report; ~ **de fondo** leader, editorial; ~**s** *nmpl* goods; ~**s de marca** (*COM*) proprietary goods.
artífice [ar'tifiθe] *nm* artist, craftsman; (*fig*) architect.
artificial [artifi'θjal] *adj* artificial.
artificio [arti'fiθjo] *nm* art, skill; (*artesanía*) craftsmanship; (*astucia*) cunning.
artillería [artiʎe'ria] *nf* artillery.
artillero [arti'ʎero] *nm* artilleryman, gunner.
artilugio [arti'luxjo] *nm* gadget.
artimaña [arti'maɲa] *nf* trap, snare; (*astucia*) cunning.
artista [ar'tista] *nm/f* (*pintor*) artist, painter; (*TEAT*) artist, artiste.
artístico, a [ar'tistiko, a] *adj* artistic.
artritis [ar'tritis] *nf* arthritis.
artrosis [ar'trosis] *nf* osteoarthritis.
arveja [ar'ßexa] *nf* (*AM*) pea.
arzobispo [arθo'ßispo] *nm* archbishop.
as [as] *nm* ace; ~ **del fútbol** star player.
asa ['asa] *nf* handle; (*fig*) lever.
asado [a'saðo] *nm* roast (meat); (*AM: barbacoa*) barbecue.
asador [asa'ðor] *nm* (*varilla*) spit; (*aparato*) spit roaster.
asadura(s) [asa'ðura(s)] *nf(pl)* entrails *pl*, offal *sg*; (*CULIN*) chitterlings *pl*.
asaetear [asaete'ar] *vt* (*fig*) to bother.
asalariado, a [asala'rjaðo, a] *adj* paid, wage-earning, salaried ♦ *nm/f* wage earner.
asaltador, a [asalta'ðor, a], **asaltante** [asal'tante] *nm/f* assailant.
asaltar [asal'tar] *vt* to attack, assault; (*fig*) to assail.
asalto [a'salto] *nm* attack, assault; (*DEPORTE*) round.
asamblea [asam'blea] *nf* assembly; (*reunión*) meeting.

asar [a'sar] *vt* to roast; ~ **al horno/a la parrilla** to bake/grill; ~**se** *vr* (*fig*): **me aso de calor** I'm roasting; **aquí se asa uno vivo** it's boiling hot here.

asbesto [as'ßesto] *nm* asbestos.

ascendencia [asθen'denθja] *nf* ancestry; **de** ~ **francesa** of French origin.

ascender [asθen'der] *vi* (*subir*) to ascend, rise; (*ser promovido*) to gain promotion ♦ *vt* to promote; ~ **a** to amount to.

ascendiente [asθen'djente] *nm* influence ♦ *nm/f* ancestor.

ascensión [asθen'sjon] *nf* ascent; **la A**~ the Ascension.

ascenso [as'θenso] *nm* ascent; (*promoción*) promotion.

ascensor [asθen'sor] *nm* lift (*BRIT*), elevator (*US*).

ascético, a [as'θetiko, a] *adj* ascetic.

ascienda [as'θjenda] *etc vb V* **ascender**.

asco ['asko] *nm*: **el ajo me da** ~ I hate *o* loathe garlic; **hacer** ~**s de algo** to turn up one's nose at sth; **estar hecho un** ~ to be filthy; **poner a algn de** ~ to call sb all sorts of names *o* every name under the sun; **¡qué** ~! how revolting *o* disgusting!

ascua ['askwa] *nf* ember; **arrimar el** ~ **a su sardina** to look after number one; **estar en** ~**s** to be on tenterhooks.

aseado, a [ase'aðo, a] *adj* clean; (*arreglado*) tidy; (*pulcro*) smart.

asear [ase'ar] *vt* (*lavar*) to wash; (*ordenar*) to tidy (up).

asechanza [ase'tʃanθa] *nf* trap, snare.

asediar [ase'ðjar] *vt* (*MIL*) to besiege, lay siege to; (*fig*) to chase, pester.

asedio [ase'ðjo] *nm* siege; (*COM*) run.

asegurado, a [aseɣu'raðo, a] *adj* insured.

asegurador, a [aseɣura'ðor, a] *nm/f* insurer.

asegurar [aseɣu'rar] *vt* (*consolidar*) to secure, fasten; (*dar garantía de*) to guarantee; (*preservar*) to safeguard; (*afirmar, dar por cierto*) to assure, affirm; (*tranquilizar*) to reassure; (*tomar un seguro*) to insure; ~**se** *vr* to assure o.s., make sure.

asemejarse [aseme'xarse] *vr* to be alike; ~ **a** to be like, resemble.

asentado, a [asen'taðo, a] *adj* established, settled.

asentar [asen'tar] *vt* (*sentar*) to seat, sit down; (*poner*) to place, establish; (*alisar*) to level, smooth down *o* out; (*anotar*) to note down ♦ *vi* to be suitable, suit.

asentimiento [asenti'mjento] *nm* assent, agreement.

asentir [asen'tir] *vi* to assent, agree.

aseo [a'seo] *nm* cleanliness; ~**s** *nmpl* toilet *sg* (*BRIT*), restroom *sg* (*US*), cloakroom *sg*.

aséptico, a [a'septiko, a] *adj* germ-free, free from infection.

asequible [ase'kiβle] *adj* (*precio*) reasonable; (*meta*) attainable; (*persona*) approachable.

aserradero [aserra'ðero] *nm* sawmill.

aserrar [ase'rrar] *vt* to saw.

asesinar [asesi'nar] *vt* to murder; (*POL*) to assassinate.

asesinato [asesi'nato] *nm* murder; assassination.

asesino, a [ase'sino, a] *nm/f* murderer, killer; (*POL*) assassin.

asesor, a [ase'sor, a] *nm/f* adviser, consultant; (*COM*) assessor, consultant; ~ **administrativo** management consultant.

asesorar [aseso'rar] *vt* (*JUR*) to advise, give legal advice to; (*COM*) to act as consultant to; ~**se** *vr*: ~**se con** *o* **de** to take advice from, consult.

asesoría [aseso'ria] *nf* (*cargo*) consultancy; (*oficina*) consultant's office.

asestar [ases'tar] *vt* (*golpe*) to deal; (*arma*) to aim; (*tiro*) to fire.

aseverar [aseße'rar] *vt* to assert.

asfaltado, a [asfal'taðo, a] *adj* asphalted ♦ *nm* (*pavimiento*) asphalt.

asfalto [as'falto] *nm* asphalt.

asfixia [as'fiksja] *nf* asphyxia, suffocation.

asfixiar [asfik'sjar] *vt* to asphyxiate, suffocate.

asga ['asɣa] *etc vb V* **asir**.

así [a'si] *adv* (*de esta manera*) in this way, like this, thus; (*aunque*) although; (*tan pronto como*) as soon as; ~ **que** so; ~ **como** as well as; ~ **y todo** even so; **¿no es** ~? isn't it?, didn't you? *etc*; ~ **de grande** this big; **¡**~ **sea!** so be it!; ~ **es la vida** such is life, that's life.

Asia ['asja] *nf* Asia.

asiático, a [a'sjatiko, a] *adj, nm/f* Asian, Asiatic.

asidero [asi'ðero] *nm* handle.

asiduidad [asiðwi'ðað] *nf* assiduousness.

asiduo, a [a'siðwo, a] *adj* assiduous; (*frecuente*) frequent ♦ *nm/f* regular (customer).

asiento [a'sjento] *etc vb V* **asentar, asentir** ♦ *nm* (*mueble*) seat, chair; (*de coche, en tribunal etc*) seat; (*localidad*) seat, place; (*fundamento*) site; ~ **delantero/trasero** front/back seat.

asierre [a'sjerre] *etc vb V* **aserrar**.

asignación [asiɣna'θjon] *nf* (*atribución*)

assignment; (*reparto*) allocation; (*COM*) allowance; ~ **(semanal)** pocket money; ~ **de presupuesto** budget appropriation.

asignar [asiɣ'nar] *vt* to assign, allocate.

asignatura [asiɣna'tura] *nf* subject; (*curso*) course; ~ **pendiente** (*fig*) matter pending.

asilado, a [asi'laðo, a] *nm/f* refugee.

asilo [a'silo] *nm* (*refugio*) asylum, refuge; (*establecimiento*) home, institution; ~ **político** political asylum.

asimilación [asimila'θjon] *nf* assimilation.

asimilar [asimi'lar] *vt* to assimilate.

asimismo [asi'mismo] *adv* in the same way, likewise.

asintiendo [asin'tjendo] *etc vb V* **asentir**.

asir [a'sir] *vt* to seize, grasp; ~**se** *vr* to take hold; ~**se a** *o* **de** to seize.

asistencia [asis'tenθja] *nf* presence; (*TEAT*) audience; (*MED*) attendance; (*ayuda*) assistance; ~ **social** social *o* welfare work.

asistente, a [asis'tente, a] *nm/f* assistant ♦ *nm* (*MIL*) orderly ♦ *nf* daily help; **los** ~**s** those present; ~ **social** social worker.

asistido, a [asis'tiðo, a] *adj* (*AUTO: dirección*) power-assisted; ~ **por ordenador** computer-assisted.

asistir [asis'tir] *vt* to assist, help ♦ *vi*: ~ **a** to attend, be present at.

asma ['asma] *nf* asthma.

asno ['asno] *nm* donkey; (*fig*) ass.

asociación [asoθja'θjon] *nf* association; (*COM*) partnership.

asociado, a [aso'θjaðo, a] *adj* associate ♦ *nm/f* associate; (*COM*) partner.

asociar [aso'θjar] *vt* to associate; ~**se** *vr* to become partners.

asolar [aso'lar] *vt* to destroy.

asolear [asole'ar] *vt* to put in the sun; ~**se** *vr* to sunbathe.

asomar [aso'mar] *vt* to show, stick out ♦ *vi* to appear; ~**se** *vr* to appear, show up; ~ **la cabeza por la ventana** to put one's head out of the window.

asombrar [asom'brar] *vt* to amaze, astonish; ~**se** *vr*: ~**se (de)** (*sorprenderse*) to be amazed (at); (*asustarse*) to be frightened (at).

asombro [a'sombro] *nm* amazement, astonishment.

asombroso, a [asom'broso, a] *adj* amazing, astonishing.

asomo [a'somo] *nm* hint, sign; **ni por** ~ by no means.

asonancia [aso'nanθja] *nf* (*LIT*) assonance; (*fig*) connection; **no tener** ~ **con** to bear no relation to.

asorocharse [asoro'tʃarse] *vr* (*AM*) to get mountain sickness.

aspa ['aspa] *nf* (*cruz*) cross; (*de molino*) sail; **en** ~ X-shaped.

aspaviento [aspa'ßjento] *nm* exaggerated display of feeling; (*fam*) fuss.

aspecto [as'pekto] *nm* (*apariencia*) look, appearance; (*fig*) aspect; **bajo ese** ~ from that point of view.

aspereza [aspe'reθa] *nf* roughness; (*de fruta*) sharpness; (*de carácter*) surliness.

áspero, a ['aspero, a] *adj* rough; sharp; harsh.

aspersión [asper'sjon] *nf* sprinkling; (*AGR*) spraying.

aspersor [asper'sor] *nm* sprinkler.

aspiración [aspira'θjon] *nf* breath, inhalation; (*MUS*) short pause; **aspiraciones** *nfpl* aspirations.

aspiradora [aspira'ðora] *nf* vacuum cleaner, Hoover ®.

aspirante [aspi'rante] *nm/f* (*candidato*) candidate; (*DEPORTE*) contender.

aspirar [aspi'rar] *vt* to breathe in ♦ *vi*: ~ **a** to aspire to.

aspirina [aspi'rina] *nf* aspirin.

asquear [aske'ar] *vt* to sicken ♦ *vi* to be sickening; ~**se** *vr* to feel disgusted.

asquerosidad [askerosi'ðað] *nf* (*suciedad*) filth; (*dicho*) obscenity; (*truco*) dirty trick.

asqueroso, a [aske'roso, a] *adj* disgusting, sickening.

asta ['asta] *nf* lance; (*arpón*) spear; (*mango*) shaft, handle; (*ZOOL*) horn; **a media** ~ at half mast.

astado, a [as'taðo, a] *adj* horned ♦ *nm* bull.

asterisco [aste'risko] *nm* asterisk.

asteroide [aste'roiðe] *nm* asteroid.

astigmatismo [astiɣma'tismo] *nm* astigmatism.

astilla [as'tiʎa] *nf* splinter; (*pedacito*) chip; ~**s** *nfpl* firewood *sg*.

astillarse [asti'ʎarse] *vr* to splinter; (*fig*) to shatter.

astillero [asti'ʎero] *nm* shipyard.

astringente [astrin'xente] *adj, nm* astringent.

astro ['astro] *nm* star.

astrología [astrolo'xia] *nf* astrology.

astrólogo, a [as'troloɣo, a] *nm/f* astrologer.

astronauta [astro'nauta] *nm/f* astronaut.

astronave [astro'naße] *nm* spaceship.

astronomía [astrono'mia] *nf* astronomy.

astronómico, a [astro'nomiko, a] *adj* (*tb fig*) astronomical.

astrónomo, a [as'tronomo, a] *nm/f*

astronomer.

astroso, a [as'troso, a] adj (*desaliñado*) untidy; (*vil*) contemptible.

astucia [as'tuθja] nf astuteness; (*destreza*) clever trick.

asturiano, a [astu'rjano, a] adj, nm/f Asturian.

Asturias [as'turjas] nfpl Asturias; **Príncipe de** ~ crown prince.

astuto, a [as'tuto, a] adj astute; (*taimado*) cunning.

asueto [a'sweto] nm holiday; (*tiempo libre*) time off; **día de** ~ day off; **tarde de** ~ (*trabajo*) afternoon off; (*ESCOL*) half-holiday.

asumir [asu'mir] vt to assume.

asunción [asun'θjon] nf assumption.

asunto [a'sunto] nm (*tema*) matter, subject; (*negocio*) business; **¡eso es** ~ **mio!** that's my business!; ~**s exteriores** foreign affairs; ~**s a tratar** agenda sg.

asustadizo, a [asusta'ðiθo, a] adj easily frightened.

asustar [asus'tar] vt to frighten; ~**se** vr to be/become frightened.

atacante [ata'kante] nm/f attacker.

atacar [ata'kar] vt to attack.

atadura [ata'ðura] nf bond, tie.

atajar [ata'xar] vt (*gen*) to stop; (*ruta de fuga*) to cut off; (*discurso*) to interrupt ♦ vi to take a short cut.

atajo [a'taxo] nm short cut; (*DEPORTE*) tackle.

atalaya [ata'laja] nf watchtower.

atañer [ata'ɲer] vi: ~ **a** to concern; **en lo que atañe a eso** with regard to that.

ataque [a'take] etc vb V **atacar** ♦ nm attack; ~ **cardíaco** heart attack.

atar [a'tar] vt to tie, tie up; ~ **la lengua a algn** (*fig*) to silence sb.

atardecer [ataðe'θer] vi to get dark ♦ nm evening; (*crepúsculo*) dusk.

atardezca [atar'ðeθka] etc vb V **atardecer**.

atareado, a [atare'aðo, a] adj busy.

atascar [atas'kar] vt to clog up; (*obstruir*) to jam; (*fig*) to hinder; ~**se** vr to stall; (*cañería*) to get blocked up; (*fig*) to get bogged down; (*en discurso*) to dry up.

atasco [a'tasko] nm obstruction; (*AUTO*) traffic jam.

atasque [a'taske] etc vb V **atascar**.

ataúd [ata'uð] nm coffin.

ataviar [ata'βjar] vt to deck, array; ~**se** vr to dress up.

atavío [ata'βio] nm attire, dress; ~**s** nmpl finery sg.

ateísmo [ate'ismo] nm atheism.

atemorice [atemo'riθe] etc vb V atemorizar.

atemorizar [atemori'θar] vt to frighten, scare; ~**se** vr to get frightened o scared.

Atenas [a'tenas] nf Athens.

atención [aten'θjon] nf attention; (*bondad*) kindness ♦ excl (be) careful!, look out!; **en** ~ **a esto** in view of this.

atender [aten'der] vt to attend to, look after; (*TEC*) to service; (*enfermo*) to care for; (*ruego*) to comply with ♦ vi to pay attention; ~ **a** to attend to.

atendré [aten'dre] etc vb V **atenerse**.

atenerse [ate'nerse] vr: ~ **a** to abide by, adhere to.

atenga [a'tenga] etc vb V **atenerse**.

ateniense [ate'njense] adj, nm/f Athenian.

atentado [aten'taðo] nm crime, illegal act; (*asalto*) assault; (*terrorista*) attack; ~ **contra la vida de algn** attempt on sb's life; ~ **golpista** attempted coup; ~ **suicida** suicide bombing, suicide attack.

atentamente [atenta'mente] adv: **le saluda** ~ Yours faithfully.

atentar [aten'tar] vi: ~ **a** o **contra** to commit an outrage against.

atento, a [a'tento, a] adj attentive, observant; (*cortés*) polite, thoughtful; **su atenta (carta)** (*COM*) your letter.

atenuante [ate'nwante] adj: **circunstancias** ~**s** extenuating o mitigating circumstances ♦ nfpl: ~**s** extenuating o mitigating circumstances.

atenuar [ate'nwar] vt to attenuate; (*disminuir*) to lessen, minimize.

ateo, a [a'teo, a] adj atheistic ♦ nm/f atheist.

aterciopelado, a [aterθjope'laðo, a] adj velvety.

aterido, a [ate'riðo, a] adj: ~ **de frío** frozen stiff.

aterrador, a [aterra'ðor, a] adj frightening.

aterrar [ate'rrar] vt to frighten; (*aterrorizar*) to terrify; ~**se** vr to be frightened; to be terrified.

aterrice [ate'rriθe] etc vb V **aterrizar**.

aterrizaje [aterri'θaxe] nm landing; ~ **forzoso** forced landing.

aterrizar [aterri'θar] vi to land.

aterrorice [aterro'riθe] etc vb V aterrorizar.

aterrorizar [aterrori'θar] vt to terrify.

atesorar [ateso'rar] vt to hoard, store up.

atestado, a [ates'taðo, a] adj packed ♦ nm (*JUR*) affidavit.

atestar [ates'tar] vt to pack, stuff; (*JUR*) to attest, testify to.

atestiguar [atesti'ɣwar] vt to testify to, bear witness to.

atestigüe [ates'tiɣwe] etc vb V **atestiguar**.

atiborrar [atiβoˈrrar] _vt_ to fill, stuff; ~**se** _vr_ to stuff o.s.

atice [aˈtiθe] _etc vb V_ **atizar**.

ático [ˈatiko] _nm_ attic; ~ **de lujo** penthouse flat.

atienda [aˈtjenda] _etc vb V_ **atender**.

atildar [atilˈdar] _vt_ to criticize; (_TIP_) to put a tilde over; ~**se** _vr_ to spruce o.s. up.

atinado, a [atiˈnaðo, a] _adj_ correct; (_sensato_) sensible.

atinar [atiˈnar] _vi_ (_acertar_) to be right; ~ **con** _o_ **en** (_solución_) to hit upon; ~ **a hacer** to manage to do.

atípico, a [aˈtipiko, a] _adj_ atypical.

atiplado, a [atiˈplaðo, a] _adj_ (_voz_) high-pitched.

atisbar [atisˈβar] _vt_ to spy on; (_echar ojeada_) to peep at.

atizar [atiˈθar] _vt_ to poke; (_horno etc_) to stoke; (_fig_) to stir up, rouse.

atlántico, a [atˈlantiko, a] _adj_ Atlantic ♦ _nm_: **el (océano) A**~ the Atlantic (Ocean).

atlas [ˈatlas] _nm inv_ atlas.

atleta [atˈleta] _nm/f_ athlete.

atlético, a [atˈletiko, a] _adj_ athletic.

atletismo [atleˈtismo] _nm_ athletics _sg_.

atmósfera [atˈmosfera] _nf_ atmosphere.

atmosférico, a [atmosˈferiko, a] _adj_ atmospheric.

atol(e) [aˈtol(e)] _nm_ (_AM_) cornflour drink.

atolladero [atoʎaˈðero] _nm_: **estar en un** ~ to be in a jam.

atollarse [atoˈʎarse] _vr_ to get stuck; (_fig_) to get into a jam.

atolondrado, a [atolonˈdraðo, a] _adj_ scatterbrained.

atolondramiento [atolondraˈmjento] _nm_ bewilderment; (_insensatez_) silliness.

atómico, a [aˈtomiko, a] _adj_ atomic.

atomizador [atomiθaˈðor] _nm_ atomizer.

átomo [ˈatomo] _nm_ atom.

atónito, a [aˈtonito, a] _adj_ astonished, amazed.

atontado, a [atonˈtaðo, a] _adj_ stunned; (_bobo_) silly, daft.

atontar [atonˈtar] _vt_ to stun; ~**se** _vr_ to become confused.

atorar [atoˈrar] _vt_ to obstruct; ~**se** _vr_ (_atragantarse_) to choke.

atormentar [atormenˈtar] _vt_ to torture; (_molestar_) to torment; (_acosar_) to plague, harass.

atornillar [atorniˈʎar] _vt_ to screw on _o_ down.

atorón [atoˈron] _nm_ (_AM_) traffic jam.

atosigar [atosiˈɣar] _vt_ to harass.

atosigue [atoˈsiɣe] _etc vb V_ **atosigar**.

atrabiliario, a [atraβiˈljarjo, a] _adj_ bad-tempered.

atracadero [atrakaˈðero] _nm_ pier.

atracador, a [atrakaˈðor, a] _nm/f_ robber.

atracar [atraˈkar] _vt_ (_NAUT_) to moor; (_robar_) to hold up, rob ♦ _vi_ to moor; ~**se** _vr_ (_hartarse_) to stuff o.s.

atracción [atrakˈθjon] _nf_ attraction.

atraco [aˈtrako] _nm_ holdup, robbery.

atracón [atraˈkon] _nm_: **darse** _o_ **pegarse un** ~ **(de)** (_fam_) to pig out (on).

atractivo, a [atrakˈtiβo, a] _adj_ attractive ♦ _nm_ attraction; (_belleza_) attractiveness.

atraer [atraˈer] _vt_ to attract; **dejarse** ~ **por** to be tempted by.

atragantarse [atraɣanˈtarse] _vr_: ~ **(con algo)** to choke (on sth); **se me ha atragantado el chico ese/el inglés** I don't take to that boy/English.

atraiga [aˈtraiɣa] _etc_, **atraje** [aˈtraxe] _etc vb V_ **atraer**.

atrancar [atranˈkar] _vt_ (_con tranca, barra_) to bar, bolt.

atranque [aˈtranke] _etc vb V_ **atrancar**.

atrapar [atraˈpar] _vt_ to trap; (_resfriado etc_) to catch.

atraque [aˈtrake] _etc vb V_ **atracar**.

atrás [aˈtras] _adv_ (_movimiento_) back(wards); (_lugar_) behind; (_tiempo_) previously; **ir hacia** ~ to go back(wards); to go to the rear; **estar** ~ to be behind _o_ at the back.

atrasado, a [atraˈsaðo, a] _adj_ slow; (_pago_) overdue, late; (_país_) backward.

atrasar [atraˈsar] _vi_ to be slow; ~**se** _vr_ to remain behind; (_llegar tarde_) to arrive late.

atraso [aˈtraso] _nm_ slowness; lateness, delay; (_de país_) backwardness; ~**s** _nmpl_ arrears.

atravesado, a [atraβeˈsaðo, a] _adj_: **un tronco** ~ **en la carretera** a tree trunk lying across the road.

atravesar [atraβeˈsar] _vt_ (_cruzar_) to cross (over); (_traspasar_) to pierce; (_período_) to go through; (_poner al través_) to lay _o_ put across; ~**se** _vr_ to come in between; (_intervenir_) to interfere.

atraviese [atraˈβjese] _etc vb V_ **atravesar**.

atrayendo [atraˈjendo] _vb V_ **atraer**.

atrayente [atraˈjente] _adj_ attractive.

atreverse [atreˈβerse] _vr_ to dare; (_insolentarse_) to be insolent.

atrevido, a [atreˈβiðo, a] _adj_ daring; insolent.

atrevimiento [atreβiˈmjento] _nm_ daring; insolence.

atribución [atriβuˈθjon] _nf_ (_LIT_) attribution; **atribuciones** _nfpl_ (_POL_) functions; (_ADMIN_) responsibilities.

atribuir [atriβu'ir] *vt* to attribute; (*funciones*) to confer.

atribular [atriβu'lar] *vt* to afflict, distress.

atributo [atri'βuto] *nm* attribute.

atribuya [atri'βuja] *etc*, **atribuyendo** [atriβu'jendo] *etc vb V* **atribuir**.

atril [a'tril] *nm* lectern; (*MUS*) music stand.

atrincherarse [atrintʃe'rarse] *vr* (*MIL*) to dig (o.s.) in; ~ **en** (*fig*) to hide behind.

atrio ['atrjo] *nm* (*REL*) porch.

atrocidad [atroθi'ðað] *nf* atrocity, outrage.

atrofiado, a [atro'fjaðo, a] *adj* (*extremidad*) withered.

atrofiarse [atro'fjarse] *vr* (*tb fig*) to atrophy.

atronador, a [atrona'ðor, a] *adj* deafening.

atropellar [atrope'ʎar] *vt* (*derribar*) to knock over *o* down; (*empujar*) to push (aside); (*AUTO*) to run over *o* down; (*agraviar*) to insult; ~**se** *vr* to act hastily.

atropello [atro'peʎo] *nm* (*AUTO*) accident; (*empujón*) push; (*agravio*) wrong; (*atrocidad*) outrage.

atroz [a'troθ] *adj* atrocious, awful.

A.T.S. *nm/f abr* (= *Ayudante Técnico Sanitario*) nurse.

atto., a. *abr* (= *atento, a*) Yours faithfully.

attrezzo [a'treθo] *nm* props *pl*.

atuendo [a'twendo] *nm* attire.

atufar [atu'far] *vt* (*suj: olor*) to overcome; (*molestar*) to irritate; ~**se** *vr* (*fig*) to get cross.

atún [a'tun] *nm* tuna, tunny.

aturdir [atur'ðir] *vt* to stun; (*suj: ruido*) to deafen; (*fig*) to dumbfound, bewilder.

atur(r)ullar [atur(r)u'ʎar] *vt* to bewilder.

atusar [atu'sar] *vt* (*cortar*) to trim; (*alisar*) to smooth (down).

atuve [a'tuβe] *etc vb V* **atenerse**.

audacia [au'ðaθja] *nf* boldness, audacity.

audaz [au'ðaθ] *adj* bold, audacious.

audible [au'ðiβle] *adj* audible.

audición [auði'θjon] *nf* hearing; (*TEAT*) audition; ~ **radiofónica** radio concert.

audiencia [au'ðjenθja] *nf* audience; (*JUR*) high court; (*POL*): ~ **pública** public inquiry.

audífono [au'ðifono] *nm* hearing aid.

audiovisual [auðjoβi'swal] *adj* audio-visual.

auditivo, a [auði'tiβo, a] *adj* hearing *cpd*; (*conducto, nervio*) auditory.

auditor [auði'tor] *nm* (*JUR*) judge-advocate; (*COM*) auditor.

auditoría [auðito'ria] *nf* audit; (*profesión*) auditing.

auditorio [auði'torjo] *nm* audience; (*sala*) auditorium.

auge ['auxe] *nm* boom; (*clímax*) climax; (*ECON*) expansion; **estar en** ~ to thrive.

augurar [auɣu'rar] *vt* to predict; (*presagiar*) to portend.

augurio [au'ɣurjo] *nm* omen.

aula ['aula] *nf* classroom.

aullar [au'ʎar] *vi* to howl, yell.

aullido [au'ʎiðo] *nm* howl, yell.

aumentar [aumen'tar] *vt* to increase; (*precios*) to put up; (*producción*) to step up; (*con microscopio, anteojos*) to magnify ♦ *vi*, ~**se** *vr* to increase, be on the increase.

aumento [au'mento] *nm* increase; rise.

aún [a'un] *adv* still, yet.

aun [a'un] *adv* even.

aunque [a'unke] *conj* though, although, even though.

aúpa [a'upa] *excl* up!, come on!; (*fam*): **una función de** ~ a slap-up do; **una paliza de** ~ a good hiding.

aupar [au'par] *vt* (*levantar*) to help up; (*fig*) to praise.

aura ['aura] *nf* (*atmósfera*) aura.

aureola [aure'ola] *nf* halo.

auricular [auriku'lar] *nm* earpiece, receiver; ~**es** *nmpl* headphones.

aurora [au'rora] *nf* dawn; ~ **boreal(is)** northern lights *pl*.

auscultar [auskul'tar] *vt* (*MED: pecho*) to listen to, sound.

ausencia [au'senθja] *nf* absence.

ausentarse [ausen'tarse] *vr* to go away; (*por poco tiempo*) to go out.

ausente [au'sente] *adj* absent ♦ *nm/f* (*ESCOL*) absentee; (*JUR*) missing person.

auspiciar [auspi'sjar] *vt* (*AM*) to back, sponsor.

auspicios [aus'piθjos] *nmpl* auspices; (*protección*) protection *sg*.

austeridad [austeri'ðað] *nf* austerity.

austero, a [aus'tero, a] *adj* austere.

austral [aus'tral] *adj* southern ♦ *nm* monetary unit of Argentina (*1985-1991*).

Australia [aus'tralja] *nf* Australia.

australiano, a [austra'ljano, a] *adj*, *nm/f* Australian.

Austria ['austrja] *nf* Austria.

austriaco, a [aus'trjako, a], **austríaco, a** [aus'triako, a] *adj*, *nm/f* Austrian.

autenticar [autenti'kar] *vt* to authenticate.

auténtico, a [au'tentiko, a] *adj* authentic.

autentificar [autentifi'kar] *vt* to authenticate.

autentique [auten'tike] *etc vb V* **autenticar**.

auto ['auto] *nm* (*coche*) car; (*JUR*) edict, decree; (: *orden*) writ; ~**s** *nmpl* (*JUR*)

proceedings; (: *acta*) court record *sg*; ~
de comparecencia summons, subpoena.
autoadhesivo, a [autoaðe'sißo, a] *adj* self-
adhesive; (*sobre*) self-sealing.
autoalimentación [autoalimenta'θjon] *nf*
(*INFORM*): ~ **de hojas** automatic paper
feed.
autobiografía [autoßjoɤra'fia] *nf*
autobiography.
autobronceador [autoßronθea'ðor] *adj*
self-tanning.
autobús [auto'ßus] *nm* bus (*BRIT*),
(passenger) bus (*US*).
autocar [auto'kar] *nm* coach; ~ **de línea**
intercity coach.
autocomprobación [autokomproßa'θjon]
nf (*INFORM*) self-test.
autóctono, a [au'toktono, a] *adj* native,
indigenous.
autodefensa [autoðe'fensa] *nf* self-
defence.
autodeterminación [autoðetermina'θjon]
nf self-determination.
autodidacta [autoði'ðakta] *adj* self-taught
♦ *nm/f*: **ser un(a)** ~ to be self-taught.
autoescuela [autoes'kwela] *nf* driving
school.
autofinanciado, a [autofinan'θjaðo, a] *adj*
self-financing.
autogestión [autoxes'tjon] *nf* self-
management.
autógrafo [au'toɤrafo] *nm* autograph.
automación [automa'θjon] *nf*
= **automatización**.
autómata [au'tomata] *nm* automaton.
automáticamente [auto'matikamente] *adv*
automatically.
automatice [automa'tiθe] *etc vb V*
automatizar.
automático, a [auto'matiko, a] *adj*
automatic ♦ *nm* press stud.
automatización [automatiθa'θjon] *nf*: ~ **de**
fábricas factory automation; ~ **de**
oficinas office automation.
automatizar [automati'θar] *vt* to automate.
automontable [automon'taßle] *adj* self-
assembly.
automotor, triz [automo'tor, 'triz] *adj*
self-propelled ♦ *nm* diesel train.
automóvil [auto'moßil] *nm* (motor) car
(*BRIT*), automobile (*US*).
automovilismo [automoßi'lismo] *nm*
(*DEPORTE*) (sports) car racing.
automovilista [automoßi'lista] *nm/f*
motorist, driver.
automovilístico, a [automoßi'listiko, a] *adj*
(*industria*) car *cpd*.
autonomía [autono'mia] *nf* autonomy; (*ESP*

POL) autonomy, self-government;
(: *comunidad*) autonomous region.
autonómico, a [auto'nomiko, a] *adj* (*ESP*
POL) relating to autonomy, autonomous;
gobierno ~ autonomous government.
autónomo, a [au'tonomo, a] *adj* autonomous; (*INFORM*) stand-alone, offline.
autopista [auto'pista] *nf* motorway (*BRIT*),
freeway (*US*).
autopsia [au'topsja] *nf* autopsy.
autor, a [au'tor, a] *nm/f* author; **los** ~**es del**
atentado those responsible for the attack.
autorice [auto'riθe] *etc vb V* **autorizar**.
autoridad [autori'ðað] *nf* authority; ~ **local**
local authority.
autoritario, a [autori'tarjo, a] *adj*
authoritarian.
autorización [autoriθa'θjon] *nf*
authorization.
autorizado, a [autori'θaðo, a] *adj*
authorized; (*aprobado*) approved.
autorizar [autori'θar] *vt* to authorize; to
approve.
autorretrato [autorre'trato] *nm* self-
portrait.
autoservicio [autoser'ßiθjo] *nm* self-
service shop *o* store; (*restaurante*) self-
service restaurant.
autostop [auto'stop] *nm* hitch-hiking;
hacer ~ to hitch-hike.
autostopista [autosto'pista] *nm/f* hitch-
hiker.
autosuficiencia [autosufi'θjenθja] *nf* self-
sufficiency.
autosuficiente [autosufi'θjente] *adj* self-
sufficient; (*pey*) smug.
autosugestión [autosuxes'tjon] *nf*
autosuggestion.
autovía [auto'ßia] *nf* ≈ dual carriageway
(*BRIT*), separated highway (*US*).
auxiliar [auksi'ljar] *vt* to help ♦ *nm/f*
assistant.
auxilio [auk'siljo] *nm* assistance, help;
primeros ~**s** first aid *sg*.
Av *abr* (= *Avenida*) Av(e).
a/v *abr* (*COM*: = *a vista*) at sight.
aval [a'ßal] *nm* guarantee; (*persona*)
guarantor.
avalancha [aßa'lantʃa] *nf* avalanche.
avalar [aßa'lar] *vt* (*COM etc*) to underwrite;
(*fig*) to endorse.
avance [a'ßanθe] *etc vb V* **avanzar** ♦ *nm*
advance; (*pago*) advance payment;
(*CINE*) trailer.
avanzado, a [aßan'θaðo, a] *adj* advanced;
de edad avanzada, ~ **de edad** elderly.
avanzar [aßan'θar] *vt, vi* to advance.
avaricia [aßa'riθja] *nf* avarice, greed.

avaricioso, a [aβari'θjoso, a] *adj* avaricious, greedy.

avaro, a [a'βaro, a] *adj* miserly, mean ♦ *nm/f* miser.

avasallar [aβasa'ʎar] *vt* to subdue, subjugate.

avatar [aβa'tar] *nm* change; **~es** ups and downs.

Avda *abr* (= *Avenida*) Av(e).

AVE ['aβe] *nm abr* (= *Alta Velocidad Española*) ≈ Bullet train.

ave ['aβe] *nf* bird; **~ de rapiña** bird of prey.

avecinarse [aβeθi'narse] *vr* (*tormenta, fig*) to approach, be on the way.

avejentar [aβexen'tar] *vt, vi*, **~se** *vr* to age.

avellana [aβe'ʎana] *nf* hazelnut.

avellano [aβe'ʎano] *nm* hazel tree.

avemaría [aβema'ria] *nm* Hail Mary, Ave Maria.

avena [a'βena] *nf* oats *pl*.

avendré [aβen'dre] *etc*, **avenga** [a'βenga] *etc vb V* **avenir**.

avenida [aβe'niða] *nf* (*calle*) avenue.

avenir [aβe'nir] *vt* to reconcile; **~se** *vr* to come to an agreement, reach a compromise.

aventado, a [aβen'taðo, a] *adj* (*AM*) daring.

aventajado, a [aβenta'xaðo, a] *adj* outstanding.

aventajar [aβenta'xar] *vt* (*sobrepasar*) to surpass, outstrip.

aventar [aβen'tar] *vt* to fan, blow; (*grano*) to winnow; (*AM fam*: *echar*) to chuck out.

aventón [aβen'ton] *nm* (*AM*) push; **pedir ~** to hitch a lift.

aventura [aβen'tura] *nf* adventure; **~ sentimental** love affair.

aventurado, a [aβentu'raðo, a] *adj* risky.

aventurar [aβentu'rar] *vt* to risk; **~se** *vr* to dare; **~se a hacer algo** to venture to do sth.

aventurero, a [aβentu'rero, a] *adj* adventurous.

avergoncé [aβerɣon'θe], **avergoncemos** [aβerɣon'θemos] *etc vb V* **avergonzar**.

avergonzar [aβerɣon'θar] *vt* to shame; (*desconcertar*) to embarrass; **~se** *vr* to be ashamed; to be embarrassed.

avergüence [aβer'ɣwenθe] *etc vb V* **avergonzar**.

avería [aβe'ria] *nf* (*TEC*) breakdown, fault.

averiado, a [aβe'rjaðo, a] *adj* broken-down.

averiar [aβe'rjar] *vt* to break; **~se** *vr* to break down.

averiguación [aβeriɣwa'θjon] *nf* investigation; (*determinación*) ascertainment.

averiguar [aβeri'ɣwar] *vt* to investigate; (*descubrir*) to find out, ascertain.

averigüe [aβe'riɣwe] *etc vb V* **averiguar**.

aversión [aβer'sjon] *nf* aversion, dislike; **cobrar ~ a** to take a strong dislike to.

avestruz [aβes'truθ] *nm* ostrich.

aviación [aβja'θjon] *nf* aviation; (*fuerzas aéreas*) air force.

aviado, a [a'βjaðo, a] *adj*: **estar ~** to be in a mess.

aviador, a [aβja'ðor, a] *nm/f* aviator, airman/woman.

aviar [a'βjar] *vt* to prepare, get ready.

avícola [a'βikola] *adj* poultry *cpd*.

avicultura [aβikul'tura] *nf* poultry farming.

avidez [aβi'ðeθ] *nf* avidity, eagerness.

ávido, a ['aβiðo, a] *adj* avid, eager.

aviente [a'βjente] *etc vb V* **aventar**.

avieso, a [a'βjeso, a] *adj* (*torcido*) distorted; (*perverso*) wicked.

avinagrado, a [aβina'ɣraðo, a] *adj* sour, acid.

avinagrarse [aβina'ɣrarse] *vr* to go o turn sour.

avine [a'βine] *etc vb V* **avenir**.

Aviñón [aβi'ɲon] *nm* Avignon.

avío [a'βio] *nm* preparation; **~s** *nmpl* gear *sg*, kit *sg*.

avión [a'βjon] *nm* aeroplane; (*ave*) martin; **~ de reacción** jet (plane); **por ~** (*CORREOS*) by air mail.

avioneta [aβjo'neta] *nf* light aircraft.

avisar [aβi'sar] *vt* (*advertir*) to warn, notify; (*informar*) to tell; (*aconsejar*) to advise, counsel.

aviso [a'βiso] *nm* warning; (*noticia*) notice; (*COM*) demand note; (*INFORM*) prompt; **~ escrito** notice in writing; **sin previo ~** without warning; **estar sobre ~** to be on the look-out.

avispa [a'βispa] *nf* wasp.

avispado, a [aβis'paðo, a] *adj* sharp, clever.

avispero [aβis'pero] *nm* wasp's nest.

avispón [aβis'pon] *nm* hornet.

avistar [aβis'tar] *vt* to sight, spot.

avitaminosis [aβitami'nosis] *nf inv* vitamin deficiency.

avituallar [aβitwa'ʎar] *vt* to supply with food.

avivar [aβi'βar] *vt* to strengthen, intensify; **~se** *vr* to revive, acquire new life.

avizor [aβi'θor] *adj*: **estar ojo ~** to be on the alert.

avizorar [aβiθo'rar] *vt* to spy on.

axila [ak'sila] *nf* armpit.

axioma [ak'sjoma] *nm* axiom.

ay [ai] *excl* (*dolor*) ow!, ouch!; (*aflicción*)

oh!, oh dear!; ¡~ **de mi!** poor me!

aya ['aja] *nf* governess; (*niñera*) nanny.

ayer [a'jer] *adv, nm* yesterday; **antes de ~** the day before yesterday; **~ por la tarde** yesterday afternoon/evening.

aymara, aymará [ai'mara, aima'ra] *adj, nm/f* Aymara.

ayo ['ajo] *nm* tutor.

ayote [a'jote] *nm* (AM) pumpkin.

Ayto. *abr* = **Ayuntamiento.**

ayuda [a'juða] *nf* help, assistance; (MED) enema ♦ *nm* page; **~ humanitaria** humanitarian aid.

ayudante, a [aju'ðante, a] *nm/f* assistant, helper; (ESCOL) assistant; (MIL) adjutant.

ayudar [aju'ðar] *vt* to help, assist.

ayunar [aju'nar] *vi* to fast.

ayunas [a'junas] *nfpl*: **estar en ~** (*no haber comido*) to be fasting; (*ignorar*) to be in the dark.

ayuno [a'juno] *nm* fasting.

ayuntamiento [ajunta'mjento] *nm* (*consejo*) town/city council; (*edificio*) town/city hall; (*cópula*) sexual intercourse.

azabache [aθa'βatʃe] *nm* jet.

azada [a'θaða] *nf* hoe.

azafata [aθa'fata] *nf* air hostess (BRIT) o stewardess.

azafate [asa'fate] *nm* (AM) tray.

azafrán [aθa'fran] *nm* saffron.

azahar [aθa'ar] *nm* orange/lemon blossom.

azalea [aθa'lea] *nf* azalea.

azar [a'θar] *nm* (*casualidad*) chance, fate; (*desgracia*) misfortune, accident; **por ~** by chance; **al ~** at random.

azaroso, a [aθa'roso, a] *adj* (*arriesgado*) risky; (*vida*) eventful.

Azerbaiyán [aθerba'jan] *nm* Azerbaijan.

azerbaiyano, a [aθerba'jano, a], **azerí** [aθe'ri] *adj, nm/f* Azerbaijani, Azeri.

azogue [a'θoxe] *nm* mercury.

azor [a'θor] *nm* goshawk.

azoramiento [aθora'mjento] *nm* alarm; (*confusión*) confusion.

azorar [aθo'rar] *vt* to alarm; **~se** *vr* to get alarmed.

Azores [a'θores] *nfpl*: **las (Islas) ~** the Azores.

azotaina [aθo'taina] *nf* beating.

azotar [aθo'tar] *vt* to whip, beat; (*pegar*) to spank.

azote [a'θote] *nm* (*látigo*) whip; (*latigazo*) lash, stroke; (*en las nalgas*) spank; (*calamidad*) calamity.

azotea [aθo'tea] *nf* (flat) roof.

azteca [aθ'teka] *adj, nm/f* Aztec.

azúcar [a'θukar] *nm* sugar.

azucarado, a [aθuka'raðo, a] *adj* sugary, sweet.

azucarero, a [aθuka'rero, a] *adj* sugar *cpd* ♦ *nm* sugar bowl.

azuce [a'θuθe] *etc vb* V **azuzar.**

azucena [aθu'θena] *nf* white lily.

azufre [a'θufre] *nm* sulphur.

azul [a'θul] *adj, nm* blue; **~ celeste/marino** sky/navy blue.

azulejo [aθu'lexo] *nm* tile.

azulgrana [aθul'ɣrana] *adj inv* of Barcelona Football Club ♦ *nm*: **los A~** the Barcelona F.C. players o team.

azuzar [aθu'θar] *vt* to incite, egg on.

B b

B, b [(ESP) be, (AM) be'larxa] *nf* (*letra*) B, b; **B de Barcelona** B for Benjamin (BRIT) o Baker (US).

baba ['baβa] *nf* spittle, saliva; **se le caía la ~** (*fig*) he was thrilled to bits.

babear [baβe'ar] *vi* (*echar saliva*) to slobber; (*niño*) to dribble; (*fig*) to drool, slaver.

babel [ba'βel] *nm o f* bedlam.

babero [ba'βero] *nm* bib.

Babia ['baβja] *nf*: **estar en ~** to be daydreaming.

bable ['baβle] *nm* Asturian (dialect).

babor [ba'βor] *nm* port (side); **a ~** to port.

babosada [baβo'saða] *nf*: **decir ~s** (AM fam) to talk rubbish.

baboso, a [ba'βoso, a] *adj* slobbering; (ZOOL) slimy; (AM) silly ♦ *nm/f* (AM) fool.

babucha [ba'βutʃa] *nf* slipper.

baca ['baka] *nf* (AUTO) luggage o roof rack.

bacalao [baka'lao] *nm* cod(fish).

bacanal [baka'nal] *nf* orgy.

bache ['batʃe] *nm* pothole, rut; (*fig*) bad patch.

bachillerato [batʃiʎe'rato] *nm* 2 *year secondary school course*; V *tb* **sistema educativo.**

bacilo [ba'θilo] *nm* bacillus, germ.

bacinica [baθi'nika] *nf*, **bacinilla** [baθi'niʎa] *nf* chamber pot.

bacteria [bak'terja] *nf* bacterium, germ.

bacteriológico, a [bakterjo'loxico, a] *adj* bacteriological; **guerra ~a** germ warfare.

báculo ['bakulo] *nm* stick, staff; (*fig*) support.

badajo [ba'ðaxo] *nm* clapper (*of a bell*).

bádminton ['baðminton] *nm* badminton.

baf(f)le ['baf(f)le] *nm* (*ELEC*) speaker.

bagaje [ba'ɣaxe] *nm* baggage; (*fig*) background.

bagatela [baɣa'tela] *nf* trinket, trifle.

Bahama [ba'ama]: **las (Islas) ~, las ~s** *nfpl* the Bahamas.

bahía [ba'ia] *nf* bay.

bailar [bai'lar] *vt, vi* to dance.

bailarín, ina [baila'rin, ina] *nm/f* dancer; (*de ballet*) ballet dancer.

baile ['baile] *nm* dance; (*formal*) ball.

baja ['baxa] *nf* drop, fall; (*ECON*) slump; (*MIL*) casualty; (*paro*) redundancy; **dar de ~** (*soldado*) to discharge; (*empleado*) to dismiss, sack; **darse de ~** (*retirarse*) to drop out; (*MED*) to go sick; (*dimitir*) to resign; **estar de ~** (*enfermo*) to be off sick; (*BOLSA*) to be dropping *o* falling; **jugar a la ~** (*ECON*) to speculate on a fall in prices; *V tb* **bajo**.

bajada [ba'xaða] *nf* descent; (*camino*) slope; (*de aguas*) ebb.

bajamar [baxa'mar] *nf* low tide.

bajar [ba'xar] *vi* to go *o* come down; (*temperatura, precios*) to drop, fall ♦ *vt* (*cabeza*) to bow; (*escalera*) to go *o* come down; (*radio etc*) to turn down; (*precio, voz*) to lower; (*llevar abajo*) to take down; **~se** *vr* (*de vehículo*) to get out; (*de autobús*) to get off; **~ de** (*coche*) to get out of; (*autobús*) to get off; **~le los humos a algn** (*fig*) to cut sb down to size; **~se algo de Internet** to download sth from the Internet.

bajeza [ba'xeθa] *nf* baseness; (*una ~*) vile deed.

bajío [ba'xio] *nm* shoal, sandbank; (*AM*) lowlands *pl*.

bajista [ba'xista] *nm/f* (*MUS*) bassist ♦ *adj* (*BOLSA*) bear *cpd*.

bajo, a ['baxo, a] *adj* (*terreno*) low(-lying); (*mueble, número, precio*) low; (*piso*) ground *cpd*; (*de estatura*) small, short; (*color*) pale; (*sonido*) faint, soft, low; (*voz, tono*) deep; (*metal*) base ♦ *adv* (*hablar*) softly, quietly; (*volar*) low ♦ *prep* under, below, underneath ♦ *nm* (*MUS*) bass; **hablar en voz baja** to whisper; **~ la lluvia** in the rain.

bajón [ba'xon] *nm* fall, drop.

bajura [ba'xura] *nf*: **pesca de ~** coastal fishing.

bakalao [baka'lao] *nm* (*MUS*) rave music.

bala ['bala] *nf* bullet; **~ de goma** plastic bullet.

balacera [bala'sera] *nf* (*AM*) shoot-out.

balada [ba'laða] *nf* ballad.

baladí [bala'ði] *adj* trivial.

baladronada [balaðro'naða] *nf* (*dicho*) boast, brag; (*hecho*) piece of bravado.

balance [ba'lanθe] *nm* (*COM*) balance; (: *libro*) balance sheet; (: *cuenta general*) stocktaking; **~ de comprobación** trial balance; **hacer ~** to take stock.

balancear [balanθe'ar] *vt* to balance ♦ *vi*, **~se** *vr* to swing (to and fro); (*vacilar*) to hesitate.

balanceo [balan'θeo] *nm* swinging.

balandro [ba'landro] *nm* yacht.

balanza [ba'lanθa] *nf* scales *pl*, balance; **~ comercial** balance of trade; **~ de pagos/de poder(es)** balance of payments/of power; (*ASTRO*): **B~ Libra**.

balar [ba'lar] *vi* to bleat.

balaustrada [balaus'traða] *nf* balustrade; (*pasamanos*) banister.

balazo [ba'laθo] *nm* (*tiro*) shot; (*herida*) bullet wound.

balboa [bal'ßoa] *nf Panamanian currency unit*.

balbucear [balßuθe'ar] *vi, vt* to stammer, stutter.

balbuceo [balßu'θeo] *nm* stammering, stuttering.

balbucir [balßu'θir] *vi, vt* to stammer, stutter.

balbuzca [bal'ßuθka] *etc vb V* **balbucir**.

Balcanes [bal'kanes] *nmpl*: **los (Montes) ~** the Balkans, the Balkan Mountains; **la Península de los ~** the Balkan Peninsula.

balcánico, a [bal'kaniko, a] *adj* Balkan.

balcón [bal'kon] *nm* balcony.

balda ['balda] *nf* (*estante*) shelf.

baldar [bal'dar] *vt* to cripple; (*agotar*) to exhaust.

balde ['balde] *nm* (*esp AM*) bucket, pail; **de ~** *adv* (for) free, for nothing; **en ~** *adv* in vain.

baldío, a [bal'dio, a] *adj* uncultivated; (*terreno*) waste; (*inútil*) vain ♦ *nm* wasteland.

baldosa [bal'dosa] *nf* (*azulejo*) floor tile; (*grande*) flagstone.

baldosín [baldo'sin] *nm* wall tile.

balear [bale'ar] *adj* Balearic, of the Balearic Islands ♦ *nm/f* native *o* inhabitant of the Balearic Islands ♦ *vt* (*AM*) to shoot (at).

Baleares [bale'ares] *nfpl*: **las (Islas) ~** the Balearics, the Balearic Islands.

balido [ba'liðo] *nm* bleat, bleating.

balín [ba'lin] *nm* pellet; **balines** *nmpl*

buckshot sg.

balística [ba'listika] nf ballistics pl.

baliza [ba'liθa] nf (AVIAT) beacon; (NAUT) buoy.

ballena [ba'ʎena] nf whale.

ballenero, a [baʎe'nero, a] adj: **industria ballenera** whaling industry ♦ nm (pescador) whaler; (barco) whaling ship.

ballesta [ba'ʎesta] nf crossbow; (AUTO) spring.

ballet, pl **ballets** [ba'le, ba'les] nm ballet.

balneario, a [balne'arjo, a] adj: **estación balnearia** (bathing) resort ♦ nm spa, health resort.

balompié [balom'pje] nm football.

balón [ba'lon] nm ball.

baloncesto [balon'θesto] nm basketball.

balonmano [balon'mano] nm handball.

balonvolea [balombo'lea] nm volleyball.

balsa ['balsa] nf raft; (BOT) balsa wood.

bálsamo ['balsamo] nm balsam, balm.

balsón [bal'son] nm (AM) swamp, bog.

báltico, a ['baltiko, a] adj Baltic; **el (Mar) B~** the Baltic (Sea).

baluarte [ba'lwarte] nm bastion, bulwark.

bambolearse [bambole'arse] vr to swing, sway; (silla) to wobble.

bamboleo [bambo'leo] nm swinging, swaying; wobbling.

bambú [bam'bu] nm bamboo.

banal [ba'nal] adj banal, trivial.

banana [ba'nana] nf (AM) banana.

bananal [bana'nal] nm (AM) banana plantation.

banano [ba'nano] nm (AM) banana tree.

banasta [ba'nasta] nf large basket, hamper.

banca ['banka] nf (asiento) bench; (COM) banking.

bancario, a [ban'karjo, a] adj banking cpd, bank cpd; **giro ~** bank draft.

bancarrota [banka'rrota] nf bankruptcy; **declararse en** o **hacer ~** to go bankrupt.

banco ['banko] nm bench; (ESCOL) desk; (COM) bank; (GEO) stratum; **~ comercial** o **mercantil** commercial bank; **~ por acciones** joint-stock bank; **~ de crédito/ de ahorros** credit/savings bank; **~ de arena** sandbank; **~ de datos** (INFORM) data bank; **~ de hielo** iceberg.

banda ['banda] nf band; (cinta) ribbon; (pandilla) gang; (MUS) brass band; (NAUT) side, edge; **~ ancha** broadband; **la B~ Oriental** Uruguay; **~ sonora** soundtrack; **~ transportadora** conveyor belt.

bandada [ban'daða] nf (de pájaros) flock;

(de peces) shoal.

bandazo [ban'daθo] nm: **dar ~s** (coche) to veer from side to side.

bandeja [ban'dexa] nf tray; **~ de entrada/ salida** in-tray/out-tray.

bandera [ban'dera] nf (de tela) flag; (estandarte) banner; (INFORM) marker, flag; **izar la ~** to hoist the flag.

banderilla [bande'riʎa] nf banderilla; (tapa) savoury appetizer (served on a cocktail stick).

banderín [bande'rin] nm pennant, small flag.

banderola [bande'rola] nf (MIL) pennant.

bandido [ban'diðo] nm bandit.

bando ['bando] nm (edicto) edict, proclamation; (facción) faction; **pasar al otro ~** to change sides; **los ~s** (REL) the banns.

bandolera [bando'lera] nf: **bolsa de ~** shoulder bag.

bandolero [bando'lero] nm bandit, brigand.

bandoneón [bandone'on] nm (AM) large accordion.

BANESTO [ba'nesto] nm abr = Banco Español de Crédito.

banquero [ban'kero] nm banker.

banqueta [ban'keta] nf stool; (AM: acera) pavement (BRIT), sidewalk (US).

banquete [ban'kete] nm banquet; (para convidados) formal dinner; **~ de boda** wedding breakfast.

banquillo [ban'kiʎo] nm (JUR) dock, prisoner's bench; (banco) bench; (para los pies) footstool.

bañadera [baɲa'ðera] nf (AM) bath(tub).

bañado [baɲa'ðo] nm (AM) swamp.

bañador [baɲa'ðor] nm swimming costume (BRIT), bathing suit (US).

bañar [ba'ɲar] vt (niño) to bath, bathe; (objeto) to dip; (de barniz) to coat; **~se** vr (en el mar) to bathe, swim; (en la bañera) to have a bath.

bañero, a [ba'ɲero, a] nmf lifeguard ♦ nf bath(tub).

bañista [ba'ɲista] nmf bather.

baño ['baɲo] nm (en bañera) bath; (en río, mar) dip, swim; (cuarto) bathroom; (bañera) bath(tub); (capa) coating; **ir a tomar los ~s** to take the waters.

baptista [bap'tista] nmf Baptist.

baqueano, a, baquiano, a [bake'ano, a, baki'ano, a] nmf (AM) guide.

baqueta [ba'keta] nf (MUS) drumstick.

bar [bar] nm bar.

barahúnda [bara'unda] nf uproar, hubbub.

baraja [ba'raxa] nf pack (of cards); see boxed note.

barbullar [barβu'ʎar] *vi* to jabber away.
barca ['barka] *nf* (small) boat; ~ **pesquera** fishing boat; ~ **de pasaje** ferry.
barcaza [bar'kaθa] *nf* barge; ~ **de desembarco** landing craft.
Barcelona [barθe'lona] *nf* Barcelona.
barcelonés, esa [barθelo'nes, esa] *adj* of o from Barcelona ♦ *nm/f* native o inhabitant of Barcelona.
barco ['barko] *nm* boat; (*buque*) ship; (*COM etc*) vessel; ~ **de carga** cargo boat; ~ **de guerra** warship; ~ **de vela** sailing ship; **ir en** ~ to go by boat.
baremo [ba'remo] *nm* scale; (*tabla de cuentas*) ready reckoner.
barítono [ba'ritono] *nm* baritone.
barman ['barman] *nm* barman.
Barna. *abr* = **Barcelona**.
barnice [bar'niθe] *etc vb V* **barnizar**.
barniz [bar'niθ] *nm* varnish; (*en la loza*) glaze; (*fig*) veneer.
barnizar [barni'θar] *vt* to varnish; (*loza*) to glaze.
barómetro [ba'rometro] *nm* barometer.
barón [ba'ron] *nm* baron.
baronesa [baro'nesa] *nf* baroness.
barquero [bar'kero] *nm* boatman.
barquilla [bar'kiʎa] *nf* (*NAUT*) log.
barquillo [bar'kiʎo] *nm* cone, cornet.
barra ['barra] *nf* bar, rod; (*JUR*) rail; (: *banquillo*) dock; (*de un bar, café*) bar; (*de pan*) French loaf; (*palanca*) lever; ~ **de carmín** o **de labios** lipstick; ~ **de herramientas** (*INFORM*) toolbar; ~ **espaciadora** (*INFORM*) space bar; ~ **inversa** backslash; ~ **libre** free bar; **no pararse en** ~**s** to stick o stop at nothing.
barrabasada [barraβa'saða] *nf* (piece of) mischief.
barraca [ba'rraka] *nf* hut, cabin; (*en Valencia*) thatched farmhouse; (*en feria*) booth.
barracón [barra'kon] *nm* (*caseta*) big hut.
barragana [barra'ɣana] *nf* concubine.
barranca [ba'rranka] *nf* ravine, gully.
barranco [ba'rranko] *nm* ravine; (*fig*) difficulty.
barrena [ba'rrena] *nf* drill.
barrenar [barre'nar] *vt* to drill (through).
barrendero, a [barren'dero, a] *nm/f* street-sweeper.
barreno [ba'rreno] *nm* large drill.
barreño [ba'rreɲo] *nm* washing-up bowl.
barrer [ba'rrer] *vt* to sweep; (*quitar*) to sweep away; (*MIL, NAUT*) to sweep, rake (with gunfire) ♦ *vi* to sweep up.
barrera [ba'rrera] *nf* barrier; (*MIL*) barricade; (*FERRO*) crossing gate; **poner** ~**s a** to hinder; ~ **arancelaria** (*COM*)

The **baraja española** *is the traditional Spanish deck of cards, which differs from a standard poker deck. The four "palos" (suits) are "oros" (golden coins), "copas" (goblets), "espadas" (swords) and "bastos" ("clubs", but not the same as the ones in a poker pack). Every suit has nine numbered cards (although for certain games only seven are used), and three face cards: "sota" (jack), "caballo" (≈ queen) and "rey" (king).*

barajar [bara'xar] *vt* (*naipes*) to shuffle; (*fig*) to jumble up.
baranda [ba'randa], **barandilla** [baran'diʎa] *nf* rail, railing.
baratija [bara'tixa] *nf* trinket; (*fig*) trifle; ~**s** *nfpl* (*COM*) cheap goods.
baratillo [bara'tiʎo] *nm* (*tienda*) junkshop; (*subasta*) bargain sale; (*conjunto de cosas*) second-hand goods *pl*.
barato, a [ba'rato, a] *adj* cheap ♦ *adv* cheap, cheaply.
baratura [bara'tura] *nf* cheapness.
baraúnda [bara'unda] *nf* = **barahúnda**.
barba ['barβa] *nf* (*mentón*) chin; (*pelo*) beard; **tener** ~ to be unshaven; **hacer algo en las** ~**s de algn** to do sth under sb's very nose; **reírse en las** ~**s de algn** to laugh in sb's face.
barbacoa [barβa'koa] *nf* (*parrilla*) barbecue; (*carne*) barbecued meat.
barbaridad [barβari'ðað] *nf* barbarity; (*acto*) barbarism; (*atrocidad*) outrage; **una** ~ **de** (*fam*) loads of; **¡qué** ~**!** (*fam*) how awful!; **cuesta una** ~ (*fam*) it costs a fortune.
barbarie [bar'βarje] *nf*, **barbarismo** [barβa'rismo] *nm* barbarism; (*crueldad*) barbarity.
bárbaro, a ['barβaro, a] *adj* barbarous, cruel; (*grosero*) rough, uncouth ♦ *nm/f* barbarian ♦ *adv*: **lo pasamos** ~ (*fam*) we had a great time; **¡qué** ~**!** (*fam*) how marvellous!; **un éxito** ~ (*fam*) a terrific success; **es un tipo** ~ (*fam*) he's a great bloke.
barbero [bar'βero] *nm* barber, hairdresser.
barbilampiño [barβilam'piɲo] *adj* smooth-faced; (*fig*) inexperienced.
barbilla [bar'βiʎa] *nf* chin, tip of the chin.
barbitúrico [barβi'turiko] *nm* barbiturate.
barbo ['barβo] *nm*: ~ **de mar** red mullet.
barbotar [barβo'tar], **barbotear** [barβote'ar] *vt, vi* to mutter, mumble.
barbudo, a [bar'βuðo, a] *adj* bearded.

tariff barrier; ~ **comercial** (*COM*) trade barrier.

barriada [ba'rrjaða] *nf* quarter, district.

barricada [barri'kaða] *nf* barricade.

barrida [ba'rriða] *nf*, **barrido** [ba'rriðo] *nm* sweep, sweeping.

barriga [ba'rriɣa] *nf* belly; (*panza*) paunch; (*vientre*) guts *pl*; **echar** ~ to get middle-age spread.

barrigón, ona [barri'ɣon, ona], **barrigudo, a** [barri'ɣuðo, a] *adj* potbellied.

barril [ba'rril] *nm* barrel, cask; **cerveza de** ~ draught beer.

barrio ['barrjo] *nm* (*vecindad*) area, neighborhood (*US*); (*en las afueras*) suburb; ~**s bajos** poor quarter *sg*; ~ **chino** red-light district.

barriobajero, a [barrjobβa'xero, a] *adj* (*vulgar*) common.

barro ['barro] *nm* (*lodo*) mud; (*objetos*) earthenware; (*MED*) pimple.

barroco, a [ba'rroko, a] *adj* Baroque; (*fig*) elaborate ♦ *nm* Baroque.

barrote [ba'rrote] *nm* (*de ventana etc*) bar.

barruntar [barrun'tar] *vt* (*conjeturar*) to guess; (*presentir*) to suspect.

barrunto [ba'rrunto] *nm* guess; suspicion.

bartola [bar'tola]: **a la** ~ *adv*: **tirarse a la** ~ to take it easy, be lazy.

bártulos ['bartulos] *nmpl* things, belongings.

barullo [ba'ruʎo] *nm* row, uproar.

basa ['basa] *nf* (*ARQ*) base.

basamento [basa'mento] *nm* base, plinth.

basar [ba'sar] *vt* to base; ~**se** *vr*: ~**se en** to be based on.

basca ['baska] *nf* nausea.

báscula ['baskula] *nf* (*platform*) scales *pl*.

bascular [basku'lar] *vt* (*INFORM*) to toggle.

base ['base] *nf* base; **a** ~ **de** on the basis of, based on; (*mediante*) by means of; **a** ~ **de bien** in abundance; ~ **de conocimiento** knowledge base; ~ **de datos** database.

básico, a ['basiko, a] *adj* basic.

Basilea [basi'lea] *nf* Basle.

basílica [ba'silika] *nf* basilica.

basilisco [basi'lisko] *nm* (*AM*) iguana; **estar hecho un** ~ to be hopping mad.

basket, básquet ['basket] *nm* basketball.

═══════════ *PALABRA CLAVE*

bastante [bas'tante] *adj* **1** (*suficiente*) enough; ~ **dinero** enough *o* sufficient money; ~**s libros** enough books
2 (*valor intensivo*): ~ **gente** quite a lot of people; **tener** ~ **calor** to be rather hot; **hace** ~ **tiempo que ocurrió** it happened quite *o* rather a long time ago
♦ *adv*: ~ **bueno/malo** quite good/rather bad; ~ **rico** pretty rich; **(lo)** ~ **inteligente (como) para hacer algo** clever enough *o* sufficiently clever to do sth; **voy a tardar** ~ I'm going to be a while *o* quite some time.

bastar [bas'tar] *vi* to be enough *o* sufficient; ~**se** *vr* to be self-sufficient; ~ **para** to be enough to; **¡basta!** (that's) enough!

bastardilla [bastar'ðiʎa] *nf* italics *pl*.

bastardo, a [bas'tarðo, a] *adj*, *nm/f* bastard.

bastidor [basti'ðor] *nm* frame; (*de coche*) chassis; (*ARTE*) stretcher; (*TEAT*) wing; **entre** ~**es** behind the scenes.

basto, a ['basto, a] *adj* coarse, rough
♦ *nmpl*: ~**s** (*NAIPES*) one of the suits in the Spanish card deck; V tb **Baraja Española**.

bastón [bas'ton] *nm* stick, staff; (*para pasear*) walking stick; ~ **de mando** baton.

bastonazo [basto'naθo] *nm* blow with a stick.

bastoncillo [baston'θiʎo] *nm* (*tb*: ~ **de algodón**) cotton bud.

basura [ba'sura] *nf* rubbish, refuse (*BRIT*), garbage (*US*) ♦ *adj*: **comida/televisión** ~ junk food/TV.

basurero [basu'rero] *nm* (*hombre*) dustman (*BRIT*), garbage collector *o* man (*US*); (*lugar*) rubbish dump; (*cubo*) (rubbish) bin (*BRIT*), trash can (*US*).

bata ['bata] *nf* (*gen*) dressing gown; (*cubretodo*) smock, overall; (*MED, TEC etc*) lab(oratory) coat.

batacazo [bata'kaθo] *nm* bump.

batalla [ba'taʎa] *nf* battle; **de** ~ for everyday use.

batallar [bata'ʎar] *vi* to fight.

batallón [bata'ʎon] *nm* battalion.

batata [ba'tata] *nf* (*AM: CULIN*) sweet potato.

bate ['bate] *nm* (*DEPORTE*) bat.

batea [ba'tea] *nf* (*AM*) washing trough.

bateador [batea'ðor] *nm* (*DEPORTE*) batter, batsman.

batería [bate'ria] *nf* battery; (*MUS*) drums *pl*; (*TEAT*) footlights *pl*; ~ **de cocina** kitchen utensils *pl*.

batiburrillo [batiβu'rriʎo] *nm* hotchpotch.

batido, a [ba'tiðo, a] *adj* (*camino*) beaten, well-trodden ♦ *nm* (*CULIN*) batter; ~ **(de leche)** milk shake ♦ *nf* (*AM*) (police) raid.

batidora [bati'ðora] *nf* beater, mixer; ~ **eléctrica** food mixer, blender.

batir [ba'tir] *vt* to beat, strike; (*vencer*) to beat, defeat; (*revolver*) to beat, mix; (*pelo*) to back-comb; **~se** *vr* to fight; **~ palmas** to clap, applaud.

baturro, a [ba'turro, a] *nm/f* Aragonese peasant.

batuta [ba'tuta] *nf* baton; **llevar la ~** (*fig*) to be the boss.

baudio ['bauðjo] *nm* (*INFORM*) baud.

baúl [ba'ul] *nm* trunk; (*AM AUTO*) boot (*BRIT*), trunk (*US*).

bautice [bau'tiθe] *etc vb V* **bautizar**.

bautismo [bau'tismo] *nm* baptism, christening.

bautista [bau'tista] *adj, nm/f* Baptist.

bautizar [bauti'θar] *vt* to baptize, christen; (*fam: diluir*) to water down; (*dar apodo*) to dub.

bautizo [bau'tiθo] *nm* baptism, christening.

bávaro, a ['baβaro, a] *adj, nm/f* Bavarian.

Baviera [ba'βjera] *nf* Bavaria.

baya ['baja] *nf* berry; *V tb* **bayo**.

bayeta [ba'jeta] *nf* (*trapo*) floorcloth; (*AM: pañal*) nappy (*BRIT*), diaper (*US*).

bayo, a ['bajo, a] *adj* bay.

bayoneta [bajo'neta] *nf* bayonet.

baza ['baθa] *nf* trick; **meter ~** to butt in.

bazar [ba'θar] *nm* bazaar.

bazo ['baθo] *nm* spleen.

bazofia [ba'θofja] *nf* pigswill (*BRIT*), hogwash (*US*); (*libro etc*) trash.

BCE *nm abr* (= *Banco Central Europeo*) ECB.

beatificar [beatifi'kar] *vt* to beatify.

beato, a [be'ato, a] *adj* blessed; (*piadoso*) pious.

bebe (*AM*), *pl* **bebes**, **bebé**, *pl* **bebés** ['beβe, 'beβes, be'βe, be'βes] *nm* baby; **~ de diseño** designer baby.

bebedero [beβe'ðero, a] *nm* (*para animales*) drinking trough.

bebedizo, a [beβe'ðiθo, a] *adj* drinkable ♦ *nm* potion.

bebedor, a [beβe'ðor, a] *adj* hard-drinking.

bebé-probeta [be'βe-pro'βeta], *pl* **bebés-probeta** *nm/f* test-tube baby.

beber [be'βer] *vt, vi* to drink; **~ a sorbos/ tragos** to sip/gulp; **se lo bebió todo** he drank it all up.

bebido, a [be'βiðo, a] *adj* drunk ♦ *nf* drink.

beca ['beka] *nf* grant, scholarship.

becado, a [be'kaðo, a] *nm/f*, **becario, a** [be'karjo, a] *nm/f* scholarship holder.

becerro [be'θerro] *nm* yearling calf.

bechamel [betʃa'mel] *nf* = **besamel**.

becuadro [be'kwaðro] *nm* natural sign.

bedel [be'ðel] *nm* porter, janitor.

beduino, a [be'ðwino, a] *adj, nm/f* Bedouin.

befarse [be'farse] *vr*: **~ de algo** to scoff at sth.

beige ['beix], **beis** ['beis] *adj, nm* beige.

béisbol ['beisβol] *nm* baseball.

bejuco [be'juko] *nm* (*AM*) reed, liana.

beldad [bel'dað] *nf* beauty.

Belén [be'len] *nm* Bethlehem; **b~** (*de Navidad*) nativity scene, crib.

belga ['belxa] *adj, nm/f* Belgian.

Bélgica ['belxika] *nf* Belgium.

Belgrado [bel'xraðo] *nm* Belgrade.

Belice [be'liθe] *nm* Belize.

bélico, a ['beliko, a] *adj* (*actitud*) warlike.

belicoso, a [beli'koso, a] *adj* (*guerrero*) warlike; (*agresivo*) aggressive, bellicose.

beligerante [belixe'rante] *adj* belligerent.

bellaco, a [be'ʎako, a] *adj* sly, cunning ♦ *nm* villain, rogue.

belladona [beʎa'ðona] *nf* deadly nightshade.

bellaquería [beʎake'ria] *nf* (*acción*) dirty trick; (*calidad*) wickedness.

belleza [be'ʎeθa] *nf* beauty.

bello, a ['beʎo, a] *adj* beautiful, lovely; **Bellas Artes** Fine Art *sg*.

bellota [be'ʎota] *nf* acorn.

bemol [be'mol] *nm* (*MUS*) flat; **esto tiene ~es** (*fam*) this is a tough one.

bencina [ben'sina] *nf* (*AM*) petrol (*BRIT*), gas (*US*).

bendecir [bende'θir] *vt* to bless; **~ la mesa** to say grace.

bendición [bendi'θjon] *nf* blessing.

bendiga [ben'dixa] *etc*, **bendije** [ben'dixe] *etc vb V* **bendecir**.

bendito, a [ben'dito, a] *pp de* **bendecir** ♦ *adj* (*santo*) blessed; (*agua*) holy; (*afortunado*) lucky; (*feliz*) happy; (*sencillo*) simple ♦ *nm/f* simple soul; **¡~ sea Dios!** thank goodness!; **es un ~** he's sweet; **dormir como un ~** to sleep like a log.

benedictino, a [beneðik'tino, a] *adj, nm* Benedictine.

benefactor, a [benefak'tor, a] *nm/f* benefactor/benefactress.

beneficencia [benefi'θenθja] *nf* charity.

beneficiar [benefi'θjar] *vt* to benefit, be of benefit to; **~se** *vr* to benefit, profit.

beneficiario, a [benefi'θjarjo, a] *nm/f* beneficiary; (*de cheque*) payee.

beneficio [bene'fiθjo] *nm* (*bien*) benefit, advantage; (*COM*) profit, gain; **a ~ de** for the benefit of; **en ~ propio** to one's own advantage; **~ bruto/neto** gross/net profit; **~ por acción** earnings *pl* per share.

beneficioso, a [benefi'θjoso, a] *adj* beneficial.

benéfico, a [be'nefiko, a] *adj* charitable;

sociedad ~**a** charity (organization).

benemérito, a [bene'merito, a] *adj* meritorious ♦ *nf*: **la Benemérita** (*ESP*) the Civil Guard; *v tb* **Guardia Civil**.

beneplácito [bene'plaθito] *nm* approval, consent.

benevolencia [beneβo'lenθja] *nf* benevolence, kindness.

benévolo, a [be'neβolo, a] *adj* benevolent, kind.

Bengala [ben'gala] *nf* Bengal; **el Golfo de** ~ the Bay of Bengal.

bengala [ben'gala] *nf* (*MIL*) flare; (*fuego*) Bengal light; (*materia*) rattan.

bengalí [benga'li] *adj*, *nm/f* Bengali.

benignidad [beniɣni'ðað] *nf* (*afabilidad*) kindness; (*suavidad*) mildness.

benigno, a [be'niɣno, a] *adj* kind; (*suave*) mild; (*MED: tumor*) benign, non-malignant.

benjamín [benxa'min] *nm* youngest child.

beodo, a [be'oðo, a] *adj* drunk ♦ *nm/f* drunkard.

berberecho [berβe'retʃo] *nm* cockle.

berenjena [beren'xena] *nf* aubergine (*BRIT*), eggplant (*US*).

berenjenal [berenxe'nal] *nm* (*AGR*) aubergine bed; (*fig*) mess; **en buen** ~ **nos hemos metido** we've got ourselves into a fine mess.

bergantín [berɣan'tin] *nm* brig(antine).

Berlín [ber'lin] *nm* Berlin.

berlinés, esa [berli'nes, esa] *adj* of *o* from Berlin ♦ *nm/f* Berliner.

bermejo, a [ber'mexo, a] *adj* red.

bermellón [berme'ʎon] *nm* vermilion.

bermudas [ber'muðas] *nfpl* Bermuda shorts.

berrear [berre'ar] *vi* to bellow, low.

berrido [be'rriðo] *nm* bellow(ing).

berrinche [be'rrintʃe] *nm* (*fam*) temper, tantrum.

berro ['berro] *nm* watercress.

berza ['berθa] *nf* cabbage; ~ **lombarda** red cabbage.

besamel [besa'mel], **besamela** [besa'mela] *nf* (*CULIN*) white sauce, bechamel sauce.

besar [be'sar] *vt* to kiss; (*fig: tocar*) to graze; ~**se** *vr* to kiss (one another).

beso ['beso] *nm* kiss.

bestia ['bestja] *nf* beast, animal; (*fig*) idiot; ~ **de carga** beast of burden; ¡~! you idiot!; ¡**no seas** ~! (*bruto*) don't be such a brute!; (*idiota*) don't be such an idiot!

bestial [bes'tjal] *adj* bestial; (*fam*) terrific.

bestialidad [bestjali'ðað] *nf* bestiality; (*fam*) stupidity.

besugo [be'suɣo] *nm* sea bream; (*fam*) idiot.

besuguera [besu'ɣera] *nf* (*CULIN*) fish pan.

besuquear [besuke'ar] *vt* to cover with kisses; ~**se** *vr* to kiss and cuddle.

bético, a ['betiko, a] *adj* Andalusian.

betún [be'tun] *nm* shoe polish; (*QUÍMICA*) bitumen, asphalt.

Bib. *abr* = **Biblioteca**.

biberón [biβe'ron] *nm* feeding bottle.

Biblia ['biβlja] *nf* Bible.

bíblico, a ['biβliko, a] *adj* biblical.

bibliografía [biβljoɣra'fia] *nf* bibliography.

biblioteca [biβljo'teka] *nf* library; (*estantes*) bookcase, bookshelves *pl*; ~ **de consulta** reference library.

bibliotecario, a [biβljote'karjo, a] *nm/f* librarian.

B.I.C. [bik] *nf abr* (= *Brigada de Investigación Criminal*) ≈ CID (*BRIT*), FBI (*US*).

bicarbonato [bikarβo'nato] *nm* bicarbonate.

bíceps ['biθeps] *nm inv* biceps.

bicho ['bitʃo] *nm* (*animal*) small animal; (*sabandija*) bug, insect; (*TAUR*) bull; ~ **raro** (*fam*) queer fish.

bici ['biθi] *nf* (*fam*) bike.

bicicleta [biθi'kleta] *nf* bicycle, cycle; ~ **estática/de montaña** exercise/mountain bike.

bicoca [bi'koka] *nf* (*ESP fam*) cushy job.

BID *n abbr* (= *Banco Interamericano de Desarrollo*) IDB.

bidé [bi'ðe] *nm* bidet.

bidireccional [biðirekθjo'nal] *adj* bidirectional.

bidón [bi'ðon] *nm* (*grande*) drum; (*pequeño*) can.

Bielorrusia [bjelo'rrusja] *nf* Belarus, Byelorussia.

bielorruso, a [bjelo'rruso, a] *adj*, *nm/f* Belarussian, Belorussian ♦ *nm* (*LING*) Belarussian, Belorussian.

═══════════════ *PALABRA CLAVE*

bien [bjen] *nm* **1** (*bienestar*) good; **te lo digo por tu** ~ I'm telling you for your own good; **el** ~ **y el mal** good and evil **2** (*posesión*): ~**es** goods; ~**es de consumo/equipo** consumer/capital goods; ~**es inmuebles** *o* **raíces**/~**es muebles** real estate *sg*/personal property *sg*

♦ *adv* **1** (*de manera satisfactoria, correcta etc*) well; **trabaja/come** ~ she works/eats well; **contestó** ~ he answered correctly; **oler** ~ to smell nice *o* good; **me siento** ~ I feel fine; **no me siento** ~ I don't feel

very well; **se está** ~ **aquí** it's nice here
2 (*frases*): **hiciste** ~ **en llamarme** you
were right to call me
3 (*valor intensivo*) very; **un cuarto** ~
caliente a nice warm room; ~ **de veces**
lots of times; ~ **se ve que** ... it's quite
clear that ...
4: estar ~: **estoy muy** ~ **aquí** I feel very
happy here; **¿te encuentras** ~? are you
all right?; **te está** ~ **la falda** (*ser la talla*)
the skirt fits you; **el libro está muy** ~ the book is
really good; **está** ~ **que vengan** it's all
right for them to come; **¡está** ~**! lo haré**
oh all right, I'll do it; **ya está** ~ **de quejas**
that's quite enough complaining
5 (*de buena gana*): **yo** ~ **que iría pero** ...
I'd gladly go but ...
♦ *excl*: **¡**~**!** (*aprobación*) O.K!; **¡muy** ~**!**
well done!; **¡qué** ~**!** great!; ~, **gracias, ¿y**
usted? fine thanks, and you?
♦ *adj inv*: **niño** ~ rich kid; **gente** ~ posh
people
♦ *conj* **1**: ~ ... ~: ~ **en coche** ~ **en tren**
either by car or by train
2: no ~ (*esp AM*): **no** ~ **llegue te llamaré**
as soon as I arrive I'll call you
3: si ~ even though; *V tb* **más**.

bienal [bje'nal] *adj* biennial.
bienaventurado, a [bjenaßentu'raðo, a]
adj (*feliz*) happy; (*afortunado*) fortunate;
(*REL*) blessed.
bienestar [bjenes'tar] *nm* well-being;
estado de ~ welfare state.
bienhechor, a [bjene'tʃor, a] *adj* benefi-
cent ♦ *nm/f* benefactor/benefactress.
bienio ['bjenjo] *nm* two-year period.
bienvenido, a [bjembe'niðo, a] *adj*
welcome ♦ *excl* welcome! ♦ *nf* welcome;
dar la bienvenida a algn to welcome sb.
bies ['bjes] *nm*: **falda al** ~ bias-cut skirt.
bifásico, a [bi'fasiko, a] *adj* (*ELEC*) two-
phase.
bife ['bife] *nm* (*AM*) steak.
bifocal [bifo'kal] *adj* bifocal.
bifurcación [bifurka'θjon] *nf* fork; (*FERRO*,
INFORM) branch.
bifurcarse [bifur'karse] *vr* to fork.
bigamia [bi'ɣamja] *nf* bigamy.
bígamo, a ['biɣamo, a] *adj* bigamous ♦ *nm/f*
bigamist.
bígaro ['biɣaro] *nm* winkle.
bigote [bi'ɣote] *nm* (*tb*: ~**s**) moustache.
bigotudo, a [biɣo'tuðo, a] *adj* with a big
moustache.
bigudí [biɣu'ði] *nm* (hair-)curler.
bikini [bi'kini] *nm* bikini; (*CULIN*) toasted

cheese and ham sandwich.
bilateral [bilate'ral] *adj* bilateral.
bilbaíno, a [bilßa'ino, a] *adj* of *o* from
Bilbao ♦ *nm/f* native *o* inhabitant of
Bilbao.
bilingüe [bi'lingwe] *adj* bilingual.
bilis ['bilis] *nf inv* bile.
billar [bi'ʎar] *nm* billiards *sg*; (*lugar*)
billiard hall; (*galería de atracciones*)
amusement arcade; ~ **americano** pool.
billete [bi'ʎete] *nm* ticket; (*de banco*)
banknote (*BRIT*), bill (*US*); (*carta*) note; ~
sencillo, ~ **de ida solamente/**~ **de ida y**
vuelta single (*BRIT*) *o* one-way (*US*)
ticket/return (*BRIT*) *o* round-trip (*US*)
ticket; **sacar (un)** ~ to get a ticket; **un** ~
de 5 libras a five-pound note.
billetera [biʎe'tera] *nf*, **billetero** [biʎe'tero]
nm wallet.
billón [bi'ʎon] *nm* billion.
bimensual [bimen'swal] *adj* twice
monthly.
bimestral [bimes'tral] *adj* bimonthly.
bimestre [bi'mestre] *nm* two-month period.
bimotor [bimo'tor] *adj* twin-engined ♦ *nm*
twin-engined plane.
binario, a [bi'narjo, a] *adj* (*INFORM*) binary.
bingo ['bingo] *nm* (*juego*) bingo; (*sala*)
bingo hall.
binóculo [bi'nokulo] *nm* pince-nez.
binomio [bi'nomjo] *nm* (*MAT*) binomial.
biodegradable [bioðeɣra'ðaßle] *adj*
biodegradable.
biodiversidad [bioðißersi'ðað] *nf*
biodiversity.
biografía [bjoɣra'fia] *nf* biography.
biográfico, a [bio'ɣrafiko, a] *adj*
biographical.
biógrafo, a [bi'oɣrafo, a] *nm/f* biographer.
biología [biolo'xia] *nf* biology.
biológico, a [bio'loxiko, a] *adj* biological;
(*cultivo, producto*) organic; **guerra**
biológica biological warfare.
biólogo, a [bi'oloɣo, a] *nm/f* biologist.
biombo ['bjombo] *nm* (folding) screen.
biopsia [bi'opsja] *nf* biopsy.
bioquímico, a [bio'kimiko, a] *adj*
biochemical ♦ *nm/f* biochemist ♦ *nf*
biochemistry.
biosfera [bios'fera] *nf* biosphere.
bioterrorismo [bioterro'rismo] *nm*
bioterrorism.
bióxido [bi'oksiðo] *nm* dioxide.
bipartidismo [biparti'ðismo] *nm* (*POL*)
two-party system.
biquini [bi'kini] *nm* = **bikini**.
birlar [bir'lar] *vt* (*fam*) to pinch.
birlibirloque [birlißir'loke] *nm*: **por arte de**

~ (as if) by magic.

Birmania [bir'manja] *nf* Burma.

birmano, a [bir'mano, a] *adj nm/f* Burmese.

birrete [bi'rrete] *nm* (*JUR*) judge's cap.

birria ['birrja] *nf* (*fam*): **ser una** ~ to be rubbish; **ir hecho una** ~ to be o look a sight.

bis [bis] *excl* encore! ♦ *nm* encore ♦ *adv* (*dos veces*) twice; **viven en el 27** ~ they live at 27a.

bisabuelo, a [bisa'ßwelo, a] *nm/f* great-grandfather/mother; ~**s** *nmpl* great-grandparents.

bisagra [bi'saɣra] *nf* hinge.

bisbisar [bisßi'sar], **bisbisear** [bisßise'ar] *vt* to mutter, mumble.

bisbiseo [bisßi'seo] *nm* muttering.

biselar [bise'lar] *vt* to bevel.

bisexual [bisek'swal] *adj, nm/f* bisexual.

bisiesto [bi'sjesto] *adj*: **año** ~ leap year.

bisnieto, a [bis'njeto, a] *nm/f* great-grandson/daughter; ~**s** *nmpl* great-grandchildren.

bisonte [bi'sonte] *nm* bison.

bisoñé [biso'ɲe] *nm* toupée.

bisoño, a [bi'soɲo, a] *adj* green, inexperienced.

bistec [bis'tek], **bisté** [bis'te] *nm* steak.

bisturí [bistu'ri] *nm* scalpel.

bisutería [bisute'ria] *nf* imitation o costume jewellery.

bit [bit] *nm* (*INFORM*) bit; ~ **de parada** stop bit; ~ **de paridad** parity bit.

bitácora [bi'takora] *nf*: **cuaderno de** ~ logbook, ship's log.

bitio ['bitjo] *nm* (*INFORM*) bit.

bizantino, a [biθan'tino, a] *adj* Byzantine; (*fig*) pointless.

bizarría [biθa'rria] *nf* (*valor*) bravery; (*generosidad*) generosity.

bizarro, a [bi'θarro, a] *adj* brave; generous.

bizco, a ['biθko, a] *adj* cross-eyed.

bizcocho [biθ'kotʃo] *nm* (*CULIN*) sponge cake.

biznieto, a [biθ'njeto, a] *nm/f* = **bisnieto**.

bizquear [biθke'ar] *vi* to squint.

blanco, a ['blanko, a] *adj* white ♦ *nm/f* white man/woman, white ♦ *nm* (*color*) white; (*en texto*) blank; (*MIL, fig*) target ♦ *nf* (*MUS*) minim; **en** ~ blank; **cheque en** ~ blank cheque; **votar en** ~ to spoil one's vote; **quedarse en** ~ to be disappointed; **noche en** ~ sleepless night; **ser el** ~ **de las burlas** to be the butt of jokes; **estar sin blanca** to be broke.

blancura [blan'kura] *nf* whiteness.

blandengue [blan'denge] *adj* (*fam*) soft, weak.

blandir [blan'dir] *vt* to brandish.

blando, a ['blando, a] *adj* soft; (*tierno*) tender, gentle; (*carácter*) mild; (*fam*) cowardly ♦ *nm/f* (*POL etc*) soft-liner.

blandura [blan'dura] *nf* softness; tenderness; mildness.

blanquear [blanke'ar] *vt* to whiten; (*fachada*) to whitewash; (*paño*) to bleach; (*dinero*) to launder ♦ *vi* to turn white.

blanquecino, a [blanke'θino, a] *adj* whitish.

blanqueo [blan'keo] *nm* (*de pared*) whitewashing; (*de dinero*) laundering.

blasfemar [blasfe'mar] *vi* to blaspheme; (*fig*) to curse.

blasfemia [blas'femja] *nf* blasphemy.

blasfemo, a [blas'femo, a] *adj* blasphemous ♦ *nm/f* blasphemer.

blasón [bla'son] *nm* coat of arms; (*fig*) honour.

blasonar [blaso'nar] *vt* to emblazon ♦ *vi* to boast, brag.

bledo ['bleðo] *nm*: **(no) me importa un** ~ I couldn't care less.

blindado, a [blin'daðo, a] *adj* (*MIL*) armour-plated; (*antibalas*) bulletproof; **coche** o (*AM*) **carro** ~ armoured car; **puertas blindadas** security doors.

blindaje [blin'daxe] *nm* armour, armour-plating.

bloc, *pl* **blocs** [blok, blos] *nm* writing pad; (*ESCOL*) jotter; ~ **de dibujos** sketch pad.

bloque ['bloke] *nm* (*tb INFORM*) block; (*POL*) bloc; ~ **de cilindros** cylinder block.

bloquear [bloke'ar] *vt* (*NAUT etc*) to blockade; (*aislar*) to cut off; (*COM, ECON*) to freeze; **fondos bloqueados** frozen assets.

bloqueo [blo'keo] *nm* blockade; (*COM*) freezing, blocking.

bluejean [blu'jin] *nm* (*AM*) jeans *pl*, denims *pl*.

blusa ['blusa] *nf* blouse.

B.º *abr* (*FINANZAS*: = *banco*) bank; (*COM*: = *beneficiario*) beneficiary.

boa ['boa] *nf* boa.

boato [bo'ato] *nm* show, ostentation.

bobada [bo'ßaða] *nf* foolish action (o statement); **decir** ~**s** to talk nonsense.

bobalicón, ona [boßali'kon, ona] *adj* utterly stupid.

bobería [boße'ria] *nf* = **bobada**.

bobina [bo'ßina] *nf* (*TEC*) bobbin; (*FOTO*) spool; (*ELEC*) coil, winding.

bobo, a ['boßo, a] *adj* (*tonto*) daft, silly; (*cándido*) naïve ♦ *nm/f* fool, idiot ♦ *nm* (*TEAT*) clown, funny man.

boca ['boka] *nf* mouth; (*de crustáceo*)

pincer; (*de cañón*) muzzle; (*entrada*) mouth, entrance; (*INFORM*) slot; ~**s** *nfpl* (*de río*) mouth *sg*; ~ **abajo/arriba** face down/up; **a ~ jarro** point-blank; **se me hace la ~ agua** my mouth is watering; **todo salió a pedir de ~** it all turned out perfectly; **en ~ de** (*esp AM*) according to; **la cosa anda de ~ en ~** the story is going the rounds; **¡cállate la ~!** (*fam*) shut up!; **quedarse con la ~ abierta** to be dumbfounded; **no abrir la ~** to keep quiet; ~ **del estómago** pit of the stomach; ~ **de metro** tube (*BRIT*) o subway (*US*) entrance.

bocacalle [boka'kaʎe] *nf* side street; **la primera ~** the first turning o street.

bocadillo [boka'ðiʎo] *nm* sandwich.

bocado [bo'kaðo] *nm* mouthful, bite; (*de caballo*) bridle; ~ **de Adán** Adam's apple.

bocajarro [boka'xarro]: **a ~** *adv* (*MIL*) at point-blank range; **decir algo a ~** to say sth bluntly.

bocanada [boka'naða] *nf* (*de vino*) mouthful, swallow; (*de aire*) gust, puff.

bocata [bo'kata] *nm* (*fam*) sandwich.

bocazas [bo'kaθas] *nm/f inv* (*fam*) bigmouth.

boceto [bo'θeto] *nm* sketch, outline.

bocha [ˈbotʃa] *nf* bowl; ~**s** *nfpl* bowls *sg*.

bochinche [bo'tʃintʃe] *nm* (*fam*) uproar.

bochorno [bo'tʃorno] *nm* (*vergüenza*) embarrassment; (*calor*): **hace ~** it's very muggy.

bochornoso, a [botʃor'noso, a] *adj* muggy; embarrassing.

bocina [bo'θina] *nf* (*MUS*) trumpet; (*AUTO*) horn; (*para hablar*) megaphone; **tocar la ~** (*AUTO*) to sound o blow one's horn.

bocinazo [boθi'naθo] *nm* (*AUTO*) toot.

bocio [ˈboθjo] *nm* (*MED*) goitre.

boda [ˈboða] *nf* (*tb*: ~**s**) wedding, marriage; (*fiesta*) wedding reception; ~**s de plata/de oro** silver/golden wedding *sg*.

bodega [bo'ðeɣa] *nf* (*de vino*) (wine) cellar; (*bar*) bar; (*restaurante*) restaurant; (*depósito*) storeroom; (*de barco*) hold.

bodegón [boðe'ɣon] *nm* (*ARTE*) still life.

bodrio [bo'ðrio] *nm*: **el libro es un ~** the book is awful o rubbish.

B.O.E. [ˈboe] *nm abr* = **Boletín Oficial del Estado**.

bofe [ˈbofe] *nm* (*tb*: ~**s**: **de res**) lights *pl*; **echar los ~s** to slave (away).

bofetada [bofe'taða] *nf* slap (in the face); **dar de ~s a algn** to punch sb.

bofetón [bofe'ton] *nm* = **bofetada**.

boga [ˈboɣa] *nf*: **en ~** in vogue.

bogar [bo'ɣar] *vi* (*remar*) to row; (*navegar*) to sail.

bogavante [boɣa'ßante] *nm* (*NAUT*) stroke, first rower; (*ZOOL*) lobster.

Bogotá [boɣo'ta] *n* Bogota.

bogotano, a [boɣo'tano, a] *adj* of o from Bogota ♦ *nm/f* native o inhabitant of Bogota.

bogue [ˈboɣe] *etc vb* V **bogar**.

bohemio, a [bo'emjo, a] *adj, nm/f* Bohemian.

boicot, *pl* **boicots** [boi'ko(t)] *nm* boycott.

boicotear [boikote'ar] *vt* to boycott.

boicoteo [boiko'teo] *nm* boycott.

boina [ˈboina] *nf* beret.

bola [ˈbola] *nf* ball; (*canica*) marble; (*NAIPES*) (grand) slam; (*betún*) shoe polish; (*mentira*) tale, story; ~**s** *nfpl* (*AM*) bolas; ~ **de billar** billiard ball; ~ **de nieve** snowball.

bolchevique [boltʃe'ßike] *adj, nm/f* Bolshevik.

boleadoras [bolea'ðoras] *nfpl* (*AM*) bolas *sg*.

bolera [bo'lera] *nf* skittle o bowling alley.

bolero [bo'lero] *nm* bolero.

boleta [bo'leta] *nf* (*AM: permiso*) pass, permit; (: *para votar*) ballot.

boletería [bolete'ria] *nf* (*AM*) ticket office.

boletero, a [bole'tero, a] *nm/f* (*AM*) ticket seller.

boletín [bole'tin] *nm* bulletin; (*periódico*) journal, review; ~ **escolar** (*ESP*) school report; ~ **de noticias** news bulletin; **B~ Oficial del Estado** (*ESP*) ≈ Hansard (*BRIT*), ≈ The Congressional Record (*US*); ~ **de pedido** application form; ~ **de precios** price list; ~ **de prensa** press release; *see boxed note.*

BOLETÍN OFICIAL DEL ESTADO

The **Boletín Oficial del Estado**, or "BOE", is the official government record of all laws and resolutions passed by "las Cortes" (the Spanish Parliament). It is widely consulted, mainly because it also publishes details of the "oposiciones" (competitive public service examinations).

---

boleto [bo'leto] *nm* (*esp AM*) ticket; ~ **de apuestas** betting slip.

boli [ˈboli] *nm* Biro ®.

boliche [bo'litʃe] *nm* (*bola*) jack; (*juego*) bowls *sg*; (*lugar*) bowling alley; (*AM: tienda*) small grocery store.

bólido [ˈboliðo] *nm* meteorite; (*AUTO*) racing car.

bolígrafo [bo'liɣrafo] *nm* ball-point pen, biro ®.

bolillo [bo'liʎo] *nm* (*COSTURA*) bobbin (for lacemaking).

bolívar [bo'liβar] nm *monetary unit of Venezuela.*

Bolivia [bo'liβja] nf Bolivia.

boliviano, a [boli'βjano, a] adj, nmf Bolivian.

bollo ['boʎo] nm (*pan*) roll; (*dulce*) scone; (*bulto*) bump, lump; (*abolladura*) dent; ~s nmpl (*AM*) troubles.

bolo ['bolo] nm skittle; (*píldora*) (large) pill; (**juego de**) ~s skittles sg.

Bolonia [bo'lonja] nf Bologna.

bolsa ['bolsa] nf (*cartera*) purse; (*saco*) bag; (*AM*) pocket; (*ANAT*) cavity, sac; (*COM*) stock exchange; (*MINERÍA*) pocket; ~ **de agua caliente** hot water bottle; ~ **de aire** air pocket; ~ **de (la) basura** bin-liner; ~ **de dormir** (*AM*) sleeping bag; ~ **de papel** paper bag; ~ **de plástico** plastic (o carrier) bag; **"B~ de la propiedad"** "Property Mart"; ~ **de trabajo** employment bureau; **jugar a la** ~ to play the market.

bolsillo [bol'siʎo] nm pocket; (*cartera*) purse; **de** ~ pocket cpd; **meterse a algn en el** ~ to get sb eating out of one's hand.

bolsista [bol'sista] nmf stockbroker.

bolso ['bolso] nm (*bolsa*) bag; (*de mujer*) handbag.

boludo, a [bo'luðo, a] (*AM fam!*) adj stupid ♦ nmf prat (!)

bomba ['bomba] nf (*MIL*) bomb; (*TEC*) pump; (*AM: borrachera*) drunkenness ♦ adj (*fam*): **noticia** ~ bombshell ♦ adv (*fam*): **pasarlo** ~ to have a great time; ~ **atómica/de humo/de retardo** atomic/ smoke/time bomb; ~ **de gasolina** petrol pump; ~ **de incendios** fire engine.

bombacho, a [bom'batʃo, a] adj baggy.

bombardear [bombarðe'ar] vt to bombard; (*MIL*) to bomb.

bombardeo [bombar'ðeo] nm bombardment; bombing.

bombardero [bombar'ðero] nm bomber.

bombear [bombe'ar] vt (*agua*) to pump (out o up); (*MIL*) to bomb; (*FÚTBOL*) to lob; ~**se** vr to warp.

bombero [bom'bero] nm fireman; (**cuerpo de**) ~s fire brigade.

bombilla [bom'biʎa] nf (*ESP*), **bombillo** [bom'biʎo] nm (*AM*) (light) bulb.

bombín [bom'bin] nm bowler hat.

bombo ['bombo] nm (*MUS*) bass drum; (*TEC*) drum; (*fam*) exaggerated praise; **hacer algo a** ~ **y platillo** to make a great song and dance about sth; **tengo la cabeza hecha un** ~ I've got a splitting headache.

bombón [bom'bon] nm chocolate; (*belleza*) gem.

bombona [bom'bona] nf: ~ **de butano** gas cylinder.

bombonería [bombone'ria] nf sweetshop.

bonachón, ona [bona'tʃon, ona] adj good-natured.

bonaerense [bonae'rense] adj of o from Buenos Aires ♦ nmf native o inhabitant of Buenos Aires.

bonancible [bonan'θiβle] adj (*tiempo*) fair, calm.

bonanza [bo'nanθa] nf (*NAUT*) fair weather; (*fig*) bonanza; (*MINERÍA*) rich pocket o vein.

bondad [bon'dað] nf goodness, kindness; **tenga la** ~ **de** (please) be good enough to.

bondadoso, a [bonda'ðoso, a] adj good, kind.

bongo ['bongo] nm large canoe.

boniato [bo'njato] nm sweet potato, yam.

bonificación [bonifika'θjon] nf (*COM*) allowance, discount; (*pago*) bonus; (*DEPORTE*) extra points pl.

bonito, a [bo'nito, a] adj (*lindo*) pretty; (*agradable*) nice ♦ adv (*AM fam*) well ♦ nm (*atún*) tuna (fish).

bono ['bono] nm voucher; (*FIN*) bond; ~ **de billetes de metro** booklet of metro tickets; ~ **del Tesoro** treasury bill.

bonobús [bono'βus] nm (*ESP*) bus pass.

Bono Loto, bonoloto [bono'loto] nm o f (*ESP*) *state-run weekly lottery*; V tb **lotería.**

boom [bum], pl **booms** ['bum, 'bums] nm boom.

boquear [boke'ar] vi to gasp.

boquerón [boke'ron] nm (*pez*) (kind of) anchovy; (*agujero*) large hole.

boquete [bo'kete] nm gap, hole.

boquiabierto, a [bokia'βjerto, a] adj open-mouthed (in astonishment); **quedar** ~ to be left aghast.

boquilla [bo'kiʎa] nf (*para riego*) nozzle; (*para cigarro*) cigarette holder; (*MUS*) mouthpiece.

borbollar [borβo'ʎar], **borbollear** [borβoʎe'ar] vi to bubble.

borbollón [borβo'ʎon] nm bubbling; **hablar a borbollones** to gabble; **salir a borbollones** (*agua*) to gush out.

borbotar [borβo'tar] vi = **borbollar.**

borbotón [borβo'ton] nm: **salir a borbotones** to gush out.

borda ['borða] nf (*NAUT*) gunwale; **echar** o **tirar algo por la** ~ to throw sth overboard.

bordado [bor'ðaðo] nm embroidery.

bordar [bor'ðar] vt to embroider.

borde ['borðe] nm edge, border; (de camino etc) side; (en la costura) hem; **al ~ de** (fig) on the verge o brink of; **ser ~** (ESP fam) to be a pain in the neck.

bordear [borðe'ar] vt to border.

bordillo [bor'ðiʎo] nm kerb (BRIT), curb (US).

bordo ['borðo] nm (NAUT) side; **a ~** on board.

Borgoña [bor'ɣoɲa] nf Burgundy.

borgoña [bor'ɣoɲa] nm burgundy.

boricua [bo'rikwa], **borinqueño, a** [borin'keɲo, a] adj, nm/f Puerto Rican.

borla ['borla] nf (gen) tassel; (de gorro) pompon.

borra ['borra] nf (pelusa) fluff; (sedimento) sediment.

borrachera [borra'tʃera] nf (ebriedad) drunkenness; (orgía) spree, binge.

borracho, a [bo'rratʃo, a] adj drunk ♦ nm/f (que bebe mucho) drunkard, drunk; (temporalmente) drunk, drunk man/ woman ♦ nm (CULIN) cake soaked in liqueur or spirit.

borrador [borra'ðor] nm (escritura) first draft, rough sketch; (cuaderno) scribbling pad; (goma) rubber (BRIT), eraser; (COM) daybook; (para pizarra) duster; **hacer un nuevo ~ de** (COM) to redraft.

borrar [bo'rrar] vt to erase, rub out; (tachar) to delete; (cinta) to wipe out; (INFORM: archivo) to delete, erase; (POL etc: eliminar) to deal with.

borrasca [bo'rraska] nf storm.

borrascoso, a [borras'koso, a] adj stormy.

borrego, a [bo'rreɣo, a] nm/f lamb; (oveja) sheep; (fig) simpleton.

borricada [borri'kaða] nf foolish action/ statement.

borrico, a [bo'rriko, a] nm donkey; (fig) stupid man ♦ nf she-donkey; (fig) stupid woman.

borrón [bo'rron] nm (mancha) stain; **~ y cuenta nueva** let bygones be bygones.

borroso, a [bo'rroso, a] adj vague, unclear; (escritura) illegible; (escrito) smudgy; (FOTO) blurred.

Bósforo ['bosforo] nm: **el (Estrecho del) ~** the Bosp(h)orus.

Bosnia ['bosnja] nf Bosnia.

bosnio, a ['bosnjo, a] adj, nm/f Bosnian.

bosque ['boske] nm wood; (grande) forest.

bosquejar [boske'xar] vt to sketch.

bosquejo [bos'kexo] nm sketch.

bosta ['bosta] nf dung, manure.

bostece [bos'teθe] etc vb V **bostezar**.

bostezar [boste'θar] vi to yawn.

bostezo [bos'teθo] nm yawn.

bota ['bota] nf (calzado) boot; (saco) leather wine bottle; **ponerse las ~s** (fam) to strike it rich.

botadura [bota'ðura] nf launching.

botanas [bo'tanas] nfpl (AM) hors d'œuvres.

botánico, a [bo'taniko, a] adj botanical ♦ nm/f botanist ♦ nf botany.

botar [bo'tar] vt to throw, hurl; (NAUT) to launch; (esp AM fam) to throw out ♦ vi to bounce.

botarate [bota'rate] nm (imbécil) idiot.

bote ['bote] nm (salto) bounce; (golpe) thrust; (vasija) tin, can; (embarcación) boat; **de ~ en ~** packed, jammed full; **~ salvavidas** lifeboat; **dar un ~** to jump; **dar ~s** (AUTO etc) to bump; **~ de la basura** (AM) dustbin (BRIT), trashcan (US).

botella [bo'teʎa] nf bottle; **~ de vino** (contenido) bottle of wine; (recipiente) wine bottle.

botellero [bote'ʎero] nm wine rack.

botellín [bote'ʎin] nm small bottle.

botellón [bote'ʎon] nm (ESP fam) outdoor drinking session (involving groups of young people).

botica [bo'tika] nf chemist's (shop) (BRIT), pharmacy.

boticario, a [boti'karjo, a] nm/f chemist (BRIT), pharmacist.

botijo [bo'tixo] nm (earthenware) jug; (tren) excursion train.

botín [bo'tin] nm (calzado) half boot; (MIL) booty; (de ladrón) loot.

botiquín [boti'kin] nm (armario) medicine chest; (portátil) first-aid kit.

botón [bo'ton] nm button; (BOT) bud; (de florete) tip; **~ de arranque** (AUTO etc) starter; **~ de oro** buttercup; **pulsar el ~** to press the button.

botones [bo'tones] nm inv bellboy, bellhop (US).

botulismo [botu'lismo] nm botulism.

bóveda ['boβeða] nf (ARQ) vault.

bovino, a [bo'βino, a] adj bovine; (AGR): **ganado ~** cattle.

box ['boks] nm (AM) boxing.

boxeador [boksea'ðor] nm boxer.

boxear [bokse'ar] vi to box.

boxeo [bok'seo] nm boxing.

boya ['boja] nf (NAUT) buoy; (flotador) float.

boyante [bo'jante] adj (NAUT) buoyant; (feliz) buoyant; (próspero) prosperous.

bozal [bo'θal] nm (de caballo) halter; (de perro) muzzle.

bozo ['boθo] nm (pelusa) fuzz; (boca) mouth.

bracear [braθe'ar] vi (agitar los brazos) to wave one's arms.

bracero [bra'θero] nm labourer; (en el campo) farmhand.

braga ['braɣa] nf (cuerda) sling, rope; (de bebé) nappy, diaper (US); ~s nfpl (de mujer) panties.

braguero [bra'ɣero] nm (MED) truss.

bragueta [bra'ɣeta] nf fly (BRIT), flies pl (BRIT), zipper (US).

braguetazo [braɣe'taθo] nm marriage of convenience.

braille [breil] nm braille.

bramante [bra'mante] nm twine, string.

bramar [bra'mar] vi to bellow, roar.

bramido [bra'miðo] nm bellow, roar.

branquias ['brankjas] nfpl gills.

brasa ['brasa] nf live o hot coal; **carne a la ~** grilled meat.

brasero [bra'sero] nm brazier; (AM: chimenea) fireplace.

Brasil [bra'sil] nm: **(el) ~** Brazil.

brasileño, a [brasi'leɲo, a] adj, nm/f Brazilian.

bravata [bra'βata] nf boast.

braveza [bra'βeθa] nf (valor) bravery; (ferocidad) ferocity.

bravío, a [bra'βio, a] adj wild; (feroz) fierce.

bravo, a ['braβo, a] adj (valiente) brave; (bueno) fine, splendid; (feroz) ferocious; (salvaje) wild; (mar etc) rough, stormy; (CULIN) hot, spicy ♦ excl bravo!

bravucón, ona [braβu'kon, ona] adj swaggering ♦ nm/f braggart.

bravura [bra'βura] nf bravery; ferocity; (pey) boast.

braza ['braθa] nf fathom; **nadar a la ~** to swim (the) breast-stroke.

brazada [bra'θaða] nf stroke.

brazalete [braθa'lete] nm (pulsera) bracelet; (banda) armband.

brazo ['braθo] nm arm; (ZOOL) foreleg; (BOT) limb, branch; ~s nmpl (braceros) hands, workers; **~ derecho** (fig) right-hand man; **a ~ partido** hand-to-hand; **cogidos etc del ~** arm in arm; **no dar su ~ a torcer** not to give way easily; **huelga de ~s caídos** sit-down strike.

brea ['brea] nf pitch, tar.

brebaje [bre'βaxe] nm potion.

brecha ['bretʃa] nf breach; (hoyo vacío) gap, opening.

brécol ['brekol] nm broccoli.

brega ['breɣa] nf (lucha) struggle; (trabajo) hard work.

bregar [bre'ɣar] vi (luchar) to struggle;

(trabajar mucho) to slog away.

bregue ['breɣe] etc vb V **bregar.**

breña ['breɲa] nf rough ground.

Bretaña [bre'taɲa] nf Brittany.

brete ['brete] nm (cepo) shackles pl; (fig) predicament; **estar en un ~** to be in a jam.

breteles [bre'teles] nmpl (AM) straps.

bretón, ona [bre'ton, ona] adj, nm/f Breton.

breva ['breβa] nf (BOT) early fig; (puro) flat cigar; **¡no caerá esa ~!** no such luck!

breve ['breβe] adj short, brief; **en ~** (pronto) shortly; (en pocas palabras) in short ♦ nf (MUS) breve.

brevedad [breβe'ðað] nf brevity, shortness; **con o a la major ~** as soon as possible.

breviario [bre'βjarjo] nm (REL) breviary.

brezal [bre'θal] nm moor(land), heath.

brezo ['breθo] nm heather.

bribón, ona [bri'βon, ona] adj idle, lazy ♦ nm/f (vagabundo) vagabond; (pícaro) rascal, rogue.

bricolaje [briko'laxe] nm do-it-yourself, DIY.

brida ['briða] nf bridle, rein; (TEC) clamp; **a toda ~** at top speed.

bridge [britʃ] nm (NAIPES) bridge.

brigada [bri'ɣaða] nf (unidad) brigade; (trabajadores) squad, gang ♦ nm warrant officer.

brigadier [briɣa'ðjer] nm brigadier (-general).

brillante [bri'ʎante] adj brilliant; (color) bright; (joya) sparkling ♦ nm diamond.

brillantez [briʎan'teθ] nf (color etc) brightness; (fig) brilliance.

brillar [bri'ʎar] vi (tb fig) to shine; (joyas) to sparkle; **~ por su ausencia** to be conspicuous by one's absence.

brillo ['briʎo] nm shine; (brillantez) brilliance; (fig) splendour; **sacar ~ a** to polish.

brilloso, a [bri'ʎoso, a] adj (AM) = **brillante.**

brincar [brin'kar] vi to skip about, hop about, jump about; **está que brinca** he's hopping mad.

brinco ['brinko] nm jump, leap; **a ~s** by fits and starts; **de un ~** at one bound.

brindar [brin'dar] vi: **~ a o por** to drink (a toast) to ♦ vt to offer, present; **le brinda la ocasión de** it offers o affords him the opportunity to; **~se** vr: **~se a hacer algo** to offer to do sth.

brindis ['brindis] nm inv toast; (TAUR) (ceremony of) dedication.

brinque ['brinke] etc vb V **brincar.**

brío ['brio] nm spirit, dash.

brioso, a [bri'oso, a] *adj* spirited, dashing.
brisa ['brisa] *nf* breeze.
británico, a [bri'taniko, a] *adj* British ♦ *nm/f*
Briton, British person; **los ~s** the
British.
brizna ['briθna] *nf* (*hebra*) strand, thread;
(*de hierba*) blade; (*trozo*) piece.
broca ['broka] *nf* (*COSTURA*) bobbin; (*TEC*)
drill bit; (*clavo*) tack.
brocado [bro'kaðo] *nm* brocade.
brocal [bro'kal] *nm* rim.
brocha ['brotʃa] *nf* (large) paintbrush; **~
de afeitar** shaving brush; **pintor de ~
gorda** painter and decorator; (*fig*) poor
painter.
brochazo [bro'tʃaθo] *nm* brush-stroke; **a
grandes ~s** (*fig*) in general terms.
broche ['brotʃe] *nm* brooch.
broma ['broma] *nf* joke; (*inocentada*)
practical joke; **en ~** in fun, as a joke;
gastar una ~ a algn to play a joke on sb;
tomar algo a ~ to take sth as a joke.
bromear [brome'ar] *vi* to joke.
bromista [bro'mista] *adj* fond of joking
♦ *nm/f* joker, wag.
bromuro [bro'muro] *nm* bromide.
bronca ['bronka] *nf* row; (*regañada*)
ticking-off; **armar una ~** to kick up a
fuss; **echar una ~ a algn** to tell sb off.
bronce ['bronθe] *nm* bronze; (*latón*) brass.
bronceado, a [bronθe'aðo, a] *adj* bronze
cpd; (*por el sol*) tanned ♦ *nm* (sun)tan;
(*TEC*) bronzing.
bronceador [bronθea'ðor] *nm* suntan
lotion.
broncearse [bronθe'arse] *vr* to get a
suntan.
bronco, a ['bronko, a] *adj* (*manera*) rude,
surly; (*voz*) harsh.
bronquios ['bronkjos] *nmpl* bronchial
tubes.
bronquitis [bron'kitis] *nf inv* bronchitis.
brotar [bro'tar] *vt* (*tierra*) to produce ♦ *vi*
(*BOT*) to sprout; (*aguas*) to gush (forth);
(*lágrimas*) to well up; (*MED*) to break out.
brote ['brote] *nm* (*BOT*) shoot; (*MED, fig*)
outbreak.
broza ['broθa] *nf* (*BOT*) dead leaves *pl*; (*fig*)
rubbish.
bruces ['bruθes]: **de ~** *adv*: **caer** *o* **dar de ~**
to fall headlong, fall flat.
bruja ['bruxa] *nf* witch.
Brujas ['bruxas] *nf* Bruges.
brujería [bruxe'ria] *nf* witchcraft.
brujo ['bruxo] *nm* wizard, magician.
brújula ['bruxula] *nf* compass.
bruma ['bruma] *nf* mist.
brumoso, a [bru'moso, a] *adj* misty.

bruñendo [bru'ɲenðo] *etc vb V* **bruñir**.
bruñido [bru'ɲiðo] *nm* polish.
bruñir [bru'ɲir] *vt* to polish.
brusco, a ['brusko, a] *adj* (*súbito*) sudden;
(*áspero*) brusque.
Bruselas [bru'selas] *nf* Brussels.
brusquedad [bruske'ðað] *nf* suddenness;
brusqueness.
brutal [bru'tal] *adj* brutal.
brutalidad [brutali'ðað] *nf* brutality.
bruto, a ['bruto, a] *adj* (*idiota*) stupid;
(*bestial*) brutish; (*peso*) gross ♦ *nm* brute;
a la bruta, a lo ~ roughly; **en ~** raw,
unworked.
Bs. *abr* = **bolívares**.
Bs.As. *abr* = **Buenos Aires**.
bucal [bu'kal] *adj* oral; **por vía ~** orally.
bucanero [buka'nero] *nm* buccaneer.
bucear [buθe'ar] *vi* to dive ♦ *vt* to explore.
buceo [bu'θeo] *nm* diving; (*fig*)
investigation.
buche ['butʃe] *nm* (*de ave*) crop; (*ZOOL*)
maw; (*fam*) belly.
bucle ['bukle] *nm* curl; (*INFORM*) loop.
budín [bu'ðin] *nm* pudding.
budismo [bu'ðismo] *nm* Buddhism.
budista [bu'ðista] *adj, nm/f* Buddhist.
buen [bwen] *adj V* **bueno**.
buenamente [bwena'mente] *adv*
(*fácilmente*) easily; (*voluntariamente*)
willingly.
buenaventura [bwenaβen'tura] *nf* (*suerte*)
good luck; (*adivinación*) fortune; **decir** *o*
echar la ~ a algn to tell sb's fortune.

══════════════════ PALABRA CLAVE

bueno, a ['bweno, a] (*antes de nmsg*: **buen**)
adj **1** (*excelente etc*) good; (*MED*) well; **es
un libro ~, es un buen libro** it's a good
book; **hace ~, hace buen tiempo** the
weather is fine, it is fine; **es ~a persona**
he's a good sort; **el ~ de Paco** good old
Paco; **fue muy ~ conmigo** he was very
nice *o* kind to me; **ya está ~** he's fine
now
2 (*apropiado*): **ser ~ para** to be good for;
creo que vamos por buen camino I think
we're on the right track
3 (*irónico*): **le di un buen rapapolvo** I
gave him a good *o* real ticking off;
¡buen conductor estás hecho! some
driver *o* a fine driver you are!; **¡estaría
~ que ...!** a fine thing it would be if ...!
4 (*atractivo, sabroso*): **está ~ este
bizcocho** this sponge is delicious; **Julio
está muy ~** (*fam*) Julio is a bit of alright
5 (*grande*) good, big; **un buen número
de ...** a good number of ...; **un buen trozo**

de ... a nice big piece of ...
6 (*saludos*): **¡buen día! (***AM***), ¡~s días!**
(**good**) morning!; **¡buenas (tardes)!** good
afternoon!; (*más tarde*) good evening!;
¡buenas noches! good night!
7 (*otras locuciones*): **estar de buenas** to
be in a good mood; **por las buenas o por
las malas** by hook or by crook; **de
buenas a primeras** all of a sudden
♦ *excl:* **¡~!** all right!; **~, ¿y qué?** well, so
what?; **~, lo que pasa es que ...** well, the
thing is ...; **pero ¡~!** well, I like that!; **~,
pues ...** right, (then) ...

Buenos Aires [bweno'saires] *nm* Buenos
Aires.
buey [bwei] *nm* ox.
búfalo ['bufalo] *nm* buffalo.
bufanda [bu'fanda] *nf* scarf.
bufar [bu'far] *vi* to snort.
bufete [bu'fete] *nm* (*despacho de abogado*)
lawyer's office; **establecer su ~** to set up
in legal practice.
buffer ['bufer] *nm* (*INFORM*) buffer.
bufón [bu'fon] *nm* clown.
bufonada [bufo'naða] *nf* (*dicho*) jest;
(*hecho*) piece of buffoonery; (*TEAT*)
farce.
buhardilla [buar'ðiʎa] *nf* attic.
búho ['buo] *nm* owl; (*fig*) hermit, recluse.
buhonero [buo'nero] *nm* pedlar.
buitre ['bwitre] *nm* vulture.
bujía [bu'xia] *nf* (*vela*) candle; (*ELEC*)
candle (power); (*AUTO*) spark plug.
bula ['bula] *nf* (*papal*) bull.
bulbo ['bulßo] *nm* (*BOT*) bulb.
bulevar [bule'ßar] *nm* boulevard.
Bulgaria [bul'xarja] *nf* Bulgaria.
búlgaro, a ['bulxaro, a] *adj, nm/f* Bulgarian.
bulimia [bu'limja] *nf* bulimia.
bulla ['buʎa] *nf* (*ruido*) uproar; (*de gente*)
crowd; **armar** *o* **meter ~** to kick up a
row.
bullendo [bu'ʎendo] *etc vb V* **bullir**.
bullicio [bu'ʎiθjo] *nm* (*ruido*) uproar;
(*movimiento*) bustle.
bullicioso, a [buʎi'θjoso, a] *adj* (*ruidoso*)
noisy; (*calle*) busy; (*situación*) turbulent.
bullir [bu'ʎir] *vi* (*hervir*) to boil; (*burbujear*)
to bubble; (*mover*) to move, stir;
(*insectos*) to swarm; **~ de** (*fig*) to teem *o*
seethe with.
bulo ['bulo] *nm* false rumour.
bulto ['bulto] *nm* (*paquete*) package; (*fardo*)
bundle; (*tamaño*) size, bulkiness; (*MED*)
swelling, lump; (*silueta*) vague shape;
(*estatua*) bust, statue; **hacer ~** to take up
space; **escurrir el ~** to make o.s. scarce;

(*fig*) to dodge the issue.
buñuelo [bu'ɲwelo] *nm* ≈ doughnut, donut
(*US*).
BUP [bup] *nm abr* (*ESP ESCOL*:= *Bachillerato
Unificado y Polivalente*) *secondary
education for 14-17 age group;* V *tb*
sistema educativo.
buque ['buke] *nm* ship, vessel; **~ de guerra**
warship; **~ mercante** merchant ship; **~
de vela** sailing ship.
burbuja [bur'ßuxa] *nf* bubble; **hacer ~s** to
bubble; (*gaseosa*) to fizz.
burbujear [burßuxe'ar] *vi* to bubble.
burdel [bur'ðel] *nm* brothel.
Burdeos [bur'ðeos] *nm* Bordeaux.
burdo, a ['burðo, a] *adj* coarse, rough.
burgalés, esa [burxa'les, esa] *adj* of *o* from
Burgos ♦ *nm/f* native *o* inhabitant of
Burgos.
burgués, esa [bur'xes, esa] *adj* middle-
class, bourgeois; **pequeño ~** lower
middle-class; (*POL, pey*) petty bourgeois.
burguesía [burxe'sia] *nf* middle class,
bourgeoisie.
burla ['burla] *nf* (*mofa*) gibe; (*broma*) joke;
(*engaño*) trick; **hacer ~ de** to make fun
of.
burladero [burla'ðero] *nm* (bullfighter's)
refuge.
burlador, a [burla'ðor, a] *adj* mocking
♦ *nm/f* mocker; (*bromista*) joker ♦ *nm*
(*libertino*) seducer.
burlar [bur'lar] *vt* (*engañar*) to deceive;
(*seducir*) to seduce ♦ *vi*, **~se** *vr* to joke;
~se de to make fun of.
burlesco, a [bur'lesko, a] *adj* burlesque.
burlón, ona [bur'lon, ona] *adj* mocking.
buró [bu'ro] *nm* bureau.
burocracia [buro'kraθja] *nf* bureaucracy.
burócrata [bu'rokrata] *nm/f* bureaucrat.
buromática [buro'matika] *nf* office
automation.
burrada [bu'rraða] *nf* stupid act; **decir ~s**
to talk nonsense.
burro, a ['burro, a] *nm/f* (*ZOOL*) donkey;
(*fig*) ass, idiot ♦ *adj* stupid; **caerse del ~**
to realise one's mistake; **no ver tres en
un ~** to be as blind as a bat.
bursátil [bur'satil] *adj* stock-exchange *cpd*.
bus [bus] *nm* bus.
busca ['buska] *nf* search, hunt ♦ *nm*
bleeper, pager; **en ~ de** in search of.
buscador, a [buska'ðor, a] *nm/f* searcher ♦
nm (*INTERNET*) search engine.
buscapiés [buska'pjes] *nm inv* jumping
jack (*BRIT*), firecracker (*US*).
buscapleitos [buska'pleitos] *nm/f inv*
troublemaker.

buscar [bus'kar] *vt* to look for; (*objeto perdido*) to have a look for; (*beneficio*) to seek; (*enemigo*) to seek out; (*traer*) to bring, fetch; (*provocar*) to provoke; (*INFORM*) to search ♦ *vi* to look, search, seek; **ven a ~me a la oficina** come and pick me up at the office; **~le 3 o 4 pies al gato** to split hairs; **"~ y reemplazar"** (*INFORM*) "search and replace"; **se busca secretaria** secretary wanted; **se la buscó** he asked for it.

buscavidas [buska'ßiðas] *nm/f inv* snooper; (*persona ambiciosa*) go-getter.

buscona [bus'kona] *nf* whore.

busilis [bu'silis] *nm inv* (*fam*) snag.

busque ['buske] *etc vb V* **buscar**.

búsqueda ['buskeða] *nf* = **busca**.

busto ['busto] *nm* (*ANAT, ARTE*) bust.

butaca [bu'taka] *nf* armchair; (*de cine, teatro*) stall, seat.

butano [bu'tano] *nm* butane (gas); **bombona de ~** gas cylinder.

butifarra [buti'farra] *nf* Catalan sausage.

buzo ['buθo] *nm* diver; (*AM: chandal*) tracksuit.

buzón [bu'θon] *nm* (*gen*) letter box; (*en la calle*) pillar box (*BRIT*); (*TELEC*) mailbox; **echar al ~** to post.

buzonear [buθone'ar] *vt* to leaflet.

byte [bait] *nm* (*INFORM*) byte.

Cc

C, c [θe, se (*esp AM*)] *nf* (*letra*) C, c; **C de Carmen** C for Charlie.

C. *abr* (= *centígrado*) C.; (= *compañía*) Co.

c. *abr* (= *capítulo*) ch.

C/ *abr* (= *calle*) St, Rd.

c/ *abr* (*COM*: = *cuenta*) a/c.

ca [ka] *excl* not a bit of it!

c.a. *abr* (= *corriente alterna*) A.C.

cabal [ka'ßal] *adj* (*exacto*) exact; (*correcto*) right, proper; (*acabado*) finished, complete; **~es** *nmpl*: **estar en sus ~es** to be in one's right mind.

cábala ['kaßala] *nf* (*REL*) cab(b)ala; (*fig*) cabal, intrigue; **~s** *nfpl* guess *sg*, supposition *sg*.

cabalgadura [kaßalɣa'ðura] *nf* mount, horse.

cabalgar [kaßal'ɣar] *vt, vi* to ride.

cabalgata [kaßal'ɣata] *nf* procession; *V tb* **Reyes Magos**.

cabalgue [ka'ßalɣe] *etc vb V* **cabalgar**.

cabalístico, a [kaßa'listiko, a] *adj* (*fig*) mysterious.

caballa [ka'ßaʎa] *nf* mackerel.

caballeresco, a [kaßaʎe'resko, a] *adj* noble, chivalrous.

caballería [kaßaʎe'ria] *nf* mount; (*MIL*) cavalry.

caballeriza [kaßaʎe'riθa] *nf* stable.

caballerizo [kaßaʎe'riθo] *nm* groom, stableman.

caballero [kaßa'ʎero] *nm* gentleman; (*de la orden de caballería*) knight; (*trato directo*) sir; **"C~s"** "Gents".

caballerosidad [kaßaʎerosi'ðað] *nf* chivalry.

caballete [kaßa'ʎete] *nm* (*AGR*) ridge; (*ARTE*) easel.

caballito [kaßa'ʎito] *nm* (*caballo pequeño*) small horse, pony; (*juguete*) rocking horse; **~s** *nmpl* merry-go-round *sg*; **~ de mar** seahorse; **~ del diablo** dragonfly.

caballo [ka'ßaʎo] *nm* horse; (*AJEDREZ*) knight; (*NAIPES*) ≈ queen; **~ de vapor** *o* **de fuerza** horsepower; **es su ~ de batalla** it's his hobby-horse; **~ blanco** (*COM*) backer; *V tb* **Baraja Española**.

cabaña [ka'ßaɲa] *nf* (*casita*) hut, cabin.

cabaré, cabaret, *pl* **cabarets** [kaßa're, kaßa'res] *nm* cabaret.

cabecear [kaßeθe'ar] *vi* to nod.

cabecera [kaße'θera] *nf* (*gen*) head; (*de distrito*) chief town; (*de cama*) headboard; (*IMPRENTA*) headline.

cabecilla [kaße'θiʎa] *nm* ringleader.

cabellera [kaße'ʎera] *nf* (head of) hair; (*de cometa*) tail.

cabello [ka'ßeʎo] *nm* (*tb: ~s*) hair *sg*.

cabelludo [kaße'ʎuðo] *adj V* **cuero**.

caber [ka'ßer] *vi* (*entrar*) to fit, go; **caben 3 más** there's room for 3 more; **cabe preguntar si...** one might ask whether...; **cabe que venga más tarde** he may come later.

cabestrillo [kaßes'triʎo] *nm* sling.

cabestro [ka'ßestro] *nm* halter.

cabeza [ka'ßeθa] *nf* head; (*POL*) chief, leader ♦ *nm/f*: **~ rapada** skinhead; **caer de ~** to fall head first; **sentar la ~** to settle down; **~ de lectura/escritura** read/write head; **~ impresora** *o* **de impresión** printhead.

cabezada [kaße'θaða] *nf* (*golpe*) butt; **dar una ~** to nod off.

cabezal [kaße'θal] *nm*: **~ impresor** print head.

cabezazo [kaße'θaθo] *nm* (*golpe*) headbutt; (*FÚTBOL*) header.

cabezón, ona [kaße'θon, ona] *adj* with a big head; (*vino*) heady; (*obstinado*) obstinate, stubborn.

cabezota [kaße'θota] *adj inv* obstinate, stubborn.

cabezudo, a [kaße'θuðo, a] *adj* with a big head; (*obstinado*) obstinate, stubborn.

cabida [ka'ßiða] *nf* space; **dar ~ a** to make room for; **tener ~ para** to have room for.

cabildo [ka'ßildo] *nm* (*de iglesia*) chapter; (*POL*) town council.

cabina [ka'ßina] *nf* (*de camión*) cabin; **~ telefónica** (tele)phone box (*BRIT*) *o* booth.

cabizbajo, a [kaßiθ'ßaxo, a] *adj* crestfallen, dejected.

cable ['kaßle] *nm* cable; (*de aparato*) lead; **~ aéreo** (*ELEC*) overhead cable; **conectar con ~** (*INFORM*) to hardwire.

cabo ['kaßo] *nm* (*de objeto*) end, extremity; (*MIL*) corporal; (*NAUT*) rope, cable; (*GEO*) cape; (*TEC*) thread; **al ~ de 3 días** after 3 days; **de ~ a rabo** *o* **~** from beginning to end; (*libro: leer*) from cover to cover; **llevar a ~** to carry out; **atar ~s** to tie up the loose ends; **C~ de Buena Esperanza** Cape of Good Hope; **C~ de Hornos** Cape Horn; **las Islas de C~ Verde** the Cape Verde Islands.

cabra ['kaßra] *nf* goat; **estar como una ~** (*fam*) to be nuts.

cabré [ka'ßre] *etc vb V* **caber.**

cabrear [kaßre'ar] *vt* to annoy; **~se** *vr* to fly off the handle.

cabrío, a [ka'ßrio, a] *adj* goatish; **macho ~** (he-)goat, billy goat.

cabriola [ka'ßrjola] *nf* caper.

cabritilla [kaßri'tiʎa] *nf* kid, kidskin.

cabrito [ka'ßrito] *nm* kid.

cabrón [ka'ßron] *nm* (*fig: fam!*) bastard (*!*).

cabronada [kaßro'naða] *nf* (*fam!*): **hacer una ~ a algn** to be a bastard to sb.

caca ['kaka] *nf* (*palabra de niños*) pooh ♦ *excl*: **no toques, ¡~**! don't touch, it's dirty!

cacahuete [kaka'wete] *nm* (*ESP*) peanut.

cacao [ka'kao] *nm* cocoa; (*BOT*) cacao.

cacarear [kakare'ar] *vi* (*persona*) to boast; (*gallina*) to cackle.

cacatúa [kaka'tua] *nf* cockatoo.

cacereño, a [kaθe'reɲo, a] *adj* of *o* from Cáceres ♦ *nmf* native *o* inhabitant of Cáceres.

cacería [kaθe'ria] *nf* hunt.

cacerola [kaθe'rola] *nf* pan, saucepan.

cacha ['katʃa] *nf* (*mango*) handle; (*nalga*) buttock.

cachalote [katʃa'lote] *nm* sperm whale.

cacharro [ka'tʃarro] *nm* (*vasija*) (earthenware) pot; (*cerámica*) piece of pottery; (*fam*) useless object; **~s** *nmpl* pots and pans.

cachear [katʃe'ar] *vt* to search, frisk.

cachemir [katʃe'mir] *nm* cashmere.

cacheo [ka'tʃeo] *nm* searching, frisking.

cachete [ka'tʃete] *nm* (*ANAT*) cheek; (*bofetada*) slap (in the face).

cachimba [ka'tʃimba] *nf*, **cachimbo** [ka'tʃimbo] *nm* (*AM*) pipe.

cachiporra [katʃi'porra] *nf* truncheon.

cachivache [katʃi'ßatʃe] *nm* piece of junk; **~s** *nmpl* trash *sg*, junk *sg*.

cacho, a ['katʃo, a] *nm* (small) bit; (*AM: cuerno*) horn.

cachondearse [katʃonde'arse] *vr*: **~ de algn** to tease sb.

cachondeo [katʃon'deo] *nm* (*fam*) farce, joke; (*guasa*) laugh.

cachondo, a [ka'tʃondo, a] *adj* (*ZOOL*) on heat; (*persona*) randy, sexy; (*gracioso*) funny.

cachorro, a [ka'tʃorro, a] *nm/f* (*perro*) pup, puppy; (*león*) cub.

cacique [ka'θike] *nm* chief, local ruler; (*POL*) local party boss; (*fig*) despot.

caco ['kako] *nm* pickpocket.

cacofonía [kakofo'nia] *nf* cacophony.

cacto ['kakto] *nm*, **cactus** ['kaktus] *nm inv* cactus.

cada ['kaða] *adj inv* each; (*antes de número*) every; **~ día** each day, every day; **~ dos días** every other day; **~ uno/a** each one, every one; **~ vez más/menos** more and more/less and less; **uno de ~ diez** one out of every ten; **¿~ cuánto?** how often?

cadalso [ka'ðalso] *nm* scaffold.

cadáver [ka'ðaßer] *nm* (dead) body, corpse.

cadavérico, a [kaða'ßeriko, a] *adj* cadaverous; (*pálido*) deathly pale.

cadena [ka'ðena] *nf* chain; (*TV*) channel; **reacción en ~** chain reaction; **trabajo en ~** assembly line work; **~ midi/mini** (*MUS*) midi/mini system; **~ perpetua** (*JUR*) life imprisonment; **~ de caracteres** (*INFORM*) character string.

cadencia [ka'ðenθja] *nf* cadence, rhythm.

cadera [ka'ðera] *nf* hip.

cadete [ka'ðete] *nm* cadet.

Cádiz ['kaðiθ] *nm* Cadiz.

caducar [kaðu'kar] *vi* to expire.

caducidad [kaðuθi'ðað] *nf*: **fecha de ~** expiry date; (*de comida*) sell-by date.

caduco, a [ka'ðuko, a] *adj* (*idea etc*) outdated, outmoded; **de hoja caduca**

deciduous.

caduque [ka'ðuke] *etc vb* V **caducar**.

C.A.E. *abr* (= *cóbrese al entregar*) COD.

caer [ka'er] *vi* to fall; (*premio*) to go; (*sitio*) to be, lie; (*pago*) to fall due; ~**se** *vr* to fall (down); **dejar** ~ to drop; **estar al** ~ to be due to happen; (*persona*) to be about to arrive; **me cae bien/mal** I like/don't like him; ~ **en la cuenta** to catch on; **su cumpleaños cae en viernes** her birthday falls on a Friday; **se me ha caído el guante** I've dropped my glove.

café, *pl* **cafés** [ka'fe, ka'fes] *nm* (*bebida, planta*) coffee; (*lugar*) café ♦ *adj* (*color*) brown; ~ **con leche** white coffee; ~ **solo**, ~ **negro** (*AM*) (small) black coffee.

cafeína [kafe'ina] *nf* caffein(e).

cafetal [kafe'tal] *nm* coffee plantation.

cafetera [kafe'tera] *nf* V **cafetero**.

cafetería [kafete'ria] *nf* cafe.

cafetero, a [kafe'tero, a] *adj* coffee *cpd* ♦ *nf* coffee pot; **ser muy** ~ to be a coffee addict.

cafre ['kafre] *nmlf*: **como** ~**s** (*fig*) like savages.

cagalera [kaɣa'lera] *nf* (*fam!*): **tener** ~ to have the runs.

cagar [ka'ɣar] (*fam!*) *vt* to shit (*!*); (*fig*) to bungle, mess up ♦ *vi* to have a shit (*!*); ~**se** *vr*: **¡me cago en diez** (*etc*)! Christ! (*!*).

cague ['kaɣe] *etc vb* V **cagar**.

caído, a [ka'iðo, a] *adj* fallen; (*INFORM*) down ♦ *nf* fall; (*declive*) slope; (*disminución*) fall, drop; ~ **del cielo** out of the blue; **a la caída del sol** at sunset; **sufrir una caída** to have a fall.

caiga ['kaiɣa] *etc vb* V **caer**.

caimán [kai'man] *nm* alligator.

Cairo ['kairo] *nm*: **el** ~ Cairo.

caja ['kaxa] *nf* box; (*ataúd*) coffin, casket (*US*); (*para reloj*) case; (*de ascensor*) shaft; (*COM*) cashbox; (*ECON*) fund; (*donde se hacen los pagos*) cashdesk; (*en supermercado*) checkout, till; (*TIP*) case; ~ **de ahorros** savings bank; ~ **de cambios** gearbox; ~ **fuerte**, ~ **de caudales** safe, strongbox; **ingresar en** ~ to be paid in.

cajero, a [ka'xero, a] *nmlf* cashier; (*en banco*) (bank) teller ♦ *nm*: ~ **automático** cash dispenser, automatic telling machine, A.T.M.

cajetilla [kaxe'tiʎa] *nf* (*de cigarrillos*) packet.

cajista [ka'xista] *nmlf* typesetter.

cajón [ka'xon] *nm* big box; (*de mueble*) drawer.

cal [kal] *nf* lime; **cerrar algo a** ~ **y canto** to shut sth firmly.

cala ['kala] *nf* (*GEO*) cove, inlet; (*de barco*) hold.

calabacín [kalaβa'θin] *nm* (*BOT*) baby marrow, courgette, zucchini (*US*).

calabaza [kala'βaθa] *nf* (*BOT*) pumpkin; **dar** ~**s a** (*candidato*) to fail.

calabozo [kala'βoθo] *nm* (*cárcel*) prison; (*celda*) cell.

calado, a [ka'laðo, a] *adj* (*prenda*) lace *cpd* ♦ *nm* (*TEC*) fretwork; (*NAUT*) draught ♦ *nf* (*de cigarrillo*) puff; **estar** ~ (*hasta los huesos*) to be soaked (to the skin).

calamar [kala'mar] *nm* squid.

calambre [ka'lambre] *nm* (*tb*: ~**s**) cramp.

calamidad [kalami'ðað] *nf* calamity, disaster; (*persona*): **es una** ~ he's a dead loss.

calamina [kala'mina] *nf* calamine.

cálamo ['kalamo] *nm* (*BOT*) stem; (*MUS*) reed.

calaña [ka'laɲa] *nf* model, pattern; (*fig*) nature, stamp.

calar [ka'lar] *vt* to soak, drench; (*penetrar*) to pierce, penetrate; (*comprender*) to see through; (*vela, red*) to lower; ~**se** *vr* (*AUTO*) to stall; ~**se las gafas** to stick one's glasses on.

calavera [kala'βera] *nf* skull.

calcañal [kalka'ɲal], **calcañar** [kalka'ɲar] *nm* heel.

calcar [kal'kar] *vt* (*reproducir*) to trace; (*imitar*) to copy.

calce ['kalθe] *etc vb* V **calzar**.

calceta [kal'θeta] *nf* (knee-length) stocking; **hacer** ~ to knit.

calcetín [kalθe'tin] *nm* sock.

calcinar [kalθi'nar] *vt* to burn, blacken.

calcio ['kalθjo] *nm* calcium.

calco ['kalko] *nm* tracing.

calcomanía [kalkoma'nia] *nf* transfer.

calculador, a [kalkula'ðor, a] *adj* calculating ♦ *nf* calculator.

calcular [kalku'lar] *vt* (*MAT*) to calculate, compute; ~ **que** ... to reckon that ....

cálculo ['kalkulo] *nm* calculation; (*MED*) (gall)stone; (*MAT*) calculus; ~ **de costo** costing; ~ **diferencial** differential calculus; **obrar con mucho** ~ to act cautiously.

caldear [kalde'ar] *vt* to warm (up), heat (up); (*metales*) to weld.

caldera [kal'dera] *nf* boiler.

calderero [kalde'rero] *nm* boilermaker.

calderilla [kalde'riʎa] *nf* (*moneda*) small change.

caldero [kal'dero] *nm* small boiler.

caldo ['kaldo] *nm* stock; (*consomé*)

consommé; ~ **de cultivo** (*BIO*) culture medium; **poner a ~ a algn** to tear sb off a strip; **los ~s jerezanos** sherries.

caldoso, a [kal'doso, a] *adj* (*guisado*) juicy; (*sopa*) thin.

calé [ka'le] *adj* gipsy *cpd*.

calefacción [kalefak'θjon] *nf* heating; ~ **central** central heating.

caleidoscopio [kaleiðos'kopjo] *nm* kaleidoscope.

calendario [kalen'darjo] *nm* calendar.

calentador [kalenta'ðor] *nm* heater.

calentamiento [kalenta'mjento] *nm* (*DEPORTE*) warm-up.

calentar [kalen'tar] *vt* to heat (up); (*fam: excitar*) to turn on; (*AM: enfurecer*) to anger; ~**se** *vr* to heat up, warm up; (*fig: discusión etc*) to get heated.

calentura [kalen'tura] *nf* (*MED*) fever, (high) temperature; (*de boca*) mouth sore.

calenturiento, a [kalentu'rjento, a] *adj* (*mente*) overactive.

calibrar [kali'ßrar] *vt* to gauge, measure.

calibre [ka'lißre] *nm* (*de cañón*) calibre, bore; (*diámetro*) diameter; (*fig*) calibre.

calidad [kali'ðað] *nf* quality; **de ~** quality *cpd*; ~ **de borrador** (*INFORM*) draft quality; ~ **de carta** *o* **de correspondencia** (*INFORM*) letter quality; ~ **texto** (*INFORM*) text quality; ~ **de vida** quality of life; **en ~ de** in the capacity of.

cálido, a ['kaliðo, a] *adj* hot; (*fig*) warm.

caliente [ka'ljente] *etc vb V* **calentar** ♦ *adj* hot; (*fig*) fiery; (*disputa*) heated; (*fam: cachondo*) randy.

califa [ka'lifa] *nm* caliph.

calificación [kalifika'θjon] *nf* qualification; (*de alumno*) grade, mark; ~ **de sobresaliente** first-class mark.

calificar [kalifi'kar] *vt* to qualify; (*alumno*) to grade, mark; ~ **de** to describe as.

calificativo, a [kalifika'tißo, a] *adj* qualifying ♦ *nm* qualifier, epithet.

califique [kali'fike] *etc vb V* **calificar**.

californiano, a [kalifor'njano, a] *adj*, *nm/f* Californian.

caligrafía [kalixra'fia] *nf* calligraphy.

calima [ka'lima] *nf* mist.

calina [ka'lina] *nf* haze.

cáliz ['kaliθ] *nm* (*BOT*) calyx; (*REL*) chalice.

caliza [ka'liθa] *nf* limestone.

callado, a [ka'ʎaðo, a] *adj* quiet, silent.

callar [ka'ʎar] *vt* (*asunto delicado*) to keep quiet about, say nothing about; (*omitir*) to pass over in silence; (*persona, oposición*) to silence ♦ *vi*, ~**se** *vr* to keep quiet, be silent; (*dejar de hablar*) to stop

talking; **¡calla!**, be quiet!; **¡cállate!**, **¡cállese!** shut up!; **¡cállate la boca!** shut your mouth!

calle ['kaʎe] *nf* street; (*DEPORTE*) lane; ~ **arriba/abajo** up/down the street; ~ **de sentido único** one-way street; **poner a algn (de patitas) en la ~** to kick sb out.

calleja [ka'ʎexa] *nf* alley, narrow street.

callejear [kaʎexe'ar] *vi* to wander (about) the streets.

callejero, a [kaʎe'xero, a] *adj* street *cpd* ♦ *nm* street map.

callejón [kaʎe'xon] *nm* alley, passage; (*GEO*) narrow pass; ~ **sin salida** cul-de-sac; (*fig*) blind alley.

callejuela [kaʎe'xwela] *nf* side-street, alley.

callista [ka'ʎista] *nm/f* chiropodist.

callo ['kaʎo] *nm* callus; (*en el pie*) corn; ~**s** *nmpl* (*CULIN*) tripe *sg*.

callosidad [kaʎosi'ðað] *nf* (*de pie*) corn; (*de mano*) callus.

calloso, a [ka'ʎoso, a] *adj* horny, rough.

calma ['kalma] *nf* calm; (*pachorra*) slowness; (*COM, ECON*) calm, lull; ~ **chicha** dead calm; **¡~!**, **¡con ~!** take it easy!

calmante [kal'mante] *adj* soothing ♦ *nm* sedative, tranquillizer.

calmar [kal'mar] *vt* to calm, calm down; (*dolor*) to relieve ♦ *vi*, ~**se** *vr* (*tempestad*) to abate; (*mente etc*) to become calm.

calmoso, a [kal'moso, a] *adj* calm, quiet.

caló [ka'lo] *nm* (*de gitanos*) gipsy language, Romany; (*argot*) slang.

calor [ka'lor] *nm* heat; (~ *agradable*) warmth; **entrar en ~** to get warm; **tener ~** to be *o* feel hot.

caloría [kalo'ria] *nf* calorie.

calorífero, a [kalo'rifero, a] *adj* heat-producing, heat-giving ♦ *nm* heating system.

calque ['kalke] *etc vb V* **calcar**.

calumnia [ka'lumnja] *nf* slander; (*por escrito*) libel.

calumniar [kalum'njar] *vt* to slander; to libel.

calumnioso, a [kalum'njoso, a] *a* slanderous; libellous.

caluroso, a [kalu'roso, a] *adj* hot; (*sin exceso*) warm; (*fig*) enthusiastic.

calva ['kalßa] *nf* bald patch; (*en bosque*) clearing.

calvario [kal'ßarjo] *nm* stations *pl* of the cross; (*fig*) cross, heavy burden.

calvicie [kal'ßiθje] *nf* baldness.

calvo, a ['kalßo, a] *adj* bald; (*terreno*) bare, barren; (*tejido*) threadbare ♦ *nm* bald man.

calza ['kalθa] nf wedge, chock.

calzado, a [kal'θaðo, a] adj shod ♦ nm footwear ♦ nf roadway, highway.

calzador [kalθa'ðor] nm shoehorn.

calzar [kal'θar] vt (zapatos etc) to wear; (un mueble) to put a wedge under; (TEC: rueda etc) to scotch; **~se** vr: **~se los zapatos** to put on one's shoes; **¿qué (número) calza?** what size do you take?

calzón [kal'θon] nm (tb: **calzones**) shorts pl; (AM: de hombre) pants pl; (: de mujer) panties pl.

calzoncillos [kalθon'θiʎos] nmpl underpants.

cama ['kama] nf bed; (GEO) stratum; **~ individual/de matrimonio** single/double bed; **guardar ~** to be ill in bed.

camada [ka'maða] nf litter; (de personas) gang, band.

camafeo [kama'feo] nm cameo.

camaleón [kamale'on] nm chameleon.

cámara ['kamara] nf (POL, TEC) chamber; (habitación) room; (sala) hall; (CINE) cine camera; (fotográfica) camera; **~ de aire** inner tube; **~ alta/baja** upper/lower house; **~ de comercio** chamber of commerce; **~ digital** digital camera; **~ de gas** gas chamber; **~ de vídeo** video camera; **a ~ lenta** in slow motion.

camarada [kama'raða] nm comrade, companion.

camaradería [kamaraðe'ria] nf comradeship.

camarero, a [kama'rero, a] nm waiter ♦ nf (en restaurante) waitress; (en casa, hotel) maid.

camarilla [kama'riʎa] nf (clan) clique; (POL) lobby.

camarín [kama'rin] nm (TEAT) dressing room.

camarón [kama'ron] nm shrimp.

camarote [kama'rote] nm (NAUT) cabin.

cambiable [kam'bjaßle] adj (variable) changeable, variable; (intercambiable) interchangeable.

cambiante [kam'bjante] adj variable.

cambiar [kam'bjar] vt to change; (trocar) to exchange ♦ vi to change; **~se** vr (mudarse) to move; (de ropa) to change; **~(se) de ...** to change one's ...; **~ de idea/de ropa** to change one's mind/ clothes.

cambiazo [kam'bjaθo] nm: **dar el ~ a algn** to swindle sb.

cambio ['kambjo] nm change; (trueque) exchange; (COM) rate of exchange; (oficina) bureau de change; (dinero menudo) small change; **en ~** on the other hand; (en lugar de eso) instead; **~ de divisas** (COM) foreign exchange; **~ de línea** (INFORM) line feed; **~ de página** (INFORM) form feed; **~ a término** (COM) forward exchange; **~ de velocidades** gear lever; **~ de vía** points pl.

cambista [kam'bista] nm (COM) exchange broker.

Camboya [kam'boja] nf Cambodia, Kampuchea.

camboyano, a [kambo'jano, a] a, nm/f Cambodian, Kampuchean.

camelar [kame'lar] vt (con mujer) to flirt with; (persuadir) to cajole.

camelia [ka'melia] nf camellia.

camello [ka'meʎo] nm camel; (fam: traficante) pusher.

camelo [ka'melo] nm: **me huele a ~** it smells fishy.

camerino [kame'rino] nm (TEAT) dressing room.

camilla [ka'miʎa] nf (MED) stretcher.

caminante [kami'nante] nm/f traveller.

caminar [kami'nar] vi (marchar) to walk, go; (viajar) to travel, journey ♦ vt (recorrer) to cover, travel.

caminata [kami'nata] nf long walk.

camino [ka'mino] nm way, road; (sendero) track; **a medio ~** halfway (there); **en el ~** on the way, en route; **~ de** on the way to; **~ particular** private road; **~ vecinal** country road; **C~s, Canales y Puertos** (UNIV) Civil Engineering; **C~ de Santiago** see boxed note; **ir por buen ~** (fig) to be on the right track.

CAMINO DE SANTIAGO

The **Camino de Santiago** is a medieval pilgrim route stretching from the Pyrenees to Santiago de Compostela in north-west Spain, where tradition has it that the body of the Apostle James is buried. Nowadays it is a popular tourist route too. The "concha" (cockleshell) symbolizes the **Camino de Santiago**, because it is said that when St James's body was found it was covered in shells.

---

camión [ka'mjon] nm lorry, truck (US); (AM: autobús) bus; **~ de bomberos** fire engine.

camionero [kamjo'nero] nm lorry o truck (US) driver, trucker (esp US).

camioneta [kamjo'neta] nf van, transit ®.

camisa [ka'misa] nf shirt; (BOT) skin; **~ de dormir** nightdress; **~ de fuerza**

straitjacket.

camisería [kamise'ria] *nf* outfitter's (shop).

camiseta [kami'seta] *nf* tee-shirt; (*ropa interior*) vest; (*de deportista*) top.

camisón [kami'son] *nm* nightdress, nightgown.

camomila [kamo'mila] *nf* camomile.

camorra [ka'morra] *nf*: **armar** ~ to kick up a row; **buscar** ~ to look for trouble.

camorrista [kamo'rrista] *nm/f* thug.

camote [ka'mote] *nm* (*AM*) sweet potato.

campal [kam'pal] *adj*: **batalla** ~ pitched battle.

campamento [kampa'mento] *nm* camp.

campana [kam'pana] *nf* bell.

campanada [kampa'naða] *nf* peal.

campanario [kampa'narjo] *nm* belfry.

campanilla [kampa'niʎa] *nf* (*campana*) small bell.

campante [kam'pante] *adj*: **siguió tan** ~ he went on as if nothing had happened.

campaña [kam'paɲa] *nf* (*MIL, POL*) campaign; **hacer** ~ (**en pro de/contra**) to campaign (for/against); ~ **de venta** sales campaign.

campechano, a [kampe'tʃano, a] *adj* open.

campeón, ona [kampe'on, ona] *nm/f* champion.

campeonato [kampeo'nato] *nm* championship.

campesino, a [kampe'sino, a] *adj* country *cpd*, rural; (*gente*) peasant *cpd* ♦ *nm/f* countryman/woman; (*agricultor*) farmer.

campestre [kam'pestre] *adj* country *cpd*, rural.

camping ['kampin] *nm* camping; (*lugar*) campsite; **ir de** *o* **hacer** ~ to go camping.

campiña [kam'piɲa] *nf* countryside.

campista [kam'pista] *nm/f* camper.

campo ['kampo] *nm* (*fuera de la ciudad*) country, countryside; (*AGR, ELEC, INFORM*) field; (*de fútbol*) pitch; (*de golf*) course; (*MIL*) camp; ~ **de batalla** battlefield; ~ **de minas** minefield; ~ **petrolífero** oilfield; ~ **visual** field of vision; ~ **de concentración/de internación/de trabajo** concentration/ internment/labour camp.

camposanto [kampo'santo] *nm* cemetery.

CAMPSA ['kampsa] *nf abr* (*ESP COM*) = *Compañía Arrendataria del Monopolio de Petróleos, S.A.*

campus ['kampus] *nm inv* (*UNIV*) campus.

camuflaje [kamu'flaxe] *nm* camouflage.

camuflar [kamu'flar] *vt* to camouflage.

can [kan] *nm* dog, mutt (*fam*).

cana ['kana] *nf V* **cano**.

Canadá [kana'ða] *nm* Canada.

canadiense [kana'ðjense] *adj, nm/f* Canadian ♦ *nf* fur-lined jacket.

canal [ka'nal] *nm* canal; (*GEO*) channel, strait; (*de televisión*) channel; (*de tejado*) gutter; **C~ de la Mancha** English Channel; **C~ de Panamá** Panama Canal.

canalice [kana'liθe] *etc vb V* **canalizar**.

canalizar [kanali'θar] *vt* to channel.

canalla [ka'naʎa] *nf* rabble, mob ♦ *nm* swine.

canallada [kana'ʎaða] *nf* (*hecho*) dirty trick.

canalón [kana'lon] *nm* (*conducto vertical*) drainpipe; (*del tejado*) gutter; **canalones** *nmpl* (*CULIN*) cannelloni.

canapé, *pl* **canapés** [kana'pe, kana'pes] *nm* sofa, settee; (*CULIN*) canapé.

Canarias [ka'narjas] *nfpl*: **las (Islas)** ~ the Canaries, the Canary Isles.

canario, a [ka'narjo, a] *adj* of *o* from the Canary Isles ♦ *nm/f* native *o* inhabitant of the Canary Isles ♦ *nm* (*ZOOL*) canary.

canasta [ka'nasta] *nf* (*round*) basket.

canastilla [kanas'tiʎa] *nf* small basket; (*de niño*) layette.

canasto [ka'nasto] *nm* large basket.

cancela [kan'θela] *nf* (wrought-iron) gate.

cancelación [kanθela'θjon] *nf* cancellation.

cancelar [kanθe'lar] *vt* to cancel; (*una deuda*) to write off.

cáncer ['kanθer] *nm* (*MED*) cancer; **C~** (*ASTRO*) Cancer.

cancerígeno, a [kanθe'rixeno, a] *adj* carcinogenic.

cancha ['kantʃa] *nf* (*de baloncesto, tenis etc*) court; (*AM: de fútbol etc*) pitch.

canciller [kanθi'ʎer] *nm* chancellor; **C~** (*AM*) Foreign Minister, ≈ Foreign Secretary (*BRIT*).

Cancillería [kansiʎe'ria] *nf* (*AM*) Foreign Ministry, ≈ Foreign Office (*BRIT*).

canción [kan'θjon] *nf* song; ~ **de cuna** lullaby.

cancionero [kanθjo'nero] *nm* song book.

candado [kan'daðo] *nm* padlock.

candela [kan'dela] *nf* candle.

candelabro [kande'laßro] *nm* candelabra.

candelero [kande'lero] *nm* (*para vela*) candlestick; (*de aceite*) oil lamp.

candente [kan'dente] *adj* red-hot; (*tema*) burning.

candidato, a [kandi'ðato, a] *nm/f* candidate; (*para puesto*) applicant.

candidatura [kandiða'tura] *nf* candidature.

candidez [kandi'ðeθ] *nf* (*sencillez*) simplicity; (*simpleza*) naiveté.

cándido, a ['kandiðo, a] *adj* simple; naive.

candil [kan'dil] *nm* oil lamp.

candilejas [kandi'lexas] *nfpl* (*TEAT*) footlights.

candor [kan'dor] *nm* (*sinceridad*) frankness; (*inocencia*) innocence.

canela [ka'nela] *nf* cinnamon.

canelo [ka'nelo] *nm*: **hacer el** ~ to act the fool.

canelones [kane'lones] *nmpl* cannelloni.

cangrejo [kan'grexo] *nm* crab.

canguro [kan'guro] *nm* (*ZOOL*) kangaroo; (*de niños*) baby-sitter; **hacer de** ~ to baby-sit.

caníbal [ka'niβal] *adj, nm/f* cannibal.

canica [ka'nika] *nf* marble.

caniche [ka'nitʃe] *nm* poodle.

canícula [ka'nikula] *nf* midsummer heat.

canijo, a [ka'nixo, a] *adj* frail, sickly.

canilla [ka'niʎa] *nf* (*TEC*) bobbin.

canino, a [ka'nino, a] *adj* canine ♦ *nm* canine (tooth).

canje [kan'xe] *nm* exchange; (*trueque*) swap.

canjear [kanxe'ar] *vt* to exchange; (*trocar*) to swap.

cano, a ['kano, a] *adj* grey-haired, white-haired ♦ *nf* (*tb*: **canas**) white o grey hair; **tener canas** to be going grey.

canoa [ka'noa] *nf* canoe.

canon ['kanon] *nm* canon; (*pensión*) rent; (*COM*) tax.

canonice [kano'niθe] *etc vb V* **canonizar**.

canónico, a [ka'noniko, a] *adj*: **derecho** ~ canon law.

canónigo [ka'nonixo] *nm* canon.

canonizar [kanoni'θar] *vt* to canonize.

canoro, a [ka'noro, a] *adj* melodious.

canoso, a [ka'noso, a] *adj* (*pelo*) grey (*BRIT*), gray (*US*); (*persona*) grey-haired.

cansado, a [kan'saðo, a] *adj* tired, weary; (*tedioso*) tedious, boring; **estoy** ~ **de hacerlo** I'm sick of doing it.

cansancio [kan'sanθjo] *nm* tiredness, fatigue.

cansar [kan'sar] *vt* (*fatigar*) to tire, tire out; (*aburrir*) to bore; (*fastidiar*) to bother; **~se** *vr* to tire, get tired; (*aburrirse*) to get bored.

cantábrico, a [kan'taβriko, a] *adj* Cantabrian; **Mar C~** Bay of Biscay; (**Montes**) **C~s, Cordillera Cantábrica** Cantabrian Mountains.

cántabro, a ['kantaβro, a] *adj, nm/f* Cantabrian.

cantante [kan'tante] *adj* singing ♦ *nm/f* singer.

cantaor, a [kanta'or, a] *nm/f* Flamenco singer.

cantar [kan'tar] *vt* to sing ♦ *vi* to sing;

(*insecto*) to chirp; (*rechinar*) to squeak; (*fam: criminal*) to squeal ♦ *nm* (*acción*) singing; (*canción*) song; (*poema*) poem; ~ **a algn las cuarenta** to tell sb a few home truths; ~ **a dos voces** to sing a duet.

cántara ['kantara] *nf* large pitcher.

cántaro ['kantaro] *nm* pitcher, jug.

cantautor, a [kantau'tor, a] *nm/f* singer-songwriter.

cante ['kante] *nm*: ~ **jondo** flamenco singing.

cantera [kan'tera] *nf* quarry.

cántico ['kantiko] *nm* (*REL*) canticle; (*fig*) song.

cantidad [kanti'ðað] *nf* quantity, amount; (*ECON*) sum ♦ *adv* (*fam*) a lot; ~ **alzada** lump sum; ~ **de** lots of.

cantilena [kanti'lena] *nf* = **cantinela**.

cantimplora [kantim'plora] *nf* (*frasco*) water bottle, canteen.

cantina [kan'tina] *nf* canteen; (*de estación*) buffet; (*esp AM*) bar.

cantinela [kanti'nela] *nf* ballad, song.

canto ['kanto] *nm* singing; (*canción*) song; (*borde*) edge, rim; (*de un cuchillo*) back; ~ **rodado** boulder.

cantón [kan'ton] *nm* canton.

cantor, a [kan'tor, a] *nm/f* singer.

canturrear [kanturre'ar] *vi* to sing softly.

canutas [ka'nutas] *nfpl*: **pasarlas** ~ (*fam*) to have a rough time (of it).

canuto [ka'nuto] *nm* (*tubo*) small tube; (*fam: droga*) joint.

caña ['kaɲa] *nf* (*BOT: tallo*) stem, stalk; (*carrizo*) reed; (*vaso*) tumbler; (*de cerveza*) glass of beer; (*ANAT*) shinbone; (*AM: aguardiente*) cane liquor; ~ **de azúcar** sugar cane; ~ **de pescar** fishing rod.

cañada [ka'ɲaða] *nf* (*entre dos montañas*) gully, ravine; (*camino*) cattle track.

cáñamo ['kaɲamo] *nm* (*BOT*) hemp.

cañaveral [kaɲaβe'ral] *nm* (*BOT*) reedbed; (*AGR*) sugar-cane field.

cañería [kaɲe'ria] *nf* piping; (*tubo*) pipe.

caño ['kaɲo] *nm* (*tubo*) tube, pipe; (*de aguas servidas*) sewer; (*MUS*) pipe; (*NAUT*) navigation channel; (*de fuente*) jet.

cañón [ka'ɲon] *nm* (*MIL*) cannon; (*de fusil*) barrel; (*GEO*) canyon, gorge.

cañonazo [kaɲo'naθo] *nm* (*MIL*) gunshot.

cañonera [kaɲo'nera] *nf* (*tb*: **lancha** ~) gunboat.

caoba [ka'oβa] *nf* mahogany.

caos ['kaos] *nm* chaos.

caótico, a [ka'otiko, a] *adj* chaotic.

C.A.P. *nm abr* (= *Certificado de Aptitud*

Pedagógica) teaching certificate.

cap. *abr* (= *capítulo*) ch.

capa ['kapa] *nf* cloak, cape; (*CULIN*) coating; (*GEO*) layer, stratum; (*de pintura*) coat; **de ~ y espada** cloak-and-dagger; **so ~ de** under the pretext of; **~ de ozono** ozone layer; **~s sociales** social groups.

capacho [ka'patʃo] *nm* wicker basket.

capacidad [kapaθi'ðað] *nf* (*medida*) capacity; (*aptitud*) capacity, ability; **una sala con ~ para 900** a hall seating 900; **~ adquisitiva** purchasing power.

capacitación [kapaθita'θjon] *nf* training.

capacitar [kapaθi'tar] *vt*: **~ a algn para algo** to qualify sb for sth; (*TEC*) to train sb for sth.

capar [ka'par] *vt* to castrate, geld.

caparazón [kapara'θon] *nm* (*ZOOL*) shell.

capataz [kapa'taθ] *nm* foreman, chargehand.

capaz [ka'paθ] *adj* able, capable; (*amplio*) capacious, roomy; **es ~ que venga mañana** (*AM*) he'll probably come tomorrow.

capcioso, a [kap'θjoso, a] *adj* wily, deceitful; **pregunta capciosa** trick question.

capea [ka'pea] *nf* (*TAUR*) bullfight with young bulls.

capear [kape'ar] *vt* (*dificultades*) to dodge; **~ el temporal** to weather the storm.

capellán [kape'ʎan] *nm* chaplain; (*sacerdote*) priest.

caperuza [kape'ruθa] *nf* hood; (*de bolígrafo*) cap.

capi ['kapi] *nf* (*esp AM fam*) capital (city).

capicúa [kapi'kua] *nm reversible number, e.g. 1441.*

capilar [kapi'lar] *adj* hair *cpd.*

capilla [ka'piʎa] *nf* chapel.

capital [kapi'tal] *adj* capital ♦ *nm* (*COM*) capital ♦ *nf* (*de nación*) capital (city); (*tb*: **~ de provincia**) provincial capital, ≈ county town; **~ activo/en acciones** working/share o equity capital; **~ arriesgado** venture capital; **~ autorizado** authorised capital; **~ emitido** issued capital; **~ improductivo** idle money; **~ invertido** o **utilizado** capital employed; **~ pagado** paid-up capital; **~ de riesgo** risk capital; **~ social** authorized o share capital; **inversión de ~es** capital investment; *V tb* **provincia.**

capitalice [kapita'liθe] *etc vb V* **capitalizar.**

capitalino, a [kapita'lino, a] *adj* (*AM*) of o from the capital ♦ *nm/f* native o inhabitant of the capital.

capitalismo [kapita'lismo] *nm* capitalism.

capitalista [kapita'lista] *adj, nm/f* capitalist.

capitalizar [kapitali'θar] *vt* to capitalize.

capitán [kapi'tan] *nm* captain; (*fig*) leader.

capitana [kapi'tana] *nf* flagship.

capitanear [kapitane'ar] *vt* to captain.

capitanía [kapita'nia] *nf* captaincy.

capitel [kapi'tel] *nm* (*ARQ*) capital.

capitolio [kapi'toljo] *nm* capitol.

capitulación [kapitula'θjon] *nf* (*rendición*) capitulation, surrender; (*acuerdo*) agreement, pact; **capitulaciones matrimoniales** marriage contract *sg.*

capitular [kapitu'lar] *vi* to come to terms, make an agreement; (*MIL*) to surrender.

capítulo [ka'pitulo] *nm* chapter.

capo [ka'po] *nm* drugs baron.

capó [ka'po] *nm* (*AUTO*) bonnet (*BRIT*), hood (*US*).

capón [ka'pon] *nm* capon.

caporal [kapo'ral] *nm* chief, leader.

capota [ka'pota] *nf* (*de mujer*) bonnet; (*AUTO*) hood (*BRIT*), top (*US*).

capote [ka'pote] *nm* (*abrigo: de militar*) greatcoat; (*de torero*) cloak.

capricho [ka'pritʃo] *nm* whim, caprice.

caprichoso, a [kapri'tʃoso, a] *adj* capricious.

Capricornio [kapri'kornjo] *nm* Capricorn.

cápsula ['kapsula] *nf* capsule; **~ espacial** space capsule.

captar [kap'tar] *vt* (*comprender*) to understand; (*RADIO*) to pick up; (*atención, apoyo*) to attract.

captura [kap'tura] *nf* capture; (*JUR*) arrest.

capturar [kaptu'rar] *vt* to capture; (*JUR*) to arrest; (*datos*) to input.

capucha [ka'putʃa] *nf* hood, cowl.

capullo [ka'puʎo] *nm* (*ZOOL*) cocoon; (*BOT*) bud; (*fam!*) berk (*BRIT*), jerk (*US*).

caqui ['kaki] *nm* khaki.

cara ['kara] *nf* (*ANAT, de moneda*) face; (*aspecto*) appearance; (*de disco*) side; (*fig*) boldness; (*descara*) cheek, nerve ♦ *prep*: **~ a** facing; **de ~ a** opposite, facing; **dar la ~** to face the consequences; **echar algo en ~ a algn** to reproach sb for sth; **¿~ o cruz?** heads or tails?; **¡qué ~ más dura!** what a nerve!; **de una ~** (*disquete*) single-sided.

carabina [kara'βina] *nf* carbine, rifle; (*persona*) chaperone.

carabinero [karaβi'nero] *nm* (*de aduana*) customs officer; (*AM*) gendarme.

Caracas [ka'rakas] *nm* Caracas.

caracol [kara'kol] *nm* (*ZOOL*) snail; (*concha*) (sea)shell; **escalera de ~** spiral staircase.

caracolear [karakole'ar] *vi* (*caballo*) to prance about.

carácter, *pl* **caracteres** [ka'rakter, karak'teres] *nm* character; ~ **de cambio de página** (*INFORM*) form feed character; **caracteres de imprenta** (*TIP*) type(face) *sg*; ~ **libre** (*INFORM*) wildcard character; **tener buen/mal** ~ to be good-natured/ bad tempered.

caracterice [karakte'riθe] *etc vb V* **caracterizar**.

característico, a [karakte'ristiko, a] *adj* characteristic ♦ *nf* characteristic.

caracterizar [karakteri'θar] *vt* (*distinguir*) to characterize, typify; (*honrar*) to confer (a) distinction on.

caradura [kara'ðura] *nm/f* cheeky person; **es un** ~ he's got a nerve.

carajillo [kara'xiʎo] *nm black coffee with brandy.*

carajo [ka'raxo] *nm* (*esp AM fam!*): **¡~!** shit!(*!*); **¡qué ~!** what the hell!; **me importa un** ~ I don't give a damn.

caramba [ka'ramba] *excl* well!, good gracious!

carámbano [ka'rambano] *nm* icicle.

carambola [karam'bola] *nf*: **por** ~ by a fluke.

caramelo [kara'melo] *nm* (*dulce*) sweet; (*azúcar fundido*) caramel.

carantoñas [karan'toɲas] *nfpl*: **hacer** ~ **a algn** to (try to) butter sb up.

caraqueño, a [kara'keɲo, a] *adj* of *o* from Caracas ♦ *nm/f* native *o* inhabitant of Caracas.

carátula [ka'ratula] *nf* (*máscara*) mask; (*TEAT*): **la** ~ the stage.

caravana [kara'ßana] *nf* caravan; (*fig*) group; (*de autos*) tailback.

carbón [kar'ßon] *nm* coal; ~ **de leña** charcoal; **papel** ~ carbon paper.

carbonatado, a [karßono'taðo, a] *adj* carbonated.

carbonato [karßo'nato] *nm* carbonate; ~ **sódico** sodium carbonate.

carboncillo [karßon'θiʎo] *nm* (*ARTE*) charcoal.

carbonice [karßo'niθe] *etc vb V* **carbonizar**.

carbonilla [karßo'niʎa] *nf* coal dust.

carbonizar [karßoni'θar] *vt* to carbonize; (*quemar*) to char; **quedar carbonizado** (*ELEC*) to be electrocuted.

carbono [kar'ßono] *nm* carbon.

carburador [karßura'ðor] *nm* carburettor.

carburante [karßu'rante] *nm* fuel.

carca ['karka] *adj*, *nm/f inv* reactionary.

carcajada [karka'xaða] *nf* (loud) laugh, guffaw.

carcajearse [karkaxe'arse] *vr* to roar with laughter.

cárcel ['karθel] *nf* prison, jail; (*TEC*) clamp.

carcelero, a [karθe'lero, a] *adj* prison *cpd* ♦ *nm/f* warder.

carcoma [kar'koma] *nf* woodworm.

carcomer [karko'mer] *vt* to bore into, eat into; (*fig*) to undermine; ~**se** *vr* to become worm-eaten; (*fig*) to decay.

carcomido, a [karko'miðo, a] *adj* worm-eaten; (*fig*) rotten.

cardar [kar'ðar] *vt* (*TEC*) to card, comb.

cardenal [karðe'nal] *nm* (*REL*) cardinal; (*MED*) bruise.

cárdeno, a ['karðeno, a] *adj* purple; (*lívido*) livid.

cardiaco, a [kar'ðjako, a], **cardíaco, a** [kar'ðiako, a] *adj* cardiac; (*ataque*) heart *cpd*.

cardinal [karði'nal] *adj* cardinal.

cardiólogo, a [karðj'oloxo, a] *nm/f* cardiologist.

cardo ['karðo] *nm* thistle.

carear [kare'ar] *vt* to bring face to face; (*comparar*) to compare; ~**se** *vr* to come face to face, meet.

carecer [kare'θer] *vi*: ~ **de** to lack, be in need of.

carencia [ka'renθja] *nf* lack; (*escasez*) shortage; (*MED*) deficiency.

carente [ka'rente] *adj*: ~ **de** lacking in, devoid of.

carestía [kares'tia] *nf* (*escasez*) scarcity, shortage; (*COM*) high cost; **época de** ~ period of shortage.

careta [ka'reta] *nf* mask.

carey [ka'rei] *nm* (*tortuga*) turtle; (*concha*) tortoiseshell.

carezca [ka'reθka] *etc vb V* **carecer**.

carga ['karxa] *nf* (*peso, ELEC*) load; (*de barco*) cargo, freight; (*FINANZAS*) tax, duty; (*MIL*) charge; (*INFORM*) loading; (*obligación, responsabilidad*) duty, obligation; ~ **aérea** (*COM*) air cargo; ~ **útil** (*COM*) payload; **la** ~ **fiscal** the tax burden.

cargadero [karxa'ðero] *nm* goods platform, loading bay.

cargado, a [kar'xaðo, a] *adj* loaded; (*ELEC*) live; (*café, té*) strong; (*cielo*) overcast.

cargador, a [karxa'ðor, a] *nm/f* loader; (*NAUT*) docker ♦ *nm* (*INFORM*): ~ **de discos** disk pack.

cargamento [karxa'mento] *nm* (*acción*) loading; (*mercancías*) load, cargo.

cargante [kar'xante] *adj* (*persona*) trying.

cargar [kar'xar] *vt* (*barco, arma*) to load; (*ELEC*) to charge; (*impuesto*) to impose;

(*COM: algo en cuenta*) to charge, debit; (*MIL: enemigo*) to charge ♦ *vi* (*AUTO*) to load (up); (*inclinarse*) to lean; (*INFORM*) to load; ~ **con** to pick up, carry away; ~**se** *vr* (*fam: estropear*) to break; (: *matar*) to bump off; (*ELEC*) to become charged.

cargo ['karɣo] *nm* (*COM etc*) charge, debit; (*puesto*) post, office; (*responsabilidad*) duty, obligation; (*fig*) weight, burden; (*JUR*) charge; **altos** ~**s** high-ranking officials; **una cantidad en** ~ **a algn** a sum chargeable to sb; **hacerse** ~ **de** to take charge of *o* responsibility for.

cargue ['karɣe] *etc vb* V **cargar.**

Caribe [ka'riβe] *nm*: **el** ~ the Caribbean.

caribeño, a [kari'βeɲo, a] *adj* Caribbean.

caricatura [karika'tura] *nf* caricature.

caricia [ka'riθja] *nf* caress; (*a animal*) pat, stroke.

caridad [kari'ðað] *nf* charity.

caries ['karjes] *nf inv* (*MED*) tooth decay.

cariño [ka'riɲo] *nm* affection, love; (*caricia*) caress; (*en carta*) love ....

cariñoso, a [kari'ɲoso, a] *adj* affectionate.

carioca [ka'rjoka] *adj* (*AM*) of *o* from Rio de Janeiro ♦ *nm/f* native *o* inhabitant of Rio de Janeiro.

carisma [ka'risma] *nm* charisma.

carismático, a [karis'matiko, a] *adj* charismatic.

caritativo, a [karita'tiβo, a] *adj* charitable.

cariz [ka'riθ] *nm*: **tener** *o* **tomar buen/mal** ~ to look good/bad.

carmesí [karme'si] *adj, nm* crimson.

carmín [kar'min] *nm* (*color*) carmine; ~ **(de labios)** lipstick.

carnal [kar'nal] *adj* carnal; **primo** ~ first cousin.

carnaval [karna'βal] *nm* carnival; *see boxed note.*

CARNAVAL

The three days before "miércoles de ceniza" (Ash Wednesday), when fasting for Lent traditionally starts, are the signal for **carnaval,** *an exuberant celebration which dates back to pre-Christian times. Although in decline during the Franco years in Spain,* **carnaval** *has recently grown in popularity, Cádiz and Tenerife being particularly well known for their celebrations. "Martes de carnaval" (Shrove Tuesday) is the most important day, with colourful street parades, fancy dress, fireworks and a general party atmosphere.*

---

carne ['karne] *nf* flesh; (*CULIN*) meat; ~ **de cerdo/de cordero/de ternera/de vaca** pork/lamb/veal/beef; ~ **picada** mince; ~ **de gallina** (*fig*) gooseflesh.

carné [kar'ne] *nm* = **carnet.**

carnero [kar'nero] *nm* sheep, ram; (*carne*) mutton.

carnet, *pl* **carnets** [kar'ne, kar'nes] *nm*: ~ **de conducir** driving licence; ~ **de identidad** identity card; V *tb* **Documento Nacional de Identidad.**

carnicería [karniθe'ria] *nf* butcher's (shop); (*fig: matanza*) carnage, slaughter.

carnicero, a [karni'θero, a] *adj* carnivorous ♦ *nm/f* (*tb fig*) butcher ♦ *nm* carnivore.

carnívoro, a [kar'niβoro, a] *adj* carnivorous ♦ *nm* carnivore.

carnoso, a [kar'noso, a] *adj* beefy, fat.

caro, a ['karo, a] *adj* dear; (*COM*) dear, expensive ♦ *adv* dear, dearly; **vender** ~ to sell at a high price.

carpa ['karpa] *nf* (*pez*) carp; (*de circo*) big top; (*AM: de camping*) tent.

carpeta [kar'peta] *nf* folder, file.

carpintería [karpinte'ria] *nf* carpentry.

carpintero [karpin'tero] *nm* carpenter; **pájaro** ~ woodpecker.

carraca [ka'rraka] *nf* (*DEPORTE*) rattle.

carraspear [karraspe'ar] *vi* (*aclararse*) to clear one's throat.

carraspera [karras'pera] *nf* hoarseness.

carrera [ka'rrera] *nf* (*acción*) run(ning); (*espacio recorrido*) run; (*certamen*) race; (*trayecto*) course; (*profesión*) career; (*ESCOL, UNIV*) course; (*de taxi*) ride; (*en medias*) ladder; **a la** ~ at (full) speed; **caballo de** ~**(s)** racehorse; ~ **de armamentos** arms race.

carrerilla [karre'riʎa] *nf*: **decir algo de** ~ to reel sth off; **tomar** ~ to get up speed.

carreta [ka'rreta] *nf* wagon, cart.

carrete [ka'rrete] *nm* reel, spool; (*TEC*) coil.

carretera [karre'tera] *nf* (*main*) road, highway; ~ **nacional** ≈ A road (*BRIT*), state highway (*US*); ~ **de circunvalación** ring road.

carretilla [karre'tiʎa] *nf* trolley; (*AGR*) (wheel)barrow.

carril [ka'rril] *nm* furrow; (*de autopista*) lane; (*FERRO*) rail.

carril bici, *pl* **carriles bici** [karil'βiθi, kariles'βiθi] *nm* cycle lane, bikeway (*US*).

carrillo [ka'rriʎo] *nm* (*ANAT*) cheek; (*TEC*) pulley.

carro ['karro] *nm* cart, wagon; (*MIL*) tank; (*AM: coche*) car; (*TIP*) carriage; ~ **blindado** armoured car.

carrocería [karroθe'ria] *nf* body, bodywork
no *pl* (*BRIT*).

carroña [ka'rroɲa] *nf* carrion no *pl*.

carroza [ka'rroθa] *nf* (*vehículo*) coach ♦ *nm/f*
(*fam*) old fogey.

carruaje [ka'rrwaxe] *nm* carriage.

carrusel [karru'sel] *nm* merry-go-round,
roundabout (*BRIT*).

carta ['karta] *nf* letter; (*CULIN*) menu;
(*naipe*) card; (*mapa*) map; (*JUR*)
document; ~ **de crédito** credit card; ~
de crédito documentaria (*COM*)
documentary letter of credit; ~ **de
crédito irrevocable** (*COM*) irrevocable
letter of credit; ~ **certificada/urgente**
registered/special delivery letter; ~
marítima chart; ~ **de pedido** (*COM*)
order; ~ **verde** (*AUTO*) green card; ~ **de
vinos** wine list; **echar una** ~ **al correo** to
post a letter; **echar las** ~**s a algn** to tell
sb's fortune.

cartabón [karta'βon] *nm* set square.

cartearse [karte'arse] *vr* to correspond.

cartel [kar'tel] *nm* (*anuncio*) poster,
placard; (*ESCOL*) wall chart; (*COM*)
cartel.

cartelera [karte'lera] *nf* hoarding,
billboard; (*en periódico etc*) listings *pl*,
entertainments guide; "**en ~**"
"showing".

cartera [kar'tera] *nf* (*de bolsillo*) wallet; (*de
colegial, cobrador*) satchel; (*AM*: *de señora*)
handbag (*BRIT*), purse (*US*); (*para
documentos*) briefcase; **ministro sin** ~
(*POL*) minister without portfolio; **ocupa
la** ~ **de Agricultura** he is Minister of
Agriculture; ~ **de pedidos** (*COM*) order
book; **efectos en** ~ (*ECON*) holdings.

carterista [karte'rista] *nm/f* pickpocket.

cartero [kar'tero] *nm* postman.

cartílago [kar'tilaɣo] *nm* cartilage.

cartilla [kar'tiʎa] *nf* (*ESCOL*) primer, first
reading book; ~ **de ahorros** bank book.

cartografía [kartoɣra'fia] *nf* cartography.

cartón [kar'ton] *nm* cardboard.

cartucho [kar'tutʃo] *nm* (*MIL*) cartridge;
(*bolsita*) paper cone.

cartulina [kartu'lina] *nf* fine cardboard,
card.

CASA ['kasa] *nf abr* (*ESP AVIAT*)
= *Construcciones Aeronáuticas S.A.*

casa ['kasa] *nf* house; (*hogar*) home;
(*edificio*) building; (*COM*) firm, company;
~ **consistorial** town hall; ~ **de huéspedes**
≈ guest house; ~ **de socorro** first aid
post; ~ **de citas** (*fam*) brothel; ~ **rural** (*de
alquiler*) holiday cottage; (*pensión*) rural
B&B; **ir a** ~ to go home; **salir de** ~ to go

out; (*para siempre*) to leave home; **echar
la** ~ **por la ventana** (*gastar*) to spare no
expense; *V tb* **hotel**.

casadero, a [kasa'ðero, a] *adj*
marriageable.

casado, a [ka'saðo, a] *a* married ♦ *nm/f*
married man/woman.

casamiento [kasa'mjento] *nm* marriage,
wedding.

casar [ka'sar] *vt* to marry; (*JUR*) to quash,
annul; ~**se** *vr* to marry, get married; ~**se
por lo civil** to have a civil wedding, get
married in a registry office (*BRIT*).

cascabel [kaska'βel] *nm* (small) bell;
(*ZOOL*) rattlesnake.

cascada [kas'kaða] *nf* waterfall.

cascajo [kas'kaxo] *nm* gravel, stone
chippings *pl*.

cascanueces [kaska'nweθes] *nm inv*: **un** ~ a
pair of nutcrackers.

cascar [kas'kar] *vt* to split; (*nuez*) to crack
♦ *vi* to chatter; ~**se** *vr* to crack, split,
break (open).

cáscara ['kaskara] *nf* (*de huevo, fruta seca*)
shell; (*de fruta*) skin; (*de limón*) peel.

cascarón [kaska'ron] *nm* (broken)
eggshell.

cascarrabias [kaska'rraβjas] *nm/f inv* (*fam*)
hothead.

casco ['kasko] *nm* (*de bombero, soldado*)
helmet; (*cráneo*) skull; (*NAUT*: *de barco*)
hull; (*ZOOL*: *de caballo*) hoof; (*botella*)
empty bottle; (*de ciudad*): **el** ~ **antiguo**
the old part; **el** ~ **urbano** the town
centre; **los** ~**s azules** the UN peacekeeping force, the blue helmets.

cascote [kas'kote] *nm* piece of rubble; ~**s**
nmpl rubble *sg*.

caserío [kase'rio] *nm* hamlet, group of
houses; (*casa*) country house.

casero, a [ka'sero, a] *adj*: **ser muy** ~
(*persona*) to be homeloving; "**comida
casera**" "home cooking" ♦ *nm/f*
(*propietario*) landlord/lady; (*COM*) house
agent.

caserón [kase'ron] *nm* large (ramshackle)
house.

caseta [ka'seta] *nf* hut; (*para bañista*)
cubicle; (*de feria*) stall.

casete [ka'sete] *nm o f* cassette: ~ **digital**
digital audio tape, DAT.

casi ['kasi] *adv* almost; ~ **nunca** hardly
ever, almost never; ~ **nada** next to
nothing; ~ **te caes** you almost *o* nearly
fell.

casilla [ka'siʎa] *nf* (*casita*) hut, cabin;
(*TEAT*) box office; (*para cartas*)
pigeonhole; (*AJEDREZ*) square; **C~ postal**

o **de Correo(s)** (*AM*) P.O. Box; **sacar a algn de sus** ~ **s** to drive sb round the bend (*fam*), make sb lose his temper.

casillero [kasi'ʎero] *nm* pigeonholes.

casino [ka'sino] *nm* club; (*de juego*) casino.

caso ['kaso] *nm* case; (*suceso*) event; **en** ~ **de** ... in case of ...; **el** ~ **es que** the fact is that; **en el mejor de los** ~**s** at best; **en ese** ~ in that case; **en todo** ~ in any case; **en último** ~ as a last resort; **hacer** ~ **a** to pay attention to; **hacer** ~ **omiso de** to fail to mention, pass over; **hacer** *o* **venir al** ~ to be relevant.

caspa ['kaspa] *nf* dandruff.

Caspio ['kaspjo] *adj*: **Mar** ~ Caspian Sea.

casque ['kaske] *etc vb V* **cascar.**

casquillo [kas'kiʎo] *nm* (*de bombilla*) fitting; (*de bala*) cartridge case.

cassette [ka'set] *nf o m* = **casete.**

casta ['kasta] *nf* caste; (*raza*) breed.

castaña [kas'taɲa] *nf V* **castaño.**

castañetear [kastaɲete'ar] *vi* (*dientes*) to chatter.

castaño, a [kas'taɲo, a] *adj* chestnut (-coloured), brown ♦ *nm* chestnut tree ♦ *nf* chestnut; (*fam: golpe*) punch; ~ **de Indias** horse chestnut tree.

castañuelas [kasta'ɲwelas] *nfpl* castanets.

castellano, a [kaste'ʎano, a] *adj* Castilian; (*fam*) Spanish ♦ *nm/f* Castilian; (*fam*) Spaniard ♦ *nm* (*LING*) Castilian, Spanish; *see boxed note.*

CASTELLANO

Castellano is now the term most widely used in Spain and Spanish America to refer to the Spanish language, since "español" is too closely associated with the concept of Spain as a nation. Some purists maintain that **castellano** *should only refer to the variety of Spanish spoken in Castille.*

---

castellonense [kasteʎo'nense] *adj* of *o* from Castellón de la Plana ♦ *nm/f* native *o* inhabitant of Castellón de la Plana.

castidad [kasti'ðað] *nf* chastity, purity.

castigar [kasti'ɣar] *vt* to punish; (*DEPORTE*) to penalize; (*afligir*) to afflict.

castigo [kas'tiɣo] *nm* punishment; (*DEPORTE*) penalty.

castigue [kas'tiɣe] *etc vb V* **castigar.**

Castilla [kas'tiʎa] *nf* Castile.

castillo [kas'tiʎo] *nm* castle.

castizo, a [kas'tiθo, a] *adj* (*LING*) pure; (*de buena casta*) purebred, pedigree; (*auténtico*) genuine.

casto, a ['kasto, a] *adj* chaste, pure.

castor [kas'tor] *nm* beaver.

castrar [kas'trar] *vt* to castrate; (*gato*) to doctor; (*BOT*) to prune.

castrense [kas'trense] *adj* army *cpd*, military.

casual [ka'swal] *adj* chance, accidental.

casualidad [kaswali'ðað] *nf* chance, accident; (*combinación de circunstancias*) coincidence; **¡qué** ~**!** what a coincidence!

casualmente [kaswal'mente] *adv* by chance.

cataclismo [kata'klismo] *nm* cataclysm.

catador [kata'ðor] *nm* taster.

catadura [kata'ðura] *nf* (*aspecto*) looks *pl*.

catalán, ana [kata'lan, ana] *adj, nm/f* Catalan ♦ *nm* (*LING*) Catalan; *V tb* **lenguas cooficiales.**

catalejo [kata'lexo] *nm* telescope.

catalizador [kataliθa'ðor] *nm* catalyst; (*AUTO*) catalytic converter.

catalogar [katalo'ɣar] *vt* to catalogue; ~ **(de)** (*fig*) to classify (as).

catálogo [ka'taloɣo] *nm* catalogue.

catalogue [kata'loɣe] *etc vb V* **catalogar.**

Cataluña [kata'luɲa] *nf* Catalonia.

cataplasma [kata'plasma] *nf* (*MED*) poultice.

catapulta [kata'pulta] *nf* catapult.

catar [ka'tar] *vt* to taste, sample.

catarata [kata'rata] *nf* (*GEO*) (water)fall; (*MED*) cataract.

catarro [ka'tarro] *nm* catarrh; (*constipado*) cold.

catarsis [ka'tarsis] *nf* catharsis.

catastro [ka'tastro] *nm* property register.

catástrofe [ka'tastrofe] *nf* catastrophe.

catear [kate'ar] *vt* (*fam*) to flunk.

catecismo [kate'θismo] *nm* catechism.

cátedra ['kateðra] *nf* (*UNIV*) chair, professorship; (*ESCOL*) principal teacher's post; **sentar** ~ **sobre un argumento** to take one's stand on an argument.

catedral [kate'ðral] *nf* cathedral.

catedrático, a [kate'ðratiko, a] *nm/f* professor; (*ESCOL*) principal teacher.

categoría [kateɣo'ria] *nf* category; (*rango*) rank, standing; (*calidad*) quality; **de** ~ (*hotel*) top-class; **de baja** ~ (*oficial*) low-ranking; **de segunda** ~ second-rate; **no tiene** ~ he has no standing.

categórico, a [kate'ɣoriko, a] *adj* categorical.

catequesis [kate'kesis] *nf* catechism lessons.

caterva [ka'terβa] *nf* throng, crowd.

cateto, a [ka'teto, a] *nm/f* yokel.

cátodo ['katoðo] *nm* cathode.

catolicismo [katoli'θismo] *nm* Catholicism.

católico, a [ka'toliko, a] *adj, nm/f* Catholic.

catorce [ka'torθe] *num* fourteen.

catre ['katre] *nm* camp bed (*BRIT*), cot (*US*); (*fam*) pit.

Cáucaso ['kaukaso] *nm* Caucasus.

cauce ['kauθe] *nm* (*de río*) riverbed; (*fig*) channel.

caucho ['kautʃo] *nm* rubber; (*AM: llanta*) tyre.

caución [kau'θjon] *nf* bail.

caucionar [kauθjo'nar] *vt* (*JUR*) to bail (out), go bail for.

caudal [kau'ðal] *nm* (*de río*) volume, flow; (*fortuna*) wealth; (*abundancia*) abundance.

caudaloso, a [kauða'loso, a] *adj* (*río*) large; (*persona*) wealthy, rich.

caudillaje [kauði'ʎaxe] *nm* leadership.

caudillo [kau'ðiʎo] *nm* leader, chief.

causa ['kausa] *nf* cause; (*razón*) reason; (*JUR*) lawsuit, case; **a o por ~ de** because of, on account of.

causar [kau'sar] *vt* to cause.

cáustico, a ['kaustiko, a] *adj* caustic.

cautela [kau'tela] *nf* caution, cautiousness.

cauteloso, a [kaute'loso, a] *adj* cautious, wary.

cautivar [kauti'βar] *vt* to capture; (*fig*) to captivate.

cautiverio [kauti'βerjo] *nm*, **cautividad** [kautiβi'ðað] *nf* captivity.

cautivo, a [kau'tiβo, a] *adj, nm/f* captive.

cauto, a ['kauto, a] *adj* cautious, careful.

cava ['kaβa] *nf* (*bodega*) (wine) cellar ♦ *nm* (*vino*) champagne-type wine.

cavar [ka'βar] *vt* to dig; (*AGR*) to dig over.

caverna [ka'βerna] *nf* cave, cavern.

cavernoso, a [kaβer'noso, a] *adj* cavernous; (*voz*) resounding.

caviar [ka'βjar] *nm* caviar(e).

cavidad [kaβi'ðað] *nf* cavity.

cavilación [kaβila'θjon] *nf* deep thought.

cavilar [kaβi'lar] *vt* to ponder.

cayado [ka'jaðo] *nm* (*de pastor*) crook; (*de obispo*) crozier.

cayendo [ka'jendo] *etc vb V* caer.

caza ['kaθa] *nf* (*acción: gen*) hunting; (: *con fusil*) shooting; (*una ~*) hunt, chase; (*animales*) game; **coto de ~** hunting estate ♦ *nm* (*AVIAT*) fighter.

cazabe [ka'saβe] *nm* (*AM*) cassava bread *o* flour.

cazador, a [kaθa'ðor, a] *nm/f* hunter/huntress ♦ *nf* jacket.

cazaejecutivos [kaθaexeku'tiβos] *nm inv* (*COM*) headhunter.

cazar [ka'θar] *vt* to hunt; (*perseguir*) to

chase; (*prender*) to catch; **~las al vuelo** to be pretty sharp. .

cazasubmarinos [kaθasuβma'rinos] *nm inv* (*NAUT*) destroyer; (*AVIAT*) anti-submarine craft.

cazo ['kaθo] *nm* saucepan.

cazuela [ka'θwela] *nf* (*vasija*) pan; (*guisado*) casserole.

cazurro, a [ka'θurro, a] *adj* surly.

CC *nm abr* (*POL*: = *Comité Central*) Central Committee.

c/c. *abr* (*COM*: = *cuenta corriente*) current account.

CC.AA. *abr* (*ESP*) = **Comunidades Autónomas**.

CCI *nf abr* (*COM*: = *Cámara de Comercio Internacional*) ICC.

CC.OO. *nfpl abr* = **Comisiones Obreras**.

CD *nm abr* (= *compact disc*) CD ♦ *abr* (*POL*: = *Cuerpo Diplomático*) CD.

c/d *abr* (= *en casa de*) c/o; (= *con descuento*) with discount.

CDN *nm abr* (= *Centro Dramático Nacional*) ≈ RADA (*BRIT*).

CDS *nm abr* (= *Centro Democrático y Social*) political party.

CE *nm abr* (= *Consejo de Europa*) Council of Europe ♦ *nf abr* (= *Comunidad Europea*) EC.

cebada [θe'βaða] *nf* barley.

cebar [θe'βar] *vt* (*animal*) to fatten (up); (*anzuelo*) to bait; (*MIL, TEC*) to prime; **~se** *vr*: **~se en** to vent one's fury on, take it out on.

cebo [θe'βo] *nm* (*para animales*) feed, food; (*para peces, fig*) bait; (*de arma*) charge.

cebolla [θe'βoʎa] *nf* onion.

cebolleta [θeβo'ʎeta] *nf* spring onion.

cebollino [θeβo'ʎino] *nm* spring onion.

cebón, ona [θe'βon, ona] *adj* fat, fattened.

cebra ['θeβra] *nf* zebra; **paso de ~** zebra crossing.

CECA ['θeka] *nf abr* (= *Comunidad Europea del Carbón y del Acero*) ECSC.

ceca ['θeka] *nf*: **andar o ir de la ~ a la Meca** to chase about all over the place.

cecear [θeθe'ar] *vi* to lisp.

ceceo [θe'θeo] *nm* lisp.

cecina [θe'θina] *nf* cured *o* smoked meat.

cedazo [θe'ðaθo] *nm* sieve.

ceder [θe'ðer] *vt* (*entregar*) to hand over; (*renunciar a*) to give up, part with ♦ *vi* (*renunciar*) to give in, yield; (*disminuir*) to diminish, decline; (*romperse*) to give way; (*viento*) to drop; (*fiebre etc*) to abate; **"ceda el paso"** (*AUTO*) "give way".

cedro ['θeðro] *nm* cedar.

cédula ['θeðula] *nf* certificate, document;

~ **de identidad** (*AM*) identity card; ~ **en blanco** blank cheque; *V tb* **Documento Nacional de Identidad**.

CEE *nf abr* (= *Comunidad Económica Europea*) EEC.

cegar [θe'ɣar] *vt* to blind; (*tubería etc*) to block up, stop up ♦ *vi* to go blind; ~**se** *vr* to be blinded (*de* by).

cegué [θe'ɣe] *etc vb V* **cegar**.

ceguemos [θe'ɣemos] *etc vb V* **cegar**.

ceguera [θe'ɣera] *nf* blindness.

CEI *nf abr* (= *Comunidad de Estados Independientes*) CIS.

Ceilán [θei'lan] *nm* Ceylon, Sri Lanka.

ceja ['θexa] *nf* eyebrow; ~**s pobladas** bushy eyebrows; **arquear las** ~**s** to raise one's eyebrows; **fruncir las** ~**s** to frown.

cejar [θe'xar] *vi* (*fig*) to back down; **no** ~ **to** keep it up, stick at it.

cejijunto, a [θexi'xunto, a] *adj* with bushy eyebrows; (*fig*) scowling.

celada [θe'laða] *nf* ambush, trap.

celador, a [θela'ðor, a] *nm/f* (*de edificio*) watchman; (*de museo etc*) attendant; (*de cárcel*) warder.

celda ['θelda] *nf* cell.

celebérrimo, a [θele'ßerrimo, a] *adj superlativo de* **célebre**.

celebración [θeleßra'θjon] *nf* celebration.

celebrar [θele'ßrar] *vt* to celebrate; (*alabar*) to praise ♦ *vi* to be glad; ~**se** *vr* to occur, take place.

célebre ['θeleßre] *adj* celebrated, renowned.

celebridad [θeleßri'ðað] *nf* fame; (*persona*) celebrity.

celeridad [θeleri'ðað] *nf*: **con** ~ promptly.

celeste [θe'leste] *adj* sky-blue; (*cuerpo etc*) heavenly ♦ *nm* sky blue.

celestial [θeles'tjal] *adj* celestial, heavenly.

celibato [θeli'ßato] *nm* celibacy.

célibe ['θeliße] *adj, nm/f* celibate.

celo ['θelo] *nm* zeal; (*REL*) fervour; (*pey*) envy; ~**s** *nmpl* jealousy *sg*; **dar** ~**s a algn** to make sb jealous; **tener** ~**s de algn** to be jealous of sb; **en** ~ (*animales*) on heat.

celofán [θelo'fan] *nm* Cellophane ®.

celosía [θelo'sia] *nf* lattice (window).

celoso, a [θe'loso, a] *adj* (*envidioso*) jealous; (*trabajador*) zealous; (*desconfiado*) suspicious.

celta ['θelta] *adj* Celtic ♦ *nm/f* Celt.

célula ['θelula] *nf* cell.

celular [θelu'lar] *adj*: **tejido** ~ cell tissue.

celulitis [θelu'litis] *nf* (*enfermedad*) cellulitis; (*grasa*) cellulite.

celuloide [θelu'loiðe] *nm* celluloid.

celulosa [θelu'losa] *nf* cellulose.

cementerio [θemen'terjo] *nm* cemetery, graveyard; ~ **de coches** scrapyard.

cemento [θe'mento] *nm* cement; (*hormigón*) concrete; (*AM: cola*) glue.

CEN *nm abr* (*ESP*) = *Consejo de Economía Nacional*.

cena ['θena] *nf* evening meal, dinner.

cenagal [θena'ɣal] *nm* bog, quagmire.

cenar [θe'nar] *vt* to have for dinner, dine on ♦ *vi* to have dinner, dine.

cencerro [θen'θerro] *nm* cowbell; **estar como un** ~ (*fam*) to be round the bend.

cenicero [θeni'θero] *nm* ashtray.

ceniciento, a [θeni'θjento, a] *adj* ash-coloured, ashen.

cenit [θe'nit] *nm* zenith.

ceniza [θe'niθa] *nf* ash, ashes *pl*.

censar [θen'sar] *vt* to take a census of.

censo ['θenso] *nm* census; ~ **electoral** electoral roll.

censor [θen'sor] *nm* censor; ~ **de cuentas** (*COM*) auditor; ~ **jurado de cuentas** chartered (*BRIT*) *ou* certified public (*US*) accountant.

censura [θen'sura] *nf* (*POL*) censorship; (*moral*) censure, criticism.

censurable [θensu'raßle] *adj* reprehensible.

censurar [θensu'rar] *vt* (*idea*) to censure; (*cortar: película*) to censor.

centavo [θen'taßo] *nm* hundredth (part); (*AM*) cent.

centella [θen'teʎa] *nf* spark.

centellear [θenteʎe'ar] *vi* (*metal*) to gleam; (*estrella*) to twinkle; (*fig*) to sparkle.

centelleo [θente'ʎeo] *nm* gleam(ing); twinkling; sparkling.

centena [θen'tena] *nf* hundred.

centenar [θente'nar] *nm* hundred.

centenario, a [θente'narjo, a] *adj* one hundred years old ♦ *nm* centenary.

centeno [θen'teno] *nm* rye.

centésimo, a [θen'tesimo, a] *adj, nm* hundredth.

centígrado [θen'tiɣraðo] *adj* centigrade.

centigramo [θenti'ɣramo] *nm* centigramme.

centilitro [θenti'litro] *nm* centilitre (*BRIT*), centiliter (*US*).

centímetro [θen'timetro] *nm* centimetre (*BRIT*), centimeter (*US*).

céntimo, a ['θentimo, a] *adj* hundredth ♦ *nm* cent.

centinela [θenti'nela] *nm* sentry, guard.

centollo, a [θen'toʎo, a] *nm/f* large (*o* spider) crab.

central [θen'tral] *adj* central ♦ *nf* head

office; (*TEC*) plant; (*TELEC*) exchange; ~ **nuclear** nuclear power station.
centralice [θentra'liθe] *etc vb V* **centralizar.**
centralita [θentra'lita] *nf* switchboard.
centralización [θentraliθa'θjon] *nf* centralization.
centralizar [θentrali'θar] *vt* to centralize.
centrar [θen'trar] *vt* to centre.
céntrico, a ['θentriko, a] *adj* central.
centrifugar [θentrifu'ɣar] *vt* (*ropa*) to spin-dry.
centrífugo, a [θent'rifuxo, a] *adj* centrifugal.
centrifugue [θentri'fuɣe] *etc vb V* **centrifugar.**
centrista [θen'trista] *adj* centre *cpd.*
centro ['θentro] *nm* centre; **ser de ~** (*POL*) to be a moderate; **~ de acogida (para niños)** children's home; **~ de beneficios** (*COM*) profit centre; **~ cívico** community centre; **~ comercial** shopping centre; **~ de computatión** computer centre; **~ (de determinación) de costos** (*COM*) cost centre; **~ delantero** (*DEPORTE*) centre forward; **~ docente** teaching institution; **~ juvenil** youth club; **~ de llamadas** call centre; **~ social** community centre.
centroafricano, a [θentroafri'kano, a] *adj*: **la República Centroafricana** the Central African Republic.
centroamericano, a [θentroameri'kano, a] *adj, nm/f* Central American.
centrocampista [θentrokam'pista] *nm/f* (*DEPORTE*) midfielder.
ceñido, a [θe'ɲiðo, a] *adj* tight.
ceñir [θe'ɲir] *vt* (*rodear*) to encircle, surround; (*ajustar*) to fit (tightly); (*apretar*) to tighten; **~se** *vr*: **~se algo** to put sth on; **~se al asunto** to stick to the matter in hand.
ceño ['θeɲo] *nm* frown, scowl; **fruncir el ~** to frown, knit one's brow.
CEOE *nf abr* (= *Confederación Española de Organizaciones Empresariales*) ≈ CBI (*BRIT*).
cepa ['θepa] *nf* (*de vid, fig*) stock; (*BIO*) strain.
CEPAL [θe'pal] *nf abr* (= *Comisión Económica de las Naciones Unidas para la América Latina*) ECLA.
cepillar [θepi'ʎar] *vt* to brush; (*madera*) to plane (down).
cepillo [θe'piʎo] *nm* brush; (*para madera*) plane; (*REL*) poorbox, alms box; **~ de dientes** toothbrush.
cepo ['θepo] *nm* (*caza*) trap.
CEPSA ['θepsa] *nf abr* (*COM*) = *Compañía Española de Petróleos, S.A.*

CEPYME *nf abr* = *Confederación Española de la Pequeña y Mediana Empresa.*
cera ['θera] *nf* wax; **~ de abejas** beeswax.
cerámica [θe'ramika] *nf* pottery; (*arte*) ceramics *sg.*
ceramista [θera'mista] *nm/f* potter.
cerbatana [θerßa'tana] *nf* blowpipe.
cerca ['θerka] *nf* fence ♦ *adv* near, nearby, close; **por aquí ~** nearby ♦ *prep*: **~ de** (*cantidad*) nearly, about; (*distancia*) near, close to ♦ *nmpl*: **~s** foreground *sg.*
cercado [θer'kaðo] *nm* enclosure.
cercanía [θerka'nia] *nf* nearness, closeness; **~s** *nfpl* outskirts, suburbs; **tren de ~s** commuter *o* local train.
cercano, a [θer'kano, a] *adj* close, near; (*pueblo etc*) nearby; **C~ Oriente** Near East.
cercar [θer'kar] *vt* to fence in; (*rodear*) to surround.
cerciorar [θerθjo'rar] *vt* (*asegurar*) to assure; **~se** *vr* (*descubrir*) to find out (*de* about); (*asegurarse*) to make sure (*de* of).
cerco ['θerko] *nm* (*AGR*) enclosure; (*AM*) fence; (*MIL*) siege.
cerda ['θerða] *nf* (*de cepillo*) bristle; (*ZOOL*) sow.
cerdada [θer'ðaða] *nf* (*fam*): **hacer una ~ a algn** to play a dirty trick on sb.
Cerdeña [θer'ðeɲa] *nf* Sardinia.
cerdo ['θerðo] *nm* pig; **carne de ~** pork.
cereal [θere'al] *nm* cereal; **~es** *nmpl* cereals, grain *sg.*
cerebral [θere'ßral] *adj* (*tb fig*) cerebral; (*tumor*) brain *cpd.*
cerebro [θe'reßro] *nm* brain; (*fig*) brains *pl*; **ser un ~** (*fig*) to be brilliant.
ceremonia [θere'monja] *nf* ceremony; **reunión de ~** formal meeting; **hablar sin ~** to speak plainly.
ceremonial [θeremo'njal] *adj, nm* ceremonial.
ceremonioso, a [θeremo'njoso, a] *adj* ceremonious; (*cumplido*) formal.
cereza [θe'reθa] *nf* cherry.
cerezo [θe'reθo] *nm* cherry tree.
cerilla [θe'riʎa] *nf*, **cerillo** [se'riʎo] *nm* (*AM*) match.
cerner [θer'ner] *vt* to sift, sieve; **~se** *vr* to hover.
cero ['θero] *nm* nothing, zero; (*DEPORTE*) nil; **8 grados bajo ~** 8 degrees below zero; **a partir de ~** from scratch.
cerque ['θerke] *etc vb V* **cercar.**
cerrado, a [θe'rraðo, a] *adj* closed, shut; (*con llave*) locked; (*tiempo*) cloudy, overcast; (*curva*) sharp; (*acento*) thick, broad; **a puerta cerrada** (*JUR*) in camera.

cerradura [θerra'ðura] *nf* (*acción*) closing; (*mecanismo*) lock.

cerrajería [θerraxe'ria] *nf* locksmith's craft; (*tienda*) locksmith's (shop).

cerrajero, a [θerra'xero, a] *nm/f* locksmith.

cerrar [θe'rrar] *vt* to close, shut; (*paso, carretera*) to close; (*grifo*) to turn off; (*trato, cuenta, negocio*) to close ♦ *vi* to close, shut; (*la noche*) to come down; ~ **con llave** to lock; ~ **el sistema** (*INFORM*) to close *o* shut down the system; ~ **un trato** to strike a bargain; ~**se** *vr* to close, shut; (*herida*) to heal.

cerro ['θerro] *nm* hill; **andar por las** ~**s de Úbeda** to wander from the point, digress.

cerrojo [θe'rroxo] *nm* (*herramienta*) bolt; (*de puerta*) latch.

certamen [θer'tamen] *nm* competition, contest.

certero, a [θer'tero, a] *adj* (*gen*) accurate.

certeza [θer'teθa], **certidumbre** [θerti'ðumbre] *nf* certainty.

certificación [θertifika'θjon] *nf* certification; (*JUR*) affidavit.

certificado, a [θertifi'kaðo, a] *adj* certified; (*CORREOS*) registered ♦ *nm* certificate.

certificar [θertifi'kar] *vt* (*asegurar, atestar*) to certify.

certifique [θerti'fike] *etc vb V* **certificar**.

cervatillo [θerβa'tiλo] *nm* fawn.

cervecería [θerβeθe'ria] *nf* (*fábrica*) brewery; (*taberna*) public house.

cerveza [θer'βeθa] *nf* beer; ~ **de barril** draught beer.

cervical [θerβi'kal] *adj* cervical.

cerviz [θer'βiθ] *nf* nape of the neck.

cesación [θesa'θjon] *nf* cessation, suspension.

cesante [θe'sante] *adj* redundant; (*AM*) unemployed; (*ministro*) outgoing; (*diplomático*) recalled ♦ *nm/f* redundant worker.

cesar [θe'sar] *vi* to cease, stop; (*de un trabajo*) to leave ♦ *vt* (*en el trabajo*) to dismiss; (*alto cargo*) to remove from office.

cesárea [θe'sarea] *nf* Caesarean (section).

cese ['θese] *nm* (*de trabajo*) dismissal; (*de pago*) suspension.

Cesid [θe'sið] *nm abr* (*ESP*: = *Centro Superior de Investigación de la Defensa Nacional*) *military intelligence service.*

cesión [θe'sjon] *nf*: ~ **de bienes** surrender of property.

césped ['θespeð] *nm* grass, lawn.

cesta ['θesta] *nf* basket.

cesto ['θesto] *nm* (large) basket, hamper.

cetrería [θetre'ria] *nf* falconry.

cetrino, a [θe'trino, a] *adj* (*tez*) sallow.

cetro ['θetro] *nm* sceptre.

Ceuta [θe'uta] *nf* Ceuta.

ceutí [θeu'ti] *adj* of *o* from Ceuta ♦ *nm/f* native *o* inhabitant of Ceuta.

C.F. *nm abr* (= *Club de Fútbol*) F.C.

CFC *nm abr* (= *clorofluorocarbono*) CFC.

cfr. *abr* (= *confróntese, compárese*) cf.

cg. *abr* (= *centígramo*) cg.

CGPJ *nm abr* (= *Consejo General del Poder Judicial*) *governing body of Spanish legal system.*

CGS *nf abr* (*Guatemala, El Salvador*) = *Confederación General de Sindicatos.*

CGT *nf abr* (*Colombia, México, Nicaragua, ESP*) = *Confederación General de Trabajadores*; (*Argentina*) = *Confederación General del Trabajo.*

Ch, ch [t∫e] *nf former letter in the Spanish alphabet.*

chabacano, a [t∫aβa'kano, a] *adj* vulgar, coarse.

chabola [t∫a'βola] *nf* shack; ~**s** *nfpl* shanty town *sg.*

chabolismo [t∫aβo'lismo] *nm*: **el problema del** ~ the problem of substandard housing, the shanty town problem.

chacal [t∫a'kal] *nm* jackal.

chacarero [t∫aka'rero] *nm* (*AM*) small farmer.

chacha ['t∫at∫a] *nf* (*fam*) maid.

cháchara ['t∫at∫ara] *nf* chatter; **estar de** ~ to chatter away.

chacra ['t∫akra] *nf* (*AM*) smallholding.

chafar [t∫a'far] *vt* (*aplastar*) to crush, flatten; (*arruinar*) to ruin.

chaflán [t∫a'flan] *nm* (*TEC*) bevel.

chal [t∫al] *nm* shawl.

chalado, a [t∫a'laðo, a] *adj* (*fam*) crazy.

chalé, *pl* **chalés** [t∫a'le, t∫a'les] *nm* = **chalet**.

chaleco [t∫a'leko] *nm* waistcoat, vest (*US*); ~ **antibala** bulletproof vest; ~ **salvavidas** life jacket.

chalet, *pl* **chalets** [t∫a'le, t∫a'les] *nm* villa, ≈ detached house; ~ **adosado** semi-detached house.

chalupa [t∫a'lupa] *nf* launch, boat.

chamaco, a [t∫a'mako, a] *nm/f* (*AM*) boy/girl.

chamarra [t∫a'marra] *nf* sheepskin jacket; (*AM*: *poncho*) blanket.

champán [t∫am'pan] *nm*, **champaña** [t∫am'paɲa] *nm* champagne.

champiñón [t∫ampi'ɲon] *nm* mushroom.

champú [t∫am'pu] (*pl* **champúes**,

champús) *nm* shampoo.

chamuscar [tʃamusˈkar] *vt* to scorch, singe.

chamusque [tʃaˈmuske] *etc vb* V **chamuscar**.

chamusquina [tʃamusˈkina] *nf* singeing.

chance [ˈtʃanθe] *nm* (*a veces nf*) (*AM*) chance, opportunity.

chanchada [tʃanˈtʃaða] *nf* (*AM fam*) dirty trick.

chancho, a [ˈtʃantʃo, a] *nm/f* (*AM*) pig.

chanchullo [tʃanˈtʃuʎo] *nm* (*fam*) fiddle, wangle.

chancla [ˈtʃankla] *nf*, **chancleta** [tʃanˈkleta] *nf* flip-flop; (*zapato viejo*) old shoe.

chandal [tʃanˈdal] *nm* tracksuit; ~ **(de tactel)** shellsuit.

chantaje [tʃanˈtaxe] *nm* blackmail; **hacer ~ a uno** to blackmail sb.

chanza [ˈtʃanθa] *nf* joke.

chao [tʃao] *excl* (*fam*) cheerio.

chapa [ˈtʃapa] *nf* (*de metal*) plate, sheet; (*de madera*) board, panel; (*de botella*) bottle top; (*insignia*) (lapel) badge; (*AM: AUTO*): ~ **de matrícula**) number (*BRIT*) o license (*US*) plate; (*AM: cerradura*) lock; **de 3 ~s** (*madera*) 3-ply.

chapado, a [tʃaˈpaðo, a] *adj* (*metal*) plated; (*muebles etc*) finished.

chaparro, a [tʃaˈparro, a] *adj* squat; (*AM: bajito*) short.

chaparrón [tʃapaˈrron] *nm* downpour, cloudburst.

chapotear [tʃapoteˈar] *vt* to sponge down ♦ *vi* (*fam*) to splash about.

chapucero, a [tʃapuˈθero, a] *adj* rough, crude ♦ *nm/f* bungler.

chapuza [tʃaˈpuθa] *nf* botched job.

chapuzón [tʃapuˈθon] *nm:* **darse un ~** to go for a dip.

chaqué [tʃaˈke] *nm* morning coat.

chaqueta [tʃaˈketa] *nf* jacket; **cambiar la ~** (*fig*) to change sides.

chaquetón [tʃakeˈton] *nm* three-quarter-length coat.

charca [ˈtʃarka] *nf* pond, pool.

charco [ˈtʃarko] *nm* pool, puddle.

charcutería [tʃarkuteˈria] *nf* (*tienda*) shop selling chiefly pork meat products; (*productos*) cooked pork meats *pl*.

charla [ˈtʃarla] *nf* talk, chat; (*conferencia*) lecture.

charlar [tʃarˈlar] *vi* to talk, chat.

charlatán, ana [tʃarlaˈtan, ana] *nm/f* chatterbox; (*estafador*) trickster.

charol[1] [tʃaˈrol] *nm* varnish; (*cuero*) patent leather.

charol[2] [tʃaˈrol] *nm* (*AM*), **charola** [tʃaˈrola] *nf* (*AM*) tray.

charqui [ˈtʃarki] *nm* (*AM*) dried beef, jerky (*US*).

charro, a [ˈtʃarro, a] *adj* Salamancan; (*AM*) Mexican; (*ropa*) loud, gaudy; (*AM: costumbres*) traditional ♦ *nm/f* Salamancan; Mexican.

chárter [ˈtʃarter] *adj inv:* **vuelo** ~ charter flight.

chascarrillo [tʃaskaˈrriʎo] *nm* (*fam*) funny story.

chasco [ˈtʃasko] *nm* (*broma*) trick, joke; (*desengaño*) disappointment.

chasis [ˈtʃasis] *nm inv* (*AUTO*) chassis; (*FOTO*) plateholder.

chasquear [tʃaskeˈar] *vt* (*látigo*) to crack; (*lengua*) to click.

chasquido [tʃasˈkiðo] *nm* (*de lengua*) click; (*de látigo*) crack.

chat [tʃat] *nm* (*INTERNET*) chat room.

chatarra [tʃaˈtarra] *nf* scrap (metal).

chatero, a [tʃaˈtero, a] *adj* chat *cpd* ♦ *nm/f* chat-room user.

chato, a [ˈtʃato, a] *adj* flat; (*nariz*) snub ♦ *nm* wine tumbler; **beber unos ~s** to have a few drinks.

chau [tʃau], **chaucito** [tʃauˈsito] *excl* (*fam*) cheerio.

chauvinismo [tʃoβiˈnismo] *nm* chauvinism.

chauvinista [tʃoβiˈnista] *adj*, *nm/f* chauvinist.

chaval, a [tʃaˈβal, a] *nm/f* kid (*fam*), lad/lass.

chavo [ˈtʃaβo] *nm* (*AM: fam*) bloke (*BRIT*), guy.

checo, a [ˈtʃeko, a] *adj*, *nm/f* Czech ♦ *nm* (*LING*) Czech.

checo(e)slovaco, a [tʃeko(e)sloˈβako, a] *adj*, *nm/f* Czech, Czechoslovak.

Checo(e)slovaquia [tʃeko(e)sloˈβakja] *nf* Czechoslovakia.

chepa [ˈtʃepa] *nf* hump.

cheque [ˈtʃeke] *nm* cheque (*BRIT*), check (*US*); ~ **abierto/en blanco/cruzado** open/blank/crossed cheque; ~ **al portador** cheque payable to bearer; ~ **de viajero** traveller's cheque.

chequeo [tʃeˈkeo] *nm* (*MED*) check-up; (*AUTO*) service.

chequera [tʃeˈkera] *nf* (*AM*) chequebook (*BRIT*), checkbook (*US*).

chévere [ˈtʃeβere] *adj* (*AM*) great, fabulous (*fam*).

chicano, a [tʃiˈkano, a] *adj*, *nm/f* chicano, Mexican-American.

chicha [ˈtʃitʃa] *nf* (*AM*) maize liquor.

chícharo ['tʃitʃaro] nm (AM) pea.
chicharra [tʃi'tʃarra] nf harvest bug, cicada.
chicharrón [tʃitʃa'rron] nm (pork) crackling.
chichón [tʃi'tʃon] nm bump, lump.
chicle ['tʃikle] nm chewing gum.
chico, a ['tʃiko, a] adj small, little ♦ nm/f child; (muchacho) boy; (muchacha) girl.
chicote [tʃi'kote] nm (AM) whip.
chiflado, a [tʃi'flaðo, a] adj (fam) crazy, round the bend ♦ nm/f nutcase.
chiflar [tʃi'flar] vt to hiss, boo ♦ vi (esp AM) to whistle.
Chile ['tʃile] nm Chile.
chile ['tʃile] nm chilli, pepper.
chileno, a [tʃi'leno, a] adj, nm/f Chilean.
chillar [tʃi'ʎar] vi (persona) to yell, scream; (animal salvaje) to howl; (cerdo) to squeal; (puerta) to creak.
chillido [tʃi'ʎiðo] nm (de persona) yell, scream; (de animal) howl; (de frenos) screech(ing).
chillón, ona [tʃi'ʎon, ona] adj (niño) noisy; (color) loud, gaudy.
chimenea [tʃime'nea] nf chimney; (hogar) fireplace.
chimpancé, pl chimpancés [tʃimpan'θe, tʃimpan'θes] nm chimpanzee.
China ['tʃina] nf: (la) ~ China.
china ['tʃina] nf pebble.
chinchar [tʃin'tʃar] (fam) vt to pester, annoy; ~se vr to get cross; ¡chínchate! tough!
chinche ['tʃintʃe] nf bug; (TEC) drawing pin (BRIT), thumbtack (US) ♦ nm/f nuisance, pest.
chincheta [tʃin'tʃeta] nf drawing pin (BRIT), thumbtack (US).
chinchorro [tʃin'tʃorro] nm (AM) hammock.
chingado, a [tʃin'gaðo, a] adj (esp AM fam!) lousy, bloody (!); hijo de la ~a bastard (!), son of a bitch (US!).
chingar [tʃin'gar] vt (AM: fam!) to fuck (up) (!), screw (up) (!); ~se vr (AM: emborracharse) to get pissed (BRIT), get plastered (!: fracasar) to fail.
chingue ['tʃinge] etc vb V chingar.
chino, a ['tʃino, a] adj, nm/f Chinese ♦ nm (LING) Chinese; (CULIN) chinois, conical strainer.
chip [tʃip] nm (INFORM) chip.
chipirón [tʃipi'ron] nm squid.
Chipre ['tʃipre] nf Cyprus.
chipriota [tʃi'prjota], **chipriote** [tʃi'prjote] adj Cypriot, Cyprian ♦ nm/f Cypriot.
chiquillada [tʃiki'ʎaða] nf childish prank;

(AM: chiquillos) kids pl.
chiquillo, a [tʃi'kiʎo, a] nm/f kid (fam), youngster, child.
chiquito, a [tʃi'kito, a] adj very small, tiny ♦ nm/f kid (fam).
chirigota [tʃiri'ɣota] nf joke.
chirimbolo [tʃirim'bolo] nm thingummyjig (fam).
chirimoya [tʃiri'moja] nf custard apple.
chiringuito [tʃirin'gito] nm refreshment stall o stand.
chiripa [tʃi'ripa] nf fluke; por ~ by chance.
chirona [tʃi'rona], (AM) **chirola** [tʃi'rola] nf (fam) clink, jail.
chirriar [tʃi'rrjar] vi (goznes) to creak, squeak; (pájaros) to chirp, sing.
chirrido [tʃi'rriðo] nm creak(ing), squeak(ing); (de pájaro) chirp(ing).
chis [tʃis] excl sh!
chisme ['tʃisme] nm (habladurías) piece of gossip; (fam: objeto) thingummyjig.
chismoso, a [tʃis'moso, a] adj gossiping ♦ nm/f gossip.
chispa ['tʃispa] nf spark; (fig) sparkle; (ingenio) wit; (fam) drunkenness.
chispeante [tʃispe'ante] adj (tb fig) sparkling.
chispear [tʃispe'ar] vi to spark; (lloviznar) to drizzle.
chisporrotear [tʃisporrote'ar] vi (fuego) to throw out sparks; (leña) to crackle; (aceite) to hiss, splutter.
chistar [tʃistar] vi: no ~ not to say a word.
chiste ['tʃiste] nm joke, funny story; ~ verde blue joke.
chistera [tʃis'tera] nf top hat.
chistoso, a [tʃis'toso, a] adj (gracioso) funny, amusing; (bromista) witty.
chistu ['tʃistu] nm = txistu.
chivarse [tʃi'ßarse] vr (fam) to grass.
chivatazo [tʃißa'taθo] nm (fam) tip-off; dar ~ to inform.
chivo, a ['tʃißo, a] nm/f (billy/nanny-)goat; ~ expiatorio scapegoat.
chocante [tʃo'kante] adj startling; (extraño) odd; (ofensivo) shocking.
chocar [tʃo'kar] vi (coches etc) to collide, crash; (MIL, fig) to clash ♦ vt to shock; (sorprender) to startle; ~ con to collide with; (fig) to run into, run up against; ¡chócala! (fam) put it there!
chochear [tʃotʃe'ar] vi to dodder, be senile.
chocho, a ['tʃotʃo, a] adj doddering, senile; (fig) soft, doting.
chocolate [tʃoko'late] adj chocolate ♦ nm chocolate; (fam) dope, marijuana.
chocolatería [tʃokolate'ria] nf chocolate

factory (o shop).

chófer ['tʃofer], **chofer** [tʃo'fer] (esp AM) nm driver.

chollo ['tʃoʎo] nm (fam) bargain, snip.

chomba ['tʃomba], **chompa** ['tʃompa] nf (AM) jumper, sweater.

chopo ['tʃopo] nm black poplar.

choque ['tʃoke] etc vb V **chocar ♦** nm (impacto) impact; (golpe) jolt; (AUTO) crash; (fig) conflict.

chorizo [tʃo'riθo] nm hard pork sausage, (type of) salami; (ladrón) crook.

chorra ['tʃorra] nf luck.

chorrada [tʃo'rraða] nf (fam): **¡es una ~!** that's crap! (!); **decir ~s** to talk crap (!).

chorrear [tʃorre'ar] vt to pour ♦ vi to gush (out), spout (out); (gotear) to drip, trickle.

chorreras [tʃo'rreras] nfpl (adorno) frill sg.

chorro ['tʃorro] nm jet; (caudalito) dribble, trickle; (fig) stream; **salir a ~s** to gush forth; **con propulsión a ~** jet-propelled.

chotearse [tʃote'arse] vr to joke.

choto ['tʃoto] nm (cabrito) kid.

chovinismo [tʃoβi'nismo] nm = **chauvinismo**.

chovinista [tʃoβi'nista] adj, nmlf = **chauvinista**.

choza ['tʃoθa] nf hut, shack.

chubasco [tʃu'βasko] nm squall.

chubasquero [tʃuβas'kero] nm oilskins pl.

chuchería [tʃutʃe'ria] nf trinket.

chucho ['tʃutʃo] nm (ZOOL) mongrel.

chufa ['tʃufa] nf chufa, earth almond, tiger nut; **horchata de ~s** drink made from chufas.

chuleta [tʃu'leta] nf chop, cutlet; (ESCOL etc: fam) crib.

chulo, a ['tʃulo, a] adj (encantador) charming; (aire) proud; (pey) fresh; (fam: estupendo) great, fantastic ♦ nm (pícaro) rascal; (madrileño) working-class Madrilenian; (rufián: tb: ~ **de putas**) pimp.

chumbera [tʃum'bera] nf prickly pear.

chungo, a ['tʃungo, a] (fam) adj lousy ♦ nf: **estar de chunga** to be in a merry mood.

chupa ['tʃupa] nf (fam) jacket.

chupado, a [tʃu'paðo, a] adj (delgado) skinny, gaunt; **está ~** (fam) it's simple, it's dead easy.

chupar [tʃu'par] vt to suck; (absorber) to absorb; **~se** vr to grow thin; **para ~se los dedos** mouthwatering.

chupatintas [tʃupa'tintas] nm inv penpusher.

chupe ['tʃupe] nm (AM) stew.

chupete [tʃu'pete] nm dummy (BRIT), pacifier (US).

chupetón [tʃupe'ton] nm suck.

churrasco [tʃu'rrasko] nm (AM) barbecue, barbecued meat.

churrería [tʃurre'ria] nf stall or shop which sells "churros".

churrete [tʃu'rrete] nm grease spot.

churretón [tʃurre'ton] nm stain.

churrigueresco, a [tʃurrige'resko, a] adj (ARQ) baroque; (fig) excessively ornate.

churro, a ['tʃurro, a] adj coarse ♦ nm (CULIN) (type of) fritter; (chapuza) botch, mess; see boxed note.

> **CHURRO**
>
> **Churros**, long golden fritters made from a flour and water batter, are very popular in much of Spain and are often eaten with very thick hot chocolate, either for breakfast or as a snack. The citizens of Madrid, eat a thicker variety of **churro** called "porra".

---

churruscar [tʃurrus'kar] vt to fry crisp.

churrusque [tʃu'rruske] etc vb V **churruscar**.

churumbel [tʃurum'bel] nm (fam) kid.

chus [tʃus] excl: **no decir ni ~ ni mus** not to say a word.

chusco, a ['tʃusko, a] adj funny.

chusma ['tʃusma] nf rabble, mob.

chutar [tʃu'tar] vi (DEPORTE) to shoot (at goal); **esto va que chuta** it's going fine.

chuzo ['tʃuθo] nm: **llueve a ~s, llueven ~s de punta** it's raining cats and dogs.

C.I. nm abr = **coeficiente intelectual** o **de inteligencia**.

Cía abr (= compañía) Co.

cianuro [θja'nuro] nm cyanide.

ciática ['θjatika] nf sciatica.

cibercafé [θiβerka'fe] nm cybercafe.

ciberespacio [θiβeres'paθjo] nm cyberspace.

cibernauta [θiβer'nauta] nmf cybernaut.

cibernética [θiβer'netika] nf cybernetics sg.

cicatrice [θika'triθe] etc vb V **cicatrizar**.

cicatriz [θika'triθ] nf scar.

cicatrizar [θikatri'θar] vt to heal; **~se** vr to heal (up), form a scar.

cíclico, a ['θikliko, a] adj cyclical.

ciclismo [θi'klismo] nm cycling.

ciclista [θi'klista] nmlf cyclist.

ciclo ['θiklo] nm cycle.

ciclomotor [θiklomo'tor] nm moped.

ciclón [θi'klon] nm cyclone.

cicloturismo [θiklotu'rismo] nm touring by bicycle.

cicuta [θi'kuta] nf hemlock.

ciego, a ['θjeγo, a] etc vb V **cegar ♦** adj blind ♦ nmlf blind man/woman; **a ciegas** blindly; **me puse ~ a mariscos** (fam) I stuffed myself with seafood.

ciegue [ˈθjeɣe] *etc vb V* **cegar.**

cielo [ˈθjelo] *nm* sky; (*REL*) heaven; (*ARQ*: *tb*: ~ **raso**) ceiling; ¡~**s**! good heavens!; **ver el** ~ **abierto** to see one's chance.

ciempiés [θjemˈpjes] *nm inv* centipede.

cien [θjen] *num V* **ciento.**

ciénaga [ˈθjenaɣa] *nf* marsh, swamp.

ciencia [ˈθjenθja] *nf* science; ~**s** *nfpl* science *sg*; **saber algo a** ~ **cierta** to know sth for certain.

ciencia-ficción [ˈθjenθjafikˈθjon] *nf* science fiction.

cieno [ˈθjeno] *nm* mud, mire.

científico, a [θjenˈtifiko, a] *adj* scientific ♦ *nm/f* scientist.

ciento [ˈθjento], **cien** *num* hundred; **pagar al 10 por ciento** to pay at 10 per cent.

cierne [ˈθjerne] *etc vb V* **cerner** ♦ *nm*: **en** ~ in blossom; **en** ~(**s**) (*fig*) in its infancy.

cierre [ˈθjerre] *etc vb V* **cerrar** ♦ *nm* closing, shutting; (*con llave*) locking; (*RADIO, TV*) close-down; ~ **de cremallera** zip (fastener); **precios de** ~ (*BOLSA*) closing prices; ~ **del sistema** (*INFORM*) system shutdown.

cierto, a [ˈθjerto, a] *adj* sure, certain; (*un tal*) a certain; (*correcto*) right, correct; ~ **hombre** a certain man; **ciertas personas** certain *o* some people; **sí, es** ~ yes, that's correct; **por** ~ by the way; **lo** ~ **es que ...** the fact is that ...; **estar en lo** ~ to be right.

ciervo [ˈθjerβo] *nm* (*ZOOL*) deer; (: *macho*) stag.

cierzo [ˈθjerθo] *nm* north wind.

CIES *nm abr* = *Consejo Interamericano Económico y Social.*

cifra [ˈθifra] *nf* number, figure; (*cantidad*) number, quantity; (*secreta*) code; ~ **global** lump sum; ~ **de negocios** (*COM*) turnover; **en** ~**s redondas** in round figures; ~ **de referencia** (*COM*) bench mark; ~ **de ventas** (*COM*) sales figures.

cifrado, a [θiˈfraðo, a] *adj* in code.

cifrar [θiˈfrar] *vt* to code, write in code; (*resumir*) to abridge; (*calcular*) to reckon.

cigala [θiˈɣala] *nf* Norway lobster.

cigarra [θiˈɣarra] *nf* cicada.

cigarrera [θiɣaˈrrera] *nf* cigar case.

cigarrillo [θiɣaˈrriʎo] *nm* cigarette.

cigarro [θiˈɣarro] *nm* cigarette; (*puro*) cigar.

cigüeña [θiˈɣweɲa] *nf* stork.

cilíndrico, a [θiˈlindriko, a] *adj* cylindrical.

cilindro [θiˈlindro] *nm* cylinder.

cima [ˈθima] *nf* (*de montaña*) top, peak; (*de árbol*) top; (*fig*) height.

címbalo [ˈθimbalo] *nm* cymbal.

cimbrear [θimbreˈar] *vt* to brandish; ~**se** *vr* to sway.

cimentar [θimenˈtar] *vt* to lay the foundations of; (*fig: reforzar*) to strengthen; (: *fundar*) to found.

cimiento [θiˈmjento] *etc vb V* **cimentar** ♦ *nm* foundation.

cinc [θink] *nm* zinc.

cincel [θinˈθel] *nm* chisel.

cincelar [θinθeˈlar] *vt* to chisel.

cincha [ˈθintʃa] *nf* girth, saddle strap.

cincho [ˈθintʃo] *nm* sash, belt.

cinco [ˈθinko] *num* five; (*fecha*) fifth; **las** ~ five o'clock; **no estar en sus** ~ (*fam*) to be off one's rocker.

cincuenta [θinˈkwenta] *num* fifty.

cincuentón, ona [θinkwenˈton, ona] *adj, nm/f* fifty-year-old.

cine [ˈθine] *nm* cinema; **el** ~ **mudo** silent films *pl*; **hacer** ~ to make films.

cineasta [θineˈasta] *nm/f* (*director de cine*) film-maker *o* director.

cine-club [ˈθineˈklub] *nm* film club.

cinéfilo, a [θiˈnefilo, a] *nm/f* film buff.

cinematográfico, a [θinematoˈɣrafiko, a] *adj* cine-, film *cpd*.

cínico, a [ˈθiniko, a] *adj* cynical; (*descarado*) shameless ♦ *nm/f* cynic.

cinismo [θiˈnismo] *nm* cynicism.

cinta [ˈθinta] *nf* band, strip; (*de tela*) ribbon; (*película*) reel; (*de máquina de escribir*) ribbon; (*métrica*) tape measure; (*magnetofónica*) tape; ~ **adhesiva** sticky tape; ~ **aislante** insulating tape; ~ **de carbón** carbon ribbon; ~ **magnética** (*INFORM*) magnetic tape; ~ **métrica** tape measure; ~ **de múltiples impactos** (*en impresora*) multistrike ribbon; ~ **de tela** (*para máquina de escribir*) fabric ribbon; ~ **transportadora** conveyor belt.

cinto [ˈθinto] *nm* belt, girdle.

cintura [θinˈtura] *nf* waist; (*medida*) waistline.

cinturón [θintuˈron] *nm* belt; (*fig*) belt, zone; ~ **salvavidas** lifebelt; ~ **de seguridad** safety belt.

ciña [ˈθiɲa] *etc*, **ciñendo** [θiˈɲendo] *etc vb V* **ceñir.**

CIP [θip] *nm abr* = *Club Internacional de Prensa* (*Madrid*).

ciprés [θiˈpres] *nm* cypress (tree).

circo [ˈθirko] *nm* circus.

circuito [θirˈkwito] *nm* circuit; (*DEPORTE*) lap; **TV por** ~ **cerrado** closed-circuit TV; ~ **experimental** (*INFORM*) breadboard; ~ **impreso** printed circuit; ~ **lógico** (*INFORM*) logical circuit.

circulación [θirkulaˈθjon] *nf* circulation;

(*AUTO*) traffic; **"cerrado a la ~ rodada"** "closed to vehicles".

circular [θirku'lar] *adj*, *nf* circular ♦ *vt* to circulate ♦ *vi* to circulate; (*dinero*) to be in circulation; (*AUTO*) to drive; (*autobús*) to run.

círculo ['θirkulo] *nm* circle; (*centro*) clubhouse; (*POL*) political group.

circuncidar [θirkunθi'dar] *vt* to circumcise.

circunciso, a [θirkun'θiso, a] *pp de* **circuncidar**.

circundante [θirkun'dante] *adj* surrounding.

circundar [θirkun'dar] *vt* to surround.

circunferencia [θirkunfe'renθja] *nf* circumference.

circunloquio [θirkun'lokjo] *nm* circumlocution.

circunscribir [θirkunskri'βir] *vt* to circumscribe; **~se** *vr* to be limited.

circunscripción [θirkunskrip'θjon] *nf* division; (*POL*) constituency.

circunscrito [θirkuns'krito] *pp de* **circunscribir**.

circunspección [θirkunspek'θjon] *nf* circumspection, caution.

circunspecto, a [θirkuns'pekto, a] *adj* circumspect, cautious.

circunstancia [θirkuns'tanθja] *nf* circumstance; **~s agravantes/ extenuantes** aggravating/extenuating circumstances; **estar a la altura de las ~s** to rise to the occasion.

circunvalación [θirkumbala'θjon] *nf*: **carretera de ~** ring road.

cirio ['θirjo] *nm* (wax) candle.

cirrosis [θi'rrosis] *nf* cirrhosis (of the liver).

ciruela [θi'rwela] *nf* plum; **~ pasa** prune.

ciruelo [θi'rwelo] *nm* plum tree.

cirugía [θiru'xia] *nf* surgery; **~ estética** o **plástica** plastic surgery.

cirujano [θiru'xano] *nm* surgeon.

cisco ['θisko] *nm*: **armar un ~** to kick up a row; **estar hecho ~** to be a wreck.

cisma ['θisma] *nm* schism; (*POL etc*) split.

cisne ['θisne] *nm* swan; **canto de ~** swan song.

cisterna [θis'terna] *nf* cistern, tank.

cistitis [θis'titis] *nf* cystitis.

cita ['θita] *nf* appointment, meeting; (*de novios*) date; (*referencia*) quotation; **acudir/faltar a una ~** to turn up for/miss an appointment.

citación [θita'θjon] *nf* (*JUR*) summons *sg*.

citadino, a [sita'ðino, a] (*AM*) *adj* urban ♦ *nm/f* urban *o* city dweller.

citar [θi'tar] *vt* to make an appointment

with, arrange to meet; (*JUR*) to summons; (*un autor, texto*) to quote; **~se** *vr*: **~se con algn** to arrange to meet sb; **se citaron en el cine** they arranged to meet at the cinema.

cítara ['θitara] *nf* zither.

citología [θitolo'xia] *nf* smear test.

cítrico, a ['θitriko, a] *adj* citric ♦ *nm*: **~s** citrus fruits.

CiU *nm abr* (*POL*) = *Convergència i Unió*.

ciudad [θju'ðað] *nf* town; (*capital de país etc*) city; **~ universitaria** university campus; **C~ del Cabo** Cape Town; **la C~ Condal** Barcelona.

ciudadanía [θjuðaða'nia] *nf* citizenship.

ciudadano, a [θjuða'ðano, a] *adj* civic ♦ *nm/f* citizen.

ciudadrealeño, a [θjuðaðrea'leɲo, a] *adj* of *o* from Ciudad Real ♦ *nm/f* native *o* inhabitant of Ciudad Real.

cívico, a ['θiβiko, a] *adj* civic; (*fig*) public-spirited.

civil [θi'βil] *adj* civil ♦ *nm* (*guardia*) policeman.

civilice [θiβi'liθe] *etc vb V* **civilizar**.

civilización [θiβiliθa'θjon] *nf* civilization.

civilizar [θiβili'θar] *vt* to civilize.

civismo [θi'βismo] *nm* public spirit.

cizaña [θi'θaɲa] *nf* (*fig*) discord; **sembrar ~** to sow discord.

cl. *abr* (= *centilitro*) cl.

clamar [kla'mar] *vt* to clamour for, cry out for ♦ *vi* to cry out, clamour.

clamor [kla'mor] *nm* (*grito*) cry, shout; (*fig*) clamour, protest.

clamoroso, a [klamo'roso, a] *adj* (*éxito etc*) resounding.

clan ['klan] *nm* clan; (*de gángsters*) gang.

clandestinidad [klandestini'ðað] *nf* secrecy.

clandestino, a [klandes'tino, a] *adj* clandestine; (*POL*) underground.

clara ['klara] *nf* (*de huevo*) eggwhite.

claraboya [klara'βoja] *nf* skylight.

clarear [klare'ar] *vi* (*el día*) to dawn; (*el cielo*) to clear up, brighten up; **~se** *vr* to be transparent.

clarete [kla'rete] *nm* rosé (wine).

claridad [klari'ðað] *nf* (*del día*) brightness; (*de estilo*) clarity.

clarificar [klarifi'kar] *vt* to clarify.

clarifique [klari'fike] *etc vb V* **clarificar**.

clarín [kla'rin] *nm* bugle.

clarinete [klari'nete] *nm* clarinet.

clarividencia [klariβi'ðenθja] *nf* clairvoyance; (*fig*) far-sightedness.

claro, a ['klaro, a] *adj* clear; (*luminoso*) bright; (*color*) light; (*evidente*) clear, evident; (*poco espeso*) thin ♦ *nm* (*en bosque*) clearing ♦ *adv* clearly ♦ *excl* of course!; **hablar** ~ (*fig*) to speak plainly; **a las claras** openly; **no sacamos nada en** ~ we couldn't get anything definite.

clase ['klase] *nf* class; (*tipo*) kind, sort; (*ESCOL etc*) class; (: *aula*) classroom; ~ **alta/media/obrera** upper/middle/working class; **dar** ~**s** to teach.

clásico, a ['klasiko, a] *adj* classical; (*fig*) classic.

clasificable [klasifi'kaßle] *adj* classifiable.

clasificación [klasifika'θjon] *nf* classification; (*DEPORTE*) league (table); (*COM*) ratings *pl*.

clasificador [klasifika'ðor] *nm* filing cabinet.

clasificar [klasifi'kar] *vt* to classify; (*INFORM*) to sort; ~**se** *vr* (*DEPORTE: torneo*) to qualify.

clasifique [klasi'fike] *etc vb V* **clasificar.**

clasista [kla'sista] *adj* (*fam: actitud*) snobbish.

claudicar [klauði'kar] *vi* (*fig*) to back down.

claudique [klau'ðike] *etc vb V* **claudicar.**

claustro ['klaustro] *nm* cloister; (*UNIV*) staff; (*junta*) senate.

claustrofobia [klaustro'foßja] *nf* claustrophobia.

cláusula ['klausula] *nf* clause; ~ **de exclusión** (*COM*) exclusion clause.

clausura [klau'sura] *nf* closing, closure.

clausurar [klausu'rar] *vt* (*congreso etc*) to close, bring to a close; (*POL etc*) to adjourn; (*cerrar*) to close (down).

clavado, a [kla'ßaðo, a] *adj* nailed ♦ *excl* exactly!, precisely!

clavar [kla'ßar] *vt* (*tablas etc*) to nail (together); (*con alfiler*) to pin; (*clavo*) to hammer in; (*cuchillo*) to stick, thrust; (*mirada*) to fix; (*fam: estafar*) to cheat.

clave ['klaße] *nf* key; (*MUS*) clef ♦ *adj inv* key *cpd*; ~ **de acceso** password.

clavel [kla'ßel] *nm* carnation.

clavicémbalo [klaßi'θembalo] *nm* harpsichord.

clavicordio [klaßikor'ðjo] *nm* clavichord.

clavícula [kla'ßikula] *nf* collar bone.

clavija [kla'ßixa] *nf* peg; (*ELEC*) plug.

clavo ['klaßo] *nm* (*de metal*) nail; (*BOT*) clove; **dar en el** ~ (*fig*) to hit the nail on the head.

claxon ['klakson], *pl* **claxons** *nm* horn; **tocar el** ~ to sound one's horn.

clemencia [kle'menθja] *nf* mercy, clemency.

clemente [kle'mente] *adj* merciful.

cleptómano, a [klep'tomano, a] *nm/f*

kleptomaniac.

clerical [kleri'kal] *adj* clerical.

clérigo ['klerixo] *nm* priest, clergyman.

clero ['klero] *nm* clergy.

clic [klik] *nm* click; **hacer** ~/**doble** ~ **en algo** to click/double-click on sth.

clicar [kli'kar] *vi* (*INFORM*) to click; **clica en el icono** click on the icon.

cliché [kli'tʃe] *nm* cliché; (*TIP*) stencil; (*FOTO*) negative.

cliente, a ['kljente, a] *nm/f* client, customer.

clientela [kljen'tela] *nf* clientele, customers *pl*; (*COM*) goodwill; (*MED*) patients *pl*.

clima ['klima] *nm* climate.

climatizado, a [klimati'θaðo, a] *adj* air-conditioned.

clímax ['klimaks] *nm inv* climax.

clínico, a ['kliniko, a] *adj* clinical ♦ *nf* clinic; (*particular*) private hospital.

clip, *pl* **clips** [klip, klis] *nm* paper clip.

cliquear [klike'ar] *vi* (*INFORM*) to click; **cliquea en el icono** click on the icon.

clítoris ['klitoris] *nm inv* clitoris.

cloaca [klo'aka] *nf* sewer, drain.

clonación [klona'θjon] *nf* cloning.

clorhídrico, a [klo'ridriko, a] *adj* hydrochloric.

cloro ['kloro] *nm* chlorine.

clorofila [kloro'fila] *nf* chlorophyl(l).

cloroformo [kloro'formo] *nm* chloroform.

cloruro [klo'ruro] *nm* chloride; ~ **sódico** sodium chloride.

club, *pl* **clubs** *o* **clubes** [klub, klus, 'klußes] *nm* club; ~ **de jóvenes** youth club.

cm *abr* (= *centímetro*) cm.

C.N.T. *nf abr* (*ESP: Confederación Nacional de Trabajo*) Anarchist Union Confederation; (*AM*) = *Confederación Nacional de Trabajadores*.

coacción [koak'θjon] *nf* coercion, compulsion.

coaccionar [koakθjo'nar] *vt* to coerce, compel.

coagular [koaɣu'lar] *vt*, ~**se** *vr* (*sangre*) to clot; (*leche*) to curdle.

coágulo [ko'aɣulo] *nm* clot.

coalición [koali'θjon] *nf* coalition.

coartada [koar'taða] *nf* alibi.

coartar [koar'tar] *vt* to limit, restrict.

coba ['koßa] *nf*: **dar** ~ **a algn** to soft-soap sb.

cobarde [ko'ßarðe] *adj* cowardly ♦ *nm/f* coward.

cobardía [koßar'ðia] *nf* cowardice.

cobaya [ko'ßaja] *nf* guinea pig.

cobertizo [koßer'tiθo] *nm* shelter.

cobertor [koßer'tor] *nm* bedspread.

cobertura [koßer'tura] *nf* cover; (*COM*)

coverage; ~ **de dividendo** (*COM*)
dividend cover; **estar fuera de** ~ to be
out of range; **no tengo** ~ I'm out of
range.
cobija [ko'βixa] *nf* (*AM*) blanket.
cobijar [koβi'xar] *vt* (*cubrir*) to cover;
(*abrigar*) to shelter; ~**se** *vr* to take
shelter.
cobijo [ko'βixo] *nm* shelter.
cobra ['koβra] *nf* cobra.
cobrador, a [koβra'ðor, a] *nm/f* (*de autobús*)
conductor/conductress; (*de impuestos,
gas*) collector.
cobrar [ko'βrar] *vt* (*cheque*) to cash;
(*sueldo*) to collect, draw; (*objeto*) to
recover; (*precio*) to charge; (*deuda*) to
collect ♦ *vi* to draw one's pay; ~**se** *vr* to
recover, get on well; **cóbrese al entregar**
cash on delivery (COD) (*BRIT*), collect on
delivery (COD) (*US*); **a** ~ (*COM*)
receivable; **cantidades por** ~ sums due.
cobre ['koβre] *nm* copper; (*AM fam*) cent.
cobrizo, a [ko'βriθo, a] *adj* coppery.
cobro ['koβro] *nm* (*de cheque*) cashing;
(*pago*) payment; **presentar al** ~ to cash;
V tb **llamada**.
coca ['koka] *nf* coca; (*droga*) coke.
cocaína [koka'ina] *nf* cocaine.
cocainómano, a [kokai'nomano, a] *nm/f*
cocaine addict.
cocción [kok'θjon] *nf* (*CULIN*) cooking; (*el
hervir*) boiling.
cocear [koθe'ar] *vi* to kick.
cocer [ko'θer] *vt, vi* to cook; (*en agua*) to
boil; (*en horno*) to bake.
coche ['kotʃe] *nm* (*AUTO*) car, automobile
(*US*); (*de tren, de caballos*) coach, carriage; (*para niños*) pram (*BRIT*), baby
carriage (*US*); ~ **de bomberos** fire
engine; ~ **celular** Black Maria, prison
van; ~ **(comedor)** (*FERRO*) (dining) car; ~
fúnebre hearse.
coche-bomba ['kotʃe'βomba], *pl* **coches-
bomba** *nm* car bomb.
coche-cama ['kotʃe'kama], *pl* **coches-
cama** *nm* (*FERRO*) sleeping car, sleeper.
cochera [ko'tʃera] *nf* garage; (*de autobuses,
trenes*) depot.
**coche-restaurante, pl coches-
restaurante** ['kotʃerestau'rante] *nm*
(*FERRO*) dining-car, diner.
cochinada [kotʃi'naða] *nf* dirty trick.
cochinillo [kotʃi'niʎo] *nm* piglet, suckling
pig.
cochino, a [ko'tʃino, a] *adj* filthy, dirty
♦ *nm/f* pig.
cocido, a [ko'θiðo, a] *adj* boiled; (*fam*)
plastered ♦ *nm* stew.

cociente [ko'θjente] *nm* quotient.
cocina [ko'θina] *nf* kitchen; (*aparato*)
cooker, stove; (*acto*) cookery; ~ **casera**
home cooking; ~ **eléctrica** electric
cooker; ~ **francesa** French cuisine; ~ **de
gas** gas cooker.
cocinar [koθi'nar] *vt, vi* to cook.
cocinero, a [koθi'nero, a] *nm/f* cook.
coco ['koko] *nm* coconut; (*fantasma*)
bogeyman; (*fam: cabeza*) nut; **comer el** ~
a algn (*fam*) to brainwash sb.
cocodrilo [koko'ðrilo] *nm* crocodile.
cocotero [koko'tero] *nm* coconut palm.
cóctel ['koktel] *nm* (*bebida*) cocktail;
(*reunión*) cocktail party; ~ **Molotov**
Molotov cocktail, petrol bomb.
coctelera [kokte'lera] *nf* cocktail shaker.
cod. *abr* (= *código*) code.
codazo [ko'ðaθo] *nm*: **dar un** ~ **a algn** to
nudge sb.
codear [koðe'ar] *vi* to elbow, jostle; ~**se** *vr*:
~**se con** to rub shoulders with.
códice ['koðiθe] *nm* manuscript, codex.
codicia [ko'ðiθja] *nf* greed; (*fig*) lust.
codiciar [koði'θjar] *vt* to covet.
codicioso, a [koði'θjoso, a] *adj* covetous.
codificador [koðifika'ðor] *nm* (*INFORM*)
encoder; ~ **digital** digitizer.
codificar [koðifi'kar] *vt* (*mensaje*) to
(en)code; (*leyes*) to codify.
código ['koðiɣo] *nm* code; ~ **de barras**
(*COM*) bar code; ~ **binario** binary code;
~ **de caracteres** (*INFORM*) character
code; ~ **de (la) circulación** highway code;
~ **civil** common law; ~ **de control**
(*INFORM*) control code; ~ **máquina**
(*INFORM*) machine code; ~ **militar**
military law; ~ **de operación** (*INFORM*)
operational *o* machine code; ~ **penal**
penal code; ~ **de práctica** code of
practice.
codillo [ko'ðiʎo] *nm* (*ZOOL*) knee; (*TEC*)
elbow (joint).
codo ['koðo] *nm* (*ANAT, de tubo*) elbow;
(*ZOOL*) knee; **hablar por los** ~**s** to talk
nineteen to the dozen.
codorniz [koðor'niθ] *nf* quail.
coeficiente [koefi'θjente] *nm* (*MAT*)
coefficient; (*ECON etc*) rate; ~ **intelectual**
o **de inteligencia** I.Q.
coerción [koer'θjon] *nf* coercion.
coercitivo, a [koerθi'tiβo, a] *adj* coercive.
coetáneo, a [koe'taneo, a] *nm/f*: ~**s**
contemporaries.
coexistencia [koeksis'tenθja] *nf*
coexistence.
coexistir [koeksis'tir] *vi* to coexist.
cofia ['kofja] *nf* (*de enfermera*) (white) cap.

cofradía [kofra'ðia] *nf* brotherhood, fraternity; V *tb* **Semana Santa**.

cofre ['kofre] *nm* (*baúl*) trunk; (*de joyas*) box; (*AM AUTO*) bonnet (*BRIT*), hood (*US*).

cogedor [koxe'ðor] *nm* dustpan.

coger [ko'xer] *vt* (*ESP*) to take (hold of); (*objeto caído*) to pick up; (*frutas*) to pick, harvest; (*resfriado, ladrón, pelota*) to catch; (*AM fam!*) to lay (*!*) ♦ *vi:* ~ **por el buen camino** to take the right road; ~**se** *vr* (*el dedo*) to catch; ~ **a algn desprevenido** to take sb unawares; ~**se a algo** to get hold of sth.

cogida [ko'xiða] *nf* gathering, harvesting; (*de peces*) catch; (*TAUR*) goring.

cogollo [ko'ɣoʎo] *nm* (*de lechuga*) heart; (*fig*) core, nucleus.

cogorza [ko'ɣorθa] *nf* (*fam*): **agarrar una** ~ to get smashed.

cogote [ko'ɣote] *nm* back of the neck.

cohabitar [koaβi'tar] *vi* to live together, cohabit.

cohecho [ko'etʃo] *nm* (*acción*) bribery; (*soborno*) bribe.

coherencia [koe'renθja] *nf* coherence.

coherente [koe'rente] *adj* coherent.

cohesión [koe'sjon] *nm* cohesion.

cohete [ko'ete] *nm* rocket.

cohibido, a [koi'βiðo, a] *adj* (*PSICO*) inhibited; (*tímido*) shy; **sentirse** ~ to feel embarrassed.

cohibir [koi'βir] *vt* to restrain, restrict; ~**se** *vr* to feel inhibited.

COI *nm abr* (= *Comité Olímpico Internacional*) IOC.

coima ['koima] *nf* (*AM fam*) bribe.

coincidencia [koinθi'ðenθja] *nf* coincidence.

coincidir [koinθi'ðir] *vi* (*en idea*) to coincide, agree; (*en lugar*) to coincide.

coito ['koito] *nm* intercourse, coitus.

cojear [koxe'ar] *vi* (*persona*) to limp, hobble; (*mueble*) to wobble, rock.

cojera [ko'xera] *nf* lameness; (*andar cojo*) limp.

cojín [ko'xin] *nm* cushion.

cojinete [koxi'nete] *nm* small cushion, pad; (*TEC*) (ball) bearing.

cojo, a ['koxo, a] *etc vb V* **coger** ♦ *adj* (*que no puede andar*) lame, crippled; (*mueble*) wobbly ♦ *nm/f* lame person, cripple.

cojón [ko'xon] *nm* (*fam!*) ball (*!*), testicle; **¡cojones!** shit! (*!*).

cojonudo, a [koxo'nuðo, a] *adj* (*ESP fam*) great, fantastic.

col [kol] *nf* cabbage; ~**es de Bruselas** Brussels sprouts.

col., col.ª *abr* (= *columna*) col.

cola ['kola] *nf* tail; (*de gente*) queue; (*lugar*)

end, last place; (*para pegar*) glue, gum; (*de vestido*) train; **hacer** ~ to queue (up).

colaboración [kolaβora'θjon] *nf* collaboration; (*en periódico*) contribution.

colaborador, a [kolaβora'ðor, a] *nm/f* collaborator; contributor.

colaborar [kolaβo'rar] *vi* to collaborate.

colación [kola'θjon] *nf*: **sacar a** ~ to bring up.

colado, a [ko'laðo, a] *adj* (*metal*) cast ♦ *nf*: **hacer la colada** to do the washing.

colador [kola'ðor] *nm* (*de té*) strainer; (*para verduras etc*) colander.

colapsar [kolap'sar] *vt* (*tráfico etc*) to bring to a standstill.

colapso [ko'lapso] *nm* collapse; ~ **nervioso** nervous breakdown.

colar [ko'lar] *vt* (*líquido*) to strain off; (*metal*) to cast ♦ *vi* to ooze, seep (through); ~**se** *vr* to jump the queue; (*en mitin*) to sneak in; (*equivocarse*) to slip up; ~**se en** to get into without paying; (*en una fiesta*) to gatecrash.

colateral [kolate'ral] *nm* collateral.

colcha ['koltʃa] *nf* bedspread.

colchón [kol'tʃon] *nm* mattress; ~ **inflable** inflatable mattress.

colchoneta [koltʃo'neta] *nf* (*en gimnasio*) mattress; ~ **hinchable** airbed.

colear [kole'ar] *vi* (*perro*) to wag its tail.

colección [kolek'θjon] *nf* collection.

coleccionar [kolekθjo'nar] *vt* to collect.

coleccionista [kolekθjo'nista] *nm/f* collector.

colecta [ko'lekta] *nf* collection.

colectivo, a [kolek'tiβo, a] *adj* collective, joint ♦ *nm* (*AM: autobús*) (small) bus; (: *taxi*) collective taxi.

colector [kolek'tor] *nm* collector; (*sumidero*) sewer.

colega [ko'leɣa] *nm/f* colleague.

colegiado, a [kole'xjaðo, a] *adj* (*profesional*) registered ♦ *nm/f* referee.

colegial, a [kole'xjal, a] *adj* (*ESCOL etc*) school *cpd*, college *cpd* ♦ *nm/f* schoolboy/girl.

colegio [ko'lexjo] *nm* college; (*escuela*) school; (*de abogados etc*) association; ~ **de internos** boarding school; **ir al** ~ to go to school; *see boxed note*.

COLEGIO

A **colegio** *is normally a private school, either primary or secondary. Within the state system, however, the word indicates primary school, although these are also referred to as "escuelas". State secondary* schools are called "institutos". Extra-curricular subjects, such as computing or foreign languages, are taught in private schools called "academias".

colegir [kole'xir] *vt* (*juntar*) to collect, gather; (*deducir*) to infer, conclude.

cólera ['kolera] *nf* (*ira*) anger; **montar en ~** to get angry ♦ *nm* (*MED*) cholera.

colérico, a [ko'leriko, a] *adj* angry, furious.

colesterol [koleste'rol] *nm* cholesterol.

coleta [ko'leta] *nf* pigtail.

coletazo [kole'taθo] *nm*: **dar un ~** (*animal*) to flap its tail; **los últimos ~s** death throes.

coletilla [kole'tiʎa] *nf* (*en carta*) postscript; (*en conversación*) filler phrase.

colgado, a [kol'xaðo, a] *pp de* **colgar** ♦ *adj* hanging; (*ahorcado*) hanged; **dejar ~ a** algn to let sb down.

colgajo [kol'xaxo] *nm* tatter.

colgante [kol'xante] *adj* hanging; *V* **puente** ♦ *nm* (*joya*) pendant.

colgar [kol'xar] *vt* to hang (up); (*tender: ropa*) to hang out ♦ *vi* to hang; (*teléfono*) to hang up.

colgué [kol'xe], **colguemos** [kol'xemos] *etc vb V* **colgar**.

colibrí [koli'ßri] *nm* hummingbird.

cólico ['koliko] *nm* colic.

coliflor [koli'flor] *nf* cauliflower.

coligiendo [koli'xjenðo] *etc vb V* **colegir**.

colija [ko'lixa] *etc vb V* **colegir**.

colilla [ko'liʎa] *nf* cigarette end, butt.

colina [ko'lina] *nf* hill.

colindante [kolin'dante] *adj* adjacent, neighbouring.

colindar [kolin'dar] *vi* to adjoin, be adjacent.

colisión [koli'sjon] *nf* collision; **~ de frente** head-on crash.

colitis [ko'litis] *nf inv*: **tener ~** to have diarrhoea.

collar [ko'ʎar] *nm* necklace; (*de perro*) collar.

colmado, a [kol'maðo, a] *adj* full ♦ *nm* grocer's (shop) (*BRIT*), grocery store (*US*).

colmar [kol'mar] *vt* to fill to the brim; (*fig*) to fulfil, realize.

colmena [kol'mena] *nf* beehive.

colmillo [kol'miʎo] *nm* (*diente*) eye tooth; (*de elefante*) tusk; (*de perro*) fang.

colmo ['kolmo] *nm* height, summit; **para ~ de desgracias** to cap it all; **¡eso es ya el ~!** that's beyond a joke!

colocación [koloka'θjon] *nf* (*acto*) placing; (*empleo*) job, position; (*situación*) place, position; (*COM*) placement.

colocar [kolo'kar] *vt* to place, put, position; (*poner en empleo*) to find a job for; **~ dinero** to invest money; **~se** *vr* to place o.s.; (*conseguir trabajo*) to find a job.

colofón [kolo'fon] *nm*: **como ~ de las conversaciones** as a sequel to *o* following the talks.

Colombia [ko'lombja] *nf* Colombia.

colombiano, a [kolom'bjano, a] *adj*, *nm/f* Colombian.

colon ['kolon] *nm* colon.

colón [ko'lon] *nm* (*AM*) *monetary unit of Costa Rica and El Salvador*.

Colonia [ko'lonja] *nf* Cologne.

colonia [ko'lonja] *nf* colony; (*de casas*) housing estate; (*agua de ~*) cologne; **~ escolar** summer camp (for schoolchildren).

colonice [kolo'niθe] *etc vb V* **colonizar**.

colonización [koloniθa'θjon] *nf* colonization.

colonizador, a [koloniθa'ðor, a] *adj* colonizing ♦ *nm/f* colonist, settler.

colonizar [koloni'θar] *vt* to colonize.

colono [ko'lono] *nm* (*POL*) colonist, settler; (*AGR*) tenant farmer.

coloque [ko'loke] *etc vb V* **colocar**.

coloquial [kolo'kjal] *adj* colloquial.

coloquio [ko'lokjo] *nm* conversation; (*congreso*) conference; (*INFORM*) handshake.

color [ko'lor] *nm* colour; **a todo ~** in full colour; **verlo todo ~ de rosa** to see everything through rose-coloured spectacles; **le salieron los ~es** she blushed.

colorado, a [kolo'raðo, a] *adj* (*rojo*) red; (*AM: chiste*) rude, blue; **ponerse ~** to blush.

colorante [kolo'rante] *nm* colouring (matter).

colorar [kolo'rar] *vt* to colour; (*teñir*) to dye.

colorear [kolore'ar] *vt* to colour.

colorete [kolo'rete] *nm* blusher.

colorido [kolo'riðo] *nm* colour(ing).

coloso [ko'loso] *nm* colossus.

columbrar [kolum'brar] *vt* to glimpse, spy.

columna [ko'lumna] *nf* column; (*pilar*) pillar; (*apoyo*) support; **~ blindada** (*MIL*) armoured column; **~ vertebral** spine, spinal column.

columpiar [kolum'pjar] *vt*, **~se** *vr* to swing.

columpio [ko'lumpjo] *nm* swing.

colza ['kolθa] *nf* rape; **aceite de ~** rapeseed oil.

coma ['koma] *nf* comma ♦ *nm* (*MED*) coma.

comadre [ko'maðre] *nf* (*madrina*)
godmother; (*vecina*) neighbour;
(*chismosa*) gossip.

comadrear [komaðre'ar] *vi* (*esp AM*) to
gossip.

comadreja [koma'ðrexa] *nf* weasel.

comadrona [koma'ðrona] *nf* midwife.

comandancia [koman'danθja] *nf*
command.

comandante [koman'dante] *nm*
commandant; (*grado*) major.

comandar [koman'dar] *vt* to command.

comando [ko'mando] *nm* (*MIL: mando*)
command; (: *grupo*) commando unit;
(*INFORM*) command; ~ **de búsqueda**
search command.

comarca [ko'marka] *nf* region; *V tb*
provincia.

comarcal [komar'kal] *adj* local.

comba ['komba] *nf* (*curva*) curve; (*en viga*)
warp; (*cuerda*) skipping rope; **saltar a la**
~ to skip.

combar [kom'bar] *vt* to bend, curve.

combate [kom'bate] *nm* fight; (*fig*) battle;
fuera de ~ out of action.

combatiente [komba'tjente] *nm*
combatant.

combatir [komba'tir] *vt* to fight, combat.

combatividad [kombatiβi'ðað] *nf* (*actitud*)
fighting spirit; (*agresividad*)
aggressiveness.

combativo, a [komba'tiβo, a] *adj* full of
fight.

combi ['kombi] *nm* fridge-freezer.

combinación [kombina'θjon] *nf*
combination; (*QUÍMICA*) compound;
(*bebida*) cocktail; (*plan*) scheme, setup;
(*prenda*) slip.

combinado, a [kombi'naðo, a] *adj*: **plato** ~
main course served with vegetables.

combinar [kombi'nar] *vt* to combine;
(*colores*) to match.

combustible [kombus'tiβle] *nm* fuel.

combustión [kombus'tjon] *nf* combustion.

comedia [ko'meðja] *nf* comedy; (*TEAT*)
play, drama; (*fig*) farce.

comediante [kome'ðjante] *nm/f* (*comic*)
actor/actress.

comedido, a [kome'ðiðo, a] *adj* moderate.

comedirse [kome'ðirse] *vr* to behave
moderately; (*ser cortés*) to be courteous.

comedor, a [kome'ðor, a] *nm/f* (*persona*)
glutton ♦ *nm* (*habitación*) dining room;
(*restaurante*) restaurant; (*cantina*)
canteen.

comencé [komen'θe], **comencemos**
[komen'θemos] *etc vb V* **comenzar**.

comensal [komen'sal] *nm/f* fellow guest/
diner.

comentar [komen'tar] *vt* to comment on;
(*fam*) to discuss; **comentó que...** he made
the comment that....

comentario [komen'tarjo] *nm* comment,
remark; (*LIT*) commentary; ~**s** *nmpl*
gossip *sg*; **dar lugar a** ~**s** to cause gossip.

comentarista [komenta'rista] *nm/f*
commentator.

comenzar [komen'θar] *vt, vi* to begin, start,
commence; ~ **a hacer algo** to begin *o*
start doing *o* to do sth.

comer [ko'mer] *vt* to eat; (*DAMAS, AJEDREZ*)
to take, capture; (*párrafo etc*) to skip ♦ *vi*
to eat; (*almorzar*) to have lunch; ~**se** *vr* to
eat up; ~ **el coco a** (*fam*) to brainwash; **¡a**
~! food's ready!

comercial [komer'θjal] *adj* commercial;
(*relativo al negocio*) business *cpd*.

comerciante [komer'θjante] *nm/f* trader,
merchant; (*tendero*) shopkeeper; ~
exclusivo (*COM*) sole trader.

comerciar [komer'θjar] *vi* to trade, do
business.

comercio [ko'merθjo] *nm* commerce, trade;
(*negocio*) business; (*grandes empresas*) big
business; (*fig*) dealings *pl*; ~ **autorizado**
(*COM*) licensed trade; ~ **electrónico**
e-commerce; ~ **exterior** foreign trade.

comestible [komes'tiβle] *adj* eatable,
edible ♦ *nm*: ~**s** food *sg*, foodstuffs;
(*COM*) groceries.

cometa [ko'meta] *nm* comet ♦ *nf* kite.

cometer [kome'ter] *vt* to commit.

cometido [kome'tiðo] *nm* (*misión*) task,
assignment; (*deber*) commitment.

comezón [kome'θon] *nf* itch, itching.

cómic, *pl* **cómics** ['komik, 'komiks] *nm*
comic.

comicios [ko'miθjos] *nmpl* elections; (*voto*)
voting *sg*.

cómico, a ['komiko, a] *adj* comic(al) ♦ *nm/f*
comedian; (*de teatro*) (comic) actor/
actress.

comida [ko'miða] *etc vb V* **comedirse** ♦ *nf*
(*alimento*) food; (*almuerzo, cena*) meal;
(*de mediodía*) lunch; (*AM*) dinner.

comidilla [komi'ðiʎa] *nf*: **ser la** ~ **de la**
ciudad to be the talk of the town.

comience [ko'mjenθe] *etc vb V* **comenzar**.

comienzo [ko'mjenθo] *etc vb V* **comenzar**
♦ *nm* beginning, start; **dar** ~ **a un acto** to
begin a ceremony; ~ **del archivo**
(*INFORM*) top-of-file.

comillas [ko'miʎas] *nfpl* quotation marks.

comilón, ona [komi'lon, ona] *adj* greedy
♦ *nf* (*fam*) blow-out.

comino [ko'mino] *nm* cumin (seed); **no me**

importa un ~ I don't give a damn.
comisaría [komisa'ria] nf police station,
precinct (US); (MIL) commissariat.
comisario [komi'sarjo] nm (MIL etc)
commissary; (POL) commissar.
comisión [komi'sjon] nf (COM: pago)
commission, rake-off (fam); (: junta)
board; (encargo) assignment; ~ **mixta/
permanente** joint/standing committee;
Comisiones Obreras (ESP) formerly
Communist Union Confederation.
comisura [komi'sura] nf: ~ **de los labios**
corner of the mouth.
comité, pl **comités** nm [komi'te, komi'tes]
committee; ~ **de empresa** works
council.
comitiva [komi'tißa] nf suite, retinue.
como ['komo] adv as; (tal ~) like;
(aproximadamente) about, approximately
♦ conj (ya que, puesto que) as, since; (en
seguida que) as soon as; (si: +subjun) if;
¡~ no! of course!; ~ **no lo haga hoy**
unless he does it today; ~ **si** as if; **es tan
alto** ~ **ancho** it is as high as it is wide.
cómo ['komo] adv how?, why? ♦ excl what?,
I beg your pardon? ♦ nm: **el** ~ **y el porqué**
the whys and wherefores; ¿~ **está Ud?**
how are you?; ¿~ **no?** why not?; ¡~ **no!**
(esp AM) of course!; ¿~ **son?** what are
they like?
cómoda ['komoða] nf chest of drawers.
comodidad [komoði'ðað] nf comfort;
venga a su ~ come at your convenience.
comodín [komo'ðin] nm joker; (INFORM)
wild card; **símbolo** ~ wild-card
character.
cómodo, a ['komoðo, a] adj comfortable;
(práctico, de fácil uso) convenient.
comodón, ona [komo'ðon, ona] adj
comfort-loving ♦ nm/f: **ser un(a)** ~ to like
one's home comforts.
comoquiera [como'kjera] conj: ~ **que**
(+ subjun) in whatever way; ~ **que sea
eso** however that may be.
comp. abr (= compárese) cp.
compacto, a [kom'pakto, a] adj compact.
compadecer [kompaðe'θer] vt to pity, be
sorry for; ~**se** vr: ~**se de** to pity, be
sorry for.
compadezca [kompa'ðeθka] etc vb V
compadecer.
compadre [kom'paðre] nm (padrino)
godfather; (esp AM: amigo) friend, pal.
compaginar [kompaxi'nar] vt: ~ **A con B** to
bring A into line with B; ~**se** vr: ~**se con**
to tally with, square with.
compañerismo [kompaɲe'rismo] nm
comradeship.

compañero, a [kompa'ɲero, a] nm/f
companion; (novio) boyfriend/girlfriend;
~ **de clase** classmate.
compañía [kompa'ɲia] nf company; ~
afiliada associated company; ~
concesionadora franchiser; ~ **(no)
cotizable** (un)listed company; ~
inversionista investment trust; **hacer** ~ **a
algn** to keep sb company.
comparación [kompara'θjon] nf
comparison; **en** ~ **con** in comparison
with.
comparar [kompa'rar] vt to compare.
comparativo, a [kompara'tißo, a] adj
comparative.
comparecencia [kompare'θenθja] nf (JUR)
appearance (in court); **orden de** ~
summons sg.
comparecer [kompare'θer] vi to appear (in
court).
comparezca [kompa'reθka] etc vb V
comparecer.
comparsa [kom'parsa] nm/f extra.
compartimento [komparti'mento],
compartimiento [komparti'mjento] nm
(FERRO) compartment; (de mueble, cajón)
section; ~ **estanco** (fig) watertight
compartment.
compartir [kompar'tir] vt to divide (up),
share (out).
compás [kom'pas] nm (MUS) beat, rhythm;
(MAT) compasses pl; (NAUT etc) compass;
al ~ in time.
compasión [kompa'sjon] nf compassion,
pity.
compasivo, a [kompa'sißo, a] adj
compassionate.
compatibilidad [kompatißili'ðað] nf (tb
INFORM) compatibility.
compatible [kompa'tißle] adj compatible.
compatriota [kompa'trjota] nm/f
compatriot, fellow countryman/woman.
compendiar [kompen'djar] vt to
summarize; (libro) to abridge.
compendio [kom'pendjo] nm summary;
abridgement.
compenetración [kompenetra'θjon] nf (fig)
mutual understanding.
compenetrarse [kompene'trarse] vr (fig):
~ **(muy) bien** to get on (very) well
together.
compensación [kompensa'θjon] nf
compensation; (JUR) damages pl; (COM)
clearing.
compensar [kompen'sar] vt to
compensate; (pérdida) to make up for.
competencia [kompe'tenθja] nf
(incumbencia) domain, field; (COM)

receipt; (*JUR*, *habilidad*) competence; (*rivalidad*) competition.

competente [kompe'tente] *adj* (*JUR*, *persona*) competent; (*conveniente*) suitable.

competer [kompe'ter] *vi*: ~ **a** to be the responsibility of, fall to.

competición [kompeti'θjon] *nf* competition.

competidor, a [kompeti'ðor, a] *nm/f* competitor.

competir [kompe'tir] *vi* to compete.

competitivo, a [kompeti'tiβo, a] *adj* competitive.

compilación [kompila'θjon] *nf* compilation; **tiempo de** ~ (*INFORM*) compile time.

compilador [kompila'ðor] *nm* compiler.

compilar [kompi'lar] *vt* to compile.

compinche [kom'pintʃe] *nm/f* (*fam*) crony.

compita [kom'pita] *etc vb V* **competir**.

complacencia [kompla'θenθja] *nf* (*placer*) pleasure; (*satisfacción*) satisfaction; (*buena voluntad*) willingness.

complacer [kompla'θer] *vt* to please; ~**se** *vr* to be pleased.

complaciente [kompla'θjente] *adj* kind, obliging, helpful.

complazca [kom'plaθka] *etc vb V* **complacer**.

complejo, a [kom'plexo, a] *adj, nm* complex.

complementario, a [komplemen'tarjo, a] *adj* complementary.

complemento [komple'mento] *nm* (*de moda, diseño*) accessory; (*LING*) complement.

completar [komple'tar] *vt* to complete.

completo, a [kom'pleto, a] *adj* complete; (*perfecto*) perfect; (*lleno*) full ♦ *nm* full complement.

complexión [komple'ksjon] *nf* constitution.

complicación [komplika'θjon] *nf* complication.

complicado, a [kompli'kaðo, a] *adj* complicated; **estar** ~ **en** to be involved in.

complicar [kompli'kar] *vt* to complicate.

cómplice ['kompliθe] *nm/f* accomplice.

complique [kom'plike] *etc vb V* **complicar**.

complot, *pl* **complots** [kom'plo(t), kom'plos] *nm* plot; (*conspiración*) conspiracy.

compondré [kompon'dre] *etc vb V* **componer**.

componenda [kompo'nenda] *nf* compromise; (*pey*) shady deal.

componente [kompo'nente] *adj, nm* component.

componer [kompo'ner] *vt* to make up, put together; (*MUS, LIT, IMPRENTA*) to compose; (*algo roto*) to mend, repair; (*adornar*) to adorn; (*arreglar*) to arrange; (*reconciliar*) to reconcile; ~**se** *vr*: ~**se de** to consist of; **componérselas para hacer algo** to manage to do sth.

componga [kom'ponga] *etc vb V* **componer**.

comportamiento [komporta'mjento] *nm* behaviour, conduct.

comportarse [kompor'tarse] *vr* to behave.

composición [komposi'θjon] *nf* composition.

compositor, a [komposi'tor, a] *nm/f* composer.

compostelano, a [kompostel'lano, a] *adj* of *o* from Santiago de Compostela ♦ *nm/f* native *o* inhabitant of Santiago de Compostela.

compostura [kompos'tura] *nf* (*reparación*) mending, repair; (*composición*) composition; (*acuerdo*) agreement; (*actitud*) composure.

compota [kom'pota] *nf* compote, preserve.

compra ['kompra] *nf* purchase; ~**s** *nfpl* purchases, shopping *sg*; **hacer la** ~/**ir de** ~**s** to do the/go shopping; ~ **a granel** (*COM*) bulk buying; ~ **proteccionista** (*COM*) support buying.

comprador, a [kompra'ðor, a] *nm/f* buyer, purchaser.

comprar [kom'prar] *vt* to buy, purchase; ~ **deudas** (*COM*) to factor.

compraventa [kompra'βenta] *nf* (*JUR*) contract of sale.

comprender [kompren'der] *vt* to understand; (*incluir*) to comprise, include.

comprensible [kompren'siβle] *adj* understandable.

comprensión [kompren'sjon] *nf* understanding; (*totalidad*) comprehensiveness.

comprensivo, a [kompren'siβo, a] *adj* comprehensive; (*actitud*) understanding.

compresa [kom'presa] *nf* compress; ~ **higiénica** sanitary towel (*BRIT*) *o* napkin (*US*).

compresión [kompre'sjon] *nf* compression.

comprimido, a [kompri'miðo] *adj* compressed ♦ *nm* (*MED*) pill, tablet; **en caracteres** ~**s** (*TIP*) condensed.

comprimir [kompri'mir] *vt* to compress;

(*fig*) to control; (*INFORM*) to pack.

comprobación [komproßa'θjon] *nf*: ~
general de cuentas (*COM*) general audit.

comprobante [kompro'ßante] *nm* proof;
(*COM*) voucher; ~ **(de pago)** receipt.

comprobar [kompro'ßar] *vt* to check;
(*probar*) to prove; (*TEC*) to check, test.

comprometedor, a [komprompete'ðor, a]
adj compromising.

comprometer [komprompe'ter] *vt* to
compromise; (*exponer*) to endanger; ~**se**
vr to compromise o.s.; (*involucrarse*) to
get involved.

comprometido, a [komprompe'tiðo, a] *a*
(*situación*) awkward; (*escritor etc*)
committed.

compromiso [kompro'miso] *nm*
(*obligación*) obligation; (*cita*)
engagement, date; (*cometido*)
commitment; (*convenio*) agreement;
(*dificultad*) awkward situation; **libre de** ~
(*COM*) without obligation.

comprueba [kom'prweßa] *etc vb* V
comprobar.

compuerta [kom'pwerta] *nf* (*en canal*)
sluice, floodgate; (*INFORM*) gate.

compuesto, a [kom'pwesto, a] *pp de* **componer** ♦ *adj*: ~ **de** composed of, made up
of ♦ *nm* compound; (*MED*) preparation.

compulsar [kompul'sar] *vt* (*cotejar*) to
collate, compare; (*JUR*) to make an
attested copy of.

compulsivo, a [kompul'sißo, a] *adj*
compulsive.

compungido, a [kompun'xiðo, a] *adj*
remorseful.

compuse [com'puse] *etc vb* V **componer**.

computador [komputa'ðor] *nm*, **computadora** [komputa'ðora] *nf* computer; ~ **central** mainframe computer; ~ **especializado** dedicated computer; ~ **personal**
personal computer.

computar [kompu'tar] *vt* to calculate,
compute.

cómputo ['komputo] *nm* calculation.

comulgar [komul'ɣar] *vi* to receive
communion.

comulgue [ko'mulɣe] *etc vb* V **comulgar**.

común [ko'mun] *adj* (*gen*) common;
(*corriente*) ordinary; **por lo** ~ generally
♦ *nm*: **el** ~ the community.

comuna [ko'muna] *nf* commune; (*AM*)
district.

comunicación [komunika'θjon] *nf*
communication; (*informe*) report.

comunicado [komuni'kaðo] *nm*
announcement; ~ **de prensa** press
release.

comunicar [komuni'kar] *vt* to
communicate; (*ARQ*) to connect ♦ *vi* to
communicate; to send a report; ~**se** *vr* to
communicate; **está comunicando** (*TELEC*)
the line's engaged (*BRIT*) o busy (*US*).

comunicativo, a [komunika'tißo, a] *adj*
communicative.

comunidad [komuni'ðað] *nf* community; ~
autónoma autonomous region; ~ **de
vecinos** residents' association; **C~ Económica Europea (CEE)** European Economic Community (EEC); *see boxed note.*

COMUNIDAD AUTÓNOMA

*The 1978 constitution provides for a
degree of self-government in the 19
regions of Spain, called* **comunidades
autónomas** *or "autonomías". Some, such
as Catalonia and the Basque Country,
which have their own language, history
and culture, have long felt separate from
the rest of Spain, and this explains why
some of the autonomous regions have
more devolved powers than others, in all
matters except foreign affairs and national
defence. The Spanish names of the
regions are: Andalucía, Aragón, Asturias,
Islas Baleares, Canarias, Cantabria, Castilla
y León, Castilla-La Mancha, Cataluña,
Extremadura, Galicia, Madrid, Murcia,
Navarra, País Vasco, La Rioja, Comunidad
Valenciana, Ceuta and Melilla.*

---

comunión [komu'njon] *nf* communion.

comunique [komu'nike] *etc vb* V
comunicar.

comunismo [komu'nismo] *nm* communism.

comunista [komu'nista] *adj, nm/f*
communist.

comunitario, a [komuni'tarjo, a] *adj* (*de la
CE*) Community *cpd*, EC *cpd*.

================== *PALABRA CLAVE*

con [kon] *prep* **1** (*medio, compañía, modo*)
with; **comer** ~ **cuchara** to eat with a
spoon; **café** ~ **leche** white coffee; **estoy**
~ **un catarro** I've got a cold; **pasear** ~
algn to go for a walk with sb; ~
habilidad skilfully
2 (*a pesar de*): ~ **todo, merece nuestros
respetos** all the same o even so, he
deserves our respect
3 (*para* ~): **es muy bueno para** ~ **los
niños** he's very good with (the) children
4 (*+infin*): ~ **llegar tan tarde se quedó
sin comer** by arriving o because he
arrived so late he missed out on eating;

~ **estudiar un poco apruebas** with a bit
of studying you should pass
5 (*queja*): ¡~ **las ganas que tenía de ir!**
and I really wanted to go (too)!
♦ *conj*: ~ **que: será suficiente ~ que le
escribas** it will be enough if you write to
her.

conato [ko'nato] *nm* attempt; ~ **de robo**
attempted robbery.
cóncavo, a ['konkaβo, a] *adj* concave.
concebir [konθe'βir] *vt* to conceive;
(*imaginar*) to imagine ♦ *vi* to conceive.
conceder [konθe'ðer] *vt* to concede.
concejal, a [konθe'xal, a] *nm/f* town
councillor.
concejo [kon'θexo] *nm* council.
concentración [konθentra'θjon] *nf*
concentration.
concentrar [konθen'trar] *vt*, ~**se** *vr* to
concentrate.
concéntrico, a [kon'θentriko, a] *adj*
concentric.
concepción [konθep'θjon] *nf* conception.
concepto [kon'θepto] *nm* concept; **por ~
de** as, by way of; **tener buen ~ de algn** to
think highly of sb; **bajo ningún ~** under
no circumstances.
conceptuar [konθep'twar] *vt* to judge.
concernir [konθer'nir] *vi*: **en lo que
concierne a** concerning.
concertar [konθer'tar] *vt* (*MUS*) to
harmonize; (*acordar: precio*) to agree;
(: *tratado*) to conclude; (*trato*) to arrange,
fix up; (*combinar: esfuerzos*) to
coordinate; (*reconciliar: personas*) to
reconcile ♦ *vi* to harmonize, be in tune.
concesión [konθe'sjon] *nf* concession;
(*COM: fabricación*) licence.
concesionario, a [konθesjo'narjo, a] *nm/f*
(*COM*) (licensed) dealer, agent,
concessionaire; (: *de venta*) franchisee;
(: *de transportes etc*) contractor.
concha ['kontʃa] *nf* shell; (*AM fam!*) cunt
(!)
conchabarse [kontʃa'βarse] *vr*: ~ **contra** to
gang up on.
conciencia [kon'θjenθja] *nf* (*moral*)
conscience; (*conocimiento*) awareness;
libertad de ~ freedom of worship;
tener/tomar ~ de to be/become aware
of; **tener la ~ limpia o tranquila** to have a
clear conscience; **tener plena ~ de** to be
fully aware of.
concienciar [konθjen'θjar] *vt* to make
aware; ~**se** *vr* to become aware.
concienzudo, a [konθjen'θuðo, a] *adj*
conscientious.

concierne [kon'θjerne] *etc vb V* **concernir**.
concierto [kon'θjerto] *etc vb V* **concertar**
♦ *nm* concert; (*obra*) concerto.
conciliación [konθilja'θjon] *nf* conciliation.
conciliar [konθi'ljar] *vt* to reconcile ♦ *adj*
(*REL*) of a council; ~ **el sueño** to get to
sleep.
concilio [kon'θiljo] *nm* council.
concisión [konθi'sjon] *nf* conciseness.
conciso, a [kon'θiso, a] *adj* concise.
conciudadano, a [konθjuða'ðano, a] *nm/f*
fellow citizen.
concluir [konklu'ir] *vt* (*acabar*) to conclude;
(*inferir*) to infer, deduce ♦ *vi*, ~**se** *vr* to
conclude; **todo ha concluido** it's all over.
conclusión [konklu'sjon] *nf* conclusion;
llegar a la ~ de que ... to come to the
conclusion that ....
concluya [kon'kluja] *etc vb V* **concluir**.
concluyente [konklu'jente] *adj* (*prueba,
información*) conclusive.
concordancia [konkor'ðanθja] *nf*
agreement.
concordar [konkor'ðar] *vt* to reconcile ♦ *vi*
to agree, tally.
concordia [kon'korðja] *nf* harmony.
concretamente [konkreta'mente] *adv*
specifically, to be exact.
concretar [konkre'tar] *vt* to make
concrete, make more specific;
(*problema*) to pinpoint; ~**se** *vr* to become
more definite.
concreto, a [kon'kreto, a] *adj, nm* (*AM*)
concrete; **en ~** (*en resumen*) to sum up;
(*específicamente*) specifically; **no hay
nada en ~** there's nothing definite.
concubina [konku'βina] *nf* concubine.
concuerde [kon'kwerðe] *etc vb V*
concordar.
concupiscencia [konkupis'θenθja] *nf*
(*avancia*) greed; (*lujuria*) lustfulness.
concurrencia [konku'rrenθja] *nf* turnout.
concurrido, a [konku'rriðo, a] *a* (*calle*)
busy; (*local, reunión*) crowded.
concurrir [konku'rrir] *vi* (*juntarse: ríos*) to
meet, come together; (: *personas*) to
gather, meet.
concursante [konkur'sante] *nm*
competitor.
concursar [konkur'sar] *vi* to compete.
concurso [kon'kurso] *nm* (*de público*)
crowd; (*ESCOL, DEPORTE, competencia*)
competition; (*COM*) invitation to tender;
(*examen*) open competition; (*TV etc*) quiz;
(*ayuda*) help, cooperation.
condado [kon'daðo] *nm* county.
condal [kon'dal] *adj*: **la ciudad ~**
Barcelona.

conde ['konde] nm count.
condecoración [kondekora'θjon] nf (MIL) medal, decoration.
condecorar [kondeko'rar] vt to decorate.
condena [kon'dena] nf sentence; **cumplir una ~** to serve a sentence.
condenación [kondena'θjon] nf condemnation; (REL) damnation.
condenado, a [konde'naðo, a] adj (JUR) condemned; (fam: maldito) damned ♦ nm/f (JUR) convicted person.
condenar [konde'nar] vt to condemn; (JUR) to convict; **~se** vr (JUR) to confess (one's guilt); (REL) to be damned.
condensar [konden'sar] vt to condense.
condesa [kon'desa] nf countess.
condescendencia [kondesθen'denθja] nf condescension; **aceptar algo por ~** to accept sth so as not to hurt feelings.
condescender [kondesθen'der] vi to acquiesce, comply.
condescienda [kondes'θjenda] etc vb V **condescender**.
condición [kondi'θjon] nf (gen) condition; (rango) social class; **condiciones** nfpl (cualidades) qualities; (estado) condition; **a ~ de que ...** on condition that ...; **las condiciones del contrato** the terms of the contract; **condiciones de trabajo** working conditions; **condiciones de venta** conditions of sale.
condicional [kondiθjo'nal] adj conditional.
condicionamiento [kondiθjona'mjento] nm conditioning.
condicionar [kondiθjo'nar] vt (acondicionar) to condition; **~ algo a algo** to make sth conditional o dependent on sth.
condimento [kondi'mento] nm seasoning.
condiscípulo, a [kondis'θipulo, a] nm/f fellow student.
condolerse [kondo'lerse] vr to sympathize.
condominio [kondo'minjo] nm (COM) joint ownership; (AM) condominium, apartment.
condón [kon'don] nm condom.
condonar [kondo'nar] vt (JUR: reo) to reprieve; (COM: deuda) to cancel.
cóndor ['kondor] nm condor.
conducente [kondu'θente] adj: **~ a** conducive to, leading to.
conducir [kondu'θir] vt to take, convey; (ELEC etc) to carry; (AUTO) to drive; (negocio) to manage ♦ vi to drive; (fig) to lead; **~se** vr to behave.
conducta [kon'dukta] nf conduct, behaviour.
conducto [kon'dukto] nm pipe, tube; (fig)

channel; (ELEC) lead; **por ~ de** through.
conductor, a [konduk'tor, a] adj leading, guiding ♦ nm (FÍSICA) conductor; (de vehículo) driver.
conduela [kon'dwela] etc vb V **condolerse**.
conduje [kon'duxe] etc vb V **conducir**.
conduzca [kon'duθka] etc vb V **conducir**.
conectado, a [konek'taðo, a] a (ELEC) connected, plugged in; (INFORM) on-line.
conectar [konek'tar] vt to connect (up), plug in; (INFORM) to toggle on; **~se** vr (INFORM) to log in (on).
conejillo [kone'xiʎo] nm: **~ de Indias** guinea pig.
conejo [ko'nexo] nm rabbit.
conexión [konek'sjon] nf connection; (INFORM) logging in (on).
confabularse [konfaβu'larse] vr: **~ (para hacer algo)** to plot, conspire (to do sth).
confección [konfek'θjon] nf (preparación) preparation, making-up; (industria) clothing industry; (producto) article; **de ~ (ropa)** off-the-peg.
confeccionar [konfe(k)θjo'nar] vt to make (up).
confederación [konfeðera'θjon] nf confederation.
conferencia [konfe'renθja] nf conference; (lección) lecture; (TELEC) call; **~ de cobro revertido** (TELEC) reversed-charge (BRIT) o collect (US) call; **~ cumbre** summit (conference).
conferenciante [konferen'θjante] nm/f lecturer.
conferir [konfe'rir] vt to award.
confesar [konfe'sar] vt (admitir) to confess, admit; (error) to acknowledge; (crimen) to own up to.
confesión [konfe'sjon] nf confession.
confesionario [konfesjo'narjo] nm confessional.
confeso, a [kon'feso, a] adj (JUR etc) self-confessed.
confeti [kon'feti] nm confetti.
confiado, a [kon'fjaðo, a] adj (crédulo) trusting; (seguro) confident; (presumido) conceited, vain.
confianza [kon'fjanθa] nf trust; (aliento, confidencia) confidence; (familiaridad) intimacy, familiarity; (pey) vanity, conceit; **margen de ~** credibility gap; **tener ~ con algn** to be on close terms with sb.
confiar [kon'fjar] vt to entrust ♦ vi (fiarse) to trust; (contar con) to rely; **~se** vr to put one's trust.
confidencia [konfi'ðenθja] nf confidence.
confidencial [konfiðen'θjal] adj

confidential.

confidente [konfi'ðente] *nm/f* confidant/e; (*policial*) informer.

confiera [kon'fjera] *etc vb V* **conferir**.

confiese [kon'fjese] *etc vb V* **confesar**.

configuración [konfiɣura'θjon] *nf* (*tb* INFORM) configuration; **la ~ del terreno** the lie of the land; **~ de bits** (INFORM) bit pattern.

configurar [konfiɣu'rar] *vt* to shape, form.

confín [kon'fin] *nm* limit; **confines** *nmpl* confines, limits.

confinar [konfi'nar] *vi* to confine; (*desterrar*) to banish.

confiriendo [konfi'rjendo] *etc vb V* **conferir**.

confirmación [konfirma'θjon] *nf* confirmation; (REL) Confirmation.

confirmar [konfir'mar] *vt* to confirm; (JUR *etc*) to corroborate; **la excepción confirma la regla** the exception proves the rule.

confiscar [konfis'kar] *vt* to confiscate.

confisque [kon'fiske] *etc vb V* **confiscar**.

confitado, a [konfi'taðo, a] *adj*: **fruta confitada** crystallized fruit.

confite [kon'fite] *nm* sweet (BRIT), candy (US).

confitería [konfite'ria] *nf* confectionery; (*tienda*) confectioner's (shop).

confitura [konfi'tura] *nf* jam.

conflagración [konflaɣra'θjon] *nf* conflagration.

conflictivo, a [konflik'tiβo, a] *adj* (*asunto, propuesta*) controversial; (*país, situación*) troubled.

conflicto [kon'flikto] *nm* conflict; (*fig*) clash; (: *dificultad*): **estar en un ~** to be in a jam; **~ laboral** labour dispute.

confluir [konflu'ir] *vi* (*ríos etc*) to meet; (*gente*) to gather.

confluya [kon'fluja] *etc vb V* **confluir**.

conformar [konfor'mar] *vt* to shape, fashion ♦ *vi* to agree; **~se** *vr* to conform; (*resignarse*) to resign o.s.

conforme [kon'forme] *adj* alike, similar; (*de acuerdo*) agreed, in agreement; (*satisfecho*) satisfied ♦ *adv* as ♦ *excl* agreed! ♦ *nm* agreement ♦ *prep*: **~ a** in accordance with.

conformidad [konformi'ðað] *nf* (*semejanza*) similarity; (*acuerdo*) agreement; (*resignación*) resignation; **de/en ~ con** in accordance with; **dar su ~** to consent.

conformismo [konfor'mismo] *nm* conformism.

conformista [konfor'mista] *nm/f* conformist.

confort, *pl* **conforts** [kon'for, kon'for(t)s] *nm* comfort.

confortable [konfor'taβle] *adj* comfortable.

confortar [konfor'tar] *vt* to comfort.

confraternidad [konfraterni'ðað] *nf* brotherhood; **espíritu de ~** feeling of unity.

confraternizar [konfraterni'θar] *vi* to fraternize.

confrontación [konfronta'θjon] *nf* confrontation.

confrontar [konfron'tar] *vt* to confront; (*dos personas*) to bring face to face; (*cotejar*) to compare ♦ *vi* to border.

confundir [konfun'dir] *vt* (*borrar*) to blur; (*equivocar*) to mistake, confuse; (*mezclar*) to mix; (*turbar*) to confuse; **~se** *vr* (*hacerse borroso*) to become blurred; (*turbarse*) to get confused; (*equivocarse*) to make a mistake; (*mezclarse*) to mix.

confusión [konfu'sjon] *nf* confusion.

confusionismo [konfusjo'nismo] *nm* confusion, uncertainty.

confuso, a [kon'fuso, a] *adj* (*gen*) confused; (*recuerdo*) hazy; (*estilo*) obscure.

congelación [konxela'θjon] *nf* freezing; **~ de créditos** credit freeze.

congelado, a [konxe'laðo, a] *adj* frozen ♦ *nmpl*: **~s** frozen food *sg o* foods.

congelador [konxela'ðor] *nm* freezer, deep freeze.

congelar [konxe'lar] *vt* to freeze; **~se** *vr* (*sangre, grasa*) to congeal.

congénere [kon'xenere] *nm/f*: **sus ~s** his peers.

congeniar [konxe'njar] *vi* to get on (BRIT) o along (US) (well).

congénito, a [kon'xenito, a] *adj* congenital.

congestión [konxes'tjon] *nf* congestion.

congestionado, a [konxestjo'naðo, a] *adj* congested.

congestionar [konxestjo'nar] *vt* to congest; **~se** *vr* to become congested; **se le congestionó la cara** his face became flushed.

conglomerado [konglome'raðo] *nm* conglomerate.

Congo ['kongo] *nm*: **el ~** the Congo.

congoja [kon'goxa] *nf* distress, grief.

congraciarse [kongra'θjarse] *vr* to ingratiate o.s.

congratular [kongratu'lar] *vt* to congratulate.

congregación [kongreɣa'θjon] *nf* congregation.

congregar [kongre'ɣar] vt, **~se** vr to gather together.
congregue [kon'ɡreɣe] etc vb V **congregar**.
congresista [kongre'sista] nm/f delegate, congressman/woman.
congreso [kon'greso] nm congress; **C~ de los Diputados** (ESP POL) ≈ House of Commons (BRIT), House of Representatives (US); V tb **Las Cortes (españolas)**.
congrio ['kongrjo] nm conger (eel).
congruente [kon'grwente] adj congruent, congruous.
conífera [ko'nifera] nf conifer.
conjetura [konxe'tura] nf guess; (COM) guesstimate.
conjeturar [konxetu'rar] vt to guess.
conjugación [konxuɣa'θjon] nf conjugation.
conjugar [konxu'ɣar] vt to combine, fit together; (LING) to conjugate.
conjugue [kon'xuɣe] etc vb V **conjugar**.
conjunción [konxun'θjon] nf conjunction.
conjuntivitis [konxunti'ßitis] nf conjunctivitis.
conjunto, a [kon'xunto, a] adj joint, united ♦ nm whole; (MUS) band; (vestido) ensemble; (INFORM) set; **en ~** as a whole; **~ integrado de programas** (INFORM) integrated software suite.
conjura [kon'xura] nf plot, conspiracy.
conjurar [konxu'rar] vt (REL) to exorcise; (peligro) to ward off ♦ vi to plot.
conjuro [kon'xuro] nm spell.
conllevar [konʎe'ßar] vt to bear; (implicar) to imply, involve.
conmemoración [konmemora'θjon] nf commemoration.
conmemorar [konmemo'rar] vt to commemorate.
conmigo [kon'miɣo] pron with me.
conminar [konmi'nar] vt to threaten.
conmiseración [konmisera'θjon] nf pity, commiseration.
conmoción [konmo'θjon] nf shock; (POL) disturbance; (fig) upheaval; **~ cerebral** (MED) concussion.
conmovedor, a [konmoße'ðor, a] adj touching, moving; (emocionante) exciting.
conmover [konmo'ßer] vt to shake, disturb; (fig) to move; **~se** vr (fig) to be moved.
conmueva [kon'mweßa] etc vb V **conmover**.
conmutación [konmuta'θjon] nf (INFORM) switching; **~ de mensajes** message switching; **~ por paquetes** packet switching.
conmutador [konmuta'ðor] nm switch; (AM TELEC) switchboard.
conmutar [konmu'tar] vt (JUR) to commute.
connivencia [konni'ßenθja] nf: **estar en ~ con** to be in collusion with.
connotación [konnota'θjon] nf connotation.
cono ['kono] nm cone; **C~ Sur** Southern Cone.
conocedor, a [konoθe'ðor, a] adj expert, knowledgeable ♦ nm/f expert, connoisseur.
conocer [kono'θer] vt to know; (por primera vez) to meet, get to know; (entender) to know about; (reconocer) to recognize; **~se** vr (una persona) to know o.s.; (dos personas) to (get to) know each other; **darse a ~** (presentarse) to make o.s. known; **se conoce que ...** (parece) apparently ....
conocido, a [kono'θiðo, a] adj (well-) known ♦ nm/f acquaintance.
conocimiento [konoθi'mjento] nm knowledge; (MED) consciousness; (NAUT: tb: **~ de embarque**) bill of lading; **~s** nmpl (personas) acquaintances; (saber) knowledge sg; **hablar con ~ de causa** to speak from experience; **~ aéreo** (COM) air waybill.
conozca [ko'noθka] etc vb V **conocer**.
conque ['konke] conj and so, so then.
conquense [kon'kense] adj of o from Cuenca ♦ nm/f native o inhabitant of Cuenca.
conquista [kon'kista] nf conquest.
conquistador, a [konkista'ðor, a] adj conquering ♦ nm conqueror.
conquistar [konkis'tar] vt (MIL) to conquer; (puesto, simpatía) to win; (enamorar) to win the heart of.
consabido, a [konsa'ßiðo, a] adj (frase etc) old; (pey): **las consabidas excusas** the same old excuses.
consagrado, a [konsa'ɣraðo, a] adj (REL) consecrated; (actor) established.
consagrar [konsa'ɣrar] vt (REL) to consecrate; (fig) to devote.
consciente [kons'θjente] adj conscious; **ser o estar ~ de** to be aware of.
consecución [konseku'θjon] nf acquisition; (de fin) attainment.
consecuencia [konse'kwenθja] nf consequence, outcome; (firmeza) consistency; **de ~** of importance.
consecuente [konse'kwente] adj consistent.

consecutivo, a [konseku'tiβo, a] *adj* consecutive.

conseguir [konse'ɣir] *vt* to get, obtain; (*sus fines*) to attain.

consejería [konsexe'ria] *nf* (*POL*) ministry (*in a regional government*).

consejero, a [konse'xero, a] *nm/f* adviser, consultant; (*POL*) minister (*in a regional government*); (*COM*) director; (*en comisión*) member.

consejo [kon'sexo] *nm* advice; (*POL*) council; (*COM*) board; **un ~** a piece of advice; **~ de administración** board of directors; **~ de guerra** court-martial; **C~ de Europa** Council of Europe.

consenso [kon'senso] *nm* consensus.

consentido, a [konsen'tiðo, a] *adj* (*mimado*) spoiled.

consentimiento [konsenti'mjento] *nm* consent.

consentir [konsen'tir] *vt* (*permitir, tolerar*) to consent to; (*mimar*) to pamper, spoil ♦ *vi* to agree, consent; **~ que algn haga algo** to allow sb to do sth.

conserje [kon'serxe] *nm* caretaker; (*portero*) porter.

conserva [kon'serβa] *nf*: **en ~** (*alimentos*) tinned (*BRIT*), canned (*US*); **~s** tinned *o* canned foods.

conservación [konserβa'θjon] *nf* conservation; (*de alimentos, vida*) preservation.

conservador, a [konserβa'ðor, a] *adj* (*POL*) conservative ♦ *nm/f* conservative.

conservadurismo [konserβaðu'rismo] *nm* (*POL etc*) conservatism.

conservante [konser'βante] *nm* preservative.

conservar [konser'βar] *vt* (*gen*) to preserve; (*recursos*) to conserve, keep; (*alimentos, vida*) to preserve; **~se** *vr* to survive.

conservas [kon'serβas] *nfpl*: **~ (alimenticias)** tinned (*BRIT*) *o* canned goods.

conservatorio [konserβa'torjo] *nm* (*MUS*) conservatoire; (*AM*) greenhouse.

considerable [konsiðe'raβle] *adj* considerable.

consideración [konsiðera'θjon] *nf* consideration; (*estimación*) respect; **de ~** important; **De mi *o* nuestra (mayor) ~** (*AM*) Dear Sir(s) *o* Madam; **tomar en ~** to take into account.

considerado, a [konsiðe'raðo, a] *adj* (*atento*) considerate; (*respetado*) respected.

considerar [konsiðe'rar] *vt* (*gen*) to consider; (*meditar*) to think about; (*tener en cuenta*) to take into account.

consienta [kon'sjenta] *etc vb V* **consentir**.

consigna [kon'siɣna] *nf* (*orden*) order, instruction; (*para equipajes*) left-luggage office (*BRIT*), checkroom (*US*).

consignación [konsiɣna'θjon] *nf* consignment; **~ de créditos** allocation of credits.

consignador [konsiɣna'ðor] *nm* (*COM*) consignor.

consignar [konsiɣ'nar] *vt* (*COM*) to send; (*créditos*) to allocate.

consignatario, a [konsiɣna'tarjo, a] *nm/f* (*COM*) consignee.

consigo [kon'siɣo] *etc vb V* **conseguir** ♦ *pron* (*m*) with him; (*f*) with her; (*usted*) with you; (*reflexivo*) with o.s.

consiguiendo [konsi'ɣjendo] *etc vb V* **conseguir**.

consiguiente [konsi'ɣjente] *adj* consequent; **por ~** and so, therefore, consequently.

consintiendo [konsin'tjendo] *etc vb V* **consentir**.

consistente [konsis'tente] *adj* consistent; (*sólido*) solid, firm; (*válido*) sound; **~ en** consisting of.

consistir [konsis'tir] *vi*: **~ en** (*componerse de*) to consist of; (*ser resultado de*) to be due to.

consola [kon'sola] *nf* console, control panel; (*mueble*) console table; **~ de juegos** games console; **~ de mando** (*INFORM*) control console; **~ de visualización** visual display console.

consolación [konsola'θjon] *nf* consolation.

consolar [konso'lar] *vt* to console.

consolidar [konsoli'ðar] *vt* to consolidate.

consomé, *pl* **consomés** [konso'me, konso'mes] *nm* consommé, clear soup.

consonancia [konso'nanθja] *nf* harmony; **en ~ con** in accordance with.

consonante [konso'nante] *adj* consonant, harmonious ♦ *nf* consonant.

consorcio [kon'sorθjo] *nm* (*COM*) consortium, syndicate.

consorte [kon'sorte] *nm/f* consort.

conspicuo, a [kons'pikwo, a] *adj* conspicuous.

conspiración [konspira'θjon] *nf* conspiracy.

conspirador, a [konspira'ðor, a] *nm/f* conspirator.

conspirar [konspi'rar] *vi* to conspire.

constancia [kons'tanθja] *nf* (*gen*) constancy; (*certeza*) certainly; **dejar ~ de algo** to put sth on record.

constante [kons'tante] *adj, nf* constant.
constar [kons'tar] *vi* (*evidenciarse*) to be clear *o* evident; ~ **(en)** to appear (in); ~ **de** to consist of; **hacer** ~ to put on record; **me consta que** ... I have evidence that ...; **que conste que lo hice por ti** believe me, I did it for your own good.
constatar [konsta'tar] *vt* (*controlar*) to check; (*observar*) to note.
constelación [konstela'θjon] *nf* constellation.
consternación [konsterna'θjon] *nf* consternation.
constipado, a [konsti'paðo, a] *adj*: **estar** ~ to have a cold ♦ *nm*: cold.
constiparse [konsti'parse] *vr* to catch a cold.
constitución [konstitu'θjon] *nf* constitution; **Día de la C~** (*ESP*) Constitution Day (*6th December*).
constitucional [konstituθjo'nal] *adj* constitutional.
constituir [konstitu'ir] *vt* (*formar, componer*) to constitute, make up; (*fundar, erigir, ordenar*) to constitute, establish; (*ser*) to be; ~**se** *vr* (*POL etc: cuerpo*) to be composed; (: *fundarse*) to be established.
constitutivo, a [konstitu'tiβo, a] *adj* constitutive, constituent.
constituya [konsti'tuja] *etc vb V* **constituir**.
constituyente [konstitu'jente] *adj* constituent.
constreñir [konstre'ɲir] *vt* (*obligar*) to compel, oblige; (*restringir*) to restrict.
constriño [kons'triɲo] *etc*, **constriñendo** [konstri'ɲendo] *etc vb V* **constreñir**.
construcción [konstruk'θjon] *nf* construction, building.
constructivo, a [konstruk'tiβo, a] *adj* constructive.
constructor, a [konstruk'tor, a] *nm/f* builder.
construir [konstru'ir] *vt* to build, construct.
construyendo [konstru'jendo] *etc vb V* **construir**.
consuelo [kon'swelo] *etc vb V* **consolar** ♦ *nm* consolation, solace.
consuetudinario, a [konswetuði'narjo, a] *adj* customary; **derecho** ~ common law.
cónsul ['konsul] *nm* consul.
consulado [konsu'laðo] *nm* (*sede*) consulate; (*cargo*) consulship.
consulta [kon'sulta] *nf* consultation; (*MED: consultorio*) consulting room; (*INFORM*) enquiry; **horas de** ~ surgery hours; **obra**

de ~ reference book.
consultar [konsul'tar] *vt* to consult; ~ **un archivo** (*INFORM*) to interrogate a file.
consultor, a [konsul'tor, a] *nm*: ~ **en dirección de empresas** management consultant.
consultorio [konsul'torjo] *nm* (*MED*) surgery.
consumado, a [konsu'maðo, a] *adj* perfect; (*bribón*) out-and-out.
consumar [konsu'mar] *vt* to complete, carry out; (*crimen*) to commit; (*sentencia*) to carry out.
consumición [konsumi'θjon] *nf* consumption; (*bebida*) drink; (*comida*) food; ~ **mínima** cover charge.
consumido, a [konsu'miðo, a] *adj* (*flaco*) skinny.
consumidor, a [konsumi'ðor, a] *nm/f* consumer.
consumir [konsu'mir] *vt* to consume; ~**se** *vr* to be consumed; (*persona*) to waste away.
consumismo [konsu'mismo] *nm* (*COM*) consumerism.
consumo [kon'sumo] *nm* consumption; **bienes de** ~ consumer goods.
contabilice [kontaβi'liθe] *etc vb V* **contabilizar**.
contabilidad [kontaβili'ðað] *nf* accounting, book-keeping; (*profesión*) accountancy; (*COM*): ~ **analítica** variable costing; ~ **de costos** cost accounting; ~ **de doble partida** double-entry book-keeping; ~ **de gestión** management accounting; ~ **por partida simple** single-entry book-keeping.
contabilizar [kontaβi'liθar] *vt* to enter in the accounts.
contable [kon'taβle] *nm/f* bookkeeper; (*licenciado*) accountant; ~ **de costos** (*COM*) cost accountant.
contactar [kontak'tar] *vi*: ~ **con algn** to contact sb.
contacto [kon'takto] *nm* contact; **lentes de** ~ contact lenses; **estar en** ~ **con** to be in touch with.
contado, a [kon'taðo, a] *adj*: ~**s** (*escasos*) numbered, scarce, few ♦ *nm*: **al** ~ for cash; **pagar al** ~ to pay (in) cash; **precio al** ~ cash price.
contador [konta'ðor] *nm* (*aparato*) meter; (*AM*: *contable*) accountant.
contaduría [kontaðu'ria] *nf* accountant's office.
contagiar [konta'xjar] *vt* (*enfermedad*) to pass on, transmit; (*persona*) to infect; ~**se** *vr* to become infected.

contagio [kon'taxjo] *nm* infection.

contagioso, a [konta'xjoso, a] *adj* infectious; (*fig*) catching.

contaminación [kontamina'θjon] *nf* (*gen*) contamination; (*del ambiente etc*) pollution.

contaminar [kontami'nar] *vt* (*gen*) to contaminate; (*aire, agua*) to pollute; (*fig*) to taint.

contante [kon'tante] *adj*: **dinero ~ (y sonante)** hard cash.

contar [kon'tar] *vt* (*páginas, dinero*) to count; (*anécdota etc*) to tell ♦ *vi* to count; **~se** *vr* to be counted, figure; **~ con** to rely on, count on; **sin ~** not to mention; **le cuento entre mis amigos** I reckon him among my friends.

contemplación [kontempla'θjon] *nf* contemplation; **no andarse con contemplaciones** not to stand on ceremony.

contemplar [kontem'plar] *vt* to contemplate; (*mirar*) to look at.

contemporáneo, a [kontempo'raneo, a] *adj, nm/f* contemporary.

contemporizar [kontempori'θar] *vi*: **~ con** to keep in with.

contención [konten'θjon] *nf* (*JUR*) suit; **muro de ~** retaining wall.

contencioso, a [konten'θjoso, a] *adj* contentious ♦ *nm* conflict, dispute.

contender [konten'der] *vi* to contend; (*en un concurso*) to compete.

contendiente [konten'djente] *nm/f* contestant.

contendrá [konten'dra] *etc vb V* **contener**.

contenedor [kontene'ðor] *nm* container; (*de escombros*) skip; **~ de (la) basura** wheelie-bin (*BRIT*); **~ de vidrio** bottle bank.

contener [konte'ner] *vt* to contain, hold; (*risa etc*) to hold back, contain; **~se** *vr* to control o restrain o.s.

contenga [kon'tenga] *etc vb V* **contener**.

contenido, a [konte'niðo, a] *adj* (*moderado*) restrained; (*risa etc*) suppressed ♦ *nm* contents *pl*, content.

contentar [konten'tar] *vt* (*satisfacer*) to satisfy; (*complacer*) to please; (*COM*) to endorse; **~se** *vr* to be satisfied.

contento, a [kon'tento, a] *adj* contented, content; (*alegre*) pleased; (*feliz*) happy.

contestación [kontesta'θjon] *nf* answer, reply; **~ a la demanda** defence plea.

contestador [kontesta'ðor] *nm*: **~ automático** answering machine.

contestar [kontes'tar] *vt* to answer (back), reply; (*JUR*) to corroborate, confirm.

contestatario, a [kontes'tarjo, a] *adj* anti-establishment, nonconformist.

contexto [kon'teksto] *nm* context.

contienda [kon'tjenda] *nf* contest, struggle.

contiene [kon'tjene] *etc vb V* **contener**.

contigo [kon'tixo] *pron* with you.

contiguo, a [kon'tixwo, a] *adj* (*de al lado*) next; (*vecino*) adjacent, adjoining.

continental [kontinen'tal] *adj* continental.

continente [konti'nente] *adj, nm* continent.

contingencia [kontin'xenθja] *nf* contingency; (*riesgo*) risk; (*posibilidad*) eventuality.

contingente [kontin'xente] *adj* contingent ♦ *nm* contingent; (*COM*) quota.

continuación [kontinwa'θjon] *nf* continuation; **a ~** then, next.

continuamente [kon'tinwamente] *adv* (*sin interrupción*) continuously; (*a todas horas*) constantly.

continuar [konti'nwar] *vt* to continue, go on with; (*reanudar*) to resume ♦ *vi* to continue, go on; **~ hablando** to continue talking o to talk.

continuidad [kontinwi'ðað] *nf* continuity.

continuo, a [kon'tinwo, a] *adj* (*sin interrupción*) continuous; (*acción perseverante*) continual.

contonearse [kontone'arse] *vr* (*hombre*) to swagger; (*mujer*) to swing one's hips.

contorno [kon'torno] *nm* outline; (*GEO*) contour; **~s** *nmpl* neighbourhood *sg*, surrounding area *sg*.

contorsión [kontor'sjon] *nf* contortion.

contra ['kontra] *prep* against; (*COM: giro*) on ♦ *adv* against ♦ *adj, nm/f* (*POL fam*) counter-revolutionary ♦ *nm* con ♦ *nf*: **la C~ (nicaragüense)** the Contras *pl*.

contraalmirante [kontraalmi'rante] *nm* rear admiral.

contraanálisis [kontraa'nalisis] *nm* follow-up test, countertest.

contraataque [kontraa'take] *nm* counterattack.

contrabajo [kontra'βaxo] *nm* double bass.

contrabandista [kontraβan'dista] *nm/f* smuggler.

contrabando [kontra'βando] *nm* (*acción*) smuggling; (*mercancías*) contraband; **~ de armas** gun-running.

contracción [kontrak'θjon] *nf* contraction.

contrachapado [kontratʃa'paðo] *nm* plywood.

contracorriente [kontrako'rrjente] *nf* cross-current.

contradecir [kontraðe'θir] *vt* to contradict.

contradicción [kontraðik'θjon] *nf*

contradiction; **espíritu de ~**
contrariness.
contradicho [kontra'ðitʃo] *pp de*
contradecir.
contradiciendo [kontraði'θjendo] *etc vb V*
contradecir.
contradictorio, a [kontraðik'torjo, a] *adj*
contradictory.
contradiga [kontra'ðiɣa] *etc*, **contradije**
[kontra'ðixe], **contradirá** [kontraði'ra] *etc*
vb V **contradecir**.
contraer [kontra'er] *vt* to contract; (*hábito*)
to acquire; (*limitar*) to restrict; **~se** *vr* to
contract; (*limitarse*) to limit o.s.
contraespionaje [kontraespjo'naxe] *nm*
counter-espionage.
contrafuerte [kontra'fwerte] *nm* (*ARQ*)
buttress.
contragolpe [kontra'ɣolpe] *nm* backlash.
contrahaga [kontra'aɣa] *etc*, **contraharé**
[kontraa're] *etc vb V* **contrahacer**.
contrahecho, a [kontra'etʃo, a] *pp de*
contrahacer ♦ *adj* fake; (*ANAT*)
hunchbacked.
contrahice [kontra'iθe] *etc vb V*
contrahacer.
contraiga [kon'traiɣa] *etc vb V* **contraer**.
contraindicaciones [kontraindika'θjones]
nfpl (*MED*) contraindications.
contraje [kon'traxe] *etc vb V* **contraer**.
contralor [kontra'lor] *nm* (*AM*) government
accounting inspector.
contraluz [kontra'luθ] *nf* (*FOTO etc*) back
lighting; **a ~** against the light.
contramaestre [kontrama'estre] *nm*
foreman.
contraofensiva [kontraofen'sißa] *nf*
counteroffensive.
contraorden [kontra'orðen] *nf* counter-
order, countermand.
contrapartida [kontrapar'tiða] *nf* (*COM*)
balancing entry; **como ~ (de)** in return
(for), as *o* in compensation (for).
contrapelo [kontra'pelo]: **a ~** *adv* the
wrong way.
contrapesar [kontrape'sar] *vt* to
counterbalance; (*fig*) to offset.
contrapeso [kontra'peso] *nm*
counterweight; (*fig*) counterbalance;
(*COM*) makeweight.
contrapondré [kontrapon'dre] *etc vb V*
contraponer.
contraponer [kontrapo'ner] *vt* (*cotejar*) to
compare; (*oponer*) to oppose.
contraponga [kontra'ponga] *etc vb V*
contraponer.
contraportada [kontrapor'taða] *nf* (*de
revista*) back page.

contraproducente [kontraproðu'θente] *adj*
counterproductive.
contrapuesto [kontra'pwesto] *pp de*
contraponer.
contrapunto [kontra'punto] *nm*
counterpoint.
contrapuse [kontra'puse] *etc vb V*
contraponer.
contrariar [kontra'rjar] *vt* (*oponerse*) to
oppose; (*poner obstáculo*) to impede;
(*enfadar*) to vex.
contrariedad [kontrarje'ðað] *nf* (*oposición*)
opposition; (*obstáculo*) obstacle, setback;
(*disgusto*) vexation, annoyance.
contrario, a [kon'trarjo, a] *adj* contrary;
(*persona*) opposed; (*sentido, lado*)
opposite ♦ *nm/f* enemy, adversary;
(*DEPORTE*) opponent; **al ~**, **por el ~** on the
contrary; **de lo ~** otherwise.
Contrarreforma [kontrarre'forma] *nf*
Counter-Reformation.
contrarreloj [kontrarre'lo(x)] *nf* (*tb:* **prueba
~**) time trial.
contrarrestar [kontrarres'tar] *vt* to
counteract.
contrarrevolución [kontrarreßolu'θjon] *nf*
counter-revolution.
contrasentido [kontrasen'tiðo] *nm*
contradiction; **es un ~ que él ...** it
doesn't make sense for him to ... .
contraseña [kontra'seɲa] *nf* countersign;
(*frase*) password.
contrastar [kontras'tar] *vt* to resist ♦ *vi* to
contrast.
contraste [kon'traste] *nm* contrast.
contrata [kon'trata] *nf* (*JUR*) written
contract; (*empleo*) hiring.
contratar [kontra'tar] *vt* (*firmar un acuerdo
para*) to contract for; (*empleados,
obreros*) to hire, engage; (*DEPORTE*) to
sign up; **~se** *vr* to sign on.
contratiempo [kontra'tjempo] *nm* (*revés*)
setback; (*accidente*) mishap; **a ~** (*MUS*)
off-beat.
contratista [kontra'tista] *nm/f* contractor.
contrato [kon'trato] *nm* contract; **~ de
compraventa** contract of sale; **~ a precio
fijo** fixed-price contract; **~ a término**
forward contract; **~ de trabajo** contract
of employment *o* service.
contravalor [kontraßa'lor] *nm* exchange
value.
contravención [kontraßen'θjon] *nf*
contravention, violation.
contravendré [kontraßen'dre] *etc*,
contravenga [kontra'ßenga] *etc vb V*
contravenir.
contravenir [kontraße'nir] *vi*: **~ a** to

contravene, violate.

contraventana [kontraßen'tana] *nf* shutter.

contraviene [kontra'ßjene] *etc,* **contraviniendo** [kontraßi'njendo] *etc vb* V **contravenir.**

contrayendo [kontra'jendo] *vb* V **contraer.**

contribución [kontrißu'θjon] *nf (municipal etc)* tax; *(ayuda)* contribution; **exento de contribuciones** tax-free.

contribuir [kontrißu'ir] *vt, vi* to contribute; *(COM)* to pay (in taxes).

contribuyendo [kontrißu'jendo] *etc vb* V **contribuir.**

contribuyente [kontrißu'jente] *nm/f (COM)* taxpayer; *(que ayuda)* contributor.

contrincante [kontrin'kante] *nm* opponent, rival.

control [kon'trol] *nm* control; *(inspección)* inspection, check; *(COM):* ~ **de calidad** quality control; ~ **de cambios** exchange control; ~ **de costos** cost control; ~ **de créditos** credit control; ~ **de existencias** stock control; ~ **de precios** price control.

controlador, a [kontrola'ðor, a] *nm/f* controller; ~ **aéreo** air-traffic controller.

controlar [kontro'lar] *vt* to control; to inspect, check; *(COM)* to audit.

controversia [kontro'ßersja] *nf* controversy.

contubernio [kontu'ßernjo] *nm* ring, conspiracy.

contumaz [kontu'maθ] *adj* obstinate, stubbornly disobedient.

contundente [kontun'dente] *adj (prueba)* conclusive; *(fig: argumento)* convincing; **instrumento** ~ blunt instrument.

contusión [kontu'sjon] *nf* bruise.

contuve [kon'tuße] *etc vb* V **contener.**

convalecencia [kombale'θenθja] *nf* convalescence.

convalecer [kombale'θer] *vi* to convalesce, get better.

convaleciente [kombale'θjente] *adj, nm/f* convalescent.

convalezca [komba'leθka] *etc vb* V **convalecer.**

convalidar [kombali'ðar] *vt (título)* to recognize.

convencer [komben'θer] *vt* to convince; *(persuadir)* to persuade.

convencimiento [kombenθi'mjento] *nm (acción)* convincing; *(persuasión)* persuasion; *(certidumbre)* conviction; **tener el** ~ **de que ...** to be convinced that ... .

convención [komben'θjon] *nf* convention.

convencional [kombenθjo'nal] *adj* conventional.

convendré [komben'dre] *etc,* **convenga** [kom'benga] *etc vb* V **convenir.**

conveniencia [kombe'njenθja] *nf* suitability; *(conformidad)* agreement; *(utilidad, provecho)* usefulness; ~**s** *nfpl* conventions; *(COM)* property *sg;* **ser de la** ~ **de algn** to suit sb.

conveniente [kombe'njente] *adj* suitable; *(útil)* useful; *(correcto)* fit, proper; *(aconsejable)* advisable.

convenio [kom'benjo] *nm* agreement, treaty; ~ **de nivel crítico** threshold agreement.

convenir [kombe'nir] *vi (estar de acuerdo)* to agree; *(ser conveniente)* to suit, be suitable; **"sueldo a** ~**"** "salary to be agreed"; **conviene recordar que ...** it should be remembered that .... .

convento [kom'bento] *nm* monastery; *(de monjas)* convent.

convenza [kom'benθa] *etc vb* V **convencer.**

convergencia [komber'xenθja] *nf* convergence.

converger [komber'xer], **convergir** [komber'xir] *vi* to converge; **sus esfuerzos convergen a un fin común** their efforts are directed towards the same objective.

converja [kom'berxa] *etc vb* V **converger, convergir.**

conversación [kombersa'θjon] *nf* conversation.

conversar [komber'sar] *vi* to talk, converse.

conversión [komber'sjon] *nf* conversion.

converso, a [kom'berso, a] *nm/f* convert.

convertir [komber'tir] *vt* to convert; *(transformar)* to transform, turn; *(COM)* to (ex)change; ~**se** *vr (REL)* to convert.

convexo, a [kom'bekso, a] *adj* convex.

convicción [kombik'θjon] *nf* conviction.

convicto , a [kom'bikto, a] *adj* convicted; *(condenado)* condemned.

convidado, a [kombi'ðaðo, a] *nm/f* guest.

convidar [kombi'ðar] *vt* to invite.

conviene [kom'bjene] *etc vb* V **convenir.**

convierta [kom'bjerta] *etc vb* V **convertir.**

convincente [kombin'θente] *adj* convincing.

conviniendo [kombi'njendo] *etc vb* V **convenir.**

convirtiendo [kombir'tjendo] *etc vb* V **convertir.**

convite [kom'bite] *nm* invitation; *(banquete)* banquet.

convivencia [kombi'βenθja] *nf* coexistence, living together.

convivir [kombi'βir] *vi* to live together; (*POL*) to coexist.

convocar [kombo'kar] *vt* to summon, call (together).

convocatoria [komboka'torja] *nf* summons *sg*; (*anuncio*) notice of meeting; (*ESCOL*) examination session.

convoque [kom'boke] *etc vb V* **convocar**.

convoy [kom'boj] *nm* (*FERRO*) train.

convulsión [kombul'sjon] *nf* convulsion; (*POL etc*) upheaval.

conyugal [konju'βal] *adj* conjugal; **vida** ~ married life.

cónyuge ['konjuxe] *nm/f* spouse, partner.

coña ['koɲa] *nf*: **tomar algo a** ~ (*fam!*) to take sth as a joke.

coñac, *pl* **coñacs** ['koɲa(k), 'koɲas] *nm* cognac, brandy.

coñazo [ko'ɲaθo] *nm* (*fam*) pain; **dar el** ~ to be a real pain.

coño ['koɲo] (*fam!*) *nm* cunt (!); (*AM pey*) Spaniard ♦ *excl* (*enfado*) shit (!); (*sorpresa*) bloody hell (!); **¡qué** ~**!** what a pain in the arse (!).

cooperación [koopera'θjon] *nf* cooperation.

cooperar [koope'rar] *vi* to cooperate.

cooperativo, a [koopera'tiβo, a] *adj* cooperative ♦ *nf* cooperative.

coordenada [koorðe'naða] *nf* (*MAT*) coordinate; (*fig*): ~**s** *nfpl* guidelines, framework *sg*.

coordinación [koorðina'θjon] *nf* coordination.

coordinador, a [koorðina'ðor, a] *nm/f* coordinator ♦ *nf* coordinating committee.

coordinar [koorði'nar] *vt* to coordinate.

copa ['kopa] *nf* (*tb DEPORTE*) cup; (*vaso*) glass; (*de árbol*) top; (*de sombrero*) crown; ~**s** *nfpl* (*NAIPES*) *one of the suits in the Spanish card deck*; (**tomar una**) ~ (to have a) drink; **ir de** ~**s** to go out for a drink; *V tb* **Baraja Española**.

copar [ko'par] *vt* (*puestos*) to monopolize.

coparticipación [kopartiθipa'θjon] *nf* (*COM*) co-ownership.

COPE *nf abr* (= *Cadena de Ondas Populares Españolas*) *Spanish radio network*.

Copenhague [kope'naɣe] *n* Copenhagen.

copete [ko'pete] *nm* tuft (of hair); **de alto** ~ aristocratic, upper-crust (*fam*).

copia ['kopja] *nf* copy; (*ARTE*) replica; (*COM etc*) duplicate; (*INFORM*): ~ **impresa** hard copy; ~ **de respaldo** *o* **de seguridad** backup copy; **hacer** ~ **de seguridad** to

back up; ~ **de trabajo** working copy; ~ **vaciada** dump.

copiadora [kopja'ðora] *nf* photocopier; ~ **al alcohol** spirit duplicator.

copiar [ko'pjar] *vt* to copy; ~ **al pie de la letra** to copy word for word.

copiloto [kopi'loto] *nm* (*AVIAT*) co-pilot; (*AUTO*) co-driver.

copioso, a [ko'pjoso, a] *adj* copious, plentiful.

copita [ko'pita] *nf* (small) glass; (*GOLF*) tee.

copla ['kopla] *nf* verse; (*canción*) (popular) song.

copo ['kopo] *nm*: ~**s de maíz** cornflakes; ~ **de nieve** snowflake.

coprocesador [koproθesa'ðor] *nm* (*INFORM*) co-processor.

coproducción [koproðuk'θjon] *nf* (*CINE etc*) joint production.

copropietarios [kopropje'tarjos] *nmpl* (*COM*) joint owners.

cópula ['kopula] *nf* copulation.

copular [kopu'lar] *vi* to copulate.

coqueta [ko'keta] *adj* flirtatious, coquettish ♦ *nf* (*mujer*) flirt.

coquetear [kokete'ar] *vi* to flirt.

coraje [ko'raxe] *nm* courage; (*ánimo*) spirit; (*ira*) anger.

coral [ko'ral] *adj* choral ♦ *nf* choir ♦ *nm* (*ZOOL*) coral.

Corán [ko'ran] *nm*: **el** ~ the Koran.

coraza [ko'raθa] *nf* (*armadura*) armour; (*blindaje*) armour-plating.

corazón [kora'θon] *nm* heart; (*BOT*) core; **corazones** *nmpl* (*NAIPES*) hearts; **de buen** ~ kind-hearted; **de todo** ~ wholeheartedly; **estar mal del** ~ to have heart trouble.

corazonada [koraθo'naða] *nf* impulse; (*presentimiento*) presentiment, hunch.

corbata [kor'βata] *nf* tie.

corbeta [kor'βeta] *nf* corvette.

Córcega ['korθeɣa] *nf* Corsica.

corcel [kor'θel] *nm* steed.

corchea [kor't∫ea] *nf* quaver.

corchete [kor't∫ete] *nm* catch, clasp; ~**s** *nmpl* (*TIP*) square brackets.

corcho [kor't∫o] *nm* cork; (*PESCA*) float.

corcovado, a [korko'βaðo, a] *adj* hunchbacked ♦ *nm/f* hunchback.

cordel [kor'ðel] *nm* cord, line.

cordero [kor'ðero] *nm* lamb; (*piel*) lambskin.

cordial [kor'ðjal] *adj* cordial ♦ *nm* cordial, tonic.

cordialidad [korðjali'ðað] *nf* warmth, cordiality.

cordillera [korði'ʎera] _nf_ range (of mountains).

Córdoba ['korðoßa] _nf_ Cordova.

cordobés, esa [korðo'ßes, esa] _adj, nm/f_ Cordovan.

cordón [kor'ðon] _nm_ (_cuerda_) cord, string; (_de zapatos_) lace; (_ELEC_) flex, wire (_US_); (_MIL etc_) cordon.

cordura [kor'ðura] _nf_ (_MED_) sanity; (_fig_) good sense.

Corea [ko'rea] _nf_ Korea; ~ **del Norte/Sur** North/South Korea.

coreano, a [kore'ano, a] _adj, nm/f_ Korean.

corear [kore'ar] _vt_ to chorus.

coreografía [koreoɣra'fia] _nf_ choreography.

corista [ko'rista] _nf_ (_TEAT etc_) chorus girl.

cornada [kor'naða] _nf_ (_TAUR etc_) butt, goring.

córner, _pl_ **córners** ['korner, 'korners] _nm_ corner (kick).

corneta [kor'neta] _nf_ bugle.

Cornualles [kor'nwaʎes] _nm_ Cornwall.

cornudo, a [kor'nuðo, a] _adj_ (_ZOOL_) horned; (_marido_) cuckolded.

coro ['koro] _nm_ chorus; (_conjunto de cantores_) choir.

corolario [koro'larjo] _nm_ corollary.

corona [ko'rona] _nf_ crown; (_de flores_) garland.

coronación [korona'θjon] _nf_ coronation.

coronar [koro'nar] _vt_ to crown.

coronel [koro'nel] _nm_ colonel.

coronilla [koro'niʎa] _nf_ (_ANAT_) crown (of the head); **estar hasta la** ~ **(de)** to be utterly fed up (with).

corpiño [korpiɲo] _nm_ bodice; (_AM: sostén_) bra.

corporación [korpora'θjon] _nf_ corporation.

corporal [korpo'ral] _adj_ corporal, bodily.

corporativo, a [korpora'tißo, a] _adj_ corporate.

corpulento, a [korpu'lento, a] _adj_ well-built.

corral [ko'rral] _nm_ (_patio_) farmyard; (_AGR: de aves_) poultry yard; (_redil_) pen.

correa [ko'rrea] _nf_ strap; (_cinturón_) belt; (_de perro_) lead, leash; ~ **transportadora** conveyor belt.

correaje [korre'axe] _nm_ (_AGR_) harness.

corrección [korrek'θjon] _nf_ correction; (_reprensión_) rebuke; (_cortesía_) good manners; (_INFORM_): ~ **por líneas** line editing; ~ **en pantalla** screen editing; ~ **(de pruebas)** (_TIP_) proofreading.

correccional [korrekθjo'nal] _nm_ reformatory.

correcto, a [ko'rrekto, a] _adj_ correct; (_persona_) well-mannered.

corrector, a [korrek'tor, a] _nm/f_: ~ **de pruebas** proofreader.

corredera [korre'ðera] _nf_: **puerta de** ~ sliding door.

corredizo, a [korre'ðiθo, a] _adj_ (_puerta etc_) sliding; (_nudo_) running.

corredor, a [korre'ðor, a] _adj_ running; (_rápido_) fast ♦ _nm/f_ (_DEPORTE_) runner ♦ _nm_ (_pasillo_) corridor; (_balcón corrido_) gallery; (_COM_) agent, broker; (_pasillo_) corridor, passage; ~ **de bienes raíces** real-estate broker; ~ **de bolsa** stockbroker; ~ **de seguros** insurance broker.

corregir [korre'xir] _vt_ (_error_) to correct; (_amonestar, reprender_) to rebuke, reprimand; ~**se** _vr_ to reform.

correo [ko'rreo] _nm_ post, mail; (_persona_) courier; **C~s** _nmpl_ Post Office _sg_; ~ **aéreo** airmail; ~ **basura** (_por carta_) junk mail; (_por Internet_) spam; ~ **certificado** registered mail; ~ **electrónico** e-mail, electronic mail; ~ **urgente** special delivery; **a vuelta de** ~ by return (of post).

correr [ko'rrer] _vt_ to run; (_viajar_) to cover, travel; (_riesgo_) to run; (_aventura_) to have; (_cortinas_) to draw; (_cerrojo_) to shoot ♦ _vi_ to run; (_líquido_) to run, flow; (_rumor_) to go round; ~**se** _vr_ to slide, move; (_colores_) to run; (_fam: tener orgasmo_) to come; **echar a** ~ to break into a run; ~ **con los gastos** to pay the expenses; **eso corre de mi cuenta** I'll take care of that.

correspondencia [korrespon'denθja] _nf_ correspondence; (_FERRO_) connection; (_reciprocidad_) return; ~ **directa** (_COM_) direct mail.

corresponder [korrespon'der] _vi_ to correspond; (_convenir_) to be suitable; (_pertenecer_) to belong; (_tocar_) to concern; (_favor_) to repay; ~**se** _vr_ (_por escrito_) to correspond; (_amarse_) to love one another; "**a quien corresponda**" "to whom it may concern".

correspondiente [korrespon'djente] _adj_ corresponding; (_respectivo_) respective.

corresponsal [korrespon'sal] _nm/f_ (newspaper) correspondent; (_COM_) agent.

corretaje [korre'taxe] _nm_ (_COM_) brokerage.

corretear [korrete'ar] _vi_ to loiter.

corrido, a [ko'rriðo, a] _adj_ (_avergonzado_) abashed; (_fluido_) fluent ♦ _nf_ run, dash; (_de toros_) bullfight; **de** ~ fluently; **3 noches corridas** 3 nights running; **un kilo** ~ a good kilo.

corriente [ko'rrjente] _adj_ (_agua_) running;

(*fig*) flowing; (*dinero, cuenta etc*) current; (*común*) ordinary, normal ♦ *nf* current; (*fig: tendencia*) course ♦ *nm* current month; ~ *f* **de aire** draught; ~ **eléctrica** electric current; **las ~s modernas del arte** modern trends in art; **estar al ~ de** to be informed about.

corrigiendo [korri'xjendo] *etc vb V* **corregir.**

corrija [ko'rrixa] *etc vb V* **corregir.**

corrillo [ko'rriʎo] *nm* ring, circle (of people); (*fig*) clique.

corro ['korro] *nm* ring, circle (of people); (*baile*) ring-a-ring-a-roses; **la gente hizo** ~ the people formed a ring.

corroborar [korroβo'rar] *vt* to corroborate.

corroer [korro'er] *vt* (*tb fig*) to corrode, eat away; (*GEO*) to erode.

corromper [korrom'per] *vt* (*madera*) to rot; (*fig*) to corrupt.

corrompido, a [korrom'piðo, a] *adj* corrupt.

corrosivo, a [korro'siβo, a] *adj* corrosive.

corroyendo [korro'jendo] *etc vb V* **corroer.**

corrupción [korrup'θjon] *nf* rot, decay; (*fig*) corruption.

corrupto, a [ko'rrupto, a] *adj* corrupt.

corsario [kor'sarjo] *nm* privateer, corsair.

corsé [kor'se] *nm* corset.

corso, a ['korso, a] *adj, nm/f* Corsican.

cortacésped [korta'θespeð] *nm* lawn mower.

cortado, a [kor'taðo, a] *adj* (*con cuchillo*) cut; (*leche*) sour; (*confuso*) confused; (*desconcertado*) embarrassed; (*tímido*) shy ♦ *nm* white coffee (with a little milk).

cortadora [korta'ðora] *nf* cutter, slicer.

cortadura [korta'ðura] *nf* cut.

cortante [kor'tante] *adj* (*viento*) biting; (*frío*) bitter.

cortapisa [korta'pisa] *nf* (*restricción*) restriction; (*traba*) snag.

cortar [kor'tar] *vt* to cut; (*suministro*) to cut off; (*un pasaje*) to cut out; (*comunicación, teléfono*) to cut off ♦ *vi* to cut; (*AM TELEC*) to hang up; ~**se** *vr* (*turbarse*) to become embarrassed; (*leche*) to turn, curdle; **por lo sano** to settle things once and for all; ~**se el pelo** to have one's hair cut; **se cortó la línea** *o* **el teléfono** I got cut off.

cortauñas [korta'uɲas] *nm inv* nail clippers *pl*.

corte ['korte] *nm* cut, cutting; (*filo*) edge; (*de tela*) piece, length; (*COSTURA*) tailoring ♦ *nf* (*real*) (royal) court; ~ **y confección** dressmaking; ~ **de corriente** *o* **luz** power cut; ~ **de pelo** haircut; **me**

da ~ **pedírselo** I'm embarrassed to ask him for it; **¡qué** ~ **le di!** I left him with no comeback!; **C~ Internacional de Justicia** International Court of Justice; **las C~s** the Spanish Parliament *sg*; **hacer la** ~ **a** to woo, court; *see boxed note.*

LAS CORTES

The Spanish Parliament, **las Cortes (Españolas),** *has a lower and an upper chamber, the "Congreso de los Diputados" and the "Senado" respectively. Members of the lower house are called "diputados" and are chosen in general elections by a system of proportional representation. Some Senate members, "senadores", are voted in during general elections, while others are appointed by the regional parliaments.*

---

cortejar [korte'xar] *vt* to court.

cortejo [kor'texo] *nm* entourage; ~ **fúnebre** funeral procession, cortège.

cortés [kor'tes] *adj* courteous, polite.

cortesano, a [korte'sano, a] *adj* courtly.

cortesía [korte'sia] *nf* courtesy.

corteza [kor'teθa] *nf* (*de árbol*) bark; (*de pan*) crust; (*de fruta*) peel, skin; (*de queso*) rind.

cortijo [kor'tixo] *nm* farmhouse.

cortina [kor'tina] *nf* curtain; ~ **de humo** smoke screen.

corto, a ['korto, a] *adj* (*breve*) short; (*tímido*) bashful; ~ **de luces** not very bright; ~ **de oído** hard of hearing; ~ **de vista** short-sighted; **estar** ~ **de fondos** to be short of funds.

cortocircuito [kortoθir'kwito] *nm* short-circuit.

cortometraje [kortome'traxe] *nm* (*CINE*) short.

Coruña [ko'ruɲa] *nf*: **La** ~ Corunna.

coruñés, esa [koru'ɲes, esa] *adj* of *o* from Corunna ♦ *nm/f* native *o* inhabitant of Corunna.

corvo, a ['korβo, a] *adj* curved; (*nariz*) hooked ♦ *nf* back of knee.

cosa ['kosa] *nf* thing; (*asunto*) affair; ~ **de** about; **eso es** ~ **mía** that's my business; **es poca** ~ it's not important; **¡qué** ~ **más rara!** how strange.

cosaco, a [ko'sako, a] *adj, nm/f* Cossack.

coscorrón [kosko'rron] *nm* bump on the head.

cosecha [ko'setʃa] *nf* (*AGR*) harvest; (*acto*) harvesting; (*de vino*) vintage; (*producción*) yield.

cosechadora [koseʧa'ðora] nf combine harvester.

cosechar [kose'tʃar] vt to harvest, gather (in).

coser [ko'ser] vt to sew; (MED) to stitch (up).

cosido [ko'siðo] nm sewing.

cosmético, a [kos'metiko, a] adj, nm cosmetic ♦ nf cosmetics pl.

cosmopolita [kosmopo'lita] adj cosmopolitan.

cosmos ['kosmos] nm cosmos.

coso ['koso] nm bullring.

cosquillas [kos'kiʎas] nfpl: **hacer ~** to tickle; **tener ~** to be ticklish.

cosquilleo [koski'ʎeo] nm tickling (sensation).

costa ['kosta] nf (GEO) coast; **C~ Brava** Costa Brava; **C~ Cantábrica** Cantabrian Coast; **C~ de Marfil** Ivory Coast; **C~ del Sol** Costa del Sol; **a ~** (COM) at cost; **a ~ de** at the expense of; **a toda ~** at any price.

costado [kos'taðo] nm side; **de ~** (dormir) on one's side; **español por los 4 ~s** Spanish through and through.

costal [kos'tal] nm sack.

costalada [kosta'laða] nf bad fall.

costanera [kosta'nera] nf (AM) (seaside) promenade.

costar [kos'tar] vt (valer) to cost; **me cuesta hablarle** I find it hard to talk to him; **¿cuánto cuesta?** how much does it cost?

Costa Rica [kosta'rika] nf Costa Rica.

costarricense [kostarri'θense], **costarriqueño, a** [kostarri'keɲo, a] adj, nm/f Costa Rican.

coste ['koste] nm (COM): **~ promedio** average cost; **~s fijos** fixed costs; V tb **costo**.

costear [koste'ar] vt to pay for; (COM etc) to finance; (NAUT) to sail along the coast of; **~se** vr (negocio) to pay for itself, cover its costs.

costeño, a [kos'teɲo, a] adj coastal.

costero, a [kos'tero, a] adj coastal, coast cpd.

costilla [kos'tiʎa] nf rib; (CULIN) cutlet.

costo ['kosto] nm cost, price; **~ directo** direct cost; **~ de expedición** shipping charges; **~ de sustitución** replacement cost; **~ unitario** unit cost; **~ de la vida** cost of living.

costoso, a [kos'toso, a] adj costly, expensive.

costra ['kostra] nf (corteza) crust; (MED) scab.

costumbre [kos'tumbre] nf custom, habit;

como de ~ as usual.

costura [kos'tura] nf sewing, needlework; (confección) dressmaking; (zurcido) seam.

costurera [kostu'rera] nf dressmaker.

costurero [kostu'rero] nm sewing box o case.

cota ['kota] nf (GEO) height above sea level; (fig) height.

cotarro [ko'tarro] nm: **dirigir el ~** (fam) to rule the roost.

cotejar [kote'xar] vt to compare.

cotejo [ko'texo] nm comparison.

cotice [ko'tiθe] etc vb V **cotizar**.

cotidiano, a [koti'ðjano, a] adj daily, day to day.

cotilla [ko'tiʎa] nf busybody, gossip.

cotillear [kotiʎe'ar] vi to gossip.

cotilleo [koti'ʎeo] nm gossip(ing).

cotización [kotiθa'θjon] nf (COM) quotation, price; (de club) dues pl.

cotizado, a [koti'θaðo, a] adj (fig) highly-prized.

cotizar [koti'θar] vt (COM) to quote, price; **~se** vr (fig) to be highly prized; **~se a** to sell at, fetch; (BOLSA) to stand at, be quoted at.

coto ['koto] nm (terreno cercado) enclosure; (de caza) reserve; (COM) price-fixing agreement; **poner ~ a** to put a stop to.

cotorra [ko'torra] nf (ZOOL: loro) parrot; (fam: persona) windbag.

COU [kou] nm abr (ESP: = Curso de Orientación Universitario) one year course leading to final school leaving certificate and university entrance examinations; V tb **sistema educativo**.

coyote [ko'jote] nm coyote, prairie wolf.

coyuntura [kojun'tura] nf (ANAT) joint; (fig) juncture, occasion; **esperar una ~ favorable** to await a favourable moment.

coz [koθ] nf kick.

CP nm abr (= computador personal) PC.

C.P. abr (ESP) = **Caja Postal**.

C.P.A. nf abr (= Caja Postal de Ahorros) Post Office Savings Bank.

CP/M nm abr (= Programa de control para microprocesadores) CP/M.

CPN nm abr (ESP) = **Cuerpo de la Policía Nacional**.

cps abr (= caracteres por segundo) c.p.s.

crac [krak] nm (ECON) crash.

cráneo ['kraneo] nm skull, cranium.

crápula ['krapula] nf drunkenness.

cráter ['krater] nm crater.

creación [krea'θjon] nf creation.

creador, a [krea'ðor, a] adj creative ♦ nm/f creator.

crear [kre'ar] *vt* to create, make; (*originar*) to originate; (*INFORM: archivo*) to create; ~**se** *vr* (*comité etc*) to be set up.

creativo, a [krea'tißo, a] *adj* creative.

crecer [kre'θer] *vi* to grow; (*precio*) to rise; ~**se** *vr* (*engreírse*) to get cocky.

creces ['kreθes]: **con** ~ *adv* amply, fully.

crecido, a [kre'θiðo, a] *adj* (*persona, planta*) full-grown; (*cantidad*) large ♦ *nf* (*de río*) spate, flood.

creciente [kre'θjente] *adj* growing; (*cantidad*) increasing; (*luna*) crescent ♦ *nm* crescent.

crecimiento [kreθi'mjento] *nm* growth; (*aumento*) increase; (*COM*) rise.

credenciales [kreðen'θjales] *nfpl* credentials.

crédito ['kreðito] *nm* credit; **a** ~ on credit; **dar** ~ **a** to believe (in); ~ **al consumidor** consumer credit; ~ **rotativo** *o* **renovable** revolving credit.

credo ['kreðo] *nm* creed.

crédulo, a ['kreðulo, a] *adj* credulous.

creencia [kre'enθja] *nf* belief.

creer [kre'er] *vt, vi* to think, believe; (*considerar*) to think, consider; ~**se** *vr* to believe o.s. (to be); ~ **en** to believe in; **¡ya lo creo!** I should think so!

creíble [kre'ißle] *adj* credible, believable.

creído, a [kre'iðo, a] *adj* (*engreído*) conceited.

crema ['krema] *adj inv* cream (coloured) ♦ *nf* cream; (*natillas*) custard; **la** ~ **de la sociedad** the cream of society.

cremallera [krema'ʎera] *nf* zip (fastener) (*BRIT*), zipper (*US*).

crematorio [krema'torjo] *nm* crematorium (*BRIT*), crematory (*US*).

cremoso, a [kre'moso, a] *adj* creamy.

crepitar [krepi'tar] *vi* (*fuego*) to crackle.

crepúsculo [kre'puskulo] *nm* twilight, dusk.

crespo, a ['krespo, a] *adj* (*pelo*) curly.

crespón [kres'pon] *nm* crêpe.

cresta ['kresta] *nf* (*GEO, ZOOL*) crest.

Creta ['kreta] *nf* Crete.

cretino, a [kre'tino, a] *adj* cretinous ♦ *nmf* cretin.

creyendo [kre'jendo] *etc vb V* **creer**.

creyente [kre'jente] *nmf* believer.

crezca ['kreθka] *etc vb V* **crecer**.

cría ['kria] *etc vb V* **criar** ♦ *nf V* **crío, a**.

criada [kri'aða] *nf V* **criado, a**.

criadero [kria'ðero] *nm* nursery; (*ZOOL*) breeding place.

criadillas [kria'ðiʎas] *nfpl* (*CULIN*) bull's (*o* sheep's) testicles.

criado, a [kri'aðo, a] *nm* servant ♦ *nf* servant, maid.

criador [kria'ðor] *nm* breeder.

crianza [kri'anθa] *nf* rearing, breeding; (*fig*) breeding; (*MED*) lactation.

criar [kri'ar] *vt* (*amamantar*) to suckle, feed; (*educar*) to bring up; (*producir*) to grow, produce; (*animales*) to breed; ~**se** *vr* to grow (up); ~ **cuervos** to nourish a viper in one's bosom; **Dios los cría y ellos se juntan** birds of a feather flock together.

criatura [kria'tura] *nf* creature; (*niño*) baby, (small) child.

criba ['krißa] *nf* sieve.

cribar [kri'ßar] *vt* to sieve.

crimen ['krimen] *nm* crime; ~ **pasional** crime of passion.

criminal [krimi'nal] *adj, nmf* criminal.

crin [krin] *nf* (*tb*: ~**es**) mane.

crío, a ['krio, a] *nm/f* (*fam: chico*) kid ♦ *nf* (*de animales*) rearing, breeding; (*animal*) young.

criollo, a [kri'oʎo, a] *adj* (*gen*) Creole; (*AM*) native (to America), national ♦ *nm/f* (*gen*) Creole; (*AM*) native American.

cripta ['kripta] *nf* crypt.

crisis ['krisis] *nf inv* crisis; ~ **nerviosa** nervous breakdown.

crisma ['krisma] *nf*: **romperle la** ~ **a algn** (*fam*) to knock sb's block off.

crisol [kri'sol] *nm* (*TEC*) crucible; (*fig*) melting pot.

crispación [krispa'θjon] *nf* tension.

crispar [kris'par] *vt* (*músculo*) to cause to contract; (*nervios*) to set on edge.

cristal [kris'tal] *nm* crystal; (*de ventana*) glass, pane; (*lente*) lens; **de** ~ glass *cpd*; ~ **ahumado/tallado** smoked/cut glass.

cristalería [kristale'ria] *nf* (*tienda*) glassware shop; (*objetos*) glassware.

cristalice [krista'liθe] *etc vb V* **cristalizar**.

cristalino, a [krista'lino, a] *adj* crystalline; (*fig*) clear ♦ *nm* lens of the eye.

cristalizar [kristali'θar] *vt, vi* to crystallize.

cristiandad [kristjan'daθ] *nf*, **cristianismo** [kristja'nismo] *nm* Christianity.

cristiano, a [kris'tjano, a] *adj, nmf* Christian; **hablar en** ~ to speak proper Spanish; (*fig*) to speak clearly.

Cristo ['kristo] *nm* (*dios*) Christ; (*crucifijo*) crucifix.

Cristóbal [kris'toßal] *nm*: ~ **Colón** Christopher Columbus.

criterio [kri'terjo] *nm* criterion; (*juicio*) judgement; (*enfoque*) attitude, approach; (*punto de vista*) view, opinion; ~ **de clasificación** (*INFORM*) sort criterion.

criticar [kriti'kar] *vt* to criticize.

crítico, a ['kritiko, a] adj critical ♦ nm critic ♦ nf criticism; (TEAT etc) review, notice; **la crítica** the critics pl.

critique [kri'tike] etc vb V **criticar**.

Croacia [kro'aθja] nf Croatia.

croar [kro'ar] vi to croak.

croata [kro'ata] adj, nmf Croat(ian) ♦ nm (LING) Croat(ian).

croissan(t) [krwa'san] nm croissant.

crol ['krol] nm crawl.

cromado [kro'maðo] nm chromium plating, chrome.

cromo ['kromo] nm chrome; (TIP) coloured print.

cromosoma [kromo'soma] nm chromosome.

crónico, a ['kroniko, a] adj chronic ♦ nf chronicle, account; (de periódico) feature, article.

cronología [kronolo'xia] nf chronology.

cronológico, a [krono'loxiko, a] adj chronological.

cronometraje [kronome'traxe] nm timing.

cronometrar [kronome'trar] vt to time.

cronómetro [kro'nometro] nm (DEPORTE) stopwatch; (TEC etc) chronometer.

croqueta [kro'keta] nf croquette, rissole.

croquis ['krokis] nm inv sketch.

cruce ['kruθe] etc vb V **cruzar** ♦ nm crossing; (de carreteras) crossroads; (AUTO etc) junction, intersection; (BIO: proceso) crossbreeding; **luces de ~** dipped headlights.

crucero [kru'θero] nm (NAUT: barco) cruise ship; (: viaje) cruise.

crucial [kru'θjal] adj crucial.

crucificar [kruθifi'kar] vt to crucify; (fig) to torment.

crucifijo [kruθi'fixo] nm crucifix.

crucifique [kruθi'fike] etc vb V **crucificar**.

crucigrama [kruθi'ɣrama] nm crossword (puzzle).

crudeza [kru'ðeθa] nf (rigor) harshness; (aspereza) crudeness.

crudo, a ['kruðo, a] adj raw; (no maduro) unripe; (petróleo) crude; (rudo, cruel) cruel; (agua) hard; (clima etc) harsh ♦ nm crude (oil).

cruel [krwel] adj cruel.

crueldad [krwel'ðað] nf cruelty.

cruento, a ['krwento, a] adj bloody.

crujido [kru'xiðo] nm (de madera etc) creak.

crujiente [kru'xjente] adj (galleta etc) crunchy.

crujir [kru'xir] vi (madera etc) to creak; (dedos) to crack; (dientes) to grind; (nieve, arena) to crunch.

cruz [kruθ] nf cross; (de moneda) tails sg; (fig) burden; ~ **gamada** swastika; **C~ Roja** Red Cross.

cruzado, a [kru'θaðo, a] adj crossed ♦ nm crusader ♦ nf crusade.

cruzar [kru'θar] vt to cross; (palabras) to exchange; ~**se** vr (líneas etc) to cross, intersect; (personas) to pass each other; ~**se de brazos** to fold one's arms; (fig) not to lift a finger to help; ~**se con algn en la calle** to pass sb in the street.

c.s.f. abr (= costo, seguro y flete) c.i.f.

CSIC [θe'sik] nm abr (ESP ESCOL) = Consejo Superior de Investigaciones Científicas.

cta, c.ta nf abr (= cuenta) a/c.

cta. cto. abr (= carta de crédito) L.C.

cte. abr (= corriente, de los corrientes) inst.

CTNE nf abr (TELEC) = Compañía Telefónica Nacional de España.

c/u abr (= cada uno) ea.

cuaco ['kwako] nm (AM) nag.

cuaderno [kwa'ðerno] nm notebook; (de escuela) exercise book; (NAUT) logbook.

cuadra ['kwaðra] nf (caballeriza) stable; (AM) (city) block.

cuadrado, a [kwa'ðraðo, a] adj square ♦ nm (MAT) square.

cuadragésimo, a [kwaðra'xesimo, a] num fortieth.

cuadrángulo [kwa'ðrangulo, a] nm quadrangle.

cuadrante [kwa'ðrante] nm quadrant.

cuadrar [kwa'ðrar] vt to square; (TIP) to justify ♦ vi: ~ **con** (cuenta) to square with, tally with; ~**se** vr (soldado) to stand to attention; ~ **por la derecha/izquierda** to right-/left-justify.

cuadrícula [kwa'ðrikula] nf (TIP etc) grid, ruled squares.

cuadriculado, a [kwaðriku'laðo, a] adj: **papel** ~ squared o graph paper.

cuadrilátero [kwaðri'latero] nm (DEPORTE) boxing ring; (GEOM) quadrilateral.

cuadrilla [kwa'ðriʎa] nf (amigos) party, group; (pandilla) gang; (obreros) team.

cuadro ['kwaðro] nm square; (PINTURA) painting; (TEAT) scene; (diagrama: tb: ~ **sinóptico**) chart, table, diagram; (DEPORTE, MED) team; (POL) executive; ~ **de mandos** control panel; **a ~s** check cpd.

cuadruplicarse [kwaðrupli'karse] vr to quadruple.

cuádruplo, a ['kwaðruplo, a], **cuádruple** ['kwaðruple] adj quadruple.

cuajado, a [kwa'xaðo, a] adj: ~ **de** (fig) full of ♦ nf (de leche) curd.

cuajar [kwa'xar] vt to thicken; (leche) to curdle; (sangre) to congeal; (adornar) to adorn; (*CULIN*) to set ♦ *vi* (*nieve*) to lie; (*fig*) to become set, become established; (*idea*) to be received, be acceptable; **~se** *vr* to curdle; to congeal; (*llenarse*) to fill up.

cuajo ['kwaxo] *nm*: **arrancar algo de ~** to tear sth out by its roots.

cual [kwal] *adv* like, as ♦ *pron*: **el ~** *etc* which; (*persona: sujeto*) who; (: *objeto*) whom; **lo ~** (*relativo*) which; **allá cada ~** every man to his own taste; **son a ~ más gandul** each is as idle as the other; **cada ~** each one ♦ *adj* such as; **tal ~** just as it is.

cuál [kwal] *pron interrogativo* which (one), what.

cualesquier(a) [kwales'kjer(a)] *pl de* **cualquier(a)**.

cualidad [kwali'ðað] *nf* quality.

cualificado, a [kwalifi'kaðo, a] *adj* (*obrero*) skilled, qualified.

cualquiera [kwal'kjera], **cualquier** [kwal'kjer], *pl* **cualesquier(a)** *adj* any ♦ *pron* anybody, anyone; (*quienquiera*) whoever; **en cualquier momento** any time; **en cualquier parte** anywhere; **cualquiera que sea** whichever it is; (*persona*) whoever it is.

cuán [kwan] *adv* how.

cuando ['kwando] *adv* when; (*aún sí*) if, even if ♦ *conj* (*puesto que*) since ♦ *prep*: **yo, ~ niño ...** when I was a child *o* as a child I ...; **~ no sea así** even if it is not so; **~ más** at (the) most; **~ menos** at least; **~ no** if not, otherwise; **de ~ en ~** from time to time; **ven ~ quieras** come when(ever) you like.

cuándo ['kwando] *adv* when; **¿desde ~?**, **¿de ~ acá?** since when?

cuantía [kwan'tia] *nf* (*alcance*) extent; (*importancia*) importance.

cuantioso, a [kwan'tjoso, a] *adj* substantial.

===================== *PALABRA CLAVE*

cuanto, a ['kwanto, a] *adj* **1** (*todo*): **tiene todo ~ desea** he's got everything he wants; **le daremos ~s ejemplares necesite** we'll give him as many copies as *o* all the copies he needs; **~s hombres la ven** all the men who see her

2: *unos* **~s**: **había unos ~s periodistas** there were (quite) a few journalists

3 (+*más*): **~ más vino bebas peor te sentirás** the more wine you drink the worse you'll feel; **~s más, mejor** the more the merrier

♦ *pron*: **tiene ~ desea** he has everything he wants; **tome ~/~s quiera** take as much/many as you want

♦ *adv*: **en ~**: **en ~ profesor** as a teacher; **en ~ a mí** as for me; *V tb* **antes**

♦ *conj* **1**: **~ más gana menos gasta** the more he earns the less he spends; **~ más joven se es más se es confiado** the younger you are the more trusting you are

2: **en ~**: **en ~ llegue/llegué** as soon as I arrive/arrived.

cuánto, a ['kwanto, a] *adj* (*exclamación*) what a lot of; (*interrogativo: sg*) how much?; (: *pl*) how many? ♦ *pron, adv* how; (*interrogativo: sg*) how much?; (: *pl*) how many? ♦ *excl*: **¡~ me alegro!** I'm so glad!; **¡cuánta gente!** what a lot of people!; **¿~ tiempo?** how long?; **¿~ cuesta?** how much does it cost?; **¿a ~s estamos?** what's the date?; **¿~ hay de aquí a Bilbao?** how far is it from here to Bilbao?; **Señor no sé ~s** Mr. So-and-So.

cuarenta [kwa'renta] *num* forty.

cuarentena [kwaren'tena] *nf* (*MED etc*) quarantine; (*conjunto*) forty(-odd).

cuarentón, ona [kwaren'ton, ona] *adj* forty-year-old, fortyish ♦ *nm/f* person of about forty.

cuaresma [kwa'resma] *nf* Lent.

cuarta ['kwarta] *nf V* **cuarto**.

cuartear [kwarte'ar] *vt* to quarter; (*dividir*) to divide up; **~se** *vr* to crack, split.

cuartel [kwar'tel] *nm* (*de ciudad*) quarter, district; (*MIL*) barracks *pl*; **~ general** headquarters *pl*.

cuartelazo [kwarte'laθo] *nm* coup, military uprising.

cuarteto [kwar'teto] *nm* quartet.

cuartilla [kwar'tiʎa] *nf* (*hoja*) sheet (of paper); **~s** *nfpl* (*TIP*) copy *sg*.

cuarto, a ['kwarto, a] *adj* fourth ♦ *nm* (*MAT*) quarter, fourth; (*habitación*) room ♦ *nf* (*MAT*) quarter, fourth; (*palmo*) span; **~ de baño** bathroom; **~ de estar** living room; **~ de hora** quarter (of an) hour; **~ de kilo** quarter kilo; **no tener un ~** to be broke (*fam*).

cuarzo ['kwarθo] *nm* quartz.

cuatrero [kwa'trero] *nm* (*AM*) rustler, stock thief.

cuatrimestre [kwatri'mestre] *nm* four-month period.

cuatro ['kwatro] *num* four; **las ~** four o'clock; **el ~ de octubre** (on) the fourth of October; *V tb* **seis**.

cuatrocientos, as [kwatro'θjentos, as] *num* four hundred; *V tb* **seiscientos**.

Cuba ['kuβa] *nf* Cuba.

cuba ['kuβa] *nf* cask, barrel; **estar como una ~** (*fam*) to be sloshed.

cubalibre [kuβa'liβre] *nm* (white) rum and coke ®.

cubano, a [ku'βano, a] *adj, nm/f* Cuban.

cubata [ku'βata] *nm* = **cubalibre**.

cubertería [kuβerte'ria] *nf* cutlery.

cúbico, a ['kuβiko, a] *adj* cubic.

cubierto, a [ku'βjerto, a] *pp de* **cubrir ♦** *adj* covered; (*cielo*) overcast **♦** *nm* cover; (*en la mesa*) place **♦** *nf* cover, covering; (*neumático*) tyre; (*NAUT*) deck; **~s** *nmpl* cutlery *sg*; **a ~ de** covered with *o* in; **precio del ~** cover charge.

cubil [ku'βil] *nm* den.

cubilete [kuβi'lete] *nm* (*en juegos*) cup.

cubito [ku'βito] *nm:* **~ de hielo** ice cube.

cubo ['kuβo] *nm* cube; (*balde*) bucket, tub; (*TEC*) drum; **~ de (la) basura** dustbin.

cubrecama [kuβre'kama] *nm* bedspread.

cubrir [ku'βrir] *vt* to cover; (*vacante*) to fill; (*BIO*) to mate with; (*gastos*) to meet; **~se** *vr* (*cielo*) to become overcast; (*COM: gastos*) to be met *o* paid; (: *deuda*) to be covered; **~ las formas** to keep up appearances; **lo cubrieron las aguas** the waters closed over it; **el agua casi me cubría** I was almost out of my depth.

cucaracha [kuka'ratʃa] *nf* cockroach.

cuchara [ku'tʃara] *nf* spoon; (*TEC*) scoop.

cucharada [kutʃa'raða] *nf* spoonful; **~ colmada** heaped spoonful.

cucharadita [kutʃara'ðita] *nf* teaspoonful.

cucharilla [kutʃa'riʎa] *nf* teaspoon.

cucharita [kutʃa'rita] *nf* teaspoon.

cucharón [kutʃa'ron] *nm* ladle.

cuchichear [kutʃitʃe'ar] *vi* to whisper.

cuchicheo [kutʃi'tʃeo] *nm* whispering.

cuchilla [ku'tʃiʎa] *nf* (large) knife; (*de arma blanca*) blade; **~ de afeitar** razor blade; **pasar a ~** to put to the sword.

cuchillada [kutʃi'ʎaða] *nf* (*golpe*) stab; (*herida*) knife *o* stab wound.

cuchillo [ku'tʃiʎo] *nm* knife.

cuchitril [kutʃi'tril] *nm* hovel; (*habitación etc*) pigsty.

cuclillas [ku'kliʎas] *nfpl:* **en ~** squatting.

cuco, a ['kuko, a] *adj* pretty; (*astuto*) sharp **♦** *nm* cuckoo.

cucurucho [kuku'rutʃo] *nm* paper cone, cornet.

cuece ['kweθe] *etc vb V* **cocer**.

cuele ['kwele] *etc vb V* **colar**.

cuelgue ['kwelɣe] *etc vb V* **colgar**.

cuello ['kweʎo] *nm* (*ANAT*) neck; (*de vestido, camisa*) collar.

cuenca ['kwenka] *nf* (*ANAT*) eye socket; (*GEO: valle*) bowl, deep valley; (: *fluvial*) basin.

cuenco ['kwenko] *nm* (earthenware) bowl.

cuenta ['kwenta] *etc vb V* **contar ♦** *nf* (*cálculo*) count, counting; (*en café, restaurante*) bill; (*COM*) account; (*de collar*) bead; (*fig*) account; **a fin de ~s** in the end; **en resumidas ~s** in short; **caer en la ~** to catch on; **dar ~ a algn de sus actos** to account to sb for one's actions; **darse ~ de** to realize; **tener en ~** to bear in mind; **echar ~s** to take stock; **~ atrás** countdown; **~ corriente/de ahorros/a plazo (fijo)** current/savings/deposit account; **~ de caja** cash account; **~ de capital** capital account; **~ por cobrar** account receivable; **~ de correo** (*INTERNET*) e-mail account; **~ de crédito** credit *o* loan account; **~ de gastos e ingresos** income and expenditure account; **~ por pagar** account payable; **abonar una cantidad en ~ a algn** to credit a sum to sb's account; **ajustar** *o* **liquidar una ~** to settle an account; **pasar la ~** to send the bill.

cuentagotas [kwenta'ɣotas] *nm inv* (*MED*) dropper; **a** *o* **con ~** (*fam, fig*) drop by drop, bit by bit.

cuentakilómetros [kwentaki'lometros] *nm inv* (*de distancias*) ≈ milometer, clock; (*velocímetro*) speedometer.

cuentista [kwen'tista] *nm/f* gossip; (*LIT*) short-story writer.

cuento ['kwento] *etc vb V* **contar ♦** *nm* story; (*LIT*) short story; **~ de hadas** fairy story; **es el ~ de nunca acabar** it's an endless business; **eso no viene a ~** that's irrelevant.

cuerda ['kwerða] *nf* rope; (*hilo*) string; (*de reloj*) spring; (*MUS: de violín etc*) string; (*MAT*) chord; (*ANAT*) cord; **~ floja** tightrope; **~s vocales** vocal cords; **dar ~ a un reloj** to wind up a clock.

cuerdo, a ['kwerðo, a] *adj* sane; (*prudente*) wise, sensible.

cuerear [kwere'ar] *vt* (*AM*) to skin.

cuerno ['kwerno] *nm* (*ZOOL: gen*) horn; (: *de ciervo*) antler; **poner los ~s a** (*fam*) to cuckold; **saber a ~ quemado** to leave a nasty taste.

cuero ['kwero] *nm* (*ZOOL*) skin, hide; (*TEC*) leather; **en ~s** stark naked; **~ cabelludo** scalp.

cuerpo ['kwerpo] *nm* body; (*cadáver*) corpse; (*fig*) main part; **~ de bomberos** fire brigade; **~ diplomático** diplomatic corps; **luchar** ~ **a** ~ to fight hand-to-hand; **tomar** ~ (*plan etc*) to take shape.

cuervo ['kwerβo] *nm* (*ZOOL*) raven, crow; *V* **criar**.

cuesta ['kwesta] *etc vb V* **costar** ♦ *nf* slope; (*en camino etc*) hill; ~ **arriba/abajo** uphill/downhill; **a** ~**s** on one's back.

cuestión [kwes'tjon] *nf* matter, question, issue; (*riña*) quarrel, dispute; **eso es otra** ~ that's another matter.

cuestionar [kwestjo'nar] *vt* to question.

cuestionario [kwestjo'narjo] *nm* questionnaire.

cueva ['kweβa] *nf* cave.

cueza ['kweθa] *etc vb V* **cocer**.

cuidado [kwi'ðaðo] *nm* care, carefulness; (*preocupación*) care, worry ♦ *excl* careful!, look out!; **eso me tiene sin** ~ I'm not worried about that.

cuidadoso, a [kwiða'ðoso, a] *adj* careful; (*preocupado*) anxious.

cuidar [kwi'ðar] *vt* (*MED*) to care for; (*ocuparse de*) to take care of, look after; (*detalles*) to pay attention to ♦ *vi*: ~ **de** to take care of, look after; ~**se** *vr* to look after o.s.; ~**se de hacer algo** to take care to do something.

cuita ['kwita] *nf* (*preocupación*) worry, trouble; (*pena*) grief.

culata [ku'lata] *nf* (*de fusil*) butt.

culatazo [kula'taθo] *nm* kick, recoil.

culebra [ku'leβra] *nf* snake; ~ **de cascabel** rattlesnake.

culebrear [kuleβre'ar] *vi* to wriggle along; (*río*) to meander.

culebrón [kule'βron] *nm* (*fam*) soap (opera).

culinario, a [kuli'narjo, a] *adj* culinary, cooking *cpd*.

culminación [kulmina'θjon] *nf* culmination.

culminante [kulmi'nante] *adj*: **momento** ~ climax, highlight, highspot.

culminar [kulmi'nar] *vi* to culminate.

culo ['kulo] *nm* (*fam: asentaderas*) bottom, backside, bum (*BRIT*); (: *ano*) arse(hole) (*BRIT!*), ass(hole) (*US!*); (*de vaso*) bottom.

culpa ['kulpa] *nf* fault; (*JUR*) guilt; ~**s** *nfpl* sins; **por** ~ **de** through, because of; **tener la** ~ (**de**) to be to blame (for).

culpabilidad [kulpaβili'ðað] *nf* guilt.

culpable [kul'paβle] *adj* guilty ♦ *nmf* culprit; **confesarse** ~ to plead guilty; **declarar** ~ **a algn** to find sb guilty.

culpar [kul'par] *vt* to blame; (*acusar*) to accuse.

cultivadora [kultiβa'ðora] *nf* cultivator.

cultivar [kulti'βar] *vt* to cultivate; (*cosecha*)

to raise; (*talento*) to develop.

cultivo [kul'tiβo] *nm* (*acto*) cultivation; (*plantas*) crop; (*BIO*) culture.

culto, a ['kulto, a] *adj* (*cultivado*) cultivated; (*que tiene cultura*) cultured, educated ♦ *nm* (*homenaje*) worship; (*religión*) cult; (*POL etc*) cult.

cultura [kul'tura] *nf* culture.

cultural [kultu'ral] *adj* cultural.

culturismo [kultu'rismo] *nm* body-building.

cumbre ['kumbre] *nf* summit, top; (*fig*) top, height; **conferencia (en la)** ~ summit (conférence).

cumpleaños [kumple'aɲos] *nm inv* birthday.

cumplido, a [kum'pliðo, a] *adj* complete, perfect; (*abundante*) plentiful; (*cortés*) courteous ♦ *nm* compliment; **visita de** ~ courtesy call.

cumplidor, a [kumpli'ðor, a] *adj* reliable.

cumplimentar [kumplimen'tar] *vt* to congratulate; (*órdenes*) to carry out.

cumplimiento [kumpli'mjento] *nm* (*de un deber*) fulfilment, execution, performance; (*acabamiento*) completion; (*COM*) expiry, end.

cumplir [kum'plir] *vt* (*orden*) to carry out, obey; (*promesa*) to carry out, fulfil; (*condena*) to serve; (*años*) to reach, attain ♦ *vi* (*pago*) to fall due; (*plazo*) to expire; ~**se** *vr* (*plazo*) to expire; (*plan etc*) to be fulfilled; (*vaticinio*) to come true; **hoy cumple dieciocho años** he is eighteen today; ~ **con** (*deberes*) to carry out, fulfil.

cúmulo ['kumulo] *nm* (*montón*) heap; (*nube*) cumulus.

cuna ['kuna] *nf* cradle, cot; **canción de** ~ lullaby.

cundir [kun'dir] *vi* (*noticia, rumor, pánico*) to spread; (*rendir*) to go a long way.

cuneta [ku'neta] *nf* ditch.

cuña ['kuɲa] *nf* (*TEC*) wedge; (*COM*) advertising spot; (*MED*) bedpan; **tener** ~**s** to have influence.

cuñado, a [ku'ɲaðo, a] *nm/f* brother/sister-in-law.

cuño ['kuɲo] *nm* (*TEC*) die-stamp; (*fig*) stamp.

cuota ['kwota] *nf* (*parte proporcional*) share; (*cotización*) fee, dues *pl*; ~ **inicial** (*COM*) down payment.

cupo ['kupo] *etc vb V* **caber** ♦ *nm* quota, share; (*COM*): ~ **de importación** import quota; ~ **de ventas** sales quota.

cupón [ku'pon] *nm* coupon; ~ **de la ONCE** *o* **de los ciegos** ONCE lottery ticket; *V tb* lotería.

cúpula ['kupula] *nf* (*ARQ*) dome.

cura ['kura] *nf* (*curación*) cure; (*método curativo*) treatment ♦ *nm* priest; ~ **de emergencia** emergency treatment.

curación [kura'θjon] *nf* cure; (*acción*) curing.

curado, a [ku'raðo, a] *adj* (*CULIN*) cured; (*pieles*) tanned.

curandero, a [kuran'dero, a] *nm/f* healer.

curar [ku'rar] *vt* (*MED: herida*) to treat, dress; (: *enfermo*) to cure; (*CULIN*) to cure, salt; (*cuero*) to tan ♦ *vi*, ~**se** *vr* to get well, recover.

curda ['kurða] (*fam*) *nm* drunk ♦ *nf*: **agarrar una/estar** ~ to get/be sloshed.

curiosear [kurjose'ar] *vt* to glance at, look over ♦ *vi* to look round, wander round; (*explorar*) to poke about.

curiosidad [kurjosi'ðað] *nf* curiosity.

curioso, a [ku'rjoso, a] *adj* curious; (*aseado*) neat ♦ *nm/f* bystander, onlooker; ¡**qué** ~! how odd!

curita [ku'rita] *nf* (*AM*) sticking plaster.

currante [ku'rrante] *nm/f* (*fam*) worker.

currar [ku'rrar] *vi* (*fam*), **currelar** [kurre'lar] *vi* (*fam*) to work.

currículo [ku'rrikulo] *nm*, **currículum** [ku'rrikulum] *nm* curriculum vitae.

curro ['kurro] *nm* (*fam*) work, job.

cursar [kur'sar] *vt* (*ESCOL*) to study.

cursi ['kursi] *adj* (*fam*) pretentious; (: *amanerado*) affected.

cursilada [kursi'laða] *nf*: ¡**qué** ~! how tacky!

cursilería [kursile'ria] *nf* (*vulgaridad*) bad taste; (*amaneramiento*) affectation.

cursillo [kur'siʎo] *nm* short course.

cursiva [kur'siβa] *nf* italics *pl*.

curso ['kurso] *nm* (*dirección*) course; (*fig*) progress; (*ESCOL*) school year; (*UNIV*) academic year; **en** ~ (*año*) current; (*proceso*) going on, under way; **moneda de** ~ **legal** legal tender.

cursor [kur'sor] *nm* (*INFORM*) cursor; (*TEC*) slide.

curtido, a [kur'tiðo, a] *adj* (*cara etc*) weather-beaten; (*fig: persona*) experienced.

curtir [kur'tir] *vt* (*piel*) to tan; (*fig*) to harden.

curvo, a ['kurßo, a] *adj* (*gen*) curved; (*torcido*) bent ♦ *nf* (*gen*) curve, bend; **curva de rentabilidad** (*COM*) break-even chart.

cúspide ['kuspiðe] *nf* (*GEO*) summit, peak; (*fig*) top, pinnacle.

custodia [kus'toðja] *nf* (*cuidado*) safekeeping; (*JUR*) custody.

custodiar [kusto'ðjar] *vt* (*conservar*) to keep, take care of; (*vigilar*) to guard.

custodio [kus'toðjo] *nm* guardian, keeper.

cutáneo, a [ku'taneo, a] *adj* skin *cpd*.

cutícula [ku'tikula] *nf* cuticle.

cutis ['kutis] *nm inv* skin, complexion.

cutre ['kutre] *adj* (*fam: lugar*) grotty; (: *persona*) naff.

cuyo, a ['kujo, a] *pron* (*de quien*) whose; (*de que*) whose, of which; **la señora en cuya casa me hospedé** the lady in whose house I stayed; **el asunto cuyos detalles conoces** the affair the details of which you know; **por** ~ **motivo** for which reason.

C.V. *abr* (= *caballos de vapor*) H.P.

C y F *abr* (= *costo y flete*) C & F.

D d

D, d [de] *nf* (*letre*) D, d; **D de Dolores** D for David (*BRIT*), D for Dog (*US*).

D. *abr* = **Don.**

D.ª *abr* = **Doña.**

dactilar [dakti'lar] *adj*: **huellas** ~**es** fingerprints.

dactilógrafo, a [dakti'loɣrafo, a] *nm/f* typist.

dádiva ['daðißa] *nf* (*donación*) donation; (*regalo*) gift.

dadivoso, a [daði'ßoso, a] *adj* generous.

dado, a ['daðo, a] *pp de* **dar** ♦ *nm* die; ~**s** *nmpl* dice ♦ *adj*: **en un momento** ~ at a certain point; **ser** ~ **a** (*hacer algo*) to be very fond of (doing sth); ~ **que** *conj* given that.

daga ['daɣa] *nf* dagger.

daltónico, a [dal'toniko, a] *adj* colour-blind.

daltonismo [dalto'nismo] *nm* colour blindness.

dama ['dama] *nf* (*gen*) lady; (*AJEDREZ*) queen; ~**s** *nfpl* draughts; **primera** ~ (*TEAT*) leading lady; (*POL*) president's wife, first lady (*US*); ~ **de honor** (*de reina*) lady-in-waiting; (*de novia*) bridesmaid.

damasco [da'masko] *nm* (*tela*) damask; (*AM: árbol*) apricot tree; (: *fruta*) apricot.

damnificado, a [damnifi'kaðo, a] *nm/f*: **los**

~s the victims.

damnificar [damnifi'kar] vt to harm; (persona) to injure.

damnifique [damni'fike] etc vb V **damnificar**.

dance ['danθe] etc vb V **danzar**.

danés, esa [da'nes, esa] adj Danish ♦ nm/f Dane ♦ nm (LING) Danish.

Danubio [da'nuβjo] nm Danube.

danza ['danθa] nf (gen) dancing; (una ~) dance.

danzar [dan'θar] vt, vi to dance.

danzarín, ina [danθa'rin, ina] nm/f dancer.

dañar [da'ɲar] vt (objeto) to damage; (persona) to hurt; (estropear) to spoil; ~se vr (objeto) to get damaged.

dañino, a [da'ɲino, a] adj harmful.

daño ['daɲo] nm (a un objeto) damage; (a una persona) harm, injury; ~s y perjuicios (JUR) damages; hacer ~ a to damage; (persona) to hurt, injure; hacerse ~ to hurt o.s.

DAO abr (=Diseño Asistido por Ordenador) CAD.

═══════════════ PALABRA CLAVE

dar [dar] vt **1** (gen) to give; (obra de teatro) to put on; (film) to show; (fiesta) to have; ~ **algo a algn** to give sb sth o sth to sb; ~ **una patada a algn/algo** to kick sb/sth, give sb/sth a kick; ~ **un susto a algn** to give sb a fright; ~ **de beber a algn** to give sb a drink

2 (producir: intereses) to yield; (fruta) to produce

3 (locuciones +n): **da gusto escucharle** it's a pleasure to listen to him; **me da pena/asco** it frightens/sickens me; V tb **paseo** y otros sustantivos

4 (considerar): ~ **algo por descontado/ entendido** to take sth for granted/as read; ~ **algo por concluido** to consider sth finished; **le dieron por desaparecido** they gave him up as lost

5 (hora): **el reloj dio las 6** the clock struck 6 (o'clock)

6: me da lo mismo it's all the same to me; V tb **igual, más**

7: ¡y dale! (¡otra vez!) not again!; **estar/ seguir dale que dale** o **dale que te pego** o (AM) **dale y dale** to go/keep on and on

♦ vi **1:** ~ **a** (habitación) to overlook, look on to; (accionar: botón etc) to press, hit

2: ~ **con: dimos con él dos horas más tarde** we came across him two hours later; **al final di con la solución** I eventually came up with the answer

3: ~ **en** (blanco, suelo) to hit; **el sol me da en la cara** the sun is shining (right) in my face

4: ~ **de sí** (zapatos etc) to stretch, give

5: ~ **para** to be enough for; **nuestro presupuesto no da para más** our budget's really tight

6: ~ **por: le ha dado por estudiar música** now he's into studying music

7: ~ **que hablar** to set people talking; **una película que da que pensar** a thought-provoking film

♦ ~se vr **1:** ~se **un baño** to have a bath; ~se **un golpe** to hit o.s.

2: ~se **por vencido** to give up; **con eso me doy por satisfecho** I'd settle for that

3 (ocurrir): **se han dado muchos casos** there have been a lot of cases

4: ~se **a: se ha dado a la bebida** he's taken to drinking

5: se me dan bien/mal las ciencias I'm good/bad at science

6: dárselas de: se las da de experto he fancies himself o poses as an expert.

dardo ['darðo] nm dart.

dársena ['darsena] nf (NAUT) dock.

datar [da'tar] vi: ~ **de** to date from.

dátil ['datil] nm date.

dativo [da'tiβo] nm (LING) dative.

dato ['dato] nm fact, piece of information; (MAT) datum; ~s nmpl (INFORM) data; ~s de entrada/salida input/output data; ~s personales personal particulars.

dcha. abr (= derecha) r.h.

d. de J. C. abr (= después de Jesucristo) A.D.

═══════════════ PALABRA CLAVE

de [de] prep (de+el = del) **1** (posesión, pertenencia) of; **la casa** ~ **Isabel/mis padres** Isabel's/my parents' house; **es** ~ **ellos/ella** it's theirs/hers; **un libro** ~ **Unamuno** a book by Unamuno

2 (origen, distancia, con números) from; **soy** ~ **Gijón** I'm from Gijón; ~ **8 a 20** from 8 to 20; **5 metros** ~ **largo** 5 metres long; **salir del cine** to go out of o leave the cinema; ~ ... **en** ... from ... to ...; ~ **2 en 2** 2 by 2, 2 at a time; **9** ~ **cada 10** 9 out of every 10

3 (valor descriptivo): **una copa** ~ **vino** a glass of wine; **una silla** ~ **madera** a wooden chair; **la mesa** ~ **la cocina** the kitchen table; **un viaje** ~ **dos días** a two-day journey; **un billete** ~ **50 euros** a 50-euro note; **un niño** ~ **tres años** a three-year-old (child); **una máquina** ~ **coser** a sewing machine; **la ciudad** ~ **Madrid** the city of Madrid; **el tonto ~ Juan** that idiot Juan; **ir vestido ~ gris** to be dressed in grey; **la niña del vestido azul** the girl in the blue dress; **la chica del pelo largo** the girl with long hair; **trabaja ~ profesora** she works as a teacher; **~ lado** sideways; **~ atrás/delante** rear/front

4 (_hora, tiempo_): **a las 8 ~ la mañana** at 8 o'clock in the morning; **~ día/noche** by day/night; **~ hoy en ocho días** a week from now; **~ niño era gordo** as a child he was fat

5 (_comparaciones_): **más/menos ~ cien personas** more/less than a hundred people; **el más caro ~ la tienda** the most expensive in the shop; **menos/más ~ lo pensado** less/more than expected

6 (_causa_): **del calor** from the heat; **~ puro tonto** out of sheer stupidity

7 (_tema_) about; **clases ~ inglés** English classes; **¿sabes algo ~ él?** do you know anything about him?; **un libro ~ física** a physics book

8 (_adj + de + infin_): **fácil ~ entender** easy to understand

9 (_oraciones pasivas_): **fue respetado ~ todos** he was loved by all

10 (_condicional + infin_) if; **~ ser posible** if possible; **~ no terminarlo hoy** if I _etc_ don't finish it today.

dé [de] _vb V_ **dar**.

deambular [deambu'lar] _vi_ to stroll, wander.

debajo [de'βaxo] _adv_ underneath; **~ de** below, under; **por ~ de** beneath.

debate [de'βate] _nm_ debate.

debatir [deβa'tir] _vt_ to debate; **~se** _vr_ to struggle.

debe ['deβe] _nm_ (_en cuenta_) debit side; **~ y haber** debit and credit.

deber [de'βer] _nm_ duty ♦ _vt_ to owe ♦ _vi_: **debe (de)** it must, it should; **~se** _vr_: **~se a** to be owing _o_ due to; **~es** _nmpl_ (_ESCOL_) homework _sg_; **debo hacerlo** I must do it; **debe de ir** he should go; **¿qué** _o_ **cuánto le debo?** how much is it?

debidamente [deβiða'mente] _adv_ properly; (_rellenar: documento, solicitud_) duly.

debido, a [de'βiðo, a] _adj_ proper, due; **~ a** due to, because of; **en debida forma** duly.

débil ['deβil] _adj_ weak; (_persona: físicamente_) feeble; (_salud_) poor; (_voz, ruido_) faint; (_luz_) dim.

debilidad [deβili'ðað] _nf_ weakness; feebleness; dimness; **tener ~ por algn** to have a soft spot for sb.

debilitar [deβili'tar] _vt_ to weaken; **~se** _vr_ to grow weak.

débito ['deβito] _nm_ debit; (_deuda_) debt.

debutante [deβu'tante] _nm/f_ beginner.

debutar [deβu'tar] _vi_ to make one's debut.

década ['dekaða] _nf_ decade.

decadencia [deka'ðenθja] _nf_ (_estado_) decadence; (_proceso_) decline, decay.

decadente [deca'ðente] _adj_ decadent.

decaer [deka'er] _vi_ (_declinar_) to decline; (_debilitarse_) to weaken; (_salud_) to fail; (_negocio_) to fall off.

decaído, a [deka'iðo, a] _adj_: **estar ~** (_persona_) to be down.

decaiga [de'kaixa] _etc vb V_ **decaer**.

decaimiento [dekai'mjento] _nm_ (_declinación_) decline; (_desaliento_) discouragement; (_MED: depresión_) depression.

decanato [deka'nato] _nm_ (_cargo_) deanship; (_despacho_) dean's office.

decano, a [de'kano, a] _nm/f_ (_UNIV etc_) dean; (_de grupo_) senior member.

decantar [dekan'tar] _vt_ (_vino_) to decant.

decapitar [dekapi'tar] _vt_ to behead.

decayendo [deka'jendo] _etc vb V_ **decaer**.

decena [de'θena] _nf_: **una ~** ten (or so).

decencia [de'θenθja] _nf_ (_modestia_) modesty; (_honestidad_) respectability.

decenio [de'θenjo] _nm_ decade.

decente [de'θente] _adj_ (_correcto_) proper; (_honesto_) respectable.

decepción [deθep'θjon] _nf_ disappointment.

decepcionante [deθepθjo'nante] _adj_ disappointing.

decepcionar [deθepθjo'nar] _vt_ to disappoint.

decibelio [deθi'βeljo] _nm_ decibel.

decidido, a [deθi'ðiðo, a] _a_ decided; (_resuelto_) resolute.

decidir [deθi'ðir] _vt_ (_persuadir_) to convince, persuade; (_resolver_) to decide ♦ _vi_ to decide; **~se** _vr_: **~se a** to make up one's mind to; **~se por** to decide _o_ settle on, choose.

decimal [deθi'mal] _adj, nm_ decimal.

décimo, a ['deθimo, a] _num_ tenth ♦ _nf_ (_MAT_) tenth; **tiene unas ~as de fiebre** he has a slight temperature.

decimoctavo, a [deθimok'taβo, a] _num_ eighteenth; _V tb_ **sexto**.

decimocuarto, a [deθimo'kwarto, a] _num_ fourteenth; _V tb_ **sexto**.

decimonoveno, a [deθimono'βeno, a] _num_ nineteenth; _V tb_ **sexto**.

decimoquinto, a [deθimo'kinto, a] _num_ fifteenth; _V tb_ **sexto**.

decimoséptimo, a [deθimo'septimo, a] *num* seventeenth; *V tb* **sexto**.

decimosexto, a [deθimo'seksto, a] *num* sixteenth; *V tb* **sexto**.

decimotercero, a [deθimoter'θero, a] *num* thirteenth; *V tb* **sexto**.

decir [de'θir] *vt* (*expresar*) to say; (*contar*) to tell; (*hablar*) to speak; (*indicar*) to show; (*revelar*) to reveal; (*fam: nombrar*) to call ♦ *nm* saying; ~**se** *vr*: **se dice** it is said, they say; (*se cuenta*) the story goes; **¿cómo se dice en inglés "cursi"?** what's the English for "cursi"?; ~ **para** *o* **entre sí** to say to o.s.; ~ **por** ~ to talk for talking's sake; **dar que** ~ **(a la gente)** to make people talk; **querer** ~ to mean; **es** ~ that is to say, namely; **ni que** ~ **tiene que ...** it goes without saying that ...; **como quien dice** so to speak; **¡quién lo diría!** would you believe it!; **el qué dirán** gossip; **¡diga!, ¡dígame!** (*en tienda etc*) can I help you?; (*TELEC*) hello?; **le dije que fuera más tarde** I told her to go later; **es un** ~ it's just a phrase.

decisión [deθi'sjon] *nf* decision; (*firmeza*) decisiveness; (*voluntad*) determination.

decisivo, a [deθi'siβo, a] *adj* decisive.

declamar [dekla'mar] *vt, vi* to declaim; (*versos etc*) to recite.

declaración [deklara'θjon] *nf* (*manifestación*) statement; (*explicación*) explanation; (*JUR: testimonio*) evidence; ~ **de derechos** (*POL*) bill of rights; ~ **de impuestos** (*COM*) tax return; ~ **de ingresos** *o* **de la renta** income tax return; ~ **jurada** affidavit; **falsa** ~ (*JUR*) misrepresentation.

declarar [dekla'rar] *vt* to declare ♦ *vi* to declare; (*JUR*) to testify; ~**se** *vr* (*opinión*) to make one's opinion known; (*a una chica*) to propose; (*guerra, incendio*) to break out; ~ **culpable/inocente a algn** to find sb guilty/not guilty; ~**se culpable/ inocente** to plead guilty/not guilty.

declinación [deklina'θjon] *nf* (*decaimiento*) decline; (*LING*) declension.

declinar [dekli'nar] *vt* (*gen, LING*) to decline; (*JUR*) to reject ♦ *vi* (*el día*) to draw to a close.

declive [de'kliβe] *nm* (*cuesta*) slope; (*inclinación*) incline; (*fig*) decline; (*COM: tb:* ~ **económico**) slump.

decodificador [dekoðifika'ðor] *nm* (*INFORM*) decoder.

decolorarse [dekolo'rarse] *vr* to become discoloured.

decomisar [dekomi'sar] *vt* to seize, confiscate.

decomiso [deko'miso] *nm* seizure.

decoración [dekora'θjon] *nf* decoration; (*TEAT*) scenery, set; ~ **de escaparates** window dressing.

decorado [deko'raðo] *nm* (*CINE, TEAT*) scenery, set.

decorador, a [dekora'ðor, a] *nm/f* (*de interiores*) (interior) decorator; (*TEAT*) stage *o* set designer.

decorar [deko'rar] *vt* to decorate.

decorativo, a [dekora'tiβo, a] *adj* ornamental, decorative.

decoro [de'koro] *nm* (*respeto*) respect; (*dignidad*) decency; (*recato*) propriety.

decoroso, a [deko'roso, a] *adj* (*decente*) decent; (*modesto*) modest; (*digno*) proper.

decrecer [dekre'θer] *vi* to decrease, diminish; (*nivel de agua*) to go down; (*días*) to draw in.

decrépito, a [de'krepito, a] *adj* decrepit.

decretar [dekre'tar] *vt* to decree.

decreto [de'kreto] *nm* decree; (*POL*) act.

decreto-ley [dekreto'lei], *pl* **decretos- leyes** *nm* decree.

decrezca [de'kreθka] *etc vb V* **decrecer**.

decúbito [de'kuβito] *nm* (*MED*): ~ **prono/ supino** prone/supine position.

dedal [de'ðal] *nm* thimble.

dedalera [deða'lera] *nf* foxglove.

dédalo ['deðalo] *nm* (*laberinto*) labyrinth; (*fig*) tangle, mess.

dedicación [deðika'θjon] *nf* dedication; **con** ~ **exclusiva** *o* **plena** full-time.

dedicar [deði'kar] *vt* (*libro*) to dedicate; (*tiempo, dinero*) to devote; ~**se** *vr*: ~**se a** to devote o.s. to (*hacer algo* doing sth); (*carrera, estudio*) to go in for, take up; **¿a qué se dedica usted?** what do you do (for a living)?

dedicatoria [deðika'torja] *nf* (*de libro*) dedication.

dedillo [de'ðiʎo] *nm*: **saber algo al** ~ to have sth at one's fingertips.

dedique [de'ðike] *etc vb V* **dedicar**.

dedo ['deðo] *nm* finger; (*de vino etc*) drop; ~ **(del pie)** toe; ~ **pulgar** thumb; ~ **índice** index finger; ~ **mayor** *o* **cordial** middle finger; ~ **anular** ring finger; ~ **meñique** little finger; **contar con los** ~**s** to count on one's fingers; **comerse los** ~**s** to get very impatient; **entrar a** ~ to get a job by pulling strings; **hacer** ~ (*fam*) to hitch (a lift); **poner el** ~ **en la llaga** to put one's finger on it; **no tiene dos** ~**s de frente** he's pretty dim.

deducción [deðuk'θjon] *nf* deduction.

deducir [deðu'θir] *vt* (*concluir*) to deduce,

infer; (*COM*) to deduct.
deduje [de'ðuxe] *etc*, **dedujera**
[deðu'xera] *etc*, **deduzca** [de'ðuθka] *etc*
vb V **deducir**.
defección [defek'θjon] *nf* defection,
desertion.
defecto [de'fekto] *nm* defect, flaw; (*de
cara*) imperfection; ~ **de pronunciación**
speech defect; **por** ~ (*INFORM*) default; ~
latente (*COM*) latent defect.
defectuoso, a [defek'twoso, a] *adj*
defective, faulty.
defender [defen'der] *vt* to defend; (*ideas*)
to uphold; (*causa*) to champion; (*amigos*)
to stand up for; ~**se** *vr* to defend o.s.;
~**se bien** to give a good account of o.s.;
me defiendo en inglés (*fig*) I can get by
in English.
defendible [defen'diβle] *adj* defensible.
defensa [de'fensa] *nf* defence; (*NAUT*)
fender ♦ *nm* (*DEPORTE*) back; **en** ~ **propia**
in self-defence.
defensivo, a [defen'siβo, a] *adj* defensive
♦ *nf*: **a la defensiva** on the defensive.
defensor, a [defen'sor, a] *adj* defending
♦ *nm/f* (*abogado* ~) defending counsel;
(*protector*) protector; ~ **del pueblo** (*ESP*)
≈ ombudsman.
deferente [defe'rente] *adj* deferential.
deferir [defe'rir] *vt* (*JUR*) to refer, delegate
♦ *vi*: ~ **a** to defer to.
deficiencia [defi'θjenθja] *nf* deficiency.
deficiente [defi'θjente] *adj* (*defectuoso*)
defective; ~ **en** lacking *o* deficient in
♦ *nm/f*: **ser un** ~ **mental** to be mentally
handicapped.
déficit, ~s ['defiθit] *nm* (*COM*) deficit; (*fig*)
lack, shortage; ~ **presupuestario** budget
deficit.
deficitario, a [defiθi'tarjo, a] *adj* (*COM*) in
deficit; (*empresa*) loss-making.
defienda [de'fjenda] *etc vb V* **defender**.
defiera [de'fjera] *etc vb V* **deferir**.
definición [defini'θjon] *nf* definition;
(*INFORM: de pantalla*) resolution.
definido, a [defi'niðo, a] *adj* (*tb LING*)
definite; **bien** ~ well *o* clearly defined; ~
por el usuario (*INFORM*) user-defined.
definir [defi'nir] *vt* (*determinar*) to
determine, establish; (*decidir, INFORM*) to
define; (*aclarar*) to clarify.
definitivo, a [defini'tiβo, a] *adj* (*edición,
texto*) definitive; (*fecha*) definite; **en
definitiva** definitively; (*en conclusión*)
finally; (*en resumen*) in short.
defiriendo [defi'rjendo] *etc vb V* **deferir**.
deflacionario, a [deflaθjo'narjo, a],
deflacionista [deflaθjo'nista] *adj*

deflationary.
deflector [deflek'tor] *nm* (*TEC*) baffle.
deforestación [deforesta'θjon] *nf*
deforestation.
deformación [deforma'θjon] *nf* (*alteración*)
deformation; (*RADIO etc*) distortion.
deformar [defor'mar] *vt* (*gen*) to deform;
~**se** *vr* to become deformed.
deforme [de'forme] *adj* (*informe*)
deformed; (*feo*) ugly; (*mal hecho*)
misshapen.
deformidad [deformi'ðað] *nf* (*forma
anormal*) deformity; (*fig: defecto*) (moral)
shortcoming.
defraudar [defrau'ðar] *vt* (*decepcionar*) to
disappoint; (*estafar*) to cheat; to defraud;
~ **impuestos** to evade tax.
defunción [defun'θjon] *nf* decease,
demise.
degeneración [dexenera'θjon] *nf* (*de las
células*) degeneration; (*moral*)
degeneracy.
degenerar [dexene'rar] *vi* to degenerate;
(*empeorar*) to get worse.
deglutir [deɣlu'tir] *vt, vi* to swallow.
degolladero [deɣoʎa'ðero] *nm* (*ANAT*)
throat; (*cadalso*) scaffold; (*matadero*)
slaughterhouse.
degollar [deɣo'ʎar] *vt* to slaughter.
degradar [deɣra'ðar] *vt* to debase,
degrade; (*INFORM: datos*) to corrupt; ~**se**
vr to demean o.s.
degüelle [de'ɣweʎe] *etc vb V* **degollar**.
degustación [deɣusta'θjon] *nf* sampling,
tasting.
deificar [deifi'kar] *vt* (*persona*) to deify.
deifique [dei'fike] *etc vb V* **deificar**.
dejadez [dexa'ðeθ] *nf* (*negligencia*) neglect;
(*descuido*) untidiness, carelessness.
dejado, a [de'xaðo, a] *adj* (*desaliñado*)
slovenly; (*negligente*) careless;
(*indolente*) lazy.
dejar [de'xar] *vt* (*gen*) to leave; (*permitir*) to
allow, let; (*abandonar*) to abandon,
forsake; (*actividad, empleo*) to give up;
(*beneficios*) to produce, yield ♦ *vi*: ~ **de**
(*parar*) to stop; ~**se** *vr* (*abandonarse*) to let
o.s. go; **no puedo** ~ **de fumar** I can't give
up smoking; **no dejes de visitarles** don't
fail to visit them; **no dejes de comprar
un billete** make sure you buy a ticket; ~
a un lado to leave *o* set aside; ~ **caer** to
drop; ~ **entrar/salir** to let in/out; ~ **pasar**
to let through; **¡déjalo!** (*no te preocupes*)
don't worry about it; **te dejo en tu casa**
I'll drop you off at your place; **deja
mucho que desear** it leaves a lot to be
desired; ~**se persuadir** to allow o.s. to *o*

let o.s. be persuaded; **¡déjate de tonterías!** stop messing about!
deje ['dexe] *nm* (trace of) accent.
dejo ['dexo] *nm* (*LING*) accent.
del [del] = **de** + **el**; *V* **de.**
del. *abr* (*ADMIN*: = *Delegación*) district office.
delantal [delan'tal] *nm* apron.
delante [de'lante] *adv* in front; (*enfrente*) opposite; (*adelante*) ahead ♦ *prep*: ~ **de** in front of, before; **la parte de** ~ the front part; **estando otros** ~ with others present.
delantero, a [delan'tero, a] *adj* front; (*patas de animal*) fore ♦ *nm* (*DEPORTE*) forward ♦ *nf* (*de vestido, casa etc*) front part; (*TEAT*) front row; (*DEPORTE*) forward line; **llevar la delantera (a algn)** to be ahead (of sb).
delatar [dela'tar] *vt* to inform on *o* against, betray; **los delató a la policía** he reported them to the police.
delator, a [dela'tor, a] *nm/f* informer.
delegación [deleɣa'θjon] *nf* (*acción, delegados*) delegation; (*COM: oficina*) district office, branch; ~ **de poderes** (*POL*) devolution; ~ **de policía** police station.
delegado, a [dele'ɣaðo, a] *nm/f* delegate; (*COM*) agent.
delegar [dele'ɣar] *vt* to delegate.
delegue [de'leɣe] *etc vb V* **delegar.**
deleitar [delei'tar] *vt* to delight; ~**se** *vr*: ~**se con** *o* **en** to delight in, take pleasure in.
deleite [de'leite] *nm* delight, pleasure.
deletrear [deletre'ar] *vt* (*tb fig*) to spell (out).
deletreo [dele'treo] *nm* spelling; (*fig*) interpretation, decipherment.
deleznable [deleθ'naβle] *adj* (*frágil*) fragile; (*fig: malo*) poor; (*excusa*) feeble.
delfín [del'fin] *nm* dolphin.
delgadez [delɣa'ðeθ] *nf* thinness, slimness.
delgado, a [del'ɣaðo, a] *adj* thin; (*persona*) slim, thin; (*tierra*) poor; (*tela etc*) light, delicate ♦ *adv*: **hilar (muy)** ~ (*fig*) to split hairs.
deliberación [deliβera'θjon] *nf* deliberation.
deliberar [deliβe'rar] *vt* to debate, discuss ♦ *vi* to deliberate.
delicadeza [delika'ðeθa] *nf* delicacy; (*refinamiento, sutileza*) refinement.
delicado, a [deli'kaðo, a] *adj* delicate; (*sensible*) sensitive; (*rasgos*) dainty; (*gusto*) refined; (*situación: difícil*) tricky; (*: violento*) embarrassing; (*punto, tema*) sore; (*persona: difícil de contentar*) hard to

please; (: *sensible*) touchy, hypersensitive; (: *atento*) considerate.
delicia [de'liθja] *nf* delight.
delicioso, a [deli'θjoso, a] *adj* (*gracioso*) delightful; (*exquisito*) delicious.
delictivo, a [delik'tiβo, a] *adj* criminal *cpd.*
delimitar [delimi'tar] *vt* to delimit.
delincuencia [delin'kwenθja] *nf*: ~ **juvenil** juvenile delinquency; **cifras de la** ~ crime rate.
delincuente [delin'kwente] *nm/f* delinquent; (*criminal*) criminal; ~ **sin antecedentes** first offender; ~ **habitual** hardened criminal.
delineante [deline'ante] *nm/f* draughtsman.
delinear [deline'ar] *vt* to delineate; (*dibujo*) to draw; (*contornos, fig*) to outline; ~ **un proyecto** to outline a project.
delinquir [delin'kir] *vi* to commit an offence.
delirante [deli'rante] *adj* delirious.
delirar [deli'rar] *vi* to be delirious, rave; (*fig: desatinar*) to talk nonsense.
delirio [de'lirjo] *nm* (*MED*) delirium; (*palabras insensatas*) ravings *pl*; ~ **de grandeza** megalomania; ~ **de persecución** persecution mania; **con** ~ (*fam*) madly; **¡fue el** ~! (*fam*) it was great!
delito [de'lito] *nm* (*gen*) crime; (*infracción*) offence.
delta ['delta] *nm* delta.
demacrado, a [dema'kraðo, a] *adj* emaciated.
demagogia [dema'ɣoxja] *nf* demagogy, demagoguery.
demagogo [dema'ɣoɣo] *nm* demagogue.
demanda [de'manda] *nf* (*pedido, COM*) demand; (*petición*) request; (*pregunta*) inquiry; (*reivindicación*) claim; (*JUR*) action, lawsuit; (*TEAT*) call; (*ELEC*) load; ~ **de pago** demand for payment; **escribir en** ~ **de ayuda** to write asking for help; **entablar** ~ (*JUR*) to sue; **presentar** ~ **de divorcio** to sue for divorce; ~ **final** final demand; ~ **indirecta** derived demand; ~ **de mercado** market demand.
demandado, a [deman'daðo, a] *nm/f* defendant; (*en divorcio*) respondent.
demandante [deman'dante] *nm/f* claimant; (*JUR*) plaintiff.
demandar [deman'dar] *vt* (*gen*) to demand; (*JUR*) to sue, file a lawsuit against, start proceedings against; ~ **a algn por calumnia/daños y perjuicios** to sue sb for libel/damages.
demarcación [demarka'θjon] *nf* (*de terreno*) demarcation.

demás [de'mas] *adj*: los ~ niños the other children, the remaining children ♦ *pron*: los/las ~ the others, the rest (of them); lo ~ the rest (of it); por ~ moreover; (*en vano*) in vain; y ~ etcetera.

demasía [dema'sia] *nf* (*exceso*) excess, surplus; comer en ~ to eat to excess.

demasiado, a [dema'sjaðo, a] *adj*: ~ vino too much wine ♦ *adv* (*antes de adj, adv*) too; ~s libros too many books; ¡es ~! it's too much!; es ~ pesado para levantar it is too heavy to lift; ~ lo sé I know it only too well; hace ~ calor it's too hot.

demencia [de'menθja] *nf* (*locura*) madness.

demencial [demen'θjal] *adj* crazy.

demente [de'mente] *adj* mad, insane ♦ *nm/f* lunatic.

democracia [demo'kraθja] *nf* democracy.

demócrata [de'mokrata] *nm/f* democrat.

democratacristiano, a [demokrata kris'tjano, a], **democristiano, a** [demokris'tjano, a] *adj, nm/f* Christian Democrat.

democrático, a [demo'kratiko, a] *adj* democratic.

demográfico, a [demo'ɣrafiko, a] *adj* demographic, population *cpd*; la explosión demográfica the population explosion.

demoledor, a [demole'ðor, a] *adj* (*fig: argumento*) overwhelming; (: *ataque*) shattering.

demoler [demo'ler] *vt* to demolish; (*edificio*) to pull down.

demolición [demoli'θjon] *nf* demolition.

demonio [de'monjo] *nm* devil, demon; ¡~s! hell!; ¿cómo ~s? how the hell?; ¿qué ~s será? what the devil can it be?; ¿dónde ~ lo habré dejado? where the devil can I have left it?; tener el ~ en el cuerpo (*no parar*) to be always on the go.

demora [de'mora] *nf* delay.

demorar [demo'rar] *vt* (*retardar*) to delay, hold back; (*dilatar*) to hold up ♦ *vi* to linger, stay on; ~se *vr* to linger, stay on; (*retrasarse*) to take a long time; ~se en hacer algo (*esp AM*) to take time doing sth.

demos ['demos] *vb V* dar.

demostración [demostra'θjon] *nf* (*gen, MAT*) demonstration; (*de cariño, fuerza*) show; (*de teorema*) proof; (*de amistad*) gesture; (*de cólera, gimnasia*) display; ~ comercial commercial exhibition.

demostrar [demos'trar] *vt* (*probar*) to prove; (*mostrar*) to show; (*manifestar*) to demonstrate.

demostrativo, a [demostra'tißo, a] *adj* demonstrative.

demudado, a [demu'ðaðo, a] *adj* (*rostro*)

pale; (*fig*) upset; tener el rostro ~ to look pale.

demudar [demu'ðar] *vt* to change, alter; ~se *vr* (*expresión*) to alter; (*perder color*) to change colour.

demuela [de'mwela] *etc vb V* demoler.

demuestre [de'mwestre] *etc vb V* demostrar.

den [den] *vb V* dar.

denegación [deneɣa'θjon] *nf* refusal.

denegar [dene'ɣar] *vt* (*rechazar*) to refuse; (*negar*) to deny; (*JUR*) to reject.

denegué [dene'ɣe], **deneguemos** [dene'ɣemos] *etc*, **deniego** [de'njeɣo] *etc*, **deniegue** [de'njeɣe] *etc vb V* denegar.

dengue ['denɣe] *nm* dengue *o* breakbone fever.

denigrante [deni'ɣrante] *adj* (*injurioso*) insulting; (*deshonroso*) degrading.

denigrar [deni'ɣrar] *vt* (*desacreditar*) to denigrate; (*injuriar*) to insult.

denodado, a [deno'ðaðo, a] *adj* bold, brave.

denominación [denomina'θjon] *nf* (*acto*) naming; (*clase*) denomination; ~ de origen *see boxed note*.

DENOMINACIÓN DE ORIGEN

The denominación de origen, *often abbreviated to DO, is a prestigious classification awarded to food and wine from designated regions by the Consejo Regulador de la Denominación de Origen. Produce must meet the required standards concerning quality and production methods. It is often associated with "manchego" cheeses and many of the wines from the Rioja and Ribera de Duero regions.*

---

denominador [denomina'ðor] *nm*: ~ común common denominator.

denostar [denos'tar] *vt* to insult.

denotar [deno'tar] *vt* (*indicar*) to indicate, denote.

densidad [densi'ðað] *nf* (*FÍSICA*) density; (*fig*) thickness.

denso, a ['denso, a] *adj* (*apretado*) solid; (*espeso, pastoso*) thick; (*fig*) heavy.

dentado, a [den'taðo, a] *adj* (*rueda*) cogged; (*filo*) jagged; (*sello*) perforated; (*BOT*) dentate.

dentadura [denta'ðura] *nf* (set of) teeth *pl*; ~ postiza false teeth *pl*.

dental [den'tal] *adj* dental.

dentellada [dente'ʎaða] *nf* (*mordisco*) bite, nip; (*señal*) tooth mark; partir algo a ~s to sever sth with one's teeth.

dentera [den'tera] *nf* (*sensación desagradable*) the shivers *pl*.

dentición [denti'θjon] *nf* (*acto*) teething; (*ANAT*) dentition; **estar con la ~** to be teething.

dentífrico, a [den'tifriko, a] *adj* dental, tooth *cpd* ♦ *nm* toothpaste; **pasta dentífrica** toothpaste.

dentista [den'tista] *nm/f* dentist.

dentro ['dentro] *adv* inside ♦ *prep*: **~ de** in, inside, within; **allí ~** in there; **mirar por ~** to look inside; **~ de lo posible** as far as possible; **~ de todo** all in all; **~ de tres meses** within three months.

denuedo [de'nweðo] *nm* boldness, daring.

denuesto [de'nwesto] *nm* insult.

denuncia [de'nunθja] *nf* (*delación*) denunciation; (*acusación*) accusation; (*de accidente*) report; **hacer o poner una ~** to report an incident to the police.

denunciable [denun'θjaβle] *adj* indictable, punishable.

denunciante [denun'θjante] *nm/f* accuser; (*delator*) informer.

denunciar [denun'θjar] *vt* to report; (*delatar*) to inform on *o* against.

Dep. *abr* (= *Departamento*) Dept.; (= *Depósito*) dep.

deparar [depa'rar] *vt* (*brindar*) to provide *o* furnish with; (*suj: futuro, destino*) to have in store for; **los placeres que el viaje nos deparó** the pleasures which the trip afforded us.

departamento [departa'mento] *nm* (*sección administrativa*) department, section; (*AM: piso*) flat (*BRIT*), apartment (*US*); (*distrito*) department, province; **~ de envíos** (*COM*) dispatch department; **~ de máquinas** (*NAUT*) engine room.

departir [depar'tir] *vi* to talk, converse.

dependencia [depen'denθja] *nf* dependence; (*POL*) dependency; (*COM*) office, section; (*sucursal*) branch office; (*ARQ: cuarto*) room; **~s** *nfpl* outbuildings.

depender [depen'der] *vi*: **~ de** to depend on; (*contar con*) to rely on; (*de autoridad*) to be under, be answerable to; **depende** it (all) depends; **no depende de mí** it's not up to me.

dependienta [depen'djenta] *nf* saleswoman, shop assistant.

dependiente [depen'djente] *adj* dependent ♦ *nm* salesman, shop assistant.

depilación [depila'θjon] *nf* hair removal.

depilar [depi'lar] *vt* (*con cera: piernas*) to wax; (*cejas*) to pluck.

depilatorio, a [depila'torjo, a] *adj* depilatory ♦ *nm* hair remover.

deplorable [deplo'raβle] *adj* deplorable.

deplorar [deplo'rar] *vt* to deplore.

depondré [depon'dre] *etc vb V* **deponer**.

deponer [depo'ner] *vt* (*armas*) to lay down; (*rey*) to depose; (*gobernante*) to oust; (*ministro*) to remove from office ♦ *vi* (*JUR*) to give evidence; (*declarar*) to make a statement.

deponga [de'ponga] *etc vb V* **deponer**.

deportación [deporta'θjon] *nf* deportation.

deportar [depor'tar] *vt* to deport.

deporte [de'porte] *nm* sport.

deportista [depor'tista] *adj* sports *cpd* ♦ *nm/f* sportsman/woman.

deportivo, a [depor'tiβo, a] *adj* (*club, periódico*) sports *cpd* ♦ *nm* sports car.

deposición [deposi'θjon] *nf* (*de funcionario etc*) removal from office; (*JUR: testimonio*) evidence.

depositante [deposi'tante] *nm/f* depositor.

depositar [deposi'tar] *vt* (*dinero*) to deposit; (*mercaderías*) to put away, store; **~se** *vr* to settle; **~ la confianza en algn** to place one's trust in sb.

depositario, a [deposi'tarjo, a] *nm/f* trustee; **~ judicial** official receiver.

depósito [de'posito] *nm* (*gen*) deposit; (*de mercaderías*) warehouse, store; (*de animales, coches*) pound; (*de agua, gasolina etc*) tank; (*en retrete*) cistern; **~ afianzado** bonded warehouse; **~ bancario** bank deposit; **~ de cadáveres** mortuary; **~ de maderas** timber yard; **~ de suministro** feeder bin.

depravar [depra'βar] *vt* to deprave, corrupt; **~se** *vr* to become depraved.

depreciación [depreθja'θjon] *nf* depreciation.

depreciar [depre'θjar] *vt* to depreciate, reduce the value of; **~se** *vr* to depreciate, lose value.

depredador, a [depreða'ðor, a] (*ZOOL*) *adj* predatory ♦ *nm* predator.

depredar [depre'ðar] *vt* to pillage.

depresión [depre'sjon] *nf* (*gen, MED*) depression; (*hueco*) hollow; (*en horizonte, camino*) dip; (*merma*) drop; (*ECON*) slump, recession; **~ nerviosa** nervous breakdown.

deprimente [depri'mente] *adj* depressing.

deprimido, a [depri'miðo, a] *adj* depressed.

deprimir [depri'mir] *vt* to depress; **~se** *vr* (*persona*) to become depressed.

deprisa [de'prisa] *adv V* **prisa**.

depuesto [de'pwesto] *pp de* **deponer**.

depuración [depura'θjon] *nf* purification; (*POL*) purge; (*INFORM*) debugging.
depurador [depura'ðor] *nm* purifier.
depuradora [depura'ðora] *nf* (*de agua*) water-treatment plant; (*tb:* ~ **de aguas residuales**) sewage farm.
depurar [depu'rar] *vt* to purify; (*purgar*) to purge; (*INFORM*) to debug.
depuse [de'puse] *etc vb V* **deponer**.
der., der.º *abr* (= *derecho*) r.
derecha [de'retʃa] *nf V* **derecho, a**.
derechazo [dere'tʃaθo] *nm* (*BOXEO*) right; (*TENIS*) forehand drive; (*TAUR*) *a pass with the cape*.
derechista [dere'tʃista] (*POL*) *adj* right-wing ♦ *nm/f* right-winger.
derecho, a [de'retʃo, a] *adj* right, right-hand ♦ *nm* (*privilegio*) right; (*título*) claim, title; (*lado*) right(-hand) side; (*leyes*) law ♦ *nf* right(-hand) side ♦ *adv* straight, directly; ~s *nmpl* dues; (*profesionales*) fees; (*impuestos*) taxes; (*de autor*) royalties; **la(s) derecha(s)** (*pl*) (*POL*) the Right; ~s **civiles** civil rights; ~s **de patente** patent rights; ~s **portuarios** (*COM*) harbour dues; ~s **de propiedad literaria** copyright; ~ **de timbre** (*COM*) stamp duty; ~ **de votar** right to vote; ~ **al voto** voting right; **Facultad de D**~ Faculty of Law; **a derechas** rightly, correctly; **de derechas** (*POL*) right-wing; "**reservados todos los** ~s" "all rights reserved"; **¡no hay** ~! it's not fair!; **tener** ~ **a** to have a right to; **a la derecha** on the right; (*dirección*) to the right; **siga todo** ~ carry *o* (*BRIT*) go straight on.
deriva [de'rißa] *nf*: **ir** *o* **estar a la** ~ to drift, be adrift.
derivación [derißa'θjon] *nf* derivation.
derivado, a [deri'ßaðo, a] *adj* derived ♦ *nm* (*LING*) derivative; (*INDUSTRIA, QUÍMICA*) by-product.
derivar [deri'ßar] *vt* to derive; (*desviar*) to direct ♦ *vi*, ~**se** *vr* to derive, be derived; ~(**se**) **de** (*consecuencia*) to spring from.
dermatólogo, a [derma'toloɣo, a] *nm/f* dermatologist.
dérmico, a ['dermiko, a] *adj* skin *cpd*.
dermoprotector, a [dermoprotek'tor, a] *adj* protective.
derogación [deroɣa'θjon] *nf* repeal.
derogar [dero'ɣar] *vt* (*ley*) to repeal; (*contrato*) to revoke.
derogue [de'roɣe] *etc vb V* **derogar**.
derramamiento [derrama'mjento] *nm* (*dispersión*) spilling; (*fig*) squandering; ~ **de sangre** bloodshed.
derramar [derra'mar] *vt* to spill; (*verter*) to

pour out; (*esparcir*) to scatter; ~**se** *vr* to pour out; ~ **lágrimas** to weep.
derrame [de'rrame] *nm* (*de líquido*) spilling; (*de sangre*) shedding; (*de tubo etc*) overflow; (*perdida*) leakage; (*MED*) discharge; (*declive*) slope; ~ **cerebral** brain haemorrhage; ~ **sinovial** water on the knee.
derrapar [derra'par] *vi* to skid.
derredor [derre'ðor] *adv*: **al** *o* **en** ~ **de** around, about.
derrengado, a [derren'gaðo, a] *adj* (*torcido*) bent; (*cojo*) crippled; **estar** ~ (*fig*) to ache all over; **dejar** ~ **a algn** (*fig*) to wear sb out.
derretido, a [derre'tiðo, a] *adj* melted; (*metal*) molten; **estar** ~ **por algn** (*fig*) to be crazy about sb.
derretir [derre'tir] *vt* (*gen*) to melt; (*nieve*) to thaw; (*fig*) to squander; ~**se** *vr* to melt.
derribar [derri'ßar] *vt* to knock down; (*construcción*) to demolish; (*persona, gobierno, político*) to bring down.
derribo [de'rrißo] *nm* (*de edificio*) demolition; (*LUCHA*) throw; (*AVIAT*) shooting down; (*POL*) overthrow; ~s *nmpl* rubble *sg*, debris *sg*.
derrita [de'rrita] *etc vb V* **derretir**.
derrocar [derro'kar] *vt* (*gobierno*) to bring down, overthrow; (*ministro*) to oust.
derrochador, a [derrotʃa'ðor, a] *adj*, *nm/f* spendthrift.
derrochar [derro'tʃar] *vt* (*dinero, recursos*) to squander; (*energía, salud*) to be bursting with *o* full of.
derroche [de'rrotʃe] *nm* (*despilfarro*) waste, squandering; (*exceso*) extravagance; **con un** ~ **de buen gusto** with a fine display of good taste.
derroque [de'rroke] *etc vb V* **derrocar**.
derrota [de'rrota] *nf* (*NAUT*) course; (*MIL*) defeat, rout; **sufrir una grave** ~ (*fig*) to suffer a grave setback.
derrotar [derro'tar] *vt* (*gen*) to defeat.
derrotero [derro'tero] *nm* (*rumbo*) course; **tomar otro** ~ (*fig*) to adopt a different course.
derrotista [derro'tista] *adj*, *nm/f* defeatist.
derruir [derru'ir] *vt* to demolish, tear down.
derrumbamiento [derrumba'mjento] *nm* (*caída*) plunge; (*demolición*) demolition; (*desplome*) collapse; ~ **de tierra** landslide.
derrumbar [derrum'bar] *vt* to throw down; (*despeñar*) to fling *o* hurl down; (*volcar*) to upset; ~**se** *vr* (*hundirse*) to collapse; (: *techo*) to fall in, cave in; (*fig: esperanzas*)

to collapse.

derrumbe [de'rrumbe] *nm*
= derrumbamiento.

derruyendo [derru'jendo] *etc vb V* **derruir.**

des [des] *vb V* **dar.**

desabastecido, a [desaβaste'θiðo, a] *adj*:
estar ~ de algo to be short of *o* out of
sth.

desabotonar [desaβoto'nar] *vt* to
unbutton, undo ♦ *vi* (*flores*) to blossom;
~se *vr* to come undone.

desabrido, a [desa'βriðo, a] *adj* (*comida*)
insipid, tasteless; (*persona: soso*) dull;
(: *antipático*) rude, surly; (*respuesta*)
sharp; (*tiempo*) unpleasant.

desabrigado, a [desaβri'ɣaðo, a] *adj* (*sin
abrigo*) not sufficiently protected; (*fig*)
exposed.

desabrigar [desaβri'ɣar] *vt* (*quitar ropa a*) to
remove the clothing of; (*descubrir*) to
uncover; (*fig*) to deprive of protection;
~se *vr*: me desabrigué en la cama the
bedclothes came off.

desabrigue [desa'βriɣe] *etc vb V*
desabrigar.

desabrochar [desaβro'tʃar] *vt* (*botones,
broches*) to undo, unfasten; ~se *vr* (*ropa
etc*) to come undone.

desacatar [desaka'tar] *vt* (*ley*) to disobey.

desacato [desa'kato] *nm* (*falta de respeto*)
disrespect; (*JUR*) contempt.

desacertado, a [desaθer'taðo, a] *adj*
(*equivocado*) mistaken; (*inoportuno*)
unwise.

desacierto [desa'θjerto] *nm* (*error*)
mistake, error; (*dicho*) unfortunate
remark.

desaconsejable [desakonse'xaβle] *adj*
inadvisable.

desaconsejado, a [desakonse'xaðo, a] *adj*
ill-advised.

desaconsejar [desakonse'xar] *vt*: ~ algo a
algn to advise sb against sth.

desacoplar [desako'plar] *vt* (*ELEC*) to
disconnect; (*TEC*) to take apart.

desacorde [desa'korðe] *adj* (*MUS*)
discordant; (*fig: opiniones*) conflicting;
estar ~ con algo to disagree with sth.

desacreditar [desakreði'tar] *vt*
(*desprestigiar*) to discredit, bring into
disrepute; (*denigrar*) to run down.

desactivar [desakti'βar] *vt* to deactivate;
(*bomba*) to defuse.

desacuerdo [desa'kwerðo] *nm* (*conflicto*)
disagreement, discord; (*error*) error,
blunder; en ~ con of keeping.

desafiante [desa'fjante] *adj* (*insolente*)
defiant; (*retador*) challenging ♦ *nm/f*

challenger.

desafiar [desa'fjar] *vt* (*retar*) to challenge;
(*enfrentarse a*) to defy.

desafilado, a [desafi'laðo, a] *adj* blunt.

desafinado, a [desafi'naðo, a] *adj*: estar ~
to be out of tune.

desafinar [desafi'nar] *vi* to be out of tune;
~se *vr* to go out of tune.

desafío [desa'fio] *nm* (*reto*) challenge;
(*combate*) duel; (*resistencia*) defiance.

desaforadamente [desaforaða'mente] *adv*:
gritar ~ to shout one's head off.

desaforado, a [desafo'raðo, a] *adj* (*grito*)
ear-splitting; (*comportamiento*)
outrageous.

desafortunadamente [desafortunaða
'mente] *adv* unfortunately.

desafortunado, a [desafortu'naðo, a] *adj*
(*desgraciado*) unfortunate, unlucky.

desagradable [desaɣra'ðaβle] *adj*
(*fastidioso, enojoso*) unpleasant; (*irritante*)
disagreeable; ser ~ con algn to be rude
to sb.

desagradar [desaɣra'ðar] *vi* (*disgustar*) to
displease; (*molestar*) to bother.

desagradecido, a [desaɣraðe'θiðo, a] *adj*
ungrateful.

desagrado [desa'ɣraðo] *nm* (*disgusto*)
displeasure; (*contrariedad*)
dissatisfaction; con ~ unwillingly.

desagraviar [desaɣra'βjar] *vt* to make
amends to.

desagravio [desa'ɣraβjo] *nm* (*satisfacción*)
amends; (*compensación*) compensation.

desaguadero [desaɣwa'ðero] *nm* drain.

desagüe [de'saɣwe] *nm* (*de un líquido*)
drainage; (*cañería: tb*: tubo de ~)
drainpipe; (*salida*) outlet, drain.

desaguisado, a [desaɣi'saðo, a] *adj* illegal
♦ *nm* outrage.

desahogado, a [desao'ɣaðo, a] *adj*
(*holgado*) comfortable; (*espacioso*)
roomy.

desahogar [desao'ɣar] *vt* (*aliviar*) to ease,
relieve; (*ira*) to vent; ~se *vr* (*distenderse*)
to relax; (*desfogarse*) to let off steam
(*fam*); (*confesarse*) to confess, get sth off
one's chest (*fam*).

desahogo [desa'oɣo] *nm* (*alivio*) relief;
(*comodidad*) comfort, ease; vivir con ~ to
be comfortably off.

desahogue [desa'oɣe] *etc vb V* **desahogar.**

desahuciado, a [desau'θjaðo, a] *adj*
hopeless.

desahuciar [desau'θjar] *vt* (*enfermo*) to
give up hope for; (*inquilino*) to evict.

desahucio [de'sauθjo] *nm* eviction.

desairado, a [desai'raðo, a] *adj*

(*menospreciado*) disregarded; (*desgarbado*) shabby; (*sin éxito*) unsuccessful; **quedar** ~ to come off badly.

desairar [desai'rar] *vt* (*menospreciar*) to slight, snub; (*cosa*) to disregard; (*COM*) to default on.

desaire [des'aire] *nm* (*menosprecio*) slight; (*falta de garbo*) unattractiveness; **dar** *o* **hacer un** ~ **a algn** to offend sb; **¿me va usted a hacer ese** ~? I won't take no for an answer!

desajustar [desaxus'tar] *vt* (*desarreglar*) to disarrange; (*desconcertar*) to throw off balance; (*fig: planes*) to upset; ~**se** *vr* to get out of order; (*aflojarse*) to loosen.

desajuste [desa'xuste] *nm* (*de máquina*) disorder; (*avería*) breakdown; (*situación*) imbalance; (*desacuerdo*) disagreement.

desalentador, a [desalenta'ðor, a] *adj* discouraging.

desalentar [desalen'tar] *vt* (*desanimar*) to discourage; ~**se** *vr* to get discouraged.

desaliento [desa'ljento] *etc vb* V **desalentar** ♦ *nm* discouragement; (*abatimiento*) depression.

desaliñado, a [desali'ɲaðo, a] *adj* (*descuidado*) slovenly; (*raído*) shabby; (*desordenado*) untidy; (*negligente*) careless.

desaliño [desa'liɲo] *nm* (*descuido*) slovenliness; (*negligencia*) carelessness.

desalmado, a [desal'maðo, a] *adj* (*cruel*) cruel, heartless.

desalojar [desalo'xar] *vt* (*gen*) to remove, expel; (*expulsar, echar*) to eject; (*abandonar*) to move out of ♦ *vi* to move out; **la policía desalojó el local** the police cleared people out of the place.

desalquilar [desalki'lar] *vt* to vacate, move out; ~**se** *vr* to become vacant.

desamarrar [desama'rrar] *vt* to untie; (*NAUT*) to cast off.

desamor [desa'mor] *nm* (*frialdad*) indifference; (*odio*) dislike.

desamparado, a [desampa'raðo, a] *adj* (*persona*) helpless; (*lugar: expuesto*) exposed; (: *desierto*) deserted.

desamparar [desampa'rar] *vt* (*abandonar*) to desert, abandon; (*JUR*) to leave defenceless; (*barco*) to abandon.

desamparo [desam'paro] *nm* (*acto*) desertion; (*estado*) helplessness.

desamueblado, a [desamwe'βlaðo, a] *adj* unfurnished.

desandar [desan'dar] *vt*: ~ **lo andado** *o* **el camino** to retrace one's steps.

desanduve [desan'duβe] *etc*,

desanduviera [desandu'βjera] *etc vb* V **desandar.**

desangelado, a [desanxe'laðo, a] *adj* (*habitación, edificio*) lifeless.

desangrar [desan'grar] *vt* to bleed; (*fig: persona*) to bleed dry; (*lago*) to drain; ~**se** *vr* to lose a lot of blood; (*morir*) to bleed to death.

desanimado, a [desani'maðo, a] *adj* (*persona*) downhearted; (*espectáculo, fiesta*) dull.

desanimar [desani'mar] *vt* (*desalentar*) to discourage; (*deprimir*) to depress; ~**se** *vr* to lose heart.

desánimo [de'sanimo] *nm* despondency; (*abatimiento*) dejection; (*falta de animación*) dullness.

desanudar [desanu'ðar] *vt* to untie; (*fig*) to clear up.

desapacible [desapa'θiβle] *adj* unpleasant.

desaparecer [desapare'θer] *vi* to disappear; (*el sol, la luz*) to vanish; (~ *de vista*) to drop out of sight; (*efectos, señales*) to wear off ♦ *vt* (*esp AM POL*) to cause to disappear; (: *eufemismo*) to murder.

desaparecido, a [desapare'θiðo, a] *adj* missing; (*especie*) extinct ♦ *nm/f* (*AM POL*) kidnapped *o* missing person.

desaparezca [desapa'reθka] *etc vb* V **desaparecer.**

desaparición [desapari'θjon] *nf* disappearance; (*de especie etc*) extinction.

desapasionado, a [desapasjo'naðo, a] *adj* dispassionate, impartial.

desapego [desa'peɣo] *nm* (*frialdad*) coolness; (*distancia*) detachment.

desapercibido, a [desaperθi'βiðo, a] *adj* unnoticed; (*desprevenido*) unprepared; **pasar** ~ to go unnoticed.

desaplicado, a [desapli'kado, a] *adj* slack, lazy.

desaprensivo, a [desapren'siβo, a] *adj* unscrupulous.

desaprobar [desapro'βar] *vt* (*reprobar*) to disapprove of; (*condenar*) to condemn; (*no consentir*) to reject.

desaprovechado, a [desaproβe't∫aðo, a] *adj* (*oportunidad, tiempo*) wasted; (*estudiante*) slack.

desaprovechar [desaproβe't∫ar] *vt* to waste; (*talento*) not to use to the full ♦ *vi* (*perder terreno*) to lose ground.

desapruebe [desa'prweβe] *etc vb* V **desaprobar.**

desarmar [desar'mar] *vt* (*MIL, fig*) to disarm; (*TEC*) to take apart, dismantle.

desarme [de'sarme] *nm* disarmament.

desarraigado, a [desarrai'ɣaðo, a] *adj* (*persona*) without roots, rootless.

desarraigar [desarrai'ɣar] *vt* to uproot; (*fig: costumbre*) to root out; (: *persona*) to banish.

desarraigo [desa'rraiɣo] *nm* uprooting.

desarraigue [desa'rraiɣe] *etc vb V* **desarraigar**.

desarreglado, a [desarre'ɣlaðo, a] *adj* (*desordenado*) disorderly, untidy; (*hábitos*) irregular.

desarreglar [desarre'ɣlar] *vt* to mess up; (*desordenar*) to disarrange; (*trastocar*) to upset, disturb.

desarreglo [desa'rreɣlo] *nm* (*de casa, persona*) untidiness; (*desorden*) disorder; (*TEC*) trouble; (*MED*) upset; **viven en el mayor** ~ they live in complete chaos.

desarrollado, a [desarro'ʎaðo, a] *adj* developed.

desarrollar [desarro'ʎar] *vt* (*gen*) to develop; (*extender*) to unfold; (*teoría*) to explain; ~**se** *vr* to develop; (*extenderse*) to open (out); (*film*) to develop; (*fig*) to grow; (*tener lugar*) to take place; **aquí desarrollan un trabajo muy importante** they carry on *o* out very important work here; **la acción se desarrolla en Roma** (*CINE etc*) the scene is set in Rome.

desarrollo [desa'rroʎo] *nm* development; (*de acontecimientos*) unfolding; (*de industria, mercado*) expansion, growth; **país en vías de** ~ developing country; **la industria está en pleno** ~ industry is expanding steadily; ~ **sostenible** sustainable development.

desarrugar [desarru'ɣar] *vt* (*alisar*) to smooth (out); (*ropa*) to remove the creases from.

desarrugue [desa'rruɣe] *etc vb V* **desarrugar**.

desarticulado, a [desartiku'laðo, a] *adj* disjointed.

desarticular [desartiku'lar] *vt* (*huesos*) to dislocate, put out of joint; (*objeto*) to take apart; (*grupo terrorista etc*) to break up.

desaseado, a [desase'aðo, a] *adj* (*sucio*) dirty; (*desaliñado*) untidy.

desaseo [desa'seo] *nm* (*suciedad*) dirtiness; (*desarreglo*) untidiness.

desasga [de'sasɣa] *etc vb V* **desasir**.

desasir [desa'sir] *vt* to loosen; ~**se** *vr* to extricate o.s.; ~**se de** to let go, give up.

desasosegar [desasose'ɣar] *vt* (*inquietar*) to disturb, make uneasy; ~**se** *vr* to become uneasy.

desasosegué [desasose'ɣe], **desasoseguemos** [desasose'ɣemos] *etc vb V* **desasosegar**.

desasosiego [desaso'sjeɣo] *etc vb V* **desasosegar ♦** *nm* (*intranquilidad*) uneasiness, restlessness; (*ansiedad*) anxiety; (*POL etc*) unrest.

desasosigue [desaso'sjeɣue] *etc vb V* **desasosegar**.

desastrado, a [desas'traðo, a] *adj* (*desaliñado*) shabby; (*sucio*) dirty.

desastre [de'sastre] *nm* disaster; ¡**un** ~! how awful!; **la función fue un** ~ the show was a shambles.

desastroso, a [desas'troso, a] *adj* disastrous.

desatado, a [desa'taðo, a] *adj* (*desligado*) untied; (*violento*) violent, wild.

desatar [desa'tar] *vt* (*nudo*) to untie; (*paquete*) to undo; (*perro, odio*) to unleash; (*misterio*) to solve; (*separar*) to detach; ~**se** *vr* (*zapatos*) to come untied; (*tormenta*) to break; (*perder control de sí*) to lose self-control; ~**se en injurias** to pour out a stream of insults.

desatascar [desatas'kar] *vt* (*cañería*) to unblock, clear; ~ **a algn** (*fig*) to get sb out of a jam.

desatasque [desa'taske] *etc vb V* **desatascar**.

desatención [desaten'θjon] *nf* (*descuido*) inattention; (*distracción*) absent-mindedness.

desatender [desaten'der] *vt* (*no prestar atención a*) to disregard; (*abandonar*) to neglect.

desatento, a [desa'tento, a] *adj* (*distraído*) inattentive; (*descortés*) discourteous.

desatienda [desa'tjenda] *etc vb V* **desatender**.

desatinado, a [desati'naðo, a] *adj* foolish, silly.

desatino [desa'tino] *nm* (*idiotez*) foolishness, folly; (*error*) blunder; ~**s** *nmpl* nonsense *sg*; ¡**qué** ~! how silly!, what rubbish!

desatornillar [desatorni'ʎar] *vt* to unscrew.

desatrancar [desatran'kar] *vt* (*puerta*) to unbolt; (*cañería*) to unblock.

desatranque [desa'tranke] *etc vb V* **desatrancar**.

desautorice [desauto'riθe] *etc vb V* **desautorizar**.

desautorizado, a [desautori'θaðo, a] *adj* unauthorized.

desautorizar [desautori'θar] *vt* (*oficial*) to

deprive of authority; (*informe*) to deny.
desavendré [desaßen'dre] *etc vb V*
desavenir.
desavenencia [desaße'nenθja] *nf*
(*desacuerdo*) disagreement;
(*discrepancia*) quarrel.
desavenga [desa'ßenga] *etc vb V*
desavenir.
desavenido, a [desaße'niðo, a] *adj*
(*opuesto*) contrary; (*reñidos*) in
disagreement; **ellos están ~s** they
are at odds.
desavenir [desaße'nir] *vt* (*enemistar*) to
make trouble between; **~se** *vr* to fall out.
desaventajado, a [desaßenta'xaðo, a] *adj*
(*inferior*) inferior; (*poco ventajoso*)
disadvantageous.
desaviene [desa'ßjene] *etc*,
desaviniendo [desaßi'njendo] *etc vb V*
desavenir.
desayunar [desaju'nar] *vi*, **~se** *vr* to have
breakfast ♦ *vt* to have for breakfast; **~
con café** to have coffee for breakfast; **~
con algo** (*fig*) to get the first news of sth.
desayuno [desa'juno] *nm* breakfast.
desazón [desa'θon] *nf* (*angustia*) anxiety;
(*MED*) discomfort; (*fig*) annoyance.
desazonar [desaθo'nar] *vt* (*fig*) to annoy,
upset; **~se** *vr* (*enojarse*) to be annoyed;
(*preocuparse*) to worry, be anxious.
desbancar [desßan'kar] *vt* (*quitar el puesto
a*) to oust; (*suplantar*) to supplant (in sb's
affections).
desbandada [desßan'daða] *nf* rush; **~
general** mass exodus; **a la ~** in disorder.
desbandarse [desßan'darse] *vr* (*MIL*) to
disband; (*fig*) to flee in disorder.
desbanque [des'ßanke] *etc vb V* **desbancar**.
desbarajuste [desßara'xuste] *nm*
confusion, disorder; **¡qué ~!** what a
mess!
desbaratar [desßara'tar] *vt* (*gen*) to mess
up; (*plan*) to spoil; (*deshacer, destruir*) to
ruin ♦ *vi* to talk nonsense; **~se** *vr*
(*máquina*) to break down; (*persona:
irritarse*) to fly off the handle (*fam*).
desbarrar [desßa'rrar] *vi* to talk nonsense.
desbloquear [desßloke'ar] *vt*
(*negociaciones, tráfico*) to get going
again; (*COM: cuenta*) to unfreeze.
desbocado, a [desßo'kaðo, a] *adj* (*caballo*)
runaway; (*herramienta*) worn.
desbocar [desßo'kar] *vt* (*vasija*) to break
the rim of; **~se** *vr* (*caballo*) to bolt;
(*persona: soltar injurias*) to let out a
stream of insults.
desboque [des'ßoke] *etc vb V* **desbocar**.
desbordamiento [desßorða'mjento] *nm*

(*de río*) overflowing; (*INFORM*) overflow;
(*de cólera*) outburst; (*de entusiasmo*)
upsurge.
desbordar [desßor'ðar] *vt* (*sobrepasar*) to
go beyond; (*exceder*) to exceed ♦ *vi*, **~se**
vr (*líquido, río*) to overflow; (*entusiasmo*)
to erupt; (*persona: exaltarse*) to get
carried away.
desbravar [desßra'ßar] *vt* (*caballo*) to break
in; (*animal*) to tame.
descabalgar [deskaßal'xar] *vi* to dismount.
descabalgue [deska'ßalxe] *etc vb V*
descabalgar.
descabellado, a [deskaße'ʎaðo, a] *adj*
(*disparatado*) wild, crazy; (*insensato*)
preposterous.
descabellar [deskaße'ʎar] *vt* to ruffle;
(*TAUR: toro*) to give the coup de grace to.
descabezado, a [deskaße'θaðo, a] *adj* (*sin
cabeza*) headless; (*insensato*) wild.
descafeinado, a [deskafei'naðo, a] *adj*
decaffeinated ♦ *nm* decaffeinated
coffee, de-caff.
descalabrar [deskala'ßrar] *vt* to smash;
(*persona*) to hit; (: *en la cabeza*) to hit on
the head; (*NAUT*) to cripple; (*dañar*) to
harm, damage; **~se** *vr* to hurt one's
head.
descalabro [deska'laßro] *nm* blow;
(*desgracia*) misfortune.
descalce [des'kalθe] *etc vb V* **descalzar**.
descalificación [deskalifika'θjon] *nf*
disqualification; **descalificaciones** *nfpl*
discrediting *sg*.
descalificar [deskalifi'kar] *vt* to disqualify;
(*desacreditar*) to discredit.
descalifique [deskali'fike] *etc vb V*
descalificar.
descalzar [deskal'θar] *vt* (*zapato*) to take
off.
descalzo, a [des'kalθo, a] *adj* barefoot(ed);
(*fig*) destitute; **estar (con los pies) ~(s)** to
be barefooted.
descambiar [deskam'bjar] *vt* to exchange.
descaminado, a [deskami'naðo, a] *adj*
(*equivocado*) on the wrong road; (*fig*)
misguided; **en eso no anda usted muy ~**
you're not far wrong there.
descamisado, a [deskami'saðo, a] *adj*
bare-chested.
descampado [deskam'paðo] *nm* open
space, piece of empty ground; **comer al
~** to eat in the open air.
descansado, a [deskan'saðo, a] *adj* (*gen*)
rested; (*que tranquiliza*) restful.
descansar [deskan'sar] *vt* (*gen*) to rest;
(*apoyar*): **~ (sobre)** to lean (on) ♦ *vi* to
rest, have a rest; (*echarse*) to lie down;

(*cadáver, restos*) to lie; ¡**que usted descanse!** sleep well!; ~ **en** (*argumento*) to be based on.

descansillo [deskanˈsiʎo] *nm* (*de escalera*) landing.

descanso [desˈkanso] *nm* (*reposo*) rest; (*alivio*) relief; (*pausa*) break; (*DEPORTE*) interval, half time; **día de** ~ day off; ~ **de enfermedad/maternidad** sick/maternity leave; **tomarse unos días de** ~ to take a few days' leave o rest.

descapitalizado, a [deskapitaliˈθaðo, a] *adj* undercapitalized.

descapotable [deskapoˈtaβle] *nm* (*tb:* **coche** ~) convertible.

descarado, a [deskaˈraðo, a] *adj* (*sin vergüenza*) shameless; (*insolente*) cheeky.

descarga [desˈkarɣa] *nf* (*ARQ, ELEC, MIL*) discharge; (*NAUT*) unloading.

descargador [deskarɣaˈðor] *nm* (*de barcos*) docker.

descargar [deskarˈɣar] *vt* to unload; (*golpe*) to let fly; (*arma*) to fire; (*ELEC*) to discharge; (*pila*) to run down; (*conciencia*) to relieve; (*COM*) to take up; (*persona: de una obligación*) to release; (: *de una deuda*) to free; (*JUR*) to clear ♦ *vi* (*río*): ~ **(en)** to flow (into); ~**se** *vr* to unburden o.s.; ~**se de algo** to get rid of sth; ~**se algo de Internet** to download sth from the Internet.

descargo [desˈkarɣo] *nm* (*de obligación*) release; (*COM: recibo*) receipt; (: *de deuda*) discharge; (*JUR*) evidence; ~ **de una acusación** acquittal on a charge.

descargue [desˈkarɣe] *etc vb V* **descargar**.

descarnado, a [deskarˈnaðo, a] *adj* scrawny; (*fig*) bare; (*estilo*) straightforward.

descaro [desˈkaro] *nm* nerve.

descarriar [deskaˈrrjar] *vt* (*descaminar*) to misdirect; (*fig*) to lead astray; ~**se** *vr* (*perderse*) to lose one's way; (*separarse*) to stray; (*pervertirse*) to err, go astray.

descarrilamiento [deskarrilaˈmjento] *nm* (*de tren*) derailment.

descarrilar [deskarriˈlar] *vi* to be derailed.

descartable [deskarˈtaβle] *adj* (*INFORM*) temporary.

descartar [deskarˈtar] *vt* (*rechazar*) to reject; (*eliminar*) to rule out; ~**se** *vr* (*NAIPES*) to discard; ~**se de** to shirk.

descascarar [deskaskaˈrar] *vt* (*naranja, limón*) to peel; (*nueces, huevo duro*) to shell; ~**se** *vr* to peel (off).

descascarillado, a [deskaskariˈʎaðo, a] *adj* (*paredes*) peeling.

descendencia [desθenˈdenθja] *nf* (*origen*)

origin, descent; (*hijos*) offspring; **morir sin dejar** ~ to die without issue.

descendente [desθenˈdente] *adj* (*cantidad*) diminishing; (*INFORM*) top-down.

descender [desθenˈder] *vt* (*bajar: escalera*) to go down ♦ *vi* to descend; (*temperatura, nivel*) to fall, drop; (*líquido*) to run; (*cortina*) to hang; (*fuerzas, persona*) to fail, get weak; ~ **de** to be descended from.

descendiente [desθenˈdjente] *nm/f* descendant.

descenso [desˈθenso] *nm* descent; (*de temperatura*) drop; (*de producción*) downturn; (*de calidad*) decline; (*MINERÍA*) collapse; (*bajada*) slope; (*fig: decadencia*) decline; (*de empleado etc*) demotion.

descentrado, a [desθenˈtraðo, a] *adj* (*pieza de una máquina*) off-centre; (*rueda*) out of true; (*persona*) bewildered; (*desequilibrado*) unbalanced; (*problema*) out of focus; **todavía está algo** ~ he is still somewhat out of touch.

descentralice [desθentraˈliθe] *etc vb V* **descentralizar**.

descentralizar [desθentraliˈθar] *vt* to decentralize.

descerrajar [desθerraˈxar] *vt* (*puerta*) to break open.

descienda [desˈθjenda] *etc vb V* **descender**.

descifrable [desθiˈfraβle] *adj* (*gen*) decipherable; (*letra*) legible.

descifrar [desθiˈfrar] *vt* (*escritura*) to decipher; (*mensaje*) to decode; (*problema*) to puzzle out; (*misterio*) to solve.

descocado, a [deskoˈkaðo, a] *adj* (*descarado*) cheeky; (*desvergonzado*) brazen.

descoco [desˈkoko] *nm* (*descaro*) cheek; (*atrevimiento*) brazenness.

descodificador [deskoðifikaˈðor] *nm* decoder.

descodificar [deskoðifiˈkar] *vt* to decode.

descolgar [deskolˈɣar] *vt* (*bajar*) to take down; (*desde una posición alta*) to lower; (*de una pared etc*) to unhook; (*teléfono*) to pick up; ~**se** *vr* to let o.s. down; ~**se por** (*bajar escurriéndose*) to slip down; (*pared*) to climb down; **dejó el teléfono descolgado** he left the phone off the hook.

descolgué [deskolˈɣe], **descolguemos** [deskolˈɣemos] *etc vb V* **descolgar**.

descollar [deskoˈʎar] *vi* (*sobresalir*) to stand out; (*montaña etc*) to rise; **la obra que más descuella de las suyas** his most outstanding work.

descolocado, a [deskoloˈkaðo, a] *adj:* **estar**

~ (*cosa*) to be out of place; (*criada*) to be unemployed.

descolorido, a [deskolo'riðo, a] *adj* (*color, tela*) faded; (*pálido*) pale; (*fig: estilo*) colourless.

descompaginar [deskompaxi'nar] *vt* (*desordenar*) to disarrange, mess up.

descompasado, a [deskompa'saðo, a] *adj* (*sin proporción*) out of all proportion; (*excesivo*) excessive; (*hora*) unearthly.

descompensar [deskompen'sar] *vt* to unbalance.

descompondré [deskompon'dre] *etc vb V* **descomponer**.

descomponer [deskompo'ner] *vt* (*gen, LING, MAT*) to break down; (*desordenar*) to disarrange, disturb; (*materia orgánica*) to rot, decompose; (*TEC*) to put out of order; (*facciones*) to distort; (*estómago etc*) to upset; (*planes*) to mess up; (*persona: molestar*) to upset; (: *irritar*) to annoy; ~**se** *vr* (*corromperse*) to rot, decompose; (*estómago*) to get upset; (*el tiempo*) to change (for the worse); (*TEC*) to break down.

descomponga [deskom'ponga] *etc vb V* **descomponer**.

descomposición [deskomposi'θjon] *nf* (*gen*) breakdown; (*de fruta etc*) decomposition; (*putrefacción*) rotting; (*de cara*) distortion; ~ **de vientre** (*MED*) stomach upset, diarrhoea.

descompostura [deskompos'tura] *nf* (*TEC*) breakdown; (*desorganización*) disorganization; (*desorden*) untidiness.

descompuesto, a [deskom'pwesto, a] *pp de* **descomponer** ♦ *adj* (*corrompido*) decomposed; (*roto*) broken (down).

descompuse [deskom'puse] *etc vb V* **descomponer**.

descomunal [deskomu'nal] *adj* (*enorme*) huge; (*fam: excelente*) fantastic.

desconcertado, a [deskonθer'taðo, a] *adj* disconcerted, bewildered.

desconcertar [deskonθer'tar] *vt* (*confundir*) to baffle; (*incomodar*) to upset, put out; (*orden*) to disturb; ~**se** *vr* (*turbarse*) to be upset; (*confundirse*) to be bewildered.

desconchado, a [deskon'tʃaðo, a] *adj* (*pintura*) peeling.

desconchar [deskon'tʃar] *vt* (*pared*) to strip off; (*loza*) to chip off.

desconcierto [deskon'θjerto] *etc vb V* **desconcertar** ♦ *nm* (*gen*) disorder; (*desorientación*) uncertainty; (*inquietud*) uneasiness; (*confusión*) bewilderment.

desconectado, a [deskonek'taðo, a] *adj* (*ELEC*) disconnected, switched off;

(*INFORM*) offline; **estar ~ de** (*fig*) to have no contact with.

desconectar [deskonek'tar] *vt* to disconnect; (*desenchufar*) to unplug; (*radio, televisión*) to switch off; (*INFORM*) to toggle off.

desconfiado, a [deskon'fjaðo, a] *adj* suspicious.

desconfianza [deskon'fjanθa] *nf* distrust.

desconfiar [deskon'fjar] *vi* to be distrustful; ~ **de** (*sospechar*) to mistrust, suspect; (*no tener confianza en*) to have no faith *o* confidence in; **desconfío de ello** I doubt it; **desconfíe de las imitaciones** (*COM*) beware of imitations.

desconforme [deskon'forme] *adj* = **disconforme**.

descongelar [deskonxe'lar] *vt* (*nevera*) to defrost; (*comida*) to thaw; (*AUTO*) to de-ice; (*COM, POL*) to unfreeze.

descongestionar [desconxestjo'nar] *vt* (*cabeza, tráfico*) to clear; (*calle, ciudad*) to relieve congestion in; (*fig: despejar*) to clear.

desconocer [deskono'θer] *vt* (*ignorar*) not to know, be ignorant of; (*no aceptar*) to deny; (*repudiar*) to disown.

desconocido, a [deskono'θiðo, a] *adj* unknown; (*que no se conoce*) unfamiliar; (*no reconocido*) unrecognized ♦ *nm/f* stranger; (*recién llegado*) newcomer; **está ~** he is hardly recognizable.

desconocimiento [deskonoθi'mjento] *nm* (*falta de conocimientos*) ignorance; (*repudio*) disregard.

desconozca [desko'noθka] *etc vb V* **desconocer**.

desconsiderado, a [deskonsiðe'raðo, a] *adj* inconsiderate; (*insensible*) thoughtless.

desconsolado, a [deskonso'laðo, a] *adj* (*afligido*) disconsolate; (*cara*) sad; (*desanimado*) dejected.

desconsolar [deskonso'lar] *vt* to distress; ~**se** *vr* to despair.

desconsuelo [deskon'swelo] *etc vb V* **desconsolar** ♦ *nm* (*tristeza*) distress; (*desesperación*) despair.

descontado, a [deskon'taðo, a] *adj*: **por ~** of course; **dar por ~ (que)** to take it for granted (that).

descontar [deskon'tar] *vt* (*deducir*) to take away, deduct; (*rebajar*) to discount.

descontento, a [deskon'tento, a] *adj* dissatisfied ♦ *nm* dissatisfaction, discontent.

descontrol [deskon'trol] *nm* (*fam*) lack of control.

descontrolado, a [deskontroˈlaðo, a] *adj* uncontrolled.

descontrolarse [deskontroˈlarse] *vr* (*persona*) to lose control.

desconvenir [deskombeˈnir] *vi* (*personas*) to disagree; (*no corresponder*) not to fit; (*no convenir*) to be inconvenient.

desconvocar [deskomboˈkar] *vt* to call off.

descorazonar [deskoraθoˈnar] *vt* to discourage, dishearten; ~**se** *vr* to get discouraged, lose heart.

descorchador [deskortʃaˈðor] *nm* corkscrew.

descorchar [deskorˈtʃar] *vt* to uncork, open.

descorrer [deskoˈrrer] *vt* (*cortina, cerrojo*) to draw back; (*velo*) to remove.

descortés [deskorˈtes] *adj* (*mal educado*) discourteous; (*grosero*) rude.

descortesía [deskorteˈsia] *nf* discourtesy; (*grosería*) rudeness.

descoser [deskoˈser] *vt* to unstitch; ~**se** *vr* to come apart (at the seams); (*fam: descubrir un secreto*) to blurt out a secret; ~**se de risa** to split one's sides laughing.

descosido, a [deskoˈsiðo, a] *adj* (*costura*) unstitched; (*desordenado*) disjointed ♦ *nm*: **como un** ~ (*obrar*) wildly; (*beber, comer*) to excess; (*estudiar*) like mad.

descoyuntar [deskojunˈtar] *vt* (*ANAT*) to dislocate; (*hechos*) to twist; ~**se** *vr*: ~**se un hueso** (*ANAT*) to put a bone out of joint; ~**se de risa** (*fam*) to split one's sides laughing; **estar descoyuntado** (*persona*) to be double-jointed.

descrédito [desˈkreðito] *nm* discredit; **caer en** ~ to fall into disrepute; **ir en** ~ **de** to be to the discredit of.

descreído, a [deskreˈiðo, a] *adj* (*incrédulo*) incredulous; (*falto de fe*) unbelieving.

descremado, a [deskreˈmaðo, a] *adj* skimmed.

descremar [deskreˈmar] *vt* (*leche*) to skim.

describir [deskriˈβir] *vt* to describe.

descripción [deskripˈθjon] *nf* description.

descrito [desˈkrito] *pp de* **describir**.

descuajar [deskwaˈxar] *vt* (*disolver*) to melt; (*planta*) to pull out by the roots; (*extirpar*) to eradicate, wipe out; (*desanimar*) to dishearten.

descuajaringarse [deskwaxarinˈgarse] *vr* to fall to bits.

descuajaringue [deskwaxaˈringe] *etc vb V* **descuajaringarse**.

descuartice [deskwarˈtiθe] *etc vb V* **descuartizar**.

descuartizar [deskwartiˈθar] *vt* (*animal*) to carve up, cut up; (*fig: hacer pedazos*) to tear apart.

descubierto, a [deskuˈβjerto, a] *pp de* **descubrir** ♦ *adj* uncovered, bare; (*persona*) bare-headed; (*cielo*) clear; (*coche*) open; (*campo*) treeless ♦ *nm* (*lugar*) open space; (*COM: en el presupuesto*) shortage; (: *bancario*) overdraft; **al** ~ in the open; **poner al** ~ to lay bare; **quedar al** ~ to be exposed; **estar en** ~ to be overdrawn.

descubridor, a [deskuˈβriðor, a] *nm/f* discoverer.

descubrimiento [deskuβriˈmjento] *nm* (*hallazgo*) discovery; (*de criminal, fraude*) detection; (*revelación*) revelation; (*de secreto etc*) disclosure; (*de estatua etc*) unveiling.

descubrir [deskuˈβrir] *vt* to discover, find; (*petróleo*) to strike; (*inaugurar*) to unveil; (*vislumbrar*) to detect; (*sacar a luz: crimen*) to bring to light; (*revelar*) to reveal, show; (*poner al descubierto*) to expose to view; (*naipes*) to lay down; (*quitar la tapa de*) to uncover; (*cacerola*) to take the lid off; (*enterarse de: causa, solución*) to find out; (*divisar*) to see, make out; (*delatar*) to give away, betray; ~**se** *vr* to reveal o.s.; (*quitarse sombrero*) to take off one's hat; (*confesar*) to confess; (*fig: salir a luz*) to come out *o* to light.

descuelga [desˈkwelɣa] *etc*, **descuelgue** [desˈkwelɣe] *etc vb V* **descolgar**.

descuelle [desˈkweʎe] *etc vb V* **descollar**.

descuento [desˈkwento] *etc vb V* **descontar** ♦ *nm* discount; ~ **del 3%** 3% off; **con** ~ at a discount; ~ **por pago al contado** (*COM*) cash discount; ~ **por volumen de compras** (*COM*) volume discount.

descuidado, a [deskwiˈðaðo, a] *adj* (*sin cuidado*) careless; (*desordenado*) untidy; (*olvidadizo*) forgetful; (*dejado*) neglected; (*desprevenido*) unprepared.

descuidar [deskwiˈðar] *vt* (*dejar*) to neglect; (*olvidar*) to overlook ♦ *vi*, ~**se** *vr* (*distraerse*) to be careless; (*estar desaliñado*) to let o.s. go; (*desprevenirse*) to drop one's guard; **¡descuida!** don't worry!

descuido [desˈkwiðo] *nm* (*dejadez*) carelessness; (*olvido*) negligence; (*un* ~) oversight; **al** ~ casually; (*sin cuidado*) carelessly; **al menor** ~ if my *etc* attention wanders for a minute; **con** ~ thoughtlessly; **por** ~ by an oversight.

════════════ *PALABRA CLAVE*

desde ['desðe] prep **1** (*lugar*) from; ~
Burgos hasta mi casa hay 30 km it's 30
kms from Burgos to my house; ~ **lejos**
from a distance
2 (*posición*): **hablaba ~ el balcón** she
was speaking from the balcony
3 (*tiempo*: +adv, n): ~ **ahora** from now
on; ~ **entonces/la boda** since then/the
wedding; ~ **niño** since I *etc* was a child;
~ **3 años atrás** since 3 years ago
4 (*tiempo*: +vb) since; for; **nos
conocemos ~ 1978/~ hace 20 años**
we've known each other since 1978/for
20 years; **no le veo ~ 1983/~ hace 5
años** I haven't seen him since 1983/for 5
years; **¿~ cuándo vives aquí?** how long
have you lived here?
5 (*gama*): ~ **los más lujosos hasta los
más económicos** from the most
luxurious to the most reasonably priced
6: ~ **luego (que no)** of course (not)
♦ *conj*: ~ **que**: ~ **que recuerdo** for as long
as I can remember; ~ **que llegó no ha
salido** he hasn't been out since he
arrived.

desdecir [desðe'θir] vi: ~ **de** (*no merecer*)
to be unworthy of; (*no corresponder*) to
clash with; ~**se de** to go back on.
desdén [des'ðen] nm scorn.
desdentado, a [desðen'taðo, a] adj
toothless.
desdeñable [desðe'ɲaβle] adj
contemptible; **nada ~** far from
negligible, considerable.
desdeñar [desðe'ɲar] vt (*despreciar*) to
scorn.
desdeñoso, a [desðe'ɲoso, a] adj scornful.
desdibujar [desðiβu'xar] vt to blur (the
outlines of); ~**se** vr to get blurred, fade
(away); **el recuerdo se ha desdibujado**
the memory has become blurred.
desdichado, a [desði'tʃaðo, a] adj (*sin
suerte*) unlucky; (*infeliz*) unhappy; (*día*)
ill-fated ♦ nm/f (*pobre desgraciado*) poor
devil.
desdicho, a [des'ðitʃo, a] pp de **desdecir**
♦ nf (*desgracia*) misfortune; (*infelicidad*)
unhappiness.
desdiciendo [desði'θjendo] etc vb V
desdecir.
desdiga [des'ðixa] etc, **desdije** [des'ðixe]
etc vb V **desdecir**.
desdoblado, a [desðo'βlaðo, a] adj
(*personalidad*) split.
desdoblar [desðo'βlar] vt (*extender*) to

spread out; (*desplegar*) to unfold.
deseable [dese'aβle] adj desirable.
desear [dese'ar] vt to want, desire, wish
for; **¿qué desea la señora?** (*tienda etc*)
what can I do for you, madam?; **estoy
deseando que esto termine** I'm longing
for this to finish.
desecar [dese'kar] vt, **desecarse** vr to dry
up.
desechable [dese'tʃaβle] adj (*envase etc*)
disposable.
desechar [dese'tʃar] vt (*basura*) to throw
out o away; (*ideas*) to reject, discard;
(*miedo*) to cast aside; (*plan*) to drop.
desecho [de'setʃo] nm (*desprecio*)
contempt; (*lo peor*) dregs pl; ~**s** nmpl
rubbish sg, waste sg; **de ~** (*hierro*) scrap;
(*producto*) waste; (*ropa*) cast-off.
desembalar [desemba'lar] vt to unpack.
desembarace [desemba'raθe] etc vb V
desembarazar.
desembarazado, a [desembara'θaðo, a]
adj (*libre*) clear, free; (*desenvuelto*) free
and easy.
desembarazar [desembara'θar] vt
(*desocupar*) to clear; (*desenredar*) to free;
~**se** vr: ~**se de** to free o.s. of, get rid of.
desembarazo [desemba'raθo] nm (*acto*)
clearing; (*AM: parto*) birth; (*desenfado*)
ease.
desembarcadero [desembarka'ðero] nm
quay.
desembarcar [desembar'kar] vt (*personas*)
to land; (*mercancías etc*) to unload ♦ vi,
~**se** vr (*de barco, avión*) to disembark.
desembarco [desem'barko] nm landing.
desembargar [desembar'xar] vt (*gen*) to
free; (*JUR*) to remove the embargo on.
desembargue [desem'βarxe] etc vb V
desembargar.
desembarque [desem'barke] etc vb V
desembarcar ♦ nm disembarkation; (*de
pasajeros*) landing; (*de mercancías*)
unloading.
desembocadura [desemboka'ðura] nf (*de
río*) mouth; (*de calle*) opening.
desembocar [desembo'kar] vi: ~ **en** to flow
into; (*fig*) to result in.
desemboce [desem'boθe] etc vb V
desembozar.
desembolsar [desembol'sar] vt (*pagar*) to
pay out; (*gastar*) to lay out.
desembolso [desem'bolso] nm payment.
desemboque [desem'boke] etc vb V
desembocar.
desembozar [desembo'θar] vt to unmask.
desembragar [desembra'xar] vt (*TEC*) to
disengage; (*embrague*) to release ♦ vi

desembrague [desem'ßraɣe] etc vb V
desembragar.

desembrollar [desembro'ʎar] vt (madeja)
to unravel; (asunto, malentendido) to sort
out.

desembuchar [desembu't∫ar] vt to
disgorge; (fig) to come out with ♦ vi
(confesar) to spill the beans (fam);
¡**desembucha**! out with it!

desemejante [deseme'xante] adj
dissimilar; ~ **de** different from, unlike.

desemejanza [deseme'xanθa] nf
dissimilarity.

desempacar [desempa'kar] vt (esp AM) to
unpack.

desempañar [desempa'ɲar] vt (cristal) to
clean, demist.

desempaque [desem'pake] etc vb V
desempacar.

desempaquetar [desempake'tar] vt to
unpack, unwrap.

desempatar [desempa'tar] vi to break a
tie; **volvieron a jugar para** ~ they held a
play-off.

desempate [desem'pate] nm (FÚTBOL)
play-off; (TENIS) tie-break(er).

desempeñar [desempe'ɲar] vt (cargo) to
hold; (papel) to play; (deber, función) to
perform, carry out; (lo empeñado) to
redeem; ~**se** vr to get out of debt; ~ **un**
papel (fig) to play (a role).

desempeño [desem'peɲo] nm occupation;
(de lo empeñado) redeeming; **de mucho**
~ very capable.

desempleado, a [desemple'aðo, a] adj
unemployed, out of work ♦ nm/f
unemployed person.

desempleo [desem'pleo] nm
unemployment.

desempolvar [desempol'ßar] vt (muebles
etc) to dust; (lo olvidado) to revive.

desencadenar [desenkaðe'nar] vt to
unchain; (ira) to unleash; (provocar) to
cause, set off; ~**se** vr to break loose;
(tormenta) to burst; (guerra) to break out;
se desencadenó una lucha violenta a
violent struggle ensued.

desencajar [desenka'xar] vt (hueso) to put
out of joint; (mandíbula) to dislocate;
(mecanismo, pieza) to disconnect,
disengage.

desencantar [desenkan'tar] vt to
disillusion, disenchant.

desencanto [desen'kanto] nm
disillusionment, disenchantment.

desenchufar [desent∫u'far] vt to unplug,
disconnect.

desenfadado, a [desenfa'ðaðo, a] adj
(desenvuelto) uninhibited; (descarado)
forward; (en el vestir) casual.

desenfado [desen'faðo] nm (libertad)
freedom; (comportamiento) free and easy
manner; (descaro) forwardness;
(desenvoltura) self-confidence.

desenfocado, a [desenfo'kaðo, a] adj
(FOTO) out of focus.

desenfrenado, a [desenfre'naðo, a] adj
(descontrolado) uncontrolled;
(inmoderado) unbridled.

desenfrenarse [desenfre'narse] vr
(persona: desmandarse) to lose all self-
control; (multitud) to run riot;
(tempestad) to burst; (viento) to rage.

desenfreno [desen'freno] nm (vicio)
wildness; (falta de control) lack of self-
control; (de pasiones) unleashing.

desenganchar [desengan't∫ar] vt (gen) to
unhook; (FERRO) to uncouple; (TEC) to
disengage.

desengañar [desenga'ɲar] vt to disillusion;
(abrir los ojos a) to open the eyes of; ~**se**
vr to become disillusioned;
¡**desengáñate**! don't you believe it!

desengaño [desen'gaɲo] nm
disillusionment; (decepción)
disappointment; **sufrir un** ~ **amoroso** to
be disappointed in love.

desengrasar [desengra'sar] vt to degrease.

desenlace [desen'laθe] etc vb V **desenlazar**
♦ nm outcome; (LIT) ending.

desenlazar [desenla'θar] vt (desatar) to
untie; (problema) to solve; (aclarar:
asunto) to unravel; ~**se** vr (desatarse) to
come undone; (LIT) to end.

desenmarañar [desenmara'ɲar] vt (fig) to
unravel.

desenmascarar [desenmaska'rar] vt to
unmask, expose.

desenredar [desenre'ðar] vt to resolve.

desenrollar [desenro'ʎar] vt to unroll,
unwind.

desenroscar [desenros'kar] vt (tornillo etc)
to unscrew.

desenrosque [desen'roske] etc vb V
desenroscar.

desentenderse [desenten'derse] vr: ~ **de**
to pretend not to know about; (apartarse)
to have nothing to do with.

desentendido, a [desenten'diðo, a] adj:
hacerse el ~ to pretend not to notice; **se**
hizo el ~ he didn't take the hint.

desenterrar [desente'rrar] vt to exhume;
(tesoro, fig) to unearth, dig up.

desentierre [desen'tjerre] etc vb V
desenterrar.

desentonar [desento'nar] *vi* (*MUS*) to sing (*o* play) out of tune; (*no encajar*) to be out of place; (*color*) to clash.

desentorpecer [desentorpe'θer] *vt* (*miembro*) to stretch; (*fam: persona*) to polish up.

desentorpezca [desentor'peθka] *etc vb V* **desentorpecer**.

desentrañar [desentra'nar] *vt* (*misterio*) to unravel.

desentrenado, a [desentre'naðo, a] *adj* out of training.

desentumecer [desentume'θer] *vt* (*pierna etc*) to stretch; (*DEPORTE*) to loosen up.

desentumezca [desentu'meθka] *etc vb V* **desentumecer**.

desenvainar [desembai'nar] *vt* (*espada*) to draw, unsheathe.

desenvoltura [desembol'tura] *nf* (*libertad, gracia*) ease; (*descaro*) free and easy manner; (*al hablar*) fluency.

desenvolver [desembol'ßer] *vt* (*paquete*) to unwrap; (*fig*) to develop; ~**se** *vr* (*desarrollarse*) to unfold, develop; (*suceder*) to go off; (*prosperar*) to prosper; (*arreglárselas*) to cope.

desenvolvimiento [desembolßi'mjento] *nm* (*desarrollo*) development; (*de idea*) exposition.

desenvuelto, a [desem'bwelto, a] *pp de* **desenvolver** ♦ *adj* (*suelto*) easy; (*desenfadado*) confident; (*al hablar*) fluent; (*pey*) forward.

desenvuelva [desem'buelßa] *etc vb V* **desenvolver**.

deseo [de'seo] *nm* desire, wish; ~ **de saber** thirst for knowledge; **buen** ~ good intentions *pl*; **arder en** ~**s de algo** to yearn for sth.

deseoso, a [dese'oso, a] *adj*: **estar** ~ **de hacer** to be anxious to do.

deseque [de'seke] *etc vb V* **desecar**.

desequilibrado, a [desekili'ßraðo, a] *adj* unbalanced ♦ *nm/f* unbalanced person; ~ **mental** mentally disturbed person.

desequilibrar [desekili'ßrar] *vt* (*mente*) to unbalance; (*objeto*) to throw out of balance; (*persona*) to throw off balance.

desequilibrio [deseki'lißrio] *nm* (*de mente*) unbalance; (*entre cantidades*) imbalance; (*MED*) unbalanced mental condition.

desertar [deser'tar] *vt* (*JUR: derecho de apelación*) to forfeit ♦ *vi* to desert; ~ **de sus deberes** to neglect one's duties.

desértico, a [de'sertiko, a] *adj* desert *cpd*; (*vacío*) deserted.

desertor, a [deser'tor, a] *nm/f* deserter.

desesperación [desespera'θjon] *nf* desperation, despair; (*irritación*) fury; **es una** ~ it's maddening; **es una** ~ **tener que** ... it's infuriating to have to ....

desesperado, a [desespe'raðo, a] *adj* (*persona: sin esperanza*) desperate; (*caso, situación*) hopeless; (*esfuerzo*) furious ♦ *nm*: **como un** ~ like mad ♦ *nf*: **hacer algo a la desesperada** to do sth as a last resort *o* in desperation.

desesperance [desespe'ranθe] *etc vb V* **desesperanzar**.

desesperante [desespe'rante] *adj* (*exasperante*) infuriating; (*persona*) hopeless.

desesperanzar [desesperan'θar] *vt* to drive to despair; ~**se** *vr* to lose hope, despair.

desesperar [desespe'rar] *vt* to drive to despair; (*exasperar*) to drive to distraction ♦ *vi*: ~ **de** to despair of; ~**se** *vr* to despair, lose hope.

desespero [deses'pero] *nm* (*AM*) despair.

desestabilice [desestaßi'liθe] *etc vb V* **desestabilizar**.

desestabilizar [desestaßili'θar] *vt* to destabilize.

desestimar [desesti'mar] *vt* (*menospreciar*) to have a low opinion of; (*rechazar*) to reject.

desfachatez [desfatʃa'teθ] *nf* (*insolencia*) impudence; (*descaro*) rudeness.

desfalco [des'falko] *nm* embezzlement.

desfallecer [desfaʎe'θer] *vi* (*perder las fuerzas*) to become weak; (*desvanecerse*) to faint.

desfallecido, a [desfaʎe'θiðo, a] *adj* (*débil*) weak.

desfallezca [desfa'ʎeθka] *etc vb V* **desfallecer**.

desfasado, a [desfa'saðo, a] *adj* (*anticuado*) old-fashioned; (*TEC*) out of phase.

desfasar [desfa'sar] *vt* to phase out.

desfase [des'fase] *nm* (*diferencia*) gap.

desfavorable [desfaßo'raßle] *adj* unfavourable.

desfavorecer [desfaßore'θer] *vt* (*sentar mal*) not to suit.

desfavorezca [desfaßo'reθka] *etc vb V* **desfavorecer**.

desfiguración [desfixura'θjon] *nf*, **desfiguramiento** [desfixura'mjento] *nm* (*de persona*) disfigurement; (*de monumento*) defacement; (*FOTO*) blurring.

desfigurar [desfixu'rar] *vt* (*cara*) to disfigure; (*cuerpo*) to deform; (*cuadro, monumento*) to deface; (*FOTO*) to blur; (*sentido*) to twist; (*suceso*) to misrepresent.

desfiladero [desfila'ðero] *nm* gorge, defile.

desfilar [desfi'lar] *vi* to parade; **desfilaron ante el general** they marched past the general.

desfile [des'file] *nm* procession; (*MIL*) parade; ~ **de modelos** fashion show.

desflorar [desflo'rar] *vt* (*mujer*) to deflower; (*arruinar*) to tarnish; (*asunto*) to touch on.

desfogar [desfo'xar] *vt* (*fig*) to vent ♦ *vi* (*NAUT: tormenta*) to burst; ~**se** *vr* (*fig*) to let off steam.

desfogue [des'foxe] *etc vb V* **desfogar**.

desgajar [desxa'xar] *vt* (*arrancar*) to tear off; (*romper*) to break off; (*naranja*) to split into segments; ~**se** *vr* to come off.

desgana [des'xana] *nf* (*falta de apetito*) loss of appetite; (*renuencia*) unwillingness; **hacer algo a** ~ to do sth unwillingly.

desganado, a [desxa'naðo, a] *adj*: **estar** ~ (*sin apetito*) to have no appetite; (*sin entusiasmo*) to have lost interest.

desgañitarse [desxaɲi'tarse] *vr* to shout o.s. hoarse.

desgarbado, a [desxar'βaðo, a] *adj* (*sin gracia*) clumsy, ungainly.

desgarrador, a [desxarra'ðor, a] *adj* heartrending.

desgarrar [desxa'rrar] *vt* to tear (up); (*fig*) to shatter.

desgarro [des'xarro] *nm* (*en tela*) tear; (*aflicción*) grief; (*descaro*) impudence.

desgastar [desxas'tar] *vt* (*deteriorar*) to wear away o down; (*estropear*) to spoil; ~**se** *vr* to get worn out.

desgaste [des'xaste] *nm* wear (and tear); (*de roca*) erosion; (*de cuerda*) fraying; (*de metal*) corrosion; ~ **económico** drain on one's resources.

desglosar [desxlo'sar] *vt* to detach.

desgobierno [desxo'βjerno] *etc vb V* **desgobernar** ♦ *nm* (*POL*) misgovernment, misrule.

desgracia [des'xraθja] *nf* misfortune; (*accidente*) accident; (*vergüenza*) disgrace; (*contratiempo*) setback; **por** ~ unfortunately; **en el accidente no hay que lamentar** ~**s personales** there were no casualties in the accident; **caer en** ~ to fall from grace; **tener la** ~ **de** to be unlucky enough to.

desgraciadamente [desxraθjaða'mente] *adv* unfortunately.

desgraciado, a [desxra'θjaðo, a] *adj* (*sin suerte*) unlucky, unfortunate; (*miserable*) wretched; (*infeliz*) miserable ♦ *nm/f* (*malo*) swine; (*infeliz*) poor creature; **¡esa radio desgraciada!** (*esp AM*) that lousy radio!

desgraciar [desxra'θjar] *vt* (*estropear*) to spoil; (*ofender*) to displease.

desgranar [desxra'nar] *vt* (*trigo*) to thresh; (*guisantes*) to shell; ~ **un racimo** to pick the grapes from a bunch; ~ **mentiras** to come out with a string of lies.

desgravación [desxraβa'θjon] *nf* (*COM*): ~ **de impuestos** tax relief; ~ **personal** personal allowance.

desgravar [desxra'βar] *vt* (*producto*) to reduce the tax o duty on.

desgreñado, a [desxre'ɲaðo, a] *adj* dishevelled.

desguace [des'xwaθe] *nm* (*de coches*) scrapping; (*lugar*) scrapyard.

desguazar [desxwa'θar] *vt* (*coche*) to scrap.

deshabitado, a [desaβi'taðo, a] *adj* uninhabited.

deshabitar [desaβi'tar] *vt* (*casa*) to leave empty; (*despoblar*) to depopulate.

deshacer [desa'θer] *vt* (*lo hecho*) to undo, unmake; (*proyectos: arruinar*) to spoil; (*casa*) to break up; (*TEC*) to take apart; (*enemigo*) to defeat; (*diluir*) to melt; (*contrato*) to break; (*intriga*) to solve; (*cama*) to strip; (*maleta*) to unpack; (*paquete*) to unwrap; (*nudo*) to untie; (*costura*) to unpick; ~**se** *vr* (*desatarse*) to come undone; (*estropearse*) to be spoiled; (*descomponerse*) to fall to pieces; (*disolverse*) to melt; (*despedazarse*) to come apart o undone; ~**se de** to get rid of; (*COM*) to dump, unload; ~**se en** (*cumplidos, elogios*) to be lavish with; ~**se en lágrimas** to burst into tears; ~**se por algo** to be crazy about sth.

deshaga [de'saxa] *etc*, **desharé** [desa're] *etc vb V* **deshacer**.

des(h)arrapado, a [desarra'paðo, a] *adj* ragged; (**de aspecto**) ~ shabby.

deshecho, a [de'setʃo, a] *pp de* **deshacer** ♦ *adj* (*lazo, nudo*) undone; (*roto*) smashed; (*despedazado*) in pieces; (*cama*) unmade; (*MED: persona*) weak, emaciated; (: *salud*) broken; **estoy** ~ I'm shattered.

deshelar [dese'lar] *vt* (*cañería*) to thaw; (*heladera*) to defrost.

desheredar [desere'ðar] *vt* to disinherit.

deshice [de'siθe] *etc vb V* **deshacer**.

deshidratación [desiðrata'θjon] *nf* dehydration.

deshidratar [desiðra'tar] *vt* to dehydrate.

deshielo [des'jelo] *etc vb V* **deshelar** ♦ *nm* thaw.

deshilachar [desila'tʃar] *vt*, **deshilacharse** *vr* to fray.

deshilar [desi'lar] *vt* (*tela*) to unravel.

deshilvanado, a [desilßa'naðo, a] *adj (fig)* disjointed, incoherent.

deshinchar [desin'tʃar] *vt (neumático)* to let down; *(herida etc)* to reduce (the swelling of); **~se** *vr (neumático)* to go flat; *(hinchazón)* to go down.

deshojar [deso'xar] *vt (árbol)* to strip the leaves off; *(flor)* to pull the petals off; **~se** *vr* to lose its leaves *etc*.

deshollinar [desoʎi'nar] *vt (chimenea)* to sweep.

deshonesto, a [deso'nesto, a] *adj (no honrado)* dishonest; *(indecente)* indecent.

deshonor [deso'nor] *nm* dishonour, disgrace; *(un ~)* insult, affront.

deshonra [de'sonra] *nf (deshonor)* dishonour; *(vergüenza)* shame.

deshonrar [deson'rar] *vt* to dishonour.

deshonroso, a [deson'roso, a] *adj* dishonourable, disgraceful.

deshora [de'sora]: **a ~** *adv* at the wrong time; *(llegar)* unexpectedly; *(acostarse)* at some unearthly hour.

deshuesar [deswe'sar] *vt (carne)* to bone; *(fruta)* to stone.

desidia [de'siðja] *nf (pereza)* idleness.

desierto, a [de'sjerto, a] *adj (casa, calle, negocio)* deserted; *(paisaje)* bleak ♦ *nm* desert.

designación [desiɣna'θjon] *nf (para un cargo)* appointment; *(nombre)* designation.

designar [desiɣ'nar] *vt (nombrar)* to designate; *(indicar)* to fix.

designio [de'siɣnjo] *nm* plan; **con el ~ de** with the intention of.

desigual [desi'ɣwal] *adj (lucha)* unequal; *(diferente)* different; *(terreno)* uneven; *(tratamiento)* unfair; *(cambiadizo: tiempo)* changeable; *(: carácter)* unpredictable.

desigualdad [desiɣwal'ðað] *nf (ECON, POL)* inequality; *(de carácter, tiempo)* unpredictability; *(de escritura)* unevenness; *(de terreno)* roughness.

desilusión [desilu'sjon] *nf* disillusionment; *(decepción)* disappointment.

desilusionar [desilusjo'nar] *vt* to disillusion; *(decepcionar)* to disappoint; **~se** *vr* to become disillusioned.

desinencia [desi'nenθja] *nf (LING)* ending.

desinfectar [desinfek'tar] *vt* to disinfect.

desinfestar [desinfes'tar] *vt* to decontaminate.

desinflación [desinfla'θjon] *nf (COM)* disinflation.

desinflar [desin'flar] *vt* to deflate; **~se** *vr (neumático)* to go down o flat.

desintegración [desinteɣra'θjon] *nf* disintegration; **~ nuclear** nuclear fission.

desintegrar [desinte'ɣrar] *vt (gen)* to disintegrate; *(átomo)* to split; *(grupo)* to break up; **~se** *vr* to disintegrate; to split; to break up.

desinterés [desinte'res] *nm (objetividad)* disinterestedness; *(altruismo)* unselfishness.

desinteresado, a [desintere'saðo, a] *adj (imparcial)* disinterested; *(altruista)* unselfish.

desintoxicar [desintoksi'kar] *vt* to detoxify; **~se** *vr (drogadicto)* to undergo treatment for drug addiction; **~se de** *(rutina, trabajo)* to get away from.

desintoxique [desintok'sike] *etc vb V* **desintoxicar.**

desistir [desis'tir] *vi (renunciar)* to stop, desist; **~ de** *(empresa)* to give up; *(derecho)* to waive.

deslavazado, a [deslaßa'θaðo, a] *adj (lacio)* limp; *(desteñido)* faded; *(insípido)* colourless; *(incoherente)* disjointed.

desleal [desle'al] *adj (infiel)* disloyal; *(COM: competencia)* unfair.

deslealtad [desleal'tað] *nf* disloyalty.

desleído, a [desle'iðo, a] *adj* weak, woolly.

desleír [desle'ir] *vt (líquido)* to dilute; *(sólido)* to dissolve.

deslenguado, a [deslen'gwaðo, a] *adj (grosero)* foul-mouthed.

deslía [des'lia] *etc vb V* **desleír.**

desliar [des'ljar] *vt (desatar)* to untie; *(paquete)* to open; **~se** *vr* to come undone.

deslice [des'liθe] *etc vb V* **deslizar.**

desliendo [desli'endo] *etc vb V* **desleír.**

desligar [desli'ɣar] *vt (desatar)* to untie, undo; *(separar)* to separate; **~se** *vr (de un compromiso)* to extricate o.s.

desligue [des'liɣe] *etc vb V* **desligar.**

deslindar [deslin'dar] *vt (señalar las lindes de)* to mark out, fix the boundaries of; *(fig)* to define.

desliz [des'liθ] *nm (fig)* lapse; **~ de lengua** slip of the tongue; **cometer un ~** to slip up.

deslizar [desli'θar] *vt* to slip, slide; **~se** *vr (escurrirse: persona)* to slip, slide; *(: coche)* to skid; *(aguas mansas)* to flow gently; *(error)* to creep in; *(tiempo)* to pass; *(persona: irse)* to slip away; **~se en un cuarto** to slip into a room.

deslomar [deslo'mar] *vt (romper el lomo de)* to break the back of; *(fig)* to wear out; **~se** *vr (fig fam)* to work one's guts out.

deslucido, a [deslu'θiðo, a] *adj* dull; *(torpe)*

awkward, graceless; (*deslustrado*) tarnished; (*fracasado*) unsuccessful; **quedar** ~ to make a poor impression.

deslucir [deslu'θir] *vt* (*deslustrar*) to tarnish; (*estropear*) to spoil, ruin; (*persona*) to discredit; **la lluvia deslució el acto** the rain ruined the ceremony.

deslumbrar [deslum'brar] *vt* (*con la luz*) to dazzle; (*cegar*) to blind; (*impresionar*) to dazzle; (*dejar perplejo a*) to puzzle, confuse.

deslustrar [deslus'trar] *vt* (*vidrio*) to frost; (*quitar lustre a*) to dull; (*reputación*) to sully.

desluzca [des'luθka] *etc vb V* **deslucir**.

desmadrarse [desma'ðrarse] *vr* (*fam*) to run wild.

desmadre [des'maðre] *nm* (*fam:* *desorganización*) chaos; (: *jaleo*) commotion.

desmán [des'man] *nm* (*exceso*) outrage; (*abuso de poder*) abuse.

desmandarse [desman'darse] *vr* (*portarse mal*) to behave badly; (*excederse*) to get out of hand; (*caballo*) to bolt.

desmano [des'mano]: **a** ~ *adv*: **me coge** o **pilla a** ~ it's out of my way.

desmantelar [desmante'lar] *vt* (*deshacer*) to dismantle; (*casa*) to strip; (*organización*) to disband; (*MIL*) to raze; (*andamio*) to take down; (*NAUT*) to unrig.

desmaquillador [desmakiʎa'ðor] *nm* make-up remover.

desmaquillarse [desmaki'ʎarse] *vr* to take off one's make up.

desmarcarse [desmar'karse] *vr*: ~ **de** (*DEPORTE*) to get clear of; (*fig*) to distance o.s. from.

desmayado, a [desma'jaðo, a] *adj* (*sin sentido*) unconscious; (*carácter*) dull; (*débil*) faint, weak; (*color*) pale.

desmayar [desma'jar] *vi* to lose heart; ~**se** *vr* (*MED*) to faint.

desmayo [des'majo] *nm* (*MED: acto*) faint; (*estado*) unconsciousness; (*depresión*) dejection; (*de voz*) faltering; **sufrir un** ~ to have a fainting fit.

desmedido, a [desme'ðiðo, a] *adj* excessive; (*ambición*) boundless.

desmejorado, a [desmexo'raðo, a] *adj*: **está muy desmejorada** (*MED*) she's not looking too well.

desmejorar [desmexo'rar] *vt* (*dañar*) to impair, spoil; (*MED*) to weaken.

desmembración [desmembra'θjon] *nf* dismemberment; (*fig*) break-up.

desmembrar [desmem'brar] *vt* (*MED*) to dismember; (*fig*) to separate.

desmemoriado, a [desmemo'rjaðo, a] *adj* forgetful, absent-minded.

desmentir [desmen'tir] *vt* (*contradecir*) to contradict; (*refutar*) to deny; (*rumor*) to scotch ♦ *vi*: ~ **de** to refute; ~**se** *vr* to contradict o.s.

desmenuce [desme'nuθe] *etc vb V* **desmenuzar**.

desmenuzar [desmenu'θar] *vt* (*deshacer*) to crumble; (*carne*) to chop; (*examinar*) to examine closely.

desmerecer [desmere'θer] *vt* to be unworthy of ♦ *vi* (*deteriorarse*) to deteriorate.

desmerezca [desme'reθka] *etc vb V* **desmerecer**.

desmesurado, a [desmesu'raðo, a] *adj* (*desmedido*) disproportionate; (*enorme*) enormous; (*ambición*) boundless; (*descarado*) insolent.

desmiembre [des'mjembre] *etc vb V* **desmembrar**.

desmienta [des'mjenta] *etc vb V* **desmentir**.

desmigajar [desmixa'xar], **desmigar** [desmi'xar] *vt* to crumble.

desmigue [des'mixe] *etc vb V* **desmigar**.

desmilitarice [desmilita'riθe] *etc vb V* **desmilitarizar**.

desmilitarizar [desmilitari'θar] *vt* to demilitarize.

desmintiendo [desmin'tjendo] *etc vb V* **desmentir**.

desmochar [desmo'tʃar] *vt* (*árbol*) to lop; (*texto*) to cut, hack about.

desmontable [desmon'taßle] *adj* (*que se quita*) detachable; (*en compartimientos*) sectional; (*que se puede plegar etc*) collapsible.

desmontar [desmon'tar] *vt* (*deshacer*) to dismantle; (*motor*) to strip down; (*máquina*) to take apart; (*escopeta*) to uncock; (*tienda de campaña*) to take down; (*tierra*) to level; (*quitar los árboles a*) to clear; (*jinete*) to throw ♦ *vi* to dismount.

desmonte [des'monte] *nm* (*de tierra*) levelling; (*de árboles*) clearing; (*terreno*) levelled ground; (*FERRO*) cutting.

desmoralice [desmora'liθe] *etc vb V* **desmoralizar**.

desmoralizador, a [desmoraliθa'ðor, a] *adj* demoralizing.

desmoralizar [desmorali'θar] *vt* to demoralize.

desmoronado, a [desmoro'naðo, a] *adj* (*casa, edificio*) dilapidated.

desmoronamiento [desmorona'mjento]

nm (*tb fig*) crumbling.

desmoronar [desmoro'nar] *vt* to wear away, erode; ~**se** *vr* (*edificio, dique*) to fall into disrepair; (*economía*) to decline.

desmovilice [desmoβi'liθe] *etc vb V* **desmovilizar.**

desmovilizar [desmoβili'θar] *vt* to demobilize.

desnacionalización [desnaθjonaliθa'θjon] *nf* denationalization.

desnacionalizado, a [desnaθjonali'θaðo, a] *adj* (*industria*) denationalized; (*persona*) stateless.

desnatado, a [desna'taðo, a] *adj* skimmed; (*yogur*) low fat.

desnatar [desna'tar] *vt* (*leche*) to skim; **leche sin** ~ whole milk.

desnaturalice [desnatura'liθe] *etc vb V* **desnaturalizar.**

desnaturalizado, a [desnaturali'θaðo, a] *adj* (*persona*) unnatural; **alcohol** ~ methylated spirits.

desnaturalizar [desnaturali'θar] *vt* (*QUIMICA*) to denature; (*corromper*) to pervert; (*sentido de algo*) to distort; ~**se** *vr* (*perder la nacionalidad*) to give up one's nationality.

desnivel [desni'βel] *nm* (*de terreno*) unevenness; (*POL*) inequality; (*diferencia*) difference.

desnivelar [desniβe'lar] *vt* (*terreno*) to make uneven; (*fig: desequilibrar*) to unbalance; (*balanza*) to tip.

desnuclearizado, a [desnukleari'θaðo, a] *adj:* **región desnuclearizada** nuclear-free zone.

desnudar [desnu'ðar] *vt* (*desvestir*) to undress; (*despojar*) to strip; ~**se** *vr* (*desvestirse*) to get undressed.

desnudez [desnu'ðeθ] *nf* (*de persona*) nudity; (*fig*) bareness.

desnudo, a [des'nuðo, a] *adj* (*cuerpo*) naked; (*árbol, brazo*) bare; (*paisaje*) flat; (*estilo*) unadorned; (*verdad*) plain ♦ *nm/f* nude; ~ **de** devoid *o* bereft of; **la retrató al** ~ he painted her in the nude; **poner al** ~ to lay bare.

desnutrición [desnutri'θjon] *nf* malnutrition.

desnutrido, a [desnu'triðo, a] *adj* undernourished.

desobedecer [desoβeðe'θer] *vt, vi* to disobey.

desobedezca [desoβe'ðeθka] *etc vb V* **desobedecer.**

desobediencia [desoβe'ðjenθja] *nf* disobedience.

desocupación [desokupa'θjon] *nf* (*AM*) unemployment.

desocupado, a [desoku'paðo, a] *adj* at leisure; (*desempleado*) unemployed; (*deshabitado*) empty, vacant.

desocupar [desoku'par] *vt* to vacate; ~**se** *vr* (*quedar libre*) to be free; **se ha desocupado aquella mesa** that table's free now.

desodorante [desoðo'rante] *nm* deodorant.

desoiga [de'soixa] *etc vb V* **desoír.**

desoír [deso'ir] *vt* to ignore, disregard.

desolación [desola'θjon] *nf* (*de lugar*) desolation; (*fig*) grief.

desolar [deso'lar] *vt* to ruin, lay waste.

desollar [deso'ʎar] *vt* (*quitar la piel a*) to skin; (*criticar*): ~ **vivo a** to criticize unmercifully.

desorbitado, a [desorβi'taðo, a] *adj* (*excesivo*) excessive; (*precio*) exorbitant; **con los ojos** ~**s** pop-eyed.

desorbitar [desorβi'tar] *vt* (*exagerar*) to exaggerate; (*interpretar mal*) to misinterpret; ~**se** *vr* (*persona*) to lose one's sense of proportion; (*asunto*) to get out of hand.

desorden [de'sorðen] *nm* confusion; (*de casa, cuarto*) mess; (*político*) disorder; **desórdenes** *nmpl* (*alborotos*) disturbances; (*excesos*) excesses; **en** ~ (*gente*) in confusion.

desordenado, a [desorðe'naðo, a] *adj* (*habitación, persona*) untidy; (*objetos: revueltos*) in a mess, jumbled; (*conducta*) disorderly.

desordenar [desorðe'nar] *vt* (*gen*) to disarrange; (*pelo*) to mess up; (*cuarto*) to make a mess in; (*causar confusión a*) to throw into confusion.

desorganice [desorxa'niθe] *etc vb V* **desorganizar.**

desorganizar [desorxani'θar] *vt* to disorganize.

desorientar [desorjen'tar] *vt* (*extraviar*) to mislead; (*confundir, desconcertar*) to confuse; ~**se** *vr* (*perderse*) to lose one's way.

desovar [deso'βar] *vi* (*peces*) to spawn; (*insectos*) to lay eggs.

desoyendo [deso'jendo] *etc vb V* **desoír.**

despabilado, a [despaβi'laðo, a] *adj* (*despierto*) wide-awake; (*fig*) alert, sharp.

despabilar [despaβi'lar] *vt* (*despertar*) to wake up; (*fig: persona*) to liven up; (*trabajo*) to get through quickly ♦ *vi*, ~**se** *vr* to wake up; (*fig*) to get a move on.

despachar [despa'tʃar] *vt* (*negocio*) to do, complete; (*resolver: problema*) to settle; (*correspondencia*) to deal with; (*fam:*

comida) to polish off; (: *bebida*) to knock back; (*enviar*) to send, dispatch; (*vender*) to sell, deal in; (*COM: cliente*) to attend to; (*billete*) to issue; (*mandar ir*) to send away ♦ *vi* (*decidirse*) to get things settled; (*apresurarse*) to hurry up; ~**se** *vr* to finish off; (*apresurarse*) to hurry up; ~**se de algo** to get rid of sth; ~**se a su gusto con algn** to give sb a piece of one's mind; **¿quién despacha?** is anybody serving?

despacho [des'patʃo] *nm* (*oficina*) office; (: *en una casa*) study; (*de paquetes*) dispatch; (*COM: venta*) sale (of goods); (*comunicación*) message; ~ **de billetes o boletos** (*AM*) booking office; ~ **de localidades** box office; **géneros sin** ~ unsaleable goods; **tener buen** ~ to find a ready sale.

despachurrar [despatʃu'rrar] *vt* (*aplastar*) to crush; (*persona*) to flatten.

despacio [des'paθjo] *adv* (*lentamente*) slowly; (*esp AM: en voz baja*) softly; ¡~! take it easy!

despacito [despa'θito] *adv* (*fam*) slowly; (*suavemente*) softly.

despampanante [despampa'nante] *adj* (*fam: chica*) stunning.

desparejado, a [despare'xaðo, a] *adj* odd.

desparpajo [despar'paxo] *nm* (*desenvoltura*) self-confidence; (*pey*) nerve.

desparramar [desparra'mar] *vt* (*esparcir*) to scatter; (*líquido*) to spill.

despatarrarse [despata'rrarse] *vr* (*abrir las piernas*) to open one's legs wide; (*caerse*) to tumble; (*fig*) to be flabbergasted.

despavorido, a [despaβo'riðo, a] *adj* terrified.

despecho [des'petʃo] *nm* spite; **a** ~ **de** in spite of; **por** ~ out of (sheer) spite.

despectivo, a [despek'tiβo, a] *adj* (*despreciativo*) derogatory; (*LING*) pejorative.

despedace [despe'ðaθe] *etc vb V* **despedazar**.

despedazar [despeða'θar] *vt* to tear to pieces.

despedida [despe'ðiða] *nf* (*adiós*) goodbye, farewell; (*antes de viaje*) send-off; (*en carta*) closing formula; (*de obrero*) sacking; (*INFORM*) logout; **cena/función de** ~ farewell dinner/performance; **regalo de** ~ parting gift; ~ **de soltero/ soltera** stag/hen party.

despedir [despe'ðir] *vt* (*visita*) to see off, show out; (*empleado*) to dismiss; (*inquilino*) to evict; (*objeto*) to hurl; (*olor etc*) to give out *o* off; ~**se** *vr* (*dejar un*

empleo) to give up one's job; (*INFORM*) to log out *o* off; ~**se de** to say goodbye to; **se despidieron** they said goodbye to each other.

despegado, a [despe'ɣaðo, a] *adj* (*separado*) detached; (*persona: poco afectuoso*) cold, indifferent ♦ *nm/f*: **es un** ~ he has cut himself off from his family.

despegar [despe'ɣar] *vt* to unstick; (*sobre*) to open ♦ *vi* (*avión*) to take off; (*cohete*) to blast off; ~**se** *vr* to come loose, come unstuck; **sin** ~ **los labios** without uttering a word.

despego [des'peɣo] *nm* detachment.

despegue [des'peɣe] *etc vb V* **despegar** ♦ *nm* takeoff; (*de cohete*) blastoff.

despeinado, a [despei'naðo, a] *adj* dishevelled, unkempt.

despeinar [despei'nar] *vt* (*pelo*) to ruffle; **¡me has despeinado todo!** you've completely ruined my hairdo!

despejado, a [despe'xaðo, a] *adj* (*lugar*) clear, free; (*cielo*) clear; (*persona*) wide-awake, bright.

despejar [despe'xar] *vt* (*gen*) to clear; (*misterio*) to clarify, clear up; (*MAT: incógnita*) to find ♦ *vi* (*el tiempo*) to clear; ~**se** *vr* (*tiempo, cielo*) to clear (up); (*misterio*) to become clearer; (*cabeza*) to clear; **¡despejen!** (*moverse*) move along!; (*salirse*) everybody out!

despeje [des'pexe] *nm* (*DEPORTE*) clearance.

despellejar [despeʎe'xar] *vt* (*animal*) to skin; (*criticar*) to criticize unmercifully; (*fam: arruinar*) to fleece.

despelotarse [despelo'tarse] *vr* (*fam*) to strip off; (*fig*) to let one's hair down.

despelote [despe'lote] (*fam*) *nm* (*AM: lío*) mess; **¡qué o vaya** ~! what a riot *o* laugh!

despenalizar [despenali'θar] *vt* to decriminalize.

despensa [des'pensa] *nf* (*armario*) larder; (*NAUT*) storeroom; (*provisión de comestibles*) stock of food.

despeñadero [despeɲa'ðero] *nm* (*GEO*) cliff, precipice.

despeñar [despe'ɲar] *vt* (*arrojar*) to fling down; ~**se** *vr* to fling o.s. down; (*caer*) to fall headlong.

desperdiciar [desperði'θjar] *vt* (*comida, tiempo*) to waste; (*oportunidad*) to throw away.

desperdicio [desper'ðiθjo] *nm* (*despilfarro*) squandering; (*residuo*) waste; ~**s** *nmpl* (*basura*) rubbish *sg*, refuse *sg*, garbage *sg*

(_US_); (_residuos_) waste _sg_; ~**s de cocina** kitchen scraps; **el libro no tiene** ~ the book is excellent from beginning to end.

desperdigar [desperði'yar] _vt_ (_esparcir_) to scatter; (_energía_) to dissipate; ~**se** _vr_ to scatter.

desperdigue [desper'ðiye] _etc vb V_ **desperdigar.**

desperece [despe'reθe] _etc vb V_ **desperezarse.**

desperezarse [despere'θarse] _vr_ to stretch.

desperfecto [desper'fekto] _nm_ (_deterioro_) slight damage; (_defecto_) flaw, imperfection.

despertador [desperta'ðor] _nm_ alarm clock; ~ **de viaje** travelling clock.

despertar [desper'tar] _vt_ (_persona_) to wake up; (_recuerdos_) to revive; (_esperanzas_) to raise; (_sentimiento_) to arouse ♦ _vi_, ~**se** _vr_ to awaken, wake up ♦ _nm_ awakening; ~**se a la realidad** to wake up to reality.

despiadado a [despja'ðaðo, a] _adj_ (_ataque_) merciless; (_persona_) heartless.

despido [des'piðo] _etc vb V_ **despedir** ♦ _nm_ dismissal, sacking; ~ **improcedente** _o_ **injustificado** wrongful dismissal; ~ **injusto** unfair dismissal; ~ **libre** right to hire and fire; ~ **voluntario** voluntary redundancy.

despierto, a [des'pjerto, a] _etc vb V_ **despertar** ♦ _adj_ awake; (_fig_) sharp, alert.

despilfarrar [despilfa'rrar] _vt_ (_gen_) to waste; (_dinero_) to squander.

despilfarro [despil'farro] _nm_ (_derroche_) squandering; (_lujo desmedido_) extravagance.

despintar [despin'tar] _vt_ (_quitar pintura a_) to take the paint off; (_hechos_) to distort ♦ _vi_: **A no despinta a B** A is in no way inferior to B; ~**se** _vr_ (_desteñir_) to fade.

despiojar [despjo'xar] _vt_ to delouse.

despistado, a [despis'taðo, a] _adj_ (_distraído_) vague, absent-minded; (_poco práctico_) unpractical; (_confuso_) confused; (_desorientado_) off the track ♦ _nm/f_ (_tipo: distraído_) scatterbrain, absent-minded person.

despistar [despis'tar] _vt_ to throw off the track _o_ scent; (_fig_) to mislead, confuse; ~**se** _vr_ to take the wrong road; (_fig_) to become confused.

despiste [des'piste] _nm_ (_AUTO etc_) swerve; (_error_) slip; (_distracción_) absent-mindedness; **tiene un terrible** ~ he's terribly absent-minded.

desplace [des'plaθe] _etc vb V_ **desplazar.**

desplante [des'plante] _nm_: **hacer un** ~ **a algn** to be rude to sb.

desplazado, a [despla'θaðo, a] _adj_ (_pieza_) wrongly placed ♦ _nm/f_ (_inadaptado_) misfit; **sentirse un poco** ~ to feel rather out of place.

desplazamiento [desplaθa'mjento] _nm_ displacement; (_viaje_) journey; (_de opinión, votos_) swing; (_INFORM_) scrolling; ~ **hacia arriba/abajo** (_INFORM_) scroll up/down.

desplazar [despla'θar] _vt_ (_gen_) to move; (_FÍSICA, NAUT, TEC_) to displace; (_tropas_) to transfer; (_suplantar_) to take the place of; (_INFORM_) to scroll; ~**se** _vr_ (_persona, vehículo_) to travel, go; (_objeto_) to move, shift; (_votos, opinión_) to shift, swing.

desplegar [desple'xar] _vt_ (_tela, papel_) to unfold, open out; (_bandera_) to unfurl; (_alas_) to spread; (_MIL_) to deploy; (_manifestar_) to display.

desplegué [desple'ye], **despleguemos** [desple'yemos] _etc vb V_ **desplegar.**

despliegue [des'pljeye] _etc vb V_ **desplegar** ♦ _nm_ unfolding, opening; deployment, display.

desplomarse [desplo'marse] _vr_ (_edificio, gobierno, persona_) to collapse; (_derrumbarse_) to topple over; (_precios_) to slump; **se ha desplomado el techo** the ceiling has fallen in.

desplumar [desplu'mar] _vt_ (_ave_) to pluck; (_fam: estafar_) to fleece.

despoblado, a [despo'βlaðo, a] _adj_ (_sin habitantes_) uninhabited; (_con pocos habitantes_) depopulated; (_con insuficientes habitantes_) underpopulated ♦ _nm_ deserted spot.

despojar [despo'xar] _vt_ (_alguien: de sus bienes_) to divest of, deprive of; (_casa_) to strip, leave bare; (_de su cargo_) to strip of; ~**se** _vr_ (_desnudarse_) to undress; ~**se de** (_ropa, hojas_) to shed; (_poderes_) to relinquish.

despojo [des'poxo] _nm_ (_acto_) plundering; (_objetos_) plunder, loot; ~**s** _nmpl_ (_de ave, res_) offal _sg._

desposado, a [despo'saðo, a] _adj, nm/f_ newly-wed.

desposar [despo'sar] _vt_ (_suj: sacerdote: pareja_) to marry; ~**se** _vr_ (_casarse_) to marry, get married.

desposeer [despose'er] _vt_ (_despojar_) to dispossess; ~ **a algn de su autoridad** to strip sb of his authority.

desposeído, a [despose'iðo, a] _nm/f_: **los** ~**s** the have-nots.

desposeyendo [despose'jendo] _etc vb V_ **desposeer.**

desposorios [despo'sorjos] _nmpl_

(*esponsales*) betrothal *sg*; (*boda*) marriage ceremony *sg*.

déspota ['despota] *nm/f* despot.

despotismo [despo'tismo] *nm* despotism.

despotricar [despotri'kar] *vi*: ~ **contra** to moan *o* complain about.

despotrique [despo'trike] *etc vb* V **despotricar.**

despreciable [despre'θjaßle] *adj* (*moralmente*) despicable; (*objeto*) worthless; (*cantidad*) negligible.

despreciar [despre'θjar] *vt* (*desdeñar*) to despise, scorn; (*afrentar*) to slight.

despreciativo, a [despreθja'tißo, a] *adj* (*observación, tono*) scornful, contemptuous; (*comentario*) derogatory.

desprecio [des'preθjo] *nm* scorn, contempt; slight.

desprender [despren'der] *vt* (*soltar*) to loosen; (*separar*) to separate; (*desatar*) to unfasten; (*olor*) to give off; ~**se** *vr* (*botón: caerse*) to fall off; (: *abrirse*) to unfasten; (*olor, perfume*) to be given off; ~**se de** to follow from; ~**se de algo** (*ceder*) to give sth up; (*desembarazarse*) to get rid of sth; **se desprende que** it transpires that.

desprendido, a [despren'dido, a] *adj* (*pieza*) loose; (*sin abrochar*) unfastened; (*desinteresado*) disinterested; (*generoso*) generous.

desprendimiento [desprendi'mjento] *nm* (*gen*) loosening; (*generosidad*) disinterestedness; (*indiferencia*) detachment; (*de gas*) leak; (*de tierra, rocas*) landslide.

despreocupado, a [despreoku'paðo, a] *adj* (*sin preocupación*) unworried, unconcerned; (*tranquilo*) nonchalant; (*en el vestir*) casual; (*negligente*) careless.

despreocuparse [despreoku'parse] *vr* to be carefree; (*dejar de inquietarse*) to stop worrying; (*ser indiferente*) to be unconcerned; ~ **de** to have no interest in.

desprestigiar [despresti'xjar] *vt* (*criticar*) to run down, disparage; (*desacreditar*) to discredit.

desprestigio [despres'tixjo] *nm* (*denigración*) disparagement; (*impopularidad*) unpopularity.

desprevenido, a [despreße'niðo, a] *adj* (*no preparado*) unprepared, unready; **coger** (*ESP*) *o* **agarrar** (*AM*) **a algn** ~ to catch sb unawares.

desproporción [despropor'θjon] *nf* disproportion, lack of proportion.

desproporcionado, a [desproporθjo'naðo, a] *adj* disproportionate, out of proportion.

despropósito [despro'posito] *nm* (*salida de tono*) irrelevant remark; (*disparate*) piece of nonsense.

desprovisto, a [despro'ßisto, a] *adj*: ~ **de** devoid of; **estar** ~ **de** to lack.

después [des'pwes] *adv* afterwards, later; (*desde entonces*) since (then); (*próximo paso*) next; **poco** ~ soon after; **un año** ~ a year later; ~ **se debatió el tema** next the matter was discussed ♦ *prep*: ~ **de** (*tiempo*) after, since; (*orden*) next (to); ~ **de comer** after lunch; ~ **de corregido el texto** after the text had been corrected; ~ **de esa fecha** (*pasado*) since that date; (*futuro*) from *o* after that date; ~ **de todo** after all; ~ **de verlo** after seeing it, after I *etc* saw it; **mi nombre está** ~ **del tuyo** my name comes next to yours ♦ *conj*: ~ **(de) que** after; ~ **(de) que lo escribí** after *o* since I wrote it, after writing it.

despuntar [despun'tar] *vt* (*lápiz*) to blunt ♦ *vi* (*BOT: plantas*) to sprout; (: *flores*) to bud; (*alba*) to break; (*día*) to dawn; (*persona: descollar*) to stand out.

desquiciar [deski'θjar] *vt* (*puerta*) to take off its hinges; (*descomponer*) to upset; (*persona: turbar*) to disturb; (: *volver loco a*) to unhinge.

desquitarse [deski'tarse] *vr* to obtain satisfaction; (*COM*) to recover a debt; (*fig: vengarse de*) to get one's own back; ~ **de una pérdida** to make up for a loss.

desquite [des'kite] *nm* (*satisfacción*) satisfaction; (*venganza*) revenge.

Dest. *abr* = **destinatario.**

destacado, a [desta'kaðo, a] *adj* outstanding.

destacamento [destaka'mento] *nm* (*MIL*) detachment.

destacar [desta'kar] *vt* (*ARTE: hacer resaltar*) to make stand out; (*subrayar*) to emphasize, point up; (*MIL*) to detach, detail; (*INFORM*) to highlight ♦ *vi*, ~**se** *vr* (*resaltarse*) to stand out; (*persona*) to be outstanding *o* exceptional; **quiero** ~ **que...** I wish to emphasize that...; ~**(se) contra** *o* **en** *o* **sobre** to stand out *o* be outlined against.

destajo [des'taxo] *nm*: **a** ~ (*por pieza*) by the job; (*con afán*) eagerly; **trabajar a** ~ to do piecework; (*fig*) to work one's fingers to the bone.

destapar [desta'par] *vt* (*botella*) to open; (*cacerola*) to take the lid off; (*descubrir*) to uncover; ~**se** *vr* (*descubrirse*) to get uncovered; (*revelarse*) to reveal one's true character.

destape [des'tape] *nm* nudity; (*fig*) permissiveness; **el ~ español** *the process of liberalization in Spain after Franco's death.*

destaque [des'take] *etc vb V* **destacar.**

destartalado, a [destarta'laðo, a] *adj* (*desordenado*) untidy; (*casa etc: grande*) rambling; (: *ruinoso*) tumbledown.

destellar [deste'ʎar] *vi* (*diamante*) to sparkle; (*metal*) to glint; (*estrella*) to twinkle.

destello [des'teʎo] *nm* (*de diamante*) sparkle; (*de metal*) glint; (*de estrella*) twinkle; (*de faro*) signal light; **no tiene un ~ de verdad** there's not a grain of truth in it.

destemplado, a [destem'plaðo, a] *adj* (*MUS*) out of tune; (*voz*) harsh; (*MED*) out of sorts; (*METEOROLOGÍA*) unpleasant, nasty.

destemplar [destem'plar] *vt* (*MUS*) to put out of tune; (*alterar*) to upset; **~se** *vr* (*MUS*) to lose its pitch; (*descomponerse*) to get out of order; (*persona: irritarse*) to get upset; (*MED*) to get out of sorts.

desteñir [deste'ɲir] *vt* to fade ♦ *vi*, **~se** *vr* to fade; **esta tela no destiñe** this fabric will not run.

desternillarse [desterni'ʎarse] *vr*: **~ de risa** to split one's sides laughing.

desterrado, a [deste'rraðo, a] *nm/f* (*exiliado*) exile.

desterrar [deste'rrar] *vt* (*exilar*) to exile; (*fig*) to banish, dismiss.

destetar [deste'tar] *vt* to wean.

destiempo [des'tjempo]: **a ~** *adv* at the wrong time.

destierro [des'tjerro] *etc vb V* **desterrar** ♦ *nm* exile; **vivir en el ~** to live in exile.

destilar [desti'lar] *vt* to distil; (*pus, sangre*) to ooze; (*fig: rebosar*) to exude; (: *revelar*) to reveal ♦ *vi* (*gotear*) to drip.

destilería [destile'ria] *nf* distillery; **~ de petróleo** oil refinery.

destinar [desti'nar] *vt* (*funcionario*) to appoint, assign; (*fondos*) to set aside; **es un libro destinado a los niños** it is a book (intended *o* meant) for children; **una carta que viene destinada a usted** a letter for you, a letter addressed to you.

destinatario, a [destina'tarjo, a] *nm/f* addressee; (*COM*) payee.

destino [des'tino] *nm* (*suerte*) destiny; (*de viajero*) destination; (*función*) use; (*puesto*) post, placement; **~ público** public appointment; **salir con ~ a** to leave for; **con ~ a Londres** (*avión, barco*) (bound) for London; (*carta*) to London.

destiña [des'tiɲa] *etc*, **destiñendo** [desti'ɲendo] *etc vb V* **desteñir.**

destitución [destitu'θjon] *nf* dismissal, removal.

destituir [destitu'ir] *vt* (*despedir*) to dismiss; (: *ministro, funcionario*) to remove from office.

destituyendo [destitu'jendo] *etc vb V* **destituir.**

destornillador [destorniʎa'ðor] *nm* screwdriver.

destornillar [destorni'ʎar] *vt*, **~se** *vr* (*tornillo*) to unscrew.

destreza [des'treθa] *nf* (*habilidad*) skill; (*maña*) dexterity.

destripar [destri'par] *vt* (*animal*) to gut; (*reventar*) to mangle.

destroce [de'stroθe] *etc vb V* **destrozar.**

destronar [destro'nar] *vt* (*rey*) to dethrone; (*fig*) to overthrow.

destroncar [destron'kar] *vt* (*árbol*) to chop off, lop; (*proyectos*) to ruin; (*discurso*) to interrupt.

destronque [des'tronke] *etc vb V* **destroncar.**

destrozar [destro'θar] *vt* (*romper*) to smash, break (up); (*estropear*) to ruin; (*nervios*) to shatter; **~ a algn en una discusión** to crush sb in an argument.

destrozo [des'troθo] *nm* (*acción*) destruction; (*desastre*) smashing; **~s** *nmpl* (*pedazos*) pieces; (*daños*) havoc *sg.*

destrucción [destruk'θjon] *nf* destruction.

destructor, a [destruk'tor, a] *adj* destructive ♦ *nm* (*NAUT*) destroyer.

destruir [destru'ir] *vt* to destroy; (*casa*) to demolish; (*equilibrio*) to upset; (*proyecto*) to spoil; (*esperanzas*) to dash; (*argumento*) to demolish.

destruyendo [destru'jendo] *etc vb V* **destruir.**

desuelle [de'sweʎe] *etc vb V* **desollar.**

desueve [de'sweβe] *etc vb V* **desovar.**

desunión [desu'njon] *nf* (*separación*) separation; (*discordia*) disunity.

desunir [desu'nir] *vt* to separate; (*TEC*) to disconnect; (*fig*) to cause a quarrel *o* rift between.

desuso [de'suso] *nm* disuse; **caer en ~** to fall into disuse, become obsolete; **una expresión caída en ~** an obsolete expression.

desvaído, a [desβa'iðo, a] *adj* (*color*) pale; (*contorno*) blurred.

desvalido, a [desβa'liðo, a] *adj* (*desprotegido*) destitute; (*sin fuerzas*) helpless; **niños ~s** waifs and strays.

desvalijar [desβali'xar] *vt* (*persona*) to rob;

(*casa, tienda*) to burgle; (*coche*) to break into.

desvalorice [desβalo'riθe] *etc vb V* **desvalorizar**.

desvalorizar [desβalori'θar] *vt* to devalue.

desván [des'βan] *nm* attic.

desvanecer [desβane'θer] *vt* (*disipar*) to dispel; (*recuerdo, temor*) to banish; (*borrar*) to blur; **~se** *vr* (*humo etc*) to vanish, disappear; (*duda*) to be dispelled; (*color*) to fade; (*recuerdo, sonido*) to fade away; (*MED*) to pass out.

desvanecido, a [desβane'θiðo, a] *adj* (*MED*) faint; **caer ~** to fall in a faint.

desvanecimiento [desβaneθi'mjento] *nm* (*desaparición*) disappearance; (*de dudas*) dispelling; (*de colores*) fading; (*evaporación*) evaporation; (*MED*) fainting fit.

desvanezca [desβa'neθka] *etc vb V* **desvanecer**.

desvariar [desβa'rjar] *vi* (*enfermo*) to be delirious; (*delirar*) to talk nonsense.

desvarío [desβa'rio] *nm* delirium; (*desatino*) absurdity; **~s** *nmpl* ravings.

desvelar [desβe'lar] *vt* to keep awake; **~se** *vr* (*no poder dormir*) to stay awake; (*vigilar*) to be vigilant *o* watchful; **~se por algo** (*inquietarse*) to be anxious about sth; (*poner gran cuidado*) to take great care over sth.

desvelo [des'βelo] *nm* lack of sleep; (*insomnio*) sleeplessness; (*fig*) vigilance; **~s** *nmpl* (*preocupación*) anxiety *sg*, effort *sg*.

desvencijado, a [desβenθi'xaðo, a] *adj* (*silla*) rickety; (*máquina*) broken-down.

desvencijar [desβenθi'xar] *vt* (*romper*) to break; (*soltar*) to loosen; (*persona: agotar*) to exhaust; **~se** *vr* to come apart.

desventaja [desβen'taxa] *nf* disadvantage; (*inconveniente*) drawback.

desventajoso, a [desβenta'xoso, a] *adj* disadvantageous, unfavourable.

desventura [desβen'tura] *nf* misfortune.

desventurado, a [desβentu'raðo, a] *adj* (*desgraciado*) unfortunate; (*de poca suerte*) ill-fated.

desvergonzado, a [desβerɣon'θaðo, a] *adj* (*sin vergüenza*) shameless; (*descarado*) insolent ♦ *nm/f* shameless person.

desvergüenza [desβer'ɣwenθa] *nf* (*descaro*) shamelessness; (*insolencia*) impudence; (*mala conducta*) effrontery; **esto es una ~** this is disgraceful; **¡qué ~!** what a nerve!

desvestir [desβes'tir] *vt*, **desvestirse** *vr* to undress.

desviación [desβja'θjon] *nf* deviation; (*AUTO: rodeo*) diversion, detour; (*: carretera de circunvalación*) ring road (*BRIT*), circular route (*US*); **~ de la circulación** traffic diversion; **es una ~ de sus principios** it is a departure from his usual principles.

desviar [des'βjar] *vt* to turn aside; (*balón, flecha, golpe*) to deflect; (*pregunta*) to parry; (*ojos*) to avert, turn away; (*río*) to alter the course of; (*navío*) to divert, reroute; (*conversación*) to sidetrack; **~se** *vr* (*apartarse del camino*) to turn aside; (*: barco*) to go off course; (*AUTO: dar un rodeo*) to make a detour; **~se de un tema** to get away from the point.

desvincular [desβinku'lar] *vt* to free, release; **~se** *vr* (*aislarse*) to be cut off; (*alejarse*) to cut o.s. off.

desvío [des'βio] *etc vb V* **desviar** ♦ *nm* (*desviación*) detour, diversion; (*fig*) indifference.

desvirgar [desβir'ɣar] *vt* to deflower.

desvirtuar [desβir'twar] *vt* (*estropear*) to spoil; (*argumento, razonamiento*) to detract from; (*efecto*) to counteract; (*sentido*) to distort; **~se** *vr* to spoil.

desvistiendo [desβis'tjendo] *etc vb V* **desvestir**.

desvitalizar [desβitali'θar] *vt* (*nervio*) to numb.

desvivirse [desβi'βirse] *vr*: **~ por** to long for, crave for; **~ por los amigos** to do anything for one's friends.

detalladamente [detaʎaða'mente] *adv* (*con detalles*) in detail; (*extensamente*) at great length.

detallar [deta'ʎar] *vt* to detail; (*asunto por asunto*) to itemize.

detalle [de'taʎe] *nm* detail; (*fig*) gesture, token; **al ~** in detail; (*COM*) retail *cpd*; **comercio al ~** retail trade; **vender al ~** to sell retail; **no pierde ~** he doesn't miss a trick; **me observaba sin perder ~** he watched my every move; **tiene muchos ~s** she is very considerate.

detallista [deta'ʎista] *nm/f* retailer ♦ *adj* (*meticuloso*) meticulous; **comercio ~** retail trade.

detectar [detek'tar] *vt* to detect.

detective [detek'tiβe] *nm/f* detective; **~ privado** private detective.

detector [detek'tor] *nm* (*NAUT, TEC etc*) detector; **~ de mentiras/de minas** lie/mine detector.

detención [deten'θjon] *nf* (*acción*) stopping; (*estancamiento*) stoppage; (*retraso*) holdup, delay; (*JUR: arresto*)

arrest; (*cuidado*) care; ~ **de juego**
(*DEPORTE*) stoppage of play; ~ **ilegal**
unlawful detention.

detendré [deten'dre] *etc vb* V **detener.**

detener [dete'ner] *vt* (*gen*) to stop; (*JUR*:
arrestar) to arrest; (: *encarcelar*) to detain;
(*objeto*) to keep; (*retrasar*) to hold up,
delay; (*aliento*) to hold; ~**se** *vr* to stop;
~**se en** (*demorarse*) to delay over, linger
over.

detenga [de'tenga] *etc vb* V **detener.**

detenidamente [deteniða'mente] *adv*
(*minuciosamente*) carefully;
(*extensamente*) at great length.

detenido, a [dete'niðo, a] *adj* (*arrestado*)
under arrest; (*minucioso*) detailed;
(*examen*) thorough; (*tímido*) timid ♦ *nm/f*
person under arrest, prisoner.

detenimiento [deteni'mjento] *nm* care;
con ~ thoroughly.

detentar [deten'tar] *vt* to hold; (*sin derecho*:
título) to hold unlawfully; (: *puesto*) to
occupy unlawfully.

detergente [deter'xente] *adj, nm*
detergent.

deteriorado, a [deterjo'raðo, a] *adj*
(*estropeado*) damaged; (*desgastado*)
worn.

deteriorar [deterjo'rar] *vt* to spoil,
damage; ~**se** *vr* to deteriorate.

deterioro [dete'rjoro] *nm* deterioration.

determinación [determina'θjon] *nf*
(*empeño*) determination; (*decisión*)
decision; (*de fecha, precio*) settling,
fixing.

determinado, a [determi'naðo, a] *adj*
(*preciso*) fixed, set; (*LING*: *artículo*)
definite; (*persona*: *resuelto*) determined;
un día ~ on a certain day; **no hay ningún
tema** ~ there is no particular theme.

determinar [determi'nar] *vt* (*plazo*) to fix;
(*precio*) to settle; (*daños, impuestos*) to
assess; (*pleito*) to decide; (*causar*) to
cause; ~**se** *vr* to decide; **el reglamento
determina que ...** the rule lays it down *o*
states that ...; **aquello determinó la caída
del gobierno** that brought about the fall
of the government; **esto le determinó**
this decided him.

detestable [detes'taßle] *adj* (*persona*)
hateful; (*acto*) detestable.

detestar [detes'tar] *vt* to detest.

detonación [detona'θjon] *nf* detonation;
(*sonido*) explosion.

detonante [deto'nante] *nm* (*fig*) trigger.

detonar [deto'nar] *vi* to detonate.

detractor, a [detrak'tor, a] *adj* disparaging
♦ *nm/f* detractor.

detrás [de'tras] *adv* behind; (*atrás*) at the
back ♦ *prep*: ~ **de** behind; **por** ~ **de algn**
(*fig*) behind sb's back; **salir de** ~ to come
out from behind; **por** ~ behind.

detrasito [detra'sito] *adv* (*AM fam*)
behind.

detrimento [detri'mento] *nm*: **en** ~ **de** to
the detriment of.

detuve [de'tuße] *etc vb* V **detener.**

deuda [de'uða] *nf* (*condición*) indebtedness,
debt; (*cantidad*) debt; ~ **a largo plazo**
long-term debt; ~ **exterior/pública**
foreign/national debt; ~ **incobrable** *o*
morosa bad debt; ~**s activas/pasivas**
assets/liabilities; **contraer** ~**s** to get
into debt.

deudor, a [deu'ðor, a] *nm/f* debtor; ~
hipotecario mortgager; ~ **moroso** slow
payer.

devaluación [deßalwa'θjon] *nf*
devaluation.

devaluar [deßalu'ar] *vt* to devalue.

devanar [deßa'nar] *vt* (*hilo*) to wind; ~**se** *vr*:
~**se los sesos** to rack one's brains.

devaneo [deßa'neo] *nm* (*MED*) delirium;
(*desatino*) nonsense; (*fruslería*) idle
pursuit; (*amorío*) flirtation.

devastar [deßas'tar] *vt* (*destruir*) to
devastate.

devendré [deßen'dre] *etc*, **devenga**
[de'ßenga] *etc vb* V **devenir.**

devengar [deßen'gar] *vt* (*salario*: *ganar*) to
earn; (: *tener que cobrar*) to be due;
(*intereses*) to bring in, accrue, earn.

devengue [de'ßenge] *etc vb* V **devengar.**

devenir [deße'nir] *vi*: ~ **en** to become, turn
into ♦ *nm* (*movimiento progresivo*) process
of development; (*transformación*)
transformation.

deviene [de'ßjene] *etc*, **deviniendo**
[deßi'njendo] *etc vb* V **devenir.**

devoción [deßo'θjon] *nf* devotion; (*afición*)
strong attachment.

devolución [deßolu'θjon] *nf* (*reenvío*)
return, sending back; (*reembolso*)
repayment; (*JUR*) devolution.

devolver [deßol'ßer] *vt* (*lo extraviado,
prestado*) to give back; (*a su sitio*) to put
back; (*carta al correo*) to send back;
(*COM*) to repay, refund; (*visita, la palabra*)
to return; (*salud, vista*) to restore; (*fam*:
vomitar) to throw up ♦ *vi* (*fam*) to be sick;
~**se** *vr* (*AM*) to return; ~ **mal por bien** to
return ill for good; ~ **la pelota a algn** to
give sb tit for tat.

devorar [deßo'rar] *vt* to devour; (*comer
ávidamente*) to gobble up; (*fig*: *fortuna*) to
run through; **todo lo devoró el fuego** the

fire consumed everything; **le devoran los celos** he is consumed with jealousy.

devoto, a [de'ßoto, a] *adj* (*REL: persona*) devout; (: *obra*) devotional; (*amigo*): ~ **(de algn)** devoted (to sb) ♦ *nm/f* admirer; **los ~s** (*REL*) the faithful; **su muy** ~ your devoted servant.

devuelto [de'ßwelto], **devuelva** [de'ßwelßa] *etc vb V* **devolver**.

D.F. *abr* (*México*) = *Distrito Federal*.

dg. *abr* (= *decigramo*) dg.

D.G. *abr* = *Dirección General*; (= *Director General*) D.G.

DGT *nf abr* = *Dirección General de Tráfico*; = *Dirección General de Turismo*.

di [di] *vb V* **dar**; **decir**.

día ['dia] *nm* day; ~ **de asueto** day off; ~ **feriado** (*AM*) *o* **festivo** (public) holiday; ~ **hábil/inhábil** working/non-working day; ~ **domingo,** ~ **lunes** (*AM*) Sunday, Monday; ~ **lectivo** teaching day; ~ **libre** day off; **D~ de Reyes** Epiphany (*6 January*); **¿qué** ~ **es?** what's the date?; **estar/poner al** ~ to be/keep up to date; **el** ~ **de hoy/de mañana** today/tomorrow; **el** ~ **menos pensado** when you least expect it; **al** ~ **siguiente** on the following day; **todos los ~s** every day; **un** ~ **sí y otro no** every other day; **vivir al** ~ to live from hand to mouth; **de** ~ during the day, by day; **es de** ~ it's daylight; **del** ~ (*estilos*) fashionable; (*menú*) today's; **de un** ~ **para otro** any day now; **en pleno** ~ in full daylight; **en su** ~ in due time; **¡hasta otro** ~! so long!

diabetes [dja'betes] *nf* diabetes *sg*.

diabético, a [dja'betiko, a] *adj, nm/f* diabetic.

diablo ['djaßlo] *nm* (*tb fig*) devil; **pobre** ~ poor devil; **hace un frío de todos los ~s** it's hellishly cold.

diablura [dja'ßlura] *nf* prank; (*travesura*) mischief.

diabólico, a [dja'ßoliko, a] *adj* diabolical.

diadema [dja'ðema] *nf* (*para el pelo*) Alice band, headband; (*joya*) tiara.

diáfano, a ['djafano, a] *adj* (*tela*) diaphanous; (*agua*) crystal-clear.

diafragma [dja'fraɣma] *nm* diaphragm.

diagnosis [djaɣ'nosis] *nf inv*, **diagnóstico** [djaɣ'nostiko] *nm* diagnosis.

diagnosticar [djaɣnosti'kar] *vt* to diagnose.

diagonal [djaɣo'nal] *adj* diagonal ♦ *nf* (*GEOM*) diagonal; **en** ~ diagonally.

diagrama [dja'ɣrama] *nm* diagram; ~ **de barras** (*COM*) bar chart; ~ **de dispersión** (*COM*) scatter diagram; ~ **de flujo**

(*INFORM*) flowchart.

dial [di'al] *nm* dial.

dialecto [dja'lekto] *nm* dialect.

dialogar [djalo'ɣar] *vt* to write in dialogue form ♦ *vi* (*conversar*) to have a conversation; ~ **con** (*POL*) to hold talks with.

diálogo ['djaloɣo] *nm* dialogue.

dialogue [dja'loɣe] *etc vb V* **dialogar**.

diamante [dja'mante] *nm* diamond.

diametralmente [djametral'mente] *adv* diametrically; ~ **opuesto a** diametrically opposed to.

diámetro [di'ametro] *nm* diameter; ~ **de giro** (*AUTO*) turning circle; **faros de gran** ~ wide-angle headlights.

diana ['djana] *nf* (*MIL*) reveille; (*de blanco*) centre, bull's-eye.

diantre ['djantre] *nm*: **¡~!** (*fam*) oh hell!

diapasón [djapa'son] *nm* (*instrumento*) tuning fork; (*de violín etc*) fingerboard; (*de voz*) tone.

diapositiva [djaposi'tißa] *nf* (*FOTO*) slide, transparency.

diario, a ['djarjo, a] *adj* daily ♦ *nm* newspaper; (*libro diario*) diary; (: *COM*) daybook; (*COM: gastos*) daily expenses; ~ **de navegación** (*NAUT*) logbook; ~ **hablado** (*RADIO*) news (bulletin); ~ **de sesiones** parliamentary report; **a** ~ daily; **de** *o* **para** ~ everyday.

diarrea [dja'rrea] *nf* diarrhoea.

diatriba [dja'trißa] *nf* diatribe, tirade.

dibujante [dißu'xante] *nm/f* (*de bosquejos*) sketcher; (*de dibujos animados*) cartoonist; (*de moda*) designer; ~ **de publicidad** commercial artist.

dibujar [dißu'xar] *vt* to draw, sketch; **~se** *vr* (*emoción*) to show; **~se contra** to be outlined against.

dibujo [di'ßuxo] *nm* drawing; (*TEC*) design; (*en papel, tela*) pattern; (*en periódico*) cartoon; (*fig*) description; **~s animados** cartoons; ~ **del natural** drawing from life.

dic., dic.ᵉ *abr* (= *diciembre*) Dec.

diccionario [dikθjo'narjo] *nm* dictionary.

dicharachero, a [ditʃara'tʃero, a] *adj* talkative ♦ *nm/f* (*ingenioso*) wit; (*parlanchín*) chatterbox.

dicho, a ['ditʃo, a] *pp de* **decir** ♦ *adj* (*susodicho*) aforementioned ♦ *nm* saying; (*proverbio*) proverb; (*ocurrencia*) bright remark ♦ *nf* (*buena suerte*) good luck; **mejor** ~ rather; ~ **y hecho** no sooner said than done.

dichoso, a [di'tʃoso, a] *adj* (*feliz*) happy; (*afortunado*) lucky; **¡aquel** ~ **coche!** (*fam*) that blessed car!

diciembre [di'θjembre] *nm* December.

diciendo [di'θjendo] *etc vb V* **decir**.

dictado [dik'taðo] *nm* dictation; **escribir al** ~ to take dictation; **los ~s de la conciencia** (*fig*) the dictates of conscience.

dictador [dikta'ðor] *nm* dictator.

dictadura [dikta'ðura] *nf* dictatorship.

dictáfono ® [dik'tafono] *nm* Dictaphone ®.

dictamen [dik'tamen] *nm* (*opinión*) opinion; (*informe*) report; ~ **contable** auditor's report; ~ **facultativo** (*MED*) medical report.

dictar [dik'tar] *vt* (*carta*) to dictate; (*JUR: sentencia*) to pass; (*decreto*) to issue; (*AM: clase*) to give; (: *conferencia*) to deliver.

didáctico, a [di'ðaktiko, a] *adj* didactic; (*material*) teaching *cpd*; (*juguete*) educational.

diecinueve [djeθinu'eβe] *num* nineteen; (*fecha*) nineteenth; *V tb* **seis**.

dieciochesco, a [djeθio'tʃesko, a] *adj* eighteenth-century.

dieciocho [djeθi'otʃo] *num* eighteen; (*fecha*) eighteenth; *V tb* **seis**.

dieciséis [djeθi'seis] *num* sixteen; (*fecha*) sixteenth; *V tb* **seis**.

diecisiete [djeθi'sjete] *num* seventeen; (*fecha*) seventeenth; *V tb* **seis**.

diente [di'ente] *nm* (*ANAT, TEC*) tooth; (*ZOOL*) fang; (: *de elefante*) tusk; (*de ajo*) clove; ~ **de león** dandelion; ~**s postizos** false teeth; **enseñar los ~s** (*fig*) to show one's claws; **hablar entre ~s** to mutter, mumble; **hincar el ~ en** (*comida*) to bite into.

diera ['djera] *etc vb V* **dar**.

diéresis [di'eresis] *nf* diaeresis.

dieron ['djeron] *vb V* **dar**.

diesel ['disel] *adj*: **motor** ~ diesel engine.

diestro, a ['djestro, a] *adj* (*derecho*) right; (*hábil*) skilful; (: *con las manos*) handy ♦ *nm* (*TAUR*) matador ♦ *nf* right hand; **a ~ y siniestro** (*sin método*) wildly.

dieta ['djeta] *nf* diet; ~**s** *nfpl* expenses; **estar a** ~ to be on a diet.

dietético, a [dje'tetiko, a] *adj* dietetic ♦ *nm/f* dietician ♦ *nf* dietetics *sg*.

dietista [dje'tista] *nm/f* dietician.

diez [djeθ] *num* ten; (*fecha*) tenth; **hacer las** ~ **de últimas** (*NAIPES*) to sweep the board; *V tb* **seis**.

diezmar [djeθ'mar] *vt* to decimate.

difamación [difama'θjon] *nf* slander; libel.

difamar [difa'mar] *vt* (*JUR: hablando*) to slander; (: *por escrito*) to libel.

difamatorio, a [difama'torjo, a] *adj*

slanderous; libellous.

diferencia [dife'renθja] *nf* difference; **a** ~ **de** unlike; **hacer** ~ **entre** to make a distinction between; ~ **salarial** (*COM*) wage differential.

diferencial [diferen'θjal] *nm* (*AUTO*) differential.

diferenciar [diferen'θjar] *vt* to differentiate between ♦ *vi* to differ; ~**se** *vr* to differ, be different; (*distinguirse*) to distinguish o.s.

diferente [dife'rente] *adj* different.

diferido [dife'riðo] *nm*: **en** ~ (*TV etc*) recorded.

diferir [dife'rir] *vt* to defer.

difícil [di'fiθil] *adj* difficult; (*tiempos, vida*) hard; (*situación*) delicate; **es un hombre** ~ he's a difficult man to get on with.

difícilmente [di'fiθilmente] *adv* (*con dificultad*) with difficulty; (*apenas*) hardly.

dificultad [difikul'tað] *nf* difficulty; (*problema*) trouble; (*objeción*) objection.

dificultar [difikul'tar] *vt* (*complicar*) to complicate, make difficult; (*estorbar*) to obstruct; **las restricciones dificultan el comercio** the restrictions hinder trade.

dificultoso, a [difikul'toso, a] *adj* (*difícil*) difficult, hard; (*fam: cara*) odd, ugly; (*persona: exigente*) fussy.

difiera [di'fjera] *etc*, **difiriendo** [difi'rjendo] *etc vb V* **diferir**.

difuminar [difumi'nar] *vt* to blur.

difundir [difun'dir] *vt* (*calor, luz*) to diffuse; (*RADIO*) to broadcast; ~**se** *vr* to spread (out); ~ **una noticia** to spread a piece of news.

difunto, a [di'funto, a] *adj* dead, deceased ♦ *nm/f*: **el** ~ the deceased.

difusión [difu'sjon] *nf* (*de calor, luz*) diffusion; (*de noticia, teoría*) dissemination; (*de programa*) broadcasting; (*programa*) broadcast.

difuso, a [di'fuso, a] *adj* (*luz*) diffused; (*conocimientos*) widespread; (*estilo, explicación*) wordy.

diga ['diɣa] *etc vb V* **decir**.

digerir [dixe'rir] *vt* to digest; (*fig*) to absorb; (*reflexionar sobre*) to think over.

digestión [dixes'tjon] *nf* digestion; **corte de** ~ indigestion.

digestivo, a [dixes'tiβo, a] *adj* digestive ♦ *nm* (*bebida*) liqueur, digestif.

digiera [di'xjera] *etc*, **digiriendo** [dixi'rjendo] *etc vb V* **digerir**.

digital [dixi'tal] *adj* (*INFORM*) digital; (*dactilar*) finger *cpd* ♦ *nf* (*BOT*) foxglove; (*droga*) digitalis.

digitalizador [dixitaliθa'ðor] *nm* (*INFORM*) digitizer.

dignarse [diɣ'narse] *vr* to deign to.

dignidad [diɣni'ðað] *nf* dignity; (*honra*) honour; (*rango*) rank; (*persona*) dignitary; **herir la ~ de algn** to hurt sb's pride.

dignificar [diɣnifi'kar] *vt* to dignify.

dignifique [diɣni'fike] *etc vb V* **dignificar**.

digno, a ['diɣno, a] *adj* worthy; (*persona*: *honesto*) honourable; **~ de elogio** praiseworthy; **~ de mención** worth mentioning; **es ~ de verse** it is worth seeing; **poco ~** unworthy.

digresión [diɣre'sjon] *nf* digression.

dije ['dixe] *etc*, **dijera** [di'xera] *etc vb V* **decir**.

dilación [dila'θjon] *nf* delay; **sin ~** without delay, immediately.

dilapidar [dilapi'ðar] *vt* to squander, waste.

dilatación [dilata'θjon] *nf* (*expansión*) dilation.

dilatado, a [dila'taðo, a] *adj* dilated; (*período*) long drawn-out; (*extenso*) extensive.

dilatar [dila'tar] *vt* (*gen*) to dilate; (*prolongar*) to prolong; (*aplazar*) to delay; **~se** *vr* (*pupila etc*) to dilate; (*agua*) to expand.

dilema [di'lema] *nm* dilemma.

diligencia [dili'xenθja] *nf* diligence; (*rapidez*) speed; (*ocupación*) errand, job; (*carruaje*) stagecoach; **~s** *nfpl* (*JUR*) formalities; **~s judiciales** judicial proceedings; **~s previas** inquest *sg*.

diligente [dili'xente] *adj* diligent; **poco ~** slack.

dilucidar [diluθi'ðar] *vt* (*aclarar*) to elucidate, clarify; (*misterio*) to clear up.

diluir [dilu'ir] *vt* to dilute; (*aguar*, *fig*) to water down.

diluviar [dilu'βjar] *vi* to pour with rain.

diluvio [di'luβjo] *nm* deluge, flood; **un ~ de cartas** (*fig*) a flood of letters.

diluyendo [dilu'jendo] *etc vb V* **diluir**.

dimanar [dima'nar] *vi*: **~ de** to arise *o* spring from.

dimensión [dimen'sjon] *nf* dimension; **dimensiones** *nfpl* size *sg*; **tomar las dimensiones de** to take the measurements of.

dimes ['dimes] *nmpl*: **andar en ~ y diretes con algn** to bicker *o* squabble with sb.

diminutivo [diminu'tiβo] *nm* diminutive.

diminuto, a [dimi'nuto, a] *adj* tiny, diminutive.

dimisión [dimi'sjon] *nf* resignation.

dimitir [dimi'tir] *vt* (*cargo*) to give up; (*despedir*) to sack ♦ *vi* to resign.

dimos ['dimos] *vb V* **dar**.

Dinamarca [dina'marka] *nf* Denmark.

dinamarqués, esa [dinamar'kes, esa] *adj* Danish ♦ *nm/f* Dane ♦ *nm* (*LING*) Danish.

dinámico, a [di'namiko, a] *adj* dynamic ♦ *nf* dynamics *sg*.

dinamita [dina'mita] *nf* dynamite.

dinamitar [dinami'tar] *vt* to dynamite.

dinamo [di'namo], **dínamo** ['dinamo] *nf* (*nm en AM*) dynamo.

dinastía [dinas'tia] *nf* dynasty.

dineral [dine'ral] *nm* fortune.

dinero [di'nero] *nm* money; (**~ en** *circulación*) currency; **~ caro** (*COM*) dear money; **~ contante (y sonante)** hard cash; **~ de curso legal** legal tender; **~ efectivo** cash, ready cash; **es hombre de ~** he is a man of means; **andar mal de ~** to be short of money; **ganar ~ a espuertas** to make money hand over fist.

dinosaurio [dino'saurjo] *nm* dinosaur.

dintel [din'tel] *nm* lintel; (*umbral*) threshold.

diñar [di'ɲar] *vt* (*fam*) to give; **~la** to kick the bucket.

dio [djo] *vb V* **dar**.

diócesis ['djoθesis] *nf inv* diocese.

Dios [djos] *nm* God; **~ mediante** God willing; **a ~ gracias** thank heaven; **a la buena de ~** any old how; **una de ~ es Cristo** an almighty row; **~ los cría y ellos se juntan** birds of a feather flock together; **como ~ manda** as is proper; **¡~ mío!** (oh,) my God!; **¡por ~!** for God's sake!; **¡válgame ~!** bless my soul!

dios [djos] *nm* god.

diosa ['djosa] *nf* goddess.

Dip. *abr* (= *Diputación*) ≈ CC.

diploma [di'ploma] *nm* diploma.

diplomacia [diplo'maθja] *nf* diplomacy; (*fig*) tact.

diplomado, a [diplo'maðo, a] *adj* qualified ♦ *nm/f* holder of a diploma; (*UNIV*) graduate; *V tb* **licenciado**.

diplomático, a [diplo'matiko, a] *adj* (*cuerpo*) diplomatic; (*que tiene tacto*) tactful ♦ *nm/f* diplomat.

diptongo [dip'tongo] *nm* diphthong.

diputación [diputa'θjon] *nf* deputation; **~ permanente** (*POL*) standing committee; **~ provincial** ≈ county council.

diputado, a [dipu'taðo, a] *nm/f* delegate; (*POL*) ≈ member of parliament (*BRIT*), ≈ representative (*US*); *V tb* **Las Cortes (españolas)**.

dique ['dike] *nm* dyke; (*rompeolas*)

breakwater; ~ **de contención** dam.

Dir. *abr* = **dirección**; (= *director*) dir.

diré [di're] *etc vb V* **decir**.

dirección [direk'θjon] *nf* direction; (*fig: tendencia*) trend; (*señas, tb INFORM*) address; (*AUTO*) steering; (*gerencia*) management; (*de periódico*) editorship; (*en escuela*) headship; (*POL*) leadership; (*junta*) board of directors; (*despacho*) director's/manager's/headmaster's/ editor's office; ~ **administrativa** office management; ~ **asistida** power-assisted steering; **D**~ **General de Seguridad/ Turismo** State Security/Tourist Office; ~ **única** *o* **prohibida** one-way; **tomar la** ~ **de una empresa** to take over the running of a company.

direccionamiento [direkθjona'mjento] *nm* (*INFORM*) addressing.

directivo, a [direk'tiβo, a] *adj* (*junta*) managing; (*función*) administrative ♦ *nm/f* (*COM*) manager ♦ *nf* (*norma*) directive; (*tb: junta directiva*) board of directors.

directo, a [di'rekto, a] *adj* direct; (*línea*) straight; (*inmediato*) immediate; (*tren*) through; (*TV*) live; **en** ~ (*INFORM*) on line; **transmitir en** ~ to broadcast live.

director, a [direk'tor, a] *adj* leading ♦ *nm/f* director; (*ESCOL*) head (teacher) (*BRIT*), principal (*US*); (*gerente*) manager(ess) (*de compañía*) president; (*jefe*) head; (*PRENSA*) editor; (*de prisión*) governor; (*MUS*) conductor; ~ **adjunto** assistant manager; ~ **de cine** film director; ~ **comercial** marketing manager; ~ **ejecutivo** executive director; ~ **de empresa** company director; ~ **general** general manager; ~ **gerente** managing director; ~ **de sucursal** branch manager.

directorio [direk'torjo] *nm* (*INFORM*) directory.

directrices [direk'triθes] *nfpl* guidelines.

dirigente [diri'xente] *adj* leading ♦ *nm/f* (*POL*) leader; **los** ~**s del partido** the party leaders.

dirigible [diri'xiβle] *adj* (*AVIAT, NAUT*) steerable ♦ *nm* airship.

dirigir [diri'xir] *vt* to direct; (*acusación*) to level; (*carta*) to address; (*obra de teatro, film*) to produce, direct; (*MUS*) to conduct; (*comercio*) to manage; (*expedición*) to lead; (*sublevación*) to head; (*periódico*) to edit; (*guiar*) to guide; ~**se** *vr*: ~**se a** to go towards, make one's way towards; (*hablar con*) to speak to; ~**se a algn solicitando algo** to apply

to sb for sth; **"diríjase a ..."** "apply to ...".

dirigismo [diri'xismo] *nm* management, control; ~ **estatal** state control.

dirija [di'rixa] *etc vb V* **dirigir**.

dirimir [diri'mir] *vt* (*contrato, matrimonio*) to dissolve.

discado [dis'kaðo] *nm*: ~ **automático** autodial.

discernir [disθer'nir] *vt* to discern ♦ *vi* to distinguish.

discierna [dis'θjerna] *etc vb V* **discernir**.

disciplina [disθi'plina] *nf* discipline.

disciplinar [disθipli'nar] *vt* to discipline; (*enseñar*) to school; (*MIL*) to drill; (*azotar*) to whip.

discípulo, a [dis'θipulo, a] *nm/f* disciple; (*seguidor*) follower; (*ESCOL*) pupil.

Discman ® ['diskman] *nm* Discman ®.

disco ['disko] *nm* disc (*BRIT*), disk (*US*); (*DEPORTE*) discus; (*TELEC*) dial; (*AUTO: semáforo*) light; (*MUS*) record; (*INFORM*) disk; ~ **de arranque** boot disk; ~ **compacto** compact disc; ~ **de densidad sencilla/doble** single/double density disk; ~ **de larga duración** long-playing record (LP); ~ **flexible** *o* **floppy** floppy disk; ~ **de freno** brake disc; ~ **maestro** master disk; ~ **de reserva** backup disk; ~ **rígido** hard disk; ~ **de una cara/dos caras** single-/double-sided disk; ~ **virtual** ramdisk.

discóbolo [dis'koβolo] *nm* discus thrower.

discográfico, a [disko'ɣrafiko, a] *adj* record *cpd*; **casa discográfica** record company; **sello** ~ label.

díscolo, a ['diskolo, a] *adj* (*rebelde*) unruly.

disconforme [diskon'forme] *adj* differing; **estar** ~ (**con**) to be in disagreement (with).

discontinuo, a [diskon'tinwo, a] *adj* discontinuous; (*AUTO: línea*) broken.

discordar [diskor'ðar] *vi* (*MUS*) to be out of tune; (*estar en desacuerdo*) to disagree; (*colores, opiniones*) to clash.

discorde [dis'korðe] *adj* (*sonido*) discordant; (*opiniones*) clashing.

discordia [dis'korðja] *nf* discord.

discoteca [disko'teka] *nf* disco(theque).

discreción [diskre'θjon] *nf* discretion; (*reserva*) prudence; **¡a** ~**!** (*MIL*) stand easy!; **añadir azúcar a** ~ (*CULIN*) add sugar to taste; **comer a** ~ to eat as much as one wishes.

discrecional [diskreθjo'nal] *adj* (*facultativo*) discretionary; **parada** ~ request stop.

discrepancia [diskre'panθja] *nf* (*diferencia*) discrepancy; (*desacuerdo*) disagreement.

discrepante [diskre'pante] *adj* divergent;
hubo varias voces ~s there were some
dissenting voices.
discrepar [diskre'par] *vi* to disagree.
discreto, a [dis'kreto, a] *adj* (*diplomático*)
discreet; (*sensato*) sensible; (*reservado*)
quiet; (*sobrio*) sober; (*mediano*) fair,
fairly good; **le daremos un plazo ~** we'll
allow him a reasonable time.
discriminación [diskrimina'θjon] *nf*
discrimination.
discriminar [diskrimi'nar] *vt* to
discriminate against; (*diferenciar*) to
discriminate between.
discuerde [dis'kwerðe] *etc vb V* **discordar**.
disculpa [dis'kulpa] *nf* excuse; (*pedir
perdón*) apology; **pedir ~s a/por** to
apologize to/for.
disculpar [diskul'par] *vt* to excuse, pardon;
~se *vr* to excuse o.s.; to apologize.
discurrir [disku'rrir] *vt* to contrive, think
up ♦ *vi* (*pensar, reflexionar*) to think,
meditate; (*recorrer*) to roam, wander;
(*río*) to flow; (*el tiempo*) to pass, flow by.
discurso [dis'kurso] *nm* speech; **~ de
clausura** closing speech; **pronunciar un
~** to make a speech; **en el ~ del tiempo**
with the passage of time.
discusión [disku'sjon] *nf* (*diálogo*)
discussion; (*riña*) argument; **tener una ~**
to have an argument.
discutible [disku'tiβle] *adj* debatable; **de
mérito ~** of dubious worth.
discutido, a [disku'tiðo, a] *adj*
controversial.
discutir [disku'tir] *vt* (*debatir*) to discuss;
(*pelear*) to argue about; (*contradecir*) to
argue against ♦ *vi* to discuss; (*disputar*)
to argue; **~ de política** to argue about
politics; **¡no discutas!** don't argue!
disecar [dise'kar] *vt* (*para conservar: animal*)
to stuff; (: *planta*) to dry.
diseminar [disemi'nar] *vt* to disseminate,
spread.
disentir [disen'tir] *vi* to dissent, disagree.
diseñador, a [diseɲa'dor, a] *nm/f* designer.
diseñar [dise'ɲar] *vt* to design.
diseño [di'seɲo] *nm* (*TEC*) design; (*ARTE*)
drawing; (*COSTURA*) pattern; **de ~
italiano** Italian-designed; **~ asistido por
ordenador** computer-assisted design,
CAD.
diseque [di'seke] *etc vb V* **disecar**.
disertar [diser'tar] *vi* to speak.
disfrace [dis'fraθe] *etc vb V* **disfrazar**.
disfraz [dis'fraθ] *nm* (*máscara*) disguise;
(*traje*) fancy dress; (*excusa*) pretext; **bajo
el ~ de** under the cloak of.

disfrazado, a [disfra'θaðo, a] *adj*
disguised; **ir ~ de** to masquerade as.
disfrazar [disfra'θar] *vt* to disguise; **~se** *vr*
to dress (o.s.) up; **~se de** to disguise o.s.
as.
disfrutar [disfru'tar] *vt* to enjoy ♦ *vi* to
enjoy o.s.; **¡que disfrutes!** have a good
time; **~ de** to enjoy, possess; **~ de buena
salud** to enjoy good health.
disfrute [dis'frute] *nm* (*goce*) enjoyment;
(*aprovechamiento*) use.
disgregar [disɣre'ɣar] *vt* (*desintegrar*) to
disintegrate; (*manifestantes*) to disperse;
~se *vr* to disintegrate, break up.
disgregue [dis'ɣreɣe] *etc vb V* **disgregar**.
disgustar [disɣus'tar] *vt* (*no gustar*) to
displease; (*contrariar, enojar*) to annoy; to
upset; **~se** *vr* to be annoyed; (*dos
personas*) to fall out; **estaba muy
disgustado con el asunto** he was very
upset about the affair.
disgusto [dis'ɣusto] *nm* (*repugnancia*)
disgust; (*contrariedad*) annoyance;
(*desagrado*) displeasure; (*tristeza*) grief;
(*riña*) quarrel; (*avería*) misfortune; **hacer
algo a ~** to do sth unwillingly; **matar a
algn a ~s** to drive sb to distraction.
disidente [disi'ðente] *nm* dissident.
disienta [di'sjenta] *etc vb V* **disentir**.
disimulado, a [disimu'laðo, a] *adj*
(*solapado*) furtive, underhand; (*oculto*)
covert; **hacerse el ~** to pretend not to
notice.
disimular [disimu'lar] *vt* (*ocultar*) to hide,
conceal ♦ *vi* to dissemble.
disimulo [disi'mulo] *nm* (*fingimiento*)
dissimulation; **con ~** cunningly.
disipar [disi'par] *vt* (*duda, temor*) to dispel;
(*esperanza*) to destroy; (*fortuna*) to
squander; **~se** *vr* (*nubes*) to vanish;
(*dudas*) to be dispelled; (*indisciplinarse*)
to dissipate.
diskette [dis'ket] *nm* (*INFORM*) diskette,
floppy disk.
dislate [dis'late] *nm* (*absurdo*) absurdity;
~s *nmpl* nonsense *sg*.
dislexia [dis'leksja] *nf* dyslexia.
dislocar [dislo'kar] *vt* (*gen*) to dislocate;
(*tobillo*) to sprain.
disloque [dis'loke] *etc vb V* **dislocar** ♦ *nm*:
es el ~ (*fam*) it's the last straw.
disminución [disminu'θjon] *nf* diminution.
disminuido, a [disminu'iðo, a] *nm/f*: **~
mental/físico** mentally/physically-
handicapped person.
disminuir [disminu'ir] *vt* to decrease,
diminish; (*estrechar*) to lessen;
(*temperatura*) to lower; (*gastos, raciones*)

to cut down; (*dolor*) to relieve; (*autoridad, prestigio*) to weaken; (*entusiasmo*) to damp ♦ *vi* (*días*) to grow shorter; (*precios, temperatura*) to drop, fall; (*velocidad*) to slacken; (*población*) to decrease; (*beneficios, número*) to fall off; (*memoria, vista*) to fail.

disminuyendo [dismiku'jendo] *etc vb V* **disminuir**.

disociar [diso'θjar] *vt* to disassociate; ~**se** *vr* to disassociate o.s.

disoluble [diso'luβle] *adj* soluble.

disolución [disolu'θjon] *nf* (*acto*) dissolution; (*QUÍMICA*) solution; (*COM*) liquidation; (*moral*) dissoluteness.

disoluto, a [diso'luto, a] *adj* dissolute.

disolvente [disol'βente] *nm* (*solvent*) thinner.

disolver [disol'βer] *vt* (*gen*) to dissolve; (*manifestación*) to break up; ~**se** *vr* to dissolve; (*COM*) to go into liquidation.

dispar [dis'par] *adj* (*distinto*) different; (*irregular*) uneven.

disparado, a [dispa'raðo, a] *adj*: **entrar** ~ to shoot in; **salir** ~ to shoot out; **ir** ~ to go like mad.

disparador [dispara'ðor] *nm* (*de arma*) trigger; (*FOTO, TEC*) release; ~ **atómico** aerosol; ~ **de bombas** bomb release.

disparar [dispa'rar] *vt, vi* to shoot, fire; ~**se** *vr* (*arma de fuego*) to go off; (*persona: marcharse*) to rush off; (*caballo*) to bolt; (*enojarse*) to lose control.

disparatado, a [dispara'taðo, a] *adj* crazy.

disparate [dispa'rate] *nm* (*tontería*) foolish remark; (*error*) blunder; **decir** ~**s** to talk nonsense; **¡qué** ~**!** how absurd!; **costar un** ~ to cost a hell of a lot.

disparo [dis'paro] *nm* shot; (*acto*) firing; ~**s** *nmpl* shooting *sg*, (exchange of) shots (*sg*); ~ **inicial** (*de cohete*) blastoff.

dispendio [dis'pendjo] *nm* waste.

dispensar [dispen'sar] *vt* to dispense; (*ayuda*) to give; (*honores*) to grant; (*disculpar*) to excuse; **¡usted dispense!** I beg your pardon!; ~ **a algn de hacer algo** to excuse sb from doing sth.

dispensario [dispen'sarjo] *nm* (*clínica*) community clinic; (*de hospital*) outpatients' department.

dispersar [disper'sar] *vt* to disperse; (*manifestación*) to break up; ~**se** *vr* to scatter.

disperso, a [dis'perso, a] *adj* scattered.

displicencia [displi'θenθja] *nf* (*mal humor*) peevishness; (*desgana*) lack of enthusiasm.

displicente [displi'θente] *adj*

(*malhumorado*) peevish; (*poco entusiasta*) unenthusiastic.

dispondré [dispon'dre] *etc vb V* **disponer**.

disponer [dispo'ner] *vt* (*arreglar*) to arrange; (*ordenar*) to put in order; (*preparar*) to prepare, get ready ♦ *vi*: ~ **de** to have, own; ~**se** *vr*: ~**se para** to prepare to, prepare for; **la ley dispone que ...** the law provides that ...; **no puede ~ de esos bienes** she cannot dispose of those properties.

disponga [dis'ponga] *etc vb V* **disponer**.

disponibilidad [disponiβili'ðað] *nf* availability; ~**es** *nfpl* (*COM*) resources, financial assets.

disponible [dispo'niβle] *adj* available; (*tiempo*) spare; (*dinero*) on hand.

disposición [disposi'θjon] *nf* arrangement, disposition; (*de casa, INFORM*) layout; (*ley*) order; (*cláusula*) provision; (*aptitud*) aptitude; ~ **de ánimo** attitude of mind; **última** ~ last will and testament; **a la** ~ **de** at the disposal of; **a su** ~ at your service.

dispositivo [disposi'tiβo] *nm* device, mechanism; ~ **de alimentación** hopper; ~ **de almacenaje** storage device; ~ **periférico** peripheral (device); ~ **de seguridad** safety catch; (*fig*) security measure.

dispuesto, a [dis'pwesto, a] *pp de* **disponer** ♦ *adj* (*arreglado*) arranged; (*preparado*) disposed; (*persona: dinámico*) bright; **estar** ~**/poco** ~ **a hacer algo** to be inclined/reluctant to do sth.

dispuse [dis'puse] *etc vb V* **disponer**.

disputa [dis'puta] *nf* (*discusión*) dispute, argument; (*controversia*) controversy.

disputar [dispu'tar] *vt* (*discutir*) to dispute, question; (*contender*) to contend for ♦ *vi* to argue.

disquete [dis'kete] *nm* (*INFORM*) diskette, floppy disk.

disquetera [diske'tera] *nf* disk drive.

Dist. *abr* (= *distancia, Distrito*) dist.

distancia [dis'tanθja] *nf* distance; (*de tiempo*) interval; ~ **de parada** braking distance; ~ **del suelo** (*AUTO etc*) height off the ground; **a gran** *o* **a larga** ~ long-distance; **mantenerse a** ~ to keep one's distance; (*fig*) to remain aloof; **guardar las** ~**s** to keep one's distance.

distanciado, a [distan'θjaðo, a] *adj* (*remoto*) remote; (*fig: alejado*) far apart; **estamos** ~**s en ideas** our ideas are poles apart.

distanciamiento [distanθja'mjento] *nm* (*acto*) spacing out; (*estado*) remoteness;

(*fig*) distance.

distanciar [distan'θjar] *vt* to space out;
~**se** *vr* to become estranged.

distante [dis'tante] *adj* distant.

distar [dis'tar] *vi*: **dista 5 kms de aquí** it is 5
kms from here; **¿dista mucho?** is it far?;
dista mucho de la verdad it's very far
from the truth.

diste ['diste], **disteis** ['disteis] *vb* V **dar**.

distensión [disten'sjon] *nf* distension;
(*POL*) détente; ~ **muscular** (*MED*)
muscular strain.

distinción [distin'θjon] *nf* distinction;
(*elegancia*) elegance; (*honor*) honour; **a** ~
de unlike; **sin** ~ indiscriminately; **sin** ~
de edades irrespective of age.

distinga [dis'tinga] *etc vb* V **distinguir**.

distinguido, a [distin'giðo, a] *adj*
distinguished; (*famoso*) prominent,
well-known; (*elegante*) elegant.

distinguir [distin'gir] *vt* to distinguish;
(*divisar*) to make out; (*escoger*) to single
out; (*caracterizar*) to mark out; ~**se** *vr* to
be distinguished; (*destacarse*) to
distinguish o.s.; **a lo lejos no se distingue**
it's not visible from a distance.

distintivo, a [distin'tiβo, a] *adj* distinctive;
(*signo*) distinguishing ♦ *nm* (*de policía etc*)
badge; (*fig*) characteristic.

distinto, a [dis'tinto, a] *adj* different;
(*claro*) clear; ~**s** several, various.

distorsión [distor'sjon] *nf* (*ANAT*) twisting;
(*RADIO etc*) distortion.

distorsionar [distorsjo'nar] *vt*, *vi* to distort.

distracción [distrak'θjon] *nf* distraction;
(*pasatiempo*) hobby, pastime; (*olvido*)
absent-mindedness, distraction.

distraer [distra'er] *vt* (*atención*) to distract;
(*divertir*) to amuse; (*fondos*) to embezzle
♦ *vi* to be relaxing; ~**se** *vr* (*entretenerse*)
to amuse o.s.; (*perder la concentración*) to
allow one's attention to wander; ~ **a**
algn de su pensamiento to divert sb
from his train of thought; **el pescar**
distrae fishing is a relaxation.

distraído, a [distra'iðo, a] *adj* (*gen*)
absent-minded; (*desatento*) inattentive;
(*entretenido*) amusing ♦ *nm*: **hacerse el** ~
to pretend not to notice; **con aire** ~ idly;
me miró distraída she gave me a casual
glance.

distraiga [dis'traiɣa] *etc*, **distraje**
[dis'traxe] *etc*, **distrajera** [distra'xera]
etc, **distrayendo** [distra'jendo] *vb* V
distraer.

distribución [distriβu'θjon] *nf* distribution;
(*entrega*) delivery; (*en estadística*)
distribution, incidence; (*ARQ*) layout; ~

de premios prize giving; **la** ~ **de los**
impuestos the incidence of taxes.

distribuidor, a [distriβui'ðor, a] *nm/f*
(*persona*: *gen*) distributor; (: *CORREOS*)
sorter; (: *COM*) dealer; **su** ~ **habitual**
your regular dealer.

distribuir [distriβu'ir] *vt* to distribute;
(*prospectos*) to hand out; (*cartas*) to
deliver; (*trabajo*) to allocate; (*premios*) to
award; (*dividendos*) to pay; (*peso*) to
distribute; (*ARQ*) to plan.

distribuyendo [distriβu'jendo] *etc vb* V
distribuir.

distrito [dis'trito] *nm* (*sector, territorio*)
region; (*barrio*) district; ~ **electoral**
constituency; ~ **postal** postal district.

disturbio [dis'turβjo] *nm* disturbance;
(*desorden*) riot; **los** ~**s** the troubles.

disuadir [diswa'ðir] *vt* to dissuade.

disuasión [diswa'sjon] *nf* dissuasion; (*MIL*)
deterrent; ~ **nuclear** nuclear deterrent.

disuasivo, a [diswa'siβo, a] *adj* dissuasive;
arma disuasiva deterrent.

disuasorio, a [diswa'sorjo, a] *adj*
= **disuasivo**.

disuelto [di'swelto] *pp de* **disolver**.

disuelva [di'swelβa] *etc vb* V **disolver**.

disuene [di'swene] *etc vb* V **disonar**.

disyuntiva [disjun'tiβa] *nf* (*dilema*)
dilemma.

DIU ['diu] *nm abr* (= *dispositivo intrauterino*)
I.U.D.

diurno, a ['djurno, a] *adj* day *cpd*, diurnal.

diva ['diβa] *nf* prima donna.

divagar [diβa'ɣar] *vi* (*desviarse*) to digress.

divague [di'βaɣe] *etc vb* V **divagar**.

diván [di'βan] *nm* divan.

divergencia [diβer'xenθja] *nf* divergence.

divergir [diβer'xir] *vi* (*líneas*) to diverge;
(*opiniones*) to differ; (*personas*) to
disagree.

diverja [di'βerxa] *etc vb* V **divergir**.

diversidad [diβersi'ðað] *nf* diversity,
variety.

diversificación [diβersifika'θjon] *nf* (*COM*)
diversification.

diversificar [diβersifi'kar] *vt* to diversify.

diversifique [diβersi'fike] *etc vb* V
diversificar.

diversión [diβer'sjon] *nf* (*gen*)
entertainment; (*actividad*) hobby,
pastime.

diverso, a [di'βerso, a] *adj* diverse;
(*diferente*) different ♦ *nm*: ~**s** (*COM*)
sundries; ~**s libros** several books.

divertido, a [diβer'tiðo, a] *adj* (*chiste*)
amusing, funny; (*fiesta etc*) enjoyable;
(*película, libro*) entertaining; **está** ~

(*irónico*) this is going to be fun.
divertir [diβer'tir] *vt* (*entretener, recrear*) to amuse; ~**se** *vr* (*pasarlo bien*) to have a good time; (*distraerse*) to amuse o.s.
dividendo [diβi'ðendo] *nm* (*COM*): ~**s** *nmpl* dividends; ~**s por acción** earnings per share; ~ **definitivo** final dividend.
dividir [diβi'ðir] *vt* (*gen*) to divide; (*separar*) to separate; (*distribuir*) to distribute.
divierta [di'βjerta] *etc vb V* **divertir**.
divinidad [diβini'ðað] *nf* (*esencia divina*) divinity; **la D~** God.
divino, a [di'βino, a] *adj* divine; (*fig*) lovely.
divirtiendo [diβir'tjendo] *etc vb V* **divertir**.
divisa [di'βisa] *nf* (*emblema, moneda*) emblem, badge; ~**s** *nfpl* currency *sg*; (*COM*) foreign exchange *sg*; **control de** ~**s** exchange control; ~ **de reserva** reserve currency.
divisar [diβi'sar] *vt* to make out.
división [diβi'sjon] *nf* division; (*de partido*) split; (*de país*) partition.
divisorio, a [diβi'sorjo, a] *adj* (*línea*) dividing; **línea divisoria de las aguas** watershed.
divorciado, a [diβor'θjaðo, a] *adj* divorced; (*opinion*) split ♦ *nm/f* divorcé(e).
divorciar [diβor'θjar] *vt* to divorce; ~**se** *vr* to get divorced.
divorcio [di'βorθjo] *nm* divorce; (*fig*) split.
divulgación [diβulxa'θjon] *nf* (*difusión*) spreading; (*popularización*) popularization.
divulgar [diβul'xar] *vt* (*desparramar*) to spread; (*popularizar*) to popularize; (*hacer circular*) to divulge, circulate; ~**se** *vr* (*secreto*) to leak out; (*rumor*) to get about.
divulgue [di'βulxe] *etc vb V* **divulgar**.
dizque ['diske] *adv* (*AM fam*) apparently.
Dls., dls *abr* (*AM*) = **dólares**.
DM *abr* = **decimal**.
dm. *abr* (= *decímetro*) dm.
DNI *nm abr* (*ESP*) = **Documento Nacional de Identidad**.
Dña. *abr* = **Doña**.
do [do] *nm* (*MUS*) C.
D.O. *abr* = **Denominación de Origen**.
dobladillo [doβla'ðiλo] *nm* (*de vestido*) hem; (*de pantalón: vuelta*) turn-up (*BRIT*), cuff (*US*).
doblaje [do'βlaxe] *nm* (*CINE*) dubbing.
doblar [do'βlar] *vt* to double; (*papel*) to fold; (*caño*) to bend; (*la esquina*) to turn, go round; (*film*) to dub ♦ *vi* to turn; (*campana*) to toll; ~**se** *vr* (*plegarse*) to fold (up), crease; (*encorvarse*) to bend.
doble ['doβle] *adj* (*gen*) double; (*de dos aspectos*) dual; (*cuerda*) thick; (*fig*) two-

faced ♦ *nm* double ♦ *nm/f* (*TEAT*) double, stand-in; ~**s** *nmpl* (*DEPORTE*) doubles *sg*; ~ **o nada** double or quits; ~ **página** double-page spread; **con** ~ **sentido** with a double meaning; **el** ~ twice the quantity *o* as much; **su sueldo es el** ~ **del mío** his salary is twice (as much as) mine; (*INFORM*): ~ **cara** double-sided; ~ **densidad** double density.
doblegar [doβle'xar] *vt* to fold, crease; ~**se** *vr* to yield.
doblegue [do'βlexe] *etc vb V* **doblegar**.
doblez [do'βleθ] *nm* (*pliegue*) fold, hem ♦ *nf* (*falsedad*) duplicity.
doc. *abr* (= *docena*) doz.; (= *documento*) doc.
doce ['doθe] *num* twelve; (*fecha*) twelfth; **las** ~ twelve o'clock; *V tb* **seis**.
docena [do'θena] *nf* dozen; **por** ~**s** by the dozen.
docente [do'θente] *adj*: **centro/personal** ~ teaching institution/staff.
dócil [do'θil] *adj* (*pasivo*) docile; (*manso*) gentle; (*obediente*) obedient.
docto, a ['dokto, a] *adj* learned, erudite ♦ *nm/f* scholar.
doctor, a [dok'tor, a] *nm/f* doctor; ~ **en filosofía** Doctor of Philosophy.
doctorado [dokto'raðo] *nm* doctorate.
doctorarse [dokto'rarse] *vr* to get a doctorate.
doctrina [dok'trina] *nf* doctrine, teaching.
documentación [dokumenta'θjon] *nf* documentation; (*de identidad etc*) papers *pl*.
documental [dokumen'tal] *adj, nm* documentary.
documentar [dokumen'tar] *vt* to document; ~**se** *vr* to gather information.
documento [doku'mento] *nm* (*certificado*) document; (*JUR*) exhibit; ~**s** *nmpl* papers; ~ **adjunto** (*INFORM*) attachment; ~ **justificativo** voucher; **D~ Nacional de Identidad** national identity card; *see boxed note*.

DOCUMENTO NACIONAL DE IDENTIDAD

A laminated plastic ID card with the holder's personal details and photograph, the **Documento Nacional de Identidad** *is renewed every ten years. People are required to carry it at all times and to produce it on request for the police. In Spain it is commonly known as a "DNI" or "carnet de identidad". In Spanish America a similar card is called a "cédula (de identidad)".*

dogma ['doɣma] *nm* dogma.
dogmático, a [doɣ'matiko, a] *adj* dogmatic.
dogo ['doɣo] *nm* bulldog.
dólar ['dolar] *nm* dollar.
dolencia [do'lenθja] *nf* (*achaque*) ailment; (*dolor*) ache.
doler [do'ler] *vt, vi* to hurt; (*fig*) to grieve; ~**se** *vr* (*de su situación*) to grieve, feel sorry; (*de las desgracias ajenas*) to sympathize; (*quejarse*) to complain; **me duele el brazo** my arm hurts; **no me duele el dinero** I don't mind about the money; **¡ahí le duele!** you've put your finger on it!
doliente [do'ljente] *adj* (*enfermo*) sick; (*dolorido*) aching; (*triste*) sorrowful; **la familia** ~ the bereaved family.
dolor [do'lor] *nm* pain; (*fig*) grief, sorrow; ~ **de cabeza** headache; ~ **de estómago** stomach ache; ~ **de oídos** earache; ~ **sordo** dull ache.
dolorido, a [dolo'riðo, a] *adj* (*MED*) sore, aching; **la parte dolorida** the part which hurts.
doloroso, a [dolo'roso, a] *adj* (*MED*) painful; (*fig*) distressing.
domar [do'mar] *vt* to tame.
domesticado, a [domesti'kaðo, a] *adj* (*amansado*) tame.
domesticar [domesti'kar] *vt* to tame.
doméstico, a [do'mestiko, a] *adj* domestic ♦ *nm/f* servant; **economía doméstica** home economy; **gastos** ~**s** household expenses.
domestique [domes'tike] *etc vb V* **domesticar**.
domiciliación [domiθilja'θjon] *nf*: ~ **de pagos** (*COM*) standing order, direct debit.
domiciliar [domiθi'ljar] *vt* to domicile; ~**se** *vr* to take up (one's) residence.
domiciliario, a [domiθi'ljarjo, a] *adj*: **arresto** ~ house arrest.
domicilio [domi'θiljo] *nm* home; ~ **particular** private residence; ~ **social** (*COM*) head office, registered office; **servicio a** ~ delivery service; **sin** ~ **fijo** of no fixed abode.
dominante [domi'nante] *adj* dominant; (*person*) domineering.
dominar [domi'nar] *vt* (*gen*) to dominate; (*países*) to rule over; (*adversario*) to overpower; (*caballo, nervios, emoción*) to control; (*incendio, epidemia*) to bring under control; (*idiomas*) to be fluent in ♦ *vi* to dominate, prevail; ~**se** *vr* to control o.s.

domingo [do'mingo] *nm* Sunday; **D**~ **de Ramos** Palm Sunday; **D**~ **de Resurrección** Easter Sunday; *V tb* **sábado**; **Semana Santa**.
dominguero, a [domin'gero, a] *adj* Sunday *cpd*.
dominical [domini'kal] *adj* Sunday *cpd*; **periódico** ~ Sunday newspaper.
dominicano, a [domini'kano, a] *adj, nm/f* Dominican.
dominio [do'minjo] *nm* (*tierras*) domain; (*POL*) dominion; (*autoridad*) power, authority; (*supremacía*) supremacy; (*de las pasiones*) grip, hold; (*de idioma*) command; **ser del** ~ **público** to be widely known.
dominó [domi'no] *nm* (*pieza*) domino; (*juego*) dominoes.
dom.º *abr* (= *domingo*) Sun.
don [don] *nm* (*talento*) gift; **D**~ **Juan Gómez** Mr Juan Gómez, Juan Gómez Esq. (*BRIT*); **tener** ~ **de gentes** to known how to handle people; ~ **de lenguas** gift for languages; ~ **de mando** (qualities of) leadership; ~ **de palabra** gift of the gab; *see boxed note*.

DON

*The title **don** or **doña** is used before a person's first name – for example, Don Diego, Doña Inés – as a mark of respect or politeness to someone of superior social standing or an older person. Its use is dying out but it continues to be found in official documents and correspondence: for example, Sr. D. Pedro Rodríguez Hernández, Sra. Dña Inés Rodríguez Hernández.*

---

donación [dona'θjon] *nf* donation.
donaire [do'naire] *nm* charm.
donante [do'nante] *nm/f* donor; ~ **de sangre** blood donor.
donar [do'nar] *vt* to donate.
donativo [dona'tiβo] *nm* donation.
doncella [don'θeʎa] *nf* (*criada*) maid.
donde ['donde] *adv* where ♦ *prep*: **el coche está allí** ~ **el farol** the car is over there by the lamppost *o* where the lamppost is; **por** ~ through which; **a** ~ to where, to which; **en** ~ where, in which; **es a** ~ **vamos nosotros** that's where we're going.
dónde ['donde] *adv interrogativo* where?; **¿a** ~ **vas?** where are you going (to)?; **¿de** ~ **vienes?** where have you come from?; **¿en** ~**?** where?; **¿por** ~**?** where?,

whereabouts?; **¿por ~ se va al estadio?** how do you get to the stadium?

dondequiera [donde'kjera] *adv* anywhere ♦ *conj*: ~ **que** wherever; **por ~** everywhere, all over the place.

donostiarra [donos'tjarra] *adj* of *o* from San Sebastián ♦ *nm/f* native *o* inhabitant of San Sebastián.

doña ['doɲa] *nf*: **D~ Carmen Gómez** Mrs Carmen Gómez; *V tb* **don.**

dopar [do'par] *vt* to dope, drug.

doping ['dopin] *nm* doping, drugging.

doquier [do'kjer] *adv*: **por ~** all over, everywhere.

dorado, a [do'raðo, a] *adj* (*color*) golden; (*TEC*) gilt.

dorar [do'rar] *vt* (*TEC*) to gild; (*CULIN*) to brown, cook lightly; ~ **la píldora** to sweeten the pill.

dormilón, ona [dormi'lon, ona] *adj* fond of sleeping ♦ *nm/f* sleepyhead.

dormir [dor'mir] *vt*: ~ **la siesta por la tarde** to have an afternoon nap ♦ *vi* to sleep; ~**se** *vr* (*persona, brazo, pierna*) to fall asleep; ~**la** (*fam*) to sleep it off; ~ **la mona** (*fam*) to sleep off a hangover; ~ **como un lirón** *o* **tronco** to sleep like a log; ~ **a pierna suelta** to sleep soundly.

dormitar [dormi'tar] *vi* to doze.

dormitorio [dormi'torjo] *nm* bedroom; ~ **común** dormitory.

dorsal [dor'sal] *adj* dorsal ♦ *nm* (*DEPORTE*) number.

dorso ['dorso] *nm* back; **escribir algo al ~** to write sth on the back; **"véase al ~"** "see other side", "please turn over".

DOS *nm abr* (= *sistema operativo de disco*) DOS.

dos [dos] *num* two; (*fecha*) second; **los ~** the two of them, both of them; **cada ~ por tres** every five minutes; **de ~ en ~** in twos; **estamos a ~** (*TENIS*) the score is deuce; *V tb* **seis.**

doscientos, as [dos'θjentos, as] *num* two hundred.

dosel [do'sel] *nm* canopy.

dosificar [dosifi'kar] *vt* (*CULIN, MED, QUÍMICA*) to measure out; (*no derrochar*) to be sparing with.

dosifique [dosi'fike] *etc vb V* **dosificar.**

dosis ['dosis] *nf inv* dose, dosage.

dossier [do'sjer] *nm* dossier, file.

dotación [dota'θjon] *nf* (*acto, dinero*) endowment; (*plantilla*) staff; (*NAUT*) crew; **la ~ es insuficiente** we are under staffed.

dotado, a [do'taðo, a] *adj* gifted; ~ **de** (*persona*) endowed with; (*máquina*) equipped with.

dotar [do'tar] *vt* to endow; (*TEC*) to fit; (*barco*) to man; (*oficina*) to staff.

dote ['dote] *nf* (*de novia*) dowry; ~**s** *nfpl* (*talentos*) gifts.

doy [doj] *vb V* **dar.**

Dpto. *abr* (= *Departamento*) dept.

Dr(a). *abr* (= *Doctor, Doctora*) Dr.

draga ['draɣa] *nf* dredge.

dragado [dra'ɣaðo] *nm* dredging.

dragar [dra'ɣar] *vt* to dredge; (*minas*) to sweep.

dragón [dra'ɣon] *nm* dragon.

drague ['draɣe] *etc vb V* **dragar.**

drama ['drama] *nm* drama; (*obra*) play.

dramático, a [dra'matiko, a] *adj* dramatic ♦ *nm/f* dramatist; (*actor*) actor; **obra dramática** play.

dramaturgo, a [drama'turɣo, a] *nm/f* dramatist, playwright.

dramón [dra'mon] *nm* (*TEAT*) melodrama; **¡qué ~!** what a scene!

drástico, a ['drastiko, a] *adj* drastic.

drenaje [dre'naxe] *nm* drainage.

drenar [dre'nar] *vt* to drain.

droga ['droɣa] *nf* drug; (*DEPORTE*) dope; **el problema de la ~** the drug problem.

drogadicto, a [droɣa'ðikto, a] *nm/f* drug addict.

drogar [dro'ɣar] *vt* to drug; (*DEPORTE*) to dope; ~**se** *vr* to take drugs.

drogodependencia [droɣoðepen'denθja] *nf* drug addiction.

drogue ['droɣe] *etc vb V* **drogar.**

droguería [droɣe'ria] *nf* ≈ hardware shop (*BRIT*) *o* store (*US*).

dromedario [drome'ðarjo] *nm* dromedary.

Dto., D.^{to} *abr* = **descuento.**

Dtor(a). *abr* (= *Director, Directora*) Dir.

ducado [du'kaðo] *nm* duchy, dukedom.

ducha ['dutʃa] *nf* (*baño*) shower; (*MED*) douche.

ducharse [du'tʃarse] *vr* to take a shower.

ducho, a ['dutʃo, a] *adj*: ~ **en** (*experimentado*) experienced in; (*hábil*) skilled at.

dúctil ['duktil] *adj* (*metal*) ductile; (*persona*) easily influenced.

duda ['duða] *nf* doubt; **sin ~** no doubt, doubtless; **¡sin ~!** of course!; **no cabe ~** there is no doubt about it; **no le quepa ~** make no mistake about it; **no quiero poner en ~ su conducta** I don't want to call his behaviour into question; **sacar a algn de la ~** to settle sb's doubts; **tengo una ~** I have a query.

dudar [du'ðar] *vt* to doubt ♦ *vi* to doubt, have doubts; ~ **acerca de algo** to be uncertain about sth; **dudó en comprarlo** he hesitated to buy it; **dudan que sea verdad** they doubt whether o if it's true.

dudoso, a [du'ðoso, a] *adj* (*incierto*) hesitant; (*sospechoso*) doubtful; (*conducta*) dubious.

duelo ['dwelo] *etc vb V* **doler** ♦ *nm* (*combate*) duel; (*luto*) mourning; **batirse en** ~ to fight a duel.

duende ['dwende] *nm* imp, goblin; **tiene** ~ he's got real soul.

dueño, a ['dweɲo, a] *nm/f* (*propietario*) owner; (*de pensión, taberna*) landlord/lady; (*de casa, perro*) master/mistress; (*empresario*) employer; **ser** ~ **de sí mismo** to have self-control; (*libre*) to be one's own boss; **eres** ~ **de hacer como te parezca** you're free to do as you think fit; **hacerse** ~ **de una situación** to take command of a situation.

duerma ['dwerma] *etc vb V* **dormir**.

duermevela [dwerme'βela] *nf* (*fam*) nap, snooze.

Duero ['dwero] *nm* Douro.

dulce ['dulθe] *adj* sweet; (*carácter, clima*) gentle, mild ♦ *adv* gently, softly ♦ *nm* sweet.

dulcificar [dulθifi'kar] *vt* (*fig*) to soften.

dulcifique [dulθi'fike] *etc vb V* **dulcificar**.

dulzón, ona [dul'θon, ona] *adj* (*alimento*) sickly-sweet, too sweet; (*canción etc*) gooey.

dulzura [dul'θura] *nf* sweetness; (*ternura*) gentleness.

duna ['duna] *nf* dune.

Dunquerque [dun'kerke] *nm* Dunkirk.

dúo ['duo] *nm* duet, duo.

duodécimo, a [duo'deθimo, a] *adj* twelfth; *V tb* **sexto, a**.

dup., dup.do *abr* (= *duplicado*) duplicated.

dúplex ['dupleks] *nm inv* (*piso*) flat on two floors; (*TELEC*) link-up; (*INFORM*): ~ **integral** full duplex.

duplicar [dupli'kar] *vt* (*hacer el doble de*) to duplicate; (*cantidad*) to double; **~se** *vr* to double.

duplique [du'plike] *etc vb V* **duplicar**.

duque ['duke] *nm* duke.

duquesa [du'kesa] *nf* duchess.

duración [dura'θjon] *nf* duration, length; (*de máquina*) life; ~ **media de la vida** average life expectancy; **de larga** ~ (*enfermedad*) lengthy; (*pila*) long-life; (*disco*) long-playing; **de poca** ~ short.

duradero, a [dura'ðero, a] *adj* (*tela*) hard-wearing; (*fe, paz*) lasting.

durante [du'rante] *adv* during; ~ **toda la noche** all night long; **habló** ~ **una hora** he spoke for an hour.

durar [du'rar] *vi* (*permanecer*) to last; (*recuerdo*) to remain; (*ropa*) to wear (well).

durazno [du'rasno] *nm* (*AM: fruta*) peach; (: *árbol*) peach tree.

durex ['dureks] *nm* (*AM: tira adhesiva*) Sellotape ® (*BRIT*), Scotch tape ® (*US*).

dureza [du'reθa] *nf* (*cualidad*) hardness; (*de carácter*) toughness.

durmiendo [dur'mjendo] *etc vb V* **dormir**.

durmiente [dur'mjente] *adj* sleeping ♦ *nm/f* sleeper.

duro, a ['duro, a] *adj* hard; (*carácter*) tough; (*pan*) stale; (*cuello, puerta*) stiff; (*clima, luz*) harsh ♦ *adv* hard ♦ *nm* (*moneda*) five peseta coin; **el sector** ~ **del partido** the hardliners *pl* in the party; **ser** ~ **con algn** to be tough with o hard on sb; ~ **de mollera** (*torpe*) dense; ~ **de oído** hard of hearing; **trabajar** ~ to work hard; **estar sin un** ~ to be broke.

DVD *nm abr* (= *disco de vídeo digital*) DVD.

E e

E, e [e] *nf* (*letra*) E, e; **E de Enrique** E for Edward (*BRIT*) o Easy (*US*).

E *abr* (= *este*) E.

e [e] *conj* (*delante de* **i-** *e* **hi-**, *pero no* **hie-**) and; *V tb* **y**.

e/ *abr* (*COM*: = *envío*) shpt.

ebanista [eβa'nista] *nm/f* cabinetmaker.

ébano ['eβano] *nm* ebony.

ebrio, a ['eβrjo, a] *adj* drunk.

Ebro ['eβro] *nm* Ebro.

ebullición [eβuʎi'θjon] *nf* boiling; **punto de** ~ boiling point.

eccema [ek'θema] *nm* (*MED*) eczema.

echar [e'tʃar] *vt* to throw; (*agua, vino*) to pour (out); (*CULIN*) to put in, add; (*dientes*) to cut; (*discurso*) to give; (*empleado: despedir*) to fire, sack; (*hojas*) to sprout; (*cartas*) to post; (*humo*) to emit, give out; (*reprimenda*) to deal out; (*cuenta*) to make up; (*freno*) to put on ♦ *vi*: ~ **a correr/llorar** to break into a run/burst into tears; ~ **a reír** to burst out laughing; **~se** *vr* to lie down; ~ **abajo** (*gobierno*) to overthrow; (*edificio*) to demolish; ~ **la buenaventura a algn** to tell sb's fortune; ~ **la culpa a** to lay the

blame on; ~ **de menos** to miss; **~se atrás**
to throw o.s. back(wards); (*fig*) to go
back on what one has said; **~se una
novia** to get o.s. a girlfriend; **~se una
siestecita** to have a nap.

echarpe [e'tʃarpe] *nm* (woman's) stole.

eclesiástico, a [ekle'sjastiko, a] *adj*
ecclesiastical; (*autoridades etc*) church
cpd ♦ *nm* clergyman.

eclipsar [eklip'sar] *vt* to eclipse; (*fig*) to
outshine, overshadow.

eclipse [e'klipse] *nm* eclipse.

eco ['eko] *nm* echo; **encontrar un ~ en** to
produce a response from; **hacerse ~ de
una opinión** to echo an opinion; **tener ~**
to catch on.

ecografía [ekoɣra'fia] *nf* ultrasound.

ecología [ekolo'xia] *nf* ecology.

ecológico, a [eko'loxiko, a] *adj* ecological;
(*producto, método*) environmentally-
friendly; (*agricultura*) organic.

ecologista [ekolo'xista] *adj* environmental, conservation *cpd* ♦ *nm/f* environmentalist.

economato [ekono'mato] *nm* cooperative
store.

economía [ekono'mia] *nf* (*sistema*)
economy; (*cualidad*) thrift; **~ dirigida**
planned economy; **~ doméstica**
housekeeping; **~ de mercado** market
economy; **~ mixta** mixed economy; **~
sumergida** black economy; **hacer ~s** to
economize; **~s de escala** economies of
scale.

economice [ekono'miθe] *etc vb V*
economizar.

económico, a [eko'nomiko, a] *adj* (*barato*)
cheap, economical; (*persona*) thrifty;
(*COM: año etc*) financial; (: *situación*)
economic.

economista [ekono'mista] *nm/f* economist.

economizar [ekonomi'θar] *vt* to economize
on ♦ *vi* (*ahorrar*) to save up; (*pey*) to be
miserly.

ecosistema [ekosis'tema] *nm* ecosystem.

ecu ['eku] *nm* ecu.

ecuación [ekwa'θjon] *nf* equation.

ecuador [ekwa'ðor] *nm* equator; **(el) E~**
Ecuador.

ecuánime [e'kwanime] *adj* (*carácter*) level-
headed; (*estado*) calm.

ecuatorial [ekwato'rjal] *adj* equatorial.

ecuatoriano, a [ekwato'rjano, a] *adj, nm/f*
Ecuador(i)an.

ecuestre [e'kwestre] *adj* equestrian.

eczema [ek'θema] *nm* = **eccema**.

ed. *abr* (= *edición*) ed.

edad [e'ðað] *nf* age; **¿qué ~ tienes?** how

old are you?; **tiene ocho años de ~** he is
eight (years old); **de ~ corta** young; **ser
de ~ mediana/avanzada** to be middle-
aged/getting on; **ser mayor de ~** to be of
age; **llegar a mayor ~** to come of age; **ser
menor de ~** to be under age; **la E~
Media** the Middle Ages; **la E~ de Oro** the
Golden Age.

Edén [e'ðen] *nm* Eden.

edición [eði'θjon] *nf* (*acto*) publication;
(*ejemplar*) edition; **"al cerrar la ~"** (*TIP*)
"stop press".

edicto [e'ðikto] *nm* edict, proclamation.

edificante [eðifi'kante] *adj* edifying.

edificar [eðifi'kar] *vt* (*ARQ*) to build.

edificio [eði'fiθjo] *nm* building; (*fig*)
edifice, structure.

edifique [eði'fike] *etc vb V* **edificar**.

Edimburgo [eðim'burɣo] *nm* Edinburgh.

editar [eði'tar] *vt* (*publicar*) to publish;
(*preparar textos, tb INFORM*) to edit.

editor, a [eði'tor, a] *nm/f* (*que publica*)
publisher; (*redactor*) editor ♦ *adj*: **casa ~a**
publishing company.

editorial [eðito'rjal] *adj* editorial ♦ *nm*
leading article, editorial ♦ *nf* (*tb*: **casa ~**)
publishers.

editorialista [eðitorja'lista] *nm/f* leader-
writer.

Edo. *abr* (*AM*) = **Estado**.

edredón [eðre'ðon] *nm* eiderdown, quilt; **~
nórdico** continental quilt, duvet.

educación [eðuka'θjon] *nf* education;
(*crianza*) upbringing; (*modales*) (good)
manners *pl*; (*formación*) training; **sin ~**
ill-mannered; **¡qué falta de ~!** how rude!

educado, a [eðu'kaðo, a] *adj* well-
mannered; **mal ~** ill-mannered.

educar [eðu'kar] *vt* to educate; (*criar*) to
bring up; (*voz*) to train.

educativo, a [eðuka'tiβo, a] *adj*
educational; (*política*) education *cpd*.

eduque [e'ðuke] *etc vb V* **educar**.

EE.UU. *nmpl abr* (= *Estados Unidos*) USA.

efectista [efek'tista] *adj* sensationalist.

efectivamente [efektiβa'mente] *adv* (*como
respuesta*) exactly, precisely; (*verdaderamente*) really; (*de hecho*) in fact.

efectivo, a [efek'tiβo, a] *adj* effective;
(*real*) actual, real ♦ *nm*: **pagar en ~** to pay
(in) cash; **hacer ~ un cheque** to cash a
cheque.

efecto [e'fekto] *nm* effect, result; (*objetivo*)
purpose, end; **~s** *nmpl* (*personales*) effects;
(*bienes*) goods; (*COM*) assets; (*ECON*) bills,
securities; **~ 2000** millennium bug; **~ de
invernadero** greenhouse effect; **~s de
consumo** consumer goods; **~s a cobrar**

bills receivable; ~**s especiales** special effects; ~**s personales** personal effects; ~**s secundarios** (*COM*) spin-off effects; ~**s sonoros** sound effects; **hacer** *o* **surtir** ~ to have the desired effect; **hacer** ~ (*impresionar*) to make an impression; **llevar algo a** ~ to carry sth out; **en** ~ in fact; (*respuesta*) exactly, indeed.

efectuar [efek'twar] *vt* to carry out; (*viaje*) to make.

efervescente [eferβes'θente] *adj* (*bebida*) fizzy, bubbly.

eficacia [efi'kaθja] *nf* (*de persona*) efficiency; (*de medicamento etc*) effectiveness.

eficaz [efi'kaθ] *adj* (*persona*) efficient; (*acción*) effective.

eficiencia [efi'θjenθja] *nf* efficiency.

eficiente [efi'θjente] *adj* efficient.

efigie [e'fixje] *nf* effigy.

efímero, a [e'fimero, a] *adj* ephemeral.

efusión [efu'sjon] *nf* outpouring; (*en el trato*) warmth; **con** ~ effusively.

efusivo, a [efu'siβo, a] *adj* effusive; **mis más efusivas gracias** my warmest thanks.

EGB *nf abr* (*ESP ESCOL*: = *Educación General Básica*) *primary education for 6-14 year olds*; *V tb* **sistema educativo**.

Egeo [e'xeo] *nm*: (**Mar**) ~ Aegean (Sea).

egipcio, a [e'xipθjo, a] *adj, nm/f* Egyptian.

Egipto [e'xipto] *nm* Egypt.

egocéntrico, a [eɣo'θentriko, a] *adj* self-centred.

egoísmo [eɣo'ismo] *nm* egoism.

egoísta [eɣo'ista] *adj* egoistical, selfish ♦ *nm/f* egoist.

ególatra [e'ɣolatra] *adj* big-headed.

egregio, a [e'ɣrexjo, a] *adj* eminent, distinguished.

egresado, a [eɣre'saðo, a] *nm/f* (*AM*) graduate.

egresar [eɣre'sar] *vi* (*AM*) to graduate.

eh [e] *excl* hey!, hi!

Eire ['eire] *nm* Eire.

ej. *abr* (= *ejemplo*) ex.

eje ['exe] *nm* (*GEO, MAT*) axis; (*POL, fig*) axis, main line; (*de rueda*) axle; (*de máquina*) shaft, spindle.

ejecución [exeku'θjon] *nf* execution; (*cumplimiento*) fulfilment; (*actuación*) performance; (*JUR: embargo de deudor*) attachment.

ejecutar [exeku'tar] *vt* to execute, carry out; (*matar*) to execute; (*cumplir*) to fulfil; (*MUS*) to perform; (*JUR: embargar*) to attach, distrain; (*deseos*) to fulfil; (*INFORM*) to run.

ejecutivo, a [exeku'tiβo, a] *adj, nm/f* executive; **el (poder)** ~ the Executive (Power).

ejecutor [exeku'tor] *nm* (*tb*: ~ **testamentario**) executor.

ejecutoria [exeku'torja] *nf* (*JUR*) final judgment.

ejemplar [exem'plar] *adj* exemplary ♦ *nm* example; (*ZOOL*) specimen; (*de libro*) copy; (*de periódico*) number, issue; ~ **de regalo** complimentary copy; **sin** ~ unprecedented.

ejemplificar [exemplifi'kar] *vt* to exemplify, illustrate.

ejemplifique [exempli'fike] *etc vb V* **ejemplificar**.

ejemplo [e'xemplo] *nm* example; (*caso*) instance; **por** ~ for example; **dar** ~ to set an example.

ejercer [exer'θer] *vt* to exercise; (*funciones*) to perform; (*negocio*) to manage; (*influencia*) to exert; (*un oficio*) to practise; (*poder*) to wield ♦ *vi*: ~ **de** to practise as.

ejercicio [exer'θiθjo] *nm* exercise; (*MIL*) drill; (*COM*) **fiscal** *o* **financial year**; (*período*) tenure; ~ **acrobático** (*AVIAT*) stunt; ~ **comercial** business year; ~**s espirituales** (*REL*) retreat *sg*; **hacer** ~ to take exercise.

ejercitar [exerθi'tar] *vt* to exercise; (*MIL*) to drill.

ejército [e'xerθito] *nm* army; **E~ del Aire/de Tierra** Air Force/Army; ~ **de ocupación** army of occupation; ~ **permanente** standing army; **entrar en el** ~ to join the army, join up.

ejerza [e'xerθa] *etc vb V* **ejercer**.

ejote [e'xote] *nm* (*AM*) green bean.

══════════════════════════ *PALABRA CLAVE*

el [el] (*f* **la**, *pl* **los, las**, *neutro* **lo**) *art def* **1** the; **el libro/la mesa/los estudiantes/las flores** the book/table/students/flowers; **me gusta el fútbol** I like football; **está en la cama** she's in bed

2 (*con n abstracto o propio: no se traduce*): **el amor/la juventud** love/youth; ~ **Conde Drácula** Count Dracula

3 (*posesión: se traduce a menudo por adj posesivo*): **romperse el brazo** to break one's arm; **levantó la mano** he put his hand up; **se puso el sombrero** she put her hat on

4 (*valor descriptivo*): **tener la boca grande/los ojos azules** to have a big mouth/blue eyes

5 (*con días*) on; **me iré el viernes** I'll leave on Friday; **los domingos suelo ir a**

nadar on Sundays I generally go swimming
6 (*lo* + *adj*): **lo difícil/caro** what is difficult/expensive; (= *cuán*): **no se da cuenta de lo pesado que es** he doesn't realise how boring he is
♦ *pron demos* **1**: **mi libro y el de usted** my book and yours; **las de Pepe son mejores** Pepe's are better; **no la(s) blanca(s) sino la(s) gris(es)** not the white one(s) but the grey one(s)
2: **lo de**: **lo de ayer** what happened yesterday; **lo de las facturas** that business about the invoices
♦ *pron relativo*: **el que** *etc* **1** (*indef*): **el (los) que quiera(n) que se vaya(n)** anyone who wants to can leave; **llévese el/la que más le guste** take the one you like best
2 (*def*): **el que compré ayer** the one I bought yesterday; **los que se van** those who leave
3: **lo que**: **lo que pienso yo/más me gusta** what I think/like most
♦ *conj*: **el que**: **el que lo diga** the fact that he says so; **el que sea tan vago me molesta** his being so lazy bothers me
♦ *excl*: **¡el susto que me diste!** what a fright you gave me!
♦ *pron personal* **1** (*persona*: *m*) him; (: *f*) her; (: *pl*) them; **lo/las veo** I can see him/them
2 (*animal, cosa*: *sg*) it; (: *pl*) them; **lo** (*o* **la**) **veo** I can see it; **los** (*o* **las**) **veo** I can see them
3: **lo** (*como sustituto de frase*): **no lo sabía** I didn't know; **ya lo entiendo** I understand now.

él [el] *pron* (*persona*) he; (*cosa*) it; (*después de prep*: *persona*) him; (: *cosa*) it; **mis libros y los de ~** my books and his.
elaboración [elaβoraˈθjon] *nf* (*producción*) manufacture; **~ de presupuestos** (*COM*) budgeting.
elaborar [elaβoˈrar] *vt* (*producto*) to make, manufacture; (*preparar*) to prepare; (*madera, metal etc*) to work; (*proyecto etc*) to work on *o* out.
elasticidad [elastiθiˈðað] *nf* elasticity.
elástico, a [eˈlastiko, a] *adj* elastic; (*flexible*) flexible ♦ *nm* elastic; (*gomita*) elastic band.
elección [elekˈθjon] *nf* election; (*selección*) choice, selection; **elecciones parciales** by-election *sg*; **elecciones generales** general election *sg*.
electo, a [eˈlekto, a] *adj* elect; **el presidente ~** the president-elect.
electorado [elektoˈraðo] *nm* electorate,

voters *pl*.
electoral [elektoˈral] *adj* electoral.
electrice [elekˈtriθe] *etc vb V* **electrizar**.
electricidad [elektriθiˈðað] *nf* electricity.
electricista [elektriˈθista] *nm/f* electrician.
eléctrico, a [eˈlektriko, a] *adj* electric.
electrificar [elektrifiˈkar] *vt* to electrify.
electrizar [elektriˈθar] *vt* (*FERRO, fig*) to electrify.
electro... [elektro] *pref* electro....
electrocardiograma [elektrokarðjoˈɣrama] *nm* electrocardiogram.
electrocución [elektrokuˈθjon] *nf* electrocution.
electrocutar [elektrokuˈtar] *vt* to electrocute.
electrodo [elekˈtroðo] *nm* electrode.
electrodomésticos [elektroðoˈmestikos] *nmpl* (electrical) household appliances; (*COM*) white goods.
electroimán [elektroiˈman] *nm* electromagnet.
electromagnético, a [elektromaɣˈnetiko, a] *adj* electromagnetic.
electrón [elekˈtron] *nm* electron.
electrónico, a [elekˈtroniko, a] *adj* electronic ♦ *nf* electronics *sg*; **proceso ~ de datos** (*INFORM*) electronic data processing.
electrotecnia [elektroˈteknja] *nf* electrical engineering.
electrotécnico, a [elektroˈtekniko, a] *nm/f* electrical engineer.
elefante [eleˈfante] *nm* elephant.
elegancia [eleˈɣanθja] *nf* elegance, grace; (*estilo*) stylishness.
elegante [eleˈɣante] *adj* elegant, graceful; (*traje etc*) smart, fashionable; (*decoración*) tasteful.
elegía [eleˈxia] *nf* elegy.
elegir [eleˈxir] *vt* (*escoger*) to choose, select; (*optar*) to opt for; (*presidente*) to elect.
elemental [elemenˈtal] *adj* (*claro, obvio*) elementary; (*fundamental*) elemental, fundamental.
elemento [eleˈmento] *nm* element; (*fig*) ingredient; (*AM*) person, individual; (*tipo raro*) odd person; (*de pila*) cell; **~s** *nmpl* elements, rudiments; **estar en su ~** to be in one's element; **vino a verle un ~** someone came to see you.
elenco [eˈlenko] *nm* catalogue, list; (*TEAT*) cast; (*AM*: *equipo*) team.
elepé [eleˈpe] *nm* LP.
elevación [eleβaˈθjon] *nf* elevation; (*acto*) raising, lifting; (*de precios*) rise; (*GEO*

etc) height, altitude.

elevador [eleβa'ðor] *nm* (*AM*) lift (*BRIT*), elevator (*US*).

elevar [ele'βar] *vt* to raise, lift (up); (*precio*) to put up; (*producción*) to step up; (*informe etc*) to present; ~**se** *vr* (*edificio*) to rise; (*precios*) to go up; (*transportarse, enajenarse*) to get carried away; **la cantidad se eleva a** ... the total amounts to ... .

eligiendo [eli'xjenðo] *etc*, **elija** [e'lixa] *etc vb V* **elegir**.

eliminar [elimi'nar] *vt* to eliminate, remove; (*olor, persona*) to get rid of; (*DEPORTE*) to eliminate, knock out.

eliminatoria [elimina'torja] *nf* heat, preliminary (round).

elite [e'lite], **élite** ['elite] *nf* elite, élite.

elitista [eli'tista] *adj* elitist.

elixir [elik'sir] *nm* elixir; (*tb:* ~ **bucal**) mouthwash.

ella ['eʎa] *pron* (*persona*) she; (*cosa*) it; (*después de prep: persona*) her; (: *cosa*) it; **de** ~ hers.

ellas ['eʎas] *pron V* **ellos**.

ello ['eʎo] *pron neutro* it; **es por** ~ **que** ... that's why ....

ellos, as ['eʎos, as] *pron personal pl* they; (*después de prep*) them; **de** ~ theirs.

elocuencia [elo'kwenθja] *nf* eloquence.

elocuente [elo'kwente] *adj* eloquent; (*fig*) significant; **un dato** ~ a fact which speaks for itself.

elogiar [elo'xjar] *vt* to praise, eulogize.

elogio [e'loxjo] *nm* praise; **queda por encima de todo** ~ it's beyond praise; **hacer** ~ **de** to sing the praises of.

elote [e'lote] *nm* (*AM*) corn on the cob.

eludir [elu'ðir] *vt* (*evitar*) to avoid, evade; (*escapar*) to escape, elude.

e-mail ['imeil] *nm* (*gen*) e-mail; (*dirección*) e-mail address; **mandar un** ~ **a algn** to e-mail sb, to send sb an e-mail.

emanar [ema'nar] *vi:* ~ **de** to emanate from, come from; (*derivar de*) to originate in.

emancipar [emanθi'par] *vt* to emancipate; ~**se** *vr* to become emancipated, free o.s.

embadurnar [embaður'nar] *vt* to smear.

embajada [emba'xaða] *nf* embassy.

embajador, a [embaxa'ðor, a] *nmlf* ambassador/ambassadress.

embaladura [embala'ðura] *nf* (*AM*), **embalaje** [emba'laxe] *nm* packing.

embalar [emba'lar] *vt* (*envolver*) to parcel, wrap (up); (*envasar*) to package ♦ *vi* to sprint.

embalsamar [embalsa'mar] *vt* to embalm.

embalsar [embal'sar] *vt* (*río*) to dam (up); (*agua*) to retain.

embalse [em'balse] *nm* (*presa*) dam; (*lago*) reservoir.

embarace [emba'raθe] *etc vb V* **embarazar**.

embarazada [embara'θaða] *adj f* pregnant ♦ *nf* pregnant woman.

embarazar [embara'θar] *vt* to obstruct, hamper; ~**se** *vr* (*aturdirse*) to become embarrassed; (*confundirse*) to get into a mess.

embarazo [emba'raθo] *nm* (*de mujer*) pregnancy; (*impedimento*) obstacle, obstruction; (*timidez*) embarrassment.

embarazoso, a [embara'θoso, a] *adj* (*molesto*) awkward; (*violento*) embarrassing.

embarcación [embarka'θjon] *nf* (*barco*) boat, craft; (*acto*) embarkation; ~ **de arrastre** trawler; ~ **de cabotaje** coasting vessel.

embarcadero [embarka'ðero] *nm* pier, landing stage.

embarcar [embar'kar] *vt* (*cargamento*) to ship, stow; (*persona*) to embark, put on board; (*fig*): ~ **a algn en una empresa** to involve sb in an undertaking; ~**se** *vr* to embark, go on board; (*marinero*) to sign on; (*AM: en tren etc*) to get on, get in.

embargar [embar'ɣar] *vt* (*frenar*) to restrain; (*sentidos*) to overpower; (*JUR*) to seize, impound.

embargo [em'barɣo] *nm* (*JUR*) seizure; (*COM etc*) embargo; **sin** ~ still, however, nonetheless.

embargue [em'barɣe] *etc vb V* **embargar**.

embarque [em'barke] *etc vb V* **embarcar** ♦ *nm* shipment, loading.

embarrancar [embarran'kar] *vt*, *vi* (*NAUT*) to run aground; (*AUTO etc*) to run into a ditch.

embarranque [emba'rranke] *etc vb V* **embarrancar**.

embarullar [embaru'ʎar] *vt* to make a mess of.

embate [em'bate] *nm* (*de mar, viento*) beating, violence.

embaucador, a [embauka'ðor, a] *nmlf* (*estafador*) trickster; (*impostor*) impostor.

embaucar [embau'kar] *vt* to trick, fool.

embauque [em'bauke] *etc vb V* **embaucar**.

embeber [embe'βer] *vt* (*absorber*) to absorb, soak up; (*empapar*) to saturate ♦ *vi* to shrink; ~**se** *vr:* ~**se en un libro** to be engrossed o absorbed in a book.

embelesado, a [embele'saðo, a] *adj* spellbound.

embelesar [embele'sar] *vt* to enchant; ~**se** *vr*: ~**se (con)** to be enchanted (by).

embellecer [embeʎe'θer] *vt* to embellish, beautify.

embellezca [embe'ʎeθka] *etc vb V* **embellecer.**

embestida [embes'tiða] *nf* attack, onslaught; (*carga*) charge.

embestir [embes'tir] *vt* to attack, assault; to charge, attack ♦ *vi* to attack.

embistiendo [embis'tjendo] *etc vb V* **embestir.**

emblanquecer [emblanke'θer] *vt* to whiten, bleach; ~**se** *vr* to turn white.

emblanquezca [emblan'keθka] *etc vb V* **emblanquecer.**

emblema [em'blema] *nm* emblem.

embobado, a [embo'ßaðo, a] *adj* (*atontado*) stunned, bewildered.

embobar [embo'ßar] *vt* (*asombrar*) to amaze; (*fascinar*) to fascinate; ~**se** *vr*: ~**se con** *o* **de** *o* **en** to be amazed at; to be fascinated by.

embocadura [emboka'ðura] *nf* narrow entrance; (*de río*) mouth; (*MUS*) mouthpiece.

embolado [embo'laðo] *nm* (*TEAT*) bit part, minor role; (*fam*) trick.

embolia [em'bolja] *nf* (*MED*) embolism; ~ **cerebral** clot on the brain.

émbolo ['embolo] *nm* (*AUTO*) piston.

embolsar [embol'sar] *vt* to pocket.

emboquillado, a [emboki'ʎaðo, a] *adj* (*cigarrillo*) tipped, filter *cpd.*

emborrachar [emborra'tʃar] *vt* to make drunk; ~**se** *vr* to get drunk.

emboscada [embos'kaða] *nf* (*celada*) ambush.

embotar [embo'tar] *vt* to blunt, dull; ~**se** *vr* (*adormecerse*) to go numb.

embotellamiento [emboteʎa'mjento] *nm* (*AUTO*) traffic jam.

embotellar [embote'ʎar] *vt* to bottle; ~**se** *vr* (*circulación*) to get into a jam.

embozo [em'boθo] *nm* muffler, mask; (*de sábana*) turn over.

embragar [embra'ɣar] *vt* (*AUTO, TEC*) to engage; (*partes*) to connect ♦ *vi* to let in the clutch.

embrague [em'braɣe] *etc vb V* **embragar** ♦ *nm* (*tb: pedal de* ~) clutch.

embravecer [embraße'θer] *vt* to enrage, infuriate; ~**se** *vr* to become furious; (*mar*) to get rough; (*tormenta*) to rage.

embravecido, a [embraße'θiðo, a] *adj* (*mar*) rough; (*persona*) furious.

embriagador, a [embrjaɣa'ðor, a] *adj* intoxicating.

embriagar [embrja'ɣar] *vt* (*emborrachar*) to make drunk; (*alegrar*) to delight; ~**se** *vr* (*emborracharse*) to get drunk.

embriague [em'brjaɣe] *etc vb V* **embriagar.**

embriaguez [embrja'ɣeθ] *nf* (*borrachera*) drunkenness.

embrión [em'brjon] *nm* embryo.

embrionario, a [embrjo'narjo, a] *adj* embryonic.

embrollar [embro'ʎar] *vt* (*asunto*) to confuse, complicate; (*persona*) to involve, embroil; ~**se** *vr* (*confundirse*) to get into a muddle *o* mess.

embrollo [em'broʎo] *nm* (*enredo*) muddle, confusion; (*aprieto*) fix, jam.

embromado, a [embro'maðo, a] *adj* (*AM fam*) tricky, difficult.

embromar [embro'mar] *vt* (*burlarse de*) to tease, make fun of; (*AM fam: molestar*) to annoy.

embrujado, a [embru'xaðo, a] *adj* (*persona*) bewitched; **casa embrujada** haunted house.

embrujo [em'bruxo] *nm* (*de mirada etc*) charm, magic.

embrutecer [embrute'θer] *vt* (*atontar*) to stupefy; ~**se** *vr* to be stupefied.

embrutezca [embru'teθka] *etc vb V* **embrutecer.**

embudo [em'buðo] *nm* funnel.

embuste [em'buste] *nm* trick; (*mentira*) lie; (*hum*) fib.

embustero, a [embus'tero, a] *adj* lying, deceitful ♦ *nm/f* (*tramposo*) cheat; (*mentiroso*) liar; (*hum*) fibber.

embutido [embu'tiðo] *nm* (*CULIN*) sausage.

embutir [embu'tir] *vt* to insert; (*TEC*) to inlay; (*llenar*) to pack tight, cram.

emergencia [emer'xenθja] *nf* emergency; (*surgimiento*) emergence.

emergente [emer'xente] *adj* resultant, consequent; (*nación*) emergent; (*INFORM*) pop-up *cpd*; **menú/ventana** ~ pop-up menu/window.

emerger [emer'xer] *vi* to emerge, appear.

emeritense [emeri'tense] *adj* of *o* from Mérida ♦ *nm/f* native *o* inhabitant of Mérida.

emerja [e'merxa] *etc vb V* **emerger.**

emigración [emiɣra'θjon] *nf* emigration; (*de pájaros*) migration.

emigrado, a [emi'ɣraðo, a] *nm/f* emigrant; (*POL etc*) émigré(e).

emigrante [emi'ɣrante] *adj, nm/f* emigrant.

emigrar [emi'ɣrar] *vi* (*personas*) to emigrate; (*pájaros*) to migrate.

eminencia [emi'nenθja] *nf* eminence; (*en títulos*): **Su E**~ His Eminence; **Vuestra**

E~ Your Eminence.
eminente [emi'nente] *adj* eminent,
distinguished; (*elevado*) high.
emisario [emi'sarjo] *nm* emissary.
emisión [emi'sjon] *nf* (*acto*) emission;
(*COM etc*) issue; (*RADIO, TV: acto*)
broadcasting; (: *programa*) broadcast,
programme, program (*US*); ~ **de
acciones** (*COM*) share issue; ~ **gratuita
de acciones** (*COM*) rights issue; ~ **de
valores** (*COM*) flotation.
emisor, a [emi'sor, a] *nm* transmitter ♦ *nf*
radio *o* broadcasting station.
emitir [emi'tir] *vt* (*olor etc*) to emit, give
off; (*moneda etc*) to issue; (*opinión*) to
express; (*voto*) to cast; (*señal*) to send
out; (*RADIO*) to broadcast; ~ **una señal
sonora** to beep.
emoción [emo'θjon] *nf* emotion;
(*excitación*) excitement; (*sentimiento*)
feeling; ¡**qué** ~! how exciting!; (*irónico*)
what a thrill!
emocionado, a [emoθjo'naðo, a] *adj*
deeply moved, stirred.
emocionante [emoθjo'nante] *adj*
(*excitante*) exciting, thrilling.
emocionar [emoθjo'nar] *vt* (*excitar*) to
excite, thrill; (*conmover*) to move, touch;
(*impresionar*) to impress; ~**se** *vr* to get
excited.
emoticón [emoti'kon] *nm* smiley, emoticon.
emotivo, a [emo'tiβo, a] *adj* emotional.
empacar [empa'kar] *vt* (*gen*) to pack; (*en
caja*) to bale, crate.
empacharse [empa't∫arse] *vr* (*MED*) to get
indigestion.
empacho [em'pat∫o] *nm* (*MED*) indigestion;
(*fig*) embarrassment.
empadronamiento [empaðrona'mjento]
nm census; (*de electores*) electoral
register.
empadronarse [empaðro'narse] *vr* (*POL:
como elector*) to register.
empalagar [empala'xar] *vt* (*suj: comida*) to
cloy; (*hartar*) to pall on ♦ *vi* to pall.
empalagoso, a [empala'xoso, a] *adj*
cloying; (*fig*) tiresome.
empalague [empa'laxe] *etc vb V*
empalagar.
empalizada [empali'θaða] *nf* fence; (*MIL*)
palisade.
empalmar [empal'mar] *vt* to join, connect
♦ *vi* (*dos caminos*) to meet, join.
empalme [em'palme] *nm* joint, connection;
(*de vías*) junction; (*de trenes*) connection.
empanada [empa'naða] *nf* pie, pasty.
empanar [empa'nar] *vt* (*CULIN*) to cook *o*
roll in breadcrumbs *o* pastry.

empantanarse [empanta'narse] *vr* to get
swamped; (*fig*) to get bogged down.
empañarse [empa'ɲarse] *vr* (*nublarse*) to
get misty, steam up.
empapar [empa'par] *vt* (*mojar*) to soak,
saturate; (*absorber*) to soak up, absorb;
~**se** *vr*: ~**se de** to soak up.
empapelar [empape'lar] *vt* (*paredes*) to
paper.
empaque [em'pake] *etc vb V* **empacar.**
empaquetar [empake'tar] *vt* to pack,
parcel up; (*COM*) to package.
emparedado [empare'ðaðo] *nm* sandwich.
emparejar [empare'xar] *vt* to pair ♦ *vi* to
catch up.
emparentar [emparen'tar] *vi*: ~ **con** to
marry into.
empariente [empa'rjente] *etc vb V*
emparentar.
empastar [empas'tar] *vt* (*embadurnar*) to
paste; (*diente*) to fill.
empaste [em'paste] *nm* (*de diente*) filling.
empatar [empa'tar] *vi* to draw, tie.
empate [em'pate] *nm* draw, tie; **un** ~ **a
cero** a no-score draw.
empecé [empe'θe], **empecemos**
[empe'θemos] *etc vb V* **empezar.**
empecinado, a [empeθi'naðo, a] *adj*
stubborn.
empedernido, a [empeðer'niðo, a] *adj*
hard, heartless; (*fijado*) hardened,
inveterate; **un fumador** ~ a heavy
smoker.
empedrado, a [empe'ðraðo, a] *adj* paved
♦ *nm* paving.
empedrar [empe'ðrar] *vt* to pave.
empeine [em'peine] *nm* (*de pie, zapato*)
instep.
empellón [empe'ʎon] *nm* push, shove;
abrirse paso a empellones to push *o*
shove one's way past *o* through.
empeñado, a [empe'ɲaðo, a] *adj* (*persona*)
determined; (*objeto*) pawned.
empeñar [empe'ɲar] *vt* (*objeto*) to pawn,
pledge; (*persona*) to compel; ~**se** *vr*
(*obligarse*) to pledge o.s.; (*endeudarse*) to
get into debt; ~**se en hacer** to be set on
doing, be determined to do.
empeño [em'peɲo] *nm* (*determinación*)
determination; (*cosa prendada*) pledge;
casa de ~**s** pawnshop; **con** ~ insistently;
(*con celo*) eagerly; **tener** ~ **en hacer algo**
to be bent on doing sth.
empeoramiento [empeora'mjento] *nm*
worsening.
empeorar [empeo'rar] *vt* to make worse,
worsen ♦ *vi* to get worse, deteriorate.
empequeñecer [empekeɲe'θer] *vt* to

dwarf; (*fig*) to belittle.

empequeñezca [empeke'neθka] *etc vb V*
empequeñecer.

emperador [empera'ðor] *nm* emperor.

emperatriz [empera'triθ] *nf* empress.

emperrarse [empe'rrarse] *vr* to get
stubborn; ~ **en algo** to persist in sth.

empezar [empe'θar] *vt, vi* to begin, start;
empezó a llover it started to rain; **bueno,
para** ~ well, to start with.

empiece [em'pjeθe] *etc vb V* **empezar.**

empiedre [em'pjeðre] *etc vb V* **empedrar.**

empiezo [em'pjeθo] *etc vb V* **empezar.**

empinado, a [empi'naðo, a] *adj* steep.

empinar [empi'nar] *vt* to raise; (*botella*) to
tip up; ~**se** *vr* (*persona*) to stand on
tiptoe; (*animal*) to rear up; (*camino*) to
climb steeply; ~ **el codo** to booze (*fam*).

empírico, a [em'piriko, a] *adj* empirical.

emplace [em'plaθe] *etc vb V* **emplazar.**

emplaste [em'plaste], **emplasto**
[em'plasto] *nm* (*MED*) plaster.

emplazamiento [emplaθa'mjento] *nm* site,
location; (*JUR*) summons *sg*.

emplazar [empla'θar] *vt* (*ubicar*) to site,
place, locate; (*JUR*) to summons;
(*convocar*) to summon.

empleado, a [emple'aðo, a] *nmf* (*gen*)
employee; (*de banco etc*) clerk; ~ **público**
civil servant.

emplear [emple'ar] *vt* (*usar*) to use,
employ; (*dar trabajo a*) to employ; ~**se** *vr*
(*conseguir trabajo*) to be employed;
(*ocuparse*) to occupy o.s.; ~ **mal el
tiempo** to waste time; **¡te está bien
empleado!** it serves you right!

empleo [em'pleo] *nm* (*puesto*) job; (*puestos:
colectivamente*) employment; (*uso*) use,
employment; "**modo de ~**"
"instructions for use".

emplumar [emplu'mar] *vt* (*estafar*) to
swindle.

empobrecer [empoβre'θer] *vt* to
impoverish; ~**se** *vr* to become poor *o*
impoverished.

empobrecimiento [empoβreθi'mjento] *nm*
impoverishment.

empobrezca [empo'βreθka] *etc vb V*
empobrecer.

empollar [empo'ʎar] *vt* to incubate; (*ESCOL
fam*) to swot (up) ♦ *vi* (*gallina*) to brood;
(*ESCOL fam*) to swot.

empollón, ona [empo'ʎon, ona] *nmf*
(*ESCOL fam*) swot.

empolvar [empol'βar] *vt* (*cara*) to powder;
~**se** *vr* to powder one's face; (*superficie*)
to get dusty.

emponzoñar [emponθo'nar] *vt* to poison.

emporio [em'porjo] *nm* emporium, trading
centre; (*AM: gran almacén*) department
store.

empotrado, a [empo'traðo, a] *adj* (*armario
etc*) built-in.

empotrar [empo'trar] *vt* to embed;
(*armario etc*) to build in.

emprendedor, a [emprende'ðor, a] *adj*
enterprising.

emprender [empren'der] *vt* to undertake;
(*empezar*) to begin, embark on;
(*acometer*) to tackle, take on; ~ **marcha a**
to set out for.

empresa [em'presa] *nf* enterprise; (*COM:
sociedad*) firm, company; (*: negocio*)
business; (*esp TEAT*) management; ~
filial (*COM*) affiliated company; ~ **matriz**
(*COM*) parent company.

empresarial [empresa'rjal] *adj* (*función,
clase*) managerial; **sector** ~ business
sector.

empresariales [empresa'rjales] *nfpl*
business studies.

empresario, a [empre'sarjo, a] *nm/f* (*COM*)
businessman/woman, entrepreneur;
(*TEC*) manager; (*MUS: de ópera etc*)
impresario; ~ **de pompas fúnebres**
undertaker (*BRIT*), mortician (*US*).

empréstito [em'prestito] *nm* (public) loan;
(*COM*) loan capital.

empujar [empu'xar] *vt* to push, shove.

empuje [em'puxe] *nm* thrust; (*presión*)
pressure; (*fig*) vigour, drive.

empujón [empu'xon] *nm* push, shove;
abrirse paso a empujones to shove one's
way through.

empuñadura [empuna'ðura] *nf* (*de espada*)
hilt; (*de herramienta etc*) handle.

empuñar [empu'nar] *vt* (*asir*) to grasp,
take (firm) hold of; ~ **las armas** (*fig*) to
take up arms.

emular [emu'lar] *vt* to emulate; (*rivalizar*) to
rival.

émulo, a ['emulo, a] *nm/f* rival, competitor.

emulsión [emul'sjon] *nf* emulsion.

═══════════════ *PALABRA CLAVE*

en [en] *prep* **1** (*posición*) in; (*: sobre*) on; **está**
~ **el cajón** it's in the drawer; ~
Argentina/La Paz in Argentina/La Paz; ~
el colegio/la oficina at school/the office;
~ **casa** at home; **está** ~ **el suelo/quinto
piso** it's on the floor/the fifth floor; ~ **el
periódico** in the paper

2 (*dirección*) into; **entró** ~ **el aula** she
went into the classroom; **meter algo** ~ **el
bolso** to put sth into one's bag; **ir de
puerta** ~ **puerta** to go from door to door

3 (*tiempo*) in; on; ~ **1605/3 semanas/ invierno** in 1605/3 weeks/winter; ~ **(el mes de) enero** in (the month of) January; ~ **aquella ocasión/época** on that occasion/at that time
4 (*precio*) for; **lo vendió ~ 20 dólares** he sold it for 20 dollars
5 (*diferencia*) by; **reducir/aumentar ~ una tercera parte/un 20 por ciento** to reduce/increase by a third/20 per cent
6 (*manera, forma*): ~ **avión/autobús** by plane/bus; **escrito ~ inglés** written in English; ~ **serio** seriously; ~ **espiral/ círculo** in a spiral/circle
7 (*después de vb que indica gastar etc*) on; **han cobrado demasiado ~ dietas** they've charged too much to expenses; **se le va la mitad del sueldo ~ comida** half his salary goes on food
8 (*tema, ocupación*): **experto ~ la materia** expert on the subject; **trabaja ~ la construcción** he works in the building industry
9 (*adj + ~ + infin*): **lento ~ reaccionar** slow to react.

enagua(s) [enaɣwa(s)] *nf(pl)* (*esp AM*) petticoat.
enajenación [enaxena'θjon] *nf*, **enajenamiento** [enaxena'mjento] *nm* alienation; (*fig: distracción*) absent-mindedness; (: *embelesamiento*) rapture, trance; ~ **mental** mental derangement.
enajenar [enaxe'nar] *vt* to alienate; (*fig*) to carry away.
enamorado, a [enamo'raðo, a] *adj* in love ♦ *nm/f* lover; **estar ~ (de)** to be in love (with).
enamorar [enamo'rar] *vt* to win the love of; ~**se** *vr*: ~**se (de)** to fall in love (with).
enano, a [e'nano, a] *adj* tiny, dwarf ♦ *nm/f* dwarf; (*pey*) runt.
enarbolar [enarβo'lar] *vt* (*bandera etc*) to hoist; (*espada etc*) to brandish.
enardecer [enarðe'θer] *vt* (*pasiones*) to fire, inflame; (*persona*) to fill with enthusiasm; ~**se** *vr* to get excited; ~**se por** to get enthusiastic about.
enardezca [enar'deθka] *etc vb V* **enardecer**.
encabece [enka'βeθe] *etc vb V* **encabezar**.
encabezado [enkaβe'θaðo] *nm* (*COM*) header.
encabezamiento [enkaβeθa'mjento] *nm* (*de carta*) heading; (*COM*) billhead, letterhead; (*de periódico*) headline; (*preámbulo*) foreword, preface; ~ **normal** (*TIP etc*) running head.
encabezar [enkaβe'θar] *vt* (*movimiento*, *revolución*) to lead, head; (*lista*) to head; (*carta*) to put a heading to; (*libro*) to entitle.
encadenar [enkaðe'nar] *vt* to chain (together); (*poner grilletes a*) to shackle.
encajar [enka'xar] *vt* (*ajustar*): ~ **en** to fit (into); (*meter a la fuerza*) to push in; (*máquina etc*) to house; (*partes*) to join; (*fam: golpe*) to give, deal; (*entrometer*) to insert ♦ *vi* to fit (well); (*fig: corresponder a*) to match; ~**se** *vr*: ~**se en un sillón** to squeeze into a chair.
encaje [en'kaxe] *nm* (*labor*) lace.
encajonar [enkaxo'nar] *vt* to box (up), put in a box.
encalar [enka'lar] *vt* (*pared*) to whitewash.
encallar [enka'ʎar] *vi* (*NAUT*) to run aground.
encaminado, a [enkami'naðo, a] *adj*: **medidas encaminadas a ...** measures designed to *o* aimed at ....
encaminar [enkami'nar] *vt* to direct, send; ~**se** *vr*: ~**se a** to set out for; ~ **por** (*expedición etc*) to route via.
encandilar [enkandi'lar] *vt* to dazzle; (*persona*) to daze, bewilder.
encanecer [enkane'θer] *vi*, **encanecerse** *vr* (*pelo*) to go grey.
encanezca [enka'neθka] *etc vb V* **encanecer**.
encantado, a [enkan'taðo, a] *adj* delighted; ¡~! how do you do!, pleased to meet you.
encantador, a [enkanta'ðor, a] *adj* charming, lovely ♦ *nm/f* magician, enchanter/enchantress.
encantar [enkan'tar] *vt* to charm, delight; (*cautivar*) to fascinate; (*hechizar*) to bewitch, cast a spell on.
encanto [en'kanto] *nm* (*magia*) spell, charm; (*fig*) charm, delight; (*expresión de ternura*) sweetheart; **como por ~** as if by magic.
encapotado, a [enkapo'taðo, a] *adj* (*cielo*) overcast.
encapricharse [enkapri'tʃarse] *vr*: **se ha encaprichado con ir** he's taken it into his head to go; **se ha encaprichado** he's digging his heels in.
encaramar [enkara'mar] *vt* (*subir*) to raise, lift up; ~**se** *vr* (*subir*) to perch; ~**se a** (*árbol etc*) to climb.
encararse [enka'rarse] *vr*: ~ **a** *o* **con** to confront, come face to face with.
encarcelar [enkarθe'lar] *vt* to imprison, jail.
encarecer [enkare'θer] *vt* to put up the price of ♦ *vi*, ~**se** *vr* to get dearer.

encarecidamente [enkareθiða'mente] *adv*
earnestly.

encarecimiento [enkareθi'mjento] *nm*
price increase.

encarezca [enka'reθka] *etc vb* V **encarecer.**

encargado, a [enkar'ɣaðo, a] *adj* in charge
♦ *nm/f* agent, representative;
(*responsable*) person in charge.

encargar [enkar'ɣar] *vt* to entrust; (*COM*)
to order; (*recomendar*) to urge,
recommend; ~**se** *vr*: ~**se de** to look
after, take charge of; ~ **algo a algn** to
put sb in charge of sth.

encargo [en'karɣo] *nm* (*pedido*)
assignment, job; (*responsabilidad*)
responsibility; (*recomendación*)
recommendation; (*COM*) order.

encargue [en'karɣe] *etc vb* V **encargar.**

encariñarse [enkari'ɲarse] *vr*: ~ **con** to
grow fond of, get attached to.

encarnación [enkarna'θjon] *nf* incarnation,
embodiment.

encarnado, a [enkar'naðo, a] *adj* (*color*)
red; **ponerse** ~ to blush.

encarnar [enkar'nar] *vt* to personify; (*TEAT*:
papel) to play ♦ *vi* (*REL etc*) to become
incarnate.

encarnizado, a [enkarni'θaðo, a] *adj* (*lucha*)
bloody, fierce.

encarrilar [enkarri'lar] *vt* (*tren*) to put back
on the rails; (*fig*) to correct, put on the
right track.

encasillar [enkasi'ʎar] *vt* (*TEAT*) to
typecast; (*clasificar. pey*) to pigeonhole.

encasquetar [enkaske'tar] *vt* (*sombrero*) to
pull down *o* on; ~**se** *vr*: ~**se el sombrero**
to pull one's hat down *o* on; ~ **algo a**
algn to offload sth onto sb.

encauce [en'kauθe] *etc vb* V **encauzar.**

encausar [enkau'sar] *vt* to prosecute, sue.

encauzar [enkau'θar] *vt* to channel; (*fig*) to
direct.

encendedor [enθende'ðor] *nm* lighter.

encender [enθen'der] *vt* (*con fuego*) to
light; (*incendiar*) to set fire to; (*luz, radio*)
to put on, switch on; (*INFORM*) to toggle
on, switch on; (*avivar. pasiones etc*) to
inflame; (*despertar. entusiasmo*) to
arouse; (*odio*) to awaken; ~**se** *vr* to catch
fire; (*excitarse*) to get excited; (*de cólera*)
to flare up; (*el rostro*) to blush.

encendidamente [enθendiða'mente] *adv*
passionately.

encendido, a [enθen'diðo, a] *adj* alight;
(*aparato*) (switched) on; (*mejillas*)
glowing; (*cara: por el vino etc*) flushed;
(*mirada*) passionate ♦ *nm* (*AUTO*) ignition;
(*de faroles*) lighting.

encerado, a [enθe'raðo, a] *adj* (*suelo*)
waxed, polished ♦ *nm* (*ESCOL*)
blackboard; (*hule*) oilcloth.

encerar [enθe'rar] *vt* (*suelo*) to wax, polish.

encerrar [enθe'rrar] *vt* (*confinar*) to shut in
o up; (*con llave*) to lock in *o* up;
(*comprender, incluir*) to include, contain;
~**se** *vr* to shut *o* lock o.s. up *o* in.

encerrona [enθe'rrona] *nf* trap.

encestar [enθes'tar] *vi* to score a basket.

encharcar [entʃar'kar] *vt* to swamp, flood;
~**se** *vr* to become flooded.

encharque [en'tʃarke] *etc vb* V **encharcar.**

enchufar [entʃu'far] *vt* (*ELEC*) to plug in;
(*TEC*) to connect, fit together; (*COM*) to
merge.

enchufe [en'tʃufe] *nm* (*ELEC: clavija*) plug;
(: *toma*) socket; (*de dos tubos*) joint,
connection; (*fam: influencia*) contact,
connection; (: *puesto*) cushy job; ~ **de**
clavija jack plug; **tiene un** ~ **en el**
ministerio he can pull strings at the
ministry.

encía [en'θia] *nf* (*ANAT*) gum.

enciclopedia [enθiklo'peðja] *nf*
encyclopaedia.

encienda [en'θjenda] *etc vb* V **encender.**

encierro [en'θjerro] *etc vb* V **encerrar** ♦ *nm*
shutting in *o* up; (*calabozo*) prison; (*AGR*)
pen; (*TAUR*) penning.

encima [en'θima] *adv* (*sobre*) above, over;
(*además*) besides; ~ **de** (*en*) on, on top of;
(*sobre*) above, over; (*además de*) besides,
on top of; **por** ~ **de** over; **¿llevas dinero**
~**?** have you (got) any money on you?;
se me vino ~ it took me by surprise.

encina [en'θina] *nf* (holm) oak.

encinta [en'θinta] *adj f* pregnant.

enclave [en'klaβe] *nm* enclave.

enclenque [en'klenke] *adj* weak, sickly.

encoger [enko'xer] *vt* (*gen*) to shrink,
contract; (*fig: asustar*) to scare;
(: *desanimar*) to discourage; ~**se** *vr* to
shrink, contract; (*fig*) to cringe; ~**se de**
hombros to shrug one's shoulders.

encoja [en'koxa] *etc vb* V **encoger.**

encolar [enko'lar] *vt* (*engomar*) to glue,
paste; (*pegar*) to stick down.

encolerice [enkoleri'θe] *etc vb* V
encolerizar.

encolerizar [enkoleri'θar] *vt* to anger,
provoke; ~**se** *vr* to get angry.

encomendar [enkomen'dar] *vt* to entrust,
commend; ~**se** *vr*: ~**se a** to put one's
trust in.

encomiar [enko'mjar] *vt* to praise, pay
tribute to.

encomienda [enko'mjenda] *etc vb* V

encomendar ♦ nf (encargo) charge, commission; (elogio) tribute; (AM) parcel, package; ~ **postal** (AM) parcel post.

encomio [en'komjo] nm praise, tribute.

encono [en'kono] nm (rencor) rancour, spite.

encontrado, a [enkon'traðo, a] adj (contrario) contrary, conflicting; (hostil) hostile.

encontrar [enkon'trar] vt (hallar) to find; (inesperadamente) to meet, run into; ~**se** vr to meet (each other); (situarse) to be (situated); (persona) to find o.s., be; (entrar en conflicto) to crash, collide; ~**se con** to meet; ~**se bien (de salud)** to feel well; **no se encuentra aquí en este momento** he's not in at the moment.

encontronazo [enkontro'naθo] nm collision, crash.

encorvar [enkor'ßar] vt to curve; (inclinar) to bend (down); ~**se** vr to bend down, bend over.

encrespado, a [enkres'paðo, a] adj (pelo) curly; (mar) rough.

encrespar [enkres'par] vt (cabellos) to curl; (fig) to anger, irritate; ~**se** vr (el mar) to get rough; (fig) to get cross o irritated.

encrucijada [enkruθi'xaða] nf crossroads sg; (empalme) junction.

encuadernación [enkwaðerna'θjon] nf binding; (taller) binder's.

encuadernador, a [enkwaðerna'ðor, a] nm/f bookbinder.

encuadrar [enkwa'ðrar] vt (retrato) to frame; (ajustar) to fit, insert; (encerrar) to contain.

encubierto [enku'ßjerto] pp de **encubrir**.

encubrir [enku'ßrir] vt (ocultar) to hide, conceal; (criminal) to harbour, shelter; (ayudar) to be an accomplice in.

encuentro [en'kwentro] etc vb V **encontrar** ♦ nm (de personas) meeting; (AUTO etc) collision, crash; (DEPORTE) match, game; (MIL) encounter.

encuesta [en'kwesta] nf inquiry, investigation; (sondeo) public opinion poll; ~ **judicial** post mortem.

encumbrado, a [enkum'braðo, a] adj eminent, distinguished.

encumbrar [enkum'brar] vt (persona) to exalt; ~**se** vr (fig) to become conceited.

endeble [en'deßle] adj (argumento, excusa, persona) weak.

endémico, a [en'demiko, a] adj endemic.

endemoniado, a [endemo'njaðo, a] adj possessed (of the devil); (travieso) devilish.

enderece [ende're θe] etc vb V **enderezar**.

enderezar [endere'θar] vt (poner derecho) to straighten (out); (: verticalmente) to set upright; (fig) to straighten o sort out; (dirigir) to direct; ~**se** vr (persona sentada) to sit up straight.

endeudarse [endeu'ðarse] vr to get into debt.

endiablado, a [endja'ßlaðo, a] adj devilish, diabolical; (hum) mischievous.

endibia [en'dißja] nf endive.

endilgar [endil'ɣar] vt (fam): ~ **algo a algn** to lumber sb with sth; ~ **un sermón a algn** to give sb a lecture.

endilgue [en'dilɣe] etc vb V **endilgar**.

endiñar [endi'ɲar] vt: ~ **algo a algn** to land sth on sb.

endomingarse [endomin'garse] vr to dress up, put on one's best clothes.

endomingue [endo'minge] etc vb V **endomingarse**.

endosar [endo'sar] vt (cheque etc) to endorse.

endulce [en'dulθe] etc vb V **endulzar**.

endulzar [endul'θar] vt to sweeten; (suavizar) to soften.

endurecer [endure'θer] vt to harden; ~**se** vr to harden, grow hard.

endurecido, a [endure'θiðo, a] adj (duro) hard; (fig) hardy, tough; **estar ~ a algo** to be hardened o used to sth.

endurezca [endu're θka] etc vb V **endurecer**.

ene. abr (= enero) Jan.

enemigo, a [ene'miɣo, a] adj enemy, hostile ♦ nm/f enemy ♦ nf enmity, hostility; **ser ~ de** (persona) to dislike; (suj: tendencia) to be inimical to.

enemistad [enemis'tað] nf enmity.

enemistar [enemis'tar] vt to make enemies of, cause a rift between; ~**se** vr to become enemies; (amigos) to fall out.

energético, a [ener'xetiko, a] adj: **política energética** energy policy.

energía [ener'xia] nf (vigor) energy, drive; (TEC, ELEC) energy, power; ~ **atómica/ eléctrica/eólica** atomic/electric/wind power.

enérgico, a [e'nerxiko, a] adj (gen) energetic; (ataque) vigorous; (ejercicio) strenuous; (medida) bold; (voz, modales) forceful.

energúmeno, a [ener'ɣumeno, a] nm/f madman/woman; **ponerse como un ~ con algn** to get furious with sb.

enero [e'nero] nm January.

enervar [ener'ßar] vt (poner nervioso a) to get on sb's nerves.

enésimo, a [e'nesimo, a] adj (MAT) nth; **por enésima vez** (fig) for the umpteenth time.

enfadado, a [enfa'ðaðo, a] *adj* angry, annoyed.

enfadar [enfa'ðar] *vt* to anger, annoy; ~**se** *vr* to get angry o annoyed.

enfado [en'faðo] *nm* (*enojo*) anger, annoyance; (*disgusto*) trouble, bother.

énfasis ['enfasis] *nm* emphasis, stress; **poner** ~ **en** to stress.

enfático, a [en'fatiko, a] *adj* emphatic.

enfatizado, a [enfati'θaðo, a] *adj*: **en caracteres** ~**s** (*INFORM*) emphasized.

enfermar [enfer'mar] *vt* to make ill ♦ *vi* to fall ill, be taken ill; **su actitud me enferma** his attitude makes me sick; ~ **del corazón** to develop heart trouble.

enfermedad [enferme'ðað] *nf* illness; ~ **venérea** venereal disease.

enfermera [enfer'mera] *nf* V **enfermero**.

enfermería [enferme'ria] *nf* infirmary; (*de colegio etc*) sick bay.

enfermero, a [enfer'mero, a] *nm* (*male*) nurse ♦ *nf* nurse; **enfermera jefa** matron.

enfermizo, a [enfer'miθo, a] *adj* (*persona*) sickly, unhealthy; (*fig*) unhealthy.

enfermo, a [en'fermo, a] *adj* ill, sick ♦ *nm/f* invalid, sick person; (*en hospital*) patient.

enfilar [enfi'lar] *vt* (*aguja*) to thread; (*calle*) to go down.

enflaquecer [enflake'θer] *vt* (*adelgazar*) to make thin; (*debilitar*) to weaken.

enflaquezca [enfla'keθka] *etc vb* V **enflaquecer**.

enfocar [enfo'kar] *vt* (*foto etc*) to focus; (*problema etc*) to consider, look at.

enfoque [en'foke] *etc vb* V **enfocar** ♦ *nm* focus; (*acto*) focusing; (*óptica*) approach.

enfrascado, a [enfras'kaðo, a] *adj*: **estar** ~ **en algo** (*fig*) to be wrapped up in sth.

enfrascarse [enfras'karse] *vr*: ~ **en un libro** to bury o.s. in a book.

enfrasque [en'fraske] *etc vb* V **enfrascar**.

enfrentamiento [enfrenta'mjento] *nm* confrontation.

enfrentar [enfren'tar] *vt* (*peligro*) to face (up to), confront; (*oponer*) to bring face to face; ~**se** *vr* (*dos personas*) to face o confront each other; (*DEPORTE: dos equipos*) to meet; ~**se a** o **con** to face up to, confront.

enfrente [en'frente] *adv* opposite; ~ **de** *prep* opposite, facing; **la casa de** ~ the house opposite, the house across the street.

enfriamiento [enfria'mjento] *nm* chilling, refrigeration; (*MED*) cold, chill.

enfriar [enfri'ar] *vt* (*alimentos*) to cool, chill; (*algo caliente*) to cool down;

(*habitación*) to air, freshen; (*entusiasmo*) to dampen; ~**se** *vr* to cool down; (*MED*) to catch a chill; (*amistad*) to cool.

enfurecer [enfure'θer] *vt* to enrage, madden; ~**se** *vr* to become furious, fly into a rage; (*mar*) to get rough.

enfurezca [enfu'reθka] *etc vb* V **enfurecer**.

engalanar [engala'nar] *vt* (*adornar*) to adorn; (*ciudad*) to decorate; ~**se** *vr* to get dressed up.

enganchar [engan'tʃar] *vt* to hook; (*ropa*) to hang up; (*dos vagones*) to hitch up; (*TEC*) to couple, connect; (*MIL*) to recruit; (*fam: atraer: persona*) to rope into; ~**se** *vr* (*MIL*) to enlist, join up; ~**se (a)** (*drogas*) to get hooked (on).

enganche [en'gantʃe] *nm* hook; (*TEC*) coupling, connection; (*acto*) hooking (up); (*MIL*) recruitment, enlistment; (*AM: depósito*) deposit.

engañar [enga'nar] *vt* to deceive; (*estafar*) to cheat, swindle ♦ *vi*: **las apariencias engañan** appearances are deceptive; ~**se** *vr* (*equivocarse*) to be wrong; (*asimismo*) to deceive o kid o.s.; **engaña a su mujer** he's unfaithful to o cheats on his wife.

engaño [en'gano] *nm* deceit; (*estafa*) trick, swindle; (*error*) mistake, misunderstanding; (*ilusión*) delusion.

engañoso, a [enga'noso, a] *adj* (*tramposo*) crooked; (*mentiroso*) dishonest, deceitful; (*aspecto*) deceptive; (*consejo*) misleading.

engarce [en'garθe] *etc vb* V **engarzar**.

engarzar [engar'θar] *vt* (*joya*) to set, mount; (*fig*) to link, connect.

engatusar [engatu'sar] *vt* (*fam*) to coax.

engendrar [enxen'drar] *vt* to breed; (*procrear*) to beget; (*fig*) to cause, produce.

engendro [en'xendro] *nm* (*BIO*) foetus; (*fig*) monstrosity; (*idea*) brainchild.

englobar [englo'βar] *vt* (*comprender*) to include, comprise; (*incluir*) to lump together.

engomar [engo'mar] *vt* to glue, stick.

engordar [engor'ðar] *vt* to fatten ♦ *vi* to get fat, put on weight.

engorro [en'gorro] *nm* bother, nuisance.

engorroso, a [engo'rroso, a] *adj* bothersome, trying.

engranaje [engra'naxe] *nm* (*AUTO*) gear; (*juego*) gears *pl*.

engrandecer [engrande'θer] *vt* to enlarge, magnify; (*alabar*) to praise, speak highly of; (*exagerar*) to exaggerate.

engrandezca [engran'deθka] *etc vb* V

engrandecer.

engrasar [engra'sar] *vt* (*TEC: poner grasa*) to grease; (*: lubricar*) to lubricate, oil; (*manchar*) to make greasy.

engrase [en'grase] *nm* greasing, lubrication.

engreído, a [engre'iðo, a] *adj* vain, conceited.

engrosar [engro'sar] *vt* (*ensanchar*) to enlarge; (*aumentar*) to increase; (*hinchar*) to swell.

engrudo [en'gruðo] *nm* paste.

engruese [en'grwese] *etc vb V* **engrosar.**

engullir [engu'ʎir] *vt* to gobble, gulp (down).

enhebrar [ene'ßrar] *vt* to thread.

enhiesto, a [e'njesto, a] *adj* (*derecho*) erect; (*bandera*) raised; (*edificio*) lofty.

enhorabuena [enora'ßwena] *excl* congratulations.

enigma [e'niɣma] *nm* enigma; (*problema*) puzzle; (*misterio*) mystery.

enigmático, a [eniɣ'matiko, a] *adj* enigmatic.

enjabonar [enxaßo'nar] *vt* to soap; (*barba*) to lather; (*fam: adular*) to soft-soap; (*: regañar*) to tick off.

enjalbegar [enxalße'ɣar] *vt* (*pared*) to whitewash.

enjalbegue [enxal'ßeɣe] *etc vb V* **enjalbegar.**

enjambre [en'xambre] *nm* swarm.

enjaular [enxau'lar] *vt* to (put in a) cage; (*fam*) to jail, lock up.

enjuagar [enxwa'ɣar] *vt* (*ropa*) to rinse (out).

enjuague [en'xwaɣe] *etc vb V* **enjuagar** ♦ *nm* (*MED*) mouthwash; (*de ropa*) rinse, rinsing.

enjugar [enxu'ɣar] *vt* to wipe (off); (*lágrimas*) to dry; (*déficit*) to wipe out.

enjugue [en'xuɣe] *etc vb V* **enjugar.**

enjuiciar [enxwi'θjar] *vt* (*JUR: procesar*) to prosecute, try; (*fig*) to judge.

enjuto, a [en'xuto, a] *adj* dry, dried up; (*fig*) lean, skinny.

enlace [en'laθe] *etc vb V* **enlazar** ♦ *nm* link, connection; (*relación*) relationship; (*tb:* ~ **matrimonial**) marriage; (*de trenes*) connection; ~ **de datos** data link; ~ **sindical** shop steward; ~ **telefónico** telephone link-up.

enlazar [enla'θar] *vt* (*unir con lazos*) to bind together; (*atar*) to tie; (*conectar*) to link, connect; (*AM*) to lasso.

enlodar [enlo'ðar] *vt* to cover in mud; (*fig: manchar*) to stain; (*: rebajar*) to debase.

enloquecer [enloke'θer] *vt* to drive mad

♦ *vi*, ~**se** *vr* to go mad.

enloquezca [enlo'keθka] *etc vb V* **enloquecer.**

enlutado, a [enlu'taðo, a] *adj* (*persona*) in mourning.

enlutar [enlu'tar] *vt* to dress in mourning; ~**se** *vr* to go into mourning.

enmarañar [enmara'nar] *vt* (*enredar*) to tangle up, entangle; (*complicar*) to complicate; (*confundir*) to confuse; ~**se** *vr* (*enredarse*) to become entangled; (*confundirse*) to get confused.

enmarcar [enmar'kar] *vt* (*cuadro*) to frame; (*fig*) to provide a setting for.

enmarque [en'marke] *etc vb V* **enmarcar.**

enmascarar [enmaska'rar] *vt* to mask; (*intenciones*) to disguise; ~**se** *vr* to put on a mask.

enmendar [enmen'dar] *vt* to emend, correct; (*constitución etc*) to amend; (*comportamiento*) to reform; ~**se** *vr* to reform, mend one's ways.

enmienda [en'mjenda] *etc vb V* **enmendar** ♦ *nf* correction; amendment; reform.

enmohecerse [enmoe'θerse] *vr* (*metal*) to rust, go rusty; (*muro, plantas*) to go mouldy.

enmohezca [enmo'eθka] *etc vb V* **enmohecerse.**

enmudecer [enmuðe'θer] *vt* to silence ♦ *vi*, ~**se** *vr* (*perder el habla*) to fall silent; (*guardar silencio*) to remain silent; (*por miedo*) to be struck dumb.

enmudezca [enmu'ðeθka] *etc vb V* **enmudecer.**

ennegrecer [enneɣre'θer] *vt* (*poner negro*) to blacken; (*oscurecer*) to darken; ~**se** *vr* to turn black; (*oscurecerse*) to get dark, darken.

ennegrezca [enne'ɣreθka] *etc vb V* **ennegrecer.**

ennoblecer [ennoße'θer] *vt* to ennoble.

ennoblezca [enno'ßleθka] *etc vb V* **ennoblecer.**

en.° *abr* (= *enero*) Jan.

enojadizo, a [enoxa'ðiθo, a] *adj* irritable, short-tempered.

enojar [eno'xar] (*esp AM*) *vt* (*encolerizar*) to anger; (*disgustar*) to annoy, upset; ~**se** *vr* to get angry; to get annoyed.

enojo [e'noxo] (*esp AM*) *nm* (*cólera*) anger; (*irritación*) annoyance; ~**s** *nmpl* trials, problems.

enojoso, a [eno'xoso, a] *adj* annoying.

enorgullecerse [enorɣuʎe'θerse] *vr* to be proud; ~ **de** to pride o.s. on, be proud of.

enorgullezca [enorɣu'ʎeθka] *etc vb V* **enorgullecerse.**

enorme [e'norme] *adj* enormous, huge; (*fig*) monstrous.

enormidad [enormi'ðað] *nf* hugeness, immensity.

enraice [en'raiθe] *etc vb* V **enraizar.**

enraizar [enrai'θar] *vi* to take root.

enrarecido, a [enrare'θiðo, a] *adj* rarefied.

enredadera [enreða'ðera] *nf* (*BOT*) creeper, climbing plant.

enredar [enre'ðar] *vt* (*cables, hilos etc*) to tangle (up), entangle; (*situación*) to complicate, confuse; (*meter cizaña*) to sow discord among o between; (*implicar*) to embroil, implicate; ~**se** *vr* to get entangled, get tangled (up); (*situación*) to get complicated; (*persona*) to get embroiled.

enredo [en'reðo] *nm* (*maraña*) tangle; (*confusión*) mix-up, confusion; (*intriga*) intrigue; (*apuro*) jam; (*amorío*) love affair.

enrejado [enre'xaðo] *nm* grating; (*de ventana*) lattice; (*en jardín*) trellis.

enrevesado, a [enreße'saðo, a] *adj* (*asunto*) complicated, involved.

enriquecer [enrike'θer] *vt* to make rich; (*fig*) to enrich; ~**se** *vr* to get rich.

enriquezca [enri'keθka] *etc vb* V **enriquecer.**

enrojecer [enroxe'θer] *vt* to redden ♦ *vi*, ~**se** *vr* (*persona*) to blush.

enrojezca [enro'xeθka] *etc vb* V **enrojecer.**

enrolar [enro'lar] *vt* (*MIL*) to enlist; (*reclutar*) to recruit; ~**se** *vr* (*MIL*) to join up; (*afiliarse*) to enrol, sign on.

enrollar [enro'ʎar] *vt* to roll (up), wind (up); ~**se** *vr*: ~**se con algn** to get involved with sb.

enroque [en'roke] *nm* (*AJEDREZ*) castling.

enroscar [enros'kar] *vt* (*torcer, doblar*) to · twist; (*arrollar*) to coil (round), wind; (*tornillo, rosca*) to screw in; ~**se** *vr* to coil, wind.

enrosque [en'roske] *etc vb* V **enroscar.**

ensalada [ensa'laða] *nf* salad; (*lío*) mix-up.

ensaladilla [ensala'ðiʎa] *nf* (*tb*: ~ **rusa**) ≈ Russian salad.

ensalce [en'salθe] *etc vb* V **ensalzar.**

ensalzar [ensal'θar] *vt* (*alabar*) to praise, extol; (*exaltar*) to exalt.

ensamblador [ensambla'ðor] *nm* (*INFORM*) assembler.

ensambladura [ensambla'ðura] *nf*, **ensamblaje** [ensam'blaxe] *nm* assembly; (*TEC*) joint.

ensamblar [ensam'blar] *vt* (*montar*) to assemble; (*madera etc*) to join.

ensanchar [ensan't∫ar] *vt* (*hacer más ancho*) to widen; (*agrandar*) to enlarge, expand; (*COSTURA*) to let out; ~**se** *vr* to get wider, expand; (*pey*) to give o.s. airs.

ensanche [en'sant∫e] *nm* (*de calle*) widening; (*de negocio*) expansion.

ensangrentado, a [ensangren'taðo, a] *adj* bloodstained, covered with blood.

ensangrentar [ensangren'tar] *vt* to stain with blood.

ensangriente [ensan'grjente] *etc vb* V **ensangrentar.**

ensañarse [ensa'ɲarse] *vr*: ~ **con** to treat brutally.

ensartar [ensar'tar] *vt* (*gen*) to string (together); (*carne*) to spit, skewer.

ensayar [ensa'jar] *vt* to test, try (out); (*TEAT*) to rehearse.

ensayista [ensa'jista] *nm/f* essayist.

ensayo [en'sajo] *nm* test, trial; (*QUÍMICA*) experiment; (*TEAT*) rehearsal; (*DEPORTE*) try; (*ESCOL, LITERATURA*) essay; **pedido de** ~ (*COM*) trial order; ~ **general** (*TEAT*) dress rehearsal; (*MUS*) full rehearsal.

enseguida [ense'ɣuiða] *adv* at once, right away; ~ **termino** I've nearly finished, I shan't be long now.

ensenada [ense'naða] *nf* inlet, cove.

enseña [en'seɲa] *nf* ensign, standard.

enseñante [ense'ɲante] *nm/f* teacher.

enseñanza [ense'ɲanθa] *nf* (*educación*) education; (*acción*) teaching; (*doctrina*) teaching, doctrine; ~ **primaria/ secundaria/superior** primary/ secondary/higher education.

enseñar [ense'ɲar] *vt* (*educar*) to teach; (*instruir*) to teach, instruct; (*mostrar, señalar*) to show.

enseres [en'seres] *nmpl* belongings.

ENSIDESA [ensi'ðesa] *abr* (*ESP COM*) = *Empresa Nacional Siderúrgica, S. A.*

ensillar [ensi'ʎar] *vt* to saddle (up).

ensimismarse [ensimis'marse] *vr* (*abstraerse*) to become lost in thought; (*estar absorto*) to be lost in thought; (*AM*) to become conceited.

ensopar [enso'par] *vt* (*AM*) to soak.

ensordecer [ensorðe'θer] *vt* to deafen ♦ *vi* to go deaf.

ensordezca [ensor'ðeθka] *etc vb* V **ensordecer.**

ensortijado, a [ensorti'xaðo, a] *adj* (*pelo*) curly.

ensuciar [ensu'θjar] *vt* (*manchar*) to dirty, soil; (*fig*) to defile; ~**se** *vr* (*mancharse*) to get dirty; (*niño*) to dirty (o wet) o.s.

ensueño [en'sweɲo] *nm* (*sueño*) dream, fantasy; (*ilusión*) illusion; (*soñando despierto*) daydream; **de** ~ dream-like.

entablado [enta'βlaðo] *nm* (*piso*) floorboards *pl*; (*armazón*) boarding.

entablar [enta'βlar] *vt* (*recubrir*) to board (up); (*AJEDREZ, DAMAS*) to set up; (*conversación*) to strike up; (*JUR*) to file ♦ *vi* to draw.

entablillar [entaβli'ʎar] *vt* (*MED*) to (put in a) splint.

entallado, a [enta'ʎaðo, a] *adj* waisted.

entallar [enta'ʎar] *vt* (*traje*) to tailor ♦ *vi*: **el traje entalla bien** the suit fits well.

ente ['ente] *nm* (*organización*) body, organization; (*compañía*) company; (*fam: persona*) odd character; (*ser*) being; ~ **público** (*ESP*) state(-owned) body.

entender [enten'der] *vt* (*comprender*) to understand; (*darse cuenta*) to realize; (*querer decir*) to mean ♦ *vi* to understand; (*creer*) to think, believe ♦ *nm*: **a mi** ~ in my opinion; ~ **de** to know all about; ~ **algo de** to know a little about; ~ **en** to deal with, have to do with; ~**se** *vr* (*comprenderse*) to be understood; (*2 personas*) to get on together; (*ponerse de acuerdo*) to agree, reach an agreement; **dar a** ~ **que** ... to lead to believe that ...; ~**se mal** to get on badly; **¿entiendes?** (do you) understand?

entendido, a [enten'diðo, a] *adj* (*comprendido*) understood; (*hábil*) skilled; (*inteligente*) knowledgeable ♦ *nm/f* (*experto*) expert ♦ *excl* agreed!

entendimiento [entendi'mjento] *nm* (*comprensión*) understanding; (*inteligencia*) mind, intellect; (*juicio*) judgement.

enterado, a [ente'raðo, a] *adj* well-informed; **estar** ~ **de** to know about, be aware of; **no darse por** ~ to pretend not to understand.

enteramente [entera'mente] *adv* entirely, completely.

enterarse [ente'rarse] *vr*: ~ (**de**) to find out (about); **para que te enteres** ... (*fam*) for your information ....

entereza [ente're θa] *nf* (*totalidad*) entirety; (*fig: carácter*) strength of mind; (*honradez*) integrity.

enternecedor, a [enterneθe'ðor, a] *adj* touching.

enternecer [enterne'θer] *vt* (*ablandar*) to soften; (*apiadar*) to touch, move; ~**se** *vr* to be touched, be moved.

enternezca [enter'neθka] *etc vb* V **enternecer**.

entero, a [en'tero, a] *adj* (*total*) whole, entire; (*fig: recto*) honest; (: *firme*) firm, resolute ♦ *nm* (*MAT*) integer; (*COM: punto*)

point; (*AM: pago*) payment; **las acciones han subido dos** ~**s** the shares have gone up two points.

enterrador [enterra'ðor] *nm* gravedigger.

enterrar [ente'rrar] *vt* to bury; (*fig*) to forget.

entibiar [enti'βjar] *vt* (*enfriar*) to cool; (*calentar*) to warm; ~**se** *vr* (*fig*) to cool.

entidad [enti'ðað] *nf* (*empresa*) firm, company; (*organismo*) body; (*sociedad*) society; (*FILOSOFÍA*) entity.

entienda [en'tjenda] *etc vb* V **entender**.

entierro [en'tjerro] *etc vb* V **enterrar** ♦ *nm* (*acción*) burial; (*funeral*) funeral.

entomología [entomolo'xia] *nf* entomology.

entomólogo, a [ento'moloxo, a] *nm/f* entomologist.

entonación [entona'θjon] *nf* (*LING*) intonation; (*fig*) conceit.

entonar [ento'nar] *vt* (*canción*) to intone; (*colores*) to tone; (*MED*) to tone up ♦ *vi* to be in tune; ~**se** *vr* (*engreírse*) to give o.s. airs.

entonces [en'tonθes] *adv* then, at that time; **desde** ~ since then; **en aquel** ~ at that time; (**pues**) ~ and so; **el** ~ **embajador de España** the then Spanish ambassador.

entornar [entor'nar] *vt* (*puerta, ventana*) to half close, leave ajar; (*los ojos*) to screw up.

entorno [en'torno] *nm* setting, environment; ~ **de redes** (*INFORM*) network environment.

entorpecer [entorpe'θer] *vt* (*entendimiento*) to dull; (*impedir*) to obstruct, hinder; (: *tránsito*) to slow down, delay.

entorpezca [entor'peθka] *etc vb* V **entorpecer**.

entrado, a [en'traðo, a] *adj*: ~ **en años** elderly; (**una vez**) ~ **el verano** in the summer(time), when summer comes ♦ *nf* (*acción*) entry, access; (*sitio*) entrance, way in; (*principio*) beginning; (*COM*) receipts *pl*, takings *pl*; (*CULIN*) entrée; (*DEPORTE*) innings *sg*; (*TEAT*) house, audience; (*para el cine etc*) ticket; (*INFORM*) input; (*ECON*): **entradas** *nfpl* income *sg*; **entradas brutas** gross receipts; **entradas y salidas** (*COM*) income and expenditure; **entrada de aire** (*TEC*) air intake o inlet; **de entrada** right away; **"entrada gratis"** "admission free"; **entrada de datos vocal** (*INFORM*) voice input; **tiene entradas** he's losing his hair.

entrante [en'trante] *adj* next, coming; (*POL*) incoming ♦ *nm* inlet; (*CULIN*) starter; **mes/año ~** next month/year.

entraña [en'traɲa] *nf* (*fig: centro*) heart, core; (*raíz*) root; **~s** *nfpl* (*ANAT*) entrails; (*fig*) heart *sg*.

entrañable [entra'ɲaßle] *adj* (*persona, lugar*) dear; (*relación*) close; (*acto*) intimate.

entrañar [entra'ɲar] *vt* to entail.

entrar [en'trar] *vt* (*introducir*) to bring in; (*persona*) to show in; (*INFORM*) to input ♦ *vi* (*meterse*) to go *o* come in, enter; (*comenzar*): **~ diciendo** to begin by saying; **entré en *o* (*AM*) la casa** I went into the house; **le entraron ganas de reír** he felt a sudden urge to laugh; **no me entra** I can't get the hang of it.

entre ['entre] *prep* (*dos*) between; (*en medio de*) among(st); (*por*): **se abrieron paso ~ la multitud** they forced their way through the crowd; **~ una cosa y otra** what with one thing and another; **~ más estudia más aprende** (*AM*) the more he studies the more he learns.

entreabierto [entrea'ßjerto] *pp de* **entreabrir**.

entreabrir [entrea'ßrir] *vt* to half-open, open halfway.

entreacto [entre'akto] *nm* interval.

entrecano, a [entre'kano, a] *a* greying; **ser ~** (*persona*) to be going grey.

entrecejo [entre'θexo] *nm*: **fruncir el ~** to frown.

entrechocar [entretʃo'kar] *vi* (*dientes*) to chatter.

entrechoque [entre'tʃoke] *etc vb V* **entrechocar**.

entrecomillado, a [entrekomi'ʎaðo, a] *adj* in inverted commas.

entrecortado, a [entrekor'taðo, a] *adj* (*respiración*) laboured, difficult; (*habla*) faltering.

entrecot [entre'ko(t)] *nm* (*CULIN*) sirloin steak.

entrecruce [entre'kruθe] *etc vb V* **entrecruzarse**.

entrecruzarse [entrekru'θarse] *vr* (*BIO*) to interbreed.

entredicho [entre'ðitʃo] *nm* (*JUR*) injunction; **poner en ~** to cast doubt on; **estar en ~** to be in doubt.

entrega [en'treɣa] *nf* (*de mercancías*) delivery; (*de premios*) presentation; (*de novela etc*) instalment; **"~ a domicilio"** "door-to-door delivery service".

entregar [entre'ɣar] *vt* (*dar*) to hand (over), deliver; (*ejercicios*) to hand in;

~se *vr* (*rendirse*) to surrender, give in, submit; **~se a** (*dedicarse*) to devote o.s. to; **a ~** (*COM*) to be supplied.

entregue [en'treɣe] *etc vb V* **entregar**.

entrelace [entre'laθe] *etc vb V* **entrelazar**.

entrelazar [entrela'θar] *vt* to entwine.

entremedias [entre'meðjas] *adv* (*en medio*) in between, halfway.

entremeses [entre'meses] *nmpl* hors d'œuvres.

entremeter [entreme'ter] *vt* to insert, put in; **~se** *vr* to meddle, interfere.

entremetido, a [entreme'tiðo, a] *adj* meddling, interfering.

entremezclar [entremeθ'klar] *vt*, **~se** *vr* to intermingle.

entrenador, a [entrena'ðor, a] *nm/f* trainer, coach.

entrenamiento [entrena'mjento] *nm* training.

entrenar [entre'nar] *vt* (*DEPORTE*) to train; (*caballo*) to exercise ♦ *vi*, **~se** *vr* to train.

entrepierna [entre'pjerna] *nf* (*tb*: **~s**) crotch, crutch.

entresacar [entresa'kar] *vt* to pick out, select.

entresaque [entre'sake] *etc vb V* **entresacar**.

entresuelo [entre'swelo] *nm* mezzanine, entresol; (*TEAT*) dress *o* first circle.

entretanto [entre'tanto] *adv* meanwhile, meantime.

entretejer [entrete'xer] *vt* to interweave.

entretela [entre'tela] *nf* (*de ropa*) interlining; **~s** *nfpl* heart-strings.

entretención [entreten'sjon] *nf* (*AM*) entertainment.

entretendré [entreten'dre] *etc vb V* **entretener**.

entretener [entrete'ner] *vt* (*divertir*) to entertain, amuse; (*detener*) to hold up, delay; (*mantener*) to maintain; **~se** *vr* (*divertirse*) to amuse o.s.; (*retrasarse*) to delay, linger; **no le entretengo más** I won't keep you any longer.

entretenga [entre'tenga] *etc vb V* **entretener**.

entretenido, a [entrete'niðo, a] *adj* entertaining, amusing.

entretenimiento [entreteni'mjento] *nm* entertainment, amusement; (*mantenimiento*) upkeep, maintenance.

entretiempo [entre'tjempo] *nm*: **ropa de ~** clothes for spring and autumn.

entretiene [entre'tjene] *etc*, **entretuve** [entre'tuße] *etc vb V* **entretener**.

entreveía [entreße'ia] *etc vb V* **entrever**.

entrever [entre'ßer] *vt* to glimpse, catch a

glimpse of.

entrevista [entre'ßista] *nf* interview.

entrevistar [entreßis'tar] *vt* to interview; ~**se** *vr*: ~**se con** to have an interview with, see.

entrevisto [entre'ßisto] *pp de* **entrever.**

entristecer [entriste'θer] *vt* to sadden, grieve; ~**se** *vr* to grow sad.

entristezca [entris'teθka] *etc vb V* **entristecer.**

entrometerse [entrome'terse] *vr*: ~ **(en)** to interfere (in *o* with).

entrometido, a [entrome'tiðo, a] *adj* interfering, meddlesome.

entroncar [entron'kar] *vi* to be connected *o* related.

entronque [en'tronke] *etc vb V* **entroncar.**

entuerto [en'twerto] *nm* wrong, injustice; ~**s** *nmpl* (*MED*) afterpains.

entumecer [entume'θer] *vt* to numb, benumb; ~**se** *vr* (*por el frío*) to go *o* become numb.

entumecido, a [entume'θiðo, a] *adj* numb, stiff.

entumezca [entu'meθka] *etc vb V* **entumecer.**

enturbiar [entur'ßjar] *vt* (*el agua*) to make cloudy; (*fig*) to confuse; ~**se** *vr* (*oscurecerse*) to become cloudy; (*fig*) to get confused, become obscure.

entusiasmar [entusjas'mar] *vt* to excite, fill with enthusiasm; (*gustar mucho*) to delight; ~**se** *vr*: ~**se con** *o* **por** to get enthusiastic *o* excited about.

entusiasmo [entu'sjasmo] *nm* enthusiasm; (*excitación*) excitement.

entusiasta [entu'sjasta] *adj* enthusiastic ♦ *nm/f* enthusiast.

enumerar [enume'rar] *vt* to enumerate.

enunciación [enunθja'θjon] *nf*, **enunciado** [enun'θjaðo] *nm* enunciation; (*declaración*) declaration, statement.

enunciar [enun'θjar] *vt* to enunciate; to declare, state.

envainar [embai'nar] *vt* to sheathe.

envalentonar [embalento'nar] *vt* to give courage to; ~**se** *vr* (*pey: jactarse*) to boast, brag.

envanecer [embane'θer] *vt* to make conceited; ~**se** *vr* to grow conceited.

envanezca [emba'neθka] *etc vb V* **envanecer.**

envasar [emba'sar] *vt* (*empaquetar*) to pack, wrap; (*enfrascar*) to bottle; (*enlatar*) to can; (*embolsar*) to pocket.

envase [em'base] *nm* packing, wrapping; bottling; canning; pocketing; (*recipiente*) container; (*paquete*) package; (*botella*)

bottle; (*lata*) tin (*BRIT*), can.

envejecer [embexe'θer] *vt* to make old, age ♦ *vi*, ~**se** *vr* (*volverse viejo*) to grow old; (*parecer viejo*) to age.

envejecido, a [embexe'θiðo, a] *adj* old, aged; (*de aspecto*) old-looking.

envejezca [embe'xeθka] *etc vb V* **envejecer.**

envenenar [embene'nar] *vt* to poison; (*fig*) to embitter.

envergadura [emberxa'ðura] *nf* (*expansión*) expanse; (*NAUT*) breadth; (*fig*) scope; **un programa de gran** ~ a wide-ranging programme.

envés [em'bes] *nm* (*de tela*) back, wrong side.

enviado, a [em'bjaðo, a] *nm/f* (*POL*) envoy; ~ **especial** (*de periódico, TV*) special correspondent.

enviar [em'bjar] *vt* to send; ~ **un mensaje a algn** (*por móvil*) to text sb, send sb a text message.

enviciar [embi'θjar] *vt* to corrupt ♦ *vi* (*trabajo etc*) to be addictive; ~**se** *vr*: ~**se (con** *o* **en)** to get addicted (to).

envidia [em'biðja] *nf* envy; **tener** ~ **a** to envy, be jealous of.

envidiar [embi'ðjar] *vt* (*desear*) to envy; (*tener celos de*) to be jealous of.

envidioso, a [embi'ðjoso, a] *adj* envious, jealous.

envío [em'bio] *nm* (*acción*) sending; (*de mercancías*) consignment; (*de dinero*) remittance; (*en barco*) shipment; **gastos de** ~ postage and packing; ~ **contra reembolso** COD shipment.

enviudar [embju'ðar] *vi* to be widowed.

envoltura [embol'tura] *nf* (*cobertura*) cover; (*embalaje*) wrapper, wrapping.

envolver [embol'ßer] *vt* to wrap (up); (*cubrir*) to cover; (*enemigo*) to surround; (*implicar*) to involve, implicate.

envuelto [em'bwelto], **envuelva** [em'bwelßa] *etc vb V* **envolver.**

enyesar [enje'sar] *vt* (*pared*) to plaster; (*MED*) to put in plaster.

enzarzarse [enθar'θarse] *vr*: ~ **en algo** to get mixed up in sth.

epa ['epa], **épale** ['epale] (*AM*) *excl* hey!, wow!

E.P.D. *abr* (= *en paz descanse*) R.I.P.

epicentro [epi'θentro] *nm* epicentre.

épico, a ['epiko, a] *adj* epic ♦ *nf* epic (poetry).

epidemia [epi'ðemja] *nf* epidemic.

epidémico, a [epi'ðemiko, a] *adj* epidemic.

epidermis [epi'ðermis] *nf* epidermis.

epifanía [epifa'nia] *nf* Epiphany.

epilepsia [epi'lepsja] *nf* epilepsy.

epiléptico, a [epi'leptiko, a] *adj, nm/f* epileptic.

epílogo [e'piloɣo] *nm* epilogue.

episcopado [episko'paðo] *nm* (*cargo*) bishopric; (*obispos*) bishops *pl* (*collectively*).

episodio [epi'soðjo] *nm* episode; (*suceso*) incident.

epístola [e'pistola] *nf* epistle.

epitafio [epi'tafjo] *nm* epitaph.

epíteto [e'piteto] *nm* epithet.

época ['epoka] *nf* period, time; (*temporada*) season; (*HISTORIA*) age, epoch; **hacer** ~ to be epoch-making.

equidad [eki'ðað] *nf* equity, fairness.

equilibrar [ekili'ßrar] *vt* to balance.

equilibrio [eki'lißrjo] *nm* balance, equilibrium; ~ **político** balance of power.

equilibrista [ekili'ßrista] *nm/f* (*funámbulo*) tightrope walker; (*acróbata*) acrobat.

equinoccio [eki'nokθjo] *nm* equinox.

equipaje [eki'paxe] *nm* luggage (*BRIT*), baggage (*US*); (*avíos*) equipment, kit; ~ **de mano** hand luggage; **hacer el** ~ to pack.

equipar [eki'par] *vt* (*proveer*) to equip.

equiparar [ekipa'rar] *vt* (*igualar*) to put on the same level; (*comparar*) to compare (*con* with); ~**se** *vr*: ~**se con** to be on a level with.

equipo [e'kipo] *nm* (*conjunto de cosas*) equipment; (*DEPORTE, grupo*) team; (*de obreros*) shift; (*de máquinas*) plant; (*turbinas etc*) set; ~ **de caza** hunting gear; ~ **físico** (*INFORM*) hardware; ~ **médico** medical team; ~ **de música** music centre.

equis ['ekis] *nf* (the letter) X.

equitación [ekita'θjon] *nf* (*acto*) riding; (*arte*) horsemanship.

equitativo, a [ekita'tißo, a] *adj* equitable, fair.

equivaldré [ekißal'dre] *etc vb V* equivaler.

equivalencia [ekißa'lenθja] *nf* equivalence.

equivalente [ekißa'lente] *adj, nm* equivalent.

equivaler [ekißa'ler] *vi*: ~ **a** to be equivalent *o* equal to; (*en rango*) to rank as.

equivalga [eki'ßalɣa] *etc vb V* equivaler.

equivocación [ekißoka'θjon] *nf* mistake, error; (*malentendido*) misunderstanding.

equivocado, a [ekißo'kaðo, a] *adj* wrong, mistaken.

equivocarse [ekißo'karse] *vr* to be wrong, make a mistake; ~ **de camino** to take the wrong road.

equívoco, a [e'kißoko, a] *adj* (*dudoso*) suspect; (*ambiguo*) ambiguous ♦ *nm* ambiguity; (*malentendido*) misunderstanding.

equivoque [eki'ßoke] *etc vb V* equivocar.

era ['era] *vb V* ser ♦ *nf* era, age; (*AGR*) threshing floor.

erais ['erais], **éramos** ['eramos], **eran** ['eran] *vb V* ser.

erario [e'rarjo] *nm* exchequer, treasury.

eras ['eras], **eres** ['eres] *vb V* ser.

erección [erek'θjon] *nf* erection.

ergonomía [erxono'mia] *nf* ergonomics *sg*, human engineering.

erguir [er'xir] *vt* to raise, lift; (*poner derecho*) to straighten; ~**se** *vr* to straighten up.

erice [e'riθe] *etc vb V* erizarse.

erigir [eri'xir] *vt* to erect, build; ~**se** *vr*: ~**se en** to set o.s. up as.

erija [e'rixa] *etc vb V* erigir.

erizado, a [eri'θaðo, a] *adj* bristly.

erizarse [eri'θarse] *vr* (*pelo: de perro*) to bristle; (: *de persona*) to stand on end.

erizo [e'riθo] *nm* hedgehog; ~ **de mar** sea urchin.

ermita [er'mita] *nf* hermitage.

ermitaño, a [ermi'taɲo, a] *nm/f* hermit.

erosión [ero'sjon] *nf* erosion.

erosionar [erosjo'nar] *vt* to erode.

erótico, a [e'rotiko, a] *adj* erotic.

erotismo [ero'tismo] *nm* eroticism.

erradicar [erraði'kar] *vt* to eradicate.

erradique [erra'ðike] *etc vb V* erradicar.

errado, a [e'rraðo, a] *adj* mistaken, wrong.

errante [e'rrante] *adj* wandering, errant.

errar [e'rrar] *vi* (*vagar*) to wander, roam; (*equivocarse*) to be mistaken ♦ *vt*: ~ **el camino** to take the wrong road; ~ **el tiro** to miss.

errata [e'rrata] *nf* misprint.

erre ['erre] *nf* (the letter) R; ~ **que** ~ stubbornly.

erróneo, a [e'rroneo, a] *adj* (*equivocado*) wrong, mistaken; (*falso*) false, untrue.

error [e'rror] *nm* error, mistake; (*INFORM*) bug; ~ **de imprenta** misprint; ~ **de lectura/escritura** (*INFORM*) read/write error; ~ **sintáctico** syntax error; ~ **judicial** miscarriage of justice.

Ertzaintza [er'tʃantʃa] *nf* Basque police; *V tb* policía.

eructar [eruk'tar] *vt* to belch, burp.

eructo [e'rukto] *nm* belch.

erudición [eruði'θjon] *nf* erudition, learning.

erudito, a [eru'ðito, a] *adj* erudite, learned ♦ *nm/f* scholar; **los** ~**s en esta materia** the experts in this field.

erupción [erup'θjon] *nf* eruption; (*MED*) rash; (*de violencia*) outbreak; (*de ira*) outburst.

es [es] *vb V* **ser.**

E/S *abr* (*INFORM: entrada/salida*) I/O.

esa ['esa], **esas** ['esas] *adj demostrativo V* **ese.**

ésa ['esa], **ésas** ['esas] *pron V* **ése.**

esbelto, a [es'βelto, a] *adj* slim, slender.

esbirro [es'βirro] *nm* henchman.

esbozar [esβo'θar] *vt* to sketch, outline.

esbozo [es'βoθo] *nm* sketch, outline.

escabeche [eska'βetʃe] *nm* brine; (*de aceitunas etc*) pickle; **en ~** pickled.

escabechina [eskaβe'tʃina] *nf* (*batalla*) massacre; **hacer una ~** (*ESCOL*) to fail a lot of students.

escabroso, a [eska'βroso, a] *adj* (*accidentado*) rough, uneven; (*fig*) tough, difficult; (: *atrevido*) risqué.

escabullirse [eskaβu'ʎirse] *vr* to slip away; (*largarse*) to clear out.

escacharrar [eskatʃa'rrar] *vt* (*fam*) to break; **~se** *vr* to get broken.

escafandra [eska'fandra] *nf* (*buzo*) diving suit; (*~ espacial*) spacesuit.

escala [es'kala] *nf* (*proporción, MUS*) scale; (*de mano*) ladder; (*AVIAT*) stopover; (*de colores etc*) range; **~ de tiempo** time scale; **~ de sueldos** salary scale; **una investigación a ~** nacional a nationwide inquiry; **reproducir a ~** to reproduce to scale; **hacer ~ en** to stop off *o* over at.

escalada [eska'laða] *nf* (*de montaña*) climb; (*de pared*) scaling.

escalafón [eskala'fon] *nm* (*escala de salarios*) salary scale, wage scale.

escalar [eska'lar] *vt* to climb, scale ♦ *vi* (*MIL, POL*) to escalate.

escaldar [eskal'dar] *vt* (*quemar*) to scald; (*escarmentar*) to teach a lesson.

escalera [eska'lera] *nf* stairs *pl*, staircase; (*escala*) ladder; (*NAIPES*) run; (*de camión*) tailboard; **~ mecánica** escalator; **~ de caracol** spiral staircase; **~ de incendios** fire escape.

escalerilla [eskale'riʎa] *nf* (*de avión*) steps *pl*.

escalfar [eskal'far] *vt* (*huevos*) to poach.

escalinata [eskali'nata] *nf* staircase.

escalofriante [eskalo'frjante] *adj* chilling.

escalofrío [eskalo'frio] *nm* (*MED*) chill; **~s** *nmpl* (*fig*) shivers.

escalón [eska'lon] *nm* step, stair; (*de escalera*) rung; (*fig: paso*) step; (*al éxito*) ladder.

escalonar [eskalo'nar] *vt* to spread out; (*tierra*) to terrace; (*horas de trabajo*) to

stagger.

escalope [eska'lope] *nm* (*CULIN*) escalope.

escama [es'kama] *nf* (*de pez, serpiente*) scale; (*de jabón*) flake; (*fig*) resentment.

escamar [eska'mar] *vt* (*pez*) to scale; (*producir recelo*) to make wary.

escamotear [eskamote'ar] *vt* (*fam: robar*) to lift, swipe; (*hacer desaparecer*) to make disappear.

escampar [eskam'par] *vb impersonal* to stop raining.

escanciar [eskan'θjar] *vt* (*vino*) to pour (out).

escandalice [eskanda'liθe] *etc vb V* **escandalizar.**

escandalizar [eskandali'θar] *vt* to scandalize, shock; **~se** *vr* to be shocked; (*ofenderse*) to be offended.

escándalo [es'kandalo] *nm* scandal; (*alboroto, tumulto*) row, uproar; **armar un ~** to make a scene; **¡es un ~!** it's outrageous!

escandaloso, a [eskanda'loso, a] *adj* scandalous, shocking; (*risa*) hearty; (*niño*) noisy.

Escandinavia [eskandi'naβja] *nf* Scandinavia.

escandinavo, a [eskandi'naβo, a] *adj, nm/f* Scandinavian.

escaneo [es'kaneo] *nm* scanning.

escáner [es'kaner] *nm* scanner.

escaño [es'kaɲo] *nm* bench; (*POL*) seat.

escapada [eska'paða] *nf* (*huida*) escape, flight; (*deportes*) breakaway; (*viaje*) quick trip.

escapar [eska'par] *vi* (*gen*) to escape, run away; (*DEPORTE*) to break away; **~se** *vr* to escape, get away; (*agua, gas, noticias*) to leak (out); **se me escapa su nombre** his name escapes me.

escaparate [eskapa'rate] *nm* shop window; (*COM*) showcase.

escapatoria [eskapa'torja] *nf*: **no tener ~** (*fig*) to have no way out.

escape [es'kape] *nm* (*huida*) escape; (*de agua, gas*) leak; (*de motor*) exhaust; **salir a ~** to rush out.

escapismo [eska'pismo] *nm* escapism.

escaquearse [eskake'arse] *vr* (*fam*) to duck out.

escarabajo [eskara'βaxo] *nm* beetle.

escaramuza [eskara'muθa] *nf* skirmish; (*fig*) brush.

escarbar [eskar'βar] *vt* (*gallina*) to scratch; (*fig*) to inquire into, investigate.

escarceos [eskar'θeos] *nmpl*: **en sus ~ con la política** in his occasional forays into politics; **~ amorosos** flirtations.

escarcha [es'kartʃa] *nf* frost.

escarlata [eskar'lata] *adj inv* scarlet.
escarlatina [eskarla'tina] *nf* scarlet fever.
escarmentar [eskarmen'tar] *vt* to punish severely ♦ *vi* to learn one's lesson; **¡para que escarmientes!** that'll teach you!
escarmiento [eskar'mjento] *etc vb* V **escarmentar** ♦ *nm* (*ejemplo*) lesson; (*castigo*) punishment.
escarnio [es'karnjo] *nm* mockery; (*injuria*) insult.
escarola [eska'rola] *nf* (*BOT*) endive.
escarpado, a [eskar'paðo, a] *adj* (*pendiente*) sheer, steep; (*rocas*) craggy.
escasamente [eskasa'mente] *adv* (*insuficientemente*) scantily; (*apenas*) scarcely.
escasear [eskase'ar] *vi* to be scarce.
escasez [eska'seθ] *nf* (*falta*) shortage, scarcity; (*pobreza*) poverty; **vivir con ~** to live on the breadline.
escaso, a [es'kaso, a] *adj* (*poco*) scarce; (*raro*) rare; (*ralo*) thin, sparse; (*limitado*) limited; (*recursos*) scanty; (*público*) sparse; (*posibilidad*) slim; (*visibilidad*) poor.
escatimar [eskati'mar] *vt* (*limitar*) to skimp (on), be sparing with; **no ~ esfuerzos (para)** to spare no effort (to).
escayola [eska'jola] *nf* plaster.
escayolar [eskajo'lar] *vt* to put in plaster.
escena [es'θena] *nf* scene; (*decorado*) scenery; (*escenario*) stage; **poner en ~** to put on.
escenario [esθe'narjo] *nm* (*TEAT*) stage; (*CINE*) set; (*fig*) scene; **el ~ del crimen** the scene of the crime; **el ~ político** the political scene.
escenografía [esθenoɣra'fia] *nf* set *o* stage design.
escepticismo [esθepti'θismo] *nm* scepticism.
escéptico, a [es'θeptiko, a] *adj* sceptical ♦ *nm/f* sceptic.
escindir [esθin'dir] *vt* to split; **~se** *vr* (*facción*) to split off; **~se en** to split into.
escisión [esθi'sjon] *nf* (*MED*) excision; (*fig, POL*) split; **~ nuclear** nuclear fission.
esclarecer [esklare'θer] *vt* (*iluminar*) to light up, illuminate; (*misterio, problema*) to shed light on.
esclarezca [eskla'reθka] *etc vb* V **esclarecer**.
esclavice [eskla'βiθe] *etc vb* V **esclavizar**.
esclavitud [esklaβi'tuð] *nf* slavery.
esclavizar [esklaβi'θar] *vt* to enslave.
esclavo, a [es'klaβo, a] *nm/f* slave.
esclusa [es'klusa] *nf* (*de canal*) lock; (*compuerta*) floodgate.

escoba [es'koβa] *nf* broom; **pasar la ~** to sweep up.
escobazo [esko'βaθo] *nm* (*golpe*) blow with a broom; **echar a algn a ~s** to kick sb out.
escobilla [esko'βiʎa] *nf* brush.
escocer [esko'θer] *vi* to burn, sting; **~se** *vr* to chafe, get chafed.
escocés, esa [esko'θes, esa] *adj* Scottish; (*whisky*) Scotch ♦ *nm/f* Scotsman/woman, Scot ♦ *nm* (*LING*) Scots *sg*; **tela escocesa** tartan.
Escocia [es'koθja] *nf* Scotland.
escoger [esko'xer] *vt* to choose, pick, select.
escogido, a [esko'xiðo, a] *adj* chosen, selected; (*calidad*) choice, select; (*persona*): **ser muy ~** to be very fussy.
escoja [es'koxa] *etc vb* V **escoger**.
escolar [esko'lar] *adj* school *cpd* ♦ *nm/f* schoolboy/girl, pupil.
escolaridad [eskolari'ðað] *nf* schooling; **libro de ~** school record.
escolarización [eskolariθa'θjon] *nf*: **~ obligatoria** compulsory education.
escolarizado, a [eskolari'θaðo, a] *adj, nm/f*: **los ~s** those in *o* attending school.
escollo [es'koʎo] *nm* (*arrecife*) reef, rock; (*fig*) pitfall.
escolta [es'kolta] *nf* escort.
escoltar [eskol'tar] *vt* to escort; (*proteger*) to guard.
escombros [es'kombros] *nmpl* (*basura*) rubbish *sg*; (*restos*) debris *sg*.
esconder [eskon'der] *vt* to hide, conceal; **~se** *vr* to hide.
escondidas [eskon'diðas] *nfpl* (*AM*) hide-and-seek *sg*; **a ~** secretly; **hacer algo a ~ de algn** to do sth behind sb's back.
escondite [eskon'dite] *nm* hiding place; (*juego*) hide-and-seek.
escondrijo [eskon'drixo] *nm* hiding place, hideout.
escopeta [esko'peta] *nf* shotgun; **~ de aire comprimido** air gun.
escoria [es'korja] *nf* (*desecho mineral*) slag; (*fig*) scum, dregs *pl*.
Escorpio [es'korpjo] *nm* (*ASTRO*) Scorpio.
escorpión [eskor'pjon] *nm* scorpion.
escotado, a [esko'taðo, a] *adj* low-cut.
escotar [esko'tar] *vt* (*vestido: ajustar*) to cut to fit; (*cuello*) to cut low.
escote [es'kote] *nm* (*de vestido*) low neck; **pagar a ~** to share the expenses.
escotilla [esko'tiʎa] *nf* (*NAUT*) hatchway.
escotillón [eskoti'ʎon] *nm* trapdoor.
escozor [esko'θor] *nm* (*dolor*) sting(ing).
escribano, a [eskri'βano, a], **escribiente**

[eskri'βjente] nm/f clerk; (secretario judicial) court o lawyer's clerk.

escribir [eskri'βir] vt, vi to write; ~ **a máquina** to type; **¿cómo se escribe?** how do you spell it?

escrito, a [es'krito, a] pp de **escribir** ♦ adj written, in writing; (examen) written ♦ nm (documento) document; (manuscrito) text, manuscript; **por** ~ in writing.

escritor, a [eskri'tor, a] nm/f writer.

escritorio [eskri'torjo] nm desk; (oficina) office.

escritura [eskri'tura] nf (acción) writing; (caligrafía) (hand)writing; (JUR: documento) deed; (COM) indenture; ~ **de propiedad** title deed; **Sagrada E~** (Holy) Scripture; ~ **social** articles pl of association.

escroto [es'kroto] nm scrotum.

escrúpulo [es'krupulo] nm scruple; (minuciosidad) scrupulousness.

escrupuloso, a [eskrupu'loso, a] adj scrupulous.

escrutar [eskru'tar] vt to scrutinize, examine; (votos) to count.

escrutinio [eskru'tinjo] nm (examen atento) scrutiny; (POL: recuento de votos) count(ing).

escuadra [es'kwaðra] nf (TEC) square; (MIL etc) squad; (NAUT) squadron; (de coches etc) fleet.

escuadrilla [eskwa'ðriʎa] nf (de aviones) squadron.

escuadrón [eskwa'ðron] nm squadron.

escuálido, a [es'kwaliðo, a] adj skinny, scraggy; (sucio) squalid.

escucha [es'kutʃa] nf (acción) listening ♦ nm (TELEC: sistema) monitor; (oyente) listener; **estar a la** ~ to listen in; **estar de** ~ to spy; ~**s telefónicas** (phone) tapping sg.

escuchar [esku'tʃar] vt to listen to; (consejo) to heed; (esp AM: oír) to hear ♦ vi to listen; ~**se** vr: **se escucha muy mal** (TELEC) it's a very bad line.

escudarse [esku'ðarse] vr: ~ **en** (fig) to hide behind.

escudería [eskuðe'ria] nf: **la** ~ **Ferrari** the Ferrari team.

escudero [esku'ðero] nm squire.

escudilla [esku'ðiʎa] nf bowl, basin.

escudo [es'kuðo] nm shield; ~ **de armas** coat of arms.

escudriñar [eskuðri'ɲar] vt (examinar) to investigate, scrutinize; (mirar de lejos) to scan.

escuece [es'kweθe] etc vb V **escocer**.

escuela [es'kwela] nf (tb fig) school; ~ **normal** teacher training college; ~

técnica superior university offering 5-year courses in engineering and technical subjects; ~ **universitaria** university offering 3-year diploma courses; ~ **de párvulos** kindergarten; V tb **colegio**.

escueto, a [es'kweto, a] adj plain; (estilo) simple; (explicación) concise.

escueza [es'kweθa] etc vb V **escocer**.

escuincle [es'kwinkle] nm (AM fam) kid.

esculpir [eskul'pir] vt to sculpt; (grabar) to engrave; (tallar) to carve.

escultor, a [eskul'tor, a] nm/f sculptor.

escultura [eskul'tura] nf sculpture.

escupidera [eskupi'ðera] nf spittoon.

escupir [esku'pir] vt to spit (out) ♦ vi to spit.

escupitajo [eskupi'taxo] nm (fam) gob of spit.

escurreplatos [eskurre'platos] nm inv plate rack.

escurridizo, a [eskurri'ðiθo, a] adj slippery.

escurrir [esku'rrir] vt (ropa) to wring out; (verduras, platos) to drain ♦ vi (los líquidos) to drip; ~**se** vr (secarse) to drain; (resbalarse) to slip, slide; (escaparse) to slip away.

ese¹ ['ese] nf (the letter) S; **hacer** ~**s** (carretera) to zigzag; (borracho) to reel about.

ese² ['ese], **esa** ['esa], **esos** ['esos], **esas** ['esas] adj demostrativo (sg) that; (pl) those.

ése ['ese], **ésa** ['esa], **ésos** ['esos], **ésas** ['esas] pron (sg) that (one); (pl) those (ones); **ése ... éste** ... the former ... the latter ...; **¡no me vengas con ésas!** don't give me any more of that nonsense!

esencia [e'senθja] nf essence.

esencial [esen'θjal] adj essential; (principal) chief; **lo** ~ the main thing.

esfera [es'fera] nf sphere; (de reloj) face; ~ **de acción** scope; ~ **terrestre** globe.

esférico, a [es'feriko, a] adj spherical.

esfinge [es'finxe] nf sphinx.

esforcé [esfor'θe], **esforcemos** [esfor'θemos] etc vb V **esforzar**.

esforzado, a [esfor'θaðo, a] adj (enérgico) energetic, vigorous.

esforzarse [esfor'θarse] vr to exert o.s., make an effort.

esfuerce [es'fwerθe] etc vb V **esforzar**.

esfuerzo [es'fwerθo] etc vb V **esforzar** ♦ nm effort; **sin** ~ effortlessly.

esfumarse [esfu'marse] vr (apoyo, esperanzas) to fade away; (persona) to vanish.

esgrima [es'ɣrima] nf fencing.

esgrimidor [esɣrimiˈðor] *nm* fencer.
esgrimir [esɣriˈmir] *vt* (*arma*) to brandish; (*argumento*) to use ♦ *vi* to fence.
esguince [esˈɣinθe] *nm* (*MED*) sprain.
eslabón [eslaˈβon] *nm* link; ~ **perdido** (*BIO, fig*) missing link.
eslabonar [eslaβoˈnar] *vt* to link, connect.
eslálom [esˈlalom] *nm* slalom.
eslavo, a [esˈlaβo, a] *adj* Slav, Slavonic ♦ *nm/f* Slav ♦ *nm* (*LING*) Slavonic.
eslogan [esˈloɣan] *nm*, *pl* **eslogans** slogan.
eslora [esˈlora] *nf* (*NAUT*) length.
eslovaco, a [esloˈβako, a] *adj, nm/f* Slovak, Slovakian ♦ *nm* (*LING*) Slovak, Slovakian.
Eslovaquia [esloˈβakja] *nf* Slovakia.
Eslovenia [esloˈβenja] *nf* Slovenia.
esloveno, a [esloˈβeno, a] *adj, nm/f* Slovene, Slovenian ♦ *nm* (*LING*) Slovene, Slovenian.
esmaltar [esmalˈtar] *vt* to enamel.
esmalte [esˈmalte] *nm* enamel; ~ **de uñas** nail varnish *o* polish.
esmerado, a [esmeˈraðo, a] *adj* careful, neat.
esmeralda [esmeˈralda] *nf* emerald.
esmerarse [esmeˈrarse] *vr* (*aplicarse*) to take great pains, exercise great care; (*afanarse*) to work hard; (*hacer lo mejor*) to do one's best.
esmero [esˈmero] *nm* (great) care.
esmirriado, a [esmiˈrrjaðo, a] *adj* puny.
esmoquin [esˈmokin] *nm* dinner jacket (*BRIT*), tuxedo (*US*).
esnob [esˈnob] *adj inv* (*persona*) snobbish; (*coche etc*) posh ♦ *nm/f* snob.
esnobismo [esnoˈβismo] *nm* snobbery.
eso [ˈeso] *pron* that, that thing *o* matter; ~ **de su coche** that business about his car; ~ **de ir al cine** all that about going to the cinema; **a** ~ **de las cinco** at about five o'clock; **en** ~ thereupon, at that point; **por** ~ therefore; ~ **es** that's it; **nada de** ~ far from it; ¡~ **sí que es vida!** now this is really living!; **por** ~ **te lo dije** that's why I told you; **y** ~ **que llovía** in spite of the fact that it was raining.
esófago [eˈsofaɣo] *nm* (*ANAT*) oesophagus.
esos [ˈesos] *adj demostrativo V* **ese**.
ésos [ˈesos] *pron V* **ése**.
esotérico, a [esoˈteriko, a] *adj* esoteric.
esp. *abr* (= *español*) Sp., Span.
espabilado, a [espaβiˈlaðo, a] *adj* quick-witted.
espabilar [espaβiˈlar] *vt*, **espabilarse** *vr* = **despabilar(se)**.
espachurrar [espatʃuˈrrar] *vt* to squash; ~**se** *vr* to get squashed.

espaciado [espaˈθjaðo] *nm* (*INFORM*) spacing.
espacial [espaˈθjal] *adj* (*del espacio*) space *cpd*.
espaciar [espaˈθjar] *vt* to space (out).
espacio [esˈpaθjo] *nm* space; (*MUS*) interval; (*RADIO, TV*) programme, program (*US*); **el** ~ space; **ocupar mucho** ~ to take up a lot of room; **a dos** ~**s, a doble** ~ (*TIP*) double-spaced; **por** ~ **de** during, for.
espacioso, a [espaˈθjoso, a] *adj* spacious, roomy.
espada [esˈpaða] *nf* sword ♦ *nm* swordsman; (*TAUR*) matador; ~**s** *nfpl* (*NAIPES*) one of the suits in the Spanish card deck; **estar entre la** ~ **y la pared** to be between the devil and the deep blue sea; *V tb* **baraja española**.
espadachín [espaðaˈtʃin] *nm* (*esgrimidor*) skilled swordsman.
espaguetis [espaˈɣetis] *nmpl* spaghetti *sg*.
espalda [esˈpalda] *nf* (*gen*) back; (*NATACIÓN*) backstroke; ~**s** *nfpl* (*hombros*) shoulders; **a** ~**s de algn** behind sb's back; **estar de** ~**s** to have one's back turned; **tenderse de** ~**s** to lie (down) on one's back; **volver la** ~ **a algn** to cold-shoulder sb.
espaldarazo [espaldaˈraθo] *nm* (*tb fig*) slap on the back.
espaldilla [espalˈdiʎa] *nf* shoulder blade.
espantadizo, a [espantaˈðiθo, a] *adj* timid, easily frightened.
espantajo [espanˈtaxo] *nm*, **espantapájaros** [espantaˈpaxaros] *nm inv* scarecrow.
espantar [espanˈtar] *vt* (*asustar*) to frighten, scare; (*ahuyentar*) to frighten off; (*asombrar*) to horrify, appal; ~**se** *vr* to get frightened *o* scared; to be appalled.
espanto [esˈpanto] *nm* (*susto*) fright; (*terror*) terror; (*asombro*) astonishment; ¡**qué** ~! how awful!
espantoso, a [espanˈtoso, a] *adj* frightening, terrifying; (*ruido*) dreadful.
España [esˈpaɲa] *nf* Spain; **la** ~ **de pandereta** touristy Spain.
español, a [espaˈɲol, a] *adj* Spanish ♦ *nm/f* Spaniard ♦ *nm* (*LING*) Spanish; *V tb* **castellano**.
españolice [espaɲoˈliθe] *etc vb V* **españolizar**.
españolizar [espaɲoliˈθar] *vt* to make Spanish, Hispanicize; ~**se** *vr* to adopt Spanish ways.
esparadrapo [esparaˈðrapo] *nm* (sticking)

plaster, Band-Aid ® (*US*).

esparcido, a [espar'θiðo, a] *adj* scattered.

esparcimiento [esparθi'mjento] *nm*
(*dispersión*) spreading; (*derramamiento*)
scattering; (*fig*) cheerfulness.

esparcir [espar'θir] *vt* to spread; (*derramar*)
to scatter; **~se** *vr* to spread (out); to
scatter; (*divertirse*) to enjoy o.s.

espárrago [es'parraɣo] *nm* (*tb*: **~s**)
asparagus; **estar hecho un ~** to be as
thin as a rake; **¡vete a freír ~s!** (*fam*) go
to hell!

esparto [es'parto] *nm* esparto (grass).

esparza [es'parθa] *etc vb V* **esparcir**.

espasmo [es'pasmo] *nm* spasm.

espátula [es'patula] *nf* (*MED*) spatula;
(*ARTE*) palette knife; (*CULIN*) fish slice.

especia [es'peθja] *nf* spice.

especial [espe'θjal] *adj* special.

especialidad [espeθjali'ðað] *nf* speciality,
specialty (*US*); (*ESCOL: ramo*) specialism.

especialista [espeθja'lista] *nm/f* specialist;
(*CINE*) stuntman/woman.

especializado, a [espeθjali'θaðo, a] *adj*
specialized; (*obrero*) skilled.

especialmente [espeθjal'mente] *adv*
particularly, especially.

especie [es'peθje] *nf* (*BIO*) species; (*clase*)
kind, sort; **pagar en ~** to pay in kind.

especificar [espeθifi'kar] *vt* to specify.

específico, a [espe'θifiko, a] *adj* specific.

especifique [espeθi'fike] *etc vb V*
especificar.

espécimen [es'peθimen], *pl* **especímenes**
nm specimen.

espectáculo [espek'takulo] *nm* (*gen*)
spectacle; (*TEAT etc*) show; (*función*)
performance; **dar un ~** to make a scene.

espectador, a [espekta'ðor, a] *nm/f*
spectator; (*de incidente*) onlooker; **los
~es** (*TEAT*) the audience *sg*.

espectro [es'pektro] *nm* ghost; (*fig*)
spectre.

especulación [espekula'θjon] *nf*
speculation; **~ bursátil** speculation on
the Stock Market.

especular [espeku'lar] *vt, vi* to speculate.

especulativo, a [espekula'tiβo, a] *adj*
speculative.

espejismo [espe'xismo] *nm* mirage.

espejo [es'pexo] *nm* mirror; (*fig*) model; **~
retrovisor** rear-view mirror; **mirarse al
~** to look (at o.s.) in the mirror.

espeleología [espeleolo'xia] *nf* potholing.

espeluznante [espeluθ'nante] *adj*
horrifying, hair-raising.

espera [es'pera] *nf* (*pausa, intervalo*) wait;
(*JUR: plazo*) respite; **en ~ de** waiting for;

(*con expectativa*) expecting; **en ~ de su
contestación** awaiting your reply.

esperance [espe'ranθe] *etc vb V*
esperanzar.

esperanza [espe'ranθa] *nf* (*confianza*) hope;
(*expectativa*) expectation; **hay pocas ~s
de que venga** there is little prospect of
his coming.

esperanzador, a [esperanθa'ðor, a] *adj*
hopeful, encouraging.

esperanzar [esperan'θar] *vt* to give hope
to.

esperar [espe'rar] *vt* (*aguardar*) to wait for;
(*tener expectativa de*) to expect; (*desear*)
to hope for ♦ *vi* to wait; to expect; to
hope; **~se** *vr*: **como podía ~se** as was to
be expected; **hacer ~ a uno** to keep sb
waiting; **ir a ~ a uno** to go and meet sb;
~ un bebé to be expecting (a baby).

esperma [es'perma] *nf* sperm.

espermatozoide [espermato'θoiðe] *nm*
spermatozoid.

esperpento [esper'pento] *nm* (*persona*)
sight (*fam*); (*disparate*) (piece of)
nonsense.

espesar [espe'sar] *vt* to thicken; **~se** *vr* to
thicken, get thicker.

espeso, a [es'peso, a] *adj* thick; (*bosque*)
dense; (*nieve*) deep; (*sucio*) dirty.

espesor [espe'sor] *nm* thickness; (*de nieve*)
depth.

espesura [espe'sura] *nf* (*bosque*) thicket.

espetar [espe'tar] *vt* (*reto, sermón*) to give.

espía [es'pia] *nm/f* spy.

espiar [espi'ar] *vt* (*observar*) to spy on ♦ *vi*:
~ para to spy for.

espiga [es'piɣa] *nf* (*BOT: de trigo etc*) ear;
(: *de flores*) spike.

espigado, a [espi'ɣaðo, a] *adj* (*BOT*) ripe;
(*fig*) tall, slender.

espigón [espi'ɣon] *nm* (*BOT*) ear; (*NAUT*)
breakwater.

espina [es'pina] *nf* thorn; (*de pez*) bone; **~
dorsal** (*ANAT*) spine; **me da mala ~** I
don't like the look of it.

espinaca [espi'naka] *nf* (*tb*: **~s**) spinach.

espinar [espi'nar] *nm* (*matorral*) thicket.

espinazo [espi'naθo] *nm* spine, backbone.

espinilla [espi'niʎa] *nf* (*ANAT: tibia*)
shin(bone); (: *en la piel*) blackhead.

espino [es'pino] *nm* hawthorn.

espinoso, a [espi'noso, a] *adj* (*planta*)
thorny, prickly; (*fig*) bony; (*problema*)
knotty.

espionaje [espjo'naxe] *nm* spying,
espionage.

espiral [espi'ral] *adj, nf* spiral; **la ~
inflacionista** the inflationary spiral.

espirar [espi'rar] *vt, vi* to breathe out, exhale.

espiritista [espiri'tista] *adj, nm/f* spiritualist.

espíritu [es'piritu] *nm* spirit; (*mente*) mind; (*inteligencia*) intelligence; (*REL*) spirit, soul; **E~ Santo** Holy Ghost; **con ~ amplio** with an open mind.

espiritual [espiri'twal] *adj* spiritual.

espita [es'pita] *nf* tap (*BRIT*), faucet (*US*).

esplendidez [esplendi'ðeθ] *nf* (*abundancia*) lavishness; (*magnificencia*) splendour.

espléndido, a [es'plendiðo, a] *adj* (*magnífico*) magnificent, splendid; (*generoso*) generous, lavish.

esplendor [esplen'dor] *nm* splendour.

espliego [es'pljeɣo] *nm* lavender.

espolear [espole'ar] *vt* to spur on.

espoleta [espo'leta] *nf* (*de bomba*) fuse.

espolvorear [espolβore'ar] *vt* to dust, sprinkle.

esponja [es'ponxa] *nf* sponge; (*fig*) sponger.

esponjoso, a [espon'xoso, a] *adj* spongy.

esponsales [espon'sales] *nmpl* betrothal *sg*.

espontaneidad [espontanei'ðað] *nf* spontaneity.

espontáneo, a [espon'taneo, a] *adj* spontaneous; (*improvisado*) impromptu; (*persona*) natural.

espora [es'pora] *nf* spore.

esporádico, a [espo'raðiko, a] *adj* sporadic.

esposa [es'posa] *nf V* **esposo**.

esposar [espo'sar] *vt* to handcuff.

esposo, a [es'poso, a] *nm* husband ♦ *nf* wife; **esposas** *nfpl* handcuffs.

espuela [es'pwela] *nf* spur; (*fam: trago*) one for the road.

espuerta [es'pwerta] *nf* basket, pannier.

espuma [es'puma] *nf* foam; (*de cerveza*) froth, head; (*de jabón*) lather; (*de olas*) surf.

espumadera [espuma'ðera] *nf* skimmer.

espumarajo [espuma'raxo] *nm* froth, foam; **echar ~s (de rabia)** to splutter with rage.

espumoso, a [espu'moso, a] *adj* frothy, foamy; (*vino*) sparkling.

esputo [es'puto] *nm* (*saliva*) spit; (*MED*) sputum.

esqueje [es'kexe] *nm* (*BOT*) cutting.

esquela [es'kela] *nf:* **~ mortuoria** announcement of death.

esquelético, a [eske'letiko, a] *adj* (*fam*) skinny.

esqueleto [eske'leto] *nm* skeleton; (*lo esencial*) bare bones (of a matter); **en ~** unfinished.

esquema [es'kema] *nm* (*diagrama*) diagram; (*dibujo*) plan; (*plan*) scheme; (*FILOSOFÍA*) schema.

esquemático, a [eske'matiko, a] *adj* schematic; **un resumen ~** a brief outline.

esquí [es'ki], *pl* **esquís** *nm* (*objeto*) ski; (*deporte*) skiing; **~ acuático** water-skiing; **hacer ~** to go skiing.

esquiador, a [eskja'ðor, a] *nm/f* skier.

esquiar [es'kjar] *vi* to ski.

esquila [es'kila] *nf* (*campanilla*) small bell; (*encerro*) cowbell.

esquilar [eski'lar] *vt* to shear.

esquimal [eski'mal] *adj, nm/f* Eskimo.

esquina [es'kina] *nf* corner; **doblar la ~** to turn the corner.

esquinazo [eski'naθo] *nm:* **dar ~ a algn** to give sb the slip.

esquirla [es'kirla] *nf* splinter.

esquirol [eski'rol] *nm* blackleg.

esquivar [eski'βar] *vt* to avoid; (*evadir*) to dodge, elude.

esquivo, a [es'kiβo, a] *adj* (*altanero*) aloof; (*desdeñoso*) scornful, disdainful.

esquizofrenia [eskiθo'frenja] *nf* schizophrenia.

esta ['esta] *adj demostrativo V* **este**.

ésta ['esta] *pron V* **éste**.

está [es'ta] *vb V* **estar**.

estabilice [estaβi'liθe] *etc vb V* **estabilizar**.

estabilidad [estaβili'ðað] *nf* stability.

estabilización [estaβiliθa'θjon] *nf* (*COM*) stabilization.

estabilizar [estaβili'θar] *vt* to stabilize; (*fijar*) to make steady; (*precios*) to peg; **~se** *vr* to become stable.

estable [es'taβle] *adj* stable.

establecer [estaβle'θer] *vt* to establish; (*fundar*) to set up; (*colonos*) to settle; (*récord*) to set (up); **~se** *vr* to establish o.s.; (*echar raíces*) to settle (down); (*COM*) to start up.

establecimiento [estaβleθi'mjento] *nm* establishment; (*fundación*) institution; (*de negocio*) start-up; (*de colonias*) settlement; (*local*) establishment; **~ comercial** business house.

establezca [esta'βleθka] *etc vb V* **establecer**.

establo [es'taβlo] *nm* (*AGR*) stall; (*: esp AM*) barn.

estaca [es'taka] *nf* stake, post; (*de tienda de campaña*) peg.

estacada [esta'kaða] *nf* (*cerca*) fence, fencing; (*palenque*) stockade; **dejar a algn en la ~** to leave sb in the lurch.

estación [esta'θjon] *nf* station; (*del año*) season; ~ **de autobuses/ferrocarril** bus/railway station; ~ **balnearia (de turistas)** seaside resort; ~ **de servicio** service station; ~ **terminal** terminus; ~ **de trabajo** (*COM*) work station; ~ **transmisora** transmitter; ~ **de visualización** display unit.

estacionamiento [estaθjona'mjento] *nm* (*AUTO*) parking; (*MIL*) stationing.

estacionar [estaθjo'nar] *vt* (*AUTO*) to park; (*MIL*) to station.

estacionario, a [estaθjo'narjo, a] *adj* stationary; (*COM: mercado*) slack.

estada [es'taða], **estadía** [esta'ðia] *nf* (*AM*) stay.

estadio [es'taðjo] *nm* (*fase*) stage, phase; (*DEPORTE*) stadium.

estadista [esta'ðista] *nm* (*POL*) statesman; (*ESTADÍSTICA*) statistician.

estadística [esta'ðistika] *nf* (*una* ~) figure, statistic; (*ciencia*) statistics *sg*.

estado [es'taðo] *nm* (*POL: condición*) state; ~ **civil** marital status; ~ **de cuenta(s)** bank statement, statement of accounts; ~ **de excepción** (*POL*) state of emergency; ~ **financiero** (*COM*) financial statement; ~ **mayor** (*MIL*) staff; ~ **de pérdidas y ganancias** (*COM*) profit and loss statement, operating statement; **E~s Unidos (EE.UU.)** United States (of America) (USA); **estar en** ~ (**de buena esperanza**) to be pregnant.

estadounidense [estaðouni'ðense] *adj* United States *cpd*, American ♦ *nm/f* United States citizen, American.

estafa [es'tafa] *nf* swindle, trick; (*COM etc*) racket.

estafar [esta'far] *vt* to swindle, defraud.

estafeta [esta'feta] *nf* (*oficina de correos*) post office; ~ **diplomática** diplomatic bag.

estalactita [estalak'tita] *nf* stalactite.

estalagmita [estalaɣ'mita] *nf* stalagmite.

estallar [esta'ʎar] *vi* to burst; (*bomba*) to explode, go off; (*volcán*) to erupt; (*vidrio*) to shatter; (*látigo*) to crack; (*epidemia, guerra, rebelión*) to break out; ~ **en llanto** to burst into tears.

estallido [esta'ʎiðo] *nm* explosion; (*de látigo, trueno*) crack; (*fig*) outbreak.

estambre [es'tambre] *nm* (*tela*) worsted; (*BOT*) stamen.

Estambul [estam'bul] *nm* Istanbul.

estamento [esta'mento] *nm* (*social*) class.

estampa [es'tampa] *nf* (*impresión, imprenta*) print, engraving; (*imagen, figura: de persona*) appearance.

estampado, a [estam'paðo, a] *adj* printed ♦ *nm* (*impresión: acción*) printing;

(: *efecto*) print; (*marca*) stamping.

estampar [estam'par] *vt* (*imprimir*) to print; (*marcar*) to stamp; (*metal*) to engrave; (*poner sello en*) to stamp; (*fig*) to stamp, imprint.

estampida [estam'piða] *nf* stampede.

estampido [estam'piðo] *nm* bang, report.

estampilla [estam'piʎa] *nf* (*sello de goma*) (rubber) stamp; (*AM*) (postage) stamp.

están [es'tan] *vb V* **estar**.

estancado, a [estan'kaðo, a] *adj* (*agua*) stagnant.

estancamiento [estanka'mjento] *nm* stagnation.

estancar [estan'kar] *vt* (*aguas*) to hold up, hold back; (*COM*) to monopolize; (*fig*) to block, hold up; ~**se** *vr* to stagnate.

estancia [es'tanθja] *nf* (*permanencia*) stay; (*sala*) room; (*AM*) farm, ranch.

estanciero [estan'sjero] *nm* (*AM*) farmer, rancher.

estanco, a [es'tanko, a] *adj* watertight ♦ *nm* tobacconist's (shop); *see boxed note*.

ESTANCO

Cigarettes, tobacco, postage stamps and official forms are all sold under a state monopoly and are usually purchased at a shop called an **estanco**. *Tobacco products are also sold in "quioscos" and bars but are generally more expensive. The number of* **estanco** *licences is regulated by the state.*

---

estándar [es'tandar] *adj, nm* standard.

estandarice [estanda'riθe] *etc vb V* **estandarizar**.

estandarizar [estandari'θar] *vt* to standardize.

estandarte [estan'darte] *nm* banner, standard.

estanque [es'tanke] *etc vb V* **estancar** ♦ *nm* (*lago*) pool, pond; (*AGR*) reservoir.

estanquero, a [estan'kero, a] *nm/f* tobacconist.

estante [es'tante] *nm* (*armario*) rack, stand; (*biblioteca*) bookcase; (*anaquel*) shelf; (*AM*) prop.

estantería [estante'ria] *nf* shelving, shelves *pl*.

estaño [es'taɲo] *nm* tin.

════════════════ *PALABRA CLAVE*

estar [es'tar] *vi* 1 (*posición*) to be; **está en la plaza** it's in the square; **¿está Juan?** is Juan in?; **estamos a 30 km de Junín** we're 30 kms from Junín

2 (+*adj o adv: estado*) to be; ~ **enfermo**

to be ill; **está muy elegante** he's looking very smart; **~ lejos** to be far (away); **¿cómo estás?** how are you keeping?
3 (+*gerundio*) to be; **estoy leyendo** I'm reading
4 (*uso pasivo*): **está condenado a muerte** he's been condemned to death; **está envasado en ...** it's packed in ...
5: **~ a**: **¿a cuántos estamos?** what's the date today?; **estamos a 5 de mayo** it's the 5th of May; **las manzanas están a 1,50 euros** apples are (selling at) 1.5 euros; **estamos a 25 grados** it's 25 degrees today
6 (*locuciones*): **¿estamos?** (*¿de acuerdo?*) okay?; (*¿listo?*) ready?; **¡ya está bien!** that's enough!; **¿está la comida?** is dinner ready?; **¡ya está!**, (*AM*) **¡ya estuvo!** that's it!
7: **~ con**: **está con gripe** he's got (the) flu
8: **~ de**: **~ de vacaciones/viaje** to be on holiday/away *o* on a trip; **está de camarero** he's working as a waiter
9: **~ para**: **está para salir** he's about to leave; **no estoy para bromas** I'm not in the mood for jokes
10: **~ por** (*propuesta etc*) to be in favour of; (*persona etc*) to support, side with; **está por limpiar** it still has to be cleaned; **¡estoy por dejarlo!** I think I'm going to leave this!
11 (+*que*): **está que rabia** (*fam*) he's hopping mad (*fam*); **estoy que me caigo de sueño** I'm terribly sleepy, I can't keep my eyes open
12: **~ sin**: **~ sin dinero** to have no money; **está sin terminar** it isn't finished yet
♦ **~se** *vr*: **se estuvo en la cama toda la tarde** he stayed in bed all afternoon; **¡estáte quieto!** stop fidgeting!

estárter [es'tarter] *nm* (*AUTO*) choke.
estas ['estas] *adj demostrativo* V **este**.
éstas ['estas] *pron* V **éste**.
estás [es'tas] *vb* V **estar**.
estatal [esta'tal] *adj* state *cpd*.
estático, a [es'tatiko, a] *adj* static.
estatua [es'tatwa] *nf* statue.
estatura [esta'tura] *nf* stature, height.
estatus [es'tatus] *nm inv* status.
estatutario, a [estatu'tarjo, a] *adj* statutory.
estatuto [esta'tuto] *nm* (*JUR*) statute; (*de ciudad*) bye-law; (*de comité*) rule; **~s sociales** (*COM*) articles of association.
este¹ ['este] *adj* (*lado*) east; (*dirección*) easterly ♦ *nm* east; **en la parte del ~** in

the eastern part.
este² ['este], **esta** ['esta], **estos** ['estos], **estas** ['estas] *adj demostrativo* (*sg*) this; (*pl*) these; (*AM*: *como muletilla*) er, um.
éste ['este], **ésta** ['esta], **éstos** ['estos], **éstas** ['estas] *pron* (*sg*) this (one); (*pl*) these (ones); **ése ... éste ...** the former ... the latter ....
esté [es'te] *vb* V **estar**.
estela [es'tela] *nf* wake, wash; (*fig*) trail.
estelar [este'lar] *adj* (*ASTRO*) stellar; (*TEAT*) star *cpd*.
estén [es'ten] *vb* V **estar**.
estenografía [estenoɣra'fia] *nf* shorthand.
estentóreo, a [esten'toreo, a] *adj* (*sonido*) strident; (*voz*) booming.
estepa [es'tepa] *nf* (*GEO*) steppe.
estera [es'tera] *nf* (*alfombra*) mat; (*tejido*) matting.
estercolero [esterko'lero] *nm* manure heap, dunghill.
estéreo [es'tereo] *adj inv*, *nm* stereo.
estereofónico, a [estereo'foniko, a] *adj* stereophonic.
estereotipar [estereoti'par] *vt* to stereotype.
estereotipo [estereo'tipo] *nm* stereotype.
estéril [es'teril] *adj* sterile, barren; (*fig*) vain, futile.
esterilice [esteri'liθe] *etc vb* V **esterilizar**.
esterilizar [esterili'θar] *vt* to sterilize.
esterilla [este'riʎa] *nf* (*alfombrilla*) small mat.
esterlina [ester'lina] *adj*: **libra ~** pound sterling.
esternón [ester'non] *nm* breastbone.
estero [es'tero] *nm* (*AM*) swamp.
estertor [ester'tor] *nm* death rattle.
estés [es'tes] *vb* V **estar**.
esteta [es'teta] *nm/f* aesthete.
esteticienne [esteti'θjen] *nf* beautician.
estético, a [es'tetiko, a] *adj* aesthetic ♦ *nf* aesthetics *sg*.
estetoscopio [estetos'kopjo] *nm* stethoscope.
estibador [estiβa'ðor] *nm* stevedore.
estibar [esti'βar] *vt* (*NAUT*) to stow.
estiércol [es'tjerkol] *nm* dung, manure.
estigma [es'tiɣma] *nm* stigma.
estigmatice [estiɣma'tiθe] *etc vb* V **estigmatizar**.
estigmatizar [estiɣmati'θar] *vt* to stigmatize.
estilarse [esti'larse] *vr* (*estar de moda*) to be in fashion; (*usarse*) to be used.
estilice [esti'liθe] *etc vb* V **estilizar**.
estilizar [estili'θar] *vt* to stylize; (*TEC*) to design.

estilo [es'tilo] *nm* style; (*TEC*) stylus; (*NATACIÓN*) stroke; ~ **de vida** lifestyle; **al** ~ **de** in the style of; **algo por el** ~ something along those lines.

estilográfica [estilo'ɣrafika] *nf* fountain pen.

estima [es'tima] *nf* esteem, respect.

estimación [estima'θjon] *nf* (*evaluación*) estimation; (*aprecio, afecto*) esteem, regard.

estimado, a [esti'maðo, a] *adj* esteemed; "E~ **Señor**" "Dear Sir".

estimar [esti'mar] *vt* (*evaluar*) to estimate; (*valorar*) to value; (*apreciar*) to esteem, respect; (*pensar, considerar*) to think, reckon.

estimulante [estimu'lante] *adj* stimulating ♦ *nm* stimulant.

estimular [estimu'lar] *vt* to stimulate; (*excitar*) to excite; (*animar*) to encourage.

estímulo [es'timulo] *nm* stimulus; (*ánimo*) encouragement; (*INFORM*) prompt.

estío [es'tio] *nm* summer.

estipendio [esti'pendjo] *nm* salary; (*COM*) stipend.

estipulación [estipula'θjon] *nf* stipulation, condition.

estipular [estipu'lar] *vt* to stipulate.

estirado, a [esti'raðo, a] *adj* (*tenso*) (stretched *o* drawn) tight; (*fig: persona*) stiff, pompous; (*engreído*) stuck-up.

estirar [esti'rar] *vt* to stretch; (*dinero, suma etc*) to stretch out; (*cuello*) to crane; (*dinero*) to eke out; (*discurso*) to spin out; ~ **la pata** (*fam*) to kick the bucket; ~**se** *vr* to stretch.

estirón [esti'ron] *nm* pull, tug; (*crecimiento*) spurt, sudden growth; **dar un** ~ (*niño*) to shoot up.

estirpe [es'tirpe] *nf* stock, lineage.

estival [esti'βal] *adj* summer *cpd*.

esto ['esto] *pron* this, this thing *o* matter; (*como muletilla*) er, um; ~ **de la boda** this business about the wedding; **en** ~ at this *o* that point; **por** ~ for this reason.

estocada [esto'kaða] *nf* (*acción*) stab; (*TAUR*) death blow.

Estocolmo [esto'kolmo] *nm* Stockholm.

estofa [es'tofa] *nf*: **de baja** ~ poor-quality.

estofado [esto'faðo] *nm* stew.

estofar [esto'far] *vt* (*bordar*) to quilt; (*CULIN*) to stew.

estoico, a [es'toiko, a] *adj* (*FILOSOFÍA*) stoic(al); (*fig*) cold, indifferent.

estomacal [estoma'kal] *adj* stomach *cpd*; **trastorno** ~ stomach upset.

estómago [es'tomaɣo] *nm* stomach; **tener** ~ to be thick-skinned.

Estonia [es'tonja] *nf* Estonia.

estonio, a [es'tonjo, a] *adj, nm/f* Estonian ♦ *nm* (*LING*) Estonian.

estoque [es'toke] *nm* rapier, sword.

estorbar [estor'βar] *vt* to hinder, obstruct; (*fig*) to bother, disturb ♦ *vi* to be in the way.

estorbo [es'torβo] *nm* (*molestia*) bother, nuisance; (*obstáculo*) hindrance, obstacle.

estornino [estor'nino] *nm* starling.

estornudar [estornu'ðar] *vi* to sneeze.

estornudo [estor'nuðo] *nm* sneeze.

estos ['estos] *adj demostrativo V* **este**.

éstos ['estos] *pron V* **éste**.

estoy [es'toi] *vb V* **estar**.

estrabismo [estra'βismo] *nm* squint.

estrado [es'traðo] *nm* (*tarima*) platform; (*MUS*) bandstand; ~**s** *nmpl* law courts.

estrafalario, a [estrafa'larjo, a] *adj* odd, eccentric; (*desarreglado*) slovenly, sloppy.

estrago [es'traɣo] *nm* ruin, destruction; **hacer** ~**s en** to wreak havoc among.

estragón [estra'ɣon] *nm* (*CULIN*) tarragon.

estrambótico, a [estram'botiko, a] *adj* odd, eccentric.

estrangulación [estrangula'θjon] *nf* strangulation.

estrangulador, a [estrangula'ðor, a] *nm/f* strangler ♦ *nm* (*TEC*) throttle; (*AUTO*) choke.

estrangulamiento [estrangula'mjento] *nm* (*AUTO*) bottleneck.

estrangular [estrangu'lar] *vt* (*persona*) to strangle; (*MED*) to strangulate.

estraperlista [estraper'lista] *nm/f* black marketeer.

estraperlo [estra'perlo] *nm* black market.

estratagema [estrata'xema] *nf* (*MIL*) stratagem; (*astucia*) cunning.

estratega [estra'teɣa] *nm/f* strategist.

estrategia [estra'texja] *nf* strategy.

estratégico, a [estra'texiko, a] *adj* strategic.

estratificar [estratifi'kar] *vt* to stratify.

estratifique [estrati'fike] *etc vb V* **estratificar**.

estrato [es'trato] *nm* stratum, layer.

estratosfera [estratos'fera] *nf* stratosphere.

estrechar [estre'tʃar] *vt* (*reducir*) to narrow; (*vestido*) to take in; (*persona*) to hug, embrace; ~**se** *vr* (*reducirse*) to narrow, grow narrow; (*2 personas*) to embrace; ~ **la mano** to shake hands.

estrechez [estre'tʃeθ] *nf* narrowness; (*de ropa*) tightness; (*intimidad*) intimacy;

(*COM*) want o shortage of money; **estrecheces** *nfpl* financial difficulties.

estrecho, a [es'tretʃo, a] *adj* narrow; (*apretado*) tight; (*íntimo*) close, intimate; (*miserable*) mean ♦ *nm* strait; ~ **de miras** narrow-minded; **E~ de Gibraltar** Straits of Gibraltar.

estrella [es'treʎa] *nf* star; ~ **fugaz** shooting star; ~ **de mar** starfish; **tener (buena)/mala** ~ to be lucky/unlucky.

estrellado, a [estre'ʎaðo, a] *adj* (*forma*) star-shaped; (*cielo*) starry; (*huevos*) fried.

estrellar [estre'ʎar] *vt* (*hacer añicos*) to smash (to pieces); (*huevos*) to fry; ~**se** *vr* to smash; (*chocarse*) to crash; (*fracasar*) to fail.

estrellato [estre'ʎato] *nm* stardom.

estremecer [estreme'θer] *vt* to shake; ~**se** *vr* to shake, tremble; ~ **de** (*horror*) to shudder with; (*frío*) to shiver with.

estremecimiento [estremeθi'mjento] *nm* (*temblor*) trembling, shaking.

estremezca [estre'meθka] *etc vb* V **estremecer**.

estrenar [estre'nar] *vt* (*vestido*) to wear for the first time; (*casa*) to move into; (*película, obra de teatro*) to present for the first time; ~**se** *vr* (*persona*) to make one's début; (*película*) to have its premiere; (*TEAT*) to open.

estreno [es'treno] *nm* (*primer uso*) first use; (*CINE etc*) premiere.

estreñido, a [estre'ɲiðo, a] *adj* constipated.

estreñimiento [estreɲi'mjento] *nm* constipation.

estreñir [estre'ɲir] *vt* to constipate.

estrépito [es'trepito] *nm* noise, racket; (*fig*) fuss.

estrepitoso, a [estrepi'toso, a] *adj* noisy; (*fiesta*) rowdy.

estrés [es'tres] *nm* stress.

estresante [estre'sante] *adj* stressful.

estría [es'tria] *nf* groove; ~**s (en el cutis)** stretchmarks.

estribación [estriβa'θjon] *nf* (*GEO*) spur; **estribaciones** *nfpl* foothills.

estribar [estri'βar] *vi*: ~ **en** to rest on, be supported by; **la dificultad estriba en el texto** the difficulty lies in the text.

estribillo [estri'βiʎo] *nm* (*LITERATURA*) refrain; (*MUS*) chorus.

estribo [es'triβo] *nm* (*de jinete*) stirrup; (*de coche, tren*) step; (*de puente*) support; (*GEO*) spur; **perder los** ~**s** to fly off the handle.

estribor [estri'βor] *nm* (*NAUT*) starboard.

estricnina [estrik'nina] *nf* strychnine.

estricto, a [es'trikto, a] *adj* (*riguroso*) strict; (*severo*) severe.

estridente [estri'ðente] *adj* (*color*) loud; (*voz*) raucous.

estro ['estro] *nm* inspiration.

estrofa [es'trofa] *nf* verse.

estropajo [estro'paxo] *nm* scourer.

estropeado, a [estrope'aðo, a] *adj*: **está** ~ it's not working.

estropear [estrope'ar] *vt* (*arruinar*) to spoil; (*dañar*) to damage; (: *máquina*) to break; ~**se** *vr* (*objeto*) to get damaged; (*coche*) to break down; (*la piel etc*) to be ruined.

estropicio [estro'piθjo] *nm* (*rotura*) breakage; (*efectos*) harmful effects *pl*.

estructura [estruk'tura] *nf* structure.

estruendo [es'trwendo] *nm* (*ruido*) racket, din; (*fig: alboroto*) uproar, turmoil.

estrujar [estru'xar] *vt* (*apretar*) to squeeze; (*aplastar*) to crush; (*fig*) to drain, bleed.

estuario [es'twarjo] *nm* estuary.

estuche [es'tutʃe] *nm* box, case.

estudiante [estu'ðjante] *nmlf* student.

estudiantil [estuðjan'til] *adj inv* student *cpd*.

estudiantina [estuðjan'tina] *nf* student music group.

estudiar [estu'ðjar] *vt* to study; (*propuesta*) to think about o over; ~ **para abogado** to study to become a lawyer.

estudio [es'tuðjo] *nm* study; (*encuesta*) research; (*proyecto*) plan; (*piso*) studio flat; (*CINE, ARTE, RADIO*) studio; ~**s** *nmpl* studies; (*erudición*) learning *sg*; **cursar** o **hacer** ~**s** to study; ~ **de casos prácticos** case study; ~ **de desplazamientos y tiempos** (*COM*) time and motion study; ~**s de motivación** motivational research *sg*; ~ **del trabajo** (*COM*) work study; ~ **de viabilidad** (*COM*) feasibility study.

estudioso, a [estu'ðjoso, a] *adj* studious.

estufa [es'tufa] *nf* heater, fire.

estulticia [estul'tiθja] *nf* foolishness.

estupefaciente [estupefa'θjente] *adj, nm* narcotic.

estupefacto, a [estupe'fakto, a] *adj* speechless, thunderstruck.

estupendamente [estupenda'mente] *adv* (*fam*): **estoy** ~ I feel great; **le salió** ~ he did it very well.

estupendo, a [estu'pendo, a] *adj* wonderful, terrific; (*fam*) great; ¡~! that's great!, fantastic!

estupidez [estupi'ðeθ] *nf* (*torpeza*) stupidity; (*acto*) stupid thing (to do); **fue una** ~ **mía** that was a silly thing for me to do o say.

estúpido, a [es'tupiðo, a] *adj* stupid, silly.

estupor [estu'por] *nm* stupor; (*fig*) astonishment, amazement.

estupro [es'tupro] *nm* rape.

estuve [es'tuße] *etc vb V* **estar**.

esvástica [es'ßastika] *nf* swastika.

ET *abr = Ejército de Tierra*.

ETA ['eta] *nf abr* (*POL*: = *Euskadi Ta Askatasuna*) ETA.

etapa [e'tapa] *nf* (*de viaje*) stage; (*DEPORTE*) leg; (*parada*) stopping place; (*fig*) stage, phase; **por ~s** gradually *o* in stages.

etarra [e'tarra] *adj* ETA *cpd* ♦ *nm/f* member of ETA.

etc. *abr* (= *etcétera*) etc.

etcétera [et'θetera] *adv* etcetera.

etéreo, a [e'tereo, a] *adj* ethereal.

eternice [eter'niθe] *etc vb V* **eternizar**.

eternidad [eterni'ðað] *nf* eternity.

eternizarse [eterni'θarse] *vr:* **~ en hacer algo** to take ages to do sth.

eterno, a [e'terno, a] *adj* eternal, everlasting; (*despectivo*) never-ending.

ético, a ['etiko, a] *adj* ethical ♦ *nf* ethics.

etimología [etimolo'xia] *nf* etymology.

etiqueta [eti'keta] *nf* (*modales*) etiquette; (*rótulo*) label, tag; **de ~** formal.

etnia ['etnja] *nf* ethnic group.

étnico, a ['etniko, a] *adj* ethnic.

EU(A) *abr* (*esp AM*) = **Estados Unidos (de América)**.

eucalipto [euka'lipto] *nm* eucalyptus.

Eucaristía [eukaris'tia] *nf* Eucharist.

eufemismo [eufe'mismo] *nm* euphemism.

euforia [eu'forja] *nf* euphoria.

eufórico, a [eu'foriko, a] *adj* euphoric.

euro ['euro] *nm* (*moneda*) euro.

eurodiputado, a [euroðipu'taðo, a] *nm/f* Euro MP, MEP.

Eurolandia [euro'landja] *nf* Euroland.

Europa [eu'ropa] *nf* Europe.

europeice [euro'peiθe] *etc vb V* **europeizar**.

europeizar [europei'θar] *vt* to Europeanize; **~se** *vr* to become Europeanized.

europeo, a [euro'peo, a] *adj, nm/f* European.

Eurotúnel [euro'tunel] *nm* (*estructura*) Channel Tunnel.

eurozona [euro'θona] *nf* Eurozone.

Euskadi [eus'kaði] *nm* the Basque Provinces *pl*.

euskera, eusquera [eus'kera] *nm* (*LING*) Basque; *V tb* **lenguas cooficiales**.

eutanasia [euta'nasja] *nf* euthanasia.

evacuación [eßakwa'θjon] *nf* evacuation.

evacuar [eßa'kwar] *vt* to evacuate.

evadir [eßa'ðir] *vt* to evade, avoid; **~se** *vr* to escape.

evaluación [eßalwa'θjon] *nf* evaluation, assessment.

evaluar [eßa'lwar] *vt* to evaluate, assess.

evangélico, a [eßan'xeliko, a] *adj* evangelical.

evangelio [eßan'xeljo] *nm* gospel.

evaporación [eßapora'θjon] *nf* evaporation.

evaporar [eßapo'rar] *vt* to evaporate; **~se** *vr* to vanish.

evasión [eßa'sjon] *nf* escape, flight; (*fig*) evasion; **~ fiscal** *o* **tributaria** tax evasion.

evasivo, a [eßa'sißo, a] *adj* evasive, non-committal ♦ *nf* (*pretexto*) excuse; **contestar con evasivas** to avoid giving a straight answer.

evento [e'ßento] *nm* event.

eventual [eßen'twal] *adj* possible, conditional (upon circumstances); (*trabajador*) casual, temporary.

Everest [eße'rest] *nm:* **el (Monte) ~** (Mount) Everest.

evidencia [eßi'ðenθja] *nf* evidence, proof; **poner en ~** to make clear; **ponerse en ~** (*persona*) to show o.s. up.

evidenciar [eßiðen'θjar] *vt* (*hacer patente*) to make evident; (*probar*) to prove, show; **~se** *vr* to be evident.

evidente [eßi'ðente] *adj* obvious, clear, evident.

evitar [eßi'tar] *vt* (*evadir*) to avoid; (*impedir*) to prevent; (*peligro*) to escape; (*molestia*) to save; (*tentación*) to shun; **si puedo ~lo** if I can help it.

evocador, a [eßoka'ðor, a] *adj* (*sugestivo*) evocative.

evocar [eßo'kar] *vt* to evoke, call forth.

evolución [eßolu'θjon] *nf* (*desarrollo*) evolution, development; (*cambio*) change; (*MIL*) manoeuvre.

evolucionar [eßoluθjo'nar] *vi* to evolve; (*MIL, AVIAT*) to manoeuvre.

evoque [e'ßoke] *etc vb V* **evocar**.

ex [eks] *adj* ex-; **el ~ ministro** the former minister, the ex-minister.

exabrupto [eksa'ßrupto] *nm* interjection.

exacción [eksak'θjon] *nf* (*acto*) exaction; (*de impuestos*) demand.

exacerbar [eksaθer'ßar] *vt* to irritate, annoy.

exactamente [eksakta'mente] *adv* exactly.

exactitud [eksakti'tuð] *nf* exactness; (*precisión*) accuracy; (*puntualidad*) punctuality.

exacto, a [ek'sakto, a] *adj* exact; accurate; punctual; ¡**~!** exactly!; **eso no es del todo ~** that's not quite right; **para ser ~** to be precise.

exageración [eksaxera'θjon] *nf* exaggeration.

exagerado, a [eksaxe'raðo, a] _adj (relato)_ exaggerated; _(precio)_ excessive; _(persona)_ over-demonstrative; _(gesto)_ theatrical.

exagerar [eksaxe'rar] _vt_ to exaggerate; _(exceder)_ to overdo.

exaltado, a [eksal'taðo, a] _adj (apasionado)_ over-excited, worked up; _(exagerado)_ extreme; _(fanático)_ hot-headed; _(discurso)_ impassioned ♦ _nm/f (fanático)_ hothead; _(POL)_ extremist.

exaltar [eksal'tar] _vt_ to exalt, glorify; **~se** _vr (excitarse)_ to get excited _o_ worked up.

examen [ek'samen] _nm_ examination; _(de problema)_ consideration; ~ **de** _(encuesta)_ inquiry into; ~ **de ingreso** entrance examination; ~ **de conducir** driving test; ~ **eliminatorio** qualifying examination.

examinar [eksami'nar] _vt_ to examine; _(poner a prueba)_ to test; _(inspeccionar)_ to inspect; **~se** _vr_ to be examined, take an examination.

exánime [ek'sanime] _adj_ lifeless; _(fig)_ exhausted.

exasperar [eksaspe'rar] _vt_ to exasperate; **~se** _vr_ to get exasperated, lose patience.

Exc.ª _abr_ = **Excelencia**.

excarcelar [ekskarθe'lar] _vt_ to release (from prison).

excavador, a [ekskaßa'ðor, a] _nm/f (persona)_ excavator ♦ _nf (TEC)_ digger.

excavar [ekska'ßar] _vt_ to excavate, dig (out).

excedencia [eksθe'ðenθja] _nf (MIL)_ leave; _(ESCOL)_ sabbatical.

excedente [eksθe'ðente] _adj, nm_ excess, surplus.

exceder [eksθe'ðer] _vt_ to exceed, surpass; **~se** _vr (extralimitarse)_ to go too far; _(sobrepasarse)_ to excel o.s.

excelencia [eksθe'lenθja] _nf_ excellence; **E~** Excellency; **por ~** par excellence.

excelente [eksθe'lente] _adj_ excellent.

excelso, a [eks'θelso, a] _adj_ lofty, sublime.

excentricidad [eksθentriθi'ðað] _nf_ eccentricity.

excéntrico, a [eks'θentriko, a] _adj, nm/f_ eccentric.

excepción [eksθep'θjon] _nf_ exception; **la ~ confirma la regla** the exception proves the rule.

excepcional [eksθepθjo'nal] _adj_ exceptional.

excepto [eks'θepto] _adv_ excepting, except (for).

exceptuar [eksθep'twar] _vt_ to except, exclude.

excesivo, a [eksθe'sißo, a] _adj_ excessive.

exceso [eks'θeso] _nm_ excess; _(COM)_ surplus; ~ **de equipaje/peso** excess luggage/weight; ~ **de velocidad** speeding; **en** _o_ **por ~** excessively.

excitación [eksθita'θjon] _nf (sensación)_ excitement; _(acción)_ excitation.

excitado, a [eksθi'taðo, a] _adj_ excited; _(emociones)_ aroused.

excitante [eksθi'tante] _adj_ exciting; _(MED)_ stimulating ♦ _nm_ stimulant.

excitar [eksθi'tar] _vt_ to excite; _(incitar)_ to urge; _(emoción)_ to stir up; _(esperanzas)_ to raise; _(pasión)_ to arouse; **~se** _vr_ to get excited.

exclamación [eksklama'θjon] _nf_ exclamation.

exclamar [ekskla'mar] _vi_ to exclaim; **~se** _vr_: **~se (contra)** to complain (about).

excluir [eksklu'ir] _vt_ to exclude; _(dejar fuera)_ to shut out; _(solución)_ to reject; _(posibilidad)_ to rule out.

exclusión [eksklu'sjon] _nf_ exclusion.

exclusiva [eksklu'sißa] _nf V_ **exclusivo**.

exclusive [eksklu'siße] _prep_ exclusive of, not counting.

exclusivo, a [eksklu'sißo, a] _adj_ exclusive ♦ _nf (PRENSA)_ exclusive, scoop; _(COM)_ sole right _o_ agency; **derecho ~** sole _o_ exclusive right.

excluyendo [eksklu'jendo] _etc vb V_ **excluir**.

Excma., Excmo. _abr_ (= _Excelentísima, Excelentísimo_) courtesy title.

excombatiente [ekskomba't jente] _nm_ ex-serviceman, war veteran _(US)_.

excomulgar [ekskomul'xar] _vt (REL)_ to excommunicate.

excomulgue [eksko'mulxe] _etc vb V_ **excomulgar**.

excomunión [ekskomu'njon] _nf_ excommunication.

excoriar [eksko'rjar] _vt_ to flay, skin.

excremento [ekskre'mento] _nm_ excrement.

exculpar [ekskul'par] _vt_ to exonerate; _(JUR)_ to acquit; **~se** _vr_ to exonerate o.s.

excursión [ekskur'sjon] _nf_ excursion, outing; **ir de ~** to go (off) on a trip.

excursionista [ekskursjo'nista] _nm/f (turista)_ sightseer.

excusa [eks'kusa] _nf_ excuse; _(disculpa)_ apology; **presentar sus ~s** to excuse o.s.

excusado, a [eksku'saðo, a] _adj_ unnecessary; _(disculpado)_ excused, forgiven.

excusar [eksku'sar] _vt_ to excuse; _(evitar)_ to avoid, prevent; **~se** _vr (disculparse)_ to apologize.

execrable [ekse'kraße] _adj_ appalling.

exención [eksen'θjon] _nf_ exemption.

exento, a [ek'sento, a] *pp de* **eximir** ♦ *adj* exempt.

exequias [ek'sekjas] *nfpl* funeral rites.

exfoliar [eksfo'ljar] *vt* to exfoliate.

exhalación [eksala'θjon] *nf* (*del aire*) exhalation; (*vapor*) fumes *pl*, vapour; (*rayo*) shooting star; **salir como una ~ to** shoot out.

exhalar [eksa'lar] *vt* to exhale, breathe out; (*olor etc*) to give off; (*suspiro*) to breathe, heave.

exhaustivo, a [eksaus'tiβo, a] *adj* exhaustive.

exhausto, a [ek'sausto, a] *adj* exhausted, worn-out.

exhibición [eksiβi'θjon] *nf* exhibition; (*demostración*) display, show; (*de película*) showing; (*de equipo*) performance.

exhibicionista [eksiβiθjo'nista] *adj, nmf* exhibitionist.

exhibir [eksi'βir] *vt* to exhibit; to display, show; (*cuadros*) to exhibit; (*artículos*) to display; (*pasaporte*) to show; (*película*) to screen; (*mostrar con orgullo*) to show off; **~se** *vr* (*mostrarse en público*) to show o.s. off, (*fam: indecentemente*) to expose o.s.

exhortación [eksorta'θjon] *nf* exhortation.

exhortar [eksor'tar] *vt:* **~ a** to exhort to.

exhumar [eksu'mar] *vt* to exhume.

exigencia [eksi'xenθja] *nf* demand, requirement.

exigente [eksi'xente] *adj* demanding; (*profesor*) strict; **ser ~ con algn** to be hard on sb.

exigir [eksi'xir] *vt* (*gen*) to demand, require; (*impuestos*) to exact, levy; **~ el pago** to demand payment.

exiguo, a [ek'siχwo, a] *adj* (*cantidad*) meagre; (*objeto*) tiny.

exija [e'ksixa] *etc vb V* **exigir**.

exiliado, a [eksi'ljaðo, a] *adj* exiled, in exile ♦ *nmf* exile.

exiliar [eksi'ljar] *vt* to exile; **~se** *vr* to go into exile.

exilio [ek'siljo] *nm* exile.

eximio, a [ek'simjo, a] *adj* (*eminente*) distinguished, eminent.

eximir [eksi'mir] *vt* to exempt.

existencia [eksis'tenθja] *nf* existence; **~s** *nfpl* stock *sg*; **~ de mercancías** (*COM*) stock-in-trade; **tener en ~** to have in stock; **amargar la ~ a algn** to make sb's life a misery.

existir [eksis'tir] *vi* to exist, be.

éxito ['eksito] *nm* (*resultado*) result, outcome; (*triunfo*) success; (*MUS, TEAT*) hit; **~ editorial** bestseller; **~ rotundo**

smash hit; **tener ~** to be successful.

exitoso, a [eksi'toso, a] *adj* (*esp AM*) successful.

éxodo ['eksoðo] *nm* exodus; **el ~ rural** the drift from the land.

ex oficio [ekso'fiθjo] *adj, adv* ex officio.

exonerar [eksone'rar] *vt* to exonerate; **~ de una obligación** to free from an obligation.

exorcice [eksor'θiθe] *etc vb V* **exorcizar**.

exorcismo [eksor'θismo] *nm* exorcism.

exorcizar [eksorθi'θar] *vt* to exorcize.

exótico, a [ek'sotiko, a] *adj* exotic.

expandido, a [ekspan'diðo, a] *adj:* **en caracteres ~s** (*INFORM*) double width.

expandir [ekspan'dir] *vt* to expand; (*COM*) to expand, enlarge; **~se** *vr* to expand, spread.

expansión [ekspan'sjon] *nf* expansion; (*recreo*) relaxation; **la ~ económica** economic growth; **economía en ~** expanding economy.

expansionarse [ekspansjo'narse] *vr* (*dilatarse*) to expand; (*recrearse*) to relax.

expansivo, a [ekspan'siβo, a] *adj* expansive; (*efusivo*) communicative.

expatriado, a [ekspa'trjaðo, a] *nmf* (*emigrado*) expatriate; (*exiliado*) exile.

expatriarse [ekspa'trjarse] *vr* to emigrate; (*POL*) to go into exile.

expectación [ekspekta'θjon] *nf* (*esperanza*) expectation; (*ilusión*) excitement.

expectativa [ekspekta'tiβa] *nf* (*espera*) expectation; (*perspectiva*) prospect; **~ de vida** life expectancy; **estar a la ~** to wait and see (what will happen).

expedición [ekspeði'θjon] *nf* (*excursión*) expedition; **gastos de ~** shipping charges.

expedientar [ekspeðjen'tar] *vt* to open a file on; (*funcionario*) to discipline, start disciplinary proceedings against.

expediente [ekspe'ðjente] *nm* expedient; (*JUR: procedimiento*) action, proceedings *pl*; (: *papeles*) dossier, file, record; **~ judicial** court proceedings *pl*; **~ académico** (student's) record.

expedir [ekspe'ðir] *vt* (*despachar*) to send, forward; (*pasaporte*) to issue; (*cheque*) to make out.

expedito, a [ekspe'ðito, a] *adj* (*libre*) clear, free.

expeler [ekspe'ler] *vt* to expel, eject.

expendedor, a [ekspende'ðor, a] *nmf* (*vendedor*) dealer; (*TEAT*) ticket agent ♦ *nm* (*aparato*) (vending) machine; **~ de cigarrillos** cigarette machine.

expendeduría [ekspendedu'ria] *nf* (*estanco*)

tobacconist's (shop) (*BRIT*), cigar store (*US*).

expendio [eks'pendjo] *nm* (*AM*) small shop (*BRIT*) o store (*US*).

expensas [eks'pensas] *nfpl* (*JUR*) costs; **a ~ de** at the expense of.

experiencia [ekspe'rjenθja] *nf* experience.

experimentado, a [eksperimen'taðo, a] *adj* experienced.

experimentar [eksperimen'tar] *vt* (*en laboratorio*) to experiment with; (*probar*) to test, try out; (*notar, observar*) to experience; (*deterioro, pérdida*) to suffer; (*aumento*) to show; (*sensación*) to feel.

experimento [eksperi'mento] *nm* experiment.

experto, a [eks'perto, a] *adj* expert ♦ *nmlf* expert.

expiar [ekspi'ar] *vt* to atone for.

expida [eks'piða] *etc vb V* **expedir.**

expirar [ekspi'rar] *vi* to expire.

explanada [ekspla'naða] *nf* (*paseo*) esplanade; (*a orillas del mar*) promenade.

explayarse [ekspla'jarse] *vr* (*en discurso*) to speak at length; **~ con algn** to confide in sb.

explicación [eksplika'θjon] *nf* explanation.

explicar [ekspli'kar] *vt* to explain; (*teoría*) to expound; (*UNIV*) to lecture in; **~se** *vr* to explain (o.s.); **no me lo explico** I can't understand it.

explícito, a [eks'pliθito, a] *adj* explicit.

explique [eks'plike] *etc vb V* **explicar.**

exploración [eksplora'θjon] *nf* exploration; (*MIL*) reconnaissance.

explorador, a [eksplora'ðor, a] *nmlf* (*pionero*) explorer; (*MIL*) scout ♦ *nm* (*MED*) probe; (*radar*) (radar) scanner.

explorar [eksplo'rar] *vt* to explore; (*MED*) to probe; (*radar*) to scan.

explosión [eksplo'sjon] *nf* explosion.

explosivo, a [eksplo'siβo, a] *adj* explosive.

explotación [eksplota'θjon] *nf* exploitation; (*de planta etc*) running; (*de mina*) working; (*de recurso*) development; **~ minera** mine; **gastos de ~** operating costs.

explotar [eksplo'tar] *vt* to exploit; (*planta*) to run, operate; (*mina*) to work ♦ *vi* (*bomba etc*) to explode, go off.

expondré [ekspon'dre] *etc vb V* **exponer.**

exponer [ekspo'ner] *vt* to expose; (*cuadro*) to display; (*vida*) to risk; (*idea*) to explain; (*teoría*) to expound; (*hechos*) to set out; **~se** *vr*: **~se a (hacer) algo** to run the risk of (doing) sth.

exponga [eks'ponga] *etc vb V* **exponer.**

exportación [eksporta'θjon] *nf* (*acción*)

export; (*mercancías*) exports *pl*.

exportador, a [eksporta'ðor, a] *adj* (*país*) exporting ♦ *nmlf* exporter.

exportar [ekspor'tar] *vt* to export.

exposición [eksposi'θjon] *nf* (*gen*) exposure; (*de arte*) show, exhibition; (*COM*) display; (*feria*) show, fair; (*explicación*) explanation; (*de teoría*) exposition; (*narración*) account, statement.

exprés [eks'pres] *adj inv* (*café*) espresso ♦ *nm* (*FERRO*) express (train).

expresamente [ekspresa'mente] *adv* (*concretamente*) expressly; (*a propósito*) on purpose.

expresar [ekspre'sar] *vt* to express; (*redactar*) to phrase, put; (*emoción*) to show; **~se** *vr* to express o.s.; (*dato*) to be stated; **como abajo se expresa** as stated below.

expresión [ekspre'sjon] *nf* expression; **~ familiar** colloquialism.

expresivo, a [ekspre'siβo, a] *adj* expressive; (*cariñoso*) affectionate.

expreso, a [eks'preso, a] *adj* (*explícito*) express; (*claro*) specific, clear; (*tren*) fast ♦ *nm* (*FERRO*) fast train ♦ *adv*: **mandar ~** to send by express (delivery).

exprimidor [eksprimi'ðor] *nm* (lemon) squeezer.

exprimir [ekspri'mir] *vt* (*fruta*) to squeeze; (*zumo*) to squeeze out.

ex profeso [ekspro'feso] *adv* expressly.

expropiar [ekspro'pjar] *vt* to expropriate.

expuesto, a [eks'pwesto, a] *pp de* **exponer** ♦ *adj* exposed; (*cuadro etc*) on show, on display; **según lo ~ arriba** according to what has been stated above.

expulsar [ekspul'sar] *vt* (*echar*) to eject, throw out; (*alumno*) to expel; (*despedir*) to sack, fire; (*DEPORTE*) to send off.

expulsión [ekspul'sjon] *nf* expulsion; sending-off.

expurgar [ekspur'yar] *vt* to expurgate.

expuse [eks'puse] *etc vb V* **exponer.**

exquisito, a [ekski'sito, a] *adj* exquisite; (*comida*) delicious; (*afectado*) affected.

Ext. *abr* (= *Exterior*) ext.; (= *Extensión*) ext.

éxtasis ['ekstasis] *nm* (*tb droga*) ecstasy.

extemporáneo, a [ekstempo'raneo, a] *adj* unseasonal.

extender [eksten'der] *vt* to extend; (*los brazos*) to stretch out, hold out; (*mapa, tela*) to spread (out), open (out); (*mantequilla*) to spread; (*certificado*) to issue; (*cheque, recibo*) to make out; (*documento*) to draw up; **~se** *vr* to extend; (*terreno*) to stretch o spread

(out); (*persona: en el suelo*) to stretch out;
(*en el tiempo*) to extend, last; (*costumbre,
epidemia*) to spread; (*guerra*) to escalate;
~**se sobre un tema** to enlarge on a
subject.

extendido, a [eksten'diðo, a] *adj* (*abierto*)
spread out, open; (*brazos*) outstretched;
(*costumbre etc*) widespread.

extensible [eksten'sißle] *adj* extending.

extensión [eksten'sjon] *nf* (*de terreno, mar*)
expanse, stretch; (*MUS*) range; (*de
conocimientos*) extent; (*de programa*)
scope; (*de tiempo*) length, duration;
(*TELEC*) extension; ~ **de plazo** (*COM*)
extension; **en toda la** ~ **de la palabra** in
every sense of the word; **de** ~ (*INFORM*)
add-on.

extenso, a [eks'tenso, a] *adj* extensive.

extenuar [ekste'nwar] *vt* (*debilitar*) to
weaken.

exterior [ekste'rjor] *adj* (*de fuera*) external;
(*afuera*) outside, exterior; (*apariencia*)
outward; (*deuda, relaciones*) foreign ♦ *nm*
exterior, outside; (*aspecto*) outward
appearance; (*DEPORTE*) wing(er); (*países
extranjeros*) abroad; **asuntos** ~**es** foreign
affairs; **al** ~ outwardly, on the outside;
en el ~ abroad; **noticias del** ~ foreign *o*
overseas news.

exteriorice [eksterjo'riθe] *etc vb V*
exteriorizar.

exteriorizar [eksterjori'θar] *vt* (*emociones*)
to show, reveal.

exteriormente [eksterjor'mente] *adv*
outwardly.

exterminar [ekstermi'nar] *vt* to
exterminate.

exterminio [ekster'minjo] *nm*
extermination.

externo, a [eks'terno, a] *adj* (*exterior*)
external, outside; (*superficial*) outward
♦ *nm/f* day pupil.

extienda [eks'tjenda] *etc vb V* **extender.**

extinción [ekstin'θjon] *nf* extinction.

extinga [eks'tinga] *etc vb V* **extinguir.**

extinguido, a [ekstin'giðo, a] *adj* (*animal,
volcán*) extinct; (*fuego*) out,
extinguished.

extinguir [ekstin'gir] *vt* (*fuego*) to
extinguish, put out; (*raza, población*) to
wipe out; ~**se** *vr* (*fuego*) to go out; (*BIO*)
to die out, become extinct.

extinto, a [eks'tinto, a] *adj* extinct.

extintor [ekstin'tor] *nm* (fire) extinguisher.

extirpar [ekstir'par] *vt* (*vicios*) to eradicate,
stamp out; (*MED*) to remove (surgically).

extorsión [ekstor'sjon] *nf* blackmail.

extra ['ekstra] *adj inv* (*tiempo*) extra; (*vino*)
vintage; (*chocolate*) good-quality;
(*gasolina*) high-octane ♦ *nm/f* extra ♦ *nm*
(*bono*) bonus; (*periódico*) special edition.

extracción [ekstrak'θjon] *nf* extraction; (*en
lotería*) draw; (*de carbón*) mining.

extracto [eks'trakto] *nm* extract.

extractor [ekstrak'tor] *nm* (*tb:* ~ **de
humos**) extractor fan.

extradición [ekstraði'θjon] *nf* extradition.

extraditar [ekstraði'tar] *vt* to extradite.

extraer [ekstra'er] *vt* to extract, take out.

extrafino, a [ekstra'fino, a] *adj* extra-fine;
azúcar ~ caster sugar.

extraiga [eks'traiɣa] *etc*, **extraje**
[eks'traxe] *etc*, **extrajera** [ekstra'xera] *etc*
vb V **extraer.**

extralimitarse [ekstralimi'tarse] *vr* to go
too far.

extranjerismo [ekstranxe'rismo] *nm*
foreign word *o* phrase *etc*.

extranjero, a [ekstran'xero, a] *adj* foreign
♦ *nm/f* foreigner ♦ *nm* foreign lands *pl*; **en
el** ~ abroad.

extrañamiento [ekstraɲa'mjento] *nm*
estrangement.

extrañar [ekstra'ɲar] *vt* (*sorprender*) to find
strange *o* odd; (*echar de menos*) to miss;
~**se** *vr* (*sorprenderse*) to be amazed, be
surprised; (*distanciarse*) to become
estranged, grow apart; **me extraña** I'm
surprised.

extrañeza [ekstra'ɲeθa] *nf* (*rareza*)
strangeness, oddness; (*asombro*)
amazement, surprise.

extraño, a [eks'traɲo, a] *adj* (*extranjero*)
foreign; (*raro, sorprendente*) strange,
odd.

extraoficial [ekstraofi'θjal] *adj* unofficial,
informal.

extraordinario, a [ekstraorði'narjo, a] *adj*
extraordinary; (*edición, número*) special
♦ *nm* (*de periódico*) special edition; **horas
extraordinarias** overtime *sg*.

extrarradio [ekstra'rraðjo] *nm* suburbs *pl*.

extrasensorial [ekstrasenso'rjal] *adj*:
percepción ~ extrasensory perception.

extraterrestre [ekstrate'rrestre] *adj* of *o*
from outer space ♦ *nm/f* creature from
outer space.

extravagancia [ekstraßa'ɣanθja] *nf*
oddness; outlandishness; (*rareza*)
peculiarity; ~**s** *nfpl* (*tonterías*) nonsense
sg.

extravagante [ekstraßa'ɣante] *adj*
(*excéntrico*) eccentric; (*estrafalario*)
outlandish.

extraviado, a [ekstra'ßjaðo, a] *adj* lost,
missing.

extraviar [ekstra'βjar] *vt* to mislead, misdirect; (*perder*) to lose, misplace; ~**se** *vr* to lose one's way, get lost; (*objeto*) to go missing, be mislaid.

extravío [ekstra'βio] *nm* loss; (*fig*) misconduct.

extrayendo [ekstra'jendo] *vb* V **extraer.**

extremado, a [ekstre'maðo, a] *adj* extreme, excessive.

Extremadura [ekstrema'ðura] *nf* Estremadura.

extremar [ekstre'mar] *vt* to carry to extremes; ~**se** *vr* to do one's utmost, make every effort.

extremaunción [ekstremaun'θjon] *nf* extreme unction, last rites *pl*.

extremidad [ekstremi'ðað] *nf* (*punta*) extremity; (*fila*) edge; ~**es** *nfpl* (*ANAT*) extremities.

extremista [ekstre'mista] *adj, nm/f* extremist.

extremo, a [eks'tremo, a] *adj* extreme; (*más alejado*) furthest; (*último*) last ♦ *nm* end; (*situación*) extreme; **E~ Oriente** Far East; **en último** ~ as a last resort; **pasar de un** ~ **a otro** (*fig*) to go from one extreme to the other; **con** ~ in the extreme; **la extrema derecha** (*POL*) the far right; ~ **derecho/izquierdo** (*DEPORTE*) outside right/left.

extrínseco, a [eks'trinseko, a] *adj* extrinsic.

extrovertido, a [ekstroβer'tiðo, a] *adj* extrovert, outgoing ♦ *nm/f* extrovert.

exuberancia [eksuβe'ranθja] *nf* exuberance.

exuberante [eksuβe'rante] *adj* exuberant; (*fig*) luxuriant, lush.

exudar [eksu'ðar] *vt, vi* to exude.

exultar [eksul'tar] *vi*: ~ **(en)** to exult (in); (*pey*) to gloat (over).

exvoto [eks'βoto] *nm* votive offering.

eyaculación [ejakula'θjon] *nf* ejaculation.

eyacular [ejaku'lar] *vt, vi* to ejaculate.

Ff

F, f ['efe] *nf* (*letra*) F, f; **F de Francia** F for Frederick (*BRIT*), F for Fox (*US*).

fa [fa] *nm* (*MUS*) F.

f.ª *abr* (*COM*: = *factura*) Inv.

f.a.b. *abr* (= *franco a bordo*) f.o.b.

fabada [fa'βaða] *nf bean and sausage stew.*

fábrica ['faβrika] *nf* factory; ~ **de moneda** mint; **marca de** ~ trademark; **precio de** ~ factory price.

fabricación [faβrika'θjon] *nf* (*manufactura*) manufacture; (*producción*) production; **de** ~ **casera** home-made; **de** ~ **nacional** home produced; ~ **en serie** mass production.

fabricante [faβri'kante] *nm/f* manufacturer.

fabricar [faβri'kar] *vt* (*manufacturar*) to manufacture, make; (*construir*) to build; (*cuento*) to fabricate, devise; ~ **en serie** to mass-produce.

fabril [fa'βril] *adj*: **industria** ~ manufacturing industry.

fabrique [fa'βrike] *etc vb* V **fabricar.**

fábula ['faβula] *nf* (*cuento*) fable; (*chisme*) rumour; (*mentira*) fib.

fabuloso, a [faβu'loso, a] *adj* fabulous, fantastic.

FACA ['faka] *nm abr* (*ESP AVIAT*) = *Futuro Avión de Combate y Ataque.*

facción [fak'θjon] *nf* (*POL*) faction; **facciones** *nfpl* (*del rostro*) features.

faceta [fa'θeta] *nf* facet.

facha ['fatʃa] (*fam*) *nm/f* fascist, right-wing extremist ♦ *nf* (*aspecto*) look; (*cara*) face; **¡qué** ~ **tienes!** you look a sight!

fachada [fa'tʃaða] *nf* (*ARQ*) façade, front; (*TIP*) title page; (*fig*) façade, outward show.

facial [fa'θjal] *adj* facial.

fácil ['faθil] *adj* (*simple*) easy; (*sencillo*) simple, straightforward; (*probable*) likely; (*respuesta*) facile; ~ **de usar** (*INFORM*) user-friendly.

facilidad [faθili'ðað] *nf* (*capacidad*) ease; (*sencillez*) simplicity; (*de palabra*) fluency; ~**es** *nfpl* facilities; "~**es de pago**" (*COM*) "credit facilities", "payment terms".

facilitar [faθili'tar] *vt* (*hacer fácil*) to make easy; (*proporcionar*) to provide; (*documento*) to issue; **le agradecería me facilitara** ... I would be grateful if you could let me have ....

fácilmente ['faθilmente] *adv* easily.

facsímil [fak'simil] *nm* (*documento*) facsimile; **enviar por ~** to fax.

factible [fak'tiβle] *adj* feasible.

factor [fak'tor] *nm* factor; (*COM*) agent; (*FERRO*) freight clerk.

factoría [fakto'ria] *nf* (*COM: agencia*) agency; (: *fábrica*) factory.

factura [fak'tura] *nf* (*cuenta*) bill; (*nota de pago*) invoice; (*hechura*) manufacture; **presentar ~ a** to invoice.

facturación [faktura'θjon] *nf* (*COM*) invoicing; (: *ventas*) turnover; **~ de equipajes** luggage check-in.

facturar [faktu'rar] *vt* (*COM*) to invoice, charge for; (*AVIAT*) to check in; (*equipaje*) to register, check (*US*).

facultad [fakul'tað] *nf* (*aptitud, ESCOL etc*) faculty; (*poder*) power.

facultativo, a [fakulta'tiβo, a] *adj* optional; (*de un oficio*) professional; **prescripción facultativa** medical prescription.

FAD *nm abr* (*ESP*) = *Fondo de Ayuda y Desarrollo*.

faena [fa'ena] *nf* (*trabajo*) work; (*quehacer*) task, job; **~s domésticas** housework *sg*.

faenar [fae'nar] *vi* to fish.

fagot [fa'xot] *nm* (*MUS*) bassoon.

faisán [fai'san] *nm* pheasant.

faja ['faxa] *nf* (*para la cintura*) sash; (*de mujer*) corset; (*de tierra*) strip.

fajo ['faxo] *nm* (*de papeles*) bundle; (*de billetes*) role, wad.

falange [fa'lanxe] *nf*: **la F~** (*POL*) the Falange.

falda ['falda] *nf* (*prenda de vestir*) skirt; (*GEO*) foothill; **~ escocesa** kilt.

fálico, a ['faliko, a] *adj* phallic.

falla ['faʎa] *nf* (*defecto*) fault, flaw.

fallar [fa'ʎar] *vt* (*JUR*) to pronounce sentence on; (*NAIPES*) to trump ♦ *vi* (*memoria*) to fail; (*plan*) to go wrong; (*motor*) to miss; **~ a algn** to let sb down.

Fallas ['faʎas] *nfpl see boxed note*.

fallecer [faʎe'θer] *vi* to pass away, die.

fallecido, a [faʎe'θiðo, a] *adj* late ♦ *nm/f* deceased.

fallecimiento [faʎeθi'mjento] *nm* decease, demise.

fallero, a [fa'ʎero, a] *nm/f* maker of "Fallas".

fallezca [fa'ʎeθka] *etc vb V* **fallecer**.

fallido, a [fa'ʎiðo, a] *adj* vain; (*intento*) frustrated, unsuccessful.

fallo ['faʎo] *nm* (*JUR*) verdict, ruling; (*decisión*) decision; (*de jurado*) findings; (*fracaso*) failure; (*DEPORTE*) miss; (*INFORM*) bug.

falo ['falo] *nm* phallus.

falsear [false'ar] *vt* to falsify; (*firma etc*) to forge ♦ *vi* (*MUS*) to be out of tune.

falsedad [false'ðað] *nf* falseness; (*hipocresía*) hypocrisy; (*mentira*) falsehood.

falsificación [falsifika'θjon] *nf* (*acto*) falsification; (*objeto*) forgery.

falsificar [falsifi'kar] *vt* (*firma etc*) to forge; (*voto etc*) to rig; (*moneda*) to counterfeit.

falsifique [falsi'fike] *etc vb V* **falsificar**.

falso, a ['falso, a] *adj* false; (*erróneo*) wrong, mistaken; (*firma, documento*) forged; (*documento, moneda etc*) fake; **en ~** falsely; **dar un paso en ~** to trip; (*fig*) to take a false step.

falta ['falta] *nf* (*defecto*) fault, flaw; (*privación*) lack, want; (*ausencia*) absence; (*carencia*) shortage; (*equivocación*) mistake; (*JUR*) default; (*DEPORTE*) foul; (*TENIS*) fault; **~ de ortografía** spelling mistake; **~ de respeto** disrespect; **echar en ~** to miss; **hacer ~ hacer algo** to be necessary to do sth; **me hace ~ una pluma** I need a pen; **sin ~** without fail; **por ~ de** through o for lack of.

faltar [fal'tar] *vi* (*escasear*) to be lacking, be wanting; (*ausentarse*) to be absent, be missing; **¿falta algo?** is anything missing?; **faita mucho todavía** there's plenty of time yet; **¿falta mucho?** is there long to go?; **faltan 2 horas para llegar** there are 2 hours to go till arrival; **~ (al respeto) a algn** to be disrespectful to sb; **~ a una cita** to miss an appointment; **~ a la verdad** to lie; **¡no faltaba más!** that's the last straw!

falto, a ['falto, a] *adj* (*desposeído*) deficient,

lacking; (_necesitado_) poor, wretched;
estar ~ de to be short of.

fama ['fama] _nf_ (_renombre_) fame;
(_reputación_) reputation.

famélico, a [fa'meliko, a] _adj_ starving.

familia [fa'milja] _nf_ family; **~ política** in-
laws _pl_.

familiar [fami'ljar] _adj_ (_relativo a la familia_)
family _cpd_; (_conocido, informal_) familiar;
(_estilo_) informal; (_LING_) colloquial ♦ _nm/f_
relative, relation.

familiarice [familja'riθe] _etc vb V_
familiarizarse.

familiaridad [familjari'ðað] _nf_ familiarity;
(_informalidad_) homeliness.

familiarizarse [familjari'θarse] _vr:_ **~ con** to
familiarize o.s. with.

famoso, a [fa'moso, a] _adj_ (_renombrado_)
famous.

fan, _pl_ **fans** [fan, fans] _nm_ fan.

fanático, a [fa'natiko, a] _adj_ fanatical
♦ _nm/f_ fanatic; (_CINE, DEPORTE etc_) fan.

fanatismo [fana'tismo] _nm_ fanaticism.

fanfarrón, ona [fanfa'rron, ona] _adj_
boastful; (_pey_) showy.

fanfarronear [fanfarrone'ar] _vi_ to boast.

fango ['fango] _nm_ mud.

fangoso, a [fan'goso, a] _adj_ muddy.

fantasear [fantase'ar] _vi_ to fantasize; **~
con una idea** to toy with an idea.

fantasía [fanta'sia] _nf_ fantasy,
imagination; (_MUS_) fantasia; (_capricho_)
whim; **joyas de ~** imitation jewellery _sg_.

fantasma [fan'tasma] _nm_ (_espectro_) ghost,
apparition; (_presumido_) show-off.

fantástico, a [fan'tastiko, a] _adj_ (_irreal,
fam_) fantastic.

fanzine [fan'θine] _nm_ fanzine.

FAO ['fao] _nf abr_ (= _Organización de las
Naciones Unidas para la Agricultura y la
Alimentación_) FAO.

faquir [fa'kir] _nm_ fakir.

faraón [fara'on] _nm_ Pharaoh.

faraónico, a [fara'oniko, a] _adj_ Pharaonic;
(_fig_) grandiose.

fardar [far'ðar] _vi_ to show off; **~ de** to
boast about.

fardo ['farðo] _nm_ bundle; (_fig_) burden.

faringe [fa'rinxe] _nf_ pharynx.

faringitis [farin'xitis] _nf_ pharyngitis.

farmacéutico, a [farma'θeutiko, a] _adj_
pharmaceutical ♦ _nm/f_ chemist (_BRIT_),
pharmacist.

farmacia [far'maθja] _nf_ (_ciencia_) pharmacy;
(_tienda_) chemist's (shop) (_BRIT_),
pharmacy, drugstore (_US_); **~ de turno**
duty chemist.

fármaco ['farmako] _nm_ medicine, drug.

faro ['faro] _nm_ (_NAUT: torre_) lighthouse;
(_señal_) beacon; (_AUTO_) headlamp; **~s
antiniebla** fog lamps; **~s delanteros/
traseros** headlights/rear lights.

farol [fa'rol] _nm_ (_luz_) lantern, lamp; (_FERRO_)
headlamp; (_poste_) lamppost; **echarse un
~** (_fam_) to show off.

farola [fa'rola] _nf_ street lamp (_BRIT_) o light
(_US_), lamppost.

farruco, a [fa'rruko, a] _adj_ (_fam_): **estar** o
ponerse ~ to get aggressive.

farsa ['farsa] _nf_ (_gen_) farce.

farsante [far'sante] _nm/f_ fraud, fake.

FASA ['fasa] _nf abr_ (_ESP AUTO_) = _Fábrica de
Automóviles, S.A._

fascículo [fas'θikulo] _nm_ (_gen_) part,
instalment (_BRIT_), installment (_US_).

fascinante [fasθi'nante] _adj_ fascinating.

fascinar [fasθi'nar] _vt_ to fascinate;
(_encantar_) to captivate.

fascismo [fas'θismo] _nm_ fascism.

fascista [fas'θista] _adj, nm/f_ fascist.

fase ['fase] _nf_ phase.

fastidiar [fasti'ðjar] _vt_ (_disgustar_) to annoy,
bother; (_estropear_) to spoil; **~se** _vr_
(_disgustarse_) to get annoyed o cross; **¡no
fastidies!** you're joking!; **¡que se
fastidie!** (_fam_) he'll just have to put up
with it!

fastidio [fas'tiðjo] _nm_ (_disgusto_)
annoyance.

fastidioso, a [fasti'ðjoso, a] _adj_ (_molesto_)
annoying.

fastuoso, a [fas'twoso, a] _adj_ (_espléndido_)
magnificent; (_banquete etc_) lavish.

fatal [fa'tal] _adj_ (_gen_) fatal; (_desgraciado_)
ill-fated; (_fam: malo, pésimo_) awful ♦ _adv_
terribly; **lo pasó ~** he had a terrible
time (of it).

fatalidad [fatali'ðað] _nf_ (_destino_) fate; (_mala
suerte_) misfortune.

fatídico, a [fa'tiðiko, a] _adj_ fateful.

fatiga [fa'tiɣa] _nf_ (_cansancio_) fatigue,
weariness; **~s** _nfpl_ hardships.

fatigar [fati'ɣar] _vt_ to tire, weary; **~se** _vr_ to
get tired.

fatigoso, a [fati'ɣoso, a] _adj_ (_cansador_)
tiring.

fatigue [fa'tiɣe] _etc vb V_ **fatigar**.

fatuo, a ['fatwo, a] _adj_ (_vano_) fatuous;
(_presuntuoso_) conceited.

fauces ['fauθes] _nfpl_ (_ANAT_) gullet _sg_; (_fam_)
jaws.

fauna ['fauna] _nf_ fauna.

favor [fa'ßor] _nm_ favour (_BRIT_), favor (_US_);
haga el ~ de ... would you be so good as
to ..., kindly ...; **por ~** please; **a ~** in
favo(u)r; **a ~ de** to be in favo(u)r of;

(*COM*) to the order of.

favorable [faβo'raβle] *adj* favourable (*BRIT*), favorable (*US*); (*condiciones etc*) advantageous.

favorecer [faβore'θer] *vt* to favour (*BRIT*), favor (*US*); (*amparar*) to help; (*vestido etc*) to become, flatter; **este peinado le favorece** this hairstyle suits him.

favorezca [faβo'reθka] *etc vb V* **favorecer**.

favorito, a [faβo'rito, a] *adj, nm/f* favourite (*BRIT*), favorite (*US*).

fax [faks] *nm inv* fax; **mandar por** ~ to fax.

faz [faθ] *nf* face; **la** ~ **de la tierra** the face of the earth.

F.C., f.c. *abr* = **ferrocarril**.

FE *nf abr* = *Falange Española*.

fe [fe] *nf* (*REL*) faith; (*confianza*) belief; (*documento*) certificate; **de buena** ~ (*JUR*) bona fide; (*prestar* ~ **a** to believe, credit; **actuar con buena/mala** ~ to act in good/bad faith; **dar** ~ **de** to bear witness to; ~ **de erratas** errata.

fealdad [feal'dað] *nf* ugliness.

feb., feb.º *abr* (= *febrero*) Feb.

febrero [fe'βrero] *nm* February.

febril [fe'βril] *adj* feverish; (*movido*) hectic.

fecha ['fetʃa] *nf* date; ~ **límite** o **tope** closing o last date; ~ **límite de venta** (*de alimentos*) sell-by date; ~ **de caducidad** (*de alimentos*) sell-by date; (*de contrato*) expiry date; **en** ~ **próxima** soon; **hasta la** ~ to date, so far; ~ **de vencimiento** (*COM*) due date; ~ **de vigencia** (*COM*) effective date.

fechar [fe'tʃar] *vt* to date.

fechoría [fetʃo'ria] *nf* misdeed.

fécula ['fekula] *nf* starch.

fecundación [fekunda'θjon] *nf* fertilization; ~ **in vitro** in vitro fertilization, I.V.F.

fecundar [fekun'dar] *vt* (*generar*) to fertilize, make fertile.

fecundidad [fekundi'ðað] *nf* fertility; (*fig*) productiveness.

fecundo, a [fe'kundo, a] *adj* (*fértil*) fertile; (*fig*) prolific; (*productivo*) productive.

FED *nm abr* (= *Fondo Europeo de Desarrollo*) EDF.

FEDER *nm abr* (= *Fondo Europeo de Desarrollo Regional*) ERDF.

federación [feðera'θjon] *nf* federation.

federal [feðe'ral] *adj* federal.

federalismo [feðera'lismo] *nm* federalism.

FEF [fef] *nf abr* = *Federación Española de Fútbol*.

felicidad [feliθi'ðað] *nf* (*satisfacción, contento*) happiness; ~**es** *nfpl* best wishes, congratulations.

felicitación [feliθita'θjon] *nf* (*tarjeta*) greetings card; **felicitaciones** *nfpl* (*enhorabuena*) congratulations; ~ **navideña** o **de Navidad** Christmas Greetings.

felicitar [feliθi'tar] *vt* to congratulate.

feligrés, esa [feli'ɣres, esa] *nm/f* parishioner.

felino, a [fe'lino, a] *adj* cat-like; (*ZOOL*) feline ♦ *nm* feline.

feliz [fe'liθ] *adj* (*contento*) happy; (*afortunado*) lucky.

felonía [felo'nia] *nf* felony, crime.

felpa ['felpa] *nf* (*terciopelo*) plush; (*toalla*) towelling.

felpudo [fel'puðo] *nm* doormat.

femenino, a [feme'nino, a] *adj* feminine; (*ZOOL etc*) female ♦ *nm* (*LING*) feminine.

feminismo [femi'nismo] *nm* feminism.

feminista [femi'nista] *adj, nm/f* feminist.

fenomenal [fenome'nal] *adj* phenomenal; (*fam*) great, terrific.

fenómeno [fe'nomeno] *nm* phenomenon; (*fig*) freak, accident ♦ *adv*: **lo pasamos** ~ we had a great time ♦ *excl* great!, marvellous!

feo, a ['feo, a] *adj* (*gen*) ugly; (*desagradable*) bad, nasty ♦ *nm* insult; **hacer un** ~ **a algn** to offend sb; **más** ~ **que Picio** as ugly as sin.

féretro ['feretro] *nm* (*ataúd*) coffin; (*sarcófago*) bier.

feria ['ferja] *nf* (*gen*) fair; (*AM: mercado*) market; (*descanso*) holiday, rest day; (*AM: cambio*) small change; ~ **comercial** trade fair; ~ **de muestras** trade show.

feriado, a [fe'rjaðo, a] (*AM*) *adj*: **día** ~ (public) holiday ♦ *nm* (public) holiday.

fermentar [fermen'tar] *vi* to ferment.

fermento [fer'mento] *nm* leaven, leavening.

ferocidad [feroθi'ðað] *nf* fierceness, ferocity.

ferocísimo, a [fero'θisimo, a] *adj superlativo de* **feroz**.

feroz [fe'roθ] *adj* (*cruel*) cruel; (*salvaje*) fierce.

férreo, a ['ferreo, a] *adj* iron *cpd*; (*TEC*) ferrous; (*fig*) (of) iron.

ferretería [ferrete'ria] *nf* (*tienda*) ironmonger's (shop) (*BRIT*), hardware store.

ferrocarril [ferroka'rril] *nm* railway, railroad (*US*); ~ **de vía estrecha/única** narrow-gauge/single-track railway o line.

ferroviario, a [ferrovja'rjo, a] *adj* rail *cpd*, railway *cpd* (*BRIT*), railroad *cpd* (*US*) ♦ *nm*:

~s railway (*BRIT*) o railroad (*US*) workers.

fértil ['fertil] *adj* (*productivo*) fertile; (*rico*) rich.

fertilice [ferti'liθe] *etc vb V* **fertilizar.**

fertilidad [fertili'ðað] *nf* (*gen*) fertility; (*productividad*) fruitfulness.

fertilizante [fertili'θante] *nm* fertilizer.

fertilizar [fertili'θar] *vt* to fertilize.

ferviente [fer'βjente] *adj* fervent.

fervor [fer'βor] *nm* fervour (*BRIT*), fervor (*US*).

fervoroso, a [ferβo'roso, a] *adj* fervent.

festejar [feste'xar] *vt* (*agasajar*) to wine and dine, fête; (*galantear*) to court; (*celebrar*) to celebrate.

festejo [fes'texo] *nm* (*diversión*) entertainment; (*galanteo*) courtship; (*fiesta*) celebration.

festín [fes'tin] *nm* feast, banquet.

festival [festi'βal] *nm* festival.

festividad [festiβi'ðað] *nf* festivity.

festivo, a [fes'tiβo, a] *adj* (*de fiesta*) festive; (*fig*) witty; (*CINE, LIT*) humorous; **día ~** holiday.

fetiche [fe'titʃe] *nm* fetish.

fetichista [feti'tʃista] *adj* fetishistic ♦ *nm/f* fetishist.

fétido, a ['fetiðo, a] *adj* (*hediondo*) foul-smelling.

feto ['feto] *nm* foetus; (*fam*) monster.

F.E.V.E. *nf abr* (= *Ferrocarriles Españoles de Vía Estrecha*) *Spanish narrow-gauge railways.*

FF.AA. *nfpl abr* (*MIL*) = **Fuerzas Armadas.**

FF.CC. *nmpl abr* = **Ferrocarriles.**

fiable [fi'aβle] *adj* (*persona*) trustworthy; (*máquina*) reliable.

fiado [fi'aðo] *nm*: **comprar al ~** to buy on credit; **en ~** on bail.

fiador, a [fia'ðor, a] *nm/f* (*JUR*) surety, guarantor; (*COM*) backer; **salir ~ por algn** to stand bail for sb.

fiambre ['fjambre] *adj* (*CULIN*) (served) cold ♦ *nm* (*CULIN*) cold meat (*BRIT*), cold cut (*US*); (*fam*) corpse, stiff.

fiambrera [fjam'brera] *nf* ≈ lunch box, dinner pail (*US*).

fianza ['fjanθa] *nf* surety; (*JUR*): **libertad bajo ~** release on bail.

fiar [fi'ar] *vt* (*salir garante de*) to guarantee; (*JUR*) to stand bail o bond (*US*) for; (*vender a crédito*) to sell on credit; (*secreto*) to confide ♦ *vi*: **~ (de)** to trust (in); **ser de ~** to be trustworthy; **~se** *vr*: **~ de** to trust (in), rely on.

fiasco ['fjasko] *nm* fiasco.

fibra ['fiβra] *nf* fibre (*BRIT*), fiber (*US*); (*fig*)

vigour (*BRIT*), vigor (*US*); **~ óptica** (*INFORM*) optical fibre (*BRIT*) o fiber (*US*).

ficción [fik'θjon] *nf* fiction.

ficha ['fitʃa] *nf* (*TELEC*) token; (*en juegos*) counter, marker; (*en casino*) chip; (*COM, ECON*) tally, check (*US*); (*INFORM*) file; (*tarjeta*) (index) card; (*ELEC*) plug; (*en hotel*) registration form; **~ policíaca** police dossier.

fichaje [fi'tʃaxe] *nm* signing(-up).

fichar [fi'tʃar] *vt* (*archivar*) to file, index; (*DEPORTE*) to sign (up) ♦ *vi* (*deportista*) to sign (up); (*obrero*) to clock in o on; **estar fichado** to have a record.

fichero [fi'tʃero] *nm* card index; (*archivo*) filing cabinet; (*COM*) box file; (*INFORM*) file, archive; (*de policía*) criminal records; **~ activo** (*INFORM*) active file; **~ archivado** (*INFORM*) archived file; **~ indexado** (*INFORM*) index file; **~ de reserva** (*INFORM*) backup file; **~ de tarjetas** card index; **nombre de ~** filename.

ficticio, a [fik'tiθjo, a] *adj* (*imaginario*) fictitious; (*falso*) fabricated.

ficus ['fikus] *nm inv* (*BOT*) rubber plant.

fidedigno, a [fiðe'ðiɣno, a] *adj* reliable.

fideicomiso [fiðeiko'miso] *nm* (*COM*) trust.

fidelidad [fiðeli'ðað] *nf* (*lealtad*) fidelity, loyalty; (*exactitud: de dato etc*) accuracy; **alta ~** high fidelity, hi-fi.

fidelísimo, a [fiðe'lisimo, a] *adj superlativo de* **fiel.**

fideos [fi'ðeos] *nmpl* noodles.

fiduciario, a [fiðu'θjarjo, a] *nm/f* fiduciary.

fiebre ['fjeβre] *nf* (*MED*) fever; (*fig*) fever, excitement; **~ amarilla/del heno** yellow/hay fever; **~ palúdica** malaria; **tener ~** to have a temperature.

fiel [fjel] *adj* (*leal*) faithful, loyal; (*fiable*) reliable; (*exacto*) accurate ♦ *nm* (*aguja*) needle, pointer; **los ~es** the faithful.

fieltro ['fjeltro] *nm* felt.

fiera ['fjera] *nf V* **fiero.**

fiereza [fje'reθa] *nf* (*ZOOL*) wildness; (*bravura*) fierceness.

fiero, a ['fjero, a] *adj* (*cruel*) cruel; (*feroz*) fierce; (*duro*) harsh ♦ *nm/f* (*fig*) fiend ♦ *nf* (*animal feroz*) wild animal o beast; (*fig*) dragon.

fierro ['fjerro] *nm* (*AM*) iron.

fiesta ['fjesta] *nf* party; (*de pueblo*) festival; **la ~ nacional** bullfighting; (**día de) la ~** (public) holiday; **mañana es ~** it's a holiday tomorrow; **~ de guardar** (*REL*) day of obligation; *see boxed note.*

FIESTA

Fiestas *can be national public holidays (such as the Día de la Constitución), or special regional ones for each autonomous region, many of which are religious feast days. All over Spain there are also special local* **fiestas** *in honour of a patron saint or the Virgin Mary. These often last several days and can include religious processions, carnival parades, bullfights, dancing and feasting on local produce.*

FIFA *nf abr* (= *Federación Internacional de Fútbol Asociación*) FIFA.

figura [fiˈɣura] *nf* (*gen*) figure; (*forma, imagen*) shape, form; (*NAIPES*) face card.

figurado, a [fiɣuˈraðo, a] *adj* figurative.

figurante [fiɣuˈrante] *nm/f* (*TEAT*) walk-on part; (*CINE*) extra.

figurar [fiɣuˈrar] *vt* (*representar*) to represent; (*fingir*) to feign ♦ *vi* to figure; ~**se** *vr* (*imaginarse*) to imagine; (*suponer*) to suppose; **ya me lo figuraba** I thought as much.

fijador [fixaˈðor] *nm* (*FOTO etc*) fixative; (*de pelo*) gel.

fijar [fiˈxar] *vt* (*gen*) to fix; (*cartel*) to post, put up; (*estampilla*) to affix, stick (on); (*pelo*) to set; (*fig*) to settle (on), decide; ~**se** *vr*: ~**se en** to notice; **¡fíjate!** just imagine!; **¿te fijas?** see what I mean?

fijo, a [ˈfixo, a] *adj* (*gen*) fixed; (*firme*) firm; (*permanente*) permanent; (*trabajo*) steady; (*color*) fast ♦ *adv*: **mirar** ~ to stare.

fila [ˈfila] *nf* row; (*MIL*) rank; (*cadena*) line; (*MIL*) rank; (*en marcha*) file; ~ **india** single file; **ponerse en** ~ to line up, get into line; **primera** ~ front row.

filántropo, a [fiˈlantropo, a] *nm/f* philanthropist.

filarmónico, a [filarˈmoniko, a] *adj, nf* philharmonic.

filatelia [filaˈtelja] *nf* philately, stamp collecting.

filatelista [filateˈlista] *nm/f* philatelist, stamp collector.

filete [fiˈlete] *nm* (*carne*) fillet steak; (*de cerdo*) tenderloin; (*pescado*) fillet; (*MEC: rosca*) thread.

filiación [filjaˈθjon] *nf* (*POL etc*) affiliation; (*señas*) particulars *pl*; (*MIL, POLICÍA*) records *pl*.

filial [fiˈljal] *adj* filial ♦ *nf* subsidiary; (*sucursal*) branch.

Filipinas [filiˈpinas] *nfpl*: **las** (**Islas**) ~ the Philippines.

filipino, a [filiˈpino, a] *adj, nm/f* Philippine.

film [film], *pl* **films** *nm* = **filme**.

filmación [filmaˈθjon] *nf* filming, shooting.

filmar [filˈmar] *vt* to film, shoot.

filme [ˈfilme] *nm* film, movie (*US*).

filmoteca [filmoˈteka] *nf* film library.

filo [ˈfilo] *nm* (*gen*) edge; **sacar** ~ **a** to sharpen; **al** ~ **del medio día** at about midday; **de doble** ~ double-edged.

filología [filoloˈxia] *nf* philology.

filólogo, a [fiˈloloɣo, a] *nm/f* philologist.

filón [fiˈlon] *nm* (*MINERÍA*) vein, lode; (*fig*) gold mine.

filoso, a [fiˈloso, a] *adj* (*AM*) sharp.

filosofía [filosoˈfia] *nf* philosophy.

filosófico, a [filoˈsofiko, a] *adj* philosophic(al).

filósofo, a [fiˈlosofo, a] *nm/f* philosopher.

filtración [filtraˈθjon] *nf* (*TEC*) filtration; (*INFORM*) sorting; (*fig: de fondos*) misappropriation; (*de datos*) leak.

filtrar [filˈtrar] *vt, vi* to filter, strain; (*información*) to leak; ~**se** *vr* to filter; (*fig: dinero*) to dwindle.

filtro [ˈfiltro] *nm* (*TEC, utensilio*) filter.

filudo, a [fiˈluðo, a] *adj* (*AM*) sharp.

fin [fin] *nm* end; (*objetivo*) aim, purpose; **a** ~ **de cuentas** at the end of the day; **al** ~ **y al cabo** when all's said and done; **a** ~ **de** in order to; **por** ~ finally; **en** ~ (*resumiendo*) in short; **¡en** ~! (*resignación*) oh, well!; ~ **de archivo** (*INFORM*) end-of-file; ~ **de semana** weekend; **sin** ~ endless(ly).

final [fiˈnal] *adj* final ♦ *nm* end, conclusion ♦ *nf* (*DEPORTE*) final.

finalice [finaˈliθe] *etc vb V* **finalizar**.

finalidad [finaliˈðað] *nf* finality; (*propósito*) purpose, aim.

finalista [finaˈlista] *nm/f* finalist.

finalizar [finaliˈθar] *vt* to end, finish ♦ *vi* to end, come to an end; ~ **la sesión** (*INFORM*) to log out *o* off.

financiación [finanθjaˈθjon] *nf* financing.

financiar [finanˈθjar] *vt* to finance.

financiero, a [finanˈθjero, a] *adj* financial ♦ *nm/f* financier.

financista [finanˈsista] *nm/f* (*AM*) financier.

finanzas [fiˈnanθas] *nfpl* finances.

finca [ˈfinka] *nf* country estate.

finde [ˈfinde] *nm abr* (*fam*) (= *fin de semana*) weekend.

fingir [finˈxir] *vt* (*simular*) to simulate, feign; (*pretextar*) to sham, fake ♦ *vi* (*aparentar*) to pretend; ~**se** *vr*: ~**se dormido** to pretend to be asleep.

finiquitar [finikiˈtar] *vt* (*ECON: cuenta*) to settle and close.

Finisterre [finis'terre] *nm*: **el cabo de ~** Cape Finisterre.

finja ['finxa] *etc vb V* **fingir**.

finlandés, esa [finlan'des, esa] *adj* Finnish ♦ *nm/f* Finn ♦ *nm* (*LING*) Finnish.

Finlandia [fin'landja] *nf* Finland.

fino, a ['fino, a] *adj* fine; (*delgado*) slender; (*de buenas maneras*) polite, refined; (*inteligente*) shrewd; (*punta*) sharp; (*gusto*) discriminating; (*oído*) sharp; (*jerez*) fino, dry ♦ *nm* (*jerez*) dry sherry.

finura [fi'nura] *nf* (*calidad*) fineness; (*cortesía*) politeness; (*elegancia*) elegance; (*agudeza*) shrewdness.

FIP [fip] *nf abr* (*ESP*) = *Formación Intensiva Profesional.*

firma ['firma] *nf* signature; (*COM*) firm, company.

firmamento [firma'mento] *nm* firmament.

firmante [fir'mante] *adj, nm/f* signatory; **los abajo ~s** the undersigned.

firmar [fir'mar] *vt* to sign; **~ un contrato** (*COM: colocarse*) to sign on; **firmado y sellado** signed and sealed.

firme ['firme] *adj* firm; (*estable*) stable; (*sólido*) solid; (*constante*) steady; (*decidido*) resolute; (*duro*) hard; **¡~s!** (*MIL*) attention!; **oferta en ~** (*COM*) firm offer ♦ *nm* road (surface).

firmemente [firme'mente] *adv* firmly.

firmeza [fir'meθa] *nf* firmness; (*constancia*) steadiness; (*solidez*) solidity.

fiscal [fis'kal] *adj* fiscal ♦ *nm* (*JUR*) ≈ Crown Prosecutor, Procurator Fiscal (*Escocia*), district attorney (*US*).

fiscalice [fiska'liθe] *etc vb V* **fiscalizar**.

fiscalizar [fiskali'θar] *vt* (*controlar*) to control; (*registrar*) to inspect (officially); (*fig*) to criticize.

fisco ['fisko] *nm* (*hacienda*) treasury, exchequer; **declarar algo al ~** to declare sth for tax purposes.

fisgar [fis'xar] *vt* to pry into.

fisgón, ona [fis'xon, ona] *adj* nosey.

fisgue ['fisxe] *etc vb V* **fisgar**.

físico, a ['fisiko, a] *adj* physical ♦ *nm* physique; (*aspecto*) appearance, looks ♦ *nm/f* physicist ♦ *nf* physics *sg*.

fisioterapeuta [fisjotera'peuta] *nm/f* physiotherapist.

fisioterapia [fisjote'rapja] *nf* physiotherapy.

fisioterapista [fisjotera'pista] *nm/f* (*AM*) physiotherapist.

fisonomía [fisono'mia] *nf* physiognomy, features *pl*.

fisonomista [fisono'mista] *nm/f*: **ser buen ~** to have a good memory for faces.

flac(c)idez [fla(k)θi'ðeθ] *nf* softness, flabbiness.

flác(c)ido, a ['fla(k)θiðo, a] *adj* flabby.

flaco, a ['flako, a] *adj* (*muy delgado*) skinny, thin; (*débil*) weak, feeble.

flagrante [fla'vrante] *adj* flagrant.

flamante [fla'mante] *adj* (*fam*) brilliant; (: *nuevo*) brand-new.

flamear [flame'ar] *vt* (*CULIN*) to flambé.

flamenco, a [fla'menko, a] *adj* (*de Flandes*) Flemish; (*baile, música*) gipsy ♦ *nm/f* Fleming; **los ~s** the Flemish ♦ *nm* (*LING*) Flemish; (*baile, música*) flamenco; (*ZOOL*) flamingo.

flan [flan] *nm* creme caramel.

flanco ['flanko] *nm* side; (*MIL*) flank.

Flandes ['flandes] *nm* Flanders.

flanquear [flanke'ar] *vt* to flank; (*MIL*) to outflank.

flaquear [flake'ar] *vi* (*debilitarse*) to weaken; (*persona*) to slack.

flaqueza [fla'keθa] *nf* (*delgadez*) thinness, leanness; (*fig*) weakness.

flaquísimo, a [fla'kisimo, a] *adj superlativo de* **flaco**.

flash [flas], *pl* **flashes** [flas] *nm* (*FOTO*) flash.

flato ['flato] *nm*: **el** (*o* **un**) **~** the (*o* a) stitch.

flauta ['flauta] (*MUS*) *nf* flute ♦ *nm/f* flautist, flute player; **¡la gran ~!** (*AM*) my God!; **hijo de la gran ~** (*AM fam!*) bastard (!), son of a bitch (*US!*).

flecha ['fletʃa] *nf* arrow.

flechazo [fle'tʃaθo] *nm* (*acción*) bowshot; (*fam*): **fue un ~** it was love at first sight.

fleco ['fleko] *nm* fringe.

flema ['flema] *nm* phlegm.

flemático, a [fle'matiko, a] *adj* phlegmatic; (*tono etc*) matter-of-fact.

flemón [fle'mon] *nm* (*MED*) gumboil.

flequillo [fle'kiʎo] *nm* (*pelo*) fringe.

fletar [fle'tar] *vt* (*COM*) to charter; (*embarcar*) to load; (*AUTO*) to lease (-purchase).

flete ['flete] *nm* (*carga*) freight; (*alquiler*) charter; (*precio*) freightage; **~ debido** (*COM*) freight forward; **~ sobre compras** (*COM*) freight inward.

flexible [flek'siβle] *adj* flexible; (*individuo*) compliant.

flexión [flek'sjon] *nf* (*DEPORTE*) bend; (: *en el suelo*) press-up.

flexo ['flekso] *nm* adjustable table lamp.

flipper ['fliper] *nm* pinball machine.

flirtear [flirte'ar] *vi* to flirt.

FLN *nm abr* (*POL: ESP, Perú, Venezuela*) = *Frente de Liberación Nacional.*

flojear [floxe'ar] *vi* (*piernas: al andar*) to

give way; (*alumno*) to do badly; (*cosecha, mercado*) to be poor.

flojera [flo'xera] *nf (AM)* laziness; **me da ~** I can't be bothered.

flojo, a ['floxo, a] *adj* (*gen*) loose; (*sin fuerzas*) limp; (*débil*) weak; (*viento*) light; (*bebida*) weak; (*trabajo*) poor; (*actitud*) slack; (*precio*) low; (*COM: mercado*) dull, slack; (*AM*) lazy.

flor [flor] *nf* flower; (*piropo*) compliment; **la ~ y nata de la sociedad** (*fig*) the cream of society; **en la ~ de la vida** in the prime of life; **a ~ de** on the surface of.

flora ['flora] *nf* flora.

florecer [flore'θer] *vi (BOT)* to flower, bloom; (*fig*) to flourish.

floreciente [flore'θjente] *adj (BOT)* in flower, flowering; (*fig*) thriving.

Florencia [flo'renθja] *nf* Florence.

florero [flo'rero] *nm* vase.

florezca [flo'reθka] *etc vb V* **florecer**.

florista [flo'rista] *nmf* florist.

floristería [floriste'ria] *nf* florist's (shop).

flota ['flota] *nf* fleet.

flotación [flota'θjon] *nf (COM)* flotation.

flotador [flota'ðor] *nm* (*gen*) float; (*para nadar*) rubber ring; (*de cisterna*) ballcock.

flotante [flo'tante] *adj* floating; (*INFORM*): **de coma ~** floating-point.

flotar [flo'tar] *vi* to float.

flote ['flote] *nm*: **a ~** afloat; **ponerse a ~** (*fig*) to get back on one's feet.

FLS *nm abr (POL: Nicaragua)* = Frente de Liberación Sandinista.

fluctuación [fluktwa'θjon] *nf* fluctuation.

fluctuante [fluk'twante] *adj* fluctuating.

fluctuar [fluk'twar] *vi* (*oscilar*) to fluctuate.

fluidez [flui'ðeθ] *nf* fluidity; (*fig*) fluency.

fluido, a ['flwiðo, a] *adj* fluid; (*lenguaje*) fluent; (*estilo*) smooth ♦ *nm* (*líquido*) fluid.

fluir [flu'ir] *vi* to flow.

flujo ['fluxo] *nm* flow; (*POL*) swing; (*NAUT*) rising tide; **~ y reflujo** ebb and flow; **~ de sangre** (*MED*) haemorrhage (*BRIT*), hemorrhage (*US*); **~ positivo/negativo de efectivo** (*COM*) positive/negative cash flow.

flúor ['fluor] *nm* fluorine; (*en dentífrico*) fluoride.

fluorescente [flwores'θente] *adj* fluorescent ♦ *nm* (*tb*: **tubo ~**) fluorescent tube.

fluoruro [flwo'ruro] *nm* fluoride.

fluvial [fluβi'al] *adj* fluvial, river *cpd*.

fluyendo [flu'jendo] *etc vb V* **fluir**.

F.M. *nf abr* (= Frecuencia Modulada) F.M.

FMI *nm abr* (= Fondo Monetario Internacional) I.M.F.

F.N. *nf abr (ESP POL)* = Fuerza Nueva ♦ *nm* = Frente Nacional.

FNPT *nm abr (ESP)* = Fondo Nacional de Protección del Trabajo.

f.º *abr* (= folio) fo., fol.

foca ['foka] *nf* seal.

foco ['foko] *nm* focus; (*centro*) focal point; (*fuente*) source; (*de incendio*) seat; (*ELEC*) floodlight; (*TEAT*) spotlight; (*AM*) (light) bulb, light.

fofo, a ['fofo, a] *adj* (*esponjoso*) soft, spongy; (*músculo*) flabby.

fogata [fo'ɣata] *nf* (*hoguera*) bonfire.

fogón [fo'ɣon] *nm* (*de cocina*) ring, burner.

fogoso, a [fo'ɣoso, a] *adj* spirited.

foja ['foxa] *nf (AM)* sheet (of paper); **~ de servicios** record (file).

fol. *abr* (= folio) fo., fol.

folder, fólder ['folder] *nm (AM)* folder.

folio ['foljo] *nm* folio; (*hoja*) leaf.

folklore [fol'klore] *nm* folklore.

folklórico, a [fol'kloriko, a] *adj* traditional.

follaje [fo'ʎaxe] *nm* foliage.

follar [fo'ʎar] *vt, vi (fam!)* to fuck (*!*).

folletinesco, a [foʎetin'esko, a] *adj* melodramatic.

folleto [fo'ʎeto] *nm* pamphlet; (*COM*) brochure; (*prospecto*) leaflet; (*ESCOL etc*) handout.

follón [fo'ʎon] *nm (fam: lío)* mess; (*: conmoción*) fuss, rumpus, shindy; **armar un ~** to kick up a fuss; **se armó un ~** there was a hell of a row.

fomentar [fomen'tar] *vt (MED)* to foment; (*fig: promover*) to promote, foster; (*odio etc*) to stir up.

fomento [fo'mento] *nm* (*fig: ayuda*) fostering; (*promoción*) promotion.

fonda ['fonda] *nf* ≈ guest house; *V tb* **hotel**.

fondear [fonde'ar] *vt (NAUT: sondear)* to sound; (*barco*) to search.

fondo ['fondo] *nm* (*de caja etc*) bottom; (*medida*) depth; (*de coche, sala*) back; (*ARTE etc*) background; (*reserva*) fund; (*fig: carácter*) nature; **~s** *nmpl* (*COM*) funds, resources; **~ de escritorio** (*INFORM*) wallpaper; **F~ Monetario Internacional** International Monetary Fund; **~ del mar** sea bed *o* floor; **una investigación a ~** a thorough investigation; **en el ~** at bottom, deep down; **tener buen ~** to be good natured.

fonética [fo'netika] *nf* phonetics *sg*.

fono ['fono] *nm (AM)* telephone (number).

fonobuzón [fonoβu'θon] *nm* voice mail.

fonógrafo [fo'noɣrafo] *nm (esp AM)* gramophone, phonograph (*US*).

fonología [fonolo'xia] *nf* phonology.

fontanería [fontane'ria] *nf* plumbing.

fontanero [fonta'nero] _nm_ plumber.

footing ['futin] _nm_ jogging; **hacer** ~ to jog.

F.O.P. [fop] _nfpl abr (ESP)_ = **Fuerzas del Orden Público.**

forajido [fora'xiðo] _nm_ outlaw.

foráneo, a [fo'raneo, a] _adj_ foreign ♦ _nm/f_ outsider.

forastero, a [foras'tero, a] _nm/f_ stranger.

forcé [for'θe] _vb V_ **forzar.**

forcejear [forθexe'ar] _vi (luchar)_ to struggle.

forcemos [for'θemos] _etc vb V_ **forzar.**

fórceps ['forθeps] _nm inv_ forceps.

forense [fo'rense] _adj_ forensic ♦ _nm/f_ pathologist.

forestal [fores'tal] _adj_ forest _cpd._

forjar [for'xar] _vt_ to forge; _(formar)_ to form.

forma ['forma] _nf (figura)_ form, shape; _(molde)_ mould, pattern; _(MED)_ fitness; _(método)_ way, means; **estar en** ~ to be fit; ~ **de pago** _(COM)_ method of payment; **las** ~**s** the conventions; **de** ~ **que** ... so that ...; **de todas** ~**s** in any case.

formación [forma'θjon] _nf (gen)_ formation; _(enseñanza)_ training; ~ **profesional** vocational training; ~ **fuera del trabajo** off-the-job training; ~ **en el trabajo** _o_ **sobre la práctica** on-the-job training.

formal [for'mal] _adj (gen)_ formal; _(fig: persona)_ serious; (: _de fiar)_ reliable; _(conducta)_ steady.

formalice [forma'liθe] _etc vb V_ **formalizar.**

formalidad [formali'ðað] _nf_ formality; seriousness; reliability; steadiness.

formalizar [formali'θar] _vt_ to formalize; _(plan)_ to draw up; _(situación)_ to put in order, regularize; ~**se** _vr_ _(situación)_ to be put in order, be regularized.

formar [for'mar] _vt (componer)_ to form, shape; _(constituir)_ to make up, constitute; _(ESCOL)_ to train, educate ♦ _vi (MIL)_ to fall in; _(DEPORTE)_ to line up; ~**se** _vr (ESCOL)_ to be trained _(o educated)_; _(cobrar forma)_ to form, take form; _(desarrollarse)_ to develop.

formatear [formate'ar] _vt (INFORM)_ to format.

formateo [forma'teo] _nm (INFORM)_ formatting.

formato [for'mato] _nm (INFORM)_: **sin** ~ _(disco, texto)_ unformatted; ~ **de registro** record format.

formidable [formi'ðaβle] _adj (temible)_ formidable; _(asombroso)_ tremendous.

fórmula ['formula] _nf_ formula.

formular [formu'lar] _vt (queja)_ to lodge; _(petición)_ to draw up; _(pregunta)_ to pose, formulate; _(idea)_ to formulate.

formulario [formu'larjo] _nm_ form; ~ **de solicitud/de pedido** _(COM)_ application/order form; **llenar un** ~ to fill in a form; ~ **contínuo desplegable** _(INFORM)_ fanfold paper.

fornicar [forni'kar] _vi_ to fornicate.

fornido, a [for'niðo, a] _adj_ well-built.

fornique [for'nike] _etc vb V_ **fornicar.**

foro ['foro] _nm (gen)_ forum; _(JUR)_ court.

forofo, a [fo'rofo, a] _nm/f_ fan.

FORPPA ['forpa] _nm abr (ESP)_ = _Fondo de Ordenación y Regulación de Productos y Precios Agrarios._

FORPRONU [for'pronu] _nf abr_ (= _Fuerza de Protección de las Naciones Unidas)_ UNPROFOR.

forrado, a [fo'rraðo, a] _adj (ropa)_ lined; _(fam)_ well-heeled.

forrar [fo'rrar] _vt (abrigo)_ to line; _(libro)_ to cover; _(coche)_ to upholster; ~**se** _vr (fam)_ to line one's pockets.

forro ['forro] _nm (de cuaderno)_ cover; _(costura)_ lining; _(de sillón)_ upholstery; ~ **polar** fleece.

fortalecer [fortale'θer] _vt_ to strengthen; ~**se** _vr_ to fortify o.s.; _(opinión etc)_ to become stronger.

fortaleza [forta'leθa] _nf (MIL)_ fortress, stronghold; _(fuerza)_ strength; _(determinación)_ resolution.

fortalezca [forta'leθka] _etc vb V_ **fortalecer.**

fortificar [fortifi'kar] _vt_ to fortify; _(fig)_ to strengthen.

fortifique [forti'fike] _etc vb V_ **fortificar.**

fortísimo, a [for'tisimo, a] _adj superlativo de_ **fuerte.**

fortuito, a [for'twito, a] _adj_ accidental, chance _cpd._

fortuna [for'tuna] _nf (suerte)_ fortune, (good) luck; _(riqueza)_ fortune, wealth.

forzar [for'θar] _vt (puerta)_ to force (open); _(compeler)_ to compel; _(violar)_ to rape; _(ojos etc)_ to strain.

forzoso, a [for'θoso, a] _adj_ necessary; _(inevitable)_ inescapable; _(obligatorio)_ compulsory.

forzudo, a [for'θuðo, a] _adj_ burly.

fosa ['fosa] _nf (sepultura)_ grave; _(en tierra)_ pit; _(MED)_ cavity; ~**s nasales** nostrils.

fosfato [fos'fato] _nm_ phosphate.

fosforescente [fosfores'θente] _adj_ phosphorescent.

fósforo ['fosforo] _nm (QUÍMICA)_ phosphorus; _(esp AM: cerilla)_ match.

fósil [fo'sil] _adj_ fossil, fossilized ♦ _nm_ fossil.

foso ['foso] _nm_ ditch; _(TEAT)_ pit; _(AUTO)_: ~

de reconocimiento inspection pit.
foto ['foto] *nf* photo, snap(shot); **sacar una**
  ~ to take a photo o picture.
fotocopia [foto'kopja] *nf* photocopy.
fotocopiadora [fotokopja'ðora] *nf*
  photocopier.
fotocopiar [fotoko'pjar] *vt* to photocopy.
fotogénico, a [foto'xeniko, a] *adj*
  photogenic.
fotografía [fotoɣra'fia] *nf* (*arte*)
  photography; (*una* ~) photograph.
fotografiar [fotoɣra'fjar] *vt* to photograph.
fotógrafo, a [fo'toɣrafo, a] *nm/f*
  photographer.
fotomatón [fotoma'ton] *nm* (*cabina*) photo
  booth.
fotómetro [fo'tometro] *nm* (*FOTO*) light
  meter.
fotonovela [fotono'ßela] *nf* photo-story.
foulard [fu'lar] *nm* (head)scarf.
FP *nf abr* (*ESP: ESCOL, COM*) = *Formación
  Profesional* ♦ *nm abr* (*POL*) = *Frente Popular*.
FPLP *nm abr* (*POL*: = *Frente Popular para la
  Liberación de Palestina*) PFLP.
Fr. *abr* (= *Fray, franco*) Fr.
frac [frak], *pl* **fracs** *o* **fraques** ['frakes] *nm*
  dress coat, tails.
fracasar [fraka'sar] *vi* (*gen*) to fail; (*plan
  etc*) to fall through.
fracaso [fra'kaso] *nm* (*desgracia, revés*)
  failure; (*de negociaciones etc*) collapse,
  breakdown.
fracción [frak'θjon] *nf* fraction; (*POL*)
  faction, splinter group.
fraccionamiento [fraksjona'mjento] *nm*
  (*AM*) housing estate.
fractura [frak'tura] *nf* fracture, break.
fragancia [fra'xanθja] *nf* (*olor*) fragrance,
  perfume.
fragante [fra'xante] *adj* fragrant, scented.
fraganti [fra'xanti]: **in** ~ *adv*: **coger a algn
  in** ~ to catch sb red-handed.
fragata [fra'xata] *nf* frigate.
frágil ['fraxil] *adj* (*débil*) fragile; (*COM*)
  breakable; (*fig*) frail, delicate.
fragilidad [fraxili'ðað] *nf* fragility; (*de
  persona*) frailty.
fragmento [fraɣ'mento] *nm* fragment;
  (*pedazo*) piece; (*de discurso*) excerpt; (*de
  canción*) snatch.
fragor [fra'xor] *nm* (*ruido intenso*) din.
fragua ['fraɣwa] *nf* forge.
fraguar [fra'xwar] *vt* to forge; (*fig*) to
  concoct ♦ *vi* to harden.
fragüe ['fraɣwe] *etc vb V* **fraguar**.
fraile ['fraile] *nm* (*REL*) friar; (: *monje*)
  monk.
frambuesa [fram'bwesa] *nf* raspberry.

francés, esa [fran'θes, esa] *adj* French
  ♦ *nm/f* Frenchman/woman ♦ *nm* (*LING*)
  French.
Francia ['franθja] *nf* France.
franco, a ['franko, a] *adj* (*cándido*) frank,
  open; (*COM: exento*) free ♦ *nm* (*moneda*)
  franc; ~ **de derechos** duty-free; ~ **al
  costado del buque** (*COM*) free alongside
  ship; ~ **puesto sobre vagón** (*COM*) free
  on rail; ~ **a bordo** free on board.
francotirador, a [frankotira'ðor, a] *nm/f*
  sniper.
franela [fra'nela] *nf* flannel.
franja ['franxa] *nf* fringe; (*de uniforme*)
  stripe; (*de tierra etc*) strip.
franquear [franke'ar] *vt* (*camino*) to clear;
  (*carta, paquete*) to frank, stamp; (*obstáculo*) to overcome; (*COM etc*) to free, exempt.
franqueo [fran'keo] *nm* postage.
franqueza [fran'keθa] *nf* frankness.
franquicia [fran'kiθja] *nf* exemption; ~ **aduanera** exemption from customs duties.
franquismo [fran'kismo] *nm*: **el** ~ (*sistema*)
  the Franco system; (*período*) the Franco
  years; *see boxed note*.

FRANQUISMO

*Both the political reign and style of
government of Francisco Franco (from the
end of the Spanish Civil War in 1939 until
his death in 1975) are commonly called*
franquismo. *The General was a powerful,
authoritarian, right-wing dictator, who
promoted traditional Catholic values and
self-sufficiency. From the 1960s on, Spain
gradually opened its doors to the outside
world and this coincided with a period of
economic growth and the rise of internal
political opposition. On Franco's death
Spain became a democratic constitutional
monarchy.*

---

franquista [fran'kista] *adj* pro-Franco
  ♦ *nm/f* supporter of Franco.
frasco ['frasko] *nm* bottle, flask; ~ **al vacío**
  (vacuum) flask.
frase ['frase] *nf* sentence; (*locución*)
  phrase, expression; ~ **hecha** set phrase.
fraternal [frater'nal] *adj* brotherly,
  fraternal.
fraude ['frauðe] *nm* (*cualidad*) dishonesty;
  (*acto*) fraud, swindle.
fraudulento, a [frauðu'lento, a] *adj*
  fraudulent.
frazada [fra'saða] *nf* (*AM*) blanket.
frecuencia [fre'kwenθja] *nf* frequency; **con**
  ~ frequently, often; ~ **de red** (*INFORM*)

mains frequency; ~ **del reloj** (*INFORM*) clock speed; ~ **telefónica** voice frequency.

frecuentar [frekwen'tar] *vt* (*lugar*) to frequent; (*persona*) to see frequently *o* often; ~ **la buena sociedad** to mix in high society.

frecuente [fre'kwente] *adj* frequent; (*costumbre*) common; (*vicio*) rife.

fregadero [freɣa'ðero] *nm* (kitchen) sink.

fregado, a [fre'gaðo, a] *adj* (*AM fam!*) damn, bloody (*!*).

fregar [fre'ɣar] *vt* (*frotar*) to scrub; (*platos*) to wash (up); (*AM*) to annoy.

fregón, ona [fre'ɣon, ona] *adj* = **fregado** ♦ *nf* (*utensilio*) mop; (*pey: sirvienta*) skivvy.

fregué [fre'ɣe], **freguemos** [fre'ɣemos] *etc vb V* **fregar**.

freidora [frei'ðora] *nf* deep-fat fryer.

freír [fre'ir] *vt* to fry.

fréjol ['frexol] *nm* = **frijol**.

frenar [fre'nar] *vt* to brake; (*fig*) to check.

frenazo [fre'naθo] *nm*: **dar un** ~ to brake sharply.

frenesí [frene'si] *nm* frenzy.

frenético, a [fre'netiko, a] *adj* frantic; **ponerse** ~ to lose one's head.

freno ['freno] *nm* (*TEC, AUTO*) brake; (*de cabalgadura*) bit; (*fig*) check.

frente ['frente] *nm* (*ARQ, MIL, POL*) front; (*de objeto*) front part ♦ *nf* forehead, brow; ~ **de batalla** battle front; **hacer** ~ **común con algn** to make common cause with sb; ~ **a** in front of; (*en situación opuesta de*) opposite; **chocar de** ~ to crash head-on; **hacer** ~ **a** to face up to.

fresa ['fresa] *nf* (*ESP: fruta*) strawberry; (*de dentista*) drill.

fresco, a ['fresko, a] *adj* (*nuevo*) fresh; (*huevo*) newly-laid; (*frío*) cool; (*descarado*) cheeky, bad-mannered ♦ *nm* (*aire*) fresh air; (*ARTE*) fresco; (*AM: bebida*) fruit juice *o* drink ♦ *nm/f* (*fam*) shameless person; (*persona insolente*) impudent person; **tomar el** ~ to get some fresh air; **¡qué** ~! what a cheek!

frescor [fres'kor] *nm* freshness.

frescura [fres'kura] *nf* freshness; (*descaro*) cheek, nerve; (*calma*) calmness.

fresno ['fresno] *nm* ash (tree).

fresón [fre'son] *nm* strawberry.

frialdad [frjal'dað] *nf* (*gen*) coldness; (*indiferencia*) indifference.

fricción [frik'θjon] *nf* (*gen*) friction; (*acto*) rub(bing); (*MED*) massage; (*POL, fig etc*) friction, trouble.

friega ['frjeɣa] *etc*, **friegue** ['frjeɣe] *etc vb V* **fregar**.

friendo [fri'endo] *etc vb V* **freír**.

frigidez [frixi'ðeθ] *nf* frigidity.

frígido, a ['frixiðo, a] *adj* frigid.

frigorífico, a [friɣo'rifiko, a] *adj* refrigerating ♦ *nm* refrigerator; (*camión*) freezer lorry *o* truck (*US*); **instalación frigorífica** cold-storage plant.

frijol [fri'xol], **fríjol** ['frixol] *nm* kidney bean.

frió [fri'o] *vb V* **freír**.

frío, a ['frio, a] *etc vb V* **freír** ♦ *adj* cold; (*fig: indiferente*) unmoved, indifferent; (*poco entusiasta*) chilly ♦ *nm* cold(ness); indifference; **¡qué** ~! how cold it is!

friolento, a [frjo'lento, a] (*AM*), **friolero, a** [frjo'lero, a] *adj* sensitive to cold.

frito, a ['frito, a] *pp de* **freír** ♦ *adj* fried ♦ *nm* fry; **me trae** ~ **ese hombre** I'm sick and tired of that man; ~**s variados** mixed grill.

frívolo, a ['friβolo, a] *adj* frivolous.

frondoso, a [fron'doso, a] *adj* leafy.

frontal [fron'tal] *nm*: **choque** ~ head-on collision.

frontera [fron'tera] *nf* frontier; (*línea divisoria*) border; (*zona*) frontier area.

fronterizo, a [fronte'riθo, a] *adj* frontier *cpd*; (*contiguo*) bordering.

frontón [fron'ton] *nm* (*DEPORTE: cancha*) pelota court; (: *juego*) pelota.

frotar [fro'tar] *vt* to rub; (*fósforo*) to strike; ~**se** *vr*: ~**se las manos** to rub one's hands.

frs. *abr* (= *francos*) fr.

fructífero, a [fruk'tifero, a] *adj* productive, fruitful.

frugal [fru'ɣal] *adj* frugal.

fruncir [frun'θir] *vt* (*COSTURA*) to gather; (*ceño*) to frown; (*labios*) to purse.

frunza ['frunθa] *etc vb V* **fruncir**.

frustración [frustra'θjon] *nf* frustration.

frustrar [frus'trar] *vt* to frustrate; ~**se** *vr* to be frustrated; (*plan etc*) to fail.

fruta ['fruta] *nf* fruit.

frutal [fru'tal] *adj* fruit-bearing, fruit *cpd* ♦ *nm*: (*árbol*) ~ fruit tree.

frutería [frute'ria] *nf* fruit shop.

frutero, a [fru'tero, a] *adj* fruit *cpd* ♦ *nm/f* fruiterer ♦ *nm* fruit dish *o* bowl.

frutilla [fru'tiʎa] *nf* (*AM*) strawberry.

fruto ['fruto] *nm* (*BOT*) fruit; (*fig: resultado*) result, outcome; ~**s secos** ≈ nuts and raisins.

FSLN *nm abr* (*POL: Nicaragua*) = *Frente Sandinista de Liberación Nacional*.

fue [fwe] *vb V* **ser**, **ir**.

fuego ['fweɣo] *nm* (*gen*) fire; (*CULIN*: *gas*) burner, ring; (*MIL*) fire; (*fig*: *pasión*) fire, passion; **~ amigo** friendly fire; **~s artificiales** *o* **de artificio** fireworks; **prender ~ a** to set fire to; **a ~ lento** on a low flame *o* gas; **¡alto el ~!** cease fire!; **estar entre dos ~s** to be in the crossfire; **¿tienes ~?** have you (got) a light?

fuelle ['fweʎe] *nm* bellows *pl*.

fuel-oil [fuel'oil] *nm* paraffin (*BRIT*), kerosene (*US*).

fuente ['fwente] *nf* fountain; (*manantial*, *fig*) spring; (*origen*) source; (*plato*) large dish; **~ de alimentación** (*INFORM*) power supply; **de ~ desconocida/fidedigna** from an unknown/reliable source.

fuera ['fwera] *etc vb V* **ser, ir** ♦ *adv* out(side); (*en otra parte*) away; (*excepto, salvo*) except, save ♦ *prep*: **~ de** outside; (*fig*) besides; **~ de alcance** out of reach; **~ de combate** out of action; (*boxeo*) knocked out; **~ de sí** beside o.s.; **por ~** (on the) outside; **los de ~** strangers, newcomers; **estar ~** (*en el extranjero*) to be abroad.

fuera-borda [fwera'βorða] *nm inv* outboard engine *o* motor.

fuerce ['fwerθe] *etc vb V* **forzar**.

fuereño, a [fwe'reɲo, a] *nm/f* (*AM*) outsider.

fuero ['fwero] *nm* (*carta municipal*) municipal charter; (*leyes locales*) local *o* regional law code; (*privilegio*) privilege; (*autoridad*) jurisdiction; (*fig*): **en mi** *etc* **~ interno** in my *etc* heart of hearts ..., deep down ....

fuerte ['fwerte] *adj* strong; (*golpe*) hard; (*ruido*) loud; (*comida*) rich; (*lluvia*) heavy; (*dolor*) intense ♦ *adv* strongly; hard; loud(ly) ♦ *nm* (*MIL*) fort, strongpoint; (*fig*): **el canto no es mi ~** singing is not my strong point.

fuerza ['fwerθa] *etc vb V* **forzar** ♦ *nf* (*fortaleza*) strength; (*TEC, ELEC*) power; (*coacción*) force; (*violencia*) violence; (*MIL*: *tb*: **~s**) forces *pl*; **~ de arrastre** (*TEC*) pulling power; **~ de brazos** manpower; **~ mayor** force majeure; **~ bruta** brute force; **~s armadas** (**FF.AA.**) armed forces; **~ de Orden Público** (**F.O.P.**) police (forces); **~ vital** vitality; **a ~ de** by (dint of); **cobrar ~s** to recover one's strength; **tener ~s para** to have the strength to; **hacer algo a la ~** to be forced to do sth; **con ~ legal** (*COM*) legally binding; **a la ~**, **por ~** of necessity; **~ de voluntad** willpower.

fuete ['fwete] *nm* (*AM*) whip.

fuga ['fuɣa] *nf* (*huida*) flight, escape; (*de enamorados*) elopement; (*de gas etc*) leak; **~ de cerebros** (*fig*) brain drain.

fugarse [fu'ɣarse] *vr* to flee, escape.

fugaz [fu'ɣaθ] *adj* fleeting.

fugitivo, a [fuxi'tiβo, a] *adj* fugitive, fleeing ♦ *nm/f* fugitive.

fugue ['fuxe] *etc vb V* **fugarse**.

fui [fwi] *etc vb V* **ser, ir.**

fulano, a [fu'lano, a] *nm/f* so-and-so, what's-his-name.

fulgor [ful'xor] *nm* brilliance.

fulminante [fulmi'nante] *adj* (*pólvora*) fulminating; (*fig*: *mirada*) withering; (*MED*) fulminant; (*fam*) terrific, tremendous.

fulminar [fulmi'nar] *vt*: **caer fulminado por un rayo** to be struck down by lightning; **~ a algn con la mirada** to look daggers at sb.

fumador, a [fuma'ðor, a] *nm/f* smoker; **no ~** non-smoker.

fumar [fu'mar] *vt, vi* to smoke; **~se** *vr* (*disipar*) to squander; **~ en pipa** to smoke a pipe.

fumigar [fumi'ɣar] *vt* to fumigate.

funámbulo, a [fu'nambulo, a],

funambulista [funambu'lista] *nm/f* tightrope walker.

función [fun'θjon] *nf* function; (*de puesto*) duties *pl*; (*TEAT etc*) show; **entrar en funciones** to take up one's duties; **~ de tarde/de noche** matinée/evening performance.

funcional [funθjo'nal] *adj* functional.

funcionamiento [funθjona'mjento] *nm* functioning; (*TEC*) working; **en ~** (*COM*) on stream; **entrar en ~** to come into operation.

funcionar [funθjo'nar] *vi* (*gen*) to function; (*máquina*) to work; **"no funciona"** "out of order".

funcionario, a [funθjo'narjo, a] *nm/f* official; (*público*) civil servant.

funda ['funda] *nf* (*gen*) cover; (*de almohada*) pillowcase; **~ protectora del disco** (*INFORM*) disk-jacket.

fundación [funda'θjon] *nf* foundation.

fundado, a [fun'daðo, a] *adj* (*justificado*) well-founded.

fundamental [fundamen'tal] *adj* fundamental, basic.

fundamentalismo [fundamenta'lismo] *nm* fundamentalism.

fundamentalista [fundamenta'lista] *adj*, *nm/f* fundamentalist.

fundamentar [fundamen'tar] *vt* (*poner base*) to lay the foundations of; (*establecer*) to found; (*fig*) to base.

fundamento [funda'mento] *nm* (*base*) foundation; (*razón*) grounds; **eso carece de** ~ that is groundless.

fundar [fun'dar] *vt* to found; (*crear*) to set up; (*fig: basar*): ~ **(en)** to base *o* found (on); ~**se** *vr:* ~**se en** to be founded on.

fundición [fundi'θjon] *nf* (*acción*) smelting; (*fábrica*) foundry; (*TIP*) fount (*BRIT*), font.

fundir [fun'dir] *vt* (*gen*) to fuse; (*metal*) to smelt, melt down; (*COM*) to merge; (*estatua*) to cast; ~**se** *vr* (*colores etc*) to merge, blend; (*unirse*) to fuse together; (*ELEC: fusible, lámpara etc*) to blow; (*nieve etc*) to melt.

fúnebre ['funeßre] *adj* funeral *cpd*, funereal.

funeral [fune'ral] *nm* funeral.

funeraria [fune'rarja] *nf* undertaker's (*BRIT*), mortician's (*US*).

funesto, a [fu'nesto, a] *adj* ill-fated; (*desastroso*) fatal.

fungir [fun'xir] *vi:* ~ **de** (*AM*) to act as.

furgón [fur'ɣon] *nm* wagon.

furgoneta [furɣo'neta] *nf* (*AUTO, COM*) (transit) van (*BRIT*), pickup (truck) (*US*).

furia ['furja] *nf* (*ira*) fury; (*violencia*) violence.

furibundo, a [furi'ßundo, a] *adj* furious.

furioso, a [fu'rjoso, a] *adj* (*iracundo*) furious; (*violento*) violent.

furor [fu'ror] *nm* (*cólera*) rage; (*pasión*) frenzy, passion; **hacer** ~ to be a sensation.

furtivo, a [fur'tißo, a] *adj* furtive ♦ *nm* poacher.

furúnculo [fu'runkulo] *nm* (*MED*) boil.

fuselaje [fuse'laxe] *nm* fuselage.

fusible [fu'sißle] *nm* fuse.

fusil [fu'sil] *nm* rifle.

fusilamiento [fusila'mjento] *nm* (*JUR*) execution by firing squad.

fusilar [fusi'lar] *vt* to shoot.

fusión [fu'sjon] *nf* (*gen*) melting; (*unión*) fusion; (*COM*) merger, amalgamation.

fusionar [fusjo'nar] *vt* to fuse (together); (*COM*) to merge; ~**se** *vr* (*COM*) to merge, amalgamate.

fusta ['fusta] *nf* (*látigo*) riding crop.

fútbol ['futßol] *nm* football.

futbolín [futßo'lin] *nm* table football.

futbolista [futßo'lista] *nm/f* footballer.

fútil ['futil] *adj* trifling.

futilidad [futili'ðað], **futileza** [futi'leθa] *nf* triviality.

futón [fu'ton] *nm* futon.

futuro, a [fu'turo, a] *adj* future ♦ *nm* future; (*LING*) future tense; ~**s** *nmpl* (*COM*) futures.

G g

G, g [xe] *nf* (*letra*) G, g; **G de Gerona** G for George.

g/ *abr* = **giro**.

gabacho, a [ga'ßatʃo, a] *adj* Pyrenean; (*fam*) Frenchified ♦ *nm/f* Pyrenean villager; (*fam*) Frenchy.

gabán [ga'ßan] *nm* overcoat.

gabardina [gaßar'ðina] *nf* (*tela*) gabardine; (*prenda*) raincoat.

gabinete [gaßi'nete] *nm* (*POL*) cabinet; (*estudio*) study; (*de abogados etc*) office; ~ **de consulta/de lectura** consulting/reading room.

gacela [ga'θela] *nf* gazelle.

gaceta [ga'θeta] *nf* gazette.

gacetilla [gaθe'tiʎa] *nf* (*en periódico*) news in brief; (*de personalidades*) gossip column.

gachas ['gatʃas] *nfpl* porridge *sg*.

gacho, a ['gatʃo, a] *adj* (*encorvado*) bent down; (*orejas*) drooping.

gaditano, a [gaði'tano, a] *adj* of *o* from Cadiz ♦ *nm/f* native *o* inhabitant of Cadiz.

GAE *nm abr* (*ESP MIL*) = **Grupo Aéreo Embarcado**.

gaélico, a [ga'eliko, a] *adj* Gaelic ♦ *nm/f* Gael ♦ *nm* (*LING*) Gaelic.

gafar [ga'far] *vt* (*fam: traer mala suerte*) to put a jinx on.

gafas ['gafas] *nfpl* glasses; ~ **oscuras** dark glasses; ~ **de sol** sunglasses.

gafe ['gafe] *adj:* **ser** ~ to be jinxed ♦ *nm* (*fam*) jinx.

gaita ['gaita] *nf* flute; (~ *gallega*) bagpipes *pl*; (*dificultad*) bother; (*cosa engorrosa*) tough job.

gajes ['gaxes] *nmpl* (*salario*) pay *sg*; **los** ~ **del oficio** occupational hazards; ~ **y emolumentos** perquisites.

gajo ['gaxo] *nm* (*gen*) bunch; (*de árbol*) bough; (*de naranja*) segment.

gala ['gala] *nf* full dress; (*fig: lo mejor*) cream, flower; ~**s** *nfpl* finery *sg*; **estar de** ~ to be in one's best clothes; **hacer** ~ **de** to display, show off; **tener algo a** ~ to be proud of sth.

galaico, a [ga'laiko, a] *adj* Galician.

galán [ga'lan] *nm* lover, gallant; (*hombre*

atractivo) ladies' man; (*TEAT*): **primer ~** leading man.

galante [ga'lante] *adj* gallant; (*atento*) charming; (*cortés*) polite.

galantear [galante'ar] *vt* (*hacer la corte a*) to court, woo.

galanteo [galan'teo] *nm* (*coqueteo*) flirting; (*de pretendiente*) wooing.

galantería [galante'ria] *nf* (*caballerosidad*) gallantry; (*cumplido*) politeness; (*piropo*) compliment.

galápago [ga'lapaɣo] *nm* (*ZOOL*) freshwater tortoise.

galardón [galar'ðon] *nm* award, prize.

galardonar [galarðo'nar] *vt* (*premiar*) to reward; (*una obra*) to award a prize for.

galaxia [ga'laksja] *nf* galaxy.

galbana [gal'ßana] *nf* (*pereza*) sloth, laziness.

galeote [gale'ote] *nm* galley slave.

galera [ga'lera] *nf* (*nave*) galley; (*carro*) wagon; (*MED*) hospital ward; (*TIP*) galley.

galería [gale'ria] *nf* (*gen*) gallery; (*balcón*) veranda(h); (*de casa*) corridor; (*fam: público*) audience; **~ secreta** secret passage.

Gales ['gales] *nm*: **(el País de) ~** Wales.

galés, esa [ga'les, esa] *adj* Welsh ♦ *nm/f* Welshman/woman ♦ *nm* (*LING*) Welsh.

galgo, a ['galɣo, a] *nm/f* greyhound.

Galia ['galja] *nf* Gaul.

Galicia [ga'liθja] *nf* Galicia.

galicismo [gali'θismo] *nm* gallicism.

Galilea [gali'lea] *nf* Galilee.

galimatías [galima'tias] *nm inv* (*asunto*) rigmarole; (*lenguaje*) gibberish, nonsense.

gallardía [gaʎar'ðia] *nf* (*galantería*) dash; (*gracia*) gracefulness; (*valor*) bravery; (*elegancia*) elegance; (*nobleza*) nobleness.

gallego, a [ga'ʎeɣo, a] *adj* Galician; (*AM pey*) Spanish ♦ *nm/f* Galician; (*AM pey*) Spaniard ♦ *nm* (*LING*) Galician; *V tb* **lenguas cooficiales**.

galleta [ga'ʎeta] *nf* biscuit; (*fam: bofetada*) whack, slap.

gallina [ga'ʎina] *nf* hen ♦ *nm* (*fam*) coward; **~ ciega** blind man's buff; **~ clueca** broody hen.

gallinazo [gaʎi'naso] *nm* (*AM*) turkey buzzard.

gallinero [gaʎi'nero] *nm* (*criadero*) henhouse; (*TEAT*) gods *sg*, top gallery; (*voces*) hubbub.

gallo ['gaʎo] *nm* cock, rooster; (*MUS*) false *o* wrong note; (*cambio de voz*) break in the voice; **en menos que canta un ~** in an instant.

galo, a ['galo, a] *adj* Gallic; (= *francés*) French ♦ *nm/f* Gaul.

galón [ga'lon] *nm* (*COSTURA*) braid; (*MIL*) stripe; (*medida*) gallon.

galopante [galo'pante] *adj* galloping.

galopar [galo'par] *vi* to gallop.

galope [ga'lope] *nm* gallop; **al ~** (*fig*) in great haste; **a ~ tendido** at full gallop.

galvanice [galßa'niθe] *etc vb V* **galvanizar**.

galvanizar [galßani'θar] *vt* to galvanize.

gama ['gama] *nf* (*MUS*) scale; (*fig*) range; (*ZOOL*) doe.

gamba ['gamba] *nf* prawn.

gamberrada [gambe'rraða] *nf* act of hooliganism.

gamberro, a [gam'berro, a] *nm/f* hooligan, lout.

gamo ['gamo] *nm* (*ZOOL*) buck.

gamuza [ga'muθa] *nf* chamois; (*bayeta*) duster; (*AM: piel*) suede.

gana ['gana] *nf* (*deseo*) desire, wish; (*apetito*) appetite; (*voluntad*) will; (*añoranza*) longing; **de buena ~** willingly; **de mala ~** reluctantly; **me dan ~s de** I feel like, I want to; **tener ~s de** to feel like; **no me da la (real) ~** I don't (damned well) want to; **son ~s de molestar** they're just trying to be awkward.

ganadería [ganaðe'ria] *nf* (*ganado*) livestock; (*ganado vacuno*) cattle *pl*; (*cría, comercio*) cattle raising.

ganadero, a [gana'ðero, a] *adj* stock *cpd* ♦ *nm* stockman.

ganado [ga'naðo] *nm* livestock; **~ caballar/cabrío** horses *pl*/goats *pl*; **~ lanar** *u* **ovejuno** sheep *pl*; **~ porcino/vacuno** pigs *pl*/cattle *pl*.

ganador, a [gana'ðor, a] *adj* winning ♦ *nm/f* winner; (*ECON*) earner.

ganancia [ga'nanθja] *nf* (*lo ganado*) gain; (*aumento*) increase; (*beneficio*) profit; **~s** *nfpl* (*ingresos*) earnings; (*beneficios*) profit *sg*, winnings; **~s y pérdidas** profit and loss; **~ bruta/líquida** gross/net profit; **~s de capital** capital gains; **sacar ~ de** to draw profit from.

ganapán [gana'pan] *nm* (*obrero casual*) odd-job man; (*individuo tosco*) lout.

ganar [ga'nar] *vt* (*obtener*) to get, obtain; (*sacar ventaja*) to gain; (*COM*) to earn; (*DEPORTE, premio*) to win; (*derrotar*) to beat; (*alcanzar*) to reach; (*MIL: objetivo*) to take; (*apoyo*) to gain, win ♦ *vi* (*DEPORTE*) to win; **~se** *vr*: **~se la vida** to earn one's living; **se lo ha ganado** he deserves it; **~ tiempo** to gain time.

ganchillo [gan'tʃiʎo] *nm* (*para croché*)

crochet hook; (*arte*) crochet work.

gancho ['gantʃo] *nm* (*gen*) hook; (*colgador*) hanger; (*pey: revendedor*) tout; (*fam: atractivo*) sex appeal; (*BOXEO: golpe*) hook.

gandul, a [gan'dul, a] *adj, nm/f* good-for-nothing.

ganga ['ganga] *nf* (*cosa*) bargain; (*buena situación*) cushy job.

Ganges ['ganxes] *nm*: **el (Río)** ~ the Ganges.

ganglio ['gangljo] *nm* (*ANAT*) ganglion; (*MED*) swelling.

gangrena [gan'grena] *nf* gangrene.

gansada [gan'saða] *nf* (*fam*) stupid thing (to do).

ganso, a ['ganso, a] *nm/f* (*ZOOL*) gander/goose; (*fam*) idiot.

Gante ['gante] *nm* Ghent.

ganzúa [gan'θua] *nf* skeleton key ♦ *nm/f* burglar.

gañán [ga'ɲan] *nm* farmhand, farm labourer.

garabatear [garaβate'ar] *vt* to scribble, scrawl.

garabato [gara'βato] *nm* (*gancho*) hook; (*garfio*) grappling iron; (*escritura*) scrawl, scribble; (*fam*) sex appeal.

garaje [ga'raxe] *nm* garage.

garante [ga'rante] *adj* responsible ♦ *nm/f* guarantor.

garantía [garan'tia] *nf* guarantee; (*seguridad*) pledge; (*compromiso*) undertaking; (*JUR: caución*) warranty; **de máxima** ~ absolutely guaranteed; ~ **de trabajo** job security.

garantice [garan'tiθe] *etc vb V* **garantizar**.

garantizar [garanti'θar] *vt* (*hacerse responsable de*) to vouch for; (*asegurar*) to guarantee.

garbanzo [gar'βanθo] *nm* chickpea.

garbeo [gar'βeo] *nm*: **darse un** ~ to go for a walk.

garbo ['garβo] *nm* grace, elegance; (*aire*) jauntiness; (*de mujer*) glamour; **andar con** ~ to walk gracefully.

garboso, a [gar'βoso, a] *adj* graceful, elegant.

garete [ga'rete] *nm*: **irse al** ~ to go to the dogs.

garfio ['garfjo] *nm* grappling iron; (*gancho*) hook; (*ALPINISMO*) climbing iron.

gargajo [gar'xaxo] *nm* phlegm, sputum.

garganta [gar'xanta] *nf* (*interna*) throat; (*externa, de botella*) neck; (*GEO: barranco*) ravine; (*desfiladero*) narrow pass.

gargantilla [garxan'tiʎa] *nf* necklace.

gárgara ['garxara] *nf* gargle, gargling;

hacer ~s to gargle; **¡vete a hacer** ~s! (*fam*) go to blazes!

gárgola ['garxola] *nf* gargoyle.

garita [ga'rita] *nf* cabin, hut; (*MIL*) sentry box; (*puesto de vigilancia*) lookout post.

garito [ga'rito] *nm* (*lugar*) gaming house *o* den.

garra ['garra] *nf* (*de gato, TEC*) claw; (*de ave*) talon; (*fam*) hand, paw; (*fig: de canción etc*) bite; **caer en las** ~**s de algn** to fall into sb's clutches.

garrafa [ga'rrafa] *nf* carafe, decanter.

garrafal [garra'fal] *adj* enormous, terrific; (*error*) terrible.

garrapata [garra'pata] *nf* (*ZOOL*) tick.

garrotazo [garro'taθo] *nm* blow with a stick *o* club.

garrote [ga'rrote] *nm* (*palo*) stick; (*porra*) club, cudgel; (*suplicio*) garrotte.

garza ['garθa] *nf* heron.

gas [gas] *nm* gas; (*vapores*) fumes *pl*; ~**es de escape** exhaust (fumes).

gasa ['gasa] *nf* gauze; (*de pañal*) nappy liner.

gaseoso, a [gase'oso, a] *adj* gassy, fizzy ♦ *nf* lemonade, pop (*fam*).

gasoducto [gaso'ðukto] *nm* gas pipeline.

gasoil [ga'soil], **gasóleo** [ga'soleo] *nm* diesel (oil).

gasolina [gaso'lina] *nf* petrol, gas(oline) (*US*); ~ **sin plomo** unleaded petrol.

gasolinera [gasoli'nera] *nf* petrol (*BRIT*) *o* gas (*US*) station.

gastado, a [gas'taðo, a] *adj* (*ropa*) worn out; (*usado: frase etc*) trite.

gastar [gas'tar] *vt* (*dinero, tiempo*) to spend; (*consumir*) to use (up), consume; (*desperdiciar*) to waste; (*llevar*) to wear; ~**se** *vr* to wear out; (*terminarse*) to run out; (*estropearse*) to waste; ~ **bromas** to crack jokes; **¿qué número gastas?** what size (shoe) do you take?

gasto ['gasto] *nm* (*desembolso*) expenditure, spending; (*cantidad gastada*) outlay, expense; (*consumo, uso*) use; (*desgaste*) waste; ~**s** *nmpl* (*desembolsos*) expenses; (*cargos*) charges, costs; ~ **corriente** (*COM*) revenue expenditure; ~ **fijo** (*COM*) fixed charge; ~**s bancarios** bank charges; ~**s corrientes** running expenses; ~**s de distribución** (*COM*) distribution costs; ~**s generales** overheads; ~**s de mantenimiento** maintenance expenses; ~**s operacionales** operating costs; ~**s de tramitación** (*COM*) handling charge *sg*; ~**s vencidos** (*COM*) accrued charges; **cubrir** ~**s** to cover expenses; **meterse en**

~**s** to incur expense.

gastronomía [gastrono'mia] *nf*
gastronomy.

gata ['gata] *nf* (*ZOOL*) she-cat; **andar a** ~**s**
to go on all fours.

gatear [gate'ar] *vi* to go on all fours.

gatillo [ga'tiʎo] *nm* (*de arma de fuego*)
trigger; (*de dentista*) forceps.

gato ['gato] *nm* (*ZOOL*) cat; (*TEC*) jack; ~ **de
Angora** Angora cat; ~ **montés** wildcat;
dar a algn ~ **por liebre** to take sb in; **aquí
hay** ~ **encerrado** there's something fishy
here.

gatuno, a [ga'tuno, a] *adj* feline.

gaucho, a ['gautʃo, a] *adj, nm/f* gaucho.

gaveta [ga'ßeta] *nf* drawer.

gavilán [gaßi'lan] *nm* sparrowhawk.

gavilla [ga'ßiʎa] *nf* sheaf.

gaviota [ga'ßjota] *nf* seagull.

gay [ge] *adj, nm* gay, homosexual.

gazapo [ga'θapo] *nm* young rabbit.

gaznate [gaθ'nate] *nm* (*pescuezo*) gullet;
(*garganta*) windpipe.

gazpacho [gaθ'patʃo] *nm* gazpacho.

gel [xel] *nm* gel.

gelatina [xela'tina] *nf* jelly; (*polvos etc*)
gelatine.

gema ['xema] *nf* gem.

gemelo, a [xe'melo, a] *adj, nm/f* twin; ~**s**
nmpl (*de camisa*) cufflinks; ~**s de campo**
field glasses, binoculars; ~**s de teatro**
opera glasses.

gemido [xe'miðo] *nm* (*quejido*) moan,
groan; (*lamento*) wail, howl.

Géminis ['xeminis] *nm* (*ASTRO*) Gemini.

gemir [xe'mir] *vi* (*quejarse*) to moan, groan;
(*animal*) to whine; (*viento*) to howl.

gen [xen] *nm* gene.

gen. *abr* (*LING*) = **género; genitivo.**

gendarme [xen'darme] *nm* (*AM*)
policeman.

genealogía [xenealoꞌxia] *nf* genealogy.

generación [xenera'θjon] *nf* generation;
primera/segunda/tercera/cuarta ~
(*INFORM*) first/second/third/fourth
generation.

generado, a [xene'raðo, a] *adj* (*INFORM*): ~
por ordenador computer generated.

generador [xenera'ðor] *nm* generator; ~
de programas (*INFORM*) program
generator.

general [xene'ral] *adj* general; (*común*)
common; (*pey: corriente*) rife; (*frecuente*)
usual ♦ *nm* general; ~ **de brigada/de
división** brigadier-/major-general; **por lo
o en** ~ in general.

generalice [xenera'liθe] *etc vb V*
generalizar.

generalidad [xenerali'ðað] *nf* generality.

Generalitat [jenerali'tat] *nf regional
government of Catalonia*; ~ **Valenciana**
regional government of Valencia.

generalización [xeneraliθa'θjon] *nf*
generalization.

generalizar [xenerali'θar] *vt* to generalize;
~**se** *vr* to become generalized, spread;
(*difundirse*) to become widely known.

generalmente [xeneral'mente] *adv*
generally.

generar [xene'rar] *vt* to generate.

genérico, a [xe'neriko, a] *adj* generic.

género ['xenero] *nm* (*clase*) kind, sort;
(*tipo*) type; (*BIO*) genus; (*LING*) gender;
(*COM*) material; ~**s** *nmpl* (*productos*)
goods; ~ **humano** human race; ~ **chico**
(*zarzuela*) Spanish operetta; ~**s de punto**
knitwear *sg.*

generosidad [xenerosi'ðað] *nf* generosity.

generoso, a [xene'roso, a] *adj* generous.

genético, a [xe'netiko, a] *adj* genetic ♦ *nf*
genetics *sg.*

genial [xe'njal] *adj* inspired; (*idea*)
brilliant; (*afable*) genial.

genialidad [xenjali'ðað] *nf* (*singularidad*)
genius; (*acto genial*) stroke of genius; **es
una** ~ **suya** it's one of his brilliant ideas.

genio ['xenjo] *nm* (*carácter*) nature,
disposition; (*humor*) temper; (*facultad
creadora*) genius; **mal** ~ bad temper; ~
vivo quick *o* hot temper; **de mal** ~ bad-
tempered.

genital [xeni'tal] *adj* genital ♦ *nm*: ~**es**
genitals, genital organs.

genocidio [xeno'θiðjo] *nm* genocide.

Génova ['xenoßa] *nf* Genoa.

genovés, esa [xeno'ßes, esa] *adj, nm/f*
Genoese.

gente ['xente] *nf* (*personas*) people *pl*; (*raza*)
race; (*nación*) nation; (*parientes*)
relatives *pl*; ~ **bien/baja** posh/lower-
class people *pl*; ~ **menuda** (*niños*)
children *pl*; **es buena** ~ (*fam: esp AM*)
he's a good sort; **una** ~ **como Vd** (*AM*) a
person like you.

gentil [xen'til] *adj* (*elegante*) graceful;
(*encantador*) charming; (*REL*) gentile.

gentileza [xenti'leθa] *nf* grace; charm;
(*cortesía*) courtesy; **por** ~ **de** by courtesy
of.

gentilicio, a [xenti'liθjo, a] *adj* (*familiar*)
family *cpd.*

gentío [xen'tio] *nm* crowd, throng.

gentuza [xen'tuθa] *nf* (*pey: plebe*) rabble;
(*: chusma*) riffraff.

genuflexión [xenuflek'sjon] *nf*
genuflexion.

genuino, a [xe'nwino, a] *adj* genuine.
GEO ['xeo] *nmpl abr* (*ESP:* = *Grupos Especiales de Operaciones*) Special Police Units used in anti-terrorist operations etc.
geografía [xeoɣra'fia] *nf* geography.
geográfico, a [xeo'ɣrafiko, a] *adj* geographic(al).
geología [xeolo'xia] *nf* geology.
geólogo, a [xe'oloɣo, a] *nm/f* geologist.
geometría [xeome'tria] *nf* geometry.
geométrico, a [xeo'metriko, a] *adj* geometric(al).
Georgia [xe'orxja] *nf* Georgia.
georgiano, a [xeor'xjano, a] *adj, nm/f* Georgian ♦ *nm* (*LING*) Georgian.
geranio [xe'ranjo] *nm* (*BOT*) geranium.
gerencia [xe'renθja] *nf* management; (*cargo*) post of manager; (*oficina*) manager's office.
gerente [xe'rente] *nm/f* (*supervisor*) manager; (*jefe*) director.
geriatría [xerja'tria] *nf* (*MED*) geriatrics *sg*.
geriátrico, a [xer'jatriko, a] *adj* geriatric.
germano, a [xer'mano, a] *adj* German, Germanic ♦ *nm/f* German.
germen ['xermen] *nm* germ.
germinar [xermi'nar] *vi* to germinate; (*brotar*) to sprout.
gerundense [xerun'dense] *adj* of *o* from Gerona ♦ *nm/f* native *o* inhabitant of Gerona.
gerundio [xe'rundjo] *nm* (*LING*) gerund.
gestación [xesta'θjon] *nf* gestation.
gesticulación [xestikula'θjon] *nf* (*ademán*) gesticulation; (*mueca*) grimace.
gesticular [xestiku'lar] *vi* (*con ademanes*) to gesture; (*con muecas*) to make faces.
gestión [xes'tjon] *nf* management; (*diligencia, acción*) negotiation; **hacer las gestiones preliminares** to do the groundwork; ~ **de cartera** (*COM*) portfolio management; ~ **financiera** (*COM*) financial management; ~ **interna** (*INFORM*) housekeeping; ~ **de personal** personnel management; ~ **de riesgos** (*COM*) risk management.
gestionar [xestjo'nar] *vt* (*lograr*) to try to arrange; (*llevar*) to manage.
gesto ['xesto] *nm* (*mueca*) grimace; (*ademán*) gesture; **hacer ~s** to make faces.
gestor, a [xes'tor, a] *adj* managing ♦ *nm/f* manager; (*promotor*) promoter; (*agente*) business agent.
gestoría [xesto'ria] *nf* agency undertaking business with government departments, insurance companies etc.

Gibraltar [xiβral'tar] *nm* Gibraltar.
gibraltareño, a [xiβralta'reɲo, a] *adj* of *o* from Gibraltar ♦ *nm/f* native *o* inhabitant of Gibraltar.
gigante [xi'ɣante] *adj, nm/f* giant.
gijonés [xixo'nes, esa] *adj* of *o* from Gijón ♦ *nm/f* native *o* inhabitant of Gijón.
gilipollas [xili'poʎas] (*fam*) *adj inv* daft ♦ *nm/f* berk.
gilipollez [xilipo'ʎez] *nf* (*fam*): **es una ~** that's a load of crap (*!*); **decir gilipolleces** to talk crap (*!*).
gima ['xima] *etc vb V* **gemir**.
gimnasia [xim'nasja] *nf* gymnastics *pl*; **confundir la ~ con la magnesia** to get things mixed up.
gimnasio [xim'nasjo] *nm* gym(nasium).
gimnasta [xim'nasta] *nm/f* gymnast.
gimotear [ximote'ar] *vi* to whine, whimper; (*lloriquear*) to snivel.
Ginebra [xi'neβra] *n* Geneva.
ginebra [xi'neβra] *nf* gin.
ginecología [xinekolo'xia] *nf* gyn(a)ecology.
ginecológico, a [xineko'loxiko, a] *adj* gyn(a)ecological.
ginecólogo, a [xine'koloɣo, a] *nm/f* gyn(a)ecologist.
gira ['xira] *nf* tour, trip.
girar [xi'rar] *vt* (*dar la vuelta*) to turn (around); (: *rápidamente*) to spin; (*COM: giro postal*) to draw; (*comerciar: letra de cambio*) to issue ♦ *vi* to turn (round); (*dar vueltas*) to rotate; (*rápido*) to spin; **la conversación giraba en torno a las elecciones** the conversation centred on the election; ~ **en descubierto** to overdraw.
giratorio, a [xira'torjo, a] *adj* (*gen*) revolving; (*puente*) swing *cpd*; (*silla*) swivel *cpd*.
giro ['xiro] *nm* (*movimiento*) turn, revolution; (*LING*) expression; (*COM*) draft; (*de sucesos*) trend, course; ~ **bancario** money order, bank giro; ~ **de existencias** (*COM*) stock turnover; ~ **postal** postal order.
gis [xis] *nm* (*AM*) chalk.
gitano, a [xi'tano, a] *adj, nm/f* gypsy.
glacial [gla'θjal] *adj* icy, freezing.
glaciar [gla'θjar] *nm* glacier.
glándula ['glandula] *nf* (*ANAT, BOT*) gland.
glicerina [gliθe'rina] *nf* (*TEC*) glycerin(e).
global [glo'βal] *adj* (*en conjunto*) global; (*completo*) total; (*investigación*) full; (*suma*) lump *cpd*.
globalización [gloβaliɣa'θjon] *nf* globalization.
globo ['gloβo] *nm* (*esfera*) globe, sphere;

(*aeróstato, juguete*) balloon.

glóbulo ['gloβulo] *nm* globule; (*ANAT*) corpuscle; ~ **blanco/rojo** white/red corpuscle.

gloria ['glorja] *nf* glory; (*fig*) delight; (*delicia*) bliss.

glorieta [glo'rjeta] *nf* (*de jardín*) bower, arbour, (*US*) arbor; (*AUTO*) roundabout (*BRIT*), traffic circle (*US*); (*plaza redonda*) circus; (*cruce*) junction.

glorificar [glorifi'kar] *vt* (*enaltecer*) to glorify, praise.

glorifique [glori'fike] *etc vb* V **glorificar**.

glorioso, a [glo'rjoso, a] *adj* glorious.

glosa ['glosa] *nf* comment; (*explicación*) gloss.

glosar [glo'sar] *vt* (*comentar*) to comment on.

glosario [glo'sarjo] *nm* glossary.

glotón, ona [glo'ton, ona] *adj* gluttonous, greedy ♦ *nm/f* glutton.

glotonería [glotone'ria] *nf* gluttony, greed.

glúteo ['gluteo] *nm* (*fam: nalga*) buttock.

gnomo ['nomo] *nm* gnome.

gobernación [goβerna'θjon] *nf* government, governing; (*POL*) Provincial Governor's office; **Ministro de la G~** Minister of the Interior, Home Secretary (*BRIT*).

gobernador, a [goβerna'ðor, a] *adj* governing ♦ *nm/f* governor.

gobernanta [goβer'nanta] *nf* (*esp AM: niñera*) governess.

gobernante [goβer'nante] *adj* governing ♦ *nm* ruler, governor ♦ *nf* (*en hotel etc*) housekeeper.

gobernar [goβer'nar] *vt* (*dirigir*) to guide, direct; (*POL*) to rule, govern ♦ *vi* to govern; (*NAUT*) to steer; ~ **mal** to misgovern.

gobierno [go'βjerno] *etc vb* V **gobernar** ♦ *nm* (*POL*) government; (*gestión*) management; (*dirección*) guidance, direction; (*NAUT*) steering; (*puesto*) governorship.

goce ['goθe] *etc vb* V **gozar** ♦ *nm* enjoyment.

godo, a ['goðo, a] *nm/f* Goth; (*AM pey*) Spaniard.

gol [gol] *nm* goal.

golear [gole'ar] *vt* (*marcar*) to score a goal against.

golf [golf] *nm* golf.

golfo, a ['golfo, a] *nm/f* (*pilluelo*) street urchin; (*vago*) tramp; (*gorrón*) loafer; (*gamberro*) lout ♦ *nm* (*GEO*) gulf ♦ *nf* (*fam: prostituta*) slut, whore, hooker (*US*).

golondrina [golon'drina] *nf* swallow.

golosina [golo'sina] *nf* titbit; (*dulce*) sweet.

goloso, a [go'loso, a] *adj* sweet-toothed; (*fam: glotón*) greedy.

golpe ['golpe] *nm* blow; (*de puño*) punch; (*de mano*) smack; (*de remo*) stroke; (*FÚTBOL*) kick; (*TENIS etc*) hit, shot; (*mala suerte*) misfortune; (*fam: atraco*) job, heist (*US*); (*fig: choque*) clash; **no dar** ~ to be bone idle; **de un** ~ with one blow; **de** ~ suddenly; ~ **(de estado)** coup (d'état); ~ **de gracia** coup de grâce (*tb fig*); ~ **de fortuna/maestro** stroke of luck/genius; **cerrar una puerta de** ~ to slam a door.

golpear [golpe'ar] *vt, vi* to strike, knock; (*asestar*) to beat; (*de puño*) to punch; (*golpetear*) to tap; (*mesa*) to bang.

golpista [gol'pista] *adj*: **intentona** ~ coup attempt ♦ *nm/f* participant in a coup (d'état).

golpiza [gol'pisa] *nf*: **dar una** ~ **a algn** (*AM*) to beat sb up.

goma ['goma] *nf* (*caucho*) rubber; (*elástico*) elastic; (*tira*) rubber o elastic (*BRIT*) band; (*fam: preservativo*) condom; (*droga*) hashish; (*explosivo*) plastic explosive; ~ **(de borrar)** eraser, rubber (*BRIT*); ~ **de mascar** chewing gum; ~ **de pegar** gum, glue.

goma-espuma [gomaes'puma] *nf* foam rubber.

gomina [go'mina] *nf* hair gel.

gomita [go'mita] *nf* rubber o elastic (*BRIT*) band.

góndola ['gondola] *nf* (*barco*) gondola; (*de tren*) goods wagon.

gordo, a ['gorðo, a] *adj* (*gen*) fat; (*persona*) plump; (*agua*) hard; (*fam*) enormous ♦ *nm/f* fat man o woman; **el (premio)** ~ (*en lotería*) first prize; **¡~!** (*fam*) fatty!

gordura [gor'ðura] *nf* fat; (*corpulencia*) fatness, stoutness.

gorgojo [gor'xoxo] *nm* (*insecto*) grub.

gorgorito [gorɣo'rito] *nm* (*gorjeo*) trill, warble.

gorila [go'rila] *nm* gorilla; (*fam*) tough, thug; (*guardaespaldas*) bodyguard.

gorjear [gorxe'ar] *vi* to twitter, chirp.

gorjeo [gor'xeo] *nm* twittering, chirping.

gorra ['gorra] *nf* (*gen*) cap; (*de niño*) bonnet; (*militar*) bearskin; ~ **de montar/ de paño/de punto/de visera** riding/ cloth/knitted/peaked cap; **andar** o **ir** o **vivir de** ~ to sponge, scrounge; **entrar de** ~ (*fam*) to gatecrash.

gorrión [go'rrjon] *nm* sparrow.

gorro ['gorro] *nm* cap; (*de niño, mujer*) bonnet; **estoy hasta el** ~ I am fed up.

gorrón, ona [go'rron, ona] *nm* pebble;

(*TEC*) pivot ♦ *nm/f* scrounger.

gorronear [gorrone'ar] *vi* (*fam*) to sponge, scrounge.

gota ['gota] *nf* (*gen*) drop; (*de pintura*) blob; (*de sudor*) bead; (*MED*) gout; ~ **a** ~ drop by drop; **caer a** ~**s** to drip.

gotear [gote'ar] *vi* to drip; (*escurrir*) to trickle; (*salirse*) to leak; (*cirio*) to gutter; (*lloviznar*) to drizzle.

gotera [go'tera] *nf* leak.

gótico, a ['gotiko, a] *adj* Gothic.

gozar [go'θar] *vi* to enjoy o.s.; ~ **de** (*disfrutar*) to enjoy; (*poseer*) to possess; ~ **de buena salud** to enjoy good health.

gozne ['goθne] *nm* hinge.

gozo ['goθo] *nm* (*alegría*) joy; (*placer*) pleasure; ¡**mi** ~ **en el pozo!** that's torn it!, just my luck!

g.p. *nm abr* (= *giro postal*) m.o.

gr. *abr* (= *gramo(s)*) g.

grabación [graβa'θjon] *nf* recording.

grabado, a [gra'βaðo, a] *adj* (*MUS*) recorded; (*en cinta*) taped, on tape ♦ *nm* print, engraving; ~ **al agua fuerte** etching; ~ **al aguatinta** aquatint; ~ **en cobre** copperplate; ~ **en madera** woodcut; ~ **rupestre** rock carving.

grabador, a [graβa'ðor, a] *nm/f* engraver ♦ *nf* tape-recorder; ~**a de cassettes** cassette recorder.

grabar [gra'βar] *vt* to engrave; (*discos, cintas*) to record; (*impresionar*) to impress.

gracejo [gra'θexo] *nm* (*humor*) wit, humour; (*elegancia*) grace.

gracia ['graθja] *nf* (*encanto*) grace, gracefulness; (*REL*) grace; (*chiste*) joke; (*humor*) humour, wit; ¡**muchas** ~**s!** thanks very much!; ~**s a** thanks to; **tener** ~ (*chiste etc*) to be funny; ¡**qué** ~! how funny!; (*irónico*) what a nerve!; **no me hace** ~ (*broma*) it's not funny; (*plan*) I am not too keen; **con** ~**s anticipadas/ repetidas** thanking you in advance/ again; **dar las** ~**s a algn por algo** to thank sb for sth.

grácil ['graθil] *adj* (*sutil*) graceful; (*delgado*) slender; (*delicado*) delicate.

gracioso, a [gra'θjoso, a] *adj* (*garboso*) graceful; (*chistoso*) funny; (*cómico*) comical; (*agudo*) witty; (*título*) ♦ *nm/f* (*TEAT*) comic character, fool; **su graciosa Majestad** His/Her Gracious Majesty.

grada ['graða] *nf* (*de escalera*) step; (*de anfiteatro*) tier, row; ~**s** *nfpl* (*de estadio*) terraces.

gradación [graða'θjon] *nf* gradation; (*serie*)

graded series.

gradería [graðe'ria] *nf* (*gradas*) (flight of) steps *pl*; (*de anfiteatro*) tiers *pl*, rows *pl*; ~ **cubierta** covered stand.

grado ['graðo] *nm* degree; (*etapa*) stage, step; (*nivel*) rate; (*de parentesco*) order of lineage; (*de aceite, vino*) grade; (*grada*) step; (*ESCOL*) class, year, grade (*US*); (*UNIV*) degree; (*LING*) degree of comparison; (*MIL*) rank; **de buen** ~ willingly; **en sumo** ~, **en** ~ **superlativo** in the highest degree.

graduación [graðwa'θjon] *nf* (*acto*) gradation; (*clasificación*) rating; (*del alcohol*) proof, strength; (*ESCOL*) graduation; (*MIL*) rank; **de alta** ~ high-ranking.

gradual [gra'ðwal] *adj* gradual.

graduar [gra'ðwar] *vt* (*gen*) to graduate; (*medir*) to gauge; (*TEC*) to calibrate; (*UNIV*) to confer a degree on; (*MIL*) to commission; ~**se** *vr* to graduate; ~**se la vista** to have one's eyes tested.

grafía [gra'fia] *nf* (*escritura*) writing; (*ortografía*) spelling.

gráfico, a ['grafiko, a] *adj* graphic; (*fig: vívido*) vivid, lively ♦ *nm* diagram ♦ *nf* graph; ~ **de barras** (*COM*) bar chart; ~ **de sectores** *o* **de tarta** (*COM*) pie chart; ~**s** *nmpl* (*tb INFORM*) graphics; ~**s empresariales** (*COM*) business graphics.

grafito [gra'fito] *nm* (*TEC*) graphite, black lead.

grafología [grafolo'xia] *nf* graphology.

gragea [gra'xea] *nf* (*MED*) pill; (*caramelo*) dragée.

grajo ['graxo] *nm* rook.

Gral. *abr* (*MIL*: = *General*) Gen.

gramático, a [gra'matiko, a] *nm/f* (*persona*) grammarian ♦ *nf* grammar.

gramo ['gramo] *nm* gramme (*BRIT*), gram (*US*).

gran [gran] *adj V* **grande**.

grana ['grana] *nf* (*BOT*) seedling; (*color*) scarlet; **ponerse como la** ~ to go as red as a beetroot.

granada [gra'naða] *nf* pomegranate; (*MIL*) grenade; ~ **de mano** hand grenade; ~ **de metralla** shrapnel shell.

granadilla [grana'ðiʎa] *nf* (*AM*) passion fruit.

granadino, a [grana'ðino, a] *adj* of *o* from Granada ♦ *nm/f* native *o* inhabitant of Granada ♦ *nf* grenadine.

granar [gra'nar] *vi* to seed.

granate [gra'nate] *adj inv* maroon ♦ *nm* garnet; (*color*) maroon.

Gran Bretaña [grambre'taɲa] *nf* Great

Britain.

Gran Canaria [granka'narja] nf Grand Canary.

grancanario, a [granka'narjo, a] adj of o from Grand Canary ♦ nm/f native o inhabitant of Grand Canary.

grande ['grande], **gran** adj (de tamaño) big, large; (alto) tall; (distinguido) great; (impresionante) grand ♦ nm grandee; ¿cómo es de ~? how big is it?, what size is it?; **pasarlo en** ~ to have a tremendous time.

grandeza [gran'deθa] nf greatness; (tamaño) bigness; (esplendidez) grandness; (nobleza) nobility.

grandioso, a [gran'djoso, a] adj magnificent, grand.

grandullón, ona [granðu'ʎon, ona] adj oversized.

granel [gra'nel] nm (montón) heap; **a** ~ (COM) in bulk.

granero [gra'nero] nm granary, barn.

granice [gra'niθe] etc vb V granizar.

granito [gra'nito] nm (AGR) small grain; (roca) granite.

granizada [grani'θaða] nf hailstorm; (fig) hail; **una** ~ **de balas** a hail of bullets.

granizado [grani'θaðo] nm iced drink; ~ **de café** iced coffee.

granizar [grani'θar] vi to hail.

granizo [gra'niθo] nm hail.

granja ['granxa] nf (gen) farm; ~ **avícola** chicken o poultry farm.

granjear [granxe'ar] vt (cobrar) to earn; (ganar) to win; (avanzar) to gain; ~**se** vr (amistad etc) to gain for o.s.

granjero, a [gran'xero, a] nm/f farmer.

grano ['grano] nm grain; (semilla) seed; (baya) berry; (MED) pimple, spot; (partícula) particle; (punto) speck; ~**s** nmpl cereals; ~ **de café** coffee bean; **ir al** ~ to get to the point.

granuja [gra'nuxa] nm rogue; (golfillo) urchin.

grapa ['grapa] nf staple; (TEC) clamp; (sujetador) clip, fastener; (ARQ) cramp.

grapadora [grapa'ðora] nf stapler.

GRAPO ['grapo] nm abr (ESP POL) = Grupo de Resistencia Antifascista Primero de Octubre.

grasa ['grasa] nf V graso.

grasiento, a [gra'sjento, a] adj greasy; (de aceite) oily; (mugriento) filthy.

graso, a ['graso, a] adj fatty; (aceitoso) greasy, oily ♦ nf (gen) grease; (de cocina) fat, lard; (sebo) suet; (mugre) filth; (AUTO) oil; (lubricante) grease; ~ **de ballena** blubber; ~ **de pescado** fish oil.

grasoso, a [gra'soso, a] adj (AM) greasy, sticky.

gratificación [gratifika'θjon] nf (propina) tip; (aguinaldo) gratuity; (bono) bonus; (recompensa) reward.

gratificar [gratifi'kar] vt (dar propina) to tip; (premiar) to reward; "**se gratificará**" "a reward is offered".

gratifique [grati'fike] etc vb V gratificar.

gratinar [grati'nar] vt to cook au gratin.

gratis ['gratis] adv free, for nothing.

gratitud [grati'tuð] nf gratitude.

grato, a ['grato, a] adj (agradable) pleasant, agreeable; (bienvenido) welcome; **nos es** ~ **informarle que** ... we are pleased to inform you that ....

gratuito, a [gra'twito, a] adj (gratis) free; (sin razón) gratuitous; (acusación) unfounded.

grava ['graβa] nf (guijos) gravel; (piedra molida) crushed stone; (en carreteras) road metal.

gravamen [gra'βamen] nm (carga) burden; (impuesto) tax; **libre de** ~ (ECON) free from encumbrances.

gravar [gra'βar] vt to burden; (COM) to tax; (ECON) to assess for tax; ~ **con impuestos** to burden with taxes.

grave ['graβe] adj heavy; (fig, MED) grave, serious; (importante) important; (herida) severe; (MUS) low, deep; (LING: acento) grave; **estar** ~ to be seriously ill.

gravedad [graβe'ðað] nf gravity; (fig) seriousness; (grandeza) importance; (dignidad) dignity; (MUS) depth.

grávido, a ['graβiðo, a] adj (preñada) pregnant.

gravilla [gra'βiʎa] nf gravel.

gravitación [graβita'θjon] nf gravitation.

gravitar [graβi'tar] vi to gravitate; ~ **sobre** to rest on.

gravoso, a [gra'βoso, a] adj (pesado) burdensome; (costoso) costly.

graznar [graθ'nar] vi (cuervo) to squawk; (pato) to quack; (hablar ronco) to croak.

graznido [graθ'niðo] nm squawk; croak.

Grecia ['greθja] nf Greece.

gregario, a [gre'xarjo, a] adj gregarious; **instinto** ~ herd instinct.

gremio ['gremjo] nm (asociación) professional association, guild.

greña ['greɲa] nf (cabellos) shock of hair; (maraña) tangle; **andar a la** ~ to bicker, squabble.

greñudo, a [gre'ɲuðo, a] adj (persona) dishevelled; (pelo) tangled.

gresca ['greska] nf uproar; (trifulca) row.

griego, a ['grjeɣo, a] adj Greek, Grecian

◆ *nm/f* Greek ◆ *nm* (*LING*) Greek.

grieta ['grjeta] *nf* crack; (*hendidura*) chink; (*quiebra*) crevice; (*MED*) chap; (*POL*) rift.

grifa ['grifa] *nf* (*fam: droga*) marijuana.

grifo ['grifo] *nm* tap (*BRIT*), faucet (*US*); (*AM*) petrol (*BRIT*) o gas (*US*) station.

grilletes [gri'ʎetes] *nmpl* fetters, shackles.

grillo ['griʎo] *nm* (*ZOOL*) cricket; (*BOT*) shoot; ~**s** *nmpl* shackles, irons.

grima ['grima] *nf* (*horror*) loathing; (*desagrado*) reluctance; (*desazón*) uneasiness; **me da** ~ it makes me sick.

gringo, a ['gringo, a] (*AM*) *adj* (*pey: extranjero*) foreign; (*: norteamericano*) Yankee; (*idioma*) foreign ◆ *nm/f* foreigner; Yank.

gripa ['gripa] *nf* (*AM*) flu, influenza.

gripe ['gripe] *nf* flu, influenza.

gris [gris] *adj* grey.

grisáceo, a [gri'saθeo, a] *adj* greyish.

grisoso, a [gri'soso, a] *adj* (*AM*) greyish, grayish (*esp US*).

gritar [gri'tar] *vt, vi* to shout, yell; **¡no grites!** stop shouting!

grito ['grito] *nm* shout, yell; (*de horror*) scream; **a** ~ **pelado** at the top of one's voice; **poner el** ~ **en el cielo** to scream blue murder; **es el último** ~ (*de moda*) it's all the rage.

groenlandés, ésa [groenlan'des, esa] *adj* Greenland *cpd* ◆ *nm/f* Greenlander.

Groenlandia [groen'landja] *nf* Greenland.

grosella [gro'seʎa] *nf* (red)currant; ~ **negra** blackcurrant.

grosería [grose'ria] *nf* (*actitud*) rudeness; (*comentario*) vulgar comment; (*palabrota*) swearword.

grosero, a [gro'sero, a] *adj* (*poco cortés*) rude, bad-mannered; (*ordinario*) vulgar, crude.

grosor [gro'sor] *nm* thickness.

grotesco, a [gro'tesko, a] *adj* grotesque; (*absurdo*) bizarre.

grúa ['grua] *nf* (*TEC*) crane; (*de petróleo*) derrick; ~ **corrediza** *o* **móvil/de pescante/puente/de torre** travelling/jib/overhead/tower crane.

grueso, a ['grweso, a] *adj* thick; (*persona*) stout; (*calidad*) coarse ◆ *nm* bulk; (*espesor*) thickness; (*densidad*) density; (*de gente*) main body, mass; **el** ~ **de** the bulk of.

grulla ['gruʎa] *nf* (*ZOOL*) crane.

grumete [gru'mete] *nm* (*NAUT*) cabin *o* ship's boy.

grumo ['grumo] *nm* (*coágulo*) clot, lump; (*masa*) dollop.

gruñido [gru'niðo] *nm* grunt, growl; (*fig*) grumble.

gruñir [gru'nir] *vi* (*animal*) to grunt, growl; (*fam*) to grumble.

gruñón, ona [gru'non, ona] *adj* grumpy ◆ *nm/f* grumbler.

grupa ['grupa] *nf* (*ZOOL*) rump.

grupo ['grupo] *nm* group; (*TEC*) unit, set; (*de árboles*) cluster; ~ **sanguíneo** blood group.

gruta ['gruta] *nf* grotto.

Gta. *abr* (*AUTO*) = **Glorieta**.

guaca ['gwaka] *nf* Indian tomb.

guacamole [gwaka'mole] *nm* (*AM*) avocado salad.

guachimán [gwatʃi'man] *nm* (*AM*) night watchman.

guadalajareño, a [gwaðalaxa'reno, a] *adj* of *o* from Guadalajara ◆ *nm/f* native *o* inhabitant of Guadalajara.

Guadalquivir [gwaðalki'ßir] *nm*: **el (Río)** ~ the Guadalquivir.

guadaña [gwa'ðana] *nf* scythe.

guadañar [gwaða'nar] *vt* to scythe, mow.

Guadiana [gwa'ðjana] *nm*: **el (Río)** ~ the Guadiana.

guagua ['gwaɣwa] *nf* (*AM, Canarias*) bus; (*AM: criatura*) baby.

guajolote [gwaxo'lote] *nm* (*AM*) turkey.

guano ['gwano] *nm* guano.

guantada [gwan'taða] *nf*, **guantazo** [gwan'taθo] *nm* slap.

guante ['gwante] *nm* glove; **se ajusta como un** ~ it fits like a glove; **echar el** ~ **a algn** to catch hold of sb; (*fig: policía*) to catch sb.

guapo, a ['gwapo, a] *adj* good-looking; (*mujer*) pretty, attractive; (*hombre*) handsome; (*elegante*) smart ◆ *nm* lover, gallant; (*AM fam*) tough guy, bully.

guaraní [gwara'ni] *adj, nm/f* Guarani ◆ *nm* (*moneda*) *monetary unit of Paraguay*.

guarapo [gwa'rapo] *nm* (*AM*) fermented cane juice.

guarda ['gwarða] *nm/f* (*persona*) warden, keeper ◆ *nf* (*acto*) guarding; (*custodia*) custody; (*TIP*) flyleaf, endpaper; ~ **forestal** game warden.

guarda(a)gujas [gwarða'ɣuxas] *nm inv* (*FERRO*) switchman.

guardabarros [gwarða'ßarros] *nm inv* mudguard (*BRIT*), fender (*US*).

guardabosques [gwarða'ßoskes] *nm inv* gamekeeper.

guardacoches [gwarða'kotʃes] *nm/f inv* (*celador*) parking attendant.

guardacostas [gwarða'kostas] *nm inv* coastguard vessel.

guardador, a [gwarða'ðor, a] *adj* protective; (*tacaño*) mean, stingy ◆ *nm/f* guardian, protector.

guardaespaldas [gwardaes'paldas] *nm/f inv* bodyguard.

guardameta [gwarða'meta] *nm* goalkeeper.

guardapolvo [gwarda'polβo] *nm* dust cover; (*prenda de vestir*) overalls *pl*.

guardar [gwar'ðar] *vt* (*gen*) to keep; (*vigilar*) to guard, watch over; (*conservar*) to put away; (*dinero: ahorrar*) to save; (*promesa etc*) to keep; (*ley*) to observe; (*rencor*) to bear, harbour; (*INFORM: archivo*) to save; **~se** *vr* (*preservarse*) to protect o.s.; **~se de algo** (*evitar*) to avoid sth; (*abstenerse*) to refrain from sth; **~se de hacer algo** to be careful not to do sth; **guardársela a algn** to have it in for sb.

guardarropa [gwarða'rropa] *nm* (*armario*) wardrobe; (*en establecimiento público*) cloakroom.

guardería [gwarðe'ria] *nf* nursery.

guardia ['gwarðja] *nf* (*MIL*) guard; (*cuidado*) care, custody ♦ *nm/f* guard; (*policía*) policeman/woman; **estar de ~** to be on guard; **montar ~** to mount guard; **la G~ Civil** the Civil Guard; **~ municipal** *o* **urbana** municipal police; **un ~ civil** a Civil Guard(sman); **un(a) ~ nacional** a policeman/woman; **~ urbano** traffic policeman; *see boxed note.*

GUARDIA CIVIL

The **Guardia Civil** *is a branch of the army, or "Ejército de Tierra", and is run along military lines. It has a policing role outside large towns and cities and comes under the joint control of the Spanish Ministry of Defence and the Ministry of the Interior. It is also known as "La Benemérita".*

---

guardián, ana [gwar'ðjan, ana] *nm/f* (*gen*) guardian, keeper.

guarecer [gware'θer] *vt* (*proteger*) to protect; (*abrigar*) to shelter; **~se** *vr* to take refuge.

guarezca [gwa'reθka] *etc vb V* **guarecer**.

guarida [gwa'riða] *nf* (*de animal*) den, lair; (*de persona*) haunt, hideout; (*refugio*) refuge.

guarnecer [gwarne'θer] *vt* (*equipar*) to provide; (*adornar*) to adorn; (*TEC*) to reinforce.

guarnezca [gwar'neθka] *etc vb V* **guarnecer**.

guarnición [gwarni'θjon] *nf* (*de vestimenta*) trimming; (*de piedra*) mount; (*CULIN*) garnish; (*arneses*) harness; (*MIL*) garrison.

guarrada [gwa'rraða] (*fam*) *nf* (*cosa sucia*) dirty mess; (*acto o dicho obsceno*) obscenity; **hacer una ~ a algn** to do the dirty on sb.

guarrería [gwarre'ria] *nf* = **guarrada**.

guarro, a ['gwarro, a] *nm/f* (*fam*) pig; (*fig*) dirty *o* slovenly person.

guasa ['gwasa] *nf* joke; **con** *o* **de ~** jokingly, in fun.

guasón, ona [gwa'son, ona] *adj* witty; (*bromista*) joking ♦ *nm/f* wit; joker.

Guatemala [gwate'mala] *nf* Guatemala.

guatemalteco, a [gwatemal'teko, a] *adj, nm/f* Guatemalan.

guateque [gwa'teke] *nm* (*fiesta*) party.

guay [gwai] *adj* (*fam*) super, great.

guayaba [gwa'jaβa] *nf* (*BOT*) guava.

Guayana [gwa'jana] *nf* Guyana, Guiana.

gubernamental [guβernamen'tal], **gubernativo, a** [guβerna'tiβo, a] *adj* governmental.

guedeja [ge'ðexa] *nf* long hair.

guerra ['gerra] *nf* war; (*arte*) warfare; (*pelea*) struggle; **~ atómica/ bacteriológica/nuclear/de guerrillas** atomic/germ/nuclear/guerrilla warfare; **Primera/Segunda G~ Mundial** First/ Second World War; **~ de precios** (*COM*) price war; **~ civil/fría** civil/cold war; **~ a muerte** fight to the death; **de ~** military, war *cpd*; **estar en ~** to be at war; **dar ~** to be annoying.

guerrear [gerre'ar] *vi* to wage war.

guerrero, a [ge'rrero, a] *adj* fighting; (*carácter*) warlike ♦ *nm/f* warrior.

guerrilla [ge'rriλa] *nf* guerrilla warfare; (*tropas*) guerrilla band *o* group.

guerrillero, a [gerri'λero, a] *nm/f* guerrilla (fighter); (*contra invasor*) partisan.

gueto ['geto] *nm* ghetto.

guía ['gia] *etc vb V* **guiar** ♦ *nm/f* (*persona*) guide ♦ *nf* (*libro*) guidebook; (*manual*) handbook; (*INFORM*) prompt; **~ de ferrocarriles** railway timetable; **~ telefónica** telephone directory; **~ del turista/del viajero** tourist/traveller's guide.

guiar [gi'ar] *vt* to guide, direct; (*dirigir*) to lead; (*orientar*) to advise; (*AUTO*) to steer; **~se** *vr*: **~se por** to be guided by.

guijarro [gi'xarro] *nm* pebble.

guillotina [giλo'tina] *nf* guillotine.

guinda ['ginda] *nf* morello cherry; (*licor*) cherry liqueur.

guindar [gin'dar] *vt* to hoist; (*fam: robar*) to nick.

guindilla [gin'diλa] *nf* chil(l)i pepper.

Guinea [gi'nea] *nf* Guinea.

guineo, a [gi'neo, a] *adj* Guinea *cpd*,
Guinean ♦ *nm/f* Guinean.
guiñapo [gi'ɲapo] *nm* (*harapo*) rag;
(*persona*) rogue.
guiñar [gi'ɲar] *vi* to wink.
guiño ['giɲo] *nm* (*parpadeo*) wink; (*muecas*)
grimace; **hacer ~s a** (*enamorados*) to
make eyes at.
guiñol [gi'ɲol] *nm* (*TEAT*) puppet theatre.
guión [gi'on] *nm* (*LING*) hyphen, dash;
(*esquema*) summary, outline; (*CINE*)
script.
guionista [gjo'nista] *nm/f* scriptwriter.
guipuzcoano, a [gipuθko'ano, a] *adj* of o
from Guipúzcoa ♦ *nm/f* native o
inhabitant of Guipúzcoa.
guiri ['giri] *nm/f* (*fam, pey*) foreigner.
guirigay [giri'gai] *nm* (*griterío*) uproar;
(*confusión*) chaos.
guirnalda [gir'nalda] *nf* garland.
guisa ['gisa] *nf*: **a ~ de** as, like.
guisado [gi'saðo] *nm* stew.
guisante [gi'sante] *nm* pea.
guisar [gi'sar] *vt, vi* to cook; (*fig*) to
arrange.
guiso ['giso] *nm* cooked dish.
guita ['gita] *nf* twine; (*fam: dinero*) dough.
guitarra [gi'tarra] *nf* guitar.
guitarrista [gita'rrista] *nm/f* guitarist.
gula ['gula] *nf* gluttony, greed.
gusano [gu'sano] *nm* maggot, worm; (*de
mariposa, polilla*) caterpillar; (*fig*) worm;
(*ser despreciable*) creep; **~ de seda** silk-
worm.
gustar [gus'tar] *vt* to taste, sample ♦ *vi* to
please, be pleasing; **~ de algo** to like o
enjoy sth; **me gustan las uvas** I like
grapes; **le gusta nadar** she likes o enjoys
swimming; **¿gusta Ud?** would you like
some?; **como Ud guste** as you wish.
gusto ['gusto] *nm* (*sentido, sabor*) taste;
(*agrado*) liking; (*placer*) pleasure; **tiene
un ~ amargo** it has a bitter taste; **tener
buen ~** to have good taste; **sobre ~s no
hay nada escrito** there's no accounting
for tastes; **de buen/mal ~** in good/bad
taste; **sentirse a ~** to feel at ease;
¡mucho o tanto ~ (en conocerle)! how do
you do?, pleased to meet you; **el ~ es
mío** the pleasure is mine; **tomar ~ a** to
take a liking to; **con ~** willingly, gladly.
gustoso, a [gus'toso, a] *adj* (*sabroso*) tasty;
(*agradable*) pleasant; (*con voluntad*)
willing, glad; **lo hizo ~** he did it gladly.
gutural [gutu'ral] *adj* guttural.
guyanés, esa [gwaja'nes, esa] *adj, nm/f*
Guyanese.

H h

H, h ['atʃe] *nf* (*letra*) H, h; **H de Historia** H
for Harry (*BRIT*) o How (*US*).
H. *abr* (*QUÍMICA*: = *Hidrógeno*) H;
(= *Hectárea(s)*) ha.; (*COM*: = *Haber*) cr.
h. *abr* (= *hora(s)*) h., hr(s).; (= *hacia*) c.
♦ *nmpl abr* (= *habitantes*) pop.
ha [a] *vb V* haber.
Ha. *abr* (= *Hectárea(s)*) ha.
haba ['aβa] *nf* bean; **son ~s contadas** it
goes without saying; **en todas partes
cuecen ~s** it's the same (story) the
whole world over.
Habana [a'βana] *nf*: **la ~** Havana.
habanero, a [aβa'nero, a] *adj* of o from
Havana ♦ *nm/f* native o inhabitant of
Havana ♦ *nf* (*MUS*) habanera.
habano [a'βano] *nm* Havana cigar.
habeas corpus [a'βeas'korpus] *nm* (*LAW*)
habeas corpus.

haber [a'βer] *vb aux* **1** (*tiempos compuestos*)
to have; **había comido** I have/had eaten;
antes/después de ~lo visto before
seeing/after seeing o having seen it; **si
lo hubiera sabido habría ido** if I had
known I would have gone
2: **¡~lo dicho antes!** you should have
said so before!; **¿habráse visto (cosa
igual)?** have you ever seen anything like
it?
3: **~ de**: **he de hacerlo** I must do it; **ha de
llegar mañana** it should arrive
tomorrow
♦ *vb impers* **1** (*existencia: sg*) there is; (*: pl*)
there are; **hay un hermano/dos
hermanos** there is one brother/there are
two brothers; **¿cuánto hay de aquí a
Sucre?** how far is it from here to
Sucre?; **habrá unos 4 grados** it must be
about 4 degrees; **no hay quien te
entienda** there's no understanding you
2 (*obligación*): **hay que hacer algo**
something must be done; **hay que
apuntarlo para acordarse** you have to
write it down to remember
3: **¡hay que ver!** well I never!
4: **¡no hay de o por (AM) qué!** don't

mention it!, not at all!
5: ¿qué hay? (¿qué pasa?) what's up?,
what's the matter?; (¿qué tal?) how's it
going?

♦ ~**se** vr: **habérselas con algn** to have it
out with sb
♦ vt: **he aquí unas sugerencias** here are
some suggestions; **todos los inventos
habidos y por** ~ all inventions present
and future; **en el encuentro habido ayer**
in yesterday's game
♦ nm (en cuenta) credit side; ~**es** nmpl
assets; **¿cuánto tengo en el** ~**?** how
much do I have in my account?; **tiene
varias novelas en su** ~ he has several
novels to his credit.

habichuela [aβiˈtʃwela] nf kidney bean.
hábil [ˈaβil] adj (listo) clever, smart; (capaz)
fit, capable; (experto) expert; **día** ~
working day.
habilidad [aβiliˈðað] nf (gen) skill, ability;
(inteligencia) cleverness; (destreza)
expertness, expertise; (JUR)
competence; ~ **(para)** fitness (for); **tener**
~ **manual** to be clever with one's hands.
habilitación [aβilitaˈθjon] nf qualification;
(colocación de muebles) fitting out;
(financiamiento) financing; (oficina)
paymaster's office.
habilitado [aβiliˈtaðo] nm paymaster.
habilitar [aβiliˈtar] vt to qualify; (autorizar)
to authorize; (capacitar) to enable; (dar
instrumentos) to equip; (financiar) to
finance.
hábilmente [aβilˈmente] adv skilfully,
expertly.
habitable [aβiˈtaβle] adj inhabitable.
habitación [aβitaˈθjon] nf (cuarto) room;
(casa) dwelling, abode; (BIO: morada)
habitat; ~ **sencilla** o **individual** single
room; ~ **doble** o **de matrimonio** double
room.
habitante [aβiˈtante] nmf inhabitant.
habitar [aβiˈtar] vt (residir en) to inhabit;
(ocupar) to occupy ♦ vi to live.
hábitat, pl **hábitats** [ˈaβitat, ˈaβitats] nm
habitat.
hábito [ˈaβito] nm habit; **tener el** ~ **de
hacer algo** to be in the habit of doing
sth.
habitual [aβiˈtwal] adj habitual.
habituar [aβiˈtwar] vt to accustom; ~**se** vr:
~**se a** to get used to.
habla [ˈaβla] nf (capacidad de hablar)
speech; (idioma) language; (dialecto)
dialect; **perder el** ~ to become
speechless; **de** ~ **francesa** French-

speaking; **estar al** ~ to be in contact;
(TELEC) to be on the line; **¡González al** ~**!**
(TELEC) Gonzalez speaking!
hablador, a [aβlaˈðor, a] adj talkative
♦ nm/f chatterbox.
habladuría [aβlaðuˈria] nf rumour; ~**s** nfpl
gossip sg.
hablante [aˈβlante] adj speaking ♦ nm/f
speaker.
hablar [aˈβlar] vt to speak, talk ♦ vi to
speak; ~**se** vr to speak to each other; ~
con to speak to; **¡hable!, ¡puede** ~**!**
(TELEC) you're through!; **de eso ni** ~ no
way, that's not on; ~ **alto/bajo/claro** to
speak loudly/quietly/plainly o bluntly; ~
de to speak of o about; **"se habla inglés"**
"English spoken here"; **no se hablan**
they are not on speaking terms.
habré [aˈβre] etc vb V **haber**.
hacedor, a [aθeˈðor, a] nm/f maker.
hacendado, a [aθenˈdaðo, a] adj property-
owning ♦ nm (terrateniente) large
landowner.
hacendoso, a [aθenˈdoso, a] adj
industrious, hard-working.

═══════════════════════ *PALABRA CLAVE*

hacer [aˈθer] vt **1** (fabricar, producir,
conseguir) to make; (construir) to build; ~
una película/un ruido to make a film/
noise; **el guisado lo hice yo** I made o
cooked the stew; ~ **amigos** to make
friends
2 (ejecutar. trabajo etc) to do; ~ **la colada**
to do the washing; ~ **la comida** to do the
cooking; **¿qué haces?** what are you
doing?; **¡eso está hecho!** you've got it!;
~ **el tonto/indio** to act the fool/clown; ~
el malo o **el papel del malo** (TEAT) to play
the villain
3 (estudios, algunos deportes) to do; ~
español/económicas to do o study
Spanish/economics; ~ **yoga/gimnasia** to
do yoga/go to gym
4 (transformar, incidir en): **esto lo hará
más difícil** this will make it more
difficult; **salir te hará sentir mejor** going
out will make you feel better; **te hace
más joven** it makes you look younger
5 (cálculo): **2 y 2 hacen 4** 2 and 2 make 4;
éste hace 100 this one makes 100
6 (+sub): **esto hará que ganemos** this
will make us win; **harás que no quiera
venir** you'll stop him wanting to come
7 (como sustituto de vb) to do; **él bebió y
yo hice lo mismo** he drank and I did
likewise
8: no hace más que criticar all he does is

criticize

♦ *vb semi-aux:* ~ + *infin* **1** (*directo*): **les hice venir** I made *o* had them come; ~ **trabajar a los demás** to get others to work

2 (*por intermedio de otros*): ~ **reparar algo** to get sth repaired

♦ *vi* **1: haz como que no lo sabes** act as if you don't know; **hiciste bien en decírmelo** you were right to tell me

2 (*ser apropiado*): **si os hace** if it's alright with you

3: ~ **de**: ~ **de madre para uno** to be like a mother to sb; (*TEAT*): ~ **de Otelo** to play Othello; **la tabla hace de mesa** the board does as a table

♦ *vb impers* **1: hace calor/frío** it's hot/cold; *V tb* **bueno; sol; tiempo**

2 (*tiempo*): **hace 3 años** 3 years ago; **hace un mes que voy/no voy** I've been going/I haven't been for a month; **no le veo desde hace mucho** I haven't seen him for a long time

3: ¿cómo has hecho para llegar tan rápido? how did you manage to get here so quickly?

♦ ~**se** *vr* **1** (*volverse*) to become; **se hicieron amigos** they became friends; ~**se viejo** to get *o* grow old; **se hace tarde** it's getting late

2: ~**se algo: me hice un traje** I got a suit made

3 (*acostumbrarse*): ~**se a** to get used to; ~**se a la idea** to get used to the idea

4: se hace con huevos y leche it's made out of eggs and milk; **eso no se hace** that's not done

5 (*obtener*): ~**se de** *o* **con algo** to get hold of sth

6 (*fingirse*): ~**se el sordo/sueco** to turn a deaf ear/pretend not to notice.

hacha ['atʃa] *nf* axe; (*antorcha*) torch.
hachazo [a'tʃaθo] *nm* axe blow.
hache ['atʃe] *nf* (the letter) H; **llámele usted** ~ call it what you will.
hachís [a'tʃis] *nm* hashish.
hacia ['aθja] *prep* (*en dirección de, actitud*) towards; (*cerca de*) near; ~ **arriba/abajo** up(wards)/down(wards); ~ **mediodía** about noon.
hacienda [a'θjenda] *nf* (*propiedad*) property; (*finca*) farm; (*AM*) ranch; ~ **pública** public finance; (**Ministerio de**) **H~** Exchequer (*BRIT*), Treasury Department (*US*).
hacinar [aθi'nar] *vt* to pile (up); (*AGR*) to stack; (*fig*) to overcrowd.

hada ['aða] *nf* fairy; ~ **madrina** fairy godmother.
hado ['aðo] *nm* fate, destiny.
haga ['aɣa] *etc vb V* **hacer**.
Haití [ai'ti] *nm* Haiti.
haitiano, a [ai'tjano, a] *adj, nm/f* Haitian.
hala ['ala] *excl* (*vamos*) come on!; (*anda*) get on with it!
halagar [ala'ɣar] *vt* (*lisonjear*) to flatter.
halago [a'laɣo] *nm* (*adulación*) flattery.
halague [a'laɣe] *etc vb V* **halagar**.
halagüeño, a [ala'ɣweɲo, a] *adj* flattering.
halcón [al'kon] *nm* falcon, hawk.
hálito ['alito] *nm* breath.
halitosis [ali'tosis] *nf* halitosis, bad breath.
hallar [a'ʎar] *vt* (*gen*) to find; (*descubrir*) to discover; (*toparse con*) to run into; ~**se** *vr* to be (situated); (*encontrarse*) to find o.s.; **se halla fuera** he is away; **no se halla** he feels out of place.
hallazgo [a'ʎaθɣo] *nm* discovery; (*cosa*) find.
halo ['alo] *nm* halo.
halógeno, a [a'loxeno, a] *adj*: **faro** ~ halogen lamp.
halterofilia [altero'filja] *nf* weightlifting.
hamaca [a'maka] *nf* hammock.
hambre ['ambre] *nf* hunger; (*carencia*) famine; (*inanición*) starvation; (*fig*) longing; **tener** ~ to be hungry.
hambriento, a [am'brjento, a] *adj* hungry, starving ♦ *nm/f* starving person; **los** ~**s** the hungry; ~ **de** hungry *o* longing for.
hambruna [am'bruna] *nf* famine.
Hamburgo [am'burɣo] *nm* Hamburg.
hamburguesa [ambur'ɣesa] *nf* hamburger, burger.
hampa ['ampa] *nf* underworld.
hampón [am'pon] *nm* thug.
han [an] *vb V* **haber**.
haragán, ana [ara'ɣan, ana] *adj, nm/f* good-for-nothing.
haraganear [araɣane'ar] *vi* to idle, loaf about.
harapiento, a [ara'pjento, a] *adj* tattered, in rags.
harapo [a'rapo] *nm* rag.
hardware ['xardwer] *nm* (*INFORM*) hardware.
haré [a're] *etc vb V* **hacer**.
harén [a'ren] *nm* harem.
harina [a'rina] *nf* flour; **eso es** ~ **de otro costal** that's another kettle of fish.
harinero, a [ari'nero, a] *nm/f* flour merchant.
harinoso, a [ari'noso, a] *adj* floury.
hartar [ar'tar] *vt* to satiate, glut; (*fig*) to tire, sicken; ~**se** *vr* (*de comida*) to fill o.s.,

gorge o.s.; (*cansarse*) to get fed up (*de* with).

hartazgo [ar'taθɣo] *nm* surfeit, glut.

harto, a ['arto, a] *adj* (*lleno*) full; (*cansado*) fed up ♦ *adv* (*bastante*) enough; (*muy*) very; **estar** ~ **de** to be fed up with; **¡estoy** ~ **de decírtelo!** I'm sick and tired of telling you (so)!

hartura [ar'tura] *nf* (*exceso*) surfeit; (*abundancia*) abundance; (*satisfacción*) satisfaction.

has [as] *vb* V **haber.**

Has. *abr* (= *Hectáreas*) ha.

hasta ['asta] *adv* even ♦ *prep* (*alcanzando a*) as far as, up/down to; (*de tiempo: a tal hora*) till, until; (: *antes de*) before ♦ *conj:* ~ **que** until; ~ **luego** o **ahora** (*fam*)/**el sábado** see you soon/on Saturday; ~ **la fecha** (up) to date; ~ **nueva orden** until further notice; ~ **en Valencia hiela a veces** even in Valencia it freezes sometimes.

hastiar [as'tjar] *vt* (*gen*) to weary; (*aburrir*) to bore; ~**se** *vr:* ~**se de** to get fed up with.

hastío [as'tio] *nm* weariness; boredom.

hatajo [a'taxo] *nm:* **un** ~ **de gamberros** a bunch of hooligans.

hatillo [a'tiʎo] *nm* belongings *pl*, kit; (*montón*) bundle, heap.

Hawai [a'wai] *nm* (*tb:* **las Islas** ~) Hawaii.

hawaianas [awa'janas] *nfpl* (*esp AM*) flip-flops (*BRIT*), thongs.

hawaiano, a [awa'jano, a] *adj, nm/f* Hawaiian.

hay [ai] *vb* V **haber.**

Haya ['aja] *nf:* **la** ~ The Hague.

haya ['aja] *etc vb* V **haber** ♦ *nf* beech tree.

hayal [a'jal] *nm* beech grove.

haz [aθ] *vb* V **hacer** ♦ *nm* bundle, bunch; (*rayo: de luz*) beam ♦ *nf:* ~ **de la tierra** face of the earth.

hazaña [a'θaɲa] *nf* feat, exploit; **sería una** ~ it would be a great achievement.

hazmerreír [aθmerre'ir] *nm inv* laughing stock.

HB *abr* (= *Herri Batasuna*) *Basque political party.*

he [e] *vb* V **haber** ♦ *adv:* ~ **aquí** here is, here are; ~ **aquí por qué** ... that is why ....

hebilla [e'βiʎa] *nf* buckle, clasp.

hebra ['eβra] *nf* thread; (*BOT: fibra*) fibre, grain.

hebreo, a [e'βreo, a] *adj, nm/f* Hebrew ♦ *nm* (*LING*) Hebrew.

Hébridas ['eβriðas] *nfpl:* **las** ~ the Hebrides.

hechice [e'tʃiθe] *etc vb* V **hechizar.**

hechicero, a [etʃi'θero, a] *nm/f* sorcerer/ sorceress.

hechizar [etʃi'θar] *vt* to cast a spell on, bewitch.

hechizo [e'tʃiθo] *nm* witchcraft, magic; (*acto de magia*) spell, charm.

hecho, a ['etʃo, a] *pp de* **hacer** ♦ *adj* complete; (*maduro*) mature; (*COSTURA*) ready-to-wear ♦ *nm* deed, act; (*dato*) fact; (*cuestión*) matter; (*suceso*) event ♦ *excl* agreed!, done!; **¡bien** ~**!** well done!; **de** ~ in fact, as a matter of fact; (*POL etc: adj, adv*) de facto; **de** ~ **y de derecho** de facto and de jure; ~ **a la medida** made-to-measure; **a lo** ~**, pecho** it's no use crying over spilt milk.

hechura [e'tʃura] *nf* making, creation; (*producto*) product; (*forma*) form, shape; (*de persona*) build; (*TEC*) craftsmanship.

hectárea [ek'tarea] *nf* hectare.

heder [e'ðer] *vi* to stink, smell; (*fig*) to be unbearable.

hediondez [eðjon'deθ] *nf* stench, stink; (*cosa*) stinking thing.

hediondo, a [e'ðjondo, a] *adj* stinking.

hedor [e'ðor] *nm* stench.

hegemonía [exemo'nia] *nf* hegemony.

helada [e'laða] *nf* frost.

heladera [ela'ðera] *nf* (*AM: refrigerador*) refrigerator.

heladería [elaðe'ria] *nf* ice-cream stall (*o* parlour).

helado, a [e'laðo, a] *adj* frozen; (*glacial*) icy; (*fig*) chilly, cold ♦ *nm* ice-cream; **dejar** ~ **a algn** to dumbfound sb.

helador, a [ela'ðor, a] *adj* (*viento etc*) icy, freezing.

helar [e'lar] *vt* to freeze, ice (up); (*dejar atónito*) to amaze; (*desalentar*) to discourage ♦ *vi,* ~**se** *vr* to freeze; (*AVIAT, FERRO etc*) to ice (up), freeze up; (*líquido*) to set.

helecho [e'letʃo] *nm* bracken, fern.

helénico, a [e'leniko, a] *adj* Hellenic, Greek.

heleno, a [e'leno, a] *nm/f* Hellene, Greek.

hélice ['eliθe] *nf* spiral; (*TEC*) propeller; (*MAT*) helix.

helicóptero [eli'koptero] *nm* helicopter.

helio ['eljo] *nm* helium.

helmántico, a [el'mantiko, a] *adj* of *o* from Salamanca.

helvético, a [el'βetiko, a] *adj, nm/f* Swiss.

hematoma [ema'toma] *nm* bruise.

hembra ['embra] *nf* (*BOT, ZOOL*) female; (*mujer*) woman; (*TEC*) nut; **un elefante** ~ a she-elephant.

hemeroteca [emero'teka] *nf* newspaper

library.
hemiciclo [emi'θiklo] *nm*: **el** ~ (*POL*) the floor.
hemisferio [emis'ferjo] *nm* hemisphere.
hemofilia [emo'filja] *nf* haemophilia (*BRIT*), hemophilia (*US*).
hemorragia [emo'rraxja] *nf* haemorrhage (*BRIT*), hemorrhage (*US*).
hemorroides [emo'rroiðes] *nfpl* haemorrhoids (*BRIT*), hemorrhoids (*US*).
hemos ['emos] *vb V* **haber**.
henar [e'nar] *nm* meadow, hayfield.
henchir [en'tʃir] *vt* to fill, stuff; ~**se** *vr* (*llenarse de comida*) to stuff o.s. (with food); (*inflarse*) to swell (up).
Hendaya [en'daja] *nf* Hendaye.
hender [en'der] *vt* to cleave, split.
hendidura [endi'ðura] *nf* crack, split; (*GEO*) fissure.
henequén [ene'ken] *nm* (*AM*) henequen.
heno ['eno] *nm* hay.
hepatitis [epa'titis] *nf inv* hepatitis.
herbario, a [er'βarjo, a] *adj* herbal ♦ *nm* (*colección*) herbarium; (*especialista*) herbalist; (*botánico*) botanist.
herbicida [erβi'θiða] *nm* weedkiller.
herbívoro, a [er'βiβoro, a] *adj* herbivorous.
herboristería [erβoriste'ria] *nf* herbalist's shop.
heredad [ere'ðað] *nf* landed property; (*granja*) farm.
heredar [ere'ðar] *vt* to inherit.
heredero, a [ere'ðero, a] *nm/f* heir(ess); ~ **del trono** heir to the throne.
hereditario, a [ereði'tarjo, a] *adj* hereditary.
hereje [e'rexe] *nm/f* heretic.
herejía [ere'xia] *nf* heresy.
herencia [e'renθja] *nf* inheritance; (*fig*) heritage; (*BIO*) heredity.
herético, a [e'retiko, a] *adj* heretical.
herido, a [e'riðo, a] *adj* injured, wounded; (*fig*) offended ♦ *nm/f* casualty ♦ *nf* wound, injury.
herir [e'rir] *vt* to wound, injure; (*fig*) to offend; (*conmover*) to touch, move.
hermana [er'mana] *nf V* **hermano**.
hermanar [erma'nar] *vt* to match; (*unir*) to join; (*ciudades*) to twin.
hermanastro, a [erma'nastro. a] *nm/f* stepbrother/sister.
hermandad [erman'dað] *nf* brotherhood; (*de mujeres*) sisterhood; (*sindicato etc*) association.
hermano, a [er'mano, a] *adj* similar ♦ *nm* brother ♦ *nf* sister; ~ **gemelo** twin brother; ~ **político** brother-in-law; ~ **primo** first cousin; **mis ~s** my brothers,

my brothers and sisters; **hermana política** sister-in-law.
hermético, a [er'metiko, a] *adj* hermetic; (*fig*) watertight.
hermoso, a [er'moso, a] *adj* beautiful, lovely; (*estupendo*) splendid; (*guapo*) handsome.
hermosura [ermo'sura] *nf* beauty; (*de hombre*) handsomeness.
hernia ['ernja] *nf* hernia, rupture; ~ **discal** slipped disc.
herniarse [er'njarse] *vr* to rupture o.s.; (*fig*) to break one's back.
héroe ['eroe] *nm* hero.
heroicidad [eroiθi'ðað] *nf* heroism; (*una* ~) heroic deed.
heroico, a [e'roiko, a] *adj* heroic.
heroína [ero'ina] *nf* (*mujer*) heroine; (*droga*) heroin.
heroinómano, a [eroi'nomano, a] *nm/f* heroin addict.
heroísmo [ero'ismo] *nm* heroism.
herpes ['erpes] *nmpl o nfpl* (*MED: gen*) herpes *sg*; (: *de la piel*) shingles *sg*.
herradura [erra'ðura] *nf* horseshoe.
herraje [e'rraxe] *nm* (*trabajos*) ironwork.
herramienta [erra'mjenta] *nf* tool.
herrería [erre'ria] *nf* smithy; (*TEC*) forge.
herrero [e'rrero] *nm* blacksmith.
herrumbre [e'rrumbre] *nf* rust.
herrumbroso, a [errum'broso, a] *adj* rusty.
hervidero [erβi'ðero] *nm* (*fig*) swarm; (*POL etc*) hotbed.
hervir [er'βir] *vi* to boil; (*burbujear*) to bubble; (*fig*): ~ **de** to teem with; ~ **a fuego lento** to simmer.
hervor [er'βor] *nm* boiling; (*fig*) ardour, fervour.
heterogéneo, a [etero'xeneo, a] *adj* heterogeneous.
heterosexual [eterosek'swal] *adj, nm/f* heterosexual.
hez [eθ] *nf* (*tb*: **heces** *pl*) dregs.
hibernar [iβer'nar] *vi* to hibernate.
híbrido, a ['iβriðo, a] *adj* hybrid.
hice ['iθe] *etc vb V* **hacer**.
hidalgo, a [i'ðalxo, a] *adj* noble; (*honrado*) honourable (*BRIT*), honorable (*US*) ♦ *nm/f* noble(man/woman).
hidratante [iðra'tante] *adj*: **crema** ~ moisturizing cream, moisturizer.
hidratar [iðra'tar] *vt* to moisturize.
hidrato [i'ðrato] *nm* hydrate; ~ **de carbono** carbohydrate.
hidráulico, a [i'ðrauliko, a] *adj* hydraulic ♦ *nf* hydraulics *sg*.
hidro... [iðro] *pref* hydro..., water-....
hidroavión [iðroa'βjon] *nm* seaplane.

hidroeléctrico, a [iðroe'lektriko, a] *adj* hydroelectric.

hidrófilo, a [i'ðrofilo, a] *adj* absorbent; **algodón** ~ cotton wool (*BRIT*), absorbent cotton (*US*).

hidrofobia [iðro'foßja] *nf* hydrophobia, rabies.

hidrófugo, a [i'ðrofuɣo, a] *adj* damp-proof.

hidrógeno [i'ðroxeno] *nm* hydrogen.

hieda ['jeða] *etc vb V* **heder.**

hiedra ['jeðra] *nf* ivy.

hiel [jel] *nf* gall, bile; (*fig*) bitterness.

hielo ['jelo] *etc vb V* **helar ♦** *nm* (*gen*) ice; (*escarcha*) frost; (*fig*) coldness, reserve; **romper el** ~ (*fig*) to break the ice.

hiena ['jena] *nf* (*ZOOL*) hyena.

hiera ['jera] *etc vb V* **herir.**

hierba ['jerßa] *nf* (*pasto*) grass; (*CULIN, MED: planta*) herb; **mala** ~ weed; (*fig*) evil influence.

hierbabuena [jerßa'ßwena] *nf* mint.

hierro ['jerro] *nm* (*metal*) iron; (*objeto*) iron object; ~ **acanalado** corrugated iron; ~ **colado** *o* **fundido** cast iron; **de** ~ iron *cpd*.

hierva ['jerßa] *etc vb V* **hervir.**

hígado ['iɣaðo] *nm* liver; ~**s** *nmpl* (*fig*) guts; **echar los** ~**s** to wear o.s. out.

higiene [i'xjene] *nf* hygiene.

higiénico, a [i'xjeniko, a] *adj* hygienic.

higo ['iɣo] *nm* fig; ~ **seco** dried fig; ~ **chumbo** prickly pear; **de** ~**s a brevas** once in a blue moon.

higuera [i'ɣera] *nf* fig tree.

hijastro, a [i'xastro, a] *nm/f* stepson/daughter.

hijo, a ['ixo, a] *nm/f* son/daughter, child; (*uso vocativo*) dear; ~**s** *nmpl* children, sons and daughters; **sin** ~**s** childless; ~**/hija político/a** son-/daughter-in-law; ~ **pródigo** prodigal son; ~ **de papá/mamá** daddy's/mummy's boy; ~ **de puta** (*fam!*) bastard (*!*), son of a bitch (*!*); **cada** ~ **de vecino** any Tom, Dick or Harry.

hilacha [i'latʃa] *nf* ravelled thread; ~ **de acero** steel wool.

hilado, a [i'laðo, a] *adj* spun.

hilandero, a [ilan'dero, a] *nm/f* spinner.

hilar [i'lar] *vt* to spin; (*fig*) to reason, infer; ~ **delgado** to split hairs.

hilera [i'lera] *nf* row, file.

hilo ['ilo] *nm* thread; (*BOT*) fibre; (*tela*) linen; (*metal*) wire; (*de agua*) trickle, thin stream; (*de luz*) beam, ray; (*de conversación*) thread, theme; (*de pensamientos*) train; ~ **dental** dental floss; **colgar de un** ~ (*fig*) to hang by a thread; **traje de** ~ linen suit.

hilvanar [ilßa'nar] *vt* (*COSTURA*) to tack

(*BRIT*), baste (*US*); (*fig*) to do hurriedly.

Himalaya [ima'laja] *nm*: **el** ~, **los Montes** ~ the Himalayas.

himno ['imno] *nm* hymn; ~ **nacional** national anthem.

hincapié [inka'pje] *nm*: **hacer** ~ **en** to emphasize, stress.

hincar [in'kar] *vt* to drive (in), thrust (in); (*diente*) to sink; ~**se** *vr*: ~**se de rodillas** (*esp AM*) to kneel down.

hincha ['intʃa] *nm/f* (*fam: DEPORTE*) fan.

hinchado, a [in'tʃaðo, a] *adj* (*gen*) swollen; (*persona*) pompous ♦ *nf* (group of) supporters *o* fans.

hinchar [in'tʃar] *vt* (*gen*) to swell; (*inflar*) to blow up, inflate; (*fig*) to exaggerate; ~**se** *vr* (*inflarse*) to swell up; (*fam: llenarse*) to stuff o.s.; (*fig*) to get conceited; ~**se de reír** to have a good laugh.

hinchazón [intʃa'θon] *nf* (*MED*) swelling; (*protuberancia*) bump, lump; (*altivez*) arrogance.

hindú [in'du] *adj, nm/f* Hindu.

hinojo [i'noxo] *nm* fennel.

hinque ['inke] *etc vb V* **hincar.**

hipar [i'par] *vi* to hiccup.

hiper... [iper] *pref* hyper....

hiperactivo, a [iperak'tißo, a] *adj* hyperactive.

hipermercado [ipermer'kaðo] *nm* hypermarket, superstore.

hipersensible [ipersen'sißle] *adj* hypersensitive.

hipertensión [iperten'sjon] *nf* high blood pressure, hypertension.

hípico, a ['ipiko, a] *adj* horse *cpd*, equine; **club** ~ riding club.

hipnosis [ip'nosis] *nf inv* hypnosis.

hipnotice [ipno'tiθe] *etc vb V* **hipnotizar.**

hipnotismo [ipno'tismo] *nm* hypnotism.

hipnotizar [ipnoti'θar] *vt* to hypnotize.

hipo ['ipo] *nm* hiccups *pl*; **quitar el** ~ **a algn** to cure sb's hiccups.

hipocondría [ipokon'dria] *nf* hypochondria.

hipocondríaco, a [ipokon'driako, a] *adj, nm/f* hypochondriac.

hipocresía [ipokre'sia] *nf* hypocrisy.

hipócrita [i'pokrita] *adj* hypocritical ♦ *nm/f* hypocrite.

hipodérmico, a [ipo'ðermiko, a] *adj*: **aguja hipodérmica** hypodermic needle.

hipódromo [i'poðromo] *nm* racetrack.

hipopótamo [ipo'potamo] *nm* hippopotamus.

hipoteca [ipo'teka] *nf* mortgage; **redimir una** ~ to pay off a mortgage.

hipotecar [ipote'kar] *vt* to mortgage; (*fig*)

to jeopardize.
hipotecario, a [ipote'karjo, a] *adj* mortgage *cpd*.
hipótesis [i'potesis] *nf inv* hypothesis; **es una ~ (nada más)** that's just a theory.
hipotético, a [ipo'tetiko, a] *adj* hypothetic(al).
hiriendo [i'rjendo] *etc vb V* **herir**.
hiriente [i'rjente] *adj* offensive, wounding.
hirsuto, a [ir'suto, a] *adj* hairy.
hirviendo [ir'ßjendo] *etc vb V* **hervir**.
hisopo [i'sopo] *nm* (*REL*) sprinkler; (*BOT*) hyssop; (*de algodón*) swab.
hispánico, a [is'paniko, a] *adj* Hispanic, Spanish.
hispanidad [ispani'ðað] *nf* (*cualidad*) Spanishness; (*POL*) Spanish o Hispanic world.
hispanista [ispa'nista] *nm/f* (*UNIV etc*) Hispan(ic)ist.
hispano, a [is'pano, a] *adj* Hispanic, Spanish, Hispano- ♦ *nm/f* Spaniard.
Hispanoamérica [ispanoa'merika] *nf* Spanish o Latin America.
hispanoamericano, a [ispanoameri'kano, a] *adj, nm/f* Spanish o Latin American.
hispanohablante [ispanoa'ßlante], **hispanoparlante** [ispanopar'lante] *adj* Spanish-speaking.
histeria [is'terja] *nf* hysteria.
histérico, a [is'teriko, a] *adj* hysterical.
histerismo [iste'rismo] *nm* (*MED*) hysteria; (*fig*) hysterics.
histograma [isto'ɣrama] *nm* histogram.
historia [is'torja] *nf* history; (*cuento*) story, tale; **~s** *nfpl* (*chismes*) gossip *sg*; **dejarse de ~s** to come to the point; **pasar a la ~** to go down in history.
historiador, a [istorja'ðor, a] *nm/f* historian.
historial [isto'rjal] *nm* record; (*profesional*) curriculum vitae, c.v., résumé (*US*); (*MED*) case history.
histórico, a [is'toriko, a] *adj* historical; (*fig*) historic.
historieta [isto'rjeta] *nf* tale, anecdote; (*dibujos*) comic strip.
histrionismo [istrjo'nismo] *nm* (*TEAT*) acting; (*fig*) histrionics *pl*.
hito ['ito] *nm* (*fig*) landmark; (*objetivo*) goal, target; (*fig*) milestone.
hizo ['iθo] *vb V* **hacer**.
Hna(s). *abr* (= *Hermana(s)*) Sr(s).
Hno(s). *abr* (= *Hermano(s)*) Bro(s).
hocico [o'θiko] *nm* snout; (*fig*) grimace.
hockey ['xoki] *nm* hockey; **~ sobre hielo** ice hockey.
hogar [o'ɣar] *nm* fireplace, hearth; (*casa*)

home; (*vida familiar*) home life.
hogareño, a [oɣa'reɲo, a] *adj* home *cpd*; (*persona*) home-loving.
hogaza [o'ɣaθa] *nf* (*pan*) large loaf.
hoguera [o'ɣera] *nf* (*gen*) bonfire; (*para herejes*) stake.
hoja ['oxa] *nf* (*gen*) leaf; (*de flor*) petal; (*de hierba*) blade; (*de papel*) sheet; (*página*) page; (*formulario*) form; (*de puerta*) leaf; **~ de afeitar** razor blade; **~ de cálculo electrónico** spreadsheet; **~ de trabajo** (*INFORM*) worksheet; **de ~ ancha** broad-leaved; **de ~ caduca/perenne** deciduous/evergreen.
hojalata [oxa'lata] *nf* tin(plate).
hojaldre [o'xaldre] *nm* (*CULIN*) puff pastry.
hojarasca [oxa'raska] *nf* (*hojas*) dead o fallen leaves *pl*; (*fig*) rubbish.
hojear [oxe'ar] *vt* to leaf through, turn the pages of.
hola ['ola] *excl* hello!
Holanda [o'landa] *nf* Holland.
holandés, esa [olan'des, esa] *adj* Dutch ♦ *nm/f* Dutchman/woman; **los holandeses** the Dutch ♦ *nm* (*LING*) Dutch.
holgado, a [ol'ɣaðo, a] *adj* loose, baggy; (*rico*) well-to-do.
holgar [ol'ɣar] *vi* (*descansar*) to rest; (*sobrar*) to be superfluous; **huelga decir que** it goes without saying that.
holgazán, ana [olɣa'θan, ana] *adj* idle, lazy ♦ *nm/f* loafer.
holgazanear [olɣaθane'ar] *vi* to laze o loaf around.
holgura [ol'ɣura] *nf* looseness, bagginess; (*TEC*) play, free movement; (*vida*) comfortable living, luxury.
hollar [o'ʎar] *vt* to tread (on), trample.
hollín [o'ʎin] *nm* soot.
hombre ['ombre] *nm* man; (*raza humana*): **el ~** man(kind) ♦ *excl*: **¡sí ~!** (*claro*) of course!; (*para énfasis*) man, old chap; **~ de negocios** businessman; **~-rana** frogman; **~ de bien** o **pro** honest man; **~ de confianza** right-hand man; **~ de estado** statesman; **el ~ medio** the average man.
hombrera [om'brera] *nf* shoulder strap.
hombro ['ombro] *nm* shoulder; **arrimar el ~** to lend a hand; **encogerse de ~s** to shrug one's shoulders.
hombruno, a [om'bruno, a] *adj* mannish.
homenaje [ome'naxe] *nm* (*gen*) homage; (*tributo*) tribute; **un partido ~** a benefit match.
homeopatía [omeopa'tia] *nf* hom(o)eopathy.
homeopático, a [omeo'patiko, a] *adj*

hom(o)eopathic.

homicida [omi'θiða] *adj* homicidal ♦ *nm/f* murderer.

homicidio [omi'θiðjo] *nm* murder, homicide; (*involuntario*) manslaughter.

homologación [omoloɣa'θjon] *nf* (*de sueldo, condiciones*) parity.

homologar [omolo'ɣar] *vt* (*COM*) to standardize; (*ESCOL*) to officially approve; (*DEPORTE*) to officially recognize; (*sueldos*) to equalize.

homólogo, a [o'moloɣo, a] *nm/f* counterpart, opposite number.

homónimo [o'monimo] *nm* (*tocayo*) namesake.

homosexual [omosek'swal] *adj*, *nm/f* homosexual.

hondo, a ['ondo, a] *adj* deep; **lo ~ the** depth(s) (*pl*), the bottom; **con ~ pesar** with deep regret.

hondonada [ondo'naða] *nf* hollow, depression; (*cañón*) ravine; (*GEO*) lowland.

hondura [on'dura] *nf* depth, profundity.

Honduras [on'duras] *nf* Honduras.

hondureño, a [ondu'reɲo, a] *adj*, *nm/f* Honduran.

honestidad [onesti'ðað] *nf* purity, chastity; (*decencia*) decency.

honesto, a [o'nesto, a] *adj* chaste; decent, honest; (*justo*) just.

hongo ['ongo] *nm* (*BOT*: *gen*) fungus; (: *comestible*) mushroom; (: *venenoso*) toadstool; (*sombrero*) bowler (hat) (*BRIT*), derby (*US*); **~s del pie** footrot *sg*, athlete's foot *sg*.

honor [o'nor] *nm* (*gen*) honour (*BRIT*), honor (*US*); (*gloria*) glory; **~ profesional** professional etiquette; **en ~ a la verdad** to be fair.

honorable [ono'raβle] *adj* honourable (*BRIT*), honorable (*US*).

honorario, a [ono'rarjo, a] *adj* honorary ♦ *nm*: **~s** fees.

honorífico, a [ono'rifiko, a] *adj* honourable (*BRIT*), honorable (*US*); **mención honorífica** hono(u)rable mention.

honra ['onra] *nf* (*gen*) honour; (*renombre*) good name; **~s fúnebres** funeral rites; **tener algo a mucha ~** to be proud of sth.

honradez [onra'ðeθ] *nf* honesty; (*de persona*) integrity.

honrado, a [on'raðo, a] *adj* honest, upright.

honrar [on'rar] *vt* to honour; **~se** *vr*: **~se con algo/de hacer algo** to be honoured by sth/to do sth.

honroso, a [on'roso, a] *adj* (*honrado*)

honourable; (*respetado*) respectable.

hora ['ora] *nf* hour; (*tiempo*) time; **¿qué ~ es?** what time is it?; **¿a qué ~?** at what time?; **media ~** half an hour; **a la ~ de comer/de recreo** at lunchtime/at playtime; **a primera ~** first thing (in the morning); **a última ~** at the last moment; **"última ~"** "stop press"; **noticias de última ~** last-minute news; **a altas ~s** in the small hours; **a la ~ en punto** on the dot; **¡a buena ~!** about time, too!; **en mala ~** unluckily; **dar la ~** to strike the hour; **poner el reloj en ~** to set one's watch; **~s de oficina/de trabajo** office/working hours; **~s de visita** visiting times; **~s extras o extraordinarias** overtime *sg*; **~s punta** rush hours; **no ver la ~ de** to look forward to; **¡ya era ~!** and about time too!

horadar [ora'ðar] *vt* to drill, bore.

horario, a [o'rarjo, a] *adj* hourly, hour *cpd* ♦ *nm* timetable; **~ comercial** business hours.

horca ['orka] *nf* gallows *sg*; (*AGR*) pitchfork.

horcajadas [orka'xaðas]: **a ~** *adv* astride.

horchata [or'tʃata] *nf* cold drink made from tiger nuts and water, tiger nut milk.

horda ['orða] *nf* horde.

horizontal [oriθon'tal] *adj* horizontal.

horizonte [ori'θonte] *nm* horizon.

horma ['orma] *nf* mould; **~ (de calzado)** last; **~ de sombrero** hat block.

hormiga [or'miɣa] *nf* ant; **~s** *nfpl* (*MED*) pins and needles.

hormigón [ormi'ɣon] *nm* concrete; **~ armado/pretensado** reinforced/ prestressed concrete.

hormigueo [ormi'ɣeo] *nm* (*comezón*) itch; (*fig*) uneasiness.

hormiguero [ormi'ɣero] *nm* (*ZOOL*) ant's nest; **era un ~** it was swarming with people.

hormona [or'mona] *nf* hormone.

hornada [or'naða] *nf* batch of loaves (*etc*).

hornillo [or'niʎo] *nm* (*cocina*) portable stove.

horno ['orno] *nm* (*CULIN*) oven; (*TEC*) furnace; (*para cerámica*) kiln; **~ microondas** microwave (oven); **alto ~** blast furnace; **~ crematorio** crematorium.

horóscopo [o'roskopo] *nm* horoscope.

horquilla [or'kiʎa] *nf* hairpin; (*AGR*) pitchfork.

horrendo, a [o'rrendo, a] *adj* horrendous,

frightful.

horrible [o'rriβle] *adj* horrible, dreadful.

horripilante [orripi'lante] *adj* hair-raising, horrifying.

horripilar [orripi'lar] *vt*: ~ **a algn** to horrify sb; ~**se** *vr* to be horrified.

horror [o'rror] *nm* horror, dread; (*atrocidad*) atrocity; ¡qué ~! (*fam*) how awful!; **estudia horrores** he studies a hell of a lot.

horrorice [orro'riθe] *etc vb V* **horrorizar**.

horrorizar [orrori'θar] *vt* to horrify, frighten; ~**se** *vr* to be horrified.

horroroso, a [orro'roso, a] *adj* horrifying, ghastly.

hortaliza [orta'liθa] *nf* vegetable.

hortelano, a [orte'lano, a] *nm/f* (market) gardener.

hortera [or'tera] *adj* (*fam*) vulgar, naff.

horterada [orte'raða] *nf* (*fam*): **es una** ~ it's really naff.

hortícola [or'tikola] *adj* horticultural.

horticultura [ortikul'tura] *nf* horticulture.

hortofrutícola [ortofru'tikola] *adj* fruit and vegetable *cpd*.

hosco, a ['osko, a] *adj* dark; (*persona*) sullen, gloomy.

hospedaje [ospe'ðaxe] *nm* (cost of) board and lodging.

hospedar [ospe'ðar] *vt* to put up; ~**se** *vr*: ~**se (con/en)** to stay *o* lodge (with/at).

hospedería [ospeðe'ria] *nf* (*edificio*) inn; (*habitación*) guest room.

hospicio [os'piθjo] *nm* (*para niños*) orphanage.

hospital [ospi'tal] *nm* hospital.

hospitalario, a [ospita'larjo, a] *adj* (*acogedor*) hospitable.

hospitalice [ospita'liθe] *etc vb V* **hospitalizar**.

hospitalidad [ospitali'ðað] *nf* hospitality.

hospitalizar [ospitali'θar] *vt* to send *o* take to hospital, hospitalize.

hosquedad [oske'ðað] *nf* sullenness.

hostal [os'tal] *nm* small hotel; *V tb* **hotel**.

hostelería [ostele'ria] *nf* hotel business *o* trade.

hostia ['ostja] *nf* (*REL*) host, consecrated wafer; (*fam*: *golpe*) whack, punch ♦ *excl*: ¡~(s)! (*fam!*) damn!

hostigar [osti'ɣar] *vt* to whip; (*fig*) to harass, pester.

hostigue [os'tiɣe] *etc vb V* **hostigar**.

hostil [os'til] *adj* hostile.

hostilidad [ostili'ðað] *nf* hostility.

hotel [o'tel] *nm* hotel; *see boxed note*.

HOTEL

In Spain you can choose from the following categories of accommodation, in descending order of quality and price: **hotel** *(from five stars down to one), "hostal", "pensión", "casa de huéspedes" or "fonda". Standards can vary widely even within these categories. The state also runs luxury hotels called "paradores", which are usually sited in places of particular historical interest and are often architecturally important buildings themselves.*

---

hotelero, a [ote'lero, a] *adj* hotel *cpd* ♦ *nm/f* hotelier.

hoy [oi] *adv* (*este día*) today; (*en la actualidad*) now(adays) ♦ *nm* present time; ~ **(en) día** now(adays); **el día de** ~, ~ **día** (*AM*) this very day; ~ **por** ~ right now; **de** ~ **en ocho días** a week today; **de** ~ **en adelante** from now on.

hoya ['oja] *nf* pit; (*sepulcro*) grave; (*GEO*) valley.

hoyo ['ojo] *nm* hole, pit; (*tumba*) grave; (*GOLF*) hole; (*MED*) pockmark.

hoyuelo [oj'welo] *nm* dimple.

hoz [oθ] *nf* sickle.

hube ['uβe] *etc vb V* **haber**.

hucha ['utʃa] *nf* money box.

hueco, a ['weko, a] *adj* (*vacío*) hollow, empty; (*resonante*) booming; (*sonido*) resonant; (*persona*) conceited; (*estilo*) pompous ♦ *nm* hollow, cavity; (*agujero*) hole; (*de escalera*) well; (*de ascensor*) shaft; (*vacante*) vacancy; ~ **de la mano** hollow of the hand.

huela ['wela] *etc vb V* **oler**.

huelga ['welɣa] *etc vb V* **holgar** ♦ *nf* strike; **declararse en** ~ to go on strike, come out on strike; ~ **general** general strike; ~ **de hambre** hunger strike; ~ **oficial** official strike.

huelgue ['welɣe] *etc vb V* **holgar**.

huelguista [wel'ɣista] *nm/f* striker.

huella ['weʎa] *nf* (*acto de pisar, pisada*) tread(ing); (*marca del paso*) footprint, footstep; (: *de animal, máquina*) track; ~ **digital** fingerprint; **sin dejar** ~ without leaving a trace.

huérfano, a ['werfano, a] *adj* orphan(ed); (*fig*) unprotected ♦ *nm/f* orphan.

huerta ['werta] *nf* market garden (*BRIT*), truck farm (*US*); (*Murcia, Valencia*) irrigated region.

huerto ['werto] *nm* kitchen garden; (*de*

árboles frutales) orchard.

hueso ['weso] *nm* (*ANAT*) bone; (*de fruta*) stone, pit (*US*); **sin ~** (*carne*) boned; **estar en los ~s** to be nothing but skin and bone; **ser un ~** (*profesor*) to be terribly strict; **un ~ duro de roer** a hard nut to crack.

huesoso, a [we'soso, a] *adj* (*esp AM*) bony.

huésped, a ['wespeð, a] *nm/f* (*invitado*) guest; (*habitante*) resident; (*anfitrión*) host(ess).

huesudo, a [we'suðo, a] *adj* bony, big-boned.

huevas ['weßas] *nfpl* eggs, roe *sg*; (*AM: fam!*) balls (*!*).

huevera [we'ßera] *nf* eggcup.

huevo ['weßo] *nm* egg; (*fam!*) ball (*!*), testicle; **~ duro/escalfado/estrellado** *o* **frito/pasado por agua** hard-boiled/poached/fried/soft-boiled egg; **~s revueltos** scrambled eggs; **me costó un ~** (*fam!*) it was hard work; **tener ~s** (*fam!*) to have guts.

huevón, ona [we'ßon, ona] *nm/f* (*AM fam!*) stupid bastard (*!*), stupid idiot.

huida [u'iða] *nf* escape, flight; **~ de capitales** (*COM*) flight of capital.

huidizo, a [ui'ðiθo, a] *adj* (*tímido*) shy; (*pasajero*) fleeting.

huir [u'ir] *vt* (*escapar*) to flee, escape; (*evadir*) to avoid ♦ *vi* to flee, run away; **~se** *vr* (*escaparse*) to escape.

hule ['ule] *nm* (*encerado*) oilskin; (*esp AM*) rubber.

hulla ['uʎa] *nf* bituminous coal.

humanice [uma'niθe] *etc vb V* **humanizar**.

humanidad [umani'ðað] *nf* (*género humano*) man(kind); (*cualidad*) humanity; (*fam: gordura*) corpulence.

humanitario, a [umani'tarjo, a] *adj* humanitarian; (*benévolo*) humane.

humanizar [umani'θar] *vt* to humanize; **~se** *vr* to become more human.

humano, a [u'mano, a] *adj* (*gen*) human; (*humanitario*) humane ♦ *nm* human; **ser ~** human being.

humareda [uma'reða] *nf* cloud of smoke.

humeante [ume'ante] *adj* smoking, smoky.

humedad [ume'ðað] *nf* (*del clima*) humidity; (*de pared etc*) dampness; **a prueba de ~** damp-proof.

humedecer [umeðe'θer] *vt* to moisten, wet; **~se** *vr* to get wet.

humedezca [ume'ðeθka] *etc vb V* **humedecer**.

húmedo, a ['umeðo, a] *adj* (*mojado*) damp, wet; (*tiempo etc*) humid.

humildad [umil'dað] *nf* humility, humbleness.

humilde [u'milde] *adj* humble, modest; (*clase etc*) low, modest.

humillación [umiʎa'θjon] *nf* humiliation.

humillante [umi'ʎante] *adj* humiliating.

humillar [umi'ʎar] *vt* to humiliate; **~se** *vr* to humble o.s., grovel.

humo ['umo] *nm* (*de fuego*) smoke; (*gas nocivo*) fumes *pl*; (*vapor*) steam, vapour; **~s** *nmpl* (*fig*) conceit *sg*; **irse todo en ~** (*fig*) to vanish without trace; **bajar los ~s a algn** to take sb down a peg or two.

humor [u'mor] *nm* (*disposición*) mood, temper; (*lo que divierte*) humour; **de buen/mal ~** in a good/bad mood.

humorismo [umo'rismo] *nm* humour.

humorista [umo'rista] *nm/f* comic.

humorístico, a [umo'ristiko, a] *adj* funny, humorous.

hundimiento [undi'mjento] *nm* (*gen*) sinking; (*colapso*) collapse.

hundir [un'dir] *vt* to sink; (*edificio, plan*) to ruin, destroy; **~se** *vr* to sink, collapse; (*fig: arruinarse*) to be ruined; (*desaparecer*) to disappear; **se hundió la economía** the economy collapsed; **se hundieron los precios** prices slumped.

húngaro, a ['ungaro, a] *adj, nm/f* Hungarian ♦ *nm* (*LING*) Hungarian, Magyar.

Hungría [un'gria] *nf* Hungary.

huracán [ura'kan] *nm* hurricane.

huraño, a [u'raɲo, a] *adj* shy; (*antisocial*) unsociable.

hurgar [ur'ɣar] *vt* to poke, jab; (*remover*) to stir (up); **~se** *vr*: **~se (las narices)** to pick one's nose.

hurgonear [urɣone'ar] *vt* to poke.

hurgue ['urɣe] *etc vb V* **hurgar**.

hurón [u'ron] *nm* (*ZOOL*) ferret.

hurra ['urra] *excl* hurray!, hurrah!

hurtadillas [urta'ðiʎas]: **a ~** *adv* stealthily, on the sly.

hurtar [ur'tar] *vt* to steal; **~se** *vr* to hide, keep out of the way.

hurto ['urto] *nm* theft, stealing; (*lo robado*) (piece of) stolen property, loot.

husmear [usme'ar] *vt* (*oler*) to sniff out, scent; (*fam*) to pry into ♦ *vi* to smell bad.

huso ['uso] *nm* (*TEC*) spindle; (*de torno*) drum.

huy ['ui] *excl* (*dolor*) ow!, ouch!; (*sorpresa*) well!; (*alivio*) phew!; ¡**~, perdona!** oops, sorry!

huyendo [u'jendo] *etc vb V* **huir**.

I i

I, i [i] nf (letra) I, i; **I de Inés** I for Isaac.
I.A. abr = **inteligencia artificial**.
iba ['iβa] etc vb V **ir**.
Iberia [i'βerja] nf Iberia.
ibérico, a [i'βeriko, a] adj Iberian; **la Península ibérica** the Iberian Peninsula.
ibero, a [i'βero, a], **íbero, a** ['iβero, a] adj, nm/f Iberian.
iberoamericano, a [iβeroameri'kano, a] adj, nm/f Latin American.
íbice ['iβiθe] nm ibex.
ibicenco, a [iβi'θenko, a] adj of o from Ibiza ♦ nm/f native o inhabitant of Ibiza.
ice ['iθe] etc vb V **izar**.
iceberg [iθe'ber] nm iceberg.
ICONA [i'kona] nm abr (ESP) = **Instituto Nacional para la Conservación de la Naturaleza**.
icono [i'kono] nm (tb INFORM) icon.
iconoclasta [ikono'klasta] adj iconoclastic ♦ nm/f iconoclast.
ictericia [ikte'riθja] nf jaundice.
íd. abr = **ídem**.
I+D abr (= Investigación y Desarrollo) R&D.
ida ['iða] nf going, departure; ~ **y vuelta** round trip, return; ~**s y venidas** comings and goings.
IDE ['iðe] nf abr (= Iniciativa de Defensa Estratégica) SDI.
idea [i'ðea] nf idea; (impresión) opinion; (propósito) intention; ~ **genial** brilliant idea; **a mala** ~ out of spite; **no tengo la menor** ~ I haven't a clue.
ideal [iðe'al] adj, nm ideal.
idealice [iðea'liθe] etc vb V **idealizar**.
idealista [iðea'lista] adj idealistic ♦ nm/f idealist.
idealizar [iðeali'θar] vt to idealize.
idear [iðe'ar] vt to think up; (aparato) to invent; (viaje) to plan.
ídem ['iðem] pron ditto.
idéntico, a [i'ðentiko, a] adj identical.
identidad [iðenti'ðað] nf identity; ~ **corporativa** corporate identity o image.
identificación [iðentifika'θjon] nf identification.
identificador de llamadas [iðentifika'ðor-] nm caller ID.

identificar [iðentifi'kar] vt to identify; ~**se** vr: ~**se con** to identify with.
identifique [iðenti'fike] etc vb V **identificar**.
ideología [iðeolo'xia] nf ideology.
ideológico, a [iðeo'loxiko, a] adj ideological.
idílico, a [i'ðiliko, a] adj idyllic.
idilio [i'ðiljo] nm love affair.
idioma [i'ðjoma] nm language.
idiomático, a [iðjo'matiko, a] adj idiomatic.
idiota [i'ðjota] adj idiotic ♦ nm/f idiot.
idiotez [iðjo'teθ] nf idiocy.
idolatrar [iðola'trar] vt (fig) to idolize.
ídolo ['iðolo] nm (tb fig) idol.
idoneidad [iðonei'ðað] nf suitability; (capacidad) aptitude.
idóneo, a [i'ðoneo, a] adj suitable.
iglesia [i'ɣlesja] nf church; ~ **parroquial** parish church; **¡con la** ~ **hemos topado!** now we're really up against it!
iglú [i'ɣlu] nm igloo; (contenedor) bottle bank.
ignición [iɣni'θjon] nf ignition.
ignominia [iɣno'minja] nf ignominy.
ignominioso, a [iɣnomi'njoso, a] adj ignominious.
ignorado, a [iɣno'raðo, a] adj unknown; (dato) obscure.
ignorancia [iɣno'ranθja] nf ignorance; **por** ~ through ignorance.
ignorante [iɣno'rante] adj ignorant, uninformed ♦ nm/f ignoramus.
ignorar [iɣno'rar] vt not to know, be ignorant of; (no hacer caso a) to ignore; **ignoramos su paradero** we don't know his whereabouts.
ignoto, a [iɣ'noto, a] adj unknown.
igual [i'ɣwal] adj equal; (similar) like, similar; (mismo) (the) same; (constante) constant; (temperatura) even ♦ nm/f equal; **al** ~ **que** prep, conj like, just like; ~ **que** the same as; **sin** ~ peerless; **me da** o **es** ~ I don't care, it makes no difference; **no tener** ~ to be unrivalled; **son** ~**es** they're the same.
iguala [i'ɣwala] nf equalization; (COM) agreement.
igualada [iɣwa'laða] nf equalizer.
igualar [iɣwa'lar] vt (gen) to equalize, make equal; (terreno) to make even; (COM) to agree upon; ~**se** vr (platos de balanza) to balance out; ~**se (a)** (equivaler) to be equal (to).
igualdad [iɣwal'dað] nf equality; (similaridad) sameness; (uniformidad) uniformity; **en** ~ **de condiciones** on an equal basis.

igualmente [iɣwal'mente] *adv* equally; (*también*) also, likewise ♦ *excl* the same to you!

iguana [i'ɣwana] *nf* iguana.

ikurriña [iku'rriɲa] *nf* Basque flag.

ilegal [ile'ɣal] *adj* illegal.

ilegitimidad [ilexitimi'ðað] *nf* illegitimacy.

ilegítimo, a [ile'xitimo, a] *adj* illegitimate.

ileso, a [i'leso, a] *adj* unhurt, unharmed.

ilícito, a [i'liθito, a] *adj* illicit.

ilimitado, a [ilimi'taðo, a] *adj* unlimited.

Ilma., Ilmo. *abr* (= *Ilustrísima, Ilustrísimo*) courtesy title.

ilógico, a [i'loxiko, a] *adj* illogical.

iluminación [ilumina'θjon] *nf* illumination; (*alumbrado*) lighting; (*fig*) enlightenment.

iluminar [ilumi'nar] *vt* to illuminate, light (up); (*fig*) to enlighten.

ilusión [ilu'sjon] *nf* illusion; (*quimera*) delusion; (*esperanza*) hope; (*emoción*) excitement, thrill; **hacerse ilusiones** to build up one's hopes; **no te hagas ilusiones** don't build up your hopes o get too excited.

ilusionado, a [ilusjo'naðo, a] *adj* excited.

ilusionar [ilusjo'nar] *vt*: ~ **a algn** (*falsamente*) to build up sb's hopes; ~**se** *vr* (*falsamente*) to build up one's hopes; (*entusiasmarse*) to get excited; **me ilusiona mucho el viaje** I'm really excited about the trip.

ilusionista [ilusjo'nista] *nm/f* conjurer.

iluso, a [i'luso, a] *adj* gullible, easily deceived ♦ *nm/f* dreamer, visionary.

ilusorio, a [ilu'sorjo, a] *adj* (*de ilusión*) illusory, deceptive; (*esperanza*) vain.

ilustración [ilustra'θjon] *nf* illustration; (*saber*) learning, erudition; **la I**~ the Enlightenment.

ilustrado, a [ilus'traðo, a] *adj* illustrated; learned.

ilustrar [ilus'trar] *vt* to illustrate; (*instruir*) to instruct; (*explicar*) to explain, make clear; ~**se** *vr* to acquire knowledge.

ilustre [i'lustre] *adj* famous, illustrious.

imagen [i'maxen] *nf* (*gen*) image; (*dibujo, TV*) picture; (*REL*) statue; **ser la viva ~ de** to be the spitting o living image of; **a su ~** in one's own image.

imaginación [imaxina'θjon] *nf* imagination; (*fig*) fancy; **ni por ~** on no account; **no se me pasó por la ~ que ...** it never even occurred to me that ....

imaginar [imaxi'nar] *vt* (*gen*) to imagine; (*idear*) to think up; (*suponer*) to suppose; ~**se** *vr* to imagine; **¡imagínate!** just imagine!, just fancy!; **imagínese que ...**

suppose that ...; **me imagino que sí** I should think so.

imaginario, a [imaxi'narjo, a] *adj* imaginary.

imaginativo, a [imaxina'tiβo, a] *adj* imaginative ♦ *nf* imagination.

imán [i'man] *nm* magnet.

iman(t)ar [ima'n(t)ar] *vt* to magnetize.

imbécil [im'beθil] *nm/f* imbecile, idiot.

imbecilidad [imbeθili'ðað] *nf* imbecility, stupidity.

imberbe [im'berβe] *adj* beardless.

imborrable [imbo'rraβle] *adj* indelible; (*inolvidable*) unforgettable.

imbuir [imbu'ir] *vi* to imbue.

imbuyendo [imbu'jendo] *etc vb* V **imbuir**.

imitación [imita'θjon] *nf* imitation; (*parodia*) mimicry; **a ~ de** in imitation of; **desconfíe de las imitaciones** (*COM*) beware of copies o imitations.

imitador, a [imita'ðor, a] *adj* imitative ♦ *nm/f* imitator; (*TEAT*) mimic.

imitar [imi'tar] *vt* to imitate; (*parodiar, remedar*) to mimic, ape; (*copiar*) to follow.

impaciencia [impa'θjenθja] *nf* impatience.

impacientar [impaθjen'tar] *vt* to make impatient; (*enfadar*) to irritate; ~**se** *vr* to get impatient; (*inquietarse*) to fret.

impaciente [impa'θjente] *adj* impatient; (*nervioso*) anxious.

impacto [im'pakto] *nm* impact; (*esp AM: fig*) shock.

impagado, a [impa'ɣaðo, a] *adj* unpaid, still to be paid.

impar [im'par] *adj* odd ♦ *nm* odd number.

imparable [impa'raβle] *adj* unstoppable.

imparcial [impar'θjal] *adj* impartial, fair.

imparcialidad [imparθjali'ðað] *nf* impartiality, fairness.

impartir [impar'tir] *vt* to impart, give.

impasible [impa'siβle] *adj* impassive.

impávido, a [im paβiðo, a] *adj* fearless, intrepid.

IMPE ['impe] *nm abr* (*ESP COM*) = *Instituto de la Mediana y Pequeña Empresa*.

impecable [impe'kaβle] *adj* impeccable.

impedido, a [impe'ðiðo, a] *adj*: **estar ~ to** be an invalid ♦ *nm/f*: **ser un ~ físico** to be an invalid.

impedimento [impeði'mento] *nm* impediment, obstacle.

impedir [impe'ðir] *vt* (*obstruir*) to impede, obstruct; (*estorbar*) to prevent; ~ **el tráfico** to block the traffic.

impeler [impe'ler] *vt* to drive, propel; (*fig*) to impel.

impenetrabilidad [impenetraβili'ðað] *nf*

impenetrability.
impenetrable [impene'traβle] *adj*
impenetrable; (*fig*) incomprehensible.
impensable [impen'saβle] *adj* unthinkable.
impepinable [impepi'naβle] *adj* (*fam*)
certain, inevitable.
imperante [impe'rante] *adj* prevailing.
imperar [impe'rar] *vi* (*reinar*) to rule, reign;
(*fig*) to prevail, reign; (*precio*) to be
current.
imperativo, a [impera'tiβo, a] *adj* (*persona*)
imperious; (*urgente, LING*) imperative.
imperceptible [imperθep'tiβle] *adj*
imperceptible.
imperdible [imper'ðiβle] *nm* safety pin.
imperdonable [imperðo'naβle] *adj*
unforgivable, inexcusable.
imperecedero, a [impereθe'ðero, a] *adj*
undying.
imperfección [imperfek'θjon] *nf*
imperfection; (*falla*) flaw, fault.
imperfecto, a [imper'fekto, a] *adj* faulty,
imperfect ♦ *nm* (*LING*) imperfect tense.
imperial [impe'rjal] *adj* imperial.
imperialismo [imperja'lismo] *nm*
imperialism.
imperialista [imperja'lista] *adj*
imperialist(ic) ♦ *nmlf* imperialist.
impericia [impe'riθja] *nf* (*torpeza*)
unskilfulness; (*inexperiencia*)
inexperience.
imperio [im'perjo] *nm* empire; (*autoridad*)
rule, authority; (*fig*) pride, haughtiness;
vale un ~ (*fig*) it's worth a fortune.
imperioso, a [impe'rjoso, a] *adj* imperious;
(*urgente*) urgent; (*imperativo*)
imperative.
impermeable [imperme'aβle] *adj* (*a prueba
de agua*) waterproof ♦ *nm* raincoat, mac
(*BRIT*).
impersonal [imperso'nal] *adj* impersonal.
impertérrito, a [imper'territo, a] *adj*
undaunted.
impertinencia [imperti'nenθja] *nf*
impertinence.
impertinente [imperti'nente] *adj*
impertinent.
imperturbable [impertur'βaβle] *adj*
imperturbable; (*sereno*) unruffled;
(*impasible*) impassive.
ímpetu ['impetu] *nm* (*impulso*) impetus,
impulse; (*impetuosidad*) impetuosity;
(*violencia*) violence.
impetuosidad [impetwosi'ðað] *nf*
impetuousness; (*violencia*) violence.
impetuoso, a [impe'twoso, a] *adj*
impetuous; (*río*) rushing; (*acto*) hasty.
impida [im'piða] *etc vb V* **impedir**.

impío, a [im'pio, a] *adj* impious, ungodly;
(*cruel*) cruel, pitiless.
implacable [impla'kaβle] *adj* implacable,
relentless.
implantación [implanta'θjon] *nf*
introduction; (*BIO*) implantation.
implantar [implan'tar] *vt* (*costumbre*) to
introduce; (*BIO*) to implant; **~se** *vr* to be
introduced.
implicar [impli'kar] *vt* to involve; (*entrañar*)
to imply; **esto no implica que ...** this does
not mean that ....
implícito, a [im'pliθito, a] *adj* (*tácito*)
implicit; (*sobreentendido*) implied.
implique [im'plike] *etc vb V* **implicar**.
implorar [implo'rar] *vt* to beg,
implore.
impondré [impon'dre] *etc vb V* **imponer**.
imponente [impo'nente] *adj*
(*impresionante*) impressive, imposing;
(*solemne*) grand ♦ *nmlf* (*COM*) depositor.
imponer [impo'ner] *vt* (*gen*) to impose;
(*tarea*) to set; (*exigir*) to exact; (*miedo*) to
inspire; (*COM*) to deposit; **~se** *vr* to
assert o.s.; (*prevalecer*) to prevail;
(*costumbre*) to grow up; **~se un deber** to
assume a duty.
imponga [im'ponga] *etc vb V* **imponer**.
imponible [impo'niβle] *adj* (*COM*) taxable,
subject to tax; (*importación*) dutiable,
subject to duty; **no ~** tax-free, tax-
exempt (*US*).
impopular [impopu'lar] *adj* unpopular.
importación [importa'θjon] *nf* (*acto*)
importing; (*mercancías*) imports *pl*.
importancia [impor'tanθja] *nf* importance;
(*valor*) value, significance; (*extensión*)
size, magnitude; **no dar ~ a** to consider
unimportant; (*fig*) to make light of; **no
tiene ~** it's nothing.
importante [impor'tante] *adj* important;
valuable, significant.
importar [impor'tar] *vt* (*del extranjero*) to
import; (*costar*) to amount to; (*implicar*)
to involve ♦ *vi* to be important, matter;
me importa un bledo I don't give a
damn; **¿le importa que fume?** do you
mind if I smoke?; **¿te importa
prestármelo?** would you mind lending it
to me?; **¿qué importa?** what difference
does it make?; **no importa** it doesn't
matter; **no le importa** he doesn't care, it
doesn't bother him; **"no importa precio"**
"cost no object".
importe [im'porte] *nm* (*total*) amount;
(*valor*) value.
importunar [importu'nar] *vt* to bother,
pester.

importuno, a [impor'tuno, a] adj
(inoportuno, molesto) inopportune;
(indiscreto) troublesome.

imposibilidad [imposiβili'ðað] nf
impossibility; **mi ~ para hacerlo** my
inability to do it.

imposibilitado, a [imposiβili'taðo, a] adj:
verse ~ para hacer algo to be unable to
do sth.

imposibilitar [imposiβili'tar] vt to make
impossible, prevent.

imposible [impo'siβle] adj impossible;
(insoportable) unbearable, intolerable; **es
~** it's out of the question; **es ~ de
predecir** it's impossible to forecast o
predict.

imposición [imposi'θjon] nf imposition;
(COM) tax; (inversión) deposit; **efectuar
una ~** to make a deposit.

impostor, a [impos'tor, a] nm/f impostor.

impostura [impos'tura] nf fraud,
imposture.

impotencia [impo'tenθja] nf impotence.

impotente [impo'tente] adj impotent.

impracticable [imprakti'kaβle] adj
(irrealizable) impracticable; (intransitable)
impassable.

imprecar [impre'kar] vi to curse.

imprecisión [impreθi'sjon] nf lack of
precision, vagueness.

impreciso, a [impre'θiso, a] adj imprecise,
vague.

impredecible [impreðe'θiβle],
impredictible [impreðik'tiβle] adj
unpredictable.

impregnar [impreɣ'nar] vt to impregnate;
(fig) to pervade; **~se** vr to become
impregnated.

imprenta [im'prenta] nf (acto) printing;
(aparato) press; (casa) printer's; (letra)
print.

impreque [im'preke] etc vb V
imprecar.

imprescindible [impresθin'diβle] adj
essential, vital.

impresión [impre'sjon] nf impression;
(IMPRENTA) printing; (edición) edition;
(FOTO) print; (marca) imprint; **~ digital**
fingerprint.

impresionable [impresjo'naβle] adj
(sensible) impressionable.

impresionado, a [impresjo'naðo, a] adj
impressed; (FOTO) exposed.

impresionante [impresjo'nante] adj
impressive; (tremendo) tremendous;
(maravilloso) great, marvellous.

impresionar [impresjo'nar] vt (conmover)
to move; (afectar) to impress, strike;

(película fotográfica) to expose; **~se** vr to
be impressed; (conmoverse) to be
moved.

impresionista [impresjo'nista] adj
impressionist(ic); (ARTE) impressionist
♦ nm/f impressionist.

impreso, a [im'preso, a] pp de **imprimir**
♦ adj printed ♦ nm printed paper/book
etc; **~s** nmpl printed matter sg; **~ de
solicitud** application form.

impresora [impre'sora] nf (INFORM)
printer; **~ de chorro de tinta** ink-jet
printer; **~ (por) láser** laser printer; **~ de
línea** line printer; **~ de matriz (de
agujas)** dot-matrix printer; **~ de rueda** o
de margarita daisy-wheel printer.

imprevisible [impreβi'siβle] adj
unforeseeable; (individuo) unpredictable.

imprevisión [impreβi'sjon] nf short-
sightedness; (irreflexión)
thoughtlessness.

imprevisto, a [impre'βisto, a] adj
unforeseen; (inesperado) unexpected
♦ nm: **~s** (dinero) incidentals, unforeseen
expenses.

imprimir [impri'mir] vt to stamp; (textos) to
print; (INFORM) to output, print out.

improbabilidad [improβaβili'ðað] nf
improbability, unlikelihood.

improbable [impro'βaβle] adj improbable;
(inverosímil) unlikely.

improcedente [improθe'ðente] adj
inappropriate; (JUR) inadmissible.

improductivo, a [improðuk'tiβo, a] adj
unproductive.

impronunciable [impronun'θjaβle] adj
unpronounceable.

improperio [impro'perjo] nm insult; **~s**
nmpl abuse sg.

impropiedad [impropje'ðað] nf
impropriety (of language).

impropio, a [im'propjo, a] adj improper;
(inadecuado) inappropriate.

improvisación [improβisa'θjon] nf
improvization.

improvisado, a [improβi'saðo, a] adj
improvised, impromptu.

improvisar [improβi'sar] vt to improvise;
(comida) to rustle up ♦ vi to improvise;
(MUS) to extemporize; (TEAT etc) to ad-
lib.

improviso [impro'βiso]: adv **de ~**
unexpectedly, suddenly; (MUS etc)
impromptu.

imprudencia [impru'denθja] nf
imprudence; (indiscreción) indiscretion;
(descuido) carelessness.

imprudente [impru'ðente] adj imprudent;

indiscreet.

Impte. *abr* (= *Importe*) amt.

impúdico, a [im'puðiko, a] *adj* shameless; (*lujurioso*) lecherous.

impudor [impu'ðor] *nm* shamelessness; (*lujuria*) lechery.

impuesto, a [im'pwesto, a] *pp de* **imponer** ♦ *adj* imposed ♦ *nm* tax; (*derecho*) duty; **anterior al** ~ pre-tax; **sujeto a** ~ taxable; ~ **de lujo** luxury tax; ~ **de plusvalía** capital gains tax; ~ **sobre la propiedad** property tax; ~ **sobre la renta** income tax; ~ **sobre la renta de las personas físicas (IRPF)** personal income tax; ~ **sobre la riqueza** wealth tax; ~ **de transferencia de capital** capital transfer tax; ~ **de venta** sales tax; ~ **sobre el valor añadido (IVA)** value added tax (VAT).

impugnar [impuɣ'nar] *vt* to oppose, contest; (*refutar*) to refute, impugn.

impulsar [impul'sar] *vt* to promote.

impulsivo, a [impul'siβo, a] *adj* impulsive.

impulso [im'pulso] *nm* impulse; (*fuerza, empuje*) thrust, drive; (*fig: sentimiento*) urge, impulse; **a ~s del miedo** driven on by fear.

impune [im'pune] *adj* unpunished.

impunemente [impune'mente] *adv* with impunity.

impureza [impu'reθa] *nf* impurity; (*fig*) lewdness.

impuro, a [im'puro, a] *adj* impure; lewd.

impuse [im'puse] *etc vb V* **imponer**.

imputación [imputa'θjon] *nf* imputation.

imputar [impu'tar] *vt*: ~ **a** to attribute to, to impute to.

inabordable [inaβor'ðaβle] *adj* unapproachable.

inacabable [inaka'βaβle] *adj* (*infinito*) endless; (*interminable*) interminable.

inaccesible [inakθe'siβle] *adj* inaccessible; (*fig: precio*) beyond one's reach, prohibitive; (*individuo*) aloof.

inacción [inak'θjon] *nf* inactivity.

inaceptable [inaθep'taβle] *adj* unacceptable.

inactividad [inaktiβi'ðað] *nf* inactivity; (*COM*) dullness.

inactivo, a [inak'tiβo, a] *adj* inactive; (*COM*) dull; (*población*) non-working.

inadaptación [inaðapta'θjon] *nf* maladjustment.

inadaptado, a [inaðap'taðo, a] *adj* maladjusted ♦ *nm/f* misfit.

inadecuado, a [inaðe'kwaðo, a] *adj* (*insuficiente*) inadequate; (*inapto*) unsuitable.

inadmisible [inaðmi'siβle] *adj* inadmissible.

inadvertido, a [inaðβer'tiðo, a] *adj* (*no visto*) unnoticed.

inagotable [inaɣo'taβle] *adj* inexhaustible.

inaguantable [inaɣwan'taβle] *adj* unbearable.

inalámbrico, a [ina'lambriko, a] *adj* cordless.

inalcanzable [inalkan'θaβle] *adj* unattainable.

inalterable [inalte'raβle] *adj* immutable, unchangeable.

inamovible [inamo'βiβle] *adj* fixed, immovable; (*TEC*) undetachable.

inanición [inani'θjon] *nf* starvation.

inanimado, a [inani'maðo, a] *adj* inanimate.

inapelable [inape'laβle] *adj* (*JUR*) unappealable; (*fig*) irremediable.

inapetencia [inape'tenθja] *nf* lack of appetite.

inaplicable [inapli'kaβle] *adj* not applicable.

inapreciable [inapre'θjaβle] *adj* invaluable.

inarrugable [inarru'ɣaβle] *adj* crease-resistant.

inasequible [inase'kiβle] *adj* unattainable.

inaudito, a [inau'ðito, a] *adj* unheard-of.

inauguración [inauɣura'θjon] *nf* inauguration; (*de exposición*) opening.

inaugurar [inauɣu'rar] *vt* to inaugurate; to open.

I.N.B. *abr* (= *Instituto Nacional de Bachillerato*) ≈ comprehensive school (*BRIT*), high school (*US*).

I.N.B.A. *abr* (*AM*) = *Instituto Nacional de Bellas Artes*.

inca ['inka] *nm/f* Inca.

INCAE [in'kae] *nm abr* = *Instituto Centroamericano de Administración de Empresas*.

incaico, a [in'kaiko, a] *adj* Inca.

incalculable [inkalku'laβle] *adj* incalculable.

incandescente [inkandes'θente] *adj* incandescent.

incansable [inkan'saβle] *adj* tireless, untiring.

incapacidad [inkapaθi'ðað] *nf* incapacity; (*incompetencia*) incompetence; ~ **física/mental** physical/mental disability.

incapacitar [inkapaθi'tar] *vt* (*inhabilitar*) to incapacitate, handicap; (*descalificar*) to disqualify.

incapaz [inka'paθ] *adj* incapable; ~ **de hacer algo** unable to do sth.

incautación [inkauta'θjon] *nf* seizure,

confiscation.

incautarse [inkau'tarse] *vr*: ~ **de** to seize, confiscate.

incauto, a [in'kauto, a] *adj (imprudente)* incautious, unwary.

incendiar [inθen'djar] *vt* to set fire to; *(fig)* to inflame; ~**se** *vr* to catch fire.

incendiario, a [inθen'djarjo, a] *adj* incendiary ♦ *nm/f* fire-raiser, arsonist.

incendio [in'θendjo] *nm* fire; ~ **intencionado** arson.

incentivo [inθen'tiβo] *nm* incentive.

incertidumbre [inθerti'ðumbre] *nf (inseguridad)* uncertainty; *(duda)* doubt.

incesante [inθe'sante] *adj* incessant.

incesto [in'θesto] *nm* incest.

incidencia [inθi'ðenθja] *nf (MAT)* incidence; *(fig)* effect.

incidente [inθi'ðente] *nm* incident.

incidir [inθi'ðir] *vi*: ~ **en** *(influir)* to influence; *(afectar)* to affect; ~ **en un error** to be mistaken.

incienso [in'θjenso] *nm* incense.

incierto, a [in'θjerto, a] *adj* uncertain.

incineración [inθinera'θjon] *nf* incineration; *(de cadáveres)* cremation.

incinerar [inθine'rar] *vt* to burn; to cremate.

incipiente [inθi'pjente] *adj* incipient.

incisión [inθi'sjon] *nf* incision.

incisivo, a [inθi'siβo, a] *adj* sharp, cutting; *(fig)* incisive.

inciso [in'θiso] *nm (LING)* clause, sentence; *(coma)* comma; *(JUR)* subsection.

incitante [inθi'tante] *adj (estimulante)* exciting; *(provocativo)* provocative.

incitar [inθi'tar] *vt* to incite, rouse.

incivil [inθi'βil] *adj* rude, uncivil.

inclemencia [inkle'menθja] *nf (severidad)* harshness, severity; *(del tiempo)* inclemency.

inclemente [inkle'mente] *adj* harsh, severe; inclement.

inclinación [inklina'θjon] *nf (gen)* inclination; *(de tierras)* slope, incline; *(de cabeza)* nod, bow; *(fig)* leaning, bent.

inclinado, a [inkli'naðo, a] *adj (objeto)* leaning; *(superficie)* sloping.

inclinar [inkli'nar] *vt* to incline; *(cabeza)* to nod, bow; ~**se** *vr* to lean, slope; *(en reverencia)* to bow; *(encorvarse)* to stoop; ~**se a** *(parecerse)* to take after, resemble; ~**se ante** to bow down to; **me inclino a pensar que** ... I'm inclined to think that ....

incluir [inklu'ir] *vt* to include; *(incorporar)* to incorporate; *(meter)* to enclose; **todo incluido** *(COM)* inclusive, all-in.

inclusive [inklu'siße] *adv* inclusive ♦ *prep* including.

incluso, a [in'kluso, a] *adj* included ♦ *adv* inclusively; *(hasta)* even.

incluyendo [inklu'jendo] *etc vb V* **incluir**.

incobrable [inko'ßraße] *adj* irrecoverable; *(deuda)* bad.

incógnita [in'koɣnita] *nf (fig)* mystery.

incógnito [in'koɣnito]: **de** ~ *adv* incognito.

incoherencia [inkoe'renθja] *nf* incoherence; *(falta de conexión)* disconnectedness.

incoherente [inkoe'rente] *adj* incoherent.

incoloro, a [inko'loro, a] *adj* colourless.

incólume [in'kolume] *adj* safe; *(indemne)* unhurt, unharmed.

incombustible [inkombus'tiße] *adj (gen)* fire-resistant; *(telas)* fireproof.

incomodar [inkomo'ðar] *vt* to inconvenience; *(molestar)* to bother, trouble; *(fastidiar)* to annoy; ~**se** *vr* to put o.s. out; *(fastidiarse)* to get annoyed; **no se incomode** don't bother.

incomodidad [inkomoði'ðað] *nf* inconvenience; *(fastidio, enojo)* annoyance; *(de vivienda)* discomfort.

incómodo, a [in'komoðo, a] *adj (inconfortable)* uncomfortable; *(molesto)* annoying; *(inconveniente)* inconvenient; **sentirse** ~ to feel ill at ease.

incomparable [inkompa'raße] *adj* incomparable.

incomparecencia [inkompare'θenθja] *nf (JUR etc)* failure to appear.

incompatible [inkompa'tiße] *adj* incompatible.

incompetencia [inkompe'tenθja] *nf* incompetence.

incompetente [inkompe'tente] *adj* incompetent.

incompleto, a [inkom'pleto, a] *adj* incomplete, unfinished.

incomprendido, a [inkompren'diðo, a] *adj* misunderstood.

incomprensible [inkompren'siße] *adj* incomprehensible.

incomunicado, a [inkomuni'kaðo, a] *adj (aislado)* cut off, isolated; *(confinado)* in solitary confinement.

incomunicar [inkomuni'kar] *vt (gen)* to cut off; *(preso)* to put into solitary confinement; ~**se** *vr (fam)* to go into one's shell.

incomunique [inkomu'nike] *etc vb V* **incomunicar**.

inconcebible [inkonθe'ßiße] *adj* inconceivable.

inconcluso, a [inkon'kluso, a] *adj*

(*inacabado*) unfinished.

incondicional [inkondi'θjo'nal] *adj*
unconditional; (*apoyo*) wholehearted;
(*partidario*) staunch.

inconexo, a [inko'nekso, a] *adj*
unconnected; (*desunido*) disconnected;
(*incoherente*) incoherent.

inconfeso, a [inkon'feso, a] *adj*
unconfessed; **un homosexual** ~ a closet
homosexual.

inconformista [inkonfor'mista] *adj, nm/f*
nonconformist.

inconfundible [inkonfun'diβle] *adj*
unmistakable.

incongruente [inkon'grwente] *adj*
incongruous.

inconmensurable [inkonmensu'raβle] *adj*
immeasurable, vast.

inconsciencia [inkons'θjenθja] *nf*
unconsciousness; (*fig*) thoughtlessness.

inconsciente [inkons'θjente] *adj*
unconscious; thoughtless; (*ignorante*)
unaware; (*involuntario*) unwitting.

inconsecuencia [inkonse'kwenθja] *nf*
inconsistency.

inconsecuente [inkonse'kwente] *adj*
inconsistent.

inconsiderado, a [inkonsiðe'raðo, a] *adj*
inconsiderate.

inconsistente [inkonsis'tente] *adj*
inconsistent; (*CULIN*) lumpy; (*endeble*)
weak; (*tela*) flimsy.

inconstancia [inkons'tanθja] *nf*
inconstancy; (*de tiempo*) changeability;
(*capricho*) fickleness.

inconstante [inkons'tante] *adj* inconstant;
changeable; fickle.

incontable [inkon'taβle] *adj* countless,
innumerable.

incontestable [inkontes'taβle] *adj*
unanswerable; (*innegable*) undeniable.

incontinencia [inkonti'nenθja] *nf*
incontinence.

incontrolado, a [inkontro'laðo, a] *adj*
uncontrolled.

incontrovertible [inkontroβer'tiβle] *adj*
undeniable, incontrovertible.

inconveniencia [inkombe'njenθja] *nf*
unsuitability, inappropriateness;
(*descortesía*) impoliteness.

inconveniente [inkombe'njente] *adj*
unsuitable; impolite ♦ *nm* obstacle;
(*desventaja*) disadvantage; **el** ~ **es que** ...
the trouble is that ...; **no hay** ~ **en** o **para
hacer eso** there is no objection to doing
that; **no tengo** ~ I don't mind.

incordiar [inkor'ðjar] *vt* (*fam*) to hassle.

incorporación [inkorpora'θjon] *nf*

incorporation; (*fig*) inclusion.

incorporado, a [inkorpo'raðo, a] *adj* (*TEC*)
built-in.

incorporar [inkorpo'rar] *vt* to incorporate;
(*abarcar*) to embody; (*CULIN*) to mix; ~**se**
vr to sit up; ~**se a** to join.

incorrección [inkorrek'θjon] *nf*
incorrectness, inaccuracy; (*descortesía*)
bad-mannered behaviour.

incorrecto, a [inko'rrekto, a] *adj* incorrect,
wrong; (*comportamiento*) bad-mannered.

incorregible [inkorre'xiβle] *adj*
incorrigible.

incorruptible [inkorrup'tiβle] *adj*
incorruptible.

incorrupto, a [inko'rrupto, a] *adj*
uncorrupted; (*fig*) pure.

incredulidad [inkreðuli'ðað] *nf* incredulity;
(*escepticismo*) scepticism.

incrédulo, a [in'kreðulo, a] *adj*
incredulous, unbelieving; sceptical.

increíble [inkre'iβle] *adj* incredible.

incrementar [inkremen'tar] *vt* (*aumentar*)
to increase; (*alzar*) to raise; ~**se** *vr* to
increase.

incremento [inkre'mento] *nm* increment;
(*aumento*) rise, increase; ~ **de precio**
rise in price.

increpar [inkre'par] *vt* to reprimand.

incriminar [inkrimi'nar] *vt* (*JUR*) to
incriminate.

incruento, a [in'krwento, a] *adj* bloodless.

incrustar [inkrus'tar] *vt* to incrust; (*piedras:
en joya*) to inlay; (*fig*) to graft; (*TEC*) to
set.

incubar [inku'βar] *vt* to incubate; (*fig*) to
hatch.

incuestionable [inkwestjo'naβle] *adj*
unchallengeable.

inculcar [inkul'kar] *vt* to inculcate.

inculpar [inkul'par] *vt*: ~ **de** (*acusar*) to
accuse of; (*achacar, atribuir*) to charge
with, blame for.

inculque [in'kulke] *etc vb V* **inculcar**.

inculto, a [in'kulto, a] *adj* (*persona*)
uneducated, uncultured; (*fig: grosero*)
uncouth ♦ *nm/f* ignoramus.

incumbencia [inkum'benθja] *nf* obligation;
no es de mi ~ it is not my field.

incumbir [inkum'bir] *vi*: ~ **a** to be
incumbent upon; **no me incumbe a mí** it
is no concern of mine.

incumplimiento [inkumpli'mjento] *nm*
non-fulfilment; (*COM*) repudiation; ~ **de
contrato** breach of contract; **por** ~ by
default.

incurable [inku'raβle] *adj* (*enfermedad*)
incurable; (*paciente*) incurably ill.

incurrir [inku'rrir] *vi*: ~ **en** to incur; (*crimen*) to commit; ~ **en un error** to make a mistake.

indagación [indaɣa'θjon] *nf* investigation; (*búsqueda*) search; (*JUR*) inquest.

indagar [inda'ɣar] *vt* to investigate; to search; (*averiguar*) to ascertain.

indague [in'daɣe] *etc vb V* **indagar**.

indebido, a [inde'βiðo, a] *adj* undue; (*dicho*) improper.

indecencia [inde'θenθja] *nf* indecency; (*dicho*) obscenity.

indecente [inde'θente] *adj* indecent, improper; (*lascivo*) obscene.

indecible [inde'θiβle] *adj* unspeakable; (*indescriptible*) indescribable.

indeciso, a [inde'θiso, a] *adj* (*por decidir*) undecided; (*vacilante*) hesitant.

indefenso, a [inde'fenso, a] *adj* defenceless.

indefinido, a [indefi'niðo, a] *adj* indefinite; (*vago*) vague, undefined.

indeleble [inde'leβle] *adj* indelible.

indemne [in'demne] *adj* (*objeto*) undamaged; (*persona*) unharmed, unhurt.

indemnice [indem'niθe] *etc vb V* **indemnizar**.

indemnización [indemniθa'θjon] *nf* (*acto*) indemnification; (*suma*) indemnity; ~ **de cese** redundancy payment; ~ **de despido** severance pay; **doble** ~ double indemnity.

indemnizar [indemni'θar] *vt* to indemnify; (*compensar*) to compensate.

independencia [indepen'denθja] *nf* independence.

independice [indepen'diθe] *etc vb V* **independizar**.

independiente [indepen'djente] *adj* (*libre*) independent; (*autónomo*) self-sufficient; (*INFORM*) stand-alone.

independizar [independi'θar] *vt* to make independent; ~**se** *vr* to become independent.

indescifrable [indesθi'fraβle] *adj* (*MIL: código*) indecipherable; (*fig: misterio*) impenetrable.

indeseable [indese'aβle] *adj, nm/f* undesirable.

indeterminado, a [indetermi'naðo, a] *adj* (*tb LING*) indefinite; (*desconocido*) indeterminate.

India ['indja] *nf*: **la** ~ India.

indiano, a [in'djano, a] *adj* (Spanish-) American ♦ *nm* Spaniard who has made good in America.

indicación [indika'θjon] *nf* indication;

(*dato*) piece of information; (*señal*) sign; (*sugerencia*) suggestion, hint; **indicaciones** *nfpl* (*COM*) instructions.

indicado, a [indi'kaðo, a] *adj* (*apto*) right, appropriate.

indicador [indika'ðor] *nm* indicator; (*TEC*) gauge, meter; (*aguja*) hand, pointer; (*de carretera*) roadsign; ~ **de encendido** (*INFORM*) power-on indicator.

indicar [indi'kar] *vt* (*mostrar*) to indicate, show; (*suj: termómetro etc*) to read, register; (*señalar*) to point to.

indicativo, a [indika'tiβo, a] *adj* indicative ♦ *nm* (*RADIO*) call sign; ~ **de nacionalidad** (*AUTO*) national identification plate.

índice ['indiθe] *nm* index; (*catálogo*) catalogue; (*ANAT*) index finger, forefinger; ~ **del coste de (la) vida** cost-of-living index; ~ **de crédito** credit rating; ~ **de materias** table of contents; ~ **de natalidad** birth rate; ~ **de precios al por menor (IPM)** (*COM*) retail price index (RPI).

indicio [in'diθjo] *nm* indication, sign; (*en pesquisa etc*) clue; (*INFORM*) marker, mark.

indiferencia [indife'renθja] *nf* indifference; (*apatía*) apathy.

indiferente [indife'rente] *adj* indifferent; **me es** ~ it makes no difference to me.

indígena [in'dixena] *adj* indigenous, native ♦ *nm/f* native.

indigencia [indi'xenθja] *nf* poverty, need.

indigenista [indixe'nista] (*AM*) *adj* pro-Indian ♦ *nm/f* (*estudiante*) student of Indian cultures; (*POL etc*) promoter of Indian cultures.

indigestar [indixes'tar] *vt* to cause indigestion to; ~**se** *vr* to get indigestion.

indigestión [indixes'tjon] *nf* indigestion.

indigesto, a [indi'xesto, a] *adj* undigested; (*indigestible*) indigestible; (*fig*) turgid.

indignación [indixna'θjon] *nf* indignation.

indignante [indix'nante] *adj* outrageous, infuriating.

indignar [indix'nar] *vt* to anger, make indignant; ~**se** *vr*: ~**se por** to get indignant about.

indigno, a [in'dixno, a] *adj* (*despreciable*) low, contemptible; (*inmerecido*) unworthy.

indio, a ['indjo, a] *adj, nm/f* Indian.

indique [in'dike] *etc vb V* **indicar**.

indirecto, a [indi'rekto, a] *adj* indirect ♦ *nf* insinuation, innuendo; (*sugerencia*) hint.

indisciplina [indisθi'plina] *nf* (*gen*) lack of discipline; (*MIL*) insubordination.

indiscreción [indiskre'θjon] *nf*

(*imprudencia*) indiscretion; (*irreflexión*) tactlessness; (*acto*) gaffe, faux pas; ..., **si no es ~ ...**, if I may say so.

indiscreto, a [indis'kreto, a] *adj* indiscreet.

indiscriminado, a [indiskrimi'naðo, a] *adj* indiscriminate.

indiscutible [indisku'tißle] *adj* indisputable, unquestionable.

indispensable [indispen'saßle] *adj* indispensable.

indispondré [indispon'dre] *etc vb V* **indisponer**.

indisponer [indispo'ner] *vt* to spoil, upset; (*salud*) to make ill; **~se** *vr* to fall ill; **~se con algn** to fall out with sb.

indisponga [indis'ponga] *etc vb V* **indisponer**.

indisposición [indisposi'θjon] *nf* indisposition; (*desgana*) unwillingness.

indispuesto, a [indis'pwesto, a] *pp de* **indisponer** ♦ *adj* indisposed; **sentirse ~** to feel unwell *o* indisposed.

indispuse [indis'puse] *etc vb V* **indisponer**.

indistinto, a [indis'tinto, a] *adj* indistinct; (*vago*) vague.

individual [indißi'ðwal] *adj* individual; (*habitación*) single ♦ *nm* (*DEPORTE*) singles *sg*.

individuo, a [indi'ßiðwo, a] *adj* individual ♦ *nm* individual.

Indochina [indo'tʃina] *nf* Indochina.

indocumentado, a [indokumen'taðo, a] *adj* without identity papers.

indoeuropeo, a [indoeuro'peo, a] *adj, nm/f* Indo-European.

índole ['indole] *nf* (*naturaleza*) nature; (*clase*) sort, kind.

indolencia [indo'lenθja] *nf* indolence, laziness.

indoloro, a [in'doloro, a] *adj* painless.

indomable [indo'maßle] *adj* (*animal*) untameable; (*espíritu*) indomitable.

indómito, a [in'domito, a] *adj* indomitable.

Indonesia [indo'nesja] *nf* Indonesia.

indonesio, a [indo'nesjo, a] *adj, nm/f* Indonesian.

inducción [induk'θjon] *nf* (*FILOSOFÍA, ELEC*) induction; **por ~** by induction.

inducir [indu'θir] *vt* to induce; (*inferir*) to infer; (*persuadir*) to persuade; **~ a algn en el error** to mislead sb.

indudable [indu'ðaßle] *adj* undoubted; (*incuestionable*) unquestionable; **es ~ que** ... there is no doubt that ....

indulgencia [indul'xenθja] *nf* indulgence; (*JUR etc*) leniency; **proceder sin ~ contra** to proceed ruthlessly against.

indultar [indul'tar] *vt* (*perdonar*) to pardon, reprieve; (*librar de pago*) to exempt.

indulto [in'dulto] *nm* pardon; exemption.

indumentaria [indumen'tarja] *nf* (*ropa*) clothing, dress.

industria [in'dustrja] *nf* industry; (*habilidad*) skill; **~ agropecuaria** farming and fishing; **~ pesada** heavy industry; **~ petrolífera** oil industry.

industrial [indus'trjal] *adj* industrial ♦ *nm* industrialist.

industrializar [industrjali'θar] *vt* to industrialize; **~se** *vr* to become industrialized.

INE ['ine] *nm abr* (*ESP*) = *Instituto Nacional de Estadística*.

inédito, a [i'neðito, a] *adj* (*libro*) unpublished; (*nuevo*) unheard-of.

inefable [ine'faßle] *adj* ineffable, indescribable.

ineficacia [inefi'kaθja] *nf* (*de medida*) ineffectiveness; (*de proceso*) inefficiency.

ineficaz [inefi'kaθ] *adj* (*inútil*) ineffective; (*ineficiente*) inefficient.

ineludible [inelu'ðißle] *adj* inescapable, unavoidable.

INEM, Inem [i'nem] *nm abr* (*ESP*: = *Instituto Nacional de Empleo*) ≈ Department of Employment (*BRIT*).

INEN ['inen] *nm abr* (*México*) = *Instituto Nacional de Energía Nuclear*.

inenarrable [inena'rraßle] *adj* inexpressible.

ineptitud [inepti'tuð] *nf* ineptitude, incompetence.

inepto, a [i'nepto, a] *adj* inept, incompetent.

inequívoco, a [ine'kißoko, a] *adj* unequivocal; (*inconfundible*) unmistakable.

inercia [i'nerθja] *nf* inertia; (*pasividad*) passivity.

inerme [i'nerme] *adj* (*sin armas*) unarmed; (*indefenso*) defenceless.

inerte [i'nerte] *adj* inert; (*inmóvil*) motionless.

inescrutable [ineskru'taßle] *adj* inscrutable.

inesperado, a [inespe'raðo, a] *adj* unexpected, unforeseen.

inestable [ines'taßle] *adj* unstable.

inestimable [inesti'maßle] *adj* inestimable; **de valor ~** invaluable.

inevitable [ineßi'taßle] *adj* inevitable.

inexactitud [ineksakti'tuð] *nf* inaccuracy.

inexacto, a [inek'sakto, a] *adj* inaccurate; (*falso*) untrue.

inexistente [ineksis'tente] *adj* non-

existent.
inexorable [inekso'raßle] *adj* inexorable.
inexperiencia [inekspe'rjenθja] *nf*
inexperience, lack of experience.
inexperto, a [ineks'perto, a] *adj* (*novato*)
inexperienced.
inexplicable [inekspli'kaßle] *adj*
inexplicable.
inexpresable [inekspre'saßle] *adj*
inexpressible.
inexpresivo, a [inekspre'sißo, a] *adj*
inexpressive; (*ojos*) dull; (*cara*) wooden.
inexpugnable [inekspuɣ'naßle] *adj* (*MIL*)
impregnable; (*fig*) firm.
infalible [infa'lißle] *adj* infallible;
(*indefectible*) certain, sure; (*plan*)
foolproof.
infame [in'fame] *adj* infamous.
infamia [in'famja] *nf* infamy; (*deshonra*)
disgrace.
infancia [in'fanθja] *nf* infancy, childhood;
jardín de la ~ nursery school.
infanta [in'fanta] *nf* (*hija del rey*) infanta,
princess.
infante [in'fante] *nm* (*hijo del rey*) infante,
prince.
infantería [infante'ria] *nf* infantry.
infantil [infan'til] *adj* child's, children's;
(*pueril, aniñado*) infantile; (*cándido*)
childlike.
infarto [in'farto] *nm* (*tb:* **~ de miocardio**)
heart attack.
infatigable [infati'ɣaßle] *adj* tireless,
untiring.
infección [infek'θjon] *nf* infection.
infeccioso, a [infek'θjoso, a] *adj*
infectious.
infectar [infek'tar] *vt* to infect; **~se** *vr:* **~se**
(de) (*tb fig*) to become infected (with).
infecundidad [infekundi'ðað] *nf* (*de tierra*)
infertility, barrenness; (*de mujer*)
sterility.
infecundo, a [infe'kundo, a] *adj* infertile,
barren; sterile.
infeliz [infe'liθ] *adj* (*desgraciado*) unhappy,
wretched; (*inocente*) gullible ♦ *nm/f*
(*desgraciado*) wretch; (*inocentón*)
simpleton.
inferior [infe'rjor] *adj* inferior; (*situación,*
MAT) lower ♦ *nm/f* inferior, subordinate;
cualquier número ~ a 9 any number less
than *o* under *o* below 9; **una cantidad ~ a**
lesser quantity.
inferioridad [inferjori'ðað] *nf* inferiority;
estar en ~ de condiciones to be at a
disadvantage.
inferir [infe'rir] *vt* (*deducir*) to infer,
deduce; (*causar*) to cause.

infernal [infer'nal] *adj* infernal.
infértil [in'fertil] *adj* infertile.
infestar [infes'tar] *vt* to infest.
infidelidad [infiðeli'ðað] *nf* (*gen*) infidelity,
unfaithfulness.
infiel [in'fjel] *adj* unfaithful, disloyal;
(*falso*) inaccurate ♦ *nm/f* infidel,
unbeliever.
infiera [in'fjera] *etc vb V* **inferir**.
infierno [in'fjerno] *nm* hell; **¡vete al ~!** go
to hell; **está en el quinto ~** it's at the
back of beyond.
infiltrar [infil'trar] *vt* to infiltrate; **~se** *vr* to
infiltrate, filter; (*líquidos*) to percolate.
ínfimo, a ['infimo, a] *adj* (*vil*) vile, mean;
(*más bajo*) lowest; (*peor*) worst;
(*miserable*) wretched.
infinidad [infini'ðað] *nf* infinity;
(*abundancia*) great quantity; **~ de** vast
numbers of; **~ de veces** countless times.
infinitivo [infini'tißo] *nm* infinitive.
infinito, a [infi'nito, a] *adj* infinite; (*fig*)
boundless ♦ *adv* infinitely ♦ *nm* infinite;
(*MAT*) infinity; **hasta lo ~** ad infinitum.
infiriendo [infi'rjendo] *etc vb V* **inferir**.
inflación [infla'θjon] *nf* (*hinchazón*)
swelling; (*monetaria*) inflation; (*fig*)
conceit.
inflacionario, a [inflaθjo'narjo, a] *adj*
inflationary.
inflacionismo [inflaθjo'nismo] *nm* (*ECON*)
inflation.
inflacionista [inflaθjo'nista] *adj*
inflationary.
inflamar [infla'mar] *vt* to set on fire; (*MED,*
fig) to inflame; **~se** *vr* to catch fire; to
become inflamed.
inflar [in'flar] *vt* (*hinchar*) to inflate, blow
up; (*fig*) to exaggerate; **~se** *vr* to swell
(up); (*fig*) to get conceited.
inflexible [inflek'sißle] *adj* inflexible; (*fig*)
unbending.
infligir [infli'xir] *vt* to inflict.
inflija [in'flixa] *etc vb V* **infligir**.
influencia [in'flwenθja] *nf* influence.
influenciar [inflwen'θjar] *vt* to influence.
influir [influ'ir] *vt* to influence ♦ *vi* to have
influence, carry weight; **~ en o sobre** to
influence, affect; (*contribuir a*) to have a
hand in.
influjo [in'fluxo] *nm* influence; **~ de**
capitales (*ECON etc*) capital influx.
influyendo [influ'jendo] *etc vb V* **influir**.
influyente [influ'jente] *adj* influential.
información [informa'θjon] *nf*
information; (*noticias*) news *sg*; (*informe*)
report; (*INFORM: datos*) data; (*JUR*)
inquiry; **I~** (*oficina*) Information; (*TELEC*)

Directory Enquiries (*BRIT*), Directory Assistance (*US*); (*mostrador*) Information Desk; **una** ~ a piece of information; **abrir una** ~ (*JUR*) to begin proceedings; ~ **deportiva** (*en periódico*) sports section.

informal [infor'mal] *adj* (*gen*) informal.

informante [infor'mante] *nmlf* informant.

informar [infor'mar] *vt* (*gen*) to inform; (*revelar*) to reveal, make known ♦ *vi* (*JUR*) to plead; (*denunciar*) to inform; (*dar cuenta de*) to report on; ~**se** *vr* to find out; ~**se de** to inquire into.

informática [infor'matika] *nf* V **informático**.

informatice [informa'tiθe] *etc vb* V **informatizar**.

informático, a [infor'matiko, a] *adj* computer *cpd* ♦ *nf* (*TEC*) information technology; computing; (*ESCOL*) computer science *o* studies; ~ **de gestión** commercial computing.

informativo, a [informa'tißo, a] *adj* (*libro*) informative; (*folleto*) information *cpd*; (*RADIO, TV*) news *cpd* ♦ *nm* (*RADIO, TV*) news programme.

informatización [informatiθa'θjon] *nf* computerization.

informatizar [informati'θar] *vt* to computerize.

informe [in'forme] *adj* shapeless ♦ *nm* report; (*dictamen*) statement; (*MIL*) briefing; (*JUR*) plea; ~**s** *nmpl* information *sg*; (*datos*) data; ~ **anual** annual report; ~ **del juez** summing-up.

infortunio [infor'tunjo] *nm* misfortune.

infracción [infrak'θjon] *nf* infraction, infringement; (*AUTO*) offence.

infraestructura [infraestruk'tura] *nf* infrastructure.

in fraganti [infra'ɣanti] *adv*: **pillar a algn** ~ to catch sb red-handed.

infranqueable [infranke'aßle] *adj* impassable; (*fig*) insurmountable.

infrarrojo, a [infra'rroxo, a] *adj* infrared.

infravalorar [infraßalo'rar] *vt* to undervalue; (*FIN*) to underestimate.

infringir [infrin'xir] *vt* to infringe, contravene.

infrinja [in'frinxa] *etc vb* V **infringir**.

infructuoso, a [infruk'twoso, a] *adj* fruitless, unsuccessful.

infundado, a [infun'daðo, a] *adj* groundless, unfounded.

infundir [infun'dir] *vt* to infuse, instil; ~ **ánimo a algn** to encourage sb; ~ **miedo a algn** to intimidate sb.

infusión [infu'sjon] *nf* infusion; ~ **de manzanilla** camomile tea.

Ing. *abr* = **Ingeniero**.

ingeniar [inxe'njar] *vt* to think up, devise; ~**se** *vr* to manage; ~**se para** to manage to.

ingeniería [inxenje'ria] *nf* engineering; ~ **genética** genetic engineering; ~ **de sistemas** (*INFORM*) systems engineering.

ingeniero, a [inxe'njero, a] *nmlf* engineer; ~ **de sonido** sound engineer; ~ **de caminos** civil engineer.

ingenio [in'xenjo] *nm* (*talento*) talent; (*agudeza*) wit; (*habilidad*) ingenuity, inventiveness; (*TEC*): ~ **azucarero** sugar refinery.

ingenioso, a [inxe'njoso, a] *adj* ingenious, clever; (*divertido*) witty.

ingente [in'xente] *adj* huge, enormous.

ingenuidad [inxenwi'ðað] *nf* ingenuousness; (*sencillez*) simplicity.

ingenuo, a [in'xenwo, a] *adj* ingenuous.

ingerir [inxe'rir] *vt* to ingest; (*tragar*) to swallow; (*consumir*) to consume.

ingiera [in'xjera] *etc*, **ingiriendo** [inxi'rjenðo] *etc vb* V **ingerir**.

Inglaterra [ingla'terra] *nf* England.

ingle ['ingle] *nf* groin.

inglés, esa [in'gles, esa] *adj* English ♦ *nmlf* Englishman/woman ♦ *nm* (*LING*) English; **los ingleses** the English.

ingratitud [ingrati'tuð] *nf* ingratitude.

ingrato, a [in'grato, a] *adj* ungrateful; (*tarea*) thankless.

ingravidez [ingraßi'ðeθ] *nf* weightlessness.

ingrediente [ingre'ðjente] *nm* ingredient; ~**s** *nmpl* (*AM*: *tapas*) titbits.

ingresar [ingre'sar] *vt* (*dinero*) to deposit ♦ *vi* to come *o* go in; ~ **a** (*esp AM*) to enter; ~ **en** (*club*) to join; (*MIL, ESCOL*) to enrol in; ~ **en el hospital** to go into hospital.

ingreso [in'greso] *nm* (*entrada*) entry; (: *en hospital etc*) admission; (*MIL, ESCOL*) enrolment; ~**s** *nmpl* (*dinero*) income *sg*; (: *COM*) takings *pl*; ~ **gravable** taxable income *sg*; ~**s accesorios** fringe benefits; ~**s brutos** gross receipts; ~**s devengados** earned income *sg*; ~**s exentos de impuestos** non-taxable income *sg*; ~**s personales disponibles** disposable personal income *sg*.

íngrimo, a ['ingrimo, a] *adj* (*AM*: *tb* ~ **y solo**) all alone.

inhábil [i'naßil] *adj* unskilful, clumsy.

inhabilitar [inaßili'tar] *vt* (*POL, MED*): ~ **a algn (para hacer algo)** to disqualify sb (from doing sth).

inhabitable [inaßi'taßle] *adj* uninhabitable.

inhabituado, a [inaßi'twaðo, a] *adj* unaccustomed.

inhalador [inala'ðor] *nm (MED)* inhaler.

inhalar [ina'lar] *vt* to inhale.

inherente [ine'rente] *adj* inherent.

inhibición [iniβi'θjon] *nf* inhibition.

inhibir [ini'βir] *vt* to inhibit; *(REL)* to restrain; **~se** *vr* to keep out.

inhospitalario, a [inospita'larjo, a], **inhóspito, a** [i'nospito, a] *adj* inhospitable.

inhumación [inuma'θjon] *nf* burial, interment.

inhumano, a [inu'mano, a] *adj* inhuman.

INI ['ini] *nm abr* = **Instituto Nacional de Industria**.

inicial [ini'θjal] *adj, nf* initial.

inicialice [iniθja'liθe] *etc vb V* **inicializar**.

inicializar [iniθjali'θar] *vt (INFORM)* to initialize.

iniciar [ini'θjar] *vt (persona)* to initiate; *(empezar)* to begin, commence; *(conversación)* to start up; **~ a algn en un secreto** to let sb into a secret; **~ la sesión** *(INFORM)* to log in o on.

iniciativa [iniθja'tiβa] *nf* initiative; *(liderazgo)* leadership; **la ~ privada** private enterprise.

inicio [i'niθjo] *nm* start, beginning.

inicuo, a [i'nikwo, a] *adj* iniquitous.

inigualado, a [inixwa'laðo, a] *adj* unequalled.

ininteligible [ininteli'xiβle] *adj* unintelligible.

ininterrumpido, a [ininterrum'piðo, a] *adj* uninterrupted; *(proceso)* continuous; *(progreso)* steady.

injerencia [inxe'renθja] *nf* interference.

injertar [inxer'tar] *vt* to graft.

injerto [in'xerto] *nm* graft; **~ de piel** skin graft.

injuria [in'xurja] *nf (agravio, ofensa)* offence; *(insulto)* insult; **~s** *nfpl* abuse *sg*.

injuriar [inxu'rjar] *vt* to insult.

injurioso, a [inxu'rjoso, a] *adj* offensive; insulting.

injusticia [inxus'tiθja] *nf* injustice, unfairness; **con ~** unjustly.

injusto, a [in'xusto, a] *adj* unjust, unfair.

inmaculado, a [inmaku'laðo, a] *adj* immaculate, spotless.

inmadurez [inmaðu'reθ] *nf* immaturity.

inmaduro, a [inma'ðuro, a] *adj* immature; *(fruta)* unripe.

inmediaciones [inmeðja'θjones] *nfpl* neighbourhood *sg*, environs.

inmediatez [inmeðja'teθ] *nf* immediacy.

inmediato, a [inme'ðjato, a] *adj* immediate; *(contiguo)* adjoining; *(rápido)* prompt; *(próximo)* neighbouring, next;

de ~ *(esp AM)* immediately.

inmejorable [inmexo'raβle] *adj* unsurpassable; *(precio)* unbeatable.

inmemorable [inmemo'raβle], **inmemorial** [inmemo'rjal] *adj* immemorial.

inmenso, a [in'menso, a] *adj* immense, huge.

inmerecido, a [inmere'θiðo, a] *adj* undeserved.

inmersión [inmer'sjon] *nf* immersion; *(buzo)* dive.

inmigración [inmixra'θjon] *nf* immigration.

inmigrante [inmi'xrante] *adj, nm/f* immigrant.

inminente [inmi'nente] *adj* imminent, impending.

inmiscuirse [inmisku'irse] *vr* to interfere, meddle.

inmiscuyendo [inmisku'jendo] *etc vb V* **inmiscuirse**.

inmobiliario, a [inmoβi'ljarjo, a] *adj* real-estate *cpd*, property *cpd* ♦ *nf* estate agency.

inmolar [inmo'lar] *vt* to immolate, sacrifice.

inmoral [inmo'ral] *adj* immoral.

inmortal [inmor'tal] *adj* immortal.

inmortalice [inmorta'liθe] *etc vb V* **inmortalizar**.

inmortalizar [inmortali'θar] *vt* to immortalize.

inmotivado, a [inmoti'βaðo, a] *adj* motiveless; *(sospecha)* groundless.

inmóvil [in'moβil] *adj* immobile.

inmovilizar [inmoβili'θar] *vt* to immobilize; *(paralizar)* to paralyse; **~se** *vr*: **se le ha inmovilizado la pierna** her leg was paralysed.

inmueble [in'mweβle] *adj*: **bienes ~s** real estate *sg*, landed property *sg* ♦ *nm* property.

inmundicia [inmun'diθja] *nf* filth.

inmundo, a [in'mundo, a] *adj* filthy.

inmune [in'mune] *adj (MED)* immune.

inmunidad [inmuni'ðað] *nf* immunity; *(fisco)* exemption; **~ diplomática/ parlamentaria** diplomatic/parliamentary immunity.

inmunitario, a [inmuni'tarjo, a] *adj*: **sistema ~** immune system.

inmunización [inmuniθa'θjon] *nf* immunization.

inmunizar [inmuni'θar] *vt* to immunize.

inmutable [inmu'taβle] *adj* immutable; **permaneció ~** he didn't flinch.

inmutarse [inmu'tarse] *vr*: **siguió sin ~** he

carried on unperturbed.

innato, a [in'nato, a] *adj* innate.

innecesario, a [inneθe'sarjo, a] *adj* unnecessary.

innegable [inne'ɣaßle] *adj* undeniable.

innoble [in'noßle] *adj* ignoble.

innovación [innoßa'θjon] *nf* innovation.

innovador, a [innoßa'ðor, a] *adj* innovatory, innovative ♦ *nm/f* innovator.

innovar [inno'ßar] *vt* to introduce.

innumerable [innume'raßle] *adj* countless.

inocencia [ino'θenθja] *nf* innocence.

inocentada [inoθen'taða] *nf* practical joke.

inocente [ino'θente] *adj* (*ingenuo*) naive, innocent; (*inculpable*) innocent; (*sin malicia*) harmless ♦ *nm/f* simpleton; **día de los (Santos) I~s** ≈ April Fool's Day; *see boxed note*.

DÍA DE LOS SANTOS INOCENTES

El día de los (Santos) Inocentes, *28 December, is when the Church commemorates Herod's slaughter of the innocent children of Judea in biblical times. On this day Spaniards play "inocentadas" (practical jokes) on each other, much like British April Fools' Day pranks, perhaps sticking a "monigote" (cut-out paper figure) on someone's back or broadcasting unlikely news stories.*

---

inocuidad [inokwi'ðað] *nf* harmlessness.

inocular [inoku'lar] *vt* to inoculate.

inocuo, a [i'nokwo, a] *adj* (*sustancia*) harmless.

inodoro, a [ino'ðoro, a] *adj* odourless ♦ *nm* toilet (*BRIT*), lavatory (*BRIT*), washroom (*US*).

inofensivo, a [inofen'sißo, a] *adj* inoffensive.

inolvidable [inolßi'ðaßle] *adj* unforgettable.

inoperante [inope'rante] *adj* ineffective.

inopinado, a [inopi'naðo, a] *adj* unexpected.

inoportuno, a [inopor'tuno, a] *adj* untimely; (*molesto*) inconvenient; (*inapropiado*) inappropriate.

inoxidable [inoksi'ðaßle] *adj* stainless; **acero ~** stainless steel.

inquebrantable [inkeßran'taßle] *adj* unbreakable; (*fig*) unshakeable.

inquiera [in'kjera] *etc vb V* **inquirir**.

inquietante [inkje'tante] *adj* worrying.

inquietar [inkje'tar] *vt* to worry, trouble; **~se** *vr* to worry, get upset.

inquieto, a [in'kjeto, a] *adj* anxious,

worried; **estar ~ por** to be worried about.

inquietud [inkje'tuð] *nf* anxiety, worry.

inquilino, a [inki'lino, a] *nm/f* tenant; (*COM*) lessee.

inquiriendo [inki'rjendo] *etc vb V* **inquirir**.

inquirir [inki'rir] *vt* to enquire into, investigate.

insaciable [insa'θjaßle] *adj* insatiable.

insalubre [insa'lußre] *adj* unhealthy; (*condiciones*) insanitary.

INSALUD [insa'luð] *nm abr* (*ESP*) = *Instituto Nacional de la Salud*.

insano, a [in'sano, a] *adj* (*loco*) insane; (*malsano*) unhealthy.

insatisfacción [insatisfak'θjon] *nf* dissatisfaction.

insatisfecho, a [insatis'fetʃo, a] *adj* (*condición*) unsatisfied; (*estado de ánimo*) dissatisfied.

inscribir [inskri'ßir] *vt* to inscribe; (*en lista*) to put; (*en censo*) to register; **~se** *vr* to register; (*ESCOL etc*) to enrol.

inscripción [inskrip'θjon] *nf* inscription; (*ESCOL etc*) enrolment; (*en censo*) registration.

inscrito, a [ins'krito] *pp de* **inscribir**.

insecticida [insekti'θiða] *nm* insecticide.

insecto [in'sekto] *nm* insect.

inseguridad [inseɣuri'ðað] *nf* insecurity.

inseguro, a [inse'ɣuro, a] *adj* insecure; (*inconstante*) unsteady; (*incierto*) uncertain.

inseminación [insemina'θjon] *nf*: **~ artificial** artificial insemination (A.I.).

inseminar [insemi'nar] *vt* to inseminate, fertilize.

insensato, a [insen'sato, a] *adj* foolish, stupid.

insensibilice [insensißi'liθe] *etc vb V* **insensibilizar**.

insensibilidad [insensißili'ðað] *nf* (*gen*) insensitivity; (*dureza de corazón*) callousness.

insensibilizar [insensißili'θar] *vt* to desensitize; (*MED*) to anaesthetize (*BRIT*), anesthetize (*US*); (*eufemismo*) to knock out o unconscious.

insensible [insen'sißle] *adj* (*gen*) insensitive; (*movimiento*) imperceptible; (*sin sentido*) numb.

inseparable [insepa'raßle] *adj* inseparable.

INSERSO [in'serso] *nm abr* (= *Instituto Nacional de Servicios Sociales*) branch of social services.

insertar [inser'tar] *vt* to insert.

inservible [inser'ßißle] *adj* useless.

insidioso, a [insi'ðjoso, a] *adj* insidious.

insigne [in'siɣne] *adj* distinguished; (*famoso*) notable.

insignia [in'siɣnja] *nf* (*señal distintiva*) badge; (*estandarte*) flag.

insignificante [insiɣnifi'kante] *adj* insignificant.

insinuar [insi'nwar] *vt* to insinuate, imply; ~**se** *vr*: ~**se con algn** to ingratiate o.s. with sb.

insípido, a [in'sipiðo, a] *adj* insipid.

insistencia [insis'tenθja] *nf* insistence.

insistir [insis'tir] *vi* to insist; ~ **en algo** to insist on sth; (*enfatizar*) to stress sth.

in situ [in'situ] *adv* on the spot, in situ.

insobornable [insoβor'naβle] *adj* incorruptible.

insociable [inso'θjaβle] *adj* unsociable.

insolación [insola'θjon] *nf* (*MED*) sunstroke.

insolencia [inso'lenθja] *nf* insolence.

insolente [inso'lente] *adj* insolent.

insólito, a [in'solito, a] *adj* unusual.

insoluble [inso'luβle] *adj* insoluble.

insolvencia [insol'βenθja] *nf* insolvency.

insomne [in'somne] *adj* sleepless ♦ *nm/f* insomniac.

insomnio [in'somnjo] *nm* insomnia.

insondable [inson'daβle] *adj* bottomless.

insonorización [insonoriθa'θjon] *nf* soundproofing.

insonorizado, a [insonori'θaðo, a] *adj* (*cuarto etc*) soundproof.

insoportable [insopor'taβle] *adj* unbearable.

insoslayable [insosla'jaβle] *adj* unavoidable.

insospechado, a [insospe't ʃaðo, a] *adj* (*inesperado*) unexpected.

insostenible [insoste'niβle] *adj* untenable.

inspección [inspek'θjon] *nf* inspection, check; **l**~ inspectorate; ~ **técnica (de vehículos)** ≈ MOT (test) (*BRIT*).

inspeccionar [inspekθjo'nar] *vt* (*examinar*) to inspect, examine; (*controlar*) to check; (*INFORM*) to peek.

inspector, a [inspek'tor, a] *nm/f* inspector.

inspectorado [inspekto'raðo] *nm* inspectorate.

inspiración [inspira'θjon] *nf* inspiration.

inspirador, a [inspira'ðor, a] *adj* inspiring.

inspirar [inspi'rar] *vt* to inspire; (*MED*) to inhale; ~**se** *vr*: ~**se en** to be inspired by.

instalación [instala'θjon] *nf* (*equipo*) fittings *pl*, equipment; ~ **eléctrica** wiring.

instalar [insta'lar] *vt* (*establecer*) to instal; (*erguir*) to set up, erect; ~**se** *vr* to establish o.s.; (*en una vivienda*) to move into.

instancia [ins'tanθja] *nf* (*solicitud*) application; (*ruego*) request; (*JUR*) petition; **a** ~ **de** at the request of; **en última** ~ in the last resort.

instantáneo, a [instan'taneo, a] *adj* instantaneous ♦ *nf* snap(shot); **café** ~ instant coffee.

instante [ins'tante] *nm* instant, moment; **en un** ~ in a flash.

instar [ins'tar] *vt* to press, urge.

instaurar [instau'rar] *vt* (*establecer*) to establish, set up.

instigador, a [instiɣa'ðor, a] *nm/f* instigator; ~ **de un delito** (*JUR*) accessory before the fact.

instigar [insti'ɣar] *vt* to instigate.

instigue [ins'tiɣe] *etc vb V* **instigar**.

instintivo, a [instin'tiβo, a] *adj* instinctive.

instinto [ins'tinto] *nm* instinct; **por** ~ instinctively.

institución [institu'θjon] *nf* institution, establishment; ~ **benéfica** charitable foundation.

instituir [institu'ir] *vt* to establish; (*fundar*) to found.

instituto [insti'tuto] *nm* (*gen*) institute; **l**~ **Nacional de Enseñanza** (*ESP*) ≈ comprehensive (*BRIT*) o high (*US*) school; **l**~ **Nacional de Industria (INI)** (*ESP COM*) ≈ National Enterprise Board (*BRIT*) .

institutriz [institu'triθ] *nf* governess.

instituyendo [institu'jendo] *etc vb V* **instituir**.

instrucción [instruk'θjon] *nf* instruction; (*enseñanza*) education, teaching; (*JUR*) proceedings *pl*; (*MIL*) training; (*DEPORTE*) coaching; (*conocimientos*) knowledge; (*INFORM*) statement; **instrucciones para el uso** directions for use; **instrucciones de funcionamiento** operating instructions.

instructivo, a [instruk'tiβo, a] *adj* instructive.

instruir [instru'ir] *vt* (*gen*) to instruct; (*enseñar*) to teach, educate; (*JUR: proceso*) to prepare, draw up; ~**se** *vr* to learn, teach o.s.

instrumento [instru'mento] *nm* (*gen, MUS*) instrument; (*herramienta*) tool, implement; (*COM*) indenture; (*JUR*) legal document; ~ **de percusión/cuerda/ viento** percussion/string(ed)/wind instrument.

instruyendo [instru'jendo] *etc vb V* **instruir**.

insubordinarse [insuβorði'narse] *vr* to rebel.

insuficiencia [insufi'θjenθja] *nf* (*carencia*)

lack; (_inadecuación_) inadequacy; ~
cardíaca/renal heart/kidney failure.
insuficiente [insufi'θjente] _adj (gen)_
insufficient; (_ESCOL: nota_)
unsatisfactory.
insufrible [insu'frißle] _adj_ insufferable.
insular [insu'lar] _adj_ insular.
insulina [insu'lina] _nf_ insulin.
insulso, a [in'sulso, a] _adj_ insipid; (_fig_)
dull.
insultar [insul'tar] _vt_ to insult.
insulto [in'sulto] _nm_ insult.
insumisión [insumi'sjon] _nf_ refusal to do
military service or community service.
insumiso, a [insu'miso, a] _adj (rebelde)_
rebellious ♦ _nm/f (POL)_ person who
_refuses to do military service or
community service; V tb_ **mili**.
insuperable [insupe'raßle] _adj (excelente)_
unsurpassable; (_problema etc_)
insurmountable.
insurgente [insur'xente] _adj, nm/f_
insurgent.
insurrección [insurrek'θjon] _nf_
insurrection, rebellion.
insustituible [insusti'twißle] _adj_
irreplaceable.
intachable [inta'tʃaßle] _adj_ irreproachable.
intacto, a [in'takto, a] _adj (sin tocar)_
untouched; (_entero_) intact.
integrado, a [inte'ɣraðo, a] _adj (INFORM)_:
circuito ~ integrated circuit.
integral [inte'ɣral] _adj_ integral; (_completo_)
complete; (_TEC_) built-in; **pan ~**
wholemeal bread.
integrante [inte'ɣrante] _adj_ integral ♦ _nm/f_
member.
integrar [inte'ɣrar] _vt_ to make up,
compose; (_MAT, fig_) to integrate.
integridad [inteɣri'ðað] _nf_ wholeness;
(_carácter, tb INFORM_) integrity; **en su ~**
completely.
integrismo [inte'ɣrismo] _nm_
fundamentalism.
integrista [inte'ɣrista] _adj, nm/f_
fundamentalist.
íntegro, a ['inteɣro, a] _adj_ whole, entire;
(_texto_) uncut, unabridged; (_honrado_)
honest.
intelectual [intelek'twal] _adj, nm/f_
intellectual.
intelectualidad [intelektwali'ðað] _nf_
intelligentsia, intellectuals _pl._
inteligencia [inteli'xenθja] _nf_ intelligence;
(_ingenio_) ability; **~ artificial** artificial
intelligence.
inteligente [inteli'xente] _adj_ intelligent.
inteligible [inteli'xißle] _adj_ intelligible.

intemperancia [intempe'ranθja] _nf_ excess,
intemperance.
intemperie [intem'perje] _nf_: **a la ~**
outdoors, in the open air.
intempestivo, a [intempes'tißo, a] _adj_
untimely.
intención [inten'θjon] _nf (gen)_ intention,
purpose; **con segundas intenciones**
maliciously; **con ~** deliberately.
intencionado, a [intenθjo'naðo, a] _adj_
deliberate; **bien ~** well-meaning;
mal ~ ill-disposed, hostile.
intendencia [inten'denθja] _nf_
management, administration; (_MIL: tb_:
cuerpo de ~) ≈ service corps.
intensidad [intensi'ðað] _nf (gen)_ intensity;
(_ELEC, TEC_) strength; (_de recuerdo_)
vividness; **llover con ~** to rain hard.
intensificar [intensifi'kar] _vt_,
intensificarse _vr_ to intensify.
intensifique [intensi'fike] _etc vb V_
intensificar.
intensivo, a [inten'sißo, a] _adj_ intensive;
curso ~ crash course.
intenso, a [in'tenso, a] _adj_ intense;
(_impresión_) vivid; (_sentimiento_) profound,
deep.
intentar [inten'tar] _vt (tratar)_ to try,
attempt.
intento [in'tento] _nm (intención)_ intention,
purpose; (_tentativa_) attempt.
intentona [inten'tona] _nf (POL)_ attempted
coup.
interaccionar [interakθjo'nar] _vi (INFORM)_
to interact.
interactivo, a [interak'tißo, a] _adj_
interactive; (_INFORM_): **computación
interactiva** interactive computing.
intercalación [interkala'θjon] _nf (INFORM)_
merging.
intercalar [interka'lar] _vt_ to insert;
(_INFORM: archivos, texto_) to merge.
intercambiable [interkam'bjaßle] _adj_
interchangeable.
intercambio [inter'kambjo] _nm (canje)_
exchange; (_trueque_) swap.
interceder [interθe'ðer] _vi_ to intercede.
interceptar [interθep'tar] _vt_ to intercept,
cut off; (_AUTO_) to hold up.
interceptor [interθep'tor] _nm_ interceptor;
(_TEC_) trap.
intercesión [interθe'sjon] _nf_ intercession.
interés [inte'res] _nm (gen, COM)_ interest;
(_importancia_) concern; (_parte_) share,
part; (_pey_) self-interest; **~ compuesto**
compound interest; **~ simple** simple
interest; **con un ~ de 9 por ciento** at an
interest of 9%; **dar a ~** to lend at

interest; **tener ~ en** (COM) to hold a share in; **intereses acumulados** accrued interest sg; **intereses por cobrar** interest receivable sg; **intereses creados** vested interests; **intereses por pagar** interest payable sg.

interesado, a [intere'saðo, a] adj interested; (prejuiciado) prejudiced; (pey) mercenary, self-seeking ♦ nm/f person concerned; (firmante) the undersigned.

interesante [intere'sante] adj interesting.

interesar [intere'sar] vt to interest, be of interest to ♦ vi to interest, be of interest; (importar) to be important; **~se** vr: **~se en** o **por** to take an interest in; **no me interesan los toros** bullfighting does not appeal to me.

interestatal [interesta'tal] adj inter-state.

interface [inter'faθe], **interfase** [inter'fase] nm (INFORM) interface; **~ hombre/máquina/por menús** man/machine/menu interface.

interfaz [inter'faθ] nm = **interface**.

interferencia [interfe'renθja] nf interference.

interferir [interfe'rir] vt to interfere with; (TELEC) to jam ♦ vi to interfere.

interfiera [inter'fjera] etc, **interfiriendo** [interfi'rjendo] etc vb V **interferir**.

interfono [inter'fono] nm intercom.

ínterin ['interin] adv meanwhile ♦ nm interim; **en el ~** in the meantime.

interino, a [inte'rino, a] adj temporary; (empleado etc) provisional ♦ nm/f temporary holder of a post; (MED) locum; (ESCOL) supply teacher; (TEAT) stand-in.

interior [inte'rjor] adj inner, inside; (COM) domestic, internal ♦ nm interior, inside; (fig) soul, mind; (DEPORTE) inside forward; **Ministerio del I~** ≈ Home Office (BRIT), Ministry of the Interior; **dije para mi ~** I said to myself.

interjección [interxek'θjon] nf interjection.

interlínea [inter'linea] nf (INFORM) line feed.

interlocutor, a [interloku'tor, a] nm/f speaker; (al teléfono) person at the other end (of the line); **mi ~** the person I was speaking to.

intermediario, a [interme'ðjarjo, a] adj (mediador) mediating ♦ nm/f intermediary, go-between; (mediador) mediator.

intermedio, a [inter'meðjo, a] adj intermediate; (tiempo) intervening ♦ nm interval; (POL) recess.

interminable [intermi'naßle] adj endless,

interminable.

intermitente [intermi'tente] adj intermittent ♦ nm (AUTO) indicator.

internacional [internaθjo'nal] adj international.

internado [inter'naðo] nm boarding school.

internamiento [interna'mjento] nm internment.

internar [inter'nar] vt to intern; (en un manicomio) to commit; **~se** vr (penetrar) to penetrate; **~se en** to go into o right inside; **~se en un estudio** to study a subject in depth.

internauta [inter'nauta] nm/f Internet user.

Internet [inter'net] nm o nf Internet.

interno, a [in'terno, a] adj internal, interior; (POL etc) domestic ♦ nm/f (alumno) boarder.

interpelación [interpela'θjon] nf appeal, plea.

interpelar [interpe'lar] vt (rogar) to implore; (hablar) to speak to; (POL) to ask for explanations, question formally.

interpondré [interpon'dre] etc vb V **interponer**.

interponer [interpo'ner] vt to interpose, put in; **~se** vr to intervene.

interponga [inter'ponga] etc vb V **interponer**.

interposición [interposi'θjon] nf insertion.

interpretación [interpreta'θjon] nf interpretation; (MUS, TEAT) performance; **mala ~** misinterpretation.

interpretar [interpre'tar] vt to interpret.

intérprete [in'terprete] nm/f (LING) interpreter, translator; (MUS, TEAT) performer, artist(e).

interpuesto, a [inter'pwesto], **interpuse** [inter'puse] etc vb V **interponer**.

interrogación [interroxa'θjon] nf interrogation; (LING: tb: **signo de ~**) question mark; (TELEC) polling.

interrogante [interro'xante] adj questioning ♦ nm question mark; (fig) question mark, query.

interrogar [interro'xar] vt to interrogate, question.

interrogatorio [interroxa'torjo] nm interrogation; (MIL) debriefing; (JUR) examination.

interrogue [inte'rroxe] etc vb V **interrogar**.

interrumpir [interrum'pir] vt to interrupt; (vacaciones) to cut short; (servicio) to cut off; (tráfico) to block.

interrupción [interrup'θjon] nf interruption.

interruptor [interrup'tor] *nm* (*ELEC*) switch.
intersección [intersek'θjon] *nf*
  intersection; (*AUTO*) junction.
interurbano, a [interur'ßano, a] *adj* inter
  city; (*TELEC*) long-distance.
intervalo [inter'ßalo] *nm* interval;
  (*descanso*) break; **a ~s** at intervals,
  every now and then.
intervención [interßen'θjon] *nf*
  supervision; (*COM*) audit(ing); (*MED*)
  operation; (*TELEC*) tapping; (*participación*)
  intervention; ~ **quirúrgica** surgical
  operation; **la política de no** ~ the policy
  of non-intervention.
intervencionista [interßenθjo'nista] *adj*: **no**
  ~ (*COM*) laissez-faire.
intervendré [interßen'dre] *etc*, **inter-
  venga** [inter'ßenga] *etc vb V* **intervenir**.
intervenir [interße'nir] *vt* (*controlar*) to
  control, supervise; (*COM*) to audit; (*MED*)
  to operate on; (*TELEC*) to tap ♦ *vi*
  (*participar*) to take part, participate;
  (*mediar*) to intervene.
interventor, a [interßen'tor, a] *nm/f*
  inspector; (*COM*) auditor.
interviniendo [interßi'njendo] *etc vb V*
  intervenir.
interviú [inter'ßju] *nf* interview.
intestino [intes'tino] *nm* intestine.
inti ['inti] *nm monetary unit of Peru.*
intimar [inti'mar] *vt* to intimate, announce;
  (*mandar*) to order ♦ *vi*, **~se** *vr* to become
  friendly.
intimidad [intimi'ðað] *nf* intimacy;
  (*familiaridad*) familiarity; (*vida privada*)
  private life; (*JUR*) privacy.
intimidar [intimi'ðar] *vt* to intimidate,
  scare.
íntimo, a ['intimo, a] *adj* intimate;
  (*pensamientos*) innermost; (*vida*)
  personal, private; **una boda íntima** a
  quiet wedding.
intolerable [intole'raßle] *adj* intolerable,
  unbearable.
intolerancia [intole'ranθja] *nf* intolerance.
intoxicación [intoksika'θjon] *nf* poisoning;
  ~ **alimenticia** food poisoning.
intraducible [intraðu'θißle] *adj*
  untranslatable.
intranet [intra'net] *nf* intranet.
intranquilice [intranki'liθe] *etc vb V*
  intranquilizarse.
intranquilizarse [intrankili'θarse] *vr* to get
  worried *o* anxious.
intranquilo, a [intran'kilo, a] *adj* worried.
intranscendente [intransθen'dente] *adj*
  unimportant.
intransferible [intransfe'rißle] *adj* not

transferable.
intransigente [intransi'xente] *adj*
  intransigent.
intransitable [intransi'taßle] *adj*
  impassable.
intransitivo, a [intransi'tißo, a] *adj*
  intransitive.
intratable [intra'taßle] *adj* (*problema*)
  intractable; (*dificultad*) awkward;
  (*individuo*) unsociable.
intrepidez [intrepi'ðeθ] *nf* courage,
  bravery.
intrépido, a [in'trepiðo, a] *adj* intrepid,
  fearless.
intriga [in'triχa] *nf* intrigue; (*plan*) plot.
intrigar [intri'χar] *vt, vi* to intrigue.
intrigue [in'triχe] *etc vb V* **intrigar**.
intrincado, a [intrin'kaðo, a] *adj* intricate.
intrínseco, a [in'trinseko, a] *adj* intrinsic.
introducción [introðuk'θjon] *nf*
  introduction; (*de libro*) foreword;
  (*INFORM*) input.
introducir [introðu'θir] *vt* (*gen*) to
  introduce; (*moneda*) to insert; (*INFORM*)
  to input, enter.
introduje [intro'ðuxe] *etc*, **introduzca**
  [intro'ðuθka] *etc vb V* **introducir**.
intromisión [intromi'sjon] *nf* interference,
  meddling.
introvertido, a [introßer'tiðo, a] *adj*, *nm/f*
  introvert.
intruso, a [in'truso, a] *adj* intrusive ♦ *nm/f*
  intruder.
intuición [intwi'θjon] *nf* intuition.
intuir [intu'ir] *vt* to know by intuition,
  intuit.
intuyendo [intu'jendo] *etc vb V* **intuir**.
inundación [inunda'θjon] *nf* flood(ing).
inundar [inun'dar] *vt* to flood; (*fig*) to
  swamp, inundate.
inusitado, a [inusi'taðo, a] *adj* unusual.
inútil [i'nutil] *adj* useless; (*esfuerzo*) vain,
  fruitless.
inutilice [inuti'liθe] *etc vb V* **inutilizar**.
inutilidad [inutili'ðað] *nf* uselessness.
inutilizar [inutili'θar] *vt* to make unusable,
  put out of action; (*incapacitar*) to disable;
  ~se *vr* to become useless.
invadir [imba'ðir] *vt* to invade.
invalidar [imbali'ðar] *vt* to invalidate.
invalidez [imbali'ðeθ] *nf* (*MED*)
  disablement; (*JUR*) invalidity.
inválido, a [im'baliðo, a] *adj* invalid; (*JUR*)
  null and void ♦ *nm/f* invalid.
invariable [imba'rjable] *adj* invariable.
invasión [imba'sjon] *nf* invasion.
invasor, a [imba'sor, a] *adj* invading ♦ *nm/f*
  invader.

invencible [imben'θiβle] *adj* invincible;
  (*timidez, miedo*) unsurmountable.
invención [imben'θjon] *nf* invention.
inventar [imben'tar] *vt* to invent.
inventario [imben'tarjo] *nm* inventory;
  (*COM*) stocktaking.
inventiva [imben'tiβa] *nf* inventiveness.
invento [im'bento] *nm* invention; (*fig*)
  brainchild; (*pey*) silly idea.
inventor, a [imben'tor, a] *nm/f* inventor.
invernadero [imberna'ðero] *nm*
  greenhouse.
invernal [imber'nal] *adj* wintry, winter *cpd*.
invernar [imber'nar] *vi* (*ZOOL*) to hibernate.
inverosímil [imbero'simil] *adj* implausible.
inversión [imber'sjon] *nf* (*COM*)
  investment; ~ **de capitales** capital
  investment; **inversiones extranjeras**
  foreign investment *sg*.
inverso, a [im'berso, a] *adj* inverse,
  opposite; **en el orden** ~ in reverse order;
  a la inversa inversely, the other way
  round.
inversor, a [imber'sor, a] *nm/f* (*COM*)
  investor.
invertebrado, a [imberte'βraðo, a] *adj, nm*
  invertebrate.
invertido, a [imber'tiðo, a] *adj* inverted; (*al
  revés*) reversed; (*homosexual*)
  homosexual ♦ *nm/f* homosexual.
invertir [imber'tir] *vt* (*COM*) to invest;
  (*volcar*) to turn upside down; (*tiempo etc*)
  to spend.
investigación [imbestiɣa'θjon] *nf*
  investigation; (*indagación*) inquiry;
  (*UNIV*) research; ~ **y desarrollo** (*COM*)
  research and development (R & D); ~
  de los medios de publicidad media
  research; ~ **del mercado** market
  research.
investigador, a [imbestiɣa'ðor, a] *nm/f*
  investigator; (*UNIV*) research fellow.
investigar [imbesti'ɣar] *vt* to investigate;
  (*estudiar*) to do research into.
investigue [imbes'tiɣe] *etc vb V* **investigar**.
investir [imbes'tir] *vt*: ~ **a algn con algo** to
  confer sth on sb; **fue investido Doctor
  Honoris Causa** he was awarded an
  honorary doctorate.
invicto, a [im'bikto, a] *adj* unconquered.
invidente [imbi'ðente] *adj* sightless ♦ *nm/f*
  blind person; **los** ~**s** the sightless.
invierno [im'bjerno] *nm* winter.
invierta [im'bjerta] *etc vb V* **invertir**.
inviolabilidad [imbjolaβili'ðað] *nf*
  inviolability; ~ **parlamentaria**
  parliamentary immunity.
invirtiendo [imbir'tjendo] *etc vb V* **invertir**.

invisible [imbi'siβle] *adj* invisible;
  exportaciones/importaciones ~**s**
  invisible exports/imports.
invitación [imbita'θjon] *nf* invitation.
invitado, a [imbi'taðo, a] *nm/f* guest.
invitar [imbi'tar] *vt* to invite; (*incitar*) to
  entice; ~ **a algn a hacer algo** to invite sb
  to do sth; ~ **a algo** to pay for sth; **nos
  invitó a cenar fuera** she took us out for
  dinner; **invito yo** it's on me.
in vitro [im'bitro] *adv* in vitro.
invocar [imbo'kar] *vt* to invoke, call on;
  (*INFORM*) to call.
involucrar [imbolu'krar] *vt*: ~ **algo en un
  discurso** to bring something irrelevant
  into a discussion; ~ **a algn en algo** to
  involve sb in sth; ~**se** *vr* (*interesarse*) to
  get involved.
involuntario, a [imbolun'tarjo, a] *adj*
  involuntary; (*ofensa etc*) unintentional.
invoque [im'boke] *etc vb V* **invocar**.
inyección [injek'θjon] *nf* injection.
inyectar [injek'tar] *vt* to inject.
ión [i'on] *nm* ion.
IPC *nm abr* (*ESP*: = *índice de precios al
  consumo*) CPI.
IPM *nm abr* (= *índice de precios al por
  menor*) RPI.

═══════════════ *PALABRA CLAVE*

ir [ir] *vi* **1** to go; (*a pie*) to walk; (*viajar*) to
  travel; ~ **caminando** to walk; **fui en tren**
  I went *o* travelled by train; **voy a la calle**
  I'm going out; ~ **en coche/en bicicleta** to
  drive/cycle; ~ **a pie** to walk, go on foot;
  ~ **de pesca** to go fishing; **¡¡ahora voy!**
  (I'm just) coming!
2: ~ **(a) por**: ~ **(a) por el médico** to fetch
  the doctor
3 (*progresar: persona, cosa*) to go; **el
  trabajo va muy bien** work is going very
  well; **¿cómo te va?** how are things
  going?; **me va muy bien** I'm getting on
  very well; **le fue fatal** it went awfully
  badly for him
4 (*funcionar*): **el coche no va muy bien**
  the car isn't running very well
5 (*sentar*): **me va estupendamente** (*ropa,
  color*) it suits me really well;
  (*medicamento*) it works really well for
  me; ~ **bien con algo** to go well with sth
6 (*aspecto*): **iba muy bien vestido** he was
  very well dressed; ~ **con zapatos negros**
  to wear black shoes
7 (*locuciones*): **¿vino? – ¡que va!** did he
  come? – of course not!; **vamos, no llores**
  come on, don't cry; **¡vaya coche!**
  (*admiración*) what a car!, that's some

car!; (_desprecio_) that's a terrible car!;
¡**vaya**! (_regular_) so so; (_desagrado_) come
on!; ¡**vamos**! come on!; ¡**que le vaya
bien**! (_adiós_) take care!
**8: no vaya a ser: tienes que correr, no
vaya a ser que pierdas el tren** you'll have
to run so as not to miss the train
9: no me _etc_ **va ni me viene** I _etc_ don't
care
♦ _vb aux_ **1**: ~ **a: voy/iba a hacerlo hoy** I
am/was going to do it today
2 (+_gerundio_): **iba anocheciendo** it was
getting dark; **todo se me iba aclarando**
everything was gradually becoming
clearer to me
3 (+_pp_ = _pasivo_): **van vendidos 300
ejemplares** 300 copies have been sold so
far
♦ ~**se** _vr_ **1**: ¿**por dónde se va al
zoológico?** which is the way to the zoo?
2 (_marcharse_) to leave; **ya se habrán ido**
they must already have left _o_ gone;
¡**vámonos**!, (_AM_) ¡**nos fuimos**! let's go!;
¡**vete**! go away!; ¡**vete a saber**! your
guess is as good as mine!, who knows!

ira ['ira] _nf_ anger, rage.
iracundo, a [ira'kundo, a] _adj_ irascible.
Irak [i'rak] _nm_ = **Iraq**.
Irán [i'ran] _nm_ Iran.
iraní [ira'ni] _adj, nm/f_ Iranian.
Iraq [i'rak] _nm_ Iraq.
iraquí [ira'ki] _adj, nm/f_ Iraqi.
irascible [iras'θiβle] _adj_ irascible.
irguiendo [ir'ɣjendo] _etc vb_ V **erguir**.
iris ['iris] _nm inv_ (_arco_ ~) rainbow; (_ANAT_)
iris.
Irlanda [ir'landa] _nf_ Ireland; ~ **del Norte**
Northern Ireland, Ulster.
irlandés, esa [irlan'des, esa] _adj_ Irish
♦ _nm/f_ Irishman/woman ♦ _nm_ (_LING_)
Gaelic, Irish; **los irlandeses** _npl_ the Irish.
ironía [iro'nia] _nf_ irony.
irónico, a [i'roniko, a] _adj_ ironic(al).
IRPF _nm abr_ (_ESP_) = _impuesto sobre la renta
de las personas físicas._
irracional [irraθjo'nal] _adj_ irrational.
irrazonable [irraθo'naβle] _adj_
unreasonable.
irreal [irre'al] _adj_ unreal.
irrealizable [irreali'θaβle] _adj_ (_gen_)
unrealizable; (_meta_) unrealistic.
irrebatible [irreβa'tiβle] _adj_ irrefutable.
irreconocible [irrekono'θiβle] _adj_
unrecognizable.
irrecuperable [irrekupe'raβle] _adj_
irrecoverable, irretrievable.
irreembolsable [irreembol'saβle] _adj_ (_COM_)

non-returnable.
irreflexión [irreflek'sjon] _nf_
thoughtlessness; (_ímpetu_) rashness.
irregular [irreɣu'lar] _adj_ irregular;
(_situación_) abnormal, anomalous; **margen
izquierdo/derecho** ~ (_texto_) ragged left/
right (margin).
irregularidad [irreɣulari'ðað] _nf_
irregularity.
irremediable [irreme'ðjaβle] _adj_
irremediable; (_vicio_) incurable.
irreprochable [irrepro't∫aβle] _adj_
irreproachable.
irresistible [irresis'tiβle] _adj_ irresistible.
irresoluto, a [irreso'luto, a] _adj_ irresolute,
hesitant; (_sin resolver_) unresolved.
irrespetuoso, a [irrespe'twoso, a] _adj_
disrespectful.
irresponsable [irrespon'saβle] _adj_
irresponsible.
irreverente [irreβe'rente] _adj_
disrespectful.
irreversible [irreβer'siβle] _adj_ irreversible.
irrevocable [irreβo'kaβle] _adj_ irrevocable.
irrigar [irri'ɣar] _vt_ to irrigate.
irrigue [i'rriɣe] _etc vb_ V **irrigar**.
irrisorio, a [irri'sorjo, a] _adj_ derisory,
ridiculous; (_precio_) bargain _cpd_.
irritación [irrita'θjon] _nf_ irritation.
irritar [irri'tar] _vt_ to irritate, annoy; ~**se** _vr_
to get angry, lose one's temper.
irrompible [irrom'piβle] _adj_ unbreakable.
irrumpir [irrum'pir] _vi_: ~ **en** to burst _o_ rush
into.
irrupción [irrup'θjon] _nf_ irruption;
(_invasión_) invasion.
IRTP _nm abr_ (_ESP_: = _impuesto sobre el
rendimiento del trabajo personal_) ≈ PAYE.
isla ['isla] _nf_ (_GEO_) island; **I~s Británicas**
British Isles; **I~s Filipinas/Malvinas/
Canarias** Philippines/Falklands/
Canaries.
Islam [is'lam] _nm_ Islam.
islámico, a [is'lamiko, a] _adj_ Islamic.
islandés, esa [islan'des, esa] _adj_ Icelandic
♦ _nm/f_ Icelander ♦ _nm_ (_LING_) Icelandic.
Islandia [is'landja] _nf_ Iceland.
isleño, a [is'leɲo, a] _adj_ island _cpd_ ♦ _nm/f_
islander.
islote [is'lote] _nm_ small island.
isotónico, a [iso'toniko, a] _adj_ isotonic.
isótopo [i'sotopo] _nm_ isotope.
Israel [isra'el] _nm_ Israel.
israelí [israe'li] _adj, nm/f_ Israeli.
istmo ['istmo] _nm_ isthmus; **el I~ de
Panamá** the Isthmus of Panama.
Italia [i'talja] _nf_ Italy.
italiano, a [ita'ljano, a] _adj, nm/f_ Italian

♦ nm (LING) Italian.
itinerante [itine'rante] adj travelling; (embajador) roving.
itinerario [itine'rarjo] nm itinerary, route.
ITV nf abr (= Inspección Técnica de Vehículos) ≈ MOT (test) (BRIT).
IVA ['iβa] nm abr (ESP COM: = Impuesto sobre el Valor Añadido) VAT.
IVP nm abr = Instituto Venezolano de Petroquímica.
izada [i'saða] nf (AM) lifting, raising.
izar [i'θar] vt to hoist.
izda, izq.ª abr = **izquierda**.
izdo, izq, izq.º abr = **izquierdo**.
izquierda [iθ'kjerða] nf V **izquierdo**.
izquierdista [iθkjer'ðista] adj leftist, left-wing ♦ nm/f left-winger, leftist.
izquierdo, a [iθ'kjerðo, a] adj left ♦ nf left; (POL) left (wing); **a la ~** on the left; **es un cero a la ~** (fam) he is a nonentity; **conducción por la ~** left-hand drive.

J j

J, j ['xota] nf (letra) J, j; **J de José** J for Jack (BRIT) o Jig (US).
jabalí [xaβa'li] nm wild boar.
jabalina [xaβa'lina] nf javelin.
jabato, a [xa'βato, a] adj brave, bold ♦ nm young wild boar.
jabón [xa'βon] nm soap; (fam: adulación) flattery; **~ de afeitar** shaving soap; **~ de tocador** toilet soap; **dar ~ a algn** to soft-soap sb.
jabonar [xaβo'nar] vt to soap.
jaca ['xaka] nf pony.
jacinto [xa'θinto] nm hyacinth.
jactancia [xak'tanθja] nf boasting, boastfulness.
jactarse [xak'tarse] vr: **~ (de)** to boast o brag (about o of).
jadear [xaðe'ar] vi to pant, gasp for breath.
jadeo [xa'ðeo] nm panting, gasping.
jaguar [xa'ɣwar] nm jaguar.
jalar [xa'lar] vt (AM) to pull.
jalbegue [xal'βeɣe] nm whitewash.
jalea [xa'lea] nf jelly.
jaleo [xa'leo] nm racket, uproar; **armar un ~** to kick up a racket.
jalón [xa'lon] nm (AM) tug.

jalonar [xalo'nar] vt to stake out; (fig) to mark.
Jamaica [xa'maika] nf Jamaica.
jamaicano, a [xamai'kano, a] adj, nm/f Jamaican.
jamás [xa'mas] adv never, not ... ever; (interrogativo) ever; **¿~ se vio tal cosa?** did you ever see such a thing?
jamón [xa'mon] nm ham; **~ (de) York** boiled ham; **~ dulce/serrano** boiled/cured ham.
Japón [xa'pon] nm: **el ~** Japan.
japonés, esa [xapo'nes, esa] adj, nm/f Japanese ♦ nm (LING) Japanese.
jaque ['xake] nm: **~ mate** checkmate.
jaqueca [xa'keka] nf (very bad) headache, migraine.
jarabe [xa'raβe] nm syrup; **~ para la tos** cough syrup o mixture.
jarana [xa'rana] nf (juerga) spree (fam); **andar/ir de ~** to be/go on a spree.
jarcia ['xarθja] nf (NAUT) ropes pl, rigging.
jardín [xar'ðin] nm garden; **~ botánico** botanical garden; **~ de (la) infancia** (ESP) o **de niños** (AM) o **infantil** (AM) kindergarten, nursery school.
jardinería [xarðine'ria] nf gardening.
jardinero, a [xarði'nero, a] nm/f gardener.
jarra ['xarra] nf jar; (jarro) jug; (de leche) churn; (de cerveza) mug; **de o en ~s** with arms akimbo.
jarro ['xarro] nm jug.
jarrón [xa'rron] nm vase; (ARQUEOLOGÍA) urn.
jaspeado, a [xaspe'ado, a] adj mottled, speckled.
jaula ['xaula] nf cage; (embalaje) crate.
jauría [xau'ria] nf pack of hounds.
jazmín [xaθ'min] nm jasmine.
J. C. abr = **Jesucristo**.
jeep, pl jeeps ® [jip, jips] nm jeep ®.
jefa ['xefa] nf V **jefe**.
jefatura [xefa'tura] nf (liderato) leadership; (sede) central office; **J~ de la aviación civil** ≈ Civil Aviation Authority; **~ de policía** police headquarters sg.
jefazo [xe'faθo] nm bigwig.
jefe, a ['xefe, a] nm/f (gen) chief, head; (patrón) boss; (POL) leader; (COM) manager(ess); **~ de camareros** head waiter; **~ de cocina** chef; **~ ejecutivo** (COM) chief executive; **~ de estación** stationmaster; **~ de estado** head of state; **~ de oficina** (COM) office manager; **~ de producción** (COM) production manager; **~ supremo** commander-in-chief; **ser el ~** (fig) to be the boss.
JEN [xen] nf abr (ESP) = Junta de Energía

Nuclear.

jengibre [xen'xiβre] *nm* ginger.

jeque ['xeke] *nm* sheik(h).

jerarquía [xerar'kia] *nf (orden)* hierarchy; *(rango)* rank.

jerárquico, a [xe'rarkiko, a] *adj* hierarchic(al).

jerez [xe'reθ] *nm* sherry; **J~ de la Frontera** Jerez.

jerezano, a [xere'θano, a] *adj* of o from Jerez ♦ *nm/f* native o inhabitant of Jerez.

jerga ['xerɣa] *nf (tela)* coarse cloth; *(lenguaje)* jargon; **~ informática** computer jargon.

jerigonza [xeri'ɣonθa] *nf (jerga)* jargon, slang; *(galimatías)* nonsense, gibberish.

jeringa [xe'ringa] *nf* syringe; *(AM)* annoyance, bother; **~ de engrase** grease gun.

jeringar [xerin'gar] *vt* to annoy, bother.

jeringue [xe'ringe] *etc vb* V **jeringar**.

jeringuilla [xerin'guiλa] *nf* hypodermic (syringe).

jeroglífico [xero'xlifiko] *nm* hieroglyphic.

jersey [xer'sei], *pl* **jerseys** *nm* jersey, pullover, jumper.

Jerusalén [xerusa'len] *n* Jerusalem.

Jesucristo [xesu'kristo] *nm* Jesus Christ.

jesuita [xe'swita] *adj, nm* Jesuit.

Jesús [xe'sus] *nm* Jesus; **¡~!** good heavens!; *(al estornudar)* bless you!

jet, *pl* **jets** [jet, jet] *nm* jet (plane) ♦ *nf*: **la ~** the jet set.

jeta ['xeta] *nf (ZOOL)* snout; *(fam: cara)* mug; **¡que ~ tienes!** *(fam: insolencia)* you've got a nerve!

jíbaro, a ['xiβaro, a] *adj, nm/f* Jíbaro (Indian).

jícara ['xikara] *nf* small cup.

jiennense [xjen'nense] *adj* of o from Jaén ♦ *nm/f* native o inhabitant of Jaén.

jilguero [xil'ɣero] *nm* goldfinch.

jinete, a [xi'nete, a] *nm/f* horseman/woman.

jipijapa [xipi'xapa] *nm (AM)* straw hat.

jira ['xira] *nf (de tela)* strip; *(excursión)* picnic.

jirafa [xi'rafa] *nf* giraffe.

jirón [xi'ron] *nm* rag, shred.

JJ.OO. *nmpl abr* = **Juegos Olímpicos**.

jocosidad [xokosi'ðað] *nf* humour; *(chiste)* joke.

jocoso, a [xo'koso, a] *adj* humorous, jocular.

joder [xo'ðer] *(fam!) vt* to fuck (!), screw (!); *(fig: fastidiar)* to piss off (!), bug; **~se** *vr (fracasar)* to fail; **¡~!** damn it!; **se jodió todo** everything was ruined.

jodido, a [xo'ðiðo, a] *adj (fam!: difícil)* awkward; **estoy ~** I'm knackered.

jofaina [xo'faina] *nf* washbasin.

jojoba [xo'xoβa] *nf* jojoba.

jolgorio [xol'ɣorjo] *nm (juerga)* fun, revelry.

jonrón [xon'ron] *nm* home run.

Jordania [xor'ðanja] *nf* Jordan.

jornada [xor'naða] *nf (viaje de un día)* day's journey; *(camino o viaje entero)* journey; *(día de trabajo)* working day; **~ de 8 horas** 8-hour day; **(trabajar a) ~ partida** (to work a) split shift.

jornal [xor'nal] *nm* (day's) wage.

jornalero, a [xorna'lero, a] *nm/f* (day) labourer.

joroba [xo'roβa] *nf* hump.

jorobado, a [xoro'βaðo, a] *adj* hunchbacked ♦ *nm/f* hunchback.

jorobar [xoro'βar] *vt* to annoy, pester, bother; **~se** *vr* to get cross; **¡hay que ~se!** to hell with it!; **esto me joroba** I'm fed up with this!

jota ['xota] *nf* letter J; *(danza)* Aragonese dance; *(fam)* jot, iota; **no saber ni ~** to have no idea.

joven ['xoβen] *adj* young ♦ *nm* young man, youth ♦ *nf* young woman, girl.

jovencito, a [xoβen'θito, a] *nm/f* youngster.

jovial [xo'βjal] *adj* cheerful, jolly.

jovialidad [xoβjali'ðað] *nf* cheerfulness.

joya ['xoja] *nf* jewel, gem; *(fig: persona)* gem; **~s de fantasía** imitation jewellery *sg*.

joyería [xoje'ria] *nf (joyas)* jewellery; *(tienda)* jeweller's (shop).

joyero [xo'jero] *nm (persona)* jeweller; *(caja)* jewel case.

Juan [xwan] *nm*: **Noche de San ~** *see boxed note.*

NOCHE DE SAN JUAN

The **Noche de San Juan** *(evening of the Feast of Saint John) on 24 June coincides with the summer solstice; the "fiesta" has in fact replaced other more ancient pagan festivals. Traditionally fire plays a major part in these festivities, which can last for days in certain areas. Celebrations, fireworks and dancing centre around "hogueras" (bonfires) in towns and villages across Spain.*

---

juanete [xwa'nete] *nm (del pie)* bunion.

jubilación [xuβila'θjon] *nf (retiro)* retirement.

jubilado, a [xuβi'laðo, a] *adj* retired ♦ *nm/f* retired person, pensioner *(BRIT)*, senior citizen.

jubilar [xuβi'lar] *vt* to pension off, retire;

(*fam*) to discard; ~**se** *vr* to retire.
jubileo [xuβi'leo] *nm* jubilee.
júbilo ['xuβilo] *nm* joy, rejoicing.
jubiloso, a [xuβi'loso, a] *adj* jubilant.
judaísmo [xuða'ismo] *nm* Judaism.
judía [xu'ðia] *nf* V **judío**.
judicatura [xuðika'tura] *nf* (*cargo de juez*)
  office of judge; (*cuerpo de jueces*)
  judiciary.
judicial [xuði'θjal] *adj* judicial.
judío, a [xu'ðio, a] *adj* Jewish ♦ *nm* Jew ♦ *nf*
  Jewess, Jewish woman; (*CULIN*) bean;
  judía blanca haricot bean; **judía verde**
  French *o* string bean.
juego ['xweɣo] *etc vb* V **jugar** ♦ *nm* (*gen*)
  play; (*pasatiempo, partido*) game; (*en
  casino*) gambling; (*deporte*) sport;
  (*conjunto*) set; (*herramientas*) kit; ~ **de
  azar** game of chance; ~ **de café** coffee
  set; ~ **de caracteres** (*INFORM*) font; ~
  limpio/sucio fair/foul *o* dirty play; **J~s
  Olímpicos** Olympic Games; ~ **de
  programas** (*INFORM*) suite of programs;
  fuera de ~ (*DEPORTE*: *persona*) offside;
  (: *pelota*) out of play; **por** ~ in fun, for fun.
juegue ['xweɣe] *etc vb* V **jugar**.
juerga ['xwerɣa] *nf* binge; (*fiesta*) party; **ir
  de** ~ to go out on a binge.
juerguista [xwer'ɣista] *nm/f* reveller.
jueves ['xweβes] *nm inv* Thursday.
juez [xweθ] *nm/f* (*f tb*: **jueza**) judge; (*TENIS*)
  umpire; ~ **de línea** linesman; ~ **de paz**
  justice of the peace; ~ **de salida** starter.
jugada [xu'ɣaða] *nf* play; **buena** ~ good
  move (*o* shot *o* stroke) *etc*.
jugador, a [xuɣa'ðor, a] *nm/f* player; (*en
  casino*) gambler.
jugar [xu'ɣar] *vt* to play; (*en casino*) to
  gamble; (*apostar*) to bet ♦ *vi* to play; to
  gamble; (*COM*) to speculate; ~**se** *vr* to
  gamble (away); ~**se el todo por el todo**
  to stake one's all, go for bust; **¿quién
  juega?** whose move is it?; **¡me la han
  jugado!** (*fam*) I've been had!
jugarreta [xuɣa'rreta] *nf* (*mala jugada*) bad
  move; (*trampa*) dirty trick; **hacer una** ~ **a
  algn** to play a dirty trick on sb.
juglar [xu'ɣlar] *nm* minstrel.
jugo ['xuɣo] *nm* (*BOT, de fruta*) juice; (*fig*)
  essence, substance; ~ **de naranja** (*esp
  AM*) orange juice.
jugoso, a [xu'ɣoso, a] *adj* juicy; (*fig*)
  substantial, important.
jugué [xu'ɣe], **juguemos** [xu'ɣemos] *etc
  vb* V **jugar**.
juguete [xu'ɣete] *nm* toy.
juguetear [xuɣete'ar] *vi* to play.
juguetería [xuɣete'ria] *nf* toyshop.

juguetón, ona [xuɣe'ton, ona] *adj* playful.
juicio ['xwiθjo] *nm* judgement; (*sana razón*)
  sanity, reason; (*opinión*) opinion; (*JUR*:
  proceso) trial; **estar fuera de** ~ to be out
  of one's mind; **a mi** ~ in my opinion.
juicioso, a [xwi'θjoso, a] *adj* wise,
  sensible.
JUJEM [xu'xem] *nf abr* (*ESP MIL*) = *Junta de
  Jefes del Estado Mayor*.
jul. *abr* (= *julio*) Jul.
julio ['xuljo] *nm* July.
jumento, a [xu'mento, a] *nm/f* donkey.
jun. *abr* (= *junio*) Jun.
junco ['xunko] *nm* rush, reed.
jungla ['xungla] *nf* jungle.
junio ['xunjo] *nm* June.
junta ['xunta] *nf* V **junto**.
juntar [xun'tar] *vt* to join, unite; (*maquinaria*) to assemble, put together; (*dinero*) to
  collect; ~**se** *vr* to join, meet; (*reunirse*:
  personas) to meet, assemble; (*arrimarse*)
  to approach, draw closer; ~**se con algn**
  to join sb.
junto, a ['xunto, a] *adj* joined; (*unido*)
  united; (*anexo*) near, close; (*contiguo,
  próximo*) next, adjacent ♦ *nf* (*asamblea*)
  meeting, assembly; (*comité, consejo*)
  board, council, committee; (*MIL, POL*)
  junta; (*articulación*) joint ♦ *adv*: **todo** ~ all
  at once ♦ *prep*: ~ **a** near (to), next to; ~**s**
  together; **junta constitutiva** (*COM*)
  statutory meeting; **junta directiva** (*COM*)
  board of management; **junta general
  extraordinaria** (*COM*) extraordinary
  general meeting.
juntura [xun'tura] *nf* (*punto de unión*) join,
  junction; (*articulación*) joint.
jura ['xura] *nf* oath, pledge; ~ **de bandera**
  (ceremony of taking the) oath of
  allegiance.
jurado [xu'raðo] *nm* (*JUR*: *individuo*) juror;
  (: *grupo*) jury; (*de concurso*: *grupo*) panel
  (of judges); (: *individuo*) member of a
  panel.
juramentar [xuramen'tar] *vt* to swear in,
  administer the oath to; ~**se** *vr* to be
  sworn in, take the oath.
juramento [xura'mento] *nm* oath;
  (*maldición*) oath, curse; **bajo** ~ on oath;
  prestar ~ to take the oath; **tomar** ~ **a** to
  swear in, administer the oath to.
jurar [xu'rar] *vt, vi* to swear; ~ **en falso** to
  commit perjury; **jurárselas a algn** to
  have it in for sb.
jurídico, a [xu'riðiko, a] *adj* legal,
  juridical.
jurisdicción [xurisðik'θjon] *nf* (*poder,
  autoridad*) jurisdiction; (*territorio*)

district.

jurisprudencia [xurispru'ðenθja] *nf* jurisprudence.

jurista [xu'rista] *nm/f* jurist.

justamente [xusta'mente] *adv* justly, fairly; (*precisamente*) just, exactly.

justicia [xus'tiθja] *nf* justice; (*equidad*) fairness, justice; **de** ~ deservedly.

justiciero, a [xusti'θjero, a] *adj* just, righteous.

justificable [xustifi'kaßle] *adj* justifiable.

justificación [xustifika'θjon] *nf* justification; ~ **automática** (*INFORM*) automatic justification.

justificado, a [xustifi'kaðo, a] *adj* (*TIP*): **(no)** ~ (un)justified.

justificante [xustifi'kante] *nm* voucher; ~ **médico** sick note.

justificar [xustifi'kar] *vt* (*tb TIP*) to justify; (*probar*) to verify.

justifique [xusti'fike] *etc vb V* **justificar.**

justo, a ['xusto, a] *adj* (*equitativo*) just, fair, right; (*preciso*) exact, correct; (*ajustado*) tight ♦ *adv* (*precisamente*) exactly, precisely; (*apenas a tiempo*) just in time; ¡~! that's it!, correct!; **llegaste muy** ~ you just made it; **vivir muy** ~ to be hard up.

juvenil [xuße'nil] *adj* youthful.

juventud [xußen'tuð] *nf* (*adolescencia*) youth; (*jóvenes*) young people *pl.*

juzgado [xuθ'yaðo] *nm* tribunal; (*JUR*) court.

juzgar [xuθ'yar] *vt* to judge; **a** ~ **por** ... to judge by ..., judging by ...; ~ **mal** to misjudge; **júzguelo usted mismo** see for yourself.

K k

K, k [ka] *nf* (*letra*) K, k; **K de Kilo** K for King.

K *abr* (= *1.000*) K; (*INFORM*: = *1.024*) K.

Kampuchea [kampu'tʃea] *nf* Kampuchea.

karaoke [kara'oke] *nm* karaoke.

kárate ['karate] *nm*, **karate** [ka'rate] *nm* karate.

KAS *nf abr* (= *Koordinadora Abertzale Sozialista*) *Basque nationalist umbrella group.*

Kazajstán [kaθaxs'tan] *nm* Kazakhstan.

k/c. *abr* (= *kilociclos*) kc.

Kenia ['kenja] *nf* Kenya.

keniata [ke'njata] *adj, nm/f* Kenyan.

kepí, kepis [ke'pi, 'kepis] *nm* (*esp AM*) kepi, military hat.

kerosene [kero'sene] *nm* kerosene.

kg. *abr* (= *kilogramo(s)*) kg.

kilate [ki'late] *nm* = **quilate.**

kilo ['kilo] *nm* kilo.

kilobyte ['kiloßait] *nm* (*INFORM*) kilobyte.

kilogramo [kilo'vramo] *nm* kilogramme (*BRIT*), kilogram (*US*).

kilolitro [kilo'litro] *nm* kilolitre (*BRIT*), kiloliter (*US*).

kilometraje [kilome'traxe] *nm* distance in kilometres, ≈ mileage.

kilométrico, a [kilo'metriko, a] *adj* kilometric; (*fam*) very long; (**billete**) ~ (*FERRO*) mileage ticket.

kilómetro [ki'lometro] *nm* kilometre (*BRIT*), kilometer (*US*).

kiloocteto [kilook'teto] *nm* (*INFORM*) kilobyte.

kilovatio [kilo'ßatjo] *nm* kilowatt.

kiosco ['kjosko] *nm* = **quiosco.**

Kirguizistán [kirviðis'tan] *nm* Kirghizia.

kiwi ['kiwi] *nm* kiwi (fruit).

km *abr* (= *kilómetro(s)*) km.

km/h *abr* (= *kilómetros por hora*) km/h.

knock-out ['nokau], **K.O.** ['kao] *nm* knockout; (*golpe*) knockout blow; **dejar** *o* **poner a algn** ~ to knock sb out.

kosovar [koso'ßar] *adj* Kosovan.

Kosovo ['kosoßo] *nm* Kosovo.

k.p.h. *abr* (= *kilómetros por hora*) km/h.

k.p.l. *abr* (= *kilómetros por litro*) ≈ m.p.g.

kurdo, a ['kurðo, a] *adj* Kurdish ♦ *nm/f* Kurd ♦ *nm* (*LING*) Kurdish.

kuwaití [kußai'ti] *adj, nm/f* Kuwaiti.

kv *abr* (= *kilovatio*) kw.

kv/h *abr* (= *kilovatios-hora*) kw-h.

L l

L, l ['ele] *nf* (*letra*) L, l; **L de Lorenzo** L for Lucy (*BRIT*) *o* Love (*US*).

l. *abr* (= *litro(s)*) l.; (*JUR*) = **ley;** (*LITERATURA*: = *libro*) bk.

L/ *abr* (*COM*) = **letra.**

la [la] *artículo definido fsg* the ♦ *pron* her; (*usted*) you; (*cosa*) it ♦ *nm* (*MUS*) A; **está en** ~ **cárcel** he's in jail; ~ **del sombrero rojo** the woman/girl/one in the red hat.

laberinto [laße'rinto] nm labyrinth.
labia ['laßja] nf fluency; (pey) glibness;
tener mucha ~ to have the gift of the
gab.
labial [la'ßjal] adj labial.
labio ['laßjo] nm lip; (de vasija etc) edge,
rim; ~ **inferior/superior** lower/upper lip.
labor [la'ßor] nf labour; (AGR) farm work;
(tarea) job, task; (COSTURA) needlework,
sewing; (punto) knitting; ~ **de equipo**
teamwork; ~ **de ganchillo** crochet.
laborable [laßo'raßle] adj (AGR) workable;
día ~ working day.
laboral [laßo'ral] adj (accidente,
conflictividad) industrial; (jornada)
working; (derecho, relaciones) labour cpd.
laboralista [laßora'lista] adj: **abogado** ~
labour lawyer.
laborar [laßo'rar] vi to work.
laboratorio [laßora'torjo] nm laboratory.
laborioso, a [laßo'rjoso, a] a (persona)
hard-working; (trabajo) tough.
laborista [laßo'rista] (BRIT POL) adj: **Partido
L~** Labour Party ♦ nm/f Labour Party
member o supporter.
labrado, a [la'ßraðo, a] adj worked;
(madera) carved; (metal) wrought ♦ nm
(AGR) cultivated field.
Labrador [laßra'ðor] nm Labrador.
labrador, a [laßra'ðor, a] nm/f farmer.
labranza [la'ßranθa] nf (AGR) cultivation.
labrar [la'ßrar] vt (gen) to work; (madera
etc) to carve; (fig) to cause, bring about.
labriego, a [la'ßrjeɣo, a] nm/f peasant.
laca ['laka] nf lacquer; (de pelo) hairspray;
~ **de uñas** nail varnish.
lacayo [la'kajo] nm lackey.
lacerar [laθe'rar] vt to lacerate.
lacio, a ['laθjo, a] adj (pelo) lank, straight.
lacón [la'kon] nm shoulder of pork.
lacónico, a [la'koniko, a] adj laconic.
lacra ['lakra] nf (defecto) blemish; ~ **social**
social disgrace.
lacrar [la'krar] vt (cerrar) to seal (with
sealing wax).
lacre ['lakre] nm sealing wax.
lacrimógeno, a [lakri'moxeno, a] adj (fig)
sentimental; **gas** ~ tear gas.
lacrimoso, a [lakri'moso, a] adj tearful.
lactancia [lak'tanθja] nf breast-feeding.
lactar [lak'tar] vt, vi to suckle, breast-feed.
lácteo, a ['lakteo, a] adj: **productos** ~**s**
dairy products.
ladear [laðe'ar] vt to tip, tilt ♦ vi to tilt; ~**se**
vr to lean; (DEPORTE) to swerve; (AVIAT)
to bank, turn.
ladera [la'ðera] nf slope.
ladino, a [la'ðino, a] adj cunning.

lado ['laðo] nm (gen) side; (fig) protection;
(MIL) flank; ~ **izquierdo** left(-hand) side;
~ **a** ~ side by side; **al** ~ **de** next to,
beside; **hacerse a un** ~ to stand aside;
poner de ~ to put on its side; **poner a un**
~ to put aside; **me da de** ~ I don't care;
por un ~ ..., **por otro** ~ ... on the one
hand ..., on the other (hand), ...; **por
todos** ~**s** on all sides, all round (BRIT).
ladrar [la'ðrar] vi to bark.
ladrido [la'ðriðo] nm bark, barking.
ladrillo [la'ðriʎo] nm (gen) brick; (azulejo)
tile.
ladrón, ona [la'ðron, ona] nm/f thief.
lagar [la'ɣar] nm (wine/oil) press.
lagartija [laɣar'tixa] nf (small) lizard, wall
lizard.
lagarto [la'ɣarto] nm (ZOOL) lizard; (AM)
alligator.
lago ['laɣo] nm lake.
Lagos ['laɣos] nm Lagos.
lágrima ['laɣrima] nf tear.
lagrimal [laɣri'mal] nm (inner) corner of
the eye.
lagrimear [laɣrime'ar] vi to weep; (ojos) to
water.
laguna [la'ɣuna] nf (lago) lagoon; (en
escrito, conocimientos) gap.
laico, a ['laiko, a] adj lay ♦ nm/f layman/
woman.
laja ['laxa] nf rock.
lamber [lam'ber] vt (AM) to lick.
lambiscón, ona [lambis'kon, ona] adj
flattering ♦ nm/f flatterer.
lameculos [lame'kulos] nm/f inv (fam)
arselicker (!), crawler.
lamentable [lamen'taßle] adj lamentable,
regrettable; (miserable) pitiful.
lamentación [lamenta'θjon] nf
lamentation; **ahora no sirven
lamentaciones** it's no good crying over
spilt milk.
lamentar [lamen'tar] vt (sentir) to regret;
(deplorar) to lament; ~**se** vr to lament; **lo
lamento mucho** I'm very sorry.
lamento [la'mento] nm lament.
lamer [la'mer] vt to lick.
lámina ['lamina] nf (plancha delgada) sheet;
(para estampar, estampa) plate; (grabado)
engraving.
laminar [lami'nar] vt (en libro) to laminate;
(TEC) to roll.
lámpara ['lampara] nf lamp; ~ **de alcohol/
gas** spirit/gas lamp; ~ **de pie** standard
lamp.
lamparilla [lampa'riʎa] nf nightlight.
lamparón [lampa'ron] nm (MED) scrofula;
(mancha) (large) grease spot.

lampiño, a [lam'piɲo, a] *adj* (*sin pelo*) hairless.

lana ['lana] *nf* wool; (*tela*) woollen (*BRIT*) o woolen (*US*) cloth; (*AM fam: dinero*) dough; **(hecho) de** ~ wool *cpd*.

lance ['lanθe] *etc vb V* **lanzar** ♦ *nm* (*golpe*) stroke; (*suceso*) event, incident.

lanceta [lan'seta] *nf* (*AM*) sting.

lancha ['lantʃa] *nf* launch; ~ **motora** motorboat; ~ **de pesca** fishing boat; ~ **salvavidas/torpedera** lifeboat/torpedo boat; ~ **neumática** rubber dinghy.

lanero, a [la'nero, a] *adj* wool *cpd*.

langosta [lan'gosta] *nf* (*insecto*) locust; (*crustáceo*) lobster (: *de río*) crayfish.

langostino [langos'tino] *nm* prawn; (*de agua dulce*) crayfish.

languidecer [langiðe'θer] *vi* to languish.

languidez [langi'ðeθ] *nf* languor.

languidezca [langi'ðeθka] *etc vb V* **languidecer**.

lánguido, a ['langiðo, a] *adj* (*gen*) languid; (*sin energía*) listless.

lanilla [la'niʎa] *nf* nap; (*tela*) thin flannel cloth.

lanolina [lano'lina] *nf* lanolin(e).

lanudo, a [la'nuðo, a] *adj* woolly, fleecy.

lanza ['lanθa] *nf* (*arma*) lance, spear; **medir** ~**s** to cross swords.

lanzacohetes [lanθako'etes] *nm inv* rocket launcher.

lanzadera [lanθa'ðera] *nf* shuttle.

lanzado, a [lan'θaðo, a] *adj* (*atrevido*) forward; (*decidido*) determined; **ir** ~ (*rápido*) to fly along.

lanzallamas [lanθa'ʎamas] *nm inv* flamethrower.

lanzamiento [lanθa'mjento] *nm* (*gen*) throwing; (*NAUT, COM*) launch, launching; ~ **de pesos** putting the shot.

lanzar [lan'θar] *vt* (*gen*) to throw; (*con violencia*) to fling; (*DEPORTE: pelota*) to bowl; (: *US*) to pitch; (*NAUT, COM*) to launch; (*JUR*) to evict; (*grito*) to give, utter; ~**se** *vr* to throw o.s.; (*fig*) to take the plunge; ~**se a** (*fig*) to embark upon.

Lanzarote [lanθa'rote] *nm* Lanzarote.

lanzatorpedos [lanθator'peðos] *nm inv* torpedo tube.

lapa ['lapa] *nf* limpet.

La Paz *nf* La Paz.

lapicero [lapi'θero] *nm* pencil; (*AM*) propelling (*BRIT*) o mechanical (*US*) pencil; (: *bolígrafo*) Biro ®.

lápida ['lapiða] *nf* stone; ~ **conmemorativa** memorial stone; ~ **mortuoria** headstone.

lapidar [lapi'ðar] *vt* to stone; (*TEC*) to

polish, lap.

lapidario, a [lapi'ðarjo, a] *adj*, *nm* lapidary.

lápiz ['lapiθ] *nm* pencil; ~ **de color** coloured pencil; ~ **de labios** lipstick; ~ **óptico** o **luminoso** light pen.

lapón, ona [la'pon, ona] *adj* Lapp ♦ *nm/f* Laplander, Lapp ♦ *nm* (*LING*) Lapp.

Laponia [la'ponja] *nf* Lapland.

lapso ['lapso] *nm* lapse; (*error*) error; ~ **de tiempo** interval of time.

lapsus ['lapsus] *nm inv* error, mistake.

LAR [lar] *nf abr* (*ESP JUR*) = *Ley de Arrendamientos Rústicos*.

largamente [larɣa'mente] *adv* for a long time; (*relatar*) at length.

largar [lar'ɣar] *vt* (*soltar*) to release; (*aflojar*) to loosen; (*lanzar*) to launch; (*fam*) to let fly; (*velas*) to unfurl; (*AM*) to throw; ~**se** *vr* (*fam*) to beat it; ~**se a** (*AM*) to start to.

largo, a ['larɣo, a] *adj* (*longitud*) long; (*tiempo*) lengthy; (*persona: alta*) tall; (: *fig*) generous ♦ *nm* length; (*MUS*) largo; **dos años** ~**s** two long years; **a** ~ **plazo** in the long term; **tiene 9 metros de** ~ it is 9 metres long; **a lo** ~ (*posición*) lengthways; **a lo** ~ **de** along; (*tiempo*) all through, throughout; **a la larga** in the long run; **me dio largas con una promesa** she put me off with a promise; **¡** ~ **de aquí!** (*fam*) clear off!

largometraje [larɣome'traxe] *nm* full-length o feature film.

largue ['larɣe] *etc vb V* **largar**.

larguero [lar'ɣero] *nm* (*ARQ*) main beam, chief support; (*de puerta*) jamb; (*DEPORTE*) crossbar; (*en cama*) bolster.

largueza [lar'ɣeθa] *nf* generosity.

larguirucho, a [larɣi'rutʃo, a] *adj* lanky, gangling.

larguísimo, a [lar'ɣisimo, a] *adj superlativo de* **largo**.

largura [lar'ɣura] *nf* length.

laringe [la'rinxe] *nf* larynx.

laringitis [larin'xitis] *nf* laryngitis.

larva ['larßa] *nf* larva.

las [las] *artículo definido fpl* the ♦ *pron* them; ~ **que cantan** the ones/women/girls who sing.

lasaña [la'saɲa] *nf* lasagne, lasagna.

lasca ['laska] *nf* chip of stone.

lascivia [las'θißja] *nf* lewdness; (*lujuria*) lust; (*fig*) playfulness.

lascivo, a [las'θißo, a] *adj* lewd.

láser ['laser] *nm* laser.

Las Palmas *nf* Las Palmas.

lástima ['lastima] *nf* (*pena*) pity; **dar** ~ to be pitiful; **es una** ~ **que** it's a pity that;

¡qué ~! what a pity!; **estar hecho una ~**
to be a sorry sight.
lastimar [lasti'mar] *vt* (*herir*) to wound;
(*ofender*) to offend; **~se** *vr* to hurt o.s.
lastimero, a [lasti'mero,‚a] *adj* pitiful,
pathetic.
lastre ['lastre] *nm* (*TEC*, *NAUT*) ballast; (*fig*)
dead weight.
lata ['lata] *nf* (*metal*) tin; (*envase*) tin, can;
(*fam*) nuisance; **en ~** tinned; **dar (la) ~** to
be a nuisance.
latente [la'tente] *adj* latent.
lateral [late'ral] *adj* side, lateral ♦ *nm*
(*TEAT*) wings *pl*.
latido [la'tiðo] *nm* (*del corazón*) beat; (*de
herida*) throb(bing).
latifundio [lati'fundjo] *nm* large estate.
latifundista [latifun'dista] *nm/f* owner of a
large estate.
latigazo [lati'ɣaθo] *nm* (*golpe*) lash;
(*sonido*) crack; (*fig: regaño*) dressing-
down.
látigo ['latiɣo] *nm* whip.
latiguillo [lati'ɣiʎo] *nm* (*TEAT*) hamming.
latín [la'tin] *nm* Latin; **saber (mucho) ~**
(*fam*) to be pretty sharp.
latinajo [lati'naxo] *nm* dog Latin; **echar ~s**
to come out with Latin words.
latino, a [la'tino, a] *adj* Latin.
Latinoamérica [latinoa'merika] *nf* Latin
America.
latinoamericano, a [latinoameri'kano, a]
adj, nm/f Latin American.
latir [la'tir] *vi* (*corazón, pulso*) to beat.
latitud [lati'tuð] *nf* (*GEO*) latitude; (*fig*)
breadth, extent.
lato, a ['lato, a] *adj* broad.
latón [la'ton] *nm* brass.
latoso, a [‚ia'toso, a] *adj* (*molesto*)
annoying; (*aburrido*) boring.
latrocinio [latro'θinjo] *nm* robbery.
LAU *nf abr* (*ESP JUR*) = *Ley de
Arrendamientos Urbanos*.
laúd [la'uð] *nm* lute.
laudatorio, a [lauða'torjo, a] *adj*
laudatory.
laudo ['lauðo] *nm* (*JUR*) decision, finding.
laurear [laure'ar] *vt* to honour, reward.
laurel [lau'rel] *nm* (*BOT*) laurel; (*CULIN*) bay.
Lausana [lau'sana] *nf* Lausanne.
lava ['laβa] *nf* lava.
lavable [la'βaβle] *adj* washable.
lavabo [la'βaβo] *nm* (*jofaina*) washbasin;
(*retrete*) lavatory (*BRIT*), toilet (*BRIT*),
washroom (*US*).
lavadero [laβa'ðero] *nm* laundry.
lavado [la'βaðo] *nm* washing; (*de ropa*)
wash, laundry; (*ARTE*) wash; **~ de**

cerebro brainwashing.
lavadora [laβa'ðora] *nf* washing machine.
lavanda [la'βanda] *nf* lavender.
lavandería [laβande'ria] *nf* laundry; **~
automática** launderette.
lavaparabrisas [laβapara'βrisas] *nm inv*
windscreen washer.
lavaplatos [laβa'platos] *nm inv* dishwasher.
lavar [la'βar] *vt* to wash; (*borrar*) to wipe
away; **~se** *vr* to wash o.s.; **~se las manos**
to wash one's hands; (*fig*) to wash one's
hands of it; **~ y marcar** (*pelo*) to
shampoo and set; **~ en seco** to dry-
clean.
lavativa [laβa'tiβa] *nf* (*MED*) enema.
lavavajillas [laβaβa'xiʎas] *nm inv*
dishwasher.
laxante [lak'sante] *nm* laxative.
laxitud [laksi'tuð] *nf* laxity, slackness.
lazada [la'θaða] *nf* bow.
lazarillo [laθa'riʎo] *nm*: **perro de ~** guide
dog.
lazo ['laθo] *nm* knot; (*lazada*) bow; (*para
animales*) lasso; (*trampa*) snare; (*vínculo*)
tie; **~ corredizo** slipknot.
LBE *nf abr* (*ESP JUR*) = *Ley Básica de Empleo*.
lb(s) *abr* = **libra(s)**.
L/C *abr* (= *Letra de Crédito*) B/E.
Lda., Ldo. *abr* = **Licenciado, a**.
le [le] *pron* (*directo*) him (*o* her); (: *usted*)
you; (*indirecto*) to him (*o* her *o* it);
(: *usted*) to you.
leal [le'al] *adj* loyal.
lealtad [leal'tað] *nf* loyalty.
lebrel [le'βrel] *nm* greyhound.
lección [iek'θjon] *nf* lesson; **~ práctica**
object lesson; **dar lecciones** to teach,
give lessons; **dar una ~ a algn** (*fig*) to
teach sb a lesson.
leche ['letʃe] *nf* milk; (*fam!*) semen,
spunk (!); **dar una ~ a algn** (*fam*) to belt
sb; **estar de mala ~** (*fam*) to be in a foul
mood; **tener mala ~** (*fam*) to be a nasty
piece of work; **~ condensada/en polvo**
condensed/powdered milk; **~ desnatada**
skimmed milk; **~ de magnesia** milk of
magnesia; ¡**~**! hell!
lechera [le'tʃera] *nf V* **lechero**.
lechería [letʃe'ria] *nf* dairy.
lechero, a [le'tʃero, a] *adj* milk *cpd* ♦ *nm*
milkman ♦ *nf* (*vendedora*) milkmaid;
(*recipiente*) milk pan; (*para servir*) milk
churn.
lecho ['letʃo] *nm* (*cama, de río*) bed; (*GEO*)
layer; **~ mortuorio** deathbed.
lechón [le'tʃon] *nm* sucking (*BRIT*) *o*
suckling (*US*) pig.
lechoso, a [le'tʃoso, a] *adj* milky.

lechuga [le'tʃuɣa] nf lettuce.
lechuza [le'tʃuθa] nf (barn) owl.
lectivo, a [lek'tiβo, a] adj (horas) teaching
cpd; **año o curso ~** (ESCOL) school year;
(UNIV) academic year.
lector, a [lek'tor, a] nm/f reader; (ESCOL,
UNIV) (conversation) assistant ♦ nm: **~
óptico de caracteres** (INFORM) optical
character reader ♦ nf: **~a de fichas**
(INFORM) card reader.
lectura [lek'tura] nf reading; **~ de marcas
sensibles** (INFORM) mark sensing.
leer [le'er] vt to read; **~ entre líneas** to
read between the lines.
legación [leɣa'θjon] nf legation.
legado [le'ɣaðo] nm (don) bequest;
(herencia) legacy; (enviado) legate.
legajo [le'ɣaxo] nm file, bundle (of papers).
legal [le'ɣal] adj legal, lawful; (persona)
trustworthy.
legalice [leɣa'liθe] etc vb V **legalizar**.
legalidad [leɣali'ðað] nf legality.
legalizar [leɣali'θar] vt to legalize;
(documento) to authenticate.
legar [le'ɣar] vt to bequeath, leave.
legatario, a [leɣa'tarjo, a] nm/f legatee.
legendario, a [lexen'darjo, a] adj
legendary.
legible [le'xiβle] adj legible; **~ por máquina**
(INFORM) machine-readable.
legión [le'xjon] nf legion.
legionario, a [lexjo'narjo, a] adj legionary
♦ nm legionnaire.
legislación [lexisla'θjon] nf legislation;
(leyes) laws pl; **~ antimonopolio** (COM)
anti-trust legislation.
legislar [lexis'lar] vt to legislate.
legislativo, a [lexisla'tiβo, a] adj: (elecciones) **legislativas** ≈ general election.
legislatura [lexisla'tura] nf (POL) period of
office.
legitimar [lexiti'mar] vt to legitimize.
legítimo, a [le'xitimo, a] adj (genuino)
authentic; (legal) legitimate, rightful.
lego, a ['leɣo, a] adj (REL) secular;
(ignorante) ignorant ♦ nm layman.
legua ['leɣwa] nf league; **se ve (o nota) a la
~** you can tell (it) a mile off.
legue ['leɣe] etc vb V **legar**.
leguleyo [leɣu'lejo] nm (pey) petty o
shyster (US) lawyer.
legumbres [le'ɣumbres] nfpl pulses.
leído, a [le'iðo, a] adj well-read.
lejanía [lexa'nia] nf distance.
lejano, a [le'xano, a] adj far-off; (en el
tiempo) distant; (fig) remote; **L~ Oriente**
Far East.
lejía [le'xia] nf bleach.

lejísimos [le'xisimos] adv a long, long way.
lejos ['lexos] adv far, far away; **a lo ~** in
the distance; **de o desde ~** from a distance; **está muy ~** it's a long way (away);
¿está ~? is it far?; **~ de** prep far from.
lelo, a ['lelo, a] adj silly ♦ nm/f idiot.
lema ['lema] nm motto; (POL) slogan.
lencería [lenθe'ria] nf (telas) linen,
drapery; (ropa interior) lingerie.
lendakari [lenda'kari] nm head of the
Basque Autonomous Government.
lengua ['lengwa] nf tongue; **~ cooficial** see
boxed note; **~ materna** mother tongue; **~
oficial** official language; **~ de tierra**
(GEO) spit o tongue of land; **dar a la ~** to
chatter; **morderse la ~** to hold one's
tongue; **sacar la ~ a algn** (fig) to cock a
snook at sb.

LENGUAS COOFICIALES

Under the Spanish constitution **lenguas
cooficiales** or **oficiales** enjoy the same
status as "castellano" in those regions
which have retained their own distinct
language: in Galicia, "gallego"; in the
Basque Country, "euskera"; in Catalonia
and the Balearic Islands, "catalán". The
regional governments actively promote
their own language through the media and
the education system. Of these three
regions, Catalonia has the highest number
of native speakers.

---

lenguado [len'gwaðo] nm sole.
lenguaje [len'gwaxe] nm language; (forma
de hablar) (mode of) speech; **~ comercial**
business language; **~ ensamblador o de
alto nivel** (INFORM) high-level language;
~ máquina (INFORM) machine language;
~ original source language; **~
periodístico** journalese; **~ de
programación** (INFORM) programming
language; **en ~ llano** ≈ in plain English.
lenguaraz [lengwa'raθ] adj talkative; (pey)
foul-mouthed.
lengüeta [len'gweta] nf (ANAT) epiglottis;
(de zapatos, MUS) tongue.
lenidad [leni'ðað] nf lenience.
Leningrado [lenin'graðo] nm Leningrad.
lente ['lente] nm o nf lens; (lupa)
magnifying glass; **~s** pl glasses; **~s de
contacto** contact lenses; **~s progresivas**
varifocal lenses.
lenteja [len'texa] nf lentil.
lentejuela [lente'xwela] nf sequin.
lentilla [len'tiʎa] nf contact lens.
lentitud [lenti'tuð] nf slowness; **con ~**

slowly.

lento, a ['lento, a] *adj* slow.

leña ['leɲa] *nf* firewood; **dar ~ a** to thrash; **echar ~ al fuego** to add fuel to the flames.

leñador, a [leɲa'ðor, a] *nm/f* woodcutter.

leño ['leɲo] *nm* (*trozo de árbol*) log; (*madera*) timber; (*fig*) blockhead.

Leo ['leo] *nm* (*ASTRO*) Leo.

león [le'on] *nm* lion; **~ marino** sea lion.

leonera [leo'nera] *nf* (*jaula*) lion's cage; **parece una ~** it's shockingly dirty.

leonés, esa [leo'nes, esa] *adj, nm/f* Leonese ♦ *nm* (*LING*) Leonese.

leonino, a [leo'nino, a] *adj* leonine.

leopardo [leo'parðo] *nm* leopard.

leotardos [leo'tarðos] *nmpl* tights.

lepra ['lepra] *nf* leprosy.

leprosería [leprose'ria] *nf* leper colony.

leproso, a [le'proso, a] *nm/f* leper.

lerdo, a ['lerðo, a] *adj* (*lento*) slow; (*patoso*) clumsy.

leridano, a [leri'ðano, a] *adj* of *o* from Lérida ♦ *nm/f* native *o* inhabitant of Lérida.

les [les] *pron* (*directo*) them; (: *ustedes*) you; (*indirecto*) to them; (: *ustedes*) to you.

lesbiana [les'βjana] *nf* lesbian.

lesión [le'sjon] *nf* wound, lesion; (*DEPORTE*) injury.

lesionado, a [lesjo'naðo, a] *adj* injured ♦ *nm/f* injured person.

lesionar [lesjo'nar] *vt* (*dañar*) to hurt; (*herir*) to wound; **~se** *vr* to get hurt.

letal [le'tal] *adj* lethal.

letanía [leta'nia] *nf* litany; (*retahíla*) long list.

letárgico, a [le'tarxiko, a] *adj* lethargic.

letargo [le'tarɣo] *nm* lethargy.

letón, ona [le'ton, ona] *adj, nm/f* Latvian ♦ *nm* (*LING*) Latvian.

Letonia [le'tonja] *nf* Latvia.

letra ['letra] *nf* letter; (*escritura*) handwriting; (*COM*) letter, bill, draft; (*MUS*) lyrics *pl*; **~s** *nfpl* (*UNIV*) arts; **~ bastardilla/negrilla** italics *pl*/bold type; **~ de cambio** bill of exchange; **~ de imprenta** print; **~ inicial/capital/minúscula** initial/capital/small letter; **lo tomó al pie de la ~** he took it literally; **~ bancaria** (*COM*) bank draft; **~ de patente** (*COM*) letters patent *pl*; **escribir 4 ~s a algn** to drop a line to sb.

letrado, a [le'traðo, a] *adj* learned; (*fam*) pedantic ♦ *nm/f* lawyer.

letrero [le'trero] *nm* (*cartel*) sign; (*etiqueta*) label.

letrina [le'trina] *nf* latrine.

leucemia [leu'θemja] *nf* leukaemia.

leucocito [leuko'θito] *nm* white blood cell, leucocyte.

leva ['leβa] *nf* (*NAUT*) weighing anchor; (*MIL*) levy; (*TEC*) lever.

levadizo, a [leβa'ðiθo, a] *adj*: **puente ~** drawbridge.

levadura [leβa'ðura] *nf* yeast, leaven; **~ de cerveza** brewer's yeast.

levantamiento [leβanta'mjento] *nm* raising, lifting; (*rebelión*) revolt, rising; (*GEO*) survey; **~ de pesos** weightlifting.

levantar [leβan'tar] *vt* (*gen*) to raise; (*del suelo*) to pick up; (*hacia arriba*) to lift (up); (*plan*) to make, draw up; (*mesa*) to clear; (*campamento*) to strike; (*fig*) to cheer up, hearten; **~se** *vr* to get up; (*enderezarse*) to straighten up; (*rebelarse*) to rebel; (*sesión*) to be adjourned; (*niebla*) to lift; (*viento*) to rise; **~se (de la cama)** to get up, get out of bed; **~ el ánimo** to cheer up.

levante [le'βante] *nm* east; (*viento*) east wind; **el L~** region of Spain extending from Castellón to Murcia.

levantino, a [leβan'tino, a] *adj* of *o* from the *Levante* ♦ *nm/f*: **los ~s** the people of the *Levante*.

levar [le'βar] *vi* to weigh anchor.

leve ['leβe] *adj* light; (*fig*) trivial; (*mínimo*) slight.

levedad [leβe'ðað] *nf* lightness; (*fig*) levity.

levita [le'βita] *nf* frock coat.

léxico, a ['leksiko, a] *adj* lexical ♦ *nm* (*vocabulario*) vocabulary; (*LING*) lexicon.

ley [lei] *nf* (*gen*) law; (*metal*) standard; **decreto-~** decree law; **de buena ~** (*fig*) genuine; **según la ~** in accordance with the law, by law, in law.

leyenda [le'jenda] *nf* legend; (*TIP*) inscription.

leyendo [le'jendo] *etc vb V* **leer**.

liar [li'ar] *vt* to tie (up); (*unir*) to bind; (*envolver*) to wrap (up); (*enredar*) to confuse; (*cigarrillo*) to roll; **~se** *vr* (*fam*) to get involved; (*confundirse*) to get mixed up; **~se a palos** to get involved in a fight.

lib. *abr* (= *libro*) bk.

libanés, esa [liβa'nes, esa] *adj, nm/f* Lebanese.

Líbano ['liβano] *nm*: **el ~** the Lebanon.

libar [li'βar] *vt* to suck.

libelo [li'βelo] *nm* satire, lampoon; (*JUR*) petition.

libélula [li'βelula] *nf* dragonfly.

liberación [liβera'θjon] *nf* liberation; (*de la cárcel*) release.

liberado, a [liße'raðo, a] adj liberated; (COM) paid-up, paid-in (US).
liberal [liße'ral] adj, nm/f liberal.
liberar [liße'rar] vt to liberate.
libertad [lißer'tað] nf liberty, freedom; ~ de asociación/de culto/de prensa/de comercio/de palabra freedom of association/of worship/of the press/of trade/of speech; ~ condicional probation; ~ bajo palabra parole; ~ bajo fianza bail; estar en ~ to be free; poner a algn en ~ to set sb free.
libertador, a [lißerta'ðor, a] adj liberating ♦ nm/f liberator; El L~ (AM) The Liberator.
libertar [lißer'tar] vt (preso) to set free; (de una obligación) to release; (eximir) to exempt.
libertinaje [lißerti'naxe] nm licentiousness.
libertino, a [lißer'tino, a] adj permissive ♦ nm/f permissive person.
Libia ['lißja] nf Libya.
libidinoso, a [lißiði'noso, a] adj lustful; (viejo) lecherous.
libido [li'ßiðo] nf libido.
libio, a ['lißjo, a] adj, nm/f Libyan.
libra ['lißra] nf pound; L~ (ASTRO) Libra; ~ esterlina pound sterling.
librador, a [lißra'ðor, a] nm/f drawer.
libranza [li'ßranθa] nf (COM) draft; (letra de cambio) bill of exchange.
librar [li'ßrar] vt (de peligro) to save; (batalla) to wage, fight; (de impuestos) to exempt; (cheque) to make out; (JUR) to exempt; ~se vr: ~se de to escape from, free o.s. from; de buena nos hemos librado we're well out of that.
libre ['lißre] adj (gen) free; (lugar) unoccupied; (tiempo) spare; (asiento) vacant; (COM): ~ a bordo free on board; ~ de franqueo post-free; ~ de impuestos free of tax; tiro ~ free kick; los 100 metros ~ the 100 metres freestyle (race); al aire ~ in the open air; ¿estás ~? are you free?
librecambio [lißre'kambjo] nm free trade.
librecambista [lißrekam'bista] adj free-trade cpd ♦ nm free-trader.
librería [lißre'ria] nf (tienda) bookshop; (estante) bookcase; ~ de ocasión secondhand bookshop.
librero, a [li'ßrero, a] nm/f bookseller.
libreta [li'ßreta] nf notebook; (pan) one-pound loaf; ~ de ahorros savings book.
libro ['lißro] nm book; ~ de actas minute book; ~ de bolsillo paperback; ~ de cabecera bedside book; ~ de caja auxiliar (COM) petty cash book; ~ de cocina

cookery book (BRIT), cookbook (US); ~ de consulta reference book; ~ de cuentas account book; ~ de cuentos storybook; ~ de cheques cheque (BRIT) o check (US) book; ~ diario journal; ~ de entradas y salidas (COM) daybook; ~ de honor visitors' book; ~ electrónico e-book; ~ mayor (COM) general ledger; ~ de reclamaciones complaints book; ~ de texto textbook.
Lic. abr = Licenciado, a.
licencia [li'θenθja] nf (gen) licence; (permiso) permission; ~ por enfermedad/con goce de sueldo sick/paid leave; ~ de armas/de caza gun/game licence; ~ de exportación (COM) export licence; ~ poética poetic licence.
licenciado, a [liθen'θjaðo, a] adj licensed ♦ nm/f graduate; L~ en Filosofía y Letras ≈ Bachelor of Arts; see boxed note.

LICENCIADO

*After an average of five years at Spanish universities, successful students are awarded a degree called a **licenciado**. If they have done a shorter three-year course, such as nursing, or if they choose not to stay on for another two years to specialize, they are awarded a "diplomado" instead. "Cursos de posgrado", postgraduate courses, are becoming increasingly popular, especially one-year specialist courses called "masters".*

---

licenciar [liθen'θjar] vt (empleado) to dismiss; (permitir) to permit, allow; (soldado) to discharge; (estudiante) to confer a degree upon; ~se vr: ~se en letras to get an arts degree.
licenciatura [liθenθja'tura] nf (título) degree; (estudios) degree course.
licencioso, a [liθen'θjoso, a] adj licentious.
liceo [li'θeo] nm (esp AM) (high) school.
licitación [liθita'θjon] nf bidding; (oferta) tender, offer.
licitador [liθita'ðor] nm bidder.
licitar [liθi'tar] vt to bid for ♦ vi to bid.
lícito, a ['liθito, a] adj (legal) lawful; (justo) fair, just; (permisible) permissible.
licor [li'kor] nm spirits pl (BRIT), liquor (US); (con hierbas etc) liqueur.
licra ® ['likra] nf Lycra ®.
licuadora [likwa'ðora] nf blender.
licuar [li'kwar] vt to liquidize.
lid [lið] nf combat; (fig) controversy.
líder ['liðer] nm/f leader.

liderato [liðeˈrato] *nm* = **liderazgo**.
liderazgo [liðeˈraθɣo] *nm* leadership.
lidia [ˈliðja] *nf* bullfighting; (*una ~*) bullfight; **toros de** ~ fighting bulls.
lidiar [liˈðjar] *vt, vi* to fight.
liebre [ˈljeßre] *nf* hare; **dar gato por** ~ to con.
Lieja [ˈljexa] *nf* Liège.
lienzo [ˈljenθo] *nm* linen; (*ARTE*) canvas; (*ARQ*) wall.
lifting [ˈliftin] *nm* facelift.
liga [ˈliɣa] *nf* (*de medias*) garter, suspender; (*confederación*) league; (*AM: gomita*) rubber band.
ligadura [liɣaˈðura] *nf* bond, tie; (*MED, MUS*) ligature.
ligamento [liɣaˈmento] *nm* (*ANAT*) ligament; (*atadura*) tie; (*unión*) bond.
ligar [liˈɣar] *vt* (*atar*) to tie; (*unir*) to join; (*MED*) to bind up; (*MUS*) to slur; (*fam*) to get off with, pick up ♦ *vi* to mix, blend; (*fam*) to get off with sb; (*2 personas*) to get off with one another; ~**se** *vr* (*fig*) to commit o.s.; ~ **con** (*fam*) to get off with, pick up; ~**se a algn** to get off with *o* pick up sb.
ligereza [lixeˈreθa] *nf* lightness; (*rapidez*) swiftness; (*agilidad*) agility; (*superficialidad*) flippancy.
ligero, a [liˈxero, a] *adj* (*de peso*) light; (*tela*) thin; (*rápido*) swift, quick; (*ágil*) agile, nimble; (*de importancia*) slight; (*de carácter*) flippant, superficial ♦ *adv* quickly, swiftly; **a la ligera** superficially; **juzgar a la ligera** to jump to conclusions.
light [ˈlait] *adj inv* (*cigarrillo*) low-tar; (*comida*) diet *cpd*.
ligón [liˈɣon] *nm* (*fam*) Romeo.
ligue [ˈliɣe] *etc vb V* **ligar** ♦ *nm/f* boyfriend/girlfriend ♦ *nm* (*persona*) pick-up.
liguero [liˈɣero] *nm* suspender (*BRIT*) *o* garter (*US*) belt.
lija [ˈlixa] *nf* (*ZOOL*) dogfish; (**papel de**) ~ sandpaper.
lijar [liˈxar] *vt* to sand.
lila [ˈlila] *adj inv, nf* lilac ♦ *nm* (*fam*) twit.
lima [ˈlima] *nf* file; (*BOT*) lime; ~ **de uñas** nail file; **comer como una** ~ to eat like a horse.
limar [liˈmar] *vt* to file; (*alisar*) to smooth over; (*fig*) to polish up.
limbo [ˈlimbo] *nm* (*REL*) limbo; **estar en el** ~ to be on another planet.
limitación [limitaˈθjon] *nf* limitation, limit; ~ **de velocidad** speed limit.
limitado, a [limiˈtaðo, a] *adj* limited; **sociedad limitada** (*COM*) limited company.

limitar [limiˈtar] *vt* to limit; (*reducir*) to reduce, cut down ♦ *vi*: ~ **con** to border on; ~**se** *vr*: ~**se a** to limit *o* confine o.s. to.
límite [ˈlimite] *nm* (*gen*) limit; (*fin*) end; (*frontera*) border; **como** ~ at (the) most; (*fecha*) at the latest; **no tener** ~**s** to know no bounds; ~ **de crédito** (*COM*) credit limit; ~ **de página** (*INFORM*) page break; ~ **de velocidad** speed limit.
limítrofe [liˈmitrofe] *adj* bordering, neighbouring.
limón [liˈmon] *nm* lemon ♦ *adj*: **amarillo** ~ lemon-yellow.
limonada [limoˈnaða] *nf* lemonade.
limonero [limoˈnero] *nm* lemon tree.
limosna [liˈmosna] *nf* alms *pl*; **pedir** ~ to beg; **vivir de** ~ to live on charity.
limpiabotas [limpjaˈßotas] *nm/f inv* bootblack (*BRIT*), shoeshine boy/girl.
limpiacristales [limpjakrisˈtales] *nm inv* (*detergente*) window cleaner.
limpiador, a [limpjaˈðor, a] *adj* cleaning, cleansing ♦ *nm/f* cleaner.
limpiaparabrisas [limpjaparaˈßrisas] *nm inv* windscreen (*BRIT*) *o* windshield (*US*) wiper.
limpiar [limˈpjar] *vt* to clean; (*con trapo*) to wipe; (*quitar*) to wipe away; (*zapatos*) to shine, polish; (*casa*) to tidy up; (*fig*) to clean up; (: *purificar*) to cleanse, purify; (*MIL*) to mop up; ~ **en seco** to dry-clean.
limpieza [limˈpjeθa] *nf* (*estado*) cleanliness; (*acto*) cleaning; (: *de las calles*) cleansing; (: *de zapatos*) polishing; (*habilidad*) skill; (*fig: POLICÍA*) clean-up; (*pureza*) purity; (*MIL*): **operación de** ~ mopping-up operation; ~ **étnica** ethnic cleansing; ~ **en seco** dry cleaning.
limpio, a [ˈlimpjo, a] *adj* clean; (*moralmente*) pure; (*ordenado*) tidy; (*despejado*) clear; (*COM*) clear, net; (*fam*) honest ♦ *adv*: **jugar** ~ to play fair; **pasar a** ~ to make a fair copy; **sacar algo en** ~ to get benefit from sth; ~ **de** free from.
linaje [liˈnaxe] *nm* lineage, family.
linaza [liˈnaθa] *nf* linseed; **aceite de** ~ linseed oil.
lince [ˈlinθe] *nm* lynx; **ser un** ~ (*fig: observador*) to be very observant; (: *astuto*) to be shrewd.
linchar [linˈtʃar] *vt* to lynch.
lindante [linˈdante] *adj* adjoining; ~ **con** bordering on.
lindar [linˈdar] *vi* to adjoin; ~ **con** to border on; (*ARQ*) to abut on.
linde [ˈlinde] *nm o nf* boundary.
lindero, a [linˈdero, a] *adj* adjoining ♦ *nm*

boundary.

lindo, a ['lindo, a] *adj* pretty, lovely ♦ *adv* (*esp AM: fam*) nicely, very well; **canta muy ~** (*AM*) he sings beautifully; **se divertían de lo ~** they enjoyed themselves enormously.

línea ['linea] *nf* (*gen, moral, POL etc*) line; (*talle*) figure; (*INFORM*): **en ~** on line; **fuera de ~** off line; **~ de estado** status line; **~ de formato** format line; **~ aérea** airline; **~ de alto el fuego** ceasefire line; **~ de fuego** firing line; **~ de meta** goal line; (*de carrera*) finishing line; **~ de montaje** assembly line; **~ dura** (*POL*) hard line; **~ recta** straight line; **la ~ de 1995** (*moda*) the 1995 look.

lineal [line'al] *adj* linear; (*INFORM*) on-line.

lingote [lin'gote] *nm* ingot.

lingüista [lin'gwista] *nmlf* linguist.

lingüística [lin'gwistika] *nf* linguistics *sg.*

linimento [lini'mento] *nm* liniment.

lino ['lino] *nm* linen; (*BOT*) flax.

linóleo [li'noleo] *nm* lino, linoleum.

linterna [lin'terna] *nf* lantern, lamp; **~ eléctrica** *o* **a pilas** torch (*BRIT*), flashlight (*US*).

lío ['lio] *nm* bundle; (*desorden*) muddle, mess; (*fam: follón*) fuss; (: *relación amorosa*) affair; **armar un ~** to make a fuss; **meterse en un ~** to get into a jam; **tener un ~ con algn** to be having an affair with sb.

lipotimia [lipo'timja] *nf* blackout.

liquen ['liken] *nm* lichen.

liquidación [likiða'θjon] *nf* liquidation; (*cuenta*) settlement; **venta de ~** clearance sale.

liquidar [liki'ðar] *vt* (*QUÍMICA*) to liquefy; (*COM*) to liquidate; (*deudas*) to pay off; (*empresa*) to wind up; **~ a algn** to bump sb off, rub sb out (*fam*).

liquidez [liki'ðeθ] *nf* liquidity.

líquido, a ['likiðo, a] *adj* liquid; (*ganancia*) net ♦ *nm* liquid; (*COM: efectivo*) ready cash *o* money; (: *ganancia*) net amount *o* profit; **~ imponible** net taxable income.

lira ['lira] *nf* (*MUS*) lyre; (*moneda*) lira.

lírico, a ['liriko, a] *adj* lyrical.

lirio ['lirjo] *nm* (*BOT*) iris.

lirismo [li'rismo] *nm* lyricism; (*sentimentalismo*) sentimentality.

lirón [li'ron] *nm* (*ZOOL*) dormouse; (*fig*) sleepyhead.

Lisboa [lis'ßoa] *nf* Lisbon.

lisboeta [lisßo'eta] *adj* of *o* from Lisbon ♦ *nmlf* native *o* inhabitant of Lisbon.

lisiado, a [li'sjaðo, a] *adj* injured ♦ *nmlf* cripple.

lisiar [li'sjar] *vt* to maim; **~se** *vr* to injure o.s.

liso, a ['liso, a] *adj* (*terreno*) flat; (*cabello*) straight; (*superficie*) even; (*tela*) plain; **lisa y llanamente** in plain language, plainly.

lisonja [li'sonxa] *nf* flattery.

lisonjear [lisonxe'ar] *vt* to flatter; (*fig*) to please.

lisonjero, a [lison'xero, a] *adj* flattering; (*agradable*) gratifying, pleasing ♦ *nmlf* flatterer.

lista ['lista] *nf* list; (*de alumnos*) school register; (*de libros*) catalogue; (*de correos*) poste restante; (*de platos*) menu; (*de precios*) price list; **pasar ~** to call the roll; (*ESCOL*) to call the register; **~ de correos** poste restante; **~ de direcciones** mailing list; **~ electoral** electoral roll; **~ de espera** waiting list; **tela a ~s** striped material.

listado, a [lis'taðo, a] *adj* striped ♦ *nm* (*COM, INFORM*) listing; **~ paginado** (*INFORM*) paged listing.

listar [lis'tar] *vt* (*INFORM*) to list.

listo, a ['listo, a] *adj* (*perspicaz*) smart, clever; (*preparado*) ready; **~ para usar** ready-to-use; **¿estás ~?** are you ready?; **pasarse de ~** to be too clever by half.

listón [lis'ton] *nm* (*tela*) ribbon; (*de madera, metal*) strip.

litera [li'tera] *nf* (*en barco, tren*) berth; (*en dormitorio*) bunk, bunk bed.

literal [lite'ral] *adj* literal.

literario, a [lite'rarjo, a] *adj* literary.

literato, a [lite'rato, a] *nmlf* writer.

literatura [litera'tura] *nf* literature.

litigante [liti'xante] *nmlf* litigant, claimant.

litigar [liti'xar] *vt* to fight ♦ *vi* (*JUR*) to go to law; (*fig*) to dispute, argue.

litigio [li'tixjo] *nm* (*JUR*) lawsuit; (*fig*): **en ~ con** in dispute with.

litigue [li'tixe] *etc vb V* **litigar.**

litografía [litoxra'fia] *nf* lithography; (*una ~*) lithograph.

litoral [lito'ral] *adj* coastal ♦ *nm* coast, seaboard.

litro ['litro] *nm* litre, liter (*US*).

Lituania [li'twanja] *nf* Lithuania.

lituano, a [li'twano, a] *adj, nmlf* Lithuanian ♦ *nm* (*LING*) Lithuanian.

liturgia [li'turxja] *nf* liturgy.

liviano, a [li'ßjano, a] *adj* (*persona*) fickle; (*cosa, objeto*) trivial; (*AM*) light.

lívido, a ['lißiðo, a] *adj* livid.

living ['lißin], *pl* **livings** *nm* (*esp AM*) sitting room.

Ll, ll ['eʎe] *nf former letter in the Spanish*

alphabet.

llaga ['ʎaɣa] _nf_ wound.

llagar [ʎa'ɣar] _vt_ to make sore; (_herir_) to wound.

llague ['ʎaɣe] _etc vb_ V **llagar**.

llama ['ʎama] _nf_ flame; (_fig_) passion; (_ZOOL_) llama; **en ~s** burning, ablaze.

llamada [ʎa'maða] _nf_ call; (_a la puerta_) knock; (: _timbre_) ring; **~ a cobro revertido** reverse-charge call; **~ al orden** call to order; **~ a pie de página** reference note; **~ a procedimiento** (_INFORM_) procedure call; **~ interurbana** trunk call.

llamado [ʎa'maðo] _nm_ (_AM_) (telephone) call; (_llamamiento_) appeal, call.

llamamiento [ʎama'mjento] _nm_ call; **hacer un ~ a algn para que haga algo** to appeal to sb to do sth.

llamar [ʎa'mar] _vt_ to call; (_convocar_) to summon; (_invocar_) to invoke; (_atraer con gesto_) to beckon; (_atención_) to attract; (_TELEC: tb:_ **~ por teléfono**) to call, ring up, telephone; (_MIL_) to call up ♦ _vi_ (_por teléfono_) to phone; (_a la puerta_) to knock (_o_ ring); (_por señas_) to beckon; **~se** _vr_ to be called, be named; **¿cómo se llama usted?** what's your name?; **¿quién llama?** (_TELEC_) who's calling?, who's that?; **no me llama la atención** (_fam_) I don't fancy it.

llamarada [ʎama'raða] _nf_ (_llamas_) blaze; (_rubor_) flush; (_fig_) flare-up.

llamativo, a [ʎama'tiβo, a] _adj_ showy; (_color_) loud.

llamear [ʎame'ar] _vi_ to blaze.

llanamente [ʎana'mente] _adv_ (_lisamente_) smoothly; (_sin ostentaciones_) plainly; (_sinceramente_) frankly; V tb **liso**.

llaneza [ʎa'neθa] _nf_ (_gen_) simplicity; (_honestidad_) straightforwardness, frankness.

llano, a ['ʎano, a] _adj_ (_superficie_) flat; (_persona_) straightforward; (_estilo_) clear ♦ _nm_ plain, flat ground.

llanta ['ʎanta] _nf_ (wheel) rim; (_AM: neumático_) tyre; (: _cámara_) (inner) tube.

llanto ['ʎanto] _nm_ weeping; (_fig_) lamentation; (_canción_) dirge, lament.

llanura [ʎa'nura] _nf_ (_lisura_) flatness, smoothness; (_GEO_) plain.

llave ['ʎaβe] _nf_ key; (_de gas, agua_) tap (_BRIT_), faucet (_US_); (_MECÁNICA_) spanner; (_de la luz_) switch; (_MUS_) key; **~ inglesa** monkey wrench; **~ maestra** master key; **~ de contacto** (_AUTO_) ignition key; **~ de paso** stopcock; **echar ~ a** to lock up.

llavero [ʎa'βero] _nm_ keyring.

llavín [ʎa'βin] _nm_ latchkey.

llegada [ʎe'ɣaða] _nf_ arrival.

llegar [ʎe'ɣar] _vt_ to bring up, bring over ♦ _vi_ to arrive; (_bastar_) to be enough; **~se** _vr_: **~se a** to approach; **~ a** (_alcanzar_) to reach; to manage to, succeed in; **~ a saber** to find out; **~ a ser famoso/el jefe** to become famous/the boss; **~ a las manos** to come to blows; **~ a las manos de** to come into the hands of; **no llegues tarde** don't be late; **esta cuerda no llega** this rope isn't long enough.

llegue ['ʎeɣe] _etc vb_ V **llegar**.

llenar [ʎe'nar] _vt_ to fill; (_superficie_) to cover; (_espacio, tiempo_) to fill, take up; (_formulario_) to fill in _o_ out; (_deber_) to fulfil; (_fig_) to heap; **~se** _vr_ to fill (up); **~se de** (_fam_) to stuff o.s. with.

lleno, a ['ʎeno, a] _adj_ full, filled; (_repleto_) full up ♦ _nm_ (_abundancia_) abundance; (_TEAT_) full house; **dar de ~ contra un muro** to hit a wall head-on.

llevadero, a [ʎeβa'ðero, a] _adj_ bearable, tolerable.

llevar [ʎe'βar] _vt_ to take; (_ropa_) to wear; (_cargar_) to carry; (_quitar_) to take away; (_en coche_) to drive; (_transportar_) to transport; (_ruta_) to follow, keep to; (_traer: dinero_) to carry; (_suj: camino etc_): **~ a** to lead to; (_MAT_) to carry; (_aguantar_) to bear; (_negocio_) to conduct, direct; to manage; **~se** _vr_ to carry off, take away; **llevamos dos días aquí** we have been here for two days; **él me lleva 2 años** he's 2 years older than me; **~ adelante** (_fig_) to carry forward; **~ por delante a uno** (_en coche etc_) to run sb over; (_fig_) to ride roughshod over sb; **~ la ventaja** to be winning _o_ in the lead; **~ los libros** (_COM_) to keep the books; **llevo las de perder** I'm likely to lose; **no las lleva todas consigo** he's not all there; **nos llevó a cenar fuera** she took us out for a meal; **~se a uno por delante** (_atropellar_) to run sb over; **~se bien** to get on well (together).

llorar [ʎo'rar] _vt_ to cry, weep ♦ _vi_ to cry, weep; (_ojos_) to water; **~ a moco tendido** to sob one's heart out; **~ de risa** to cry with laughter.

lloriquear [ʎorike'ar] _vi_ to snivel, whimper.

lloro ['ʎoro] _nm_ crying, weeping.

llorón, ona [ʎo'ron, ona] _adj_ tearful ♦ _nm/f_ cry-baby.

lloroso, a [ʎo'roso, a] _adj_ (_gen_) weeping, tearful; (_triste_) sad, sorrowful.

llover [ʎo'ßer] _vi_ to rain; ~ **a cántaros** _o_ **a cubos** _o_ **a mares** to rain cats and dogs, pour (down); **ser una cosa llovida del cielo** to be a godsend; **llueve sobre mojado** it never rains but it pours.

llovizna [ʎo'ßiθna] _nf_ drizzle.

lloviznar [ʎoßiθ'nar] _vi_ to drizzle.

llueve ['ʎweße] _etc vb_ V **llover**.

lluvia ['ʎußja] _nf_ rain; (_cantidad_) rainfall; (_fig: balas etc_) hail, shower; ~ **radioactiva** radioactive fallout; **día de** ~ rainy day; **una** ~ **de regalos** a shower of gifts.

lluvioso, a [ʎu'ßjoso, a] _adj_ rainy.

lo [lo] _artículo definido neutro_: ~ **bueno** the good ♦ _pron_ (_persona_) him; (_cosa_) it; ~ **mío** what is mine; ~ **difícil es que** ... the difficult thing about it is that ...; **no saben** ~ **aburrido que es** they don't know how boring it is; **viste a** ~ **americano** he dresses in the American style; ~ **de** that matter of; ~ **que** what, that which; **toma** ~ **que quieras** take what(ever) you want; ~ **que sea** whatever; **¡toma** ~ **que he dicho!** I stand by what I said!

loa ['loa] _nf_ praise.

loable [lo'aßle] _adj_ praiseworthy.

LOAPA [lo'apa] _nf abr_ (_ESP JUR_) = _Ley Orgánica de Armonización del Proceso Autónomo_.

loar [lo'ar] _vt_ to praise.

lobato [lo'ßato] _nm_ (_ZOOL_) wolf cub.

lobo ['loßo] _nm_ wolf; ~ **de mar** (_fig_) sea dog; ~ **marino** seal.

lóbrego, a ['loßreɣo, a] _adj_ dark; (_fig_) gloomy.

lóbulo ['loßulo] _nm_ lobe.

LOC _nm abr_ (= _lector óptico de caracteres_) OCR.

local [lo'kal] _adj_ local ♦ _nm_ place, site; (_oficinas_) premises _pl_.

localice [loka'liθe] _etc vb_ V **localizar**.

localidad [lokali'ðað] _nf_ (_barrio_) locality; (_lugar_) location; (_TEAT_) seat, ticket.

localizar [lokali'θar] _vt_ (_ubicar_) to locate, find; (_encontrar_) to find, track down; (_restringir_) to localize; (_situar_) to place.

loción [lo'θjon] _nf_ lotion, wash.

loco, a ['loko, a] _adj_ mad; (_fig_) wild, mad ♦ _nm/f_ lunatic, madman/woman; ~ **de atar**, ~ **de remate**, ~ **rematado** raving mad; **a lo** ~ without rhyme or reason; **ando** ~ **con el examen** the exam is driving me crazy; **estar** ~ **de alegría** to be overjoyed _o_ over the moon.

locomoción [lokomo'θjon] _nf_ locomotion.

locomotora [lokomo'tora] _nf_ engine, locomotive.

locuaz [lo'kwaθ] _adj_ loquacious, talkative.

locución [loku'θjon] _nf_ expression.

locura [lo'kura] _nf_ madness; (_acto_) crazy act.

locutor, a [loku'tor, a] _nm/f_ (_RADIO_) announcer; (_comentarista_) commentator; (_TV_) newscaster, newsreader.

locutorio [loku'torjo] _nm_ (_TELEC_) telephone box _o_ booth.

lodo ['lodo] _nm_ mud.

logia ['loxja] _nf_ (_MIL, de masones_) lodge; (_ARQ_) loggia.

lógico, a ['loxiko, a] _adj_ logical; (_correcto_) natural; (_razonable_) reasonable ♦ _nm_ logician ♦ _nf_ logic; **es** ~ **que** ... it stands to reason that ...; **ser de una lógica aplastante** to be as clear as day.

logístico, a [lo'xistiko, a] _adj_ logistical ♦ _nf_ logistics _pl_.

logotipo [loxo'tipo] _nm_ logo.

logrado, a [lo'ɣrado, a] _adj_ accomplished.

lograr [lo'ɣrar] _vt_ (_obtener_) to get, obtain; (_conseguir_) to achieve, attain; ~ **hacer** to manage to do; ~ **que algn venga** to manage to get sb to come; ~ **acceso a** (_INFORM_) to access.

logro ['loɣro] _nm_ achievement, success; (_COM_) profit.

logroñés, esa [loɣro'ɲes, esa] _adj_ of _o_ from Logroño ♦ _nm/f_ native _o_ inhabitant of Logroño.

LOGSE _nf abr_ (= _Ley Orgánica de Ordenación General del Sistema Educativo_) _educational reform act_.

Loira ['loira] _nm_ Loire.

loma ['loma] _nf_ hillock, low ridge.

Lombardía [lombar'ðia] _nf_ Lombardy.

lombriz [lom'briθ] _nf_ (earth)worm.

lomo ['lomo] _nm_ (_de animal_) back; (_CULIN: de cerdo_) pork loin; (: _de vaca_) rib steak; (_de libro_) spine.

lona ['lona] _nf_ canvas.

loncha ['lontʃa] _nf_ = **lonja**.

lonche ['lontʃe] _nm_ (_AM_) lunch.

lonchería [lontʃe'ria] _nf_ (_AM_) snack bar, diner (_US_).

londinense [londi'nense] _adj_ London _cpd_, of _o_ from London ♦ _nm/f_ Londoner.

Londres ['londres] _nm_ London.

longaniza [longa'niθa] _nf_ pork sausage.

longevidad [lonxeßi'ðað] _nf_ longevity.

longitud [lonxi'tuð] _nf_ length; (_GEO_) longitude; **tener 3 metros de** ~ to be 3 metres long; ~ **de onda** wavelength; **salto de** ~ long jump.

longitudinal [lonxituði'nal] _adj_ longitudinal.

lonja ['lonxa] _nf_ slice; (_de tocino_) rasher; (_COM_) market, exchange; ~ **de pescado**

fish market.

lontananza [lonta'nanθa] *nf* background;
en ~ far away, in the distance.

Lorena [lo'rena] *nf* Lorraine.

loro ['loro] *nm* parrot.

los [los] *artículo definido mpl* the ♦ *pron* them;
(*ustedes*) you; **mis libros y** ~ **de usted** my
books and yours.

losa ['losa] *nf* stone; ~ **sepulcral**
gravestone.

lote ['lote] *nm* portion, share; (*COM*) lot;
(*INFORM*) batch.

lotería [lote'ria] *nf* lottery; (*juego*) lotto; **le
tocó la** ~ he won a big prize in the
lottery; (*fig*) he struck lucky; ~ **nacional**
national lottery; ~ **primitiva** (*ESP*) *type
of state-run lottery; see boxed note.*

LOTERÍA

*Millions of pounds are spent in Spain
every year on* **loterías,** *or lotteries. The
weekly "Lotería Nacional" is very popular,
especially at Christmas. Other weekly
lotteries include the Bono Loto and the
(Lotería) Primitiva. One of the best known
is run by the wealthy and influential
society for the blind, "la ONCE"; their form
is called "el cupón de la ONCE" or "el
cupón de los ciegos".*

---

lotero, a [lo'tero, a] *nm/f* seller of lottery
tickets.

Lovaina [lo'βaina] *nf* Louvain.

loza ['loθa] *nf* crockery; ~ **fina** china.

lozanía [loθa'nia] *nf* (*lujo*) luxuriance.

lozano, a [lo'θano, a] *adj* luxuriant;
(*animado*) lively.

lubina [lu'βina] *nf* (*ZOOL*) sea bass.

lubricante [luβri'kante] *adj, nm* lubricant.

lubricar [luβri'kar], **lubrificar** [luβrifi'kar]
vt to lubricate.

lubrifique [luβri'fike] *etc vb* V **lubrificar.**

lubrique [lu'βrike] *etc vb* V **lubricar.**

lucense [lu'θense] *adj* of *o* from Lugo ♦ *nm/f*
native *o* inhabitant of Lugo.

Lucerna [lu'θerna] *nf* Lucerne.

lucero [lu'θero] *nm* (*ASTRO*) bright star;
(*fig*) brilliance; ~ **del alba/de la tarde**
morning/evening star.

luces ['luθes] *nfpl de* **luz.**

lucha ['lutʃa] *nf* fight, struggle; ~ **de clases**
class struggle; ~ **libre** wrestling.

luchar [lu'tʃar] *vi* to fight.

lucidez [luθi'ðeθ] *nf* lucidity.

lucido, a [lu'θiðo, a] *adj* (*espléndido*)
splendid, brilliant; (*elegante*) elegant;
(*exitoso*) successful.

lúcido, a ['luθiðo, a] *adj* lucid.

luciérnaga [lu'θjernaɣa] *nf* glow-worm.

lucimiento [luθi'mjento] *nm* (*brillo*)
brilliance; (*éxito*) success.

lucio ['luθjo] *nm* (*ZOOL*) pike.

lucir [lu'θir] *vt* to illuminate, light (up);
(*ostentar*) to show off ♦ *vi* (*brillar*) to
shine; (*AM: parecer*) to look, seem; ~**se** *vr*
(*irónico*) to make a fool of o.s.;
(*ostentarse*) to show off; **la casa luce
limpia** the house looks clean.

lucrativo, a [lukra'tiβo, a] *adj* lucrative,
profitable; **institución no lucrativa** non
profit-making institution.

lucro ['lukro] *nm* profit, gain; ~**s y daños**
(*COM*) profit and loss *sg.*

luctuoso, a [luk'twoso, a] *adj* mournful.

lúdico, a ['luðiko, a] *adj* playful; (*actividad*)
recreational.

ludopatía [luðopa'tia] *nf* addiction to
gambling (*o* videogames).

luego ['lweɣo] *adv* (*después*) next; (*más
tarde*) later, afterwards; (*AM fam: en
seguida*) at once, immediately; **desde** ~
of course; **¡hasta** ~**!** see you later!, so
long!; **¿y** ~**?** what next?

lugar [lu'ɣar] *nm* place; (*sitio*) spot; (*pueblo*)
village, town; **en** ~ **de** instead of; **en
primer** ~ in the first place, firstly; **dar** ~
a to give rise to; **hacer** ~ to make room;
fuera de ~ out of place; **tener** ~ to take
place; ~ **común** commonplace; **yo en su**
~ if I were him; **no hay** ~ **para preocupaciones** there is no cause for concern.

lugareño, a [luɣa'reɲo, a] *adj* village *cpd*
♦ *nm/f* villager.

lugarteniente [luɣarte'njente] *nm* deputy.

lúgubre ['luɣuβre] *adj* mournful.

lujo ['luxo] *nm* luxury; (*fig*) profusion,
abundance; **de** ~ luxury *cpd*, de luxe.

lujoso, a [lu'xoso, a] *adj* luxurious.

lujuria [lu'xurja] *nf* lust.

lumbago [lum'baɣo] *nm* lumbago.

lumbre ['lumbre] *nf* (*luz*) light; (*fuego*) fire;
cerca de la ~ near the fire, at the
fireside; **¿tienes** ~**?** (*para cigarro*) have
you got a light?

lumbrera [lum'brera] *nf* luminary; (*fig*)
leading light.

luminoso, a [lumi'noso, a] *adj* luminous,
shining; (*idea*) bright, brilliant.

luna ['luna] *nf* moon; (*vidrio: escaparate*)
plate glass; (: *de un espejo*) glass; (: *de
gafas*) lens; (*fig*) crescent; ~ **creciente/
llena/menguante/nueva** crescent/full/
waning/new moon; ~ **de miel**
honeymoon; **estar en la** ~ to have one's
head in the clouds.

lunar [lu'nar] *adj* lunar ♦ *nm* (*ANAT*) mole;
tela a ~es spotted material.
lunes ['lunes] *nm inv* Monday.
luneta [lu'neta] *nf* lens.
lupa ['lupa] *nf* magnifying glass.
lusitano, a [lusi'tano, a], **luso, a** ['luso, a]
adj, nm/f Portuguese.
lustrador [lustra'ðor] *nm* (*AM*) bootblack.
lustrar [lus'trar] *vt* (*esp AM*) (*mueble*) to
polish; (*zapatos*) to shine.
lustre ['lustre] *nm* polish; (*fig*) lustre; **dar ~
a** to polish.
lustro ['lustro] *nm* period of five years.
lustroso, a [lus'troso, a] *adj* shining.
luterano, a [lute'rano, a] *adj* Lutheran.
luto ['luto] *nm* mourning; (*congoja*) grief,
sorrow; **llevar el o vestirse de ~** to be in
mourning.
luxación [luksa'θjon] *nf* (*MED*) dislocation;
tener una ~ de tobillo to have a
dislocated ankle.
Luxemburgo [luksem'burɣo] *nm*
Luxembourg.
luz [luθ], *pl* **luces** *nf* (*tb fig*) light; (*fam*)
electricity; **dar a ~ un niño** to give birth
to a child; **sacar a la ~** to bring to light;
dar la ~ to switch on the light; **encender**
(*ESP*) *o* **prender** (*AM*)/**apagar la ~** to
switch the light on/off; **les cortaron la ~**
their (electricity) supply was cut off; **a
la ~ de** in the light of; **a todas luces** by
any reckoning; **hacer la ~ sobre** to shed
light on; **tener pocas luces** to be dim *o*
stupid; **~ de la luna/del sol** *o* **solar**
moonlight/sunlight; **~ eléctrica** electric
light; **~ roja/verde** red/green light; **~ de
cruce** (*AUTO*) dipped headlight; **~ de
freno** brake light; **~ intermitente/trasera**
flashing/rear light; **luces de tráfico**
traffic lights; **el Siglo de las Luces** the
Age of Enlightenment; **traje de luces**
bullfighter's costume.

M m

M, m ['eme] *nf* (*letra*) M, m; **M de Madrid** M
for Mike.
M. *abr* (*FERRO*) = **Metro**.
m. *abr* (= *metro(s)*) m; (= *minuto(s)*) min.,
m; (= *masculino*) m., masc.
M.ª *abr* = **María**.
macabro, [ma'kaßro, a] *adj* macabre.
macaco [ma'kako] *nm* (*ZOOL*) rhesus
monkey; (*fam*) runt, squirt.
macana [ma'kana] *nf* (*AM: porra*) club;
(: *mentira*) lie, fib; (: *tontería*) piece of
nonsense.
macanudo, a [maka'nuðo, a] *adj* (*AM fam*)
great.
macarra [ma'karra] *nm* (*fam*) thug.
macarrones [maka'rrones] *nmpl* macaroni
sg.
Macedonia [maθe'ðonja] *nf* Macedonia.
macedonia [maθe'ðonja] *nf*: **~ de frutas**
fruit salad.
macedonio [maθe'ðonjo] *adj, nm/f*
Macedonian ♦ *nm* (*LING*) Macedonian.
macerar [maθe'rar] *vt* (*CULIN*) to soak,
macerate; **~se** *vr* to soak, soften.
maceta [ma'θeta] *nf* (*de flores*) pot of
flowers; (*para plantas*) flowerpot.
macetero [maθe'tero] *nm* flowerpot stand
o holder.
machacar [matʃa'kar] *vt* to crush, pound;
(*moler*) to grind (up); (*aplastar*) to mash
♦ *vi* (*insistir*) to go on, keep on.
machacón, ona [matʃa'kon, ona] *adj*
(*pesado*) tiresome; (*insistente*) insistent;
(*monótono*) monotonous.
machamartillo [matʃamar'tiʎo]: **a ~** *adv*:
creer a ~ (*firmemente*) to believe
firmly.
machaque [ma'tʃake] *etc vb V* **machacar**.
machete [ma'tʃete] *nm* machete, (large)
knife.
machismo [ma'tʃismo] *nm* sexism; male
chauvinism.
machista [ma'tʃista] *adj, nm* sexist; male
chauvinist.
macho ['matʃo] *adj* male; (*fig*) virile ♦ *nm*
male; (*fig*) he-man, tough guy (*US*); (*TEC:
perno*) pin, peg; (*ELEC*) pin, plug;
(*COSTURA*) hook.

macilento – magnetofónico

macilento, a [maθi'lento, a] *adj (pálido)*
pale; *(ojeroso)* haggard.

macizo, a [ma'θiθo, a] *adj (grande)*
massive; *(fuerte, sólido)* solid ♦ *nm* mass,
chunk; *(GEO)* massif.

macramé [makra'me] *nm* macramé.

macrobiótico, a [makro'ßjotiko, a] *adj*
macrobiotic.

macro-comando [makroko'mando] *nm*
(INFORM) macro (command).

macroeconomía [makroekono'mia] *nf*
(COM) macroeconomics *sg.*

mácula ['makula] *nf* stain, blemish.

macuto [ma'kuto] *nm (MIL)* knapsack.

Madagascar [maðaɣas'kar] *nm*
Madagascar.

madeja [ma'ðexa] *nf (de lana)* skein, hank.

madera [ma'ðera] *nf* wood; *(fig)* nature,
character; (: *aptitud)* aptitude; **una ~** a
piece of wood; **~ contrachapada** *o*
laminada plywood; **tiene buena ~** he's
made of solid stuff; **tiene ~ de futbolista**
he's got the makings of a footballer.

maderaje [maðe'raxe], **maderamen**
[maðe'ramen] *nm* timber; *(trabajo)*
woodwork, timbering.

maderero [maðe'rero] *nm* timber
merchant.

madero [ma'ðero] *nm* beam; *(fig)* ship.

madrastra [ma'ðrastra] *nf* stepmother.

madre ['maðre] *adj* mother *cpd; (AM)*
tremendous ♦ *nf* mother; *(de vino etc)*
dregs *pl;* **~ adoptiva/política/soltera**
foster mother/mother-in-law/unmarried
mother; **la M~ Patria** the Mother
Country; **sin ~** motherless; **¡~ mía!** oh
dear!; **¡tu ~!** *(fam!)* fuck off! *(!)*; **salirse
de ~** *(río)* to burst its banks; *(persona)* to
lose all self-control.

madreperla [maðre'perla] *nf* mother-of-
pearl.

madreselva [maðre'selßa] *nf* honeysuckle.

Madrid [ma'ðrið] *n* Madrid.

madriguera [maðri'ɣera] *nf* burrow.

madrileño, a [maðri'leɲo, a] *adj* of *o* from
Madrid ♦ *nm/f* native *o* inhabitant of
Madrid.

Madriles [ma'ðriles] *nmpl:* **Los ~** *(fam)*
Madrid *sg.*

madrina [ma'ðrina] *nf* godmother; *(ARQ)*
prop, shore; *(TEC)* brace; **~ de boda**
bridesmaid.

madroño [ma'ðroɲo] *nm (BOT)* strawberry
tree, arbutus.

madrugada [maðru'ɣaða] *nf* early
morning, small hours; *(alba)* dawn,
daybreak; **a las 4 de la ~** at 4 o'clock in
the morning.

madrugador, a [maðruɣa'ðor, a] *adj*
early-rising.

madrugar [maðru'ɣar] *vi* to get up early;
(fig) to get a head start.

madrugue [ma'ðruɣe] *etc vb V* **madrugar.**

madurar [maðu'rar] *vt, vi (fruta)* to ripen;
(fig) to mature.

madurez [maðu're θ] *nf* ripeness; *(fig)*
maturity.

maduro, a [ma'ðuro, a] *adj* ripe; *(fig)*
mature; **poco ~** unripe.

MAE *nm abr (ESP POL)* = Ministerio de
Asuntos Exteriores.

maestra [ma'estra] *nf V* **maestro.**

maestría [maes'tria] *nf* mastery; *(habilidad)*
skill, expertise; *(AM)* Master's Degree.

maestro, a [ma'estro, a] *adj* masterly;
(perito) skilled, expert; *(principal)* main;
(educado) trained ♦ *nm/f* master/mistress;
(profesor) teacher ♦ *nm (autoridad)*
authority; *(MUS)* maestro; *(obrero)*
skilled workman; **~ albañil** master
mason; **~ de obras** foreman.

mafia ['mafja] *nf* mafia; **la M~** the Mafia.

mafioso [ma'fjoso] *nm* gangster.

Magallanes [maɣa'ʎanes] *nm:* **Estrecho de
~** Strait of Magellan.

magia ['maxja] *nf* magic.

mágico, a ['maxiko, a] *adj* magic(al) ♦ *nm/f*
magician.

magisterio [maxis'terjo] *nm (enseñanza)*
teaching; *(profesión)* teaching
profession; *(maestros)* teachers *pl.*

magistrado [maxis'traðo] *nm* magistrate;
Primer M~ *(AM)* President, Prime
Minister.

magistral [maxis'tral] *adj* magisterial; *(fig)*
masterly.

magistratura [maxistra'tura] *nf*
magistracy; **M~ del Trabajo** *(ESP)*
≈ Industrial Tribunal.

magnánimo, a [maɣ'nanimo, a] *adj*
magnanimous.

magnate [maɣ'nate] *nm* magnate, tycoon;
~ de la prensa press baron.

magnesio [maɣ'nesjo] *nm (QUÍMICA)*
magnesium.

magnetice [maɣne'tiθe] *etc vb V*
magnetizar.

magnético, a [maɣ'netiko, a] *adj*
magnetic.

magnetismo [maɣne'tismo] *nm*
magnetism.

magnetizar [maɣneti'θar] *vt* to magnetize.

magnetofón [maɣneto'fon],
magnetófono [maɣne'tofono] *nm* tape
recorder.

magnetofónico, a [maɣneto'foniko, a] *adj:*

cinta magnetofónica recording tape.
magnicidio [maɣniˈθiðjo] _nm_ assassination (of an important person).
magnífico, a [maɣˈnifiko, a] _adj_ splendid, magnificent.
magnitud [maɣniˈtuð] _nf_ magnitude.
mago, a [ˈmaɣo, a] _nm/f_ magician, wizard; **los Reyes M~s** the Magi, the Three Wise Men; _v tb_ **Reyes Magos.**
magrear [maɣreˈar] _vt_ (fam) to touch up.
magro, a [ˈmaɣro, a] _adj_ (persona) thin, lean; (carne) lean.
maguey [maˈɣei] _nm_ (BOT) agave.
magulladura [maɣuʎaˈðura] _nf_ bruise.
magullar [maɣuˈʎar] _vt_ (amoratar) to bruise; (dañar) to damage; (fam: golpear) to bash, beat.
mahometano, a [maomeˈtano, a] _adj_ Mohammedan.
mahonesa [maoˈnesa] _nf_ = **mayonesa.**
maicena [maiˈθena] _nf_ cornflour, corn starch (US).
mail [meil] _nm_ (fam) e-mail.
maillot [maˈjot] _nm_ swimming costume; (DEPORTE) vest.
maître [ˈmetre] _nm_ head waiter.
maíz [maˈiθ] _nm_ maize (BRIT), corn (US); sweet corn.
maizal [maiˈθal] _nm_ maize field, cornfield.
majadero, a [maxaˈðero, a] _adj_ silly, stupid.
majar [maˈxar] _vt_ to crush, grind.
majareta [maxaˈreta] _adj_ (fam) cracked, potty.
majestad [maxesˈtað] _nf_ majesty; **Su M~** His/Her Majesty; **(Vuestra) M~** Your Majesty.
majestuoso, a [maxesˈtwoso, a] _adj_ majestic.
majo, a [ˈmaxo, a] _adj_ nice; (guapo) attractive, good-looking; (elegante) smart.
mal [mal] _adv_ badly; (equivocadamente) wrongly; (con dificultad) with difficulty ♦ _adj_ = **malo, a** ♦ _nm_ evil; (desgracia) misfortune; (daño) harm, damage; (MED) illness ♦ _conj:_ **~ que le pese** whether he likes it or not; **me entendió ~** he misunderstood me; **hablar ~ de algn** to speak ill of sb; **huele ~** it smells bad; **ir de ~ en peor** to go from bad to worse; **oigo/veo ~** I can't hear/see very well; **si ~ no recuerdo** if my memory serves me right; **¡menos ~!** just as well!; **~ que bien** rightly or wrongly; **no hay ~ que por bien no venga** every cloud has a silver lining; **~ de ojo** evil eye.
malabarismo [malaβaˈrismo] _nm_ juggling.

malabarista [malaβaˈrista] _nm/f_ juggler.
malaconsejado, a [malakonseˈxaðo, a] _adj_ ill-advised.
malacostumbrado, a [malakostumˈbraðo, a] _adj_ (consentido) spoiled.
malacostumbrar [malakostumˈbrar] _vt:_ **~ a algn** to get sb into bad habits.
malagueño, a [malaˈɣeɲo, a] _adj_ of o from Málaga ♦ _nm/f_ native o inhabitant of Málaga.
Malaisia [maˈlaisja] _nf_ Malaysia.
malaria [maˈlarja] _nf_ malaria.
Malasia [maˈlasja] _nf_ Malaysia.
malavenido, a [malaβeˈniðo, a] _adj_ incompatible.
malayo, a [maˈlajo, a] _adj_ Malay(an) ♦ _nm/f_ Malay ♦ _nm_ (LING) Malay.
Malaysia [maˈlaisja] _nf_ Malaysia.
malcarado, a [malkaˈraðo, a] _adj_ ugly, grim-faced.
malcriado, a [malˈkrjaðo, a] _adj_ (consentido) spoiled.
malcriar [malˈkrjar] _vt_ to spoil, pamper.
maldad [malˈdað] _nf_ evil, wickedness.
maldecir [maldeˈθir] _vt_ to curse ♦ _vi:_ **~ de** to speak ill of.
maldiciendo [maldiˈθjendo] _etc vb_ V **maldecir.**
maldición [maldiˈθjon] _nf_ curse; **¡~!** curse it!, damn!
maldiga [malˈdiɣa] _etc_, **maldije** [malˈdixe] _etc vb_ V **maldecir.**
maldito, a [malˈdito, a] _adj_ (condenado) damned; (perverso) wicked ♦ _nm:_ **el ~** the devil; **¡~ sea!** damn it!; **no le hace ~ (el) caso** he doesn't take a blind bit of notice.
maleable [maleˈaβle] _adj_ malleable.
maleante [maleˈante] _adj_ wicked ♦ _nm/f_ criminal, crook.
malecón [maleˈkon] _nm_ pier, jetty.
maledicencia [maleðiˈθenθja] _nf_ slander, scandal.
maleducado, a [maleðuˈkaðo, a] _adj_ bad-mannered, rude.
maleficio [maleˈfiθjo] _nm_ curse, spell.
malentendido [malentenˈdiðo] _nm_ misunderstanding.
malestar [malesˈtar] _nm_ (gen) discomfort; (enfermedad) indisposition; (fig: inquietud) uneasiness; (POL) unrest; **siento un ~ en el estómago** my stomach is upset.
maleta [maˈleta] _nf_ case, suitcase; (AUTO) boot (BRIT), trunk (US); **hacer la ~** to pack.
maletera [maleˈtera] _nf_ (AM AUTO) boot (BRIT), trunk (US).
maletero [maleˈtero] _nm_ (AUTO) boot

(*BRIT*), trunk (*US*); (*persona*) porter.

maletín [male'tin] *nm* small case, bag; (*portafolio*) briefcase.

malevolencia [maleßo'lenθja] *nf* malice, spite.

malévolo, a [ma'leßolo, a] *adj* malicious, spiteful.

maleza [ma'leθa] *nf* (*hierbas malas*) weeds *pl*; (*arbustos*) thicket.

malgache [mal'ɣatʃe] *adj* of *o* from Madagascar ♦ *nm/f* native *o* inhabitant of Madagascar.

malgastar [malɣas'tar] *vt* (*tiempo, dinero*) to waste; (*recursos*) to squander; (*salud*) to ruin.

malhaya [ma'laja] *excl* (*espAM: fam!*) damn (it)! (*!*); ¡~ **sea/sean!** damn it/them! (*!*).

malhechor, a [male'tʃor, a] *nm/f* delinquent; (*criminal*) criminal.

malherido, a [male'riðo, a] *adj* badly injured.

malhumorado, a [malumo'raðo, a] *adj* bad-tempered.

malicia [ma'liθja] *nf* (*maldad*) wickedness; (*astucia*) slyness, guile; (*mala intención*) malice, spite; (*carácter travieso*) mischievousness.

malicioso, a [mali'θjoso, a] *adj* wicked, evil; sly, crafty; malicious, spiteful; mischievous.

malignidad [maliɣni'ðað] *nf* (*MED*) malignancy; (*malicia*) malice.

maligno, a [ma'livno, a] *adj* evil; (*dañino*) pernicious, harmful; (*malévolo*) malicious; (*MED*) malignant ♦ *nm*: **el** ~ the devil.

malintencionado, a [malintenθjo'naðo, a] *adj* (*comentario*) hostile; (*persona*) malicious.

malla ['maʎa] *nf* (*de una red*) mesh; (*red*) network; (*AM: de baño*) swimsuit; (*de ballet, gimnasia*) leotard; ~**s** *nfpl* tights; ~ **de alambre** wire mesh.

Mallorca [ma'ʎorka] *nf* Majorca.

mallorquín, ina [maʎor'kin, ina] *adj, nm/f* Majorcan ♦ *nm* (*LING*) Majorcan.

malnutrido, a [malnu'triðo, a] *adj* undernourished.

malo, a ['malo, a] *adj* (**mal** *before nmsg*) bad; (*calidad*) poor; (*falso*) false; (*espantoso*) dreadful; (*niño*) naughty ♦ *nm/f* villain ♦ *nm* (*CINE fam*) bad guy ♦ *nf* spell of bad luck; **estar** ~ to be ill; **andar a malas con algn** to be on bad terms with sb; **estar de malas** (*mal humor*) to be in a bad mood; **lo** ~ **es que** ... the trouble is that ....

malograr [malo'ɣrar] *vt* to spoil; (*plan*) to

upset; (*ocasión*) to waste; ~**se** *vr* (*plan etc*) to fail, come to grief; (*persona*) to die before one's time.

maloliente [malo'ljente] *adj* stinking, smelly.

malparado, a [malpa'raðo, a] *adj*: **salir** ~ to come off badly.

malpensado, a [malpen'saðo, a] *adj* evil-minded.

malquerencia [malke'renθja] *nf* dislike.

malquistar [malkis'tar] *vt*: ~ **a dos personas** to cause a rift between two people; ~**se** *vr* to fall out.

malsano, a [mal'sano, a] *adj* unhealthy.

malsonante [malso'nante] *adj* (*palabra*) nasty, rude.

Malta ['malta] *nf* Malta.

malta ['malta] *nf* malt.

malteada [malte'aða] *nf* (*AM*) milk shake.

maltés, esa [mal'tes, esa] *adj, nm/f* Maltese.

maltraer [maltra'er] *vt* (*abusar*) to insult, abuse; (*maltratar*) to ill-treat.

maltratar [maltra'tar] *vt* to ill-treat, mistreat.

maltrecho, a [mal'tretʃo, a] *adj* battered, damaged.

malva ['malßa] *nf* mallow; ~ **loca** hollyhock; (**de color de**) ~ mauve.

malvado, a [mal'ßaðo, a] *adj* evil, villainous.

malvavisco [malßa'ßisko] *nm* marshmallow.

malvender [malßen'der] *vt* to sell off cheap *o* at a loss.

malversación [malßersa'θjon] *nf* embezzlement, misappropriation.

malversar [malßer'sar] *vt* to embezzle, misappropriate.

Malvinas [mal'ßinas] *nfpl*: **Islas** ~ Falkland Islands.

mama ['mama], *pl* **mamás** *nf* (*de animal*) teat; (*de mujer*) breast.

mamá [ma'ma] *nf* (*fam*) mum, mummy.

mamacita [mama'sita] *nf* (*AM fam*) mum, mummy.

mamadera [mama'dera] *nf* (*AM*) baby's bottle.

mamagrande [mama'grande] *nf* (*AM*) grandmother.

mamar [ma'mar] *vt* (*pecho*) to suck; (*fig*) to absorb, assimilate ♦ *vi* to suck; **dar de** ~ to (breast-)feed; (*animal*) to suckle.

mamarracho [mama'rratʃo] *nm* sight, mess.

mambo ['mambo] *nf* (*MUS*) mambo.

mamífero, a [ma'mifero, a] *adj* mammalian, mammal *cpd* ♦ *nm* mammal.

mamón, ona [ma'mon, ona] *adj* small,

baby _cpd_ ♦ _nm/f_ small baby; (_fam!_)
wanker (_!_).

mamotreto [mamo'treto] _nm_ hefty
volume; (_fam_) whacking great thing.

mampara [mam'para] _nf_ (_entre
habitaciones_) partition; (_biombo_) screen.

mamporro [mam'porro] _nm_ (_fam_): **dar un ~
a** to clout.

mampostería [mamposte'ria] _nf_ masonry.

mamut [ma'mut] _nm_ mammoth.

maná [ma'na] _nm_ manna.

manada [ma'naða] _nf_ (_ZOOL_) herd; (: _de
leones_) pride; (: _de lobos_) pack; **llegaron
en ~s** (_fam_) they came in droves.

Managua [ma'naɣwa] _n_ Managua.

manantial [manan'tjal] _nm_ spring; (_fuente_)
fountain; (_fig_) source.

manar [ma'nar] _vt_ to run with, flow with
♦ _vi_ to run, flow; (_abundar_) to abound.

manaza [ma'naθa] _nf_ big hand ♦ _adj, nm/f inv_:
~s: ser un ~s to be clumsy.

mancebo [man'θeβo] _nm_ (_joven_) young
man.

mancha ['mantʃa] _nf_ stain, mark; (_de tinta_)
blot; (_de vegetación_) patch; (_imperfección_)
stain, blemish, blot; (_boceto_) sketch,
outline; **la M~** La Mancha.

manchado, a [man'tʃaðo, a] _adj_ (_sucio_)
dirty; (_animal_) spotted; (_ave_) speckled;
(_tinta_) smudged.

manchar [man'tʃar] _vt_ to stain, mark;
(_ZOOL_) to patch; (_ensuciar_) to soil, dirty;
~se _vr_ to get dirty; (_fig_) to dirty one's
hands.

manchego, a [man'tʃeɣo, a] _adj_ of _o_ from
La Mancha ♦ _nm/f_ native _o_ inhabitant of
La Mancha.

mancilla [man'θiʎa] _nf_ stain, blemish.

mancillar [manθi'ʎar] _vt_ to stain, sully.

manco, a ['manko, a] _adj_ one-armed; one-
handed; (_fig_) defective, faulty; **no ser ~**
to be useful _o_ active.

mancomunar [mankomu'nar] _vt_ to unite,
bring together; (_recursos_) to pool; (_JUR_)
to make jointly responsible.

mancomunidad [mankomuni'ðað] _nf_
union, association; (_comunidad_)
community; (_JUR_) joint responsibility.

mandado [man'daðo] _nm_ (_orden_) order;
(_recado_) commission, errand.

mandamás [manda'mas] _adj, nm/f inv_ boss;
ser un ~ to be very bossy.

mandamiento [manda'mjento] _nm_ (_orden_)
order, command; (_REL_) commandment;
~ judicial warrant.

mandar [man'dar] _vt_ (_ordenar_) to order;
(_dirigir_) to lead, command; (_país_) to rule
over; (_enviar_) to send; (_pedir_) to order,

ask for ♦ _vi_ to be in charge; (_pey_) to be
bossy; **~se** _vr_: **~se mudar** (_AM fam_) to go
away, clear off; **¿mande?** pardon?,
excuse me? (_US_); **¿manda usted algo
más?** is there anything else?; **~ a algn a
paseo** _o_ **a la porra** to tell sb to go to hell;
se lo mandaremos por correo we'll post
it to you; **~ hacer un traje** to have a suit
made.

mandarín [manda'rin] _nm_ petty
bureaucrat.

mandarina [manda'rina] _nf_ (_fruta_)
tangerine, mandarin (orange).

mandatario, a [manda'tarjo, a] _nm/f_
(_representante_) agent; **primer ~** (_esp AM_)
head of state.

mandato [man'dato] _nm_ (_orden_) order;
(_POL: período_) term of office; (: _territorio_)
mandate; (_INFORM_) command; **~ judicial**
(_search_) warrant.

mandíbula [man'diβula] _nf_ jaw.

mandil [man'dil] _nm_ (_delantal_) apron.

Mandinga [man'dinɣa] _nm_ (_AM_) Devil.

mandioca [man'djoka] _nf_ cassava.

mando ['mando] _nm_ (_MIL_) command; (_de
país_) rule; (_el primer lugar_) lead; (_POL_)
term of office; (_TEC_) control; **~ a la
izquierda** left-hand drive; **los altos ~s**
the high command _sg_; **~ por botón**
push-button control; **al ~ de** in charge
of; **tomar el ~** to take the lead.

mandolina [mando'lina] _nf_ mandolin(e).

mandón, ona [man'don, ona] _adj_ bossy,
domineering.

manecilla [mane'θiʎa] _nf_ (_TEC_) pointer; (_de
reloj_) hand.

manejable [mane'xaβle] _adj_ manageable;
(_fácil de usar_) handy.

manejar [mane'xar] _vt_ to manage;
(_máquina_) to work, operate; (_caballo etc_)
to handle; (_casa_) to run, manage; (_AM
AUTO_) to drive ♦ _vi_ (_AM AUTO_) to drive;
~se _vr_ (_comportarse_) to act, behave;
(_arreglárselas_) to manage; "**~ con
cuidado**" "handle with care".

manejo [ma'nexo] _nm_ management;
handling; running; driving; (_facilidad de
trato_) ease, confidence; (_de idioma_)
command; **~s** _nmpl_ intrigues; **tengo ~
del francés** I have a good command of
French.

manera [ma'nera] _nf_ way, manner,
fashion; (_ARTE, LITERATURA etc: estilo_)
manner, style; **~s** _nfpl_ (_modales_)
manners; **su ~ de ser** the way he is;
(_aire_) his manner; **de mala ~** (_fam_) badly,
unwillingly; **de ninguna ~** no way, by no
means; **de otra ~** otherwise; **de todas ~s**

at any rate; **en gran** ~ to a large extent; **sobre** ~ exceedingly; **a mi** ~ **de ver** in my view; **no hay** ~ **de persuadirle** there's no way of convincing him.

manga ['manga] *nf* (*de camisa*) sleeve; (*de riego*) hose; **de** ~ **corta/larga** short-/ long-sleeved; **andar** ~ **por hombro** (*desorden*) to be topsy-turvy; **tener** ~ **ancha** to be easy-going.

mangante [man'gante] *adj* (*descarado*) brazen ♦ *nm* (*mendigo*) beggar.

mangar [man'gar] *vt* (*unir*) to plug in; (*fam: birlar*) to pinch, nick, swipe; (*mendigar*) to beg.

mango ['mango] *nm* handle; (*BOT*) mango; ~ **de escoba** broomstick.

mangonear [mangone'ar] *vt* to boss about ♦ *vi* to be bossy.

mangue ['mange] *etc vb V* **mangar.**

manguera [man'gera] *nf* (*de riego*) hose; (*tubo*) pipe; ~ **de incendios** fire hose.

maní [ma'ni] *nm, pl* **maníes** *o* **manises** (*AM: cacahuete*) peanut; (: *planta*) groundnut plant.

manía [ma'nia] *nf* (*MED*) mania; (*fig: moda*) rage, craze; (*disgusto*) dislike; (*malicia*) spite; **tiene** ~**s** she's a bit fussy; **tener** ~ **a algn** to dislike sb.

maníaco, a [ma'niako, a] *adj* maniac(al) ♦ *nm/f* maniac.

maniatar [manja'tar] *vt* to tie the hands of.

maniático, a [ma'njatiko, a] *adj* maniac(al); (*loco*) crazy; (*tiquismiquis*) fussy ♦ *nm/f* maniac.

manicomio [mani'komjo] *nm* mental hospital (*BRIT*), insane asylum (*US*).

manicuro, a [mani'kuro, a] *nm/f* manicurist ♦ *nf* manicure.

manido, a [ma'niðo, a] *adj* (*tema etc*) trite, stale.

manifestación [manifesta'θjon] *nf* (*declaración*) statement, declaration; (*demostración*) show, display; (*POL*) demonstration.

manifestante [manifes'tante] *nm/f* demonstrator.

manifestar [manifes'tar] *vt* to show, manifest; (*declarar*) to state, declare; ~**se** *vr* to show, become apparent; (*POL: desfilar*) to demonstrate; (: *reunirse*) to hold a mass meeting.

manifiesto, a [mani'fjesto, a] *etc vb V* **manifestar** ♦ *adj* clear, manifest ♦ *nm* manifesto; (*ANAT, NAUT*) manifest; **poner algo de** ~ (*aclarar*) to make sth clear; (*revelar*) to reveal sth; **quedar** ~ to be plain *o* clear.

manija [ma'nixa] *nf* handle.

manilla [ma'niʎa] *nf* (*de reloj*) hand; (*AM*) handle, lever; ~**s (de hierro)** *nfpl* handcuffs.

manillar [mani'ʎar] *nm* handlebars *pl.*

maniobra [ma'njoβra] *nf* manœuvring; (*maneja*) handling; (*fig: movimiento*) manœuvre, move; (: *estratagema*) trick, stratagem; ~**s** *nfpl* manœuvres.

maniobrar [manio'βrar] *vt* to manœuvre; (*manejar*) to handle ♦ *vi* to manœuvre.

manipulación [manipula'θjon] *nf* manipulation; (*COM*) handling.

manipular [manipu'lar] *vt* to manipulate; (*manejar*) to handle.

maniquí [mani'ki] *nm/f* model ♦ *nm* dummy.

manirroto, a [mani'rroto, a] *adj* lavish, extravagant ♦ *nm/f* spendthrift.

manita [ma'nita] *nf* little hand; ~**s de plata** artistic hands.

manitas [ma'nitas] *adj inv* good with one's hands ♦ *nm/f inv*: **ser un** ~ to be very good with one's hands.

manito [ma'nito] *nm* (*AM: en conversación*) mate (*fam*), chum.

manivela [mani'βela] *nf* crank.

manjar [man'xar] *nm* (tasty) dish.

mano¹ ['mano] *nf* hand; (*ZOOL*) foot, paw; (*de pintura*) coat; (*serie*) lot, series; **a** ~ by hand; **a** ~ **derecha/izquierda** on (*o* to) the right(-hand side)/left(-hand side); **hecho a** ~ handmade; **a** ~**s llenas** lavishly, generously; **de primera** ~ (at) first hand; **de segunda** ~ (at) second hand; **robo a** ~ **armada** armed robbery; **Pedro es mi** ~ **derecha** Pedro is my right-hand man; ~ **de obra** labour, manpower; ~ **de santo** sure remedy; **darse la(s)** ~**(s)** to shake hands; **echar una** ~ to lend a hand; **echar una** ~ **a** to lay hands on; **echar** ~ **de** to make use of; **estrechar la** ~ **a algn** to shake sb's hand; **traer** *o* **llevar algo entre** ~**s** to deal *o* be busy with sth; **está en tus** ~**s** it's up to you; **se le fue la** ~ his hand slipped; (*fig*) he went too far; **¡** ~**s a la obra!** to work!

mano² ['mano] *nm* (*AM fam*) friend, mate.

manojo [ma'noxo] *nm* handful, bunch; ~ **de llaves** bunch of keys.

manómetro [ma'nometro] *nm* (pressure) gauge.

manopla [ma'nopla] *nf* (*paño*) flannel; ~**s** *nfpl* mittens.

manoseado, a [manose'aðo, a] *adj* well-worn.

manosear [manose'ar] *vt* (*tocar*) to handle, touch; (*desordenar*) to mess up, rumple; (*insistir en*) to overwork; (*acariciar*) to caress, fondle; (*pey: persona*) to feel *o* touch up.

manotazo [mano'taθo] *nm* slap, smack.

mansalva [man'salβa]: **a ~** *adv* indiscriminately.

mansedumbre [manse'ðumbre] *nf* gentleness, meekness; (*de animal*) tameness.

mansión [man'sjon] *nf* mansion.

manso, a ['manso, a] *adj* gentle, mild; (*animal*) tame.

manta ['manta] *nf* blanket; (*AM*) poncho.

manteca [man'teka] *nf* fat; (*AM*) butter; **~ de cacahuete/cacao** peanut/cocoa butter; **~ de cerdo** lard.

mantecado [mante'kaðo] *nm* ice cream.

mantecoso, a [mante'koso, a] *adj* fat, greasy; **queso ~** soft cheese.

mantel [man'tel] *nm* tablecloth.

mantelería [mantele'ria] *nf* table linen.

mantendré [manten'dre] *etc vb V* **mantener.**

mantener [mante'ner] *vt* to support, maintain; (*alimentar*) to sustain; (*conservar*) to keep; (*TEC*) to maintain, service; **~se** *vr* (*seguir de pie*) to be still standing; (*no ceder*) to hold one's ground; (*subsistir*) to sustain o.s., keep going; **~ algo en equilibrio** to keep sth balanced; **~se a distancia** to keep one's distance; **~se firme** to hold one's ground.

mantenga [man'tenga] *etc vb V* **mantener.**

mantenimiento [manteni'mjento] *nm* maintenance; sustenance; (*sustento*) support.

mantequería [manteke'ria] *nf* (*ultramarinos*) grocer's (shop).

mantequilla [mante'kiʎa] *nf* butter.

mantilla [man'tiʎa] *nf* mantilla; **~s** *nfpl* baby clothes; **estar en ~s** (*persona*) to be terribly innocent; (*proyecto*) to be in its infancy.

manto ['manto] *nm* (*capa*) cloak; (*de ceremonia*) robe, gown.

mantón [man'ton] *nm* shawl.

mantuve [man'tuβe] *etc vb V* **mantener.**

manual [ma'nwal] *adj* manual ♦ *nm* manual, handbook; **habilidad ~** manual skill.

manubrio [ma'nuβrio] *nm* (*AM AUTO*) steering wheel.

manufactura [manufak'tura] *nf* manufacture; (*fábrica*) factory.

manufacturado, a [manufaktu'raðo, a] *adj* manufactured.

manuscrito, a [manus'krito, a] *adj* handwritten ♦ *nm* manuscript.

manutención [manuten'θjon] *nf* maintenance; (*sustento*) support.

manzana [man'θana] *nf* apple; (*ARQ*) block; **~ de la discordia** (*fig*) bone of contention.

manzanal [manθa'nal] *nm* apple orchard.

manzanilla [manθa'niʎa] *nf* (*planta*) camomile; (*infusión*) camomile tea; (*vino*) manzanilla.

manzano [man'θano] *nm* apple tree.

maña ['maɲa] *nf* (*gen*) skill, dexterity; (*pey*) guile; (*costumbre*) habit; (*una ~*) trick, knack; **con ~** craftily.

mañana [ma'ɲana] *adv* tomorrow ♦ *nm* future ♦ *nf* morning; **de o por la ~** in the morning; **¡hasta ~!** see you tomorrow!; **pasado ~** the day after tomorrow; **~ por la ~** tomorrow morning.

mañanero, a [maɲa'nero, a] *adj* early-rising.

maño, a ['maɲo, a] *adj* Aragonese ♦ *nm/f* native *o* inhabitant of Aragon.

mañoso, a [ma'ɲoso, a] *adj* (*hábil*) skilful; (*astuto*) smart, clever.

mapa ['mapa] *nm* map.

mapuche, a [ma'putʃe, a] *adj*, *nm/f* Mapuche, Araucanian.

maqueta [ma'keta] *nf* (*scale*) model.

maquiavélico, a [makja'βeliko, a] *adj* Machiavellian.

maquillador, a [makiʎa'ðor, a] *nm/f* (*TEAT etc*) make-up artist.

maquillaje [maki'ʎaxe] *nm* make-up; (*acto*) making up.

maquillar [maki'ʎar] *vt* to make up; **~se** *vr* to put on (some) make-up.

máquina ['makina] *nf* machine; (*de tren*) locomotive, engine; (*FOTO*) camera; (*AM: coche*) car; (*fig*) machinery; (: *proyecto*) plan, project; **a toda ~** at full speed; **escrito a ~** typewritten; **~ de escribir** typewriter; **~ de coser/lavar** sewing/washing machine; **~ de facsímil** facsimile (machine), fax; **~ de franqueo** franking machine; **~ tragaperras** fruit machine; (*COM*) slot machine.

maquinación [makina'θjon] *nf* machination, plot.

maquinal [maki'nal] *adj* (*fig*) mechanical, automatic.

maquinar [maki'nar] *vt, vi* to plot.

maquinaria [maki'narja] *nf* (*máquinas*) machinery; (*mecanismo*) mechanism, works *pl*.

maquinilla [maki'niʎa] *nf* small machine; (*torno*) winch; **~ de afeitar** razor; **~ eléctrica** electric razor.

maquinista [maki'nista] *nm* (*FERRO*) engine driver (*BRIT*), engineer (*US*); (*TEC*) operator; (*NAUT*) engineer.

mar [mar] *nm* sea; ~ **de fondo**
groundswell; ~ **llena** high tide; ~
adentro *o* **afuera** out at sea; **en alta** ~ on
the high seas; **por** ~ by sea *o* boat;
hacerse a la ~ to put to sea; **a** ~**es** in
abundance; **un** ~ **de** lots of; **es la** ~ **de
guapa** she is ever so pretty; **el M**~
Negro/Báltico the Black/Baltic Sea; **el
M**~ **Muerto/Rojo** the Dead/Red Sea; **el
M**~ **del Norte** the North Sea.

mar. *abr* (= *marzo*) Mar.

maraca [ma'raka] *nf* maraca.

maraña [ma'raɲa] *nf* (*maleza*) thicket;
(*confusión*) tangle.

maravilla [mara'βiʎa] *nf* marvel, wonder;
(*BOT*) marigold; **hacer** ~**s** to work
wonders; **a (las mil)** ~**s** wonderfully
well.

maravillar [maraβi'ʎar] *vt* to astonish,
amaze; ~**se** *vr* to be astonished, be
amazed.

maravilloso, a [maraβi'ʎoso, a] *adj*
wonderful, marvellous.

marbellí [marβe'ʎi] *adj* of *o* from Marbella
♦ *nm/f* native *o* inhabitant of Marbella.

marca ['marka] *nf* mark; (*sello*) stamp;
(*COM*) make, brand; (*de ganado*) brand;
(: *acto*) branding; (*NAUT*) seamark;
(: *boya*) marker; (*DEPORTE*) record; **de** ~
excellent, outstanding; ~ **de fábrica**
trademark; ~ **propia** own brand; ~
registrada registered trademark.

marcación [marka'θjon] *nf* (*TELEC*): ~
automática autodial.

marcado, a [mar'kaðo, a] *adj* marked,
strong.

marcador [marka'ðor] *nm* marker;
(*rotulador*) marker (pen); (*de libro*)
bookmark; (*DEPORTE*) scoreboard;
(: *persona*) scorer.

marcapasos [marka'pasos] *nm inv*
pacemaker.

marcar [mar'kar] *vt* to mark; (*número de
teléfono*) to dial; (*gol*) to score; (*números*)
to record, keep a tally of; (*el pelo*) to set;
(*ganado*) to brand; (*suj: termómetro*) to
read, register; (: *reloj*) to show; (*tarea*) to
assign; (*COM*) to put a price on ♦ *vi*
(*DEPORTE*) to score; (*TELEC*) to dial; **mi
reloj marca las 2** it's 2 o'clock by my
watch; ~ **el compás** (*MUS*) to keep time;
~ **el paso** (*MIL*) to mark time.

marcha ['martʃa] *nf* march; (*DEPORTE*)
walk; (*TEC*) running, working; (*AUTO*)
gear; (*velocidad*) speed; (*fig*) progress;
(*dirección*) course; **dar** ~ **atrás** to
reverse, put into reverse; **estar en** ~ to

be under way, be in motion; **hacer algo
sobre la** ~ to do sth as you *etc* go along;
poner en ~ to put into gear; **ponerse en**
~ to start, get going; **a** ~**s forzadas** (*fig*)
with all speed; **¡en** ~**!** (*MIL*) forward
march!; (*fig*) let's go!; "~ **moderada**"
(*AUTO*) "drive slowly"; **que tiene** *o* **de
mucha** ~ (*fam*) very lively.

marchante, a [mar'tʃante, a] *nm/f* dealer,
merchant.

marchar [mar'tʃar] *vi* (*ir*) to go; (*funcionar*)
to work, go; (*fig*) to go, proceed; ~**se** *vr*
to go (away), leave; **todo marcha bien**
everything is going well.

marchitar [martʃi'tar] *vt* to wither, dry up;
~**se** *vr* (*BOT*) to wither; (*fig*) to fade away.

marchito, a [mar'tʃito, a] *adj* withered,
faded; (*fig*) in decline.

marchoso, a [mar'tʃoso, a] *adj* (*fam:
animado*) lively; (: *moderno*) modern.

marcial [mar'θjal] *adj* martial, military.

marciano, a [mar'θjano, a] *adj* Martian, of
o from Mars.

marco ['marko] *nm* frame; (*DEPORTE*)
goalposts *pl*; (*moneda*) mark; (*fig*)
setting; (*contexto*) framework; ~ **de
chimenea** mantelpiece.

marea [ma'rea] *nf* tide; (*llovizna*) drizzle; ~
alta/baja high/low tide; ~ **negra** oil slick.

mareado, a [mare'aðo, a] *adj*: **estar** ~ (*con
náuseas*) to feel sick; (*aturdido*) to feel
dizzy.

marear [mare'ar] *vt* (*fig: irritar*) to annoy,
upset; (*MED*): ~ **a algn** to make sb feel
sick; ~**se** *vr* (*tener náuseas*) to feel sick;
(*desvanecerse*) to feel faint; (*aturdirse*) to
feel dizzy; (*fam: emborracharse*) to get
tipsy.

marejada [mare'xaða] *nf* (*NAUT*) swell,
heavy sea.

maremágnum [mare'maɣnum] *nm* (*fig*)
ocean, abundance.

maremoto [mare'moto] *nm* tidal wave.

mareo [ma'reo] *nm* (*náusea*) sick feeling;
(*aturdimiento*) dizziness; (*fam: lata*)
nuisance.

marfil [mar'fil] *nm* ivory.

margarina [marɣa'rina] *nf* margarine.

margarita [marɣa'rita] *nf* (*BOT*) daisy;
(*rueda*) ~ (*en máquina impresora*) daisy
wheel.

margen ['marxen] *nm* (*borde*) edge,
border; (*fig*) margin, space ♦ *nf* (*de río
etc*) bank; ~ **de beneficio** *o* **de ganancia**
profit margin; ~ **comercial** mark-up; ~
de confianza credibility gap; **dar** ~ **para**
to give an opportunity for; **dejar a algn
al** ~ to leave sb out (in the cold);

mantenerse al ~ to keep out (of things); **al** ~ **de lo que digas** despite what you say.

marginado, a [marxi'naðo, a] _nm/f_ outcast.

marginal [marxi'nal] _adj_ (_tema, error_) minor; (_grupo_) fringe _cpd_; (_anotación_) marginal.

marginar [marxi'nar] _vt_ to exclude.

maría [ma'ria] _nf_ (_fam: mujer_) housewife.

mariachi [ma'rjatʃi] _nm_ (_música_) mariachi music; (_grupo_) mariachi band; (_persona_) mariachi player.

marica [ma'rika] _nm_ (_fam_) sissy; (_homosexual_) queer.

Maricastaña [marikas'taɲa] _nf_: **en los días** _o_ **en tiempos de** ~ way back, in the good old days.

maricón [mari'kon] _nm_ (_fam_) queer.

marido [ma'riðo] _nm_ husband.

marihuana [mari'wənə] _nf_ marijuana, cannabis.

marimacho [mari'matʃo] _nf_ (_fam_) mannish woman.

marimorena [marimo'rena] _nf_ fuss, row; **armar una** ~ to kick up a row.

marina [ma'rina] _nf_ navy; ~ **mercante** merchant navy.

marinero, a [mari'nero, a] _adj_ sea _cpd_; (_barco_) seaworthy ♦ _nm_ sailor, seaman.

marino, a [ma'rino, a] _adj_ sea _cpd_, marine ♦ _nm_ sailor; ~ **de agua dulce/de cubierta/de primera** landlubber/ deckhand/able seaman.

marioneta [marjo'neta] _nf_ puppet.

mariposa [mari'posa] _nf_ butterfly.

mariposear [maripose'ar] _vi_ (_revolotear_) to flutter about; (_ser inconstante_) to be fickle; (_coquetear_) to flirt.

mariquita [mari'kita] _nm_ (_fam_) sissy; (_homosexual_) queer ♦ _nf_ (_ZOOL_) ladybird (_BRIT_), ladybug (_US_).

marisco [ma'risko] _nm_ (_tb:_ ~**s**) shellfish, seafood.

marisma [ma'risma] _nf_ marsh, swamp.

marisquería [mariske'ria] _nf_ shellfish bar, seafood restaurant.

marítimo, a [ma'ritimo, a] _adj_ sea _cpd_, maritime.

marmita [mar'mita] _nf_ pot.

mármol ['marmol] _nm_ marble.

marmóreo, a [mar'moreo, a] _adj_ marble.

marmota [mar'mota] _nf_ (_ZOOL_) marmot; (_fig_) sleepyhead.

maroma [ma'roma] _nf_ rope.

marque ['marke] _etc vb V_ **marcar**.

marqués, esa [mar'kes, esa] _nm/f_ marquis/marchioness.

marquesina [marke'sina] _nf_ (_de parada_) bus-shelter.

marquetería [markete'ria] _nf_ marquetry, inlaid work.

marranada [marra'naða] _nf_ (_fam_): **es una** ~ that's disgusting; **hacer una** ~ **a algn** to do the dirty on sb.

marrano, a [ma'rrano, a] _adj_ filthy, dirty ♦ _nm_ (_ZOOL_) pig; (_malo_) swine; (_sucio_) dirty pig.

marras ['marras]: **de** ~ _adv_: **es el problema de** ~ it's the same old problem.

marrón [ma'rron] _adj_ brown.

marroquí [marro'ki] _adj, nm/f_ Moroccan ♦ _nm_ Morocco (leather).

Marruecos [ma'rrwekos] _nm_ Morocco.

marta ['marta] _nf_ (_animal_) (pine) marten; (_piel_) sable.

Marte ['marte] _nm_ Mars.

martes ['martes] _nm inv_ Tuesday; ~ **de carnaval** Shrove Tuesday; _V tb_ **Carnaval**.

martillar [marti'ʎar], **martillear** [martiʎe'ar] _vt_ to hammer.

martilleo [marti'ʎeo] _nm_ hammering.

martillo [mar'tiʎo] _nm_ hammer; (_de presidente de asamblea, comité_) gavel; ~ **neumático** pneumatic drill (_BRIT_), jackhammer (_US_).

Martinica [marti'nika] _nf_ Martinique.

mártir ['martir] _nm/f_ martyr.

martirice [marti'riθe] _etc vb V_ **martirizar**.

martirio [mar'tirjo] _nm_ martyrdom; (_fig_) torture, torment.

martirizar [martiri'θar] _vt_ (_REL_) to martyr; (_fig_) to torture, torment.

maruja [ma'ruxa] _nf_ (_fam_) = **maría**.

marxismo [mark'sismo] _nm_ Marxism.

marxista [mark'sista] _adj, nm/f_ Marxist.

marzo ['marθo] _nm_ March.

mas [mas] _conj_ but.

─────────────── _PALABRA CLAVE_

más [mas] _adj, adv_ **1**: ~ (**que, de**) (_compar_) more (than), ...+er (than); ~ **grande/ inteligente** bigger/more intelligent; **trabaja** ~ (**que yo**) he works more (than me); ~ **de 6** more than 6; **es** ~ **de medianoche** it's after midnight; **durar** ~ to last longer; _V tb_ **cada**

2 (_superl_): **el** ~ the most, ...+est; **el** ~ **grande/inteligente** (**de**) the biggest/most intelligent (in)

3 (_negativo_): **no tengo** ~ **dinero** I haven't got any more money; **no viene** ~ **por aquí** he doesn't come round here any more; **no sé** ~ I don't know any more, that's all I know

4 (_adicional_): **un kilómetro** ~ one more kilometre; **no le veo** ~ **solución que** ... I

see no other solution than to ...; **¿algo ~?** anything else?; (*en tienda*) will that be all?; **¿quién ~?** anybody else?
5 (*+adj: valor intensivo*): **¡qué perro ~ sucio!** what a filthy dog!; **¡es ~ tonto!** he's so stupid!
6 (*locuciones*): **~ o menos** more or less; **los ~** most people; **es ~** in fact, furthermore; **~ bien** rather; **¡qué ~ da!** what does it matter!; *V tb* **no**
7: por ~: por ~ que lo intento no matter how much *o* hard I try; **por ~ que quisiera ayudar** much as I should like to help
8: de ~: veo que aquí estoy de ~ I can see I'm not needed here; **tenemos uno de ~** we've got one extra
9: (*AM*): **no ~** only, just; **ayer no ~** just yesterday
♦ *prep*: **2 ~ 2 son 4** 2 and *o* plus 2 are 4
♦ *nm inv*: **este trabajo tiene sus ~ y sus menos** this job's got its good points and its bad points.

masa ['masa] *nf* (*mezcla*) dough; (*volumen*) volume, mass; (*FÍSICA*) mass; **en ~ en masse**; **las ~s** (*POL*) the masses.
masacrar [masa'krar] *vt* to massacre.
masacre [ma'sakre] *nf* massacre.
masaje [ma'saxe] *nm* massage; **dar ~ a** to massage.
masajista [masa'xista] *nm/f* masseur/masseuse.
mascar [mas'kar] *vt, vi* to chew; (*fig*) to mumble, mutter.
máscara ['maskara] *nf* (*tb INFORM*) mask ♦ *nm/f* masked person; **~ antigás** gas mask.
mascarada [maska'raða] *nf* masquerade.
mascarilla [maska'riʎa] *nf* mask; (*vaciado*) deathmask; (*maquillaje*) face pack.
mascarón [maska'ron] *nm* large mask; **~ de proa** figurehead.
mascota [mas'kota] *nf* mascot.
masculino, a [masku'lino, a] *adj* masculine; (*BIO*) male ♦ *nm* (*LING*) masculine.
mascullar [masku'ʎar] *vt* to mumble, mutter.
masificación [masifika'θjon] *nf* overcrowding.
masilla [ma'siʎa] *nf* putty.
masivo, a [ma'siβo, a] *adj* (*en masa*) mass.
masón [ma'son] *nm* (free)mason.
masonería [masone'ria] *nf* (free)masonry.
masoquista [maso'kista] *adj* masochistic ♦ *nm/f* masochist.
masque ['maske] *etc vb V* **mascar**.
mastectomía [mastekto'mia] *nf*

mastectomy.
máster, r, *pl* **masters** ['master, 'masters] *nm* postgraduate degree; *V tb* **licenciado**.
masticar [masti'kar] *vt* to chew; (*fig*) to ponder over.
mástil ['mastil] *nm* (*de navío*) mast; (*de guitarra*) neck.
mastín [mas'tin] *nm* mastiff.
mastique [mas'tike] *etc vb V* **masticar**.
masturbación [masturβa'θjon] *nf* masturbation.
masturbarse [mastur'βarse] *vr* to masturbate.
Mat. *abr =* **Matemáticas**.
mata ['mata] *nf* (*arbusto*) bush, shrub; (*de hierbas*) tuft; (*campo*) field; (*manojo*) tuft, blade; **~s** *nfpl* scrub *sg*; **~ de pelo** mop of hair; **a salto de ~** (*día a día*) from day to day; (*al azar*) haphazardly.
matadero [mata'ðero] *nm* slaughterhouse, abattoir.
matador, a [mata'ðor, a] *adj* killing ♦ *nm/f* killer ♦ *nm* (*TAUR*) matador, bullfighter.
matamoscas [mata'moskas] *nm inv* (*palo*) fly swat.
matanza [ma'tanθa] *nf* slaughter.
matar [ma'tar] *vt* to kill; (*tiempo, pelota*) to kill ♦ *vi* to kill; **~se** *vr* (*suicidarse*) to kill o.s., commit suicide; (*morir*) to be *o* get killed; (*gastarse*) to wear o.s. out; **~ el hambre** to stave off hunger; **~ a algn a disgustos** to make sb's life a misery; **~las callando** to go about things slyly; **~se trabajando** to kill o.s. with work; **~se por hacer algo** to struggle to do sth.
matarife [mata'rife] *nm* slaughterman.
matasanos [mata'sanos] *nm inv* quack.
matasellos [mata'seʎos] *nm inv* postmark.
mate ['mate] *adj* (*sin brillo: color*) dull, matt ♦ *nm* (*en ajedrez*) (check)mate; (*AM: hierba*) maté; (: *vasija*) gourd.
matemático, a [mate'matiko, a] *adj* mathematical ♦ *nm/f* mathematician ♦ **matemáticas** *nfpl* mathematics *sg*.
materia [ma'terja] *nf* (*gen*) matter; (*TEC*) material; (*ESCOL*) subject; **en ~ de** on the subject of; (*en cuanto a*) as regards; **~ prima** raw material; **entrar en ~** to get down to business.
material [mate'rjal] *adj* material; (*dolor*) physical; (*real*) real; (*literal*) literal ♦ *nm* material; (*TEC*) equipment; **~ de construcción** building material; **~es de derribo** rubble *sg*.
materialismo [materja'lismo] *nm* materialism.
materialista [materja'lista] *adj* materialist(ic).

materialmente [materjal'mente] *adv* materially; (*fig*) absolutely.

maternal [mater'nal] *adj* motherly, maternal.

maternidad [materni'ðað] *nf* motherhood, maternity.

materno, a [ma'terno, a] *adj* maternal; (*lengua*) mother *cpd*.

matice [ma'tiθe] *etc vb* V **matizar**.

matinal [mati'nal] *adj* morning *cpd*.

matiz [ma'tiθ] *nm* shade; (*de sentido*) shade, nuance; (*ironía etc*) touch.

matizar [mati'θar] *vt* (*variar*) to vary; (*ARTE*) to blend; ~ **de** to tinge with.

matón [ma'ton] *nm* bully.

matorral [mato'rral] *nm* thicket.

matraca [ma'traka] *nf* rattle; (*fam*) nuisance.

matraz [ma'traθ] *nm* (*QUÍMICA*) flask.

matriarcado [matrjar'kaðo] *nm* matriarchy.

matrícula [ma'trikula] *nf* (*registro*) register; (*ESCOL*: *inscripción*) registration; (*AUTO*) registration number; (: *placa*) number plate.

matricular [matriku'lar] *vt* to register, enrol.

matrimonial [matrimo'njal] *adj* matrimonial.

matrimonio [matri'monjo] *nm* (*pareja*) (married) couple; (*acto*) marriage; ~ **civil/clandestino** civil/secret marriage; **contraer** ~ (**con**) to marry.

matriz [ma'triθ] *nf* (*ANAT*) womb; (*TEC*) mould; (*MAT*) matrix; **casa** ~ (*COM*) head office.

matrona [ma'trona] *nf* (*persona de edad*) matron.

matutino, a [matu'tino, a] *adj* morning *cpd*.

maula ['maula] *adj* (*persona*) good-for-nothing ♦ *nm/f* (*vago*) idler, slacker ♦ *nf* (*persona*) dead loss (*fam*).

maullar [mau'ʎar] *vi* to mew, miaow.

maullido [mau'ʎiðo] *nm* mew(ing), miaow(ing).

Mauricio [mau'riθjo] *nm* Mauritius.

Mauritania [mauri'tanja] *nf* Mauritania.

mausoleo [mauso'leo] *nm* mausoleum.

maxilar [maksi'lar] *nm* jaw(bone).

máxima ['maksima] *nf* V **máximo**.

máxime ['maksime] *adv* especially.

máximo, a ['maksimo, a] *adj* maximum; (*más alto*) highest; (*más grande*) greatest ♦ *nm* maximum ♦ *nf* maxim; ~ **jefe** o **líder** (*AM*) President, leader; **como** ~ at most; **al** ~ to the utmost.

maxisingle [maksi'singel] *nm* twelve-inch (single).

maya ['maja] *adj* Mayan ♦ *nm/f* Maya(n).

mayo ['majo] *nm* May.

mayonesa [majo'nesa] *nf* mayonnaise.

mayor [ma'jor] *adj* main, chief; (*adulto*) grown-up, adult; (*JUR*) of age; (*de edad avanzada*) elderly; (*MUS*) major; (*comparativo*: *de tamaño*) bigger; (: *de edad*) older; (*superlativo*: *de tamaño*) biggest; (*tb*: *fig*) greatest; (: *de edad*) oldest ♦ *nm* chief, boss; (*adulto*) adult; **al por** ~ wholesale; ~ **de edad** adult; V *tb* **mayores**.

mayoral [majo'ral] *nm* foreman.

mayordomo [major'ðomo] *nm* butler.

mayoreo [majo'reo] *nm* (*AM*) wholesale (trade).

mayores [ma'jores] *nmpl* grown-ups; **llegar a** ~**es** to get out of hand.

mayoría [majo'ria] *nf* majority, greater part; **en la** ~ **de los casos** in most cases; **en su** ~ on the whole.

mayorista [majo'rista] *nm/f* wholesaler.

mayoritario, a [majori'tarjo, a] *adj* majority *cpd*; **gobierno** ~ majority government.

mayúsculo, a [ma'juskulo, a] *adj* (*fig*) big, tremendous ♦ *nf* capital (letter); **mayúsculas** *nfpl* capitals; (*TIP*) upper case *sg*.

maza ['maθa] *nf* (*arma*) mace; (*DEPORTE*) bat; (*POLO*) stick.

mazacote [maθa'kote] *nm* hard mass; (*CULIN*) dry doughy food; (*ARTE, LITERATURA etc*) mess, hotchpotch.

mazapán [maθa'pan] *nm* marzipan.

mazmorra [maθ'morra] *nf* dungeon.

mazo ['maθo] *nm* (*martillo*) mallet; (*de mortero*) pestle; (*de flores*) bunch; (*DEPORTE*) bat.

mazorca [ma'θorka] *nf* (*BOT*) spike; (*de maíz*) cob, ear.

MCAC *nm abr* = **Mercado Común de la América Central**.

MCI *nm abr* = **Mercado Común Iberoamericano**.

me [me] *pron* (*directo*) me; (*indirecto*) (to) me; (*reflexivo*) (to) myself; **¡dámelo!** give it to me!; ~ **lo compró** (*de mí*) he bought it from me; (*para mí*) he bought it for me.

meandro [me'andro] *nm* meander.

mear [me'ar] (*fam*) *vt* to piss on (*!*) ♦ *vi* to pee, piss (*!*), have a piss (*!*); ~**se** *vr* to wet o.s.

Meca ['meka] *nf*: **La** ~ Mecca.

mecánica [me'kanika] *nf* V **mecánico**.

mecanice [meka'niθe] *etc vb* V **mecanizar**.

mecánico, a [me'kaniko, a] *adj*

mechanical; (*repetitivo*) repetitive ♦ *nm/f*
mechanic ♦ *nf* (*estudio*) mechanics *sg*;
(*mecanismo*) mechanism.

mecanismo [meka'nismo] *nm* mechanism;
(*engranaje*) gear.

mecanizar [mekani'θar] *vt* to mechanize.

mecanografía [mekanoɣra'fia] *nf*
typewriting.

mecanografiado, a [mekanoɣra'fjaðo, a]
adj typewritten ♦ *nm* typescript.

mecanógrafo, a [meka'noɣrafo, a] *nm/f*
(*copy*) typist.

mecate [me'kate] *nm* (*AM*) rope.

mecedor [mese'ðor] *nm* (*AM*), **mecedora**
[meθe'ðora] *nf* rocking chair.

mecenas [me'θenas] *nm inv* patron.

mecenazgo [meθe'naθɣo] *nm* patronage.

mecer [me'θer] *vt* (*cuna*) to rock; ~**se** *vr* to
rock; (*rama*) to sway.

mecha ['metʃa] *nf* (*de vela*) wick; (*de
bomba*) fuse; **a toda** ~ at full speed;
ponerse ~**s** to streak one's hair.

mechero [me'tʃero] *nm* (*cigarette*) lighter.

mechón [me'tʃon] *nm* (*gen*) tuft; (*manojo*)
bundle; (*de pelo*) lock.

medalla [me'ðaʎa] *nf* medal.

media ['meðja] *nf* V **medio**.

mediación [meða'θjon] *nf* mediation; **por**
~ **de** through.

mediado, a [me'ðjaðo, a] *adj* half-full;
(*trabajo*) half-completed; **a** ~**s de** in the
middle of, halfway through.

medianamente [meðjana'mente] *adv*
(*moderadamente*) moderately, fairly;
(*regularmente*) moderately well.

mediano, a [me'ðjano, a] *adj* (*regular*)
medium, average; (*mediocre*) mediocre
♦ *nf* (*AUT*) central reservation, median
(*US*); (*de tamaño*) ~ medium-sized.

medianoche [meðja'notʃe] *nf* midnight.

mediante [me'ðjante] *adv* by (means of),
through.

mediar [me'ðjar] *vi* (*tiempo*) to elapse;
(*interceder*) to mediate, intervene;
(*existir*) to exist; **media el hecho de que**
... there is the fact that ....

medicación [meðika'θjon] *nf* medication,
treatment.

medicamento [meðika'mento] *nm*
medicine, drug.

medicina [meði'θina] *nf* medicine.

medicinal [meðiθi'nal] *adj* medicinal.

medición [meði'θjon] *nf* measurement.

médico, a ['meðiko, a] *adj* medical ♦ *nm/f*
doctor; ~ **de cabecera** family doctor; ~
pediatra paediatrician; ~ **residente**
house physician, intern (*US*).

medida [me'ðiða] *nf* measure; (*medición*)

measurement; (*de camisa, zapato etc*) size,
fitting; (*prudencia*) moderation, prudence;
en cierta/gran ~ up to a point/to a great
extent; **un traje a la** ~ made-to-measure
suit; ~ **de cuello** collar size; **a** ~ **de** in
proportion to; (*de acuerdo con*) in keeping
with; **con** ~ with restraint; **sin** ~
immoderately; **a** ~ **que** ... (at the same
time) as ...; **tomar** ~**s** to take steps.

medieval [meðje'ßal] *adj* medieval.

medio, a ['meðjo, a] *adj* half (a); (*punto*)
mid, middle; (*promedio*) average ♦ *adv*
half-; (*esp AM: un tanto*) rather, quite
♦ *nm* (*centro*) middle, centre; (*promedio*)
average; (*método*) means, way;
(*ambiente*) environment ♦ *nf* (*prenda de
vestir*) stocking, (*AM*) sock; (*promedio*)
average; ~**s** *nfpl* tights; **media hora** half
an hour; ~ **litro** half a litre; **las tres y
media** half past three; **M**~ **Oriente**
Middle East; **a** ~ **camino** halfway
(there); ~ **dormido** half asleep; ~
enojado (*esp AM*) rather annoyed; **lo dejó
a** ~**s** he left it half-done; **ir a** ~**s** to go
fifty-fifty; **a** ~ **terminar** half finished; **en**
~ in the middle; (*entre*) in between; **por**
~ **de** by (means of), through; **en los** ~**s
financieros** in financial circles;
encontrarse en su ~ to be in one's
element; ~ **ambiente** environment; ~
circulante (*COM*) money supply; *V tb*
medios.

medioambiental [meðjoambjen'tal] *adj*
environmental.

mediocre [me'ðjokre] *adj* middling,
average; (*pey*) mediocre.

mediocridad [meðjokri'ðað] *nf* middling
quality; (*pey*) mediocrity.

mediodía [meðjo'ðia] *nm* midday, noon.

mediopensionista [meðjopensjo'nista]
nm/f day boy/girl.

medios ['meðjos] *nmpl* means, resources;
los ~ **de comunicación** the media.

medir [me'ðir] *vt* (*gen*) to measure ♦ *vi* to
measure; ~**se** *vr* (*moderarse*) to be
moderate, act with restraint; **¿cuánto
mides? — mido 1.50 m** how tall are you?
— I am 1.50 m tall.

meditabundo, a [meðita'ßundo, a] *adj*
pensive.

meditar [meði'tar] *vt* to ponder, think
over, meditate on; (*planear*) to think out
♦ *vi* to ponder, think, meditate.

mediterráneo, a [meðite'rraneo, a] *adj*
Mediterranean ♦ *nm*: **el** (**mar**) **M**~ the
Mediterranean (Sea).

medrar [me'ðrar] *vi* to increase, grow;
(*mejorar*) to improve; (*prosperar*) to

prosper, thrive; (*animal, planta etc*) to grow.

medroso, a [me'ðroso, a] *adj* fearful, timid.

médula ['meðula] *nf* (*ANAT*) marrow; (*BOT*) pith; ~ **espinal** spinal cord; **hasta la** ~ (*fig*) to the core.

medusa [me'ðusa] *nf* (*ESP*) jellyfish.

megabyte ['meɣaßait] *nm* (*INFORM*) megabyte.

megafonía [meɣafo'nia] *nf* PA *o* public address system.

megáfono [me'ɣafono] *nm* public address system.

megalomanía [meɣaloma'nia] *nf* megalomania.

megalómano, a [meɣa'lomano, a] *nm/f* megalomaniac.

megaocteto [meɣaok'teto] *nm* (*INFORM*) megabyte.

mejicano, a [mexi'kano, a] *adj, nm/f* Mexican.

Méjico ['mexiko] *nm* Mexico.

mejilla [me'xiʎa] *nf* cheek.

mejillón [mexi'ʎon] *nm* mussel.

mejor [me'xor] *adj, adv* (*comparativo*) better; (*superlativo*) best; **lo** ~ **the** best thing; **lo** ~ **de la vida** the prime of life; **a lo** ~ probably; (*quizá*) maybe; ~ **dicho** rather; **tanto** ~ so much the better; **es el** ~ **de todos** he's the best of all.

mejora [me'xora] *nf*, **mejoramiento** [mexora'mjento] *nm* improvement.

mejorar [mexo'rar] *vt* to improve, make better ♦ *vi*, ~**se** *vr* to improve, get better; (*COM*) to do well, prosper; ~ **a** to be better than; **los negocios mejoran** business is picking up.

mejoría [mexo'ria] *nf* improvement; (*restablecimiento*) recovery.

mejunje [me'xunxe] *nm* (*pey*) concoction.

melancolía [melanko'lia] *nf* melancholy.

melancólico, a [melan'koliko, a] *adj* (*triste*) sad, melancholy; (*soñador*) dreamy.

melena [me'lena] *nf* (*de persona*) long hair; (*ZOOL*) mane.

melillense [meli'ʎense] *adj* of *o* from Melilla ♦ *nm/f* native *o* inhabitant of Melilla.

mella ['meʎa] *nf* (*rotura*) notch, nick; **hacer** ~ (*fig*) to make an impression.

mellizo, a [me'ʎiθo, a] *adj, nm/f* twin.

melocotón [meloko'ton] *nm* (*ESP*) peach.

melodía [melo'ðia] *nf* melody; (*aire*) tune.

melodrama [melo'ðrama] *nm* melodrama.

melodramático, a [meloðra'matiko, a] *adj* melodramatic.

melón [me'lon] *nm* melon.

melopea [melo'pea] *nf* (*fam*): **tener una** ~ to be sloshed.

meloso, a [me'loso, a] *adj* honeyed, sweet; (*empalagoso*) sickly, cloying; (*voz*) sweet; (*zalamero*) smooth.

membrana [mem'brana] *nf* membrane.

membrete [mem'brete] *nm* letterhead; **papel con** ~ headed notepaper.

membrillo [mem'briʎo] *nm* quince; **carne de** ~ quince jelly.

memo, a ['memo, a] *adj* silly, stupid ♦ *nm/f* idiot.

memorable [memo'raßle] *adj* memorable.

memorándum [memo'randum] *nm* (*libro*) notebook; (*comunicación*) memorandum.

memoria [me'morja] *nf* (*gen*) memory; (*artículo*) (learned) paper; ~**s** *nfpl* (*de autor*) memoirs; ~ **anual** annual report; **aprender algo de** ~ to learn sth by heart; **si tengo buena** ~ if my memory serves me right; **venir a la** ~ to come to mind; (*INFORM*): ~ **de acceso aleatorio** random access memory, RAM; ~ **auxiliar** backing storage; ~ **fija** read-only memory, ROM; ~ **fija programable** programmable memory; ~ **del teclado** keyboard memory.

memorice [memo'riθe] *etc vb V* **memorizar**.

memorizar [memori'θar] *vt* to memorize.

menaje [me'naxe] *nm* (*muebles*) furniture; (*utensilios domésticos*) household equipment; ~ **de cocina** kitchenware.

mención [men'θjon] *nf* mention; **digno de** ~ noteworthy; **hacer** ~ **de** to mention.

mencionar [menθjo'nar] *vt* to mention; (*nombrar*) to name; **sin** ~ ... let alone ....

mendicidad [mendiθi'ðað] *nf* begging.

mendigar [mendi'ɣar] *vt* to beg (for).

mendigo, a [men'diɣo, a] *nm/f* beggar.

mendigue [men'diɣe] *etc vb V* **mendigar**.

mendrugo [men'druɣo] *nm* crust.

menear [mene'ar] *vt* to move; (*cola*) to wag; (*cadera*) to swing; (*fig*) to handle; ~**se** *vr* to shake; (*balancearse*) to sway; (*moverse*) to move; (*fig*) to get a move on.

menester [menes'ter] *nm* (*necesidad*) necessity; ~**es** *nmpl* (*deberes*) duties; **es** ~ **hacer algo** it is necessary to do sth, sth must be done.

menestra [me'nestra] *nf*: ~ **de verduras** vegetable stew.

mengano, a [men'gano, a] *nm/f* Mr (*o* Mrs *o* Miss) So-and-so.

mengua ['mengwa] *nf* (*disminución*) decrease; (*falta*) lack; (*pobreza*) poverty; (*fig*) discredit; **en** ~ **de** to the detriment of.

menguante [men'gwante] *adj* decreasing, diminishing; (*luna*) waning; (*marea*) ebb *cpd*.

menguar [men'gwar] *vt* to lessen, diminish; (*fig*) to discredit ♦ *vi* to diminish, decrease; (*fig*) to decline.

mengüe ['mengwe] *etc vb V* **menguar.**

menopausia [meno'pausja] *nf* menopause.

menor [me'nor] *adj* (*más pequeño*: *comparativo*) smaller; (*número*) less, lesser; (: *superlativo*) smallest; (*número*) least; (*más joven*: *comparativo*) younger; (: *superlativo*) youngest; (*MUS*) minor ♦ *nm/f* (*joven*) young person, juvenile; **Juanito es ~ que Pepe** Juanito is younger than Pepe; **ella es la ~ de todas** she is the youngest of all; **no tengo la ~ idea** I haven't the faintest idea; **al por ~** retail; **~ de edad** under age.

Menorca [me'norka] *nf* Minorca.

menorquín, ina [menor'kin, ina] *adj, nm/f* Minorcan.

═══════════ *PALABRA CLAVE* ═══════════

menos [menos] *adj* 1: **~ (que, de)** (*compar*: *cantidad*) less (than); (: *número*) fewer (than); **con ~ entusiasmo** with less enthusiasm; **~ gente** fewer people; *V tb* **cada**

2 (*superl*): **es el que ~ culpa tiene** he is the least to blame; **donde ~ problemas hay** where there are fewest problems

♦ *adv* 1 (*compar*): **~ (que, de)** less (than); **me gusta ~ que el otro** I like it less than the other one; **~ de 5** less than 5; **~ de lo que piensas** less than you think

2 (*superl*): **es el ~ listo (de su clase)** he's the least bright (in his class); **de todas ellas es la que ~ me agrada** out of all of them she's the one I like least; **(por) lo ~** at (the very) least; **es lo ~ que puedo hacer** it's the least I can do; **lo ~ posible** as little as possible

3 (*locuciones*): **no quiero verle y ~ visitarle** I don't want to see him let alone visit him; **tenemos 7 (de) ~** we're 7 short; **eso es lo de ~** that's the least of it; **¡todo ~ eso!** anything but that!; **al/por lo ~** at (the very) only

♦ *prep* except; (*cifras*) minus; **todos ~ él** everyone except (for) him; **5 ~ 2** 5 minus 2; **las 7 ~ 20** (*hora*) 20 to 7

♦ *conj*: **a ~ que**: **a ~ que venga mañana** unless he comes tomorrow.

menoscabar [menoska'ßar] *vt* (*estropear*) to damage, harm; (*fig*) to discredit.

menospreciar [menospre'θjar] *vt* to underrate, undervalue; (*despreciar*) to scorn, despise.

menosprecio [menos'preθjo] *nm* (*subestimación*) underrating, undervaluation; (*desdén*) scorn, contempt.

mensaje [men'saxe] *nm* message; **~ de error** (*INFORM*) error message; **~ de texto** text message.

mensajero, a [mensa'xero, a] *nm/f* messenger.

menstruación [menstrwa'θjon] *nf* menstruation.

menstruar [mens'trwar] *vi* to menstruate.

mensual [men'swal] *adj* monthly; **10 euros ~es** 10 euros a month.

mensualidad [menswali'ðað] *nf* (*salario*) monthly salary; (*COM*) monthly payment *o* instalment.

menta ['menta] *nf* mint.

mentado, a [men'taðo, a] *adj* (*mencionado*) aforementioned; (*famoso*) well-known ♦ *nf*: **hacerle una mentada a algn** (*AM fam*) to (seriously) insult sb.

mental [men'tal] *adj* mental.

mentalidad [mentali'ðað] *nf* mentality.

mentalizar [mentali'θar] *vt* (*sensibilizar*) to make aware; (*convencer*) to convince; (*preparar mentalmente*) to psych up; **~se** *vr* (*concienciarse*) to become aware; (*prepararse mentalmente*) to get psyched up; **~se de que ...** (*convencerse*) to get it into one's head that ...

mentar [men'tar] *vt* to mention, name; **~ la madre a algn** to swear at sb.

mente ['mente] *nf* mind; (*inteligencia*) intelligence; **no tengo en ~ hacer eso** it is not my intention to do that.

mentecato, a [mente'kato, a] *adj* silly, stupid ♦ *nm/f* fool, idiot.

mentir [men'tir] *vi* to lie; **¡miento!** sorry, I'm wrong!

mentira [men'tira] *nf* (*una ~*) lie; (*acto*) lying; (*invención*) fiction; **~ piadosa** white lie; **una ~ como una casa** a whopping great lie (*fam*); **parece ~ que ...** it seems incredible that ..., I can't believe that ....

mentiroso, a [menti'roso, a] *adj* lying; (*falso*) deceptive ♦ *nm/f* liar.

mentís [men'tis] *nm inv* denial; **dar el ~ a** to deny.

mentón [men'ton] *nm* chin.

menú [me'nu] *nm* (*tb INFORM*) menu; (*tb*: **~ del día**) set meal; **guiado por ~** (*INFORM*) menu-driven.

menudear [menuðe'ar] *vt* (*repetir*) to repeat frequently ♦ *vi* (*ser frecuente*) to be frequent; (*detallar*) to go into great detail.

menudencia [menu'ðenθja] *nf* (*bagatela*) trifle; ~**s** *nfpl* odds and ends.

menudeo [menu'ðeo] *nm* retail sales *pl*.

menudillos [menu'ðiʎos] *nmpl* giblets.

menudo, a [me'nuðo, a] *adj* (*pequeño*) small, tiny; (*sin importancia*) petty, insignificant; ¡~ **negocio!** (*fam*) some deal!; **a** ~ often, frequently.

meñique [me'ɲike] *nm* little finger.

meollo [me'oʎo] *nm* (*fig*) essence, core.

mequetrefe [meke'trefe] *nm* good-for-nothing, whippersnapper.

mercader [merka'ðer] *nm* merchant.

mercadería [merkaðe'ria] *nf* commodity; ~**s** *nfpl* goods, merchandise *sg*.

mercado [mer'kaðo] *nm* market; ~ **en baja** falling market; **M~ Común** Common Market; ~ **de demanda/de oferta** seller's/buyer's market; ~ **laboral** labour market; ~ **objetivo** target market; ~ **de productos básicos** commodity market; ~ **de valores** stock market; ~ **exterior/interior** *o* **nacional/ libre** overseas/home/free market.

mercancía [merkan'θia] *nf* commodity; ~**s** *nfpl* goods, merchandise *sg*; ~**s en depósito** bonded goods; ~**s perecederas** perishable goods.

mercancías [merkan'θias] *nm inv* goods train, freight train (*US*).

mercantil [merkan'til] *adj* mercantile, commercial.

mercenario, a [merθe'narjo, a] *adj, nm* mercenary.

mercería [merθe'ria] *nf* (*artículos*) haberdashery (*BRIT*), notions *pl* (*US*); (*tienda*) haberdasher's shop (*BRIT*), drapery (*BRIT*), notions store (*US*).

Mercosur [merko'sur] *nm abr* = *Mercado Común del Sur*.

mercurio [mer'kurjo] *nm* mercury.

merecedor, a [mereθe'ðor, a] *adj* deserving; ~ **de confianza** trustworthy.

merecer [mere'θer] *vt* to deserve, merit ♦ *vi* to be deserving, be worthy; **merece la pena** it's worthwhile.

merecido, a [mere'θiðo, a] *adj* (well) deserved; **llevarse su** ~ to get one's deserts.

merendar [meren'dar] *vt* to have for tea ♦ *vi* to have tea; (*en el campo*) to have a picnic.

merendero [meren'dero] *nm* (*café*) tearoom; (*en el campo*) picnic spot.

merengue [me'renge] *nm* meringue.

merezca [me'reθka] *etc vb V* **merecer.**

meridiano [meri'ðjano] *nm* (*ASTRO, GEO*) meridian; **la explicación es de una claridad meridiana** the explanation is as clear as day.

meridional [meriðjo'nal] *adj* Southern ♦ *nm/f* Southerner.

merienda [me'rjenda] *etc vb V* **merendar** ♦ *nf* (light) tea, afternoon snack; (*de campo*) picnic; ~ **de negros** free-for-all.

mérito ['merito] *nm* merit; (*valor*) worth, value; **hacer** ~**s** to make a good impression; **restar** ~ **a** to detract from.

meritorio, a [meri'torjo, a] *adj* deserving.

merluza [mer'luθa] *nf* hake; **coger una** ~ (*fam*) to get sozzled.

merma ['merma] *nf* decrease; (*pérdida*) wastage.

mermar [mer'mar] *vt* to reduce, lessen ♦ *vi* to decrease, dwindle.

mermelada [merme'laða] *nf* jam; ~ **de naranja** marmalade.

mero, a ['mero, a] *adj* mere, simple; (*AM fam*) real ♦ *adv* (*AM*) just, right ♦ *nm* (*ZOOL*) grouper; **el** ~ ~ (*AM fam*) the boss.

merodear [meroðe'ar] *vi* (*MIL*) to maraud; (*de noche*) to prowl (about); (*curiosear*) to snoop around.

mes [mes] *nm* month; (*salario*) month's pay; **el** ~ **corriente** this *o* the current month.

mesa ['mesa] *nf* table; (*de trabajo*) desk; (*COM*) counter; (*en mitin*) platform; (*GEO*) plateau; (*ARQ*) landing; ~ **de noche/de tijera/de operaciones** *u* **operatoria** bedside/folding/operating table; ~ **redonda** (*reunión*) round table; ~ **digitalizadora** (*INFORM*) graph pad; ~ **directiva** board; ~ **y cama** bed and board; **poner/quitar la** ~ to lay/clear the table.

mesarse [me'sarse] *vr*: ~ **el pelo** *o* **los cabellos** to tear one's hair.

mesera [me'sera] *nf* (*AM*) waitress.

mesero [me'sero] *nm* (*AM*) waiter.

meseta [me'seta] *nf* (*GEO*) meseta, tableland; (*ARQ*) landing.

mesilla [me'siʎa], **mesita** [me'sita] *nf*: ~ **de noche** bedside table.

mesón [me'son] *nm* inn.

mestizo, a [mes'tiθo, a] *adj* half-caste, of mixed race; (*ZOOL*) crossbred ♦ *nm/f* half-caste.

mesura [me'sura] *nf* (*calma*) calm; (*moderación*) moderation, restraint; (*cortesía*) courtesy.

mesurar [mesu'rar] *vt* (*contener*) to restrain; ~**se** *vr* to restrain o.s.

meta ['meta] *nf* goal; (*de carrera*) finish; (*fig*) goal, aim, objective.

metabolismo [metaßo'lismo] *nm* metabolism.

metafísico, a [meta'fisiko, a] *adj* metaphysical ♦ *nf* metaphysics *sg*.

metáfora [me'tafora] *nf* metaphor.

metafórico, a [meta'foriko, a] *adj* metaphorical.

metal [me'tal] *nm* (*materia*) metal; (*MUS*) brass.

metálico, a [me'taliko, a] *adj* metallic; (*de metal*) metal ♦ *nm* (*dinero contante*) cash.

metalurgia [meta'lurxja] *nf* metallurgy.

metalúrgico, a [meta'lurxiko, a] *adj* metallurgic(al); **industria ~a** engineering industry.

metamorfosear [metamorfose'ar] *vt*: ~ (**en**) to metamorphose *o* transform (into).

metamorfosis [metamor'fosis] *nf inv* metamorphosis, transformation.

metedura [mete'ðura] *nf*: ~ **de pata** (*fam*) blunder.

meteorito [meteo'rito] *nm* meteorite.

meteoro [mete'oro] *nm* meteor.

meteorología [meteorolo'xia] *nf* meteorology.

meteorólogo, a [meteo'roloxo, a] *nm/f* meteorologist; (*RADIO, TV*) weather reporter.

meter [me'ter] *vt* (*colocar*) to put, place; (*introducir*) to put in, insert; (*involucrar*) to involve; (*causar*) to make, cause; ~**se** *vr*: ~**se en** to go into, enter; (*fig*) to interfere in, meddle in; ~**se a** to start; ~**se a escritor** to become a writer; ~**se con algn** to provoke sb, pick a quarrel with sb; ~ **prisa a algn** to hurry sb up.

meticuloso, a [metiku'loso, a] *adj* meticulous, thorough.

metido, a [me'tiðo, a] *adj*: **estar muy ~ en un asunto** to be deeply involved in a matter; ~ **en años** elderly; ~ **en carne** plump.

metódico, a [me'toðiko, a] *adj* methodical.

metodismo [meto'ðismo] *nm* Methodism.

método [me'toðo] *nm* method.

metodología [metoðolo'xia] *nf* methodology.

metomentodo [metomen'toðo] *nm inv* meddler, busybody.

metraje [me'traxe] *nm* (*CINE*) length; **cinta de largo/corto ~** full-length film/short.

metralla [me'traʎa] *nf* shrapnel.

metralleta [metra'ʎeta] *nf* sub-machine-gun.

métrico, a ['metriko, a] *adj* metric ♦ *nf* metrics *pl*; **cinta métrica** tape measure.

metro ['metro] *nm* metre; (*tren*: *tb*: **metropolitano**) underground (*BRIT*), subway (*US*); (*instrumento*) rule; ~ **cuadrado/cúbico** square/cubic metre.

metrópoli [me'tropoli], **metrópolis** [me'tropolis] *nf* (*ciudad*) metropolis; (*colonial*) mother country.

mexicano, a [mexi'kano, a] *adj*, *nm/f* (*AM*) Mexican.

México ['mexiko] *nm* (*AM*) Mexico; **Ciudad de ~** Mexico City.

mezcla ['meθkla] *nf* mixture; (*fig*) blend.

mezclar [meθ'klar] *vt* to mix (up); (*armonizar*) to blend; (*combinar*) to merge; ~**se** *vr* to mix, mingle; ~ **en** to get mixed up in, get involved in.

mezcolanza [meθko'lanθa] *nf* hotchpotch, jumble.

mezquindad [meθkin'dað] *nf* (*cicatería*) meanness; (*miras estrechas*) pettiness; (*acto*) mean action.

mezquino, a [meθ'kino, a] *adj* (*cicatero*) mean ♦ *nm/f* (*avaro*) mean person; (*miserable*) petty individual.

mezquita [meθ'kita] *nf* mosque.

MF *abr* (= *Modulación de Frecuencia*) FM.

mg. *abr* (= *miligramo(s)*) mg.

mi [mi] *adj posesivo* my ♦ *nm* (*MUS*) E.

mí [mi] *pron* me, myself; **¿y a ~ qué?** so what?

miaja ['mjaxa] *nf* crumb; **ni una ~** (*fig*) not the least little bit.

miau [mjau] *nm* miaow.

michelín [mitʃe'lin] *nm* (*fam*) spare tyre.

mico ['miko] *nm* monkey.

micro ['mikro] *nm* (*RADIO*) mike, microphone; (*AM*: *pequeño*) minibus; (: *grande*) coach, bus.

microbio [mi'kroßjo] *nm* microbe.

microbús [mikro'ßus] *nm* minibus.

microchip [mikro'tʃip] *nm* microchip.

microcomputador [mikrokomputa'ðor] *nm*, **microcomputadora** [mikrokomputa'ðora] *nf* micro(computer).

microeconomía [mikroekono'mia] *nf* microeconomics *sg*.

microficha [mikro'fitʃa] *nf* microfiche.

microfilm, *pl* **microfilms** [mikro'film, mikro'films] *nm* microfilm.

micrófono [mi'krofono] *nm* microphone.

microinformática [mikroinfor'matika] *nf* microcomputing.

micrómetro [mi'krometro] *nm* micrometer.

microonda [mikro'onda] *nf* microwave; (**horno**) ~**s** microwave (oven).

microordenador [mikroordena'ðor] *nm*

microcomputer.

micropastilla [mikropas'tiʎa],
microplaqueta [mikropla'keta] *nf*
(*INFORM*) chip, wafer.

microplaquita [mikropla'kita] *nf*: ~ **de**
silicio silicon chip.

microprocesador [mikroprocesa'ðor] *nm*
microprocessor.

microscópico, a [mikros'kopiko, a] *adj*
microscopic.

microscopio [mikros'kopjo] *nm*
microscope.

midiendo [mi'ðjendo] *etc vb V* **medir**.

miedo ['mjeðo] *nm* fear; (*nerviosismo*)
apprehension, nervousness; **meter ~ a**
to scare, frighten; **tener ~** to be afraid;
de ~ wonderful, marvellous; **¡qué ~!**
(*fam*) how awful!; **me da ~** it scares me;
hace un frío de ~ (*fam*) it's terribly cold.

miedoso, a [mje'ðoso, a] *adj* fearful,
timid.

miel [mjel] *nf* honey; **no hay ~ sin hiel**
there's no rose without a thorn.

miembro ['mjembro] *nm* limb; (*socio*)
member; (*de institución*) fellow; **~ viril**
penis.

mientes ['mjentes] *etc vb V* **mentar; mentir**
♦ *nfpl*: **no parar ~ en** to pay no attention
to; **traer a las ~** to recall.

mientras ['mjentras] *conj* while; (*duración*)
as long as ♦ *adv* meanwhile; **~ (que)**
whereas; **~ tanto** meanwhile; **~ más**
tiene, más quiere the more he has, the
more he wants.

miérc. *abr* (= **miércoles**) Wed.

miércoles ['mjerkoles] *nm inv* Wednesday;
~ de ceniza Ash Wednesday; *V tb*
Carnaval.

mierda ['mjerða] *nf* (*fam!*) shit (*!*), crap (*!*);
(*fig*) filth, dirt; **¡vete a la ~!** go to hell!

mies [mjes] *nf* (ripe) corn, wheat, grain.

miga ['miɣa] *nf* crumb; (*fig*: *meollo*)
essence; **hacer buenas ~s** (*fam*) to get on
well; **esto tiene su ~** there's more to this
than meets the eye.

migaja [mi'ɣaxa] *nf*: **una ~ de** (*un poquito*)
a little; **~s** *nfpl* crumbs; (*pey*) left-overs.

migración [miɣra'θjon] *nf* migration.

migratorio, a [miɣra'torjo, a] *adj*
migratory.

mil [mil] *num* thousand; **dos ~ libras** two
thousand pounds.

milagro [mi'laɣro] *nm* miracle; **hacer ~s**
(*fig*) to work wonders.

milagroso, a [mila'ɣroso, a] *adj*
miraculous.

Milán [mi'lan] *nm* Milan.

milenario, a [mile'narjo, a] *adj* millennial;

(*fig*) very ancient.

milenio [mi'lenjo] *nm* millennium.

milésimo, a [mi'lesimo, a] *num* thousandth.

mili ['mili] *nf*: **hacer la ~** (*fam*) to do one's
military service; *see boxed note.*

MILI

La mili, *military service, is compulsory in
Spain, although the number of months'
service has been reduced and recruits are
now posted close to their home town.
There continues to be strong opposition
from conscientious objectors, who are
obliged to do "Prestación Social
Sustitutoria" instead; this usually involves
doing some form of community service
and lasts longer. Those who refuse to do
either of these, "los insumisos", can be
sent to prison.*

---

milicia [mi'liθja] *nf* (*MIL*) militia; (*servicio
militar*) military service.

miligramo [mili'ɣramo] *nm* milligram.

milímetro [mi'limetro] *nm* millimetre
(*BRIT*), millimeter (*US*).

militante [mili'tante] *adj* militant.

militar [mili'tar] *adj* military ♦ *nm/f* soldier
♦ *vi* to serve in the army; (*fig*) to
militate, fight.

militarismo [milita'rismo] *nm* militarism.

milla ['miʎa] *nf* mile; **~ marina** nautical
mile.

millar [mi'ʎar] *num* thousand; **a ~es** in
thousands.

millón [mi'ʎon] *num* million.

millonario, a [miʎo'narjo, a] *nm/f*
millionaire.

millonésimo, a [miʎo'nesimo, a] *num*
millionth.

mimado, a [mi'maðo, a] *adj* spoiled.

mimar [mi'mar] *vt* to spoil, pamper.

mimbre ['mimbre] *nm* wicker; **de ~** wicker
cpd, wickerwork.

mimetismo [mime'tismo] *nm* mimicry.

mímica ['mimika] *nf* (*para comunicarse*)
sign language; (*imitación*) mimicry.

mimo ['mimo] *nm* (*caricia*) caress; (*de niño*)
spoiling; (*TEAT*) mime; (: *actor*) mime
artist.

mina ['mina] *nf* mine; (*pozo*) shaft; (*de
lápiz*) lead refill; **hullera o ~ de carbón**
coalmine.

minar [mi'nar] *vt* to mine; (*fig*) to
undermine.

mineral [mine'ral] *adj* mineral ♦ *nm* (*GEO*)
mineral; (*mena*) ore.

minería [mine'ria] *nf* mining.

minero, a [mi'nero, a] *adj* mining *cpd* ♦ *nm/f* miner.

miniatura [minja'tura] *adj inv*, *nf* miniature.

minicadena [minika'ðena] *nf* (*MUS*) mini hi-fi.

minicomputador [minikomputa'ðor] *nm* minicomputer.

MiniDisc ® [mini'ðisk] *nm* MiniDisc ®.

minidisco [mini'ðisko] *nm* diskette.

minifalda [mini'falda] *nf* miniskirt.

minifundio [mini'fundjo] *nm* smallholding, small farm.

minimizar [minimi'θar] *vt* to minimize.

mínimo, a ['minimo, a] *adj* minimum; (*insignificante*) minimal ♦ *nm* minimum; **precio/salario** ~ minimum price/wage; **lo** ~ **que pueden hacer** the least they can do.

minino, a [mi'nino, a] *nm/f* (*fam*) puss, pussy.

ministerio [minis'terjo] *nm* ministry (*BRIT*), department (*US*); **M~ de Asuntos Exteriores** Foreign Office (*BRIT*), State Department (*US*); **M~ del Comercio e Industria** Department of Trade and Industry; **M~ de (la) Gobernación** *o* **del Interior** ≈ Home Office (*BRIT*), Ministry of the Interior; **M~ de Hacienda** Treasury (*BRIT*), Treasury Department (*US*).

ministro, a [mi'nistro, a] *nm/f* minister, secretary (*esp US*); **M~ de Hacienda** Chancellor of the Exchequer, Secretary of the Treasury (*US*); **M~ de (la) Gobernación** *o* **del Interior** ≈ Home Secretary (*BRIT*), Secretary of the Interior (*US*).

minoría [mino'ria] *nf* minority.

minorista [mino'rista] *nm* retailer.

mintiendo [min't jendo] *etc vb V* **mentir**.

minucia [mi'nuθja] *nf* (*detalle insignificante*) trifle; (*bagatela*) mere nothing.

minuciosidad [minuθjosi'ðað] *nf* (*meticulosidad*) thoroughness, meticulousness.

minucioso, a [minu'θjoso, a] *adj* thorough, meticulous; (*prolijo*) very detailed.

minúsculo, a [mi'nuskulo, a] *adj* tiny, minute ♦ *nf* small letter; **minúsculas** *nfpl* (*TIP*) lower case *sg*.

minusvalía [minusßa'lia] *nf* physical handicap; (*COM*) depreciation, capital loss.

minusválido, a [minus'ßaliðo, a] *adj* (physically) handicapped *o* disabled ♦ *nm/f* disabled person.

minuta [mi'nuta] *nf* (*de comida*) menu; (*de abogado etc*) fee.

minutero [minu'tero] *nm* minute hand.

minuto [mi'nuto] *nm* minute.

Miño ['mino] *nm*: **el (río)** ~ the Miño.

mío, a ['mio, a] *adj*, *pron*: **el** ~ mine; **un amigo** ~ a friend of mine; **lo** ~ what is mine; **los** ~**s** my people, my relations.

miope ['mjope] *adj* short-sighted.

miopía [mjo'pia] *nf* near- *o* short-sightedness.

MIR [mir] *nm abr* (*POL*) = *Movimiento de Izquierda Revolucionaria*; (*ESP MED*) = *Médico Interno y Residente*.

mira ['mira] *nf* (*de arma*) sight(s) (*pl*); (*fig*) aim, intention; **de amplias/estrechas** ~**s** broad-/narrow-minded.

mirada [mi'raða] *nf* look, glance; (*expresión*) look, expression; ~ **de soslayo** sidelong glance; ~ **fija** stare, gaze; ~ **perdida** distant look; **echar una** ~ **a** to glance at; **levantar/bajar la** ~ to look up/down; **resistir la** ~ **de algn** to stare sb out.

mirado, a [mi'raðo, a] *adj* (*sensato*) sensible; (*considerado*) considerate; **bien/mal** ~ well/not well thought of.

mirador [mira'ðor] *nm* viewpoint, vantage point.

miramiento [mira'mjento] *nm* (*consideración*) considerateness; **tratar sin** ~**s a algn** to ride roughshod over sb.

mirar [mi'rar] *vt* to look at; (*observar*) to watch; (*considerar*) to consider, think over; (*vigilar, cuidar*) to watch, look after ♦ *vi* to look; (*ARQ*) to face; ~**se** *vr* (*dos personas*) to look at each other; ~ **algo/a algn de reojo** *o* **de través** to look askance at sth/sb; ~ **algo/a algn por encima del hombro** to look down on sth/sb; ~ **bien/mal** to think highly of/have a poor opinion of; ~ **fijamente** to stare *o* gaze at; ~ **por** (*fig*) to look after; ~ **por la ventana** to look out of the window; ~**se al espejo** to look at o.s. in the mirror; ~**se a los ojos** to look into each other's eyes.

mirilla [mi'riʎa] *nf* (*agujero*) spyhole, peephole.

mirlo ['mirlo] *nm* blackbird.

misa ['misa] *nf* mass; ~ **del gallo** midnight mass (*on Christmas Eve*); ~ **de difuntos** requiem mass; **como en** ~ in dead silence; **estos datos van a** ~ (*fig*) these facts are utterly trustworthy.

misántropo [mi'santropo] *nm* misanthrope, misanthropist.

miscelánea [misθe'lanea] *nf* miscellany.

miserable [mise'raßle] *adj* (*avaro*) mean, stingy; (*nimio*) miserable, paltry; (*lugar*) squalid; (*fam*) vile, despicable ♦ *nm/f* (*malvado*) rogue.

miseria [mi'serja] *nf* misery; (*pobreza*) poverty; (*tacañería*) meanness, stinginess; (*condiciones*) squalor; **una ~** a pittance.

misericordia [miseri'korðja] *nf* (*compasión*) compassion, pity; (*perdón*) forgiveness, mercy.

misil [mi'sil] *nm* missile.

misión [mi'sjon] *nf* mission; (*tarea*) job, duty; (*POL*) assignment; **misiones** *nfpl* (*REL*) overseas missions.

misionero, a [misjo'nero, a] *nm/f* missionary.

mismamente [misma'mente] *adv* (*fam*: *sólo*) only, just.

mismísimo, a [mis'misimo, a] *adj superlativo* selfsame, very (same).

mismo, a ['mismo, a] *adj* (*semejante*) same; (*después de pronombre*) -self; (*para énfasis*) very ♦ *adv*: **aquí/ayer/hoy ~** right here/only yesterday/this very day; **ahora ~** right now ♦ *conj*: **lo ~ que** just like, just as; **por lo ~** for the same reason; **el ~ traje** the same suit; **en ese ~ momento** at that very moment; **vino el ~ Ministro** the Minister himself came; **yo ~ lo vi** I saw it myself; **lo hizo por sí ~** he did it by himself; **lo ~ the same (thing); **da lo ~** it's all the same; **quedamos en las mismas** we're no further forward.

misógino [mi'soxino] *nm* misogynist.

miss [mis] *nf* beauty queen.

misterio [mis'terjo] *nm* mystery; (*lo secreto*) secrecy.

misterioso, a [miste'rjoso, a] *adj* mysterious; (*inexplicable*) puzzling.

misticismo [misti'θismo] *nm* mysticism.

místico, a ['mistiko, a] *adj* mystic(al) ♦ *nm/f* mystic ♦ *nf* mysticism.

mitad [mi'tað] *nf* (*medio*) half; (*centro*) middle; **~ (y) ~** half-and-half; (*fig*) yes and no; **a ~ de precio** (at) half-price; **en o a ~ del camino** halfway along the road; **cortar por la ~** to cut through the middle.

mítico, a ['mitiko, a] *adj* mythical.

mitigar [miti'xar] *vt* to mitigate; (*dolor*) to relieve; (*sed*) to quench; (*ira*) to appease; (*preocupación*) to allay; (*soledad*) to alleviate.

mitigue [mi'tixe] *etc vb V* **mitigar**.

mitin ['mitin] *nm* (*esp POL*) meeting.

mito ['mito] *nm* myth.

mitología [mitolo'xia] *nf* mythology.

mitológico, a [mito'loxiko, a] *adj* mythological.

mixto, a ['miksto, a] *adj* mixed; (*comité*) joint.

ml. *abr* (= *mililitro*) ml.

mm. *abr* (= *milímetro*) mm.

m/n *abr* (*ECON*) = *moneda nacional*.

M.º *abr* (*POL*: = *Ministerio*) Min.

m/o *abr* (*COM*) = *mi orden*.

mobiliario [moßi'ljarjo] *nm* furniture.

MOC *nm abr* = *Movimiento de Objeción de Conciencia*.

mocasín [moka'sin] *nm* moccasin.

mocedad [moθe'ðað] *nf* youth.

mochila [mo'tʃila] *nf* rucksack (*BRIT*), backpack.

moción [mo'θjon] *nf* motion; **~ compuesta** (*POL*) composite motion.

moco ['moko] *nm* mucus; **limpiarse los ~s** to blow one's nose; **no es ~ de pavo** it's no trifle.

mocoso, a [mo'koso, a] *adj* snivelling; (*fig*) ill-bred ♦ *nm/f* (*fam*) brat.

moda ['moða] *nf* fashion; (*estilo*) style; **de o a la ~** in fashion, fashionable; **pasado de ~** out of fashion; **vestido a la última ~** trendily dressed.

modal [mo'ðal] *adj* modal ♦ *nm*: **~es** *nmpl* manners.

modalidad [moðali'ðað] *nf* (*clase*) kind, variety; (*manera*) way; (*INFORM*) mode; **~ de texto** (*INFORM*) text mode.

modelar [moðe'lar] *vt* to model.

modelo [mo'ðelo] *adj inv* model ♦ *nm/f* model ♦ *nm* (*patrón*) pattern; (*norma*) standard.

módem ['moðem] *nm* (*INFORM*) modem.

moderado, a [moðe'raðo, a] *adj* moderate.

moderar [moðe'rar] *vt* to moderate; (*violencia*) to restrain, control; (*velocidad*) to reduce; **~se** *vr* to restrain o.s., control o.s.

modernice [moðer'niθe] *etc vb V* **modernizar**.

modernizar [moðerni'θar] *vt* to modernize; (*INFORM*) to upgrade.

moderno, a [mo'ðerno, a] *adj* modern; (*actual*) present-day; (*equipo etc*) up-to-date.

modestia [mo'ðestja] *nf* modesty.

modesto, a [mo'ðesto, a] *adj* modest.

módico, a ['moðiko, a] *adj* moderate, reasonable.

modificar [moðifi'kar] *vt* to modify.

modifique [moði'fike] *etc vb V* **modificar**.

modismo [mo'ðismo] *nm* idiom.

modisto, a [mo'ðisto, a] *nm/f* dressmaker.

modo ['moðo] *nm* (*manera, forma*) way, manner; (*INFORM, MUS*) mode; (*LING*) mood; **~s** *nmpl* manners; **"~ de empleo"** "instructions for use"; **~ de gobierno**

form of government; **a ~ de** like; **de este ~** in this way; **de ningún ~** in no way; **de todos ~s** at any rate; **de un ~ u otro** (in) one way or another.

modorra [mo'ðorra] *nf* drowsiness.

modoso, a [mo'ðoso, a] *adj* (*educado*) quiet, well-mannered.

modulación [moðula'θjon] *nf* modulation; **~ de frecuencia** (*RADIO*) frequency modulation, FM.

módulo ['moðulo] *nm* module; (*de mueble*) unit.

mofarse [mo'farse] *vr*: **~ de** to mock, scoff at.

moflete [mo'flete] *nm* fat cheek, chubby cheek.

mogollón [moɣo'ʎon] (*fam*) *nm*: **~ de discos** *etc* loads of records *etc* ♦ *adv*: **un ~ a hell of a lot.**

mohín [mo'in] *nm* (*mueca*) (wry) face; (*pucheros*) pout.

mohino, a [mo'ino, a] *adj* (*triste*) gloomy, depressed; (*enojado*) sulky.

moho ['moo] *nm* (*BOT*) mould, mildew; (*en metal*) rust.

mohoso, a [mo'oso, a] *adj* mouldy; rusty.

mojado, a [mo'xaðo, a] *adj* wet; (*húmedo*) damp; (*empapado*) drenched.

mojar [mo'xar] *vt* to wet; (*humedecer*) to damp(en), moisten; (*calar*) to soak; **~se** *vr* to get wet; **~ el pan en el café** to dip o dunk one's bread in one's coffee.

mojigato, a [moxi'ɣato, a] *adj* (*hipócrita*) hypocritical; (*santurrón*) sanctimonious; (*gazmoño*) prudish ♦ *nm/f* hypocrite; sanctimonious person; prude.

mojón [mo'xon] *nm* (*hito*) landmark; (*en un camino*) signpost; (**~ kilométrico**) milestone.

mol. *abr* (= *molécula*) mol.

molar [mo'lar] *nm* molar ♦ *vt* (*fam*): **lo que más me mola es ...** what I'm really into is ...; **¿te mola un pitillo?** do you fancy a smoke?

Moldavia [mol'ðaβja], **Moldova** [mol'ðoβa] *nf* Moldavia, Moldova.

moldavo, a [mol'ðaβo, a] *adj, nm/f* Moldavian, Moldovan.

molde ['molde] *nm* mould; (*vaciado*) cast; (*de costura*) pattern; (*fig*) model.

moldear [molde'ar] *vt* to mould; (*en yeso etc*) to cast.

mole ['mole] *nf* mass, bulk; (*edificio*) pile.

molécula [mo'lekula] *nf* molecule.

moler [mo'ler] *vt* to grind, crush; (*pulverizar*) to pound; (*trigo etc*) to mill; (*cansar*) to tire out, exhaust; **~ a algn a palos** to give sb a beating.

molestar [moles'tar] *vt* to bother; (*fastidiar*) to annoy; (*incomodar*) to inconvenience, put out; (*perturbar*) to trouble, upset ♦ *vi* to be a nuisance; **~se** *vr* to bother; (*incomodarse*) to go to a lot of trouble; (*ofenderse*) to take offence; **¿le molesta el ruido?** do you mind the noise?; **siento ~le** I'm sorry to trouble you.

molestia [mo'lestja] *nf* bother, trouble; (*incomodidad*) inconvenience; (*MED*) discomfort; **no es ninguna ~** it's no trouble at all.

molesto, a [mo'lesto, a] *adj* (*que fastidia*) annoying; (*incómodo*) inconvenient; (*inquieto*) uncomfortable, ill at ease; (*enfadado*) annoyed; **estar ~** (*MED*) to be in some discomfort; **estar ~ con algn** (*fig*) to be cross with sb; **me sentí ~** I felt embarrassed.

molido, a [mo'liðo, a] *adj* (*machacado*) ground; (*pulverizado*) powdered; **estar ~** (*fig*) to be exhausted o dead beat.

molinero [moli'nero] *nm* miller.

molinillo [moli'niʎo] *nm* hand mill; **~ de carne/café** mincer/coffee grinder.

molino [mo'lino] *nm* (*edificio*) mill; (*máquina*) grinder.

mollera [mo'ʎera] *nf* (*ANAT*) crown of the head; (*fam: seso*) brains *pl*; **duro de ~** (*estúpido*) thick.

Molucas [mo'lukas] *nfpl*: **las (Islas) ~** the Moluccas, the Molucca Islands.

molusco [mo'lusko] *nm* mollusc.

momentáneo, a [momen'taneo, a] *adj* momentary.

momento [mo'mento] *nm* (*gen*) moment; (*TEC*) momentum; **de ~** at the moment, for the moment; **en ese ~** at that moment, just then; **por el ~** for the time being.

momia ['momja] *nf* mummy.

mona ['mona] *nf V* mono.

Mónaco ['monako] *nm* Monaco.

monada [mo'naða] *nf* (*de niño*) charming habit; (*cosa primorosa*) lovely thing; (*chica*) pretty girl; **¡qué ~!** isn't it cute?

monaguillo [mona'ɣiʎo] *nm* altar boy.

monarca [mo'narka] *nm/f* monarch, ruler.

monarquía [monar'kia] *nf* monarchy.

monárquico, a [mo'narkiko, a] *nm/f* royalist, monarchist.

monasterio [monas'terjo] *nm* monastery.

Moncloa [mon'kloa] *nf*: **la ~** *official residence of the Spanish Prime Minister.*

monda ['monda] *nf* (*poda*) pruning; (: *de árbol*) lopping; (: *de fruta*) peeling; (*cáscara*) skin; **¡es la ~!** (*fam: fantástico*)

it's great!; (: *el colmo*) it's the limit!;
(: *persona*: *gracioso*) he's a knockout!

mondadientes [monda'ðjentes] *nm inv*
toothpick.

mondar [mon'dar] *vt* (*limpiar*) to clean;
(*pelar*) to peel; ~**se** *vr*: ~**se de risa** (*fam*)
to split one's sides laughing.

moneda [mo'neða] *nf* (*tipo de dinero*)
currency, money; (*pieza*) coin; **una ~ de
50 céntimos** a 50-cent coin; ~ **de curso
legal** legal tender; ~ **extranjera** foreign
exchange; ~ **única** single currency; **es ~
corriente** (*fig*) it's common knowledge.

monedero [mone'ðero] *nm* purse.

monegasco, a [mone'ɣasko, a] *adj cpd* of *o*
from Monaco, Monegasque ♦ *nm/f*
Monegasque.

monetario, a [mone'tarjo, a] *adj*
monetary, financial.

monetarista [moneta'rista] *adj, nm/f*
monetarist.

mongólico, a [mon'goliko, a] *adj, nm/f*
Mongol.

monigote [moni'ɣote] *nm* (*dibujo*) doodle;
(*de papel*) cut-out figure; (*pey*) wimp; *V tb*
Día de los (Santos) Inocentes.

monitor [moni'tor] *nm* (*INFORM*) monitor;
~ **en color** colour monitor; ~ **fósfor
verde** green screen.

monja ['monxa] *nf* nun.

monje ['monxe] *nm* monk.

mono, a ['mono, a] *adj* (*bonito*) lovely,
pretty; (*gracioso*) nice, charming ♦ *nm/f*
monkey, ape ♦ *nm* dungarees *pl*; (*overo-
les*) overalls *pl*; (*fam*: *de droges*) cold
turkey; **una chica muy mona** a very pretty girl; **dormir la mona** to sleep it off.

monóculo [mo'nokulo] *nm* monocle.

monografía [monoɣra'fia] *nf* monograph.

monolingüe [mono'lingwe] *adj*
monolingual.

monólogo [mo'noloɣo] *nm* monologue.

monomando [mono'mando] *nm* (*tb*: **grifo
~**) mixer tap.

monoparental [monoparen'tal] *adj*: **familia
~** single-parent family.

monopatín [monopa'tin] *nm* skateboard.

monopolice [monopo'liθe] *etc vb V*
monopolizar.

monopolio [mono'poljo] *nm* monopoly; ~
total absolute monopoly.

monopolista [monopo'lista] *adj, nm/f*
monopolist.

monopolizar [monopoli'θar] *vt* to
monopolize.

monosílabo, a [mono'silaβo, a] *adj*
monosyllabic ♦ *nm* monosyllable.

monotonía [monoto'nia] *nf* (*sonido*)

monotone; (*fig*) monotony.

monótono, a [mo'notono, a] *adj*
monotonous.

mono-usuario, a [monou'swarjo, a] *adj*
(*INFORM*) single-user.

monóxido [mo'noksiðo] *nm* monoxide; ~
de carbono carbon monoxide.

Mons. *abr* (*REL*) = **Monseñor**.

monseñor [monse'ɲor] *nm* monsignor.

monserga [mon'serɣa] *nf* (*lenguaje
confuso*) gibberish; (*tonterías*) drivel.

monstruo ['monstrwo] *nm* monster ♦ *adj
inv* fantastic.

monstruoso, a [mons'trwoso, a] *adj*
monstrous.

monta ['monta] *nf* total, sum; **de poca ~**
unimportant, of little account.

montacargas [monta'karɣas] *nm inv*
service lift (*BRIT*), freight elevator (*US*).

montador [monta'ðor] *nm* (*para montar*)
mounting block; (*profesión*) fitter; (*CINE*)
film editor.

montaje [mon'taxe] *nm* assembly;
(*organización*) fitting up; (*TEAT*) décor;
(*CINE*) montage.

montante [mon'tante] *nm* (*poste*) upright;
(*soporte*) stanchion; (*ARQ*: *de puerta*)
transom; (: *de ventana*) mullion; (*suma*)
amount, total.

montaña [mon'taɲa] *nf* (*monte*) mountain;
(*sierra*) mountains *pl*, mountainous area;
(*AM*: *selva*) forest; ~ **rusa** roller coaster.

montañero, a [monta'ɲero, a] *adj*
mountain *cpd* ♦ *nm/f* mountaineer,
climber.

montañés, esa [monta'ɲes, esa] *adj*
mountain *cpd*; (*de Santander*) of *o* from
the Santander region ♦ *nm/f* highlander;
native *o* inhabitant of the Santander
region.

montañismo [monta'ɲismo] *nm*
mountaineering, climbing.

montañoso, a [monta'ɲoso, a] *adj*
mountainous.

montar [mon'tar] *vt* (*subir a*) to mount, get
on; (*caballo etc*) to ride; (*TEC*) to
assemble, put together; (*negocio*) to set
up; (*colocar*) to lift on to; (*CINE*: *película*)
to edit; (*TEAT*: *obra*) to stage, put on;
(*CULIN*: *batir*) to whip, beat
♦ *vi* to mount, get on; (*sobresalir*) to
overlap; ~ **en cólera** to get angry; ~ **un
número** *o* **numerito** to make a scene;
tanto monta it makes no odds.

montaraz [monta'raθ] *adj* mountain *cpd*,
highland *cpd*; (*pey*) uncivilized.

monte ['monte] *nm* (*montaña*) mountain;
(*bosque*) woodland; (*área sin cultivar*) wild

area, wild country; ~ **de piedad** pawnshop; ~ **alto** forest; ~ **bajo** scrub(land).

montera [mon'tera] *nf (sombrero)* cloth cap; *(de torero)* bullfighter's hat.

monto ['monto] *nm* total, amount.

montón [mon'ton] *nm* heap, pile; **un ~ de** *(fig)* heaps of, lots of; **a montones** by the score, galore.

montura [mon'tura] *nf (cabalgadura)* mount; *(silla)* saddle; *(arreos)* harness; *(de gafas)* frame.

monumental [monumen'tal] *adj (tb fig)* monumental; **zona ~** area of historical interest.

monumento [monu'mento] *nm* monument; *(de conmemoración)* memorial.

monzón [mon'θon] *nm* monsoon.

moña ['moɲa] *nf* hair ribbon.

moño ['moɲo] *nm (de pelo)* bun; **estar hasta el ~** *(fam)* to be fed up to the back teeth.

MOPTMA *nm abr* = *Ministerio de Obras Públicas, Transporte y Medio Ambiente.*

moqueta [mo'keta] *nf* fitted carpet.

moquillo [mo'kiʎo] *nm (enfermedad)* distemper.

mora ['mora] *nf (BOT)* mulberry; (: *zarzamora)* blackberry; *(COM)*: **en ~** in arrears.

morado, a [mo'raðo, a] *adj* purple, violet ♦ *nm* bruise ♦ *nf (casa)* dwelling, abode; **pasarlas moradas** to have a tough time of it.

moral [mo'ral] *adj* moral ♦ *nf (ética)* ethics *pl*; *(moralidad)* morals *pl*, morality; *(ánimo)* morale; **tener baja la ~** to be in low spirits.

moraleja [mora'lexa] *nf* moral.

moralice [mora'liθe] *etc vb V* **moralizar.**

moralidad [morali'ðað] *nf* morals *pl*, morality.

moralizar [morali'θar] *vt* to moralize.

morar [mo'rar] *vi* to live, dwell.

moratón [mora'ton] *nm* bruise.

moratoria [mora'torja] *nf* moratorium.

morbo ['morβo] *nm (fam)* morbid pleasure.

morbosidad [morβosi'ðað] *nf* morbidity.

morboso, a [mor'βoso, a] *adj* morbid.

morcilla [mor'θiʎa] *nf* blood sausage, ≈ black pudding *(BRIT)*.

mordaz [mor'ðaθ] *adj (crítica)* biting, scathing.

mordaza [mor'ðaθa] *nf (para la boca)* gag; *(TEC)* clamp.

morder [mor'ðer] *vt* to bite; *(mordisquear)* to nibble; *(fig: consumir)* to eat away, eat into ♦ *vi*, ~**se** *vr* to bite; **está que muerde**

he's hopping mad; ~**se la lengua** to hold one's tongue.

mordida [mor'ðiða] *nf (AM fam)* bribe.

mordisco [mor'ðisko] *nm* bite.

mordisquear [morðiske'ar] *vt* to nibble at.

moreno, a [mo'reno, a] *adj (color)* (dark) brown; *(de tez)* dark; *(de pelo ~)* dark-haired; *(negro)* black ♦ *nm/f (de tez)* dark-skinned man/woman; *(de pelo)* dark-haired man/woman.

morfina [mor'fina] *nf* morphine.

morfinómano, a [morfi'nomano, a] *adj* addicted to hard drugs ♦ *nm/f* drug addict.

morgue ['morɣe] *nf (AM)* mortuary *(BRIT)*, morgue *(US)*.

moribundo, a [mori'βundo, a] *adj* dying ♦ *nm/f* dying person.

morir [mo'rir] *vi* to die; *(fuego)* to die down; *(luz)* to go out; ~**se** *vr* to die; *(fig)* to be dying; *(FERRO etc: vías)* to end; *(calle)* to come out; **fue muerto a tiros/en un accidente** he was shot (dead)/was killed in an accident; ~ **de frío/hambre** to die of cold/starve to death; **¡me muero de hambre!** *(fig)* I'm starving!; ~**se por algo** to be dying for sth; ~**se por algn** to be crazy about sb.

mormón, ona [mor'mon, ona] *nm/f* Mormon.

moro, a ['moro, a] *adj* Moorish ♦ *nm/f* Moor; **¡hay ~s en la costa!** watch out!

moroso, a [mo'roso, a] *adj (lento)* slow ♦ *nm (COM)* bad debtor, defaulter; **deudor ~** *(COM)* slow payer.

morral [mo'rral] *nm* haversack.

morriña [mo'rriɲa] *nf* homesickness; **tener ~** to be homesick.

morro ['morro] *nm (ZOOL)* snout, nose; *(AUTO, AVIAT)* nose; *(fam: labio)* (thick) lip; **beber a ~** to drink from the bottle; **caer de ~** to nosedive; **estar de ~s (con algn)** to be in a bad mood (with sb); **tener ~** to have a nerve.

morrocotudo, a [morroko'tuðo, a] *adj (fam) (fantástico)* smashing; *(riña, golpe)* tremendous; *(fuerte)* strong; *(pesado)* heavy; *(difícil)* awkward.

morsa ['morsa] *nf* walrus.

morse ['morse] *nm* Morse (code).

mortadela [morta'ðela] *nf* mortadella, bologna sausage.

mortaja [mor'taxa] *nf* shroud; *(TEC)* mortise; *(AM)* cigarette paper.

mortal [mor'tal] *adj* mortal; *(golpe)* deadly.

mortalidad [mortali'ðað], **mortandad** [mortan'dað] *nf* mortality.

mortecino, a [morte'θino, a] *adj (débil)*

weak; (_luz_) dim; (_color_) dull.

mortero [mor'tero] _nm_ mortar.

mortífero, a [mor'tifero, a] _adj_ deadly, lethal.

mortificar [mortifi'kar] _vt_ to mortify; (_atormentar_) to torment.

mortifique [morti'fike] _etc vb_ V **mortificar.**

mortuorio, a [mor'tworjo, a] _adj_ mortuary, death _cpd._

mosaico [mo'saiko] _nm_ mosaic.

mosca ['moska] _nf_ fly; **por si las ~s** just in case; **estar ~** (_desconfiar_) to smell a rat; **tener la ~ en** o **detrás de la oreja** to be wary.

moscovita [mosko'ßita] _adj_ Muscovite, Moscow _cpd_ ♦ _nm/f_ Muscovite.

Moscú [mos'ku] _nm_ Moscow.

mosquear [moske'ar] (_fam_) _vt_ (_hacer sospechar_) to make suspicious; (_fastidiar_) to annoy; **~se** _vr_ (_enfadarse_) to get annoyed; (_ofenderse_) to take offence.

mosquita [mos'kita] _nf_: **parece una ~ muerta** he looks as though butter wouldn't melt in his mouth.

mosquitero [moski'tero] _nm_ mosquito net.

mosquito [mos'kito] _nm_ mosquito.

Mossos ['mosos] _nmpl_: **~ d'Esquadra** Catalan police; V _tb_ **policía.**

mostaza [mos'taθa] _nf_ mustard.

mosto ['mosto] _nm_ unfermented grape juice.

mostrador [mostra'ðor] _nm_ (_de tienda_) counter; (_de café_) bar.

mostrar [mos'trar] _vt_ to show; (_exhibir_) to display, exhibit; (_explicar_) to explain; **~se** _vr_: **~se amable** to be kind; to prove to be kind; **no se muestra muy inteligente** he doesn't seem (to be) very intelligent; **~ en pantalla** (_INFORM_) to display.

mota ['mota] _nf_ speck, tiny piece; (_en diseño_) dot.

mote ['mote] _nm_ (_apodo_) nickname.

motín [mo'tin] _nm_ (_del pueblo_) revolt, rising; (_del ejército_) mutiny.

motivación [motißa'θjon] _nf_ motivation.

motivar [moti'ßar] _vt_ (_causar_) to cause, motivate; (_explicar_) to explain, justify.

motivo [mo'tißo] _nm_ motive, reason; (_ARTE, MUS_) motif; **con ~ de** (_debido a_) because of; (_en ocasión de_) on the occasion of; (_con el fin de_) in order to; **sin ~** for no reason at all.

moto ['moto] _nf_, **motocicleta** [motoθi'kleta] _nf_ motorbike (_BRIT_), motorcycle.

motoneta [moto'neta] _nf_ (_AM_) Vespa ®.

motor, a [mo'tor, a] _adj_ (_TEC_) motive; (_ANAT_) motor ♦ _nm_ motor, engine; **~ a chorro** o **de reacción/de explosión** jet engine/internal combustion engine; **~ de búsqueda** (_INTERNET_) search engine ♦ _nf_ motorboat.

motorismo [moto'rismo] _nm_ motorcycling.

motorista [moto'rista] _nm/f_ (_esp AM_: _automovilista_) motorist; (: _motociclista_) motorcyclist.

motorizado, a [motori'θaðo, a] _adj_ motorized.

motosierra [moto'sjerra] _nf_ mechanical saw.

motriz [mo'triz] _adj_: **fuerza ~** motive power; (_fig_) driving force.

movedizo, a [moße'ðiθo, a] _adj_ (_inseguro_) unsteady; (_fig_) unsettled, changeable; (_persona_) fickle.

mover [mo'ßer] _vt_ to move; (_cambiar de lugar_) to shift; (_cabeza: para negar_) to shake; (: _para asentir_) to nod; (_accionar_) to drive; (_fig_) to cause, provoke; **~se** _vr_ to move; (_mar_) to get rough; (_viento_) to rise; (_fig: apurarse_) to get a move on; (: _transformarse_) to be on the move.

movible [mo'ßißle] _adj_ (_no fijo_) movable; (_móvil_) mobile; (_cambiadizo_) changeable.

movido, a [mo'ßiðo, a] _adj_ (_FOTO_) blurred; (_persona: activo_) active; (_mar_) rough; (_día_) hectic ♦ _nf_ move; **la movida madrileña** the Madrid scene.

móvil ['moßil] _adj_ mobile; (_pieza de máquina_) moving; (_mueble_) movable ♦ _nm_ (_motivo_) motive; (_teléfono_) mobile.

movilice [moßi'liθe] _etc vb_ V **movilizar.**

movilidad [moßili'ðað] _nf_ mobility.

movilizar [moßili'θar] _vt_ to mobilize.

movimiento [moßi'mjento] _nm_ (_gen, LITERATURA, POL_) movement; (_TEC_) motion; (_actividad_) activity; (_MUS_) tempo; **el M~** the Falangist Movement; **~ de bloques** (_INFORM_) block move; **~ de mercancías** (_COM_) turnover, volume of business; **~ obrero/sindical** workers'/ trade union movement; **~ sísmico** earth tremor.

Mozambique [moθam'bike] _nm_ Mozambique.

mozambiqueño, a [moθambi'keɲo, a] _adj, nm/f_ Mozambican.

mozo, a ['moθo, a] _adj_ (_joven_) young; (_soltero_) single, unmarried ♦ _nm/f_ (_joven_) youth, young man/girl; (_camarero_) waiter; (_camarera_) waitress; **~ de**

estación porter.
MP3 *nm* MP3; **reproductor (de) MP3** MP3
player.
MPAIAC [emepa'jak] *nm abr* (*ESP POL*)
= *Movimiento para la Autodeterminación y
la Independencia del Archipiélago
Canario.*
mucama [mu'kama] *nf* (*AM*) maid.
muchacho, a [mu'tʃatʃo, a] *nm/f* (*niño*)
boy/girl; (*criado*) servant/servant *o*
maid.
muchedumbre [mutʃe'ðumbre] *nf* crowd.
muchísimo, a [mu'tʃisimo, a] *adj*
(*superlativo de* **mucho**) lots and lots of,
ever so much ♦ *adv* ever so much.

═══════════ *PALABRA CLAVE*

mucho, a ['mutʃo, a] *adj* **1** (*cantidad*) a lot
of, much; (*número*) lots of, a lot of,
many; ~ **dinero** a lot of money; **hace** ~
calor it's very hot; **muchas amigas** lots *o*
a lot of *o* many friends
2 (*sg: fam*): **ésta es mucha casa para él**
this house is much too big for him;
había ~ **borracho** there were a lot *o* lots
of drunks
♦ *pron*: **tengo** ~ **que hacer** I've got a lot to
do; ~**s dicen que ...** a lot of people say
that ...; *V tb* **tener**
♦ *adv* **1**: **me gusta** ~ I like it a lot *o* very
much; **lo siento** ~ I'm very sorry; **come**
~ he eats a lot; **trabaja** ~ he works hard;
¿te vas a quedar ~? are you going to be
staying long?; ~ **más/menos** much *o* a
lot more/less
2 (*respuesta*) very; **¿estás cansado? – ¡**~**!**
are you tired? – very!
3 (*locuciones*): **como** ~ at (the) most; **el
mejor con** ~ by far the best; **¡ni** ~
menos! far from it!; **no es rico ni** ~
menos he's far from being rich
4: por ~ **que: por** ~ **que le creas** however
much *o* no matter how much you
believe him.

muda ['muða] *nf* (*de ropa*) change of
clothing; (*ZOOL*) moult; (*de serpiente*)
slough.
mudanza [mu'ðanθa] *nf* (*cambio*) change;
(*de casa*) move; **estar de** ~ to be moving.
mudar [mu'ðar] *vt* to change; (*ZOOL*) to
shed ♦ *vi* to change; ~**se** *vr* (*la ropa*) to
change; ~**se de casa** to move house.
mudo, a ['muðo, a] *adj* dumb; (*callado,
película*) silent; (*LING: letra*) mute;
(: *consonante*) voiceless; **quedarse** ~ (**de**)
(*fig*) to be dumb with; **quedarse** ~ **de
asombro** to be speechless.

mueble ['mweβle] *nm* piece of furniture;
~**s** *nmpl* furniture *sg.*
mueble-bar [mweβle'βar] *nm* cocktail
cabinet.
mueca ['mweka] *nf* face, grimace; **hacer**
~**s a** to make faces at.
muela ['mwela] *etc vb V* **moler** ♦ *nf* (*diente*)
tooth; (: *de atrás*) molar; (*de molino*)
millstone; (*de afilar*) grindstone; ~ **del
juicio** wisdom tooth.
muelle ['mweʎe] *adj* (*blando*) soft; (*fig*)
soft, easy ♦ *nm* spring; (*NAUT*) wharf;
(*malecón*) jetty.
muera ['mwera] *etc vb V* **morir**.
muerda ['mwerða] *etc vb V* **morder**.
muermo ['mwermo] *nm* (*fam*) wimp.
muerte ['mwerte] *nf* death; (*homicidio*)
murder; **dar** ~ **a** to kill; **de mala** ~ (*fam*)
lousy, rotten; **es la** ~ (*fam*) it's deadly
boring.
muerto, a ['mwerto, a] *pp de* **morir** ♦ *adj*
dead; (*color*) dull ♦ *nm/f* dead man/
woman; (*difunto*) deceased; (*cadáver*)
corpse; **cargar con el** ~ (*fam*) to carry
the can; **echar el** ~ **a algn** to pass the
buck; **hacer el** ~ (*nadando*) to float; **estar**
~ **de cansancio** to be dead tired.
muesca ['mweska] *nf* nick.
muestra ['mwestra] *etc vb V* **mostrar** ♦ *nf*
(*señal*) indication, sign; (*demostración*)
demonstration; (*prueba*) proof;
(*estadística*) sample; (*modelo*) model,
pattern; (*testimonio*) token; **dar** ~**s de** to
show signs of; ~ **al azar** (*COM*) random
sample.
muestrario [mwes'trarjo] *nm* collection of
samples; (*exposición*) showcase.
muestreo [mwes'treo] *nm* sample,
sampling.
mueva [mweβa] *etc vb V* **mover**.
mugir [mu'xir] *vi* (*vaca*) to moo.
mugre ['muxre] *nf* dirt, filth, muck.
mugriento, a [mu'xrjento, a] *adj* dirty,
filthy mucky.
mugroso, a [mux'roso, a] *adj* (*AM*) filthy,
grubby.
muja ['muxa] *etc vb V* **mugir**.
mujer [mu'xer] *nf* woman; (*esposa*) wife.
mujeriego [muxe'rjeɣo] *nm* womaniser.
mula ['mula] *nf* mule.
mulato, a [mu'lato, a] *adj, nm/f* mulatto.
muleta [mu'leta] *nf* (*para andar*) crutch;
(*TAUR*) stick with red cape attached.
muletilla [mule'tiʎa] *nf* (*palabra*) pet word,
tag; (*de cómico*) catch phrase.
mullido, a [mu'ʎiðo, a] *adj* (*cama*) soft;
(*hierba*) soft, springy.
multa ['multa] *nf* fine; **echar** *o* **poner una** ~

a to fine.

multar [mul'tar] *vt* to fine; (*DEPORTE*) to penalize.

multiacceso [multjak'θeso] *adj* (*INFORM*) multi-access.

multicine [multi'θine] *nm* multiscreen cinema.

multicolor [multiko'lor] *adj* multicoloured.

multimillonario, a [multimiʎo'narjo, a] *adj* (*contrato*) multimillion pound o dollar *cpd* ♦ *nm/f* multimillionaire/-millionairess.

multinacional [multinaθjo'nal] *adj, nf* multinational.

múltiple ['multiple] *adj* multiple; (*pl*) many, numerous; **de tarea** ~ (*INFORM*) multi-tasking; **de usuario** ~ (*INFORM*) multi-user.

multiplicar [multipli'kar] *vt* (*MAT*) to multiply; (*fig*) to increase; ~**se** *vr* (*BIO*) to multiply; (*fig*) to be everywhere at once.

multiplique [multi'plike] *etc vb V* **multiplicar**.

múltiplo ['multiplo] *adj, nm* multiple.

multitud [multi'tuð] *nf* (*muchedumbre*) crowd; ~ **de** lots of.

multitudinario, a [multituði'narjo, a] *adj* (*numeroso*) multitudinous; (*de masa*) mass *cpd*.

mundanal [munda'nal] *adj* worldly; **alejarse del** ~ **ruido** to get away from it all.

mundano, a [mun'dano, a] *adj* worldly; (*de moda*) fashionable.

mundial [mun'djal] *adj* world-wide, universal; (*guerra, récord*) world *cpd*.

mundialización [mundjaliθa'θjon] *nf* globalization.

mundialmente [mundjal'mente] *adv* worldwide; ~ **famoso** world-famous.

mundo ['mundo] *nm* world; (*ámbito*) world, circle; **el otro** ~ the next world; **el** ~ **del espectáculo** show business; **todo el** ~ everybody; **tener** ~ to be experienced, know one's way around; **el** ~ **es un pañuelo** it's a small world; **no es nada del otro** ~ it's nothing special; **se le cayó el** ~ (**encima**) his world fell apart.

Munich ['munitʃ] *nm* Munich.

munición [muni'θjon] *nf* (*MIL: provisiones*) stores *pl*, supplies *pl*; (: *de armas*) ammunition.

municipal [muniθi'pal] *adj* (*elección*) municipal; (*concejo*) town *cpd*, local; (*piscina etc*) public ♦ *nm* (*guardia*) policeman.

municipio [muni'θipjo] *nm* (*ayuntamiento*) town council, corporation; (*territorio administrativo*) town, municipality.

muñeca [mu'ɲeka] *nf* (*ANAT*) wrist; (*juguete*) doll.

muñeco [mu'ɲeko] *nm* (*figura*) figure; (*marioneta*) puppet; (*fig*) puppet, pawn; (*niño*) pretty little boy; ~ **de nieve** snowman.

muñequera [muɲe'kera] *nf* wristband.

muñón [mu'ɲon] *nm* (*ANAT*) stump.

mural [mu'ral] *adj* mural, wall *cpd* ♦ *nm* mural.

muralla [mu'raʎa] *nf* (*city*) wall(s) (*pl*).

murciano, a [mur'θjano, a] *adj* of o from Murcia ♦ *nm/f* native o inhabitant of Murcia.

murciélago [mur'θjelaɣo] *nm* bat.

murga ['murɣa] *nf* (*banda*) band of street musicians; **dar la** ~ to be a nuisance.

murmullo [mur'muʎo] *nm* murmur(ing); (*cuchicheo*) whispering; (*de arroyo*) murmur, rippling; (*de hojas, viento*) rustle, rustling; (*ruido confuso*) hum(ming).

murmuración [murmura'θjon] *nf* gossip; (*críticas*) backbiting.

murmurador, a [murmura'ðor, a] *adj* gossiping; (*criticón*) backbiting ♦ *nm/f* gossip; backbiter.

murmurar [murmu'rar] *vi* to murmur, whisper; (*criticar*) to criticize; (*cotillear*) to gossip.

muro ['muro] *nm* wall; ~ **de contención** retaining wall.

mus [mus] *nm* card game.

musaraña [musa'raɲa] *nf* (*ZOOL*) shrew; (*insecto*) creepy-crawly; **pensar en las** ~**s** to daydream.

muscular [musku'lar] *adj* muscular.

músculo ['muskulo] *nm* muscle.

musculoso, a [musku'loso, a] *adj* muscular.

museo [mu'seo] *nm* museum; ~ **de arte** o **de pintura** art gallery; ~ **de cera** waxworks.

musgo ['musɣo] *nm* moss.

musical [musi'kal] *adj, nm* musical.

músico, a ['musiko, a] *adj* musical ♦ *nm/f* musician ♦ *nf* music; **irse con la música a otra parte** to clear off.

musitar [musi'tar] *vt, vi* to mutter, mumble.

muslo ['muslo] *nm* thigh; (*de pollo*) leg, drumstick.

mustio, a ['mustjo, a] *adj* (*persona*) depressed, gloomy; (*planta*) faded, withered.

musulmán, ana [musul'man, ana] *nm/f* Moslem, Muslim.

mutación [muta'θjon] *nf* (*BIO*) mutation;

(: *cambio*) (sudden) change.

mutilar [muti'lar] *vt* to mutilate; (*a una persona*) to maim.

mutis ['mutis] *nm inv* (*TEAT*) exit; **hacer ~** (*TEAT: retirarse*) to exit, go off; (*fig*) to say nothing.

mutismo [mu'tismo] *nm* silence.

mutualidad [mutwali'ðað] *nf* (*reciprocidad*) mutual character; (*asociación*) friendly *o* benefit (*US*) society.

mutuamente [mutwa'mente] *adv* mutually.

mutuo, a ['mutwo, a] *adj* mutual.

muy [mwi] *adv* very; (*demasiado*) too; **M~ Señor mío** Dear Sir; **~ bien** (*de acuerdo*) all right; **~ de noche** very late at night; **eso es ~ de él** that's just like him; **eso es ~ español** that's typically Spanish.

Nn

N, n ['ene] *nf* (*letra*) N, n; **N de Navarra** N for Nellie (*BRIT*) *o* Nan (*US*).

N *abr* (= *norte*) N.

N. *abr* (= *noviembre*) Nov; (*AM*: = *moneda nacional*) local currency; **le entregaron sólo N.$2.000** they only gave him $2000 pesos.

N.º *abr* (= *número*) No.

n. *abr* (*LING*: = *nombre*) n; (= *nacido*) b.

n/ *abr* = **nuestro, a.**

nabo ['naßo] *nm* turnip.

nácar ['nakar] *nm* mother-of-pearl.

nacer [na'θer] *vi* to be born; (*huevo*) to hatch; (*vegetal*) to sprout; (*río*) to rise; (*fig*) to begin, originate, have its origins; **nació para poeta** he was born to be a poet; **nadie nace enseñado** we all have to learn; **nació una sospecha en su mente** a suspicion formed in her mind.

nacido, a [na'θiðo, a] *adj* born; **recién ~** newborn.

naciente [na'θjente] *adj* new, emerging; (*sol*) rising.

nacimiento [naθi'mjento] *nm* birth; (*fig*) birth, origin; (*de Navidad*) Nativity; (*linaje*) descent, family; (*de río*) source; **ciego de ~** blind from birth.

nación [na'θjon] *nf* nation; (*pueblo*) people; **Naciones Unidas** United Nations.

nacional [naθjo'nal] *adj* national; (*COM*, *ECON*) domestic, home *cpd*.

nacionalice [naθjona'liθe] *etc vb V* **nacionalizar.**

nacionalidad [naθjonali'ðað] *nf* nationality; (*ESP POL*) autonomous region.

nacionalismo [naθjona'lismo] *nm* nationalism.

nacionalista [naθjona'lista] *adj, nm/f* nationalist.

nacionalizar [naθjonali'θar] *vt* to nationalize; **~se** *vr* (*persona*) to become naturalized.

nada ['naða] *pron* nothing ♦ *adv* not at all, in no way ♦ *nf* nothingness; **no decir ~** (*más*) to say nothing (else), not to say anything (else); **¡~ más!** that's all; **de ~** don't mention it; **~ de eso** nothing of the kind; **antes de ~** right away; **como si ~** as if it didn't matter; **no ha sido ~** it's nothing; **la ~** the void.

nadador, a [naða'ðor, a] *nm/f* swimmer.

nadar [na'ðar] *vi* to swim; **~ en abundancia** (*fig*) to be rolling in money.

nadie ['naðje] *pron* nobody, no-one; **~ habló** nobody spoke; **no había ~** there was nobody there, there wasn't anybody there; **es un don ~** he's a nobody *o* nonentity.

nadita [na'ðita] (*esp AM: fam*) = **nada.**

nado ['naðo]: **a ~** *adv*: **pasar a ~** to swim across.

nafta ['nafta] *nf* (*AM*) petrol (*BRIT*), gas(oline) (*US*).

naftalina [nafta'lina] *nf*: **bolas de ~** mothballs.

náhuatl ['nawatl] *adj, nm* Nahuatl.

naipe ['naipe] *nm* (playing) card; **~s** *nmpl* cards.

nal. *abr* (= *nacional*) nat.

nalgas ['nalɣas] *nfpl* buttocks.

Namibia [na'mißja] *nf* Namibia.

nana ['nana] *nf* lullaby.

napias ['napjas] *nfpl* (*fam*) conk *sg*.

Nápoles ['napoles] *nf* Naples.

napolitano, a [napoli'tano, a] *adj of o* from Naples, Neapolitan ♦ *nm/f* Neapolitan.

naranja [na'ranxa] *adj inv, nf* orange; **media ~** (*fam*) better half; **¡~s de la China!** nonsense!

naranjada [naran'xaða] *nf* orangeade.

naranjo [na'ranxo] *nm* orange tree.

Narbona [nar'ßona] *nf* Narbonne.

narcisista [narθi'sista] *adj* narcissistic.

narciso [nar'θiso] *nm* narcissus.

narcotice [narko'tiθe] *etc vb V* **narcotizar.**

narcótico, a [nar'kotiko, a] *adj, nm* narcotic.

narcotizar [narkoti'θar] *vt* to drug.
narcotraficante [narkotrafi'kante] *nm/f* narcotics *o* drug trafficker.
narcotráfico [narko'trafiko] *nm* narcotics *o* drug trafficking.
nardo ['narðo] *nm* lily.
narices [na'riθes] *nfpl V* **nariz**.
narigón, ona [nari'ɣon, ona], **narigudo, a** [nari'ɣuðo, a] *adj* big-nosed.
nariz [na'riθ] *nf* nose; **narices** *nfpl* nostrils; **¡narices!** *(fam)* rubbish!; **delante de las narices de algn** under one's (very) nose; **estar hasta las narices** to be completely fed up; **meter las narices en algo** to poke one's nose into sth.
narración [narra'θjon] *nf* narration.
narrador, a [narra'ðor, a] *nm/f* narrator.
narrar [na'rrar] *vt* to narrate, recount.
narrativo, a [narra'tiβo, a] *adj* narrative
♦ *nf* narrative, story.
nasal [na'sal] *adj* nasal.
N.ª S.ra *abr = Nuestra Señora*.
nata ['nata] *nf* cream *(tb fig)*; *(en leche cocida etc)* skin; **~ batida** whipped cream.
natación [nata'θjon] *nf* swimming.
natal [na'tal] *adj* natal; *(país)* native; **ciudad ~** home town.
natalicio [nata'liθjo] *nm* birthday.
natalidad [natali'ðað] *nf* birth rate.
natillas [na'tiʎas] *nfpl* (egg) custard *sg*.
natividad [natiβi'ðað] *nf* nativity.
nativo, a [na'tiβo, a] *adj, nm/f* native.
nato, a ['nato, a] *adj* born; **un músico ~** a born musician.
natural [natu'ral] *adj* natural; *(fruta etc)* fresh ♦ *nm/f* native ♦ *nm* disposition, temperament; **buen ~** good nature; **fruta al ~** fruit in its own juice.
naturaleza [natura'leθa] *nf* nature; *(género)* nature, kind; **~ muerta** still life.
naturalice [natura'liθe] *etc vb V* **naturalizarse**.
naturalidad [naturali'ðað] *nf* naturalness.
naturalización [naturaliθa'θjon] *nf* naturalization.
naturalizarse [naturali'θarse] *vr* to become naturalized; *(aclimatarse)* to become acclimatized.
naturalmente [natural'mente] *adv* naturally; **¡~!** of course!
naturista [natu'rista] *adj (MED)* naturopathic ♦ *nm/f* naturopath.
naufragar [naufra'ɣar] *vi (barco)* to sink; *(gente)* to be shipwrecked; *(fig)* to fail.
naufragio [nau'fraxjo] *nm* shipwreck.
náufrago, a ['naufraɣo, a] *nm/f* castaway, shipwrecked person.
naufrague [nau'fraɣe] *etc vb V* **naufragar**.

náusea ['nausea] *nf* nausea; **me da ~s** it makes me feel sick.
nauseabundo, a [nausea'βundo, a] *adj* nauseating, sickening.
náutico, a ['nautiko, a] *adj* nautical; **club ~** sailing *o* yacht club ♦ *nf* navigation, seamanship.
navaja [na'βaxa] *nf (cortaplumas)* clasp knife *(BRIT)*, penknife; **~ (de afeitar)** razor.
navajazo [naβa'xaθo] *nm (herida)* gash; *(golpe)* slash.
naval [na'βal] *adj (MIL)* naval; **construcción ~** shipbuilding; **sector ~** shipbuilding industry.
Navarra [na'βarra] *nf* Navarre.
navarro, a [na'βarro, a] *adj* of *o* from Navarre, Navarrese ♦ *nm/f* Navarrese ♦ *nm (LING)* Navarrese.
nave ['naβe] *nf (barco)* ship, vessel; *(ARQ)* nave; **~ espacial** spaceship; **quemar las ~s** to burn one's boats.
navegación [naβeɣa'θjon] *nf* navigation; *(viaje)* sea journey; **~ aérea** air traffic; **~ costera** coastal shipping; **~ fluvial** river navigation.
navegador [naβeɣa'ðor] *nm (INFORM)* browser.
navegante [naβe'ɣante] *nm/f* navigator.
navegar [naβe'ɣar] *vi (barco)* to sail; *(avión)* to fly ♦ *vt* to sail; to fly; *(dirigir el rumbo de)* to navigate.
navegue [na'βeɣe] *etc vb V* **navegar**.
Navidad [naβi'ðað] *nf* Christmas; **~es** *nfpl* Christmas time *sg*; **día de ~** Christmas Day; **por ~es** at Christmas (time); **¡felices ~es!** Merry Christmas.
navideño, a [naβi'ðeɲo, a] *adj* Christmas *cpd*.
navío [na'βio] *nm* ship.
nazi ['naθi] *adj, nm/f* Nazi.
nazismo [na'θismo] *nm* Nazism.
n/cta *abr (COM) = nuestra cuenta*.
N. de la R. *abr (= nota de la redacción)* editor's note.
N. de la T./del T. *abr (= nota de la traductora/del traductor)* translator's note.
NE *abr (= nor(d)este)* NE.
neblina [ne'βlina] *nf* mist.
nebuloso, a [neβu'loso, a] *adj* foggy; *(calinoso)* misty; *(indefinido)* nebulous, vague ♦ *nf* nebula.
necedad [neθe'ðað] *nf* foolishness; *(una ~)* foolish act.
necesario, a [neθe'sarjo, a] *adj* necessary; **si fuera *o* fuese ~** if need(s) be.
neceser [neθe'ser] *nm* vanity case; *(bolsa grande)* holdall.
necesidad [neθesi'ðað] *nf* need; *(lo*

inevitable) necessity; (*miseria*) poverty, need; **en caso de** ~ in case of need *o* emergency; **hacer sus ~es** to relieve o.s.

necesitado, a [neθesi'taðo, a] *adj* needy, poor; ~ **de** in need of.

necesitar [neθesi'tar] *vt* to need, require ♦ *vi*: ~ **de** to have need of; ~**se** *vr* to be needed; (*anuncios*) **"necesítase coche"** "car wanted".

necio, a ['neθjo, a] *adj* foolish ♦ *nm/f* fool.

necrología [nekrolo'xia] *nf* obituary.

necrópolis [ne'kropolis] *nf inv* cemetery.

néctar ['nektar] *nm* nectar.

nectarina [nekta'rina] *nf* nectarine.

neerlandés, esa [neerlan'des, esa] *adj* Dutch ♦ *nm/f* Dutchman/woman ♦ *nm* (*LING*) Dutch; **los neerlandeses** the Dutch.

nefando, a [ne'fando, a] *adj* unspeakable.

nefasto, a [ne'fasto, a] *adj* ill-fated, unlucky.

negación [neɣa'θjon] *nf* negation; (*LING*) negative; (*rechazo*) refusal, denial.

negado, a [ne'ɣaðo, a] *adj*: ~ **para** inept at, unfitted for.

negar [ne'ɣar] *vt* (*renegar, rechazar*) to refuse; (*prohibir*) to refuse, deny; (*desmentir*) to deny; ~**se** *vr*: ~**se a hacer algo** to refuse to do sth.

negativo, a [neɣa'tiβo, a] *adj* negative ♦ *nm* (*FOTO*) negative; (*MAT*) minus ♦ *nf* (*gen*) negative; (*rechazo*) refusal, denial; **negativa rotunda** flat refusal.

negligencia [neɣli'xenθja] *nf* negligence.

negligente [neɣli'xente] *adj* negligent.

negociable [neɣo'θjaβle] *adj* negotiable.

negociación [neɣoθja'θjon] *nf* negotiation.

negociado [neɣo'θjaðo] *nm* department, section.

negociante [neɣo'θjante] *nm/f* businessman/woman.

negociar [neɣo'θjar] *vt, vi* to negotiate; ~ **en** to deal in, trade in.

negocio [ne'ɣoθjo] *nm* (*COM*) business; (*asunto*) affair, business; (*operación comercial*) deal, transaction; (*AM*) shop, store; (*lugar*) place of business; **los ~s** business *sg*; **hacer** ~ to do business; **el ~ del libro** the book trade; ~ **autorizado** licensed trade; **hombre de ~s** businessman; ~ **sucio** shady deal; **hacer un buen** ~ to pull off a profitable deal; **¡mal ~!** it looks bad!

negra ['neɣra] *nf V* **negro** ♦ *nf* (*MUS*) crotchet.

negrita [ne'ɣrita] *nf* (*TIP*) bold face; **en** ~ in bold (type).

negro, a ['neɣro, a] *adj* black; (*suerte*)

awful, atrocious; (*humor etc*) sad; (*lúgubre*) gloomy ♦ *nm* (*color*) black ♦ *nm/f* Negro/Negress, black ♦ *nf* (*MUS*) crotchet; ~ **como la boca del lobo** pitch-black; **estoy** ~ **con esto** I'm getting desperate about it; **ponerse** ~ (*fam*) to get cross.

negrura [ne'ɣrura] *nf* blackness.

negué [ne'ɣe], **neguemos** [ne'ɣemos] *etc vb V* **negar**.

nene, a ['nene, a] *nm/f* baby, small child.

nenúfar [ne'nufar] *nm* water lily.

neologismo [neolo'xismo] *nm* neologism.

neón [ne'on] *nm* neon.

neoyorquino, a [neojor'kino, a] *adj* New York *cpd* ♦ *nm/f* New Yorker.

neozelandés, esa [neoθelan'des, esa] *adj* New Zealand *cpd* ♦ *nm/f* New Zealander.

nepotismo [nepo'tismo] *nm* nepotism.

nervio ['nerβjo] *nm* (*ANAT*) nerve; (: *tendón*) tendon; (*fig*) vigour; (*TEC*) rib; **crispar los ~s a algn, poner los ~s de punta a algn** to get on sb's nerves.

nerviosismo [nerβjo'sismo] *nm* nervousness, nerves *pl*.

nervioso, a [ner'βjoso, a] *adj* nervous; (*sensible*) nervy, highly-strung; (*impaciente*) restless; **¡no te pongas ~!** take it easy!

nervudo, a [ner'βuðo, a] *adj* tough; (*mano*) sinewy.

neto, a ['neto, a] *adj* clear; (*limpio*) clean; (*COM*) net.

neumático, a [neu'matiko, a] *adj* pneumatic ♦ *nm* (*ESP*) tyre (*BRIT*), tire (*US*); ~ **de recambio** spare tyre.

neumonía [neumo'nia] *nf* pneumonia; ~ **asiática** SARS.

neura ['neura] (*fam*) *nm/f* (*persona*) neurotic ♦ *nf* (*obsesión*) obsession.

neuralgia [neu'ralxja] *nf* neuralgia.

neurálgico, a [neu'ralxiko, a] *adj* neuralgic; (*fig: centro*) nerve *cpd*.

neurastenia [neuras'tenja] *nf* neurasthenia; (*fig*) excitability.

neurasténico, a [neuras'teniko, a] *adj* neurasthenic; excitable.

neurólogo, a [neu'roloɣo, a] *nm/f* neurologist.

neurona [neu'rona] *nf* neuron.

neurosis [neu'rosis] *nf inv* neurosis.

neurótico, a [neu'rotiko, a] *adj, nm/f* neurotic.

neutral [neu'tral] *adj* neutral.

neutralice [neutra'liθe] *etc vb V* **neutralizar**.

neutralizar [neutrali'θar] *vt* to neutralize; (*contrarrestar*) to counteract.

neutro, a ['neutro, a] *adj* (*BIO, LING*) neuter.

neutrón [neu'tron] _nm_ neutron.

nevado, a [ne'ßaðo, a] _adj_ snow-covered; (_montaña_) snow-capped; (_fig_) snowy, snow-white ♦ _nf_ snowstorm; (_caída de nieve_) snowfall.

nevar [ne'ßar] _vi_ to snow ♦ _vt_ (_fig_) to whiten.

nevera [ne'ßera] _nf_ (_ESP_) refrigerator (_BRIT_), icebox (_US_).

nevisca [ne'ßiska] _nf_ flurry of snow.

nexo [ˈnekso] _nm_ link, connection.

n/f _abr_ (_COM_) = _nuestro favor._

ni [ni] _conj_ nor, neither; (_tb:_ ~ **siquiera**) not even; ~ **que** not even if; ~ **blanco** ~ **negro** neither white nor black; ~ **el uno** ~ **el otro** neither one nor the other.

Nicaragua [nika'raɣwa] _nf_ Nicaragua.

nicaragüense [nikara'ɣwense] _adj, nm/f_ Nicaraguan.

nicho [ˈnitʃo] _nm_ niche.

nick [nik] _nm_ (_INTERNET_) nickname, user name, nick.

nicotina [niko'tina] _nf_ nicotine.

nido [ˈniðo] _nm_ nest; (_fig_) hiding place; ~ **de ladrones** den of thieves.

niebla [ˈnjeßla] _nf_ fog; (_neblina_) mist; **hay** ~ it is foggy.

niego [ˈnjeɣo] _etc_, **niegue** [ˈnjeɣe] _etc vb V_ **negar**.

nieto, a [ˈnjeto, a] _nm/f_ grandson/daughter; ~**s** _nmpl_ grandchildren.

nieve [ˈnjeße] _etc vb V_ **nevar** ♦ _nf_ snow; (_AM_) ice cream; **copo de** ~ snowflake.

N.I.F. _nm abr_ (= _Número de Identificación Fiscal_) ID number used for tax purposes.

Nigeria [niˈxerja] _nf_ Nigeria.

nigeriano, a [nixe'rjano, a] _adj, nm/f_ Nigerian.

nigromancia [nixro'manθja] _nf_ necromancy, black magic.

nihilista [nii'lista] _adj_ nihilistic ♦ _nm_ nihilist.

Nilo [ˈnilo] _nm:_ **el (Río)** ~ the Nile.

nimbo [ˈnimbo] _nm_ (_aureola_) halo; (_nube_) nimbus.

nimiedad [nimje'ðað] _nf_ small-mindedness; (_trivialidad_) triviality; (_una_ ~) trifle, tiny detail.

nimio, a [ˈnimjo, a] _adj_ trivial, insignificant.

ninfa [ˈninfa] _nf_ nymph.

ninfómana [nin'fomana] _nf_ nymphomaniac.

ninguno, a [nin'ɡuno, a] _adj_ (**ningún** _delante de nmsg_) no ♦ _pron_ (_nadie_) nobody; (_ni uno_) none, not one; (_ni uno ni otro_) neither; **de ninguna manera** by no means, not at all; **no voy a ninguna parte** I'm not going

anywhere.

niña [ˈnina] _nf V_ **niño.**

niñera [ni'nera] _nf_ nursemaid, nanny.

niñería [nine'ria] _nf_ childish act.

niñez [ni'neθ] _nf_ childhood; (_infancia_) infancy.

niño, a [ˈnino, a] _adj_ (_joven_) young; (_inmaduro_) immature ♦ _nm_ (_chico_) boy, child ♦ _nf_ girl, child; (_ANAT_) pupil; **los** ~**s** the children; ~ **bien** rich kid; ~ **expósito** foundling; ~ **de pecho** babe-in-arms; ~ **prodigio** child prodigy; **de** ~ as a child; **ser el** ~ **mimado de algn** to be sb's pet; **ser la niña de los ojos de algn** to be the apple of sb's eye.

nipón, ona [ni'pon, ona] _adj, nm/f_ Japanese; **los nipones** the Japanese.

níquel [ˈnikel] _nm_ nickel.

niquelar [nike'lar] _vt_ (_TEC_) to nickel-plate.

níspero [ˈnispero] _nm_ medlar.

nitidez [niti'ðeθ] _nf_ (_claridad_) clarity; (: _de atmósfera_) brightness; (: _de imagen_) sharpness.

nítido, a [ˈnitiðo, a] _adj_ bright; (_fig_) pure; (_imagen_) clear, sharp.

nitrato [ni'trato] _nm_ nitrate.

nitrógeno [ni'troxeno] _nm_ nitrogen.

nitroglicerina [nitroxliθe'rina] _nf_ nitroglycerine.

nivel [ni'ßel] _nm_ (_GEO_) level; (_norma_) level, standard; (_altura_) height; ~ **de aceite** oil level; ~ **de aire** spirit level; ~ **de vida** standard of living; **al** ~ **de** on a level with, at the same height as; (_fig_) on a par with; **a 900m sobre el** ~ **del mar** at 900m above sea level.

nivelado, a [niße'laðo, a] _adj_ level, flat; (_TEC_) flush.

nivelar [niße'lar] _vt_ to level out; (_fig_) to even up; (_COM_) to balance.

n/l. _abr_ (_COM_) = _nuestra letra._

NNE _abr_ (= _nornordeste_) NNE.

NNO _abr_ (= _nornoroeste_) NNW.

NN.UU. _nfpl abr_ (= _Naciones Unidas_) UN _sg._

NO _abr_ (= _noroeste_) NW.

no [no] _adv_ no; (_con verbo_) not ♦ _excl_ no!; ~ **tengo nada** I don't have anything, I have nothing; ~ **es el mío** it's not mine; **ahora** ~ not now; ¿~ **lo sabes?** don't you know?; ~ **mucho** not much; ~ **bien termine, lo entregaré** as soon as I finish I'll hand it over; **¡a que** ~ **lo sabes!** I bet you don't know!; **¡cómo** ~**!** of course!; **pacto de** ~ **agresión** non-aggression pact; **los países** ~ **alineados** the non-aligned countries; **el** ~ **va más** the ultimate; **la** ~ **intervención** non-intervention.

n/o *abr* (*COM*) = *nuestra orden*.
noble ['noβle] *adj*, *nmf* noble; **los ~s** the
    nobility *sg*.
nobleza [noβ'leθa] *nf* nobility.
noche ['notʃe] *nf* night, night-time; (*la
    tarde*) evening; (*fig*) darkness; **de ~, por
    la ~** at night; **ayer por la ~** last night;
    esta ~ tonight; **(en) toda la ~** all night;
    hacer ~ en un sitio to spend the night in
    a place; **se hace de ~** it's getting dark.
Nochebuena [notʃe'βwena] *nf* Christmas
    Eve; *see boxed note*.

NOCHEBUENA

*On **Nochebuena** in Spanish homes family
members normally gather together for a
large supper and the more religiously
inclined attend "la misa del gallo" at
midnight. The tradition of receiving
Christmas presents from Santa Claus on
Christmas Eve is becoming more and
more widespread and is gradually
replacing the visit of "los Reyes Magos"
(the Three Wise Men) who bring gifts on 6
January.*

Nochevieja [notʃe'βjexa] *nf* New Year's
    Eve; *V tb* **uvas**.
noción [no'θjon] *nf* notion; **nociones** *nfpl*
    elements, rudiments.
nocivo, a [no'θiβo, a] *adj* harmful.
noctambulismo [noktambu'lismo] *nm*
    sleepwalking.
noctámbulo, a [nok'tambulo, a] *nmf*
    sleepwalker.
nocturno, a [nok'turno, a] *adj* (*de la noche*)
    nocturnal, night *cpd*; (*de la tarde*) evening
    cpd ♦ *nm* nocturne.
Noé [no'e] *nm* Noah.
nogal [no'ɣal] *nm* walnut tree; (*madera*)
    walnut.
nómada ['nomaða] *adj* nomadic ♦ *nmf*
    nomad.
nomás [no'mas] *adv*: (*AM: gen*) just; (: *tan
    sólo*) only; **así ~** (*AM fam*) just like that;
    ayer ~ only yesterday ♦ *conj* (*AM: en
    cuanto*) **~ se fue se acordó** no sooner had
    she left than she remembered.
nombramiento [nombra'mjento] *nm*
    naming; (*a un empleo*) appointment; (*POL
    etc*) nomination; (*MIL*) commission.
nombrar [nom'brar] *vt* (*gen*) to name;
    (*mencionar*) to mention; (*designar*) to
    appoint, nominate; (*MIL*) to commission.
nombre ['nombre] *nm* name; (*sustantivo*)
    noun; (*fama*) renown; **~ y apellidos** name
    in full; **~ común/propio** common/proper

noun; **~ de pila/de soltera** Christian/
    maiden name; **~ de fichero** (*INFORM*) file
    name; **en ~ de** in the name of, on behalf
    of; **sin ~** nameless; **su conducta no tiene
    ~** his behaviour is utterly despicable.
nomenclatura [nomenkla'tura] *nf*
    nomenclature.
nomeolvides [nomeol'βiðes] *nm inv*
    forget-me-not.
nómina ['nomina] *nf* (*lista*) list; (*COM: tb:
    ~s*) payroll.
nominal [nomi'nal] *adj* nominal; (*valor*)
    face *cpd*; (*LING*) noun *cpd*, substantival.
nominar [nomi'nar] *vt* to nominate.
nominativo, a [nomina'tiβo, a] *adj* (*LING*)
    nominative; (*COM*): **un cheque ~ a X** a
    cheque made out to X.
non [non] *adj* odd, uneven ♦ *nm* odd
    number; **pares y ~es** odds and evens.
nonagésimo, a [nona'xesimo, a] *num*
    ninetieth.
nono, a ['nono, a] *num* ninth.
nordeste [nor'ðeste] *adj* north-east,
    north-eastern, north-easterly ♦ *nm*
    north-east; (*viento*) north-east wind,
    north-easterly.
nórdico, a ['norðiko, a] *adj* (*del norte*)
    northern, northerly; (*escandinavo*)
    Nordic, Norse ♦ *nmf* northerner;
    (*escandinavo*) Norseman/woman ♦ *nm*
    (*LING*) Norse.
noreste [no'reste] *adj, nm* = **nordeste**.
noria ['norja] *nf* (*AGR*) waterwheel; (*de
    carnaval*) big (*BRIT*) o Ferris (*US*) wheel.
norma ['norma] *nf* standard, norm, rule;
    (*patrón*) pattern; (*método*) method.
normal [nor'mal] *adj* (*corriente*) normal;
    (*habitual*) usual, natural; (*TEC*) standard;
    Escuela N~ teacher training college;
    (gasolina) ~ two-star petrol.
normalice [norma'liθe] *etc vb V* **normalizar**.
normalidad [normali'ðað] *nf* normality.
normalización [normaliθa'θjon] *nf* (*COM*)
    standardization.
normalizar [normali'θar] *vt* (*reglamentar*) to
    normalize; (*COM, TEC*) to standardize;
    ~se *vr* to return to normal.
normalmente [normal'mente] *adv* (*con
    normalidad*) normally; (*habitualmente*)
    usually.
Normandía [norman'dia] *nf* Normandy.
normando, a [nor'mando, a] *adj, nmf*
    Norman.
normativo, a [norma'tiβo, a] *adj*: **es ~ en
    todos los coches nuevos** it is standard in
    all new cars ♦ *nf* regulations *pl*.
noroeste [noro'este] *adj* north-west,
    north-western, north-westerly ♦ *nm*

north-west; (*viento*) north-west wind, north-westerly.

norte ['norte] *adj* north, northern, northerly ♦ *nm* north; (*fig*) guide.

Norteamérica [nortea'merika] *nf* North America.

norteamericano, a [norteameri'kano, a] *adj, nm/f* (North) American.

norteño, a [nor'teɲo, a] *adj* northern ♦ *nm/f* northerner.

Noruega [no'rweɣa] *nf* Norway.

noruego, a [no'rweɣo, a] *adj, nm/f* Norwegian ♦ *nm* (*LING*) Norwegian.

nos [nos] *pron* (*directo*) us; (*indirecto*) (to) us; (*reflexivo*) (to) ourselves; (*recíproco*) (to) each other; ~ **levantamos a las 7** we get up at 7.

nosocomio [noso'komio] *nm* (*AM*) hospital.

nosotros, as [no'sotros, as] *pron* (*sujeto*) we; (*después de prep*) us; ~ (**mismos**) ourselves.

nostalgia [nos'talxja] *nf* nostalgia, homesickness.

nostálgico, a [nos'talxiko, a] *adj* nostalgic, homesick.

nota ['nota] *nf* note; (*ESCOL*) mark; (*de fin de año*) report; (*UNIV etc*) footnote; (*COM*) account; ~ **de aviso** advice note; ~ **de crédito/débito** credit/debit note; ~ **de gastos** expenses claim; ~ **de sociedad** gossip column; **tomar** ~**s** to take notes.

notable [no'taßle] *adj* noteworthy, notable; (*ESCOL etc*) outstanding ♦ *nm/f* notable.

notar [no'tar] *vt* to notice, note; (*percibir*) to feel; (*ver*) to see; ~**se** *vr* to be obvious; **se nota que** ... one observes that ....

notaría [nota'ria] *nf* (*profesión*) profession of notary; (*despacho*) notary's office.

notarial [nota'rjal] *adj* (*estilo*) legal; **acta** ~ affidavit.

notario [no'tarjo] *nm* notary; (*abogado*) solicitor.

noticia [no'tiθja] *nf* (*información*) piece of news; (*TV etc*) news item; **las** ~**s** the news *sg*; **según nuestras** ~**s** according to our information; **tener** ~**s de algn** to hear from sb.

noticiario [noti'θjarjo] *nm* (*CINE*) newsreel; (*TV*) news bulletin.

noticiero [noti'θjero] *nm* newspaper, gazette; (*AM*: *tb*: ~ **telediario**) news bulletin.

notificación [notifika'θjon] *nf* notification.

notificar [notifi'kar] *vt* to notify, inform.

notifique [noti'fike] *etc vb V* **notificar.**

notoriedad [notorje'ðað] *nf* fame, renown.

notorio, a [no'torjo, a] *adj* (*público*) well-known; (*evidente*) obvious.

nov. *abr* (= *noviembre*) Nov.

novatada [noßa'taða] *nf* (*burla*) teasing, hazing (*US*); **pagar la** ~ to learn the hard way.

novato, a [no'ßato, a] *adj* inexperienced ♦ *nm/f* beginner, novice.

novecientos, as [noße'θjentos, as] *num* nine hundred.

novedad [noße'ðað] *nf* (*calidad de nuevo*) newness, novelty; (*noticia*) piece of news; (*cambio*) change, (new) development; (*sorpresa*) surprise; ~**es** *nfpl* (*noticia*) latest (news) *sg*.

novedoso, a [noße'ðoso, a] *adj* novel.

novel [no'ßel] *adj* new; (*inexperto*) inexperienced ♦ *nm/f* beginner.

novela [no'ßela] *nf* novel; ~ **policíaca** detective story.

novelero, a [noße'lero, a] *adj* highly imaginative.

novelesco, a [noße'lesko, a] *adj* fictional; (*romántico*) romantic; (*fantástico*) fantastic.

novelista [noße'lista] *nm/f* novelist.

novelística [noße'listika] *nf*: **la** ~ fiction, the novel.

noveno, a [no'ßeno, a] *num* ninth.

noventa [no'ßenta] *num* ninety.

novia ['noßja] *nf V* **novio.**

noviazgo [no'ßjaθɣo] *nm* engagement.

novicio, a [no'ßiθjo, a] *nm/f* novice.

noviembre [no'ßjembre] *nm* November.

novilla [no'ßiʎa] *nf* heifer.

novillada [noßi'ʎaða] *nf* (*TAUR*) *bullfight with young bulls.*

novillero [noßi'ʎero] *nm* novice bullfighter.

novillo [no'ßiʎo] *nm* young bull, bullock; **hacer** ~**s** (*fam*) to play truant (*BRIT*) o hooky (*US*).

novio, a ['noßjo, a] *nm/f* boyfriend/girlfriend; (*prometido*) fiancé/fiancée; (*recién casado*) bridegroom/bride; **los** ~**s** the newly-weds.

novísimo, a [no'ßisimo, a] *adj superlativo de* **nuevo, a.**

NPI *nm abr* (*INFORM*: = *número personal de identificación*) PIN.

N. S. *abr* = *Nuestro Señor.*

ntra., ntro. *abr* = **nuestra, nuestro.**

NU *nfpl abr* (= *Naciones Unidas*) UN *sg*.

nubarrón [nußa'rron] *nm* storm cloud.

nube ['nuße] *nf* cloud; (*MED*: *ocular*) cloud, film; (*fig*) mass; **una** ~ **de críticas** a storm of criticism; **los precios están por las** ~**s** prices are sky-high; **estar en las** ~**s** to be away with the fairies.

nublado, a [nu'ßlaðo, a] *adj* cloudy ♦ *nm* storm cloud.

nublar [nu'ßlar] *vt* (*oscurecer*) to darken;

(*confundir*) to cloud; ~**se** *vr* to cloud over.

nuca ['nuka] *nf* nape of the neck.

nuclear [nukle'ar] *adj* nuclear.

nuclearizado, a [nukleari'θaðo, a] *adj*: **países ~s** countries possessing nuclear weapons.

núcleo ['nukleo] *nm* (*centro*) core; (*FÍSICA*) nucleus.

nudillo [nu'ðiʎo] *nm* knuckle.

nudista [nu'dista] *adj, nm/f* nudist.

nudo ['nuðo] *nm* knot; (*unión*) bond; (*de problema*) crux; (*FERRO*) junction; (*fig*) lump; ~ **corredizo** slipknot; **con un ~ en la garganta** with a lump in one's throat.

nudoso, a [nu'ðoso, a] *adj* knotty; (*tronco*) gnarled; (*bastón*) knobbly.

nueces ['nweθes] *nfpl de* **nuez**.

nuera ['nwera] *nf* daughter-in-law.

nuestro, a ['nwestro, a] *adj posesivo* our ♦ *pron* ours; ~ **padre** our father; **un amigo ~** a friend of ours; **es el ~** it's ours; **los ~s** our people; (*DEPORTE*) our *o* the local team *o* side.

nueva ['nweβa] *nf* V **nuevo**.

Nueva Escocia *nf* Nova Scotia.

nuevamente [nweβa'mente] *adv* (*otra vez*) again; (*de nuevo*) anew.

Nueva York [-'jork] *nf* New York.

Nueva Zeland(i)a [-θe'land(j)a] *nf* New Zealand.

nueve ['nweβe] *num* nine.

nuevo, a ['nweβo, a] *adj* (*gen*) new ♦ *nf* piece of news; **¿qué hay de ~?** (*fam*) what's new?; **de ~** again.

Nuevo Méjico *nm* New Mexico.

nuez [nweθ], *pl* **nueces** *nf* (*del nogal*) walnut; (*fruto*) nut; ~ **de Adán** Adam's apple; ~ **moscada** nutmeg.

nulidad [nuli'ðað] *nf* (*incapacidad*) incompetence; (*abolición*) nullity; (*individuo*) nonentity; **es una ~** he's a dead loss.

nulo, a ['nulo, a] *adj* (*inepto, torpe*) useless; (*inválido*) (null and) void; (*DEPORTE*) drawn, tied.

núm. *abr* (= *número*) no.

numen ['numen] *nm* inspiration.

numeración [numera'θjon] *nf* (*cifras*) numbers *pl*; (*arábiga, romana etc*) numerals *pl*; ~ **de línea** (*INFORM*) line numbering.

numerador [numera'ðor] *nm* (*MAT*) numerator.

numeral [nume'ral] *nm* numeral.

numerar [nume'rar] *vt* to number; ~**se** *vr* (*MIL etc*) to number off.

numerario, a [nume'rarjo, a] *adj* numerary; **profesor ~** permanent *o*

tenured member of teaching staff ♦ *nm* hard cash.

numérico, a [nu'meriko, a] *adj* numerical.

número ['numero] *nm* (*gen*) number; (*tamaño: de zapato*) size; (*ejemplar: de diario*) number, issue; (*TEAT etc*) turn, act, number; **sin ~** numberless, unnumbered; ~ **binario** (*INFORM*) binary number; ~ **de matrícula/de teléfono** registration/telephone number; ~ **personal de identificación** (*INFORM etc*) personal identification number; ~ **de serie** (*COM*) serial number; ~ **atrasado** back number.

numeroso, a [nume'roso, a] *adj* numerous; **familia numerosa** large family.

numerus ['numerus] *nm*: ~ **clausus** (*UNIV*) restricted *o* selective entry.

nunca ['nunka] *adv* (*jamás*) never; (*con verbo negativo*) ever; ~ **lo pensé** I never thought it; **no viene ~** he never comes; ~ **más** never again.

nuncio ['nunθjo] *nm* (*REL*) nuncio.

nupcial [nup'θjal] *adj* wedding *cpd*.

nupcias ['nupθjas] *nfpl* wedding *sg*, nuptials.

nutria ['nutrja] *nf* otter.

nutrición [nutri'θjon] *nf* nutrition.

nutrido, a [nu'triðo, a] *adj* (*alimentado*) nourished; (*fig: grande*) large; (*abundante*) abundant; **mal ~** undernourished; ~ **de** full of.

nutrir [nu'trir] *vt* to feed, nourish; (*fig*) to feed, strengthen.

nutritivo, a [nutri'tiβo, a] *adj* nourishing, nutritious.

nylon [ni'lon] *nm* nylon.

Ñ ñ

Ñ, ñ ['eɲe] *nf* (*letra*) Ñ, ñ.

ñato, a ['ɲato, a] *adj* (*AM*) snub-nosed.

ñoñería [ɲoɲe'ria], **ñoñez** [ɲo'ɲeθ] *nf* insipidness.

ñoño, a ['ɲoɲo, a] *adj* (*soso*) insipid; (*persona: débil*) spineless.

ñoquis ['ɲokis] *nmpl* (*CULIN*) gnocchi.

Oo

O, o [o] *nf* (*letra*) O, o; **O de Oviedo** O for Oliver (*BRIT*) *o* Oboe (*US*).

O *abr* (= *oeste*) W.

o [o] *conj* or; ~ ... ~ either ... or; ~ **sea** that is.

ó [o] *conj* (*en números para evitar confusión*) or; **5 ~ 6** 5 or 6.

o/ *nm* (*COM*: = *orden*) o.

OACI *nf abr* (= *Organización de la Aviación Civil Internacional*) ICAO.

oasis [o'asis] *nm inv* oasis.

obcecado, a [oβθe'kaðo, a] *adj* blind; (*terco*) stubborn.

obcecarse [oββe'karse] *vr* to be obstinate; ~ **en hacer** to insist on doing.

obceque [oβ'θeke] *etc vb V* **obcecarse**.

obedecer [oβeðe'θer] *vt* to obey; ~ **a** (*MED etc*) to yield to; (*fig*) ~ **a** ..., ~ **al hecho de que** ... to be due to ..., arise from ....

obedezca [oβe'ðeθka] *etc vb V* **obedecer**.

obediencia [oβe'ðjenθja] *nf* obedience.

obediente [oβe'ðjente] *adj* obedient.

obertura [oβer'tura] *nf* overture.

obesidad [oβesi'ðað] *nf* obesity.

obeso, a [o'βeso, a] *adj* obese.

óbice ['oβiθe] *nm* obstacle, impediment.

obispado [oβis'paðo] *nm* bishopric.

obispo [o'βispo] *nm* bishop.

óbito ['oβito] *nm* demise.

objeción [oβxe'θjon] *nf* objection; **hacer una ~, poner objeciones** to raise objections, object.

objetar [oβxe'tar] *vt, vi* to object.

objetivo, a [oβxe'tiβo, a] *adj* objective ♦ *nm* objective; (*fig*) aim; (*FOTO*) lens.

objeto [oβ'xeto] *nm* (*cosa*) object; (*fin*) aim.

objetor, a [oβxe'tor, a] *nm/f* objector; ~ **de conciencia** conscientious objector; *V tb* **mili**.

oblea [o'βlea] *nf* (*REL, fig*) wafer; (*INFORM*) chip, wafer.

oblicuo, a [o'βlikwo, a] *adj* oblique; (*mirada*) sidelong.

obligación [oβliγa'θjon] *nf* obligation; (*COM*) bond, debenture.

obligar [oβli'xar] *vt* to force; ~**se** *vr*: ~**se a** to commit o.s. to.

obligatorio, a [oβliγa'torjo, a] *adj* compulsory, obligatory.

obligue [o'βliγe] *etc vb V* **obligar**.

oboe [o'βoe] *nm* oboe; (*músico*) oboist.

Ob.ᵖᵒ *abr* (= *Obispo*) Bp.

obra ['oβra] *nf* work; (*hechura*) piece of work; (*ARQ*) construction, building; (*libro*) book; (*MUS*) opus; (*TEAT*) play; ~ **de arte** work of art; ~ **maestra** masterpiece; ~ **de consulta** reference book; ~**s completas** complete works; ~ **benéfica** charity; "~**s**" (*en carretera*) "men at work"; ~**s públicas** public works; **por ~ de** thanks to (the efforts of); ~**s son amores y no buenas razones** actions speak louder than words.

obrar [o'βrar] *vt* to work; (*tener efecto*) to have an effect on ♦ *vi* to act, behave; (*tener efecto*) to have an effect; **la carta obra en su poder** the letter is in his/her possession.

obr. cit. *abr* (= *obra citada*) op. cit.

obrero, a [o'βrero, a] *adj* working; (*movimiento*) labour *cpd*; **clase obrera** working class ♦ *nm/f* (*gen*) worker; (*sin oficio*) labourer.

obscenidad [oββθeni'ðað] *nf* obscenity.

obsceno, a [oββ'θeno, a] *adj* obscene.

obscu... = oscu...

obsequiar [oββe'kjar] *vt* (*ofrecer*) to present; (*agasajar*) to make a fuss of, lavish attention on.

obsequio [oβ'sekjo] *nm* (*regalo*) gift; (*cortesía*) courtesy, attention.

obsequioso, a [oββe'kjoso, a] *adj* attentive.

observación [oββerβa'θjon] *nf* observation; (*reflexión*) remark; (*objeción*) objection.

observador, a [oββerβa'ðor, a] *adj* observant ♦ *nm/f* observer.

observancia [oββer'βanθja] *nf* observance.

observar [oββer'βar] *vt* to observe; (*notar*) to notice; (*leyes*) to observe, respect; (*reglas*) to abide by.

observatorio [oββerβa'torjo] *nm* observatory; ~ **del tiempo** weather station.

obsesión [oββe'sjon] *nf* obsession.

obsesionar [oββesjo'nar] *vt* to obsess.

obseso, a [oβ'seso, a] *nm/f* (*sexual*) sex maniac.

obsolescencia [oββoles'θenθja] *nf*: ~ **incorporada** (*COM*) built-in obsolescence.

obsoleto, a [oββo'leto, a] *adj* obsolete.

obstaculice [oββstaku'liθe] *etc vb V* **obstaculizar**.

obstaculizar [oββstakuli'θar] *vt* (*dificultar*) to hinder, hamper.

obstáculo [oββ'takulo] *nm* (*gen*) obstacle;

(*impedimento*) hindrance, drawback.

obstante [oßs'tante]: **no** ~ *adv*
nevertheless; (*de todos modos*) all the
same ♦ *prep* in spite of.

obstetra [oßs'tetra] *nm/f* obstetrician.

obstetricia [oßste'triθja] *nf* obstetrics *sg*.

obstinado, a [oßsti'naðo, a] *adj* (*gen*)
obstinate; (*terco*) stubborn.

obstinarse [oßsti'narse] *vr* to dig one's
heels in; ~ **en** to persist in.

obstrucción [oßstruk'θjon] *nf* obstruction.

obstruir [oßstru'ir] *vt* to obstruct;
(*bloquear*) to block; (*estorbar*) to hinder.

obstruyendo [oßstru'jendo] *etc vb V*
obstruir.

obtención [oßten'θjon] *nf* (*COM*)
procurement.

obtendré [oßten'dre] *etc vb V* **obtener**.

obtener [oßte'ner] *vt* (*conseguir*) to obtain;
(*ganar*) to gain.

obtenga [oß'tenga] *etc vb V* **obtener**.

obturación [oßtura'θjon] *nf* plugging,
stopping; (*FOTO*): **velocidad de** ~ shutter
speed.

obturador [oßtura'ðor] *nm* (*FOTO*) shutter.

obtuso, a [oß'tuso, a] *adj* (*filo*) blunt; (*MAT,
fig*) obtuse.

obtuve [oß'tuße] *etc vb V* **obtener**.

obús [o'ßus] *nm* (*MIL*) shell.

obviar [oß'ßjar] *vt* to obviate, remove.

obvio, a ['oßßjo, a] *adj* obvious.

oca ['oka] *nf* goose; (*tb*: **juego de la** ~)
≈ snakes and ladders.

ocasión [oka'sjon] *nf* (*oportunidad*)
opportunity, chance; (*momento*)
occasion, time; (*causa*) cause; **de** ~
secondhand; **con** ~ **de** on the occasion
of; **en algunas ocasiones** sometimes;
aprovechar la ~ to seize one's
opportunity.

ocasionar [okasjo'nar] *vt* to cause.

ocaso [o'kaso] *nm* sunset; (*fig*) decline.

occidental [okθiðen'tal] *adj* western ♦ *nm/f*
westerner ♦ *nm* west.

occidente [okθi'ðente] *nm* west; **el O**~ the
West.

occiso, a [ok'θiso, a] *nm/f*: **el** ~ the
deceased; (*de asesinato*) the victim.

O.C.D.E. *nf abr* (= *Organización de
Cooperación y Desarrollo Económicos*)
OECD.

océano [o'θeano] *nm* ocean; **el** ~ **Índico** the
Indian Ocean.

ochenta [o't∫enta] *num* eighty.

ocho ['ot∫o] *num* eight; (*fecha*) eighth; ~
días a week.

ochocientos, as [ot∫o'θjentos, as] *num*
eight hundred.

OCI ['oθi] *nf abr* (*POL: Venezuela, Perú*)
= Oficina Central de Información.

ocio ['oθjo] *nm* (*tiempo*) leisure; (*pey*)
idleness; "**guía del** ~" "what's on".

ociosidad [oθjosi'ðað] *nf* idleness.

ocioso, a [o'θjoso, a] *adj* (*inactivo*) idle;
(*inútil*) useless.

oct. *abr* (= *octubre*) Oct.

octanaje [okta'naxe] *nm*: **de alto** ~ high
octane.

octano [ok'tano] *nm* octane.

octavilla [okta'ßiʎa] *nm* leaflet, pamphlet.

octavo, a [ok'taßo, a] *num* eighth.

octeto [ok'teto] *nm* (*INFORM*) byte.

octogenario, a [oktoxe'narjo, a] *adj, nm/f*
octogenarian.

octubre [ok'tußre] *nm* October.

OCU ['oku] *nf abr* (*ESP*. = *Organización de
Consumidores y Usuarios*) ≈ Consumers'
Association.

ocular [oku'lar] *adj* ocular, eye *cpd*; **testigo**
~ eyewitness.

oculista [oku'lista] *nm/f* oculist.

ocultar [okul'tar] *vt* (*esconder*) to hide;
(*callar*) to conceal; (*disfrazar*) to screen;
~**se** *vr* to hide (o.s.); ~**se a la vista** to
keep out of sight.

oculto, a [o'kulto, a] *adj* hidden; (*fig*)
secret.

ocupación [okupa'θjon] *nf* occupation;
(*tenencia*) occupancy.

ocupado, a [oku'paðo, a] *adj* (*persona*)
busy; (*plaza*) occupied, taken; (*teléfono*)
engaged; **¿está ocupada la silla?** is that
seat taken?

ocupar [oku'par] *vt* (*gen*) to occupy;
(*puesto*) to hold, fill; (*individuo*) to
engage; (*obreros*) to employ; (*confiscar*)
to seize; ~**se** *vr*: ~**se de** *o* **en** to concern
o.s. with; (*cuidar*) to look after; ~**se de lo
suyo** to mind one's own business.

ocurrencia [oku'rrenθja] *nf* (*ocasión*)
occurrence; (*agudeza*) witticism.

ocurrir [oku'rrir] *vi* to happen; ~**se** *vr*: **se
me ocurrió que** ... it occurred to me that
...; **¿se te ocurre algo?** can you think of *o*
come up with anything? **¿qué ocurre?**
what's going on?

oda ['oða] *nf* ode.

ODECA [o'ðeka] *nf abr* = *Organización de
Estados Centroamericanos*.

odiar [o'ðjar] *vt* to hate.

odio ['oðjo] *nm* (*gen*) hate, hatred;
(*disgusto*) dislike.

odioso, a [o'ðjoso, a] *adj* (*gen*) hateful;
(*malo*) nasty.

odisea [oði'sea] *nf* odyssey.

odontología [oðontolo'xia] *nf* dentistry,

dental surgery.

odontólogo, a [oðon'toloɣo, a] *nm/f* dentist, dental surgeon.

odre ['oðre] *nm* wineskin.

O.E.A. *nf abr* (= *Organización de Estados Americanos*) O.A.S.

OECE *nf abr* (= *Organización Europea de Cooperación Económica*) OEEC.

OELA [o'ela] *nf abr* = *Organización de Estados Latinoamericanos.*

oeste [o'este] *nm* west; **una película del** ~ a western.

ofender [ofen'der] *vt* (*agraviar*) to offend; (*insultar*) to insult; ~**se** *vr* to take offence.

ofensa [o'fensa] *nf* offence; (*insulto*) slight.

ofensivo, a [ofen'siβo, a] *adj* (*insultante*) insulting; (*MIL*) offensive ♦ *nf* offensive.

oferta [o'ferta] *nf* offer; (*propuesta*) proposal; (*para contrato*) bid, tender; **la** ~ **y la demanda** supply and demand; **artículos en** ~ goods on offer; ~ **excedentaria** (*COM*) excess supply; ~ **monetaria** money supply; ~ **pública de adquisición (OPA)** (*COM*) takeover bid; ~**s de trabajo** (*en periódicos*) situations vacant column.

offset ['ofset] *nm* offset.

oficial [ofi'θjal] *adj* official ♦ *nm* official; (*MIL*) officer.

oficialista [ofisja'lista] *adj* (*AM*) (pro-) government; **el candidato** ~ the governing party's candidate.

oficiar [ofi'θjar] *vt* to inform officially ♦ *vi* (*REL*) to officiate.

oficina [ofi'θina] *nf* office; ~ **de colocación** employment agency; ~ **de información** information bureau; ~ **de objetos perdidos** lost property office (*BRIT*), lost-and-found department (*US*); ~ **de turismo** tourist office.

oficinista [ofiθi'nista] *nm/f* clerk; **los** ~**s** white-collar workers.

oficio [o'fiθjo] *nm* (*profesión*) profession; (*puesto*) post; (*REL*) service; (*función*) function; (*comunicado*) official letter; **ser del** ~ to be an old hand; **tener mucho** ~ to have a lot of experience; ~ **de difuntos** funeral service; **de** ~ officially.

oficioso, a [ofi'θjoso, a] *adj* (*pey*) officious; (*no oficial*) unofficial, informal.

ofimática [ofi'matika] *nf* office automation.

ofrecer [ofre'θer] *vt* (*dar*) to offer; (*proponer*) to propose; ~**se** *vr* (*persona*) to offer o.s., volunteer; (*situación*) to present itself; **¿qué se le ofrece?, ¿se le ofrece algo?** what can I do for you?, can I get you anything?

ofrecimiento [ofreθi'mjento] *nm* offer, offering.

ofrendar [ofren'dar] *vt* to offer, contribute.

ofrezca [o'freθka] *etc vb V* **ofrecer.**

oftalmología [oftalmolo'xia] *nf* ophthalmology.

oftalmólogo, a [oftal'moloɣo, a] *nm/f* ophthalmologist.

ofuscación [ofuska'θjon] *nf,* **ofuscamiento** [ofuska'mjento] *nm* (*fig*) bewilderment.

ofuscar [ofus'kar] *vt* (*confundir*) to bewilder; (*enceguecer*) to dazzle, blind.

ofusque [o'fuske] *etc vb V* **ofuscar.**

ogro ['oɣro] *nm* ogre.

OIC *nf abr* = *Organización Interamericana del Café*; (*COM*) = *Organización Internacional del Comercio.*

oída [o'iða] *nf:* **de** ~**s** by hearsay.

oído [o'iðo] *nm* (*ANAT, MUS*) ear; (*sentido*) hearing; ~ **interno** inner ear; **de** ~ by ear; **apenas pude dar crédito a mis** ~**s** I could scarcely believe my ears; **hacer** ~**s sordos a** to turn a deaf ear to.

OIEA *nm abr* (= *Organismo Internacional de Energía Atómica*) IAEA.

oiga ['oiɣa] *etc vb V* **oír.**

OIR [o'ir] *nf abr* (= *Organización Internacional para los Refugiados*) IRO.

oír [o'ir] *vt* (*gen*) to hear; (*esp AM: escuchar*) to listen to; **¡oye!** (*sorpresa*) I say!, say! (*US*); **¡oiga!** (*TELEC*) hullo?; ~ **misa** to attend mass; **como quien oye llover** without paying (the slightest) attention.

O.I.T. *nf abr* (= *Organización Internacional del Trabajo*) ILO.

ojal [o'xal] *nm* buttonhole.

ojalá [oxa'la] *excl* if only (it were so)!, some hope! ♦ *conj* if only...!, would that...!; ~ **que venga hoy** I hope he comes today; **¡**~ **pudiera!** I wish I could!

ojeada [oxe'aða] *nf* glance; **echar una** ~ a to take a quick look at.

ojera [o'xera] *nf:* **tener** ~**s** to have bags under one's eyes.

ojeriza [oxe'riθa] *nf* ill-will; **tener** ~ **a** to have a grudge against, have it in for.

ojeroso, a [oxe'roso, a] *adj* haggard.

ojete [o'xete] *nm* eye(let).

ojo ['oxo] *nm* eye; (*de puente*) span; (*de cerradura*) keyhole ♦ *excl* careful!; **tener** ~ **para** to have an eye for; ~**s saltones** bulging *o* goggle eyes; ~ **de buey** porthole; ~ **por** ~ an eye for an eye; **en un abrir y cerrar de** ~**s** in the twinkling of an eye; **a** ~**s vistas** openly; (*crecer etc*)

before one's (very) eyes; **a ~ (de buen
cubero)** roughly; **~s que no ven, corazón
que no siente** out of sight, out of mind;
ser el ~ derecho de algn (*fig*) to be the
apple of sb's eye.

okupa [o'kupa] *nm/f* (*fam*) squatter.

ola ['ola] *nf* wave; **~ de calor/frío**
heatwave/cold spell; **la nueva ~** the
latest fashion; (*CINE, MUS*) (the) new
wave.

OLADE [o'laðe] *nf abr* = *Organización
Latinoamericana de Energía*.

olé [o'le] *excl* bravo!, olé!

oleada [ole'aða] *nf* big wave, swell; (*fig*)
wave.

oleaje [ole'axe] *nm* swell.

óleo ['oleo] *nm* oil.

oleoducto [oleo'ðukto] *nm* (oil) pipeline.

oler [o'ler] *vt* (*gen*) to smell; (*inquirir*) to
pry into; (*fig: sospechar*) to sniff out ♦ *vi*
to smell; **~ a** to smell of; **huele mal** it
smells bad, it stinks.

olfatear [olfate'ar] *vt* to smell; (*fig:
sospechar*) to sniff out; (*inquirir*) to pry
into.

olfato [ol'fato] *nm* sense of smell.

oligarquía [oliɣar'kia] *nf* oligarchy.

olimpiada [olim'piaða] *nf*: **la ~ o las ~s** the
Olympics.

olímpicamente [o'limpikamente] *adv*:
pasar ~ de algo to totally ignore sth.

olímpico, a [o'limpiko, a] *adj* Olympian;
(*deportes*) Olympic.

oliva [o'liβa] *nf* (*aceituna*) olive; **aceite de ~**
olive oil.

olivar [oli'βar] *nm* olive grove *o* plantation.

olivo [o'liβo] *nm* olive tree.

olla ['oʎa] *nf* pan; (*para hervir agua*) kettle;
(*comida*) stew; **~ a presión** pressure
cooker.

olmo ['olmo] *nm* elm (tree).

olor [o'lor] *nm* smell.

oloroso, a [olo'roso, a] *adj* scented.

OLP *nf abr* (= *Organización para la Liberación
de Palestina*) PLO.

olvidadizo, a [olβiða'ðiθo, a] *adj*
(*desmemoriado*) forgetful; (*distraído*)
absent-minded.

olvidar [olβi'ðar] *vt* to forget; (*omitir*) to
omit; (*abandonar*) to leave behind; **~se** *vr*
(*fig*) to forget o.s.; **se me olvidó** I forgot.

olvido [ol'βiðo] *nm* oblivion; (*acto*)
oversight; (*descuido*) slip; **caer en el ~** to
fall into oblivion.

O.M. *abr* (*POL*) = *Orden Ministerial*.

ombligo [om'bliɣo] *nm* navel.

OMI *nf abr* (= *Organización Marítima
Internacional*) IMO.

ominoso, a [omi'noso, a] *adj* ominous.

omisión [omi'sjon] *nf* (*abstención*)
omission; (*descuido*) neglect.

omiso, a [o'miso, a] *adj*: **hacer caso ~ de** to
ignore, pass over.

omitir [omi'tir] *vt* to leave *o* miss out, omit.

ómnibus ['omniβus] *nm* (*AM*) bus.

omnipotente [omnipo'tente] *adj*
omnipotent.

omnipresente [omnipre'sente] *adj*
omnipresent.

omnívoro, a [om'niβoro, a] *adj*
omnivorous.

omoplato [omo'plato], **omóplato**
[o'moplato] *nm* shoulder-blade.

OMS *nf abr* (= *Organización Mundial de la
Salud*) WHO.

ONCE ['onθe] *nf abr* (= *Organización
Nacional de Ciegos Españoles*) *charity for
the blind*.

once ['onθe] *num* eleven ♦ *nm* (*AM*): **~s** *nfpl*
tea break *sg*.

onda ['onda] *nf* wave; **~ corta/larga/media**
short/long/medium wave; **~s acústicas/
hertzianas** acoustic/Hertzian waves; **~
sonora** sound wave.

ondear [onde'ar] *vi* to wave; (*tener ondas*)
to be wavy; (*agua*) to ripple; **~se** *vr* to
swing, sway.

ondulación [ondula'θjon] *nf* undulation.

ondulado, a [ondu'laðo, a] *adj* wavy ♦ *nm*
wave.

ondulante [ondu'lante] *adj* undulating.

ondular [ondu'lar] *vt* (*el pelo*) to wave ♦ *vi*,
~se *vr* to undulate.

oneroso, a [one'roso, a] *adj* onerous.

ONG *nf abr* (= *organización no
gubernamental*) NGO.

onomástico, a [ono'mastiko, a] *adj*: **fiesta
onomástica** saint's day ♦ *nm* saint's day.

ONU ['onu] *nf abr* V **Organización de las
Naciones Unidas**.

onubense [onu'βense] *adj* of *o* from
Huelva ♦ *nm/f* native *o* inhabitant of
Huelva.

ONUDI [o'nuði] *nf abr* (= *Organización de las
Naciones Unidas para el Desarrollo
Industrial*) UNIDO (*United Nations
Industrial Development Organization*).

onza ['onθa] *nf* ounce.

O.P. *nfpl abr* = **obras públicas**; (*COM*)
= *Oficina Principal*.

OPA *nf abr* (= *oferta pública de adquisición*)
takeover bid.

opaco, a [o'pako, a] *adj* opaque; (*fig*) dull.

ópalo ['opalo] *nm* opal.

opción [op'θjon] *nf* (*gen*) option; (*derecho*)
right, option; **no hay ~** there is no

alternative.

opcional [opθjo'nal] *adj* optional.

O.P.E.P. [o'pep] *nf abr* (= *Organización de Países Exportadores de Petróleo*) OPEC.

ópera ['opera] *nf* opera; ~ **bufa** *o* **cómica** comic opera.

operación [opera'θjon] *nf* (*gen*) operation; (*COM*) transaction, deal; ~ **"llave en manos"** (*INFORM*) turnkey operation; ~ **a plazo** (*COM*) forward transaction; **operaciones accesorias** (*INFORM*) housekeeping; **operaciones a término** (*COM*) futures.

operador, a [opera'ðor, a] *nm/f* operator; (*CINE*: *proyección*) projectionist; (: *rodaje*) cameraman.

operar [ope'rar] *vt* (*producir*) to produce, bring about; (*MED*) to operate on ♦ *vi* (*COM*) to operate, deal; ~**se** *vr* to occur; (*MED*) to have an operation; **se han operado grandes cambios** great changes have been made *o* have taken place.

operario, a [ope'rarjo, a] *nm/f* worker.

opereta [ope'reta] *nf* operetta.

opinar [opi'nar] *vt* (*estimar*) to think ♦ *vi* (*enjuiciar*) to give one's opinion; ~ **bien de** to think well of.

opinión [opi'njon] *nf* (*creencia*) belief; (*criterio*) opinion; **la ~ pública** public opinion.

opio ['opjo] *nm* opium.

opíparo, a [o'piparo, a] *adj* sumptuous.

opondré [opon'dre] *etc vb V* **oponer**.

oponente [opo'nente] *nm/f* opponent.

oponer [opo'ner] *vt* (*resistencia*) to put up, offer; (*negativa*) to raise; ~**se** *vr* (*objetar*) to object; (*estar frente a frente*) to be opposed; (*dos personas*) to oppose each other; ~ **A a B** to set A against B; **me opongo a pensar que ...** I refuse to believe *o* think that ....

oponga [o'ponga] *etc vb V* **oponer**.

Oporto [o'porto] *nm* Oporto.

oporto [o'porto] *nm* port.

oportunidad [oportuni'ðað] *nf* (*ocasión*) opportunity; (*posibilidad*) chance.

oportunismo [oportu'nismo] *nm* opportunism.

oportunista [oportu'nista] *nm/f* opportunist; (*infección*) opportunistic.

oportuno, a [opor'tuno, a] *adj* (*en su tiempo*) opportune, timely; (*respuesta*) suitable; **en el momento ~** at the right moment.

oposición [oposi'θjon] *nf* opposition; **oposiciones** *nfpl* public examinations; **ganar un puesto por oposiciones** to win a post by public competitive examination; **hacer oposiciones a, presentarse a**

unas oposiciones a to sit a competitive examination for; *see boxed note.*

OPOSICIONES

Oposiciones *are examinations which are held every year in Spain in which candidates compete, both nationally and locally, for posts in the public sector, state education, the judiciary and so on. These posts are permanent and the number of entrants is high, so the examinations are correspondingly tough. The candidates, "opositores", have to study a wide range of subjects relating to their field and must also know and understand the constitution. People can spend years studying for* **oposiciones** *and resitting them if necessary.*

---

opositar [oposi'tar] *vi* to sit a public entrance examination.

opositor, a [oposi'tor, a] *nm/f* (*ADMIN*) candidate to a public examination; (*adversario*) opponent.

opresión [opre'sjon] *nf* oppression.

opresivo, a [opre'sißo, a] *adj* oppressive.

opresor, a [opre'sor, a] *nm/f* oppressor.

oprimir [opri'mir] *vt* to squeeze; (*asir*) to grasp; (*pulsar*) to press; (*fig*) to oppress.

optar [op'tar] *vi* (*elegir*) to choose; ~ **a** *o* **por** to opt for.

optativo, a [opta'tißo, a] *adj* optional.

óptico, a ['optiko, a] *adj* optic(al) ♦ *nm/f* optician ♦ *nf* optics *sg*; (*fig*) viewpoint.

optimismo [opti'mismo] *nm* optimism.

optimista [opti'mista] *nm/f* optimist.

óptimo, a ['optimo, a] *adj* (*el mejor*) very best.

opuesto, a [o'pwesto, a] *pp de* **oponer** ♦ *adj* (*contrario*) opposite; (*antagónico*) opposing.

opulencia [opu'lenθja] *nf* opulence.

opulento, a [opu'lento, a] *adj* opulent.

opuse [o'puse] *etc vb V* **oponer**.

ORA ['ora] *nf abr* (*ESP*: = *Operación de Regulación de Aparcamientos*) *parking regulations.*

ora ['ora] *adv*: ~ **tú** ~ **yo** now you, now me.

oración [ora'θjon] *nf* (*discurso*) speech; (*REL*) prayer; (*LING*) sentence.

oráculo [o'rakulo] *nm* oracle.

orador, a [ora'ðor, a] *nm/f* orator; (*conferenciante*) speaker.

oral [o'ral] *adj* oral; **por vía ~** (*MED*) orally.

orangután [orangu'tan] *nm* orang-utan.

orar [o'rar] *vi* (*REL*) to pray.

oratoria [ora'torja] *nf* oratory.

orbe ['orße] nm orb, sphere; (fig) world; **en todo el** ~ all over the globe.

órbita ['orßita] nf orbit; (ANAT: ocular) (eye-)socket.

orden ['orðen] nm (gen) order; (INFORM) command; ~ **público** public order, law and order; (números) del ~ **de** about; **de primer** ~ first-rate; **en** ~ **de prioridad** in order of priority ♦ nf (gen) order; ~ **bancaria** banker's order; ~ **de compra** (COM) purchase order; ~ **del día** agenda; **eso ahora está a la** ~ **del día** that is now the order of the day; **a la** ~ **de usted** at your service; **dar la** ~ **de hacer algo** to give the order to do sth.

ordenación [orðena'θjon] nf (estado) order; (acto) ordering; (REL) ordination.

ordenado, a [orðe'naðo, a] adj (metódico) methodical; (arreglado) orderly.

ordenador [orðena'ðor] nm computer; ~ **central** mainframe computer; ~ **de gestión** business computer; ~ **portátil** laptop (computer); ~ **de sobremesa** desktop computer.

ordenamiento [orðena'mjento] nm legislation.

ordenanza [orðe'nanθa] nf ordinance; ~**s municipales** by-laws ♦ nm (COM etc) messenger; (MIL) orderly; (bedel) porter.

ordenar [orðe'nar] vt (mandar) to order; (poner orden) to put in order, arrange; ~**se** vr (REL) to be ordained.

ordeñadora [orðeɲa'ðora] nf milking machine.

ordeñar [orðe'ɲar] vt to milk.

ordinariez [orðina'rjeθ] nf (cualidad) coarseness, vulgarity; (una ~) coarse remark o joke etc.

ordinario, a [orði'narjo, a] adj (común) ordinary, usual; (vulgar) vulgar, common.

ordinograma [orðino'ɣrama] nm flowchart.

orear [ore'ar] vt to air; ~**se** vr (ropa) to air.

orégano [o'reɣano] nm oregano.

oreja [o'rexa] nf ear; (MECÁNICA) lug, flange.

orensano, a [oren'sano, a] adj of o from Orense ♦ nm/f native o inhabitant of Orense.

orfanato [orfa'nato] nm, **orfanatorio** [orfana'torjo] nm orphanage.

orfandad [orfan'dað] nf orphanhood.

orfebre [or'feßre] nm gold-/silversmith.

orfebrería [orfeßre'ria] nf gold/silver work.

orfelinato [orfeli'nato] nm orphanage.

orfeón [orfe'on] nm (MUS) choral society.

organice [orɣa'niθe] etc vb V **organizar**.

orgánico, a [or'ɣaniko, a] adj organic.

organigrama [orɣani'ɣrama] nm flow chart; (de organización) organization chart.

organillo [orɣa'niʎo] nm barrel organ.

organismo [orɣa'nismo] nm (BIO) organism; (POL) organization; **O~ Internacional de Energía Atómica** International Atomic Energy Agency.

organista [orɣa'nista] nm/f organist.

organización [orɣaniθa'θjon] nf organization; **O~ de las Naciones Unidas (ONU)** United Nations Organization **O~ del Tratado del Atlántico Norte (OTAN)** North Atlantic Treaty Organization (NATO).

organizador, a [orɣaniθa'ðor, a] adj organizing; **el comité** ~ the organizing committee ♦ nm/f organizer.

organizar [orɣani'θar] vt to organize.

órgano ['orɣano] nm organ.

orgasmo [or'ɣasmo] nm orgasm.

orgía [or'xia] nf orgy.

orgullo [or'ɣuʎo] nm (altanería) pride; (autorespeto) self-respect.

orgulloso, a [orɣu'ʎoso, a] adj (gen) proud; (altanero) haughty.

orientación [orjenta'θjon] nf (posición) position; (dirección) direction; ~ **profesional** occupational guidance.

oriental [orjen'tal] adj oriental; (región etc) eastern ♦ nm/f oriental.

orientar [orjen'tar] vt (situar) to orientate; (señalar) to point; (dirigir) to direct; (guiar) to guide; ~**se** vr to get one's bearings; (decidirse) to decide on a course of action.

oriente [o'rjente] nm east; **el O~** the East, the Orient; **Cercano/Medio/Lejano O~** Near/ Middle/Far East.

orificio [ori'fiθjo] nm orifice.

origen [o'rixen] nm origin; (nacimiento) lineage, birth; **dar** ~ **a** to cause, give rise to.

original [orixi'nal] adj (nuevo) original; (extraño) odd, strange ♦ nm original; (TIP) manuscript; (TEC) master (copy).

originalidad [orixinali'ðað] nf originality.

originar [orixi'nar] vt to originate; ~**se** vr to originate.

originario, a [orixi'narjo, a] adj (nativo) native; (primordial) original; **ser** ~ **de** to originate from; **país** ~ country of origin.

orilla [o'riʎa] nf (borde) border; (de río) bank; (de bosque, tela) edge; (de mar) shore; **a** ~**s de** on the banks of.

orillar [ori'ʎar] vt (bordear) to skirt, go round; (COSTURA) to edge; (resolver) to

wind up; (*tocar. asunto*) to touch briefly
on; (*dificultad*) to avoid.

orín [o'rin] *nm* ı ust.

orina [o'rina] *nf* ırine.

orinal [ori'nal] *nm* (chamber) pot.

orinar [ori'nar] *vi* to urinate; ~**se** *vr* to wet
o.s.

orines [o'rines] *nmpl* urine *sg.*

oriundo, a [o'rjundo, a] *adj*: ~ **de** native
of.

orla ['orla] *nf* edge, border; (*ESCOL*)
graduation photograph.

ornamentar [ornamen'tar] *vt* (*adornar,
ataviar*) to adorn; (*revestir*) to bedeck.

ornar [or'nar] *vt* to adorn.

ornitología [ornitolo'xia] *nf* ornithology,
bird watching.

ornitólogo, a [orni'toloɣo, a] *nm/f*
ornithologist.

oro ['oro] *nm* gold; ~ **en barras** gold ingots;
de ~ gold, golden; **no es** ~ **todo lo que
reluce** all that glitters is not gold;
hacerse de ~ to make a fortune; *V tb*
oros.

orondo, a [o'rondo, a] *adj* (*vasija*) rounded;
(*individuo*) smug, self-satisfied.

oropel [oro'pel] *nm* tinsel.

oros ['oros] *nmpl* (*NAIPES*) *one of the suits
in the Spanish card deck*; *V tb* **Baraja
Española**.

orquesta [or'kesta] *nf* orchestra; ~ **de
cámara/sinfónica** chamber/symphony
orchestra; ~ **de jazz** jazz band.

orquestar [orkes'tar] *vt* to orchestrate.

orquídea [or'kiðea] *nf* orchid.

ortiga [or'tiɣa] *nf* nettle.

ortodoncia [orto'ðonθja] *nf* orthodontics
sg.

ortodoxo, a [orto'ðokso, a] *adj* orthodox.

ortografía [ortoɣra'fia] *nf* spelling.

ortopedia [orto'peðja] *nf* orthop(a)edics
sg.

ortopédico, a [orto'peðiko, a] *adj*
orthop(a)edic.

oruga [o'ruɣa] *nf* caterpillar.

orujo [o'ruxo] *nm type of strong grape
liqueur made from grape pressings.*

orzuelo [or'θwelo] *nm* (*MED*) stye.

os [os] *pron* (*gen*) you; (*a vosotros*) (to) you;
(*reflexivo*) (to) yourselves; (*mutuo*) (to)
each other; **vosotros** ~ **laváis** you wash
yourselves; **¡callar**~! (*fam*) shut up!

osa ['osa] *nf* (she-)bear; **O**~ **Mayor/Menor**
Great/Little Bear, Ursa Major/Minor.

osadía [osa'ðia] *nf* daring; (*descaro*)
impudence.

osamenta [osa'menta] *nf* skeleton.

osar [o'sar] *vi* to dare.

oscense [os'θense] *adj* of *o* from Huesca
♦ *nm/f* native *o* inhabitant of Huesca.

oscilación [osθila'θjon] *nf* (*movimiento*)
oscillation; (*fluctuación*) fluctuation;
(*vacilación*) hesitation; (*columpio*)
swinging, movement to and fro.

oscilar [osθi'lar] *vi* to oscillate; to
fluctuate; to hesitate.

ósculo ['oskulo] *nm* kiss.

oscurecer [oskure'θer] *vt* to darken ♦ *vi* to
grow dark; ~**se** *vr* to grow *o* get dark.

oscurezca [osku'reθka] *etc vb V* **oscurecer**.

oscuridad [oskuri'ðað] *nf* obscurity;
(*tinieblas*) darkness.

oscuro, a [os'kuro, a] *adj* dark; (*fig*)
obscure; (*indefinido*) confused; (*cielo*)
overcast, cloudy; (*futuro etc*) uncertain;
a oscuras in the dark.

óseo, a ['oseo, a] *adj* bony; (*MED etc*) bone
cpd.

oso ['oso] *nm* bear; ~ **blanco/gris/pardo**
polar/grizzly/brown bear; ~ **de peluche**
teddy bear; ~ **hormiguero** anteater;
hacer el ~ to play the fool.

Ostende [os'tende] *nm* Ostend.

ostensible [osten'siβle] *adj* obvious.

ostensiblemente [ostensiβle'mente] *adv*
perceptibly, visibly.

ostentación [ostenta'θjon] *nf* (*gen*)
ostentation; (*acto*) display.

ostentar [osten'tar] *vt* (*gen*) to show; (*pey*)
to flaunt, show off; (*poseer*) to have,
possess.

ostentoso, a [osten'toso, a] *adj*
ostentatious, showy.

osteópata [oste'opata] *nm/f* osteopath.

ostra ['ostra] *nf* oyster ♦ *excl*: **¡**~**s!** (*fam*)
sugar!

ostracismo [ostra'θismo] *nm* ostracism.

OTAN ['otan] *nf abr V* **Organización del
Tratado del Atlántico Norte**.

OTASE [o'tase] *nf abr* (= *Organización del
Tratado del Sudeste Asiático*) SEATO.

otear [ote'ar] *vt* to observe; (*fig*) to look
into.

otero [o'tero] *nm* low hill, hillock.

otitis [o'titis] *nf* earache.

otoñal [oto'ɲal] *adj* autumnal.

otoño [o'toɲo] *nm* autumn, fall (*US*).

otorgamiento [otorɣa'mjento] *nm*
conferring, granting; (*JUR*) execution.

otorgar [otor'ɣar] *vt* (*conceder*) to concede;
(*dar*) to grant; (*poderes*) to confer;
(*premio*) to award.

otorgue [o'torɣe] *etc vb V* **otorgar**.

otorrinolaringólogo, a [otorrinolarin'go
loɣo, a] *nm/f* (*MED: tb*: **otorrino**) ear, nose
and throat specialist.

═══════════ *PALABRA CLAVE*

otro, a ['otro, a] *adj* **1** (*distinto: sg*) another;
(: *pl*) other; **otra cosa/persona**
something/someone else; **con ~s amigos**
with other *o* different friends; **a/en otra
parte** elsewhere, somewhere else
2 (*adicional*): **tráigame ~ café (más), por
favor** can I have another coffee please;
~s 10 días más another 10 days
♦ *pron* **1** (*sg*) another one; **el ~** the other
one; **(los) ~s** (the) others; **¡otra!** (*MUS*)
more!; **de ~** somebody *o* someone else's;
que lo haga ~ let somebody *o* someone
else do it; **ni uno ni ~** neither one nor
the other
2 (*recíproco*): **se odian (la) una a (la) otra**
they hate one another *o* each other
3: **~ tanto: comer ~ tanto** to eat the
same *o* as much again; **recibió una
decena de telegramas y otras tantas
llamadas** he got about ten telegrams and
as many calls.

otrora [o'trora] *adv* formerly; **el ~ señor
del país** the one-time ruler of the
country.
ovación [oβa'θjon] *nf* ovation.
ovacionar [oβaθjo'nar] *vt* to cheer.
oval [o'βal], **ovalado, a** [oβa'laðo, a] *adj*
oval.
óvalo ['oβalo] *nm* oval.
ovario [o'βarjo] *nm* ovary.
oveja [o'βexa] *nf* sheep; **~ negra** (*fig*) black
sheep (of the family).
overol [oβe'rol] *nm* (*AM*) overalls *pl*.
ovetense [oβe'tense] *adj* of *o* from Oviedo
♦ *nm/f* native *o* inhabitant of Oviedo.
ovillo [o'βiʎo] *nm* (*de lana*) ball; (*fig*) tangle;
hacerse un ~ to curl up (into a ball).
OVNI ['oβni] *nm abr* (= *objeto volante no
identificado*) UFO.
ovulación [oβula'θjon] *nf* ovulation.
óvulo ['oβulo] *nm* ovum.
oxidación [oksiða'θjon] *nf* rusting.
oxidar [oksi'ðar] *vt* to rust; **~se** *vr* to go
rusty; (*TEC*) to oxidize.
óxido ['oksiðo] *nm* oxide.
oxigenado, a [oksixe'naðo, a] *adj*
(*QUÍMICA*) oxygenated; (*pelo*) bleached.
oxigenar [oksixe'nar] *vt* to oxygenate; **~se**
vr to become oxygenated; (*fam*) to get
some fresh air.
oxígeno [ok'sixeno] *nm* oxygen.
oyendo [o'jendo] *etc vb V* **oír.**
oyente [o'jente] *nm/f* listener, hearer;
(*ESCOL*) unregistered *o* occasional
student.

P p

P, p [pe] *nf* (*letra*) P, p; **P de París** P for
Peter.
P *abr* (*REL*: = *padre*) Fr.; = **papa.**
p. *abr* (= *página*) p.
p.a. *abr* = **por autorización.**
pabellón [paβe'ʎon] *nm* bell tent; (*ARQ*)
pavilion; (*de hospital etc*) block, section;
(*bandera*) flag; **~ de conveniencia** (*COM*)
flag of convenience; **~ de la oreja** outer
ear.
pábilo ['paβilo] *nm* wick.
pábulo ['paβulo] *nm* food; **dar ~ a** to feed,
encourage.
PAC *nf abr* (= *Política Agrícola Común*) CAP.
pacense [pa'θense] *adj* of *o* from Badajoz
♦ *nm/f* native *o* inhabitant of Badajoz.
paceño, a [pa'θeɲo, a] *adj* of *o* from La
Paz ♦ *nm/f* native *o* inhabitant of La Paz.
pacer [pa'θer] *vi* to graze ♦ *vt* to graze on.
pachá [pa'tʃa] *nm*: **vivir como un ~** to live
like a king.
pachanguero, a [patʃan'gero, a] *adj* (*pey:
música*) noisy and catchy.
pachorra [pa'tʃorra] *nf* (*indolencia*)
slowness; (*tranquilidad*) calmness.
pachucho, a [pa'tʃutʃo, a] *adj* (*fruta*)
overripe; (*persona*) off-colour, poorly.
paciencia [pa'θjenθja] *nf* patience; **¡~!** be
patient!; **¡~ y barajar!** don't give up!;
perder la ~ to lose one's temper.
paciente [pa'θjente] *adj, nm/f* patient.
pacificación [paθifika'θjon] *nf* pacification.
pacificar [paθifi'kar] *vt* to pacify;
(*tranquilizar*) to calm.
pacífico, a [pa'θifiko, a] *adj* peaceful;
(*persona*) peace-loving; (*existencia*)
pacific; **el (Océano) P~** the Pacific
(Ocean).
pacifique [paθi'fike] *etc vb V* **pacificar.**
pacifismo [paθi'fismo] *nm* pacifism.
pacifista [paθi'fista] *nm/f* pacifist.
pack [pak] *nm* (*de yogures, latas*) pack; (*de
vacaciones*) package.
pacotilla [pako'tiʎa] *nf* trash; **de ~** shoddy.
pactar [pak'tar] *vt* to agree to, agree on
♦ *vi* to come to an agreement.
pacto ['pakto] *nm* (*tratado*) pact; (*acuerdo*)
agreement.

padecer [paðe'θer] *vt* (*sufrir*) to suffer; (*soportar*) to endure, put up with; (*ser víctima de*) to be a victim of ♦ *vi*: ~ **de** to suffer from.

padecimiento [paðeθi'mjento] *nm* suffering.

pádel ['paðel] *nm* paddle tennis.

padezca [pa'ðeθka] *etc vb* V **padecer**.

padrastro [pa'ðrastro] *nm* stepfather.

padre ['paðre] *nm* father ♦ *adj* (*fam*): **un éxito** ~ a tremendous success; ~**s** *nmpl* parents; ~ **espiritual** confessor; **P~ Nuestro** Lord's Prayer; ~ **político** father-in-law; **García** ~ García senior; **¡tu** ~**!** (*fam!*) up yours! (*!*).

padrino [pa'ðrino] *nm* godfather; (*fig*) sponsor, patron; ~**s** *nmpl* godparents; ~ **de boda** best man.

padrón [pa'ðron] *nm* (*censo*) census, roll; (*de socios*) register.

paella [pa'eʎa] *nf* paella, *dish of rice with meat, shellfish etc*.

paga ['paɣa] *nf* (*dinero pagado*) payment; (*sueldo*) pay, wages *pl*.

pagadero, a [paɣa'ðero, a] *adj* payable; ~ **a la entrega/a plazos** payable on delivery/in instalments.

pagano, a [pa'ɣano, a] *adj, nm/f* pagan, heathen.

pagar [pa'ɣar] *vt* (*gen*) to pay; (*las compras, crimen*) to pay for; (*deuda*) to pay (off); (*fig: favor*) to repay ♦ *vi* to pay; ~**se** *vr*: ~**se con algo** to be content with sth; **¡me las pagarás!** I'll get you for this!

pagaré [paɣa're] *nm* I.O.U.

página ['paxina] *nf* page; ~ **de inicio** (*INFORM*) home page; ~**s amarillas** Yellow Pages ®; ~ **web** web page.

paginación [paxina'θjon] *nf* pagination.

paginar [paxi'nar] *vt* (*INFORM, TIP*) to paginate.

pago ['paɣo] *nm* (*dinero*) payment; (*fig*) return; ~ **anticipado/a cuenta/a la entrega/en especie/inicial** advance payment/payment on account/cash on delivery/payment in kind/down payment; ~ **a título gracioso** ex gratia payment; **en** ~ **de** in return for.

pág(s). *abr* (= *página(s)*) p(p).

pague ['paɣe] *etc vb* V **pagar**.

paila ['paila] *nf* (*AM*) frying pan.

país [pa'is] *nm* (*gen*) country; (*región*) land; **los Países Bajos** the Low Countries; **el P~ Vasco** the Basque Country.

paisaje [pai'saxe] *nm* countryside, landscape; (*vista*) scenery.

paisano, a [pai'sano, a] *adj* of the same country ♦ *nm/f* (*compatriota*) fellow

countryman/woman; **vestir de** ~ (*soldado*) to be in civilian clothes; (*guardia*) to be in plain clothes.

paja ['paxa] *nf* straw; (*fig*) trash, rubbish; (*en libro, ensayo*) padding, waffle; **riñeron por un quítame allá esas** ~**s** they quarrelled over a trifle.

pajar [pa'xar] *nm* hay loft.

pajarita [paxa'rita] *nf* bow tie.

pájaro ['paxaro] *nm* bird; (*fam: astuto*) clever fellow; **tener la cabeza a** ~**s** to be featherbrained.

pajita [pa'xita] *nf* (drinking) straw.

pajizo, a [pa'xiθo, a] *adj* (*de paja*) straw *cpd*; (*techo*) thatched; (*color*) straw-coloured.

pakistaní [pakista'ni] *adj, nm/f* Pakistani.

pala ['pala] *nf* (*de mango largo*) spade; (*de mango corto*) shovel; (*raqueta etc*) bat; (: *de tenis*) racquet; (*CULIN*) slice; ~ **matamoscas** fly swat.

palabra [pa'laβra] *nf* (*gen, promesa*) word; (*facultad*) (power of) speech; (*derecho de hablar*) right to speak; **faltar a su** ~ to go back on one's word; **quedarse con la** ~ **en la boca** to stop short; (*en reunión, comité etc*) **tomar la** ~ to speak, take the floor; **pedir la** ~ to ask to be allowed to speak; **tener la** ~ to have the floor; **no encuentro** ~**s para expresarme** words fail me.

palabrería [palaβre'ria] *nf* hot air.

palabrota [pala'βrota] *nf* swearword.

palacio [pa'laθjo] *nm* palace; (*mansión*) mansion, large house; ~ **de justicia** courthouse; ~ **municipal** town/city hall.

palada [pa'laða] *nf* shovelful, spadeful; (*de remo*) stroke.

paladar [pala'ðar] *nm* palate.

paladear [palaðe'ar] *vt* to taste.

palanca [pa'lanka] *nf* lever; (*fig*) pull, influence; ~ **de cambio** (*AUTO*) gear lever, gearshift (*US*); ~ **de freno** (*AUTO*) brake lever; ~ **de gobierno** *o* **de control** (*INFORM*) joystick.

palangana [palan'gana] *nf* washbasin.

palco ['palko] *nm* box.

palenque [pa'lenke] *nm* (*cerca*) stockade, fence; (*área*) arena, enclosure; (*de gallos*) pit.

palentino, a [palen'tino, a] *adj* of *o* from Palencia ♦ *nm/f* native *o* inhabitant of Palencia.

paleolítico, a [paleo'litiko, a] *adj* paleolithic.

paleontología [paleontolo'xia] *nf* paleontology.

Palestina [pales'tina] *nf* Palestine.

palestino, a [pales'tino, a] *adj, nm/f* Palestinian.

palestra [pa'lestra] *nf*: **salir** *o* **saltar a la** ~ to come into the spotlight.

paleto, a [pa'leto, a] *nm/f* yokel, hick (*US*); ♦ *nf* (*pala*) small shovel; (*ARTE*) palette; (*ANAT*) shoulder blade; (*AM*) ice lolly.

paliar [pa'ljar] *vt* (*mitigar*) to mitigate; (*disfrazar*) to conceal.

paliativo [palja'tiβo] *nm* palliative.

palidecer [paliðe'θer] *vi* to turn pale.

palidez [pali'ðeθ] *nf* paleness.

palidezca [pali'ðeθka] *etc vb V* **palidecer**.

pálido, a [pa'liðo, a] *adj* pale.

palillo [pa'liʎo] *nm* small stick; (*para dientes*) toothpick; ~**s (chinos)** chopsticks; **estar hecho un** ~ to be as thin as a rake.

palio ['paljo] *nm* canopy.

palique [pa'like] *nm*: **estar de** ~ (*fam*) to have a chat.

paliza [pa'liθa] *nf* beating, thrashing; **dar** *o* **propinar** (*fam*) **una** ~ **a algn** to give sb a thrashing.

palma ['palma] *nf* (*ANAT*) palm; (*árbol*) palm tree; **batir** *o* **dar** ~**s** to clap, applaud; **llevarse la** ~ to triumph, win.

palmada [pal'maða] *nf* slap; ~**s** *nfpl* clapping *sg*, applause *sg*.

palmar [pal'mar] *vi* (*tb*: ~**la**) to die, kick the bucket.

palmarés [palma'res] *nm* (*lista*) list of winners; (*historial*) track record.

palmear [palme'ar] *vi* to clap.

palmero, a [pal'mero, a] *adj* of the island of Palma ♦ *nm/f* native *o* inhabitant of the island of Palma ♦ *nm* (*AM*), *nf* palm tree.

palmo ['palmo] *nm* (*medida*) span; (*fig*) small amount; ~ **a** ~ inch by inch.

palmotear [palmote'ar] *vi* to clap, applaud.

palmoteo [palmo'teo] *nm* clapping, applause.

palo ['palo] *nm* stick; (*poste*) post, pole; (*mango*) handle, shaft; (*golpe*) blow, hit; (*de golf*) club; (*de béisbol*) bat; (*NAUT*) mast; (*NAIPES*) suit; **vermut a** ~ **seco** straight vermouth; **de tal** ~ **tal astilla** like father like son.

paloma [pa'loma] *nf* dove, pigeon; ~ **mensajera** carrier *o* homing pigeon.

palomilla [palo'miʎa] *nf* moth; (*TEC: tuerca*) wing nut; (*soporte*) bracket.

palomitas [palo'mitas] *nfpl* popcorn *sg*.

palpable [pal'paβle] *adj* palpable; (*fig*) tangible.

palpar [pal'par] *vt* to touch, feel.

palpitación [palpita'θjon] *nf* palpitation.

palpitante [palpi'tante] *adj* palpitating; (*fig*) burning.

palpitar [palpi'tar] *vi* to palpitate; (*latir*) to

beat.

palta ['palta] *nf* (*AM*) avocado.

palúdico, a [pa'luðiko, a] *adj* marshy.

paludismo [palu'ðismo] *nm* malaria.

palurdo, a [pa'lurðo, a] *adj* coarse, uncouth ♦ *nm/f* yokel, hick (*US*).

pamela [pa'mela] *nf* sun hat.

pampa ['pampa] *nf* (*AM*) pampa(s), prairie.

pamplinas [pam'plinas] *nfpl* nonsense *sg*.

pamplonés, esa [pamplo'nes, esa], **pamplonica** [pamplo'nika] *adj* of *o* from Pamplona ♦ *nm/f* native *o* inhabitant of Pamplona.

pan [pan] *nm* bread; (*una barra*) loaf; ~ **de molde** sliced loaf; ~ **integral** wholemeal bread; ~ **rallado** breadcrumbs *pl*; **eso es** ~ **comido** it's a cinch; **llamar al** ~ ~ **y al vino vino** to call a spade a spade.

pana ['pana] *nf* corduroy.

panadería [panaðe'ria] *nf* baker's (shop).

panadero, a [pana'ðero, a] *nm/f* baker.

panal [pa'nal] *nm* honeycomb.

Panamá [pana'ma] *nm* Panama.

panameño, a [pana'meɲo, a] *adj* Panamanian.

pancarta [pan'karta] *nf* placard, banner.

pancho, a ['pantʃo, a] *adj*: **estar tan** ~ to remain perfectly calm.

pancito [pan'sito] *nm* (*AM*) (bread) roll.

páncreas ['pankreas] *nm* pancreas.

panda ['panda] *nm* panda ♦ *nf* gang.

pandereta [pande'reta] *nf* tambourine.

pandilla [pan'diʎa] *nf* set, group; (*de criminales*) gang; (*pey*) clique.

pando, a ['pando, a] *adj* sagging.

panecillo [pane'θiʎo] *nm* (bread) roll.

panel [pa'nel] *nm* panel; ~ **acústico** acoustic screen.

panera [pa'nera] *nf* bread basket.

panfleto [pan'fleto] *nm* (*POL etc*) pamphlet; lampoon.

pánico ['paniko] *nm* panic.

panificadora [panifika'ðora] *nf* bakery.

panorama [pano'rama] *nm* panorama; (*vista*) view.

panqué [pan'ke] *nm* (*AM*) pancake.

pantaletas [panta'letas] *nfpl* (*AM*) panties.

pantalla [pan'taʎa] *nf* (*de cine*) screen; (*cubreluz*) lampshade; (*INFORM*) screen, display; **servir de** ~ **a** to be a blind for; ~ **de cristal líquido** liquid crystal display; ~ **táctil** touch-sensitive screen; ~ **de ayuda** help screen.

pantalón [panta'lon] *nm*, **pantalones** [panta'lones] *nmpl* trousers *pl*, pants *pl* (*US*); **pantalones cortos** shorts; **pantalones vaqueros** jeans *pl*.

pantano [pan'tano] *nm* (*ciénaga*) marsh,

swamp; (*depósito: de agua*) reservoir; (*fig*) jam, fix, difficulty.

pantera [pan'tera] *nf* panther.

pantis ['pantis] *nmpl* tights.

pantomima [panto'mima] *nf* pantomime.

pantorrilla [panto'rriʎa] *nf* calf (of the leg).

pantufla [pan'tufla] *nf* slipper.

panty ['panti] *nm* = **pantis**.

panza ['panθa] *nf* belly, paunch.

panzón, ona [pan'θon, ona], **panzudo, a** [pan'θuðo, a] *adj* fat, potbellied.

pañal [pa'ɲal] *nm* nappy, diaper (*US*); **estar todavía en ~es** to be still wet behind the ears.

pañería [paɲe'ria] *nf* (*artículos*) drapery; (*tienda*) draper's (shop), dry-goods store (*US*).

paño ['paɲo] *nm* (*tela*) cloth; (*pedazo de tela*) (piece of) cloth; (*trapo*) duster, rag; **~ de cocina** dishcloth; **~ higiénico** sanitary towel; **~s menores** underclothes; **~s calientes** (*fig*) half-measures; **no andarse con ~s calientes** to pull no punches.

pañuelo [pa'ɲwelo] *nm* handkerchief, hanky (*fam*); (*para la cabeza*) (head)scarf.

papa ['papa] *nf* (*AM*) potato ♦ *nm*: **el P~** the Pope.

papá [pa'pa] *nm, pl* **papás** (*fam*) dad, daddy, pop (*US*); **~s** *nmpl* parents; **hijo de ~** Hooray Henry (*fam*).

papada [pa'paða] *nf* double chin.

papagayo [papa'ɣajo] *nm* parrot.

papanatas [papa'natas] *nm inv* (*fam*) sucker, simpleton.

paparrucha [papa'rrutʃa] *nf* (*tontería*) piece of nonsense.

papaya [pa'paja] *nf* papaya.

papear [pape'ar] *vt, vi* (*fam*) to eat.

papel [pa'pel] *nm* (*gen*) paper; (*hoja de papel*) sheet of paper; (*TEAT*) part, role; **~es** *nmpl* identification papers; **~ de calco/carbón/de cartas** tracing paper/carbon paper/stationery; **~ continuo** (*INFORM*) continuous stationery; **~ de envolver/de empapelar** brown paper, wrapping paper/wallpaper; **~ de aluminio/higiénico** tinfoil/toilet paper; **~ del** *o* **de pagos al Estado** government bonds *pl*; **~ de lija** sandpaper; **~ moneda** paper money; **~ plegado** (**en abanico** *o* **en acordeón**) fanfold paper; **~ secante** blotting paper.

papeleo [pape'leo] *nm* red tape.

papelera [pape'lera] *nf* (*cesto*) wastepaper basket; (*escritorio*) desk; **~ de reciclaje** (*INFORM*) wastebasket.

papelería [papele'ria] *nf* (*tienda*) stationer's (shop).

papeleta [pape'leta] *nf* (*pedazo de papel*) slip *o* bit of paper; (*POL*) ballot paper; (*ESCOL*) report; **¡vaya ~!** this is a tough one!

paperas [pa'peras] *nfpl* mumps *sg*.

papilla [pa'piʎa] *nf* (*de bebé*) baby food; (*pey*) mush; **estar hecho ~** to be dog-tired.

paquete [pa'kete] *nm* (*caja*) packet; (*bulto*) parcel; (*AM fam*) nuisance, bore; (*INFORM*) package (*of software*); (*vacaciones*) package tour; **~ de aplicaciones** (*INFORM*) applications package; **~ integrado** (*INFORM*) integrated package; **~ de gestión integrado** combined management suite; **~s postales** parcel post *sg*.

paquistaní [pakista'ni] = **pakistaní**.

par [par] *adj* (*igual*) like, equal; (*MAT*) even ♦ *nm* equal; (*de guantes*) pair; (*de veces*) couple; (*dignidad*) peer; (*GOLF, COM*) par ♦ *nf* par; **~es o nones** odds or evens; **abrir de ~ en ~** to open wide; **a la ~** par; **sobre/bajo la ~** above/below par.

para ['para] *prep* (*gen*) for; **no es ~ comer** it's not for eating; **decir ~ sí** to say to o.s.; **¿~ qué lo quieres?** what do you want it for?; **se casaron ~ separarse otra vez** they married only to separate again; **~ entonces** by then *o* that time; **lo tendré ~ mañana** I'll have it for tomorrow; **ir ~ casa** to go home, head for home; **~ profesor es muy estúpido** he's very stupid for a teacher; **¿quién es usted ~ gritar así?** who are you to shout like that?; **tengo bastante ~ vivir** I have enough to live on.

parabellum [paraße'lum] *nm* (automatic) pistol.

parabién [para'ßjen] *nm* congratulations *pl*.

parábola [pa'raßola] *nf* parable; (*MAT*) parabola.

parabólica [para'ßolika] *nf* (*tb:* **antena ~**) satellite dish.

parabrisas [para'ßrisas] *nm inv* windscreen, windshield (*US*).

paracaídas [paraka'iðas] *nm inv* parachute.

paracaidista [parakai'ðista] *nm/f* parachutist; (*MIL*) paratrooper.

parachoques [para'tʃokes] *nm inv* bumper, fender (*US*); shock absorber.

parada [pa'raða] *nf V* **parado**.

paradero [para'ðero] *nm* stopping-place; (*situación*) whereabouts.

parado, a [pa'raðo, a] *adj* (*persona*) motionless, standing still; (*fábrica*) closed, at a standstill; (*coche*) stopped; (*AM*: *de pie*) standing (up); (*sin empleo*) unemployed, idle; (*confuso*) confused ♦ *nf* (*gen*) stop; (*acto*) stopping; (*de industria*) shutdown, stoppage; (*lugar*) stopping-place; **salir bien** ~ to come off well; **parada de autobús** bus stop; **parada discrecional** request stop; **parada en seco** sudden stop; **parada de taxis** taxi rank.

paradoja [para'ðoxa] *nf* paradox.

paradójico, a [para'ðoxiko, a] *adj* paradoxical.

parador [para'ðor] *nm* (luxury) hotel.

parafrasear [parafrase'ar] *vt* to paraphrase.

paráfrasis [pa'rafrasis] *nf inv* paraphrase.

paraguas [pa'raɣwas] *nm inv* umbrella.

Paraguay [para'ɣwai] *nm*: **el** ~ Paraguay.

paraguayo, a [para'ɣwajo, a] *adj, nm/f* Paraguayan.

paraíso [para'iso] *nm* paradise, heaven; ~ **fiscal** (*COM*) tax haven.

paraje [pa'raxe] *nm* place, spot.

paralelo, a [para'lelo, a] *adj, nm* parallel; **en** ~ (*ELEC, INFORM*) (in) parallel.

paralice [para'liθe] *etc vb V* **paralizar**.

parálisis [pa'ralisis] *nf inv* paralysis; ~ **cerebral** cerebral palsy; ~ **progresiva** creeping paralysis.

paralítico, a [para'litiko, a] *adj, nm/f* paralytic.

paralizar [parali'θar] *vt* to paralyse; ~**se** *vr* to become paralysed; (*fig*) to come to a standstill.

parámetro [pa'rametro] *nm* parameter.

paramilitar [paramili'tar] *adj* paramilitary.

páramo ['paramo] *nm* bleak plateau.

parangón [paran'gon] *nm*: **sin** ~ incomparable.

paraninfo [para'ninfo] *nm* (*ESCOL*) assembly hall.

paranoia [para'noia] *nf* paranoia.

paranoico, a [para'noiko, a] *adj, nm/f* paranoid.

paranormal [paranor'mal] *adj* paranormal.

parapetarse [parape'tarse] *vr* to shelter.

parapléjico, a [para'plexiko, a] *adj, nm/f* paraplegic.

parar [pa'rar] *vt* to stop; (*progreso etc*) to check, halt; (*golpe*) to ward off ♦ *vi* to stop; (*hospedarse*) to stay, put up; ~**se** *vr* to stop; (*AM*) to stand up; **no** ~ **de hacer algo** to keep on doing sth; **ha parado de llover** it has stopped raining; **van a** ~ **en la comisaría** they're going to end up in the police station; **no sabemos en qué va a** ~ **todo esto** we don't know where all

this is going to end; ~**se a hacer algo** to stop to do sth; ~**se en** to pay attention to.

pararrayos [para'rrajos] *nm inv* lightning conductor.

parásito, a [pa'rasito, a] *nm/f* parasite.

parasol [para'sol] *nm* parasol, sunshade.

parcela [par'θela] *nf* plot, piece of ground, smallholding.

parche ['partʃe] *nm* patch.

parchís [par'tʃis] *nm* ludo.

parcial [par'θjal] *adj* (*pago*) part-; (*eclipse*) partial; (*juez*) prejudiced, biased.

parcialidad [parθjali'ðað] *nf* (*prejuicio*) prejudice, bias.

parco, a ['parko, a] *adj* (*frugal*) sparing; (*moderado*) moderate.

pardillo, a [par'ðiʎo, a] *adj* (*pey*) provincial ♦ *nm/f* (*pey*) country bumpkin ♦ *nm* (*ZOOL*) linnet.

pardo, a ['parðo, a] *adj* (*color*) brown; (*cielo*) overcast; (*voz*) flat, dull.

parear [pare'ar] *vt* (*juntar, hacer par*) to match, put together; (*calcetines*) to put into pairs; (*BIO*) to mate, pair.

parecer [pare'θer] *nm* (*opinión*) opinion, view; (*aspecto*) looks *pl* ♦ *vi* (*tener apariencia*) to seem, look; (*asemejarse*) to look like, seem like; (*aparecer, llegar*) to appear; ~**se** *vr* to look alike, resemble each other; ~**se a** to look like, resemble; **al** ~ apparently; **me parece que** I think (that), it seems to me that.

parecido, a [pare'θiðo, a] *adj* similar ♦ *nm* similarity, likeness, resemblance; ~ **a** like, similar to; **bien** ~ good-looking, nice-looking.

pared [pa'reð] *nf* wall; ~ **divisoria/ medianera** dividing/party wall; **subirse por las** ~**es** (*fam*) to go up the wall.

paredón [pare'ðon] *nm*: **llevar a algn al** ~ to put sb up against a wall, shoot sb.

parejo, a [pa'rexo, a] *adj* (*igual*) equal; (*liso*) smooth, even ♦ *nf* (*dos*) pair; (: *de personas*) couple; (*el otro: de un par*) other one (of a pair); (: *persona*) partner; (*Guardias*) Civil Guard patrol.

parentela [paren'tela] *nf* relations *pl*.

parentesco [paren'tesko] *nm* relationship.

paréntesis [pa'rentesis] *nm inv* parenthesis; (*digresión*) digression; (*en escrito*) bracket.

parezca [pa'reθka] *etc vb V* **parecer**.

parida [pa'riða] *nf*: ~ **mental** (*fam*) dumb idea.

paridad [pari'ðað] *nf* (*ECON*) parity.

pariente, a [pa'rjente, a] *nm/f* relative, relation.

parihuela [pari'wela] *nf* stretcher.

paripé [pari'pe] *nm*: **hacer el ~** to put on an act.

parir [pa'rir] *vt* to give birth to ♦ *vi* (*mujer*) to give birth, have a baby; (*yegua*) to foal; (*vaca*) to calve.

París [pa'ris] *nm* Paris.

parisiense [pari'sjense] *adj, nm/f* Parisian.

paritario, a [pari'tarjo, a] *adj* equal.

parking ['parkin] *nm* car park, parking lot (US).

parlamentar [parlamen'tar] *vi* (*negociar*) to parley.

parlamentario, a [parlamen'tarjo, a] *adj* parliamentary ♦ *nm/f* member of parliament.

parlamento [parla'mento] *nm* (*POL*) parliament; (*JUR*) speech.

parlanchín, ina [parlan't∫in, ina] *adj* loose-tongued, indiscreet ♦ *nm/f* chatterbox.

parlante [par'lante] *nm* (*AM*) loudspeaker.

parlar [par'lar] *vi* to chatter (away).

parlotear [parlote'ar] *vi* to chatter, prattle.

parloteo [parlo'teo] *nm* chatter, prattle.

paro ['paro] *nm* (*huelga*) stoppage (of work), strike; (*desempleo*) unemployment; **~ cardiaco** cardiac arrest; **subsidio de ~** unemployment benefit; **hay ~ en la industria** work in the industry is at a standstill; **~ del sistema** (*INFORM*) system shutdown.

parodia [pa'roðja] *nf* parody.

parodiar [paro'ðjar] *vt* to parody.

parpadear [parpaðe'ar] *vi* (*los ojos*) to blink; (*luz*) to flicker.

parpadeo [parpa'ðeo] *nm* (*de ojos*) blinking, winking; (*de luz*) flickering.

párpado ['parpaðo] *nm* eyelid.

parque ['parke] *nm* (*lugar verde*) park; **~ de atracciones/de bomberos/zoológico** fairground/fire station/zoo; **~ infantil** children's playground; **~ temático** theme park.

parqué, parquet [par'ke] *nm* parquet.

parqueadero [parkea'ðero] *nm* (*AM*) car park, parking lot (US).

parquímetro [par'kimetro] *nm* parking meter.

parra ['parra] *nf* grapevine.

párrafo ['parrafo] *nm* paragraph; **echar un ~** (*fam*) to have a chat.

parranda [pa'rranda] *nf* (*fam*) spree, binge.

parrilla [pa'rriʎa] *nf* (*CULIN*) grill; (*AM AUTO*) roof-rack; **~ (de salida)** (*AUTO*) starting grid; **carne a la ~** grilled meat.

parrillada [parri'ʎaða] *nf* barbecue.

párroco ['parroko] *nm* parish priest.

parroquia [pa'rrokja] *nf* parish; (*iglesia*) parish church; (*COM*) clientele, customers *pl*.

parroquiano, a [parro'kjano, a] *nm/f* parishioner; client, customer.

parsimonia [parsi'monja] *nf* (*frugalidad*) sparingness; (*calma*) deliberateness; **con ~** calmly.

parte ['parte] *nm* message; (*informe*) report; **~ meteorológico** weather forecast ♦ *nf* part; (*lado, cara*) side; (*de reparto*) share; (*JUR*) party; **en alguna ~ de Europa** somewhere in Europe; **en cualquier ~** anywhere; **por ahí no se va a ninguna ~** that leads nowhere; (*fig*) this is getting us nowhere; **en o por todas ~s** everywhere; **en gran ~** to a large extent; **la mayor ~ de los españoles** most Spaniards; **de algún tiempo a esta ~** for some time past; **de ~ de algn** on sb's behalf; **¿de ~ de quién?** (*TELEC*) who is speaking?; **por ~ de** on the part of; **yo por mi ~** I for my part; **por una ~ ... por otra ~** on the one hand, ... on the other (hand); **dar ~ a algn** to report to sb; **tomar ~** to take part.

partera [par'tera] *nf* midwife.

parterre [par'terre] *nm* (flower)bed.

partición [parti'θjon] *nf* division, sharing-out; (*POL*) partition.

participación [partiθipa'θjon] *nf* (*acto*) participation, taking part; (*parte*) share; (*COM*) share, stock (US); (*de lotería*) shared prize; (*aviso*) notice, notification; **~ en los beneficios** profit-sharing; **~ minoritaria** minority interest.

participante [partiθi'pante] *nm/f* participant.

participar [partiθi'par] *vt* to notify, inform ♦ *vi* to take part, participate; **~ en una empresa** (*COM*) to invest in an enterprise; **le participo que ...** I have to tell you that ....

partícipe [par'tiθipe] *nm/f* participant; **hacer ~ a algn de algo** to inform sb of sth.

participio [parti'θipjo] *nm* participle; **~ de pasado/presente** past/present participle.

partícula [par'tikula] *nf* particle.

particular [partiku'lar] *adj* (*especial*) particular, special; (*individual, personal*) private, personal ♦ *nm* (*punto, asunto*) particular, point; (*individuo*) individual; **tiene coche ~** he has a car of his own; **no dijo mucho sobre el ~** he didn't say much about the matter.

particularice [partikula'riθe] *etc vb V* **particularizar**.

particularidad [partikulari'ðað] *nf*
peculiarity; **tiene la ~ de que ...** one of
its special features is (that) ....

particularizar [partikulari'θar] *vt* to
distinguish; (*especificar*) to specify;
(*detallar*) to give details about.

partida [par'tiða] *nf* (*salida*) departure;
(*COM*) entry, item; (*juego*) game; (*grupo,
bando*) band, group; **mala ~** dirty trick;
~ de nacimiento/matrimonio/defunción
birth/marriage/death certificate; **echar
una ~** to have a game.

partidario, a [parti'ðarjo, a] *adj* partisan
♦ *nm/f* (*DEPORTE*) supporter; (*POL*) partisan.

partidismo [parti'ðismo] *nm* (*JUR*)
partisanship, bias; (*POL*) party politics.

partido [par'tiðo] *nm* (*POL*) party;
(*encuentro*) game, match; (*apoyo*)
support; (*equipo*) team; **~ amistoso**
(*DEPORTE*) friendly (game); **~ de fútbol**
football match; **sacar ~ de** to profit
from, benefit from; **tomar ~** to take
sides.

partir [par'tir] *vt* (*dividir*) to split, divide;
(*compartir, distribuir*) to share (out),
distribute; (*romper*) to break open, split
open; (*rebanada*) to cut (off) ♦ *vi* (*tomar
camino*) to set off, set out; (*comenzar*) to
start (off *o* out); **~se** *vr* to crack *o* split *o*
break (in two *etc*); **a ~ de** (starting)
from; **~se de risa** to split one's sides
(laughing).

partitura [parti'tura] *nf* score.

parto ['parto] *nm* birth, delivery; (*fig*)
product, creation; **estar de ~** to be in
labour.

parvulario [parβu'larjo] *nm* nursery
school, kindergarten.

párvulo, a ['parβulo, a] *nm/f* infant.

pasa ['pasa] *nf* V **paso**.

pasable [pa'saβle] *adj* passable.

pasada [pa'saða] *nf* V **pasado**.

pasadizo [pasa'ðiθo] *nm* (*pasillo*) passage,
corridor; (*callejuela*) alley.

pasado, a [pa'saðo, a] *adj* past; (*malo:
comida, fruta*) bad; (*muy cocido*)
overdone; (*anticuado*) out of date ♦ *nm*
past; (*LING*) past (tense) ♦ *nf* passing,
passage; (*acción de pulir*) rub, polish; **~
mañana** the day after tomorrow; **el mes
~** last month; **~s dos días** after two
days; **lo ~, ~** let bygones be bygones; **~
de moda** old-fashioned; **~ por agua**
(*huevo*) boiled; **estar ~ de vueltas** *o* **de
rosca** (*grifo, tuerca*) to be worn; **de
pasada** in passing, incidentally; **una
mala pasada** a dirty trick.

pasador [pasa'ðor] *nm* (*gen*) bolt; (*de pelo*)

pin, grip, slide.

pasaje [pa'saxe] *nm* (*gen*) passage; (*pago
de viaje*) fare; (*los pasajeros*) passengers
pl; (*pasillo*) passageway.

pasajero, a [pasa'xero, a] *adj* passing;
(*ave*) migratory ♦ *nm/f* passenger;
(*viajero*) traveller.

pasamanos [pasa'manos] *nm inv* rail,
handrail; (*de escalera*) banister.

pasamontañas [pasamon'taɲas] *nm inv*
balaclava (helmet).

pasaporte [pasa'porte] *nm* passport.

pasar [pa'sar] *vt* (*gen*) to pass; (*tiempo*) to
spend; (*durezas*) to suffer, endure;
(*noticia*) to give, pass on; (*película*) to
show; (*persona*) to take, conduct; (*río*) to
cross; (*barrera*) to pass through; (*falta*) to
overlook, tolerate; (*contrincante*) to
surpass, do better than; (*coche*) to
overtake; (*contrabando*) to smuggle (in/
out); (*enfermedad*) to give, infect with
♦ *vi* (*gen*) to pass, go; (*terminarse*) to be
over; (*ocurrir*) to happen; **~se** *vr* (*efectos*)
to pass, be over; (*flores*) to fade; (*comida*)
to go bad, go off; (*fig*) to overdo it, go
too far *o* over the top; **~ de** to go
beyond, exceed; **¡pase!** come in!; **nos
hicieron ~** they showed us in; **~ por** to
fetch; **~ por alto** to skip; **~ por una crisis**
to go through a crisis; **se hace ~ por
médico** he passes himself off as a
doctor; **~lo bien/bomba** *o* **de maravilla**
to have a good/great time; **~se al
enemigo** to go over to the enemy; **~se
de la raya** to go too far; **¡no te pases!**
don't try me!; **se me pasó** I forgot; **se
me pasó el turno** I missed my turn; **no
se le pasa nada** nothing escapes him, he
misses nothing; **ya se te pasará** you'll
get over it; **¿qué pasa?** what's
happening?, what's going on?, what's
up?; **¡cómo pasa el tiempo!** time just
flies!; **pase lo que pase** come what may;
el autobús pasa por nuestra casa the bus
goes past our house.

pasarela [pasa'rela] *nf* footbridge; (*en
barco*) gangway.

pasatiempo [pasa'tjempo] *nm* pastime,
hobby; (*distracción*) amusement.

Pascua, pascua ['paskwa] *nf*: **(de
Resurrección)** Easter; **~ de Navidad**
Christmas; **~s** *nfpl* Christmas time *sg*;
¡felices ~s! Merry Christmas; **de ~s a
Ramos** once in a blue moon; **hacer la ~ a**
(*fam*) to annoy, bug.

pase ['pase] *nm* pass; (*CINE*) performance,
showing; (*COM*) permit; (*JUR*) licence.

pasear [pase'ar] *vt* to take for a walk;

(*exhibir*) to parade, show off ♦ *vi*, ~**se** *vr*
to walk, go for a walk; ~ **en coche** to go
for a drive.

paseo [pa'seo] *nm* (*avenida*) avenue;
(*distancia corta*) short walk; ~ **marítimo**
promenade; **dar un** ~ to go for a walk; ~
en bicicleta (bike) ride; ~ **en barco** boat
trip; **mandar a algn a** ~ to tell sb to go to
blazes; ¡**vete a** ~! get lost!

pasillo [pa'siʎo] *nm* passage, corridor.

pasión [pa'sjon] *nf* passion.

pasional [pasjo'nal] *adj* passionate; **crimen**
~ crime of passion.

pasivo, a [pa'siβo, a] *adj* passive; (*inactivo*)
inactive ♦ *nm* (*COM*) liabilities *pl*, debts *pl*;
(*de cuenta*) debit side; ~ **circulante**
current liabilities.

pasma ['pasma] *nm* (*fam*) cop.

pasmado, a [pas'maðo, a] *adj* (*asombrado*)
astonished; (*atontado*) bewildered.

pasmar [pas'mar] *vt* (*asombrar*) to amaze,
astonish; ~**se** *vr* to be amazed *o*
astonished.

pasmo ['pasmo] *nm* amazement,
astonishment; (*fig*) wonder, marvel.

pasmoso, a [pas'moso, a] *adj* amazing,
astonishing.

paso, a ['paso, a] *adj* dried ♦ *nm* (*gen, de
baile*) step; (*modo de andar*) walk; (*huella*)
footprint; (*rapidez*) speed, pace, rate;
(*camino accesible*) way through, passage;
(*cruce*) crossing; (*pasaje*) passing,
passage; (*REL*) *religious float or
sculpture*; (*GEO*) pass; (*estrecho*) strait;
(*fig*) step, measure; (*apuro*) difficulty ♦ *nf*
raisin; **pasa de Corinto/de Esmirna**
currant/sultana; ~ **a** ~ step by step; **a
ese** ~ (*fig*) at that rate; **salir al** ~ **de** *o* **a**
to waylay; **salir del** ~ to get out of
trouble; **dar un** ~ **en falso** to trip; (*fig*) to
take a false step; **estar de** ~ to be
passing through; ~ **atrás** step
backwards; (*fig*) backward step; ~
elevado/subterráneo flyover/subway,
underpass (*US*); **prohibido el** ~ no entry;
ceda el ~ give way; *V tb* **Semana Santa**.

pasota [pa'sota] *adj, nm/f* (*fam*) ≈ dropout;
ser un (tipo) ~ to be a bit of a dropout;
(*ser indiferente*) not to care about
anything.

pasotismo [paso'tismo] *nm* underground *o*
alternative culture.

pasta ['pasta] *nf* (*gen*) paste; (*CULIN: masa*)
dough; (: *de bizcochos etc*) pastry; (*fam*)
money, dough; (*encuadernación*)
hardback; ~**s** *nfpl* (*bizcochos*) pastries,
small cakes; (*espaguetis etc*) pasta; ~ **de
dientes** *o* **dentífrica** toothpaste; ~ **de**

madera wood pulp.

pastar [pas'tar] *vt, vi* to graze.

pastel [pas'tel] *nm* (*dulce*) cake; (*de carne*)
pie; (*ARTE*) pastel; (*fig*) plot; ~**es** *nmpl*
pastry *sg*, confectionery *sg*.

pastelería [pastele'ria] *nf* cake shop,
pastry shop.

pasteurizado, a [pasteuri'θaðo, a] *adj*
pasteurized.

pastilla [pas'tiʎa] *nf* (*de jabón, chocolate*)
cake, bar; (*píldora*) tablet, pill.

pastizal [pasti'θal] *nm* pasture.

pasto ['pasto] *nm* (*hierba*) grass; (*lugar*)
pasture, field; (*fig*) food, nourishment.

pastor, a [pas'tor, a] *nm/f* shepherd(ess)
♦ *nm* clergyman, pastor; (*ZOOL*)
sheepdog; ~ **alemán** Alsatian.

pastoso, a [pas'toso, a] *adj* (*material*)
doughy, pasty; (*lengua*) furry; (*voz*)
mellow.

pat. *abr* (= *patente*) pat.

pata ['pata] *nf* (*pierna*) leg; (*pie*) foot; (*de
muebles*) leg; ~**s arriba** upside down; **a
cuatro** ~**s** on all fours; **meter la** ~ to put
one's foot in it; ~ **de cabra** (*TEC*)
crowbar; ~**s de gallo** crow's feet; **tener
buena/mala** ~ to be lucky/unlucky.

patada [pa'taða] *nf* stamp; (*puntapié*) kick;
a ~**s** in abundance; (*trato*) roughly; **echar
a algn a** ~**s** to kick sb out.

patagón, ona [pata'ɣon, ona] *adj, nm/f*
Patagonian.

Patagonia [pata'ɣonja] *nf*: **la** ~ Patagonia.

patalear [patale'ar] *vi* to stamp one's feet.

pataleo [pata'leo] *nm* stamping.

patán [pa'tan] *nm* rustic, yokel.

patata [pa'tata] *nf* potato; ~**s fritas** *o* **a la
española** chips, French fries; ~**s a la
inglesa** crisps; **ni** ~ (*fam*) nothing at all;
no entendió ni ~ he didn't understand a
single word.

paté [pa'te] *nm* pâté.

patear [pate'ar] *vt* (*pisar*) to stamp on,
trample (on); (*pegar con el pie*) to kick
♦ *vi* to stamp (with rage), stamp one's foot.

patentar [paten'tar] *vt* to patent.

patente [pa'tente] *adj* obvious, evident;
(*COM*) patent ♦ *nf* patent.

patera [pa'tera] *nf* boat.

paternal [pater'nal] *adj* fatherly, paternal.

paternalista [paterna'lista] *adj* (*tono,
actitud etc*) patronizing.

paternidad [paterni'ðað] *nf* fatherhood,
parenthood; (*JUR*) paternity.

paterno, a [pa'terno, a] *adj* paternal.

patético, a [pa'tetiko, a] *adj* pathetic,
moving.

patíbulo [pa'tiβulo] *nm* scaffold,

gallows sg.

patilla [pa'tiʎa] nf (de gafas) arm; (de pelo) sideburn.

patín [pa'tin] nm skate; (de tobogán) runner; ~ **de hielo** ice skate; ~ **de ruedas** roller skate.

patinaje [pati'naxe] nm skating.

patinar [pati'nar] vi to skate; (resbalarse) to skid, slip; (fam) to slip up, blunder.

patinazo [pati'naθo] nm (AUTO) skid; **dar un** ~ (fam) to blunder.

patio [p'patjo] nm (de casa) patio, courtyard; ~ **de recreo** playground.

pato ['pato] nm duck; **pagar el** ~ (fam) to take the blame, carry the can.

patológico, a [pato'loxiko, a] adj pathological.

patoso, a [pa'toso, a] adj awkward, clumsy.

patraña [pa'traɲa] nf story, fib.

patria ['patrja] nf native land, mother country; ~ **chica** home town.

patrimonio [patri'monjo] nm inheritance; (fig) heritage; (COM) net worth.

patriota [pa'trjota] nm/f patriot.

patriotero, a [patrjo'tero, a] adj chauvinistic.

patriótico, a [pa'trjotiko, a] adj patriotic.

patriotismo [patrjo'tismo] nm patriotism.

patrocinador, a [patroθina'ðor, a] nm/f sponsor.

patrocinar [patroθi'nar] vt to sponsor; (apoyar) to back, support.

patrocinio [patro'θinjo] nm sponsorship; backing, support.

patrón, ona [pa'tron, ona] nm/f (jefe) boss, chief, master/mistress; (propietario) landlord/lady; (REL) patron saint ♦ nm (COSTURA) pattern; (TEC) standard; ~ **oro** gold standard.

patronal [patro'nal] adj: **la clase** ~ management; **cierre** ~ lockout.

patronato [patro'nato] nm sponsorship; (acto) patronage; (COM) employers' association; (fundación) trust; **el** ~ **de turismo** the tourist board.

patrulla [pa'truʎa] nf patrol.

patrullar [patru'ʎar] vi to patrol.

paulatino, a [paula'tino, a] adj gradual, slow.

paupérrimo, a [pau'perrimo, a] adj very poor, poverty-stricken.

pausa ['pausa] nf pause; (intervalo) break; (interrupción) interruption; (TEC: en videograbadora) hold; **con** ~ slowly.

pausado, a [pau'saðo, a] adj slow, deliberate.

pauta ['pauta] nf line, guide line.

pavimento [paβi'mento] nm (ARQ) flooring.

pavo ['paβo] nm turkey; (necio) silly thing, idiot; ~ **real** peacock; ¡**no seas** ~! don't be silly!

pavonearse [paβone'arse] vr to swagger, show off.

pavor [pa'βor] nm dread, terror.

payasada [paja'saða] nf ridiculous thing (to do); ~**s** nfpl clowning sg.

payaso, a [pa'jaso, a] nm/f clown.

payo, a ['pajo, a] adj, nm/f non-gipsy.

paz [paθ] nf peace; (tranquilidad) peacefulness, tranquillity; **dejar a algn en** ~ to leave sb alone o in peace; **hacer las paces** to make peace; (fig) to make up; ¡**haya** ~! stop it!

pazca ['paθka] etc vb V **pacer**.

PC nm abr (POL: = Partido Comunista) CP.

P.C.E. nm abr = Partido Comunista Español.

PCL nf abr (= pantalla de cristal líquido) LCD.

PCUS [pe'kus] nm abr (= Partido Comunista de la Unión Soviética) Soviet Communist Party.

P.D. abr (= posdata) P.S.

pdo. abr (= pasado) ult.

peaje [pe'axe] nm toll; **autopista de** ~ toll motorway, turnpike (US).

peatón [pea'ton] nm pedestrian; **paso de peatones** pedestrian crossing, crosswalk (US).

peca ['peka] nf freckle.

pecado [pe'kaðo] nm sin.

pecador, a [peka'ðor, a] adj sinful ♦ nm/f sinner.

pecaminoso, a [pekami'noso, a] adj sinful.

pecar [pe'kar] vi (REL) to sin; (fig): ~ **de generoso** to be too generous.

pecera [pe'θera] nf goldfish bowl.

pecho ['petʃo] nm (ANAT) chest; (de mujer) breast(s) (pl), bosom; (corazón) heart, breast; (valor) courage, spirit; **dar el** ~ **a** to breast-feed; **tomar algo a** ~ to take sth to heart; **no le cabía en el** ~ he was bursting with happiness.

pechuga [pe'tʃuɣa] nf breast (of chicken etc).

pecoso, a [pe'koso, a] adj freckled.

peculiar [peku'ljar] adj special, peculiar; (característico) typical, characteristic.

peculiaridad [pekuljari'ðað] nf peculiarity; special feature, characteristic.

pedagogía [peðaɣo'xia] nf education.

pedagogo [peða'ɣoɣo] nm pedagogue, teacher.

pedal [pe'ðal] nm pedal; ~ **de embrague** clutch (pedal); ~ **de freno** footbrake.

pedalear [peðale'ar] vi to pedal.

pedante [pe'ðante] *adj* pedantic ♦ *nm/f* pedant.

pedantería [peðante'ria] *nf* pedantry.

pedazo [pe'ðaθo] *nm* piece, bit; **hacerse ~s** to fall to pieces; (*romperse*) to smash, shatter; **un ~ de pan** a scrap of bread; (*fig*) a terribly nice person.

pedernal [peðer'nal] *nm* flint.

pedestal [peðes'tal] *nm* base; **tener/poner a algn en un ~** to put sb on a pedestal.

pedestre [pe'ðestre] *adj* pedestrian; **carrera ~** foot race.

pediatra [pe'ðjatra] *nm/f* paediatrician (*BRIT*), pediatrician (*US*).

pediatría [peðja'tria] *nf* paediatrics *sg* (*BRIT*), pediatrics *sg* (*US*).

pedicuro, a [peði'kuro, a] *nm/f* chiropodist (*BRIT*), podiatrist (*US*).

pedido [pe'ðiðo] *nm* (*COM: mandado*) order; (*petición*) request; **~s en cartera** (*COM*) backlog *sg*.

pedigrí [peði'ɣri] *nm* pedigree.

pedir [pe'ðir] *vt* to ask for, request; (*comida, COM: mandar*) to order; (*exigir: precio*) to ask; (*necesitar*) to need, demand, require ♦ *vi* to ask; **~ prestado** to borrow; **~ disculpas** to apologize; **me pidió que cerrara la puerta** he asked me to shut the door; **¿cuánto piden por el coche?** how much are they asking for the car?

pedo ['peðo] (*fam*) *adj inv*: **estar ~** to be pissed (*!*) ♦ *nm* fart (*!*).

pedrada [pe'ðraða] *nf* throw of a stone; (*golpe*) blow from a stone; **herir a algn de una ~** to hit sb with a stone.

pedrea [pe'ðrea] *nf* (*granizada*) hailstorm; (*de lotería*) minor prizes.

pedrisco [pe'ðrisko] *nm* (*granizo*) hail; (*granizada*) hailstorm.

Pedro ['peðro] *nm* Peter; **entrar como ~ por su casa** to come in as if one owned the place.

pega ['peɣa] *nf* (*dificultad*) snag; **de ~** false, dud; **poner ~s** to raise objections.

pegadizo, a [peɣa'ðiθo, a] *adj* (*canción etc*) catchy.

pegajoso, a [peɣa'xoso, a] *adj* sticky.

pegamento [peɣa'mento] *nm* gum.

pegar [pe'ɣar] *vt* (*papel, sellos*) to stick (on); (*con cola*) to glue; (*cartel*) to post, stick up; (*coser*) to sew (on); (*unir: partes*) to join, fix together; (*INFORM*) to paste; (*MED*) to give, infect with; (*dar: golpe*) to give, deal ♦ *vi* (*adherirse*) to stick, adhere; (*INFORM*) to paste; (*ir juntos: colores*) to match, go together; (*golpear*) to hit; (*quemar: el sol*) to strike hot, burn

(*fig*); **~se** *vr* (*gen*) to stick; (*dos personas*) to hit each other, fight; **~le a algo** to be a great one for sth; **~ un grito** to let out a yell; **~ un salto** to jump (with fright); **~ fuego** to catch fire; **~ en** to touch; **~se un tiro** to shoot o.s.; **no pega** that doesn't seem right; **ese sombrero no pega con el abrigo** that hat doesn't go with the coat.

pegatina [peɣa'tina] *nf* (*POL etc*) sticker.

pego ['peɣo] *nm*: **dar el ~** (*pasar por verdadero*) to look like the real thing.

pegote [pe'ɣote] *nm* (*fig*) patch, ugly mend; **tirarse ~s** (*fam*) to come on strong.

pegue ['peɣe] *etc vb V* **pegar**.

peinado [pei'naðo] *nm* (*en peluquería*) hairdo; (*estilo*) hair style.

peinar [pei'nar] *vt* to comb sb's hair; (*hacer estilo*) to style; **~se** *vr* to comb one's hair.

peine ['peine] *nm* comb.

peineta [pei'neta] *nf* ornamental comb.

p.ej. *abr* (= *por ejemplo*) e.g.

Pekín [pe'kin] *n* Peking.

pela ['pela] *nf* (*ESP fam*) peseta; *V tb* **pelas**.

pelado, a [pe'laðo, a] *adj* (*cabeza*) shorn; (*fruta*) peeled; (*campo, fig*) bare; (*fam: sin dinero*) broke.

pelaje [pe'laxe] *nm* (*ZOOL*) fur, coat; (*fig*) appearance.

pelambre [pe'lambre] *nm* long hair, mop.

pelar [pe'lar] *vt* (*fruta, patatas*) to peel; (*cortar el pelo a*) to cut the hair of; (*quitar la piel: animal*) to skin; (*ave*) to pluck; (*habas etc*) to shell; **~se** *vr* (*la piel*) to peel off; **corre que se las pela** (*fam*) he runs like nobody's business.

pelas ['pelas] *nfpl* (*ESP fam*) dough.

peldaño [pel'daɲo] *nm* step; (*de escalera portátil*) rung.

pelea [pe'lea] *nf* (*lucha*) fight; (*discusión*) quarrel, row.

peleado, a [pele'aðo, a] *adj*: **estar ~ (con algn)** to have fallen out (with sb).

pelear [pele'ar] *vi* to fight; **~se** *vr* to fight; (*reñirse*) to fall out, quarrel.

pelele [pe'lele] *nm* (*figura*) guy, dummy; (*fig*) puppet.

peletería [pelete'ria] *nf* furrier's, fur shop.

peliagudo, a [pelja'ɣuðo, a] *adj* tricky.

pelícano [pe'likano] *nm* pelican.

película [pe'likula] *nf* (*CINE*) film, movie (*US*); (*cobertura ligera*) film, thin covering; (*FOTO: rollo*) roll *o* reel of film; **~ de dibujos (animados)** cartoon film; **~ muda** silent film; **de ~** (*fam*) astonishing, out of this world.

peligrar [peli'ɣrar] *vi* to be in danger.

peligro [pe'liɣro] *nm* danger; (*riesgo*) risk;

"~ **de muerte**" "danger"; **correr** ~ **de** to be in danger of; **con** ~ **de la vida** at the risk of one's life.

peligrosidad [peliɣrosi'ðað] *nf* danger, riskiness.

peligroso, a [peli'ɣroso, a] *adj* dangerous; risky.

pelirrojo, a [peli'rroxo, a] *adj* red-haired, red-headed.

pellejo [pe'ʎexo] *nm* (*de animal*) skin, hide; **salvar el** ~ to save one's skin.

pellizcar [peʎiθ'kar] *vt* to pinch, nip.

pellizco [pe'ʎiθko] *nm* (*gen*) pinch.

pellizque [pe'ʎiθke] *etc vb V* **pellizcar**.

pelma ['pelma] *nmf*, **pelmazo** [pel'maθo] *nm* (*fam*) pest.

pelo ['pelo] *nm* (*cabellos*) hair; (*de barba, bigote*) whisker; (*de animal: pellejo*) fur, coat; (*de perro etc*) hair, coat; (*de ave*) down; (*de tejido*) nap; (*TEC*) fibre; **a** ~ bareheaded; (*desnudo*) naked; **al** ~ just right; **venir al** ~ to be exactly what one needs; **por los** ~**s** by the skin of one's teeth; **escaparse por un** ~ to have a close shave; **se me pusieron los** ~**s de punta** my hair stood on end; **no tener** ~**s en la lengua** to be outspoken, not mince words; **tomar el** ~ **a algn** to pull sb's leg.

pelón, ona [pe'lon, ona] *adj* hairless, bald.

pelota [pe'lota] *nf* ball; (*fam: cabeza*) nut (*fam*); **en** ~(**s**) stark naked; ~ **vasca** pelota; **devolver la** ~ **a algn** (*fig*) to turn the tables on sb; **hacer la** ~ (**a algn**) to creep (to sb).

pelotera [pelo'tera] *nf* (*fam*) barney.

pelotón [pelo'ton] *nm* (*MIL*) squad, detachment.

peluca [pe'luka] *nf* wig.

peluche [pe'lutʃe] *nm*: **muñeco de** ~ soft toy.

peludo, a [pe'luðo, a] *adj* hairy, shaggy.

peluquería [peluke'ria] *nf* hairdresser's; (*para hombres*) barber's (shop).

peluquero, a [pelu'kero, a] *nm/f* hairdresser; barber.

peluquín [pelu'kin] *nm* toupée.

pelusa [pe'lusa] *nf* (*BOT*) down; (*COSTURA*) fluff.

pelvis ['pelβis] *nf* pelvis.

PEMEX [pe'meks] *nm abr* = *Petróleos Mejicanos*.

PEN [pen] *nm abr* (*ESP*) = *Plan Energético Nacional*.

pena ['pena] *nf* (*congoja*) grief, sadness; (*remordimiento*) regret; (*dificultad*) trouble; (*dolor*) pain; (*AM: vergüenza*) shame; (*JUR*) sentence; (*DEPORTE*) penalty; ~ **capital** capital punishment; ~

de muerte death penalty; ~ **pecuniaria** fine; **merecer** *o* **valer la** ~ to be worthwhile; **a duras** ~**s** with great difficulty; **so** ~ **de** on pain of; **me dan** ~ I feel sorry for them; **¿no te da** ~ **hacerlo?** (*AM*) aren't you embarrassed doing that?; **¡qué** ~! what a shame *o* pity!

penal [pe'nal] *adj* penal ♦ *nm* (*cárcel*) prison.

penalidad [penali'ðað] *nf* (*problema, dificultad*) trouble, hardship; (*JUR*) penalty, punishment.

penalizar [penali'θar] *vt* to penalize.

penalti, penalty [pe'nalti] *nm* (*DEPORTE*) penalty.

penar [pe'nar] *vt* to penalize; (*castigar*) to punish ♦ *vi* to suffer.

pendejo, a [pen'dexo, a] *nm/f* (*AM fam!*) wanker (*BRIT!*), jerk (*US!*).

pender [pen'der] *vi* (*colgar*) to hang; (*JUR*) to be pending.

pendiente [pen'djente] *adj* pending, unsettled ♦ *nm* earring ♦ *nf* hill, slope; **tener una asignatura** ~ to have to resit a subject.

pendón [pen'don] *nm* banner, standard.

péndulo ['pendulo] *nm* pendulum.

pene ['pene] *nm* penis.

penene [pe'nene] *nm/f* = **PNN**.

penetración [penetra'θjon] *nf* (*acto*) penetration; (*agudeza*) sharpness, insight.

penetrante [pene'trante] *adj* (*herida*) deep; (*persona, arma*) sharp; (*sonido*) penetrating, piercing; (*mirada*) searching; (*viento, ironía*) biting.

penetrar [pene'trar] *vt* to penetrate, pierce; (*entender*) to grasp ♦ *vi* to penetrate, go in; (*líquido*) to soak in; (*emoción*) to pierce.

penicilina [peniθi'lina] *nf* penicillin.

península [pe'ninsula] *nf* peninsula; **P~ Ibérica** Iberian Peninsula.

peninsular [peninsu'lar] *adj* peninsular.

penique [pe'nike] *nm* penny; ~**s** *nmpl* pence.

penitencia [peni'tenθja] *nf* (*remordimiento*) penitence; (*castigo*) penance; **en** ~ as a penance.

penitencial [peniten'θjal] *adj* penitential.

penitenciaría [penitenθja'ria] *nf* prison, penitentiary.

penitenciario, a [peniten'θjarjo, a] *adj* prison *cpd*.

penoso, a [pe'noso, a] *adj* laborious, difficult.

pensado, a [pen'saðo, a] *adj*: **bien/mal** ~

well intentioned/cynical; **en el momento menos** ~ when least expected.
pensador, a [pensa'ðor, a] *nm/f* thinker.
pensamiento [pensa'mjento] *nm* (*gen*) thought; (*mente*) mind; (*idea*) idea; (*BOT*) pansy; **no se le pasó por el** ~ it never occurred to him.
pensar [pen'sar] *vt* to think; (*considerar*) to think over, think out; (*proponerse*) to intend, plan, propose; (*imaginarse*) to think up, invent ♦ *vi* to think; ~ **en** to think of o about; (*anhelar*) to aim at, aspire to; **dar que** ~ **a algn** to give sb food for thought.
pensativo, a [pensa'tiβo, a] *adj* thoughtful, pensive.
pensión [pen'sjon] *nf* (*casa*) ≈ guest house; (*dinero*) pension; (*cama y comida*) board and lodging; ~ **de jubilación** retirement pension; ~ **escalada** graduated pension; ~ **completa** full board; **media** ~ half board.
pensionista [pensjo'nista] *nm/f* (*jubilado*) (old-age) pensioner; (*quien vive en pensión*) lodger; (*ESCOL*) boarder.
pentágono [pen'taɣono] *nm* pentagon: **el P**~ (*US*) the Pentagon.
pentagrama [penta'ɣrama] *nm* (*MUS*) stave, staff.
penúltimo, a [pe'nultimo, a] *adj* penultimate, second last.
penumbra [pe'numbra] *nf* half-light, semi-darkness.
penuria [pe'nurja] *nf* shortage, want.
peña ['peɲa] *nf* (*roca*) rock; (*cuesta*) cliff, crag; (*grupo*) group, circle; (*DEPORTE*) supporters' club.
peñasco [pe'ɲasko] *nm* large rock, boulder.
peñón [pe'ɲon] *nm* crag; **el P**~ the Rock (of Gibraltar).
peón [pe'on] *nm* labourer; (*AM*) farm labourer, farmhand; (*TEC*) spindle, shaft; (*AJEDREZ*) pawn.
peonza [pe'onθa] *nf* spinning top.
peor [pe'or] *adj* (*comparativo*) worse; (*superlativo*) worst ♦ *adv* worse; worst; **de mal en** ~ from bad to worse; **tanto** ~ so much the worse; **A es** ~ **que B** A is worse than B; **Z es el** ~ **de todos** Z is the worst of all.
pepenar [pepe'nar] *vi* (*AM*) to sift through rubbish o garbage.
pepinillo [pepi'niʎo] *nm* gherkin.
pepino [pe'pino] *nm* cucumber; **(no) me importa un** ~ I don't care two hoots.
pepita [pe'pita] *nf* (*BOT*) pip; (*MINERÍA*) nugget.

pepito [pe'pito] *nm* meat sandwich.
peque ['peke] *etc vb* V **pecar**.
pequeñez [peke'neθ] *nf* smallness, littleness; (*trivialidad*) trifle, triviality.
pequeño, a [pe'keɲo, a] *adj* small, little; (*cifra*) small, low; (*bajo*) short; ~ **burgués** lower middle-class.
pequinés, esa [peki'nes, esa] *adj, nm/f* Pekinese.
pera ['pera] *adj inv* classy; **niño** ~ spoiled upper-class brat ♦ *nf* pear; **eso es pedir** ~**s al olmo** that's asking the impossible.
peral [pe'ral] *nm* pear tree.
percance [per'kanθe] *nm* setback, misfortune.
per cápita [per'kapita] *adj*: **renta** ~ per capita income.
percatarse [perka'tarse] *vr*: ~ **de** to notice, take note of.
percebe [per'θeβe] *nm* (*ZOOL*) barnacle; (*fam*) idiot.
percepción [perθep'θjon] *nf* (*vista*) perception; (*idea*) notion, idea; (*COM*) collection.
perceptible [perθep'tiβle] *adj* perceptible, noticeable; (*COM*) payable, receivable.
percha ['pertʃa] *nf* (*poste*) pole, support; (*gancho*) peg; (*de abrigos*) coat stand; (*colgador*) coat hanger; (*de ave*) perch.
perchero [per'tʃero] *nm* clothes rack.
percibir [perθi'βir] *vt* to perceive, notice; (*ver*) to see; (*peligro etc*) to sense; (*COM*) to earn, receive, get.
percusión [perku'sjon] *nf* percussion.
percusor [perku'sor], **percutor** [perku'tor] *nm* (*TEC*) hammer; (*de arma*) firing pin.
perdedor, a [perðe'ðor, a] *adj* losing ♦ *nm/f* loser.
perder [per'ðer] *vt* to lose; (*tiempo, palabras*) to waste; (*oportunidad*) to lose, miss; (*tren*) to miss ♦ *vi* to lose; ~**se** *vr* (*extraviarse*) to get lost; (*desaparecer*) to disappear, be lost to view; (*arruinarse*) to be ruined; **echar a** ~ (*comida*) to spoil, ruin; (*oportunidad*) to waste; **tener buen** ~ to be a good loser; **¡no te lo pierdas!** don't miss it!; **he perdido la costumbre** I have got out of the habit.
perdición [perði'θjon] *nf* perdition; (*fig*) ruin.
pérdida ['perðiða] *nf* loss; (*de tiempo*) waste; (*COM*) net loss; ~**s** *nfpl* (*COM*) losses; **¡no tiene** ~! you can't go wrong!; ~ **contable** (*COM*) book loss.
perdido, a [per'ðiðo, a] *adj* lost; **estar** ~ **por** to be crazy about; **es un caso** ~ he is a hopeless case.
perdigón [perði'ɣon] *nm* pellet.

perdiz [per'ðiθ] *nf* partridge.

perdón [per'ðon] *nm* (*disculpa*) pardon, forgiveness; (*clemencia*) mercy; ¡~! sorry!, I beg your pardon!; **con** ~ if I may, if you don't mind.

perdonar [perðo'nar] *vt* to pardon, forgive; (*la vida*) to spare; (*excusar*) to exempt, excuse ♦ *vi* to pardon, forgive; **¡perdone (usted)!** sorry!, I beg your pardon!; **perdone, pero me parece que ...** excuse me, but I think ...

perdurable [perðu'raβle] *adj* lasting; (*eterno*) everlasting.

perdurar [perðu'rar] *vi* (*resistir*) to last, endure; (*seguir existiendo*) to stand, still exist.

perecedero, a [pereθe'ðero, a] *adj* perishable.

perecer [pere'θer] *vi* to perish, die.

peregrinación [pereɣrina'θjon] *nf* (*REL*) pilgrimage.

peregrino, a [pere'ɣrino] *adj* (*extraño*) strange; (*singular*) rare ♦ *nm/f* pilgrim.

perejil [pere'xil] *nm* parsley.

perenne [pe'renne] *adj* perennial.

perentorio, a [peren'torjo, a] *adj* (*urgente*) urgent; (*terminante*) peremptory; (*fijo*) set, fixed.

pereza [pe'reθa] *nf* (*flojera*) laziness; (*lentitud*) sloth, slowness.

perezca [pe'reθka] *etc vb V* **perecer.**

perezoso, a [pere'θoso, a] *adj* lazy; slow, sluggish.

perfección [perfek'θjon] *nf* perfection; **a la** ~ to perfection.

perfeccionar [perfekθjo'nar] *vt* to perfect; (*acabar*) to complete, finish.

perfecto, a [per'fekto, a] *adj* perfect ♦ *nm* (*LING*) perfect (tense).

perfidia [per'fiðja] *nf* perfidy, treachery.

pérfido, a ['perfiðo, a] *adj* perfidious, treacherous.

perfil [per'fil] *nm* (*parte lateral*) profile; (*silueta*) silhouette, outline; (*TEC*) (cross) section; **~es** *nmpl* features; (*fig*) social graces; ~ **del cliente** (*COM*) customer profile; **en** ~ from the side, in profile.

perfilado, a [perfi'laðo, a] *adj* (*bien formado*) well-shaped; (*largo: cara*) long.

perfilar [perfi'lar] *vt* (*trazar*) to outline; (*dar carácter a*) to shape, give character to; **~se** *vr* to be silhouetted (*en* against); **el proyecto se va perfilando** the project is taking shape.

perforación [perfora'θjon] *nf* perforation; (*con taladro*) drilling.

perforadora [perfora'ðora] *nf* drill; ~ **de fichas** card-punch.

perforar [perfo'rar] *vt* to perforate; (*agujero*) to drill, bore; (*papel*) to punch a hole in ♦ *vi* to drill, bore.

perfumar [perfu'mar] *vt* to scent, perfume.

perfume [per'fume] *nm* perfume, scent.

perfumería [perfume'ria] *nf* perfume shop.

pergamino [perɣa'mino] *nm* parchment.

pericia [pe'riθja] *nf* skill, expertise.

periferia [peri'ferja] *nf* periphery; (*de ciudad*) outskirts *pl*.

periférico, a [peri'feriko, a] *adj* peripheral ♦ *nm* (*INFORM*) peripheral; (*AM: AUTO*) ring road; **barrio** ~ outlying district.

perilla [pe'riʎa] *nf* goatee.

perímetro [pe'rimetro] *nm* perimeter.

periódico, a [pe'rjoðiko, a] *adj* periodic(al) ♦ *nm* (news)paper; ~ **dominical** Sunday (news)paper.

periodismo [perjo'ðismo] *nm* journalism.

periodista [perjo'ðista] *nm/f* journalist.

periodístico, a [perjo'ðistiko, a] *adj* journalistic.

periodo [pe'rjoðo], **período** [pe'rioðo] *nm* period; ~ **contable** (*COM*) accounting period.

peripecias [peri'peθjas] *nfpl* adventures.

peripuesto, a [peri'pwesto, a] *adj* dressed up; **tan** ~ all dressed up (to the nines).

periquito [peri'kito] *nm* budgerigar, budgie (*fam*).

perito, a [pe'rito, a] *adj* (*experto*) expert; (*diestro*) skilled, skilful ♦ *nm/f* expert; skilled worker; (*técnico*) technician.

perjudicar [perxuði'kar] *vt* (*gen*) to damage, harm; (*fig*) to prejudice.

perjudicial [perxuði'θjal] *adj* damaging, harmful; (*en detrimento*) detrimental.

perjudique [perxu'ðike] *etc vb V* **perjudicar.**

perjuicio [per'xwiθjo] *nm* damage, harm; **en/sin** ~ **de** to the detriment of/without prejudice to.

perjurar [perxu'rar] *vi* to commit perjury.

perla ['perla] *nf* pearl; **me viene de** ~**s** it suits me fine.

permanecer [permane'θer] *vi* (*quedarse*) to stay, remain; (*seguir*) to continue to be.

permanencia [perma'nenθja] *nf* (*duración*) permanence; (*estancia*) stay.

permanente [perma'nente] *adj* (*que queda*) permanent; (*constante*) constant; (*comisión etc*) standing ♦ *nf* perm; **hacerse una** ~ to have one's hair permed.

permanezca [perma'neθka] *etc vb V* **permanecer.**

permisible [permi'siβle] *adj* permissible, allowable.

permiso [per'miso] *nm* permission; (*licencia*) permit, licence (*BRIT*), license (*US*); **con** ~ excuse me; **estar de** ~ (*MIL*) to be on leave; ~ **de conducir** *o* **conductor** driving licence (*BRIT*), driver's license (*US*); ~ **de exportación/ importación** export/import licence; ~ **por asuntos familiares** compassionate leave.

permitir [permi'tir] *vt* to permit, allow; ~**se** *vr*: ~**se algo** to allow o.s. sth; **no me puedo** ~ **ese lujo** I can't afford that; **¿me permite?** may I?; **si lo permite el tiempo** weather permitting.

permuta [per'muta] *nf* exchange.

permutar [permu'tar] *vt* to switch, exchange; ~ **destinos con algn** to swap *o* exchange jobs with sb.

pernicioso, a [perni'θjoso, a] *adj* (*maligno, MED*) pernicious; (*persona*) wicked.

perno ['perno] *nm* bolt.

pernoctar [pernok'tar] *vi* to stay for the night.

pero ['pero] *conj* but; (*aún*) yet ♦ *nm* (*defecto*) flaw, defect; (*reparo*) objection; **¡no hay** ~ **que valga!** there are no buts about it.

perogrullada [peroɣru'ʎaða] *nf* platitude, truism.

perol [pe'rol] *nm*, **perola** [pe'rola] *nf* pan.

peronista [pero'nista] *adj*, *nm/f* Peronist.

perorata [pero'rata] *nf* long-winded speech.

perpendicular [perpendiku'lar] *adj* perpendicular; **el camino es** ~ **al río** the road is at right angles to the river.

perpetrar [perpe'trar] *vt* to perpetrate.

perpetuamente [perpetwa'mente] *adv* perpetually.

perpetuar [perpe'twar] *vt* to perpetuate.

perpetuo, a [per'petwo, a] *adj* perpetual; (*JUR etc: condena*) life *cpd*.

Perpiñán [perpi'ɲan] *nm* Perpignan.

perplejo, a [per'plexo, a] *adj* perplexed, bewildered.

perra ['perra] *nf* bitch; (*fam: dinero*) money; (: *manía*) mania, crazy idea; (: *rabieta*) tantrum; **estar sin una** ~ to be flat broke.

perrera [pe'rrera] *nf* kennel.

perro ['perro] *nm* dog; ~ **caliente** hot dog; "~ **peligroso**" "beware of the dog"; **ser** ~ **viejo** to be an old hand; **tiempo de** ~**s** filthy weather; ~ **que ladra no muerde** his bark is worse than his bite.

persa ['persa] *adj*, *nm/f* Persian ♦ *nm* (*LING*) Persian.

persecución [perseku'θjon] *nf* pursuit, hunt, chase; (*REL, POL*) persecution.

perseguir [perse'ɣir] *vt* to pursue, hunt; (*cortejar*) to chase after; (*molestar*) to pester, annoy; (*REL, POL*) to persecute; (*JUR*) to prosecute.

perseverante [perseße'rante] *adj* persevering, persistent.

perseverar [perseve'rar] *vi* to persevere, persist; ~ **en** to persevere in, persist with.

persiana [per'sjana] *nf* (Venetian) blind.

persiga [per'siɣa] *etc vb V* **perseguir**.

persignarse [persiɣ'narse] *vr* to cross o.s.

persiguiendo [persi'xjenðo] *etc vb V* **perseguir**.

persistente [persis'tente] *adj* persistent.

persistir [persis'tir] *vi* to persist.

persona [per'sona] *nf* person; **10 ~s** 10 people; **tercera** ~ third party; (*LING*) third person; **en** ~ in person *o* the flesh; **por** ~ a head; **es buena** ~ he's a good sort.

personaje [perso'naxe] *nm* important person, celebrity; (*TEAT*) character.

personal [perso'nal] *adj* (*particular*) personal; (*para una persona*) single, for one person ♦ *nm* (*plantilla*) personnel, staff; (*NAUT*) crew; (*fam: gente*) people.

personalidad [personali'ðað] *nf* personality; (*JUR*) status.

personalizar [personali'θar] *vt* to personalize ♦ *vi* (*al hablar*) to name names.

personarse [perso'narse] *vr* to appear in person; ~ **en** to present o.s. at, report to.

personero, a [perso'nero, a] *nm/f* (*AM*) (government) official.

personificar [personifi'kar] *vt* to personify.

personifique [personi'fike] *etc vb V* **personificar**.

perspectiva [perspek'tißa] *nf* perspective; (*vista, panorama*) view, panorama; (*posibilidad futura*) outlook, prospect; **tener algo en** ~ to have sth in view.

perspicacia [perspi'kaθja] *nf* discernment, perspicacity.

perspicaz [perspi'kaθ] *adj* shrewd.

persuadir [perswa'ðir] *vt* (*gen*) to persuade; (*convencer*) to convince; ~**se** *vr* to become convinced.

persuasión [perswa'sjon] *nf* (*acto*) persuasion; (*convicción*) conviction.

persuasivo, a [perwa'sißo, a] *adj* persuasive; convincing.

pertenecer [pertene'θer] *vi*: ~ **a** to belong to; (*fig*) to concern.

perteneciente [pertene'θjente] *adj*: ~ **a** belonging to.

pertenencia [perte'nenθja] *nf* ownership;

~s *nfpl* possessions, property *sg.*

pertenezca [perte'neθka] *etc vb V*
pertenecer.

pértiga ['pertiɣa] *nf* pole; **salto de** ~ pole
vault.

pertinaz [perti'naθ] *adj* (*persistente*)
persistent; (*terco*) obstinate.

pertinente [perti'nente] *adj* relevant,
pertinent; (*apropiado*) appropriate; ~ **a**
concerning, relevant to.

pertrechar [pertre't∫ar] *vt* (*gen*) to supply;
(*MIL*) to supply with ammunition and
stores; ~**se** *vr*: ~**se de algo** to provide
o.s. with sth.

pertrechos [per'tret∫os] *nmpl* (*gen*)
implements; (*MIL*) supplies and stores.

perturbación [perturßa'θjon] *nf* (*POL*)
disturbance; (*MED*) upset, disturbance;
~ **del orden público** breach of the peace.

perturbador, a [perturßa'ðor, a] *adj* (*que
perturba*) perturbing, disturbing;
(*subversivo*) subversive.

perturbar [pertur'ßar] *vt* (*el orden*) to
disturb; (*MED*) to upset, disturb;
(*mentalmente*) to perturb.

Perú [pe'ru] *nm*: **el** ~ Peru.

peruano, a [pe'rwano, a] *adj, nm/f* Peruvian.

perversión [perßer'sjon] *nf* perversion.

perverso, a [perßerso, a] *adj* perverse;
(*depravado*) depraved.

pervertido, a [perßer'tiðo, a] *adj* perverted
♦ *nm/f* pervert.

pervertir [perßer'tir] *vt* to pervert,
corrupt.

pervierta [per'ßjerta] *etc*, **pervirtiendo**
[perßir't jendo] *etc vb V* pervertir.

pesa ['pesa] *nf* weight; (*DEPORTE*) shot.

pesadez [pesa'ðeθ] *nf* (*calidad de pesado*)
heaviness; (*lentitud*) slowness;
(*aburrimiento*) tediousness; **es una** ~
tener que ... it's a bind having to ....

pesadilla [pesa'ðiʎa] *nf* nightmare, bad
dream; (*fig*) worry, obsession.

pesado, a [pe'saðo, a] *adj* (*gen*) heavy;
(*lento*) slow; (*difícil, duro*) tough, hard;
(*aburrido*) tedious, boring; (*bochornoso*)
sultry ♦ *nm/f* bore; **tener el estómago** ~
to feel bloated; **¡no seas** ~**!** come off it!

pesadumbre [pesa'ðumbre] *nf* grief,
sorrow.

pésame ['pesame] *nm* expression of
condolence, message of sympathy; **dar
el** ~ to express one's condolences.

pesar [pe'sar] *vt* to weigh; (*fig*) to weigh
heavily on; (*afligir*) to grieve ♦ *vi* to
weigh; (*ser pesado*) to weigh a lot, be
heavy; (*fig: opinión*) to carry weight ♦ *nm*
(*sentimiento*) regret; (*pena*) grief,

sorrow; **a** ~ **de (que)** in spite of, despite;
no me pesa haberlo hecho I'm not sorry
I did it.

pesca ['peska] *nf* (*acto*) fishing; (*cantidad de
pescado*) catch; ~ **de altura/en bajura**
deep sea/coastal fishing; **ir de** ~ to go
fishing.

pescadería [peskaðe'ria] *nf* fish shop,
fishmonger's.

pescadilla [peska'ðiʎa] *nf* whiting.

pescado [pes'kaðo] *nm* fish.

pescador, a [peska'ðor, a] *nm/f* fisherman/
woman.

pescar [pes'kar] *vt* (*coger*) to catch; (*tratar
de coger*) to fish for; (*fam: lograr*) to get
hold of, land; (*conseguir: trabajo*) to
manage to get; (*sorprender*) to catch
unawares ♦ *vi* to fish, go fishing.

pescuezo [pes'kweθo] *nm* neck.

pese ['pese] *prep*: ~ **a** despite, in spite of.

pesebre [pe'seßre] *nm* manger.

peseta [pe'seta] *nf* peseta.

pesetero, a [pese'tero, a] *adj* money-
grubbing.

pesimismo [pesi'mismo] *nm* pessimism.

pesimista [pesi'mista] *adj* pessimistic
♦ *nm/f* pessimist.

pésimo, a ['pesimo, a] *adj* abominable,
vile.

peso ['peso] *nm* weight; (*balanza*) scales *pl*;
(*AM COM*) *monetary unit*; (*moneda*) peso;
(*DEPORTE*) shot; ~ **bruto/neto** gross/net
weight; ~ **mosca/pesado** fly-/
heavyweight; **de poco** ~ light(weight);
levantamiento de ~**s** weightlifting;
vender a ~ to sell by weight; **argumento
de** ~ weighty argument; **eso cae de su** ~
that goes without saying.

pesque ['peske] *etc vb V* pescar.

pesquero, a [pes'kero, a] *adj* fishing *cpd.*

pesquisa [pes'kisa] *nf* inquiry,
investigation.

pestaña [pes'taɲa] *nf* (*ANAT*) eyelash;
(*borde*) rim.

pestañear [pestaɲe'ar] *vi* to blink.

peste ['peste] *nf* plague; (*fig*) nuisance;
(*mal olor*) stink, stench; ~ **negra** Black
Death; **echar** ~**s** to swear, fume.

pesticida [pesti'θiða] *nf* pesticide.

pestilencia [pesti'lenθja] *nf* (*mal olor*)
stink, stench.

pestillo [pes'tiʎo] *nm* bolt, latch; (*cerrojo*)
catch; (*picaporte*) (door) handle.

petaca [pe'taka] *nf* (*de cigarrillos*) cigarette
case; (*de pipa*) tobacco pouch; (*AM:
maleta*) suitcase.

pétalo ['petalo] *nm* petal.

petanca [pe'tanka] *nf a game in which*

metal bowls are thrown at a target bowl.

petardo [pe'tarðo] *nm* firework, firecracker.

petición [peti'θjon] *nf (pedido)* request, plea; *(memorial)* petition; *(JUR)* plea; **a ~ de** at the request of; **~ de aumento de salarios** wage demand *o* claim.

petirrojo [peti'rroxo] *nm* robin.

peto ['peto] *nm (corpiño)* bodice; *(TAUR)* horse's padding.

pétreo, a ['petreo, a] *adj* stony, rocky.

petrificar [petrifi'kar] *vt* to petrify.

petrifique [petri'fike] *etc vb V* **petrificar**.

petrodólar [petro'ðolar] *nm* petrodollar.

petróleo [pe'troleo] *nm* oil, petroleum.

petrolero, a [petro'lero, a] *adj* petroleum *cpd ♦ nm (COM)* oil man; *(buque)* (oil) tanker.

petulancia [petu'lanθja] *nf (insolencia)* vanity, opinionated nature.

peyorativo, a [pejora'tiβo, a] *adj* pejorative.

pez [peθ] *nm* fish; **~ de colores** goldfish; **~ espada** swordfish; **estar como ~ en el agua** to feel completely at home.

pezón [pe'θon] *nm* teat, nipple.

pezuña [pe'θuɲa] *nm* hoof.

piadoso, a [pja'ðoso, a] *adj (devoto)* pious, devout; *(misericordioso)* kind, merciful.

Piamonte [pja'monte] *nm* Piedmont.

pianista [pja'nista] *nmf* pianist.

piano ['pjano] *nm* piano; **~ de cola** grand piano.

piar [pjar] *vi* to cheep.

piara ['pjara] *nf (manada)* herd, drove.

PIB *nm abr (ESP COM: = Producto Interno Bruto)* GDP.

pibe, a ['piβe, a] *nm/f (AM)* boy/girl, kid, child.

pica ['pika] *nf (MIL)* pike; *(TAUR)* goad; **poner una ~ en Flandes** to bring off something difficult.

picadero [pika'ðero] *nm* riding school.

picadillo [pika'ðiʎo] *nm* mince, minced meat.

picado, a [pi'kaðo, a] *adj* pricked, punctured; *(mar)* choppy; *(diente)* bad; *(tabaco)* cut; *(enfadado)* cross.

picador [pika'ðor] *nm (TAUR)* picador; *(minero)* faceworker.

picadora [pika'ðora] *nf* mincer.

picadura [pika'ðura] *nf (pinchazo)* puncture; *(de abeja)* sting; *(de mosquito)* bite; *(tabaco picado)* cut tobacco.

picana [pi'kana] *(AM) nf (AGR)* cattle prod; *(POL: para tortura)* electric prod.

picante [pi'kante] *adj (comida, sabor)* hot;

(comentario) racy, spicy.

picaporte [pika'porte] *nm (tirador)* handle; *(pestillo)* latch.

picar [pi'kar] *vt (agujerear, perforar)* to prick, puncture; *(billete)* to punch, clip; *(abeja)* to sting; *(mosquito, serpiente)* to bite; *(persona)* to nibble (at); *(incitar)* to incite, goad; *(dañar, irritar)* to annoy, bother; *(quemar: lengua)* to burn, sting ♦ *vi (pez)* to bite, take the bait; *(el sol)* to burn, scorch; *(abeja, MED)* to sting; *(mosquito)* to bite; **~se** *vr (agriarse)* to turn sour, go off; *(mar)* to get choppy; *(ofenderse)* to take offence; **me pican los ojos** my eyes sting; **me pica el brazo** my arm itches.

picardía [pikar'ðia] *nf* villainy; *(astucia)* slyness, craftiness; *(una ~)* dirty trick; *(palabra)* rude/bad word *o* expression.

picaresco, a [pika'resko, a] *adj (travieso)* roguish, rascally; *(LIT)* picaresque.

pícaro, a ['pikaro, a] *adj (malicioso)* villainous; *(travieso)* mischievous ♦ *nm (astuto)* sly sort; *(sinvergüenza)* rascal, scoundrel.

picazón [pika'θon] *nf (comezón)* itch; *(ardor)* sting(ing feeling); *(remordimiento)* pang of conscience.

pichón, ona [pi'tʃon, ona] *nm/f (paloma)* young pigeon; *(apelativo)* darling, dearest.

pico ['piko] *nm (de ave)* beak; *(punto agudo)* peak, sharp point; *(TEC)* pick, pickaxe; *(GEO)* peak, summit; *(labia)* talkativeness; **no abrir el ~** to keep quiet; **~ parásito** *(ELEC)* spike; **y ~** and a bit; **son las 3 y ~** it's just after 3; **tiene 50 libros y ~** he has 50-odd books; **me costó un ~** it cost me quite a bit.

picor [pi'kor] *nm* itch; *(ardor)* sting(ing feeling).

picota [pi'kota] *nf* pillory; **poner a algn en la ~** *(fig)* to ridicule sb.

picotada [piko'taða] *nf*, **picotazo** [piko'taθo] *nm (de pájaro)* peck; *(de insecto)* sting, bite.

picotear [pikote'ar] *vt* to peck ♦ *vi* to nibble, pick.

pictórico, a [pik'toriko, a] *adj* pictorial; **tiene dotes pictóricas** she has a talent for painting.

picudo, a [pi'kuðo, a] *adj* pointed, with a point.

pidiendo [pi'ðjendo] *etc vb V* **pedir**.

pie [pje] *(pl ~s) nm (gen, MAT)* foot; *(de cama, página, escalera)* foot, bottom; *(TEAT)* cue; *(fig: motivo)* motive, basis; *(: fundamento)* foothold; **~s planos** flat feet; **ir a** ~ to go on foot, walk; **estar de** ~ to be standing (up); **ponerse de** ~ to stand up; **al** ~ **de la letra** (*citar*) literally, verbatim; (*copiar*) exactly, word for word; **de** ~**s a cabeza** from head to foot; **en** ~ **de guerra** on a war footing; **sin** ~**s ni cabeza** pointless, absurd; **dar** ~ **a** to give cause for; **no dar** ~ **con bola** to be no good at anything; **saber de qué** ~ **cojea algn** to know sb's weak spots.

piedad [pje'ðað] *nf* (*lástima*) pity, compassion; (*clemencia*) mercy; (*devoción*) piety, devotion; **tener** ~ **de** to take pity on.

piedra ['pjeðra] *nf* stone; (*roca*) rock; (*de mechero*) flint; (*METEOROLOGÍA*) hailstone; **primera** ~ foundation stone; ~ **de afilar** grindstone; ~ **arenisca/caliza** sand-/limestone.

piel [pjel] *nf* (*ANAT*) skin; (*ZOOL*) skin, hide; (*de oso*) fur; (*cuero*) leather; (*BOT*) skin, peel ♦ *nm/f*: ~ **roja** redskin.

pienso ['pjenso] *etc vb V* **pensar** ♦ *nm* (*AGR*) feed.

piercing ['pirsiŋ] *nm* piercing.

pierda ['pjerða] *etc vb V* **perder**.

pierna ['pjerna] *nf* leg; **en** ~**s** bare-legged.

pieza ['pjeθa] *nf* piece; (*esp AM: habitación*) room; (*MUS*) piece, composition; (*TEAT*) work, play; ~ **de recambio** *o* **repuesto** spare (part), extra (*US*); ~ **de ropa** article of clothing; **quedarse de una** ~ to be dumbfounded.

pigmento [pig'mento] *nm* pigment.

pigmeo, a [pig'meo, a] *adj, nm/f* pigmy.

pijama [pi'xama] *nm* pyjamas *pl*.

pijo, a ['pixo, a] *nm/f* (*fam*) upper-class twit.

pijotada [pixo'taða] *nf* nuisance.

pila ['pila] *nf* (*ELEC*) battery; (*montón*) heap, pile; (*fuente*) sink; (*REL: tb:* ~ **bautismal**) font; **nombre de** ~ Christian *o* first name; **tengo una** ~ **de cosas que hacer** (*fam*) I have heaps *o* stacks of things to do.

pilar [pi'lar] *nm* pillar; (*de puente*) pier; (*fig*) prop, mainstay.

píldora ['pildora] *nf* pill; **la** ~ **(anticonceptiva)** the pill; **tragarse la** ~ to be taken in.

pileta [pi'leta] *nf* basin, bowl; (*AM: de cocina*) sink; (: *piscina*) swimming pool.

pillaje [pi'ʎaxe] *nm* pillage, plunder.

pillar [pi'ʎar] *vt* (*fam: coger*) to catch; (: *agarrar*) to grasp, seize; (: *entender*) to grasp, catch on to; (*suj: coche etc*) to run over; ~ **un resfriado** (*fam*) to catch a cold.

pillo, a ['piʎo, a] *adj* villainous; (*astuto*) sly, crafty ♦ *nm/f* rascal, rogue, scoundrel.

pilón [pi'lon] *nm* pillar, post; (*ELEC*) pylon; (*bebedero*) drinking trough; (*de fuente*) basin.

pilotar [pilo'tar] *vt* (*avión*) to pilot; (*barco*) to steer.

piloto [pi'loto] *nm* pilot; (*AUTO*) rear light, tail light; (*conductor*) driver ♦ *adj inv*: **planta** ~ pilot plant; **luz** ~ side light.

piltrafa [pil'trafa] *nf* (*carne*) poor quality meat; (*fig*) worthless object; (: *individuo*) wretch.

pimentón [pimen'ton] *nm* (*polvo*) paprika.

pimienta [pi'mjenta] *nf* pepper.

pimiento [pi'mjento] *nm* pepper, pimiento.

pimpante [pim'pante] *adj* (*encantador*) charming; (*tb:* **tan** ~) smug, self-satisfied.

PIN *nm abr* (*ESP COM*: = *Producto Interior Neto*) net domestic product.

pin, *pl* **pins** [pin, pins] *nm* badge.

pinacoteca [pinako'teka] *nf* art gallery.

pinar [pi'nar] *nm* pinewood.

pincel [pin'θel] *nm* paintbrush.

pincelada [pinθe'laða] *nf* brushstroke; **última** ~ (*fig*) finishing touch.

pinchadiscos [pintʃa'diskos] *nm/f inv* disc jockey, DJ.

pinchar [pin'tʃar] *vt* (*perforar*) to prick, pierce; (*neumático*) to puncture; (*incitar*) to prod ♦ *vi* (*MUS fam*) to be DJ; ~**se** *vr* (*con droga*) to inject o.s.; (*neumático*) to burst, puncture; **no** ~ **ni cortar** (*fam*) to cut no ice; **tener un neumático pinchado** to have a puncture *o* a flat tyre.

pinchazo [pin'tʃaθo] *nm* (*perforación*) prick; (*de llanta*) puncture, flat (*US*).

pinche ['pintʃe] *nm* (*de cocina*) kitchen boy, scullion.

pinchito [pin'tʃito] *nm* shish kebab.

pincho ['pintʃo] *nm* point; (*aguijón*) spike; (*CULIN*) savoury (snack); ~ **moruno** shish kebab; ~ **de tortilla** small slice of omelette.

ping-pong ['pimpon] *nm* table tennis.

pingüe ['pingwe] *adj* (*cosecha*) bumper *cpd*; (*negocio*) lucrative.

pingüino [pin'gwino] *nm* penguin.

pinitos [pi'nitos] *nmpl*: **hacer sus primeros** ~ to take one's first steps.

pino ['pino] *nm* pine (tree); **vivir en el quinto** ~ to live at the back of beyond.

pinta ['pinta] *nf* spot; (*gota*) spot, drop; (*aspecto*) appearance, look(s) (*pl*); (*medida*) pint; **tener buena** ~ to look good, look well; **por la** ~ by the look of it.

pintado, a [pin'taðo, a] *adj* spotted; (*de muchos colores*) colourful ♦ *nf* piece of political graffiti; ~**s** *nfpl* political graffiti *sg*; **me sienta que ni** ~, **me viene que ni** ~ it suits me a treat.

pintar [pin'tar] *vt* to paint ♦ *vi* to paint; (*fam*) to count, be important; ~**se** *vr* to put on make-up; **pintárselas solo para hacer algo** to manage to do sth by o.s.; **no pinta nada** (*fam*) he has no say.

pintor, a [pin'tor, a] *nm/f* painter; ~ **de brocha gorda** house painter; (*fig*) bad painter.

pintoresco, a [pinto'resko, a] *adj* picturesque.

pintura [pin'tura] *nf* painting; ~ **a la acuarela** watercolour; ~ **al óleo** oil painting; ~ **rupestre** cave painting.

pinza ['pinθa] *nf* (*ZOOL*) claw; (*para colgar ropa*) clothes peg, clothespin (*US*); (*TEC*) pincers *pl*; ~**s** *nfpl* (*para depilar*) tweezers.

piña ['piɲa] *nf* (*fruto del pino*) pine cone; (*fruta*) pineapple; (*fig*) group.

piñón [pi'ɲon] *nm* (*BOT*) pine nut; (*TEC*) pinion.

PIO *nm abr* (*ESP*: = *Patronato de Igualdad de Oportunidades*) ≈ Equal Opportunities Board.

pío, a ['pio, a] *adj* (*devoto*) pious, devout; (*misericordioso*) merciful ♦ *nm*: **no decir ni** ~ not to breathe a word.

piojo ['pjoxo] *nm* louse.

piojoso, a [pjo'xoso, a] *adj* lousy; (*sucio*) dirty.

piolet [pjo'le], *pl* ~**s** [-s] *nm* ice axe.

pionero, a [pjo'nero, a] *adj* pioneering ♦ *nm/f* pioneer.

pipa ['pipa] *nf* pipe; (*BOT*) seed, pip.

pipí [pi'pi] *nm* (*fam*): **hacer** ~ to have a wee-(wee).

pipiolo [pi'pjolo] *nm* youngster; (*novato*) novice, greenhorn.

pique ['pike] *etc vb V* **picar** ♦ *nm* (*resentimiento*) pique, resentment; (*rivalidad*) rivalry, competition; **irse a** ~ to sink; (*familia*) to be ruined; **tener un** ~ **con algn** to have a grudge against sb.

piqueta [pi'keta] *nf* pick(axe).

piquete [pi'kete] *nm* (*agujerito*) small hole; (*MIL*) squad, party; (*de obreros*) picket; ~ **secundario** secondary picket.

pirado, a [pi'raðo, a] *adj* (*fam*) round the bend.

piragua [pi'raɣwa] *nf* canoe.

piragüismo [piraˈɣwismo] *nm* (*DEPORTE*) canoeing.

pirámide [pi'ramiðe] *nf* pyramid.

piraña [pi'raɲa] *nf* piranha.

pirarse [pi'rarse] *vr*: ~**(las)** (*largarse*) to beat it (*fam*); (*ESCOL*) to cut class.

pirata [pi'rata] *adj*: **edición/disco** ~ pirate edition/bootleg record ♦ *nm* pirate; (*tb*: ~ **informático**) hacker.

pirenaico, a [pire'naiko, a] *adj* Pyrenean.

Pirineo(s) [piri'neo(s)] *nm(pl)* Pyrenees *pl*.

pirómano, a [pi'romano, a] *nm/f* (*PSICO*) pyromaniac; (*JUR*) arsonist.

piropo [pi'ropo] *nm* compliment, (piece of) flattery; **echar** ~**s a** to make flirtatious remarks to.

pirueta [pi'rweta] *nf* pirouette.

piruleta [piru'leta] *nf* lollipop.

pirulí [piru'li] *nm* lollipop.

pis [pis] *nm* (*fam*) pee; **hacer** ~ to have a pee.

pisada [pi'saða] *nf* (*paso*) footstep; (*huella*) footprint.

pisar [pi'sar] *vt* (*caminar sobre*) to walk on, tread on; (*apretar con el pie*) to press; (*fig*) to trample on, walk all over ♦ *vi* to tread, step, walk; ~ **el acelerador** to step on the accelerator; ~ **fuerte** (*fig*) to act determinedly.

piscifactoría [pisθifakto'ria] *nf* fish farm.

piscina [pis'θina] *nf* swimming pool.

Piscis ['pisθis] *nm* (*ASTRO*) Pisces.

piso ['piso] *nm* (*suelo, de edificio*) floor; (*AM*) ground; (*apartamento*) flat, apartment; **primer** ~ (*ESP*) first *o* second (*US*) floor; (*AM*) ground *o* first (*US*) floor.

pisotear [pisote'ar] *vt* to trample (on *o* underfoot); (*fig: humillar*) to trample on.

pisotón [piso'ton] *nm* (*con el pie*) stamp.

pista ['pista] *nf* track, trail; (*indicio*) clue; (*INFORM*) track; ~ **de auditoría** (*COM*) audit trail; ~ **de aterrizaje** runway; ~ **de baile** dance floor; ~ **de tenis** tennis court; ~ **de hielo** ice rink; **estar sobre la** ~ **de algn** to be on sb's trail.

pisto ['pisto] *nm* (*CULIN*) ratatouille; **darse** ~ (*fam*) to show off.

pistola [pis'tola] *nf* pistol; (*TEC*) spray-gun.

pistolero, a [pisto'lero, a] *nm/f* gunman, gangster ♦ *nf* holster.

pistón [pis'ton] *nm* (*TEC*) piston; (*MUS*) key.

pitar [pi'tar] *vt* (*hacer sonar*) to blow; (*partido*) to referee; (*rechiflar*) to whistle at, boo; (*actor, obra*) to hiss ♦ *vi* to whistle; (*AUTO*) to sound *o* toot one's horn; (*AM*) to smoke; **salir pitando** to beat it.

pitido [pi'tiðo] *nm* whistle; (*sonido agudo*) beep; (*sonido corto*) pip.

pitillera [piti'ʎera] *nf* cigarette case.

pitillo [pi'tiʎo] *nm* cigarette.

pito ['pito] *nm* whistle; (*de coche*) horn;

(*cigarrillo*) cigarette; (*fam: de marijuana*) joint; (*fam!*) prick (*!*); **me importa un** ~ I don't care two hoots.

pitón [pi'ton] *nm* (*ZOOL*) python.

pitonisa [pito'nisa] *nf* fortune-teller.

pitorrearse [pitorre'arse] *vr*: ~ **de** to scoff at, make fun of.

pitorreo [pito'rreo] *nm* joke, laugh; **estar de** ~ to be in a joking mood.

píxel ['piksel] *nm* (*INFORM*) pixel.

piyama [pi'jama] *nm* (*AM*) pyjamas *pl*, pajamas (*US*) *pl*.

pizarra [pi'θarra] *nf* (*piedra*) slate; (*encerado*) blackboard.

pizca ['piθka] *nf* pinch, spot; (*fig*) spot, speck, trace; **ni** ~ not a bit.

pizza ['pitsa] *nf* pizza.

placa ['plaka] *nf* plate; (*MED*) dental plate; (*distintivo*) badge; ~ **de matrícula** number plate; ~ **madre** (*INFORM*) mother board.

placaje [pla'kaxe] *nm* tackle.

placard [pla'kar] *nm* (*AM*) built-in cupboard, (*clothes*) closet (*US*).

placenta [pla'θenta] *nf* placenta; (*tras el parto*) afterbirth.

placentero, a [plaθen'tero, a] *adj* pleasant, agreeable ♦ *vt* to please.

placer [pla'θer] *nm* pleasure; **a** ~ at one's pleasure.

plácido, a ['plaθiðo, a] *adj* placid.

plafón [pla'fon] *nm* (*AM*) ceiling.

plaga ['plaɣa] *nf* (*MED*) plague; (*fig*) swarm.

plagar [pla'ɣar] *vt* to infest, plague; (*llenar*) to fill; **plagado de** riddled with; **han plagado la ciudad de carteles** they have plastered the town with posters.

plagiar [pla'ɣjar] *vt* to plagiarize; (*AM*) to kidnap.

plagiario, a [pla'ɣjario, a] *nm/f* plagiarist; (*AM*) kidnapper.

plagio ['plaxjo] *nm* plagiarism; (*AM*) kidnap.

plague ['plaɣe] *etc vb V* **plagar**.

plan [plan] *nm* (*esquema, proyecto*) plan; (*idea, intento*) idea, intention; (*de curso*) programme; ~ **cotizable de jubilación** contributory pension scheme; ~ **de estudios** curriculum, syllabus; ~ **de incentivos** (*COM*) incentive scheme; **tener** ~ (*fam*) to have a date; **tener un** ~ (*fam*) to have an affair; **en** ~ **de cachondeo** for a laugh; **en** ~ **económico** (*fam*) on the cheap; **vamos en** ~ **de turismo** we're going as tourists; **si te pones en ese** ~ ... if that's your attitude ...

plana ['plana] *nf V* **plano**.

plancha ['plantʃa] *nf* (*para planchar*) iron; (*rótulo*) plate, sheet; (*NAUT*) gangway; (*CULIN*) grill; **pescado a la** ~ grilled fish.

planchado, a [plan'tʃaðo, a] *adj* (*ropa*) ironed; (*traje*) pressed ♦ *nm* ironing.

planchar [plan'tʃar] *vt* to iron ♦ *vi* to do the ironing.

planeador [planea'ðor] *nm* glider.

planear [plane'ar] *vt* to plan ♦ *vi* to glide.

planeta [pla'neta] *nm* planet.

planetario, a [plane'tarjo, a] *adj* planetary ♦ *nm* planetarium.

planicie [pla'niθje] *nf* plain.

planificación [planifika'θjon] *nf* planning; ~ **corporativa** (*COM*) corporate planning; ~ **familiar** family planning; **diagrama de** ~ (*COM*) planner.

planilla [pla'niʎa] *nf* (*AM*) form.

plano, a ['plano, a] *adj* flat, level, even; (*liso*) smooth ♦ *nm* (*MAT, TEC, AVIAT*) plane; (*FOTO*) shot; (*ARQ*) plan; (*GEO*) map; (*de ciudad*) map, street plan ♦ *nf* sheet of paper, page; (*TEC*) trowel **primer** ~ close-up; **caer de** ~ to fall flat; **rechazar algo de** ~ to turn sth down flat; **le daba el sol de** ~ (*fig*) the sun shone directly on it; **en primera plana** on the front page; **plana mayor** staff.

planta ['planta] *nf* (*BOT, TEC*) plant; (*ANAT*) sole of the foot, foot; ~ **baja** ground floor.

plantación [planta'θjon] *nf* (*AGR*) plantation; (*acto*) planting.

plantar [plan'tar] *vt* (*BOT*) to plant; (*puesto*) to put in; (*levantar*) to erect, set up; ~**se** *vr* to stand firm; ~ **a algn en la calle** to chuck sb out; **dejar plantado a algn** (*fam*) to stand sb up; ~**se en** to reach, get to.

plantear [plante'ar] *vt* (*problema*) to pose; (*dificultad*) to raise; **se lo plantearé** I'll put it to him.

plantel [plan'tel] *nm* (*fig*) group, set.

plantilla [plan'tiʎa] *nf* (*de zapato*) insole; (*personal*) personnel; **ser de** ~ to be on the staff.

plantío [plan'tio] *nm* (*acto*) planting; (*lugar*) plot, bed, patch.

plantón [plan'ton] *nm* (*MIL*) guard, sentry; (*fam*) long wait; **dar (un)** ~ **a algn** to stand sb up.

plañir [pla'ɲir] *vi* to mourn.

plasma ['plasma] *nm* plasma.

plasmar [plas'mar] *vt* (*dar forma*) to mould, shape; (*representar*) to represent ♦ *vi*: ~ **en** to take the form of.

plasta ['plasta] *nf* soft mass, lump; (*desastre*) botch, mess.

plasticidad [plastiθi'ðað] *nf* (*fig*) expressiveness.

plástico, a ['plastiko, a] *adj* plastic ♦ *nf* (art of) sculpture, modelling ♦ *nm* plastic.

plastificar [plastifi'kar] *vt* (*documento*) to laminate.

plastifique [plasti'fike] *etc vb V* **plastificar**.

plastilina [plasti'lina] *nf* Plasticine ®.

plata ['plata] *nf* (*metal*) silver; (*cosas hechas de plata*) silverware; (*AM*) cash, dough (*fam*); **hablar en** ~ to speak bluntly *o* frankly.

plataforma [plata'forma] *nf* platform; ~ **de lanzamiento/perforación** launch(ing) pad/drilling rig.

plátano ['platano] *nm* (*fruta*) banana; (*árbol*) plane tree.

platea [pla'tea] *nf* (*TEAT*) pit.

plateado, a [plate'aðo, a] *adj* silver; (*TEC*) silver-plated.

platense [pla'tense] (*fam*) = **ríoplatense**.

plática ['platika] *nf* (*AM*) talk, chat; (*REL*) sermon.

platicar [plati'kar] *vi* (*AM*) to talk, chat.

platillo [pla'tiʎo] *nm* saucer; (*de limosnas*) collecting bowl; ~**s** *nmpl* cymbals; ~ **volador** *o* **volante** flying saucer; **pasar el** ~ to pass the hat round.

platina [pla'tina] *nf* (*MUS*) tape deck.

platino [pla'tino] *nm* platinum; ~**s** *nmpl* (*AUTO*) (contact) points.

platique [pla'tike] *etc vb V* **platicar**.

plato ['plato] *nm* plate, dish; (*parte de comida*) course; (*guiso*) dish; ~ **frutero/ sopero** fruit/soup dish; **pagar los** ~**s rotos** (*fam*) to carry the can (*fam*).

plató [pla'to] *nm* set.

platónico, a [pla'toniko, a] *adj* platonic.

playa ['plaja] *nf* beach; (*costa*) seaside; ~ **de estacionamiento** (*AM*) car park.

playero, a [pla'jero, a] *adj* beach *cpd* ♦ *nf* (*AM: camiseta*) T-shirt; ~**s** *nfpl* canvas shoes; (*TENIS*) tennis shoes.

plaza ['plaθa] *nf* square; (*mercado*) market(place); (*sitio*) room, space; (*en vehículo*) seat, place; (*colocación*) post, job; ~ **de abastos** food market; ~ **mayor** main square; ~ **de toros** bullring; **hacer la** ~ to do the daily shopping; **reservar una** ~ to reserve a seat; **el hotel tiene 100** ~**s** the hotel has 100 beds.

plazca ['plaθka] *etc vb V* **placer**.

plazo ['plaθo] *nm* (*lapso de tiempo*) time, period, term; (*fecha de vencimiento*) expiry date; (*pago parcial*) instalment; **a corto/largo** ~ short-/long-term; **comprar a** ~**s** to buy on hire purchase, pay for in instalments; **nos dan un** ~ **de 8 días** they

allow us a week.

plazoleta [plaθo'leta], **plazuela** [pla'θwela] *nf* small square.

pleamar [plea'mar] *nf* high tide.

plebe ['pleβe] *nf*: **la** ~ the common people *pl*, the masses *pl*; (*pey*) the plebs *pl*.

plebeyo, a [ple'βejo, a] *adj* plebeian; (*pey*) coarse, common.

plebiscito [pleβis'θito] *nm* plebiscite.

pleca ['pleka] *nf* (*INFORM*) backslash.

plegable [ple'ɣaβle] *adj* pliable; (*silla*) folding.

plegar [ple'ɣar] *vt* (*doblar*) to fold, bend; (*COSTURA*) to pleat; ~**se** *vr* to yield, submit.

plegaria [ple'ɣarja] *nf* (*oración*) prayer.

plegué [ple'ɣe], **pleguemos** [ple'ɣemos] *etc vb V* **plegar**.

pleitear [pleite'ar] *vi* (*JUR*) to plead, conduct a lawsuit; (*litigar*) to go to law.

pleito ['pleito] *nm* (*JUR*) lawsuit, case; (*fig*) dispute, feud; ~**s** *nmpl* litigation *sg*; **entablar** ~ to bring an action *o* a lawsuit; **poner** ~ to sue.

plenario, a [ple'narjo, a] *adj* plenary, full.

plenilunio [pleni'lunjo] *nm* full moon.

plenitud [pleni'tuð] *nf* plenitude, fullness; (*abundancia*) abundance.

pleno, a ['pleno, a] *adj* full; (*completo*) complete ♦ *nm* plenum; **en** ~ as a whole; (*por unanimidad*) unanimously; **en** ~ **día** in broad daylight; **en** ~ **verano** at the height of summer; **en plena cara** full in the face.

pletina *nf* (*MUS*) tape deck.

pleuresía [pleure'sia] *nf* pleurisy.

plexiglás [pleksi'ɣlas] *nm* acrylic.

pliego ['pljeɣo] *etc vb V* **plegar** ♦ *nm* (*hoja*) sheet (of paper); (*carta*) sealed letter/ document; ~ **de condiciones** details *pl*, specifications *pl*.

pliegue ['pljeɣe] *etc vb V* **plegar** ♦ *nm* fold, crease; (*de vestido*) pleat.

plisado [pli'saðo] *nm* pleating.

plomero [plo'mero] *nm* (*AM*) plumber.

plomizo, a [plo'miθo, a] *adj* leaden, lead-coloured.

plomo ['plomo] *nm* (*metal*) lead; (*ELEC*) fuse; **caer a** ~ to fall heavily *o* flat.

pluma ['pluma] *nf* (*ZOOL*) feather; ~ **estilográfica**, ~ **fuente** (*AM*) fountain pen.

plumazo [plu'maθo] *nm* (*lit, fig*) stroke of the pen.

plumero [plu'mero] *nm* (*quitapolvos*) feather duster; **ya te veo el** ~ I know what you're up to.

plumón [plu'mon] *nm* (*AM*) felt-tip pen.

plural [plu'ral] *adj* plural ♦ *nm*: **en** ~ in the plural.

pluralidad [plurali'ðað] *nf* plurality; **una** ~ **de votos** a majority of votes.

pluriempleo [pluriem'pleo] *nm* moonlighting.

plus [plus] *nm* bonus.

plusmarquista [plusmar'kista] *nm/f* (*DEPORTE*) record holder.

plusvalía [plusßa'lia] *nf* (*mayor valor*) appreciation, added value; (*COM*) goodwill.

plutocracia [pluto'kraθja] *nf* plutocracy.

PM *nf abr* (*MIL*: = *Policía Militar*) MP.

p.m. *abr* (= *post meridiem*) p.m.; (= *por minuto*) per minute.

PMA *nm abr* (= *Programa Mundial de Alimentos*) World Food Programme.

pmo. *abr* (= *próximo*) prox.

PN *nf abr* (*MIL*: = *Policía Naval*) Naval Police.

PNB *nm abr* (*ESP COM*: = *producto nacional bruto*) GNP.

P.N.D. *nm abr* (*ESCOL*: = *personal no docente*) non-teaching staff.

PNN *nm/f abr* (= *profesor no numerario*) untenured teacher; (*ESP COM*: = *producto nacional neto*) net national product.

PNUD *nm abr* (= *Programa de las Naciones Unidas para el Desarrollo*) United Nations Development Programme.

PNV *nm abr* (*ESP POL*) = *Partido Nacional Vasco*.

P.º *abr* (= *Paseo*) Av(e).

p.o. *abr* = **por orden**.

p.º n.º *abr* (= *peso neto*) nt. wt.

población [poßla'θjon] *nf* population; (*pueblo, ciudad*) town, city; ~ **activa** working population.

poblado, a [po'ßlaðo, a] *adj* inhabited; (*barba*) thick; (*cejas*) bushy ♦ *nm* (*aldea*) village; (*pueblo*) (small) town; ~ **de** (*lleno*) filled with; **densamente** ~ densely populated.

poblador, a [poßla'ðor, a] *nm/f* settler, colonist.

poblar [po'ßlar] *vt* (*colonizar*) to colonize; (*fundar*) to found; (*habitar*) to inhabit; ~**se** *vr*: ~**se de** to fill up with; (*irse cubriendo*) to become covered with.

pobre ['poßre] *adj* poor ♦ *nm/f* poor person; (*mendigo*) beggar; **los** ~**s** the poor; ¡~! poor thing!; ~ **diablo** (*fig*) poor wretch *o* devil.

pobreza [po'ßreθa] *nf* poverty.

pocho, a ['potʃo, a] *adj* (*flor, color*) faded, discoloured; (*persona*) pale; (*fruta*) overripe; (*deprimido*) depressed.

pocilga [po'θilɣa] *nf* pigsty.

pocillo [po'siʎo] *nm* (*AM*) coffee cup.

pócima ['poθima], **poción** [po'θjon] *nf* potion; (*brebaje*) concoction, nasty drink.

━━━━━━━━━━━━ *PALABRA CLAVE*

poco, a ['poko, a] *adj* **1** (*sg*) little, not much; ~ **tiempo** little *o* not much time; **de** ~ **interés** of little interest, not very interesting; **poca cosa** not much
2 (*pl*) few, not many; **unos** ~**s** a few, some; ~**s niños comen lo que les conviene** few children eat what they should
♦ *adv* **1** little, not much; **cuesta** ~ it doesn't cost much; ~ **más o menos** more or less
2 (+*adj*: = *negativo, antónimo*): ~ **amable/inteligente** not very nice/intelligent
3: **por** ~ **me caigo** I almost fell
4 (*tiempo*): ~ **después** soon after that; **dentro de** ~ shortly; **hace** ~ a short time ago, not long ago; **a** ~ **de haberse casado** shortly after getting married
5: ~ **a** ~ little by little
6 (*AM*): **¿a** ~ **no está divino?** isn't it just divine?; **de a** ~ gradually
♦ *nm* a little, a bit; **un** ~ **triste/de dinero** a little sad/money.

poda ['poða] *nf* (*acto*) pruning; (*temporada*) pruning season.

podar [po'ðar] *vt* to prune.

podenco [po'ðenko] *nm* hound.

━━━━━━━━━━━━ *PALABRA CLAVE*

poder [po'ðer] *vi* **1** (*capacidad*) can, be able to; **no puedo hacerlo** I can't do it, I'm unable to do it
2 (*permiso*) can, may, be allowed to; **¿se puede?** may I (*o* we)?; **puedes irte ahora** you may go now; **no se puede fumar en este hospital** smoking is not allowed in this hospital
3 (*posibilidad*) may, might, could; **puede llegar mañana** he may *o* might arrive tomorrow; **pudiste haberte hecho daño** you might *o* could have hurt yourself; **¡podías habérmelo dicho antes!** you might have told me before!
4: **puede (ser)** perhaps; **puede que lo sepa Tomás** Tomás may *o* might know
5: **¡no puedo más!** I've had enough!; **no pude menos que dejarlo** I couldn't help but leave it; **es tonto a más no** ~ he's as stupid as they come
6: ~ **con: ¿puedes con eso?** can you manage that?; **no puedo con este crío**

this kid's too much for me
7: **él me puede** (*fam*) he's stronger than
me
♦ *nm* power; **el** ~ the Government; ~
adquisitivo purchasing power; **detentar**
u **ocupar** *o* **estar en el** ~ to be in power *o*
office; **estar** *u* **obrar en** ~ **de** to be in the
hands *o* possession of; **por** ~**(es)** by proxy.

poderío [poðe'rio] *nm* power; (*autoridad*)
authority.
poderoso, a [poðe'roso, a] *adj* powerful.
podio ['poðjo] *nm* podium.
podólogo, a [po'ðoloɣo, a] *nm/f*
chiropodist (*BRIT*), podiatrist (*US*).
podré [po'ðre] *etc vb V* **poder**.
podrido, a [po'ðriðo, a] *adj* rotten, bad;
(*fig*) rotten, corrupt.
podrir [po'ðrir] = **pudrir**.
poema [po'ema] *nm* poem.
poesía [poe'sia] *nf* poetry.
poeta [po'eta] *nm* poet.
poético, a [po'etiko, a] *adj* poetic(al).
poetisa [poe'tisa] *nf* (woman) poet.
póker ['poker] *nm* poker.
polaco, a [po'lako, a] *adj* Polish ♦ *nm/f* Pole
♦ *nm* (*LING*) Polish.
polar [po'lar] *adj* polar.
polarice [pola'riθe] *etc vb V* **polarizar**.
polaridad [polari'ðað] *nf* polarity.
polarizar [polari'θar] *vt* to polarize.
polea [po'lea] *nf* pulley.
polémica [po'lemika] *nf* polemics *sg*; (*una*
~) controversy.
polemice [pole'miθe] *etc vb V* **polemizar**.
polémico, a [po'lemiko, a] *adj* polemic(al).
polemizar [polemi'θar] *vi* to argue.
polen ['polen] *nm* pollen.
poleo [po'leo] *nm* pennyroyal.
poli ['poli] *nm* (*fam*) cop (*fam*) ♦ *nf*: **la** ~ the
cops *pl* (*fam*).
policía [poli'θia] *nm/f* policeman/woman
♦ *nf* police; ~ **municipal** local police; ~
nacional national police; *see boxed note*.

---

policíaco, a [poli'θiako, a] *adj* police *cpd*;
novela policíaca detective story.
polideportivo [poliðepor'tiβo] *nm* sports
centre.
poliéster [poli'ester] *nm* polyester.
polietileno [polieti'leno] *nm* polythene
(*BRIT*), polyethylene (*US*).
polifacético, a [polifa'θetiko, a] *adj*
(*persona, talento*) many-sided, versatile.
poligamia [poli'ɣamja] *nf* polygamy.
polígamo, a [po'liɣamo, a] *adj* polygamous
♦ *nm* polygamist.
polígono [po'liɣono] *nm* (*MAT*) polygon;
(*solar*) building lot; (*zona*) area; (*unidad
vecina*) housing estate; ~ **industrial**
industrial estate.
polígrafo [po'liɣrafo] *nm* polygraph.
polilla [po'liʎa] *nf* moth.
Polinesia [poli'nesja] *nf* Polynesia.
polinesio, a [poli'nesjo, a] *adj, nm/f*
Polynesian.
polio ['poljo] *nf* polio.
Polisario [poli'sarjo] *nm abr* (*POL: tb:* **Frente**
~) = *Frente Político de Liberación del
Sáhara y Río de Oro*.
politécnico [poli'tekniko] *nm* polytechnic.
político, a [po'litiko, a] *adj* political;
(*discreto*) tactful; (*pariente*) in-law ♦ *nm/f*
politician ♦ *nf* politics *sg*; (*económica,
agraria*) policy; **padre** ~ father-in-law;
política exterior/de ingresos y precios
foreign/prices and incomes policy.
póliza ['poliθa] *nf* certificate, voucher;
(*impuesto*) tax *o* fiscal stamp; ~ **de
seguro(s)** insurance policy.
polizón [poli'θon] *nm* (*AVIAT, NAUT*)
stowaway.
pollera [po'ʎera] *nf* (*criadero*) hencoop;
(*AM*) skirt, overskirt.
pollería [poʎe'ria] *nf* poulterer's (shop).
pollo ['poʎo] *nm* chicken; (*joven*) young
man; (*señorito*) playboy; ~ **asado** roast
chicken.
polo ['polo] *nm* (*GEO, ELEC*) pole; (*helado*)
ice lolly; (*DEPORTE*) polo; (*suéter*) polo-
neck; **P**~ **Norte/Sur** North/South Pole;
esto es el ~ **opuesto de lo que dijo antes**
this is the exact opposite of what he
said before.
Polonia [po'lonja] *nf* Poland.
poltrona [pol'trona] *nf* reclining chair,
easy chair.
polución [polu'θjon] *nf* pollution; ~
ambiental environmental pollution.
polvera [pol'βera] *nf* powder compact.
polvo ['polβo] *nm* dust; (*QUÍMICA, CULIN,
MED*) powder; (*fam!*) screw(!); **en** ~
powdered; ~ **de talco** talcum powder;

estar hecho ~ to be worn out o
exhausted; **hacer algo** ~ to smash sth;
hacer ~ **a algn** to shatter sb; V tb **polvos.**
pólvora ['polβora] nf gunpowder; (*fuegos
artificiales*) fireworks pl; **propagarse
como la** ~ (*noticia*) to spread like
wildfire.
polvoriento, a [polβo'rjento, a] adj
(*superficie*) dusty; (*sustancia*) powdery.
polvorín [polβo'rin] nm (*fig*) powder keg.
polvorosa [polβo'rosa] adj (*fam*): **poner
pies en** ~ to beat it.
polvos ['polβos] nmpl powder sg.
polvoso, a [pol'βoso, a] adj (*AM*) dusty.
pomada [po'maða] nf pomade.
pomelo [po'melo] nm grapefruit.
pómez ['pomeθ] nf: **piedra** ~ pumice
stone.
pomo ['pomo] nm handle.
pompa ['pompa] nf (*burbuja*) bubble;
(*bomba*) pump; (*esplendor*) pomp,
splendour; ~**s fúnebres** funeral sg.
pomposo, a [pom'poso, a] adj splendid,
magnificent; (*pey*) pompous.
pómulo ['pomulo] nm cheekbone.
ponche ['pontʃe] nm punch.
poncho ['pontʃo] nm (*AM*) poncho, cape.
ponderar [ponde'rar] vt (*considerar*) to
weigh up, consider; (*elogiar*) to praise
highly, speak in praise of.
pondré [pon'dre] etc vb V **poner.**
ponencia [po'nenθja] nf (*exposición*)
(learned) paper, communication;
(*informe*) report.

=========== *PALABRA CLAVE* ===========

poner [po'ner] vt **1** to put; (*colocar*) to
place, set; (*ropa*) to put on; (*problema, la
mesa*) to set; (*interés*) to show;
(*telegrama*) to send; (*obra de teatro*) to put
on; (*película*) to show; **ponlo más alto**
turn it up; **¿qué ponen en el Excelsior?**
what's on at the Excelsior?; ~ **algo a
secar** to put sth (out) to dry; **¡no pongas
esa cara!** don't look at me like that!
2 (*tienda*) to open; (*instalar: gas etc*) to
put in; (*radio, TV*) to switch o turn on
3 (*suponer*): **pongamos que** ... let's
suppose that ...
4 (*contribuir*): **el gobierno ha puesto otro
millón** the government has contributed
another million
5 (*TELEC*): **póngame con el Sr. López** can
you put me through to Mr. López?
6 (*estar escrito*) to say; **¿qué pone aquí?**
what does it say here?
7: ~ **de: le han puesto de director general**
they've appointed him general manager

8 (+*adj*) to make; **me estás poniendo
nerviosa** you're making me nervous
9 (*dar nombre*): **al hijo le pusieron Diego**
they called their son Diego
♦ vi (*gallina*) to lay
♦ ~**se** vr **1** (*colocarse*): **se puso a mi lado**
he came and stood beside me; **tú ponte
en esa silla** you go and sit on that chair
2 (*vestido, cosméticos*) to put on; **¿por
qué no te pones el vestido nuevo?** why
don't you put on o wear your new dress?
3 (*sol*) to set
4 (+*adj*) to get, become; to turn; ~**se
enfermo/gordo/triste** to get ill/fat/sad;
se puso muy serio he got very serious;
después de lavarla la tela se puso azul
after washing it the material turned
blue; **¡no te pongas así!** don't be like
that!; ~**se cómodo** to make o.s.
comfortable
5: ~**se a: se puso a llorar** he started to
cry; **tienes que ~te a estudiar** you must
get down to studying
6: ~**se a bien con algn** to make it up with
sb; ~**se a mal con algn** to get on the
wrong side of sb
7 (*AM*): **se me pone que** ... it seems to
me that ..., I think that ....

ponga ['ponga] etc vb V **poner.**
poniente [po'njente] nm west.
pontevedrés, esa [ponteβe'ðres, esa] adj
of o from Pontevedra ♦ nm/f native o
inhabitant of Pontevedra.
pontificado [pontifi'kaðo] nm papacy,
pontificate.
pontífice [pon'tifiθe] nm pope, pontiff; **el
Sumo P**~ His Holiness the Pope.
pontón [pon'ton] nm pontoon.
ponzoña [pon'θoɲa] nf poison,
venom.
ponzoñoso, a [ponθo'ɲoso, a] adj
poisonous, venomous.
pop [pop] adj inv, nm (*MUS*) pop.
popa ['popa] nf stern; **a** ~ astern, abaft; **de**
~ **a proa** fore and aft.
popular [popu'lar] adj popular; (*del pueblo*)
of the people.
popularice [popula'riθe] etc vb V
popularizarse.
popularidad [populari'ðað] nf popularity.
popularizarse [populari'θarse] vr to
become popular.
poquísimo, a [po'kisimo, a] adj (*superlativo
de poco*) very little; (*pl*) very few; (*casi
nada*) hardly any.
poquito [po'kito] nm: **un** ~ a little bit ♦ adv
a little, a bit; **a** ~**s** bit by bit.

========================= *PALABRA CLAVE*

por [por] *prep* **1** (*objetivo*) for; **luchar ~ la patria** to fight for one's country; **hazlo ~ mí** do it for my sake

2 (*+infin*): **~ no llegar tarde** so as not to arrive late; **~ citar unos ejemplos** to give a few examples

3 (*causa*) out of, because of; **no es ~ eso** that's not the reason; **~ escasez de fondos** through *o* for lack of funds

4 (*tiempo*): **~ la mañana/noche** in the morning/at night; **se queda ~ una semana** she's staying (for) a week

5 (*lugar*): **pasar ~ Madrid** to pass through Madrid; **ir a Guayaquil ~ Quito** to go to Guayaquil via Quito; **caminar ~ la calle** to walk along the street; **~ allí** over there; **se va ~ ahí** we have to go that way; **¿~ dónde?** which way?; **está ~ el norte** it's somewhere in the north; **~ todo el país** throughout the country

6 (*cambio, precio*): **te doy uno nuevo ~ el que tienes** I'll give you a new one (in return) for the one you've got; **lo vendí ~ 15 dólares** I sold it for 15 dollars

7 (*valor distributivo*): **30 euros ~ hora/cabeza** 30 euros an *o* per hour/a *o* per head; **10 ~ ciento** 10 per cent; **80 (kms) ~ hora** 80 (km) an *o* per hour

8 (*modo, medio*) by; **~ correo/avión** by post/air; **día ~ día** day by day; **~ orden** in order; **entrar ~ la entrada principal** to go in through the main entrance

9 (*agente*) by; **hecho ~ él** done by him; "dirigido ~" "directed by"

10: **10 ~ 10 son 100** 10 by 10 is 100

11 (*en lugar de*): **vino él ~ su jefe** he came instead of his boss

12: **~ mí que revienten** as far as I'm concerned they can drop dead

13 (*evidencia*): **~ lo que dicen** judging by *o* from what they say

14: **estar/quedar ~ hacer** to be still *o* remain to be done

15: **~ (muy) difícil que sea** however hard it is *o* may be; **~ más que lo intente** no matter how *o* however hard I try

16: **~ qué** why; **¿~ qué?** why?; **¿~?** (*fam*) why (do you ask)?

porcelana [porθe'lana] *nf* porcelain; (*china*) china.

porcentaje [porθen'taxe] *nm* percentage; **~ de actividad** (*INFORM*) hit rate.

porche ['portʃe] *nm* (*de una plaza*) arcade; (*de casa*) porch.

porción [por'θjon] *nf* (*parte*) portion, share;

(*cantidad*) quantity, amount.

pordiosero, a [porðjo'sero, a] *nm/f* beggar.

porfía [por'fia] *nf* persistence; (*terquedad*) obstinacy.

porfiado, a [por'fjaðo, a] *adj* persistent; obstinate.

porfiar [por'fjar] *vi* to persist, insist; (*disputar*) to argue stubbornly.

pormenor [porme'nor] *nm* detail, particular.

pormenorice [pormeno'riθe] *etc vb V* **pormenorizar**.

pormenorizar [pormenori'θar] *vt* to (set out in) detail ♦ *vi* to go into detail.

porno ['porno] *adj inv* porno ♦ *nm* porn.

pornografía [pornoɣra'fia] *nf* pornography.

poro ['poro] *nm* pore.

poroso, a [po'roso, a] *adj* porous.

poroto [po'roto] *nm* (*AM*) kidney bean.

porque ['porke] *conj* (*a causa de*) because; (*ya que*) since; **~ sí** because I feel like it.

porqué [por'ke] *nm* reason, cause.

porquería [porke'ria] *nf* (*suciedad*) filth, muck, dirt; (*acción*) dirty trick; (*objeto*) small thing, trifle; (*fig*) rubbish.

porqueriza [porke'riθa] *nf* pigsty.

porra ['porra] *nf* (*arma*) stick, club; (*cachiporra*) truncheon; **¡~s!** oh heck!; **¡vete a la ~!** go to heck!

porrazo [po'rraθo] *nm* (*golpe*) blow; (*caída*) bump; **de un ~** in one go.

porro ['porro] *nm* joint.

porrón [po'rron] *nm glass wine jar with a long spout.*

port [por(t)] *nm* (*INFORM*) port.

portaaviones [port(a)a'βjones] *nm inv* aircraft carrier.

portada [por'taða] *nf* (*TIP*) title page; (: *de revista*) cover.

portador, a [porta'ðor, a] *nm/f* carrier, bearer; (*COM*) bearer, payee; (*MED*) carrier; **ser ~ del virus del sida** to be HIV-positive.

portaequipajes [portaeki'paxes] *nm inv* boot (*BRIT*), trunk (*US*); (*baca*) luggage rack.

portafolio(s) [porta'foljo(s)] *nm* (*AM*) briefcase; **~ de inversiones** (*COM*) investment portfolio.

portal [por'tal] *nm* (*entrada*) vestibule, hall; (*pórtico*) porch, doorway; (*puerta de entrada*) main door; (*DEPORTE*) goal; **~es** *nmpl* arcade *sg*.

portaligas [porta'liɣas] *nm inv* (*AM*) suspender belt.

portamaletas [portama'letas] *nm inv* roof rack.

portamonedas [portamo'neðas] *nm inv* purse.

portar [por'tar] *vt* to carry, bear; ~**se** *vr* to behave, conduct o.s.; ~**se mal** to misbehave; **se portó muy bien conmigo** he treated me very well.

portátil [por'tatil] *adj* portable.

portaviones [porta'ßjones] *nm inv* aircraft carrier.

portavoz [porta'ßoθ] *nm/f* spokesman/woman.

portazo [por'taθo] *nm*: **dar un ~** to slam the door.

porte ['porte] *nm* (*COM*) transport; (*precio*) transport charges *pl*; (*CORREOS*) postage; ~ **debido** (*COM*) carriage forward; ~ **pagado** (*COM*) carriage paid, post-paid.

portento [por'tento] *nm* marvel, wonder.

portentoso, a [porten'toso, a] *adj* marvellous, extraordinary.

porteño, a [por'teɲo, a] *adj* of *o* from Buenos Aires ♦ *nm/f* native *o* inhabitant of Buenos Aires.

portería [porte'ria] *nf* (*oficina*) porter's office; (*gol*) goal.

portero, a [por'tero, a] *nm/f* porter; (*conserje*) caretaker; (*DEPORTE*) goalkeeper.

pórtico ['portiko] *nm* (*porche*) portico, porch; (*fig*) gateway; (*arcada*) arcade.

portilla [por'tiʎa] *nf*, **portillo** [por'tiʎo] *nm* gate.

portón [por'ton] *nm* proton.

portorriqueño, a [portorri'keɲo, a] *adj*, *nm/f* Puerto Rican.

portuario, a [por'twarjo] *adj* (*del puerto*) port *cpd*, harbour *cpd*; (*del muelle*) dock *cpd*; **trabajador ~** docker.

Portugal [portu'ɣal] *nm* Portugal.

portugués, esa [portu'ɣes, esa] *adj*, *nm/f* Portuguese ♦ *nm* (*LING*) Portuguese.

porvenir [porße'nir] *nm* future.

pos [pos]: **en ~ de:** *prep* after, in pursuit of.

posada [po'saða] *nf* (*refugio*) shelter, lodging; (*mesón*) guest house; **dar ~ a** to give shelter to, take in.

posaderas [posa'ðeras] *nfpl* backside *sg*, buttocks.

posar [po'sar] *vt* (*en el suelo*) to lay down, put down; (*la mano*) to place, put gently ♦ *vi* to sit, pose; ~**se** *vr* to settle; (*pájaro*) to perch; (*avión*) to land, come down.

posdata [pos'ðata] *nf* postscript.

pose ['pose] *nf* (*ARTE, afectación*) pose.

poseedor, a [posee'ðor, a] *nm/f* owner, possessor; (*de récord, puesto*) holder.

poseer [pose'er] *vt* to have, possess, own; (*ventaja*) to enjoy; (*récord, puesto*) to hold.

poseído, a [pose'iðo, a] *adj* possessed; **estar muy ~ de** to be very vain about.

posesión [pose'sjon] *nf* possession; **tomar ~ (de)** to take over.

posesionarse [posesjo'narse] *vr*: ~ **de** to take possession of, take over.

posesivo, a [pose'sißo, a] *adj* possessive.

poseyendo [pose'jendo] *etc vb V* **poseer.**

posgrado [pos'ɣraðo] *nm* = **postgrado.**

posgraduado, a [posɣra'ðwaðo, a] *adj*, *nm/f* = **postgraduado.**

posibilidad [posißili'ðað] *nf* possibility; (*oportunidad*) chance.

posibilitar [posißili'tar] *vt* to make possible, permit; (*hacer factible*) to make feasible.

posible [po'sißle] *adj* possible; (*factible*) feasible ♦ *nm*: ~**s** means; (*bienes*) funds, assets; **de ser ~** if possible; **en o dentro de lo ~** as far as possible; **lo antes ~** as quickly as possible.

posición [posi'θjon] *nf* (*gen*) position; (*rango social*) status.

positivo, a [posi'tißo, a] *adj* positive ♦ *nf* (*FOTO*) print.

poso ['poso] *nm* sediment.

posoperatorio, a [posopera'torjo, a] *adj*, *nm* = **postoperatorio.**

posponer [pospo'ner] *vt* to put behind *o* below; (*aplazar*) to postpone.

posponga [pos'ponga] *etc*, **pospuesto** [pos'pwesto], **pospuse** [pos'puse] *etc vb V* **posponer.**

posta ['posta] *nf* (*de caballos*) relay, team; **a ~ on purpose**, deliberately.

postal [pos'tal] *adj* postal ♦ *nf* postcard.

poste ['poste] *nm* (*de telégrafos*) post, pole; (*columna*) pillar.

póster ['poster], *pl* **posters** ['posters] *nm* poster.

postergar [poster'ɣar] *vt* (*esp AM*) to put off, postpone, delay.

postergue [pos'terɣe] *etc vb V* **postergar.**

posteridad [posteri'ðað] *nf* posterity.

posterior [poste'rjor] *adj* back, rear; (*siguiente*) following, subsequent; (*más tarde*) later; **ser ~ a** to be later than.

posterioridad [posterjori'ðað] *nf*: **con ~** later, subsequently.

postgrado [post'ɣraðo] *nm*: **curso de ~** postgraduate course.

postgraduado, a [postɣra'ðwaðo, a] *adj*, *nm/f* postgraduate.

pos(t)guerra [pos(t)'ɣerra] *nf* postwar period; **en la ~** after the war.

postigo [pos'tiɣo] *nm* (*portillo*) postern;

(*contraventana*) shutter.

postín [pos'tin] *nm* (*fam*) elegance; **de ~** posh; **darse ~** to show off.

postizo, a [pos'tiθo, a] *adj* false, artificial; (*sonrisa*) false, phoney ♦ *nm* hairpiece.

postoperatorio, a [postopera'torjo, a] *adj* postoperative ♦ *nm* postoperative period.

postor, a [pos'tor, a] *nm/f* bidder; **mejor ~** highest bidder.

postrado, a [pos'traðo, a] *adj* prostrate.

postrar [pos'trar] *vt* (*derribar*) to cast down, overthrow; (*humillar*) to humble; (*MED*) to weaken, exhaust; **~se** *vr* to prostrate o.s.

postre ['postre] *nm* sweet, dessert ♦ *nf*: **a la ~** in the end, when all is said and done; **para ~** (*fam*) to crown it all; **llegar a los ~s** (*fig*) to come too late.

postrero, a [pos'trero, a] *adj* (*delante de nmsg*: **postrer**: *último*) last; (: *que viene detrás*) rear.

postrimerías [postrime'rias] *nfpl* final stages.

postulado [postu'laðo] *nm* postulate.

postulante [postu'lante] *nm/f* petitioner; (*REL*) postulant.

póstumo, a ['postumo, a] *adj* posthumous.

postura [pos'tura] *nf* (*del cuerpo*) posture, position; (*fig*) attitude, position.

post-venta [pos'ßenta] *adj* (*COM*) after-sales.

potable [po'taßle] *adj* drinkable.

potaje [po'taxe] *nm* thick vegetable soup.

pote ['pote] *nm* pot, jar.

potencia [po'tenθja] *nf* power; (*capacidad*) capacity; **~ (en caballos)** horsepower; **en ~** potential, in the making; **las grandes ~s** the great powers.

potencial [poten'θjal] *adj*, *nm* potential.

potenciar [poten'θjar] *vt* (*promover*) to promote; (*fortalecer*) to boost.

potente [po'tente] *adj* powerful.

potestad [potes'tað] *nf* authority; **patria ~** paternal authority.

potosí [poto'si] *nm* fortune; **cuesta un ~** it costs the earth.

potra ['potra] *nf* (*ZOOL*) filly; **tener ~** to be lucky.

potro ['potro] *nm* (*ZOOL*) colt; (*DEPORTE*) vaulting horse.

pozo ['poθo] *nm* well; (*de río*) deep pool; (*de mina*) shaft; **~ negro** cesspool; **ser un ~ de ciencia** (*fig*) to be deeply learned.

PP *abr* (= *por poderes*) pp; (= *porte pagado*) carriage paid.

p.p.m. *abr* (= *palabras por minuto*) wpm.

práctica ['praktika] *nf* V **práctico**.

practicable [prakti'kaßle] *adj* practicable; (*camino*) passable, usable.

prácticamente ['praktikamente] *adv* practically.

practicante [prakti'kante] *nm/f* (*MED*: *ayudante de doctor*) medical assistant; (: *enfermero*) nurse; (*quien practica algo*) practitioner ♦ *adj* practising.

practicar [prakti'kar] *vt* to practise; (*deporte*) to go in for, play; (*ejecutar*) to carry out, perform.

práctico, a ['praktiko, a] *adj* (*gen*) practical; (*conveniente*) handy; (*instruido*: *persona*) skilled, expert ♦ *nf* practice; (*método*) method; (*arte, capacidad*) skill; **en la práctica** in practice.

practique [prak'tike] *etc vb* V **practicar**.

pradera [pra'ðera] *nf* meadow; (*de Canadá*) prairie.

prado ['praðo] *nm* (*campo*) meadow, field; (*pastizal*) pasture; (*AM*) lawn.

Praga ['praɣa] *nf* Prague.

pragmático, a [praɣ'matiko, a] *adj* pragmatic.

preámbulo [pre'ambulo] *nm* preamble, introduction; **decir algo sin ~s** to say sth without beating about the bush.

precalentamiento [prekalenta'mjento] *nm* (*DEPORTE*) warm-up.

precalentar [prekalen'tar] *vt* to preheat.

precaliente [preka'ljente] *etc vb* V **precalentar**.

precario, a [pre'karjo, a] *adj* precarious.

precaución [prekau'θjon] *nf* (*medida preventiva*) preventive measure, precaution; (*prudencia*) caution, wariness.

precaver [preka'ßer] *vt* to guard against; (*impedir*) to forestall; **~se** *vr*: **~se de** *o* **contra algo** to (be on one's) guard against sth.

precavido, a [preka'ßiðo, a] *adj* cautious, wary.

precedencia [preθe'ðenθja] *nf* precedence; (*prioridad*) priority; (*superioridad*) greater importance, superiority.

precedente [preθe'ðente] *adj* preceding; (*anterior*) former ♦ *nm* precedent; **sin ~(s)** unprecedented; **establecer** *o* **sentar un ~** to establish *o* set a precedent.

preceder [preθe'ðer] *vt, vi* to precede, go/come before.

precepto [pre'θepto] *nm* precept.

preceptor [preθep'tor] *nm* (*maestro*) teacher; (: *particular*) tutor.

preciado, a [pre'θjaðo, a] *adj* (*estimado*) esteemed, valuable.

preciar [pre'θjar] *vt* to esteem, value; **~se**

vr to boast; ~**se de** to pride o.s. on.
precintar [preθin'tar] *vt* (*local*) to seal off;
(*producto*) to seal.
precinto [pre'θinto] *nm* (COM: *tb*: ~ **de
garantía**) seal.
precio ['preθjo] *nm* (*de mercado*) price;
(*costo*) cost; (*valor*) value, worth; (*de
viaje*) fare; ~ **de coste** *o* **de cobertura**
cost price; ~ **al contado** cash price; ~ **al
detalle** *o* **al por menor** retail price; ~ **al
detallista** trade price; ~ **de entrega
inmediata** spot price; ~ **de oferta** offer
price; ~ **de oportunidad** bargain price;
~ **de salida** upset price; ~ **tope** top
price; ~ **unitario** unit price; **no tener** ~
(*fig*) to be priceless; "**no importa** ~"
"cost no object".
preciosidad [preθjosi'ðað] *nf* (*valor*) (high)
value, (great) worth; (*encanto*) charm;
(*cosa bonita*) beautiful thing; **es una** ~
it's lovely, it's really beautiful.
precioso, a [pre'θjoso, a] *adj* precious; (*de
mucho valor*) valuable; (*fam*) lovely,
beautiful.
precipicio [preθi'piθjo] *nm* cliff, precipice;
(*fig*) abyss.
precipitación [preθipita'θjon] *nf* (*prisa*)
haste; (*lluvia*) rainfall; (QUÍMICA)
precipitation.
precipitado, a [preθipi'taðo, a] *adj* hasty,
rash; (*salida*) hasty, sudden ♦ *nm*
(QUÍMICA) precipitate.
precipitar [preθipi'tar] *vt* (*arrojar*) to hurl,
throw; (*apresurar*) to hasten; (*acelerar*) to
speed up, accelerate; (QUÍMICA) to
precipitate; ~**se** *vr* to throw o.s.;
(*apresurarse*) to rush; (*actuar sin pensar*)
to act rashly; ~**se hacia** to rush towards.
precisado, a [preθi'saðo, a] *adj*: **verse** ~ **a
hacer algo** to be obliged to do sth.
precisamente [preθisa'mente] *adv*
precisely; (*justo*) precisely, exactly,
just; ~ **por eso** for that very reason; ~
fue él quien lo dijo as a matter of fact he
said it; **no es eso** ~ it's not really that.
precisar [preθi'sar] *vt* (*necesitar*) to need,
require; (*fijar*) to determine exactly, fix;
(*especificar*) to specify; (*señalar*) to
pinpoint.
precisión [preθi'sjon] *nf* (*exactitud*)
precision.
preciso, a [pre'θiso, a] *adj* (*exacto*) precise;
(*necesario*) necessary, essential; (*estilo,
lenguaje*) concise; **es** ~ **que lo hagas** you
must do it.
precocidad [prekoθi'ðað] *nf*
precociousness, precocity.
preconcebido, a [prekonθe'βiðo, a] *adj*
preconceived.

preconice [preko'niθe] *etc vb* V **preconizar**.
preconizar [prekoni'θar] *vt* (*aconsejar*) to
advise; (*prever*) to foresee.
precoz [pre'koθ] *adj* (*persona*) precocious;
(*calvicie*) premature.
precursor, a [prekur'sor, a] *nm/f*
precursor.
predecesor, a [preðeθe'sor, a] *nm/f*
predecessor.
predecir [preðe'θir] *vt* to predict, foretell,
forecast.
predestinado, a [preðesti'naðo, a] *adj*
predestined.
predeterminar [preðetermi'nar] *vt* to
predetermine.
predicado [preði'kaðo] *nm* predicate.
predicador, a [preðika'ðor, a] *nm/f*
preacher.
predicar [preði'kar] *vt, vi* to preach.
predicción [preðik'θjon] *nf* prediction;
(*pronóstico*) forecast; ~ **del tiempo**
weather forecast(ing).
predicho [pre'ðitʃo], **prediga** [pre'ðiɣa]
etc, **predije** [pre'ðixe] *etc vb* V **predecir**.
predilecto, a [preði'lekto, a] *adj* favourite.
predique [pre'ðike] *etc vb* V **predicar**.
prediré [preði're] *etc vb* V **predecir**.
predispondré [preðispon'dre] *etc vb* V
predisponer.
predisponer [preðispo'ner] *vt* to
predispose; (*pey*) to prejudice.
predisponga [preðis'ponga] *etc vb* V
predisponer.
predisposición [preðisposi'θjon] *nf*
predisposition, inclination; prejudice,
bias; (MED) tendency.
predispuesto [preðis'pwesto],
predispuse [preðis'puse] *etc vb* V
predisponer.
predominante [preðomi'nante] *adj*
predominant; (*preponderante*) prevailing;
(*interés*) controlling.
predominar [preðomi'nar] *vt* to dominate
♦ *vi* to predominate; (*prevalecer*) to
prevail.
predominio [preðo'minjo] *nm*
predominance; prevalence.
preescolar [preesko'lar] *adj* preschool.
preestreno [prees'treno] *nm* preview,
press view.
prefabricado, a [prefaβri'kaðo, a] *adj*
prefabricated.
prefacio [pre'faθjo] *nm* preface.
preferencia [prefe'renθja] *nf* preference;
de ~ preferably, for preference;
localidad de ~ reserved seat.
preferible [prefe'riβle] *adj* preferable.

preferido, a [prefeˈriðo, a] *adj, nm/f* favourite, (*US*) favorite.
preferir [prefeˈrir] *vt* to prefer.
prefiera [preˈfjera] *etc vb V* **preferir**.
prefijo [preˈfixo] *nm* prefix.
prefiriendo [prefiˈrjendo] *etc vb V* **preferir**.
pregón [preˈɣon] *nm* proclamation, announcement.
pregonar [preɣoˈnar] *vt* to proclaim, announce; (*mercancía*) to hawk.
pregonero [preɣoˈnero] *nm* town crier.
pregunta [preˈɣunta] *nf* question; ~ **capciosa** catch question; **hacer una** ~ to ask a question; ~**s frecuentes** FAQs, frequently asked questions.
preguntar [preɣunˈtar] *vt* to ask; (*cuestionar*) to question ♦ *vi* to ask; ~**se** *vr* to wonder; ~ **por algn** to ask for sb; ~ **por la salud de algn** to ask after sb's health.
preguntón, ona [preɣunˈton, ona] *adj* inquisitive.
prehistórico, a [preisˈtoriko, a] *adj* prehistoric.
prejuicio [preˈxwiθjo] *nm* prejudgement; (*preconcepción*) preconception; (*pey*) prejudice, bias.
prejuzgar [prexuθˈɣar] *vt* (*predisponer*) to prejudge.
prejuzgue [preˈxuθɣe] *etc vb V* **prejuzgar**.
preliminar [prelimiˈnar] *adj, nm* preliminary.
preludio [preˈluðjo] *nm* (*MUS, fig*) prelude.
premamá [premaˈma] *adj*: **vestido** ~ maternity dress.
prematrimonial [prematrimoˈnjal] *adj*: **relaciones** ~**es** premarital sex.
prematuro, a [premaˈturo, a] *adj* premature.
premeditación [premeðitaˈθjon] *nf* premeditation.
premeditado, a [premeðiˈtaðo, a] *adj* premeditated, deliberate; (*intencionado*) wilful.
premeditar [premeðiˈtar] *vt* to premeditate.
premiar [preˈmjar] *vt* to reward; (*en un concurso*) to give a prize to.
premio [ˈpremjo] *nm* reward; prize; (*COM*) premium; ~ **gordo** first prize.
premisa [preˈmisa] *nf* premise.
premonición [premoniˈθjon] *nf* premonition.
premura [preˈmura] *nf* (*prisa*) haste, urgency.
prenatal [prenaˈtal] *adj* antenatal, prenatal.
prenda [ˈprenda] *nf* (*ropa*) garment, article of clothing; (*garantía*) pledge; (*fam*)

darling!; ~**s** *nfpl* talents, gifts; **dejar algo en** ~ to pawn sth; **no soltar** ~ to give nothing away; (*fig*) not to say a word.
prendar [prenˈdar] *vt* to captivate, enchant; ~**se de algo** to fall in love with sth.
prendedor [prendeˈðor] *nm* brooch.
prender [prenˈder] *vt* (*captar*) to catch, capture; (*detener*) to arrest; (*coser*) to pin, attach; (*sujetar*) to fasten; (*AM*) to switch on ♦ *vi* to catch; (*arraigar*) to take root; ~**se** *vr* (*encenderse*) to catch fire.
prendido, a [prenˈdiðo, a] *adj* (*AM: luz*) on.
prensa [ˈprensa] *nf* press; **la P**~ the press; **tener mala** ~ to have *o* get a bad press.
prensar [prenˈsar] *vt* to press.
preñado, a [preˈɲaðo, a] *adj* (*mujer*) pregnant; ~ **de** pregnant with, full of.
preocupación [preokupaˈθjon] *nf* worry, concern; (*ansiedad*) anxiety.
preocupado, a [preokuˈpaðo, a] *adj* worried, concerned; anxious.
preocupar [preokuˈpar] *vt* to worry; ~**se** *vr* to worry; ~**se de algo** (*hacerse cargo*) to take care of sth; ~**se por algo** to worry about sth.
preparación [preparaˈθjon] *nf* (*acto*) preparation; (*estado*) preparedness, readiness; (*entrenamiento*) training.
preparado, a [prepaˈraðo, a] *adj* (*dispuesto*) prepared; (*CULIN*) ready (to serve) ♦ *nm* (*MED*) preparation; ¡~**s, listos, ya!** ready, steady, go!
preparar [prepaˈrar] *vt* (*disponer*) to prepare, get ready; (*TEC: tratar*) to prepare, process, treat; (*entrenar*) to teach, train; ~**se** *vr*: ~**se a** *o* **para hacer algo** to prepare *o* get ready to do sth.
preparativo, a [preparaˈtiβo] *adj* preparatory, preliminary ♦ *nm*: ~**s** *nmpl* preparations.
preparatoria [preparaˈtorja] *nf* (*AM*) sixth form college (*BRIT*), senior high school (*US*).
preposición [preposiˈθjon] *nf* preposition.
prepotencia [prepoˈtenθja] *nf* abuse of power; (*POL*) high-handedness; (*soberbia*) arrogance.
prepotente [prepoˈtente] *adj* (*POL*) high-handed; (*soberbio*) arrogant.
prerrogativa [prerroɣaˈtiβa] *nf* prerogative, privilege.
presa [ˈpresa] *nf* (*cosa apresada*) catch; (*víctima*) victim; (*de animal*) prey; (*de agua*) dam; **hacer** ~ **en** to clutch (on to), seize; **ser** ~ **de** (*fig*) to be a prey to.
presagiar [presaˈxjar] *vt* to threaten.
presagio [preˈsaxjo] *nm* omen.

presbítero [pres'ßitero] *nm* priest.
prescindir [presθin'dir] *vi*: ~ **de** (*privarse de*) to do without, go without; (*descartar*) to dispense with; **no podemos** ~ **de él** we can't manage without him.
prescribir [preskri'ßir] *vt* to prescribe.
prescripción [preskrip'θjon] *nf* prescription; ~ **facultativa** medical prescription.
prescrito [pres'krito] *pp de* **prescribir**.
preseleccionar [preselekθjo'nar] *vt* (*DEPORTE*) to seed.
presencia [pre'senθja] *nf* presence; **en** ~ **de** in the presence of.
presencial [presen'θjal] *adj*: **testigo** ~ eyewitness.
presenciar [presen'θjar] *vt* to be present at; (*asistir a*) to attend; (*ver*) to see, witness.
presentación [presenta'θjon] *nf* presentation; (*introducción*) introduction.
presentador, a [presenta'ðor, a] *nm/f* compère.
presentar [presen'tar] *vt* to present; (*ofrecer*) to offer; (*mostrar*) to show, display; (*renuncia*) to tender; (*moción*) to propose; (*a una persona*) to introduce; ~**se** *vr* (*llegar inesperadamente*) to appear, turn up; (*ofrecerse: como candidato*) to run, stand; (*aparecer*) to show, appear; (*solicitar empleo*) to apply; ~ **al cobro** (*COM*) to present for payment; ~**se a la policía** to report to the police.
presente [pre'sente] *adj* present ♦ *nm* present; (*LING*) present (tense); (*regalo*) gift; **los** ~**s** those present; **hacer** ~ to state, declare; **tener** ~ to remember, bear in mind; **la carta** ~, **la** ~ this letter.
presentimiento [presenti'mjento] *nm* premonition, presentiment.
presentir [presen'tir] *vt* to have a premonition of.
preservación [preserßa'θjon] *nf* protection, preservation.
preservar [preser'ßar] *vt* to protect, preserve.
preservativo [preserßa'tißo] *nm* sheath, condom.
presidencia [presi'ðenθja] *nf* presidency; (*de comité*) chairmanship; **ocupar la** ~ to preside, be in *o* take the chair.
presidente [presi'ðente] *nm/f* president; chairman/woman; (*en parlamento*) speaker; (*JUR*) presiding magistrate.
presidiario [presi'ðjarjo] *nm* convict.
presidio [pre'siðjo] *nm* prison, penitentiary.
presidir [presi'ðir] *vt* (*dirigir*) to preside at,

preside over; (: *comité*) to take the chair at; (*dominar*) to dominate, rule ♦ *vi* to preside; to take the chair.
presienta [pre'sjenta] *etc*, **presintiendo** [presin'tjendo] *etc vb* V **presentir**.
presión [pre'sjon] *nf* pressure; ~ **arterial** *o* **sanguínea** blood pressure; **a** ~ under pressure.
presionar [presjo'nar] *vt* to press; (*botón*) to push, press; (*fig*) to press, put pressure on ♦ *vi*: ~ **para** *o* **por** to press for.
preso, a ['preso, a] *adj*: **estar** ~ **de terror** *o* **pánico** to be panic-stricken ♦ *nm/f* prisoner; **tomar** *o* **llevar** ~ **a algn** to arrest sb, take sb prisoner.
prestación [presta'θjon] *nf* (*aportación*) lending; (*INFORM*) capability; (*servicio*) service; (*subsidio*) benefit; **prestaciones** *nfpl* (*AUTO*) performance features; ~ **de juramento** oath-taking; ~ **personal** obligatory service; **P~ Social Sustitutoria** community service for conscientious objectors; *V tb* **mili**.
prestado, a [pres'taðo, a] *adj* on loan; **dar algo** ~ to lend sth; **pedir** ~ to borrow.
prestamista [presta'mista] *nm/f* moneylender.
préstamo ['prestamo] *nm* loan; ~ **con garantía** loan against collateral; ~ **hipotecario** mortgage.
prestar [pres'tar] *vt* to lend, loan; (*atención*) to pay; (*ayuda*) to give; (*servicio*) to do, render; (*juramento*) to take, swear; ~**se** *vr* (*ofrecerse*) to offer *o* volunteer.
prestatario, a [presta'tarjo, a] *nm/f* borrower.
presteza [pres'teθa] *nf* speed, promptness.
prestidigitador [prestiðixita'ðor] *nm* conjurer.
prestigio [pres'tixjo] *nm* prestige; (*reputación*) face; (*renombre*) good name.
prestigioso, a [presti'xjoso, a] *adj* (*honorable*) prestigious; (*famoso, renombrado*) renowned, famous.
presto, a ['presto, a] *adj* (*rápido*) quick, prompt; (*dispuesto*) ready ♦ *adv* at once, right away.
presumido, a [presu'miðo, a] *adj* conceited.
presumir [presu'mir] *vt* to presume ♦ *vi* (*tener aires*) to be conceited; **según cabe** ~ as may be presumed, presumably; ~ **de listo** to think o.s. very smart.
presunción [presun'θjon] *nf* presumption; (*sospecha*) suspicion; (*vanidad*) conceit.
presunto, a [pre'sunto, a] *adj* (*supuesto*)

supposed, presumed; (*así llamado*) so-called.

presuntuoso, a [presun'twoso, a] *adj* conceited, presumptuous.

presupondré [presupon'dre] *etc vb V* **presuponer.**

presuponer [presupo'ner] *vt* to presuppose.

presuponga [presu'ponga] *etc vb V* **presuponer.**

presupuestar [presupwes'tar] *vi* to budget ♦ *vt:* ~ **algo** to budget for sth.

presupuestario, a [presupwes'tarjo, a] *adj* (*FINANZAS*) budgetary, budget *cpd*.

presupuesto [presu'pwesto] *pp de* **presuponer** ♦ *nm* (*FINANZAS*) budget; (*estimación: de costo*) estimate; **asignación de** ~ (*COM*) budget appropriation.

presupuse [presu'puse] *etc vb V* **presuponer.**

presuroso, a [presu'roso, a] *adj* (*rápido*) quick, speedy; (*que tiene prisa*) hasty.

pretencioso, a [preten'θjoso, a] *adj* pretentious.

pretender [preten'der] *vt* (*intentar*) to try to, seek to; (*reivindicar*) to claim; (*buscar*) to seek, try for; (*cortejar*) to woo, court; ~ **que** to expect that; **¿qué pretende usted?** what are you after?

pretendiente [preten'djente] *nm/f* (*candidato*) candidate, applicant; (*amante*) suitor.

pretensión [preten'sjon] *nf* (*aspiración*) aspiration; (*reivindicación*) claim; (*orgullo*) pretension.

pretérito, a [pre'terito, a] *adj* (*LING*) past; (*fig*) past, former.

pretextar [preteks'tar] *vt* to plead, use as an excuse.

pretexto [pre'teksto] *nm* pretext; (*excusa*) excuse; **so** ~ **de** under pretext of.

pretil [pre'til] *nm* (*valla*) parapet; (*baranda*) handrail.

prevalecer [preβale'θer] *vi* to prevail.

prevaleciente [preβale'θjente] *adj* prevailing, prevalent.

prevalezca [preβa'leθka] *etc vb V* **prevalecer.**

prevención [preβen'θjon] *nf* (*preparación*) preparation; (*estado*) preparedness, readiness; (*medida*) prevention; (*previsión*) foresight, forethought; (*precaución*) precaution.

prevendré [preβen'dre] *etc,* **prevenga** [pre'βenga] *etc vb V* **prevenir.**

prevenido, a [preβe'niðo, a] *adj* prepared, ready; (*cauteloso*) cautious; **estar** ~

(*preparado*) to be ready; **ser** ~ (*cuidadoso*) to be cautious; **hombre** ~ **vale por dos** forewarned is forearmed.

prevenir [preβe'nir] *vt* (*impedir*) to prevent; (*prever*) to foresee, anticipate; (*predisponer*) to prejudice, bias; (*avisar*) to warn; (*preparar*) to prepare, get ready; ~**se** *vr* to get ready, prepare; ~**se contra** to take precautions against.

preventivo, a [preβen'tiβo, a] *adj* preventive, precautionary.

prever [pre'βer] *vt* to foresee; (*anticipar*) to anticipate.

previniendo [preβi'njendo] *etc vb V* **prevenir.**

previo, a ['preβjo, a] *adj* (*anterior*) previous, prior ♦ *prep:* ~ **acuerdo de los otros** subject to the agreement of the others; ~ **pago de los derechos** on payment of the fees.

previsible [preβi'siβle] *adj* foreseeable.

previsión [preβi'sjon] *nf* (*perspicacia*) foresight; (*predicción*) forecast; (*prudencia*) caution; ~ **de ventas** (*COM*) sales forecast.

previsor, a [preβi'sor, a] *adj* (*precavido*) far-sighted; (*prudente*) thoughtful.

previsto [pre'βisto] *pp de* **prever.**

P.R.I. *nm abr* (*AM*) = **Partido Revolucionario Institucional.**

prieto, a ['prjeto, a] *adj* (*oscuro*) dark; (*AM*) dark(-skinned); (*fig*) mean; (*comprimido*) tight, compressed.

prima ['prima] *nf V* **primo.**

primacía [prima'θia] *nf* primacy.

primar [pri'mar] *vi* (*tener primacía*) to occupy first place; ~ **sobre** to have priority over.

primario, a [pri'marjo, a] *adj* primary ♦ *nf* primary education; *V tb* **sistema educativo.**

primavera [prima'βera] *nf* (*temporada*) spring; (*período*) springtime.

primaveral [primaβe'ral] *adj* spring *cpd*, springlike.

primero, a [pri'mero, a] *adj* (*delante de nmsg:* **primer**) first; (*fig*) prime; (*anterior*) former; (*básico*) fundamental ♦ *adv* first; (*más bien*) sooner, rather ♦ *nf* (*AUTO*) first gear; (*FERRO*) first class; **de primera** (*fam*) first-class, first-rate; **de buenas a primeras** suddenly; **primera dama** (*TEAT*) leading lady.

primicia [pri'miθja] *nf* (*PRENSA*) scoop; ~**s** *nfpl* (*tb fig*) first fruits.

primitivo, a [primi'tiβo, a] *adj* primitive; (*original*) original; (*COM: acción*) ordinary ♦ *nf:* **(Lotería) Primitiva** *weekly state-run* *lottery*; V *tb* **lotería**.

primo, a ['primo, a] *adj* (*MAT*) prime ♦ *nm/f*
cousin; (*fam*) fool, dupe ♦ *nf* (*COM*) bonus;
(*seguro*) premium; (*a la exportación*)
subsidy; ~ **hermano** first cousin;
materias primas raw materials; **hacer el**
~ to be taken for a ride.

primogénito, a [primo'xenito, a] *adj* first-
born.

primor [pri'mor] *nm* (*cuidado*) care; **es un**
~ it's lovely.

primordial [primor'ðjal] *adj* basic,
fundamental.

primoroso, a [primo'roso, a] *adj* exquisite,
fine.

princesa [prin'θesa] *nf* princess.

principado [prinθi'paðo] *nm* principality.

principal [prinθi'pal] *adj* principal, main;
(*más destacado*) foremost; (*piso*) first,
second (*US*); (*INFORM*) foreground ♦ *nm*
(*jefe*) chief, principal.

príncipe ['prinθipe] *nm* prince; ~ **heredero**
crown prince; **P~ de Asturias** *King's son*
and heir to the Spanish throne; ~ **de**
gales (*tela*) check.

principiante [prinθi'pjante] *nm/f* beginner;
(*novato*) novice.

principio [prin'θipjo] *nm* (*comienzo*)
beginning, start; (*origen*) origin; (*base*)
rudiment, basic idea; (*moral*) principle;
a ~s de at the beginning of; **desde el** ~
from the first; **en un** ~ at first.

pringar [prin'gar] *vt* (*CULIN: pan*) to dip;
(*ensuciar*) to dirty; ~**se** *vr* to get splashed
o soiled; ~ **a algn en un asunto** (*fam*) to
involve sb in a matter.

pringoso, a [prin'goso, a] *adj* greasy;
(*pegajoso*) sticky.

pringue ['pringe] *etc vb* V **pringar** ♦ *nm*
(*grasa*) grease, fat, dripping.

prioridad [priori'ðað] *nf* priority; (*AUTO*)
right of way.

prioritario, a [priori'tarjo, a] *adj* (*INFORM*)
foreground.

prisa ['prisa] *nf* (*apresuramiento*) hurry,
haste; (*rapidez*) speed; (*urgencia*) (sense
of) urgency; **correr** ~ to be urgent; **darse**
~ to hurry up; **estar de** *o* **tener** ~ to be in
a hurry.

prisión [pri'sjon] *nf* (*cárcel*) prison; (*período*
de cárcel) imprisonment.

prisionero, a [prisjo'nero, a] *nm/f* prisoner.

prismáticos [pris'matikos] *nmpl*
binoculars.

privación [priβa'θjon] *nf* deprivation;
(*falta*) want, privation; **privaciones** *nfpl*
hardships, privations.

privado, a [pri'βaðo, a] *adj* (*particular*)
private; (*POL: favorito*) favourite (*BRIT*),
favorite (*US*); **en** ~ privately, in private;
"~ **y confidencial**" "private and
confidential".

privar [pri'βar] *vt* to deprive; ~**se** *vr*: ~**se**
de (*abstenerse*) to deprive o.s. of;
(*renunciar*) to give up.

privativo, a [priβa'tiβo, a] *adj* exclusive.

privatizar [priβati'θar] *vt* to privatize.

privilegiado, a [priβile'xjaðo, a] *adj*
privileged; (*memoria*) very good ♦ *nm/f*
(*afortunado*) privileged person.

privilegiar [priβile'xjar] *vt* to grant a
privilege to; (*favorecer*) to favour.

privilegio [priβi'lexjo] *nm* privilege;
(*concesión*) concession.

pro [pro] *nm o nf* profit, advantage ♦ *prep*:
asociación ~ **ciegos** association for the
blind ♦ *pref*: ~ **soviético/americano** pro-
Soviet/-American; **en** ~ **de** on behalf of,
for; **los** ~**s y los contras** the pros and
cons.

proa ['proa] *nf* (*NAUT*) bow, prow.

probabilidad [proβaβili'ðað] *nf* probability,
likelihood; (*oportunidad, posibilidad*)
chance, prospect.

probable [pro'βaβle] *adj* probable, likely;
es ~ que + *subjun* it is probable *o* likely
that; **es ~ que no venga** he probably
won't come.

probador [proβa'ðor] *nm* (*persona*) taster
(*of wine etc*); (*en una tienda*) fitting room.

probar [pro'βar] *vt* (*demostrar*) to prove;
(*someter a prueba*) to test, try out; (*ropa*)
to try on; (*comida*) to taste ♦ *vi* to try;
~**se** *vr*: ~**se un traje** to try on a suit.

probeta [pro'βeta] *nf* test tube.

problema [pro'βlema] *nm* problem.

procaz [pro'kaθ] *adj* insolent, impudent.

procedencia [proθe'ðenθja] *nf* (*principio*)
source, origin; (*lugar de salida*) point of
departure.

procedente [proθe'ðente] *adj* (*razonable*)
reasonable; (*conforme a derecho*) proper,
fitting; ~ **de** coming from, originating
in.

proceder [proθe'ðer] *vi* (*avanzar*) to
proceed; (*actuar*) to act; (*ser correcto*) to
be right (and proper), be fitting ♦ *nm*
(*comportamiento*) behaviour, conduct; **no**
procede obrar así it is not right to act
like that; ~ **de** to come from, originate
in.

procedimiento [proθeði'mjento] *nm*
procedure; (*proceso*) process; (*método*)
means, method; (*trámite*) proceedings *pl.*

prócer ['proθer] *nm* (*persona eminente*)
worthy; (*líder*) great man, leader; (*esp*

_AM_) national hero.
procesado, a [proθe'saðo, a] _nm/f_ accused (person).
procesador [proθesa'ðor] _nm_: ~ **de textos** (_INFORM_) word processor.
procesamiento [proθesa'mjento] _nm_ (_INFORM_) processing; ~ **de datos** data processing; ~ **por lotes** batch processing; ~ **solapado** multiprogramming; ~ **de textos** word processing.
procesar [proθe'sar] _vt_ to try, put on trial; (_INFORM_) to process.
procesión [proθe'sjon] _nf_ procession; **la** ~ **va por dentro** he keeps his troubles to himself.
proceso [pro'θeso] _nm_ process; (_JUR_) trial; (_lapso_) course (of time); (_INFORM_): ~ (**automático**) **de datos** (automatic) data processing; ~ **no prioritario** background process; ~ **por pasadas** batch processing; ~ **en tiempo real** real-time programming.
proclama [pro'klama] _nf_ (_acto_) proclamation; (_cartel_) poster.
proclamar [prokla'mar] _vt_ to proclaim.
proclive [pro'kliβe] _adj_: ~ (**a**) inclined _o_ prone (to).
procreación [prokrea'θjon] _nf_ procreation.
procrear [prokre'ar] _vt, vi_ to procreate.
procurador, a [prokura'ðor, a] _nm/f_ attorney, solicitor.
procurar [proku'rar] _vt_ (_intentar_) to try, endeavour; (_conseguir_) to get, obtain; (_asegurar_) to secure; (_producir_) to produce.
prodigar [proði'ɣar] _vt_ to lavish; ~**se** _vr_: ~**se en** to be lavish with.
prodigio [pro'ðixjo] _nm_ prodigy; (_milagro_) wonder, marvel; **niño** ~ child prodigy.
prodigioso, a [proði'xjoso, a] _adj_ prodigious, marvellous.
pródigo, a ['proðiɣo, a] _adj_ (_rico_) rich, productive; **hijo** ~ prodigal son.
producción [proðuk'θjon] _nf_ production; (_suma de productos_) output; (_producto_) product; ~ **en serie** mass production.
producir [proðu'θir] _vt_ to produce; (_generar_) to cause, bring about; (_impresión_) to give; (_COM: interés_) to bear; ~**se** _vr_ (_gen_) to come about, happen; (_hacerse_) to be produced, be made; (_estallar_) to break out; (_accidente_) to take place.
productividad [proðuktiβi'ðað] _nf_ productivity.
productivo, a [proðuk'tiβo, a] _adj_ productive; (_provechoso_) profitable.
producto [pro'ðukto] _nm_ (_resultado_)

product; _producción_) production; ~ **alimenticio** foodstuff; ~ (**nacional**) **bruto** gross (national) product; ~ **interno bruto** gross domestic product.
productor, a [proðuk'tor, a] _adj_ productive, producing ♦ _nm/f_ producer.
produje [pro'ðuxe], **produjera** [proðu'xera], **produzca** [pro'ðuθka] _etc vb_ _V_ **producir**.
proeza [pro'eθa] _nf_ exploit, feat.
profanar [profa'nar] _vt_ to desecrate, profane.
profano, a [pro'fano, a] _adj_ profane ♦ _nm/f_ (_inexperto_) layman/woman; **soy** ~ **en música** I don't know anything about music.
profecía [profe'θia] _nf_ prophecy.
proferir [profe'rir] _vt_ (_palabra, sonido_) to utter; (_injuria_) to hurl, let fly.
profesar [profe'sar] _vt_ (_declarar_) to profess; (_practicar_) to practise.
profesión [profe'sjon] _nf_ profession; (_confesión_) avowal; **abogado de** ~, **de** ~ **abogado** a lawyer by profession.
profesional [profesjo'nal] _adj_ professional.
profesor, a [profe'sor, a] _nm/f_ teacher; (_instructor_) instructor; (~ **de universidad**) lecturer; ~ **adjunto** assistant lecturer, associate professor (_US_).
profesorado [profeso'raðo] _nm_ (_profesión_) teaching profession; (_cuerpo_) teaching staff, faculty (_US_); (_cargo_) professorship.
profeta [pro'feta] _nm/f_ prophet.
profetice [profe'tiθe] _etc vb_ _V_ **profetizar**.
profetizar [profeti'θar] _vt, vi_ to prophesy.
profiera [pro'fjera] _etc_, **profiriendo** [profi'rjendo] _etc vb_ _V_ **proferir**.
profilaxis [profi'laksis] _nf inv_ prevention.
prófugo, a ['profuɣo, a] _nm/f_ fugitive; (_desertor_) deserter.
profundice [profun'diθe] _etc vb_ _V_ **profundizar**.
profundidad [profundi'ðað] _nf_ depth; **tener una** ~ **de 30 cm** to be 30 cm deep.
profundizar [profundi'θar] _vt_ (_fig_) to go deeply into, study in depth.
profundo, a [pro'fundo, a] _adj_ deep; (_misterio, pensador_) profound; **poco** ~ shallow.
profusión [profu'sjon] _nf_ (_abundancia_) profusion; (_prodigalidad_) wealth.
progenie [pro'xenje] _nf_ offspring.
progenitor [proxeni'tor] _nm_ ancestor; ~**es** _nmpl_ (_fam_) parents.
programa [pro'ɣrama] _nm_ programme; (_INFORM_) program; ~ **de estudios** curriculum, syllabus; ~ **verificador de**

ortografía (*INFORM*) spelling checker.

programación [proɣrama'θjon] *nf*
(*INFORM*) programming; ~ **estructurada**
structured programming.

programador, a [proɣrama'ðor, a] *nm/f*
(computer) programmer; ~ **de**
aplicaciones applications programmer.

programar [proɣra'mar] *vt* (*INFORM*) to
programme.

programería [proɣrame'ria] *nf* (*INFORM*): ~
fija firmware.

progre ['proɣre] *adj* (*fam*) liberal.

progresar [proɣre'sar] *vi* to progress,
make progress.

progresión [proɣre'sjon] *nf*: ~
geométrica/aritmética geometric/
arithmetic progression.

progresista [proɣre'sista] *adj, nm/f*
progressive.

progresivo, a [proɣre'siβo, a] *adj*
progressive; (*gradual*) gradual;
(*continuo*) continuous.

progreso [pro'ɣreso] *nm* (*tb*: ~**s**) progress;
hacer ~**s** to progress, advance.

prohibición [proiβi'θjon] *nf* prohibition,
ban; **levantar la** ~ **de** to remove the ban
on.

prohibir [proi'βir] *vt* to prohibit, ban,
forbid; **se prohíbe fumar** no smoking.

prohibitivo, a [proiβi'tiβo, a] *adj*
prohibitive.

prójimo, a ['proximo, a] *nm* fellow man
♦ *nm/f* (*vecino*) neighbour.

prole ['prole] *nf* (*descendencia*) offspring.

proletariado [proleta'rjaðo] *nm*
proletariat.

proletario, a [prole'tarjo, a] *adj, nm/f*
proletarian.

proliferación [prolifera'θjon] *nf*
proliferation; ~ **de armas nucleares**
spread of nuclear arms.

proliferar [prolife'rar] *vi* to proliferate.

prolífico, a [pro'lifiko, a] *adj* prolific.

prolijo, a [pro'lixo, a] *adj* long-winded,
tedious; (*AM*) neat.

prólogo ['proloɣo] *nm* prologue;
(*preámbulo*) preface, introduction.

prolongación [prolonga'θjon] *nf*
extension.

prolongado, a [prolon'gaðo, a] *adj* (*largo*)
long; (*alargado*) lengthy.

prolongar [prolon'gar] *vt* (*gen*) to extend;
(*en el tiempo*) to prolong; (*calle, tubo*) to
make longer, extend; ~**se** *vr* (*alargarse*)
to extend, go on.

prolongue [pro'longe] *etc vb V* **prolongar**.

prom. *abr* (= *promedio*) av.

promedio [pro'meðjo] *nm* average; (*de*
distancia) middle, mid-point.

promesa [pro'mesa] *nf* promise ♦ *adj*:
jugador ~ promising player; **faltar a una**
~ to break a promise.

prometer [prome'ter] *vt* to promise ♦ *vi* to
show promise; ~**se** *vr* (*dos personas*) to
get engaged.

prometido, a [prome'tiðo, a] *adj* promised;
engaged ♦ *nm/f* fiancé/fiancée.

prominente [promi'nente] *adj* prominent.

promiscuidad [promiskwi'ðað] *nf*
promiscuity.

promiscuo, a [pro'miskwo, a] *adj*
promiscuous.

promoción [promo'θjon] *nf* promotion;
(*año*) class, year; ~ **por correspondencia**
directa (*COM*) direct mailshot; ~ **de**
ventas sales promotion *o* drive.

promocionar [promoθjo'nar] *vt* (*COM*: *dar*
publicidad) to promote.

promontorio [promon'torjo] *nm*
promontory.

promotor [promo'tor] *nm* promoter;
(*instigador*) instigator.

promover [promo'βer] *vt* to promote;
(*causar*) to cause; (*juicio*) to bring;
(*motín*) to instigate, stir up.

promueva [pro'mweβa] *etc vb V* **promover**.

promulgar [promul'ɣar] *vt* to promulgate;
(*fig*) to proclaim.

promulgue [pro'mulɣe] *etc vb V*
promulgar.

pronombre [pro'nombre] *nm* pronoun.

pronosticar [pronosti'kar] *vt* to predict,
foretell, forecast.

pronóstico [pro'nostiko] *nm* prediction,
forecast; (*profecía*) omen; (*MED*:
diagnóstico) prognosis; **de** ~ **leve** slight,
not serious; ~ **del tiempo** weather
forecast.

pronostique [pronos'tike] *etc vb V*
pronosticar.

prontitud [pronti'tuð] *nf* speed, quickness.

pronto, a ['pronto, a] *adj* (*rápido*) prompt,
quick; (*preparado*) ready ♦ *adv* quickly,
promptly; (*en seguida*) at once, right
away; (*dentro de poco*) soon; (*temprano*)
early ♦ *nm* urge, sudden feeling; **tener**
~**s de enojo** to be quick-tempered; **al** ~
at first; **de** ~ suddenly; **¡hasta** ~**!** see
you soon!; **lo más** ~ **posible** as soon as
possible; **por lo** ~ meanwhile, for the
present; **tan** ~ **como** as soon as.

pronunciación [pronunθja'θjon] *nf*
pronunciation.

pronunciado, a [pronun'θjaðo, a] *adj*
(*marcado*) pronounced; (*curva etc*) sharp;
(*facciones*) marked.

pronunciamiento [pronunθja'mjento] *nm* (*rebelión*) insurrection.

pronunciar [pronun'θjar] *vt* to pronounce; (*discurso*) to make, deliver; (*JUR: sentencia*) to pass, pronounce; ~**se** *vr* to revolt, rise, rebel; (*declararse*) to declare o.s.; ~**se sobre** to pronounce on.

propagación [propaɣa'θjon] *nf* propagation; (*difusión*) spread(ing).

propaganda [propa'ɣanda] *nf* (*política*) propaganda; (*comercial*) advertising; **hacer** ~ **de** (*COM*) to advertise.

propagar [propa'ɣar] *vt* to propagate; (*difundir*) to spread, disseminate; ~**se** *vr* (*BIO*) to propagate; (*fig*) to spread.

propague [pro'paɣe] *etc vb V* **propagar**.

propalar [propa'lar] *vt* (*divulgar*) to divulge; (*publicar*) to publish an account of.

propano [pro'pano] *nm* propane.

propasarse [propa'sarse] *vr* (*excederse*) to go too far; (*sexualmente*) to take liberties.

propensión [propen'sjon] *nf* inclination, propensity.

propenso, a [pro'penso, a] *adj*: ~ **a** prone *o* inclined to; **ser** ~ **a hacer algo** to be inclined *o* have a tendency to do sth.

propiamente [propja'mente] *adv* properly; (*realmente*) really, exactly; ~ **dicho** real, true.

propicio, a [pro'piθjo, a] *adj* favourable, propitious.

propiedad [propje'ðað] *nf* property; (*posesión*) possession, ownership; (*conveniencia*) suitability; (*exactitud*) accuracy; ~ **particular** private property; ~ **pública** (*COM*) public ownership; **ceder algo a algn en** ~ to transfer to sb the full rights over sth.

propietario, a [propje'tarjo, a] *nm/f* owner, proprietor.

propina [pro'pina] *nf* tip; **dar algo de** ~ to give something extra.

propinar [propi'nar] *vt* (*golpe*) to strike; (*azotes*) to give.

propio, a ['propjo, a] *adj* own, of one's own; (*característico*) characteristic, typical; (*conveniente*) proper; (*mismo*) selfsame, very; **el** ~ **ministro** the minister himself; **¿tienes casa propia?** have you a house of your own?; **eso es muy** ~ **de él** that's just like him; **tiene un olor muy** ~ it has a smell of its own.

propondré [propon'dre] *etc vb V* **proponer**.

proponente [propo'nente] *nm* proposer, mover.

proponer [propo'ner] *vt* to propose, put forward; (*candidato*) to propose, nominate; (*problema*) to pose; ~**se** *vr* to propose, plan, intend.

proponga [pro'ponga] *etc vb V* **proponer**.

proporción [propor'θjon] *nf* proportion; (*MAT*) ratio; (*razón, porcentaje*) rate; **proporciones** *nfpl* dimensions; (*fig*) size *sg*; **en** ~ **con** in proportion to.

proporcionado, a [proporθjo'naðo, a] *adj* proportionate; (*regular*) medium, middling; (*justo*) just right; **bien** ~ well-proportioned.

proporcional [proporθjo'nal] *adj* proportional; ~ **a** proportional to.

proporcionar [proporθjo'nar] *vt* (*dar*) to give, supply, provide; **esto le proporciona una renta anual de ...** this brings him in a yearly income of ....

proposición [proposi'θjon] *nf* proposition; (*propuesta*) proposal.

propósito [pro'posito] *nm* (*intención*) purpose; (*intento*) aim, intention ♦ *adv*: **a** ~ by the way, incidentally; **a** ~ **de** about, with regard to.

propuesto, a [pro'pwesto, a] *pp de* **proponer** ♦ *nf* proposal.

propugnar [propuɣ'nar] *vt* to uphold.

propulsar [propul'sar] *vt* to drive, propel; (*fig*) to promote, encourage.

propulsión [propul'sjon] *nf* propulsion; ~ **a chorro** *o* **por reacción** jet propulsion.

propuse [pro'puse] *etc vb V* **proponer**.

prorrata [pro'rrata] *nf* (*porción*) share, quota, prorate (*US*) ♦ *adv* (*COM*) pro rata.

prorratear [prorrate'ar] *vt* (*dividir*) to share out, prorate (*US*).

prórroga ['prorroɣa] *nf* (*gen*) extension; (*JUR*) stay; (*COM*) deferment.

prorrogable [prorro'ɣaßle] *adj* which can be extended.

prorrogar [prorro'ɣar] *vt* (*período*) to extend; (*decisión*) to defer, postpone.

prorrogue [pro'rroɣe] *etc vb V* **prorrogar**.

prorrumpir [prorrum'pir] *vi* to burst forth, break out; ~ **en gritos** to start shouting; ~ **en lágrimas** to burst into tears.

prosa ['prosa] *nf* prose.

prosaico, a [pro'saiko, a] *adj* prosaic, dull.

proscribir [proskri'ßir] *vt* to prohibit, ban; (*desterrar*) to exile, banish; (*partido*) to proscribe.

proscripción [proskrip'θjon] *nf* prohibition, ban; banishment; proscription.

proscrito, a [pros'krito, a] *pp de* **proscribir** ♦ *adj* (*prohibido*) banned; (*desterrado*) outlawed ♦ *nm/f* (*exilado*) exile; (*bandido*) outlaw.

prosecución [proseku'θjon] *nf*
continuation; (*persecución*) pursuit.

proseguir [prose'ɣir] *vt* to continue, carry
on, proceed with; (*investigación, estudio*)
to pursue ♦ *vi* to continue, go on.

prosiga [pro'siɣa] *etc*, **prosiguiendo**
[prosi'ɣjenðo] *etc vb V* **proseguir**.

prosista [pro'sista] *nm/f* (*escritor*) prose
writer.

prospección [prospek'θjon] *nf* exploration;
(*del petróleo, del oro*) prospecting.

prospecto [pros'pekto] *nm* prospectus;
(*folleto*) leaflet, sheet of instructions.

prosperar [prospe'rar] *vi* to prosper,
thrive, flourish.

prosperidad [prosperi'ðað] *nf* prosperity;
(*éxito*) success.

próspero, a ['prospero, a] *adj* prosperous;
(*que tiene éxito*) successful.

prostíbulo [pros'tiβulo] *nm* brothel.

prostitución [prostitu'θjon] *nf*
prostitution.

prostituir [prosti'twir] *vt* to prostitute; ~**se**
vr to prostitute o.s., become a prostitute.

prostituta [prosti'tuta] *nf* prostitute.

prostituyendo [prostitu'jendo] *etc vb V*
prostituir.

protagonice [protaɣo'niθe] *etc vb V*
protagonizar.

protagonista [protaɣo'nista] *nm/f*
protagonist; (*LIT: personaje*) main
character, hero(ine).

protagonizar [protaɣoni'θar] *vt* to head,
take the chief role in.

protección [protek'θjon] *nf* protection.

proteccionismo [protekθjo'nismo] *nm*
(*COM*) protectionism.

protector, a [protek'tor, a] *adj* protective,
protecting; (*tono*) patronizing ♦ *nm/f*
protector; (*bienhechor*) patron; (*de la
tradición*) guardian.

proteger [prote'xer] *vt* to protect; ~ **contra
grabación** o **contra escritura** (*INFORM*) to
write-protect.

protegido, a [prote'xiðo, a] *nm/f* protégé/
protégée.

proteína [prote'ina] *nf* protein.

proteja [pro'texa] *etc vb V* **proteger**.

prótesis ['protesis] *nf* (*MED*) prosthesis.

protesta [pro'testa] *nf* protest.

protestante [protes'tante] *adj* Protestant.

protestar [protes'tar] *vt* to protest,
declare; (*fe*) to protest ♦ *vi* to protest;
(*objetar*) to object; **cheque protestado
por falta de fondos** cheque referred to
drawer.

protocolo [proto'kolo] *nm* protocol; **sin** ~**s**
(*formalismo*) informal(ly).

protón [pro'ton] *nm* proton.

prototipo [proto'tipo] *nm* prototype; (*ideal*)
model.

protuberancia [protuβe'ranθja] *nf*
protuberance.

prov. *abr* (= *provincia*) prov.

provecho [pro'βetʃo] *nm* advantage,
benefit; (*FINANZAS*) profit; ¡**buen** ~! bon
appétit!; **en** ~ **de** to the benefit of; **sacar**
~ **de** to benefit from, profit by.

provechoso, a [proβe'tʃoso, a] *adj*
(*ventajoso*) advantageous; (*beneficioso*)
beneficial, useful; (*FINANZAS: lucrativo*)
profitable.

proveedor, a [proβee'ðor, a] *nm/f*
(*abastecedor*) supplier; (*distribuidor*)
dealer; ~ **de (acceso a) Internet** Internet
Service Provider.

proveer [proβe'er] *vt* to provide, supply;
(*preparar*) to provide, get ready;
(*vacante*) to fill; (*negocio*) to transact,
dispatch ♦ *vi*: ~ **a** to provide for; ~**se** *vr*:
~**se de** to provide o.s. with.

provendré [proβen'dre] *etc*, **provenga**
[pro'βenga] *etc vb V* **provenir**.

provenir [proβe'nir] *vi*: ~ **de** to come from.

Provenza [pro'βenθa] *nf* Provence.

proverbial [proβer'βjal] *adj* proverbial;
(*fig*) notorious.

proverbio [pro'βerβjo] *nm* proverb.

proveyendo [proβe'jendo] *etc vb V* **proveer**.

providencia [proβi'ðenθja] *nf* providence;
(*previsión*) foresight; ~**s** *nfpl* measures,
steps.

provincia [pro'βinθja] *nf* province; (*ESP:
ADMIN*) ≈ county, ≈ region (*Scot*); **un
pueblo de** ~**(s)** a country town; *see boxed
note*.

PROVINCIA

Spain is divided up into 55 administrative
provincias, *including the islands and also
the territories in North Africa. Each one
has a "capital de provincia", which
generally bears the same name. Provinces
are grouped together by way of
geographical, historical and cultural links
into "comunidades autónomas". The term
"comarca" (region) normally has purely
geographical connotations, but in
Catalonia designates administrative
boundaries.*

---

provinciano, a [proβin'θjano, a] *adj*
provincial; (*del campo*) country *cpd*.

proviniendo [proβi'njendo] *etc vb V*
provenir.

provisión [proßi'sjon] *nf* provision;
(*abastecimiento*) provision, supply;
(*medida*) measure, step.
provisional [proßisjo'nal] *adj* provisional.
provisorio, a [proßi'sorjo, a] *adj* (*esp AM*)
provisional.
provisto, a [pro'ßisto, a] *adj*: ~ **de**
provided *o* supplied with; (*que tiene*)
having, possessing.
provocación [proßoka'θjon] *nf*
provocation.
provocador, a [proßoka'ðor, a] *adj*
provocative, provoking.
provocar [proßo'kar] *vt* to provoke;
(*alentar*) to tempt, invite; (*causar*) to
bring about, lead to; (*promover*) to
promote; (*estimular*) to rouse, stir,
stimulate; (*protesta, explosión*) to cause,
spark off; (*AM*): **¿te provoca un café?**
would you like a coffee?
provocativo, a [proßoka'tißo, a] *adj*
provocative.
provoque [pro'ßoke] *etc vb* V **provocar**.
proxeneta [prokse'neta] *nm/f* go-between;
(*de prostitutas*) pimp/procuress.
próximamente [proksima'mente] *adv*
shortly, soon.
proximidad [proksimi'ðað] *nf* closeness,
proximity.
próximo, a ['proksimo, a] *adj* near, close;
(*vecino*) neighbouring; (*el que viene*)
next; **en fecha próxima** at an early date;
el mes ~ next month.
proyección [projek'θjon] *nf* projection;
(*CINE*) showing; (*diapositiva*) slide,
transparency; (*influencia*) influence; **el
tiempo de** ~ **es de 35 minutos** the film
runs for 35 minutes.
proyectar [projek'tar] *vt* (*objeto*) to hurl,
throw; (*luz*) to cast, shed; (*CINE*) to
screen, show; (*planear*) to plan.
proyectil [projek'til] *nm* projectile,
missile; ~ **(tele)dirigido** guided missile.
proyecto [pro'jekto] *nm* plan; (*idea*)
project; (*estimación de costo*) detailed
estimate; **tener algo en** ~ to be planning
sth; ~ **de ley** (*POL*) bill.
proyector [projek'tor] *nm* (*CINE*) projector.
prudencia [pru'ðenθja] *nf* (*sabiduría*)
wisdom, prudence; (*cautela*) care.
prudente [pru'ðente] *adj* sensible, wise,
prudent; (*cauteloso*) careful.
prueba ['prweßa] *etc vb* V **probar** ♦ *nf* proof;
(*ensayo*) test, trial; (*cantidad*) taste,
sample; (*saboreo*) testing, sampling; (*de
ropa*) fitting; (*DEPORTE*) event; **a** ~ **on**
trial; (*COM*) on approval; **a** ~ **de** proof
against; **a** ~ **de agua/fuego** waterproof/

fireproof; ~ **de capacitación** (*COM*)
proficiency test; ~ **de fuego** (*fig*) acid
test; ~ **de vallas** hurdles; **someter a** ~ **to**
put to the test; **¿tiene usted** ~ **de ello?**
can you prove it?, do you have proof?
prurito [pru'rito] *nm* itch; (*de bebé*) nappy
rash; (*anhelo*) urge.
psico... [siko] *pref* psycho...
psicoanálisis [sikoa'nalisis] *nm*
psychoanalysis.
psicoanalista [sikoana'lista] *nm/f*
psychoanalyst.
psicología [sikolo'xia] *nf* psychology.
psicológico, a [siko'loxiko, a] *adj*
psychological.
psicólogo, a [si'koloxo, a] *nm/f*
psychologist.
psicópata [si'kopata] *nm/f* psychopath.
psicosis [si'kosis] *nf inv* psychosis.
psicosomático, a [sikoso'matiko, a] *adj*
psychosomatic.
psicoterapia [sikote'rapja] *nf*
psychotherapy.
psiquiatra [si'kjatra] *nm/f* psychiatrist.
psiquiátrico, a [si'kjatriko, a] *adj*
psychiatric ♦ *nm* mental hospital.
psíquico, a ['sikiko, a] *adj* psychic(al).
PSOE [pe'soe] *nm abr* = *Partido Socialista
Obrero Español.*
PSS *nf abr* (= *Prestación Social Sustitutoria*)
*community service for conscientious
objectors.*
Pta. *abr* (*GEO*: = *Punta*) Pt.
pta(s). *abr* = **peseta(s)**.
ptmo. *abr* (*COM*) = **préstamo**.
pts. *abr* = **pesetas**.
púa ['pua] *nf* sharp point; (*para guitarra*)
plectrum; **alambre de** ~**s** barbed wire.
pub [puß/paß/paf] *nm* bar.
púber, a ['pußer, a] *adj, nm/f* adolescent.
pubertad [pußer'tað] *nf* puberty.
publicación [pußlika'θjon] *nf* publication.
publicar [pußli'kar] *vt* (*editar*) to publish;
(*hacer público*) to publicize; (*divulgar*) to
make public, divulge.
publicidad [pußliθi'ðað] *nf* publicity; (*COM*)
advertising; **dar** ~ **a** to publicize, give
publicity to; ~ **gráfica** display
advertising; ~ **en el punto de venta**
point-of-sale advertising.
publicitar [pußliθi'tar] *vt* to publicize.
publicitario, a [pußliθi'tarjo, a] *adj*
publicity *cpd*; advertising *cpd*.
público, a ['pußliko, a] *adj* public ♦ *nm*
public; (*TEAT etc*) audience; (*DEPORTE*)
spectators *pl*, crowd; (*restaurantes etc*)
clients *pl*; **el gran** ~ the general public;
hacer ~ to publish; (*difundir*) to disclose;

~ **objetivo** (*COM*) target audience.
publique [pu'ßlike] *etc vb* V **publicar.**
pucherazo [putʃe'raθo] *nm* (*fraude*)
electoral fiddle; **dar** ~ to rig an election.
puchero [pu'tʃero] *nm* (*CULIN*: *olla*) cooking
pot; (: *guiso*) stew; **hacer** ~s to pout.
pudibundo, a [puði'ßundo, a] *adj* bashful.
púdico, a ['puðiko, a] *adj* modest;
(*pudibundo*) bashful.
pudiendo [pu'ðjendo] *etc vb* V **poder.**
pudiente [pu'ðjente] *adj* (*opulento*)
wealthy; (*poderoso*) powerful.
pudín [pu'ðin] *nm* pudding.
pudor [pu'ðor] *nm* modesty; (*vergüenza*)
(sense of) shame.
pudoroso, a [puðo'roso, a] *adj* (*modesto*)
modest; (*casto*) chaste.
pudrir [pu'ðrir] *vt* to rot; (*fam*) to upset,
annoy; ~**se** *vr* to rot, decay; (*fig*) to rot,
languish.
pueblerino, a [pweßle'rino, a] *adj*
(*lugareño*) small-town *cpd*; (*persona*)
rustic, provincial ♦ *nm/f* (*aldeano*)
country person.
pueblo ['pweßlo] *etc vb* V **poblar** ♦ *nm*
people; (*nación*) nation; (*aldea*) village;
(*plebe*) common people; (*población
pequeña*) small town, country town.
pueda ['pweða] *etc vb* V **poder.**
puente ['pwente] *nm* (*gen*) bridge; (*NAUT*:
tb: ~ **de mando**) bridge; (: *cubierta*) deck;
~ **aéreo** airlift; ~ **colgante** suspension
bridge; ~ **levadizo** drawbridge; **hacer**
(el) ~ (*fam*) to take a long weekend.
puenting ['pwentin] *nm* bungee jumping.
puerco, a ['pwerko, a] *adj* (*sucio*) dirty,
filthy; (*obsceno*) disgusting ♦ *nm/f* pig/
sow.
pueril [pwe'ril] *adj* childish.
puerro ['pwerro] *nm* leek.
puerta ['pwerta] *nf* door; (*de jardín*) gate;
(*portal*) doorway; (*fig*) gateway; (*gol*)
goal; (*INFORM*) port; **a la** ~ at the door; **a**
~ **cerrada** behind closed doors; ~
corredera/giratoria sliding/swing *o*
revolving door; ~ **principal/trasera** *o* **de**
servicio front/back door; ~ **(de**
transmisión en) paralelo/serie (*INFORM*)
parallel/serial port; **tomar la** ~ (*fam*) to
leave.
puerto ['pwerto] *nm* (*tb INFORM*) port; (*de
mar*) seaport; (*paso*) pass; (*fig*) haven,
refuge; **llegar a** ~ (*fig*) to get over a
difficulty.
Puerto Rico [pwerto'riko] *nm* Puerto Rico.
puertorriqueño, a [pwertorri'keɲo, a] *adj*,
nm/f Puerto Rican.
pues [pwes] *adv* (*entonces*) then;

(¡*entonces!*) well, well then; (*así que*) so
♦ *conj* (*porque*) since; ~ ... **no sé** well ... I
don't know.
puesto, a ['pwesto, a] *pp de* **poner** ♦ *adj*
dressed ♦ *nm* (*lugar, posición*) place;
(*trabajo*) post, job; (*MIL*) post; (*COM*) stall;
(*quiosco*) kiosk ♦ *conj*: ~ **que** since, as ♦ *nf*
(*apuesta*) bet, stake; ~ **de mercado**
market stall; ~ **de policía** police station;
~ **de socorro** first aid post; **puesta en**
escena staging; **puesta en marcha**
starting; **puesta del sol** sunset; **puesta a**
cero (*INFORM*) reset.
pugna ['puɣna] *nf* battle, conflict.
pugnar [puɣ'nar] *vi* (*luchar*) to struggle,
fight; (*pelear*) to fight.
puja ['puxa] *nf* (*esfuerzo*) attempt; (*en una
subasta*) bid.
pujante [pu'xante] *adj* strong, vigorous.
pujar [pu'xar] *vt* (*precio*) to raise, push up
♦ *vi* (*en licitación*) to bid, bid up; (*fig:
esforzarse*) to struggle, strain.
pulcro, a ['pulkro, a] *adj* neat, tidy.
pulga ['pulɣa] *nf* flea; **tener malas** ~s to be
short-tempered.
pulgada [pul'ɣaða] *nf* inch.
pulgar [pul'ɣar] *nm* thumb.
pulgón [pul'ɣon] *nm* plant louse, greenfly.
pulir [pu'lir] *vt* to polish; (*alisar*) to smooth;
(*fig*) to polish up, touch up.
pulla ['puʎa] *nf* cutting remark.
pulmón [pul'mon] *nm* lung; **a pleno** ~
(*respirar*) deeply; (*gritar*) at the top of
one's voice; ~ **de acero** iron lung.
pulmonía [pulmo'nia] *nf* pneumonia.
pulpa ['pulpa] *nf* pulp; (*de fruta*) flesh, soft
part.
pulpería [pulpe'ria] *nf* (*AM*) small grocery
store.
púlpito ['pulpito] *nm* pulpit.
pulpo ['pulpo] *nm* octopus.
pulsación [pulsa'θjon] *nf* beat, pulsation;
(*ANAT*) throb(bing); (*en máquina de
escribir*) touch; (*de pianista, mecanógrafo*)
touch; ~ (**de una tecla**) (*INFORM*)
keystroke; ~ **doble** (*INFORM*) strikeover.
pulsador [pulsa'ðor] *nm* button, push
button.
pulsar [pul'sar] *vt* (*tecla*) to touch, tap;
(*MUS*) to play; (*botón*) to press, push ♦ *vi*
to pulsate; (*latir*) to beat, throb.
pulsera [pul'sera] *nf* bracelet; **reloj de** ~
wristwatch.
pulso ['pulso] *nm* (*MED*) pulse; **hacer algo a**
~ to do sth unaided *o* by one's own
efforts.
pulular [pulu'lar] *vi* (*estar plagado*): ~ **(de)**
to swarm (with).

pulverice [pulße'riθe] _etc vb_ V **pulverizar**.
pulverizador [pulßeriθa'ðor] _nm_ spray,
spray gun.
pulverizar [pulßeri'θar] _vt_ to pulverize;
(_líquido_) to spray.
puna ['puna] _nf_ (_AM MED_) mountain
sickness.
punce ['punθe] _etc vb_ V **punzar**.
punción [pun'θjon] _nf_ (_MED_) puncture.
pundonor [pundo'nor] _nm_ self-respect.
punición [puni'θjon] _nf_ punishment.
punitivo, a [puni'tißo, a] _adj_ punitive.
punki ['punki] _adj, nm/f_ punk.
punta ['punta] _nf_ point, tip; (_extremidad_)
end; (_promontorio_) headland; (_COSTURA_)
corner; (_TEC_) small nail; (_fig_) touch,
trace; **horas ~s** peak hours, rush hours;
sacar ~ a to sharpen; **de ~** on end; **de ~
a ~** from one end to the other; **estar de
~** to be edgy; **ir de ~ en blanco** to be all
dressed up to the nines; **tener algo en la
~ de la lengua** to have sth on the tip of
one's tongue; **se le pusieron los pelos de
~** her hair stood on end.
puntada [pun'taða] _nf_ (_COSTURA_) stitch.
puntal [pun'tal] _nm_ prop, support.
puntapié [punta'pje], _pl_ **puntapiés** _nm_
kick; **echar a algn a ~s** to kick sb out.
punteado, a [punte'aðo, a] _adj_ (_moteado_)
dotted; (_diseño_) of dots ♦ _nm_ (_MUS_)
twang.
puntear [punte'ar] _vt_ to tick, mark; (_MUS_)
to pluck.
puntería [punte'ria] _nf_ (_de arma_) aim,
aiming; (_destreza_) marksmanship.
puntero, a [pun'tero, a] _adj_ leading ♦ _nm_
(_señal, INFORM_) pointer; (_dirigente_)
leader.
puntiagudo, a [puntja'ɣuðo, a] _adj_ sharp,
pointed.
puntilla [pun'tiʎa] _nf_ (_TEC_) tack, braid;
(_COSTURA_) lace edging; (**andar**) **de ~s** (to
walk) on tiptoe.
puntilloso, a [punti'ʎoso, a] _adj_
(_pundonoroso_) punctilious; (_susceptible_)
touchy.
punto ['punto] _nm_ (_gen_) point; (_señal
diminuta_) spot, dot; (_lugar_) spot, place;
(_momento_) point, moment; (_en un
examen_) mark; (_tema_) item; (_COSTURA_)
stitch; (_INFORM: impresora_) pitch;
(: _pantalla_) pixel; **a ~** ready; **estar a ~ de**
to be on the point of o about to; **llegar a
~** to come just at the right moment; **al ~**
at once; **en ~** on the dot; **estar en su ~**
(_CULIN_) to be done to a turn; **hasta cierto
~** to some extent; **hacer ~** to knit; **poner
un motor en ~** to tune an engine; **~ de**

partida/de congelación/de fusión
starting/freezing/melting point; **~ de
vista** point of view, viewpoint; **~ muerto**
dead centre; (_AUTO_) neutral (gear); **~s a
tratar** matters to be discussed, agenda
_sg_; **~ final** full stop; **dos ~s** colon; **~ y
coma** semicolon; **~ acápite** (_AM_) full
stop, new paragraph; **~ de interrogación**
question mark; **~s suspensivos**
suspension points; **~ de equilibrio/de
pedido** (_COM_) breakeven/reorder point;
~ inicial o **de partida** (_INFORM_) home; **~
de referencia/de venta** (_COM_) benchmark
point/point-of-sale.
puntocom [punto'kom] _nf inv, adj inv_
dotcom, dot.com.
puntuación [puntwa'θjon] _nf_ punctuation;
(_puntos: en examen_) mark(s) (_pl_);
(: _DEPORTE_) score.
puntual [pun'twal] _adj_ (_a tiempo_) punctual;
(_cálculo_) exact, accurate; (_informe_)
reliable.
puntualice [puntwa'liθe] _etc vb_ V
puntualizar.
puntualidad [puntwali'ðað] _nf_ punctuality;
exactness, accuracy; reliability.
puntualizar [puntwali'θar] _vt_ to fix, specify.
puntuar [pun'twar] _vt_ (_LING, TIP_) to
punctuate; (_examen_) to mark ♦ _vi_
(_DEPORTE_) to score, count.
punzada [pun'θaða] _nf_ (_puntura_) prick;
(_MED_) stitch; (_dolor_) twinge (of pain).
punzante [pun'θante] _adj_ (_dolor_) shooting,
sharp; (_herramienta_) sharp; (_comentario_)
biting.
punzar [pun'θar] _vt_ to prick, pierce ♦ _vi_ to
shoot, stab.
punzón [pun'θon] _nm_ (_TEC_) punch.
puñado [pu'ɲaðo] _nm_ handful (_tb fig_); **a ~s**
by handfuls.
puñal [pu'ɲal] _nm_ dagger.
puñalada [puɲa'laða] _nf_ stab.
puñeta [pu'ɲeta] _nf_: **¡~!**, **¡qué ~(s)!** (_fam!_)
hell!; **mandar a algn a hacer ~s** (_fam_) to
tell sb to go to hell.
puñetazo [puɲe'taθo] _nm_ punch.
puño ['puɲo] _nm_ (_ANAT_) fist; (_cantidad_)
fistful, handful; (_COSTURA_) cuff; (_de
herramienta_) handle; **como un ~** (_verdad_)
obvious; (_palpable_) tangible, visible; **de
~ y letra del poeta** in the poet's own
handwriting.
pupila [pu'pila] _nf_ (_ANAT_) pupil.
pupitre [pu'pitre] _nm_ desk.
puré [pu're], _pl_ **purés** _nm_ puree; (_sopa_)
(thick) soup; **~ de patatas** mashed
potatoes; **estar hecho ~** (_fig_) to be
knackered.

pureza [pu'reθa] *nf* purity.
purga ['purɣa] *nf* purge.
purgante [pur'ɣante] *adj, nm* purgative.
purgar [pur'ɣar] *vt* to purge; (*POL: depurar*)
to purge, liquidate; **~se** *vr* (*MED*) to take
a purge.
purgatorio [purɣa'torjo] *nm* purgatory.
purgue ['purɣe] *etc vb V* **purgar**.
purificar [purifi'kar] *vt* to purify; (*refinar*)
to refine.
purifique [puri'fike] *etc vb V* **purificar**.
puritano, a [puri'tano, a] *adj* (*actitud*)
puritanical; (*iglesia, tradición*) puritan
♦ *nm/f* puritan.
puro, a ['puro, a] *adj* pure; (*depurado*)
unadulterated; (*oro*) solid; (*cielo*) clear;
(*verdad*) simple, plain ♦ *adv*: **de ~
cansado** out of sheer tiredness ♦ *nm*
cigar; **por pura casualidad** by sheer
chance.
púrpura ['purpura] *nf* purple.
purpúreo, a [pur'pureo, a] *adj* purple.
pus [pus] *nm* pus.
puse ['puse] *etc vb V* **poner**.
pústula ['pustula] *nf* pimple, sore.
puta ['puta] *nf* whore, prostitute.
putada [pu'taða] *nf* (*fam!*): **hacer una ~ a
algn** to play a dirty trick on sb; **¡qué ~**!
what a pain in the arse!(*!*).
putería [pute'ria] *nf* (*prostitución*)
prostitution; (*prostíbulo*) brothel.
putrefacción [putrefak'θjon] *nf* rotting,
putrefaction.
pútrido, a ['putriðo, a] *adj* rotten.
puzzle ['puθle] *nm* puzzle.
PVP *abr* (*ESP*: = *Precio Venta al Público*)
≈ RRP.
PYME *nf abr* (= *Pequeña y Mediana
Empresa*) SME.

Q q

Q, q [ku] *nf* (*letra*) Q, q; **Q de Querido** Q for
Queen.
q.e.g.e. *abr* (= *que en gloria esté*) R.I.P.
q.e.p.d. *abr* (= *que en paz descanse*)
R.I.P.
q.e.s.m. *abr* (= *que estrecha su mano*)
courtesy formula.
qm. *abr* = **quintal(es) métrico(s)**.
qts. *abr* = **quilates**.

────────── *PALABRA CLAVE*

que [ke] *conj* **1** (*con oración subordinada*:
muchas veces no se traduce) that; **dijo ~
vendría** he said (that) he would come;
espero ~ lo encuentres I hope (that) you
find it; **dile ~ me llame** ask him to call
me; *V tb* **el**
2 (*en oración independiente*): **¡~ entre!**
send him in; **¡que se mejore tu padre!** I
hope your father gets better; **¡~ lo haga
él!** he can do it!; (*orden*) get him to do it!
3 (*enfático*): **¿me quieres? – ¡~ sí!** do you
love me? – of course!; **te digo ~ sí** I'm
telling you
4 (*consecutivo: muchas veces no se
traduce*) that; **es tan grande ~ no lo
puedo levantar** it's so big (that) I can't
lift it
5 (*comparaciones*) than; **yo ~ tú/él** if I
were you/him; *V tb* **más; menos**
6 (*valor disyuntivo*): **~ le guste o no**
whether he likes it or not; **~ venga o ~
no venga** whether he comes or not
7 (*porque*): **no puedo, ~ tengo ~
quedarme en casa** I can't, I've got to
stay in
8: siguió toca ~ toca he kept on playing
♦ *pron* **1** (*cosa*) that, which; (+*prep*)
which; **el sombrero ~ te compraste** the
hat (that *o* which) you bought; **la cama
en ~ dormí** the bed (that *o* which) I
slept in; **el día (en) ~ ella nació** the day
(when) she was born
2 (*persona: suj*) that, who; (: *objeto*) that,
whom; **el amigo ~ me acompañó al
museo** the friend that *o* who went to the
museum with me: **la chica ~ invité** the
girl (that *o* whom) I invited.

qué [ke] *adj* what?, which? ♦ *pron* what?; **¡~
divertido/asco!** how funny/revolting!; **¡~
día más espléndido!** what a glorious
day!; **¿~ edad tienes?** how old are you?;
¿de ~ me hablas? what are you saying
to me?; **¿~ tal?** how are you?, how are
things?; **¿~ hay (de nuevo)?** what's
new?; **¿~ más?** anything else?
quebrada [ke'βraða] *nf V* **quebrado**.
quebradero [keβra'ðero] *nm*: **~ de cabeza**
headache, worry.
quebradizo, a [keβra'ðiθo, a] *adj* fragile;
(*persona*) frail.
quebrado, a [ke'βraðo, a] *adj* (*roto*)
broken; (*terreno*) rough, uneven ♦ *nm/f*
bankrupt ♦ *nm* (*MAT*) fraction ♦ *nf* ravine;
~ rehabilitado discharged bankrupt.
quebradura [keβra'ðura] *nf* (*fisura*) fissure;

(*MED*) rupture.

quebrantamiento [keßranta'mjento] *nm* (*acto*) breaking; (*de ley*) violation; (*estado*) exhaustion.

quebrantar [keßran'tar] *vt* (*infringir*) to violate, transgress; **~se** *vr* (*persona*) to fail in health.

quebranto [ke'ßranto] *nm* damage, harm; (*decaimiento*) exhaustion; (*dolor*) grief, pain.

quebrar [ke'ßrar] *vt* to break, smash ♦ *vi* to go bankrupt; **~se** *vr* to break, get broken; (*MED*) to be ruptured.

quechua ['ketʃua] *adj, nm/f* Quechua.

queda ['keða] *nf*: (**toque de**) **~** curfew.

quedar [ke'ðar] *vi* to stay, remain; (*encontrarse*) to be; (*restar*) to remain, be left; **~se** *vr* to remain, stay (behind); **~ en** (*acordar*) to agree on/to; (*acabar siendo*) to end up as; **~ por hacer** to be still to be done; **~ ciego/mudo** to be left blind/dumb; **no te queda bien ese vestido** that dress doesn't suit you; **quedamos a las seis** we agreed to meet at six; **eso queda muy lejos** that's a long way (away); **nos quedan 12 kms para llegar al pueblo** there are still 12 kms before we get to the village; **no queda otra** there's no alternative; **~se (con) algo** to keep sth; **~se con algn** (*fam*) to swindle sb; **~se en nada** to come to nothing *o* nought; **~se sin** to run out of.

quedo, a ['keðo, a] *adj* still ♦ *adv* softly, gently.

quehacer [kea'θer] *nm* task, job; **~es (domésticos)** household chores.

queja ['kexa] *nf* complaint.

quejarse [ke'xarse] *vr* (*enfermo*) to moan, groan; (*protestar*) to complain; **~ de que** ... to complain (about the fact) that ....

quejica [ke'xika] *adj* grumpy, complaining ♦ *nm/f* grumbler, whinger.

quejido [ke'xiðo] *nm* moan.

quejoso, a [ke'xoso, a] *adj* complaining.

quema ['kema] *nf* fire; (*combustión*) burning.

quemado, a [ke'maðo, a] *adj* burnt; (*irritado*) annoyed.

quemadura [kema'ðura] *nf* burn, scald; (*de sol*) sunburn; (*de fusible*) blow-out.

quemar [ke'mar] *vt* to burn; (*fig: malgastar*) to burn up, squander; (*COM: precios*) to slash, cut; (*fastidiar*) to annoy, bug ♦ *vi* to be burning hot; **~se** *vr* (*consumirse*) to burn (up); (*del sol*) to get sunburnt.

quemarropa [kema'rropa]: **a ~** *adv* point-blank.

quemazón [kema'θon] *nf* burn; (*calor*)

intense heat; (*sensación*) itch.

quena ['kena] *nf* (*AM*) Indian flute.

quepo ['kepo] *etc vb* V **caber**.

querella [ke'reʎa] *nf* (*JUR*) charge; (*disputa*) dispute.

querellarse [kere'ʎarse] *vr* to file a complaint.

querencia [ke'renθja] *nf* (*ZOOL*) homing instinct; (*fig*) homesickness.

═══════════════ *PALABRA CLAVE*

querer [ke'rer] *vt* **1** (*desear*) to want; **quiero más dinero** I want more money; **quisiera** *o* **querría un té** I'd like a tea; **quiero ayudar/que vayas** I want to help/you to go; **como Vd quiera** as you wish, as you please; **ven cuando quieras** come when you like; **lo hizo sin ~** he didn't mean to do it; **no quiero** I don't want to; **le pedí que me dejara ir pero no quiso** I asked him to let me go but he refused

2 (*preguntas: para pedir u ofrecer algo*): **¿quiere abrir la ventana?** could you open the window?; **¿quieres echarme una mano?** can you give me a hand?; **¿quiere un café?** would you like some coffee?

3 (*amar*) to love; (*tener cariño a*) to be fond of; **quiere mucho a sus hijos** he's very fond of his children

4 (*requerir*): **esta planta quiere más luz** this plant needs more light

5: **~ decir** to mean; **¿qué quieres decir?** what do you mean?

querido, a [ke'riðo, a] *adj* dear ♦ *nm/f* darling; (*amante*) lover; **nuestra querida patria** our beloved country.

querosén [kero'sen], **querosene** [kero'sene] *nm* (*AM*) kerosene, paraffin.

querré [ke'rre] *etc vb* V **querer**.

quesería [kese'ria] *nf* dairy; (*fábrica*) cheese factory.

quesero, a [ke'sero, a] *adj*: **la industria quesera** the cheese industry ♦ *nm/f* cheesemaker ♦ *nf* cheese dish.

queso ['keso] *nm* cheese; **~ rallado** grated cheese; **~ crema** cream cheese; **dárselas con ~ a algn** (*fam*) to take sb in.

quetzal [ket'sal] *nm* monetary unit of Guatemala.

quicio ['kiθjo] *nm* hinge; **estar fuera de ~** to be beside o.s.; **sacar a algn de ~** to drive sb up the wall.

quid [kið] *nm* gist, crux; **dar en el ~** to hit the nail on the head.

quiebra ['kjeßra] *nf* break, split; (*COM*) bankruptcy; (*ECON*) slump.

quiebro ['kjeßro] *etc vb* V **quebrar** ♦ *nm* (*del*

cuerpo) swerve.

quien [kjen] *pron relativo (suj)* who; *(complemento)* whom; *(indefinido)*: ~ **dice eso es tonto** whoever says that is a fool; **hay ~ piensa que** there are those who think that; **no hay ~ lo haga** no-one will do it; ~ **más,** ~ **menos tiene sus problemas** everybody has problems.

quién [kjen] *pron interrogativo* who; *(complemento)* whom; ¿~ **es?** who is it?, who's there?; *(TELEC)* who's calling?

quienquiera [kjen'kjera] *(pl* **quienesquiera)** *pron* whoever.

quiera ['kjera] *etc vb V* **querer.**

quieto, a ['kjeto, a] *adj* still; *(carácter)* placid; ¡**estáte** ~! keep still!

quietud [kje'tuð] *nf* stillness.

quijada [ki'xaða] *nf* jaw, jawbone.

quijote [ki'xote] *nm* dreamer; **Don Q**~ Don Quixote.

quil. *abr* = **quilates.**

quilate [ki'late] *nm* carat.

quilla ['kiʎa] *nf* keel.

quilo... ['kilo] = **kilo...**

quimera [ki'mera] *nf (sueño)* pipe dream.

quimérico, a [ki'meriko, a] *adj* fantastic.

químico, a ['kimiko, a] *adj* chemical ♦ *nm/f* chemist ♦ *nf* chemistry.

quimioterapia [kimiote'rapia] *nf* chemotherapy.

quina ['kina] *nf* quinine.

quincallería [kinkaʎe'ria] *nf* ironmonger's *(shop)*, hardware store *(US)*.

quince ['kinθe] *num* fifteen; ~ **días** a fortnight.

quinceañero, a [kinθea'ɲero, a] *adj* fifteen-year-old; *(adolescente)* teenage ♦ *nm/f* fifteen-year-old; *(adolescente)* teenager.

quincena [kin'θena] *nf* fortnight; *(pago)* fortnightly pay.

quincenal [kinθe'nal] *adj* fortnightly.

quincuagésimo, a [kinkwa'xesimo, a] *num* fiftieth.

quiniela [ki'njela] *nf* football pools *pl*; ~**s** *nfpl* pools coupon *sg*.

quinientos, as [ki'njentos, as] *num* five hundred.

quinina [ki'nina] *nf* quinine.

quinqué [kin'ke] *nm* oil lamp.

quinquenal [kinke'nal] *adj* five-year *cpd*.

quinqui ['kinki] *nm* delinquent.

quinta ['kinta] *nf V* **quinto.**

quintaesencia [kintae'senθja] *nf* quintessence.

quintal [kin'tal] *nm (Castilla: peso)* = 46kg; ~ **métrico** = 100kg.

quinteto [kin'teto] *nm* quintet.

quinto, a ['kinto, a] *adj* fifth ♦ *nm (MIL)* conscript, draftee ♦ *nf* country house; *(MIL)* call-up, draft.

quíntuplo, a ['kintuplo, a] *adj* quintuple, five-fold.

quiosco ['kjosko] *nm (de música)* bandstand; *(de periódicos)* news stand *(also selling sweets, cigarettes etc).*

quirófano [ki'rofano] *nm* operating theatre.

quiromancia [kiro'manθja] *nf* palmistry.

quirúrgico, a [ki'rurxiko, a] *adj* surgical.

quise ['kise] *etc vb V* **querer.**

quisque ['kiske] *pron (fam)*: **cada** *o* **todo** ~ *(absolutely)* everyone.

quisquilloso, a [kiski'ʎoso, a] *adj (susceptible)* touchy; *(meticuloso)* pernickety.

quiste ['kiste] *nm* cyst.

quitaesmalte [kitaes'malte] *nm* nail polish remover.

quitamanchas [kita'mantʃas] *nm inv* stain remover.

quitanieves [kita'njeßes] *nm inv* snowplough *(BRIT)*, snowplow *(US)*.

quitar [ki'tar] *vt* to remove, take away; *(ropa)* to take off; *(dolor)* to relieve; *(vida)* to take; *(valor)* to reduce; *(hurtar)* to remove, steal ♦ *vi*: ¡**quita de ahí!** get away!; ~**se** *vr* to withdraw; *(mancha)* to come off *o* out; *(ropa)* to take off; **me quita mucho tiempo** it takes up a lot of my time; **el café me quita el sueño** coffee stops me sleeping; ~ **de en medio a algn** to get rid of sb; ~**se algo de encima** to get rid of sth; ~**se del tabaco** to give up smoking; **se quitó el sombrero** he took off his hat.

quitasol [kita'sol] *nm* sunshade *(BRIT)*, parasol.

quite ['kite] *nm (esgrima)* parry; *(evasión)* dodge; **estar al** ~ to be ready to go to sb's aid.

Quito ['kito] *n* Quito.

quizá(s) [ki'θa(s)] *adv* perhaps, maybe.

quórum ['kworum] *pl* **quórums** ['kworum] *nm* quorum.

R r

R, r ['erre] *nf* (*letra*) R, r; **R de Ramón** R for Robert (*BRIT*) o Roger (*US*).

R. *abr* = **Remite, Remitente.**

rabadilla [raβa'ðiʎa] *nf* base of the spine.

rábano ['raβano] *nm* radish; **me importa un** ~ I don't give a damn.

rabia ['raβja] *nf* (*MED*) rabies *sg*; (*fig: ira*) fury, rage; **¡qué ~!** isn't it infuriating!; **me da ~** it maddens me; **tener ~ a algn** to have a grudge against sb.

rabiar [ra'βjar] *vi* to have rabies; to rage, be furious; ~ **por algo** to long for sth.

rabieta [ra'βjeta] *nf* tantrum, fit of temper.

rabino [ra'βino] *nm* rabbi.

rabioso, a [ra'βjoso, a] *adj* rabid; (*fig*) furious.

rabo ['raβo] *nm* tail.

racanear [rakane'ar] *vi* (*fam*) to skive.

rácano ['rakano] *nm* (*fam*) slacker, skiver.

RACE *nm abr* (= *Real Automóvil Club de España*) ≈ RAC.

racha ['ratʃa] *nf* gust of wind; (*serie*) string, series; **buena/mala ~** spell of good/bad luck.

racial [ra'θjal] *adj* racial, race *cpd*.

racimo [ra'θimo] *nm* bunch.

raciocinio [raθjo'θinjo] *nm* reason; (*razonamiento*) reasoning.

ración [ra'θjon] *nf* portion; **raciones** *nfpl* rations.

racional [raθjo'nal] *adj* (*razonable*) reasonable; (*lógico*) rational.

racionalice [raθjona'liθe] *etc vb V* **racionalizar.**

racionalizar [raθjonali'θar] *vt* to rationalize; (*COM*) to streamline.

racionamiento [raθjona'mjento] *nm* (*COM*) rationing.

racionar [raθjo'nar] *vt* to ration (out).

racismo [ra'θismo] *nm* racialism, racism.

racista [ra'θista] *adj*, *nm/f* racist.

radar [ra'ðar] *nm* radar.

radiación [raðja'θjon] *nf* radiation; (*TELEC*) broadcasting.

radiactividad [raðjaktiβi'ðað] *nf* radioactivity.

radiado, a [ra'ðjaðo, a] *adj* radio *cpd*, broadcast.

radiador [raðja'ðor] *nm* radiator.

radial [ra'ðjal] *adj* (*AM*) radio *cpd*.

radiante [ra'ðjante] *adj* radiant.

radiar [ra'ðjar] *vt* to radiate; (*TELEC*) to broadcast; (*MED*) to give radiotherapy to.

radical [raði'kal] *adj*, *nm/f* radical ♦ *nm* (*LING*) root; (*MAT*) square-root sign.

radicar [raði'kar] *vi* to take root; ~ **en** to lie o consist in; **~se** *vr* to establish o.s., put down (one's) roots.

radio ['raðjo] *nf* radio; (*aparato*) radio (set) ♦ *nm* (*MAT*) radius; (*AM*) radio; (*QUÍMICA*) radium; ~ **de acción** extent of one's authority, sphere of influence.

radioactivo, a [raðjoak'tiβo, a] *adj* radioactive.

radioaficionado, a [raðjoafiθjo'naðo, a] *nm/f* radio ham.

radiocasete [raðjoka'sete] *nm* radiocassette (player).

radiodifusión [raðjodifu'sjon] *nf* broadcasting.

radioemisora [raðjoemi'sora] *nf* transmitter, radio station.

radiofónico, a [raðjo'foniko, a] *adj* radio *cpd*.

radiografía [raðjoɤra'fia] *nf* X-ray.

radiólogo, a [ra'ðjoloɤo, a] *nm/f* radiologist.

radionovela [raðjono'βela] *nf* radio series.

radiotaxi [raðjo'taksi] *nm* radio taxi.

radioterapia [raðjote'rapja] *nf* radiotherapy.

radioyente [raðjo'jente] *nm/f* listener.

radique [ra'ðike] *etc vb V* **radicar.**

RAE *nf abr* = **Real Academia Española.**

ráfaga ['rafaɤa] *nf* gust; (*de luz*) flash; (*de tiros*) burst.

raído, a [ra'iðo, a] *adj* (*ropa*) threadbare; (*persona*) shabby.

raigambre [rai'ɤambre] *nf* (*BOT*) roots *pl*; (*fig*) tradition.

raíz [ra'iθ] (*pl* **raíces**) *nf* root; ~ **cuadrada** square root; **a ~ de** as a result of; (*después de*) immediately after.

raja ['raxa] *nf* (*de melón etc*) slice; (*hendedura*) slit, split; (*grieta*) crack.

rajar [ra'xar] *vt* to split; (*fam*) to slash; **~se** *vr* to split, crack; **~se de** to back out of.

rajatabla [raxa'taβla]: **a ~** *adv* (*estrictamente*) strictly, to the letter.

ralea [ra'lea] *nf* (*pey*) kind, sort.

ralenti [ra'lenti] *nm* (*TV etc*) slow motion; (*AUTO*) neutral; **al ~** in slow motion; (*AUTO*) ticking over.

rallador [raʎa'ðor] *nm* grater.

rallar [ra'ʎar] *vt* to grate.

ralo, a ['ralo, a] *adj* thin, sparse.
RAM [ram] *nf abr* (= *random access memory*) RAM.
rama ['rama] *nf* bough, branch; **andarse por las ~s** (*fig, fam*) to beat about the bush.
ramaje [ra'maxe] *nm* branches *pl*, foliage.
ramal [ra'mal] *nm* (*de cuerda*) strand; (*FERRO*) branch line; (*AUTO*) branch (road).
rambla ['rambla] *nf* (*avenida*) avenue.
ramera [ra'mera] *nf* whore, hooker (*US*).
ramificación [ramifika'θjon] *nf* ramification.
ramificarse [ramifi'karse] *vr* to branch out.
ramifique [rami'fike] *etc vb V* **ramificarse.**
ramillete [rami'ʎete] *nm* bouquet; (*fig*) select group.
ramo ['ramo] *nm* branch, twig; (*sección*) department, section; (*sector*) field, sector.
rampa ['rampa] *nf* ramp.
ramplón, ona [ram'plon, ona] *adj* uncouth, coarse.
rana ['rana] *nf* frog; **salto de ~** leapfrog; **cuando las ~s críen pelos** when pigs fly.
ranchero [ran'tʃero] *nm* (*AM*) rancher; (*pequeño propietario*) smallholder.
rancho ['rantʃo] *nm* (*MIL*) food; (*AM: grande*) ranch; (: *pequeño*) small farm.
rancio, a ['ranθjo, a] *adj* (*comestibles*) stale, rancid; (*vino*) aged, mellow; (*fig*) ancient.
rango ['rango] *nm* rank; (*prestigio*) standing.
ranura [ra'nura] *nf* groove; (*de teléfono etc*) slot; **~ de expansión** (*INFORM*) expansion slot.
rap [rap] *nm* (*MUS*) rap.
rapacidad [rapaθi'ðað] *nf* rapacity.
rapapolvo [rapa'polβo] *nm*: **echar un ~ a algn** to give sb a ticking off.
rapar [ra'par] *vt* to shave; (*los cabellos*) to crop.
rapaz [ra'paθ] *adj* (*ZOOL*) predatory ♦ *nm/f* (*f*: **rapaza**) young boy/girl.
rape ['rape] *nm* quick shave; (*pez*) angler (fish); **al ~** cropped.
rapé [ra'pe] *nm* snuff.
rapidez [rapi'ðeθ] *nf* speed, rapidity.
rápido, a ['rapiðo, a] *adj* fast, quick ♦ *adv* quickly ♦ *nm* (*FERRO*) express; **~s** *nmpl* rapids.
rapiña [ra'piɲa] *nm* robbery; **ave de ~** bird of prey.
rap(p)el [ra'pel] *nm* (*DEPORTE*) abseiling.
raptar [rap'tar] *vt* to kidnap.
rapto ['rapto] *nm* kidnapping; (*impulso*)

sudden impulse; (*éxtasis*) ecstasy, rapture.
raqueta [ra'keta] *nf* racquet.
raquítico, a [ra'kitiko, a] *adj* stunted; (*fig*) poor, inadequate.
raquitismo [raki'tismo] *nm* rickets *sg.*
rareza [ra'reθa] *nf* rarity; (*fig*) eccentricity.
raro, a ['raro, a] *adj* (*poco común*) rare; (*extraño*) odd, strange; (*excepcional*) remarkable; **¡qué ~!** how (very) odd!; **¡qué cosa más rara!** how strange!
ras [ras] *nm*: **a ~ de** level with; **a ~ de tierra** at ground level.
rasar [ra'sar] *vt* to level.
rascacielos [raska'θjelos] *nm inv* skyscraper.
rascar [ras'kar] *vt* (*con las uñas etc*) to scratch; (*raspar*) to scrape; **~se** *vr* to scratch (o.s.).
rasgar [ras'ɣar] *vt* to tear, rip (up).
rasgo ['rasɣo] *nm* (*con pluma*) stroke; **~s** *nmpl* features, characteristics; **a grandes ~s** in outline, broadly.
rasgue ['rasɣe] *etc vb V* **rasgar.**
rasguear [rasɣe'ar] *vt* (*MUS*) to strum.
rasguñar [rasɣu'ɲar] *vt* to scratch; (*bosquejar*) to sketch.
rasguño [ras'ɣuɲo] *nm* scratch.
raso, a ['raso, a] *adj* (*liso*) flat, level; (*a baja altura*) very low ♦ *nm* satin; (*campo llano*) flat country; **cielo ~** clear sky; **al ~** in the open.
raspado [ras'paðo] *nm* (*MED*) scrape.
raspador [raspa'ðor] *nm* scraper.
raspadura [raspa'ðura] *nf* (*acto*) scrape, scraping; (*marca*) scratch; **~s** *nfpl* scrapings.
raspar [ras'par] *vt* to scrape; (*arañar*) to scratch; (*limar*) to file ♦ *vi* (*manos*) to be rough; (*vino*) to be sharp, have a rough taste.
rasque ['raske] *etc vb V* **rascar.**
rastra ['rastra] *nf*: **a ~s** by dragging; (*fig*) unwillingly.
rastreador [rastrea'ðor] *nm* tracker; **~ de minas** minesweeper.
rastrear [rastre'ar] *vt* (*seguir*) to track; (*minas*) to sweep.
rastrero, a [ras'trero, a] *adj* (*BOT, ZOOL*) creeping; (*fig*) despicable, mean.
rastrillar [rastri'ʎar] *vt* to rake.
rastrillo [ras'triʎo] *nm* rake; (*AM*) safety razor.
rastro ['rastro] *nm* (*AGR*) rake; (*pista*) track, trail; (*vestigio*) trace; (*mercado*) fleamarket; **el R~** *the Madrid fleamarket*; **perder el ~** to lose the scent; **desaparecer sin ~** to vanish without

trace.

rastrojo [ras'troxo] _nm_ stubble.

rasurador [rasura'ðor] _nm_, (_AM_)
rasuradora [rasura'ðora] _nf_ electric
shaver _o_ razor.

rasurarse [rasu'rarse] _vr_ to shave.

rata ['rata] _nf_ rat.

ratear [rate'ar] _vt_ (_robar_) to steal.

ratero, a [ra'tero, a] _adj_ light-fingered
♦ _nm/f_ pickpocket; (_AM: de casas_) burglar.

ratificar [ratifi'kar] _vt_ to ratify.

ratifique [rati'fike] _etc vb V_ **ratificar**.

rato ['rato] _nm_ while, short time; **a ~s**
from time to time; **al poco ~** shortly
after, soon afterwards; **~s libres** _o_ **de
ocio** leisure _sg_, spare _o_ free time _sg_; **hay
para ~** there's still a long way to go;
pasar el ~ to kill time; **pasar un buen/
mal ~** to have a good/rough time.

ratón [ra'ton] _nm_ (_tb INFORM_) mouse.

ratonera [rato'nera] _nf_ mousetrap.

RAU _nf abr_ (= _República Árabe Unida_) UAR.

raudal [rau'ðal] _nm_ torrent; **a ~es** in
abundance; **entrar a ~es** to pour in.

raya ['raja] _nf_ line; (_marca_) scratch; (_en
tela_) stripe; (_TIP_) hyphen; (_de pelo_)
parting; (_límite_) boundary; (_pez_) ray; **a
~s** striped; **pasarse de la ~** to overstep
the mark; **tener a ~** to keep in check.

rayado, a [ra'jaðo, a] _adj_ (_papel_) ruled;
(_tela, diseño_) striped.

rayar [ra'jar] _vt_ to line; to scratch;
(_subrayar_) to underline ♦ _vi_: **~ en** _o_ **con** to
border on; **al ~ el alba** at first light.

rayo ['rajo] _nm_ (_del sol_) ray, beam; (_de luz_)
shaft; (_en una tormenta_) (flash of)
lightning; **~ solar** _o_ **de sol** sunbeam; **~s
infrarrojos** infrared rays; **~s X** X-rays;
como un ~ like a shot; **la noticia cayó
como un ~** the news was a bombshell;
pasar como un ~ to flash past.

raza ['raθa] _nf_ race; (_de animal_) breed; **~
humana** human race; **de pura ~** (_caballo_)
thoroughbred; (_perro etc_) pedigree.

razón [ra'θon] _nf_ reason; (_justicia_) right,
justice; (_razonamiento_) reasoning;
(_motivo_) reason, motive; (_proporción_)
rate; (_MAT_) ratio; **a ~ de 10 cada día** at
the rate of 10 a day; **"~: ..."** "inquiries
to ..."; **en ~ de** with regard to; **perder la
~** to go out of one's mind; **dar ~ a algn**
to agree that sb is right; **dar ~ de** to
give an account of, report on; **tener/no
tener ~** to be right/wrong; **~ directa/
inversa** direct/inverse proportion; **~ de
ser** raison d'être.

razonable [raθo'naβle] _adj_ reasonable;
(_justo, moderado_) fair.

razonamiento [raθona'mjento] _nm_ (_juicio_)
judgement; (_argumento_) reasoning.

razonar [raθo'nar] _vt_, _vi_ to reason, argue.

RDA _nf_ = **República Democrática Alemana**.

Rdo. _abr_ (_REL:_ = _Reverendo_) Rev.

RDSI _nf abr_ (= _Red Digital de Servicios
Integrados_) ISDN.

re [re] _nm_ (_MUS_) D.

reabierto [rea'βjerto] _pp de_ **reabrir**.

reabrir [rea'βrir] _vt_, **~se** _vr_ to reopen.

reacción [reak'θjon] _nf_ reaction; **avión a ~**
jet plane; **~ en cadena** chain reaction.

reaccionar [reakθjo'nar] _vi_ to react.

reaccionario, a [reakθjo'narjo, a] _adj_
reactionary.

reacio, a [re'aθjo, a] _adj_ stubborn; **ser** _o_
estar ~ a to be opposed to.

reactivar [reakti'βar] _vt_ to reactivate; **~se**
_vr_ (_economía_) to be on the upturn.

reactor [reak'tor] _nm_ reactor; (_avión_) jet
plane; **~ nuclear** nuclear reactor.

readaptación [reaðapta'θjon] _nf_: **~
profesional** industrial retraining.

readmitir [reaðmi'tir] _vt_ to readmit.

reafirmar [reafir'mar] _vt_ to reaffirm.

reagrupar [reaɣru'par] _vt_ to regroup.

reajustar [reaxus'tar] _vt_ (_INFORM_) to reset.

reajuste [rea'xuste] _nm_ readjustment; **~
salarial** wage increase; **~ de plantilla**
rationalization.

real [re'al] _adj_ real; (_del rey, fig_) royal;
(_espléndido_) grand ♦ _nm_ (_de feria_)
fairground; **la R~ Academia Española** _see
boxed note_.

┌───┐
│ **REAL ACADEMIA ESPAÑOLA**

The **Real Academia Española** (_RAE_), dating
back to 1713, is the regulatory body for the
Spanish language in Spain. It produces its
own dictionaries and grammars, and is
considered to be the leading authority on
the language, although it has been
criticized in the past for being too
conservative. In 1994, along with the
Spanish American "_academias_", it
approved a fundamental change to the
Spanish alphabet: "_ch_" and "_ll_" are no
longer treated as separate letters,
although. "_ñ_" continues to follow "_n_" as a
new letter.
└───┘

realce [re'alθe] _etc vb V_ **realzar** ♦ _nm_ (_TEC_)
embossing; **poner de ~** to emphasize.

real-decreto [re'alde'kreto] (_pl_ **~es-~s**) _nm_
royal decree.

realeza [rea'leθa] _nf_ royalty.

realice [rea'liθe] _etc vb V_ **realizar**.

realidad [reali'ðað] *nf* reality; (*verdad*) truth; ~ **virtual** virtual reality; **en** ~ in fact.

realismo [rea'lismo] *nm* realism.

realista [rea'lista] *nmlf* realist.

realización [realiθa'θjon] *nf* fulfilment, realization; (*COM*) selling up (*BRIT*), conversion into money (*US*); ~ **de plusvalías** profit-taking.

realizador, a [realiθa'ðor, a] *nmlf* (*TV etc*) producer.

realizar [reali'θar] *vt* (*objetivo*) to achieve; (*plan*) to carry out; (*viaje*) to make, undertake; (*COM*) to realize; ~**se** *vr* to come about, come true; ~**se como persona** to fulfil one's aims in life.

realmente [real'mente] *adv* really.

realojar [realo'xar] *vt* to rehouse.

realquilar [realki'lar] *vt* (*subarrendar*) to sublet; (*alquilar de nuevo*) to relet.

realzar [real'θar] *vt* (*TEC*) to raise; (*embellecer*) to enhance; (*acentuar*) to highlight.

reanimar [reani'mar] *vt* to revive; (*alentar*) to encourage; ~**se** *vr* to revive.

reanudar [reanu'ðar] *vt* (*renovar*) to renew; (*historia, viaje*) to resume.

reaparición [reapari'θjon] *nf* reappearance; (*vuelta*) return.

reapertura [reaper'tura] *nf* reopening.

rearme [re'arme] *nm* rearmament.

reata [re'ata] *nf* (*AM*) lasso.

reavivar [reaβi'βar] *vt* (*persona*) to revive; (*fig*) to rekindle.

rebaja [re'βaxa] *nf* reduction, lowering; (*COM*) discount; "**grandes ~s**" "big reductions", "sale".

rebajar [reβa'xar] *vt* (*bajar*) to lower; (*reducir*) to reduce; (*precio*) to cut; (*disminuir*) to lessen; (*humillar*) to humble; ~**se** *vr*: ~**se a hacer algo** to stoop to doing sth.

rebanada [reβa'naða] *nf* slice.

rebañar [reβa'nar] *vt* to scrape clean.

rebaño [re'βano] *nm* herd; (*de ovejas*) flock.

rebasar [reβa'sar] *vt* (*tb*: ~ **de**) to exceed; (*AUTO*) to overtake.

rebatir [reβa'tir] *vt* to refute; (*rebajar*) to reduce; (*ataque*) to repel.

rebato [re'βato] *nm* alarm; (*ataque*) surprise attack; **llamar** *o* **tocar a** ~ (*fig*) to sound the alarm.

rebeca [re'βeka] *nf* cardigan.

rebelarse [reβe'larse] *vr* to rebel, revolt.

rebelde [re'βelde] *adj* rebellious; (*niño*) unruly ♦ *nmlf* rebel; **ser** ~ **a** to be in revolt against, rebel against.

rebeldía [reβel'dia] *nf* rebelliousness; (*desobediencia*) disobedience; (*JUR*) default.

rebelión [reβe'ljon] *nf* rebellion.

rebenque [re'βenke] *nm* (*AM*) whip.

reblandecer [reβlande'θer] *vt* to soften.

reblandezca [reβlan'deθka] *etc vb V* **reblandecer**.

rebobinar [reβoβi'nar] *vt* to rewind.

reboce [re'βoθe] *etc vb V* **rebozar**.

rebosante [reβo'sante] *adj*: ~ **de** (*fig*) brimming *o* overflowing with.

rebosar [reβo'sar] *vi* to overflow; (*abundar*) to abound, be plentiful; ~ **de salud** to be bursting *o* brimming with health.

rebotar [reβo'tar] *vt* to bounce; (*rechazar*) to repel.

rebote [re'βote] *nm* rebound; **de** ~ on the rebound.

rebozado, a [reβo'θaðo, a] *adj* (*CULIN*) fried in batter *o* breadcrumbs *o* flour.

rebozar [reβo'θar] *vt* to wrap up; (*CULIN*) to fry in batter *etc*.

rebozo [reβo'θo] *nm*: **sin** ~ openly.

rebuscado, a [reβus'kaðo, a] *adj* affected.

rebuscar [reβus'kar] *vi* (*en bolsillo, cajón*) to fish; (*en habitación*) to search high and low.

rebuznar [reβuθ'nar] *vi* to bray.

recabar [reka'βar] *vt* (*obtener*) to manage to get; ~ **fondos** to collect money.

recadero [reka'ðero] *nm* messenger.

recado [re'kaðo] *nm* message; **dejar/tomar un** ~ (*TELEC*) to leave/take a message.

recaer [reka'er] *vi* to relapse; ~ **en** to fall to *o* on; (*criminal etc*) to fall back into, relapse into; (*premio*) to go to.

recaída [reka'iða] *nf* relapse.

recaiga [re'kaiɣa] *etc vb V* **recaer**.

recalcar [rekal'kar] *vt* (*fig*) to stress, emphasize.

recalcitrante [rekalθi'trante] *adj* recalcitrant.

recalentamiento [rekalenta'mjento] *nm*: ~ **global** global warming.

recalentar [rekalen'tar] *vt* (*comida*) to warm up, reheat; (*demasiado*) to overheat; ~**se** *vr* to overheat, get too hot.

recaliente [reka'ljente] *etc vb V* **recalentar**.

recalque [re'kalke] *etc vb V* **recalcar**.

recámara [re'kamara] *nf* side room; (*AM*) bedroom.

recamarera [rekama'rera] *nf* (*AM*) maid.

recambio [re'kambjo] *nm* spare; (*de pluma*) refill; **piezas de** ~ spares.

recapacitar [rekapaθi'tar] *vi* to reflect.

recapitular [rekapitu'lar] *vt* to recap.

recargable [rekar'ɣaβle] *adj* (*batería, pila*)

rechargeable; (_mechero, pluma_) refillable.

recargado, a [rekar'ɣaðo, a] _adj_ overloaded; (_exagerado_) over-elaborate.

recargar [rekar'ɣar] _vt_ to overload; (_batería_) to recharge; (_mechero, pluma_) to refill.

recargo [re'karɣo] _nm_ surcharge; (_aumento_) increase.

recargue [re'karɣe] _etc vb V_ **recargar**.

recatado, a [reka'taðo, a] _adj_ (_modesto_) modest, demure; (_prudente_) cautious.

recato [re'kato] _nm_ (_modestia_) modesty, demureness; (_cautela_) caution.

recauchutado, a [rekautʃu'taðo, a] _adj_ remould _cpd._

recaudación [rekauða'θjon] _nf_ (_acción_) collection; (_cantidad_) takings _pl_; (_en deporte_) gate; (_oficina_) tax office.

recaudador, a [rekauða'ðor, a] _nm/f_ tax collector.

recaudar [rekau'ðar] _vt_ to collect.

recaudo [re'kauðo] _nm_ **estar a buen ~** to be in safekeeping; **poner algo a buen ~** to put sth in a safe place.

recayendo [reka'jendo] _etc vb V_ **recaer**.

rece ['reθe] _etc vb V_ **rezar**.

recelar [reθe'lar] _vt_: **~ que** (_sospechar_) to suspect that; (_temer_) to fear that ♦ _vi_: **~(se) de** to distrust.

recelo [re'θelo] _nm_ distrust, suspicion.

receloso, a [reθe'loso, a] _adj_ distrustful, suspicious.

recepción [reθep'θjon] _nf_ reception; (_acto de recibir_) receipt.

recepcionista [reθepθjo'nista] _nm/f_ receptionist.

receptáculo [reθep'takulo] _nm_ receptacle.

receptivo, a [reθep'tißo, a] _adj_ receptive.

receptor, a [reθep'tor, a] _nm/f_ recipient ♦ _nm_ (_TELEC_) receiver; **descolgar el ~** to pick up the receiver.

recesión [reθe'sjon] _nf_ (_COM_) recession.

receta [re'θeta] _nf_ (_CULIN_) recipe; (_MED_) prescription.

recetar [reθe'tar] _vt_ to prescribe.

rechace [re'tʃaθe] _etc vb V_ **rechazar**.

rechazar [retʃa'θar] _vt_ to repel, drive back; (_idea_) to reject; (_oferta_) to turn down.

rechazo [re'tʃaθo] _nm_ (_de fusil_) recoil; (_rebote_) rebound; (_negación_) rebuff.

rechifla [re'tʃifla] _nf_ hissing, booing; (_fig_) derision.

rechinar [retʃi'nar] _vi_ to creak; (_dientes_) to grind; (_máquina_) to clank, clatter; (_metal seco_) to grate; (_motor_) to hum.

rechistar [retʃis'tar] _vi_: **sin ~** without

complaint.

rechoncho, a [re'tʃontʃo, a] _adj_ (_fam_) stocky, thickset (_BRIT_), heavy-set (_US_).

rechupete [retʃu'pete]: **de ~** _adj_ (_comida_) delicious.

recibidor [reθißi'ðor] _nm_ entrance hall.

recibimiento [reθißi'mjento] _nm_ reception, welcome.

recibir [reθi'ßir] _vt_ to receive; (_dar la bienvenida_) to welcome; (_salir al encuentro de_) to go and meet ♦ _vi_ to entertain; **~se** _vr_: **~se de** to qualify as.

recibo [re'θißo] _nm_ receipt; **acusar ~ de** to acknowledge receipt of.

reciclable [reθi'klaßle] _adj_ recyclable.

reciclaje [reθi'klaxe] _nm_ recycling; (_de trabajadores_) retraining; **cursos de ~** refresher courses.

reciclar [reθi'klar] _vt_ to recycle; (_trabajador_) to retrain.

recién [re'θjen] _adv_ recently, newly; (_AM_) just, recently; **~ casado** newly-wed; **el ~ llegado** the newcomer; **el ~ nacido** the newborn child; **~ a las seis** only at six o'clock.

reciente [re'θjente] _adj_ recent; (_fresco_) fresh.

recientemente [reθjente'mente] _adv_ recently.

recinto [re'θinto] _nm_ enclosure; (_área_) area, place.

recio, a ['reθjo, a] _adj_ strong, tough; (_voz_) loud ♦ _adv_ hard; loud(ly).

recipiente [reθi'pjente] _nm_ (_objeto_) container, receptacle; (_persona_) recipient.

reciprocidad [reθiproθi'ðað] _nf_ reciprocity.

recíproco, a [re'θiproko, a] _adj_ reciprocal.

recital [reθi'tal] _nm_ (_MUS_) recital; (_LIT_) reading.

recitar [reθi'tar] _vt_ to recite.

reclamación [reklama'θjon] _nf_ claim, demand; (_queja_) complaint; **~ salarial** pay claim.

reclamar [rekla'mar] _vt_ to claim, demand ♦ _vi_: **~ contra** to complain about; **~ a algn en justicia** to take sb to court.

reclamo [re'klamo] _nm_ (_anuncio_) advertisement; (_tentación_) attraction.

reclinar [rekli'nar] _vt_ to recline, lean; **~se** _vr_ to lean back.

recluir [reklu'ir] _vt_ to intern, confine.

reclusión [reklu'sjon] _nf_ (_prisión_) prison; (_refugio_) seclusion; **~ perpetua** life imprisonment.

recluso, a [re'kluso, a] _adj_ imprisoned; **población reclusa** prison population ♦ _nm/f_ (_solitario_) recluse; (_JUR_) prisoner.

recluta [re'kluta] _nm/f_ recruit ♦ _nf_

recruitment.

reclutamiento [rekluta'mjento] *nm*
recruitment.

recluyendo [reklu'jendo] *etc vb V* **recluir**.

recobrar [reko'ßrar] *vt* (*recuperar*) to
recover; (*rescatar*) to get back; (*ciudad*)
to recapture; (*tiempo*) to make up (for);
~**se** *vr* to recover.

recochineo [rekotʃi'neo] *nm* (*fam*)
mickey-taking.

recodo [re'koðo] *nm* (*de río, camino*) bend.

recogedor, a [rekoxe'ðor, a] *nm/f* picker,
harvester.

recoger [reko'xer] *vt* to collect; (*AGR*) to
harvest; (*fruta*) to pick; (*levantar*) to pick
up; (*juntar*) to gather; (*pasar a buscar*) to
come for, get; (*dar asilo*) to give shelter
to; (*faldas*) to gather up; (*mangas*) to roll
up; (*pelo*) to put up; ~**se** *vr* (*retirarse*) to
retire; **me recogieron en la estación** they
picked me up at the station.

recogido, a [reko'xiðo, a] *adj* (*lugar*) quiet,
secluded; (*pequeño*) small ♦ *nf* (*CORREOS*)
collection; (*AGR*) harvest; **recogida de
datos** (*INFORM*) data capture.

recogimiento [rekoxi'mjento] *nm*
collection; (*AGR*) harvesting.

recoja [re'koxa] *etc vb V* **recoger**.

recolección [rekolek'θjon] *nf* (*AGR*)
harvesting; (*colecta*) collection.

recomencé [rekomen'θe],
recomencemos [rekomen'θemos] *etc vb*
V **recomenzar**.

recomendable [rekomen'daßle] *adj*
recommendable; **poco** ~ inadvisable.

recomendación [rekomenda'θjon] *nf*
(*sugerencia*) suggestion,
recommendation; (*referencia*) reference;
carta de ~ **para** letter of introduction to.

recomendar [rekomen'dar] *vt* to suggest,
recommend; (*confiar*) to entrust.

recomenzar [rekomen'θar] *vt, vi* to begin
again, recommence.

recomience [reko'mjenθe] *etc vb V*
recomenzar.

recomiende [reko'mjende] *etc vb V*
recomendar.

recomienzo [reko'mjenθo] *etc vb V*
recomenzar.

recompensa [rekom'pensa] *nf* reward,
recompense; (*compensación*): ~ **(de una
pérdida)** compensation (for a loss);
como *o* **en** ~ **por** in return for.

recompensar [rekompen'sar] *vt* to reward,
recompense.

recompondré [rekompon'dre] *etc vb V*
recomponer.

recomponer [rekompo'ner] *vt* to mend;

(*INFORM*: *texto*) to reformat.

recomponga [rekom'ponga] *etc*,
recompuesto [rekom'pwesto],
récompuse [rekom'puse] *etc vb V*
recomponer.

reconciliación [rekonθilja'θjon] *nf*
reconciliation.

reconciliar [rekonθi'ljar] *vt* to reconcile;
~**se** *vr* to become reconciled.

recóndito, a [re'kondito, a] *adj* (*lugar*)
hidden, secret.

reconfortar [rekonfor'tar] *vt* to comfort.

reconocer [rekono'θer] *vt* to recognize; ~
los hechos to face the facts.

reconocido, a [rekono'θiðo, a] *adj*
recognized; (*agradecido*) grateful.

reconocimiento [rekonoθi'mjento] *nm*
recognition; (*registro*) search;
(*inspección*) examination; (*gratitud*)
gratitude; (*confesión*) admission; ~
óptico de caracteres (*INFORM*) optical
character recognition; ~ **de la voz**
(*INFORM*) speech recognition.

reconozca [reko'noθka] *etc vb V* **reconocer**.

reconquista [rekon'kista] *nf* reconquest.

reconquistar [rekonkis'tar] *vt* (*MIL*) to
reconquer; (*fig*) to recover, win back.

reconstituyente [rekonstitu'jente] *nm*
tonic.

reconstruir [rekonstru'ir] *vt* to reconstruct.

reconstruyendo [rekonstru'jendo] *etc vb V*
reconstruir.

reconversión [rekomber'sjon] *nf*
restructuring, reorganization; (*tb*: ~
industrial) rationalization.

recopilación [rekopila'θjon] *nf* (*resumen*)
summary; (*compilación*) compilation.

recopilar [rekopi'lar] *vt* to compile.

récord ['rekorð] *adj inv* record; **cifras** ~
record figures ♦ *nm, pl* **records**, **récords**
['rekorð] record; **batir el** ~ to break the
record.

recordar [rekor'ðar] *vt* (*acordarse de*) to
remember; (*traer a la memoria*) to recall;
(*acordar a otro*) to remind ♦ *vi* to
remember; **recuérdale que me debe 5
dólares** remind him that he owes me 5
dollars; **que yo recuerde** as far as I can
remember; **creo** ~, **si mal no recuerdo** if
my memory serves me right.

recordatorio [rekorða'torjo] *nm* (*de
fallecimiento*) in memoriam card; (*de
bautizo, comunión*) *commemorative card*.

recorrer [reko'rrer] *vt* (*país*) to cross,
travel through; (*distancia*) to cover;
(*registrar*) to search; (*repasar*) to look
over.

recorrido [reko'rriðo] *nm* run, journey;

tren de largo ~ main-line o inter-city (*BRIT*) train.

recortado, a [rekor'taðo, a] *adj* uneven, irregular.

recortar [rekor'tar] *vt* (*papel*) to cut out; (*el pelo*) to trim; (*dibujar*) to draw in outline; ~**se** *vr* to stand out, be silhouetted.

recorte [re'korte] *nm* (*acción, de prensa*) cutting; (*de telas, chapas*) trimming; ~ **presupuestario** budget cut; ~ **salarial** wage cut.

recostado, a [rekos'taðo, a] *adj* leaning; **estar** ~ to be lying down.

recostar [rekos'tar] *vt* to lean; ~**se** *vr* to lie down.

recoveco [reko'ßeko] *nm* (*de camino, río etc*) bend; (*en casa*) cubbyhole.

recreación [rekrea'θjon] *nf* recreation.

recrear [rekre'ar] *vt* (*entretener*) to entertain; (*volver a crear*) to recreate.

recreativo, a [rekrea'tißo, a] *adj* recreational.

recreo [re'kreo] *nm* recreation; (*ESCOL*) break, playtime.

recriminar [rekrimi'nar] *vt* to reproach ♦ *vi* to recriminate; ~**se** *vr* to reproach each other.

recrudecer [rekruðe'θer] *vt, vi,* **recrudecerse** *vr* to worsen.

recrudecimiento [rekruðeθi'mjento] *nm* upsurge.

recrudezca [recru'ðeθka] *etc vb V* **recrudecer**.

recta ['rekta] *nf V* **recto**.

rectangular [rektangu'lar] *adj* rectangular.

rectángulo, a [rek'tangulo, a] *adj* rectangular ♦ *nm* rectangle.

rectificable [rektifi'kaßle] *adj* rectifiable; **fácilmente** ~ easily rectified.

rectificación [rektifika'θjon] *nf* correction.

rectificar [rektifi'kar] *vt* to rectify; (*volverse recto*) to straighten ♦ *vi* to correct o.s.

rectifique [rekti'fike] *etc vb V* **rectificar**.

rectitud [rekti'tuð] *nf* straightness; (*fig*) rectitude.

recto, a ['rekto, a] *adj* straight; (*persona*) honest, upright; (*estricto*) strict; (*juez*) fair; (*juicio*) sound ♦ *nm* rectum; (*ATLETISMO*) straight ♦ *nf* straight line; **en el sentido** ~ **de la palabra** in the proper sense of the word; **recta final** o **de llegada** home straight.

rector, a [rek'tor, a] *adj* governing ♦ *nm/f* head, chief; (*ESCOL*) rector, president (*US*).

rectorado [rekto'raðo] *nm* (*cargo*) rectorship, presidency (*US*); (*oficina*)

rector's office.

recuadro [re'kwaðro] *nm* box; (*TIP*) inset.

recubrir [reku'ßir] *vt* to cover.

recuento [re'kwento] *nm* inventory; **hacer el** ~ **de** to count o reckon up.

recuerdo [re'kwerðo] *etc vb V* **recordar** ♦ *nm* souvenir; ~**s** *nmpl* memories; **¡~s a tu madre!** give my regards to your mother!; "**R~ de Mallorca**" "a present from Majorca"; **contar los** ~**s** to reminisce.

recueste [re'kweste] *etc vb V* **recostar**.

recular [reku'lar] *vi* to back down.

recuperable [rekupe'raßle] *adj* recoverable.

recuperación [rekupera'θjon] *nf* recovery; ~ **de datos** (*INFORM*) data retrieval.

recuperar [rekupe'rar] *vt* to recover; (*tiempo*) to make up; (*INFORM*) to retrieve; ~**se** *vr* to recuperate.

recurrir [reku'rrir] *vi* (*JUR*) to appeal; ~ **a** to resort to; (*persona*) to turn to.

recurso [re'kurso] *nm* resort; (*medio*) means *pl,* resource; (*JUR*) appeal; **como último** ~ as a last resort; ~**s económicos** economic resources; ~**s naturales** natural resources.

recusar [reku'sar] *vt* to reject, refuse.

red [reð] *nf* net, mesh; (*FERRO, INFORM*) network; (*ELEC, de agua*) mains, supply system; (*de tiendas*) chain; (*trampa*) trap; **la R~** (*Internet*) the Net; **estar conectado con la** ~ to be connected to the mains; ~ **local** (*INFORM*) local area network; ~ **de transmisión** (*INFORM*) data network.

redacción [reðak'θjon] *nf* (*acción*) writing; (*ESCOL*) essay, composition; (*limpieza de texto*) editing; (*personal*) editorial staff.

redactar [reðak'tar] *vt* to draw up, draft; (*periódico, INFORM*) to edit.

redactor, a [reðak'tor, a] *nm/f* writer; (*en periódico*) editor.

redada [re'ðaða] *nf* (*PESCA*) cast, throw; (*fig*) catch; ~ **policial** police raid, round-up.

redención [reðen'θjon] *nf* redemption.

redentor, a [reðen'tor, a] *adj* redeeming ♦ *nm/f* (*COM*) redeemer.

redescubierto [reðesku'ßjerto] *pp de* **redescubrir**.

redescubrir [reðesku'ßrir] *vt* to rediscover.

redesignar [reðesix'nar] *vt* (*INFORM*) to rename.

redicho, a [re'ðitʃo, a] *adj* affected.

redil [re'ðil] *nm* sheepfold.

redimir [reði'mir] *vt* to redeem; (*rehén*) to ransom.

redistribución [reðistrißu'θjon] *nf* (*COM*)

redeployment.

rédito ['reðito] *nm* interest, yield.

redoblar [reðo'βlar] *vt* to redouble ♦ *vi* (*tambor*) to play a roll on the drums.

redoble [re'ðoβle] *nm* (*MUS*) drumroll, drumbeat; (*de trueno*) roll.

redomado, a [reðo'maðo, a] *adj* (*astuto*) sly, crafty; (*perfecto*) utter.

redonda [re'ðonda] *nf* V **redondo**.

redondear [reðonde'ar] *vt* to round, round off; (*cifra*) to round up.

redondel [reðon'del] *nm* (*círculo*) circle; (*TAUR*) bullring, arena; (*AUTO*) roundabout.

redondo, a [re'ðondo, a] *adj* (*circular*) round; (*completo*) complete ♦ *nf*: **a la redonda** around, round about; **en muchas millas a la redonda** for many miles around; **rehusar en ~** to give a flat refusal.

reducción [reðuk'θjon] *nf* reduction; **~ del activo** (*COM*) divestment; **~ de precios** (*COM*) price-cutting.

reducido, a [reðu'θiðo, a] *adj* reduced; (*limitado*) limited; (*pequeño*) small; **quedar ~ a** to be reduced to.

reducir [reðu'θir] *vt* to reduce, limit; (*someter*) to bring under control; **~se** *vr* to diminish; (*MAT*): **~ (a)** to reduce (to), convert (into); **~ las millas a kilómetros** to convert miles into kilometres; **~se a** (*fig*) to come o boil down to.

reducto [re'ðukto] *nm* redoubt.

reduje [re'ðuxe] *etc vb* V **reducir**.

redundancia [reðun'danθja] *nf* redundancy.

reduzca [re'ðuθka] *etc vb* V **reducir**.

reedición [re(e)ði'θjon] *nf* reissue.

reeditar [re(e)ði'tar] *vt* to reissue.

reelección [re(e)lek'θjon] *nf* re-election.

reelegir [re(e)le'xir] *vt* to re-elect.

reembolsable [re(e)mbol'saβle] *adj* (*COM*) redeemable, refundable.

reembolsar [re(e)mbol'sar] *vt* (*persona*) to reimburse; (*dinero*) to repay, pay back; (*depósito*) to refund.

reembolso [re(e)m'bolso] *nm* reimbursement; refund; **enviar algo contra ~** to send sth cash on delivery; **contra ~ del flete** freight forward; **~ fiscal** tax rebate.

reemplace [re(e)m'plaθe] *etc vb* V **reemplazar**.

reemplazar [re(e)mpla'θar] *vt* to replace.

reemplazo [re(e)m'plaθo] *nm* replacement; **de ~** (*MIL*) reserve.

reencuentro [re(e)n'kwentro] *nm* reunion.

reengancharse [re(e)ngan'tʃarse] *vr* (*MIL*)

to re-enlist.

reestreno [re(e)s'treno] *nm* rerun.

reestructurar [re(e)struktu'rar] *vt* to restructure.

reexportación [re(e)ksporta'θjon] *nf* (*COM*) re-export.

reexportar [re(e)kspor'tar] *vt* (*COM*) to re-export.

REF *nm abr* (*ESP ECON*) = **Régimen Económico Fiscal**.

Ref.ª *abr* (= *referencia*) ref.

refacción [refak'θjon] *nf* (*AM*) repair(s); **refacciones** *nfpl* (*piezas de repuesto*) spare parts.

referencia [refe'renθja] *nf* reference; **con ~ a** with reference to; **hacer ~ a** to refer o allude to; **~ comercial** (*COM*) trade reference.

referéndum [refe'rendum], *pl* **referéndums** *nm* referendum.

referente [refe'rente] *adj*: **~ a** concerning, relating to.

referir [refe'rir] *vt* (*contar*) to tell, recount; (*relacionar*) to refer, relate; **~se** *vr*: **~se a** to refer to; **~ al lector a un apéndice** to refer the reader to an appendix; **~ a** (*COM*) to convert into; **por lo que se refiere a eso** as for that, as regards that.

refiera [re'fjera] *etc vb* V **referir**.

refilón [refi'lon]: **de ~** *adv* obliquely; **mirar a algn de ~** to look out of the corner of one's eye at sb.

refinado, a [refi'naðo, a] *adj* refined.

refinamiento [refina'mjento] *nm* refinement; **~ por pasos** (*INFORM*) stepwise refinement.

refinar [refi'nar] *vt* to refine.

refinería [refine'ria] *nf* refinery.

refiriendo [refi'rjendo] *etc vb* V **referir**.

reflector [reflek'tor] *nm* reflector; (*ELEC*) spotlight; (*AVIAT, MIL*) searchlight.

reflejar [refle'xar] *vt* to reflect; **~se** *vr* to be reflected.

reflejo, a [re'flexo, a] *adj* reflected; (*movimiento*) reflex ♦ *nm* reflection; (*ANAT*) reflex; (*en el pelo*): **~s** *nmpl* highlights; **tiene el pelo castaño con ~s rubios** she has chestnut hair with blond streaks.

reflexión [reflek'sjon] *nf* reflection.

reflexionar [refleksjo'nar] *vt* to reflect on ♦ *vi* to reflect; (*detenerse*) to pause (to think); **¡reflexione!** you think it over!

reflexivo, a [reflek'siβo, a] *adj* thoughtful; (*LING*) reflexive.

refluir [reflu'ir] *vi* to flow back.

reflujo [re'fluxo] *nm* ebb.

refluyendo [reflu'jendo] *etc vb* V **refluir**.

reforcé [refor'θe], **reforcemos** [refor'θemos] *etc vb V* **reforzar**.

reforma [re'forma] *nf* reform; (*ARQ etc*) repair; ~ **agraria** agrarian reform.

reformar [refor'mar] *vt* to reform; (*modificar*) to change, alter; (*texto*) to revise; (*ARQ*) to repair; ~**se** *vr* to mend one's ways.

reformatear [reformate'ar] *vt* (*INFORM*: *disco*) to reformat.

reformatorio [reforma'torjo] *nm* reformatory; ~ **de menores** remand home.

reformista [refor'mista] *adj*, *nm/f* reformist.

reforzamiento [reforθa'mjento] *nm* reinforcement.

reforzar [refor'θar] *vt* to strengthen; (*ARQ*) to reinforce; (*fig*) to encourage.

refractario, a [refrak'tarjo, a] *adj* (*TEC*) heat-resistant; **ser** ~ **a una reforma** to resist *o* be opposed to a reform.

refrán [re'fran] *nm* proverb, saying.

refregar [refre'ɣar] *vt* to scrub.

refrenar [refre'nar] *vt* to check, restrain.

refrendar [refren'dar] *vt* (*firma*) to endorse, countersign; (*ley*) to approve.

refrescante [refres'kante] *adj* refreshing, cooling.

refrescar [refres'kar] *vt* to refresh ♦ *vi* to cool down; ~**se** *vr* to get cooler; (*tomar aire fresco*) to go out for a breath of fresh air; (*beber*) to have a drink.

refresco [re'fresko] *nm* soft drink, cool drink; "~**s**" "refreshments".

refresque [re'freske] *etc vb V* **refrescar**.

refriega [re'frjeɣa] *etc vb V* **refregar** ♦ *nf* scuffle, brawl.

refriegue [re'frjeɣe] *etc vb V* **refregar**.

refrigeración [refrixera'θjon] *nf* refrigeration; (*de casa*) air-conditioning.

refrigerado, a [refrixe'raðo, a] *adj* cooled; (*sala*) air-conditioned.

refrigerador [refrixera'ðor] *nm*, (*AM*) **refrigeradora** [refrixera'ðora] *nf* refrigerator, icebox (*US*).

refrigerar [refrixe'rar] *vt* to refrigerate; (*sala*) to air-condition.

refrito [re'frito] *nm* (*CULIN*): **un** ~ **de cebolla y tomate** sautéed onions and tomatoes; **un** ~ (*fig*) a rehash.

refuerce [re'fwerθe] *etc vb V* **reforzar**.

refuerzo [re'fwerθo] *etc vb V* **reforzar** ♦ *nm* reinforcement; (*TEC*) support.

refugiado, a [refu'xjaðo, a] *nm/f* refugee.

refugiarse [refu'xjarse] *vr* to take refuge, shelter.

refugio [re'fuxjo] *nm* refuge; (*protección*) shelter; (*AUTO*) street *o* traffic island; ~

alpino *o* **de montaña** mountain hut; ~ **subterráneo** (*MIL*) underground shelter.

refulgencia [reful'xenθja] *nf* brilliance.

refulgir [reful'xir] *vi* to shine, be dazzling.

refulja [re'fulxa] *etc vb V* **refulgir**.

refundir [refun'dir] *vt* to recast; (*escrito etc*) to adapt, rewrite.

refunfuñar [refunfu'ɲar] *vi* to grunt, growl; (*quejarse*) to grumble.

refunfuñón, ona [refunfu'ɲon, ona] (*fam*) *adj* grumpy ♦ *nm/f* grouch.

refutación [refuta'θjon] *nf* refutation.

refutar [refu'tar] *vt* to refute.

regadera [reɣa'ðera] *nf* watering can; (*AM*) shower; **estar como una** ~ (*fam*) to be as mad as a hatter.

regadío [reɣa'ðio] *nm* irrigated land.

regalado, a [reɣa'laðo, a] *adj* comfortable, luxurious; (*gratis*) free, for nothing; **lo tuvo** ~ it was handed to him on a plate.

regalar [reɣa'lar] *vt* (*dar*) to give (as a present); (*entregar*) to give away; (*mimar*) to pamper, make a fuss of; ~**se** *vr* to treat o.s. to.

regalía [reɣa'lia] *nf* privilege, prerogative; (*COM*) bonus; (*de autor*) royalty.

regaliz [reɣa'liθ] *nm* liquorice.

regalo [re'ɣalo] *nm* (*obsequio*) gift, present; (*gusto*) pleasure; (*comodidad*) comfort.

regañadientes [reɣaɲa'ðjentes]: **a** ~ *adv* reluctantly.

regañar [reɣa'ɲar] *vt* to scold ♦ *vi* to grumble; (*dos personas*) to fall out, quarrel.

regañón, ona [reɣa'ɲon, ona] *adj* nagging.

regar [re'ɣar] *vt* to water, irrigate; (*fig*) to scatter, sprinkle.

regata [re'ɣata] *nf* (*NAUT*) race.

regatear [reɣate'ar] *vt* (*COM*) to bargain over; (*escatimar*) to be mean with ♦ *vi* to bargain, haggle; (*DEPORTE*) to dribble; **no** ~ **esfuerzo** to spare no effort.

regateo [reɣa'teo] *nm* bargaining; (*DEPORTE*) dribbling; (*del cuerpo*) swerve, dodge.

regazo [re'ɣaθo] *nm* lap.

regencia [re'xenθja] *nf* regency.

regeneración [rexenera'θjon] *nf* regeneration.

regenerar [rexene'rar] *vt* to regenerate.

regentar [rexen'tar] *vt* to direct, manage; (*puesto*) to hold in an acting capacity; (*negocio*) to be in charge of.

regente, a [re'xente, a] *adj* (*príncipe*) regent; (*director*) managing ♦ *nm* (*COM*) manager; (*POL*) regent.

régimen ['reximen], *pl* **regímenes**

[re'ximenes] *nm* regime; (*reinado*) rule; (*MED*) diet; (*reglas*) (set of) rules *pl*; (*manera de vivir*) lifestyle; **estar a** ~ to be on a diet.

regimiento [rexi'mjento] *nm* regiment.

regio, a ['rexjo, a] *adj* royal, regal; (*fig: suntuoso*) splendid; (*AM fam*) great, terrific.

región [re'xjon] *nf* region; (*área*) area.

regional [rexjo'nal] *adj* regional.

regir [re'xir] *vt* to govern, rule; (*dirigir*) to manage, run; (*ECON, JUR, LING*) to govern ♦ *vi* to apply, be in force.

registrador [rexistra'ðor] *nm* registrar, recorder.

registrar [rexis'trar] *vt* (*buscar*) to search; (*en cajón*) to look through; (*inspeccionar*) to inspect; (*anotar*) to register, record; (*INFORM, MUS*) to record; ~**se** *vr* to register; (*ocurrir*) to happen.

registro [re'xistro] *nm* (*acto*) registration; (*MUS, libro*) register; (*lista*) list, record; (*INFORM*) record; (*inspección*) inspection, search; ~ **civil** registry office; ~ **electoral** voting register; ~ **de la propiedad** land registry (office).

regla ['rexla] *nf* (*ley*) rule, regulation; (*de medir*) ruler; (*MED: período*) period; (~ *científica*) law, principle; **no hay** ~ **sin excepción** every rule has its exception.

reglamentación [rexlamenta'θjon] *nf* (*acto*) regulation; (*lista*) rules *pl*.

reglamentar [rexlamen'tar] *vt* to regulate.

reglamentario, a [rexlamen'tarjo, a] *adj* statutory; **en la forma reglamentaria** in the properly established way.

reglamento [rexla'mento] *nm* rules *pl*, regulations *pl*; ~ **del tráfico** highway code.

reglar [re'xlar] *vt* (*acciones*) to regulate; ~**se** *vr*: ~**se por** to be guided by.

regocijarse [rexoθi'xarse] *vr*: ~ **de** *o* **por** to rejoice at, be glad about.

regocijo [rexo'θixo] *nm* joy, happiness.

regodearse [rexoðe'arse] *vr* to be glad, be delighted; (*pey*): ~ **con** *o* **en** to gloat over.

regodeo [rexo'ðeo] *nm* delight; (*pey*) perverse pleasure.

regresar [rexre'sar] *vi* to come/go back, return; ~**se** *vr* (*AM*) to return.

regresivo, a [rexre'sißo, a] *adj* backward; (*fig*) regressive.

regreso [re'xreso] *nm* return; **estar de** ~ to be back, be home.

regué [re'xe], **reguemos** [re'xemos] *etc vb V* **regar**.

reguero [re'xero] *nm* (*de sangre*) trickle;

(*de humo*) trail.

regulación [rexula'θjon] *nf* regulation; (*TEC*) adjustment; (*control*) control; ~ **de empleo** redundancies *pl*; ~ **del tráfico** traffic control.

regulador [rexula'ðor] *nm* (*TEC*) regulator; (*de radio etc*) knob, control.

regular [rexu'lar] *adj* regular; (*normal*) normal, usual; (*común*) ordinary; (*organizado*) regular, orderly; (*mediano*) average; (*fam*) not bad, so-so ♦ *adv*: **estar** ~ to be so-so *o* alright ♦ *vt* (*controlar*) to control, regulate; (*TEC*) to adjust; **por lo** ~ as a rule.

regularice [rexula'riθe] *etc vb V* **regularizar**.

regularidad [rexulari'ðað] *nf* regularity; **con** ~ regularly.

regularizar [rexulari'θar] *vt* to regularize.

regusto [re'xusto] *nm* aftertaste.

rehabilitación [reaßilita'θjon] *nf* rehabilitation; (*ARQ*) restoration.

rehabilitar [reaßili'tar] *vt* to rehabilitate; (*ARQ*) to restore; (*reintegrar*) to reinstate.

rehacer [rea'θer] *vt* (*reparar*) to mend, repair; (*volver a hacer*) to redo, repeat; ~**se** *vr* (*MED*) to recover.

rehaga [re'axa] *etc*, **reharé** [rea're] *etc*, **rehaz** [re'aθ], **rehecho** [re'etʃo] *vb V* **rehacer**.

rehén [re'en] *nm/f* hostage.

rehice [re'iθe] *etc*, **rehizo** [re'iθo] *vb V* **rehacer**.

rehogar [reo'xar] *vt* to sauté, toss in oil.

rehuir [reu'ir] *vt* to avoid, shun.

rehusar [reu'sar] *vt, vi* to refuse.

rehuyendo [reu'jendo] *etc vb V* **rehuir**.

reina ['reina] *nf* queen.

reinado [rei'naðo] *nm* reign.

reinante [rei'nante] *adj* (*fig*) prevailing.

reinar [rei'nar] *vi* to reign; (*fig: prevalecer*) to prevail, be general.

reincidir [reinθi'ðir] *vi* to relapse; (*criminal*) to repeat an offence.

reincorporarse [reinkorpo'rarse] *vr*: ~ **a** to rejoin.

reinicializar [reiniθjali'θar] *vt* (*INFORM*) to reset.

reino ['reino] *nm* kingdom; **el R**~ **Unido** the United Kingdom.

reinserción [reinser'θjon] *nf* rehabilitation.

reinsertar [reinser'tar] *vt* to rehabilitate.

reintegración [reintexra'θjon] *nf* (*COM*) reinstatement.

reintegrar [reinte'xrar] *vt* (*reconstituir*) to reconstruct; (*persona*) to reinstate; (*dinero*) to refund, pay back; ~**se** *vr*: ~**se a** to return to.

reintegro [rein'texro] *nm* refund,

reimbursement; (*en banco*) withdrawal.

reír [re'ir] *vi*, **reírse** *vr* to laugh; **~se de** to laugh at.

reiterado, a [reite'raðo, a] *adj* repeated.

reiterar [reite'rar] *vt* to reiterate; (*repetir*) to repeat.

reivindicación [reißindika'θjon] *nf* (*demanda*) claim, demand; (*justificación*) vindication.

reivindicar [reißindi'kar] *vt* to claim.

reivindique [reißin'dike] *etc vb V* **reivindicar**.

reja ['rexa] *nf* (*de ventana*) grille, bars *pl*; (*en la calle*) grating.

rejamos [re'xamos] *etc vb V* **regir**.

rejilla [re'xiʎa] *nf* grating, grille; (*muebles*) wickerwork; (*de ventilación*) vent; (*de coche etc*) luggage rack.

rejuvenecer [rexußene'θer] *vt, vi* to rejuvenate.

rejuvenezca [rexuße'neθka] *etc vb V* **rejuvenecer**.

relación [rela'θjon] *nf* relation, relationship; (*MAT*) ratio; (*lista*) list; (*narración*) report; **~ costo-efectivo** *o* **costo-rendimiento** (*COM*) cost-effectiveness; **relaciones** *nfpl* (*enchufes*) influential friends, connections; **relaciones carnales** sexual relations; **relaciones comerciales** business connections; **relaciones empresariales/humanas** industrial/human relations; **relaciones laborales/públicas** labour/public relations; **con ~ a, en ~ con** in relation to; **estar en** *o* **tener buenas relaciones con** to be on good terms with.

relacionar [relaθjo'nar] *vt* to relate, connect; **~se** *vr* to be connected *o* linked.

relajación [relaxa'θjon] *nf* relaxation.

relajado, a [rela'xaðo, a] *adj* (*disoluto*) loose; (*cómodo*) relaxed; (*MED*) ruptured.

relajante [rela'xante] *adj* relaxing; (*MED*) sedative.

relajar [rela'xar] *vt*, **relajarse** *vr* to relax.

relamerse [rela'merse] *vr* to lick one's lips.

relamido, a [rela'miðo, a] *adj* (*pulcro*) overdressed; (*afectado*) affected.

relámpago [re'lampaɣo] *nm* flash of lightning ♦ *adj* lightning *cpd*; **como un ~** as quick as lightning, in a flash; **visita/huelga ~** lightning visit/strike.

relampaguear [relampaɣe'ar] *vi* to flash.

relanzar [relan'θar] *vt* to relaunch.

relatar [rela'tar] *vt* to tell, relate.

relatividad [relatißi'ðað] *nf* relativity.

relativo, a [rela'tißo, a] *adj* relative; **en lo ~ a** concerning.

relato [re'lato] *nm* (*narración*) story, tale.

relax [re'las] *nm* rest; "R~" (*en anuncio*) "Personal services".

relegar [rele'xar] *vt* to relegate; **~ algo al olvido** to banish sth from one's mind.

relegue [re'leɣe] *etc vb V* **relegar**.

relevante [rele'ßante] *adj* eminent, outstanding.

relevar [rele'ßar] *vt* (*sustituir*) to relieve; **~se** *vr* to relay; **~ a algn de un cargo** to relieve sb of his post.

relevo [re'leßo] *nm* relief; **carrera de ~s** relay race; **~ con cinta** (*INFORM*) tape relay; **coger** *o* **tomar el ~** to take over, stand in.

relieve [re'ljeße] *nm* (*ARTE, TEC*) relief; (*fig*) prominence, importance; **bajo ~** bas-relief; **un personaje de ~** an important man; **dar ~ a** to highlight.

religión [reli'xjon] *nf* religion.

religioso, a [reli'xjoso, a] *adj* religious ♦ *nm/f* monk/nun.

relinchar [relin'tʃar] *vi* to neigh.

relincho [re'lintʃo] *nm* neigh; (*acto*) neighing.

reliquia [re'likja] *nf* relic; **~ de familia** heirloom.

rellano [re'ʎano] *nm* (*ARQ*) landing.

rellenar [reʎe'nar] *vt* (*llenar*) to fill up; (*CULIN*) to stuff; (*COSTURA*) to pad; (*formulario etc*) to fill in *o* out.

relleno, a [re'ʎeno, a] *adj* full up; (*CULIN*) stuffed ♦ *nm* stuffing; (*de tapicería*) padding.

reloj [re'lo(x)] *nm* clock; **~ de pie** grandfather clock; **~ (de pulsera)** wristwatch; **~ de sol** sundial; **~ despertador** alarm (clock); **como un ~** like clockwork; **contra (el) ~** against the clock.

relojería [reloxe'ria] *nf* (*tienda*) watchmaker's (shop); **aparato de ~** clockwork; **bomba de ~** time bomb.

relojero, a [relo'xero, a] *nm/f* clockmaker; watchmaker.

reluciente [relu'θjente] *adj* brilliant, shining.

relucir [relu'θir] *vi* to shine; (*fig*) to excel; **sacar algo a ~** to show sth off.

relumbrante [relum'brante] *adj* dazzling.

relumbrar [relum'brar] *vi* to dazzle, shine brilliantly.

reluzca [re'luθka] *etc vb V* **relucir**.

remachar [rema'tʃar] *vt* to rivet; (*fig*) to hammer home, drive home.

remache [re'matʃe] *nm* rivet.

remanente [rema'nente] *nm* remainder; (*COM*) balance; (*de producto*) surplus.

remangarse [reman'garse] *vr* to roll one's

sleeves up.

remanso [re'manso] *nm* pool.

remar [re'mar] *vi* to row.

rematado, a [rema'taðo, a] *adj* complete, utter; **es un loco ~** he's a raving lunatic.

rematar [rema'tar] *vt* to finish off; (*animal*) to put out of its misery; (*COM*) to sell off cheap ♦ *vi* to end, finish off; (*DEPORTE*) to shoot.

remate [re'mate] *nm* end, finish; (*punta*) tip; (*DEPORTE*) shot; (*ARQ*) top; (*COM*) auction sale; **de** *o* **para ~** to crown it all (*BRIT*), to top it off.

remediable [reme'ðjaßle] *adj*: **fácilmente ~** easily remedied.

remediar [reme'ðjar] *vt* (*gen*) to remedy; (*subsanar*) to make good, repair; (*evitar*) to avoid; **sin poder ~lo** without being able to prevent it.

remedio [re'meðjo] *nm* remedy; (*JUR*) recourse, remedy; **poner ~ a** to correct, stop; **no tener más ~** to have no alternative; **¡qué ~!** there's no other way; **como último ~** as a last resort; **sin ~ inevitable**; (*MED*) hopeless.

remedo [re'meðo] *nm* imitation; (*pey*) parody.

remendar [remen'dar] *vt* to repair; (*con parche*) to patch; (*fig*) to correct.

remesa [re'mesa] *nf* remittance; (*COM*) shipment.

remiendo [re'mjendo] *etc vb V* **remendar** ♦ *nm* mend; (*con parche*) patch; (*cosido*) darn; (*fig*) correction.

remilgado, a [remil'ɣaðo, a] *adj* prim; (*afectado*) affected.

remilgo [re'milɣo] *nm* primness; (*afectación*) affectation.

reminiscencia [reminis'θenθja] *nf* reminiscence.

remirar [remi'rar] *vt* (*volver a mirar*) to look at again; (*examinar*) to look hard at.

remisión [remi'sjon] *nf* (*acto*) sending, shipment; (*REL*) forgiveness, remission; **sin ~** hopelessly.

remiso, a [re'miso, a] *adj* remiss.

remite [re'mite] *nm* (*en sobre*) name and address of sender.

remitente [remi'tente] *nm/f* (*CORREOS*) sender.

remitir [remi'tir] *vt* to remit, send ♦ *vi* to slacken.

remo ['remo] *nm* (*de barco*) oar; (*DEPORTE*) rowing; **cruzar un río a ~** to row across a river.

remoce [re'moθe] *etc vb V* **remozar**.

remodelación [remodela'θjon] *nf* (*POL*): **~ del gobierno** cabinet reshuffle.

remojar [remo'xar] *vt* to steep, soak; (*galleta etc*) to dip, dunk; (*fam*) to celebrate with a drink.

remojo [re'moxo] *nm* steeping, soaking; (*por la lluvia*) drenching, soaking; **dejar la ropa en ~** to leave clothes to soak.

remojón [remo'xon] *nm* soaking; **darse un ~** (*fam*) to go (in) for a dip.

remolacha [remo'latʃa] *nf* beet, beetroot (*BRIT*).

remolcador [remolka'ðor] *nm* (*NAUT*) tug; (*AUTO*) breakdown lorry.

remolcar [remol'kar] *vt* to tow.

remolino [remo'lino] *nm* eddy; (*de agua*) whirlpool; (*de viento*) whirlwind; (*de gente*) crowd.

remolón, ona [remo'lon, ona] *adj* lazy ♦ *nm/f* slacker, shirker.

remolque [re'molke] *etc vb V* **remolcar** ♦ *nm* tow, towing; (*cuerda*) towrope; **llevar a ~** to tow.

remontar [remon'tar] *vt* to mend; (*obstáculo*) to negotiate, get over; **~se** *vr* to soar; **~se a** (*COM*) to amount to; (*en tiempo*) to go back to, date from; **~ el vuelo** to soar.

rémora ['remora] *nf* hindrance.

remorder [remor'ðer] *vt* to distress, disturb.

remordimiento [remorði'mjento] *nm* remorse.

remotamente [remota'mente] *adv* vaguely.

remoto, a [re'moto, a] *adj* remote.

remover [remo'ßer] *vt* to stir; (*tierra*) to turn over; (*objetos*) to move round.

remozar [remo'θar] *vt* (*ARQ*) to refurbish; (*fig*) to brighten *o* polish up.

remuerda [re'mwerða] *etc vb V* **remorder**.

remueva [re'mweßa] *etc vb V* **remover**.

remuneración [remunera'θjon] *nf* remuneration.

remunerado, a [remune'raðo, a] *adj*: **trabajo bien/mal ~** well-/badly-paid job.

remunerar [remune'rar] *vt* to remunerate; (*premiar*) to reward.

renacer [rena'θer] *vi* to be reborn; (*fig*) to revive.

renacimiento [renaθi'mjento] *nm* rebirth; **el R~** the Renaissance.

renacuajo [rena'kwaxo] *nm* (*ZOOL*) tadpole.

renal [re'nal] *adj* renal, kidney *cpd*.

Renania [re'nanja] *nf* Rhineland.

renazca [re'naθka] *etc vb V* **renacer**.

rencilla [ren'θiʎa] *nf* quarrel; **~s** *nfpl* bickering *sg*.

rencor [ren'kor] *nm* rancour, bitterness; (*resentimiento*) ill feeling, resentment;

guardar ~ **a** to have a grudge against.
rencoroso, a [renko'roso, a] *adj* spiteful.
rendición [rendi'θjon] *nf* surrender.
rendido, a [ren'diðo, a] *adj* (*sumiso*)
submissive; (*agotado*) worn-out,
exhausted; (*enamorado*) devoted.
rendija [ren'dixa] *nf* (*hendedura*) crack;
(*abertura*) aperture; (*fig*) rift, split; (*JUR*)
loophole.
rendimiento [rendi'mjento] *nm*
(*producción*) output; (*COM*) yield,
profit(s) (*pl*); (*TEC, COM*) efficiency; ~ **de**
capital (*COM*) return on capital.
rendir [ren'dir] *vt* (*vencer*) to defeat;
(*producir*) to produce; (*dar beneficio*) to
yield; (*agotar*) to exhaust ♦ *vi* to pay;
(*COM*) to yield, produce; ~**se** *vr*
(*someterse*) to surrender; (*ceder*) to
yield; (*cansarse*) to wear o.s. out; ~
homenaje o **culto a** to pay homage to; **el**
negocio no rinde the business doesn't
pay.
renegado, a [rene'xaðo, a] *adj, nm/f*
renegade.
renegar [rene'xar] *vt* (*negar*) to deny
vigorously ♦ *vi* (*blasfemar*) to blaspheme;
~ **de** (*renunciar*) to renounce; (*quejarse*)
to complain about.
renegué [rene'xe], **reneguemos**
[rene'xemos] *etc vb V* **renegar**.
RENFE ['renfe] *nf abr ESP.* = *Red Nacional de*
Ferrocarriles Españoles.
renglón [ren'glon] *nm* (*línea*) line; (*COM*)
item, article; **a ~ seguido** immediately
after.
rengo, a ['rengo, a] *adj* (*AM*) lame.
reniego [re'njexo] *etc*, **reniegue**
[re'njexe] *etc vb V* **renegar**.
reno ['reno] *nm* reindeer.
renombrado, a [renom'braðo, a] *adj*
renowned.
renombre [re'nombre] *nm* renown.
renovable [reno'ßaßle] *adj* renewable.
renovación [renoßa'θjon] *nf* (*de contrato*)
renewal; (*ARQ*) renovation.
renovar [reno'ßar] *vt* to renew; (*ARQ*) to
renovate; (*sala*) to redecorate.
renquear [renke'ar] *vi* to limp; (*fam*) to get
along, scrape by.
renta ['renta] *nf* (*ingresos*) income;
(*beneficio*) profit; (*alquiler*) rent; ~
gravable o **imponible** taxable income; ~
nacional (bruta) (gross) national income;
~ **no salarial** unearned income; ~ **sobre**
el terreno (*COM*) ground rent; ~ **vitalicia**
annuity; **política de ~s** incomes policy;
vivir de sus ~s to live on one's private
income.

rentabilizar [rentaßili'θar] *vt* to make
profitable.
rentable [ren'taßle] *adj* profitable; **no ~**
unprofitable.
rentar [ren'tar] *vt* to produce, yield; (*AM*)
to rent.
rentista [ren'tista] *nm/f* (*accionista*)
shareholder (*BRIT*), stockholder (*US*).
renuencia [re'nwenθja] *nf* reluctance.
renuente [re'nwente] *adj* reluctant.
renueve [re'nweße] *etc vb V* **renovar**.
renuncia [re'nunθja] *nf* resignation.
renunciar [renun'θjar] *vt* to renounce, give
up ♦ *vi* to resign; ~ **a hacer algo** to give
up doing sth.
reñido, a [re'ɲiðo, a] *adj* (*batalla*) bitter,
hard-fought; **estar ~ con algn** to be on
bad terms with sb; **está ~ con su familia**
he has fallen out with his family.
reñir [re'ɲir] *vt* (*regañar*) to scold ♦ *vi* (*estar*
peleado) to quarrel, fall out; (*combatir*) to
fight.
reo ['reo] *nm/f* culprit, offender; (*JUR*)
accused.
reojo [re'oxo]: **de ~** *adv* out of the corner
of one's eye.
reorganice [reorxa'niθe] *etc vb V*
reorganizar.
reorganizar [reorxani'θar] *vt* to
reorganize.
Rep *abr* = **República**.
reparación [repara'θjon] *nf* (*acto*) mending,
repairing; (*TEC*) repair; (*fig*) amends,
reparation; **"reparaciones en el acto"**
"repairs while you wait".
reparar [repa'rar] *vt* to repair; (*fig*) to make
amends for; (*suerte*) to retrieve;
(*observar*) to observe ♦ *vi*: ~ **en** (*darse*
cuenta de) to notice; (*poner atención en*) to
pay attention to; **sin ~ en los gastos**
regardless of the cost.
reparo [re'paro] *nm* (*advertencia*)
observation; (*duda*) doubt; (*dificultad*)
difficulty; (*escrúpulo*) scruple, qualm;
poner ~s (a) to raise objections (to);
(*criticar*) to criticize; **no tuvo ~ en**
hacerlo he did not hesitate to do it.
repartición [reparti'θjon] *nf* distribution;
(*división*) division.
repartidor, a [reparti'ðor, a] *nm/f*
distributor; ~ **de leche** milkman.
repartir [repar'tir] *vt* to distribute, share
out; (*COM, CORREOS*) to deliver; (*MIL*) to
partition; (*libros*) to give out; (*comida*) to
serve out; (*NAIPES*) to deal.
reparto [re'parto] *nm* distribution; (*COM,*
CORREOS) delivery; (*TEAT, CINE*) cast;
(*AM: urbanización*) housing estate (*BRIT*),

real estate development (*US*); *"~ a*
domicilio" "home delivery service".

repasar [repa'sar] *vt* (*ESCOL*) to revise;
(*MECÁNICA*) to check, overhaul;
(*COSTURA*) to mend.

repaso [re'paso] *nm* revision; (*MECÁNICA*)
overhaul, checkup; (*COSTURA*) mending;
~ **general** servicing, general overhaul;
curso de ~ refresher course.

repatriar [repa'trjar] *vt* to repatriate; *~se*
vr to return home.

repelente [repe'lente] *adj* repellent,
repulsive.

repeler [repe'ler] *vt* to repel; (*idea, oferta*)
to reject.

repensar [repen'sar] *vt* to reconsider.

repente [re'pente] *nm* sudden movement;
(*fig*) impulse; **de** ~ suddenly; ~ **de ira** fit
of anger.

repentice [repen'tiθe] *etc vb V* **repentizar**.

repentino, a [repen'tino, a] *adj* sudden;
(*imprevisto*) unexpected.

repentizar [repenti'θar] *vi* (*MUS*) to sight-
read.

repercusión [reperku'sjon] *nf*
repercussion; **de amplia** *o* **ancha** ~ far-
reaching.

repercutir [reperku'tir] *vi* (*objeto*) to
rebound; (*sonido*) to echo; ~ **en** (*fig*) to
have repercussions *o* effects on.

repertorio [reper'torjo] *nm* list; (*TEAT*)
repertoire.

repesca [re'peska] *nf* (*ESCOL fam*) resit.

repetición [repeti'θjon] *nf* repetition.

repetido, a [repe'tiðo, a] *adj* repeated;
repetidas veces repeatedly.

repetir [repe'tir] *vt* to repeat; (*plato*) to
have a second helping of; (*TEAT*) to give
as an encore, sing *etc* again ♦ *vi* to
repeat; (*sabor*) to come back; *~se vr* to
repeat o.s.; (*suceso*) to recur.

repetitivo, a [repeti'tiβo, a] *adj* repetitive,
repetitious.

repicar [repi'kar] *vi* (*campanas*) to ring
(out).

repiense [re'pjense] *etc vb V* **repensar**.

repipi [re'pipi] *adj* la-di-da ♦ *nf*: **es una** ~
she's a little madam.

repique [re'pike] *etc vb V* **repicar** ♦ *nm*
pealing, ringing.

repiqueteo [repike'teo] *nm* pealing; (*de
tambor*) drumming.

repisa [re'pisa] *nf* ledge, shelf; ~ **de
chimenea** mantelpiece; ~ **de ventana**
windowsill.

repitiendo [repi'tjendo] *etc vb V* **repetir**.

replantear [replante'ar] *vt* (*cuestión
pública*) to readdress; (*problema personal*)

to reconsider; (*en reunión*) to raise
again; *~se vr*: *~se algo* to reconsider
sth.

replegarse [reple'ɣarse] *vr* to fall back,
retreat.

replegué [reple'ɣe], **repleguemos**
[reple'ɣemos] *etc vb V* **replegarse**.

repleto, a [re'pleto, a] *adj* replete, full up;
~ **de** filled *o* crammed with.

réplica ['replika] *nf* answer; (*ARTE*) replica;
derecho de ~ right of *o* to reply.

replicar [repli'kar] *vi* to answer; (*objetar*) to
argue, answer back.

repliego [re'pljeɣo] *etc vb V* **replegarse**.

repliegue [re'pljeɣe] *etc vb V* **replegarse**
♦ *nm* (*MIL*) withdrawal.

replique [re'plike] *etc vb V* **replicar**.

repoblación [repoßla'θjon] *nf*
repopulation; (*de río*) restocking; ~
forestal reafforestation.

repoblar [repo'ßlar] *vt* to repopulate; to
restock.

repollo [re'poʎo] *nm* cabbage.

repondré [repon'dre] *etc vb V* **reponer**.

reponer [repo'ner] *vt* to replace, put back;
(*máquina*) to re-set; (*TEAT*) to revive; *~se*
vr to recover; ~ **que** to reply that.

reponga [re'ponga] *etc vb V* **reponer**.

reportaje [repor'taxe] *nm* report, article; ~
gráfico illustrated report.

reportar [repor'tar] *vt* (*traer*) to bring,
carry; (*conseguir*) to obtain; (*fig*) to
check; *~se vr* (*contenerse*) to control o.s.;
(*calmarse*) to calm down; **la cosa no le
reportó sino disgustos** the affair
brought him nothing but trouble.

reportero, a [repor'tero, a] *nm/f* reporter;
~ **gráfico/a** news photographer.

reposacabezas [reposaka'ßeθas] *nm inv*
headrest.

reposado, a [repo'saðo, a] *adj* (*descansado*)
restful; (*tranquilo*) calm.

reposar [repo'sar] *vi* to rest, repose;
(*muerto*) to lie, rest.

reposición [reposi'θjon] *nf* replacement;
(*CINE*) second showing; (*TEAT*) revival.

reposo [re'poso] *nm* rest.

repostar [repos'tar] *vt* to replenish; (*AUTO*)
to fill up (with petrol *o* gasoline).

repostería [reposte'ria] *nf* (*arte*)
confectionery, pastry-making; (*tienda*)
confectioner's (shop).

repostero, a [repos'tero, a] *nm/f*
confectioner.

reprender [repren'der] *vt* to reprimand;
(*niño*) to scold.

reprensión [repren'sjon] *nf* rebuke,
reprimand; (*de niño*) telling-off,

scolding.

represa [re'presa] *nf* dam; (*lago artificial*) lake, pool.

represalia [repre'salja] *nf* reprisal; **tomar ~s** to take reprisals, retaliate.

representación [representa'θjon] *nf* representation; (*TEAT*) performance; **en ~ de** representing; **por ~** by proxy; **~ visual** (*INFORM*) display.

representante [represen'tante] *nm/f* (*POL, COM*) representative; (*TEAT*) performer.

representar [represen'tar] *vt* to represent; (*significar*) to mean; (*TEAT*) to perform; (*edad*) to look; **~se** *vr* to imagine; **tal acto representaría la guerra** such an act would mean war.

representativo, a [representa'tiβo, a] *adj* representative.

represión [repre'sjon] *nf* repression.

represivo, a [repre'siβo, a] *adj* repressive.

reprimenda [repri'menda] *nf* reprimand, rebuke.

reprimir [repri'mir] *vt* to repress; **~se** *vr*: **~se de hacer algo** to stop o.s. from doing sth.

reprobación [reproβa'θjon] *nf* reproval; (*culpa*) blame.

reprobar [repro'βar] *vt* to censure, reprove.

réprobo, a [ˈreproβo, a] *nm/f* reprobate.

reprochar [repro'tʃar] *vt* to reproach; (*censurar*) to condemn, censure.

reproche [re'protʃe] *nm* reproach.

reproducción [reproðuk'θjon] *nf* reproduction.

reproducir [reproðu'θir] *vt* to reproduce; **~se** *vr* to breed; (*situación*) to recur.

reproductor, a [reproðuk'tor, a] *adj* reproductive ♦ *nm*: **~ de discos compactos** CD player.

reproduje [repro'ðuxe], **reprodujera** [reproðu'xera] *etc*, **reproduzca** [repro'ðuθka] *etc vb V* **reproducir**.

repruebe [re'prweβe] *etc vb V* **reprobar**.

reptar [rep'tar] *vi* to creep, crawl.

reptil [rep'til] *nm* reptile.

república [re'puβlika] *nf* republic; **R~ Dominicana** Dominican Republic; **R~ Democrática Alemana (RDA)** German Democratic Republic; **R~ Federal Alemana (RFA)** Federal Republic of Germany; **R~ Árabe Unida** United Arab Republic.

republicano, a [repuβli'kano, a] *adj, nm/f* republican.

repudiar [repu'ðjar] *vt* to repudiate; (*fe*) to renounce.

repudio [re'puðjo] *nm* repudiation.

repueble [re'pweβle] *etc vb V* **repoblar**.

repuesto [re'pwesto] *pp de* **reponer** ♦ *nm* (*pieza de recambio*) spare (part); (*abastecimiento*) supply; **rueda de ~** spare wheel; **y llevamos otro de ~** and we have another as a spare *o* in reserve.

repugnancia [repuɣ'nanθja] *nf* repugnance.

repugnante [repuɣ'nante] *adj* repugnant, repulsive.

repugnar [repuɣ'nar] *vt* to disgust ♦ *vi*, **~se** *vr* (*contradecirse*) to contradict each other; (*dar asco*) to be disgusting.

repujar [repu'xar] *vt* to emboss.

repulsa [re'pulsa] *nf* rebuff.

repulsión [repul'sjon] *nf* repulsion, aversion.

repulsivo, a [repul'siβo, a] *adj* repulsive.

repuse [re'puse] *etc vb V* **reponer**.

reputación [reputa'θjon] *nf* reputation.

reputar [repu'tar] *vt* to consider, deem.

requemado, a [reke'maðo, a] *adj* (*quemado*) scorched; (*bronceado*) tanned.

requemar [reke'mar] *vt* (*quemar*) to scorch; (*secar*) to parch; (*CULIN*) to overdo, burn; (*la lengua*) to burn, sting.

requerimiento [rekeri'mjento] *nm* request; (*demanda*) demand; (*JUR*) summons.

requerir [reke'rir] *vt* (*pedir*) to ask, request; (*exigir*) to require; (*ordenar*) to call for; (*llamar*) to send for, summon.

requesón [reke'son] *nm* cottage cheese.

requete... [rekete] *pref* extremely.

requiebro [re'kjeβro] *nm* (*piropo*) compliment, flirtatious remark.

réquiem [ˈrekjem] *nm* requiem.

requiera [re'kjera] *etc*, **requiriendo** [reki'rjendo] *etc vb V* **requerir**.

requisa [re'kisa] *nf* (*inspección*) survey, inspection; (*MIL*) requisition.

requisar [reki'sar] *vt* (*MIL*) to requisition; (*confiscar*) to seize, confiscate.

requisito [reki'sito] *nm* requirement, requisite; **~ previo** prerequisite; **tener los ~s para un cargo** to have the essential qualifications for a post.

res [res] *nf* beast, animal.

resabio [re'saβjo] *nm* (*maña*) vice, bad habit; (*dejo*) (unpleasant) aftertaste.

resaca [re'saka] *nf* (*en el mar*) undertow, undercurrent; (*fig*) backlash; (*fam*) hangover.

resaltar [resal'tar] *vi* to project, stick out; (*fig*) to stand out.

resarcir [resar'θir] *vt* to compensate; (*pagar*) to repay; **~se** *vr* to make up for; **~ a algn de una pérdida** to compensate sb for a loss; **~ a algn de una cantidad** to repay sb a sum.

resarza [re'sarθa] *etc vb V* **resarcir**.

resbalada [resßa'laða] *nf (AM)* slip.

resbaladizo, a [resßala'ðiθo, a] *adj* slippery.

resbalar [resßa'lar] *vi*, **resbalarse** *vr* to slip, slide; *(fig)* to slip (up); **le resbalaban las lágrimas por las mejillas** tears were trickling down his cheeks.

resbalón [resßa'lon] *nm (acción)* slip; *(deslizamiento)* slide; *(fig)* slip.

rescatar [reska'tar] *vt (salvar)* to save, rescue; *(objeto)* to get back, recover; *(cautivos)* to ransom.

rescate [res'kate] *nm* rescue; *(objeto)* recovery; **pagar un ~** to pay a ransom.

rescindir [resθin'dir] *vt (contrato)* to annul, rescind.

rescisión [resθi'sjon] *nf* cancellation.

rescoldo [res'koldo] *nm* embers *pl*.

resecar [rese'kar] *vt* to dry off, dry thoroughly; *(MED)* to cut out, remove; **~se** *vr* to dry up.

reseco, a [re'seko, a] *adj* very dry; *(fig)* skinny.

resentido, a [resen'tiðo, a] *adj* resentful; **es un ~** he's bitter.

resentimiento [resenti'mjento] *nm* resentment, bitterness.

resentirse [resen'tirse] *vr (debilitarse*: *persona)* to suffer; **~ con** to resent; **~ de** *(consecuencias)* to feel the effects of.

reseña [re'seɲa] *nf (cuenta)* account; *(informe)* report; *(LIT)* review.

reseñar [rese'ɲar] *vt* to describe; *(LIT)* to review.

reseque [re'seke] *etc vb V* **resecar**.

reserva [re'serßa] *nf* reserve; *(reservación)* reservation; **a ~ de que ... unless ...; con toda ~** in strictest confidence; **de ~** spare; **tener algo de ~** to have sth in reserve; **~ de indios** Indian reservation; *(COM):* **~ para amortización** depreciation allowance; **~ de caja** *o* **en efectivo** cash reserves; **~s del Estado** government stock; **~s en oro** gold reserves.

reservado, a [reser'ßaðo, a] *adj* reserved; *(retraído)* cold, distant ♦ *nm* private room; *(FERRO)* reserved compartment.

reservar [reser'ßar] *vt (guardar)* to keep; *(FERRO, TEAT etc)* to reserve, book; **~se** *vr* to save o.s.; *(callar)* to keep to o.s.; **~ con exceso** to overbook.

resfriado [res'friaðo] *nm* cold.

resfriarse [res'friarse] *vr* to cool off; *(MED)* to catch (a) cold.

resfrío [resf'rio] *nm (esp AM)* cold.

resguardar [resɣwar'ðar] *vt* to protect, shield; **~se** *vr*: **~se de** to guard against.

resguardo [res'ɣwarðo] *nm* defence; *(vale)* voucher; *(recibo)* receipt, slip.

residencia [resi'ðenθja] *nf* residence; *(UNIV)* hall of residence; **~ para ancianos** *o* **jubilados** rest home.

residencial [resiðen'θjal] *adj* residential ♦ *nf (urbanización)* housing estate *(BRIT)*, real estate development *(US)*.

residente [resi'ðente] *adj*, *nm/f* resident.

residir [resi'ðir] *vi* to reside, live; **~ en** to reside *o* lie in; *(consistir en)* to consist of.

residual [resi'ðwal] *adj* residual; **aguas ~es** sewage.

residuo [re'siðwo] *nm* residue; **~s atmosféricos** *o* **radiactivos** fallout *sg*.

resienta [re'sjenta] *etc vb V* **resentir**.

resignación [resiɣna'θjon] *nf* resignation.

resignarse [resiɣ'narse] *vr*: **~ a** *o* **con** to resign o.s. to, be resigned to.

resina [re'sina] *nf* resin.

resintiendo [resin'tjendo] *etc vb V* **resentir**.

resistencia [resis'tenθja] *nf (dureza)* endurance, strength; *(oposición, ELEC)* resistance; **la R~** *(MIL)* the Resistance.

resistente [resis'tente] *adj* strong, hardy; *(TEC)* resistant; **~ al calor** heat-resistant.

resistir [resis'tir] *vt (soportar)* to bear; *(oponerse a)* to resist, oppose; *(aguantar)* to put up with ♦ *vi* to resist; *(aguantar)* to last, endure; **~se** *vr*: **~se a** to refuse to, resist; **no puedo ~ este frío** I can't bear *o* stand this cold; **me resisto a creerlo** I refuse to believe it; **se le resiste la química** chemistry escapes her.

resol [re'sol] *nm* glare of the sun.

resollar [reso'ʎar] *vi* to breathe noisily, wheeze.

resolución [resolu'θjon] *nf* resolution; *(decisión)* decision; *(moción)* motion; **~ judicial** legal ruling; **tomar una ~** to take a decision.

resoluto, a [reso'luto, a] *adj* resolute.

resolver [resol'ßer] *vt* to resolve; *(solucionar)* to solve, resolve; *(decidir)* to decide, settle; **~se** *vr* to make up one's mind.

resonancia [reso'nanθja] *nf (del sonido)* resonance; *(repercusión)* repercussion; *(fig)* wide effect, impact.

resonante [reso'nante] *adj* resonant, resounding; *(fig)* tremendous.

resonar [reso'nar] *vi* to ring, echo.

resoplar [reso'plar] *vi* to snort; *(por cansancio)* to puff.

resoplido [reso'pliðo] *nm* heavy breathing.

resorte [re'sorte] *nm* spring; *(fig)* lever.

respaldar [respal'dar] *vt* to back (up),

support; (*INFORM*) to back up; ~**se** *vr* to lean back; ~**se con** *o* **en** (*fig*) to take one's stand on.

respaldo [res'paldo] *nm* (*de sillón*) back; (*fig*) support, backing.

respectivo, a [respek'tiβo, a] *adj* respective; **en lo** ~ **a** with regard to.

respecto [res'pekto] *nm*: **al** ~ on this matter; **con** ~ **a**, ~ **de** with regard to, in relation to.

respetable [respe'taβle] *adj* respectable.

respetar [respe'tar] *vt* to respect.

respeto [res'peto] *nm* respect; (*acatamiento*) deference; ~**s** *nmpl* respects; **por** ~ **a** out of consideration for; **presentar sus** ~**s a** to pay one's respects to.

respetuoso, a [respe'twoso, a] *adj* respectful.

respingo [res'pingo] *nm* start, jump.

respiración [respira'θjon] *nf* breathing; (*MED*) respiration; (*ventilación*) ventilation.

respirar [respi'rar] *vt, vi* to breathe; **no dejar** ~ **a algn** to keep on at sb; **estuvo escuchándole sin** ~ he listened to him in complete silence.

respiratorio, a [respira'torjo, a] *adj* respiratory.

respiro [res'piro] *nm* breathing; (*fig: descanso*) respite, rest; (*COM*) period of grace.

resplandecer [resplande'θer] *vi* to shine.

resplandeciente [resplande'θjente] *adj* resplendent, shining.

resplandezca [resplan'deθka] *etc vb V* **resplandecer**.

resplandor [resplan'dor] *nm* brilliance, brightness; (*del fuego*) blaze.

responder [respon'der] *vt* to answer ♦ *vi* to answer; (*fig*) to respond; (*pey*) to answer back; (*corresponder*) to correspond; ~ **a** (*situación etc*) to respond to; ~ **a una pregunta** to answer a question; ~ **a una descripción** to fit a description; ~ **de** *o* **por** to answer for.

respondón, ona [respon'don, ona] *adj* cheeky.

responsabilice [responsaβi'liθe] *etc vb V* **responsabilizarse**.

responsabilidad [responsaβili'ðað] *nf* responsibility; **bajo mi** ~ on my authority; ~ **ilimitada** (*COM*) unlimited liability.

responsabilizarse [responsaβili'θarse] *vr* to make o.s. responsible, take charge.

responsable [respon'saβle] *adj* responsible; **la persona** ~ the person in

charge; **hacerse** ~ **de algo** to assume responsibility for sth.

respuesta [res'pwesta] *nf* answer, reply; (*reacción*) response.

resquebrajar [reskeβra'xar] *vt*, **resquebrajarse** *vr* to crack, split.

resquemor [reske'mor] *nm* resentment.

resquicio [res'kiθjo] *nm* chink; (*hendedura*) crack.

resta ['resta] *nf* (*MAT*) remainder.

restablecer [restaβle'θer] *vt* to re-establish, restore; ~**se** *vr* to recover.

restablecimiento [restaβleθi'mjento] *nm* re-establishment; (*restauración*) restoration; (*MED*) recovery.

restablezca [resta'βleθka] *etc vb V* **restablecer**.

restallar [resta'ʎar] *vi* to crack.

restante [res'tante] *adj* remaining; **lo** ~ the remainder; **los** ~**s** the rest, those left (over).

restar [res'tar] *vt* (*MAT*) to subtract; (*descontar*) to deduct; (*fig*) to take away ♦ *vi* to remain, be left.

restauración [restaura'θjon] *nf* restoration.

restaurador, a [restaura'ðor, a] *nm/f* (*persona*) restorer.

restaurante [restau'rante] *nm* restaurant.

restaurar [restau'rar] *vt* to restore.

restitución [restitu'θjon] *nf* return, restitution.

restituir [restitu'ir] *vt* (*devolver*) to return, give back; (*rehabilitar*) to restore.

restituyendo [restitu'jendo] *etc vb V* **restituir**.

resto ['resto] *nm* (*residuo*) rest, remainder; (*apuesta*) stake; ~**s** *nmpl* remains; (*CULIN*) leftovers, scraps; ~**s mortales** mortal remains.

restregar [restre'xar] *vt* to scrub, rub.

restregué [restre'xe], **restreguemos** [restre'xemos] *etc vb V* **restregar**.

restricción [restrik'θjon] *nf* restriction; **sin** ~ **de** without restrictions on *o* as to; **hablar sin restricciones** to talk freely.

restrictivo, a [restrik'tiβo, a] *adj* restrictive.

restriego [res'trjexo] *etc*, **restriegue** [res'trjexe] *etc vb V* **restregar**.

restringir [restrin'xir] *vt* to restrict, limit.

restrinja [res'trinxa] *etc vb V* **restringir**.

resucitar [resuθi'tar] *vt, vi* to resuscitate, revive.

resuello [re'sweʎo] *etc vb V* **resollar** ♦ *nm* (*aliento*) breath.

resuelto, a [re'swelto, a] *pp de* **resolver** ♦ *adj* resolute, determined; **estar** ~ **a**

algo to be set on sth; **estar ~ a hacer algo** to be determined to do sth.
resuelva [re'swelβa] *etc vb V* **resolver**.
resuene [re'swene] *etc vb V* **resonar**.
resulta [re'sulta] *nf* result; **de ~s de** as a result of.
resultado [resul'taðo] *nm* result; (*conclusión*) outcome; **~s** *nmpl* (*INFORM*) output *sg*; **dar ~** to produce results.
resultante [resul'tante] *adj* resulting, resultant.
resultar [resul'tar] *vi* (*ser*) to be; (*llegar a ser*) to turn out to be; (*salir bien*) to turn out well; (*seguir*) to ensue; **~ a** (*COM*) to amount to; **~ de** to stem from; **~ en** to result in, produce; **resulta que ...** (*por consecuencia*) it follows that ...; (*parece que*) it seems that ...; **el conductor resultó muerto** the driver was killed; **no resultó** it didn't work *o* come off; **me resulta difícil hacerlo** it's difficult for me to do it.
resumen [re'sumen] *nm* summary, résumé; **en ~** in short.
resumir [resu'mir] *vt* to sum up; (*condensar*) to summarize; (*cortar*) to abridge, cut down; (*condensar*) to summarize; **~se** *vr*: **la situación se resume en pocas palabras** the situation can be summed up in a few words.
resurgir [resur'xir] *vi* (*reaparecer*) to reappear.
resurrección [resurrek'θjon] *nf* resurrection.
retablo [re'taβlo] *nm* altarpiece.
retaguardia [reta'xwarðja] *nf* rearguard.
retahíla [reta'ila] *nf* series, string; (*de injurias*) volley, stream.
retal [re'tal] *nm* remnant.
retar [re'tar] *vt* (*gen*) to challenge; (*desafiar*) to defy, dare.
retardar [retar'ðar] *vt* (*demorar*) to delay; (*hacer más lento*) to slow down; (*retener*) to hold back.
retardo [re'tarðo] *nm* delay.
retazo [re'taθo] *nm* snippet (*BRIT*), fragment.
RETD *nf abr* (*ESP TELEC*) = Red Especial de Transmisión de Datos.
rete... ['rete] *pref* very, extremely.
retén [re'ten] *nm* (*AM*) roadblock, checkpoint.
retención [reten'θjon] *nf* retention; (*de pago*) deduction; **~ de llamadas** (*TELEC*) hold facility.
retendré [reten'dre] *etc vb V* **retener**.
retener [rete'ner] *vt* (*guardar*) to retain, keep; (*intereses*) to withhold.

retenga [re'tenga] *etc vb V* **retener**.
reticencia [reti'θenθja] *nf* (*sugerencia*) insinuation, (malevolent) suggestion; (*engaño*) half-truth.
reticente [reti'θente] *adj* (*insinuador*) insinuating; (*engañoso*) deceptive.
retiene [re'tjene] *etc vb V* **retener**.
retina [re'tina] *nf* retina.
retintín [retin'tin] *nm* jangle, jingle; **decir algo con ~** to say sth sarcastically.
retirado, a [reti'raðo, a] *adj* (*lugar*) remote; (*vida*) quiet; (*jubilado*) retired ♦ *nf* (*MIL*) retreat; (*de dinero*) withdrawal; (*de embajador*) recall; (*refugio*) safe place; **batirse en retirada** to retreat.
retirar [reti'rar] *vt* to withdraw; (*la mano*) to draw back; (*quitar*) to remove; (*dinero*) to take out, withdraw; (*jubilar*) to retire, pension off; **~se** *vr* to retreat, withdraw; (*jubilarse*) to retire; (*acostarse*) to retire, go to bed.
retiro [re'tiro] *nm* retreat; (*jubilación, tb DEPORTE*) retirement; (*pago*) pension; (*lugar*) quiet place.
reto ['reto] *nm* dare, challenge.
retocar [reto'kar] *vt* to touch up, retouch.
retoce [re'toθe] *etc vb V* **retozar**.
retoño [re'topo] *nm* sprout, shoot; (*fig*) offspring, child.
retoque [re'toke] *etc vb V* **retocar** ♦ *nm* retouching.
retorcer [retor'θer] *vt* to twist; (*argumento*) to turn, twist; (*manos, lavado*) to wring; **~se** *vr* to become twisted; (*persona*) to writhe; **~se de dolor** to writhe in *o* squirm with pain.
retorcido, a [retor'θiðo, a] *adj* (*tb fig*) twisted.
retorcimiento [retorθi'mjento] *nm* twist, twisting; (*fig*) deviousness.
retórico, a [re'toriko, a] *adj* rhetorical; (*pey*) affected, windy ♦ *nf* rhetoric; (*pey*) affectedness.
retornable [retor'naβle] *adj* returnable.
retornar [retor'nar] *vt* to return, give back ♦ *vi* to return, go/come back.
retorno [re'torno] *nm* return; **~ del carro** (*INFORM, TIP*) carriage return; **~ del carro automático** (*INFORM*) wordwrap, word wraparound.
retortero [retor'tero] *nm*: **andar al ~** to bustle about, have heaps of things to do; **andar al ~ por algn** to be madly in love with sb.
retortijón [retorti'xon] *nm* twist, twisting; **~ de tripas** stomach cramp.
retorzamos [retor'θamos] *etc vb V* **retorcer**.

retozar [reto'θar] *vi* (*juguetear*) to frolic, romp; (*saltar*) to gambol.

retozón, ona [reto'θon, ona] *adj* playful.

retracción [retrak'θjon] *nf* retraction.

retractarse [retrak'tarse] *vr* to retract; **me retracto** I take that back.

retraerse [retra'erse] *vr* to retreat, withdraw.

retraído, a [retra'iðo, a] *adj* shy, retiring.

retraiga [re'traixa] *etc vb V* **retraerse**.

retraimiento [retrai'mjento] *nm* retirement; (*timidez*) shyness.

retraje [re'traxe] *etc*, **retrajera** [retra'xera] *etc vb V* **retraerse**.

retransmisión [retransmi'sjon] *nf* repeat (broadcast).

retransmitir [retransmi'tir] *vt* (*mensaje*) to relay; (*TV etc*) to repeat, retransmit; (: *en vivo*) to broadcast live.

retrasado, a [retra'saðo, a] *adj* late; (*MED*) mentally retarded; (*país etc*) backward, underdeveloped; **estar** ~ (*reloj*) to be slow; (*persona, industria*) to be o lag behind.

retrasar [retra'sar] *vt* (*demorar*) to postpone, put off; (*retardar*) to slow down ♦ *vi*, ~**se** *vr* (*atrasarse*) to be late; (*reloj*) to be slow; (*producción*) to fall (away); (*quedarse atrás*) to lag behind.

retraso [re'traso] *nm* (*demora*) delay; (*lentitud*) slowness; (*tardanza*) lateness; (*atraso*) backwardness; ~**s** *nmpl* (*COM*) arrears; (*deudas*) deficit *sg*, debts; **llegar con** ~ to arrive late; **llegar con 25 minutos de** ~ to be 25 minutes late; **llevo un** ~ **de 6 semanas** I'm 6 weeks behind (with my work *etc*); ~ **mental** mental deficiency.

retratar [retra'tar] *vt* (*ARTE*) to paint the portrait of; (*fotografiar*) to photograph; (*fig*) to depict, describe; ~**se** *vr* to have one's portrait painted; to have one's photograph taken.

retratista [retra'tista] *nm/f* (*pintura*) (portrait) painter; (*FOTO*) photographer.

retrato [re'trato] *nm* portrait; (*FOTO*) photograph; (*descripción*) portrayal, depiction; (*fig*) likeness; **ser el vivo** ~ **de** to be the spitting image of.

retrato-robot [re'tratoro'ßo(t)], *pl* **retratos-robot** *nm* identikit picture.

retrayendo [retra'jendo] *etc vb V* **retraerse**.

retreta [re'treta] *nf* retreat.

retrete [re'trete] *nm* toilet.

retribución [retrißu'θjon] *nf* (*recompensa*) reward; (*pago*) pay, payment.

retribuir [retrißu'ir] *vt* (*recompensar*) to reward; (*pagar*) to pay.

retribuyendo [retrißu'jendo] *etc vb V* **retribuir**.

retro... [retro] *pref* retro....

retroactivo, a [retroak'tißo, a] *adj* retroactive, retrospective; **dar efecto** ~ **a un pago** to backdate a payment.

retroalimentación [retroalimenta'θjon] *nf* (*INFORM*) feedback.

retroceder [retroθe'ðer] *vi* (*echarse atrás*) to move back(wards); (*fig*) to back down; **no** ~ to stand firm; **la policía hizo** ~ **a la multitud** the police forced the crowd back.

retroceso [retro'θeso] *nm* backward movement; (*MED*) relapse; (*COM*) recession, depression; (*fig*) backing down.

retrógrado, a [re'troɣraðo, a] *adj* retrograde, retrogressive; (*POL*) reactionary.

retropropulsión [retropropul'sjon] *nf* jet propulsion.

retrospectivo, a [retrospek'tißo, a] *adj* retrospective; **mirada retrospectiva** backward glance.

retrovisor [retroßi'sor] *nm* rear-view mirror.

retuerce [re'twerθe] *etc*, **retuerza** [re'twerθa] *etc vb V* **retorcer**.

retumbante [retum'bante] *adj* resounding.

retumbar [retum'bar] *vi* to echo, resound; (*continuamente*) to reverberate.

retuve [re'tuße] *etc vb V* **retener**.

reuma ['reuma] *nm* rheumatism.

reumático, a [reu'matiko, a] *adj* rheumatic.

reumatismo [reuma'tismo] *nm* rheumatism.

reunificar [reunifi'kar] *vt* to reunify.

reunifique [reuni'fike] *etc vb V* **reunificar**.

reunión [reu'njon] *nf* (*asamblea*) meeting; (*fiesta*) party; ~ **en la cumbre** summit meeting; ~ **de ventas** (*COM*) sales meeting.

reunir [reu'nir] *vt* (*juntar*) to reunite, join (together); (*recoger*) to gather (together); (*personas*) to bring o get together; (*cualidades*) to combine; ~**se** *vr* (*personas: en asamblea*) to meet, gather; **reunió a sus amigos para discutirlo** he got his friends together to talk it over.

reválida [re'ßaliða] *nf* (*ESCOL*) final examination.

revalidar [reßali'ðar] *vt* (*ratificar*) to confirm, ratify.

revalorar [reßalo'rar] *vt* to revalue, reassess.

revalor(iz)ación [reßalor(iθ)a'θjon] *nf*

revaluation; (*ECON*) reassessment.
revancha [re'ßantʃa] *nf* revenge; (*DEPORTE*) return match; (*BOXEO*) return fight.
revelación [reßela'θjon] *nf* revelation.
revelado [reße'laðo] *nm* developing.
revelador, a [reßela'ðor, a] *adj* revealing.
revelar [reße'lar] *vt* to reveal; (*secreto*) to disclose; (*mostrar*) to show; (*FOTO*) to develop.
revendedor, a [reßende'ðor, a] *nm/f* retailer; (*pey*) ticket tout.
revendré [reßen'dre] *etc*, **revenga** [re'ßenga] *etc vb V* **revenirse**.
revenirse [reße'nirse] *vr* to shrink; (*comida*) to go bad *o* off; (*vino*) to sour; (*CULIN*) to get tough.
reventa [re'ßenta] *nf* resale; (*especulación*) speculation; (*de entradas*) touting.
reventar [reßen'tar] *vt* to burst, explode; (*molestar*) to annoy, rile ♦ *vi*, ~**se** *vr* (*estallar*) to burst, explode; **me revienta tener que ponérmelo** I hate having to wear it; ~ **de** (*fig*) to be bursting with; ~ **por** to be bursting to.
reventón [reßen'ton] *nm* (*AUTO*) blow-out (*BRIT*), flat (*US*).
reverberación [reßerßera'θjon] *nf* reverberation.
reverberar [reßerße'rar] *vi* (*luz*) to play, be reflected; (*superficie*) to shimmer; (*nieve*) to glare; (*sonido*) to reverberate.
reverbero [reßer'ßero] *nm* play; shimmer, shine; glare; reverberation.
reverencia [reße'renθja] *nf* reverence; (*inclinación*) bow.
reverenciar [reßeren'θjar] *vt* to revere.
reverendo, a [reße'rendo, a] *adj* reverend; (*fam*) big, awful; **un ~ imbécil** an awful idiot.
reverente [reße'rente] *adj* reverent.
reversible [reßer'sißle] *adj* reversible.
reverso [re'ßerso] *nm* back, other side; (*de moneda*) reverse.
revertir [reßer'tir] *vi* to revert; ~ **en beneficio de** to be to the advantage of; ~ **en perjuicio de** to be to the detriment of.
revés [re'ßes] *nm* back, wrong side; (*fig*) reverse, setback; (*DEPORTE*) backhand; **al ~** the wrong way round; (*de arriba abajo*) upside down; (*ropa*) inside out; **y al ~** and vice versa; **volver algo al ~** to turn sth round; (*ropa*) to turn sth inside out; **los reveses de la fortuna** the blows of fate.
revestir [reßes'tir] *vt* (*poner*) to put on; (*cubrir*) to cover, coat; (*cualidad*) to have, possess; ~**se** *vr* (*REL*) to put on one's vestments; (*ponerse*) to put on; ~ **con** *o*

de to arm o.s. with; **el acto revestía gran solemnidad** the ceremony had great dignity.
reviejo, a [re'ßjexo, a] *adj* very old, ancient.
reviene [re'ßjene] *etc vb V* **revenirse**.
reviente [re'ßjente] *etc vb V* **reventar**.
revierta [re'ßjerta] *etc vb V* **revertir**.
reviniendo [reßi'njendo] *etc vb V* **revenirse**.
revirtiendo [reßir'tjendo] *etc vb V* **revertir**.
revisar [reßi'sar] *vt* (*examinar*) to check; (*texto etc*) to revise; (*JUR*) to review.
revisión [reßi'sjon] *nf* revision; ~ **aduanera** customs inspection; ~ **de cuentas** audit.
revisor, a [reßi'sor, a] *nm/f* inspector; (*FERRO*) ticket collector; ~ **de cuentas** auditor.
revista [re'ßista] *etc vb V* **revestir** ♦ *nf* magazine, review; (*sección*) section, page; (*TEAT*) revue; (*inspección*) inspection; ~ **literaria** literary review; ~ **de libros** book reviews (page); **pasar ~ a** to review, inspect.
revivir [reßi'ßir] *vt* (*recordar*) to revive memories of ♦ *vi* to revive.
revocación [reßoka'θjon] *nf* repeal.
revocar [reßo'kar] *vt* (*decisión*) to revoke; (*ARQ*) to plaster.
revolcar [reßol'kar] *vt* to knock down, send flying; ~**se** *vr* to roll about.
revolcón [reßol'kon] *nm* tumble.
revolotear [reßolote'ar] *vi* to flutter.
revoloteo [reßolo'teo] *nm* fluttering.
revolqué [reßol'ke], **revolquemos** [reßol'kemos] *etc vb V* **revolcar**.
revoltijo [reßol'tixo] *nm* mess, jumble.
revoltoso, a [reßol'toso, a] *adj* (*travieso*) naughty, unruly.
revolución [reßolu'θjon] *nf* revolution.
revolucionar [reßoluθjo'nar] *vt* to revolutionize.
revolucionario, a [reßoluθjo'narjo, a] *adj*, *nm/f* revolutionary.
revolver [reßol'ßer] *vt* (*desordenar*) to disturb, mess up; (*agitar*) to shake; (*líquido*) to stir; (*mover*) to move about; (*POL*) to stir up ♦ *vi*: ~ **en** to go through, rummage (about) in; ~**se** *vr* (*en cama*) to toss and turn; (*METEOROLOGÍA*) to break, turn stormy; ~**se contra** to turn on *o* against; **han revuelto toda la casa** they've turned the whole house upside down.
revólver [re'ßolßer] *nm* revolver.
revoque [re'ßoke] *etc vb V* **revocar**.
revuelco [re'ßwelko] *etc vb V* **revolcar**.
revuelo [re'ßwelo] *nm* fluttering; (*fig*) commotion; **armar** *o* **levantar un gran ~**

to cause a great stir.

revuelque [reˈβwelke] *etc vb V* **revolcar**.

revuelto, a [reˈβwelto, a] *pp de* **revolver**
♦ *adj* (*mezclado*) mixed-up, in disorder;
(*mar*) rough; (*tiempo*) unsettled ♦ *nf*
(*motín*) revolt; (*agitación*) commotion;
todo estaba ~ everything was in
disorder *o* was topsy-turvy.

revuelva [reˈβwelβa] *etc vb V* **revolver**.

revulsivo [reβulˈsiβo] *nm*: **servir de** ~ to
have a salutary effect.

rey [rei] *nm* king; **los R~es** the King and
Queen; **los R~es Magos** the Magi; *see
boxed note.*

REYES MAGOS

*On the night before 6 January (Epiphany),
a holiday in Spain, children go to bed
expecting* **los Reyes Magos**, *the Three
Wise Men, to bring them presents. Twelfth
Night processions, known as "cabal-
gatas", take place that evening too; three
people dressed as* **los Reyes Magos** *arrive
in town by land or sea to the delight of the
local children.*

---

reyerta [reˈjerta] *nf* quarrel, brawl.

rezagado, a [reθaˈɣaðo, a] *adj*: **quedar** ~ to
be left behind; (*estar retrasado*) to be
late, be behind ♦ *nm/f* straggler.

rezagar [reθaˈɣar] *vt* (*dejar atrás*) to leave
behind; (*retrasar*) to delay, postpone; ~**se**
vr (*atrasarse*) to fall behind.

rezague [reˈθaɣe] *etc vb V* **rezagar**.

rezar [reˈθar] *vi* to pray; ~ **con** (*fam*) to
concern, have to do with.

rezo [ˈreθo] *nm* prayer.

rezongar [reθonˈɡar] *vi* to grumble; (*murmurar*) to mutter; (*refunfuñar*) to growl.

rezongue [reˈθonɡe] *etc vb V* **rezongar**.

rezumar [reθuˈmar] *vt* to ooze ♦ *vi* to leak;
~**se** *vr* to leak out.

RFA *nf abr* = **República Federal Alemana**.

ría [ˈria] *nf* estuary.

riachuelo [rjaˈtʃwelo] *nm* stream.

riada [riˈaða] *nf* flood.

ribera [riˈβera] *nf* (*de río*) bank; (: *área*)
riverside.

ribete [riˈβete] *nm* (*de vestido*) border; (*fig*)
addition.

ribetear [riβeteˈar] *vt* to edge, border.

rice [ˈriθe] *etc vb V* **rizar**.

ricino [riˈθino] *nm*: **aceite de** ~ castor oil.

rico, a [ˈriko, a] *adj* (*adinerado*) rich,
wealthy; (*lujoso*) luxurious; (*comida*)
delicious; (*niño*) lovely, cute ♦ *nm/f* rich
person; **nuevo** ~ nouveau riche.

rictus [ˈriktus] *nm* (*mueca*) sneer, grin; ~
de amargura bitter smile.

ridiculez [riðikuˈleθ] *nf* absurdity.

ridiculice [riðikuˈliθe] *etc vb V* **ridiculizar**.

ridiculizar [riðikuliˈθar] *vt* to ridicule.

ridículo, a [riˈðikulo, a] *adj* ridiculous;
hacer el ~ to make a fool of o.s.; **poner a
algn en** ~ to make a fool of sb; **ponerse
en** ~ to make a fool of o.s.

riego [ˈrjeɣo] *etc vb V* **regar** ♦ *nm*
(*aspersión*) watering; (*irrigación*)
irrigation.

riegue [ˈrjeɣe] *etc vb V* **regar**.

riel [rjel] *nm* rail.

rienda [ˈrjenda] *nf* rein; (*fig*) restraint,
moderating influence; **dar** ~ **suelta a** to
give free rein to; **llevar las** ~**s** to be in
charge.

riendo [ˈrjendo] *vb V* **reír**.

riesgo [ˈrjesɣo] *nm* risk; **seguro a** *o* **contra
todo** ~ comprehensive insurance; ~
para la salud health hazard; **correr el** ~
de to run the risk of.

Rif [rif] *nm* Rif(f).

rifa [ˈrifa] *nf* (*lotería*) raffle.

rifar [riˈfar] *vt* to raffle.

rifeño, a [riˈfeɲo, a] *adj* of the Rif(f),
Rif(f)ian ♦ *nm/f* Rif(f)ian, Rif(f).

rifle [ˈrifle] *nm* rifle.

rigidez [rixiˈðeθ] *nf* rigidity, stiffness; (*fig*)
strictness.

rígido, a [ˈrixiðo, a] *adj* rigid, stiff;
(*moralmente*) strict, inflexible; (*cara*)
wooden, expressionless.

rigiendo [riˈxjendo] *etc vb V* **regir**.

rigor [riˈɣor] *nm* strictness, rigour; (*dureza*)
toughness; (*inclemencia*) harshness;
(*meticulosidad*) accuracy; **el** ~ **del verano**
the hottest part of the summer; **con
todo** ~ **científico** with scientific
precision; **de** ~ de rigueur, essential;
después de los saludos de ~ after the
inevitable greetings.

riguroso, a [riɣuˈroso, a] *adj* rigorous;
(*METEOROLOGÍA*) harsh; (*severo*) severe.

rija [ˈrixa] *etc vb V* **regir** ♦ *nf* quarrel.

rima [ˈrima] *nf* rhyme; ~**s** *nfpl* verse *sg*; ~
imperfecta assonance; ~ **rimando** (*fam*)
merrily.

rimar [riˈmar] *vi* to rhyme.

rimbombante [rimbomˈbante] *adj* (*fig*)
pompous.

rímel, rímmel [ˈrimel] *nm* mascara.

rimero [riˈmero] *nm* stack, pile.

Rin [rin] *nm* Rhine.

rincón [rinˈkon] *nm* corner (*inside*).

rindiendo [rinˈdjendo] *etc vb V* **rendir**.

ring [riŋ] *nm* (*BOXEO*) ring.

rinoceronte [rinoθe'ronte] *nm* rhinoceros.

riña ['riɲa] *nf* (*disputa*) argument; (*pelea*) brawl.

riñendo [ri'ɲendo] *etc vb V* **reñir.**

riñón [ri'ɲon] *nm* kidney; **me costó un ~** (*fam*) it cost me an arm and a leg; **tener riñones** to have guts.

río ['rio] *etc vb V* **reír ♦** *nm* river; (*fig*) torrent, stream; **~ abajo/arriba** downstream/upstream; **cuando el ~ suena, agua lleva** there's no smoke without fire.

rió [ri'o] *vb V* **reír.**

Río de Janeiro ['rioðexa'neiro] *nm* Rio de Janeiro.

Río de la Plata ['rioðela'plata] *nm* Rio de la Plata, River Plate.

Rioja [ri'oxa] *nf*: **La ~** La Rioja ♦ *nm*: **r~** rioja wine.

riojano, a [rjo'xano, a] *adj, nm/f* Riojan.

rioplatense [riopla'tense] *adj* of *o* from the River Plate region ♦ *nm/f* native *o* inhabitant of the River Plate region.

riqueza [ri'keθa] *nf* wealth, riches *pl*; (*cualidad*) richness.

risa ['risa] *nf* laughter; (*una ~*) laugh; **¡qué ~!** what a laugh!; **caerse *o* morirse de ~** to split one's sides laughing, die laughing; **tomar algo a ~** to laugh sth off.

risco ['risko] *nm* crag, cliff.

risible [ri'siβle] *adj* ludicrous, laughable.

risotada [riso'taða] *nf* guffaw, loud laugh.

ristra ['ristra] *nf* string.

ristre ['ristre] *nm*: **en ~** at the ready.

risueño, a [ri'sweɲo, a] *adj* (*sonriente*) smiling; (*contento*) cheerful.

ritmo ['ritmo] *nm* rhythm; **a ~ lento** slowly; **trabajar a ~ lento** to go slow.

rito ['rito] *nm* rite.

ritual [ri'twal] *adj, nm* ritual.

rival [ri'βal] *adj, nm/f* rival.

rivalice [riβa'liθe] *etc vb V* **rivalizar.**

rivalidad [riβali'ðað] *nf* rivalry, competition.

rivalizar [riβali'θar] *vi*: **~ con** to rival, compete with.

rizado, a [ri'θaðo, a] *adj* (*pelo*) curly; (*superficie*) ridged; (*terreno*) undulating; (*mar*) choppy ♦ *nm* curls *pl*.

rizar [ri'θar] *vt* to curl; **~se** *vr* (*el pelo*) to curl; (*agua*) to ripple; (*el mar*) to become choppy.

rizo ['riθo] *nm* curl; (*agua*) ripple.

Rma. *abr* (= *Reverendísima*) *courtesy title.*

Rmo. *abr* (= *Reverendísimo*) Rt. Rev.

RNE *nf abr* = *Radio Nacional de España.*

R. O. *abr* (= *Real Orden*) royal order.

robar [ro'βar] *vt* to rob; (*objeto*) to steal; (*casa etc*) to break into; (*NAIPES*) to draw; (*atención*) to steal, capture; (*paciencia*) to exhaust.

roble ['roβle] *nm* oak.

robledal [roβle'ðal], **robledo** [ro'βleðo] *nm* oakwood.

robo ['roβo] *nm* robbery, theft; (*objeto robado*) stolen article *o* goods *pl*; **¡esto es un ~!** this is daylight robbery!

robot [ro'βo(t)], *pl* **robots** *adj, nm* robot ♦ *nm* (*tb*: **~ de cocina**) food processor.

robótica [ro'βotika] *nf* robotics *sg*.

robustecer [roβuste'θer] *vt* to strengthen.

robustezca [roβus'teθka] *etc vb V* **robustecer.**

robusto, a [ro'βusto, a] *adj* robust, strong.

ROC *abr* (*INFORM*: = *reconocimiento óptico de caracteres*) OCR.

roca ['roka] *nf* rock; **la R~** the Rock (of Gibraltar).

roce ['roθe] *etc vb V* **rozar ♦** *nm* rub, rubbing; (*caricia*) brush; (*TEC*) friction; (*en la piel*) graze; **tener ~ con** to have a brush with.

rociar [ro'θjar] *vt* to sprinkle, spray.

rocín [ro'θin] *nm* nag, hack.

rocío [ro'θio] *nm* dew.

rock [rok] *adj inv, nm* (*MUS*) rock (*cpd*).

rockero, a [ro'kero, a] *adj* rock *cpd* ♦ *nm/f* rocker.

rocoso, a [ro'koso, a] *adj* rocky.

rodado, a [ro'ðaðo, a] *adj* (*con ruedas*) wheeled ♦ *nf* rut.

rodaja [ro'ðaxa] *nf* (*raja*) slice.

rodaje [ro'ðaxe] *nm* (*CINE*) shooting, filming; (*AUTO*): **en ~** running in.

rodamiento [roða'mjento] *nm* (*AUTO*) tread.

Ródano ['roðano] *nm* Rhône.

rodar [ro'ðar] *vt* (*vehículo*) to wheel (along); (*escalera*) to roll down; (*viajar por*) to travel (over) ♦ *vi* to roll; (*coche*) to go, run; (*CINE*) to shoot, film; (*persona*) to move about (from place to place), drift; **echarlo todo a ~** (*fig*) to mess it all up.

Rodas ['roðas] *nf* Rhodes.

rodear [roðe'ar] *vt* to surround ♦ *vi* to go round; **~se** *vr*: **~se de amigos** to surround o.s. with friends.

rodeo [ro'ðeo] *nm* (*ruta indirecta*) long way round, roundabout way; (*desvío*) detour; (*evasión*) evasion; (*AM*) rodeo; **dejarse de ~s** to talk straight; **hablar sin ~s** to come to the point, speak plainly.

rodilla [ro'ðiʎa] *nf* knee; **de ~s** kneeling.

rodillo [ro'ðiʎo] *nm* roller; (*CULIN*) rolling-pin; (*en máquina de escribir, impresora*) platen.

rododendro [roðo'ðendro] *nm* rhododendron.

roedor, a [roe'ðor, a] *adj* gnawing ♦ *nm* rodent.

roer [ro'er] *vt* (*masticar*) to gnaw; (*corroer, fig*) to corrode.

rogar [ro'ɣar] *vt* (*pedir*) to beg, ask for ♦ *vi* (*suplicar*) to beg, plead; ~**se** *vr*: **se ruega no fumar** please do not smoke; ~ **que** + *subjun* to ask to ...; **ruegue a este señor que nos deje en paz** please ask this gentleman to leave us alone; **no se hace de** ~ he doesn't have to be asked twice.

rogué [ro'ɣe], **roguemos** [ro'ɣemos] *etc vb V* rogar.

rojizo, a [ro'xiθo, a] *adj* reddish.

rojo, a ['roxo, a] *adj* red ♦ *nm* red (colour); (*POL*) red; **ponerse** ~ to turn red, blush; **al** ~ **vivo** red-hot.

rol [rol] *nm* list, roll; (*esp AM: papel*) role.

rollizo, a [ro'ʎiθo, a] *adj* (*objeto*) cylindrical; (*persona*) plump.

rollo, a ['roʎo, a] *adj* (*fam*) boring, tedious ♦ *nm* roll; (*de cuerda*) coil; (*madera*) log; (*fam*) bore; (*discurso*) boring speech; **¡qué** ~**!** what a carry-on!; **la conferencia fue un** ~ the lecture was a big drag.

ROM [rom] *nf abr* (= *memoria de sólo lectura*) ROM.

Roma ['roma] *nf* Rome; **por todas partes se va a** ~ all roads lead to Rome.

romance [ro'manθe] *nm* (*LING*) Romance language; (*LIT*) ballad; **hablar en** ~ to speak plainly.

románico, a [ro'maniko, a] *adj, nm* Romanesque.

romano, a [ro'mano, a] *adj* Roman, of Rome ♦ *nm/f* Roman.

romanticismo [romanti'θismo] *nm* romanticism.

romántico, a [ro'mantiko, a] *adj* romantic.

rombo ['rombo] *nm* (*GEOM*) rhombus; (*diseño*) diamond; (*TIP*) lozenge.

romería [rome'ria] *nf* (*REL*) pilgrimage; (*excursión*) trip, outing; *see boxed note.*

ROMERÍA

Originally a pilgrimage to a shrine or church to express devotion to the Virgin Mary or a local saint, the term **romería** *has been extended to describe the rural "fiesta" which accompanies the pilgrimage. People come from all over the country to spend the day in celebration, bringing copious amounts of food and drink with them.*

---

romero, a [ro'mero, a] *nm/f* pilgrim ♦ *nm* rosemary.

romo, a ['romo, a] *adj* blunt; (*fig*) dull.

rompecabezas [rompeka'βeθas] *nm inv* riddle, puzzle; (*juego*) jigsaw (puzzle).

rompehielos [rompe'jelos] *nm inv* icebreaker.

rompeolas [rompe'olas] *nm inv* breakwater.

romper [rom'per] *vt* to break; (*hacer pedazos*) to smash; (*papel, tela etc*) to tear, rip; (*relaciones*) to break off ♦ *vi* (*olas*) to break; (*sol, diente*) to break through; ~ **un contrato** to break a contract; ~ **a** to start (suddenly) to; ~ **a llorar** to burst into tears; ~ **con algn** to fall out with sb; **ha roto con su novio** she has broken up with her fiancé.

rompimiento [rompi'mjento] *nm* (*acto*) breaking; (*fig*) break; (*quiebra*) crack; ~ **de relaciones** breaking off of relations.

ron [ron] *nm* rum.

roncar [ron'kar] *vi* (*al dormir*) to snore; (*animal*) to roar.

roncha ['rontʃa] *nf* (*cardenal*) bruise; (*hinchazón*) swelling.

ronco, a ['ronko, a] *adj* (*afónico*) hoarse; (*áspero*) raucous.

ronda ['ronda] *nf* (*de bebidas etc*) round; (*patrulla*) patrol; (*de naipes*) hand, game; **ir de** ~ to do one's round.

rondar [ron'dar] *vt* to patrol; (*a una persona*) to hang round; (*molestar*) to harass; (*a una chica*) to court ♦ *vi* to patrol; (*fig*) to prowl round; (*MUS*) to go serenading.

rondeño, a [ron'deɲo, a] *adj* of *o* from Ronda ♦ *nm/f* native *o* inhabitant of Ronda.

ronque ['ronke] *etc vb V* roncar.

ronquido [ron'kiðo] *nm* snore, snoring.

ronronear [ronrone'ar] *vi* to purr.

ronroneo [ronro'neo] *nm* purr.

roña ['roɲa] *nf* (*veterinaria*) mange; (*mugre*) dirt, grime; (*óxido*) rust.

roñica [ro'ɲika] *nm/f* (*fam*) skinflint.

roñoso, a [ro'ɲoso, a] *adj* (*mugriento*) filthy; (*tacaño*) mean.

ropa ['ropa] *nf* clothes *pl*, clothing; ~ **blanca** linen; ~ **de cama** bed linen; ~ **interior** underwear; ~ **lavada** *o* **para lavar** washing; ~ **planchada** ironing; ~ **sucia** dirty clothes *pl*, washing; ~ **usada** secondhand clothes.

ropaje [ro'paxe] *nm* gown, robes *pl*.

ropero [ro'pero] *nm* linen cupboard; (*guardarropa*) wardrobe.

rosa ['rosa] *adj inv* pink ♦ *nf* rose; (*ANAT*)

red birthmark; ~ **de los vientos** the compass; **estar como una** ~ to feel as fresh as a daisy; **(color) de** ~ pink.
rosado, a [ro'saðo, a] *adj* pink ♦ *nm* rosé.
rosal [ro'sal] *nm* rosebush.
rosaleda [rosa'leða] *nf* rose bed *o* garden.
rosario [ro'sarjo] *nm* (*REL*) rosary; (*fig: serie*) string; **rezar el** ~ to say the rosary.
rosbif [ros'ßif] *nm* roast beef.
rosca ['roska] *nf* (*de tornillo*) thread; (*de humo*) coil, spiral; (*pan, postre*) ring-shaped roll/pastry; **hacer la** ~ **a algn** (*fam*) to suck up to sb; **pasarse de** ~ (*fig*) to go too far.
Rosellón [rose'ʎon] *nm* Roussillon.
rosetón [rose'ton] *nm* rosette; (*ARQ*) rose window.
rosquilla [ros'kiʎa] *nf* small ring-shaped cake; (*de humo*) ring.
rosticería [rostise'ria] *nf* (*AM*) roast chicken shop.
rostro ['rostro] *nm* (*cara*) face; (*fig*) cheek.
rotación [rota'θjon] *nf* rotation; ~ **de cultivos** crop rotation.
rotativo, a [rota'tißo, a] *adj* rotary ♦ *nm* newspaper.
roto, a ['roto, a] *pp de* **romper** ♦ *adj* broken; (*en pedazos*) smashed; (*tela, papel*) torn; (*vida*) shattered ♦ *nm* (*en vestido*) hole, tear.
rótula ['rotula] *nf* kneecap; (*TEC*) ball-and-socket joint.
rotulador [rotula'ðor] *nm* felt-tip pen.
rotular [rotu'lar] *vt* (*carta, documento*) to head, entitle; (*objeto*) to label.
rótulo ['rotulo] *nm* (*título*) heading, title; (*etiqueta*) label; (*letrero*) sign.
rotundo, a [ro'tundo, a] *adj* round; (*enfático*) emphatic.
rotura [ro'tura] *nf* (*rompimiento*) breaking; (*MED*) fracture.
roturar [rotu'rar] *vt* to plough.
roulote [ru'lote] *nf* caravan (*BRIT*), trailer (*US*).
rozado, a [ro'θaðo, a] *adj* worn.
rozadura [roθa'ðura] *nf* abrasion, graze.
rozar [ro'θar] *vt* (*frotar*) to rub; (*ensuciar*) to dirty; (*MED*) to graze; (*tocar ligeramente*) to shave, skim; (*fig*) to touch *o* border on; ~**se** *vr* to rub (together); ~ **con** (*fam*) to rub shoulders with.
Rte. *abr* = **remite, remitente.**
RTVE *nf abr* (*TV*) = **Radiotelevisión Española.**
Ruán [ru'an] *nm* Rouen.
rubéola [ru'ßeola] *nf* German measles, rubella.
rubí [ru'ßi] *nm* ruby; (*de reloj*) jewel.
rubio, a ['rußjo, a] *adj* fair-haired, blond(e)

♦ *nm/f* blond/blonde; **tabaco** ~ Virginia tobacco; (*cerveza*) **rubia** lager.
rubor [ru'ßor] *nm* (*sonrojo*) blush; (*timidez*) bashfulness.
ruborice [rußo'riθe] *etc vb V* **ruborizarse.**
ruborizarse [rußori'θarse] *vr* to blush.
ruboroso, a [rußo'roso, a] *adj* blushing.
rúbrica ['rußrika] *nf* (*título*) title, heading; (*de la firma*) flourish; **bajo la** ~ **de** under the heading of.
rubricar [rußri'kar] *vt* (*firmar*) to sign with a flourish; (*concluir*) to sign and seal.
rubrique [ru'ßrike] *etc vb V* **rubricar.**
rudeza [ru'ðeθa] *nf* (*tosquedad*) coarseness, (*sencillez*) simplicity.
rudimentario, a [ruðimen'tarjo, a] *adj* rudimentary, basic.
rudo, a ['ruðo, a] *adj* (*sin pulir*) unpolished; (*grosero*) coarse; (*violento*) violent; (*sencillo*) simple.
rueda ['rweða] *nf* wheel; (*círculo*) ring, circle; (*rodaja*) slice, round; (*en impresora etc*) sprocket; ~ **delantera/trasera/de repuesto** front/back/spare wheel; ~ **impresora** (*INFORM*) print wheel; ~ **de prensa** press conference.
ruedo ['rweðo] *etc vb V* **rodar** ♦ *nm* (*contorno*) edge, border; (*de vestido*) hem; (*círculo*) circle; (*TAUR*) arena, bullring; (*esterilla*) (round) mat.
ruego ['rweɣo] *etc vb V* **rogar** ♦ *nm* request; **a** ~ **de** at the request of; "~**s y preguntas"** "question and answer session".
ruegue ['rweɣe] *etc vb V* **rogar.**
rufián [ru'fjan] *nm* scoundrel.
rugby ['ruɣßi] *nm* rugby.
rugido [ru'xiðo] *nm* roar.
rugir [ru'xir] *vi* to roar; (*toro*) to bellow; (*estómago*) to rumble.
rugoso, a [ru'ɣoso, a] *adj* (*arrugado*) wrinkled; (*áspero*) rough; (*desigual*) ridged.
ruibarbo [rwi'ßarßo] *nm* rhubarb.
ruido ['rwiðo] *nm* noise; (*sonido*) sound; (*alboroto*) racket, row; (*escándalo*) commotion, rumpus; ~ **de fondo** background noise; **hacer** *o* **meter** ~ to cause a stir.
ruidoso, a [rwi'ðoso, a] *adj* noisy, loud; (*fig*) sensational.
ruin [rwin] *adj* contemptible, mean.
ruina ['rwina] *nf* ruin; (*colapso*) collapse; (*de persona*) ruin, downfall; **estar hecho una** ~ to be a wreck; **la empresa le llevó a la** ~ the venture ruined him (financially).
ruindad [rwin'dað] *nf* lowness, meanness;

(*acto*) low *o* mean act.
ruinoso, a [rwi'noso, a] *adj* ruinous;
(*destartalado*) dilapidated, tumbledown;
(*COM*) disastrous.
ruiseñor [rwise'ɲor] *nm* nightingale.
ruja ['ruxa] *etc vb V* **rugir**.
ruleta [ru'leta] *nf* roulette.
rulo ['rulo] *nm* (*para el pelo*) curler.
rulot(e) [ru'lot(e)] *nf* caravan (*BRIT*), trailer
(*US*).
Rumanía [ruma'nia] *nf* Rumania.
rumano, a [ru'mano, a] *adj, nm/f* Rumanian.
rumba ['rumba] *nf* rumba.
rumbo ['rumbo] *nm* (*ruta*) route, direction;
(*ángulo de dirección*) course, bearing;
(*fig*) course of events; **con ~ a** in the
direction of; **ir con ~ a** to be heading
for; (*NAUT*) to be bound for.
rumboso, a [rum'boso, a] *adj* (*generoso*)
generous.
rumiante [ru'mjante] *nm* ruminant.
rumiar [ru'mjar] *vt* to chew; (*fig*) to chew
over ♦ *vi* to chew the cud.
rumor [ru'mor] *nm* (*ruido sordo*) low sound;
(*murmuración*) murmur, buzz.
rumorearse [rumore'arse] *vr*: **se rumorea
que** it is rumoured that.
rumoroso, a [rumo'roso, a] *adj* full of
sounds; (*arroyo*) murmuring.
runrún [run'run] *nm* (*voces*) murmur,
sound of voices; (*fig*) rumour; (*de una
máquina*) whirr.
rupestre [ru'pestre] *adj* rock *cpd*; **pintura ~**
cave painting.
ruptura [rup'tura] *nf* (*gen*) rupture;
(*disputa*) split; (*de contrato*) breach; (*de
relaciones*) breaking-off.
rural [ru'ral] *adj* rural.
Rusia ['rusja] *nf* Russia.
ruso, a ['ruso, a] *adj, nm/f* Russian ♦ *nm*
(*LING*) Russian.
rústico, a ['rustiko, a] *adj* rustic; (*ordinario*)
coarse, uncouth ♦ *nm/f* yokel ♦ *nf*: **libro en
rústica** paperback (book).
ruta ['ruta] *nf* route.
rutina [ru'tina] *nf* routine; **~ diaria** daily
routine; **por ~** as a matter of course.
rutinario, a [ruti'narjo, a] *adj* routine.

S s

S, s ['ese] *nf* S, s; **S de Sábado** S for Sugar.
S *abr* (= *san, santo, a*) St.; (= *sur*) S.
s. *abr* (= *siglo*) c.; (= *siguiente*) foll.
s/ *abr* (*COM*) = **su(s)**.
S.ª *abr* (= *Sierra*) Mts.
S.A. *abr* (= *Sociedad Anónima*) Ltd., Inc.
(*US*); (= *Su Alteza*) H.H.
sáb. *abr* (= *sábado*) Sat.
sábado ['saβaðo] *nm* Saturday; (*de los
judíos*) Sabbath; **del ~ en ocho días** a
week on Saturday; **un ~ sí y otro no,
cada dos ~s** every other Saturday; **S~
Santo** Holy Saturday; *V tb* **Semana
Santa**.
sabana [sa'βana] *nf* savannah.
sábana ['saβana] *nf* sheet; **se le pegan las
~s** he can't get up in the morning.
sabandija [saβan'dixa] *nf* (*bicho*) bug; (*fig*)
louse.
sabañón [saβa'ɲon] *nm* chilblain.
sabático, a [sa'βatiko, a] *adj* (*REL, UNIV*)
sabbatical.
sabelotodo [saβelo'toðo] *nm/f inv* know-all.
saber [sa'βer] *vt* to know; (*llegar a conocer*)
to find out, learn; (*tener capacidad de*) to
know how to ♦ *vi*: **~ a** to taste of, taste
like ♦ *nm* knowledge, learning; **~se** *vr*: **se
sabe que ...** it is known that ...; **no se
sabe** nobody knows; **a ~** namely; **¿sabes
conducir/nadar?** can you drive/swim?;
¿sabes francés? do you *o* can you speak
French?; **~ de memoria** to know by
heart; **lo sé** I know; **hacer ~** to inform,
let know; **que yo sepa** as far as I know;
vete *o* anda a ~ your guess is as good as
mine, who knows!; **¿sabe?** (*fam*) you
know (what I mean)?; **le sabe mal que
otro la saque a bailar** it upsets him that
anybody else should ask her to dance.
sabido, a [sa'βiðo, a] *adj* (*consabido*) well-
known; **como es ~** as we all know.
sabiduría [saβiðu'ria] *nf* (*conocimientos*)
wisdom; (*instrucción*) learning; **~ popular**
folklore.
sabiendas [sa'βjendas]: **a ~** *adv*
knowingly; **a ~ de que ...** knowing full
well that ....
sabihondo, a [sa'βjondo, a] *adj, nm/f*

know-all, know-it-all (US).
sabio, a ['saβjo,a] adj (docto) learned;
(prudente) wise, sensible.
sablazo [sa'βlaθo] nm (herida) sword
wound; (fam) sponging; **dar un ~ a algn**
to tap sb for money.
sable [sa'βle] nm sabre.
sabor [sa'βor] nm taste, flavour; (fig)
flavour; **sin ~** flavourless.
saborear [saβore'ar] vt to taste, savour;
(fig) to relish.
sabotaje [saβo'taxe] nm sabotage.
saboteador, a [saβotea'ðor, a] nm/f
saboteur.
sabotear [saβote'ar] vt to sabotage.
Saboya [sa'βoja] nf Savoy.
sabré [sa'βre] etc vb V **saber**.
sabroso, a [sa'βroso, a] adj tasty; (fig fam)
racy, salty.
saca ['saka] nf big sack; **~ de correo(s)**
mailbag; (COM) withdrawal.
sacacorchos [saka'kortʃos] nm inv
corkscrew.
sacapuntas [saka'puntas] nm inv pencil
sharpener.
sacar [sa'kar] vt to take out; (fig: extraer) to
get (out); (quitar) to remove, get out;
(hacer salir) to bring out; (fondos: de
cuenta) to draw out, withdraw; (obtener:
legado etc) to get; (demostrar) to show;
(conclusión) to draw; (novela etc) to
publish, bring out; (ropa) to take off;
(obra) to make; (premio) to receive;
(entradas) to get; (TENIS) to serve;
(FÚTBOL) to put into play; **~ adelante**
(niño) to bring up; **~ a algn a bailar** to
dance with sb; **~ a algn de sí** to infuriate
sb; **~ una foto** to take a photo; **~ la
lengua** to stick out one's tongue; **~
buenas/malas notas** to get good/bad
marks.
sacarina [saka'rina] nf saccharin(e).
sacerdote [saθer'ðote] nm priest.
saciar [sa'θjar] vt (hartar) to satiate; (fig) to
satisfy; **~se** vr (fig) to be satisfied.
saciedad [saθje'ðað] nf satiety; **hasta la ~**
(comer) one's fill; (repetir) ad nauseam.
saco ['sako] nm bag; (grande) sack; (su
contenido) bagful; (AM: chaqueta) jacket;
~ de dormir sleeping bag.
sacramento [sakra'mento] nm sacrament.
sacrificar [sakrifi'kar] vt to sacrifice;
(animal) to slaughter; (perro etc) to put to
sleep; **~se** vr to sacrifice o.s.
sacrificio [sakri'fiθjo] nm sacrifice.
sacrifique [sakri'fike] etc vb V **sacrificar**.
sacrilegio [sakri'lexjo] nm sacrilege.
sacrílego, a [sa'krileɣo, a] adj sacrilegious.

sacristán [sakris'tan] nm verger.
sacristía [sakris'tia] nf sacristy.
sacro, a ['sakro, a] adj sacred.
sacudida [saku'ðiða] nf (agitación) shake,
shaking; (sacudimiento) jolt, bump; (fig)
violent change; (POL etc) upheaval; **~
eléctrica** electric shock.
sacudir [saku'ðir] vt to shake; (golpear) to
hit; (ala) to flap; (alfombra) to beat; **~ a
algn** (fam) to belt sb.
sádico, a ['saðiko, a] adj sadistic ♦ nm/f
sadist.
sadismo [sa'ðismo] nm sadism.
sadomasoquismo [saðomaso'kismo] nm
sadomasochism, S & M.
sadomasoquista [saðomaso'kista] adj
sadomasochistic ♦ nm/f sadomasochist.
saeta [sa'eta] nf (flecha) arrow; (MUS)
sacred song in flamenco style.
safari [sa'fari] nm safari.
sagacidad [saɣaθi'ðað] nf shrewdness,
cleverness.
sagaz [sa'ɣaθ] adj shrewd, clever.
Sagitario [saxi'tarjo] nm (ASTRO)
Sagittarius.
sagrado, a [sa'ɣraðo, a] adj sacred, holy.
Sáhara ['saara] nm: **el ~** the Sahara
(desert).
saharaui [saxa'rawi] adj Saharan ♦ nm/f
native o inhabitant of the Sahara.
sajón, ona [sa'xon, 'xona] adj, nm/f Saxon.
Sajonia [sa'xonja] nf Saxony.
sal [sal] vb ver **salir** ♦ nf salt; (gracia) wit;
(encanto) charm; **~es de baño** bath salts;
~ gorda o **de cocina** kitchen o cooking
salt.
sala ['sala] nf (cuarto grande) large room;
(~ de estar) living room; (TEAT) house,
auditorium; (de hospital) ward; **~ de
apelación** court; **~ de conferencias**
lecture hall; **~ de espera** waiting room;
~ de embarque departure lounge; **~ de
estar** living room; **~ de fiestas** function
room; **~ de juntas** (COM) boardroom.
salado, a [sa'laðo, a] adj salty; (fig) witty,
amusing; **agua salada** salt water.
salar [sa'lar] vt to salt, add salt to.
salarial [sala'rjal] adj (aumento, revisión)
wage cpd, salary cpd, pay cpd.
salario [sa'larjo] nm wage, pay.
salchicha [sal'tʃitʃa] nf (pork) sausage.
salchichón [saltʃi'tʃon] nm (salami-type)
sausage.
saldar [sal'dar] vt to pay; (vender) to sell
off; (fig) to settle, resolve.
saldo ['saldo] nm (pago) settlement; (de
una cuenta) balance; (lo restante)
remnant(s) (pl), remainder; (liquidación)

sale; (*COM*): ~ **anterior** balance brought forward; ~ **acreedor/deudor** *o* **pasivo** credit/debit balance; ~ **final** final balance.

saldré [sal'dre] *etc vb V* **salir**.

salero [sa'lero] *nm* salt cellar; (*ingenio*) wit; (*encanto*) charm.

salga ['salɣa] *etc vb V* **salir**.

salida [sa'liða] *nf* (*puerta etc*) exit, way out; (*acto*) leaving, going out; (*de tren, AVIAT*) departure; (*COM, TEC*) output, production; (*fig*) way out; (*resultado*) outcome; (*COM: oportunidad*) opening; (*GEO, válvula*) outlet; (*de gas*) escape; (*ocurrencia*) joke; **calle sin** ~ cul-de-sac; **a la** ~ **del teatro** after the theatre; **dar la** ~ (*DEPORTE*) to give the starting signal; ~ **de incendios** fire escape; ~ **impresa** (*INFORM*) hard copy; **no hay** ~ there's no way out of it; **no tenemos otra** ~ we have no option; **tener** ~**s** to be witty.

salido, a [sa'liðo, a] *adj* (*fam*) randy.

saliente [sa'ljente] *adj* (*ARQ*) projecting; (*sol*) rising; (*fig*) outstanding.

salina [sa'lina] *nf* salt mine; ~**s** *nfpl* saltworks *sg*.

════════════ *PALABRA CLAVE*

salir [sa'lir] *vi* **1** (*persona*) to come *o* go out; (*tren, avión*) to leave; **Juan ha salido** Juan has gone out; **salió de la cocina** he came out of the kitchen; **salimos de Madrid a las 8** we left Madrid at 8 (o'clock); **salió corriendo (del cuarto)** he ran out (of the room); ~ **de un apuro** to get out of a jam
2 (*pelo*) to grow; (*diente*) to come through; (*disco, libro*) to come out; (*planta, número de lotería*) to come up; ~ **a la superficie** to come to the surface; **anoche salió en la tele** she appeared *o* was on TV last night; **salió en todos los periódicos** it was in all the papers; **le salió un trabajo** he got a job
3 (*resultar*): **la muchacha nos salió muy trabajadora** the girl turned out to be a very hard worker; **la comida te ha salido exquisita** the food was delicious; **sale muy caro** it's very expensive; **la entrevista que hice me salió bien/mal** the interview I did turned out *o* went well/badly; **nos salió a 30 euros cada uno** it worked out at 30 euros each; **no salen las cuentas** it doesn't work out *o* add up; ~ **ganando** to come out on top; ~ **perdiendo** to lose out
4 (*DEPORTE*) to start; (*NAIPES*) to lead
5: ~ **con algn** to go out with sb
6: ~ **adelante: no sé como haré para** ~ **adelante** I don't know how I'll get by
♦ ~**se** *vr* **1** (*líquido*) to spill; (*animal*) to escape
2 (*desviarse*): ~**se de la carretera** to leave *o* go off the road; ~**se de lo normal** to be unusual; ~**se del tema** to get off the point
3: ~**se con la suya** to get one's own way

saliva [sa'liβa] *nf* saliva.

salivadera [saliβa'ðera] *nf* (*AM*) spittoon.

salmantino, a [salman'tino, a] *adj* of *o* from Salamanca ♦ *nm/f* native *o* inhabitant of Salamanca.

salmo ['salmo] *nm* psalm.

salmón [sal'mon] *nm* salmon.

salmonete [salmo'nete] *nm* red mullet.

salmuera [sal'mwera] *nf* pickle, brine.

salón [sa'lon] *nm* (*de casa*) living-room, lounge; (*muebles*) lounge suite; ~ **de belleza** beauty parlour; ~ **de baile** dance hall; ~ **de sesiones** assembly hall.

salpicadero [salpika'ðero] *nm* (*AUTO*) dashboard.

salpicar [salpi'kar] *vt* (*de barro, pintura*) to splash; (*rociar*) to sprinkle, spatter; (*esparcir*) to scatter.

salpicón [salpi'kon] *nm* (*acto*) splashing; (*CULIN*) meat *o* fish salad.

salpimentar [salpimen'tar] *vt* (*CULIN*) to season.

salpique [sal'pike] *etc vb V* **salpicar**.

salsa ['salsa] *nf* sauce; (*con carne asada*) gravy; (*fig*) spice; ~ **mayonesa** mayonnaise; **estar en su** ~ (*fam*) to be in one's element.

saltamontes [salta'montes] *nm inv* grasshopper.

saltar [sal'tar] *vt* to jump (over), leap (over); (*dejar de lado*) to skip, miss out ♦ *vi* to jump, leap; (*pelota*) to bounce; (*al aire*) to fly up; (*quebrarse*) to break; (*al agua*) to dive; (*fig*) to explode, blow up; (*botón*) to come off; (*corcho*) to pop out; ~**se** *vr* (*omitir*) to skip, miss; **salta a la vista** it's obvious; ~**se todas las reglas** to break all the rules.

salteado, a [salte'aðo, a] *adj* (*CULIN*) sauté(ed).

salteador [saltea'ðor] *nm* (*tb*: ~ **de caminos**) highwayman.

saltear [salte'ar] *vt* (*robar*) to rob (in a holdup); (*asaltar*) to assault, attack; (*CULIN*) to sauté.

saltimbanqui [saltim'banki] *nm/f* acrobat.

salto ['salto] *nm* jump, leap; (*al agua*) dive; **a** ~**s** by jumping; ~ **de agua** waterfall; ~ **de altura** high jump; ~ **de cama**

negligee; ~ **mortal** somersault; (*INFORM*):
~ **de línea** line feed; ~ **de línea automático**
wordwrap; ~ **de página** formfeed.
saltón, ona [sal'ton, ona] *adj* (*ojos*)
bulging, popping; (*dientes*) protruding.
salubre [sa'luβre] *adj* healthy, salubrious.
salud [sa'luð] *nf* health; **estar bien/mal de**
~ to be in good/poor health; **¡(a su) ~!**
cheers!, good health!; **beber a la ~ de** to
drink (to) the health of.
saludable [salu'ðaβle] *adj* (*de buena salud*)
healthy; (*provechoso*) good, beneficial.
saludar [salu'ðar] *vt* to greet; (*MIL*) to
salute; **ir a ~ a algn** to drop in to see sb;
salude de mi parte a X give my regards
to X; **le saluda atentamente** (*en carta*)
yours faithfully.
saludo [sa'luðo] *nm* greeting; ~**s** (*en carta*)
best wishes, regards; **un ~ afectuoso o**
cordial yours sincerely.
salva ['salβa] *nf* (*MIL*) salvo; **una ~ de**
aplausos thunderous applause.
salvación [salβa'θjon] *nf* salvation;
(*rescate*) rescue.
salvado [sal'βaðo] *nm* bran.
salvador [salβa'ðor] *nm* rescuer, saviour;
el S~ the Saviour; **El S~** El Salvador;
San S~ San Salvador.
salvadoreño, a [salβaðo'reɲo, a] *adj, nm/f*
Salvadoran, Salvadorian.
salvaguardar [salβaɣwar'ðar] *vt* to
safeguard; (*INFORM*) to back up, make a
backup copy of.
salvajada [salβa'xaða] *nf* savage deed,
atrocity.
salvaje [sal'βaxe] *adj* wild; (*tribu*) savage.
salvajismo [salβa'xismo] *nm* savagery.
salvamento [salβa'mento] *nm* (*acción*)
rescue; (*de naufragio*) salvage; ~ **y**
socorrismo life-saving.
salvapantallas [salβapan'taʎas] *nm inv*
screen saver.
salvar [sal'βar] *vt* (*rescatar*) to save, rescue;
(*resolver*) to overcome, resolve; (*cubrir*
distancias) to cover, travel; (*hacer excep-*
ción) to except, exclude; (*un barco*) to salvage; ~**se** *vr* to save o.s., escape; **¡sálvese**
el que pueda! every man for himself!
salvavidas [salβa'βiðas] *adj inv*: **bote/**
chaleco/cinturón ~ lifeboat/lifejacket/
lifebelt.
salvedad [salβe'ðað] *nf* reservation,
qualification; **con la ~ de que ...** with the
proviso that ....
salvia ['salβja] *nf* sage.
salvo, a ['salβo, a] *adj* safe ♦ *prep* except
(for), save; ~ **error u omisión** (*COM*)
errors and omissions excepted; **a ~ out**

of danger; ~ **que** unless.
salvoconducto [salβokon'dukto] *nm* safe-
conduct.
samba ['samba] *nf* samba.
san [san] *nm* (*apócope de* **santo**) saint; ~
Juan St. John; *V tb* **Juan.**
sanar [sa'nar] *vt* (*herida*) to heal; (*persona*)
to cure ♦ *vi* (*persona*) to get well,
recover; (*herida*) to heal.
sanatorio [sana'torjo] *nm* sanatorium.
sanción [san'θjon] *nf* sanction.
sancionar [sanθjo'nar] *vt* to sanction.
sancocho [san'kotʃo] *nm* (*AM*) stew.
sandalia [san'dalja] *nf* sandal.
sándalo ['sandalo] *nm* sandal(wood).
sandez [san'deθ] *nf* (*cualidad*) foolishness;
(*acción*) stupid thing; **decir sandeces** to
talk nonsense.
sandía [san'dia] *nf* watermelon.
sandinista [sandi'nista] *adj, nm/f*
Sandinist(a).
sandwich ['sandwitʃ], *pl* **sandwichs** *o*
sandwiches *nm* sandwich.
saneamiento [sanea'mjento] *nm* sanitation.
sanear [sane'ar] *vt* to drain; (*indemnizar*) to
compensate; (*ECON*) to reorganize.
sanfermines [sanfer'mines] *nmpl see boxed*
note.

SANFERMINES

The **sanfermines** *are week-long "fiestas"*
which take place in Pamplona, the capital
of Navarre. They were made famous by
the American writer Ernest Hemingway.
From 7 July, the feast of San Fermín,
onwards, crowds of mainly young people
take to the streets, drinking, singing and
dancing. Early in the morning bulls are
released along the narrow streets which
lead to the bullring, and people risk
serious injury by running in front of them,
a custom which is also typical of many
Spanish villages.

---

sangrar [san'grar] *vt, vi* to bleed; (*texto*) to
indent.
sangre ['sangre] *nf* blood; ~ **fría** sangfroid;
a ~ fría in cold blood.
sangría [san'gria] *nf* (*MED*) bleeding;
(*CULIN*) sangria, sweetened drink of red
wine with fruit, ≈ fruit cup.
sangriento, a [san'grjento, a] *adj* bloody.
sanguijuela [sangi'xwela] *nf* (*ZOOL*, *fig*)
leech.
sanguinario, a [sangi'narjo, a] *adj*
bloodthirsty.
sanguíneo, a [san'gineo, a] *adj* blood *cpd.*

sanidad [sani'ðað] *nf* sanitation; (*calidad de sano*) health, healthiness; ~ **pública** public health (department).

sanitario, a [sani'tarjo, a] *adj* sanitary; (*de la salud*) health *cpd* ♦ *nm*: ~**s** *nmpl* toilets (*BRIT*), restroom *sg* (*US*).

San Marino [sanma'rino] *nm*: **(La República de)** ~ San Marino.

sano, a ['sano, a] *adj* healthy; (*sin daños*) sound; (*comida*) wholesome; (*entero*) whole, intact; ~ **y salvo** safe and sound.

santanderino, a [santande'rino, a] *adj* of o from Santander ♦ *nm/f* native o inhabitant of Santander.

Santiago [san'tjaɣo] *nm*: ~ **(de Chile)** Santiago.

santiamén [santja'men] *nm*: **en un** ~ in no time at all.

santidad [santi'ðað] *nf* holiness, sanctity.

santificar [santifi'kar] *vt* to sanctify.

santifique [santi'fike] *etc vb V* **santificar**.

santiguarse [santi'ɣwarse] *vr* to make the sign of the cross.

santigüe [san'tiɣwe] *etc vb V* **santiguarse**.

santo, a ['santo, a] *adj* holy; (*fig*) wonderful, miraculous ♦ *nm/f* saint ♦ *nm* saint's day; **hacer su santa voluntad** to do as one jolly well pleases; **¿a** ~ **de qué ...?** why on earth ...?; **se le fue el** ~ **al cielo** he forgot what he was about to say; ~ **y seña** password; *see boxed note.*

SANTO

As well as having a birthday, Spaniards have traditionally celebrated **el santo**, *their saint's day, when the saint they were called after — San Pedro or la Virgen de los Dolores, for example — is honoured in the Christian calendar. The custom is gradually dying out.*

---

santuario [san'twarjo] *nm* sanctuary, shrine.

saña ['saɲa] *nf* rage, fury.

sapo ['sapo] *nm* toad.

saque ['sake] *etc vb V* **sacar** ♦ *nm* (*TENIS*) service, serve; (*FÚTBOL*) throw-in; ~ **inicial** kick-off; ~ **de esquina** corner (kick); **tener buen** ~ to eat heartily.

saquear [sake'ar] *vt* (*MIL*) to sack; (*robar*) to loot, plunder; (*fig*) to ransack.

saqueo [sa'keo] *nm* sacking; looting, plundering; ransacking.

S.A.R. *abr* (= *Su Alteza Real*) HRH.

sarampión [saram'pjon] *nm* measles *sg.*

sarape [sa'rape] *nm* (*AM*) blanket.

sarcasmo [sar'kasmo] *nm* sarcasm.

sarcástico, a [sar'kastiko, a] *adj* sarcastic.

sarcófago [sar'kofaɣo] *nm* sarcophagus.

sardina [sar'ðina] *nf* sardine.

sardo, a ['sarðo, a] *adj*, *nm/f* Sardinian.

sardónico, a [sar'ðoniko, a] *adj* sardonic; (*irónico*) ironical, sarcastic.

sargento [sar'xento] *nm* sergeant.

sarmiento [sar'mjento] *nm* vine shoot.

sarna ['sarna] *nf* itch; (*MED*) scabies.

sarpullido [sarpu'ʎiðo] *nm* (*MED*) rash.

sarro ['sarro] *nm* deposit; (*en dientes*) tartar.

sarta ['sarta] *nf* (*fig*): **una** ~ **de mentiras** a pack of lies.

sartén [sar'ten] *nf* frying pan; **tener la** ~ **por el mango** to rule the roost.

sastre ['sastre] *nm* tailor.

sastrería [sastre'ria] *nf* (*arte*) tailoring; (*tienda*) tailor's (shop).

Satanás [sata'nas] *nm* Satan.

satélite [sa'telite] *nm* satellite.

satinado, a [sati'naðo, a] *adj* glossy ♦ *nm* gloss, shine.

sátira ['satira] *nf* satire.

satírico, a [sa'tiriko, a] *adj* satiric(al).

sátiro ['satiro] *nm* (*MITOLOGÍA*) satyr; (*fig*) sex maniac.

satisfacción [satisfak'θjon] *nf* satisfaction.

satisfacer [satisfa'θer] *vt* to satisfy; (*gastos*) to meet; (*deuda*) to pay; (*COM: letra de cambio*) to honour (*BRIT*), honor (*US*); (*pérdida*) to make good; ~**se** *vr* to satisfy o.s., be satisfied; (*vengarse*) to take revenge.

satisfaga [satis'faɣa] *etc*, **satisfaré** [satisfa're] *etc vb V* **satisfacer**.

satisfecho, a [satis'fetʃo, a] *pp de* **satisfacer** ♦ *adj* satisfied; (*contento*) content(ed), happy; (*tb*: ~ **de sí mismo**) self-satisfied, smug.

satisfice [satis'fiθe] *etc vb V* **satisfacer**.

saturación [satura'θjon] *nf* saturation; **llegar a la** ~ to reach saturation point.

saturar [satu'rar] *vt* to saturate; ~**se** *vr* (*mercado, aeropuerto*) to reach saturation point; **¡estoy saturado de tanta televisión!** I can't take any more television!

sauce ['sauθe] *nm* willow; ~ **llorón** weeping willow.

saúco [sa'uko] *nm* (*BOT*) elder.

saudí [sau'ði] *adj*, *nm/f* Saudi.

sauna ['sauna] *nf* sauna.

savia ['saβja] *nf* sap.

saxo ['sakso] *nm* sax.

saxofón [sakso'fon] *nm* saxophone.

saya ['saja] *nf* (*falda*) skirt; (*enagua*) petticoat.

sayo ['sajo] *nm* smock.

sazón [sa'θon] *nf* (*de fruta*) ripeness; **a la ~** then, at that time.

sazonado, a [saθo'naðo, a] *adj* (*fruta*) ripe; (*CULIN*) flavoured, seasoned.

sazonar [saθo'nar] *vt* to ripen; (*CULIN*) to flavour, season.

s/c *abr* (*COM*: = *su casa*) your firm; (: = *su cuenta*) your account.

Sdo. *abr* (*COM*: = *Saldo*) bal.

SE *abr* (= *sudeste*) SE.

===================== *PALABRA CLAVE*

se [se] *pron* **1** (*reflexivo*: *sg*: *m*) himself; (: *f*) herself; (: *pl*) themselves; (: *cosa*) itself; (: *de Vd*) yourself; (: *de Vds*) yourselves; (*indefinido*) oneself; **~ mira en el espejo** he looks at himself in the mirror; **¡siénte~!** sit down!; **~ durmió** he fell asleep; **~ está preparando** she's getting (herself) ready; *para usos léxicos del pron ver el vb en cuestión, p.ej.* **arrepentirse**

2 (*como complemento indirecto*) to him; to her; to them; to it; to you; **~ lo dije ayer** (*a Vd*) I told you yesterday; **~ compró un sombrero** he bought himself a hat; **~ rompió la pierna** he broke his leg; **cortar~ el pelo** to get one's hair cut; (*uno mismo*) to cut one's hair; **~ comió un pastel** he ate a cake

3 (*uso recíproco*) each other, one another; **~ miraron (el uno al otro)** they looked at each other *o* one another

4 (*en oraciones pasivas*): **se han vendido muchos libros** a lot of books have been sold; **"~ vende coche"** "car for sale"

5 (*impers*): **~ dice que** people say that, it is said that; **allí ~ come muy bien** the food there is very good, you can eat very well there.

sé [se] *vb V* **saber, ser.**

sea ['sea] *etc vb V* **ser.**

SEAT ['seat] *nf abr = Sociedad Española de Automóviles de Turismo.*

sebo ['seβo] *nm* fat, grease.

Sec. *abr* (= *Secretario*) Sec.

seca ['seka] *nf V* **seco.**

secado [se'kaðo] *nm* drying; **~ a mano** blow-dry.

secador [seka'ðor] *nm*: **~ para el pelo** hairdryer.

secadora [seka'ðora] *nf* tumble dryer; **~ centrífuga** spin-dryer.

secano [se'kano] *nm* (*AGR*: *tb*: **tierra de ~**) dry land *o* region; **cultivo de ~** dry farming.

secante [se'kante] *adj* (*viento*) drying ♦ *nm*

blotting paper.

secar [se'kar] *vt* to dry; (*superficie*) to wipe dry; (*frente, suelo*) to mop; (*líquido*) to mop up; (*tinta*) to blot; **~se** *vr* to dry (off); (*río, planta*) to dry up.

sección [sek'θjon] *nf* section; (*COM*) department; **~ deportiva** (*en periódico*) sports page(s).

seco, a ['seko, a] *adj* dry; (*fruta*) dried; (*persona: magro*) thin, skinny; (*carácter*) cold; (*antipático*) disagreeable; (*respuesta*) sharp, curt ♦ *nf* dry season; **habrá pan a secas** there will be just bread; **decir algo a secas** to say sth curtly; **parar en ~** to stop dead.

secreción [sekre'θjon] *nf* secretion.

secretaría [sekreta'ria] *nf* secretariat; (*oficina*) secretary's office.

secretariado [sekreta'rjaðo] *nm* (*oficina*) secretariat; (*cargo*) secretaryship; (*curso*) secretarial course.

secretario, a [sekre'tarjo, a] *nm/f* secretary; **~ adjunto** (*COM*) assistant secretary.

secreto, a [se'kreto, a] *adj* secret; (*información*) confidential; (*persona*) secretive ♦ *nm* secret; (*calidad*) secrecy.

secta ['sekta] *nf* sect.

sectario, a [sek'tarjo, a] *adj* sectarian.

sector [sek'tor] *nm* sector (*tb INFORM*); (*de opinión*) section; (*fig: campo*) area, field; **~ privado/público** (*COM, ECON*) private/ public sector.

secuela [se'kwela] *nf* consequence.

secuencia [se'kwenθja] *nf* sequence.

secuestrar [sekwes'trar] *vt* to kidnap; (*avión*) to hijack; (*bienes*) to seize, confiscate.

secuestro [se'kwestro] *nm* kidnapping; hijack; seizure, confiscation.

secular [seku'lar] *adj* secular.

secundar [sekun'dar] *vt* to second, support.

secundario, a [sekun'darjo, a] *adj* secondary; (*carretera*) side *cpd*; (*INFORM*) background *cpd* ♦ *nf* secondary education; *V tb* **sistema educativo.**

sed [seð] *nf* thirst; (*fig*) thirst, craving; **tener ~** to be thirsty.

seda ['seða] *nf* silk; **~ dental** dental floss.

sedal [se'ðal] *nm* fishing line.

sedante [se'ðante] *nm* sedative.

sede ['seðe] *nf* (*de gobierno*) seat; (*de compañía*) headquarters *pl*, head office; **Santa S~** Holy See.

sedentario, a [seðen'tarjo, a] *adj* sedentary.

SEDIC [se'ðik] *nf abr = Sociedad Española de*

Documentación e Información Científica.
sedición [seði'θjon] *nf* sedition.
sediento, a [se'ðjento, a] *adj* thirsty.
sedimentar [seðimen'tar] *vt* to deposit;
~**se** *vr* to settle.
sedimento [seði'mento] *nm* sediment.
sedoso, a [se'ðoso, a] *adj* silky, silken.
seducción [seðuk'θjon] *nf* seduction.
seducir [seðu'θir] *vt* to seduce; (*sobornar*)
to bribe; (*cautivar*) to charm, fascinate;
(*atraer*) to attract.
seductor, a [seðuk'tor, a] *adj* seductive;
charming, fascinating; attractive;
(*engañoso*) deceptive, misleading ♦ *nm/f*
seducer.
seduje [se'ðuxe] *etc*, **seduzca** [se'ðuθka]
etc vb V **seducir**.
sefardí [sefar'ði], **sefardita** [sefar'ðita] *adj*
Sephardi(c) ♦ *nm/f* Sephardi.
segador, a [seɣa'ðor, a] *nm/f* (*persona*)
harvester ♦ *nf* (*TEC*) mower, reaper.
segadora-trilladora [seɣa'ðoratriʎa'ðora]
nf combine harvester.
segar [se'ɣar] *vt* (*mies*) to reap, cut;
(*hierba*) to mow, cut; (*esperanzas*) to
ruin.
seglar [se'ɣlar] *adj* secular, lay.
segoviano, a [seɣo'ßjano, a] *adj* of *o* from
Segovia ♦ *nm/f* native *o* inhabitant of
Segovia.
segregación [seɣreɣa'θjon] *nf*
segregation; ~ **racial** racial segregation.
segregar [seɣre'ɣar] *vt* to segregate,
separate.
segregue [se'ɣreɣe] *etc vb V* **segregar**.
segué [se'ɣe], **seguemos** [se'ɣemos] *etc*
vb V **segar**.
seguidamente [seɣiða'mente] *adv* (*sin*
parar) without a break; (*inmediatamente*
después) immediately after.
seguido, a [se'ɣiðo, a] *adj* (*continuo*)
continuous, unbroken; (*recto*) straight
♦ *adv* (*directo*) straight (on); (*después*)
after; (*AM: a menudo*) often ♦ *nf:* **en**
seguida at once, right away; **5 días** ~**s** 5
days running, 5 days in a row; **en**
seguida termino I've nearly finished, I
shan't be long now.
seguimiento [seɣi'mjento] *nm* chase,
pursuit; (*continuación*) continuation.
seguir [se'ɣir] *vt* to follow; (*venir después*)
to follow on, come after; (*proseguir*) to
continue; (*perseguir*) to chase, pursue;
(*indicio*) to follow up; (*mujer*) to court ♦ *vi*
(*gen*) to follow; (*continuar*) to continue,
carry *o* go on; ~**se** *vr* to follow; **a** ~ to be
continued; **sigo sin comprender** I still
don't understand; **sigue lloviendo** it's

still raining; **sigue** (*en carta*) P.T.O.; (*en*
libro, TV) continued; "**hágase** ~" "please
forward"; ¡**siga!** (*AM: pase*) come in!
según [se'ɣun] *prep* according to ♦ *adv:* ~ (**y**
conforme) it all depends ♦ *conj* as; ~ **esté**
el tiempo depending on the weather; ~
me consta as far as I know; **está** ~ **lo**
dejaste it is just as you left it.
segundo, a [se'ɣundo, a] *adj* second; (*en*
discurso) secondly ♦ *nm* (*gen, medida de*
tiempo) second; (*piso*) second floor ♦ *nf*
(*sentido*) second meaning; ~ (**de a bordo**)
(*NAUT*) first mate; **segunda** (**clase**)
(*FERRO*) second class; **segunda** (**marcha**)
(*AUTO*) second (gear); **de segunda mano**
second hand.
seguramente [seɣura'mente] *adv* surely;
(*con certeza*) for sure, with certainty;
(*probablemente*) probably; ¿**lo va a**
comprar? — ~ is he going to buy it? — I
should think so.
seguridad [seɣuri'ðað] *nf* safety; (*del*
estado, de casa etc) security;
(*certidumbre*) certainty; (*confianza*)
confidence; (*estabilidad*) stability; ~
social social security; ~ **contra**
incendios fire precautions *pl*; ~ **en sí**
mismo (self-) confidence.
seguro, a [se'ɣuro, a] *adj* (*cierto*) sure,
certain; (*fiel*) trustworthy; (*libre de*
peligro) safe; (*bien defendido, firme*)
secure; (*datos etc*) reliable; (*fecha*) firm
♦ *adv* for sure, certainly ♦ *nm* (*dispositivo*)
safety device; (*de cerradura*) tumbler; (*de*
arma) safety catch; (*COM*) insurance; ~
contra accidentes/incendios fire/-
accident insurance; ~ **contra terceros/a**
todo riesgo third party/comprehensive
insurance; ~ **dotal con beneficios** with-
profits endowment assurance; **S**~ **de**
Enfermedad ≈ National Insurance; ~ **de**
marítimo marine insurance; ~ **mixto**
endowment assurance; ~ **temporal** term
insurance; ~ **de vida** life insurance.
seis [seis] *num* six; ~ **mil** six thousand;
tiene ~ **años** she is six (years old); **unos**
~ about six; **hoy es el** ~ today is the
sixth.
seiscientos, as [seis'θjentos, as] *num* six
hundred.
seísmo [se'ismo] *nm* tremor, earthquake.
selección [selek'θjon] *nf* selection; ~
múltiple multiple choice; ~ **nacional**
(*DEPORTE*) national team.
seleccionador, a [selekθjona'ðor, a] *nm/f*
(*DEPORTE*) selector.
seleccionar [selekθjo'nar] *vt* to pick,
choose, select.

selectividad [selektiβi'ðað] *nf* (*UNIV*) entrance examination; *see boxed note*.

SELECTIVIDAD

School-leavers wishing to go on to university sit the dreaded entrance examination, the **selectividad***, in June, with resits in September. When student numbers are too high for a particular course, only the best candidates get through. The others must wait a year to sit the examination again.*

---

selecto, a [se'lekto, a] *adj* select, choice; (*escogido*) selected.

sellado, a [se'ʎaðo, a] *adj* (*documento oficial*) sealed; (*pasaporte*) stamped.

sellar [se'ʎar] *vt* (*documento oficial*) to seal; (*pasaporte, visado*) to stamp; (*marcar*) to brand; (*pacto, labios*) to seal.

sello ['seʎo] *nm* stamp; (*precinto*) seal; (*fig: tb:* ~ **distintivo**) hallmark; ~ **fiscal** revenue stamp; ~**s de prima** (*COM*) trading stamps.

selva ['selβa] *nf* (*bosque*) forest, woods *pl*; (*jungla*) jungle; **la S~ Negra** the Black Forest.

semáforo [se'maforo] *nm* (*AUTO*) traffic lights *pl*; (*FERRO*) signal.

semana [se'mana] *nf* week; ~ **inglesa** 5-day (working) week; ~ **laboral** working week; **S~ Santa** Holy Week; **entre** ~ during the week; *see boxed note*.

SEMANA

Semana Santa *is an important national holiday in Spain. The whole country takes "Viernes Santo" (Good Friday) "Sábado Santo", (Holy Saturday), and "Domingo de Resurrección" (Easter Sunday) off, while other days around this time of year vary according to region. There are spectacular processions all over the country, with members of "cofradías" (brotherhoods) dressing in hooded robes and parading their "pasos" (religious floats or sculptures) through the streets. Holy Week in Seville is very famous, on account of the religious fervour shown by the locals.*

---

semanal [sema'nal] *adj* weekly.

semanario [sema'narjo] *nm* weekly (magazine).

semántica [se'mantika] *nf* semantics *sg*.

semblante [sem'blante] *nm* face; (*fig*) look.

sembrar [sem'brar] *vt* to sow; (*objetos*) to sprinkle, scatter about; (*noticias etc*) to spread.

semejante [seme'xante] *adj* (*parecido*) similar; (*tal*) such; ~**s alike, similar ♦ *nm* fellow man, fellow creature; **son muy** ~**s** they are very much alike; **nunca hizo cosa** ~ he never did such a thing.

semejanza [seme'xanθa] *nf* similarity, resemblance; **a** ~ **de** like, as.

semejar [seme'xar] *vi* to seem like; ~**se** *vr* to look alike, be similar.

semen ['semen] *nm* semen.

semental [semen'tal] *nm* (*macho*) stud.

sementera [semen'tera] *nf* (*acto*) sowing; (*temporada*) seedtime; (*tierra*) sown land.

semestral [semes'tral] *adj* half-yearly, bi-annual.

semestre [se'mestre] *nm* period of six months; (*US UNIV*) semester; (*COM*) half-yearly payment.

semicírculo [semi'θirkulo] *nm* semicircle.

semiconductor [semikonduk'tor] *nm* semiconductor.

semiconsciente [semikons'θjente] *adj* semiconscious.

semidesnatado, a [semiðesna'taðo, a] *adj* semi-skimmed.

semifinal [semifi'nal] *nf* semifinal.

semiinconsciente [semi(i)nkons'θjente] *adj* semiconscious.

semilla [se'miʎa] *nf* seed.

semillero [semi'ʎero] *nm* (*AGR etc*) seedbed; (*fig*) hotbed.

seminario [semi'narjo] *nm* (*REL*) seminary; (*ESCOL*) seminar.

semiseco [semi'seko] *nm* medium-dry.

semita [se'mita] *adj* Semitic ♦ *nm/f* Semite.

sémola ['semola] *nf* semolina.

sempiterno, a [sempi'terno, a] *adj* everlasting.

Sena ['sena] *nm*: **el** ~ the (river) Seine.

senado [se'naðo] *nm* senate; *V tb* **Las Cortes (españolas).**

senador, a [sena'ðor, a] *nm/f* senator.

sencillez [senθi'ʎeθ] *nf* simplicity; (*de persona*) naturalness.

sencillo, a [sen'θiʎo, a] *adj* simple; (*carácter*) natural, unaffected; (*billete*) single ♦ *nm* (*disco*) single; (*AM*) small change.

senda ['senda] *nf*, **sendero** [sen'dero] *nm* path, track; **Sendero Luminoso** the Shining Path (guerrilla movement).

senderismo [sende'rismo] *nm* trekking.

sendos, as ['sendos, as] *adj pl*: **les dio** ~ **golpes** he hit both of them.

senil [se'nil] *adj* senile.

seno ['seno] *nm* (*ANAT*) bosom, bust; (*fig*)

bosom; ~s *nmpl* breasts; ~ **materno** womb.

sensación [sensa'θjon] *nf* sensation; (*sentido*) sense; (*sentimiento*) feeling; **causar** *o* **hacer** ~ to cause a sensation.

sensacional [sensaθjo'nal] *adj* sensational.

sensatez [sensa'teθ] *nf* common sense.

sensato, a [sen'sato, a] *adj* sensible.

sensibilidad [sensiβili'ðað] *nf* sensitivity; (*para el arte*) feel.

sensibilizar [sensiβili'θar] *vt*: ~ **a la población/opinión pública** to raise public awareness.

sensible [sen'sible] *adj* sensitive; (*apreciable*) perceptible, appreciable; (*pérdida*) considerable.

sensiblero, a [sensi'βlero, a] *adj* sentimental, slushy.

sensitivo, a [sensi'tiβo, a], **sensorial** [senso'rjal] *adj* sense *cpd*.

sensor [sen'sor] *nm*: ~ **de fin de papel** paper out sensor.

sensual [sen'swal] *adj* sensual.

sentado, a [sen'taðo, a] *adj* (*establecido*) settled; (*carácter*) sensible ♦ *nf* sitting; (*POL*) sit-in, sit-down protest; **dar por** ~ to take for granted, assume; **dejar algo** ~ to establish sth firmly; **estar** ~ to sit, be sitting (down); **de una sentada** at one sitting.

sentar [sen'tar] *vt* to sit, seat; (*fig*) to establish ♦ *vi* (*vestido*) to suit; (*alimento*): ~ **bien/mal a** to agree/disagree with; ~**se** *vr* (*persona*) to sit, sit down; (*el tiempo*) to settle (down); (*los depósitos*) to settle; **¡siéntese!** (do) sit down, take a seat.

sentencia [sen'tenθja] *nf* (*máxima*) maxim, saying; (*JUR*) sentence; (*INFORM*) statement; ~ **de muerte** death sentence.

sentenciar [senten'θjar] *vt* to sentence.

sentido, a [sen'tiðo, a] *adj* (*pérdida*) regrettable; (*carácter*) sensitive ♦ *nm* sense; (*sentimiento*) feeling; (*significado*) sense, meaning; (*dirección*) direction; **mi más** ~ **pésame** my deepest sympathy; ~ **del humor** sense of humour; ~ **común** common sense; **en el buen** ~ **de la palabra** in the best sense of the word; **sin** ~ meaningless; **tener** ~ to make sense; ~ **único** one-way (street).

sentimental [sentimen'tal] *adj* sentimental; **vida** ~ love life.

sentimiento [senti'mjento] *nm* (*emoción*) feeling, emotion; (*sentido*) sense; (*pesar*) regret, sorrow.

sentir [sen'tir] *vt* to feel; (*percibir*) to perceive, sense; (*esp AM*: *oír*) to hear; (*lamentar*) to regret, be sorry for; (*música etc*) to have a feeling for ♦ *vi* to feel; (*lamentarse*) to feel sorry ♦ *nm* opinion, judgement; ~**se** *vr* to feel; **lo siento** I'm sorry; ~**se mejor/mal** to feel better/ill; ~**se como en su casa** to feel at home.   •

seña ['sena] *nf* sign; (*MIL*) password; ~**s** *nfpl* address *sg*; ~**s personales** personal description *sg*; **por más** ~**s** moreover; **dar** ~**s de** to show signs of.

señal [se'nal] *nf* sign; (*síntoma*) symptom; (*indicio*) indication; (*FERRO, TELEC*) signal; (*marca*) mark; (*COM*) deposit; (*INFORM*) marker, mark; **en** ~ **de** as a token of, as a sign of; **dar** ~**es de** to show signs of; ~ **de auxilio/de peligro** distress/danger signal; ~ **de llamada** ringing tone; ~ **para marcar** dialling tone.

señalado, a [sena'laðo, a] *adj* (*persona*) distinguished; (*pey*) notorious.

señalar [sena'lar] *vt* to mark; (*indicar*) to point out, indicate; (*significar*) to denote; (*referirse a*) to allude to; (*fijar*) to fix, settle; (*pey*) to criticize.

señalice [sena'liθe] *etc vb* V **señalizar**.

señalización [senaliθa'θjon] *nf* signposting; signals *pl*.

señalizar [senali'θar] *vt* (*AUTO*) to put up road signs on; (*FERRO*) to put signals on; (*AUTO*: *ruta*): **está bien señalizada** it's well signposted.

señas ['senas] *nfpl* V **seña**.

señor, a [se'nor, a] *adj* (*fam*) lordly ♦ *nm* (*hombre*) man; (*caballero*) gentleman; (*dueño*) owner, master; (*trato*: *antes de nombre propio*) Mr; (: *hablando directamente*) sir ♦ *nf* (*dama*) lady; (*trato*: *antes de nombre propio*) Mrs; (: *hablando directamente*) madam; (*esposa*) wife; **los** ~**es González** Mr and Mrs González; **S~ Don Jacinto Benavente** (*en sobre*) Mr J. Benavente, J. Benavente Esq.; **S~ Director ...** (*de periódico*) Dear Sir ...; ~ **juez** my lord, your worship (*US*); ~ **Presidente** Mr Chairman *o* President; **Muy** ~ **mío** Dear Sir; **Muy** ~**es nuestros** Dear Sirs; **Nuestro S~** (*REL*) Our Lord; **¿está la señora?** is the lady of the house in?; **la señora de Smith** Mrs Smith; **Nuestra Señora** (*REL*) Our Lady.

señoría [seno'ria] *nf* rule; **su** *o* **vuestra S~** your *o* his/her lordship/ladyship.

señorío [seno'rio] *nm* manor; (*fig*) rule.

señorita [seno'rita] *nf* (*gen*) Miss; (*mujer joven*) young lady; (*maestra*) schoolteacher.

señorito [seno'rito] *nm* young gentleman;

(*lenguaje de criados*) master; (*pey*) toff.
señuelo [se'ɲwelo] *nm* decoy.
Sep. *abr* (= *septiembre*) Sept.
sepa ['sepa] *etc vb* V **saber**.
separable [sepa'raßle] *adj* separable; (*TEC*)
detachable.
separación [separa'θjon] *nf* separation;
(*división*) division; (*distancia*) gap,
distance; ~ **de bienes** division of
property.
separado, a [sepa'raðo, a] *adj* separate;
(*TEC*) detached; **vive** ~ **de su mujer** he is
separated from his wife; **por** ~
separately.
separador [separa'ðor] *nm* (*INFORM*)
delimiter.
separadora [separa'ðora] *nf*: ~ **de hojas**
burster.
separar [sepa'rar] *vt* to separate; (*silla de la
mesa*) to move away; (*TEC*: *pieza*) to
detach; (*persona*: *de un cargo*) to remove,
dismiss; (*dividir*) to divide; ~**se** *vr* (*parte*)
to come away; (*partes*) to come apart;
(*persona*) to leave, go away; (*matrimonio*)
to separate.
separata [sepa'rata] *nf* offprint.
separatismo [separa'tismo] *nm* (*POL*)
separatism.
sepelio [se'peljo] *nm* burial, interment.
sepia ['sepja] *nf* cuttlefish.
Sept. *abr* (= *septiembre*) Sept.
septentrional [septentrjo'nal] *adj* north
cpd, northern.
septiembre [sep'tjembre] *nm* September.
séptimo, a ['septimo, a] *adj, nm* seventh.
septuagésimo, a [septwa'xesimo, a] *adj*
seventieth.
sepulcral [sepul'kral] *adj* sepulchral; (*fig*)
gloomy, dismal.
sepulcro [se'pulkro] *nm* tomb, grave,
sepulchre.
sepultar [sepul'tar] *vt* to bury; (*en
accidente*) to trap; **quedaban sepultados
en la caverna** they were trapped in the
cave.
sepultura [sepul'tura] *nf* (*acto*) burial;
(*tumba*) grave, tomb; **dar** ~ **a** to bury;
recibir ~ to be buried.
sepulturero, a [sepultu'rero, a] *nm/f*
gravedigger.
seque ['seke] *etc vb* V **secar**.
sequedad [seke'ðað] *nf* dryness; (*fig*)
brusqueness, curtness.
sequía [se'kia] *nf* drought.
séquito ['sekito] *nm* (*de rey etc*) retinue;
(*POL*) followers *pl*.
SER *nf abr* (= *Sociedad Española de
Radiodifusión*) Spanish radio network.

ser [ser] *vi* **1** (*descripción, identidad*) to be;
es médica/muy alta she's a doctor/very
tall; **la familia es de Cuzco** his (*o* her *etc*)
family is from Cuzco; ~ **de madera** to be
made of wood; **soy Ana** it's Ana
2 (*propiedad*): **es de Joaquín** it's
Joaquín's, it belongs to Joaquín
3 (*horas, fechas, números*): **es la una** it's
one o'clock; **son las seis y media** it's
half-past six; **es el 1 de junio** it's the
first of June; **somos/son seis** there are
six of us/them; **2 y 2 son 4** 2 and 2 are *o*
make 4
4 (*suceso*): **¿qué ha sido eso?** what was
that?; **la fiesta es en mi casa** the party's
at my house; **¿qué será de mí?** what will
become of me?; **"érase una vez ..."**
"once upon a time ..."
5 (*en oraciones pasivas*): **ha sido
descubierto ya** it's already been
discovered
6: **es de esperar que ...** it is to be hoped *o*
I *etc* hope that ...
7 (*locuciones con sub*): **o sea** that is to
say; **sea él sea su hermana** either him or
his sister; **tengo que irme, no sea que
mis hijos estén esperándome** I have to
go in case my children are waiting for
me
8: **a** *o* **de no** ~ **por él ...** but for him ...
9: **a no** ~ **que: a no** ~ **que tenga uno ya**
unless he's got one already
♦ *nm* being; ~ **humano** human being; ~
vivo living creature.

Serbia ['serßja] *nf* Serbia.
serbio, a ['serßjo, a] *adj* Serbian ♦ *nm/f*
Serb.
serenarse [sere'narse] *vr* to calm down;
(*mar*) to grow calm; (*tiempo*) to clear up.
serenidad [sereni'ðað] *nf* calmness.
sereno, a [se'reno, a] *adj* (*persona*) calm,
unruffled; (*el tiempo*) fine, settled; (*ambiente*) calm, peaceful ♦ *nm* night watchman.
serial [se'rjal] *nm* serial.
serie ['serje] *nf* series; (*cadena*) sequence,
succession; (*TV etc*) serial; (*de
inyecciones*) course; **fuera de** ~ out of
order; (*fig*) special, out of the ordinary;
fabricación en ~ mass production;
(*INFORM*): **interface/impresora en** ~
serial interface/printer.
seriedad [serje'ðað] *nf* seriousness;
(*formalidad*) reliability; (*de crisis*)
gravity, seriousness.

serigrafía [seriɣra'fia] *nf* silk screen printing.

serio, a ['serjo, a] *adj* serious; reliable, dependable; grave, serious; **poco ~** (*actitud*) undignified; (*carácter*) unreliable; **en ~** seriously.

sermón [ser'mon] *nm* (*REL*) sermon.

sermonear [sermone'ar] *vt* (*fam*) to lecture ♦ *vi* to sermonize.

seropositivo, a [seroposi'tiβo, a] *adj* HIV-positive.

serpentear [serpente'ar] *vi* to wriggle; (*camino, río*) to wind, snake.

serpentina [serpen'tina] *nf* streamer.

serpiente [ser'pjente] *nf* snake; **~ boa** boa constrictor; **~ de cascabel** rattlesnake.

serranía [serra'nia] *nf* mountainous area.

serrano, a [se'rrano, a] *adj* highland *cpd*, hill *cpd* ♦ *nm/f* highlander.

serrar [se'rrar] *vt* to saw.

serrín [se'rrin] *nm* sawdust.

serrucho [se'rrutʃo] *nm* handsaw.

Servia ['serßja] *nf* Serbia.

servicial [serßi'θjal] *adj* helpful, obliging.

servicio [ser'ßiθjo] *nm* service; (*CULIN etc*) set; **~s** *nmpl* toilet(s) (*pl*); **estar de ~** to be on duty; **~ aduanero** o **de aduana** customs service; **~ a domicilio** home delivery service; **~ incluido** (*en hotel etc*) service charge included; **~ militar** military service; **~ público** (*COM*) public utility.

servidor, a [serßi'ðor, a] *nm/f* servant ♦ *nm* (*INFORM*) server; **su seguro ~ (s.s.s.)** yours faithfully; **un ~** (*el que habla o escribe*) your humble servant.

servidumbre [serßi'ðumbre] *nf* (*sujeción*) servitude; (*criados*) servants *pl*, staff.

servil [ser'ßil] *adj* servile.

servilleta [serßi'ʎeta] *nf* serviette, napkin.

servilletero [serßiʎe'tero] *nm* napkin ring.

servir [ser'ßir] *vt* to serve; (*comida*) to serve out o up; (*TENIS etc*) to serve ♦ *vi* to serve; (*camarero*) to serve, wait; (*tener utilidad*) to be of use, be useful; **~se** *vr* to serve o help o.s.; **¿en qué puedo ~le?** how can I help you?; **~ vino a algn** to pour out wine for sb; **~ de guía** to act o serve as a guide; **no sirve para nada** it's no use at all; **~se de algo** to make use of sth, use sth; **sírvase pasar** please come in.

sesantía [θesan'tia] *nf* (*AM*) unemployment.

sesenta [se'senta] *num* sixty.

sesentón, ona [sesen'ton, ona] *adj, nm/f* sixty-year-old.

sesgado, a [ses'ɣaðo, a] *adj* slanted, slanting.

sesgo ['sesɣo] *nm* slant; (*fig*) slant, twist.

sesión [se'sjon] *nf* (*POL*) session, sitting; (*CINE*) showing; (*TEAT*) performance; **abrir/levantar la ~** to open/close o adjourn the meeting; **la segunda ~** the second house.

seso ['seso] *nm* brain; (*fig*) intelligence; **~s** *nmpl* (*CULIN*) brains; **devanarse los ~s** to rack one's brains.

sesudo, a [se'suðo, a] *adj* sensible, wise.

set, *pl* sets [set, sets] *nm* (*TENIS*) set.

Set. *abr* (= **setiembre**) Sept.

seta ['seta] *nf* mushroom; **~ venenosa** toadstool.

setecientos, as [sete'θjentos, as] *num* seven hundred.

setenta [se'tenta] *num* seventy.

setiembre [se'tjembre] *nm* = **septiembre**.

seto ['seto] *nm* fence; **~ vivo** hedge.

seudo... [seuðo] *pref* pseudo....

seudónimo [seu'ðonimo] *nm* pseudonym.

Seúl [se'ul] *nm* Seoul.

s.e.u.o. *abr* (= *salvo error u omisión*) E & O E.

severidad [seßeri'ðað] *nf* severity.

severo, a [se'ßero, a] *adj* severe; (*disciplina*) strict; (*frío*) bitter.

Sevilla [se'ßiʎa] *nf* Seville.

sevillano, a [seßi'ʎano, a] *adj* of o from Seville ♦ *nm/f* native o inhabitant of Seville.

sexagenario, a [seksaxe'narjo, a] *adj* sixty-year-old ♦ *nm/f* person in his/her sixties.

sexagésimo, a [seksa'xesimo, a] *num* sixtieth.

sexo ['sekso] *nm* sex; **el ~ femenino/masculino** the female/male sex.

sexto, a ['seksto, a] *num* sixth; **Juan S~** John the Sixth.

sexual [sek'swal] *adj* sexual; **vida ~** sex life.

sexualidad [sekswali'ðað] *nf* sexuality.

s.f. *abr* (= *sin fecha*) no date.

s/f *abr* (*COM*: = *su favor*) your favour.

sgte(s). *abr* (= *siguiente(s)*) foll.

si [si] *conj* if; (*en pregunta indirecta*) if, whether ♦ *nm* (*MUS*) B; **~ ... ~ ...** whether ... or ...; **me pregunto ~ ...** I wonder if o whether ...; **~ no** if not, otherwise; **¡~ fuera verdad!** if only it were true!; **por ~ viene** in case he comes.

sí [si] *adv* yes ♦ *nm* consent ♦ *pron* (*uso impersonal*) oneself; (*sg: m*) himself; (: *f*) herself; (: *de cosa*) itself; (: *de usted*) yourself; (*pl*) themselves; (: *de ustedes*) yourselves; (: *recíproco*) each other; **él no**

quiere pero yo ~ he doesn't want to but I do; **ella** ~ **vendrá** she will certainly come, she is sure to come; **claro que** ~ of course; **creo que** ~ I think so; **porque** ~ because that's the way it is; (*porque lo digo yo*) because I say so; ¡~ **que lo es!** I'll say it is!; ¡**eso** ~ **que no!** never; **se ríe de** ~ **misma** she laughs at herself; **cambiaron una mirada entre** ~ they gave each other a look; **de por** ~ in itself.

siamés, esa [sja'mes, esa] *adj, nm/f* Siamese.

sibarita [siβa'rita] *adj* sybaritic ♦ *nm/f* sybarite.

sicario [si'karjo] *nm* hired killer.

Sicilia [si'θilja] *nf* Sicily.

siciliano, a [siθi'ljano, a] *adj, nm/f* Sicilian ♦ *nm* (*LING*) Sicilian.

SIDA ['siða] *nm abr* (= *síndrome de inmunodeficiencia adquirida*) AIDS.

sida ['siða] *nm* AIDS.

siderurgia [siðe'rurxja] *nf* iron and steel industry.

siderúrgico, a [siðe'rurxico, a] *adj* iron and steel *cpd*.

sidra ['siðra] *nf* cider.

siega ['sjeɣa] *etc vb V* **segar** ♦ *nf* (*cosechar*) reaping; (*segar*) mowing; (*época*) harvest (time).

siegue ['sjeɣe] *etc vb V* **segar**.

siembra ['sjembra] *etc vb V* **sembrar** ♦ *nf* sowing.

siempre ['sjempre] *adv* always; (*todo el tiempo*) all the time; (*AM: así y todo*) still ♦ *conj*: ~ **que ...** (+ *indic*) whenever ...; (+ *subjun*) provided that ...; **es lo de** ~ it's the same old story; **como** ~ as usual; **para** ~ forever; ~ **me voy mañana** (*AM*) I'm still leaving tomorrow.

sien [sjen] *nf* (*ANAT*) temple.

siento ['sjento] *etc vb V* **sentar, sentir**.

sierra ['sjerra] *etc vb V* **serrar** ♦ *nf* (*TEC*) saw; (*GEO*) mountain range; **S~ Leona** Sierra Leone.

siervo, a ['sjerβo, a] *nm/f* slave.

siesta ['sjesta] *nf* siesta, nap; **dormir la** *o* **echarse una** *o* **tomar una** ~ to have an afternoon nap *o* a doze.

siete ['sjete] *num* seven ♦ *excl* (*AM fam*): **¡la gran ~!** wow!, hell!; **hijo de la gran ~** (*fam!*) bastard(*!*), son of a bitch (*US!*).

sífilis ['sifilis] *nf* syphilis.

sifón [si'fon] *nm* syphon; **whisky con** ~ whisky and soda.

siga ['siɣa] *etc vb V* **seguir**.

sigilo [si'xilo] *nm* secrecy; (*discreción*) discretion.

sigla ['siɣla] *nf* initial, abbreviation.

siglo ['siɣlo] *nm* century; (*fig*) age; **S~ de las Luces** Age of Enlightenment; **S~ de Oro** Golden Age.

significación [siɣnifika'θjon] *nf* significance.

significado [siɣnifi'kaðo] *nm* significance; (*de palabra etc*) meaning.

significar [siɣnifi'kar] *vt* to mean, signify; (*notificar*) to make known, express.

significativo, a [siɣnifika'tiβo, a] *adj* significant.

signifique [siɣni'fike] *etc vb V* **significar**.

signo ['siɣno] *nm* sign; ~ **de admiración** *o* **exclamación** exclamation mark; ~ **igual** equals sign; ~ **de interrogación** question mark; ~ **de más/de menos** plus/minus sign; ~s **de puntuación** punctuation marks.

siguiendo [si'ɣjendo] *etc vb V* **seguir**.

siguiente [si'ɣjente] *adj* following; (*próximo*) next.

silbar [sil'βar] *vt, vi* to whistle; (*silbato*) to blow; (*TEAT etc*) to hiss.

silbato [sil'βato] *nm* (*instrumento*) whistle.

silbido [sil'βiðo] *nm* whistle, whistling; (*abucheo*) hiss.

silenciador [silenθja'ðor] *nm* silencer.

silenciar [silen'θjar] *vt* (*persona*) to silence; (*escándalo*) to hush up.

silencio [si'lenθjo] *nm* silence, quiet; **en el** ~ **más absoluto** in dead silence; **guardar** ~ to keep silent.

silencioso, a [silen'θjoso, a] *adj* silent, quiet.

sílfide ['silfiðe] *nf* sylph.

silicio [si'liθjo] *nm* silicon.

silla ['siʎa] *nf* (*asiento*) chair; (*tb*: ~ **de montar**) saddle; ~ **de ruedas** wheelchair.

sillería [siʎe'ria] *nf* (*asientos*) chairs *pl*, set of chairs; (*REL*) choir stalls *pl*; (*taller*) chairmaker's workshop.

sillín [si'ʎin] *nm* saddle, seat.

sillón [si'ʎon] *nm* armchair, easy chair.

silueta [si'lweta] *nf* silhouette; (*de edificio*) outline; (*figura*) figure.

silvestre [sil'βestre] *adj* (*BOT*) wild; (*fig*) rustic, rural.

sima ['sima] *nf* abyss, chasm.

simbolice [simbo'liθe] *etc vb V* **simbolizar**.

simbólico, a [sim'boliko, a] *adj* symbolic(al).

simbolizar [simboli'θar] *vt* to symbolize.

símbolo ['simbolo] *nm* symbol; ~ **gráfico** (*INFORM*) icon.

simetría [sime'tria] *nf* symmetry.

simétrico, a [si'metriko, a] *adj* symmetrical.

simiente [si'mjente] *nf* seed.

similar [simiˈlar] *adj* similar.
similitud [similiˈtuð] *nf* similarity, resemblance.
simio [ˈsimjo] *nm* ape.
simpatía [simpaˈtia] *nf* liking; (*afecto*) affection; (*amabilidad*) kindness; (*de ambiente*) friendliness; (*de persona, lugar*) charm, attractiveness; (*solidaridad*) mutual support, solidarity; **tener ~ a** to like; **la famosa ~ andaluza** that well-known Andalusian charm.
simpatice [simpaˈtiθe] *etc vb V* **simpatizar**.
simpático, a [simˈpatiko, a] *adj* nice, pleasant; (*bondadoso*) kind; **no le hemos caído muy ~s** she didn't much take to us.
simpatiquísimo, a [simpatiˈkisimo, a] *adj* (*superl de* **simpático**) ever so nice; ever so kind.
simpatizante [simpatiˈθante] *nm/f* sympathizer.
simpatizar [simpatiˈθar] *vi:* **~ con** to get on well with.
simple [ˈsimple] *adj* simple; (*elemental*) simple, easy; (*mero*) mere; (*puro*) pure, sheer ♦ *nm/f* simpleton; **un ~ soldado** an ordinary soldier.
simpleza [simˈpleθa] *nf* simpleness; (*necedad*) silly thing.
simplicidad [simpliθiˈðað] *nf* simplicity.
simplificar [simplifiˈkar] *vt* to simplify.
simplifique [simpliˈfike] *etc vb V* **simplificar**.
simplón, ona [simˈplon, ona] *adj* simple, gullible ♦ *nm/f* simple soul.
simposio [simˈposjo] *nm* symposium.
simulacro [simuˈlakro] *nm* (*apariencia*) semblance; (*fingimiento*) sham.
simular [simuˈlar] *vt* to simulate; (*fingir*) to feign, sham.
simultanear [simultaneˈar] *vt:* **~ dos cosas** to do two things simultaneously.
simultáneo, a [simulˈtaneo, a] *adj* simultaneous.
sin [sin] *prep* without; (*a no ser por*) but for ♦ *conj:* **~ que** (+ *subjun*) without; **~ decir nada** without a word; **~ verlo yo** without my seeing it; **platos ~ lavar** unwashed *o* dirty dishes; **la ropa está ~ lavar** the clothes are unwashed; **~ que lo sepa él** without his knowing; **~ embargo** however.
sinagoga [sinaˈɣoɣa] *nf* synagogue.
Sinaí [sinaˈi] *nm:* **El ~** Sinai, the Sinai Peninsula; **el Monte ~** Mount Sinai.
sinceridad [sinθeriˈðað] *nf* sincerity.
sincero, a [sinˈθero, a] *adj* sincere; (*persona*) genuine; (*opinión*) frank; (*felicitaciones*) heartfelt.

síncope [ˈsinkope] *nm* (*desmayo*) blackout; **~ cardíaco** (*MED*) heart failure.
sincronice [sinkroˈniθe] *etc vb V* **sincronizar**.
sincronizar [sinkroniˈθar] *vt* to synchronize.
sindical [sindiˈkal] *adj* (trade-)union *cpd*.
sindicalista [sindikaˈlista] *adj* trade-union *cpd* ♦ *nm/f* trade unionist.
sindicar [sindiˈkar] *vt* (*obreros*) to organize, unionize; **~se** *vr* (*obrero*) to join a union.
sindicato [sindiˈkato] *nm* (*de trabajadores*) trade(s) *o* labor (*US*) union; (*de negociantes*) syndicate.
sindique [sinˈdike] *etc vb V* **sindicar**.
síndrome [ˈsindrome] *nm* syndrome; **~ de abstinencia** withdrawal symptoms; **~ de la clase turista** economy class syndrome.
sine qua non [sineˈkwanon] *adj:* **condición ~** sine qua non.
sinfín [sinˈfin] *nm:* **un ~ de** a great many, no end of.
sinfonía [sinfoˈnia] *nf* symphony.
sinfónico, a [sinˈfoniko, a] *adj* (*música*) symphonic; **orquesta sinfónica** symphony orchestra.
Singapur [singaˈpur] *nm* Singapore.
singular [singuˈlar] *adj* singular; (*fig*) outstanding, exceptional; (*pey*) peculiar, odd ♦ *nm* (*LING*) singular; **en ~** in the singular.
singularice [singulaˈriθe] *etc vb V* **singularizar**.
singularidad [singulariˈðað] *nf* singularity, peculiarity.
singularizar [singulariˈθar] *vt* to single out; **~se** *vr* to distinguish o.s., stand out.
siniestro, a [siˈnjestro, a] *adj* left; (*fig*) sinister ♦ *nm* (*accidente*) accident; (*desastre*) natural disaster.
sinnúmero [sinˈnumero] *nm* = **sinfín**.
sino [ˈsino] *nm* fate, destiny ♦ *conj* (*pero*) but; (*salvo*) except, save; **no son 8 ~ 9** there are not 8 but 9; **todos ~ él** all except him.
sinónimo, a [siˈnonimo, a] *adj* synonymous ♦ *nm* synonym.
sinrazón [sinraˈθon] *nf* wrong, injustice.
sinsabor [sinsaˈβor] *nm* (*molestia*) trouble; (*dolor*) sorrow; (*preocupación*) uneasiness.
sintaxis [sinˈtaksis] *nf* syntax.
síntesis [ˈsintesis] *nf inv* synthesis.
sintetice [sinteˈtiθe] *etc vb V* **sintetizar**.
sintético, a [sinˈtetiko, a] *adj* synthetic.
sintetizador [sintetiθaˈðor] *nm* synthesizer.
sintetizar [sintetiˈθar] *vt* to synthesize.
sintiendo [sinˈtjendo] *etc vb V* **sentir**.
síntoma [ˈsintoma] *nm* symptom.
sintomático, a [sintoˈmatiko, a] *adj*

symptomatic.

sintonía [sinto'nia] *nf* (*RADIO*) tuning; (*melodía*) signature tune.

sintonice [sinto'niθe] *etc vb V* **sintonizar**.

sintonizador [sintoniθa'ðor] *nm* (*RADIO*) tuner.

sintonizar [sintoni'θar] *vt* (*RADIO*) to tune (in) to, pick up.

sinuoso, a [si'nwoso, a] *adj* (*camino*) winding; (*rumbo*) devious.

sinvergüenza [simber'ɣwenθa] *nm/f* rogue, scoundrel.

sionismo [sjo'nismo] *nm* Zionism.

siquiera [si'kjera] *conj* even if, even though ♦ *adv* (*esp AM*) at least; **ni** ~ not even; ~ **bebe algo** at least drink something.

sirena [si'rena] *nf* siren, mermaid; (*bocina*) siren, hooter.

Siria ['sirja] *nf* Syria.

sirio, a ['sirjo, a] *adj, nm/f* Syrian.

sirviendo [sir'ßjendo] *etc vb V* **servir**.

sirviente, a [sir'ßjente, a] *nm/f* servant.

sisa ['sisa] *nf* petty theft; (*COSTURA*) dart; (*sobaquera*) armhole.

sisar [si'sar] *vt* (*robar*) to thieve; (*COSTURA*) to take in.

sisear [sise'ar] *vt, vi* to hiss.

sísmico, a ['sismiko, a] *adj*: **movimiento** ~ earthquake.

sismógrafo [sis'moɣrafo] *nm* seismograph.

sistema [sis'tema] *nm* system; (*método*) method; ~ **educativo** education system; ~ **impositivo** *o* **tributario** taxation, tax system; ~ **pedagógico** educational system; ~ **de alerta inmediata** early-warning system; ~ **binario** (*INFORM*) binary system; ~ **experto** expert system; ~ **de facturación** (*COM*) invoicing system; ~ **de fondo fijo** (*COM*) imprest system; ~ **métrico** metric system; ~ **operativo (en disco)** (*INFORM*) (disk-based) operating system; *see boxed note.*

SISTEMA EDUCATIVO

The reform of the Spanish **sistema educativo** (*education system*) *begun in the early 1990s, has replaced the old EGB, BUP and COU courses with the following: six years of compulsory primary education* (*"primaria"*); *four years of compulsory secondary education* (*"secundaria"*); *and a two-year "bachillerato", which is optional but a prerequisite for entry into higher education.*

---

sistemático, a [siste'matiko, a] *adj*

systematic.

sitiar [si'tjar] *vt* to besiege, lay siege to.

sitio ['sitjo] *nm* (*lugar*) place; (*espacio*) room, space; (*MIL*) siege; ~ **Web** website; **¿hay** ~**?** is there any room?; **hay** ~ **de sobra** there's plenty of room.

situación [sitwa'θjon] *nf* situation, position; (*estatus*) position, standing.

situado, a [si'twaðo, a] *adj* situated, placed; **estar** ~ (*COM*) to be financially secure.

situar [si'twar] *vt* to place, put; (*edificio*) to locate, situate.

S.L. *abr* (*COM*: = *Sociedad Limitada*) Ltd.

slip [es'lip], *pl* **slips** *nm* pants *pl*, briefs *pl*.

slot [es'lot], *pl* **slots** *nm*: ~ **de expansión** expansion slot.

S.M. *abr* (= *Su Majestad*) HM.

SME *nm abr* (= *Sistema Monetario Europeo*) EMS; **(mecanismo de cambios del)** ~ ERM.

smoking [(e)'smokin] (*pl* ~**s**) *nm* dinner jacket (*BRIT*), tuxedo (*US*).

SMS *nm* (*mensaje*) text (message), SMS (message).

s/n *abr* (= *sin número*) no number.

snob [es'nob] = **esnob**.

SO *abr* (= *suroeste*) SW.

so [so] *excl* whoa!; **¡**~ **burro!** you idiot! ♦ *prep* under.

s/o *abr* (*COM*: = *su orden*) your order.

sobaco [so'ßako] *nm* armpit.

sobado, a [so'ßaðo, a] *adj* (*ropa*) worn; (*arrugado*) crumpled; (*libro*) well-thumbed; (*CULIN*: *masa*) short.

sobar [so'ßar] *vt* (*tela*) to finger; (*ropa*) to rumple, mess up; (*músculos*) to rub, massage.

soberanía [soßera'nia] *nf* sovereignty.

soberano, a [soße'rano, a] *adj* sovereign; (*fig*) supreme ♦ *nm/f* sovereign; **los** ~**s** the king and queen.

soberbio, a [so'ßerßjo, a] *adj* (*orgulloso*) proud; (*altivo*) haughty, arrogant; (*fig*) magnificent, superb ♦ *nf* pride; haughtiness, arrogance; magnificence.

sobornar [soßor'nar] *vt* to bribe.

soborno [so'ßorno] *nm* (*un* ~) bribe; (*el* ~) bribery.

sobra ['soßra] *nf* excess, surplus; ~**s** *nfpl* left-overs, scraps; **de** ~ surplus, extra; **lo sé de** ~ I'm only too aware of it; **tengo de** ~ I've more than enough.

sobradamente [soßraða'mente] *adv* amply; (*saber*) only too well.

sobrado, a [so'ßraðo, a] *adj* (*más que suficiente*) more than enough; (*superfluo*) excessive ♦ *adv* too, exceedingly;

sobradas veces repeatedly.
sobrante [so'βrante] *adj* remaining, extra
♦ *nm* surplus, remainder.
sobrar [so'βrar] *vt* to exceed, surpass ♦ *vi*
(*tener de más*) to be more than enough;
(*quedar*) to remain, be left (over).
sobrasada [soβra'saða] *nf* ≈ sausage
spread.
sobre ['soβre] *prep* (*gen*) on; (*encima*) on
(top of); (*por encima de, arriba de*) over,
above; (*más que*) more than; (*además*) in
addition to, besides; (*alrededor de*) about;
(*porcentaje*) in, out of; (*tema*) about, on
♦ *nm* envelope; ~ **todo** above all; **3** ~ **100**
3 in a 100, 3 out of every 100; **un libro** ~
Tirso a book about Tirso; ~ **de ventanilla**
window envelope.
sobrecama [soβre'kama] *nf* bedspread.
sobrecapitalice [soβrekapita'liθe] *etc vb V*
sobrecapitalizar.
sobrecapitalizar [soβrekapitali'θar] *vi* to
overcapitalize.
sobrecargar [soβrekar'ɣar] *vt* (*camión*) to
overload; (*COM*) to surcharge.
sobrecargue [soβre'karɣe] *etc vb V*
sobrecargar.
sobrecoger [soβreko'xer] *vt* (*sobresaltar*) to
startle; (*asustar*) to scare; ~**se** *vr*
(*sobresaltarse*) to be startled; (*asustarse*)
to get scared; (*quedar impresionado*): ~**se**
(**de**) to be overawed (by).
sobrecoja [soβre'koxa] *etc vb V*
sobrecoger.
sobredosis [soβre'ðosis] *nf inv* overdose.
sobre(e)ntender [soβre(e)nten'der] *vt* to
understand; (*adivinar*) to deduce, infer;
~**se** *vr*: **se sobre(e)ntiende que ...** it is
implied that ....
sobreescribir [soβreeskri'βir] *vt* (*INFORM*)
to overwrite.
sobre(e)stimar [soβre(e)sti'mar] *vt* to
overestimate.
sobregiro [soβre'xiro] *nm* (*COM*) overdraft.
sobrehumano, a [soβreu'mano, a] *adj*
superhuman.
sobreimprimir [soβreimpri'mir] *vt* (*COM*) to
merge.
sobrellevar [soβreʎe'βar] *vt* (*fig*) to bear,
endure.
sobremesa [soβre'mesa] *nf* (*después de
comer*) sitting on after a meal; (*INFORM*)
desktop; **conversación de** ~ table talk.
sobremodo [soβre'moðo] *adv* very much,
enormously.
sobrenatural [soβrenatu'ral] *adj*
supernatural.
sobrenombre [soβre'nombre] *nm*
nickname.

sobrepasar [soβrepa'sar] *vt* to exceed,
surpass.
sobrepondré [soβrepon'dre] *etc vb V*
sobreponer.
sobreponer [soβrepo'ner] *vt* (*poner encima*)
to put on top; (*añadir*) to add; ~**se** *vr*: ~**se
a** to overcome.
sobreponga [soβre'ponga] *etc vb V*
sobreponer.
sobreprima [soβre'prima] *nf* (*COM*)
loading.
sobreproducción [soβreproðuk'θjon] *nf*
overproduction.
sobrepuesto [soβre'pwesto], **sobrepuse**
[soβre'puse] *etc vb V* **sobreponer**.
sobresaldré [soβresal'dre] *etc*,
sobresalga [soβre'salɣa] *etc vb V*
sobresalir.
sobresaliente [soβresa'ljente] *adj*
projecting; (*fig*) outstanding, excellent;
(*UNIV etc*) first class ♦ *nm* (*UNIV etc*) first
class (mark), distinction.
sobresalir [soβresa'lir] *vi* to project, jut
out; (*fig*) to stand out, excel.
sobresaltar [soβresal'tar] *vt* (*asustar*) to
scare, frighten; (*sobrecoger*) to startle.
sobresalto [soβre'salto] *nm* (*movimiento*)
start; (*susto*) scare; (*turbación*) sudden
shock.
sobreseer [soβrese'er] *vt*: ~ **una causa**
(*JUR*) to stop a case.
sobrestadía [soβresta'ðia] *nf* (*COM*)
demurrage.
sobretensión [soβreten'sjon] *nf* (*ELEC*): ~
transitoria surge.
sobretiempo [soβre'tjempo] *nm* (*AM*)
overtime.
sobretodo [soβre'toðo] *nm* overcoat.
sobrevendré [soβreβen'dre] *etc*,
sobrevenga [soβre'βenga] *etc vb V*
sobrevenir.
sobrevenir [soβreβe'nir] *vi* (*ocurrir*) to
happen (unexpectedly); (*resultar*) to
follow, ensue.
sobreviene [soβre'βjene] *etc*, **sobrevine**
[soβre'βine] *etc vb V* **sobrevenir**.
sobreviviente [soβreβi'βjente] *adj*
surviving ♦ *nm/f* survivor.
sobrevivir [soβreβi'βir] *vi* to survive;
(*persona*) to outlive; (*objeto etc*) to
outlast.
sobrevolar [soβreβo'lar] *vt* to fly over.
sobrevuele [soβre'βwele] *etc vb V*
sobrevolar.
sobriedad [soβrje'ðað] *nf* sobriety,
soberness; (*moderación*) moderation,
restraint.
sobrino, a [so'βrino, a] *nm/f* nephew/niece.

sobrio, a ['soβrjo, a] *adj* (*moderado*) moderate, restrained.

socarrón, ona [soka'rron, ona] *adj* (*sarcástico*) sarcastic, ironic(al).

socavar [soka'βar] *vt* to undermine; (*excavar*) to dig underneath o below.

socavón [soka'βon] *nm* (*en mina*) gallery; (*hueco*) hollow; (*en la calle*) hole.

sociable [so'θjaβle] *adj* (*persona*) sociable, friendly; (*animal*) social.

social [so'θjal] *adj* social; (*COM*) company *cpd*.

socialdemócrata [soθjalde'mokrata] *adj* social-democratic ♦ *nm/f* social democrat.

socialice [soθja'liθe] *etc vb V* **socializar**.

socialista [soθja'lista] *adj, nm/f* socialist.

socializar [soθjali'θar] *vt* to socialize.

sociedad [soθje'ðað] *nf* society; (*COM*) company; ~ **de ahorro y préstamo** savings and loan society; ~ **anónima** (**S.A.**) limited company (Ltd) (*BRIT*), incorporated company (Inc) (*US*); ~ **de beneficiencia** friendly society (*BRIT*), benefit association (*US*); ~ **de cartera** investment trust; ~ **comanditaria** (*COM*) co-ownership; ~ **conjunta** (*COM*) joint venture; ~ **inmobiliaria** building society (*BRIT*), savings and loan (society) (*US*); ~ **de responsabilidad limitada** (*COM*) private limited company.

socio, a ['soθjo, a] *nm/f* (*miembro*) member; (*COM*) partner; ~ **activo** active partner; ~ **capitalista** o **comanditario** sleeping o silent (*US*) partner.

socioeconómico, a [soθjoeko'nomiko, a] *adj* socio-economic.

sociología [soθjolo'xia] *nf* sociology.

sociólogo, a [so'θjoloɣo, a] *nm/f* sociologist.

socorrer [soko'rrer] *vt* to help.

socorrido, a [soko'rriðo, a] *adj* (*tienda*) well-stocked; (*útil*) handy; (*persona*) helpful.

socorrismo [soko'rrismo] *nm* life-saving.

socorrista [soko'rrista] *nm/f* first aider; (*en piscina, playa*) lifeguard.

socorro [so'korro] *nm* (*ayuda*) help, aid; (*MIL*) relief; ¡~! help!

soda ['soða] *nf* (*sosa*) soda; (*bebida*) soda (water).

sódico, a ['soðiko, a] *adj* sodium *cpd*.

soez [so'eθ] *adj* dirty, obscene.

sofá [so'fa] *nm* sofa, settee.

sofá-cama [so'fakama] *nm* studio couch, sofa bed.

Sofia ['sofja] *nf* Sofia.

sofisticación [sofistika'θjon] *nf* sophistication.

sofisticado, a [sofisti'kaðo, a] *adj* sophisticated.

sofocado, a [sofo'kaðo, a] *adj*: **estar** ~ (*fig*) to be out of breath; (*ahogarse*) to feel stifled.

sofocar [sofo'kar] *vt* to suffocate; (*apagar*) to smother, put out; ~**se** *vr* to suffocate; (*fig*) to blush, feel embarrassed.

sofoco [so'foko] *nm* suffocation; (*azoro*) embarrassment.

sofocón [sofo'kon] *nm*: **llevarse** o **pasar un** ~ to have a sudden shock.

sofreír [sofre'ir] *vt* to fry lightly.

sofría [so'fria] *etc*, **sofriendo** [so'frjendo] *etc*, **sofrito** [so'frito] *vb V* **sofreír**.

soft(ware) ['sof(wer)] *nm* (*INFORM*) software.

soga ['soɣa] *nf* rope.

sois [sois] *vb V* **ser**.

soja ['soxa] *nf* soya.

sojuzgar [soxuθ'ɣar] *vt* to subdue, rule despotically.

sojuzgue [so'xuθɣe] *etc vb V* **sojuzgar**.

sol [sol] *nm* sun; (*luz*) sunshine, sunlight; (*MUS*) G; ~ **naciente/poniente** rising/setting sun; **tomar el** ~ to sunbathe; **hace** ~ it is sunny.

solace [so'laθe] *etc vb V* **solazar**.

solamente [sola'mente] *adv* only, just.

solapa [so'lapa] *nf* (*de chaqueta*) lapel; (*de libro*) jacket.

solapado, a [sola'paðo, a] *adj* sly, underhand.

solar [so'lar] *adj* solar, sun *cpd* ♦ *nm* (*terreno*) plot (of ground); (*local*) undeveloped site.

solaz [so'laθ] *nm* recreation, relaxation.

solazar [sola'θar] *vt* (*divertir*) to amuse; ~**se** *vr* to enjoy o.s., relax.

soldada [sol'daða] *nf* pay.

soldado [sol'daðo] *nm* soldier; ~ **raso** private.

soldador [solda'ðor] *nm* soldering iron; (*persona*) welder.

soldar [sol'dar] *vt* to solder, weld; (*unir*) to join, unite.

soleado, a [sole'aðo, a] *adj* sunny.

soledad [sole'ðað] *nf* solitude; (*estado infeliz*) loneliness.

solemne [so'lemne] *adj* solemn; (*tontería*) utter; (*error*) complete.

solemnidad [solemni'ðað] *nf* solemnity.

soler [so'ler] *vi* to be in the habit of, be accustomed to; **suele salir a las ocho** she usually goes out at 8 o'clock; **solíamos ir todos los años** we used to go every year.

solera [so'lera] *nf (tradición)* tradition; **vino de** ~ vintage wine.

solfeo [sol'feo] *nm* singing of scales; **ir a clases de** ~ to take singing lessons.

solicitar [soliθi'tar] *vt (permiso)* to ask for, seek; *(puesto)* to apply for; *(votos)* to canvass for; *(atención)* to attract; *(persona)* to pursue, chase after.

solícito, a [so'liθito, a] *adj (diligente)* diligent; *(cuidadoso)* careful.

solicitud [soliθi'tuð] *nf (calidad)* great care; *(petición)* request; *(a un puesto)* application.

solidaridad [soliðari'ðað] *nf* solidarity; **por ~ con** *(POL etc)* out of *o* in solidarity with.

solidario, a [soli'ðarjo, a] *adj (participación)* joint, common; *(compromiso)* mutually binding; **hacerse** ~ **de** to declare one's solidarity with.

solidarizarse [soliðari'θarse] *vr:* ~ **con algn** to support sb, sympathize with sb.

solidez [soli'ðeθ] *nf* solidity.

sólido, a ['soliðo, a] *adj* solid; *(TEC)* solidly made; *(bien construido)* well built.

soliloquio [soli'lokjo] *nm* soliloquy.

solista [so'lista] *nmf* soloist.

solitario, a [soli'tarjo, a] *adj (persona)* lonely, solitary; *(lugar)* lonely, desolate ♦ *nmlf (reclusa)* recluse; *(en la sociedad)* loner ♦ *nm* solitaire ♦ *nf* tapeworm.

soliviantar [solißjan'tar] *vt* to stir up, rouse (to revolt); *(enojar)* to anger; *(sacar de quicio)* to exasperate.

solloce [so'ʎoθe] *etc vb* V **sollozar.**

sollozar [soʎo'θar] *vi* to sob.

sollozo [so'ʎoθo] *nm* sob.

solo, a ['solo, a] *adj (único)* single, sole; *(sin compañía)* alone; *(MUS)* solo; *(solitario)* lonely; **hay una sola dificultad** there is just one difficulty; **a solas** alone, by o.s.

sólo ['solo] *adv* only, just; *(exclusivamente)* solely; **tan** ~ only just.

solomillo [solo'miʎo] *nm* sirloin.

solsticio [sols'tiθjo] *nm* solstice.

soltar [sol'tar] *vt (dejar ir)* to let go of; *(desprender)* to unfasten, loosen; *(librar)* to release, set free; *(amarras)* to cast off; *(AUTO: freno etc)* to release; *(suspiro)* to heave; *(risa etc)* to let out; ~**se** *vr (desanudarse)* to come undone; *(desprenderse)* to come off; *(adquirir destreza)* to become expert; *(en idioma)* to become fluent.

soltero, a [sol'tero, a] *adj* single, unmarried ♦ *nm* bachelor ♦ *nf* single woman, spinster.

solterón [solte'ron] *nm* confirmed bachelor.

solterona [solte'rona] *nf* spinster, maiden lady; *(pey)* old maid.

soltura [sol'tura] *nf* looseness, slackness; *(de los miembros)* agility, ease of movement; *(en el hablar)* fluency, ease.

soluble [so'lußle] *adj (QUÍMICA)* soluble; *(problema)* solvable; ~ **en agua** soluble in water.

solución [solu'θjon] *nf* solution; ~ **de continuidad** break in continuity.

solucionar [soluθjo'nar] *vt (problema)* to solve; *(asunto)* to settle, resolve.

solvencia [sol'ßenθja] *nf (COM: estado)* solvency; *(: acción)* settlement, payment.

solventar [solßen'tar] *vt (pagar)* to settle, pay; *(resolver)* to resolve.

solvente [sol'ßente] *adj* solvent, free of debt.

Somalia [so'malja] *nf* Somalia.

sombra ['sombra] *nf* shadow; *(como protección)* shade; ~**s** *nfpl* darkness *sg,* shadows; **sin** ~ **de duda** without a shadow of doubt; **tener buena/mala** ~ *(suerte)* to be lucky/unlucky; *(carácter)* to be likeable/disagreeable.

sombrero [som'brero] *nm* hat; ~ **hongo** bowler (hat), derby *(US)*; ~ **de copa** *o* **de pelo** *(AM)* top hat.

sombrilla [som'briʎa] *nf* parasol, sunshade.

sombrío, a [som'brio, a] *adj (oscuro)* shady; *(fig)* sombre, sad; *(persona)* gloomy.

somero, a [so'mero, a] *adj* superficial.

someter [some'ter] *vt (país)* to conquer; *(persona)* to subject to one's will; *(informe)* to present, submit; ~**se** *vr* to give in, yield, submit; ~**se a** to submit to; ~**se a una operación** to undergo an operation.

sometimiento [someti'mjento] *nm (estado)* submission; *(acción)* presentation.

somier [so'mjer], *pl* **somiers** *nm* spring mattress.

somnífero [som'nifero] *nm* sleeping pill *o* tablet.

somnolencia [somno'lenθja] *nf* sleepiness, drowsiness.

somos ['somos] *vb* V **ser.**

son [son] *vb* V **ser** ♦ *nm* sound; **en** ~ **de broma** as a joke.

sonado, a [so'naðo, a] *adj (comentado)* talked-of; *(famoso)* famous; *(COM: pey)* hyped(-up).

sonajero [sona'xero] *nm* (baby's) rattle.

sonambulismo [sonambu'lismo] *nm*

sleepwalking.

sonámbulo, a [so'nambulo, a] *nm/f* sleepwalker.

sonar [so'nar] *vt* (*campana*) to ring; (*trompeta, sirena*) to blow ♦ *vi* to sound; (*hacer ruido*) to make a noise; (*LING*) to be sounded, be pronounced; (*ser conocido*) to sound familiar; (*campana*) to ring; (*reloj*) to strike, chime; **~se** *vr*: **~se (la nariz)** to blow one's nose; **es un nombre que suena** it's a name that's in the news; **me suena ese nombre** that's name rings a bell.

sonda ['sonda] *nf* (*NAUT*) sounding; (*TEC*) bore, drill; (*MED*) probe.

sondear [sonde'ar] *vt* to sound; to bore (into), drill; to probe, sound; (*fig*) to sound out.

sondeo [son'deo] *nm* sounding; boring, drilling; (*encuesta*) poll, enquiry; **~ de la opinión pública** public opinion poll.

sónico, a ['soniko, a] *adj* sonic, sound *cpd*.

sonido [so'niðo] *nm* sound.

sonoro, a [so'noro, a] *adj* sonorous; (*resonante*) loud, resonant; (*LING*) voiced; **efectos ~s** sound effects.

sonreír [sonre'ir] *vi*, **sonreírse** *vr* to smile.

sonría [son'ria] *etc*, **sonriendo** [son'rjendo] *etc vb V* **sonreír**.

sonriente [son'rjente] *adj* smiling.

sonrisa [son'risa] *nf* smile.

sonrojar [sonro'xar] *vt*: **~ a algn** to make sb blush; **~se** *vr*: **~se (de)** to blush (at).

sonrojo [son'roxo] *nm* blush.

sonsacar [sonsa'kar] *vt* to wheedle, coax; **~ a algn** to pump sb for information.

sonsaque [son'sake] *etc vb V* **sonsacar**.

sonsonete [sonso'nete] *nm* (*golpecitos*) tap(ping); (*voz monótona*) monotonous delivery, singsong (voice).

soñador, a [sona'ðor, a] *nm/f* dreamer.

soñar [so'nar] *vt*, *vi* to dream; **~ con** to dream about *o* of; **soñé contigo anoche** I dreamed about you last night.

soñoliento, a [sono'ljento, a] *adj* sleepy, drowsy.

sopa ['sopa] *nf* soup; **~ de fideos** noodle soup.

sopero, a [so'pero, a] *adj* (*plato, cuchara*) soup *cpd* ♦ *nm* soup plate ♦ *nf* soup tureen.

sopesar [sope'sar] *vt* to try the weight of; (*fig*) to weigh up.

sopetón [sope'ton] *nm*: **de ~** suddenly, unexpectedly.

soplar [so'plar] *vt* (*polvo*) to blow away, blow off; (*inflar*) to blow up; (*vela*) to blow out; (*ayudar a recordar*) to prompt; (*birlar*) to nick; (*delatar*) to split on ♦ *vi* to

blow; (*delatar*) to squeal; (*beber*) to booze, bend the elbow.

soplete [so'plete] *nm* blowlamp; **~ soldador** welding torch.

soplo ['soplo] *nm* blow, puff; (*de viento*) puff, gust.

soplón, ona [so'plon, ona] *nm/f* (*fam: chismoso*) telltale; (: *de policía*) informer, grass.

soponcio [so'ponθjo] *nm* dizzy spell.

sopor [so'por] *nm* drowsiness.

soporífero, a [sopo'rifero, a] *adj* sleep-inducing; (*fig*) soporific ♦ *nm* sleeping pill.

soportable [sopor'taßle] *adj* bearable.

soportal [sopor'tal] *nm* porch; **~es** *nmpl* arcade *sg*.

soportar [sopor'tar] *vt* to bear, carry; (*fig*) to bear, put up with.

soporte [so'porte] *nm* support; (*fig*) pillar, support; (*INFORM*) medium; **~ de entrada/salida** input/output medium.

soprano [so'prano] *nf* soprano.

sor [sor] *nf*: **S~ María** Sister Mary.

sorber [sor'ßer] *vt* (*chupar*) to sip; (*inhalar*) to sniff, inhale; (*absorber*) to soak up, absorb.

sorbete [sor'ßete] *nm* sherbet.

sorbo ['sorßo] *nm* (*trago*) gulp, swallow; (*chupada*) sip; **beber a ~s** to sip.

sordera [sor'ðera] *nf* deafness.

sórdido, a ['sorðiðo, a] *adj* dirty, squalid.

sordo, a ['sorðo, a] *adj* (*persona*) deaf; (*ruido*) dull; (*LING*) voiceless ♦ *nm/f* deaf person; **quedarse ~** to go deaf.

sordomudo, a [sorðo'muðo, a] *adj* deaf and dumb ♦ *nm/f* deaf-mute.

soriano, a [so'rjano, a] *adj* of *o* from Soria ♦ *nm/f* native *o* inhabitant of Soria.

sorna ['sorna] *nf* (*malicia*) slyness; (*tono burlón*) sarcastic tone.

soroche [so'rotʃe] *nm* (*AM MED*) mountain sickness.

sorprendente [sorpren'dente] *adj* surprising.

sorprender [sorpren'der] *vt* to surprise; (*asombrar*) to amaze; (*sobresaltar*) to startle; (*coger desprevenido*) to catch unawares; **~se** *vr*: **~se (de)** to be surprised *o* amazed (at).

sorpresa [sor'presa] *nf* surprise.

sorpresivo, a [sorpre'sißo, a] *adj* (*AM*) surprising; (*imprevisto*) sudden.

sortear [sorte'ar] *vt* to draw lots for; (*rifar*) to raffle; (*dificultad*) to dodge, avoid.

sorteo [sor'teo] *nm* (*en lotería*) draw; (*rifa*) raffle.

sortija [sor'tixa] *nf* ring; (*rizo*) ringlet, curl.

sortilegio [sorti'lexjo] *nm* (*hechicería*) sorcery; (*hechizo*) spell.

sosegado, a [sose'ɣaðo, a] *adj* quiet, calm.

sosegar [sose'ɣar] *vt* to quieten, calm; (*el ánimo*) to reassure ♦ *vi* to rest.

sosegué [sose'ɣe], **soseguemos** [sose'ɣemos] *etc vb* V **sosegar**.

sosiego [so'sjeɣo] *etc vb* V **sosegar** ♦ *nm* quiet(ness), calm(ness).

sosiegue [so'sjeɣe] *etc vb* V **sosegar**.

soslayar [sosla'jar] *vt* (*preguntas*) to get round.

soslayo [sos'lajo]: **de ~** *adv* obliquely, sideways; **mirar de ~** to look out of the corner of one's eye (at).

soso, a ['soso, a] *adj* (*CULIN*) tasteless; (*fig*) dull, uninteresting.

sospecha [sos'petʃa] *nf* suspicion.

sospechar [sospe'tʃar] *vt* to suspect ♦ *vi*: **~ de** to be suspicious of.

sospechoso, a [sospe'tʃoso, a] *adj* suspicious; (*testimonio, opinión*) suspect ♦ *nm/f* suspect.

sostén [sos'ten] *nm* (*apoyo*) support; (*sujetador*) bra; (*alimentación*) sustenance, food.

sostendré [sosten'dre] *etc vb* V **sostener**.

sostener [soste'ner] *vt* to support; (*mantener*) to keep up, maintain; (*alimentar*) to sustain, keep going; **~se** *vr* to support o.s.; (*seguir*) to continue, remain.

sostenga [sos'tenga] *etc vb* V **sostener**.

sostenido, adj [soste'niðo, a] *adj* continuous, constant; (*prolongado*) prolonged; (*MUS*) sharp ♦ *nm* (*MUS*) sharp.

sostuve [sos'tuβe] *etc vb* V **sostener**.

sota ['sota] *nf* (*NAIPES*) ≈ jack; V *tb* **baraja española**.

sotana [so'tana] *nf* (*REL*) cassock.

sótano ['sotano] *nm* basement.

sotavento [sota'βento] *nm* (*NAUT*) lee, leeward.

soterrar [sote'rrar] *vt* to bury; (*esconder*) to hide away.

sotierre [so'tjerre] *etc vb* V **soterrar**.

soviético, a [so'βjetiko, a] *adj, nm/f* Soviet; **los ~s** the Soviets, the Russians.

soy [soi] *vb* V **ser**.

soya ['soja] *nf* (*AM*) soya (bean).

SP *abr* (*AUTO*) = **servicio público**.

SPM *nm abr* (= *síndrome premenstrual*) PMS.

spooling [es'pulin] *nm* (*INFORM*) spooling.

sport [es'por(t)] *nm* sport.

spot [es'pot], *pl* **spot** *nm* (*publicitario*) ad.

squash [es'kwas] *nm* (*DEPORTE*) squash.

Sr. *abr* (= *Señor*) Mr.

Sra. *abr* (= *Señora*) Mrs.

S.R.C. *abr* (= *se ruega contestación*) R.S.V.P.

Sres., Srs. *abr* (= *Señores*) Messrs.

Sri Lanka [sri'lanka] *nm* Sri Lanka.

Srta. *abr* = **Señorita**.

SS *abr* (= *Santos, Santas*) SS.

ss. *abr* (= *siguientes*) foll.

S.S. *abr* (*REL*: = *Su Santidad*) H.H.

SS.MM. *abr* (= *Sus Majestades*) Their Royal Highnesses.

Sta. *abr* (= *Santa*) St; (= *Señorita*) Miss.

stand, *pl* **stands** [es'tan, es'tan(s)] *nm* (*COM*) stand.

stárter [es'tarter] *nm* (*AUTO*) self-starter, starting motor.

status ['status, es'tatus] *nm inv* status.

statu(s) quo [es'tatu(s)'kuo] *nm* status quo.

Sto. *abr* (= *Santo*) St.

stop, *pl* **stops** [es'top, es'top(s)] *nm* (*AUTO*) stop sign.

su [su] *pron* (*de él*) his; (*de ella*) her; (*de una cosa*) its; (*de ellos, ellas*) their; (*de usted, ustedes*) your.

suave ['swaβe] *adj* gentle; (*superficie*) smooth; (*trabajo*) easy; (*música, voz*) soft, sweet; (*clima, sabor*) mild.

suavice [swa'βiθe] *etc vb* V **suavizar**.

suavidad [swaβi'ðað] *nf* gentleness; (*de superficie*) smoothness; (*de música*) softness, sweetness.

suavizante [swaβi'θante] *nm* conditioner.

suavizar [swaβi'θar] *vt* to soften; (*quitar la aspereza*) to smooth (out); (*pendiente*) to ease; (*colores*) to tone down; (*carácter*) to mellow; (*dureza*) to temper.

subalimentado, a [suβalimen'taðo, a] *adj* undernourished.

subalterno, a [suβal'terno, a] *adj* (*importancia*) secondary; (*personal*) minor, auxiliary ♦ *nm* subordinate.

subarrendar [suβarren'dar] *vt* (*COM*) to lease back.

subarriendo [suβa'rrjendo] *nm* (*COM*) leaseback.

subasta [su'βasta] *nf* auction; **poner en** o **sacar a pública ~** to put up for public auction; **~ a la rebaja** Dutch auction.

subastador, a [suβasta'ðor, a] *nm/f* auctioneer.

subastar [suβas'tar] *vt* to auction (off).

subcampeón, ona [suβkampe'on, ona] *nm/f* runner-up.

subconsciente [suβkons'θjente] *adj* subconscious.

subcontratar [suβkontra'tar] *vt* (*COM*) to

subcontract.

subcontrato [sußkon'trato] *nm* (*COM*)
subcontract.

subdesarrollado, a [sußðesarro'ʎaðo, a]
adj underdeveloped.

subdesarrollo [sußðesa'rroʎo] *nm*
underdevelopment.

subdirector, a [sußðirek'tor, a] *nm/f*
assistant *o* deputy manager.

subdirectorio [sußðirek'torjo] *nm* (*INFORM*)
subdirectory.

súbdito, a ['sußðito, a] *nm/f* subject.

subdividir [sußðißi'ðir] *vt* to subdivide.

subempleo [sußem'pleo] *nm*
underemployment.

subestimar [sußesti'mar] *vt* to
underestimate, underrate.

subido, a [su'ßiðo, a] *adj* (*color*) bright,
strong; (*precio*) high ♦ *nf* (*de montaña etc*)
ascent, climb; (*de precio*) rise, increase;
(*pendiente*) slope, hill.

subíndice [su'ßindiθe] *nm* (*INFORM*, *TIP*)
subscript.

subir [su'ßir] *vt* (*objeto*) to raise, lift up;
(*cuesta, calle*) to go up; (*colina, montaña*)
to climb; (*precio*) to raise, put up;
(*empleado etc*) to promote ♦ *vi* to go/come
up; (*a un coche*) to get in; (*a un autobús,
tren*) to get on; (*precio*) to rise, go up; (*en
el empleo*) to be promoted; (*río, marea*) to
rise; ~**se** *vr* to get up, climb; ~**se a un
coche** to get in(to) a car.

súbito, a ['sußito, a] *adj* (*repentino*) sudden;
(*imprevisto*) unexpected.

subjetivo, a [sußxe'tißo, a] *adj* subjective.

subjuntivo [sußxun'tißo] *nm* subjunctive
(mood).

sublevación [sußleßa'θjon] *nf* revolt,
rising.

sublevar [sußle'ßar] *vt* to rouse to revolt;
~**se** *vr* to revolt, rise.

sublimar [sußli'mar] *vt* (*persona*) to exalt;
(*deseos etc*) to sublimate.

sublime [su'ßlime] *adj* sublime.

subliminal [sußlimi'nal] *adj* subliminal.

submarinista [sußmari'nista] *nm/f*
underwater explorer.

submarino, a [sußma'rino, a] *adj*
underwater ♦ *nm* submarine.

subnormal [sußnor'mal] *adj* subnormal
♦ *nm/f* subnormal person.

suboficial [sußofi'θjal] *nm* non-commissioned officer.

subordinado, a [sußorði'naðo, a] *adj*, *nm/f*
subordinate.

subproducto [sußpro'ðukto] *nm* by-
product.

subrayado [sußra'jaðo] *nm* underlining.

subrayar [sußra'jar] *vt* to underline;
(*recalcar*) to underline, emphasize.

subrepticio, a [sußrep'tiθjo, a] *adj*
surreptitious.

subrutina [sußru'tina] *nf* (*INFORM*) subroutine.

subsanar [sußsa'nar] *vt* (*reparar*) to make
good; (*perdonar*) to excuse; (*sobreponerse
a*) to overcome.

subscribir [sußskri'ßir] *vt* = **suscribir**.

subscrito [sußs'krito] *pp de* **subscribir**.

subsecretario, a [sußsekre'tarjo, a] *nm/f*
undersecretary, assistant secretary.

subsidiariedad [sußsiðjarie'ðað] *nf* (*POL*)
subsidiarity.

subsidiario, a [sußsi'ðjarjo, a] *adj*
subsidiary.

subsidio [suß'siðjo] *nm* (*ayuda*) aid,
financial help; (*subvención*) subsidy,
grant; (*de enfermedad, paro etc*) benefit,
allowance.

subsistencia [sußsis'tenθja] *nf*
subsistence.

subsistir [sußsis'tir] *vi* to subsist; (*vivir*) to
live; (*sobrevivir*) to survive, endure.

subsuelo [suß'swelo] *nm* subsoil.

subterfugio [sußter'fuxjo] *nm* subterfuge.

subterráneo, a [sußte'rraneo, a] *adj*
underground, subterranean ♦ *nm*
underpass, underground passage; (*AM*)
underground railway, subway (*US*).

subtítulo [suß'titulo] *nm* subtitle,
subheading.

suburbano, a [sußur'ßano, a] *adj*
suburban.

suburbio [su'ßurßjo] *nm* (*barrio*) slum
quarter; (*afueras*) suburbs *pl*.

subvención [sußßen'θjon] *nf* subsidy,
subvention, grant; ~ **estatal** state
subsidy *o* support; ~ **para la inversión**
(*COM*) investment grant.

subvencionar [sußßenθjo'nar] *vt* to
subsidize.

subversión [sußßer'sjon] *nf* subversion.

subversivo, a [sußßer'sißo, a] *adj*
subversive.

subyacente [sußja'θente] *adj* underlying.

subyugar [sußju'ʝar] *vt* (*país*) to
subjugate, subdue; (*enemigo*) to
overpower; (*voluntad*) to dominate.

subyugue [sub'juʝe] *etc vb V* **subyugar**.

succión [suk'θjon] *nf* suction.

succionar [sukθjo'nar] *vt* (*sorber*) to suck;
(*TEC*) to absorb, soak up.

sucedáneo, a [suθe'ðaneo, a] *adj*
substitute ♦ *nm* substitute (food).

suceder [suθe'ðer] *vi* to happen; ~ **a**
(*seguir*) to succeed, follow; **lo que sucede**

es que ... the fact is that ...; **~ al trono** to succeed to the throne.

sucesión [suθe'sjon] *nf* succession; (*serie*) sequence, series; (*hijos*) issue, offspring.

sucesivamente [suθesiβa'mente] *adv*: **y así ~** and so on.

sucesivo, a [suθe'siβo, a] *adj* successive, following; **en lo ~** in future, from now on.

suceso [su'θeso] *nm* (*hecho*) event, happening; (*incidente*) incident.

sucesor, a [suθe'sor, a] *nm/f* successor; (*heredero*) heir/heiress.

suciedad [suθje'ðað] *nf* (*estado*) dirtiness; (*mugre*) dirt, filth.

sucinto, a [su'θinto, a] *adj* (*conciso*) succinct, concise.

sucio, a ['suθjo, a] *adj* dirty; (*mugriento*) grimy; (*manchado*) grubby; (*borroso*) smudged; (*conciencia*) bad; (*conducta*) vile; (*táctica*) dirty, unfair.

Sucre ['sukre] *n* Sucre.

sucre ['sukre] *nm Ecuadorean monetary unit*.

suculento, a [suku'lento, a] *adj* (*sabroso*) tasty; (*jugoso*) succulent.

sucumbir [sukum'bir] *vi* to succumb.

sucursal [sukur'sal] *nf* branch (office); (*filial*) subsidiary.

Sudáfrica [su'ðafrika] *nf* South Africa.

sudafricano, a [suðafri'kano, a] *adj*, *nm/f* South African.

Sudamérica [suða'merika] *nf* South America.

sudamericano, a [suðameri'kano, a] *adj*, *nm/f* South American.

sudanés, esa [suða'nes, esa] *adj*, *nm/f* Sudanese.

sudar [su'ðar] *vt*, *vi* to sweat; (*BOT*) to ooze, give out *o* off.

sudeste [su'ðeste] *adj* south-east(ern); (*rumbo, viento*) south-easterly ♦ *nm* south-east; (*viento*) south-east wind.

sudoeste [suðo'este] *adj* south-west(ern); (*rumbo, viento*) south-westerly ♦ *nm* south-west; (*viento*) south-west wind.

sudor [su'ðor] *nm* sweat.

sudoroso, a [suðo'roso, a] *adj* sweaty, sweating.

Suecia ['sweθja] *nf* Sweden.

sueco, a ['sweko, a] *adj* Swedish ♦ *nm/f* Swede ♦ *nm* (*LING*) Swedish; **hacerse el ~** to pretend not to hear *o* understand.

suegro, a ['sweɣro, a] *nm/f* father-/mother-in-law; **los ~s** one's in-laws.

suela ['swela] *nf* (*de zapato, tb pescado*) sole.

sueldo ['sweldo] *etc vb V* **soldar** ♦ *nm* pay, wage(s) (*pl*).

suelo ['swelo] *etc vb V* **soler** ♦ *nm* (*tierra*) ground; (*de casa*) floor.

suelto, a ['swelto, a] *etc vb V* **soltar** ♦ *adj* loose; (*libre*) free; (*separado*) detached; (*ágil*) quick, agile; (*corriente*) fluent, flowing ♦ *nm* (loose) change, small change; **está muy ~ en inglés** he is very good at *o* fluent in English.

suene ['swene] *etc vb V* **sonar**.

sueño ['sweɲo] *etc vb V* **soñar** ♦ *nm* sleep; (*somnolencia*) sleepiness, drowsiness; (*lo soñado, fig*) dream; **~ pesado** *o* **profundo** deep *o* heavy sleep; **tener ~** to be sleepy.

suero ['swero] *nm* (*MED*) serum; (*de leche*) whey.

suerte ['swerte] *nf* (*fortuna*) luck; (*azar*) chance; (*destino*) fate, destiny; (*condición*) lot; (*género*) sort, kind; **lo echaron a ~s** they drew lots *o* tossed up for it; **tener ~** to be lucky; **de otra ~** otherwise, if not; **de ~ que** so that, in such a way that.

suéter ['sweter], *pl* **suéters** *nm* sweater.

suficiencia [sufi'θjenθja] *nf* (*cabida*) sufficiency; (*idoneidad*) suitability; (*aptitud*) adequacy.

suficiente [sufi'θjente] *adj* enough, sufficient.

sufijo [su'fixo] *nm* suffix.

sufragar [sufra'ɣar] *vt* (*ayudar*) to help; (*gastos*) to meet; (*proyecto*) to pay for.

sufragio [su'fraxjo] *nm* (*voto*) vote; (*derecho de voto*) suffrage.

sufrague [su'fraɣe] *etc vb V* **sufragar**.

sufrido, a [su'friðo, a] *adj* (*de carácter fuerte*) tough; (*paciente*) long-suffering; (*tela*) hard-wearing; (*color*) that does not show the dirt; (*marido*) complaisant.

sufrimiento [sufri'mjento] *nm* suffering.

sufrir [su'frir] *vt* (*padecer*) to suffer; (*soportar*) to bear, stand, put up with; (*apoyar*) to hold up, support ♦ *vi* to suffer.

sugerencia [suxe'renθja] *nf* suggestion.

sugerir [suxe'rir] *vt* to suggest; (*sutilmente*) to hint; (*idea: incitar*) to prompt.

sugestión [suxes'tjon] *nf* suggestion; (*sutil*) hint; (*poder*) hypnotic power.

sugestionar [suxestjo'nar] *vt* to influence.

sugestivo, a [suxes'tiβo, a] *adj* stimulating; (*atractivo*) attractive; (*fascinante*) fascinating.

sugiera [su'xjera] *etc*, **sugiriendo** [suxi'rjendo] *etc vb V* **sugerir**.

suicida [sui'θiða] *adj* suicidal ♦ *nm/f*

suicidal person; (*muerto*) suicide, person who has committed suicide.

suicidarse [suiθi'ðarse] *vr* to commit suicide, kill o.s.

suicidio [sui'θiðjo] *nm* suicide.

Suiza ['swiθa] *nf* Switzerland.

suizo, a ['swiθo, a] *adj, nm/f* Swiss ♦ *nm* sugared bun.

sujeción [suxe'θjon] *nf* subjection.

sujetador [suxeta'ðor] *nm* fastener, clip; (*prenda femenina*) bra, brassiere.

sujetapapeles [suxetapa'peles] *nm inv* paper clip.

sujetar [suxe'tar] *vt* (*fijar*) to fasten; (*detener*) to hold down; (*fig*) to subject, subjugate; (*pelo etc*) to keep *o* hold in place; (*papeles*) to fasten together; ~se *vr* to subject o.s.

sujeto, a [su'xeto, a] *adj* fastened, secure ♦ *nm* subject; (*individuo*) individual; (*fam: tipo*) fellow, character, type, guy (*US*); ~ a subject to.

sulfurar [sulfu'rar] *vt* (*TEC*) to sulphurate; (*sacar de quicio*) to annoy; ~se *vr* (*enojarse*) to get riled, see red, blow up.

sulfuro [sul'furo] *nm* sulphide.

suma ['suma] *nf* (*cantidad*) total, sum; (*de dinero*) sum; (*acto*) adding (up), addition; **en** ~ in short; ~ **y sigue** (*COM*) carry forward.

sumador [suma'ðor] *nm* (*INFORM*) adder.

sumamente [suma'mente] *adv* extremely, exceedingly.

sumar [su'mar] *vt* to add (up); (*reunir*) to collect, gather ♦ *vi* to add up.

sumario, a [su'marjo, a] *adj* brief, concise ♦ *nm* summary.

sumergir [sumer'xir] *vt* to submerge; (*hundir*) to sink; (*bañar*) to immerse, dip; ~se *vr* (*hundirse*) to sink beneath the surface.

sumerja [su'merxa] *etc vb V* **sumergir**.

sumidero [sumi'ðero] *nm* drain, sewer; (*TEC*) sump.

suministrador, a [suministra'ðor, a] *nm/f* supplier.

suministrar [suminis'trar] *vt* to supply, provide.

suministro [sumi'nistro] *nm* supply; (*acto*) supplying, providing.

sumir [su'mir] *vt* to sink, submerge; (*fig*) to plunge; ~se *vr* (*objeto*) to sink; ~se **en el estudio** to become absorbed in one's studies.

sumisión [sumi'sjon] *nf* (*acto*) submission; (*calidad*) submissiveness, docility.

sumiso, a [su'miso, a] *adj* submissive, docile.

súmmum ['sumum] *nm inv* (*fig*) height.

sumo, a ['sumo, a] *adj* great, extreme; (*mayor*) highest, supreme ♦ *nm* sumo (wrestling); **a lo** ~ at most.

suntuoso, a [sun'twoso, a] *adj* sumptuous, magnificent; (*lujoso*) lavish.

sup. *abr* (= *superior*) sup.

supe ['supe] *etc vb V* **saber**.

supeditar [supeði'tar] *vt* to subordinate; (*sojuzgar*) to subdue; (*oprimir*) to oppress; ~se *vr*: ~se **a** to subject o.s. to.

super... [super] *pref* super..., over....

súper ['super] *adj* (*fam*) super, great.

superable [supe'raβle] *adj* (*dificultad*) surmountable; (*tarea*) that can be performed.

superación [supera'θjon] *nf* (*tb*: ~ **personal**) self-improvement.

superar [supe'rar] *vt* (*sobreponerse a*) to overcome; (*rebasar*) to surpass, do better than; (*pasar*) to go beyond; (*marca, récord*) to break; (*etapa: dejar atrás*) to get past; ~se *vr* to excel o.s.

superávit [supe'raβit] *pl* **superávits** *nm* surplus.

superchería [supertʃe'ria] *nf* fraud, trick, swindle.

superficial [superfi'θjal] *adj* superficial; (*medida*) surface *cpd*.

superficie [super'fiθje] *nf* surface; (*área*) area; **grandes** ~s (*COM*) superstores.

superfluo, a [su'perflwo, a] *adj* superfluous.

superíndice [supe'rindiθe] *nm* (*INFORM, TIP*) superscript.

superintendente [superinten'dente] *nm/f* supervisor, superintendent.

superior [supe'rjor] *adj* (*piso, clase*) upper; (*temperatura, número, nivel*) higher; (*mejor: calidad, producto*) superior, better ♦ *nm* superior.

superiora [supe'rjora] *nf* (*REL*) mother superior.

superioridad [superjori'ðað] *nf* superiority.

superlativo, a [superla'tiβo, a] *adj, nm* superlative.

supermercado [supermer'kaðo] *nm* supermarket.

superpoblación [superpoβla'θjon] *nf* overpopulation; (*congestionamiento*) overcrowding.

superponer [superpo'ner] *vt* (*INFORM*) to overstrike.

superposición [superposi'θjon] *nf* (*en impresora*) overstrike.

superpotencia [superpo'tenθja] *nf* superpower, great power.

superproducción [superproðuk'θjon] *nf* overproduction.

supersónico, a [super'soniko, a] *adj* supersonic.

superstición [supersti'θjon] *nf* superstition.

supersticioso, a [supersti'θjoso, a] *adj* superstitious.

supervisar [superßi'sar] *vt* to supervise; (*COM*) to superintend.

supervisor, a [superßi'sor, a] *nm/f* supervisor.

supervivencia [superßi'ßenθja] *nf* survival.

superviviente [superßi'ßjente] *adj* surviving ♦ *nm/f* survivor.

suplantar [suplan'tar] *vt* (*persona*) to supplant; (*hacerse pasar por otro*) to take the place of.

suplementario, a [suplemen'tarjo, a] *adj* supplementary.

suplemento [suple'mento] *nm* supplement.

suplencia [su'plenθja] *nf* substitution, replacement; (*etapa*) period during which one deputizes *etc.*

suplente [su'plente] *adj* substitute; (*disponible*) reserve ♦ *nm/f* substitute.

supletorio, a [suple'torjo, a] *adj* supplementary; (*adicional*) extra ♦ *nm* supplement; **mesa supletoria** spare table.

súplica ['suplika] *nf* request; (*REL*) supplication; (*JUR: instancia*) petition; **~s** *nfpl* entreaties.

suplicar [supli'kar] *vt* (*cosa*) to beg (for), plead for; (*persona*) to beg, plead with; (*JUR*) to appeal to, petition.

suplicio [su'pliθjo] *nm* torture; (*tormento*) torment; (*emoción*) anguish; (*experiencia penosa*) ordeal.

suplique [su'plike] *etc vb V* **suplicar**.

suplir [su'plir] *vt* (*compensar*) to make good, make up for; (*reemplazar*) to replace, substitute ♦ *vi*: **~ a** to take the place of, substitute for.

supo ['supo] *etc vb V* **saber**.

supondré [supon'dre] *etc vb V* **suponer**.

suponer [supo'ner] *vt* to suppose; (*significar*) to mean; (*acarrear*) to involve ♦ *vi* to count, have authority; **era de ~ que ...** it was to be expected that ....

suponga [su'ponga] *etc vb V* **suponer**.

suposición [suposi'θjon] *nf* supposition.

supositorio [suposi'torjo] *nm* suppository.

supremacía [suprema'θia] *nf* supremacy.

supremo, a [su'premo, a] *adj* supreme.

supresión [supre'sjon] *nf* suppression; (*de derecho*) abolition; (*de dificultad*)

removal; (*de palabra etc*) deletion; (*de restricción*) cancellation, lifting.

suprimir [supri'mir] *vt* to suppress; (*derecho, costumbre*) to abolish; (*dificultad*) to remove; (*palabra etc, INFORM*) to delete; (*restricción*) to cancel, lift.

supuestamente [supwesta'mente] *adv* supposedly.

supuesto, a [su'pwesto, a] *pp de* **suponer** ♦ *adj* (*hipotético*) supposed; (*falso*) false ♦ *nm* assumption, hypothesis ♦ *conj*: **~ que** since; **dar por ~ algo** to take sth for granted; **por ~** of course.

supurar [supu'rar] *vi* to fester, suppurate.

supuse [su'puse] *etc vb V* **suponer**.

sur [sur] *adj* southern; (*rumbo*) southerly ♦ *nm* south; (*viento*) south wind.

Suráfrica [su'rafrika] *etc* = **Sudáfrica** *etc.*

Suramérica [sura'merika] *etc* = **Sudamérica** *etc.*

surcar [sur'kar] *vt* to plough; (*superficie*) to cut, score.

surco ['surko] *nm* (*en metal, disco*) groove; (*AGR*) furrow.

surcoreano, a [surkore'ano, a] *adj, nm/f* South Korean.

sureño, a [su'reɲo, a] *adj* southern ♦ *nm/f* southerner.

sureste [su'reste] = **sudeste**.

surf [surf] *nm* surfing.

surgir [sur'xir] *vi* to arise, emerge; (*dificultad*) to come up, crop up.

surja ['surxa] *etc vb V* **surgir**.

suroeste [suro'este] = **sudoeste**.

surque ['surke] *etc vb V* **surcar**.

surrealismo [surrea'lismo] *nm* surrealism.

surrealista [surrea'lista] *adj, nm/f* surrealist.

surtido, a [sur'tiðo, a] *adj* mixed, assorted ♦ *nm* (*selección*) selection, assortment; (*abastecimiento*) supply, stock.

surtidor [surti'ðor] *nm* (*chorro*) jet, spout; (*fuente*) fountain; **~ de gasolina** petrol (*BRIT*) *o* gas (*US*) pump.

surtir [sur'tir] *vt* to supply, provide; (*efecto*) to have, produce ♦ *vi* to spout, spurt; **~se** *vr*: **~se de** to provide o.s. with.

susceptible [susθep'tißle] *adj* susceptible; (*sensible*) sensitive; **~ de** capable of.

suscitar [susθi'tar] *vt* to cause, provoke; (*discusión*) to start; (*duda, problema*) to raise; (*interés, sospechas*) to arouse.

suscribir [suskri'ßir] *vt* (*firmar*) to sign; (*respaldar*) to subscribe to, endorse; (*COM: acciones*) to take out an option on; **~se** *vr* to subscribe; **~ a algn a una revista** to take out a subscription to a journal for sb.

suscripción [suskrip'θjon] *nf* subscription.

suscrito, a [sus'krito, a] *pp de* **suscribir**
♦ *adj*: ~ **en exceso** oversubscribed.

sushi ['suʃi] *nm* sushi.

susodicho, a [suso'ditʃo, a] *adj* above-
mentioned.

suspender [suspen'der] *vt* (*objeto*) to hang
(up), suspend; (*trabajo*) to stop, suspend;
(*ESCOL*) to fail.

suspense [sus'pense] *nm* suspense.

suspensión [suspen'sjon] *nf* suspension;
(*fig*) stoppage, suspension; (*JUR*) stay; ~
de fuego *o* **de hostilidades** ceasefire,
cessation of hostilities; ~ **de pagos**
suspension of payments.

suspensivo, a [suspen'siβo, a] *adj*: **puntos**
~**s** dots, suspension points.

suspenso, a [sus'penso, a] *adj* hanging,
suspended; (*ESCOL*) failed ♦ *nm* (*ESCOL*)
fail(ure); **quedar** *o* **estar en** ~ to be
pending.

suspicacia [suspi'kaθja] *nf* suspicion,
mistrust.

suspicaz [suspi'kaθ] *adj* suspicious,
distrustful.

suspirar [suspi'rar] *vi* to sigh.

suspiro [sus'piro] *nm* sigh.

sustancia [sus'tanθja] *nf* substance; ~ **gris**
(*ANAT*) grey matter; **sin** ~ lacking in
substance, shallow.

sustancial [sustan'θjal] *adj* substantial.

sustancioso, a [sustan'θjoso, a] *adj*
substantial; (*discurso*) solid.

sustantivo, a [sustan'tiβo, a] *adj*
substantive; (*LING*) substantival, noun
cpd ♦ *nm* noun, substantive.

sustentar [susten'tar] *vt* (*alimentar*) to
sustain, nourish; (*objeto*) to hold up,
support; (*idea, teoría*) to maintain,
uphold; (*fig*) to sustain, keep going.

sustento [sus'tento] *nm* support; (*alimento*)
sustenance, food.

sustituir [sustitu'ir] *vt* to substitute,
replace.

sustituto, a [susti'tuto, a] *nm/f* substitute,
replacement.

sustituyendo [sustitu'jendo] *etc vb V*
sustituir.

susto ['susto] *nm* fright, scare; **dar un** ~ **a**
algn to give sb a fright; **darse** *o* **pegarse**
un ~ (*fam*) to get a fright.

sustraer [sustra'er] *vt* to remove, take
away; (*MAT*) to subtract.

sustraiga [sus'traiɣa] *etc*, **sustraje**
[sus'traxe] *etc vb V* **sustraer**.

sustrato [sus'trato] *nm* substratum.

sustrayendo [sustra'jendo] *etc vb V*
sustraer.

susurrar [susu'rrar] *vi* to whisper.

susurro [su'surro] *nm* whisper.

sutil [su'til] *adj* (*aroma*) subtle; (*tenue*) thin;
(*hilo, hebra*) fine; (*olor*) delicate; (*brisa*)
gentle; (*diferencia*) fine, subtle;
(*inteligencia*) sharp, keen.

sutileza [suti'leθa] *nf* subtlety; (*delgadez*)
thinness; (*delicadeza*) delicacy; (*agudeza*)
keenness.

sutura [su'tura] *nf* suture.

suturar [sutu'rar] *vt* to suture; (*juntar con*
puntos) to stitch.

suyo, a ['sujo, a] *adj* (*con artículo o después*
del verbo ser: de él) his; (: *de ella*) hers;
(: *de ellos, ellas*) theirs; (: *de usted,*
ustedes) yours; (*después de un nombre: de*
él) of his; (: *de ella*) of hers; (: *de ellos,*
ellas) of theirs; (: *de usted, ustedes*) of
yours; **lo** ~ (= what is) his; (*su parte*) his
share, what he deserves; **los** ~**s** (*familia*)
one's family *o* relations; (*partidarios*)
one's own people *o* supporters; ~
afectísimo (*en carta*) yours faithfully *o*
sincerely; **de** ~ in itself; **eso es muy** ~
that's just like him; **hacer de las suyas** to
get up to one's old tricks; **ir a la suya, ir**
a lo ~ to go one's own way; **salirse con la**
suya to get one's way.

T t

T, t [te] *nf* (*letra*) T, t; **T de Tarragona** T for
Tommy.

t *abr* = **tonelada**.

T. *abr* (= *Teléfono, Telégrafo*) tel.; (*COM*)
= **Tarifa**; **Tasa**.

t. *abr* (= *tomo(s)*) vol(s).

Tabacalera [taβaka'lera] *nf Spanish state*
tobacco monopoly.

tabaco [ta'βako] *nm* tobacco; (*fam*)
cigarettes *pl*.

tábano ['taβano] *nm* horsefly.

tabaquería [tabake'ria] *nf* tobacconist's
(*BRIT*), cigar store (*US*).

tabarra [ta'βarra] *nf* (*fam*) nuisance; **dar la**
~ to be a pain in the neck.

taberna [ta'βerna] *nf* bar.

tabernero, a [taβer'nero, a] *nm/f*
(*encargado*) publican; (*camarero*)
barman/barmaid.

tabique [ta'βike] *nm* (*pared*) thin wall; (*para dividir*) partition.

tabla ['taβla] *nf* (*de madera*) plank; (*estante*) shelf; (*de anuncios*) board; (*lista, catálogo*) list; (*mostrador*) counter; (*de vestido*) pleat; (*ARTE*) panel; ~**s** *nfpl* (*TAUR, TEAT*) boards; **hacer** ~**s** to draw; ~ **de consulta** (*INFORM*) lookup table.

tablado [ta'βlaðo] *nm* (*plataforma*) platform; (*suelo*) plank floor; (*TEAT*) stage.

tablao [ta'βlao] *nm* (*tb:* ~ **flamenco**) flamenco show.

tablero [ta'βlero] *nm* (*de madera*) plank, board; (*pizarra*) blackboard; (*de ajedrez, damas*) board; (*AUTO*) dashboard; ~ **de gráficos** (*INFORM*) graph pad.

tableta [ta'βleta] *nf* (*MED*) tablet; (*de chocolate*) bar.

tablilla [ta'βliʎa] *nf* small board; (*MED*) splint.

tablón [ta'βlon] *nm* (*de suelo*) plank; (*de techo*) beam; (*de anuncios*) notice board.

tabú [ta'βu] *nm* taboo.

tabulación [taβula'θjon] *nf* (*INFORM*) tab(bing).

tabulador [taβula'ðor] *nm* (*INFORM, TIP*) tab.

tabuladora [taβula'ðora] *nf:* ~ **eléctrica** electric accounting machine.

tabular [taβu'lar] *vt* to tabulate; (*INFORM*) to tab.

taburete [taβu'rete] *nm* stool.

tacaño, a [ta'kaɲo, a] *adj* (*avaro*) mean; (*astuto*) crafty.

tacha ['tatʃa] *nf* (*defecto*) flaw, defect; (*TEC*) stud; **poner** ~ **a** to find fault with; **sin** ~ flawless.

tachar [ta'tʃar] *vt* (*borrar*) to cross out; (*corregir*) to correct; (*criticar*) to criticize; ~ **de** to accuse of.

tacho ['tatʃo] *nm* (*AM*) bucket, pail.

tachón [ta'tʃon] *nm* erasure; (*tachadura*) crossing-out; (*TEC*) ornamental stud; (*COSTURA*) trimming.

tachuela [ta'tʃwela] *nf* (*clavo*) tack.

tácito, a ['taθito, a] *adj* tacit; (*acuerdo*) unspoken; (*LING*) understood; (*ley*) unwritten.

taciturno, a [taθi'turno, a] *adj* (*callado*) silent; (*malhumorado*) sullen.

taco ['tako] *nm* (*BILLAR*) cue; (*libro de billetes*) book; (*manojo de billetes*) wad; (*AM*) heel; (*tarugo*) peg; (*fam: bocado*) snack; (: *palabrota*) swear word; (: *trago de vino*) swig; (*Méjico*) filled tortilla; **armarse** *o* **hacerse un** ~ to get into a mess.

tacógrafo [ta'koɣrafo] *nm* (*COM*) tachograph.

tacón [ta'kon] *nm* heel; **de** ~ **alto** high-heeled.

taconear [takone'ar] *vi* (*dar golpecitos*) to tap with one's heels; (*MIL etc*) to click one's heels.

taconeo [tako'neo] *nm* (heel) tapping *o* clicking.

táctico, a ['taktiko, a] *adj* tactical ♦ *nf* tactics *pl*.

tacto ['takto] *nm* touch; (*acción*) touching; (*fig*) tact.

TAE *nf abr* (= *tasa anual equivalente*) APR.

tafetán [tafe'tan] *nm* taffeta; **tafetanes** *nmpl* (*fam*) frills; ~ **adhesivo** *o* **inglés** sticking plaster.

tafilete [tafi'lete] *nm* morocco leather.

tahona [ta'ona] *nf* (*panadería*) bakery; (*molino*) flourmill.

tahúr [ta'ur] *nm* gambler; (*pey*) cheat.

tailandés, esa [tailan'des, esa] *adj, nm/f* Thai ♦ *nm* (*LING*) Thai.

Tailandia [tai'landja] *nf* Thailand.

taimado, a [tai'maðo, a] *adj* (*astuto*) sly; (*resentido*) sullen.

taita ['taita] *nm* dad, daddy.

tajada [ta'xaða] *nf* slice; (*fam*) rake-off; **sacar** ~ to get one's share.

tajante [ta'xante] *adj* sharp; (*negativa*) emphatic; **es una persona** ~ he's an emphatic person.

tajar [ta'xar] *vt* to cut, slice.

Tajo ['taxo] *nm* Tagus.

tajo ['taxo] *nm* (*corte*) cut; (*filo*) cutting edge; (*GEO*) cleft.

tal [tal] *adj* such; **un** ~ **García** a man called García; ~ **vez** perhaps ♦ *pron* (*persona*) someone, such a one; (*cosa*) something, such a thing; ~ **como** such as; ~ **para cual** tit for tat; (*dos iguales*) two of a kind; **hablábamos de que si** ~ **si cual** we were talking about this, that and the other ♦ *adv*: ~ **como** (*igual*) just as; ~ **cual** (*como es*) just as it is; ~ **el padre, cual el hijo** like father, like son; **¿qué** ~**?** how are things?; **¿qué** ~ **te gusta?** how do you like it? ♦ *conj*: **con** ~ **(de) que** provided that.

tala ['tala] *nf* (*de árboles*) tree felling.

taladradora [talaðra'ðora] *nf* drill; ~ **neumática** pneumatic drill.

taladrar [tala'ðrar] *vt* to drill; (*fig: suj: ruido*) to pierce.

taladro [ta'laðro] *nm* (*gen*) drill; (*hoyo*) drill hole; ~ **neumática** pneumatic drill.

talante [ta'lante] *nm* (*humor*) mood; (*voluntad*) will, willingness.

talar [ta'lar] *vt* to fell, cut down; (*fig*) to devastate.

talco ['talko] *nm* (*polvos*) talcum powder; (*MINERALOGÍA*) talc.

talega [ta'leɣa] *nf* sack.

talego [ta'leɣo] *nm* sack; **tener ~** (*fam*) to have money.

talento [ta'lento] *nm* talent; (*capacidad*) ability; (*don*) gift.

Talgo ['talɣo] *nm abr* (*FERRO* = *tren articulado ligero Goicoechea-Oriol*) high-speed train.

talidomida [taliðo'miða] *nm* thalidomide.

talismán [talis'man] *nm* talisman.

talla ['taʎa] *nf* (*estatura, fig, MED*) height, stature; (*de ropa*) size, fitting; (*palo*) measuring rod; (*ARTE: de madera*)) carving; (*de piedra*) sculpture.

tallado, a [ta'ʎaðo, a] *adj* carved ♦ *nm* (*de madera*) carving; (*de piedra*) sculpture.

tallar [ta'ʎar] *vt* (*trabajar*) to work, carve; (*grabar*) to engrave; (*medir*) to measure; (*repartir*) to deal ♦ *vi* to deal.

tallarín [taʎa'rin] *nm* noodle.

talle ['taʎe] *nm* (*ANAT*) waist; (*medida*) size; (*física*) build; (: *de mujer*) figure; (*fig*) appearance; **de ~ esbelto** with a slim figure.

taller [ta'ʎer] *nm* (*TEC*) workshop; (*fábrica*) factory; (*AUTO*) garage; (*de artista*) studio.

tallo ['taʎo] *nm* (*de planta*) stem; (*de hierba*) blade; (*brote*) shoot; (*col*) cabbage; (*CULIN*) candied peel.

talmente [tal'mente] *adv* (*de esta forma*) in such a way; (*hasta tal punto*) to such an extent; (*exactamente*) exactly.

talón [ta'lon] *nm* (*gen*) heel; (*COM*) counterfoil; (*TEC*) rim; **~ de Aquiles** Achilles heel.

talonario [talo'narjo] *nm* (*de cheques*) cheque book; (*de billetes*) book of tickets; (*de recibos*) receipt book.

tamaño, a [ta'maɲo, a] *adj* (*tan grande*) such a big; (*tan pequeño*) such a small ♦ *nm* size; **de ~ natural** full-size; **¿de qué ~ es?** what size is it?

tamarindo [tama'rindo] *nm* tamarind.

tambaleante [tambale'ante] *adj* (*persona*) staggering; (*mueble*) wobbly; (*vehículo*) swaying.

tambalearse [tambale'arse] *vr* (*persona*) to stagger; (*mueble*) to wobble; (*vehículo*) to sway.

también [tam'bjen] *adv* (*igualmente*) also, too, as well; (*además*) besides; **estoy cansado — yo ~** I'm tired — so am I *o* me too.

tambor [tam'bor] *nm* drum; (*ANAT*) eardrum; **~ del freno** brake drum; **~**

magnético (*INFORM*) magnetic drum.

tamboril [tambo'ril] *nm* small drum.

tamborilear [tamborile'ar] *vi* (*MUS*) to drum; (*con los dedos*) to drum with one's fingers.

tamborilero [tambori'lero] *nm* drummer.

Támesis ['tamesis] *nm* Thames.

tamice [ta'miθe] *etc vb V* **tamizar**.

tamiz [ta'miθ] *nm* sieve.

tamizar [tami'θar] *vt* to sieve.

tampoco [tam'poko] *adv* nor, neither; **yo ~ lo compré** I didn't buy it either.

tampón [tam'pon] *nm* plug; (*MED*) tampon.

tan [tan] *adv* so; **~ es así que** so much so that; **¡qué cosa ~ rara!** how strange!; **no es una idea ~ buena** it is not such a good idea.

tanatorio [tana'torjo] *nm* (*privado*) funeral home *o* parlour; (*público*) mortuary.

tanda ['tanda] *nf* (*gen*) series; (*de inyecciones*) course; (*juego*) set; (*turno*) shift; (*grupo*) gang.

tándem ['tandem] *nm* tandem; (*POL*) duo.

tanga ['tanga] *nm* (*bikini*) tanga; (*ropa interior*) tanga briefs.

tangente [tan'xente] *nf* tangent; **salirse por la ~** to go off at a tangent.

Tánger ['tanxer] *n* Tangier.

tangerino, a [tanxe'rino, a] *adj* of *o* from Tangier ♦ *nm/f* native *o* inhabitant of Tangier.

tangible [tan'xiβle] *adj* tangible.

tango ['tango] *nm* tango.

tanino [ta'nino] *nm* tannin.

tanque ['tanke] *nm* (*gen*) tank; (*AUTO, NAUT*) tanker.

tanqueta [tan'keta] *nf* (*MIL*) small tank, armoured vehicle.

tantear [tante'ar] *vt* (*calcular*) to reckon (up); (*medir*) to take the measure of; (*probar*) to test, try out; (*tomar la medida: persona*) to take the measurements of; (*considerar*) to weigh up ♦ *vi* (*DEPORTE*) to score.

tanteo [tan'teo] *nm* (*cálculo*) (rough) calculation; (*prueba*) test, trial; (*DEPORTE*) scoring; (*adivinanzas*) guesswork; **al ~** by trial and error.

tantísimo, a [tan'tisimo, a] *adj* so much; **~s** so many.

tanto, a ['tanto, a] *adj* (*cantidad*) so much, as much; **~s** so many, as many; **20 y ~s** 20-odd ♦ *adv* (*cantidad*) so much, as much; (*tiempo*) so long, as long; **~ tú como yo** both you and I; **~ como eso** it's not as bad as that; **~ más ... cuanto que** it's all the more ... because; **~ mejor/ peor** so much the better/the worse; **~ si**

viene como si va whether he comes or
whether he goes; ~ es así que so much
so that; por ~, por lo ~ therefore; me he
vuelto ronco de *o* con ~ hablar I have
become hoarse with so much talking
♦ *conj*: con ~ que provided (that); en ~
que while; hasta ♦ *pron*: **(que)** until such time
as ♦ *nm* (*suma*) certain amount;
(*proporción*) so much; (*punto*) point; (*gol*)
goal; ~ **alzado** agreed price; ~ **por
ciento** percentage; **al** ~ up to date; **estar
al** ~ **de los acontecimientos** to be fully
abreast of events; **un** ~ **perezoso**
somewhat lazy; **al** ~ **de que** because of
the fact that ♦ *pron*: **cado uno paga** ~
each one pays so much; **uno de** ~**s** one
of many; **a** ~**s de agosto** on such and
such a day in August; **entre** ~
meanwhile.
tañer [ta'ɲer] *vt* (*MUS*) to play; (*campana*)
to ring.
T/año *abr = toneladas por año.*
TAO *nf abr* (= *traducción asistida por
ordenador*) MAT.
tapa ['tapa] *nf* (*de caja, olla*) lid; (*de botella*)
top; (*de libro*) cover; (*comida*) snack.
tapacubos [tapa'kuβos] *nm inv* hub cap.
tapadera [tapa'ðera] *nf* lid, cover.
tapado [ta'paðo] *nm* (*AM: abrigo*) coat.
tapar [ta'par] *vt* (*cubrir*) to cover; (*envolver*)
to wrap *o* cover up; (*la vista*) to obstruct;
(*persona, falta*) to conceal; (*AM*) to fill;
~**se** *vr* to wrap o.s. up.
tapete [ta'pete] *nm* table cover; **estar
sobre el** ~ (*fig*) to be under discussion.
tapia ['tapja] *nf* (*garden*) wall.
tapiar [ta'pjar] *vt* to wall in.
tapice [ta'piθe] *etc vb V* **tapizar**.
tapicería [tapiθe'ria] *nf* tapestry; (*para
muebles*) upholstery; (*tienda*)
upholsterer's (shop).
tapicero, a [tapi'θero, a] *nm/f* (*de muebles*)
upholsterer.
tapiz [ta'piθ] *nm* (*alfombra*) carpet; (*tela
tejida*) tapestry.
tapizar [tapi'θar] *vt* (*pared*) to wallpaper;
(*suelo*) to carpet; (*muebles*) to upholster.
tapón [ta'pon] *nm* (*corcho*) stopper; (*TEC*)
plug; (*MED*) tampon; ~ **de rosca** *o* **de
tuerca** screw-top.
taponar [tapo'nar] *vt* (*botella*) to cork;
(*tubería*) to block.
taponazo [tapo'naθo] *nm* (*de tapón*) pop.
tapujo [ta'puxo] *nm* (*embozo*) muffler;
(*engaño*) deceit; **sin** ~**s** honestly.
taquigrafía [takiɣra'fia] *nf* shorthand.
taquígrafo, a [ta'kiɣrafo, a] *nm/f* shorthand
writer.

taquilla [ta'kiʎa] *nf* (*de estación etc*)
booking office; (*de teatro*) box office;
(*suma recogida*) takings *pl*; (*archivador*)
filing cabinet.
taquillero, a [taki'ʎero, a] *adj*: **función
taquillera** box office success ♦ *nm/f* ticket
clerk.
taquimecanografía [takimekanoɣra'fia] *nf*
shorthand and typing.
taquímetro [ta'kimetro] *nm* speedometer;
(*de control*) tachymeter.
tara ['tara] *nf* (*defecto*) defect; (*COM*) tare.
tarado, a [ta'raðo, a] *adj* (*COM*) defective,
imperfect; (*idiota*) stupid; (*loco*) crazy,
nuts ♦ *nm/f* idiot, cretin.
tarántula [ta'rantula] *nf* tarantula.
tararear [tarare'ar] *vi* to hum.
tardanza [tar'ðanθa] *nf* (*demora*) delay;
(*lentitud*) slowness.
tardar [tar'ðar] *vi* (*tomar tiempo*) to take a
long time; (*llegar tarde*) to be late;
(*demorar*) to delay; ¿**tarda mucho el tren?**
does the train take long?; **a más** ~ at the
(very) latest; ~ **en hacer algo** to be slow
o take a long time to do sth; **no tardes en
venir** come soon, come before long.
tarde ['tarðe] *adv* (*hora*) late; (*fuera de
tiempo*) too late ♦ *nf* (*de día*) afternoon;
(*de noche*) evening; ~ **o temprano**
sooner or later; **de** ~ **en** ~ from time to
time; ¡**buenas** ~**s!** (*de día*) good
afternoon!; (*de noche*) good evening!; **a** *o*
por la ~ in the afternoon; in the
evening.
tardío, a [tar'ðio, a] *adj* (*retrasado*) late;
(*lento*) slow (to arrive).
tardo, a ['tarðo, a] *adj* (*lento*) slow; (*torpe*)
dull; ~ **de oído** hard of hearing.
tarea [ta'rea] *nf* task; ~**s** *nfpl* (*ESCOL*)
homework *sg*; ~ **de ocasión** chore.
tarifa [ta'rifa] *nf* (*lista de precios*) price list;
(*COM*) tariff; ~ **básica** basic rate; ~
completa all-in cost; ~ **a destajo** piece
rate; ~ **doble** double time.
tarima [ta'rima] *nf* (*plataforma*) platform;
(*taburete*) stool; (*litera*) bunk.
tarjeta [tar'xeta] *nf* card; ~ **postal/de
crédito/de Navidad** postcard/credit
card/Christmas card; ~ **de circuitos**
(*INFORM*) circuit board; ~ **cliente** loyalty
card; ~ **comercial** (*COM*) calling card; ~
dinero cash card; ~ **gráficos** (*INFORM*)
graphics card; ~ **monedero** electronic
purse *o* wallet; ~ **SIM** SIM card.
tarot [ta'rot] *nm* tarot.
tarraconense [tarrako'nense] *adj* of *o* from
Tarragona ♦ *nm/f* native *o* inhabitant of
Tarragona.

tarro ['tarro] nm jar, pot.

tarta ['tarta] nf (pastel) cake; (torta) tart.

tartajear [tartaxe'ar] vi to stammer.

tartamudear [tartamuðe'ar] vi to stutter, stammer.

tartamudo, a [tarta'muðo, a] adj stuttering, stammering ♦ nm/f stutterer, stammerer.

tartárico, a [tar'tariko, a] adj: **ácido** ~ tartaric acid.

tártaro ['tartaro] adj, nm Tartar ♦ nm (QUIMICA) tartar.

tarugo, a [ta'ruɣo, a] adj stupid ♦ nm (de madera) lump.

tarumba [ta'rumba] adj (confuso) confused.

tasa ['tasa] nf (precio) (fixed) price, rate; (valoración) valuation; (medida, norma) measure, standard; ~ **básica** (COM) basic rate; ~ **de cambio** exchange rate; **de** ~ **cero** (COM) zero-rated; ~ **de crecimiento** growth rate; ~ **de interés/de nacimiento** rate of interest/birth rate; ~ **de rendimiento** (COM) rate of return; ~**s universitarias** university fees.

tasación [tasa'θjon] nf assessment, valuation; (fig) appraisal.

tasador, a [tasa'ðor, a] nm/f valuer; (COM: de impuestos) assessor.

tasar [ta'sar] vt (arreglar el precio) to fix a price for; (valorar) to value, assess; (limitar) to limit.

tasca ['taska] nf (fam) pub.

tata ['tata] nm (fam) dad(dy) ♦ nf (niñera) nanny, maid.

tatarabuelo, a [tatara'ßwelo, a] nm/f great-great-grandfather/mother; **los** ~**s** one's great-great-grandparents.

tatuaje [ta'twaxe] nm (dibujo) tattoo; (acto) tattooing.

tatuar [ta'twar] vt to tattoo.

taumaturgo [tauma'turɣo] nm miracle-worker.

taurino, a [tau'rino, a] adj bullfighting cpd.

Tauro ['tauro] nm Taurus.

tauromaquia [tauro'makja] nf (art of) bullfighting.

tautología [tautolo'xia] nf tautology.

taxativo, a [taksa'tißo, a] adj (restringido) limited; (sentido) specific.

taxi ['taksi] nm taxi.

taxidermia [taksi'ðermja] nf taxidermy.

taxímetro [tak'simetro] nm taximeter.

taxista [tak'sista] nm/f taxi driver.

Tayikistán [tajikis'tan] nm Tajikistan.

taza ['taθa] nf cup; (de retrete) bowl; ~ **para café** coffee cup.

tazón [ta'θon] nm mug, large cup; (escudilla) basin.

TCI nf abr (= tarjeta de circuito impreso) PCB.

te [te] pron (complemento de objeto) you; (complemento indirecto) (to) you; (reflexivo) (to) yourself; ¿~ **duele mucho el brazo?** does your arm hurt a lot?; ~ **equivocas** you're wrong; ¡**cálma**~! calm yourself!

té [te], pl **tés** nm tea; (reunión) tea party.

tea ['tea] nf (antorcha) torch.

teatral [tea'tral] adj theatre cpd; (fig) theatrical.

teatro [te'atro] nm theatre; (LITERATURA) plays pl, drama; **el** ~ (carrera) the theatre, acting; ~ **de aficionados/de variedades** amateur/variety theatre, vaudeville theater (US); **hacer** ~ (fig) to make a fuss.

tebeo [te'ßeo] nm children's comic.

techado [te't∫aðo] nm (techo) roof; **bajo** ~ under cover.

techo ['tet∫o] nm (externo) roof; (interno) ceiling.

techumbre [te't∫umbre] nf roof.

tecla ['tekla] nf (INFORM, MUS, TIP) key; (INFORM): ~ **de anulación/de borrar** cancel/delete key; ~ **de control/de edición** control/edit key; ~ **con flecha** arrow key; ~ **programable** user-defined key; ~ **de retorno/de tabulación** return/tab key; ~ **del cursor** cursor key; ~**s de control direccional del cursor** cursor control keys.

teclado [te'klaðo] nm keyboard (tb INFORM); ~ **numérico** (INFORM) numeric keypad.

teclear [tekle'ar] vi to strum; (fam) to drum ♦ vt (INFORM) to key (in), type in, keyboard.

tecleo [te'kleo] nm (MUS: sonido) strumming; (: forma de tocar) fingering; (fam) drumming.

tecnicismo [tekni'θismo] nm (carácter técnico) technical nature; (LING) technical term.

técnico, a ['tekniko, a] adj technical ♦ nm technician; (experto) expert ♦ nf (procedimientos) technique; (arte, oficio) craft.

tecnicolor [tekniko'lor] nm Technicolor ®.

tecnócrata [tek'nokrata] nm/f technocrat.

tecnología [teknolo'xia] nf technology; ~ **de estado sólido** (INFORM) solid-state technology; ~ **de la información** information technology.

tecnológico, a [tekno'loxiko, a] adj technological.

tecnólogo, a [tek'noloxo, a] *nm/f*
technologist.

tedio ['teðjo] *nm* (*aburrimiento*) boredom;
(*apatía*) apathy; (*fastidio*) depression.

tedioso, a [te'ðjoso, a] *adj* boring;
(*cansado*) wearisome, tedious.

Teherán [tee'ran] *nm* Teheran.

teja ['texa] *nf* (*azulejo*) tile; (*BOT*) lime (tree).

tejado [te'xaðo] *nm* (tiled) roof.

tejano, a [te'xano, a] *adj, nm/f* Texan ♦ *nmpl*:
~**s** (*vaqueros*) jeans.

Tejas ['texas] *nm* Texas.

tejemaneje [texema'nexe] *nm* (*actividad*)
bustle; (*lío*) fuss, to-do; (*intriga*) intrigue.

tejer [te'xer] *vt* to weave; (*tela de araña*) to
spin; (*AM*) to knit; (*fig*) to fabricate ♦ *vi*:
~ **y destejer** to chop and change.

tejido [te'xiðo] *nm* fabric; (*estofa, tela*)
(knitted) material; (*ANAT*) tissue;
(*textura*) texture.

tejo ['texo] *nm* (*BOT*) yew (tree).

tel. *abr* (= *teléfono*) tel.

tela ['tela] *nf* (*material*) material; (*de fruta,
en líquido*) skin; (*del ojo*) film; **hay** ~ **para
rato** there's lots to talk about; **poner en**
~ **de juicio** to (call in) question; ~ **de
araña** cobweb, spider's web.

telar [te'lar] *nm* (*máquina*) loom; (*de teatro*)
gridiron; ~**es** *nmpl* textile mill *sg*.

telaraña [tela'rana] *nf* cobweb, spider's web.

tele... [tele] *pref* tele...

tele ['tele] *nf* (*fam*) TV.

telecargar [telekar'xar] *vt* (*INFORM*) to
download.

telecomunicación [telekomunika'θjon] *nf*
telecommunication.

teleconferencia [telekonfe'renθja] *nf*
(*reunión*) teleconference; (*sistema*)
teleconferencing.

telecontrol [telekon'trol] *nm* remote
control.

telecopiadora [telekopja'ðora] *nf*: ~
facsímil fax copier.

telediario [tele'ðjarjo] *nm* television news.

teledifusión [teleðifu'sjon] *nf* (television)
broadcast.

teledirigido, a [teleðiri'xiðo, a] *adj*
remote-controlled.

teléf. *abr* (= *teléfono*) tel.

teleférico [tele'feriko] *nm* (*tren*) cable-
railway; (*de esquí*) ski-lift.

telefilm [tele'film], **telefilme** [tele'filme]
nm TV film.

telefonazo [telefo'naθo] *nm* (*fam*) telephone
call; **te daré un** ~ I'll give you a ring.

telefonear [telefone'ar] *vi* to telephone.

telefónicamente [tele'fonikamente] *adv* by
(tele)phone.

telefónico, a [tele'foniko, a] *adj* telephone
cpd ♦ *nf*: **Telefónica** (*ESP*) Spanish national
telephone company, ≈ British Telecom.

telefonista [telefo'nista] *nm/f* telephonist.

teléfono [te'lefono] *nm* (tele)phone; ~
móvil mobile phone; **está hablando por**
~ he's on the phone.

telefoto [tele'foto] *nf* telephoto.

telegrafía [telexra'fia] *nf* telegraphy.

telégrafo [te'lexrafo] *nm* telegraph; (*fam:
persona*) telegraph boy.

telegrama [tele'xrama] *nm* telegram.

teleimpresor [teleimpre'sor] *nm*
teleprinter.

telemática [tele'matika] *nf* telematics *sg*.

telémetro [te'lemetro] *nm* rangefinder.

telenovela [teleno'ßela] *nf* soap (opera).

teleobjetivo [teleobxe'tißo] *nm* telephoto
lens.

telepatía [telepa'tia] *nf* telepathy.

telepático, a [tele'patiko, a] *adj* telepathic.

teleproceso [telepro'θeso] *nm*
teleprocessing.

telescópico, a [teles'kopiko, a] *adj*
telescopic.

telescopio [teles'kopjo] *nm* telescope.

telesilla [tele'siʎa] *nm* chairlift.

telespectador, a [telespekta'ðor, a] *nm/f*
viewer.

telesquí [teles'ki] *nm* ski-lift.

teletex(to) [tele'teks(to)] *nm* teletext.

teletipista [teleti'pista] *nm/f* teletypist.

teletipo [tele'tipo] *nm* teletype(writer).

teletrabajo [teletra'ßaxo] *nm* teleworking.

televentas [tele'ßentas] *nfpl* telesales.

televidente [teleßi'ðente] *nm/f* viewer.

televisar [teleßi'sar] *vt* to televise.

televisión [teleßi'sjon] *nf* television; ~ **en
color/por satélite** colour/satellite
television; ~ **digital** digital television.

televisivo, a [teleßi'sißo, a] *adj* television
cpd.

televisor [teleßi'sor] *nm* television set.

télex ['teleks] *nm* telex; **máquina** ~ telex
(machine); **enviar por** ~ to telex.

telón [te'lon] *nm* curtain; ~ **de boca/
seguridad** front/safety curtain; ~ **de
acero** (*POL*) iron curtain; ~ **de fondo**
backcloth, background.

telonero, a [telo'nero, a] *nm/f* support act;
los ~**s** (*MUS*) the support band.

tema ['tema] *nm* (*asunto*) subject, topic;
(*MUS*) theme; ~**s de actualidad** current
affairs ♦ *nf* (*obsesión*) obsession; (*manía*)
ill-will; **tener** ~ **a algn** to have a grudge
against sb.

temario [te'marjo] *nm* (*ESCOL*) set of top-
ics; (*de una conferencia*) agenda.

temático, a [te'matiko, a] adj thematic ♦ nf subject matter.

tembladera [tembla'ðera] nf shaking; (AM) quagmire.

temblar [tem'blar] vi to shake, tremble; (de frío) to shiver.

tembleque [tem'bleke] adj shaking ♦ nm shaking.

temblón, ona [tem'blon, ona] adj shaking.

temblor [tem'blor] nm trembling; (AM: de tierra) earthquake.

tembloroso, a [temblo'roso, a] adj trembling.

temer [te'mer] vt to fear ♦ vi to be afraid; **temo que Juan llegue tarde** I am afraid Juan may be late.

temerario, a [teme'rarjo, a] adj (imprudente) rash; (descuidado) reckless; (arbitrario) hasty.

temeridad [temeri'ðað] nf (imprudencia) rashness; (audacia) boldness.

temeroso, a [teme'roso, a] adj (miedoso) fearful; (que inspira temor) frightful.

temible [te'mißle] adj fearsome.

temor [te'mor] nm (miedo) fear; (duda) suspicion.

témpano ['tempano] nm (MUS) kettledrum; ~ **de hielo** ice floe.

temperamento [tempera'mento] nm temperament; **tener** ~ to be temperamental.

temperar [tempe'rar] vt to temper, moderate.

temperatura [tempera'tura] nf temperature.

tempestad [tempes'tað] nf storm; ~ **en un vaso de agua** (fig) storm in a teacup.

tempestuoso, a [tempes'twoso, a] adj stormy.

templado, a [tem'plaðo, a] adj (moderado) moderate; (: en el comer) frugal; (: en el beber) abstemious; (agua) lukewarm; (clima) mild; (MUS) in tune, well-tuned.

templanza [tem'planθa] nf moderation; (en el beber) abstemiousness; (del clima) mildness.

templar [tem'plar] vt (moderar) to moderate; (furia) to restrain; (calor) to reduce; (solución) to dilute; (afinar) to tune (up); (acero) to temper ♦ vi to moderate; ~**se** vr to be restrained.

temple ['temple] nm (humor) mood; (coraje) courage; (ajuste) tempering; (afinación) tuning; (pintura) tempera.

templo ['templo] nm (iglesia) church; (pagano etc) temple; ~ **metodista** Methodist chapel.

temporada [tempo'raða] nf time, period;

(estación, social, DEPORTE) season; **en plena** ~ at the height of the season.

temporal [tempo'ral] adj (no permanente) temporary; (REL) temporal ♦ nm storm.

temporario, a [tempo'rarjo, a] adj (AM) temporary.

tempranero, a [tempra'nero, a] adj (BOT) early; (persona) early-rising.

temprano, a [tem'prano, a] adj early ♦ adv early; (demasiado pronto) too soon, too early; **lo más** ~ **posible** as soon as possible.

ten [ten] vb V tener.

tenacidad [tenaθi'ðað] nf (gen) tenacity; (dureza) toughness; (terquedad) stubbornness.

tenacillas [tena'θiλas] nfpl (gen) tongs; (para el pelo) curling tongs; (MED) forceps.

tenaz [te'naθ] adj (material) tough; (persona) tenacious; (pegajoso) sticky; (terco) stubborn.

tenaza(s) [te'naθa(s)] nf(pl) (MED) forceps; (TEC) pliers; (ZOOL) pincers.

tendal [ten'dal] nm awning.

tendedero [tende'ðero] nm (para ropa) drying-place; (cuerda) clothes line.

tendencia [ten'denθja] nf tendency; (proceso) trend; ~ **imperante** prevailing tendency; ~ **del mercado** run of the market; **tener** ~ **a** to tend o have a tendency to.

tendenciosidad [tendenθosi'ðað] nf tendentiousness.

tendencioso, a [tenden'θjoso, a] adj tendentious.

tender [ten'der] vt (extender) to spread out; (ropa) to hang out; (vía férrea, cable) to lay; (cuerda) to stretch; (trampa) to set ♦ vi to tend; ~**se** vr to lie down; (fig: dejarse llevar) to let o.s. go; (: dejar ir) to let things go; ~ **la cama/la mesa** (AM) to make the bed/lay the table.

ténder ['tender] nm (FERRO) tender.

tenderete [tende'rete] nm (puesto) stall; (carretilla) barrow; (exposición) display of goods.

tendero, a [ten'dero, a] nm/f shopkeeper.

tendido, a [ten'diðo, a] adj (acostado) lying down, flat; (colgado) hanging ♦ nm (ropa) washing; (TAUR) front rows pl of seats; (colocación) laying; (ARQ: enyesado) coat of plaster; **a galope** ~ flat out.

tendón [ten'don] nm tendon.

tendré [ten'dre] etc vb V tener.

tenducho [ten'dutʃo] nm small dirty shop.

tenebroso, a [tene'ßroso, a] adj (oscuro) dark; (fig) gloomy; (siniestro) sinister.

tenedor [tene'ðor] *nm* (*CULIN*) fork; (*poseedor*) holder; ~ **de libros** bookkeeper; ~ **de acciones** shareholder; ~ **de póliza** policyholder.

teneduría [teneðu'ria] *nf* keeping; ~ **de libros** book-keeping.

tenencia [te'nenθja] *nf* (*de casa*) tenancy; (*de oficio*) tenure; (*de propiedad*) possession; ~ **asegurada** security of tenure; ~ **ilícita de armas** illegal possession of weapons.

═══════════════════ *PALABRA CLAVE*

tener [te'ner] *vt* **1** (*poseer, gen*) to have; (*en la mano*) to hold; **¿tienes un boli?** have you got a pen?; **va a ~ un niño** she's going to have a baby; **tiene los ojos azules** he's got blue eyes; **¡ten (*o* tenga)!, ¡aquí tienes (*o* tiene)!** here you are!

2 (*edad, medidas*) to be; **tiene 7 años** she's 7 (years old); **tiene 15 cm de largo** it's 15 cm long

3 (*sentimientos, sensaciones*): ~ **sed/hambre/frío/calor** to be thirsty/hungry/cold/hot; ~ **celos** to be jealous; ~ **cuidado** to be careful; ~ **razón** to be right; ~ **suerte** to be lucky

4 (*considerar*): **lo tengo por brillante** I consider him to be brilliant; ~ **en mucho a algn** to think very highly of sb

5 (*+pp, +adj, +gerundio*): **tengo terminada ya la mitad del trabajo** I've done half the work already; **tenía el sombrero puesto** he had his hat on; **tenía pensado llamarte** I had been thinking of phoning you; **nos tiene hartos** we're fed up with him; **me ha tenido tres horas esperando** he kept me waiting three hours

6: ~ **que hacer algo** to have to do sth; **tengo que acabar este trabajo hoy** I have to finish this job today

7: **¿qué tienes, estás enfermo?** what's the matter with you, are you ill?

8 (*locuciones*): **¿conque ésas tenemos?** so it's like that, then?; **no las tengo todas conmigo** I'm a bit unsure (about it); **lo tiene difícil** he'll have a hard job

♦ ~**se** *vr* **1**: ~**se en pie** to stand up

2: ~**se por** to think o.s.; **se tiene por un gran cantante** he thinks himself a great singer.

tenga ['tenga] *etc vb V* **tener.**

tenia ['tenja] *nf* tapeworm.

teniente [te'njente] *nm* lieutenant; ~ **coronel** lieutenant colonel.

tenis ['tenis] *nm* tennis; ~ **de mesa** table tennis.

tenista [te'nista] *nm/f* tennis player.

tenor [te'nor] *nm* (*tono*) tone; (*sentido*) meaning; (*MUS*) tenor; **a ~ de** on the lines of.

tenorio [te'norjo] *nm* (*fam*) ladykiller, Don Juan.

tensar [ten'sar] *vt* to tauten; (*arco*) to draw.

tensión [ten'sjon] *nf* tension; (*TEC*) stress; (*MED*): ~ **arterial** blood pressure; ~ **nerviosa** nervous strain; **tener la ~ alta** to have high blood pressure.

tenso, a ['tenso, a] *adj* tense; (*relaciones*) strained.

tentación [tenta'θjon] *nf* temptation.

tentáculo [ten'takulo] *nm* tentacle.

tentador, a [tenta'ðor, a] *adj* tempting ♦ *nm/f* tempter/temptress.

tentar [ten'tar] *vt* (*tocar*) to touch, feel; (*seducir*) to tempt; (*atraer*) to attract; (*probar*) to try (out); (*MED*) to probe; ~ **hacer algo** to try to do sth.

tentativa [tenta'tißa] *nf* attempt; ~ **de asesinato** attempted murder.

tentempié [tentem'pje] *nm* (*fam*) snack.

tenue ['tenwe] *adj* (*delgado*) thin, slender; (*alambre*) fine; (*insustancial*) tenuous; (*sonido*) faint; (*neblina*) light; (*lazo, vínculo*) slight.

teñir [te'ɲir] *vt* to dye; (*fig*) to tinge; ~**se el pelo** to dye one's hair.

teología [teolo'xia] *nf* theology.

teólogo, a [te'oloxo, a] *nm/f* theologist, theologian.

teorema [teo'rema] *nm* theorem.

teoría [teo'ria] *nf* theory; **en ~** in theory.

teóricamente [te'orikamente] *adv* theoretically.

teorice [teo'riθe] *etc vb V* **teorizar.**

teórico, a [te'oriko, a] *adj* theoretic(al) ♦ *nm/f* theoretician, theorist.

teorizar [teori'θar] *vi* to theorize.

tequila [te'kila] *nm o f* tequila.

TER [ter] *nm abr* (*FERRO*) = **tren español rápido.**

terapeuta [tera'peuta] *nm/f* therapist.

terapéutico, a [tera'peutiko, a] *adj* therapeutic(al) ♦ *nf* therapeutics *sg*.

terapia [te'rapja] *nf* therapy; ~ **laboral** occupational therapy.

tercer [ter'θer] *adj V* **tercero.**

tercermundista [terθermun'dista] *adj* Third World *cpd*.

tercero, a [ter'θero, a] *adj* third (*delante de nmsg*: **tercer**) ♦ *nm* (*árbitro*) mediator; (*JUR*) third party.

terceto [ter'θeto] *nm* trio.

terciado, a [ter'θjaðo, a] *adj* slanting;

azúcar ~ brown sugar.
terciar [terˈθjar] vt (MAT) to divide into three; (inclinarse) to slope; (llevar) to wear across one's chest ♦ vi (participar) to take part; (hacer de árbitro) to mediate; **~se** vr to arise.
terciario, a [terˈθjarjo, a] adj tertiary.
tercio [ˈterθjo] nm third.
terciopelo [terθjoˈpelo] nm velvet.
terco, a [ˈterko, a] adj obstinate, stubborn; (material) tough.
tergal ® [terˈɣal] nm Terylene ®.
tergiversación [terxiβersaˈθjon] nf (deformación) distortion; (evasivas) prevarication.
tergiversar [terxiβerˈsar] vt to distort ♦ vi to prevaricate.
termal [terˈmal] adj thermal.
termas [ˈtermas] nfpl hot springs.
térmico, a [ˈtermiko, a] adj thermic, thermal, heat cpd.
terminación [terminaˈθjon] nf (final) end; (conclusión) conclusion, ending.
terminal [termiˈnal] adj terminal ♦ nm (ELEC, INFORM) terminal; ~ **conversacional** interactive terminal; ~ **de pantalla** visual display unit ♦ nf (AVIAT, FERRO) terminal.
terminante [termiˈnante] adj (final) final, definitive; (tajante) categorical.
terminar [termiˈnar] vt (completar) to complete, finish; (concluir) to end ♦ vi (llegar a su fin) to end; (parar) to stop; (acabar) to finish; **~se** vr to come to an end; ~ **por hacer algo** to end up (by) doing sth.
término [ˈtermino] nm end, conclusion; (parada) terminus; (límite) boundary; (en discusión) point; (LING, COM) term; ~ **medio** average; (fig) middle way; **en otros ~s** in other words; **en último** ~ (a fin de cuentas) in the last analysis; (como último recurso) as a last resort; **en ~s de** in terms of; **según los ~s del contrato** according to the terms of the contract.
terminología [terminoloˈxia] nf terminology.
termita [terˈmita] nf termite.
termo [ˈtermo] nm Thermos ® (flask).
termodinámico, a [termoðiˈnamiko, a] adj thermodynamic ♦ nf thermodynamics sg.
termoimpresora [termoimpreˈsora] nf thermal printer.
termómetro [terˈmometro] nm thermometer.
termonuclear [termonukleˈar] adj thermonuclear.
termostato [termosˈtato] nm thermostat.

ternero, a [terˈnero, a] nm/f (animal) calf ♦ nf (carne) veal.
terneza [terˈneθa] nf tenderness.
ternilla [terˈniʎa] nf gristle; (cartílago) cartilage.
terno [ˈterno] nm (traje) three-piece suit; (conjunto) set of three.
ternura [terˈnura] nf (trato) tenderness; (palabra) endearment; (cariño) fondness.
terquedad [terkeˈðað] nf obstinacy; (dureza) harshness.
terrado [teˈrraðo] nm terrace.
Terranova [terraˈnoβa] nf Newfoundland.
terraplén [terraˈplen] nm (AGR) terrace; (FERRO) embankment; (MIL) rampart; (cuesta) slope.
terráqueo, a [teˈrrakeo, a] adj: **globo** ~ globe.
terrateniente [terrateˈnjente] nm landowner.
terraza [teˈrraθa] nf (balcón) balcony; (techo) flat roof; (AGR) terrace.
terremoto [terreˈmoto] nm earthquake.
terrenal [terreˈnal] adj earthly.
terreno, a [teˈrreno, a] adj (de la tierra) earthly, worldly ♦ nm (tierra) land; (parcela) plot; (suelo) soil; (fig) field; **un** ~ a piece of land; **sobre el** ~ on the spot; **ceder/perder** ~ to give/lose ground; **preparar el** ~ (a) (fig) to pave the way (for).
terrestre [teˈrrestre] adj terrestrial; (ruta) land cpd.
terrible [teˈrriβle] adj (espantoso) terrible; (aterrador) dreadful; (tremendo) awful.
territorial [territoˈrjal] adj territorial.
territorio [territoˈrjo] nm territory; ~ **bajo mandato** mandated territory.
terrón [teˈrron] nm (de azúcar) lump; (de tierra) clod, lump; **terrones** nmpl land sg.
terror [teˈrror] nm terror.
terrorífico, a [terroˈrifiko, a] adj terrifying.
terrorismo [terroˈrismo] nm terrorism.
terrorista [terroˈrista] adj, nm/f terrorist.
terroso, a [teˈrroso, a] adj earthy.
terruño [teˈrruɲo] nm (pedazo) clod; (parcela) plot; (fig) native soil; **apego al** ~ attachment to one's native soil.
terso, a [ˈterso, a] adj (liso) smooth; (pulido) polished; (fig: estilo) flowing.
tersura [terˈsura] nf smoothness; (brillo) shine.
tertulia [terˈtulja] nf (reunión informal) social gathering; (grupo) group, circle; (sala) clubroom; ~ **literaria** literary circle.
tesina [teˈsina] nf dissertation.

tesis ['tesis] *nf inv* thesis.
tesón [te'son] *nm* (*firmeza*) firmness; (*tenacidad*) tenacity.
tesorería [tesore'ria] *nf* treasurership.
tesorero, a [teso'rero, a] *nm/f* treasurer.
tesoro [te'soro] *nm* treasure; **T~ público** (*POL*) Exchequer.
test, *pl* **tests** [tes(t), tes(t)] *nm* test.
testaferro [testa'ferro] *nm* figurehead.
testamentaría [testamenta'ria] *nf* execution of a will.
testamentario, a [testamen'tarjo, a] *adj* testamentary ♦ *nm/f* executor/executrix.
testamento [testa'mento] *nm* will.
testar [tes'tar] *vi* to make a will.
testarada [testa'raða] *nf*, **testarazo** [testa'raθo] *nm*: **darse un(a) ~** (*fam*) to bump one's head.
testarudo, a [testa'ruðo, a] *adj* stubborn.
testículo [tes'tikulo] *nm* testicle.
testificar [testifi'kar] *vt* to testify; (*fig*) to attest ♦ *vi* to give evidence.
testifique [testi'fike] *etc vb* V **testificar**.
testigo [tes'tiɣo] *nm/f* witness; **~ de cargo/descargo** witness for the prosecution/defence; **~ ocular** eye witness; **poner a algn por ~** to cite sb as a witness.
testimonial [testimo'njal] *adj* (*prueba*) testimonial; (*gesto*) token.
testimoniar [testimo'njar] *vt* to testify to; (*fig*) to show.
testimonio [testi'monjo] *nm* testimony; **en ~ de** as a token *o* mark of; **falso ~** perjured evidence, false witness.
teta ['teta] *nf* (*de biberón*) teat; (*ANAT*) nipple; (*fam*) breast; (*fam!*) tit (*!*).
tétanos ['tetanos] *nm* tetanus.
tetera [te'tera] *nf* teapot; **~ eléctrica** (electric) kettle.
tetilla [te'tiʎa] *nf* (*ANAT*) nipple; (*de biberón*) teat.
tétrico, a ['tetriko, a] *adj* gloomy, dismal.
textil [teks'til] *adj* textile.
texto ['teksto] *nm* text.
textual [teks'twal] *adj* textual; **palabras ~es** exact words.
textura [teks'tura] *nf* (*de tejido*) texture; (*de mineral*) structure.
tez [teθ] *nf* (*cutis*) complexion; (*color*) colouring.
tfno. *abr* (= *teléfono*) tel.
ti [ti] *pron* you; (*reflexivo*) yourself.
tía ['tia] *nf* (*pariente*) aunt; (*fam: mujer*) girl.
Tibet [ti'ßet] *nm*: **El ~** Tibet.
tibetano, a [tiße'tano, a] *adj, nm/f* Tibetan

♦ *nm* (*LING*) Tibetan.
tibia ['tißja] *nf* tibia.
tibieza [ti'ßjeθa] *nf* (*temperatura*) tepidness; (*fig*) coolness.
tibio, a ['tißjo, a] *adj* lukewarm, tepid.
tiburón [tißu'ron] *nm* shark.
tic [tik] *nm* (*de reloj*) tick; **~ nervioso** (*MED*) nervous tic.
tico, a ['tiko, a] *adj, nm/f* (*AM fam*) Costa Rican.
tictac [tik'tak] *nm* (*de reloj*) tick tock.
tiemble ['tjemble] *etc vb* V **temblar**.
tiempo ['tjempo] *nm* (*gen*) time; (*época, período*) age, period; (*METEOROLOGÍA*) weather; (*LING*) tense; (*edad*) age; (*de juego*) half; **a ~** in time; **a un** *o* **al mismo ~** at the same time; **al poco ~** very soon (after); **andando el ~** in due course; **cada cierto ~** every so often; **con ~** in time; **con el ~** eventually; **de ~ en ~** from time to time; **en mis ~s** in my time; **en los buenos ~s** in the good old days; **hace buen/mal ~** the weather is fine/bad; **estar a ~** to be in time; **hace ~** some time ago; **hacer ~** to while away the time; **¿qué ~ tiene?** how old is he?; **motor de 2 ~s** two-stroke engine; **~ compartido** (*INFORM*) time sharing; **~ de ejecución** (*INFORM*) run time; **~ inactivo** (*COM*) downtime; **~ libre** spare time; **~ de paro** (*COM*) idle time; **a ~ partido** (*trabajar*) part-time; **~ preferencial** (*COM*) prime time; **en ~ real** (*INFORM*) real time.
tienda ['tjenda] *etc vb* V **tender** ♦ *nf* shop; (*más grande*) store; (*NAUT*) awning; **~ de campaña** tent; **~ de comestibles** grocer's (shop) (*esp BRIT*), grocery (*US*).
tiene ['tjene] *etc vb* V **tener**.
tienta ['tjenta] *nf* (*MED*) probe; (*fig*) tact; **andar a ~s** to grope one's way along.
tiento ['tjento] *etc vb* V **tentar** ♦ *nm* (*tacto*) touch; (*precaución*) wariness; (*pulso*) steady hand; (*ZOOL*) feeler, tentacle.
tierno, a ['tjerno, a] *adj* (*blando, dulce*) tender; (*fresco*) fresh.
tierra ['tjerra] *nf* earth; (*suelo*) soil; (*mundo*) world; (*país*) country, land; (*ELEC*) earth, ground (*US*); **~ adentro** inland; **~ natal** native land; **echar ~ a un asunto** to hush an affair up; **no es de estas ~s** he's not from these parts; **la T~ Santa** the Holy Land.
tieso, a ['tjeso, a] *adj* (*rígido*) rigid; (*duro*) stiff; (*fig: testarudo*) stubborn; (*fam: orgulloso*) conceited ♦ *adv* strongly.
tiesto ['tjesto] *nm* flowerpot; (*pedazo*)

piece of pottery.

tifoidea [tifoi'ðea] *nf* typhoid.

tifón [ti'fon] *nm* (*huracán*) typhoon; (*de mar*) tidal wave.

tifus ['tifus] *nm* typhus; ~ **icteroides** yellow fever.

tigre ['tixre] *nm* tiger; (*AM*) jaguar.

tijera [ti'xera] *nf* (*una* ~) (pair of) scissors *pl*; (*ZOOL*) claw; (*persona*) gossip; **de** ~ folding; ~**s** *nfpl* scissors; (*para plantas*) shears; **unas** ~**s** a pair of scissors.

tijeretear [tixerete'ar] *vt* to snip ♦ *vi* (*fig*) to meddle.

tila ['tila] *nf* (*BOT*) lime tree; (*CULIN*) lime flower tea.

tildar [til'dar] *vt*: ~ **de** to brand as.

tilde ['tilde] *nf* (*defecto*) defect; (*trivialidad*) triviality; (*TIP*) tilde.

tilín [ti'lin] *nm* tinkle.

tilo ['tilo] *nm* lime tree.

timador, a [tima'ðor, a] *nm/f* swindler.

timar [ti'mar] *vt* (*robar*) to steal; (*estafar*) to swindle; (*persona*) to con; ~**se** *vr* (*fam*) to make eyes (con algn at sb).

timbal [tim'bal] *nm* small drum.

timbrar [tim'brar] *vt* to stamp; (*sellar*) to seal; (*carta*) to postmark.

timbrazo [tim'braθo] *nm* ring; **dar un** ~ to ring the bell.

timbre ['timbre] *nm* (*sello*) stamp; (*campanilla*) bell; (*tono*) timbre; (*COM*) stamp duty.

timidez [timi'ðeθ] *nf* shyness.

tímido, a ['timiðo, a] *adj* shy, timid.

timo ['timo] *nm* swindle; **dar un** ~ **a algn** to swindle sb.

timón [ti'mon] *nm* helm, rudder; (*AM*) steering wheel; **coger el** ~ (*fig*) to take charge.

timonel [timo'nel] *nm* helmsman.

timorato, a [timo'rato, a] *adj* God-fearing; (*mojigato*) sanctimonious.

tímpano ['timpano] *nm* (*ANAT*) eardrum; (*MUS*) small drum.

tina ['tina] *nf* tub; (*AM: baño*) bath(tub).

tinaja [ti'naxa] *nf* large earthen jar.

tinerfeño, a [tiner'feɲo, a] *adj* of *o* from Tenerife ♦ *nm/f* native *o* inhabitant of Tenerife.

tinglado [tin'glaðo] *nm* (*cobertizo*) shed; (*fig: truco*) trick; (*intriga*) intrigue; **armar un** ~ to lay a plot.

tinieblas [ti'njeβlas] *nfpl* darkness *sg*; (*sombras*) shadows; **estamos en** ~ **sobre sus proyectos** (*fig*) we are in the dark about his plans.

tino ['tino] *nm* (*habilidad*) skill; (*MIL*) marksmanship; (*juicio*) insight;

(*moderación*) moderation; **sin** ~ immoderately; **coger el** ~ to get the feel *o* hang of it.

tinta ['tinta] *nf* ink; (*TEC*) dye; (*ARTE*) colour; ~ **china** Indian ink; ~**s** *nfpl* (*fig*) shades; **medias** ~**s** (*fig*) half measures; **saber algo de buena** ~ to have sth on good authority.

tinte ['tinte] *nm* (*acto*) dyeing; (*fig*) tinge; (*barniz*) veneer.

tintero [tin'tero] *nm* inkwell; **se le quedó en el** ~ he clean forgot about it.

tintinear [tintine'ar] *vt* to tinkle.

tinto, a ['tinto, a] *adj* (*teñido*) dyed; (*manchado*) stained ♦ *nm* red wine.

tintorera [tinto'rera] *nf* shark.

tintorería [tintore'ria] *nf* dry cleaner's.

tintorero [tinto'rero] *nm* dry cleaner('s).

tintura [tin'tura] *nf* (*acto*) dyeing; (*QUÍMICA*) dye; (*farmacéutico*) tincture.

tiña ['tiɲa] *etc vb V* **teñir** ♦ *nf* (*MED*) ringworm.

tío ['tio] *nm* (*pariente*) uncle; (*fam: hombre*) bloke, guy (*US*).

tiovivo [tio'βiβo] *nm* roundabout.

típico, a ['tipiko, a] *adj* typical; (*pintoresco*) picturesque.

tiple ['tiple] *nm* soprano (voice) ♦ *nf* soprano.

tipo ['tipo] *nm* (*clase*) type, kind; (*norma*) norm; (*patrón*) pattern; (*fam: hombre*) fellow, bloke, guy (*US*); (*ANAT*) build; (: *de mujer*) figure; (*IMPRENTA*) type; ~ **bancario/de descuento** bank/discount rate; ~ **de interés** interest rate; ~ **de interés vigente** (*COM*) standard rate; ~ **de cambio** exchange rate; ~ **base** (*COM*) base rate; ~ **a término** (*COM*) forward rate; **dos** ~**s sospechosos** two suspicious characters; ~ **de letra** (*INFORM, TIP*) typeface; ~ **de datos** (*INFORM*) data type.

tipografía [tipoɣra'fia] *nf* (*tipo*) printing; (*lugar*) printing press.

tipográfico, a [tipo'ɣrafiko, a] *adj* printing.

tipógrafo, a [ti'poɣrafo, a] *nm/f* printer.

tíque(t) ['tike], *pl* **tíque(t)s** ['tikes] *nm* ticket; (*en tienda*) cash slip.

tiquismiquis [tikis'mikis] *nm* fussy person ♦ *nmpl* (*querellas*) squabbling *sg*; (*escrúpulos*) silly scruples.

tira ['tira] *nf* strip; (*fig*) abundance ♦ *nm*: ~ **y afloja** give and take; (*cautela*) caution; **la** ~ **de ...** (*fam*) lots of ....

tirabuzón [tiraβu'θon] *nm* corkscrew; (*rizo*) curl.

tiradero [tira'ðero] *nm* (*AM*) rubbish dump.

tirado, a [ti'raðo, a] *adj* (*barato*) dirt-cheap; (*fam: fácil*) very easy ♦ *nf* (*acto*) cast, throw; (*distancia*) distance; (*serie*) series; (*TIP*) printing, edition; **de una tirada** at one go; **está ~** (*fam*) it's a cinch.

tirador, a [tira'ðor, a] *nm/f* (*persona*) shooter ♦ *nm* (*mango*) handle; (*ELEC*) flex; **~ certero** sniper.

tiralíneas [tira'lineas] *nm inv* ruling-pen.

tiranía [tira'nia] *nf* tyranny.

tiránico, a [ti'raniko, a] *adj* tyrannical.

tiranizar [tirani'θar] *vt* (*pueblo, empleado*) to tyrannize.

tirano, a [ti'rano, a] *adj* tyrannical ♦ *nm/f* tyrant.

tirante [ti'rante] *adj* (*cuerda*) tight, taut; (*relaciones*) strained ♦ *nm* (*ARQ*) brace; (*TEC*) stay; (*correa*) shoulder strap; **~s** *nmpl* braces, suspenders (*US*).

tirantez [tiran'teθ] *nf* tightness; (*fig*) tension.

tirar [ti'rar] *vt* to throw; (*volcar*) to upset; (*derribar*) to knock down *o* over; (*tiro*) to fire; (*cohete*) to launch; (*bomba*) to drop; (*edificio*) to pull down; (*desechar*) to throw out *o* away; (*disipar*) to squander; (*imprimir*) to print; (*dar: golpe*) to deal ♦ *vi* (*disparar*) to shoot; (*jalar*) to pull; (*fig*) to draw; (*interesar*) to appeal; (*fam: andar*) to go; (*tender a, buscar realizar*) to tend to; (*DEPORTE*) to shoot; **~se** *vr* to throw o.s.; (*fig*) to demean o.s.; (*fam !*) to screw (*!*); **~ abajo** to bring down, destroy; **tira más a su padre** he takes more after his father; **~ de algo** to pull *o* tug (on) sth; **ir tirando** to manage; **~ a la derecha** to turn *o* go right; **a todo ~** at the most.

tirita [ti'rita] *nf* (sticking) plaster, bandaid (*US*).

tiritar [tiri'tar] *vi* to shiver.

tiritona [tiri'tona] *nf* shivering (fit).

tiro ['tiro] *nm* (*lanzamiento*) throw; (*disparo*) shot; (*tiroteo*) shooting; (*DEPORTE*) shot; (*TENIS, GOLF*) drive; (*alcance*) range; (*de escalera*) flight (of stairs); (*golpe*) blow; (*engaño*) hoax; **~ al blanco** target practice; **caballo de ~** cart-horse; **andar de ~s largos** to be all dressed up; **al ~** (*AM*) at once; **de a ~** (*AM fam*) completely; **se pegó un ~** he shot himself; **le salió el ~ por la culata** it backfired on him.

tiroides [ti'roiðes] *nm inv* thyroid.

Tirol [ti'rol] *nm:* **El ~** the Tyrol.

tirolés, esa [tiro'les, esa] *adj, nm/f* Tyrolean.

tirón [ti'ron] *nm* (*sacudida*) pull, tug; **de un**
~ in one go; dar un ~ a to pull at, tug at.

tirotear [tirote'ar] *vt* to shoot at; **~se** *vr* to exchange shots.

tiroteo [tiro'teo] *nm* exchange of shots, shooting; (*escaramuza*) skirmish.

tirria ['tirrja] *nf:* **tener una ~ a algn** to have a grudge against sb.

tísico, a ['tisiko, a] *adj, nm/f* consumptive.

tisis ['tisis] *nf* consumption, tuberculosis.

tít. *abr* = **título.**

titánico, a [ti'taniko, a] *adj* titanic.

títere ['titere] *nm* puppet; **no dejar ~ con cabeza** to turn everything upside-down.

titilar [titi'lar] *vi* (*luz, estrella*) to twinkle; (*parpado*) to flutter.

titiritero, a [titiri'tero, a] *nm/f* (*acróbata*) acrobat; (*malabarista*) juggler.

titubeante [tituße'ante] *adj* (*inestable*) shaky, tottering; (*farfullante*) stammering; (*dudoso*) hesitant.

titubear [tituße'ar] *vi* to stagger; (*tartamudear*) to stammer; (*vacilar*) to hesitate.

titubeo [titu'ßeo] *nm* staggering; stammering; hesitation.

titulado, a [titu'laðo, a] *adj* (*libro*) entitled; (*persona*) titled.

titular [titu'lar] *adj* titular ♦ *nm/f* (*de oficina*) occupant; (*de pasaporte*) holder ♦ *nm* headline ♦ *vt* to title; **~se** *vr* to be entitled.

título ['titulo] *nm* (*gen*) title; (*de diario*) headline; (*certificado*) professional qualification; (*universitario*) university degree; (*COM*) bond; (*fig*) right; **~s** *nmpl* qualifications; **a ~ de** by way of; (*en calidad de*) in the capacity of; **a ~ de curiosidad** as a matter of interest; **~ de propiedad** title deed; **~s convertibles de interés fijo** (*COM*) convertible loan stock *sg*.

tiza ['tiθa] *nf* chalk; **una ~** a piece of chalk.

tizna ['tiθna] *nf* grime.

tiznar [tiθ'nar] *vt* to blacken; (*manchar*) to smudge, stain; (*fig*) to tarnish.

tizón [ti'θon], **tizo** ['tiθo] *nm* brand; (*fig*) stain.

TLC *nm abr* (= *Tratado de Libre Comercio*) NAFTA.

Tm. *abr* = **tonelada(s) métrica(s).**

toalla [to'aʎa] *nf* towel.

tobillo [to'ßiʎo] *nm* ankle.

tobogán [toßo'ɣan] *nm* toboggan; (*montaña rusa*) switchback; (*resbaladilla*) chute, slide.

toca ['toka] *nf* headdress.

tocadiscos [toka'ðiskos] *nm inv* record player.

tocado, a [to'kaðo, a] *adj* (*fruta etc*) rotten;
♦ *nm* headdress; **estar ~ de la cabeza**
(*fam*) to be weak in the head.

tocador [toka'ðor] *nm* (*mueble*) dressing
table; (*cuarto*) boudoir; (*neceser*) toilet
case; (*fam*) ladies' room.

tocante [to'kante]: **~ a** *prep* with regard
to; **en lo ~ a** as for, so far as concerns.

tocar [to'kar] *vt* to touch; (*sentir*) to feel;
(*con la mano*) to handle; (*MUS*) to play;
(*campana*) to ring; (*tambor*) to beat;
(*trompeta*) to blow; (*topar con*) to run
into, strike; (*referirse a*) to allude to; (*ser
emparentado con*) to be related to ♦ *vi* (*a
la puerta*) to knock (on *o* at the door); (*ser
de turno*) to fall to, be the turn of; (*ser
hora*) to be due; (*atañer*) to concern; **~se**
vr (*cubrirse la cabeza*) to cover one's head;
(*tener contacto*) to touch (each other);
~le a algn to fall to sb's lot; **~ en** (*NAUT*)
to call at; **por lo que a mí me toca** as far
as I am concerned; **esto toca en la locura**
this verges on madness.

tocateja [toka'texa] (*fam*): **a ~** *adv* in
readies.

tocayo, a [to'kajo, a] *nm/f* namesake.

tocino [to'θino] *nm* (bacon) fat; **~ de
panceta** bacon.

todavía [toða'βia] *adv* (*aun*) even; (*aún*)
still, yet; **~ más** yet *o* still more; **~ no**
not yet; **~ en 1970** as late as 1970; **está
lloviendo ~** it's still raining.

todito, a [to'ði'tito, a], **todito, a** [to'ðito,
a] *adj* (*AM fam*) (absolutely) all.

══════════════ *PALABRA CLAVE*

todo, a ['toðo, a] *adj* **1** (*sg*) all; **toda la
carne** all the meat; **toda la noche** all
night, the whole night; **~ el libro** the
whole book; **toda una botella** a whole
bottle; **~ lo contrario** quite the opposite;
está toda sucia she's all dirty; **a toda
velocidad** at full speed; **por ~ el país**
throughout the whole country; **es ~ un
hombre** he's every inch a man; **soy ~
oídos** I'm all ears

2 (*pl*) all; every; **~s los libros** all the
books; **todas las noches** every night; **~s
los que quieran salir** all those who want
to leave; **~s vosotros** all of you

♦ *pron* **1** everything, all; **~s** everyone,
everybody; **lo sabemos ~** we know
everything; **~s querían más tiempo**
everybody *o* everyone wanted more
time; **nos marchamos ~s** all of us left;
corriendo y ~, no llegaron a tiempo even
though they ran, they still didn't arrive
in time

2 (*con preposición*): **a pesar de ~** even so,
in spite of everything; **con ~ él me sigue
gustando** even so I still like him; **le
llamaron de todo** they called him all the
names under the sun; **no me agrada del
~** I don't entirely like it

♦ *adv* all; **vaya ~ seguido** keep straight
on *o* ahead

♦ *nm*: **como un ~** as a whole; **arriba del ~**
at the very top; **~ a cien** ≈ pound store
(*BRIT*), ≈ dollar store (*US*)

todopoderoso, a [toðopoðe'roso, a] *adj* all
powerful; (*REL*) almighty.

todoterreno [toðote'rreno] *nm* (*tb:
vehículo ~*) four-by-four.

toga ['toxa] *nf* toga; (*ESCOL*) gown.

Tokio ['tokjo] *n* Tokyo.

toldo ['toldo] *nm* (*para el sol*) sunshade;
(*tienda*) marquee; (*fig*) pride.

tole ['tole] *nm* (*fam*) commotion.

toledano, a [tole'ðano, a] *adj* of *o* from
Toledo ♦ *nm/f* native *o* inhabitant of
Toledo.

tolerable [tole'raβle] *adj* tolerable.

tolerancia [tole'ranθja] *nf* tolerance.

tolerante [tole'rante] *adj* tolerant; (*fig*)
open-minded.

tolerar [tole'rar] *vt* to tolerate; (*resistir*) to
endure.

toma ['toma] *nf* (*gen*) taking; (*MED*) dose;
(*ELEC*: *tb*: **~ de corriente**) socket; (*MEC*)
inlet; **~ de posesión** (*por presidente*)
taking up office; **~ de tierra** (*AVIAT*)
landing.

tomadura [toma'ðura] *nf*: **~ de pelo** hoax.

tomar [to'mar] *vt* (*gen, CINE, FOTO, TV*) to
take; (*actitud*) to adopt; (*aspecto*) to take
on; (*notas*) to take down; (*beber*) to drink
♦ *vi* to take; (*AM*) to drink; **~se** *vr* to take;
~se por to consider o.s. to be; **¡toma!**
here you are!; **~ asiento** to sit down; **~ a
algn por loco** to think sb mad; **~ a bien/a
mal** to take well/badly; **~ en serio** to
take seriously; **~ el pelo a algn** to pull
sb's leg; **~la con algn** to pick a quarrel
with sb; **~ por escrito** to write down;
toma y daca give and take.

tomate [to'mate] *nm* tomato.

tomatera [toma'tera] *nf* tomato plant.

tomavistas [toma'βistas] *nm inv* movie
camera.

tomillo [to'miʎo] *nm* thyme.

tomo ['tomo] *nm* (*libro*) volume; (*fig*)
importance.

ton [ton] *abr* = **tonelada** ♦ *nm*: **sin ~ ni son**
without rhyme or reason.

tonada [to'naða] *nf* tune.

tonalidad [tonaliˈðað] *nf* tone.

tonel [toˈnel] *nm* barrel.

tonelada [toneˈlaða] *nf* ton; ~ **métrica** metric ton.

tonelaje [toneˈlaxe] *nm* tonnage.

tonelero [toneˈlero] *nm* cooper.

tongo [ˈtongo] *nm* (*DEPORTE*) fix.

tónico, a [ˈtoniko, a] *adj* tonic ♦ *nm* (*MED*) tonic ♦ *nf* (*MUS*) tonic; (*fig*) keynote.

tonificador, a [tonifikaˈðor, a], **tonificante** [tonifiˈkante] *adj* invigorating, stimulating.

tonificar [tonifiˈkar] *vt* to tone up.

tonifique [toniˈfike] *etc vb V* **tonificar**.

tonillo [toˈniʎo] *nm* monotonous voice.

tono [ˈtono] *nm* (*MUS*) tone; (*altura*) pitch; (*color*) shade; **fuera de** ~ inappropriate; ~ **de marcar** (*TELEC*) dialling tone; **darse** ~ to put on airs.

tontear [tonteˈar] *vi* (*fam*) to fool about; (*enamorados*) to flirt.

tontería [tonteˈria] *nf* (*estupidez*) foolishness; (*una* ~) silly thing; ~**s** *nfpl* rubbish *sg*, nonsense *sg*.

tonto, a [ˈtonto, a] *adj* stupid; (*ridículo*) silly ♦ *nm/f* fool; (*payaso*) clown; **a tontas y a locas** anyhow; **hacer(se) el** ~ to act the fool.

topacio [toˈpaθjo] *nm* topaz.

topar [toˈpar] *vt* (*tropezar*) to bump into; (*encontrar*) to find, come across; (*cabra etc*) to butt ♦ *vi*: ~ **contra** *o* **en** to run into; ~ **con** to run up against; **el problema topa en eso** that's where the problem lies.

tope [ˈtope] *adj* maximum ♦ *nm* (*fin*) end; (*límite*) limit; (*riña*) quarrel; (*FERRO*) buffer; (*AUTO*) bumper; **al** ~ end to end; **fecha** ~ closing date; **precio** ~ top price; **sueldo** ~ maximum salary; ~ **de tabulación** tab stop.

tópico, a [ˈtopiko, a] *adj* topical; (*MED*) local ♦ *nm* platitude, cliché; **de uso** ~ for external application.

topo [ˈtopo] *nm* (*ZOOL*) mole; (*fig*) blunderer.

topografía [topoɣraˈfia] *nf* topography.

topógrafo, a [toˈpoɣrafo, a] *nm/f* topographer; (*agrimensor*) surveyor.

toponimia [topoˈnimja] *nf* place names *pl*; (*estudio*) study of place names.

toque [ˈtoke] *etc vb V* **tocar** ♦ *nm* touch; (*MUS*) beat; (*de campana*) ring, chime; (*MIL*) bugle call; (*fig*) crux; **dar un** ~ **a** to test; **dar el último** ~ **a** to put the final touch to; ~ **de queda** curfew.

toquetear [toketeˈar] *vt* to handle; (*fam!*) to touch up.

toquilla [toˈkiʎa] *nf* (*chal*) shawl.

tórax [ˈtoraks] *nm inv* thorax.

torbellino [torbeˈʎino] *nm* whirlwind; (*fig*) whirl.

torcedura [torθeˈðura] *nf* twist; (*MED*) sprain.

torcer [torˈθer] *vt* to twist; (*la esquina*) to turn; (*MED*) to sprain; (*cuerda*) to plait; (*ropa, manos*) to wring; (*persona*) to corrupt; (*sentido*) to distort ♦ *vi* (*cambiar de dirección*) to turn; ~**se** *vr* to twist; (*doblar*) to bend; (*desviarse*) to go astray; (*fracasar*) to go wrong; ~ **el gesto** to scowl; ~**se un pie** to twist one's foot; **el coche torció a la derecha** the car turned right.

torcido, a [torˈθiðo, a] *adj* twisted; (*fig*) crooked ♦ *nm* curl.

tordo, a [ˈtorðo, a] *adj* dappled ♦ *nm* thrush.

torear [toreˈar] *vt* (*fig: evadir*) to dodge; (*toro*) to fight ♦ *vi* to fight bulls.

toreo [toˈreo] *nm* bullfighting.

torero, a [toˈrero, a] *nm/f* bullfighter.

toril [toˈril] *nm* bullpen.

tormenta [torˈmenta] *nf* storm; (*fig: confusión*) turmoil.

tormento [torˈmento] *nm* torture; (*fig*) anguish.

tormentoso, a [tormenˈtoso, a] *adj* stormy.

tornar [torˈnar] *vt* (*devolver*) to return, give back; (*transformar*) to transform ♦ *vi* to go back; ~**se** *vr* (*ponerse*) to become; (*volver*) to return.

tornasol [tornaˈsol] *nm* (*BOT*) sunflower; **papel de** ~ litmus paper.

tornasolado, a [tornasoˈlaðo, a] *adj* (*brillante*) iridescent; (*reluciente*) shimmering.

torneo [torˈneo] *nm* tournament.

tornero, a [torˈnero, a] *nm/f* machinist.

tornillo [torˈniʎo] *nm* screw; **apretar los** ~**s a algn** to apply pressure on sb; **le falta un** ~ (*fam*) he's got a screw loose.

torniquete [torniˈkete] *nm* (*puerta*) turnstile; (*MED*) tourniquet.

torno [ˈtorno] *nm* (*TEC: grúa*) winch; (: *de carpintero*) lathe; (*tambor*) drum; ~ **de banco** vice, vise (*US*); **en** ~ (**a**) round, about.

toro [ˈtoro] *nm* bull; (*fam*) he-man; **los** ~**s** bullfighting *sg*.

toronja [toˈronxa] *nf* grapefruit.

torpe [ˈtorpe] *adj* (*poco hábil*) clumsy, awkward; (*movimiento*) sluggish; (*necio*) dim; (*lento*) slow; (*indecente*) crude; (*no honrado*) dishonest.

torpedo [tor'peðo] nm torpedo.

torpemente [torpe'mente] adv (sin destreza) clumsily; (lentamente) slowly.

torpeza [tor'peθa] nf (falta de agilidad) clumsiness; (lentitud) slowness; (rigidez) stiffness; (error) mistake; (crudeza) obscenity.

torre ['torre] nf tower; (de petróleo) derrick; (de electricidad) pylon; (AJEDREZ) rook; (AVIAT, MIL, NAUT) turret.

torrefacto, a [torre'fakto, a] adj: **café ~** high roast coffee.

torrencial [torren'θjal] adj torrential.

torrente [to'rrente] nm torrent.

tórrido, a ['torriðo, a] adj torrid.

torrija [to'rrixa] nf fried bread; **~s** French toast sg.

torsión [tor'sjon] nf twisting.

torso ['torso] nm torso.

torta ['torta] nf cake; (fam) slap; **~ de huevos** (AM) omelette; **no entendió ni ~** he didn't understand a word of it.

tortazo [tor'taθo] nm (bofetada) slap; (de coche) crash.

tortícolis [tor'tikolis] nm inv stiff neck.

tortilla [tor'tiʎa] nf omelette; (AM) maize pancake; **~ francesa/española** plain/ potato omelette; **cambiar o volver la ~ a algn** to turn the tables on sb.

tortillera [torti'ʎera] nf (fam!) lesbian.

tórtola ['tortola] nf turtledove.

tortuga [tor'tuxa] nf tortoise; **~ marina** turtle.

tortuoso, a [tor'twoso, a] adj winding.

tortura [tor'tura] nf torture.

torturar [tortu'rar] vt to torture.

torvo, a ['torβo, a] adj grim, fierce.

torzamos [tor'θamos] etc vb V **torcer**.

tos [tos] nf inv cough; **~ ferina** whooping cough.

Toscana [tos'kana] nf: **La ~** Tuscany.

tosco, a ['tosko, a] adj coarse.

toser [to'ser] vi to cough; **no hay quien le tosa** he's in a class by himself.

tostado, a [tos'taðo, a] adj toasted; (por el sol) dark brown; (piel) tanned ♦ nf tan; (pan) piece of toast; **tostadas** nfpl toast sg.

tostador [tosta'ðor] nm toaster.

tostar [tos'tar] vt to toast; (café) to roast; (al sol) to tan; **~se** vr to get brown.

tostón [tos'ton] nm: **ser un ~** to be a drag.

total [to'tal] adj total ♦ adv in short; (al fin y al cabo) when all is said and done ♦ nm total; **en ~** in all; **~ que** to cut a long story short; **~ de comprobación** (INFORM) hash total; **~ debe/haber** (COM) debit/assets total.

totalidad [totali'ðað] nf whole.

totalitario, a [totali'tarjo, a] adj totalitarian.

totalmente [to'talmente] adv totally.

tóxico, a ['toksiko, a] adj toxic ♦ nm poison.

toxicómano, a [toksi'komano, a] adj addicted to drugs ♦ nm/f drug addict.

toxina [to'ksina] nf toxin.

tozudo, a [to'θuðo, a] adj obstinate.

traba ['traβa] nf bond, tie; (cadena) fetter; **poner ~s a** to restrain.

trabajador, a [traβaxa'ðor, a] nm/f worker ♦ adj hard-working.

trabajar [traβa'xar] vt to work; (arar) to till; (empeñarse en) to work at; (empujar: persona) to push; (convencer) to persuade ♦ vi to work; (esforzarse) to strive; **¡a ~!** let's get to work!; **~ por hacer algo** to strive to do sth.

trabajo [tra'βaxo] nm work; (tarea) task; (POL) labour; (fig) effort; **tomarse el ~ de** to take the trouble to; **~ por turno/a destajo** shift work/piecework; **~ en proceso** (COM) work-in-progress.

trabajoso, a [traβa'xoso, a] adj hard; (MED) pale.

trabalenguas [traβa'lengwas] nm inv tongue twister.

trabar [tra'βar] vt (juntar) to join, unite; (atar) to tie down, fetter; (agarrar) to seize; (amistad) to strike up; **~se** vr to become entangled; (reñir) to squabble; **se le traba la lengua** he gets tongue-tied.

trabazón [traβa'θon] nf (TEC) joining, assembly; (fig) bond, link.

trabucar [traβu'kar] vt (confundir) to confuse, mix up; (palabras) to misplace.

trabuque [tra'βuke] etc vb V **trabucar**.

tracción [trak'θjon] nf traction; **~ delantera/trasera** front-wheel/rear-wheel drive.

trace ['traθe] etc vb V **trazar**.

tractor [trak'tor] nm tractor.

trad. abr (= traducido) trans.

tradición [traði'θjon] nf tradition.

tradicional [traðiθjo'nal] adj traditional.

traducción [traðuk'θjon] nf translation; **~ asistida por ordenador** computer-assisted translation.

traducible [traðu'θiβle] adj translatable.

traducir [traðu'θir] vt to translate; **~se** vr: **~se en** (fig) to entail, result in.

traductor, a [traðuk'tor, a] nm/f translator.

traduzca [tra'ðuθka] etc vb V **traducir**.

traer [tra'er] vt to bring; (llevar) to carry; (ropa) to wear; (incluir) to carry; (fig) to cause; **~se** vr: **~se algo** to be up to sth; **~se bien/mal** to dress well/badly; **traérselas** to be annoying; **~ consigo** to involve, entail; **es un problema que se**

las trae it's a difficult problem.
traficante [trafiˈkante] *nm/f* trader, dealer.
traficar [trafiˈkar] *vi* to trade; ~ **con** (*pey*)
   to deal illegally in.
tráfico [ˈtrafiko] *nm* (*COM*) trade; (*AUTO*)
   traffic.
trafique [traˈfike] *etc vb* V **traficar**.
tragaderas [traɣaˈðeras] *nfpl* (*garganta*)
   throat *sg*, gullet *sg*; (*credulidad*) gullibility
   sg.
tragaluz [traɣaˈluθ] *nm* skylight.
tragamonedas [traɣamoˈneðas] *nm inv*,
tragaperras [traɣaˈperras] *nm inv* slot
   machine.
tragar [traˈɣar] *vt* to swallow; (*devorar*) to
   devour, bolt down; ~**se** *vr* to swallow;
   (*tierra*) to absorb, soak up; **no le puedo** ~
   (*persona*) I can't stand him.
tragedia [traˈxeðja] *nf* tragedy.
trágico, a [ˈtraxiko, a] *adj* tragic.
trago [ˈtraɣo] *nm* (*líquido*) drink; (*comida
   de golpe*) gulp; (*fam: de bebida*) swig;
   (*desgracia*) blow; ~ **amargo** (*fig*) hard
   time.
trague [ˈtraɣe] *etc vb* V **tragar**.
traición [traiˈθjon] *nf* treachery; (*JUR*)
   treason; (*una* ~) act of treachery.
traicionar [traiθjoˈnar] *vt* to betray.
traicionero, a [traiθjoˈnero, a] = **traidor, a**.
traída [traˈiða] *nf* carrying; ~ **de aguas**
   water supply.
traidor, a [traiˈðor, a] *adj* treacherous
   ♦ *nm/f* traitor.
traiga [ˈtraiɣa] *etc vb* V **traer**.
trailer, *pl* **trailers** [ˈtrailer, ˈtrailer(s)] *nm*
   trailer.
traje [ˈtraxe] *etc vb* V **traer** ♦ *nm* (*gen*)
   dress; (*de hombre*) suit; (~ *típico*)
   costume; (*fig*) garb; ~ **de baño** swimsuit;
   ~ **de luces** bullfighter's costume; ~
   hecho a la medida made-to-measure
   suit.
trajera [traˈxera] *etc vb* V **traer**.
trajín [traˈxin] *nm* haulage; (*fam:
   movimiento*) bustle; **trajines** *nmpl* goings-
   on.
trajinar [traxiˈnar] *vt* (*llevar*) to carry,
   transport ♦ *vi* (*moverse*) to bustle about;
   (*viajar*) to travel around.
trama [ˈtrama] *nf* (*fig*) link; (: *intriga*) plot;
   (*de tejido*) weft.
tramar [traˈmar] *vt* to plot; (*TEC*) to weave;
   ~**se** *vr* (*fig*): **algo se está tramando**
   there's something going on.
tramitar [tramiˈtar] *vt* (*asunto*) to transact;
   (*negociar*) to negotiate; (*manejar*) to handle.
trámite [ˈtramite] *nm* (*paso*) step; (*JUR*)

transaction; ~**s** *nmpl* (*burocracia*)
   paperwork *sg*, procedures; (*JUR*)
   proceedings.
tramo [ˈtramo] *nm* (*de tierra*) plot; (*de
   escalera*) flight; (*de vía*) section.
tramoya [traˈmoja] *nf* (*TEAT*) piece of
   stage machinery; (*fig*) trick.
tramoyista [tramoˈjista] *nm/f* scene
   shifter; (*fig*) trickster.
trampa [ˈtrampa] *nf* trap; (*en el suelo*)
   trapdoor; (*prestidigitación*) conjuring
   trick; (*engaño*) trick; (*fam*) fiddle; (*de
   pantalón*) fly; **caer en la** ~ to fall into the
   trap; **hacer** ~**s** (*hacer juegos de manos*) to
   juggle, conjure; (*trampear*) to cheat.
trampear [trampeˈar] *vt, vi* to cheat.
trampilla [tramˈpiʎa] *nf* trap, hatchway.
trampolín [trampoˈlin] *nm* trampoline; (*de
   piscina etc*) diving board.
tramposo, a [tramˈposo, a] *adj* crooked,
   cheating ♦ *nm/f* crook, cheat.
tranca [ˈtranka] *nf* (*palo*) stick; (*viga*)
   beam; (*de puerta, ventana*) bar;
   (*borrachera*) binge; **a** ~**s y barrancas** with
   great difficulty.
trancar [tranˈkar] *vt* to bar ♦ *vi* to stride
   along.
trancazo [tranˈkaθo] *nm* (*golpe*) blow.
trance [ˈtranθe] *nm* (*momento difícil*)
   difficult moment; (*situación crítica*)
   critical situation; (*estado hipnotizado*)
   trance; **estar en** ~ **de muerte** to be at
   death's door.
tranco [ˈtranko] *nm* stride.
tranque [ˈtranke] *etc vb* V **trancar**.
tranquilamente [tranˈkilamente] *adv* (*sin
   preocupaciones: leer, trabajar*) peacefully;
   (*sin enfadarse: hablar, discutir*) calmly.
tranquilice [trankiˈliθe] *etc vb* V
   tranquilizar.
tranquilidad [trankiliˈðað] *nf* (*calma*)
   calmness, stillness; (*paz*) peacefulness.
tranquilizador, a [trankiliθaˈðor, a] *adj*
   (*música*) soothing; (*hecho*) reassuring.
tranquilizante [trankiliˈθante] *nm*
   tranquillizer.
tranquilizar [trankiliˈθar] *vt* (*calmar*) to
   calm (down); (*asegurar*) to reassure.
tranquilo, a [tranˈkilo, a] *adj* (*calmado*)
   calm; (*apacible*) peaceful; (*mar*) calm;
   (*mente*) untroubled.
Trans. *abr* (*COM*) = **transferencia**.
transacción [transakˈθjon] *nf* transaction.
transar [tranˈsar] *vi* (*AM*) = **transigir**.
transatlántico, a [transatˈlantiko, a] *adj*
   transatlantic ♦ *nm* (ocean) liner.
transbordador [transβorðaˈðor] *nm* ferry.
transbordar [transβorˈðar] *vt* to transfer;

~**se** *vr* to change.
transbordo [trans'βorðo] *nm* transfer;
hacer ~ to change (trains).
transcender [transθen'der] *vt* = **trascender**.
transcribir [transkri'βir] *vt* to transcribe.
transcurrir [transku'rrir] *vi* (*tiempo*) to
pass; (*hecho*) to turn out.
transcurso [trans'kurso] *nm* passing, lapse;
en el ~ **de 8 días** in the course of a week.
transeúnte [transe'unte] *adj* transient
♦ *nm/f* passer-by.
transexual [transe'kswal] *adj, nm/f*
transsexual.
transferencia [transfe'renθja] *nf*
transference; (*COM*) transfer; ~
bancaria banker's order; ~ **de crédito**
(*COM*) credit transfer; ~ **electrónica de**
fondos (*COM*) electronic funds transfer.
transferir [transfe'rir] *vt* to transfer;
(*aplazar*) to postpone.
transfiera [trans'fjera] *etc vb V* **transferir**.
transfigurar [transfiɣu'rar] *vt* to
transfigure.
transfiriendo [transfi'rjendo] *etc vb V*
transferir.
transformación [transforma'θjon] *nf*
transformation.
transformador [transforma'ðor] *nm*
transformer.
transformar [transfor'mar] *vt* to
transform; (*convertir*) to convert.
tránsfuga ['transfuɣa] *nm/f* (*MIL*) deserter;
(*POL*) turncoat.
transfusión [transfu'sjon] *nf* (*tb:* ~ **de**
sangre) (blood) transfusion.
transgénico, a [trans'xeniko, a] *adj*
genetically modified.
transgredir [transɣre'dir] *vt* to transgress.
transgresión [transɣre'sjon] *nf*
transgression.
transición [transi'θjon] *nf* transition;
período de ~ transitional period.
transido, a [tran'siðo, a] *adj* overcome; ~
de angustia beset with anxiety; ~ **de**
dolor racked with pain.
transigir [transi'xir] *vi* to compromise;
(*ceder*) to make concessions.
transija [tran'sixa] *etc vb V* **transigir**.
Transilvania [transil'βanja] *nf*
Transylvania.
transistor [transis'tor] *nm* transistor.
transitable [transi'taβle] *adj* (*camino*)
passable.
transitar [transi'tar] *vi* to go (from place to
place).
transitivo, a [transi'tiβo, a] *adj* transitive.
tránsito ['transito] *nm* transit; (*AUTO*)
traffic; (*parada*) stop; **horas de máximo** ~

rush hours; "**se prohíbe el** ~" "no
thoroughfare."
transitorio, a [transi'torjo, a] *adj*
transitory.
transmisión [transmi'sjon] *nf* (*RADIO, TV*)
transmission, broadcast(ing);
(*transferencia*) transfer; ~ **en circuito**
hookup; ~ **en directo/exterior** live/
outside broadcast; ~ **de datos (en**
paralelo/en serie) (*INFORM*) (parallel/
serial) data transfer *o* transmission;
plena/media ~ **bidireccional** (*INFORM*)
full/half duplex.
transmitir [transmi'tir] *vt* to transmit;
(*RADIO, TV*) to broadcast; (*enfermedad*) to
give, pass on.
transparencia [transpa'renθja] *nf*
transparency; (*claridad*) clearness,
clarity; (*foto*) slide.
transparentar [transparen'tar] *vt* to reveal
♦ *vi* to be transparent.
transparente [transpa'rente] *adj*
transparent; (*aire*) clear; (*ligero*)
diaphanous ♦ *nm* curtain.
transpirar [transpi'rar] *vi* to perspire; (*fig*)
to transpire.
transpondré [transpon'dre] *etc vb V*
transponer.
transponer [transpo'ner] *vt* to transpose;
(*cambiar de sitio*) to move about ♦ *vi*
(*desaparecer*) to disappear; (*ir más allá*) to
go beyond; ~**se** *vr* to change places;
(*ocultarse*) to hide; (*sol*) to go down.
transponga [trans'ponga] *etc vb V*
transponer.
transportador [transporta'ðor] *nm*
(*MECÁNICA*): ~ **de correa** belt conveyor.
transportar [transpor'tar] *vt* to transport;
(*llevar*) to carry.
transporte [trans'porte] *nm* transport;
(*COM*) haulage; **Ministerio de T**~**s**
Ministry of Transport.
transpuesto [trans'pwesto], **transpuse**
[trans'puse] *etc vb V* **transponer**.
transversal [transβer'sal] *adj* transverse,
cross ♦ *nf* (*tb:* **calle** ~) cross street.
transversalmente [transβersal'mente] *adv*
obliquely.
tranvía [tram'bia] *nm* tram, streetcar (*US*).
trapecio [tra'peθjo] *nm* trapeze.
trapecista [trape'θista] *nm/f* trapeze artist.
trapero, a [tra'pero, a] *nm/f* ragman.
trapicheos [trapi'tʃeos] *nmpl* (*fam*)
schemes, fiddles.
trapisonda [trapi'sonda] *nf* (*jaleo*) row;
(*estafa*) swindle.
trapo ['trapo] *nm* (*tela*) rag; (*de cocina*)
cloth; ~**s** *nmpl* (*fam: de mujer*) clothes,

tráquea – tratamiento

dresses; **a todo** ~ under full sail; **soltar el** ~ (*llorar*) to burst into tears.

tráquea ['trakea] *nf* trachea, windpipe.

traqueteo [trake'teo] *nm* (*crujido*) crack; (*golpeteo*) rattling.

tras [tras] *prep* (*detrás*) behind; (*después*) after; ~ **de** besides; **día** ~ **día** day after day; **uno** ~ **otro** one after the other.

trascendencia [trasθen'denθja] *nf* (*importancia*) importance; (*filosofía*) transcendence.

trascendental [trasθenden'tal] *adj* important; transcendental.

trascender [trasθen'der] *vi* (*oler*) to smell; (*noticias*) to come out, leak out; (*eventos, sentimientos*) to spread, have a wide effect; ~ **a** (*afectar*) to reach, have an effect on; (*oler a*) to smack of; **en su novela todo trasciende a romanticismo** everything in his novel smacks of romanticism.

trascienda [tras'θjenda] *etc vb V* **trascender**.

trasegar [trase'ɣar] *vt* (*mover*) to move about; (*vino*) to decant.

trasegué [trase'ɣe], **traseguemos** [trase'ɣemos] *etc vb V* **trasegar**.

trasero, a [tra'sero, a] *adj* back, rear ♦ *nm* (*ANAT*) bottom; ~s *nmpl* ancestors.

trasfondo [tras'fondo] *nm* background.

trasgo ['trasɣo] *nm* (*duende*) goblin.

trasgredir [trasɣre'ðir] *vt* to contravene.

trashumante [trasu'mante] *adj* migrating.

trasiego [tra'sjeɣo] *etc vb V* **trasegar** ♦ *nm* (*cambiar de sitio*) move, switch; (*de vino*) decanting; (*trastorno*) upset.

trasiegue [tra'sjeɣe] *etc vb V* **trasegar**.

trasladar [trasla'ðar] *vt* to move; (*persona*) to transfer; (*postergar*) to postpone; (*copiar*) to copy; (*interpretar*) to interpret; ~**se** *vr* (*irse*) to go; (*mudarse*) to move; ~**se a otro puesto** to move to a new job.

traslado [tras'laðo] *nm* move; (*mudanza*) move, removal; (*de persona*) transfer; (*copia*) copy; ~ **de bloque** (*INFORM*) block move, cut-and-paste.

traslucir [traslu'θir] *vt* to show; ~**se** *vr* to be translucent; (*fig*) to be revealed.

trasluz [tras'luθ] *nm* reflected light; **al** ~ against *o* up to the light.

trasluzca [tras'luθka] *etc vb V* **traslucir**.

trasmano [tras'mano]: **a** ~ *adv* (*fuera de alcance*) out of reach; (*apartado*) out of the way.

trasnochado, a [trasno'tʃaðo, a] *adj* dated.

trasnochador, a [trasnotʃa'ðor, a] *adj* given to staying up late ♦ *nm/f* (*fig*) night bird.

trasnochar [trasno'tʃar] *vi* (*acostarse tarde*) to stay up late; (*no dormir*) to have a sleepless night; (*pasar la noche*) to stay the night.

traspasar [traspa'sar] *vt* (*bala*) to pierce, go through; (*propiedad*) to sell, transfer; (*calle*) to cross over; (*límites*) to go beyond; (*ley*) to break; **"traspaso negocio"** "business for sale".

traspaso [tras'paso] *nm* transfer; (*fig*) anguish.

traspié [tras'pje], *pl* **traspiés** *nm* (*caída*) stumble; (*tropezón*) trip; (*fig*) blunder.

trasplantar [trasplan'tar] *vt* to transplant.

trasplante [tras'plante] *nm* transplant.

traspuesto, a [tras'pwesto, a] *adj*: **quedarse** ~ to doze off.

trastada [tras'taða] *nf* (*fam*) prank.

trastazo [tras'taθo] *nm* (*fam*) bump; **darse un** ~ (*persona*) to bump o.s.; (*en coche*) to have a bump.

traste ['traste] *nm* (*MUS*) fret; **dar al** ~ **con algo** to ruin sth; **ir al** ~ to fall through.

trastero [tras'tero] *nm* lumber room.

trastienda [tras'tjenda] *nf* backshop; **obtener algo por la** ~ to get sth by underhand means.

trasto ['trasto] *nm* (*mueble*) piece of furniture; (*tarro viejo*) old pot; (*pey: cosa*) piece of junk; (: *persona*) dead loss; ~s *nmpl* (*TEAT*) scenery *sg*; **tirar los** ~s **a la cabeza** to have a blazing row.

trastocar [trasto'kar] *vt* (*papeles*) to mix up.

trastornado, a [trastor'naðo, a] *adj* (*loco*) mad; (*agitado*) crazy.

trastornar [trastor'nar] *vt* to overturn, upset; (*fig: ideas*) to confuse; (: *nervios*) to shatter; (: *persona*) to drive crazy; ~**se** *vr* (*plan*) to fall through.

trastorno [tras'torno] *nm* (*acto*) overturning; (*confusión*) confusion; (*POL*) disturbance, upheaval; (*MED*) upset; ~ **estomacal** stomach upset; ~ **mental** mental disorder, breakdown.

trasunto [tra'sunto] *nm* copy.

trasvase [tras'βase] *nm* (*de río*) diversion.

tratable [tra'taβle] *adj* friendly.

tratado [tra'taðo] *nm* (*POL*) treaty; (*COM*) agreement; (*LITERATURA*) treatise.

tratamiento [trata'mjento] *nm* treatment; (*TEC*) processing; (*de problema*) handling; ~ **de datos** (*INFORM*) data processing; ~ **de gráficos** (*INFORM*) graphics; ~ **de márgenes** margin settings; ~ **de textos** (*INFORM*) word processing; ~ **por lotes** (*INFORM*) batch processing; ~ **de tú** familiar address.

tratante [tra'tante] *nm/f* dealer, merchandizer.

tratar [tra'tar] *vt* (*ocuparse de*) to treat; (*manejar, TEC*) to handle; (*INFORM*) to process; (*MED*) to treat; (*dirigirse a: persona*) to address ♦ *vi:* ~ **de** (*hablar sobre*) to deal with, be about; (*intentar*) to try to; ~ **con** (*COM*) to trade in; (*negociar*) to negotiate with; (*tener contactos*) to have dealings with; ~**se** *vr* to treat each other; **se trata de la nueva piscina** it's about the new pool; **¿de qué se trata?** what's it about?

trato ['trato] *nm* dealings *pl*; (*relaciones*) relationship; (*comportamiento*) manner; (*COM, JUR*) agreement, contract; (*título*) (form of) address; **de** ~ **agradable** pleasant; **de fácil** ~ easy to get on with; ~ **equitativo** fair deal; **¡**~ **hecho!** it's a deal!; **malos** ~**s** ill-treatment *sg*.

trauma ['trauma] *nm* trauma.

traumático, a [trau'matiko, a] *adj* traumatic.

través [tra'ßes] *nm* (*contratiempo*) reverse; **al** ~ across, crossways; **a** ~ **de** across; (*sobre*) over; (*por*) through; **de** ~ across; (*de lado*) sideways.

travesaño [traße'saɲo] *nm* (*ARQ*) crossbeam; (*DEPORTE*) crossbar.

travesía [traße'sia] *nf* (*calle*) cross-street; (*NAUT*) crossing.

travesti [tra'ßesti] *nm/f* transvestite.

travesura [traße'sura] *nf* (*broma*) prank; (*ingenio*) wit.

travieso, a [tra'ßjeso, a] *adj* (*niño*) naughty; (*adulto*) restless; (*ingenioso*) witty ♦ *nf* crossing; (*ARQ*) crossbeam; (*FERRO*) sleeper.

trayecto [tra'jekto] *nm* (*ruta*) road, way; (*viaje*) journey; (*tramo*) stretch; (*curso*) course; **final del** ~ end of the line.

trayectoria [trajek'torja] *nf* trajectory; (*desarrollo*) development, path; **la** ~ **actual del partido** the party's present line.

trayendo [tra'jendo] *etc vb V* **traer**.

traza ['traθa] *nf* (*ARQ*) plan, design; (*aspecto*) looks *pl*; (*señal*) sign; (*engaño*) trick; (*habilidad*) skill; (*INFORM*) trace.

trazado, a [tra'θaðo, a] *adj:* **bien** ~ shapely, well-formed ♦ *nm* (*ARQ*) plan, design; (*fig*) outline; (*de carretera etc*) line, route.

trazador [traθa'ðor] *nm* plotter; ~ **plano** flatbed plotter.

trazar [tra'θar] *vt* (*ARQ*) to plan; (*ARTE*) to sketch; (*fig*) to trace; (*itinerario: hacer*) to plot; (*plan*) to follow.

trazo ['traθo] *nm* (*línea*) line; (*bosquejo*) sketch; ~**s** *nmpl* (*de cara*) lines, features.

TRB *abr = toneladas de registro bruto.*

trébol ['treßol] *nm* (*BOT*) clover; ~**es** *nmpl* (*NAIPES*) clubs.

trece ['treθe] *num* thirteen; **estar en sus** ~ to stand firm.

trecho ['tretʃo] *nm* (*distancia*) distance; (*de tiempo*) while; (*fam*) piece; **de** ~ **en** ~ at intervals.

tregua ['treɣwa] *nf* (*MIL*) truce; (*fig*) lull; **sin** ~ without respite.

treinta ['treinta] *num* thirty.

treintena [trein'tena] *nf* (about) thirty.

tremendo, a [tre'mendo, a] *adj* (*terrible*) terrible; (*imponente: cosa*) imposing; (*fam: fabuloso*) tremendous; (*divertido*) entertaining.

trémulo, a ['tremulo, a] *adj* quivering; (*luz*) flickering.

tren [tren] *nm* (*FERRO*) train; ~ **de aterrizaje** undercarriage; ~ **directo/expreso/(de) mercancías/de pasajeros/suplementario** through/fast/goods *o* freight/passenger/ relief train; ~ **de vida** way of life.

trenca ['trenka] *nf* duffel coat.

trence ['trenθe] *etc vb V* **trenzar**.

trenza ['trenθa] *nf* (*de pelo*) plait.

trenzar [tren'θar] *vt* (*el pelo*) to plait ♦ *vi* (*en baile*) to weave in and out; ~**se** *vr* (*AM*) to become involved.

trepa ['trepa] *nf* (*subida*) climb; (*ardid*) trick.

trepador(a) [trepa'ðor(a)] *nm/f* (*fam*): **ser un(a)** ~ to be on the make ♦ *nf* (*BOT*) climber.

trepar [tre'par] *vt, vi* to climb; (*TEC*) to drill.

trepidación [trepiða'θjon] *nf* shaking, vibration.

trepidar [trepi'ðar] *vi* to shake, vibrate.

tres [tres] *num* three; (*fecha*) third; **las** ~ three o'clock.

trescientos, as [tres'θjentos, as] *num* three hundred.

tresillo [tre'siʎo] *nm* three-piece suite; (*MUS*) triplet.

treta ['treta] *nf* (*COM etc*) gimmick; (*fig*) trick.

tri... [tri] *pref* tri..., three-....

tríada ['triaða] *nf* triad.

triangular [trjaŋgu'lar] *adj* triangular.

triángulo [tri'aŋgulo] *nm* triangle.

tribal [tri'ßal] *adj* tribal.

tribu ['trißu] *nf* tribe.

tribuna [tri'ßuna] *nf* (*plataforma*) platform; (*DEPORTE*) stand; (*fig*) public speaking; ~ **de la prensa** press box; ~ **del acusado** (*JUR*) dock; ~ **del jurado** jury box.

tribunal [triβu'nal] *nm* (*juicio*) court; (*comisión*, *fig*) tribunal; (*ESCOL: examinadores*) board of examiners; **T~ Supremo** High Court, (*US*) Supreme Court; **T~ de Justicia de las Comunidades Europeas** European Court of Justice; ~ **popular** jury.

tributar [triβu'tar] *vt* to pay; (*las gracias*) to give; (*cariño*) to show.

tributario, a [triβu'tarjo, a] *adj* (*GEO, POL*) tributary *cpd*; (*ECON*) tax *cpd*, taxation *cpd* ♦ *nm* (*GEO*) tributary ♦ *nm/f* (*COM*) taxpayer; **sistema** ~ tax system.

tributo [tri'βuto] *nm* (*COM*) tax.

trice ['triθe] *etc vb V* **trizar**.

triciclo [tri'θiklo] *nm* tricycle.

tricornio [tri'kornjo] *nm* three-cornered hat.

tricota [tri'kota] *nf* (*AM*) knitted sweater.

tricotar [triko'tar] *vi* to knit.

tridimensional [triðimensjo'nal] *adj* three-dimensional.

trienal [trje'nal] *adj* three-year.

trifulca [tri'fulka] *nf* (*fam*) row, shindy.

trigal [tri'ɣal] *nm* wheat field.

trigésimo, a [tri'xesimo, a] *num* thirtieth.

trigo ['triɣo] *nm* wheat; ~**s** *nmpl* wheat field(s) (*pl*).

trigueño, a [tri'ɣeɲo, a] *adj* (*pelo*) corn-coloured; (*piel*) olive-skinned.

trillado, a [tri'ʎaðo, a] *adj* threshed; (*fig*) trite, hackneyed.

trilladora [triʎa'ðora] *nf* threshing machine.

trillar [tri'ʎar] *vt* (*AGR*) to thresh; (*fig*) to frequent.

trillizos, as [tri'ʎiθos, as] *nmpl/nfpl* triplets.

trilogía [trilo'xia] *nf* triology.

trimestral [trimes'tral] *adj* quarterly; (*ESCOL*) termly.

trimestre [tri'mestre] *nm* (*ESCOL*) term; (*COM*) quarter, financial period; (: *pago*) quarterly payment.

trinar [tri'nar] *vi* (*MUS*) to trill; (*ave*) to sing, warble; **está que trina** he's hopping mad.

trincar [trin'kar] *vt* (*atar*) to tie up; (*NAUT*) to lash; (*agarrar*) to pinion.

trinchante [trin'tʃante] *nm* (*para cortar carne*) carving knife; (*tenedor*) meat fork.

trinchar [trin'tʃar] *vt* to carve.

trinchera [trin'tʃera] *nf* (*fosa*) trench; (*para vía*) cutting; (*impermeable*) trench-coat.

trineo [tri'neo] *nm* sledge.

trinidad [trini'ðað] *nf* trio; (*REL*): **la T~** the Trinity.

trino ['trino] *nm* trill.

trinque ['trinke] *etc vb V* **trincar**.

trinquete [trin'kete] *nm* (*TEC*) pawl; (*NAUT*) foremast.

trío ['trio] *nm* trio.

tripa ['tripa] *nf* (*ANAT*) intestine; (*fig, fam*) belly; ~**s** *nfpl* (*ANAT*) insides; (*CULIN*) tripe *sg*; **tener mucha** ~ to be fat; **me duelen las** ~**s** I have a stomach ache.

tripartito, a [tripar'tito, a] *adj* tripartite.

triple ['triple] *adj* triple; (*tres veces*) threefold.

triplicado, a [tripli'kaðo, a] *adj*: **por** ~ in triplicate.

triplicar [tripli'kar] *vt* to treble.

triplo ['triplo] *adj* = **triple**.

trípode ['tripoðe] *nm* tripod.

Trípoli ['tripoli] *nm* Tripoli.

tríptico ['triptiko] *nm* (*ARTE*) triptych; (*documento*) three-part document.

tripulación [tripula'θjon] *nf* crew.

tripulante [tripu'lante] *nm/f* crewman/woman.

tripular [tripu'lar] *vt* (*barco*) to man; (*AUTO*) to drive.

triquiñuela [triki'ɲwela] *nf* trick.

tris [tris] *nm* crack; **en un** ~ in an instant; **estar en un** ~ **de hacer algo** to be within an inch of doing sth.

triste ['triste] *adj* (*afligido*) sad; (*sombrío*) melancholy, gloomy; (*desolado*) desolate; (*lamentable*) sorry, miserable; (*viejo*) old; (*único*) single; **no queda sino un** ~ **penique** there's just one miserable penny left.

tristeza [tris'teθa] *nf* (*aflicción*) sadness; (*melancolía*) melancholy; (*de lugar*) desolation; (*pena*) misery.

tristón, ona [tris'ton, ona] *adj* sad, downhearted.

trituradora [tritura'ðora] *nf* shredder.

triturar [tritu'rar] *vt* (*moler*) to grind; (*mascar*) to chew; (*documentos*) to shred.

triunfador, a [triunfa'ðor, a] *adj* triumphant; (*ganador*) winning ♦ *nm/f* winner.

triunfal [triun'fal] *adj* triumphant; (*arco*) triumphal.

triunfante [triun'fante] *adj* triumphant; (*ganador*) winning.

triunfar [triun'far] *vi* (*tener éxito*) to triumph; (*ganar*) to win; (*NAIPES*) to be trumps; **triunfan corazones** hearts are trumps; ~ **en la vida** to succeed in life.

triunfo [tri'unfo] *nm* triumph; (*NAIPES*) trump.

trivial [tri'βjal] *adj* trivial.

trivialice [triβja'liθe] *etc vb V* **trivializar**.

trivializar [triβjali'θar] *vt* to minimize, play

down.

triza ['triθa] *nf* bit, piece; **hacer algo ~s** to smash sth to bits; (*papel*) to tear sth to shreds.

trocar [tro'kar] *vt* (*COM*) to exchange; (*dinero, de lugar*) to change; (*palabras*) to exchange; (*confundir*) to confuse; (*vomitar*) to vomit; **~se** *vr* (*confundirse*) to get mixed up; (*transformarse*): **~se (en)** to change (into).

trocear [troθe'ar] *vt* to cut up.

trocha ['trotʃa] *nf* (*sendero*) by-path; (*atajo*) short cut.

troche ['trotʃe]: **a ~ y moche** *adv* helter-skelter, pell-mell.

trofeo [tro'feo] *nm* (*premio*) trophy; (*éxito*) success.

trola ['trola] *nf* (*fam*) fib.

tromba ['tromba] *nf* whirlwind; **~ de agua** cloudburst.

trombón [trom'bon] *nm* trombone.

trombosis [trom'bosis] *nf inv* thrombosis.

trompa ['trompa] *nf* (*MUS*) horn; (*de elefante*) trunk; (*trompo*) humming top; (*hocico*) snout; (*ANAT*) tube, duct ♦ *nm* (*MUS*) horn player; **~ de Falopio** Fallopian tube; **cogerse una ~** (*fam*) to get tight.

trompada [trom'paða] *nf*, **trompazo** [trom'paθo] *nm* (*choque*) bump, bang; (*puñetazo*) punch.

trompeta [trom'peta] *nf* trumpet; (*clarín*) bugle ♦ *nm* trumpeter.

trompetilla [trompe'tiʎa] *nf* ear trumpet.

trompicón [trompi'kon]: **a trompicones** *adv* in fits and starts.

trompo ['trompo] *nm* spinning top.

trompón [trom'pon] *nm* bump.

tronado, a [tro'naðo, a] *adj* broken-down.

tronar [tro'nar] *vt* (*AM*) to shoot, execute ♦ *vi* to thunder; (*fig*) to rage; (*fam*) to go broke.

tronchar [tron'tʃar] *vt* (*árbol*) to chop down; (*fig: vida*) to cut short; (*esperanza*) to shatter; (*persona*) to tire out; **~se** *vr* to fall down; **~se de risa** to split one's sides with laughter.

tronco ['tronko] *nm* (*de árbol, ANAT*) trunk; (*de planta*) stem; **estar hecho un ~** to be sound asleep.

tronera [tro'nera] *nf* (*MIL*) loophole; (*ARQ*) small window.

trono ['trono] *nm* throne.

tropa ['tropa] *nf* (*MIL*) troop; (*soldados*) soldiers *pl*; (*soldados rasos*) ranks *pl*; (*gentío*) mob.

tropecé [trope'θe], **tropecemos** [trope'θemos] *etc vb V* **tropezar**.

tropel [tro'pel] *nm* (*muchedumbre*) crowd; (*prisa*) rush; (*montón*) throng; **acudir** *etc* **en ~** to come *etc* in a mad rush.

tropelía [trope'lia] *nm* outrage.

tropezar [trope'θar] *vi* to trip, stumble; (*fig*) to slip up; **~se** *vr* (*dos personas*) to run into each other; **~ con** (*encontrar*) to run into; (*topar con*) to bump into.

tropezón [trope'θon] *nm* trip; (*fig*) blunder; (*traspié*): **dar un ~** to trip.

tropical [tropi'kal] *adj* tropical.

trópico ['tropiko] *nm* tropic.

tropiece [tro'pjeθe] *etc vb V* **tropezar**.

tropiezo [tro'pjeθo] *etc vb V* **tropezar** ♦ *nm* (*error*) slip, blunder; (*desgracia*) misfortune; (*revés*) setback; (*obstáculo*) snag; (*discusión*) quarrel.

troqué [tro'ke], **troquemos** [tro'kemos] *etc vb V* **trocar**.

trotamundos [trota'mundos] *nm inv* globetrotter.

trotar [tro'tar] *vi* to trot; (*viajar*) to travel about.

trote ['trote] *nm* trot; (*fam*) travelling; **de mucho ~** hard-wearing.

Troya ['troja] *nf* Troy; **aquí fue ~** now there's nothing but ruins.

trozo ['troθo] *nm* bit, piece; (*LITERATURA, MUS*) passage; **a ~s** in bits.

trucha ['trutʃa] *nf* (*pez*) trout; (*TEC*) crane.

truco ['truko] *nm* (*habilidad*) knack; (*engaño*) trick; (*CINE*) trick effect *o* photography; **~s** *nmpl* billiards *sg*; **~ publicitario** advertising gimmick.

trueco ['trweko] *etc vb V* **trocar**.

trueno ['trweno] *etc vb V* **tronar** ♦ *nm* (*gen*) thunder; (*estampido*) boom; (*de arma*) bang.

trueque ['trweke] *etc vb V* **trocar** ♦ *nm* exchange; (*COM*) barter.

trufa ['trufa] *nf* (*BOT*) truffle; (*fig: fam*) fib.

truhán, ana [tru'an, ana] *nm/f* rogue.

truncado, a [trun'kaðo, a] *adj* truncated.

truncar [trun'kar] *vt* (*cortar*) to truncate; (*la vida etc*) to cut short; (*el desarrollo*) to stunt.

trunque ['trunke] *etc vb V* **truncar**.

tu [tu] *adj* your.

tú [tu] *pron* you.

tubérculo [tu'βerkulo] *nm* (*BOT*) tuber.

tuberculosis [tußerku'losis] *nf inv* tuberculosis.

tubería [tuße'ria] *nf* pipes *pl*, piping; (*conducto*) pipeline.

tubo ['tußo] *nm* tube, pipe; **~ de desagüe** drainpipe; **~ de ensayo** test-tube; **~ de escape** exhaust (pipe); **~ digestivo** alimentary canal.

tuerca ['twerka] *nf (TEC)* nut.
tuerce ['twerθe] *etc vb V* **torcer.**
tuerto, a ['twerto, a] *adj (torcido)* twisted; *(ciego)* blind in one eye ♦ *nm/f* one-eyed person ♦ *nm (ofensa)* wrong; **a tuertas** upside-down.
tuerza ['twerθa] *etc vb V* **torcer.**
tueste ['tweste] *etc vb V* **tostar.**
tuétano ['twetano] *nm (ANAT: médula)* marrow; *(BOT)* pith; **hasta los ~s** through and through, utterly.
tufo ['tufo] *nm* vapour; *(fig: pey)* stench.
tugurio [tu'ɣurjo] *nm* slum.
tul [tul] *nm* tulle.
tulipán [tuli'pan] *nm* tulip.
tullido, a [tu'ʎiðo, a] *adj* crippled; *(cansado)* exhausted.
tumba ['tumba] *nf (sepultura)* tomb; *(sacudida)* shake; *(voltereta)* somersault; **ser (como) una ~** to keep one's mouth shut.
tumbar [tum'bar] *vt* to knock down; *(doblar)* to knock over; *(fam: suj: olor)* to overpower ♦ *vi* to fall down; **~se** *vr (echarse)* to lie down; *(extenderse)* to stretch out.
tumbo ['tumbo] *nm (caída)* fall; *(de vehículo)* jolt; *(momento crítico)* critical moment.
tumbona [tum'bona] *nf* lounger.
tumor [tu'mor] *nm* tumour.
tumulto [tu'multo] *nm* turmoil; *(POL: motín)* riot.
tuna ['tuna] *nf (MUS)* student music group; *V tb* **tuno;** *see boxed note.*

TUNA

*A **tuna** is a musical group made up of university students, or quite often former students, who dress up in costumes from the "Edad de Oro", the Spanish Golden Age. These musical troupes wander through town, playing guitars, lutes and tambourines and serenading young women in the halls of residence. Sometimes they make impromptu appearances at weddings or parties, singing traditional songs in exchange for a few donations.*

---

tunante [tu'nante] *adj* rascally ♦ *nm* rogue, villain; **¡~!** you villain!
tunda ['tunda] *nf (de tela)* shearing; *(golpeo)* beating.
tundir [tun'dir] *vt (tela)* to shear; *(hierba)* to mow; *(fig)* to exhaust; *(fam: golpear)* to beat.
tunecino, a [tune'θino, a] *adj, nm/f* Tunisian.

túnel ['tunel] *nm* tunnel.
Túnez ['tuneθ] *nm* Tunis.
túnica ['tunika] *nf* tunic; *(vestido largo)* long dress; *(ANAT, BOT)* tunic.
Tunicia [tu'niθja] *nf* Tunisia.
tuno, a ['tuno, a] *nm/f (fam)* rogue ♦ *nm (MUS)* member of a "tuna".
tuntún [tun'tun]: **al ~** *adv* thoughtlessly.
tupamaro, a [tupa'maro, a] *adj, nm/f (AM)* urban guerrilla.
tupé [tu'pe] *nm* quiff.
tupí [tu'pi], **tupí-guaraní** [tupiɣwara'ni] *adj, nm/f* Tupi-Guarani.
tupido, a [tu'piðo, a] *adj (denso)* dense; *(fig: torpe)* dim; *(tela)* close-woven.
turba ['turßa] *nf (combustible)* turf; *(muchedumbre)* crowd.
turbación [turßa'θjon] *nf (molestia)* disturbance; *(preocupación)* worry.
turbado, a [tur'ßaðo, a] *adj (molesto)* disturbed; *(preocupado)* worried.
turbante [tur'ßante] *nm* turban.
turbar [tur'ßar] *vt (molestar)* to disturb; *(incomodar)* to upset; **~se** *vr* to be disturbed.
turbina [tur'ßina] *nf* turbine.
turbio, a ['turßjo, a] *adj (agua etc)* cloudy; *(vista)* dim, blurred; *(tema)* unclear, confused; *(negocio)* shady ♦ *adv* indistinctly.
turbión [tur'ßjon] *nf* downpour; *(fig)* shower, hail.
turbo ['turßo] *adj inv* turbo(-charged) ♦ *nm (tb coche)* turbo.
turbulencia [turßu'lenθja] *nf* turbulence; *(fig)* restlessness.
turbulento, a [turßu'lento, a] *adj* turbulent; *(fig: intranquilo)* restless; *(: ruidoso)* noisy.
turco, a ['turko, a] *adj* Turkish ♦ *nm/f* Turk ♦ *nm (LING)* Turkish.
Turena [tu'rena] *nf* Touraine.
turgente [tur'xente], **túrgido, a** ['turxiðo, a] *adj (hinchado)* turgid, swollen.
Turín [tu'rin] *nm* Turin.
turismo [tu'rismo] *nm* tourism; *(coche)* saloon car; **hacer ~** to go travelling (abroad).
turista [tu'rista] *nm/f* tourist; *(vacacionista)* holidaymaker *(BRIT)*, vacationer *(US)*.
turístico, a [tu'ristiko, a] *adj* tourist *cpd.*
Turkmenistán [turkmeni'stan] *nm* Turkmenistan.
turnar [tur'nar] *vi*, **turnarse** *vr* to take (it in) turns.
turno ['turno] *nm (oportunidad, orden de prioridad)* opportunity; *(DEPORTE etc)* turn; **es su ~** it's his turn (next); **~ de**

día/de noche (*INDUSTRIA*) day/night shift.

turolense [turo'lense] *adj* of *o* from Teruel ♦ *nm/f* native *o* inhabitant of Teruel.

turquesa [tur'kesa] *nf* turquoise.

Turquía [tur'kia] *nf* Turkey.

turrón [tu'rron] *nm* (*dulce*) nougat; (*fam*) sinecure, cushy job *o* number.

tute ['tute] *nm* (*NAIPES*) *card game*; **darse un** ~ to break one's back.

tutear [tute'ar] *vt* to address as familiar "tú"; ~**se** *vr* to be on familiar terms.

tutela [tu'tela] *nf* (*legal*) guardianship; (*instrucción*) guidance; **estar bajo la** ~ **de** (*fig*) to be under the protection of.

tutelar [tute'lar] *adj* tutelary ♦ *vt* to protect.

tutor, a [tu'tor, a] *nm/f* (*legal*) guardian; (*ESCOL*) tutor; ~ **de curso** form master/mistress.

tuve ['tuβe] *etc vb V* **tener**.

tuyo, a ['tujo, a] *adj* yours, of yours ♦ *pron* yours; **los** ~**s** (*fam*) your relations, your family.

TVE *nf abr = Televisión Española.*

U u

U, u [u] *nf* (*letra*) U, u; **viraje en U** U-turn; **U de Ulises** U for Uncle.

u [u] *conj* or.

UAR [war] *nfpl abr* (*ESP*) = *Unidades Antiterroristas Rurales.*

ubérrimo, a [u'βerrimo, a] *adj* very rich, fertile.

ubicación [uβika'θjon] *nf* (*esp AM*) place, position, location.

ubicado, a [uβi'kaðo, a] *adj* (*esp AM*) situated.

ubicar [uβi'kar] *vt* (*esp AM*) to place, situate; (: *fig*) to install in a post; (: *encontrar*) to find; ~**se** *vr* to be situated, be located.

ubicuo, a [u'βikwo, a] *adj* ubiquitous.

ubique [u'βike] *etc vb V* **ubicar**.

ubre ['uβre] *nf* udder.

Ucrania [u'kranja] *nf* Ukraine.

ucraniano, a [ukra'njano, a] *adj, nm/f* Ukrainian ♦ *nm* (*LING*) Ukrainian.

ucranio [u'kranjo] *nm* (*LING*) Ukrainian.

Ud(s) *abr* = **usted(es)**.

UE *nf abr* (= *Unión Europea*) EU.

UEFA *nf abr* (= *Unión de Asociaciones de Fútbol Europeo*) UEFA.

UEO *nf abr* (= *Unión Europea Occidental*) WEU.

UEP *nf abr* = *Unión Europea de Pagos*.

uf [uf] *excl* (*cansancio*) phew!; (*repugnancia*) ugh!

ufanarse [ufa'narse] *vr* to boast; ~ **de** to pride o.s. on.

ufano, a [u'fano, a] *adj* (*arrogante*) arrogant; (*presumido*) conceited.

UGT *nf abr V* **Unión General de Trabajadores**.

ujier [u'xjer] *nm* usher; (*portero*) doorkeeper.

úlcera ['ulθera] *nf* ulcer.

ulcerar [ulθe'rar] *vt* to make sore; ~**se** *vr* to ulcerate.

ulterior [ulte'rjor] *adj* (*más allá*) farther, further; (*subsecuente, siguiente*) subsequent.

ulteriormente [ulterjor'mente] *adv* later, subsequently.

últimamente ['ultimamente] *adv* (*recientemente*) lately, recently; (*finalmente*) finally; (*como último recurso*) as a last resort.

ultimar [ulti'mar] *vt* to finish; (*finalizar*) to finalize; (*AM*: *rematar*) to finish off, murder.

ultimátum [ulti'matum] *nm, pl* **ultimátums** ultimatum.

último, a ['ultimo, a] *adj* last; (*más reciente*) latest, most recent; (*más bajo*) bottom; (*más alto*) top; (*fig*) final, extreme; **en las últimas** on one's last legs; **por** ~ finally.

ultra ['ultra] *adj* ultra ♦ *nm/f* extreme right-winger.

ultracongelar [ultrakonxe'lar] *vt* to deep-freeze.

ultraderecha [ultraðe'retʃa] *nf* extreme right (wing).

ultrajar [ultra'xar] *vt* (*escandalizar*) to outrage; (*insultar*) to insult, abuse.

ultraje [ul'traxe] *nm* outrage; insult.

ultraligero [ultrali'xero] *nm* microlight (*BRIT*), microlite (*US*).

ultramar [ultra'mar] *nm*: **de** *o* **en** ~ abroad, overseas; **los países de** ~ the overseas countries.

ultramarino, a [ultrama'rino, a] *adj* overseas, foreign ♦ *nmpl*: ~**s** groceries; **tienda de** ~**s** grocer's (shop).

ultranza [ul'tranθa]: **a** ~ *adv* to the death; (*a todo trance*) at all costs; (*completo*) outright; (*POL etc*) out-and-out, extreme; **un nacionalista a** ~ a rabid nationalist.

ultrarrojo, a [ultra'rroxo, a] *adj*

= **infrarrojo, a.**

ultrasónico, a [ultra'soniko, a] adj ultrasonic.

ultratumba [ultra'tumba] nf: **la vida de ~** the next life; **una voz de ~** a ghostly voice.

ultravioleta [ultraßjo'leta] adj inv ultraviolet.

ulular [ulu'lar] vi to howl; (búho) to hoot.

umbilical [umbili'kal] adj: **cordón ~** umbilical cord.

umbral [um'bral] nm (gen) threshold; **~ de rentabilidad** (COM) break-even point.

umbrío, a [um'brio, a] adj shady.

UME nf abr (= Unión Monetaria y Económica) EMU.

============== PALABRA CLAVE

un, una [un, 'una] art indef a; (antes de vocal) an; **una mujer/naranja** a woman/an orange ♦ adj **1: unos (o unas): hay unos regalos para ti** there are some presents for you; **hay unas cervezas en la nevera** there are some beers in the fridge

2 (enfático): **¡hace un frío!** it's so cold!; **¡tiene una casa!** he's got some house!

U.N.A.M. ['unam] nf abr = Universidad Nacional Autónoma de México.

unánime [u'nanime] adj unanimous.

unanimidad [unanimi'ðað] nf unanimity; **por ~** unanimously.

unción [un'θjon] nf anointing.

uncir [un'θir] vt to yoke.

undécimo, a [un'deθimo, a] adj, nmf eleventh.

UNED [u'ned] nf abr (ESP UNIV: = Universidad Nacional de Enseñanza a Distancia) ≈ Open University (BRIT).

ungir [un'xir] vt to rub with ointment; (REL) to anoint.

ungüento [un'gwento] nm ointment; (fig) salve, balm.

únicamente ['unikamente] adv solely; (solamente) only.

unicidad [uniθi'ðað] nf uniqueness.

único, a ['uniko, a] adj only; (solo) sole, single; (sin par) unique; **hijo ~** only child.

unidad [uni'ðað] nf unity; (TEC) unit; **~ móvil** (TV) mobile unit; (INFORM): **~ central** system unit, central processing unit; **~ de control** control unit; **~ de disco** disk drive; **~ de entrada/salida** input/output device; **~ de información** data item; **~ periférica** peripheral device; **~ de presentación visual o de visualización** visual display unit; **~ procesadora central** central processing unit.

unido, a [u'niðo, a] adj joined, linked; (fig) united.

unifamiliar [unifamil'jar] adj: **vivienda ~** single-family home.

unificar [unifi'kar] vt to unite, unify.

unifique [uni'fike] etc vb V **unificar.**

uniformado, a [unifor'maðo, a] adj uniformed, in uniform.

uniformar [unifor'mar] vt to make uniform; (TEC) to standardize.

uniforme [uni'forme] adj uniform, equal; (superficie) even ♦ nm uniform.

uniformidad [uniformi'ðað] nf uniformity; (llaneza) levelness, evenness.

unilateral [unilate'ral] adj unilateral.

unión [u'njon] nf (gen) union; (acto) uniting, joining; (calidad) unity; (TEC) joint; (fig) closeness, togetherness; **en ~ con** (together) with, accompanied by; **~ aduanera** customs union; **U~ General de Trabajadores (UGT)** (ESP) Socialist Union Confederation; **U~ Europea** European Union; **la U~ Soviética** the Soviet Union; **punto de ~** (TEC) junction.

unir [u'nir] vt (juntar) to join, unite; (atar) to tie, fasten; (combinar) to combine ♦ vi (ingredientes) to mix well; **~se** vr to join together, unite; (empresas) to merge; **les une una fuerte simpatía** they are bound by (a) strong affection; **~se en matrimonio** to marry.

unisex [uni'seks] adj inv unisex.

unísono [u'nisono] nm: **al ~** in unison.

unitario, a [uni'tarjo, a] adj unitary; (REL) Unitarian ♦ nmf (REL) Unitarian.

universal [unißer'sal] adj universal; (mundial) world cpd; **historia ~** world history.

universidad [unißersi'ðað] nf university; **~ laboral** polytechnic, poly.

universitario, a [unißersi'tarjo, a] adj university cpd ♦ nmf (profesor) lecturer; (estudiante) (university) student.

universo [uni'ßerso] nm universe.

unja ['unxa] etc vb V **ungir.**

============== PALABRA CLAVE

uno, a ['uno, a] adj one; **es todo ~** it's all one and the same; **~s pocos** a few; **~s cien** about a hundred

♦ pron **1** one; **quiero sólo uno** I only want one; **~ de ellos** one of them; **una de dos** either one or the other; **no doy una hoy** I can't do anything right today

2 (alguien) somebody, someone; **conozco a ~ que se te parece** I know somebody o someone who looks like you; **~s querían quedarse** some (people) wanted to stay

3 (*impersonal*) one; ~ **mismo** oneself; ~
nunca sabe qué hacer one never knows
what to do
4: ~**s ... otros ...** some ... others; **una y
otra son muy agradables** they're both
very nice; **(los) ~(s) a (los) otro(s)** each
other, one another
♦ *nf* one; **es la una** it's one o'clock
♦ *num* (number) one; **el día** ~ the first.

untar [un'tar] *vt* (*gen*) to rub; (*engrasar*) to
grease, oil; (*MED*) to rub (with
ointment); (*fig*) to bribe; ~**se** *vr* (*fig*) to be
crooked; ~ **el pan con mantequilla** to
spread butter on one's bread.
unto ['unto] *nm* animal fat; (*MED*)
ointment.
unza ['unθa] *etc vb V* **uncir.**
uña ['uɲa] *nf* (*ANAT*) nail; (*del pie*) toenail;
(*garra*) claw; (*casco*) hoof; (*arrancaclavos*)
claw; **ser ~ y carne** to be as thick as
thieves; **enseñar o mostrar o sacar las ~s**
to show one's claws.
UOE *nf abr* (*ESP MIL*) = *Unidad de
Operaciones Especiales.*
UPA *nf abr* = *Unión Panamericana.*
UPC *nf abr* (= *unidad procesadora central*)
CPU.
uperizado, a [uperi'θaðo, a] *adj*: **leche
uperizada** UHT milk.
Urales [u'rales] *nmpl* (*tb*: **Montes ~**) Urals.
uralita ® [ura'lita] *nf* corrugated asbestos
cement.
uranio [u'ranjo] *nm* uranium.
urbanidad [urßani'ðað] *nf* courtesy,
politeness.
urbanismo [urßa'nismo] *nm* town
planning.
urbanista [urßa'nista] *nm/f* town planner.
urbanización [urßaniθa'θjon] *nf* (*colonia,
barrio*) estate, housing scheme.
urbanizar [urßani'θar] *vt* to develop.
urbano, a [ur'ßano, a] *adj* (*de ciudad*)
urban, town *cpd*; (*cortés*) courteous,
polite.
urbe ['urße] *nf* large city, metropolis.
urdimbre [ur'ðimbre] *nf* (*de tejido*) warp;
(*intriga*) intrigue.
urdir [ur'ðir] *vt* to warp; (*fig*) to plot,
contrive.
urgencia [ur'xenθja] *nf* urgency; (*prisa*)
haste, rush; **salida de ~** emergency exit;
servicios de ~ emergency services.
urgente [ur'xente] *adj* urgent; (*insistente*)
insistent; **carta ~** registered (*BRIT*) *o*
special delivery (*US*) letter.
urgir [ur'xir] *vi* to be urgent; **me urge** I'm
in a hurry for it; **me urge terminarlo** I

must finish it as soon as I can.
urinario, a [uri'narjo, a] *adj* urinary ♦ *nm*
urinal, public lavatory, comfort station
(*US*).
urja ['urxa] *etc vb V* **urgir.**
urna ['urna] *nf* urn; (*POL*) ballot box; **acudir
a las ~s** (*fig*: *persona*) to (go and) vote;
(: *gobierno*) to go to the country.
urología [urolo'xia] *nf* urology.
urólogo, a [u'roloɣo, a] *nm/f* urologist.
urraca [u'rraka] *nf* magpie.
URSS *nf abr* (= *Unión de Repúblicas
Socialistas Soviéticas*) USSR.
Uruguay [uru'ɣwai] *nm*: **El ~** Uruguay.
uruguayo, a [uru'ɣwajo, a] *adj, nm/f*
Uruguayan.
usado, a [u'saðo, a] *adj* (*gen*) used; (*ropa
etc*) worn; **muy ~** worn out.
usanza [u'sanθa] *nf* custom, usage.
usar [u'sar] *vt* to use; (*ropa*) to wear; (*tener
costumbre*) to be in the habit of ♦ *vi*: ~ **de**
to make use of; ~**se** *vr* to be used; (*ropa*)
to be worn *o* in fashion.
USO *nf abr* (*ESP*: = *Unión Sindical Obrera*)
workers' union.
uso ['uso] *nm* use; (*MECÁNICA etc*) wear;
(*costumbre*) usage, custom; (*moda*)
fashion; **al ~** in keeping with custom; **al
~ de** in the style of; **de ~ externo** (*MED*)
for external application; **estar en el ~ de
la palabra** to be speaking, have the floor;
~ **y desgaste** (*COM*) wear and tear.
usted [us'teð] *pron* (*sg*: *abr* Ud *o* Vd: *formal*)
you *sg*; ~**es** (*pl*: *abr* Uds *o* Vds: *formal*)
you *pl*; (*AM*: *formal y fam*) you *pl*.
usual [u'swal] *adj* usual.
usuario, a [usw'arjo, a] *nm/f* user; ~ **final**
(*COM*) end user.
usufructo [usu'frukto] *nm* use; ~ **vitalicio
(de)** life interest (in).
usura [u'sura] *nf* usury.
usurero, a [usu'rero, a] *nm/f* usurer.
usurpar [usur'par] *vt* to usurp.
utensilio [uten'siljo] *nm* tool; (*CULIN*)
utensil.
útero ['utero] *nm* uterus, womb.
útil ['util] *adj* useful; (*servible*) usable,
serviceable ♦ *nm* tool; **día ~** working
day, weekday; **es muy ~ tenerlo aquí
cerca** it's very handy having it here
close by.
utilice [uti'liθe] *etc vb V* **utilizar.**
utilidad [utili'ðað] *nf* usefulness, utility;
(*COM*) profit; ~**es líquidas** net profit *sg*.
utilitario [utili'tarjo] *nm* (*INFORM*) utility.
utilizar [utili'θar] *vt* to use, utilize;
(*explotar*) to harness.
utopía [uto'pia] *nf* Utopia.

utópico, a [u'topiko, a] *adj* Utopian.
uva ['uβa] *nf* grape; ~ **pasa** raisin; ~ **de Corinto** currant; **estar de mala** ~ to be in a bad mood; **las (doce)** ~**s** *see boxed note.*

LAS UVAS

Las uvas *play an important part in the New Years' Eve ("Nochevieja") celebrations; on the stroke of midnight people from every part of Spain, at home, in restaurants or in the "plaza mayor", eat a grape for each stroke of the clock at the Puerta del Sol in Madrid. It is said to bring luck for the coming year.*

---

uve ['uβe] *nf name of the letter V;* **en forma de** ~ V-shaped; ~ **doble** *name of the letter W.*
UVI ['uβi] *nf abr (ESP MED:* = *unidad de vigilancia intensiva)* ICU.

V v

V, v [(*ESP*) 'uβe, (*AM*) be'lkorta, bet∫ika] *nf* (*letra*) V, v; **V de Valencia** V for Victor.
V. *abr* (= *visto*) approved, passed.
v. *abr* (= *voltio*) v.; (= *véase*) v.; (= *verso*) v.
va [ba] *vb V* **ir.**
V.A. *abr* = *Vuestra Alteza.*
vaca ['baka] *nf* (*animal*) cow; (*carne*) beef; (*cuero*) cowhide; ~**s flacas/gordas** (*fig*) bad/good times.
vacaciones [baka'θjones] *nfpl* holiday(s); **estar/irse** *o* **marcharse de** ~ to be/go (away) on holiday.
vacante [ba'kante] *adj* vacant, empty ♦ *nf* vacancy.
vaciado, a [ba'θjaðo, a] *adj* (*hecho en molde*) cast in a mould; (*hueco*) hollow ♦ *nm* cast, mould(ing).
vaciar [ba'θjar] *vt* to empty (out); (*ahuecar*) to hollow out; (*moldear*) to cast; (*INFORM*) to dump ♦ *vi* (*río*) to flow (*en into*); ~**se** *vr* to empty; (*fig*) to blab, spill the beans.
vaciedad [baθje'ðað] *nf* emptiness.
vacilación [baθila'θjon] *nf* hesitation.
vacilante [baθi'lante] *adj* unsteady; (*habla*) faltering; (*luz*) flickering; (*fig*) hesitant.
vacilar [baθi'lar] *vi* to be unsteady; to falter; to flicker; to hesitate, waver;

(*persona*) to stagger, stumble; (*memoria*) to fail; (*esp AM: divertirse*) to have a great time.
vacilón [baθi'lon] *nm* (*esp AM*): **estar** *o* **ir de** ~ to have a great time.
vacío, a [ba'θio, a] *adj* empty; (*puesto*) vacant; (*desocupado*) idle; (*vano*) vain; (*charla etc*) light, superficial ♦ *nm* emptiness; (*FÍSICA*) vacuum; (*un* ~) (empty) space; **hacer el** ~ **a algn** to send sb to Coventry.
vacuna [ba'kuna] *nf* vaccine.
vacunar [baku'nar] *vt* to vaccinate; ~**se** *vr* to get vaccinated.
vacuno, a [ba'kuno, a] *adj* bovine.
vacuo, a ['bakwo, a] *adj* empty.
vadear [baðe'ar] *vt* (*río*) to ford; (*problema*) to overcome; (*persona*) to sound out.
vado ['baðo] *nm* ford; (*solución*) solution; (*descanso*) respite.
vagabundo, a [baɣa'βundo, a] *adj* wandering; (*pey*) vagrant ♦ *nm/f* (*errante*) wanderer; (*vago*) tramp, bum (*US*).
vagamente [baɣa'mente] *adv* vaguely.
vagancia [ba'ɣanθja] *nf* vagrancy.
vagar [ba'ɣar] *vi* to wander; (*pasear*) to saunter up and down; (*no hacer nada*) to idle ♦ *nm* leisure.
vagido [ba'xiðo] *nm* wail.
vagina [ba'xina] *nf* vagina.
vago, a ['baɣo, a] *adj* vague; (*perezoso*) lazy; (*ambulante*) wandering ♦ *nm/f* (*vagabundo*) tramp, bum (*US*); (*flojo*) lazybones *sg*, idler.
vagón [ba'ɣon] *nm* (*de pasajeros*) carriage; (*de mercancías*) wagon; ~ **cama/restaurante** sleeping/dining car.
vague ['baɣe] *etc vb V* **vagar.**
vaguear [baɣe'ar] *vi* to laze around.
vaguedad [baɣe'ðað] *nf* vagueness.
vahído [ba'iðo] *nm* dizzy spell.
vaho ['bao] *nm* (*vapor*) vapour, steam; (*olor*) smell; (*respiración*) breath; ~**s** *nmpl* (*MED*) inhalation *sg*.
vaina ['baina] *nf* sheath ♦ *nm* (*AM*) nuisance.
vainilla [bai'niʎa] *nf* vanilla.
vainita [bai'nita] *nf* (*AM*) green *o* French bean.
vais [bais] *vb V* **ir.**
vaivén [bai'βen] *nm* to-and-fro movement; (*de tránsito*) coming and going; **vaivenes** *nmpl* (*fig*) ups and downs.
vajilla [ba'xiʎa] *nf* crockery, dishes *pl*; (*una* ~) service; ~ **de porcelana** chinaware.
val [bal], **valdré** [bal'dre] *etc vb V* **valer.**
vale ['bale] *nm* voucher; (*recibo*) receipt; (*pagaré*) I.O.U.; ~ **de compra** voucher; ~

de regalo gift voucher *o* token.
valedero, a [bale'ðero, a] *adj* valid.
valenciano, a [balen'θjano, a] *adj, nm/f*
Valencian ♦ *nm (LING)* Valencian.
valentía [balen'tia] *nf* courage, bravery;
(*pey*) boastfulness; (*acción*) heroic deed.
valentísimo, a [balen'tisimo, a] *adj (superl
de valiente*) very brave, courageous.
valentón, ona [balen'ton, ona] *adj*
blustering.
valer [ba'ler] *vt* to be worth; (*MAT*) to
equal; (*costar*) to cost; (*amparar*) to aid,
protect ♦ *vi (ser útil)* to be useful; (*ser
válido*) to be valid; ~**se** *vr* to defend o.s.
♦ *nm* worth, value; ~ **la pena** to be
worthwhile; **¿vale?** O.K.?; **¡vale!** (*¡basta!*)
that'll do!; **¡eso no vale!** that doesn't
count!; **no vale nada** it's no good;
(*mercancía*) it's worthless; (*argumento*)
it's no use; **no vale para nada** he's no
good at all; **más vale tarde que nunca**
better late than never; **más vale que nos
vayamos** we'd better go; ~**se de** to make
use of, take advantage of; ~**se por sí
mismo** to help *o* manage by o.s.
valga ['balɣa] *etc vb V* **valer**.
valía [ba'lia] *nf* worth; **de gran ~** (*objeto*)
very valuable.
validar [bali'ðar] *vt* to validate; (*POL*) to
ratify.
validez [bali'ðeθ] *nf* validity; **dar ~ a** to
validate.
válido, a ['baliðo, a] *adj* valid.
valiente [ba'ljente] *adj* brave, valiant;
(*audaz*) bold; (*pey*) boastful; (*con ironía*)
fine, wonderful ♦ *nm/f* brave man/
woman.
valija [ba'lixa] *nf* case; (*AM*) suitcase;
(*mochila*) satchel; (*CORREOS*) mailbag; ~
diplomática diplomatic bag.
valioso, a [ba'ljoso, a] *adj* valuable; (*rico*)
wealthy.
valla ['baʎa] *nf* fence; (*DEPORTE*) hurdle;
(*fig*) barrier; ~ **publicitaria** billboard.
vallar [ba'ʎar] *vt* to fence in.
valle ['baʎe] *nm* valley, vale.
vallisoletano, a [baʎisole'tano, a] *adj* of *o*
from Valladolid ♦ *nm/f* native *o*
inhabitant of Valladolid.
valor [ba'lor] *nm* value, worth; (*precio*)
price; (*valentía*) valour, courage;
(*importancia*) importance; (*cara*) nerve,
cheek (*fam*); **sin ~** worthless; ~
adquisitivo *o* **de compra** purchasing
power; **dar ~ a** to attach importance to;
quitar ~ a to minimize the importance
of; (*COM*): ~ **según balance** book value;
~ **comercial** *o* **de mercado** market value;

~ **contable/desglosado** asset/break-up
value; ~ **de escasez** scarcity value; ~
intrínseco intrinsic value; ~ **a la par** par
value; ~ **neto** net worth; ~ **de rescate/de
sustitución** surrender/replacement
value; *V tb* **valores**.
valoración [balora'θjon] *nf* valuation.
valorar [balo'rar] *vt* to value; (*tasar*) to
price; (*fig*) to assess.
valores [ba'lores] *nmpl (COM)* securities; ~
en cartera *o* **habidos** investments.
vals [bals] *nm* waltz.
válvula ['balßula] *nf* valve.
vamos ['bamos] *vb V* **ir**.
vampiro, iresa [bam'piro, i'resa] *nm/f*
vampire ♦ *nf (CINE)* vamp, femme fatale.
van [ban] *vb V* **ir**.
vanagloriarse [banaɣlo'rjarse] *vr* to boast.
vandalismo [banda'lismo] *nm* vandalism.
vándalo, a ['bandalo, a] *nm/f* vandal.
vanguardia [ban'gwardja] *nf* vanguard; **de
~** (*ARTE*) avant-garde; **estar en** *o* **ir a la ~
de** (*fig*) to be in the forefront of.
vanguardista [bangwar'ðista] *adj* avant-
garde.
vanidad [bani'ðað] *nf* vanity; (*inutilidad*)
futility; (*irrealidad*) unreality.
vanidoso, a [bani'ðoso, a] *adj* vain,
conceited.
vano, a ['bano, a] *adj (irreal*) unreal;
(*irracional*) unreasonable; (*inútil*) vain,
useless; (*persona*) vain, conceited;
(*frívolo*) frivolous.
vapor [ba'por] *nm* vapour; (*vaho*) steam;
(*de gas*) fumes *pl*; (*neblina*) mist; ~**es**
nmpl (MED) hysterics; **al ~** (*CULIN*)
steamed.
vaporice [bapo'riθe] *etc vb V* **vaporizar**.
vaporizador [bapori'θaðor] *nm (perfume
etc*) spray.
vaporizar [bapori'θar] *vt* to vaporize;
(*perfume*) to spray.
vaporoso, a [bapo'roso, a] *adj* vaporous;
(*vahoso*) steamy; (*tela*) light, airy.
vapulear [bapule'ar] *vt* to thrash; (*fig*) to
slate.
vaque ['bake] *etc vb V* **vacar**.
vaquería [bake'ria] *nf* dairy.
vaquero, a [ba'kero, a] *adj* cattle *cpd* ♦ *nm*
cowboy; ~**s** *nmpl* jeans.
vaquilla [ba'kiʎa] *nf* heifer.
vara ['bara] *nf* stick, pole; (*TEC*) rod; ~
mágica magic wand.
varado, a [ba'raðo, a] *adj (NAUT*) stranded;
estar ~ to be aground.
varar [ba'rar] *vt* to beach ♦ *vi*, ~**se** *vr* to be
beached.
varear [bare'ar] *vt* to hit, beat; (*frutas*) to

knock down (with poles).

variable [ba'rjaßle] adj, nf variable (tb INFORM).

variación [barja'θjon] nf variation; **sin ~** unchanged.

variado, a [ba'rjaðo, a] adj varied; (dulces, galletas) assorted; **entremeses ~s** a selection of starters.

variante [ba'rjante] adj variant ♦ nf (alternativa) alternative; (AUTO) bypass.

variar [ba'rjar] vt (cambiar) to change; (poner variedad) to vary; (modificar) to modify; (cambiar de posición) to switch around ♦ vi to vary; **~ de** to differ from; **~ de opinión** to change one's mind; **para ~** just for a change.

varicela [bari'θela] nf chicken pox.

varices [ba'riθes] nfpl varicose veins.

variedad [barje'ðað] nf variety.

varilla [ba'riʎa] nf stick; (BOT) twig; (TEC) rod; (de rueda) spoke; **~ mágica** magic wand.

vario, a ['barjo, a] adj (variado) varied; (multicolor) motley; (cambiable) changeable; **~s** various, several.

variopinto, a [barjo'pinto, a] adj diverse; **un público ~** a mixed audience.

varita [ba'rita] nf: **~ mágica** magic wand.

varón [ba'ron] nm male, man.

varonil [baro'nil] adj manly.

Varsovia [bar'soßja] nf Warsaw.

vas [bas] vb V **ir**.

vasco, a ['basko, a], **vascongado, a** [baskon'gaðo, a] adj, nm/f Basque ♦ nm (LING) Basque ♦ nfpl: **las Vascongadas** the Basque Country sg o Provinces.

vascuence [bas'kwenθe] nm (LING) Basque.

vasectomía [basekto'mia] nf vasectomy.

vaselina [base'lina] nf Vaseline ®.

vasija [ba'sixa] nf (earthenware) vessel.

vaso ['baso] nm glass, tumbler; (ANAT) vessel; (cantidad) glass(ful); **~ de vino** glass of wine; **~ para vino** wineglass.

vástago ['bastaʝo] nm (BOT) shoot; (TEC) rod; (fig) offspring.

vasto, a ['basto, a] adj vast, huge.

váter ['bater] nm lavatory, W.C.

Vaticano [bati'kano] nm: **el ~** the Vatican; **la Ciudad del ~** the Vatican City.

vaticinar [batiθi'nar] vt to prophesy, predict.

vaticinio [bati'θinjo] nm prophecy.

vatio ['batjo] nm (ELEC) watt.

vaya ['baja] etc vb V **ir**.

Vda. abr = **viuda**.

Vd(s) abr = **usted(es)**.

ve [be] vb V **ir**, **ver**.

vea ['bea] etc vb V **ver**.

vecinal [beθi'nal] adj (camino, impuesto etc) local.

vecindad [beθin'dað] nf, **vecindario** [beθin'darjo] nm neighbourhood; (habitantes) residents pl.

vecino, a [be'θino, a] adj neighbouring ♦ nm/f neighbour; (residente) resident; **somos ~s** we live next door to one another.

vector [bek'tor] nm vector.

veda ['beða] nf prohibition; (temporada) close season.

vedado [be'ðaðo] nm preserve.

vedar [be'ðar] vt (prohibir) to ban, prohibit; (idea, plan) to veto; (impedir) to stop, prevent.

vedette [be'ðet] nf (TEAT, CINE) star(let).

vega ['beʝa] nf fertile plain o valley.

vegetación [bexeta'θjon] nf vegetation.

vegetal [bexe'tal] adj, nm vegetable.

vegetar [bexe'tar] vi to vegetate.

vegetariano, a [bexeta'rjano, a] adj, nm/f vegetarian.

vegetativo, a [bexeta'tißo, a] adj vegetative.

vehemencia [bee'menθja] nf (insistencia) vehemence; (pasión) passion; (fervor) fervour; (violencia) violence.

vehemente [bee'mente] adj vehement; passionate; fervent; violent.

vehículo [be'ikulo] nm vehicle; (MED) carrier; **~ de servicio público** public service vehicle; **~ espacial** spacecraft.

veinte ['beinte] num twenty; (orden, fecha) twentieth; **el siglo ~** the twentieth century.

veintena [bein'tena] nf: **una ~** (about) twenty, a score.

vejación [bexa'θjon] nf vexation; (humillación) humiliation.

vejamen [be'xamen] nm satire.

vejar [be'xar] vt (irritar) to annoy, vex; (humillar) to humiliate.

vejatorio, a [bexa'torjo, a] adj humiliating, degrading.

vejez [be'xeθ] nf old age.

vejiga [be'xiʝa] nf (ANAT) bladder.

vela ['bela] nf (de cera) candle; (NAUT) sail; (insomnio) sleeplessness; (vigilia) vigil; (MIL) sentry duty; (fam) snot; **a toda ~** (NAUT) under full sail; **estar a dos ~s** (fam) to be skint; **pasar la noche en ~** to have a sleepless night.

velado, a [be'laðo, a] adj veiled; (sonido) muffled; (FOTO) blurred ♦ nf soirée.

velador [bela'ðor] nm watchman; (candelero) candlestick; (AM) bedside table.

velar [be'lar] *vt* (*vigilar*) to keep watch over; (*cubrir*) to veil ♦ *vi* to stay awake; ~ **por** to watch over, look after.

velatorio [bela'torjo] *nm* (*funeral*) wake.

veleidad [belei'ðað] *nf* (*ligereza*) fickleness; (*capricho*) whim.

velero [be'lero] *nm* (*NAUT*) sailing ship; (*AVIAT*) glider.

veleta [be'leta] *nmf* fickle person ♦ *nf* weather vane.

veliz [be'lis] *nm* (*AM*) suitcase.

vello ['beʎo] *nm* down, fuzz.

vellón [be'ʎon] *nm* fleece.

velloso, a [be'ʎoso, a] *adj* fuzzy.

velludo, a [be'ʎuðo, a] *adj* shaggy ♦ *nm* plush, velvet.

velo ['belo] *nm* veil; ~ **de paladar** (*ANAT*) soft palate.

velocidad [beloθi'ðað] *nf* speed; (*TEC*) rate, pace, velocity; (*MECÁNICA, AUTO*) gear; **¿a qué ~?** how fast?; **de alta ~** high-speed; **cobrar ~** to pick up *o* gather speed; **meter la segunda ~** to change into second gear; **~ máxima de impresión** (*INFORM*) maximum print speed.

velocímetro [belo'θimetro] *nm* speedometer.

velódromo [be'loðromo] *nm* cycle track.

veloz [be'loθ] *adj* fast, swift.

ven [ben] *vb V* **venir**.

vena ['bena] *nf* vein; (*fig*) vein, disposition; (*GEO*) seam, vein.

venablo [be'naβlo] *nm* javelin.

venado [be'naðo] *nm* deer; (*CULIN*) venison.

venal [be'nal] *adj* (*ANAT*) venous; (*pey*) venal.

venalidad [benali'ðað] *nf* venality.

vencedor, a [benθe'ðor, a] *adj* victorious ♦ *nmf* victor, winner.

vencer [ben'θer] *vt* (*dominar*) to defeat, beat; (*derrotar*) to vanquish; (*superar, controlar*) to overcome, master ♦ *vi* (*triunfar*) to win (through), triumph; (*pago*) to fall due; (*plazo*) to expire; **dejarse ~** to yield, give in.

vencido, a [ben'θiðo, a] *adj* (*derrotado*) defeated, beaten; (*COM*) payable, due ♦ *adv*: **pagar ~** to pay in arrears; **le pagan por meses ~s** he is paid at the end of the month; **darse por ~** to give up.

vencimiento [benθi'mjento] *nm* collapse; (*COM: plazo*) expiration; **a su ~** when it falls due.

venda ['benda] *nf* bandage.

vendaje [ben'daxe] *nm* bandage, dressing.

vendar [ben'dar] *vt* to bandage; ~ **los ojos** to blindfold.

vendaval [benda'βal] *nm* (*viento*) gale; (*huracán*) hurricane.

vendedor, a [bende'ðor, a] *nmf* seller; ~ **ambulante** hawker, pedlar (*BRIT*), peddler (*US*).

vender [ben'der] *vt* to sell; (*comerciar*) to market; (*traicionar*) to sell out, betray; **~se** *vr* to be sold; ~ **al contado/al por mayor/al por menor/a plazos** to sell for cash/wholesale/retail/on credit; **"se vende"** "for sale"; **"véndese coche"** "car for sale"; ~ **al descubierto** to sell short.

vendimia [ben'dimja] *nf* grape harvest; **la ~ de 1973** the 1973 vintage.

vendimiar [bendi'mjar] *vi* to pick grapes.

vendré [ben'dre] *etc vb V* **venir**.

Venecia [be'neθja] *nf* Venice.

veneciano, a [bene'θjano, a] *adj, nmf* Venetian.

veneno [be'neno] *nm* poison, venom.

venenoso, a [bene'noso, a] *adj* poisonous.

venerable [bene'raβle] *adj* venerable.

veneración [benera'θjon] *nf* veneration.

venerar [bene'rar] *vt* (*reconocer*) to venerate; (*adorar*) to worship.

venéreo, a [be'nereo, a] *adj* venereal.

venezolano, a [beneθo'lano, a] *adj, nmf* Venezuelan.

Venezuela [bene'θwela] *nf* Venezuela.

venga ['benga] *etc vb V* **venir**.

vengador, a [benga'ðor, a] *adj* avenging ♦ *nmf* avenger.

venganza [ben'ganθa] *nf* vengeance, revenge.

vengar [ben'gar] *vt* to avenge; **~se** *vr* to take revenge.

vengativo, a [benga'tiβo, a] *adj* (*persona*) vindictive.

vengue ['benge] *etc vb V* **vengar**.

venia ['benja] *nf* (*perdón*) pardon; (*permiso*) consent; **con su ~** by your leave.

venial [be'njal] *adj* venial.

venida [be'niða] *nf* (*llegada*) arrival; (*regreso*) return; (*fig*) rashness.

venidero, a [beni'ðero, a] *adj* coming, future; **en lo ~** in (the) future.

venir [be'nir] *vi* to come; (*llegar*) to arrive; (*ocurrir*) to happen; **~se** *vr*: **~se abajo** to collapse; ~ **a menos** (*persona*) to lose status; (*empresa*) to go downhill; ~ **bien** to be suitable, come just right; (*ropa, gusto*) to suit; ~ **mal** to be unsuitable *o* inconvenient, come awkwardly; **el año que viene** next year; **¡ven acá!** come (over) here!; **¡venga!** (*fam*) come on!

venta ['benta] *nf* (*COM*) sale; (*posada*) inn; ~ **a plazos** hire purchase; ~ **al contado/**

al por mayor/al por menor *o* **al detalle**
cash sale/wholesale/retail; **~ a domicilio**
door-to-door selling; **~ y arrendamiento**
al vendedor sale and lease back; **~ de**
liquidación clearance sale; **estar de** *o* **en**
~ to be (up) for sale *o* on the market; **~s**
brutas gross sales; **~s a término**
forward sales.

ventaja [ben'taxa] *nf* advantage; **llevar la ~**
(*en carrera*) to be leading *o* ahead.

ventajoso, a [benta'xoso, a] *adj*
advantageous.

ventana [ben'tana] *nf* window; **~ de**
guillotina/galería sash/bay window; **~ de**
la nariz nostril.

ventanilla [venta'niʎa] *nf* (*de taquilla, tb*
INFORM) window.

ventearse [bente'arse] *vr* (*romperse*) to
crack; (*ANAT*) to break wind.

ventilación [bentila'θjon] *nf* ventilation;
(*corriente*) draught; (*fig*) airing.

ventilador [bentila'ðor] *nm* ventilator;
(*eléctrico*) fan.

ventilar [benti'lar] *vt* to ventilate; (*a secar*)
to put out to dry; (*fig*) to air, discuss.

ventisca [ben'tiska] *nf* blizzard.

ventisquero [bentis'kero] *nm* snowdrift.

ventolera [bento'lera] *nf* (*ráfaga*) gust of
wind; (*idea*) whim, wild idea; **le dio la ~**
de comprarlo he had a sudden notion to
buy it.

ventosear [bentose'ar] *vi* to break wind.

ventosidad [bentosi'ðað] *nf* flatulence.

ventoso, a [ben'toso, a] *adj* windy ♦ *nf*
(*ZOOL*) sucker; (*instrumento*) suction pad.

ventrículo [ben'trikulo] *nm* ventricle.

ventrílocuo, a [ben'trilokwo, a] *nm/f*
ventriloquist.

ventriloquia [bentri'lokja] *nf*
ventriloquism.

ventura [ben'tura] *nf* (*felicidad*) happiness;
(*buena suerte*) luck; (*destino*) fortune; **a la**
(buena) ~ at random.

venturoso, a [bentu'roso, a] *adj* happy;
(*afortunado*) lucky, fortunate.

venza ['benθa] *etc vb V* **vencer.**

ver [ber] *vt, vi* to see; (*mirar*) to look at,
watch; (*investigar*) to look into; (*entender*)
to see, understand; **~se** *vr* (*encontrarse*)
to meet; (*dejarse ~*) to be seen; (*hallarse:*
en un apuro) to find o.s., be ♦ *nm* looks *pl*,
appearance; **a ~** let's see; **a ~ si ...** I
wonder if ...; **por lo que veo** apparently;
dejarse ~ to become apparent; **no tener**
nada que ~ con to have nothing to do
with; **a mi modo de ~** as I see it; **merece**
~se it's worth seeing; **no lo veo** I can't
see it; **¡nos vemos!** see you (later)!;

¡habráse visto! did you ever! (*fam*);
¡viera(n) *o* **hubiera(n) visto qué casa!** (*AM*
fam) if only you'd seen the house!, what
a house!; **ya se ve que ...** it is obvious
that ...; **si te vi no me acuerdo** they *etc*
just don't want to know.

vera ['bera] *nf* edge, verge; (*de río*) bank; **a**
la ~ de near, next to.

veracidad [beraθi'ðað] *nf* truthfulness.

veraneante [berane'ante] *nm/f*
holidaymaker, (summer) vacationer
(*US*).

veranear [berane'ar] *vi* to spend the
summer.

veraneo [bera'neo] *nm*: **estar de ~** to be
away on (one's summer) holiday; **lugar**
de ~ holiday resort.

veraniego, a [bera'njeɣo, a] *adj* summer
cpd.

verano [be'rano] *nm* summer.

veras ['beras] *nfpl* truth *sg*; **de ~** really,
truly; **esto va de ~** this is serious.

veraz [be'raθ] *adj* truthful.

verbal [ber'ßal] *adj* verbal; (*mensaje etc*)
oral.

verbena [ber'ßena] *nf* street party.

verbigracia [berßi'ɣraθja] *adv* for example.

verbo ['berßo] *nm* verb.

verborrea [berßo'rrea] *nf* verbosity, verbal
diarrhoea.

verboso, a [ber'ßoso, a] *adj* verbose.

verdad [ber'ðað] *nf* (*lo verídico*) truth;
(*fiabilidad*) reliability ♦ *adv* really; **¿~?,**
¿no es ~? isn't it?, aren't you?, don't
you? *etc*; **de ~** *adj* real, proper; **a decir ~,**
no quiero to tell (you) the truth, I don't
want to; **la pura ~** the plain truth.

verdaderamente [berðaðera'mente] *adv*
really, indeed, truly.

verdadero, a [berða'ðero, a] *adj* (*veraz*)
true, truthful; (*fiable*) reliable; (*fig*) real.

verde ['berðe] *adj* green; (*fruta etc*) green,
unripe; (*chiste etc*) blue, smutty, dirty
♦ *nm* green; **viejo ~** dirty old man; **poner**
~ a algn to give sb a dressing-down.

verdear [berðe'ar], **verdecer** [berðe'θer] *vi*
to turn green.

verdezca [ber'ðeθka] *etc vb V* **verdecer.**

verdor [ber'ðor] *nm* (*lo verde*) greenness;
(*BOT*) verdure; (*fig*) youthful vigour.

verdugo [ber'ðuxo] *nm* executioner; (*BOT*)
shoot; (*cardenal*) weal.

verdulero, a [berðu'lero, a] *nm/f* greengrocer.

verdura [ber'ðura] *nf* greenness; **~s** *nfpl*
(*CULIN*) greens.

vereda [be'reða] *nf* path; (*AM*) pavement,
sidewalk (*US*); **meter a algn en ~** to

bring sb into line.
veredicto [bere'ðikto] *nm* verdict.
vergel [ber'xel] *nm* lush garden.
vergonzoso, a [berɣon'θoso, a] *adj*
shameful; (*tímido*) timid, bashful.
vergüenza [ber'ɣwenθa] *nf* shame, sense
of shame; (*timidez*) bashfulness; (*pudor*)
modesty; **tener ~ to** be ashamed; **me da
~ decírselo** I feel too shy *o* it
embarrasses me to tell him; **¡qué ~!** (*de
situación*) what a disgrace!; (*a persona*)
shame on you!
vericueto [beri'kweto] *nm* rough track.
verídico, a [be'riðiko, a] *adj* true, truthful.
verificar [berifi'kar] *vt* to check; (*corroborar*) to verify (*tb INFORM*); (*testamento*) to
prove; (*llevar a cabo*) to carry out; **~se** *vr*
to occur, happen; (*mitin etc*) to be held;
(*profecía etc*) to come *o* prove true.
verifique [beri'fike] *etc vb V* **verificar**.
verja ['berxa] *nf* iron gate; (*cerca*) railing(s)
(*pl*); (*rejado*) grating.
vermut [ber'mu], *pl* **vermuts** *nm*
vermouth ♦ *nf* (*esp AM*) matinée.
verosímil [bero'simil] *adj* likely, probable;
(*relato*) credible.
verosimilitud [berosimili'tuð] *nf* likeliness,
probability.
verruga [be'rruɣa] *nf* wart.
versado, a [ber'saðo, a] *adj*: **~ en** versed
in.
Versalles [ber'saʎes] *nm* Versailles.
versar [ber'sar] *vi* to go round, turn; **~
sobre** to deal with, be about.
versátil [ber'satil] *adj* versatile.
versículo [ber'sikulo] *nm* (*REL*) verse.
versión [ber'sjon] *nf* version; (*traducción*)
translation.
verso ['berso] *nm* (*gen*) verse; **un ~** a line
of poetry; **~ libre/suelto** free/blank
verse.
vértebra ['berteβra] *nf* vertebra.
vertebrado, a [berte'βraðo, a] *adj, nm/f*
vertebrate.
vertebral [berte'βral] *adj* vertebral;
columna ~ spine.
vertedero [berte'ðero] *nm* rubbish dump,
tip.
verter [ber'ter] *vt* (*vaciar*) to empty, pour
(out); (*tirar*) to dump ♦ *vi* to flow.
vertical [berti'kal] *adj* vertical; (*postura,
piano etc*) upright ♦ *nf* vertical.
vértice ['bertiθe] *nm* vertex, apex.
vertiente [ber'tjente] *nf* slope.
vertiginoso, a [bertixi'noso, a] *adj* giddy,
dizzy.
vértigo ['bertiɣo] *nm* vertigo; (*mareo*)
dizziness; (*actividad*) intense activity; **de**

~ (*fam*: *velocidad*) giddy; (: *ruido*)
tremendous; (: *talento*) fantastic.
vesícula [be'sikula] *nf* blister; **~ biliar** gall
bladder.
vespa ® ['bespa] *nf* (*motor*) scooter.
vespertino, a [besper'tino, a] *adj* evening
cpd.
vespino ® [bes'pino] *nm o f* ≈ moped.
vestíbulo [bes'tiβulo] *nm* hall; (*de teatro*)
foyer.
vestido [bes'tiðo] *nm* (*ropa*) clothes *pl*,
clothing; (*de mujer*) dress, frock.
vestigio [bes'tixjo] *nm* (*trazo*) trace; (*señal*)
sign; **~s** *nmpl* remains.
vestimenta [besti'menta] *nf* clothing.
vestir [bes'tir] *vt* (*poner: ropa*) to put on;
(*llevar: ropa*) to wear; (*cubrir*) to clothe,
cover; (*pagar: la ropa*) to clothe, pay for
the clothing of; (*sastre*) to make clothes
for ♦ *vi* (*ponerse: ropa*) to dress; (*verse
bien*) to look good; **~se** *vr* to get dressed,
dress o.s.; **traje de ~** (*formal*) formal
suit; **estar vestido de** to be dressed *o*
clad in; (*como disfraz*) to be dressed as.
vestuario [bes'twarjo] *nm* clothes *pl*,
wardrobe; (*TEAT: para actores*) dressing
room; (: *para público*) cloakroom;
(*DEPORTE*) changing room.
Vesubio [be'suβjo] *nm* Vesuvius.
veta ['beta] *nf* (*vena*) vein, seam; (*raya*)
streak; (*de madera*) grain.
vetar [be'tar] *vt* to veto.
veterano, a [bete'rano, a] *adj, nm/f* veteran.
veterinario, a [beteri'narjo, a] *nm/f*
vet(erinary surgeon) ♦ *nf* veterinary
science.
veto ['beto] *nm* veto.
vetusto, a [be'tusto, a] *adj* ancient.
vez [beθ] *nf* time; (*turno*) turn; **a la ~ que** at
the same time as; **a su ~** in its turn;
cada ~ más/menos more and more/less
and less; **una ~** once; **dos veces** twice;
de una ~ in one go; **de una ~ para
siempre** once and for all; **en ~ de**
instead of; **a veces** sometimes; **otra ~**
again; **una y otra ~** repeatedly; **muchas
veces** often; **pocas veces** seldom; **de ~
en cuando** from time to time; **7 veces 9** 7
times 9; **hacer las veces de** to stand in
for; **tal ~** perhaps; **¿lo viste alguna ~?**
did you ever see it?; **¿cuántas veces?**
how often?; **érase una ~** once upon a
time (there was).
v. g., v. gr. *abr* (= *verbigracia*) viz.
vía ['bia] *nf* (*calle*) road; (*ruta*) track, route;
(*FERRO*) line; (*fig*) way; (*ANAT*) passage,
tube ♦ *prep* via, by way of; **por ~ bucal**
orally; **por ~ judicial** by legal means; **por**

~ **oficial** through official channels; **por** ~ **de** by way of; **en** ~**s de** in the process of; **un país en** ~**s de desarrollo** a developing country; ~ **aérea** airway; **V**~ **Láctea** Milky Way; ~ **pública** public highway *o* thoroughfare; ~ **única** one-way street; **el tren está en la** ~ **8** the train is (standing) at platform 8.

viable ['bjaßle] *adj* (*COM*) viable; (*plan etc*) feasible.

viaducto [bja'ðukto] *nm* viaduct.

viajante [bja'xante] *nm* commercial traveller, traveling salesman (*US*).

viajar [bja'xar] *vi* to travel, journey.

viaje ['bjaxe] *nm* journey; (*gira*) tour; (*NAUT*) voyage; (*COM*: *carga*) load; **los** ~**s** travel *sg*; **estar de** ~ to be on a journey; ~ **de ida y vuelta** round trip; ~ **de novios** honeymoon.

viajero, a [bja'xero, a] *adj* travelling (*BRIT*), traveling (*US*); (*ZOOL*) migratory ♦ *nm/f* (*quien viaja*) traveller; (*pasajero*) passenger.

vial [bjal] *adj* road *cpd*, traffic *cpd*.

vianda ['bjanda] *nf* (*tb*: ~**s**) food.

viáticos ['bjatikos] *nmpl* (*COM*) travelling (*BRIT*) *o* traveling (*US*) expenses.

víbora ['bißora] *nf* viper.

vibración [bißra'θjon] *nf* vibration.

vibrador [bißra'ðor] *nm* vibrator.

vibrante [bi'ßrante] *adj* vibrant, vibrating.

vibrar [bi'ßrar] *vt* to vibrate ♦ *vi* to vibrate; (*pulsar*) to throb, beat, pulsate.

vicario [bi'karjo] *nm* curate.

vicecónsul [biθe'konsul] *nm* vice-consul.

vicegerente [biθexe'rente] *nm/f* assistant manager.

vicepresidente [biθepresi'ðente] *nm/f* vice president; (*de comité etc*) vice-chairman.

viceversa [biθe'ßersa] *adv* vice versa.

viciado, a [bi'θjaðo, a] *adj* (*corrompido*) corrupt; (*contaminado*) foul, contaminated.

viciar [bi'θjar] *vt* (*pervertir*) to pervert; (*adulterar*) to adulterate; (*falsificar*) to falsify; (*JUR*) to nullify; (*estropear*) to spoil; (*sentido*) to twist; ~**se** *vr* to become corrupted; (*aire, agua*) to be(come) polluted.

vicio ['biθjo] *nm* (*libertinaje*) vice; (*mala costumbre*) bad habit; (*mimo*) spoiling; (*alabeo*) warp, warping; **de** *o* **por** ~ out of sheer habit.

vicioso, a [bi'θjoso, a] *adj* (*muy malo*) vicious; (*corrompido*) depraved; (*mimado*) spoiled ♦ *nm/f* depraved person; (*adicto*) addict.

vicisitud [biθisi'tuð] *nf* vicissitude.

víctima ['biktima] *nf* victim; (*de accidente etc*) casualty.

victimario [bikti'marjo] *nm* (*AM*) killer, murderer.

victoria [bik'torja] *nf* victory.

victorioso, a [bikto'rjoso, a] *adj* victorious.

vicuña [bi'kuɲa] *nf* vicuna.

vid [bið] *nf* vine.

vida ['biða] *nf* life; (*duración*) lifetime; (*modo de vivir*) way of life; ¡~!, ¡~ **mía!** (*saludo cariñoso*) my love!; **de por** ~ for life; **de** ~ **airada** *o* **libre** loose-living; **en la/mi** ~ never; **estar con** ~ to be still alive; **ganarse la** ~ to earn one's living; ¡**esto es** ~! this is the life!; **le va la** ~ **en esto** his life depends on it.

vidente [bi'ðente] *nm/f* (*adivino*) clairvoyant; (*no ciego*) sighted person.

vídeo ['biðeo] *nm* video; (*aparato*) video (recorder); **cinta de** ~ videotape; **película de** ~ videofilm; **grabar en** ~ to record, (video)tape; ~ **compuesto/ inverso** (*INFORM*) composite/reverse video.

videocámara [biðeo'kamara] *nf* video camera; (*pequeña*) camcorder.

videocassette [biðeoka'set] *nm* video cassette.

videoclip [biðeo'klip] *nm* (music) video.

videoclub [biðeo'klub] *nm* video club; (*tienda*) video shop.

videodatos [biðeo'ðatos] *nmpl* (*COM*) viewdata.

videojuego [biðeo'xweɣo] *nm* video game.

videotex(o) [biðeo'teks(o)] *nm* Videotex ®.

vidriero, a [bi'ðrjero, a] *nm/f* glazier ♦ *nf* (*ventana*) stained-glass window; (*AM*: *de tienda*) shop window; (*puerta*) glass door.

vidrio ['biðrjo] *nm* glass; (*AM*) window; ~ **cilindrado/inastillable** plate/splinter-proof glass.

vidrioso, a [bi'ðrjoso, a] *adj* glassy; (*frágil*) fragile, brittle; (*resbaladizo*) slippery.

viejo, a ['bjexo, a] *adj* old ♦ *nm/f* old man/ woman; **mi** ~/**vieja** (*fam*) my old man/ woman; **hacerse** *o* **ponerse** ~ to grow *o* get old.

Viena ['bjena] *nf* Vienna.

viene ['bjene] *etc vb V* **venir**.

vienés, esa [bje'nes, esa] *adj, nm/f* Viennese.

viento ['bjento] *nm* wind; (*olfato*) scent; **contra** ~ **y marea** at all costs; **ir** ~ **en popa** to go splendidly; (*negocio*) to prosper.

vientre ['bjentre] *nm* belly; (*matriz*) womb; ~**s** *nmpl* bowels; **hacer de** ~ to have a movement of the bowels.

vier. *abr* (= *viernes*) Fri.

viernes ['bjernes] *nm inv* Friday; **V~ Santo** Good Friday; *V tb* **Semana Santa.**

vierta ['bjerta] *etc vb V* **verter.**

Vietnam [bjet'nam] *nm*: **el ~** Vietnam.

vietnamita [bjetna'mita] *adj, nm/f* Vietnamese.

viga ['biɣa] *nf* beam, rafter; (*de metal*) girder.

vigencia [bi'xenθja] *nf* validity; (*de contrato etc*) term, life; **estar/entrar en ~** to be in/come into effect *o* force.

vigente [bi'xente] *adj* valid, in force; (*imperante*) prevailing.

vigésimo, a [bi'xesimo, a] *num* twentieth.

vigía [bi'xia] *nm* look-out ♦ *nf* (*atalaya*) watchtower; (*acción*) watching.

vigilancia [bixi'lanθja] *nf* vigilance.

vigilante [bixi'lante] *adj* vigilant ♦ *nm* caretaker; (*en cárcel*) warder; (*en almacén*) shopwalker (*BRIT*), floor-walker (*US*); **~ jurado** security guard (*licensed to carry a gun*); **~ nocturno** night watchman.

vigilar [bixi'lar] *vt* to watch over; (*cuidar*) to look after, keep an eye on ♦ *vi* to be vigilant; (*hacer guardia*) to keep watch.

vigilia [vi'xilja] *nf* wakefulness; (*REL*) fast; **comer de ~** to fast.

vigor [bi'ɣor] *nm* vigour, vitality; **en ~** in force; **entrar/poner en ~** to take/put into effect.

vigoroso, a [biɣo'roso, a] *adj* vigorous.

VIH *nm abr* (= *virus de inmunodeficiencia humana*) HIV.

vil [bil] *adj* vile, low.

vileza [bi'leθa] *nf* vileness; (*acto*) base deed.

vilipendiar [bilipen'djar] *vt* to vilify, revile.

villa ['biʎa] *nf* (*pueblo*) small town; (*municipalidad*) municipality; **la V~** (*ESP*) Madrid; **~ miseria** shanty town.

villancico [biʎan'θiko] *nm* (Christmas) carol.

villorrio [bi'ʎorrjo] *nm* one-horse town, dump; (*AM*: *barrio pobre*) shanty town.

vilo ['bilo]: **en ~** *adv* in the air, suspended; (*fig*) on tenterhooks, in suspense; **estar** *o* **quedar en ~** to be left in suspense.

vinagre [bi'naɣre] *nm* vinegar.

vinagrera [bina'ɣrera] *nf* vinegar bottle; **~s** *nfpl* cruet stand *sg.*

vinagreta [bina'ɣreta] *nf* French dressing.

vinatería [binate'ria] *nf* wine shop.

vinatero, a [bina'tero, a] *adj* wine *cpd* ♦ *nm* wine merchant.

vinculación [binkula'θjon] *nf* (*lazo*) link, bond; (*acción*) linking.

vincular [binku'lar] *vt* to link, bind.

vínculo ['binkulo] *nm* link, bond.

vindicar [bindi'kar] *vt* to vindicate; (*vengar*) to avenge; (*JUR*) to claim.

vinícola [bi'nikola] *adj* (*industria*) wine *cpd*; (*región*) wine-growing *cpd.*

vinicultura [binikul'tura] *nf* wine growing.

vino ['bino] *etc vb V* **venir** ♦ *nm* wine; **~ de solera/seco/tinto** vintage/dry/red wine; **~ de Jerez** sherry; **~ de Oporto** port (wine).

viña ['biɲa] *nf*, **viñedo** [bi'ɲeðo] *nm* vineyard.

viñeta [bi'ɲeta] *nf* (*en historieta*) cartoon.

viola ['bjola] *nf* viola.

violación [bjola'θjon] *nf* violation; (*JUR*) offence, infringement; (*estupro*): **~ (sexual)** rape; **~ de contrato** (*COM*) breach of contract.

violar [bjo'lar] *vt* to violate; (*JUR*) to infringe; (*cometer estupro*) to rape.

violencia [bjo'lenθja] *nf* (*fuerza*) violence, force; (*embarazo*) embarrassment; (*acto injusto*) unjust act.

violentar [bjolen'tar] *vt* to force; (*casa*) to break into; (*agredir*) to assault; (*violar*) to violate.

violento, a [bjo'lento, a] *adj* violent; (*furioso*) furious; (*situación*) embarrassing; (*acto*) forced, unnatural; (*difícil*) awkward; **me es muy ~** it goes against the grain with me.

violeta [bjo'leta] *nf* violet.

violín [bjo'lin] *nm* violin.

violón [bjo'lon] *nm* double bass.

violoncelo [bjolon'θelo] *nm* cello.

virador [bira'ðor] *nm* (*para fotocopiadora*) toner.

viraje [bi'raxe] *nm* turn; (*de vehículo*) swerve; (*de carretera*) bend; (*fig*) change of direction.

virar [bi'rar] *vi* to turn; to swerve; to change direction.

virgen ['birxen] *adj* virgin; (*cinta*) blank ♦ *nm/f* virgin; **la Santísima V~** (*REL*) the Blessed Virgin.

virginidad [birxini'ðað] *nf* virginity.

Virgo ['birɣo] *nm* Virgo.

viril [bi'ril] *adj* virile.

virilidad [birili'ðað] *nf* virility.

virrey [bi'rrei] *nm* viceroy.

virtual [bir'twal] *adj* (*real*) virtual; (*en potencia*) potential.

virtud [bir'tuð] *nf* virtue; **en ~ de** by virtue of.

virtuoso, a [bir'twoso, a] *adj* virtuous

♦ nm/f virtuoso.

viruela [bi'rwela] nf smallpox; **~s** nfpl pockmarks; **~s locas** chickenpox sg.

virulento, a [biru'lento, a] adj virulent.

virus ['birus] nm inv virus.

viruta [bi'ruta] nf wood o metal shaving.

vis [bis] nf: **~ cómica** sense of humour.

visa ['bisa] nf (AM), **visado** [bi'saðo] nm visa; **~ de permanencia** residence permit.

visar [bi'sar] vt (pasaporte) to visa; (documento) to endorse.

víscera ['bisθera] nf internal organ; **~s** nfpl entrails.

visceral [bisθe'ral] adj (odio) deep-rooted; **reacción ~** gut reaction.

viscoso, a [bis'koso, a] adj viscous.

visera [bi'sera] nf visor.

visibilidad [bisiβili'ðað] nf visibility.

visible [bi'siβle] adj visible; (fig) obvious; **exportaciones/importaciones ~s** (COM) visible exports/imports.

visillo [bi'siʎo] nm lace curtain.

visión [bi'sjon] nf (ANAT) vision, (eye)sight; (fantasía) vision, fantasy; (panorama) view; **ver visiones** to see o be seeing things.

visionario, a [bisjo'narjo, a] adj (que prevé) visionary; (alucinado) deluded ♦ nm/f visionary; (chalado) lunatic.

visita [bi'sita] nf call, visit; (persona) visitor; **horas/tarjeta de ~** visiting hours/card; **~ de cortesía/de cumplido/de despedida** courtesy/formal/farewell visit; **hacer una ~** to pay a visit; **ir de ~** to go visiting.

visitar [bisi'tar] vt to visit, call on; (inspeccionar) to inspect.

vislumbrar [bislum'brar] vt to glimpse, catch a glimpse of.

vislumbre [bis'lumbre] nf glimpse; (centelleo) gleam; (idea vaga) glimmer.

viso ['biso] nm (de metal) glint, gleam; (de tela) sheen; (aspecto) appearance; **hay un ~ de verdad en esto** there is an element of truth in this.

visón [bi'son] nm mink.

visor [bi'sor] nm (FOTO) viewfinder.

víspera ['bispera] nf eve, day before; **la ~ o en ~s de** on the eve of.

vista ['bista] nf sight, vision; (capacidad de ver) (eye)sight; (mirada) look(s) (pl); (FOTO etc) view; (JUR) hearing ♦ nm customs officer; **a primera ~** at first glance; **~ general** overview; **fijar o clavar la ~ en** to stare at; **hacer la ~ gorda** to turn a blind eye; **volver la ~** to look back; **está a la ~ que** it's obvious that; **a**

la ~ (COM) at sight; **en ~ de** in view of; **en ~ de que** in view of the fact that; **¡hasta la ~!** so long!, see you!; **con ~s a** with a view to; V tb **visto, a.**

vistazo [bis'taθo] nm glance; **dar o echar un ~ a** to glance at.

visto, a ['bisto, a] etc vb V **vestir** ♦ pp de **ver** ♦ adj seen; (considerado) considered ♦ nm: **~ bueno** approval; "**~ bueno**" "approved"; **por lo ~** evidently; **dar el ~ bueno a algo** to give sth the go-ahead; **está ~ que** it's clear that; **está bien/mal ~** it's acceptable/unacceptable; **está muy ~** it is very common; **estaba ~** it had to be; **~ que** conj since, considering that.

vistoso, a [bis'toso, a] adj colourful; (alegre) gay; (pey) gaudy.

visual [bi'swal] adj visual.

visualice [biswa'liθe] etc vb V **visualizar.**

visualizador [biswali'θa'ðor] nm (INFORM) display screen, VDU.

visualizar [biswali'θar] vt (imaginarse) to visualize; (INFORM) to display.

vital [bi'tal] adj life cpd, living cpd; (fig) vital; (persona) lively, vivacious.

vitalicio, a [bita'liθjo, a] adj for life.

vitalidad [bitali'ðað] nf vitality.

vitamina [bita'mina] nf vitamin.

vitaminado, a [bitami'naðo, a] adj with added vitamins.

vitamínico, a [bita'miniko, a] adj vitamin cpd; **complejos ~s** vitamin compounds.

viticultor, a [bitikul'tor, a] nm/f vine grower.

viticultura [bitikul'tura] nf vine growing.

vitorear [bitore'ar] vt to cheer, acclaim.

vítores ['bitores] nmpl cheers.

vitoriano, a [bito'rjano, a] adj of o from Vitoria ♦ nm/f native o inhabitant of Vitoria.

vítreo, a ['bitreo, a] adj vitreous.

vitrina [bi'trina] nf glass case; (en casa) display cabinet; (AM) shop window.

vituperar [bitupe'rar] vt to condemn.

vituperio [bitu'perjo] nm (condena) condemnation; (censura) censure; (insulto) insult.

viudez [bju'ðeθ] nf widowhood.

viudo, a ['bjuðo, a] adj widowed ♦ nm widower ♦ nf widow.

viva ['biβa] excl hurrah! ♦ nm cheer; **¡~ el rey!** long live the King!

vivacidad [biβaθi'ðað] nf (vigor) vigour; (vida) vivacity.

vivamente [biβa'mente] adv in lively fashion; (descripción etc) vividly; (protesta) sharply; (emoción) acutely.

vivaracho, a [biβa'ratʃo, a] *adj* jaunty, lively; (*ojos*) bright, twinkling.

vivaz [bi'βaθ] *adj* (*que dura*) enduring; (*vigoroso*) vigorous; (*vivo*) lively.

vivencia [bi'βenθja] *nf* experience.

víveres ['biβeres] *nmpl* provisions.

vivero [bi'βero] *nm* (*HORTICULTURA*) nursery; (*para peces*) fishpond; (: *COM*) fish farm.

viveza [bi'βeθa] *nf* liveliness; (*agudeza*) sharpness.

vividor, a [biβi'ðor, a] *adj* (*pey*) opportunistic ♦ *nm* (*aprovechado*) hustler.

vivienda [bi'βjenda] *nf* (*alojamiento*) housing; (*morada*) dwelling; **~s protegidas** *o* **sociales** council housing *sg* (*BRIT*), public housing *sg* (*US*).

viviente [bi'βjente] *adj* living.

vivificar [biβifi'kar] *vt* to give life to.

vivifique [biβi'fike] *etc vb V* vivificar.

vivir [bi'βir] *vt* (*experimentar*) to live *o* go through ♦ *vi* (*gen*, *COM*): ~ **(de)** to live (by, off, on) ♦ *nm* life, living; **¡viva!** hurray!; **¡viva el rey!** long live the king!

vivo, a ['biβo, a] *adj* living, live, alive; (*fig*) vivid; (*movimiento*) quick; (*color*) bright; (*protesta etc*) strong; (*astuto*) smart, clever; **en ~** (*TV etc*) live; **llegar a lo ~** to cut to the quick.

vizcaíno, a [biθka'ino, a] *adj*, *nm/f* Biscayan.

Vizcaya [biθ'kaja] *nf* Biscay; **el Golfo de ~** the Bay of Biscay.

V.M. *abr* = **Vuestra Majestad**.

V.O. *abr* = *versión original*.

V.ºB.º *abr* = **visto bueno**.

vocablo [bo'kaβlo] *nm* (*palabra*) word; (*término*) term.

vocabulario [bokaβu'larjo] *nm* vocabulary, word list.

vocación [boka'θjon] *nf* vocation.

vocacional [bokasjo'nal] *nf* (*AM*) ≈ technical college.

vocal [bo'kal] *adj* vocal ♦ *nm/f* member (of a committee *etc*) ♦ *nm* non-executive director ♦ *nf* vowel.

vocalice [boka'liθe] *etc vb V* vocalizar.

vocalizar [bokali'θar] *vt* to vocalize.

voceador [bosea'ðor] *nm* (*AM*): ~ **de periódicos** newspaper vendor *o* seller.

vocear [boθe'ar] *vt* (*para vender*) to cry; (*aclamar*) to acclaim; (*fig*) to proclaim ♦ *vi* to yell.

vocerío [boθe'rio] *nm* shouting; (*escándalo*) hullabaloo.

vocero, a [bo'sero, a] *nm/f* (*AM*) spokesman/woman.

vociferar [boθife'rar] *vt* to shout; (*jactarse*) to proclaim boastfully ♦ *vi* to yell.

vocinglero, a [boθin'glero, a] *adj* vociferous; (*gárrulo*) garrulous; (*fig*) blatant.

vodevil [boðe'βil] *nm* music hall, variety, (*US*) vaudeville.

vodka ['boðka] *nm* vodka.

vodú [bo'ðu] *nm* voodoo.

vol *abr* = **volumen**.

volado, a [bo'laðo, a] *adj*: **estar ~** (*fam*: *inquieto*) to be worried; (: *loco*) to be crazy.

volador, a [bola'ðor, a] *adj* flying.

voladura [bola'ðura] *nf* blowing up, demolition; (*MINERÍA*) blasting.

volandas [bo'landas]: **en ~** *adv* in *o* through the air; (*fig*) swiftly.

volante [bo'lante] *adj* flying ♦ *nm* (*de máquina*, *coche*) steering wheel; (*de reloj*) balance; (*nota*) note; **ir al ~** to be at the wheel, be driving.

volar [bo'lar] *vt* (*demolir*) to blow up, demolish ♦ *vi* to fly; (*fig*: *correr*) to rush, hurry; (*fam*: *desaparecer*) to disappear; **voy volando** I must dash; **¡cómo vuela el tiempo!** how time flies!

volátil [bo'latil] *adj* volatile; (*fig*) changeable.

volcán [bol'kan] *nm* volcano.

volcánico, a [bol'kaniko, a] *adj* volcanic.

volcar [bol'kar] *vt* to upset, overturn; (*tumbar*, *derribar*) to knock over; (*vaciar*) to empty out ♦ *vi* to overturn; **~se** *vr* to tip over; (*barco*) to capsize.

voleibol [bolei'βol] *nm* volleyball.

voleo [bo'leo] *nm* volley; **a(l) ~** haphazardly; **de un ~** quickly.

Volga ['bolɣa] *nm* Volga.

volición [boli'θjon] *nf* volition.

volqué [bol'ke], **volquemos** [bol'kemos] *etc vb V* volcar.

volquete [bol'kete] *nm* dumper, dump truck (*US*).

voltaje [bol'taxe] *nm* voltage.

voltear [bolte'ar] *vt* to turn over; (*volcar*) to knock over; (*doblar*) to peal ♦ *vi* to roll over; **~se** *vr* (*AM*) to turn round; **~ a hacer algo** (*AM*) to do sth again.

voltereta [bolte'reta] *nf* somersault; **~ sobre las manos** handspring; **~ lateral** cartwheel.

voltio ['boltjo] *nm* volt.

voluble [bo'luβle] *adj* fickle.

volumen [bo'lumen] *nm* volume; **~ monetario** money supply; **~ de negocios** turnover; **bajar el ~** to turn down the volume; **poner la radio a todo ~** to turn the radio up full.

voluminoso, a [bolumi'noso, a] adj voluminous; (*enorme*) massive.

voluntad [bolun'tað] nf will, willpower; (*deseo*) desire, wish; (*afecto*) fondness; **a ~ at** will; (*cantidad*) as much as one likes; **buena ~** goodwill; **mala ~** ill will, malice; **por causas ajenas a mi ~** for reasons beyond my control.

voluntario, a [bolun'tarjo, a] adj voluntary ♦ nm/f volunteer.

voluntarioso, a [bolunta'rjoso, a] adj headstrong.

voluptuoso, a [bolup'twoso, a] adj voluptuous.

volver [bol'ßer] vt to turn; (*boca abajo*) to turn (over); (*voltear*) to turn round, turn upside down; (*poner al revés*) to turn inside out; (*devolver*) to return; (*transformar*) to change, transform; (*manga*) to roll up ♦ vi to return, go/come back; **~se** vr to turn round; (*llegar a ser*) to become; **~ la espalda** to turn one's back; **~ bien por mal** to return good for evil; **~ a hacer** to do again; **~ en sí** to come to o round, regain consciousness; **~ la vista atrás** to look back; **~ loco a algn** to drive sb mad; **~se loco** to go mad.

vomitar [bomi'tar] vt, vi to vomit.

vómito ['bomito] nm (*acto*) vomiting; (*resultado*) vomit.

voracidad [boraθi'ðað] nf voracity.

vorágine [bo'raxine] nf whirlpool; (*fig*) maelstrom.

voraz [bo'raθ] adj voracious; (*fig*) fierce.

vórtice ['bortiθe] nm whirlpool; (*de aire*) whirlwind.

vos [bos] pron (*AM*) you.

voseo [bo'seo] nm (*AM*) addressing a person as "vos", *familiar usage.*

Vosgos ['bosɣos] nmpl Vosges.

vosotros, as [bo'sotros, as] pron you pl; (*reflexivo*) yourselves; **entre ~** among yourselves.

votación [bota'θjon] nf (*acto*) voting; (*voto*) vote; **~ a mano alzada** show of hands; **someter algo a ~** to put sth to the vote.

votar [bo'tar] vt (*POL: partido etc*) to vote for; (*proyecto: aprobar*) to pass; (*REL*) to vow ♦ vi to vote.

voto ['boto] nm vote; (*promesa*) vow; (*maldición*) oath, curse; **~s** nmpl (good) wishes; **~ de bloque/de grupo** block/card vote; **~ de censura/de (des)confianza/de gracias** vote of censure/(no) confidence/thanks; **dar su ~** to cast one's vote.

voy [boi] vb V **ir**.

voz [boθ] nf voice; (*grito*) shout; (*chisme*)

rumour; (*LING: palabra*) word; (*: forma*) voice; **dar voces** to shout, yell; **llamar a algn a voces** to shout to sb; **llevar la ~ cantante** (*fig*) to be the boss; **tener la ~ tomada** to be hoarse; **tener ~ y voto** to have the right to speak; **a media ~** in a low voice; **a ~ en cuello** o **en grito** at the top of one's voice; **de viva ~** verbally; **en ~ alta** aloud; **~ de mando** command.

vozarrón [boθa'rron] nm booming voice.

vra., vro. abr = **vuestra, vuestro.**

Vto. abr (*COM*) = **vencimiento.**

vudú [bu'ðu] nm voodoo.

vuelco ['bwelko] etc vb V **volcar** ♦ nm spill, overturning; (*fig*) collapse; **mi corazón dio un ~** my heart missed a beat.

vuelo ['bwelo] etc vb V **volar** ♦ nm flight; (*encaje*) lace, frill; (*de falda etc*) loose part; (*fig*) importance; **de altos ~s** (*fig: plan*) grandiose; (*: persona*) ambitious; **alzar el ~** to take flight; (*fig*) to dash off; **coger al ~** to catch in flight; **~ en picado** dive; **~ libre** hang-gliding; **~ regular** scheduled flight; **falda de mucho ~** full o wide skirt.

vuelque ['bwelke] etc vb V **volcar.**

vuelta ['bwelta] nf turn; (*curva*) bend, curve; (*regreso*) return; (*revolución*) revolution; (*paseo*) stroll; (*circuito*) lap; (*de papel, tela*) reverse; (*de pantalón*) turn-up (*BRIT*), cuff (*US*); (*dinero*) change; **~ a empezar** back to square one; **~ al mundo** world trip; **V~ de Francia** Tour de France; **~ cerrada** hairpin bend; **a la ~** (*ESP*) on one's return; **a la ~ de la esquina, a la ~** (*AM*) round the corner; **a ~ de correo** by return of post; **dar ~s** to turn, revolve; **dar ~s a una idea** to turn over an idea (in one's mind); **dar una ~** to go for a walk; **dar media ~** (*AUTO*) to do a U-turn; (*fam*) to beat it; **estar de ~** (*fam*) to be back; **poner a algn de ~ y media** to heap abuse on sb; **no tiene ~ de hoja** there's no alternative.

vueltita [bwel'tita] nf (*esp AM fam*) (little) walk; (*: en coche*) (little) drive.

vuelto ['bwelto] pp de **volver** ♦ nm (*AM: moneda*) change.

vuelva ['bwelßa] etc vb V **volver.**

vuestro, a ['bwestro, a] adj your; (*después de n*) of yours ♦ pron: **el ~/la vuestra/los ~s/las vuestras** yours; **lo ~** (what is) yours; **un amigo ~** a friend of yours; **una idea vuestra** an idea of yours.

vulgar [bul'ɣar] adj (*ordinario*) vulgar; (*común*) common.

vulgarice [bulɣa'riθe] etc vb V **vulgarizar.**

vulgaridad [bulɣari'ðað] *nf* commonness;
(*acto*) vulgarity; (*expresión*) coarse
expression; ~**es** *nfpl* banalities.
vulgarismo [bulɣa'rismo] *nm* popular form
of a word.
vulgarizar [bulɣari'θar] *vt* to popularize.
vulgo ['bulɣo] *nm* common people.
vulnerable [bulne'raßle] *adj* vulnerable.
vulnerar [bulne'rar] *vt* to harm, damage;
(*derechos*) to interfere with; (*JUR, COM*)
to violate.
vulva ['bulßa] *nf* vulva.

W w

W, w ['ußе'doßle, (*AM*) 'doßleße] *nf* (*letra*) W,
w; **W de Washington** W for William.
walkie-talkie [walki'talki] *nm* walkie-
talkie.
walkman ® ['wal(k)man] *nm* Walkman ®.
WAP [wap] *adj, nm* WAP; **teléfono** ~ WAP
phone.
wáter ['bater] *nm* lavatory.
waterpolo [water'polo] *nm* waterpolo.
wátman ['watman] *adj inv* (*fam*) cool.
web [web] *nm o nf* (*página*) website: (*red*)
(World Wide) Web.
webcam ['webkam] *nf* webcam.
webmaster ['webmaster] *nm/f* webmaster.
web site ['websait] *nm* website.
whisky ['wiski] *nm* whisky.
Winchester ['wintʃester] *nm* (*INFORM*):
disco ~ Winchester disk.
windsurf ['winsurf] *nm* windsurfing.
WWW *nm o nf abr* (*INFORM*: = *World Wide
Web*) WWW.

X x

X, x ['ekis] *nf* (*letra*) X, x; **X de Xiquena** X
for Xmas.
xenofobia [seno'foßja] *nf* xenophobia.
xenófobo, a [se'nofoßo, a] *adj* xenophobic
♦ *nm/f* xenophobe.
xerografía [seroxra'fia] *nf* xerography.
xilófono [si'lofono] *nm* xylophone.
Xunta ['ʃunta] *nf* (*tb* ~ **de Galicia**)
regional government of Galicia.

Y y

Y, y [i'ɣrjeɣa] *nf* (*letra*) Y, y; **Y de Yegua** Y
for Yellow (*BRIT*) o Yoke (*US*).
y [i] *conj* and; (*AM fam: pues*) well; *¿*~ **eso?**
why?, how so?; **¡**~ **los demás?** what
about the others?; ~ **bueno, ...** (*AM*)
well ...
ya [ja] *adv* (*gen*) already; (*ahora*) now; (*en
seguida*) at once; (*pronto*) soon ♦ *excl* all
right!; (*por supuesto*) of course! ♦ *conj*
(*ahora que*) now that; ~ **no** not any more,
no longer; ~ **lo sé** I know; ~ **dice que sí,**
~ **dice que no** first he says yes, then he
says no; **¡**~, ~! yes, yes!; (*con
impaciencia*) all right!, O.K.!; **¡**~ **voy!**
(*enfático: no se suele traducir*) coming!; ~
que since.
yacer [ja'θer] *vi* to lie.
yacimiento [jaθi'mjento] *nm* bed, deposit;
~ **petrolífero** oilfield.
Yakarta [ja'karta] *nf* Jakarta.
yanqui ['janki] *adj* Yankee ♦ *nm/f* Yank,
Yankee.
yate ['jate] *nm* yacht.
yazca ['jaθka] *etc vb V* **yacer.**
yedra ['jeðra] *nf* ivy.
yegua ['jeɣwa] *nf* mare.
yema ['jema] *nf* (*del huevo*) yolk; (*BOT*)
leaf bud; (*fig*) best part; ~ **del dedo**
fingertip.

Yemen ['jemen] nm: el ~ del Norte Yemen;
el ~ del Sur Southern Yemen.
yemení [jeme'ni] adj, nm/f Yemeni.
yendo ['jendo] vb V ir.
yerba ['jerßa] nf = hierba.
yerbatero, a [jerßa'tero, a] adj (AM) maté
♦ nm/f (AM) herbal healer.
yerga ['jerɣa] etc, yergue ['jerɣe] etc vb V
erguir.
yermo, a ['jermo, a] adj barren; (de gente)
uninhabited ♦ nm waste land.
yerno ['jerno] nm son-in-law.
yerre ['jerre] etc vb V errar.
yerto, a ['jerto, a] adj stiff.
yesca ['jeska] nf tinder.
yeso ['jeso] nm (GEO) gypsum; (ARQ)
plaster.
yo ['jo] pron personal I; soy ~ it's me, it is I;
~ que tú/usted if I were you.
yodo ['joðo] nm iodine.
yoga ['joɣa] nm yoga.
yogur(t) [jo'ɣur(t)] nm yogurt.
yogurtera [joɣur'tera] nf yogurt maker.
yuca ['juka] nf yucca.
yudo ['juðo] nm judo.
yugo ['juɣo] nm yoke.
Yugoslavia [juɣos'laßja] nf Yugoslavia.
yugoslavo, a [juɣos'laßo, a] adj
Yugoslavian ♦ nm/f Yugoslav.
yugular [juɣu'lar] adj jugular.
yunque ['junke] nm anvil.
yunta ['junta] nf yoke.
yuntero [jun'tero] nm ploughman.
yute ['jute] nm jute.
yuxtapondré [jukstapond're] etc vb V
yuxtaponer.
yuxtaponer [jukstapo'ner] vt to juxtapose.
yuxtaponga [juksta'ponga] etc vb V
yuxtaponer.
yuxtaposición [jukstaposi'θjon] nf
juxtaposition.
yuxtapuesto [juksta'pwesto], yuxtapuse
[juksta'puse] etc vb V yuxtaponer.

Z z

Z, z ['θeta, (esp AM) 'seta] nf (letra) Z, z; Z de
Zaragoza Z for Zebra.
zafar [θa'far] vt (soltar) to untie; (superficie)
to clear; ~se vr (escaparse) to escape;
(ocultarse) to hide o.s. away; (TEC) to slip
off; ~se de (persona) to get away from.
zafio, a ['θafjo, a] adj coarse.
zafiro [θa'firo] nm sapphire.
zaga ['θaɣa] nf rear; a la ~ behind, in the
rear.
zagal [θa'ɣal] nm boy, lad.
zagala [θa'ɣala] nf girl, lass.
zaguán [θa'ɣwan] nm hallway.
zaherir [θae'rir] vt (criticar) to criticize; (fig:
herir) to wound.
zahiera etc, zahiriendo [θa'jera,
θai'rjendo] etc vb V zaherir.
zahorí [θao'ri] nm clairvoyant.
zaino, a ['θaino, a] adj (color de caballo)
chestnut; (pérfido) treacherous; (animal)
vicious.
zalamería [θalame'ria] nf flattery.
zalamero, a [θala'mero, a] adj flattering;
(relamido) suave.
zamarra [θa'marra] nf (piel) sheepskin;
(saco) sheepskin jacket.
Zambeze [θam'beθe] nm Zambezi.
zambo, a ['θambo, a] adj knock-kneed
♦ nm/f (AM) half-breed (of Negro and
Indian parentage); (mulato) mulatto ♦ nf
samba.
zambullida [θambu'ʎiða] nf dive, plunge.
zambullirse [θambu'ʎirse] vr to dive;
(ocultarse) to hide o.s.
zamorano, a [θamo'rano, a] adj of o from
Zamora ♦ nm/f native o inhabitant of
Zamora.
zampar [θam'par] vt (esconder) to hide o
put away (hurriedly); (comer) to gobble;
(arrojar) to hurl ♦ vi to eat voraciously;
~se vr (chocar) to bump; (fig) to
gatecrash.
zanahoria [θana'orja] nf carrot.
zancada [θan'kaða] nf stride.
zancadilla [θanka'ðiʎa] nf trip; (fig)
stratagem; echar la ~ a algn to trip sb up.
zancajo [θan'kaxo] nm (ANAT) heel; (fig)
dwarf.

zanco ['θanko] nm stilt.
zancudo, a [θan'kuðo, a] adj long-legged
♦ nm (AM) mosquito.
zángano ['θangano] nm drone; (holgazán)
idler, slacker.
zanja ['θanxa] nf (fosa) ditch; (tumba)
grave.
zanjar [θan'xar] vt (fosa) to ditch, trench;
(problema) to surmount; (conflicto) to
resolve.
zapapico [θapa'piko] nm pick, pickaxe.
zapata [θa'pata] nf half-boot; (MECÁNICA)
shoe.
zapateado [θapate'aðo] nm (flamenco) tap
dance.
zapatear [θapate'ar] vt (tocar) to tap with
one's foot; (patear) to kick; (fam) to ill-
treat ♦ vi to tap with one's feet.
zapatería [θapate'ria] nf (oficio)
shoemaking; (tienda) shoe-shop; (fábrica)
shoe factory.
zapatero, a [θapa'tero, a] nmf shoemaker;
~ **remendón** cobbler.
zapatilla [θapa'tiʎa] nf slipper; (TEC)
washer; (para deporte) training shoe.
zapato [θa'pato] nm shoe.
zapear [θape'ar] vi to flick through the
channels.
zapping ['θapin] nm channel-hopping;
hacer ~ to channel-hop.
zar [θar] nm tsar, czar.
zarabanda [θara'ßanda] nf saraband; (fig)
whirl.
Zaragoza [θara'xoθa] nf Saragossa.
zaragozano, a [θaraxo'θano, a] adj of o
from Saragossa ♦ nmf native o
inhabitant of Saragossa.
zaranda [θa'randa] nf sieve.
zarandear [θarande'ar] vt to sieve; (fam) to
shake vigorously.
zarpa ['θarpa] nf (garra) claw, paw; **echar la**
~ **a** to claw at; (fam) to grab.
zarpar [θar'par] vi to weigh anchor.
zarpazo [θar'paθo] nm: **dar un** ~ to claw.
zarza ['θarθa] nf (BOT) bramble.
zarzal [θar'θal] nm (matorral) bramble
patch.
zarzamora [θarθa'mora] nf blackberry.
zarzuela [θar'θwela] nf Spanish light
opera; **la Z~** home of the Spanish Royal
Family.
zigzag [θiɣ'θaɣ] adj zigzag.
zigzaguear [θiɣðaɣe'ar] vi to zigzag.
zinc [θink] nm zinc.
zíper ['siper] nm (AM) zip, zipper (US).

zócalo ['θokalo] nm (ARQ) plinth, base; (de
pared) skirting board.
zoco ['θoko] nm (Arab) market, souk.
zodíaco [θo'ðiako] nm zodiac; **signo del** ~
star sign.
zona ['θona] nf zone; ~ **cero** Ground Zero;
~ **euro** Eurozone; **los países de la** ~ **euro**
the Eurozone countries; ~ **fronteriza**
border area; ~ **del dólar** (COM) dollar
area; ~ **de fomento** o **de desarrollo**
development area.
zonzo, a ['sonso, a] adj (AM) silly.
zoología [θoolo'xia] nf zoology.
zoológico, a [θoo'loxiko, a] adj zoological
♦ nm (tb: **parque** ~) zoo.
zoólogo, a [θo'oloxo, a] nmf zoologist.
zoom [θum] nm zoom lens.
zopenco, a [θo'penko, a] (fam) adj dull,
stupid ♦ nmf clot, nitwit.
zopilote [sopi'lote] nm (AM) buzzard.
zoquete [θo'kete] nm (madera) block; (pan)
crust; (fam) blockhead.
zorro, a ['θorro, a] adj crafty ♦ nmf fox/
vixen ♦ nf (fam) whore, tart, hooker
(US).
zote ['θote] (fam) adj dim, stupid ♦ nmf
dimwit.
zozobra [θo'θoßra] nf (fig) anxiety.
zozobrar [θoθo'ßrar] vi (hundirse) to
capsize; (fig) to fail.
zueco ['θweko] nm clog.
zulo ['θulo] nm (de armas) cache.
zumbar [θum'bar] vt (burlar) to tease;
(golpear) to hit ♦ vi to buzz; (fam) to be
very close; ~**se** vr: ~**se de** to tease; **me**
zumban los oídos I have a buzzing o
ringing in my ears.
zumbido [θum'biðo] nm buzzing; (fam)
punch; ~ **de oídos** buzzing o ringing in
the ears.
zumo ['θumo] nm juice; (ganancia) profit; ~
de naranja (fresh) orange juice.
zurcir [θur'θir] vt (coser) to darn; (fig) to
put together; **¡que las zurzan!** to blazes
with them!
zurdo, a ['θurðo, a] adj (mano) left;
(persona) left-handed.
zurrar [θu'rrar] vt (TEC) to dress; (fam:
pegar duro) to wallop; (: aplastar) to
flatten; (: criticar) to criticize harshly.
zurriagazo [θurrja'xaθo] nm lash, stroke;
(desgracia) stroke of bad luck.
zurrón [θu'rron] nm pouch.
zurza ['θurθa] etc vb V **zurcir**.
zutano, a [θu'tano, a] nmf so-and-so.

English-Spanish
Inglés-Español

Aa

A, a [eɪ] n (*letter*) A, a; (*SCOL: mark*) ≈ sobresaliente; (*MUS*): **A** la m; **A for Andrew**, (*US*) **A for Able** A de Antonio; **A road** n (*BRIT AUT*) ≈ carretera nacional.

━━━━━━━━━━━━━━━━━━ *KEYWORD*

a [ə] *indef art* (*before vowel or silent h*: **an**) **1** un(a); ~ **book** un libro; **an apple** una manzana; **she's** ~ **nurse** (ella) es enfermera; **I haven't got** ~ **car** no tengo coche

2 (*instead of the number "one"*) un(a); ~ **year ago** hace un año; ~ **hundred/ thousand pounds** cien/mil libras

3 (*in expressing ratios, prices etc*): **3** ~ **day/week** 3 al día/a la semana; **10 km an hour** 10 km por hora; **£5** ~ **person** £5 por persona; **30p** ~ **kilo** 30p el kilo; **3 times** ~ **month** 3 veces al mes.

a. *abbr* = **acre**.

A2 n (*BRIT SCOL*) segunda parte de los "A levels" (*módulos 4–6*).

AA n *abbr* (*BRIT*: = *Automobile Association*) ≈ RACE m (*SP*); (= *Alcoholics Anonymous*; (*US*: = *Associate in/of Arts*) título universitario; (= *anti-aircraft*) A.A.

AAA n *abbr* (= *American Automobile Association*) ≈ RACE m (*SP*); ['θriː'eɪz] (*BRIT*: = *Amateur Athletics Association*) asociación de atletismo amateur.

A & R n *abbr* (*MUS*) (= *artists and repertoire*) nuevos artistas y canciones; ~ **man** descubridor de jóvenes talentos.

AAUP n *abbr* (= *American Association of University Professors*) asociación de profesores universitarios.

AB *abbr* (*BRIT*) = **able-bodied seaman**;

(*Canada*) = Alberta.

aback [ə'bæk] *adv*: **to be taken** ~ quedar(se) desconcertado.

abandon [ə'bændən] *vt* abandonar; (*renounce*) renunciar a ♦ n abandono; (*wild behaviour*): **with** ~ con desenfreno; **to** ~ **ship** abandonar el barco.

abandoned [ə'bændənd] *adj* (*child, house etc*) abandonado; (*unrestrained: manner*) desinhibido.

abase [ə'beɪs] *vt*: **to** ~ **o.s. (so far as to do ...)** rebajarse (hasta el punto de hacer ...).

abashed [ə'bæʃt] *adj* avergonzado.

abate [ə'beɪt] *vi* moderarse; (*lessen*) disminuir; (*calm down*) calmarse.

abatement [ə'beɪtmənt] n (*of pollution, noise*) disminución f.

abattoir ['æbətwɑː*] n (*BRIT*) matadero.

abbey ['æbɪ] n abadía.

abbot ['æbət] n abad m.

abbreviate [ə'briːvɪeɪt] *vt* abreviar.

abbreviation [əbriːvɪ'eɪʃən] n (*short form*) abreviatura; (*act*) abreviación f.

ABC n *abbr* (= *American Broadcasting Company*) cadena de televisión.

abdicate ['æbdɪkeɪt] *vt*, *vi* abdicar.

abdication [æbdɪ'keɪʃən] n abdicación f.

abdomen ['æbdəmən] n abdomen m.

abdominal [æb'dɔmɪnl] *adj* abdominal.

abduct [æb'dʌkt] *vt* raptar, secuestrar.

abductor [æb'dʌktə*] n raptor(a) m/f, secuestrador(a) m/f.

abduction [æb'dʌkʃən] n rapto, secuestro.

Aberdonian [æbə'dəunɪən] *adj* de Aberdeen ♦ n nativo/a or habitante m/f de Aberdeen.

aberration [æbə'reɪʃən] n aberración f; **in a moment of mental** ~ en un momento de enajenación mental.

abet [ə'bɛt] *vt see* **aid.**

abeyance [ə'beɪəns] *n*: **in** ~ (*law*) en desuso; (*matter*) en suspenso.

abhor [əb'hɔː*] *vt* aborrecer, abominar (de).

abhorrent [əb'hɔrənt] *adj* aborrecible, detestable.

abide [ə'baɪd] *vt*: **I can't** ~ **it/him** no lo/le puedo ver *or* aguantar; **to** ~ **by** *vt fus* atenerse a.

abiding [ə'baɪdɪŋ] *adj* (*memory etc*) perdurable.

ability [ə'bɪlɪtɪ] *n* habilidad *f*, capacidad *f*; (*talent*) talento; **to the best of my** ~ lo mejor que pueda *etc*.

abject ['æbdʒɛkt] *adj* (*poverty*) sórdido; (*apology*) rastrero; (*coward*) vil.

ablaze [ə'bleɪz] *adj* en llamas, ardiendo.

able ['eɪbl] *adj* capaz; (*skilled*) hábil; **to be** ~ **to do sth** poder hacer algo.

able-bodied ['eɪbl'bɔdɪd] *adj* sano; ~ **seaman** marinero de primera.

ably ['eɪblɪ] *adv* hábilmente.

ABM *n abbr* = **anti-ballistic missile.**

abnormal [æb'nɔːməl] *adj* anormal.

abnormality [æbnɔː'mælɪtɪ] *n* (*condition*) anormalidad *f*; (*instance*) anomalía.

aboard [ə'bɔːd] *adv* a bordo ♦ *prep* a bordo de; ~ **the train** en el tren.

abode [ə'bəʊd] *n* (*old*) morada; (*LAW*) domicilio; **of no fixed** ~ sin domicilio fijo.

abolish [ə'bɔlɪʃ] *vt* suprimir, abolir.

abolition [æbəʊ'lɪʃən] *n* supresión *f*, abolición *f*.

abominable [ə'bɔmɪnəbl] *adj* abominable.

aborigine [æbə'rɪdʒɪnɪ] *n* aborigen *m/f*.

abort [ə'bɔːt] *vt* abortar; (*COMPUT*) interrumpir ♦ *vi* (*COMPUT*) interrumpir el programa.

abortion [ə'bɔːʃən] *n* aborto (*provocado*); **to have an** ~ abortar.

abortionist [ə'bɔːʃənɪst] *n* persona que practica abortos.

abortive [ə'bɔːtɪv] *adj* fracasado.

abound [ə'baʊnd] *vi*: **to** ~ (**in** *or* **with**) abundar (de *or* en).

================== *KEYWORD*

about [ə'baʊt] *adv* **1** (*approximately*) más o menos, aproximadamente; ~ **a hundred/ thousand** *etc* unos(unas) *or* como cien/ mil *etc*; **it takes** ~ **10 hours** se tarda unas *or* más o menos 10 horas; **at** ~ **2 o'clock** sobre las dos; **I've just** ~ **finished** casi he terminado

2 (*referring to place*) por todas partes; **to leave things lying** ~ dejar las cosas (tiradas) por ahí; **to run** ~ correr por

todas partes; **to walk** ~ pasearse, ir y venir; **is Paul** ~? ¿está por aquí Paul?; **it's the other way** ~ es al revés

3: **to be** ~ **to do sth** estar a punto de hacer algo; **I'm not** ~ **to do all that for nothing** no pienso hacer todo eso para nada

♦ *prep* **1** (*relating to*) de, sobre, acerca de; **a book** ~ **London** un libro sobre *or* acerca de Londres; **what is it** ~? (*book, film*) ¿de qué se trata?; **we talked** ~ **it** hablamos de eso *or* ello; **what** *or* **how** ~ **doing this?** ¿qué tal si hacemos esto?

2 (*referring to place*) por; **to walk** ~ **the town** caminar por la ciudad.

about face, about turn *n* (*MIL*) media vuelta; (*fig*) cambio radical.

above [ə'bʌv] *adv* encima, por encima, arriba ♦ *prep* encima de; **mentioned** ~ susodicho; ~ **all** sobre todo; **he's not** ~ **a bit of blackmail** es capaz hasta de hacer chantaje.

above board *adj* legítimo.

above-mentioned [əbʌv'mɛnʃnd] *adj* susodicho.

abrasion [ə'breɪʒən] *n* (*on skin*) abrasión *f*.

abrasive [ə'breɪzɪv] *adj* abrasivo.

abreast [ə'brɛst] *adv* uno al lado de otro; **to keep** ~ **of** mantenerse al corriente de.

abridge [ə'brɪdʒ] *vt* abreviar.

abroad [ə'brɔːd] *adv* (*to be*) en el extranjero; (*to go*) al extranjero; **there is a rumour** ~ **that ...** corre el rumor de que ...

abrupt [ə'brʌpt] *adj* (*sudden: departure*) repentino; (*manner*) brusco.

abruptly [ə'brʌptlɪ] *adv* (*leave*) repentinamente; (*speak*) bruscamente.

abscess ['æbsɪs] *n* absceso.

abscond [əb'skɔnd] *vi* fugarse.

absence ['æbsəns] *n* ausencia; **in the** ~ **of** (*person*) en ausencia de; (*thing*) a falta de.

absent ['æbsənt] *adj* ausente; ~ **without leave** (*AWOL*) ausente sin permiso.

absentee [æbsən'tiː] *n* ausente *m/f*.

absenteeism [æbsən'tiːɪzəm] *n* absentismo.

absent-minded [æbsənt'maɪndɪd] *adj* distraído.

absolute ['æbsəluːt] *adj* absoluto; ~ **monopoly** monopolio total.

absolutely [æbsə'luːtlɪ] *adv* totalmente; **oh yes,** ~! ¡claro *or* por supuesto que sí!

absolution [æbsə'luːʃən] *n* (*REL*) absolución *f*.

absolve [əb'zɔlv] *vt*: **to** ~ **sb (from)** absolver a alguien (de).

absorb [əb'zɔːb] *vt* absorber; **to be** ~**ed in a**

book estar enfrascado en un libro.
absorbent [əb'zɔːbənt] *adj* absorbente.
absorbent cotton *n* (*US*) algodón *m* hidrófilo.
absorbing [əb'zɔːbɪŋ] *adj* absorbente; (*book etc*) interesantísimo.
absorption [əb'zɔːpʃən] *n* absorción *f*.
abstain [əb'steɪn] *vi*: **to ~ (from)** abstenerse (de).
abstemious [əb'stiːmɪəs] *adj* abstemio.
abstention [əb'stenʃən] *n* abstención *f*.
abstinence ['æbstɪnəns] *n* abstinencia.
abstract ['æbstrækt] *adj* abstracto.
abstruse [æb'struːs] *adj* abstruso, oscuro.
absurd [əb'səːd] *adj* absurdo.
absurdity [əb'səːdɪtɪ] *n* absurdo.
ABTA ['æbtə] *n abbr* = *Association of British Travel Agents*.
abundance [ə'bʌndəns] *n* abundancia.
abundant [ə'bʌndənt] *adj* abundante.
abuse [ə'bjuːs] *n* (*insults*) insultos *mpl*, improperios *mpl*; (*misuse*) abuso ♦ *vt* [ə'bjuːz] (*ill-treat*) maltratar; (*take advantage of*) abusar de; **open to ~** sujeto al abuso.
abusive [ə'bjuːsɪv] *adj* ofensivo.
abysmal [ə'bɪzməl] *adj* pésimo; (*ignorance*) supino.
abyss [ə'bɪs] *n* abismo.
AC *abbr* (= *alternating current*) corriente *f* alterna ♦ *n abbr* (*US*) = *athletic club*.
a/c *abbr* (*BANKING etc*) = *account, account current*.
academic [ækə'dɛmɪk] *adj* académico, universitario; (*pej: issue*) puramente teórico/a; (*lecturer*) profesor(a) *m/f* universitario/a; **~ year** (*UNIV*) año académico.
academy [ə'kædəmɪ] *n* (*learned body*) academia; (*school*) instituto, colegio; **~ of music** conservatorio.
ACAS ['eɪkæs] *n abbr* (*BRIT*: = *Advisory, Conciliation and Arbitration Service*) ≈ Instituto de Mediación, Arbitraje y Conciliación.
accede [æk'siːd] *vi*: **to ~ to** acceder a.
accelerate [æk'sɛləreɪt] *vt* acelerar ♦ *vi* acelerarse.
acceleration [ækselə'reɪʃən] *n* aceleración *f*.
accelerator [æk'sɛləreɪtə*] *n* (*BRIT*) acelerador *m*.
accent ['æksɛnt] *n* acento.
accentuate [æk'sɛntjueɪt] *vt* (*syllable*) acentuar; (*need, difference etc*) recalcar, subrayar.
accept [ək'sɛpt] *vt* aceptar; (*approve*) aprobar; (*concede*) admitir.
acceptable [ək'sɛptəbl] *adj* aceptable;

admisible.
acceptance [ək'sɛptəns] *n* aceptación *f*; aprobación *f*; **to meet with general ~** recibir la aprobación general.
access ['æksɛs] *n* acceso ♦ *vt* (*COMPUT*) acceder a; **the burglars gained ~ through a window** los ladrones lograron entrar por una ventana; **to have ~ to** tener acceso a.
accessible [æk'sɛsəbl] *adj* accesible.
accession [æk'sɛʃən] (*of monarch*) subida, ascenso; (*addition*) adquisición *f*.
accessory [æk'sɛsərɪ] *n* accesorio; **toilet accessories** artículos *mpl* de tocador.
access road *n* carretera de acceso; (*to motorway*) carril *m* de acceso.
access time *n* (*COMPUT*) tiempo de acceso.
accident ['æksɪdənt] *n* accidente *m*; (*chance*) casualidad *f*; **by ~** (*unintentionally*) sin querer; (*by coincidence*) por casualidad; **~s at work** accidentes *mpl* de trabajo; **to meet with** *or* **to have an ~** tener *or* sufrir un accidente.
accidental [æksɪ'dɛntl] *adj* accidental, fortuito.
accidentally [æksɪ'dɛntəlɪ] *adv* sin querer; por casualidad.
accident insurance *n* seguro contra accidentes.
accident-prone ['æksɪdənt'prəun] *adj* propenso a los accidentes.
acclaim [ə'kleɪm] *vt* aclamar, aplaudir ♦ *n* aclamación *f*, aplausos *mpl*.
acclamation [æklə'meɪʃən] *n* (*approval*) aclamación *f*; (*applause*) aplausos *mpl*; **by ~** por aclamación.
acclimatize [ə'klaɪmətaɪz], (*US*) **acclimate** [ə'klaɪmət] *vt*: **to become ~d** aclimatarse.
accolade ['ækəuleɪd] *n* (*prize*) premio; (*praise*) alabanzas *fpl*, homenaje *m*.
accommodate [ə'kɔmədeɪt] *vt* alojar, hospedar; (*oblige, help*) complacer; **this car ~s 4 people comfortably** en este coche caben 4 personas cómodamente.
accommodating [ə'kɔmədeɪtɪŋ] *adj* servicial, complaciente.
accommodation *n*, (*US*) **accommodations** *npl* [əkɔmə'deɪʃən(z)] alojamiento; **"~ to let"** "se alquilan habitaciones"; **seating ~** asientos *mpl*.
accompaniment [ə'kʌmpənɪmənt] *n* acompañamiento.
accompanist [ə'kʌmpənɪst] *n* (*MUS*) acompañante *m/f*.
accompany [ə'kʌmpənɪ] *vt* acompañar.
accomplice [ə'kʌmplɪs] *n* cómplice *m/f*.
accomplish [ə'kʌmplɪʃ] *vt* (*finish*) acabar;

(*aim*) realizar; (*task*) llevar a cabo.

accomplished [əˈkʌmplɪʃt] *adj* experto, hábil.

accomplishment [əˈkʌmplɪʃmənt] *n* (*ending*) conclusión *f*; (*bringing about*) realización *f*; (*skill*) talento.

accord [əˈkɔːd] *n* acuerdo ♦ *vt* conceder; **of his own** ~ espontáneamente; **with one** ~ de *or* por común acuerdo.

accordance [əˈkɔːdəns] *n*: **in** ~ **with** de acuerdo con.

according [əˈkɔːdɪŋ]: ~ **to** *prep* según; (*in accordance with*) conforme a; **it went** ~ **to plan** salió según lo previsto.

accordingly [əˈkɔːdɪŋlɪ] *adv* (*thus*) por consiguiente.

accordion [əˈkɔːdɪən] *n* acordeón *m*.

accordionist [əˈkɔːdɪənɪst] *n* acordeonista *m/f*.

accost [əˈkɔst] *vt* abordar, dirigirse a.

account [əˈkaunt] *n* (*COMM*) cuenta, factura; (*report*) informe *m*; ~**s** *npl* (*COMM*) cuentas *fpl*; "~ **payee only**" "únicamente en cuenta del beneficiario"; **your** ~ **is still outstanding** su cuenta está todavía pendiente; **of little** ~ de poca importancia; **on** ~ a crédito; **to buy sth on** ~ comprar algo a crédito; **on no** ~ bajo ningún concepto; **on** ~ **of** a causa de, por motivo de; **to take into** ~, **take** ~ **of** tener en cuenta; **to keep an** ~ **of** llevar la cuenta de; **to bring sb to** ~ **for sth/for having done sth** pedirle cuentas a algn por algo/por haber hecho algo.

▶**account for** *vt fus* (*explain*) explicar; **all the children were** ~**ed for** no faltaba ningún niño.

accountability [əkauntəˈbɪlɪtɪ] *n* responsabilidad *f*.

accountable [əˈkauntəbl] *adj*: ~ **(for)** responsable (de).

accountancy [əˈkauntənsɪ] *n* contabilidad *f*.

accountant [əˈkauntənt] *n* contable *m/f*, contador(a) *m/f* (*LAM*).

accounting [əˈkauntɪŋ] *n* contabilidad *f*.

accounting period *n* período contable, ejercicio financiero.

account number *n* (*at bank etc*) número de cuenta.

account payable *n* cuenta por pagar.

account receivable *n* cuenta por cobrar.

accoutrements [əˈkuːtrəmənts] *npl* equipo, pertrechos *mpl*.

accredited [əˈkredɪtɪd] *adj* (*agent etc*) autorizado, acreditado.

accretion [əˈkriːʃən] *n* acumulación *f*.

accrue [əˈkruː] *vi* (*mount up*) aumentar, incrementarse; (*interest*) acumularse; **to**

~ **to** corresponder a; ~**d charges** gastos *mpl* vencidos; ~**d interest** interés *m* acumulado.

accumulate [əˈkjuːmjuleɪt] *vt* acumular ♦ *vi* acumularse.

accumulation [əkjuːmjuˈleɪʃən] *n* acumulación *f*.

accuracy [ˈækjurəsɪ] *n* exactitud *f*, precisión *f*.

accurate [ˈækjurɪt] *adj* (*number*) exacto; (*answer*) acertado; (*shot*) certero.

accurately [ˈækjurɪtlɪ] *adv* (*count, shoot, answer*) con precisión.

accursed [əˈkəːst] *adj* maldito.

accusation [ækjuˈzeɪʃən] *n* acusación *f*.

accusative [əˈkjuːzətɪv] *n* acusativo.

accuse [əˈkjuːz] *vt* acusar; (*blame*) echar la culpa a.

accused [əˈkjuːzd] *n* acusado/a.

accuser [əˈkjuːzə*] *n* acusador(a) *m/f*.

accustom [əˈkʌstəm] *vt* acostumbrar; **to** ~ **o.s. to sth** acostumbrarse a algo.

accustomed [əˈkʌstəmd] *adj*: ~ **to** acostumbrado a.

AC/DC *abbr* = *alternating current/direct current*.

ACE [eɪs] *n abbr* = *American Council on Education*.

ace [eɪs] *n* as *m*.

acerbic [əˈsəːbɪk] *adj* acerbo; (*fig*) mordaz.

acetate [ˈæsɪteɪt] *n* acetato.

ache [eɪk] *n* dolor *m* ♦ *vi* doler; (*yearn*): **to** ~ **to do sth** ansiar hacer algo; **i've got stomach** ~ *or* (*US*) **a stomach** ~ tengo dolor de estómago, me duele el estómago; **my head** ~**s** me duele la cabeza.

achieve [əˈtʃiːv] *vt* (*reach*) alcanzar; (*realize*) realizar; (*victory, success*) lograr, conseguir.

achievement [əˈtʃiːvmənt] *n* (*completion*) realización *f*; (*success*) éxito.

Achilles heel [əˈkɪliːz-] *n* talón *m* de Aquiles.

acid [ˈæsɪd] *adj* ácido; (*bitter*) agrio ♦ *n* ácido.

acidity [əˈsɪdɪtɪ] *n* acidez *f*; (*MED*) acedía.

acid rain *n* lluvia ácida.

acid test *n* (*fig*) prueba de fuego.

acknowledge [əkˈnɔlɪdʒ] *vt* (*letter: also*: ~ **receipt of**) acusar recibo de; (*fact*) reconocer.

acknowledgement [əkˈnɔlɪdʒmənt] *n* acuse *m* de recibo; reconocimiento; ~**s** (*in book*) agradecimientos *mpl*.

ACLU *n abbr* (= *American Civil Liberties Union*) unión *americana por libertades civiles*.

acme ['ækmɪ] n súmmum m.

acne ['æknɪ] n acné m.

acorn ['eɪkɔːn] n bellota.

acoustic [ə'kuːstɪk] adj acústico.

acoustic coupler [-'kʌplə*] n (COMPUT) acoplador m acústico.

acoustics [ə'kuːstɪks] n, npl acústica sg.

acquaint [ə'kweɪnt] vt: **to ~ sb with sth** (inform) poner a algn al corriente de algo; **to be ~ed with** (person) conocer; (fact) estar al corriente de.

acquaintance [ə'kweɪntəns] n conocimiento; (person) conocido/a; **to make sb's ~** conocer a algn.

acquiesce [ækwɪ'ɛs] vi (agree): **to ~ (in)** consentir (en), conformarse (con).

acquire [ə'kwaɪə*] vt adquirir.

acquired [ə'kwaɪəd] adj adquirido; **it's an ~ taste** es algo a lo que uno se aficiona poco a poco.

acquisition [ækwɪ'zɪʃən] n adquisición f.

acquisitive [ə'kwɪzɪtɪv] adj codicioso.

acquit [ə'kwɪt] vt absolver, exculpar; **to ~ o.s. well** defenderse bien.

acquittal [ə'kwɪtl] n absolución f, exculpación f.

acre ['eɪkə*] n acre m.

acreage ['eɪkərɪdʒ] n extensión f.

acrid ['ækrɪd] adj (smell) acre; (fig) mordaz, sarcástico.

acrimonious [ækrɪ'məunɪəs] adj (remark) mordaz; (argument) reñido.

acrobat ['ækrəbæt] n acróbata m/f.

acrobatic [ækrə'bætɪk] adj acrobático.

acrobatics [ækrə'bætɪks] npl acrobacias fpl.

acronym ['ækrənɪm] n siglas fpl.

across [ə'krɔs] prep (on the other side of) al otro lado de; (crosswise) a través de ♦ adv de un lado a otro, de una parte a otra; a través, al través; **to run/swim ~** atravesar corriendo/nadando; **~ from** enfrente de; **the lake is 12 km ~** el lago tiene 12 km de ancho; **to get sth ~ to sb** (fig) hacer comprender algo a algn.

acrylic [ə'krɪlɪk] adj acrílico.

act [ækt] n acto, acción f; (THEAT) acto; (in music-hall etc) número; (LAW) decreto, ley f ♦ vi (behave) comportarse; (THEAT) actuar; (pretend) fingir; (take action) tomar medidas ♦ vt (part) hacer, representar; **~ of God** fuerza mayor; **it's only an ~** es cuento; **to catch sb in the ~** coger a algn in fraganti or con las manos en la masa; **to ~ Hamlet** hacer el papel de Hamlet; **to ~ as** actuar or hacer de; **~ing in my capacity as chairman, I ...** en mi calidad de presidente, yo ...; **it ~s as a deterrent** sirve para disuadir; **he's only ~ing** está

fingiendo nada más.

►**act on** vt: **to ~ on sth** actuar or obrar sobre algo.

►**act out** vt (event) representar; (fantasies) realizar.

acting ['æktɪŋ] adj suplente ♦ n: **to do some ~** hacer algo de teatro; **he is the ~ manager** es el gerente en funciones.

action ['ækʃən] n acción f, acto; (MIL) acción f; (LAW) proceso, demanda; **to put a plan into ~** poner un plan en acción or en marcha; **killed in ~** (MIL) muerto en acto de servicio or en combate; **out of ~** (person) fuera de combate; (thing) averiado, descompuesto; **to take ~** tomar medidas; **to bring an ~ against sb** entablar or presentar demanda contra algn.

action replay n (TV) repetición f.

activate ['æktɪveɪt] vt activar.

active ['æktɪv] adj activo, enérgico; (volcano) en actividad; **to play an ~ part in** colaborar activamente en; **~ file** (COMPUT) fichero activo.

active duty (AD) n (US MIL) servicio activo.

actively ['æktɪvlɪ] adv (participate) activamente; (discourage, dislike) enérgicamente.

active partner n (COMM) socio activo.

activist ['æktɪvɪst] n activista m/f.

activity [æk'tɪvɪtɪ] n actividad f.

actor ['æktə*] n actor m.

actress ['æktrɪs] n actriz f.

ACTT n abbr (BRIT: = Association of Cinematographic, Television and Allied Technicians) sindicato de técnicos de cine y televisión.

actual ['æktjuəl] adj verdadero, real.

actually ['æktjuəlɪ] adv realmente, en realidad.

actuary ['æktjuərɪ] n (COMM) actuario/a (de seguros).

actuate ['æktjueɪt] vt mover, impulsar.

acumen ['ækjumən] n perspicacia; **business ~** talento para los negocios.

acupuncture ['ækjupʌŋktʃə*] n acupuntura.

acute [ə'kjuːt] adj agudo.

acutely [ə'kjuːtlɪ] adv profundamente, extremadamente.

AD adv abbr (= Anno Domini) A.C. ♦ n abbr (US MIL) see **active duty**.

ad [æd] n abbr = **advertisement**.

adage ['ædɪdʒ] n refrán m, adagio.

Adam ['ædəm] n Adán m; **~'s apple** n nuez f (de la garganta).

adamant ['ædəmənt] adj firme, inflexible.

adapt [ə'dæpt] vt adaptar; (reconcile) acomodar ♦ vi: **to** ~ **(to)** adaptarse (a), ajustarse (a).

adaptability [ədæptə'bɪlɪtɪ] n (of person, device etc) adaptabilidad f.

adaptable [ə'dæptəbl] adj (device) adaptable; (person) acomodadizo, que se adapta.

adaptation [ædæp'teɪʃən] n adaptación f.

adapter, adaptor [ə'dæptə*] n (ELEC) adaptador m.

ADC n abbr (MIL) = aide-de-camp; (US: = Aid to Dependent Children) ayuda para niños dependientes.

add [æd] vt añadir, agregar (esp LAM); (figures: also: ~ **up**) sumar ♦ vi: **to** ~ **to** (increase) aumentar, acrecentar.

▶**add on** vt añadir.

▶**add up** vt (figures) sumar ♦ vi (fig): **it doesn't** ~ **up** no tiene sentido; **it doesn't** ~ **up to much** es poca cosa, no tiene gran or mucha importancia.

addendum [ə'dɛndəm] n ad(d)enda m or f.

adder ['ædə*] n víbora.

addict ['ædɪkt] n (to drugs etc) adicto/a; (enthusiast) aficionado/a, entusiasta m/f; **heroin** ~ heroinómano/a.

addicted [ə'dɪktɪd] adj: **to be** ~ **to** ser adicto a; ser aficionado a.

addiction [ə'dɪkʃən] n (dependence) hábito morboso; (enthusiasm) afición f.

addictive [ə'dɪktɪv] adj que causa adicción.

adding machine ['ædɪŋ-] n calculadora.

Addis Ababa ['ædɪs'æbəbə] n Addis Abeba m.

addition [ə'dɪʃən] n (adding up) adición f; (thing added) añadidura, añadido; **in** ~ además, por añadidura; **in** ~ **to** además de.

additional [ə'dɪʃənl] adj adicional.

additive ['ædɪtɪv] n aditivo.

addled ['ædld] adj (BRIT: rotten) podrido; (: fig) confuso.

address [ə'drɛs] n dirección f, señas fpl; (speech) discurso; (COMPUT) dirección f ♦ vt (letter) dirigir; (speak to) dirigirse a, dirigir la palabra a; **form of** ~ tratamiento; **absolute/relative** ~ (COMPUT) dirección f absoluta/relativa; **to** ~ **o.s. to sth** (issue, problem) abordar.

address book n agenda (de direcciones).

addressee [ædrɛ'siː] n destinatario/a.

Aden ['eɪdn] n Adén m.

adenoids ['ædɪnɔɪdz] npl vegetaciones fpl (adenoideas).

adept ['ædɛpt] adj: ~ **at** experto or ducho en.

adequacy ['ædɪkwəsɪ] n idoneidad f.

adequate ['ædɪkwɪt] adj (satisfactory) adecuado; (enough) suficiente; **to feel** ~ **to a task** sentirse con fuerzas para una tarea.

adequately ['ædɪkwɪtlɪ] adv adecuadamente.

adhere [əd'hɪə*] vi: **to** ~ **to** adherirse a; (fig: abide by) observar.

adherent [əd'hɪərənt] n partidario/a.

adhesion [əd'hiːʒən] n adherencia.

adhesive [əd'hiːzɪv] adj, n adhesivo.

adhesive tape n (BRIT) cinta adhesiva; (US: MED) esparadrapo.

ad hoc [æd'hɔk] adj (decision) ad hoc; (committee) formado con fines específicos ♦ adv ad hoc.

adieu [ə'djuː] excl ¡vaya con Dios!

ad inf ['æd'ɪnf] adv hasta el infinito.

adjacent [ə'dʒeɪsənt] adj: ~ **to** contiguo a, inmediato a.

adjective ['ædʒɛktɪv] n adjetivo.

adjoin [ə'dʒɔɪn] vt estar contiguo a; (land) lindar con.

adjoining [ə'dʒɔɪnɪŋ] adj contiguo, vecino.

adjourn [ə'dʒɜːn] vt aplazar; (session) suspender, levantar; (US: end) terminar ♦ vi suspenderse; **the meeting has been** ~**ed till next week** se ha levantado la sesión hasta la semana que viene; **they** ~**ed to the pub** (col) se trasladaron al bar.

adjournment [ə'dʒɜːnmənt] n (period) suspensión f; (postponement) aplazamiento.

Adjt. abbr = **adjutant**.

adjudicate [ə'dʒuːdɪkeɪt] vi sentenciar; (contest) hacer de árbitro en, juzgar; (claim) decidir.

adjudication [ədʒuːdɪ'keɪʃən] n fallo.

adjudicator [ə'dʒuːdɪkeɪtə*] n juez m, árbitro.

adjust [ə'dʒʌst] vt (change) modificar; (arrange) arreglar; (machine) ajustar ♦ vi: **to** ~ **(to)** adaptarse (a).

adjustable [ə'dʒʌstəbl] adj ajustable.

adjuster [ə'dʒʌstə*] n see **loss adjuster**.

adjustment [ə'dʒʌstmənt] n modificación f; arreglo; (of prices, wages) ajuste m.

adjutant ['ædʒətənt] n ayudante m.

ad-lib [æd'lɪb] vt, vi improvisar ♦ adv: **ad lib** a voluntad, a discreción.

adman ['ædmæn] n (col) publicista m.

admin ['ædmɪn] n abbr (col) = **administration**.

administer [əd'mɪnɪstə*] vt proporcionar; (justice) administrar.

administration [ædmɪnɪ'streɪʃən] n administración f; (government) gobierno;

the A~ (*US*) la Administración.
administrative [əd'mınıstrətɪv] *adj* administrativo.
administrator [əd'mınıstreɪtə*] *n* administrador(a) *m/f*.
admirable ['ædmərəbl] *adj* admirable.
admiral ['ædmərəl] *n* almirante *m*.
Admiralty ['ædmərəltɪ] *n* (*BRIT*) Ministerio de Marina, Almirantazgo.
admiration [ædmə'reɪʃən] *n* admiración *f*.
admire [əd'maɪə*] *vt* admirar.
admirer [əd'maɪərə*] *n* admirador(a) *m/f*; (*suitor*) pretendiente *m*.
admiring [əd'maɪərɪŋ] *adj* (*expression*) de admiración.
admissible [əd'mɪsəbl] *adj* admisible.
admission [əd'mɪʃən] *n* (*exhibition, nightclub*) entrada; (*enrolment*) ingreso; (*confession*) confesión *f*; "**~ free**" "entrada gratis *or* libre"; **by his own** ~ él mismo reconoce que.
admit [əd'mɪt] *vt* dejar entrar, dar entrada a; (*permit*) admitir; (*acknowledge*) reconocer; "**this ticket ~s two**" "entrada para 2 personas"; **children not ~ted** se prohíbe la entrada a (los) menores de edad; **I must ~ that** ... debo reconocer que ...
▶**admit of** *vt fus* admitir, permitir.
▶**admit to** *vt fus* confesarse culpable de.
admittance [əd'mɪtəns] *n* entrada; "**no ~**" "se prohíbe la entrada", "prohibida la entrada".
admittedly [əd'mɪtədlɪ] *adv* de acuerdo que.
admonish [əd'mɔnɪʃ] *vt* amonestar (*advise*) aconsejar.
ad nauseam [æd'nɔːsɪæm] *adv* hasta la saciedad.
ado [ə'duː] *n*: **without (any) more** ~ sin más (ni más).
adolescence [ædəu'lɛsns] *n* adolescencia.
adolescent [ædəu'lɛsnt] *adj, n* adolescente *m/f*.
adopt [ə'dɔpt] *vt* adoptar.
adopted [ə'dɔptɪd] *adj* adoptivo.
adoption [ə'dɔpʃən] *n* adopción *f*.
adoptive [ə'dɔptɪv] *adj* adoptivo.
adorable [ə'dɔːrəbl] *adj* adorable.
adoration [ædə'reɪʃən] *n* adoración *f*.
adore [ə'dɔː*] *vt* adorar.
adoring [ə'dɔːrɪŋ] *adj*: **to his ~ public** a un público que le adora *or* le adoraba *etc*.
adorn [ə'dɔːn] *vt* adornar.
adornment [ə'dɔːnmənt] *n* adorno.
adrenalin [ə'drɛnəlɪn] *n* adrenalina.
Adriatic [eɪdrɪ'ætɪk] *n*: **the ~ (Sea)** el (Mar) Adriático.

adrift [ə'drɪft] *adv* a la deriva; **to come** ~ (*boat*) ir a la deriva, soltarse; (*wire, rope etc*) soltarse.
adroit [ə'drɔɪt] *adj* diestro, hábil.
ADT *abbr* (*US*: = *Atlantic Daylight Time*) hora de verano de Nueva York.
adulation [ædju'leɪʃən] *n* adulación *f*.
adult ['ædʌlt] *n* adulto/a ♦ *adj*: ~ **education** educación *f* para adultos.
adulterate [ə'dʌltəreɪt] *vt* adulterar.
adulterer [ə'dʌltərə*] *n* adúltero.
adulteress [ə'dʌltrɪs] *n* adúltera.
adultery [ə'dʌltərɪ] *n* adulterio.
adulthood ['ædʌlthud] *n* edad *f* adulta.
advance [əd'vɑːns] *n* adelanto, progreso; (*money*) anticipo; (*MIL*) avance *m* ♦ *vt* avanzar, adelantar; (*money*) anticipar ♦ *vi* avanzar, adelantarse; **in** ~ por adelantado; (*book*) con antelación; **to make ~s to sb** (*gen*) ponerse en contacto con algn; (*amorously*) insinuarse a algn.
advanced *adj* avanzado; (*SCOL: studies*) adelantado; ~ **in years** entrado en años.
Advanced Higher *n* (*SCOT SCOL*) titulación que sigue al "*Higher*", ≈ Bachillerato.
advancement [əd'vɑːnsmənt] *n* progreso; (*in rank*) ascenso.
advance notice *n* previo aviso.
advance payment *n* (*part sum*) anticipo.
advantage [əd'vɑːntɪdʒ] *n* (*also TENNIS*) ventaja; **to take ~ of** aprovecharse de; **it's to our** ~ es ventajoso para nosotros.
advantageous [ædvən'teɪdʒəs] *adj* ventajoso, provechoso.
advent ['ædvənt] *n* advenimiento; **A~** Adviento.
adventure [əd'vɛntʃə*] *n* aventura.
adventure playground *n* parque *m* infantil.
adventurous [əd'vɛntʃərəs] *adj* aventurero; (*bold*) arriesgado.
adverb ['ædvəːb] *n* adverbio.
adversary ['ædvəsərɪ] *n* adversario, contrario.
adverse ['ædvəːs] *adj* adverso, contrario; ~ **to** adverso a.
adversity [əd'vəːsɪtɪ] *n* infortunio.
advert ['ædvəːt] *n abbr* (*BRIT*) = **advertisement**.
advertise ['ædvətaɪz] *vi* hacer propaganda; (*in newspaper etc*) poner un anuncio, anunciarse; **to ~ for** (*staff*) buscar por medio de anuncios ♦ *vt* anunciar.
advertisement [əd'vəːtɪsmənt] *n* anuncio.
advertiser ['ædvətaɪzə*] *n* anunciante *m/f*.
advertising ['ædvətaɪzɪŋ] *n* publicidad *f*, propaganda; anuncios *mpl*.
advertising agency *n* agencia de

publicidad.
advertising campaign *n* campaña de publicidad.
advice [əd'vaɪs] *n* consejo, consejos *mpl*; (*notification*) aviso; **a piece of** ~ un consejo; **to take legal** ~ consultar a un abogado; **to ask (sb) for** ~ pedir consejo (a algn).
advice note *n* (*BRIT*) nota de aviso.
advisable [əd'vaɪzəbl] *adj* aconsejable, conveniente.
advise [əd'vaɪz] *vt* aconsejar; **to** ~ **sb of sth** (*inform*) informar a algn de algo; **to** ~ **sb against sth/doing sth** desaconsejar algo a algn/aconsejar a algn que no haga algo; **you will be well/ill** ~**d to go** deberías/no deberías ir.
advisedly [əd'vaɪzɪdlɪ] *adv* deliberadamente.
adviser [əd'vaɪzə*] *n* consejero/a; (*business adviser*) asesor(a) *m/f*.
advisory [əd'vaɪzərɪ] *adj* consultivo; **in an** ~ **capacity** como asesor.
advocate ['ædvəkeɪt] *vt* (*argue for*) abogar por; (*give support to*) ser partidario de ♦ *n* ['ædvəkɪt] abogado/a.
AEA *n abbr* (*BRIT:* = *Atomic Energy Authority*) consejo de energía nuclear; (*BRIT SCOL:* = *Advanced Extension Award*) titulación opcional para los alumnos mejor preparados de los "*A levels*".
AEC *n abbr* (*US:* = *Atomic Energy Commission*) AEC *f*.
AEEU *n abbr* (*BRIT:* = *Amalgamated Engineering and Electrical Union*) sindicato mixto de ingenieros y electricistas.
Aegean [iː'dʒiːən] *n:* **the** ~ **(Sea)** el (Mar) Egeo.
aegis ['iːdʒɪs] *n:* **under the** ~ **of** bajo la tutela de.
aeon ['iːən] *n* eón *m*.
aerial ['ɛərɪəl] *n* antena ♦ *adj* aéreo.
aerie ['ɛərɪ] *n* (*US*) aguilera.
aero- ['ɛərəu] *pref* aero-.
aerobatics [ɛərəu'bætɪks] *npl* acrobacia aérea.
aerobics [ɛə'rəubɪks] *nsg* aerobic *m*, aerobismo (*LAM*).
aerodrome ['ɛərədrəum] *n* (*BRIT*) aeródromo.
aerodynamic [ɛərəudaɪ'næmɪk] *adj* aerodinámico.
aeronautics [ɛərəu'nɔːtɪks] *nsg* aeronáutica.
aeroplane ['ɛərəpleɪn] *n* (*BRIT*) avión *m*.
aerosol ['ɛərəsɔl] *n* aerosol *m*.
aerospace industry ['ɛərəuspeɪs-] *n* industria aerospacial.
aesthetic [iːs'θetɪk] *adj* estético.

aesthetics [iːs'θetɪks] *npl* estética.
afar [ə'fɑː*] *adv* lejos; **from** ~ desde lejos.
AFB *n abbr* (*US*) = *Air Force Base*.
AFDC *n abbr* (*US:* = *Aid to Families with Dependent Children*) ayuda a familias con hijos menores.
affable ['æfəbl] *adj* afable.
affair [ə'fɛə*] *n* asunto; (*also:* **love** ~) aventura *f* amorosa; ~**s** (*business*) asuntos *mpl*; **the Watergate** ~ el asunto (de) Watergate.
affect [ə'fɛkt] *vt* afectar, influir en; (*move*) conmover.
affectation [æfɛk'teɪʃən] *n* afectación *f*.
affected [ə'fɛktɪd] *adj* afectado.
affection [ə'fɛkʃən] *n* afecto, cariño.
affectionate [ə'fɛkʃənɪt] *adj* afectuoso, cariñoso.
affectionately [ə'fɛkʃənɪtlɪ] *adv* afectuosamente.
affidavit [æfɪ'deɪvɪt] *n* (*LAW*) declaración *f* jurada.
affiliated [ə'fɪlɪeɪtɪd] *adj* afiliado; ~ **company** empresa *or* compañía filial *or* subsidiaria.
affinity [ə'fɪnɪtɪ] *n* afinidad *f*.
affirm [ə'fəːm] *vt* afirmar.
affirmation [æfə'meɪʃən] *n* afirmación *f*.
affirmative [ə'fəːmətɪv] *adj* afirmativo.
affix [ə'fɪks] *vt* (*signature*) estampar; (*stamp*) pegar.
afflict [ə'flɪkt] *vt* afligir.
affliction [ə'flɪkʃən] *n* enfermedad *f*, aflicción *f*.
affluence ['æfluəns] *n* opulencia, riqueza.
affluent ['æfluənt] *adj* adinerado, acaudalado; **the** ~ **society** la sociedad opulenta.
afford [ə'fɔːd] *vt* poder permitirse; (*provide*) proporcionar; **can we** ~ **a car?** ¿podemos permitirnos el gasto de comprar un coche?
affordable [ə'fɔːdəbl] *adj* asequible.
affray [ə'freɪ] *n* refriega, reyerta.
affront [ə'frʌnt] *n* afrenta, ofensa.
affronted [ə'frʌntɪd] *adj* ofendido.
Afghan ['æfgæn] *adj*, *n* afgano/a *m/f*.
Afghanistan [æf'gænɪstæn] *n* Afganistán *m*.
afield [ə'fiːld] *adv:* **far** ~ muy lejos.
AFL-CIO *n abbr* (*US:* = *American Federation of Labor and Congress of Industrial Organizations*) confederación sindicalista.
afloat [ə'fləut] *adv* (*floating*) a flote; (*at sea*) en el mar.
afoot [ə'fut] *adv:* **there is something** ~ algo se está tramando.
aforesaid [ə'fɔːsɛd] *adj* susodicho; (*COMM*) mencionado anteriormente.

afraid [ə'freɪd] *adj*: **to be ~ of** (*person*) tener miedo a; (*thing*) tener miedo de; **to be ~ to** tener miedo de, temer; **I am ~ that we** temo que; **I'm ~ so** ¡me temo que sí!, ¡lo siento, pero es así!; **I'm ~ not** me temo que no.

afresh [ə'freʃ] *adv* de nuevo, otra vez.

Africa ['æfrɪkə] *n* África.

African ['æfrɪkən] *adj*, *n* africano/a *m/f*.

Afrikaans [æfrɪ'kɑːns] *n* africaans *m*.

Afrikaner [æfrɪ'kɑːnə*] *n* africánder *m/f*.

Afro-American ['æfrəuə'merɪkən] *adj*, *n* afroamericano/a *m/f*.

AFT *n abbr* (= *American Federation of Teachers*) *sindicato de profesores*.

aft [ɑːft] *adv* (*to be*) en popa; (*to go*) a popa.

after ['ɑːftə*] *prep* (*time*) después de; (*place, order*) detrás de, tras ♦ *adv* después ♦ *conj* después (de) que; **what/who are you ~?** ¿qué o quién buscas?; **the police are ~ him** la policía le está buscando; **~ having done/he left** después de haber hecho/ después de que se marchó; **~ dinner** después de cenar o comer; **the day ~ tomorrow** pasado mañana; **to ask ~ sb** preguntar por algn; **~ all** después de todo, al fin y al cabo; **~ you!** ¡Vd primero!; **quarter ~ two** (*US*) las 2 y cuarto.

afterbirth ['ɑːftəbəːθ] *n* placenta.

aftercare ['ɑːftəkeə*] *n* (*MED*) asistencia postoperatoria.

after-effects ['ɑːftərɪfekts] *npl* secuelas *fpl*, efectos *mpl*.

afterlife ['ɑːftəlaɪf] *n* vida después de la muerte.

aftermath ['ɑːftəmɑːθ] *n* consecuencias *fpl*, resultados *mpl*.

afternoon [ɑːftə'nuːn] *n* tarde *f*; **good ~!** ¡buenas tardes!

afters ['ɑːftəz] *n* (*col*: *dessert*) postre *m*.

after-sales service [ɑːftə'seɪlz-] *n* (*BRIT COMM*: *for car, washing machine etc*) servicio de asistencia pos-venta.

after-shave (lotion) ['ɑːftəʃeɪv-] *n* loción *f* para después del afeitado, aftershave *m*.

aftershock ['ɑːftəʃɔk] *n* (*of earthquake*) pequeño temblor *m* posterior.

aftertaste ['ɑːftəteɪst] *n* regusto.

afterthought ['ɑːftəθɔːt] *n* ocurrencia (tardía).

afterwards ['ɑːftəwədz] *adv* después, más tarde.

again [ə'gen] *adv* otra vez, de nuevo; **to do sth ~** volver a hacer algo; **~ and ~** una y otra vez; **now and ~** de vez en cuando.

against [ə'genst] *prep* (*opposed*) en contra de; (*close to*) contra, junto a; **I was leaning ~ the desk** estaba apoyado en el escritorio; **(as) ~** frente a.

age [eɪdʒ] *n* edad *f*; (*old ~*) vejez *f*; (*period*) época ♦ *vi* envejecer(se) ♦ *vt* envejecer; **what ~ is he?** ¿qué edad o cuántos años tiene?; **he is 20 years of ~** tiene 20 años; **under ~** menor de edad; **to come of ~** llegar a la mayoría de edad; **it's been ~s since I saw you** hace siglos que no te veo.

aged [eɪdʒd] *adj*: **~ 10** de 10 años de edad ♦ *npl* ['eɪdʒɪd]: **the ~** los ancianos.

age group *n*: **to be in the same ~** tener la misma edad; **the 40 to 50 ~** las personas de 40 a 50 años.

ageing ['eɪdʒɪŋ] *adj* que envejece; (*pej*) en declive ♦ *n* envejecimiento.

ageless ['eɪdʒlɪs] *adj* (*eternal*) eterno; (*ever young*) siempre joven.

age limit *n* límite *m* de edad, edad *f* tope.

agency ['eɪdʒənsɪ] *n* agencia; **through o by the ~ of** por medio de.

agenda [ə'dʒendə] *n* orden *m* del día; **on the ~** (*COMM*) en el orden del día.

agent ['eɪdʒənt] *n* (*gen*) agente *m/f*; (*representative*) representante *m/f*, delegado/a.

aggravate ['ægrəveɪt] *vt* agravar; (*annoy*) irritar, exasperar.

aggravating ['ægrəveɪtɪŋ] *adj* irritante, molesto.

aggravation [ægrə'veɪʃən] *n* agravamiento.

aggregate ['ægrɪgeɪt] *n* conjunto.

aggression [ə'greʃən] *n* agresión *f*.

aggressive [ə'gresɪv] *adj* agresivo; (*vigorous*) enérgico.

aggressiveness [ə'gresɪvnɪs] *n* agresividad *f*.

aggressor [ə'gresə*] *n* agresor(a) *m/f*.

aggrieved [ə'griːvd] *adj* ofendido, agraviado.

aggro ['ægrəu] *n* (*col*) (*physical violence*) bronca; (*bad feeling*) mal rollo; (*hassle*) rollo, movida.

aghast [ə'gɑːst] *adj* horrorizado.

agile ['ædʒaɪl] *adj* ágil.

agility [ə'dʒɪlɪtɪ] *n* agilidad *f*.

agitate ['ædʒɪteɪt] *vt* (*shake*) agitar; (*trouble*) inquietar; **to ~ for** hacer campaña en pro de o en favor de.

agitated ['ædʒɪteɪtɪd] *adj* agitado.

agitator ['ædʒɪteɪtə*] *n* agitador(a) *m/f*.

AGM *n abbr see* **annual general meeting**.

agnostic [æg'nɔstɪk] *adj*, *n* agnóstico/a *m/f*.

ago [ə'gəu] *adv*: **2 days ~** hace 2 días; **not long ~** hace poco; **how long ~?** ¿hace cuánto tiempo?; **as long ~ as 1960** ya en 1960.

agog [ə'gɔg] *adj* (*anxious*) ansioso; (*excited*):

(all) ~ **(for)** (todo) emocionado (por).
agonize ['ægənaɪz] *vi:* **to** ~ **(over)** atormentarse (por).
agonized ['ægənaɪzd] *adj* angustioso.
agonizing ['ægənaɪzɪŋ] *adj* (*pain*) atroz; (*suspense*) angustioso.
agony ['ægənɪ] *n* (*pain*) dolor *m* atroz; (*distress*) angustia; **to be in** ~ retorcerse de dolor.
agony aunt *n* (*BRIT col*) consejera sentimental.
agony column *n* consultorio sentimental.
agree [ə'griː] *vt* (*price*) acordar, quedar en ♦ *vi* (*statements etc*) coincidir, concordar; **to** ~ **(with)** (*person*) estar de acuerdo (con), ponerse de acuerdo (con); **to** ~ **to do** aceptar hacer; **to** ~ **to sth** consentir en algo; **to** ~ **that** (*admit*) estar de acuerdo en que; **it was** ~**d that** ... se acordó que ...; **garlic doesn't** ~ **with me** el ajo no me sienta bien.
agreeable [ə'griːəbl] *adj* agradable; (*person*) simpático; (*willing*) de acuerdo, conforme.
agreeably [ə'griːəblɪ] *adv* agradablemente.
agreed [ə'griːd] *adj* (*time, place*) convenido.
agreement [ə'griːmənt] *n* acuerdo; (*COMM*) contrato; **in** ~ de acuerdo, conforme; **by mutual** ~ de común acuerdo.
agricultural [ægrɪ'kʌltʃərəl] *adj* agrícola.
agriculture ['ægrɪkʌltʃə*] *n* agricultura.
aground [ə'graund] *adv:* **to run** ~ encallar, embarrancar.
ahead [ə'hɛd] *adv* delante; ~ **of** delante de; (*fig: schedule etc*) antes de; ~ **of time** antes de la hora; **to be** ~ **of sb** (*fig*) llevar ventaja *or* la delantera a algn; **go right** *or* **straight** ~ siga adelante; **they were (right)** ~ **of us** iban (justo) delante de nosotros.
ahoy [ə'hɔɪ] *excl* ¡oiga!
AI *n abbr* = *Amnesty International*; (*COMPUT*) = **artificial intelligence**.
AIB *n abbr* (*BRIT*: = *Accident Investigation Bureau*) oficina de investigación de accidentes.
AID *n abbr* (= *artificial insemination by donor*) inseminación artificial por donante; (*US*: = *Agency for International Development*) Agencia Internacional para el Desarrollo.
aid [eɪd] *n* ayuda, auxilio ♦ *vt* ayudar, auxiliar; **in** ~ **of** a beneficio de; **with the** ~ **of** con la ayuda de; **to** ~ **and abet** (*LAW*) ser cómplice.
aide [eɪd] *n* (*POL*) ayudante *m/f*.
AIDS [eɪdz] *n abbr* (= *acquired immune* (*or* *immuno-*)*deficiency syndrome*) SIDA *m*, sida *m*.

AIH *abbr* (= *artificial insemination by husband*) inseminación artificial por esposo.
ailing ['eɪlɪŋ] *adj* (*person, economy*) enfermizo.
ailment ['eɪlmənt] *n* enfermedad *f*, achaque *m*.
aim [eɪm] *vt* (*gun*) apuntar; (*missile, remark*) dirigir; (*blow*) asestar ♦ *vi* (*also:* **take** ~) apuntar ♦ *n* puntería; (*objective*) propósito, meta; **to** ~ **at** (*objective*) aspirar a, pretender; **to** ~ **to do** tener como objetivo hacer, aspirar a hacer.
aimless ['eɪmlɪs] *adj* sin propósito, sin objeto.
aimlessly ['eɪmlɪslɪ] *adv* sin rumbo fijo.
ain't [eɪnt] (*col*) = **am not**; **aren't**; **isn't**.
air [ɛə*] *n* aire *m*; (*appearance*) aspecto ♦ *vt* (*room*) ventilar; (*clothes, bed, grievances, ideas*) airear; (*views*) hacer público ♦ *cpd* aéreo; **to throw sth into the** ~ (*ball etc*) lanzar algo al aire; **by** ~ (*travel*) en avión; **to be on the** ~ (*RADIO, TV: programme*) estarse emitiendo; (*: station*) estar emitiendo.
airbag ['ɛəbæg] *n* airbag *m inv*.
air base *n* (*MIL*) base *f* aérea.
air bed *n* (*BRIT*) colcheta inflable *or* neumática.
airborne ['ɛəbɔːn] *adj* (*in the air*) en el aire; (*MIL*) aerotransportado; **as soon as the plane was** ~ tan pronto como el avión estuvo en el aire.
air cargo *n* carga aérea.
air-conditioned ['ɛəkən'dɪʃənd] *adj* climatizado.
air conditioning [-kən'dɪʃənɪŋ] *n* aire *m* acondicionado.
air-cooled ['ɛəkuːld] *adj* refrigerado por aire.
aircraft ['ɛəkrɑːft] *n*, *pl inv* avión *m*.
aircraft carrier *n* porta(a)viones *m inv*.
air cushion *n* cojín *m* de aire; (*AVIAT*) colchón *m* de aire.
airdrome ['ɛədrəum] *n* (*US*) aeródromo.
airfield ['ɛəfiːld] *n* campo de aviación.
Air Force *n* fuerzas aéreas *fpl*, aviación *f*.
air freight *n* flete *m* por avión.
air freshener *n* ambientador *m*.
air gun *n* escopeta de aire comprimido.
air hostess (*BRIT*) *n* azafata, aeromoza (*LAM*).
airily ['ɛərɪlɪ] *adv* muy a la ligera.
airing ['ɛərɪŋ] *n:* **to give an** ~ **to** (*linen*) airear; (*room*) ventilar; (*fig: ideas etc*) airear, someter a discusión.
air letter *n* (*BRIT*) carta aérea.
airlift ['ɛəlɪft] *n* puente *m* aéreo.

airline ['ɛəlaɪn] n línea aérea.
airliner ['ɛəlaɪnə*] n avión m de pasajeros.
airlock ['ɛəlɔk] n (in pipe) esclusa de aire.
airmail ['ɛəmeɪl] n: **by** ~ por avión.
air mattress n colchón m inflable.
airplane ['ɛəpleɪn] n (US) avión m.
air pocket n bolsa de aire.
airport ['ɛəpɔːt] n aeropuerto.
air rage n conducta agresiva de pasajeros a bordo de un avión.
air raid n ataque m aéreo.
air rifle n escopeta de aire comprimido.
airsick ['ɛəsɪk] adj: **to be** ~ marearse (en avión).
airspeed ['ɛəspiːd] n velocidad f de vuelo.
airstrip ['ɛəstrɪp] n pista de aterrizaje.
air terminal n terminal f.
airtight ['ɛətaɪt] adj hermético.
air time n (RADIO, TV) tiempo en antena.
air traffic control n control m de tráfico aéreo.
air traffic controller n controlador(a) m/f aéreo/a.
airway ['ɛəweɪ] n (AVIAT) vía aérea; (ANAT) vía respiratoria.
airy ['ɛərɪ] adj (room) bien ventilado; (manners) despreocupado.
aisle [aɪl] n (of church) nave f lateral; (of theatre, plane) pasillo.
ajar [ə'dʒɑː*] adj entreabierto.
AK abbr (US) = Alaska.
aka abbr (= also known as) alias.
akin [ə'kɪn] adj: ~ **to** semejante a.
AL abbr (US) = Alabama.
Ala. abbr (US) = Alabama.
alabaster ['æləbɑːstə*] n alabastro.
à la carte [ælæ'kɑːt] adv a la carta.
alacrity [ə'lækrɪtɪ] n: **with** ~ con la mayor prontitud.
alarm [ə'lɑːm] n alarma; (anxiety) inquietud f ♦ vt asustar, alarmar.
alarm clock n despertador m.
alarmed [ə'lɑːmd] adj (person) alarmado, asustado; (house, car etc) con alarma.
alarming [ə'lɑːmɪŋ] adj alarmante.
alarmingly [ə'lɑːmɪŋlɪ] adv de forma alarmante; ~ **quickly** a una velocidad alarmante.
alarmist [ə'lɑːmɪst] n alarmista m/f.
alas [ə'læs] adv desgraciadamente ♦ excl ¡ay!
Alas. abbr (US) = Alaska.
Alaska [ə'læskə] n Alaska.
Albania [æl'beɪnɪə] n Albania.
Albanian [æl'beɪnɪən] adj albanés/esa ♦ n albanés/esa m/f; (LING) albanés m.
albatross ['ælbətrɔs] n albatros m.
albeit [ɔːl'biːɪt] conj (although) aunque.

album ['ælbəm] n álbum m; (L.P.) elepé m.
albumen ['ælbjumɪn] n albúmina f.
alchemy ['ælkɪmɪ] n alquimia.
alcohol ['ælkəhɔl] n alcohol m.
alcohol-free adj sin alcohol.
alcoholic [ælkə'hɔlɪk] adj, n alcohólico/a m/f.
alcoholism ['ælkəhɔlɪzəm] n alcoholismo.
alcove ['ælkəuv] n nicho, hueco.
Ald. abbr = **alderman**.
alderman ['ɔːldəmən] n concejal m.
ale [eɪl] n cerveza.
alert [ə'lɜːt] adj alerta inv; (sharp) despierto, despabilado ♦ n alerta m, alarma ♦ vt poner sobre aviso; **to** ~ **sb (to sth)** poner sobre aviso or alertar a algn (de algo); **to** ~ **sb to the dangers of sth** poner sobre aviso or alertar a algn de los peligros de algo; **to be on the** ~ estar alerta or sobre aviso.
alertness [ə'lɜːtnɪs] n vigilancia.
Aleutian Islands [ə'luːʃən-] npl Islas fpl Aleutianas.
A level n (BRIT SCOL) ≈ Bachillerato.
Alexandria [ælɪg'zɑːndrɪə] n Alejandría.
alfresco [æl'frɛskəu] adj, adv al aire libre.
algebra ['ældʒɪbrə] n álgebra.
Algeria [æl'dʒɪərɪə] n Argelia.
Algerian [æl'dʒɪərɪən] adj, n argelino/a m/f.
Algiers [æl'dʒɪəz] n Argel m.
algorithm ['ælgərɪðəm] n algoritmo.
alias ['eɪlɪəs] adv alias, conocido por ♦ n alias m.
alibi ['ælɪbaɪ] n coartada.
alien ['eɪlɪən] n (foreigner) extranjero/a ♦ adj: ~ **to** ajeno a.
alienate ['eɪlɪəneɪt] vt enajenar, alejar.
alienation [eɪlɪə'neɪʃən] n alejamiento m.
alight [ə'laɪt] adj ardiendo ♦ vi apearse.
align [ə'laɪn] vt alinear.
alignment [ə'laɪnmənt] n alineación f; **the desks are out of** ~ los pupitres no están bien alineados.
alike [ə'laɪk] adj semejantes, iguales ♦ adv igualmente, del mismo modo; **to look** ~ parecerse.
alimony ['ælɪmənɪ] n (LAW) pensión f alimenticia.
alive [ə'laɪv] adj (gen) vivo; (lively) activo.
alkali ['ælkəlaɪ] n álcali m.

═══════════════════ KEYWORD

all [ɔːl] adj (sg) todo/a; (pl) todos/as; ~ **day** todo el día; ~ **night** toda la noche; ~ **men** todos los hombres; ~ **five came** vinieron los cinco; ~ **the books** todos los libros; ~ **the time/his life** todo el tiempo/toda su vida; **for** ~ **their efforts** a pesar de todos sus esfuerzos

♦ *pron* **1** todo; **I ate it ~, I ate ~ of it** me lo comí todo; **~ of them** todos (ellos); **~ of us went** fuimos todos; **~ the boys went** fueron todos los chicos; **is that ~?** ¿eso es todo?, ¿algo más?; (*in shop*) ¿algo más?, ¿alguna cosa más?
2 (*in phrases*): **above ~** sobre todo; **after ~** después de todo; **at ~: anything at ~** lo que sea; **not at ~** (*in answer to question*) en absoluto; (*in answer to thanks*) ¡de nada!, ¡no hay de qué!; **I'm not at ~ tired** no estoy nada cansado/a; **anything at ~ will do** cualquier cosa viene bien; **~ in** ~ a fin de cuentas
♦ *adv*: **~ alone** completamente solo/a; **to be/feel ~ in** estar rendido; **it's not as hard as ~ that** no es tan difícil como lo pintas; **~ the more/the better** tanto más/mejor; **~ but** casi; **the score is 2 ~** están empatados a 2.

all-around [ˈɔːləˈraund] *adj* (*US*) = **all-round**.
allay [əˈleɪ] *vt* (*fears*) aquietar; (*pain*) aliviar.
all clear *n* (*after attack etc*) fin *m* de la alerta; (*fig*) luz *f* verde.
allegation [ælɪˈgeɪʃən] *n* alegato.
allege [əˈlɛdʒ] *vt* pretender; **he is ~d to have said** ... se afirma que él dijo ....
alleged [əˈlɛdʒd] *adj* supuesto, presunto.
allegedly [əˈlɛdʒɪdlɪ] *adv* supuestamente, según se afirma.
allegiance [əˈliːdʒəns] *n* lealtad *f.*
allegory [ˈælɪgərɪ] *n* alegoría.
all-embracing [ˈɔːləmˈbreɪsɪŋ] *adj* universal.
allergic [əˈlɜːdʒɪk] *adj*: **~ to** alérgico a.
allergy [ˈælədʒɪ] *n* alergia.
alleviate [əˈliːvɪeɪt] *vt* aliviar.
alleviation [əliːvɪˈeɪʃən] *n* alivio.
alley [ˈælɪ] *n* (*street*) callejuela; (*in garden*) paseo.
alleyway [ˈælɪweɪ] *n* callejón *m.*
alliance [əˈlaɪəns] *n* alianza.
allied [ˈælaɪd] *adj* aliado; (*related*) relacionado.
alligator [ˈælɪgeɪtə*] *n* caimán *m.*
all-important [ˈɔːlɪmˈpɔːtənt] *adj* de suma importancia.
all-in [ˈɔːlɪn] *adj* (*BRIT*) (*also adv: charge*) todo incluido.
all-in wrestling *n* lucha libre.
alliteration [əlɪtəˈreɪʃən] *n* aliteración *f.*
all-night [ˈɔːlnaɪt] *adj* (*café*) abierto toda la noche; (*party*) que dura toda la noche.
allocate [ˈæləkeɪt] *vt* (*share out*) repartir; (*devote*) asignar.
allocation [æləˈkeɪʃən] *n* (*of money*) ración

f, cuota; (*distribution*) reparto.
allot [əˈlɒt] *vt* asignar; **in the ~ted time** en el tiempo asignado.
allotment [əˈlɒtmənt] *n* porción *f*; (*garden*) parcela.
all-out [ˈɔːlaut] *adj* (*effort etc*) supremo ♦ *adv*: **all out** con todas las fuerzas, a fondo.
allow [əˈlau] *vt* (*permit*) permitir, dejar; (*a claim*) admitir; (*sum to spend, time estimated*) dar, conceder; (*concede*): **to ~ that** reconocer que; **to ~ sb to do** permitir a alguien hacer; **smoking is not ~ed** prohibido *or* se prohíbe fumar; **he is ~ed to ...** se le permite ...; **we must ~ 3 days for the journey** debemos dejar 3 días para el viaje.
▶**allow for** *vt fus* tener en cuenta.
allowance [əˈlauəns] *n* concesión *f*; (*payment*) subvención *f*, pensión *f*; (*discount*) descuento, rebaja; **to make ~s for** (*person*) disculpar a; (*thing: take into account*) tener en cuenta.
alloy [ˈælɔɪ] *n* aleación *f.*
all right *adv* (*feel, work*) bien; (*as answer*) ¡de acuerdo!, ¡está bien!
all-round [ˈɔːlˈraund] *adj* completo; (*view*) amplio.
all-rounder [ˈɔːlˈraundə*] *n*: **to be a good ~** ser una persona que hace de todo.
allspice [ˈɔːlspaɪs] *n* pimienta inglesa *or* de Jamaica.
all-time [ˈɔːlˈtaɪm] *adj* (*record*) de todos los tiempos.
allude [əˈluːd] *vi*: **to ~ to** aludir a.
alluring [əˈljuərɪŋ] *adj* seductor(a), atractivo.
allusion [əˈluːʒən] *n* referencia, alusión *f.*
ally *n* [ˈælaɪ] aliado/a ♦ *vt* [əˈlaɪ]: **to ~ o.s. with** aliarse con.
almanac [ˈɔːlmənæk] *n* almanaque *m.*
almighty [ɔːlˈmaɪtɪ] *adj* todopoderoso.
almond [ˈɑːmənd] *n* (*fruit*) almendra; (*tree*) almendro.
almost [ˈɔːlməust] *adv* casi; **he ~ fell** casi *or* por poco se cae.
alms [ɑːmz] *npl* limosna *sg.*
aloft [əˈlɒft] *adv* arriba.
alone [əˈləun] *adj* solo ♦ *adv* sólo, solamente; **to leave sb ~** dejar a algn en paz; **to leave sth ~** no tocar algo; **let ~ ...** y mucho menos, y no digamos ...
along [əˈlɒŋ] *prep* a lo largo de, por ♦ *adv*: **is he coming ~ with us?** ¿viene con nosotros?; **he was limping ~** iba cojeando; **~ with** junto con; **all ~** (*all the time*) desde el principio.
alongside [əˈlɒŋˈsaɪd] *prep* al lado de ♦ *adv* (*NAUT*) de costado; **we brought our boat**

~ atracamos nuestro barco.
aloof [ə'luːf] *adj* distante ♦ *adv*: **to stand ~** mantenerse a distancia.
aloud [ə'laud] *adv* en voz alta.
alphabet ['ælfəbet] *n* alfabeto.
alphabetical [ælfə'betɪkəl] *adj* alfabético; **in ~ order** por orden alfabético.
alphanumeric [ælfənjuː'merɪk] *adj* alfanumérico.
alpine ['ælpaɪn] *adj* alpino, alpestre.
Alps [ælps] *npl*: **the ~** los Alpes.
already [ɔːl'redɪ] *adv* ya.
alright ['ɔːl'raɪt] *adv* (*BRIT*) = **all right**.
Alsatian [æl'seɪʃən] *n* (*dog*) pastor *m* alemán.
also ['ɔːlsəu] *adv* también, además.
Alta. *abbr* (*Canada*) = *Alberta*.
altar ['ɔːltə*] *n* altar *m*.
alter ['ɔːltə*] *vt* cambiar, modificar ♦ *vi* cambiarse, modificarse.
alteration [ɔːltə'reɪʃən] *n* cambio, modificación *f*; **~s** *npl* (*ARCH*) reformas *fpl*; (*SEWING*) arreglos *mpl*; **timetable subject to ~** el horario puede cambiar.
altercation [ɔːltə'keɪʃən] *n* altercado.
alternate [ɔl'tɜːnɪt] *adj* alterno ♦ *vi* ['ɔltəneɪt]: **to ~ (with)** alternar (con); **on ~ days** en días alternos.
alternately [ɔl'tɜːnɪtlɪ] *adv* alternativamente, por turno.
alternating ['ɔltəneɪtɪŋ] *adj* (*current*) alterno.
alternative [ɔl'tɜːnətɪv] *adj* alternativo ♦ *n* alternativa.
alternatively [ɔl'tɜːnətɪvlɪ] *adv*: **~ one could ...** por otra parte se podría....
alternative medicine *n* medicina alternativa.
alternator ['ɔltəneɪtə*] *n* (*AUT*) alternador *m*.
although [ɔːl'ðəu] *conj* aunque, si bien.
altitude ['æltɪtjuːd] *n* altitud *f*, altura.
altitude sickness *n* mal *m* de altura, soroche *m* (*LAM*).
alto ['æltəu] *n* (*female*) contralto *f*; (*male*) alto.
altogether [ɔːltə'geðə*] *adv* completamente, del todo; (*on the whole, in all*) en total, en conjunto; **how much is that ~?** ¿cuánto es todo *or* en total?
altruism ['æltruɪzəm] *n* altruismo.
altruistic [æltru'ɪstɪk] *adj* altruista.
aluminium [ælju'mɪnɪəm], (*US*) **aluminum** [ə'luːmɪnəm] *n* aluminio.
always ['ɔːlweɪz] *adv* siempre.
Alzheimer's ['æltshaɪməz] (*also*: **~ disease**) enfermedad *f* de Alzheimer.
AM *abbr* (= *amplitude modulation*) A.M. *f*;

(*POL*) = **Assembly Member**.
am [æm] *vb see* **be**.
a.m. *adv abbr* (= *ante meridiem*) de la mañana.
AMA *n abbr* = *American Medical Association*.
amalgam [ə'mælgəm] *n* amalgama.
amalgamate [ə'mælgəmeɪt] *vi* amalgamarse ♦ *vt* amalgamar.
amalgamation [əmælgə'meɪʃən] *n* (*COMM*) fusión *f*.
amass [ə'mæs] *vt* amontonar, acumular.
amateur ['æmətə*] *n* aficionado/a, amateur *m/f*; **~ dramatics** dramas *mpl* presentados por aficionados.
amateurish ['æmətərɪʃ] *adj* (*pej*) torpe, inexperto.
amaze [ə'meɪz] *vt* asombrar, pasmar; **to be ~d (at)** asombrarse (de).
amazement [ə'meɪzmənt] *n* asombro, sorpresa; **to my ~** para mi sorpresa.
amazing [ə'meɪzɪŋ] *adj* extraordinario, asombroso; (*bargain, offer*) increíble.
amazingly [ə'meɪzɪŋlɪ] *adv* extraordinariamente.
Amazon ['æməzən] *n* (*GEO*) Amazonas *m*; (*MYTHOLOGY*) amazona ♦ *cpd*: **the ~ basin/jungle** la cuenca/selva del Amazonas.
Amazonian [æmə'zəunɪən] *adj* amazónico.
ambassador [æm'bæsədə*] *n* embajador(a) *m/f*.
amber ['æmbə*] *n* ámbar *m*; **at ~** (*BRIT AUT*) en amarillo.
ambidextrous [æmbɪ'dekstrəs] *adj* ambidextro.
ambience ['æmbɪəns] *n* ambiente *m*.
ambiguity [æmbɪ'gjuɪtɪ] *n* ambigüedad *f*; (*of meaning*) doble sentido *m*.
ambiguous [æm'bɪgjuəs] *adj* ambiguo.
ambition [æm'bɪʃən] *n* ambición *f*; **to achieve one's ~** realizar su ambición.
ambitious [æm'bɪʃəs] *adj* ambicioso; (*plan*) grandioso.
ambivalent [æm'bɪvələnt] *adj* ambivalente; (*pej*) equívoco.
amble ['æmbl] *vi* (*gen*: **~ along**) deambular, andar sin prisa.
ambulance ['æmbjuləns] *n* ambulancia.
ambulanceman/woman ['æmbjulənsmən/ wumən] *n* ambulanciero/a.
ambush ['æmbuʃ] *n* emboscada ♦ *vt* tender una emboscada a; (*fig*) coger (*SP*) *or* agarrar (*LAM*) por sorpresa.
ameba [ə'miːbə] *n* (*US*) = **amoeba**.
ameliorate [ə'miːlɪəreɪt] *vt* mejorar.
amelioration [əmiːlɪə'reɪʃən] *n* mejora.
amen [ɑː'men] *excl* amén.
amenable [ə'miːnəbl] *adj*: **~ to** (*advice etc*)

sensible a.

amend [ə'mɛnd] vt (*law, text*) enmendar; **to make ~s** (*apologize*) enmendarlo, dar cumplida satisfacción.

amendment [ə'mɛndmənt] n enmienda.

amenities [ə'miːnɪtɪz] npl comodidades *fpl*.

amenity [ə'miːnɪtɪ] n servicio.

America [ə'mɛrɪkə] n América (del Norte).

American [ə'mɛrɪkən] adj, n (norte)americano/a *m/f*, estadounidense *m/f*.

Americanism [ə'mɛrɪkənɪzəm] n americanismo.

americanize [ə'mɛrɪkənaɪz] vt americanizar.

Amerindian [æmər'ɪndɪən] adj, n amerindio/a.

amethyst ['æmɪθɪst] n amatista.

Amex ['æmɛks] n abbr = *American Stock Exchange*.

amiable ['eɪmɪəbl] adj (*kind*) amable, simpático.

amicable ['æmɪkəbl] adj amistoso, amigable.

amicably ['æmɪkəblɪ] adv amigablemente, amistosamente; **to part ~** separarse amistosamente.

amid(st) [ə'mɪd(st)] prep entre, en medio de.

amiss [ə'mɪs] adv: **to take sth ~** tomar algo a mal; **there's something ~** pasa algo.

ammo ['æməʊ] n abbr (*col*) = **ammunition**.

ammonia [ə'məʊnɪə] n amoníaco.

ammunition [æmju'nɪʃən] n municiones *fpl*; (*fig*) argumentos *mpl*.

ammunition dump n depósito de municiones.

amnesia [æm'niːzɪə] n amnesia.

amnesty ['æmnɪstɪ] n amnistía; **to grant an ~ to** amnistiar (a); **A~ International** Amnistía Internacional.

amoeba, (*US*) **ameba** [ə'miːbə] n amiba.

amok [ə'mɔk] adv: **to run ~** enloquecerse, desbocarse.

among(st) [ə'mʌŋ(st)] prep entre, en medio de.

amoral [æ'mɔrəl] adj amoral.

amorous ['æmərəs] adj cariñoso.

amorphous [ə'mɔːfəs] adj amorfo.

amortization [əmɔːtaɪ'zeɪʃən] n amortización *f*.

amount [ə'maʊnt] n (*gen*) cantidad *f*; (*of bill etc*) suma, importe *m* ♦ vi: **to ~ to** (*total*) sumar; (*be same as*) equivaler a, significar; **this ~s to a refusal** esto equivale a una negativa; **the total ~** (*of money*) la suma total.

amp(ère) ['æmp(ɛə*)] n amperio; **a 13 amp**

plug un enchufe de 13 amperios.

ampersand ['æmpəsænd] n signo &, "y" comercial.

amphetamine [æm'fɛtəmiːn] n anfetamina.

amphibian [æm'fɪbɪən] n anfibio.

amphibious [æm'fɪbɪəs] adj anfibio.

amphitheatre, (*US*) **amphitheater** ['æmfɪθɪətə*] n anfiteatro.

ample ['æmpl] adj (*spacious*) amplio; (*abundant*) abundante; **to have ~ time** tener tiempo de sobra.

amplifier ['æmplɪfaɪə*] n amplificador *m*.

amplify ['æmplɪfaɪ] vt amplificar, aumentar; (*explain*) explicar.

amply ['æmplɪ] adv ampliamente.

ampoule, (*US*) **ampule** ['æmpuːl] n (*MED*) ampolla.

amputate ['æmpjuteɪt] vt amputar.

amputee [æmpju'tiː] n persona que ha sufrido una amputación.

Amsterdam ['æmstədæm] n Amsterdam *m*.

amt abbr = **amount**.

amuck [ə'mʌk] adv = **amok**.

amuse [ə'mjuːz] vt divertir; (*distract*) distraer, entretener; **to ~ o.s. with sth/ by doing sth** distraerse con algo/ haciendo algo; **he was ~d at the joke** le divirtió el chiste.

amusement [ə'mjuːzmənt] n diversión *f*; (*pastime*) pasatiempo; (*laughter*) risa; **much to my ~** con gran regocijo mío.

amusement arcade n salón *m* de juegos.

amusement park n parque *m* de atracciones.

amusing [ə'mjuːzɪŋ] adj divertido.

an [æn, ən, n] indef art see **a**.

ANA n abbr = *American Newspaper Association; American Nurses Association*.

anachronism [ə'nækrənɪzəm] n anacronismo.

anaemia [ə'niːmɪə] n anemia.

anaemic [ə'niːmɪk] adj anémico; (*fig*) flojo.

anaesthetic [ænɪs'θɛtɪk] n anestesia; **local/ general ~** anestesia local/general.

anaesthetist [æ'niːsθɪtɪst] n anestesista *m/f*.

anagram ['ænəgræm] n anagrama *m*.

anal ['eɪnl] adj anal.

analgesic [ænæl'dʒiːsɪk] adj, n analgésico.

analogous [ə'næləgəs] adj: **~ to** or **with** análogo a.

analog(ue) ['ænəlɔg] adj (*computer, watch*) analógico.

analogy [ə'nælədʒɪ] n analogía; **to draw an ~ between** señalar la analogía entre.

analyse ['ænəlaɪz] vt (*BRIT*) analizar.

analysis, pl **analyses** [ə'næləsɪs, -siːz] n análisis *m inv*.

analyst ['ænəlɪst] n (*political ~*) analista *m/f*,

(*psycho~*) psicoanalista *m/f*.

analytic(al) [ænə'lɪtɪk(əl)] *adj* analítico.

analyze ['ænəlaɪz] *vt* (*US*) = **analyse**.

anarchic [æ'nɑːkɪk] *adj* anárquico.

anarchist ['ænəkɪst] *adj*, *n* anarquista *m/f*.

anarchy ['ænəkɪ] *n* anarquía, desorden *m*.

anathema [ə'næθɪmə] *n*: **that is ~ to him** eso es pecado para él.

anatomical [ænə'tɔmɪkəl] *adj* anatómico.

anatomy [ə'nætəmɪ] *n* anatomía.

ANC *n abbr* = *African National Congress*.

ancestor ['ænsɪstə*] *n* antepasado.

ancestral [æn'sɛstrəl] *adj* ancestral.

ancestry ['ænsɪstrɪ] *n* ascendencia, abolengo.

anchor ['æŋkə*] *n* ancla, áncora ♦ *vi* (*also*: **to drop ~**) anclar, echar el ancla ♦ *vt* (*fig*) sujetar, afianzar; **to weigh ~** levar anclas.

anchorage ['æŋkərɪdʒ] *n* ancladero.

anchor man, anchor woman *n* (*RADIO, TV*) presentador(a) *m/f*.

anchovy ['æntʃəvɪ] *n* anchoa.

ancient ['eɪnʃənt] *adj* antiguo; **~ monument** monumento histórico.

ancillary [æn'sɪlərɪ] *adj* (*worker, staff*) auxiliar.

and [ænd] *conj* y; (*before i, hi*) e; **~ so on** etcétera; **try ~ come** procure *or* intente venir; **better ~ better** cada vez mejor.

Andalusia [ændə'luːzɪə] *n* Andalucía.

Andean ['ændɪən] *adj* andino/a; **~ high plateau** altiplanicie *f*, altiplano (*LAM*).

Andes ['ændiːz] *npl*: **the ~** los Andes.

anecdote ['ænɪkdəʊt] *n* anécdota.

anemia [ə'niːmɪə] *n* (*US*) = **anaemia**.

anemic [ə'niːmɪk] *adj* (*US*) = **anaemic**.

anemone [ə'nɛmənɪ] *n* (*BOT*) anémone *f*; **sea ~** anémona.

anesthetic [ænɪs'θɛtɪk] *adj*, *n* (*US*) = **anaesthetic**.

anesthetist [æ'niːsθɪtɪst] *n* (*US*) = **anaesthetist**.

anew [ə'njuː] *adv* de nuevo, otra vez.

angel ['eɪndʒəl] *n* ángel *m*.

angel dust *n* polvo de ángel.

angelic [æn'dʒɛlɪk] *adj* angélico.

anger ['æŋgə*] *n* ira, cólera, enojo (*LAM*) ♦ *vt* enojar, enfurecer.

angina [æn'dʒaɪnə] *n* angina (del pecho).

angle ['æŋgl] *n* ángulo; **from their ~** desde su punto de vista.

angler ['æŋglə*] *n* pescador(a) *m/f* (de caña).

Anglican ['æŋglɪkən] *adj*, *n* anglicano/a.

anglicize ['æŋglɪsaɪz] *vt* anglicanizar.

angling ['æŋglɪŋ] *n* pesca con caña.

Anglo- [æŋgləʊ] *pref* anglo... .

Angola [æŋ'gəʊlə] *n* Angola.

Angolan [æŋ'gəʊlən] *adj*, *n* angoleño/a *m/f*.

angrily ['æŋgrɪlɪ] *adv* enojado, enfadado.

angry ['æŋgrɪ] *adj* enfadado, enojado (*esp LAM*); **to be ~ with sb/at sth** estar enfadado con algn/por algo; **to get ~** enfadarse, enojarse (*esp LAM*).

anguish ['æŋgwɪʃ] *n* (*physical*) tormentos *mpl*; (*mental*) angustia.

anguished ['æŋgwɪʃt] *adj* angustioso.

angular ['æŋgjulə*] *adj* (*shape*) angular; (*features*) anguloso.

animal ['ænɪməl] *adj*, *n* animal *m*.

animal rights [-raɪts] *npl* derechos *mpl* de los animales.

animate ['ænɪmeɪt] *vt* (*enliven*) animar; (*encourage*) estimular, alentar ♦ ['ænɪmɪt] *adj* vivo, animado.

animated ['ænɪmeɪtɪd] *adj* vivo, animado.

animation [ænɪ'meɪʃən] *n* animación *f*.

animosity [ænɪ'mɔsɪtɪ] *n* animosidad *f*, rencor *m*.

aniseed ['ænɪsiːd] *n* anís *m*.

Ankara ['æŋkərə] *n* Ankara.

ankle ['æŋkl] *n* tobillo *m*.

ankle sock *n* calcetín *m*.

annex ['ænɛks] *n* (*also*: *Brit*: **annexe**) (*building*) edificio anexo ♦ *vt* [æ'nɛks] (*territory*) anexar.

annihilate [ə'naɪəleɪt] *vt* aniquilar.

annihilation [ənaɪə'leɪʃən] *n* aniquilación *f*.

anniversary [ænɪ'vɔːsərɪ] *n* aniversario.

annotate ['ænəuteɪt] *vt* anotar.

announce [ə'nauns] *vt* (*gen*) anunciar; (*inform*) comunicar; **he ~d that he wasn't going** declaró que no iba.

announcement [ə'naunsmənt] *n* (*gen*) anuncio; (*declaration*) declaración *f*; **I'd like to make an ~** quisiera anunciar algo.

announcer [ə'naunsə*] *n* (*RADIO, TV*) locutor(a) *m/f*.

annoy [ə'nɔɪ] *vt* molestar, fastidiar, fregar (*LAM*), embromar (*LAM*); **to be ~ed (at sth/with sb)** estar enfadado *or* molesto (por algo/con algn); **don't get ~ed!** ¡no se enfade!

annoyance [ə'nɔɪəns] *n* enojo; (*thing*) molestia.

annoying [ə'nɔɪɪŋ] *adj* molesto, fastidioso, fregado (*LAM*), embromado (*LAM*); (*person*) pesado.

annual ['ænjuəl] *adj* anual ♦ *n* (*BOT*) anual *m*; (*book*) anuario.

annual general meeting (AGM) *n* junta general anual.

annually ['ænjuəlɪ] *adv* anualmente, cada año.

annual report *n* informe *m or* memoria

anual.

annuity [ə'njuːɪtɪ] *n* renta *or* pensión *f* vitalicia.

annul [ə'nʌl] *vt* anular; (*law*) revocar.

annulment [ə'nʌlmənt] *n* anulación *f*.

annum ['ænəm] *n see* **per annum**.

Annunciation [ənʌnsɪ'eɪʃən] *n* Anunciación *f*.

anode ['ænəud] *n* ánodo.

anoint [ə'nɔɪnt] *vt* untar.

anomalous [ə'nɒmələs] *adj* anómalo.

anomaly [ə'nɒməlɪ] *n* anomalía.

anon. [ə'nɒn] *abbr* = **anonymous**.

anonymity [ænə'nɪmɪtɪ] *n* anonimato.

anonymous [ə'nɒnɪməs] *adj* anónimo; **to remain ~** quedar en el anonimato.

anorak ['ænəræk] *n* anorak *m*.

anorexia [ænə'rɛksɪə] *n* (*MED*) anorexia.

anorexic [ænə'rɛksɪk] *adj, n* anoréxico/a *m/f*.

another [ə'nʌðə*] *adj*: ~ **book** otro libro; ~ **beer?** ¿(quieres) otra cerveza?; **in ~ 5 years** en cinco años más ♦ *pron* otro; *see also* **one**.

ANSI *n abbr* (= *American National Standards Institution*) oficina de normalización de *EEUU*.

answer ['ɑːnsə*] *n* respuesta, contestación *f*; (*to problem*) solución *f* ♦ *vi* contestar, responder ♦ *vt* (*reply to*) contestar a, responder a; (*problem*) resolver; **to ~ the phone** contestar el teléfono; **in ~ to your letter** contestando *or* en contestación a su carta; **to ~ the door** abrir la puerta.

▶**answer back** *vi* replicar, ser respondón/ona.

▶**answer for** *vt fus* responder de *or* por.

▶**answer to** *vt fus* (*description*) corresponder a.

answerable ['ɑːnsərəbl] *adj*: ~ **to sb for sth** responsable ante algn de algo.

answering machine ['ɑːnsərɪŋ-] *n* contestador *m* automático.

ant [ænt] *n* hormiga.

antagonism [æn'tægənɪzəm] *n* antagonismo *m*.

antagonist [æn'tægənɪst] *n* antagonista *m/f*, adversario/a.

antagonistic [æntægə'nɪstɪk] *adj* antagónico; (*opposed*) contrario, opuesto.

antagonize [æn'tægənaɪz] *vt* provocar la enemistad de.

Antarctic [ænt'ɑːktɪk] *adj* antártico ♦ *n*: **the ~** el Antártico.

Antarctica [ænt'ɑːktɪkə] *n* Antártida.

Antarctic Circle *n* Círculo Polar Antártico.

Antarctic Ocean *n* Océano Antártico.

ante ['æntɪ] *n*: **to up the ~** subir la apuesta.

ante... ['æntɪ] *pref* ante....

anteater ['æntiːtə*] *n* oso hormiguero.

antecedent [æntɪ'siːdənt] *n* antecedente *m*.

antechamber ['æntɪtʃeɪmbə*] *n* antecámara.

antelope ['æntɪləup] *n* antílope *m*.

antenatal [æntɪ'neɪtl] *adj* prenatal.

antenatal clinic *n* clínica prenatal.

antenna [æn'tɛnə], *pl* **~e** [-niː] *n* antena.

anteroom ['æntɪrum] *n* antesala.

anthem ['ænθəm] *n*: **national ~** himno nacional.

anthology [æn'θɒlədʒɪ] *n* antología.

anthropologist [ænθrə'pɒlədʒɪst] *n* antropólogo/a.

anthropology [ænθrə'pɒlədʒɪ] *n* antropología.

anti... [æntɪ] *pref* anti....

anti-aircraft ['æntɪ'ɛəkrɑːft] *adj* antiaéreo.

antiballistic [æntɪbə'lɪstɪk] *adj* antibalístico.

antibiotic [æntɪbaɪ'ɔtɪk] *adj, n* antibiótico.

antibody ['æntɪbɒdɪ] *n* anticuerpo.

anticipate [æn'tɪsɪpeɪt] *vt* (*foresee*) prever; (*expect*) esperar, contar con; (*forestall*) anticiparse a, adelantarse a; **this is worse than I ~d** esto es peor de lo que esperaba; **as ~d** según se esperaba.

anticipation [æntɪsɪ'peɪʃən] *n* previsión *f*; esperanza; anticipación *f*.

anticlimax [æntɪ'klaɪmæks] *n* decepción *f*.

anticlockwise [æntɪ'klɒkwaɪz] *adv* en dirección contraria a la de las agujas del reloj.

antics ['æntɪks] *npl* payasadas *fpl*.

anticyclone [æntɪ'saɪkləun] *n* anticiclón *m*.

antidepressant ['æntɪdɪ'prɛsnt] *n* antidepresivo.

antidote ['æntɪdəut] *n* antídoto.

antifreeze ['æntɪfriːz] *n* anticongelante *m*.

anti-globalization ['æntɪgləubəlaɪ'zeɪʃən] *n* antiglobalización *f*; ~ **protesters** manifestantes *m/fpl* antiglobalización.

antihistamine [æntɪ'hɪstəmiːn] *n* antihistamínico.

Antilles [æn'tɪliːz] *npl*: **the ~** las Antillas.

antipathy [æn'tɪpəθɪ] *n* (*between people*) antipatía; (*to person, thing*) aversión *f*.

antiperspirant ['æntɪpə:spɪrənt] *n* antitranspirante *m*.

Antipodean [æntɪpə'diːən] *adj* antípoda.

Antipodes [æn'tɪpədiːz] *npl*: **the ~** las Antípodas.

antiquarian [æntɪ'kwɛərɪən] *n* anticuario/a.

antiquated ['æntɪkweɪtɪd] *adj* anticuado.

antique [æn'tiːk] *n* antigüedad *f* ♦ *adj* antiguo.

antique dealer *n* anticuario/a.

antique shop *n* tienda de antigüedades.

antiquity [æn'tɪkwɪtɪ] *n* antigüedad *f*.

anti-Semitic ['æntɪsɪ'mɪtɪk] *adj* antisemita.

anti-Semitism [ænti'semitizəm] *n* antisemitismo.

antiseptic [ænti'septik] *adj, n* antiséptico.

antisocial [ænti'səuʃəl] *adj* antisocial.

antitank [ænti'tæŋk] *adj* antitanque.

antithesis, *pl* **antitheses** [æn'tiθisis, -si:z] *n* antítesis *f inv*.

antitrust [ænti'trʌst] *adj*: ~ **legislation** legislación *f* antimonopolio.

antlers ['æntləz] *npl* cornamenta.

anus ['einəs] *n* ano.

anvil ['ænvil] *n* yunque *m*.

anxiety [æŋ'zaiəti] *n* (*worry*) inquietud *f*; (*eagerness*) ansia, anhelo.

anxious ['æŋkʃəs] *adj* (*worried*) inquieto; (*keen*) deseoso; **I'm very ~ about you** me tienes muy preocupado.

anxiously ['æŋkʃəsli] *adv* con inquietud, de manera angustiada.

———————— *KEYWORD*

any ['eni] *adj* **1** (*in questions etc*) algún/alguna; **have you ~ butter/children?** ¿tienes mantequilla/hijos?; **if there are ~ tickets left** si quedan billetes, si queda algún billete

2 (*with negative*): **I haven't ~ money/books** no tengo dinero/libros

3 (*no matter which*) cualquier; ~ **excuse will do** valdrá *or* servirá cualquier excusa; **choose ~ book you like** escoge el libro que quieras; ~ **teacher you ask will tell you** cualquier profesor al que preguntes te lo dirá

4 (*in phrases*): **in ~ case** de todas formas, en cualquier caso; ~ **day now** cualquier día (de estos); **at ~ moment** en cualquier momento, de un momento a otro; **at ~ rate** en todo caso; ~ **time: come (at) ~ time** ven cuando quieras; **he might come (at) ~ time** podría llegar de un momento a otro

♦ *pron* **1** (*in questions etc*): **have you got ~?** ¿tienes alguno/a?; **can ~ of you sing?** ¿sabe cantar alguno de vosotros/ustedes?

2 (*with negative*): **I haven't ~ (of them)** no tengo ninguno

3 (*no matter which one(s)*): **take ~ of those books (you like)** toma el libro que quieras de ésos

♦ *adv* **1** (*in questions etc*): **do you want ~ more soup/sandwiches?** ¿quieres más sopa/bocadillos?; **are you feeling ~ better?** ¿te sientes algo mejor?

2 (*with negative*): **I can't hear him ~ more** ya no le oigo; **don't wait ~ longer** no esperes más.

anybody ['enibɔdi] *pron* cualquiera, cualquier persona; (*in interrogative sentences*) alguien; (*in negative sentences*): **I don't see ~** no veo a nadie.

anyhow ['enihau] *adv* de todos modos, de todas maneras; (*carelessly*) de cualquier manera; (*haphazardly*) de cualquier modo; **I shall go ~** iré de todas maneras.

anyone ['eniwʌn] = **anybody**.

anyplace ['enipleis] *adv* (*US*) = **anywhere**.

anything ['eniθiŋ] *pron* (*see anybody*) cualquier cosa; (*in interrogative sentences*) algo; (*in negative sentences*) nada; (*everything*) todo; ~ **else?** ¿algo más?; **it can cost ~ between £15 and £20** puede costar entre 15 y 20 libras.

anytime ['enitaim] *adv* (*at any moment*) en cualquier momento, de un momento a otro; (*whenever*) no importa cuándo, cuando quiera.

anyway ['eniwei] *adv* de todas maneras; de cualquier modo.

anywhere ['eniweə*] *adv* (*see anybody*) dondequiera; (*interrogative*) en algún sitio; (*negative sense*) en ningún sitio; (*everywhere*) en *or* por todas partes; **I don't see him ~** no le veo en ningún sitio; ~ **in the world** en cualquier parte del mundo.

Anzac ['ænzæk] *n abbr* (= *Australia-New Zealand Army Corps*).

apace [ə'peis] *adv* aprisa.

apart [ə'pɑ:t] *adv* aparte, separadamente; **10 miles ~** separados por 10 millas; **to take ~** desmontar; ~ **from** *prep* aparte de.

apartheid [ə'pɑ:teit] *n* apartheid *m*.

apartment [ə'pɑ:tmənt] *n* (*US*) piso, departamento (*LAM*), apartamento; (*room*) cuarto.

apartment block *or* **building** (*US*) bloque *m* de pisos.

apathetic [æpə'θetik] *adj* apático, indiferente.

apathy ['æpəθi] *n* apatía, indiferencia.

APB *n abbr* (*US*: = *all points bulletin*) *expresión usada por la policía que significa* "*descubrir y aprehender al sospechoso*".

ape [eip] *n* mono ♦ *vt* imitar, remedar.

Apennines ['æpənainz] *npl*: **the ~** los Apeninos *mpl*.

aperitif [ə'peritiːf] *n* aperitivo.

aperture ['æpətʃuə*] *n* rendija, resquicio; (*PHOT*) abertura.

APEX ['eipeks] *n abbr* (*AVIAT* = *advance purchase excursion*) APEX *m*.

apex ['eipeks] *n* ápice *m*; (*fig*) cumbre *f*.

aphid ['eifid] *n* pulgón *m*.

aphorism ['æfərɪzəm] *n* aforismo.
aphrodisiac [æfrəu'dɪzɪæk] *adj, n* afrodisíaco.
API *n abbr = American Press Institute.*
apiece [ə'piːs] *adv* cada uno.
aplomb [ə'plɔm] *n* aplomo, confianza.
APO *n abbr (US: = Army Post Office) servicio postal del ejército.*
Apocalypse [ə'pɔkəlɪps] *n* Apocalipsis *m.*
apocryphal [ə'pɔkrɪfəl] *adj* apócrifo.
apolitical [eɪpə'lɪtɪkl] *adj* apolítico.
apologetic [əpɔlə'dʒɛtɪk] *adj (look, remark)* de disculpa.
apologetically [əpɔlə'dʒɛtɪkəlɪ] *adv* con aire de disculpa, excusándose, disculpándose.
apologize [ə'pɔlədʒaɪz] *vi:* to ~ (for sth to sb) disculparse (con algn por algo).
apology [ə'pɔlədʒɪ] *n* disculpa, excusa; **please accept my apologies** le ruego me disculpe.
apoplectic [æpə'plɛktɪk] *adj (MED)* apoplético; *(col):* ~ **with rage** furioso.
apoplexy ['æpəplɛksɪ] *n* apoplegía.
apostle [ə'pɔsl] *n* apóstol *m/f.*
apostrophe [ə'pɔstrəfɪ] *n* apóstrofo *m.*
appal [ə'pɔːl] *vt* horrorizar, espantar.
Appalachian Mountains [æpə'leɪʃən-] *npl:* the ~ los (Montes) Apalaches.
appalling [ə'pɔːlɪŋ] *adj* espantoso; *(awful)* pésimo; **she's an** ~ **cook** es una cocinera malísima.
apparatus [æpə'reɪtəs] *n* aparato; *(in gymnasium)* aparatos *mpl.*
apparel [ə'pærl] *n (US)* indumentaria.
apparent [ə'pærənt] *adj* aparente; *(obvious)* manifiesto, evidente; **it is** ~ **that** está claro que.
apparently [ə'pærəntlɪ] *adv* por lo visto, al parecer, dizque *(LAM).*
apparition [æpə'rɪʃən] *n* aparición *f.*
appeal [ə'piːl] *vi (LAW)* apelar ♦ *n (LAW)* apelación *f;* *(request)* llamamiento, llamado *(LAM);* *(plea)* súplica; *(charm)* atractivo, encanto; **to** ~ **for** solicitar; **to** ~ **to** *(subj: person)* rogar a, suplicar a; *(: thing)* atraer, interesar; **to** ~ **to sb for mercy** rogarle misericordia a alguien; **it doesn't** ~ **to me** no me atrae, no me llama la atención; **right of** ~ derecho de apelación.
appealing [ə'piːlɪŋ] *adj (nice)* atractivo; *(touching)* conmovedor(a), emocionante.
appear [ə'pɪə*] *vi* aparecer, presentarse; *(LAW)* comparecer; *(publication)* salir (a luz), publicarse; *(seem)* parecer; **it would** ~ **that** parecería que.
appearance [ə'pɪərəns] *n* aparición *f;* *(look, aspect)* apariencia, aspecto; **to keep up** ~**s** salvar las apariencias; **to all** ~**s** al parecer.

appease [ə'piːz] *vt (pacify)* apaciguar; *(satisfy)* satisfacer.
appeasement [ə'piːzmənt] *n (POL)* apaciguamiento.
append [ə'pɛnd] *vt (COMPUT)* añadir (al final).
appendage [ə'pɛndɪdʒ] *n* añadidura.
appendicitis [əpɛndɪ'saɪtɪs] *n* apendicitis *f.*
appendix, *pl* **appendices** [ə'pɛndɪks, -dɪsiːz] *n* apéndice *m;* **to have one's** ~ **out** operarse de apendicitis.
appetite ['æpɪtaɪt] *n* apetito; *(fig)* deseo, anhelo; **that walk has given me an** ~ ese paseo me ha abierto el apetito.
appetizer ['æpɪtaɪzə*] *n (drink)* aperitivo; *(food)* tapas *fpl (SP).*
appetizing ['æpɪtaɪzɪŋ] *adj* apetitoso.
applaud [ə'plɔːd] *vt, vi* aplaudir.
applause [ə'plɔːz] *n* aplausos *mpl.*
apple ['æpl] *n* manzana.
apple tree *n* manzano.
appliance [ə'plaɪəns] *n* aparato; **electrical** ~**s** electrodomésticos *mpl.*
applicable [ə'plɪkəbl] *adj* aplicable, pertinente; **the law is** ~ **from January** la ley es aplicable *or* se pone en vigor a partir de enero; **to be** ~ **to** referirse a.
applicant ['æplɪkənt] *n* candidato/a; solicitante *m/f.*
application [æplɪ'keɪʃən] *n* aplicación *f;* *(for a job, a grant etc)* solicitud *f.*
application form *n* solicitud *f.*
applications package *n (COMPUT)* paquete *m* de programas de aplicación.
applied [ə'plaɪd] *adj (science, art)* aplicado.
apply [ə'plaɪ] *vt:* to ~ (to) aplicar (a); *(fig)* emplear (para) ♦ *vi:* to ~ to *(ask)* dirigirse a; *(be suitable for)* ser aplicable a; *(be relevant to)* tener que ver con; **to** ~ **for** *(permit, grant, job)* solicitar; **to** ~ **the brakes** echar el freno; **to** ~ **o.s. to** aplicarse a, dedicarse a.
appoint [ə'pɔɪnt] *vt (to post)* nombrar; *(date, place)* fijar, señalar.
appointee [əpɔɪn'tiː] *n* persona nombrada.
appointment [ə'pɔɪntmənt] *n (engagement)* cita; *(date)* compromiso; *(act)* nombramiento; *(post)* puesto; **to make an** ~ **(with)** *(doctor)* pedir hora (con); *(friend)* citarse (con); "~**s (vacant)"** "ofertas de trabajo"; **by** ~ mediante cita.
apportion [ə'pɔːʃən] *vt* repartir.
appraisal [ə'preɪzl] *n* evaluación *f.*
appraise [ə'preɪz] *vt (value)* tasar, valorar; *(situation etc)* evaluar.
appreciable [ə'priːʃəbl] *adj* sensible.

appreciably [ə'priːʃəblɪ] *adv* sensiblemente, de manera apreciable.

appreciate [ə'priːʃɪeɪt] *vt* (*like*) apreciar, tener en mucho; (*be grateful for*) agradecer; (*be aware of*) comprender ♦ *vi* (*COMM*) aumentar en valor; **I ~d your help** agradecí tu ayuda.

appreciation [əpriːʃɪ'eɪʃən] *n* aprecio; reconocimiento, agradecimiento; aumento en valor.

appreciative [ə'priːʃɪətɪv] *adj* agradecido.

apprehend [æprɪ'hɛnd] *vt* percibir; (*arrest*) detener.

apprehension [æprɪ'hɛnʃən] *n* (*fear*) aprensión *f*.

apprehensive [æprɪ'hɛnsɪv] *adj* aprensivo.

apprentice [ə'prɛntɪs] *n* aprendiz(a) *m/f*.

apprenticeship [ə'prɛntɪʃɪp] *n* aprendizaje *m*; **to serve one's ~** hacer el aprendizaje.

appro. ['æprəu] *abbr* (*BRIT COMM: col*) = **approval**.

approach [ə'prəutʃ] *vi* acercarse ♦ *vt* acercarse a; (*be approximate*) aproximarse a; (*ask, apply to*) dirigirse a; (*problem*) abordar ♦ *n* acercamiento; aproximación *f*; (*access*) acceso; (*proposal*) proposición *f*; (*to problem etc*) enfoque *m*; **to ~ sb about sth** hablar con algn sobre algo.

approachable [ə'prəutʃəbl] *adj* (*person*) abordable; (*place*) accesible.

approach road *n* vía de acceso.

approbation [æprə'beɪʃən] *n* aprobación *f*.

appropriate [ə'prəuprɪt] *adj* apropiado, conveniente ♦ *vt* [-rɪeɪt] (*take*) apropiarse de; (*allot*): **to ~ sth for** destinar algo a; **~ for or to** apropiado para; **it would not be ~ for me to comment** no estaría bien *or* sería pertinente que yo diera mi opinión.

appropriation [əprəuprɪ'eɪʃən] *n* asignación *f*.

approval [ə'pruːvəl] *n* aprobación *f*, visto bueno; **on ~** (*COMM*) a prueba; **to meet with sb's ~** obtener la aprobación de algn.

approve [ə'pruːv] *vt* aprobar.

▶ **approve of** *vt fus* aprobar.

approved school *n* (*BRIT*) correccional *m*.

approx. *abbr* (= *approximately*) aprox.

approximate [ə'prɒksɪmɪt] *adj* aproximado.

approximately [ə'prɒksɪmɪtlɪ] *adv* aproximadamente, más o menos.

approximation [əprɒksɪ'meɪʃən] *n* aproximación *f*.

Apr. *abbr* (= *April*) abr.

apr *n abbr* (= *annual percentage rate*) tasa de interés anual.

apricot ['eɪprɪkɒt] *n* albaricoque *m* (*SP*), damasco (*LAM*).

April ['eɪprəl] *n* abril *m*; **~ Fools' Day** *n* ≈ día *m* de los (Santos) Inocentes; *ver recuadro*.

APRIL FOOLS' DAY

El 1 de abril es **April Fools' Day** en la tradición anglosajona. Tal día se les gastan bromas a los más desprevenidos, quienes reciben la denominación de "April Fool" (≈ inocente), y tanto la prensa escrita como la televisión difunden alguna historia falsa con la que sumarse al espíritu del día.

---

apron ['eɪprən] *n* delantal *m*; (*AVIAT*) pista.

apse [æps] *n* (*ARCH*) ábside *m*.

APT *n abbr* (*BRIT*) = *advanced passenger train*.

Apt. *abbr* = **apartment**.

apt [æpt] *adj* (*to the point*) acertado, oportuno; (*appropriate*) apropiado; **~ to do** (*likely*) propenso a hacer.

aptitude ['æptɪtjuːd] *n* aptitud *f*, capacidad *f*.

aptitude test *n* prueba de aptitud.

aptly ['æptlɪ] *adj* acertadamente.

aqualung ['ækwəlʌŋ] *n* escafandra autónoma.

aquarium [ə'kwɛərɪəm] *n* acuario.

Aquarius [ə'kwɛərɪəs] *n* Acuario.

aquatic [ə'kwætɪk] *adj* acuático.

aqueduct ['ækwɪdʌkt] *n* acueducto.

AR *abbr* (*US*) = *Arkansas*.

ARA *n abbr* (*BRIT*)= *Associate of the Royal Academy*.

Arab ['ærəb] *adj*, *n* árabe *m/f*.

Arabia [ə'reɪbɪə] *n* Arabia.

Arabian [ə'reɪbɪən] *adj* árabe, arábigo.

Arabian Desert *n* Desierto de Arabia.

Arabian Sea *n* Mar *m* de Omán.

Arabic ['ærəbɪk] *adj* (*language, manuscripts*) árabe, arábigo ♦ *n* árabe *m*; **~ numerals** numeración *f* arábiga.

arable ['ærəbl] *adj* cultivable.

Aragon ['ærəgən] *n* Aragón *m*.

ARAM *n abbr* (*BRIT*) = *Associate of the Royal Academy of Music*.

arbitrary ['ɑːbɪtrərɪ] *adj* arbitrario.

arbitrate ['ɑːbɪtreɪt] *vi* arbitrar.

arbitration [ɑːbɪ'treɪʃən] *n* arbitraje *m*; **the dispute went to ~** el conflicto laboral fue sometido al arbitraje.

arbitrator ['ɑːbɪtreɪtə*] *n* árbitro.

ARC *n abbr* = *American Red Cross*.

arc [ɑːk] *n* arco.

arcade [ɑː'keɪd] *n* (*ARCH*) arcada; (*round a square*) soportales *mpl*; (*shopping ~*) galería comercial.

arch [ɑːtʃ] *n* arco; (*vault*) bóveda; (*of foot*) empeine *m* ♦ *vt* arquear.
archaeological [ɑːkɪə'lɔdʒɪkl] *adj* arqueológico.
archaeologist [ɑːkɪ'ɔlədʒɪst] *n* arqueólogo/a.
archaeology [ɑːkɪ'ɔlədʒɪ] *n* arqueología.
archaic [ɑː'keɪɪk] *adj* arcaico.
archangel ['ɑːkeɪndʒəl] *n* arcángel *m*.
archbishop [ɑːtʃ'bɪʃəp] *n* arzobispo.
arched [ɑːtʃt] *adj* abovedado.
archenemy ['ɑːtʃ'ɛnəmɪ] *n* enemigo jurado.
archeology [ɑːkɪ'ɔlədʒɪ] *etc* (*US*) = **archaeology** *etc.*
archer ['ɑːtʃə*] *n* arquero/a.
archery ['ɑːtʃərɪ] *n* tiro al arco.
archetypal ['ɑːkɪtaɪpəl] *adj* arquetípico.
archetype ['ɑːkɪtaɪp] *n* arquetipo.
archipelago [ɑːkɪ'pɛlɪɡəu] *n* archipiélago.
architect ['ɑːkɪtɛkt] *n* arquitecto/a.
architectural [ɑːkɪ'tɛktʃərəl] *adj* arquitectónico.
architecture ['ɑːkɪtɛktʃə*] *n* arquitectura.
archive ['ɑːkaɪv] *n* (*often pl: also COMPUT*) archivo.
archive file *n* (*COMPUT*) fichero archivado.
archives ['ɑːkaɪvz] *npl* archivo *sg.*
archivist ['ɑːkɪvɪst] *n* archivero/a.
archway ['ɑːtʃweɪ] *n* arco, arcada.
ARCM *n abbr* (*BRIT*) = *Associate of the Royal College of Music.*
Arctic ['ɑːktɪk] *adj* ártico ♦ *n*: **the** ~ el Ártico.
Arctic Circle *n* Círculo Polar Ártico.
Arctic Ocean *n* Océano (Glacial) Ártico.
ARD *n abbr* (*US MED*) = *acute respiratory disease.*
ardent ['ɑːdənt] *adj* (*desire*) ardiente; (*supporter, lover*) apasionado.
ardour, (*US*) **ardor** ['ɑːdə*] *n* ardor *m*, pasión *f*.
arduous ['ɑːdjuəs] *adj* (*gen*) arduo; (*journey*) penoso.
are [ɑː*] *vb see* **be**.
area ['ɛərɪə] *n* área; (*MATH etc*) superficie *f*, extensión *f*; (*zone*) región *f*, zona; **the London** ~ la zona de Londres.
area code *n* (*US TEL*) prefijo.
arena [ə'riːnə] *n* arena; (*of circus*) pista; (*for bullfight*) plaza, ruedo.
aren't [ɑːnt] = **are not**.
Argentina [ɑːdʒən'tiːnə] *n* Argentina.
Argentinian [ɑːdʒən'tɪnɪən] *adj, n* argentino/a *m/f.*
arguable ['ɑːgjuəbl] *adj*: **it is** ~ **whether ...** es dudoso que + *subjun.*
arguably ['ɑːgjuəblɪ] *adv*: **it is** ~ **...** es discutiblemente ....

argue ['ɑːgjuː] *vt* (*debate: case, matter*) mantener, argüir ♦ *vi* (*quarrel*) discutir; (*reason*) razonar, argumentar; **to** ~ **that** sostener que; **to** ~ **about sth (with sb)** pelearse (con algn) por algo.
argument ['ɑːgjumənt] *n* (*reasons*) argumento; (*quarrel*) discusión *f*; (*debate*) debate *m*; ~ **for/against** argumento en pro/contra de.
argumentative [ɑːgju'mɛntətɪv] *adj* discutidor(a).
aria ['ɑːrɪə] *n* (*MUS*) aria.
ARIBA *n abbr* (*BRIT*) = *Associate of the Royal Institute of British Architects.*
arid ['ærɪd] *adj* árido.
aridity [ə'rɪdɪtɪ] *n* aridez *f.*
Aries ['ɛərɪz] *n* Aries *m.*
arise [ə'raɪz], *pt* **arose**, *pp* **arisen** [ə'rɪzn] *vi* (*rise up*) levantarse, alzarse; (*emerge*) surgir, presentarse; **to** ~ **from** derivar de; **should the need** ~ si fuera necesario.
aristocracy [ærɪs'tɔkrəsɪ] *n* aristocracia.
aristocrat ['ærɪstəkræt] *n* aristócrata *m/f.*
aristocratic [ærɪstə'krætɪk] *adj* aristocrático.
arithmetic [ə'rɪθmətɪk] *n* aritmética.
arithmetical [ærɪθ'mɛtɪkl] *adj* aritmético.
Ariz. *abbr* (*US*) = *Arizona.*
Ark [ɑːk] *n*: **Noah's** ~ el Arca *f* de Noé.
Ark. *abbr* (*US*) = *Arkansas.*
arm [ɑːm] *n* (*ANAT*) brazo ♦ *vt* armar; ~ **in** ~ cogidos del brazo; *see also* **arms**.
armaments ['ɑːməmənts] *npl* (*weapons*) armamentos *mpl.*
armchair ['ɑːmtʃɛə*] *n* sillón *m*, butaca.
armed [ɑːmd] *adj* armado; **the** ~ **forces** las fuerzas armadas.
armed robbery *n* robo a mano armada.
Armenia [ɑː'miːnɪə] *n* Armenia.
Armenian [ɑː'miːnɪən] *adj* armenio ♦ *n* armenio/a; (*LING*) armenio.
armful ['ɑːmful] *n* brazada.
armistice ['ɑːmɪstɪs] *n* armisticio.
armour, (*US*) **armor** ['ɑːmə*] *n* armadura.
armo(u)red car *n* coche *m or* carro (*LAM*) blindado.
armo(u)ry ['ɑːmərɪ] *n* arsenal *m.*
armpit ['ɑːmpɪt] *n* sobaco, axila.
armrest ['ɑːmrɛst] *n* reposabrazos *m inv*, brazo.
arms [ɑːmz] *npl* (*weapons*) armas *fpl*; (*HERALDRY*) escudo *sg.*
arms control *n* control *m* de armamentos.
arms race *n* carrera de armamentos.
army ['ɑːmɪ] *n* ejército.
aroma [ə'rəumə] *n* aroma *m*, fragancia.
aromatherapy [ərəumə'θɛrəpɪ] *n* aromaterapia.

aromatic [ærə'mætık] *adj* aromático, fragante.

arose [ə'rəuz] *pt of* **arise**.

around [ə'raund] *adv* alrededor, (*in the area*) a la redonda ♦ *prep* alrededor de.

arousal [ə'rauzəl] *n* (*sexual*) excitación *f*; (*of feelings, interest*) despertar *m*.

arouse [ə'rauz] *vt* despertar.

arrange [ə'reındʒ] *vt* arreglar, ordenar; (*programme*) organizar; (*appointment*) concertar ♦ *vi*: **we have ~d for a taxi to pick you up** hemos organizado todo para que le recoja un taxi; **to ~ to do sth** quedar en hacer algo; **it was ~d that ...** se quedó en que ....

arrangement [ə'reındʒmənt] *n* arreglo; (*agreement*) acuerdo; **~s** *npl* (*plans*) planes *mpl*, medidas *fpl*; (*preparations*) preparativos *mpl*; **to come to an ~ (with sb)** llegar a un acuerdo (con algn); **by ~ a** convenir; **I'll make ~s for you to be met** haré los preparativos para que le estén esperando.

arrant ['ærənt] *adj*: **~ nonsense** una verdadera tontería.

array [ə'reı] *n* (*COMPUT*) matriz *f*; **~ of** (*things*) serie *f or* colección *f* de; (*people*) conjunto de.

arrears [ə'rıəz] *npl* atrasos *mpl*; **in ~** (*COMM*) en mora; **to be in ~ with one's rent** estar retrasado en el pago del alquiler.

arrest [ə'rɛst] *vt* detener; (*sb's attention*) llamar ♦ *n* detención *f*; **under ~** detenido.

arresting [ə'rɛstıŋ] *adj* (*fig*) llamativo.

arrival [ə'raıvəl] *n* llegada, arribo (*LAM*); **new ~** recién llegado/a.

arrive [ə'raıv] *vi* llegar, arribar (*LAM*).

arrogance ['ærəgəns] *n* arrogancia, prepotencia (*LAM*).

arrogant ['ærəgənt] *adj* arrogante, prepotente (*LAM*).

arrow ['ærəu] *n* flecha.

arse [ɑːs] *n* (*BRIT col!*) culo, trasero.

arsenal ['ɑːsınl] *n* arsenal *m*.

arsenic ['ɑːsnık] *n* arsénico.

arson ['ɑːsn] *n* incendio provocado.

art [ɑːt] *n* arte *m*; (*skill*) destreza; (*technique*) técnica; **A~s** *npl* (*SCOL*) Letras *fpl*; **work of ~** obra de arte.

art and design *n* (*BRIT SCOL*) arte *m* y diseño, dibujo.

artefact ['ɑːtıfækt] *n* artefacto.

arterial [ɑː'tıərıəl] *adj* (*ANAT*) arterial; (*road etc*) principal.

artery ['ɑːtərı] *n* (*MED, road etc*) arteria.

artful ['ɑːtful] *adj* (*cunning: person, trick*) mañoso.

art gallery *n* pinacoteca, museo de pintura; (*COMM*) galería de arte.

arthritis [ɑː'θraıtıs] *n* artritis *f*.

artichoke ['ɑːtıtʃəuk] *n* alcachofa; **Jerusalem ~** aguaturma.

article ['ɑːtıkl] *n* artículo, objeto, cosa; (*in newspaper*) artículo; (*BRIT LAW: training*): **~s** *npl* contrato *sg* de aprendizaje; **~s of clothing** prendas *fpl* de vestir.

articles of association *npl* (*COMM*) estatutos *mpl* sociales, escritura social.

articulate *adj* [ɑː'tıkjulıt] (*speech*) claro; (*person*) que se expresa bien ♦ *vi* [ɑː'tıkjuleıt] articular.

articulated lorry *n* (*BRIT*) trailer *m*.

artifice ['ɑːtıfıs] *n* artificio, truco.

artificial [ɑːtı'fıʃəl] *adj* artificial; (*teeth etc*) postizo.

artificial insemination *n* inseminación *f* artificial.

artificial intelligence (A.I.) *n* inteligencia artificial (I.A.).

artificial respiration *n* respiración *f* artificial.

artillery [ɑː'tılərı] *n* artillería.

artisan ['ɑːtızæn] *n* artesano/a.

artist ['ɑːtıst] *n* artista *m/f*; (*MUS*) intérprete *m/f*.

artistic [ɑː'tıstık] *adj* artístico.

artistry ['ɑːtıstrı] *n* arte *m*, habilidad *f* (*artística*).

artless ['ɑːtlıs] *adj* (*innocent*) natural, sencillo; (*clumsy*) torpe.

art school *n* escuela de bellas artes.

artwork ['ɑːtwəːk] *n* material *m* gráfico.

arty ['ɑːtı] *adj* artistoide.

ARV *n abbr* (= *American Revised Version*) *traducción americana de la Biblia*.

═══════════════════════ — *KEYWORD*

as [æz] *conj* **1** (*referring to time: while*) mientras; (: *when*) cuando; **she wept ~ she told her story** lloraba mientras contaba lo que le ocurrió; **~ the years go by** a medida que pasan los años, con el paso de los años; **he came in ~ I was leaving** entró cuando me marchaba; **~ from tomorrow** a partir de *or* desde mañana

2 (*in comparisons*): **~ big ~** tan grande como; **twice ~ big ~** el doble de grande que; **~ much money/many books ~** tanto dinero/tantos libros como; **~ soon ~** en cuanto, no bien (*LAM*)

3 (*since, because*) como, ya que; **~ I don't**

speak German I can't understand him
como no hablo alemán no le entiendo, no
le entiendo ya que no hablo alemán
4 (*although*): **much ~ I like them, ...**
aunque me gustan, ...
5 (*referring to manner, way*): **do ~ you
wish** haz lo que quieras; **~ she said** como
dijo; **he gave it to me ~ a present** me lo
dio de regalo; **it's on the left ~ you go in**
según se entra, a la izquierda
6 (*concerning*): **~ for** *or* **to that** por *or* en
lo que respecta a eso
7: **~ if** *or* **though** como si; **he looked ~ if
he was ill** parecía como si estuviera
enfermo, tenía aspecto de enfermo; *see
also* **long; such; well**
♦ *prep* (*in the capacity of*): **he works ~ a
barman** trabaja de barman; **~ chairman
of the company, he ...** como presidente de
la compañía, ...

ASA *n abbr* (= *American Standards
Association*) *instituto de normalización*;
(*BRIT*: = *Advertising Standards Authority*)
*departamento de control de la
publicidad.*
a.s.a.p. *abbr* (= *as soon as possible*) cuanto
antes, lo más pronto posible.
asbestos [æz'bɛstəs] *n* asbesto, amianto.
ascend [ə'sɛnd] *vt* subir, ascender.
ascendancy [ə'sɛndənsɪ] *n* ascendiente *m*,
dominio.
ascendant [ə'sɛndənt] *n*: **to be in the ~**
estar en auge, ir ganando predominio.
Ascension [ə'sɛnʃən] *n*: **the ~** la Ascensión.
Ascension Island *n* Isla Ascensión.
ascent [ə'sɛnt] *n* subida; (*slope*) cuesta,
pendiente *f*; (*of plane*) ascenso.
ascertain [æsə'teɪn] *vt* averiguar.
ascetic [ə'sɛtɪk] *adj* ascético.
asceticism [ə'sɛtɪsɪzəm] *n* ascetismo.
ASCII ['æski:] *n abbr* (= *American Standard
Code for Information Interchange*) ASCII.
ascribe [ə'skraɪb] *vt*: **to ~ sth to** atribuir
algo a.
ASCU *n abbr* (*US*) = *Association of State
Colleges and Universities.*
ASE *n abbr* = *American Stock Exchange.*
ASH [æʃ] *n abbr* (*BRIT*: = *Action on Smoking
and Health*) *organización anti-tabaco.*
ash [æʃ] *n* ceniza; (*tree*) fresno.
ashamed [ə'ʃeɪmd] *adj* avergonzado; **to be
~ of** avergonzarse de.
ashcan ['æʃkæn] *n* (*US*) cubo *or* bote *m*
(*LAM*) de la basura.
ashen ['æʃn] *adj* pálido.
ashore [ə'ʃɔː*] *adv* en tierra.
ashtray ['æʃtreɪ] *n* cenicero.

Ash Wednesday *n* miércoles *m* de ceniza.
Asia ['eɪʃə] *n* Asia.
Asian ['eɪʃən], **Asiatic** [eɪsɪ'ætɪk] *adj*, *n*
asiático/a *m/f*.
aside [ə'saɪd] *adv* a un lado ♦ *n* aparte *m*; **~
from** *prep* (*as well as*) aparte *or* además de.
ask [ɑːsk] *vt* (*question*) preguntar; (*demand*)
pedir; (*invite*) invitar ♦ *vi*: **to ~ about sth**
preguntar acerca de algo; **to ~ sb sth/to
do sth** preguntar algo a algn/pedir a algn
que haga algo; **to ~ sb about sth**
preguntar algo a algn; **to ~ (sb) a
question** hacer una pregunta (a algn); **to
~ sb the time** preguntar la hora a algn;
to ~ sb out to dinner invitar a cenar a
algn.
▶**ask after** *vt fus* preguntar por.
▶**ask for** *vt fus* pedir; **it's just ~ing for
trouble** *or* **for it** es buscarse problemas.
askance [ə'skɑːns] *adv*: **to look ~ at sb**
mirar con recelo a algn.
askew [ə'skjuː] *adv* sesgado, ladeado.
asking price *n* (*COMM*) precio inicial.
asleep [ə'sliːp] *adj* dormido; **to fall ~**
dormirse, quedarse dormido.
ASLEF ['æzlɛf] *n abbr* (*BRIT*: = *Associated
Society of Locomotive Engineers and
Firemen*) *sindicato de ferroviarios.*
AS level *n abbr* (*BRIT SCOL*: *Advanced
Subsidiary level*) *título intermedio entre
los "GCSEs" y los "A Levels".*
asp [æsp] *n* áspid *m*.
asparagus [əs'pærəgəs] *n* espárragos *mpl*.
ASPCA *n abbr* = *American Society for the
Prevention of Cruelty to Animals.*
aspect ['æspɛkt] *n* aspecto, apariencia;
(*orientation*) orientación *f*.
aspersions [əs'pɔːʃənz] *npl*: **to cast ~ on**
difamar a, calumniar a.
asphalt ['æsfælt] *n* asfalto.
asphyxiate [æs'fɪksɪeɪt] *vt* asfixiar.
asphyxiation [æsfɪksɪ'eɪʃən] *n* asfixia.
aspirate ['æspəreɪt] *vt* aspirar ♦ *adj*
['æspərɪt] aspirado.
aspirations [æspə'reɪʃənz] *npl* aspiraciones
fpl; (*ambition*) ambición *f*.
aspire [əs'paɪə*] *vi*: **to ~ to** aspirar a,
ambicionar.
aspirin ['æsprɪn] *n* aspirina.
aspiring [əs'paɪərɪŋ] *adj*: **an ~ actor** un
aspirante a actor.
ass [æs] *n* asno, burro; (*col*) imbécil *m/f*; (*US
col!*) culo, trasero.
assailant [ə'seɪlənt] *n* agresor(a) *m/f*.
assassin [ə'sæsɪn] *n* asesino/a.
assassinate [ə'sæsɪneɪt] *vt* asesinar.
assassination [əsæsɪ'neɪʃən] *n* asesinato.
assault [ə'sɔːlt] *n* (*gen: attack*) asalto,

agresión *f* ♦ *vt* asaltar, agredir; (*sexually*) violar.

assemble [ə'sɛmbl] *vt* reunir, juntar; (*TECH*) montar ♦ *vi* reunirse, juntarse.

assembler [ə'sɛmblə*] *n* (*COMPUT*) ensamblador *m*.

assembly [ə'sɛmblɪ] *n* (*meeting*) reunión *f*, asamblea; (*construction*) montaje *m*.

assembly language *n* (*COMPUT*) lenguaje *m* ensamblador.

assembly line *n* cadena de montaje.

Assembly Member *n* (*in Wales*) miembro *mf* de la Asamblea Nacional (de Gales).

assent [ə'sɛnt] *n* asentimiento, aprobación *f* ♦ *vi* consentir, asentir; **to** ~ **(to sth)** consentir (en algo).

assert [ə'səːt] *vt* afirmar; (*insist on*) hacer valer; **to** ~ **o.s.** imponerse.

assertion [ə'səːʃən] *n* afirmación *f*.

assertive [ə'səːtɪv] *adj* enérgico, agresivo, perentorio.

assess [ə'sɛs] *vt* valorar, calcular; (*tax, damages*) fijar; (*property etc: for tax*) gravar.

assessment [ə'sɛsmənt] *n* valoración *f*; gravamen *m*; (*judgment*): ~ **(of)** juicio (sobre).

assessor [ə'sɛsə*] *n* asesor(a) *m/f*; (*of tax*) tasador(a) *m/f*.

asset ['æsɛt] *n* posesión *f*; (*quality*) ventaja; ~**s** *npl* (*funds*) activo *sg*, fondos *mpl*.

asset-stripping ['æsɛt'strɪpɪŋ] *n* (*COMM*) acaparamiento de activos.

assiduous [ə'sɪdjuəs] *adj* asiduo.

assign [ə'saɪn] *vt* (*date*) fijar; (*task*) asignar; (*resources*) destinar; (*property*) traspasar.

assignment [ə'saɪnmənt] *n* asignación *f*; (*task*) tarea.

assimilate [ə'sɪmɪleɪt] *vt* asimilar.

assimilation [əsɪmɪ'leɪʃən] *n* asimilación *f*.

assist [ə'sɪst] *vt* ayudar.

assistance [ə'sɪstəns] *n* ayuda, auxilio.

assistant [ə'sɪstənt] *n* ayudante *m/f*; (*BRIT: also*: **shop** ~) dependiente/a *m/f*.

assistant manager *n* subdirector(a) *m/f*.

assizes [ə'saɪzɪz] *npl* sesión *f* de un tribunal.

associate [ə'səʊʃɪɪt] *adj* asociado ♦ *n* socio/a, colega *m/f*; (*in crime*) cómplice *m/f*; (*member*) miembro/a ♦ *vb* [ə'səʊʃɪeɪt] *vt* asociar; (*ideas*) relacionar ♦ *vi*: **to** ~ **with sb** tratar con alguien; ~ **director** subdirector/a *m/f*; ~**d company** compañía afiliada.

association [əsəʊsɪ'eɪʃən] *n* asociación *f*; (*COMM*) sociedad *f*; **in** ~ **with** en asociación con.

association football *n* (*BRIT*) fútbol *m*.

assorted [ə'sɔːtɪd] *adj* surtido, variado; **in**

~ **sizes** en distintos tamaños.

assortment [ə'sɔːtmənt] *n* surtido.

Asst. *abbr* = **Assistant**.

assuage [ə'sweɪdʒ] *vt* mitigar.

assume [ə'sjuːm] *vt* (*suppose*) suponer; (*responsibilities etc*) asumir; (*attitude, name*) adoptar, tomar.

assumed name *n* nombre *m* falso.

assumption [ə'sʌmpʃən] *n* (*supposition*) suposición *f*, presunción *f*; (*act*) asunción *f*; **on the** ~ **that** suponiendo que.

assurance [ə'ʃuərəns] *n* garantía, promesa; (*confidence*) confianza, aplomo; (*BRIT: insurance*) seguro; **I can give you no** ~**s** no puedo hacerle ninguna promesa.

assure [ə'ʃuə*] *vt* asegurar.

assured [ə'ʃuəd] *adj* seguro.

assuredly [ə'ʃuərɪdlɪ] *adv* indudablemente.

AST *n abbr* (= *Atlantic Standard Time*) hora oficial del este del Canadá.

asterisk ['æstərɪsk] *n* asterisco.

astern [ə'stəːn] *adv* a popa.

asteroid ['æstərɔɪd] *n* asteroide *m*.

asthma ['æsmə] *n* asma.

asthmatic [æs'mætɪk] *adj, n* asmático/a *m/f*.

astigmatism [ə'stɪgmətɪzəm] *n* astigmatismo.

astir [ə'stəː*] *adv* en acción.

astonish [ə'stɔnɪʃ] *vt* asombrar, pasmar.

astonishing [ə'stɔnɪʃɪŋ] *adj* asombroso, pasmoso; **I find it** ~ **that** ... me asombra *or* pasma que ....

astonishingly [ə'stɔnɪʃɪŋlɪ] *adv* increíblemente, asombrosamente.

astonishment [ə'stɔnɪʃmənt] *n* asombro, sorpresa; **to my** ~ con gran sorpresa mía.

astound [ə'staʊnd] *vt* asombrar, pasmar.

astounding [ə'staʊndɪŋ] *adj* asombroso.

astray [ə'streɪ] *adv*: **to go** ~ extraviarse; **to lead** ~ llevar por mal camino; **to go** ~ **in one's calculations** equivocarse en sus cálculos.

astride [ə'straɪd] *prep* a caballo *or* horcajadas sobre.

astringent [əs'trɪndʒənt] *adj, n* astringente *m*.

astrologer [əs'trɔlədʒə*] *n* astrólogo/a.

astrology [əs'trɔlədʒɪ] *n* astrología.

astronaut ['æstrənɔːt] *n* astronauta *m/f*.

astronomer [əs'trɔnəmə*] *n* astrónomo/a.

astronomical [æstrə'nɔmɪkəl] *adj* astronómico.

astronomy [aes'trɔnəmɪ] *n* astronomía.

astrophysics ['æstrəʊ'fɪzɪks] *n* astrofísica.

astute [əs'tjuːt] *adj* astuto.

asunder [ə'sʌndə*] *adv*: **to tear** ~ hacer pedazos.

asylum [ə'saɪləm] *n* (*refuge*) asilo; (*hospital*) manicomio; **to seek political** ~ pedir asilo político.

asymmetric(al) [eɪsɪ'mɛtrɪk(l)] *adj* asimétrico.

================= *KEYWORD* =================

at [æt] *prep* **1** (*referring to position*) en; (*direction*) a; ~ **the top** en lo alto; ~ **home/school** en casa/la escuela; **to look** ~ **sth/sb** mirar algo/a algn

2 (*referring to time*): ~ **4 o'clock** a las 4; ~ **night** por la noche; ~ **Christmas** en Navidad; ~ **times** a veces

3 (*referring to rates, speed etc*): ~ **£1 a kilo** a una libra el kilo; **two** ~ **a time** de dos en dos; ~ **50 km/h** a 50 km/h

4 (*referring to manner*): ~ **a stroke** de un golpe; ~ **peace** en paz

5 (*referring to activity*): **to be** ~ **work** estar trabajando; (*in office*) estar en el trabajo; **to play** ~ **cowboys** jugar a los vaqueros; **to be good** ~ **sth** ser bueno en algo

6 (*referring to cause*): **shocked/surprised/ annoyed** ~ **sth** asombrado/sorprendido/ fastidiado por algo; **I went** ~ **his suggestion** fui a instancias suyas.

──────────────────────────────

ate [ɛt, eɪt] *pt of* **eat**.

atheism ['eɪθɪɪzəm] *n* ateísmo.

atheist ['eɪθɪɪst] *n* ateo/a.

Athenian [ə'θiːnɪən] *adj*, *n* ateniense *m/f*.

Athens ['æθɪnz] *n* Atenas *f*.

athlete ['æθliːt] *n* atleta *m/f*.

athletic [æθ'lɛtɪk] *adj* atlético.

athletics [æθ'lɛtɪks] *n* atletismo.

Atlantic [ət'læntɪk] *adj* atlántico ♦ *n*: **the** ~ **(Ocean)** el (Océano) Atlántico.

atlas ['ætləs] *n* atlas *m inv*.

Atlas Mountains *npl*: **the** ~ el Atlas.

A.T.M. *n abbr* (= *Automated Telling Machine*) cajero automático.

atmosphere ['ætməsfɪə*] *n* (*air*) atmósfera; (*fig*) ambiente *m*.

atom ['ætəm] *n* átomo.

atomic [ə'tɒmɪk] *adj* atómico.

atom(ic) bomb *n* bomba atómica.

atomic power *n* energía atómica.

atomizer ['ætəmaɪzə*] *n* atomizador *m*.

atone [ə'təun] *vi*: **to** ~ **for** expiar.

atonement [ə'təunmənt] *n* expiación *f*.

A to Z ® *n* guía alfabética; (*map*) callejero.

ATP *n abbr* (= *Association of Tennis Professionals*) sindicato de jugadores de tenis profesionales.

atrocious [ə'trəuʃəs] *adj* atroz; (*fig*) horrible, infame.

atrocity [ə'trɒsɪtɪ] *n* atrocidad *f*.

atrophy ['ætrəfɪ] *n* atrofia ♦ *vi* atrofiarse.

attach [ə'tætʃ] *vt* sujetar; (*stick*) pegar; (*document, letter*) adjuntar; **to be** ~**ed to sb/sth** (*to like*) tener cariño a algn/algo; **the** ~**ed letter** la carta adjunta.

attaché [ə'tæʃeɪ] *n* agregado/a.

attaché case *n* (*BRIT*) maletín *m*.

attachment [ə'tætʃmənt] *n* (*tool*) accesorio; (*COMPUT*) archivo *o* documento adjunto; (*love*): ~ **(to)** apego (a), cariño (a).

attack [ə'tæk] *vt* (*MIL*) atacar; (*criminal*) agredir, asaltar; (*task etc*) emprender ♦ *n* ataque *m*, asalto; (*on sb's life*) atentado; **heart** ~ infarto (de miocardio).

attacker [ə'tækə*] *n* agresor(a) *m/f*, asaltante *m/f*.

attain [ə'teɪn] *vt* (*also*: ~ **to**) alcanzar; (*achieve*) lograr, conseguir.

attainments [ə'teɪnmənts] *npl* (*skill*) talento *sg*.

attempt [ə'tɛmpt] *n* tentativa, intento; (*attack*) atentado ♦ *vt* intentar, tratar de; **he made no** ~ **to help** ni siquiera intentó ayudar.

attempted [ə'tɛmptɪd] *adj*: ~ **murder/ burglary/suicide** tentativa *or* intento de asesinato/robo/suicidio.

attend [ə'tɛnd] *vt* asistir a; (*patient*) atender.

▶**attend to** *vt fus* (*needs, affairs etc*) ocuparse de; (*speech etc*) prestar atención a; (*customer*) atender a.

attendance [ə'tɛndəns] *n* asistencia, presencia; (*people present*) concurrencia.

attendant [ə'tɛndənt] *n* sirviente/a *m/f*, mozo/a; (*THEAT*) acomodador(a) *m/f* ♦ *adj* concomitante.

attention [ə'tɛnʃən] *n* atención *f* ♦ *excl* (*MIL*) ¡firme(s)!; **for the** ~ **of...** (*ADMIN*) a la atención de...; **it has come to my** ~ **that ...** me he enterado de que ....

attentive [ə'tɛntɪv] *adj* atento; (*polite*) cortés.

attenuate [ə'tɛnjueɪt] *vt* atenuar.

attest [ə'tɛst] *vi*: **to** ~ **to** dar fe de.

attic ['ætɪk] *n* desván *m*, altillo (*LAM*), entretecho (*LAM*).

attitude ['ætɪtjuːd] *n* (*gen*) actitud *f*; (*disposition*) disposición *f*.

attorney [ə'tɜːnɪ] *n* (*US: lawyer*) abogado/a; (*having proxy*) apoderado.

Attorney General *n* (*BRIT*) ≈ Presidente *m* del Consejo del Poder Judicial (*SP*); (*US*) ≈ ministro de justicia.

attract [ə'trækt] *vt* atraer; (*attention*) llamar.

attraction [ə'trækʃən] *n* (*gen*) encanto, atractivo; (*PHYSICS, towards sth*) atracción f.

attractive [ə'træktɪv] adj atractivo.

attribute ['ætrɪbjuːt] n atributo ♦ vt [ə'trɪbjuːt]: **to ~ sth to** atribuir algo a; (accuse) achacar algo a.

attrition [ə'trɪʃən] n: **war of ~** guerra de agotamiento or desgaste.

Atty. Gen. abbr = **Attorney General**.

ATV n abbr (= all terrain vehicle) vehículo todo terreno.

atypical [eɪ'tɪpɪkl] adj atípico.

aubergine ['əubəʒiːn] n (BRIT) berenjena.

auburn ['ɔːbən] adj color castaño rojizo.

auction ['ɔːkʃən] n (also: **sale by ~**) subasta ♦ vt subastar.

auctioneer [ɔːkʃə'nɪə*] n subastador(a) m/f.

auction room n sala de subastas.

audacious [ɔː'deɪʃəs] adj (bold) audaz, osado; (impudent) atrevido, descarado.

audacity [ɔː'dæsɪtɪ] n audacia, atrevimiento; (pej) descaro.

audible ['ɔːdɪbl] adj audible, que se puede oír.

audience ['ɔːdɪəns] n auditorio; (gathering) público; (interview) audiencia.

audio-typist ['ɔːdɪəu'taɪpɪst] n mecanógrafo/a de dictáfono.

audiovisual [ɔːdɪəu'vɪzjuəl] adj audiovisual.

audiovisual aid n ayuda or medio audiovisual.

audit ['ɔːdɪt] vt revisar, intervenir.

audition [ɔː'dɪʃən] n audición f ♦ vi: **to ~ for the part of** hacer una audición para el papel de.

auditor ['ɔːdɪtə*] n interventor(a) m/f, censor(a) m/f de cuentas.

auditorium [ɔːdɪ'tɔːrɪəm] n auditorio.

Aug. abbr (= August) ag.

augment [ɔːg'mɛnt] vt, vi aumentar.

augur ['ɔːgə*] vi: **it ~s well** es de buen agüero.

August ['ɔːgəst] n agosto.

august [ɔː'gʌst] adj augusto.

aunt [ɑːnt] n tía.

auntie, aunty ['ɑːntɪ] n diminutive of **aunt**.

au pair ['əu'pɛə*] n (also: **~ girl**) chica f au pair.

aura ['ɔːrə] n aura; (atmosphere) ambiente m.

auspices ['ɔːspɪsɪz] npl: **under the ~ of** bajo los auspicios de.

auspicious [ɔːs'pɪʃəs] adj propicio, de buen augurio.

austere [ɔs'tɪə*] adj austero; (manner) adusto.

austerity [ɔ'stɛrɪtɪ] n austeridad f.

Australasia [ɔːstrə'leɪzɪə] n Australasia.

Australia [ɔs'treɪlɪə] n Australia.

Australian [ɔs'treɪlɪən] adj, n australiano/a m/f.

Austria ['ɔstrɪə] n Austria.

Austrian ['ɔstrɪən] adj, n austríaco/a m/f.

AUT n abbr (BRIT: = Association of University Teachers) sindicato de profesores de universidad.

authentic [ɔː'θɛntɪk] adj auténtico.

authenticate [ɔː'θɛntɪkeɪt] vt autentificar.

authenticity [ɔːθɛn'tɪsɪtɪ] n autenticidad f.

author ['ɔːθə*] n autor(a) m/f.

authoritarian [ɔːθɔrɪ'tɛərɪən] adj autoritario.

authoritative [ɔː'θɔrɪtətɪv] adj autorizado; (manner) autoritario.

authority [ɔː'θɔrɪtɪ] n autoridad f; **the authorities** npl las autoridades; **to have ~ to do sth** tener autoridad para hacer algo.

authorization [ɔːθəraɪ'zeɪʃən] n autorización f.

authorize ['ɔːθəraɪz] vt autorizar.

authorized capital n (COMM) capital m autorizado or social.

autistic [ɔː'tɪstɪk] adj autista.

auto ['ɔːtəu] n (US) coche m, carro (LAM), auto (LAM), automóvil m.

autobiographical [ɔːtəbaɪə'græfɪkəl] adj autobiográfico.

autobiography [ɔːtəbaɪ'ɔgrəfɪ] n autobiografía.

autocratic [ɔːtə'krætɪk] adj autocrático.

Autocue ® ['ɔːtəukjuː] n autocue m, teleapuntador m.

autograph ['ɔːtəgrɑːf] n autógrafo ♦ vt firmar; (photo etc) dedicar.

autoimmune [ɔːtəuɪ'mjuːn] adj autoinmune.

automat ['ɔːtəmæt] n (US) restaurante m de autoservicio.

automate ['ɔːtəmeɪt] vt automatizar.

automated ['ɔːtəmeɪtɪd] adj automatizado.

automatic [ɔːtə'mætɪk] adj automático ♦ n (gun) pistola automática; (washing machine) lavadora.

automatically [ɔːtə'mætɪklɪ] adv automáticamente.

automatic data processing (ADP) n proceso automático de datos.

automation [ɔːtə'meɪʃən] n automatización f.

automaton, pl **automata** [ɔː'tɔmətən, -tə] n autómata.

automobile ['ɔːtəməbiːl] n (US) coche m, carro (LAM), automóvil m.

autonomous [ɔː'tɔnəməs] adj autónomo.

autonomy [ɔː'tɔnəmɪ] n autonomía.

autopsy ['ɔːtɔpsɪ] n autopsia.

autumn ['ɔːtəm] n otoño.

auxiliary [ɔːg'zɪlɪərɪ] adj auxiliar.

AV *n abbr* (= *Authorized Version*) traducción inglesa de la Biblia ♦ *abbr* = **audiovisual**.

Av. *abbr* (= *avenue*) Av., Avda.

avail [ə'veɪl] *vt*: **to ~ o.s. of** aprovechar(se) de, valerse de ♦ *n*: **to no ~ en** vano, sin resultado.

availability [əveɪlə'bɪlɪtɪ] *n* disponibilidad *f*.

available [ə'veɪləbl] *adj* disponible; (*obtainable*) asequible; **to make sth ~ to sb** poner algo a la disposición de algn; **is the manager ~?** ¿está libre el gerente?

avalanche ['ævəlɑːnʃ] *n* alud *m*, avalancha.

avant-garde ['ævāŋ'gɑːd] *adj* de vanguardia.

avarice ['ævərɪs] *n* avaricia.

avaricious [ævə'rɪʃəs] *adj* avaricioso.

avdp. *abbr* = *avoirdupois*.

Ave. *abbr* (= *avenue*) Av., Avda.

avenge [ə'vɛndʒ] *vt* vengar.

avenue ['ævənjuː] *n* avenida; (*fig*) camino, vía.

average ['ævərɪdʒ] *n* promedio, media ♦ *adj* (*mean*) medio; (*ordinary*) regular, corriente ♦ *vt* calcular el promedio de; **on ~** por término medio.

▶**average out** *vi*: **to ~ out at** salir a un promedio de.

averse [ə'vɜːs] *adj*: **to be ~ to sth/doing** sentir aversión *or* antipatía por algo/por hacer.

aversion [ə'vɜːʃən] *n* aversión *f*, repugnancia.

avert [ə'vɜːt] *vt* prevenir; (*blow*) desviar; (*one's eyes*) apartar.

aviary ['eɪvɪərɪ] *n* pajarera.

aviation [eɪvɪ'eɪʃən] *n* aviación *f*.

aviator ['eɪvɪeɪtə*] *n* aviador(a) *m/f*.

avid ['ævɪd] *adj* ávido, ansioso.

avidly ['ævɪdlɪ] *adv* ávidamente, con avidez.

avocado [ævə'kɑːdəu] *n* (*also: Brit: ~ pear*) aguacate *m*, palta (*LAM*).

avoid [ə'vɔɪd] *vt* evitar, eludir.

avoidable [ə'vɔɪdəbl] *adj* evitable, eludible.

avoidance [ə'vɔɪdəns] *n* evasión *f*.

avow [ə'vau] *vt* prometer.

avowal [ə'vauəl] *n* promesa, voto.

avowed [ə'vaud] *adj* declarado.

AVP *n abbr* (*US*) = *assistant vice-president*.

avuncular [ə'vʌŋkjulə*] *adj* paternal.

AWACS ['eɪwæks] *n abbr* (= *airborne warning and control system*) AWACS *m*.

await [ə'weɪt] *vt* esperar, aguardar; **long ~ed** largamente esperado.

awake [ə'weɪk] *adj* despierto ♦ (*vb: pt* **awoke**, *pp* **awoken** *or* **awaked**) *vt* despertar ♦ *vi* despertarse; **to be ~** estar despierto.

awakening [ə'weɪknɪŋ] *n* despertar *m*.

award [ə'wɔːd] *n* (*prize*) premio; (*medal*) condecoración *f*; (*LAW*) fallo, sentencia; (*act*) concesión *f* ♦ *vt* (*prize*) otorgar, conceder; (*LAW: damages*) adjudicar.

aware [ə'wɛə*] *adj* consciente; (*awake*) despierto; (*informed*) enterado; **to become ~ of** darse cuenta de, enterarse de; **I am fully ~ that** sé muy bien que.

awareness [ə'wɛənɪs] *n* conciencia, conocimiento.

awash [ə'wɔʃ] *adj* inundado.

away [ə'weɪ] *adv* (*gen*) fuera; (*far ~*) lejos; **two kilometres ~** a dos kilómetros (de distancia); **two hours ~ by car** a dos horas en coche; **the holiday was two weeks ~** faltaban dos semanas para las vacaciones; **~ from** lejos de, fuera de; **he's ~ for a week** estará ausente una semana; **he's ~ in Barcelona** está en Barcelona; **to take ~** llevar(se); **to work/pedal ~** seguir trabajando/pedaleando; **to fade ~** desvanecerse; (*sound*) apagarse.

away game *n* (*SPORT*) partido de fuera.

awe [ɔː] *n* respeto, temor *m* reverencial.

awe-inspiring ['ɔːɪnspaɪərɪŋ], **awesome** ['ɔːsəm] *adj* imponente, pasmoso.

awestruck ['ɔːstrʌk] *adj* pasmado.

awful ['ɔːfəl] *adj* terrible; **an ~ lot of** (*people, cars, dogs*) la mar de, muchísimos.

awfully ['ɔːfəlɪ] *adv* (*very*) terriblemente.

awhile [ə'waɪl] *adv* (durante) un rato, algún tiempo.

awkward ['ɔːkwəd] *adj* (*clumsy*) desmañado, torpe; (*shape, situation*) incómodo; (*difficult: question*) difícil; (*problem*) complicado.

awkwardness ['ɔːkwədnɪs] *n* (*clumsiness*) torpeza; (*of situation*) incomodidad *f*.

awl [ɔːl] *n* lezna, subilla.

awning ['ɔːnɪŋ] *n* (*of shop*) toldo; (*of window etc*) marquesina.

awoke [ə'wəuk], **awoken** [ə'wəukən] *pt*, *pp* *of* **awake**.

AWOL ['eɪwɔl] *abbr* (*MIL*) *see* **absent without leave**.

awry [ə'raɪ] *adv*: **to be ~** estar descolocado *or* atravesado; **to go ~** salir mal, fracasar.

axe, (*US*) **ax** [æks] *n* hacha ♦ *vt* (*employee*) despedir; (*project etc*) cortar; (*jobs*) reducir; **to have an ~ to grind** (*fig*) tener un interés creado *or* algún fin interesado.

axes ['æksiːz] *npl of* **axis**.

axiom ['æksɪəm] *n* axioma *m*.

axiomatic [æksɪə'mætɪk] *adj* axiomático.

axis, *pl* **axes** ['æksɪs, -siːz] *n* eje *m*.

axle ['æksl] n eje m, árbol m.
ay(e) [aɪ] excl (yes) sí; **the ayes** npl los que votan a favor.
AYH n abbr = American Youth Hostels.
AZ abbr (US) = Arizona.
Azerbaijan [æzəbaɪ'dʒɑ:n] n Azerbaiyán m.
Azerbaijani [æzəbaɪ'dʒɑ:nɪ], **Azeri** [ə'zɛərɪ] adj, n azerbaiyano/a, azerí m/f.
Azores [ə'zɔːz] npl: **the ~** las (Islas) Azores.
Aztec ['æztɛk] adj, n azteca m/f.
azure ['eɪʒə*] adj celeste.

B b

B, b [biː] n (letter) B, b f; (SCOL: mark) N; (MUS) si m; **B for Benjamin**, (US) **B for Baker** B de Barcelona; **B road** (BRIT AUT) ≈ carretera secundaria.
BA n abbr = British Academy; (SCOL) = **Bachelor of Arts**; see also **bachelor's degree**.
babble ['bæbl] vi farfullar.
baboon [bə'buːn] n mandril m.
baby ['beɪbɪ] n bebé m/f.
baby carriage n (US) cochecito.
babyish ['beɪbɪʃ] adj infantil.
baby-sit ['beɪbɪsɪt] vi hacer de canguro.
baby-sitter ['beɪbɪsɪtə*] n canguro m/f.
bachelor ['bætʃələ*] n soltero; **B~ of Arts/Science (BA/BSc)** licenciado/a en Filosofía y Letras/Ciencias.
bachelor's degree n licenciatura; ver recuadro.

BACHELOR'S DEGREE

Se denomina **bachelor's degree** a la titulación que se recibe al finalizar el primer ciclo universitario, normalmente después de un período de estudio de tres o cuatro años. Las titulaciones más frecuentes son las de Letras, "BA (Bachelor of Arts)", Ciencias, "BSc (Bachelor of Science)", Educación, "BEd (Bachelor of Education)" y Derecho, "LLB (Bachelor of Laws)".

---

back [bæk] n (of person) espalda; (of animal) lomo; (of hand, page) dorso; (as opposed to front) parte f de atrás; (of room) fondo; (of chair) respaldo; (FOOTBALL) defensa m; **to have one's ~ to the wall** (fig) estar entre la espada y la pared; **to break the ~ of a** job hacer lo más difícil de un trabajo; **~ to front** al revés; **at the ~ of my mind was the thought that ...** en el fondo tenía la idea de que ... ♦ vt (candidate: also: **~ up**) respaldar, apoyar; (horse: at races) apostar a; (car) dar marcha atrás a or con ♦ vi (car etc) dar marcha atrás ♦ adj (in compounds) de atrás; **~ seats/wheels** (AUT) asientos mpl/ruedas fpl traseros/as; **~ garden/room** jardín m/habitación f de atrás; **~ payments** pagos mpl con efecto retroactivo; **~ rent** renta atrasada; **to take a ~ seat** (fig) pasar a segundo plano ♦ adv (not forward) (hacia) atrás; **he's ~** (returned) ha vuelto; **he ran ~** volvió corriendo; **throw the ball ~** (restitution) devuelve la pelota; **can I have it ~?** ¿me lo devuelve?; **he called ~** (again) volvió a llamar; **~ and forth** de acá para allá; **as far ~ as the 13th century** ya en el siglo XIII; **when will you be ~?** ¿cuándo volverá?
▶**back down** vi echarse atrás.
▶**back on to** vt fus: **the house ~s on to the golf course** por atrás la casa da al campo de golf.
▶**back out** vi (of promise) volverse atrás.
▶**back up** vt (support: person) apoyar, respaldar; (: theory) defender; (car) dar marcha atrás a; (COMPUT) hacer una copia de reserva de.
backache ['bækeɪk] n dolor m de espalda.
backbencher ['bæk'bɛntʃə*] n (BRIT) diputado sin cargo oficial en el gobierno o la oposición.
back benches npl (BRIT) ver recuadro.

BACK BENCHES

Reciben el nombre genérico de **the back benches** los escaños más alejados del pasillo central en la Cámara de los Comunes del Parlamento británico, que son ocupados por los "backbenchers", los miembros de la cámara que no tienen cargo en el gobierno o en la oposición.

---

backbiting ['bækbaɪtɪŋ] n murmuración f.
backbone ['bækbəʊn] n columna vertebral; **the ~ of the organization** el pilar de la organización.
backchat ['bæktʃæt] n réplicas fpl.
backcloth ['bækklɒθ] n telón m de fondo.
backcomb ['bækkəʊm] vt cardar.
backdate [bæk'deɪt] vt (letter) poner fecha atrasada a; **~d pay rise** aumento de sueldo con efecto retroactivo.
backdrop ['bækdrɒp] n = **backcloth**.
backer ['bækə*] n partidario/a; (COMM)

promotor(a) *m/f.*

backfire [bæk'faɪə*] *vi* (*AUT*) petardear; (*plans*) fallar, salir mal.

backgammon ['bækgæmən] *n* backgammon *m.*

background ['bækgraund] *n* fondo; (*of events*) antecedentes *mpl*; (*basic knowledge*) bases *fpl*; (*experience*) conocimientos *mpl*, educación *f ♦ cpd* (*noise, music*) de fondo; (*COMPUT*) secundario; ~ **reading** lectura de preparación; **family** ~ origen *m*, antecedentes *mpl* familiares.

backhand ['bækhænd] *n* (*TENNIS: also:* ~ **stroke**) revés *m.*

backhanded ['bæk'hændɪd] *adj* (*fig*) ambiguo, equívoco.

backhander ['bæk'hændə*] *n* (*BRIT: bribe*) soborno.

backing ['bækɪŋ] *n* (*fig*) apoyo, respaldo; (*COMM*) respaldo financiero; (*MUS*) acompañamiento.

backlash ['bæklæʃ] *n* reacción *f* (en contra).

backlog ['bæklɔg] *n:* ~ **of work** trabajo atrasado.

back number *n* (*of magazine etc*) número atrasado.

backpack ['bækpæk] *n* mochila.

backpacker ['bækpækə*] *n* mochilero/a.

back pay *n* atrasos *mpl.*

backpedal ['bækpedl] *vi* (*fig*) volverse/ echarse atrás.

backseat driver ['bæksiːt-] *n* pasajero que se empeña en aconsejar al conductor.

backside ['bæksaɪd] *n* (*col*) trasero.

backslash ['bækslæʃ] *n* pleca, barra inversa.

backslide ['bækslaɪd] *vi* reincidir, recaer.

backspace ['bækspeɪs] *vi* (*in typing*) retroceder.

backstage [bæk'steɪdʒ] *adv* entre bastidores.

back-street ['bækstriːt] *adj* de barrio; ~ **abortionist** persona que practica abortos clandestinos.

backstroke ['bækstrəuk] *n* espalda.

backtrack ['bæktræk] *vi* (*fig*) = **backpedal.**

backup ['bækʌp] *adj* (*train, plane*) suplementario; (*COMPUT: disk, file*) de reserva *♦ n* (*support*) apoyo; (*also:* ~ **file**) copia de reserva; (*US: congestion*) embotellamiento, retención *f.*

back-up lights *npl* (*US*) luces *fpl* de marcha atrás.

backward ['bækwəd] *adj* (*movement*) hacia atrás; (*person, country*) atrasado; (*shy*) tímido.

backwardness ['bækwədnɪs] *n* atraso.

backwards ['bækwədz] *adv* (*move, go*) hacia atrás; (*read a list*) al revés; (*fall*) de espaldas; **to know sth** ~ *or* (*US*) ~ **and forwards** (*col*) saberse algo al dedillo.

backwater ['bækwɔːtə*] *n* (*fig*) lugar *m* atrasado *or* apartado.

backyard [bæk'jaːd] *n* patio trasero.

bacon ['beɪkən] *n* tocino, bacon *m*, beicon *m.*

bacteria [bæk'tɪərɪə] *npl* bacterias *fpl.*

bacteriology [bæktɪərɪ'ɔlədʒɪ] *n* bacteriología.

bad [bæd] *adj* malo; (*serious*) grave; (*meat, food*) podrido, pasado; **to go** ~ pasarse; **to have a** ~ **time of it** pasarlo mal; **I feel** ~ **about it** (*guilty*) me siento culpable; ~ **debt** (*COMM*) cuenta incobrable; **in** ~ **faith** de mala fe.

baddie, baddy ['bædɪ] *n* (*col: CINE etc*) malo/a.

bade [bæd, beɪd] *pt of* **bid.**

badge [bædʒ] *n* insignia; (*metal* ~) chapa; (*of policeman*) placa; (*stick-on*) pegatina.

badger ['bædʒə*] *n* tejón *m.*

badly ['bædlɪ] *adv* (*work, dress etc*) mal; ~ **wounded** gravemente herido; **he needs it** ~ le hace mucha falta; **to be** ~ **off (for money)** andar mal de dinero; **things are going** ~ las cosas van muy mal.

bad-mannered ['bæd'mænəd] *adj* mal educado.

badminton ['bædmɪntən] *n* bádminton *m.*

bad-tempered ['bæd'tempəd] *adj* de mal genio *or* carácter; (*temporary*) de mal humor.

baffle ['bæfl] *vt* desconcertar, confundir.

baffling ['bæflɪŋ] *adj* incomprensible.

bag [bæg] *n* bolsa; (*handbag*) bolso; (*satchel*) mochila; (*case*) maleta; (*of hunter*) caza *♦ vt* (*col: take*) coger (*SP*), agarrar (*LAM*), pescar; ~**s of** (*col: lots of*) un montón de; **to pack one's** ~**s** hacer las maletas.

bagful ['bægful] *n* saco (lleno).

baggage ['bægɪdʒ] *n* equipaje *m.*

baggage claim *n* recogida de equipajes.

baggy ['bægɪ] *adj* (*trousers*) ancho, holgado.

Baghdad [bæg'dæd] *n* Bagdad *m.*

bag lady *n* (*col*) *mujer sin hogar cargada de bolsas.*

bagpipes ['bægpaɪps] *npl* gaita *sg.*

bag-snatcher ['bægsnætʃə*] *n* (*BRIT*) ladrón/ona *m/f* de bolsos.

bag-snatching ['bægsnætʃɪŋ] *n* (*BRIT*) tirón *m* (de bolsos).

Bahamas [bə'hɑːməz] *npl:* **the** ~ las (Islas) Bahama.

Bahrain [baː'reɪn] *n* Bahrein *m.*

bail [beɪl] *n* fianza *♦ vt* (*prisoner: also: grant*

~ **to**) poner en libertad bajo fianza; (*boat:
also*: ~ **out**) achicar; **on** ~ (*prisoner*) bajo
fianza; **to be released on** ~ ser puesto en
libertad bajo fianza; **to** ~ **sb out** pagar la
fianza de algn; *see also* **bale**.

bailiff ['beɪlɪf] *n* alguacil *m*.

bait [beɪt] *n* cebo ♦ *vt* poner el cebo en.

bake [beɪk] *vt* cocer (al horno) ♦ *vi* (*cook*)
cocerse; (*be hot*) hacer un calor terrible.

baked beans *npl* judías *fpl* en salsa de
tomate.

baker ['beɪkə*] *n* panadero/a.

baker's dozen *n* docena del fraile.

bakery ['beɪkərɪ] *n* (*for bread*) panadería;
(*for cakes*) pastelería.

baking ['beɪkɪŋ] *n* (*act*) cocción *f*; (*batch*)
hornada.

baking powder *n* levadura (en polvo).

baking tin *n* molde *m* (para horno).

balaclava [bælə'klɑːvə] *n* (*also*: ~ **helmet**)
pasamontañas *m inv*.

balance ['bæləns] *n* equilibrio; (*COMM*: *sum*)
balance *m*; (*remainder*) resto; (*scales*)
balanza ♦ *vt* equilibrar; (*budget*) nivelar;
(*account*) saldar; (*compensate*)
compensar; ~ **of trade/payments** balanza
de comercio/pagos; ~ **carried forward**
balance *m* pasado a cuenta nueva; ~
brought forward saldo de hoja anterior;
to ~ **the books** hacer el balance.

balanced ['bælənst] *adj* (*personality*, *diet*)
equilibrado.

balance sheet *n* balance *m*.

balcony ['bælkənɪ] *n* (*open*) balcón *m*;
(*closed*) galería.

bald [bɔːld] *adj* calvo; (*tyre*) liso.

baldness ['bɔːldnɪs] *n* calvicie *f*.

bale [beɪl] *n* (*AGR*) paca, fardo.

▶**bale out** *vi* (*of a plane*) lanzarse en
paracaídas ♦ *vt* (*NAUT*) achicar; **to** ~ **sb
out of a difficulty** sacar a algn de un
apuro.

Balearic Islands [bælɪ'ærɪk-] *npl*: **the** ~ las
(Islas) Baleares.

baleful ['beɪlful] *adj* (*look*) triste; (*sinister*)
funesto, siniestro.

balk [bɔːk] *vi*: **to** ~ (**at**) resistirse (a);
(*horse*) plantarse (ante).

Balkan ['bɔːlkən] *adj* balcánico ♦ *n*: **the** ~**s**
los Balcanes.

ball [bɔːl] *n* (*sphere*) bola; (*football*) balón *m*;
(*for tennis, golf etc*) pelota; (*dance*) baile *m*;
to be on the ~ (*fig*: *competent*) ser un
enterado; (: *alert*) estar al tanto; **to play** ~
(**with sb**) jugar a la pelota (con algn); (*fig*)
cooperar; **to start the** ~ **rolling** (*fig*)
empezar; **the** ~ **is in your court** (*fig*) le
toca a usted.

ballad ['bæləd] *n* balada, romance *m*.

ballast ['bæləst] *n* lastre *m*.

ball bearing *n* cojinete *m* de bolas.

ballcock ['bɔːlkɔk] *n* llave *f* de bola *or* de
flotador.

ballerina [bælə'riːnə] *n* bailarina.

ballet ['bæleɪ] *n* ballet *m*.

ballet dancer *n* bailarín/ina *m/f* (de ballet).

ballistic [bə'lɪstɪk] *adj* balístico;
intercontinental ~ **missile** misil *m*
balístico intercontinental.

ballistics [bə'lɪstɪks] *n* balística.

balloon [bə'luːn] *n* globo; (*in comic strip*)
bocadillo ♦ *vi* dispararse.

balloonist [bə'luːnɪst] *n* aeróstata *m/f*.

ballot ['bælət] *n* votación *f*.

ballot box *n* urna (electoral).

ballot paper *n* papeleta.

ballpark ['bɔːlpɑːk] *n* (*US*) estadio de
béisbol.

ball-point pen ['bɔːlpɔɪnt-] *n* bolígrafo.

ballroom ['bɔːlrum] *n* salón *m* de baile.

balm [bɑːm] *n* (*also fig*) bálsamo.

balmy ['bɑːmɪ] *adj* (*breeze*, *air*) suave; (*col*)
= **barmy**.

BALPA ['bælpə] *n abbr* (= *British Airline
Pilots' Association*) sindicato de pilotos de
líneas aéreas.

balsa (wood) ['bɔːlsə-] *n* (madera de)
balsa.

Baltic ['bɔːltɪk] *adj* báltico ♦ *n*: **the** ~ (**Sea**) el
(Mar) Báltico.

balustrade ['bæləstreɪd] *n* barandilla.

bamboo [bæm'buː] *n* bambú *m*.

bamboozle [bæm'buːzl] *vt* (*col*) embaucar,
engatusar.

ban [bæn] *n* prohibición *f* ♦ *vt* prohibir;
(*exclude*) excluir; **he was** ~**ned from
driving** le retiraron el carnet de
conducir.

banal [bə'nɑːl] *adj* banal, vulgar.

banana [bə'nɑːnə] *n* plátano, banana (*LAM*).

band [bænd] *n* (*group*) banda; (*gang*)
pandilla; (*strip*) faja, tira; (*at a dance*)
orquesta; (*MIL*) banda; (*rock* ~) grupo.

▶**band together** *vi* juntarse, asociarse.

bandage ['bændɪdʒ] *n* venda, vendaje *m* ♦ *vt*
vendar.

Band-Aid ® ['bændeɪd] *n* (*US*) tirita, curita
(*LAM*).

bandit ['bændɪt] *n* bandido; **one-armed** ~
máquina tragaperras.

bandstand ['bændstænd] *n* quiosco de
música.

bandwagon ['bændwægən] *n*: **to jump on
the** ~ (*fig*) subirse al carro.

bandy ['bændɪ] *vt* (*jokes*, *insults*)
intercambiar.

bandy-legged ['bændı'lɛgd] *adj* patizambo.
bane [beın] *n*: **it** (*or* **he** *etc*) **is the ~ of my life** me amarga la vida.
bang [bæŋ] *n* estallido; (*of door*) portazo; (*blow*) golpe *m* ♦ *vt* golpear ♦ *vi* estallar ♦ *adv*: **to be ~ on time** (*col*) llegar en punto; **to ~ the door** dar un portazo; **to ~ into sth** chocar con algo, golpearse contra algo; *see also* **bangs.**
banger ['bæŋə*] *n* (*BRIT: car: also*: **old ~**) armatoste *m*, cacharro; (*BRIT col: sausage*) salchicha; (*firework*) petardo.
Bangkok [bæŋ'kɔk] *n* Bangkok *m*.
Bangladesh [bæŋglə'dɛʃ] *n* Bangladesh *f*.
bangle ['bæŋgl] *n* brazalete *m*, ajorca.
bangs [bæŋz] *npl* (*US*) flequillo *sg*.
banish ['bænıʃ] *vt* desterrar.
banister(s) ['bænıstə(z)] *n*(*pl*) barandilla *f*, pasamanos *m inv*.
banjo, *pl* **~es** *or* **~s** ['bændʒəu] *n* banjo.
bank [bæŋk] *n* (*COMM*) banco; (*of river, lake*) ribera, orilla; (*of earth*) terraplén *m*.
▶**bank on** *vt fus* contar con.
bank account *n* cuenta bancaria.
bank balance *n* saldo.
bank card *n* = **banker's card.**
bank charges *npl* comisión *fsg*.
bank draft *n* letra de cambio.
banker ['bæŋkə*] *n* banquero; **~'s card** (*BRIT*) tarjeta bancaria; **~'s order** orden *f* bancaria.
bank giro *n* giro bancario.
bank holiday *n* (*BRIT*) día *m* festivo *or* de fiesta; *ver recuadro.*

BANK HOLIDAY

El término **bank holiday** *se aplica en el Reino Unido a todo día festivo oficial en el que cierran bancos y comercios. Los más destacados coinciden con Navidad, Semana Santa, finales de mayo y finales de agosto. Al contrario que en los países de tradición católica, no se celebran las festividades dedicadas a los santos.*

---

banking ['bæŋkıŋ] *n* banca.
bank loan *n* préstamo bancario.
bank manager *n* director(a) *m/f* (de sucursal) de banco.
banknote ['bæŋknəut] *n* billete *m* de banco.
bank rate *n* tipo de interés bancario.
bankrupt ['bæŋkrʌpt] *n* quebrado/a ♦ *adj* quebrado, insolvente; **to go ~** quebrar, hacer bancarrota; **to be ~** estar en quiebra.
bankruptcy ['bæŋkrʌptsı] *n* quiebra, bancarrota.

bank statement *n* extracto de cuenta.
banned substance [bænd-] *n* (*SPORT*) sustancia prohibida.
banner ['bænə*] *n* bandera; (*in demonstration*) pancarta.
banns [bænz] *npl* amonestaciones *fpl*.
banquet ['bæŋkwıt] *n* banquete *m*.
banter ['bæntə*] *n* guasa, bromas *fpl*.
baptism ['bæptızəm] *n* bautismo; (*act*) bautizo.
baptize [bæp'taız] *vt* bautizar.
bar [bɑ:*] *n* barra; (*on door*) tranca; (*of window, cage*) reja; (*of soap*) pastilla; (*fig: hindrance*) obstáculo; (*prohibition*) prohibición *f*; (*pub*) bar *m*, cantina (*esp LAM*); (*counter: in pub*) barra, mostrador *m*; (*MUS*) barra ♦ *vt* (*road*) obstruir; (*window, door*) atrancar; (*person*) excluir; (*activity*) prohibir; **behind ~s** entre rejas; **the B~** (*LAW: profession*) la abogacía; (*: people*) el cuerpo de abogados; **~ none** sin excepción.
Barbados [bɑ:'beıdɔs] *n* Barbados *m*.
barbarian [bɑ:'bɛərıən] *n* bárbaro/a.
barbaric [bɑ:'bærık] *adj* bárbaro.
barbarity [bɑ:'bærıtı] *n* barbaridad *f*.
barbarous ['bɑ:bərəs] *adj* bárbaro.
barbecue ['bɑ:bıkju:] *n* barbacoa, asado (*LAM*).
barbed wire ['bɑ:bd-] *n* alambre *m* de espino.
barber ['bɑ:bə*] *n* peluquero, barbero.
barbiturate [bɑ:'bıtjurıt] *n* barbitúrico.
Barcelona [bɑ:sı'ləunə] *n* Barcelona.
bar chart *n* gráfico de barras.
bar code *n* código de barras.
bare [bɛə*] *adj* desnudo; (*head*) descubierto ♦ *vt* desnudar; **to ~ one's teeth** enseñar los dientes.
bareback ['bɛəbæk] *adv* a pelo.
barefaced ['bɛəfeıst] *adj* descarado.
barefoot ['bɛəfut] *adj, adv* descalzo.
bareheaded [bɛə'hɛdıd] *adj* descubierto, sin sombrero.
barely ['bɛəlı] *adv* apenas.
bareness ['bɛənıs] *n* desnudez *f*.
Barents Sea ['bærənts-] *n*: **the ~** el Mar de Barents.
bargain ['bɑ:gın] *n* pacto; (*transaction*) negocio; (*good buy*) ganga ♦ *vi* negociar; (*haggle*) regatear; **into the ~** además, por añadidura.
▶**bargain for** *vt fus* (*col*): **he got more than he ~ed for** le resultó peor de lo que esperaba.
bargaining ['bɑ:gənıŋ] *n* negociación *f*; regateo; **~ table** mesa de negociaciones.
bargaining position *n*: **to be in a strong/**

weak ~ estar/no estar en una posición de fuerza para negociar.
barge [bɑːdʒ] n barcaza.
►**barge in** vi irrumpir; (*conversation*) entrometerse.
►**barge into** vt fus dar contra.
baritone ['bærɪtəʊn] n barítono.
barium meal ['bɛərɪəm-] n (*MED*) sulfato de bario.
bark [bɑːk] n (*of tree*) corteza; (*of dog*) ladrido ♦ vi ladrar.
barley ['bɑːlɪ] n cebada.
barley sugar n azúcar m cande.
barmaid ['bɑːmeɪd] n camarera.
barman ['bɑːmən] n camarero, barman m.
barmy ['bɑːmɪ] adj (*col*) chiflado, chalado.
barn [bɑːn] n granero; (*for animals*) cuadra.
barnacle ['bɑːnəkl] n percebe m.
barn owl n lechuza.
barometer [bə'rɒmɪtə*] n barómetro.
baron ['bærən] n barón m; (*fig*) magnate m; **the press** ~**s** los magnates de la prensa.
baroness ['bærənɪs] n baronesa.
baroque [bə'rɒk] adj barroco.
barrack ['bærək] vt (*BRIT*) abuchear.
barracks ['bærəks] npl cuartel msg.
barrage ['bærɑːʒ] n (*MIL*) cortina de fuego; (*dam*) presa; (*fig: of criticism etc*) lluvia, aluvión m; **a** ~ **of questions** una lluvia de preguntas.
barrel ['bærəl] n barril m; (*of wine*) tonel m, cuba; (*of gun*) cañón m.
barren ['bærən] adj estéril.
barricade [bærɪ'keɪd] n barricada ♦ vt cerrar con barricadas.
barrier ['bærɪə*] n barrera; (*crash* ~) barrera.
barrier cream n crema protectora.
barring ['bɑːrɪŋ] prep excepto, salvo.
barrister ['bærɪstə*] n (*BRIT*) abogado/a; *ver recuadro*.

BARRISTER

En el sistema legal inglés **barrister** *es el abogado que se ocupa de defender los casos de sus clientes en los tribunales superiores. El equivalente escocés es "advocate". Normalmente actúan según instrucciones de un "solicitor", abogado de despacho que no toma parte activa en los juicios de dichos tribunales. El título de* **barrister** *lo otorga el órgano colegiado correspondiente, "the Inns of Court".*

---

barrow ['bærəʊ] n (*cart*) carretilla.
barstool ['bɑːstuːl] n taburete m (de bar).
Bart. abbr (*BRIT*) = baronet.

bartender ['bɑːtɛndə*] n (*US*) camarero, barman m.
barter ['bɑːtə*] vt: **to** ~ **sth for sth** trocar algo por algo.
base [beɪs] n base f ♦ vt: **to** ~ **sth on** basar or fundar algo en ♦ adj bajo, infame; **to** ~ **at** (*troops*) estacionar en; **I'm** ~**d in London** (*work*) trabajo en Londres.
baseball ['beɪsbɔːl] n béisbol m.
base camp n campamento base.
Basel ['bɑːzəl] n Basilea.
baseless ['beɪslɪs] adj infundado.
baseline ['beɪslaɪn] n (*TENNIS*) línea de fondo.
basement ['beɪsmənt] n sótano.
base rate n tipo base.
bases ['beɪsiːz] npl of **basis**; ['beɪsɪz] npl of **base**.
bash [bæʃ] n: **I'll have a** ~ (**at it**) lo intentaré ♦ vt (*col*) golpear.
►**bash up** vt (*col: car*) destrozar; (: *person*) aporrear, vapulear.
bashful ['bæʃful] adj tímido, vergonzoso.
bashing ['bæʃɪŋ] n (*col*) paliza.
BASIC ['beɪsɪk] n BASIC m.
basic ['beɪsɪk] adj (*salary etc*) básico; (*elementary: principles*) fundamental.
basically ['beɪsɪklɪ] adv fundamentalmente, en el fondo.
basic rate n (*of tax*) base f mínima imponible.
basil ['bæzl] n albahaca.
basin ['beɪsn] n (*vessel*) cuenco, tazón m; (*GEO*) cuenca; (*also:* **wash**~) palangana, jofaina; (*in bathroom*) lavabo.
basis ['beɪsɪs], pl **-ses** [-siːz] n base f; **on the** ~ **of what you've said** en base a lo que has dicho.
bask [bɑːsk] vi: **to** ~ **in the sun** tomar el sol.
basket ['bɑːskɪt] n cesta, cesto.
basketball ['bɑːskɪtbɔːl] n baloncesto.
basketball player n jugador(a) m/f de baloncesto.
basketwork ['bɑːskɪtwəːk] n cestería.
Basle [bɑːl] n Basilea.
basmati rice [bəz'mætɪ-] n arroz m basmati.
Basque [bæsk] adj, n vasco/a m/f.
Basque Country n Euskadi m, País m Vasco.
bass [beɪs] n (*MUS*) bajo.
bass clef n clave f de fa.
bassoon [bə'suːn] n fagot m.
bastard ['bɑːstəd] n bastardo/a; (*col!*) cabrón m, hijo de puta (*!*).
baste [beɪst] vt (*CULIN*) rociar (con su salsa).

bastion ['bæstɪən] *n* bastión *m*, baluarte *m*.

bat [bæt] *n* (*ZOOL*) murciélago; (*for ball games*) palo; (*for cricket, baseball*) bate *m*; (*BRIT: for table tennis*) pala; **he didn't ~ an eyelid** ni pestañeó, ni se inmutó.

batch [bætʃ] *n* lote *m*, remesa; (*of bread*) hornada.

batch processing *n* (*COMPUT*) proceso por lotes.

bated ['beɪtɪd] *adj*: **with ~ breath** sin respirar.

bath [bɑːθ, *pl* bɑːðz] *n* (*action*) baño; (*~tub*) bañera, tina (*esp LAM*) ♦ *vt* bañar; **to have a ~** bañarse, darse un baño; *see also* **baths**.

bathchair ['bɑːθtʃɛə*] *n* silla de ruedas.

bathe [beɪð] *vi* bañarse; (*US*) darse un baño, bañarse ♦ *vt* (*wound etc*) lavar; (*US*) bañar, dar un baño a.

bather ['beɪðə*] *n* bañista *m/f*.

bathing ['beɪðɪŋ] *n* baño.

bathing cap *n* gorro de baño.

bathing costume, (*US*) **bathing suit** *n* bañador *m*, traje *m* de baño.

bathing trunks *npl* bañador *msg*.

bathmat ['bɑːθmæt] *n* alfombrilla de baño.

bathrobe ['bɑːθrəub] *n* albornoz *m*.

bathroom ['bɑːθrum] *n* (cuarto de) baño.

baths [bɑːðz] *npl* piscina *sg*.

bath towel *n* toalla de baño.

bathtub ['bɑːθtʌb] *n* bañera.

batman ['bætmən] *n* (*BRIT*) ordenanza *m*.

baton ['bætən] *n* (*MUS*) batuta.

battalion [bə'tælɪən] *n* batallón *m*.

batten ['bætn] *n* (*CARPENTRY*) listón *m*; (*NAUT*) junquillo, sable *m*.

▶**batten down** *vt* (*NAUT*): **to ~ down the hatches** atrancar las escotillas.

batter ['bætə*] *vt* maltratar, apalear; (*subj: wind, rain*) azotar ♦ *n* batido.

battered ['bætəd] *adj* (*hat, pan*) estropeado.

battery ['bætərɪ] *n* batería; (*of torch*) pila.

battery charger *n* cargador *m* de baterías.

battery farming *n* cría intensiva.

battle ['bætl] *n* batalla; (*fig*) lucha ♦ *vi* luchar; **that's half the ~** (*col*) ya hay medio camino andado; **to fight a losing ~** (*fig*) luchar por una causa perdida.

battlefield ['bætlfiːld] *n* campo *m* de batalla.

battlements ['bætlmənts] *npl* almenas *fpl*.

battleship ['bætlʃɪp] *n* acorazado.

batty ['bætɪ] *adj* (*col: person*) chiflado; (: *idea*) de chiflado.

bauble ['bɔːbl] *n* chuchería.

baud [bɔːd] *n* (*COMPUT*) baudio.

baud rate *n* (*COMPUT*) velocidad *f* (de transmisión) en baudios.

bauxite ['bɔːksaɪt] *n* bauxita.

Bavaria [bə'vɛərɪə] *n* Baviera.

Bavarian [bə'vɛərɪən] *adj*, *n* bávaro/a *m/f*.

bawdy ['bɔːdɪ] *adj* indecente; (*joke*) verde.

bawl [bɔːl] *vi* chillar, gritar.

bay [beɪ] *n* (*GEO*) bahía; (*for parking*) parking *m*, estacionamiento; (*loading ~*) patio de carga; (*BOT*) laurel *m* ♦ *vi* aullar; **to hold sb at ~** mantener a alguien a raya.

bay leaf *n* (hoja de) laurel *m*.

bayonet ['beɪənɪt] *n* bayoneta.

bay window *n* ventana salediza.

bazaar [bə'zɑː*] *n* bazar *m*.

bazooka [bə'zuːkə] *n* bazuca.

BB *n abbr* (*BRIT*: = *Boys' Brigade*) organización juvenil para chicos.

B. & B. *n abbr* = **bed and breakfast**.

BBB *n abbr* (*US*: = *Better Business Bureau*) organismo para la defensa del consumidor.

BBC *n abbr* (= *British Broadcasting Corporation*) BBC *f*; *ver recuadro*.

BBC

La **BBC** es el organismo público británico de radio y televisión, autónomo en cuanto a su política de programas pero subvencionado por un estatuto ("BBC charter") que ha de aprobar el Parlamento. Además de cadenas nacionales de televisión y de radio, transmite también un servicio informativo mundial ("BBC World Service"). A no tener publicidad, se financia a través de operaciones comerciales paralelas y del cobro de una licencia anual obligatoria ("TV licence") para los que tienen aparato de televisión.

BC *ad abbr* (= *before Christ*) a. de J.C. ♦ *abbr* (*Canada*) = *British Columbia*.

BCG *n abbr* (= *Bacillus Calmette-Guérin*) vacuna de la tuberculosis.

BD *n abbr* (= *Bachelor of Divinity*) Licenciado/a en Teología.

B/D *abbr* = **bank draft**.

BDS *n abbr* (= *Bachelor of Dental Surgery*) título universitario.

―――――――――――――― *KEYWORD*

be [biː] (*pt* **was, were**, *pp* **been**) *aux vb* **1** (*with present participle: forming continuous tenses*): **what are you doing?** ¿qué estás haciendo?, ¿qué haces?; **they're coming tomorrow** vienen mañana; **I've been waiting for you for hours** llevo horas esperándote

2 (*with pp: forming passives*) ser (*but often*

B/E – bearing

replaced by active or reflexive constructions);
to ~ **murdered** ser asesinado; **the box
had been opened** habían abierto la caja;
the thief was nowhere to ~ **seen** no se
veía al ladrón por ninguna parte
3 (in tag questions): **it was fun, wasn't it?**
fue divertido, ¿no? or ¿verdad?; **he's
good-looking, isn't he?** es guapo, ¿no te
parece?; **she's back again, is she?**
entonces, ¿ha vuelto?
4 (+to +infin): **the house is to** ~ **sold**
(necessity) hay que vender la casa;
(future) van a vender la casa; **he's not to
open it** no tiene que abrirlo; **he was to
have come yesterday** debía de haber
venido ayer; **am I to understand that ...?**
¿debo entender que ...?
♦ vb +complement **1** (with n or num
complement) ser; **he's a doctor** es médico;
2 and 2 are 4 2 y 2 son 4
2 (with adj complement: expressing
permanent or inherent quality) ser;
(: expressing state seen as temporary or
reversible) estar; **I'm English** soy inglés/
esa; **she's tall/pretty** es alta/bonita; **he's
young** es joven; ~ **careful/good/quiet** ten
cuidado/pórtate bien/cállate; **I'm tired**
estoy cansado/a; **I'm warm** tengo calor;
it's dirty está sucio/a
3 (of health) estar; **how are you?** ¿cómo
estás?; **he's very ill** está muy enfermo;
I'm better now ya estoy mejor
4 (of age) tener; **how old are you?**
¿cuántos años tienes?; **I'm sixteen (years
old)** tengo dieciséis años
5 (cost) costar; ser; **how much was the
meal?** ¿cuánto fue or costó la comida?;
that'll ~ **£5.75, please** son £5.75, por
favor; **this shirt is £17** esta camisa cuesta
£17
♦ vi **1** (exist, occur etc) existir, haber; **the
best singer that ever was** el mejor
cantante que existió jamás; **is there a
God?** ¿hay un Dios?, ¿existe Dios?; ~
that as it may sea como sea; **so** ~ **it** así
sea
2 (referring to place) estar; **I won't** ~ **here
tomorrow** no estaré aquí mañana
3 (referring to movement): **where have you
been?** ¿dónde has estado?
♦ impers vb **1** (referring to time): **it's 5
o'clock** son las 5; **it's the 28th of April**
estamos a 28 de abril
2 (referring to distance): **it's 10 km to the
village** el pueblo está a 10 km
3 (referring to the weather): **it's too hot/
cold** hace demasiado calor/frío; **it's
windy today** hace viento hoy

4 (emphatic): **it's me** soy yo; **it was Maria
who paid the bill** fue María la que pagó la
cuenta.

B/E abbr = **bill of exchange**.
beach [biːtʃ] n playa ♦ vt varar.
beach buggy [-bʌgɪ] n buggy m.
beachcomber ['biːtʃkəumə*] n raquero/a.
beachwear ['biːtʃwɛə*] n ropa de playa.
beacon ['biːkən] n (lighthouse) faro;
(marker) guía; (radio ~) radiofaro.
bead [biːd] n cuenta, abalorio; (of dew,
sweat) gota; ~**s** npl (necklace) collar m.
beady ['biːdɪ] adj (eyes) pequeño y
brillante.
beagle ['biːgl] n sabueso pequeño, beagle
m.
beak [biːk] n pico.
beaker ['biːkə*] n vaso.
beam [biːm] n (ARCH) viga; (of light) rayo,
haz m de luz; (RADIO) rayo ♦ vi brillar;
(smile) sonreír; **to drive on full** or **main** ~
conducir con las luces largas.
beaming ['biːmɪŋ] adj (sun, smile) radiante.
bean [biːn] n judía, fríjol/frijol m (esp LAM);
runner/broad ~ habichuela/haba; **coffee**
~ grano de café.
beanpole ['biːnpəul] n (col) espárrago.
beansprouts ['biːnsprauts] npl brotes mpl
de soja.
bear [bɛə*] n oso; (STOCK EXCHANGE) bajista
m ♦ (vb: pt **bore**, pp **borne**) vt (weight etc)
llevar; (cost) pagar; (responsibility) tener;
(traces, signs) mostrar; (produce: fruit) dar;
(COMM: interest) devengar; (endure)
soportar, aguantar; (stand up to) resistir
a; (children) tener, dar a luz ♦ vi: **to** ~
right/left torcer a la derecha/izquierda; **I
can't** ~ **him** no le puedo ver, no lo
soporto; **to bring pressure to** ~ **on sb**
ejercer presión sobre algn.
►**bear on** vt fus tener que ver con,
referirse a.
►**bear out** vt fus (suspicions) corroborar,
confirmar; (person) confirmar lo dicho
por.
►**bear up** vi (cheer up) animarse; **he bore
up well under the strain** resistió bien la
presión.
►**bear with** vt fus (sb's moods, temper)
tener paciencia con.
bearable ['bɛərəbl] adj soportable,
aguantable.
beard [bɪəd] n barba.
bearded ['bɪədɪd] adj con barba.
bearer ['bɛərə*] n (of news, cheque)
portador(a) m/f; (of passport) titular m/f.
bearing ['bɛərɪŋ] n porte m; (connection)

relación *f*; **(ball)** ~**s** *npl* cojinetes *mpl* a
bolas; **to take a** ~ marcarse; **to find one's**
~**s** orientarse.
bearskin ['bɛəskɪn] *n* (*MIL*) gorro militar
(*de piel de oso*).
beast [biːst] *n* bestia; (*col*) bruto, salvaje *m*.
beastly ['biːstlɪ] *adj* bestial; (*awful*)
horrible.
beat [biːt] *n* (*of heart*) latido; (*MUS*) ritmo,
compás *m*; (*of policeman*) ronda ♦ (*vb: pt*
beat, *pp* **beaten**) *vt* (*hit*) golpear; (*eggs*)
batir; (*defeat*) vencer, derrotar; (*better*)
sobrepasar; (*drum*) tocar; (*rhythm*)
marcar ♦ *vi* (*heart*) latir; **off the** ~**en track**
aislado; **to** ~ **about the bush** andarse con
rodeos; **to** ~ **it** largarse; **that** ~**s**
everything! (*col*) ¡eso es el colmo!; **to** ~
on a door dar golpes en una puerta.
▶**beat down** *vt* (*door*) derribar a golpes;
(*price*) conseguir rebajar, regatear;
(*seller*) hacer rebajar el precio ♦ *vi* (*rain*)
llover a cántaros; (*sun*) caer de plomo.
▶**beat off** *vt* rechazar.
▶**beat up** *vt* (*col: person*) dar una paliza a.
beater ['biːtə*] *n* (*for eggs, cream*) batidora.
beating ['biːtɪŋ] *n* paliza, golpiza (*LAM*); **to**
take a ~ recibir una paliza.
beat-up ['biːt'ʌp] *adj* (*col*) destartalado.
beautiful ['bjuːtɪful] *adj* hermoso, bello,
lindo (*esp LAM*).
beautifully ['bjuːtɪfəlɪ] *adv* de maravilla.
beautify ['bjuːtɪfaɪ] *vt* embellecer.
beauty ['bjuːtɪ] *n* belleza, hermosura;
(*concept, person*) belleza; **the** ~ **of it is**
that ... lo mejor de esto es que ....
beauty contest *n* concurso de belleza.
beauty queen *n* reina de la belleza.
beauty salon *n* salón *m* de belleza.
beauty sleep *n*: **to get one's** ~ *no perder*
horas de sueño.
beauty spot *n* lunar *m* postizo; (*BRIT:*
TOURISM) lugar *m* pintoresco.
beaver ['biːvə*] *n* castor *m*.
becalmed [bɪ'kɑːmd] *adj* encalmado.
became [bɪ'keɪm] *pt of* **become**.
because [bɪ'kɔz] *conj* porque; ~ **of** *prep*
debido a, a causa de.
beck [bɛk] *n*: **to be at the** ~ **and call of** estar
a disposición de.
beckon ['bɛkən] *vt* (*also:* ~ **to**) llamar con
señas.
become [bɪ'kʌm] (*irreg: like* **come**) *vi*
(+ *noun*) hacerse, llegar a ser; (+ *adj*)
ponerse, volverse ♦ *vt* (*suit*) favorecer,
sentar bien a; **to** ~ **fat** engordar; **to** ~
angry enfadarse; **it became known that ...**
se descubrió que ....
becoming [bɪ'kʌmɪŋ] *adj* (*behaviour*)

decoroso; (*clothes*) favorecedor(a).
becquerel [bɛkə'rɛl] *n* becquerelio.
BEd *n abbr* (= *Bachelor of Education*) título
universitario; *see also* **Bachelor's Degree**.
bed [bɛd] *n* cama; (*of flowers*) macizo; (*of*
sea, lake) fondo; (*of coal, clay*) capa; **to go**
to ~ acostarse.
▶**bed down** *vi* acostarse.
bed and breakfast (B & B) *n* ≈ pensión *f*;
ver recuadro.

BED AND BREAKFAST

Se llama **bed and breakfast** *a la casa de*
hospedaje particular, o granja si es en el
campo, que ofrece cama y desayuno a
tarifas inferiores a las de un hotel. El
servicio se suele anunciar con carteles
colocados en las ventanas del
establecimiento, en el jardín o en la
carretera y en ellos aparece a menudo
únicamente el símbolo "B & B".

---

bedbug ['bɛdbʌg] *n* chinche *f*.
bedclothes ['bɛdkləuðz] *npl* ropa de cama.
bedding ['bɛdɪŋ] *n* ropa de cama.
bedeck [bɪ'dɛk] *vt* engalanar, adornar.
bedevil [bɪ'dɛvl] *vt* (*dog*) acosar; (*trouble*)
fastidiar.
bedfellow ['bɛdfɛləu] *n*: **they are strange**
~**s** (*fig*) hacen una pareja rara.
bedlam ['bɛdləm] *n* confusión *f*.
bedpan ['bɛdpæn] *n* cuña.
bedraggled [bɪ'drægld] *adj* desastrado.
bedridden ['bɛdrɪdn] *adj* postrado (en
cama).
bedrock ['bɛdrɔk] *n* (*GEO*) roca firme; (*fig*)
pilar *m*.
bedroom ['bɛdrum] *n* dormitorio, alcoba.
Beds *abbr* (*BRIT*) = *Bedfordshire*.
bed settee *n* sofá-cama *m*.
bedside ['bɛdsaɪd] *n*: **at sb's** ~ a la
cabecera de alguien.
bedside lamp *n* lámpara de noche.
bedsit(ter) ['bɛdsɪt(ə*)] *n* (*BRIT*) estudio.
bedspread ['bɛdsprɛd] *n* cubrecama *m*,
colcha.
bedtime ['bɛdtaɪm] *n* hora de acostarse;
it's ~ es hora de acostarse *or* de irse a la
cama.
bee [biː] *n* abeja; **to have a** ~ **in one's**
bonnet (about sth) tener una idea fija (de
algo).
beech [biːtʃ] *n* haya.
beef [biːf] *n* carne *f* de vaca; **roast** ~ rosbif
m.
▶**beef up** *vt* (*col*) reforzar.
beefburger ['biːfbəːgə*] *n* hamburguesa.

beefeater ['biːfiːtə*] n alabardero de la Torre de Londres.

beehive ['biːhaɪv] n colmena.

bee-keeping ['biːkiːpɪŋ] n apicultura.

beeline ['biːlaɪn] n: **to make a ~ for** ir derecho a.

been [biːn] pp of **be**.

beep [biːp] n pitido ♦ vi pitar.

beeper ['biːpə*] n (of doctor etc) busca m inv.

beer [bɪə*] n cerveza.

beer belly n (col) barriga (de bebedor de cerveza).

beer can n bote m or lata de cerveza.

beet [biːt] n (US) remolacha.

beetle ['biːtl] n escarabajo.

beetroot ['biːtruːt] n (BRIT) remolacha.

befall [bɪ'fɔːl] vi (vt) (irreg: like **fall**) acontecer (a).

befit [bɪ'fɪt] vt convenir a, corresponder a.

before [bɪ'fɔː*] prep (of time) antes de; (of space) delante de ♦ conj antes (de) que ♦ adv (time) antes; (space) delante, adelante; ~ **going** antes de marcharse; ~ **she goes** antes de que se vaya; **the week** ~ la semana anterior; **I've never seen it** ~ no lo he visto nunca.

beforehand [bɪ'fɔːhænd] adv de antemano, con anticipación.

befriend [bɪ'frɛnd] vt ofrecer amistad a.

befuddled [bɪ'fʌdld] adj aturdido, atontado.

beg [bɛg] vi pedir limosna, mendigar ♦ vt pedir, rogar; (entreat) suplicar; **I ~ your pardon** (apologising) perdóneme; (not hearing) ¿perdón?

began [bɪ'gæn] pt of **begin**.

beggar ['bɛgə*] n mendigo/a.

begin, pt **began**, pp **begun** [bɪ'gɪn, -gæn, -gʌn] vt, vi empezar, comenzar; **to ~ doing** or **to do sth** empezar a hacer algo; **I can't ~ to thank you** no encuentro palabras para agradecerle; **to ~ with**, **I'd like to know** ... en primer lugar, quisiera saber ...; **~ning from Monday** a partir del lunes.

beginner [bɪ'gɪnə*] n principiante m/f.

beginning [bɪ'gɪnɪŋ] n principio, comienzo; **right from the** ~ desde el principio.

begrudge [bɪ'grʌdʒ] vt: **to ~ sb sth** tenerle envidia a alguien por algo.

beguile [bɪ'gaɪl] vt (enchant) seducir.

beguiling [bɪ'gaɪlɪŋ] adj seductor(a), atractivo.

begun [bɪ'gʌn] pp of **begin**.

behalf [bɪ'hɑːf] n: **on** ~ **of**, (US) **in** ~ **of** en nombre de; (for benefit of) por.

behave [bɪ'heɪv] vi (person) portarse, comportarse; (thing) funcionar; (well: also: ~ **o.s.**) portarse bien.

behaviour, (US) **behavior** [bɪ'heɪvjə*] n comportamiento, conducta.

behead [bɪ'hɛd] vt decapitar.

beheld [bɪ'hɛld] pt, pp of **behold**.

behind [bɪ'haɪnd] prep detrás de ♦ adv detrás, por detrás, atrás ♦ n trasero; **to be** ~ **(schedule)** ir retrasado; ~ **the scenes** (fig) entre bastidores; **we're** ~ **them in technology** (fig) nos dejan atrás en tecnología; **to leave sth** ~ olvidar or dejarse algo; **to be** ~ **with sth** estar atrasado en algo; **to be** ~ **with payments (on sth)** estar atrasado en el pago (de algo).

behold [bɪ'həuld] (irreg: like **hold**) vt contemplar.

beige [beɪʒ] adj (color) beige.

being ['biːɪŋ] n ser m; **to come into** ~ nacer, aparecer.

Beirut [beɪ'ruːt] n Beirut m.

Belarus [bɛlə'rus] n Bielorrusia.

Belarussian [bɛlə'rʌʃən] adj, n bielorruso/a ♦ n (LING) bielorruso.

belated [bɪ'leɪtɪd] adj atrasado, tardío.

belch [bɛltʃ] vi eructar ♦ vt (also: ~ **out**: smoke etc) vomitar, arrojar.

beleaguered [bɪ'liːgəd] adj asediado.

Belfast ['bɛlfaːst] n Belfast m.

belfry ['bɛlfrɪ] n campanario.

Belgian ['bɛldʒən] adj, n belga m/f.

Belgium ['bɛldʒəm] n Bélgica.

Belgrade [bɛl'greɪd] n Belgrado.

belie [bɪ'laɪ] vt (give false impression of) desmentir, contradecir.

belief [bɪ'liːf] n (opinion) opinión f; (trust, faith) fe f; (acceptance as true) creencia; **it's beyond** ~ es increíble; **in the** ~ **that** creyendo que.

believable [bɪ'liːvəbl] adj creíble.

believe [bɪ'liːv] vt, vi creer; **to ~ (that)** creer (que); **to ~ in** (God, ghosts) creer en; (method) ser partidario de; **he is ~d to be abroad** se cree que está en el extranjero; **I don't ~ in corporal punishment** no soy partidario del castigo corporal.

believer [bɪ'liːvə*] n (in idea, activity) partidario/a; (REL) creyente m/f, fiel m/f.

belittle [bɪ'lɪtl] vt despreciar.

Belize [bɛ'liːz] n Belice f.

bell [bɛl] n campana; (small) campanilla; (on door) timbre m; (animal's) cencerro; (on toy etc) cascabel m; **that rings a** ~ (fig) eso me suena.

bellboy ['bɛlbɔɪ] n, (US) **bellhop** ['bɛlhɔp] n botones m inv.

belligerent [bɪ'lɪdʒərənt] adj (at war) beligerante; (fig) agresivo.

bellow ['bɛləu] *vi* bramar; (*person*) rugir
♦ *vt* (*orders*) gritar.
bellows ['bɛləuz] *npl* fuelle *msg*.
bell push *n* pulsador *m* de timbre.
belly ['bɛlɪ] *n* barriga, panza.
bellyache ['bɛlɪeɪk] *n* dolor *m* de barriga *or*
de tripa ♦ *vi* (*col*) gruñir.
bellyful ['bɛlɪful] *n*: **to have had a ~ of**
(*col*) estar más que harto de ....
belong [bɪ'lɔŋ] *vi*: **to ~ to** pertenecer a;
(*club etc*) ser socio de; **this book ~s here**
este libro va aquí.
belongings [bɪ'lɔŋɪŋz] *npl*: **personal ~**
pertenencias *fpl*.
Belorussia [bɛləu'rʌʃə] *n* Bielorrusia.
Belorussian [bɛləu'rʌʃən] *adj, n* =
Belarussian.
beloved [bɪ'lʌvɪd] *adj, n* querido/a *m/f*,
amado/a *m/f*.
below [bɪ'ləu] *prep* bajo, debajo de ♦ *adv*
abajo, (por) debajo; **see ~** véase más
abajo.
belt [bɛlt] *n* cinturón *m*; (*TECH*) correa,
cinta ♦ *vt* (*thrash*) golpear con correa;
industrial ~ cinturón industrial.
▶**belt out** *vt* (*song*) cantar a voz en grito *or*
a grito pelado.
▶**belt up** *vi* (*AUT*) ponerse el cinturón de
seguridad; (*fig, col*) cerrar el pico.
beltway ['bɛltweɪ] *n* (*US AUT*) carretera de
circunvalación.
bemoan [bɪ'məun] *vt* lamentar.
bemused [bɪ'mju:zd] *adj* perplejo.
bench [bɛntʃ] *n* banco; **the B~** (*LAW*) el
tribunal; (*people*) la judicatura.
bench mark *n* punto de referencia.
bend [bɛnd] *vb* (*pt, pp* **bent** [bɛnt]) *vt* doblar;
(*body, head*) inclinar ♦ *vi* inclinarse; (*road*)
curvarse ♦ *n* (*BRIT: in road, river*) recodo;
(*in pipe*) codo; *see also* **bends**.
▶**bend down** *vi* inclinarse, doblarse.
▶**bend over** *vi* inclinarse.
bends [bɛndz] *npl* (*MED*) apoplejía por
cambios bruscos de presión.
beneath [bɪ'ni:θ] *prep* bajo, debajo de;
(*unworthy of*) indigno de ♦ *adv* abajo, (por)
debajo.
benefactor ['bɛnɪfæktə*] *n* bienhechor *m*.
benefactress ['bɛnɪfæktrɪs] *n* bienhechora.
beneficial [bɛnɪ'fɪʃəl] *adj*: **~ to** beneficioso
para.
beneficiary [bɛnɪ'fɪʃərɪ] *n* (*LAW*)
beneficiario/a.
benefit ['bɛnɪfɪt] *n* beneficio, provecho;
(*allowance of money*) subsidio ♦ *vt*
beneficiar ♦ *vi*: **he'll ~ from it** lo sacará
provecho; **unemployment ~** subsidio de
desempleo.

Benelux ['bɛnɪlʌks] *n* Benelux *m*.
benevolence [bɪ'nɛvələns] *n* benevolencia.
benevolent [bɪ'nɛvələnt] *adj* benévolo.
BEng *n abbr* (= *Bachelor of Engineering*)
título universitario.
benign [bɪ'naɪn] *adj* (*person, MED*) benigno;
(*smile*) afable.
bent [bɛnt] *pt, pp of* **bend** ♦ *n* inclinación *f*
♦ *adj* (*wire, pipe*) doblado, torcido; **to be**
~ on estar empeñado en.
bequeath [bɪ'kwi:ð] *vt* legar.
bequest [bɪ'kwɛst] *n* legado.
bereaved [bɪ'ri:vd] *adj* afligido ♦ *n*: **the ~**
los afligidos *mpl*.
bereavement [bɪ'ri:vmənt] *n* aflicción *f*.
beret ['bɛreɪ] *n* boina.
Bering Sea ['bɛərɪŋ-] *n*: **the ~** el Mar de
Bering.
berk [bə:k] *n* (*BRIT col*) capullo/a (*!*).
Berks *abbr* (*BRIT*) = *Berkshire*.
Berlin [bə:'lɪn] *n* Berlín *m*; **East/West ~**
Berlín del Este/Oeste.
berm [bə:m] *n* (*US AUT*) arcén *m*.
Bermuda [bə:'mju:də] *n* las (Islas)
Bermudas.
Bermuda shorts *npl* bermudas *mpl or fpl*.
Bern [bə:n] *n* Berna.
berry ['bɛrɪ] *n* baya.
berserk [bə'sə:k] *adj*: **to go ~** perder los
estribos.
berth [bə:θ] *n* (*bed*) litera; (*cabin*) camarote
m; (*for ship*) amarradero ♦ *vi* atracar,
amarrar; **to give sb a wide ~** (*fig*) evitar
encontrarse con algn.
beseech, *pt, pp* **besought** [bɪ'si:tʃ, -'sɔ:t] *vt*
suplicar.
beset, *pt, pp* **beset** [bɪ'sɛt] *vt* (*person*) acosar
♦ *adj*: **a policy ~ with dangers** una política
rodeada de peligros.
besetting [bɪ'sɛtɪŋ] *adj*: **his ~ sin** su
principal falta.
beside [bɪ'saɪd] *prep* junto a, al lado de;
(*compared with*) comparado con; **to be ~**
o.s. with anger estar fuera de sí; **that's ~**
the point eso no tiene nada que ver con
el asunto.
besides [bɪ'saɪdz] *adv* además ♦ *prep* (*as well*
as) además de; (*except*) excepto.
besiege [bɪ'si:dʒ] *vt* (*town*) sitiar; (*fig*)
asediar.
besmirch [bɪ'smə:tʃ] *vt* (*fig*) manchar,
mancillar.
besotted [bɪ'sɔtɪd] *adj*: **~ with** chiflado por.
bespoke [bɪ'spəuk] *adj* (*garment*) hecho a la
medida; **~ tailor** sastre *m* que
confecciona a la medida.
best [bɛst] *adj* (el/la) mejor ♦ *adv* (lo) mejor;
the ~ part of (*quantity*) la mayor parte de;

at ~ en el mejor de los casos; **to make the ~ of sth** sacar el mejor partido de algo; **to do one's ~** hacer todo lo posible; **to the ~ of my knowledge** que yo sepa; **to the ~ of my ability** como mejor puedo; **the ~ thing to do is ...** lo mejor (que se puede hacer) es ...; **he's not exactly patient at the ~ of times** no es que tenga mucha paciencia precisamente.

bestial ['bɛstɪəl] *adj* bestial.

best man *n* padrino *m* de boda.

bestow [bɪ'stəu] *vt* otorgar; (*honour, praise*) dispensar; **to ~ sth on sb** conceder *or* dar algo a algn.

bestseller ['bɛst'sɛlə*] *n* éxito de ventas, best-seller *m*.

bet [bɛt] *n* apuesta ♦ *vt, vi* (*pt, pp* **bet** *or* **betted**) apostar (*on* a); **it's a safe ~** (*fig*) es cosa segura.

Bethlehem ['bɛθlɪhɛm] *n* Belén *m*.

betray [bɪ'treɪ] *vt* traicionar; (*inform on*) delatar.

betrayal [bɪ'treɪəl] *n* traición *f*.

better ['bɛtə*] *adj* mejor ♦ *adv* mejor ♦ *vt* mejorar; (*record etc*) superar ♦ *n*: **to get the ~ of sb** quedar por encima de algn; **you had ~ do it** más vale que lo hagas; **he thought ~ of it** cambió de parecer; **to get ~** mejorar(se); (*MED*) reponerse; **that's ~!** ¡eso es!; **I had ~ go** tengo que irme; **a change for the ~** una mejora; **~ off** *adj* más acomodado.

betting ['bɛtɪŋ] *n* juego, apuestas *fpl*.

betting shop *n* (*BRIT*) casa de apuestas.

between [bɪ'twi:n] *prep* entre ♦ *adv* (*also* **in ~**: *time*) mientras tanto; (: *place*) en medio; **the road ~ here and London** la carretera de aquí a Londres; **we only had 5 ~ us** teníamos sólo 5 entre todos.

bevel ['bɛvəl] *n* (*also*: ~ **edge**) bisel *m*, chaflán *m*.

beverage ['bɛvərɪdʒ] *n* bebida.

bevy ['bɛvɪ] *n*: **a ~ of** una bandada de.

bewail [bɪ'weɪl] *vt* lamentar.

beware [bɪ'wɛə*] *vi*: **to ~ (of)** tener cuidado (con) ♦ *excl* ¡cuidado!

bewildered [bɪ'wɪldəd] *adj* aturdido, perplejo.

bewildering [bɪ'wɪldərɪŋ] *adj* desconcertante.

bewitching [bɪ'wɪtʃɪŋ] *adj* hechicero, encantador(a).

beyond [bɪ'jɔnd] *prep* más allá de; (*exceeding*) además de, fuera de; (*above*) superior a ♦ *adv* más allá, más lejos; **~ doubt** fuera de toda duda; **~ repair** irreparable.

b/f *abbr* (= *brought forward*) saldo previo.

BFPO *n abbr* (= *British Forces Post Office*) servicio postal del ejército.

bhp *n abbr* (= *brake horsepower*) potencia al freno.

bi ... [baɪ] *pref* bi ....

biannual [baɪ'ænjuəl] *adj* semestral.

bias ['baɪəs] *n* (*prejudice*) prejuicio; (*preference*) predisposición *f*.

bias(s)ed ['baɪəst] *adj* parcial; **to be ~ against** tener perjuicios contra.

biathlon [baɪ'æθlən] *n* biatlón *m*.

bib [bɪb] *n* babero *m*.

Bible ['baɪbl] *n* Biblia.

biblical ['bɪblɪkəl] *adj* bíblico.

bibliography [bɪblɪ'ɔgrəfɪ] *n* bibliografía.

bicarbonate of soda [baɪ'kɑ:bənɪt-] *n* bicarbonato de soda.

bicentenary [baɪsɛn'ti:nərɪ], (*US*) **bicentennial** [baɪsɛn'tɛnɪəl] *n* bicentenario.

biceps ['baɪsɛps] *n* bíceps *m*.

bicker ['bɪkə*] *vi* reñir.

bickering ['bɪkərɪŋ] *n* riñas *fpl*, altercados *mpl*.

bicycle ['baɪsɪkl] *n* bicicleta.

bicycle path *n* camino para ciclistas.

bicycle pump *n* bomba de bicicleta.

bid [bɪd] *n* (*at auction*) oferta, puja, postura; (*attempt*) tentativa, conato ♦ *vi* (*pt, pp* **bid**) hacer una oferta ♦ *vt* (*pt* **bade** [bæd], *pp* **bidden** ['bɪdn]) mandar, ordenar; **to ~ sb good day** dar a algn los buenos días.

bidder ['bɪdə*] *n*: **the highest ~** el mejor postor.

bidding ['bɪdɪŋ] *n* (*at auction*) ofertas *fpl*, puja; (*order*) orden *f*, mandato.

bide [baɪd] *vt*: **to ~ one's time** esperar el momento adecuado.

bidet ['bi:deɪ] *n* bidet *m*.

bidirectional ['baɪdɪ'rɛkʃənl] *adj* bidireccional.

biennial [baɪ'ɛnɪəl] *adj, n* bienal *f*.

bier [bɪə*] *n* féretro.

bifocals [baɪ'fəuklz] *npl* gafas *fpl or* anteojos *mpl* (*LAM*) bifocales.

big [bɪg] *adj* grande; **~ business** gran negocio; **to do things in a ~ way** hacer las cosas en grande.

bigamy ['bɪgəmɪ] *n* bigamia.

big dipper [-'dɪpə*] *n* montaña rusa.

big end *n* (*AUT*) cabeza de biela.

biggish ['bɪgɪʃ] *adj* más bien grande; (*man*) más bien alto.

bigheaded ['bɪg'hɛdɪd] *adj* engreído.

bigot ['bɪgət] *n* fanático/a, intolerante *m/f*.

bigoted ['bɪgətɪd] *adj* fanático, intolerante.

bigotry ['bɪgətrɪ] *n* fanatismo, intolerancia.

big toe *n* dedo gordo (del pie).

big top *n* (*circus*) circo; (*main tent*) carpa principal.
big wheel *n* (*at fair*) noria.
bigwig ['bɪgwɪg] *n* (*col*) pez *m* gordo.
bike [baɪk] *n* bici *f*.
bike lane *n* carril *m* de bicicleta, carril *m* bici.
bikini [bɪ'kiːnɪ] *n* bikini *m*.
bilateral [baɪ'lætərl] *adj* (*agreement*) bilateral.
bile [baɪl] *n* bilis *f*.
bilge [bɪldʒ] *n* (*water*) agua de sentina.
bilingual [baɪ'lɪŋgwəl] *adj* bilingüe.
bilious ['bɪlɪəs] *adj* bilioso (*also fig*).
bill [bɪl] *n* (*gen*) cuenta; (*invoice*) factura; (*POL*) proyecto de ley; (*US*: *banknote*) billete *m*; (*of bird*) pico; (*notice*) cartel *m*; (*THEAT*) programa *m* ♦ *vt* extender *or* pasar la factura a; **may I have the ~ please?** ¿puede traerme la cuenta, por favor?; **~ of exchange** letra de cambio; **~ of lading** conocimiento de embarque; **~ of sale** escritura de venta; **"post no ~s"** "prohibido fijar carteles".
billboard ['bɪlbɔːd] *n* valla publicitaria.
billet ['bɪlɪt] *n* alojamiento ♦ *vt*: **to ~ sb (on sb)** alojar a algn (con algn).
billfold ['bɪlfəʊld] *n* (*US*) cartera.
billiards ['bɪljədz] *n* billar *m*.
billion ['bɪljən] *n* (*BRIT*) billón *m*; (*US*) mil millones *mpl*.
billow ['bɪləʊ] *n* (*of smoke*) nube *f*; (*of sail*) ondulación *f* ♦ *vi* (*smoke*) salir en nubes; (*sail*) ondear, ondular.
billy ['bɪlɪ] *n* (*US*) porra.
billy goat *n* macho cabrío.
bimbo ['bɪmbəʊ] *n* (*col*) tía buena sin seso.
bin [bɪn] *n* (*gen*) cubo *or* bote *m* (*LAM*) de la basura; **litter~** *n* (*BRIT*) papelera.
binary ['baɪnərɪ] *adj* (*MATH*) binario; **~ code** código binario.
bind, *pt, pp* **bound** [baɪnd, baʊnd] *vt* atar, liar; (*wound*) vendar; (*book*) encuadernar; (*oblige*) obligar.
▶**bind over** *vt* (*LAW*) obligar por vía legal.
▶**bind up** *vt* (*wound*) vendar; **to be bound up in** (*work, research etc*) estar absorto en; **to be bound up with** (*person*) estar estrechamente ligado a.
binder ['baɪndə*] *n* (*file*) archivador *m*.
binding ['baɪndɪŋ] *adj* (*contract*) vinculante.
binge [bɪndʒ] *n* borrachera, juerga; **to go on a ~** ir de juerga.
bingo ['bɪŋgəʊ] *n* bingo *m*.
bin-liner ['bɪnlaɪnə*] *n* bolsa de la basura.
binoculars [bɪ'nɒkjuləz] *npl* prismáticos *mpl*, gemelos *mpl*.
biochemistry [baɪə'kemɪstrɪ] *n* bioquímica.

biodegradable ['baɪəʊdɪ'greɪdəbl] *adj* biodegradable.
biodiversity ['baɪəʊdaɪ'vɜːsɪtɪ] *n* biodiversidad *f*.
biographer [baɪ'ɒgrəfə*] *n* biógrafo/a.
biographical [baɪə'græfɪkəl] *adj* biográfico.
biography [baɪ'ɒgrəfɪ] *n* biografía.
biological [baɪə'lɒdʒɪkəl] *adj* biológico.
biological clock *n* reloj *m* biológico.
biologist [baɪ'ɒlədʒɪst] *n* biólogo/a.
biology [baɪ'ɒlədʒɪ] *n* biología.
biophysics ['baɪəʊ'fɪzɪks] *nsg* biofísica.
biopic ['baɪəʊpɪk] *n* filme *m* biográfico.
biopsy ['baɪɒpsɪ] *n* biopsia.
biosphere ['baɪəsfɪə*] *n* biosfera.
biotechnology ['baɪəʊtek'nɒlədʒɪ] *n* biotecnología.
bioterrorism ['baɪəʊ'terərɪzəm] *n* bioterrorismo.
biped ['baɪped] *n* bípedo.
birch [bɜːtʃ] *n* abedul *m*; (*cane*) vara.
bird [bɜːd] *n* ave *f*, pájaro; (*BRIT col*: *girl*) chica.
birdcage ['bɜːdkeɪdʒ] *n* jaula.
bird of prey *n* ave *f* de presa.
bird's-eye view ['bɜːdzaɪ-] *n* vista de pájaro.
bird watcher *n* ornitólogo/a.
Biro ® ['baɪrəʊ] *n* bolígrafo.
birth [bɜːθ] *n* nacimiento; (*MED*) parto; **to give ~ to** parir, dar a luz a; (*fig*) dar origen a.
birth certificate *n* partida de nacimiento.
birth control *n* control *m* de natalidad; (*methods*) métodos *mpl* anticonceptivos.
birthday ['bɜːθdeɪ] *n* cumpleaños *m inv*.
birthplace ['bɜːθpleɪs] *n* lugar *m* de nacimiento.
birth rate *n* (tasa de) natalidad *f*.
Biscay ['bɪskeɪ] *n*: **the Bay of ~** el Mar Cantábrico, el golfo de Vizcaya.
biscuit ['bɪskɪt] *n* (*BRIT*) galleta.
bisect [baɪ'sekt] *vt* (*also MATH*) bisecar.
bisexual ['baɪ'seksjuəl] *adj, n* bisexual *m/f*.
bishop ['bɪʃəp] *n* obispo; (*CHESS*) alfil *m*.
bistro ['biːstrəʊ] *n* café-bar *m*.
bit [bɪt] *pt of* **bite** ♦ *n* trozo, pedazo, pedacito; (*COMPUT*) bit *m*; (*for horse*) freno, bocado; **a ~ of** un poco de; **a ~ mad** algo loco; **~ by ~** poco a poco; **to come to ~s** (*break*) hacerse pedazos; **to do one's ~** aportar su granito de arena; **bring all your ~s and pieces** trae todas tus cosas.
bitch [bɪtʃ] *n* (*dog*) perra; (*col!*) zorra (*!*).
bite [baɪt] *vt, vi* (*pt* **bit** [bɪt], *pp* **bitten** ['bɪtn]) morder; (*insect etc*) picar ♦ *n* (*wound*: *of dog, snake etc*) mordedura; (*of insect*)

picadura; (*mouthful*) bocado; **to ~ one's nails** morderse las uñas; **let's have a ~ (to eat)** comamos algo.

biting ['baɪtɪŋ] *adj* (*wind*) que traspasa los huesos; (*criticism*) mordaz.

bit part *n* (*THEAT*) papel *m* sin importancia, papelito.

bitten ['bɪtn] *pp of* **bite.**

bitter ['bɪtə*] *adj* amargo; (*wind, criticism*) cortante, penetrante; (*icy: weather*) glacial; (*battle*) encarnizado ♦ *n* (*BRIT: beer*) cerveza típica británica a base de lúpulos.

bitterly ['bɪtəlɪ] *adv* (*disappoint, complain, weep*) desconsoladamente; (*oppose, criticise*) implacablemente; (*jealous*) agriamente; **it's ~ cold** hace un frío glacial.

bitterness ['bɪtənɪs] *n* amargura; (*anger*) rencor *m*.

bitty ['bɪtɪ] *adj* deshilvanado.

bitumen ['bɪtjumɪn] *n* betún *m*.

bivouac ['bɪvuæk] *n* vivac *m*, vivaque *m*.

bizarre [bɪ'zɑ:*] *adj* raro, estrafalario.

bk *abbr* = **bank, book.**

BL *n abbr* (= *Bachelor of Law(s), Bachelor of Letters*) título universitario; (*US:* = *Bachelor of Literature*) título universitario.

bl *abbr* = **bill of lading.**

blab [blæb] *vi* cantar ♦ *vt* (*also:* ~ **out**) soltar, contar.

black [blæk] *adj* (*colour*) negro; (*dark*) oscuro ♦ *n* (*colour*) color *m* negro; (*person*): **B~** negro/a ♦ *vt* (*shoes*) lustrar; (*BRIT: INDUSTRY*) boicotear; **to give sb a ~ eye** ponerle a algn el ojo morado; ~ **coffee** café *m* solo; **there it is in ~ and white** (*fig*) ahí está bien claro; **to be in the ~** (*in credit*) tener saldo positivo; ~ **and blue** *adj* amoratado.

▶**black out** *vi* (*faint*) desmayarse.

black belt *n* (*SPORT*) cinturón *m* negro; (*US: area*) zona negra.

blackberry ['blækbərɪ] *n* zarzamora.

blackbird ['blækbɜ:d] *n* mirlo.

blackboard ['blækbɔ:d] *n* pizarra.

black box *n* (*AVIAT*) caja negra.

Black Country *n* (*BRIT*): **the ~** región industrial del centro de Inglaterra.

blackcurrant ['blæk'kʌrənt] *n* grosella negra.

black economy *n* economía sumergida.

blacken ['blækən] *vt* ennegrecer; (*fig*) denigrar.

Black Forest *n:* **the ~** la Selva Negra.

blackguard ['blægɑːd] *n* canalla *m*, pillo.

black hole *n* (*ASTRO*) agujero negro.

black ice *n* hielo invisible en la carretera.

blackjack ['blækdʒæk] *n* (*US*) veintiuna.

blackleg ['blækleg] *n* (*BRIT*) esquirol *m/f.*

blacklist ['blæklɪst] *n* lista negra ♦ *vt* poner en la lista negra.

blackmail ['blækmeɪl] *n* chantaje *m* ♦ *vt* chantajear.

blackmailer ['blækmeɪlə*] *n* chantajista *m/f.*

black market *n* mercado negro, estraperlo.

blackness ['blæknɪs] *n* negrura.

blackout ['blækaut] *n* (*TV, ELEC*) apagón *m*; (*fainting*) desmayo, pérdida de conocimiento.

Black Sea *n:* **the ~** el Mar Negro.

black sheep *n* oveja negra.

blacksmith ['blæksmɪθ] *n* herrero.

black spot *n* (*AUT*) punto negro.

bladder ['blædə*] *n* vejiga.

blade [bleɪd] *n* hoja; (*cutting edge*) filo; **a ~ of grass** una brizna de hierba.

Blairite ['bleəraɪt] *n, adj* blairista *m/f.*

blame [bleɪm] *n* culpa ♦ *vt:* **to ~ sb for sth** echar a algn la culpa de algo; **to be to ~ (for)** tener la culpa (de); **I'm not to ~** yo no tengo la culpa; **and I don't ~ him** y lo comprendo perfectamente.

blameless ['bleɪmlɪs] *adj* (*person*) inocente.

blanch [blɑːntʃ] *vi* (*person*) palidecer; (*CULIN*) escaldar.

bland [blænd] *adj* suave; (*taste*) soso.

blank [blæŋk] *adj* en blanco; (*shot*) de fogueo; (*look*) sin expresión ♦ *n* blanco, espacio en blanco; cartucho de fogueo; **to draw a ~** (*fig*) no conseguir nada.

blank cheque, (*US*) **blank check** *n* cheque *m* en blanco.

blanket ['blæŋkɪt] *n* manta, frazada (*LAM*), cobija (*LAM*) ♦ *adj* (*statement, agreement*) comprensivo, general; **to give ~ cover** (*subj: insurance policy*) dar póliza a todo riesgo.

blankly ['blæŋklɪ] *adv:* **she looked at me ~** me miró sin comprender.

blare [bleə*] *vi* (*brass band, horns, radio*) resonar.

blasé ['blɑːzeɪ] *adj* de vuelta de todo.

blaspheme [blæs'fiːm] *vi* blasfemar.

blasphemous ['blæsfɪməs] *adj* blasfemo.

blasphemy ['blæsfɪmɪ] *n* blasfemia.

blast [blɑːst] *n* (*of wind*) ráfaga, soplo; (*of whistle*) toque *m*; (*of explosive*) carga explosiva; (*force*) choque *m* ♦ *vt* (*blow up*) volar; (*blow open*) abrir con carga explosiva ♦ *excl* (*BRIT col*) ¡maldito sea!; **(at) full ~** (*also fig*) a toda marcha.

▶**blast off** *vi* (*spacecraft etc*) despegar.

blast furnace *n* alto horno.

blast-off ['blɑːstɔf] *n* (*SPACE*) lanzamiento.

blatant ['bleɪtənt] *adj* descarado.
blatantly ['bleɪtəntlɪ] *adv*: **it's ~ obvious** está clarísimo.
blather ['blæðə*] *vi* decir tonterías.
blaze [bleɪz] *n* (*fire*) fuego; (*flames*) llamarada; (*glow: of fire, sun etc*) resplandor *m*; (*fig*) arranque *m* ♦ *vi* (*fire*) arder con llamaradas; (*fig*) brillar ♦ *vt*: **to ~ a trail** (*fig*) abrir (un) camino; **in a ~ of publicity** bajo los focos de la publicidad.
blazer ['bleɪzə*] *n* chaqueta de uniforme de colegial o de socio de club.
bleach [bliːtʃ] *n* (*also*: **household ~**) lejía ♦ *vt* (*linen*) blanquear.
bleached [bliːtʃt] *adj* (*hair*) de colorado; (*clothes*) blanqueado.
bleachers ['bliːtʃəz] *npl* (*US SPORT*) gradas *fpl*.
bleak [bliːk] *adj* (*countryside*) desierto; (*landscape*) desolado, desierto; (*weather*) desapacible; (*smile*) triste; (*prospect, future*) poco prometedor(a).
bleary-eyed ['blɪərɪ'aɪd] *adj*: **to be ~** tener ojos de cansado.
bleat [bliːt] *vi* balar.
bleed, *pt, pp* **bled** [bliːd, blɛd] *vt* sangrar; (*brakes, radiator*) desaguar ♦ *vi* sangrar.
bleeding ['bliːdɪŋ] *adj* sangrante.
bleep [bliːp] *n* pitido ♦ *vi* pitar ♦ *vt* llamar por el busca.
bleeper ['bliːpə*] *n* (*of doctor etc*) busca *m*.
blemish ['blɛmɪʃ] *n* mancha, tacha.
blench [blɛntʃ] *vi* (*shrink back*) acobardarse; (*grow pale*) palidecer.
blend [blɛnd] *n* mezcla ♦ *vt* mezclar ♦ *vi* (*colours etc*) combinarse, mezclarse.
blender ['blɛndə*] *n* (*CULIN*) batidora.
bless, *pt, pp* **blessed** *or* **blest** [blɛs, blɛst] *vt* bendecir.
blessed ['blɛsɪd] *adj* (*REL: holy*) santo, bendito; (: *happy*) dichoso; **every ~ day** cada santo día.
blessing ['blɛsɪŋ] *n* bendición *f*; (*advantage*) beneficio, ventaja; **to count one's ~s** agradecer lo que se tiene; **it was a ~ in disguise** no hay mal que por bien no venga.
blew [bluː] *pt of* **blow**.
blight [blaɪt] *vt* (*hopes etc*) frustrar, arruinar.
blimey ['blaɪmɪ] *excl* (*BRIT col*) ¡caray!
blind [blaɪnd] *adj* ciego ♦ *n* (*for window*) persiana ♦ *vt* cegar; (*dazzle*) deslumbrar.
blind alley *n* callejón *m* sin salida.
blind corner *n* (*BRIT*) esquina *or* curva sin visibilidad.
blind date *n* cita a ciegas.
blinders ['blaɪndəz] *npl* (*US*) anteojeras *fpl*.

blindfold ['blaɪndfəuld] *n* venda ♦ *adj, adv* con los ojos vendados ♦ *vt* vendar los ojos a.
blinding ['blaɪndɪŋ] *adj* (*flash, light*) cegador; (*pain*) intenso.
blindingly ['blaɪndɪŋlɪ] *adv*: **it's ~ obvious** salta a la vista.
blindly ['blaɪndlɪ] *adv* a ciegas, ciegamente.
blindness ['blaɪndnɪs] *n* ceguera.
blind spot *n* (*AUT*) ángulo muerto; **to have a ~ about sth** estar ciego para algo.
blink [blɪŋk] *vi* parpadear, pestañear; (*light*) oscilar; **to be on the ~** (*col*) estar estropeado.
blinkers ['blɪŋkəz] *npl* (*esp BRIT*) anteojeras *fpl*.
blinking ['blɪŋkɪŋ] *adj* (*col*): **this ~...** este condenado....
blip [blɪp] *n* señal *f* luminosa; (*on graph*) pequeña desviación *f*; (*fig*) pequeña anomalía.
bliss [blɪs] *n* felicidad *f*.
blissful ['blɪsful] *adj* dichoso; **in ~ ignorance** feliz en la ignorancia.
blissfully ['blɪsfulɪ] *adv* (*sigh, smile*) con felicidad; **~ happy** sumamente feliz.
blister ['blɪstə*] *n* (*on skin, paint*) ampolla ♦ *vi* ampollarse.
blistering ['blɪstərɪŋ] *adj* (*heat*) abrasador(a).
blithely ['blaɪðlɪ] *adv* alegremente, despreocupadamente.
blithering ['blɪðərɪŋ] *adj* (*col*): **this ~ idiot** este tonto perdido.
BLit(t) *n abbr* (= *Bachelor of Literature*) título universitario.
blitz [blɪts] *n* bombardeo aéreo; **to have a ~ on sth** (*fig*) emprenderla con algo.
blizzard ['blɪzəd] *n* ventisca.
BLM *n abbr* (*US*) = *Bureau of Land Management*.
bloated ['bləutɪd] *adj* hinchado.
blob [blɔb] *n* (*drop*) gota; (*stain, spot*) mancha.
bloc [blɔk] *n* (*POL*) bloque *m*.
block [blɔk] *n* bloque *m* (*also COMPUT*); (*in pipes*) obstáculo; (*of buildings*) manzana ♦ *vt* (*gen*) obstruir, cerrar; (*progress*) estorbar; (*COMPUT*) agrupar; **~ of flats** (*BRIT*) bloque *m* de pisos; **mental ~** amnesia temporal; **~ and tackle** (*TECH*) aparejo de polea; **3 ~s from here** a 3 manzanas *or* cuadras (*LAM*) de aquí.
▶**block up** *vt* tapar, obstruir; (*pipe*) atascar.
blockade [blɔ'keɪd] *n* bloqueo ♦ *vt* bloquear.
blockage ['blɔkɪdʒ] *n* estorbo, obstrucción *f*.

block booking n reserva en grupo.
blockbuster ['blɔkbʌstə*] n (book) best-seller m; (film) éxito de público.
block capitals npl mayúsculas fpl.
block letters npl letras fpl de molde.
block release n (BRIT) exención f por estudios.
block vote n (BRIT) voto por delegación.
bloke [bləuk] n (BRIT col) tipo, tío.
blond(e) [blɔnd] adj, n rubio/a m/f.
blood [blʌd] n sangre f; **new ~** (fig) gente f nueva.
blood bank n banco de sangre.
blood count n recuento de glóbulos rojos y blancos.
blood donor n donante m/f de sangre.
blood group n grupo sanguíneo.
bloodhound ['blʌdhaund] n sabueso.
bloodless ['blʌdlɪs] adj (pale) exangüe; (revolt etc) sin derramamiento de sangre, incruento.
bloodletting ['blʌdletɪŋ] n (MED) sangría; (fig) sangría, carnicería.
blood poisoning n septicemia de la sangre.
blood pressure n tensión f sanguínea; **to have high/low ~** tener la tensión alta/baja.
bloodshed ['blʌdʃed] n baño de sangre.
bloodshot ['blʌdʃɔt] adj inyectado en sangre.
bloodstained ['blʌdsteɪnd] adj manchado de sangre.
bloodstream ['blʌdstri:m] n corriente f sanguínea.
blood test n análisis m de sangre.
bloodthirsty ['blʌdθə:stɪ] adj sanguinario.
blood transfusion n transfusión f de sangre.
blood type n grupo sanguíneo.
blood vessel n vaso sanguíneo.
bloody ['blʌdɪ] adj sangriento; (BRIT col!): **this ~...** este condenado or puñetero or fregado (LAM) ... (!) ♦ adv (BRIT col!): **~ strong/good** terriblemente fuerte/bueno.
bloody-minded ['blʌdɪ'maɪndɪd] adj (BRIT col) con malas pulgas.
bloom [blu:m] n floración f; **in ~** en flor ♦ vi florecer.
blooming ['blu:mɪŋ] adj (col): **this ~...** este condenado....
blossom ['blɔsəm] n flor f ♦ vi florecer; (fig) desarrollarse; **to ~ into** (fig) convertirse en.
blot [blɔt] n borrón m ♦ vt (dry) secar; (stain) manchar; **to ~ out** vt (view) tapar; (memories) borrar; **to be a ~ on the landscape** estropear el paisaje; **to ~**

one's copy book (fig) manchar su reputación.
blotchy ['blɔtʃɪ] adj (complexion) lleno de manchas.
blotter ['blɔtə*] n secante m.
blotting paper ['blɔtɪŋ-] n papel m secante.
blotto ['blɔtəu] adj (col) mamado.
blouse [blauz] n blusa.
blow [bləu] n golpe m ♦ vb (pt blew, pp blown [blu:, bləun]) vi soplar; (fuse) fundirse ♦ vt (glass) soplar; (fuse) quemar; (instrument) tocar; **to come to ~s** llegar a golpes; **to ~ one's nose** sonarse.
▶**blow away** vt llevarse, arrancar.
▶**blow down** vt derribar.
▶**blow off** vt arrebatar.
▶**blow out** vt apagar ♦ vi apagarse; (tyre) reventar.
▶**blow over** vi amainar.
▶**blow up** vi estallar ♦ vt volar; (tyre) inflar; (PHOT) ampliar.
blow-dry ['bləudraɪ] n secado con secador de mano ♦ vt secar con secador de mano.
blowlamp ['bləulæmp] n (BRIT) soplete m, lámpara de soldar.
blow-out ['bləuaut] n (of tyre) pinchazo; (col: big meal) banquete m, festín m.
blowtorch ['bləutɔ:tʃ] n = **blowlamp**.
blow-up ['bləuʌp] n (PHOT) ampliación f.
BLS n abbr (US) = Bureau of Labor Statistics.
blubber ['blʌbə*] n grasa de ballena ♦ vi (pej) lloriquear.
bludgeon ['blʌdʒən] vt: **to ~ sb into doing sth** coaccionar a algn a hacer algo.
blue [blu:] adj azul; **~ film** película porno; **~ joke** chiste verde; **once in a ~ moon** de higos a brevas; **to come out of the ~** (fig) ser completamente inesperado; see also **blues.**
blue baby n niño azul or cianótico.
bluebell ['blu:bel] n campanilla, campánula azul.
blue-blooded [blu:'blʌdɪd] adj de sangre azul.
bluebottle ['blu:bɔtl] n moscarda, mosca azul.
blue cheese n queso azul.
blue-chip ['blu:tʃɪp] n: **~ investment** inversión f asegurada.
blue-collar worker ['blu:kɔlə*-] n obrero/a.
blue jeans npl tejanos mpl, vaqueros mpl.
blueprint ['blu:prɪnt] n proyecto; **~ (for)** (fig) anteproyecto (de).
blues [blu:z] npl: **the ~** (MUS) el blues; **to have the ~** estar triste.
Bluetooth ® ['blu:tu:θ] n Bluetooth ® f; **~ technology** tecnología Bluetooth ®.
bluff [blʌf] vi tirarse un farol, farolear ♦ n

bluff *m*, farol *m*; (*GEO*) precipicio, despeñadero; **to call sb's** ~ coger a algn en un renuncio.

bluish ['bluːɪʃ] *adj* azulado.

blunder ['blʌndə*] *n* patinazo, metedura de pata ♦ *vi* cometer un error, meter la pata; **to** ~ **into sb/sth** tropezar con algn/algo.

blunt [blʌnt] *adj* (*knife*) desafilado; (*person*) franco, directo ♦ *vt* embotar, desafilar; **this pencil is** ~ este lápiz está despuntado; ~ **instrument** (*LAW*) instrumento contundente.

bluntly ['blʌntlɪ] *adv* (*speak*) francamente, de modo terminante.

bluntness ['blʌntnɪs] *n* (*of person*) franqueza, brusquedad *f*.

blur [bləː*] *n* aspecto borroso ♦ *vt* (*vision*) enturbiar; (*memory*) empañar.

blurb [bləːb] *n* propaganda.

blurred [bləːd] *adj* borroso.

blurt [bləːt]: **to** ~ **out** *vt* (*say*) descolgarse con, dejar escapar.

blush [blʌʃ] *vi* ruborizarse, ponerse colorado ♦ *n* rubor *m*.

blusher ['blʌʃə*] *n* colorete *m*.

bluster ['blʌstə*] *n* fanfarronada, bravata ♦ *vi* fanfarronear, echar bravatas.

blustering ['blʌstərɪŋ] *adj* (*person*) fanfarrón/ona.

blustery ['blʌstərɪ] *adj* (*weather*) tempestuoso, tormentoso.

Blvd *abbr* = **boulevard**.

BM *n abbr* = *British Museum*; (*UNIV*: = *Bachelor of Medicine*) título universitario.

BMA *n abbr* = *British Medical Association*.

BMJ *n abbr* = *British Medical Journal*.

BMus *n abbr* (= *Bachelor of Music*) título universitario.

BMX *n abbr* (= *bicycle motocross*) BMX *f*; ~ **bike** bici(cleta) *f* BMX.

BO *n abbr* (*col*: = *body odour*) olor *m* a sudor; (*US*) = **box office**.

boa ['bəuə] *n* boa.

boar [bɔː*] *n* verraco, cerdo.

board [bɔːd] *n* tabla, tablero; (*on wall*) tablón *m*; (*for chess etc*) tablero; (*committee*) junta, consejo; (*in firm*) mesa *or* junta directiva; (*NAUT*, *AVIAT*): **on** ~ a bordo ♦ *vt* (*ship*) embarcarse en; (*train*) subir a; **full** ~ (*BRIT*) pensión *f* completa; **half** ~ (*BRIT*) media pensión; ~ **and lodging** alojamiento y comida; **to go by the** ~ (*fig*) irse por la borda; **above** ~ (*fig*) sin tapujos; **across the** ~ (*fig*: *adv*) en todos los niveles; (: *adj*) general.

▶**board up** *vt* (*door*) tapar, cegar.

boarder ['bɔːdə*] *n* huésped(a) *m/f*; (*SCOL*) interno/a.

board game *n* juego de tablero.

boarding card ['bɔːdɪŋ-] *n* (*BRIT*: *AVIAT*, *NAUT*) tarjeta de embarque.

boarding house ['bɔːdɪŋ-] *n* casa de huéspedes.

boarding party ['bɔːdɪŋ-] *n* brigada de inspección.

boarding pass ['bɔːdɪŋ-] *n* (*US*) = **boarding card**.

boarding school ['bɔːdɪŋ-] *n* internado.

board meeting *n* reunión *f* de la junta directiva.

board room *n* sala de juntas.

boardwalk ['bɔːdwɔːk] *n* (*US*) paseo entablado.

boast [bəust] *vi*: **to** ~ (**about** *or* **of**) alardear (de) ♦ *vt* ostentar ♦ *n* alarde *m*, baladronada.

boastful ['bəustfəl] *adj* presumido, jactancioso.

boastfulness ['bəustfulnɪs] *n* fanfarronería, jactancia.

boat [bəut] *n* barco, buque *m*; (*small*) barca, bote *m*; **to go by** ~ ir en barco.

boater ['bəutə*] *n* (*hat*) canotié *m*.

boating ['bəutɪŋ] *n* canotaje *m*.

boatman ['bəutmən] *n* barquero.

boat people *npl refugiados que huyen en barca*.

boatswain ['bəusn] *n* contramaestre *m*.

bob [bɔb] *vi* (*boat, cork on water: also*: ~ **up and down**) menearse, balancearse ♦ *n* (*BRIT col*) = **shilling**.

▶**bob up** *vi* (re)aparecer de repente.

bobbin ['bɔbɪn] *n* (*of sewing machine*) carrete *m*, bobina.

bobby ['bɔbɪ] *n* (*BRIT col*) poli *m/f*.

bobsleigh ['bɔbsleɪ] *n* bob *m*, trineo de competición *f*.

bode [bəud] *vi*: **to** ~ **well/ill (for)** ser de buen/mal agüero (para).

bodice ['bɔdɪs] *n* corpiño.

-bodied ['bɔdɪd] *adj suff* de cuerpo ....

bodily ['bɔdɪlɪ] *adj* (*comfort, needs*) corporal; (*pain*) corpóreo ♦ *adv* (*in person*) en persona; (*carry*) corporalmente; (*lift*) en peso.

body ['bɔdɪ] *n* cuerpo; (*corpse*) cadáver *m*; (*of car*) caja, carrocería; (*also*: ~ **stocking**) body *m*; (*fig*: *organization*) organización *f*; (: *public* ~) organismo; (: *quantity*) masa; (: *of speech, document*) parte *f* principal; **ruling** ~ directiva; **in a** ~ todos juntos, en masa.

body blow *n* (*fig*) palo.

body-building ['bɔdɪ'bɪldɪŋ] *n* culturismo.

bodyguard ['bɔdɪgɑːd] *n* guardaespaldas *m inv*.

body language n lenguaje m gestual.
body search n cacheo; **to carry out a ~ on sb** registrar a algn; **to submit to** or **undergo a ~** ser registrado.
bodywork ['bɔdɪwɔːk] n carrocería.
boffin ['bɔfɪn] n (BRIT) científico/a.
bog [bɔg] n pantano, ciénaga ♦ vt: **to get ~ged down** (fig) empantanarse, atascarse.
boggle ['bɔgl] vi: **the mind ~s!** ¡no puedo creerlo!
Bogotá [bəugə'taː] n Bogotá.
bogus ['bəugəs] adj falso, fraudulento; (person) fingido.
Bohemia [bə'hiːmɪə] n Bohemia.
Bohemian [bə'hiːmɪən] adj, n bohemio/a m/f.
boil [bɔɪl] vt cocer; (eggs) pasar por agua ♦ vi hervir ♦ n (MED) furúnculo, divieso; **to bring to the ~** calentar hasta que hierva; **to come to the** (BRIT) or **a** (US) **~** comenzar a hervir; **~ed egg** huevo pasado por agua; **~ed potatoes** patatas fpl or papas fpl (LAM) cocidas.
▶**boil down** vi (fig): **to ~ down to** reducirse a.
▶**boil over** vi (liquid) rebosar; (anger, resentment) llegar al colmo.
boiler ['bɔɪlə*] n caldera.
boiler suit n (BRIT) mono, overol m (LAM).
boiling ['bɔɪlɪŋ] adj: **I'm ~ (hot)** (col) estoy asado.
boiling point n punto de ebullición f.
boil-in-the-bag [bɔɪlɪnðə'bæg] adj: **~ meals** platos que se cuecen en su misma bolsa.
boisterous ['bɔɪstərəs] adj (noisy) bullicioso; (excitable) exuberante; (crowd) tumultuoso.
bold [bəuld] adj (brave) valiente, audaz; (pej) descarado; (outline) grueso; (colour) vivo; **~ type** (TYP) negrita.
boldly ['bəuldlɪ] adv audazmente.
boldness ['bəuldnɪs] n valor m, audacia; (cheek) descaro.
Bolivia [bə'lɪvɪə] n Bolivia.
Bolivian [bə'lɪvɪən] adj, n boliviano/a m/f.
bollard ['bɔləd] n (BRIT AUT) poste m.
bolshy ['bɔlʃɪ] adj (BRIT col) protestón/ona; **to be in a ~ mood** tener el día protestón.
bolster ['bəulstə*] n travesero, cabezal m.
▶**bolster up** vt reforzar; (fig) alentar.
bolt [bəult] n (lock) cerrojo; (with nut) perno, tornillo ♦ adv: **~ upright** rígido, erguido ♦ vt (door) echar el cerrojo a; (food) engullir ♦ vi fugarse; (horse) desbocarse.
bomb [bɔm] n bomba ♦ vt bombardear.
bombard [bɔm'baːd] vt bombardear; (fig) asediar.

bombardment [bɔm'baːdmənt] n bombardeo.
bombastic [bɔm'bæstɪk] adj rimbombante; (person) pomposo.
bomb disposal n desactivación f de explosivos.
bomb disposal expert n artificiero/a.
bomber ['bɔmə*] n (AVIAT) bombardero; (terrorist) persona que pone bombas.
bombing ['bɔmɪŋ] n bombardeo.
bomb scare n amenaza de bomba.
bombshell ['bɔmʃɛl] n obús m, granada; (fig) bomba.
bomb site n lugar m donde estalló una bomba.
bona fide ['bəunə'faɪdɪ] adj genuino, auténtico.
bonanza [bə'nænzə] n bonanza.
bond [bɔnd] n (binding promise) fianza; (FINANCE) bono; (link) vínculo, lazo; **in ~** (COMM) en depósito bajo fianza.
bondage ['bɔndɪdʒ] n esclavitud f.
bonded goods ['bɔndɪd-] npl mercancías fpl en depósito de aduanas.
bonded warehouse ['bɔndɪd-] n depósito de aduanas.
bone [bəun] n hueso; (of fish) espina ♦ vt deshuesar; quitar las espinas a; **~ of contention** manzana de la discordia.
bone china n porcelana fina.
bone-dry ['bəun'draɪ] adj completamente seco.
bone idle adj gandul.
bone marrow n médula; **~ transplant** transplante m de médula.
boner ['bəunə*] n (US col) plancha, patochada.
bonfire ['bɔnfaɪə*] n hoguera, fogata.
bonk [bɔŋk] vt, vi (hum, col) chingar (!).
bonkers ['bɔŋkəz] adj (BRIT col) majareta.
Bonn [bɔn] n Bonn m.
bonnet ['bɔnɪt] n gorra; (BRIT: of car) capó m.
bonny ['bɔnɪ] adj (esp Scottish) bonito, hermoso, lindo.
bonus ['bəunəs] n (at Christmas etc) paga extraordinaria; (merit award) sobrepaga, prima.
bony ['bəunɪ] adj (arm, face, MED: tissue) huesudo; (meat) lleno de huesos; (fish) lleno de espinas; (thin: person) flaco, delgado.
boo [buː] vt abuchear.
boob [buːb] n (col: mistake) disparate m, sandez f; (: breast) teta.
booby prize ['buːbɪ-] n premio de consolación (al último).
booby trap ['buːbɪ-] n (MIL etc) trampa

explosiva.

book [buk] *n* libro; (*notebook*) libreta; (*of stamps etc*) librillo; ~**s** (*COMM*) cuentas *fpl*, contabilidad *f* ♦ *vt* (*ticket, seat, room*) reservar; (*driver*) fichar; (*FOOTBALL*) amonestar; **to keep the** ~**s** llevar las cuentas *or* los libros; **by the** ~ según las reglas; **to throw the** ~ **at sb** echar un rapapolvo a algn.

▶**book in** *vi* (*at hotel*) registrarse.

▶**book up** *vt*: **all seats are** ~**ed up** todas las plazas están reservadas; **the hotel is** ~**ed up** el hotel está lleno.

bookable ['bukəbl] *adj*: **seats are** ~ los asientos se pueden reservar (de antemano).

bookcase ['bukkeɪs] *n* librería, estante *m* para libros.

booking office ['bukɪŋ-] *n* (*BRIT: RAIL*) despacho de billetes *or* boletos (*LAM*); (: *THEAT*) taquilla, boletería (*LAM*).

book-keeping ['buk'ki:pɪŋ] *n* contabilidad *f*.

booklet ['buklɪt] *n* folleto.

bookmaker ['bukmeɪkə*] *n* corredor *m* de apuestas.

bookseller ['buksɛlə*] *n* librero/a.

bookshelf ['bukʃɛlf] *n* estante *m*.

bookshop ['bukʃɔp] *n* librería.

bookstall ['bukstɔ:l] *n* quiosco de libros.

book store *n* = **bookshop**.

book token *n* vale *m* para libros.

book value *n* (*COMM*) valor *m* contable.

bookworm ['bukwə:m] *n* (*fig*) ratón *m* de biblioteca.

boom [bu:m] *n* (*noise*) trueno, estampido; (*in prices etc*) alza rápida; (*ECON*) boom *m*, auge *m* ♦ *vi* (*cannon*) hacer gran estruendo, retumbar; (*ECON*) estar en alza.

boomerang ['bu:məræŋ] *n* bumerang *m* (*also fig*) ♦ *vi*: **to** ~ **on sb** (*fig*) ser contraproducente para algn.

boom town *n* ciudad *f* de crecimiento rápido.

boon [bu:n] *n* favor *m*, beneficio.

boorish ['buərɪʃ] *adj* grosero.

boost [bu:st] *n* estímulo, empuje *m* ♦ *vt* estimular, empujar; (*increase: sales, production*) aumentar; **to give a** ~ **to** (*morale*) levantar; **it gave a** ~ **to his confidence** le dio confianza en sí mismo.

booster ['bu:stə*] *n* (*MED*) reinyección *f*; (*TV*) repetidor *m*; (*ELEC*) elevador *m* de tensión; (*also*: ~ **rocket**) cohete *m*.

boot [bu:t] *n* bota; (*ankle* ~) botín *m*, borceguí *m*; (*BRIT: of car*) maleta, maletero, baúl *m* (*LAM*) ♦ *vt* dar un

puntapié a; (*COMPUT*) arrancar; **to** ~ (*in addition*) además, por añadidura; **to give sb the** ~ (*col*) despedir a algn, poner a algn en la calle.

booth [bu:ð] *n* (*at fair*) barraca; (*telephone* ~, *voting* ~) cabina.

bootleg ['bu:tlɛg] *adj* de contrabando; ~ **record** disco pirata.

booty ['bu:tɪ] *n* botín *m*.

booze [bu:z] (*col*) *n* bebida ♦ *vi* emborracharse.

boozer ['bu:zə*] *n* (*col*: *person*) bebedor(a) *m/f*; (: *BRIT: pub*) bar *m*.

border ['bɔ:də*] *n* borde *m*, margen *m*; (*of a country*) frontera ♦ *adj* fronterizo; **the B**~**s** región fronteriza entre Escocia e Inglaterra.

▶**border on** *vt fus* lindar con; (*fig*) rayar en.

borderline ['bɔ:dəlaɪn] *n* (*fig*) frontera.

bore [bɔ:*] *pt of* **bear** ♦ *vt* (*hole*) taladrar; (*person*) aburrir ♦ *n* (*person*) pelmazo, pesado; (*of gun*) calibre *m*.

bored [bɔ:d] *adj* aburrido; **he's** ~ **to tears** *or* **to death** *or* **stiff** está aburrido como una ostra, está muerto de aburrimiento.

boredom ['bɔ:dəm] *n* aburrimiento.

boring ['bɔ:rɪŋ] *adj* aburrido, pesado.

born [bɔ:n] *adj*: **to be** ~ nacer; **I was** ~ **in 1960** nací en 1960.

born-again [bɔ:nə'gɛn] *adj*: ~ **Christian** evangelista *m/f*.

borne [bɔ:n] *pp of* **bear**.

Borneo ['bɔ:nɪəu] *n* Borneo.

borough ['bʌrə] *n* municipio.

borrow ['bɔrəu] *vt*: **to** ~ **sth (from sb)** tomar algo prestado (a alguien); **may I** ~ **your car?** ¿me prestas tu coche?

borrower ['bɔrəuə*] *n* prestatario/a.

borrowing ['bɔrəuɪŋ] *n* préstamos *mpl*.

borstal ['bɔ:stl] *n* (*BRIT*) reformatorio (de menores).

Bosnia ['bɔznɪə] *n* Bosnia.

Bosnia-Herzegovina, Bosnia-Hercegovina ['bɔːsnɪəherzə'gəuvɪːnə] *n* Bosnia-Herzegovina.

Bosnian ['bɔznɪən] *adj, n* bosnio/a.

bosom ['buzəm] *n* pecho; (*fig*) seno; ~ **friend** *n* amigo/a íntimo/a *or* del alma.

boss [bɔs] *n* jefe/a *m/f*; (*employer*) patrón/ona *m/f*; (*political etc*) cacique *m* ♦ *vt* (*also*: ~ **about** *or* **around**) mangonear; **stop** ~**ing everyone about!** ¡deja de dar órdenes *or* de mangonear a todos!

bossy ['bɔsɪ] *adj* mandón/ona.

bosun ['bəusn] *n* contramaestre *m*.

botanical [bə'tænɪkl] *adj* botánico.

botanist ['bɔtənɪst] *n* botanista *m/f*.

botany ['bɔtənɪ] *n* botánica.

botch [bɔtʃ] vt (also: ~ **up**) arruinar, estropear.

both [bəuθ] adj, pron ambos/as, los/las dos; ~ **of us went, we ~ went** fuimos los dos, ambos fuimos ♦ adv: ~ **A and B** tanto A como B.

bother ['bɔðə*] vt (worry) preocupar; (disturb) molestar, fastidiar, fregar (LAM), embromar (LAM) ♦ vi (gen: ~ **o.s.**) molestarse ♦ n: **what a ~!** ¡qué lata! ♦ excl ¡maldita sea!, ¡caramba!; **I'm sorry to ~ you** perdona que te moleste; **to ~ doing** tomarse la molestia de hacer; **please don't ~** no te molestes.

Botswana [bɔt'swɑːnə] n Botswana.

bottle ['bɔtl] n botella; (small) frasco; (baby's) biberón m ♦ vt embotellar; ~ **of wine/milk** botella de vino/de leche; **wine/milk ~** botella de vino/de leche.

▶**bottle up** vt (fig) contener, reprimir.

bottle bank n contenedor m de vidrio, iglú m.

bottleneck ['bɔtlnɛk] n embotellamiento.

bottle-opener ['bɔtləupnə*] n abrebotellas m inv.

bottom ['bɔtəm] n (of box, sea) fondo; (buttocks) trasero, culo; (of page, mountain, tree) pie m; (of list) final m ♦ adj (lowest) más bajo; (last) último; **to get to the ~ of sth** (fig) llegar al fondo de algo.

bottomless ['bɔtəmlɪs] adj sin fondo, insondable.

bottom line n: **the ~** lo fundamental; **the ~ is he has to go** el caso es que tenemos que despedirle.

bough [bau] n rama.

bought [bɔːt] pt, pp of **buy**.

bouillon cube ['buːjɔn-] n (US) cubito de caldo.

boulder ['bəuldə*] n canto rodado.

bounce [bauns] vi (ball) (re)botar; (cheque) ser rechazado ♦ vt hacer (re)botar ♦ n (rebound) (re)bote m; **he's got plenty of ~** (fig) tiene mucha energía.

bouncer ['baunsə*] n (col) forzudo, gorila m.

bouncy castle ® ['baunsɪ-] n castillo inflable.

bound [baund] pt, pp of **bind** ♦ n (leap) salto; (gen pl: limit) límite m ♦ vi (leap) saltar ♦ adj: ~ **by** rodeado de; **to be ~ to do sth** (obliged) tener el deber de hacer algo; **he's ~ to come** es seguro que vendrá; **"out of ~s to the public"** "prohibido el paso"; ~ **for** con destino a.

boundary ['baundrɪ] n límite m, lindero.

boundless ['baundlɪs] adj ilimitado.

bountiful ['bauntɪful] adj (person) liberal, generoso; (God) bondadoso; (supply) abundante.

bouquet ['bukeɪ] n (of flowers) ramo, ramillete m; (of wine) aroma m.

bourbon ['buəbən] n (US: also: ~ **whiskey**) whisky m americano, bourbon m.

bourgeois ['buəʒwɑː] adj, n burgués/esa m/f.

bout [baut] n (of malaria etc) ataque m; (BOXING etc) combate m, encuentro.

boutique [buː'tiːk] n boutique f, tienda de ropa.

bow [bəu] n (knot) lazo; (weapon, MUS) arco; [bau] (of the head) reverencia; (NAUT: also: ~**s**) proa ♦ vi [bau] inclinarse, hacer una reverencia; (yield): **to ~ to** or **before** ceder ante, someterse a; **to ~ to the inevitable** resignarse a lo inevitable.

bowels ['bauəlz] npl intestinos mpl, vientre m.

bowl [bəul] n tazón m, cuenco; (for washing) palangana, jofaina; (ball) bola; (US: stadium) estadio ♦ vi (CRICKET) arrojar la pelota; see also **bowls**.

bow-legged ['bəu'lɛgɪd] adj estevado.

bowler ['bəulə*] n (CRICKET) lanzador m (de la pelota); (BRIT: also: ~ **hat**) hongo, bombín m.

bowling ['bəulɪŋ] n (game) bolos mpl, bochas fpl.

bowling alley n bolera.

bowling green n pista para bochas.

bowls [bəulz] n juego de los bolos, bochas fpl.

bow tie ['bəu-] n corbata de lazo, pajarita.

box [bɔks] n (also: **cardboard ~**) caja, cajón m; (for jewels) estuche m; (for money) cofre m; (crate) cofre m, arca; (THEAT) palco ♦ vt encajonar ♦ vi (SPORT) boxear.

boxer ['bɔksə*] n (person) boxeador m; (dog) bóxer m.

box file n fichero.

boxing ['bɔksɪŋ] n (SPORT) boxeo, box m (LAM).

Boxing Day n (BRIT) día m de San Esteban; ver recuadro.

BOXING DAY

El día después de Navidad es **Boxing Day**, fiesta en todo el Reino Unido, aunque si el 26 de diciembre cae en domingo el día de descanso se traslada al lunes. En dicho día solía ser tradición entregar "Christmas boxes" (aguinaldos) a empleados, proveedores a domicilio, carteros etc.

---

boxing gloves npl guantes mpl de boxeo.

boxing ring n ring m, cuadrilátero.

box number *n* (*for advertisements*) apartado.

box office *n* taquilla, boletería (*LAM*).

boxroom ['bɔksrum] *n* trastero.

boy [bɔɪ] *n* (*young*) niño; (*older*) muchacho.

boycott ['bɔɪkɔt] *n* boicot *m* ♦ *vt* boicotear.

boyfriend ['bɔɪfrɛnd] *n* novio.

boyish ['bɔɪɪʃ] *adj* de muchacho, inmaduro.

boy scout *n* boy scout *m*.

Bp *abbr* = **bishop**.

BPOE *n abbr* (*US*: = *Benevolent and Protective Order of Elks*) *organización benéfica.*

BR *abbr see* **British Rail**.

bra [brɑː] *n* sostén *m*, sujetador *m*, corpiño (*LAM*).

brace [breɪs] *n* refuerzo, abrazadera; (*BRIT*: *on teeth*) corrector *m*; (*tool*) berbiquí *m* ♦ *vt* asegurar, reforzar; **to ~ o.s. (for)** (*fig*) prepararse (para); *see also* **braces**.

bracelet ['breɪslɪt] *n* pulsera, brazalete *m*, pulso (*LAM*).

braces ['breɪsɪz] *npl* (*BRIT*) tirantes *mpl*, suspensores *mpl* (*LAM*); (*US*: *on teeth*) corrector *m*.

bracing ['breɪsɪŋ] *adj* vigorizante, tónico.

bracken ['brækən] *n* helecho.

bracket ['brækɪt] *n* (*TECH*) soporte *m*, puntal *m*; (*group*) clase *f*, categoría; (*also*: **brace** ~) soporte *m*, abrazadera; (*also*: **round** ~) paréntesis *m inv*; (*gen*: **square** ~) corchete *m* ♦ *vt* (*fig*: *also*: ~ **together**) agrupar; **income** ~ nivel *m* económico; **in** ~**s** entre paréntesis.

brackish ['brækɪʃ] *adj* (*water*) salobre.

brag [bræg] *vi* jactarse.

braid [breɪd] *n* (*trimming*) galón *m*; (*of hair*) trenza.

Braille [breɪl] *n* Braille *m*.

brain [breɪn] *n* cerebro; ~**s** *npl* sesos *mpl*; **she's got** ~**s** es muy lista.

brainchild ['breɪntʃaɪld] *n* invención *f*.

braindead ['breɪndɛd] *adj* (*MED*) clínicamente muerto; (*col*) subnormal, tarado.

brainless ['breɪnlɪs] *adj* estúpido, insensato.

brainstorm ['breɪnstɔːm] *n* (*fig*) ataque *m* de locura, frenesí *m*; (*US*: *brainwave*) idea luminosa *or* genial, inspiración *f*.

brainstorming ['breɪnstɔːmɪŋ] *n discusión intensa para solucionar problemas.*

brainwash ['breɪnwɔʃ] *vt* lavar el cerebro a.

brainwave ['breɪnweɪv] *n* idea luminosa *or* genial, inspiración *f*.

brainy ['breɪnɪ] *adj* muy listo *or* inteligente.

braise [breɪz] *vt* cocer a fuego lento.

brake [breɪk] *n* (*on vehicle*) freno ♦ *vt*, *vi* frenar.

brake drum *n* tambor *m* de freno.

brake fluid *n* líquido de frenos.

brake light *n* luz *f* de frenado.

brake pedal *n* pedal *m* de freno.

bramble ['bræmbl] *n* (*fruit*) zarza.

bran [bræn] *n* salvado.

branch [brɑːntʃ] *n* rama; (*fig*) ramo; (*COMM*) sucursal *f* ♦ *vi* ramificarse; (*fig*) extenderse.

▶**branch out** *vi* ramificarse.

branch line *n* (*RAIL*) ramal *m*, línea secundaria.

branch manager *n* director(a) *m/f* de sucursal.

brand [brænd] *n* marca; (*iron*) hierro de marcar ♦ *vt* (*cattle*) marcar con hierro candente.

brandish ['brændɪʃ] *vt* blandir.

brand name *n* marca.

brand-new ['brænd'njuː] *adj* flamante, completamente nuevo.

brandy ['brændɪ] *n* coñac *m*, brandy *m*.

brash [bræʃ] *adj* (*rough*) tosco; (*cheeky*) descarado.

Brasilia [brə'zɪlɪə] *n* Brasilia.

brass [brɑːs] *n* latón *m*; **the** ~ (*MUS*) los cobres.

brass band *n* banda de metal.

brassière ['bræsɪə*] *n* sostén *m*, sujetador *m*.

brass tacks *npl*: **to get down to** ~ ir al grano.

brat [bræt] *n* (*pej*) mocoso/a.

bravado [brə'vɑːdəu] *n* fanfarronería.

brave [breɪv] *adj* valiente, valeroso ♦ *n* guerrero indio ♦ *vt* (*challenge*) desafiar; (*resist*) aguantar.

bravely ['breɪvlɪ] *adv* valientemente, con valor.

bravery ['breɪvərɪ] *n* valor *m*, valentía.

bravo [brɑː'vəu] *excl* ¡bravo!, ¡olé!

brawl [brɔːl] *n* pendencia, reyerta ♦ *vi* pelearse.

brawn [brɔːn] *n* fuerza muscular; (*meat*) carne *f* en gelatina.

brawny ['brɔːnɪ] *adj* fornido, musculoso.

bray [breɪ] *n* rebuzno ♦ *vi* rebuznar.

brazen ['breɪzn] *adj* descarado, cínico ♦ *vt*: **to** ~ **it out** echarle cara al asunto.

brazier ['breɪzɪə*] *n* brasero.

Brazil [brə'zɪl] *n* (el) Brasil.

Brazilian [brə'zɪlɪən] *adj*, *n* brasileño/a *m/f*.

breach [briːtʃ] *vt* abrir brecha en ♦ *n* (*gap*) brecha; (*estrangement*) ruptura; (*breaking*): ~ **of confidence** abuso de confianza; ~ **of contract** infracción *f* de contrato; ~ **of the peace** perturbación *f* del órden público; **in** ~ **of** por incumplimiento or infracción de.

bread [brɛd] n pan m; (col: money) pasta, lana (LAM); ~ **and butter** n pan con mantequilla; (fig) pan (de cada día) ♦ adj común y corriente; **to earn one's daily** ~ ganarse el pan; **to know which side one's** ~ **is buttered (on)** saber dónde aprieta el zapato.

breadbin ['brɛdbɪn] n panera.

breadboard ['brɛdbɔːd] n (COMPUT) circuito experimental.

breadbox ['brɛdbɔks] n (US) panera.

breadcrumbs ['brɛdkrʌmz] npl migajas fpl; (CULIN) pan msg rallado.

breadline ['brɛdlaɪn] n: **on the** ~ en la miseria.

breadth [brɛtθ] n anchura; (fig) amplitud f.

breadwinner ['brɛdwɪnə*] n sostén m de la familia.

break [breɪk] vb (pt **broke** [brəuk], pp **broken** ['brəukən]) vt (gen) romper; (promise) no cumplir; (fall) amortiguar; (journey) interrumpir; (law) violar, infringir; (record) batir; (news) comunicar ♦ vi romperse, quebrarse; (storm) estallar; (weather) cambiar ♦ n (gap) abertura; (crack) grieta; (fracture) fractura; (in relations) ruptura; (rest) descanso; (time) intervalo; (: at school) (período de) recreo; (holiday) vacaciones fpl; (chance) oportunidad f; (escape) evasión f, fuga; **to** ~ **with sb** (fig) romper con algn; **to** ~ **even** vi cubrir los gastos; **to** ~ **free** or **loose** vi escaparse; **lucky** ~ (col) chiripa, racha de buena suerte; **to have** or **take a** ~ (few minutes) descansar; **without a** ~ sin descanso or descansar.

▶**break down** vt (door etc) echar abajo, derribar; (resistance) vencer, acabar con; (figures, data) analizar, descomponer; (undermine) acabar con ♦ vi estropearse; (MED) sufrir un colapso; (AUT) averiarse, descomponerse (LAM); (person) romper a llorar.

▶**break in** vt (horse etc) domar ♦ vi (burglar) forzar una entrada.

▶**break into** vt fus (house) forzar.

▶**break off** vi (speaker) pararse, detenerse; (branch) partir ♦ vt (talks) suspender; (engagement) romper.

▶**break open** vt (door etc) abrir por la fuerza, forzar.

▶**break out** vi estallar; **to** ~ **out in spots** salir a algn granos.

▶**break through** vi: **the sun broke through** asomó el sol ♦ vt fus (defences, barrier) abrirse paso por; (crowd) abrirse paso por.

▶**break up** vi (partnership) disolverse; (friends) romper ♦ vt (rocks, ice etc) partir; (crowd) disolver.

breakable ['breɪkəbl] adj quebradizo ♦ n: ~**s** cosas fpl frágiles.

breakage ['breɪkɪdʒ] n rotura; **to pay for** ~**s** pagar por los objetos rotos.

breakaway ['breɪkəweɪ] adj (group etc) disidente.

break-dancing ['breɪkdɑːnsɪŋ] n break m.

breakdown ['breɪkdaun] n (AUT) avería; (in communications) interrupción f; (MED: also: **nervous** ~) colapso, crisis f nerviosa; (of figures) desglose m.

breakdown van n (BRIT) (camión m) grúa.

breaker ['breɪkə*] n rompiente m, ola grande.

breakeven ['breɪk'iːvn] cpd: ~ **chart** gráfico del punto de equilibrio; ~ **point** punto de break-even or de equilibrio.

breakfast ['brɛkfəst] n desayuno.

breakfast cereal n cereales mpl para el desayuno.

break-in ['breɪkɪn] n robo con allanamiento de morada.

breaking and entering ['breɪkɪŋənd 'ɛntərɪŋ] n (LAW) violación f de domicilio, allanamiento de morada.

breaking point ['breɪkɪŋ-] n punto de ruptura.

breakthrough ['breɪkθruː] n ruptura; (fig) avance m, adelanto.

break-up ['breɪkʌp] n (of partnership, marriage) disolución f.

break-up value n (COMM) valor m de liquidación.

breakwater ['breɪkwɔːtə*] n rompeolas m inv.

breast [brɛst] n (of woman) pecho, seno; (chest) pecho; (of bird) pechuga.

breast-feed ['brɛstfiːd] vt, vi (irreg: like **feed**) amamantar, dar el pecho.

breaststroke ['brɛststrəuk] n braza de pecho.

breath [brɛθ] n aliento, respiración f; **out of** ~ sin aliento, sofocado; **to go out for a** ~ **of air** salir a tomar el fresco.

Breathalyser ® ['brɛθəlaɪzə*] n (BRIT) alcoholímetro m; ~ **test** n prueba de alcoholemia.

breathe [briːð] vt, vi respirar; (noisily) resollar; **I won't** ~ **a word about it** no diré ni una palabra de ello.

▶**breathe in** vt, vi aspirar.

▶**breathe out** vt, vi espirar.

breather ['briːðə*] n respiro, descanso.

breathing ['briːðɪŋ] n respiración f.

breathing space n (fig) respiro, pausa.

breathless ['brεθlıs] *adj* sin aliento, jadeante; (*with excitement*) pasmado.
breathtaking ['brεθteıkıŋ] *adj* imponente, pasmoso.
breath test *n* prueba de la alcoholemia.
-bred [brεd] *suff*: **to be well/ill~** estar bien/mal criado.
breed [briːd] *vb* (*pt, pp* **bred** [brεd]) *vt* criar; (*fig: hate, suspicion*) crear, engendrar ♦ *vi* reproducirse, procrear ♦ *n* raza, casta.
breeder ['briːdə*] *n* (*person*) criador(a) *m/f*; (*PHYSICS: also:* ~ **reactor**) reactor *m*.
breeding ['briːdıŋ] *n* (*of person*) educación *f*.
breeze [briːz] *n* brisa.
breezeblock ['briːzblɔk] *n* (*BRIT*) bovedilla.
breezy ['briːzı] *adj* de mucho viento, ventoso; (*person*) despreocupado.
Breton ['brεtən] *adj* bretón/ona ♦ *n* bretón/ona *m/f*; (*LING*) bretón *m*.
brevity ['brεvıtı] *n* brevedad *f*.
brew [bruː] *vt* (*tea*) hacer; (*beer*) elaborar; (*plot*) tramar ♦ *vi* hacerse; elaborarse; tramarse; (*storm*) amenazar.
brewer ['bruːə*] *n* cervecero, fabricante *m* de cerveza.
brewery ['bruːərı] *n* fábrica de cerveza.
briar ['braıə*] *n* (*thorny bush*) zarza; (*wild rose*) escaramujo, rosa silvestre.
bribe [braıb] *n* soborno ♦ *vt* sobornar, cohechar; **to ~ sb to do sth** sobornar a algn para que haga algo.
bribery ['braıbərı] *n* soborno, cohecho.
bric-a-brac ['brıkəbræk] *n inv* baratijas *fpl*.
brick [brık] *n* ladrillo.
bricklayer ['brıkleıə*] *n* albañil *m*.
brickwork ['brıkwɔːk] *n* enladrillado.
brickworks ['brıkwəːks] *n* ladrillar *m*.
bridal ['braıdl] *adj* nupcial.
bride [braıd] *n* novia.
bridegroom ['braıdgruːm] *n* novio.
bridesmaid ['braıdzmeıd] *n* dama de honor.
bridge [brıdʒ] *n* puente *m*; (*NAUT*) puente *m* de mando; (*of nose*) caballete *m*; (*CARDS*) bridge *m* ♦ *vt* (*river*) tender un puente sobre.
bridgehead ['brıdʒhεd] *n* cabeza de puente.
bridging loan ['brıdʒıŋ-] *n* crédito provisional.
bridle ['braıdl] *n* brida, freno ♦ *vt* poner la brida a; (*fig*) reprimir, refrenar ♦ *vi* (*in anger etc*) picarse.
bridle path *n* camino de herradura.
brief [briːf] *adj* breve, corto ♦ *n* (*LAW*) escrito ♦ *vt* (*inform*) informar; (*instruct*) dar instrucciones a; **in ~ ...** en resumen ...; **to ~ sb (about sth)** informar a algn (sobre algo).

briefcase ['briːfkeıs] *n* cartera, portafolio(s) *m inv* (*LAM*).
briefing ['briːfıŋ] *n* (*PRESS*) informe *m*.
briefly *adv* (*smile, glance*) brevemente; (*explain, say*) brevemente, en pocas palabras.
briefs [briːfs] *npl* (*for men*) calzoncillos *mpl*; (*for women*) bragas *fpl*.
Brig. *abbr* = **brigadier**.
brigade [brı'geıd] *n* (*MIL*) brigada.
brigadier [brıgə'dıə*] *n* general *m* de brigada.
bright [braıt] *adj* claro; (*room*) luminoso; (*day*) de sol; (*person: clever*) listo, inteligente; (: *lively*) alegre, animado; (*colour*) vivo; **to look on the** ~ **side** mirar el lado bueno.
brighten ['braıtn] (*also:* ~ **up**) *vt* (*room*) hacer más alegre ♦ *vi* (*weather*) despejarse; (*person*) animarse, alegrarse.
brill [brıl] *adj* (*BRIT col*) guay.
brilliance ['brıljəns] *n* brillo, brillantez *f*; (*fig: of person*) inteligencia.
brilliant ['brıljənt] *adj* (*light, idea, person, success*) brillante; (*clever*) genial.
brilliantly ['brıljəntlı] *adv* brillantemente.
brim [brım] *n* borde *m*; (*of hat*) ala.
brimful ['brım'ful] *adj* lleno hasta el borde; (*fig*) rebosante.
brine [braın] *n* (*CULIN*) salmuera.
bring, *pt, pp* **brought** [brıŋ, brɔːt] *vt* (*thing*) traer; (*person*) conducir; **to ~ sth to an end** terminar con algo; **I can't ~ myself to sack him** no soy capaz de echarle.
►**bring about** *vt* ocasionar, producir.
►**bring back** *vt* volver a traer; (*return*) devolver.
►**bring down** *vt* bajar; (*price*) rebajar.
►**bring forward** *vt* adelantar; (*BOOKKEEPING*) sumar y seguir.
►**bring in** *vt* (*harvest*) recoger; (*person*) hacer entrar *or* pasar; (*object*) traer; (*POL: bill, law*) presentar; (*LAW: verdict*) pronunciar; (*produce: income*) producir, rendir.
►**bring off** *vt* (*task, plan*) lograr, conseguir; (*deal*) cerrar.
►**bring out** *vt* (*object*) sacar; (*new product*) sacar; (*book*) publicar.
►**bring round** *vt* (*unconscious person*) hacer volver en sí; (*convince*) convencer.
►**bring up** *vt* (*person*) educar, criar; (*carry up*) subir; (*question*) sacar a colación; (*food: vomit*) devolver, vomitar.
brink [brıŋk] *n* borde *m*; **on the ~ of doing sth** a punto de hacer algo; **she was on the** ~ **of tears** estaba al borde de las lágrimas.

brisk [brɪsk] *adj* (*walk*) enérgico, vigoroso; (*speedy*) rápido; (*wind*) fresco; (*trade*) activo, animado; (*abrupt*) brusco; **business is** ~ el negocio va bien.

brisket ['brɪskɪt] *n* falda de vaca.

bristle ['brɪsl] *n* cerda ♦ *vi* erizarse.

bristly ['brɪslɪ] *adj* (*beard, hair*) erizado; **to have a** ~ **chin** tener la barba crecida.

Brit [brɪt] *n abbr* (*col*: = *British person*) británico/a.

Britain ['brɪtən] *n* (*also*: **Great** ~) Gran Bretaña.

British ['brɪtɪʃ] *adj* británico; **the** ~ *npl* los británicos; **the** ~ **Isles** *npl* las Islas Británicas.

British Rail (BR) *n* ≈ RENFE *f* (*SP*).

British Summer Time *n* hora de verano *británica*.

Briton ['brɪtən] *n* británico/a.

brittle ['brɪtl] *adj* quebradizo, frágil.

Br(o). *abbr* (*REL*) = **brother**.

broach [brəʊtʃ] *vt* (*subject*) abordar.

broad [brɔːd] *adj* ancho, amplio; (*accent*) cerrado ♦ *n* (*US col*) tía; **in** ~ **daylight** en pleno día; **the** ~ **outlines** las líneas generales.

broadband ['brɔːdbænd] *n* banda ancha.

broad bean *n* haba.

broadcast ['brɔːdkɑːst] *n* emisión *f* ♦ *vb* (*pt, pp* **broadcast**) *vt* (*RADIO*) emitir; (*TV*) transmitir ♦ *vi* emitir; transmitir.

broadcaster ['brɔːdkɑːstə*] *n* locutor(a) *m/f*.

broadcasting ['brɔːdkɑːstɪŋ] *n* radiodifusión *f*, difusión *f*.

broadcasting station *n* emisora.

broaden ['brɔːdn] *vt* ensanchar ♦ *vi* ensancharse.

broadly ['brɔːdlɪ] *adv* en general.

broad-minded ['brɔːd'maɪndɪd] *adj* tolerante, liberal.

broadsheet ['brɔːdʃiːt] *n* (*BRIT*) periódico de gran formato (*no sensacionalista*); *see also* **quality press**.

brocade [brə'keɪd] *n* brocado.

broccoli ['brɔkəlɪ] *n* brécol *m*, bróculi, *m*.

brochure ['brəʊʃjʊə*] *n* folleto.

brogue [brəʊg] *n* (*accent*) acento regional; (*shoe*) (*tipo de*) zapato de cuero grueso.

broil [brɔɪl] *vt* (*US*) asar a la parrilla.

broiler ['brɔɪlə*] *n* (*fowl*) pollo (para asar).

broke [brəʊk] *pt of* **break** ♦ *adj* (*col*) pelado, sin una perra; **to go** ~ quebrar.

broken ['brəʊkən] *pp of* **break** ♦ *adj* (*stick*) roto; (*fig: marriage*) deshecho; (: *promise, vow*) violado; ~ **leg** pierna rota; **in** ~ **English** en un inglés chapurreado.

broken-down ['brəʊkn'daʊn] *adj* (*car*) averiado; (*machine*) estropeado; (*house*)

destartalado.

broken-hearted ['brəʊkn'hɑːtɪd] *adj* con el corazón destrozado.

broker ['brəʊkə*] *n* corredor(a) *m/f* de bolsa.

brokerage ['brəʊkərɪdʒ] *n* corretaje *m*.

brolly ['brɔlɪ] *n* (*BRIT col*) paraguas *m inv*.

bronchitis [brɔŋ'kaɪtɪs] *n* bronquitis *f*.

bronze [brɔnz] *n* bronce *m*.

bronzed [brɔnzd] *adj* bronceado.

brooch [brəʊtʃ] *n* broche *m*.

brood [bruːd] *n* camada, cría; (*children*) progenie *f* ♦ *vi* (*hen*) empollar; **to** ~ **over** dar vueltas a, rumiar.

broody ['bruːdɪ] *adj* (*fig*) triste, melancólico.

brook [bruk] *n* arroyo.

broom [brum] *n* escoba; (*BOT*) retama.

broomstick ['brumstɪk] *n* palo de escoba.

Bros. *abbr* (*COMM*: = *Brothers*) Hnos.

broth [brɔθ] *n* caldo.

brothel ['brɔθl] *n* burdel *m*.

brother ['brʌðə*] *n* hermano.

brotherhood ['brʌðəhʊd] *n* hermandad *f*.

brother-in-law ['brʌðərɪn'lɔː] *n* cuñado.

brotherly ['brʌðəlɪ] *adj* fraternal.

brought [brɔːt] *pt, pp of* **bring**.

brow [brau] *n* (*forehead*) frente *f*; (*of hill*) cumbre *f*.

browbeat ['braubiːt] *vt* (*irreg: like* **beat**) intimidar.

brown [braun] *adj* marrón; (*hair*) castaño; (*tanned*) moreno ♦ *n* (*colour*) marrón *m* ♦ *vt* (*tan*) poner moreno; (*CULIN*) dorar; **to go** ~ (*person*) ponerse moreno; (*leaves*) dorarse.

brown bread *n* pan *m* moreno.

brownie ['braunɪ] *n* niña exploradora.

brown paper *n* papel *m* de estraza.

brown rice *n* arroz *m* integral.

brown sugar *n* azúcar *m* moreno.

browse [brauz] *vi* (*animal*) pacer; (*among books*) hojear libros; **to** ~ **through a book** hojear un libro.

browser ['brauzə*] *n* (*COMPUT*) navegador *m*.

bruise [bruːz] *n* (*on person*) cardenal *m*, hematoma *m* ♦ *vt* (*leg etc*) magullar; (*fig: feelings*) herir.

Brum [brʌm] *n abbr* (*col*) = **Birmingham**.

Brummie ['brʌmɪ] *n* (*col*) habitante *m/f* de Birmingham.

brunch [brʌntʃ] *n* desayuno-almuerzo.

brunette [bruː'net] *n* morena, morocha (*LAM*).

brunt [brʌnt] *n*: **to bear the** ~ **of** llevar el peso de.

brush [brʌʃ] *n* cepillo, escobilla (*LAM*); (*large*) escoba; (*for painting, shaving etc*)

brocha; (_artist's_) pincel _m_; (_BOT_) maleza
♦ _vt_ cepillar; (_gen_: ~ **past**, ~ **against**)
rozar al pasar; **to have a ~ with the
police** tener un roce con la policía.
▶**brush aside** _vt_ rechazar, no hacer caso
a.
▶**brush up** _vt_ (_knowledge_) repasar,
refrescar.
brushed [brʌʃt] _adj_ (_nylon, denim etc_)
afelpado; (_TECH: steel, chrome etc_)
cepillado.
brushwood ['brʌʃwud] _n_ (_bushes_) maleza;
(_sticks_) leña.
brusque [bruːsk] _adj_ (_person, manner_)
brusco; (_tone_) áspero.
Brussels ['brʌslz] _n_ Bruselas.
Brussels sprout _n_ col _f_ de Bruselas.
brutal ['bruːtl] _adj_ brutal.
brutality [bruː'tælɪtɪ] _n_ brutalidad _f_.
brutalize ['bruːtəlaɪz] _vt_ (_harden_) embrutecer; (_ill-treat_) tratar brutalmente a.
brute [bruːt] _n_ bruto; (_person_) bestia ♦ _adj_:
by ~ force por la fuerza bruta.
BS _n abbr_ (_US_: = _Bachelor of Science_) _título
universitario_.
bs _abbr_ = **bill of sale**.
BSA _n abbr_ = **Boy Scouts of America**.
BSc _abbr_ = **Bachelor of Science**; _see also_
Bachelor's Degree.
BSE _n abbr_ (= _bovine spongiform
encephalopathy_) encefalopatía
espongiforme bovina.
BSI _n abbr_ (= _British Standards Institution_)
institución británica de normalización.
BST _n abbr_ (= _British Summer Time_) hora de
verano británica.
btu _n abbr_ (= _British thermal unit_) ≈ _1054.2
julios_.
BTW _abbr_ (= _by the way_) por cierto.
bubble ['bʌbl] _n_ burbuja; (_in paint_) ampolla
♦ _vi_ burbujear, borbotar.
bubble bath _n_ espuma para el baño.
bubble gum _n_ chicle _m_.
bubblejet printer ['bʌbldʒet-] _n_ impresora
de inyección por burbujas.
bubbly ['bʌblɪ] _adj_ (_person_) vivaracho;
(_liquid_) con burbujas ♦ _n_ (_col_) champán _m_.
Bucharest [buːkə'rest] _n_ Bucarest _m_.
buck [bʌk] _n_ macho; (_US col_) dólar _m_ ♦ _vi_
corcovear; **to pass the ~** (**to sb**) echar (a
algn) el muerto.
▶**buck up** _vi_ (_cheer up_) animarse, cobrar
ánimo ♦ _vt_: **to ~ one's ideas up** poner más
empeño.
bucket ['bʌkɪt] _n_ cubo, balde _m_ (_esp LAM_)
♦ _vi_: **the rain is ~ing (down)** (_col_) está
lloviendo a cántaros.
Buckingham Palace ['bʌkɪŋəm-] _n_ el

Palacio de Buckingham; _ver recuadro_.

BUCKINGHAM PALACE

Buckingham Palace _es la residencia oficial
del monarca británico en Londres. Data de
1703 y fue en principio el palacio del Duque
de Buckingham, para pasar a manos de
Jorge III en 1762. Fue reconstruido el siglo
pasado y reformado después a principios
de este siglo. Hoy en día parte del palacio
está abierto al público._

---

buckle ['bʌkl] _n_ hebilla ♦ _vt_ abrochar con
hebilla ♦ _vi_ torcerse, combarse.
▶**buckle down** _vi_ poner empeño.
Bucks [bʌks] _abbr_ (_BRIT_) = **Buckinghamshire**.
bud [bʌd] _n_ brote _m_, yema; (_of flower_)
capullo ♦ _vi_ brotar, echar brotes.
Budapest [bjuːdə'pest] _n_ Budapest _m_.
Buddhism ['budɪzm] _n_ Budismo.
Buddhist ['budɪst] _adj, n_ budista _m/f_.
budding ['bʌdɪŋ] _adj_ en ciernes, en
embrión.
buddy ['bʌdɪ] _n_ (_US_) compañero,
compinche _m_.
budge [bʌdʒ] _vt_ mover; (_fig_) hacer ceder
♦ _vi_ moverse.
budgerigar ['bʌdʒərɪgɑː*] _n_ periquito.
budget ['bʌdʒɪt] _n_ presupuesto ♦ _vi_: **to ~
for sth** presupuestar algo; **I'm on a tight
~** no puedo gastar mucho; **she works out
her ~ every month** planea su
presupuesto todos los meses.
budgie ['bʌdʒɪ] _n_ = **budgerigar**.
Buenos Aires ['bweɪnɔs'aɪrɪz] _n_ Buenos
Aires _m_ ♦ _adj_ bonaerense, porteño (_LAM_).
buff [bʌf] _adj_ (_colour_) color _m_ de ante ♦ _n_
(_enthusiast_) entusiasta _m/f_.
buffalo ['bʌfələu], _pl_ ~ _or_ **buffaloes** _n_
(_BRIT_) búfalo; (_US: bison_) bisonte _m_.
buffer ['bʌfə*] _n_ amortiguador _m_; (_COMPUT_)
memoria intermedia, buffer _m_.
buffer zone _n_ zona (que sirve de) colchón.
buffet ['bufeɪ] _n_ (_BRIT: bar_) bar _m_, cafetería;
(_food_) buffet _m_ ♦ _vt_ ['bʌfɪt] (_strike_)
abofetear; (_wind etc_) golpear.
buffet car _n_ (_BRIT RAIL_) coche-restaurante
_m_.
buffet lunch _n_ buffet _m_ (almuerzo).
buffoon [bə'fuːn] _n_ bufón _m_.
bug [bʌg] _n_ (_insect_) chinche _m_; (: _gen_) bicho,
sabandija; (_germ_) microbio, bacilo; (_spy
device_) micrófono oculto; (_COMPUT_) fallo,
error _m_ ♦ _vt_ (_annoy_) fastidiar; (_room_)
poner un micrófono oculto en; (_phone_)
pinchar; **I've got the travel ~** (_fig_) me
encanta viajar; **it really ~s me** me

fastidia or molesta mucho.

bugbear ['bʌgbɛə*] n pesadilla.

bugle ['bjuːgl] n corneta, clarín m.

build [bɪld] n (of person) talle m, tipo ♦ vt (pt, pp **built** [bɪlt]) construir, edificar.

▶**build on** vt fus (fig) basar en.

▶**build up** vt (MED) fortalecer; (stocks) acumular; (establish: business) fomentar, desarrollar; (: reputation) crear(se); (increase: production) aumentar; **don't ~ your hopes up too soon** no te hagas demasiadas ilusiones.

builder ['bɪldə*] n constructor(a) m/f; (contractor) contratista m/f.

building ['bɪldɪŋ] n (act of) construcción f; (habitation, offices) edificio.

building contractor n contratista m/f de obras.

building industry n construcción f.

building site n solar m (SP), obra (LAM).

building society n (BRIT) sociedad f de préstamo inmobiliario; ver recuadro.

BUILDING SOCIETY

En el Reino Unido existe un tipo de entidad financiera llamada **building society** de la que sus clientes son también propietarios y cuyos servicios son similares a los de los bancos, aunque se centran fundamental-mente en créditos hipotecarios y cuentas de ahorro. Son una entidad más utilizada por el público en general a la hora de pedir créditos para la compra de la vivienda.

---

building trade n = **building industry**.

build-up ['bɪldʌp] n (publicity): **to give sb/ sth a good ~** hacer mucha propaganda de algn/algo.

built [bɪlt] pt, pp of **build**.

built-in ['bɪlt'ɪn] adj (cupboard) empotrado; (device) interior, incorporado; ~ **obsolescence** caducidad f programada.

built-up ['bɪltʌp] adj (area) urbanizado.

bulb [bʌlb] n (BOT) bulbo; (ELEC) bombilla, bombillo (LAM), foco (LAM).

Bulgaria [bʌl'gɛərɪə] n Bulgaria.

Bulgarian [bʌl'gɛərɪən] adj búlgaro ♦ n búlgaro/a; (LING) búlgaro.

bulge [bʌldʒ] n bombeo, pandeo; (in birth rate, sales) alza, aumento ♦ vi bombearse, pandearse; (pocket etc) hacer bulto.

bulimia [bə'lɪmɪə] n bulimia.

bulk [bʌlk] n (mass) bulto, volumen m; (major part) grueso; **in ~** (COMM) a granel; **the ~ of** la mayor parte de; **to buy in ~** comprar en grandes cantidades.

bulk buying n compra a granel.

bulk carrier n (buque m) granelero.

bulkhead ['bʌlkhɛd] n mamparo.

bulky ['bʌlkɪ] adj voluminoso, abultado.

bull [bul] n toro; (STOCK EXCHANGE) alcista m/f de bolsa; (REL) bula.

bulldog ['buldɔg] n dogo.

bulldoze ['buldəuz] vt mover con excavadora; **I was ~d into doing it** (fig col) me obligaron a hacerlo.

bulldozer ['buldəuzə*] n buldozer m, excavadora.

bullet ['bulɪt] n bala; ~ **wound** balazo.

bulletin ['bulɪtɪn] n comunicado, parte m; (journal) boletín m.

bulletin board n (US) tablón m de anuncios; (COMPUT) tablero de noticias.

bulletproof ['bulɪtpruːf] adj a prueba de balas; ~ **vest** chaleco anti-balas.

bullfight ['bulfaɪt] n corrida de toros.

bullfighter ['bulfaɪtə*] n torero.

bullfighting ['bulfaɪtɪŋ] n los toros mpl, el toreo; (art of ~) tauromaquia.

bullion ['buljən] n oro or plata en barras.

bullock ['bulək] n novillo.

bullring ['bulrɪŋ] n plaza de toros.

bull's-eye ['bulzaɪ] n blanco, diana.

bullshit ['bulʃɪt] (col!) excl chorradas ♦ n chorradas fpl ♦ vi decir chorradas ♦ vt: **to ~ sb** quedarse con algn.

bully ['bulɪ] n valentón m, matón m ♦ vt intimidar, tiranizar.

bum [bʌm] n (BRIT: col: backside) culo; (: tramp) vagabundo; (col: esp US: idler) holgazán/ana m/f, flojo/a.

bumble ['bʌmbl] vi (walk unsteadily) andar de forma vacilante; (fig) farfullar, trastabillar.

bumblebee ['bʌmblbiː] n abejorro.

bumbling ['bʌmblɪŋ] n divagación f.

bumf [bʌmf] n (col: forms etc) papeleo.

bump [bʌmp] n (blow) tope m, choque m; (jolt) sacudida; (noise) choque m, topetón m; (on road etc) bache m; (on head) chichón m ♦ vt (strike) chocar contra, topetar ♦ vi dar sacudidas.

▶**bump into** vt fus chocar contra, tropezar con; (person) topar con; (col: meet) tropezar con, toparse con.

bumper ['bʌmpə*] n (BRIT) parachoques m inv ♦ adj: ~ **crop/harvest** cosecha abundante.

bumper cars npl (US) autos or coches mpl de choque.

bumph [bʌmf] n = **bumf**.

bumptious ['bʌmpʃəs] adj engreído, presuntuoso.

bumpy ['bʌmpɪ] adj (road) lleno de baches; (journey, flight) agitado.

bun [bʌn] *n* (*BRIT: cake*) pastel *m*; (*US: bread*) bollo; (*of hair*) moño.

bunch [bʌntʃ] *n* (*of flowers*) ramo; (*of keys*) manojo; (*of bananas*) piña; (*of people*) grupo; (*pej*) pandilla.

bundle ['bʌndl] *n* (*gen*) bulto, fardo; (*of sticks*) haz *m*; (*of papers*) legajo ♦ *vt* (*also*: ~ **up**) atar, envolver; **to ~ sth/sb into** meter algo/a algn precipitadamente en.

bun fight *n* (*BRIT col: tea party*) merienda; (: *function*) fiesta oficial.

bung [bʌŋ] *n* tapón *m*, bitoque *m* ♦ *vt* (*throw: also*: ~ **into**) arrojar; (*also*: ~ **up**: *pipe, hole*) tapar; **my nose is ~ed up** (*col*) tengo la nariz atascada *or* taponada.

bungalow ['bʌŋgələu] *n* bungalow *m*, chalé *m*.

bungee jumping ['bʌndʒiː'dʒʌmpiŋ] *n* puenting *m*, banyi *m*.

bungle ['bʌŋgl] *vt* chapucear.

bunion ['bʌnjən] *n* juanete *m*.

bunk [bʌŋk] *n* litera; ~ **beds** *npl* literas *fpl*.

bunker ['bʌŋkə*] *n* (*coal store*) carbonera; (*MIL*) refugio; (*GOLF*) bunker *m*.

bunk off *vi*: **to ~ school** (*BRIT col*) pirarse las clases; **I'll ~ at 3 this afternoon** me voy a pirar a las 3 esta tarde.

bunny ['bʌnɪ] *n* (*also*: ~ **rabbit**) conejito.

Bunsen burner ['bʌnsn-] *n* mechero Bunsen.

bunting ['bʌntɪŋ] *n* empavesada, banderas *fpl*.

buoy [bɔɪ] *n* boya.

▶**buoy up** *vt* mantener a flote; (*fig*) animar.

buoyancy ['bɔɪənsɪ] *n* (*of ship*) flotabilidad *f*.

buoyant ['bɔɪənt] *adj* (*carefree*) boyante, optimista; (*COMM: market, prices etc*) sostenido.

BUPA ['buːpə] *n abbr* (= *British United Provident Association*) *seguro médico privado*.

burden ['bəːdn] *n* carga ♦ *vt* cargar; **to be a ~ to sb** ser una carga para algn.

bureau, *pl* ~**x** ['bjuərəu, -z] *n* (*BRIT: writing desk*) escritorio, buró *m*; (*US: chest of drawers*) cómoda; (*office*) oficina, agencia.

bureaucracy [bjuə'rɔkrəsɪ] *n* burocracia.

bureaucrat ['bjuərəkræt] *n* burócrata *m/f*.

bureaucratic [bjuərə'krætɪk] *adj* burocrático.

burgeon ['bəːdʒən] *vi* (*develop rapidly*) crecer, incrementarse; (*trade etc*) florecer.

burger ['bəːgə*] *n* hamburguesa.

burglar ['bəːglə*] *n* ladrón/ona *m/f*.

burglar alarm *n* alarma *f* contra robo.

burglarize ['bəːgləraɪz] *vt* (*US*) robar (con allanamiento).

burglary ['bəːglərɪ] *n* robo con allanamiento *or* fractura, robo de una casa.

burgle ['bəːgl] *vt* robar (con allanamiento).

burial ['bɛrɪəl] *n* entierro.

burial ground *n* cementerio.

burlesque [bəː'lɛsk] *n* parodia.

burly ['bəːlɪ] *adj* fornido, membrudo.

Burma ['bəːmə] *n* Birmania; *see also* **Myanmar.**

Burmese [bəː'miːz] *adj* birmano ♦ *n* (*pl inv*) birmano/a; (*LING*) birmano.

burn [bəːn] *vb* (*pt, pp* **burned** *or* **burnt** [bəːnt]) *vt* quemar; (*house*) incendiar ♦ *vi* quemarse, arder; incendiarse; (*sting*) escocer ♦ *n* (*MED*) quemadura; **the cigarette ~t a hole in her dress** se ha quemado el vestido con el cigarrillo; **I've ~t myself!** ¡me he quemado!

▶**burn down** *vt* incendiar.

▶**burn out** *vt* (*subj: writer etc*): **to ~ o.s. out** agotarse.

burner ['bəːnə*] *n* (*gas*) quemador *m*.

burning ['bəːnɪŋ] *adj* ardiente; (*building, forest*) en llamas.

Burns' Night [bəːnz-] *n ver recuadro.*

burp [bəːp] (*col*) *n* eructo ♦ *vi* eructar.

burqa ['bəːkə] *n* burka *m*, burqa *m*.

burrow ['bʌrəu] *n* madriguera ♦ *vt* hacer una madriguera.

bursar ['bəːsə*] *n* tesorero; (*BRIT: student*) becario/a.

bursary ['bəːsərɪ] *n* (*BRIT*) beca.

burst [bəːst] *vb* (*pt, pp* **burst**) *vt* (*balloon, pipe*) reventar; (*banks etc*) romper ♦ *vi* reventarse; romperse; (*tyre*) pincharse; (*bomb*) estallar ♦ *n* (*explosion*) estallido; (*also*: ~ **pipe**) reventón *m*; **the river has ~ its banks** el río se ha desbordado; **to ~ into flames** estallar en llamas; **to ~ out laughing** soltar la carcajada; **to ~ into tears** deshacerse en lágrimas; **to be ~ing with** reventar de; **a ~ of energy** una explosión de energía; **a ~ of applause** una salva de aplausos; **a ~ of speed** una escapada; **to ~ open** *vi* abrirse de golpe.

▶**burst into** *vt fus* (*room etc*) irrumpir en.

bury ['bɛrɪ] *vt* enterrar; (*body*) enterrar, sepultar; **to ~ the hatchet** enterrar el hacha (de guerra), echar pelillos a la mar.

bus [bʌs] *n* autobús *m*, camión *m* (*LAM*).

bus boy *n* (*US*) ayudante *m/f* de camarero.

bush [buʃ] *n* arbusto; (*scrub land*) monte *m* bajo; **to beat about the ~** andar(se) con rodeos.

bushed [buʃt] *adj* (*col*) molido.

bushel ['buʃl] *n* (*measure: Brit*) = 36,36 *litros*; (*: US*) = 35,24 *litros*.

bush fire *n* incendio en el monte.

bushy ['buʃɪ] *adj* (*beard, eyebrows*) poblado; (*hair*) espeso; (*fur*) tupido.

busily ['bɪzɪlɪ] *adv* afanosamente.

business ['bɪznɪs] *n* (*matter, affair*) asunto; (*trading*) comercio, negocios *mpl*; (*firm*) empresa, casa; (*occupation*) oficio; **to be away on ~** estar en viaje de negocios; **it's my ~ to...** me toca *or* corresponde...; **it's none of my ~** no es asunto mío; **he means ~** habla en serio; **he's in the insurance ~** se dedica a los seguros; **I'm here on ~** estoy aquí por mi trabajo; **to do ~ with sb** hacer negocios con algn.

business address *n* dirección *f* comercial.

business card *n* tarjeta de visita.

businesslike ['bɪznɪslaɪk] *adj* (*company*) serio; (*person*) eficiente.

businessman ['bɪznɪsmən] *n* hombre *m* de negocios.

business trip *n* viaje *m* de negocios.

businesswoman ['bɪznɪswumən] *n* mujer *f* de negocios.

busker ['bʌskə*] *n* (*BRIT*) músico/a ambulante.

bus route *n* recorrido del autobús.

bus station *n* estación *f* or terminal *f* de autobuses.

bus-stop ['bʌsstɔp] *n* parada de autobús, paradero (*LAM*).

bust [bʌst] *n* (*ANAT*) pecho ♦ *adj* (*col: broken*) roto, estropeado ♦ *vt* (*col: POLICE: arrest*) detener; **to go ~** quebrar.

bustle ['bʌsl] *n* bullicio, movimiento ♦ *vi* menearse, apresurarse.

bustling ['bʌslɪŋ] *adj* (*town*) animado, bullicioso.

bust-up ['bʌstʌp] *n* (*col*) riña.

busty ['bʌstɪ] *adj* (*col*) pechugona, con buena delantera.

busy ['bɪzɪ] *adj* ocupado, atareado; (*shop, street*) concurrido, animado ♦ *vt*: **to ~ o.s.**

with ocuparse en; **he's a ~ man** (*normally*) es un hombre muy ocupado; (*temporarily*) está muy ocupado; **the line's ~** (*esp US*) está comunicando.

busybody ['bɪzɪbɔdɪ] *n* entrometido/a.

busy signal *n* (*US TEL*) señal *f* de comunicando.

══════════ *KEYWORD*

but [bʌt] *conj* **1** pero; **he's not very bright, ~ he's hard-working** no es muy inteligente, pero es trabajador

2 (*in direct contradiction*) sino; **he's not English ~ French** no es inglés sino francés; **he didn't sing ~ he shouted** no cantó sino que gritó

3 (*showing disagreement, surprise etc*): **~ that's far too expensive!** ¡pero eso es carísimo!; **~ it does work!** ¡(pero) sí que funciona!

♦ *prep* (*apart from, except*) menos, salvo; **we've had nothing ~ trouble** no hemos tenido más que problemas; **no-one ~ him can do it** nadie más que él puede hacerlo; **the last ~ one** el penúltimo; **who ~ a lunatic would do such a thing?** ¡sólo un loco haría una cosa así!; **~ for you/your help** si no fuera por ti/tu ayuda; **anything ~ that** cualquier cosa menos eso

♦ *adv* (*just, only*): **she's ~ a child** no es más que una niña; **had I ~ known** si lo hubiera sabido; **I can ~ try** al menos lo puedo intentar; **it's all ~ finished** está casi acabado.

butane ['bjuːteɪn] *n* (*also: ~ gas*) (gas *m*) butano.

butch [butʃ] *adj* (*pej: woman*) machirula, marimacho; (*col: man*) muy macho.

butcher ['butʃə*] *n* carnicero/a ♦ *vt* hacer una carnicería con; (*cattle etc for meat*) matar; **~'s (shop)** carnicería.

butler ['bʌtlə*] *n* mayordomo.

butt [bʌt] *n* (*cask*) tonel *m*; (*for rain*) tina; (*thick end*) cabo, extremo; (*of gun*) culata; (*of cigarette*) colilla; (*BRIT fig: target*) blanco ♦ *vt* dar cabezadas contra, topetar.

▶**butt in** *vi* (*interrupt*) interrumpir.

butter ['bʌtə*] *n* mantequilla, manteca (*LAM*) ♦ *vt* untar con mantequilla.

butter bean *n* judía blanca.

buttercup ['bʌtəkʌp] *n* ranúnculo.

butterfingers ['bʌtəfɪŋgəz] *n* (*col*) torpe *m/f*.

butterfly ['bʌtəflaɪ] *n* mariposa; (*SWIMMING: also: ~ stroke*) (braza de) mariposa.

buttocks ['bʌtəks] *npl* nalgas *fpl*.

button ['bʌtn] *n* botón *m* ♦ *vt* (*also: ~ up*)

abotonar, abrochar ♦ vi abrocharse.
buttonhole ['bʌtnhəul] n ojal m; (flower) flor f que se lleva en el ojal.
buttress ['bʌtrɪs] n contrafuerte m; (fig) apoyo, sostén m.
buy [baɪ] vb (pt, pp **bought** [bɔːt]) vt comprar ♦ n compra; **to ~ sb sth/sth from sb** comprarle algo a algn; **to ~ sb a drink** invitar a algn a una copa; **a good/bad ~** una buena/mala compra.
▶**buy back** vt volver a comprar.
▶**buy in** vt proveerse or abastecerse de.
▶**buy into** vt fus comprar acciones en.
▶**buy off** vt (col: bribe) sobornar.
▶**buy out** vt (partner) comprar la parte de.
buyer ['baɪə*] n comprador(a) m/f; **~'s market** mercado favorable al comprador.
buy-out ['baɪaut] n (COMM) adquisición f de (la totalidad de) las acciones.
buzz [bʌz] n zumbido; (col: phone call) llamada (telefónica) ♦ vt (call on intercom) llamar; (with buzzer) hacer sonar; (AVIAT: plane, building) pasar rozando ♦ vi zumbar; **my head is ~ing** me zumba la cabeza.
▶**buzz off** vi (BRIT col) largarse.
buzzard ['bʌzəd] n (BRIT) águila ratonera; (US) buitre m, gallinazo (LAM).
buzzer ['bʌzə*] n timbre m.
buzz word n palabra que está de moda.

=================== KEYWORD

by [baɪ] prep **1** (referring to cause, agent) por; de; **abandoned ~ his mother** abandonado por su madre; **surrounded ~ enemies** rodeado de enemigos; **a painting ~ Picasso** un cuadro de Picasso
2 (referring to method, manner, means): **~ bus/car/train** en autobús/coche/tren; **to pay ~ cheque** pagar con cheque(s); **~ moonlight/candlelight** a la luz de la luna/ una vela; **~ saving hard, he ...** ahorrando, ...
3 (via, through) por; **we came ~ Dover** vinimos por Dover
4 (close to, past): **the house ~ the river** la casa junto al río; **she rushed ~ me** pasó a mi lado como una exhalación; **I go ~ the post office every day** paso por delante de Correos todos los días
5 (time: not later than) para; (: during): **~ daylight** de día; **~ 4 o'clock** para las cuatro; **~ this time tomorrow** mañana a estas horas; **~ the time I got here it was too late** cuando llegué ya era demasiado tarde
6 (amount): **~ the metre/kilo** por metro/ kilo; **paid ~ the hour** pagado por hora

7 (MATH, measure): **to divide/multiply ~ 3** dividir/multiplicar por 3; **a room 3 metres ~ 4** una habitación de 3 metros por 4; **it's broader ~ a metre** es un metro más ancho; **the bus missed me ~ inches** no me pilló el autobús por un pelo
8 (according to) según, de acuerdo con; **it's 3 o'clock ~ my watch** según mi reloj, son las tres; **it's all right ~ me** por mí, está bien
9: (all) **~ oneself** etc todo solo; **he did it (all) ~ himself** lo hizo él solo; **he was standing (all) ~ himself in a corner** estaba de pie solo en un rincón
10: **~ the way** a propósito, por cierto; **this wasn't my idea, ~ the way** pues, no fue idea mía
♦ adv **1** see **go**; **pass** etc
2: **~ and ~** finalmente; **they'll come back ~ and ~** acabarán volviendo; **~ and large** en líneas generales, en general.

bye(-bye) ['baɪ('baɪ)] excl adiós, hasta luego, chao (esp LAM).
by(e)-law ['baɪlɔː] n ordenanza municipal.
by-election ['baɪɪlekʃən] n (BRIT) elección f parcial; ver recuadro.

┌─────────────────────────┐
│ **BY-ELECTION** │
│ │
│ Se celebra una **by-election** en el Reino │
│ Unido y otros países de la "Common- │
│ wealth" cuando es necesario reemplazar a │
│ un parlamentario ("Member of Parlia- │
│ ment") cesado o fallecido durante una │
│ legislatura. Dichas elecciones tienen lugar │
│ únicamente en el área electoral represen- │
│ tada por el citado parlamentario, su │
│ "constituency". │
└─────────────────────────┘

bygone ['baɪgɔn] adj pasado, del pasado ♦ n: **let ~s be ~s** lo pasado, pasado está.
Byelorussia [bjɛləu'rʌʃə] n Bielorrusia.
Byelorussian [bjɛləu'rʌʃən] adj, n = **Belorussian**.
bypass ['baɪpɑːs] n carretera de circunvalación; (MED) (operación f de) by-pass m ♦ vt evitar.
by-product ['baɪprɔdʌkt] n subproducto, derivado.
bystander ['baɪstændə*] n espectador(a) m/ f.
byte [baɪt] n (COMPUT) byte m, octeto.
byway ['baɪweɪ] n camino poco frecuentado.
byword ['baɪwəːd] n: **to be a ~ for** ser sinónimo de.
by-your-leave ['baɪjɔː'liːv] n: **without so**

much as a ~ sin decir nada, sin dar
ningún tipo de explicación.

C c

C, c [siː] n (letter) C, c f; (MUS): **C do** m; **C for
Charlie** C de Carmen.
C abbr (= Celsius, centigrade) C.
c abbr (= century) S.; (= circa) hacia; (US etc)
= **cent(s)**.
CA n abbr = **Central America**; (BRIT) =
chartered accountant; (US) = **California**.
ca. abbr (= circa) c.
c/a abbr = **capital account, credit account,
current account**.
CAA n abbr (BRIT: = Civil Aviation Authority)
organismo de control y desarrollo de la
aviación civil.
CAB n abbr (BRIT: = Citizens' Advice Bureau)
≈ Servicio de Información Ciudadana.
cab [kæb] n taxi m; (of truck) cabina.
cabaret ['kæbəreɪ] n cabaret m.
cabbage ['kæbɪdʒ] n col f, berza.
cabbie, cabby ['kæbɪ] n (col) taxista m/f.
cab driver n taxista m/f.
cabin ['kæbɪn] n cabaña; (on ship) camarote
m.
cabin cruiser n yate m de motor.
cabinet ['kæbɪnɪt] n (POL) consejo de
ministros; (furniture) armario; (also:
display ~) vitrina.
cabinet-maker ['kæbɪnɪt'meɪkə*] n
ebanista m.
cabinet minister n ministro/a (del
gabinete).
cable ['keɪbl] n cable m ♦ vt cablegrafiar.
cable-car ['keɪblkɑː*] n teleférico.
cablegram ['keɪblgræm] n cablegrama m.
cable television n televisión f por cable.
cache [kæʃ] n (drugs) alijo; (arms) zulo.
cackle ['kækl] vi cacarear.
cactus, pl **cacti** ['kæktəs, -taɪ] n cacto.
CAD n abbr (= computer-aided design) DAO
m.
caddie, caddy ['kædɪ] n (GOLF) cadi m.
cadence ['keɪdəns] n ritmo; (MUS)
cadencia.
cadet [kə'dɛt] n (MIL) cadete m; **police ~**
cadete m de policía.
cadge [kædʒ] vt gorronear.
cadger ['kædʒə*] n gorrón/ona m/f.

cadre ['kædrɪ] n cuadro.
Caesarean, (US) Cesarean [siː'zɛərɪən] adj:
~ (section) cesárea.
CAF abbr (BRIT: = cost and freight) C y F.
café ['kæfeɪ] n café m.
cafeteria [kæfɪ'tɪərɪə] n cafetería (con
autoservicio para comer).
caffein(e) ['kæfiːn] n cafeína.
cage [keɪdʒ] n jaula ♦ vt enjaular.
cagey ['keɪdʒɪ] adj (col) cauteloso,
reservado.
cagoule [kə'guːl] n canguro.
cahoots [kə'huːts] n: **to be in ~ (with sb)**
estar conchabado (con algn).
CAI n abbr (= computer-aided instruction)
enseñanza asistida por ordenador.
Cairo ['kaɪərəu] n El Cairo.
cajole [kə'dʒəul] vt engatusar.
cake [keɪk] n pastel m; (of soap) pastilla; **he
wants to have his ~ and eat it** (fig) quiere
estar en misa y repicando; **it's a piece of
~** (col) es pan comido.
caked [keɪkt] adj: **~ with** cubierto de.
cake shop n pastelería.
Cal. abbr (US) = California.
calamine ['kæləmaɪn] n calamina.
calamitous [kə'læmɪtəs] adj calamitoso.
calamity [kə'læmɪtɪ] n calamidad f.
calcium ['kælsɪəm] n calcio.
calculate ['kælkjuleɪt] vt (estimate: chances,
effect) calcular.
▶**calculate on** vt fus: **to ~ on sth/on doing
sth** contar con algo/con hacer algo.
calculated ['kælkjuleɪtɪd] adj: **we took a ~
risk** calculamos el riesgo.
calculating ['kælkjuleɪtɪŋ] adj (scheming)
calculador(a).
calculation [kælkju'leɪʃən] n cálculo,
cómputo.
calculator ['kælkjuleɪtə*] n calculadora.
calculus ['kælkjuləs] n cálculo.
calendar ['kæləndə*] n calendario; **~
month/year** n mes m/año civil.
calf, pl **calves** [kɑːf, kɑːvz] n (of cow)
ternero, becerro; (of other animals) cría;
(also: **~skin**) piel f de becerro; (ANAT)
pantorrilla, canilla (LAM).
caliber ['kælɪbə*] n (US) = **calibre**.
calibrate ['kælɪbreɪt] vt (gun etc) calibrar;
(scale of measuring instrument) graduar.
calibre, (US) caliber ['kælɪbə*] n calibre m.
calico ['kælɪkəu] n calicó m.
Calif. abbr (US) = California.
California [kælɪ'fɔːnɪə] n California.
calipers ['kælɪpəz] npl (US) = **callipers**.
call [kɔːl] vt (gen, also TEL) llamar;
(announce: flight) anunciar; (meeting,
strike) convocar ♦ vi (shout) llamar;

(*telephone*) llamar (por teléfono), telefonear; (*visit: also:* ~ **in**, ~ **round**) hacer una visita ♦ *n* (*shout, TEL*) llamada, llamado (*LAM*); (*of bird*) canto; (*appeal*) llamamiento, llamado (*LAM*); (*summons: for flight etc*) llamada; (*fig: lure*) llamada; **to be** ~**ed** (*person, object*) llamarse; **to** ~ **sb names** poner verde a algn; **let's** ~ **it a day** (*col*) ¡dejémoslo!, ¡ya está bien!; **who is** ~**ing?** ¿de parte de quién?; **London** ~**ing** (*RADIO*) aquí Londres; **on** ~ (*nurse, doctor etc*) de guardia; **please give me a** ~ **at 7** llámeme a las 7, por favor; **long-distance** ~ conferencia (interurbana); **to make a** ~ llamar por teléfono; **port of** ~ puerto de escala; **to pay a** ~ **on sb** pasarse a ver a algn; **there's not much** ~ **for these items** estos artículos no tienen mucha demanda.

▶**call at** *vt fus* (*ship*) hacer escala en, tocar en; (*train*) parar en.
▶**call back** *vi* (*return*) volver; (*TEL*) volver a llamar.
▶**call for** *vt fus* (*demand*) pedir, exigir; (*fetch*) venir por.
▶**call in** *vt* (*doctor, expert, police*) llamar.
▶**call off** *vt* suspender; **the strike was** ~**ed off** se desconvocó la huelga.
▶**call on** *vt fus* (*visit*) ir a ver; (*turn to*) acudir a.
▶**call out** *vi* gritar, dar voces ♦ *vt* (*doctor*) llamar; (*police, troops*) hacer intervenir.
▶**call up** *vt* (*MIL*) llamar a filas.

Callanetics ® [kælə'nɛtɪks] *nsg gimnasia de repetición de pequeños ejercicios musculares.*
callbox ['kɔːlbɔks] *n* (*BRIT*) cabina telefónica.
call centre *n* (*BRIT*) centro de llamadas.
caller ['kɔːlə*] *n* visita *f*; (*TEL*) usuario/a; **hold the line,** ~! ¡no cuelgue!
call girl *n* prostituta.
call-in ['kɔːlɪn] *n* (*US*) *programa de línea abierta al público.*
calling ['kɔːlɪŋ] *n* vocación *f*; (*profession*) profesión *f*.
calling card *n* tarjeta de visita.
callipers, (*US*) **calipers** ['kælɪpəz] *npl* (*MED*) aparato ortopédico; (*MATH*) calibrador *m*.
callous ['kæləs] *adj* insensible, cruel.
callousness ['kæləsnɪs] *n* insensibilidad, crueldad *f*.
callow ['kæləʊ] *adj* inexperto, novato.
calm [kɑːm] *adj* tranquilo; (*sea*) tranquilo, en calma ♦ *n* calma, tranquilidad *f* ♦ *vt* calmar, tranquilizar.
▶**calm down** *vi* calmarse, tranquilizarse ♦ *vt* calmar, tranquilizar.

calmly ['kɑːmlɪ] *adv* tranquilamente, con calma.
calmness ['kɑːmnɪs] *n* calma.
Calor gas ® ['kælə*-] *n* butano.
calorie ['kælərɪ] *n* caloría *f*; **low-**~ **product** producto bajo en calorías.
calve [kɑːv] *vi* parir.
calves [kɑːvz] *npl of* **calf**.
CAM *n abbr* (= *computer-aided manufacturing*) producción *f* asistida por ordenador.
camber ['kæmbə*] *n* (*of road*) combadura.
Cambodia [kæm'bəʊdjə] *n* Camboya.
Cambodian [kæm'bəʊdjən] *adj, n* camboyano/a *m/f*.
Cambs *abbr* (*BRIT*) = *Cambridgeshire*.
camcorder ['kæmkɔːdə*] *n* videocámara.
came [keɪm] *pt of* **come**.
camel ['kæməl] *n* camello.
cameo ['kæmɪəʊ] *n* camafeo.
camera ['kæmərə] *n* cámara *or* máquina fotográfica; (*CINE, TV*) cámara; (*movie* ~) cámara, tomavistas *m inv*; **in** ~ a puerta cerrada.
cameraman ['kæmərəmən] *n* cámara *m*.
Cameroon, Cameroun [kæme'ruːn] *n* Camerún *m*.
camomile tea ['kæməmaɪl-] *n* manzanilla.
camouflage ['kæməflɑːʒ] *n* camuflaje *m* ♦ *vt* camuflar.
camp [kæmp] *n* campo, campamento ♦ *vi* acampar ♦ *adj* afectado, afeminado; **to go** ~**ing** ir de *or* hacer camping.
campaign [kæm'peɪn] *n* (*MIL, POL etc*) campaña ♦ *vi*: **to** ~ (**for/against**) hacer campaña (a favor de/en contra de).
campaigner [kæm'peɪnə*] *n*: ~ **for** defensor(a) *m/f* de; ~ **against** persona que hace campaña contra.
campbed ['kæmpbɛd] *n* (*BRIT*) cama plegable.
camper ['kæmpə*] *n* campista *m/f*; (*vehicle*) caravana.
camping ['kæmpɪŋ] *n* camping *m*.
campsite ['kæmpsaɪt] *n* camping *m*.
campus ['kæmpəs] *n* campus *m*.
camshaft ['kæmʃɑːft] *n* árbol *m* de levas.
can [kæn] *aux vb see next headword* ♦ *n* (*of oil, water*) bidón *m*; (*tin*) lata, bote *m* ♦ *vt* enlatar; (*preserve*) conservar en lata; **a** ~ **of beer** una lata *or* un bote de cerveza; **to carry the** ~ (*col*) pagar el pato.

═══════════════════════════ *KEYWORD*

can (*negative* **cannot, can't**; *conditional and pt* **could**) *aux vb* **1** (*be able to*) poder; **you** ~ **do it if you try** puedes hacerlo si lo intentas; **I** ~**'t see you** no te veo; ~ **you hear me?**

(*not translated*) ¿me oyes?
2 (*know how to*) saber; **I ~ swim/play tennis/drive** sé nadar/jugar al tenis/ conducir; **~ you speak French?** ¿hablas *or* sabes hablar francés?
3 (*may*) poder; **~ I use your phone?** ¿me dejas *or* puedo usar tu teléfono?; **could I have a word with you?** ¿podría hablar contigo un momento?
4 (*expressing disbelief, puzzlement etc*): **it ~'t be true!** ¡no puede ser (verdad)!; **what** CAN **he want?** ¿qué querrá?
5 (*expressing possibility, suggestion etc*): **he could be in the library** podría estar en la biblioteca; **she could have been delayed** puede que se haya retrasado.

Canada ['kænədə] n Canadá m.
Canadian [kə'neɪdɪən] adj, n canadiense m/f.
canal [kə'næl] n canal m.
canary [kə'nɛərɪ] n canario.
Canary Islands, Canaries [kə'nɛərɪz] npl las (Islas) Canarias.
Canberra ['kænbərə] n Canberra.
cancel ['kænsəl] vt cancelar; (*train*) suprimir; (*appointment, cheque*) anular; (*cross out*) tachar.
▶**cancel out** vt (MATH) anular; (*fig*) contrarrestar; **they ~ each other out** se anulan mutuamente.
cancellation [kænsə'leɪʃən] n cancelación f; supresión f.
cancer ['kænsə*] n cáncer m; **C~** (ASTRO) Cáncer m.
cancerous ['kænsərəs] adj canceroso.
cancer patient n enfermo/a m/f de cáncer.
cancer research n investigación f del cáncer.
C and F abbr (= *cost and freight*) C y F.
candid ['kændɪd] adj franco, abierto.
candidacy ['kændɪdəsɪ] n candidatura.
candidate ['kændɪdeɪt] n candidato/a.
candidature ['kændɪdətʃə*] n (BRIT) = **candidacy**.
candidly ['kændɪdlɪ] adv francamente, con franqueza.
candle ['kændl] n vela; (*in church*) cirio.
candle holder n see **candlestick**.
candlelight ['kændllaɪt] n: **by ~** a la luz de una vela.
candlestick ['kændlstɪk] n (*also*: **candle holder**: *single*) candelero; (: *low*) palmatoria; (*bigger, ornate*) candelabro.
candour, (US) **candor** ['kændə*] n franqueza.
candy ['kændɪ] n azúcar m cande; (US) caramelo ♦ vt (*fruit*) escarchar.
candy-floss ['kændɪflɔs] n (BRIT) algodón m

(azucarado).
cane [keɪn] n (BOT) caña; (*for baskets, chairs etc*) mimbre m; (*stick*) vara, palmeta; (: *for walking*) bastón m ♦ vt (BRIT SCOL) castigar (con palmeta); **~ liquor** caña.
canine ['kænaɪn] adj canino.
canister ['kænɪstə*] n bote m.
cannabis ['kænəbɪs] n canabis m.
canned [kænd] adj en lata, de lata; (col: *music*) grabado; (: *drunk*) mamado.
cannibal ['kænɪbəl] n caníbal m/f, antropófago/a.
cannibalism ['kænɪbəlɪzəm] n canibalismo.
cannon, pl **~** or **~s** ['kænən] n cañón m.
cannonball ['kænənbɔːl] n bala (de cañón).
cannon fodder n carne f de cañón.
cannot ['kænɔt] = **can not**.
canny ['kænɪ] adj avispado.
canoe [kə'nuː] n canoa; (SPORT) piragua.
canoeing [kə'nuːɪŋ] n (SPORT) piragüismo.
canoeist [kə'nuːɪst] n piragüista m/f.
canon ['kænən] n (*clergyman*) canónigo; (*standard*) canon m.
canonize ['kænənaɪz] vt canonizar.
can opener n abrelatas m inv.
canopy ['kænəpɪ] n dosel m, toldo.
can't [kænt] = **can not**.
Cantab. abbr (BRIT: = *cantabrigiensis*) = of Cambridge.
cantankerous [kæn'tæŋkərəs] adj arisco, malhumorado.
canteen [kæn'tiːn] n (*eating place*) comedor m; (BRIT: *of cutlery*) juego.
canter ['kæntə*] n medio galope ♦ vi ir a medio galope.
cantilever ['kæntɪliːvə*] n viga voladiza.
canvas ['kænvəs] n (*material*) lona; (*painting*) lienzo; (NAUT) velamen m; **under ~** (*camping*) en tienda de campaña.
canvass ['kænvəs] vt (POL: *district*) hacer campaña (puerta a puerta) en; (: *person*) hacer campaña (puerta a puerta) a favor de; (COMM: *district*) sondear el mercado en; (: *citizens, opinions*) sondear.
canvasser ['kænvəsə*] n (POL) representante m/f electoral; (COMM) corredor(a) m/f.
canyon ['kænjən] n cañón m.
CAP n abbr (= *Common Agricultural Policy*) PAC f.
cap [kæp] n (*hat*) gorra; (*for swimming*) gorro; (*of pen*) capuchón m; (*of bottle*) tapón m; (: *metal*) chapa; (*contraceptive*) diafragma m ♦ vt (*outdo*) superar; (BRIT SPORT) seleccionar (para el equipo nacional); **and to ~ it all, he ...** y para colmo, él ....
capability [keɪpə'bɪlɪtɪ] n capacidad f.

capable ['keɪpəbl] *adj* capaz.
capacity [kə'pæsɪtɪ] *n* capacidad *f*; (*position*) calidad *f*; **filled to** ~ lleno a reventar; **this work is beyond my** ~ este trabajo es superior a mí; **in an advisory** ~ como asesor.
cape [keɪp] *n* capa; (*GEO*) cabo.
Cape of Good Hope *n* Cabo de Buena Esperanza.
caper ['keɪpə*] *n* (*CULIN: also:* ~**s**) alcaparra; (*prank*) travesura.
Cape Town *n* Ciudad *f* del Cabo.
capital ['kæpɪtl] *n* (*also:* ~ **city**) capital *f*; (*money*) capital *m*; (*also:* ~ **letter**) mayúscula.
capital account *n* cuenta de capital.
capital allowance *n* desgravación *f* sobre bienes del capital.
capital assets *n* activo fijo.
capital expenditure *n* inversión *f* de capital.
capital gains tax *n* impuesto sobre la plusvalía.
capital goods *npl* bienes *mpl* de capital.
capital-intensive [kæpɪtlɪn'tɛnsɪv] *adj* de utilización intensiva de capital.
capital investment *n* inversión *f* de capital.
capitalism ['kæpɪtəlɪzəm] *n* capitalismo.
capitalist ['kæpɪtəlɪst] *adj, n* capitalista *m/f*.
capitalize ['kæpɪtəlaɪz] *vt* (*COMM: provide with capital*) capitalizar.
▶**capitalize on** *vt fus* (*fig*) sacar provecho de, aprovechar.
capital punishment *n* pena de muerte.
capital transfer tax *n* impuesto sobre plusvalía de cesión.
Capitol ['kæpɪtl] *n*: **the** ~ el Capitolio; *ver recuadro*.

CAPITOL

*El Capitolio (**Capitol**) es el edificio en el que se reúne el Congreso de los Estados Unidos ("Congress"), situado en la ciudad de Washington. Por extensión, también se suele llamar así al edificio en el que tienen lugar las sesiones parlamentarias de la cámara de representantes de muchos de los estados.*

---

capitulate [kə'pɪtjuleɪt] *vi* capitular, rendirse.
capitulation [kəpɪtju'leɪʃən] *n* capitulación *f*, rendición *f*.
capricious [kə'prɪʃəs] *adj* caprichoso.
Capricorn ['kæprɪkɔːn] *n* Capricornio.
caps [kæps] *abbr* (= *capital letters*) may.

capsize [kæp'saɪz] *vt* volcar, hacer zozobrar ♦ *vi* volcarse, zozobrar.
capstan ['kæpstən] *n* cabrestante *m*.
capsule ['kæpsjuːl] *n* cápsula.
Capt. *abbr* = **Captain**.
captain ['kæptɪn] *n* capitán *m* ♦ *vt* capitanear, ser el capitán de.
caption ['kæpʃən] *n* (*heading*) título; (*to picture*) leyenda, pie *m*.
captivate ['kæptɪveɪt] *vt* cautivar, encantar.
captive ['kæptɪv] *adj, n* cautivo/a *m/f*.
captivity [kæp'tɪvɪtɪ] *n* cautiverio.
captor ['kæptə*] *n* captor(a) *m/f*.
capture ['kæptʃə*] *vt* capturar; (*place*) tomar; (*attention*) captar, llamar ♦ *n* captura; toma; (*data* ~) formulación *f* de datos.
car [kɑː*] *n* coche *m*, carro (*LAM*), automóvil *m*, auto (*LAM*); (*US RAIL*) vagón *m*; **by** ~ en coche.
Caracas [kə'rækəs] *n* Caracas *m*.
carafe [kə'ræf] *n* garrafa.
caramel ['kærəməl] *n* caramelo.
carat ['kærət] *n* quilate *m*; **18-**~ **gold** oro de 18 quilates.
caravan ['kærəvæn] *n* (*BRIT*) caravana, remolque *m*; (*of camels*) caravana.
caravan site *n* (*BRIT*) camping *m* para caravanas.
caraway ['kærəweɪ] *n*: ~ **seed** carvi *m*.
carbohydrates [kɑːbəu'haɪdreɪts] *npl* (*foods*) hidratos *mpl* de carbono.
car bomb *n* coche-bomba *m*.
carbon ['kɑːbən] *n* carbono.
carbonated ['kɑːbəneɪtɪd] *adj* (*drink*) con gas.
carbon copy *n* copia al carbón.
carbon dioxide *n* dióxido de carbono, anhídrido carbónico.
carbon monoxide *n* monóxido de carbono.
carbon paper *n* papel *m* carbón.
carbon ribbon *n* cinta de carbón.
car boot sale *n* mercadillo (*de objetos usados expuestos en el maletero del coche*).
carburettor, (*US*) **carburetor** [kɑːbju'rɛtə*] *n* carburador *m*.
carcass ['kɑːkəs] *n* (*animal*) res *f* muerta; (*dead body*) cadáver *m*.
carcinogenic [kɑːsɪnə'dʒɛnɪk] *adj* cancerígeno.
card [kɑːd] *n* (*thin cardboard*) cartulina; (*playing* ~) carta, naipe *m*; (*visiting* ~, *greetings* ~ *etc*) tarjeta; (*index* ~) ficha; **membership** ~ carnet *m*; **to play** ~**s** jugar a las cartas *or* los naipes.
cardamom ['kɑːdəməm] *n* cardamomo.

cardboard ['kɑːdbɔːd] n cartón m, cartulina.

cardboard box n caja de cartón.

cardboard city n zona de marginados sin hogar (*que se refugian entre cartones*).

card-carrying member ['kɑːdkærɪŋ-] n miembro con carnet.

card game n juego de naipes or cartas.

cardiac ['kɑːdɪæk] adj cardíaco.

cardigan ['kɑːdɪgən] n chaqueta (de punto), rebeca.

cardinal ['kɑːdɪnl] adj cardinal ♦ n cardenal m.

cardinal number n número cardinal.

card index n fichero.

cardphone ['kɑːdfəun] n *cabina que funciona con tarjetas telefónicas.*

cardsharp ['kɑːdʃɑːp] n fullero/a.

card vote n voto por delegación.

CARE [kɛə*] n abbr (= Cooperative for American Relief Everywhere) *sociedad benéfica.*

care [kɛə*] n cuidado; (*worry*) preocupación f; (*charge*) cargo, custodia ♦ vi: **to ~ about** preocuparse por; **~ of (c/o)** en casa de, al cuidado de; (: *on letter*) para (entregar a); **in sb's ~** a cargo de algn; **the child has been taken into ~** pusieron al niño bajo custodia del gobierno; "**with ~**" "¡frágil!"; **to take ~ to** cuidarse de, tener cuidado de; **to take ~ of** vt cuidar; (*details, arrangements*) encargarse de; **I don't ~** no me importa; **I couldn't ~ less** me trae sin cuidado.

▶**care for** vt fus cuidar; (*like*) querer.

careen [kə'riːn] vi (*ship*) inclinarse, escorar ♦ vt carenar.

career [kə'rɪə*] n carrera (profesional); (*occupation*) profesión f ♦ vi (*also:* **~ along**) correr a toda velocidad.

career girl n mujer f dedicada a su profesión.

careers officer n consejero/a de orientación profesional.

carefree ['kɛəfriː] adj despreocupado.

careful ['kɛəful] adj cuidadoso; (*cautious*) cauteloso; **(be) ~!** ¡ten cuidado!; **he's very ~ with his money** mira mucho el dinero; (*pej*) es muy tacaño.

carefully ['kɛəfəlɪ] adv con cuidado, cuidadosamente.

careless ['kɛəlɪs] adj descuidado; (*heedless*) poco atento.

carelessly ['kɛəlɪslɪ] adv sin cuidado, a la ligera.

carelessness ['kɛəlɪsnɪs] n descuido, falta de atención.

carer ['kɛərə*] n *persona que cuida de*

enfermos, ancianos o disminuidos.

caress [kə'rɛs] n caricia ♦ vt acariciar.

caretaker ['kɛəteɪkə*] n portero/a, conserje m/f.

caretaker government n gobierno provisional.

car-ferry ['kɑːfɛrɪ] n transbordador m para coches.

cargo, pl ~es ['kɑːgəu] n cargamento, carga.

cargo boat n buque m de carga, carguero.

cargo plane n avión m de carga.

car hire n alquiler m de coches.

Caribbean [kærɪ'biːən] adj caribe, caribeño; **the ~ (Sea)** el (Mar) Caribe.

caricature ['kærɪkətjuə*] n caricatura.

caring ['kɛərɪŋ] adj humanitario.

carnage ['kɑːnɪdʒ] n matanza, carnicería.

carnal ['kɑːnl] adj carnal.

carnation [kɑː'neɪʃən] n clavel m.

carnival ['kɑːnɪvəl] n carnaval m; (*US*) parque m de atracciones.

carnivore ['kɑːnɪvɔː*] n carnívoro/a.

carnivorous [kɑː'nɪvrəs] adj carnívoro.

carol ['kærəl] n: **(Christmas) ~** villancico.

carouse [kə'rauz] vi estar de juerga.

carousel [kærə'sɛl] n (*US*) tiovivo, caballitos mpl.

carp [kɑːp] n (*fish*) carpa.

▶**carp at** or **about** vt fus sacar faltas de.

car park n (*BRIT*) aparcamiento, parking m, playa de estacionamiento (*LAM*).

carpenter ['kɑːpɪntə*] n carpintero.

carpentry ['kɑːpɪntrɪ] n carpintería.

carpet ['kɑːpɪt] n alfombra ♦ vt alfombrar; **fitted ~** moqueta.

carpet bombing n bombardeo de arrasamiento.

carpet slippers npl zapatillas fpl.

carpet sweeper [-'swiːpə*] n cepillo mecánico.

car phone n teléfono de coche.

carping ['kɑːpɪŋ] adj (*critical*) criticón/ona.

carriage ['kærɪdʒ] n coche m; (*BRIT RAIL*) vagón m; (*for goods*) transporte m; (*of typewriter*) carro; (*bearing*) porte m; **~ forward** porte m debido; **~ free** franco de porte; **~ paid** porte pagado; **~ inwards/outwards** gastos mpl de transporte a cargo del comprador/vendedor.

carriage return n (*on typewriter etc*) tecla de regreso.

carriageway ['kærɪdʒweɪ] n (*BRIT: part of road*) calzada; **dual ~** autovía.

carrier ['kærɪə*] n transportista m/f; (*company*) empresa de transportes; (*MED*) portador(a) m/f.

carrier bag n (*BRIT*) bolsa de papel or

plástico.
carrier pigeon *n* paloma mensajera.
carrion ['kærɪən] *n* carroña.
carrot ['kærət] *n* zanahoria.
carry ['kærɪ] *vt* (*subj*: *person*) llevar;
(*transport*) transportar; (*a motion, bill*)
aprobar; (*involve*: *responsibilities etc*)
entrañar, conllevar; (*COMM*: *stock*) tener
en existencia; (: *interest*) llevar; (*MATH*:
figure) llevarse ♦ *vi* (*sound*) oírse; **to get
carried away** (*fig*) entusiasmarse; **this
loan carries 10% interest** este empréstito
devenga un interés del 10 por ciento.
▶**carry forward** *vt* (*MATH, COMM*) pasar a
la página/columna siguiente.
▶**carry on** *vi* (*continue*) seguir (adelante),
continuar; (*fam*: *complain*) montar el
número ♦ *vt* seguir, continuar.
▶**carry out** *vt* (*orders*) cumplir;
(*investigation*) llevar a cabo, realizar.
carrycot ['kærɪkɔt] *n* (*BRIT*) cuna portátil,
capazo.
carry-on ['kærɪ'ɔn] *n* (*col*) follón *m*.
cart [kɑːt] *n* carro, carreta ♦ *vt* cargar con.
carte blanche ['kɑːt'blɒnʃ] *n*: **to give sb** ~
dar carta blanca a algn.
cartel [kɑː'tɛl] *n* (*COMM*) cartel *m*.
cartilage ['kɑːtɪlɪdʒ] *n* cartílago.
cartographer [kɑː'tɔgrəfə*] *n* cartógrafo/a.
carton ['kɑːtən] *n* caja (de cartón); (*of
cigarettes*) cartón *m*.
cartoon [kɑː'tuːn] *n* (*PRESS*) chiste *m*;
(*comic strip*) historieta, tira cómica; (*film*)
dibujos *mpl* animados.
cartoonist [kɑː'tuːnɪst] *n* humorista *m/f*
gráfico.
cartridge ['kɑːtrɪdʒ] *n* cartucho.
cartwheel ['kɑːtwiːl] *n*: **to turn a** ~ dar una
voltereta lateral.
carve [kɑːv] *vt* (*meat*) trinchar; (*wood*)
tallar; (*stone*) cincelar, esculpir; (*on tree*)
grabar.
▶**carve up** *vt* dividir, repartir; (*meat*)
trinchar.
carving ['kɑːvɪŋ] *n* (*in wood etc*) escultura,
talla.
carving knife *n* trinchante *m*.
car wash *n* túnel *m* de lavado.
Casablanca [kæsə'blæŋkə] *n* Casablanca.
cascade [kæs'keɪd] *n* salto de agua,
cascada; (*fig*) chorro ♦ *vi* caer a chorros.
case [keɪs] *n* (*container*) caja; (*MED*) caso;
(*for jewels etc*) estuche *m*; (*LAW*) causa,
proceso; (*BRIT*: *also*: **suit**~) maleta;
lower/upper ~ (*TYP*) caja baja/alta; **in** ~
of en caso de; **in any** ~ en todo caso; **just
in** ~ por si acaso; **to have a good** ~ tener
buenas razones; **there's a strong** ~ **for**

reform hay razones sólidas para exigir
una reforma.
case history *n* (*MED*) historial *m* médico,
historia clínica.
case study *n* estudio de casos prácticos.
cash [kæʃ] *n* (dinero) efectivo; (*col*: *money*)
dinero ♦ *vt* cobrar, hacer efectivo; **to pay
(in)** ~ pagar al contado; ~ **on delivery
(COD)** entrega contra reembolso; ~ **with
order** paga al hacer el pedido; **to be short
of** ~ estar pelado, estar sin blanca.
▶**cash in** *vt* (*insurance policy etc*) cobrar
♦ *vi*: **to** ~ **in on sth** sacar partido *or*
aprovecharse de algo.
cash account *n* cuenta de caja.
cash and carry *n* cash and carry *m*,
autoservicio mayorista.
cashbook ['kæʃbuk] *n* libro de caja.
cash box *n* hucha.
cash card *n* tarjeta *f* de(l) cajero
(automático).
cash desk *n* (*BRIT*) caja.
cash discount *n* descuento por pago al
contado.
cash dispenser *n* cajero automático.
cashew [kæ'ʃuː] *n* (*also*: ~ **nut**) anacardo.
cash flow *n* flujo de fondos, cash-flow *m*,
movimiento de efectivo.
cashier [kæ'ʃɪə*] *n* cajero/a ♦ *vt* (*MIL*)
destituir, expulsar.
cashmere ['kæʃmɪə*] *n* cachemir *m*,
cachemira.
cash payment *n* pago al contado.
cash price *n* precio al contado.
cash register *n* caja.
cash reserves *npl* reserva en efectivo.
cash sale *n* venta al contado.
casing ['keɪsɪŋ] *n* revestimiento.
casino [kə'siːnəu] *n* casino.
cask [kɑːsk] *n* tonel *m*, barril *m*.
casket ['kɑːskɪt] *n* cofre *m*, estuche *m*; (*US*:
coffin) ataúd *m*.
Caspian Sea ['kæspɪən-] *n*: **the** ~ el Mar
Caspio.
cassava [kə'sɑːvə] *n* mandioca.
casserole ['kæsərəul] *n* (*food, pot*) cazuela.
cassette [kæ'sɛt] *n* cas(s)et(t)e *m or f*.
cassette deck *n* platina.
cassette player, cassette recorder *n*
cas(s)et(t)e *m*.
cassock ['kæsək] *n* sotana.
cast [kɑːst] *vb* (*pt, pp* **cast**) *vt* (*throw*) echar,
arrojar, lanzar; (*skin*) mudar, perder;
(*metal*) fundir; (*THEAT*): **to** ~ **sb as Othello**
dar a algn el papel de Otelo ♦ *n* (*THEAT*)
reparto; (*mould*) forma, molde *m*; (*also*:
plaster ~) vaciado; **to** ~ **loose** soltar; **to** ~
one's vote votar.

►**cast aside** vt (reject) descartar, desechar.
►**cast away** vt desechar.
►**cast down** vt derribar.
►**cast off** vi (NAUT) soltar amarras; (KNITTING) cerrar los puntos ♦ vt (KNITTING) cerrar; **to ~ sb off** abandonar a algn, desentenderse de algn.
►**cast on** vt (KNITTING) montar.
castanets [kæstə'nɛts] npl castañuelas fpl.
castaway ['kɑːstəwəɪ] n náufrago/a.
caste [kɑːst] n casta.
caster sugar ['kɑːstə*-] n (BRIT) azúcar m en polvo.
Castile [kæs'tiːl] n Castilla.
Castilian [kæs'tɪlɪən] adj, n castellano/a ♦ n (LING) castellano.
casting vote ['kɑːstɪŋ-] n (BRIT) voto decisivo.
cast iron n hierro fundido or colado ♦ adj (fig: alibi) irrebatible; (will) férreo.
castle ['kɑːsl] n castillo; (CHESS) torre f.
castor ['kɑːstə*] n (wheel) ruedecilla.
castor oil n aceite m de ricino.
castrate [kæs'treɪt] vt castrar.
casual ['kæʒjul] adj (by chance) fortuito; (irregular: work etc) eventual, temporero; (unconcerned) despreocupado; (informal: clothes) de sport.
casually ['kæʒjulɪ] adv por casualidad; de manera despreocupada.
casualty ['kæʒjultɪ] n víctima, herido; (dead) muerto; (MIL) baja; **heavy casualties** numerosas bajas fpl.
casualty ward n urgencias fpl.
cat [kæt] n gato.
catacombs ['kætəkuːmz] npl catacumbas fpl.
Catalan ['kætəlæn] adj, n catalán/ana m/f.
catalogue, (US) **catalog** ['kætəlɔg] n catálogo ♦ vt catalogar.
Catalonia [kætə'ləunɪə] n Cataluña.
catalyst ['kætəlɪst] n catalizador m.
catalytic converter [kætə'lɪtɪkkən'vɔːtə*] n catalizador m.
catapult ['kætəpʌlt] n tirachinas m inv.
cataract ['kætərækt] n (MED) cataratas fpl.
catarrh [kə'tɑː*] n catarro.
catastrophe [kə'tæstrəfɪ] n catástrofe f.
catastrophic [kætə'strɔfɪk] adj catastrófico.
catcall ['kætkɔːl] n (at meeting etc) rechifla, silbido.
catch [kætʃ] vb (pt, pp **caught** [kɔːt]) vt coger (SP), agarrar (LAM); (arrest) atrapar, coger (SP); (grasp) asir; (breath) recobrar; (person: by surprise) pillar; (attract: attention) captar; (MED) pillar, coger; (also: ~ **up**) alcanzar ♦ vi (fire)

encenderse; (in branches etc) engancharse ♦ n (fish etc) captura; (act of catching) cogida; (trick) trampa; (of lock) pestillo, cerradura; **to ~ fire** prenderse; (house) incendiarse; **to ~ sight of** divisar.
►**catch on** vi (understand) caer en la cuenta; (grow popular) tener éxito, cuajar.
►**catch out** vt (fig: with trick question) hundir.
►**catch up** vi (fig) ponerse al día.
catching ['kætʃɪŋ] adj (MED) contagioso.
catchment area ['kætʃmənt-] n (BRIT) zona de captación.
catch phrase n frase f de moda.
catch-22 ['kætʃtwɛntɪ'tuː] n: **it's a ~ situation** es un callejón sin salida, es un círculo vicioso.
catchy ['kætʃɪ] adj (tune) pegadizo.
catechism ['kætɪkɪzəm] n (REL) catecismo.
categoric(al) [kætɪ'gɔrɪk(əl)] adj categórico, terminante.
categorically [kætɪ'gɔrɪkəlɪ] adv categóricamente, terminantemente.
categorize ['kætɪgəraɪz] vt clasificar.
category ['kætɪgərɪ] n categoría.
cater ['keɪtə*] vi: **to ~ for** (BRIT) abastecer a; (needs) atender a; (consumers) proveer a.
caterer ['keɪtərə*] n abastecedor(a) m/f, proveedor(a) m/f.
catering ['keɪtərɪŋ] n (trade) hostelería.
caterpillar ['kætəpɪlə*] n oruga.
caterpillar track n rodado de oruga.
cat flap n gatera.
cathedral [kə'θiːdrəl] n catedral f.
cathode-ray tube ['kæθəudreɪ'tjuːb] n tubo de rayos catódicos.
catholic ['kæθəlɪk] adj católico; **C~** adj, n (REL) católico/a m/f.
CAT scanner [kæt-] (MED) n abbr (= computerized axial tomography scanner) escáner m TAC.
cat's-eye ['kætsaɪ] n (BRIT AUT) catafaro.
catsup ['kætsəp] n (US) ketchup, catsup m.
cattle ['kætl] npl ganado sg.
catty ['kætɪ] adj malicioso.
catwalk ['kætwɔːk] n pasarela.
Caucasian [kɔː'keɪzɪən] adj, n caucásico/a m/f.
Caucasus ['kɔːkəsəs] n Cáucaso.
caucus ['kɔːkəs] n (POL: local committee) comité m local; (: US: to elect candidates) comité m electoral; (: group) camarilla política.
caught [kɔːt] pt, pp of **catch**.
cauliflower ['kɔlɪflauə*] n coliflor f.
cause [kɔːz] n causa; (reason) motivo,

razón *f* ♦ *vt* causar; (*provoke*) provocar; **to ~ sb to do sth** hacer que algn haga algo.

causeway ['kɔːzweɪ] *n* (*road*) carretera elevada; (*embankment*) terraplén *m*.

caustic ['kɔːstɪk] *adj* cáustico; (*fig*) mordaz.

cauterize ['kɔːtəraɪz] *vt* cauterizar.

caution ['kɔːʃən] *n* cautela, prudencia; (*warning*) advertencia, amonestación *f* ♦ *vt* amonestar.

cautious ['kɔːʃəs] *adj* cauteloso, prudente, precavido.

cautiously ['kɔːʃəslɪ] *adv* con cautela.

cautiousness ['kɔːʃəsnɪs] *n* cautela.

cavalcade [kævəl'keɪd] *n* cabalgata.

cavalier [kævə'lɪə*] *n* (*knight*) caballero ♦ *adj* (*pej: offhand: person, attitude*) arrogante, desdeñoso.

cavalry ['kævəlrɪ] *n* caballería.

cave [keɪv] *n* cueva, caverna ♦ *vi*: **to go caving** ir en una expedición espeleológica.

▶**cave in** *vi* (*roof etc*) derrumbarse, hundirse.

caveman ['keɪvmæn] *n* cavernícola *m*.

cavern ['kævən] *n* caverna.

cavernous ['kævənəs] *adj* (*cheeks, eyes*) hundido.

caviar(e) ['kævɪɑː*] *n* caviar *m*.

cavity ['kævɪtɪ] *n* hueco, cavidad *f*.

cavity wall insulation *n* aislamiento térmico.

cavort [kə'vɔːt] *vi* hacer cabriolas.

cayenne [keɪ'ɛn] *n*: **~ pepper** pimentón *m* picante.

CB *n abbr* (= *Citizens' Band (Radio)*) *frecuencias de radio usadas para la comunicación privada*; (BRIT: = *Companion of (the Order of) the Bath*) *título de nobleza*.

CBC *n abbr* (= *Canadian Broadcasting Corporation*) *cadena de radio y televisión*.

CBE *n abbr* (= *Companion of (the Order of) the British Empire*) *título de nobleza*.

CBI *n abbr* (= *Confederation of British Industry*) ≈ C.E.O.E. *f* (SP).

CBS *n abbr* (US: = *Columbia Broadcasting System*) *cadena de radio y televisión*.

cc *abbr* (= *cubic centimetres*) cc, cm³; (*on letter etc*) = **carbon copy.**

CCA *n abbr* (US: = *Circuit Court of Appeals*) *tribunal de apelación itinerante*.

CCTV *n abbr* = **closed-circuit television.**

CCU *n abbr* (US: = *coronary care unit*) unidad *f* de cuidados cardiológicos.

CD *n abbr* (= *compact disc*) CD *m*; **~ player** reproductor *m* de compact disc; (MIL) = *Civil Defence (Corps)* (BRIT), *Civil Defense* (US) ♦ *abbr* (BRIT: = *Corps Diplomatique*)

CD.

CDC *n abbr* (US) = *center for disease control.*

CD-I ® *n* (= *Compact Disc Interactive*) CD-I *m*, disco *m* compacto interactivo.

CD-ROM *n abbr* (= *compact disc read-only memory*) CD-ROM *m*.

CDT *n abbr* (US: = *Central Daylight Time*) *hora de verano del centro*; (BRIT: = *Craft, Design and Technology*) *artesanía, diseño y tecnología*.

cease [siːs] *vt* cesar.

ceasefire ['siːsfaɪə*] *n* alto *m* el fuego.

ceaseless ['siːslɪs] *adj* incesante.

ceaselessly ['siːslɪslɪ] *adv* sin cesar.

CED *n abbr* (US) = *Committee for Economic Development.*

cedar ['siːdə*] *n* cedro.

cede [siːd] *vt* ceder.

CEEB *n abbr* (US: = *College Entrance Examination Board*) *tribunal para las pruebas de acceso a la universidad*.

ceilidh ['keɪlɪ] *n baile con música y danzas tradicionales escocesas o irlandesas*.

ceiling ['siːlɪŋ] *n* techo; (*fig: upper limit*) límite *m*, tope *m*.

celebrate ['sɛlɪbreɪt] *vt* celebrar; (*have a party*) festejar ♦ *vi*: **let's ~!** ¡vamos a celebrarlo!

celebrated ['sɛlɪbreɪtɪd] *adj* célebre.

celebration [sɛlɪ'breɪʃən] *n* celebración *f*.

celebrity [sɪ'lɛbrɪtɪ] *n* celebridad *f*.

celeriac [sə'lɛrɪæk] *n* apio-nabo.

celery ['sɛlərɪ] *n* apio.

celestial [sɪ'lɛstɪəl] *adj* (*of sky*) celeste; (*divine*) celestial.

celibacy ['sɛlɪbəsɪ] *n* celibato.

cell [sɛl] *n* celda; (BIOL) célula; (ELEC) elemento.

cellar ['sɛlə*] *n* sótano; (*for wine*) bodega.

cellist ['tʃɛlɪst] *n* violoncelista *m/f*.

cello ['tʃɛləu] *n* violoncelo.

cellophane ['sɛləfeɪn] *n* celofán *m*.

cellphone ['sɛlfəun] *n* teléfono celular.

cellular ['sɛljulə*] *adj* celular.

celluloid ['sɛljulɔɪd] *n* celuloide *m*.

cellulose ['sɛljuləus] *n* celulosa.

Celsius ['sɛlsɪəs] *adj* centígrado.

Celt [kɛlt, sɛlt] *n* celta *m/f*.

Celtic ['kɛltɪk, 'sɛltɪk] *adj* celta, céltico ♦ *n* (LING) celta *m*.

cement [sə'mɛnt] *n* cemento ♦ *vt* cementar; (*fig*) cimentar.

cement mixer *n* hormigonera.

cemetery ['sɛmɪtrɪ] *n* cementerio.

cenotaph ['sɛnətɑːf] *n* cenotafio.

censor ['sɛnsə*] *n* censor(a) *m/f* ♦ *vt* (*cut*) censurar.

censorship ['sɛnsəʃɪp] *n* censura.

censure ['sɛnʃə*] *vt* censurar.

census ['sɛnsəs] *n* censo.

cent [sɛnt] *n* (*unit of dollar*) centavo; (*unit of euro*) céntimo; *see also* **per**.

centenary [sen'ti:nərɪ], (*US*) **centennial** [sen'tenɪəl] *n* centenario.

center ['sentə*] *n* (*US*) = **centre**.

centigrade ['sentɪgreɪd] *adj* centígrado.

centilitre, (*US*) **centiliter** ['sentɪli:tə*] *n* centilitro.

centimetre, (*US*) **centimeter** ['sentɪmi:tə*] *n* centímetro.

centipede ['sentɪpi:d] *n* ciempiés *m inv*.

central ['sentrəl] *adj* central; (*of house etc*) céntrico.

Central African Republic *n* República Centroafricana.

Central America *n* Centroamérica.

Central American *adj, n* centroamericano/a *m/f*.

central heating *n* calefacción *f* central.

centralize ['sentrəlaɪz] *vt* centralizar.

central processing unit (CPU) *n* (*COMPUT*) unidad *f* procesadora central, unidad *f* central de proceso.

central reservation *n* (*BRIT AUT*) mediana.

centre, (*US*) **center** ['sentə*] *n* centro ♦ *vt* centrar; **to ~ (on)** (*concentrate*) concentrar (en).

centrefold, (*US*) **centerfold** ['sentəfəuld] *n* página central plegable.

centre-forward ['sentə'fɔ:wəd] *n* (*SPORT*) delantero centro.

centre-half ['sentə'hɑ:f] *n* (*SPORT*) medio centro.

centrepiece, (*US*) **centerpiece** ['sentəpi:s] *n* punto central.

centre spread *n* (*BRIT*) páginas *fpl* centrales.

centre-stage *n*: **to take ~** pasar a primer plano.

centrifuge ['sentrɪfju:dʒ] *n* centrifugadora.

century ['sentjurɪ] *n* siglo; **in the twentieth ~** en el siglo veinte.

CEO *n abbr* (*US*) = **chief executive officer**.

ceramic [sɪ'ræmɪk] *adj* de cerámica.

ceramics [sɪ'ræmɪks] *n* cerámica.

cereal ['si:rɪəl] *n* cereal *m*.

cerebral ['serɪbrəl] *adj* cerebral.

ceremonial [serɪ'məunɪəl] *n* ceremonial.

ceremony ['serɪmənɪ] *n* ceremonia; **to stand on ~** hacer ceremonias, andarse con cumplidos.

cert [sə:t] *n* (*BRIT col*): **it's a dead ~** ¡es cosa segura!

certain ['sə:tən] *adj* seguro; (*correct*) cierto; (*particular*) cierto; **for ~** a ciencia cierta.

certainly ['sə:tənlɪ] *adv* desde luego, por supuesto.

certainty ['sə:təntɪ] *n* certeza, certidumbre *f*, seguridad *f*.

certificate [sə'tɪfɪkɪt] *n* certificado.

certified ['sə:tɪfaɪd] *adj*: **~ mail** (*US*) correo certificado.

certified public accountant (CPA) *n* (*US*) contable *m/f* diplomado/a.

certify ['sə:tɪfaɪ] *vt* certificar.

cervical ['sə:vɪkl] *adj*: **~ cancer** cáncer *m* cervical; **~ smear** citología.

cervix ['sə:vɪks] *n* cerviz *f*, cuello del útero.

Cesarean [sɪ'zɛərɪən] *adj, n* (*US*) = **Caesarean**.

cessation [sə'seɪʃən] *n* cese *m*, suspensión *f*.

cesspit ['sespɪt] *n* pozo negro.

CET *n abbr* (= *Central European Time*) *hora de Europa central*.

Ceylon [sɪ'lɔn] *n* Ceilán *m*.

cf. *abbr* (= *compare*) cfr.

CFC *n abbr* (= *chlorofluorocarbon*) CFC *m*.

c/f *abbr* (*COMM*) = *carried forward*.

CG *n abbr* (*US*) = **coastguard**.

cg *abbr* (= *centigram*) cg.

CH *n abbr* (*BRIT*: = *Companion of Honour*) *título de nobleza*.

ch *abbr* (*BRIT*: = *central heating*) cal. cen.

ch. *abbr* (= *chapter*) cap.

Chad [tʃæd] *n* Chad *m*.

chafe [tʃeɪf] *vt* (*rub*) rozar; (*irritate*) irritar; **to ~ (against)** (*fig*) irritarse *or* enojarse (con).

chaffinch ['tʃæfɪntʃ] *n* pinzón *m* (vulgar).

chagrin ['ʃægrɪn] *n* (*annoyance*) disgusto; (*disappointment*) desazón *f*.

chain [tʃeɪn] *n* cadena ♦ *vt* (*also*: **~ up**) encadenar.

chain reaction *n* reacción *f* en cadena.

chain-smoke ['tʃeɪnsməuk] *vi* fumar un cigarrillo tras otro.

chain store *n* tienda de una cadena, ≈ grandes almacenes *mpl*.

chair [tʃɛə*] *n* silla; (*armchair*) sillón *m*; (*of university*) cátedra ♦ *vt* (*meeting*) presidir; **the ~** (*US*: *electric ~*) la silla eléctrica; **please take a ~** siéntese *or* tome asiento, por favor.

chairlift ['tʃɛəlɪft] *n* telesilla *m*.

chairman ['tʃɛəmən] *n* presidente *m*.

chairperson ['tʃɛəpə:sn] *n* presidente/a *m/f*.

chairwoman ['tʃɛəwumən] *n* presidenta.

chalet ['ʃæleɪ] *n* chalet *m* (de madera).

chalice ['tʃælɪs] *n* cáliz *m*.

chalk [tʃɔ:k] *n* (*GEO*) creta; (*for writing*) tiza, gis *m* (*LAM*).

▶**chalk up** *vt* apuntar; (*fig: success, victory*) apuntarse.

challenge ['tʃælɪndʒ] *n* desafío, reto ♦ *vt*

desafiar, retar; (*statement, right*) poner en duda; **to ~ sb to do sth** retar a algn a que haga algo.

challenger ['tʃælɪndʒə*] *n* (*SPORT*) contrincante *m/f*.

challenging ['tʃælɪndʒɪŋ] *adj* que supone un reto; (*tone*) de desafío.

chamber ['tʃeɪmbə*] *n* cámara, sala; **~ of commerce** cámara de comercio.

chambermaid ['tʃeɪmbəmeɪd] *n* camarera.

chamber music *n* música de cámara.

chamberpot ['tʃeɪmbəpɔt] *n* orinal *m*.

chameleon [kə'miːliən] *n* camaleón *m*.

chamois ['ʃæmwɑː] *n* gamuza.

champagne [ʃæm'peɪn] *n* champaña *m*, champán *m*.

champers ['ʃæmpəz] *nsg* (*col*) champán *m*.

champion ['tʃæmpɪən] *n* campeón/ona *m/f*; (*of cause*) defensor(a) *m/f*, paladín *m/f* ♦ *vt* defender, apoyar.

championship ['tʃæmpɪənʃɪp] *n* campeonato.

chance [tʃɑːns] *n* (*coincidence*) casualidad *f*; (*luck*) suerte *f*; (*fate*) azar *m*; (*opportunity*) ocasión *f*, oportunidad *f*, chance *m or f* (*LAM*); (*likelihood*) posibilidad *f*; (*risk*) riesgo ♦ *vt* arriesgar, probar ♦ *adj* fortuito, casual; **to ~ it** arriesgarse, intentarlo; **to take a ~** arriesgarse; **by ~** por casualidad; **it's the ~ of a lifetime** es la oportunidad de su vida; **the ~s are that ...** lo más probable es que ...; **to ~ to do sth** (*happen*) hacer algo por casualidad.

▶**chance (up)on** *vt fus* tropezar(se) con.

chancel ['tʃɑːnsəl] *n* coro y presbiterio.

chancellor ['tʃɑːnsələ*] *n* canciller *m*; **C~ of the Exchequer** (*BRIT*) Ministro de Economía y Hacienda; *see also* **Downing Street**.

chancy ['tʃɑːnsɪ] *adj* (*col*) arriesgado.

chandelier [ʃændə'lɪə*] *n* araña (de luces).

change [tʃeɪndʒ] *vt* cambiar; (*clothes, house*) cambiarse de, mudarse de; (*transform*) transformar ♦ *vi* cambiar(se); (*trains*) hacer transbordo; (*be transformed*): **to ~ into** transformarse en ♦ *n* cambio; (*alteration*) modificación *f*, transformación *f*; (*coins*) suelto; (*money returned*) vuelta, vuelto (*LAM*); **to ~ one's mind** cambiar de opinión *or* idea; **to ~ gear** (*AUT*) cambiar de marcha; **she ~d into an old skirt** se puso una falda vieja; **for a ~** para variar; **can you give me ~ for £1?** ¿tiene cambio de una libra?; **keep the ~** quédese con la vuelta.

changeable ['tʃeɪndʒəbl] *adj* (*weather*) cambiable; (*person*) variable.

changeless ['tʃeɪndʒlɪs] *adj* inmutable.

change machine *n* máquina de cambio.

changeover ['tʃeɪndʒəuvə*] *n* (*to new system*) cambio.

changing ['tʃeɪndʒɪŋ] *adj* cambiante.

changing room *n* (*BRIT*) vestuario.

channel ['tʃænl] *n* (*TV*) canal *m*; (*of river*) cauce *m*; (*of sea*) estrecho; (*groove, fig: medium*) conducto, medio ♦ *vt* (*river etc*) encauzar; **to ~ into** (*fig: interest, energies*) encauzar a, dirigir a; **the (English) C~** el Canal (de la Mancha); **the C~ Islands** las Islas Anglonormandas; **~s of communication** canales *mpl* de comunicación; **green/red ~** (*CUSTOMS*) pasillo verde/rojo.

Channel Tunnel *n*: **the ~** el túnel del Canal de la Mancha, el Eurotúnel.

chant [tʃɑːnt] *n* canto; (*of crowd*) gritos *mpl* ♦ *vt* cantar; **the demonstrators ~ed their disapproval** los manifestantes corearon su desaprobación.

chaos ['keɪɔs] *n* caos *m*.

chaos theory *n* teoría del caos.

chaotic [keɪ'ɔtɪk] *adj* caótico.

chap [tʃæp] *n* (*BRIT col: man*) tío, tipo; **old ~** amigo (mío).

chapel ['tʃæpəl] *n* capilla.

chaperone ['ʃæpərəun] *n* carabina.

chaplain ['tʃæplɪn] *n* capellán *m*.

chapped [tʃæpt] *adj* agrietado.

chapter ['tʃæptə*] *n* capítulo.

char [tʃɑː*] *vt* (*burn*) carbonizar, chamuscar ♦ *n* (*BRIT*) = **charlady**.

character ['kærɪktə*] *n* carácter *m*, naturaleza, índole *f*; (*in novel, film*) personaje *m*; (*role*) papel *m*; (*individuality, COMPUT*) carácter *m*; **a person of good ~** una persona de buena reputación.

character code *n* código de caracteres.

characteristic [kærɪktə'rɪstɪk] *adj* característico ♦ *n* característica.

characterize ['kærɪktəraɪz] *vt* caracterizar.

charade [ʃə'rɑːd] *n* farsa, comedia; **~s** (*game*) charadas *fpl*.

charcoal ['tʃɑːkəul] *n* carbón *m* vegetal; (*ART*) carboncillo.

charge [tʃɑːdʒ] *n* carga; (*LAW*) cargo, acusación *f*; (*cost*) precio, coste *m*; (*responsibility*) cargo; (*task*) encargo ♦ *vt* (*LAW*) acusar (*with* de); (*gun, battery, MIL: enemy*) cargar; (*price*) pedir; (*customer*) cobrar; (*sb with task*) encargar ♦ *vi* precipitarse; (*make pay*) cobrar; **~s** *npl*: **bank ~s** comisiones *fpl* bancarias; **extra ~** recargo, suplemento; **free of ~** gratis; **to reverse the ~s** (*BRIT TEL*) llamar a cobro revertido; **to take ~ of** hacerse cargo de, encargarse de; **to be in ~ of** estar

encargado de; **how much do you ~?**
¿cuánto cobra usted?; **to ~ an expense
(up) to sb's account** cargar algo a cuenta
de algn; **~ it to my account** póngalo *or*
cárguelo a mi cuenta.
charge account *n* (*US*) cuenta abierta *or* a
crédito.
charge card *n* tarjeta de cuenta.
chargé d'affaires ['ʃɑːʒeɪdæ'fɛə*] *n*
encargado de negocios.
chargehand ['tʃɑːdʒhænd] *n* capataz *m*.
charger ['tʃɑːdʒə*] *n* (*also:* **battery ~**)
cargador *m* (de baterías).
chariot ['tʃærɪət] *n* carro.
charisma [kæ'rɪzmə] *n* carisma *m*.
charitable ['tʃærɪtəbl] *adj* caritativo.
charity ['tʃærɪtɪ] *n* (*gen*) caridad *f*;
(*organization*) organización *f* benéfica.
charlady ['tʃɑːleɪdɪ] *n* (*BRIT*) mujer *f* de la
limpieza.
charlatan ['ʃɑːlətən] *n* charlatán *m*.
charm [tʃɑːm] *n* encanto, atractivo; (*spell*)
hechizo; (*object*) amuleto ♦ *vt* encantar;
hechizar.
charm bracelet *n* pulsera amuleto.
charming ['tʃɑːmɪŋ] *adj* encantador(a);
(*person*) simpático.
chart [tʃɑːt] *n* (*table*) cuadro; (*graph*)
gráfica; (*map*) carta de navegación;
(*weather* ~) mapa *m* meteorológico ♦ *vt*
(*course*) trazar; (*sales, progress*) hacer una
gráfica de; **to be in the ~s** (*record, pop
group*) estar en la lista de éxitos.
charter ['tʃɑːtə*] *vt* (*bus*) alquilar; (*plane,
ship*) fletar ♦ *n* (*document*) estatuto, carta;
on ~ en alquiler, alquilado.
chartered accountant (CA) *n* (*BRIT*)
contable *m/f* diplomado/a.
charter flight *n* vuelo chárter.
charwoman ['tʃɑːwumən] *n* = **charlady**.
chase [tʃeɪs] *vt* (*pursue*) perseguir; (*hunt*)
cazar ♦ *n* persecución *f*; caza; **to ~ after**
correr tras.
►**chase up** *vt* (*information*) tratar de
conseguir; **to ~ sb up about sth** recordar
algo a algn.
chasm ['kæzəm] *n* abismo.
chassis ['ʃæsɪ] *n* chasis *m*.
chaste [tʃeɪst] *adj* casto.
chastened ['tʃeɪsənd] *adj* escarmentado.
chastening ['tʃeɪsnɪŋ] *adj* aleccionador(a).
chastity ['tʃæstɪtɪ] *n* castidad *f*.
chat [tʃæt] *vi* (*also:* **have a ~**) charlar ♦ *n*
charla.
►**chat up** *vt* (*col: girl*) ligar con, enrollarse
con.
chatline ['tʃætlaɪn] *n* línea (telefónica)
múltiple, party line *f*.

chat room *n* (*INTERNET*) chat *m*, canal *m* de
charla.
chat show *n* (*BRIT*) programa *m* de
entrevistas.
chatter ['tʃætə*] *vi* (*person*) charlar; (*teeth*)
castañetear ♦ *n* (*of birds*) parloteo; (*of
people*) charla, cháchara.
chatterbox ['tʃætəbɔks] *n* parlanchín/ina
m/f.
chattering classes ['tʃætərɪŋ'klɑːsɪz] *npl*:
the ~ (*col: pej*) los intelectualillos.
chatty ['tʃætɪ] *adj* (*style*) informal; (*person*)
hablador(a).
chauffeur ['ʃəufə*] *n* chófer *m*.
chauvinist ['ʃəuvɪnɪst] *n* (*male* ~) machista
m; (*nationalist*) chovinista *m/f*, patriotero/a
m/f.
ChE *abbr* = **chemical engineer**.
cheap [tʃiːp] *adj* barato; (*joke*) de mal
gusto, chabacano; (*poor quality*) malo;
(*reduced: ticket*) económico, (: *fare*) barato
♦ *adv* barato.
cheapen ['tʃiːpn] *vt* rebajar el precio de,
abaratar.
cheaply ['tʃiːplɪ] *adv* barato, a bajo precio.
cheat [tʃiːt] *vi* hacer trampa; (*in exam*)
copiar ♦ *vt* estafar, timar ♦ *n* trampa;
estafa; (*person*) tramposo/a; **he's been
~ing on his wife** ha estado engañando a
su esposa.
cheating ['tʃiːtɪŋ] *n* trampa.
check [tʃɛk] *vt* comprobar; (*count*) contar;
(*halt*) frenar; (*restrain*) refrenar,
restringir ♦ *vi*: **to ~ with sb** consultar con
algn; (*official etc*) informarse por ♦ *n*
(*inspection*) control *m*, inspección *f*; (*curb*)
freno; (*bill*) nota, cuenta; (*US*) = **cheque**;
(*pattern: gen pl*) cuadro ♦ *adj* (*also:* **~ed**:
pattern, cloth) a cuadros; **to keep a ~ on
sth/sb** controlar algo/a algn.
►**check in** *vi* (*in hotel*) registrarse; (*at
airport*) facturar ♦ *vt* (*luggage*) facturar.
►**check out** *vi* (*of hotel*) desocupar la
habitación ♦ *vt* (*investigate: story*)
comprobar; (: *person*) informarse sobre.
►**check up** *vi*: **to ~ up on sth** comprobar
algo; **to ~ up on sb** investigar a algn.
checkbook ['tʃɛkbuk] *n* (*US*) =
chequebook.
checkered ['tʃɛkəd] *adj* (*US*) = **chequered**.
checkers ['tʃɛkəz] *n* (*US*) damas *fpl*.
check-in ['tʃɛkɪn] *n* (*also:* **~ desk**: *at airport*)
mostrador *m* de facturación.
checking account ['tʃɛkɪŋ-] *n* (*US*) cuenta
corriente.
checklist ['tʃɛklɪst] *n* lista.
checkmate ['tʃɛkmeɪt] *n* jaque *m* mate.
checkout ['tʃɛkaut] *n* (*in supermarket*) caja.

checkpoint ['tʃɛkpɔɪnt] n (punto de) control m, retén m (LAM).
checkroom ['tʃɛkrum] n (US) consigna.
checkup ['tʃɛkʌp] n (MED) reconocimiento general; (of machine) revisión f.
cheek [tʃiːk] n mejilla; (impudence) descaro.
cheekbone ['tʃiːkbəun] n pómulo.
cheeky ['tʃiːkɪ] adj fresco, descarado.
cheep [tʃiːp] n (of bird) pío ♦ vi piar.
cheer [tʃɪə*] vt vitorear, ovacionar; (gladden) alegrar, animar ♦ vi dar vivas ♦ n viva m; ~s npl vítores mpl; ~s! ¡salud!
▶**cheer on** vt (person etc) animar con aplausos or gritos.
▶**cheer up** vi animarse ♦ vt alegrar, animar.
cheerful ['tʃɪəful] adj alegre.
cheerfulness ['tʃɪəfulnɪs] n alegría.
cheering ['tʃɪərɪŋ] n ovaciones fpl, vítores mpl.
cheerio [tʃɪərɪ'əu] excl (BRIT) ¡hasta luego!
cheerleader ['tʃɪəliːdə*] n animador(a) m/f.
cheerless ['tʃɪəlɪs] adj triste, sombrío.
cheese [tʃiːz] n queso.
cheeseboard ['tʃiːzbɔːd] n tabla de quesos.
cheeseburger ['tʃiːzbɜːgə*] n hamburguesa con queso.
cheesecake ['tʃiːzkeɪk] n pastel m de queso.
cheetah ['tʃiːtə] n guepardo.
chef [ʃɛf] n jefe/a m/f de cocina.
chemical ['kɛmɪkəl] adj químico ♦ n producto químico.
chemist ['kɛmɪst] n (BRIT: pharmacist) farmacéutico/a; (scientist) químico/a; ~'s (shop) n (BRIT) farmacia.
chemistry ['kɛmɪstrɪ] n química.
chemotherapy [kiːməu'θɛrəpɪ] n quimioterapia.
cheque, (US) **check** [tʃɛk] n (BRIT) cheque m; **to pay by** ~ pagar con cheque.
chequebook, (US) **checkbook** ['tʃɛkbuk] n talonario (de cheques), chequera (LAM).
cheque card n (BRIT) tarjeta de identificación bancaria.
chequered, (US) **checkered** ['tʃɛkəd] adj (fig) accidentado; (pattern) de cuadros.
cherish ['tʃɛrɪʃ] vt (love) querer, apreciar; (protect) cuidar; (hope etc) abrigar.
cheroot [ʃə'ruːt] n puro (cortado en los dos extremos).
cherry ['tʃɛrɪ] n cereza.
Ches abbr (BRIT) = Cheshire.
chess [tʃɛs] n ajedrez m.
chessboard ['tʃɛsbɔːd] n tablero (de ajedrez).
chessman ['tʃɛsmən] n pieza (de ajedrez).

chest [tʃɛst] n (ANAT) pecho; (box) cofre m; **to get sth off one's** ~ (col) desahogarse; ~ **of drawers** n cómoda.
chest measurement n talla (de chaqueta etc).
chestnut ['tʃɛsnʌt] n castaña; (also: ~ **tree**) castaño; (colour) castaño ♦ adj (color) castaño inv.
chesty ['tʃɛstɪ] adj (cough) de bronquios, de pecho.
chew [tʃuː] vt mascar, masticar.
chewing gum ['tʃuːɪŋ-] n chicle m.
chic [ʃiːk] adj elegante.
chicanery [ʃɪ'keɪnərɪ] n embustes mpl, sofismas mpl.
Chicano [tʃɪ'kɑːnəu] adj, n chicano/a.
chick [tʃɪk] n pollito, polluelo; (US col) chica.
chicken ['tʃɪkɪn] n gallina, pollo; (food) pollo; (col: coward) gallina m/f.
▶**chicken out** vi (col) rajarse; **to** ~ **out of doing sth** rajarse y no hacer algo.
chickenpox ['tʃɪkɪnpɔks] n varicela.
chickpea ['tʃɪkpiː] n garbanzo.
chicory ['tʃɪkərɪ] n (for coffee) achicoria; (salad) escarola.
chide [tʃaɪd] vt: **to** ~ **sb for sth** reprender a algn por algo.
chief [tʃiːf] n jefe/a m/f ♦ adj principal, máximo (esp LAM); **C**~ **of Staff** (MIL) Jefe m del Estado mayor.
chief executive, (US) **chief executive officer** n director m general.
chiefly ['tʃiːflɪ] adv principalmente.
chieftain ['tʃiːftən] n jefe m, cacique m.
chiffon ['ʃɪfɔn] n gasa.
chilblain ['tʃɪlbleɪn] n sabañón m.
child, pl ~**ren** [tʃaɪld, 'tʃɪldrən] n niño/a; (offspring) hijo/a.
child benefit n (BRIT) subsidio por cada hijo pequeño.
childbirth ['tʃaɪldbɜːθ] n parto.
childhood ['tʃaɪldhud] n niñez f, infancia.
childish ['tʃaɪldɪʃ] adj pueril, infantil.
childless ['tʃaɪldlɪs] adj sin hijos.
childlike ['tʃaɪldlaɪk] adj de niño, infantil.
child minder n (BRIT) niñera, madre f de día.
child prodigy n niño/a prodigio inv.
children's home n centro de acogida para niños.
child's play n (fig): **this is** ~ esto es coser y cantar.
Chile ['tʃɪlɪ] n Chile m.
Chilean ['tʃɪlɪən] adj, n chileno/a m/f.
chill [tʃɪl] n frío; (MED) resfriado ♦ adj frío ♦ vt enfriar; (CULIN) refrigerar.
▶**chill out** vi (esp US col) tranquilizarse.

chil(l)i ['tʃɪlɪ] n (*BRIT*) chile m, ají m (*LAM*).
chilling ['tʃɪlɪŋ] *adj* escalofriante.
chilly ['tʃɪlɪ] *adj* frío.
chime [tʃaɪm] n repique m, campanada ♦ vi repicar, sonar.
chimney ['tʃɪmnɪ] n chimenea.
chimney sweep n deshollinador m.
chimpanzee [tʃɪmpæn'ziː] n chimpancé m.
chin [tʃɪn] n mentón m, barbilla.
China ['tʃaɪnə] n China.
china ['tʃaɪnə] n porcelana; (*crockery*) loza.
Chinese [tʃaɪ'niːz] *adj* chino ♦ n (*pl inv*) chino/a; (*LING*) chino.
chink [tʃɪŋk] n (*opening*) rendija, hendedura; (*noise*) tintineo.
chintz [tʃɪnts] n cretona.
chip [tʃɪp] n (*gen pl*: *CULIN*: *BRIT*) patata *or* papa (*LAM*) frita; (: *US*: *also*: **potato ~**) patata *or* papa (*LAM*) frita; (*of wood*) astilla; (*stone*) lasca; (*in gambling*) ficha; (*COMPUT*) chip m ♦ vt (*cup, plate*) desconchar; **when the ~s are down** (*fig*) a la hora de la verdad.
▶**chip in** vi (*col*: *interrupt*) interrumpir, meterse; (: *contribute*) contribuir.
chipboard ['tʃɪpbɔːd] n madera aglomerada.
chipmunk ['tʃɪpmʌŋk] n ardilla listada.
chip shop n ver recuadro.

CHIP SHOP

*Se denomina **chip shop** o "fish-and-chip shop" a un tipo de tienda popular de comida rápida en la que se despachan platos tradicionales británicos, principalmente filetes de pescado rebozado frito y patatas fritas.*

---

chiropodist [kɪ'rɔpədɪst] n (*BRIT*) podólogo/a.
chiropody [kɪ'rɔpədɪ] n podología.
chirp [tʃəːp] vi gorjear; (*cricket*) cantar ♦ n (*of cricket*) canto.
chirpy ['tʃəːpɪ] *adj* alegre, animado.
chisel ['tʃɪzl] n (*for wood*) escoplo; (*for stone*) cincel m.
chit [tʃɪt] n nota.
chitchat ['tʃɪttʃæt] n chismes mpl, habladurías fpl.
chivalrous ['ʃɪvəlrəs] *adj* caballeroso.
chivalry ['ʃɪvəlrɪ] n caballerosidad f.
chives [tʃaɪvz] npl cebollinos mpl.
chloride ['klɔːraɪd] n cloruro.
chlorine ['klɔːriːn] n cloro.
chock-a-block ['tʃɔkə'blɔk], **chock-full** [tʃɔk'ful] *adj* atestado.
chocolate ['tʃɔklɪt] n chocolate m.

choice [tʃɔɪs] n elección f; (*preference*) preferencia ♦ *adj* escogido; **I did it by** *or* **from ~** lo hice de buena gana; **a wide ~** un gran surtido, una gran variedad.
choir ['kwaɪə*] n coro.
choirboy ['kwaɪəbɔɪ] n niño de coro.
choke [tʃəuk] vi ahogarse; (*on food*) atragantarse ♦ vt ahogar; (*block*) atascar ♦ n (*AUT*) estárter m.
choker ['tʃəukə*] n (*necklace*) gargantilla.
cholera ['kɔlərə] n cólera m.
cholesterol [kə'lɛstərəl] n colesterol m.
choose, pt chose, pp chosen [tʃuːz, tʃəuz, 'tʃəuzn] vt escoger, elegir; (*team*) seleccionar; **to ~ between** elegir *or* escoger entre; **to ~ from** escoger entre.
choosy ['tʃuːzɪ] *adj* remilgado.
chop [tʃɔp] vt (*wood*) cortar, talar; (*CULIN*: *also*: ~ **up**) picar ♦ n tajo, golpe m cortante; (*CULIN*) chuleta; **~s** npl (*jaws*) boca sg; **to get the ~** (*col*: *project*) ser suprimido; (: *person*: *be sacked*) ser despedido.
chopper ['tʃɔpə*] n (*helicopter*) helicóptero.
choppy ['tʃɔpɪ] *adj* (*sea*) picado, agitado.
chopsticks ['tʃɔpstɪks] npl palillos mpl.
choral ['kɔːrəl] *adj* coral.
chord [kɔːd] n (*MUS*) acorde m.
chore [tʃɔː*] n faena, tarea; (*routine task*) trabajo rutinario.
choreographer [kɔrɪ'ɔgrəfə*] n coreógrafo/a.
choreography [kɔrɪ'ɔgrəfɪ] n coreografía.
chorister ['kɔrɪstə*] n corista m/f; (*US*) director(a) m/f de un coro.
chortle ['tʃɔːtl] vi reírse satisfecho.
chorus ['kɔːrəs] n coro; (*repeated part of song*) estribillo.
chose [tʃəuz] pt of **choose**.
chosen ['tʃəuzn] pp of **choose**.
chow [tʃau] n (*dog*) perro chino.
chowder ['tʃaudə*] n (*esp US*) sopa de pescado.
Christ [kraɪst] n Cristo.
christen ['krɪsn] vt bautizar.
christening ['krɪsnɪŋ] n bautizo.
Christian ['krɪstɪən] *adj*, n cristiano/a m/f.
Christianity [krɪstɪ'ænɪtɪ] n cristianismo.
Christian name n nombre m de pila.
Christmas ['krɪsməs] n Navidad f; **Merry ~!** ¡Felices Navidades!, ¡Felices Pascuas!
Christmas card n crismas m inv, tarjeta de Navidad.
Christmas Day n día m de Navidad.
Christmas Eve n Nochebuena.
Christmas Island n Isla Christmas.
Christmas tree n árbol m de Navidad.
chrome [krəum] n = **chromium plating**.

chromium ['krəumɪəm] *n* cromo; (*also*: ~ **plating**) cromado.

chromosome ['krəuməsəum] *n* cromosoma *m*.

chronic ['krɔnɪk] *adj* crónico; (*fig*: *liar, smoker*) empedernido.

chronicle ['krɔnɪkl] *n* crónica.

chronological [krɔnə'lɔdʒɪkəl] *adj* cronológico.

chrysalis ['krɪsəlɪs] *n* (*BIO*) crisálida.

chrysanthemum [krɪ'sænθəməm] *n* crisantemo.

chubby ['tʃʌbɪ] *adj* rechoncho.

chuck [tʃʌk] *vt* tirar; **to ~ (up or in)** *vt* (*BRIT*) dejar, mandar a paseo.

chuckle ['tʃʌkl] *vi* reírse entre dientes.

chuffed [tʃʌft] *adj* (*col*): **to be ~ (about sth)** estar encantado (con algo).

chug [tʃʌg] *vi* (*also*: ~ **along**: *train*) ir despacio; (: *fig*) ir tirando.

chum [tʃʌm] *n* amiguete/a *m/f*, coleguilla *m/f*.

chump [tʃʌmp] *n* (*col*) tonto/a, estúpido/a.

chunk [tʃʌŋk] *n* pedazo, trozo.

chunky ['tʃʌŋkɪ] *adj* (*furniture etc*) achaparrado; (*person*) fornido; (*knitwear*) de lana gorda, grueso.

Chunnel [tʃʌnl] *n* = **Channel Tunnel**.

church [tʃəːtʃ] *n* iglesia; **the C~ of England** la Iglesia Anglicana.

churchyard ['tʃəːtʃjɑːd] *n* cementerio, camposanto.

churlish ['tʃəːlɪʃ] *adj* grosero; (*mean*) arisco.

churn [tʃəːn] *n* (*for butter*) mantequera; (*for milk*) lechera.

▶**churn out** *vt* producir en serie.

chute [ʃuːt] *n* (*also*: **rubbish** ~) vertedero; (*BRIT*: *children's slide*) tobogán *m*.

chutney ['tʃʌtnɪ] *n* *salsa picante de frutas y especias*.

CIA *n abbr* (*US*: = *Central Intelligence Agency*) CIA *f*, Agencia Central de Inteligencia.

cicada [sɪ'kɑːdə] *n* cigarra.

CID *n abbr* (*BRIT*: = *Criminal Investigation Department*) ≈ B.I.C. *f* (*SP*).

cider ['saɪdə*] *n* sidra.

C.I.F. *abbr* (= *cost, insurance and freight*) c.s.f.

cigar [sɪ'gɑː*] *n* puro.

cigarette [sɪgə'ret] *n* cigarrillo, pitillo.

cigarette case *n* pitillera.

cigarette end *n* colilla.

cigarette holder *n* boquilla.

cinch [sɪntʃ] *n*: **it's a ~** está tirado.

Cinderella [sɪndə'relə] *n* Cenicienta.

cinders ['sɪndəz] *npl* cenizas *fpl*.

cine-camera ['sɪnɪ'kæmərə] *n* (*BRIT*) cámara cinematográfica.

cine-film ['sɪnɪfɪlm] *n* (*BRIT*) película de cine.

cinema ['sɪnəmə] *n* cine *m*.

cinnamon ['sɪnəmən] *n* canela.

cipher ['saɪfə*] *n* clave *f*; (*fig*) cero; **in ~** en clave.

circle ['səːkl] *n* círculo; (*in theatre*) anfiteatro ♦ *vi* dar vueltas ♦ *vt* (*surround*) rodear, cercar; (*move round*) dar la vuelta a.

circuit ['səːkɪt] *n* circuito; (*track*) pista; (*lap*) vuelta.

circuit board *n* tarjeta de circuitos.

circuitous [səː'kjuɪtəs] *adj* indirecto.

circular ['səːkjulə*] *adj* circular ♦ *n* circular *f*; (*as advertisement*) panfleto.

circulate ['səːkjuleɪt] *vi* circular; (*person*: *socially*) alternar, circular ♦ *vt* poner en circulación.

circulation [səːkju'leɪʃən] *n* circulación *f*; (*of newspaper etc*) tirada.

circumcise ['səːkəmsaɪz] *vt* circuncidar.

circumference [sə'kʌmfərəns] *n* circunferencia.

circumscribe ['səːkəmskraɪb] *vt* circunscribir.

circumspect ['səːkəmspɛkt] *adj* circunspecto, prudente.

circumstances ['səːkəmstənsɪz] *npl* circunstancias *fpl*; (*financial condition*) situación *f* económica; **in the ~** en or dadas las circunstancias; **under no ~** de ninguna manera, bajo ningún concepto.

circumstantial [səːkəm'stænʃəl] *adj* detallado; ~ **evidence** prueba indiciaria.

circumvent [səːkəm'vɛnt] *vt* (*rule etc*) burlar.

circus ['səːkəs] *n* circo; (*also*: **C~**: *in place names*) Plaza.

cirrhosis [sɪ'rəusɪs] *n* (*also*: ~ **of the liver**) cirrosis *f inv*.

CIS *n abbr* (= *Commonwealth of Independent States*) CEI *f*.

cissy ['sɪsɪ] *n* = **sissy**.

cistern ['sɪstən] *n* tanque *m*, depósito; (*in toilet*) cisterna.

citation [saɪ'teɪʃən] *n* cita; (*LAW*) citación *f*; (*MIL*) mención *f*.

cite [saɪt] *vt* citar.

citizen ['sɪtɪzn] *n* (*POL*) ciudadano/a; (*of city*) habitante *m/f*.

Citizens' Advice Bureau *n* (*BRIT*) *organización voluntaria británica que aconseja especialmente en temas legales o financieros*.

citizenship ['sɪtɪznʃɪp] *n* ciudadanía; (*BRIT SCOL*) civismo.

citric ['sɪtrɪk] adj: ~ **acid** ácido cítrico.
citrus fruits ['sɪtrəs-] npl cítricos mpl.
city ['sɪtɪ] n ciudad f; **the C~** centro financiero de Londres.
city centre n centro de la ciudad.
City Hall n (US) ayuntamiento.
City Technology College n (BRIT) ≈ Centro de formación profesional.
civic ['sɪvɪk] adj cívico; (authorities) municipal.
civic centre n (BRIT) centro de administración municipal.
civil ['sɪvɪl] adj civil; (polite) atento, cortés; (well-bred) educado.
civil defence n protección f civil.
civil engineer n ingeniero/a de caminos.
civil engineering n ingeniería de caminos.
civilian [sɪ'vɪlɪən] adj civil; (clothes) de paisano ♦ n civil m/f.
civilization [sɪvɪlaɪ'zeɪʃən] n civilización f.
civilized ['sɪvɪlaɪzd] adj civilizado.
civil law n derecho civil.
civil liberties npl libertades fpl civiles.
civil rights npl derechos mpl civiles.
civil servant n funcionario/a (del Estado).
Civil Service n administración f pública.
civil war n guerra civil.
civvies ['sɪvɪz] npl: **in** ~ (col) de paisano.
cl abbr (= centilitre) cl.
clad [klæd] adj: ~ **(in)** vestido (de).
claim [kleɪm] vt exigir, reclamar; (rights etc) reivindicar; (assert) pretender ♦ vi (for insurance) reclamar ♦ n (for expenses) reclamación f; (LAW) demanda; (pretension) pretensión f; **to put in a** ~ **for sth** presentar una demanda por algo.
claimant ['kleɪmənt] n (ADMIN, LAW) demandante m/f.
claim form n solicitud f.
clairvoyant [klɛə'vɔɪənt] n clarividente m/f.
clam [klæm] n almeja.
▶**clam up** vi (col) cerrar el pico.
clamber ['klæmbə*] vi trepar.
clammy ['klæmɪ] adj (cold) frío y húmedo; (sticky) pegajoso.
clamour, (US) **clamor** ['klæmə*] n (noise) clamor m; (protest) protesta ♦ vi: **to** ~ **for sth** clamar por algo, pedir algo a voces.
clamp [klæmp] n abrazadera; (laboratory ~) grapa; (wheel ~) cepo ♦ vt afianzar (con abrazadera).
▶**clamp down on** vt fus (subj: government, police) poner coto a.
clampdown ['klæmpdaun] n restricción f; **there has been a** ~ **on terrorism** se ha puesto coto al terrorismo.
clan [klæn] n clan m.

clandestine [klæn'dɛstɪn] adj clandestino.
clang [klæŋ] n estruendo ♦ vi sonar con estruendo.
clanger [klæŋə*] n: **to drop a** ~ (BRIT col) meter la pata.
clansman ['klænzmən] n miembro del clan.
clap [klæp] vi aplaudir ♦ vt (hands) batir ♦ n (of hands) palmada; **to** ~ **one's hands** dar palmadas, batir las palmas; **a** ~ **of thunder** un trueno.
clapping ['klæpɪŋ] n aplausos mpl.
claptrap ['klæptræp] n (col) gilipolleces fpl.
claret ['klærət] n burdeos m inv.
clarification [klærɪfɪ'keɪʃən] n aclaración f.
clarify ['klærɪfaɪ] vt aclarar.
clarinet [klærɪ'nɛt] n clarinete m.
clarity ['klærɪtɪ] n claridad f.
clash [klæʃ] n estruendo; (fig) choque m ♦ vi enfrentarse; (personalities, interests) oponerse, chocar; (colours) desentonar; (dates, events) coincidir.
clasp [klɑːsp] n broche m; (on jewels) cierre m ♦ vt abrochar; (hand) apretar; (embrace) abrazar.
class [klɑːs] n (gen) clase f; (group, category) clase f, categoría ♦ cpd de clase ♦ vt clasificar.
class-conscious ['klɑːs'kɔnʃəs] adj clasista, con conciencia de clase.
classic ['klæsɪk] adj clásico ♦ n (work) obra clásica, clásico; ~**s** npl (UNIV) clásicas fpl.
classical ['klæsɪkəl] adj clásico; ~ **music** música clásica.
classification [klæsɪfɪ'keɪʃən] n clasificación f.
classified ['klæsɪfaɪd] adj (information) reservado.
classified advertisement n anuncio por palabras.
classify ['klæsɪfaɪ] vt clasificar.
classless ['klɑːslɪs] adj: ~ **society** sociedad f sin clases.
classmate ['klɑːsmeɪt] n compañero/a de clase.
classroom ['klɑːsrum] n aula.
classy ['klɑːsɪ] adj (col) elegante, con estilo.
clatter ['klætə*] n ruido, estruendo; (of hooves) trápala ♦ vi hacer ruido or estruendo.
clause [klɔːz] n cláusula; (LING) oración f.
claustrophobia [klɔːstrə'fəubɪə] n claustrofobia.
claustrophobic [klɔːstrə'fəubɪk] adj claustrofóbico; **I feel** ~ me entra claustrofobia.
claw [klɔː] n (of cat) uña; (of bird of prey) garra; (of lobster) pinza; (TECH) garfio ♦ vi: **to** ~ **at** arañar; (tear) desgarrar.

clay [kleɪ] *n* arcilla.

clean [kli:n] *adj* limpio; (*copy*) en limpio; (*lines*) bien definido ♦ *vt* limpiar ♦ *adv*: **he ~ forgot** lo olvidó por completo; **to come ~** (*col: admit guilt*) confesarlo todo; **to have a ~ driving licence** tener el carnet de conducir sin sanciones; **to ~ one's teeth** lavarse los dientes.

▸**clean off** *vt* limpiar.

▸**clean out** *vt* limpiar (a fondo).

▸**clean up** *vt* limpiar, asear ♦ *vi* (*fig: make profit*): **to ~ up on** sacar provecho de.

clean-cut ['kli:n'kʌt] *adj* bien definido; (*outline*) nítido; (*person*) de buen parecer.

cleaner ['kli:nə*] *n* encargado/a *m/f* de la limpieza; (*also: dry ~*) tintorero/a.

cleaning ['kli:nɪŋ] *n* limpieza.

cleaning lady *n* señora de la limpieza, asistenta.

cleanliness ['klɛnlɪnɪs] *n* limpieza.

cleanse [klɛnz] *vt* limpiar.

cleanser ['klɛnzə*] *n* detergente *m*; (*cosmetic*) loción *f* or crema limpiadora.

clean-shaven ['kli:n'ʃeɪvn] *adj* bien afeitado.

cleansing department ['klɛnzɪŋ-] *n* (*BRIT*) servicio municipal de limpieza.

clean sweep *n*: **to make a ~** (*SPORT*) arrasar, barrer.

clear [klɪə*] *adj* claro; (*road, way*) libre; (*profit*) neto; (*majority*) absoluto ♦ *vt* (*space*) despejar, limpiar; (*LAW: suspect*) absolver; (*obstacle*) salvar, saltar por encima de; (*debt*) liquidar; (*cheque*) aceptar; (*site, woodland*) desmontar ♦ *vi* (*fog etc*) despejarse ♦ *n*: **to be in the ~** (*out of debt*) estar libre de deudas; (*out of suspicion*) estar fuera de toda sospecha; (*out of danger*) estar fuera de peligro ♦ *adv*: **~ of** a distancia de; **to make o.s. ~** explicarse claramente; **to make it ~ to sb that ...** hacer entender a algn que ...; **I have a ~ day tomorrow** mañana tengo el día libre; **to keep ~ of sth/sb** evitar algo/a algn; **to ~ a profit of ...** sacar una ganancia de ...; **to ~ the table** recoger *or* quitar la mesa.

▸**clear off** *vi* (*col: leave*) marcharse, mandarse mudar (*LAM*).

▸**clear up** *vt* limpiar; (*mystery*) aclarar, resolver.

clearance ['klɪərəns] *n* (*removal*) despeje *m*; (*permission*) acreditación *f*.

clear-cut ['klɪə'kʌt] *adj* bien definido, claro.

clearing ['klɪərɪŋ] *n* (*in wood*) claro.

clearing bank *n* (*BRIT*) banco central.

clearing house *n* (*COMM*) cámara de compensación.

clearly ['klɪəlɪ] *adv* claramente.

clearway ['klɪəweɪ] *n* (*BRIT*) *carretera en la que no se puede estacionar.*

cleaver ['kli:və] *n* cuchilla (de carnicero).

clef [klɛf] *n* (*MUS*) clave *f*.

cleft [klɛft] *n* (*in rock*) grieta, hendedura.

clemency ['klɛmənsɪ] *n* clemencia.

clench [klɛntʃ] *vt* apretar, cerrar.

clergy ['klɜ:dʒɪ] *n* clero.

clergyman ['klɜ:dʒɪmən] *n* clérigo.

clerical ['klɛrɪkəl] *adj* de oficina; (*REL*) clerical; (*error*) de copia.

clerk [klɑ:k, (*US*) klɜːrk] *n* oficinista *m/f*; (*US*) dependiente/a *m/f*, vendedor(a) *m/f*; **C~ of the Court** secretario/a de juzgado.

clever ['klɛvə*] *adj* (*mentally*) inteligente, listo; (*skilful*) hábil; (*device, arrangement*) ingenioso.

cleverly ['klɛvəlɪ] *adv* ingeniosamente.

clew [klu:] *n* (*US*) = **clue.**

cliché ['kli:ʃeɪ] *n* cliché *m*, frase *f* hecha.

click [klɪk] *vt* (*tongue*) chasquear ♦ *vi* (*COMPUT*) hacer clic; **to ~ one's heels** taconear.

clickable ['klɪkəbl] *adj* (*COMPUT*) cliqueable.

client ['klaɪənt] *n* cliente *m/f*.

clientele [kli:ɑ:n'tɛl] *n* clientela.

cliff [klɪf] *n* acantilado.

cliffhanger ['klɪfhæŋə*] *n*: **it was a ~** estuvimos *etc* en ascuas hasta el final.

climactic [klaɪˈmæktɪk] *adj* culminante.

climate ['klaɪmɪt] *n* clima *m*; (*fig*) clima *m*, ambiente *m*.

climax ['klaɪmæks] *n* punto culminante; (*of play etc*) clímax *m*; (*sexual ~*) orgasmo.

climb [klaɪm] *vi* subir, trepar; (*plane*) elevarse, remontar el vuelo ♦ *vt* (*stairs*) subir; (*tree*) trepar a; (*mountain*) escalar ♦ *n* subida, ascenso; **to ~ over a wall** saltar una tapia.

▸**climb down** *vi* (*fig*) volverse atrás.

climbdown ['klaɪmdaun] *n* vuelta atrás.

climber ['klaɪmə*] *n* escalador(a) *m/f*.

climbing ['klaɪmɪŋ] *n* escalada.

clinch [klɪntʃ] *vt* (*deal*) cerrar; (*argument*) rematar.

clincher ['klɪntʃə*] *n* (*col*): **that was the ~ for me** eso me hizo decidir.

cling, *pt, pp* **clung** [klɪŋ, klʌŋ] *vi*: **to ~ (to)** agarrarse (a); (*clothes*) pegarse (a).

clingfilm ['klɪŋfɪlm] *n* plástico adherente.

clinic ['klɪnɪk] *n* clínica.

clinical ['klɪnɪkl] *adj* clínico; (*fig*) frío, impasible.

clink [klɪŋk] *vi* tintinear.

clip [klɪp] *n* (*for hair*) horquilla; (*also: paper ~*) sujetapapeles *m inv*, clip *m*; (*clamp*) grapa ♦ *vt* (*cut*) cortar; (*hedge*) podar;

(*also*: ~ **together**) unir.

clippers ['klɪpəz] *npl* (*for gardening*) tijeras *fpl* de podar; (*for hair*) maquinilla *sg*; (*for nails*) cortauñas *m inv*.

clipping ['klɪpɪŋ] *n* (*from newspaper*) recorte *m*.

clique [kliːk] *n* camarilla.

cloak [kləuk] *n* capa, manto ♦ *vt* (*fig*) encubrir, disimular.

cloakroom ['kləukrum] *n* guardarropa *m*; (*BRIT*: *WC*) lavabo, aseos *mpl*, baño (*esp LAM*).

clobber ['klɔbə*] *n* (*col*) bártulos *mpl*, trastos *mpl* ♦ *vt* dar una paliza a.

clock [klɔk] *n* reloj *m*; (*in taxi*) taxímetro; **to work against the** ~ trabajar contra reloj; **around the** ~ las veinticuatro horas; **to sleep round the** ~ dormir un día entero; **30,000 on the** ~ (*AUT*) treinta mil millas en el cuentakilómetros.

▶**clock in, clock on** *vi* fichar, picar.

▶**clock off, clock out** *vi* fichar *or* picar la salida.

▶**clock up** *vt* hacer.

clockwise ['klɔkwaɪz] *adv* en el sentido de las agujas del reloj.

clockwork ['klɔkwəːk] *n* aparato de relojería ♦ *adj* (*toy, train*) de cuerda.

clog [klɔg] *n* zueco, chanclo ♦ *vt* atascar ♦ *vi* atascarse.

cloister ['klɔɪstə*] *n* claustro.

clone [kləun] *n* clon *m*.

close *adj, adv and derivatives* [kləus] *adj* cercano, próximo; (*near*): ~ **(to)** cerca (de); (*print, weave*) tupido, compacto; (*friend*) íntimo; (*connection*) estrecho; (*examination*) detallado, minucioso; (*weather*) bochornoso; (*atmosphere*) sofocante; (*room*) mal ventilado ♦ *adv* cerca; ~ **by**, ~ **at hand** *adj, adv* muy cerca; ~ **to** *prep* cerca de; **to have a** ~ **shave** (*fig*) escaparse por un pelo; **how** ~ **is Edinburgh to Glasgow?** ¿qué distancia hay de Edimburgo a Glasgow?; **at** ~ **quarters** de cerca ♦ *vb and derivatives* [kləuz] *vt* cerrar; (*end*) concluir, terminar ♦ *vi* (*shop etc*) cerrar; (*end*) concluir(se), terminar(se) ♦ *n* (*end*) fin *m*, final *m*, conclusión *f*; **to bring sth to a** ~ terminar algo.

▶**close down** *vi* cerrar definitivamente.

▶**close in** *vi* (*hunters*) acercarse rodeando, rodear; (*evening, night*) caer; (*fog*) cerrarse; **to** ~ **in on sb** rodear *or* cercar a algn; **the days are closing in** los días son cada vez más cortos.

▶**close off** *vt* (*area*) cerrar al tráfico *or* al público.

closed [kləuzd] *adj* (*shop etc*) cerrado.

closed-circuit ['kləuzd'səːkɪt] *adj*: ~ **television** televisión *f* por circuito cerrado.

closed shop *n* empresa en la que todo el personal está afiliado a un sindicato.

close-knit ['kləus'nɪt] *adj* (*fig*) muy unido.

closely ['kləuslɪ] *adv* (*study*) con detalle; (*listen*) con atención; (*watch*: *person, events*) de cerca; **we are** ~ **related** somos parientes cercanos; **a** ~ **guarded secret** un secreto rigurosamente guardado.

close season [kləuz-] *n* (*FOOTBALL*) temporada de descanso; (*HUNTING*) veda.

closet ['klɔzɪt] *n* (*cupboard*) armario, placar(d) *m* (*LAM*).

close-up ['kləusʌp] *n* primer plano.

closing ['kləuzɪŋ] *adj* (*stages, remarks*) último, final; ~ **price** (*STOCK EXCHANGE*) cotización *f* de cierre.

closing time *n* hora de cierre.

closure ['kləuʒə*] *n* cierre *m*.

clot [klɔt] *n* (*gen*: *blood* ~) embolia; (*col*: *idiot*) imbécil *m/f* ♦ *vi* (*blood*) coagularse.

cloth [klɔθ] *n* (*material*) tela, paño; (*table* ~) mantel *m*; (*rag*) trapo.

clothe [kləuð] *vt* vestir; (*fig*) revestir.

clothes [kləuðz] *npl* ropa *sg*; **to put one's** ~ **on** vestirse, ponerse la ropa; **to take one's** ~ **off** desvestirse, desnudarse.

clothes brush *n* cepillo (para la ropa).

clothes line *n* cuerda (para tender la ropa).

clothes peg, (*US*) **clothes pin** *n* pinza.

clothing ['kləuðɪŋ] *n* = **clothes**.

clotted cream ['klɔtɪd-] *n* nata muy espesa.

cloud [klaud] *n* nube *f*; (*storm* ~) nubarrón *m* ♦ *vt* (*liquid*) enturbiar; **every** ~ **has a silver lining** no hay mal que por bien no venga; **to** ~ **the issue** empañar el problema.

▶**cloud over** *vi* (*also fig*) nublarse.

cloudburst ['klaudbəːst] *n* chaparrón *m*.

cloud-cuckoo-land ['klaud'kukuːlænd] *n* Babia.

cloudy ['klaudɪ] *adj* nublado; (*liquid*) turbio.

clout [klaut] *n* (*fig*) influencia, peso ♦ *vt* dar un tortazo a.

clove [kləuv] *n* clavo; ~ **of garlic** diente *m* de ajo.

clover ['kləuvə*] *n* trébol *m*.

clown [klaun] *n* payaso ♦ *vi* (*also*: ~ **about,** ~ **around**) hacer el payaso.

cloying ['klɔɪɪŋ] *adj* (*taste*) empalagoso.

club [klʌb] *n* (*society*) club *m*; (*weapon*) porra, cachiporra; (*also*: **golf** ~) palo ♦ *vt* aporrear ♦ *vi*: **to** ~ **together** (*join forces*)

unir fuerzas; ~s npl (CARDS) tréboles mpl.
club car n (US RAIL) coche m salón.
club class n (AVIAT) clase f preferente.
clubhouse ['klʌbhaus] n local social, sobre todo en clubs deportivos.
club soda n (US) soda.
cluck [klʌk] vi cloquear.
clue [kluː] n pista; (in crosswords) indicación f; **I haven't a** ~ no tengo ni idea.
clued up, (US) **clued in** [kluːd-] adj (col) al tanto, al corriente.
clueless ['kluːlɪs] adj (col) desorientado.
clump [klʌmp] n (of trees) grupo.
clumsy ['klʌmzɪ] adj (person) torpe; (tool) difícil de manejar.
clung [klʌŋ] pt, pp of **cling.**
cluster ['klʌstə*] n grupo; (BOT) racimo ♦ vi agruparse, apiñarse.
clutch [klʌtʃ] n (AUT) embrague m; (pedal) (pedal m de) embrague m; **to fall into sb's** ~es caer en las garras de algn ♦ vt agarrar.
clutter ['klʌtə*] vt (also: ~ up) atestar, llenar desordenadamente ♦ n desorden m, confusión f.
CM abbr (US) = North Mariana Islands.
cm abbr (= centimetre) cm.
CNAA n abbr (BRIT: = Council for National Academic Awards) organismo no universitario que otorga diplomas.
CND n abbr (= Campaign for Nuclear Disarmament) plataforma pro desarme nuclear.
CO n abbr = **commanding officer;** (BRIT) = Commonwealth Office ♦ abbr (US) = Colorado.
Co. abbr = **county;** = **company.**
c/o abbr (= care of) c/a, a/c.
coach [kəutʃ] n (bus) autocar m (SP), autobús m; (horse-drawn) coche m; (ceremonial) carroza; (of train) vagón m, coche m; (SPORT) entrenador(a) m/f, instructor(a) m/f ♦ vt (SPORT) entrenar; (student) preparar, enseñar.
coach trip n excursión f en autocar.
coagulate [kəu'ægjuleɪt] vi coagularse.
coal [kəul] n carbón m.
coal face n frente m de carbón.
coalfield ['kəulfiːld] n yacimiento de carbón.
coalition [kəuə'lɪʃən] n coalición f.
coal man n carbonero.
coalmine ['kəulmaɪn] n mina de carbón.
coalminer ['kəulmaɪnə*] n minero (de carbón).
coalmining ['keulmaɪnɪŋ] n minería (de carbón).

coarse [kɔːs] adj basto, burdo; (vulgar) grosero, ordinario.
coast [kəust] n costa, litoral m ♦ vi (AUT) ir en punto muerto.
coastal ['kəustl] adj costero.
coaster ['kəustə*] n buque m costero, barco de cabotaje.
coastguard ['kəustgɑːd] n guardacostas m inv.
coastline ['kəustlaɪn] n litoral m.
coat [kəut] n (jacket) chaqueta, saco (LAM); (overcoat) abrigo; (of animal) pelo, lana; (of paint) mano f, capa ♦ vt cubrir, revestir.
coat hanger n percha, gancha (LAM).
coating ['kəutɪŋ] n capa, baño.
coat of arms n escudo de armas.
co-author ['kəu'ɔːθə*] n coautor(a) m/f.
coax [kəuks] vt engatusar.
cob [kɔb] n see **corn.**
cobbler ['kɔblə*] n zapatero (remendón).
cobbles ['kɔblz], **cobblestones** ['kɔblstəunz] npl adoquines mpl.
COBOL ['kəubɔl] n COBOL m.
cobra ['kəubrə] n cobra.
cobweb ['kɔbwɛb] n telaraña.
cocaine [kə'keɪn] n cocaína.
cock [kɔk] n (rooster) gallo; (male bird) macho ♦ vt (gun) amartillar.
cock-a-hoop [kɔkə'huːp] adj: **to be** ~ estar más contento que unas pascuas.
cockatoo [kɔkə'tuː] n cacatúa.
cockerel ['kɔkərl] n gallito, gallo joven.
cock-eyed ['kɔkaɪd] adj bizco; (fig: crooked) torcido; (: idea) disparatado.
cockle ['kɔkl] n berberecho.
cockney ['kɔknɪ] n habitante de ciertos barrios de Londres.
cockpit ['kɔkpɪt] n (in aircraft) cabina.
cockroach ['kɔkrəutʃ] n cucaracha.
cocktail ['kɔkteɪl] n combinado, cóctel m; **prawn** ~ cóctel m de gambas.
cocktail cabinet n mueble-bar m.
cocktail party n cóctel m.
cocktail shaker [-ʃeɪkə*] n coctelera.
cocky ['kɔkɪ] adj farruco, flamenco.
cocoa ['kəukəu] n cacao; (drink) chocolate m.
coconut ['kəukənʌt] n coco.
cocoon [kə'kuːn] n capullo.
cod [kɔd] n bacalao.
COD abbr see **cash on delivery, collect on delivery** (US).
code [kəud] n código; (cipher) clave f; (TEL) prefijo; ~ **of behaviour** código de conducta; ~ **of practice** código profesional.
codeine ['kəudiːn] n codeína.

codger [kɔdʒə*] n (BRIT col): **an old** ~ un abuelo.

codicil ['kɔdɪsɪl] n codicilo.

codify ['kəudɪfaɪ] vt codificar.

cod-liver oil ['kɔdlɪvə*-] n aceite m de hígado de bacalao.

co-driver ['kəu'draɪvə*] n (in race) copiloto m/f; (of lorry) segundo conductor m.

co-ed ['kəued] adj abbr = **coeducational** ♦ n abbr (US: = female student) alumna de una universidad mixta; (BRIT: school) colegio mixto.

coeducational [kəuɛdju'keɪʃənl] adj mixto.

coerce [kəu'əːs] vt forzar, coaccionar.

coercion [kəu'əːʃən] n coacción f.

coexistence ['kəuɪg'zɪstəns] n coexistencia.

C. of C. n abbr = **chamber of commerce.**

C of E abbr = **Church of England.**

coffee ['kɔfɪ] n café m; **white** ~, (US) ~ **with cream** café con leche.

coffee bar n (BRIT) cafetería.

coffee bean n grano de café.

coffee break n descanso (para tomar café).

coffee cup n taza de café, pocillo (LAM).

coffeepot ['kɔfɪpɔt] n cafetera.

coffee table n mesita baja.

coffin ['kɔfɪn] n ataúd m.

C of I abbr = **Church of Ireland.**

C of S abbr = **Church of Scotland.**

cog [kɔg] n diente m.

cogent ['kəudʒənt] adj lógico, convincente.

cognac ['kɔnjæk] n coñac m.

cogwheel ['kɔgwiːl] n rueda dentada.

cohabit [kəu'hæbɪt] vi (formal): **to** ~ **(with sb)** cohabitar (con algn).

coherent [kəu'hɪərənt] adj coherente.

cohesion [kəu'hiːʒen] n cohesión f.

cohesive [kəu'hiːsɪv] adj (fig) cohesivo, unido.

COI n abbr (BRIT: = Central Office of Information) servicio de información gubernamental.

coil [kɔɪl] n rollo; (of rope) vuelta; (of smoke) espiral f; (AUT, ELEC) bobina, carrete m; (contraceptive) DIU m ♦ vt enrollar.

coin [kɔɪn] n moneda ♦ vt acuñar; (word) inventar, acuñar.

coinage ['kɔɪnɪdʒ] n moneda.

coin-box ['kɔɪnbɔks] n (BRIT) caja recaudadora.

coincide [kəuɪn'saɪd] vi coincidir.

coincidence [kəu'ɪnsɪdəns] n casualidad f, coincidencia.

coin-operated ['kɔɪn'ɔpəreɪtɪd] adj (machine) que funciona con monedas.

Coke ® [kəuk] n Coca Cola ® f.

coke [kəuk] n (coal) coque m.

Col. abbr (= colonel) col; (US) = Colorado.

COLA n abbr (US: = cost-of-living adjustment) reajuste salarial de acuerdo con el coste de la vida.

colander ['kɔləndə*] n escurridor m.

cold [kəuld] adj frío ♦ n frío; (MED) resfriado; **it's** ~ hace frío; **to be** ~ tener frío; **to catch a** ~ coger un catarro, resfriarse, acatarrarse; **in** ~ **blood** a sangre fría; **the room's getting** ~ está empezando a hacer frío en la habitación; **to give sb the** ~ **shoulder** tratar a algn con frialdad.

cold-blooded ['kəuld'blʌdɪd] adj (ZOOL) de sangre fría.

cold cream n crema.

coldly ['kəuldlɪ] adj fríamente.

cold sore n calentura, herpes m labial.

cold sweat n: **to be in a** ~ **(about sth)** tener sudores fríos (por algo).

cold turkey n (col) mono.

Cold War n: **the** ~ la guerra fría.

coleslaw ['kəulslɔː] n ensalada de col con zanahoria.

colic ['kɔlɪk] n cólico.

colicky ['kɔlɪkɪ] adj: **to be** ~ tener un cólico.

collaborate [kə'læbəreɪt] vi colaborar.

collaboration [kəlæbə'reɪʃən] n colaboración f; (POL) colaboracionismo.

collaborator [kə'læbəreɪtə*] n colaborador(a) m/f; (POL) colaboracionista m/f.

collage [kɔ'lɑːʒ] n collage m.

collagen ['kɔlədʒən] n colágeno.

collapse [kə'læps] vi (gen) hundirse, derrumbarse; (MED) sufrir un colapso ♦ n (gen) hundimiento; (MED) colapso; (of government) caída; (of plans, scheme) fracaso; (of business) ruina.

collapsible [kə'læpsəbl] adj plegable.

collar ['kɔlə*] n (of coat, shirt) cuello; (for dog, TECH) collar m ♦ vt (col: person) agarrar; (: object) birlar.

collarbone ['kɔləbəun] n clavícula.

collate [kɔ'leɪt] vt cotejar.

collateral [kɔ'lætərəl] n (COMM) garantía subsidiaria.

collation [kə'leɪʃən] n colación f.

colleague ['kɔliːg] n colega m/f, compañero/a m/f.

collect [kə'lɛkt] vt reunir; (as a hobby) coleccionar; (BRIT: call and pick up) recoger; (wages) cobrar; (debts) recaudar; (donations, subscriptions) colectar ♦ vi (crowd) reunirse ♦ adv: **to call** ~ (US TEL) llamar a cobro revertido; **to** ~ **one's thoughts** reponerse, recobrar el dominio de sí mismo; ~ **on delivery (COD)** (US) entrega contra reembolso.

collection [kə'lɛkʃən] *n* colección *f*; (*of fares, wages*) cobro; (*of post*) recogida.

collective [kə'lɛktɪv] *adj* colectivo.

collective bargaining *n* negociación *f* del convenio colectivo.

collector [kə'lɛktə*] *n* coleccionista *m/f*; (*of taxes etc*) recaudador(a) *m/f*; ~**'s item** or **piece** pieza de coleccionista.

college ['kɔlɪdʒ] *n* colegio; (*of technology, agriculture etc*) escuela.

collide [kə'laɪd] *vi* chocar.

collie ['kɔlɪ] *n* (*dog*) collie *m*, perro pastor escocés.

colliery ['kɔlɪərɪ] *n* (*BRIT*) mina de carbón.

collision [kə'lɪʒən] *n* choque *m*, colisión *f*; **to be on a** ~ **course** (*also fig*) ir rumbo al desastre.

colloquial [kə'ləukwɪəl] *adj* coloquial.

collusion [kə'luːʒən] *n* confabulación *f*, connivencia; **in** ~ **with** en connivencia con.

Colo. *abbr* (*US*) = *Colorado.*

cologne [kə'ləun] *n* (*also*: **eau de** ~) (agua de) colonia.

Colombia [kə'lɔmbɪə] *n* Colombia.

Colombian [kə'lɔmbɪən] *adj, n* colombiano/a *m/f*.

colon ['kəulən] *n* (*sign*) dos puntos; (*MED*) colon *m*.

colonel ['kɜːnl] *n* coronel *m*.

colonial [kə'ləunɪəl] *adj* colonial.

colonize ['kɔlənaɪz] *vt* colonizar.

colonnade [kɔlə'neɪd] *n* columnata.

colony ['kɔlənɪ] *n* colonia.

color ['kʌlə*] *etc* (*US*) = **colour.**

Colorado beetle [kɔlə'rɑːdəu-] *n* escarabajo de la patata.

colossal [kə'lɔsl] *adj* colosal.

colour, (*US*) **color** ['kʌlə*] *n* color *m* ♦ *vt* colorear, pintar; (*dye*) teñir ♦ *vi* (*blush*) sonrojarse; ~**s** *npl* (*of party, club*) colores *mpl*.

colo(u)r bar *n* segregación *f* racial.

colo(u)r-blind ['kʌləblaɪnd] *adj* daltónico.

colo(u)red ['kʌləd] *adj* de color; (*photo*) en color; (*of race*) de color.

colo(u)r film *n* película en color.

colo(u)rful ['kʌləful] *adj* lleno de color; (*person*) pintoresco.

colo(u)ring ['kʌlərɪŋ] *n* colorido, color; (*substance*) colorante *m*.

colo(u)rless ['kʌləlɪs] *adj* incoloro, sin color.

colo(u)r scheme *n* combinación *f* de colores.

colour supplement *n* (*BRIT PRESS*) suplemento semanal *or* dominical.

colo(u)r television *n* televisión *f* en color.

colt [kəult] *n* potro.

column ['kɔləm] *n* columna; (*fashion* ~, *sports* ~ *etc*) sección *f*, columna; **the** ~ el editorial.

columnist ['kɔləmnɪst] *n* columnista *m/f*.

coma ['kəumə] *n* coma *m*.

comb [kəum] *n* peine *m*; (*ornamental*) peineta ♦ *vt* (*hair*) peinar; (*area*) registrar a fondo, peinar.

combat ['kɔmbæt] *n* combate *m* ♦ *vt* combatir.

combination [kɔmbɪ'neɪʃən] *n* (*gen*) combinación *f*.

combination lock *n* cerradura de combinación.

combine [kəm'baɪn] *vt* combinar; (*qualities*) reunir ♦ *vi* combinarse ♦ *n* ['kɔmbaɪn] (*ECON*) cartel *m*; **a** ~**d effort** un esfuerzo conjunto.

combine (harvester) *n* cosechadora.

combo ['kɔmbəu] *n* (*JAZZ etc*) conjunto.

combustion [kəm'bʌstʃən] *n* combustión *f*.

═══════════════════════════ *KEYWORD*

come [kʌm] (*pt* **came**, *pp* **come**) *vi* **1** (*movement towards*) venir; **to** ~ **running** venir corriendo; ~ **with me** ven conmigo
2 (*arrive*) llegar; **he's** ~ **here to work** ha venido aquí para trabajar; **to** ~ **home** volver a casa; **we've just** ~ **from Seville** acabamos de llegar de Sevilla; **coming!** ¡voy!
3 (*reach*): **to** ~ **to** llegar a; **the bill came to £40** la cuenta ascendía a cuarenta libras
4 (*occur*): **an idea came to me** se me ocurrió una idea; **if it** ~**s to it** llegado el caso
5 (*be, become*): **to** ~ **loose/undone** *etc* aflojarse/desabrocharse, desatarse *etc*; **I've** ~ **to like him** por fin ha llegado a gustarme

►**come about** *vi* suceder, ocurrir

►**come across** *vt fus* (*person*) encontrarse con; (*thing*) encontrar ♦ *vi*: **to** ~ **across well/badly** causar buena/mala impresión

►**come away** *vi* (*leave*) marcharse; (*become detached*) desprenderse

►**come back** *vi* (*return*) volver; (*reply*): **can I** ~ **back to you on that one?** volvamos sobre ese punto

►**come by** *vt fus* (*acquire*) conseguir

►**come down** *vi* (*price*) bajar; (*building*) derrumbarse; (: *be demolished*) ser derribado

►**come forward** *vi* presentarse

►**come from** *vt fus* (*place, source*) ser de

►**come in** *vi* (*visitor*) entrar; (*train, report*)

llegar; (*fashion*) ponerse de moda; (*on deal etc*) entrar
▶**come in for** *vt fus* (*criticism etc*) recibir
▶**come into** *vt fus* (*money*) heredar; (*be involved*) tener que ver con; **to ~ into fashion** ponerse de moda
▶**come off** *vi* (*button*) soltarse, desprenderse; (*attempt*) salir bien
▶**come on** *vi* (*pupil, work, project*) marchar; (*lights*) encenderse; (*electricity*) volver; **~ on!** ¡vamos!
▶**come out** *vi* (*fact*) salir a la luz; (*book, sun*) salir; (*stain*) quitarse; **to ~ out (on strike)** declararse en huelga; **to ~ out for/against** declararse a favor/en contra de
▶**come over** *vt fus*: **I don't know what's ~ over him!** ¡no sé lo que le pasa!
▶**come round** *vi* (*after faint, operation*) volver en sí
▶**come through** *vi* (*survive*) sobrevivir; (*telephone call*): **the call came through** recibimos la llamada
▶**come to** *vi* (*wake*) volver en sí; (*total*) sumar; **how much does it ~ to?** ¿cuánto es en total?, ¿a cuánto asciende?
▶**come under** *vt fus* (*heading*) entrar dentro de; (*influence*) estar bajo
▶**come up** *vi* (*sun*) salir; (*problem*) surgir; (*event*) aproximarse; (*in conversation*) mencionarse
▶**come up against** *vt fus* (*resistance etc*) tropezar con
▶**come up to** *vt fus* llegar hasta; **the film didn't ~ up to our expectations** la película no fue tan buena como esperábamos
▶**come up with** *vt fus* (*idea*) sugerir; (*money*) conseguir
▶**come upon** *vt fus* (*find*) dar con.

comeback ['kʌmbæk] *n* (*reaction*) reacción *f*; (*response*) réplica; **to make a ~** (*THEAT*) volver a las tablas.
Comecon ['kɔmɪkɔn] *n abbr* (= *Council for Mutual Economic Aid*) COMECON *m*.
comedian [kə'miːdɪən] *n* humorista *m*.
comedienne [kəmiːdɪ'ɛn] *n* humorista.
comedown ['kʌmdaun] *n* revés *m*.
comedy ['kɔmɪdɪ] *n* comedia.
comet ['kɔmɪt] *n* cometa *m*.
comeuppance [kʌm'ʌpəns] *n*: **to get one's ~** llevar su merecido.
comfort ['kʌmfət] *n* comodidad *f*, confort *m*; (*well-being*) bienestar *m*; (*solace*) consuelo; (*relief*) alivio ♦ *vt* consolar; *see also* **comforts.**
comfortable ['kʌmfətəbl] *adj* cómodo;

(*income*) adecuado; (*majority*) suficiente; **I don't feel very ~ about it** la cosa me tiene algo preocupado.
comfortably ['kʌmfətəblɪ] *adv* (*sit*) cómodamente; (*live*) holgadamente.
comforter ['kʌmfətə*] *n* (*US: pacifier*) chupete *m*; (: *bed cover*) colcha.
comforts ['kʌmfəts] *npl* comodidades *fpl*.
comfort station *n* (*US*) servicios *mpl*.
comic ['kɔmɪk] *adj* (*also*: ~**al**) cómico, gracioso ♦ *n* (*magazine*) tebeo; (*for adults*) cómic *m*.
comic strip *n* tira cómica.
coming ['kʌmɪŋ] *n* venida, llegada ♦ *adj* que viene; (*next*) próximo; (*future*) venidero; ~**(s) and going(s)** *n(pl)* ir y venir *m*, ajetreo; **in the ~ weeks** en las próximas semanas.
Comintern ['kɔmɪntɔːn] *n* Comintern *m*.
comma ['kɔmə] *n* coma.
command [kə'mɑːnd] *n* orden *f*, mandato; (*MIL: authority*) mando; (*mastery*) dominio; (*COMPUT*) orden *f*, comando ♦ *vt* (*troops*) mandar; (*give orders to*) mandar, ordenar; (*be able to get*) disponer de; (*deserve*) merecer; **to have at one's ~** (*money, resources etc*) disponer de; **to have/take ~ of** estar al/asumir el mando de.
command economy *n* economía dirigida.
commandeer [kɔmən'dɪə*] *vt* requisar.
commander [kə'mɑːndə*] *n* (*MIL*) comandante *m/f*, jefe/a *m/f*.
commanding [kə'mɑːndɪŋ] *adj* (*appearance*) imponente; (*voice, tone*) imperativo; (*lead*) abrumador(a); (*position*) dominante.
commanding officer *n* comandante *m*.
commandment [kə'mɑːndmənt] *n* (*REL*) mandamiento.
command module *n* módulo de mando.
commando [kə'mɑːndəu] *n* comando.
commemorate [kə'mɛməreɪt] *vt* conmemorar.
commemoration [kəmɛmə'reɪʃən] *n* conmemoración *f*.
commemorative [kə'mɛmərətɪv] *adj* conmemorativo.
commence [kə'mɛns] *vt, vi* comenzar.
commend [kə'mɛnd] *vt* (*praise*) elogiar, alabar; (*recommend*) recomendar; (*entrust*) encomendar.
commendable [kə'mɛndəbl] *adj* encomiable.
commendation [kɔmɛn'deɪʃən] *n* (*for bravery etc*) elogio, encomio.
commensurate [kə'mɛnʃərɪt] *adj*: ~ **with** en proporción a.
comment ['kɔmɛnt] *n* comentario ♦ *vt*: **to ~**

that comentar *or* observar que ♦ *vi*: **to ~ (on)** comentar, hacer comentarios (sobre); "**no ~**" "no tengo nada que decir", "sin comentarios".

commentary ['kɔməntərɪ] *n* comentario.

commentator ['kɔmənteɪtə*] *n* comentarista *m/f*.

commerce ['kɔmə:s] *n* comercio.

commercial [kə'mə:ʃəl] *adj* comercial ♦ *n* (*TV*) anuncio.

commercial bank *n* banco comercial.

commercial break *n* intermedio para publicidad.

commercialism [kə'mə:ʃəlɪzəm] *n* comercialismo.

commercial television *n* televisión *f* comercial.

commercial vehicle *n* vehículo comercial.

commiserate [kə'mɪzəreɪt] *vi*: **to ~ with** compadecerse de, condolerse de.

commission [kə'mɪʃən] *n* (*committee, fee, order for work of art etc*) comisión *f*; (*act*) perpetración *f* ♦ *vt* (*MIL*) nombrar; (*work of art*) encargar; **out of ~** (*machine*) fuera de servicio; **~ of inquiry** comisión *f* investigadora; **I get 10% ~** me dan el diez por ciento de comisión; **to ~ sb to do sth** encargar a algn que haga algo; **to ~ sth from sb** (*painting etc*) encargar algo a algn.

commissionaire [kəmɪʃə'nɛə*] *n* (*BRIT*) portero, conserje *m*.

commissioner [kə'mɪʃənə*] *n* comisario; (*POLICE*) comisario *m* de policía.

commit [kə'mɪt] *vt* (*act*) cometer; (*to sb's care*) entregar; **to ~ o.s. (to do)** comprometerse (a hacer); **to ~ suicide** suicidarse; **to ~ sb for trial** remitir a algn al tribunal.

commitment [kə'mɪtmənt] *n* compromiso.

committed [kə'mɪtɪd] *adj* (*writer, politician etc*) comprometido.

committee [kə'mɪtɪ] *n* comité *m*; **to be on a ~** ser miembro/a de un comité.

committee meeting *n* reunión *f* del comité.

commodious [kə'məudɪəs] *adj* grande, espacioso.

commodity [kə'mɔdɪtɪ] *n* mercancía.

commodity exchange *n* bolsa de productos *or* de mercancías.

commodity market *n* mercado de productos básicos.

commodore ['kɔmədɔ:*] *n* comodoro.

common ['kɔmən] *adj* (*gen*) común; (*pej*) ordinario ♦ *n* campo común; **in ~** en común; **in ~ use** de uso corriente.

common cold *n*: **the ~** el resfriado.

common denominator *n* común denominador *m*.

commoner ['kɔmənə*] *n* plebeyo/a.

common land *n* campo comunal, ejido.

common law *n* ley *f* consuetudinaria.

common-law ['kɔmənlɔ:] *adj*: **~ wife** esposa de hecho.

commonly ['kɔmənlɪ] *adv* comúnmente.

Common Market *n* Mercado Común.

commonplace ['kɔmənpleɪs] *adj* corriente.

commonroom ['kɔmənrum] *n* sala de reunión.

Commons ['kɔmənz] *npl* (*BRIT POL*): **the ~** (la Cámara de) los Comunes.

common sense *n* sentido común.

Commonwealth ['kɔmənwɛlθ] *n*: **the ~** la Comunidad (Británica) de Naciones, la Commonwealth; *ver recuadro.*

COMMONWEALTH

La **Commonwealth** es la asociación de estados soberanos independientes y territorios asociados que formaban parte del antiguo Imperio Británico. Éste pasó a llamarse así después de la Segunda Guerra Mundial, aunque ya desde 1931 se le conocía como "British Commonwealth of Nations". Todos los estados miembros reconocen al monarca británico como "Head of the Commonwealth".

---

commotion [kə'məuʃən] *n* tumulto, confusión *f*.

communal ['kɔmju:nl] *adj* comunal; (*kitchen*) común.

commune ['kɔmju:n] *n* (*group*) comuna ♦ *vi* [kə'mju:n]: **to ~ with** comunicarse con.

communicate [kə'mju:nɪkeɪt] *vt* comunicar ♦ *vi*: **to ~ (with)** comunicarse (con).

communication [kəmju:nɪ'keɪʃən] *n* comunicación *f*.

communications network *n* red *f* de comunicaciones.

communications satellite *n* satélite *m* de comunicaciones.

communicative [kə'mju:nɪkətɪv] *adj* comunicativo.

communion [kə'mju:nɪən] *n* (*also*: **Holy C~**) comunión *f*.

communiqué [kə'mju:nɪkeɪ] *n* comunicado, parte *m*.

communism ['kɔmjunɪzəm] *n* comunismo.

communist ['kɔmjunɪst] *adj, n* comunista *m/f*.

community [kə'mju:nɪtɪ] *n* comunidad *f*; (*large group*) colectividad *f*; (*local*)

vecindario.
community centre n centro social.
community chest n (US) fondo social.
community health centre n centro médico, casa de salud.
community spirit n civismo.
commutation ticket [kɔmju'teɪʃən-] n (US) billete m de abono.
commute [kə'mjuːt] vi viajar a diario de casa al trabajo ♦ vt conmutar.
commuter [kə'mjuːtə*] n persona que viaja a diario de casa al trabajo.
compact [kəm'pækt] adj compacto; (style) conciso; (packed) apretado ♦ n ['kɔmpækt] (pact) pacto; (also: **powder** ~) polvera.
compact disc n compact disc m, disco compacto.
compact disc player n lector m or reproductor m de discos compactos.
companion [kəm'pænɪən] n compañero/a.
companionship [kəm'pænjənʃɪp] n compañerismo.
companionway [kəm'pænjənweɪ] n (NAUT) escalerilla.
company ['kʌmpənɪ] n (gen) compañía; (COMM) empresa, compañía; **to keep sb** ~ acompañar a algn; **Smith and C**~ Smith y Compañía.
company car n coche m de la empresa.
company director n director(a) m/f de empresa.
company secretary n (BRIT) administrador(a) m/f de empresa.
comparable ['kɔmpərəbl] adj comparable.
comparative [kəm'pærətɪv] adj (freedom, luxury, cost) relativo; (study, linguistics) comparado.
comparatively [kəm'pærətɪvlɪ] adv (relatively) relativamente.
compare [kəm'pɛə*] vt comparar ♦ vi: **to** ~ **(with)** poder compararse (con); ~**d with** or **to** comparado con or a; **how do the prices** ~? ¿cómo son los precios en comparación?
comparison [kəm'pærɪsn] n comparación f; **in** ~ **(with)** en comparación (con).
compartment [kəm'pɑːtmənt] n compartim(i)ento; (RAIL) departamento, compartimiento.
compass ['kʌmpəs] n brújula; ~**es** npl compás m; **within the** ~ **of** al alcance de.
compassion [kəm'pæʃən] n compasión f.
compassionate [kəm'pæʃənɪt] adj compasivo; **on** ~ **grounds** por compasión.
compassionate leave n permiso por asuntos familiares.
compatibility [kəmpætɪ'bɪlɪtɪ] n compatibilidad f.

compatible [kəm'pætɪbl] adj compatible.
compel [kəm'pɛl] vt obligar.
compelling [kəm'pɛlɪŋ] adj (fig: argument) convincente.
compendium [kəm'pɛndɪəm] n compendio.
compensate ['kɔmpənseɪt] vt compensar ♦ vi: **to** ~ **for** compensar.
compensation [kɔmpən'seɪʃən] n (for loss) indemnización f.
compère ['kɔmpɛə*] n presentador(a) m/f.
compete [kəm'piːt] vi (take part) competir; (vie with) competir, hacer la competencia.
competence ['kɔmpɪtəns] n capacidad f, aptitud f.
competent ['kɔmpɪtənt] adj competente, capaz.
competing [kəm'piːtɪŋ] adj (rival) competidor(a); (ideas) contrapuesto.
competition [kɔmpɪ'tɪʃən] n (contest) concurso; (SPORT) competición f; (ECON, rivalry) competencia; **in** ~ **with** en competencia con.
competitive [kəm'pɛtɪtɪv] adj (ECON, SPORT) competitivo; (spirit) competidor(a), de competencia; (selection) por concurso.
competitor [kəm'pɛtɪtə*] n (rival) competidor(a) m/f; (participant) concursante m/f.
compile [kəm'paɪl] vt recopilar.
complacency [kəm'pleɪsnsɪ] n autosatisfacción f.
complacent [kəm'pleɪsənt] adj autocomplaciente.
complain [kəm'pleɪn] vi (gen) quejarse; (COMM) reclamar.
complaint [kəm'pleɪnt] n (gen) queja; (COMM) reclamación f; (LAW) demanda, querella; (MED) enfermedad f.
complement ['kɔmplɪmənt] n complemento; (esp ship's crew) dotación f ♦ vt ['kɔmplɪmɛnt] (enhance) complementar.
complementary [kɔmplɪ'mɛntərɪ] adj complementario.
complete [kəm'pliːt] adj (full) completo; (finished) acabado ♦ vt (fulfil) completar; (finish) acabar; (a form) rellenar; **it's a** ~ **disaster** es un desastre total.
completely [kəm'pliːtlɪ] adv completamente.
completion [kəm'pliːʃən] n (gen) conclusión f, terminación f; **to be nearing** ~ estar a punto de terminarse; **on** ~ **of contract** cuando se realice el contrato.
complex ['kɔmplɛks] adj complejo ♦ n (gen) complejo.
complexion [kəm'plɛkʃən] n (of face) tez f,

cutis *m*; (*fig*) aspecto.
complexity [kəm'plɛksɪtɪ] *n* complejidad *f*.
compliance [kəm'plaɪəns] *n* (*submission*) sumisión *f*; (*agreement*) conformidad *f*; **in ~ with** de acuerdo con.
compliant [kəm'plaɪənt] *adj* sumiso; conforme.
complicate ['kɒmplɪkeɪt] *vt* complicar.
complicated ['kɒmplɪkeɪtɪd] *adj* complicado.
complication [kɒmplɪ'keɪʃən] *n* complicación *f*.
complicity [kəm'plɪsɪtɪ] *n* complicidad *f*.
compliment ['kɒmplɪmənt] *n* (*formal*) cumplido; (*flirtation*) piropo ♦ *vt* felicitar; ~**s** *npl* saludos *mpl*; **to pay sb a ~** (*formal*) hacer cumplidos a algn; (*flirt*) piropear, echar piropos a algn; **to ~ sb (on sth/on doing sth)** felicitar a algn (por algo/por haber hecho algo).
complimentary [kɒmplɪ'mɛntərɪ] *adj* elogioso; (*copy*) de regalo; ~ **ticket** invitación *f*.
compliments slip *n* saluda *m*.
comply [kəm'plaɪ] *vi*: **to ~ with** acatar.
component [kəm'pəʊnənt] *adj* componente ♦ *n* (*TECH*) pieza, componente *m*.
compose [kəm'pəʊz] *vt* componer; **to be ~d of** componerse de, constar de; **to ~ o.s.** tranquilizarse.
composed [kəm'pəʊzd] *adj* sosegado.
composer [kəm'pəʊzə*] *n* (*MUS*) compositor(a) *m/f*.
composite ['kɒmpəzɪt] *adj* compuesto; ~ **motion** (*COMM*) moción *f* compuesta.
composition [kɒmpə'zɪʃən] *n* composición *f*.
compos mentis ['kɒmpəs'mɛntɪs] *adj*: **to be ~** estar en su sano juicio.
compost ['kɒmpɒst] *n* abono.
compost heap *n montón de basura orgánica para abono*.
composure [kəm'pəʊʒə*] *n* serenidad *f*, calma.
compound ['kɒmpaʊnd] *n* (*CHEM*) compuesto; (*LING*) término compuesto; (*enclosure*) recinto ♦ *adj* (*gen*) compuesto; (*fracture*) complicado ♦ *vt* [kəm'paʊnd] (*fig: problem, difficulty*) agravar.
comprehend [kɒmprɪ'hɛnd] *vt* comprender.
comprehension [kɒmprɪ'hɛnʃən] *n* comprensión *f*.
comprehensive [kɒmprɪ'hɛnsɪv] *adj* (*broad*) extenso; (*general*) de conjunto; ~ (**school**) *n centro estatal de enseñanza secundaria*, ≈ Instituto Nacional de Bachillerato (*SP*); *ver recuadro*.

COMPREHENSIVE SCHOOL

En los años 60 se creó un nuevo tipo de centro educativo de enseñanza secundaria (aproximadamente de los once años en adelante) denominado **comprehensive school**, *abierto a todos los alumnos independientemente de sus capacidades, con el que se intentó poner fin a la división tradicional entre centros de enseñanzas teóricas para acceder a la educación superior (*"grammar schools"*) y otros de enseñanzas básicamente profesionales (*"secondary modern schools"*).*

comprehensive insurance policy *n* seguro a todo riesgo.
compress [kəm'prɛs] *vt* comprimir ♦ *n* ['kɒmprɛs] (*MED*) compresa.
comprise [kəm'praɪz] *vt* (*also*: **be ~d of**) comprender, constar de.
compromise ['kɒmprəmaɪz] *n* solución *f* intermedia; (*agreement*) arreglo ♦ *vt* comprometer ♦ *vi* transigir, transar (*LAM*) ♦ *cpd* (*decision, solution*) de término medio.
compulsion [kəm'pʌlʃən] *n* obligación *f*; **under ~** a la fuerza, por obligación.
compulsive [kəm'pʌlsɪv] *adj* compulsivo.
compulsory [kəm'pʌlsərɪ] *adj* obligatorio.
compulsory purchase *n* expropiación *f*.
compunction [kəm'pʌŋkʃən] *n* escrúpulo; **to have no ~ about doing sth** no tener escrúpulos en hacer algo.
computer [kəm'pjuːtə*] *n* ordenador *m*, computador *m*, computadora.
computer game *n* juego de ordenador.
computerize [kəm'pjuːtəraɪz] *vt* (*data*) computerizar; (*system*) informatizar.
computer language *n* lenguaje *m* de ordenador *or* computadora.
computer literate *adj*: **to be ~** tener conocimientos de informática a nivel de usuario.
computer peripheral *n* periférico.
computer program *n* programa *m* informático *or* de ordenador.
computer programmer *n* programador(a) *m/f*.
computer programming *n* programación *f*.
computer science *n* informática.
computing [kəm'pjuːtɪŋ] *n* (*activity*) informática.
comrade ['kɒmrɪd] *n* compañero/a.
comradeship ['kɒmrɪdʃɪp] *n* camaradería, compañerismo.
comsat ® ['kɒmsæt] *n abbr*

= **communications satellite**.
con [kɔn] *vt* timar, estafar ♦ *n* timo, estafa;
  to ~ sb into doing sth (*col*) engañar a
  algn para que haga algo.
concave ['kɔn'keɪv] *adj* cóncavo.
conceal [kən'siːl] *vt* ocultar; (*thoughts etc*)
  disimular.
concede [kən'siːd] *vt* reconocer; (*game*)
  darse por vencido en; (*territory*) ceder ♦ *vi*
  darse por vencido.
conceit [kən'siːt] *n* orgullo,
  presunción *f*.
conceited [kən'siːtɪd] *adj* orgulloso.
conceivable [kən'siːvəbl] *adj* concebible; **it
  is ~ that** ... es posible que ....
conceivably [kən'siːvəblɪ] *adv*: **he may ~ be
  right** es posible que tenga razón.
conceive [kən'siːv] *vt, vi* concebir; **to ~ of
  sth/of doing sth** imaginar algo/
  imaginarse haciendo algo.
concentrate ['kɔnsəntreɪt] *vi* concentrarse
  ♦ *vt* concentrar.
concentration [kɔnsən'treɪʃən] *n*
  concentración *f*.
concentration camp *n* campo de
  concentración.
concentric [kən'sɛntrɪk] *adj* concéntrico.
concept ['kɔnsɛpt] *n* concepto.
conception [kən'sɛpʃən] *n* (*idea*) concepto,
  idea; (*BIOL*) concepción *f*.
concern [kən'səːn] *n* (*matter*) asunto;
  (*COMM*) empresa; (*anxiety*) preocupación *f*
  ♦ *vt* tener que ver con; (*affect*) atañer,
  concernir; **to be ~ed (about)** interesarse
  (por), preocuparse (por); **to be ~ed with**
  tratar de; **"to whom it may ~"** "a quien
  corresponda"; **the department ~ed**
  (*under discussion*) el departamento en
  cuestión; (*relevant*) el departamento
  competente; **as far as I am ~ed** en cuanto
  a mí, por lo que a mí se refiere.
concerning [kən'səːnɪŋ] *prep* sobre, acerca
  de.
concert ['kɔnsət] *n* concierto.
concerted [kən'səːtəd] *adj* (*efforts etc*)
  concertado.
concert hall *n* sala de conciertos.
concertina [kɔnsə'tiːnə] *n* concertina.
concerto [kən'tʃəːtəu] *n* concierto.
concession [kən'sɛʃən] *n* concesión *f*; (*price
  ~*) descuento; **tax ~** privilegio fiscal.
concessionaire [kənsɛʃə'nɛə*] *n*
  concesionario/a.
concessionary [kən'sɛʃənərɪ] *adj* (*ticket,
  fare*) con descuento, a precio reducido.
conciliation [kənsɪlɪ'eɪʃən] *n* conciliación *f*.
conciliatory [kən'sɪlɪətrɪ] *adj*
  conciliador(a).

concise [kən'saɪs] *adj* conciso.
conclave ['kɔnkleɪv] *n* cónclave *m*.
conclude [kən'kluːd] *vt* (*finish*) concluir;
  (*treaty etc*) firmar; (*agreement*) llegar a;
  (*decide*): **to ~ that** ... llegar a la
  conclusión de que ... ♦ *vi* (*events*)
  concluir, terminar.
concluding [kən'kluːdɪŋ] *adj* (*remarks etc*)
  final.
conclusion [kən'kluːʒən] *n* conclusión *f*; **to
  come to the ~ that** llegar a la conclusión
  de que.
conclusive [kən'kluːsɪv] *adj* decisivo,
  concluyente.
conclusively [kən'kluːsɪvlɪ] *adv*
  concluyentemente.
concoct [kən'kɔkt] *vt* (*food, drink*) preparar;
  (*story*) inventar; (*plot*) tramar.
concoction [kən'kɔkʃən] *n* (*food*) mezcla;
  (*drink*) brebaje *m*.
concord ['kɔnkɔːd] *n* (*harmony*) concordia;
  (*treaty*) acuerdo.
concourse ['kɔŋkɔːs] *n* (*hall*) vestíbulo.
concrete ['kɔnkriːt] *n* hormigón *m* ♦ *adj*
  concreto.
concrete mixer *n* hormigonera.
concur [kən'kəː*] *vi* estar de acuerdo.
concurrently [kən'kʌrntlɪ] *adv* al mismo
  tiempo.
concussion [kən'kʌʃən] *n* conmoción *f*
  cerebral.
condemn [kən'dɛm] *vt* condenar.
condemnation [kɔndɛm'neɪʃən] *n* (*gen*)
  condena; (*blame*) censura.
condensation [kɔndɛn'seɪʃən] *n*
  condensación *f*.
condense [kən'dɛns] *vi* condensarse ♦ *vt*
  condensar; (*text*) abreviar.
condensed milk *n* leche *f* condensada.
condescend [kɔndɪ'sɛnd] *vi* condescender;
  to ~ to sb tratar a algn con
  condescendencia; **to ~ to do sth** dignarse
  hacer algo.
condescending [kɔndɪ'sɛndɪŋ] *adj*
  superior.
condition [kən'dɪʃən] *n* condición *f*; (*of
  health*) estado; (*disease*) enfermedad *f* ♦ *vt*
  condicionar; **on ~ that** a condición (de)
  que; **weather ~s** condiciones
  atmosféricas; **in good/poor ~** en buenas/
  malas condiciones, en buen/mal estado;
  ~s of sale condiciones de venta.
conditional [kən'dɪʃənl] *adj* condicional.
conditioned reflex [kən'dɪʃənd-] *n* reflejo
  condicionado.
conditioner [kən'dɪʃənə*] *n* (*for hair*)
  suavizante *m*, acondicionador *m*.
condo ['kɔndəu] *n* (*US col*) = **condominium**.

condolences [kən'dəulənsɪz] *npl* pésame *msg*.

condom ['kɔndəm] *n* condón *m*.

condominium [kɔndə'mɪnɪəm] *n* (*US*: *building*) bloque *m* de pisos *or* apartamentos (*propiedad de quienes lo habitan*), condominio (*LAM*); (: *apartment*) piso *or* apartamento (en propiedad), condominio (*LAM*).

condone [kən'dəun] *vt* condonar.

conducive [kən'djuːsɪv] *adj*: ~ **to** conducente a.

conduct ['kɔndʌkt] *n* conducta, comportamiento ♦ *vt* [kən'dʌkt] (*lead*) conducir; (*manage*) llevar, dirigir; (*MUS*) dirigir ♦ *vi* (*MUS*) llevar la batuta; **to ~ o.s.** comportarse.

conducted tour *n* (*BRIT*) visita con guía.

conductor [kən'dʌktə*] *n* (*of orchestra*) director(a) *m/f*; (*US*: *on train*) revisor(a) *m/ f*; (*on bus*) cobrador *m*; (*ELEC*) conductor *m*.

cone [kəun] *n* cono; (*pine* ~) piña; (*for ice cream*) cucurucho.

confectioner [kən'fɛkʃənə*] *n* (*of cakes*) pastelero/a; (*of sweets*) confitero/a; ~'**s (shop)** *n* pastelería; confitería.

confectionery [kən'fɛkʃənrɪ] *n* pasteles *mpl*; dulces *mpl*.

confederate [kən'fɛdrɪt] *adj* confederado ♦ *n* (*pej*) cómplice *m/f*; (*US*: *HISTORY*) confederado/a.

confederation [kənfɛdə'reɪʃən] *n* confederación *f*.

confer [kən'fəː*] *vt* otorgar (*on* a) ♦ *vi* conferenciar; **to ~ (with sb about sth)** consultar (con algn sobre algo).

conference ['kɔnfərns] *n* (*meeting*) reunión *f*; (*convention*) congreso; **to be in ~** estar en una reunión.

conference room *n* sala de conferencias.

confess [kən'fɛs] *vt* confesar ♦ *vi* confesar; (*REL*) confesarse.

confession [kən'fɛʃən] *n* confesión *f*.

confessional [kən'fɛʃənl] *n* confesionario.

confessor [kən'fɛsə*] *n* confesor *m*.

confetti [kən'fɛtɪ] *n* confeti *m*.

confide [kən'faɪd] *vi*: **to ~ in** confiar en.

confidence ['kɔnfɪdns] *n* (*gen, also*: **self-**~) confianza; (*secret*) confidencia; **in ~ (*speak, write*) en confianza; **to have (every) ~ that** estar seguro *or* confiado de que; **motion of no ~** moción *f* de censura; **to tell sb sth in strict ~** decir algo a algn de manera confidencial.

confidence trick *n* timo.

confident ['kɔnfɪdənt] *adj* seguro de sí mismo.

confidential [kɔnfɪ'dɛnʃəl] *adj* confidencial; (*secretary*) de confianza.

confidentiality [kɔnfɪdɛnʃɪ'ælɪtɪ] *n* confidencialidad *f*.

configuration [kənfɪɡju'reɪʃən] *n* (*also COMPUT*) configuración *f*.

confine [kən'faɪn] *vt* (*limit*) limitar; (*shut up*) encerrar; **to ~ o.s. to doing sth** limitarse a hacer algo.

confined [kən'faɪnd] *adj* (*space*) reducido.

confinement [kən'faɪnmənt] *n* (*prison*) reclusión *f*; (*MED*) parto; **in solitary ~** incomunicado.

confines ['kɔnfaɪnz] *npl* confines *mpl*.

confirm [kən'fəːm] *vt* confirmar.

confirmation [kɔnfə'meɪʃən] *n* confirmación *f*.

confirmed [kən'fəːmd] *adj* empedernido.

confiscate ['kɔnfɪskeɪt] *vt* confiscar.

confiscation [kɔnfɪs'keɪʃən] *n* incautación *f*.

conflagration [kɔnflə'ɡreɪʃən] *n* conflagración *f*.

conflict ['kɔnflɪkt] *n* conflicto ♦ *vi* [kən'flɪkt] (*opinions*) estar reñido; (*reports, evidence*) contradecirse.

conflicting [kən'flɪktɪŋ] *adj* (*reports, evidence, opinions*) contradictorio.

conform [kən'fɔːm] *vi*: **to ~ to** (*laws*) someterse a; (*usages, mores*) amoldarse a; (*standards*) ajustarse a.

conformist [kən'fɔːmɪst] *n* conformista *m/f*.

confound [kən'faund] *vt* confundir; (*amaze*) pasmar.

confounded [kən'faundɪd] *adj* condenado.

confront [kən'frʌnt] *vt* (*problems*) hacer frente a; (*enemy, danger*) enfrentarse con.

confrontation [kɔnfrən'teɪʃən] *n* enfrentamiento, confrontación *f*.

confrontational [kɔnfrən'teɪʃənl] *adj* conflictivo.

confuse [kən'fjuːz] *vt* (*perplex*) desconcertar; (*mix up*) confundir.

confused [kən'fjuːzd] *adj* confuso; (*person*) desconcertado; **to get ~** desconcertarse; (*muddled up*) hacerse un lío.

confusing [kən'fjuːzɪŋ] *adj* confuso.

confusion [kən'fjuːʒən] *n* confusión *f*.

congeal [kən'dʒiːl] *vi* coagularse.

congenial [kən'dʒiːnɪəl] *adj* agradable.

congenital [kən'dʒɛnɪtl] *adj* congénito.

congested [kən'dʒɛstɪd] *adj* (*gen*) atestado; (*telephone lines*) saturado.

congestion [kən'dʒɛstʃən] *n* congestión *f*.

congestion charge(s) *n(pl)* tasa por congestión.

conglomerate [kən'ɡlɔmərət] *n* (*COMM, GEO*) conglomerado.

conglomeration [kəngləmə'reɪʃən] *n* conglomeración *f*.

Congo ['kɔŋgəu] *n* (*state*) Congo.

congratulate [kən'grætjuleɪt] *vt* felicitar.

congratulations [kəngrætju'leɪʃənz] *npl*: ~ **(on)** felicitaciones *fpl* (por); ~! ¡enhorabuena!, ¡felicidades!

congregate ['kɔŋgrɪgeɪt] *vi* congregarse.

congregation [kɔŋgrɪ'geɪʃən] *n* (*in church*) fieles *mpl*.

congress ['kɔŋgrɛs] *n* congreso; (*US POL*): **C~** el Congreso (de los Estados Unidos); *ver recuadro*.

CONGRESS

En el Congreso de los Estados Unidos (**Congress**) *se elaboran y aprueban las leyes federales. Consta de dos cámaras: la Cámara de Representantes* (*"House of Representatives"*), *cuyos 435 miembros son elegidos cada dos años por voto popular directo y en número proporcional a los habitantes de cada estado, y el Senado* (*"Senate"*), *con 100 senadores* (*"senators"*), *2 por estado, de los que un tercio se elige cada dos años y el resto cada seis.*

---

congressman ['kɔŋgrɛsmən] *n* (*US*) diputado, miembro del Congreso.

congresswoman ['kɔŋgrɛswumən] *n* (*US*) diputada, miembro *f* del Congreso.

conical ['kɔnɪkl] *adj* cónico.

conifer ['kɔnɪfə*] *n* conífera.

coniferous [kə'nɪfərəs] *adj* (*forest*) conífero.

conjecture [kən'dʒɛktʃə*] *n* conjetura.

conjugal ['kɔndʒugl] *adj* conyugal.

conjugate ['kɔndʒugeɪt] *vt* conjugar.

conjunction [kən'dʒʌŋkʃən] *n* conjunción *f*; **in ~ with** junto con.

conjunctivitis [kəndʒʌŋktɪ'vaɪtɪs] *n* conjuntivitis *f*.

conjure ['kʌndʒə*] *vi* hacer juegos de manos.

▶**conjure up** *vt* (*ghost, spirit*) hacer aparecer; (*memories*) evocar.

conjurer ['kʌndʒərə*] *n* ilusionista *m/f*.

conjuring trick ['kʌndʒərɪŋ-] *n* juego de manos.

conker ['kɔŋkə*] *n* (*BRIT*) castaño de Indias.

conk out [kɔŋk-] *vi* (*col*) estropearse, fastidiarse, descomponerse (*LAM*).

con man *n* timador *m*.

Conn. *abbr* (*US*) = *Connecticut*.

connect [kə'nɛkt] *vt* juntar, unir; (*ELEC*) conectar; (*pipes*) empalmar; (*fig*) relacionar, asociar ♦ *vi*: **to ~ with** (*train*)

enlazar con; **to be ~ed with** (*associated*) estar relacionado con; (*related*) estar emparentado con; **I am trying to ~ you** (*TEL*) estoy intentando ponerle al habla.

connection [kə'nɛkʃən] *n* juntura, unión *f*; (*ELEC*) conexión *f*; (*TECH*) empalme *m*; (*RAIL*) enlace *m*; (*TEL*) comunicación *f*; (*fig*) relación *f*; **what is the ~ between them?** ¿qué relación hay entre ellos?; **in ~ with** con respecto a, en relación a; **she has many business ~s** tiene muchos contactos profesionales; **to miss/make a ~** perder/coger el enlace.

connoisseur [kɔnɪ'sɜː*] *n* experto/a, entendido/a.

connotation [kɔnə'teɪʃən] *n* connotación *f*.

conquer ['kɔŋkə*] *vt* (*territory*) conquistar; (*enemy, feelings*) vencer.

conqueror ['kɔŋkərə*] *n* conquistador(a) *m/f*.

conquest ['kɔŋkwɛst] *n* conquista.

cons [kɔnz] *npl see* **convenience, pro.**

conscience ['kɔnʃəns] *n* conciencia; **in all ~** en conciencia.

conscientious [kɔnʃɪ'ɛnʃəs] *adj* concienzudo; (*objection*) de conciencia.

conscientious objector *n* objetor *m* de conciencia.

conscious ['kɔnʃəs] *adj* consciente; (*deliberate: insult, error*) premeditado, intencionado; **to become ~ of sth/that** darse cuenta de algo/de que.

consciousness ['kɔnʃəsnɪs] *n* conciencia; (*MED*) conocimiento.

conscript ['kɔnskrɪpt] *n* recluta *m/f*.

conscription [kən'skrɪpʃən] *n* servicio militar (obligatorio).

consecrate ['kɔnsɪkreɪt] *vt* consagrar.

consecutive [kən'sɛkjutɪv] *adj* consecutivo; **on 3 ~ occasions** en 3 ocasiones consecutivas.

consensus [kən'sɛnsəs] *n* consenso; **the ~ of opinion** el consenso general.

consent [kən'sɛnt] *n* consentimiento ♦ *vi*: **to ~ to** consentir en; **by common ~** de común acuerdo.

consequence ['kɔnsɪkwəns] *n* consecuencia; **in ~** por consiguiente.

consequently ['kɔnsɪkwəntlɪ] *adv* por consiguiente.

conservation [kɔnsə'veɪʃən] *n* conservación *f*; (*of nature*) conservación, protección *f*.

conservationist [kɔnsə'veɪʃnɪst] *n* conservacionista *m/f*.

conservative [kən'sɜːvətɪv] *adj* conservador(a); (*cautious*) moderado; **C~** *adj, n* (*BRIT POL*) conservador(a) *m/f*; **the**

C~ Party el partido conservador (británico).

conservatory [kən'sɔ:vətrɪ] *n* (*greenhouse*) invernadero.

conserve [kən'sɔ:v] *vt* conservar ♦ *n* conserva.

consider [kən'sɪdə*] *vt* considerar; (*take into account*) tomar en cuenta; (*study*) estudiar, examinar; **to ~ doing sth** pensar en (la posibilidad de) hacer algo; **all things ~ed** pensándolo bien; **~ yourself lucky** ¡date por satisfecho!

considerable [kən'sɪdərəbl] *adj* considerable.

considerably [kən'sɪdərəblɪ] *adv* bastante, considerablemente.

considerate [kən'sɪdərɪt] *adj* considerado.

consideration [kənsɪdə'reɪʃən] *n* consideración *f*; (*reward*) retribución *f*; **to be under ~** estar estudiándose; **my first ~ is my family** mi primera consideración es mi familia.

considered [kən'sɪdəd] *adj*: **it's my ~ opinion that ...** depués de haber reflexionado mucho, pienso que ....

considering [kən'sɪdərɪŋ] *prep*: **~ (that)** teniendo en cuenta (que).

consign [kən'saɪn] *vt* consignar.

consignee [kɔnsaɪ'ni:] *n* consignatario/a.

consignment [kɔn'saɪnmənt] *n* envío.

consignment note *n* (*COMM*) talón *m* de expedición.

consist [kən'sɪst] *vi*: **to ~ of** consistir en.

consistency [kən'sɪstənsɪ] *n* (*of person etc*) consecuencia, coherencia; (*thickness*) consistencia.

consistent [kən'sɪstənt] *adj* (*person, argument*) consecuente, coherente; (*results*) constante.

consolation [kɔnsə'leɪʃən] *n* consuelo.

console [kən'səul] *vt* consolar ♦ *n* ['kɔnsəul] (*control panel*) consola.

consolidate [kən'sɔlɪdeɪt] *vt* consolidar.

consols ['kɔnsɔlz] *npl* (*BRIT STOCK EXCHANGE*) valores *mpl* consolidados.

consommé [kən'sɔmeɪ] *n* consomé *m*, caldo.

consonant ['kɔnsənənt] *n* consonante *f*.

consort ['kɔnsɔ:t] *n* consorte *m/f* ♦ *vi* [kən'sɔ:t]: **to ~ with sb** (*often pej*) asociarse con algn; **prince ~** príncipe *m* consorte.

consortium [kən'sɔ:tɪəm] *n* consorcio.

conspicuous [kən'spɪkjuəs] *adj* (*visible*) visible; (*garish etc*) llamativo; (*outstanding*) notable; **to make o.s. ~** llamar la atención.

conspiracy [kən'spɪrəsɪ] *n* conjura, complot

m.

conspire [kən'spaɪə*] *vi* conspirar.

constable ['kʌnstəbl] *n* (*BRIT*) agente *m/f* (de policía); **chief ~** ≈ jefe *m/f* de policía.

constabulary [kən'stæbjulərɪ] *n* ≈ policía.

constancy ['kɔnstənsɪ] *n* constancia; fidelidad *f*.

constant ['kɔnstənt] *adj* (*gen*) constante; (*loyal*) leal, fiel.

constantly ['kɔnstəntlɪ] *adv* constantemente.

constellation [kɔnstə'leɪʃən] *n* constelación *f*.

consternation [kɔnstə'neɪʃən] *n* consternación *f*.

constipated ['kɔnstɪpeɪtəd] *adj* estreñido.

constipation [kɔnstɪ'peɪʃən] *n* estreñimiento.

constituency [kən'stɪtjuənsɪ] *n* (*POL*) distrito electoral; (*people*) electorado; *ver recuadro.*

CONSTITUENCY

Constituency *es la denominación que recibe un distrito o circunscripción electoral y el grupo de electores registrados en ella en el sistema electoral británico. Cada circunscripción elige a un diputado ("Member of Parliament"), el cual se halla disponible semanalmente para las consultas y peticiones de sus electores durante ciertas horas a la semana, tiempo al que se llama "surgery".*

---

constituency party *n* partido local.

constituent [kən'stɪtjuənt] *n* (*POL*) elector(a) *m/f*; (*part*) componente *m*.

constitute ['kɔnstɪtju:t] *vt* constituir.

constitution [kɔnstɪ'tju:ʃən] *n* constitución *f*.

constitutional [kɔnstɪ'tju:ʃənl] *adj* constitucional; **~ monarchy** monarquía constitucional.

constrain [kən'streɪn] *vt* obligar.

constrained [kən'streɪnd] *adj*: **to feel ~ to ...** sentirse obligado a ....

constraint [kən'streɪnt] *n* (*force*) fuerza; (*limit*) restricción *f*; (*restraint*) reserva; (*embarrassment*) cohibición *f*.

constrict [kən'strɪkt] *vt* oprimir.

constriction [kən'strɪkʃən] *n* constricción *f*, opresión *f*.

construct [kən'strʌkt] *vt* construir.

construction [kən'strʌkʃən] *n* construcción *f*; (*fig: interpretation*) interpretación *f*; **under ~** en construcción.

construction industry *n* industria de la

construcción.
constructive [kən'strʌktɪv] *adj*
constructivo.
construe [kən'struː] *vt* interpretar.
consul ['kɔnsl] *n* cónsul *m/f*.
consulate ['kɔnsjulɪt] *n* consulado.
consult [kən'sʌlt] *vt, vi* consultar; **to ~ sb
(about sth)** consultar a algn (sobre algo).
consultancy [kən'sʌltənsɪ] *n* (*COMM*)
consultoría; (*MED*) puesto de especialista.
consultant [kən'sʌltənt] *n* (*BRIT MED*)
especialista *m/f*; (*other specialist*) asesor(a)
m/f, consultor(a) *m/f*.
consultation [kɔnsəl'teɪʃən] *n* consulta; **in
~ with** en consulta con.
consultative [kən'sʌltətɪv] *adj* consultivo.
consulting room *n* (*BRIT*) consulta,
consultorio.
consume [kən'sjuːm] *vt* (*eat*) comerse;
(*drink*) beberse; (*fire etc, COMM*) consumir.
consumer [kən'sjuːmə*] *n* (*of electricity, gas
etc*) consumidor(a) *m/f*.
consumer association *n* asociación *f* de
consumidores.
consumer credit *n* crédito al consumidor.
consumer durables *npl* bienes *mpl* de
consumo duraderos.
consumer goods *npl* bienes *mpl* de
consumo.
consumerism [kən'sjuːmərɪzəm] *n*
consumismo.
consumer society *n* sociedad *f* de
consumo.
consumer watchdog *n* organización *f*
protectora del consumidor.
consummate ['kɔnsʌmeɪt] *vt* consumar.
consumption [kən'sʌmpʃən] *n* consumo;
(*MED*) tisis *f*; **not fit for human ~** no apto
para el consumo humano.
cont. *abbr* (= *continued*) sigue.
contact ['kɔntækt] *n* contacto; (*person: pej*)
enchufe *m* ♦ *vt* ponerse en contacto con;
~ lenses *npl* lentes *fpl* de contacto; **to be in
~ with sb/sth** estar en contacto con
algn/algo; **business ~s** relaciones *fpl*
comerciales.
contagious [kən'teɪdʒəs] *adj* contagioso.
contain [kən'teɪn] *vt* contener; **to ~ o.s.**
contenerse.
container [kən'teɪnə*] *n* recipiente *m*; (*for
shipping etc*) contenedor *m*.
containerize [kən'teɪnəraɪz] *vt* transportar
en contenedores.
container ship *n* buque *m* contenedor,
portacontenedores *m inv*.
contaminate [kən'tæmɪneɪt] *vt* contaminar.
contamination [kəntæmɪ'neɪʃən] *n*
contaminación *f*.

cont'd *abbr* (= *continued*) sigue.
contemplate ['kɔntəmpleɪt] *vt* (*gen*)
contemplar; (*reflect upon*) considerar;
(*intend*) pensar.
contemplation [kɔntəm'pleɪʃən] *n*
contemplación *f*.
contemporary [kən'tɛmpərərɪ] *adj, n* (*of the
same age*) contemporáneo/a *m/f*.
contempt [kən'tɛmpt] *n* desprecio; **~ of
court** (*LAW*) desacato (a los tribunales *or*
a la justicia).
contemptible [kən'tɛmptɪbl] *adj*
despreciable, desdeñable.
contemptuous [kən'tɛmptjuəs] *adj*
desdeñoso.
contend [kən'tɛnd] *vt* (*argue*) afirmar ♦ *vi*
(*struggle*) luchar; **he has a lot to ~ with**
tiene que hacer frente a muchos
problemas.
contender [kən'tɛndə*] *n* (*SPORT*)
contendiente *m/f*.
content [kən'tɛnt] *adj* (*happy*) contento;
(*satisfied*) satisfecho ♦ *vt* contentar;
satisfacer ♦ *n* ['kɔntɛnt] contenido; **~s** *npl*
contenido *msg*; (**table of**) **~s** índice *m* de
materias; (*in magazine*) sumario; **to be ~
with** conformarse con; **to ~ o.s. with
sth/with doing sth** conformarse con
algo/con hacer algo.
contented [kən'tɛntɪd] *adj* contento;
satisfecho.
contentedly [kən'tɛntɪdlɪ] *adv* con aire
satisfecho.
contention [kən'tɛnʃən] *n* discusión *f*;
(*belief*) argumento; **bone of ~** manzana de
la discordia.
contentious [kən'tɛnʃəs] *adj* discutible.
contentment [kən'tɛntmənt] *n* satisfacción
f.
contest ['kɔntɛst] *n* contienda; (*competition*)
concurso ♦ *vt* [kən'tɛst] (*dispute*)
impugnar; (*LAW*) disputar, litigar; (*POL:
election, seat*) presentarse como
candidato/a a.
contestant [kən'tɛstənt] *n* concursante *m/f*;
(*in fight*) contendiente *m/f*.
context ['kɔntɛkst] *n* contexto; **in/out of ~**
en/fuera de contexto.
continent ['kɔntɪnənt] *n* continente *m*; **the
C~** (*BRIT*) el continente europeo, Europa;
on the C~ en el continente europeo, en
Europa.
continental [kɔntɪ'nɛntl] *adj* continental;
(*BRIT: European*) europeo.
continental breakfast *n* desayuno estilo
europeo.
continental quilt *n* (*BRIT*) edredón *m*.
contingency [kən'tɪndʒənsɪ] *n*

contingencia.
contingent [kən'tɪndʒənt] *n* (*group*)
representación *f*.
continual [kən'tɪnjuəl] *adj* continuo.
continually [kən'tɪnjuəlɪ] *adv*
continuamente.
continuation [kəntɪnju'eɪʃən] *n*
prolongación *f*; (*after interruption*)
reanudación *f*; (*story, episode*)
continuación *f*.
continue [kən'tɪnjuː] *vi, vt* seguir,
continuar; ~**d on page 10** sigue en la
página 10.
continuing education [kən'tɪnjuɪŋ] *n*
educación *f* continua de adultos.
continuity [kɒntɪ'njuːɪtɪ] *n* (*also CINE*)
continuidad *f*.
continuity girl *n* (*CINE*) secretaria de
continuidad.
continuous [kən'tɪnjuəs] *adj* continuo; ~
performance (*CINE*) sesión *f* continua; ~
stationery papel *m* continuo.
continuously [kən'tɪnjuəslɪ] *adv*
continuamente.
contort [kən'tɔːt] *vt* retorcer.
contortion [kən'tɔːʃən] *n* (*movement*)
contorsión *f*.
contortionist [kən'tɔːʃənɪst] *n*
contorsionista *m/f*.
contour ['kɒntuə*] *n* contorno; (*also:* ~ **line**)
curva de nivel.
contraband ['kɒntrəbænd] *n* contrabando
♦ *adj* de contrabando.
contraception [kɒntrə'sɛpʃən] *n*
contracepción *f*.
contraceptive [kɒntrə'sɛptɪv] *adj, n*
anticonceptivo.
contract ['kɒntrækt] *n* contrato ♦ *cpd*
['kɒntrækt] (*price, date*) contratado, de
contrato; (*work*) bajo contrato ♦ *vb*
[kən'trækt] *vi* (*COMM*): **to** ~ **to do sth**
comprometerse por contrato a hacer
algo; (*become smaller*) contraerse,
encogerse ♦ *vt* contraer; **to be under** ~ **to
do sth** estar bajo contrato para hacer
algo; ~ **of employment** *or* **of service**
contrato de trabajo.
▶**contract in** *vi* tomar parte.
▶**contract out** *vi*: **to** ~ **out (of)** optar por
no tomar part (en); **to** ~ **out of a pension
scheme** dejar de cotizar en un plan de
jubilación.
contraction [kən'trækʃən] *n* contracción *f*.
contractor [kən'træktə*] *n* contratista *m/f*.
contractual [kən'træktjuəl] *adj* contractual.
contradict [kɒntrə'dɪkt] *vt* (*declare to be
wrong*) desmentir; (*be contrary to*)
contradecir.

contradiction [kɒntrə'dɪkʃən] *n*
contradicción *f*; **to be in** ~ **with**
contradecir.
contradictory [kɒntrə'dɪktərɪ] *adj*
(*statements*) contradictorio; **to be** ~ **to**
contradecir.
contralto [kən'træltəu] *n* contralto *f*.
contraption [kən'træpʃən] *n* (*pej*) artilugio
m.
contrary ['kɒntrərɪ] *adj* (*opposite, different*)
contrario; [kən'trɛərɪ] (*perverse*) terco ♦ *n*:
on the ~ al contrario; **unless you hear to
the** ~ a no ser que le digan lo contrario;
~ **to what we thought** al contrario de lo
que pensábamos.
contrast ['kɒntrɑːst] *n* contraste *m* ♦ *vt*
[kən'trɑːst] contrastar; **in** ~ **to** *or* **with** a
diferencia de.
contrasting [kən'trɑːstɪŋ] *adj* (*opinion*)
opuesto; (*colour*) que hace contraste.
contravene [kɒntrə'viːn] *vt* contravenir.
contravention [kɒntrə'vɛnʃən] *n*: ~ **(of)**
contravención *f* (de).
contribute [kən'trɪbjuːt] *vi* contribuir ♦ *vt*:
to ~ **to** (*gen*) contribuir a; (*newspaper*)
colaborar en; (*discussion*) intervenir en.
contribution [kɒntrɪ'bjuːʃən] *n* (*money*)
contribución *f*; (*to debate*) intervención *f*;
(*to journal*) colaboración *f*.
contributor [kən'trɪbjutə*] *n* (*to newspaper*)
colaborador(a) *m/f*.
contributory [kən'trɪbjutərɪ] *adj* (*cause*)
contribuyente; **it was a** ~ **factor in** ... fue
un factor que contribuyó en ....
contributory pension scheme *n* plan *m*
cotizable de jubilación.
contrivance [kən'traɪvəns] *n* (*machine,
device*) aparato, dispositivo.
contrive [kən'traɪv] *vt* (*invent*) idear ♦ *vi*: **to**
~ **to do** lograr hacer; (*try*) procurar
hacer.
control [kən'trəul] *vt* controlar; (*traffic etc*)
dirigir; (*machinery*) manejar; (*temper*)
dominar; (*disease, fire*) dominar,
controlar ♦ *n* (*command*) control *m*; (*of
car*) conducción *f*; (*check*) freno; ~**s** *npl*
mandos *mpl*; **to** ~ **o.s.** controlarse,
dominarse; **everything is under** ~ todo
está bajo control; **to be in** ~ **of** estar al
mando de; **the car went out of** ~ el coche
se descontroló.
control group *n* (*MED, PSYCH etc*) grupo de
control.
control key *n* (*COMPUT*) tecla de control.
controlled economy *n* economía dirigida.
controller [kən'trəulə*] *n* controlador(a)
m/f.
controlling interest [kən'trəulɪŋ-] *n*

participación *f* mayoritaria.

control panel *n* (*on aircraft, ship, TV etc*) tablero de instrumentos.

control point *n* (puesto de) control *m*.

control room *n* (*NAUT, MIL*) sala de mandos; (*RADIO, TV*) sala de control.

control tower *n* (*AVIAT*) torre *f* de control.

control unit *n* (*COMPUT*) unidad *f* de control.

controversial [kɔntrə'vəːʃl] *adj* polémico.

controversy ['kɔntrəvəːsɪ] *n* polémica.

conurbation [kɔnəː'beɪʃən] *n* conurbación *f*.

convalesce [kɔnvə'lɛs] *vi* convalecer.

convalescence [kɔnvə'lɛsns] *n* convalecencia.

convalescent [kɔnvə'lɛsnt] *adj, n* convaleciente *m/f*.

convector [kən'vɛktə*] *n* calentador *m* de convección.

convene [kən'viːn] *vt* (*meeting*) convocar ♦ *vi* reunirse.

convenience [kən'viːnɪəns] *n* (*comfort*) comodidad *f*; (*advantage*) ventaja; **at your earliest ~** (*COMM*) tan pronto como le sea posible; **all modern ~s**, (*BRIT*) **all mod cons** todo confort.

convenience foods *npl* platos *mpl* preparados.

convenient [kən'viːnɪənt] *adj* (*useful*) útil; (*place*) conveniente; (*time*) oportuno; **if it is ~ for you** si le viene bien.

conveniently [kən'viːnɪəntlɪ] *adv* (*happen*) oportunamente; (*situated*) convenientemente.

convent ['kɔnvənt] *n* convento.

convent school *n* colegio de monjas.

convention [kən'vɛnʃən] *n* convención *f*; (*meeting*) asamblea.

conventional [kən'vɛnʃənl] *adj* convencional.

converge [kən'vəːdʒ] *vi* converger.

conversant [kən'vəːsnt] *adj*: **to be ~ with** estar familiarizado con.

conversation [kɔnvə'seɪʃən] *n* conversación *f*.

conversational [kɔnvə'seɪʃənl] *adj* (*familiar*) familiar; (*talkative*) locuaz; **~ mode** (*COMPUT*) modo de conversación.

converse ['kɔnvəːs] *n* inversa ♦ *vi* [kən'vəːs] conversar; **to ~ (with sb about sth)** conversar *or* platicar (*LAM*) (con algn de algo).

conversely [kɔn'vəːslɪ] *adv* a la inversa.

conversion [kən'vəːʃən] *n* conversión *f*; (*house ~*) reforma, remodelación *f*.

conversion table *n* tabla de equivalencias.

convert [kən'vəːt] *vt* (*REL, COMM*) convertir; (*alter*) transformar ♦ *n* ['kɔnvəːt] converso/a.

convertible [kən'vəːtəbl] *adj* convertible ♦ *n* descapotable *m*; **~ loan stock** obligaciones *fpl* convertibles.

convex ['kɔn'vɛks] *adj* convexo.

convey [kən'veɪ] *vt* transportar; (*thanks*) comunicar; (*idea*) expresar.

conveyance [kən'veɪəns] *n* (*of goods*) transporte *m*; (*vehicle*) vehículo, medio de transporte.

conveyancing [kən'veɪənsɪŋ] *n* (*LAW*) preparación *f* de escrituras de traspaso.

conveyor belt [kən'veɪə*-] *n* cinta transportadora.

convict [kən'vɪkt] *vt* (*gen*) condenar; (*find guilty*) declarar culpable a ♦ *n* ['kɔnvɪkt] presidiario/a.

conviction [kən'vɪkʃən] *n* condena; (*belief*) creencia, convicción *f*.

convince [kən'vɪns] *vt* convencer; **to ~ sb (of sth/that)** convencer a algn (de algo/de que).

convinced [kən'vɪnst] *adj*: **~ of/that** convencido de/de que.

convincing [kən'vɪnsɪŋ] *adj* convincente.

convincingly [kən'vɪnsɪŋlɪ] *adv* de modo convincente, convincentemente.

convivial [kən'vɪvɪəl] *adj* (*person*) sociable; (*atmosphere*) alegre.

convoluted ['kɔnvəluːtɪd] *adj* (*argument etc*) enrevesado; (*shape*) enrollado, enroscado.

convoy ['kɔnvɔɪ] *n* convoy *m*.

convulse [kən'vʌls] *vt* convulsionar; **to be ~d with laughter** dislocarse de risa.

convulsion [kən'vʌlʃən] *n* convulsión *f*.

coo [kuː] *vi* arrullar.

cook [kuk] *vt* cocinar; (*stew etc*) guisar; (*meal*) preparar ♦ *vi* hacerse; (*person*) cocinar ♦ *n* cocinero/a.

▶**cook up** *vt* (*col: excuse, story*) inventar.

cookbook ['kukbuk] *n* libro de cocina.

cooker ['kukə*] *n* cocina.

cookery ['kukərɪ] *n* cocina.

cookery book *n* (*BRIT*) = **cookbook**.

cookie ['kukɪ] *n* (*US*) galleta.

cooking ['kukɪŋ] *n* cocina ♦ *cpd* (*apples*) para cocinar; (*utensils, salt, foil*) de cocina.

cooking chocolate *n* chocolate *m* fondant *or* de hacer.

cookout ['kukaut] *n* (*US*) comida al aire libre.

cool [kuːl] *adj* fresco; (*not hot*) tibio; (*not afraid*) tranquilo; (*unfriendly*) frío ♦ *vt* enfriar ♦ *vi* enfriarse; **it is ~** (*weather*) hace fresco; **to keep sth ~** *or* **in a ~ place** conservar algo fresco *or* en un sitio fresco.

▶**cool down** *vi* enfriarse; (*fig: person, situation*) calmarse.

coolant ['ku:lənt] *n* refrigerante *m*.

cool box, (*US*) **cooler** ['ku:lə*] *n* nevera portátil.

cooling ['ku:lɪŋ] *adj* refrescante.

cooling-off period [ku:lɪŋ'ɔf-] *n* (*INDUSTRY*) plazo de negociaciones.

cooling tower *n* torre *f* de refrigeración.

coolly ['ku:lɪ] *adv* (*calmly*) con tranquilidad; (*audaciously*) descaradamente; (*unenthusiastically*) fríamente, con frialdad.

coolness ['ku:lnɪs] *n* frescura; tranquilidad *f*; (*hostility*) frialdad *f*; (*indifference*) falta de entusiasmo.

coop [ku:p] *n* gallinero ♦ *vt*: **to ~ up** (*fig*) encerrar.

co-op ['kəuɔp] *n abbr* (= *Cooperative* (*Society*)) cooperativa.

cooperate [kəu'ɔpəreɪt] *vi* cooperar, colaborar; **will he ~?** ¿querrá cooperar?

cooperation [kəuɔpə'reɪʃən] *n* cooperación *f*, colaboración *f*.

cooperative [kəu'ɔpərətɪv] *adj* cooperativo; (*person*) dispuesto a colaborar ♦ *n* cooperativa.

co-opt [kəu'ɔpt] *vt*: **to ~ sb into sth** nombrar a algn para algo.

coordinate [kəu'ɔːdɪneɪt] *vt* coordinar ♦ *n* [kəu'ɔːdɪnət] (*MATH*) coordenada; **~s** *npl* (*clothes*) coordinados *mpl*.

coordination [kəuɔːdɪ'neɪʃən] *n* coordinación *f*.

coot [ku:t] *n* focha *f* (común).

co-ownership [kəu'əunəʃɪp] *n* copropiedad *f*.

cop [kɔp] *n* (*col*) poli *m*.

cope [kəup] *vi*: **to ~ with** poder con; (*problem*) hacer frente a.

Copenhagen [kəupən'heɪgən] *n* Copenhague *m*.

copier ['kɔpɪə*] *n* (*photo~*) (foto)copiadora.

co-pilot ['kəu'paɪlət] *n* copiloto *m/f*.

copious ['kəupɪəs] *adj* copioso, abundante.

copper ['kɔpə*] *n* (*metal*) cobre *m*; (*col: policeman*) poli *m*; **~s** *npl* perras *fpl*; (*small change*) calderilla.

coppice ['kɔpɪs], **copse** [kɔps] *n* bosquecillo.

copulate ['kɔpjuleɪt] *vi* copular.

copulation [kɔpju'leɪʃən] *n* cópula.

copy ['kɔpɪ] *n* copia; (*of book*) ejemplar *m*; (*of magazine*) número; (*material: for printing*) original *m* ♦ *vt* copiar (*also COMPUT*); (*imitate*) copiar, imitar; **to make good ~** (*fig*) ser una noticia de interés;

rough ~ borrador *m*; **fair ~** copia en limpio.

▶**copy out** *vt* copiar.

copycat ['kɔpɪkæt] *n* (*pej*) imitador(a) *m/f*.

copyright ['kɔpɪraɪt] *n* derechos *mpl* de autor.

copy typist *n* mecanógrafo/a.

coral ['kɔrəl] *n* coral *m*.

coral reef *n* arrecife *m* (de coral).

Coral Sea *n*: **the ~** el Mar del Coral.

cord [kɔːd] *n* cuerda; (*ELEC*) cable *m*; (*fabric*) pana; **~s** *npl* (*trousers*) pantalones *mpl* de pana.

cordial ['kɔːdɪəl] *adj* cordial ♦ *n* cordial *m*.

cordless ['kɔːdlɪs] *adj* sin hilos.

cordon ['kɔːdn] *n* cordón *m*.

▶**cordon off** *vt* acordonar.

Cordova ['kɔːdəvə] *n* Córdoba.

corduroy ['kɔːdərɔɪ] *n* pana.

CORE [kɔː*] *n abbr* (*US*) = *Congress of Racial Equality*.

core [kɔː*] *n* (*of earth, nuclear reactor*) centro, núcleo; (*of fruit*) corazón *m*; (*of problem etc*) esencia, meollo ♦ *vt* quitar el corazón de.

Corfu [kɔː'fu] *n* Corfú *m*.

coriander [kɔrɪ'ændə*] *n* culantro, cilantro.

cork [kɔːk] *n* corcho; (*tree*) alcornoque *m*.

corkage ['kɔːkɪdʒ] *n* precio que se cobra en un restaurante por una botella de vino traída de fuera.

corked [kɔːkt] *adj* (*wine*) con sabor a corcho.

corkscrew ['kɔːkskru:] *n* sacacorchos *m inv*.

cormorant ['kɔːmərnt] *n* cormorán *m*.

Corn *abbr* (*BRIT*) = Cornwall.

corn [kɔːn] *n* (*BRIT: wheat*) trigo; (*US: maize*) maíz *m*, choclo (*LAM*); (*on foot*) callo; **~ on the cob** (*CULIN*) maíz en la mazorca.

cornea ['kɔːnɪə] *n* córnea.

corned beef ['kɔːnd-] *n* carne *f* de vaca acecinada.

corner ['kɔːnə*] *n* (*outside*) esquina; (*inside*) rincón *m*; (*in road*) curva; (*FOOTBALL*) córner *m*, saque *m* de esquina ♦ *vt* (*trap*) arrinconar; (*COMM*) acaparar ♦ *vi* (*in car*) tomar las curvas; **to cut ~s** atajar.

corner flag *n* (*FOOTBALL*) banderola de esquina.

corner kick *n* (*FOOTBALL*) córner *m*, saque *m* de esquina.

cornerstone ['kɔːnəstəun] *n* piedra angular.

cornet ['kɔːnɪt] *n* (*MUS*) corneta; (*BRIT: of ice cream*) cucurucho.

cornflakes ['kɔːnfleɪks] *npl* copos *mpl* de maíz, cornflakes *mpl*.

cornflour ['kɔːnflauə*] *n* (*BRIT*) harina de

maíz.

cornice ['kɔːnɪs] *n* cornisa.

Cornish ['kɔːnɪʃ] *adj* de Cornualles.

corn oil *n* aceite *m* de maíz.

cornstarch ['kɔːnstɑːtʃ] *n* (*US*) = **cornflour**.

cornucopia [kɔːnju'kəupɪə] *n* cornucopia.

Cornwall ['kɔːnwəl] *n* Cornualles *m*.

corny ['kɔːnɪ] *adj* (*col*) gastado.

corollary [kə'rɔlərɪ] *n* corolario.

coronary ['kɔrənərɪ] *n*: ~ **(thrombosis)** infarto.

coronation [kɔrə'neɪʃən] *n* coronación *f*.

coroner ['kɔrənə*] *n* juez *m/f* de instrucción.

coronet ['kɔrənɪt] *n* corona.

Corp. *abbr* = **corporation**.

corporal ['kɔːpərl] *n* cabo ♦ *adj*: ~ **punishment** castigo corporal.

corporate ['kɔːpərɪt] *adj* corporativo.

corporate hospitality *n* obsequios a los clientes por cortesía de la empresa.

corporate identity, corporate image *n* (*of organization*) identidad *f* corporativa.

corporation [kɔːpə'reɪʃən] *n* (*of town*) ayuntamiento; (*COMM*) corporación *f*.

corps [kɔː*], *pl* **corps** [kɔːz] *n* cuerpo; **press** ~ gabinete *m* de prensa.

corpse [kɔːps] *n* cadáver *m*.

corpulent ['kɔːpjulənt] *adj* corpulento/a.

Corpus Christi ['kɔːpəs'krɪstɪ] *n* Corpus *m* (Christi).

corpuscle ['kɔːpʌsl] *n* corpúsculo.

corral [kə'rɑːl] *n* corral *m*.

correct [kə'rɛkt] *adj* correcto, (*accurate*) exacto ♦ *vt* corregir; **you are** ~ tiene razón.

correction [kə'rɛkʃən] *n* rectificación *f*; (*erasure*) tachadura.

correlate ['kɔrɪleɪt] *vi*: **to** ~ **with** tener correlación con.

correlation [kɔrɪ'leɪʃən] *n* correlación *f*.

correspond [kɔrɪs'pɔnd] *vi* (*write*) escribirse; (*be equal to*) corresponder.

correspondence [kɔrɪs'pɔndəns] *n* correspondencia.

correspondence course *n* curso por correspondencia.

correspondent [kɔrɪs'pɔndənt] *n* corresponsal *m/f*.

corresponding [kɔrɪs'pɔndɪŋ] *adi* correspondiente.

corridor ['kɔrɪdɔː*] *n* pasillo.

corroborate [kə'rɔbəreɪt] *vt* corroborar.

corroboration [kərɔbə'reɪʃən] *n* corroboración *f*, confirmación *f*.

corrode [kə'rəud] *vt* corroer ♦ *vi* corroerse.

corrosion [kə'rəuʒən] *n* corrosión *f*.

corrosive [kə'rəusɪv] *adj* corrosivo.

corrugated ['kɔrəgeɪtɪd] *adj* ondulado.

corrugated cardboard *n* cartón *m* ondulado.

corrugated iron *n* chapa ondulada.

corrupt [kə'rʌpt] *adj* corrompido; (*person*) corrupto ♦ *vt* corromper; (*bribe*) sobornar; (*data*) degradar; ~ **practices** (*dishonesty, bribery*) corrupción *f*.

corruption [kə'rʌpʃən] *n* corrupción *f*; (*of data*) alteración *f*.

corset ['kɔːsɪt] *n* faja; (*old-style*) corsé *m*.

Corsica ['kɔːsɪkə] *n* Córcega.

Corsican ['kɔːsɪkən] *adj*, *n* corso/a *m/f*.

cortège [kɔː'teɪʒ] *n* cortejo, comitiva.

cortisone ['kɔːtɪzəun] *n* cortisona.

c.o.s. *abbr* (= *cash on shipment*) pago al embarcar.

cosh [kɔʃ] *n* (*BRIT*) cachiporra.

cosignatory ['kəu'sɪgnətərɪ] *n* cosignatario/a.

cosine ['kəusaɪn] *n* coseno.

cosiness ['kəuzɪnɪs] *n* comodidad *f*; (*atmosphere*) lo acogedor.

cos lettuce [kɔs–] *n* lechuga romana.

cosmetic [kɔz'mɛtɪk] *n* cosmético ♦ *adj* (*also fig*) cosmético; (*surgery*) estético.

cosmic ['kɔzmɪk] *adj* cósmico.

cosmonaut ['kɔzmənɔːt] *n* cosmonauta *m/f*.

cosmopolitan [kɔzmə'pɔlɪtn] *adj* cosmopolita.

cosmos ['kɔzmɔs] *n* cosmos *m*.

cosset ['kɔsɪt] *vt* mimar.

cost [kɔst] *n* (*gen*) coste *m*, costo; (*price*) precio; ~**s** *npl* (*LAW*) costas *fpl* ♦ *vb* (*pt, pp* **cost**) *vi* costar, valer ♦ *vt* preparar el presupuesto de; **how much does it** ~**?** ¿cuánto cuesta?, ¿cuánto vale?; **what will it** ~ **to have it repaired?** ¿cuánto costará repararlo?; **the** ~ **of living** el coste *or* costo de la vida; **at all** ~**s** cueste lo que cueste.

cost accountant *n* contable *m* de costos.

co-star ['kəustɑː*] *n* coprotagonista *m/f*.

Costa Rica ['kɔstə'riːkə] *n* Costa Rica.

Costa Rican ['kɔstə'riːkən] *adj*, *n* costarriqueño/a *m/f*, costarricense *m/f*.

cost centre *n* centro (de determinación) de coste.

cost control *n* control *m* de costes.

cost-effective [kɔstɪ'fɛktɪv] *adj* (*COMM*) rentable.

cost-effectiveness ['kɔstɪ'fɛktɪvnɪs] *n* relación *f* coste-rendimiento.

costing ['kɔstɪŋ] *n* cálculo del coste.

costly ['kɔstlɪ] *adj* (*expensive*) costoso.

cost-of-living [kɔstəv'lɪvɪŋ] *adj*: ~ **allowance** *n* plus *m* de carestía de vida; ~ **index** *n* índice *m* del coste de vida.

cost price *n* (*BRIT*) precio de coste.

costume ['kɔstjuːm] n traje m; (BRIT: also: swimming ~) traje de baño.

costume jewellery n bisutería.

cosy, (US) **cozy** ['kəuzɪ] adj cómodo, a gusto; (room, atmosphere) acogedor(a).

cot [kɔt] n (BRIT: child's) cuna; (US: folding bed) cama plegable.

cot death n muerte f en la cuna.

Cotswolds ['kɔtswəuldz] npl región de colinas del suroeste inglés.

cottage ['kɔtɪdʒ] n casita de campo.

cottage cheese n requesón m.

cottage industry n industria artesanal.

cottage pie n pastel de carne cubierta de puré de patatas.

cotton ['kɔtn] n algodón m; (thread) hilo.

►**cotton on** vi (col): **to ~ on (to sth)** caer en la cuenta (de algo).

cotton candy n (US) algodón m (azucarado).

cotton wool n (BRIT) algodón m (hidrófilo).

couch [kautʃ] n sofá m; (in doctor's surgery) camilla.

couchette [kuːʃɛt] n litera.

couch potato n (col) persona comodona que no se mueve en todo el día.

cough [kɔf] vi toser ♦ n tos f.

►**cough up** vt escupir.

cough drop n pastilla para la tos.

cough mixture n jarabe m para la tos.

could [kud] pt of **can**.

couldn't ['kudnt] = **could not**.

council ['kaunsl] n consejo; **city** or **town ~** ayuntamiento; **C~ of Europe** Consejo de Europa.

council estate n (BRIT) barriada de viviendas sociales de alquiler.

council house n (BRIT) vivienda social de alquiler.

councillor ['kaunslə*] n concejal m/f.

council tax n (BRIT) contribución f municipal (dependiente del valor de la vivienda).

counsel ['kaunsl] n (advice) consejo; (lawyer) abogado/a ♦ vt aconsejar; **~ for the defence/the prosecution** abogado/a defensor(a)/fiscal; **to ~ sth/sb to do sth** aconsejar algo/a algn que haga algo.

counsellor, (US) **counselor** ['kaunslə*] n consejero/a; (US LAW) abogado/a.

count [kaunt] vt (gen) contar; (include) incluir ♦ vi contar ♦ n cuenta; (of votes) escrutinio; (nobleman) conde m; (sum) total m, suma; **to ~ the cost of** calcular el coste de; **not ~ing the children** niños aparte; **10 ~ing him** diez incluyéndolo a él, diez con él; **~ yourself lucky** date por satisfecho; **that doesn't ~!** ¡eso no vale!;

to ~ (up) to 10 contar hasta diez; **it ~s for very little** cuenta poco; **to keep ~ of sth** llevar la cuenta de algo.

►**count on** vt fus contar con; **to ~ on doing sth** contar con hacer algo.

►**count up** vt contar.

countdown ['kauntdaun] n cuenta atrás.

countenance ['kauntɪnəns] n semblante m, rostro ♦ vt (tolerate) aprobar, consentir.

counter ['kauntə*] n (in shop) mostrador m; (position: in post office, bank) ventanilla; (in games) ficha; (TECH) contador m ♦ vt contrarrestar; (blow) parar; (attack) contestar a ♦ adv: **~ to** contrario a; **to buy under the ~** (fig) comprar de estraperlo or bajo mano; **to ~ sth with sth/by doing sth** contestar algo con algo/haciendo algo.

counteract ['kauntər'ækt] vt contrarrestar.

counterattack ['kauntərə'tæk] n contraataque m ♦ vi contraatacar.

counterbalance ['kauntə'bæləns] n contrapeso.

counter-clockwise ['kauntə'klɔkwaɪz] adv en sentido contrario al de las agujas del reloj.

counter-espionage ['kauntər'ɛspɪənɑːʒ] n contraespionaje m.

counterfeit ['kauntəfɪt] n falsificación f ♦ vt falsificar ♦ adj falso, falsificado.

counterfoil ['kauntəfɔɪl] n (BRIT) matriz f, talón m.

counterintelligence ['kauntərɪn'tɛlɪdʒəns] n contraespionaje m.

countermand ['kauntəmɑːnd] vt revocar.

counter-measure ['kauntəmeʒə*] n contramedida.

counteroffensive ['kauntərə'fɛnsɪv] n contraofensiva.

counterpane ['kauntəpeɪn] n colcha.

counterpart ['kauntəpɑːt] n (of person) homólogo/a.

counter-productive [kauntəprə'dʌktɪv] adj contraproducente.

counterproposal ['kauntəprə'pəuzl] n contrapropuesta.

countersign ['kauntəsaɪn] vt ratificar, refrendar.

countess ['kauntɪs] n condesa.

countless ['kauntlɪs] adj innumerable.

countrified ['kʌntrɪfaɪd] adj rústico.

country ['kʌntrɪ] n país m; (native land) patria; (as opposed to town) campo; (region) región f, tierra; **in the ~** en el campo; **mountainous ~** región f montañosa.

country and western (music) n música country.

country dancing n (BRIT) baile m regional.
country house n casa de campo.
countryman ['kʌntrɪmən] n (national) compatriota m; (rural) hombre m del campo.
countryside ['kʌntrɪsaɪd] n campo.
countrywide ['kʌntrɪ'waɪd] adj nacional ♦ adv por todo el país.
county ['kauntɪ] n condado; see also **district council**.
county council n (BRIT) ≈ diputación f provincial.
county town n cabeza de partido.
coup, ~s [kuː, -z] n golpe m; (triumph) éxito; (also: ~ **d'état**) golpe de estado.
coupé ['kuːpeɪ] n cupé m.
couple ['kʌpl] n (of things) par m; (of people) pareja; (married ~) matrimonio ♦ vt (ideas, names) unir, juntar; (machinery) acoplar; **a ~ of** un par de.
couplet ['kʌplɪt] n pareado.
coupling ['kʌplɪŋ] n (RAIL) enganche m.
coupon ['kuːpɔn] n cupón m; (pools ~) boleto (de quiniela).
courage ['kʌrɪdʒ] n valor m, valentía.
courageous [kə'reɪdʒəs] adj valiente.
courgette [kuə'ʒet] n (BRIT) calabacín m.
courier ['kurɪə*] n mensajero/a; (diplomatic) correo; (for tourists) guía m/f (de turismo).
course [kɔːs] n (direction) dirección f; (of river, SCOL) curso; (of ship) rumbo; (fig) proceder m; (GOLF) campo; (part of meal) plato; **of ~** adv desde luego, naturalmente; **of ~!** ¡claro!, ¡cómo no! (LAM); **(no) of ~ not!** ¡claro que no!, ¡por supuesto que no!; **in due ~** a su debido tiempo; **in the ~ of the next few days** durante los próximos días; **we have no other ~ but to ...** no tenemos más remedio que ...; **there are 2 ~s open to us** se nos ofrecen dos posibilidades; **the best ~ would be to ...** lo mejor sería ...; **~ of treatment** (MED) tratamiento.
court [kɔːt] n (royal) corte f; (LAW) tribunal m, juzgado; (TENNIS) pista, cancha (LAM) ♦ vt (woman) cortejar; (fig: favour, popularity) solicitar, buscar; (: death, disaster, danger etc) buscar; **to take to ~** demandar; **~ of appeal** tribunal m de apelación.
courteous ['kɔːtɪəs] adj cortés.
courtesan [kɔːtɪ'zæn] n cortesana.
courtesy ['kɔːtəsɪ] n cortesía; **by ~ of** (por) cortesía de.
courtesy light n (AUT) luz f interior.
court-house ['kɔːthaus] n (US) palacio de justicia.
courtier ['kɔːtɪə*] n cortesano.

court martial, pl **courts martial** ['kɔːt'mɑːʃəl] n consejo de guerra ♦ vt someter a consejo de guerra.
courtroom ['kɔːtrum] n sala de justicia.
court shoe n zapato de mujer de estilo clásico.
courtyard ['kɔːtjɑːd] n patio.
cousin ['kʌzn] n primo/a; **first ~** primo/a carnal.
cove [kəuv] n cala, ensenada.
covenant ['kʌvənənt] n convenio ♦ vt: **to ~ £20 per year to a charity** concertar el pago de veinte libras anuales a una sociedad benéfica.
Coventry ['kɔvəntrɪ] n: **to send sb to ~** (fig) hacer el vacío a algn.
cover ['kʌvə*] vt cubrir; (with lid) tapar; (chairs etc) revestir; (distance) cubrir, recorrer; (include) abarcar; (protect) abrigar; (journalist) investigar; (issues) tratar ♦ n cubierta; (lid) tapa; (for chair etc) funda; (for bed) cobertor m; (envelope) sobre m; (of magazine) portada; (shelter) abrigo; (insurance) cobertura; **to take ~** (shelter) protegerse, resguardarse; **under ~** (indoors) bajo techo; **under ~ of darkness** al amparo de la oscuridad; **under separate ~** (COMM) por separado; **£10 will ~ everything** con diez libras cubriremos todos los gastos.
▶**cover up** vt (child, object) cubrir completamente, tapar; (fig: hide: truth, facts) ocultar; **to ~ up for sb** (fig) encubrir a algn.
coverage ['kʌvərɪdʒ] n alcance m; (in media) reportaje m; (INSURANCE) cobertura.
coveralls ['kʌvərɔːlz] npl (US) mono sg.
cover charge n precio del cubierto.
covering ['kʌvərɪŋ] n cubierta, envoltura.
covering letter, (US) **cover letter** n carta de explicación.
cover note n (INSURANCE) póliza provisional.
cover price n precio de cubierta.
covert ['kəuvət] adj (secret) secreto, encubierto; (dissembled) furtivo.
cover-up ['kʌvərʌp] n encubrimiento.
covet ['kʌvɪt] vt codiciar.
covetous ['kʌvɪtəs] adj codicioso.
cow [kau] n vaca ♦ vt intimidar.
coward ['kauəd] n cobarde m/f.
cowardice ['kauədɪs] n cobardía.
cowardly ['kauədlɪ] adj cobarde.
cowboy ['kaubɔɪ] n vaquero.
cower ['kauə*] vi encogerse (de miedo).
co-worker ['kəuwəːkə*] n colaborador(a) m/f.

cowshed ['kauʃɛd] *n* establo.
cowslip ['kauslɪp] *n* (*BOT*) primavera, prímula.
coxswain ['kɔksn] *n* (*abbr*: **cox**) timonel *m*.
coy [kɔɪ] *adj* tímido.
coyote [kɔɪ'əutɪ] *n* coyote *m*.
cozy ['kəuzɪ] *adj* (*US*) = **cosy**.
CP *n abbr* (= *Communist Party*) PC *m*.
cp. *abbr* (= *compare*) cfr.
c/p *abbr* (*BRIT*) = **carriage paid**.
CPA *n abbr* (*US*) = **certified public accountant**.
CPI *n abbr* (= *Consumer Price Index*) IPC *m*.
Cpl. *abbr* (*MIL*) = **corporal**.
CP/M *n abbr* (= *Central Program for Microprocessors*) CP/M *m*.
c.p.s. *abbr* (= *characters per second*) c.p.s.
CPSA *n abbr* (*BRIT*: = *Civil and Public Services Association*) sindicato de funcionarios.
CPU *n abbr* = **central processing unit**.
cr. *abbr* = **credit, creditor**.
crab [kræb] *n* cangrejo.
crab apple *n* manzana silvestre.
crack [kræk] *n* grieta; (*noise*) crujido; (: *of whip*) chasquido; (*joke*) chiste *m*; (*col*: *drug*) crack *m*; (*attempt*): **to have a ~ at sth** intentar algo ♦ *vt* agrietar, romper; (*nut*) cascar; (*safe*) forzar; (*whip etc*) chasquear; (*knuckles*) crujir; (*joke*) contar; (*case*: *solve*) resolver; (*code*) descifrar ♦ *adj* (*athlete*) de primera clase; **to ~ jokes** (*col*) bromear.
►**crack down on** *vt fus* reprimir fuertemente, adoptar medidas severas contra.
►**crack up** *vi* sufrir una crisis nerviosa.
crackdown ['krækdaun] *n*: ~ **(on)** (*on crime*) campaña (contra); (*on spending*) reducción *f* (en).
cracker ['krækə*] *n* (*biscuit*) galleta salada, crácker *m*; (*Christmas ~*) sorpresa (navideña).
crackle ['krækl] *vi* crepitar.
crackling ['kræklɪŋ] *n* (*on radio, telephone*) interferencia; (*of fire*) chisporroteo, crepitación *f*; (*of leaves etc*) crujido; (*of pork*) chicharrón *m*.
crackpot ['krækpɔt] (*col*) *n* pirado/a ♦ *adj* de pirado.
cradle ['kreɪdl] *n* cuna ♦ *vt* (*child*) mecer, acunar; (*object*) abrazar.
craft [krɑːft] *n* (*skill*) arte *m*; (*trade*) oficio; (*cunning*) astucia; (*boat*) embarcación *f*.
craftsman ['krɑːftsmən] *n* artesano.
craftsmanship ['krɑːftsmənʃɪp] *n* artesanía.
crafty ['krɑːftɪ] *adj* astuto.
crag [kræg] *n* peñasco.

craggy ['krægɪ] *adj* escarpado.
cram [kræm] *vt* (*fill*): **to ~ sth with** llenar algo (a reventar) de; (*put*): **to ~ sth into** meter algo a la fuerza en ♦ *vi* (*for exams*) empollar.
crammed [kræmd] *adj* atestado.
cramp [kræmp] *n* (*MED*) calambre *m*; (*TECH*) grapa ♦ *vt* (*limit*) poner trabas a.
cramped [kræmpt] *adj* apretado; (*room*) minúsculo.
crampon ['kræmpən] *n* crampón *m*.
cranberry ['krænbərɪ] *n* arándano.
crane [kreɪn] *n* (*TECH*) grúa; (*bird*) grulla ♦ *vt*, *vi*: **to ~ forward, to ~ one's neck** estirar el cuello.
cranium ['kreɪnɪəm] *n* cráneo.
crank [kræŋk] *n* manivela; (*person*) chiflado/a.
crankshaft ['kræŋkʃɑːft] *n* cigüeñal *m*.
cranky ['kræŋkɪ] *adj* (*eccentric*) maniático; (*bad-tempered*) de mal genio.
cranny ['krænɪ] *n see* **nook**.
crap [kræp] *n* (*col!*) mierda (!).
crappy ['kræpɪ] *adj* (*col*) chungo.
craps [kræps] *n* (*US*) dados *mpl*.
crash [kræʃ] *n* (*noise*) estrépito; (*of cars, plane*) accidente *m*; (*of business*) quiebra; (*STOCK EXCHANGE*) crac *m* ♦ *vt* (*plane*) estrellar ♦ *vi* (*plane*) estrellarse; (*two cars*) chocar; (*fall noisily*) caer con estrépito; **he ~ed the car into a wall** estrelló el coche contra una pared o tapia.
crash barrier *n* (*AUT*) barrera de protección.
crash course *n* curso acelerado.
crash helmet *n* casco (protector).
crash landing *n* aterrizaje *m* forzoso.
crass [kræs] *adj* grosero, maleducado.
crate [kreɪt] *n* caja, cajón *m* de embalaje; (*col*) armatoste *m*.
crater ['kreɪtə*] *n* cráter *m*.
cravat(e) [krə'væt] *n* pañuelo.
crave [kreɪv] *vt*, *vi*: **to ~ (for)** ansiar, anhelar.
craving ['kreɪvɪŋ] *n* (*for food, cigarettes, etc*) ansias *fpl*; (*during pregnancy*) antojo.
crawl [krɔːl] *vi* (*drag o.s.*) arrastrarse; (*child*) andar a gatas, gatear; (*vehicle*) avanzar (lentamente); (*col*): **to ~ to sb** dar coba a algn, hacerle la pelota a algn ♦ *n* (*SWIMMING*) crol *m*.
crawler lane [krɔːlə-] *n* (*BRIT AUT*) carril *m* para tráfico lento.
crayfish ['kreɪfɪʃ] *n*, *pl inv* (*freshwater*) cangrejo (de río); (*saltwater*) cigala.
crayon ['kreɪən] *n* lápiz *m* de color.
craze [kreɪz] *n* manía; (*fashion*) moda.
crazed [kreɪzd] *adj* (*look, person*) loco,

demente; (*pottery, glaze*) agrietado, cuarteado.

crazy ['kreɪzɪ] *adj* (*person*) loco; (*idea*) disparatado; **to go** ~ volverse loco; **to be** ~ **about sb/sth** (*col*) estar loco por algn/algo.

crazy paving *n* pavimento de baldosas *irregulares*.

creak [kriːk] *vi* crujir; (*hinge etc*) chirriar, rechinar.

cream [kriːm] *n* (*of milk*) nata, crema; (*lotion*) crema; (*fig*) flor *f* y nata ♦ *adj* (*colour*) color *m* crema; **whipped** ~ nata batida.

▶**cream off** *vt* (*fig*) (*best talents, part of profits*) separar lo mejor de.

cream cake *n* pastel *m* de nata.

cream cheese *n* queso fresco cremoso.

creamery ['kriːmərɪ] *n* (*shop*) quesería; (*factory*) central *f* lechera.

creamy ['kriːmɪ] *adj* cremoso.

crease [kriːs] *n* (*fold*) pliegue *m*; (*in trousers*) raya; (*wrinkle*) arruga ♦ *vt* (*fold*) doblar, plegar; (*wrinkle*) arrugar ♦ *vi* (*wrinkle up*) arrugarse.

crease-resistant ['kriːsrɪzɪstənt] *adj* inarrugable.

create [kriː'eɪt] *vt* (*also COMPUT*) crear; (*impression*) dar; (*fuss, noise*) hacer.

creation [kriː'eɪʃən] *n* creación *f*.

creative [kriː'eɪtɪv] *adj* creativo.

creativity [kriːeɪ'tɪvɪtɪ] *n* creatividad *f*.

creator [kriː'eɪtə*] *n* creador(a) *m/f*.

creature ['kriːtʃə*] *n* (*living thing*) criatura; (*animal*) animal *m*; (*insect*) bicho.

creature comforts *npl* comodidades *fpl* materiales.

crèche, creche [krɛʃ] *n* (*BRIT*) guardería (infantil).

credence ['kriːdəns] *n*: **to lend** *or* **give** ~ **to** creer en, dar crédito a.

credentials [krɪ'denʃlz] *npl* credenciales *fpl*; (*letters of reference*) referencias *fpl*.

credibility [krɛdɪ'bɪlɪtɪ] *n* credibilidad *f*.

credible ['krɛdɪbl] *adj* creíble; (*witness, source*) fidedigno.

credit ['krɛdɪt] *n* (*gen*) crédito; (*merit*) honor *m*, mérito ♦ *vt* (*COMM*) abonar; (*believe*) creer, dar crédito a ♦ *adj* crediticio; **to be in** ~ (*person, bank account*) tener saldo a favor; **on** ~ a crédito; (*col*) al fiado; **he's a** ~ **to his family** hace honor a su familia; **to** ~ **sb with** (*fig*) reconocer a algn el mérito de; *see also* **credits**.

creditable ['krɛdɪtəbl] *adj* estimable, digno de elogio.

credit account *n* cuenta de crédito.

credit agency *n* agencia de informes comerciales.

credit balance *n* saldo acreedor.

credit card *n* tarjeta de crédito.

credit control *n* control *m* de créditos.

credit facilities *npl* facilidades *fpl* de crédito.

credit limit *n* límite *m* de crédito.

credit note *n* nota de crédito.

creditor ['krɛdɪtə*] *n* acreedor(a) *m/f*.

credits ['krɛdɪts] *npl* (*CINE*) títulos *mpl or* rótulos *mpl* de crédito, créditos *mpl*.

credit transfer *n* transferencia de crédito.

creditworthy ['krɛdɪtwɜːðɪ] *adj* solvente.

credulity [krɪ'djuːlɪtɪ] *n* credulidad *f*.

creed [kriːd] *n* credo.

creek [kriːk] *n* cala, ensenada; (*US*) riachuelo.

creel [kriːl] *n* nasa.

creep, pt, pp crept [kriːp, krɛpt] *vi* (*animal*) deslizarse; (*plant*) trepar; **to** ~ **up on sb** acercarse sigilosamente a algn; (*fig: old age etc*) acercarse ♦ *n* (*col*): **he's a** ~ ¡qué lameculos es!; **it gives me the** ~**s** me da escalofríos.

creeper ['kriːpə*] *n* enredadera.

creepers ['kriːpəz] *npl* (*US: for baby*) pelele *msg*.

creepy ['kriːpɪ] *adj* (*frightening*) horripilante.

creepy-crawly ['kriːpɪ'krɔːlɪ] *n* (*col*) bicho.

cremate [krɪ'meɪt] *vt* incinerar.

cremation [krɪ'meɪʃən] *n* incineración *f*, cremación *f*.

crematorium, pl crematoria [krɛmə'tɔːrɪəm, -'tɔːrɪə] *n* crematorio.

creosote ['krɪəsəut] *n* creosota.

crêpe [kreɪp] *n* (*fabric*) crespón *m*; (*also:* ~ **rubber**) crep(é) *m*.

crêpe bandage *n* (*BRIT*) venda elástica.

crêpe paper *n* papel *m* crep(é).

crêpe sole *n* (*on shoes*) suela de crep(é).

crept [krɛpt] *pt, pp of* **creep**.

crescent ['krɛsnt] *n* media luna; (*street*) calle *f* (*en forma de semicírculo*).

cress [krɛs] *n* berro.

crest [krɛst] *n* (*of bird*) cresta; (*of hill*) cima, cumbre *f*; (*of helmet*) cimera; (*of coat of arms*) blasón *m*.

crestfallen ['krɛstfɔːlən] *adj* alicaído.

Crete [kriːt] *n* Creta.

cretin ['krɛtɪn] *n* cretino/a.

crevasse [krɪ'væs] *n* grieta.

crevice ['krɛvɪs] *n* grieta, hendedura.

crew [kruː] *n* (*of ship etc*) tripulación *f*; (*CINE etc*) equipo; (*gang*) pandilla, banda; (*MIL*) dotación *f*.

crew-cut ['kruːkʌt] *n* corte *m* al rape.

crew-neck ['kruːnɛk] n cuello de caja.
crib [krɪb] n pesebre m ♦ vt (col) plagiar; (SCOL) copiar.
crick [krɪk] n: ~ **in the neck** tortícolis f inv.
cricket ['krɪkɪt] n (insect) grillo; (game) críquet m.
cricketer ['krɪkɪtə*] n jugador(a) m/f de críquet.
crime [kraɪm] n crimen m; (less serious) delito.
crime wave n ola de crímenes or delitos.
criminal ['krɪmɪnl] n criminal m/f, delincuente m/f ♦ adj criminal; (law) penal.
Criminal Investigation Department (CID) n ≈ Brigada de Investigación Criminal (B.I.C. f) (SP).
crimp [krɪmp] vt (hair) rizar.
crimson ['krɪmzn] adj carmesí.
cringe [krɪndʒ] vi encogerse.
crinkle ['krɪŋkl] vt arrugar.
crinkly ['krɪŋklɪ] adj (hair) rizado, crespo.
cripple ['krɪpl] n lisiado/a, cojo/a ♦ vt lisiar, mutilar; (ship, plane) inutilizar; (production, exports) paralizar; ~d with arthritis paralizado por la artritis.
crippling ['krɪplɪŋ] adj (injury etc) debilitador(a); (prices, taxes) devastador(a).
crisis, pl **crises** ['kraɪsɪs, -siːz] n crisis f.
crisp [krɪsp] adj fresco; (toast, snow) crujiente; (manner) seco.
crisps [krɪsps] npl (BRIT) patatas fpl fritas.
crisscross ['krɪskrɔs] adj entrelazado, entrecruzado ♦ vt entrecruzar(se).
criterion, pl **criteria** [kraɪ'tɪərɪən, -'tɪərɪə] n criterio.
critic ['krɪtɪk] n crítico/a.
critical ['krɪtɪkl] adj (gen) crítico; (illness) grave; **to be** ~ **of sb/sth** criticar a algn/algo.
critically ['krɪtɪklɪ] adv (speak etc) en tono crítico; (ill) gravemente.
criticism ['krɪtɪsɪzm] n crítica.
criticize ['krɪtɪsaɪz] vt criticar.
critique [krɪ'tiːk] n crítica.
croak [krəuk] vi (frog) croar; (raven) graznar ♦ n (of raven) graznido.
Croat ['krəuæt] adj, n = **Croatian**.
Croatia [krəu'eɪʃə] n Croacia.
Croatian [krəu'eɪʃən] adj, n croata m/f ♦ n (LING) croata m.
crochet ['krəuʃeɪ] n ganchillo.
crock [krɔk] n cántaro; (col: person: also: old ~) carcamal m/f, vejestorio; (: car etc) cacharro.
crockery ['krɔkərɪ] n (plates, cups etc) loza, vajilla.
crocodile ['krɔkədaɪl] n cocodrilo.

crocus ['krəukəs] n azafrán m.
croft [krɔft] n granja pequeña.
crofter ['krɔftə*] n pequeño granjero.
croissant ['krwasã] n croissant m, medialuna (esp LAM).
crone [krəun] n arpía, bruja.
crony ['krəunɪ] n compinche m/f.
crook [kruk] n (fam) ladrón/ona m/f; (of shepherd) cayado; (of arm) pliegue m.
crooked ['krukɪd] adj torcido; (path) tortuoso; (fam) sucio.
crop [krɔp] n (produce) cultivo; (amount produced) cosecha; (riding ~) látigo de montar; (of bird) buche m ♦ vt cortar, recortar; (subj: animals: grass) pacer.
▶**crop up** vi surgir, presentarse.
crop spraying [-'spreɪŋ] n fumigación f de los cultivos.
croquet ['krəukeɪ] n croquet m.
croquette [krə'kɛt] n croqueta (de patata).
cross [krɔs] n cruz f ♦ vt (street etc) cruzar, atravesar; (thwart: person) contrariar, ir contra ♦ vi: **the boat ~es from Santander to Plymouth** el barco hace la travesía de Santander a Plymouth ♦ adj de mal humor, enojado; **it's a ~ between geography and sociology** es una mezcla de geografía y sociología; **to ~ o.s.** santiguarse; **they've got their lines ~ed** (fig) hay un malentendido entre ellos; **to be/get ~ with sb (about sth)** estar enfadado/enfadarse con algn (por algo).
▶**cross out** vt tachar.
▶**cross over** vi cruzar.
crossbar ['krɔsbɑː*] n travesaño; (of bicycle) barra.
crossbow ['krɔsbəu] n ballesta.
cross-Channel ferry ['krɔs'tʃænl-] n transbordador m que cruza el Canal de la Mancha.
cross-check ['krɔstʃɛk] n verificación f ♦ vt verificar.
cross-country (race) ['krɔs'kʌntrɪ-] n carrera a campo traviesa, cross m.
cross-dressing [krɔs'drɛsɪŋ] n travestismo.
cross-examination ['krɔsɪgzæmɪ'neɪʃən] n interrogatorio.
cross-examine ['krɔsɪg'zæmɪn] vt interrogar.
cross-eyed ['krɔsaɪd] adj bizco.
crossfire ['krɔsfaɪə*] n fuego cruzado.
crossing ['krɔsɪŋ] n (road) cruce m; (rail) paso a nivel; (sea passage) travesía; (also: **pedestrian** ~) paso de peatones.
crossing guard n (US) persona encargada de ayudar a los niños a cruzar la calle.
crossing point n paso; (at border) paso fronterizo.

cross purposes *npl*: **to be at ~ with sb** tener un malentendido con algn.

cross-question ['krɔs'kwɛstʃən] *vt* interrogar.

cross-reference ['krɔs'rɛfrəns] *n* remisión *f*.

crossroads ['krɔsrəudz] *nsg* cruce *m*; (*fig*) encrucijada.

cross section *n* corte *m* transversal; (*of population*) muestra (representativa).

crosswalk ['krɔswɔːk] *n* (*US*) paso de peatones.

crosswind ['krɔswɪnd] *n* viento de costado.

crossword ['krɔswɔːd] *n* crucigrama *m*.

crotch [krɔtʃ] *n* (*of garment*) entrepierna.

crotchet ['krɔtʃɪt] *n* (*BRIT MUS*) negra.

crotchety ['krɔtʃɪtɪ] *adj* (*person*) arisco.

crouch [krautʃ] *vi* agacharse.

crouton ['kruːtɔn] *n* cubito de pan frito.

crow [krəu] *n* (*bird*) cuervo; (*of cock*) canto, cacareo ♦ *vi* (*cock*) cantar; (*fig*) jactarse.

crowbar ['krəubɑː*] *n* palanca.

crowd [kraud] *n* muchedumbre *f*; (*SPORT*) público; (*common herd*) vulgo ♦ *vt* (*gather*) amontonar; (*fill*) llenar ♦ *vi* (*gather*) reunirse; (*pile up*) amontonarse; **~s of people** gran cantidad de gente.

crowded ['kraudɪd] *adj* (*full*) atestado; (*well-attended*) concurrido.

crowd scene *n* (*CINE*, *THEAT*) escena con muchos comparsas.

crown [kraun] *n* corona; (*of head*) coronilla; (*of hat*) copa; (*of hill*) cumbre *f* ♦ *vt* (*also tooth*) coronar; **and to ~ it all ...** (*fig*) y para colmo *or* remate ....

crown court *n* (*LAW*) tribunal *m* superior; *ver recuadro*.

CROWN COURT

En el sistema legal inglés los delitos graves como asesinato, violación o atraco son juzgados por un jurado en un tribunal superior llamado **crown court** *con sede en noventa ciudades. Los jueces de paz ("Justice of the Peace", juzgan delitos menores e infracciones de la ley en juzgados llamados "Magistrates' Courts". Es el juez de paz quien decide remitir los casos pertinentes a la* **crown court**, *que en caso de recursos se remite al tribunal de apelación, "Court of Appeal".*

---

crowning ['kraunɪŋ] *adj* (*achievement*, *glory*) máximo.

crown jewels *npl* joyas *fpl* reales.

crown prince *n* príncipe *m* heredero.

crow's feet ['krəuzfiːt] *npl* patas *fpl* de gallo.

crucial ['kruːʃl] *adj* crucial, decisivo; **his approval is ~ to the success of the project** su aprobación es crucial para el éxito del proyecto.

crucifix ['kruːsɪfɪks] *n* crucifijo.

crucifixion [kruːsɪ'fɪkʃən] *n* crucifixión *f*.

crucify ['kruːsɪfaɪ] *vt* crucificar; (*fig*) martirizar.

crude [kruːd] *adj* (*materials*) bruto; (*fig*: *basic*) tosco; (: *vulgar*) ordinario.

crude (oil) *n* (petróleo) crudo.

cruel ['kruəl] *adj* cruel.

cruelty ['kruəltɪ] *n* crueldad *f*.

cruet ['kruːɪt] *n* vinagreras *fpl*.

cruise [kruːz] *n* crucero ♦ *vi* (*ship*) navegar; (*holidaymakers*) hacer un crucero; (*car*) ir a velocidad constante.

cruise missile *n* misil *m* de crucero.

cruiser ['kruːzə*] *n* crucero.

cruising speed ['kruːzɪŋ-] *n* velocidad *f* de crucero.

crumb [krʌm] *n* miga, migaja.

crumble ['krʌmbl] *vt* desmenuzar ♦ *vi* (*gen*) desmenuzarse; (*building*) desmoronarse.

crumbly ['krʌmblɪ] *adj* desmenuzable.

crummy ['krʌmɪ] *adj* (*col*: *poor quality*) pésimo, cutre (*SP*); (: *unwell*) fatal.

crumpet ['krʌmpɪt] *n* ≈ bollo para tostar.

crumple ['krʌmpl] *vt* (*paper*) estrujar; (*material*) arrugar.

crunch [krʌntʃ] *vt* (*with teeth*) ronzar; (*underfoot*) hacer crujir ♦ *n* (*fig*) hora de la verdad.

crunchy ['krʌntʃɪ] *adj* crujiente.

crusade [kruː'seɪd] *n* cruzada ♦ *vi*: **to ~ for/ against** (*fig*) hacer una campaña en pro de/en contra de.

crusader [kruː'seɪdə*] *n* (*fig*) paladín *m/f*.

crush [krʌʃ] *n* (*crowd*) aglomeración *f* ♦ *vt* (*gen*) aplastar; (*paper*) estrujar; (*cloth*) arrugar; (*grind*, *break up*: *garlic*, *ice*) picar; (*fruit*) exprimir; (*grapes*) exprimir, prensar; **to have a ~ on sb** estar enamorado de algn.

crushing ['krʌʃɪŋ] *adj* aplastante; (*burden*) agobiante.

crust [krʌst] *n* corteza.

crustacean [krʌs'teɪʃən] *n* crustáceo.

crusty ['krʌstɪ] *adj* (*bread*) crujiente; (*person*) de mal carácter; (*remark*) brusco.

crutch [krʌtʃ] *n* (*MED*) muleta; (*support*) apoyo.

crux [krʌks] *n*: **the ~** lo esencial, el quid.

cry [kraɪ] *vi* llorar; (*shout*: *also*: *~ out*) gritar ♦ *n* grito; (*of animal*) aullido; (*weep*): **she had a good ~** lloró a lágrima viva; **what are you ~ing about?** ¿por qué lloras?; **to ~ for help** pedir socorro a voces; **it's a far**

~ **from** ... (fig) dista mucho de ....
▶**cry off** vi retirarse.
crypt [krɪpt] n cripta.
cryptic ['krɪptɪk] adj enigmático.
crystal ['krɪstl] n cristal m.
crystal-clear ['krɪstl'klɪə*] adj claro como el agua; (fig) cristalino.
crystallize ['krɪstəlaɪz] vt (fig) cristalizar
♦ vi cristalizarse; ~**d fruits** frutas fpl escarchadas.
CSA n abbr = Confederate States of America; (= Child Support Agency) organismo que supervisa el pago de la pensión a hijos de padres separados.
CSC n abbr (= Civil Service Commission) comisión para la contratación de funcionarios.
CSE n abbr (BRIT: = Certificate of Secondary Education) ≈ título de BUP.
CS gas n (BRIT) gas m lacrimógeno.
CST n abbr (US: = Central Standard Time) huso horario.
CT, Ct. abbr (US) = Connecticut.
ct abbr = **carat**.
CTC n abbr (BRIT: city technology college) ≈ centro de formación profesional.
cu. abbr = **cubic**.
cub [kʌb] n cachorro; (also: ~ **scout**) niño explorador.
Cuba ['kju:bə] n Cuba.
Cuban ['kju:bən] adj, n cubano/a m/f.
cubbyhole ['kʌbɪhəul] n cuchitril m.
cube [kju:b] n cubo; (of sugar) terrón m ♦ vt (MATH) elevar al cubo.
cube root n raíz f cúbica.
cubic ['kju:bɪk] adj cúbico; ~ **capacity** (AUT) capacidad f cúbica.
cubicle ['kju:bɪkl] n (at pool) caseta; (for bed) cubículo.
cubism ['kju:bɪzəm] n cubismo.
cuckoo ['kuku:] n cuco.
cuckoo clock n reloj m de cuco.
cucumber ['kju:kʌmbə*] n pepino.
cuddle ['kʌdl] vt abrazar ♦ vi abrazarse.
cuddly ['kʌdlɪ] adj mimoso; (toy) de peluche.
cudgel ['kʌdʒəl] vt: **to** ~ **one's brains** devanarse los sesos.
cue [kju:] n (snooker ~) taco; (THEAT etc) entrada.
cuff [kʌf] n (BRIT: of shirt, coat etc) puño; (US: of trousers) vuelta; (blow) bofetada ♦ vt bofetear; **off the** ~ adv improvisado.
cufflinks ['kʌflɪŋks] npl gemelos mpl.
cu. in. abbr = **cubic inches**.
cuisine [kwɪ'zi:n] n cocina.
cul-de-sac ['kʌldəsæk] n callejón m sin salida.

culinary ['kʌlɪnərɪ] adj culinario.
cull [kʌl] vt (select) entresacar; (kill selectively: animals) matar selectivamente
♦ n matanza selectiva; **seal** ~ matanza selectiva de focas.
culminate ['kʌlmɪneɪt] vi: **to** ~ **in** culminar en.
culmination [kʌlmɪ'neɪʃən] n culminación f, colmo.
culottes [ku:'lɒts] npl falda f pantalón.
culpable ['kʌlpəbl] adj culpable.
culprit ['kʌlprɪt] n culpable m/f.
cult [kʌlt] n culto; **a** ~ **figure** un ídolo.
cultivate ['kʌltɪveɪt] vt (also fig) cultivar.
cultivated ['kʌltɪveɪtɪd] adj culto.
cultivation [kʌltɪ'veɪʃən] n cultivo; (fig) cultura.
cultural ['kʌltʃərəl] adj cultural.
culture ['kʌltʃə*] n (also fig) cultura.
cultured ['kʌltʃəd] adj culto.
cumbersome ['kʌmbəsəm] adj voluminoso.
cumin ['kʌmɪn] n (spice) comino.
cummerbund ['kʌməbʌnd] n faja, fajín m.
cumulative ['kju:mjulətɪv] adj cumulativo.
cunning ['kʌnɪŋ] n astucia ♦ adj astuto; (clever: device, idea) ingenioso.
cunt [kʌnt] n (col!) n coño (!); (insult) mamonazo/a (!).
cup [kʌp] n taza; (prize, event) copa; **a** ~ **of tea** una taza de té.
cupboard ['kʌbəd] n armario, placar(d) m (LAM).
cup final n (FOOTBALL) final f de copa.
cupful ['kʌpful] n taza.
Cupid ['kju:pɪd] n Cupido.
cupola ['kju:pələ] n cúpula.
cuppa ['kʌpə] n (BRIT col) (taza de) té m.
cup-tie ['kʌptaɪ] n (BRIT) partido de copa.
cur [kə:*] n perro de mala raza; (person) canalla m.
curable ['kjuərəbl] adj curable.
curate ['kjuərɪt] n coadjutor m.
curator [kjuə'reɪtə*] n director(a) m/f.
curb [kə:b] vt refrenar; (powers, spending) limitar ♦ n freno; (US: kerb) bordillo.
curd cheese [kə:d-] n requesón m.
curdle ['kə:dl] vi cuajarse.
curds [kə:dz] npl requesón msg.
cure [kjuə*] vt curar ♦ n cura, curación f; **to be** ~**d of sth** curarse de algo; **to take a** ~ tomar un remedio.
cure-all ['kjuərɔ:l] n (also fig) panacea.
curfew ['kə:fju:] n toque m de queda.
curio ['kjuərɪəu] n curiosidad f.
curiosity [kjuərɪ'ɒsɪtɪ] n curiosidad f.
curious ['kjuərɪəs] adj curioso; **I'm** ~ **about him** me intriga.
curiously ['kjuərɪəslɪ] adv curiosamente; ~

enough, ... aunque parezca extraño ....

curl [kə:l] *n* rizo; (*of smoke etc*) espiral *f*, voluta ♦ *vt* (*hair*) rizar; (*paper*) arrollar; (*lip*) fruncir ♦ *vi* rizarse; arrollarse.

►**curl up** *vi* arrollarse; (*person*) hacerse un ovillo; (*fam*) morirse de risa.

curler ['kə:lə*] *n* bigudí *m*.

curlew ['kə:lu:] *n* zarapito.

curling tongs, (*US*) **curling irons** ['kə:lɪŋ-] *npl* tenacillas *fpl*.

curly ['kə:lɪ] *adj* rizado.

currant ['kʌrnt] *n* pasa; (*black, red*) grosella.

currency ['kʌrnsɪ] *n* moneda; **to gain ~** (*fig*) difundirse.

current ['kʌrnt] *n* corriente *f* ♦ *adj* actual; **direct/alternating ~** corriente directa/ alterna; **the ~ issue of a magazine** el último número de una revista; **in ~ use** de uso corriente.

current account *n* (*BRIT*) cuenta corriente.

current affairs *npl* (noticias *fpl* de) actualidad *f*.

current assets *npl* (*COMM*) activo disponible.

current liabilities *npl* (*COMM*) pasivo circulante.

currently ['kʌrntlɪ] *adv* actualmente.

curriculum, *pl* **~s** *or* **curricula** [kə'rɪkjuləm, -lə] *n* plan *m* de estudios.

curriculum vitae (CV) [-'vi:taɪ] *n* currículum *m* (vitae).

curry ['kʌrɪ] *n* curry *m* ♦ *vt*: **to ~ favour with** buscar el favor de.

curry powder *n* curry *m* en polvo.

curse [kə:s] *vi* echar pestes ♦ *vt* maldecir ♦ *n* maldición *f*; (*swearword*) palabrota.

cursor ['kə:sə*] *n* (*COMPUT*) cursor *m*.

cursory ['kə:sərɪ] *adj* rápido, superficial.

curt [kə:t] *adj* seco.

curtail [kə:'teɪl] *vt* (*cut short*) acortar; (*restrict*) restringir.

curtain ['kə:tn] *n* cortina; (*THEAT*) telón *m*; **to draw the ~s** (*together*) cerrar las cortinas; (*apart*) abrir las cortinas.

curtain call *n* (*THEAT*) llamada a escena.

curtain ring *n* anilla.

curts(e)y ['kə:tsɪ] *n* reverencia ♦ *vi* hacer una reverencia.

curve [kə:v] *n* curva ♦ *vt, vi* torcer.

curved [kə:vd] *adj* curvo.

cushion ['kuʃən] *n* cojín *m*; (*SNOOKER*) banda ♦ *vt* (*seat*) acolchar; (*shock*) amortiguar.

cushy ['kuʃɪ] *adj* (*col*): **a ~ job** un chollo; **to have a ~ time** tener la vida arreglada.

custard ['kʌstəd] *n* (*for pouring*) natillas *fpl*.

custard powder *n* polvos *mpl* para natillas.

custodial sentence [kʌs'təudɪəl-] *n* pena de prisión.

custodian [kʌs'təudɪən] *n* guardián/ana *m/f*; (*of museum etc*) conservador(a) *m/f*.

custody ['kʌstədɪ] *n* custodia; **to take sb into ~** detener a algn; **in the ~ of** al cuidado *or* cargo de.

custom ['kʌstəm] *n* costumbre *f*; (*COMM*) clientela; *see also* **customs.**

customary ['kʌstəmərɪ] *adj* acostumbrado; **it is ~ to do** ... es la costumbre hacer ....

custom-built ['kʌstəm'bɪlt] *adj* = **custom-made.**

customer ['kʌstəmə*] *n* cliente *m/f*; **he's an awkward ~** (*col*) es un tipo difícil.

customer profile *n* perfil *m* del cliente.

customized ['kʌstəmaɪzd] *adj* (*car etc*) hecho a encargo.

custom-made ['kʌstəm'meɪd] *adj* hecho a la medida.

customs ['kʌstəmz] *npl* aduana *sg*; **to go through (the) ~** pasar la aduana.

Customs and Excise *n* (*BRIT*) Aduanas *fpl* y Arbitrios.

customs officer *n* aduanero/a, funcionario/a de aduanas.

cut [kʌt] *vb* (*pt, pp* **cut**) *vt* cortar; (*price*) rebajar; (*record*) grabar; (*reduce*) reducir; (*col: avoid: class, lecture*) fumarse, faltar a ♦ *vi* cortar; (*intersect*) cruzarse ♦ *n* corte *m*; (*in skin*) corte, cortadura; (*with sword*) tajo; (*of knife*) cuchillada; (*in salary etc*) recorte *m*; (*slice of meat*) tajada; **to ~ one's finger** cortarse un dedo; **to get one's hair ~** cortarse el pelo; **to ~ and paste** (*COMPUT*) cortar y pegar; **to ~ sb dead** negarle el saludo *or* cortarle (*LAM*) a algn; **it ~s both ways** (*fig*) tiene doble filo; **to ~ a tooth** echar un diente; **power ~** (*BRIT*) apagón *m*.

►**cut back** *vt* (*plants*) podar; (*production, expenditure*) reducir.

►**cut down** *vt* (*tree*) cortar, derribar; (*consumption, expenses*) reducir; **to ~ sb down to size** (*fig*) bajarle los humos a algn.

►**cut in** *vi*: **to ~ in (on)** (*interrupt: conversation*) interrumpir, intervenir (en); (*AUT*) cerrar el paso (a).

►**cut off** *vt* cortar; (*fig*) aislar; (*troops*) cercar; **we've been ~ off** (*TEL*) nos han cortado la comunicación.

►**cut out** *vt* (*shape*) recortar; (*delete*) suprimir.

►**cut up** *vt* cortar (en pedazos); (*chop: food*) trinchar, cortar.

cut-and-dried ['kʌtən'draɪd] *adj* (*also*: **cut-and-dry**) arreglado de antemano, seguro.

cutback ['kʌtbæk] n reducción f.
cute [kjuːt] adj lindo, mono; (*shrewd*) listo.
cuticle ['kjuːtɪkl] n cutícula.
cutlery ['kʌtlərɪ] n cubiertos mpl.
cutlet ['kʌtlɪt] n chuleta.
cutoff ['kʌtɔf] n (*also:* ~ **point**) límite m.
cutout ['kʌtaut] n (*shape*) recortable m.
cut-price ['kʌt'praɪs], (*US*) **cut-rate** ['kʌt'reɪt] adj a precio reducido.
cutthroat ['kʌtθrəut] n asesino/a ♦ adj feroz; ~ **competition** competencia encarnizada or despiadada.
cutting ['kʌtɪŋ] adj (*gen*) cortante; (*remark*) mordaz ♦ n (*BRIT: from newspaper*) recorte m; (: *RAIL*) desmonte m; (*CINE*) montaje m.
cutting edge n (*of knife*) filo; (*fig*) vanguardia; **a country on** or **at the ~ of space technology** un país puntero en tecnología del espacio.
CV n abbr see **curriculum vitae**.
C & W n abbr = **country and western (music)**.
cwo abbr (*COMM*) = **cash with order**.
cwt. abbr = **hundredweight(s)**.
cyanide ['saɪənaɪd] n cianuro.
cybercafé ['saɪbə,kæfeɪ] n cibercafé m.
cybernetics [saɪbə'netɪks] nsg cibernética.
cyberspace ['saɪbəspeɪs] n ciberespacio.
cyberterrorism ['saɪbətɛrərɪzəm] n ciberterrorismo m.
cyclamen ['sɪkləmən] n ciclamen m.
cycle ['saɪkl] n ciclo; (*bicycle*) bicicleta ♦ vi ir en bicicleta.
cycle lane n carril m de bicicleta, carril m bici.
cycle race n carrera ciclista.
cycle rack n soporte m para bicicletas.
cycling ['saɪklɪŋ] n ciclismo.
cycling holiday n vacaciones fpl en bicicleta.
cyclist ['saɪklɪst] n ciclista m/f.
cyclone ['saɪkləun] n ciclón m.
cygnet ['sɪgnɪt] n pollo de cisne.
cylinder ['sɪlɪndə*] n cilindro.
cylinder block n bloque m de cilindros.
cylinder head n culata de cilindro.
cylinder-head gasket n junta de culata.
cymbals ['sɪmblz] npl platillos mpl, címbalos mpl.
cynic ['sɪnɪk] n cínico/a.
cynical ['sɪnɪkl] adj cínico.
cynicism ['sɪnɪsɪzəm] n cinismo.
cypress ['saɪprɪs] n ciprés m.
Cypriot ['sɪprɪət] adj, n chipriota m/f.
Cyprus ['saɪprəs] n Chipre f.
cyst [sɪst] n quiste m.
cystitis [sɪs'taɪtɪs] n cistitis f.
CZ n abbr (*US*: = *Central Zone*) zona del

Canal de Panamá.
czar [zɑː*] n zar m.
czarina [zɑː'riːnə] n zarina.
Czech [tʃɛk] adj checo ♦ n checo/a; (*LING*) checo; **the ~ Republic** la República Checa.
Czechoslovak [tʃɛkə'sləuvæk] adj, n = **Czechoslovakian**.
Czechoslovakia [tʃɛkəslə'vækɪə] n Checoslovaquia.
Czechoslovakian [tʃɛkəslə'vækɪən] adj, n checoslovaco/a m/f.

D d

D, d [diː] n (*letter*) D, d; (*MUS*): **D** re m; **D for David**, (*US*) **D for Dog** D de Dolores.
D abbr (*US POL*) = **democrat(ic)**.
d abbr (*BRIT: old*) = **penny**.
d. abbr = **died**.
DA n abbr (*US*) = **district attorney**.
dab [dæb] v: **to ~ ointment onto a wound** aplicar pomada sobre una herida; **to ~ with paint** dar unos toques de pintura ♦ n (*light stroke*) toque m; (*small amount*) pizca.
dabble ['dæbl] vi: **to ~ in** hacer por afición.
Dacca ['dækə] n Dacca.
dachshund ['dækshund] n perro tejonero.
Dacron ® ['deɪkrɔn] n (*US*) terylene m.
dad [dæd], **daddy** ['dædɪ] n papá m.
daddy-long-legs [dædɪ'lɔŋlɛgz] n típula.
daffodil ['dæfədɪl] n narciso.
daft [dɑːft] adj chiflado.
dagger ['dægə*] n puñal m, daga; **to look ~s at sb** fulminar a algn con la mirada.
dahlia ['deɪljə] n dalia.
daily ['deɪlɪ] adj diario, cotidiano ♦ n (*paper*) diario; (*domestic help*) asistenta ♦ adv todos los días, cada día; **twice ~** dos veces al día.
dainty ['deɪntɪ] adj delicado.
dairy ['dɛərɪ] n (*shop*) lechería; (*on farm*) vaquería ♦ adj (*cow etc*) lechero.
dairy cow n vaca lechera.
dairy farm n vaquería.
dairy produce n productos mpl lácteos.
dais ['deɪɪs] n estrado.
daisy ['deɪzɪ] n margarita.
daisy-wheel printer n impresora de

margarita.

dale [deɪl] n valle m.

dally ['dælɪ] vi entretenerse.

dalmatian [dæl'meɪʃən] n (dog) (perro) dálmata m.

dam [dæm] n presa; (reservoir) embalse ♦ vt embalsar.

damage ['dæmɪdʒ] n daño; (fig) perjuicio; (to machine) avería ♦ vt dañar; perjudicar; averiar; ~ **to property** daños materiales.

damages ['dæmɪdʒɪz] npl (LAW) daños y perjuicios; **to pay £5000 in** ~ pagar £5000 por daños y perjuicios.

damaging ['dæmɪdʒɪŋ] adj: ~ **(to)** perjudicial (a).

Damascus [də'mɑːskəs] n Damasco.

dame [deɪm] n (title) dama; (US col) tía; (THEAT) vieja; see also **pantomime**.

damn [dæm] vt condenar; (curse) maldecir ♦ n (col): **I don't give a** ~ me importa un pito ♦ adj (col: also: ~**ed**) maldito, fregado (LAM); ~ **(it)!** ¡maldito sea!

damnable ['dæmnəbl] adj (col: behaviour) detestable; (: weather) horrible.

damnation [dæm'neɪʃən] n (REL) condenación f ♦ excl (col) ¡maldición!, ¡maldito sea!

damning ['dæmɪŋ] adj (evidence) irrecusable.

damp [dæmp] adj húmedo, mojado ♦ n humedad f ♦ vt (also: ~**en**) (cloth, rag) mojar; (enthusiasm) enfriar.

dampcourse ['dæmpkɔːs] n aislante m hidrófugo.

damper ['dæmpə*] n (MUS) sordina; (of fire) regulador m de tiro; **to put a** ~ **on things** ser un jarro de agua fría.

dampness ['dæmpnɪs] n humedad f.

damson ['dæmzən] n ciruela damascena.

dance [dɑːns] n baile m ♦ vi bailar; **to** ~ **about** saltar.

dance hall n salón m de baile.

dancer ['dɑːnsə*] n bailador(a) m/f; (professional) bailarín/ina m/f.

dancing ['dɑːnsɪŋ] n baile m.

D and C n abbr (MED: = dilation and curettage) raspado.

dandelion ['dændɪlaɪən] n diente m de león.

dandruff ['dændrəf] n caspa.

D and T n abbr (BRIT SCOL) = design and technology.

dandy ['dændɪ] n dandi m ♦ adj (US col) estupendo.

Dane [deɪn] n danés/esa m/f.

danger ['deɪndʒə*] n peligro; (risk) riesgo; ~**!** (on sign) ¡peligro!; **to be in** ~ **of** correr riesgo de; **out of** ~ fuera de peligro.

danger list n (MED): **to be on the** ~ estar

grave.

dangerous ['deɪndʒərəs] adj peligroso.

dangerously ['deɪndʒərəslɪ] adv peligrosamente; ~ **ill** gravemente enfermo.

danger zone n área or zona de peligro.

dangle ['dæŋgl] vt colgar ♦ vi pender, estar colgado.

Danish ['deɪnɪʃ] adj danés/esa ♦ n (LING) danés m.

Danish pastry n pastel m de almendra.

dank [dæŋk] adj húmedo y malsano.

dapper ['dæpə*] adj pulcro, apuesto.

Dardanelles [dɑːdə'nelz] npl Dardanelos mpl.

dare [dɛə*] vt: **to** ~ **sb to do** desafiar a algn a hacer ♦ vi: **to** ~ **(to) do sth** atreverse a hacer algo; **I** ~ **say** (I suppose) puede ser, a lo mejor; **I** ~ **say he'll turn up** puede ser que or quizás venga; **I** ~**n't tell him** no me atrevo a decírselo.

daredevil ['dɛədevl] n temerario/a, atrevido/a.

Dar-es-Salaam ['dɑːressə'lɑːm] n Dar es Salaam m.

daring ['dɛərɪŋ] adj (person) osado; (plan, escape) atrevido ♦ n atrevimiento, osadía.

dark [dɑːk] adj oscuro; (hair, complexion) moreno; (fig: cheerless) triste, sombrío ♦ n (gen) oscuridad f; (night) tinieblas fpl; ~ **chocolate** chocolate m amargo; **it is/is getting** ~ es de noche/está oscureciendo; **in the** ~ **about** (fig) ignorante de; **after** ~ después del anochecer.

darken ['dɑːkn] vt oscurecer; (colour) hacer más oscuro ♦ vi oscurecerse; (cloud over) nublarse.

dark glasses npl gafas fpl oscuras.

dark horse n (fig) incógnita.

darkly ['dɑːklɪ] adv (gloomily) tristemente; (sinisterly) siniestramente.

darkness ['dɑːknɪs] n (in room) oscuridad f; (night) tinieblas fpl.

darkroom ['dɑːkrum] n cuarto oscuro.

darling ['dɑːlɪŋ] adj, n querido/a m/f.

darn [dɑːn] vt zurcir.

dart [dɑːt] n dardo; (in sewing) pinza ♦ vi precipitarse; **to** ~ **away/along** vi salir/marchar disparado.

dartboard ['dɑːtbɔːd] n diana.

darts [dɑːts] n dardos mpl.

dash [dæʃ] n (small quantity: of liquid) gota, chorrito; (: of solid) pizca; (sign) guión m; (: long) raya ♦ vt (break) romper, estrellar; (hopes) defraudar ♦ vi precipitarse, ir de prisa; **a** ~ **of soda** un poco or chorrito de sifón or soda.

▶**dash away, dash off** vi marcharse

apresuradamente.

dashboard ['dæʃbɔːd] *n* (*AUT*) salpicadero.

dashing ['dæʃɪŋ] *adj* gallardo.

dastardly ['dæstədlɪ] *adj* ruin, vil.

DAT *n abbr* (= *digital audio tape*) cas(s)et(t)e *m or f* digital.

data ['deɪtə] *npl* datos *mpl*.

database ['deɪtəbeɪs] *n* base *f* de datos.

data capture *n* recogida de datos.

data link *n* enlace *m* de datos.

data processing *n* proceso *or* procesamiento de datos.

data transmission *n* transmisión *f* de datos.

date [deɪt] *n* (*day*) fecha; (*with friend*) cita; (*fruit*) dátil *m* ♦ *vt* fechar; (*col: girl etc*) salir con; **what's the ~ today?** ¿qué fecha es hoy?; **~ of birth** fecha de nacimiento; **closing ~** fecha tope; **to ~** *adv* hasta la fecha; **out of ~** pasado de moda; **up to ~** moderno; puesto al día; **to bring up to ~** (*correspondence, information*) poner al día; (*method*) actualizar; **to bring sb up to ~** poner a algn al corriente; **letter ~d 5th July** *or* (*US*) **July 5th** carta fechada el 5 de julio.

dated ['deɪtɪd] *adj* anticuado.

date rape *n* violación ocurrida durante una cita con un conocido.

date stamp *n* matasellos *m inv*; (*on fresh foods*) sello de fecha.

dative ['deɪtɪv] *n* dativo.

daub [dɔːb] *vt* embadurnar.

daughter ['dɔːtə*] *n* hija.

daughter-in-law ['dɔːtərɪnlɔː] *n* nuera, hija política.

daunting ['dɔːntɪŋ] *adj* desalentador(a).

davenport ['dævnpɔːt] *n* escritorio; (*US: sofa*) sofá *m*.

dawdle ['dɔːdl] *vi* (*waste time*) perder el tiempo; (*go slowly*) andar muy despacio; **to ~ over one's work** trabajar muy despacio.

dawn [dɔːn] *n* alba, amanecer *m* ♦ *vi* amanecer; (*fig*): **it ~ed on him that ...** cayó en la cuenta de que ...; **at ~** al amanecer; **from ~ to dusk** de sol a sol.

dawn chorus *n* canto de los pájaros al amanecer.

day [deɪ] *n* día *m*; (*working ~*) jornada; **the ~ before** el día anterior; **the ~ after tomorrow** pasado mañana; **the ~ before yesterday** anteayer, antes de ayer; **the ~ after, the following ~** el día siguiente; **by ~** de día; **~ by ~** día a día; **(on) the ~ that ...** el día que ...; **to work an 8-hour ~** trabajar 8 horas diarias *or* al día; **he works 8 hours a ~** trabaja 8 horas al día;

paid by the ~ pagado por día; **these ~s, in the present** ~ hoy en día.

daybook ['deɪbuk] *n* (*BRIT*) diario *or* libro de entradas y salidas.

daybreak ['deɪbreɪk] *n* amanecer *m*.

day-care centre ['deɪkɛə-] *n* centro de día; (*for children*) guardería infantil.

daydream ['deɪdriːm] *n* ensueño ♦ *vi* soñar despierto.

daylight ['deɪlaɪt] *n* luz *f* (del día).

daylight robbery *n*: **it's ~!** (*fig, col*) ¡es un robo descarado!

Daylight Saving Time *n* (*US*) hora de verano.

day-release course [deɪrɪ'liːs-] *n* curso de formación de un día a la semana.

day return (ticket) *n* (*BRIT*) billete *m* de ida y vuelta (en un día).

day shift *n* turno de día.

daytime ['deɪtaɪm] *n* día *m*.

day-to-day ['deɪtə'deɪ] *adj* cotidiano, diario; (*expenses*) diario; **on a ~ basis** día por día.

day trip *n* excursión *f* (de un día).

day tripper *n* excursionista *m/f*.

daze [deɪz] *vt* (*stun*) aturdir ♦ *n*: **in a ~** aturdido.

dazed [deɪzd] *adj* aturdido.

dazzle ['dæzl] *vt* deslumbrar.

dazzling ['dæzlɪŋ] *adj* (*light, smile*) deslumbrante; (*colour*) fuerte.

DBS *n abbr* (= *direct broadcasting by satellite*) transmisión vía satélite.

DC *abbr* (*ELEC*) = **direct current**; (*US*) = District of Columbia.

DCC ® *n abbr* (= *digital compact cassette*) cas(s)et(t)e *m* digital compacto.

DD *n abbr* (= *Doctor of Divinity*) título universitario.

dd. *abbr* (*COMM*) = **delivered**.

D/D *abbr* = **direct debit**.

D-day ['diːdeɪ] *n* (*fig*) día *m* clave.

DDS *n abbr* (*US*: = *Doctor of Dental Science*; *Doctor of Dental Surgery*) títulos universitarios.

DDT *n abbr* (= *dichlorodiphenyltri-chloroethane*) DDT *m*.

DE *abbr* (*US*) = Delaware.

DEA *n abbr* (*US*: = *Drug Enforcement Administration*) *brigada especial dedicada a la lucha contra el tráfico de estupefacientes*.

deacon ['diːkən] *n* diácono.

dead [dɛd] *adj* muerto; (*limb*) dormido; (*battery*) agotado ♦ *adv* totalmente; (*exactly*) justo; **he was ~ on arrival** ingresó cadáver; **to shoot sb ~** matar a algn a tiros; **~ tired** muerto (de cansancio); **to stop ~** parar en seco; **the line has gone ~** (*TEL*) se ha cortado la línea; **the ~** *npl* los muertos.

dead beat *adj*: **to be ~** (*col*) estar hecho polvo.

deaden ['dɛdn] *vt* (*blow, sound*) amortiguar; (*pain*) calmar, aliviar.

dead end *n* callejón *m* sin salida.

dead-end ['dɛdɛnd] *adj*: **a ~ job** un trabajo sin porvenir.

dead heat *n* (*SPORT*) empate *m*.

deadline ['dɛdlaɪn] *n* fecha tope; **to work to a ~** trabajar con una fecha tope.

deadlock ['dɛdlɔk] *n* punto muerto.

dead loss *n* (*col*): **to be a ~** (*person*) ser un inútil; (*thing*) ser una birria.

deadly ['dɛdlɪ] *adj* mortal, fatal; **~ dull** aburridísimo.

deadly nightshade [-'naɪtʃeɪd] *n* belladona.

deadpan ['dɛdpæn] *adj* sin expresión.

Dead Sea *n*: **the ~** el Mar Muerto.

dead season *n* (*TOURISM*) temporada baja.

deaf [dɛf] *adj* sordo; **to turn a ~ ear to sth** hacer oídos sordos a algo.

deaf-aid ['dɛfeɪd] *n* audífono.

deaf-and-dumb ['dɛfən'dʌm] *adj* (*person*) sordomudo; (*alphabet*) para sordomudos.

deafen ['dɛfn] *vt* ensordecer.

deafening ['dɛfnɪŋ] *adj* ensordecedor(a).

deaf-mute ['dɛfmjuːt] *n* sordomudo/a.

deafness ['dɛfnɪs] *n* sordera.

deal [diːl] *n* (*agreement*) pacto, convenio; (*business*) negocio, transacción *f*; (*CARDS*) reparto ♦ *vt* (*pt, pp* **dealt**) (*gen*) dar; **a great ~ (of)** bastante, mucho; **it's a ~!** (*col*) ¡trato hecho!, ¡de acuerdo!; **to do a ~ with sb** hacer un trato con algn; **he got a bad/fair ~ from them** le trataron mal/bien.

►**deal in** *vt fus* tratar en, comerciar en.

►**deal with** *vt fus* (*people*) tratar con; (*problem*) ocuparse de; (*subject*) tratar de.

dealer ['diːlə*] *n* comerciante *m/f*; (*CARDS*) mano *f*.

dealership ['diːləʃɪp] *n* concesionario.

dealings ['diːlɪŋz] *npl* (*COMM*) transacciones *fpl*; (*relations*) relaciones *fpl*.

dealt [dɛlt] *pt, pp of* **deal**.

dean [diːn] *n* (*REL*) deán *m*; (*SCOL*) decano/a.

dear [dɪə*] *adj* querido; (*expensive*) caro ♦ *n*: **my ~** querido/a, **~ me!** ¡Dios mío!; **D~ Sir/Madam** (*in letter*) Muy señor mío, Estimado señor/Estimada señora, De mi/nuestra (mayor) consideración (*esp LAM*); **D~ Mr/Mrs X** Estimado/a señor(a) X.

dearly ['dɪəlɪ] *adv* (*love*) mucho; (*pay*) caro.

dearth [dɜːθ] *n* (*of food, resources, money*) escasez *f*.

death [dɛθ] *n* muerte *f*.

deathbed ['dɛθbɛd] *n* lecho de muerte.

death certificate *n* partida de defunción.

death duties *npl* (*BRIT*) derechos *mpl* de sucesión.

deathly ['dɛθlɪ] *adj* mortal; (*silence*) profundo.

death penalty *n* pena de muerte.

death rate *n* tasa de mortalidad.

death row *n*: **to be on ~** (*US*) estar condenado a muerte.

death sentence *n* condena a muerte.

death squad *n* escuadrón *m* de la muerte.

deathtrap ['dɛθtræp] *n* lugar *m* (*or* vehículo *etc*) muy peligroso.

deb [dɛb] *n abbr* (*col*) = **debutante**.

debacle [deɪ'bɑːkl] *n* desastre *m*, catástrofe *f*.

debar [dɪ'bɑː*] *vt*: **to ~ sb from doing** prohibir a algn hacer.

debase [dɪ'beɪs] *vt* degradar.

debatable [dɪ'beɪtəbl] *adj* discutible; **it is ~ whether ...** es discutible si ....

debate [dɪ'beɪt] *n* debate *m* ♦ *vt* discutir.

debauched [dɪ'bɔːtʃt] *adj* vicioso.

debauchery [dɪ'bɔːtʃərɪ] *n* libertinaje *m*.

debenture [dɪ'bɛntʃə*] *n* (*COMM*) bono, obligación *f*.

debenture capital *n* capital *m* hipotecario.

debilitate [dɪ'bɪlɪteɪt] *vt* debilitar.

debilitating [dɪ'bɪlɪteɪtɪŋ] *adj* (*illness etc*) debilitante.

debit ['dɛbɪt] *n* debe *m* ♦ *vt*: **to ~ a sum to sb or to sb's account** cargar una suma en cuenta a algn.

debit balance *n* saldo deudor *or* pasivo.

debit note *n* nota de débito *or* cargo.

debonair [dɛbə'nɛə*] *adj* jovial, cortés/esa.

debrief [diː'briːf] *vt* hacer dar parte.

debriefing [diː'briːfɪŋ] *n* relación *f* (de un informe).

debris ['dɛbriː] *n* escombros *mpl*.

debt [dɛt] *n* deuda; **to be in ~** tener deudas; **~s of £5000** deudas de cinco mil libras; **bad ~** deuda incobrable.

debt collector *n* cobrador(a) *m/f* de deudas.

debtor ['dɛtə*] *n* deudor(a) *m/f*.

debug ['diː'bʌg] *vt* (*COMPUT*) depurar.

debunk [diː'bʌŋk] *vt* (*col: theory*) desprestigiar, desacreditar; (: *claim*) desacreditar; (: *person, institution*) desenmascarar.

début ['deɪbjuː] *n* presentación *f*.

debutante ['dɛbjutænt] *n* debutante *f*.

Dec. *abbr* (= *December*) dic.

decade ['dɛkeɪd] *n* década, decenio.
decadence ['dɛkədəns] *n* decadencia.
decadent ['dɛkədənt] *adj* decadente.
de-caff ['di:kæf] *n* (*col*) descafeinado.
decaffeinated [dɪ'kæfɪneɪtɪd] *adj* descafeinado.
decamp [dɪ'kæmp] *vi* (*col*) escaparse, largarse, rajarse (*LAM*).
decant [dɪ'kænt] *vt* decantar.
decanter [dɪ'kæntə*] *n* jarra, decantador *m*.
decathlon [dɪ'kæθlən] *n* decatlón *m*.
decay [dɪ'keɪ] *n* (*fig*) decadencia; (*of building*) desmoronamiento; (*of tooth*) caries *f inv* ♦ *vi* (*rot*) pudrirse; (*fig*) decaer.
decease [dɪ'si:s] *n* fallecimiento ♦ *vi* fallecer.
deceased [dɪ'si:st] *adj* difunto.
deceit [dɪ'si:t] *n* engaño.
deceitful [dɪ'si:tful] *adj* engañoso.
deceive [dɪ'si:v] *vt* engañar.
decelerate [di:'sɛləreɪt] *vt* moderar la marcha de ♦ *vi* decelerar.
December [dɪ'sɛmbə*] *n* diciembre *m*.
decency ['di:sənsɪ] *n* decencia.
decent ['di:sənt] *adj* (*proper*) decente; (*person*) amable, bueno.
decently ['di:səntlɪ] *adv* (*respectably*) decentemente; (*kindly*) amablemente.
decentralization [di:sɛntrəlaɪ'zeɪʃən] *n* descentralización *f*.
decentralize [di:'sɛntrəlaɪz] *vt* descentralizar.
deception [dɪ'sɛpʃən] *n* engaño.
deceptive [dɪ'sɛptɪv] *adj* engañoso.
decibel ['dɛsɪbɛl] *n* decibel(io) *m*.
decide [dɪ'saɪd] *vt* (*person*) decidir; (*question, argument*) resolver ♦ *vi*: **to ~ to do/that** decidir hacer/que; **to ~ on sth** tomar una decisión sobre algo; **to ~ against doing sth** decidir en contra de hacer algo.
decided [dɪ'saɪdɪd] *adj* (*resolute*) decidido; (*clear, definite*) indudable.
decidedly [dɪ'saɪdɪdlɪ] *adv* decididamente.
deciding [dɪ'saɪdɪŋ] *adj* decisivo.
deciduous [dɪ'sɪdjuəs] *adj* de hoja caduca.
decimal ['dɛsɪməl] *adj* decimal ♦ *n* decimal *f*; **to 3 ~ places** con 3 cifras decimales.
decimalize ['dɛsɪməlaɪz] *vt* convertir al sistema decimal.
decimal point *n* coma decimal.
decimal system *n* sistema *m* métrico decimal.
decimate ['dɛsɪmeɪt] *vt* diezmar.
decipher [dɪ'saɪfə*] *vt* descifrar.
decision [dɪ'sɪʒən] *n* decisión *f*; **to make a ~** tomar una decisión.
decisive [dɪ'saɪsɪv] *adj* (*influence*) decisivo;

(*manner, person*) decidido; (*reply*) tajante.
deck [dɛk] *n* (*NAUT*) cubierta; (*of bus*) piso; (*of cards*) baraja; **cassette ~** platina; **to go up on ~** subir a (la) cubierta; **below ~** en la bodega.
deckchair ['dɛktʃɛə*] *n* tumbona.
deckhand ['dɛkhænd] *n* marinero de cubierta.
declaration [dɛklə'reɪʃən] *n* declaración *f*.
declare [dɪ'klɛə*] *vt* (*gen*) declarar.
declassify [di:'klæsɪfaɪ] *vt* permitir que salga a la luz.
decline [dɪ'klaɪn] *n* decaimiento, decadencia; (*lessening*) disminución *f* ♦ *vt* rehusar ♦ *vi* decaer; disminuir; **~ in living standards** disminución *f* del nivel de vida; **to ~ to do sth** rehusar hacer algo.
declutch ['di:'klʌtʃ] *vi* desembragar.
decode [di:'kəud] *vt* descifrar.
decoder [di:'kəudə*] *n* (*COMPUT, TV*) de(s)codificador *m*.
decompose [di:kəm'pəuz] *vi* descomponerse.
decomposition [di:kɔmpə'zɪʃən] *n* descomposición *f*.
decompression [di:kəm'prɛʃən] *n* descompresión *f*.
decompression chamber *n* cámara de descompresión.
decongestant [di:kən'dʒɛstənt] *n* descongestionante.
decontaminate [di:kən'tæmɪneɪt] *vt* descontaminar.
decontrol [di:kən'trəul] *vt* (*trade*) quitar controles a; (*prices*) descongelar.
décor ['deɪkɔ:*] *n* decoración *f*; (*THEAT*) decorado.
decorate ['dɛkəreɪt] *vt* (*paint*) pintar; (*paper*) empapelar; (*adorn*): **to ~ (with)** adornar (de), decorar (de).
decoration [dɛkə'reɪʃən] *n* adorno; (*act*) decoración *f*; (*medal*) condecoración *f*.
decorative ['dɛkərətɪv] *adj* decorativo.
decorator ['dɛkəreɪtə*] *n* (*workman*) pintor *m* decorador.
decorum [dɪ'kɔ:rəm] *n* decoro.
decoy ['di:kɔɪ] *n* señuelo; **police ~** trampa *or* señuelo policial.
decrease ['di:kri:s] *n* disminución *f* ♦ (*vb*: [dɪ'kri:s]) *vt* disminuir, reducir ♦ *vi* reducirse; **to be on the ~** ir disminuyendo.
decreasing [dɪ'kri:sɪŋ] *adj* decreciente.
decree [dɪ'kri:] *n* decreto ♦ *vt*: **to ~ (that)** decretar (que); **~ absolute/nisi** sentencia absoluta/provisional de divorcio.
decrepit [dɪ'krɛpɪt] *adj* (*person*) decrépito; (*building*) ruinoso.

decry [dɪˈkraɪ] *vt* criticar, censurar.
dedicate [ˈdɛdɪkeɪt] *vt* dedicar.
dedicated [ˈdɛdɪkeɪtɪd] *adj* dedicado; (*COMPUT*) especializado; ~ **word processor** procesador *m* de textos especializado *or* dedicado.
dedication [dɛdɪˈkeɪʃən] *n* (*devotion*) dedicación *f*, (*in book*) dedicatoria.
deduce [dɪˈdjuːs] *vt* deducir.
deduct [dɪˈdʌkt] *vt* restar; (*from wage etc*) descontar, deducir.
deduction [dɪˈdʌkʃən] *n* (*amount deducted*) descuento; (*conclusion*) deducción *f*, conclusión *f*.
deed [diːd] *n* hecho, acto; (*feat*) hazaña; (*LAW*) escritura; ~ **of covenant** escritura de contrato.
deem [diːm] *vt* (*formal*) juzgar, considerar; **to ~ it wise to do** considerar prudente hacer.
deep [diːp] *adj* profundo; (*voice*) bajo; (*breath*) profundo, a pleno pulmón ♦ *adv*: **the spectators stood 20 ~** los espectadores se formaron de 20 en fondo; **to be 4 metres ~** tener 4 metros de profundidad.
deepen [ˈdiːpn] *vt* ahondar, profundizar ♦ *vi* (*darkness*) intensificarse.
deep-freeze [ˈdiːpˈfriːz] *n* arcón *m* congelador.
deep-fry [ˈdiːpˈfraɪ] *vt* freír en aceite abundante.
deeply [ˈdiːplɪ] *adv* (*breathe*) profundamente, a pleno pulmón; (*interested, moved, grateful*) profundamente, hondamente; **to regret sth ~** sentir algo profundamente.
deep-rooted [ˈdiːpˈruːtɪd] *adj* (*prejudice, habit*) profundamente arraigado; (*affection*) profundo.
deep-sea [ˈdiːpˈsiː] *adj*: ~ **diver** buzo; ~ **diving** buceo de altura.
deep-seated [ˈdiːpˈsiːtɪd] *adj* (*beliefs*) (profundamente) arraigado.
deep-set [ˈdiːpsɛt] *adj* (*eyes*) hundido.
deep vein thrombosis *n* (*MED*) trombosis *f* venosa profunda.
deer [dɪə*] *n, pl inv* ciervo.
deface [dɪˈfeɪs] *vt* desfigurar, mutilar.
defamation [dɛfəˈmeɪʃən] *n* difamación *f*.
defamatory [dɪˈfæmətrɪ] *adj* difamatorio.
default [dɪˈfɔːlt] *vi* faltar al pago; (*SPORT*) no presentarse, no comparecer ♦ *n* (*COMPUT*) defecto; **by ~** (*LAW*) en rebeldía; (*SPORT*) por incomparecencia; **to ~ on a debt** dejar de pagar una deuda.
defaulter [dɪˈfɔːltə*] *n* (*in debt*) moroso/a.
default option *n* (*COMPUT*) opción *f* por

defecto.
defeat [dɪˈfiːt] *n* derrota ♦ *vt* derrotar, vencer; (*fig: efforts*) frustrar.
defeatism [dɪˈfiːtɪzəm] *n* derrotismo.
defeatist [dɪˈfiːtɪst] *adj, n* derrotista *m/f*.
defecate [ˈdɛfəkeɪt] *vi* defecar.
defect [ˈdiːfɛkt] *n* defecto ♦ *vi* [dɪˈfɛkt]: **to ~ to the enemy** pasarse al enemigo; **physical ~** defecto físico; **mental ~** deficiencia mental.
defective [dɪˈfɛktɪv] *adj* (*gen*) defectuoso; (*person*) anormal.
defector [dɪˈfɛktə*] *n* tránsfuga *m/f*.
defence, (*US*) **defense** [dɪˈfɛns] *n* defensa; **the Ministry of D~** el Ministerio de Defensa; **witness for the ~** testigo de descargo.
defenceless [dɪˈfɛnslɪs] *adj* indefenso.
defence spending *n* gasto militar.
defend [dɪˈfɛnd] *vt* defender; (*decision, action*) defender; (*opinion*) mantener.
defendant [dɪˈfɛndənt] *n* acusado/a; (*in civil case*) demandado/a.
defender [dɪˈfɛndə*] *n* defensor(a) *m/f*.
defending champion [dɪˈfɛndɪŋ-] *n* (*SPORT*) defensor(a) *m/f* del título.
defending counsel *n* (*LAW*) abogado defensor.
defense [dɪˈfɛns] *n* (*US*) = **defence**.
defensive [dɪˈfɛnsɪv] *adj* defensivo ♦ *n* defensiva; **on the ~** a la defensiva.
defer [dɪˈfəː*] *vt* (*postpone*) aplazar; **to ~ to** diferir a; (*submit*): **to ~ to sb/sb's opinion** someterse a algn/a la opinión de algn.
deference [ˈdɛfərəns] *n* deferencia, respeto; **out of** *or* **in ~ to** por respeto a.
deferential [dɛfəˈrɛnʃəl] *adj* respetuoso.
deferred [dɪˈfəːd] *adj*: ~ **creditor** acreedor *m* diferido.
defiance [dɪˈfaɪəns] *n* desafío; **in ~ of** en contra de.
defiant [dɪˈfaɪənt] *adj* (*insolent*) insolente; (*challenging*) retador(a).
defiantly [dɪˈfaɪəntlɪ] *adv* con aire de desafío.
deficiency [dɪˈfɪʃənsɪ] *n* (*lack*) falta; (*COMM*) déficit *m*; (*defect*) defecto.
deficient [dɪˈfɪʃənt] *adj* (*lacking*) insuficiente; (*incomplete*) incompleto; (*defective*) defectuoso; (*mentally*) anormal; ~ **in** deficiente en.
deficit [ˈdɛfɪsɪt] *n* déficit *m*.
defile [dɪˈfaɪl] *vt* manchar; (*violate*) violar.
define [dɪˈfaɪn] *vt* (*also COMPUT*) definir.
definite [ˈdɛfɪnɪt] *adj* (*fixed*) determinado; (*clear, obvious*) claro; **he was ~ about it** no dejó lugar a dudas (sobre ello).
definitely [ˈdɛfɪnɪtlɪ] *adv*: **he's ~ mad** no

cabe duda de que está loco.
definition [dɛfɪ'nɪʃən] *n* definición *f*.
definitive [dɪ'fɪnɪtɪv] *adj* definitivo.
deflate [di:'fleɪt] *vt* (*gen*) desinflar;
(*pompous person*) quitar *or* rebajar los
humos a; (*ECON*) deflacionar.
deflation [di:'fleɪʃən] *n* (*ECON*) deflación *f*.
deflationary [di:'fleɪʃənrɪ] *adj* (*ECON*)
deflacionario.
deflect [dɪ'flɛkt] *vt* desviar.
defog [di:'fɔg] *vt* desempañar.
defogger [di:fɔgə*] *n* (*US AUT*) dispositivo
antivaho.
deform [dɪ'fɔ:m] *vt* deformar.
deformed [dɪ'fɔ:md] *adj* deformado.
deformity [dɪ'fɔ:mɪtɪ] *n* deformación *f*.
defraud [dɪ'frɔ:d] *vt* estafar; **to ~ sb of sth**
estafar algo a algn.
defray [dɪ'freɪ] *vt*: **to ~ sb's expenses**
reembolsar a algn los gastos.
defrost [di:'frɔst] *vt* (*frozen food*, *fridge*)
descongelar.
defroster [di:'frɔstə*] *n* (*US*) eliminador *m*
de vaho.
deft [dɛft] *adj* diestro, hábil.
defunct [dɪ'fʌŋkt] *adj* difunto; (*organization*
etc) ya desaparecido.
defuse [di:'fju:z] *vt* desarmar; (*situation*)
calmar, apaciguar.
defy [dɪ'faɪ] *vt* (*resist*) oponerse a;
(*challenge*) desafiar; (*order*) contravenir.
degenerate [dɪ'dʒɛnəreɪt] *vi* degenerar
♦ *adj* [dɪ'dʒɛnərɪt] degenerado.
degradation [dɛgrə'deɪʃən] *n* degradación
f.
degrade [dɪ'greɪd] *vt* degradar.
degrading [dɪ'greɪdɪŋ] *adj* degradante.
degree [dɪ'gri:] *n* grado; (*SCOL*) título; **10**
~s below freezing 10 grados bajo cero; **to**
have a ~ in maths ser licenciado/a en
matemáticas; **by ~s** (*gradually*) poco a
poco, por etapas; **to some ~, to a certain**
~ hasta cierto punto; **a considerable ~ of**
risk un gran índice de riesgo.
dehydrated [di:haɪ'dreɪtɪd] *adj*
deshidratado; (*milk*) en polvo.
dehydration [di:haɪ'dreɪʃən] *n*
deshidratación *f*.
de-ice [di:'aɪs] *vt* (*windscreen*) deshelar.
de-icer [di:'aɪsə*] *n* descongelador *m*.
deign [deɪn] *vi*: **to ~ to do** dignarse hacer.
deity ['di:ɪtɪ] *n* deidad *f*, divinidad *f*.
déjà vu [deɪʒɑː'vuː] *n*: **I had a sense of ~**
sentía como si ya lo hubiera vivido.
dejected [dɪ'dʒɛktɪd] *adj* abatido,
desanimado.
dejection [dɪ'dʒɛkʃən] *n* abatimiento.
Del. *abbr* (*US*) = *Delaware*.

del. *abbr* = **delete**.
delay [dɪ'leɪ] *vt* demorar, aplazar; (*person*)
entretener; (*train*) retrasar; (*payment*)
aplazar ♦ *vi* tardar ♦ *n* demora, retraso;
without ~ en seguida, sin tardar.
delayed-action [dɪleɪd'ækʃən] *adj* (*bomb*
etc) de acción retardada.
delectable [dɪ'lɛktəbl] *adj* (*person*)
encantador(a); (*food*) delicioso.
delegate ['dɛlɪgɪt] *n* delegado/a ♦ *vt*
['dɛlɪgeɪt] delegar; **to ~ sth to sb/sb to do**
sth delegar algo en algn/en algn para
hacer algo.
delegation [dɛlɪ'geɪʃən] *n* (*of work etc*)
delegación *f*.
delete [dɪ'liːt] *vt* suprimir, tachar;
(*COMPUT*) suprimir, borrar.
Delhi ['dɛlɪ] *n* Delhi *m*.
deli ['dɛlɪ] *n* = **delicatessen**.
deliberate [dɪ'lɪbərɪt] *adj* (*intentional*)
intencionado; (*slow*) pausado, lento ♦ *vi*
[dɪ'lɪbəreɪt] deliberar.
deliberately [dɪ'lɪbərɪtlɪ] *adv* (*on purpose*) a
propósito; (*slowly*) pausadamente.
deliberation [dɪlɪbə'reɪʃən] *n* (*consideration*)
reflexión *f*; (*discussion*) deliberación *f*,
discusión *f*.
delicacy ['dɛlɪkəsɪ] *n* delicadeza; (*choice*
food) manjar *m*.
delicate ['dɛlɪkɪt] *adj* (*gen*) delicado;
(*fragile*) frágil.
delicately ['dɛlɪkɪtlɪ] *adv* con delicadeza,
delicadamente; (*act*, *express*) con
discreción.
delicatessen [dɛlɪkə'tɛsn] *n* tienda
especializada en comida exótica.
delicious [dɪ'lɪʃəs] *adj* delicioso, rico.
delight [dɪ'laɪt] *n* (*feeling*) placer *m*, deleite
m; (*object*) encanto, delicia ♦ *vt* encantar,
deleitar; **to take ~ in** deleitarse en.
delighted [dɪ'laɪtɪd] *adj*: **~ (at or with/to**
do) encantado (con/de hacer); **to be ~**
that estar encantado de que; **I'd be ~** con
mucho *or* todo gusto.
delightful [dɪ'laɪtful] *adj* encantador(a),
delicioso.
delimit [di:'lɪmɪt] *vt* delimitar.
delineate [dɪ'lɪnɪeɪt] *vt* delinear.
delinquency [dɪ'lɪŋkwənsɪ] *n* delincuencia.
delinquent [dɪ'lɪŋkwənt] *adj*, *n* delincuente
m/f.
delirious [dɪ'lɪrɪəs] *adj* (*MED*, *fig*) delirante;
to be ~ delirar, desvariar.
delirium [dɪ'lɪrɪəm] *n* delirio.
deliver [dɪ'lɪvə*] *vt* (*distribute*) repartir;
(*hand over*) entregar; (*message*)
comunicar; (*speech*) pronunciar; (*blow*)
lanzar, dar; (*MED*) asistir al parto de.

deliverance [dɪ'lɪvrəns] n liberación f.
delivery [dɪ'lɪvərɪ] n reparto; entrega; (of speaker) modo de expresarse; (MED) parto, alumbramiento; **to take ~ of** recibir.
delivery note n nota de entrega.
delivery van n furgoneta de reparto.
delta ['dɛltə] n delta m.
delude [dɪ'luːd] vt engañar.
deluge ['dɛljuːdʒ] n diluvio ♦ vt (fig): **to ~ (with)** inundar (de).
delusion [dɪ'luːʒən] n ilusión f, engaño.
de luxe [də'lʌks] adj de lujo.
delve [dɛlv] vi: **to ~ into** hurgar en.
Dem. abbr (US POL) = **democrat(ic)**.
demand [dɪ'mɑːnd] vt (gen) exigir; (rights) reclamar; (need) requerir ♦ n (gen) exigencia; (claim) reclamación f; (ECON) demanda; **to ~ sth (from or of sb)** exigir algo (a algn); **to be in ~** ser muy solicitado; **on ~** a solicitud.
demanding [dɪ'mɑːndɪŋ] adj (boss) exigente; (work) absorbente.
demarcation [diːmɑː'keɪʃən] n demarcación f.
demarcation dispute n conflicto de definición or demarcación del trabajo.
demean [dɪ'miːn] vt: **to ~ o.s.** rebajarse.
demeanour, (US) **demeanor** [dɪ'miːnə*] n porte m, conducta, comportamiento.
demented [dɪ'mɛntɪd] adj demente.
demi- ['dɛmɪ] pref semi..., medio....
demilitarize [diː'mɪlɪtəraɪz] vt desmilitarizar; **~d zone** zona desmilitarizada.
demise [dɪ'maɪz] n (death) fallecimiento.
demist [diː'mɪst] vt (AUT) eliminar el vaho de.
demister [diː'mɪstə*] n (AUT) eliminador m de vaho.
demo ['dɛməu] n abbr (col: = demonstration) manifestación f.
demobilization [diː'məubɪlaɪ'zeɪʃən] n desmovilización f.
democracy [dɪ'mɔkrəsɪ] n democracia.
democrat ['dɛməkræt] n demócrata m/f.
democratic [dɛmə'krætɪk] adj democrático; **the D~ Party** el partido demócrata (estadounidense).
demography [dɪ'mɔgrəfɪ] n demografía.
demolish [dɪ'mɔlɪʃ] vt derribar, demoler.
demolition [dɛmə'lɪʃən] n derribo, demolición f.
demon ['diːmən] n (evil spirit) demonio ♦ cpd temible.
demonstrate ['dɛmənstreɪt] vt demostrar ♦ vi manifestarse; **to ~ (for/against)** manifestarse (a favor de/en contra de).

demonstration [dɛmən'streɪʃən] n (POL) manifestación f; (proof) prueba, demostración f; **to hold a ~ (POL)** hacer una manifestación.
demonstrative [dɪ'mɔnstrətɪv] adj (person) expresivo; (LING) demostrativo.
demonstrator ['dɛmənstreɪtə*] n (POL) manifestante m/f.
demoralize [dɪ'mɔrəlaɪz] vt desmoralizar.
demote [dɪ'məut] vt degradar.
demotion [dɪ'məuʃən] n degradación f; (COMM) descenso.
demur [dɪ'mə:*] vi: **to ~ (at)** hacer objeciones (a), vacilar (ante) ♦ n: **without ~** sin objeción.
demure [dɪ'mjuə*] adj recatado.
demurrage [dɪ'mʌrɪdʒ] n sobrestadía.
den [dɛn] n (of animal) guarida; (study) estudio.
denationalization [diːnæʃnəlaɪ'zeɪʃən] n desnacionalización f.
denationalize [diː'næʃnəlaɪz] vt desnacionalizar.
denatured alcohol [diː'neɪtʃəd-] n (US) alcohol m desnaturalizado.
denial [dɪ'naɪəl] n (refusal) negativa; (of report etc) denegación f.
denier ['dɛnɪə*] n denier m.
denim ['dɛnɪm] n tela vaquera; see also **denims**.
denim jacket n chaqueta vaquera, saco vaquero (LAM).
denims ['dɛnɪms] npl vaqueros mpl.
denizen ['dɛnɪzn] n (inhabitant) habitante m/f; (foreigner) residente m/f extranjero/a.
Denmark ['dɛnmɑːk] n Dinamarca.
denomination [dɪnɔmɪ'neɪʃən] n valor m; (REL) confesión f.
denominator [dɪ'nɔmɪneɪtə*] n denominador m.
denote [dɪ'nəut] vt indicar, significar.
denounce [dɪ'nauns] vt denunciar.
dense [dɛns] adj (thick) espeso; (: foliage etc) tupido; (stupid) torpe.
densely ['dɛnslɪ] adv: **~ populated** con una alta densidad de población.
density ['dɛnsɪtɪ] n densidad f; **single/double-~ disk** n disco de densidad sencilla/de doble densidad.
dent [dɛnt] n abolladura ♦ vt (also: **make a ~ in**) abollar.
dental ['dɛntl] adj dental.
dental floss [-flɔs] n seda dental.
dental surgeon n odontólogo/a.
dentifrice ['dɛntɪfrɪs] n dentífrico.
dentist ['dɛntɪst] n dentista m/f; **~'s surgery** (BRIT) consultorio dental.
dentistry ['dɛntɪstrɪ] n odontología.

dentures ['dɛntʃəz] *npl* dentadura *sg* (postiza).

denude [dɪ'njuːd] *vt*: **to ~ of** despojar de.

denunciation [dɪnʌnsɪ'eɪʃən] *n* denuncia, denunciación *f*.

deny [dɪ'naɪ] *vt* negar; (*charge*) rechazar; (*report*) desmentir; **to ~ o.s.** privarse (de); **he denies having said it** niega haberlo dicho.

deodorant [diː'əudərənt] *n* desodorante *m*.

depart [dɪ'pɑːt] *vi* irse, marcharse; (*train*) salir; **to ~ from** (*fig: differ from*) apartarse de.

departed [dɪ'pɑːtɪd] *adj* (*bygone: days, glory*) pasado; (*dead*) difunto ♦ *n*: **the (dear) ~** el/la/los/las difunto/a/os/as.

department [dɪ'pɑːtmənt] *n* (*COMM*) sección *f*; (*SCOL*) departamento; (*POL*) ministerio; **that's not my ~** (*fig*) no tiene que ver conmigo; **D~ of State** (*US*) Ministerio de Asuntos Exteriores.

departmental [diːpɑːt'mɛntl] *adj* (*dispute*) departamental; (*meeting*) departamental, de departamento; **~ manager** jefe/a *m/f* de sección *or* de departamento *or* de servicio.

department store *n* gran almacén *m*.

departure [dɪ'pɑːtʃə*] *n* partida, ida; (*of train*) salida; **a new ~** un nuevo rumbo.

departure lounge *n* (*at airport*) sala de embarque.

depend [dɪ'pɛnd] *vi*: **to ~ (up)on** (*be dependent upon*) depender de; (*rely on*) contar con; **it ~s** depende, según; **~ing on the result** según el resultado.

dependable [dɪ'pɛndəbl] *adj* (*person*) formal, serio.

dependant [dɪ'pɛndənt] *n* dependiente *m/f*.

dependence [dɪ'pɛndəns] *n* dependencia.

dependent [dɪ'pɛndənt] *adj*: **to be ~ (on)** depender (de) ♦ *n* = **dependant**.

depict [dɪ'pɪkt] *vt* (*in picture*) pintar; (*describe*) representar.

depilatory [dɪ'pɪlətrɪ] *n* (*also*: **~ cream**) depilatorio.

depleted [dɪ'pliːtɪd] *adj* reducido.

deplorable [dɪ'plɔːrəbl] *adj* deplorable.

deplore [dɪ'plɔː*] *vt* deplorar.

deploy [dɪ'plɔɪ] *vt* desplegar.

depopulate [diː'pɒpjuleɪt] *vt* despoblar.

depopulation ['diːpɒpju'leɪʃən] *n* despoblación *f*.

deport [dɪ'pɔːt] *vt* deportar.

deportation [diːpɔː'teɪʃən] *n* deportación *f*.

deportation order *n* orden *f* de expulsión *or* deportación.

deportee [diːpɔː'tiː] *n* deportado/a.

deportment [dɪ'pɔːtmənt] *n*

comportamiento.

depose [dɪ'pəuz] *vt* deponer.

deposit [dɪ'pɒzɪt] *n* depósito; (*CHEM*) sedimento; (*of ore, oil*) yacimiento ♦ *vt* (*gen*) depositar; **to put down a ~ of £50** dejar un depósito de 50 libras.

deposit account *n* (*BRIT*) cuenta de ahorros.

depositor [dɪ'pɒzɪtə*] *n* depositante *m/f*, cuentacorrentista *m/f*.

depository [dɪ'pɒzɪtərɪ] *n* almacén *m* depositario.

depot ['dɛpəu] *n* (*storehouse*) depósito; (*for vehicles*) parque *m*.

deprave [dɪ'preɪv] *vt* depravar.

depraved [dɪ'preɪvd] *adj* depravado, vicioso.

depravity [dɪ'prævɪtɪ] *n* depravación *f*, vicio.

deprecate ['dɛprɪkeɪt] *vt* desaprobar, lamentar.

deprecating ['dɛprɪkeɪtɪŋ] *adj* (*disapproving*) de desaprobación; (*apologetic*): **a ~ smile** una sonrisa de disculpa.

depreciate [dɪ'priːʃɪeɪt] *vi* depreciarse, perder valor.

depreciation [dɪpriːʃɪ'eɪʃən] *n* depreciación *f*.

depress [dɪ'prɛs] *vt* deprimir; (*press down*) apretar.

depressant [dɪ'prɛsnt] *n* (*MED*) calmante *m*, sedante *m*.

depressed [dɪ'prɛst] *adj* deprimido; (*COMM: market, economy*) deprimido; (*area*) deprimido (económicamente); **to get ~** deprimirse.

depressing [dɪ'prɛsɪŋ] *adj* deprimente.

depression [dɪ'prɛʃən] *n* depresión *f*; **the economy is in a state of ~** la economía está deprimida.

deprivation [dɛprɪ'veɪʃən] *n* privación *f*; (*loss*) pérdida.

deprive [dɪ'praɪv] *vt*: **to ~ sb of** privar a algn de.

deprived [dɪ'praɪvd] *adj* necesitado.

dept. *abbr* (= *department*) dto.

depth [dɛpθ] *n* profundidad *f*; **at a ~ of 3 metres** a 3 metros de profundidad; **to be out of one's ~** (*swimmer*) perder pie; (*fig*) estar perdido; **to study sth in ~** estudiar algo a fondo; **in the ~s of** en lo más hondo de.

depth charge *n* carga de profundidad.

deputation [dɛpju'teɪʃən] *n* delegación *f*.

deputize ['dɛpjutaɪz] *vi*: **to ~ for sb** sustituir a algn.

deputy ['dɛpjutɪ] *adj*: **~ head**

subdirector(a) *m/f* ♦ *n* sustituto/a,
suplente *m/f*; (*POL*) diputado/a; (*agent*)
representante *m/f*.
deputy leader *n* vicepresidente/a *m/f*.
derail [dɪˈreɪl] *vt*: **to be ~ed** descarrilarse.
derailment [dɪˈreɪlmənt] *n*
descarrilamiento.
deranged [dɪˈreɪndʒd] *adj* trastornado.
derby [ˈdəːbɪ] *n* (*US*) hongo.
deregulate [diːˈrɛgjuleɪt] *vt*
desreglamentar.
deregulation [diːrɛgjuˈleɪʃən] *n*
desreglamentación *f*.
derelict [ˈdɛrɪlɪkt] *adj* abandonado.
deride [dɪˈraɪd] *vt* ridiculizar, mofarse de.
derision [dɪˈrɪʒən] *n* irrisión *f*, mofas *fpl*.
derisive [dɪˈraɪsɪv] *adj* burlón/ona.
derisory [dɪˈraɪzərɪ] *adj* (*sum*) irrisorio;
(*laughter, person*) burlón/ona, irónico.
derivation [dɛrɪˈveɪʃən] *n* derivación *f*.
derivative [dɪˈrɪvətɪv] *n* derivado ♦ *adj*
(*work*) poco original.
derive [dɪˈraɪv] *vt* derivar ♦ *vi*: **to ~ from**
derivarse de.
derived [dɪˈraɪvd] *adj* derivado.
dermatitis [dəːməˈtaɪtɪs] *n* dermatitis *f*.
dermatology [dəːməˈtɔlədʒɪ] *n*
dermatología.
derogatory [dɪˈrɔgətərɪ] *adj* despectivo.
derrick [ˈdɛrɪk] *n* torre *f* de perforación.
derv [dəːv] *n* (*BRIT*) gasoil *m*.
DES *n abbr* (*BRIT*: = *Department of Education
and Science*) ministerio de educación y
ciencia.
descend [dɪˈsɛnd] *vt, vi* descender, bajar; **to
~ from** descender de; **in ~ing order of
importance** de mayor a menor
importancia.
▶**descend on** *vt fus* (*subj: enemy, angry
person*) caer sobre; (: *misfortune*)
sobrevenir; (*gloom, silence*) invadir; **visitors ~ed on us** las visitas nos invadieron.
descendant [dɪˈsɛndənt] *n* descendiente
m/f.
descent [dɪˈsɛnt] *n* descenso; (*GEO*)
pendiente *f*, declive *m*; (*origin*)
descendencia.
describe [dɪsˈkraɪb] *vt* describir.
description [dɪsˈkrɪpʃən] *n* descripción *f*;
(*sort*) clase *f*, género; **of every ~** de toda
clase.
descriptive [dɪsˈkrɪptɪv] *adj* descriptivo.
desecrate [ˈdɛsɪkreɪt] *vt* profanar.
desegregation [diːsɛgrɪˈgeɪʃən] *n*
desegregación *f*.
desert [ˈdɛzət] *n* desierto ♦ *vb* [dɪˈzəːt] *vt*
abandonar, desamparar ♦ *vi* (*MIL*)
desertar; *see also* **deserts**.

deserter [dɪˈzəːtə*] *n* desertor(a) *m/f*.
desertion [dɪˈzəːʃən] *n* deserción *f*.
desert island *n* isla desierta.
deserts [dɪˈzəːts] *npl*: **to get one's just ~**
llevarse su merecido.
deserve [dɪˈzəːv] *vt* merecer, ser digno de,
ameritar (*LAM*).
deservedly [dɪˈzəːvɪdlɪ] *adv* con razón.
deserving [dɪˈzəːvɪŋ] *adj* (*person*) digno;
(*action, cause*) meritorio.
desiccated [ˈdɛsɪkeɪtɪd] *adj* desecado.
design [dɪˈzaɪn] *n* (*sketch*) bosquejo; (*of
dress, car*) diseño; (*pattern*) dibujo ♦ *vt*
(*gen*) diseñar; **industrial ~** diseño
industrial; **to have ~s on sb** tener la(s)
mira(s) puesta(s) en algn; **to be ~ed for
sb/sth** estar hecho para algn/algo.
design and technology *n* diseño y
tecnología.
designate [ˈdɛzɪgneɪt] *vt* (*appoint*)
nombrar; (*destine*) designar ♦ *adj*
[ˈdɛzɪgnɪt] designado.
designation [dɛzɪgˈneɪʃən] *n* (*appointment*)
nombramiento; (*name*) denominación *f*.
designer [dɪˈzaɪnə*] *n* diseñador(a) *m/f*;
(*fashion ~*) modisto/a.
designer baby *n* bebé *m* de diseño.
desirability [dɪzaɪərəˈbɪlɪtɪ] *n* ventaja,
atractivo.
desirable [dɪˈzaɪərəbl] *adj* (*proper*) deseable;
(*attractive*) atractivo; **it is ~ that** es
conveniente que.
desire [dɪˈzaɪə*] *n* deseo ♦ *vt* desear; **to ~
sth/to do sth/that** desear algo/hacer
algo/que.
desirous [dɪˈzaɪərəs] *adj* deseoso.
desist [dɪˈzɪst] *vi*: **to ~ (from)** desistir (de).
desk [dɛsk] *n* (*in office*) escritorio; (*for pupil*)
pupitre *m*; (*in hotel, at airport*) recepción *f*;
(*BRIT: in shop, restaurant*) caja.
desktop computer [ˈdɛsktɔp-] *n*
ordenador *m* de sobremesa.
desktop publishing [ˈdɛsktɔp-] *n*
autoedición *f*.
desolate [ˈdɛsəlɪt] *adj* (*place*) desierto;
(*person*) afligido.
desolation [dɛsəˈleɪʃən] *n* (*of place*)
desolación *f*; (*of person*) aflicción *f*.
despair [dɪsˈpɛə*] *n* desesperación *f* ♦ *vi*: **to
~ of** desesperar de; **in ~** desesperado.
despatch [dɪsˈpætʃ] *n, vt* = **dispatch**.
desperate [ˈdɛspərɪt] *adj* desesperado;
(*fugitive*) peligroso; (*measures*) extremo;
we are getting ~ estamos al borde de
desesperación.
desperately [ˈdɛspərɪtlɪ] *adv*
desesperadamente; (*very*) terriblemente,
gravemente; **~ ill** gravemente enfermo.

desperation [dɛspə'reɪʃən] *n* desesperación *f*; **in ~** desesperado.

despicable [dɪs'pɪkəbl] *adj* vil, despreciable.

despise [dɪs'paɪz] *vt* despreciar.

despite [dɪs'paɪt] *prep* a pesar de, pese a.

despondent [dɪs'pɔndənt] *adj* deprimido, abatido.

despot ['dɛspɔt] *n* déspota *m/f*.

dessert [dɪ'zə:t] *n* postre *m*.

dessertspoon [dɪ'zə:tspu:n] *n* cuchara (de postre).

destabilize [diː'steɪbɪlaɪz] *vt* desestabilizar.

destination [dɛstɪ'neɪʃən] *n* destino.

destine ['dɛstɪn] *vt* destinar.

destined ['dɛstɪnd] *adj*: **~ for London** con destino a Londres.

destiny ['dɛstɪnɪ] *n* destino.

destitute ['dɛstɪtjuːt] *adj* desamparado, indigente.

destitution [dɛstɪ'tjuːʃən] *n* indigencia, miseria.

destroy [dɪs'trɔɪ] *vt* destruir; (*finish*) acabar con.

destroyer [dɪs'trɔɪə*] *n* (*NAUT*) destructor *m*.

destruction [dɪs'trʌkʃən] *n* destrucción *f*; (*fig*) ruina.

destructive [dɪs'trʌktɪv] *adj* destructivo, destructor(a).

desultory ['dɛsəltərɪ] *adj* (*reading*) poco metódico; (*conversation*) inconexo; (*contact*) intermitente.

detach [dɪ'tætʃ] *vt* separar; (*unstick*) despegar.

detachable [dɪ'tætʃəbl] *adj* separable; (*TECH*) desmontable.

detached [dɪ'tætʃt] *adj* (*attitude*) objetivo, imparcial.

detached house *n* chalé *m*, chalet *m*.

detachment [dɪ'tætʃmənt] *n* separación *f*; (*MIL*) destacamento; (*fig*) objetividad *f*, imparcialidad *f*.

detail ['diːteɪl] *n* detalle *m*; (*MIL*) destacamento ♦ *vt* detallar; (*MIL*) destacar; **in ~** detalladamente; **to go into ~(s)** entrar en detalles.

detailed ['diːteɪld] *adj* detallado.

detain [dɪ'teɪn] *vt* retener; (*in captivity*) detener.

detainee [diːteɪ'niː] *n* detenido/a.

detect [dɪ'tɛkt] *vt* (*discover*) descubrir; (*MED, POLICE*) identificar; (*MIL, RADAR, TECH*) detectar; (*notice*) percibir.

detection [dɪ'tɛkʃən] *n* descubrimiento; identificación *f*; **crime ~** investigación *f*; **to escape ~** (*criminal*) escaparse sin ser descubierto; (*mistake*) pasar inadvertido.

detective [dɪ'tɛktɪv] *n* detective *m*.

detective story *n* novela policíaca.

detector [dɪ'tɛktə*] *n* detector *m*.

détente [deɪ'tɑːnt] *n* distensión *f*, detente *f*.

detention [dɪ'tɛnʃən] *n* detención *f*, arresto.

deter [dɪ'tə:*] *vt* (*dissuade*) disuadir; (*prevent*) impedir; **to ~ sb from doing sth** disuadir a algn de que haga algo.

detergent [dɪ'tə:dʒənt] *n* detergente *m*.

deteriorate [dɪ'tɪərɪəreɪt] *vi* deteriorarse.

deterioration [dɪtɪərɪə'reɪʃən] *n* deterioro.

determination [dɪtə:mɪ'neɪʃən] *n* resolución *f*.

determine [dɪ'tə:mɪn] *vt* determinar; **to ~ to do sth** decidir hacer algo.

determined [dɪ'tə:mɪnd] *adj*: **to be ~ to do sth** estar decidido *or* resuelto a hacer algo; **a ~ effort** un esfuerzo enérgico.

deterrence [dɪ'tɛrns] *n* disuasión *f*.

deterrent [dɪ'tɛrənt] *n* fuerza de disuasión; **to act as a ~** servir para prevenir.

detest [dɪ'tɛst] *vt* aborrecer.

detestable [dɪ'tɛstəbl] *adj* aborrecible.

dethrone [diː'θrəun] *vt* destronar.

detonate ['dɛtəneɪt] *vi* estallar ♦ *vt* hacer detonar.

detonator ['dɛtəneɪtə*] *n* detonador *m*, fulminante *m*.

detour ['diːtuə*] *n* (*gen, US AUT: diversion*) desvío ♦ *vt* (*US: traffic*) desviar; **to make a ~** dar un rodeo.

detract [dɪ'trækt] *vt*: **to ~ from** quitar mérito a, restar valor a.

detractor [dɪ'træktə*] *n* detractor(a) *m/f*.

detriment ['dɛtrɪmənt] *n*: **to the ~ of** en perjuicio de; **without ~ to** sin detrimento de, sin perjuicio para.

detrimental [dɛtrɪ'mɛntl] *adj* perjudicial.

deuce [djuːs] *n* (*TENNIS*) cuarenta iguales.

devaluation [dɪvælju'eɪʃən] *n* devaluación *f*.

devalue [dɪ'væljuː] *vt* devaluar.

devastate ['dɛvəsteɪt] *vt* devastar; **he was ~d by the news** las noticias le dejaron desolado.

devastating ['dɛvəsteɪtɪŋ] *adj* devastador(a); (*fig*) arrollador(a).

devastation [dɛvəs'teɪʃən] *n* devastación *f*, ruina.

develop [dɪ'vɛləp] *vt* desarrollar; (*PHOT*) revelar; (*disease*) contraer; (*habit*) adquirir ♦ *vi* desarrollarse; (*advance*) progresar; **this land is to be ~ed** se va a construir en este terreno; **to ~ a taste for sth** tomar gusto a algo; **to ~ into** transformarse *or* convertirse en.

developer [dɪ'vɛləpə*] *n* (*property ~*)

promotor(a) *m/f*.
developing country *n* país *m* en (vías de) desarrollo.
development [dɪ'vɛləpmənt] *n* desarrollo; (*advance*) progreso; (*of affair, case*) desenvolvimiento; (*of land*) urbanización *f*.
development area *n* zona de fomento *or* desarrollo.
deviant ['diːvɪənt] *adj* anómalo, pervertido.
deviate ['diːvɪeɪt] *vi*: **to ~ (from)** desviarse (de).
deviation [diːvɪ'eɪʃən] *n* desviación *f*.
device [dɪ'vaɪs] *n* (*scheme*) estratagema, recurso; (*apparatus*) aparato, mecanismo; (*explosive ~*) artefacto explosivo.
devil ['dɛvl] *n* diablo, demonio.
devilish ['dɛvlɪʃ] *adj* diabólico.
devil-may-care ['dɛvlmeɪ'kɛə*] *adj* despreocupado.
devil's advocate *n*: **to play (the) ~** hacer de abogado del diablo.
devious ['diːvɪəs] *adj* intricado, enrevesado; (*person*) taimado.
devise [dɪ'vaɪz] *vt* idear, inventar.
devoid [dɪ'vɔɪd] *adj*: **~ of** desprovisto de.
devolution [diːvə'luːʃən] *n* (*POL*) descentralización *f*.
devolve [dɪ'vɔlv] *vi*: **to ~ (up)on** recaer sobre.
devote [dɪ'vəut] *vt*: **to ~ sth to** dedicar algo a.
devoted [dɪ'vəutɪd] *adj* (*loyal*) leal, fiel; **the book is ~ to politics** el libro trata de política.
devotee [dɛvəu'tiː] *n* devoto/a.
devotion [dɪ'vəuʃən] *n* dedicación *f*; (*REL*) devoción *f*.
devour [dɪ'vauə*] *vt* devorar.
devout [dɪ'vaut] *adj* devoto.
dew [djuː] *n* rocío.
dexterity [dɛks'tɛrɪtɪ] *n* destreza.
dext(e)rous ['dɛkstrəs] *adj* (*skilful*) diestro, hábil; (*movement*) ágil.
dg *abbr* (= *decigram*) dg.
diabetes [daɪə'biːtiːz] *n* diabetes *f*.
diabetic [daɪə'bɛtɪk] *n* diabético/a ♦ *adj* diabético; (*chocolate, jam*) para diabéticos.
diabolical [daɪə'bɔlɪkəl] *adj* diabólico; (*col: dreadful*) horrendo, horroroso.
diagnose ['daɪəgnəuz] *vt* diagnosticar.
diagnosis, *pl* **diagnoses** [daɪəg'nəusɪs, -siːz] *n* diagnóstico.
diagonal [daɪ'ægənl] *adj* diagonal ♦ *n* diagonal *f*.
diagram ['daɪəgræm] *n* diagrama *m*, esquema *m*.

dial ['daɪəl] *n* esfera; (*of radio*) dial *m*; (: *tuner*) sintonizador *m*; (*of phone*) disco ♦ *vt* (*number*) marcar, discar (*LAM*); **to ~ a wrong number** equivocarse de número; **can I ~ London direct?** ¿puedo marcar un número de Londres directamente?
dial. *abbr* = **dialect**.
dial code *n* (*US*) prefijo.
dialect ['daɪəlɛkt] *n* dialecto.
dialling code ['daɪəlɪŋ-] *n* (*BRIT*) prefijo.
dialling tone *n* (*BRIT*) señal *f or* tono de marcar.
dialogue, (*US*) **dialog** ['daɪələg] *n* diálogo.
dial tone *n* (*US*) señal *f or* tono de marcar.
dialysis [daɪ'ælɪsɪs] *n* diálisis *f*.
diameter [daɪ'æmɪtə*] *n* diámetro.
diametrically [daɪə'mɛtrɪklɪ] *adv*: **~ opposed (to)** diametralmente opuesto (a).
diamond ['daɪəmənd] *n* diamante *m*; **~s** *npl* (*CARDS*) diamantes *mpl*.
diamond ring *n* anillo *or* sortija de diamantes.
diaper ['daɪəpə*] *n* (*US*) pañal *m*.
diaphragm ['daɪəfræm] *n* diafragma *m*.
diarrhoea, (*US*) **diarrhea** [daɪə'riːə] *n* diarrea.
diary ['daɪərɪ] *n* (*daily account*) diario; (*book*) agenda; **to keep a ~** escribir un diario.
diatribe ['daɪətraɪb] *n*: **~ (against)** diatriba (contra).
dice [daɪs] *n, pl inv* dados *mpl* ♦ *vt* (*CULIN*) cortar en cuadritos.
dicey ['daɪsɪ] *adj* (*col*): **it's a bit ~** (*risky*) es un poco arriesgado; (*doubtful*) es un poco dudoso.
dichotomy [daɪ'kɔtəmɪ] *n* dicotomía.
dickhead ['dɪkhɛd] *n* (*BRIT col!*) gilipollas *m inv*.
Dictaphone ® ['dɪktəfəun] *n* dictáfono ®.
dictate [dɪk'teɪt] *vt* dictar ♦ *n* ['dɪkteɪt] dictado.
▶**dictate to** *vt fus* (*person*) dar órdenes a; **I won't be ~d to** no recibo órdenes de nadie.
dictation [dɪk'teɪʃən] *n* (*to secretary etc*) dictado; **at ~ speed** para tomar al dictado.
dictator [dɪk'teɪtə*] *n* dictador *m*.
dictatorship [dɪk'teɪtəʃɪp] *n* dictadura.
diction ['dɪkʃən] *n* dicción *f*.
dictionary ['dɪkʃənrɪ] *n* diccionario.
did [dɪd] *pt of* **do**.
didactic [daɪ'dæktɪk] *adj* didáctico.
diddle ['dɪdl] *vt* estafar, timar.
didn't ['dɪdənt] = **did not**.
die [daɪ] *vi* morir; **to ~ (of *or* from)** morirse (de); **to be dying** morirse, estar muriéndose; **to be dying for sth/to do sth**

morirse por algo/de ganas de hacer algo.
▶**die away** vi (sound, light) desvanecerse.
▶**die down** vi (gen) apagarse; (wind)
amainar.
▶**die out** vi desaparecer, extinguirse.
diehard ['daɪhɑːd] n intransigente m/f.
diesel ['diːzl] n diesel m.
diesel engine n motor m diesel.
diesel fuel, diesel oil n gas-oil m.
diet ['daɪət] n dieta; (restricted food)
régimen m ♦ vi (also: **be on a ~**) estar a
dieta, hacer régimen; **to live on a ~ of**
alimentarse de.
dietician [daɪə'tɪʃən] n dietista m/f.
differ ['dɪfə*] vi (be different) ser distinto,
diferenciarse; (disagree) discrepar.
difference ['dɪfrəns] n diferencia; (quarrel)
desacuerdo; **it makes no ~ to me** me da
igual or lo mismo; **to settle one's ~s**
arreglarse.
different ['dɪfrənt] adj diferente, distinto.
differential [dɪfə'renʃəl] n diferencial f.
differentiate [dɪfə'renʃɪeɪt] vt distinguir
♦ vi diferenciarse; **to ~ between**
distinguir entre.
differently ['dɪfrəntlɪ] adv de otro modo, en
forma distinta.
difficult ['dɪfɪkəlt] adj difícil; **~ to
understand** difícil de entender.
difficulty ['dɪfɪkəltɪ] n dificultad f; **to have
difficulties with** (police, landlord etc) tener
problemas con; **to be in ~** estar en
apuros.
diffidence ['dɪfɪdəns] n timidez f, falta de
confianza en sí mismo.
diffident ['dɪfɪdənt] adj tímido.
diffuse [dɪ'fjuːs] adj difuso ♦ vt [dɪ'fjuːz]
difundir.
dig [dɪg] vt (pt, pp **dug** [dʌg]) (hole) cavar;
(ground) remover; (coal) extraer; (nails
etc) hincar ♦ n (prod) empujón m;
(archaeological) excavación f; (remark)
indirecta; **to ~ into** (savings) consumir; **to
~ into one's pockets for sth** hurgar en el
bolsillo buscando algo; **to ~ one's nails
into** clavar las uñas en; see also **digs**.
▶**dig in** vi (also: **~ o.s. in**: MIL)
atrincherarse; (col: eat) hincar los
dientes ♦ vt (compost) añadir al suelo;
(knife, claw) clavar; **to ~ in one's heels**
(fig) mantenerse en sus trece.
▶**dig out** vt (hole) excavar; (survivors, car
from snow) sacar.
▶**dig up** vt desenterrar; (plant)
desarraigar.
digest [daɪ'dʒest] vt (food) digerir; (facts)
asimilar ♦ n ['daɪdʒest] resumen m.
digestible [daɪ'dʒestəbl] adj digerible.

digestion [dɪ'dʒestʃən] n digestión f.
digestive [daɪ'dʒestɪv] adj (juices, system)
digestivo.
digit ['dɪdʒɪt] n (number) dígito; (finger)
dedo.
digital ['dɪdʒɪtl] adj digital.
digital camera n cámara digital.
digital compact cassette n cas(s)et(t)e m
or f digital compacto.
digital TV n televisión f digital.
dignified ['dɪgnɪfaɪd] adj grave, solemne;
(action) decoroso.
dignify ['dɪgnɪfaɪ] vt dignificar.
dignitary ['dɪgnɪtərɪ] n dignatario/a.
dignity ['dɪgnɪtɪ] n dignidad f.
digress [daɪ'gres] vi: **to ~ from** apartarse
de.
digression [daɪ'greʃən] n digresión f.
digs [dɪgz] npl (BRIT: col) alojamiento.
dike [daɪk] n = **dyke**.
dilapidated [dɪ'læpɪdeɪtɪd] adj
desmoronado, ruinoso.
dilate [daɪ'leɪt] vt dilatar ♦ vi dilatarse.
dilatory ['dɪlətərɪ] adj (person) lento; (action)
dilatorio.
dilemma [daɪ'lemə] n dilema m; **to be in a ~**
estar en un dilema.
dilettante [dɪlɪ'tæntɪ] n diletante m/f.
diligence ['dɪlɪdʒəns] n diligencia.
diligent ['dɪlɪdʒənt] adj diligente.
dill [dɪl] n eneldo.
dilly-dally ['dɪlɪ'dælɪ] vi (hesitate) vacilar;
(dawdle) entretenerse.
dilute [daɪ'luːt] vt diluir.
dim [dɪm] adj (light) débil; (sight) turbio;
(outline) borroso; (stupid) lerdo; (room)
oscuro ♦ vt (light) bajar; **to take a ~ view
of sth** tener una pobre opinión de algo.
dime [daɪm] n (US) moneda de diez
centavos.
dimension [dɪ'menʃən] n dimensión f.
-dimensional [dɪ'menʃənl] adj suff: **two~** de
dos dimensiones.
dimensions [dɪ'menʃənz] npl dimensiones
fpl.
diminish [dɪ'mɪnɪʃ] vt, vi disminuir.
diminished [dɪ'mɪnɪʃt] adj: **~ responsibility**
(LAW) responsabilidad f disminuida.
diminutive [dɪ'mɪnjutɪv] adj diminuto ♦ n
(LING) diminutivo.
dimly ['dɪmlɪ] adv débilmente; (not clearly)
vagamente.
dimmer ['dɪmə*] n (also: **~ switch**)
regulador m (de intensidad); (US AUT)
interruptor m.
dimple ['dɪmpl] n hoyuelo.
dimwitted ['dɪm'wɪtɪd] adj (col) lerdo, de
pocas luces.

din [dɪn] n estruendo, estrépito ♦ vt: **to ~ sth into sb** (col) meter algo en la cabeza a algn.

dine [daɪn] vi cenar.

diner ['daɪnə*] n (person: in restaurant) comensal m/f; (BRIT RAIL) = **dining car;** (US) restaurante económico.

dinghy ['dɪŋgɪ] n bote m; (also: **rubber ~**) lancha (neumática).

dingy ['dɪndʒɪ] adj (room) sombrío; (dirty) sucio; (dull) deslucido.

dining car ['daɪnɪŋ-] n (BRIT) coche-restaurante m.

dining room ['daɪnɪŋ-] n comedor m.

dinner ['dɪnə*] n (evening meal) cena, comida (LAM); (lunch) comida; (public) cena, banquete m; **~'s ready!** ¡la cena está servida!

dinner jacket n smoking m.

dinner party n cena.

dinner time n hora de cenar or comer.

dinosaur ['daɪnəsɔː*] n dinosaurio.

dint [dɪnt] n: **by ~ of (doing) sth** a fuerza de (hacer) algo.

diocese ['daɪəsɪs] n diócesis f.

dioxide [daɪ'ɔksaɪd] n bióxido; **carbon ~** bióxido de carbono.

Dip. abbr (BRIT) = **diploma.**

dip [dɪp] n (slope) pendiente f; (in sea) chapuzón m ♦ vt (in water) mojar; (ladle etc) meter; (BRIT AUT): **to ~ one's lights** poner la luz de cruce ♦ vi inclinarse hacia abajo.

diphtheria [dɪf'θɪərɪə] n difteria.

diphthong ['dɪfθɒŋ] n diptongo.

diploma [dɪ'pləumə] n diploma m.

diplomacy [dɪ'pləuməsɪ] n diplomacia.

diplomat ['dɪpləmæt] n diplomático/a m/f.

diplomatic [dɪplə'mætɪk] adj diplomático; **to break off ~ relations** romper las relaciones diplomáticas.

diplomatic corps n cuerpo diplomático.

diplomatic immunity n inmunidad f diplomática.

dipstick ['dɪpstɪk] n (AUT) varilla de nivel (del aceite).

dipswitch ['dɪpswɪtʃ] n (BRIT AUT) interruptor m.

dire [daɪə*] adj calamitoso.

direct [daɪ'rɛkt] adj (gen) directo; (manner, person) franco ♦ vt dirigir; **can you ~ me to...?** ¿puede indicarme dónde está...?; **to ~ sb to do sth** mandar a algn hacer algo.

direct access n (COMPUT) acceso directo.

direct cost n costo directo.

direct current n corriente f continua.

direct debit n domiciliación f bancaria de recibos; **to pay by ~** domiciliar el pago.

direct dialling n servicio automático de llamadas.

direction [dɪ'rɛkʃən] n dirección f; **sense of ~** sentido de la orientación; **~s** npl (advice) órdenes fpl, instrucciones fpl; (to a place) señas fpl; **in the ~ of** hacia, en dirección a; **~s for use** modo de empleo; **to ask for ~s** preguntar el camino.

directional [dɪ'rɛkʃənl] adj direccional.

directive [daɪ'rɛktɪv] n orden f, instrucción f; **a government ~** una orden del gobierno.

direct labour n mano f de obra directa.

directly [dɪ'rɛktlɪ] adv (in straight line) directamente; (at once) en seguida.

direct mail n correspondencia personalizada.

direct mailshot n (BRIT) promoción f por correspondencia personalizada.

directness [dɪ'rɛktnɪs] n (of person, speech) franqueza.

director [dɪ'rɛktə*] n director(a) m/f; **managing ~** director(a) m/f gerente.

Director of Public Prosecutions n ≈ fiscal m/f general del Estado.

directory [dɪ'rɛktərɪ] n (TEL) guía (telefónica); (street ~) callejero; (trade ~) directorio de comercio; (COMPUT) directorio.

directory enquiries, (US) **directory assistance** n (service) (servicio de) información f.

dirt [dəːt] n suciedad f.

dirt-cheap ['dəːt'tʃiːp] adj baratísimo.

dirt road n (US) camino sin firme.

dirty ['dəːtɪ] adj sucio; (joke) verde, colorado (LAM) ♦ vt ensuciar; (stain) manchar.

dirty trick n mala jugada, truco sucio.

disability [dɪsə'bɪlɪtɪ] n incapacidad f.

disability allowance n pensión f de invalidez.

disable [dɪs'eɪbl] vt (subj: illness, accident) dejar incapacitado or inválido; (tank, gun) inutilizar; (LAW: disqualify) incapacitar.

disabled [dɪs'eɪbld] adj minusválido.

disabuse [dɪsə'bjuːz] vt desengañar.

disadvantage [dɪsəd'vɑːntɪdʒ] n desventaja, inconveniente m.

disadvantaged [dɪsəd'vɑːntɪdʒd] adj (person) desventajado.

disadvantageous [dɪsædvən'teɪdʒəs] adj desventajoso.

disaffected [dɪsə'fɛktɪd] adj descontento; **to be ~ (to or towards)** estar descontento (de).

disaffection [dɪsə'fɛkʃən] n desafecto, descontento.

disagree [dɪsə'griː] _vi (differ)_ discrepar; **to ~ (with)** no estar de acuerdo (con); **I ~ with you** no estoy de acuerdo contigo.
disagreeable [dɪsə'grɪəbl] _adj_ desagradable.
disagreement [dɪsə'griːmənt] _n (gen)_ desacuerdo; _(quarrel)_ riña; **to have a ~ with sb** estar en desacuerdo con algn.
disallow ['dɪsə'lau] _vt (goal)_ anular; _(claim)_ rechazar.
disappear [dɪsə'pɪə*] _vi_ desaparecer.
disappearance [dɪsə'pɪərəns] _n_ desaparición _f_.
disappoint [dɪsə'pɔɪnt] _vt_ decepcionar; _(hopes)_ defraudar.
disappointed [dɪsə'pɔɪntɪd] _adj_ decepcionado.
disappointing [dɪsə'pɔɪntɪŋ] _adj_ decepcionante.
disappointment [dɪsə'pɔɪntmənt] _n_ decepción _f_.
disapproval [dɪsə'pruːvəl] _n_ desaprobación _f_.
disapprove [dɪsə'pruːv] _vi:_ **to ~ of** desaprobar.
disapproving [dɪsə'pruːvɪŋ] _adj_ de desaprobación, desaprobador(a).
disarm [dɪs'ɑːm] _vt_ desarmar.
disarmament [dɪs'ɑːməmənt] _n_ desarme _m_.
disarmament talks _npl_ conversaciones _fpl_ de _or_ sobre desarme.
disarming [dɪs'ɑːmɪŋ] _adj (smile)_ que desarma, encantador(a).
disarray [dɪsə'reɪ] _n:_ **in ~** _(troops)_ desorganizado; _(thoughts)_ confuso; _(hair, clothes)_ desarreglado; **to throw into ~** provocar el caos.
disaster [dɪ'zɑːstə*] _n_ desastre _m_.
disaster area _n_ zona catastrófica.
disastrous [dɪ'zɑːstrəs] _adj_ desastroso.
disband [dɪs'bænd] _vt_ disolver ♦ _vi_ desbandarse.
disbelief [dɪsbə'liːf] _n_ incredulidad _f_; **in ~** con incredulidad.
disbelieve ['dɪsbə'liːv] _vt (person, story)_ poner en duda, no creer.
disc [dɪsk] _n_ disco; _(COMPUT)_ = **disk**.
disc. _abbr (COMM)_ = **discount**.
discard [dɪs'kɑːd] _vt_ tirar; _(fig)_ descartar.
discern [dɪ'sɜːn] _vt_ percibir, discernir; _(understand)_ comprender.
discernible [dɪ'sɜːnəbl] _adj_ perceptible.
discerning [dɪ'sɜːnɪŋ] _adj_ perspicaz.
discharge [dɪs'tʃɑːdʒ] _vt (task, duty)_ cumplir; _(ship etc)_ descargar; _(patient)_ dar de alta; _(employee)_ despedir; _(soldier)_ licenciar; _(defendant)_ poner en libertad; _(settle: debt)_ saldar ♦ _n_ ['dɪstʃɑːdʒ] _(ELEC)_

descarga; _(vaginal ~)_ emisión _f_ vaginal; _(dismissal)_ despedida; _(of duty)_ desempeño; _(of debt)_ pago, descargo; _(of gas, chemicals)_ escape _m_; **~d bankrupt** quebrado/a rehabilitado/a.
disciple [dɪ'saɪpl] _n_ discípulo/a.
disciplinary ['dɪsɪplɪnərɪ] _adj:_ **to take ~ action against sb** disciplinar a algn.
discipline ['dɪsɪplɪn] _n_ disciplina ♦ _vt_ disciplinar; **to ~ o.s. to do sth** obligarse a hacer algo.
disc jockey (DJ) _n_ pinchadiscos _m/f inv_.
disclaim [dɪs'kleɪm] _vt_ negar tener.
disclaimer [dɪs'kleɪmə*] _n_ rectificación _f_; **to issue a ~** hacer una rectificación.
disclose [dɪs'kləuz] _vt_ revelar.
disclosure [dɪs'kləuʒə*] _n_ revelación _f_.
Discman ® ['dɪskmən] _n_ Discman ® _m_.
disco ['dɪskəu] _n abbr_ = **discothèque**.
discolouration, _(US)_ **discoloration** [dɪskʌlə'reɪʃən] _n_ descoloramiento, decoloración _f_.
discolo(u)red [dɪs'kʌləd] _adj_ descolorido.
discomfort [dɪs'kʌmfət] _n_ incomodidad _f_; _(unease)_ inquietud _f_; _(physical)_ malestar _m_.
disconcert [dɪskən'sɜːt] _vt_ desconcertar.
disconnect [dɪskə'nɛkt] _vt (gen)_ separar; _(ELEC etc)_ desconectar; _(supply)_ cortar (el suministro) a.
disconsolate [dɪs'kɒnsəlɪt] _adj_ desconsolado.
discontent [dɪskən'tɛnt] _n_ descontento.
discontented [dɪskən'tɛntɪd] _adj_ descontento.
discontinue [dɪskən'tɪnjuː] _vt_ interrumpir; _(payments)_ suspender.
discord ['dɪskɔːd] _n_ discordia; _(MUS)_ disonancia.
discordant [dɪs'kɔːdənt] _adj_ disonante.
discothèque ['dɪskəutɛk] _n_ discoteca.
discount ['dɪskaunt] _n_ descuento ♦ _vt_ [dɪs'kaunt] descontar; _(report etc)_ descartar; **at a ~** con descuento; **~ for cash** descuento por pago en efectivo; **to give sb a ~ on sth** hacer un descuento a algn en algo.
discount house _n (FINANCE)_ banco de descuento; _(COMM: also:_ **discount store**) ≈ tienda de saldos.
discount rate _n (COMM)_ tipo de descuento.
discount store _n_ ≈ tienda de saldos.
discourage [dɪs'kʌrɪdʒ] _vt_ desalentar; _(oppose)_ oponerse a; _(dissuade, deter)_ desanimar, disuadir.
discouragement [dɪs'kʌrɪdʒmənt] _n_ _(dissuasion)_ disuasión _f_; _(depression)_ desánimo, desaliento; **to act as a ~ to**

servir para disuadir.

discouraging [dɪsˈkʌrɪdʒɪŋ] *adj* desalentador(a).

discourteous [dɪsˈkəːtɪəs] *adj* descortés.

discover [dɪsˈkʌvə*] *vt* descubrir.

discovery [dɪsˈkʌvərɪ] *n* descubrimiento.

discredit [dɪsˈkrɛdɪt] *vt* desacreditar.

discreet [dɪˈskriːt] *adj* (*tactful*) discreto; (*careful*) circunspecto, prudente.

discreetly [dɪˈskriːtlɪ] *adv* discretamente.

discrepancy [dɪˈskrɛpənsɪ] *n* (*difference*) diferencia; (*disagreement*) discrepancia.

discretion [dɪˈskrɛʃən] *n* (*tact*) discreción *f*; (*care*) prudencia, circunspección *f*; **use your own** ~ haz lo que creas oportuno.

discretionary [dɪˈskrɛʃənrɪ] *adj* (*powers*) discrecional.

discriminate [dɪˈskrɪmɪneɪt] *vi*: **to** ~ **between** distinguir entre; **to** ~ **against** discriminar contra.

discriminating [dɪˈskrɪmɪneɪtɪŋ] *adj* entendido.

discrimination [dɪskrɪmɪˈneɪʃən] *n* (*discernment*) perspicacia; (*bias*) discriminación *f*; **racial/sexual** ~ discriminación racial/sexual.

discus [ˈdɪskəs] *n* disco.

discuss [dɪˈskʌs] *vt* (*gen*) discutir; (*a theme*) tratar.

discussion [dɪˈskʌʃən] *n* discusión *f*; **under** ~ en discusión.

disdain [dɪsˈdeɪn] *n* desdén *m* ♦ *vt* desdeñar.

disease [dɪˈziːz] *n* enfermedad *f*.

diseased [dɪˈziːzd] *adj* enfermo.

disembark [dɪsɪmˈbɑːk] *vt*, *vi* desembarcar.

disembarkation [dɪsɛmbɑːˈkeɪʃən] *n* desembarque *m*.

disenchanted [dɪsɪnˈtʃɑːntɪd] *adj*: ~ **(with)** desilusionado (con).

disenfranchise [ˈdɪsɪnˈfræntʃaɪz] *vt* privar del derecho al voto; (*COMM*) privar de franquicias.

disengage [dɪsɪnˈgeɪdʒ] *vt* soltar; **to** ~ **the clutch** (*AUT*) desembragar.

disentangle [dɪsɪnˈtæŋgl] *vt* desenredar.

disfavour, (*US*) **disfavor** [dɪsˈfeɪvə*] *n* desaprobación *f*.

disfigure [dɪsˈfɪgə*] *vt* desfigurar.

disgorge [dɪsˈgɔːdʒ] *vt* verter.

disgrace [dɪsˈgreɪs] *n* ignominia; (*downfall*) caída; (*shame*) vergüenza, escándalo ♦ *vt* deshonrar.

disgraceful [dɪsˈgreɪsful] *adj* vergonzoso; (*behaviour*) escandaloso.

disgruntled [dɪsˈgrʌntld] *adj* disgustado, descontento.

disguise [dɪsˈgaɪz] *n* disfraz *m* ♦ *vt* disfrazar; (*voice*) disimular; (*feelings etc*) ocultar; **in** ~ disfrazado; **to** ~ **o.s. as** disfrazarse de; **there's no disguising the fact that** ... no puede ocultarse el hecho de que ....

disgust [dɪsˈgʌst] *n* repugnancia ♦ *vt* repugnar, dar asco a.

disgusting [dɪsˈgʌstɪŋ] *adj* repugnante, asqueroso.

dish [dɪʃ] *n* (*gen*) plato; **to do** *or* **wash the** ~**es** fregar los platos.

▶**dish out** *vt* (*money, exam papers*) repartir; (*food*) servir; (*advice*) dar.

▶**dish up** *vt* servir.

dishcloth [ˈdɪʃklɔθ] *n* paño de cocina, bayeta.

dishearten [dɪsˈhɑːtn] *vt* desalentar.

dishevelled, (*US*) **disheveled** [dɪˈʃɛvəld] *adj* (*hair*) despeinado; (*clothes, appearance*) desarreglado.

dishonest [dɪsˈɔnɪst] *adj* (*person*) poco honrado, tramposo; (*means*) fraudulento.

dishonesty [dɪsˈɔnɪstɪ] *n* falta de honradez.

dishonour, (*US*) **dishonor** [dɪsˈɔnə*] *n* deshonra.

dishono(u)rable [dɪsˈɔnərəbl] *adj* deshonroso.

dish soap *n* (*US*) lavavajillas *m inv*.

dishtowel [ˈdɪʃtauəl] *n* (*US*) trapo de fregar.

dishwasher [ˈdɪʃwɔʃə*] *n* lavaplatos *m inv*; (*person*) friegaplatos *m/f inv*.

dishy [ˈdɪʃɪ] *adj* (*BRIT col*) buenón/ona.

disillusion [dɪsɪˈluːʒən] *vt* desilusionar; **to become** ~**ed (with)** quedar desilusionado (con).

disillusionment [dɪsɪˈluːʒənmənt] *n* desilusión *f*.

disincentive [dɪsɪnˈsɛntɪv] *n* freno; **to act as a** ~ **(to)** actuar de freno (a); **to be a** ~ **to** ser un freno a.

disinclined [ˈdɪsɪnˈklaɪnd] *adj*: **to be** ~ **to do sth** estar poco dispuesto a hacer algo.

disinfect [dɪsɪnˈfɛkt] *vt* desinfectar.

disinfectant [dɪsɪnˈfɛktənt] *n* desinfectante *m*.

disinflation [dɪsɪnˈfleɪʃən] *n* desinflación *f*.

disinformation [dɪsɪnfəˈmeɪʃən] *n* desinformación *f*.

disingenuous [dɪsɪnˈdʒɛnjuəs] *adj* poco sincero, falso.

disinherit [dɪsɪnˈhɛrɪt] *vt* desheredar.

disintegrate [dɪsˈɪntɪgreɪt] *vi* disgregarse, desintegrarse.

disinterested [dɪsˈɪntrəstɪd] *adj* desinteresado.

disjointed [dɪsˈdʒɔɪntɪd] *adj* inconexo.

disk [dɪsk] *n* (*COMPUT*) disco, disquete *m*; **single-/double-sided** ~ disco de una

cara/dos caras.
disk drive n disc drive m.
diskette [dɪs'kɛt] n diskette m, disquete m,
disco flexible.
disk operating system (DOS) n sistema
m operativo de discos (DOS).
dislike [dɪs'laɪk] n antipatía, aversión f ♦ vt
tener antipatía a; **to take a ~ to sb/sth**
cogerle or agarrarle (_LAM_) antipatía a
algn/algo; **I ~ the idea** no me gusta la
idea.
dislocate ['dɪsləkeɪt] vt dislocar; **he ~d his
shoulder** se dislocó el hombro.
dislodge [dɪs'lɔdʒ] vt sacar; (_enemy_)
desalojar.
disloyal [dɪs'lɔɪəl] adj desleal.
dismal ['dɪzml] adj (_dark_) sombrío;
(_depressing_) triste; (_very bad_) fatal.
dismantle [dɪs'mæntl] vt desmontar,
desarmar.
dismay [dɪs'meɪ] n consternación f ♦ vt
consternar; **much to my ~** para gran
consternación mía.
dismiss [dɪs'mɪs] vt (_worker_) despedir;
(_official_) destituir; (_idea, LAW_) rechazar;
(_possibility_) descartar ♦ vi (_MIL_) romper
filas.
dismissal [dɪs'mɪsl] n despedida;
destitución f.
dismount [dɪs'maunt] vi apearse; (_rider_)
desmontar.
disobedience [dɪsə'biːdɪəns] n
desobediencia.
disobedient [dɪsə'biːdɪənt] adj
desobediente.
disobey [dɪsə'beɪ] vt desobedecer; (_rule_)
infringir.
disorder [dɪs'ɔːdə*] n desorden m; (_rioting_)
disturbio; (_MED_) trastorno; (_disease_)
enfermedad f; **civil ~** desorden m civil.
disorderly [dɪs'ɔːdəlɪ] adj (_untidy_)
desordenado; (_meeting_) alborotado; **~
conduct** (_LAW_) conducta escandalosa.
disorganized [dɪs'ɔːgənaɪzd] adj
desorganizado.
disorientated [dɪs'ɔːrɪenteɪtəd] adj
desorientado.
disown [dɪs'əun] vt renegar de.
disparaging [dɪs'pærɪdʒɪŋ] adj
despreciativo; **to be ~ about sth/sb**
menospreciar algo/a algn.
disparate ['dɪspərɪt] adj dispar.
disparity [dɪs'pærɪtɪ] n disparidad f.
dispassionate [dɪs'pæʃənɪt] adj (_unbiased_)
imparcial; (_unemotional_) desapasionado.
dispatch [dɪs'pætʃ] vt enviar; (_kill_)
despachar; (_deal with: business_)
despachar ♦ n (_sending_) envío; (_speed_)

prontitud f; (_PRESS_) informe m; (_MIL_)
parte m.
dispatch department n (_COMM_)
departamento de envíos.
dispatch rider n (_MIL_) correo.
dispel [dɪs'pɛl] vt disipar, dispersar.
dispensary [dɪs'pɛnsərɪ] n dispensario.
dispensation [dɪspɛn'seɪʃən] n (_REL_)
dispensa.
dispense [dɪs'pɛns] vt dispensar, repartir;
(_medicine_) preparar.
▶**dispense with** vt fus (_make unnecessary_)
prescindir de.
dispenser [dɪs'pɛnsə*] n (_container_)
distribuidor m automático.
dispensing chemist [dɪs'pɛnsɪŋ-] n (_BRIT_)
farmacia.
dispersal [dɪs'pəːsl] n dispersión f.
disperse [dɪs'pəːs] vt dispersar ♦ vi
dispersarse.
dispirited [dɪ'spɪrɪtɪd] adj desanimado,
desalentado.
displace [dɪs'pleɪs] vt (_person_) desplazar;
(_replace_) reemplazar.
displaced person n (_POL_) desplazado/a.
displacement [dɪs'pleɪsmənt] n cambio de
sitio.
display [dɪs'pleɪ] n (_exhibition_) exposición f;
(_COMPUT_) visualización f; (_MIL_) desfile m;
(_of feeling_) manifestación f; (_pej_) aparato,
pompa ♦ vt exponer; manifestar;
(_ostentatiously_) lucir; **on ~** (_exhibits_)
expuesto, exhibido; (_goods_) en el
escaparate.
display advertising n publicidad f gráfica.
displease [dɪs'pliːz] vt (_offend_) ofender;
(_annoy_) fastidiar; **~d with** disgustado
con.
displeasure [dɪs'plɛʒə*] n disgusto.
disposable [dɪs'pəuzəbl] adj (_not reusable_)
desechable; **~ personal income** ingresos
mpl personales disponibles.
disposable nappy n pañal m desechable.
disposal [dɪs'pəuzl] n (_sale_) venta; (_of
house_) traspaso; (_by giving away_)
donación f; (_arrangement_) colocación f; (_of
rubbish_) destrucción f; **at one's ~** a la
disposición de algn; **to put sth at sb's ~**
poner algo a disposición de algn.
disposed [dɪs'pəuzd] adj: **~ to do** dispuesto
a hacer.
dispose of [dɪs'pəuz] vt fus (_time, money_)
disponer de; (_unwanted goods_)
deshacerse de; (_COMM: sell_) traspasar,
vender; (_throw away_) tirar.
disposition [dɪspə'zɪʃən] n disposición f;
(_temperament_) carácter m.
dispossess ['dɪspə'zɛs] vt: **to ~ sb (of)**

desposeer a algn (de).
disproportion [dɪsprə'pɔːʃən] n
desproporción f.
disproportionate [dɪsprə'pɔːʃənət] adj
desproporcionado.
disprove [dɪs'pruːv] vt refutar.
dispute [dɪs'pjuːt] n disputa; (verbal)
discusión f; (also: **industrial** ~) conflicto
(laboral) ♦ vt (argue) disputar; (question)
cuestionar; **to be in** or **under** ~ (matter)
discutirse; (territory) estar en disputa;
(JUR) estar en litigio.
disqualification [dɪskwɔlɪfɪ'keɪʃən] n
inhabilitación f; (SPORT, from driving)
descalificación f.
disqualify [dɪs'kwɔlɪfaɪ] vt (SPORT)
desclasificar; **to** ~ **sb for sth/from doing
sth** incapacitar a algn para algo/hacer
algo.
disquiet [dɪs'kwaɪət] n preocupación f,
inquietud f.
disquieting [dɪs'kwaɪətɪŋ] adj inquietante.
disregard [dɪsrɪ'gɑːd] vt desatender;
(ignore) no hacer caso de ♦ n (indifference:
to feelings, danger, money): ~ **(for)**
indiferencia (a); ~ **(of)** (non-observance: of
law, rules) violación f (de).
disrepair [dɪsrɪ'pɛə*] n: **to fall into** ~
(building) desmoronarse; (street)
deteriorarse.
disreputable [dɪs'rɛpjutəbl] adj (person,
area) de mala fama; (behaviour)
vergonzoso.
disrepute ['dɪsrɪ'pjuːt] n descrédito,
ignominia; **to bring into** ~ desacreditar.
disrespectful [dɪsrɪ'spɛktful] adj
irrespetuoso.
disrupt [dɪs'rʌpt] vt (meeting, public
transport, conversation) interrumpir;
(plans) desbaratar, alternar, trastornar.
disruption [dɪs'rʌpʃən] n trastorno;
desbaratamiento; interrupción f.
disruptive [dɪs'rʌptɪv] adj (influence)
disruptivo; (strike action) perjudicial.
dissatisfaction [dɪssætɪs'fækʃən] n
disgusto, descontento.
dissatisfied [dɪs'sætɪsfaɪd] adj insatisfecho.
dissect [dɪ'sɛkt] vt (also fig) disecar.
disseminate [dɪ'sɛmɪneɪt] vt divulgar,
difundir.
dissent [dɪ'sɛnt] n disensión f.
dissenter [dɪ'sɛntə*] n (REL, POL etc)
disidente m/f.
dissertation [dɪsə'teɪʃən] n (UNIV) tesina;
see also **master's degree**.
disservice [dɪs'səːvɪs] n: **to do sb a** ~
perjudicar a alguien.
dissident ['dɪsɪdnt] adj, n disidente m/f.

dissimilar [dɪ'sɪmɪlə*] adj distinto.
dissipate ['dɪsɪpeɪt] vt disipar; (waste)
desperdiciar.
dissipated ['dɪsɪpeɪtɪd] adj disoluto.
dissipation [dɪsɪ'peɪʃən] n disipación f;
(moral) libertinaje m, vicio; (waste)
derroche m.
dissociate [dɪ'səuʃɪeɪt] vt disociar; **to** ~ **o.s.
from** disociarse de.
dissolute ['dɪsəluːt] adj disoluto.
dissolution [dɪsə'luːʃən] n (of organization,
marriage, POL) disolución f.
dissolve [dɪ'zɔlv] vt (gen, COMM) disolver
♦ vi disolverse.
dissuade [dɪ'sweɪd] vt: **to** ~ **sb (from)**
disuadir a algn (de).
distaff ['dɪstæf] n: ~ **side** rama femenina.
distance ['dɪstns] n distancia; **in the** ~ a lo
lejos; **what** ~ **is it to London?** ¿qué
distancia hay de aquí a Londres?; **it's
within walking** ~ se puede ir andando.
distant ['dɪstnt] adj lejano; (manner)
reservado, frío.
distaste [dɪs'teɪst] n repugnancia.
distasteful [dɪs'teɪstful] adj repugnante,
desagradable.
Dist. Atty. abbr (US) = **district attorney**.
distemper [dɪs'tempə*] n (of dogs)
moquillo.
distend [dɪ'stɛnd] vt dilatar, hinchar ♦ vi
dilatarse, hincharse.
distended [dɪ'stɛndɪd] adj (stomach)
hinchado.
distil, (US) **distill** [dɪs'tɪl] vt destilar.
distillery [dɪs'tɪlərɪ] n destilería.
distinct [dɪs'tɪŋkt] adj (different) distinto;
(clear) claro; (unmistakeable) inequívoco;
as ~ **from** a diferencia de.
distinction [dɪs'tɪŋkʃən] n distinción f; (in
exam) sobresaliente m; **a writer of** ~ un
escritor destacado; **to draw a** ~ **between**
hacer una distinción entre.
distinctive [dɪs'tɪŋktɪv] adj distintivo.
distinctly [dɪs'tɪŋktlɪ] adv claramente.
distinguish [dɪs'tɪŋgwɪʃ] vt distinguir ♦ vi:
to ~ **(between)** distinguir (entre).
distinguished [dɪs'tɪŋgwɪʃt] adj (eminent)
distinguido; (career) eminente; (refined)
distinguido, de categoría.
distinguishing [dɪs'tɪŋgwɪʃɪŋ] adj (feature)
distintivo.
distort [dɪs'tɔːt] vt torcer, retorcer;
(account, news) desvirtuar, deformar.
distortion [dɪs'tɔːʃən] n deformación f; (of
sound) distorsión f; (of truth etc)
tergiversación f; (of facts) falseamiento.
distract [dɪs'trækt] vt distraer.
distracted [dɪs'træktɪd] adj distraído.

distracting [dɪs'træktɪŋ] *adj* que distrae la atención, molesto.

distraction [dɪs'trækʃən] *n* distracción *f*; (*confusion*) aturdimiento; (*amusement*) diversión *f*; **to drive sb to** ~ (*distress, anxiety*) volver loco a algn.

distraught [dɪs'trɔːt] *adj* turbado, enloquecido.

distress [dɪs'trɛs] *n* (*anguish*) angustia; (*want*) miseria; (*pain*) dolor *m*; (*danger*) peligro ♦ *vt* afligir; (*pain*) doler; **in** ~ (*ship etc*) en peligro.

distressing [dɪs'trɛsɪŋ] *adj* angustioso; doloroso.

distress signal *n* señal *f* de socorro.

distribute [dɪs'trɪbjuːt] *vt* (*gen*) distribuir; (*share out*) repartir.

distribution [dɪstrɪ'bjuːʃən] *n* distribución *f*.

distribution cost *n* gastos *mpl* de distribución.

distributor [dɪs'trɪbjutə*] *n* (*AUT*) distribuidor *m*; (*COMM*) distribuidora.

district ['dɪstrɪkt] *n* (*of country*) zona, región *f*; (*of town*) barrio; (*ADMIN*) distrito.

district attorney *n* (*US*) fiscal *m/f*.

district council *n* ≈ municipio; *ver recuadro*.

DISTRICT COUNCIL

En Inglaterra y Gales, con la excepción de Londres, la administración local corre a cargo del **district council***, responsable de los servicios municipales como vivienda, urbanismo, recolección de basuras, salud medioambiental etc. La mayoría de sus miembros son elegidos a nivel local cada cuatro años. Hay un total de 369 "districts" (distritos), repartidos en 53 "counties" (condados), que se financian a través de los impuestos municipales y partidas presupuestarias del Estado. Éste controla sus gastos a través de una comisión independiente.*

---

district manager *n* representante *m/f* regional.

district nurse *n* (*BRIT*) *enfermera que atiende a pacientes a domicilio.*

distrust [dɪs'trʌst] *n* desconfianza ♦ *vt* desconfiar de.

distrustful [dɪs'trʌstful] *adj* desconfiado.

disturb [dɪs'təːb] *vt* (*person: bother, interrupt*) molestar; (*meeting*) interrumpir; (*disorganize*) desordenar; **sorry to** ~ **you** perdone la molestia.

disturbance [dɪs'təːbəns] *n* (*political etc*) disturbio; (*violence*) alboroto; (*of mind*)

trastorno; **to cause a** ~ causar alboroto; ~ **of the peace** alteración *f* del orden público.

disturbed [dɪs'təːbd] *adj* (*worried, upset*) preocupado, angustiado; **to be emotionally/mentally** ~ tener problemas emocionales/ser un trastornado mental.

disturbing [dɪs'təːbɪŋ] *adj* inquietante, perturbador(a).

disuse [dɪs'juːs] *n*: **to fall into** ~ caer en desuso.

disused [dɪs'juːzd] *adj* abandonado.

ditch [dɪtʃ] *n* zanja; (*irrigation* ~) acequia ♦ *vt* (*col*) deshacerse de.

dither ['dɪðə*] *vi* vacilar.

ditto ['dɪtəu] *adv* ídem, lo mismo.

divan [dɪ'væn] *n* diván *m*.

divan bed *n* cama turca.

dive [daɪv] *n* (*from board*) salto; (*underwater*) buceo; (*of submarine*) inmersión *f*; (*AVIAT*) picada ♦ *vi* saltar; bucear; sumergirse; picar.

diver ['daɪvə*] *n* (*SPORT*) saltador(a) *m/f*; (*underwater*) buzo.

diverge [daɪ'vəːdʒ] *vi* divergir.

divergent [daɪ'vəːdʒənt] *adj* divergente.

diverse [daɪ'vəːs] *adj* diversos/as, varios/as.

diversification [daɪvəːsɪfɪ'keɪʃən] *n* diversificación *f*.

diversify [daɪ'vəːsɪfaɪ] *vt* diversificar.

diversion [daɪ'vəːʃən] *n* (*BRIT AUT*) desviación *f*; (*distraction, MIL*) diversión *f*.

diversity [daɪ'vəːsɪtɪ] *n* diversidad *f*.

divert [daɪ'vəːt] *vt* (*BRIT: train, plane, traffic*) desviar; (*amuse*) divertir.

divest [daɪ'vɛst] *vt*: **to** ~ **sb of sth** despojar a alguien de algo.

divide [dɪ'vaɪd] *vt* dividir; (*separate*) separar ♦ *vi* dividirse; (*road*) bifurcarse; **to** ~ (**between, among**) repartir *or* dividir (entre); **40** ~**d by 5** 40 dividido por 5.

▶**divide out** *vt*: **to** ~ **out** (**between, among**) (*sweets, tasks etc*) repartir (entre).

divided [dɪ'vaɪdɪd] *adj* (*country, couple*) dividido, separado; (*opinions*) en desacuerdo.

divided highway *n* (*US*) carretera de doble calzada.

dividend ['dɪvɪdɛnd] *n* dividendo; (*fig*) beneficio.

dividend cover *n* cobertura de dividendo.

dividers [dɪ'vaɪdəz] *npl* compás *m* de puntas.

divine [dɪ'vaɪn] *adj* divino ♦ *vt* (*future*) vaticinar; (*truth*) alumbrar; (*water, metal*) descubrir, detectar.

diving ['daɪvɪŋ] *n* (*SPORT*) salto; (*underwater*) buceo.

diving board n trampolín m.

diving suit n escafandra.

divinity [dɪ'vɪnɪtɪ] n divinidad f; (SCOL) teología.

divisible [dɪ'vɪzɪbl] adj divisible.

division [dɪ'vɪʒən] n (also BRIT FOOTBALL) división f; (sharing out) repartimiento; (BRIT POL) votación f; ~ **of labour** división f del trabajo.

divisive [dɪ'vaɪsɪv] adj divisivo.

divorce [dɪ'vɔːs] n divorcio ♦ vt divorciarse de.

divorced [dɪ'vɔːst] adj divorciado.

divorcee [dɪvɔː'siː] n divorciado/a.

divot ['dɪvət] n (GOLF) chuleta.

divulge [daɪ'vʌldʒ] vt divulgar, revelar.

D.I.Y. adj, n abbr (BRIT) = **do-it-yourself.**

dizziness ['dɪzɪnɪs] n vértigo.

dizzy ['dɪzɪ] adj (person) mareado; (height) vertiginoso; **to feel ~** marearse; **I feel ~** estoy mareado.

DJ n abbr see **disc jockey.**

d.j. n abbr = **dinner jacket.**

Djakarta [dʒə'kɑːtə] n Yakarta.

DJIA n abbr (US STOCK EXCHANGE) = Dow Jones Industrial Average.

dl abbr (= decilitre(s)) dl.

DLit(t) abbr (= Doctor of Literature, Doctor of Letters) título universitario.

DLO n abbr (= dead-letter office) oficina de Correos que se encarga de las cartas que no llegan a su destino.

dm abbr (= decimetre(s)) dm.

DMus abbr (= Doctor of Music) título universitario.

DMZ n abbr (= demilitarized zone) zona desmilitarizada.

DNA n abbr = (deoxyribonucleic acid) ADN m.

================= *KEYWORD*

do [duː] (pt **did**, pp **done**) n **1** (inf: party etc): **we're having a little ~ on Saturday** damos una fiestecita el sábado; **it was rather a grand ~** fue un acontecimiento a lo grande

2: the ~s and don'ts lo que se debe y no se debe hacer

♦ aux vb **1** (in negative constructions: not translated) **I don't understand** no entiendo

2 (to form questions: not translated) **~ you speak English?** ¿habla (usted) inglés?; **didn't you know?** ¿no lo sabías?; **what ~ you think?** ¿qué opinas?

3 (for emphasis, in polite expressions): **people ~ make mistakes sometimes** a veces sí se cometen errores; **she does seem rather late** a mí también me parece que se ha retrasado; **~ sit down/help**

yourself siéntate/sírvete por favor; **~ take care!** ¡ten cuidado! ¿eh?; **I DO wish I could ...** ojalá (que) pudiera ...; **but I DO like it** pero, sí (que) me gusta

4 (used to avoid repeating vb): **she sings better than I ~** canta mejor que yo; **~ you agree? — yes, I ~/no, I don't** ¿estás de acuerdo? — sí (lo estoy)/no (lo estoy); **she lives in Glasgow — so ~ I** vive en Glasgow — yo también; **he didn't like it and neither did we** no le gustó y a nosotros tampoco; **who made this mess? — I did** ¿quién hizo esta chapuza? — yo; **he asked me to help him and I did** me pidió que le ayudara y lo hice

5 (in question tags): **you like him, don't you?** te gusta, ¿verdad? or ¿no?; **I don't know him, ~ I?** creo que no le conozco; **he laughed, didn't he?** se rió ¿no?

♦ vt **1** (gen, carry out, perform etc): **what are you ~ing tonight?** ¿qué haces esta noche?; **what can I ~ for you?** (in shop) ¿en qué puedo servirle?; **what does he ~ for a living?** ¿a qué se dedica?; **I'll ~ all I can** haré todo lo que pueda; **what have you done with my slippers?** ¿qué has hecho con mis zapatillas?; **to ~ the washing-up/cooking** fregar los platos/cocinar; **to ~ one's teeth/hair/nails** lavarse los dientes/arreglarse el pelo/arreglarse las uñas

2 (AUT etc): **the car was ~ing 100** el coche iba a 100; **we've done 200 km already** ya hemos hecho 200 km; **he can ~ 100 in that car** puede ir a 100 en ese coche

3 (visit: city, museum) visitar, recorrer

4 (cook): **a steak – well done please** un filete bien hecho, por favor

♦ vi **1** (act, behave) hacer; **~ as I ~** haz como yo

2 (get on, fare): **he's ~ing well/badly at school** va bien/mal en la escuela; **the firm is ~ing well** la empresa anda or va bien; **how ~ you ~?** mucho gusto; (less formal) ¿qué tal?

3 (suit): **will it ~?** ¿sirve?, ¿está or va bien?; **it doesn't ~ to upset her** cuidado en ofenderla

4 (be sufficient) bastar; **will £10 ~?** ¿será bastante con £10?; **that'll ~** así está bien; **that'll ~!** (in annoyance) ¡ya está bien!, ¡basta ya!; **to make ~ (with)** arreglárselas (con)

▶**do away with** vt fus (kill, disease) eliminar; (abolish: law etc) abolir; (withdraw) retirar

▶**do out of** vt fus: **to ~ sb out of sth** pisar

algo a algn
► **do up** *vt* (*laces*) atar; (*zip, dress, shirt*) abrochar; (*renovate: room, house*) renovar
► **do with** *vt fus* (*need*): **I could ~ with a drink/some help** no me vendría mal un trago/un poco de ayuda; (*be connected*) tener que ver con; **what has it got to ~ with you?** ¿qué tiene que ver contigo?
► **do without** *vi*: **if you're late for dinner then you'll ~ without** si llegas tarde tendrás que quedarte sin cenar ♦ *vt fus* pasar sin; **I can ~ without a car** puedo pasar sin coche.

do. *abbr* = **ditto**.
DOA *abbr* = *dead on arrival*.
d.o.b. *abbr* = *date of birth*.
doc [dɔk] *n* (*col*) médico/a.
docile ['dəusaɪl] *adj* dócil.
dock [dɔk] *n* (*NAUT: wharf*) dársena, muelle *m*; (*LAW*) banquillo (de los acusados); **~s** *npl* muelles *mpl*, puerto *sg* ♦ *vi* (*enter~*) atracar (en el muelle) ♦ *vt* (*pay etc*) descontar.
dock dues *npl* derechos *mpl* de muelle.
docker ['dɔkə*] *n* trabajador *m* portuario, estibador *m*.
docket ['dɔkɪt] *n* (*on parcel etc*) etiqueta.
dockyard ['dɔkjɑːd] *n* astillero.
doctor ['dɔktə*] *n* médico; (*Ph.D. etc*) doctor(a) *m/f* ♦ *vt* (*fig*) arreglar, falsificar; (*drink etc*) adulterar.
doctorate ['dɔktərɪt] *n* doctorado; *ver recuadro*.

DOCTORATE

*El grado más alto que conceden las universidades es el doctorado (**doctorate**), tras un período de estudio e investigación original no inferior a tres años que culmina con la presentación de una tesis ("thesis") en la que se exponen los resultados. El título más frecuente es el de "PhD" ("Doctor of Philosophy"), que se obtiene en Letras, Ciencias e Ingeniería, aunque también existen otros doctorados específicos en Música, Derecho etc.*

Doctor of Philosophy (Ph.D.) *n* Doctor *m* (en Filosofía y Letras).
doctrinaire [dɔktrɪ'neə*] *adj* doctrinario.
doctrine ['dɔktrɪn] *n* doctrina.
docudrama [dɔkju'drɑːmə] *n* (*TV*) docudrama *m*.
document ['dɔkjumənt] *n* documento ♦ *vt* documentar.
documentary [dɔkju'mentərɪ] *adj* documental ♦ *n* documental *m*.

documentation [dɔkjumen'teɪʃən] *n* documentación *f*.
DOD *n abbr* (*US: = Department of Defense*) Ministerio de Defensa.
doddering ['dɔdərɪŋ] *adj*, **doddery** ['dɔdərɪ] *adj* vacilante.
doddle ['dɔdl] *n*: **it's a ~** (*BRIT col*) es pan comido.
dodge [dɔdʒ] *n* (*of body*) regate *m*; (*fig*) truco ♦ *vt* (*gen*) evadir; (*blow*) esquivar ♦ *vi* escabullirse; (*SPORT*) hacer una finta; **to ~ out of the way** echarse a un lado; **to ~ through the traffic** esquivar el tráfico.
dodgems ['dɔdʒəmz] *npl* (*BRIT*) autos *or* coches *mpl* de choque.
dodgy ['dɔdʒɪ] (*col*) *adj* (*uncertain*) dudoso; (*shady*) sospechoso; (*risky*) arriesgado.
DOE *n abbr* (*BRIT*) = *Department of the Environment*; (*US*) = *Department of Energy*.
doe [dəu] *n* (*deer*) cierva, gama; (*rabbit*) coneja.
does [dʌz] *vb see* **do**.
doesn't ['dʌznt] = **does not**.
dog [dɔg] *n* perro ♦ *vt* seguir (de cerca); (*fig: memory etc*) perseguir; **to go to the ~s** (*person*) echarse a perder; (*nation etc*) ir a la ruina.
dog biscuit *n* galleta de perro.
dog collar *n* collar *m* de perro; (*fig*) alzacuello(s) *msg*.
dog-eared ['dɔgɪəd] *adj* sobado; (*page*) con la esquina doblada.
dogfish ['dɔgfɪʃ] *n* cazón *m*, perro marino.
dog food *n* comida para perros.
dogged ['dɔgɪd] *adj* tenaz, obstinado.
doggy ['dɔgɪ] *n* (*col*) perrito.
doggy bag *n* bolsa para llevarse las sobras de la comida.
dogma ['dɔgmə] *n* dogma *m*.
dogmatic [dɔg'mætɪk] *adj* dogmático.
do-gooder [du:'gudə*] *n* (*col pej*): **to be a ~** ser una persona bien intencionada *or* un filantropista.
dogsbody ['dɔgzbɔdɪ] *n* (*BRIT*) burro de carga.
doily ['dɔɪlɪ] *n* pañito de adorno.
doing ['duɪŋ] *n*: **this is your ~** esto es obra tuya.
doings ['duɪŋz] *npl* (*events*) sucesos *mpl*; (*acts*) hechos *mpl*.
do-it-yourself [du:ɪtjɔː'self] *n* bricolaje *m*.
doldrums ['dɔldrəmz] *npl*: **to be in the ~** (*person*) estar abatido; (*business*) estar estancado.
dole [dəul] *n* (*BRIT: payment*) subsidio de paro; **on the ~** parado.
► **dole out** *vt* repartir.
doleful ['dəulful] *adj* triste, lúgubre.

doll – double-breasted

doll [dɔl] n muñeca.
▶**doll up** vt: **to ~ o.s. up** ataviarse.
dollar ['dɔlə*] n dólar m.
dollop ['dɔləp] n buena cucharada.
dolphin ['dɔlfɪn] n delfín m.
domain [də'meɪn] n (fig) campo,
competencia; (land) dominios mpl.
dome [dəum] n (ARCH) cúpula; (shape)
bóveda.
domestic [də'mɛstɪk] adj (animal, duty)
doméstico; (flight, news, plane) nacional.
domesticated [də'mɛstɪkeɪtɪd] adj
domesticado; (person: home-loving)
casero, hogareño.
domesticity [dəumɛs'tɪsɪtɪ] n vida casera.
domestic servant n sirviente/a m/f.
domicile ['dɔmɪsaɪl] n domicilio.
dominant ['dɔmɪnənt] adj dominante.
dominate ['dɔmɪneɪt] vt dominar.
domination [dɔmɪ'neɪʃən] n dominación f.
domineering [dɔmɪ'nɪərɪŋ] adj dominante.
Dominican Republic [də'mɪnɪkən-] n
República Dominicana.
dominion [də'mɪnɪən] n dominio.
domino, pl ~es ['dɔmɪnəu] n ficha de
dominó.
dominoes ['dɔmɪnəuz] n (game) dominó.
don [dɔn] n (BRIT) profesor(a) m/f de
universidad.
donate [də'neɪt] vt donar.
donation [də'neɪʃən] n donativo.
done [dʌn] pp of **do**.
donkey ['dɔŋkɪ] n burro.
donkey-work ['dɔŋkɪwə:k] n (BRIT col)
trabajo pesado.
donor ['dəunə*] n donante m/f.
donor card n carnet m de donante de
órganos.
don't [dəunt] = **do not**.
donut ['dəunʌt] n (US) = **doughnut**.
doodle ['du:dl] n garabato ♦ vi pintar
dibujitos or garabatos.
doom [du:m] n (fate) suerte f; (death)
muerte f ♦ vt: **to be ~ed to failure** estar
condenado al fracaso.
doomsday ['du:mzdeɪ] n día m del juicio
final.
door [dɔ:*] n puerta; (of car) portezuela;
(entry) entrada; **from ~ to ~** de puerta en
puerta.
doorbell ['dɔ:bɛl] n timbre m.
door handle n tirador m; (of car) manija.
door knocker n aldaba.
doorman ['dɔ:mən] n (in hotel) portero.
doormat ['dɔ:mæt] n felpudo, estera.
doorstep ['dɔ:stɛp] n peldaño; **on your ~**
en la puerta de casa; (fig) al lado de casa.
door-to-door ['dɔ:tə'dɔ:*] adj: **~ selling**

venta a domicilio.
doorway ['dɔ:weɪ] n entrada, puerta; **in the
~** en la puerta.
dope [dəup] n (col: person) imbécil m/f;
(: information) información f, informes mpl
♦ vt (horse etc) drogar.
dopey ['dəupɪ] adj atontado.
dormant ['dɔ:mənt] adj inactivo; (latent)
latente.
dormer ['dɔ:mə*] n (also: ~ **window**)
buhardilla.
dormitory ['dɔ:mɪtrɪ] n (BRIT) dormitorio;
(US: hall of residence) residencia, colegio
mayor.
dormouse, pl dormice ['dɔ:maus, -maɪs] n
lirón m.
Dors abbr (BRIT) = **Dorset**.
DOS n abbr see **disk operating system**.
dosage ['dəusɪdʒ] n (on medicine bottle)
dosis f inv, dosificación f.
dose [dəus] n (of medicine) dosis f inv; **a ~ of
flu** un ataque de gripe ♦ vt: **to ~ o.s. with**
automedicarse con.
dosser ['dɔsə*] n (BRIT col) mendigo/a; (lazy
person) vago/a.
doss house ['dɔs-] n (BRIT) pensión f de
mala muerte.
dossier ['dɔsɪeɪ] n: ~ **(on)** expediente m
(sobre).
DOT n abbr (US: = Department of
Transportation) ministerio de transporte.
dot [dɔt] n punto; ~**ted with** salpicado de;
on the ~ en punto.
dotcom ['dɔtkɔm] puntocom f.
dot command n (COMPUT) instrucción f
(precedida) de punto.
dote [dəut]: **to ~ on** vt fus adorar, idolatrar.
dot-matrix printer [dɔt'meɪtrɪks-] n
impresora matricial or de matriz.
dotted line ['dɔtɪd-] n línea de puntos; **to
sign on the ~** firmar.
dotty ['dɔtɪ] adj (col) disparatado, chiflado.
double ['dʌbl] adj doble ♦ adv (twice): **to
cost ~** costar el doble ♦ n (gen) doble m
♦ vt doblar; (efforts) redoblar ♦ vi
doblarse; (have two uses etc): **to ~ as**
hacer las veces de; ~ **five two six (5526)**
(TELEC) cinco cinco dos seis; **spelt with a
~ "s"** escrito con dos "eses"; **on the ~**,
(BRIT) **at the ~** corriendo.
▶**double back** vi (person) volver sobre sus
pasos.
▶**double up** vi (bend over) doblarse; (share
bedroom) compartir.
double bass n contrabajo.
double bed n cama matrimonial.
double-breasted ['dʌbl'brɛstɪd] adj
cruzado.

double-check ['dʌbltʃɛk] *vt* volver a revisar ♦ *vi*: **I'll** ~ voy a revisarlo otra vez.

double-click ['dʌbl,klɪk] *vi* (*COMPUT*) hacer doble clic.

double cream *n* nata enriquecida.

doublecross ['dʌbl'krɔs] *vt* (*trick*) engañar; (*betray*) traicionar.

doubledecker ['dʌbl'dɛkə*] *n* autobús *m* de dos pisos.

double glazing *n* (*BRIT*) doble acristalamiento.

double indemnity *n* doble indemnización *f*.

double-page ['dʌblpeɪdʒ] *adj*: ~ **spread** doble página.

double room *n* cuarto para dos.

doubles ['dʌblz] *n* (*TENNIS*) juego de dobles.

double time *n* tarifa doble.

double whammy [-'wæmɪ] *n* (*col*) palo doble.

doubly ['dʌblɪ] *adv* doblemente.

doubt [daut] *n* duda ♦ *vt* dudar; (*suspect*) dudar de; **to** ~ **that** dudar que; **there is no** ~ **that** no cabe duda de que; **without (a)** ~ sin duda (alguna); **beyond** ~ fuera de duda; **I** ~ **it very much** lo dudo mucho.

doubtful ['dautful] *adj* dudoso; (*person*) sospechoso; **to be** ~ **about sth** tener dudas sobre algo; **I'm a bit** ~ no estoy convencido.

doubtless ['dautlɪs] *adv* sin duda.

dough [dəu] *n* masa, pasta; (*col*: *money*) pasta, lana (*LAM*).

doughnut ['dəunʌt] *n* buñuelo.

douse [daus] *vt* (*drench*: *with water*) mojar; (*extinguish*: *flames*) apagar.

dove [dʌv] *n* paloma.

dovetail ['dʌvteɪl] *vi* (*fig*) encajar.

dowager ['dauɪdʒə*] *n*: ~ **duchess** duquesa viuda.

dowdy ['daudɪ] *adj* desaliñado; (*inelegant*) poco elegante.

Dow-Jones average ['daudʒəunz-] *n* (*US*) índice *m* Dow-Jones.

down [daun] *n* (*fluff*) pelusa; (*feathers*) plumón *m*, flojel *m*; (*hill*) loma ♦ *adv* (~*wards*) abajo, hacia abajo; (*on the ground*) por/en tierra ♦ *prep* abajo ♦ *vt* (*col*: *drink*) beberse, tragar(se); ~ **with X!** ¡abajo X!; ~ **there** allí abajo; ~ **here** aquí abajo; **I'll be** ~ **in a minute** ahora bajo; **England is two goals** ~ Inglaterra está perdiendo por dos tantos; **I've been** ~ **with flu** he estado con gripe; **the price of meat is** ~ ha bajado el precio de la carne; **I've got it** ~ **in my diary** lo he apuntado en mi agenda; **to pay £2** ~ dejar £2 de depósito; **he went** ~ **the hill** fue cuesta abajo; ~ **under** (*in Australia etc*) en Australia/Nueva Zelanda; **to** ~ **tools** (*fig*) declararse en huelga.

down-and-out ['daunəndaut] *n* (*tramp*) vagabundo/a.

down-at-heel ['daunət'hiːl] *adj* venido a menos; (*appearance*) desaliñado.

downbeat ['daunbiːt] *n* (*MUS*) compás *m* ♦ *adj* (*gloomy*) pesimista.

downcast ['daunkɑːst] *adj* abatido.

downfall ['daunfɔːl] *n* caída, ruina.

downgrade [daun'greɪd] *vt* (*job*) degradar; (*hotel*) bajar de categoría a.

downhearted [daun'hɑːtɪd] *adj* desanimado.

downhill [daun'hɪl] *adv*: **to go** ~ ir cuesta abajo; (*business*) estar en declive.

Downing Street ['daunɪŋ-] *n* (*BRIT*) Downing Street *f*; *ver recuadro*.

DOWNING STREET

Downing Street *es la calle de Londres en la que tienen su residencia oficial tanto el Primer Ministro* ("*Prime Minister*") *como el Ministro de Economía* ("*Chancellor of the Exchequer*"). *El primero vive en el nº10 y el segundo en el nº11. Es una calle cerrada al público que se encuentra en el barrio de Westminster, en el centro de Londres.* **Downing Street** *se usa también en lenguaje periodístico para referirse al jefe del gobierno británico.*

---

download ['daunləud] *vt* (*COMPUT*) transferir, telecargar.

down-market ['daun'mɑːkɪt] *adj* de escasa calidad.

down payment *n* entrada, pago al contado.

downplay ['daunpleɪ] *vt* (*US*) quitar importancia a.

downpour ['daunpɔː*] *n* aguacero.

downright ['daunraɪt] *adj* (*nonsense*, *lie*) manifiesto; (*refusal*) terminante.

downsize [daun'saɪz] *vt* reducir la plantilla de.

Down's syndrome [daunz-] *n* síndrome *m* de Down.

downstairs [daun'stɛəz] *adv* (*below*) (en el piso de) abajo; (*motion*) escaleras abajo; **to come** (*or* **go**) ~ bajar la escalera.

downstream [daun'striːm] *adv* aguas *or* río abajo.

downtime ['dauntaɪm] *n* (*COMM*) tiempo inactivo.

down-to-earth [dauntu'ə:θ] *adj* práctico.
downtown [daun'taun] *adv* en el centro de la ciudad.
downtrodden ['dauntrɔdn] *adj* oprimido.
downward ['daunwəd] *adv* hacia abajo
♦ *adj*: **a ~ trend** una tendencia descendente.
downward(s) ['daunwəd(z)] *adv* hacia abajo; **face ~s** (*person*) boca abajo; (*object*) cara abajo.
dowry ['dauri] *n* dote *f*.
doz. *abbr* = **dozen**.
doze [dəuz] *vi* dormitar.
▶**doze off** *vi* echar una cabezada.
dozen ['dʌzn] *n* docena; **a ~ books** una docena de libros; **~s of** cantidad de; **~s of times** cantidad de veces; **80p a ~** 80 peniques la docena.
DPh., D. Phil. *n abbr* (= *Doctor of Philosophy*) título universitario.
DPP *n abbr* (*BRIT*) = **Director of Public Prosecutions.**
DPT *n abbr* (= *diphtheria, pertussis, tetanus*) vacuna trivalente.
DPW *n abbr* (*US*: = *Department of Public Works*) ministerio de obras públicas.
Dr, Dr. *abbr* (= *doctor*) Dr.
Dr. *abbr* (*in street names*) = **Drive.**
dr *abbr* (*COMM*) = **debtor.**
drab [dræb] *adj* gris, monótono.
draft [drɑ:ft] *n* (*first copy: of document, report*) borrador *m*; (*COMM*) giro; (*US: call-up*) quinta ♦ *vt* (*write roughly*) hacer un borrador de; *see also* **draught.**
draftsman ['drɑ:ftsmən] *etc* (*US*) = **draughtsman** *etc*.
drag [dræg] *vt* arrastrar; (*river*) dragar, rastrear ♦ *vi* arrastrarse por el suelo ♦ *n* (*AVIAT: resistance*) resistencia aerodinámica; (*col*) lata; (*women's clothing*): **in ~** travestido.
▶**drag away** *vt*: **to ~ away (from)** separar a rastras (de).
▶**drag on** *vi* ser interminable.
dragnet ['drægnet] *n* (*NAUT*) rastra; (*fig*) emboscada.
dragon ['drægən] *n* dragón *m*.
dragonfly ['drægənflai] *n* libélula.
dragoon [drə'gu:n] *n* (*cavalryman*) dragón *m*
♦ *vt*: **to ~ sb into doing sth** forzar a algn a hacer algo.
drain [drein] *n* desaguadero; (*in street*) sumidero; (*~ cover*) rejilla del sumidero ♦ *vt* (*land, marshes*) desecar; (*MED*) drenar; (*reservoir*) desecar; (*fig*) agotar ♦ *vi* escurrirse; **to be a ~ on** consumir, agotar; **to feel ~ed (of energy)** (*fig*) sentirse agotado.
drainage ['dreinidʒ] *n* (*act*) desagüe *m*;

(*MED, AGR*) drenaje *m*; (*sewage*) alcantarillado.
draining board ['dreiniŋ-], (*US*)
drainboard ['dreinbɔ:d] *n* escurridero, escurridor *m*.
drainpipe ['dreinpaip] *n* tubo de desagüe.
drake [dreik] *n* pato (macho).
dram [dræm] *n* (*drink*) traguito, copita.
drama ['drɑ:mə] *n* (*art*) teatro; (*play*) drama *m*.
dramatic [drə'mætik] *adj* dramático.
dramatist ['dræmətist] *n* dramaturgo/a.
dramatize ['dræmətaiz] *vt* (*events etc*) dramatizar; (*adapt: novel: for TV, cinema*) adaptar.
drank [dræŋk] *pt of* **drink.**
drape [dreip] *vt* cubrir.
draper ['dreipə*] *n* (*BRIT*) pañero, mercero.
drapes [dreips] *npl* (*US*) cortinas *fpl*.
drastic ['dræstik] *adj* (*measure, reduction*) severo; (*change*) radical.
draught, (*US*) **draft** [drɑ:ft] *n* (*of air*) corriente *f* de aire; (*drink*) trago; (*NAUT*) calado; **on ~** (*beer*) de barril.
draught beer *n* cerveza de barril.
draughtboard ['drɑ:ftbɔ:d] (*BRIT*) *n* tablero de damas.
draughts [drɑ:fts] *n* (*BRIT*) juego de damas.
draughtsman, (*US*) **draftsman**
['drɑ:ftsmən] *n* proyectista *m*, delineante *m*.
draughtsmanship, (*US*) **draftsmanship**
['drɑ:ftsmənʃip] *n* (*drawing*) dibujo lineal; (*skill*) habilidad *f* para el dibujo.
draw [drɔ:] *vb* (*pt* **drew,** *pp* **drawn** [dru:, drɔ:n]) *vt* (*pull*) tirar; (*take out*) sacar; (*attract*) atraer; (*picture*) dibujar; (*money*) retirar; (*formulate: conclusion*): **to ~ (from)** sacar (de); (*comparison, distinction*): **to ~ (between)** hacer (entre) ♦ *vi* (*SPORT*) empatar ♦ *n* (*SPORT*) empate *m*; (*lottery*) sorteo; (*attraction*) atracción *f*; **to ~ near** *vi* acercarse.
▶**draw back** *vi*: **to ~ back (from)** echarse atrás (de).
▶**draw in** *vi* (*car*) aparcar; (*train*) entrar en la estación.
▶**draw on** *vt* (*resources*) utilizar, servirse de; (*imagination, person*) recurrir a.
▶**draw out** *vi* (*lengthen*) alargarse.
▶**draw up** *vi* (*stop*) pararse ♦ *vt* (*document*) redactar; (*plans*) trazar.
drawback ['drɔ:bæk] *n* inconveniente *m*, desventaja.
drawbridge ['drɔ:bridʒ] *n* puente *m* levadizo.
drawee [drɔ:'i:] *n* girado, librado.
drawer [drɔ:*] *n* cajón *m*; (*of cheque*)

librador(a) _m/f._
drawing ['drɔːɪŋ] _n_ dibujo.
drawing board _n_ tablero (de dibujante).
drawing pin _n_ (_BRIT_) chincheta _m._
drawing room _n_ salón _m._
drawl [drɔːl] _n_ habla lenta y cansina.
drawn [drɔːn] _pp of_ draw ♦ _adj_ (_haggard_: _with tiredness_) ojeroso; (: _with pain_) macilento.
drawstring ['drɔːstrɪŋ] _n_ cordón _m._
dread [drɛd] _n_ pavor _m_, terror _m_ ♦ _vt_ temer, tener miedo _or_ pavor a.
dreadful ['drɛdful] _adj_ espantoso; **I feel ~!**
(_ill_) ¡me siento fatal _or_ malísimo!;
(_ashamed_) ¡qué vergüenza!
dream [driːm] _n_ sueño ♦ _vt, vi_ (_pt, pp_
dreamed _or_ **dreamt** [drɛmt]) soñar; **to
have a ~ about sb/sth** soñar con algn/
algo; **sweet ~s!** ¡que sueñes con los
angelitos!
▶**dream up** _vt_ (_reason, excuse_) inventar;
(_plan, idea_) idear.
dreamer ['driːmə*] _n_ soñador(a) _m/f._
dream world _n_ mundo imaginario _or_ de
ensueño.
dreamy ['driːmɪ] _adj_ (_person_) soñador(a),
distraído; (_music_) de sueño.
dreary ['drɪərɪ] _adj_ monótono, aburrido.
dredge [drɛdʒ] _vt_ dragar.
▶**dredge up** _vt_ sacar con draga; (_fig:
unpleasant facts_) pescar, sacar a luz.
dredger ['drɛdʒə*] _n_ (_ship, machine_) draga;
(_CULIN_) tamiz _m._
dregs [drɛgz] _npl_ heces _fpl._
drench [drɛntʃ] _vt_ empapar; **~ed to the
skin** calado hasta los huesos.
dress [drɛs] _n_ vestido; (_clothing_) ropa ♦ _vt_
vestir; (_wound_) vendar; (_CULIN_) aliñar;
(_shop window_) decorar, arreglar ♦ _vi_
vestirse; **to ~ o.s., get ~ed** vestirse; **she
~es very well** se viste muy bien.
▶**dress up** _vi_ vestirse de etiqueta; (_in fancy
dress_) disfrazarse.
dress circle _n_ (_BRIT_) principal _m._
dress designer _n_ modista/o.
dresser ['drɛsə*] _n_ (_furniture_) aparador _m;_
(: _US_) tocador _m;_ (_THEAT_) camarero/a.
dressing ['drɛsɪŋ] _n_ (_MED_) vendaje _m;_
(_CULIN_) aliño.
dressing gown _n_ (_BRIT_) bata.
dressing room _n_ (_THEAT_) camarín _m;_
(_SPORT_) vestidor _m._
dressing table _n_ tocador _m._
dressmaker ['drɛsmeɪkə*] _n_ modista,
costurera.
dressmaking ['drɛsmeɪkɪŋ] _n_ costura.
dress rehearsal _n_ ensayo general.
dress shirt _n_ camisa de frac.
dressy ['drɛsɪ] _adj_ (_col_) elegante.

drew [druː] _pt of_ draw.
dribble ['drɪbl] _vi_ gotear, caer gota a gota;
(_baby_) babear ♦ _vt_ (_ball_) driblar, regatear.
dried [draɪd] _adj_ (_gen_) seco; (_fruit_) paso;
(_milk_) en polvo.
drier ['draɪə*] _n_ = dryer.
drift [drɪft] _n_ (_of current etc_) velocidad _f;_ (_of
sand_) montón _m;_ (_of snow_) ventisquero;
(_meaning_) significado ♦ _vi_ (_boat_) ir a la
deriva; (_sand, snow_) amontonarse; **to
catch sb's ~** cogerle el hilo a algn; **to let
things ~** dejar las cosas como están; **to ~
apart** (_friends_) seguir su camino; (_lovers_)
disgustarse, romper.
drifter ['drɪftə*] _n_ vagabundo/a.
driftwood ['drɪftwud] _n_ madera flotante.
drill [drɪl] _n_ taladro; (_bit_) broca; (_of dentist_)
fresa; (_for mining etc_) perforadora,
barrena; (_MIL_) instrucción _f_ ♦ _vt_ perforar,
taladrar; (_soldiers_) ejercitar; (_pupils: in
grammar_) hacer ejercicios con ♦ _vi_ (_for oil_)
perforar.
drilling ['drɪlɪŋ] _n_ (_for oil_) perforación _f._
drilling rig _n_ (_on land_) torre _f_ de
perforación; (_at sea_) plataforma de
perforación.
drily ['draɪlɪ] _adv_ secamente.
drink [drɪŋk] _n_ bebida ♦ _vt, vi_ (_pt_ **drank**, _pp_
drunk) beber, tomar (_LAM_); **to have a ~**
tomar algo; tomar una copa _or_ un trago;
a ~ of water un trago de agua; **to invite
sb for ~s** invitar a algn a tomar unas
copas; **there's food and ~ in the kitchen**
hay de comer y de beber en la cocina;
would you like something to ~? ¿quieres
beber _or_ tomar algo?
▶**drink in** _vt_ (_subj: person: fresh air_)
respirar; (_story, sight_) beberse.
drinkable ['drɪŋkəbl] _adj_ (_not poisonous_)
potable; (_palatable_) aguantable.
drink-driving [drɪŋk'draɪvɪŋ] _n:_ **to be
charged with ~** ser acusado de conducir
borracho _or_ en estado de embriaguez.
drinker ['drɪŋkə*] _n_ bebedor(a) _m/f._
drinking ['drɪŋkɪŋ] _n_ (_drunkenness_) beber _m._
drinking fountain _n_ fuente _f_ de agua
potable.
drinking water _n_ agua potable.
drip [drɪp] _n_ (_act_) goteo; (_one ~_) gota; (_MED_)
gota a gota _m;_ (_sound: of water etc_) goteo;
(_col: spineless person_) soso/a ♦ _vi_ gotear,
caer gota a gota.
drip-dry ['drɪp'draɪ] _adj_ (_shirt_) de lava y pon.
dripping ['drɪpɪŋ] _n_ (_animal fat_) pringue _m_
♦ _adj:_ **~ wet** calado.
drive [draɪv] _n_ paseo (en coche); (_journey_)
viaje _m_ (en coche); (_also:_ **~way**) entrada;
(_street_) calle; (_energy_) energía, vigor _m;_

(*PSYCH*) impulso; (*SPORT*) ataque *m*; (*COMPUT: also*: **disk** ~) disc drive *m* ♦ *vb* (*pt* **drove**, *pp* **driven** [drəuv, 'drɪvn]) *vt* (*car*) conducir, manejar (*LAM*); (*nail*) clavar; (*push*) empujar; (*TECH: motor*) impulsar ♦ *vi* (*AUT: at controls*) conducir; (: *travel*) pasearse en coche; **to go for a** ~ dar una vuelta en coche; **it's 3 hours'** ~ **from London** es un viaje de 3 horas en coche desde Londres; **left-/right-hand** ~ conducción *f* a la izquierda/derecha; **front-/rear-wheel** ~ tracción *f* delantera/trasera; **sales** ~ promoción *f* de ventas; **to** ~ **sb mad** volverle loco a algn; **to** ~ **sb to (do) sth** empujar a algn a (hacer) algo; **he** ~**s a taxi** es taxista; **he** ~**s a Mercedes** tiene un Mercedes; **can you** ~? ¿sabes conducir *or* (*LAM*) manejar?; **to** ~ **at 50 km an hour** ir a 50km por hora.
▶**drive at** *vt fus* (*fig: intend, mean*) querer decir, insinuar.
▶**drive on** *vi* no parar, seguir adelante ♦ *vt* (*incite, encourage*) empujar.
drive-by ['draɪvbaɪ] *n*: ~ **shooting** tiroteo desde el coche.
drive-in ['draɪvɪn] *adj* (*esp US*): ~ **cinema** autocine *m*.
drivel ['drɪvl] *n* (*col*) tonterías *fpl*.
driven ['drɪvn] *pp of* **drive**.
driver ['draɪvə*] *n* conductor(a) *m/f*, chofer *m* (*LAM*); (*of taxi*) taxista *m/f*.
driver's license *n* (*US*) carnet *m or* permiso de conducir.
driveway ['draɪvweɪ] *n* camino de entrada.
driving ['draɪvɪŋ] *n* conducir *m*, manejar *m* (*LAM*) ♦ *adj* (*force*) impulsor(a).
driving instructor *n* instructor(a) *m/f* de autoescuela.
driving lesson *n* clase *f* de conducir.
driving licence *n* (*BRIT*) carnet *m or* permiso de conducir.
driving school *n* autoescuela.
driving test *n* examen *m* de conducir.
drizzle ['drɪzl] *n* llovizna, garúa (*LAM*) ♦ *vi* lloviznar.
droll [drəul] *adj* gracioso.
dromedary ['drɒmɪdərɪ] *n* dromedario.
drone [drəun] *vi* (*bee, aircraft, engine*) zumbar; (*also*: ~ **on**) murmurar sin interrupción ♦ *n* zumbido; (*male bee*) zángano.
drool [druːl] *vi* babear; **to** ~ **over sb/sth** caérsele la baba por algn/algo.
droop [druːp] *vi* (*fig*) decaer, desanimarse.
drop [drɒp] *n* (*of water*) gota; (*fall: in price*) bajada; (: *in salary*) disminución *f* ♦ *vt* (*allow to fall*) dejar caer; (*voice, eyes, price*) bajar ♦ *vi* (*price*,

temperature) bajar; (*wind*) calmarse, amainar; (*numbers, attendance*) disminuir; ~**s** *npl* (*MED*) gotas *fpl*; **cough** ~**s** pastillas *fpl* para la tos; **a** ~ **of 10%** una bajada del 10 por ciento; **to** ~ **anchor** echar el ancla; **to** ~ **sb a line** mandar unas líneas a algn.
▶**drop in** *vi* (*col: visit*): **to** ~ **in (on)** pasar por casa (de).
▶**drop off** *vi* (*sleep*) dormirse ♦ *vt* (*passenger*) bajar, dejar.
▶**drop out** *vi* (*withdraw*) retirarse.
droplet ['drɒplɪt] *n* gotita.
dropout ['drɒpaut] *n* (*from society*) marginado/a; (*from university*) estudiante *m/f* que ha abandonado los estudios.
dropper ['drɒpə*] *n* (*MED*) cuentagotas *m inv*.
droppings ['drɒpɪŋz] *npl* excremento *sg*.
dross [drɒs] *n* (*coal, fig*) escoria.
drought [draut] *n* sequía.
drove [drəuv] *pt of* **drive**.
drown [draun] *vt* (*also*: ~ **out**: *sound*) ahogar ♦ *vi* ahogarse.
drowse [drauz] *vi* estar medio dormido.
drowsy ['drauzɪ] *adj* soñoliento; **to be** ~ tener sueño.
drudge [drʌdʒ] *n* esclavo del trabajo.
drudgery ['drʌdʒərɪ] *n* trabajo pesado *or* monótono.
drug [drʌg] *n* (*MED*) medicamento, droga; (*narcotic*) droga ♦ *vt* drogar; **to be on** ~**s** drogarse; **he's on** ~**s** se droga.
drug addict *n* drogadicto/a.
druggist ['drʌgɪst] *n* (*US*) farmacéutico/a.
drug peddler *n* traficante *m/f* de drogas.
drugstore ['drʌgstɔː*] *n* (*US*) tienda (*de comestibles, periódicos y medicamentos*).
drug trafficker *n* narcotraficante *m/f*.
drum [drʌm] *n* tambor *m*; (*large*) bombo; (*for oil, petrol*) bidón *m* ♦ *vi* tocar el tambor; (*with fingers*) tamborilear ♦ *vt*: **to** ~ **one's fingers on the table** tamborilear con los dedos sobre la mesa; ~**s** *npl* batería *sg*.
▶**drum up** *vt* (*enthusiasm, support*) movilizar, fomentar.
drummer ['drʌmə*] *n* (*in military band*) tambor *m/f*; (*in jazz/pop group*) batería *m/f*.
drumstick ['drʌmstɪk] *n* (*MUS*) palillo, baqueta; (*chicken leg*) muslo (*de pollo*).
drunk [drʌŋk] *pp of* **drink** ♦ *adj* borracho ♦ *n* (*also*: ~**ard**) borracho/a; **to get** ~ emborracharse.
drunken ['drʌŋkən] *adj* borracho.
drunkenness ['drʌŋkənnɪs] *n* embriaguez *f*.
dry [draɪ] *adj* seco; (*day*) sin lluvia; (*climate*) árido, seco; (*humour*) agudo; (*uninteresting: lecture*) aburrido, pesado

♦ *vt* secar; (*tears*) enjugarse ♦ *vi* secarse; **on ~ land** en tierra firme; **to ~ one's hands/hair/eyes** secarse las manos/el pelo/las lágrimas.

▶**dry up** *vi* (*supply, imagination etc*) agotarse; (*in speech*) atascarse.

dry-clean ['draɪ'kliːn] *vt* limpiar *or* lavar en seco; "*~ only*" (*on label*) "limpieza *or* lavado en seco".

dry-cleaner's ['draɪ'kliːnəz] *n* tintorería.

dry-cleaning ['draɪ'kliːnɪŋ] *n* lavado en seco.

dry dock *n* (*NAUT*) dique *m* seco.

dryer ['draɪə*] *n* (*for hair*) secador *m*; (*for clothes*) secadora.

dry goods *npl* (*COMM*) mercería *sg*.

dry goods store *n* (*US*) mercería.

dry ice *n* nieve *f* carbónica, hielo seco.

dryness ['draɪnɪs] *n* sequedad *f*.

dry rot *n* putrefacción *f*.

dry run *n* (*fig*) ensayo.

dry ski slope *n* pista artificial de esquí.

DSc *n abbr* (= *Doctor of Science*) título universitario.

DST *n abbr* (*US*: = *Daylight Saving Time*) hora de verano.

DT *n abbr* (*COMPUT*) = **data transmission**.

DTI *n abbr* (*BRIT*) = *Department of Trade and Industry*.

DTP *n abbr* = **desktop publishing**.

DT's *n abbr* (*col*: = *delirium tremens*) delirium *m* tremens.

dual ['djuəl] *adj* doble.

dual carriageway *n* (*BRIT*) ≈ autovía.

dual-control ['djuəlkən'trəul] *adj* de doble mando.

dual nationality *n* doble nacionalidad *f*.

dual-purpose ['djuəl'pəːpəs] *adj* de doble uso.

dubbed [dʌbd] *adj* (*CINE*) doblado.

dubious ['djuːbɪəs] *adj* indeciso; (*reputation, company*) dudoso; (*character*) sospechoso; **I'm very ~ about it** tengo mis dudas sobre ello.

Dublin ['dʌblɪn] *n* Dublín.

Dubliner ['dʌblɪnə*] *n* dublinés/esa *m/f*.

duchess ['dʌtʃɪs] *n* duquesa.

duck [dʌk] *n* pato ♦ *vi* agacharse ♦ *vt* (*plunge in water*) zambullir.

duckling ['dʌklɪŋ] *n* patito.

duct [dʌkt] *n* conducto, canal *m*.

dud [dʌd] *n* (*shell*) obús *m* que no estalla; (*object, tool*): **it's a ~** es una filfa ♦ *adj*: **~ cheque** (*BRIT*) cheque *m* sin fondos.

due [djuː] *adj* (*proper*) debido; (*fitting*) conveniente, oportuno ♦ *adv*: **~ north** derecho al norte; **~s** *npl* (*for club, union*) cuota *sg*; (*in harbour*) derechos *mpl*; **in ~**

course a su debido tiempo; **~ to** debido a; **to be ~ to** deberse a; **the train is ~ to arrive at 8.00** el tren tiene (prevista) la llegada a las ocho; **the rent's ~ on the 30th** hay que pagar el alquiler el día 30; **I am ~ 6 days' leave** me deben 6 días de vacaciones; **she is ~ back tomorrow** ella debe volver mañana.

due date *n* fecha de vencimiento.

duel ['djuəl] *n* duelo.

duet [djuː'ɛt] *n* dúo.

duff [dʌf] *adj* sin valor.

duffel bag ['dʌfl-] *n* macuto.

duffel coat ['dʌfl-] *n* trenca.

dug [dʌg] *pt, pp of* **dig**.

dugout ['dʌgaut] *n* (*canoe*) piragua (*hecha de un solo tronco*); (*SPORT*) banquillo; (*MIL*) refugio subterráneo.

duke [djuːk] *n* duque *m*.

dull [dʌl] *adj* (*light*) apagado; (*stupid*) torpe; (*boring*) pesado; (*sound, pain*) sordo; (*weather, day*) gris ♦ *vt* (*pain, grief*) aliviar; (*mind, senses*) entorpecer.

duly ['djuːlɪ] *adv* debidamente; (*on time*) a su debido tiempo.

dumb [dʌm] *adj* mudo; (*stupid*) estúpido; **to be struck ~** (*fig*) quedar boquiabierto.

dumbbell ['dʌmbɛl] *n* (*SPORT*) pesa.

dumbfounded [dʌm'faundɪd] *adj* pasmado.

dummy ['dʌmɪ] *n* (*tailor's model*) maniquí *m*; (*BRIT: for baby*) chupete *m* ♦ *adj* falso, postizo; **~ run** ensayo.

dump [dʌmp] *n* (*heap*) montón *m* de basura; (*place*) basurero, vertedero; (*col*) tugurio; (*MIL*) depósito; (*COMPUT*) copia vaciada ♦ *vt* (*put down*) dejar; (*get rid of*) deshacerse de; (*COMPUT*) vaciar; (*COMM: goods*) inundar el mercado de; **to be (down) in the ~s** (*col*) tener murria, estar deprimido.

dumping ['dʌmpɪŋ] *n* (*ECON*) dumping *m*; (*of rubbish*): "**no ~**" "prohibido verter basura".

dumpling ['dʌmplɪŋ] *n* bola de masa hervida.

dumpy ['dʌmpɪ] *adj* regordete/a.

dunce [dʌns] *n* zopenco.

dune [djuːn] *n* duna.

dung [dʌŋ] *n* estiércol *m*.

dungarees [dʌŋgə'riːz] *npl* mono *sg*, overol *msg* (*LAM*).

dungeon ['dʌndʒən] *n* calabozo.

dunk [dʌŋk] *vt* mojar.

duo ['djuːəu] *n* (*gen, MUS*) dúo.

duodenal [djuːə'diːnl] *adj* (*ulcer*) de duodeno.

duodenum [djuːə'diːnəm] *n* duodeno.

dupe [djuːp] *n* (*victim*) víctima ♦ *vt* engañar.

duplex – each

duplex ['djuːplɛks] n (US: also: ~
apartment) dúplex m.
duplicate ['djuːplɪkət] n duplicado; (copy of
letter etc) copia ♦ adj (copy) duplicado ♦ vt
['djuːplɪkeɪt] duplicar; (on machine)
multicopiar; **in** ~ por duplicado.
duplicate key n duplicado de una llave.
duplicating machine ['djuːplɪkeɪtɪŋ-],
duplicator ['djuːplɪkeɪtə*] n multicopista
m.
duplicity [djuː'plɪsɪtɪ] n doblez f.
Dur abbr (BRIT) = Durham.
durability [djuərə'bɪlɪtɪ] n durabilidad f.
durable ['djuərəbl] adj duradero.
duration [djuə'reɪʃən] n duración f.
duress [djuə'rɛs] n: **under** ~ por coacción.
Durex ® ['djuərɛks] n (BRIT) preservativo.
during ['djuərɪŋ] prep durante.
dusk [dʌsk] n crepúsculo, anochecer m.
dusky ['dʌskɪ] adj oscuro; (complexion)
moreno.
dust [dʌst] n polvo ♦ vt (furniture)
desempolvar; (cake etc): **to** ~ **with**
espolvorear de.
▶**dust off** vt (also fig) desempolvar, quitar
el polvo de.
dustbin ['dʌstbɪn] n (BRIT) cubo de la
basura, balde m (LAM).
dustbin liner n bolsa de basura.
duster ['dʌstə*] n paño, trapo; (feather ~)
plumero.
dust jacket n sobrecubierta.
dustman ['dʌstmən] n (BRIT) basurero.
dustpan ['dʌstpæn] n cogedor m.
dust storm n vendaval m de polvo.
dusty ['dʌstɪ] adj polvoriento.
Dutch [dʌtʃ] adj holandés/esa ♦ n (LING)
holandés m ♦ adv: **to go** ~ pagar a escote;
the ~ npl los holandeses.
Dutch auction n subasta a la rebaja.
Dutchman ['dʌtʃmən], **Dutchwoman**
['dʌtʃwumən] n holandés/esa m/f.
dutiful ['djuːtɪful] adj (child) obediente;
(husband) sumiso; (employee) cumplido.
duty ['djuːtɪ] n deber m; (tax) derechos mpl
de aduana; **on** ~ de servicio; (at night etc)
de guardia; **off** ~ libre (de servicio); **to
make it one's** ~ **to do sth** encargarse de
hacer algo sin falta; **to pay** ~ **on sth**
pagar los derechos sobre algo.
duty-free [djuːtɪ'friː] adj libre de derechos
de aduana; ~ **shop** tienda libre de
impuestos.
duty officer n (MIL etc) oficial m/f de
guardia.
duvet ['duːveɪ] n (BRIT) edredón m
(nórdico).
DV abbr (= Deo volente) Dios mediante.

DVD n abbr (= digital versatile or video disc)
DVD m.
DVLA n abbr (BRIT: = Driver and Vehicle
Licensing Agency) organismo encargado
de la expedición de permisos de conducir
y matriculación de vehículos.
DVM n abbr (US: = Doctor of Veterinary
Medicine) título universitario.
dwarf [dwɔːf], pl **dwarves** [dwɔːvz] n enano
♦ vt empequeñecer.
dwell [dwɛl], pt, pp **dwelt** [dwɛlt] vi morar.
▶**dwell on** vt fus explayarse en.
dweller ['dwɛlə*] n habitante m; **city** ~
habitante m de la ciudad.
dwelling ['dwɛlɪŋ] n vivienda.
dwelt [dwɛlt] pt, pp of **dwell**.
dwindle ['dwɪndl] vi menguar, disminuir.
dwindling ['dwɪndlɪŋ] adj (strength, interest)
menguante; (resources, supplies) en
disminución.
dye [daɪ] n tinte m ♦ vt teñir; **hair** ~ tinte m
para el pelo.
dying ['daɪɪŋ] adj moribundo, agonizante;
(moments) final; (words) último.
dyke [daɪk] n (BRIT) dique m; (channel)
arroyo, acequia; (causeway) calzada.
dynamic [daɪ'næmɪk] adj dinámico.
dynamics [daɪ'næmɪks] n or npl dinámica sg.
dynamite ['daɪnəmaɪt] n dinamita ♦ vt
dinamitar.
dynamo ['daɪnəməu] n dinamo f or m (LAM).
dynasty ['dɪnəstɪ] n dinastía.
dysentery ['dɪsɪntrɪ] n disentería.
dyslexia [dɪs'lɛksɪə] n dislexia.
dyslexic [dɪs'lɛksɪk] adj, n disléxico/a m/f.
dyspepsia [dɪs'pepsɪə] n dispepsia.
dystrophy ['dɪstrəfɪ] n distrofia; **muscular**
~ distrofia muscular.

E e

E, e [iː] n (letter) E, e f; (MUS) mi m; **E for
Edward**, (US) **E for Easy** E de Enrique.
E abbr (= east) E ♦ n abbr (= Ecstasy) éxtasis
m.
E111 n abbr (also: **form** ~) impreso E111.
ea. abbr = **each**.
E.A. abbr (US: = educational age) nivel
escolar.
each [iːtʃ] adj cada inv ♦ pron cada uno; ~
other el uno al otro; **they hate** ~ **other** se

odian (entre ellos *or* mutuamente); ~ **day** cada día; **they have 2 books** ~ tienen 2 libros cada uno; **they cost £5** ~ cuestan cinco libras cada uno; ~ **of us** cada uno de nosotros.

eager ['iːgə*] *adj* (*gen*) impaciente; (*hopeful*) ilusionado; (*keen*) entusiasmado; (: *pupil*) apasionado; **to be** ~ **to do sth** estar deseoso de hacer algo; **to be** ~ **for** ansiar, anhelar.

eagerly ['iːgəlɪ] *adv* con impaciencia; con ilusión; con entusiasmo.

eagerness ['iːgənɪs] *n* impaciencia; ilusión *f*; entusiasmo.

eagle ['iːgl] *n* águila.

E and OE *abbr* = **errors and omissions excepted**.

ear [ɪə*] *n* oreja; (*sense of hearing*) oído; (*of corn*) espiga; **up to the** ~**s in debt** abrumado de deudas.

earache ['ɪəreɪk] *n* dolor *m* de oídos.

eardrum ['ɪədrʌm] *n* tímpano.

earful ['ɪəful] *n*: **to give sb an** ~ (*col*) echar una bronca a algn.

earl [əːl] *n* conde *m*.

early ['əːlɪ] *adv* (*gen*) temprano; (*ahead of time*) con tiempo, con anticipación ♦ *adj* (*gen*) temprano; (*reply*) pronto; (*man*) primitivo; (*first: Christians, settlers*) primero; **to have an** ~ **night** acostarse temprano; **in the** ~ *or* ~ **in the spring/ 19th century** a principios de primavera/ del siglo diecinueve; **you're** ~! ¡has llegado temprano *or* pronto!; ~ **in the morning/afternoon** a primeras horas de la mañana/tarde; **she's in her** ~ **forties** tiene poco más de cuarenta años; **at your earliest convenience** (*COMM*) con la mayor brevedad posible; **I can't come any earlier** no puedo llegar antes.

early retirement *n* jubilación *f* anticipada.

early warning system *n* sistema *m* de alerta inmediata.

earmark ['ɪəmɑːk] *vt*: **to** ~ **for** reservar para, destinar a.

earn [əːn] *vt* (*gen*) ganar; (*interest*) devengar; (*praise*) ganarse; **to** ~ **one's living** ganarse la vida.

earned income *n* renta del trabajo.

earnest ['əːnɪst] *adj* serio, formal ♦ *n* (*also*: ~ **money**) anticipo, señal *f*; **in** ~ *adv* en serio.

earnings ['əːnɪŋz] *npl* (*personal*) ingresos *mpl*; (*of company etc*) ganancias *fpl*.

earphones ['ɪəfəunz] *npl* auriculares *mpl*.

earplugs ['ɪəplʌgz] *npl* tapones *mpl* para los oídos.

earring ['ɪərɪŋ] *n* pendiente *m*, arete *m* (*esp*

LAM).

earshot ['ɪəʃɔt] *n*: **out of/within** ~ fuera del/al alcance del oído.

earth [əːθ] *n* (*gen*) tierra; (*BRIT: ELEC*) toma de tierra ♦ *vt* (*BRIT: ELEC*) conectar a tierra.

earthenware ['əːθnwɛə*] *n* loza (de barro).

earthly ['əːθlɪ] *adj* terrenal, mundano; ~ **paradise** paraíso terrenal; **there is no** ~ **reason to think** ... no existe razón para pensar ....

earthquake ['əːθkweɪk] *n* terremoto.

earth-shattering ['əːθʃætərɪŋ] *adj* trascendental.

earthworm ['əːθwəːm] *n* lombriz *f*.

earthy ['əːθɪ] *adj* (*fig: uncomplicated*) sencillo; (: *coarse*) grosero.

earwig ['ɪəwɪg] *n* tijereta.

ease [iːz] *n* facilidad *f*; (*comfort*) comodidad *f* ♦ *vt* (*task*) facilitar; (*pain*) aliviar; (*loosen*) soltar; (*relieve: pressure, tension*) aflojar; (*weight*) aligerar; (*help pass*): **to** ~ **sth in/ out** meter/sacar algo con cuidado ♦ *vi* (*situation*) relajarse; **with** ~ con facilidad; **to feel at** ~/**ill at** ~ sentirse a gusto/a disgusto; **at** ~! (*MIL*) ¡descansen!

►**ease off, ease up** *vi* (*work, business*) aflojar; (*person*) relajarse.

easel ['iːzl] *n* caballete *m*.

easily ['iːzɪlɪ] *adv* fácilmente.

easiness ['iːzɪnɪs] *n* facilidad *f*; (*of manners*) soltura.

east [iːst] *n* este *m*, oriente *m* ♦ *adj* del este, oriental ♦ *adv* al este, hacia el este; **the** E~ el Oriente; (*POL*) el Este.

Easter ['iːstə*] *n* Pascua (de Resurrección).

Easter egg *n* huevo de Pascua.

Easter holidays *npl* Semana Santa *sg*.

Easter Island *n* Isla de Pascua.

easterly ['iːstəlɪ] *adj* (*to the east*) al este; (*from the east*) del este.

Easter Monday *n* lunes *m* de Pascua.

eastern ['iːstən] *adj* del este, oriental; **E**~ **Europe** Europa del Este; **the E**~ **bloc** (*POL*) los países del Este.

Easter Sunday *n* Domingo de Resurrección.

East Germany *n* (*formerly*) Alemania Oriental *or* del Este.

eastward(s) ['iːstwəd(z)] *adv* hacia el este.

easy ['iːzɪ] *adj* fácil; (*life*) holgado, cómodo; (*relaxed*) natural ♦ *adv*: **to take it** *or* **things** ~ (*not worry*) no preocuparse; (*go slowly*) tomarlo con calma; (*rest*) descansar; **payment on** ~ **terms** (*COMM*) facilidades de pago; **I'm** ~ (*col*) me da igual, no me importa; **easier said than done** del dicho al hecho hay buen trecho.

easy chair n butaca.

easy-going ['i:zɪ'gəuɪŋ] adj acomodadizo.

easy touch [i:zɪ'tʌtʃ] n: **he's an** ~ (col) es fácil de convencer.

eat, pt **ate**, pp **eaten** [i:t, eɪt, 'i:tn] vt comer.

►**eat away** vt (subj: sea) desgastar; (: acid) corroer.

►**eat into, eat away at** vt fus corroer.

►**eat out** vi comer fuera.

►**eat up** vt (meal etc) comerse; **it** ~**s up electricity** devora la electricidad.

eatable ['i:təbl] adj comestible.

eau de Cologne [əudəkə'ləun] n (agua de) colonia.

eaves [i:vz] npl alero sg.

eavesdrop ['i:vzdrɒp] vi: **to** ~ **(on sb)** escuchar a escondidas (a algn).

ebb [ɛb] n reflujo ♦ vi bajar; (fig: also: ~ **away**) decaer; ~ **and flow** el flujo y reflujo; **to be at a low** ~ (fig: person) estar de capa caída.

ebb tide n marea menguante.

ebony ['ɛbənɪ] n ébano.

e-book ['i:buk] n libro electrónico.

ebullient [ɪ'bʌlɪənt] adj entusiasta, animado.

e-business ['i:bɪznɪs] n (commerce) comercio electrónico, comercio E; (company) negocio electrónico.

EC n abbr (= European Community) CE f.

ECB n abbr (= European Central Bank) BCE m.

eccentric [ɪk'sɛntrɪk] adj, n excéntrico/a.

ecclesiastical [ɪkli:zɪ'æstɪkəl] adj eclesiástico.

ECG n abbr (= electrocardiogram) E.C. m.

echo, ~**es** ['ɛkəu] n eco m ♦ vt (sound) repetir ♦ vi resonar, hacer eco.

ECLA n abbr (= Economic Commission for Latin America) CEPAL f.

éclair ['eɪkleə*] n petisú m.

eclipse [ɪ'klɪps] n eclipse m ♦ vt eclipsar.

ECM n abbr (US: = European Common Market) MCE m.

eco- ['i:kəu] pref eco-.

eco-friendly ['i:kəufrendlɪ] adj ecológico.

ecological [i:kə'lɒdʒɪkl] adj ecológico.

ecologist [ɪ'kɒlədʒɪst] n ecologista m/f; (scientist) ecólogo/a m/f.

ecology [ɪ'kɒlədʒɪ] n ecología.

e-commerce ['i:,kɒmə:s] n comercio electrónico.

economic [i:kə'nɒmɪk] adj (profitable: price) económico; (: business etc) rentable.

economical [i:kə'nɒmɪkl] adj económico.

economically [i:kə'nɒmɪklɪ] adv económicamente.

economics [i:kə'nɒmɪks] n economía ♦ npl (financial aspects) finanzas fpl.

economist [ɪ'kɒnəmɪst] n economista m/f.

economize [ɪ'kɒnəmaɪz] vi economizar, ahorrar.

economy [ɪ'kɒnəmɪ] n economía; **economies of scale** economías fpl de escala.

economy class n (AVIAT etc) clase f turista.

economy class syndrome n síndrome m de la clase turista.

economy size n tamaño familiar.

ecosystem ['i:kəusɪstəm] n ecosistema m.

eco-tourism [i:kəu'tuərɪzm] n turismo verde or ecológico.

ECSC n abbr (= European Coal and Steel Community) CECA f.

ecstasy ['ɛkstəsɪ] n éxtasis m inv.

ecstatic [eks'tætɪk] adj extático, extasiado.

ECT n abbr see **electroconvulsive therapy.**

Ecuador ['ɛkwədɔ:*] n Ecuador m.

Ecuador(i)an [ɛkwə'dɔ:r(ɪ)ən] adj, n ecuatoriano/a m/f.

ecumenical [i:kju'mɛnɪkl] adj ecuménico.

eczema ['ɛksɪmə] n eczema m.

eddy ['ɛdɪ] n remolino.

edge [ɛdʒ] n (of knife etc) filo; (of object) borde m; (of lake etc) orilla ♦ vt (SEWING) ribetear ♦ vi: **to** ~ **past** pasar con dificultad; **on** ~ (fig) = **edgy**; **to** ~ **away from** alejarse poco a poco de; **to** ~ **forward** avanzar poco a poco.

edgeways ['ɛdʒweɪz] adv: **he couldn't get a word in** ~ no pudo meter baza.

edging ['ɛdʒɪŋ] n (SEWING) ribete m; (of path) borde m.

edgy ['ɛdʒɪ] adj nervioso, inquieto.

edible ['ɛdɪbl] adj comestible.

edict ['i:dɪkt] n edicto.

edifice ['ɛdɪfɪs] n edificio.

edifying ['ɛdɪfaɪɪŋ] adj edificante.

Edinburgh ['ɛdɪnbərə] n Edimburgo.

edit ['ɛdɪt] vt (be editor of) dirigir; (re-write) redactar; (cut) cortar; (COMPUT) editar.

edition [ɪ'dɪʃən] n (gen) edición f; (number printed) tirada.

editor ['ɛdɪtə*] n (of newspaper) director(a) m/f; (of book) redactor(a) m/f; (film ~) montador(a) m/f.

editorial [ɛdɪ'tɔ:rɪəl] adj editorial ♦ n editorial m; ~ **staff** redacción f.

EDP n abbr (= electronic data processing) PED m.

EDT n abbr (US: = Eastern Daylight Time) hora de verano de Nueva York.

educate ['ɛdjukeɪt] vt (gen) educar; (instruct) instruir.

educated guess ['ɛdjukeɪtɪd-] n hipótesis f sólida.

education [ɛdju'keɪʃən] n educación f;

(*schooling*) enseñanza; (*SCOL: subject etc*) pedagogía; **primary/secondary** ~ enseñanza primaria/secundaria.

educational [ɛdju'keɪʃənl] *adj* (*policy etc*) de educación, educativo; (*teaching*) docente; (*instructive*) educativo; ~ **technology** tecnología educacional.

Edwardian [ɛd'wɔːdɪən] *adj* eduardiano.

E.E. *abbr* = **electrical engineer.**

EEC *n abbr* (= *European Economic Community*) CEE *f.*

EEG *n abbr see* **electroencephalogram.**

eel [iːl] *n* anguila.

EENT *n abbr* (*US MED*) = *eye, ear, nose and throat.*

EEOC *n abbr* (*US*: = *Equal Employment Opportunities Commission*) comisión que investiga discriminación racial o sexual en el empleo.

eerie ['ɪərɪ] *adj* (*sound, experience*) espeluznante.

EET *n abbr* (= *Eastern European Time*) hora de Europa oriental.

efface [ɪ'feɪs] *vt* borrar.

effect [ɪ'fɛkt] *n* efecto ♦ *vt* efectuar, llevar a cabo; ~**s** *npl* (*property*) efectos *mpl*; **to take** ~ (*law*) entrar en vigor *or* vigencia; (*drug*) surtir efecto; **in** ~ en realidad; **to have an** ~ **on sb/sth** hacerle efecto a algn/afectar algo; **to put into** ~ (*plan*) llevar a la práctica; **his letter is to the** ~ **that...** su carta viene a decir que....

effective [ɪ'fɛktɪv] *adj* (*gen*) eficaz; (*striking: display, outfit*) impresionante; (*real*) efectivo; **to become** ~ (*LAW*) entrar en vigor; ~ **date** fecha de vigencia.

effectively [ɪ'fɛktɪvlɪ] *adv* (*efficiently*) eficazmente; (*strikingly*) de manera impresionante; (*in reality*) en efecto.

effectiveness [ɪ'fɛktɪvnɪs] *n* eficacia.

effeminate [ɪ'fɛmɪnɪt] *adj* afeminado.

effervescent [ɛfə'vɛsnt] *adj* efervescente.

efficacy ['ɛfɪkəsɪ] *n* eficacia.

efficiency [ɪ'fɪʃənsɪ] *n* (*gen*) eficiencia; (*of machine*) rendimiento.

efficient [ɪ'fɪʃənt] *adj* eficiente; (*remedy, product, system*) eficaz; (*machine, car*) de buen rendimiento.

effigy ['ɛfɪdʒɪ] *n* efigie *f.*

effluent ['ɛfluənt] *n* vertidos *mpl.*

effort ['ɛfət] *n* esfuerzo; **to make an** ~ **to do sth** estar deseoso de hacer algo.

effortless ['ɛfətlɪs] *adj* sin ningún esfuerzo.

effrontery [ɪ'frʌntərɪ] *n* descaro.

effusive [ɪ'fjuːsɪv] *adj* efusivo.

EFL *n abbr* (*SCOL*) = *English as a foreign language.*

EFTA ['ɛftə] *n abbr* (= *European Free Trade*

Association) EFTA *f.*

e.g. *adv abbr* (= *exempli gratia*) p.ej.

egg [ɛg] *n* huevo; **hard-boiled/soft-boiled/ poached** ~ huevo duro *or* a la copa (*LAM*) *or* tibio (*LAM*)/pasado por agua/escalfado; **scrambled** ~**s** huevos revueltos.

►**egg on** *vt* incitar.

eggcup ['ɛgkʌp] *n* huevera.

eggnog [ɛg'nɔg] *n* ponche *m* de huevo.

eggplant ['ɛgplɑːnt] *n* (*esp US*) berenjena.

eggshell ['ɛgʃɛl] *n* cáscara de huevo.

egg-timer ['ɛgtaɪmə*] *n* reloj *m* de arena (*para cocer huevos*).

egg white *n* clara de huevo.

egg yolk *n* yema de huevo.

ego ['iːgəu] *n* ego.

egotism ['ɛgəutɪzəm] *n* egoísmo.

egotist ['ɛgəutɪst] *n* egoísta *m/f.*

ego trip *n*: **to be on an** ~ creerse el centro del mundo.

Egypt ['iːdʒɪpt] *n* Egipto.

Egyptian [ɪ'dʒɪpʃən] *adj*, *n* egipcio/a *m/f.*

eiderdown ['aɪdədaun] *n* edredón *m.*

eight [eɪt] *num* ocho.

eighteen [eɪ'tiːn] *num* dieciocho.

eighth [eɪtθ] *num* octavo.

eighty ['eɪtɪ] *num* ochenta.

Eire ['ɛərə] *n* Eire *m.*

EIS *n abbr* (= *Educational Institute of Scotland*) sindicato de profesores escoceses.

either ['aɪðə*] *adj* cualquiera de los dos ...; (*both, each*) cada ♦ *pron:* ~ (**of them**) cualquiera (de los dos) ♦ *adv* tampoco ♦ *conj:* ~ **yes or no** o sí o no; **on** ~ **side** en ambos lados; **I don't like** ~ no me gusta ninguno de los dos; **no, I don't** ~ no, yo tampoco.

eject [ɪ'dʒɛkt] *vt* echar; (*tenant*) desahuciar ♦ *vi* eyectarse.

ejector seat [ɪ'dʒɛktə-] *n* asiento proyectable.

eke out [iːk-] *vt fus* (*money*) hacer que llegue.

EKG *n abbr* (*US*) *see* **electrocardiogram.**

el [ɛl] *n abbr* (*US col*) = **elevated railroad.**

elaborate *adj* [ɪ'læbərɪt] (*design, pattern*) complicado ♦ *vb* [ɪ'læbəreɪt] *vt* elaborar ♦ *vi* explicarse con muchos detalles.

elaborately [ɪ'læbərɪtlɪ] *adv* de manera complicada; (*decorated*) profusamente.

elaboration [ɪlæbə'reɪʃən] *n* elaboración *f.*

elapse [ɪ'læps] *vi* transcurrir.

elastic [ɪ'læstɪk] *adj*, *n* elástico.

elastic band *n* (*BRIT*) gomita.

elated [ɪ'leɪtɪd] *adj:* **to be** ~ estar eufórico.

elation [ɪ'leɪʃən] *n* euforia.

elbow ['ɛlbəu] *n* codo ♦ *vt:* **to** ~ **one's way through the crowd** abrirse paso a

codazos por la muchedumbre.
elbow grease n (col): **to use some** or **a bit of ~** menearse.
elder ['ɛldə*] adj mayor ♦ n (tree) saúco; (person) mayor; (of tribe) anciano.
elderly ['ɛldəlɪ] adj de edad, mayor ♦ npl: **the ~** la gente mayor, los ancianos.
eldest ['ɛldɪst] adj, n el/la mayor.
elect [ɪ'lɛkt] vt elegir; (choose): **to ~ to do** optar por hacer.
election [ɪ'lɛkʃən] n elección f; **to hold an ~** convocar elecciones.
election campaign n campaña electoral.
electioneering [ɪlɛkʃə'nɪərɪŋ] n campaña electoral.
elector [ɪ'lɛktə*] n elector(a) m/f.
electoral [ɪ'lɛktərəl] adj electoral.
electoral college n colegio electoral.
electoral roll n censo electoral.
electorate [ɪ'lɛktərɪt] n electorado.
electric [ɪ'lɛktrɪk] adj eléctrico.
electrical [ɪ'lɛktrɪkl] adj eléctrico.
electrical engineer n ingeniero/a electricista.
electrical failure n fallo eléctrico.
electric blanket n manta eléctrica.
electric chair n silla eléctrica.
electric cooker n cocina eléctrica.
electric current n corriente f eléctrica.
electric fire n estufa eléctrica.
electrician [ɪlɛk'trɪʃən] n electricista m/f.
electricity [ɪlɛk'trɪsɪtɪ] n electricidad f; **to switch on/off the ~** conectar/desconectar la electricidad.
electricity board n (BRIT) compañía eléctrica (estatal).
electric light n luz f eléctrica.
electric shock n electrochoque m.
electrify [ɪ'lɛktrɪfaɪ] vt (RAIL) electrificar; (fig: audience) electrizar.
electro... [ɪ'lɛktrəu] pref electro....
electrocardiogram (ECG, (US) **EKG)** [ɪ'lɛktrə'kɑːdɪəgræm] n electro-cardiograma m.
electrocardiograph [ɪ'lɛktrəu'kɑːdɪəgræf] n electrocardiógrafo.
electro-convulsive therapy (ECT) [ɪ'lɛktrəkən'vʌlsɪv-] n electroterapia.
electrocute [ɪ'lɛktrəukjuːt] vt electrocutar.
electrode [ɪ'lɛktrəud] n electrodo.
electroencephalogram (EEG) [ɪ'lɛktrəuɛn'sɛfələgræm] n electroencefalograma m.
electrolysis [ɪlɛk'trɔlɪsɪs] n electrólisis f inv.
electromagnetic [ɪ'lɛktrəmæg'nɛtɪk] adj electromagnético.
electron [ɪ'lɛktrɔn] n electrón m.
electronic [ɪlɛk'trɔnɪk] adj electrónico.

electronic data processing (EDP) n tratamiento or proceso electrónico de datos.
electronic mail n correo electrónico.
electronics [ɪlɛk'trɔnɪks] n electrónica.
electron microscope n microscopio electrónico.
electroplated [ɪ'lɛktrə'pleɪtɪd] adj galvanizado.
electrotherapy [ɪ'lɛktrə'θɛrəpɪ] n electroterapia.
elegance ['ɛlɪgəns] n elegancia.
elegant ['ɛlɪgənt] adj elegante.
elegy ['ɛlɪdʒɪ] n elegía.
element ['ɛlɪmənt] n (gen) elemento; (of heater, kettle etc) resistencia.
elementary [ɛlɪ'mɛntərɪ] adj elemental; (primitive) rudimentario; (school, education) primario.
elementary school n (US) escuela de enseñanza primaria; ver recuadro.

ELEMENTARY SCHOOL

En Estados Unidos y Canadá se llama **elementary school** al centro estatal en el que los niños reciben los primeros seis u ocho años de su educación, también llamado "grade school" o "grammar school".

---

elephant ['ɛlɪfənt] n elefante m.
elevate ['ɛlɪveɪt] vt (gen) elevar; (in rank) ascender.
elevated railroad n (US) ferrocarril m urbano elevado.
elevation [ɛlɪ'veɪʃən] n elevación f; (rank) ascenso; (height) altitud f.
elevator ['ɛlɪveɪtə*] n (US) ascensor m, elevador m (LAM).
eleven [ɪ'lɛvn] num once.
elevenses [ɪ'lɛvnzɪz] npl (BRIT) ≈ café m de media mañana.
eleventh [ɪ'lɛvnθ] adj undécimo; **at the ~ hour** (fig) a última hora.
elf, pl **elves** [ɛlf, ɛlvz] n duende m.
elicit [ɪ'lɪsɪt] vt: **to ~ sth (from sb)** obtener algo (de algn).
eligible ['ɛlɪdʒəbl] adj cotizado; **to be ~ for a pension** tener derecho a una pensión.
eliminate [ɪ'lɪmɪneɪt] vt eliminar; (score out) suprimir; (a suspect, possibility) descartar.
elimination [ɪlɪmɪ'neɪʃən] n eliminación f; supresión f; **by process of ~** por eliminación.
elite [eɪ'liːt] n élite f.
elitist [eɪ'liːtɪst] adj (pej) elitista.

elixir [ɪ'lɪksɪə*] *n* elixir *m*.
Elizabethan [ɪlɪzə'biːθən] *adj* isabelino.
elm [ɛlm] *n* olmo.
elocution [ɛlə'kjuːʃən] *n* elocución *f*.
elongated ['iːlɔŋgeɪtɪd] *adj* alargado.
elope [ɪ'ləup] *vi* fugarse.
elopement [ɪ'ləupmənt] *n* fuga.
eloquence ['ɛləkwəns] *n* elocuencia.
eloquent ['ɛləkwənt] *adj* elocuente.
else [ɛls] *adv*: **or ~** si no; **something ~** otra cosa *or* algo más; **somewhere ~** en otra parte; **everywhere ~** en los demás sitios; **everyone ~** todos los demás; **nothing ~** nada más; **is there anything ~ I can do?** ¿puedo hacer algo más?; **where ~?** ¿dónde más?, ¿en qué otra parte?; **there was little ~ to do** apenas quedaba otra cosa que hacer; **nobody ~** nadie más.
elsewhere [ɛls'wɛə*] *adv* (*be*) en otra parte; (*go*) a otra parte.
ELT *n abbr* = *English Language Teaching*.
elucidate [ɪ'luːsɪdeɪt] *vt* esclarecer, elucidar.
elude [ɪ'luːd] *vt* eludir; (*blow, pursuer*) esquivar.
elusive [ɪ'luːsɪv] *adj* escurridizo; (*answer*) difícil de encontrar; **he is very ~** no es fácil encontrarlo.
elves [ɛlvz] *npl of* elf.
emaciated [ɪ'meɪsɪeɪtɪd] *adj* escuálido.
e-mail ['iːmeɪl] *n* e-mail *m*, correo electrónico ♦ *vt*: **to ~ sb** mandar un e-mail *or* un correo electrónico a algn; **to ~ sb sth** mandar algo a algn por Internet, mandar algo a algn en un e-mail *or* un correo electrónico.
e-mail account *n* cuenta de correo.
e-mail address *n* dirección *f* electrónica, e-mail *m*.
emanate ['eməneɪt] *vi* emanar, provenir.
emancipate [ɪ'mænsɪpeɪt] *vt* emancipar.
emancipated [ɪ'mænsɪpeɪtɪd] *adj* liberado.
emancipation [ɪmænsɪ'peɪʃən] *n* emancipación *f*, liberación *f*.
emasculate [ɪ'mæskjuleɪt] *vt* castrar; (*fig*) debilitar.
embalm [ɪm'baːm] *vt* embalsamar.
embankment [ɪm'bæŋkmənt] *n* (*of railway*) terraplén *m*; (*riverside*) dique *m*.
embargo, *pl* **~es** [ɪm'baːgəu] *n* prohibición *f*; (*COMM, NAUT*) embargo; **to put an ~ on sth** poner un embargo en algo.
embark [ɪm'baːk] *vi* embarcarse ♦ *vt* embarcar; **to ~ on** (*journey*) comenzar, iniciar; (*fig*) emprender.
embarkation [embaː'keɪʃən] *n* (*people*) embarco; (*goods*) embarque *m*.
embarrass [ɪm'bærəs] *vt* avergonzar, dar

vergüenza a; (*financially etc*) poner en un aprieto.
embarrassed [ɪm'bærəst] *adj* azorado, violento; **to be ~** sentirse azorado *or* violento.
embarrassing [ɪm'bærəsɪŋ] *adj* (*situation*) violento; (*question*) embarazoso.
embarrassment [ɪm'bærəsmənt] *n* vergüenza, azoramiento; (*financial*) apuros *mpl*.
embassy ['embəsɪ] *n* embajada.
embed [ɪm'bɛd] *vt* (*jewel*) empotrar; (*teeth etc*) clavar.
embellish [ɪm'belɪʃ] *vt* embellecer; (*fig: story, truth*) adornar.
embers ['embəz] *npl* rescoldo *sg*, ascuas.
embezzle [ɪm'bɛzl] *vt* desfalcar, malversar.
embezzlement [ɪm'bɛzlmənt] *n* desfalco, malversación *f*.
embezzler [ɪm'bɛzlə*] *n* malversador(a) *m/f*.
embitter [ɪm'bɪtə*] *vt* (*person*) amargar; (*relationship*) envenenar.
embittered [ɪm'bɪtəd] *adj* resentido, amargado.
emblem ['embləm] *n* emblema *m*.
embody [ɪm'bɔdɪ] *vt* (*spirit*) encarnar; (*ideas*) expresar.
embolden [ɪm'bəuldən] *vt* envalentonar.
embolism ['embəlɪzəm] *n* embolia.
emboss [ɪm'bɔs] *vt* estampar en relieve; (*metal, leather*) repujar.
embossed [ɪm'bɔst] *adj* realzado; **~ with ...** con ... en relieve.
embrace [ɪm'breɪs] *vt* abrazar, dar un abrazo a; (*include*) abarcar; (*adopt: idea*) adherirse a ♦ *vi* abrazarse ♦ *n* abrazo.
embroider [ɪm'brɔɪdə*] *vt* bordar; (*fig: story*) adornar, embellecer.
embroidery [ɪm'brɔɪdərɪ] *n* bordado.
embroil [ɪm'brɔɪl] *vt*: **to become ~ed (in sth)** enredarse (en algo).
embryo ['embrɪəu] *n* (*also fig*) embrión *m*.
emcee [em'siː] *n* (*US*) presentador(a) *m/f*.
emend [ɪ'mend] *vt* (*text*) enmendar.
emerald ['emərəld] *n* esmeralda.
emerge [ɪ'məːdʒ] *vi* (*gen*) salir; (*arise*) surgir; **it ~s that** resulta que.
emergence [ɪ'məːdʒəns] *n* (*of nation*) surgimiento.
emergency [ɪ'məːdʒənsɪ] *n* (*event*) emergencia; (*crisis*) crisis *f inv*; **in an ~** en caso de urgencia; **(to declare a) state of ~** (declarar) estado de emergencia *or* de excepción.
emergency cord *n* (*US*) timbre *m* de alarma.

emergency exit n salida de emergencia.
emergency landing n aterrizaje m
forzoso.
emergency lane n (*US*) arcén m.
emergency meeting n reunión f
extraordinaria.
emergency service n servicio de
urgencia.
emergency stop n (*AUT*) parada en seco.
emergent [ɪ'mɜːdʒənt] adj (*nation*)
recientemente independizado.
emery board ['emərɪ-] n lima de uñas.
emetic [ɪ'metɪk] n vomitivo, emético.
emigrant ['emɪgrənt] n emigrante m/f.
emigrate ['emɪgreɪt] vi emigrar.
emigration [emɪ'greɪʃən] n emigración f.
émigré ['emɪgreɪ] n emigrado/a.
eminence ['emɪnəns] n eminencia; **to gain**
or **win** ~ ganarse fama.
eminent ['emɪnənt] adj eminente.
eminently ['emɪnəntlɪ] adv eminentemente.
emirate ['emɪrɪt] n emirato.
emission [ɪ'mɪʃən] n emisión f.
emit [ɪ'mɪt] vt emitir; (*smell, smoke*)
despedir.
emolument [ɪ'mɔljumənt] n (*often pl*:
formal) honorario, emolumento.
emotion [ɪ'məʊʃən] n emoción f.
emotional [ɪ'məʊʃənl] adj (*person*)
sentimental; (*scene*) conmovedor(a),
emocionante.
emotionally [ɪ'məʊʃnəlɪ] adv (*behave, speak*)
con emoción; (*be involved*)
sentimentalmente.
emotive [ɪ'məʊtɪv] adj emotivo.
empathy ['empəθɪ] n empatía; **to feel** ~
with sb sentirse identificado con algn.
emperor ['empərə*] n emperador m.
emphasis, pl **emphases** ['emfəsɪs, -siːz] n
énfasis m inv; **to lay** or **place** ~ **on sth** (*fig*)
hacer hincapié en algo; **the** ~ **is on sport**
se da mayor importancia al deporte.
emphasize ['emfəsaɪz] vt (*word, point*)
subrayar, recalcar; (*feature*) hacer
resaltar.
emphatic [em'fætɪk] adj (*condemnation*)
enérgico; (*denial*) rotundo.
emphatically [em'fætɪklɪ] adv con énfasis.
emphysema [emfɪ'siːmə] n (*MED*) enfisema
m.
empire ['empaɪə*] n imperio.
empirical [em'pɪrɪkl] adj empírico.
employ [ɪm'plɔɪ] vt (*give job to*) emplear;
(*make use of: thing, method*) emplear, usar;
he's ~**ed in a bank** está empleado en un
banco.
employee [ɪmplɔɪ'iː] n empleado/a.
employer [ɪm'plɔɪə*] n patrón/ona m/f;

(*businessman*) empresario/a.
employment [ɪm'plɔɪmənt] n empleo; **full** ~
pleno empleo; **without** ~ sin empleo; **to**
find ~ encontrar trabajo; **place of** ~
lugar m de trabajo.
employment agency n agencia de
colocaciones or empleo.
employment exchange n bolsa de
trabajo.
empower [ɪm'pauə*] vt: **to** ~ **sb to do sth**
autorizar a algn para hacer algo.
empress ['emprɪs] n emperatriz f.
emptiness ['emptɪnɪs] n vacío.
empty ['emptɪ] adj vacío; (*street, area*)
desierto; (*threat*) vano ◆ n (*bottle*) envase
m ◆ vt vaciar; (*place*) dejar vacío ◆ vi
vaciarse; (*house*) quedar(se) vacío or
desocupado; (*place*) quedar(se) desierto;
to ~ **into** (*river*) desembocar en.
empty-handed ['emptɪ'hændɪd] adj con las
manos vacías.
empty-headed ['emptɪ'hedɪd] adj
casquivano.
EMS n abbr (= *European Monetary System*)
SME m.
EMT n abbr = *emergency medical technician*.
EMU n abbr (= *Economic and Monetary*
Union) UME f.
emulate ['emjuleɪt] vt emular.
emulsion [ɪ'mʌlʃən] n emulsión f.
enable [ɪ'neɪbl] vt: **to** ~ **sb to do sth** (*allow*)
permitir a algn hacer algo; (*prepare*)
capacitar a algn para hacer algo.
enact [ɪn'ækt] vt (*law*) promulgar; (*play,*
scene, role) representar.
enamel [ɪ'næməl] n esmalte m.
enamel paint n esmalte m.
enamoured [ɪ'næməd] adj: **to be** ~ **of**
(*person*) estar enamorado de; (*activity etc*)
tener gran afición a; (*idea*) aferrarse a.
encampment [ɪn'kæmpmənt] n
campamento.
encase [ɪn'keɪs] vt: **to** ~ **in** (*contain*)
encajar; (*cover*) cubrir.
encased [ɪn'keɪst] adj: ~ **in** (*covered*)
revestido de.
enchant [ɪn'tʃɑːnt] vt encantar.
enchanting [ɪn'tʃɑːntɪŋ] adj encantador(a).
encircle [ɪn'sɜːkl] vt (*gen*) rodear; (*waist*)
ceñir.
encl. abbr (= *enclosed*) adj.
enclave ['enkleɪv] n enclave m.
enclose [ɪn'kləʊz] vt (*land*) cercar; (*with*
letter etc) adjuntar; (*in receptacle*): **to** ~
(with) encerrar (con); **please find** ~**d** le
mandamos adjunto.
enclosure [ɪn'kləʊʒə*] n cercado, recinto;
(*COMM*) carta adjunta.

encoder [ɪn'kəudə*] n (*COMPUT*) codificador m.

encompass [ɪn'kʌmpəs] vt abarcar.

encore [ɔŋ'kɔː*] excl ¡otra!, ¡bis! ♦ n bis m.

encounter [ɪn'kauntə*] n encuentro ♦ vt encontrar, encontrarse con; (*difficulty*) tropezar con.

encourage [ɪn'kʌrɪdʒ] vt alentar, animar; (*growth*) estimular; **to ~ sb (to do sth)** animar a algn (a hacer algo).

encouragement [ɪn'kʌrɪdʒmənt] n estímulo; (*of industry*) fomento.

encouraging [ɪn'kʌrɪdʒɪŋ] adj alentador(a).

encroach [ɪn'krəutʃ] vi: **to ~ (up)on** (*gen*) invadir; (*time*) adueñarse de.

encrust [ɪn'krʌst] vt incrustar.

encrusted [ɪn'krʌstəd] adj: **~ with** recubierto de.

encumber [ɪn'kʌmbə*] vt: **to be ~ed with** (*carry*) estar cargado de; (*debts*) estar gravado de.

encyclop(a)edia [ɛnsaɪkləu'piːdɪə] n enciclopedia.

end [ɛnd] n (*gen, also aim*) fin m; (*of table*) extremo; (*of line, rope etc*) cabo; (*of pointed object*) punta; (*of town*) barrio; (*of street*) final m; (*SPORT*) lado ♦ vt terminar, acabar; (*also:* **bring to an ~, put an ~ to**) acabar con ♦ vi terminar, acabar; **to ~ (with)** terminar (con); **in the ~** al final; **to be at an ~** llegar a su fin; **at the ~ of the day** (*fig*) al fin y al cabo, a fin de cuentas; **to this ~, with this ~ in view** con este propósito; **from ~ to ~** de punta a punta; **on ~** (*object*) de punta, de cabeza; **to stand on ~** (*hair*) erizarse, ponerse de punta; **for hours on ~** hora tras hora.

▶**end up** vi: **to ~ up in** terminar en; (*place*) ir a parar a.

endanger [ɪn'deɪndʒə*] vt poner en peligro; **an ~ed species** (*of animal*) una especie en peligro de extinción.

endear [ɪn'dɪə*] vt: **to ~ o.s. to sb** ganarse la simpatía de algn.

endearing [ɪn'dɪərɪŋ] adj entrañable.

endearment [ɪn'dɪərmənt] n cariño, palabra cariñosa; **to whisper ~s** decir unas palabras cariñosas al oído; **term of ~** nombre m cariñoso.

endeavour, (*US*) **endeavor** [ɪn'dɛvə*] n esfuerzo; (*attempt*) tentativa ♦ vi: **to ~ to do** esforzarse por hacer; (*try*) procurar hacer.

endemic [ɛn'dɛmɪk] adj (*poverty, disease*) endémico.

ending ['ɛndɪŋ] n fin m, final m; (*of book*) desenlace m; (*LING*) terminación f.

endive ['ɛndaɪv] n (*curly*) escarola; (*smooth, flat*) endibia.

endless ['ɛndlɪs] adj interminable, inacabable; (*possibilities*) infinito.

endorse [ɪn'dɔːs] vt (*cheque*) endosar; (*approve*) aprobar.

endorsee [ɪndɔː'siː] n endorsatario/a.

endorsement [ɪn'dɔːsmənt] n (*approval*) aprobación f; (*signature*) endoso; (*BRIT: on driving licence*) nota de sanción.

endorser [ɪn'dɔːsə*] n avalista m/f.

endow [ɪn'dau] vt (*provide with money*) dotar; (*found*) fundar; **to be ~ed with** (*fig*) estar dotado de.

endowment [ɪn'daumənt] adj (*amount*) donación f.

endowment mortgage n hipoteca dotal.

endowment policy n póliza dotal.

end product n (*INDUSTRY*) producto final; (*fig*) resultado.

end result n resultado.

endurable [ɪn'djuərəbl] adj soportable, tolerable.

endurance [ɪn'djuərəns] n resistencia.

endurance test n prueba de resistencia.

endure [ɪn'djuə*] vt (*bear*) aguantar, soportar; (*resist*) resistir ♦ vi (*last*) perdurar; (*resist*) resistir.

enduring [ɪn'djuərɪŋ] adj duradero.

end user n (*COMPUT*) usuario final.

enema ['ɛnɪmə] n (*MED*) enema m.

enemy ['ɛnəmɪ] adj, n enemigo/a m/f; **to make an ~ of sb** enemistarse con algn.

energetic [ɛnə'dʒɛtɪk] adj enérgico.

energy ['ɛnədʒɪ] n energía.

energy crisis n crisis f energética.

energy-saving ['ɛnədʒɪseɪvɪŋ] adj (*policy*) para ahorrar energía; (*device*) que ahorra energía ♦ n ahorro de energía.

enervating ['ɛnəveɪtɪŋ] adj deprimente.

enforce [ɪn'fɔːs] vt (*LAW*) hacer cumplir.

enforced [ɪn'fɔːst] adj forzoso, forzado.

enfranchise [ɪn'fræntʃaɪz] vt (*give vote to*) conceder el derecho de voto a; (*set free*) emancipar.

engage [ɪn'geɪdʒ] vt (*attention*) captar; (*in conversation*) abordar; (*worker, lawyer*) contratar ♦ vi (*TECH*) engranar; **to ~ in** dedicarse a, ocuparse en; **to ~ sb in conversation** entablar conversación con algn; **to ~ the clutch** embragar.

engaged [ɪn'geɪdʒd] adj (*BRIT: busy, in use*) ocupado; (*betrothed*) prometido; **to get ~** prometerse; **he is ~ in research** se dedica a la investigación.

engaged tone n (*BRIT TEL*) señal f de comunicando.

engagement [ɪn'geɪdʒmənt] n

(*appointment*) compromiso, cita; (*battle*) combate *m*; (*to marry*) compromiso; (*period*) noviazgo; **I have a previous** ~ ya tengo un compromiso.
engagement ring *n* anillo de pedida.
engaging [ɪn'geɪdʒɪŋ] *adj* atractivo, simpático.
engender [ɪn'dʒɛndə*] *vt* engendrar.
engine ['ɛndʒɪn] *n* (*AUT*) motor *m*; (*RAIL*) locomotora.
engine driver *n* (*BRIT: of train*) maquinista *m/f*.
engineer [ɛndʒɪ'nɪə*] *n* ingeniero/a; (*BRIT: for repairs*) técnico/a; (*US RAIL*) maquinista *m/f*; **civil/mechanical** ~ ingeniero/a de caminos, canales y puertos/industrial.
engineering [ɛndʒɪ'nɪərɪŋ] *n* ingeniería ♦ *cpd* (*works, factory*) de componentes mecánicos.
engine failure, engine trouble *n* avería del motor.
England ['ɪŋglənd] *n* Inglaterra.
English ['ɪŋglɪʃ] *adj* inglés/esa ♦ *n* (*LING*) el inglés; **the** ~ *npl* los ingleses.
English Channel *n*: **the** ~ el Canal de la Mancha.
Englishman ['ɪŋglɪʃmən], **Englishwoman** ['ɪŋglɪʃwumən] *n* inglés/esa *m/f*.
English-speaker ['ɪŋglɪʃspiːkə*] *n* persona de habla inglesa.
English-speaking ['ɪŋglɪʃspiːkɪŋ] *adj* de habla inglesa.
engraving [ɪn'greɪvɪŋ] *n* grabado.
engrossed [ɪn'grəust] *adj*: ~ **in** absorto en.
engulf [ɪn'gʌlf] *vt* sumergir, hundir; (*subj: fire*) devorar.
enhance [ɪn'hɑːns] *vt* (*gen*) aumentar; (*beauty*) realzar; (*position, reputation*) mejorar.
enigma [ɪ'nɪgmə] *n* enigma *m*.
enigmatic [ɛnɪg'mætɪk] *adj* enigmático.
enjoy [ɪn'dʒɔɪ] *vt* (*have: health, fortune*) disfrutar de, gozar de; (*food*) comer con gusto; **I** ~ **doing...** me gusta hacer...; **to** ~ **o.s.** divertirse, pasarlo bien.
enjoyable [ɪn'dʒɔɪəbl] *adj* (*pleasant*) agradable; (*amusing*) divertido.
enjoyment [ɪn'dʒɔɪmənt] *n* (*use*) disfrute *m*; (*joy*) placer *m*.
enlarge [ɪn'lɑːdʒ] *vt* aumentar; (*broaden*) extender; (*PHOT*) ampliar ♦ *vi*: **to** ~ **on** (*subject*) tratar con más detalles.
enlarged [ɪn'lɑːdʒd] *adj* (*edition*) aumentado; (*MED: organ, gland*) dilatado.
enlargement [ɪn'lɑːdʒmənt] *n* (*PHOT*) ampliación *f*.
enlighten [ɪn'laɪtn] *vt* informar, instruir.
enlightened [ɪn'laɪtnd] *adj* iluminado;

(*tolerant*) comprensivo.
enlightening [ɪn'laɪtnɪŋ] *adj* informativo, instructivo.
Enlightenment [ɪn'laɪtnmənt] *n* (*HISTORY*): **the** ~ la Ilustración, el Siglo de las Luces.
enlist [ɪn'lɪst] *vt* alistar; (*support*) conseguir ♦ *vi* alistarse; ~**ed man** (*US: MIL*) soldado raso.
enliven [ɪn'laɪvn] *vt* (*people*) animar; (*events*) avivar, animar.
enmity ['ɛnmɪtɪ] *n* enemistad *f*.
ennoble [ɪ'nəubl] *vt* ennoblecer.
enormity [ɪ'nɔːmɪtɪ] *n* enormidad *f*.
enormous [ɪ'nɔːməs] *adj* enorme.
enough [ɪ'nʌf] *adj*: ~ **time/books** bastante tiempo/bastantes libros ♦ *n*: **have you got** ~? ¿tiene usted bastante? ♦ *adv*: **big** ~ bastante grande; **he has not worked** ~ no ha trabajado bastante; (*that's*) ~! ¡basta ya!, ¡ya está bien!; **that's** ~, **thanks** con eso basta, gracias; **will 5 be** ~? ¿bastará con 5?; **I've had** ~ estoy harto; **he was kind** ~ **to lend me the money** tuvo la bondad *or* amabilidad de prestarme el dinero; ... **which, funnily** ~ ... ... lo que, por extraño que parezca ... .
enquire [ɪn'kwaɪə*] *vt, vi* = **inquire**.
enrage [ɪn'reɪdʒ] *vt* enfurecer.
enrich [ɪn'rɪtʃ] *vt* enriquecer.
enrol, (*US*) **enroll** [ɪn'rəul] *vt* (*members*) inscribir; (*SCOL*) matricular ♦ *vi* inscribirse; (*SCOL*) matricularse.
enrol(l)ment [ɪn'rəulmənt] *n* inscripción *f*; matriculación *f*.
en route [ɔn'ruːt] *adv* durante el viaje; ~ **for/from/to** camino de/de/a.
ensconce [ɪn'skɔns] *vt*: **to** ~ **o.s.** instalarse cómodamente, acomodarse.
ensemble [ɔn'sɔmbl] *n* (*MUS*) conjunto.
enshrine [ɪn'ʃraɪn] *vt* recoger.
ensign ['ɛnsaɪn] *n* (*flag*) bandera; (*NAUT*) alférez *m*.
enslave [ɪn'sleɪv] *vt* esclavizar.
ensue [ɪn'sjuː] *vi* seguirse; (*result*) resultar.
ensuing [ɪn'sjuːɪŋ] *adj* subsiguiente.
ensure [ɪn'ʃuə*] *vt* asegurar.
ENT *n abbr* (= *Ear, Nose and Throat*) otorrinolaringología.
entail [ɪn'teɪl] *vt* (*imply*) suponer; (*result in*) acarrear.
entangle [ɪn'tæŋgl] *vt* (*thread etc*) enredar, enmarañar; **to become** ~**d in sth** (*fig*) enredarse en algo.
entanglement [ɪn'tæŋglmənt] *n* enredo.
enter ['ɛntə*] *vt* (*room, profession*) entrar en; (*club*) hacerse socio de; (*army*) alistarse en; (*sb for a competition*)

inscribir; (*write down*) anotar, apuntar; (*COMPUT*) introducir ♦ *vi* entrar; **to ~ for** *vt fus* presentar a; **to ~ into** *vt fus* (*relations*) establecer; (*plans*) formar parte de; (*debate*) tomar parte en; (*negotiations*) entablar; (*agreement*) llegar a, firmar; **to ~ (up)on** *vt fus* (*career*) emprender.

enteritis [ɛntə'raɪtɪs] *n* enteritis *f*.

enterprise ['ɛntəpraɪz] *n* empresa; (*spirit*) iniciativa; **free ~** la libre empresa; **private ~** la iniciativa privada.

enterprising ['ɛntəpraɪzɪŋ] *adj* emprendedor(a).

entertain [ɛntə'teɪn] *vt* (*amuse*) divertir; (*receive: guest*) recibir (en casa); (*idea*) abrigar.

entertainer [ɛntə'teɪnə*] *n* artista *m/f*.

entertaining [ɛntə'teɪnɪŋ] *adj* divertido, entretenido ♦ *n*: **to do a lot of ~** dar muchas fiestas, tener muchos invitados.

entertainment [ɛntə'teɪnmənt] *n* (*amusement*) diversión *f*; (*show*) espectáculo; (*party*) fiesta.

entertainment allowance *n* (*COMM*) gastos *mpl* de representación.

enthral [ɪn'θrɔːl] *vt* embelesar, cautivar.

enthralled [ɪn'θrɔːld] *adj* cautivado.

enthralling [ɪn'θrɔːlɪŋ] *adj* cautivador(a).

enthuse [ɪn'θuːz] *vi*: **to ~ about or over** entusiasmarse por.

enthusiasm [ɪn'θuːzɪæzəm] *n* entusiasmo.

enthusiast [ɪn'θuːzɪæst] *n* entusiasta *m/f*.

enthusiastic [ɪnθuːzɪ'æstɪk] *adj* entusiasta; **to be ~ about sb/sth** estar entusiasmado con algn/algo.

entice [ɪn'taɪs] *vt* tentar; (*seduce*) seducir.

entire [ɪn'taɪə*] *adj* entero, todo.

entirely [ɪn'taɪəlɪ] *adv* totalmente.

entirety [ɪn'taɪərətɪ] *n*: **in its ~** en su totalidad.

entitle [ɪn'taɪtl] *vt*: **to ~ sb to sth** dar a algn derecho a algo.

entitled [ɪn'taɪtld] *adj* (*book*) titulado; **to be ~ to sth/to do sth** tener derecho a algo/a hacer algo.

entity ['ɛntɪtɪ] *n* entidad *f*.

entourage [ɔntu'rɑːʒ] *n* séquito.

entrails ['ɛntreɪlz] *npl* entrañas *fpl*; (*US*) asadura *sg*, menudos *mpl*.

entrance ['ɛntrəns] *n* entrada ♦ *vt* [ɪn'trɑːns] encantar, hechizar; **to gain ~ to** (*university etc*) ingresar en.

entrance examination *n* (*to school*) examen *m* de ingreso.

entrance fee *n* entrada.

entrance ramp *n* (*US AUT*) rampa de acceso.

entrancing [ɪn'trɑːnsɪŋ] *adj* encantador(a).

entrant ['ɛntrənt] *n* (*in race, competition*) participante *m/f*; (*in exam*) candidato/a.

entreat [ɛn'triːt] *vt* rogar, suplicar.

entrenched [ɛn'trɛntʃd] *adj*: **~ interests** intereses *mpl* creados.

entrepreneur [ɔntrəprə'nəː*] *n* empresario/a, capitalista *m/f*.

entrepreneurial [ɔntrəprə'nəːrɪəl] *adj* empresarial.

entrust [ɪn'trʌst] *vt*: **to ~ sth to sb** confiar algo a algn.

entry ['ɛntrɪ] *n* entrada; (*permission to enter*) acceso; (*in register, diary, ship's log*) apunte *m*; (*in account book, ledger, list*) partida; **no ~** prohibido el paso; (*AUT*) dirección prohibida; **single/double ~ book-keeping** contabilidad *f* simple/por partida doble.

entry form *n* boletín *m* de inscripción.

entry phone *n* (*BRIT*) portero automático.

E-number ['iːnʌmbə*] *n* número E.

enumerate [ɪ'njuːməreɪt] *vt* enumerar.

enunciate [ɪ'nʌnsɪeɪt] *vt* pronunciar; (*principle etc*) enunciar.

envelop [ɪn'vɛləp] *vt* envolver.

envelope ['ɛnvələup] *n* sobre *m*.

enviable ['ɛnvɪəbl] *adj* envidiable.

envious ['ɛnvɪəs] *adj* envidioso; (*look*) de envidia.

environment [ɪn'vaɪərnmənt] *n* medio ambiente; (*surroundings*) entorno; **Department of the E~** ministerio del medio ambiente.

environmental [ɪnvaɪərn'mɛntl] *adj* (medio) ambiental; **~ studies** (*in school etc*) ecología *sg*.

environmentalist [ɪnvaɪərn'mɛntlɪst] *n* ecologista *m/f*.

environmentally [ɪnvaɪərn'mɛntlɪ] *adv*: **~ sound/friendly** ecológico.

envisage [ɪn'vɪzɪdʒ] *vt* (*foresee*) prever; (*imagine*) concebir.

envision [ɪn'vɪʒən] *vt* imaginar.

envoy [ɪn'vɔɪ] *n* enviado/a.

envy ['ɛnvɪ] *n* envidia ♦ *vt* tener envidia a; **to ~ sb sth** envidiar algo a algn.

enzyme ['ɛnzaɪm] *n* enzima *m or f*.

EPA *n abbr* (*US*: = *Environmental Protection Agency*) Agencia del Medio Ambiente.

ephemeral [ɪ'fɛmərl] *adj* efímero.

epic ['ɛpɪk] *n* epopeya ♦ *adj* épico.

epicentre, (*US*) **epicenter** ['ɛpɪsɛntə*] *n* epicentro.

epidemic [ɛpɪ'dɛmɪk] *n* epidemia.

epigram ['ɛpɪgræm] *n* epigrama *m*.

epilepsy ['ɛpɪlɛpsɪ] *n* epilepsia.

epileptic [ɛpɪ'lɛptɪk] *adj, n* epiléptico/a *m/f*.

epilogue ['ɛpɪlɔg] *n* epílogo.

episcopal [ɪˈpɪskəpl] *adj* episcopal.
episode [ˈɛpɪsəud] *n* episodio.
epistle [ɪˈpɪsl] *n* epístola.
epitaph [ˈɛpɪtɑːf] *n* epitafio.
epithet [ˈɛpɪθɛt] *n* epíteto.
epitome [ɪˈpɪtəmɪ] *n* arquetipo.
epitomize [ɪˈpɪtəmaɪz] *vt* representar.
epoch [ˈiːpɔk] *n* época.
eponymous [ɪˈpɔnɪməs] *adj* epónimo.
equable [ˈɛkwəbl] *adj* (*climate*) estable; (*character*) ecuánime.
equal [ˈiːkwl] *adj* (*gen*) igual; (*treatment*) equitativo ♦ *n* igual *m/f* ♦ *vt* ser igual a; (*fig*) igualar; **to be ~ to** (*task*) estar a la altura de; **the E~ Opportunities Commission** (*BRIT*) *comisión para la igualdad de la mujer en el trabajo.*
equality [iːˈkwɔlɪtɪ] *n* igualdad *f.*
equalize [ˈiːkwəlaɪz] *vt, vi* igualar; (*SPORT*) empatar.
equalizer [ˈiːkwəlaɪzə*] *n* igualada.
equally [ˈiːkwəlɪ] *adv* igualmente; (*share etc*) a partes iguales; **they are ~ clever** son tan listos uno como otro.
equals sign *n* signo igual.
equanimity [ɛkwəˈnɪmɪtɪ] *n* ecuanimidad *f.*
equate [ɪˈkweɪt] *vt*: **to ~ sth with** equiparar algo con.
equation [ɪˈkweɪʒən] *n* (*MATH*) ecuación *f.*
equator [ɪˈkweɪtə*] *n* ecuador *m.*
equatorial [ɛkwəˈtɔːrɪəl] *adj* ecuatorial.
Equatorial Guinea *n* Guinea Ecuatorial.
equestrian [ɪˈkwɛstrɪən] *adj* ecuestre ♦ *n* jinete *m/f.*
equilibrium [iːkwɪˈlɪbrɪəm] *n* equilibrio.
equinox [ˈiːkwɪnɔks] *n* equinoccio.
equip [ɪˈkwɪp] *vt* (*gen*) equipar; (*person*) proveer; **~ped with** (*machinery etc*) provisto de; **to be well ~ped** estar bien equipado; **he is well ~ped for the job** está bien preparado para este puesto.
equipment [ɪˈkwɪpmənt] *n* equipo.
equitable [ˈɛkwɪtəbl] *adj* equitativo.
equities [ˈɛkwɪtɪz] *npl* (*BRIT COMM*) acciones *fpl* ordinarias.
equity [ˈɛkwɪtɪ] *n* (*fairness*) equidad *f*; (*ECON: of debtor*) valor *m* líquido.
equity capital *n* capital *m* propio, patrimonio neto.
equivalent [ɪˈkwɪvəlnt] *adj, n* equivalente *m*; **to be ~ to** equivaler a.
equivocal [ɪˈkwɪvəkl] *adj* equívoco.
equivocate [ɪˈkwɪvəkeɪt] *vi* andarse con ambigüedades.
equivocation [ɪkwɪvəˈkeɪʃən] *n* ambigüedad *f.*
ER *abbr* (*BRIT: = Elizabeth Regina*) *la reina Isabel.*

er [əː] *interj* (*col: in hesitation*) esto, este (*LAM*).
ERA *n abbr* (*US POL: = Equal Rights Amendment*) *enmienda sobre la igualdad de derechos de la mujer.*
era [ˈɪərə] *n* era, época.
eradicate [ɪˈrædɪkeɪt] *vt* erradicar, extirpar.
erase [ɪˈreɪz] *vt* (*also COMPUT*) borrar.
eraser [ɪˈreɪzə*] *n* goma de borrar.
erect [ɪˈrɛkt] *adj* erguido ♦ *vt* erigir, levantar; (*assemble*) montar.
erection [ɪˈrɛkʃən] *n* (*of building*) construcción *f*; (*of machinery*) montaje *m*; (*structure*) edificio; (*MED*) erección *f.*
ergonomics [əːgəˈnɔmɪks] *n* ergonomía.
ERISA *n abbr* (*US: = Employee Retirement Income Security Act*) *ley que regula las pensiones de jubilados.*
Eritrea [ɛrɪˈtreɪə] *n* Eritrea.
ERM *n abbr* (*= Exchange Rate Mechanism*) (mecanismo de cambios del) SME *m.*
ermine [ˈəːmɪn] *n* armiño.
ERNIE [ˈəːnɪ] *n abbr* (*BRIT: = Electronic Random Number Indicating Equipment*) *ordenador que elige al azar los números ganadores de los bonos del Estado.*
erode [ɪˈrəud] *vt* (*GEO*) erosionar; (*metal*) corroer, desgastar.
erogenous zone [ɪˈrɔdʒənəs-] *n* zona erógena.
erosion [ɪˈrəuʒən] *n* erosión *f*; desgaste *m.*
erotic [ɪˈrɔtɪk] *adj* erótico.
eroticism [ɪˈrɔtɪsɪzm] *n* erotismo.
err [əː*] *vi* errar; (*REL*) pecar.
errand [ˈɛrnd] *n* recado, mandado; **to run ~s** hacer recados; **~ of mercy** misión *f* de caridad.
errand boy *n* recadero.
erratic [ɪˈrætɪk] *adj* variable; (*results etc*) desigual, poco uniforme.
erroneous [ɪˈrəunɪəs] *adj* erróneo.
error [ˈɛrə*] *n* error *m*, equivocación *f*; **typing/spelling ~** error *m* de mecanografía/ortografía; **in ~** por equivocación; **~s and omissions excepted** salvo error u omisión.
error message *n* (*COMPUT*) mensaje *m* de error.
erstwhile [ˈəːstwaɪl] *adj* antiguo, previo.
erudite [ˈɛrudaɪt] *adj* erudito.
erudition [ɛruˈdɪʃən] *n* erudición *f.*
erupt [ɪˈrʌpt] *vi* entrar en erupción; (*MED*) hacer erupción; (*fig*) estallar.
eruption [ɪˈrʌpʃən] *n* erupción *f*; (*fig: of anger, violence*) explosión *f*, estallido.
ESA *n abbr* (*= European Space Agency*) Agencia Espacial Europea.

escalate ['ɛskəleɪt] vi extenderse, intensificarse; (costs) aumentar vertiginosamente.

escalation clause [ɛskə'leɪʃən-] n cláusula de reajuste de los precios.

escalator ['ɛskəleɪtə*] n escalera mecánica.

escapade [ɛskə'peɪd] n aventura.

escape [ɪ'skeɪp] n (gen) fuga; (TECH) escape m; (from duties) escapatoria; (from chase) evasión f ♦ vi (gen) escaparse; (flee) huir, evadirse ♦ vt evitar, eludir; (consequences) escapar a; **to ~ from** (place) escaparse de; (person) huir de; (clutches) librarse de; **to ~ to** (another place, freedom, safety) huir a; **to ~ notice** pasar desapercibido.

escape artist n artista m/f de la evasión.

escape clause n (fig: in agreement) cláusula de excepción.

escapee [ɪskeɪ'piː] n fugado/a.

escape hatch n (in submarine, space rocket) escotilla de salvamento.

escape key n (COMPUT) tecla de escape.

escape route n (from fire) vía de escape.

escapism [ɪ'skeɪpɪzəm] n escapismo, evasión f.

escapist [ɪ'skeɪpɪst] adj escapista, de evasión ♦ n escapista m/f.

escapologist [ɛskə'pɔlədʒɪst] n (BRIT) = escape artist.

escarpment [ɪ'skɑːpmənt] n escarpa.

eschew [ɪs'tʃuː] vt evitar, abstenerse de.

escort ['ɛskɔːt] n acompañante m/f; (MIL) escolta; (NAUT) convoy m ♦ vt [ɪ'skɔːt] acompañar; (MIL, NAUT) escoltar.

escort agency n agencia de acompañantes.

Eskimo ['ɛskɪməu] adj esquimal ♦ n esquimal m/f; (LING) esquimal m.

ESL n abbr (SCOL) = English as a Second Language.

esophagus [iː'sɔfəgəs] n (US) = oesophagus.

esoteric [ɛsəu'tɛrɪk] adj esotérico.

ESP n abbr = extrasensory perception; (SCOL: = English for Special Purposes) inglés especializado.

esp. abbr = especially.

especially [ɪ'spɛʃlɪ] adv (gen) especialmente; (above all) sobre todo; (particularly) en especial.

espionage ['ɛspɪənɑːʒ] n espionaje m.

esplanade [ɛsplə'neɪd] n (by sea) paseo marítimo.

espouse [ɪ'spauz] vt adherirse a.

Esq. abbr (= Esquire) D.

Esquire [ɪ'skwaɪə*] n: **J. Brown, ~**

Sr. D. J. Brown.

essay ['ɛseɪ] n (SCOL) redacción f; (: longer) trabajo.

essayist ['ɛseɪɪst] n ensayista m/f.

essence ['ɛsns] n esencia; **in ~** esencialmente; **speed is of the ~** es esencial hacerlo con la mayor prontitud.

essential [ɪ'sɛnʃl] adj (necessary) imprescindible; (basic) esencial ♦ n (often pl) lo esencial; **it is ~ that** es imprescindible que.

essentially [ɪ'sɛnʃlɪ] adv esencialmente.

EST n abbr (US: = Eastern Standard Time) hora de invierno de Nueva York.

est. abbr (= established) fundado; (= estimated) aprox.

establish [ɪ'stæblɪʃ] vt establecer; (prove: fact, identity) comprobar, verificar; (prove) demostrar; (relations) entablar.

established [ɪ'stæblɪʃt] adj (business) de buena reputación; (staff) de plantilla.

establishment [ɪ'stæblɪʃmənt] n (also business) establecimiento; **the E~** la clase dirigente; **a teaching ~** un centro de enseñanza.

estate [ɪ'steɪt] n (land) finca, hacienda; (property) propiedad f; (inheritance) herencia; (POL) estado; **housing ~** (BRIT) urbanización f; **industrial ~** polígono industrial.

estate agency n (BRIT) agencia inmobiliaria.

estate agent n (BRIT) agente m/f inmobiliario/a.

estate car n (BRIT) ranchera.

esteem [ɪ'stiːm] n: **to hold sb in high ~** estimar en mucho a algn ♦ vt estimar.

esthetic [iːs'θɛtɪk] adj (US) = aesthetic.

estimate ['ɛstɪmət] n estimación f; (assessment) tasa, cálculo; (COMM) presupuesto ♦ vt ['ɛstɪmeɪt] estimar; tasar, calcular; **to give sb an ~ of** presentar a algn un presupuesto de; **at a rough ~** haciendo un cálculo aproximado; **to ~ for** (COMM) hacer un presupuesto de, presupuestar.

estimation [ɛstɪ'meɪʃən] n opinión f, juicio; (esteem) aprecio; **in my ~** a mi juicio.

Estonia [ɛ'stəunɪə] n Estonia.

Estonian [ɛ'stəunɪən] adj estonio ♦ n estonio/a; (LING) estonio.

estranged [ɪ'streɪndʒd] adj separado.

estrangement [ɪ'streɪndʒmənt] n alejamiento, distanciamiento.

estrogen ['iːstrəudʒən] n (US) = oestrogen.

estuary ['ɛstjuərɪ] n estuario, ría.

ET n abbr (BRIT: = Employment Training) plan estatal de formación para los

desempleados ♦ *abbr* (*US*) = *Eastern Time.*
e-tailing [ˈiːteɪlɪŋ] *n* venta en línea, venta vía *or* por Internet.
et al. *abbr* (= *et alii: and others*) et al.
etc *abbr* (= *et cetera*) etc.
etch [etʃ] *vt* grabar al aguafuerte.
etching [ˈetʃɪŋ] *n* aguafuerte *m or f.*
ETD *n abbr* = *estimated time of departure.*
eternal [ɪˈtɜːnl] *adj* eterno.
eternity [ɪˈtɜːnɪtɪ] *n* eternidad *f.*
ether [ˈiːθə*] *n* éter *m.*
ethereal [ɪˈθɪərɪəl] *adj* etéreo.
ethical [ˈeθɪkl] *adj* ético; (*honest*) honrado.
ethics [ˈeθɪks] *n* ética ♦ *npl* moralidad *f.*
Ethiopia [iːθɪˈəʊpɪə] *n* Etiopía.
Ethiopian [iːθɪˈəʊpɪən] *adj, n* etíope *m/f.*
ethnic [ˈeθnɪk] *adj* étnico.
ethnic cleansing [-klenzɪŋ] *n* limpieza étnica.
ethos [ˈiːθɒs] *n* (*of culture, group*) sistema *m* de valores.
etiquette [ˈetɪket] *n* etiqueta.
ETV *n abbr* (*US*: = *Educational Television*) televisión *f* escolar.
etymology [etɪˈmɒlədʒɪ] *n* etimología.
EU *n abbr* (= *European Union*) UE *f.*
eucalyptus [juːkəˈlɪptəs] *n* eucalipto.
Eucharist [ˈjuːkərɪst] *n* Eucaristía.
eulogy [ˈjuːlədʒɪ] *n* elogio, encomio.
euphemism [ˈjuːfəmɪzm] *n* eufemismo.
euphemistic [juːfəˈmɪstɪk] *adj* eufemístico.
euphoria [juːˈfɔːrɪə] *n* euforia.
Eurasia [jʊəˈreɪʃə] *n* Eurasia.
Eurasian [jʊəˈreɪʃən] *adj, n* eurasiático/a *m/f.*
Euratom [jʊəˈrætəm] *n abbr* (= *European Atomic Energy Commission*) Euratom *m.*
Euro- *pref* euro-.
euro [ˈjʊərəʊ] *n* (*currency*) euro.
Eurocheque [ˈjʊərəʊtʃek] *n* Eurocheque *m.*
Eurocrat [ˈjʊərəʊkræt] *n* eurócrata *m/f.*
Eurodollar [ˈjʊərəʊdɒlə*] *n* eurodólar *m.*
Euroland [ˈjʊərəʊlænd] *n* Eurolandia.
Europe [ˈjʊərəp] *n* Europa.
European [jʊərəˈpiːən] *adj, n* europeo/a *m/f.*
European Court of Justice *n* Tribunal *m* de Justicia de las Comunidades Europeas.
Euro-sceptic [jʊərəʊˈskeptɪk] *n* euroescéptico/a.
Eurozone [ˈjʊərəʊzəʊn] *n* eurozona, zona euro.
euthanasia [juːθəˈneɪzɪə] *n* eutanasia.
evacuate [ɪˈvækjueɪt] *vt* evacuar; (*place*) desocupar.
evacuation [ɪvækjuˈeɪʃən] *n* evacuación *f.*
evacuee [ɪvækjuˈiː] *n* evacuado/a.
evade [ɪˈveɪd] *vt* evadir, eludir.
evaluate [ɪˈvæljueɪt] *vt* evaluar; (*value*)

tasar; (*evidence*) interpretar.
evangelical [iːvænˈdʒelɪkəl] *adj* evangélico.
evangelist [ɪˈvændʒəlɪst] *n* evangelista *m*; (*preacher*) evangelizador(a) *m/f.*
evaporate [ɪˈvæpəreɪt] *vi* evaporarse; (*fig*) desvanecerse ♦ *vt* evaporar.
evaporation [ɪvæpəˈreɪʃən] *n* evaporación *f.*
evasion [ɪˈveɪʒən] *n* evasión *f.*
evasive [ɪˈveɪsɪv] *adj* evasivo.
eve [iːv] *n*: **on the ~ of** en vísperas de.
even [ˈiːvn] *adj* (*level*) llano; (*smooth*) liso; (*speed, temperature*) uniforme; (*number*) par; (*SPORT*) igual(es) ♦ *adv* hasta, incluso; **~ if**, **~ though** aunque + *subjun*, así + *subjun* (*LAM*); **~ more** aun más; **so** aun así; **not ~** ni siquiera; **~ he was there** hasta él estaba allí; **~ on Sundays** incluso los domingos; **~ faster** aún más rápido; **to break ~** cubrir los gastos; **to get ~ with sb** ajustar cuentas con algn; **to ~ out** *vi* nivelarse.
even-handed [iːvnˈhændɪd] *adj* imparcial.
evening [ˈiːvnɪŋ] *n* tarde *f*; (*dusk*) atardecer *m*; (*night*) noche *f*; **in the ~** por la tarde; **this ~** esta tarde *or* noche; **tomorrow/yesterday ~** mañana/ayer por la tarde *or* noche.
evening class *n* clase *f* nocturna.
evening dress *n* (*man's*) traje *m* de etiqueta; (*woman's*) traje *m* de noche.
evenly [ˈiːvnlɪ] *adv* de modo uniforme; (*divide*) equitativamente.
evensong [ˈiːvnsɒŋ] *n* vísperas *fpl.*
event [ɪˈvent] *n* suceso, acontecimiento; (*SPORT*) prueba; **in the ~ of** en caso de; **in the ~** en realidad; **in the course of ~s** en el curso de los acontecimientos; **at all ~s, in any ~** en cualquier caso.
eventful [ɪˈventful] *adj* azaroso; (*game etc*) lleno de emoción.
eventing [ɪˈventɪŋ] *n* (*HORSERIDING*) competición *f.*
eventual [ɪˈventʃuəl] *adj* final.
eventuality [ɪventʃuˈælɪtɪ] *n* eventualidad *f.*
eventually [ɪˈventʃuəlɪ] *adv* (*finally*) por fin; (*in time*) con el tiempo.
ever [ˈevə*] *adv* nunca, jamás; (*at all times*) siempre; **for ~** (para) siempre; **the best ~** lo nunca visto; **did you ~ meet him?** ¿llegaste a conocerle?; **have you ~ been there?** ¿has estado allí alguna vez?; **have you ~ seen it?** ¿lo has visto alguna vez?; **better than ~** mejor que nunca; **thank you ~ so much** muchísimas gracias; **yours ~** (*in letters*) un abrazo de; **~ since** *adv* desde entonces ♦ *conj* después de que.
Everest [ˈevərɪst] *n* (*also*: **Mount ~**) el Everest *m.*

evergreen ['ɛvəgriːn] *n* árbol *m* de hoja perenne.
everlasting [ɛvə'lɑːstɪŋ] *adj* eterno, perpetuo.

=============================== KEYWORD

every ['ɛvrɪ] *adj* **1** (*each*) cada; ~ **one of them** (*persons*) todos ellos/as; (*objects*) cada uno de ellos/as; ~ **shop in the town was closed** todas las tiendas de la ciudad estaban cerradas
2 (*all possible*) todo/a; **I gave you** ~ **assistance** te di toda la ayuda posible; **I have** ~ **confidence in him** tiene toda mi confianza; **we wish you** ~ **success** te deseamos toda suerte de éxitos
3 (*showing recurrence*) todo/a; ~ **day/ week** todos los días/todas las semanas; ~ **other car had been broken into** habían forzado uno de cada dos coches; **she visits me** ~ **other/third day** me visita cada dos/tres días; ~ **now and then** de vez en cuando.

everybody ['ɛvrɪbədɪ] *pron* todos *pl*, todo el mundo; ~ **knows about it** todo el mundo lo sabe; ~ **else** todos los demás.
everyday ['ɛvrɪdeɪ] *adj* (*daily: use, occurrence, experience*) diario, cotidiano; (*usual: expression*) corriente; (*common*) vulgar; (*routine*) rutinario.
everyone ['ɛvrɪwʌn] = **everybody**.
everything ['ɛvrɪθɪŋ] *pron* todo; ~ **is ready** todo está dispuesto; **he did** ~ **possible** hizo todo lo posible.
everywhere ['ɛvrɪwɛə*] *adv* (*be*) en todas partes; (*go*) a *or* por todas partes; ~ **you go you meet...** en todas partes encontrarás....
evict [ɪ'vɪkt] *vt* desahuciar.
eviction [ɪ'vɪkʃən] *n* desahucio.
eviction notice *n* orden *f* de desahucio *or* desalojo (*LAM*).
evidence ['ɛvɪdəns] *n* (*proof*) prueba; (*of witness*) testimonio; (*facts*) datos *mpl*, hechos *mpl*; **to give** ~ prestar declaración, dar testimonio.
evident ['ɛvɪdənt] *adj* evidente, manifiesto.
evidently ['ɛvɪdəntlɪ] *adv* (*obviously*) obviamente, evidentemente; (*apparently*) por lo visto.
evil ['iːvl] *adj* malo; (*influence*) funesto; (*smell*) horrible ♦ *n* mal *m*.
evildoer ['iːvlduːə*] *n* malhechor(a) *m/f*.
evince [ɪ'vɪns] *vt* mostrar, dar señales de.
evocative [ɪ'vɔkətɪv] *adj* sugestivo, evocador(a).
evoke [ɪ'vəuk] *vt* evocar; (*admiration*) provocar.
evolution [iːvə'luːʃən] *n* evolución *f*, desarrollo.
evolve [ɪ'vɔlv] *vt* desarrollar ♦ *vi* evolucionar, desarrollarse.
ewe [juː] *n* oveja.
ex- [ɛks] *pref* (*former: husband, president etc*) ex-; (*out of*): **the price** ~ **works** precio de fábrica.
exacerbate [ɛk'sæsəbeɪt] *vt* exacerbar.
exact [ɪg'zækt] *adj* exacto ♦ *vt*: **to** ~ **sth (from)** exigir algo (de).
exacting [ɪg'zæktɪŋ] *adj* exigente; (*conditions*) arduo.
exactitude [ɪg'zæktɪtjuːd] *n* exactitud *f*.
exactly [ɪg'zæktlɪ] *adv* exactamente; (*time*) en punto; ~! ¡exacto!
exactness [ɪg'zæktnɪs] *n* exactitud *f*.
exaggerate [ɪg'zædʒəreɪt] *vt*, *vi* exagerar.
exaggerated [ɪg'zædʒəreɪtɪd] *adj* exagerado.
exaggeration [ɪgzædʒə'reɪʃən] *n* exageración *f*.
exalt [ɪg'zɔːlt] *vt* (*praise*) ensalzar; (*elevate*) elevar.
exalted [ɪg'zɔːltɪd] *adj* (*position*) elevado; (*elated*) enardecido.
exam [ɪg'zæm] *n abbr* (*SCOL*) = **examination**.
examination [ɪgzæmɪ'neɪʃən] *n* (*gen*) examen *m*; (*LAW*) interrogación *f*; (*inquiry*) investigación *f*; **to take** *or* **sit an** ~ hacer un examen; **the matter is under** ~ se está examinando el asunto.
examine [ɪg'zæmɪn] *vt* (*gen*) examinar; (*inspect: machine, premises*) inspeccionar; (*SCOL, LAW: person*) interrogar; (*at customs: luggage, passport*) registrar; (*MED*) hacer un reconocimiento médico de, examinar.
examiner [ɪg'zæmɪnə*] *n* examinador(a) *m/f*.
example [ɪg'zɑːmpl] *n* ejemplo; **for** ~ por ejemplo; **to set a good/bad** ~ dar buen/ mal ejemplo.
exasperate [ɪg'zɑːspəreɪt] *vt* exasperar, irritar; ~**d by** *or* **at** *or* **with** exasperado por *or* con.
exasperating [ɪg'zɑːspəreɪtɪŋ] *adj* irritante.
exasperation [ɪgzɑːspə'reɪʃən] *n* exasperación *f*, irritación *f*.
excavate ['ɛkskəveɪt] *vt* excavar.
excavation [ɛkskə'veɪʃən] *n* excavación *f*.
excavator ['ɛkskəveɪtə*] *n* excavadora.
exceed [ɪk'siːd] *vt* exceder; (*number*) pasar de; (*speed limit*) sobrepasar; (*limits*) rebasar; (*powers*) excederse en; (*hopes*) superar.
exceedingly [ɪk'siːdɪŋlɪ] *adv* sumamente,

sobremanera.

excel [ɪk'sɛl] *vi* sobresalir; **to ~ o.s.** lucirse.

excellence ['ɛksələns] *n* excelencia.

Excellency ['ɛksələnsɪ] *n*: **His ~** Su Excelencia.

excellent ['ɛksələnt] *adj* excelente.

except [ɪk'sɛpt] *prep (also*: **~ for, ~ing)** excepto, salvo ♦ *vt* exceptuar, excluir; **~ if/when** excepto si/cuando; **~ that** salvo que.

exception [ɪk'sɛpʃən] *n* excepción *f*; **to take ~ to** ofenderse por; **with the ~ of a** excepción de; **to make an ~** hacer una excepción.

exceptional [ɪk'sɛpʃənl] *adj* excepcional.

excerpt ['ɛksə:pt] *n* extracto.

excess [ɪk'sɛs] *n* exceso; **in ~ of** superior a; *see also* **excesses.**

excess baggage *n* exceso de equipaje.

excesses *npl* excesos *mpl*.

excess fare *n* suplemento.

excessive [ɪk'sɛsɪv] *adj* excesivo.

excess supply *n* exceso de oferta.

excess weight *n* exceso de peso.

exchange [ɪks'tʃeɪndʒ] *n* cambio; (*of prisoners*) canje *m*; (*of ideas*) intercambio; (*also*: **telephone ~**) central *f* (telefónica) ♦ *vt* intercambiar; **to ~ (for)** cambiar (por); **in ~ for** a cambio de; **foreign ~** (*COMM*) divisas *fpl*.

exchange control *n* control *m* de divisas.

exchange rate *n* tipo de cambio.

exchequer [ɪks'tʃɛkə*] *n*: **the ~** (*BRIT*) Hacienda.

excisable [ɛk'saɪzəbl] *adj* sujeto al pago de impuestos sobre el consumo.

excise ['ɛksaɪz] *n* impuestos *mpl* sobre el consumo interior.

excitable [ɪk'saɪtəbl] *adj* excitable.

excite [ɪk'saɪt] *vt* (*stimulate*) entusiasmar; (*anger*) suscitar, provocar; (*move*) emocionar; **to get ~d** emocionarse.

excitement [ɪk'saɪtmənt] *n* emoción *f*.

exciting [ɪk'saɪtɪŋ] *adj* emocionante.

excl. *abbr* = **excluding; exclusive (of).**

exclaim [ɪk'skleɪm] *vi* exclamar.

exclamation [ɛksklə'meɪʃən] *n* exclamación *f*.

exclamation mark *n* signo de admiración.

exclude [ɪk'sklu:d] *vt* excluir; (*except*) exceptuar.

excluding [ɪks'klu:dɪŋ] *prep*: **~ VAT** IVA no incluido.

exclusion [ɪk'sklu:ʒən] *n* exclusión *f*; **to the ~ of** con exclusión de.

exclusion clause *n* cláusula de exclusión.

exclusion zone *n* zona de exclusión.

exclusive [ɪk'sklu:sɪv] *adj* exclusivo; (*club*, *district*) selecto; **~ of tax** excluyendo impuestos; **~ of postage/service** franqueo/servicio no incluido; **from 1st to 13th March ~** del 1 al 13 de marzo exclusive.

exclusively [ɪk'sklu:sɪvlɪ] *adv* únicamente.

excommunicate [ɛkskə'mju:nɪkeɪt] *vt* excomulgar.

excrement ['ɛkskrəmənt] *n* excremento.

excrete [ɪk'skri:t] *vi* excretar.

excruciating [ɪk'skru:ʃɪeɪtɪŋ] *adj* (*pain*) agudísimo, atroz.

excursion [ɪk'skə:ʃən] *n* excursión *f*.

excursion ticket *n* billete *m* (especial) de excursión.

excusable [ɪk'skju:səbl] *adj* perdonable.

excuse *n* [ɪk'skju:s] disculpa, excusa; (*evasion*) pretexto ♦ *vt* [ɪk'skju:z] disculpar, perdonar; (*justify*) justificar; **to make ~s for sb** presentar disculpas por algn; **to ~ sb from doing sth** dispensar a algn de hacer algo; **to ~ o.s. (for (doing) sth)** pedir disculpas a algn (por (hacer) algo); **~ me!** ¡perdone!; (*attracting attention*) ¡oiga(, por favor)!; **if you will ~ me** con su permiso.

ex-directory ['ɛksdɪ'rɛktərɪ] *adj* (*BRIT*): **~ (phone) number** número que no figura en la guía (telefónica).

execrable ['ɛksɪkrəbl] *adj* execrable, abominable; (*manners*) detestable.

execute ['ɛksɪkju:t] *vt* (*plan*) realizar, (*order*) cumplir; (*person*) ajusticiar, ejecutar.

execution [ɛksɪ'kju:ʃən] *n* realización *f*; cumplimiento; ejecución *f*.

executioner [ɛksɪ'kju:ʃənə*] *n* verdugo.

executive [ɪg'zɛkjutɪv] *n* (*COMM*) ejecutivo/a; (*POL*) poder *m* ejecutivo ♦ *adj* ejecutivo; (*car, plane, position*) de ejecutivo; (*offices, suite*) de la dirección; (*secretary*) de dirección.

executive director *n* director(a) *m/f* ejecutivo/a.

executor [ɪg'zɛkjutə*] *n* albacea *m*, testamentario.

exemplary [ɪg'zɛmplərɪ] *adj* ejemplar.

exemplify [ɪg'zɛmplɪfaɪ] *vt* ejemplificar.

exempt [ɪg'zɛmpt] *adj*: **~ from** exento de ♦ *vt*: **to ~ sb from** eximir a algn de.

exemption [ɪg'zɛmpʃən] *n* exención *f*; (*immunity*) inmunidad *f*.

exercise ['ɛksəsaɪz] *n* ejercicio ♦ *vt* ejercer; (*patience etc*) proceder con; (*dog*) sacar de paseo ♦ *vi* hacer ejercicio.

exercise bike *n* bicicleta estática.

exercise book *n* cuaderno de ejercicios.

exert [ɪg'zə:t] *vt* ejercer; (*strength, force*)

emplear; **to** ~ **o.s.** esforzarse.
exertion [ɪg'zəːʃən] *n* esfuerzo.
exfoliant [ɛks'fəʊlɪənt] *n* exfoliante *m*.
ex gratia ['ɛks'greɪʃə] *adj*: ~ **payment** pago a título voluntario.
exhale [ɛks'heɪl] *vt* despedir, exhalar ♦ *vi* espirar.
exhaust [ɪg'zɔːst] *n* (*pipe*) (tubo de) escape *m*; (*fumes*) gases *mpl* de escape ♦ *vt* agotar; **to** ~ **o.s.** agotarse.
exhausted [ɪg'zɔːstɪd] *adj* agotado.
exhausting [ɪg'zɔːstɪŋ] *adj*: **an** ~ **journey/ day** un viaje/día agotador.
exhaustion [ɪg'zɔːstʃən] *n* agotamiento; **nervous** ~ agotamiento nervioso.
exhaustive [ɪg'zɔːstɪv] *adj* exhaustivo.
exhibit [ɪg'zɪbɪt] *n* (*ART*) obra expuesta; (*LAW*) objeto expuesto ♦ *vt* (*show: emotions*) manifestar; (: *courage, skill*) demostrar; (*paintings*) exponer.
exhibition [ɛksɪ'bɪʃən] *n* exposición *f*.
exhibitionist [ɛksɪ'bɪʃənɪst] *n* exhibicionista *m/f*.
exhibitor [ɪg'zɪbɪtə*] *n* expositor(a) *m/f*.
exhilarating [ɪg'zɪləreɪtɪŋ] *adj* estimulante, tónico.
exhilaration [ɪgzɪlə'reɪʃən] *n* júbilo.
exhort [ɪg'zɔːt] *vt* exhortar.
exile ['ɛksaɪl] *n* exilio; (*person*) exiliado/a ♦ *vt* desterrar, exiliar.
exist [ɪg'zɪst] *vi* existir.
existence [ɪg'zɪstəns] *n* existencia.
existentialism [ɛgzɪs'tɛnʃəlɪzəm] *n* existencialismo.
existing [ɪg'zɪstɪŋ] *adj* existente, actual.
exit ['ɛksɪt] *n* salida ♦ *vi* (*THEAT*) hacer mutis; (*COMPUT*) salir (del sistema).
exit poll *n* encuesta a la salida de los colegios electorales.
exit ramp *n* (*US AUT*) vía de acceso.
exit visa *n* visado de salida.
exodus ['ɛksədəs] *n* éxodo.
ex officio ['ɛksə'fɪʃɪəu] *adj* de pleno derecho ♦ *adv* ex oficio.
exonerate [ɪg'zɔnəreɪt] *vt*: **to** ~ **from** exculpar de.
exorbitant [ɪg'zɔːbɪtənt] *adj* (*price, demands*) exorbitante, excesivo.
exorcize ['ɛksɔːsaɪz] *vt* exorcizar.
exotic [ɪg'zɔtɪk] *adj* exótico.
expand [ɪk'spænd] *vt* ampliar, extender; (*number*) aumentar ♦ *vi* (*trade etc*) ampliarse, expandirse; (*gas, metal*) dilatarse; **to** ~ **on** (*notes, story etc*) ampliar.
expanse [ɪk'spæns] *n* extensión *f*.
expansion [ɪk'spænʃən] *n* ampliación *f*; aumento; (*of trade*) expansión *f*.

expansionism [ɪk'spænʃənɪzəm] *n* expansionismo.
expansionist [ɪk'spænʃənɪst] *adj* expansionista.
expatriate [ɛks'pætrɪət] *n* expatriado/a.
expect [ɪk'spɛkt] *vt* (*gen*) esperar; (*count on*) contar con; (*suppose*) suponer ♦ *vi*: **to be** ~**ing** estar encinta; **to** ~ **to do sth** esperar hacer algo; **as** ~**ed** como era de esperar; **I** ~ **so** supongo que sí.
expectancy [ɪk'spɛktənsɪ] *n* (*anticipation*) expectación *f*; **life** ~ esperanza de vida.
expectantly [ɪk'spɛktəntlɪ] *adv* (*look, listen*) con expectación.
expectant mother [ɪk'spɛktənt-] *n* futura madre *f*.
expectation [ɛkspɛk'teɪʃən] *n* esperanza, expectativa; **in** ~ **of** esperando; **against** *or* **contrary to all** ~(**s**) en contra de todas las previsiones; **to come** *or* **live up to sb's** ~**s** resultar tan bueno como se esperaba; **to fall short of sb's** ~**s** no cumplir las esperanzas de algn, decepcionar a algn.
expedience [ɪk'spiːdɪəns], **expediency** [ɪk'spiːdɪənsɪ] *n* conveniencia.
expedient [ɪk'spiːdɪənt] *adj* conveniente, oportuno ♦ *n* recurso, expediente *m*.
expedite ['ɛkspɪdaɪt] *vt* (*speed up*) acelerar; (: *progress*) facilitar.
expedition [ɛkspə'dɪʃən] *n* expedición *f*.
expeditionary force [ɛkspə'dɪʃnrɪ-] *n* cuerpo expedicionario.
expel [ɪk'spɛl] *vt* expulsar.
expend [ɪk'spɛnd] *vt* gastar; (*use up*) consumir.
expendable [ɪk'spɛndəbl] *adj* prescindible.
expenditure [ɪk'spɛndɪtʃə*] *n* gastos *mpl*, desembolso; (*of time, effort*) gasto.
expense [ɪk'spɛns] *n* gasto, gastos *mpl*; (*high cost*) coste *m*; ~**s** *npl* (*COMM*) gastos *mpl*; **at the** ~ **of** a costa de; **to meet the** ~ **of** hacer frente a los gastos de.
expense account *n* cuenta de gastos (de representación).
expensive [ɪk'spɛnsɪv] *adj* caro, costoso.
experience [ɪk'spɪərɪəns] *n* experiencia ♦ *vt* experimentar; (*suffer*) sufrir; **to learn by** ~ aprender con la experiencia.
experienced [ɪk'spɪərɪənst] *adj* experimentado.
experiment [ɪk'spɛrɪmənt] *n* experimento ♦ *vi* hacer experimentos, experimentar; **to perform** *or* **carry out an** ~ realizar un experimento; **as an** ~ como experimento; **to** ~ **with a new vaccine** experimentar con una vacuna nueva.
experimental [ɪkspɛrɪ'mɛntl] *adj* experimental; **the process is still at the** ~

stage el proceso está todavía en prueba.
expert ['ɛkspəːt] adj experto, perito ♦ n experto/a, perito/a; (specialist) especialista m/f; ~ **witness** (LAW) testigo pericial; ~ **in** or **at doing sth** experto or perito en hacer algo; **an** ~ **on sth** un experto en algo.
expertise [ɛkspəː'tiːz] n pericia.
expiration [ɛkspɪ'reɪʃən] n (gen) expiración f, vencimiento.
expire [ɪk'spaɪə*] vi (gen) caducar, vencerse.
expiry [ɪk'spaɪərɪ] n caducidad f, vencimiento.
explain [ɪk'spleɪn] vt explicar; (mystery) aclarar.
▶**explain away** vt justificar.
explanation [ɛksplə'neɪʃən] n explicación f; aclaración f; **to find an** ~ **for sth** encontrarle una explicación a algo.
explanatory [ɪk'splænətrɪ] adj explicativo; aclaratorio.
expletive [ɪk'spliːtɪv] n imprecación f.
explicable [ɪk'splɪkəbl] adj explicable.
explicit [ɪk'splɪsɪt] adj explícito.
explicitly [ɪk'splɪsɪtlɪ] adv explícitamente.
explode [ɪk'spləud] vi estallar, explotar; (with anger) reventar ♦ vt hacer explotar; (fig: theory, myth) demoler.
exploit ['ɛksplɔɪt] n hazaña ♦ vt [ɪk'splɔɪt] explotar.
exploitation [ɛksplɔɪ'teɪʃən] n explotación f.
exploration [ɛksplə'reɪʃən] n exploración f.
exploratory [ɪk'splɔrətrɪ] adj (fig: talks) exploratorio, preliminar.
explore [ɪk'splɔː*] vt explorar; (fig) examinar, sondear.
explorer [ɪk'splɔːrə*] n explorador(a) m/f.
explosion [ɪk'spləuʒən] n explosión f.
explosive [ɪk'spləusɪv] adj, n explosivo.
exponent [ɪk'spəunənt] n partidario/a; (of skill, activity) exponente m/f.
export vt [ɛk'spɔːt] exportar ♦ n ['ɛkspɔːt] exportación f ♦ cpd de exportación.
exportation [ɛkspɔː'teɪʃən] n exportación f.
export drive n campaña de exportación.
exporter [ɛk'spɔːtə*] n exportador(a) m/f.
export licence n licencia de exportación.
export manager n gerente m/f de exportación.
export trade n comercio exterior.
expose [ɪk'spəuz] vt exponer; (unmask) desenmascarar.
exposé [ɪk'spəuzeɪ] n relevación f.
exposed [ɪk'spəuzd] adj expuesto; (land, house) desprotegido; (ELEC: wire) al aire; (pipe, beam) al descubierto.

exposition [ɛkspə'zɪʃən] n exposición f.
exposure [ɪk'spəuʒə*] n exposición f; (PHOT: speed) (tiempo m de) exposición f; (: shot) fotografía; **to die from** ~ (MED) morir de frío.
exposure meter n fotómetro.
expound [ɪk'spaund] vt exponer; (theory, text) comentar; (one's views) explicar.
express [ɪk'sprɛs] adj (definite) expreso, explícito; (BRIT: letter etc) urgente ♦ n (train) rápido ♦ adv (send) por correo extraordinario ♦ vt expresar; (squeeze) exprimir; **to send sth** ~ enviar algo por correo urgente; **to** ~ **o.s.** expresarse.
expression [ɪk'sprɛʃən] n expresión f.
expressionism [ɪk'sprɛʃənɪzm] n expresionismo.
expressive [ɪk'sprɛsɪv] adj expresivo.
expressly [ɪk'sprɛslɪ] adv expresamente.
expressway [ɪk'sprɛsweɪ] n (US: urban motorway) autopista.
expropriate [ɛks'prəuprɪeɪt] vt expropiar.
expulsion [ɪk'spʌlʃən] n expulsión f.
expurgate ['ɛkspəgeɪt] vt expurgar.
exquisite [ɛk'skwɪzɪt] adj exquisito.
exquisitely [ɛk'skwɪzɪtlɪ] adv exquisitamente.
ex-serviceman ['ɛks'səːvɪsmən] n ex-combatiente m.
ext. abbr (TEL) = **extension**.
extemporize [ɪk'stɛmpəraɪz] vi improvisar.
extend [ɪk'stɛnd] vt (visit, street) prolongar; (building) ampliar; (thanks, friendship etc) extender; (COMM: credit) conceder; (deadline) prorrogar ♦ vi (land) extenderse; **the contract** ~**s to/for ...** el contrato se prolonga hasta/por ....
extension [ɪk'stɛnʃən] n extensión f; (building) ampliación f; (TEL: line) extensión f; (: telephone) supletorio m; (of deadline) prórroga; ~ **3718** extensión 3718.
extension cable n (ELEC) alargador m.
extensive [ɪk'stɛnsɪv] adj (gen) extenso; (damage) importante; (knowledge) amplio.
extensively [ɪk'stɛnsɪvlɪ] adv (altered, damaged etc) extensamente; **he's travelled** ~ ha viajado por muchos países.
extent [ɪk'stɛnt] n (breadth) extensión f; (scope: of knowledge, activities) alcance m; (degree: of damage, loss) grado; **to some** ~ hasta cierto punto; **to a certain** ~ hasta cierto punto; **to a large** ~ en gran parte; **to the** ~ **of...** hasta el punto de...; **to such an** ~ **that...** hasta tal punto que...; **to what** ~**?** ¿hasta qué punto?; **debts to the** ~ **of £5000** deudas por la cantidad de £5000.
extenuating [ɪk'stɛnjueɪtɪŋ] adj: ~

circumstances circunstancias *fpl*
atenuantes.

exterior [ɛk'stɪərɪə*] *adj* exterior, externo
♦ *n* exterior *m*.

exterminate [ɪk'stə:mɪneɪt] *vt* exterminar.

extermination [ɪkstə:mɪ'neɪʃən] *n*
exterminio.

external [ɛk'stə:nl] *adj* externo, exterior
♦ *n*: **the ~s** la apariencia exterior; **~
affairs** asuntos *mpl* exteriores; **for ~ use
only** (*MED*) para uso tópico.

externally [ɛk'stə:nəlɪ] *adv* por fuera.

extinct [ɪk'stɪŋkt] *adj* (*volcano*) extinguido,
apagado; (*race*) extinguido.

extinction [ɪk'stɪŋkʃən] *n* extinción *f*.

extinguish [ɪk'stɪŋgwɪʃ] *vt* extinguir,
apagar.

extinguisher [ɪk'stɪŋgwɪʃə*] *n* extintor *m*.

extol, (*US*) **extoll** [ɪk'stəul] *vt* (*merits,
virtues*) ensalzar, alabar; (*person*) alabar,
elogiar.

extort [ɪk'stɔ:t] *vt* sacar a la fuerza;
(*confession*) arrancar.

extortion [ɪk'stɔ:ʃən] *n* extorsión *f*.

extortionate [ɪk'stɔ:ʃnət] *adj* excesivo,
exorbitante.

extra ['ɛkstrə] *adj* adicional ♦ *adv* (*in
addition*) más ♦ *n* (*addition*) extra *m*,
suplemento; (*THEAT*) extra *m/f*, comparsa
m/f; (*newspaper*) edición *f* extraordinaria;
wine will cost ~ el vino se paga aparte; **~
large sizes** tallas extragrandes; *see also*
extras.

extra... ['ɛkstrə] *pref* extra... .

extract *vt* [ɪk'strækt] sacar; (*tooth*) extraer;
(*confession*) arrancar ♦ *n* ['ɛkstrækt]
fragmento; (*CULIN*) extracto.

extraction [ɪk'strækʃən] *n* extracción *f*;
(*origin*) origen *m*.

extractor fan [ɪk'stræktə-] *n* extractor *m* de
humos.

extracurricular [ɛkstrəkə'rɪkjulə*] *adj*
(*SCOL*) extraescolar.

extradite ['ɛkstrədaɪt] *vt* extraditar.

extradition [ɛkstrə'dɪʃən] *n* extradición *f*.

extramarital [ɛkstrə'mærɪtl] *adj*
extramatrimonial.

extramural [ɛkstrə'mjuərl] *adj* extra-
académico.

extraneous [ɪk'streɪnɪəs] *adj* extraño,
ajeno.

extraordinary [ɪk'strɔ:dnrɪ] *adj*
extraordinario; (*odd*) raro; **the ~ thing is
that ...** lo más extraordinario es que ....

extraordinary general meeting *n* junta
general extraordinaria.

extrapolation [ɪkstræpə'leɪʃən] *n*
extrapolación *f*.

extras *npl* (*additional expense*) extras *mpl*.

extrasensory perception (ESP)
['ɛkstrə'sɛnsərɪ-] *n* percepción *f*
extrasensorial.

extra time *n* (*FOOTBALL*) prórroga.

extravagance [ɪk'strævəgəns] *n* (*excessive
spending*) derroche *m*; (*thing bought*)
extravagancia.

extravagant [ɪk'strævəgənt] *adj* (*wasteful*)
derrochador(a); (*taste, gift*)
excesivamente caro; (*price*) exorbitante;
(*praise*) excesivo.

extreme [ɪk'stri:m] *adj* extremo; (*poverty
etc*) extremado; (*case*) excepcional ♦ *n*
extremo; **the ~ left/right** (*POL*) la
extrema izquierda/derecha; **~s of
temperature** temperaturas extremas.

extremely [ɪk'stri:mlɪ] *adv* sumamente,
extremadamente.

extremist [ɪk'stri:mɪst] *adj, n* extremista *m/f*.

extremity [ɪk'strɛmətɪ] *n* extremidad *f*,
punta; (*need*) apuro, necesidad *f*;
extremities *npl* (*hands and feet*)
extremidades *fpl*.

extricate ['ɛkstrɪkeɪt] *vt*: **to ~ o.s. from**
librarse de.

extrovert ['ɛkstrəvə:t] *n* extrovertido/a.

exuberance [ɪg'zju:bərns] *n* exuberancia.

exuberant [ɪg'zju:bərnt] *adj* (*person*)
eufórico; (*style*) exuberante.

exude [ɪg'zju:d] *vt* rezumar.

exult [ɪg'zʌlt] *vi* regocijarse.

exultant [ɪg'zʌltənt] *adj* (*person*)
regocijado, jubiloso; (*shout, expression,
smile*) de júbilo.

exultation [ɛgzʌl'teɪʃən] *n* regocijo, júbilo.

eye [aɪ] *n* ojo ♦ *vt* mirar; **to keep an ~ on**
vigilar; **as far as the ~ can see** hasta
donde alcanza la vista; **with an ~ to
doing sth** con vistas *or* miras a hacer
algo; **to have an ~ for sth** tener mucha
vista *or* buen ojo para algo; **there's more
to this than meets the ~** esto tiene su
miga.

eyeball ['aɪbɔ:l] *n* globo ocular.

eyebath ['aɪbɑ:θ] *n* baño ocular, lavaojos *m
inv*.

eyebrow ['aɪbrau] *n* ceja.

eyebrow pencil *n* lápiz *m* de cejas.

eye-catching ['aɪkætʃɪŋ] *adj* llamativo.

eye cup *n* (*US*) = **eyebath.**

eyedrops ['aɪdrɒps] *npl* gotas *fpl* para los
ojos.

eyeful ['aɪful] *n* (*col*): **to get an ~ of sth** ver
bien algo.

eyelash ['aɪlæʃ] *n* pestaña.

eyelet ['aɪlɪt] *n* ojete *m*.

eye-level ['aɪlɛvl] *adj* a la altura de los ojos.

eyelid ['aɪlɪd] n párpado.
eyeliner ['aɪlaɪnə*] n lápiz m de ojos.
eye-opener ['aɪəupnə*] n revelación f, gran sorpresa.
eyeshadow ['aɪʃædəu] n sombra de ojos.
eyesight ['aɪsaɪt] n vista.
eyesore ['aɪsɔː*] n monstruosidad f.
eyestrain ['aɪstreɪn] n: **to get** ~ cansar la vista or los ojos.
eyetooth, pl **eyeteeth** ['aɪtuːθ, -tiːθ] n colmillo; **to give one's eyeteeth for sth/to do sth** (col, fig) dar un ojo de la cara por algo/por hacer algo.
eyewash ['aɪwɔʃ] n (fig) disparates mpl, tonterías fpl.
eye witness n testigo m/f ocular.
eyrie ['ɪərɪ] n aguilera.

Ff

F, f [ɛf] n (letter) F, f f; (MUS) fa m; **F for Frederick**, (US) **F for Fox** F de Francia.
F. abbr = **Fahrenheit**.
FA n abbr (BRIT: = Football Association) ≈ AFE f (SP).
FAA n abbr (US) = Federal Aviation Administration.
fable ['feɪbl] n fábula.
fabric ['fæbrɪk] n tejido, tela.
fabricate ['fæbrɪkeɪt] vt fabricar; (fig) inventar.
fabrication [fæbrɪ'keɪʃən] n fabricación f; (fig) invención f.
fabric ribbon n (for typewriter) cinta de tela.
fabulous ['fæbjuləs] adj fabuloso.
façade [fə'sɑːd] n fachada.
face [feɪs] n (ANAT) cara, rostro; (of clock) esfera, cara; (side) cara; (surface) superficie f ♦ vt mirar a; (fig) enfrentarse a; ~ **down** (person, card) boca abajo; **to lose** ~ desprestigiarse; **to save** ~ salvar las apariencias; **to make** or **pull a** ~ hacer muecas; **in the** ~ **of** (difficulties etc) en vista de, ante; **on the** ~ **of** it a primera vista; ~ **to** ~ cara a cara; **to** ~ **the fact that ...** reconocer que ....
▶**face up to** vt fus hacer frente a, enfrentarse a.
face cloth n (BRIT) toallita.
face cream n crema (de belleza).

faceless ['feɪslɪs] adj (fig) anónimo.
face lift n lifting m, estirado facial.
face powder n polvos mpl para la cara.
face-saving ['feɪsseɪvɪŋ] adj para salvar las apariencias.
facet ['fæsɪt] n faceta.
facetious [fə'siːʃəs] adj chistoso.
facetiously [fə'siːʃəslɪ] adv chistosamente.
face value n (of stamp) valor m nominal; **to take sth at** ~ (fig) tomar algo en sentido literal, aceptar las apariencias de algo.
facial ['feɪʃəl] adj de la cara ♦ n (also: **beauty** ~) tratamiento facial, limpieza.
facile ['fæsaɪl] adj superficial.
facilitate [fə'sɪlɪteɪt] vt facilitar.
facility [fə'sɪlɪtɪ] n facilidad f; **facilities** npl instalaciones fpl; **credit** ~ facilidades de crédito.
facing ['feɪsɪŋ] prep frente a ♦ adj de enfrente.
facsimile [fæk'sɪmɪlɪ] n facsímil(e) m.
fact [fækt] n hecho; **in** ~ en realidad; **to know for a** ~ **that ...** saber a ciencia cierta que ....
fact-finding ['fæktfaɪndɪŋ] adj: **a** ~ **tour/ mission** un viaje/una misión de reconocimiento.
faction ['fækʃən] n facción f.
factional ['fækʃənl] adj (fighting) entre distintas facciones.
factor ['fæktə*] n factor m; (COMM: person) agente m/f comisionado/a ♦ vi (COMM) comprar deudas; **safety** ~ factor de seguridad.
factory ['fæktərɪ] n fábrica.
factory farming n cría industrial.
factory floor n (workers) trabajadores mpl, mano f de obra directa; (area) talleres mpl.
factory ship n buque m factoría.
factual ['fæktjuəl] adj basado en los hechos.
faculty ['fækəltɪ] n facultad f; (US: teaching staff) personal m docente.
fad [fæd] n novedad f, moda.
fade [feɪd] vi descolorarse, desteñirse; (sound, hope) desvanecerse; (light) apagarse; (flower) marchitarse.
▶**fade away** vi (sound) apagarse.
▶**fade in** vt (TV, CINE) fundir; (RADIO: sound) mezclar ♦ vi (TV, CINE) fundirse; (RADIO) oírse por encima.
▶**fade out** vt (TV, CINE) fundir; (RADIO) apagar, disminuir el volumen de ♦ vi (TV, CINE) desvanecerse; (RADIO) apagarse, dejarse de oír.
faded ['feɪdɪd] adj (clothes, colour) descolorido; (flower) marchito.
faeces, (US) **feces** ['fiːsiːz] npl excremento

sg, heces *fpl*.

fag [fæg] *n* (*BRIT col*: *cigarette*) pitillo (*SP*), cigarro; (*US col*: *homosexual*) maricón *m*.

fag end *n* (*BRIT col*) colilla.

fagged [fægd] *adj* (*BRIT col*: *exhausted*) rendido, agotado.

Fahrenheit ['fɑ:rənhaɪt] *n* Fahrenheit *m*.

fail [feɪl] *vt* suspender; (*subj*: *memory etc*) fallar a ♦ *vi* suspender; (*be unsuccessful*) fracasar; (*strength, brakes, engine*) fallar; **to ~ to do sth** (*neglect*) dejar de hacer algo; (*be unable*) no poder hacer algo; **without ~** sin falta; **words ~ me!** ¡no sé qué decir!

failing ['feɪlɪŋ] *n* falta, defecto ♦ *prep* a falta de; **~ that** de no ser posible eso.

failsafe ['feɪlseɪf] *adj* (*device etc*) de seguridad.

failure ['feɪljə*] *n* fracaso; (*person*) fracasado/a; (*mechanical etc*) fallo; (*in exam*) suspenso; (*of crops*) pérdida, destrucción *f*; **it was a complete ~** fue un fracaso total.

faint [feɪnt] *adj* débil; (*smell, breeze, trace*) leve; (*recollection*) vago; (*mark*) apenas visible ♦ *n* desmayo ♦ *vi* desmayarse; **to feel ~** estar mareado, marearse.

faintest ['feɪntɪst] *adj*: **I haven't the ~ idea** no tengo la más remota idea.

faint-hearted ['feɪnt'hɑ:tɪd] *adj* apocado.

faintly ['feɪntlɪ] *adv* débilmente; (*vaguely*) vagamente.

faintness ['feɪntnɪs] *n* debilidad *f*; vaguedad *f*.

fair [fɛə*] *adj* justo; (*hair, person*) rubio; (*weather*) bueno; (*good enough*) suficiente; (*sizeable*) considerable ♦ *adv*: **to play ~** jugar limpio ♦ *n* feria; (*BRIT*: *funfair*) parque *m* de atracciones; **it's not ~!** ¡no es justo!, ¡no hay derecho!; **~ copy** copia en limpio; **~ play** juego limpio; **a ~ amount of** bastante; **~ wear and tear** desgaste *m* natural; **trade ~** feria de muestras.

fair game *n*: **to be ~** ser presa fácil.

fairground ['fɛəgraund] *n* recinto ferial.

fair-haired [fɛə'hɛəd] *adj* (*person*) rubio.

fairly ['fɛəlɪ] *adv* (*justly*) con justicia; (*equally*) equitativamente; (*quite*) bastante; **I'm ~ sure** estoy bastante seguro.

fairness ['fɛənɪs] *n* justicia; (*impartiality*) imparcialidad *f*; **in all ~** a decir verdad.

fairy ['fɛərɪ] *n* hada.

fairy godmother *n* hada madrina.

fairyland ['fɛərɪlænd] *n* el país de ensueño.

fairy lights *npl* bombillas *fpl* de colores.

fairy tale *n* cuento de hadas.

faith [feɪθ] *n* fe *f*; (*trust*) confianza; (*sect*) religión *f*; **to have ~ in sb/sth** confiar en algn/algo.

faithful ['feɪθful] *adj* fiel.

faithfully ['feɪθfulɪ] *adv* fielmente; **yours ~** (*BRIT*: *in letters*) le saluda atentamente.

faith healer *n* curador(a) *m/f* por fe.

fake [feɪk] *n* (*painting etc*) falsificación *f*; (*person*) impostor(a) *m/f* ♦ *adj* falso ♦ *vt* fingir; (*painting etc*) falsificar.

falcon ['fɔ:lkən] *n* halcón *m*.

Falkland Islands ['fɔ:klkənd-] *npl* Islas *fpl* Malvinas.

fall [fɔ:l] *n* caída; (*US*) otoño; (*decrease*) disminución *f* ♦ *vi*, *pt* **fell**, *pp* **fallen** ['fɔ:lən] caer; (*accidentally*) caerse; (*price*) bajar; **~s** *npl* (*waterfall*) cataratas *fpl*, salto *sg* de agua; **a ~ of earth** un desprendimiento de tierra; **a ~ of snow** una nevada; **to ~ flat** *vi* (*on one's face*) caerse de bruces; (*joke, story*) no hacer gracia; **to ~ short of sb's expectations** decepcionar a algn; **to ~ in love (with sb/sth)** enamorarse (de algn/algo).

▶**fall apart** *vi* deshacerse.

▶**fall back** *vi* retroceder.

▶**fall back on** *vt fus* (*remedy etc*) recurrir a; **to have sth to ~ back on** tener algo a que recurrir.

▶**fall behind** *vi* quedarse atrás; (*fig*: *with payments*) retrasarse.

▶**fall down** *vi* (*person*) caerse; (*building, hopes*) derrumbarse.

▶**fall for** *vt fus* (*trick*) tragar; (*person*) enamorarse de.

▶**fall in** *vi* (*roof*) hundirse; (*MIL*) alinearse.

▶**fall in with** *vt fus*: **to ~ in with sb's plans** acomodarse con los planes de algn.

▶**fall off** *vi* caerse; (*diminish*) disminuir.

▶**fall out** *vi* (*friends etc*) reñir; (*MIL*) romper filas.

▶**fall over** *vi* caer(se).

▶**fall through** *vi* (*plan, project*) fracasar.

fallacy ['fæləsɪ] *n* error *m*.

fallback position ['fɔ:lbæk-] *n* posición *f* de repliegue.

fallen ['fɔ:lən] *pp of* **fall**.

fallible ['fæləbl] *adj* falible.

falling ['fɔ:lɪŋ] *adj*: **~ market** mercado en baja.

falling-off ['fɔ:lɪŋ'ɔf] *n* (*reduction*) disminución *f*.

Fallopian tube [fə'ləupɪən-] *n* (*ANAT*) trompa de Falopio.

fallout ['fɔ:laut] *n* lluvia radioactiva.

fallout shelter *n* refugio antinuclear.

fallow ['fæləu] *adj* (*land, field*) en barbecho.

false [fɔ:ls] *adj* (*gen*) falso; (*teeth etc*)

postizo; (*disloyal*) desleal, traidor(a);
under ~ **pretences** con engaños.
false alarm *n* falsa alarma.
falsehood ['fɔːlshud] *n* falsedad *f*.
falsely ['fɔːlslɪ] *adv* falsamente.
false teeth *npl* (*BRIT*) dentadura *sg* postiza.
falsify ['fɔːlsɪfaɪ] *vt* falsificar.
falter ['fɔːltə*] *vi* vacilar.
fame [feɪm] *n* fama.
familiar [fə'mɪlɪə*] *adj* familiar; (*well-known*) conocido; (*tone*) de confianza; **to be ~ with** (*subject*) estar enterado de; **to make o.s. ~ with** familiarizarse con; **to be on ~ terms with sb** tener confianza con algn.
familiarity [fəmɪlɪ'ærɪtɪ] *n* familiaridad *f*.
familiarize [fə'mɪlɪəraɪz] *vt*: **to ~ o.s. with** familiarizarse con.
family ['fæmɪlɪ] *n* familia.
family allowance *n subsidio que se recibe por cada hijo*.
family business *n* negocio familiar.
family credit *n* (*BRIT*) ≈ ayuda familiar.
family doctor *n* médico/a de cabecera.
family life *n* vida doméstica *or* familiar.
family man *n* (*home-loving*) hombre *m* casero; (*having family*) padre *m* de familia.
family planning *n* planificación *f* familiar.
family planning clinic *n* clínica de planificación familiar.
family tree *n* árbol *m* genealógico.
famine ['fæmɪn] *n* hambre *f*, hambruna.
famished ['fæmɪʃt] *adj* hambriento; **I'm ~!** (*col*) ¡estoy muerto de hambre!, ¡tengo un hambre canina!
famous ['feɪməs] *adj* famoso, célebre.
famously ['feɪməslɪ] *adv* (*get on*) estupendamente.
fan [fæn] *n* abanico; (*ELEC*) ventilador *m*; (*person*) aficionado/a; (*SPORT*) hincha *m/f*; (*of pop star*) fan *m/f* ♦ *vt* abanicar; (*fire, quarrel*) atizar.
▶**fan out** *vi* desplegarse.
fanatic [fə'nætɪk] *n* fanático/a.
fanatical [fə'nætɪkəl] *adj* fanático.
fan belt *n* correa de ventilador.
fancied ['fænsɪd] *adj* imaginario.
fanciful ['fænsɪful] *adj* (*gen*) fantástico; (*imaginary*) fantasioso; (*design*) rebuscado.
fan club *n* club *m* de fans.
fancy ['fænsɪ] *n* (*whim*) capricho, antojo; (*imagination*) imaginación *f* ♦ *adj* (*luxury*) de lujo; (*price*) exorbitado ♦ *vt* (*feel like, want*) tener ganas de; (*imagine*) imaginarse, figurarse; **to take a ~ to sb** tomar cariño a algn; **when the ~ takes him** cuando se le antoja; **it took** *or* **caught**

my ~ me cayó en gracia; **to ~ that** ... imaginarse que ...; **he fancies her** le gusta (ella) mucho.
fancy dress *n* disfraz *m*.
fancy-dress ball ['fænsɪdrɛs-] *n* baile *m* de disfraces.
fancy goods *n* artículos *mpl* de fantasía.
fanfare ['fænfɛə*] *n* fanfarria (de trompeta).
fanfold paper ['fænfəuld-] *n* papel *m* plegado en abanico *or* en acordeón.
fang [fæŋ] *n* colmillo.
fan heater *n* calefactor *m* de aire.
fanlight ['fænlaɪt] *n* (montante *m* en) abanico.
fanny ['fænɪ] *n* (*BRIT col!*) chocho (*!*); (*US col*) pompis *m*, culo.
fantasize ['fæntəsaɪz] *vi* fantasear, hacerse ilusiones.
fantastic [fæn'tæstɪk] *adj* fantástico.
fantasy ['fæntəzɪ] *n* fantasía.
fanzine ['fænziːn] *n* fanzine *m*.
FAQ *abbr* (= *free alongside quay*) franco sobre muelle.
FAQs *npl abbr* (= *frequently asked questions*) preguntas *fpl* frecuentes.
far [fɑː*] *adj* (*distant*) lejano ♦ *adv* lejos; **the ~ left/right** (*POL*) la extrema izquierda/derecha; **~ away, ~ off** (a lo) lejos; **~ better** mucho mejor; **~ from** lejos de; **by ~ con** mucho; **it's by ~ the best** es con mucho el mejor; **go as ~ as the farm** vaya hasta la granja; **is it ~ to London?** ¿a cuánto está Londres?; **it's not ~ (from here)** no está lejos (de aquí); **as ~ as I know** que yo sepa; **how ~ have you got with your work?** ¿hasta dónde has llegado en tu trabajo?
faraway ['fɑːrəweɪ] *adj* remoto; (*look*) ausente, perdido.
farce [fɑːs] *n* farsa.
farcical ['fɑːsɪkəl] *adj* absurdo.
fare [fɛə*] *n* (*on trains, buses*) precio (del billete); (*in taxi: cost*) tarifa; (: *passenger*) pasajero; (*food*) comida; **half/full ~** medio billete *m*/billete *m* completo.
Far East *n*: **the ~** el Extremo *or* Lejano Oriente.
farewell [fɛə'wɛl] *excl, n* adiós *m*.
far-fetched [fɑː'fetʃt] *adj* inverosímil.
farm [fɑːm] *n* granja, finca, estancia (*LAM*), chacra (*LAM*), rancho (*LAM*) ♦ *vt* cultivar.
▶**farm out** *vt* (*work*): **to ~ out (to sb)** mandar hacer fuera (a algn).
farmer ['fɑːmə*] *n* granjero/a, estanciero/a (*LAM*).
farmhand ['fɑːmhænd] *n* peón *m*.
farmhouse ['fɑːmhaus] *n* granja, casa de

hacienda (*LAM*).

farming ['fɑːmɪŋ] *n* (*gen*) agricultura; (*tilling*) cultivo; **sheep** ~ cría de ovejas.

farm labourer *n* = **farmhand**.

farmland ['fɑːmlænd] *n* tierra de cultivo.

farm produce *n* productos *mpl* agrícolas.

farm worker *n* = **farmhand**.

farmyard ['fɑːmjɑːd] *n* corral *m*.

Faroe Islands ['fɛərəu-], **Faroes** ['fɛərəuz] *npl*: **the** ~ las Islas Feroe.

far-reaching [fɑːˈriːtʃɪŋ] *adj* (*reform, effect*) de gran alcance.

far-sighted [fɑːˈsaɪtɪd] *adj* previsor(a).

fart [fɑːt] (*col!*) *n* pedo (*!*) ♦ *vi* tirarse un pedo (*!*).

farther ['fɑːðə*] *adv* más lejos, más allá ♦ *adj* más lejano.

farthest ['fɑːðɪst] *superlative of* **far**.

FAS *abbr* (= *free alongside ship*) franco al costado del buque.

fascinate ['fæsɪneɪt] *vt* fascinar.

fascinating ['fæsɪneɪtɪŋ] *adj* fascinante.

fascination [fæsɪˈneɪʃən] *n* fascinación *f*.

fascism ['fæʃɪzəm] *n* fascismo.

fascist ['fæʃɪst] *adj, n* fascista *m/f*.

fashion ['fæʃən] *n* moda; (*manner*) manera ♦ *vt* formar; **in** ~ a la moda; **out of** ~ pasado de moda; **in the Greek** ~ a la griega, al estilo griego; **after a** ~ (*finish, manage etc*) en cierto modo.

fashionable ['fæʃnəbl] *adj* de moda; (*writer*) de moda, popular; **it is** ~ **to do ...** está de moda hacer ....

fashion designer *n* diseñador(a) *m/f* de modas, modisto/a.

fashion show *n* desfile *m* de modelos.

fast [fɑːst] *adj* (*also PHOT: film*) rápido; (*dye, colour*) sólido; (*clock*): **to be** ~ estar adelantado ♦ *adv* rápidamente, de prisa; (*stuck, held*) firmemente ♦ *n* ayuno ♦ *vi* ayunar; ~ **asleep** profundamente dormido; **in the** ~ **lane** (*AUT*) en el carril de adelantamiento; **my watch is 5 minutes** ~ mi reloj está adelantado 5 minutos; **as** ~ **as I** *etc* **can** lo más rápido posible; **to make a boat** ~ amarrar una barca.

fasten ['fɑːsn] *vt* asegurar, sujetar; (*coat, belt*) abrochar ♦ *vi* cerrarse.

▶**fasten (up)on** *vt fus* (*idea*) aferrarse a.

fastener ['fɑːsnə*] *n* cierre *m*; (*of door etc*) cerrojo; (*BRIT: zip* ~) cremallera.

fastening ['fɑːsnɪŋ] *n* = **fastener**.

fast food *n* comida rápida, platos *mpl* preparados.

fastidious [fæsˈtɪdɪəs] *adj* (*fussy*) delicado; (*demanding*) exigente.

fat [fæt] *adj* gordo; (*meat*) con mucha grasa;

(*greasy*) grasiento ♦ *n* grasa; (*on person*) carnes *fpl*; (*lard*) manteca; **to live off the** ~ **of the land** vivir a cuerpo de rey.

fatal ['feɪtl] *adj* (*mistake*) fatal; (*injury*) mortal; (*consequence*) funesto.

fatalism ['feɪtəlɪzəm] *n* fatalismo.

fatality [fəˈtælɪtɪ] *n* (*road death etc*) víctima *f* mortal.

fatally ['feɪtəlɪ] *adv*: ~ **injured** herido de muerte.

fate [feɪt] *n* destino, sino.

fated ['feɪtɪd] *adj* predestinado.

fateful ['feɪtful] *adj* fatídico.

fat-free ['fætfriː] *adj* sin grasa.

father ['fɑːðə*] *n* padre *m*.

Father Christmas *n* Papá *m* Noel.

fatherhood ['fɑːðəhud] *n* paternidad *f*.

father-in-law ['fɑːðərɪnlɔː] *n* suegro.

fatherland ['fɑːðəlænd] *n* patria.

fatherly ['fɑːðəlɪ] *adj* paternal.

fathom ['fæðəm] *n* braza ♦ *vt* (*unravel*) desentrañar; (*understand*) explicarse.

fatigue [fəˈtiːg] *n* fatiga, cansancio; **metal** ~ fatiga del metal.

fatness ['fætnɪs] *n* gordura.

fatten ['fætn] *vt, vi* engordar; **chocolate is** ~**ing** el chocolate engorda.

fatty ['fætɪ] *adj* (*food*) graso ♦ *n* (*fam*) gordito/a, gordinflón/ona *m/f*.

fatuous ['fætjuəs] *adj* fatuo, necio.

faucet ['fɔːsɪt] *n* (*US*) grifo, llave *f*, canilla (*LAM*).

fault [fɔːlt] *n* (*blame*) culpa; (*defect: in character*) defecto; (*in manufacture*) desperfecto; (*GEO*) falla ♦ *vt* criticar; **it's my** ~ es culpa mía; **to find** ~ **with** criticar, poner peros a; **at** ~ culpable.

faultless ['fɔːltlɪs] *adj* (*action*) intachable; (*person*) sin defectos.

faulty ['fɔːltɪ] *adj* defectuoso.

fauna ['fɔːnə] *n* fauna.

faux pas ['fəuˈpɑː] *n* desacierto.

favour, (*US*) **favor** ['feɪvə*] *n* favor *m*; (*approval*) aprobación *f* ♦ *vt* (*proposition*) estar a favor de, aprobar; (*person etc*) preferir; (*assist*) favorecer; **to ask a** ~ **of** pedir un favor a; **to do sb a** ~ hacer un favor a algn; **to find** ~ **with sb** (*subj: person*) caerle bien a algn; (: *suggestion*) tener buena acogida por parte de algn; **in** ~ **of** a favor de; **to be in** ~ **of sth/of doing sth** ser partidario *or* estar a favor de algo/de hacer algo.

favo(u)rable ['feɪvərəbl] *adj* favorable.

favo(u)rably ['feɪvərəblɪ] *adv* favorablemente.

favo(u)rite ['feɪvərɪt] *adj, n* favorito/a *m/f*, preferido/a *m/f*.

favo(u)ritism ['feɪvərɪtɪzəm] n favoritismo.
fawn [fɔːn] n cervato ♦ adj (also: ~-
coloured) de color cervato, leonado ♦ vi:
to ~ (up)on adular.
fax [fæks] n fax m ♦ vt mandar or enviar por
fax.
FBI n abbr (US: =Federal Bureau of
Investigation) FBI m.
FCC n abbr (US) = Federal Communications
Commission.
FCO n abbr (BRIT: = Foreign and
Commonwealth Office) ≈ Min. de AA. EE.
FD n abbr (US) = **fire department**.
FDA n abbr (US: = Food and Drug
Administration) oficina que se ocupa del
control de los productos alimentarios y
farmacéuticos.
FE n abbr = **further education**.
fear [fɪə*] n miedo, temor m ♦ vt temer; **for
~ of** por temor a; **~ of heights** vértigo; **to
~ for/that** temer por/que.
fearful ['fɪəful] adj temeroso; (awful)
espantoso; **to be ~ of** (frightened) tener
miedo de.
fearfully ['fɪəfulɪ] adv (timidly) con miedo;
(col: very) terriblemente.
fearless ['fɪəlɪs] adj (gen) sin miedo or
temor; (bold) audaz.
fearlessly ['fɪəlɪslɪ] adv temerariamente.
fearlessness ['fɪəlɪsnɪs] n temeridad f.
fearsome ['fɪəsəm] adj (opponent) temible;
(sight) espantoso.
feasibility [fiːzə'bɪlɪtɪ] n factibilidad f,
viabilidad f.
feasibility study n estudio de viabilidad.
feasible ['fiːzəbl] adj factible, viable.
feast [fiːst] n banquete m; (REL: also: ~ **day**)
fiesta ♦ vi banquetear.
feat [fiːt] n hazaña.
feather ['fɛðə*] n pluma ♦ vt: **to ~ one's
nest** (fig) hacer su agosto, sacar tajada
♦ cpd (mattress, bed, pillow) de plumas.
feather-weight ['fɛðəweɪt] n (BOXING) peso
pluma.
feature ['fiːtʃə*] n (gen) característica;
(ANAT) rasgo; (article) reportaje m ♦ vt
(subj: film) presentar ♦ vi figurar; **~s** npl
(of face) facciones fpl; **a (special) ~ on**
sth/sb un reportaje (especial) sobre
algo/algn; **it ~d prominently in ...** tuvo un
papel destacado en ....
feature film n largometraje m.
Feb. abbr (= February) feb.
February ['fɛbruərɪ] n febrero.
feces ['fiːsiːz] npl (US) = **faeces**.
feckless ['fɛklɪs] adj irresponsable,
irreflexivo.
Fed abbr (US) = **federal, federation**.

fed [fɛd] pt, pp of **feed**.
Fed. [fɛd] n abbr (US col) = Federal Reserve
Board.
federal ['fɛdərəl] adj federal.
Federal Republic of Germany n
República Federal de Alemania.
federation [fɛdə'reɪʃən] n federación f.
fed-up [fɛd'ʌp] adj: **to be ~ (with)** estar
harto (de).
fee [fiː] n (professional) honorarios mpl; (for
examination) derechos mpl; (of school)
matrícula; (membership ~) cuota;
(entrance ~) entrada; **for a small ~** por
poco dinero.
feeble ['fiːbl] adj débil.
feeble-minded [fiːbl'maɪndɪd] adj imbécil.
feed [fiːd] n (gen, of baby) comida; (of
animal) pienso; (on printer) dispositivo de
alimentación ♦ vt (pt, pp **fed**) (gen)
alimentar; (BRIT: breastfeed) dar el pecho
a; (animal, baby) dar de comer a ♦ vi (baby,
animal) comer.
▶**feed back** vt (results) pasar.
▶**feed in** vt (COMPUT) introducir.
▶**feed into** vt (data, information)
suministrar a; **to ~ sth into a machine**
introducir algo en una máquina.
▶**feed on** vt fus alimentarse de.
feedback ['fiːdbæk] n (from person)
reacción f; (TECH) realimentación f,
feedback m.
feeder ['fiːdə*] n (bib) babero.
feeding bottle ['fiːdɪŋ-] n (BRIT) biberón m.
feel [fiːl] n (sensation) sensación f; (sense of
touch) tacto ♦ vt (pt, pp **felt**) tocar; (cold,
pain etc) sentir; (think, believe) creer; **to
get the ~ of sth** (fig) acostumbrarse a
algo; **to ~ hungry/cold** tener hambre/
frío; **to ~ lonely/better** sentirse solo/
mejor; **I don't ~ well** no me siento bien; **it
~s soft** es suave al tacto; **it ~s colder out
here** se siente más frío aquí fuera; **to ~
like** (want) tener ganas de; **I'm still ~ing
my way** (fig) todavía me estoy
orientando; **I ~ that you ought to do it**
creo que debes hacerlo; **to ~ about or
around** vi tantear.
feeler ['fiːlə*] n (of insect) antena; **to put out
~s** (fig) tantear el terreno.
feeling ['fiːlɪŋ] n (physical) sensación f;
(foreboding) presentimiento; (impression)
impresión f; (emotion) sentimiento; **what
are your ~s about the matter?** ¿qué
opinas tú del asunto?; **to hurt sb's ~s**
herir los sentimientos de algn; **~s ran
high about it** causó mucha controversia; **I
got the ~ that ...** me dio la impresión de
que ...; **there was a general ~ that ...** la

opinión general fue que ....

fee-paying school ['fiːpeɪɪŋ-] n colegio de pago.

feet [fiːt] npl of **foot**.

feign [feɪn] vt fingir.

feigned [feɪnd] adj fingido.

feline ['fiːlaɪn] adj felino.

fell [fɛl] pt of **fall** ♦ vt (tree) talar ♦ adj: **with one ~ blow** con un golpe feroz; **at one ~ swoop** de un solo golpe ♦ n (BRIT: mountain) montaña; (: moorland): **the ~s** los páramos.

fellow ['fɛləu] n tipo, tío (SP); (of learned society) socio/a; (UNIV) miembro de la junta de gobierno de un colegio ♦ cpd: **~ students** compañeros/as m/fpl de curso, condiscípulos/as m/fpl.

fellow citizen n conciudadano/a.

fellow countryman n compatriota m.

fellow feeling n compañerismo.

fellow men npl semejantes mpl.

fellowship ['fɛləuʃɪp] n compañerismo; (grant) beca.

fellow traveller n compañero/a de viaje; (POL: with communists) simpatizante m/f.

fellow worker n colega m/f.

felon ['fɛlən] n criminal m/f.

felony ['fɛlənɪ] n crimen m, delito mayor.

felt [fɛlt] pt, pp of **feel** ♦ n fieltro.

felt-tip pen ['fɛlttɪp-] n rotulador m.

female ['fiːmeɪl] n (woman) mujer f; (ZOOL) hembra ♦ adj femenino.

feminine ['fɛmɪnɪn] adj femenino.

femininity [fɛmɪ'nɪnɪtɪ] n feminidad f.

feminism ['fɛmɪnɪzəm] n feminismo.

feminist ['fɛmɪnɪst] n feminista m/f.

fence [fɛns] n valla, cerca; (RACING) valla ♦ vt (also: **~ in**) cercar ♦ vi hacer esgrima; **to sit on the ~** (fig) nadar entre dos aguas.

▶**fence in** vt cercar.

▶**fence off** vt separar con cerca.

fencing ['fɛnsɪŋ] n esgrima.

fend [fɛnd] vi: **to ~ for o.s.** valerse por sí mismo.

▶**fend off** vt (attack, attacker) rechazar, repeler; (blow) desviar; (awkward question) esquivar.

fender ['fɛndə*] n pantalla; (US: AUT) parachoques m inv; (: RAIL) trompa.

fennel ['fɛnl] n hinojo.

Fens [fɛnz] npl (BRIT): **the ~** las tierras bajas de Norfolk (antiguamente zona de marismas).

ferment vi [fə'mɛnt] fermentar ♦ n ['fɔːmɛnt] (fig) agitación f.

fermentation [fɔːmɛn'teɪʃən] n fermentación f.

fern [fɔːn] n helecho.

ferocious [fə'rəuʃəs] adj feroz.

ferociously [fə'rəuʃəslɪ] adv ferozmente, con ferocidad.

ferocity [fə'rɔsɪtɪ] n ferocidad f.

ferret ['fɛrɪt] n hurón m.

▶**ferret about, ferret around** vi rebuscar.

▶**ferret out** vt (secret, truth) desentrañar.

ferry ['fɛrɪ] n (small) barca (de pasaje), balsa; (large: also: **~boat**) transbordador m, ferry m ♦ vt transportar; **to ~ sth/sb across** or **over** transportar algo/a algn a la otra orilla; **to ~ sb to and fro** llevar a algn de un lado para otro.

ferryman ['fɛrɪmən] n barquero.

fertile ['fɔːtaɪl] adj fértil; (BIOL) fecundo.

fertility [fə'tɪlɪtɪ] n fertilidad f; fecundidad f.

fertility drug n medicamento contra la infertilidad.

fertilization [fɔːtɪlaɪ'zeɪʃən] n fertilización f; (BIOL) fecundación f.

fertilize ['fɔːtɪlaɪz] vt fertilizar; (BIOL) fecundar; (AGR) abonar.

fertilizer ['fɔːtɪlaɪzə*] n abono, fertilizante m.

fervent ['fɔːvənt] adj ferviente.

fervour, (US) fervor ['fɔːvə*] n fervor m, ardor m.

fester ['fɛstə*] vi supurar.

festival ['fɛstɪvəl] n (REL) fiesta; (ART, MUS) festival m.

festive ['fɛstɪv] adj festivo; **the ~ season** (BRIT: Christmas) las Navidades.

festivities [fɛs'tɪvɪtɪz] npl festejos mpl.

festoon [fɛs'tuːn] vt: **to ~ with** festonear or engalanar de.

fetch [fɛtʃ] vt ir a buscar; (BRIT: sell for) venderse por; **how much did it ~?** ¿por cuánto se vendió?

▶**fetch up** vi ir a parar.

fetching ['fɛtʃɪŋ] adj atractivo.

fête [feɪt] n fiesta.

fetid ['fɛtɪd] adj fétido.

fetish ['fɛtɪʃ] n fetiche m.

fetter ['fɛtə*] vt (person) encadenar, poner grillos a; (horse) trabar; (fig) poner trabas a.

fetters ['fɛtəz] npl grillos mpl.

fettle ['fɛtl] n: **in fine ~** en buenas condiciones.

fetus ['fiːtəs] n (US) = **foetus**.

feud [fjuːd] n (hostility) enemistad f; (quarrel) disputa; **a family ~** una pelea familiar.

feudal ['fjuːdl] adj feudal.

feudalism ['fjuːdəlɪzəm] n feudalismo.

fever ['fiːvə*] n fiebre f; **he has a ~** tiene

fiebre.

feverish ['fiːvərɪʃ] *adj* febril.

feverishly ['fiːvərɪʃlɪ] *adv* febrilmente.

few [fjuː] *adj* (*not many*) pocos; (*some*) algunos, unos ♦ *pron* algunos; **a ~** *adj* unos pocos; **~ people** poca gente; **a good ~**, **quite a ~** bastantes; **in** *or* **over the next ~ days** en los próximos días; **every ~ weeks** cada 2 o 3 semanas; **a ~ more days** unos días más.

fewer ['fjuːə*] *adj* menos.

fewest ['fjuːɪst] *adj* los/las menos.

FFA *n abbr* = *Future Farmers of America*.

FH *abbr* (*BRIT*) = **fire hydrant**.

FHA *n abbr* (*US*: = *Federal Housing Association*) *oficina federal de la vivienda*.

fiancé [fɪˈɑːŋseɪ] *n* novio, prometido.

fiancée [fɪˈɑːŋseɪ] *n* novia, prometida.

fiasco [fɪˈæskəu] *n* fiasco.

fib [fɪb] *n* mentirijilla ♦ *vi* decir mentirijillas.

fibre, (*US*) **fiber** ['faɪbə*] *n* fibra.

fibreboard, (*US*) **fiberboard** ['faɪbəbɔːd] *n* fibra vulcanizada.

fibreglass, (*US*) **fiberglass** ['faɪbəglɑːs] *n* fibra de vidrio.

fibrositis [faɪbrəˈsaɪtɪs] *n* fibrositis *f inv*.

FICA *n abbr* (*US*) = *Federal Insurance Contributions Act*.

fickle ['fɪkl] *adj* inconstante.

fiction ['fɪkʃən] *n* (*gen*) ficción *f*.

fictional ['fɪkʃənl] *adj* novelesco.

fictionalize ['fɪkʃənəlaɪz] *vt* novelar.

fictitious [fɪkˈtɪʃəs] *adj* ficticio.

fiddle ['fɪdl] *n* (*MUS*) violín *m*; (*cheating*) trampa ♦ *vt* (*BRIT: accounts*) falsificar; **tax ~** evasión *f* fiscal; **to work a ~** hacer trampa.

►**fiddle with** *vt fus* juguetear con.

fiddler ['fɪdlə*] *n* violinista *m/f*.

fiddly ['fɪdlɪ] *adj* (*task*) delicado, mañoso; (*object*) enrevesado.

fidelity [fɪˈdɛlɪtɪ] *n* fidelidad *f*.

fidget ['fɪdʒɪt] *vi* moverse (nerviosamente).

fidgety ['fɪdʒɪtɪ] *adj* nervioso.

fiduciary [fɪˈduːʃɪərɪ] *n* fiduciario/a.

field [fiːld] *n* (*gen*, *COMPUT*) campo; (*fig*) campo, esfera; (*SPORT*) campo, cancha (*LAM*); (*competitors*) competidores *mpl* ♦ *cpd*: **to have a ~ day** (*fig*) ponerse las botas; **to lead the ~** (*SPORT*, *COMM*) llevar la delantera; **to give sth a year's trial in the ~** (*fig*) sacar algo al mercado a prueba por un año; **my particular ~** mi especialidad.

field glasses *npl* gemelos *mpl*.

field hospital *n* hospital *m* de campaña.

field marshal *n* mariscal *m*.

fieldwork ['fiːldwɜːk] *n* (*ARCHAEOLOGY*, *GEO*) trabajo de campo.

fiend [fiːnd] *n* demonio.

fiendish ['fiːndɪʃ] *adj* diabólico.

fierce [fɪəs] *adj* feroz; (*wind, attack*) violento; (*heat*) intenso; (*fighting, enemy*) encarnizado.

fiercely ['fɪəslɪ] *adv* con ferocidad; violentamente; intensamente; encarnizadamente.

fierceness ['fɪəsnɪs] *n* ferocidad *f*; violencia; intensidad *f*; encarnizamiento.

fiery ['faɪərɪ] *adj* (*burning*) ardiente; (*temperament*) apasionado.

FIFA ['fiːfə] *n abbr* (= *Fédération Internationale de Football Association*) FIFA *f*.

fifteen [fɪfˈtiːn] *num* quince.

fifth [fɪfθ] *num* quinto.

fiftieth ['fɪftɪɪθ] *num* quincuagésimo.

fifty ['fɪftɪ] *num* cincuenta; **the fifties** los años cincuenta; **to be in one's fifties** andar por los cincuenta.

fifty-fifty ['fɪftɪ'fɪftɪ] *adv*: **to go ~ with sb** ir a medias con algn ♦ *adj*: **we have a ~ chance of success** tenemos un cincuenta por ciento de posibilidades de tener éxito.

fig [fɪg] *n* higo.

fight [faɪt] *n* (*gen*) pelea; (*MIL*) combate *m*; (*struggle*) lucha ♦ *vb* (*pt, pp* **fought**) *vt* luchar contra; (*cancer, alcoholism*) combatir; (*LAW*): **to ~ a case** defenderse; (*quarrel*): **to ~ (with sb)** pelear (con algn) ♦ *vi* pelear, luchar; (*fig*): **to ~ (for/against)** luchar por/contra.

►**fight back** *vi* defenderse; (*after illness*) recuperarse ♦ *vt* (*tears*) contener.

►**fight down** *vt* (*anger, anxiety, urge*) reprimir.

►**fight off** *vt* (*attack, attacker*) rechazar; (*disease, sleep, urge*) luchar contra.

►**fight out** *vt*: **to ~ it out** decidirlo en una pelea.

fighter ['faɪtə*] *n* combatiente *m/f*; (*fig*) luchador(a) *m/f*; (*plane*) caza *m*.

fighter-bomber ['faɪtəbɒmə*] *n* cazabombardero.

fighter pilot *n* piloto de caza.

fighting ['faɪtɪŋ] *n* (*gen*) el luchar; (*battle*) combate *m*; (*in streets*) disturbios *mpl*.

figment ['fɪgmənt] *n*: **a ~ of the imagination** un producto de la imaginación.

figurative ['fɪgjurətɪv] *adj* (*meaning*) figurado; (*ART*) figurativo.

figure ['fɪgə*] *n* (*DRAWING, GEOM*) figura,

dibujo; (*number, cipher*) cifra; (*person, outline*) figura; (*body shape*) línea; (: *attractive*) tipo ♦ *vt* (*esp US: think, calculate*) calcular, imaginarse ♦ *vi* (*appear*) figurar; (*esp US: make sense*) ser lógico; ~ **of speech** (*LING*) figura retórica; **public** ~ personaje *m*.
▶**figure on** *vt fus* (*US*) contar con.
▶**figure out** *vt* (*understand*) comprender.
figurehead ['fɪɡəhɛd] *n* (*fig*) figura decorativa.
figure skating *n* patinaje *m* artístico.
Fiji (Islands) ['fi:dʒi:-] *n*(*pl*) (Islas *fpl*) Fiji *fpl*.
filament ['fɪləmənt] *n* (*ELEC*) filamento.
filch [fɪltʃ] *vt* (*col: steal*) birlar.
file [faɪl] *n* (*tool*) lima; (*for nails*) lima de uñas; (*dossier*) expediente *m*; (*folder*) carpeta; (*in cabinet*) archivo; (*COMPUT*) fichero; (*row*) fila ♦ *vt* limar; (*papers*) clasificar; (*LAW: claim*) presentar; (*store*) archivar; **to open/close a** ~ (*COMPUT*) abrir/cerrar un fichero; **to** ~ **in/out** *vi* entrar/salir en fila; **to** ~ **a suit against sb** entablar pleito contra algn; **to** ~ **past** desfilar ante.
file name *n* (*COMPUT*) nombre *m* de fichero.
filibuster ['fɪlɪbʌstə*] (*esp US: POL*) *n* obstruccionista *m/f*, filibustero/a ♦ *vi* usar maniobras obstruccionistas.
filing ['faɪlɪŋ] *n*: **to do the** ~ llevar los archivos.
filing cabinet *n* fichero, archivo.
filing clerk *n* oficinista *m/f*.
fill [fɪl] *vt* llenar; (*tooth*) empastar; (*vacancy*) cubrir ♦ *n*: **to eat one's** ~ comer hasta hartarse; **we've already** ~**ed that vacancy** ya hemos cubierto esa vacante; ~**ed with admiration (for)** lleno de admiración (por).
▶**fill in** *vt* rellenar; (*details, report*) completar; **to** ~ **sb in on sth** (*col*) poner a algn al corriente *or* al día sobre algo.
▶**fill out** *vt* (*form, receipt*) rellenar.
▶**fill up** *vt* llenar (hasta el borde) ♦ *vi* (*AUT*) echar gasolina.
fillet ['fɪlɪt] *n* filete *m*.
fillet steak *n* filete *m* de ternera.
filling ['fɪlɪŋ] *n* (*CULIN*) relleno; (*for tooth*) empaste *m*.
filling station *n* estación *f* de servicio.
fillip ['fɪlɪp] *n* estímulo.
filly ['fɪlɪ] *n* potra.
film [fɪlm] *n* película ♦ *vt* (*scene*) filmar ♦ *vi* rodar.
film script *n* guión *m*.
film star *n* estrella de cine.
filmstrip ['fɪlmstrɪp] *n* tira de diapositivas.

film studio *n* estudio de cine.
Filofax ® ['faɪləufæks] *n* agenda (profesional).
filter ['fɪltə*] *n* filtro ♦ *vt* filtrar.
▶**filter in, filter through** *vi* filtrarse.
filter coffee *n* café *m* (molido) para filtrar.
filter lane *n* (*BRIT*) carril *m* de selección.
filter-tipped ['fɪltətɪpt] *adj* con filtro.
filth [fɪlθ] *n* suciedad *f*.
filthy ['fɪlθɪ] *adj* sucio; (*language*) obsceno.
fin [fɪn] *n* (*gen*) aleta.
final ['faɪnl] *adj* (*last*) final, último; (*definitive*) definitivo ♦ *n* (*SPORT*) final *f*; ~**s** *npl* (*SCOL*) exámenes *mpl* finales; ~ **demand** (*on invoice etc*) último aviso; ~ **dividend** dividendo final.
finale [fɪˈnɑːlɪ] *n* final *m*.
finalist ['faɪnəlɪst] *n* (*SPORT*) finalista *m/f*.
finality [faɪˈnælɪtɪ] *n* finalidad *f*; **with an air of** ~ en tono resuelto, de modo terminante.
finalize ['faɪnəlaɪz] *vt* ultimar.
finally ['faɪnəlɪ] *adv* (*lastly*) por último, finalmente; (*eventually*) por fin; (*irrevocably*) de modo definitivo; (*once and for all*) definitivamente.
finance [faɪˈnæns] *n* (*money, funds*) fondos *mpl*; ~**s** *npl* finanzas *fpl* ♦ *cpd* (*page, section, company*) financiero ♦ *vt* financiar.
financial [faɪˈnænʃəl] *adj* financiero.
financially [faɪˈnænʃəlɪ] *adv* económicamente.
financial management *n* gestión *f* financiera.
financial statement *n* estado financiero.
financial year *n* ejercicio (financiero).
financier [faɪˈnænsɪə*] *n* financiero/a.
find [faɪnd] *vt* (*pt, pp* **found** [faund]) (*gen*) encontrar, hallar; (*come upon*) descubrir ♦ *n* hallazgo; descubrimiento; **to** ~ **sb guilty** (*LAW*) declarar culpable a algn; **I** ~ **it easy** me resulta fácil.
▶**find out** *vt* averiguar; (*truth, secret*) descubrir ♦ *vi*: **to** ~ **out about** enterarse de.
findings ['faɪndɪŋz] *npl* (*LAW*) veredicto *sg*, fallo *sg*; (*of report*) recomendaciones *fpl*.
fine [faɪn] *adj* (*delicate*) fino; (*beautiful*) hermoso ♦ *adv* (*well*) bien ♦ *n* (*LAW*) multa ♦ *vt* (*LAW*) multar; **the weather is** ~ hace buen tiempo; **he's** ~ está muy bien; **you're doing** ~ lo estás haciendo muy bien; **to cut it** ~ (*of time, money*) calcular muy justo; **to get a** ~ **for (doing) sth** recibir una multa por (hacer) algo.
fine arts *npl* bellas artes *fpl*.
finely ['faɪnlɪ] *adv* (*splendidly*) con elegancia; (*chop*) en trozos pequeños,

fino; (*adjust*) con precisión.
fineness ['faɪnnɪs] *n* (*of cloth*) finura.
fine print *n*: **the** ~ la letra pequeña *or* menuda.
finery ['faɪnərɪ] *n* galas *fpl*.
finesse [fɪ'nɛs] *n* sutileza.
fine-tooth comb ['faɪntuːθ-] *n*: **to go through sth with a** ~ revisar algo a fondo.
finger ['fɪŋgə*] *n* dedo ♦ *vt* (*touch*) manosear; (*MUS*) puntear; **little/index** ~ (dedo) meñique *m*/índice *m*.
fingernail ['fɪŋgəneɪl] *n* uña.
fingerprint ['fɪŋgəprɪnt] *n* huella dactilar ♦ *vt* tomar las huellas dactilares de.
fingertip ['fɪŋgətɪp] *n* yema del dedo; **to have sth at one's** ~**s** saberse algo al dedillo.
finicky ['fɪnɪkɪ] *adj* (*fussy*) delicado.
finish ['fɪnɪʃ] *n* (*end*) fin *m*; (*SPORT*) meta; (*polish etc*) acabado ♦ *vt, vi* acabar, terminar; **to** ~ **doing sth** acabar de hacer algo; **to** ~ **first/second/third** (*SPORT*) llegar el primero/segundo/tercero; **I've** ~**ed with the paper** he terminado con el periódico; **she's** ~**ed with him** ha roto *or* acabado con él.
▶**finish off** *vt* acabar, terminar; (*kill*) rematar.
▶**finish up** *vt* acabar, terminar ♦ *vi* ir a parar, terminar.
finished ['fɪnɪʃt] *adj* (*product*) acabado; (*performance*) pulido; (*col: tired*) rendido, hecho polvo.
finishing ['fɪnɪʃɪŋ] *adj*: ~ **touches** toque *m* final.
finishing line *n* línea de llegada *or* meta.
finishing school *n* colegio para la educación social de señoritas.
finite ['faɪnaɪt] *adj* finito.
Finland ['fɪnlənd] *n* Finlandia.
Finn [fɪn] *n* finlandés/esa *m/f*.
Finnish ['fɪnɪʃ] *adj* finlandés/esa ♦ *n* (*LING*) finlandés *m*.
fiord [fjɔːd] *n* fiordo.
fir [fəː*] *n* abeto.
fire ['faɪə*] *n* fuego; (*accidental, damaging*) incendio ♦ *vt* (*gun*) disparar; (*set fire to*) incendiar; (*excite*) exaltar; (*interest*) despertar; (*dismiss*) despedir ♦ *vi* encenderse; (*AUT: subj: engine*) encender; **electric/gas** ~ estufa eléctrica/de gas; **on** ~ ardiendo, en llamas; **to be on** ~ estar ardiendo; **to catch** ~ prenderse fuego; **to set** ~ **to sth, set sth on** ~ prender fuego a algo; **insured against** ~ asegurado contra incendios; **to be/come under** ~ estar/caer bajo el fuego enemigo.

fire alarm *n* alarma de incendios.
firearm ['faɪərɑːm] *n* arma de fuego.
fire brigade, (*US*) **fire department** *n* (cuerpo de) bomberos *mpl*.
fire door *n* puerta contra incendios.
fire drill *n* (ejercicio de) simulacro de incendio.
fire engine *n* coche *m* de bomberos.
fire escape *n* escalera de incendios.
fire extinguisher *n* extintor *m*.
fireguard ['faɪəgɑːd] *n* pantalla (guardallama).
fire hazard *n* = **fire risk**.
fire hydrant *n* boca de incendios.
fire insurance *n* seguro contra incendios.
fireman ['faɪəmən] *n* bombero.
fireplace ['faɪəpleɪs] *n* chimenea.
fireplug ['faɪəplʌg] *n* (*US*) boca de incendios.
fire practice *n* = **fire drill**.
fireproof ['faɪəpruːf] *adj* a prueba de fuego; (*material*) incombustible.
fire regulations *npl* reglamentos *mpl* contra incendios.
fire risk *n* peligro de incendio.
firescreen ['faɪəskriːn] *n* pantalla refractaria.
fireside ['faɪəsaɪd] *n*: **by the** ~ al lado de la chimenea.
fire station *n* parque *m* de bomberos.
firewall ['faɪəwɔːl] *n* (*INTERNET*) firewall *m*.
firewood ['faɪəwud] *n* leña.
fireworks ['faɪəwəːks] *npl* fuegos *mpl* artificiales.
firing ['faɪərɪŋ] *n* (*MIL*) disparos *mpl*, tiroteo.
firing line *n* línea de fuego; **to be in the** ~ (*fig: liable to be criticised*) estar en la línea de fuego.
firing squad *n* pelotón *m* de ejecución.
firm [fəːm] *adj* firme; (*offer, decision*) en firme ♦ *n* empresa; **to be a** ~ **believer in sth** ser un partidario convencido de algo; **to stand** ~ *or* **take a** ~ **stand on sth** (*fig*) mantenerse firme ante algo.
firmly ['fəːmlɪ] *adv* firmemente.
firmness ['fəːmnɪs] *n* firmeza.
first [fəːst] *adj* primero ♦ *adv* (*before others*) primero; (*when listing reasons etc*) en primer lugar, primeramente ♦ *n* (*person: in race*) primero/a; (*AUT: also:* ~ **gear**) primera; **at** ~ al principio; ~ **of all** ante todo; **the** ~ **of January** el uno *or* primero de enero; **in the** ~ **instance** en primer lugar; **I'll do it** ~ **thing tomorrow** lo haré mañana a primera hora; **for the** ~ **time** por primera vez; **head** ~ de cabeza; **from the (very)** ~ desde el principio.
first aid *n* primeros auxilios *mpl*.

first aid kit *n* botiquín *m*.
first aid post, (*US*) **first aid station** *n* puesto de auxilio.
first-class ['fəːstklɑːs] *adj* de primera clase; ~ **ticket** (*RAIL etc*) billete *m or* boleto (*LAM*) de primera clase; ~ **mail** correo de primera clase.
first-hand [fəːst'hænd] *adj* de primera mano.
first lady *n* (*esp US*) primera dama.
firstly ['fəːstlɪ] *adv* en primer lugar.
first name *n* nombre *m* de pila.
first night *n* estreno.
first-rate [fəːst'reɪt] *adj* de primera (clase).
first-time buyer [fəːsttaɪm-] *n persona que compra su primera vivienda*.
fir tree *n* abeto.
FIS *n abbr* (*BRIT*: = *Family Income Supplement*) *ayuda estatal familiar*.
fiscal ['fɪskəl] *adj* fiscal; ~ **year** año fiscal, ejercicio.
fish [fɪʃ] *n*, *pl inv* pez *m*; (*food*) pescado ♦ *vt* pescar en ♦ *vi* pescar; **to go ~ing** ir de pesca.
►**fish out** *vt* (*from water, box etc*) sacar.
fish-and-chip shop *n* = **chip shop**.
fishbone ['fɪʃbəun] *n* espina.
fisherman ['fɪʃəmən] *n* pescador *m*.
fishery ['fɪʃərɪ] *n* pesquería.
fish factory *n* fábrica de elaboración de pescado.
fish farm *n* piscifactoría.
fish fingers *npl* (*BRIT*) palitos *mpl* de pescado (empanado).
fishing boat ['fɪʃɪŋ-] *n* barca de pesca.
fishing industry *n* industria pesquera.
fishing line *n* sedal *m*.
fishing net *n* red *f* de pesca.
fishing rod *n* caña (de pescar).
fishing tackle *n* aparejo (de pescar).
fish market *n* mercado de pescado.
fishmonger ['fɪʃmʌŋgə*] *n* (*BRIT*) pescadero/a.
fishmonger's (shop) *n* (*BRIT*) pescadería.
fishseller ['fɪʃselə*] *n* (*US*) = **fishmonger**.
fish slice *n* paleta para pescado.
fish sticks *npl* (*US*) = **fish fingers**.
fishstore ['fɪʃstɔː*] *n* (*US*) = **fishmonger's (shop)**.
fishy ['fɪʃɪ] *adj* (*fig*) sospechoso.
fission ['fɪʃən] *n* fisión *f*; **atomic/nuclear ~** fisión *f* atómica/nuclear.
fissure ['fɪʃə*] *n* fisura.
fist [fɪst] *n* puño.
fistfight ['fɪstfaɪt] *n* lucha a puñetazos.
fit [fɪt] *adj* (*MED, SPORT*) en (buena) forma; (*proper*) adecuado, apropiado ♦ *vt* (*subj: clothes*) quedar bien a; (*try on: clothes*)

probar; (*match: facts*) cuadrar *or* corresponder *or* coincidir con; (*description*) estar de acuerdo con; (*accommodate*) ajustar, adaptar ♦ *vi* (*clothes*) quedar bien; (*in space, gap*) caber; (*facts*) coincidir ♦ *n* (*MED*) ataque *m*; (*outburst*) arranque *m*; ~ **to** apto para; ~ **for** apropiado para; **do as you think** *or* **see** ~ haz lo que te parezca mejor; **to keep** ~ mantenerse en forma; **to be** ~ **for work** (*after illness*) estar en condiciones para trabajar; ~ **of coughing** acceso de tos; ~ **of anger/enthusiasm** arranque de cólera/entusiasmo; **to have** *or* **suffer a** ~ tener un ataque *or* acceso; **this dress is a good** ~ este vestido me queda bien; **by** ~**s and starts** a rachas.
►**fit in** *vi* encajar ♦ *vt* (*object*) acomodar; (*fig: appointment, visitor*) encontrar un hueco para; **to** ~ **in with sb's plans** acomodarse a los planes de algn.
►**fit out** *vt* (*BRIT: also:* **fit up**) equipar.
fitful ['fɪtful] *adj* espasmódico, intermitente.
fitfully ['fɪtfəlɪ] *adv* irregularmente; **to sleep** ~ dormir a rachas.
fitment ['fɪtmənt] *n* mueble *m*.
fitness ['fɪtnɪs] *n* (*MED*) forma física; (*of remark*) conveniencia.
fitted carpet ['fɪtɪd-] *n* moqueta.
fitted cupboards ['fɪtɪd-] *npl* armarios *mpl* empotrados.
fitted kitchen ['fɪtɪd-] *n* cocina amueblada.
fitter ['fɪtə*] *n* ajustador(a) *m/f*.
fitting ['fɪtɪŋ] *adj* apropiado ♦ *n* (*of dress*) prueba; *see also* **fittings**.
fitting room *n* (*in shop*) probador *m*.
fittings ['fɪtɪŋz] *npl* instalaciones *fpl*.
five [faɪv] *num* cinco; **she is** ~ **(years old)** tiene cinco años (de edad); **it costs** ~ **pounds** cuesta cinco libras; **it's** ~ **(o'clock)** son las cinco.
five-day week ['faɪvdeɪ] *n* semana inglesa.
fiver ['faɪvə*] *n* (*col: BRIT*) billete *m* de cinco libras; (: *US*) billete *m* de cinco dólares.
fix [fɪks] *vt* (*secure*) fijar, asegurar; (*mend*) arreglar; (*make ready: meal, drink*) preparar ♦ *n*: **to be in a** ~ estar en un aprieto; **to** ~ **sth in one's mind** fijar algo en la memoria; **the fight was a** ~ (*col*) la pelea estaba amañada.
►**fix on** *vt* (*decide on*) fijar.
►**fix up** *vt* (*arrange: date, meeting*) arreglar; **to** ~ **sb up with sth** conseguirle algo a algn.
fixation [fɪk'seɪʃən] *n* (*PSYCH, fig*) fijación *f*.
fixative ['fɪksətɪv] *n* fijador *m*.
fixed [fɪkst] *adj* (*prices etc*) fijo; **how are you**

~ **for money?** (col) ¿qué tal andas de dinero?

fixed assets npl activo sg fijo.

fixed charge n gasto fijo.

fixture ['fɪkstʃə*] n (SPORT) encuentro; ~**s** npl instalaciones fpl fijas.

fizz [fɪz] vi burbujear.

fizzle out ['fɪzl-] vi apagarse; (enthusiasm, interest) decaer; (plan) quedar en agua de borrajas.

fizzy ['fɪzɪ] adj (drink) gaseoso.

fjord [fjɔːd] n = **fiord**.

FL, Fla. abbr (US) = Florida.

flabbergasted ['flæbəgɑːstɪd] adj pasmado.

flabby ['flæbɪ] adj flojo (de carnes); (skin) fofo.

flag [flæg] n bandera; (stone) losa ♦ vi decaer; ~ **of convenience** pabellón m de conveniencia.

▶**flag down** vt: **to ~ sb down** hacer señas a algn para que se pare.

flagpole ['flægpəul] n asta de bandera.

flagrant ['fleɪgrənt] adj flagrante.

flagship ['flægʃɪp] n buque m insignia or almirante.

flagstone ['flægstəun] n losa.

flag stop n (US) parada discrecional.

flair [fleə*] n aptitud f especial.

flak [flæk] n (MIL) fuego antiaéreo; (col: criticism) lluvia de críticas.

flake [fleɪk] n (of rust, paint) desconchón m; (of snow) copo; (of soap powder) escama ♦ vi (also: ~ **off**) (paint) desconcharse; (skin) descamarse.

flaky ['fleɪkɪ] adj (paintwork) desconchado; (skin) escamoso.

flaky pastry n (CULIN) hojaldre m.

flamboyant [flæm'bɔɪənt] adj (dress) vistoso; (person) extravagante.

flame [fleɪm] n llama; **to burst into ~s** incendiarse; **old ~** (col) antiguo amor m/f.

flamingo [flə'mɪŋgəu] n flamenco.

flammable ['flæməbl] adj inflamable.

flan [flæn] n (BRIT) tarta.

flank [flæŋk] n flanco; (of person) costado ♦ vt flanquear.

flannel ['flænl] n (BRIT: also: **face ~**) toallita; (fabric) franela; ~**s** npl pantalones mpl de franela.

flannelette [flænə'lɛt] n franela de algodón.

flap [flæp] n (of pocket, envelope) solapa; (of table) hoja (plegadiza); (wing movement) aletazo; (AVIAT) flap m ♦ vt (wings) batir ♦ vi (sail, flag) ondear.

flapjack ['flæpdʒæk] n (US: pancake) torta, panqueque m (LAM).

flare [fleə*] n llamarada; (MIL) bengala; (in skirt etc) vuelo.

▶**flare up** vi encenderse; (fig: person) encolerizarse; (: revolt) estallar.

flash [flæʃ] n relámpago; (also: **news ~**) noticias fpl de última hora; (PHOT) flash m; (US: torch) linterna ♦ vt (light, headlights) lanzar destellos con; (torch) encender ♦ vi destellar; **in a ~** en un santiamén; ~ **of inspiration** ráfaga de inspiración; **to ~ sth about** (fig, col: flaunt) ostentar algo, presumir con algo; **he ~ed by** or **past** pasó como un rayo.

flashback ['flæʃbæk] n flashback m, escena retrospectiva.

flashbulb ['flæʃbʌlb] n bombilla de flash.

flash card n (SCOL) tarjeta.

flasher ['flæʃə*] n exhibicionista m.

flashlight ['flæʃlaɪt] n (US: torch) linterna.

flashpoint ['flæʃpɔɪnt] n punto de inflamación; (fig) punto de explosión.

flashy ['flæʃɪ] adj (pej) ostentoso.

flask [flɑːsk] n petaca; (also: **vacuum ~**) termo.

flat [flæt] adj llano; (smooth) liso; (tyre) desinflado; (battery) descargado; (beer) sin gas; (MUS: instrument) desafinado ♦ n (BRIT: apartment) piso (SP), departamento (LAM), apartamento; (AUT) pinchazo; (MUS) bemol m; (to work) ~ **out** (trabajar) a tope; ~ **rate of pay** sueldo fijo.

flatfooted [flæt'futɪd] adj de pies planos.

flatly ['flætlɪ] adv rotundamente, de plano.

flatmate ['flætmeɪt] n compañero/a de piso.

flatness ['flætnɪs] n (of land) llanura, lo llano.

flat pack n: **it comes in a ~** viene en un paquete plano para su automontaje.

flat-pack adj: ~ **furniture** muebles mpl automontables (embalados en paquetes planos).

flat-screen ['flætskriːn] adj de pantalla plana.

flatten ['flætn] vt (also: ~ **out**) allanar; (smooth out) alisar; (house, city) arrasar.

flatter ['flætə*] vt adular, halagar; (show to advantage) favorecer.

flatterer ['flætərə*] n adulador(a) m/f.

flattering ['flætərɪŋ] adj halagador(a); (clothes etc) que favorece, favorecedor(a).

flattery ['flætərɪ] n adulación f.

flatulence ['flætjuləns] n flatulencia.

flaunt [flɔːnt] vt ostentar, lucir.

flavour, (US) **flavor** ['fleɪvə*] n sabor m, gusto ♦ vt sazonar, condimentar; **strawberry ~ed** con sabor a fresa.

flavo(u)ring ['fleɪvərɪŋ] n (in product) aromatizante m.

flaw [flɔː] *n* defecto.
flawless ['flɔːlɪs] *adj* intachable.
flax [flæks] *n* lino.
flaxen ['flæksən] *adj* muy rubio.
flea [fliː] *n* pulga.
flea market *n* rastro, mercadillo.
fleck [flɛk] *n* mota ♦ *vt* (*with blood, mud etc*) salpicar; **brown ~ed with white** marrón con motas blancas.
fledg(e)ling ['flɛdʒlɪŋ] *n* (*fig*) novato/a, principiante *m/f.*
flee [fliː], *pt, pp* **fled** [flɛd] *vt* huir de, abandonar ♦ *vi* huir.
fleece [fliːs] *n* (*of sheep*) vellón *m*; (*wool*) lana; (*top*) forro polar ♦ *vt* (*col*) desplumar.
fleecy ['fliːsɪ] *adj* (*blanket*) lanoso, lanudo; (*cloud*) aborregado.
fleet [fliːt] *n* flota; (*of cars, lorries etc*) parque *m.*
fleeting ['fliːtɪŋ] *adj* fugaz.
Flemish ['flɛmɪʃ] *adj* flamenco ♦ *n* (*LING*) flamenco; **the ~** los flamencos.
flesh [flɛʃ] *n* carne *f*; (*of fruit*) pulpa; **of ~ and blood** de carne y hueso.
flesh wound *n* herida superficial.
flew [fluː] *pt of* **fly**.
flex [flɛks] *n* cable *m* ♦ *vt* (*muscles*) tensar.
flexibility [flɛksɪ'bɪlɪtɪ] *n* flexibilidad *f.*
flexible ['flɛksəbl] *adj* (*gen, disk*) flexible; **~ working hours** horario *sg* flexible.
flexitime ['flɛksɪtaɪm] *n* horario flexible.
flick [flɪk] *n* golpecito; (*with finger*) capirotazo; (*BRIT: col: film*) película ♦ *vt* dar un golpecito a.
▶**flick off** *vt* quitar con el dedo.
▶**flick through** *vt fus* hojear.
flicker ['flɪkə*] *vi* (*light*) parpadear; (*flame*) vacilar ♦ *n* parpadeo.
flick knife *n* navaja de muelle.
flier ['flaɪə*] *n* aviador(a) *m/f.*
flies [flaɪz] *npl of* **fly**.
flight [flaɪt] *n* vuelo; (*escape*) huida, fuga; (*also: ~ of steps*) tramo (de escaleras); **to take ~** huir, darse a la fuga; **to put to ~** ahuyentar; **how long does the ~ take?** ¿cuánto dura el vuelo?
flight attendant *n* (*US*) auxiliar *m/f* de vuelo.
flight deck *n* (*AVIAT*) cabina de mandos.
flight path *n* trayectoria de vuelo.
flight recorder *n* registrador *m* de vuelo.
flighty ['flaɪtɪ] *adj* caprichoso.
flimsy ['flɪmzɪ] *adj* (*thin*) muy ligero; (*excuse*) flojo.
flinch [flɪntʃ] *vi* encogerse.
fling [flɪŋ] *vt* (*pt, pp* **flung** [flʌŋ]) arrojar ♦ *n* (*love affair*) aventura amorosa.

flint [flɪnt] *n* pedernal *m*; (*in lighter*) piedra.
flip [flɪp] *vt*: **to ~ a coin** echar a cara o cruz.
▶**flip over** *vt* dar la vuelta a.
▶**flip through** *vt fus* (*book*) hojear; (*records*) ver de pasada.
flippancy ['flɪpənsɪ] *n* ligereza.
flippant ['flɪpənt] *adj* poco serio.
flipper ['flɪpə*] *n* aleta.
flip side *n* (*of record*) cara B.
flirt [flɜːt] *vi* coquetear, flirtear ♦ *n* coqueta *f.*
flirtation [flɜː'teɪʃən] *n* coqueteo, flirteo.
flit [flɪt] *vi* revolotear.
float [fləʊt] *n* flotador *m*; (*in procession*) carroza; (*sum of money*) (dinero suelto para) cambio ♦ *vi* (*also COMM: currency*) flotar ♦ *vt* (*gen*) hacer flotar; (*company*) lanzar; **to ~ an idea** plantear una idea.
floating ['fləʊtɪŋ] *adj*: **~ vote** voto indeciso; **~ voter** votante *m/f* indeciso/a.
flock [flɒk] *n* (*of sheep*) rebaño; (*of birds*) bandada; (*of people*) multitud *f.*
floe [fləʊ] *n*: **ice ~** témpano de hielo.
flog [flɒg] *vt* azotar; (*col*) vender.
flood [flʌd] *n* inundación *f*; (*of words, tears etc*) torrente *m* ♦ *vt* (*also AUT: carburettor*) inundar; **to ~ the market** (*COMM*) inundar el mercado.
flooding ['flʌdɪŋ] *n* inundación *f.*
floodlight ['flʌdlaɪt] *n* foco ♦ *vt* (*irreg: like* **light**) iluminar con focos.
floodlit ['flʌdlɪt] *pt, pp of* **floodlight** ♦ *adj* iluminado.
flood tide *n* pleamar *f.*
floodwater ['flʌdwɔːtə*] *n* aguas *fpl* (de la inundación).
floor [flɔː*] *n* suelo, piso (*LAM*); (*storey*) piso; (*of sea, valley*) fondo; (*dance ~*) pista ♦ *vt* (*fig: baffle*) dejar anonadado; **ground ~,** (*US*) **first ~** planta baja; **first ~,** (*US*) **second ~** primer piso; **top ~** último piso; **to have the ~** (*speaker*) tener la palabra.
floorboard ['flɔːbɔːd] *n* tabla.
flooring ['flɔːrɪŋ] *n* suelo; (*material*) solería.
floor lamp *n* (*US*) lámpara de pie.
floor show *n* cabaret *m.*
floorwalker ['flɔːwɔːkə*] *n* (*US COMM*) supervisor(a) *m/f.*
flop [flɒp] *n* fracaso ♦ *vi* (*fail*) fracasar.
floppy ['flɒpɪ] *adj* flojo ♦ *n* = **floppy disk**.
floppy disk *n* (*COMPUT*) floppy *m*, floppy-disk *m*, disco flexible.
flora ['flɔːrə] *n* flora.
floral ['flɔːrl] *adj* floral; (*dress, wallpaper*) de flores.
Florence ['flɒrəns] *n* Florencia.
Florentine ['flɒrəntaɪn] *adj, n* florentino/a *m/f.*

florid ['flɔrɪd] *adj* (*style*) florido.
florist ['flɔrɪst] *n* florista *m/f*; ~'s **(shop)** *n* floristería.
flotation [fləu'teɪʃən] *n* (*of shares*) emisión *f*; (*of company*) lanzamiento.
flounce [flauns] *n* volante *m*.
▶**flounce in** *vi* entrar con gesto exagerado.
▶**flounce out** *vi* salir con gesto airado.
flounder ['flaundə*] *vi* tropezar ♦ *n* (*ZOOL*) platija.
flour ['flauə*] *n* harina.
flourish ['flʌrɪʃ] *vi* florecer ♦ *n* ademán *m*, movimiento (ostentoso).
flourishing ['flʌrɪʃɪŋ] *adj* floreciente.
flout [flaut] *vt* burlarse de; (*order*) no hacer caso de, hacer caso omiso de.
flow [fləu] *n* (*movement*) flujo; (*direction*) curso; (*of river, also ELEC*) corriente *f* ♦ *vi* correr, fluir.
flow chart *n* organigrama *m*.
flow diagram *n* organigrama *m*.
flower ['flauə*] *n* flor *f* ♦ *vi* florecer; **in** ~ en flor.
flower bed *n* macizo.
flowerpot ['flauəpɔt] *n* tiesto.
flowery ['flauərɪ] *adj* florido; (*perfume, pattern*) de flores.
flowing ['fləuɪŋ] *adj* (*hair, clothes*) suelto; (*style*) fluido.
flown [fləun] *pp of* **fly**.
flu [fluː] *n* gripe *f*.
fluctuate ['flʌktjueɪt] *vi* fluctuar.
fluctuation [flʌktju'eɪʃən] *n* fluctuación *f*.
flue [fluː] *n* cañón *m*.
fluency ['fluːənsɪ] *n* fluidez *f*, soltura.
fluent ['fluːənt] *adj* (*speech*) elocuente; **he speaks** ~ **French, he's** ~ **in French** domina el francés.
fluently ['fluːəntlɪ] *adv* con soltura.
fluff [flʌf] *n* pelusa.
fluffy ['flʌfɪ] *adj* lanoso.
fluid ['fluːɪd] *adj, n* fluido, líquido; (*in diet*) líquido.
fluke [fluːk] *n* (*col*) chiripa.
flummox ['flʌməks] *vt* desconcertar.
flung [flʌŋ] *pt, pp of* **fling**.
flunky ['flʌŋkɪ] *n* lacayo.
fluorescent [fluə'rɛsnt] *adj* fluorescente.
fluoride ['fluəraɪd] *n* fluoruro.
fluoride toothpaste *n* pasta de dientes con flúor.
flurry ['flʌrɪ] *n* (*of snow*) ventisca; (*haste*) agitación *f*; ~ **of activity** frenesí *m* de actividad.
flush [flʌʃ] *n* (*on face*) rubor *m*; (*fig: of youth, beauty*) resplandor *m* ♦ *vt* limpiar con agua; (*also:* ~ **out**) (*game, birds*) levantar;

(*fig: criminal*) poner al descubierto ♦ *vi* ruborizarse ♦ *adj:* ~ **with** a ras de; **to** ~ **the toilet** tirar de la cadena (del wáter); **hot** ~**es** (*MED*) sofocos *mpl*.
flushed [flʌʃt] *adj* ruborizado.
fluster ['flʌstə*] *n* aturdimiento ♦ *vt* aturdir.
flustered ['flʌstəd] *adj* aturdido.
flute [fluːt] *n* flauta travesera.
flutter ['flʌtə*] *n* (*of wings*) revoloteo, aleteo; (*fam: bet*) apuesta ♦ *vi* revolotear; **to be in a** ~ estar nervioso.
flux [flʌks] *n* flujo; **in a state of** ~ cambiando continuamente.
fly [flaɪ] *n* (*insect*) mosca; (*on trousers: also:* **flies**) bragueta ♦ *vb* (*pt* **flew**, *pp* **flown**) *vt* (*plane*) pilotar; (*cargo*) transportar (en avión); (*distances*) recorrer (en avión) ♦ *vi* volar; (*passengers*) ir en avión; (*escape*) evadirse; (*flag*) ondear.
▶**fly away** *vi* (*bird, insect*) irse volando.
▶**fly in** *vi* (*person*) llegar en avión; (*plane*) aterrizar; **he flew in from Bilbao** llegó en avión desde Bilbao.
▶**fly off** *vi* irse volando.
▶**fly out** *vi* irse en avión.
fly-fishing ['flaɪfɪʃɪŋ] *n* pesca con mosca.
flying ['flaɪɪŋ] *n* (*activity*) (el) volar ♦ *adj:* ~ **visit** visita relámpago; **with** ~ **colours** con lucimiento.
flying buttress *n* arbotante *m*.
flying picket *n* piquete *m* volante.
flying saucer *n* platillo volante.
flying squad *n* (*POLICE*) brigada móvil.
flying start *n:* **to get off to a** ~ empezar con buen pie.
flyleaf, *pl* **flyleaves** ['flaɪliːf, -liːvz] *n* (hoja de) guarda.
flyover ['flaɪəuvə*] *n* (*BRIT: bridge*) paso elevado *or* a desnivel (*LAM*).
flypast ['flaɪpɑːst] *n* desfile *m* aéreo.
flysheet ['flaɪʃiːt] *n* (*for tent*) doble techo.
flyswatter ['flaɪswɔtə*] *n* matamoscas *m inv*.
flyweight ['flaɪweɪt] *adj* de peso mosca ♦ *n* peso mosca.
flywheel ['flaɪwiːl] *n* volante *m* (de motor).
FM *abbr* (*BRIT MIL*) = **field marshal**; (*RADIO:* = *frequency modulation*) FM.
FMB *n abbr* (*US*) = *Federal Maritime Board*.
FMCS *n abbr* (*US:* = *Federal Mediation and Conciliation Services*) organismo de conciliación en conflictos laborales.
FO *n abbr* (*BRIT:* = *Foreign Office*) ≈ Min. de AA. EE.
foal [fəul] *n* potro.
foam [fəum] *n* espuma ♦ *vi* hacer espuma.
foam rubber *n* goma espuma.

FOB *abbr* (= *free on board*) f.a.b.

fob [fɔb] *n* (*also*: **watch ~**) leontina ♦ *vt*: **to ~ sb off with sth** deshacerse de algn con algo.

foc *abbr* (*BRIT*: = *free of charge*) gratis.

focal ['fəukəl] *adj* focal; **~ point** punto focal; (*fig*) centro de atención.

focus ['fəukəs] (*pl*: **~es**) *n* foco ♦ *vt* (*field glasses etc*) enfocar ♦ *vi*: **to ~ (on)** enfocar (a); (*issue etc*) centrarse en; **in/out of ~** enfocado/desenfocado.

focus group *n* grupo de muestra elegido.

fodder ['fɔdə*] *n* pienso.

FOE *n abbr* (= *Friends of the Earth*) Amigos *mpl* de la Tierra; (*US*: = *Fraternal Order of Eagles*) organización benéfica.

foe [fəu] *n* enemigo.

foetus, (*US*) **fetus** ['fi:təs] *n* feto.

fog [fɔg] *n* niebla.

fogbound ['fɔgbaund] *adj* inmovilizado por la niebla.

foggy ['fɔgɪ] *adj*: **it's ~** hay niebla.

fog lamp, (*US*) **fog light** *n* (*AUT*) faro antiniebla.

foible ['fɔɪbl] *n* manía.

foil [fɔɪl] *vt* frustrar ♦ *n* hoja; (*kitchen ~*) papel *m* (de) aluminio; (*FENCING*) florete *m*.

foist [fɔɪst] *vt*: **to ~ sth on sb** endilgarle algo a algn.

fold [fəuld] *n* (*bend, crease*) pliegue *m*; (*AGR*) redil *m* ♦ *vt* doblar; (*map etc*) plegar; **to ~ one's arms** cruzarse de brazos.

▶**fold up** *vi* plegarse, doblarse; (*business*) quebrar.

folder ['fəuldə*] *n* (*for papers*) carpeta; (*binder*) carpeta de anillas; (*brochure*) folleto.

folding ['fəuldɪŋ] *adj* (*chair, bed*) plegable.

foliage ['fəulɪɪdʒ] *n* follaje *m*.

folio ['fəulɪəu] *n* folio.

folk [fəuk] *npl* gente *f* ♦ *adj* popular, folklórico; **~s** *npl* familia, parientes *mpl*.

folklore ['fəuklɔ:*] *n* folklore *m*.

folk music *n* música folk.

folk singer *n* cantante *m/f* de música folk.

folk song *n* canción *f* popular *or* folk.

follow ['fɔləu] *vt* seguir ♦ *vi* seguir; (*result*) resultar; **he ~ed suit** hizo lo mismo; **to ~ sb's advice** seguir el consejo de algn; **I don't quite ~ you** no te comprendo muy bien; **to ~ in sb's footsteps** seguir los pasos de algn; **it doesn't ~ that ...** no se deduce que ....

▶**follow on** *vi* seguir; (*continue*): **to ~ on from** ser la consecuencia lógica de.

▶**follow out** *vt* (*implement: idea, plan*) realizar, llevar a cabo.

▶**follow through** *vt* llevar hasta el fin.

▶**follow up** *vt* (*letter, offer*) responder a; (*case*) investigar.

follower ['fɔləuə*] *n* seguidor(a) *m/f*; (*POL*) partidario/a.

following ['fɔləuɪŋ] *adj* siguiente ♦ *n* seguidores *mpl*.

follow-up ['fɔləuʌp] *n* continuación *f*.

follow-up letter *n* carta recordatoria.

folly ['fɔlɪ] *n* locura.

fond [fɔnd] *adj* (*loving*) cariñoso; **to be ~ of sb** tener cariño a algn; **she's ~ of swimming** tiene afición a la natación, le gusta nadar.

fondle ['fɔndl] *vt* acariciar.

fondly ['fɔndlɪ] *adv* (*lovingly*) con cariño; **he ~ believed that ...** creía ingenuamente que ....

fondness ['fɔndnɪs] *n* (*for things*) afición *f*; (*for people*) cariño.

font [fɔnt] *n* pila bautismal.

food [fu:d] *n* comida.

food chain *n* cadena alimenticia.

food mixer *n* batidora.

food poisoning *n* intoxicación *f* alimentaria.

food processor *n* robot *m* de cocina.

food stamp *n* (*US*) vale *m* para comida.

foodstuffs ['fu:dstʌfs] *npl* comestibles *mpl*.

fool [fu:l] *n* tonto/a; (*CULIN*) mousse *m* de frutas ♦ *vt* engañar; **to make a ~ of o.s.** ponerse en ridículo; **you can't ~ me** a mí no me engañas; *see also* **April Fool's Day.**

▶**fool about, fool around** *vi* hacer el tonto.

foolhardy ['fu:lhɑ:dɪ] *adj* temerario.

foolish ['fu:lɪʃ] *adj* tonto; (*careless*) imprudente.

foolishly ['fu:lɪʃlɪ] *adv* tontamente, neciamente.

foolproof ['fu:lpru:f] *adj* (*plan etc*) infalible.

foolscap ['fu:lskæp] *n* ≈ papel *m* tamaño folio.

foot [fut], *pl* **feet** *n* (*gen, also: of page, stairs etc*) pie *m*; (*measure*) pie (= 304 mm); (*of animal, table*) pata ♦ *vt* (*bill*) pagar; **on ~** a pie; **to find one's feet** acostumbrarse; **to put one's ~ down** (*say no*) plantarse; (*AUT*) pisar el acelerador.

footage ['futɪdʒ] *n* (*CINE*) imágenes *fpl*.

foot-and-mouth (disease) [futənd'mauθ-] *n* fiebre *f* aftosa.

football ['futbɔ:l] *n* balón *m*; (*game: BRIT*) fútbol *m*; (: *US*) fútbol *m* americano.

footballer ['futbɔ:lə*] *n* (*BRIT*) = **football player.**

football match *n* partido de fútbol.

football player *n* futbolista *m/f*, jugador(a)

m/f de fútbol.
footbrake ['futbreɪk] *n* freno de pie.
footbridge ['futbrɪdʒ] *n* pasarela, puente *m* para peatones.
foothills ['futhɪlz] *npl* estribaciones *fpl*.
foothold ['futhəuld] *n* pie *m* firme.
footing ['futɪŋ] *n* (*fig*) nivel *m*; **to lose one's** ~ perder el equilibrio; **on an equal** ~ en pie de igualdad.
footlights ['futlaɪts] *npl* candilejas *fpl*.
footman ['futmən] *n* lacayo.
footnote ['futnəut] *n* nota (de pie de página).
footpath ['futpɑːθ] *n* sendero.
footprint ['futprɪnt] *n* huella, pisada.
footrest ['futrest] *n* apoyapiés *m inv*.
footsie ['futsɪ] *n*: **to play** ~ **with sb** (*col*) juguetear con los pies de algn.
footsore ['futsɔː*] *adj* con los pies doloridos.
footstep ['futstep] *n* paso.
footwear ['futwɛə*] *n* calzado.
FOR *abbr* (= *free on rail*) franco (puesto sobre) vagón.

──────────── *KEYWORD*

for [fɔː] *prep* **1** (*indicating destination, intention*) para; **the train** ~ **London** el tren para Londres; (*in announcements*) el tren con destino a Londres; **he left** ~ **Rome** marchó para Roma; **he went** ~ **the paper** fue por el periódico; **is this** ~ **me?** ¿es esto para mí?; **it's time** ~ **lunch** es la hora de comer
2 (*indicating purpose*) para; **what('s it)** ~? ¿para qué (es)?; **what's this button** ~? ¿para qué sirve este botón?; **to pray** ~ **peace** rezar por la paz
3 (*on behalf of, representing*): **the MP** ~ **Hove** el diputado por Hove; **he works** ~ **the government/a local firm** trabaja para el gobierno/en una empresa local; **I'll ask him** ~ **you** se lo pediré por ti; **G** ~ **George** G de Gerona
4 (*because of*) por esta razón; ~ **fear of being criticized** por temor a ser criticado
5 (*with regard to*) para; **it's cold** ~ **July** hace frío para julio; **he has a gift** ~ **languages** tiene don de lenguas
6 (*in exchange for*) por; **I sold it** ~ **£5** lo vendí por £5; **to pay 50 pence** ~ **a ticket** pagar 50 peniques por un billete
7 (*in favour of*): **are you** ~ **or against us?** ¿estás con nosotros o contra nosotros?; **I'm all** ~ **it** estoy totalmente a favor; **vote** ~ **X** vote (a) X
8 (*referring to distance*): **there are roadworks** ~ **5 km** hay obras en 5 km; **we**
walked ~ **miles** caminamos kilómetros y kilómetros
9 (*referring to time*): **he was away** ~ **2 years** estuvo fuera (durante) dos años; **it hasn't rained** ~ **3 weeks** no ha llovido durante *or* en 3 semanas; **I have known her** ~ **years** la conozco desde hace años; **can you do it** ~ **tomorrow?** ¿lo podrás hacer para mañana?
10 (*with infinitive clauses*): **it is not** ~ **me to decide** la decisión no es cosa mía; **it would be best** ~ **you to leave** sería mejor que te fueras; **there is still time** ~ **you to do it** todavía te queda tiempo para hacerlo; ~ **this to be possible** ... para que esto sea posible ...
11 (*in spite of*) a pesar de; ~ **all his complaints** a pesar de sus quejas
♦ *conj* (*since, as: rather formal*) puesto que.

forage ['fɔrɪdʒ] *n* forraje *m*.
foray ['fɔreɪ] *n* incursión *f*.
forbid, *pt* **forbad(e)**, *pp* **forbidden** [fə'bɪd, -'bæd, -'bɪdn] *vt* prohibir; **to** ~ **sb to do sth** prohibir a algn hacer algo.
forbidding [fə'bɪdɪŋ] *adj* (*landscape*) inhóspito; (*severe*) severo.
force [fɔːs] *n* fuerza ♦ *vt* obligar, forzar; **to** ~ **o.s. to do** hacer un esfuerzo por hacer; **the F**~**s** *npl* (*BRIT*) las Fuerzas Armadas; **sales** ~ (*COMM*) personal *m* de ventas; **a** ~ **5 wind** un viento fuerza 5; **to join** ~**s** unir fuerzas; **in** ~ (*law etc*) en vigor; **to** ~ **sb to do sth** obligar a algn a hacer algo.
▶**force back** *vt* (*crowd, enemy*) hacer retroceder; (*tears*) reprimir.
▶**force down** *vt* (*food*) tragar con esfuerzo.
forced [fɔːst] *adj* (*smile*) forzado; (*landing*) forzoso.
force-feed ['fɔːsfiːd] *vt* (*animal, prisoner*) alimentar a la fuerza.
forceful ['fɔːsful] *adj* enérgico.
forcemeat ['fɔːsmiːt] *n* (*CULIN*) relleno.
forceps ['fɔːseps] *npl* fórceps *m inv*.
forcible ['fɔːsəbl] *adj* (*violent*) a la fuerza; (*telling*) convincente.
forcibly ['fɔːsəblɪ] *adv* a la fuerza.
ford [fɔːd] *n* vado ♦ *vt* vadear.
fore [fɔː*] *n*: **to bring to the** ~ sacar a la luz pública; **to come to the** ~ empezar a destacar.
forearm ['fɔːrɑːm] *n* antebrazo.
forebear ['fɔːbɛə*] *n* antepasado.
foreboding [fɔː'bəudɪŋ] *n* presentimiento.
forecast ['fɔːkɑːst] *n* pronóstico ♦ *vt* (*irreg: like* **cast**) pronosticar; **weather** ~ previsión *f* meteorológica.

foreclose [fɔː'kləuz] *vt* (*LAW: also:* ~ **on**) extinguir el derecho de redimir.

foreclosure [fɔː'kləuʒə*] *n* apertura de un juicio hipotecario.

forecourt ['fɔːkɔːt] *n* (*of garage*) área de entrada.

forefathers ['fɔːfɑːðəz] *npl* antepasados *mpl*.

forefinger ['fɔːfɪŋgə*] *n* (dedo) índice *m*.

forefront ['fɔːfrʌnt] *n*: **in the** ~ **of** en la vanguardia de.

forego, *pt* **forewent**, *pp* **foregone** [fɔː'gəu, -'wɛnt, -'gɔn] *vt* = **forgo**.

foregoing ['fɔːgəuɪŋ] *adj* anterior, precedente.

foregone ['fɔːgɔn] *pp of* **forego** ♦ *adj*: **it's a** ~ **conclusion** es una conclusión inevitable.

foreground ['fɔːgraund] *n* primer plano.

forehand ['fɔːhænd] *n* (*TENNIS*) derechazo directo.

forehead ['fɔrɪd] *n* frente *f*.

foreign ['fɔrɪn] *adj* extranjero; (*trade*) exterior.

foreign currency *n* divisas *fpl*.

foreigner ['fɔrɪnə*] *n* extranjero/a.

foreign exchange *n* (*system*) cambio de divisas; (*money*) divisas *fpl*, moneda extranjera.

foreign investment *n* inversión *f* en el extranjero; (*money, stock*) inversiones *fpl* extranjeras.

Foreign Minister *n* Ministro/a de Asuntos Exteriores, Canciller *m* (*LAM*).

Foreign Office *n* Ministerio de Asuntos Exteriores.

Foreign Secretary *n* (*BRIT*) Ministro/a de Asuntos Exteriores, Canciller *m* (*LAM*).

foreleg ['fɔːlɛg] *n* pata delantera.

foreman ['fɔːmən] *n* capataz *m*; (*LAW: of jury*) presidente *m/f*.

foremost ['fɔːməust] *adj* principal ♦ *adv*: **first and** ~ ante todo, antes que nada.

forename ['fɔːneɪm] *n* nombre *m* (de pila).

forensic [fə'rɛnsɪk] *adj* forense; ~ **scientist** forense *m/f*.

foreplay ['fɔːpleɪ] *n* preámbulos *mpl* (*de estimulación sexual*).

forerunner ['fɔːrʌnə*] *n* precursor(a) *m/f*.

foresee, *pt* **foresaw**, *pp* **foreseen** [fɔː'siː, -'sɔː, -'siːn] *vt* prever.

foreseeable [fɔː'siːəbl] *adj* previsible.

foreshadow [fɔː'ʃædəu] *vt* prefigurar, anunciar.

foreshore ['fɔːʃɔː*] *n* playa.

foreshorten [fɔː'ʃɔːtn] *vt* (*figure, scene*) escorzar.

foresight ['fɔːsaɪt] *n* previsión *f*.

foreskin ['fɔːskɪn] *n* (*ANAT*) prepucio.

forest ['fɔrɪst] *n* bosque *m*.

forestall [fɔː'stɔːl] *vt* anticiparse a.

forestry ['fɔrɪstrɪ] *n* silvicultura.

foretaste ['fɔːteɪst] *n* anticipo.

foretell, *pt, pp* **foretold** [fɔː'tɛl, -'təuld] *vt* predecir, pronosticar.

forethought ['fɔːθɔːt] *n* previsión *f*.

forever [fə'rɛvə*] *adv* siempre; (*for good*) para siempre.

forewarn [fɔː'wɔːn] *vt* avisar, advertir.

forewent [fɔː'wɛnt] *pt of* **forego**.

foreword ['fɔːwəːd] *n* prefacio.

forfeit ['fɔːfɪt] *n* (*in game*) prenda ♦ *vt* perder (derecho a).

forgave [fə'geɪv] *pt of* **forgive**.

forge [fɔːdʒ] *n* fragua; (*smithy*) herrería ♦ *vt* (*signature: BRIT: money*) falsificar; (*metal*) forjar.

►**forge ahead** *vi* avanzar mucho.

forger ['fɔːdʒə*] *n* falsificador(a) *m/f*.

forgery ['fɔːdʒərɪ] *n* falsificación *f*.

forget, *pt* **forgot**, *pp* **forgotten** [fə'gɛt, -'gɔt, -'gɔtn] *vt* olvidar, olvidarse de ♦ *vi* olvidarse.

forgetful [fə'gɛtful] *adj* olvidadizo.

forget-me-not [fə'gɛtmɪnɔt] *n* nomeolvides *f inv*.

forgive, *pt* **forgave**, *pp* **forgiven** [fə'gɪv, -'geɪv, -'gɪvn] *vt* perdonar; **to** ~ **sb for sth/ for doing sth** perdonar algo a algn/a algn por haber hecho algo.

forgiveness [fə'gɪvnɪs] *n* perdón *m*.

forgiving [fə'gɪvɪŋ] *adj* compasivo.

forgo, *pt* **forwent**, *pp* **forgone** [fɔː'gəu, -'wɛnt, -'gɔn] *vt* (*give up*) renunciar a; (*go without*) privarse de.

forgot [fə'gɔt] *pt of* **forget**.

forgotten [fə'gɔtn] *pp of* **forget**.

fork [fɔːk] *n* (*for eating*) tenedor *m*; (*for gardening*) horca; (*of roads*) bifurcación *f*; (*in tree*) horcadura ♦ *vi* (*road*) bifurcarse.

►**fork out** *vt* (*col: pay*) soltar.

forked [fɔːkt] *adj* (*lightning*) en zigzag.

fork-lift truck ['fɔːklɪft-] *n* máquina elevadora.

forlorn [fə'lɔːn] *adj* (*person*) triste, melancólico; (*deserted: cottage*) abandonado; (*desperate: attempt*) desesperado.

form [fɔːm] *n* forma; (*BRIT SCOL*) curso; (*document*) formulario, planilla (*LAM*) ♦ *vt* formar; **in the** ~ **of** en forma de; **in top** ~ en plena forma; **to be in good** ~ (*SPORT, fig*) estar en plena forma; **to** ~ **part of sth** formar parte de algo; **to** ~ **a circle/a queue** hacer una curva/una cola.

formal ['fɔːməl] *adj* (*offer, receipt*) por escrito; (*person etc*) correcto; (*occasion, dinner*) ceremonioso; ~ **dress** traje *m* de

vestir; (*evening dress*) traje *m* de etiqueta.
formalities [fɔː'mælɪtɪz] *npl* formalidades
fpl.
formality [fɔː'mælɪtɪ] *n* ceremonia.
formalize ['fɔːməlaɪz] *vt* formalizar.
formally ['fɔːməlɪ] *adv* oficialmente.
format ['fɔːmæt] *n* formato ♦ *vt* (*COMPUT*)
formatear.
formation [fɔː'meɪʃən] *n* formación *f.*
formative ['fɔːmətɪv] *adj* (*years*) de
formación.
format line *n* (*COMPUT*) línea de formato.
former ['fɔːmə*] *adj* anterior; (*earlier*)
antiguo; (*ex*) ex; **the ~ ... the latter ...**
aquél ... éste ...; **the ~ president** el
antiguo *or* ex presidente; **the ~
Yugoslavia/Soviet Union** la antigua *or* ex
Yugoslavia/Unión Soviética.
formerly ['fɔːməlɪ] *adv* antiguamente.
form feed *n* (*on printer*) salto de página.
Formica ® [fɔː'maɪkə] *n* formica ®.
formidable ['fɔːmɪdəbl] *adj* formidable.
formula ['fɔːmjulə] *n* fórmula; **F~ One**
(*AUT*) Fórmula Uno.
formulate ['fɔːmjuleɪt] *vt* formular.
fornicate ['fɔːnɪkeɪt] *vi* fornicar.
forsake, *pt* **forsook**, *pp* **forsaken** [fə'seɪk,
-'suk, -'seɪkən] *vt* (*gen*) abandonar; (*plan*)
renunciar a.
fort [fɔːt] *n* fuerte *m*; **to hold the ~** (*fig*)
quedarse a cargo.
forte ['fɔːtɪ] *n* fuerte *m.*
forth [fɔːθ] *adv*: **back and ~** de acá para
allá; **and so ~** y así sucesivamente.
forthcoming [fɔːθ'kʌmɪŋ] *adj* próximo,
venidero; (*character*) comunicativo.
forthright ['fɔːθraɪt] *adj* franco.
forthwith ['fɔːθ'wɪθ] *adv* en el acto, acto
seguido.
fortification [fɔːtɪfɪ'keɪʃən] *n* fortificación *f.*
fortified wine ['fɔːtɪfaɪd-] *n* vino
encabezado.
fortify ['fɔːtɪfaɪ] *vt* fortalecer.
fortitude ['fɔːtɪtjuːd] *n* fortaleza.
fortnight ['fɔːtnaɪt] *n* (*BRIT*) quincena; **it's a
~ since** ... hace quince días que ....
fortnightly ['fɔːtnaɪtlɪ] *adj* quincenal ♦ *adv*
quincenalmente.
FORTRAN ['fɔːtræn] *n* FORTRAN *m.*
fortress ['fɔːtrɪs] *n* fortaleza.
fortuitous [fɔː'tjuːɪtəs] *adj* fortuito.
fortunate ['fɔːtʃənɪt] *adj*: **it is ~ that** ... (es
una) suerte que ....
fortunately ['fɔːtʃənɪtlɪ] *adv*
afortunadamente.
fortune ['fɔːtʃən] *n* suerte *f*; (*wealth*)
fortuna; **to make a ~** hacer un dineral.
fortuneteller ['fɔːtʃəntɛlə*] *n* adivino/a.

forty ['fɔːtɪ] *num* cuarenta.
forum ['fɔːrəm] *n* (*also fig*) foro.
forward ['fɔːwəd] *adj* (*position*) avanzado;
(*movement*) hacia delante; (*front*)
delantero; (*not shy*) atrevido ♦ *n* (*SPORT*)
delantero ♦ *vt* (*letter*) remitir; (*career*)
promocionar; **to move ~** avanzar;
"please ~" "remítase al destinatario".
forward contract *n* contrato a término.
forward exchange *n* cambio a término.
forward planning *n* planificación *f* por
anticipado.
forward rate *n* tipo a término.
forward(s) ['fɔːwəd(z)] *adv* (hacia)
adelante.
forward sales *npl* ventas *fpl* a término.
forwent [fɔː'wɛnt] *pt of* **forgo.**
fossil ['fɔsl] *n* fósil *m*; **~ fuel** combustible *m*
fósil.
foster ['fɔstə*] *vt* (*child*) acoger en familia;
(*idea*) fomentar.
foster brother *n* hermano de leche.
foster child *n* hijo/a adoptivo/a.
foster mother *n* madre *f* adoptiva.
fought [fɔːt] *pt, pp of* **fight.**
foul [faul] *adj* (*gen*) sucio, puerco; (*weather,
smell etc*) asqueroso ♦ *n* (*FOOTBALL*) falta
♦ *vt* (*dirty*) ensuciar; (*block*) atascar;
(*entangle: anchor, propeller*) atascar,
enredarse en; (*football player*) cometer
una falta contra.
foul play *n* (*SPORT*) mala jugada; (*LAW*)
muerte *f* violenta.
found [faund] *pt, pp of* **find** ♦ *vt* (*establish*)
fundar.
foundation [faun'deɪʃən] *n* (*act*) fundación
f; (*basis*) base *f*; (*also: ~ cream*) base *f* de
maquillaje.
foundations [faun'deɪʃənz] *npl* (*of building*)
cimientos *mpl*; **to lay the ~** poner los
cimientos.
foundation stone *n*: **to lay the ~** poner la
primera piedra.
founder ['faundə*] *n* fundador(a) *m/f* ♦ *vi*
irse a pique.
founding ['faundɪŋ] *adj*: **~ fathers** (*esp US*)
fundadores *mpl*, próceres *mpl*; **~ member**
miembro fundador.
foundry ['faundrɪ] *n* fundición *f.*
fountain ['fauntɪn] *n* fuente *f.*
fountain pen *n* (pluma) estilográfica,
(*LAM*) plumafuente *f.*
four [fɔː*] *num* cuatro; **on all ~s** a gatas.
four-footed [fɔː'futɪd] *adj* cuadrúpedo.
four-letter word ['fɔːletə-] *n* taco.
four-poster ['fɔː'pəustə*] *n* (*also: ~ bed*)
cama de columnas.
foursome ['fɔːsəm] *n* grupo de cuatro

personas.
fourteen [ˈfɔːˈtiːn] *num* catorce.
fourteenth [ˈfɔːˈtiːnθ] *num* decimocuarto.
fourth [fɔːθ] *num* cuarto ♦ *n* (AUT: also: ~
 gear) cuarta (velocidad).
four-wheel drive [ˈfɔːwiːl-] *n* tracción *f* a
 las cuatro ruedas.
fowl [faul] *n* ave *f* (de corral).
fox [fɔks] *n* zorro ♦ *vt* confundir.
fox fur *n* piel *f* de zorro.
foxglove [ˈfɔksglʌv] *n* (BOT) dedalera.
fox-hunting [ˈfɔkshʌntɪŋ] *n* caza de zorros.
foxtrot [ˈfɔkstrɔt] *n* fox(trot) *m*.
foyer [ˈfɔɪeɪ] *n* vestíbulo.
FP *n abbr* (BRIT) = former pupil; (US)
 = fireplug.
FPA *n abbr* (BRIT: = Family Planning
 Association) asociación de planificación
 familiar.
Fr. *abbr* (REL) (= Father) P.; (= friar) Fr.
fr. *abbr* (= franc) f.
fracas [ˈfrækɑː] *n* gresca, refriega.
fraction [ˈfrækʃən] *n* fracción *f*.
fractionally [ˈfrækʃnəlɪ] *adv* ligeramente.
fractious [ˈfrækʃəs] *adj* (person, mood)
 irascible.
fracture [ˈfræktʃə*] *n* fractura ♦ *vt*
 fracturar.
fragile [ˈfrædʒaɪl] *adj* frágil.
fragment [ˈfrægmənt] *n* fragmento.
fragmentary [frægˈmentərɪ] *adj*
 fragmentario.
fragrance [ˈfreɪgrəns] *n* fragancia.
fragrant [ˈfreɪgrənt] *adj* fragante, oloroso.
frail [freɪl] *adj* (fragile) frágil, quebradizo;
 (weak) delicado.
frame [freɪm] *n* (TECH) armazón *f*; (of
 picture, door etc) marco; (of spectacles:
 also: ~s) montura ♦ *vt* encuadrar; (picture)
 enmarcar; (reply) formular; **to ~ sb** (col)
 inculpar por engaños a algn.
frame of mind *n* estado de ánimo.
framework [ˈfreɪmwəːk] *n* marco.
France [frɑːns] *n* Francia.
franchise [ˈfræntʃaɪz] *n* (POL) derecho al
 voto, sufragio; (COMM) licencia,
 concesión *f*.
franchisee [fræntʃaɪˈziː] *n* concesionario/a.
franchiser [ˈfræntʃaɪzə*] *n* compañía
 concesionaria.
frank [fræŋk] *adj* franco ♦ *vt* (BRIT: letter)
 franquear.
frankfurter [ˈfræŋkfəːtə*] *n* salchicha de
 Frankfurt.
frankincense [ˈfræŋkɪnsɛns] *n* incienso.
franking machine [ˈfræŋkɪŋ-] *n* máquina
 de franqueo.
frankly [ˈfræŋklɪ] *adv* francamente.

frankness [ˈfræŋknɪs] *n* franqueza.
frantic [ˈfræntɪk] *adj* (desperate: need, desire)
 desesperado; (: search) frenético;
 (: person) desquiciado.
fraternal [frəˈtəːnl] *adj* fraterno.
fraternity [frəˈtəːnɪtɪ] *n* (club) fraternidad *f*;
 (US) club *m* de estudiantes; (guild)
 gremio.
fraternization [frætənaɪˈzeɪʃən] *n*
 fraternización *f*.
fraternize [ˈfrætənaɪz] *vi* confraternizar.
fraud [frɔːd] *n* fraude *m*; (person)
 impostor(a) *m/f*.
fraudulent [ˈfrɔːdjulənt] *adj* fraudulento.
fraught [frɔːt] *adj* (tense) tenso; ~ **with**
 cargado de.
fray [freɪ] *n* combate *m*, lucha, refriega ♦ *vi*
 deshilacharse; **tempers were ~ed** el
 ambiente se ponía tenso.
FRB *n abbr* (US) = Federal Reserve Board.
FRCM *n abbr* (BRIT) = Fellow of the Royal
 College of Music.
FRCO *n abbr* (BRIT) = Fellow of the Royal
 College of Organists.
FRCP *n abbr* (BRIT) = Fellow of the Royal
 College of Physicians.
FRCS *n abbr* (BRIT) = Fellow of the Royal
 College of Surgeons.
freak [friːk] *n* (person) fenómeno; (event)
 suceso anormal; (col: enthusiast) adicto/a
 ♦ *adj* (storm, conditions) anormal; **health** ~
 (col) maniático/a en cuestión de salud.
▶**freak out** *vi* (col: on drugs) flipar.
freakish [ˈfriːkɪʃ] *adj* (result) inesperado;
 (appearance) estrambótico; (weather)
 cambiadizo.
freckle [ˈfrɛkl] *n* peca.
freckled [ˈfrɛkld] *adj* pecoso, lleno de
 pecas.
free [friː] *adj* (person: at liberty) libre; (not
 fixed) suelto; (gratis) gratuito;
 (unoccupied) desocupado; (liberal)
 generoso ♦ *vt* (prisoner etc) poner en
 libertad; (jammed object) soltar; **to give sb
 a ~ hand** dar carta blanca a algn; ~ **and
 easy** despreocupado; **is this seat ~?** ¿está
 libre este asiento?; ~ **of tax** libre de
 impuestos; **admission** ~ entrada libre; ~
 (**of charge**), **for** ~ *adv* gratis.
freebie [ˈfriːbɪ] *n* (col): **it's a** ~ es gratis.
freedom [ˈfriːdəm] *n* libertad *f*; ~ **of
 association** libertad *f* de asociación.
freedom fighter *n* luchador(a) *m/f* por la
 libertad.
free enterprise *n* libre empresa.
Freefone ® [ˈfriːfəun] *n* (BRIT) número
 gratuito.
free-for-all [ˈfriːfərɔːl] *n* riña general.

free gift n regalo.
freehold ['fri:həuld] n propiedad f absoluta.
free kick n tiro libre.
freelance ['fri:lɑ:ns] adj, adv por cuenta propia; **to do ~ work** trabajar por su cuenta.
freely ['fri:lɪ] adv libremente; (liberally) generosamente.
free-market economy ['fri:'mɑ:kɪt-] n economía de libre mercado.
freemason ['fri:meɪsn] n francmasón m.
freemasonry ['fri:meɪsnrɪ] n (franc)masonería.
freepost ['fri:pəust] n porte m pagado.
free-range ['fri:'reɪndʒ] adj (hen, eggs) de granja.
free sample n muestra gratuita.
freesia ['fri:ʒə] n fresia.
free speech n libertad f de expresión.
free trade n libre comercio.
freeway ['fri:weɪ] n (US) autopista.
freewheel [fri:'wi:l] vi ir en punto muerto.
freewheeling [fri:'wi:lɪŋ] adj libre, espontáneo; (careless) irresponsable.
free will n libre albedrío; **of one's own ~** por su propia voluntad.
freeze [fri:z] vb (pt **froze**, pp **frozen** [frəuz, frəuzn]) vi helarse, congelarse ♦ vt helar; (prices, food, salaries) congelar ♦ n helada; congelación f.
▶**freeze over** vi (lake, river) helarse, congelarse; (window, windscreen) cubrirse de escarcha.
▶**freeze up** vi helarse, congelarse.
freeze-dried ['fri:zdraɪd] adj liofilizado.
freezer ['fri:zə*] n congelador m, congeladora.
freezing ['fri:zɪŋ] adj helado.
freezing point n punto de congelación; **3 degrees below ~** tres grados bajo cero.
freight [freɪt] n (goods) carga; (money charged) flete m; **~ forward** contra reembolso del flete, flete por pagar; **~ inward** flete sobre compras.
freight car n vagón m de mercancías.
freighter ['freɪtə*] n buque m de carga; (AVIAT) avión m de transporte de mercancías.
freight forwarder [-'fɔ:wədə*] n agente m expedidor.
freight train n (US) tren m de mercancías.
French [frentʃ] adj francés/esa ♦ n (LING) francés m; **the ~** npl los franceses.
French bean n judía verde.
French bread n pan m francés.
French Canadian adj, n francocanadiense m/f.
French dressing n (CULIN) vinagreta.

French fried potatoes, (US) **French fries** npl patatas fpl or papas fpl (LAM) fritas.
French Guiana [-gaɪ'ænə] n la Guayana Francesa.
French loaf n barra de pan.
Frenchman ['frentʃmən] n francés m.
French Riviera n: **the ~** la Riviera, la Costa Azul.
French stick n barra de pan.
French window n puertaventana.
Frenchwoman ['frentʃwumən] n francesa.
frenetic [frə'netɪk] adj frenético.
frenzy ['frenzɪ] n frenesí m.
frequency ['fri:kwənsɪ] n frecuencia.
frequency modulation (FM) n frecuencia modulada.
frequent adj ['fri:kwənt] frecuente ♦ vt [frɪ'kwent] frecuentar.
frequently ['fri:kwəntlɪ] adv frecuentemente, a menudo.
fresco ['freskəu] n fresco.
fresh [freʃ] adj (gen) fresco; (new) nuevo; (water) dulce; **to make a ~ start** empezar de nuevo.
freshen ['freʃən] vi (wind) arreciar; (air) refrescar.
▶**freshen up** vi (person) refrescarse.
freshener ['freʃnə*] n: **air ~** ambientador m; **skin ~** tónico.
fresher ['freʃə*] n (BRIT SCOL: col) estudiante m/f de primer año.
freshly ['freʃlɪ] adv: **~ painted/arrived** recién pintado/llegado.
freshman ['freʃmən] n (US: SCOL) = **fresher**.
freshness ['freʃnɪs] n frescura.
freshwater ['freʃwɔ:tə*] adj (fish) de agua dulce.
fret [fret] vi inquietarse.
fretful ['fretful] adj (child) quejumbroso.
Freudian ['frɔɪdɪən] adj freudiano; **~ slip** lapsus m (freudiano).
FRG n abbr (= Federal Republic of Germany) RFA f.
Fri. abbr (= Friday) vier.
friar ['fraɪə*] n fraile m; (before name) fray.
friction ['frɪkʃən] n fricción f.
friction feed n (on printer) avance m por fricción.
Friday ['fraɪdɪ] n viernes m inv.
fridge [frɪdʒ] n (BRIT) nevera, frigo, refrigeradora (LAM), heladera (LAM).
fridge-freezer ['frɪdʒ'fri:zə*] n frigorífico-congelador m, combi m.
fried [fraɪd] pt, pp of **fry** ♦ adj: **~ egg** huevo frito, huevo estrellado.
friend [frend] n amigo/a.
friendliness ['frendlɪnɪs] n simpatía.
friendly ['frendlɪ] adj simpático.

friendly fire *n* fuego amigo, disparos *mpl* del propio bando.

friendship ['frɛndʃɪp] *n* amistad *f.*

frieze [friːz] *n* friso.

frigate ['frɪgɪt] *n* fragata.

fright [fraɪt] *n* susto; **to take** ~ asustarse.

frighten ['fraɪtn] *vt* asustar.

▶**frighten away, frighten off** *vt* (*birds, children etc*) espantar, ahuyentar.

frightened ['fraɪtnd] *adj* asustado.

frightening ['fraɪtnɪŋ] *adj*: **it's** ~ da miedo.

frightful ['fraɪtful] *adj* espantoso, horrible.

frightfully ['fraɪtfulɪ] *adv* terriblemente; **I'm** ~ **sorry** lo siento muchísimo.

frigid ['frɪdʒɪd] *adj* (*MED*) frígido.

frigidity [frɪ'dʒɪdɪtɪ] *n* (*MED*) frigidez *f.*

frill [frɪl] *n* volante *m*; **without** ~s (*fig*) sin adornos.

frilly ['frɪlɪ] *adj* con volantes.

fringe [frɪndʒ] *n* (*BRIT: of hair*) flequillo; (*edge: of forest etc*) borde *m*, margen *m.*

fringe benefits *npl* ventajas *fpl* complementarias.

fringe theatre *n* teatro experimental.

Frisbee ® ['frɪzbɪ] *n* frisbee ® *m.*

frisk [frɪsk] *vt* cachear, registrar.

frisky ['frɪskɪ] *adj* juguetón/ona.

fritter ['frɪtə*] *n* buñuelo.

▶**fritter away** *vt* desperdiciar.

frivolity [frɪ'vɔlɪtɪ] *n* frivolidad *f.*

frivolous ['frɪvələs] *adj* frívolo.

frizzy ['frɪzɪ] *adj* crespo.

fro [frəu] *see* **to.**

frock [frɔk] *n* vestido.

frog [frɔg] *n* rana; **to have a** ~ **in one's throat** tener carraspera.

frogman ['frɔgmən] *n* hombre-rana *m.*

frogmarch ['frɔgmɑːtʃ] *vt*: **to** ~ **sb in/out** meter/sacar a algn a rastras.

frolic ['frɔlɪk] *vi* juguetear.

═══════════════════ *KEYWORD*

from [frɔm] *prep* **1** (*indicating starting place*) de, desde; **where do you come** ~?, **where are you** ~? ¿de dónde eres?; **where has he come** ~? ¿de dónde ha venido?; ~ **London to Glasgow** de Londres a Glasgow; **to escape** ~ **sth/sb** escaparse de algo/algn

2 (*indicating origin etc*) de; **a letter/ telephone call** ~ **my sister** una carta/ llamada de mi hermana; **tell him** ~ **me that ...** dígale de mi parte que ...

3 (*indicating time*): ~ **one o'clock to** *or* **until** *or* **till nine** de la una a las nueve, desde la una hasta las nueve; ~ **January (on)** a partir de enero; **(as)** ~ **Friday** a partir del viernes

4 (*indicating distance*) de; **the hotel is 1 km from the beach** el hotel está a 1 km de la playa

5 (*indicating price, number etc*) de; **prices range** ~ **£10 to £50** los precios van desde £10 a *or* hasta £50; **the interest rate was increased** ~ **9% to 10%** el tipo de interés fue incrementado de un 9% a un 10%

6 (*indicating difference*) de; **he can't tell red** ~ **green** no sabe distinguir el rojo del verde; **to be different** ~ **sb/sth** ser diferente a algn/algo

7 (*because of, on the basis of*): ~ **what he says** por lo que dice; **weak** ~ **hunger** debilitado por el hambre.

═══════════════════

frond [frɔnd] *n* fronda.

front [frʌnt] *n* (*foremost part*) parte *f* delantera; (*of house*) fachada; (*promenade: also:* **sea** ~) paseo marítimo; (*MIL, POL, METEOROLOGY*) frente *m*; (*fig: appearances*) apariencia ♦ *adj* (*wheel, leg*) delantero; (*row, line*) primero ♦ *vi*: **to** ~ **onto sth** dar a algo; **in** ~ **(of)** delante (de).

frontage ['frʌntɪdʒ] *n* (*of building*) fachada.

front bench *n* (*BRIT POL*) *ver recuadro.*

┌─────────────────────────────┐
│ **FRONT BENCH** │
└─────────────────────────────┘

El término genérico **front bench** *se usa para referirse a los escaños situados en primera fila a ambos lados del Presidente (*"Speaker"*) de la Cámara de los Comunes (*"House of Commons"*) del Parlamento británico. Dichos escaños son ocupados por los miembros del gobierno a un lado y los del gobierno en la oposición (*"shadow cabinet"*) al otro. Por esta razón a todos ellos se les denomina* "frontbenchers".

frontbencher ['frʌnt'bentʃə*] *n* (*BRIT*) *see* **front bench.**

front desk *n* (*US*) recepción *f.*

front door *n* puerta principal.

frontier ['frʌntɪə*] *n* frontera.

front page *n* primera plana.

front room *n* (*BRIT*) salón *m*, sala.

front runner *n* favorito/a.

front-wheel drive ['frʌntwiːl-] *n* tracción *f* delantera.

frost [frɔst] *n* (*gen*) helada; (*also:* **hoar**~) escarcha ♦ *vt* (*US CULIN*) escarchar.

frostbite ['frɔstbaɪt] *n* congelación *f.*

frosted ['frɔstɪd] *adj* (*glass*) esmerilado; (*esp US: cake*) glaseado.

frosting ['frɔstɪŋ] *n* (*esp US: icing*) glaseado.

frosty ['frɔstɪ] *adj* (*surface*) cubierto de

escarcha; (*welcome etc*) glacial.
froth [froθ] *n* espuma.
frothy ['froθɪ] *adj* espumoso.
frown [fraun] *vi* fruncir el ceño ♦ *n*: **with a**
  ~ frunciendo el entrecejo.
▶**frown on** *vt fus* desaprobar.
froze [frəuz] *pt of* **freeze**.
frozen ['frəuzn] *pp of* **freeze** ♦ *adj* (*food*)
  congelado; (*COMM*): ~ **assets** activos *mpl*
  congelados *or* bloqueados.
FRS *n* (*BRIT*: = *Fellow of the Royal Society*)
  miembro de la principal asociación de
  investigación científica; (*US*: = *Federal
  Reserve System*) banco central de
  los EE. UU.
frugal ['fru:gəl] *adj* (*person*) frugal.
fruit [fru:t] *n* (*pl inv*) fruta.
fruiterer ['fru:tərə*] *n* frutero/a; ~'**s** (**shop**)
  frutería.
fruit fly *n* mosca de la fruta.
fruitful ['fru:tful] *adj* provechoso.
fruition [fru:'ɪʃən] *n*: **to come to** ~
  realizarse.
fruit juice *n* jugo *or* zumo (*SP*) de fruta.
fruitless ['fru:tlɪs] *adj* (*fig*) infructuoso,
  inútil.
fruit machine *n* (*BRIT*) máquina
  tragaperras.
fruit salad *n* macedonia *or* ensalada (*LAM*)
  de frutas.
frump [frʌmp] *n* espantajo, adefesio.
frustrate [frʌs'treɪt] *vt* frustrar.
frustrated [frʌs'treɪtɪd] *adj* frustrado.
frustrating [frʌs'treɪtɪŋ] *adj* (*job, day*)
  frustrante.
frustration [frʌs'treɪʃən] *n* frustración *f*.
fry, *pt, pp* **fried** [fraɪ, -d] *vt* freír ♦ *n*: **small** ~
  gente *f* menuda.
frying pan ['fraɪŋ-] *n* sartén *f or m* (*LAM*).
FT *n abbr* (*BRIT*: = *Financial Times*) periódico
  financiero; **the** ~ **index** el índice de
  valores del Financial Times.
ft. *abbr* = **foot, feet**.
FTC *n abbr* (*US*) = *Federal Trade Commission*.
FTSE 100 Index *n abbr* (= *Financial Times
  Stock Exchange 100 Index*) índice bursátil
  del Financial Times.
fuchsia ['fju:ʃə] *n* fucsia.
fuck [fʌk] (*col!*) *vt* joder (*SP!*), coger (*LAM!*)
  ♦ *vi* joder (*SP!*), coger (*LAM!*); ~ **off!** ¡vete
  a tomar por culo! (*!*).
fuddled ['fʌdld] *adj* (*muddled*) confuso,
  aturdido; (*col: tipsy*) borracho.
fuddy-duddy ['fʌdɪdʌdɪ] (*pej*) *n* carcamal
  m, carroza *m/f* ♦ *adj* chapado a la antigua.
fudge [fʌdʒ] *n* (*CULIN*) caramelo blando ♦ *vt*
  (*issue, problem*) rehuir, esquivar.
fuel [fjuəl] *n* (*for heating*) combustible *m*;

(*coal*) carbón *m*; (*wood*) leña; (*for engine*)
  carburante *m* ♦ *vt* (*furnace etc*) alimentar;
  (*aircraft, ship etc*) aprovisionar de
  combustible.
fuel oil *n* fuel oil *m*.
fuel pump *n* (*AUT*) surtidor *m* de gasolina.
fuel tank *n* depósito de combustible.
fug [fʌg] *n* aire *m* viciado.
fugitive ['fju:dʒɪtɪv] *n* (*from prison*)
  fugitivo/a.
fulfil, (*US*) **fulfill** [ful'fɪl] *vt* (*function*)
  desempeñar; (*condition*) cumplir; (*wish,
  desire*) realizar.
fulfilled [ful'fɪld] *adj* (*person*) realizado.
fulfil(l)ment [ful'fɪlmənt] *n* realización *f*; (*of
  promise*) cumplimiento.
full [ful] *adj* lleno; (*fig*) pleno; (*complete*)
  completo; (*information*) detallado; (*price*)
  íntegro, sin descuento ♦ *adv*: ~ **well**
  perfectamente; **we're** ~ **up for July**
  estamos completos para julio; **I'm** ~ (**up**)
  estoy lleno; ~ **employment** pleno empleo;
  ~ **name** nombre *m* completo; **a** ~ **two
  hours** dos horas enteras; **at** ~ **speed** a
  toda velocidad; **in** ~ (*reproduce, quote*)
  íntegramente; **to write sth in** ~ escribir
  algo por extenso; **to pay in** ~ pagar la
  deuda entera.
fullback ['fulbæk] *n* (*FOOTBALL*) defensa *m*;
  (*RUGBY*) zaguero.
full-blooded ['ful'blʌdɪd] *adj* (*vigorous:
  attack*) vigoroso; (*pure*) puro.
full-cream ['ful'kri:m] *adj*: ~ **milk** leche *f*
  entera.
full driving licence *n* (*BRIT AUT*) carnet *m*
  de conducir (*definitivo*); *see also* **L-plates**.
full-fledged ['fulfledʒd] *adj* (*US*) = **fully-
  fledged**.
full-grown ['ful'grəun] *adj* maduro.
full-length ['ful'leŋθ] *adj* (*portrait*) de
  cuerpo entero; (*film*) de largometraje.
full moon *n* luna llena, plenilunio.
fullness ['fulnɪs] *n* plenitud *f*, amplitud *f*.
full-scale ['fulskeɪl] *adj* (*attack, war, search,
  retreat*) en gran escala; (*plan, model*) de
  tamaño natural.
full stop *n* punto.
full-time ['fultaɪm] *adj* (*work*) de tiempo
  completo ♦ *adv*: **to work** ~ trabajar a
  tiempo completo.
fully ['fulɪ] *adv* completamente; (*at least*) al
  menos.
fully-fledged ['fulɪ'fledʒd], (*US*) **full-
  fledged** *adj* (*teacher, barrister*) diplomado;
  (*bird*) con todas sus plumas, capaz de
  volar; (*fig*) de pleno derecho.
fully-paid ['fulɪpeɪd] *adj*: ~ **share** acción *f*
  liberada.

fulsome ['fulsəm] _adj_ (_pej: praise, gratitude_) excesivo, exagerado; (: _manner_) obsequioso.

fumble with ['fʌmbl-] _vt fus_ manosear.

fume [fjuːm] _vi_ humear, echar humo.

fumes [fjuːmz] _npl_ humo _sg_, gases _mpl_.

fumigate ['fjuːmɪgeɪt] _vt_ fumigar.

fun [fʌn] _n_ (_amusement_) diversión _f_; (_joy_) alegría; **to have** ~ divertirse; **for** ~ por gusto; **to make** ~ **of** reírse de.

function ['fʌŋkʃən] _n_ función _f_ ♦ _vi_ funcionar; **to** ~ **as** hacer (las veces) de, fungir de (_LAM_).

functional ['fʌŋkʃənl] _adj_ funcional.

function key _n_ (_COMPUT_) tecla de función.

fund [fʌnd] _n_ fondo; (_reserve_) reserva; ~**s** _npl_ fondos _mpl_.

fundamental [fʌndə'mentl] _adj_ fundamental ♦ _n_: ~**s** fundamentos _mpl_.

fundamentalism [fʌndə'mentəlɪzəm] _n_ fundamentalismo, integrismo.

fundamentalist [fʌndə'mentəlɪst] _n_ fundamentalista _m/f_, integrista _m/f_.

fundamentally [fʌndə'mentəlɪ] _adv_ fundamentalmente.

funding ['fʌndɪŋ] _n_ financiación _f_.

fund-raising ['fʌndreɪzɪŋ] _n_ recaudación _f_ de fondos.

funeral ['fjuːnərəl] _n_ (_burial_) entierro; (_ceremony_) funerales _mpl_.

funeral director _n_ director(a) _m/f_ de pompas fúnebres.

funeral parlour _n_ (_BRIT_) funeraria.

funeral service _n_ misa de cuerpo presente.

funereal [fjuː'nɪərɪəl] _adj_ fúnebre.

funfair ['fʌnfɛə*] _n_ (_BRIT_) parque _m_ de atracciones; (_travelling_) feria.

fungus, _pl_ **fungi** ['fʌŋgəs, -gaɪ] _n_ hongo.

funicular [fjuː'nɪkjulə*] _n_ (_also:_ ~ **railway**) funicular _m_.

funky ['fʌŋkɪ] _adj_ (_music_) funky; (_col: good_) guay.

funnel ['fʌnl] _n_ embudo; (_of ship_) chimenea.

funnily ['fʌnɪlɪ] _adv_ de modo divertido, graciosamente; (_oddly_) de una manera rara; ~ **enough** aunque parezca extraño.

funny ['fʌnɪ] _adj_ gracioso, divertido; (_strange_) curioso, raro.

funny bone _n_ hueso de la alegría.

fun run _n_ maratón _m_ popular.

fur [fəː*] _n_ piel _f_; (_BRIT: on tongue etc_) sarro.

fur coat _n_ abrigo de pieles.

furious ['fjuərɪəs] _adj_ furioso; (_effort, argument_) violento; **to be** ~ **with sb** estar furioso con algn.

furiously ['fjuərɪəslɪ] _adv_ con furia.

furl [fəːl] _vt_ (_sail_) recoger.

furlong ['fəːlɔŋ] _n_ octava parte de una milla.

furlough ['fəːləu] _n_ (_MIL, US_) permiso.

furnace ['fəːnɪs] _n_ horno.

furnish ['fəːnɪʃ] _vt_ amueblar; (_supply_) proporcionar; (_information_) facilitar.

furnished ['fəːnɪʃt] _adj_: ~ **flat** _or_ (_US_) **apartment** piso amueblado.

furnishings ['fəːnɪʃɪŋz] _npl_ mobiliario _sg_.

furniture ['fəːnɪtʃə*] _n_ muebles _mpl_; **piece of** ~ mueble _m_.

furniture polish _n_ cera para muebles.

furore [fjuə'rɔːrɪ] _n_ (_protests_) escándalo.

furrier ['fʌrɪə*] _n_ peletero/a.

furrow ['fʌrəu] _n_ surco ♦ _vt_ (_forehead_) arrugar.

furry ['fəːrɪ] _adj_ peludo; (_toy_) de peluche.

further ['fəːðə*] _adj_ (_new_) nuevo; (_place_) más lejano ♦ _adv_ más lejos; (_more_) más; (_moreover_) además ♦ _vt_ hacer avanzar; **how much** ~ **is it?** ¿a qué distancia queda?; ~ **to your letter of ...** (_COMM_) con referencia a su carta de ...; **to** ~ **one's interests** fomentar sus intereses.

further education _n_ educación _f_ postescolar.

furthermore [fəːðə'mɔː*] _adv_ además.

furthermost ['fəːðəməust] _adj_ más lejano.

furthest ['fəːðɪst] _superlative of_ **far**.

furtive ['fəːtɪv] _adj_ furtivo.

furtively ['fəːtɪvlɪ] _adv_ furtivamente, a escondidas.

fury ['fjuərɪ] _n_ furia.

fuse, (_US_) **fuze** [fjuːz] _n_ fusible _m_; (_for bomb etc_) mecha ♦ _vt_ (_metal_) fundir; (_fig_) fusionar ♦ _vi_ fundirse; fusionarse; (_BRIT: ELEC_): **to** ~ **the lights** fundir los plomos; **a** ~ **has blown** se ha fundido un fusible.

fuse box _n_ caja de fusibles.

fuselage ['fjuːzəlɑːʒ] _n_ fuselaje _m_.

fuse wire _n_ hilo fusible.

fusillade [fjuːzɪ'leɪd] _n_ descarga cerrada; (_fig_) lluvia.

fusion ['fjuːʒən] _n_ fusión _f_.

fuss [fʌs] _n_ (_noise_) bulla; (_dispute_) lío, jaleo; (_complaining_) protesta ♦ _vi_ preocuparse (por pequeñeces) ♦ _vt_ (_person_) molestar; **to make a** ~ armar jaleo.

▶**fuss over** _vt fus_ (_person_) contemplar, mimar.

fusspot ['fʌspɔt] _n_ (_col_) quisquilloso/a.

fussy ['fʌsɪ] _adj_ (_person_) quisquilloso; **I'm not** ~ (_col_) me da igual.

fusty ['fʌstɪ] _adj_ (_pej_) rancio; **to smell** ~ oler a cerrado.

futile ['fjuːtaɪl] _adj_ vano.

futility [fjuː'tɪlɪtɪ] _n_ inutilidad _f_.

futon ['fuːtɔn] _n_ futón _m_.

future ['fjuːtʃə*] adj (gen) futuro; (coming) venidero ♦ n futuro, porvenir; **in ~ de ahora en adelante.**

futures ['fjuːtʃəz] npl (COMM) operaciones fpl a término, futuros mpl.

futuristic [fjuːtʃə'rɪstɪk] adj futurista.

fuze [fjuːz] (US) = **fuse.**

fuzzy ['fʌzɪ] adj (PHOT) borroso; (hair) muy rizado.

fwd. abbr = **forward.**

fwy abbr (US) = **freeway.**

FY abbr = **fiscal year.**

FYI abbr = **for your information.**

G g

G, g [dʒiː] n (letter) G, g f; **G** (MUS) sol m; **G for George** G de Gerona.

G n abbr (BRIT SCOL: = good) N; (US CINE: = general audience) todos los públicos.

g. abbr (= gram(s), gravity) g.

G7 n abbr (POL = Group of Seven) G7 m.

GA abbr (US) = **Georgia.**

gab [gæb] n: **to have the gift of the ~** (col) tener mucha labia.

gabble ['gæbl] vi hablar atropelladamente; (gossip) cotorrear.

gaberdine [gæbə'diːn] n gabardina.

gable ['geɪbl] n aguilón m.

Gabon [gə'bɔn] n Gabón m.

gad about [gæd-] vi (col) moverse mucho.

gadget ['gædʒɪt] n aparato.

gadgetry ['gædʒɪtrɪ] n chismes mpl.

Gaelic ['geɪlɪk] adj, n (LING) gaélico.

gaffe [gæf] n plancha, patinazo, metedura de pata.

gaffer ['gæfə*] n (BRIT col) jefe m; ((old) man) vejete m.

gag [gæg] n (on mouth) mordaza; (joke) chiste m ♦ vt (prisoner etc) amordazar ♦ vi (choke) tener arcadas.

gaga ['gɑːgɑː] adj: **to go ~** (senile) chochear; (ecstatic) caérsele a algn la baba.

gage [geɪdʒ] n, vt (US) = **gauge.**

gaiety ['geɪtɪ] n alegría.

gaily ['geɪlɪ] adv alegremente.

gain [geɪn] n ganancia ♦ vt ganar ♦ vi (watch) adelantarse; **to ~ by sth** ganar con algo; **to ~ ground** ganar terreno; **to ~ 3 lbs (in weight)** engordar 3 libras.

▶**gain (up)on** vt fus alcanzar.

gainful ['geɪnful] adj (employment) remunerado.

gainfully ['geɪnfulɪ] adv: **to be ~ employed** tener un trabajo remunerado.

gait [geɪt] n forma de andar, andares mpl.

gala ['gɑːlə] n gala; **swimming ~** certamen m de natación.

Galapagos Islands [gə'læpəgəs-] npl: **the ~** las Islas Galápagos.

galaxy ['gæləksɪ] n galaxia.

gale [geɪl] n (wind) vendaval m; **~ force 10** vendaval de fuerza 10.

gall [gɔːl] n (ANAT) bilis f, hiel f; (fig: impudence) descaro, caradura ♦ vt molestar.

gal(l). abbr = **gallon(s).**

gallant ['gælənt] adj valeroso; (towards ladies) galante.

gallantry ['gæləntrɪ] n valentía; (courtesy) galantería.

gall bladder n vesícula biliar.

galleon ['gælɪən] n galeón m.

gallery ['gælərɪ] n (also THEAT) galería; (for spectators) tribuna; (also: **art ~**: state-owned) pinacoteca or museo de arte; (: private) galería de arte.

galley ['gælɪ] n (ship's kitchen) cocina; (ship) galera.

galley proof n (TYP) prueba de galera, galerada.

Gallic ['gælɪk] adj galo.

gallon ['gæln] n galón m (= 8 pints; BRIT = 4,546 litros, US = 3,785 litros).

gallop ['gæləp] n galope m ♦ vi galopar; **~ing inflation** inflación f galopante.

gallows ['gæləuz] n horca.

gallstone ['gɔːlstəun] n cálculo biliar.

Gallup poll ['gæləp-] n sondeo de opinión.

galore [gə'lɔː*] adv en cantidad, en abundancia.

galvanize ['gælvənaɪz] vt (metal) galvanizar; (fig): **to ~ sb into action** mover or impulsar a algn a actuar.

Gambia ['gæmbɪə] n Gambia.

gambit ['gæmbɪt] n (fig): **opening ~** táctica inicial.

gamble ['gæmbl] n (risk) jugada arriesgada; (bet) apuesta ♦ vt: **to ~ on** apostar a; (fig) confiar en por ♦ vi jugar; (COMM) especular; **to ~ on the Stock Exchange** jugar a la bolsa.

gambler ['gæmblə*] n jugador(a) m/f.

gambling ['gæmblɪŋ] n juego.

gambol ['gæmbl] vi brincar, juguetear.

game [geɪm] n (gen) juego; (match) partido; (of cards) partida; (HUNTING) caza ♦ adj valiente; (ready): **to be ~ for anything**

estar dispuesto a todo; **~s** (*SCOL*)
deportes *mpl*; **big ~** caza mayor.
game bird *n* ave *f* de caza.
gamekeeper ['geɪmkiːpə*] *n* guardabosque
m/f.
gamely ['geɪmlɪ] *adv* con decisión.
game reserve *n* coto de caza.
games console [geɪmz-] *n* consola de
juegos.
game show *n* programa *m* concurso *inv*,
concurso.
gamesmanship ['geɪmzmənʃɪp] *n* (uso de)
artimañas *fpl* para ganar.
gammon ['gæmən] *n* (*bacon*) tocino
ahumado; (*ham*) jamón *m* ahumado.
gamut ['gæmət] *n* (*MUS*) gama; **to run the
(whole) ~ of emotions** (*fig*) recorrer toda
la gama de emociones.
gander ['gændə*] *n* ganso.
gang [gæŋ] *n* pandilla; (*of criminals etc*)
banda; (*of kids*) pandilla; (*of colleagues*)
peña; (*of workmen*) brigada ♦ *vi*: **to ~ up
on sb** conchabarse contra algn.
Ganges ['gændʒiːz] *n*: **the ~** el Ganges.
gangland ['gæŋglænd] *adj*: **~ bosses**
cabecillas mafiosos; **~ killings** asesinatos
entre bandas.
gangling ['gæŋglɪŋ] *adj* larguirucho.
gangly ['gæŋglɪ] *adj* desgarbado.
gangplank ['gæŋplæŋk] *n* pasarela,
plancha.
gangrene ['gæŋgriːn] *n* gangrena.
gangster ['gæŋstə*] *n* gángster *m*.
gang warfare *n* guerra entre bandas.
gangway ['gæŋweɪ] *n* (*BRIT: in theatre, bus
etc*) pasillo; (*on ship*) pasarela.
gantry ['gæntrɪ] *n* (*for crane, railway signal*)
pórtico; (*for rocket*) torre *f* de
lanzamiento.
GAO *n abbr* (*US*: = *General Accounting Office*)
tribunal de cuentas.
gaol [dʒeɪl] *n, vt* (*BRIT*) = **jail**.
gap [gæp] *n* hueco; (*in trees, traffic*) claro; (*in
market, records*) laguna; (*in time*)
intervalo.
gape [geɪp] *vi* mirar boquiabierto.
gaping ['geɪpɪŋ] *adj* (*hole*) muy abierto.
gap year *n* año sabático.
garage ['gærɑːʒ] *n* garaje *m*.
garb [gɑːb] *n* atuendo.
garbage ['gɑːbɪdʒ] *n* (*US*) basura;
(*nonsense*) bobadas *fpl*; (*fig: film, book etc*)
basura.
garbage can *n* (*US*) cubo *or* balde *m* (*LAM*)
or bote *m* (*LAM*) de la basura.
garbage collector *n* (*US*) basurero/a.
garbage disposal unit *n* triturador *m* (de
basura).

garbage man *n* basurero.
garbage truck *n* (*US*) camión *m* de la
basura.
garbled ['gɑːbld] *adj* (*account, explanation*)
confuso.
garden ['gɑːdn] *n* jardín *m*; **~s** *npl* (*public*)
parque *m*, jardines *mpl*; (*private*) huertos
mpl.
garden centre *n* centro de jardinería.
garden city *n* (*BRIT*) ciudad *f* jardín.
gardener ['gɑːdnə*] *n* jardinero/a.
gardening ['gɑːdnɪŋ] *n* jardinería.
garden party *n* recepción *f* al aire libre.
gargle ['gɑːgl] *vi* hacer gárgaras,
gargarear (*LAM*).
gargoyle ['gɑːgɔɪl] *n* gárgola.
garish ['gɛərɪʃ] *adj* chillón/ona.
garland ['gɑːlənd] *n* guirnalda.
garlic ['gɑːlɪk] *n* ajo.
garment ['gɑːmənt] *n* prenda (de vestir).
garner ['gɑːnə*] *vt* hacer acopio de.
garnish ['gɑːnɪʃ] *vt* adornar; (*CULIN*)
aderezar.
garret ['gærɪt] *n* desván *m*, buhardilla.
garrison ['gærɪsn] *n* guarnición *f* ♦ *vt*
guarnecer.
garrulous ['gærjuləs] *adj* charlatán/ana.
garter ['gɑːtə*] *n* (*US*) liga.
garter belt *n* (*US*) liguero, portaligas *m inv*.
gas [gæs] *n* gas *m*; (*US: gasoline*) gasolina
♦ *vt* asfixiar con gas; **Calor ~** ® (gas *m*)
butano.
gas chamber *n* cámara de gas.
Gascony ['gæskənɪ] *n* Gascuña.
gas cooker *n* (*BRIT*) cocina de gas.
gas cylinder *n* bombona de gas.
gaseous ['gæsɪəs] *adj* gaseoso.
gas fire *n* estufa de gas.
gas-fired ['gæsfaɪəd] *adj* de gas.
gash [gæʃ] *n* brecha, raja; (*from knife*)
cuchillada ♦ *vt* rajar; (*with knife*)
acuchillar.
gasket ['gæskɪt] *n* (*AUT*) junta.
gas mask *n* careta antigás.
gas meter *n* contador *m* de gas.
gasoline ['gæsəliːn] *n* (*US*) gasolina.
gasp [gɑːsp] *n* grito sofocado ♦ *vi* (*pant*)
jadear.
► **gasp out** *vt* (*say*) decir jadeando.
gas pedal *n* (*esp US*) acelerador *m*.
gas ring *n* hornillo de gas.
gas station *n* (*US*) gasolinera.
gas stove *n* cocina de gas.
gassy ['gæsɪ] *adj* con mucho gas.
gas tank *n* (*US AUT*) depósito (de gasolina).
gas tap *n* llave *f* del gas.
gastric ['gæstrɪk] *adj* gástrico.
gastric ulcer *n* úlcera gástrica.

gastroenteritis ['gæstrəuɛntə'raɪtɪs] n
gastroenteritis f.
gasworks ['gæswɔːks] nsg or npl fábrica de
gas.
gate [geɪt] n (also at airport) puerta; (RAIL: at
level crossing) barrera; (metal) verja.
gâteau, pl ~**x** ['gætəu, z] n tarta.
gatecrash ['geɪtkræʃ] vt colarse en.
gatecrasher ['geɪtkræʃə*] n intruso/a.
gatehouse ['geɪthaus] n casa del guarda.
gateway ['geɪtweɪ] n puerta.
gather ['gæðə*] vt (flowers, fruit) coger (SP),
recoger (LAM); (assemble) reunir; (pick
up) recoger; (SEWING) fruncir;
(understand) sacar en consecuencia ♦ vi
(assemble) reunirse; (dust) acumularse;
(clouds) cerrarse; **to ~ speed** ganar
velocidad; **to ~ (from/that)** deducir (por/
que); **as far as I can ~** por lo que tengo
entendido.
gathering ['gæðərɪŋ] n reunión f, asamblea.
GATT [gæt] n abbr (= General Agreement on
Tariffs and Trade) GATT m.
gauche [gəuʃ] adj torpe.
gaudy ['gɔːdɪ] adj chillón/ona.
gauge, (US) **gage** [geɪdʒ] n calibre m; (RAIL)
ancho de vía, entrevía; (instrument)
indicador m ♦ vt medir; (fig: sb's
capabilities, character) juzgar, calibrar;
petrol ~ indicador m (del nivel) de
gasolina; **to ~ the right moment** elegir el
momento (oportuno).
gaunt [gɔːnt] adj descarnado; (fig) adusto.
gauntlet ['gɔːntlɪt] n (fig): **to run the ~ of**
sth exponerse a algo; **to throw down the**
~ arrojar el guante.
gauze [gɔːz] n gasa.
gave [geɪv] pt of **give**.
gawk [gɔːk] vi mirar pasmado.
gawky ['gɔːkɪ] adj desgarbado.
gay [geɪ] adj (colour, person) alegre;
(homosexual) gay.
gaze [geɪz] n mirada fija ♦ vi: **to ~ at sth**
mirar algo fijamente.
gazelle [gə'zɛl] n gacela.
gazette [gə'zɛt] n (newspaper) gaceta;
(official publication) boletín m oficial.
gazetteer [gæzə'tɪə*] n índice geográfico.
gazump [gə'zʌmp] vti (BRIT) echarse atrás
en la venta ya acordada de una casa por
haber una oferta más alta.
GB abbr (= Great Britain) G.B.
GBH n abbr (BRIT LAW: col) = **grievous bodily**
harm.
GC n abbr (BRIT: = George Cross) distinción
honorífica.
GCE n abbr (BRIT: =General Certificate of
Education) ≈ certificado de bachillerato.

GCHQ n abbr (BRIT: = Government
Communications Headquarters) centro de
intercepción de las telecomunicaciones
internacionales.
GCSE n abbr (BRIT: =General Certificate of
Secondary Education) certificado del
último ciclo de la enseñanza secundaria
obligatoria.
Gdns. abbr (= gardens) jdns.
GDP n abbr (= gross domestic product) PIB
m.
GDR n abbr (= German Democratic Republic)
RDA f.
gear [gɪə*] n equipo; (TECH) engranaje m;
(AUT) velocidad f, marcha ♦ vt (fig: adapt):
to ~ sth to adaptar or ajustar algo a; **top**
or (US) **high/low ~** cuarta/primera; **in ~**
con la marcha metida; **our service is ~ed**
to meet the needs of the disabled nuestro
servicio va enfocado a responder a las
necesidades de los minusválidos.
▶**gear up** vi prepararse.
gear box n caja de cambios.
gear lever, (US) **gear shift** n palanca de
cambio.
gear wheel n rueda dentada.
GED n abbr (US SCOL) = general educational
development.
geese [giːs] npl of **goose**.
geezer ['giːzə*] n (BRIT col) tipo, maromo
(SP).
Geiger counter ['gaɪgə-] n contador m
Geiger.
gel [dʒɛl] n gel m.
gelatin(e) ['dʒɛlətiːn] n gelatina.
gelignite ['dʒɛlɪgnaɪt] n gelignita.
gem [dʒɛm] n gema, piedra preciosa; (fig)
joya.
Gemini ['dʒɛmɪnaɪ] n Géminis m.
gen [dʒɛn] n (BRIT col): **to give sb the ~ on**
sth poner a algn al tanto de algo.
Gen. abbr (MIL: = General) Gen., Gral.
gen. abbr (= general) grl.; = **generally**.
gender ['dʒɛndə*] n género.
gene [dʒiːn] n gen(e) m.
genealogy [dʒiːnɪ'ælədʒɪ] n genealogía.
general ['dʒɛnərl] n general m ♦ adj general;
in ~ en general; **~ audit** auditoría
general; **the ~ public** el gran público.
general anaesthetic, (US) **general**
anesthetic n anestesia general.
general delivery n (US) lista de correos.
general election n elecciones fpl
generales.
generalization [dʒɛnrəlaɪ'zeɪʃən] n
generalización f.
generalize ['dʒɛnrəlaɪz] vi generalizar.
generally ['dʒɛnrəlɪ] adv generalmente, en

general.
general manager n director(a) m/f
general.
general practitioner (GP) n médico/a de
medicina general.
general strike n huelga general.
generate ['dʒenəreɪt] vt generar.
generation [dʒenə'reɪʃən] n (of electricity
etc) generación f.
generator ['dʒenəreɪtə*] n generador m.
generic [dʒɪ'nerɪk] adj genérico.
generosity [dʒenə'rɒsɪtɪ] n generosidad f.
generous ['dʒenərəs] adj generoso;
(copious) abundante.
generously ['dʒenərəslɪ] adv
generosamente; abundantemente.
genesis ['dʒenɪsɪs] n génesis f.
genetic [dʒɪ'netɪk] adj genético.
genetically modified organism
[dʒɪ'netɪkəlɪ] n organismo genéticamente
modificado, organismo transgénico.
genetic engineering n ingeniería
genética.
genetic fingerprinting [-'fɪŋɡəprɪntɪŋ] n
identificación f genética.
genetics [dʒɪ'netɪks] n genética.
Geneva [dʒɪ'niːvə] n Ginebra.
genial ['dʒiːnɪəl] adj afable.
genitals ['dʒenɪtlz] npl (órganos mpl)
genitales mpl.
genitive ['dʒenɪtɪv] n genitivo.
genius ['dʒiːnɪəs] n genio.
Genoa ['dʒenəuə] n Génova.
genocide ['dʒenəusaɪd] n genocidio.
gent [dʒent] n abbr (BRIT col) = **gentleman**.
genteel [dʒen'tiːl] adj fino, distinguido.
gentle ['dʒentl] adj (sweet) dulce; (touch etc)
ligero, suave.
gentleman ['dʒentlmən] n señor m; (well-
bred man) caballero; ~'s agreement
acuerdo entre caballeros.
gentlemanly ['dʒentlmənlɪ] adj caballeroso.
gentleness ['dʒentlnɪs] n dulzura; (of touch)
suavidad f.
gently ['dʒentlɪ] adv suavemente.
gentrification [dʒentrɪfɪ'keɪʃən] n
aburguesamiento.
gentry ['dʒentrɪ] npl pequeña nobleza sg.
gents [dʒents] n servicios mpl (de
caballeros).
genuine ['dʒenjuɪn] adj auténtico; (person)
sincero.
genuinely ['dʒenjuɪnlɪ] adv sinceramente.
geographer [dʒɪ'ɒɡrəfə*] n geográfo/a.
geographic(al) [dʒɪə'ɡræfɪk(l)] adj
geográfico.
geography [dʒɪ'ɒɡrəfɪ] n geografía.
geological [dʒɪə'lɒdʒɪkl] adj geológico.

geologist [dʒɪ'ɒlədʒɪst] n geólogo/a.
geology [dʒɪ'ɒlədʒɪ] n geología.
geometric(al) [dʒɪə'metrɪk(l)] adj
geométrico.
geometry [dʒɪ'ɒmətrɪ] n geometría.
Geordie ['dʒɔːdɪ] n habitante m/f de
Tyneside.
Georgia ['dʒɔːdʒə] n Georgia.
Georgian ['dʒɔːdʒən] adj georgiano ♦ n
georgiano/a; (LING) georgiano.
geranium [dʒɪ'reɪnjəm] n geranio.
geriatric [dʒerɪ'ætrɪk] adj, n geriátrico/a m/f.
germ [dʒɜːm] n (microbe) microbio,
bacteria; (seed, fig) germen m.
German ['dʒɜːmən] adj alemán/ana ♦ n
alemán/ana m/f; (LING) alemán m.
German Democratic Republic n
República Democrática Alemana.
germane [dʒɜː'meɪn] adj: ~ (to) pertinente
(a).
German measles n rubeola, rubéola.
German Shepherd n (dog) pastor m
alemán.
Germany ['dʒɜːmənɪ] n Alemania; East/
West ~ Alemania Oriental or
Democrática/Occidental or Federal.
germination [dʒɜːmɪ'neɪʃən] n
germinación f.
germ warfare n guerra bacteriológica.
gesticulate [dʒes'tɪkjuleɪt] vi gesticular.
gesticulation [dʒestɪkju'leɪʃən] n
gesticulación f.
gesture ['dʒestjə*] n gesto; as a ~ of
friendship en señal de amistad.

══════════════════ KEYWORD

get [ɡet] (pt, pp got, pp gotten (US)) vi 1
(become, be) ponerse, volverse; to ~ old/
tired envejecer/cansarse; to ~ drunk
emborracharse; to ~ dirty ensuciarse; to
~ ready/washed prepararse/lavarse; to
~ married casarse; when do I ~ paid?
¿cuándo me pagan or se me paga?; it's
~ting late se está haciendo tarde
2 (go): to ~ to/from llegar a/de; to ~
home llegar a casa; he got under the
fence pasó por debajo de la barrera
3 (begin) empezar a; to ~ to know sb
(llegar a) conocer a algn; I'm ~ting to
like him me está empezando a gustar;
let's ~ going or started ¡vamos (a
empezar)!
4 (modal aux vb): you've got to do it
tienes que hacerlo
♦ vt 1: to ~ sth done (finish) hacer algo;
(have done) mandar hacer algo; to ~
one's hair cut cortarse el pelo; to ~ the
car going or to go arrancar el coche; to ~

sb to do sth conseguir or hacer que algn haga algo; **to ~ sth/sb ready** preparar algo/a algn
2 (*obtain*: *money, permission, results*) conseguir; (*find*: *job, flat*) encontrar; (*fetch*: *person, doctor*) buscar; (*object*) ir a buscar, traer; **to ~ sth for sb** conseguir algo para algn; **~ me Mr Jones, please** (*TEL*) póngame or comuníqueme (*LAM*) con el Sr. Jones, por favor; **can I ~ you a drink?** ¿quieres algo de beber?
3 (*receive*: *present, letter*) recibir; (*acquire*: *reputation*) alcanzar; (: *prize*) ganar; **what did you ~ for your birthday?** ¿qué te regalaron por tu cumpleaños?; **how much did you ~ for the painting?** ¿cuánto sacaste por el cuadro?
4 (*catch*) coger (*SP*), agarrar (*LAM*); (*hit*: *target etc*) dar en; **to ~ sb by the arm/ throat** coger or agarrar a algn por el brazo/cuello; **~ him!** ¡cógelo! (*SP*), ¡atrápalo! (*LAM*); **the bullet got him in the leg** la bala le dio en la pierna
5 (*take, move*) llevar; **to ~ sth to sb** hacer llegar algo a algn; **do you think we'll ~ it through the door?** ¿crees que lo podremos meter por la puerta?
6 (*catch, take*: *plane, bus etc*) coger (*SP*), tomar (*LAM*); **where do I ~ the train for Birmingham?** ¿dónde se coge or se toma el tren para Birmingham?
7 (*understand*) entender; (*hear*) oír; **I've got it!** ¡ya lo tengo!, ¡eureka!; **I don't ~ your meaning** no te entiendo; **I'm sorry, I didn't ~ your name** lo siento, no me he enterado de tu nombre
8 (*have, possess*): **to have got** tener
9 (*col*: *annoy*) molestar; (: *thrill*) chiflar
▶**get about** *vi* salir mucho; (*news*) divulgarse
▶**get across** *vt* (*message, meaning*) lograr comunicar ♦ *vi*: **to ~ across to sb** hacer que algn comprenda
▶**get along** *vi* (*agree*) llevarse bien; (*depart*) marcharse; (*manage*) = **get by**
▶**get at** *vt fus* (*attack*) meterse con; (*reach*) alcanzar; (*the truth*) descubrir; **what are you ~ting at?** ¿qué insinúas?
▶**get away** *vi* marcharse; (*escape*) escaparse
▶**get away with** *vt fus* hacer impunemente
▶**get back** *vi* (*return*) volver ♦ *vt* recobrar
▶**get back at** *vt fus* (*col*): **to ~ back at sb** (*for sth*) vengarse de algn (por algo)
▶**get by** *vi* (*pass*) (*lograr*) pasar; (*manage*) arreglárselas; **I can ~ by in Dutch** me defiendo en holandés
▶**get down** *vi* bajar(se) ♦ *vt fus* bajar ♦ *vt*

bajar; (*depress*) deprimir
▶**get down to** *vt fus* (*work*) ponerse a
▶**get in** *vi* entrar; (*train*) llegar; (*arrive home*) volver a casa, regresar; (*political party*) salir ♦ *vt* (*bring in*: *harvest*) recoger; (: *coal, shopping, supplies*) comprar, traer; (*insert*) meter
▶**get into** *vt fus* entrar en; (*vehicle*) subir a; **to ~ into a rage** enfadarse
▶**get off** *vi* (*from train etc*) bajar(se); (*depart*: *person, car*) marcharse ♦ *vt* (*remove*) quitar; (*send off*) mandar; (*have as leave*: *day, time*) tener libre ♦ *vt fus* (*train, bus*) bajar(se) de; **to ~ off to a good start** (*fig*) empezar muy bien or con buen pie
▶**get on** *vi* (*at exam etc*): **how are you ~ting on?** ¿cómo te va?; (*agree*): **to ~ on (with)** llevarse bien (con) ♦ *vt fus* subir(se) a
▶**get on to** *vt fus* (*deal with*) ocuparse de; (*col*: *contact*: *on phone etc*) hablar con
▶**get out** *vi* salir; (*of vehicle*) bajar(se); (*news*) saberse ♦ *vt* sacar
▶**get out of** *vt fus* salir de; (*duty etc*) escaparse de; (*gain from*: *pleasure, benefit*) sacar de
▶**get over** *vt fus* (*illness*) recobrarse de
▶**get round** *vt fus* rodear; (*fig*: *person*) engatusar a ♦ *vi*: **to ~ round to doing sth** encontrar tiempo para hacer algo
▶**get through** *vt fus* (*finish*) acabar ♦ *vi* (*TEL*) (*lograr*) comunicar
▶**get through to** *vt fus* (*TEL*) comunicar con
▶**get together** *vi* reunirse ♦ *vt* reunir, juntar
▶**get up** *vi* (*rise*) levantarse ♦ *vt fus* subir; **to ~ up enthusiasm for sth** cobrar entusiasmo por algo
▶**get up to** *vt fus* (*reach*) llegar a; (*prank*) hacer.

getaway ['gɛtəweɪ] *n* fuga.
getaway car *n*: **the thieves' ~** el coche en que huyeron los ladrones.
get-together ['gɛttəgɛðə*] *n* reunión *f*; (*party*) fiesta.
get-up ['gɛtʌp] *n* (*BRIT col*: *outfit*) atavío, atuendo.
get-well card [gɛt'wɛl-] *n* tarjeta en la que se desea a un enfermo que se mejore.
geyser ['giːzə*] *n* (*water heater*) calentador *m* de agua; (*GEO*) géiser *m*.
Ghana ['gɑːnə] *n* Ghana.
Ghanaian [gɑːˈneɪən] *adj, n* ghanés/esa *m/f*.
ghastly ['gɑːstlɪ] *adj* horrible; (*pale*) pálido.
gherkin ['gɜːkɪn] *n* pepinillo.
ghetto ['gɛtəu] *n* gueto.

ghetto blaster [-'blɑːstə*] *n*
radiocas(s)et(t)e *m* portátil (*de gran
tamaño*).

ghost [gəust] *n* fantasma *m* ♦ *vt* (*book*)
escribir por otro.

ghostly ['gəustlɪ] *adj* fantasmal.

ghost story *n* cuento de fantasmas.

ghostwriter ['gəustraɪtə*] *n* negro/a.

ghoul [guːl] *n* espíritu *m* necrófago.

GHQ *n abbr* (*MIL*: = *general headquarters*)
E.M.

GI *n abbr* (*US col*: = *government issue*)
soldado del ejército norteamericano.

giant ['dʒaɪənt] *n* gigante *m/f* ♦ *adj*
gigantesco, gigante; ~ (**size**) **packet**
paquete *m* (de tamaño) gigante *or*
familiar.

giant killer *n* (*SPORT*) matagigantes *m inv.*

gibber ['dʒɪbə*] *vi* farfullar.

gibberish ['dʒɪbərɪʃ] *n* galimatías *m.*

gibe [dʒaɪb] *n* pulla.

giblets ['dʒɪblɪts] *npl* menudillos *mpl.*

Gibraltar [dʒɪ'brɔːltə*] *n* Gibraltar *m.*

giddiness ['gɪdɪnɪs] *n* mareo.

giddy ['gɪdɪ] *adj* (*dizzy*) mareado; (*height,
speed*) vertiginoso; **it makes me** ~ me
marea; **I feel** ~ me siento mareado.

gift [gɪft] *n* (*gen*) regalo; (*COMM*: *also*: **free**
~) obsequio; (*ability*) don *m*; **to have a** ~
for sth tener dotes para algo.

gifted ['gɪftɪd] *adj* dotado.

gift token, gift voucher *n* vale-regalo *m.*

gig [gɪg] *n* (*col*: *concert*) actuación *f.*

gigabyte ['dʒɪgəbaɪt] *n* gigabyte *m.*

gigantic [dʒaɪ'gæntɪk] *adj* gigantesco.

giggle ['gɪgl] *vi* reírse tontamente ♦ *n*
risilla.

GIGO ['gaɪgəu] *abbr* (*COMPUT*: *col*) = *garbage
in, garbage out.*

gill [dʒɪl] *n* (*measure*) = 0.25 *pints* (*BRIT*
= 0.148 *l*, *US* = 0.118 *l*).

gills [gɪlz] *npl* (*of fish*) branquias *fpl*, agallas
fpl.

gilt [gɪlt] *adj, n* dorado.

gilt-edged ['gɪltedʒd] *adj* (*COMM*: *stocks,
securities*) de máxima garantía.

gimlet ['gɪmlɪt] *n* barrena de mano.

gimmick ['gɪmɪk] *n* reclamo; **sales** ~
reclamo promocional.

gimmicky ['gɪmɪkɪ] *adj* de reclamo.

gin [dʒɪn] *n* (*liquor*) ginebra.

ginger ['dʒɪndʒə*] *n* jengibre *m.*

ginger ale *n* ginger ale *m.*

ginger beer *n* refresco *m* de jengibre.

gingerbread ['dʒɪndʒəbred] *n* pan *m* de
jengibre.

ginger-haired [dʒɪndʒə'heəd] *adj* pelirrojo.

gingerly ['dʒɪndʒəlɪ] *adv* con pies de plomo.

ginseng ['dʒɪnseŋ] *n* ginseng *m.*

gipsy ['dʒɪpsɪ] *n* gitano/a.

giraffe [dʒɪ'rɑːf] *n* jirafa.

girder ['gəːdə*] *n* viga.

girdle ['gəːdl] *n* (*corset*) faja ♦ *vt* ceñir.

girl [gəːl] *n* (*small*) niña; (*young woman*)
chica, joven *f*, muchacha; **an English** ~
una (chica) inglesa.

girlfriend ['gəːlfrend] *n* (*of girl*) amiga; (*of
boy*) novia.

Girl Guide *n* exploradora.

girlish ['gəːlɪʃ] *adj* de niña.

Girl Scout *n* (*US*) = **Girl Guide**.

giro ['dʒaɪrəu] *n* (*BRIT*: *bank* ~) giro
bancario; (*post office* ~) giro postal.

girth [gəːθ] *n* circunferencia; (*of saddle*)
cincha.

gist [dʒɪst] *n* lo esencial.

give [gɪv] *vb* (*pt* **gave**, *pp* **given** [geɪv, 'gɪvn])
vt dar; (*deliver*) entregar; (*as gift*) regalar
♦ *vi* (*break*) romperse; (*stretch*: *fabric*) dar
de sí; **to** ~ **sb sth**, ~ **sth to sb** dar algo a
algn; **how much did you** ~ **for it?** ¿cuánto
pagaste por él?; **12 o'clock,** ~ **or take a
few minutes** más o menos las doce; ~
them my regards dales recuerdos de mi
parte; **I can** ~ **you 10 minutes** le puedo
conceder 10 minutos; **to** ~ **way** (*BRIT AUT*)
ceder el paso; **to** ~ **way to despair** ceder
a la desesperación.

▶**give away** *vt* (*give free*) regalar; (*betray*)
traicionar; (*disclose*) revelar.

▶**give back** *vt* devolver.

▶**give in** *vi* ceder ♦ *vt* entregar.

▶**give off** *vt* despedir.

▶**give out** *vt* distribuir ♦ *vi* (*be exhausted*:
supplies) agotarse; (*fail*: *engine*) averiarse;
(*strength*) fallar.

▶**give up** *vi* rendirse, darse por vencido
♦ *vt* renunciar a; **to** ~ **up smoking** dejar
de fumar; **to** ~ **o.s. up** entregarse.

give-and-take ['gɪvənd'teɪk] *n* (*col*) toma y
daca *m.*

giveaway ['gɪvəweɪ] *n* (*col*): **her expression
was a** ~ su expresión la delataba; **the
exam was a** ~! ¡el examen estaba tirado!
♦ *cpd*: ~ **prices** precios *mpl* de regalo.

given ['gɪvn] *pp* of **give** ♦ *adj* (*fixed*: *time,
amount*) determinado ♦ *conj*: ~ (**that**) ...
dado (que) ...; ~ **the circumstances** ...
dadas las circunstancias ....

glacial ['gleɪsɪəl] *adj* glacial.

glacier ['glæsɪə*] *n* glaciar *m.*

glad [glæd] *adj* contento; **to be** ~ **about
sth/that** alegrarse de algo/de que; **I was**
~ **of his help** agradecí su ayuda.

gladden ['glædn] *vt* alegrar.

glade [gleɪd] *n* claro.

gladiator ['glædɪeɪtə*] n gladiador m.
gladioli [glædɪ'əʊlaɪ] npl gladiolos mpl.
gladly ['glædlɪ] adv con mucho gusto.
glamorous ['glæmərəs] adj con encanto,
atractivo.
glamour ['glæmə*] n encanto, atractivo.
glance [glɑːns] n ojeada, mirada ♦ vi: **to ~
at** echar una ojeada a.
▶**glance off** vt fus (bullet) rebotar en.
glancing ['glɑːnsɪŋ] adj (blow) oblicuo.
gland [glænd] n glándula.
glandular ['glændjʊlə*] adj: **~ fever**
mononucleosis f infecciosa.
glare [glɛə*] n deslumbramiento, brillo ♦ vi
deslumbrar; **to ~ at** mirar con odio.
glaring ['glɛərɪŋ] adj (mistake) manifiesto.
glass [glɑːs] n vidrio, cristal m; (for
drinking) vaso; (: with stem) copa; (also:
looking ~) espejo.
glass-blowing ['glɑːsbləʊɪŋ] n soplado de
vidrio.
glass ceiling n (fig) techo or barrera
invisible (que impide ascender
profesionalmente a las mujeres o miembros
de minorías étnicas).
glasses ['glɑːsəs] npl gafas fpl, anteojos mpl
(LAM).
glass fibre, (US) **glass fiber** n fibra de
vidrio.
glasshouse ['glɑːshaʊs] n invernadero.
glassware ['glɑːswɛə*] n cristalería.
glassy ['glɑːsɪ] adj (eyes) vidrioso.
Glaswegian [glæs'wiːdʒən] adj de Glasgow
♦ n nativo/a (or habitante m/f) de Glasgow.
glaze [gleɪz] vt (window) acristalar;
(pottery) vidriar; (CULIN) glasear ♦ n
barniz m; (CULIN) vidriado.
glazed [gleɪzd] adj (eye) vidrioso; (pottery)
vidriado.
glazier ['gleɪzɪə*] n vidriero/a.
gleam [gliːm] n destello ♦ vi relucir; **a ~ of**
hope un rayo de esperanza.
gleaming ['gliːmɪŋ] adj reluciente.
glean [gliːn] vt (gather: information) recoger.
glee [gliː] n alegría, regocijo.
gleeful ['gliːfʊl] adj alegre.
glen [glɛn] n cañada.
glib [glɪb] adj (person) de mucha labia;
(comment) fácil.
glibly ['glɪblɪ] adv (explain) con mucha labia.
glide [glaɪd] vi deslizarse; (AVIAT, birds)
planear.
glider ['glaɪdə*] n (AVIAT) planeador m.
gliding ['glaɪdɪŋ] n (AVIAT) vuelo sin motor.
glimmer ['glɪmə*] n luz f tenue.
glimpse [glɪmps] n vislumbre m ♦ vt
vislumbrar, entrever; **to catch a ~ of**
vislumbrar.

glint [glɪnt] n destello; (in the eye) chispa
♦ vi centellear.
glisten ['glɪsn] vi relucir, brillar.
glitter ['glɪtə*] vi relucir, brillar ♦ n brillo.
glittering ['glɪtərɪŋ] adj reluciente,
brillante.
glitz [glɪts] n (col) vistosidad f.
gloat [gləʊt] vi: **to ~ over** regodearse con.
global ['gləʊbl] adj (world-wide) mundial;
(comprehensive) global.
globalization [ˌgləʊbəlaɪ'zeɪʃən] n
globalización f, mundialización f.
global warming [-'wɔːmɪŋ] n
(re)calentamiento global or de la tierra.
globe [gləʊb] n globo, esfera; (model) bola
del mundo; globo terráqueo.
globetrotter ['gləʊbtrɒtə*] n trotamundos
m inv.
globule ['glɒbjuːl] n glóbulo.
gloom [gluːm] n penumbra; (sadness)
desaliento, melancolía.
gloomily ['gluːmɪlɪ] adv tristemente; de
modo pesimista.
gloomy ['gluːmɪ] adj (dark) oscuro; (sad)
triste; (pessimistic) pesimista; **to feel ~**
sentirse pesimista.
glorification [glɔːrɪfɪ'keɪʃən] n glorificación f.
glorify ['glɔːrɪfaɪ] vt glorificar.
glorious ['glɔːrɪəs] adj glorioso; (weather,
sunshine) espléndido.
glory ['glɔːrɪ] n gloria.
Glos abbr (BRIT) = Gloucestershire.
gloss [glɒs] n (shine) brillo; (also: **~ paint**)
(pintura) esmalte m.
▶**gloss over** vt fus restar importancia a;
(omit) pasar por alto.
glossary ['glɒsərɪ] n glosario.
glossy ['glɒsɪ] adj (hair) brillante;
(photograph) con brillo; (magazine) de
papel satinado or cuché.
glove [glʌv] n guante m.
glove compartment n (AUT) guantera m.
glow [gləʊ] vi (shine) brillar ♦ n brillo.
glower ['glaʊə*] vi: **to ~ at** mirar con
ceño.
glowing ['gləʊɪŋ] adj (fire) vivo;
(complexion) encendido; (fig: report,
description) entusiasta.
glow-worm ['gləʊwəːm] n luciérnaga.
glucose ['gluːkəʊs] n glucosa.
glue [gluː] n pegamento, cemento (LAM) ♦ vt
pegar.
glue-sniffing ['gluːsnɪfɪŋ] n inhalación f de
pegamento or cemento (LAM).
glum [glʌm] adj (mood) abatido; (person,
tone) melancólico.
glut [glʌt] n superabundancia.
glutinous ['gluːtɪnəs] adj glutinoso,

pegajoso.

glutton ['glʌtn] *n* glotón/ona *m/f*; ~ **for punishment** masoquista *m/f*.

gluttony ['glʌtənɪ] *n* gula, glotonería.

glycerin(e) ['glɪsəri:n] *n* glicerina.

GM *adj abbr* (= *genetically modified*) transgénico.

gm *abbr* (= *gram*) g.

GMAT *n abbr* (*US*: = *Graduate Management Admissions Test*) *examen de admisión al segundo ciclo de la enseñanza superior.*

GMO *n abbr* (= *genetically modified organism*) organismo transgénico, OGM *m*.

GMT *abbr* (= *Greenwich Mean Time*) GMT.

gnarled [nɑ:ld] *adj* nudoso.

gnash [næʃ] *vt*: **to ~ one's teeth** hacer rechinar los dientes.

gnat [næt] *n* mosquito.

gnaw [nɔ:] *vt* roer.

gnome [nəum] *n* gnomo.

GNP *n abbr* (= *gross national product*) PNB *m*.

GNVQ *n abbr* (*BRIT*: = *General National Vocational Qualification*) *título general de formación profesional.*

go [gəu] *vb* (*pt* **went**, *pp* **gone** [wɛnt, gɔn]) *vi* ir; (*travel*) viajar; (*depart*) irse, marcharse; (*work*) funcionar, marchar; (*be sold*) venderse; (*time*) pasar; (*become*) ponerse; (*break etc*) estropearse, romperse; (*fit, suit*): **to ~ with** hacer juego con ♦ *n* (*pl* ~**es**): **to have a ~ (at)** probar suerte (con); **to be on the ~** no parar; **whose ~ is it?** ¿a quién le toca?; **to ~ by car/on foot** ir en coche/a pie; **he's ~ing to do it** va a hacerlo; **to ~ for a walk** ir a dar un paseo; **to ~ dancing** ir a bailar; **to ~ looking for sth/sb** ir a buscar algo/a algn; **to make sth ~, get sth ~ing** poner algo en marcha; **my voice has gone** he perdido la voz; **the cake is all gone** se acabó la tarta; **the money will ~ towards our holiday** el dinero es para (ayuda de) nuestras vacaciones; **how did it ~?** ¿qué tal salió *or* resultó?, ¿cómo ha ido?; **the meeting went well** la reunión salió bien; **to ~ and see sb** ir a ver a algn; **to ~ to sleep** dormirse; **I'll take whatever is ~ing** acepto lo que haya; ... **to ~** (*US*: *food*) ... para llevar; **to ~ round the back** pasar por detrás.

▶**go about** *vi* (*rumour*) propagarse; (*also*: ~ **round**: *wander about*) andar (de un sitio para otro) ♦ *vt fus*: **how do I ~ about this?** ¿cómo me las arreglo para hacer esto?; **to ~ about one's business** ocuparse de sus asuntos.

▶**go after** *vt fus* (*pursue*) perseguir; (*job, record etc*) andar tras.

▶**go against** *vt fus* (*be unfavourable to*:

results) ir en contra de; (*be contrary to*: *principles*) ser contrario a.

▶**go ahead** *vi* seguir adelante.

▶**go along** *vi* ir; **as you ~ along** sobre la marcha ♦ *vt fus* bordear.

▶**go along with** *vt fus* (*accompany*) acompañar; (*agree with*: *idea*) estar de acuerdo con.

▶**go around** *vi* = **go round**.

▶**go away** *vi* irse, marcharse.

▶**go back** *vi* volver.

▶**go back on** *vt fus* (*promise*) faltar a.

▶**go by** *vi* (*time*) pasar ♦ *vt fus* guiarse por.

▶**go down** *vi* bajar; (*ship*) hundirse; (*sun*) ponerse ♦ *vt fus* bajar por; **that should ~ down well with him** eso le va a gustar; **he's gone down with flu** ha cogido la gripe.

▶**go for** *vt fus* (*fetch*) ir por; (*like*) gustar; (*attack*) atacar.

▶**go in** *vi* entrar.

▶**go in for** *vt fus* (*competition*) presentarse a.

▶**go into** *vt fus* entrar en; (*investigate*) investigar; (*embark on*) dedicarse a.

▶**go off** *vi* irse, marcharse; (*food*) pasarse; (*lights etc*) apagarse; (*explode*) estallar; (*event*) realizarse ♦ *vt fus* perder el interés por; **the party went off well** la fiesta salió bien.

▶**go on** *vi* (*continue*) seguir, continuar; (*lights*) encenderse; (*happen*) pasar, ocurrir; (*be guided by*) partir de; **to ~ on doing sth** seguir haciendo algo; **what's ~ing on here?** ¿qué pasa aquí?

▶**go on at** *vt fus* (*nag*) soltarle el rollo a.

▶**go out** *vi* salir; (*fire, light*) apagarse; (*ebb*: *tide*) bajar, menguar; **to ~ out with sb** salir con algn.

▶**go over** *vi* (*ship*) zozobrar ♦ *vt fus* (*check*) revisar; **to ~ over sth in one's mind** repasar algo mentalmente.

▶**go round** *vi* (*circulate*: *news, rumour*) correr; (*suffice*) alcanzar, bastar; (*revolve*) girar, dar vueltas; (*visit*): **to ~ round (to sb's)** pasar a ver (a algn); **to ~ round (by)** (*make a detour*) dar la vuelta (por).

▶**go through** *vt fus* (*town etc*) atravesar; (*search through*) revisar; (*perform*: *ceremony*) realizar; (*examine*: *list, book*) repasar.

▶**go through with** *vt fus* (*plan, crime*) llevar a cabo; **I couldn't ~ through with it** no pude llevarlo a cabo.

▶**go together** *vi* entenderse.

▶**go under** *vi* (*sink*: *ship, person*) hundirse; (*fig*: *business, firm*) quebrar.

▶**go up** *vi* subir; **to ~ up in flames** estallar

en llamas.

▶**go without** *vt fus* pasarse sin.

goad [gəud] *vt* aguijonear.

go-ahead ['gəuəhɛd] *adj* emprendedor(a) ♦ *n* luz *f* verde; **to give sth/sb the ~** dar luz verde a algo/algn.

goal [gəul] *n* meta, arco (*LAM*); (*score*) gol *m*.

goal difference *n* diferencia por goles.

goalie ['gəulɪ] *n* (*col*) portero, guardameta *m/f*, arquero (*LAM*).

goalkeeper ['gəulki:pə*] *n* portero, guardameta *m/f*, arquero (*LAM*).

goal post *n* poste *m* (de la portería).

goat [gəut] *n* cabra *f*.

gobble ['gɔbl] *vt* (*also*: ~ **down**, ~ **up**) engullir.

go-between ['gəubɪtwi:n] *n* intermediario/a.

Gobi Desert ['gəubɪ-] *n* Desierto de Gobi.

goblet ['gɔblɪt] *n* copa.

goblin ['gɔblɪn] *n* duende *m*.

go-cart ['gəukɑ:t] *n* = **go-kart**.

god [gɔd] *n* dios *m*; **G~** Dios *m*.

god-awful [gɔd'ɔ:fəl] *adj* (*col*) de puta pena.

godchild ['gɔdtʃaɪld] *n* ahijado/a.

goddamn ['gɔddæm] *adj* (*col*: *also*: **goddamned**) maldito, puñetero ♦ *excl*: ~! ¡cagüen diez!

goddess ['gɔdɪs] *n* diosa.

godfather ['gɔdfɑ:ðə*] *n* padrino.

god-fearing ['gɔdfɪərɪŋ] *adj* temeroso de Dios.

god-forsaken ['gɔdfəseɪkən] *adj* dejado de la mano de Dios.

godmother ['gɔdmʌðə*] *n* madrina.

godparents ['gɔdpɛərənts] *npl*: **the ~** los padrinos.

godsend ['gɔdsɛnd] *n*: **to be a ~** venir como llovido del cielo.

godson ['gɔdsʌn] *n* ahijado.

goes [gəuz] *vb see* **go**.

gofer ['gəufə*] *n* (*col*) chico/a para todo.

go-getter ['gəugɛtə*] *n* ambicioso/a.

goggle ['gɔgl] *vi*: **to ~ (at)** mirar con ojos desorbitados.

goggles ['gɔglz] *npl* (*AUT*) gafas *fpl*, anteojos *mpl* (*LAM*); (*diver's*) gafas *fpl* submarinas.

going ['gəuɪŋ] *n* (*conditions*) cosas *fpl* ♦ *adj*: **the ~ rate** la tarifa corriente *or* en vigor; **it was slow ~** las cosas iban lentas.

going-over [gəuɪŋ'əuvə*] *n* revisión *f*; (*col*: *beating*) paliza.

goings-on ['gəuɪŋz'ɔn] *npl* (*col*) tejemanejes *mpl*.

go-kart ['gəukɑ:t] *n* kart *m*.

gold [gəuld] *n* oro ♦ *adj* (*reserves*) de oro.

golden ['gəuldn] *adj* (*made of gold*) de oro; (~ *in colour*) dorado.

Golden Age *n* Siglo de Oro.

golden handshake *n* cuantiosa gratificación por los servicios prestados.

golden rule *n* regla de oro.

goldfish ['gəuldfɪʃ] *n* pez *m* de colores.

gold leaf *n* pan *m* de oro.

gold medal *n* (*SPORT*) medalla de oro.

goldmine ['gəuldmaɪn] *n* mina de oro.

gold-plated ['gəuld'pleɪtɪd] *adj* chapado en oro.

goldsmith ['gəuldsmɪθ] *n* orfebre *m/f*.

gold standard *n* patrón *m* oro.

golf [gɔlf] *n* golf *m*.

golf ball *n* (*for game*) pelota de golf; (*on typewriter*) esfera impresora.

golf club *n* club *m* de golf; (*stick*) palo (de golf).

golf course *n* campo de golf.

golfer ['gɔlfə*] *n* jugador(a) *m/f* de golf, golfista *m/f*.

golfing ['gɔlfɪŋ] *n*: **to go ~** jugar al golf.

gondola ['gɔndələ] *n* góndola.

gondolier [gɔndə'lɪə*] *n* gondolero.

gone [gɔn] *pp of* **go**.

goner ['gɔnə*] *n* (*col*): **to be a ~** estar en las últimas.

gong [gɔŋ] *n* gong *m*.

gonorrhea [gɔnə'rɪə] *n* gonorrea.

good [gud] *adj* bueno, (*before m sing n* **buen**); (*well-behaved*) educado ♦ *n* bien *m*; ~! ¡qué bien!; **he's ~ at it** se le da bien; **to be ~ for** servir para; **it's ~ for you** te hace bien; **would you be ~ enough to...?** ¿podría hacerme el favor de...?, ¿sería tan amable de...?; **that's very ~ of you** es usted muy amable; **to feel ~** sentirse bien; **it's ~ to see you** me alegro de verte; **a ~ deal (of)** mucho; **a ~ many** muchos; **to make ~** reparar; **it's no ~ complaining** no sirve de nada quejarse; **is this any ~?** (*will it do?*) ¿sirve esto?; (*what's it like?*) ¿qué tal es esto?; **it's a ~ thing you were there** menos mal que estabas allí; **for ~** (*for ever*) para siempre, definitivamente; ~ **morning/afternoon** ¡buenos días/buenas tardes!; ~ **evening!** ¡buenas noches!; ~ **night!** ¡buenas noches!; **he's up to no ~** está tramando algo; **for the common ~** para el bien común; *see also* **goods**.

goodbye [gud'baɪ] *excl* ¡adiós!; **to say ~ (to)** (*person*) despedirse (de).

good faith *n* buena fe *f*.

good-for-nothing ['gudfənʌθɪŋ] *n* inútil *m/f*.

Good Friday *n* Viernes *m* Santo.

good-humoured ['gud'hju:məd] *adj* (*person*) afable, de buen humor; (*remark, joke*) bien intencionado.

good-looking ['gud'lukɪŋ] *adj* guapo.

good-natured ['gud'neɪtʃəd] *adj* (*person*) de buen carácter; (*discussion*) cordial.

goodness ['gudnɪs] *n* (*of person*) bondad *f*; **for ~ sake!** ¡por Dios!; **~ gracious!** ¡madre mía!

goods [gudz] *npl* bienes *mpl*; (*COMM etc*) géneros *mpl*, mercancías *fpl*, artículos *mpl*; **all his ~ and chattels** todos sus bienes.

goods train *n* (*BRIT*) tren *m* de mercancías.

goodwill [gud'wɪl] *n* buena voluntad *f*; (*COMM*) fondo de comercio; (*customer connections*) clientela.

goody-goody ['gudɪgudɪ] *n* (*pej*) santurrón/ona *m/f*.

gooey ['gu:ɪ] *adj* (*BRIT col*) pegajoso; (*cake, behaviour*) empalagoso.

goose, *pl* **geese** [gu:s, gi:s] *n* ganso, oca.

gooseberry ['guzbərɪ] *n* grosella espinosa *or* silvestre.

gooseflesh ['gu:sfleʃ] *n*, **goosepimples** ['gu:spɪmplz] *npl* carne *f* de gallina.

goose step *n* (*MIL*) paso de la oca.

GOP *n abbr* (*US POL: col* = *Grand Old Party*) *Partido Republicano.*

gopher ['gəufə*] *n* = **gofer**.

gore [gɔ:*] *vt* dar una cornada a, cornear ♦ *n* sangre *f*.

gorge [gɔ:dʒ] *n* garganta ♦ *vr*: **to ~ o.s. (on)** atracarse (de).

gorgeous ['gɔ:dʒəs] *adj* precioso; (*weather*) estupendo; (*person*) guapísimo.

gorilla [gə'rɪlə] *n* gorila *m*.

gormless ['gɔ:mlɪs] *adj* (*col*) ceporro, zoquete.

gorse [gɔ:s] *n* tojo.

gory ['gɔ:rɪ] *adj* sangriento.

go-slow ['gəu'sləu] *n* (*BRIT*) huelga de celo.

gospel ['gɔspl] *n* evangelio.

gossamer ['gɔsəmə*] *n* gasa.

gossip ['gɔsɪp] *n* cotilleo; (*person*) cotilla *m/f* ♦ *vi* cotillear, comadrear (*LAM*); **a piece of ~** un cotilleo.

gossip column *n* ecos *mpl* de sociedad.

got [gɔt] *pt, pp of* **get**.

Gothic ['gɔθɪk] *adj* gótico.

gotten ['gɔtn] (*US*) *pp of* **get**.

gouge [gaudʒ] *vt* (*also:* ~ **out:** *hole etc*) excavar; (: *initials*) grabar; **to ~ sb's eyes out** sacar los ojos a algn.

goulash ['gu:læʃ] *n* g(o)ulash *m*.

gourd [guəd] *n* calabaza.

gourmet ['guəmeɪ] *n* gastrónomo/a *m/f*.

gout [gaut] *n* gota.

govern ['gʌvən] *vt* (*gen*) gobernar; (*event,*

conduct) regir.

governess ['gʌvənɪs] *n* institutriz *f*.

governing ['gʌvənɪŋ] *adj* (*POL*) de gobierno, gubernamental; **~ body** organismo de gobierno.

government ['gʌvnmənt] *n* gobierno; **local ~** administración *f* municipal.

governmental [gʌvn'mɛntl] *adj* gubernamental.

government stock *n* papel *m* del Estado.

governor ['gʌvənə*] *n* gobernador(a) *m/f*; (*of jail*) director(a) *m/f*.

Govt. *abbr* (= *Government*) gobno.

gown [gaun] *n* vestido; (*of teacher*; *BRIT*: *of judge*) toga.

GP *n abbr see* **general practitioner**.

GPMU *n abbr* (*BRIT*: = *Graphical, Paper and Media Union*) *sindicato de trabajadores del sector editorial*.

GPO *n abbr* (*BRIT*: *old*) = *General Post Office*; (*US*) = *Government Printing Office*.

gr. *abbr* (*COMM*: = *gross*) bto.

grab [græb] *vt* coger (*SP*) *or* agarrar; **to ~ at** intentar agarrar.

grace [greɪs] *n* (*REL*) gracia; (*gracefulness*) elegancia, gracia; (*graciousness*) cortesía, gracia ♦ *vt* (*favour*) honrar; (*adorn*) adornar; **5 days' ~** un plazo de 5 días; **to say ~** bendecir la mesa; **his sense of humour is his saving ~** lo que le salva es su sentido del humor.

graceful ['greɪsful] *adj* elegante.

gracious ['greɪʃəs] *adj* amable ♦ *excl*: **good ~!** ¡Dios mío!

grade [greɪd] *n* (*quality*) clase *f*, calidad *f*; (*in hierarchy*) grado; (*US: SCOL*) curso (: *gradient*) pendiente *f*, cuesta ♦ *vt* clasificar; **to make the ~** (*fig*) dar el nivel; *see also* **high school**.

grade crossing *n* (*US*) paso a nivel.

grade school *n* (*US*) escuela primaria; *see also* **elementary school**.

gradient ['greɪdɪənt] *n* pendiente *f*.

gradual ['grædjuəl] *adj* gradual.

gradually ['grædjuəlɪ] *adv* gradualmente.

graduate *n* ['grædjuɪt] licenciado/a, graduado/a, egresado/a (*LAM*); (*US: SCOL*) bachiller *m/f* ♦ *vi* ['grædjueɪt] licenciarse, graduarse, recibirse (*LAM*); (*US*) obtener el título de bachillerato.

graduated pension ['grædjueɪtɪd-] *n* pensión *f* escalonada.

graduation [grædju'eɪʃən] *n* graduación *f*; (*US SCOL*) entrega de los títulos de bachillerato.

graffiti [grə'fi:tɪ] *npl* pintadas *fpl*.

graft [grɑ:ft] *n* (*AGR, MED*) injerto; (*bribery*) corrupción *f* ♦ *vt* injertar; **hard ~** (*col*) trabajo duro.

grain [greɪn] n (*single particle*) grano; (*no pl: cereals*) cereales mpl; (*US: corn*) trigo; (*in wood*) veta.

gram [græm] n (*US*) gramo.

grammar ['græmə*] n gramática.

grammar school n (*BRIT*) ≈ instituto (de segunda enseñanza); (*US*) escuela primaria; *see also* **comprehensive school.**

grammatical [grə'mætɪkl] adj gramatical.

gramme [græm] n = **gram.**

gramophone ['græməfəun] n (*BRIT*) gramófono.

granary ['grænərɪ] n granero.

grand [grænd] adj grandioso ♦ n (*US: col*) mil dólares mpl.

grandchildren ['grænt∫ɪldrən] npl nietos mpl.

granddad ['grændæd] n yayo, abuelito.

granddaughter ['grændɔːtə*] n nieta.

grandeur ['grændjə*] n grandiosidad f.

grandfather ['grænfɑːðə*] n abuelo.

grandiose ['grændɪəuz] adj grandioso; (*pej*) pomposo.

grand jury n (*US*) jurado de acusación.

grandma ['grænmɑː] n yaya, abuelita.

grandmother ['grænmʌðə*] n abuela.

grandpa ['grænpɑː] n = **granddad.**

grandparents ['grændpɛərənts] npl abuelos mpl.

grand piano n piano de cola.

Grand Prix ['grɑ̃ː'priː] n (*AUT*) gran premio, Grand Prix m.

grandson ['grænsʌn] n nieto.

grandstand ['grændstænd] n (*SPORT*) tribuna.

grand total n suma total, total m.

granite ['grænɪt] n granito.

granny ['grænɪ] n abuelita, yaya.

grant [grɑːnt] vt (*concede*) conceder; (*admit*): **to ~ (that)** reconocer (que) ♦ n (*SCOL*) beca; **to take sth for ~ed** dar algo por sentado.

granulated sugar ['grænjuleɪtɪd-] n (*BRIT*) azúcar m granulado.

granule ['grænjuːl] n gránulo.

grape [greɪp] n uva; **sour ~s** (*fig*) envidia sg; **a bunch of ~s** un racimo de uvas.

grapefruit ['greɪpfruːt] n pomelo, toronja.

grape juice n jugo *or* zumo (*SP*) de uva.

grapevine ['greɪpvaɪn] n vid f, parra; **I heard it on the ~** (*fig*) me enteré, me lo contaron.

graph [grɑːf] n gráfica.

graphic ['græfɪk] adj gráfico.

graphic designer n diseñador(a) m/f gráfico/a.

graphic equalizer n ecualizador m gráfico.

graphics ['græfɪks] n (*art, process*) artes fpl gráficas ♦ npl (*drawings: also COMPUT*) gráficos mpl.

graphite ['græfaɪt] n grafito.

graph paper n papel m cuadriculado.

grapple ['græpl] vi: **to ~ with a problem** enfrentarse a un problema.

grappling iron ['græplɪŋ-] n (*NAUT*) rezón m.

grasp [grɑːsp] vt agarrar, asir; (*understand*) comprender ♦ n (*grip*) asimiento; (*reach*) alcance m; (*understanding*) comprensión f; **to have a good ~ of** (*subject*) dominar.

▶**grasp at** vt fus (*rope etc*) tratar de agarrar; (*fig: opportunity*) aprovechar.

grasping ['grɑːspɪŋ] adj avaro.

grass [grɑːs] n hierba, grama (*LAM*); (*lawn*) césped m; (*pasture*) pasto; (*col: informer*) soplón/ona m/f.

grasshopper ['grɑːshɔpə*] n saltamontes m inv.

grassland ['grɑːslænd] n pradera, pampa (*LAM*).

grass roots adj de base ♦ npl (*POL*) bases fpl.

grass snake n culebra.

grassy ['grɑːsɪ] adj cubierto de hierba.

grate [greɪt] n parrilla ♦ vi chirriar, rechinar ♦ vt (*CULIN*) rallar.

grateful ['greɪtful] adj agradecido.

gratefully ['greɪtfəlɪ] adv con agradecimiento.

grater ['greɪtə*] n rallador m.

gratification [grætɪfɪ'keɪ∫ən] n satisfacción f.

gratify ['grætɪfaɪ] vt complacer; (*whim*) satisfacer.

gratifying ['grætɪfaɪɪŋ] adj gratificante.

grating ['greɪtɪŋ] n (*iron bars*) rejilla ♦ adj (*noise*) chirriante.

gratitude ['grætɪtjuːd] n agradecimiento.

gratuitous [grə'tjuːɪtəs] adj gratuito.

gratuity [grə'tjuːɪtɪ] n gratificación f.

grave [greɪv] n tumba ♦ adj serio, grave.

gravedigger ['greɪvdɪgə*] n sepulturero/a.

gravel ['grævl] n grava.

gravely ['greɪvlɪ] adv seriamente; **~ ill** muy grave.

gravestone ['greɪvstəun] n lápida.

graveyard ['greɪvjɑːd] n cementerio, camposanto.

gravitate ['grævɪteɪt] vi gravitar.

gravitation [grævɪ'teɪ∫ən] n gravitación f.

gravity ['grævɪtɪ] n gravedad f; (*seriousness*) seriedad f.

gravy ['greɪvɪ] n salsa de carne.

gravy boat n salsera.

gravy train n (*esp US: col*): **to get on the ~** coger un chollo.

gray [greɪ] *adj* (*US*) = **grey**.

graze [greɪz] *vi* pacer ♦ *vt* (*touch lightly, scrape*) rozar ♦ *n* (*MED*) rozadura.

grazing ['greɪzɪŋ] *n* (*for livestock*) pastoreo.

grease [griːs] *n* (*fat*) grasa; (*lubricant*) lubricante *m* ♦ *vt* engrasar; **to ~ the skids** (*US: fig*) engrasar el mecanismo.

grease gun *n* pistola engrasadora.

greasepaint ['griːspeɪnt] *n* maquillaje *m*.

greaseproof ['griːspruːf] *adj* a prueba de grasa; (*BRIT: paper*) de grasa.

greasy ['griːsɪ] *adj* (*hands, clothes*) grasiento; (*road, surface*) resbaladizo.

great [greɪt] *adj* grande, (*before n sing*) gran; (*col*) estupendo, macanudo (*LAM*), regio (*LAM*), chévere (*LAM*); (*pain, heat*) intenso; **we had a ~ time** nos lo pasamos muy bien; **they're ~ friends** son íntimos *or* muy amigos; **the ~ thing is that** ... lo bueno es que ...; **it was ~!** ¡fue estupendo!

Great Barrier Reef *n* Gran Barrera de Coral.

Great Britain *n* Gran Bretaña.

greater ['greɪtə*] *adj* mayor; **G~ London** el área metropolitana de Londres.

greatest ['greɪtɪst] *adj* (el/la) mayor.

great-grandchild, *pl* **-children** [greɪt'grændtʃaɪld, 'tʃɪldrən] *n* bisnieto/a.

great-grandfather [greɪt'grændfɑːðə*] *n* bisabuelo.

great-grandmother [greɪt'grændmʌðə*] *n* bisabuela.

Great Lakes *npl*: **the ~** los Grandes Lagos.

greatly ['greɪtlɪ] *adv* sumamente, muy.

greatness ['greɪtnɪs] *n* grandeza.

Greece [griːs] *n* Grecia.

greed [griːd] *n* (*also*: **~iness**) codicia; (*for food*) gula.

greedily ['griːdɪlɪ] *adv* con avidez.

greedy ['griːdɪ] *adj* codicioso; (*for food*) glotón/ona.

Greek [griːk] *adj* griego ♦ *n* griego/a; (*LING*) griego; **ancient/modern ~** griego antiguo/moderno.

green [griːn] *adj* verde; (*inexperienced*) novato ♦ *n* verde *m*; (*stretch of grass*) césped *m*; (*of golf course*) campo, "green" *m*; **the G~ party** (*POL*) el partido verde; **~s** *npl* verduras *fpl*; **to have ~ fingers** (*fig*) tener buena mano para las plantas.

green belt *n* cinturón *m* verde.

green card *n* (*AUT*) carta verde.

greenery ['griːnərɪ] *n* vegetación *f*.

greenfly ['griːnflaɪ] *n* pulgón *m*.

greengage ['griːngeɪdʒ] *n* (ciruela) claudia.

greengrocer ['griːngrəʊsə*] *n* (*BRIT*)

frutero/a, verdulero/a.

greenhouse ['griːnhaʊs] *n* invernadero.

greenhouse effect *n*: **the ~** el efecto invernadero.

greenhouse gas *n* gas *m* que produce el efecto invernadero.

greenish ['griːnɪʃ] *adj* verdoso.

Greenland ['griːnlənd] *n* Groenlandia.

Greenlander ['griːnləndə*] *n* groenlandés/esa *m/f*.

green light *n* luz *f* verde.

green pepper *n* pimiento verde.

greet [griːt] *vt* saludar; (*news*) recibir.

greeting ['griːtɪŋ] *n* (*gen*) saludo; (*welcome*) bienvenida; **~s** saludos *mpl*; **season's ~s** Felices Pascuas.

greeting(s) card *n* tarjeta de felicitación.

gregarious [grə'gɛərɪəs] *adj* gregario.

grenade [grə'neɪd] *n* (*also*: **hand ~**) granada.

grew [gruː] *pt of* **grow**.

grey [greɪ] *adj* gris; **to go ~** salirle canas.

grey-haired [greɪ'hɛəd] *adj* canoso.

greyhound ['greɪhaʊnd] *n* galgo.

grid [grɪd] *n* rejilla; (*ELEC*) red *f*.

griddle ['grɪdl] *n* (*esp US*) plancha.

gridiron ['grɪdaɪən] *n* (*CULIN*) parrilla.

gridlock ['grɪdlɒk] *n* (*esp US*) retención *f*.

grief [griːf] *n* dolor *m*, pena; **to come to ~** (*plan*) fracasar, ir al traste; (*person*) acabar mal, desgraciarse.

grievance ['griːvəns] *n* (*cause for complaint*) motivo de queja, agravio.

grieve [griːv] *vi* afligirse, acongojarse ♦ *vt* afligir, apenar; **to ~ for** llorar por; **to ~ for sb** (*dead person*) llorar la pérdida de algn.

grievous ['griːvəs] *adj* grave; (*loss*) cruel; **~ bodily harm** (*LAW*) daños *mpl* corporales graves.

grill [grɪl] *n* (*on cooker*) parrilla ♦ *vt* (*BRIT*) asar a la parrilla; (*question*) interrogar; **~ed meat** carne *f* (asada) a la parrilla *or* plancha.

grille [grɪl] *n* rejilla.

grim [grɪm] *adj* (*place*) lúgubre; (*person*) adusto.

grimace [grɪ'meɪs] *n* mueca ♦ *vi* hacer muecas.

grime [graɪm] *n* mugre *f*.

grimly ['grɪmlɪ] *adv* (*say*) sombríamente.

grimy ['graɪmɪ] *adj* mugriento.

grin [grɪn] *n* sonrisa abierta ♦ *vi*: **to ~ (at)** sonreír abiertamente (a).

grind [graɪnd] *vb* (*pt, pp* **ground** [graʊnd]) *vt* (*coffee, pepper etc*) moler; (*US: meat*) picar; (*make sharp*) afilar; (*polish: gem, lens*) esmerilar ♦ *vi* (*car gears*) rechinar

♦ *n*: **the daily** ~ (*col*) la rutina diaria; **to** ~ **one's teeth** hacer rechinar los dientes; **to** ~ **to a halt** (*vehicle*) pararse con gran estruendo de frenos; (*fig: talks, scheme*) interrumpirse; (*work, production*) paralizarse.

grinder ['graɪndə*] *n* (*machine: for coffee*) molinillo.

grindstone ['graɪndstəʊn] *n*: **to keep one's nose to the** ~ trabajar sin descanso.

grip [grɪp] *n* (*hold*) asimiento; (*of hands*) apretón *m*; (*handle*) asidero; (*of racquet etc*) mango; (*understanding*) comprensión *f* ♦ *vt* agarrar; **to get to** ~**s with** enfrentarse con; **to lose one's** ~ (*fig*) perder el control; **he lost his** ~ **of the situation** la situación se le fue de las manos.

gripe [graɪp] *n* (*col: complaint*) queja ♦ *vi* (*col: complain*): **to** ~ (**about**) quejarse (de); ~**s** *npl* retortijones *mpl*.

gripping ['grɪpɪŋ] *adj* absorbente.

grisly ['grɪzlɪ] *adj* horripilante, horrible.

gristle ['grɪsl] *n* cartílago.

grit [grɪt] *n* gravilla; (*courage*) valor *m* ♦ *vt* (*road*) poner gravilla en; **I've got a piece of** ~ **in my eye** tengo una arenilla en el ojo; **to** ~ **one's teeth** apretar los dientes.

grits [grɪts] *npl* (*US*) maíz *msg* a medio moler.

grizzle ['grɪzl] *vi* (*cry*) lloriquear.

grizzly ['grɪzlɪ] *n* (*also:* ~ **bear**) oso pardo.

groan [grəʊn] *n* gemido, quejido ♦ *vi* gemir, quejarse.

grocer ['grəʊsə*] *n* tendero (de ultramarinos); ~**'s (shop)** *n* tienda de ultramarinos *or* de abarrotes (*LAM*).

groceries ['grəʊsərɪz] *npl* comestibles *mpl*.

grocery ['grəʊsərɪ] *n* (*shop*) tienda de ultramarinos.

grog [grɒg] *n* (*BRIT*) grog *m*.

groggy ['grɒgɪ] *adj* atontado.

groin [grɔɪn] *n* ingle *f*.

groom [gruːm] *n* mozo/a de cuadra; (*also:* **bride**~) novio ♦ *vt* (*horse*) almohazar; **well-**~**ed** acicalado.

groove [gruːv] *n* ranura; (*of record*) surco.

grope [grəʊp] *vi* ir a tientas; **to** ~ **for** buscar a tientas.

gross [grəʊs] *adj* grueso; (*COMM*) bruto ♦ *vt* (*COMM*) recaudar en bruto.

gross domestic product (GDP) *n* producto interior bruto (PIB).

gross income *n* ingresos *mpl* brutos.

grossly ['grəʊslɪ] *adv* (*greatly*) enormemente.

gross national product (GNP) *n* producto nacional bruto (PNB).

gross profit *n* beneficios *mpl* brutos.

gross sales *npl* ventas *fpl* brutas.

grotesque [grə'tɛsk] *adj* grotesco.

grotto ['grɒtəʊ] *n* gruta.

grotty ['grɒtɪ] *adj* asqueroso.

grouch [grautʃ] *vi* (*col*) refunfuñar ♦ *n* (*col: person*) refunfuñón/ona *m/f*.

ground [graʊnd] *pt, pp of* **grind** ♦ *n* suelo, tierra; (*SPORT*) campo, terreno; (*reason: gen pl*) motivo, razón *f*; (*US: also:* ~ **wire**) tierra ♦ *vt* (*plane*) mantener en tierra; (*US: ELEC*) conectar con tierra ♦ *vi* (*ship*) varar, encallar ♦ *adj* (*coffee etc*) molido; ~**s** *npl* (*of coffee etc*) poso *sg*; (*gardens etc*) jardines *mpl*, parque *m*; **on the** ~ en el suelo; **common** ~ terreno común; **to gain/lose** ~ ganar/perder terreno; **to the** ~ al suelo; **below** ~ bajo tierra; **he covered a lot of** ~ **in his lecture** abarcó mucho en la clase.

ground cloth *n* (*US*) = **groundsheet.**

ground control *n* control *m* desde tierra.

ground floor *n* (*BRIT*) planta baja.

grounding ['graʊndɪŋ] *n* (*in education*) conocimientos *mpl* básicos.

groundkeeper ['graʊndkiːpə*] *n* = **groundsman.**

groundless ['graʊndlɪs] *adj* infundado, sin fundamento.

groundnut ['graʊndnʌt] *n* cacahuete *m*.

ground rent *n* alquiler *m* del terreno.

ground rules *npl* normas básicas.

groundsheet ['graʊndʃiːt] (*BRIT*) *n* tela impermeable.

groundsman ['graʊndzmən], (*US*) **groundskeeper** ['graʊndzkiːpə*] *n* (*SPORT*) encargado de pista de deportes.

ground staff *n* personal *m* de tierra.

ground swell *n* mar *m or f* de fondo; (*fig*) ola.

ground-to-air ['graʊntə'ɛə] *adj* tierra-aire.

ground-to-ground ['graʊntə'graʊnd] *adj* tierra-tierra.

groundwork ['graʊndwɔːk] *n* trabajo preliminar.

Ground Zero *n* zona cero.

group [gruːp] *n* grupo; (*MUS: pop* ~) conjunto, grupo ♦ (*vb: also:* ~ **together**) *vt* agrupar ♦ *vi* agruparse.

groupie ['gruːpɪ] *n* groupie *f*.

group therapy *n* terapia de grupo.

grouse [graʊs] *n* (*pl inv*) (*bird*) urogallo ♦ *vi* (*complain*) quejarse.

grove [grəʊv] *n* arboleda.

grovel ['grɒvl] *vi* (*fig*) arrastrarse.

grow, *pt* **grew,** *pp* **grown** [grəʊ, gruː, grəʊn] *vi* crecer; (*increase*) aumentar; (*expand*) desarrollarse; (*become*) volverse ♦ *vt* cultivar; (*hair*, *beard*) dejar crecer; **to ~ rich/weak** enriquecerse/debilitarse; **to ~ tired of waiting** cansarse de esperar.

▶**grow apart** *vi* (*fig*) alejarse uno del otro.

▶**grow away from** *vt fus* (*fig*) alejarse de.

▶**grow on** *vt fus*: **that painting is ~ing on me** ese cuadro me gusta cada vez más.

▶**grow out of** *vt fus*: **I've grown out of this shirt** esta camisa se me ha quedado pequeña; (*habit*) perder.

▶**grow up** *vi* crecer, hacerse hombre/mujer.

grower ['grəuə*] *n* (*AGR*) cultivador(a) *m/f*, productor(a) *m/f*.

growing ['grəuɪŋ] *adj* creciente; **~ pains** (*also fig*) problemas *mpl* de crecimiento.

growl [graul] *vi* gruñir.

grown [grəun] *pp of* **grow**.

grown-up [grəun'ʌp] *n* adulto/a, mayor *m/f*.

growth [grəuθ] *n* crecimiento, desarrollo; (*what has grown*) brote *m*; (*MED*) tumor *m*.

growth rate *n* tasa de crecimiento.

GRSM *n abbr* (*BRIT*) = *Graduate of the Royal Schools of Music*.

grub [grʌb] *n* gusano; (*col: food*) comida.

grubby ['grʌbɪ] *adj* sucio, mugriento, mugroso (*LAM*).

grudge [grʌdʒ] *n* rencor ♦ *vt*: **to ~ sb sth** dar algo a algn de mala gana; **to bear sb a ~** guardar rencor a algn; **he ~s (giving) the money** da el dinero de mala gana.

grudgingly ['grʌdʒɪŋlɪ] *adv* de mala gana.

gruelling, (*US*) **grueling** ['gruəlɪŋ] *adj* agotador.

gruesome ['gru:səm] *adj* horrible.

gruff [grʌf] *adj* (*voice*) ronco; (*manner*) brusco.

grumble ['grʌmbl] *vi* refunfuñar, quejarse.

grumpy ['grʌmpɪ] *adj* gruñón/ona.

grunge [grʌndʒ] *n* (*MUS, fashion*) grunge *m*.

grunt [grʌnt] *vi* gruñir ♦ *n* gruñido.

G-string ['dʒi:strɪŋ] *n* tanga *m*.

GSUSA *n abbr* = *Girl Scouts of the United States of America*.

GT *abbr* (*AUT*: = *gran turismo*) GT.

GU *abbr* (*US*) = *Guam*.

guarantee [gærən'ti:] *n* garantía ♦ *vt* garantizar; **he can't ~ (that) he'll come** no está seguro de poder venir.

guarantor [gærən'tɔ:*] *n* garante *m/f*, fiador(a) *m/f*.

guard [gɑ:d] *n* guardia; (*person*) guarda *m/f*; (*BRIT RAIL*) jefe *m* de tren; (*safety device: on machine*) cubierta de protección; (*protection*) protección *f*; (*fire~*) pantalla; (*mud~*) guardabarros *m inv* ♦ *vt* guardar; **to ~ (against or from)** proteger (de); **to be on one's ~** (*fig*) estar en guardia.

▶**guard against** *vi*: **to ~ against doing sth** guardarse de hacer algo.

guard dog *n* perro guardián.

guarded ['gɑ:dɪd] *adj* (*fig*) cauteloso.

guardian ['gɑ:dɪən] *n* guardián/ana *m/f*; (*of minor*) tutor(a) *m/f*.

guardrail ['gɑ:dreɪl] *n* pretil *m*.

guard's van *n* (*BRIT RAIL*) furgón *m* del jefe de tren.

Guatemala [gwɑ:tə'mɑ:lə] *n* Guatemala.

Guatemalan [gwɑ:tə'mɑ:lən] *adj*, *n* guatemalteco/a *m/f*.

Guernsey ['gɜ:nzɪ] *n* Guernsey *m*.

guerrilla [gə'rɪlə] *n* guerrillero/a.

guerrilla warfare *n* guerra de guerrillas.

guess [gɛs] *vi*, *vt* (*gen*) adivinar; (*suppose*) suponer ♦ *n* suposición *f*, conjetura; **I ~ you're right** (*esp US*) supongo que tienes razón; **to keep sb ~ing** mantener a algn a la expectativa; **to take** *or* **have a ~** tratar de adivinar; **my ~ is that ...** yo creo que ....

guesstimate ['gɛstɪmɪt] *n* cálculo aproximado.

guesswork ['gɛswɜ:k] *n* conjeturas *fpl*; **I got the answer by ~** acerté a ojo de buen cubero.

guest [gɛst] *n* invitado/a; (*in hotel*) huésped(a) *m/f*; **be my ~** (*col*) estás en tu casa.

guest-house ['gɛsthaus] *n* casa de huéspedes, pensión *f*.

guest room *n* cuarto de huéspedes.

guff [gʌf] *n* (*col*) bobadas *fpl*.

guffaw [gʌ'fɔ:] *n* carcajada ♦ *vi* reírse a carcajadas.

guidance ['gaɪdəns] *n* (*gen*) dirección *f*; (*advice*) consejos *mpl*; **marriage/vocational ~** orientación *f* matrimonial/profesional.

guide [gaɪd] *n* (*person*) guía *m/f*; (*book, fig*) guía *f*; (*also: girl ~*) exploradora ♦ *vt* guiar; **to be ~d by sb/sth** dejarse guiar por algn/algo.

guidebook ['gaɪdbuk] *n* guía.

guided missile ['gaɪdɪd-] *n* misil *m* teledirigido.

guide dog *n* perro guía.

guidelines ['gaɪdlaɪnz] *npl* (*fig*) directrices *fpl*.

guild [gɪld] *n* gremio.

guildhall ['gɪldhɔ:l] *n* (*BRIT: town hall*) ayuntamiento.

guile [gaɪl] *n* astucia.

guileless ['gaɪlɪs] *adj* cándido.

guillotine ['gɪlətiːn] *n* guillotina.

guilt [gɪlt] *n* culpabilidad *f*.

guilty ['gɪltɪ] *adj* culpable; **to feel ~ (about)** sentirse culpable (de); **to plead ~/not ~**

declararse culpable/inocente.

Guinea ['gɪnɪ] *n*: **Republic of** ~ República de Guinea.

guinea ['gɪnɪ] *n* (*BRIT*: *old*) guinea (= *21 chelines*: *en la actualidad ya no se usa esta moneda*).

guinea pig *n* cobaya; (*fig*) conejillo de Indias.

guise [gaɪz] *n*: **in** *or* **under the** ~ **of** bajo la apariencia de.

guitar [gɪ'tɑ:*] *n* guitarra.

guitarist [gɪ'tɑ:rɪst] *n* guitarrista *m/f*.

gulch [gʌltʃ] *n* (*US*) barranco.

gulf [gʌlf] *n* golfo; (*abyss*) abismo; **the G~** el Golfo (Pérsico).

Gulf States *npl*: **the** ~ los países del Golfo.

Gulf Stream *n*: **the** ~ la Corriente del Golfo.

gull [gʌl] *n* gaviota.

gullet ['gʌlɪt] *n* esófago.

gullibility [gʌlɪ'bɪlɪtɪ] *n* credulidad *f*.

gullible ['gʌlɪbl] *adj* crédulo.

gully ['gʌlɪ] *n* barranco.

gulp [gʌlp] *vi* tragar saliva ♦ *vt* (*also*: ~ **down**) tragarse ♦ *n* (*of liquid*) trago; (*of food*) bocado; **in** *or* **at one** ~ de un trago.

gum [gʌm] *n* (*ANAT*) encía; (*glue*) goma, cemento (*LAM*); (*sweet*) gominola; (*also*: **chewing-~**) chicle *m* ♦ *vt* pegar con goma.

▶**gum up** *vt*: **to** ~ **up the works** (*col*) entorpecerlo todo.

gumboots ['gʌmbu:ts] *npl* (*BRIT*) botas *fpl* de goma.

gum tree *n* árbol *m* gomero.

gun [gʌn] *n* (*small*) pistola; (*shotgun*) escopeta; (*rifle*) fusil *m*; (*cannon*) cañón *m* ♦ *vt* (*also*: ~ **down**) abatir a tiros; **to stick to one's ~s** (*fig*) mantenerse firme *or* en sus trece.

gunboat ['gʌnbəut] *n* cañonero.

gun dog *n* perro de caza.

gunfire ['gʌnfaɪə*] *n* disparos *mpl*.

gung-ho [gʌŋ'həu] *adj* (*col*) patriotero.

gunk [gʌŋk] *n* (*col*) masa viscosa.

gunman ['gʌnmən] *n* pistolero.

gunner ['gʌnə*] *n* artillero.

gunpoint ['gʌnpɔɪnt] *n*: **at** ~ a mano armada.

gunpowder ['gʌnpaudə*] *n* pólvora.

gunrunning ['gʌnrʌnɪŋ] *n* tráfico de armas.

gunshot ['gʌnʃɔt] *n* disparo.

gunsmith ['gʌnsmɪθ] *n* armero.

gurgle ['gə:gl] *vi* gorgotear.

guru ['guru:] *n* guru *m*.

gush [gʌʃ] *vi* chorrear; (*fig*) deshacerse en efusiones.

gushing ['gʌʃɪŋ] *adj* efusivo.

gusset ['gʌsɪt] *n* (*in tights, pants*) escudete

m.

gust [gʌst] *n* (*of wind*) ráfaga.

gusto ['gʌstəu] *n* entusiasmo.

gusty ['gʌstɪ] *adj* racheado.

gut [gʌt] *n* intestino; (*MUS etc*) cuerda de tripa ♦ *vt* (*poultry, fish*) destripar; (*building*): **the blaze** ~**ted the entire building** el fuego destruyó el edificio entero.

gut reaction *n* reacción *f* instintiva.

guts [gʌts] *npl* (*courage*) agallas *fpl*, valor *m*; (*col*: *innards*: *of people, animals*) tripas *fpl*; **to hate sb's** ~ odiar a algn (a muerte).

gutsy ['gʌtsɪ] *adj*: **to be** ~ (*col*) tener agallas.

gutted ['gʌtɪd] *adj* (*col*: *disappointed*): **I was** ~ me quedé hecho polvo.

gutter ['gʌtə*] *n* (*of roof*) canalón *m*; (*in street*) cuneta; **the** ~ (*fig*) el arroyo.

gutter press *n* (*col*): **the** ~ la prensa sensacionalista *or* amarilla; *see also* **tabloid press.**

guttural ['gʌtərl] *adj* gutural.

guy [gaɪ] *n* (*also*: ~**rope**) viento, cuerda; (*col*: *man*) tío (*SP*), tipo.

Guyana [gaɪ'ænə] *n* Guayana.

Guy Fawkes' Night [gaɪ'fɔ:ks-] *n ver recuadro.*

GUY FAWKES' NIGHT

La noche del cinco de noviembre, **Guy Fawkes' Night**, *se celebra el fracaso de la conspiración de la pólvora ("Gunpowder Plot"), el intento fallido de volar el parlamento de Jaime 1 en 1605. Esa noche se lanzan fuegos artificiales y se queman en muchas hogueras muñecos de trapo que representan a "Guy Fawkes", uno de los cabecillas. Días antes los niños tienen por costumbre pedir a los viandantes "a penny for the guy", dinero para comprar los cohetes.*

---

guzzle ['gʌzl] *vi* tragar ♦ *vt* engullir.

gym [dʒɪm] *n* (*also*: **gymnasium**) gimnasio; (*also*: **gymnastics**) gimnasia.

gymkhana [dʒɪm'kɑ:nə] *n* gincana.

gymnast ['dʒɪmnæst] *n* gimnasta *m/f*.

gymnastics [dʒɪm'næstɪks] *n* gimnasia.

gym shoes *npl* zapatillas *fpl* de gimnasia.

gym slip *n* (*BRIT*) pichi *m*.

gynaecologist, (*US*) **gynecologist** [gaɪnɪ'kɔlədʒɪst] *n* ginecólogo/a.

gynaecology, (*US*) **gynecology** [gaɪnə'kɔlədʒɪ] *n* ginecología.

gypsy ['dʒɪpsɪ] *n* = **gipsy.**

gyrate [dʒaɪ'reɪt] *vi* girar.

gyroscope ['dʒaɪrəskəup] *n* giroscopio.

H h

H, h [eɪtʃ] n (*letter*) H, h f; **H for Harry,** (*US*) **H for How** H de Historia.

habeas corpus ['heɪbɪəs'kɔːpəs] n (*LAW*) hábeas corpus m.

haberdashery ['hæbə'dæʃərɪ] n (*BRIT*) mercería; (*US: men's clothing*) prendas fpl de caballero.

habit ['hæbɪt] n hábito, costumbre f; **to get out of/into the ~ of doing sth** perder la costumbre de/acostumbrarse a hacer algo.

habitable ['hæbɪtəbl] adj habitable.

habitat ['hæbɪtæt] n hábitat m.

habitation [hæbɪ'teɪʃən] n habitación f.

habitual [hə'bɪtjuəl] adj acostumbrado, habitual; (*drinker, liar*) empedernido.

habitually [hə'bɪtjuəlɪ] adv por costumbre.

hack [hæk] vt (*cut*) cortar; (*slice*) tajar ♦ n corte m; (*axe blow*) hachazo; (*pej: writer*) escritor(a) m/f a sueldo; (*old horse*) jamelgo.

hacker ['hækə*] n (*COMPUT*) pirata m informático.

hackles ['hæklz] npl: **to make sb's ~ rise** (*fig*) poner furioso a algn.

hackney cab ['hæknɪ-] n coche m de alquiler.

hackneyed ['hæknɪd] adj trillado, gastado.

hacksaw ['hæksɔː] n sierra para metales.

had [hæd] pt, pp of **have**.

haddock, pl **~** or **~s** ['hædək] n especie de merluza.

hadn't ['hædnt] = **had not**.

haematology, (*US*) **hematology** ['hiːmə'tɔlədʒɪ] n hematología.

haemoglobin, (*US*) **hemoglobin** ['hiːmə'gləubɪn] n hemoglobina.

haemophilia, (*US*) **hemophilia** ['hiːmə'fɪlɪə] n hemofilia.

haemorrhage, (*US*) **hemorrhage** ['hɛmərɪdʒ] n hemorragia.

haemorrhoids, (*US*) **hemorrhoids** ['hɛmərɔɪdz] npl hemorroides fpl, almorranas fpl.

hag [hæg] n (*ugly*) vieja fea, tarasca; (*nasty*) bruja; (*witch*) hechicera.

haggard ['hægəd] adj ojeroso.

haggis ['hægɪs] n (*Scottish*) asadura de cordero cocida; see also **Burns' Night**.

haggle ['hægl] vi (*argue*) discutir; (*bargain*) regatear.

haggling ['hæglɪŋ] n regateo.

Hague [heɪg] n: **The ~** La Haya.

hail [heɪl] n (*weather*) granizo ♦ vt saludar; (*call*) llamar a ♦ vi granizar; **to ~ (as)** aclamar (como), celebrar (como); **he ~s from Scotland** es natural de Escocia.

hailstone ['heɪlstəun] n (piedra de) granizo.

hailstorm ['heɪlstɔːm] n granizada.

hair [hɛə*] n (*gen*) pelo, cabellos mpl; (*one ~*) pelo, cabello; (*head of ~*) pelo, cabellera; (*on legs etc*) vello; **to do one's ~** arreglarse el pelo; **grey ~** canas fpl.

hairbrush ['hɛəbrʌʃ] n cepillo (para el pelo).

haircut ['hɛəkʌt] n corte m de pelo.

hairdo ['hɛəduː] n peinado.

hairdresser ['hɛədrɛsə*] n peluquero/a; **~'s** peluquería.

hair-dryer ['hɛədraɪə*] n secador m (de pelo).

-haired [hɛəd] adj suff: **fair/long~** (de pelo) rubio or güero (*LAM*)/de pelo largo.

hairgrip ['hɛəgrɪp] n horquilla.

hairline ['hɛəlaɪn] n nacimiento del pelo.

hairline fracture n fractura muy fina.

hairnet ['hɛənɛt] n redecilla.

hair oil n brillantina.

hairpiece ['hɛəpiːs] n trenza postiza.

hairpin ['hɛəpɪn] n horquilla.

hairpin bend, (*US*) **hairpin curve** n curva muy cerrada.

hair-raising ['hɛəreɪzɪŋ] adj espeluznante.

hair remover n depilatorio.

hair's breadth n: **by a ~** por un pelo.

hair spray n laca.

hairstyle ['hɛəstaɪl] n peinado.

hairy ['hɛərɪ] adj peludo, velludo.

Haiti ['heɪtɪ] n Haití m.

hake [heɪk] n merluza.

halcyon ['hælsɪən] adj feliz.

hale [heɪl] adj: **~ and hearty** sano y fuerte.

half [hɑːf] n (pl **halves** [hɑːvz]) mitad f; (*SPORT: of match*) tiempo, parte f; (: *of ground*) campo ♦ adj medio ♦ adv medio, a medias; **~-an-hour** media hora; **two and a ~** dos y media; **~ a dozen** media docena; **~ a pound** media libra, ≈ 250 gr.; **to cut sth in ~** cortar algo por la mitad; **to go halves (with sb)** ir a medias (con algn); **~empty/closed** medio vacío/ entreabierto; **~ asleep** medio dormido; **~ past 3** las 3 y media.

half-back ['hɑːfbæk] n (*SPORT*) medio.

half-baked ['hɑːf'beɪkt] adj (*col: idea,*

half-breed – handicap

scheme) mal concebido *or* pensado.
half-breed ['hɑːfbriːd] *n* = **half-caste**.
half-brother ['hɑːfbrʌðə*] *n* hermanastro.
half-caste ['hɑːfkɑːst] *n* mestizo/a.
half-hearted ['hɑːf'hɑːtɪd] *adj* indiferente,
poco entusiasta.
half-hour [hɑːf'auə*] *n* media hora.
half-mast ['hɑːf'mɑːst] *n*: **at ~** (*flag*) a
media asta.
halfpenny ['heɪpnɪ] *n* medio penique
m.
half-price ['hɑːf'praɪs] *adj* a mitad de
precio.
half term *n* (*BRIT SCOL*) vacaciones de
mediados del trimestre.
half-time [hɑːf'taɪm] *n* descanso.
halfway ['hɑːf'weɪ] *adv* a medio camino; **to
meet sb ~** (*fig*) llegar a un acuerdo con
algn.
halfway house *n* centro de readaptación
de antiguos presos; (*fig*) solución *f*
intermedia.
half-wit ['hɑːfwɪt] *n* (*col*) zoquete *m*.
half-yearly [hɑːf'jɪəlɪ] *adv* semestralmente
♦ *adj* semestral.
halibut ['hælɪbət] *n*, *pl inv* halibut *m*.
halitosis [hælɪ'təusɪs] *n* halitosis *f*.
hall [hɔːl] *n* (*for concerts*) sala; (*entrance
way*) entrada, vestíbulo.
hallmark ['hɔːlmɑːk] *n* (*mark*) rasgo
distintivo; (*seal*) sello.
hallo [hə'ləu] *excl* = **hello**.
hall of residence *n* (*BRIT*) colegio mayor,
residencia universitaria.
Hallowe'en [hæləu'iːn] *n* víspera de Todos
los Santos; *ver recuadro*.

HALLOWE'EN

La tradición anglosajona dice que en la
noche del 31 de octubre, **Hallowe'en**,
víspera de Todos los Santos, es fácil ver a
brujas y fantasmas. Es una ocasión festiva
en la que los niños se disfrazan y van de
puerta en puerta llevando un farol hecho
con una calabaza en forma de cabeza
humana. Cuando se les abre la puerta
gritan "trick or treat" para indicar que
gastarán una broma a quien no les dé un
pequeño regalo (como golosinas o dinero).

---

hallucination [həluːsɪ'neɪʃən] *n* alucinación *f*.
hallway ['hɔːlweɪ] *n* vestíbulo.
halo ['heɪləu] *n* (*of saint*) aureola.
halt [hɔːlt] *n* (*stop*) alto, parada; (*RAIL*)
apeadero ♦ *vt* parar ♦ *vi* pararse; (*process*)
interrumpirse; **to call a ~ (to sth)** (*fig*)
poner fin (a algo).

halter ['hɔːltə*] *n* (*for horse*) cabestro.
halterneck ['hɔːltənɛk] *adj* de espalda
escotada.
halve [hɑːv] *vt* partir por la mitad.
halves [hɑːvz] *pl of* **half**.
ham [hæm] *n* jamón *m* (cocido); (*col: also*:
radio ~) radioaficionado/a *m/f*; (: *also*: **~
actor**) comicastro.
hamburger ['hæmbəːgə*] *n* hamburguesa.
ham-fisted ['hæm'fɪstɪd] *adj* torpe,
desmañado.
hamlet ['hæmlɪt] *n* aldea.
hammer ['hæmə*] *n* martillo ♦ *vt* (*nail*)
clavar; **to ~ a point home to sb**
remacharle un punto a algn.
►**hammer out** *vt* (*metal*) forjar a martillo;
(*fig: solution, agreement*) elaborar
(trabajosamente).
hammock ['hæmək] *n* hamaca.
hamper ['hæmpə*] *vt* estorbar ♦ *n* cesto.
hamster ['hæmstə*] *n* hámster *m*.
hand [hænd] *n* mano *f*; (*of clock*) aguja,
manecilla; (*writing*) letra; (*worker*) obrero;
(*measurement: of horse*) palmo ♦ *vt* (*give*)
dar, pasar; (*deliver*) entregar; **to give sb a
~** echar una mano a algn, ayudar a algn;
to force sb's ~ forzarle la mano a algn; **at
~** a mano; **in ~** entre manos; **we have the
matter in ~** tenemos el asunto entre
manos; **to have in one's ~** (*knife, victory*)
tener en la mano; **to have a free ~** tener
carta blanca; **on ~** (*person, services*) a
mano, al alcance; **to ~** (*information etc*) a
mano; **on the one ~ ..., on the other ~ ...**
por una parte ... por otra (parte) ....
►**hand down** *vt* pasar, bajar; (*tradition*)
transmitir; (*heirloom*) dejar en herencia;
(*US: sentence, verdict*) imponer.
►**hand in** *vt* entregar.
►**hand out** *vt* (*leaflets, advice*) repartir,
distribuir.
►**hand over** *vt* (*deliver*) entregar;
(*surrender*) ceder.
►**hand round** *vt* (*BRIT: information, papers*)
pasar (de mano en mano); (: *chocolates
etc*) ofrecer.
handbag ['hændbæg] *n* bolso, cartera
(*LAM*).
hand baggage *n* = **hand luggage**.
handball ['hændbɔːl] *n* balonmano.
handbasin ['hændbeɪsn] *n* lavabo.
handbook ['hændbuk] *n* manual *m*.
handbrake ['hændbreɪk] *n* freno de mano.
hand cream *n* crema para las manos.
handcuffs ['hændkʌfs] *npl* esposas *fpl*.
handful ['hændful] *n* puñado.
hand-held ['hænd'hɛld] *adj* de mano.
handicap ['hændɪkæp] *n* desventaja;

(*SPORT*) hándicap *m* ♦ *vt* estorbar.

handicapped ['hændɪkæpt] *adj*: **to be mentally ~** ser deficiente *m/f* mental; **to be physically ~** ser minusválido/a.

handicraft ['hændɪkrɑːft] *n* artesanía.

handiwork ['hændɪwəːk] *n* manualidad(es) *f(pl)*; (*fig*) obra; **this looks like his ~** (*pej*) es obra de él, parece.

handkerchief ['hæŋkətʃɪf] *n* pañuelo.

handle ['hændl] *n* (*of door etc*) pomo; (*of cup etc*) asa; (*of knife etc*) mango; (*for winding*) manivela ♦ *vt* (*touch*) tocar; (*deal with*) encargarse de; (*treat: people*) manejar; "**~ with care**" "(manéjese) con cuidado"; **to fly off the ~** perder los estribos.

handlebar(s) ['hændlbɑː(z)] *n(pl)* manillar *msg.*

handling ['hændlɪŋ] *n* (*AUT*) conducción *f*; **his ~ of the matter** su forma de llevar el asunto.

handling charges *npl* gastos *mpl* de tramitación.

hand luggage *n* equipaje *m* de mano.

handmade ['hændmeɪd] *adj* hecho a mano.

handout ['hændaut] *n* (*distribution*) repartición *f*; (*charity*) limosna; (*leaflet*) folleto, octavilla; (*press ~*) nota.

hand-picked ['hænd'pɪkt] *adj* (*produce*) escogido a mano; (*staff etc*) seleccionado cuidadosamente.

handrail ['hændreɪl] *n* (*on staircase etc*) pasamanos *m inv*, barandilla.

handset ['hændsɛt] *n* (*TEL*) auricular *m*.

handshake ['hændʃeɪk] *n* apretón *m* de manos; (*COMPUT*) coloquio.

handsome ['hænsəm] *adj* guapo.

hands-on ['hændz'ɔn] *adj* práctico; **she has a very ~ approach** le gusta tomar parte activa; **~ experience** (*COMPUT*) experiencia práctica.

handstand ['hændstænd] *n* voltereta, salto mortal.

hand-to-mouth ['hændtə'mauθ] *adj* (*existence*) precario.

handwriting ['hændraɪtɪŋ] *n* letra.

handwritten ['hændrɪtn] *adj* escrito a mano, manuscrito.

handy ['hændɪ] *adj* (*close at hand*) a mano; (*useful: machine, tool etc*) práctico; (*skilful*) hábil, diestro; **to come in ~** venir bien.

handyman ['hændɪmæn] *n* manitas *m inv*.

hang, *pt, pp* **hung** [hæŋ, hʌŋ] *vt* colgar; (*head*) bajar; (*criminal: pt, pp* **hanged**) ahorcar; **to get the ~ of sth** (*col*) coger el tranquillo a algo.

▶**hang about** *vi* haraganear.

▶**hang back** *vi* (*hesitate*): **to ~ back (from doing)** vacilar (en hacer).

▶**hang on** *vi* (*wait*) esperar ♦ *vt fus* (*depend on: decision etc*) depender de; **to ~ on to** (*keep hold of*) agarrarse or aferrarse a; (*keep*) guardar, quedarse con.

▶**hang out** *vt* (*washing*) tender, colgar ♦ *vi* (*col: live*) vivir; (: *often be found*) moverse; **to ~ out of sth** colgar fuera de algo.

▶**hang together** *vi* (*cohere: argument etc*) sostenerse.

▶**hang up** *vt* (*coat*) colgar ♦ *vi* (*TEL*) colgar; **to ~ up on sb** colgarle a algn.

hangar ['hæŋə*] *n* hangar *m*.

hangdog ['hæŋdɔg] *adj* (*guilty: look, expression*) avergonzado.

hanger ['hæŋə*] *n* percha.

hanger-on [hæŋər'ɔn] *n* parásito.

hang-glider ['hæŋglaɪdə*] *n* ala delta.

hang-gliding ['hæŋglaɪdɪŋ] *n* vuelo con ala delta.

hanging ['hæŋɪŋ] *n* (*execution*) ejecución *f* (en la horca).

hangman ['hæŋmən] *n* verdugo.

hangover ['hæŋəuvə*] *n* (*after drinking*) resaca.

hang-up ['hæŋʌp] *n* complejo.

hanker ['hæŋkə*] *vi*: **to ~ after** (*miss*) echar de menos; (*long for*) añorar.

hankie, hanky ['hæŋkɪ] *n abbr* = **handkerchief.**

Hansard ['hænsɑːd] *n actas oficiales de las sesiones del parlamento británico.*

Hants *abbr* (*BRIT*) = **Hampshire.**

haphazard [hæp'hæzəd] *adj* fortuito.

hapless ['hæplɪs] *adj* desventurado.

happen ['hæpən] *vi* suceder, ocurrir; (*take place*) tener lugar, realizarse; **as it ~s** da la casualidad de que; **what's ~ing?** ¿qué pasa?

▶**happen (up)on** *vt fus* tropezar or dar con.

happening ['hæpnɪŋ] *n* suceso, acontecimiento.

happily ['hæpɪlɪ] *adv* (*luckily*) afortunadamente; (*cheerfully*) alegremente.

happiness ['hæpɪnɪs] *n* (*contentment*) felicidad *f*; (*joy*) alegría.

happy ['hæpɪ] *adj* feliz; (*cheerful*) alegre; **to be ~ (with)** estar contento (con); **yes, I'd be ~ to** sí, con mucho gusto; **H~ Christmas/New Year!** ¡Feliz Navidad!/ ¡Feliz Año Nuevo!; **~ birthday!** ¡felicidades!, ¡feliz cumpleaños!

happy-go-lucky ['hæpɪgəu'lʌkɪ] *adj* despreocupado.

happy hour *n horas en las que la bebida es más barata en un bar.*

harangue [hə'ræŋ] *vt* arengar.

harass ['hærəs] *vt* acosar, hostigar.
harassed ['hærəst] *adj* agobiado, presionado.
harassment ['hærəsmənt] *n* persecución *f*, acoso; (*worry*) preocupación *f*.
harbour, (*US*) **harbor** ['hɑːbə*] *n* puerto ♦ *vt* (*hope etc*) abrigar; (*hide*) dar abrigo a; (*retain: grudge etc*) guardar.
harbo(u)r dues *npl* derechos *mpl* portuarios.
hard [hɑːd] *adj* duro; (*difficult*) difícil; (*person*) severo ♦ *adv* (*work*) mucho, duro; (*think*) profundamente; **to look ~ at sb/ sth** clavar los ojos en algn/algo; **to try ~** esforzarse; **no ~ feelings!** ¡sin rencor(es)!; **to be ~ of hearing** ser duro de oído; **to be ~ done by** ser tratado injustamente; **to be ~ on sb** ser muy duro con algn; **I find it ~ to believe that ...** me cuesta trabajo creer que ....
hard-and-fast ['hɑːdən'fɑːst] *adj* rígido, definitivo.
hardback ['hɑːdbæk] *n* libro de tapas duras.
hard cash *n* dinero en efectivo.
hard copy *n* (*COMPUT*) copia impresa.
hard-core ['hɑːd'kɔː*] *adj* (*pornography*) duro; (*supporters*) incondicional.
hard court *n* (*TENNIS*) pista *or* cancha (de tenis) de cemento.
hard disk *n* (*COMPUT*) disco duro.
harden ['hɑːdn] *vt* endurecer; (*steel*) templar; (*fig*) curtir; (: *determination*) fortalecer ♦ *vi* (*substance*) endurecerse.
hardened ['hɑːdnd] *adj* (*criminal*) habitual; **to be ~ to sth** estar acostumbrado a algo.
hard-headed ['hɑːd'hedɪd] *adj* poco sentimental, realista.
hard-hearted ['hɑːd'hɑːtɪd] *adj* insensible.
hard-hitting ['hɑːd'hɪtɪŋ] *adj* (*speech, article*) contundente.
hard labour *n* trabajos *mpl* forzados.
hardliner [hɑːd'laɪnə*] *n* partidario/a de la línea dura.
hard-luck story ['hɑːdlʌk-] *n* dramón *m*.
hardly ['hɑːdlɪ] *adv* (*scarcely*) apenas; **that can ~ be true** eso difícilmente puede ser cierto; **~ ever** casi nunca; **I can ~ believe it** apenas me lo puedo creer.
hardness ['hɑːdnɪs] *n* dureza.
hard-nosed ['hɑːd'nəuzd] *adj* duro, sin contemplaciones.
hard-pressed ['hɑːd'prest] *adj* en apuros.
hard sell *n* publicidad *f* agresiva; **~ techniques** técnicas *fpl* agresivas de venta.
hardship ['hɑːdʃɪp] *n* (*troubles*) penas *fpl*; (*financial*) apuro.

hard shoulder *n* (*AUT*) arcén *m*.
hard-up [hɑːd'ʌp] *adj* (*col*) sin un duro (*SP*) *or* plata (*LAM*).
hardware ['hɑːdwɛə*] *n* ferretería; (*COMPUT*) hardware *m*.
hardware shop *n* ferretería.
hard-wearing [hɑːd'wɛərɪŋ] *adj* resistente, duradero; (*shoes*) resistente.
hard-won ['hɑːd'wʌn] *adj* ganado con esfuerzo.
hard-working [hɑːd'wɔːkɪŋ] *adj* trabajador(a).
hardy ['hɑːdɪ] *adj* fuerte; (*plant*) resistente.
hare [hɛə*] *n* liebre *f*.
hare-brained ['hɛəbreɪnd] *adj* atolondrado.
harelip ['hɛəlɪp] *n* labio leporino.
harem [hɑː'riːm] *n* harén *m*.
haricot (bean) ['hærɪkəu-] *n* alubia.
hark back [hɑːk-] *vi*: **to ~ back to** (*former days, earlier occasion*) recordar.
harm [hɑːm] *n* daño, mal *m* ♦ *vt* (*person*) hacer daño a; (*health, interests*) perjudicar; (*thing*) dañar; **out of ~'s way** a salvo; **there's no ~ in trying** no se pierde nada con intentar.
harmful ['hɑːmful] *adj* (*gen*) dañino; (*reputation*) perjudicial.
harmless ['hɑːmlɪs] *adj* (*person*) inofensivo; (*drugs*) inocuo.
harmonica [hɑː'mɔnɪkə] *n* armónica.
harmonious [hɑː'məunɪəs] *adj* armonioso.
harmonize ['hɑːmənaɪz] *vt*, *vi* armonizar.
harmony ['hɑːmənɪ] *n* armonía.
harness ['hɑːnɪs] *n* arreos *mpl* ♦ *vt* (*horse*) enjaezar; (*resources*) aprovechar.
harp [hɑːp] *n* arpa ♦ *vi*: **to ~ on (about)** machacar (con).
harpoon [hɑː'puːn] *n* arpón *m*.
harrow ['hærəu] *n* grada ♦ *vt* gradar.
harrowing ['hærəuɪŋ] *adj* angustioso.
harry ['hærɪ] *vt* (*MIL*) acosar; (*person*) hostigar.
harsh [hɑːʃ] *adj* (*cruel*) duro, cruel; (*severe*) severo; (*words*) hosco; (*colour*) chillón/ ona; (*contrast*) violento.
harshly ['hɑːʃlɪ] *adv* (*say*) con aspereza; (*treat*) con mucha dureza.
harshness ['hɑːʃnɪs] *n* dureza.
harvest ['hɑːvɪst] *n* cosecha; (*of grapes*) vendimia ♦ *vt*, *vi* cosechar.
harvester ['hɑːvɪstə*] *n* (*machine*) cosechadora; (*person*) segador(a) *m/f*; **combine ~** segadora trilladora.
has [hæz] *vb see* **have**.
has-been ['hæzbiːn] *n* (*col: person*) persona acabada; (: *thing*) vieja gloria.
hash [hæʃ] *n* (*CULIN*) picadillo; (*fig: mess*) lío.

hashish ['hæʃɪʃ] n hachís m.
hasn't ['hæznt] = **has not**.
hassle ['hæsl] n (col) lío, rollo ♦ vt incordiar.
haste [heɪst] n prisa.
hasten ['heɪsn] vt acelerar ♦ vi darse prisa; I ~ **to add that...** me apresuro a añadir que ....
hastily ['heɪstɪlɪ] adv de prisa.
hasty ['heɪstɪ] adj apresurado.
hat [hæt] n sombrero.
hatbox ['hætbɔks] n sombrerera.
hatch [hætʃ] n (NAUT: also: ~**way**) escotilla ♦ vi salir del cascarón ♦ vt incubar; (fig: scheme, plot) idear, tramar.
hatchback ['hætʃbæk] n (AUT) tres or cinco puertas m.
hatchet ['hætʃɪt] n hacha.
hatchet job n (col) varapalo.
hatchet man n (col) ejecutor m de faenas desagradables por cuenta de otro.
hate [heɪt] vt odiar, aborrecer ♦ n odio; I ~ **to trouble you, but ...** siento or lamento molestarle, pero ....
hateful ['heɪtful] adj odioso.
hatred ['heɪtrɪd] n odio.
hat trick n: **to score a** ~ (BRIT SPORT) marcar tres tantos (or triunfos) seguidos.
haughtily ['hɔːtɪlɪ] adv con arrogancia.
haughty ['hɔːtɪ] adj altanero, arrogante.
haul [hɔːl] vt tirar, jalar (LAM); (by lorry) transportar ♦ n (of fish) redada; (of stolen goods etc) botín m.
haulage ['hɔːlɪdʒ] n (BRIT) transporte m; (costs) gastos mpl de transporte.
haulage contractor n (firm) empresa de transportes; (person) transportista m/f.
haulier ['hɔːlɪə*], (US) **hauler** ['hɔːlə*] n transportista m/f.
haunch [hɔːntʃ] n anca; (of meat) pierna.
haunt [hɔːnt] vt (subj: ghost) aparecer en; (frequent) frecuentar; (obsess) obsesionar ♦ n guarida.
haunted ['hɔːntɪd] adj (castle etc) embrujado; (look) de angustia.
haunting ['hɔːntɪŋ] adj (sight, music) evocativo.
Havana [hə'vɑːnə] n La Habana.

═══════════════════════════ KEYWORD

have [hæv] (pt, pp **had**) aux vb 1 (gen) haber; **to** ~ **arrived/eaten** haber llegado/comido; **having finished** or **when he had finished, he left** cuando hubo acabado, se fue

2 (in tag questions): **you've done it,** ~**n't you?** lo has hecho, ¿verdad? or ¿no?
3 (in short answers and questions): I ~**n't** no; **so I** ~ pues, es verdad; **we** ~**n't paid** — **yes we** ~! no hemos pagado — ¡sí que hemos pagado!; **I've been there before,** ~ **you?** he estado allí antes, ¿y tú?
♦ modal aux vb (be obliged): **to** ~ **(got) to do sth** tener que hacer algo; **you** ~**n't to tell her** no hay que or no debes decírselo
♦ vt 1 (possess) tener; **he has (got) blue eyes/dark hair** tiene los ojos azules/el pelo negro
2 (referring to meals etc): **to** ~ **breakfast/ lunch/dinner** desayunar/comer/cenar; **to** ~ **a drink/a cigarette** tomar algo/fumar un cigarrillo
3 (receive) recibir; (obtain) obtener; **may I** ~ **your address?** ¿puedes darme tu dirección?; **you can** ~ **it for £5** te lo puedes quedar por £5; **I must** ~ **it by tomorrow** lo necesito para mañana; **to** ~ **a baby** tener un niño or bebé
4 (maintain, allow): **I won't** ~ **it/this nonsense!** ¡no lo permitiré!/¡no permitiré estas tonterías!; **we can't** ~ **that** no podemos permitir eso
5: **to** ~ **sth done** hacer or mandar hacer algo; **to** ~ **one's hair cut** cortarse el pelo; **to** ~ **sb do sth** hacer que algn haga algo
6 (experience, suffer): **to** ~ **a cold/flu** tener un resfriado/la gripe; **she had her bag stolen/her arm broken** le robaron el bolso/se rompió un brazo; **to** ~ **an operation** operarse
7 (+noun): **to** ~ **a swim/walk/bath/rest** nadar/dar un paseo/darse un baño/ descansar; **let's** ~ **a look** vamos a ver; **to** ~ **a meeting/party** celebrar una reunión/ una fiesta; **let me** ~ **a try** déjame intentarlo
▶**have in** vt: **to** ~ **it in for sb** (col) tenerla tomada con algn
▶**have on** vt: ~ **you anything on tomorrow?** ¿vas a hacer algo mañana?; **I don't** ~ **any money on me** no llevo dinero (encima); **to** ~ **sb on** (BRIT col) tomarle el pelo a algn
▶**have out** vt: **to** ~ **it out with sb** (settle a problem etc) dejar las cosas en claro con algn.

haven ['heɪvn] n puerto; (fig) refugio.
haven't ['hævnt] = **have not**.
haversack ['hævəsæk] n macuto.
haves [hævz] npl: **the** ~ **and the have-nots** los ricos y los pobres.
havoc ['hævək] n estragos mpl; **to play** ~

with sth hacer estragos en algo.
Hawaii [hə'waɪiː] n (Islas fpl) Hawai m.
Hawaiian [hə'waɪjən] adj, n hawaiano/a m/f.
hawk [hɔːk] n halcón m ♦ vt (goods for sale) pregonar.
hawkish ['hɔːkɪʃ] adj beligerante.
hawthorn ['hɔːθɔːn] n espino.
hay [heɪ] n heno.
hay fever n fiebre f del heno.
haystack ['heɪstæk] n almiar m.
haywire ['heɪwaɪə*] adj (col): **to go ~** (person) volverse loco; (plan) irse al garete.
hazard ['hæzəd] n riesgo; (danger) peligro ♦ vt (remark) aventurar; (one's life) arriesgar; **to be a health ~** ser un peligro para la salud; **to ~ a guess** aventurar una respuesta or hipótesis.
hazardous ['hæzədəs] adj (dangerous) peligroso; (risky) arriesgado.
hazard warning lights npl (AUT) señales fpl de emergencia.
haze [heɪz] n neblina.
hazel ['heɪzl] n (tree) avellano ♦ adj (eyes) color m de avellano.
hazelnut ['heɪzlnʌt] n avellana.
hazy ['heɪzɪ] adj brumoso; (idea) vago.
H-bomb ['eɪtʃbɔm] n bomba H.
h & c abbr (BRIT) = hot and cold (water).
HE abbr = high explosive; (REL, DIPLOMACY: = His (or Her) Excellency) S. Excª.
he [hiː] pron él; **~ who...** aquél que..., quien....
head [hed] n cabeza; (leader) jefe/a m/f; (COMPUT) cabeza (grabadora) ♦ vt (list) encabezar; (group) capitanear; **~s (or tails)** cara (o cruz); **~ first** de cabeza; **~ over heels** patas arriba; **~ over heels in love** perdidamente enamorado; **on your ~ be it!** ¡allá tú!; **they went over my ~ to the manager** fueron directamente al gerente sin hacerme caso; **it was above or over their ~s** no alcanzaron a entenderlo; **to come to a ~** (fig: situation etc) llegar a un punto crítico; **to have a ~ for business** tener talento para los negocios; **to have no ~ for heights** no resistir las alturas; **to lose/keep one's ~** perder la cabeza/mantener la calma; **to sit at the ~ of the table** sentarse a la cabecera de la mesa; **to ~ the ball** cabecear (el balón).
▶**head for** vt fus dirigirse a.
▶**head off** vt (threat, danger) evitar.
headache ['hedeɪk] n dolor m de cabeza; **to have a ~** tener dolor de cabeza.
headband ['hedbænd] n cinta (para la cabeza), vincha (LAM).

headboard ['hedbɔːd] n cabecera.
headdress ['heddres] n (of bride, Indian) tocado.
headed notepaper ['hedɪd-] n papel m con membrete.
header ['hedə*] n (BRIT col: FOOTBALL) cabezazo; (: fall) caída de cabeza.
headfirst [hed'fɜːst] adv de cabeza.
headhunt ['hedhʌnt] vt: **to be ~ed** ser seleccionado por un cazatalentos.
headhunter ['hedhʌntə*] n (fig) cazaejecutivos m inv.
heading ['hedɪŋ] n título.
headlamp ['hedlæmp] n (BRIT) = **headlight**.
headland ['hedlənd] n promontorio.
headlight ['hedlaɪt] n faro.
headline ['hedlaɪn] n titular m.
headlong ['hedlɔŋ] adv (fall) de cabeza; (rush) precipitadamente.
headmaster/mistress [hed'mɑːstə*/ mɪstrɪs] n director(a) m/f (de escuela).
head office n oficina central, central f.
head-on [hed'ɔn] adj (collision) de frente.
headphones ['hedfəunz] npl auriculares mpl.
headquarters (HQ) ['hedkwɔːtəz] npl sede f central; (MIL) cuartel m general.
head-rest ['hedrest] n reposa-cabezas m inv.
headroom ['hedrum] n (in car) altura interior; (under bridge) (límite m de) altura.
headscarf ['hedskɑːf] n pañuelo.
headset ['hedset] n cascos mpl.
headstone ['hedstəun] n lápida.
headstrong ['hedstrɔŋ] adj testarudo.
head waiter n maître m.
headway ['hedweɪ] n: **to make ~** (fig) hacer progresos.
headwind ['hedwɪnd] n viento contrario.
heady ['hedɪ] adj (experience, period) apasionante; (wine) fuerte.
heal [hiːl] vt curar ♦ vi cicatrizar.
health [helθ] n salud f.
health care n asistencia sanitaria.
health centre n ambulatorio, centro médico.
health food(s) n(pl) alimentos mpl orgánicos.
health hazard n riesgo para la salud.
Health Service n (BRIT) servicio de salud pública, ≈ Insalud m (SP).
healthy ['helθɪ] adj (gen) sano; (economy, bank balance) saludable.
heap [hiːp] n montón m ♦ vt amontonar; (plate) colmar; **~s (of)** (col: lots) montones (de); **to ~ favours/praise/gifts etc on sb** colmar a algn de favores/elogios/regalos etc.

hear, *pt, pp* **heard** [hɪə*, hɜːd] *vt* oír; (*perceive*) sentir; (*listen to*) escuchar; (*lecture*) asistir a; (*LAW: case*) ver ♦ *vi* oír; **to ~ about** oír hablar de; **to ~ from sb** tener noticias de alguien; **I've never heard of that book** nunca he oído hablar de ese libro.

▶**hear out** *vt:* **to ~ sb out** dejar que algn termine de hablar.

hearing ['hɪərɪŋ] *n* (*sense*) oído; (*LAW*) vista; **to give sb a ~** dar a algn la oportunidad de hablar, escuchar a algn.

hearing aid *n* audífono.

hearsay ['hɪəseɪ] *n* rumores *mpl*, habladurías *fpl*.

hearse [hɜːs] *n* coche *m* fúnebre.

heart [hɑːt] *n* corazón *m*; **~s** *npl* (*CARDS*) corazones *mpl*; **at ~** en el fondo; **by ~** (*learn, know*) de memoria; **to have a weak ~** tener el corazón débil; **to set one's ~ on sth/on doing sth** anhelar algo/hacer algo; **I did not have the ~ to tell her** no tuve valor para decírselo; **to take ~** cobrar ánimos; **the ~ of the matter** lo esencial *or* el meollo del asunto.

heartache ['hɑːteɪk] *n* angustia.

heart attack *n* infarto (de miocardio).

heartbeat ['hɑːtbiːt] *n* latido (del corazón).

heartbreak ['hɑːtbreɪk] *n* angustia, congoja.

heartbreaking ['hɑːtbreɪkɪŋ] *adj* desgarrador(a).

heartbroken ['hɑːtbrəukən] *adj:* **she was ~ about it** le partió el corazón.

heartburn ['hɑːtbɜːn] *n* acedía.

-hearted ['hɑːtɪd] *adj suff:* **a kind~ person** una persona bondadosa.

heartening ['hɑːtnɪŋ] *adj* alentador(a).

heart failure *n* (*MED*) paro cardíaco.

heartfelt ['hɑːtfɛlt] *adj* (*cordial*) cordial; (*deeply felt*) sincero.

hearth [hɑːθ] *n* (*gen*) hogar *m*; (*fireplace*) chimenea.

heartily ['hɑːtɪlɪ] *adv* sinceramente, cordialmente; (*laugh*) a carcajadas; (*eat*) con buen apetito; **to be ~ sick of** estar completamente harto de.

heartland ['hɑːtlænd] *n* zona interior *or* central; (*fig*) corazón *m*.

heartless ['hɑːtlɪs] *adj* despiadado.

heartstrings ['hɑːtstrɪŋz] *npl:* **to tug (at) sb's ~** tocar la fibra sensible de algn.

heart-throb ['hɑːtθrɔb] *n* ídolo.

heart-to-heart ['hɑːttə'hɑːt] *n* (*also:* **~ talk**) conversación *f* íntima.

heart transplant *n* transplante *m* de corazón.

hearty ['hɑːtɪ] *adj* cordial.

heat [hiːt] *n* (*gen*) calor *m*; (*SPORT: also:* **qualifying ~**) prueba eliminatoria; (*ZOOL*): **in** *or* **on ~** en celo ♦ *vt* calentar.

▶**heat up** *vi* (*gen*) calentarse.

heated ['hiːtɪd] *adj* caliente; (*fig*) acalorado.

heater ['hiːtə*] *n* calentador *m*.

heath [hiːθ] *n* (*BRIT*) brezal *m*.

heathen ['hiːðn] *adj, n* pagano/a *m/f*.

heather ['hɛðə*] *n* brezo.

heating ['hiːtɪŋ] *n* calefacción *f*.

heat-resistant ['hiːtrɪzɪstənt] *adj* refractario.

heat-seeking ['hiːtsiːkɪŋ-] *adj* guiado por infrarrojos, termoguiado.

heatstroke ['hiːtstrəuk] *n* insolación *f*.

heatwave ['hiːtweɪv] *n* ola de calor.

heave [hiːv] *vt* (*pull*) tirar; (*push*) empujar con esfuerzo; (*lift*) levantar (con esfuerzo) ♦ *vi* (*water*) subir y bajar ♦ *n* tirón *m*; empujón *m*; (*effort*) esfuerzo; (*throw*) echada; **to ~ a sigh** dar *or* echar un suspiro, suspirar.

▶**heave to** *vi* (*NAUT*) ponerse al pairo.

heaven ['hɛvn] *n* cielo; (*REL*) paraíso; **thank ~!** ¡gracias a Dios!; **for ~'s sake!** (*pleading*) ¡por el amor de Dios!, ¡por lo que más quiera!; (*protesting*) ¡por Dios!

heavenly ['hɛvnlɪ] *adj* celestial; (*REL*) divino.

heavenly body *n* cuerpo celeste.

heavily ['hɛvɪlɪ] *adv* pesadamente; (*drink, smoke*) en exceso; (*sleep, sigh*) profundamente.

heavy ['hɛvɪ] *adj* pesado; (*work*) duro; (*sea, rain, meal*) fuerte; (*drinker, smoker*) empedernido; (*eater*) comilón/ona.

heavy-duty ['hɛvɪ'djuːtɪ] *adj* resistente.

heavy goods vehicle (HGV) *n* (*BRIT*) vehículo pesado.

heavy-handed ['hɛvɪ'hændɪd] *adj* (*clumsy, tactless*) torpe.

heavy industry *n* industria pesada.

heavy metal *n* (*MUS*) heavy *m* (metal).

heavy-set [hɛvɪ'sɛt] *adj* (*esp US*) corpulento, fornido.

heavy user *n* consumidor *m* intensivo.

heavyweight ['hɛvɪweɪt] *n* (*SPORT*) peso pesado.

Hebrew ['hiːbruː] *adj, n* (*LING*) hebreo.

Hebrides ['hɛbrɪdiːz] *npl:* **the ~** las Hébridas.

heck [hɛk] *n* (*col*): **why the ~ ...?** ¿por qué porras ...?; **a ~ of a lot of** cantidad de.

heckle ['hɛkl] *vt* interrumpir.

heckler ['hɛklə*] *n* el/la que interrumpe a un orador.

hectare ['hɛktɑː*] *n* (*BRIT*) hectárea.

hectic ['hɛktɪk] *adj* agitado; (*busy*) ocupado.

hector ['hɛktə*] vt intimidar con bravatas.

he'd [hi:d] = **he would**; **he had**.

hedge [hɛdʒ] n seto ♦ vt cercar (con un seto) ♦ vi contestar con evasivas; **as a ~ against inflation** como protección contra la inflación; **to ~ one's bets** (fig) cubrirse.

hedgehog ['hɛdʒhɔg] n erizo.

hedgerow ['hɛdʒrəu] n seto vivo.

hedonism ['hi:dənɪzəm] n hedonismo.

heed [hi:d] vt (also: **take ~ of**) (pay attention) hacer caso de; (bear in mind) tener en cuenta; **to pay (no) ~ to, take (no) ~ of** (no) hacer caso a, (no) tener en cuenta.

heedless ['hi:dlɪs] adj desatento.

heel [hi:l] n talón m ♦ vt (shoe) poner tacón a; **to take to one's ~s** (col) poner pies en polvorosa; **to bring to ~** meter en cintura.

hefty ['hɛftɪ] adj (person) fornido; (piece) grande; (price) alto.

heifer ['hɛfə*] n novilla, ternera.

height [haɪt] n (of person) talla f; (of building) altura; (high ground) cerro; (altitude) altitud f; **what ~ are you?** ¿cuánto mides?; **of average ~** de estatura mediana; **to be afraid of ~s** tener miedo a las alturas; **it's the ~ of fashion** es el último grito en moda.

heighten ['haɪtn] vt elevar; (fig) aumentar.

heinous ['heɪnəs] adj atroz, nefasto.

heir [ɛə*] n heredero.

heir apparent n presunto heredero.

heiress ['ɛərɛs] n heredera.

heirloom ['ɛəlu:m] n reliquia de familia.

heist [haɪst] n (col: hold-up) atraco a mano armada.

held [hɛld] pt, pp of **hold**.

helicopter ['hɛlɪkɔptə*] n helicóptero.

heliport ['hɛlɪpɔ:t] n (AVIAT) helipuerto.

helium ['hi:lɪəm] n helio.

hell [hɛl] n infierno; **oh ~!** (col) ¡demonios!, ¡caramba!

he'll [hi:l] = **he will, he shall**.

hellbent [hɛl'bɛnt] adj (col): **he was ~ on going** se le metió entre ceja y ceja ir.

hellish ['hɛlɪʃ] adj infernal; (col) horrible.

hello [hə'ləu] excl ¡hola!; (surprise) ¡caramba!; (TEL) ¡dígame! (esp SP), ¡aló! (LAM).

helm [hɛlm] n (NAUT) timón m.

helmet ['hɛlmɪt] n casco.

helmsman ['hɛlmzmən] n timonel m.

help [hɛlp] n ayuda; (charwoman) criada, asistenta ♦ vt ayudar; **~!** ¡socorro!; **with the ~ of** con la ayuda de; **can I ~ you?** (in shop) ¿qué desea?; **to be of ~ to sb** servir a algn; **to ~ sb (to) do sth** echarle una mano or ayudar a algn a hacer algo; **~**

yourself sírvete; **he can't ~ it** no lo puede evitar.

helper ['hɛlpə*] n ayudante m/f.

helpful ['hɛlpful] adj útil; (person) servicial.

helping ['hɛlpɪŋ] n ración f.

helping hand n: **to give sb a ~** echar una mano a algn.

helpless ['hɛlplɪs] adj (incapable) incapaz; (defenceless) indefenso.

helpline ['hɛlplaɪn] n teléfono de asistencia al público.

Helsinki ['hɛlsɪŋkɪ] n Helsinki m.

helter-skelter ['hɛltə'skɛltə*] n (in funfair) tobogán m.

hem [hɛm] n dobladillo ♦ vt poner or coser el dobladillo a.

▶**hem in** vt cercar; **to feel ~med in** (fig) sentirse acosado.

he-man ['hi:mæn] n macho.

hematology [hi:mə'tɔlədʒɪ] n (US) = **haematology**.

hemisphere ['hɛmɪsfɪə*] n hemisferio.

hemline ['hɛmlaɪn] n bajo (del vestido).

hemlock ['hɛmlɔk] n cicuta.

hemoglobin [hi:mə'gləubɪn] n (US) = **haemoglobin**.

hemophilia [hi:mə'fɪlɪə] n (US) = **haemophilia**.

hemorrhage ['hɛmərɪdʒ] n (US) = **haemorrhage**.

hemorrhoids ['hɛmərɔɪdz] npl (US) = **haemorrhoids**.

hemp [hɛmp] n cáñamo.

hen [hɛn] n gallina; (female bird) hembra.

hence [hɛns] adv (therefore) por lo tanto; **2 years ~** de aquí a 2 años.

henceforth [hɛns'fɔ:θ] adv de hoy en adelante.

henchman ['hɛntʃmən] n (pej) secuaz m.

henna ['hɛnə] n alheña.

hen night n (col) despedida de soltera.

hen party n (col) reunión f de mujeres.

henpecked ['hɛnpɛkt] adj: **to be ~** ser un calzonazos.

hepatitis [hɛpə'taɪtɪs] n hepatitis f inv.

her [hə:*] pron (direct) la; (indirect) le; (stressed, after prep) ella ♦ adj su; see also **me; my**.

herald ['hɛrəld] n (forerunner) precursor(a) m/f ♦ vt anunciar.

heraldic [hɛ'rældɪk] adj heráldico.

heraldry ['hɛrəldrɪ] n heráldica.

herb [hə:b] n hierba.

herbaceous [hə:'beɪʃəs] adj herbáceo.

herbal ['hə:bl] adj de hierbas.

herbicide ['hə:bɪsaɪd] n herbicida m.

herd [hə:d] n rebaño; (of wild animals, swine) piara ♦ vt (drive, gather: animals) llevar en manada; (: *people*) reunir.

▶**herd together** *vt* agrupar, reunir ♦ *vi* apiñarse, agruparse.

here [hɪə*] *adv* aquí; ~! (*present*) ¡presente!; ~ **is/are** aquí está/están; ~ **she is** aquí está; **come** ~! ¡ven aquí *or* acá!; ~ **and there** aquí y allá.

hereabouts ['hɪərə'bauts] *adv* por aquí (cerca).

hereafter [hɪər'ɑːftə*] *adv* en el futuro ♦ *n*: **the** ~ el más allá.

hereby [hɪə'baɪ] *adv* (*in letter*) por la presente.

hereditary [hɪ'rɛdɪtrɪ] *adj* hereditario.

heredity [hɪ'rɛdɪtɪ] *n* herencia.

heresy ['hɛrəsɪ] *n* herejía.

heretic ['hɛrətɪk] *n* hereje *m/f*.

heretical [hɪ'rɛtɪkəl] *adj* herético.

herewith [hɪə'wɪð] *adv*: **I send you** ~ ... le mando adjunto ....

heritage ['hɛrɪtɪdʒ] *n* (*gen*) herencia; (*fig*) patrimonio; **our national** ~ nuestro patrimonio nacional.

hermetically [həː'mɛtɪkəlɪ] *adv*: ~ **sealed** herméticamente cerrado.

hermit ['həːmɪt] *n* ermitaño/a.

hernia ['həːnɪə] *n* hernia.

hero, *pl* ~**es** ['hɪərəu] *n* héroe *m*; (*in book, film*) protagonista *m*.

heroic [hɪ'rəuɪk] *adj* heroico.

heroin ['hɛrəuɪn] *n* heroína.

heroin addict *n* heroinómano/a, adicto/a a la heroína.

heroine ['hɛrəuɪn] *n* heroína; (*in book, film*) protagonista.

heroism ['hɛrəuɪzm] *n* heroísmo.

heron ['hɛrən] *n* garza.

hero worship *n* veneración *f*.

herring ['hɛrɪŋ] *n* arenque *m*.

hers [həːz] *pron* (el) suyo/(la) suya *etc*; **a friend of** ~ un amigo suyo; **this is** ~ esto es suyo *or* de ella; *see also* **mine**.

herself [həː'sɛlf] *pron* (*reflexive*) se; (*emphatic*) ella misma; (*after prep*) sí (misma); *see also* **oneself**.

Herts *abbr* (*BRIT*) = *Hertfordshire*.

he's [hiːz] = **he is; he has.**

hesitant ['hɛzɪtənt] *adj* indeciso; **to be** ~ **about doing sth** no decidirse a hacer algo.

hesitate ['hɛzɪteɪt] *vi* dudar, vacilar; **don't** ~ **to ask (me)** no dudes en pedírmelo.

hesitation [hɛzɪ'teɪʃən] *n* indecisión *f*; **I have no** ~ **in saying (that)** ... no tengo el menor reparo en afirmar que ....

hessian ['hɛsɪən] *n* arpillera.

heterogeneous ['hɛtərə'dʒiːnɪəs] *adj* heterogéneo.

heterosexual [hɛtərəu'sɛksjuəl] *adj, n* heterosexual *m/f*.

het up [hɛt'ʌp] *adj* (*col*) agitado, nervioso.

HEW *n abbr* (*US*: = *Department of Health, Education and Welfare*) *ministerio de sanidad, educación y bienestar público*.

hew [hjuː] *vt* cortar.

hex [hɛks] (*US*) *n* maleficio, mal *m* de ojo ♦ *vt* embrujar.

hexagon ['hɛksəgən] *n* hexágono.

hexagonal [hɛk'sægənl] *adj* hexagonal.

hey [heɪ] *excl* ¡oye!, ¡oiga!

heyday ['heɪdeɪ] *n*: **the** ~ **of** el apogeo de.

HF *n abbr* = *high frequency*.

HGV *n abbr see* **heavy goods vehicle.**

HI *abbr* (*US*) = *Hawaii.*

hi [haɪ] *excl* ¡hola!

hiatus [haɪ'eɪtəs] *n* vacío, interrupción *f*; (*LING*) hiato.

hibernate ['haɪbəneɪt] *vi* invernar.

hibernation [haɪbə'neɪʃən] *n* hibernación *f*.

hiccough, hiccup ['hɪkʌp] *vi* hipar; ~**s** *npl* hipo *sg*.

hid [hɪd] *pt of* **hide.**

hick [hɪk] *n* (*US col*) paleto/a.

hidden ['hɪdn] *pp of* **hide** ♦ *adj*: **there are no** ~ **extras** no hay suplementos ocultos; ~ **agenda** plan *m* encubierto.

hide [haɪd] *n* (*skin*) piel *f* ♦ *vb* (*pt* **hid,** *pp* **hidden** [hɪd, 'hɪdn]) *vt* esconder, ocultar; (*feelings, truth*) encubrir, ocultar ♦ *vi*: **to** ~ (**from sb**) esconderse *or* ocultarse (de algn).

hide-and-seek ['haɪdən'siːk] *n* escondite *m*.

hideaway ['haɪdəweɪ] *n* escondite *m*.

hideous ['hɪdɪəs] *adj* horrible.

hideously ['hɪdɪəslɪ] *adv* horriblemente.

hide-out ['haɪdaut] *n* escondite *m*, refugio.

hiding ['haɪdɪŋ] *n* (*beating*) paliza; **to be in** ~ (*concealed*) estar escondido.

hiding place *n* escondrijo.

hierarchy ['haɪərɑːkɪ] *n* jerarquía.

hieroglyphic [haɪərə'glɪfɪk] *adj* jeroglífico ♦ *n*: ~**s** jeroglíficos *mpl*.

hi-fi ['haɪfaɪ] *abbr* (= *high fidelity*) *n* estéreo, hifi *m* ♦ *adj* de alta fidelidad.

higgledy-piggledy ['hɪgldɪ'pɪgldɪ] *adv* en desorden, de cualquier modo.

high [haɪ] *adj* alto; (*speed, number*) grande, alto; (*price*) elevado; (*wind*) fuerte; (*voice*) agudo; (*col: on drugs*) colocado; (: *on drink*) borracho; (*CULIN: meat, game*) pasado; (: *spoilt*) estropeado ♦ *adv* alto, a gran altura ♦ *n*: **exports have reached a new** ~ las exportaciones han alcanzado niveles inusitados; **it is 20 m** ~ tiene 20 m de altura; ~ **in the air** en las alturas; **to pay a** ~ **price for sth** pagar algo muy caro.

highball ['haɪbɔːl] n (US: drink) whisky m soda, highball m (LAM), jaibol m (LAM).

highboy ['haɪbɔɪ] n (US) cómoda alta.

highbrow ['haɪbraʊ] adj culto.

highchair ['haɪtʃɛə*] n silla alta (para niños).

high-class ['haɪ'klɑːs] adj (neighbourhood) de alta sociedad; (hotel) de lujo; (person) distinguido; (food) de alta categoría.

High Court n (LAW) tribunal m supremo; ver recuadro.

HIGH COURT

En el sistema legal de Inglaterra y Gales **High Court** es la forma abreviada de "High Court of Justice", tribunal superior que junto con el de apelación ("Court of Appeal") forma el Tribunal Supremo ("Supreme Court of Judicature").
En el sistema legal escocés es la forma abreviada de "High Court of Justiciary" tribunal con jurado que juzga los delitos más serios, que pueden dar lugar a una pena de gran severidad.

---

higher ['haɪə*] adj (form of life, study etc) superior ♦ adv más alto ♦ n (SCOT SCOL): **H~** cada una de las asignaturas que se estudian entre los 16 y los 17 años generalmente, así como el certificado de haberlas probado.

higher education n educación f or enseñanza superior.

high explosive n explosivo de gran potencia.

highfalutin [haɪfə'luːtɪn] adj (col) de altos vuelos, encopetado.

high finance n altas finanzas fpl.

high-flier, high-flyer [haɪ'flaɪə*] n ambicioso/a.

high-handed [haɪ'hændɪd] adj despótico.

high-heeled [haɪ'hiːld] adj de tacón alto.

highjack ['haɪdʒæk] = **hijack**.

high jump n (SPORT) salto de altura.

highlands ['haɪləndz] npl tierras fpl altas; **the H~** (in Scotland) las Tierras Altas de Escocia.

high-level ['haɪlɛvl] adj (talks etc) de alto nivel.

highlight ['haɪlaɪt] n (fig: of event) punto culminante ♦ vt subrayar.

highly ['haɪlɪ] adv sumamente; ~ **paid** muy bien pagado; **to speak** ~ **of** hablar muy bien de; **highly strung** muy excitable.

highness ['haɪnɪs] n altura; **Her** or **His H~** Su Alteza.

high-pitched [haɪ'pɪtʃt] adj agudo.

high point n: **the** ~ el punto culminante.

high-powered ['haɪ'paʊəd] adj (engine) de gran potencia; (fig: person) importante.

high-pressure ['haɪprɛʃə*] adj de alta presión; (fig: salesman etc) enérgico.

high-rise ['haɪraɪz] n (also: ~ **block**, ~ **building**) torre f de pisos.

high school n centro de enseñanza secundaria, ≈ Instituto Nacional de Bachillerato (SP), liceo (LAM); ver recuadro.

HIGH SCHOOL

El término **high school** se aplica en Estados Unidos a dos tipos de centros de educación secundaria: "Junior High Schools", en los que se imparten normalmente del 7o al 9o curso (llamado "grade") y "Senior High Schools", que abarcan los cursos 10o, 11o y 12o y en ocasiones el 9o. Aquí pueden estudiarse asignaturas tanto de contenido académico como profesional. En Gran Bretaña también se llaman **high school** algunos centros de enseñanza secundaria.

---

high season n (BRIT) temporada alta.

high-speed ['haɪspiːd] adj de alta velocidad.

high-spirited [haɪ'spɪrɪtɪd] adj animado.

high spirits npl ánimos mpl.

high street n (BRIT) calle f mayor.

high tide n marea alta.

highway ['haɪweɪ] n carretera; (US) autopista.

Highway Code n (BRIT) código de la circulación.

hijack ['haɪdʒæk] vt secuestrar ♦ n (also: ~ing) secuestro.

hijacker ['haɪdʒækə*] n secuestrador(a) m/f.

hike [haɪk] vi (go walking) ir de excursión (a pie); (tramp) caminar ♦ n caminata; (col: in prices etc) aumento.

▶**hike up** vt (raise) aumentar.

hiker ['haɪkə*] n excursionista m/f.

hilarious [hɪ'lɛərɪəs] adj divertidísimo.

hilarity [hɪ'lærɪtɪ] n (laughter) risas fpl, carcajadas fpl.

hill [hɪl] n colina; (high) montaña; (slope) cuesta.

hillbilly ['hɪlbɪlɪ] n (US) rústico/a montañés/esa; (pej) palurdo/a.

hillside ['hɪlsaɪd] n ladera.

hilltop ['hɪltɔp] n cumbre f.

hilly ['hɪlɪ] adj montañoso; (uneven) accidentado.

hilt [hɪlt] n (of sword) empuñadura; **to the** ~ (fig: support) incondicionalmente; **to be in debt up to the** ~ estar hasta el cuello de deudas.

him [hɪm] *pron* (*direct*) le, lo; (*indirect*) le;
(*stressed, after prep*) él; *see also* **me.**

Himalayas [hɪmə'leɪəz] *npl:* **the ~** el
Himalaya.

himself [hɪm'sɛlf] *pron* (*reflexive*) se;
(*emphatic*) él mismo; (*after prep*) sí
(mismo); *see also* **oneself.**

hind [haɪnd] *adj* posterior ♦ *n* cierva.

hinder ['hɪndə*] *vt* estorbar, impedir.

hindquarters ['haɪndkwɔːtəz] *npl* (*ZOOL*)
cuartos *mpl* traseros.

hindrance ['hɪndrəns] *n* estorbo, obstáculo.

hindsight ['haɪndsaɪt] *n* percepción *f* tardía
or retrospectiva; **with the benefit of ~**
con la perspectiva del tiempo
transcurrido.

Hindu ['hɪnduː] *n* hindú *m/f.*

hinge [hɪndʒ] *n* bisagra, gozne *m* ♦ *vi* (*fig*):
to ~ on depender de.

hint [hɪnt] *n* indirecta; (*advice*) consejo ♦ *vt:*
to ~ that insinuar que ♦ *vi:* **to ~ at** aludir
a; **to drop a ~** soltar *or* tirar una
indirecta; **give me a ~** dame una pista.

hip [hɪp] *n* cadera; (*BOT*) escaramujo.

hip flask *n* petaca.

hip-hop ['hɪphɔp] *n* hip hop *m.*

hippie ['hɪpɪ] *n* hippie *m/f,* jipi *m/f.*

hip pocket *n* bolsillo de atrás.

hippopotamus, *pl* **~es** *or* **hippopotami**
[hɪpə'pɔtəməs, -'pɔtəmaɪ] hipopótamo.

hippy ['hɪpɪ] *n* = **hippie.**

hire ['haɪə*] *vt* (*BRIT: car, equipment*)
alquilar; (*worker*) contratar ♦ *n* alquiler *m;*
for ~ se alquila; (*taxi*) libre; **on ~** de
alquiler.

►**hire out** *vt* alquilar, arrendar.

hire(d) car *n* (*BRIT*) coche *m* de alquiler.

hire purchase (H.P.) *n* (*BRIT*) compra a
plazos; **to buy sth on ~** comprar algo a
plazos.

his [hɪz] *pron* (el) suyo/(la) suya *etc* ♦ *adj* su;
this is ~ esto es suyo *or* de él; *see also* **my,
mine.**

Hispanic [hɪs'pænɪk] *adj* hispánico.

hiss [hɪs] *vi* sisear; (*in protest*) silbar ♦ *n*
siseo; silbido.

histogram ['hɪstəgræm] *n* histograma *m.*

historian [hɪ'stɔːrɪən] *n* historiador(a) *m/f.*

historic(al) [hɪ'stɔrɪk(l)] *adj* histórico.

history ['hɪstərɪ] *n* historia; **there's a long ~**
of that illness in his family esa
enfermedad corre en su familia.

histrionics [hɪstrɪ'ɔnɪks] *npl* histrionismo.

hit [hɪt] *vt* (*pt, pp* **hit**) (*strike*) golpear, pegar;
(*reach: target*) alcanzar; (*collide with: car*)
chocar contra; (*fig: affect*) afectar ♦ *n*
golpe *m;* (*success*) éxito; **to ~ the**

headlines salir en primera plana; **to ~**
the road (*col*) largarse; **to ~ it off with sb**
llevarse bien con algn.

►**hit back** *vi* defenderse; (*fig*) devolver
golpe por golpe.

►**hit out at** *vt fus* asestar un golpe a; (*fig*)
atacar.

►**hit (up)on** *vt fus* (*answer*) dar con;
(*solution*) hallar, encontrar.

hit and miss *adj:* **it's very ~, it's a ~ affair**
es cuestión de suerte.

hit-and-run driver ['hɪtən'rʌn-] *n*
conductor(a) que tras atropellar a algn
se da a la fuga.

hitch [hɪtʃ] *vt* (*fasten*) atar, amarrar; (*also:*
~ up) arremangarse ♦ *n* (*difficulty*)
problema, pega; **to ~ a lift** hacer
autostop; **technical ~** problema *m* técnico.

►**hitch up** *vt* (*horse, cart*) enganchar, uncir.

hitch-hike ['hɪtʃhaɪk] *vi* hacer autostop.

hitch-hiker ['hɪtʃhaɪkə*] *n* autostopista *m/f.*

hi-tech [haɪ'tɛk] *adj* de alta tecnología.

hitherto ['hɪðə'tuː] *adv* hasta ahora, hasta
aquí.

hit list *n* lista negra.

hitman ['hɪtmæn] *n* asesino a sueldo.

hit or miss ['hɪtə'mɪs] *adj* = **hit and miss.**

hit parade *n:* **the ~** los cuarenta
principales.

HIV *n abbr* (= *human immunodeficiency virus*)
VIH *m;* **~-negative** no portador(a) del
virus del sida, no seropositivo; **~-positive**
portador(a) del virus del sida,
seropositivo.

hive [haɪv] *n* colmena; **the shop was a ~ of**
activity (*fig*) la tienda era una colmena
humana.

►**hive off** *vt* (*col: separate*) separar;
(*: privatize*) privatizar.

hl *abbr* (= *hectolitre*) hl.

HM *abbr* (= *His* (*or Her*) *Majesty*) S.M.

HMG *abbr* = *His* (*or Her*) *Majesty's*
Government.

HMI *n abbr* (*BRIT SCOL*) = *His* (*or Her*)
Majesty's Inspector.

HMO *n abbr* (*US:* = *health maintenance*
organization) *seguro médico global.*

HMS *abbr* = *His* (*or Her*) *Majesty's Ship.*

HMSO *n abbr* (*BRIT* = *His* (*or Her*) *Majesty's*
Stationery Office) *distribuidor oficial de*
las publicaciones del gobierno del Reino
Unido.

HNC *n abbr* (*BRIT:* = *Higher National*
Certificate) *título académico.*

HND *n abbr* (*BRIT:* = *Higher National Diploma*)
título académico.

hoard [hɔːd] *n* (*treasure*) tesoro; (*stockpile*)
provisión *f* ♦ *vt* acumular.

hoarding ['hɔːdɪŋ] n (for posters) valla
publicitaria.
hoarfrost ['hɔːfrɔst] n escarcha.
hoarse [hɔːs] adj ronco.
hoax [həuks] n engaño.
hob [hɔb] n quemador m.
hobble ['hɔbl] vi cojear.
hobby ['hɔbɪ] n pasatiempo, afición f.
hobby-horse ['hɔbɪhɔːs] n (fig) tema
preferido.
hobnob ['hɔbnɔb] vi: **to ~ (with)** alternar
(con).
hobo ['həubəu] n (US) vagabundo.
hock [hɔk] n (of animal, CULIN) corvejón m;
(col): **to be in ~** (person) estar empeñado
or endeudado; (object) estar empeñado.
hockey ['hɔkɪ] n hockey m.
hocus-pocus [həukəs'pəukəs] n (trickery)
engañifa; (words: of magician)
abracadabra m.
hod [hɔd] n capacho.
hodge-podge ['hɔdʒpɔdʒ] n (US)
= **hotchpotch.**
hoe [həu] n azadón m ♦ vt azadonar.
hog [hɔg] n cerdo, puerco ♦ vt (fig)
acaparar; **to go the whole ~** echar el
todo por el todo.
Hogmanay [hɔgmə'neɪ] n (Scottish)
Nochevieja.
hoist [hɔɪst] n (crane) grúa ♦ vt levantar,
alzar.
hoity-toity [hɔɪtɪ'tɔɪtɪ] adj (col): **to be ~**
darse humos.
hold [həuld] vb (pt, pp **held** [hɛld]) vt tener;
(contain) contener; (keep back) retener;
(believe) sostener; (take ~ of) coger (SP),
agarrar (LAM); (take weight) soportar;
(meeting) celebrar ♦ vi (withstand pressure)
resistir; (be valid) ser válido; (stick) pegarse ♦ n (grasp) asimiento; (fig) dominio;
(WRESTLING) presa; (NAUT) bodega; **~ the
line!** (TEL) ¡no cuelgue!; **to ~ one's own**
(fig) defenderse; **to ~ office** (POL) ocupar
un cargo; **to ~ firm** or **fast** mantenerse
firme; **he ~s the view that ...** opina or es
su opinión que ...; **to ~ sb responsible for
sth** culpar or echarle la culpa a algn de
algo; **where can I get ~ of ...?** ¿dónde
puedo encontrar (a) ...?; **to catch** or **get
(a) ~ of** agarrarse or asirse de.
▶**hold back** vt retener; (secret) ocultar; **to
~ sb back from doing sth** impedir a algn
hacer algo, impedir que algn haga algo.
▶**hold down** vt (person) sujetar; (job)
mantener.
▶**hold forth** vi perorar.
▶**hold off** vt (enemy) rechazar ♦ vi: **if the
rain ~s off** si no llueve.

▶**hold on** vi agarrarse bien; (wait) esperar.
▶**hold on to** vt fus agarrarse a; (keep)
guardar.
▶**hold out** vt ofrecer ♦ vi (resist) resistir; **to
~ out (against)** resistir (a), sobrevivir.
▶**hold over** vt (meeting etc) aplazar.
▶**hold up** vt (raise) levantar; (support)
apoyar; (delay) retrasar; (: traffic)
demorar; (rob: bank) asaltar, atracar.
holdall ['həuldɔːl] n (BRIT) bolsa.
holder ['həuldə*] n (of ticket, record)
poseedor(a) m/f; (of passport, post, office,
title etc) titular m/f.
holding ['həuldɪŋ] n (share) participación f.
holding company n holding m.
holdup ['həuldʌp] n (robbery) atraco; (delay)
retraso; (BRIT: in traffic) embotellamiento.
hole [həul] n agujero ♦ vt agujerear; **~ in
the heart** (MED) boquete m en el corazón;
to pick ~s in (fig) encontrar defectos en;
the ship was ~d se abrió una vía de agua
en el barco.
▶**hole up** vi esconderse.
holiday ['hɔlədɪ] n vacaciones fpl; (day off)
(día m de) fiesta, día m festivo or feriado
(LAM); **on ~** de vacaciones; **to be on ~**
estar de vacaciones.
holiday camp n colonia or centro
vacacional; (for children) colonia
veraniega infantil.
holiday job n (BRIT) trabajo para las
vacaciones.
holidaymaker ['hɔlədɪmeɪkə*] n (BRIT)
turista m/f.
holiday pay n paga de las vacaciones.
holiday resort n centro turístico.
holiday season n temporada de
vacaciones.
holiness ['həulɪnɪs] n santidad f.
holistic [həu'lɪstɪk] adj holístico.
Holland ['hɔlənd] n Holanda.
holler ['hɔlə*] vi (col) gritar, vocear.
hollow ['hɔləu] adj hueco; (fig) vacío; (eyes)
hundido; (sound) sordo ♦ n (gen) hueco;
(in ground) hoyo ♦ vt: **to ~ out** ahuecar.
holly ['hɔlɪ] n acebo.
hollyhock ['hɔlɪhɔk] n malva loca.
holocaust ['hɔləkɔːst] n holocausto.
hologram ['hɔləgræm] n holograma m.
holster ['həulstə*] n pistolera.
holy ['həulɪ] adj (gen) santo, sagrado;
(water) bendito; **the H~ Father** el Santo
Padre.
Holy Communion n Sagrada Comunión f.
Holy Ghost, Holy Spirit n Espíritu m
Santo.
homage ['hɔmɪdʒ] n homenaje m; **to pay ~
to** rendir homenaje a.

home [həum] *n* casa; (*country*) patria; (*institution*) asilo; (*COMPUT*) punto inicial ♦ *adj* (*domestic*) casero, de casa; (*ECON, POL*) nacional; (*SPORT: team*) de casa; (: *match, win*) en casa ♦ *adv* (*direction*) a casa; **at ~** en casa; **to go/come ~** ir/volver a casa; **make yourself at ~** ¡estás en tu casa!; **it's near my ~** está cerca de mi casa.

►**home in on** *vt fus* (*missiles*) dirigirse hacia.

home address *n* domicilio.

home-brew [həum'bru:] *n* cerveza *etc* casera.

homecoming ['həumkʌmɪŋ] *n* regreso (al hogar).

home computer *n* ordenador *m* doméstico.

Home Counties *npl* *condados que rodean Londres*.

home economics *n* economía doméstica.

home ground *n*: **to be on ~** estar en su *etc* terreno.

home-grown ['həumgrəun] *adj* de cosecha propia.

home help *n* (*BRIT*) trabajador(a) *m/f* del servicio de atención domiciliaria.

homeland ['həumlænd] *n* tierra natal.

homeless ['həumlɪs] *adj* sin hogar, sin casa ♦ *npl*: **the ~** las personas sin hogar.

home loan *n* préstamo para la vivienda.

homely ['həumlɪ] *adj* (*domestic*) casero; (*simple*) sencillo.

home-made [həum'meɪd] *adj* hecho en casa.

Home Office *n* (*BRIT*) Ministerio del Interior.

homeopathy [həumɪ'ɔpəθɪ] *etc* (*US*) = **homoeopathy** *etc*.

home page *n* (*COMPUT*) página de inicio.

home rule *n* autonomía.

Home Secretary *n* (*BRIT*) Ministro del Interior.

homesick ['həumsɪk] *adj*: **to be ~** tener morriña *or* nostalgia.

home town *n* ciudad *f* natal.

home truth *n*: **to tell sb a few ~s** decir cuatro verdades a algn.

homeward ['həumwəd] *adj* (*journey*) de vuelta.

homeward(s) ['həumwəd(z)] *adv* hacia casa.

homework ['həumwə:k] *n* deberes *mpl*.

homicidal [hɔmɪ'saɪdl] *adj* homicida.

homicide ['hɔmɪsaɪd] *n* (*US*) homicidio.

homing ['həumɪŋ] *adj* (*device, missile*) buscador(a); **~ pigeon** paloma mensajera.

homoeopath, (*US*) **homeopath** ['həumɪəupæθ] *n* homeópata *m/f*.

homoeopathic, (*US*) **homeopathic** [həumɪəu'pæθɪk] *adj* homeopático.

homoeopathy, (*US*) **homeopathy** [həumɪ'ɔpəθɪ] *n* homeopatía.

homogeneous [hɔmə'dʒi:nɪəs] *adj* homogéneo.

homogenize [hə'mɔdʒənaɪz] *vt* homogeneizar.

homosexual [hɔməu'sɛksjuəl] *adj, n* homosexual *m/f*.

Hon. *abbr* (= *honourable, honorary*) en *títulos*.

Honduras [hɔn'djuərəs] *n* Honduras *fpl*.

hone [həun] *vt* (*sharpen*) afilar; (*fig*) perfeccionar.

honest ['ɔnɪst] *adj* honrado; (*sincere*) franco, sincero; **to be quite ~ with you ...** para serte franco ....

honestly ['ɔnɪstlɪ] *adv* honradamente; francamente, de verdad.

honesty ['ɔnɪstɪ] *n* honradez *f*.

honey ['hʌnɪ] *n* miel *f*; (*US col*) cariño; (: *to strangers*) guapo, linda.

honeycomb ['hʌnɪkəum] *n* panal *m*; (*fig*) laberinto.

honeymoon ['hʌnɪmu:n] *n* luna de miel.

honeysuckle ['hʌnɪsʌkl] *n* madreselva.

Hong Kong ['hɔŋ'kɔŋ] *n* Hong-Kong *m*.

honk [hɔŋk] *vi* (*AUT*) tocar la bocina.

Honolulu [hɔnə'lu:lu:] *n* Honolulú *m*.

honorary ['ɔnərərɪ] *adj* no remunerado; (*duty, title*) honorario.

honour, (*US*) **honor** ['ɔnə*] *vt* honrar ♦ *n* honor *m*, honra; **in ~ of** en honor de; **it's a great ~** es un gran honor.

hono(u)rable ['ɔnərəbl] *adj* honrado, honorable.

hono(u)r-bound ['ɔnə'baund] *adj* moralmente obligado.

honours degree *n* (*UNIV*) licenciatura superior; *ver recuadro*.

HONOURS DEGREE

Tras un período de estudios de tres años normalmente (cuatro en Escocia), los universitarios obtienen una licenciatura llamada **honours degree**. *La calificación global que se recibe, en una escala de mayor a menor es la siguiente: "first class" (I), "upper-second class" (II:1), "lower-second class" (II:2) y "third class" (III). El licenciado puede añadir las letras "Hons" al título obtenido tras su nombre y apellidos, por ejemplo "BA Hons"; ver también "ordinary degree".*

honours list n (*BRIT*) lista de distinciones honoríficas que entrega la reina; *ver* recuadro.

HONOURS LIST

A la lista con los títulos honoríficos y condecoraciones que el monarca británico otorga en Año Nuevo y en el día de su cumpleaños se la conoce con el nombre de **honours list.** *Las personas que reciben dichas distinciones suelen ser miembros destacados de la vida pública (ámbito empresarial, ejército, deportes, espectáculos), aunque últimamente también se reconoce con ellas el trabajo abnegado y anónimo de la gente de la calle.*

Hons. *abbr* (*UNIV*) = **hono(u)rs degree.**

hood [hud] n capucha; (*BRIT AUT*) capota; (*US AUT*) capó m; (*US col*) matón m.

hooded ['hudɪd] *adj* (*robber*) encapuchado.

hoodlum ['huːdləm] n matón m.

hoodwink ['hudwɪŋk] vt (*BRIT*) timar.

hoof, *pl* ~**s** *or* **hooves** [huːf, huːvz] n pezuña.

hook [huk] n gancho; (*on dress*) corchete m, broche m; (*for fishing*) anzuelo ♦ vt enganchar; ~**s and eyes** corchetes mpl, macho y hembra m; **by** ~ **or by crook** por las buenas o por las malas, cueste lo que cueste; **to be** ~**ed on** (*col*) estar enganchado a.

▶**hook up** vt (*RADIO, TV*) transmitir en cadena.

hooligan ['huːlɪɡən] n gamberro.

hooliganism ['huːlɪɡənɪzəm] n gamberrismo.

hoop [huːp] n aro.

hoot [huːt] vi (*BRIT AUT*) tocar la bocina; (*siren*) sonar la sirena; (*owl*) ulular ♦ n bocinazo, toque m de sirena; **to** ~ **with laughter** morirse de risa.

hooter ['huːtə*] n (*BRIT AUT*) bocina; (*of ship, factory*) sirena.

hoover ® ['huːvə*] (*BRIT*) n aspiradora ♦ vt pasar la aspiradora por.

hooves [huːvz] *pl of* **hoof.**

hop [hɔp] vi saltar, brincar; (*on one foot*) saltar con un pie ♦ n salto, brinco; *see also* **hops.**

hope [həup] vt, vi esperar ♦ n esperanza; **I** ~ **so/not** espero que sí/no.

hopeful ['həupful] *adj* (*person*) optimista; (*situation*) prometedor(a); **I'm** ~ **that she'll manage to come** confío en que podrá venir.

hopefully ['həupfulɪ] *adv* con optimismo, con esperanza.

hopeless ['həuplɪs] *adj* desesperado.

hopelessly ['həuplɪslɪ] *adv* (*live etc*) sin esperanzas; **I'm** ~ **confused/lost** estoy totalmente despistado/perdido.

hopper ['hɔpə*] n (*chute*) tolva.

hops [hɔps] *npl* lúpulo *sg.*

horde [hɔːd] n horda.

horizon [hə'raɪzn] n horizonte m.

horizontal [hɔrɪ'zɔntl] *adj* horizontal.

hormone ['hɔːməun] n hormona.

hormone replacement therapy n terapia hormonal sustitutiva.

horn [hɔːn] n cuerno, cacho (*LAM*); (*MUS*: *also*: **French** ~) trompa; (*AUT*) bocina, claxon m.

horned [hɔːnd] *adj* con cuernos.

hornet ['hɔːnɪt] n avispón m.

horny ['hɔːnɪ] *adj* (*material*) córneo; (*hands*) calloso; (*US col*) cachondo.

horoscope ['hɔrəskəup] n horóscopo.

horrendous [hɔ'rɛndəs] *adj* horrendo.

horrible ['hɔrɪbl] *adj* horrible.

horribly ['hɔrɪblɪ] *adv* horriblemente.

horrid ['hɔrɪd] *adj* horrible, horroroso.

horridly ['hɔrɪdlɪ] *adv* (*behave*) tremendamente mal.

horrific [hɔ'rɪfɪk] *adj* (*accident*) horroroso; (*film*) horripilante.

horrify ['hɔrɪfaɪ] vt horrorizar.

horrifying ['hɔrɪfaɪɪŋ] *adj* horroroso.

horror ['hɔrə*] n horror m.

horror film n película de terror or miedo.

horror-struck ['hɔrəstrʌk], **horror-stricken** ['hɔrəstrɪkn] *adj* horrorizado.

hors d'œuvre [ɔː'dəːvrə] n entremeses mpl.

horse [hɔːs] n caballo.

horseback ['hɔːsbæk] n: **on** ~ a caballo.

horsebox ['hɔːsbɔks] n remolque m para transportar caballos.

horse chestnut n (*tree*) castaño de Indias.

horsedrawn ['hɔːsdrɔːn] *adj* de tracción animal.

horsefly ['hɔːsflaɪ] n tábano.

horseman ['hɔːsmən] n jinete m.

horseplay ['hɔːspleɪ] n pelea amistosa.

horsepower (hp) ['hɔːspauə*] n caballo (de fuerza), potencia en caballos.

horse-racing ['hɔːsreɪsɪŋ] n carreras fpl de caballos.

horseradish ['hɔːsrædɪʃ] n rábano picante.

horseshoe ['hɔːsʃuː] n herradura.

horse show n concurso hípico.

horse-trader ['hɔːstreɪdə*] n chalán/ana m/f.

horse trials npl = **horse show.**

horsewhip ['hɔːswɪp] vt azotar.

horsewoman ['hɔːswumən] n amazona.

horsey ['hɔːsɪ] *adj* (*col*: *person*) aficionado a los caballos.

horticulture ['hɔːtɪkʌltʃə*] *n* horticultura.
hose [həuz] *n* (*also*: ~**pipe**) manguera.
▶**hose down** *vt* limpiar con manguera.
hosiery ['həuzɪərɪ] *n* calcetería.
hospice ['hɔspɪs] *n* hospicio.
hospitable ['hɔspɪtəbl] *adj* hospitalario.
hospital ['hɔspɪtl] *n* hospital *m*.
hospitality [hɔspɪ'tælɪtɪ] *n* hospitalidad *f*.
hospitalize ['hɔspɪtəlaɪz] *vt* hospitalizar.
host [həust] *n* anfitrión *m*; (*TV, RADIO*) presentador(a) *m/f*; (*of inn etc*) mesonero; (*REL*) hostia; (*large number*): **a** ~ **of** multitud de.
hostage ['hɔstɪdʒ] *n* rehén *m*.
hostel ['hɔstl] *n* hostal *m*; (*for students, nurses etc*) residencia; (*also*: **youth** ~) albergue *m* juvenil; (*for homeless people*) hospicio.
hostelling ['hɔstlɪŋ] *n*: **to go (youth)** ~ hospedarse en albergues.
hostess ['həustɪs] *n* anfitriona; (*BRIT*: *air* ~) azafata; (*in night-club*) señorita de compañía.
hostile ['hɔstaɪl] *adj* hostil.
hostility [hɔ'stɪlɪtɪ] *n* hostilidad *f*.
hot [hɔt] *adj* caliente; (*weather*) caluroso, de calor; (*as opposed to only warm*) muy caliente; (*spicy*) picante; (*also*: **youth** ~) ardiente, acalorado; **to be** ~ (*person*) tener calor; (*object*) estar caliente; (*weather*) hacer calor.
▶**hot up** *vi* (*col*: *situation*) ponerse difícil *or* apurado; (: *party*) animarse ♦ *vt* (*col*: *pace*) apretar; (: *engine*) aumentar la potencia de.
hot air *n* (*col*) palabras *fpl* huecas.
hot-air balloon [hɔt'ɛə-] *n* (*AVIAT*) globo aerostático *or* de aire caliente.
hotbed ['hɔtbɛd] *n* (*fig*) semillero.
hot-blooded [hɔt'blʌdɪd] *adj* impetuoso.
hotchpotch ['hɔtʃpɔtʃ] *n* mezcolanza, baturrillo.
hot dog *n* perrito caliente.
hotel [həu'tɛl] *n* hotel *m*.
hotelier [həu'tɛlɪə*] *n* hotelero.
hotel industry *n* industria hotelera.
hotel room *n* habitación *f* de hotel.
hot flush *n* (*BRIT*) sofoco.
hotfoot ['hɔtfut] *adv* a toda prisa.
hothead ['hɔthɛd] *n* (*fig*) exaltado/a.
hotheaded [hɔt'hɛdɪd] *adj* exaltado.
hothouse ['hɔthaus] *n* invernadero.
hot line *n* (*POL*) teléfono rojo, línea directa.
hotly ['hɔtlɪ] *adv* con pasión, apasionadamente.
hotplate ['hɔtpleɪt] *n* (*on cooker*) hornillo.
hotpot ['hɔtpɔt] *n* (*BRIT CULIN*) estofado.

hot potato *n* (*BRIT col*) asunto espinoso; **to drop sth/sb like a** ~ no querer saber ya nada de algo/algn.
hot seat *n* primera fila.
hot spot *n* (*trouble spot*) punto caliente; (*night club etc*) lugar *m* popular.
hot spring *n* terma, fuente *f* de aguas termales.
hot-tempered ['hɔt'tɛmpəd] *adj* de mal genio *or* carácter.
hot-water bottle [hɔt'wɔːtə-] *n* bolsa de agua caliente.
hot-wire ['hɔtwaɪə*] *vt* (*col*: *car*) hacer el puente en.
hound [haund] *vt* acosar ♦ *n* perro de caza.
hour ['auə*] *n* hora; **at 30 miles an** ~ a 30 millas por hora; **lunch** ~ la hora del almuerzo *or* de comer; **to pay sb by the** ~ pagar a algn por horas.
hourly ['auəlɪ] *adj* (de) cada hora; (*rate*) por hora ♦ *adv* cada hora.
house *n* [haus] (*pl* ~**s** ['hauzɪz]) (*also firm*) casa; (*POL*) cámara; (*THEAT*) sala ♦ *vt* [hauz] (*person*) alojar; **at/to my** ~ en/a mi casa; **the H**~ (**of Commons/Lords**) (*BRIT*) la Cámara de los Comunes/Lores; **the H**~ (**of Representatives**) (*US*) la Cámara de Representantes; **on the** ~ (*fig*) la casa invita.
house arrest *n* arresto domiciliario.
houseboat ['hausbəut] *n* casa flotante.
housebound ['hausbaund] *adj* confinado en casa.
housebreaking ['hausbreɪkɪŋ] *n* allanamiento de morada.
house-broken ['hausbrəukən] *adj* (*US*) = **house-trained.**
housecoat ['hauskəut] *n* bata.
household ['haushəuld] *n* familia.
householder ['haushəuldə*] *n* propietario/a; (*head of house*) cabeza de familia.
househunting ['haushʌntɪŋ] *n*: **to go** ~ ir en busca de vivienda.
housekeeper ['hauskiːpə*] *n* ama de llaves.
housekeeping ['hauskiːpɪŋ] *n* (*work*) trabajos *mpl* domésticos; (*COMPUT*) gestión *f* interna; (*also*: ~ **money**) dinero para gastos domésticos.
houseman ['hausmən] *n* (*BRIT MED*) médico residente.
house-owner ['hausəunə*] *n* propietario/a de una vivienda.
house plant *n* planta de interior.
house-proud ['hauspraud] *adj* preocupado por el embellecimiento de la casa.
house-to-house ['haustə'haus] *adj* (*collection*) de casa en casa; (*search*) casa por casa.

house-train ['haustreɪn] vt (pet) enseñar (a hacer sus necesidades en el sitio apropiado).

house-trained ['haustreɪnd] adj (BRIT: animal) enseñado.

house-warming ['hauswɔːmɪŋ] n (also: ~ party) fiesta de estreno de una casa.

housewife ['hauswaɪf] n ama de casa.

housework ['hauswɜːk] n faenas fpl (de la casa).

housing ['hauzɪŋ] n (act) alojamiento; (houses) viviendas fpl ♦ cpd (problem, shortage) de (la) vivienda.

housing association n asociación f de la vivienda.

housing benefit n (BRIT) subsidio por alojamiento.

housing conditions npl condiciones fpl de habitabilidad.

housing development, (BRIT) **housing estate** n urbanización f.

hovel ['hɔvl] n casucha.

hover ['hɔvə*] vi flotar (en el aire); (helicopter) cernerse; **to ~ on the brink of disaster** estar al borde mismo del desastre.

hovercraft ['hɔvəkrɑːft] n aerodeslizador m, hovercraft m.

hoverport ['hɔvəpɔːt] n puerto de aerodeslizadores.

how [hau] adv cómo; **~ are you?** ¿cómo está usted?, ¿cómo estás?; **~ do you do?** encantado, mucho gusto; **~ far is it to ...?** ¿qué distancia hay de aquí a ...?; **~ long have you been here?** ¿cuánto (tiempo) hace que estás aquí?, ¿cuánto (tiempo) llevas aquí?; **~ lovely!** ¡qué bonito!; **~ many/much?** ¿cuántos/cuánto?; **~ old are you?** ¿cuántos años tienes?; **~ is school?** ¿qué tal la escuela?; **~ about a drink?** ¿te gustaría algo de beber?, ¿qué te parece una copa?

however [hau'ɛvə*] adv de cualquier manera; (+ adjective) por muy ... que; (in questions) cómo ♦ conj sin embargo, no obstante.

howitzer ['hauɪtsə*] n (MIL) obús m.

howl [haul] n aullido ♦ vi aullar.

howler ['haulə*] n plancha, falta garrafal.

howling ['haulɪŋ] adj (wind) huracanado.

HP n abbr see **hire purchase.**

hp abbr see **horsepower.**

HQ n abbr see **headquarters.**

HR n abbr (US) = House of Representatives.

HRH abbr (= His (or Her) Royal Highness) S.A.R.

hr(s) abbr (= hour(s)) h.

HRT n abbr see **hormone replacement therapy.**

HS abbr (US) = high school.

HST abbr (US: = Hawaiian Standard Time) hora de Hawai.

HTML n abbr (= Hypertext Mark-up Language) HTML m.

hub [hʌb] n (of wheel) cubo; (fig) centro.

hubbub ['hʌbʌb] n barahúnda, barullo.

hubcap ['hʌbkæp] n tapacubos m inv.

HUD n abbr (US: = Department of Housing and Urban Development) ministerio de la vivienda y urbanismo.

huddle ['hʌdl] vi: **to ~ together** amontonarse.

hue [hjuː] n color m, matiz m; **~ and cry** n protesta.

huff [hʌf] n: **in a ~** enojado.

huffy ['hʌfɪ] adj (col) mosqueado.

hug [hʌg] vt abrazar ♦ n abrazo.

huge [hjuːdʒ] adj enorme.

hulk [hʌlk] n (ship) barco viejo; (person, building etc) mole f.

hulking ['hʌlkɪŋ] adj pesado.

hull [hʌl] n (of ship) casco.

hullabaloo ['hʌləbə'luː] n (col: noise) algarabía, jaleo.

hullo [hə'ləu] excl = **hello.**

hum [hʌm] vt tararear, canturrear ♦ vi tararear, canturrear; (insect) zumbar ♦ n (also ELEC) zumbido; (of traffic, machines) zumbido, ronroneo; (of voices etc) murmullo.

human ['hjuːmən] adj humano ♦ n (also: ~ being) ser m humano.

humane [hjuː'meɪn] adj humano, humanitario.

humanism ['hjuːmənɪzəm] n humanismo.

humanitarian [hjuːmænɪ'tɛərɪən] adj humanitario.

humanity [hjuː'mænɪtɪ] n humanidad f.

humanly ['hjuːmənlɪ] adv humanamente.

human relations npl relaciones fpl humanas.

human rights npl derechos mpl humanos.

humble ['hʌmbl] adj humilde ♦ vt humillar.

humbly ['hʌmblɪ] adv humildemente.

humbug ['hʌmbʌg] n patrañas fpl; (BRIT: sweet) caramelo de menta.

humdrum ['hʌmdrʌm] adj (boring) monótono, aburrido; (routine) rutinario.

humid ['hjuːmɪd] adj húmedo.

humidifier [hjuː'mɪdɪfaɪə*] n humectador m.

humidity [hjuː'mɪdɪtɪ] n humedad f.

humiliate [hjuː'mɪlɪeɪt] vt humillar.

humiliation [hjuːmɪlɪ'eɪʃən] n humillación f.

humility [hjuː'mɪlɪtɪ] n humildad f.

humorist ['hjuːmərɪst] n humorista m/f.

humorous ['hjuːmərəs] adj gracioso,

humour, (*US*) **humor** ['hju:mə*] *n*
humorismo, sentido del humor; (*mood*)
humor *m* ♦ *vt* (*person*) complacer; **sense of**
~ sentido del humor; **to be in a good/bad**
~ estar de buen/mal humor.

humo(u)rless ['hju:məlɪs] *adj* serio.

hump [hʌmp] *n* (*in ground*) montículo;
(*camel's*) giba.

humus ['hju:məs] *n* (*BIO*) humus *m*.

hunch [hʌntʃ] *n* (*premonition*)
presentimiento; **I have a** ~ **that** tengo la
corazonada *or* el presentimiento de que.

hunchback ['hʌntʃbæk] *n* jorobado/a.

hunched [hʌntʃt] *adj* jorobado.

hundred ['hʌndrəd] *num* ciento; (*before n*)
cien; **about a** ~ **people** unas cien
personas, alrededor de cien personas; ~**s**
of centenares de; ~**s of people**
centenares de personas; **I'm a** ~ **per cent**
sure estoy completamente seguro.

hundredweight ['hʌndrədweɪt] *n* (*BRIT*)
= 50.8 kg; 112 lb; (*US*) = 45.3 kg; 100 lb.

hung [hʌŋ] *pt, pp of* **hang**.

Hungarian [hʌŋˈgɛərɪən] *adj* húngaro ♦ *n*
húngaro/a *m/f*; (*LING*) húngaro.

Hungary ['hʌŋgərɪ] *n* Hungría.

hunger ['hʌŋgə*] *n* hambre *f* ♦ *vi*: **to** ~ **for**
(*fig*) tener hambre de, anhelar.

hunger strike *n* huelga de hambre.

hungover [hʌŋˈəuvə*] *adj* (*col*): **to be** ~
tener resaca.

hungrily ['hʌŋgrəlɪ] *adv* ávidamente, con
ganas.

hungry ['hʌŋgrɪ] *adj* hambriento; **to be** ~
tener hambre; ~ **for** (*fig*) sediento de.

hunk [hʌŋk] *n* (*of bread etc*) trozo, pedazo.

hunt [hʌnt] *vt* (*seek*) buscar; (*SPORT*) cazar
♦ *vi* cazar ♦ *n* caza, cacería.

►**hunt down** *vt* acorralar, seguir la pista
a.

hunter ['hʌntə*] *n* cazador(a) *m/f*; (*horse*)
caballo de caza.

hunting ['hʌntɪŋ] *n* caza.

hurdle ['hə:dl] *n* (*SPORT*) valla; (*fig*)
obstáculo.

hurl [hə:l] *vt* lanzar, arrojar.

hurling ['hə:lɪŋ] *n* (*SPORT*) *juego irlandés*
semejante al hockey.

hurly-burly ['hə:lɪ'bə:lɪ] *n* jaleo, follón *m*.

hurrah [hu'rɑ:], **hurray** [hu'reɪ] *n* ¡viva!,
¡hurra!

hurricane ['hʌrɪkən] *n* huracán *m*.

hurried ['hʌrɪd] *adj* (*fast*) apresurado;
(*rushed*) hecho de prisa.

hurriedly ['hʌrɪdlɪ] *adv* con prisa,
apresuradamente.

hurry ['hʌrɪ] *n* prisa ♦ *vb* (*also:* ~ **up**) *vi*
apresurarse, darse prisa, apurarse (*LAM*)
♦ *vt* (*person*) dar prisa a; (*work*)
apresurar, hacer de prisa; **to be in a** ~
tener prisa, tener apuro (*LAM*), estar
apurado (*LAM*); **to** ~ **back/home** darse
prisa en volver/volver a casa.

►**hurry along** *vi* pasar de prisa.

►**hurry away, hurry off** *vi* irse corriendo.

►**hurry on** *vi*: **to** ~ **on to say** apresurarse a
decir.

►**hurry up** *vi* darse prisa, apurarse (*esp*
LAM).

hurt [hə:t] *vb* (*pt, pp* **hurt**) *vt* hacer daño a;
(*business, interests etc*) perjudicar ♦ *vi*
doler ♦ *adj* lastimado; **I** ~ **my arm** me
lastimé el brazo; **where does it** ~?
¿dónde te duele?

hurtful ['hə:tful] *adj* (*remark etc*) hiriente,
dañino.

hurtle ['hə:tl] *vi*: **to** ~ **past** pasar como un
rayo.

husband ['hʌzbənd] *n* marido.

hush [hʌʃ] *n* silencio ♦ *vt* hacer callar;
(*cover up*) encubrir; ~! ¡chitón!, ¡cállate!

►**hush up** *vt* (*fact*) encubrir, callar.

hushed [hʌʃt] *adj* (*voice*) bajo.

hush-hush [hʌʃ'hʌʃ] *adj* (*col*) muy secreto.

husk [hʌsk] *n* (*of wheat*) cáscara.

husky ['hʌskɪ] *adj* ronco; (*burly*) fornido ♦ *n*
perro esquimal.

hustings ['hʌstɪŋz] *npl* (*POL*) mítin *msg*
preelectoral.

hustle ['hʌsl] *vt* (*push*) empujar; (*hurry*) dar
prisa a ♦ *n* bullicio, actividad *f* febril; ~
and bustle ajetreo.

hut [hʌt] *n* cabaña; (*shed*) cobertizo.

hutch [hʌtʃ] *n* conejera.

hyacinth ['haɪəsɪnθ] *n* jacinto.

hybrid ['haɪbrɪd] *adj, n* híbrido.

hydrant ['haɪdrənt] *n* (*also:* **fire** ~) boca de
incendios.

hydraulic [haɪ'drɔ:lɪk] *adj* hidráulico.

hydraulics [haɪ'drɔ:lɪks] *n* hidráulica.

hydrochloric ['haɪdrəu'klɔrɪk] *adj*: ~ **acid**
ácido clorhídrico.

hydroelectric [haɪdrəuɪ'lektrɪk] *adj*
hidroeléctrico.

hydrofoil ['haɪdrəfɔɪl] *n* aerodeslizador *m*.

hydrogen ['haɪdrədʒən] *n* hidrógeno.

hydrogen bomb *n* bomba de hidrógeno.

hydrophobia [haɪdrə'fəubɪə] *n* hidrofobia.

hydroplane ['haɪdrəpleɪn] *n* hidroavión *m*,
hidroavioneta.

hyena [haɪ'i:nə] *n* hiena.

hygiene ['haɪdʒi:n] *n* higiene *f*.

hygienic [haɪ'dʒi:nɪk] *adj* higiénico.

hymn [hɪm] *n* himno.

hype [haɪp] *n* (*col*) bombo.

hyperactive [haɪpər'æktɪv] adj hiperactivo.
hypermarket ['haɪpəmɑːkɪt] n
hipermercado.
hypertension ['haɪpə'tɛnʃən] n
hipertensión f.
hyphen ['haɪfn] n guión m.
hypnosis [hɪp'nəusɪs] n hipnosis f.
hypnotic [hɪp'nɔtɪk] adj hipnótico.
hypnotism ['hɪpnətɪzəm] n hipnotismo.
hypnotist ['hɪpnətɪst] hipnotista m/f.
hypnotize ['hɪpnətaɪz] vt hipnotizar.
hypoallergenic ['haɪpəuælə'dʒɛnɪk] adj
hipoalérgeno.
hypochondriac [haɪpəu'kɔndrɪæk] n
hipocondríaco/a.
hypocrisy [hɪ'pɔkrɪsɪ] n hipocresía.
hypocrite ['hɪpəkrɪt] n hipócrita m/f.
hypocritical [hɪpə'krɪtɪkl] adj hipócrita.
hypodermic [haɪpə'dɔːmɪk] adj
hipodérmico ♦ n (syringe) aguja
hipodérmica.
hypotenuse [haɪ'pɔtɪnjuːz] n hipotenusa.
hypothermia [haɪpəu'θɔːmɪə] n hipotermia.
hypothesis, pl **hypotheses** [haɪ'pɔθɪsɪs,
-siːz] n hipótesis f inv.
hypothetical [haɪpə'θɛtɪkl] adj hipotético.
hysterectomy [hɪstə'rɛktəmɪ] n
histerectomía.
hysteria [hɪ'stɪərɪə] n histeria.
hysterical [hɪ'stɛrɪkl] adj histérico.
hysterics [hɪ'stɛrɪks] npl histeria sg,
histerismo sg; **to have** ~ ponerse
histérico.
Hz abbr (= Hertz) Hz.

I i

I, i [aɪ] n (letter) I, i f; **I for Isaac,** (US) **I for
Item** I de Inés, I de Israel.
I [aɪ] pron yo ♦ abbr = **island; isle.**
IA, Ia. abbr (US) = Iowa.
IAEA n abbr see **International Atomic Energy
Agency.**
IBA n abbr (BRIT) = **Independent
Broadcasting Authority;** see **ITV.**
Iberian [aɪ'bɪərɪən] adj ibero, ibérico.
Iberian Peninsula n: **the** ~ la Península
Ibérica.
ib(id). abbr (= ibidem: from the same source)

ibídem.
ICBM n abbr (= intercontinental ballistic
missile) misil m balístico intercontinental.
ICC n abbr (= International Chamber of
Commerce) CCI f; (US) = Interstate
Commerce Commission.
ice [aɪs] n hielo ♦ vt (cake) alcorzar ♦ vi (also:
~ **over,** ~ **up**) helarse; **to keep sth on** ~
(fig: plan, project) tener algo en reserva.
ice age n período glaciar.
ice axe n piqueta (de alpinista).
iceberg ['aɪsbəːg] n iceberg m; **the tip of the**
~ la punta del iceberg.
icebox ['aɪsbɔks] n (BRIT) congelador m;
(US) nevera, refrigeradora (LAM).
icebreaker ['aɪsbreɪkə*] n rompehielos m
inv.
ice bucket n cubo para el hielo.
icecap ['aɪskæp] n casquete m polar.
ice-cold [aɪs'kəuld] adj helado.
ice cream n helado.
ice-cream soda n soda mezclada con
helado.
ice cube n cubito de hielo.
iced [aɪst] adj (drink) con hielo; (cake)
escarchado.
ice hockey n hockey m sobre hielo.
Iceland ['aɪslənd] n Islandia.
Icelander ['aɪsləndə*] n islandés/esa m/f.
Icelandic [aɪs'lændɪk] adj islandés/esa ♦ n
(LING) islandés m.
ice lolly n (BRIT) polo.
ice pick n piolet m.
ice rink n pista de hielo.
ice-skate ['aɪsskeɪt] n patín m de hielo ♦ vi
patinar sobre hielo.
ice-skating ['aɪsskeɪtɪŋ] n patinaje m sobre
hielo.
icicle ['aɪsɪkl] n carámbano.
icing ['aɪsɪŋ] n (CULIN) alcorza; (AVIAT etc)
formación f de hielo.
icing sugar n (BRIT) azúcar m glas(eado).
ICJ n abbr see **International Court of Justice.**
icon ['aɪkɔn] n (gen, COMPUT) icono.
ICR n abbr (US) = Institute for Cancer
Research.
ICT n abbr (= information and
communication(s) technology) TIC f,
tecnología de la información y de las
comunicaciones; (BRIT SCOL) informática.
ICU n abbr (= intensive care unit) UVI f.
icy ['aɪsɪ] adj (road) helado; (fig) glacial.
ID abbr (US) = Idaho.
I'd [aɪd] = **I would; I had.**
Ida. abbr (US) = Idaho.
ID card n (= identity card) DNI m.
IDD n abbr (BRIT TEL: = international direct
dialling) servicio automático

internacional.

idea [aɪ'dɪə] *n* idea; **good** ~! ¡buena idea!; **to have an** ~ **that** ... tener la impresión de que ...; **I haven't the least** ~ no tengo ni (la más remota) idea.

ideal [aɪ'dɪəl] *n* ideal *m* ♦ *adj* ideal.

idealism [aɪ'dɪəlɪzəm] *n* idealismo.

idealist [aɪ'dɪəlɪst] *n* idealista *m/f*.

ideally [aɪ'dɪəlɪ] *adv* perfectamente; ~, **the book should have** ... idealmente, el libro debería tener ....

identical [aɪ'dɛntɪkl] *adj* idéntico.

identification [aɪdɛntɪfɪ'keɪʃən] *n* identificación *f*; **means of** ~ documentos *mpl* personales.

identify [aɪ'dɛntɪfaɪ] *vt* identificar ♦ *vi*: **to** ~ **with** identificarse con.

Identikit ® [aɪ'dɛntɪkɪt] *n*: ~ **(picture)** retrato-robot *m*.

identity [aɪ'dɛntɪtɪ] *n* identidad *f*.

identity card *n* carnet *m* de identidad, cédula (de identidad) (*LAM*).

identity papers *npl* documentos *mpl* (de identidad), documentación *fsg*.

identity parade *n* identificación *f* de acusados.

ideological [aɪdɪə'lɔdʒɪkəl] *adj* ideológico.

ideology [aɪdɪ'ɔlədʒɪ] *n* ideología.

idiocy ['ɪdɪəsɪ] *n* idiotez *f*; (*stupid act*) estupidez *f*.

idiom ['ɪdɪəm] *n* modismo; (*style of speaking*) lenguaje *m*.

idiomatic [ɪdɪə'mætɪk] *adj* idiomático.

idiosyncrasy [ɪdɪəʊ'sɪŋkrəsɪ] *n* idiosincrasia.

idiot ['ɪdɪət] *n* (*gen*) idiota *m/f*; (*fool*) tonto/a.

idiotic [ɪdɪ'ɔtɪk] *adj* idiota; tonto.

idle ['aɪdl] *adj* (*lazy*) holgazán/ana; (*unemployed*) parado, desocupado; (*talk*) frívolo ♦ *vi* (*machine*) funcionar *or* marchar en vacío; ~ **capacity** (*COMM*) capacidad *f* sin utilizar; ~ **money** (*COMM*) capital *m* improductivo; ~ **time** (*COMM*) tiempo de paro.

▶**idle away** *vt*: **to** ~ **away one's time** malgastar *or* desperdiciar el tiempo.

idleness ['aɪdlnɪs] *n* holgazanería; paro, desocupación *f*.

idler ['aɪdlə*] *n* holgazán/ana *m/f*, vago/a.

idol ['aɪdl] *n* ídolo.

idolize ['aɪdəlaɪz] *vt* idolatrar.

idyllic [ɪ'dɪlɪk] *adj* idílico.

i.e. *abbr* (= *id est: that is*) es decir.

if [ɪf] *conj* si ♦ *n*: **there are a lot of** ~s **and buts** hay muchas dudas sin resolver; **(even)** ~ aunque, si bien; **I'd be pleased** ~ **you could do it** yo estaría contento si pudieras hacerlo; ~ **necessary** si

resultase necesario; ~ **only** si solamente; **as** ~ como si.

iffy ['ɪfɪ] *adj* (*col*) dudoso.

igloo ['ɪgluː] *n* iglú *m*.

ignite [ɪg'naɪt] *vt* (*set fire to*) encender ♦ *vi* encenderse.

ignition [ɪg'nɪʃən] *n* (*AUT*) encendido; **to switch on/off the** ~ arrancar/apagar el motor.

ignition key *n* (*AUT*) llave *f* de contacto.

ignoble [ɪg'nəʊbl] *adj* innoble, vil.

ignominious [ɪgnə'mɪnɪəs] *adj* ignominioso, vergonzoso.

ignoramus [ɪgnə'reɪməs] *n* ignorante *m/f*, inculto/a.

ignorance ['ɪgnərəns] *n* ignorancia; **to keep sb in** ~ **of sth** ocultarle algo a algn.

ignorant ['ɪgnərənt] *adj* ignorante; **to be** ~ **of** (*subject*) desconocer; (*events*) ignorar.

ignore [ɪg'nɔː*] *vt* (*person*) no hacer caso de; (*fact*) pasar por alto.

ikon ['aɪkɔn] *n* = **icon**.

IL *abbr* (*US*) = *Illinois*.

ILA *n abbr* (*US*: = *International Longshoremen's Association*) *sindicato internacional de trabajadores portuarios*.

ill [ɪl] *adj* enfermo, malo ♦ *n* mal *m*; (*fig*) infortunio ♦ *adv* mal; **to take** *or* **be taken** ~ caer *or* ponerse enfermo; **to feel** ~ **(with)** encontrarse mal (de); **to speak/ think** ~ **of sb** hablar/pensar mal de algn; *see also* **ills**.

Ill. *abbr* (*US*) = *Illinois*.

I'll [aɪl] = **I will, I shall**.

ill-advised [ɪləd'vaɪzd] *adj* poco recomendable; **he was** ~ **to go** se equivocaba al ir.

ill-at-ease [ɪlət'iːz] *adj* incómodo.

ill-considered [ɪlkən'sɪdəd] *adj* (*plan*) poco pensado.

ill-disposed [ɪldɪs'pəʊzd] *adj*: **to be** ~ **towards sb/sth** estar maldispuesto hacia algn/algo.

illegal [ɪ'liːgl] *adj* ilegal.

illegible [ɪ'lɛdʒɪbl] *adj* ilegible.

illegitimate [ɪlɪ'dʒɪtɪmət] *adj* ilegítimo.

ill-fated [ɪl'feɪtɪd] *adj* malogrado.

ill-favoured, (*US*) **ill-favored** [ɪl'feɪvəd] *adj* poco agraciado.

ill feeling *n* rencor *m*.

ill-gotten ['ɪlgɔtn] *adj* (*gains etc*) mal adquirido.

ill health *n* mala salud *f*; **to be in** ~ estar mal de salud.

illicit [ɪ'lɪsɪt] *adj* ilícito.

ill-informed [ɪlɪn'fɔːmd] *adj* (*judgement*) erróneo; (*person*) mal informado.

illiterate [ɪ'lɪtərət] adj analfabeto.
ill-mannered [ɪl'mænəd] adj mal educado.
illness ['ɪlnɪs] n enfermedad f.
illogical [ɪ'lɒdʒɪkl] adj ilógico.
ills [ɪlz] npl males mpl.
ill-suited [ɪl'suːtɪd] adj (couple) incompatible; **he is ~ to the job** no es la persona indicada para el trabajo.
ill-timed [ɪl'taɪmd] adj inoportuno.
ill-treat [ɪl'triːt] vt maltratar.
ill-treatment [ɪl'triːtmənt] n malos tratos mpl.
illuminate [ɪ'luːmɪneɪt] vt (room, street) iluminar, alumbrar; (subject) aclarar; **~d sign** letrero luminoso.
illuminating [ɪ'luːmɪneɪtɪŋ] adj revelador(a).
illumination [ɪluːmɪ'neɪʃən] n alumbrado; **~s** npl luminarias fpl, luces fpl.
illusion [ɪ'luːʒən] n ilusión f; **to be under the ~ that**... estar convencido de que ....
illusive [ɪ'luːsɪv], **illusory** [ɪ'luːsərɪ] adj ilusorio.
illustrate ['ɪləstreɪt] vt ilustrar.
illustration [ɪlə'streɪʃən] n (example) ejemplo, ilustración f; (in book) lámina, ilustración f.
illustrator ['ɪləstreɪtə*] n ilustrador(a) m/f.
illustrious [ɪ'lʌstrɪəs] adj ilustre.
ill will n rencor m.
ILO n abbr (= International Labour Organization) OIT f.
ILWU n abbr (US: = International Longshoremen's and Warehousemen's Union) sindicato internacional de trabajadores portuarios y almacenistas.
I'm [aɪm] = **I am.**
image ['ɪmɪdʒ] n imagen f.
imagery ['ɪmɪdʒərɪ] n imágenes fpl.
imaginable [ɪ'mædʒɪnəbl] adj imaginable.
imaginary [ɪ'mædʒɪnərɪ] adj imaginario.
imagination [ɪmædʒɪ'neɪʃən] n imaginación f; (inventiveness) inventiva; (illusion) fantasía.
imaginative [ɪ'mædʒɪnətɪv] adj imaginativo.
imagine [ɪ'mædʒɪn] vt imaginarse; (suppose) suponer.
imbalance [ɪm'bæləns] n desequilibrio.
imbecile ['ɪmbəsiːl] n imbécil m/f.
imbue [ɪm'bjuː] vt: **to ~ sth with** imbuir algo de.
IMF n abbr see **International Monetary Fund.**
imitate ['ɪmɪteɪt] vt imitar.
imitation [ɪmɪ'teɪʃən] n imitación f; (copy) copia; (pej) remedo.
imitator ['ɪmɪteɪtə*] n imitador(a) m/f.
immaculate [ɪ'mækjulət] adj limpísimo,

inmaculado; (REL) inmaculado.
immaterial [ɪmə'tɪərɪəl] adj incorpóreo; **it is ~ whether**... no importa si... .
immature [ɪmə'tjuə*] adj (person) inmaduro; (of one's youth) joven.
immaturity [ɪmə'tjuərɪtɪ] n inmadurez f.
immeasurable [ɪ'meʒrəbl] adj inconmensurable.
immediacy [ɪ'miːdɪəsɪ] n urgencia, proximidad f.
immediate [ɪ'miːdɪət] adj inmediato; (pressing) urgente, apremiante; **in the ~ future** en un futuro próximo.
immediately [ɪ'miːdɪətlɪ] adv (at once) en seguida; **~ next to** justo al lado de.
immense [ɪ'mens] adj inmenso, enorme.
immensely [ɪ'menslɪ] adv enormemente.
immensity [ɪ'mensɪtɪ] n (of size, difference) inmensidad f; (of problem) enormidad f.
immerse [ɪ'məːs] vt (submerge) sumergir; **to be ~d in** (fig) estar absorto en.
immersion heater [ɪ'məːʃən-] n (BRIT) calentador m de inmersión.
immigrant ['ɪmɪgrənt] n inmigrante m/f.
immigrate ['ɪmɪgreɪt] vi inmigrar.
immigration [ɪmɪ'greɪʃən] n inmigración f.
immigration authorities npl servicio sg de inmigración.
immigration laws npl leyes fpl de inmigración.
imminent ['ɪmɪnənt] adj inminente.
immobile [ɪ'məubaɪl] adj inmóvil.
immobilize [ɪ'məubɪlaɪz] vt inmovilizar.
immoderate [ɪ'mɒdərɪt] adj (person) desmesurado; (opinion, reaction, demand) excesivo.
immodest [ɪ'mɒdɪst] adj (indecent) desvergonzado, impúdico; (boasting) jactancioso.
immoral [ɪ'mɒrl] adj inmoral.
immorality [ɪmɔ'rælɪtɪ] n inmoralidad f.
immortal [ɪ'mɔːtl] adj inmortal.
immortality [ɪmɔ'tælɪtɪ] n inmortalidad f.
immortalize [ɪ'mɔːtlaɪz] vt inmortalizar.
immovable [ɪ'muːvəbl] adj (object) imposible de mover; (person) inconmovible.
immune [ɪ'mjuːn] adj: **~ (to)** inmune (a).
immune system n sistema m inmunitario.
immunity [ɪ'mjuːnɪtɪ] n (MED, of diplomat) inmunidad f; (COMM) exención f.
immunization [ɪmjunaɪ'zeɪʃən] n inmunización f.
immunize ['ɪmjunaɪz] vt inmunizar.
imp [ɪmp] n (small devil, also fig: child) diablillo.
impact ['ɪmpækt] n (gen) impacto.
impair [ɪm'pɛə*] vt perjudicar.

-impaired [ɪmˈpɛəd] *suff:* **visually~** con defectos de visión.

impale [ɪmˈpeɪl] *vt (with sword)* atravesar.

impart [ɪmˈpɑːt] *vt* comunicar; *(make known)* participar; *(bestow)* otorgar.

impartial [ɪmˈpɑːʃl] *adj* imparcial.

impartiality [ɪmpɑːʃɪˈælɪtɪ] *n* imparcialidad *f*.

impassable [ɪmˈpɑːsəbl] *adj (barrier)* infranqueable; *(road)* intransitable.

impasse [ɪmˈpɑːs] *n* callejón *m* sin salida; **to reach an ~** llegar a un punto muerto.

impassioned [ɪmˈpæʃənd] *adj* apasionado, exaltado.

impassive [ɪmˈpæsɪv] *adj* impasible.

impatience [ɪmˈpeɪʃəns] *n* impaciencia.

impatient [ɪmˈpeɪʃənt] *adj* impaciente; **to get** *or* **grow ~** impacientarse.

impatiently [ɪmˈpeɪʃəntlɪ] *adv* con impaciencia.

impeachment [ɪmˈpiːtʃmənt] *n* denuncia, acusación *f*.

impeccable [ɪmˈpɛkəbl] *adj* impecable.

impecunious [ɪmpɪˈkjuːnɪəs] *adj* sin dinero.

impede [ɪmˈpiːd] *vt* estorbar, dificultar.

impediment [ɪmˈpɛdɪmənt] *n* obstáculo, estorbo; *(also:* **speech ~)** defecto (del habla).

impel [ɪmˈpɛl] *vt (force)*: **to ~ sb (to do sth)** obligar a algn (a hacer algo).

impending [ɪmˈpɛndɪŋ] *adj* inminente.

impenetrable [ɪmˈpɛnɪtrəbl] *adj (jungle, fortress)* impenetrable; *(unfathomable)* insondable.

imperative [ɪmˈpɛrətɪv] *adj (tone)* imperioso; *(necessary)* imprescindible ♦ *n (LING)* imperativo.

imperceptible [ɪmpəˈsɛptɪbl] *adj* imperceptible.

imperfect [ɪmˈpəːfɪkt] *adj* imperfecto; *(goods etc)* defectuoso.

imperfection [ɪmpəˈfɛkʃən] *n (blemish)* desperfecto; *(fault, flaw)* defecto.

imperial [ɪmˈpɪərɪəl] *adj* imperial.

imperialism [ɪmˈpɪərɪəlɪzəm] *n* imperialismo.

imperil [ɪmˈpɛrɪl] *vt* poner en peligro.

imperious [ɪmˈpɪərɪəs] *adj* señorial, apremiante.

impersonal [ɪmˈpəːsənl] *adj* impersonal.

impersonate [ɪmˈpəːsəneɪt] *vt* hacerse pasar por.

impersonation [ɪmpəːsəˈneɪʃən] *n* imitación *f*.

impersonator [ɪmˈpəːsəneɪtə*] *n (THEAT etc)* imitador(a) *m/f*.

impertinence [ɪmˈpəːtɪnəns] *n* impertinencia, insolencia.

impertinent [ɪmˈpəːtɪnənt] *adj* impertinente, insolente.

imperturbable [ɪmpəˈtəːbəbl] *adj* imperturbable, impasible.

impervious [ɪmˈpəːvɪəs] *adj* impermeable; *(fig)*: **~ to** insensible a.

impetuous [ɪmˈpɛtjuəs] *adj* impetuoso.

impetus [ˈɪmpətəs] *n* ímpetu *m*; *(fig)* impulso.

impinge [ɪmˈpɪndʒ]: **to ~ on** *vt fus (affect)* afectar a.

impish [ˈɪmpɪʃ] *adj* travieso.

implacable [ɪmˈplækəbl] *adj* implacable.

implant [ɪmˈplɑːnt] *vt (MED)* injertar, implantar; *(fig: idea, principle)* inculcar.

implausible [ɪmˈplɔːzɪbl] *adj* implausible.

implement *n* [ˈɪmplɪmənt] instrumento, herramienta ♦ *vt* [ˈɪmplɪmɛnt] hacer efectivo; *(carry out)* realizar.

implicate [ˈɪmplɪkeɪt] *vt (compromise)* comprometer; *(involve)* enredar; **to ~ sb in sth** comprometer a algn en algo.

implication [ɪmplɪˈkeɪʃən] *n* consecuencia; **by ~** indirectamente.

implicit [ɪmˈplɪsɪt] *adj (gen)* implícito; *(complete)* absoluto.

implicitly [ɪmˈplɪsɪtlɪ] *adv* implícitamente.

implore [ɪmˈplɔː*] *vt (person)* suplicar.

imploring [ɪmˈplɔːrɪŋ] *adj* de súplica.

imply [ɪmˈplaɪ] *vt (involve)* implicar, suponer; *(hint)* insinuar.

impolite [ɪmpəˈlaɪt] *adj* mal educado.

impolitic [ɪmˈpɒlɪtɪk] *adj* poco diplomático.

imponderable [ɪmˈpɒndərəbl] *adj* imponderable.

import *vt* [ɪmˈpɔːt] importar ♦ *n* [ˈɪmpɔːt] *(COMM)* importación *f*; *(meaning)* significado, sentido ♦ *cpd (duty, licence etc)* de importación.

importance [ɪmˈpɔːtəns] *n* importancia; **to be of great/little ~** tener mucha/poca importancia.

important [ɪmˈpɔːtənt] *adj* importante; **it's not ~** no importa, no tiene importancia; **it is ~ that** es importante que.

importantly [ɪmˈpɔːtəntlɪ] *adv (pej)* dándose importancia; **but, more ~ ...** pero, lo que es aún más importante ....

import duty *n* derechos *mpl* de importación.

imported [ɪmˈpɔːtɪd] *adj* importado.

importer [ɪmˈpɔːtə*] *n* importador(a) *m/f*.

import licence, *(US)* **import license** *n* licencia de importación.

impose [ɪmˈpəuz] *vt* imponer ♦ *vi*: **to ~ on sb** abusar de algn.

imposing [ɪmˈpəuzɪŋ] *adj* imponente, impresionante.

imposition [ɪmpə'zɪʃn] n (of tax etc)
imposición f; **to be an ~** (on person)
molestar.
impossibility [ɪmpɔsə'bɪlɪtɪ] n
imposibilidad f.
impossible [ɪm'pɔsɪbl] adj imposible;
(person) insoportable; **it is ~ for me to
leave now** me es imposible salir ahora.
impossibly [ɪm'pɔsɪblɪ] adv
imposiblemente.
impostor [ɪm'pɔstə*] n impostor(a) m/f.
impotence ['ɪmpətəns] n impotencia.
impotent ['ɪmpətənt] adj impotente.
impound [ɪm'paund] vt embargar.
impoverished [ɪm'pɔvərɪʃt] adj necesitado;
(land) agotado.
impracticable [ɪm'præktɪkəbl] adj no
factible, irrealizable.
impractical [ɪm'præktɪkl] adj (person) poco
práctico.
imprecise [ɪmprɪ'saɪs] adj impreciso.
impregnable [ɪm'prɛgnəbl] adj
invulnerable; (castle) inexpugnable.
impregnate ['ɪmprɛgneɪt] vt (gen)
impregnar; (soak) empapar; (fertilize)
fecundar.
impresario [ɪmprɪ'sɑːrɪəu] n empresario/a.
impress [ɪm'prɛs] vt impresionar; (mark)
estampar ♦ vi causar buena impresión; **to
~ sth on sb** convencer a algn de la
importancia de algo.
impression [ɪm'prɛʃən] n impresión f;
(footprint etc) huella; (print run) edición f;
to be under the ~ that tener la idea de
que; **to make a good/bad ~ on sb** causar
buena/mala impresión a algn.
impressionable [ɪm'prɛʃnəbl] adj
impresionable.
impressionist [ɪm'prɛʃənɪst] n
impresionista m/f.
impressive [ɪm'prɛsɪv] adj impresionante.
imprint ['ɪmprɪnt] n (PUBLISHING) pie m de
imprenta; (fig) sello.
imprison [ɪm'prɪzn] vt encarcelar.
imprisonment [ɪm'prɪznmənt] n
encarcelamiento; (term of ~) cárcel f; **life
~** cadena perpetua.
improbable [ɪm'prɔbəbl] adj improbable,
inverosímil.
impromptu [ɪm'prɔmptjuː] adj improvisado
♦ adv de improviso.
improper [ɪm'prɔpə*] adj (incorrect)
impropio; (unseemly) indecoroso;
(indecent) indecente.
impropriety [ɪmprə'praɪətɪ] n falta de
decoro; (indecency) indecencia; (of
language) impropiedad f.
improve [ɪm'pruːv] vt mejorar; (foreign

language) perfeccionar ♦ vi mejorar.
▶**improve (up)on** vt fus (offer) mejorar.
improvement [ɪm'pruːvmənt] n mejora;
perfeccionamiento; **to make ~s to**
mejorar.
improvise ['ɪmprəvaɪz] vt, vi improvisar.
imprudence [ɪm'pruːdns] n imprudencia.
imprudent [ɪm'pruːdnt] adj imprudente.
impudent ['ɪmpjudnt] adj descarado,
insolente.
impugn [ɪm'pjuːn] vt impugnar.
impulse ['ɪmpʌls] n impulso; **to act on ~**
sin reflexión dejarse llevar por el
impulso.
impulse buying n compra impulsiva.
impulsive [ɪm'pʌlsɪv] adj irreflexivo,
impulsivo.
impunity [ɪm'pjuːnɪtɪ] n: **with ~**
impunemente.
impure [ɪm'pjuə*] adj (adulterated)
adulterado; (morally) impuro.
impurity [ɪm'pjuərɪtɪ] n impureza.
IN abbr (US) = Indiana.

================= **KEYWORD**

in [ɪn] prep **1** (indicating place, position, with
place names) en; **~ the house/garden** en
(la) casa/el jardín; **~ here/there** aquí/ahí
or allí dentro; **~ London/England** en
Londres/Inglaterra; **~ town** en el centro
(de la ciudad)
2 (indicating time) en; **~ spring** en (la)
primavera; **in 1888/May** en 1888/mayo; **~
the afternoon** por la tarde; **at 4 o'clock ~
the afternoon** a las 4 de la tarde; **I did it ~
3 hours/days** lo hice en 3 horas/días; **I'll
see you ~ 2 weeks** or **~ 2 weeks' time** te
veré dentro de 2 semanas; **once ~ a
hundred years** una vez cada cien años
3 (indicating manner etc) en; **~ a loud/soft
voice** en voz alta/baja; **~ pencil/ink** a
lápiz/bolígrafo; **the boy ~ the blue shirt**
el chico de la camisa azul; **~ writing** por
escrito; **to pay ~ dollars** pagar en dólares
4 (indicating circumstances): **~ the sun/
shade** al sol/a la sombra; **~ the rain** bajo
la lluvia; **a change ~ policy** un cambio de
política; **a rise ~ prices** un aumento de
precios
5 (indicating mood, state): **~ tears**
llorando; **~ anger/despair** enfadado/
desesperado; **to live ~ luxury** vivir
lujosamente
6 (with ratios, numbers): **1 ~ 10
households, 1 household ~ 10** una de
cada 10 familias; **20 pence ~ the pound**
20 peniques por libra; **they lined up ~
twos** se alinearon de dos en dos; **~**

hundreds a *or* por centenares
7 (*referring to people, works*) en; entre; **the
disease is common ~ children** la
enfermedad es común entre los niños; **~
(the works of) Dickens** en (las obras de)
Dickens
8 (*indicating profession etc*): **to be ~
teaching** dedicarse a la enseñanza
9 (*after superlative*) de; **the best pupil ~
the class** el/la mejor alumno/a de la clase
10 (*with present participle*): **~ saying this**
al decir esto
♦ *adv*: **to be ~** (*person: at home*) estar en
casa; (: *work*) estar; (*train, ship, plane*)
haber llegado; (*in fashion*) estar de moda;
she'll be ~ later today llegará más tarde
hoy; **to ask sb ~** hacer pasar a algn; **to
run/limp** *etc* **~** entrar corriendo/
cojeando *etc*
♦ **~ that** *conj* ya que
♦ *npl*: **the ~s and outs** (*of proposal,
situation etc*) los detalles.

in., ins *abbr* = **inch(es)**.
inability [ɪnə'bɪlɪtɪ] *n* incapacidad *f*; **~ to
pay** insolvencia en el pago.
inaccessible [ɪnək'sɛsɪbl] *adj* inaccesible.
inaccuracy [ɪn'ækjurəsɪ] *n* inexactitud *f*.
inaccurate [ɪn'ækjurət] *adj* inexacto,
incorrecto.
inaction [ɪn'ækʃən] *n* inacción *f*.
inactive [ɪn'æktɪv] *adj* inactivo.
inactivity [ɪnæk'tɪvɪtɪ] *n* inactividad *f*.
inadequacy [ɪn'ædɪkwəsɪ] *n* insuficiencia;
incapacidad *f*.
inadequate [ɪn'ædɪkwət] *adj* (*insufficient*)
insuficiente; (*unsuitable*) inadecuado;
(*person*) incapaz.
inadmissible [ɪnəd'mɪsəbl] *adj*
improcedente, inadmisible.
inadvertent [ɪnəd'vɜːtənt] *adj* descuidado,
involuntario.
inadvertently [ɪnəd'vɜːtntlɪ] *adv* por
descuido.
inadvisable [ɪnəd'vaɪzəbl] *adj* poco
aconsejable.
inane [ɪ'neɪn] *adj* necio, fatuo.
inanimate [ɪn'ænɪmət] *adj* inanimado.
inapplicable [ɪn'æplɪkəbl] *adj* inaplicable.
inappropriate [ɪnə'prəuprɪət] *adj*
inadecuado.
inapt [ɪn'æpt] *adj* impropio.
inaptitude [ɪn'æptɪtjuːd] *n* incapacidad *f*.
inarticulate [ɪnɑː'tɪkjulət] *adj* (*person*)
incapaz de expresarse; (*speech*) mal
pronunciado.
inartistic [ɪnɑː'tɪstɪk] *adj* antiestético.
inasmuch as [ɪnəz'mʌtʃ-] *adv* en la medida

en que.
inattention [ɪnə'tɛnʃən] *n* desatención *f*.
inattentive [ɪnə'tɛntɪv] *adj* distraído.
inaudible [ɪn'ɔːdɪbl] *adj* inaudible.
inaugural [ɪ'nɔːgjurəl] *adj* inaugural;
(*speech*) de apertura.
inaugurate [ɪ'nɔːgjureɪt] *vt* inaugurar;
(*president, official*) investir.
inauguration [ɪnɔːgju'reɪʃən] *n*
inauguración *f*; (*of official*) investidura; (*of
event*) ceremonia de apertura.
inauspicious [ɪnɔːs'pɪʃəs] *adj* poco
propicio, inoportuno.
in-between [ɪnbɪ'twiːn] *adj* intermedio.
inborn [ɪn'bɔːn] *adj* (*feeling*) innato.
inbred [ɪn'brɛd] *adj* innato; (*family*)
consanguíneo.
inbreeding [ɪn'briːdɪŋ] *n* endogamia.
Inc. *abbr* = **incorporated**.
Inca ['ɪŋkə] *adj* (*also*: **~n**) inca, de los incas
♦ *n* inca *m/f*.
incalculable [ɪn'kælkjuləbl] *adj*
incalculable.
incapability [ɪnkeɪpə'bɪlɪtɪ] *n* incapacidad *f*.
incapable [ɪn'keɪpəbl] *adj*: **~ (of doing sth)**
incapaz (de hacer algo).
incapacitate [ɪnkə'pæsɪteɪt] *vt*: **to ~ sb**
incapacitar a algn.
incapacitated [ɪnkə'pæsɪteɪtɪd] *adj*
incapacitado.
incapacity [ɪnkə'pæsɪtɪ] *n* (*inability*)
incapacidad *f*.
incarcerate [ɪn'kɑːsəreɪt] *vt* encarcelar.
incarnate *adj* [ɪn'kɑːnɪt] en persona ♦ *vt*
['ɪnkɑːneɪt] encarnar.
incarnation [ɪnkɑː'neɪʃən] *n* encarnación *f*.
incendiary [ɪn'sɛndɪərɪ] *adj* incendiario ♦ *n*
(*bomb*) bomba incendiaria.
incense *n* ['ɪnsɛns] incienso ♦ *vt* [ɪn'sɛns]
(*anger*) indignar, encolerizar.
incentive [ɪn'sɛntɪv] *n* incentivo, estímulo.
incentive bonus *n* prima.
incentive scheme *n* plan *m* de incentivos.
inception [ɪn'sɛpʃən] *n* comienzo,
principio.
incessant [ɪn'sɛsnt] *adj* incesante,
continuo.
incessantly [ɪn'sɛsntlɪ] *adv*
constantemente.
incest ['ɪnsɛst] *n* incesto.
inch [ɪntʃ] *n* pulgada; **to be within an ~ of**
estar a dos dedos de; **he didn't give an ~**
no hizo la más mínima concesión; **a few
~es** unas pulgadas.
▶**inch forward** *vi* avanzar palmo a palmo.
incidence ['ɪnsɪdns] *n* (*of crime, disease*)
incidencia.
incident ['ɪnsɪdnt] *n* incidente *m*; (*in book*)

episodio.

incidental [ɪnsɪ'dɛntl] *adj* circunstancial, accesorio; (*unplanned*) fortuito; ~ **to** relacionado con; ~ **expenses** (gastos *mpl*) imprevistos *mpl*.

incidentally [ɪnsɪ'dɛntəlɪ] *adv* (*by the way*) por cierto.

incidental music *n* música de fondo.

incident room *n* (*POLICE*) centro de coordinación.

incinerate [ɪn'sɪnəreɪt] *vt* incinerar, quemar.

incinerator [ɪn'sɪnəreɪtə*] *n* incinerador *m*, incineradora.

incipient [ɪn'sɪpɪənt] *adj* incipiente.

incision [ɪn'sɪʒən] *n* incisión *f*.

incisive [ɪn'saɪsɪv] *adj* (*mind*) penetrante; (*remark etc*) incisivo.

incisor [ɪn'saɪzə*] *n* incisivo.

incite [ɪn'saɪt] *vt* provocar, incitar.

incl. *abbr* = **including; inclusive (of)**.

inclement [ɪn'klɛmənt] *adj* inclemente.

inclination [ɪnklɪ'neɪʃən] *n* (*tendency*) tendencia, inclinación *f*.

incline *n* ['ɪnklaɪn] pendiente *f*, cuesta ♦ *vb* [ɪn'klaɪn] *vt* (*slope*) inclinar; (*head*) poner de lado ♦ *vi* inclinarse; **to be** ~**d to** (*tend*) ser propenso a; (*be willing*) estar dispuesto a.

include [ɪn'kluːd] *vt* incluir, comprender; (*in letter*) adjuntar; **the tip is/is not** ~**d** la propina está/no está incluida.

including [ɪn'kluːdɪŋ] *prep* incluso, inclusive; ~ **tip** propina incluida.

inclusion [ɪn'kluːʒən] *n* inclusión *f*.

inclusive [ɪn'kluːsɪv] *adj* inclusivo ♦ *adv* inclusive; ~ **of tax** incluidos los impuestos; **$50,** ~ **of all surcharges** 50 dólares, incluidos todos los recargos.

incognito [ɪnkɔg'niːtəu] *adv* de incógnito.

incoherent [ɪnkəu'hɪərənt] *adj* incoherente.

income ['ɪnkʌm] *n* (*personal*) ingresos *mpl*; (*from property etc*) renta; (*profit*) rédito; **gross/net** ~ ingresos *mpl* brutos/netos; ~ **and expenditure account** cuenta de gastos e ingresos.

income bracket *n* categoría económica.

income support *n* (*BRIT*) ≈ ayuda familiar.

income tax *n* impuesto sobre la renta.

income tax inspector *n* inspector(a) *m/f* de Hacienda.

income tax return *n* declaración *f* de ingresos.

incoming ['ɪnkʌmɪŋ] *adj* (*passengers, flight*) de llegada; (*government*) entrante; (*tenant*) nuevo.

incommunicado ['ɪnkəmjunɪ'kɑːdəu] *adj*: **to**

hold sb ~ mantener incomunicado a algn.

incomparable [ɪn'kɔmpərəbl] *adj* incomparable, sin par.

incompatible [ɪnkəm'pætɪbl] *adj* incompatible.

incompetence [ɪn'kɔmpɪtəns] *n* incompetencia.

incompetent [ɪn'kɔmpɪtənt] *adj* incompetente.

incomplete [ɪnkəm'pliːt] *adj* incompleto; (*unfinished*) sin terminar.

incomprehensible [ɪnkɔmprɪ'hɛnsɪbl] *adj* incomprensible.

inconceivable [ɪnkən'siːvəbl] *adj* inconcebible.

inconclusive [ɪnkən'kluːsɪv] *adj* sin resultado (definitivo); (*argument*) poco convincente.

incongruity [ɪnkɔŋ'gruːɪtɪ] *n* incongruencia.

incongruous [ɪn'kɔŋgruəs] *adj* discordante.

inconsequential [ɪnkɔnsɪ'kwɛnʃl] *adj* intrascendente.

inconsiderable [ɪnkən'sɪdərəbl] *adj* insignificante.

inconsiderate [ɪnkən'sɪdərət] *adj* desconsiderado; **how** ~ **of him!** ¡qué falta de consideración (de su parte)!

inconsistency [ɪnkən'sɪstənsɪ] *n* inconsecuencia; (*of actions etc*) falta de lógica; (*of work*) carácter *m* desigual, inconsistencia; (*of statement etc*) contradicción *f*.

inconsistent [ɪnkən'sɪstnt] *adj* inconsecuente; ~ **with** que no concuerda con.

inconsolable [ɪnkən'səuləbl] *adj* inconsolable.

inconspicuous [ɪnkən'spɪkjuəs] *adj* (*discreet*) discreto; (*person*) que llama poco la atención.

inconstancy [ɪn'kɔnstənsɪ] *n* inconstancia.

inconstant [ɪn'kɔnstənt] *adj* inconstante.

incontinence [ɪn'kɔntɪnəns] *n* incontinencia.

incontinent [ɪn'kɔntɪnənt] *adj* incontinente.

incontrovertible [ɪnkɔntrə'vəːtəbl] *adj* incontrovertible.

inconvenience [ɪnkən'viːnjəns] *n* (*gen*) inconvenientes *mpl*; (*trouble*) molestia ♦ *vt* incomodar; **to put sb to great** ~ causar mucha molestia a algn; **don't** ~ **yourself** no se moleste.

inconvenient [ɪnkən'viːnjənt] *adj* incómodo, poco práctico; (*time, place*) inoportuno; **that time is very** ~ **for me** esa hora me es muy inconveniente.

incorporate [ɪnˈkɔːpəreɪt] _vt_ incorporar;
(_contain_) comprender; (_add_) agregar.
incorporated [ɪnˈkɔːpəreɪtɪd] _adj_: ~
company (_US: abbr_ **Inc.**) ≈ Sociedad _f_
Anónima (S.A.).
incorrect [ɪnkəˈrɛkt] _adj_ incorrecto.
incorrigible [ɪnˈkɔrɪdʒəbl] _adj_ incorregible.
incorruptible [ɪnkəˈrʌptɪbl] _adj_
incorruptible.
increase _n_ [ˈɪnkriːs] aumento ♦ _vb_ [ɪnˈkriːs] _vi_
aumentar; (_grow_) crecer; (_price_) subir ♦ _vt_
aumentar; **an ~ of 5%** un aumento de 5%;
to be on the ~ ir en aumento.
increasing [ɪnˈkriːsɪŋ] _adj_ (_number_)
creciente, que va en aumento.
increasingly [ɪnˈkriːsɪŋlɪ] _adv_ cada vez más.
incredible [ɪnˈkrɛdɪbl] _adj_ increíble.
incredibly [ɪnˈkrɛdɪblɪ] _adv_ increíblemente.
incredulous [ɪnˈkrɛdjuləs] _adj_ incrédulo.
increment [ˈɪnkrɪmənt] _n_ aumento,
incremento.
incriminate [ɪnˈkrɪmɪneɪt] _vt_ incriminar.
incriminating [ɪnˈkrɪmɪneɪtɪŋ] _adj_
incriminatorio.
incrust [ɪnˈkrʌst] _vt_ = **encrust.**
incubate [ˈɪnkjubeɪt] _vt_ (_eggs_) incubar,
empollar ♦ _vi_ (_egg, disease_) incubar.
incubation [ɪnkjuˈbeɪʃən] _n_ incubación _f._
incubation period _n_ período de
incubación.
incubator [ˈɪnkjubeɪtə*] _n_ incubadora.
inculcate [ˈɪnkʌlkeɪt] _vt_: **to ~ sth in sb**
inculcar algo en algn.
incumbent [ɪnˈkʌmbənt] _n_ ocupante _m/f_
♦ _adj_: **it is ~ on him to...** le incumbe....
incur [ɪnˈkəː*] _vt_ (_expenses_) incurrir en;
(_loss_) sufrir.
incurable [ɪnˈkjuərəbl] _adj_ incurable.
incursion [ɪnˈkəːʃən] _n_ incursión _f._
Ind. _abbr_ (_US_) = Indiana.
indebted [ɪnˈdɛtɪd] _adj_: **to be ~ to sb** estar
agradecido a algn.
indecency [ɪnˈdiːsnsɪ] _n_ indecencia.
indecent [ɪnˈdiːsnt] _adj_ indecente.
indecent assault _n_ (_BRIT_) atentado contra
el pudor.
indecent exposure _n_ exhibicionismo.
indecipherable [ɪndɪˈsaɪfərəbl] _adj_
indescifrable.
indecision [ɪndɪˈsɪʒən] _n_ indecisión _f._
indecisive [ɪndɪˈsaɪsɪv] _adj_ indeciso;
(_discussion_) no resuelto, inconcluyente.
indeed [ɪnˈdiːd] _adv_ efectivamente, en
realidad; **yes ~!** ¡claro que sí!
indefatigable [ɪndɪˈfætɪgəbl] _adj_
incansable, infatigable.
indefensible [ɪndɪˈfɛnsəbl] _adj_ (_conduct_)
injustificable.

indefinable [ɪndɪˈfaɪnəbl] _adj_ indefinible.
indefinite [ɪnˈdɛfɪnɪt] _adj_ indefinido;
(_uncertain_) incierto.
indefinitely [ɪnˈdɛfɪnɪtlɪ] _adv_ (_wait_)
indefinidamente.
indelible [ɪnˈdɛlɪbl] _adj_ imborrable.
indelicate [ɪnˈdɛlɪkɪt] _adj_ (_tactless_)
indiscreto, inoportuno; (_not polite_) poco
delicado.
indemnify [ɪnˈdɛmnɪfaɪ] _vt_ indemnizar,
resarcir.
indemnity [ɪnˈdɛmnɪtɪ] _n_ (_insurance_)
indemnidad _f_; (_compensation_)
indemnización _f._
indent [ɪnˈdɛnt] _vt_ (_text_) sangrar.
indentation [ɪndɛnˈteɪʃən] _n_ mella; (_TYP_)
sangría.
independence [ɪndɪˈpɛndns] _n_
independencia.
Independence Day _n_ Día _m_ de la
Independencia; _ver recuadro._

INDEPENDENCE DAY

_El cuatro de julio es la fiesta nacional de los
Estados Unidos,_ **Independence Day,** _en
conmemoración de la Declaración de
Independencia escrita por Thomas
Jefferson y adoptada en 1776. En ella se
proclamaba la ruptura total con Gran
Bretaña de las trece colonias americanas
que fueron el origen de los Estados Unidos
de América._

---

independent [ɪndɪˈpɛndənt] _adj_ independiente; **to become ~** independizarse.
in-depth [ˈɪndɛpθ] _adj_ en profundidad, a
fondo.
indescribable [ɪndɪˈskraɪbəbl] _adj_
indescriptible.
indestructible [ɪndɪsˈtrʌktəbl] _adj_
indestructible.
indeterminate [ɪndɪˈtəːmɪnɪt] _adj_
indeterminado.
index [ˈɪndɛks] _n_ (_pl_: ~**es**: _in book_)
índice _m_; (: _in library etc_) catálogo; (_pl_:
indices [ˈɪndɪsiːz]): _ratio, sign_) exponente _m._
index card _n_ ficha.
index finger _n_ índice _m._
index-linked [ˈɪndɛksˈlɪŋkt], (_US_) **indexed**
[ˈɪndɛkst] _adj_ indexado.
India [ˈɪndɪə] _n_ la India.
Indian [ˈɪndɪən] _adj, n_ indio/a
_m/f_; (_American_ ~) indio/a _m/f_ de América,
amerindio/a _m/f_; **Red ~** piel roja _m/f._
Indian Ocean _n_: **the ~** el Océano Índico, el
Mar de las Indias.
Indian summer _n_ (_fig_) veranillo de San

Martín.
india rubber n caucho.
indicate ['ɪndɪkeɪt] vt indicar ♦ vi (BRIT AUT):
to ~ left/right indicar a la izquierda/a la
derecha.
indication [ɪndɪ'keɪʃən] n indicio, señal f.
indicative [ɪn'dɪkətɪv] adj: **to be ~ of sth**
indicar algo ♦ n (LING) indicativo.
indicator ['ɪndɪkeɪtə*] n (gen) indicador m;
(AUT) intermitente m, direccional m
(LAM).
indices ['ɪndɪsiːz] npl of **index**.
indict [ɪn'daɪt] vt acusar.
indictable [ɪn'daɪtəbl] adj: ~ **offence** delito
procesable.
indictment [ɪn'daɪtmənt] n acusación f.
indifference [ɪn'dɪfrəns] n indiferencia.
indifferent [ɪn'dɪfrənt] adj indiferente;
(poor) regular.
indigenous [ɪn'dɪdʒɪnəs] adj indígena.
indigestible [ɪndɪ'dʒestɪbl] adj indigesto.
indigestion [ɪndɪ'dʒestʃən] n indigestión f.
indignant [ɪn'dɪgnənt] adj: **to be ~ about**
sth indignarse por algo.
indignation [ɪndɪg'neɪʃən] n indignación f.
indignity [ɪn'dɪgnɪtɪ] n indignidad f.
indigo ['ɪndɪgəʊ] adj (colour) (de color) añil
♦ n añil m.
indirect [ɪndɪ'rekt] adj indirecto.
indirectly [ɪndɪ'rektlɪ] adv indirectamente.
indiscernible [ɪndɪ'sə:nəbl] adj
imperceptible.
indiscreet [ɪndɪ'skriːt] adj indiscreto,
imprudente.
indiscretion [ɪndɪ'skreʃən] n indiscreción f,
imprudencia.
indiscriminate [ɪndɪ'skrɪmɪnət] adj
indiscriminado.
indispensable [ɪndɪ'spensəbl] adj
indispensable, imprescindible.
indisposed [ɪndɪ'spəʊzd] adj (unwell)
indispuesto.
indisposition [ɪndɪspə'zɪʃən] n
indisposición f.
indisputable [ɪndɪ'spjuːtəbl] adj
incontestable.
indistinct [ɪndɪ'stɪŋkt] adj indistinto.
indistinguishable [ɪndɪ'stɪŋgwɪʃəbl] adj
indistinguible.
individual [ɪndɪ'vɪdjuəl] n individuo ♦ adj
individual; (personal) personal; (for/of one
only) particular.
individualist [ɪndɪ'vɪdjuəlɪst] n
individualista m/f.
individuality [ɪndɪvɪdju'ælɪtɪ] n
individualidad f.
individually [ɪndɪ'vɪdjuəlɪ] adv
individualmente; particularmente.

indivisible [ɪndɪ'vɪzəbl] adj indivisible.
Indo-China ['ɪndəu'tʃaɪnə] n Indochina.
indoctrinate [ɪn'dɒktrɪneɪt] vt adoctrinar.
indoctrination [ɪndɒktrɪ'neɪʃən] n
adoctrinamiento.
indolence ['ɪndələns] n indolencia.
indolent ['ɪndələnt] adj indolente, perezoso.
Indonesia [ɪndə'niːzɪə] n Indonesia.
Indonesian [ɪndə'niːzɪən] adj indonesio ♦ n
indonesio/a; (LING) indonesio.
indoor ['ɪndɔː*] adj (swimming pool)
cubierto; (plant) de interior; (sport) bajo
cubierta.
indoors [ɪn'dɔːz] adv dentro; (at home) en
casa.
indubitable [ɪn'djuːbɪtəbl] adj indudable.
indubitably [ɪn'djuːbɪtəblɪ] adv
indudablemente.
induce [ɪn'djuːs] vt inducir, persuadir;
(bring about) producir; **to ~ sb to do sth**
persuadir a algn a que haga algo.
inducement [ɪn'djuːsmənt] n (incentive)
incentivo, aliciente m.
induct [ɪn'dʌkt] vt iniciar; (in job, rank,
position) instalar.
induction [ɪn'dʌkʃən] n (MED: of birth)
inducción f.
induction course n (BRIT) cursillo
introductorio or de iniciación.
indulge [ɪn'dʌldʒ] vt (whim) satisfacer;
(person) complacer; (child) mimar ♦ vi: **to
~ in** darse el gusto de.
indulgence [ɪn'dʌldʒəns] n vicio.
indulgent [ɪn'dʌldʒənt] adj indulgente.
industrial [ɪn'dʌstrɪəl] adj industrial.
industrial action n huelga.
industrial estate n (BRIT) polígono or zona
(LAM) industrial.
industrial goods npl bienes mpl de
producción.
industrialist [ɪn'dʌstrɪəlɪst] n industrial m/f.
industrialize [ɪn'dʌstrɪəlaɪz] vt
industrializar.
industrial park n (US) = **industrial estate**.
industrial relations npl relaciones fpl
empresariales.
industrial tribunal n magistratura de
trabajo, tribunal m laboral.
industrial unrest n (BRIT) agitación f
obrera.
industrious [ɪn'dʌstrɪəs] adj (gen)
trabajador(a); (student) aplicado.
industry ['ɪndəstrɪ] n industria; (diligence)
aplicación f.
inebriated [ɪ'niːbrɪeɪtɪd] adj borracho.
inedible [ɪn'edɪbl] adj incomible; (plant etc)
no comestible.
ineffective [ɪnɪ'fektɪv], **ineffectual**

[ɪnɪ'fɛktʃuəl] *adj* ineficaz, inútil.
inefficiency [ɪnɪ'fɪʃənsɪ] *n* ineficacia.
inefficient [ɪnɪ'fɪʃənt] *adj* ineficaz,
ineficiente.
inelegant [ɪn'ɛlɪgənt] *adj* poco elegante.
ineligible [ɪn'ɛlɪdʒɪbl] *adj* inelegible.
inept [ɪ'nɛpt] *adj* incompetente, incapaz.
ineptitude [ɪ'nɛptɪtjuːd] *n* incapacidad *f*,
ineptitud *f*.
inequality [ɪnɪ'kwɒlɪtɪ] *n* desigualdad *f*.
inequitable [ɪn'ɛkwɪtəbl] *adj* injusto.
ineradicable [ɪnɪ'rædɪkəbl] *adj* inextirpable.
inert [ɪ'nɜːt] *adj* inerte, inactivo; (*immobile*)
inmóvil.
inertia [ɪ'nɜːʃə] *n* inercia; (*laziness*) pereza.
inertia-reel seat-belt [ɪ'nɜːʃə'riːl-] *n*
cinturón *m* de seguridad retráctil.
inescapable [ɪnɪ'skeɪpəbl] *adj* ineludible,
inevitable.
inessential [ɪnɪ'sɛnʃl] *adj* no esencial.
inestimable [ɪn'ɛstɪməbl] *adj* inestimable.
inevitability [ɪnɛvɪtə'bɪlɪtɪ] *n* inevitabilidad
f.
inevitable [ɪn'ɛvɪtəbl] *adj* inevitable;
(*necessary*) forzoso.
inevitably [ɪn'ɛvɪtəblɪ] *adv*
inevitablemente; **as ~ happens ...** como
siempre pasa ....
inexact [ɪnɪg'zækt] *adj* inexacto.
inexcusable [ɪnɪks'kjuːzəbl] *adj*
imperdonable.
inexhaustible [ɪnɪg'zɔːstɪbl] *adj* inagotable.
inexorable [ɪn'ɛksərəbl] *adj* inexorable,
implacable.
inexpensive [ɪnɪk'spɛnsɪv] *adj* económico.
inexperience [ɪnɪk'spɪərɪəns] *n* falta de
experiencia.
inexperienced [ɪnɪk'spɪərɪənst] *adj*
inexperto; **to be ~ in sth** no tener
experiencia en algo.
inexplicable [ɪnɪk'splɪkəbl] *adj*
inexplicable.
inexpressible [ɪnɪk'sprɛsəbl] *adj*
inexpresable.
inextricable [ɪnɪks'trɪkəbl] *adj* inseparable.
inextricably [ɪnɪks'trɪkəblɪ] *adv*
indisolublemente.
infallibility [ɪnfælə'bɪlɪtɪ] *n* infalibilidad *f*.
infallible [ɪn'fælɪbl] *adj* infalible.
infamous ['ɪnfəməs] *adj* infame.
infamy ['ɪnfəmɪ] *n* infamia.
infancy ['ɪnfənsɪ] *n* infancia.
infant ['ɪnfənt] *n* niño/a.
infantile ['ɪnfəntaɪl] *adj* infantil; (*pej*)
aniñado.
infant mortality *n* mortalidad *f* infantil.
infantry ['ɪnfəntrɪ] *n* infantería.
infantryman ['ɪnfəntrɪmən] *n* soldado de
infantería.
infant school *n* (*BRIT*) escuela de párvulos;
see also **primary school**.
infatuated [ɪn'fætjueɪtɪd] *adj*: **~ with** (*in
love*) loco por; **to become ~ (with sb)**
enamoriscarse (de algn), encapricharse
(con algn).
infatuation [ɪnfætju'eɪʃən] *n*
enamoramiento.
infect [ɪn'fɛkt] *vt* (*wound*) infectar; (*person*)
contagiar; (*fig: pej*) corromper; **~ed with**
(*illness*) contagiado de; **to become ~ed**
(*wound*) infectarse.
infection [ɪn'fɛkʃən] *n* infección *f*; (*fig*)
contagio.
infectious [ɪn'fɛkʃəs] *adj* contagioso; (*also
fig*) infeccioso.
infer [ɪn'fɜː*] *vt* deducir, inferir; **to ~
(from)** inferir (de), deducir (de).
inference ['ɪnfərəns] *n* deducción *f*,
inferencia.
inferior [ɪn'fɪərɪə*] *adj*, *n* inferior *m/f*; **to feel
~** sentirse inferior.
inferiority [ɪnfɪərɪ'ɔrɪtɪ] *n* inferioridad *f*.
inferiority complex *n* complejo de
inferioridad.
infernal [ɪn'fɜːnl] *adj* infernal.
inferno [ɪn'fɜːnəu] *n* infierno; (*fig*) hoguera.
infertile [ɪn'fɜːtaɪl] *adj* estéril; (*person*)
infecundo.
infertility [ɪnfəː'tɪlɪtɪ] *n* esterilidad *f*;
infecundidad *f*.
infest [ɪn'fɛst] *vt* infestar.
infested [ɪn'fɛstɪd] *adj*: **~ (with)** plagado
(de).
infidel ['ɪnfɪdəl] *n* infiel *m/f*.
infidelity [ɪnfɪ'dɛlɪtɪ] *n* infidelidad *f*.
in-fighting ['ɪnfaɪtɪŋ] *n* (*fig*) lucha(s) *f(pl)*
interna(s).
infiltrate ['ɪnfɪltreɪt] *vt* (*troops etc*)
infiltrarse en ♦ *vi* infiltrarse.
infinite ['ɪnfɪnɪt] *adj* infinito; **an ~ amount
of money/time** un sinfín de dinero/
tiempo.
infinitely ['ɪnfɪnɪtlɪ] *adv* infinitamente.
infinitesimal [ɪnfɪnɪ'tɛsɪməl] *adj*
infinitésimo.
infinitive [ɪn'fɪnɪtɪv] *n* infinitivo.
infinity [ɪn'fɪnɪtɪ] *n* (*also MATH*) infinito; (*an
~*) infinidad *f*.
infirm [ɪn'fɜːm] *adj* enfermizo, débil.
infirmary [ɪn'fɜːmərɪ] *n* hospital *m*.
infirmity [ɪn'fɜːmɪtɪ] *n* debilidad *f*; (*illness*)
enfermedad *f*, achaque *m*.
inflame [ɪn'fleɪm] inflamar.
inflamed [ɪn'fleɪmd] *adj*: **to become ~**
inflamarse.
inflammable [ɪn'flæməbl] *adj* (*BRIT*)

inflamable; (*situation etc*) explosivo.
inflammation [ɪnfləˈmeɪʃən] *n* inflamación *f*.
inflammatory [ɪnˈflæmətərɪ] *adj* (*speech*) incendiario.
inflatable [ɪnˈfleɪtəbl] *adj* inflable.
inflate [ɪnˈfleɪt] *vt* inflar; (*fig*) hinchar.
inflated [ɪnˈfleɪtɪd] *adj* (*tyre etc*) inflado; (*price, self-esteem etc*) exagerado.
inflation [ɪnˈfleɪʃən] *n* (*ECON*) inflación *f*.
inflationary [ɪnˈfleɪʃnərɪ] *adj* inflacionario.
inflationary spiral *n* espiral *f* inflacionista.
inflexible [ɪnˈflɛksɪbl] *adj* inflexible.
inflict [ɪnˈflɪkt] *vt*: **to ~ on** infligir en; (*tax etc*) imponer a.
in-flight [ˈɪnflaɪt] *adj* durante el vuelo.
inflow [ˈɪnfləu] *n* afluencia.
influence [ˈɪnfluəns] *n* influencia ♦ *vt* influir en, influenciar; **under the ~ of alcohol** en estado de embriaguez.
influential [ɪnfluˈɛnʃl] *adj* influyente.
influenza [ɪnfluˈɛnzə] *n* gripe *f*.
influx [ˈɪnflʌks] *n* afluencia.
inform [ɪnˈfɔːm] *vt*: **to ~ sb of sth** informar a algn sobre *or* de algo; (*warn*) avisar a algn de algo; (*communicate*) comunicar algo a algn ♦ *vi*: **to ~ on sb** delatar a algn.
informal [ɪnˈfɔːml] *adj* (*manner, tone*) desenfadado; (*dress, occasion*) informal.
informality [ɪnfɔːˈmælɪtɪ] *n* falta de ceremonia; (*intimacy*) intimidad *f*; (*familiarity*) familiaridad *f*; (*ease*) afabilidad *f*.
informally [ɪnˈfɔːməlɪ] *adv* sin ceremonia; (*invite*) informalmente.
informant [ɪnˈfɔːmənt] *n* informante *m/f*.
informatics [ɪnfɔːˈmætɪks] *n* informática.
information [ɪnfəˈmeɪʃən] *n* información *f*; (*news*) noticias *fpl*; (*knowledge*) conocimientos *mpl*; (*LAW*) delación *f*; **a piece of ~** un dato; **for your ~** para su información.
information and communication(s) technology *n* (*gen*) tecnología de la información y de las comunicaciones; (*BRIT SCOL*) informática.
information bureau *n* oficina de información.
information processing *n* procesamiento de datos.
information retrieval *n* recuperación *f* de información.
information science *n* gestión *f* de la información.
information technology (IT) *n* informática.
informative [ɪnˈfɔːmətɪv] *adj* informativo.
informed [ɪnˈfɔːmd] *adj* (*observer*) informado, al corriente; **an ~ guess** una opinión bien fundamentada.
informer [ɪnˈfɔːmə*] *n* delator(a) *m/f*; (*also*: **police ~**) soplón/ona *m/f*.
infra dig [ˈɪnfrəˈdɪg] *adj abbr* (*col*: = *infra dignitatem*) denigrante.
infra-red [ɪnfrəˈred] *adj* infrarrojo.
infrastructure [ˈɪnfrəstrʌktʃə*] *n* (*of system etc, ECON*) infraestructura.
infrequent [ɪnˈfriːkwənt] *adj* infrecuente.
infringe [ɪnˈfrɪndʒ] *vt* infringir, violar ♦ *vi*: **to ~ on** invadir.
infringement [ɪnˈfrɪndʒmənt] *n* infracción *f*; (*of rights*) usurpación *f*; (*SPORT*) falta.
infuriate [ɪnˈfjuərɪeɪt] *vt*: **to become ~d** ponerse furioso.
infuriating [ɪnˈfjuərɪeɪtɪŋ] *adj*: **I find it ~** me saca de quicio.
infuse [ɪnˈfjuːz] *vt* (*with courage, enthusiasm*): **to ~ sb with sth** infundir algo a algn.
infusion [ɪnˈfjuːʒən] *n* (*tea etc*) infusión *f*.
ingenious [ɪnˈdʒiːnjəs] *adj* ingenioso.
ingenuity [ɪndʒɪˈnjuːɪtɪ] *n* ingeniosidad *f*.
ingenuous [ɪnˈdʒɛnjuəs] *adj* ingenuo.
ingot [ˈɪŋgət] *n* lingote *m*, barra.
ingrained [ɪnˈgreɪnd] *adj* arraigado.
ingratiate [ɪnˈgreɪʃɪeɪt] *vt*: **to ~ o.s. with** congraciarse con.
ingratiating [ɪnˈgreɪʃɪeɪtɪŋ] *adj* (*smile, speech*) insinuante; (*person*) zalamero, congraciador(a).
ingratitude [ɪnˈgrætɪtjuːd] *n* ingratitud *f*.
ingredient [ɪnˈgriːdɪənt] *n* ingrediente *m*.
ingrowing [ˈɪngrəuɪŋ] *adj*: **~ (toe)nail** uña encarnada.
inhabit [ɪnˈhæbɪt] *vt* vivir en; (*occupy*) ocupar.
inhabitable [ɪnˈhæbɪtəbl] *adj* habitable.
inhabitant [ɪnˈhæbɪtənt] *n* habitante *m/f*.
inhale [ɪnˈheɪl] *vt* inhalar ♦ *vi* (*in smoking*) tragar.
inhaler [ɪnˈheɪlə*] *n* inhalador *m*.
inherent [ɪnˈhɪərənt] *adj*: **~ in or to** inherente a.
inherently [ɪnˈhɪərəntlɪ] *adv* intrínsecamente.
inherit [ɪnˈhɛrɪt] *vt* heredar.
inheritance [ɪnˈhɛrɪtəns] *n* herencia; (*fig*) patrimonio.
inhibit [ɪnˈhɪbɪt] *vt* inhibir, impedir; **to ~ sb from doing sth** impedir a algn hacer algo.
inhibited [ɪnˈhɪbɪtɪd] *adj* (*person*) cohibido.
inhibition [ɪnhɪˈbɪʃən] *n* cohibición *f*.
inhospitable [ɪnhɔsˈpɪtəbl] *adj* (*person*) inhospitalario; (*place*) inhóspito.
in-house [ˈɪnhaus] *adj* dentro de la empresa.
inhuman [ɪnˈhjuːmən] *adj* inhumano.

inhumane [ɪnhjuː'meɪn] _adj_ inhumano.

inimitable [ɪ'nɪmɪtəbl] _adj_ inimitable.

iniquity [ɪ'nɪkwɪtɪ] _n_ iniquidad _f_; (_injustice_) injusticia.

initial [ɪ'nɪʃl] _adj_ inicial; (_first_) primero ♦ _n_ inicial _f_ ♦ _vt_ firmar con las iniciales; **~s** _npl_ iniciales _fpl_; (_abbreviation_) siglas _fpl_.

initialize [ɪ'nɪʃəlaɪz] _vt_ (_COMPUT_) inicializar.

initially [ɪ'nɪʃəlɪ] _adv_ en un principio.

initiate [ɪ'nɪʃɪeɪt] _vt_ (_start_) iniciar; **to ~ sb into a secret** iniciar a algn en un secreto; **to ~ proceedings against sb** (_LAW_) poner una demanda contra algn.

initiation [ɪnɪʃɪ'eɪʃən] _n_ (_into secret etc_) iniciación _f_; (_beginning_) comienzo.

initiative [ɪ'nɪʃətɪv] _n_ iniciativa; **to take the ~** tomar la iniciativa.

inject [ɪn'dʒɛkt] _vt_ inyectar; (_money, enthusiasm_) aportar.

injection [ɪn'dʒɛkʃən] _n_ inyección _f_; **to have an ~** ponerse una inyección.

injudicious [ɪndʒu'dɪʃəs] _adj_ imprudente, indiscreto.

injunction [ɪn'dʒʌŋkʃən] _n_ entredicho, interdicto.

injure ['ɪndʒə*] _vt_ herir; (_hurt_) lastimar; (_fig: reputation etc_) perjudicar; (_feelings_) herir; **to ~ o.s** hacerse daño, lastimarse.

injured ['ɪndʒəd] _adj_ (_also fig_) herido; **~ party** (_LAW_) parte _f_ perjudicada.

injurious [ɪn'dʒuərɪəs] _adj_: **~ (to)** perjudicial (para).

injury ['ɪndʒərɪ] _n_ herida, lesión _f_; (_wrong_) perjuicio, daño; **to escape without ~** salir ileso.

injury time _n_ (_SPORT_) descuento.

injustice [ɪn'dʒʌstɪs] _n_ injusticia; **you do me an ~** usted es injusto conmigo.

ink [ɪŋk] _n_ tinta.

ink-jet printer ['ɪŋkdʒɛt-] _n_ impresora de chorro de tinta.

inkling ['ɪŋklɪŋ] _n_ sospecha; (_idea_) idea.

inkpad ['ɪŋkpæd] _n_ almohadilla.

inlaid ['ɪnleɪd] _adj_ (_wood_) taraceado; (_tiles_) entarimado.

inland _adj_ ['ɪnlənd] interior; (_town_) del interior ♦ _adv_ [ɪn'lænd] tierra adentro.

Inland Revenue _n_ (_BRIT_) Hacienda.

in-laws ['ɪnlɔːz] _npl_ suegros _mpl_.

inlet ['ɪnlɛt] _n_ (_GEO_) ensenada, cala; (_TECH_) admisión _f_, entrada.

inmate ['ɪnmeɪt] _n_ (_in prison_) preso/a, presidiario/a; (_in asylum_) internado/a.

inmost ['ɪnməust] _adj_ más íntimo, más secreto.

inn [ɪn] _n_ posada, mesón _m_; **the I~s of Court** _see_ **barrister**.

innards ['ɪnədz] _npl_ (_col_) tripas _fpl_.

innate [ɪ'neɪt] _adj_ innato.

inner ['ɪnə*] _adj_ interior, interno.

inner city _n_ barrios deprimidos del centro de una ciudad.

innermost ['ɪnəməust] _adj_ más íntimo, más secreto.

inner tube _n_ (_of tyre_) cámara, llanta (_LAM_).

innings ['ɪnɪŋz] _n_ (_CRICKET_) entrada, turno.

innocence ['ɪnəsns] _n_ inocencia.

innocent ['ɪnəsnt] _adj_ inocente.

innocuous [ɪ'nɔkjuəs] _adj_ inocuo.

innovation [ɪnəu'veɪʃən] _n_ novedad _f_.

innuendo, **~es** [ɪnju'ɛndəu] _n_ indirecta.

innumerable [ɪ'njuːmrəbl] _adj_ innumerable.

inoculate [ɪ'nɔkjuleɪt] _vt_: **to ~ sb with sth/ against sth** inocular _or_ vacunar a algn con algo/contra algo.

inoculation [ɪnɔkju'leɪʃən] _n_ inoculación _f_.

inoffensive [ɪnə'fɛnsɪv] _adj_ inofensivo.

inopportune [ɪn'ɔpətjuːn] _adj_ inoportuno.

inordinate [ɪ'nɔːdɪnət] _adj_ excesivo, desmesurado.

inordinately [ɪ'nɔːdɪnətlɪ] _adv_ excesivamente, desmesuradamente.

inorganic [ɪnɔː'gaenɪk] _adj_ inorgánico.

in-patient ['ɪnpeɪʃənt] _n_ (_paciente m/f_) interno/a.

input ['ɪnput] _n_ (_ELEC_) entrada; (_COMPUT_) entrada de datos ♦ _vt_ (_COMPUT_) introducir, entrar.

inquest ['ɪnkwɛst] _n_ (_coroner's_) investigación _f_ post-mortem.

inquire [ɪn'kwaɪə*] _vi_ preguntar ♦ _vt_: **to ~ when/where/whether** preguntar cuándo/dónde/si; **to ~ about** (_person_) preguntar por; (_fact_) informarse de.

▶**inquire into** _vt fus_: **to ~ into sth** investigar _or_ indagar algo.

inquiring [ɪn'kwaɪərɪŋ] _adj_ (_mind_) inquieto; (_look_) interrogante.

inquiry [ɪn'kwaɪərɪ] _n_ pregunta; (_LAW_) investigación _f_, pesquisa; (_commission_) comisión _f_ investigadora; **to hold an ~ into sth** emprender una investigación sobre algo.

inquiry desk _n_ mesa de información.

inquiry office _n_ (_BRIT_) oficina de información.

inquisition [ɪnkwɪ'zɪʃən] _n_ inquisición _f_.

inquisitive [ɪn'kwɪzɪtɪv] _adj_ (_mind_) inquisitivo; (_person_) fisgón/ona.

inroad ['ɪnrəud] _n_ incursión _f_; (_fig_) invasión _f_; **to make ~s into** (_time_) ocupar parte de; (_savings, supplies_) agotar parte de.

insane [ɪn'seɪn] _adj_ loco; (_MED_) demente.

insanitary [ɪn'sænɪtərɪ] _adj_ insalubre.

insanity [ɪn'sænɪtɪ] _n_ demencia, locura.

insatiable [ɪn'seɪʃəbl] *adj* insaciable.
inscribe [ɪn'skraɪb] *vt* inscribir; (*book etc*):
to ~ **(to sb)** dedicar (a algn).
inscription [ɪn'skrɪpʃən] *n* (*gen*) inscripción
f; (*in book*) dedicatoria.
inscrutable [ɪn'skruːtəbl] *adj* inescrutable,
insondable.
inseam measurement ['ɪnsiːm-] *n* (*US*)
= **inside leg measurement.**
insect ['ɪnsɛkt] *n* insecto.
insect bite *n* picadura.
insecticide [ɪn'sɛktɪsaɪd] *n* insecticida *m*.
insect repellent *n* loción *f* contra los
insectos.
insecure [ɪnsɪ'kjuə*] *adj* inseguro.
insecurity [ɪnsɪ'kjuərɪtɪ] *n* inseguridad *f*.
insemination [ɪnsɛmɪ'neɪʃn] *n*: **artificial** ~
inseminación *f* artificial.
insensible [ɪn'sɛnsɪbl] *adj* inconsciente;
(*unconscious*) sin conocimiento.
insensitive [ɪn'sɛnsɪtɪv] *adj* insensible.
insensitivity [ɪnsɛnsɪ'tɪvɪtɪ] *n*
insensibilidad *f*.
inseparable [ɪn'sɛprəbl] *adj* inseparable;
they were ~ **friends** los unía una estrecha
amistad.
insert *vt* [ɪn'səːt] (*into sth*) introducir;
(*COMPUT*) insertar ♦ *n* ['ɪnsəːt] encarte *m*.
insertion [ɪn'səːʃən] *n* inserción *f*.
in-service [ɪn'səːvɪs] *adj* (*training, course*) en
el trabajo, a cargo de la empresa.
inshore [ɪn'ʃɔː*] *adj*: ~ **fishing** pesca *f*
costera ♦ *adv* (*fish*) a lo largo de la costa;
(*move*) hacia la orilla.
inside ['ɪn'saɪd] *n* interior *m*; (*lining*) forro;
(*of road: BRIT*) izquierdo; (: *US, Europe etc*)
derecho ♦ *adj* interior, interno;
(*information*) confidencial ♦ *adv* (*within*)
(por) dentro, adentro (*esp LAM*); (*with
movement*) hacia dentro; (*fam: in prison*)
en chirona ♦ *prep* dentro de; (*of time*): ~
10 minutes en menos de 10 minutos; ~**s**
npl (*col*) tripas *fpl*; ~ **out** *adv* (*turn*) al
revés; (*know*) a fondo.
inside forward *n* (*SPORT*) interior *m*.
inside information *n* información *f*
confidencial.
inside lane *n* (*AUT: in Britain*) carril *m*
izquierdo; (: *in US, Europe*) carril *m*
derecho.
inside leg measurement *n* medida de
pernera.
insider [ɪn'saɪdə*] *n* enterado/a.
insider dealing, insider trading *n* (*STOCK
EXCHANGE*) abuso de información
privilegiada.
inside story *n* historia íntima.
insidious [ɪn'sɪdɪəs] *adj* insidioso.

insight ['ɪnsaɪt] *n* perspicacia, percepción *f*;
to gain *or* **get an** ~ **into sth** comprender
algo mejor.
insignia [ɪn'sɪɡnɪə] *npl* insignias *fpl*.
insignificant [ɪnsɪɡ'nɪfɪknt] *adj*
insignificante.
insincere [ɪnsɪn'sɪə*] *adj* poco sincero.
insincerity [ɪnsɪn'sɛrɪtɪ] *n* falta de
sinceridad, doblez *f*.
insinuate [ɪn'sɪnjueɪt] *vt* insinuar.
insinuation [ɪnsɪnju'eɪʃən] *n* insinuación *f*.
insipid [ɪn'sɪpɪd] *adj* soso, insulso.
insist [ɪn'sɪst] *vi* insistir; **to** ~ **on doing**
empeñarse en hacer; **to** ~ **that** insistir en
que; (*claim*) exigir que.
insistence [ɪn'sɪstəns] *n* insistencia;
(*stubbornness*) empeño.
insistent [ɪn'sɪstənt] *adj* insistente;
empeñado.
insofar as [ɪnsəu'fɑː-] *conj* en la medida en
que, en tanto que.
insole ['ɪnsəul] *n* plantilla.
insolence ['ɪnsələns] *n* insolencia, descaro.
insolent ['ɪnsələnt] *adj* insolente,
descarado.
insoluble [ɪn'sɔljubl] *adj* insoluble.
insolvency [ɪn'sɔlvənsɪ] *n* insolvencia.
insolvent [ɪn'sɔlvənt] *adj* insolvente.
insomnia [ɪn'sɔmnɪə] *n* insomnio.
insomniac [ɪn'sɔmnɪæk] *n* insomne *m/f*.
inspect [ɪn'spɛkt] *vt* inspeccionar,
examinar; (*troops*) pasar revista a.
inspection [ɪn'spɛkʃən] *n* inspección *f*,
examen *m*.
inspector [ɪn'spɛktə*] *n* inspector(a) *m/f*;
(*BRIT: on buses, trains*) revisor(a) *m/f*.
inspiration [ɪnspə'reɪʃən] *n* inspiración *f*.
inspire [ɪn'spaɪə*] *vt* inspirar; **to** ~ **sb (to
do sth)** alentar a algn (a hacer algo).
inspired [ɪn'spaɪəd] *adj* (*writer, book etc*)
inspirado, genial, iluminado; **in an** ~
moment en un momento de inspiración.
inspiring [ɪn'spaɪərɪŋ] *adj* inspirador(a).
inst. *abbr* (*BRIT COMM:* = *instant, of the
present month*) cte.
instability [ɪnstə'bɪlɪtɪ] *n* inestabilidad *f*.
install [ɪn'stɔːl] *vt* instalar.
installation [ɪnstə'leɪʃən] *n* instalación *f*.
installment plan *n* (*US*) compra a plazos.
instalment, (*US*) **installment**
[ɪn'stɔːlmənt] *n* plazo; (*of story*) entrega; (*of
TV serial etc*) capítulo; **in** ~**s** (*pay, receive*)
a plazos; **to pay in** ~**s** pagar a plazos *or*
por abonos.
instance ['ɪnstəns] *n* ejemplo, caso; **for** ~
por ejemplo; **in the first** ~ en primer
lugar; **in that** ~ en ese caso.
instant ['ɪnstənt] *n* instante *m*, momento

♦ *adj* inmediato; (*coffee*) instantáneo.

instantaneous [ɪnstən'teɪnɪəs] *adj* instantáneo.

instantly ['ɪnstəntlɪ] *adv* en seguida, al instante.

instant replay *n* (*US TV*) repetición *f* de la jugada.

instead [ɪn'stɛd] *adv* en cambio; ~ **of** en lugar de, en vez de.

instep ['ɪnstɛp] *n* empeine *m*.

instigate ['ɪnstɪgeɪt] *vt* (*rebellion, strike, crime*) instigar; (*new ideas etc*) fomentar.

instigation [ɪnstɪ'geɪʃən] *n* instigación *f*; **at sb's** ~ a instigación de algn.

instil [ɪn'stɪl] *vt*: **to** ~ **into** inculcar a.

instinct ['ɪnstɪŋkt] *n* instinto.

instinctive [ɪn'stɪŋktɪv] *adj* instintivo.

instinctively [ɪn'stɪŋktɪvlɪ] *adv* por instinto.

institute ['ɪnstɪtjuːt] *n* instituto; (*professional body*) colegio ♦ *vt* (*begin*) iniciar, empezar; (*proceedings*) entablar.

institution [ɪnstɪ'tjuːʃən] *n* institución *f*; (*beginning*) iniciación *f*; (*MED: home*) asilo; (*asylum*) manicomio; (*custom*) costumbre *f* arraigada.

institutional [ɪnstɪ'tjuːʃənl] *adj* institucional.

instruct [ɪn'strʌkt] *vt*: **to** ~ **sb in sth** instruir a algn en *or* sobre algo; **to** ~ **sb to do sth** dar instrucciones a algn de *or* mandar a algn hacer algo.

instruction [ɪn'strʌkʃən] *n* (*teaching*) instrucción *f*; ~**s** *npl* órdenes *fpl*; ~**s (for use)** modo *sg* de empleo.

instruction book *n* manual *m*.

instructive [ɪn'strʌktɪv] *adj* instructivo.

instructor [ɪn'strʌktə*] *n* instructor(a) *m/f*.

instrument ['ɪnstrəmənt] *n* instrumento.

instrumental [ɪnstrə'mɛntl] *adj* (*MUS*) instrumental; **to be** ~ **in** ser el artífice de; **to be** ~ **in sth/in doing sth** ser responsable de algo/de hacer algo.

instrumentalist [ɪnstrə'mɛntəlɪst] *n* instrumentista *m/f*.

instrument panel *n* tablero (de instrumentos).

insubordinate [ɪnsə'bɔːdənɪt] *adj* insubordinado.

insubordination [ɪnsəbɔːdə'neɪʃən] *n* insubordinación *f*.

insufferable [ɪn'sʌfrəbl] *adj* insoportable.

insufficient [ɪnsə'fɪʃənt] *adj* insuficiente.

insufficiently [ɪnsə'fɪʃəntlɪ] *adv* insuficientemente.

insular ['ɪnsjulə*] *adj* insular; (*outlook*) estrecho de miras.

insularity [ɪnsju'lærɪtɪ] *n* insularidad *f*.

insulate ['ɪnsjuleɪt] *vt* aislar.

insulating tape ['ɪnsjuleɪtɪŋ-] *n* cinta aislante.

insulation [ɪnsju'leɪʃən] *n* aislamiento.

insulator ['ɪnsjuleɪtə*] *n* aislante *m*.

insulin ['ɪnsjulɪn] *n* insulina.

insult *n* ['ɪnsʌlt] insulto; (*offence*) ofensa ♦ *vt* [ɪn'sʌlt] insultar; ofender.

insulting [ɪn'sʌltɪŋ] *adj* insultante; ofensivo.

insuperable [ɪn'sjuːprəbl] *adj* insuperable.

insurance [ɪn'ʃuərəns] *n* seguro; **fire/life** ~ seguro de incendios/vida; **to take out** ~ **(against)** hacerse un seguro (contra).

insurance agent *n* agente *m/f* de seguros.

insurance broker *n* corredor(a) *m/f or* agente *m/f* de seguros.

insurance policy *n* póliza (de seguros).

insurance premium *n* prima de seguros.

insure [ɪn'ʃuə*] *vt* asegurar; **to** ~ **sb or sb's life** hacer un seguro de vida a algn; **to** ~ **(against)** asegurar (contra); **to be** ~**d for £5000** tener un seguro de 5000 libras.

insured [ɪn'ʃuəd] *n*: **the** ~ el/la asegurado/a.

insurer [ɪn'ʃuərə*] *n* asegurador(a).

insurgent [ɪn'sɔːdʒənt] *adj, n* insurgente *m/f*, insurrecto/a *m/f*.

insurmountable [ɪnsə'mauntəbl] *adj* insuperable.

insurrection [ɪnsə'rɛkʃən] *n* insurrección *f*.

intact [ɪn'tækt] *adj* íntegro; (*untouched*) intacto.

intake ['ɪnteɪk] *n* (*TECH*) entrada, toma; (: *pipe*) tubo de admisión; (*of food*) ingestión *f*; (*BRIT SCOL*): **an** ~ **of 200 a year** 200 matriculados al año.

intangible [ɪn'tændʒɪbl] *adj* intangible.

integer ['ɪntɪdʒə*] *n* (*número*) entero.

integral ['ɪntɪgrəl] *adj* (*whole*) íntegro; (*part*) integrante.

integrate ['ɪntɪgreɪt] *vt* integrar ♦ *vi* integrarse.

integrated circuit ['ɪntɪgreɪtɪd-] *n* (*COMPUT*) circuito integrado.

integration [ɪntɪ'greɪʃən] *n* integración *f*; **racial** ~ integración de razas.

integrity [ɪn'tɛgrɪtɪ] *n* honradez *f*, rectitud *f*; (*COMPUT*) integridad *f*.

intellect ['ɪntəlɛkt] *n* intelecto.

intellectual [ɪntə'lɛktjuəl] *adj, n* intelectual *m/f*.

intelligence [ɪn'tɛlɪdʒəns] *n* inteligencia.

intelligence quotient (IQ) *n* coeficiente *m* intelectual.

Intelligence Service *n* Servicio de Inteligencia.

intelligence test *n* prueba de inteligencia.

intelligent [ɪn'tɛlɪdʒənt] *adj* inteligente.

intelligently [ɪn'tɛlɪdʒəntlɪ] *adv*

inteligentemente.

intelligentsia [ɪntelɪ'dʒentsɪə] *n* intelectualidad *f*.

intelligible [ɪn'telɪdʒɪbl] *adj* inteligible, comprensible.

intemperate [ɪn'tempərət] *adj* inmoderado.

intend [ɪn'tend] *vt* (*gift etc*): **to ~ sth for** destinar algo a; **to ~ to do sth** tener intención de *or* pensar hacer algo.

intended [ɪn'tendɪd] *adj* (*effect*) deseado.

intense [ɪn'tens] *adj* intenso; **to be ~** (*person*) tomárselo todo muy en serio.

intensely [ɪn'tenslɪ] *adv* intensamente; (*very*) sumamente.

intensify [ɪn'tensɪfaɪ] *vt* intensificar; (*increase*) aumentar.

intensity [ɪn'tensɪtɪ] *n* (*gen*) intensidad *f*.

intensive [ɪn'tensɪv] *adj* intensivo.

intensive care *n*: **to be in ~** estar bajo cuidados intensivos; **~ unit** *n* unidad *f* de vigilancia intensiva.

intensively [ɪn'tensɪvlɪ] *adv* intensivamente.

intent [ɪn'tent] *n* propósito ♦ *adj* (*absorbed*) absorto; (*attentive*) atento; **to all ~s and purposes** a efectos prácticos; **to be ~ on doing sth** estar resuelto *or* decidido a hacer algo.

intention [ɪn'tenʃən] *n* intención *f*, propósito.

intentional [ɪn'tenʃənl] *adj* deliberado.

intentionally [ɪn'tenʃnəlɪ] *adv* a propósito.

intently [ɪn'tentlɪ] *adv* atentamente, fijamente.

inter [ɪn'tə:*] *vt* enterrar, sepultar.

inter- ['ɪntə*] *pref* inter-.

interact [ɪntər'ækt] *vi* (*substances*) influirse mutuamente; (*people*) relacionarse.

interaction [ɪntər'ækʃən] *n* interacción *f*, acción *f* recíproca.

interactive [ɪntər'æktɪv] *adj* (*also* COMPUT) interactivo.

intercede [ɪntə'si:d] *vi*: **to ~ (with)** interceder (con); **to ~ with sb/on behalf of sb** interceder con algn/en nombre de algn.

intercept [ɪntə'sept] *vt* interceptar; (*stop*) detener.

interception [ɪntə'sepʃən] *n* interceptación *f*; detención *f*.

interchange *n* ['ɪntətʃeɪndʒ] intercambio; (*on motorway*) intersección *f* ♦ *vt* [ɪntə'tʃeɪndʒ] intercambiar.

interchangeable [ɪntə'tʃeɪndʒəbl] *adj* intercambiable.

intercity [ɪntə'sɪtɪ] *adj*: **~ (train)** (tren *m*) intercity *m*.

intercom ['ɪntəkɔm] *n* interfono.

interconnect [ɪntəkə'nekt] *vi* (*rooms*) comunicar(se).

intercontinental ['ɪntəkɔntɪ'nentl] *adj* intercontinental.

intercourse ['ɪntəkɔ:s] *n* (*sexual* ~) relaciones *fpl* sexuales, contacto sexual; (*social*) trato.

interdependence [ɪntədɪ'pendəns] *n* interdependencia.

interdependent [ɪntədɪ'pendənt] *adj* interdependiente.

interest ['ɪntrɪst] *n* (*also* COMM) interés *m* ♦ *vt* interesar; **compound/simple ~** interés compuesto/simple; **business ~s** negocios *mpl*; **British ~s in the Middle East** los intereses británicos en el Medio Oriente.

interested ['ɪntrɪstɪd] *adj* interesado; **to be ~ in** interesarse por.

interest-free ['ɪntrɪst'fri:] *adj* libre de interés.

interesting ['ɪntrɪstɪŋ] *adj* interesante.

interest rate *n* tipo de interés.

interface ['ɪntəfeɪs] *n* (COMPUT) junción *f*, interface *m*.

interfere [ɪntə'fɪə*] *vi*: **to ~ in** (*quarrel, other people's business*) entrometerse en; **to ~ with** (*hinder*) estorbar; (*damage*) estropear; (*radio*) interferir con.

interference [ɪntə'fɪərəns] *n* (*gen*) intromisión *f*; (RADIO, TV) interferencia.

interfering [ɪntə'fɪərɪŋ] *adj* entrometido.

interim ['ɪntərɪm] *adj*: **~ dividend** dividendo parcial ♦ *n*: **in the ~** en el ínterin.

interior [ɪn'tɪərɪə*] *n* interior *m* ♦ *adj* interior.

interior decorator, interior designer *n* interiorista *m/f*, diseñador(a) *m/f* de interiores.

interjection [ɪntə'dʒekʃən] *n* interrupción *f*.

interlock [ɪntə'lɔk] *vi* entrelazarse; (*wheels etc*) endentarse.

interloper ['ɪntələupə*] *n* intruso/a.

interlude ['ɪntəlu:d] *n* intervalo; (*rest*) descanso; (THEAT) intermedio.

intermarriage [ɪntə'mærɪdʒ] *n* endogamia.

intermarry [ɪntə'mærɪ] *vi* casarse (entre parientes).

intermediary [ɪntə'mi:dɪərɪ] *n* intermediario/a.

intermediate [ɪntə'mi:dɪət] *adj* intermedio.

interminable [ɪn'tə:mɪnəbl] *adj* inacabable.

intermission [ɪntə'mɪʃən] *n* (THEAT) descanso.

intermittent [ɪntə'mɪtnt] *adj* intermitente.

intermittently [ɪntə'mɪtntlɪ] *adv* intermitentemente.

intern *vt* [ɪn'tə:n] internar; (*enclose*) encerrar ♦ *n* ['ɪntə:n] (US) médico/a *m/f* interno/a.

internal [ɪn'təːnl] *adj* interno, interior; ~
injuries heridas *fpl or* lesiones *fpl* internas.

internally [ɪn'təːnəlɪ] *adv* interiormente;
"not to be taken ~" "uso externo".

Internal Revenue Service (IRS) *n* (*US*)
Hacienda.

international [ɪntə'næʃənl] *adj*
internacional; ~ **(game)** partido
internacional; ~ **(player)** jugador(a) *m/f*
internacional.

**International Atomic Energy Agency
(IAEA)** *n* Organismo Internacional de
Energía Atómica.

**International Chamber of Commerce
(ICC)** *n* Cámara de Comercio
Internacional (CCI *f*).

International Court of Justice (ICJ) *n*
Corte *f* Internacional de Justicia (CIJ *f*).

international date line *n* línea de cambio
de fecha.

internationally [ɪntə'næʃnəlɪ] *adv*
internacionalmente.

International Monetary Fund (IMF) *n*
Fondo Monetario Internacional (FMI *m*).

internee [ɪntəː'niː] *n* interno/a, recluso/a.

Internet ['ɪntənɛt] *n*: **the** ~ (el *or* la) Internet.

Internet café *n* cibercafé *m*.

Internet Service Provider *n* proveedor *m*
de (acceso a) Internet.

Internet user *n* internauta *m/f*.

internment [ɪn'təːnmənt] *n* internamiento.

interplanetary [ɪntə'plænɪtərɪ] *adj*
interplanetario.

interplay ['ɪntəpleɪ] *n* interacción *f*.

Interpol ['ɪntəpɔl] *n* Interpol *f*.

interpret [ɪn'təːprɪt] *vt* interpretar;
(*translate*) traducir; (*understand*) entender
♦ *vi* hacer de intérprete.

interpretation [ɪntəːprɪ'teɪʃən] *n*
interpretación *f*; traducción *f*.

interpreter [ɪn'təːprɪtə*] *n* intérprete *m/f*.

interrelated [ɪntərɪ'leɪtɪd] *adj*
interrelacionado.

interrogate [ɪn'tɛrəʊgeɪt] *vt* interrogar.

interrogation [ɪntɛrəʊ'geɪʃən] *n*
interrogatorio.

interrogative [ɪntə'rɔgətɪv] *adj*
interrogativo.

interrupt [ɪntə'rʌpt] *vt, vi* interrumpir.

interruption [ɪntə'rʌpʃən] *n* interrupción *f*.

intersect [ɪntə'sɛkt] *vt* cruzar ♦ *vi* (*roads*)
cruzarse.

intersection [ɪntə'sɛkʃən] *n* intersección *f*;
(*of roads*) cruce *m*.

intersperse [ɪntə'spəːs] *vt*: **to** ~ **with**
salpicar de.

intertwine [ɪntə'twaɪn] *vt* entrelazar ♦ *vi*

entrelazarse.

interval ['ɪntəvl] *n* intervalo; (*BRIT: THEAT,
SPORT*) descanso; **at** ~**s** a ratos, de vez en
cuando; **sunny** ~**s** (*in weather*) claros *mpl*.

intervene [ɪntə'viːn] *vi* intervenir; (*take
part*) participar; (*occur*) sobrevenir.

intervening [ɪntə'viːnɪŋ] *adj* intermedio.

intervention [ɪntə'vɛnʃən] *n* intervención *f*.

interview ['ɪntəvjuː] *n* (*RADIO, TV etc*)
entrevista ♦ *vt* entrevistar a.

interviewee [ɪntəvjuː'iː] *n* entrevistado/a.

interviewer ['ɪntəvjuːə*] *n*
entrevistador(a) *m/f*.

intestate [ɪn'tɛsteɪt] *adj* intestado.

intestinal [ɪn'tɛstɪn] *adj* intestinal.

intestine [ɪn'tɛstɪn] *n*: **large/small** ~
intestino grueso/delgado.

intimacy ['ɪntɪməsɪ] *n* intimidad *f*;
(*relations*) relaciones *fpl* íntimas.

intimate *adj* ['ɪntɪmət] íntimo; (*friendship*)
estrecho; (*knowledge*) profundo ♦ *vt*
['ɪntɪmeɪt] (*announce*) dar a entender.

intimately ['ɪntɪmətlɪ] *adv* íntimamente.

intimidate [ɪn'tɪmɪdeɪt] *vt* intimidar.

intimidation [ɪntɪmɪ'deɪʃən] *n* intimidación
f.

into ['ɪntuː] *prep* (*gen*) en; (*towards*) a;
(*inside*) hacia el interior de; ~ **3 pieces/
French** en 3 pedazos/al francés; **to change
pounds** ~ **euros** cambiar libras por euros.

intolerable [ɪn'tɔlərəbl] *adj* intolerable,
insoportable.

intolerance [ɪn'tɔlərəns] *n* intolerancia.

intolerant [ɪn'tɔlərənt] *adj*: ~ **(of)**
intolerante (con).

intonation [ɪntəʊ'neɪʃən] *n* entonación *f*.

intoxicate [ɪn'tɔksɪkeɪt] *vt* embriagar.

intoxicated [ɪn'tɔksɪkeɪtɪd] *adj* embriagado.

intoxication [ɪntɔksɪ'keɪʃən] *n* embriaguez *f*.

intractable [ɪn'træktəbl] *adj* (*person*)
intratable; (*problem*) irresoluble; (*illness*)
incurable.

intranet ['ɪntrənɛt] *n* intranet *f*.

intransigence [ɪn'trænsɪdʒəns] *n*
intransigencia.

intransigent [ɪn'trænsɪdʒənt] *adj*
intransigente.

intransitive [ɪn'trænsɪtɪv] *adj* intransitivo.

intravenous [ɪntrə'viːnəs] *adj* intravenoso.

in-tray ['ɪntreɪ] *n* bandeja de entrada.

intrepid [ɪn'trepɪd] *adj* intrépido.

intricacy ['ɪntrɪkəsɪ] *n* complejidad *f*.

intricate ['ɪntrɪkət] *adj* intrincado; (*plot,
problem*) complejo.

intrigue [ɪn'triːg] *n* intriga ♦ *vt* fascinar ♦ *vi*
andar en intrigas.

intriguing [ɪn'triːgɪŋ] *adj* fascinante.

intrinsic [ɪn'trɪnsɪk] *adj* intrínseco.

introduce [ɪntrə'djuːs] *vt* introducir, meter; **to ~ sb (to sb)** presentar algn (a otro); **to ~ sb to** (*pastime, technique*) introducir a algn a; **may I ~ ...?** permítame presentarle a ....

introduction [ɪntrə'dʌkʃən] *n* introducción *f*; (*of person*) presentación *f*; **a letter of ~** una carta de recomendación.

introductory [ɪntrə'dʌktərɪ] *adj* introductorio; **an ~ offer** una oferta introductoria; **~ remarks** comentarios *mpl* preliminares.

introspection [ɪntrəu'spɛkʃən] *n* introspección *f*.

introspective [ɪntrəu'spɛktɪv] *adj* introspectivo.

introvert ['ɪntrəuvɜːt] *adj, n* introvertido/a *m/f*.

intrude [ɪn'truːd] *vi* (*person*) entrometerse; **to ~ on** estorbar.

intruder [ɪn'truːdə*] *n* intruso/a.

intrusion [ɪn'truːʒən] *n* invasión *f*.

intrusive [ɪn'truːsɪv] *adj* intruso.

intuition [ɪntjuː'ɪʃən] *n* intuición *f*.

intuitive [ɪn'tjuːɪtɪv] *adj* intuitivo.

intuitively [ɪn'tjuːɪtɪvlɪ] *adv* por intuición, intuitivamente.

inundate ['ɪnʌndeɪt] *vt*: **to ~ with** inundar de.

inure [ɪn'juə*] *vt*: **to ~ (to)** acostumbrar *or* habituar (a).

invade [ɪn'veɪd] *vt* invadir.

invader [ɪn'veɪdə*] *n* invasor(a) *m/f*.

invalid *n* ['ɪnvəlɪd] minusválido/a ♦ *adj* [ɪn'vælɪd] (*not valid*) inválido, nulo.

invalidate [ɪn'vælɪdeɪt] *vt* invalidar, anular.

invalid chair *n* silla de ruedas.

invaluable [ɪn'væljuəbl] *adj* inestimable.

invariable [ɪn'vɛərɪəbl] *adj* invariable.

invariably [ɪn'vɛərɪəblɪ] *adv* sin excepción, siempre; **she is ~ late** siempre llega tarde.

invasion [ɪn'veɪʒən] *n* invasión *f*.

invective [ɪn'vɛktɪv] *n* invectiva.

inveigle [ɪn'viːgl] *vt*: **to ~ sb into (doing) sth** embaucar *or* engatusar a algn para (que haga) algo.

invent [ɪn'vɛnt] *vt* inventar.

invention [ɪn'vɛnʃən] *n* invento; (*inventiveness*) inventiva; (*lie*) invención *f*.

inventive [ɪn'vɛntɪv] *adj* inventivo.

inventiveness [ɪn'vɛntɪvnɪs] *n* ingenio, inventiva.

inventor [ɪn'vɛntə*] *n* inventor(a) *m/f*.

inventory ['ɪnvəntrɪ] *n* inventario.

inventory control *n* control *m* de existencias.

inverse [ɪn'vɜːs] *adj, n* inverso; **in ~ proportion (to)** en proporción inversa (a).

inversely [ɪn'vɜːslɪ] *adv* a la inversa.

invert [ɪn'vɜːt] *vt* invertir.

invertebrate [ɪn'vɜːtɪbrət] *n* invertebrado.

inverted commas [ɪn'vɜːtɪd] *npl* (*BRIT*) comillas *fpl*.

invest [ɪn'vɛst] *vt* invertir; (*fig: time, effort*) dedicar ♦ *vi* invertir; **to ~ sb with sth** conferir algo a algn.

investigate [ɪn'vɛstɪgeɪt] *vt* investigar; (*study*) estudiar, examinar.

investigation [ɪnvɛstɪ'geɪʃən] *n* investigación *f*, pesquisa; examen *m*.

investigative journalism [ɪn'vɛstɪgətɪv-] *n* periodismo de investigación.

investigator [ɪn'vɛstɪgeɪtə*] *n* investigador(a) *m/f*; **private ~** investigador(a) *m/f* privado/a.

investiture [ɪn'vɛstɪtʃə*] *n* investidura.

investment [ɪn'vɛstmənt] *n* inversión *f*.

investment grant *n* subvención *f* para la inversión.

investment income *n* ingresos *mpl* procedentes de inversiones.

investment portfolio *n* cartera de inversiones.

investment trust *n* compañía inversionista, sociedad *f* de cartera.

investor [ɪn'vɛstə*] *n* inversor(a) *m/f*.

inveterate [ɪn'vɛtərət] *adj* empedernido.

invidious [ɪn'vɪdɪəs] *adj* odioso.

invigilate [ɪn'vɪdʒɪleɪt] *vt, vi* (*in exam*) vigilar.

invigilator [ɪn'vɪdʒɪleɪtə*] *n* celador(a) *m/f*.

invigorating [ɪn'vɪgəreɪtɪŋ] *adj* vigorizante.

invincible [ɪn'vɪnsɪbl] *adj* invencible.

inviolate [ɪn'vaɪələt] *adj* inviolado.

invisible [ɪn'vɪzɪbl] *adj* invisible.

invisible assets *npl* activo invisible.

invisible ink *n* tinta simpática.

invisible mending *n* puntada invisible.

invitation [ɪnvɪ'teɪʃən] *n* invitación *f*; **at sb's ~** a invitación de algn; **by ~ only** solamente por invitación.

invite [ɪn'vaɪt] *vt* invitar; (*opinions etc*) solicitar, pedir; (*trouble*) buscarse; **to ~ sb (to do)** invitar a algn (a hacer); **to ~ sb to dinner** invitar a algn a cenar.
▶**invite out** *vt* invitar a salir.
▶**invite over** *vt* invitar a casa.

inviting [ɪn'vaɪtɪŋ] *adj* atractivo; (*look*) provocativo; (*food*) apetitoso.

invoice ['ɪnvɔɪs] *n* factura ♦ *vt* facturar; **to ~ sb for goods** facturar a algn las mercancías.

invoicing ['ɪnvɔɪsɪŋ] *n* facturación *f*.

invoke [ɪn'vəuk] *vt* invocar; (*aid*) pedir; (*law*) recurrir a.

involuntary [ɪn'vɔləntrɪ] *adj* involuntario.
involve [ɪn'vɔlv] *vt* (*entail*) suponer, implicar; **to ~ sb (in)** involucrar a algn (en).
involved [ɪn'vɔlvd] *adj* complicado; **to be/ become ~ in sth** estar involucrado/ involucrarse en algo.
involvement [ɪn'vɔlvmənt] *n* (*gen*) enredo; (*obligation*) compromiso; (*difficulty*) apuro.
invulnerable [ɪn'vʌlnərəbl] *adj* invulnerable.
inward ['ɪnwəd] *adj* (*movement*) interior, interno; (*thought, feeling*) íntimo.
inwardly ['ɪnwədlɪ] *adv* (*feel, think etc*) para sí, para dentro.
inward(s) ['ɪnwəd(z)] *adv* hacia dentro.
I/O *abbr* (*COMPUT = input/output*) E/S; **~ error** error *m* de E/S.
IOC *n abbr* (*= International Olympic Committee*) COI *m*.
iodine ['aɪəudiːn] *n* yodo.
ion ['aɪən] *n* ion *m*.
Ionian Sea [aɪ'əunɪən-] *n*: **the ~** el Mar Jónico.
ioniser ['aɪənaɪzə*] *n* ionizador *m*.
iota [aɪ'əutə] *n* (*fig*) jota, ápice *m*.
IOU *n abbr* (*= I owe you*) pagaré *m*.
IOW *abbr* (*BRIT*) = *Isle of Wight*.
IPA *n abbr* (*= International Phonetic Alphabet*) AFI *m*.
IQ *n abbr* (*= intelligence quotient*) C.I. *m*.
IRA *n abbr* (*= Irish Republican Army*) IRA *m*; (*US*) = *individual retirement account*.
Iran [ɪ'rɑːn] *n* Irán *m*.
Iranian [ɪ'reɪnɪən] *adj* iraní ♦ *n* iraní *m/f*; (*LING*) iraní *m*.
Iraq [ɪ'rɑːk] *n* Irak *m*.
Iraqi [ɪ'rɑːkɪ] *adj*, *n* irakí *m/f*.
irascible [ɪ'ræsɪbl] *adj* irascible.
irate [aɪ'reɪt] *adj* enojado, airado.
Ireland ['aɪələnd] *n* Irlanda; **Republic of ~** República de Irlanda.
iris, ~es ['aɪrɪs, -ɪz] *n* (*ANAT*) iris *m*; (*BOT*) lirio.
Irish ['aɪrɪʃ] *adj* irlandés/esa ♦ *n* (*LING*) irlandés *m*; **the ~** *npl* los irlandeses.
Irishman ['aɪrɪʃmən] *n* irlandés *m*.
Irish Sea *n*: **the ~** el Mar de Irlanda.
Irishwoman ['aɪrɪʃwumən] *n* irlandesa.
irk [əːk] *vt* fastidiar.
irksome ['əːksəm] *adj* fastidioso.
IRN *n abbr* (*= Independent Radio News*) *servicio de noticias en las cadenas de radio privadas*.
IRO *n abbr* (*US*) = *International Refugee Organization*.
iron ['aɪən] *n* hierro; (*for clothes*) plancha ♦ *adj* de hierro ♦ *vt* (*clothes*) planchar; **~s** *npl* (*chains*) grilletes *mpl*.

▶**iron out** *vt* (*crease*) quitar; (*fig*) allanar, resolver.
Iron Curtain *n*: **the ~** el Telón de Acero.
iron foundry *n* fundición *f*, fundidora.
ironic(al) [aɪ'rɔnɪk(l)] *adj* irónico.
ironically [aɪ'rɔnɪklɪ] *adv* irónicamente.
ironing ['aɪənɪŋ] *n* (*act*) planchado; (*ironed clothes*) ropa planchada; (*to be ironed*) ropa por planchar.
ironing board *n* tabla de planchar.
iron lung *n* (*MED*) pulmón *m* de acero.
ironmonger ['aɪənmʌŋgə*] *n* (*BRIT*) ferretero/a; **~'s (shop)** ferretería.
iron ore *n* mineral *m* de hierro.
ironworks ['aɪənwəːks] *n* fundición *f*.
irony ['aɪrənɪ] *n* ironía; **the ~ of it is that ...** lo irónico del caso es que ....
irrational [ɪ'ræʃənl] *adj* irracional.
irreconcilable [ɪrekən'saɪləbl] *adj* inconciliable; (*enemies*) irreconciliable.
irredeemable [ɪrɪ'diːməbl] *adj* irredimible.
irrefutable [ɪrɪ'fjuːtəbl] *adj* irrefutable.
irregular [ɪ'regjulə*] *adj* irregular; (*surface*) desigual.
irregularity [ɪregju'lærɪtɪ] *n* irregularidad *f*; desigualdad *f*.
irrelevance [ɪ'reləvəns] *n* irrelevancia.
irrelevant [ɪ'reləvənt] *adj* irrelevante; **to be ~** estar fuera de lugar, no venir al caso.
irreligious [ɪrɪ'lɪdʒəs] *adj* irreligioso.
irreparable [ɪ'reprəbl] *adj* irreparable.
irreplaceable [ɪrɪ'pleɪsəbl] *adj* irremplazable.
irrepressible [ɪrɪ'presəbl] *adj* incontenible.
irreproachable [ɪrɪ'prəutʃəbl] *adj* irreprochable.
irresistible [ɪrɪ'zɪstɪbl] *adj* irresistible.
irresolute [ɪ'rezəluːt] *adj* indeciso.
irrespective [ɪrɪ'spektɪv]: **~ of** *prep* sin tener en cuenta, no importa.
irresponsibility [ɪrɪspɔnsɪ'bɪlɪtɪ] *n* irresponsabilidad *f*.
irresponsible [ɪrɪ'spɔnsɪbl] *adj* (*act*) irresponsable; (*person*) poco serio.
irretrievable [ɪrɪ'triːvəbl] *adj* (*object*) irrecuperable; (*loss, damage*) irremediable, irreparable.
irretrievably [ɪrɪ'triːvəblɪ] *adv* irremisiblemente.
irreverence [ɪ'revərns] *n* irreverencia.
irreverent [ɪ'revərnt] *adj* irreverente, irrespetuoso.
irrevocable [ɪ'revəkəbl] *adj* irrevocable.
irrigate ['ɪrɪgeɪt] *vt* regar.
irrigation [ɪrɪ'geɪʃən] *n* riego.
irritability [ɪrɪtə'bɪlɪtɪ] *n* irritabilidad *f*.
irritable ['ɪrɪtəbl] *adj* (*person: temperament*) irritable; (*: mood*) de mal humor.

irritant ['ɪrɪtənt] *n* agente *m* irritante.
irritate ['ɪrɪteɪt] *vt* fastidiar; (*MED*) picar.
irritating ['ɪrɪteɪtɪŋ] *adj* fastidioso.
irritation [ɪrɪ'teɪʃən] *n* fastidio; picazón *f*.
IRS *n abbr* (*US*) *see* **Internal Revenue Service.**
is [ɪz] *vb see* **be.**
ISA ['aɪsə] *n abbr* (*BRIT* = *Individual Savings Account*) plan de ahorro personal para pequeños inversores con fiscalidad cero.
ISBN *n abbr* (= *International Standard Book Number*) ISBN *m*.
ISDN *n abbr* (= *Integrated Services Digital Network*) RDSI *f*.
Islam ['ɪzlɑːm] *n* Islam *m*.
island ['aɪlənd] *n* isla; (*also*: **traffic** ~) isleta.
islander ['aɪləndə*] *n* isleño/a.
isle [aɪl] *n* isla.
isn't ['ɪznt] = **is not.**
isobar ['aɪsəubɑː*] *n* isobara.
isolate ['aɪsəleɪt] *vt* aislar.
isolated ['aɪsəleɪtɪd] *adj* aislado.
isolation [aɪsə'leɪʃən] *n* aislamiento.
isolation ward *n* pabellón *m* de aislamiento.
isotope ['aɪsəutəup] *n* isótopo.
ISP *n abbr* = *Internet service provider.*
Israel ['ɪzreɪl] *n* Israel *m*.
Israeli [ɪz'reɪlɪ] *adj, n* israelí *m/f*.
issue ['ɪsjuː] *n* cuestión *f*, asunto; (*outcome*) resultado; (*of banknotes etc*) emisión *f*, (*of newspaper etc*) número; (*offspring*) sucesión *f*, descendencia ♦ *vt* (*rations, equipment*) distribuir, repartir; (*orders*) dar; (*certificate, passport*) expedir; (*decree*) promulgar; (*magazine*) publicar; (*cheques*) extender; (*banknotes, stamps*) emitir ♦ *vi*: **to** ~ **(from)** derivar (de), brotar (de); **at** ~ en cuestión; **to take** ~ **with sb (over)** disentir con algn (en); **to avoid the** ~ andarse con rodeos; **to make an** ~ **of sth** dar a algo más importancia de lo necesario; **to** ~ **sth to sb,** ~ **sb with sth** entregar algo a algn.
Istanbul [ɪstæn'buːl] *n* Estambul *m*.
isthmus ['ɪsməs] *n* istmo.
IT *n abbr* = **information technology.**

———————— *KEYWORD*

it [ɪt] *pron* **1** (*specific: subject: not generally translated*) él/ella; (: *direct object*) lo, la; (: *indirect object*) le; (*after prep*) él/ella; (*abstract concept*) ello; ~'s **on the table** está en la mesa; **I can't find** ~ no lo (*or* la) encuentro; **give** ~ **to me** dámelo (*or* dámela); **I spoke to him about** ~ le hablé del asunto; **what did you learn from** ~**?** ¿qué aprendiste de él (*or* ella)?; **did you go to** ~**?** (*party, concert*) ¿fuiste?

2 (*impersonal*): ~'s **raining** llueve, está lloviendo; ~'s **6 o'clock/the 10th of August** son las 6/es el 10 de agosto; **how far is** ~**?** — ~'s **10 miles/2 hours on the train** ¿a qué distancia está? — a 10 millas/2 horas en tren; **who is** ~**?** — ~'s **me** ¿quién es? — soy yo.

Italian [ɪ'tæljən] *adj* italiano ♦ *n* italiano/a; (*LING*) italiano.
italic [ɪ'tælɪk] *adj* cursivo; ~s *npl* cursiva *sg*.
Italy ['ɪtəlɪ] *n* Italia.
itch [ɪtʃ] *n* picazón *f*; (*fig*) prurito ♦ *vi* (*person*) sentir *or* tener comezón; (*part of body*) picar; **to be** ~**ing to do sth** rabiar por *or* morirse de ganas de hacer algo.
itching ['ɪtʃɪŋ] *n* picazón *f*, comezón *f*.
itchy ['ɪtʃɪ] *adj*: **to be** ~ picar.
it'd ['ɪtd] = **it would; it had.**
item ['aɪtəm] *n* artículo; (*on agenda*) asunto (a tratar); (*in programme*) número; (*also*: **news** ~) noticia; ~s **of clothing** prendas *fpl* de vestir.
itemize ['aɪtəmaɪz] *vt* detallar.
itemized bill ['aɪtəmaɪzd-] *n* recibo detallado.
itinerant [ɪ'tɪnərənt] *adj* ambulante.
itinerary [aɪ'tɪnərərɪ] *n* itinerario.
it'll ['ɪtl] = **it will, it shall.**
ITN *n abbr see* **ITV.**
its [ɪts] *adj* su.
it's [ɪts] = **it is; it has.**
itself [ɪt'sɛlf] *pron* (*reflexive*) sí mismo/a; (*emphatic*) él mismo/ella misma.
ITV *n abbr* (*BRIT*: = *Independent Television*) *ver recuadro.*

ITV

En el Reino Unido la **ITV** (*"Independent Television"*) *es una cadena de emisoras comerciales regionales con licencia exclusiva para emitir en su región. Suelen producir sus propios programas, se financian con publicidad y están bajo el control del organismo oficial independiente "Independent Broadcasting Authority" ("IBA"). El servicio de noticias nacionales e internacionales, "ITN" ("Independent Television News"), funciona como una compañía productora para toda la cadena.*

IUD *n abbr* (= *intra-uterine device*) DIU *m*.
I've [aɪv] = **I have.**
ivory ['aɪvərɪ] *n* marfil *m*.
Ivory Coast *n*: **the** ~ la Costa de Marfil.
ivory tower *n* (*fig*) torre *f* de marfil.
ivy ['aɪvɪ] *n* hiedra.

Ivy League n (*US*) ver recuadro.

> **IVY LEAGUE**
>
> Las ocho universidades más prestigiosas del nordeste de los Estados Unidos reciben el nombre colectivo de **Ivy League**, por sus muros cubiertos de hiedra. Son: *Brown, Columbia, Cornell, Dartmouth College, Harvard, Princeton*, la universidad de *Pennsylvania* y *Yale*. También se llaman así las competiciones deportivas que celebran entre ellas.

J j

J, j [dʒeɪ] n (*letter*) J, j *f*; **J for Jack**, (*US*) **J for Jig** J de José.
JA n abbr = **judge advocate**.
J/A abbr = **joint account**.
jab [dʒæb] vt (*elbow*) dar un codazo a; (*punch*) dar un golpe rápido a ♦ vi: **to ~ at** intentar golpear a; **to ~ sth into sth** clavar algo en algo ♦ n codazo; golpe m (rápido); (*MED col*) pinchazo.
jabber ['dʒæbə*] vt, vi farfullar.
jack [dʒæk] n (*AUT*) gato; (*BOWLS*) boliche m; (*CARDS*) sota.
►**jack in** vt (*col*) dejar.
►**jack up** vt (*AUT*) levantar con el gato.
jackal ['dʒækl] n (*ZOOL*) chacal m.
jackass ['dʒækæs] n (*also fig*) asno, burro.
jackdaw ['dʒækdɔː] n grajo/a, chova.
jacket ['dʒækɪt] n chaqueta, americana, saco (*LAM*); (*of boiler etc*) camisa; (*of book*) sobrecubierta.
jacket potato n patata asada (con piel).
jack-in-the-box ['dʒækɪnðəbɔks] n caja sorpresa, caja de resorte.
jack-knife ['dʒæknaɪf] vi colear.
jack-of-all-trades ['dʒækəv'ɔːltreɪdz] n aprendiz m de todo.
jack plug n (*ELEC*) enchufe m de clavija.
jackpot ['dʒækpɔt] n premio gordo.
Jacuzzi ® [dʒə'kuːzɪ] n jacuzzi ® m.
jade [dʒeɪd] n (*stone*) jade m.
jaded ['dʒeɪdɪd] adj (*tired*) cansado; (*fed up*) hastiado.
jagged ['dʒægɪd] adj dentado.
jaguar ['dʒægjuə*] n jaguar m.

jail [dʒeɪl] n cárcel f ♦ vt encarcelar.
jailbird ['dʒeɪlbɜːd] n preso/a reincidente.
jailbreak ['dʒeɪlbreɪk] n fuga or evasión f (de la cárcel).
jailer ['dʒeɪlə*] n carcelero/a.
jam [dʒæm] n mermelada; (*also*: **traffic ~**) atasco, embotellamiento; (*difficulty*) apuro ♦ vt (*passage etc*) obstruir; (*mechanism, drawer etc*) atascar; (*RADIO*) interferir ♦ vi atascarse, trabarse; **to get sb out of a ~** sacar a algn del paso or de un apuro; **to ~ sth into sth** meter algo a la fuerza en algo; **the telephone lines are ~med** las líneas están saturadas.
Jamaica [dʒə'meɪkə] n Jamaica.
Jamaican [dʒə'meɪkən] adj, n jamaicano/a m/f.
jamb [dʒæm] n jamba.
jamboree [dʒæmbə'riː] n congreso de niños exploradores.
jam-packed [dʒæm'pækt] adj: **~ (with)** atestado (de).
jam session n concierto improvisado de jazz/rock etc.
Jan. abbr (= *January*) ene.
jangle ['dʒæŋgl] vi sonar (de manera) discordante.
janitor ['dʒænɪtə*] n (*caretaker*) portero, conserje m.
January ['dʒænjuərɪ] n enero.
Japan [dʒə'pæn] n (el) Japón.
Japanese [dʒæpə'niːz] adj japonés/esa ♦ n (pl inv) japonés/esa m/f; (*LING*) japonés m.
jar [dʒɑː*] n (*glass: large*) jarra; (: *small*) tarro ♦ vi (*sound*) chirriar; (*colours*) desentonar.
jargon ['dʒɑːgən] n jerga.
jarring ['dʒɑːrɪŋ] adj (*sound*) discordante, desafinado; (*colour*) chocante.
Jas. abbr = *James*.
jasmin(e) ['dʒæzmɪn] n jazmín m.
jaundice ['dʒɔːndɪs] n ictericia.
jaundiced ['dʒɔːndɪst] adj (*fig: embittered*) amargado; (: *disillusioned*) desilusionado.
jaunt [dʒɔːnt] n excursión f.
jaunty ['dʒɔːntɪ] adj alegre; (*relaxed*) desenvuelto.
javelin ['dʒævlɪn] n jabalina.
jaw [dʒɔː] n mandíbula; **~s** npl (*TECH: of vice etc*) mordaza sg.
jawbone ['dʒɔːbəun] n mandíbula, quijada.
jay [dʒeɪ] n (*ZOOL*) arrendajo.
jaywalker ['dʒeɪwɔːkə*] n peatón/ona m/f imprudente.
jazz [dʒæz] n jazz m.
►**jazz up** vt (*liven up*) animar.
jazz band n orquesta de jazz.
jazzy ['dʒæzɪ] adj de colores llamativos.

JCB ® *n abbr* excavadora.
JCS *n abbr* (*US*) = *Joint Chiefs of Staff.*
JD *n abbr* (*US:* = *Doctor of Laws*) título
universitario; (: = *Justice Department*)
Ministerio de Justicia.
jealous ['dʒɛləs] *adj* (*gen*) celoso; (*envious*)
envidioso; **to be** ~ tener celos.
jealously ['dʒɛləslɪ] *adv* (*enviously*)
envidiosamente; (*watchfully*)
celosamente.
jealousy ['dʒɛləsɪ] *n* celos *mpl*; envidia.
jeans [dʒiːnz] *npl* (pantalones *mpl*) vaqueros
mpl or tejanos *mpl*, bluejean *m inv* (*LAM*).
Jeep ® [dʒiːp] *n* jeep *m*.
jeer [dʒɪə*] *vi:* **to** ~ **(at)** (*boo*) abuchear;
(*mock*) mofarse (de).
jeering ['dʒɪərɪŋ] *adj* (*crowd*) insolente,
ofensivo ♦ *n* protestas *fpl*; (*mockery*)
burlas *fpl.*
jelly ['dʒɛlɪ] *n* gelatina, jalea.
jellyfish ['dʒɛlɪfɪʃ] *n* medusa.
jemmy ['dʒɛmɪ] *n* palanqueta.
jeopardize ['dʒɛpədaɪz] *vt* arriesgar, poner
en peligro.
jeopardy ['dʒɛpədɪ] *n:* **to be in** ~ estar en
peligro.
jerk [dʒəːk] *n* (*jolt*) sacudida; (*wrench*) tirón
m; (*US col*) imbécil *m/f*, pendejo/a (*LAM*) ♦
vt dar una sacudida a; tirar bruscamente
de ♦ *vi* (*vehicle*) dar una sacudida.
jerkin ['dʒəːkɪn] *n* chaleco.
jerky ['dʒəːkɪ] *adj* espasmódico.
jerry-built ['dʒɛrɪbɪlt] *adj* mal construido.
jerry can ['dʒɛrɪ-] *n* bidón *m*.
Jersey ['dʒəːzɪ] *n* Jersey *m.*
jersey ['dʒəːzɪ] *n* jersey *m*; (*fabric*) tejido de
punto.
Jerusalem [dʒə'ruːsləm] *n* Jerusalén *m.*
jest [dʒɛst] *n* broma.
jester ['dʒɛstə*] *n* bufón *m.*
Jesus ['dʒiːzəs] *n* Jesús *m*; ~ **Christ**
Jesucristo.
jet [dʒɛt] *n* (*of gas, liquid*) chorro; (*AVIAT*)
avión *m* a reacción.
jet-black ['dʒɛt'blæk] *adj* negro como el
azabache.
jet engine *n* motor *m* a reacción.
jet lag *n* desorientación *f* por desfase
horario.
jetsam ['dʒɛtsəm] *n* echazón *f.*
jet-setter ['dʒɛtsɛtə*] *n* personaje *m* de la
jet.
jettison ['dʒɛtɪsn] *vt* desechar.
jetty ['dʒɛtɪ] *n* muelle *m*, embarcadero.
Jew [dʒuː] *n* judío.
jewel ['dʒuːəl] *n* joya; (*in watch*) rubí *m.*
jeweller, (*US*) **jeweler** ['dʒuːələ*] *n*
joyero/a; ~**'s (shop)** joyería.

jewellery, (*US*) **jewelry** ['dʒuːəlrɪ] *n* joyas
fpl, alhajas *fpl.*
Jewess ['dʒuːɪs] *n* judía.
Jewish ['dʒuːɪʃ] *adj* judío.
JFK *n abbr* (*US*) = *John Fitzgerald Kennedy
International Airport.*
jib [dʒɪb] *vi* (*horse*) plantarse; **to** ~ **at doing
sth** resistirse a hacer algo.
jibe [dʒaɪb] *n* mofa.
jiffy ['dʒɪfɪ] *n* (*col*): **in a** ~ en un santiamén.
jig [dʒɪg] *n* (*dance, tune*) giga.
jigsaw ['dʒɪgsɔː] *n* (*also:* ~ **puzzle**)
rompecabezas *m inv*; (*tool*) sierra de
vaivén.
jilt [dʒɪlt] *vt* dejar plantado a.
jingle ['dʒɪŋgl] *n* (*advert*) musiquilla ♦ *vi*
tintinear.
jingoism ['dʒɪŋgəʊɪzəm] *n* patriotería,
jingoísmo.
jinx [dʒɪŋks] *n:* **there's a** ~ **on it** está gafado.
jitters ['dʒɪtəz] *npl* (*col*): **to get the** ~
ponerse nervioso.
jittery ['dʒɪtərɪ] *adj* (*col*) agitado.
jiujitsu [dʒuː'dʒɪtsuː] *n* ju-jitsu *m.*
job [dʒɔb] *n* trabajo; (*task*) tarea; (*duty*)
deber *m*; (*post*) empleo; (*fam: difficulty*)
dificultad *f*; **it's a good** ~ **that...** menos
mal que...; **just the** ~**!** ¡justo lo que
necesito!; **a part-time/full-time** ~ un
trabajo a tiempo parcial/tiempo
completo; **that's not my** ~ eso no me
incumbe *or* toca a mí; **he's only doing his**
~ está cumpliendo nada más.
job centre *n* (*BRIT*) oficina de empleo.
job creation scheme *n* plan *m* de
creación de puestos de trabajo.
job description *n* descripción *f* del puesto
de trabajo.
jobless ['dʒɔblɪs] *adj* sin trabajo ♦ *n:* **the** ~
los parados.
job lot *n* lote *m* de mercancías, saldo.
job satisfaction *n* satisfacción *f* en el
trabajo.
job security *n* garantía de trabajo.
job specification *n* especificación *f* del
trabajo, profesiograma *m.*
Jock *n* (*col: Scotsman*) escocés *m.*
jockey ['dʒɔkɪ] *n* jockey *m/f* ♦ *vi:* **to** ~ **for
position** maniobrar para sacar delantera.
jockey box *n* (*US AUT*) guantera.
jockstrap ['dʒɔkstræp] *n* suspensorio.
jocular ['dʒɔkjulə*] *adj* (*humorous*)
gracioso; (*merry*) alegre.
jodhpurs ['dʒɔdpəz] *npl* pantalón *msg* de
montar.
jog [dʒɔg] *vt* empujar (ligeramente) ♦ *vi*
(*run*) hacer footing; **to** ~ **along** (*fig*) ir
tirando; **to** ~ **sb's memory** refrescar la

memoria a algn.
jogger ['dʒɔgə*] *n* corredor(a) *m/f*.
jogging ['dʒɔgɪŋ] *n* footing *m*.
john [dʒɔn] *n* (*US col*) wáter *m*.
join [dʒɔɪn] *vt* (*things*) unir, juntar; (*become member of: club*) hacerse socio de; (*POL: party*) afiliarse a; (*meet: people*) reunirse con; (*fig*) unirse a ♦ *vi* (*roads*) empalmar; (*rivers*) confluir ♦ *n* juntura; **will you ~ us for dinner?** ¿quieres cenar con nosotros?; **I'll ~ you later** me reuniré contigo luego; **to ~ forces (with)** aliarse (con).
▶**join in** *vi* tomar parte, participar ♦ *vt fus* tomar parte *or* participar en.
▶**join up** *vi* unirse; (*MIL*) alistarse.
joiner ['dʒɔɪnə*] *n* carpintero/a.
joinery ['dʒɔɪnərɪ] *n* carpintería.
joint [dʒɔɪnt] *n* (*TECH*) juntura, unión *f*; (*ANAT*) articulación *f*; (*BRIT CULIN*) pieza de carne (para asar); (*col: place*) garito ♦ *adj* (*common*) común; (*combined*) conjunto; (*responsibility*) compartido; (*committee*) mixto.
joint account (J/A) *n* (*with bank etc*) cuenta común.
jointly ['dʒɔɪntlɪ] *adv* (*gen*) en común; (*together*) conjuntamente.
joint owners *npl* copropietarios *mpl*.
joint ownership *n* copropiedad *f*, propiedad *f* común.
joint-stock bank ['dʒɔɪntstɔk-] *n* banco por acciones.
joint-stock company ['dʒɔɪntstɔk-] *n* sociedad *f* anónima.
joint venture *n* empresa conjunta.
joist [dʒɔɪst] *n* viga.
joke [dʒəuk] *n* chiste *m*; (*also:* **practical ~**) broma ♦ *vi* bromear; **to play a ~ on** gastar una broma a.
joker ['dʒəukə*] *n* chistoso/a, bromista *m/f*; (*CARDS*) comodín *m*.
joking ['dʒəukɪŋ] *n* bromas *fpl*.
jokingly ['dʒəukɪŋlɪ] *adv* en broma.
jollity ['dʒɔlɪtɪ] *n* alegría.
jolly ['dʒɔlɪ] *adj* (*merry*) alegre; (*enjoyable*) divertido ♦ *adv* (*col*) muy, la mar de ♦ *vt*: **to ~ sb along** animar *or* darle ánimos a algn; **~ good!** ¡estupendo!
jolt [dʒəult] *n* (*shake*) sacudida; (*blow*) golpe *m*; (*shock*) susto ♦ *vt* sacudir.
Jordan ['dʒɔːdən] *n* (*country*) Jordania; (*river*) Jordán *m*.
joss stick [dʒɔs-] *n* barrita de incienso, pebete *m*.
jostle ['dʒɔsl] *vt* dar empujones *or* empellones a.
jot [dʒɔt] *n*: **not one ~** ni pizca, ni un ápice.
▶**jot down** *vt* apuntar.

jotter ['dʒɔtə*] *n* (*BRIT*) bloc *m*.
journal ['dʒɜːnl] *n* (*paper*) periódico; (*magazine*) revista; (*diary*) diario.
journalese [dʒɜːnə'liːz] *n* (*pej*) lenguaje *m* periodístico.
journalism ['dʒɜːnəlɪzəm] *n* periodismo.
journalist ['dʒɜːnəlɪst] *n* periodista *m/f*.
journey ['dʒɜːnɪ] *n* viaje *m*; (*distance covered*) trayecto ♦ *vi* viajar; **return ~** viaje de regreso; **a 5-hour ~** un viaje de 5 horas.
jovial ['dʒəuvɪəl] *adj* risueño, alegre.
jowl [dʒaul] *n* quijada.
joy [dʒɔɪ] *n* alegría.
joyful ['dʒɔɪful] *adj* alegre.
joyfully ['dʒɔɪfulɪ] *adv* alegremente.
joyous ['dʒɔɪəs] *adj* alegre.
joyride ['dʒɔɪraɪd] *n*: **to go for a ~** darse una vuelta en un coche robado.
joyrider ['dʒɔɪraɪdə*] *n* persona que se da una vuelta en un coche robado.
joystick ['dʒɔɪstɪk] *n* (*AVIAT*) palanca de mando; (*COMPUT*) palanca de control.
JP *n abbr see* **Justice of the Peace.**
Jr. *abbr* = **junior.**
JTPA *n abbr* (*US:* = *Job Training Partnership Act*) *programa gubernamental de formación profesional.*
jubilant ['dʒuːbɪlnt] *adj* jubiloso.
jubilation [dʒuːbɪ'leɪʃən] *n* júbilo.
jubilee ['dʒuːbɪliː] *n* aniversario; **silver ~** vigésimo quinto aniversario.
judge [dʒʌdʒ] *n* juez *m/f* ♦ *vt* juzgar; (*competition*) actuar de *or* ser juez en; (*estimate*) considerar; (: *weight, size etc*) calcular ♦ *vi*: **judging** *or* **to ~ by his expression** a juzgar por su expresión; **as far as I can ~** por lo que puedo entender, a mi entender; **I ~d it necessary to inform him** consideré necesario informarle.
judge advocate *n* (*MIL*) auditor *m* de guerra.
judg(e)ment ['dʒʌdʒmənt] *n* juicio; (*punishment*) sentencia, fallo; **to pass ~ (on)** (*LAW*) pronunciar *or* dictar sentencia (sobre); (*fig*) emitir un juicio crítico *or* dictaminar (sobre); **in my ~** a mi juicio.
judicial [dʒuː'dɪʃl] *adj* judicial.
judiciary [dʒuː'dɪʃɪərɪ] *n* poder *m* judicial, magistratura.
judicious [dʒuː'dɪʃəs] *adj* juicioso.
judo ['dʒuːdəu] *n* judo.
jug [dʒʌg] *n* jarro.
jugged hare [dʒʌgd-] *n* (*BRIT*) estofado de liebre.
juggernaut ['dʒʌgənɔːt] *n* (*BRIT: huge truck*) camión *m* de carga pesada.
juggle ['dʒʌgl] *vi* hacer juegos malabares.

juggler ['dʒʌglə*] n malabarista m/f.
Jugoslav ['juːgəuslɑːv] etc = **Yugoslav** etc.
jugular ['dʒʌgjulə*] adj: ~ **vein** (vena)
   yugular f.
juice [dʒuːs] n jugo, zumo (SP); (of meat)
   jugo; (col: petrol): **we've run out of** ~ se
   nos acabó la gasolina.
juicy ['dʒuːsɪ] adj jugoso.
jujitsu [dʒuː'dʒɪtsuː] n = **juijitsu**.
jukebox ['dʒuːkbɒks] n máquina de discos.
Jul. abbr (= July) jul.
July [dʒuː'laɪ] n julio; **the first of** ~ el uno or
   primero de julio; **during** ~ en el mes de
   julio; **in** ~ **of next year** en julio del año
   que viene.
jumble ['dʒʌmbl] n revoltijo ♦ vt (also: ~
   together, ~ **up**: mix up) revolver;
   (: disarrange) mezclar.
jumble sale n (BRIT) mercadillo; ver
   recuadro.

JUMBLE SALE

En cada **jumble sale** pueden comprarse
todo tipo de objetos baratos de segunda
mano, especialmente ropa, juguetes, libros,
vajillas y muebles. Suelen organizarse en
los locales de un colegio, iglesia,
ayuntamiento o similar, con fines
benéficos, bien en ayuda de una
organización benéfica conocida o para
solucionar problemas más concretos de la
comunidad.

---

jumbo (jet) ['dʒʌmbəu-] n jumbo.
jump [dʒʌmp] vi saltar, dar saltos; (start)
   sobresaltarse; (increase) aumentar ♦ vt
   saltar ♦ n salto; (fence) obstáculo;
   (increase) aumento; **to** ~ **the queue** (BRIT)
   colarse.
▶**jump about** vi dar saltos, brincar.
▶**jump at** vt fus (fig) apresurarse a
   aprovechar; **he** ~**ed at the offer** se
   apresuró a aceptar la oferta.
▶**jump down** vi bajar de un salto, saltar a
   tierra.
▶**jump up** vi levantarse de un salto.
jumped-up ['dʒʌmptʌp] adj (pej) engreído.
jumper ['dʒʌmpə*] n (BRIT: pullover)
   jersey m, suéter m; (US: pinafore dress)
   pichi m; (SPORT) saltador(a) m/f.
jump leads, (US) **jumper cables** npl
   cables mpl puente de batería.
jump-start ['dʒʌmpstɑːt] vt (car) arrancar
   con ayuda de otra batería or empujando;
   (fig: economy) reactivar.
jump suit n mono.
jumpy ['dʒʌmpɪ] adj nervioso.

Jun. abbr = **junior**; (= June) jun.
junction ['dʒʌŋkʃən] n (BRIT: of roads) cruce
   m; (RAIL) empalme m.
juncture ['dʒʌŋktʃə*] n: **at this** ~ en este
   momento, en esta coyuntura.
June [dʒuːn] n junio.
jungle ['dʒʌŋgl] n selva, jungla.
junior ['dʒuːnɪə*] adj (in age) menor, más
   joven; (competition) juvenil; (position)
   subalterno ♦ n menor m/f, joven m/f; **he's** ~
   to me es menor que yo.
junior high school n (US) centro de educación secundaria; see also **high school**.
junior school n (BRIT) escuela primaria;
   see also **primary school**.
junk [dʒʌŋk] n (cheap goods) baratijas fpl;
   (lumber) trastos mpl viejos; (rubbish)
   basura; (ship) junco ♦ vt (esp US)
   deshacerse de.
junk bond n (COMM) obligación f basura
   inv.
junk dealer n vendedor(a) m/f de objetos
   usados.
junket ['dʒʌŋkɪt] n (CULIN) dulce de leche
   cuajada; (BRIT col): **to go on a** ~, **go** ~**ing**
   viajar a costa ajena or del erario público.
junk food n comida basura or de plástico.
junkie ['dʒʌŋkɪ] n (col) yonqui m/f,
   heroinómano/a.
junk mail n propaganda (buzoneada).
junk room n trastero.
junk shop n tienda de objetos usados.
junta ['dʒʌntə] n junta militar.
Jupiter ['dʒuːpɪtə*] n (MYTHOLOGY, ASTRO)
   Júpiter m.
jurisdiction [dʒuərɪs'dɪkʃən] n jurisdicción
   f; **it falls** or **comes within/outside our** ~
   es/no es de nuestra competencia.
jurisprudence [dʒuərɪs'pruːdəns] n
   jurisprudencia.
juror ['dʒuərə*] n jurado.
jury ['dʒuərɪ] n jurado.
jury box n tribuna del jurado.
juryman ['dʒuərɪmən] n miembro del
   jurado.
just [dʒʌst] adj justo ♦ adv (exactly)
   exactamente; (only) sólo, solamente, no
   más (LAM); **he's** ~ **done it/left** acaba de
   hacerlo/irse; **I've** ~ **seen him** acabo de
   verle; ~ **right** perfecto; ~ **two o'clock** las
   dos en punto; **she's** ~ **as clever as you** es
   tan lista como tú; ~ **as well that...** menos
   mal que...; **it's** ~ **as well you didn't go**
   menos mal que no fuiste; **it's** ~ **as good
   (as)** es igual (que), es tan bueno (como);
   ~ **as he was leaving** en el momento en
   que se marchaba; **we were** ~ **going** ya
   nos íbamos; **I was** ~ **about to phone**

estaba a punto de llamar; ~ **before/
enough** justo antes/lo suficiente; ~ **here**
aquí mismo; **he** ~ **missed** falló por poco;
~ **listen to this** escucha esto un
momento; ~ **ask someone the way**
simplemente pregúntale a algn por
dónde se va; **not** ~ **now** ahora no.

justice ['dʒʌstɪs] *n* justicia; **this photo
doesn't do you** ~ esta foto no te
favorece.

Justice of the Peace (JP) *n* juez *m/f* de
paz; *see also* **Crown Court**.

justifiable [dʒʌstɪ'faɪəbl] *adj* justificable,
justificado.

justifiably [dʒʌstɪ'faɪəblɪ] *adv*
justificadamente, con razón.

justification [dʒʌstɪfɪ'keɪʃən] *n*
justificación *f*.

justify ['dʒʌstɪfaɪ] *vt* justificar; (*text*)
alinear, justificar; **to be justified in doing
sth** tener motivo para *or* razón al hacer
algo.

justly ['dʒʌstlɪ] *adv* (*gen*) justamente; (*with
reason*) con razón.

justness ['dʒʌstnɪs] *n* justicia.

jut [dʒʌt] *vi* (*also*: ~ **out**) sobresalir.

jute [dʒuːt] *n* yute *m*.

juvenile ['dʒuːvənaɪl] *adj* juvenil; (*court*) de
menores ♦ *n* joven *m/f*, menor *m/f* de edad.

juvenile delinquency *n* delincuencia
juvenil.

juvenile delinquent *n* delincuente *m/f*
juvenil.

juxtapose ['dʒʌkstəpəuz] *vt* yuxtaponer.

juxtaposition ['dʒʌkstəpə'zɪʃən] *n*
yuxtaposición *f*.

Kk

K, k [keɪ] *n* (*letter*) K, k *f*; **K for King** K de
Kilo.

K *abbr* (= *one thousand*) K; = **kilobyte**; (*BRIT*:
= *Knight*) *caballero de una orden*.

kaftan ['kæftæn] *n* caftán *m*.

Kalahari Desert [kælə'hɑːrɪ-] *n* desierto de
Kalahari.

kale [keɪl] *n* col *f* rizada.

kaleidoscope [kə'laɪdəskəup] *n*
calidoscopio.

kamikaze [kæmɪ'kɑːzɪ] *adj* kamikaze.

Kampala [kæm'pɑːlə] *n* Kampala.

Kampuchea [kæmpuː'tʃɪə] *n* Kampuchea.

kangaroo [kæŋgə'ruː] *n* canguro.

Kans. *abbr* (*US*) = *Kansas*.

kaput [kə'put] *adj* (*col*) roto, estropeado.

karaoke [kɑːrə'əukɪ] *n* karaoke.

karate [kə'rɑːtɪ] *n* karate *m*.

Kashmir [kæʃ'mɪə*] *n* Cachemira.

kayak ['kaɪæk] *n* kayak *m*.

Kazakhstan [kɑːzɑːk'stæn] *n* Kazajstán *m*.

KC *n abbr* (*BRIT LAW*: = *King's Counsel*) *título
concedido a determinados abogados*.

kd *abbr* (*US*: = *knocked down*) desmontado.

kebab [kə'bæb] *n* pincho moruno, brocheta.

keel [kiːl] *n* quilla; **on an even** ~ (*fig*) en
equilibrio.

▶**keel over** *vi* (*NAUT*) zozobrar, volcarse;
(*person*) desplomarse.

keen [kiːn] *adj* (*interest, desire*) grande, vivo;
(*eye, intelligence*) agudo; (*competition*)
intenso; (*BRIT*: *eager*)
entusiasta; **to be** ~ **to do** *or* **doing sth**
tener muchas ganas de hacer algo; **to be**
~ **on sth/sb** interesarse por algo/uno; **I'm
not** ~ **on going** no tengo ganas de ir.

keenly ['kiːnlɪ] *adv* (*enthusiastically*) con
entusiasmo; (*acutely*) vivamente;
(*intensely*) intensamente.

keenness ['kiːnnɪs] *n* (*eagerness*)
entusiasmo, interés *m*.

keep [kiːp] *vb* (*pt, pp* **kept** [kɛpt]) *vt* (*retain,
preserve*) guardar; (*hold back*) quedarse
con; (*shop*) ser propietario de; (*feed:
family etc*) mantener; (*promise*) cumplir;
(*chickens, bees etc*) criar ♦ *vi* (*food*)
conservarse; (*remain*) seguir, continuar
♦ *n* (*of castle*) torreón *m*; (*food etc*) comida,
sustento; **to** ~ **doing sth** seguir haciendo
algo; **to** ~ **sb from doing sth** impedir a
algn hacer algo; **to** ~ **sth from happening**
impedir que algo ocurra; **to** ~ **sb happy**
tener a algn contento; **to** ~ **sb waiting**
hacer esperar a algn; **to** ~ **a place tidy**
mantener un lugar limpio; **to** ~ **sth to
o.s.** no decirle algo a nadie; **to** ~ **time**
(*clock*) mantener la hora exacta; ~ **the
change** quédese con la vuelta; **to** ~ **an
appointment** acudir a una cita; **to** ~ **a
record** *or* **note of sth** tomar nota de *or*
apuntar algo; *see also* **keeps**.

▶**keep away** *vt*: **to** ~ **sth/sb away from sb**
mantener algo/a algn apartado de algn
♦ *vi*: **to** ~ **away (from)** mantenerse
apartado de (.).

▶**keep back** *vt* (*crowd, tears*) contener;
(*money*) quedarse con; (*conceal:
information*): **to** ~ **sth back from sb**
ocultar algo a algn ♦ *vi* hacerse a un lado.

▶**keep down** *vt* (*control: prices, spending*)

controlar; (*retain: food*) retener ♦ *vi* seguir agachado, no levantar la cabeza.

►**keep in** *vt* (*invalid, child*) impedir que salga, no dejar salir; (*SCOL*) castigar (a quedarse en el colegio) ♦ *vi* (*col*): **to ~ in with sb** mantener la relación con algn.

►**keep off** *vt* (*dog, person*) mantener a distancia ♦ *vi* evitar; **~ your hands off!** ¡no toques!; **"~ off the grass"** "prohibido pisar el césped".

►**keep on** *vi* seguir, continuar.

►**keep out** *vi* (*stay out*) permanecer fuera; **"~ out"** "prohibida la entrada".

►**keep up** *vt* mantener, conservar ♦ *vi* no rezagarse; (*fig: in comprehension*) seguir (el hilo); **to ~ up with** (*pace*) ir al paso de; (*level*) mantenerse a la altura de; **to ~ up with sb** seguir el ritmo a algn; (*fig*) seguir a algn.

keeper ['ki:pə*] *n* guarda *m/f*.

keep-fit [ki:p'fɪt] *n* gimnasia (de mantenimiento).

keeping ['ki:pɪŋ] *n* (*care*) cuidado; **in ~ with** de acuerdo con.

keeps [ki:ps] *n*: **for ~** (*col*) para siempre.

keepsake ['ki:pseɪk] *n* recuerdo.

keg [kɛg] *n* barrilete *m*, barril *m*.

Ken. *abbr* (*US*) = Kentucky.

kennel ['kɛnl] *n* perrera; **~s** *npl* perrera.

Kenya ['ki:njə] *n* Kenia.

Kenyan ['ki:njən] *adj*, *n* keniata *m/f*, keniano/a *m/f*.

kept [kɛpt] *pt*, *pp* of **keep**.

kerb [kə:b] *n* (*BRIT*) bordillo.

kerb crawler [-krɔ:lə*] *n* *conductor en busca de prostitutas desde su coche*.

kernel ['kə:nl] *n* (*nut*) fruta; (*fig*) meollo.

kerosene ['kɛrəsi:n] *n* keroseno.

kestrel ['kɛstrəl] *n* cernícalo.

ketchup ['kɛtʃəp] *n* salsa de tomate, ketchup *m*.

kettle ['kɛtl] *n* hervidor *m*.

kettle drum *n* (*MUS*) timbal *m*.

key [ki:] *n* (*gen*) llave *f*; (*MUS*) tono; (*of piano, typewriter*) tecla; (*on map*) clave *f* ♦ *cpd* (*vital: position, industry etc*) clave ♦ *vt* (*also*: **~ in**) teclear.

keyboard ['ki:bɔ:d] *n* teclado ♦ *vt* (*text*) teclear.

keyboarder ['ki:bɔ:də*] *n* teclista *m/f*.

keyed up [ki:d-] *adj* (*person*) nervioso; **to be (all) ~** estar nervioso *or* emocionado.

keyhole ['ki:həul] *n* ojo (de la cerradura).

keyhole surgery *n* cirugía cerrada *or* no invasiva.

key man *n* hombre *m* clave.

keynote ['ki:nəut] *n* (*MUS*) tónica; (*fig*) idea fundamental.

keynote speech *n* discurso de apertura.

keypad ['ki:pæd] *n* teclado numérico.

keyring ['ki:rɪŋ] *n* llavero.

keystone ['ki:stəun] *n* piedra clave.

keystroke ['ki:strəuk] *n* pulsación *f* (de una tecla).

kg *abbr* (= *kilogram*) kg.

KGB *n* *abbr* KGB *m*.

khaki ['kɑ:kɪ] *n* caqui.

kibbutz, **~im** [kɪ'buts, -ɪm] *n* kibutz *m*.

kick [kɪk] *vt* (*person*) dar una patada a; (*ball*) dar un puntapié a ♦ *vi* (*horse*) dar coces ♦ *n* patada; puntapié *m*, tiro; (*of rifle*) culetazo; (*col: thrill*): **he does it for ~s** lo hace por pura diversión.

►**kick around** *vt* (*idea*) dar vueltas a; (*person*) tratar a patadas a.

►**kick off** *vi* (*SPORT*) hacer el saque inicial.

kick-start ['kɪkstɑ:t] *n* (*also*: **~er**) (pedal *m* de) arranque *m*.

kid [kɪd] *n* (*col: child*) niño/a, chiquillo/a; (*animal*) cabrito; (*leather*) cabritilla ♦ *vi* (*col*) bromear.

kid gloves *npl*: **to treat sb with ~** andarse con pies de plomo con algn.

kidnap ['kɪdnæp] *vt* secuestrar.

kidnapper ['kɪdnæpə*] *n* secuestrador(a) *m/f*.

kidnapping ['kɪdnæpɪŋ] *n* secuestro.

kidney ['kɪdnɪ] *n* riñón *m*.

kidney bean *n* judía, alubia.

kidney machine *n* riñón *m* artificial.

kill [kɪl] *vt* matar; (*murder*) asesinar; (*fig: rumour, conversation*) acabar con ♦ *n* matanza; **to ~ time** matar el tiempo.

►**kill off** *vt* exterminar, terminar con; (*fig*) echar por tierra.

killer ['kɪlə*] *n* asesino/a.

killer app [-'æp] *n* *abbr* (*col*) (= *killer application*) aplicación *f* rompedora, aplicación *f* de excelente rendimiento.

killer instinct *n*: **to have the ~** ir a por todas.

killing ['kɪlɪŋ] *n* (*one*) asesinato; (*several*) matanza; (*COMM*): **to make a ~** tener un gran éxito financiero.

killjoy ['kɪldʒɔɪ] *n* (*BRIT*) aguafiestas *m/f inv*.

kiln [kɪln] *n* horno.

kilo ['ki:ləu] *n* (*abbr*. = *kilogram(me)*) kilo.

kilobyte ['kɪləubaɪt] *n* (*COMPUT*) kilobyte *m*, kilocteto.

kilogram(me) ['kɪləugræm] *n* kilogramo.

kilometre, (*US*) **kilometer** ['kɪləmi:tə*] *n* kilómetro.

kilowatt ['kɪləuwɔt] *n* kilovatio.

kilt [kɪlt] *n* falda escocesa.

kilter ['kɪltə*] *n*: **out of ~** desbaratado.

kimono [kɪ'məunəu] *n* quimono.

kin [kɪn] *n* parientes *mpl*.

kind [kaɪnd] *adj* (*treatment*) bueno, cariñoso; (*person, act, word*) amable, atento ♦ *n* clase *f*, especie *f*; (*species*) género; **in ~** (*COMM*) en especie; **a ~ of** una especie de; **to be two of a ~** ser tal para cual; **would you be ~ enough to ...?, would you be so ~ as to ...?** ¿me hace el favor de ...?; **it's very ~ of you (to do)** le agradezco mucho (el que haya hecho).

kindergarten ['kɪndəgɑːtn] *n* jardín *m* de infancia.

kind-hearted [kaɪnd'hɑːtɪd] *adj* bondadoso, de buen corazón.

kindle ['kɪndl] *vt* encender.

kindliness ['kaɪndlɪnəs] *n* bondad *f*, amabilidad *f*.

kindling ['kɪndlɪŋ] *n* leña (menuda).

kindly ['kaɪndlɪ] *adj* bondadoso; (*gentle*) cariñoso ♦ *adv* bondadosamente, amablemente; **will you ~ ...** sería usted tan amable de ....

kindness ['kaɪndnɪs] *n* bondad *f*, amabilidad *f*.

kindred ['kɪndrɪd] *n* familia, parientes *mpl* ♦ *adj*: **~ spirits** almas *fpl* gemelas.

kinetic [kɪ'nɛtɪk] *adj* cinético.

king [kɪŋ] *n* rey *m*.

kingdom ['kɪŋdəm] *n* reino.

kingfisher ['kɪŋfɪʃə*] *n* martín *m* pescador.

kingpin ['kɪŋpɪn] *n* (*TECH*) perno real *or* pinzote; (*fig*) persona clave.

king-size(d) ['kɪŋsaɪz(d)] *adj* de tamaño gigante; (*cigarette*) extra largo.

kink [kɪŋk] *n* (*in rope etc*) enroscadura; (*in hair*) rizo; (*fig: emotional, psychological*) manía.

kinky ['kɪŋkɪ] *adj* (*pej*) perverso.

kinship ['kɪnʃɪp] *n* parentesco; (*fig*) afinidad *f*.

kinsman ['kɪnzmən] *n* pariente *m*.

kinswoman ['kɪnzwumən] *n* parienta.

kiosk ['kiːɔsk] *n* quiosco; (*BRIT TEL*) cabina; **newspaper ~** quiosco, kiosco.

kipper ['kɪpə*] *n* arenque *m* ahumado.

Kirghizia [kəːˈɡɪzɪə] *n* Kirguizistán *m*.

kiss [kɪs] *n* beso ♦ *vt* besar; **~ of life** (*artificial respiration*) respiración *f* artificial; **to ~ sb goodbye** dar un beso de despedida a algn; **to ~ (each other)** besarse.

kissogram ['kɪsəgræm] *n* servicio de felicitaciones mediante el que se envía a una persona vestida de manera sugerente para besar a algn.

kit [kɪt] *n* equipo; (*set of tools etc*) (caja de) herramientas *fpl*; (*assembly ~*) juego de armar; **tool ~** juego *or* estuche *m* de herramientas.

►**kit out** *vt* equipar.

kitbag ['kɪtbæg] *n* (*MIL*) macuto.

kitchen ['kɪtʃɪn] *n* cocina.

kitchen garden *n* huerto.

kitchen sink *n* fregadero.

kitchen unit *n* módulo de cocina.

kitchenware ['kɪtʃɪnwɛə*] *n* batería de cocina.

kite [kaɪt] *n* (*toy*) cometa.

kith [kɪθ] *n*: **~ and kin** parientes *mpl* y allegados.

kitten ['kɪtn] *n* gatito/a.

kitty ['kɪtɪ] *n* (*pool of money*) fondo común; (*CARDS*) bote *m*.

kiwi ['kiːwiː] *n* (*col: New Zealander*) neozelandés/esa *m/f*; (*also:* **~ fruit**) kiwi *m*.

KKK *n abbr* (*US*) = **Ku Klux Klan**.

kleptomaniac [klɛptəuˈmeɪnɪæk] *n* cleptómano/a.

km *abbr* (= *kilometre*) km.

km/h *abbr* (= *kilometres per hour*) km/h.

knack [næk] *n*: **to have the ~ of doing sth** tener facilidad para hacer algo.

knackered ['nækəd] *adj* (*col*) hecho polvo.

knapsack ['næpsæk] *n* mochila.

knead [niːd] *vt* amasar.

knee [niː] *n* rodilla.

kneecap ['niːkæp] *vt* destrozar a tiros la rótula de ♦ *n* rótula.

knee-deep ['niːˈdiːp] *adj*: **the water was ~** el agua llegaba hasta la rodilla.

kneel, *pt, pp* **knelt** [niːl, nɛlt] *vi* (*also:* **~ down**) arrodillarse.

kneepad ['niːpæd] *n* rodillera.

knell [nɛl] *n* toque *m* de difuntos.

knelt [nɛlt] *pt, pp of* **kneel**.

knew [njuː] *pt of* **know**.

knickers ['nɪkəz] *npl* (*BRIT*) bragas *fpl*, calzones *mpl* (*LAM*).

knick-knack ['nɪknæk] *n* chuchería, baratija.

knife [naɪf] *n* (*pl* **knives**) *n* cuchillo ♦ *vt* acuchillar; **~, fork and spoon** cubiertos *mpl*.

knife edge *n*: **to be on a ~** estar en la cuerda floja.

knight [naɪt] *n* caballero; (*CHESS*) caballo.

knighthood ['naɪthud] *n* (*title*): **to get a ~** recibir el título de Sir.

knit [nɪt] *vt* tejer, tricotar; (*brows*) fruncir; (*fig*): **to ~ together** unir, juntar ♦ *vi* hacer punto, tejer, tricotar; (*bones*) soldarse.

knitted ['nɪtɪd] *adj* de punto.

knitting ['nɪtɪŋ] *n* labor *f* de punto.

knitting machine *n* máquina de tricotar.

knitting needle, (*US*) **knit pin** *n* aguja de hacer punto *or* tejer.

knitting pattern *n* patrón *m* para tricotar.

knitwear ['nɪtwɛə*] *n* prendas *fpl* de punto.

knives [naɪvz] *pl of* **knife.**
knob [nɔb] *n* (*of door*) pomo; (*of stick*) puño; (*lump*) bulto; (*fig*): **a ~ of butter** (*BRIT*) un pedazo de mantequilla.
knobbly ['nɔblɪ], (*US*) **knobby** ['nɔbɪ] *adj* (*wood, surface*) nudoso; (*knee*) huesudo.
knock [nɔk] *vt* (*strike*) golpear; (*bump into*) chocar contra; (*fig: col*) criticar ♦ *vi* (*at door etc*): **to ~ at/on** llamar a ♦ *n* golpe *m*; (*on door*) llamada; **he ~ed at the door** llamó a la puerta.
▶**knock down** *vt* (*pedestrian*) atropellar; (*price*) rebajar.
▶**knock off** *vi* (*col: finish*) salir del trabajo ♦ *vt* (*col: steal*) birlar; (*strike off*) quitar; (*fig: from price, record*): **to ~ off £10** rebajar en £10.
▶**knock out** *vt* dejar sin sentido; (*BOXING*) poner fuera de combate, dejar K.O.; (*stop*) estropear, dejar fuera de servicio.
▶**knock over** *vt* (*object*) derribar, tirar; (*pedestrian*) atropellar.
knockdown ['nɔkdaun] *adj* (*price*) de saldo.
knocker ['nɔkə*] *n* (*on door*) aldaba.
knocking ['nɔkɪŋ] *n* golpes *mpl*, golpeteo.
knock-kneed [nɔk'niːd] *adj* patizambo.
knockout ['nɔkaut] *n* (*BOXING*) K.O. *m*, knockout *m*.
knock-up ['nɔkʌp] *n* (*TENNIS*) peloteo.
knot [nɔt] *n* (*gen*) nudo ♦ *vt* anudar; **to tie a ~** hacer un nudo.
knotted ['nɔtɪd] *adj* anudado.
knotty ['nɔtɪ] *adj* (*fig*) complicado.
know [nəu] *vb* (*pt* **knew**, *pp* **known** [njuː, nəun]) *vt* (*gen*) saber; (*person, author, place*) conocer ♦ *vi*: **as far as I ~** ... que yo sepa ...; **yes, I ~** sí, ya lo sé; **I don't ~** no lo sé; **to ~ how to do** saber hacer; **to ~ how to swim** saber nadar; **to ~ about or of sb/sth** saber de algn/algo; **to get to ~ sth** enterarse de algo; **I ~ nothing about it** no sé nada de eso; **I don't ~ him** no lo *or* le conozco; **to ~ right from wrong** saber distinguir el bien del mal.
know-all ['nəuɔːl] *n* (*BRIT pej*) sabelotodo *m/f inv*, sabihondo/a.
know-how ['nəuhau] *n* conocimientos *mpl*.
knowing ['nəuɪŋ] *adj* (*look*) de complicidad.
knowingly ['nəuɪŋlɪ] *adv* (*purposely*) a sabiendas; (*smile, look*) con complicidad.
know-it-all ['nəutɔːl] *n* (*US*) = **know-all.**
knowledge ['nɔlɪdʒ] *n* (*gen*) conocimiento; (*learning*) saber *m*, conocimientos *mpl*; **to have no ~ of** no saber nada de; **with my ~** con mis conocimientos, sabiéndolo; **to (the best of) my ~** a mi entender, que yo sepa; **not to my ~** que yo sepa, no; **it is common ~ that** ... es del dominio público

que ...; **it has come to my ~ that** ... me he enterado de que ...; **to have a working ~ of Spanish** defenderse con el español.
knowledgeable ['nɔlɪdʒəbl] *adj* entendido.
known [nəun] *pp of* **know** ♦ *adj* (*thief, facts*) conocido; (*expert*) reconocido.
knuckle ['nʌkl] *n* nudillo.
▶**knuckle down** *vi* (*col*) ponerse a trabajar en serio.
▶**knuckle under** *vi* someterse.
knuckleduster ['nʌkldʌstə*] *n* puño de hierro.
KO *abbr n* (= *knockout*) K.O. *m* ♦ *vt* (= *knock out*) dejar K.O.
kook [kuːk] *n* (*US col*) chiflado/a *m/f*, majareta *m/f*.
Koran [kɔ'rɑːn] *n* Corán *m*.
Korea [kə'rɪə] *n* Corea; **North/South ~** Corea del Norte/Sur.
Korean [kə'rɪən] *adj*, *n* coreano/a *m/f*.
kosher ['kəuʃə*] *adj* autorizado por la ley judía.
Kosovan ['kɒsəvən], **Kosovar** ['kɒsəvɑː*] *adj* Kosovar.
Kosovo ['kɒsəvəu] *n* Kosovo *m*.
kowtow ['kau'tau] *vi*: **to ~ to sb** humillarse ante algn.
KS *abbr* (*US*) = *Kansas.*
Kt *abbr* (*BRIT*: = *Knight*) *caballero de una orden.*
Kuala Lumpur ['kwɑːlə'lumpuə*] *n* Kuala Lumpur *m*.
kudos ['kjuːdɔs] *n* gloria, prestigio.
Kurd [kəːd] *n* kurdo/a.
Kuwait [ku'weɪt] *n* Kuwait *m*.
Kuwaiti [ku'weɪtɪ] *adj*, *n* Kuwaití *m/f*.
kW *abbr* (= *kilowatt*) Kv.
KY, Ky. *abbr* (*US*) = *Kentucky.*

L l

L, l [ɛl] *n* (*letter*) L, l *f*; **L for Lucy**, (*US*) **L for Love** L de Lorenzo.
L *abbr* (*on maps etc*) = **lake; large;** (= *left*) izq.; (*BRIT AUT*: = *learner*) L.
l. *abbr* = **litre.**
LA *n abbr* (*US*) = *Los Angeles* ♦ *abbr* (*US*) = *Louisiana.*
La. *abbr* (*US*) = *Louisiana.*
lab [læb] *n abbr* = **laboratory.**
Lab. *abbr* (*Canada*) = *Labrador.*

label ['leɪbl] *n* etiqueta; (*brand: of record*) sello (discográfico) ♦ *vt* poner una etiqueta a, etiquetar.

labor *etc* ['leɪbə*] (*US*) = **labour.**

laboratory [lə'bɒrətərɪ] *n* laboratorio.

Labor Day *n* (*US*) día *m* de los trabajadores (*primer lunes de septiembre*).

laborious [lə'bɔːrɪəs] *adj* penoso.

laboriously [lə'bɔːrɪəslɪ] *adv* penosamente.

labor union *n* (*US*) sindicato.

labor unrest *n* (*US*) conflictividad *f* laboral.

Labour ['leɪbə*] *n* (*BRIT POL: also:* **the ~ Party**) el partido laborista, los laboristas.

labour, (*US*) **labor** ['leɪbə*] *n* (*task*) trabajo; (~ *force*) mano *f* de obra; (*workers*) trabajadores *mpl*; (*MED*) (dolores *mpl* de) parto ♦ *vi:* **to ~ (at)** trabajar (en) ♦ *vt* insistir en; **hard ~** trabajos *mpl* forzados; **to be in ~** estar de parto.

labo(u)r cost *n* costo de la mano de obra.

labo(u)r dispute *n* conflicto laboral.

labo(u)red ['leɪbəd] *adj* (*breathing*) fatigoso; (*style*) forzado, pesado.

labo(u)rer ['leɪbərə*] *n* peón *m*; (*on farm*) peón *m*, obrero; (*day ~*) jornalero.

labo(u)r force *n* mano *f* de obra.

labo(u)r-intensive [leɪbərɪn'tensɪv] *adj* que necesita mucha mano de obra.

labo(u)r relations *npl* relaciones *fpl* laborales.

labo(u)r-saving ['leɪbəseɪvɪŋ] *adj* que ahorra trabajo.

laburnum [lə'bɜːnəm] *n* codeso.

labyrinth ['læbɪrɪnθ] *n* laberinto.

lace [leɪs] *n* encaje *m*; (*of shoe etc*) cordón *m* ♦ *vt* (*shoes: also:* ~ **up**) atarse; (*drink: fortify with spirits*) echar licor a.

lacemaking ['leɪsmeɪkɪŋ] *n* obra de encaje.

lacerate ['læsəreɪt] *vt* lacerar.

laceration [læsə'reɪʃən] *n* laceración *f*.

lace-up ['leɪsʌp] *adj* (*shoes etc*) con cordones.

lack [læk] *n* (*absence*) falta, carencia; (*scarcity*) escasez *f* ♦ *vt* faltarle a algn, carecer de; **through** *or* **for ~ of** por falta de; **to be ~ing** faltar, no haber.

lackadaisical [lækə'deɪzɪkl] *adj* (*careless*) descuidado; (*indifferent*) indiferente.

lackey ['lækɪ] *n* (*also fig*) lacayo.

lacklustre, (*US*) **lackluster** ['læklʌstə*] *adj* (*surface*) deslustrado, deslucido; (*style*) inexpresivo; (*eyes*) apagado.

laconic [lə'kɒnɪk] *adj* lacónico.

lacquer ['lækə*] *n* laca; **hair ~** laca para el pelo.

lacrosse [lə'krɒs] *n* lacrosse *f*.

lacy ['leɪsɪ] *adj* (*like lace*) parecido al encaje.

lad [læd] *n* muchacho, chico; (*in stable etc*) mozo.

ladder ['lædə*] *n* escalera (de mano); (*BRIT: in tights*) carrera ♦ *vt* (*BRIT: tights*) hacer una carrera en.

laden ['leɪdn] *adj:* ~ **(with)** cargado (de); **fully ~** (*truck, ship*) cargado hasta el tope.

ladle ['leɪdl] *n* cucharón *m*.

lady ['leɪdɪ] *n* señora; (*distinguished, noble*) dama; **young ~** señorita; **the ladies' (room)** los servicios de señoras.

ladybird ['leɪdɪbɜːd], (*US*) **ladybug** ['leɪdɪbʌg] *n* mariquita.

lady doctor *n* médica, doctora.

lady-in-waiting ['leɪdɪɪn'weɪtɪŋ] *n* dama de honor.

ladykiller ['leɪdɪkɪlə*] *n* robacorazones *m inv*.

ladylike ['leɪdɪlaɪk] *adj* fino.

Ladyship ['leɪdɪʃɪp] *n:* **your ~** su Señoría.

LAFTA *n abbr* (= *Latin American Free Trade Association*) ALALC *f*.

lag [læg] *vi* (*also:* ~ **behind**) retrasarse, quedarse atrás ♦ *vt* (*pipes*) revestir.

lager ['lɑːgə*] *n* cerveza (rubia).

lager lout *n* (*BRIT col*) gamberro borracho.

lagging ['lægɪŋ] *n* revestimiento.

lagoon [lə'guːn] *n* laguna.

Lagos ['leɪgɒs] *n* Lagos *m*.

laid [leɪd] *pt, pp of* **lay.**

laid-back [leɪd'bæk] *adj* (*col*) tranquilo, relajado.

laid up *adj:* **to be ~** (*person*) tener que guardar cama.

lain [leɪn] *pp of* **lie.**

lair [lɛə*] *n* guarida.

laissez-faire [leseɪ'fɛə*] *n* laissez-faire *m*.

laity ['leɪtɪ] *n* laicado.

lake [leɪk] *n* lago.

Lake District *n* (*BRIT*): **the ~** la Región de los Lagos.

lamb [læm] *n* cordero; (*meat*) carne *f* de cordero.

lamb chop *n* chuleta de cordero.

lambswool ['læmzwul] *n* lana de cordero.

lame [leɪm] *adj* cojo, rengo (*LAM*); (*weak*) débil, poco convincente; ~ **duck** (*fig: person*) inútil *m/f*; (: *firm*) empresa en quiebra.

lamely ['leɪmlɪ] *adv* (*fig*) sin convicción.

lament [lə'mɛnt] *n* lamento ♦ *vt* lamentarse de.

lamentable ['læməntəbl] *adj* lamentable.

lamentation [læmən'teɪʃən] *n* lamento.

laminated ['læmɪneɪtɪd] *adj* laminado.

lamp [læmp] *n* lámpara.

lamplight ['læmplaɪt] *n:* **by ~** a la luz de la lámpara.

lampoon [læm'puːn] *vt* satirizar.
lamppost ['læmppəust] *n* (*BRIT*) farola.
lampshade ['læmpʃeɪd] *n* pantalla.
lance [lɑːns] *n* lanza ♦ *vt* (*MED*) abrir con lanceta.
lance corporal *n* (*BRIT*) soldado de primera clase.
lancet ['lɑːnsɪt] *n* (*MED*) lanceta.
Lancs [læŋks] *abbr* (*BRIT*) = *Lancashire*.
land [lænd] *n* tierra; (*country*) país *m*; (*piece of* ~) terreno; (*estate*) tierras *fpl*, finca; (*AGR*) campo ♦ *vi* (*from ship*) desembarcar; (*AVIAT*) aterrizar; (*fig: fall*) caer ♦ *vt* (*obtain*) conseguir; (*passengers, goods*) desembarcar; **to go/travel by** ~ ir/viajar por tierra; **to own** ~ ser dueño de tierras; **to** ~ **on one's feet** caer de pie; (*fig: to be lucky*) salir bien parado.
▶**land up** *vi*: **to** ~ **up in/at** ir a parar a/en.
landed ['lændɪd] *adj*: ~ **gentry** terratenientes *mpl*.
landfill site ['lændfɪl-] *n* vertedero.
landing ['lændɪŋ] *n* desembarco; aterrizaje *m*; (*of staircase*) rellano.
landing card *n* tarjeta de desembarque.
landing craft *n* lancha de desembarco.
landing gear *n* (*AVIAT*) tren *m* de aterrizaje.
landing stage *n* (*BRIT*) desembarcadero.
landing strip *n* pista de aterrizaje.
landlady ['lændleɪdɪ] *n* (*of boarding house*) patrona; (*owner*) dueña.
landlocked ['lændlɔkt] *adj* cercado de tierra.
landlord ['lændlɔːd] *n* propietario; (*of pub etc*) patrón *m*.
landlubber ['lændlʌbə*] *n* marinero de agua dulce.
landmark ['lændmɑːk] *n* lugar *m* conocido; **to be a** ~ (*fig*) hacer época.
landowner ['lændəunə*] *n* terrateniente *m/f*.
landscape ['lænskeɪp] *n* paisaje *m*.
landscape architecture *n* arquitectura paisajista.
landscaped ['lænskeɪpt] *adj* reformado artísticamente.
landscape gardener *n* diseñador(a) *m/f* de paisajes.
landscape gardening *n* jardinería paisajista.
landscape painting *n* (*ART*) paisaje *m*.
landslide ['lændslaɪd] *n* (*GEO*) corrimiento de tierras; (*fig: POL*) victoria arrolladora.
lane [leɪn] *n* (*in country*) camino; (*in town*) callejón *m*; (*AUT*) carril *m*; (*in race*) calle *f*; (*for air or sea traffic*) ruta; **shipping** ~ ruta marina.

language ['læŋgwɪdʒ] *n* lenguaje *m*; (*national tongue*) idioma *m*, lengua; **bad** ~ palabrotas *fpl*.
language laboratory *n* laboratorio de idiomas.
language studies *npl* estudios *mpl* filológicos.
languid ['læŋgwɪd] *adj* lánguido.
languish ['læŋgwɪʃ] *vi* languidecer.
languor ['læŋgə*] *n* languidez *f*.
languorous ['læŋgərəs] *adj* lánguido.
lank [læŋk] *adj* (*hair*) lacio.
lanky ['læŋkɪ] *adj* larguirucho.
lanolin(e) ['lænəlɪn] *n* lanolina.
lantern ['læntn] *n* linterna, farol *m*.
lanyard ['lænjed] *n* acollador *m*.
Laos [laus] *n* Laos *m*.
lap [læp] *n* (*of track*) vuelta; (*of body*): **to sit on sb's** ~ sentarse en las rodillas de algn ♦ *vt* (*also*: ~ **up**) beber a lengüetadas *or* con la lengua ♦ *vi* (*waves*) chapotear.
▶**lap up** *vt* beber a lengüetadas *or* con la lengua; (*fig: compliments, attention*) disfrutar; (*lies etc*) tragarse.
La Paz [læ'pæz] *n* La Paz.
lapdog ['læpdɔg] *n* perro faldero.
lapel [lə'pɛl] *n* solapa.
Lapland ['læplænd] *n* Laponia.
Laplander ['læplændə*] *n* lapón/ona *m/f*.
lapse [læps] *n* (*fault*) error *m*, fallo; (*moral*) desliz *m* ♦ *vi* (*expire*) caducar; (*morally*) cometer un desliz; (*time*) pasar, transcurrir; **to** ~ **into bad habits** volver a las andadas; ~ **of time** lapso, período; **a** ~ **of memory** un lapsus de memoria.
laptop ['læptɔp] *n* (*also*: ~ **computer**) (ordenador *m*) portátil *m*.
larceny ['lɑːsənɪ] *n* latrocinio.
lard [lɑːd] *n* manteca (de cerdo).
larder ['lɑːdə*] *n* despensa.
large [lɑːdʒ] *adj* grande ♦ *adv*: **by and** ~ en general, en términos generales; **at** ~ (*free*) en libertad; (*generally*) en general; **to make** ~(r) hacer mayor *or* más extenso; **a** ~ **number of people** una gran cantidad de personas; **on a** ~ **scale** a gran escala.
largely ['lɑːdʒlɪ] *adv* en gran parte.
large-scale ['lɑːdʒ'skeɪl] *adj* (*map, drawing*) a gran escala; (*reforms, business activities*) importante.
largesse [lɑː'ʒɛs] *n* generosidad *f*.
lark [lɑːk] *n* (*bird*) alondra; (*joke*) broma.
▶**lark about** *vi* bromear, hacer el tonto.
larva, *pl* **larvae** ['lɑːvə, -iː] *n* larva.
laryngitis [lærɪn'dʒaɪtɪs] *n* laringitis *f*.
larynx ['lærɪŋks] *n* laringe *f*.
lasagne [lə'zænjə] *n* lasaña.

lascivious [lə'sɪvɪəs] adj lascivo.
laser ['leɪzə*] n láser m.
laser beam n rayo láser.
laser printer n impresora láser.
lash [læʃ] n latigazo; (punishment) azote m; (also: eye~) pestaña ♦ vt azotar; (tie) atar.
▶**lash down** vt sujetar con cuerdas ♦ vi (rain) caer a trombas.
▶**lash out** vi (col: spend) gastar a la loca; **to ~ out at** or **against sb** lanzar invectivas contra algn.
lashing ['læʃɪŋ] n (beating) azotaina, flagelación f; **~s of** (col) montones mpl de.
lass [læs] n chica.
lassitude ['læsɪtjuːd] n lasitud f.
lasso [læ'suː] n lazo ♦ vt coger con lazo.
last [lɑːst] adj (gen) último; (final) último, final ♦ adv por último ♦ vi (endure) durar; (continue) continuar, seguir; **~ night** anoche; **~ week** la semana pasada; **at ~** por fin; **~ but one** penúltimo; **~ time** la última vez; **it ~s (for) 2 hours** dura dos horas.
last-ditch ['lɑːst'dɪtʃ] adj (attempt) de último recurso, último, desesperado.
lasting ['lɑːstɪŋ] adj duradero.
lastly ['lɑːstlɪ] adv por último, finalmente.
last-minute ['lɑːstmɪnɪt] adj de última hora.
latch [lætʃ] n picaporte m, pestillo.
▶**latch on to** vt fus (cling to: person) pegarse a; (: idea) agarrarse de.
latchkey ['lætʃkiː] n llavín m.
latchkey child n niño cuyos padres trabajan.
late [leɪt] adj (not on time) tarde, atrasado; (towards end of period, life) tardío; (hour) avanzado; (dead) fallecido ♦ adv tarde; (behind time, schedule) con retraso; **to be (10 minutes) ~** llegar con (diez minutos de) retraso; **to be ~ with** estar atrasado con; **~ delivery** entrega tardía; **~ in life** a una edad avanzada; **of ~** últimamente; **in ~ May** hacia fines de mayo; **the ~ Mr X** el difunto Sr X; **to work ~** trabajar hasta tarde.
latecomer ['leɪtkʌmə*] n recién llegado/a.
lately ['leɪtlɪ] adv últimamente.
lateness ['leɪtnɪs] n (of person) demora; (of event) tardanza.
latent ['leɪtnt] adj latente; **~ defect** defecto latente.
later ['leɪtə*] adj (date etc) posterior; (version etc) más reciente ♦ adv más tarde, después; **~ on today** hoy más tarde.
lateral ['lætərl] adj lateral.
latest ['leɪtɪst] adj último; **at the ~** a más tardar.

latex ['leɪtɛks] n látex m.
lathe [leɪð] n torno.
lather ['lɑːðə*] n espuma (de jabón) ♦ vt enjabonar.
Latin ['lætɪn] n latín m ♦ adj latino.
Latin America n América Latina, Latinoamérica.
Latin American adj, n latinoamericano/a m/f.
Latino [læ'tiːnəu] adj, n latino/a m/f.
latitude ['lætɪtjuːd] n latitud f; (fig: freedom) libertad f.
latrine [lə'triːn] n letrina.
latter ['lætə*] adj último; (of two) segundo ♦ n: **the ~** el último, éste.
latter-day ['lætədeɪ] adj moderno.
latterly ['lætəlɪ] adv últimamente.
lattice ['lætɪs] n enrejado.
lattice window n ventana enrejada or de celosía.
lattice work n enrejado.
Latvia ['lætvɪə] n Letonia.
Latvian ['lætvɪən] adj letón/ona ♦ n letón/ona m/f; (LING) letón m.
laudable ['lɔːdəbl] adj loable.
laugh [lɑːf] n risa; (loud) carcajada ♦ vi reírse, reír; reírse a carcajadas.
▶**laugh at** vt fus reírse de.
▶**laugh off** vt tomar a risa.
laughable ['lɑːfəbl] adj ridículo.
laughing ['lɑːfɪŋ] adj risueño ♦ n: **it's no ~ matter** no es cosa de risa.
laughing gas n gas m hilarante.
laughing stock n: **to be the ~ of the town** ser el hazmerreír de la ciudad.
laughter ['lɑːftə*] n risa.
launch [lɔːntʃ] n (boat) lancha; see also **launching** ♦ vt (ship) botar; (rocket, plan) lanzar.
▶**launch forth** vi: **to ~ forth (into)** lanzarse a or en, emprender.
▶**launch out** vi = **launch forth**.
launching ['lɔːntʃɪŋ] n (of rocket etc) lanzamiento; (inauguration) estreno.
launch(ing) pad n plataforma de lanzamiento.
launder ['lɔːndə*] vt lavar.
Launderette ® [lɔːn'drɛt], (US) **Laundromat** ® ['lɔːndrəmæt] n lavandería (automática).
laundry ['lɔːndrɪ] n lavandería; (clothes) ropa sucia; **to do the ~** hacer la colada.
laureate ['lɔːrɪət] adj see **poet**.
laurel ['lɔrl] n laurel m; **to rest on one's ~s** dormirse en or sobre los laureles.
lava ['lɑːvə] n lava.
lavatory ['lævətərɪ] n wáter m; **lavatories** npl servicios mpl, aseos mpl, sanitarios mpl

(*LAM*).
lavatory paper *n* papel *m* higiénico.
lavender ['lævəndə*] *n* lavanda.
lavish ['lævɪʃ] *adj* abundante; (*giving freely*):
  ~ **with** pródigo en ♦ *vt*: **to ~ sth on sb**
  colmar a algn de algo.
lavishly ['lævɪʃlɪ] *adv* (*give, spend*)
  generosamente; (*furnished*) lujosamente.
law [lɔː] *n* ley *f*; (*study*) derecho; (*of game*)
  regla; **against the ~** contra la ley; **to**
  study ~ estudiar derecho; **to go to ~**
  recurrir a la justicia.
law-abiding ['lɔːəbaɪdɪŋ] *adj* respetuoso
  con la ley.
law and order *n* orden *m* público.
lawbreaker ['lɔːbreɪkə*] *n* infractor(a) *m/f*
  de la ley.
law court *n* tribunal *m* (de justicia).
lawful ['lɔːful] *adj* legítimo, lícito.
lawfully ['lɔːfulɪ] *adv* legalmente.
lawless ['lɔːlɪs] *adj* (*act*) ilegal; (*person*)
  rebelde; (*country*) ingobernable.
Law Lord *n* (*BRIT*) *miembro de la Cámara*
  de los Lores y del más alto tribunal de
  apelación.
lawmaker ['lɔːmeɪkə*] *n* legislador(a) *m/f*.
lawn [lɔːn] *n* césped *m*.
lawnmower ['lɔːnməuə*] *n* cortacésped *m*.
lawn tennis *n* tenis *m* sobre hierba.
law school *n* (*US*) facultad *f* de derecho.
law student *n* estudiante *m/f* de derecho.
lawsuit ['lɔːsuːt] *n* pleito; **to bring a ~**
  against entablar un pleito contra.
lawyer ['lɔːjə*] *n* abogado/a; (*for sales, wills*
  etc) notario/a.
lax [læks] *adj* (*discipline*) relajado; (*person*)
  negligente.
laxative ['læksətɪv] *n* laxante *m*.
laxity ['læksɪtɪ] *n* flojedad *f*; (*moral*)
  relajamiento; (*negligence*) negligencia.
lay [leɪ] *pt of* **lie** ♦ *adj* laico; (*not expert*) lego
  ♦ *vt* (*pt, pp* **laid** [leɪd]) (*place*) colocar; (*eggs,*
  table) poner; (*trap*) tender; **to ~ the facts/**
  one's proposals before sb presentar los
  hechos/sus propuestas a algn.
►**lay aside, lay by** *vt* dejar a un lado.
►**lay down** *vt* (*pen etc*) dejar; (*arms*)
  rendir; (*policy*) trazar; **to ~ down the law**
  imponer las normas.
►**lay in** *vt* abastecerse de.
►**lay into** *vt fus* (*col: attack, scold*) arremeter
  contra.
►**lay off** *vt* (*workers*) despedir.
►**lay on** *vt* (*water, gas*) instalar; (*meal,*
  facilities) proveer.
►**lay out** *vt* (*plan*) trazar; (*display*) exponer;
  (*spend*) gastar.
►**lay up** *vt* (*store*) guardar; (*ship*)

desarmar; (*subj: illness*) obligar a guardar
  cama.
layabout ['leɪəbaut] *n* vago/a.
lay-by ['leɪbaɪ] *n* (*BRIT AUT*) apartadero.
lay days *npl* días *mpl* de inactividad.
layer ['leɪə*] *n* capa.
layette [leɪ'ɛt] *n* ajuar *m* (de niño).
layman ['leɪmən] *n* lego.
lay-off ['leɪɔf] *n* despido, paro forzoso.
layout ['leɪaut] *n* (*design*) plan *m*, trazado;
  (*disposition*) disposición *f*; (*PRESS*)
  composición *f*.
laze [leɪz] *vi* no hacer nada; (*pej*)
  holgazanear.
lazily ['leɪzɪlɪ] *adv* perezosamente.
laziness ['leɪzɪnɪs] *n* pereza.
lazy ['leɪzɪ] *adj* perezoso, vago, flojo (*LAM*).
LB *abbr* (*Canada*) = Labrador.
lb. *abbr* = **pound** (*weight*).
lbw *abbr* (*CRICKET*) = leg before wicket.
LC *n abbr* (*US*) = Library of Congress.
lc *abbr* (*TYP*: = lower case) min.
L/C *abbr* = **letter of credit**.
LCD *n abbr see* **liquid crystal display**.
Ld *abbr* (= Lord) título de nobleza.
LDS *n abbr* (= Licentiate in Dental Surgery)
  diploma universitario; (= Latter-day
  Saints) Iglesia de Jesucristo de los Santos
  del último día.
LEA *n abbr* (*BRIT*: = local education authority)
  organismos locales encargados de la
  enseñanza.
lead [liːd] *n* (*front position*) delantera;
  (*distance, time ahead*) ventaja; (*clue*) pista;
  (*ELEC*) cable *m*; (*for dog*) correa; (*THEAT*)
  papel *m* principal; [lɛd] (*metal*) plomo; (*in*
  pencil) mina ♦ *vb* (*pt, pp* **led** [lɛd]) *vt*
  conducir; (*life*) llevar; (*be leader of*)
  dirigir; (*SPORT*) ir en cabeza de;
  (*orchestra: BRIT*) ser el primer violín en;
  (*: US*) dirigir ♦ *vi* ir primero; **to be in the**
  ~ (*SPORT*) llevar la delantera; (*fig*) ir a la
  cabeza; **to take the ~** (*SPORT*) tomar la
  delantera; (*fig*) tomar la iniciativa; **to ~**
  sb to believe that ... hacer creer a algn
  que ...; **to ~ sb to do sth** llevar a algn a
  hacer algo.
►**lead astray** *vt* llevar por mal camino.
►**lead away** *vt* llevar.
►**lead back** *vt* hacer volver.
►**lead off** *vt* llevar ♦ *vi* (*in game*) abrir.
►**lead on** *vt* (*tease*) engañar; **to ~ sb on to**
  (*induce*) incitar a algn a.
►**lead to** *vt fus* producir, provocar.
►**lead up to** *vt fus* conducir a.
leaded ['lɛdɪd] *adj*: ~ **windows** ventanas *fpl*
  emplomadas.
leaden ['lɛdn] *adj* (*sky, sea*) plomizo; (*heavy*:

footsteps) pesado.
leader ['liːdə*] *n* jefe/a *m/f*, líder *m*; (*of union etc*) dirigente *m/f*; (*guide*) guía *m/f*; (*of newspaper*) editorial *m*; **they are ~s in their field** (*fig*) llevan la delantera en su especialidad.
leadership ['liːdəʃɪp] *n* dirección *f*; **qualities of ~** iniciativa *sg*; **under the ~ of ...** bajo la dirección de ..., al mando de ....
lead-free ['lɛdfriː] *adj* sin plomo.
leading ['liːdɪŋ] *adj* (*main*) principal; (*outstanding*) destacado; (*first*) primero; (*front*) delantero; **a ~ question** una pregunta tendenciosa.
leading lady *n* (*THEAT*) primera actriz *f*.
leading light *n* (*fig: person*) figura principal.
leading man *n* (*THEAT*) primer actor *m*.
leading role *n* papel *m* principal.
lead pencil *n* lápiz *m*.
lead poisoning *n* envenenamiento plúmbico.
lead time *n* (*COMM*) plazo de entrega.
lead-up ['liːdʌp] *n*: **in the ~ to the election** cuando falta *etc* poco para las elecciones.
lead weight *n* peso de plomo.
leaf, *pl* **leaves** [liːf, liːvz] *n* hoja; **to turn over a new ~** (*fig*) volver la hoja, hacer borrón y cuenta nueva; **to take a ~ out of sb's book** (*fig*) seguir el ejemplo de algn.
▶**leaf through** *vt fus* (*book*) hojear.
leaflet ['liːflɪt] *n* folleto.
leafy ['liːfɪ] *adj* frondoso.
league [liːg] *n* sociedad *f*; (*FOOTBALL*) liga; **to be in ~ with** estar confabulado con.
league table *n* clasificación *f*.
leak [liːk] *n* (*of liquid, gas*) escape *m*, fuga; (*in pipe*) agujero; (*in roof*) gotera; (*fig: of information, in security*) filtración *f* ♦ *vi* (*ship*) hacer agua; (*shoes*) tener un agujero; (*pipe*) tener un escape; (*roof*) tener goteras; (*also: ~ out: liquid, gas*) escaparse, salirse; (*fig: news*) trascender, divulgarse ♦ *vt* (*gen*) dejar escapar; (*fig: information*) filtrar.
leakage ['liːkɪdʒ] *n* (*of water, gas etc*) escape *m*, fuga.
leaky ['liːkɪ] *adj* (*roof*) con goteras; (*bucket, shoe*) con agujeros; (*pipe*) con un escape; (*boat*) que hace agua.
lean [liːn] *adj* (*thin*) flaco; (*meat*) magro ♦ *vb* (*pt, pp* **leaned** *or* **leant** [lɛnt]) *vt*: **to ~ sth on sth** apoyar algo en algo ♦ *vi* (*slope*) inclinarse; (*rest*): **to ~ against** apoyarse contra; **to ~ on** apoyarse en.
▶**lean back** *vi* inclinarse hacia atrás.
▶**lean forward** *vi* inclinarse hacia

adelante.
▶**lean out** *vi*: **to ~ out (of)** asomarse (a).
▶**lean over** *vi* inclinarse.
leaning ['liːnɪŋ] *adj* inclinado ♦ *n*: **~ (towards)** inclinación *f* (hacia); **the L~ Tower of Pisa** la Torre Inclinada de Pisa.
leant [lɛnt] *pt, pp of* **lean**.
lean-to ['liːntuː] *n* (*roof*) tejado de una sola agua; (*building*) cobertizo.
leap [liːp] *n* salto ♦ *vi* (*pt, pp* **leaped** *or* **leapt** [lɛpt]) saltar; **to ~ at an offer** apresurarse a aceptar una oferta.
▶**leap up** *vi* (*person*) saltar.
leapfrog ['liːpfrɒg] *n* pídola ♦ *vi*: **to ~ over sb/sth** saltar por encima de algn/algo.
leapt [lɛpt] *pt, pp of* **leap**.
leap year *n* año bisiesto.
learn, *pt, pp* **learned** *or* **learnt** [ləːn, -t] *vt* (*gen*) aprender; (*come to know of*) enterarse de ♦ *vi* aprender; **to ~ how to do sth** aprender a hacer algo; **to ~ that ...** enterarse *or* informarse de que ...; **to ~ about sth** (*SCOL*) aprender algo; (*hear*) enterarse *or* informarse de algo; **we were sorry to ~ that ...** nos dio tristeza saber que ....
learned ['ləːnɪd] *adj* erudito.
learner ['ləːnə*] *n* principiante *m/f*; (*BRIT: also:* **~ driver**) conductor(a) *m/f* en prácticas; *see also* **L-plates**.
learning ['ləːnɪŋ] *n* saber *m*, conocimientos *mpl*.
learnt [ləːnt] *pp of* **learn**.
lease [liːs] *n* arriendo ♦ *vt* arrendar; **on ~** en arriendo.
▶**lease back** *vt* subarrendar.
leaseback ['liːsbæk] *n* subarriendo.
leasehold ['liːshəuld] *n* (*contract*) derechos *mpl* de arrendamiento ♦ *adj* arrendado.
leash [liːʃ] *n* correa.
least [liːst] *adj* (*slightest*) menor, más pequeño; (*smallest amount of*) mínimo ♦ *adv* menos ♦ *n*: **the ~** lo menos; **the ~ expensive car** el coche menos caro; **at ~** por lo menos, al menos; **not in the ~** en absoluto.
leather ['lɛðə*] *n* cuero ♦ *cpd*: **~ goods** artículos *mpl* de cuero *or* piel.
leathery ['lɛðərɪ] *adj* (*skin*) curtido.
leave [liːv] *vb* (*pt, pp* **left** [lɛft]) *vt* dejar; (*go away from*) abandonar ♦ *vi* irse; (*train*) salir ♦ *n* permiso; **to ~ school** dejar la escuela *or* el colegio; **~ it to me!** ¡yo me encargo!; **he's already left for the airport** ya se ha marchado al aeropuerto; **to be left** quedar, sobrar; **there's some milk left over** sobra *or* queda algo de leche; **on ~**

de permiso; **to take one's ~ of** despedirse de.
▶**leave behind** vt (on purpose) dejar (atrás); (accidentally) olvidar.
▶**leave off** vt (lid) no poner; (switch) no encender; (col: stop): **to ~ off doing sth** dejar de hacer algo.
▶**leave on** vt (lid) dejar puesto; (light, fire, cooker) dejar encendido.
▶**leave out** vt omitir.
▶**leave over** vt (postpone) dejar, aplazar.
leave of absence n excedencia.
leaves [liːvz] pl of **leaf.**
leavetaking ['liːvteɪkɪŋ] n despedida.
Lebanon ['lɛbənən] n: **the ~** el Líbano.
lecherous ['lɛtʃərəs] adj lascivo.
lectern ['lɛktəːn] n atril m.
lecture ['lɛktʃə*] n conferencia; (SCOL) clase f ♦ vi dar clase(s) ♦ vt (scold) sermonear; (reprove) echar una reprimenda a; **to give a ~ on** dar una conferencia sobre.
lecture hall n sala de conferencias; (UNIV) aula.
lecturer ['lɛktʃərə*] n conferenciante m/f; (BRIT: at university) profesor(a) m/f.
lecture theatre n = **lecture hall.**
LED n abbr (= light-emitting diode) LED m.
led [lɛd] pt, pp of **lead.**
ledge [lɛdʒ] n (of window, on wall) repisa, reborde m; (of mountain) saliente m.
ledger ['lɛdʒə*] n libro mayor.
lee [liː] n sotavento; **in the ~ of** al abrigo de.
leech [liːtʃ] n sanguijuela.
leek [liːk] n puerro.
leer [lɪə*] vi: **to ~ at sb** mirar de manera lasciva a algn.
leeway ['liːweɪ] n (fig): **to have some ~** tener cierta libertad de acción.
left [lɛft] pt, pp of **leave** ♦ adj izquierdo ♦ n izquierda ♦ adv a la izquierda; **on** or **to the ~** a la izquierda; **the L~** (POL) la izquierda.
left-click ['lɛftklɪk] vi clicar con el botón izquierdo del ratón ♦ vt: **to ~ an icon** clicar en un icono con el botón izquierdo del ratón.
left-hand drive ['lɛfthænd-] n conducción f por la izquierda.
left-handed [lɛft'hændɪd] adj zurdo; **~ scissors** tijeras fpl zurdas or para zurdos.
left-hand side ['lɛfthænd-] n izquierda.
leftie ['lɛftɪ] n = **lefty.**
leftist ['lɛftɪst] adj (POL) izquierdista.
left-luggage (office) [lɛft'lʌgɪdʒ(-)] n (BRIT) consigna.
left-overs ['lɛftəuvəz] npl sobras fpl.

left-wing [lɛft'wɪŋ] adj (POL) de izquierda(s), izquierdista.
left-winger ['lɛft'wɪŋə*] n (POL) izquierdista m/f.
lefty ['lɛftɪ] n (col: POL) rojillo/a.
leg [lɛg] n pierna; (of animal, chair) pata; (CULIN: of meat) pierna; (of journey) etapa; **1st/2nd ~** (SPORT) partido de ida/de vuelta; **to pull sb's ~** tomar el pelo a algn; **to stretch one's ~s** dar una vuelta.
legacy ['lɛgəsɪ] n herencia; (fig) herencia, legado.
legal ['liːgl] adj (permitted by law) lícito; (of law) legal; (inquiry etc) jurídico; **to take ~ action** or **proceedings against sb** entablar or levantar un pleito contra algn.
legal adviser n asesor(a) m/f jurídico/a.
legal holiday n (US) fiesta oficial.
legality [lɪ'gælɪtɪ] n legalidad f.
legalize ['liːgəlaɪz] vt legalizar.
legally ['liːgəlɪ] adv legalmente; **~ binding** con fuerza legal.
legal tender n moneda de curso legal.
legend ['lɛdʒənd] n leyenda.
legendary ['lɛdʒəndərɪ] adj legendario.
-legged ['lɛgɪd] suff: **two-~** (table etc) de dos patas.
leggings ['lɛgɪŋz] npl mallas fpl, leggins mpl.
leggy ['lɛgɪ] adj de piernas largas.
legibility [lɛdʒɪ'bɪlɪtɪ] n legibilidad f.
legible ['lɛdʒəbl] adj legible.
legibly ['lɛdʒəblɪ] adv legiblemente.
legion ['liːdʒən] n legión f.
legionnaire [liːdʒə'nɛə*] n legionario.
legionnaire's disease n enfermedad f del legionario.
legislation [lɛdʒɪs'leɪʃən] n legislación f; **a piece of ~** (bill) un proyecto de ley; (act) una ley.
legislative ['lɛdʒɪslətɪv] adj legislativo.
legislator ['lɛdʒɪsleɪtə*] n legislador(a) m/f.
legislature ['lɛdʒɪslətʃə*] n cuerpo legislativo.
legitimacy [lɪ'dʒɪtɪməsɪ] n legitimidad f.
legitimate [lɪ'dʒɪtɪmət] adj legítimo.
legitimize [lɪ'dʒɪtɪmaɪz] vt legitimar.
legless ['lɛglɪs] adj (BRIT col) mamado.
leg-room ['lɛgruːm] n espacio para las piernas.
Leics abbr (BRIT) = **Leicestershire.**
leisure ['lɛʒə*] n ocio, tiempo libre; **at ~** con tranquilidad.
leisure centre n centro recreativo.
leisurely ['lɛʒəlɪ] adj sin prisa; lento.
leisure suit n conjunto tipo chandal.
lemon ['lɛmən] n limón m.
lemonade [lɛmə'neɪd] n (fruit juice) limonada; (fizzy) gaseosa.

lemon cheese, lemon curd *n* queso de limón.
lemon juice *n* zumo de limón.
lemon tea *n* té *m* con limón.
lend, *pt, pp* **lent** [lɛnd, lɛnt] *vt:* **to ~ sth to sb** prestar algo a algn.
lender ['lɛndə*] *n* prestamista *m/f*.
lending library ['lɛndɪŋ-] *n* biblioteca de préstamo.
length [lɛŋθ] *n* (*size*) largo, longitud *f*; (*section: of road, pipe*) tramo; (: *of rope etc*) largo; **at ~** (*at last*) por fin, finalmente; (*lengthily*) largamente; **it is 2 metres in ~** tiene dos metros de largo; **what ~ is it?** ¿cuánto tiene de largo?; **to fall full ~** caer de bruces; **to go to any ~(s) to do sth** ser capaz de hacer cualquier cosa para hacer algo.
lengthen ['lɛŋθn] *vt* alargar ♦ *vi* alargarse.
lengthways ['lɛŋθweɪz] *adv* a lo largo.
lengthy ['lɛŋθɪ] *adj* largo, extenso; (*meeting*) prolongado.
lenient ['liːnɪənt] *adj* indulgente.
lens [lɛnz] *n* (*of spectacles*) lente *f*; (*of camera*) objetivo.
Lent [lɛnt] *n* Cuaresma.
lent [lɛnt] *pt, pp of* **lend.**
lentil ['lɛntl] *n* lenteja.
Leo ['liːəu] *n* Leo.
leopard ['lɛpəd] *n* leopardo.
leotard ['liːətɑːd] *n* leotardo.
leper ['lɛpə*] *n* leproso/a.
leper colony *n* colonia de leprosos.
leprosy ['lɛprəsɪ] *n* lepra.
lesbian ['lɛzbɪən] *adj* lesbiano ♦ *n* lesbiana.
lesion ['liːʒən] *n* (*MED*) lesión *f*.
Lesotho [lɪ'suːtuː] *n* Lesotho.
less [lɛs] *adj* (*in size, degree etc*) menor; (*in quantity*) menos ♦ *pron, adv* menos; **~ than half** menos de la mitad; **~ than £1/a kilo/3 metres** menos de una libra/un kilo/tres metros; **~ than ever** menos que nunca; **~ 5%** menos el cinco por ciento; **~ and ~** cada vez menos; **the ~ he works...** cuanto menos trabaja ....
lessee [lɛ'siː] *n* inquilino/a, arrendatario/a.
lessen ['lɛsn] *vi* disminuir, reducirse ♦ *vt* disminuir, reducir.
lesser ['lɛsə*] *adj* menor; **to a ~ extent** *or* **degree** en menor grado.
lesson ['lɛsn] *n* clase *f*; **a maths ~** una clase de matemáticas; **to give ~s in** dar clases de; **it taught him a ~** (*fig*) le sirvió de lección.
lessor ['lɛsɔ:* *or* lɛ'sɔ:*] *n* arrendador(a) *m/f*.
lest [lɛst] *conj:* **~ it happen** para que no pase.
let, *pt, pp* **let** [lɛt] *vt* (*allow*) dejar, permitir;

(*BRIT: lease*) alquilar; **to ~ sb do sth** dejar que algn haga algo; **to ~ sb have sth** dar algo a algn; **to ~ sb know sth** comunicar algo a algn; **~'s go** ¡vamos!; **~ him come** que venga; **"to ~"** "se alquila".
▶**let down** *vt* (*lower*) bajar; (*dress*) alargar; (*tyre*) desinflar; (*hair*) soltar; (*disappoint*) defraudar.
▶**let go** *vi* soltar; (*fig*) dejarse ir ♦ *vt* soltar.
▶**let in** *vt* dejar entrar; (*visitor etc*) hacer pasar; **what have you ~ yourself in for?** ¿en qué te has metido?
▶**let off** *vt* dejar escapar; (*firework etc*) disparar; (*bomb*) accionar; (*passenger*) dejar, bajar; **to ~ off steam** (*fig, col*) desahogarse, desfogarse.
▶**let on** *vi:* **to ~ on that ...** revelar que ...
▶**let out** *vt* dejar salir; (*dress*) ensanchar; (*rent out*) alquilar.
▶**let up** *vi* disminuir; (*rain etc*) amainar.
let-down ['lɛtdaun] *n* (*disappointment*) decepción *f*.
lethal ['liːθl] *adj* (*weapon*) mortífero; (*poison, wound*) mortal.
lethargic [lɛ'θɑːdʒɪk] *adj* aletargado.
lethargy ['lɛθədʒɪ] *n* letargo.
letter ['lɛtə*] *n* (*of alphabet*) letra; (*correspondence*) carta; **~s** *npl* (*literature, learning*) letras *fpl*; **small/capital ~** minúscula/mayúscula; **covering ~** carta adjunta.
letter bomb *n* carta-bomba.
letterbox ['lɛtəbɔks] *n* (*BRIT*) buzón *m*.
letterhead ['lɛtəhɛd] *n* membrete *m*, encabezamiento.
lettering ['lɛtərɪŋ] *n* letras *fpl*.
letter of credit *n* carta de crédito; **documentary ~** carta de crédito documentaria; **irrevocable ~** carta de crédito irrevocable.
letter-opener ['lɛtərəupnə*] *n* abrecartas *m inv*.
letterpress ['lɛtəprɛs] *n* (*method*) prensa de copiar; (*printed page*) impresión *f* tipográfica.
letter quality *n* calidad *f* de correspondencia.
letters patent *npl* letra *sg* de patente.
lettuce ['lɛtɪs] *n* lechuga.
let-up ['lɛtʌp] *n* descanso, tregua.
leukaemia, (*US*) **leukemia** [luː'kiːmɪə] *n* leucemia.
level ['lɛvl] *adj* (*flat*) llano; (*flattened*) nivelado; (*uniform*) igual ♦ *adv* a nivel ♦ *n* nivel *m* ♦ *vt* nivelar, allanar; (*gun*) apuntar; (*accusation*): **to ~ (against)** levantar (contra) ♦ *vi* (*col*): **to ~ with sb** ser franco con algn; **to be ~ with** estar a

nivel de; **a ~ spoonful** (*CULIN*) una cucharada rasa; **to draw ~ with** (*team*) igualar; (*runner, car*) alcanzar a; **O ~s** *npl* (*BRIT: formerly*) ≈ bachillerato *sg* elemental, octavo *sg* de Básica; **on the ~** (*fig: honest*) en serio; **talks at ministerial ~** charlas *fpl* a nivel ministerial.

▶**level off** *or* **out** *vi* (*prices etc*) estabilizarse; (*ground*) nivelarse; (*aircraft*) ponerse en una trayectoria horizontal.

level crossing *n* (*BRIT*) paso a nivel.

level-headed ['levl'hedɪd] *adj* sensato.

levelling, (*US*) **leveling** ['levlɪŋ] *adj* (*process, effect*) de nivelación ♦ *n* igualación *f*, allanamiento.

level playing field *n* situación *f* de igualdad; **to compete on a ~** competir en igualdad de condiciones.

lever ['liːvə*] *n* palanca ♦ *vt*: **to ~ up** levantar con palanca.

leverage ['liːvərɪdʒ] *n* (*fig: influence*) influencia.

levity ['levɪtɪ] *n* frivolidad *f*, informalidad *f*.

levy ['levɪ] *n* impuesto ♦ *vt* exigir, recaudar.

lewd [luːd] *adj* lascivo; obsceno, colorado (*LAM*).

lexicographer [leksɪ'kɔgrəfə*] *n* lexicógrafo/a *m/f*.

lexicography [leksɪ'kɔgrəfɪ] *n* lexicografía *f*.

LGV *n abbr* (= *Large Goods Vehicle*) vehículo pesado.

LI *abbr* (*US*) = *Long Island*.

liabilities [laɪə'bɪlətɪz] *npl* obligaciones *fpl*; pasivo *sg*.

liability [laɪə'bɪlətɪ] *n* responsabilidad *f*; (*handicap*) desventaja.

liable ['laɪəbl] *adj* (*subject*): **~ to** sujeto a; (*responsible*): **~ for** responsable de; (*likely*): **~ to do** propenso a hacer; **to be ~ to a fine** exponerse a una multa.

liaise [liː'eɪz] *vi*: **to ~ (with)** colaborar (con); **to ~ with sb** mantener informado a algn.

liaison [liː'eɪzɔn] *n* (*coordination*) enlace *m*; (*affair*) relación *f*.

liar ['laɪə*] *n* mentiroso/a.

libel ['laɪbl] *n* calumnia ♦ *vt* calumniar.

libellous ['laɪbləs] *adj* difamatorio, calumnioso.

liberal ['lɪbərl] *adj* (*gen*) liberal; (*generous*): **~ with** generoso con ♦ *n*: **L~** (*POL*) liberal *m/f*.

Liberal Democrat *n* (*BRIT*) demócrata *m/f* liberal.

liberality [lɪbə'rælɪtɪ] *n* (*generosity*) liberalidad *f*, generosidad *f*.

liberalize ['lɪbərəlaɪz] *vt* liberalizar.

liberally ['lɪbərəlɪ] *adv* liberalmente.

liberal-minded ['lɪbərl'maɪndɪd] *adj* de miras anchas, liberal.

liberate ['lɪbəreɪt] *vt* liberar.

liberation [lɪbə'reɪʃən] *n* liberación *f*.

liberation theology *n* teología de la liberación.

Liberia [laɪ'bɪərɪə] *n* Liberia.

Liberian [laɪ'bɪərɪən] *adj, n* liberiano/a *m/f*.

liberty ['lɪbətɪ] *n* libertad *f*; **to be at ~ to do** estar libre para hacer; **to take the ~ of doing sth** tomarse la libertad de hacer algo.

libido [lɪ'biːdəu] *n* libido.

Libra ['liːbrə] *n* Libra.

librarian [laɪ'breərɪən] *n* bibliotecario/a.

library ['laɪbrərɪ] *n* biblioteca.

library book *n* libro de la biblioteca.

libretto [lɪ'bretəu] *n* libreto.

Libya ['lɪbɪə] *n* Libia.

Libyan ['lɪbɪən] *adj, n* libio/a *m/f*.

lice [laɪs] *pl of* **louse**.

licence, (*US*) **license** ['laɪsns] *n* licencia; (*permit*) permiso; (*also*: **driving licence**, (*US*) **driver's license**) carnet *m* de conducir; (*excessive freedom*) libertad *f*; **import ~** licencia *or* permiso de importación; **produced under ~** elaborado bajo licencia.

licence number *n* (número de) matrícula.

licence plate *n* (placa de) matrícula.

license ['laɪsns] (*US*) = **licence** ♦ *vt* autorizar, dar permiso a; (*car*) sacar la matrícula de *or* la patente (*LAM*) de.

licensed ['laɪsnst] *adj* (*for alcohol*) autorizado para vender bebidas alcohólicas.

licensed trade *n* comercio *or* negocio autorizado.

licensee [laɪsən'siː] *n* (*in a pub*) concesionario/a, dueño/a de un bar.

licentious [laɪ'senʃəs] *adj* licencioso.

lichen ['laɪkən] *n* liquen *m*.

lick [lɪk] *vt* lamer; (*col: defeat*) dar una paliza a ♦ *n* lamedura; **a ~ of paint** una mano de pintura.

licorice ['lɪkərɪs] *n* = **liquorice**.

lid [lɪd] *n* (*of box, case*) tapa; (*of pan*) cobertera; **to take the ~ off sth** (*fig*) exponer algo a la luz pública.

lido ['laɪdəu] *n* (*BRIT*) piscina, alberca (*LAM*).

lie [laɪ] *n* mentira ♦ *vi* mentir; (*pt* **lay**, *pp* **lain** [leɪ, leɪn]) (*rest*) estar echado, estar acostado; (*of object: be situated*) estar, encontrarse; **to tell ~s** mentir; **to ~ low** (*fig*) mantenerse a escondidas.

▶**lie about**, **lie around** *vi* (*things*) estar

tirado; (*BRIT: people*) estar acostado *or* tumbado.

▶**lie back** *vi* recostarse.

▶**lie down** *vi* echarse, tumbarse.

▶**lie up** *vi* (*hide*) esconderse.

Liechtenstein ['lɪktənstaɪn] *n* Liechtenstein *m*.

lie detector *n* detector *m* de mentiras.

lie-down ['laɪdaun] *n* (*BRIT*): **to have a ~** echarse (una siesta).

lie-in ['laɪɪn] *n* (*BRIT*): **to have a ~** quedarse en la cama.

lieu [luː]: **in ~ of** *prep* en lugar de.

Lieut *abbr* = **lieutenant**.

lieutenant [lɛf'tɛnənt, (*US*) luː'tɛnənt] *n* (*MIL*) teniente *m*.

lieutenant colonel *n* teniente *m* coronel.

life, *pl* **lives** [laɪf, laɪvz] *n* vida; (*of licence etc*) vigencia; **to be sent to prison for ~** ser condenado a cadena perpetua; **country/city ~** la vida en el campo/en la ciudad; **true to ~** fiel a la realidad; **to paint from ~** pintar del natural; **to put** *or* **breathe new ~ into** (*person*) reanimar; (*project, area etc*) infundir nueva vida a.

life assurance *n* (*BRIT*) seguro de vida.

lifebelt ['laɪfbɛlt] *n* (*BRIT*) salvavidas *m inv*.

lifeblood ['laɪfblʌd] *n* (*fig*) alma, nervio.

lifeboat ['laɪfbəut] *n* lancha de socorro.

life-buoy ['laɪfbɔɪ] *n* boya *or* guindola salvavidas.

life coach *n* profesional encargado de mejorar la situación laboral y personal de sus clientes.

life expectancy *n* esperanza de vida.

lifeguard ['laɪfgɑːd] *n* vigilante *m/f*.

life imprisonment *n* cadena perpetua.

life insurance *n* = **life assurance**.

life jacket *n* chaleco salvavidas.

lifeless ['laɪflʌs] *adj* sin vida; (*dull*) soso.

lifelike ['laɪflaɪk] *adj* natural.

lifeline ['laɪflaɪn] *n* (*fig*) cordón *m* umbilical.

lifelong ['laɪflɔŋ] *adj* de toda la vida.

life preserver *n* (*US*) = **lifebelt**.

lifer ['laɪfə*] *n* (*col*) condenado/a *m/f* a cadena perpetua.

life-saver ['laɪfseɪvə*] *n* socorrista *m/f*.

life sentence *n* cadena perpetua.

life-sized ['laɪfsaɪzd] *adj* de tamaño natural.

life span *n* vida.

lifestyle ['laɪfstaɪl] *n* estilo de vida.

life support system *n* (*MED*) sistema *m* de respiración asistida.

lifetime ['laɪftaɪm] *n*: **in his ~** durante su vida; **once in a ~** una vez en la vida; **the chance of a ~** una oportunidad única.

lift [lɪft] *vt* levantar; (*copy*) plagiar ♦ *vi* (*fog*) disiparse ♦ *n* (*BRIT: elevator*) ascensor *m*,

elevador *m* (*LAM*); **to give sb a ~** (*BRIT*) llevar a algn en coche.

▶**lift off** *vt* levantar, quitar ♦ *vi* (*rocket, helicopter*) despegar.

▶**lift out** *vt* sacar; (*troops, evacuees etc*) evacuar.

▶**lift up** *vt* levantar.

lift-off ['lɪftɔf] *n* despegue *m*.

ligament ['lɪgəmənt] *n* ligamento.

light [laɪt] *n* luz *f*; (*flame*) lumbre *f*; (*lamp*) luz *f*, lámpara; (*daylight*) luz *f* del día; (*headlight*) faro; (*rear ~*) luz *f* trasera; (*for cigarette etc*): **have you got a ~?** ¿tienes fuego? ♦ *vt* (*pt, pp* **lighted** *or* **lit** [lɪt]) (*candle, cigarette, fire*) encender; (*room*) alumbrar ♦ *adj* (*colour*) claro; (*not heavy, also fig*) ligero, liviano (*esp LAM*); (*room*) alumbrado ♦ *adv* (*travel*) con poco equipaje; **to turn the ~ on/off** encender/ apagar la luz; **in the ~ of** a la luz de; **to come to ~** salir a la luz; **to cast** *or* **shed** *or* **throw ~ on** arrojar luz sobre; **to make ~ of sth** (*fig*) no dar importancia a algo.

▶**light up** *vi* (*smoke*) encender un cigarrillo; (*face*) iluminarse ♦ *vt* (*illuminate*) iluminar, alumbrar.

light bulb *n* bombilla, bombillo (*LAM*), foco (*LAM*).

lighten ['laɪtn] *vi* (*grow light*) clarear ♦ *vt* (*give light to*) iluminar; (*make lighter*) aclarar; (*make less heavy*) aligerar.

lighter ['laɪtə*] *n* (*also*: **cigarette ~**) encendedor *m* (*esp LAM*), mechero.

light-fingered [laɪt'fɪŋgəd] *adj* de manos largas.

light-headed [laɪt'hɛdɪd] *adj* (*dizzy*) mareado; (*excited*) exaltado; (*by nature*) atolondrado.

light-hearted [laɪt'hɑːtɪd] *adj* alegre.

lighthouse ['laɪthaus] *n* faro.

lighting ['laɪtɪŋ] *n* (*act*) iluminación *f*; (*system*) alumbrado.

lighting-up time [laɪtɪŋ'ʌp-] *n* (*BRIT*) hora de encendido del alumbrado.

lightly ['laɪtlɪ] *adv* ligeramente; (*not seriously*) con poca seriedad; **to get off ~** ser castigado con poca severidad.

light meter *n* (*PHOT*) fotómetro.

lightness ['laɪtnɪs] *n* claridad *f*; (*in weight*) ligereza.

lightning ['laɪtnɪŋ] *n* relámpago, rayo.

lightning conductor, (*US*) **lightning rod** *n* pararrayos *m inv*.

lightning strike *n* huelga relámpago.

lightweight ['laɪtweɪt] *adj* (*suit*) ligero ♦ *n* (*BOXING*) peso ligero.

light year *n* año luz.

like [laɪk] *vt* (*person*) querer a; (*thing*): **I ~**

swimming/apples me gusta nadar/me gustan las manzanas ♦ *prep* como ♦ *adj* parecido, semejante ♦ *n*: **did you ever see the ~ (of it)?** ¿has visto cosa igual?; **his ~s and dislikes** sus gustos y aversiones; **the ~s of him** personas como él; **I would ~, I'd ~** me gustaría; (*for purchase*) quisiera; **would you ~ a coffee?** ¿te apetece un café?; **to be** *or* **look ~ sb/sth** parecerse a algn/algo; **that's just ~ him** es muy de él, es típico de él; **do it ~ this** hazlo así; **it is nothing ~...** no tiene parecido alguno con...; **what's he ~?** ¿cómo es (él)?; **what's the weather ~?** ¿qué tiempo hace?; **something ~ that** algo así *or* por el estilo; **I feel ~ a drink** me apetece algo de beber; **if you ~** si quieres.

likeable ['laɪkəbl] *adj* simpático, agradable.

likelihood ['laɪklɪhud] *n* probabilidad *f*; **in all ~** según todas las probabilidades.

likely ['laɪklɪ] *adj* probable, capaz (*LAM*); **he's ~ to leave** es probable *or* capaz (*LAM*) que se vaya; **not ~!** ¡ni hablar!

like-minded [laɪk'maɪndɪd] *adj* de la misma opinión.

liken ['laɪkən] *vt*: **to ~ to** comparar con.

likeness ['laɪknɪs] *n* (*similarity*) semejanza, parecido.

likewise ['laɪkwaɪz] *adv* igualmente.

liking ['laɪkɪŋ] *n*: **~ (for)** (*person*) cariño (a); (*thing*) afición (a); **to take a ~ to sb** tomar cariño a algn; **to be to sb's ~** ser del gusto de algn.

lilac ['laɪlək] *n* lila ♦ *adj* (*colour*) de color lila.

Lilo ® ['laɪləu] *n* colchoneta inflable.

lilt [lɪlt] *n* deje *m*.

lilting ['lɪltɪŋ] *adj* melodioso.

lily ['lɪlɪ] *n* lirio, azucena.

lily of the valley *n* lirio de los valles.

Lima ['liːmə] *n* Lima.

limb [lɪm] *n* miembro; (*of tree*) rama; **to be out on a ~** (*fig*) estar aislado.

limber up ['lɪmbə*-*] *vi* (*fig*) entrenarse; (*SPORT*) hacer (ejercicios de) precalentamiento.

limbo ['lɪmbəu] *n*: **to be in ~** (*fig*) quedar a la expectativa.

lime [laɪm] *n* (*tree*) limero; (*fruit*) lima; (*GEO*) cal *f*.

lime juice *n* zumo (*SP*) *or* jugo de lima.

limelight ['laɪmlaɪt] *n*: **to be in the ~** (*fig*) ser el centro de atención.

limerick ['lɪmərɪk] *n* quintilla humorística.

limestone ['laɪmstəun] *n* piedra caliza.

limit ['lɪmɪt] *n* límite *m* ♦ *vt* limitar; **weight/speed ~** peso máximo/velocidad *f* máxima; **within ~s** entre límites.

limitation [lɪmɪ'teɪʃən] *n* limitación *f*.

limited ['lɪmɪtɪd] *adj* limitado; **to be ~ to** limitarse a; **~ edition** edición limitada.

limited (liability) company (Ltd) *n* (*BRIT*) sociedad *f* anónima (SA).

limitless ['lɪmɪtlɪs] *adj* sin límites.

limousine ['lɪməziːn] *n* limusina.

limp [lɪmp] *n*: **to have a ~** tener cojera ♦ *vi* cojear, renguear (*LAM*) ♦ *adj* flojo.

limpet ['lɪmpɪt] *n* lapa.

limpid ['lɪmpɪd] *adj* (*poetic*) límpido, cristalino.

limply ['lɪmplɪ] *adv* desmayadamente; **to say ~** decir débilmente.

linchpin ['lɪntʃpɪn] *n* pezonera; (*fig*) eje *m*.

Lincs [lɪŋks] *abbr* (*BRIT*) = Lincolnshire.

line [laɪn] *n* (*also COMM*) línea; (*straight ~*) raya; (*rope*) cuerda; (*for fishing*) sedal *m*; (*wire*) hilo; (*row, series*) fila, hilera; (*of writing*) renglón *m*; (*on face*) arruga; (*speciality*) rama ♦ *vt* (*SEWING*): **to ~ (with)** forrar (de); **to ~ the streets** ocupar las aceras; **in ~ with** de acuerdo con; **she's in ~ for promotion** (*fig*) tiene muchas posibilidades de que la asciendan; **to bring sth into ~ with sth** poner algo de acuerdo con algo; **~ of research/business** campo de investigación/comercio; **to take the ~ that ...** ser de la opinión que ...; **hold the ~ please** (*TEL*) no cuelgue usted, por favor; **to draw the ~ at doing sth** negarse a hacer algo; no permitir que se haga algo; **on the right ~s** por buen camino; **a new ~ in cosmetics** una nueva línea en cosméticos; *see also* **lines**.

▶**line up** *vi* hacer cola ♦ *vt* alinear, poner en fila; **to have sth ~d up** tener algo arreglado.

linear ['lɪnɪə*] *adj* lineal.

lined [laɪnd] *adj* (*face*) arrugado; (*paper*) rayado; (*clothes*) forrado.

line editing *n* (*COMPUT*) corrección *f* por líneas.

line feed *n* (*COMPUT*) avance *m* de línea.

lineman ['laɪnmən] *n* (*US*) técnico de las líneas; (*FOOTBALL*) delantero.

linen ['lɪnɪn] *n* ropa blanca; (*cloth*) lino.

line printer *n* impresora *f* de línea.

liner ['laɪnə*] *n* vapor *m* de línea, transatlántico; **dustbin ~** bolsa de la basura.

lines [laɪnz] *npl* (*RAIL*) vía *sg*, raíles *mpl*.

linesman ['laɪnzmən] *n* (*SPORT*) juez *m* de línea.

line-up ['laɪnʌp] *n* alineación *f*.

linger ['lɪŋgə*] *vi* retrasarse, tardar en marcharse; (*smell, tradition*) persistir.

lingerie ['lænʒəri] *n* ropa interior *or* íntima

(de mujer).

lingering ['lɪŋgərɪŋ] *adj* persistente; (*death*) lento.

lingo, ~**es** ['lɪŋgəʊ] *n* (*pej*) jerga.

linguist ['lɪŋgwɪst] *n* lingüista *m/f*.

linguistic [lɪŋ'gwɪstɪk] *adj* lingüístico.

linguistics [lɪŋ'gwɪstɪks] *n* lingüística.

liniment ['lɪnɪmənt] *n* linimento.

lining ['laɪnɪŋ] *n* forro; (*TECH*) revestimiento; (*of brake*) guarnición *f*.

link [lɪŋk] *n* (*of a chain*) eslabón *m*; (*connection*) conexión *f*; (*bond*) vínculo, lazo; (*INTERNET*) enlace *m* ♦ *vt* vincular, unir; **rail** ~ línea de ferrocarril, servicio de trenes.

▶**link up** *vt* acoplar ♦ *vi* unirse.

links [lɪŋks] *npl* (*GOLF*) campo *sg* de golf.

link-up ['lɪŋkʌp] *n* (*gen*) unión *f*; (*meeting*) encuentro, reunión *f*; (*of roads*) empalme *m*; (*of spaceships*) acoplamiento; (*RADIO, TV*) enlace *m*.

lino ['laɪnəʊ] (*BRIT*), **linoleum** [lɪ'nəʊlɪəm] *n* linóleo.

linseed oil ['lɪnsiːd-] *n* aceite *m* de linaza.

lint [lɪnt] *n* gasa.

lintel ['lɪntl] *n* dintel *m*.

lion ['laɪən] *n* león *m*.

lioness ['laɪənɪs] *n* leona.

lip [lɪp] *n* labio; (*of jug*) pico; (*of cup etc*) borde *m*.

liposuction ['lɪpəʊsʌkʃən] *n* liposucción *f*.

lipread ['lɪpriːd] *vi* leer los labios.

lip salve *n* crema protectora para labios.

lip service *n*: **to pay** ~ **to sth** alabar algo pero sin hacer nada.

lipstick ['lɪpstɪk] *n* lápiz *m or* barra de labios, carmín *m*.

liquefy ['lɪkwɪfaɪ] *vt* licuar ♦ *vi* licuarse.

liqueur [lɪ'kjʊə*] *n* licor *m*.

liquid ['lɪkwɪd] *adj, n* líquido.

liquidate ['lɪkwɪdeɪt] *vt* liquidar.

liquidation [lɪkwɪ'deɪʃən] *n* liquidación *f*; **to go into** ~ entrar en liquidación.

liquid crystal display (LCD) *n* pantalla de cristal líquido.

liquidity [lɪ'kwɪdɪtɪ] *n* (*COMM*) liquidez *f*.

liquidize ['lɪkwɪdaɪz] *vt* (*CULIN*) licuar.

liquidizer ['lɪkwɪdaɪzə*] *n* (*CULIN*) licuadora.

liquor ['lɪkə*] *n* licor *m*, bebidas *fpl* alcohólicas.

liquorice ['lɪkərɪs] *n* regaliz *m*.

liquor store *n* (*US*) bodega, *tienda de vinos y bebidas alcohólicas*.

Lisbon ['lɪzbən] *n* Lisboa.

lisp [lɪsp] *n* ceceo.

lissom ['lɪsəm] *adj* ágil.

list [lɪst] *n* lista; (*of ship*) inclinación *f* ♦ *vt* (*write down*) hacer una lista de;

(*enumerate*) catalogar; (*COMPUT*) hacer un listado de ♦ *vi* (*ship*) inclinarse; **shopping** ~ lista de las compras; *see also* **lists**.

listed building ['lɪstɪd-] *n* (*ARCHIT*) edificio de interés histórico-artístico.

listed company ['lɪstɪd-] *n* compañía cotizable.

listen ['lɪsn] *vi* escuchar, oír; (*pay attention*) atender.

listener ['lɪsnə*] *n* oyente *m/f*.

listeria [lɪs'tɪərɪə] *n* listeria.

listing ['lɪstɪŋ] *n* (*COMPUT*) listado.

listless ['lɪstlɪs] *adj* apático, indiferente.

listlessly ['lɪstlɪslɪ] *adv* con indiferencia.

listlessness ['lɪstlɪsnɪs] *n* indiferencia, apatía.

list price *n* precio de catálogo.

lists [lɪsts] *npl* (*HISTORY*) liza *sg*; **to enter the** ~ (**against sb/sth**) salir a la palestra (contra algn/algo).

lit [lɪt] *pt, pp of* **light**.

litany ['lɪtənɪ] *n* letanía.

liter ['liːtə*] *n* (*US*) = **litre**.

literacy ['lɪtərəsɪ] *n* capacidad *f* de leer y escribir; ~ **campaign** campaña de alfabetización.

literal ['lɪtərl] *adj* literal.

literally ['lɪtrəlɪ] *adv* literalmente.

literary ['lɪtərərɪ] *adj* literario.

literate ['lɪtərət] *adj* que sabe leer y escribir; (*fig*) culto.

literature ['lɪtərɪtʃə*] *n* literatura; (*brochures etc*) folletos *mpl*.

lithe [laɪð] *adj* ágil.

litho(graph) ['lɪθəʊ(grɑːf)] *n* litografía.

Lithuania [lɪθju'eɪnɪə] *n* Lituania.

Lithuanian [lɪθju'eɪnɪən] *adj* lituano ♦ *n* lituano/a; (*LING*) lituano.

litigate ['lɪtɪgeɪt] *vi* litigar.

litigation [lɪtɪ'geɪʃən] *n* litigio.

litmus paper ['lɪtməs-] *n* papel *m* de tornasol.

litre, (*US*) **liter** ['liːtə*] *n* litro.

litter ['lɪtə*] *n* (*rubbish*) basura; (*paper*) papeles *mpl* (tirados); (*young animals*) camada, cría.

litter bin *n* (*BRIT*) papelera.

littered ['lɪtəd] *adj*: ~ **with** lleno de.

litter lout, (*US*) **litterbug** ['lɪtəbʌg] *n* *persona que tira papeles usados en la vía pública*.

little ['lɪtl] *adj* (*small*) pequeño, chico (*esp LAM*); (*not much*) poco; (*often translated by suffix, eg*): ~ **house** casita ♦ *adv* poco; **a** ~ un poco (de); ~ **by** ~ poco a poco; ~ **finger** (dedo) meñique *m*; **for a** ~ **while** (durante) un rato; **with** ~ **difficulty** sin problema *or* dificultad; **as** ~ **as possible**

lo menos posible.

little-known ['lɪtl'nəun] *adj* poco conocido.

liturgy ['lɪtədʒɪ] *n* liturgia.

live *vb* [lɪv] *vi* vivir ♦ *vt* (*a life*) llevar; (*experience*) vivir ♦ *adj* [laɪv] (*animal*) vivo; (*wire*) conectado; (*broadcast*) en directo; (*issue*) de actualidad; (*unexploded*) sin explotar; **to ~ in London** vivir en Londres; **to ~ together** vivir juntos.

▶**live down** *vt* hacer olvidar.

▶**live off** *vt fus* (*land, fish etc*) vivir de; (*pej: parents etc*) vivir a costa de.

▶**live on** *vt fus* (*food*) vivir de, alimentarse de; **to ~ on £50 a week** vivir con 50 libras semanales *or* a la semana.

▶**live out** *vi* (*students*) ser externo ♦ *vt*: **to ~ out one's days** *or* **life** pasar el resto de la vida.

▶**live up** *vt*: **to ~ it up** (*col*) tirarse la gran vida.

▶**live up to** *vt fus* (*fulfil*) cumplir con; (*justify*) justificar.

live-in ['lɪvɪn] *adj*: **~ partner** pareja, compañero/a sentimental; **~ maid** asistenta interna.

livelihood ['laɪvlɪhud] *n* sustento.

liveliness ['laɪvlɪnɪs] *n* viveza.

lively ['laɪvlɪ] *adj* (*gen*) vivo; (*talk*) animado; (*pace*) rápido; (*party, tune*) alegre.

liven up ['laɪvn-] *vt* (*discussion, evening*) animar.

liver ['lɪvə*] *n* hígado.

liverish ['lɪvərɪʃ] *adj*: **to feel ~** sentirse *or* encontrarse mal, no estar muy católico.

Liverpudlian [lɪvə'pʌdlɪən] *adj* de Liverpool ♦ *n* nativo/a (*or* habitante *m/f*) de Liverpool.

livery ['lɪvərɪ] *n* librea.

lives [laɪvz] *npl of* **life**.

livestock ['laɪvstɔk] *n* ganado.

live wire [laɪv-] *n* (*fig, col*): **he's a real ~!** ¡tiene una marcha!

livid ['lɪvɪd] *adj* lívido; (*furious*) furioso.

living ['lɪvɪŋ] *adj* (*alive*) vivo ♦ *n*: **to earn** *or* **make a ~** ganarse la vida; **cost of ~** coste *m* de la vida; **in ~ memory** que se recuerde *or* recuerda.

living conditions *npl* condiciones *fpl* de vida.

living expenses *npl* gastos *mpl* de mantenimiento.

living room *n* sala (de estar), living *m* (*LAM*).

living standards *npl* nivel *msg* de vida.

living wage *n* sueldo suficiente para vivir.

lizard ['lɪzəd] *n* lagartija.

llama ['lɑːmə] *n* llama.

LLB *n abbr* (= *Bachelor of Laws*) Ldo./a. en

Dcho; *see also* **Bachelor's Degree**.

LLD *n abbr* (= *Doctor of Laws*) Dr(a). en Dcho.

LMT *n abbr* (*US*: = *Local Mean Time*) *hora local*.

load [ləud] *n* (*gen*) carga; (*weight*) peso ♦ *vt* (*COMPUT*) cargar; (*also*: **~ up**): **to ~ (with)** cargar (con *or* de); **a ~ of**, **~s of** (*fig*) (gran) cantidad de, montones de.

loaded ['ləudɪd] *adj* (*dice*) cargado; (*question*) intencionado; (*col: rich*) forrado (de dinero).

loading ['ləudɪŋ] *n* (*COMM*) sobreprima.

loading bay *n* área de carga y descarga.

loaf, *pl* **loaves** [ləuf, ləuvz] *n* (barra de) pan *m* ♦ *vi* (*also*: **~ about**, **~ around**) holgazanear.

loam [ləum] *n* marga.

loan [ləun] *n* préstamo; (*COMM*) empréstito ♦ *vt* prestar; **on ~** (*book, painting*) prestado; **to raise a ~** (*money*) procurar un empréstito.

loan account *n* cuenta de crédito.

loan capital *n* empréstito.

loan shark *n* (*col: pej*) prestamista *m/f* sin escrúpulos.

loath [ləuθ] *adj*: **to be ~ to do sth** ser reacio a hacer algo.

loathe [ləuð] *vt* aborrecer; (*person*) odiar.

loathing ['ləuðɪŋ] *n* aversión *f*; odio.

loathsome ['ləuðsəm] *adj* asqueroso, repugnante; (*person*) odioso.

loaves [ləuvz] *pl of* **loaf**.

lob [lɔb] *vt* (*ball*) volear por alto.

lobby ['lɔbɪ] *n* vestíbulo, sala de espera; (*POL: pressure group*) grupo de presión ♦ *vt* presionar.

lobbyist ['lɔbɪɪst] *n* cabildero/a.

lobe [ləub] *n* lóbulo.

lobster ['lɔbstə*] *n* langosta.

lobster pot *n* nasa, langostera.

local ['ləukl] *adj* local ♦ *n* (*pub*) bar *m*; **the ~s** *npl* los vecinos, los del lugar.

local anaesthetic *n* (*MED*) anestesia local.

local authority *n* municipio, ayuntamiento (*SP*).

local call *n* (*TEL*) llamada local.

local government *n* gobierno municipal.

locality [ləu'kælɪtɪ] *n* localidad *f*.

localize ['ləukəlaɪz] *vt* localizar.

locally ['ləukəlɪ] *adv* en la vecindad.

locate [ləu'keɪt] *vt* (*find*) localizar; (*situate*) situar, ubicar (*LAM*).

location [ləu'keɪʃən] *n* situación *f*; **on ~** (*CINE*) en exteriores, fuera del estudio.

loch [lɔx] *n* lago.

lock [lɔk] *n* (*of door, box*) cerradura, chapa (*LAM*); (*of canal*) esclusa; (*of hair*) mechón

_m_ ♦ _vt_ (_with key_) cerrar con llave;
(_immobilize_) inmovilizar ♦ _vi_ (_door etc_)
cerrarse con llave; (_wheels_) trabarse; ~
stock and barrel (_fig_) por completo _or_
entero; **on full** ~ (_AUT_) con el volante
girado al máximo.
▶**lock away** _vt_ (_valuables_) guardar bajo
llave; (_criminal_) encerrar.
▶**lock out** _vt_: **the workers were** ~**ed out** los
trabajadores tuvieron que enfrentarse
con un cierre patronal.
▶**lock up** _vi_ echar la llave.
locker ['lɔkə*] _n_ casillero.
locker-room ['lɔkərum] _n_ (_US SPORT_)
vestuario.
locket ['lɔkɪt] _n_ medallón _m_.
lockout ['lɔkaut] _n_ (_INDUSTRY_) paro _or_
cierre _m_ patronal, lockout _m_.
locksmith ['lɔksmɪθ] _n_ cerrajero/a.
lock-up ['lɔkʌp] _n_ (_prison_) cárcel _f_; (_cell_)
jaula; (~ _garage_) jaula, cochera.
locomotive [ləukə'məutɪv] _n_ locomotora.
locum ['ləukəm] _n_ (_MED_) (médico/a)
suplente _m/f_.
locust ['ləukəst] _n_ langosta.
lodge [lɔdʒ] _n_ casa del guarda; (_porter's_)
portería; (_FREEMASONRY_) logia ♦ _vi_
(_person_): **to** ~ (**with**) alojarse (en casa de)
♦ _vt_ (_complaint_) presentar.
lodger ['lɔdʒə*] _n_ huésped(a) _m/f_.
lodgings ['lɔdʒɪŋz] _npl_ alojamiento _sg_;
(_house_) casa _sg_ de huéspedes.
loft [lɔft] _n_ desván _m_.
lofty ['lɔftɪ] _adj_ alto; (_haughty_) altivo,
arrogante; (_sentiments, aims_) elevado,
noble.
log [lɔg] _n_ (_of wood_) leño, tronco; (_book_)
= **logbook** ♦ _n abbr_ (= _logarithm_) log. ♦ _vt_
anotar, registrar.
▶**log in, log on** _vi_ (_COMPUT_) iniciar la (_or_
una) sesión.
▶**log off, log out** _vi_ (_COMPUT_) finalizar la
sesión.
logarithm ['lɔgərɪðəm] _n_ logaritmo.
logbook ['lɔgbuk] _n_ (_NAUT_) diario de a
bordo; (_AVIAT_) libro de vuelo; (_of car_)
documentación _f_ (del coche).
log cabin _n_ cabaña de troncos.
log fire _n_ fuego de leña.
logger ['lɔgə*] _n_ leñador(a) _m/f_.
loggerheads ['lɔgəhɛdz] _npl_: **at** ~ (**with**) de
pique (con).
logic ['lɔdʒɪk] _n_ lógica.
logical ['lɔdʒɪkl] _adj_ lógico.
logically ['lɔdʒɪkəlɪ] _adv_ lógicamente.
login ['lɔgɪn] _n_ login _m_.
logistics [lɔ'dʒɪstɪks] _n_ logística.
log jam _n_: **to break the** ~ poner fin al

estancamiento.
logo ['ləugəu] _n_ logotipo.
loin [lɔɪn] _n_ (_CULIN_) lomo, solomillo; ~**s** _npl_
lomos _mpl_.
loin cloth _n_ taparrabos _m inv_.
loiter ['lɔɪtə*] _vi_ vagar; (_pej_) merodear.
loll [lɔl] _vi_ (_also_: ~ **about**) repantigarse.
lollipop ['lɔlɪpɔp] _n_ pirulí _m_; (_iced_)
polo.
lollipop lady _n_ (_BRIT_) ver recuadro.
lollipop man _n_ (_BRIT_) ver recuadro.

LOLLIPOP LADY, LOLLIPOP MAN

_Se llama **lollipop lady** o **lollipop man** a la
persona encargada de parar el tráfico en las
carreteras cercanas a los colegios
británicos para que los niños las crucen sin
peligro. Suelen ser personas ya jubiladas,
vestidas con un abrigo de color luminoso y
llevando una señal de stop en un poste
portátil, la cual recuerda por su forma a un
pirulí, de ahí su nombre._

---

lolly ['lɔlɪ] _n_ (_col: ice cream_) polo; (: _lollipop_)
piruleta; (: _money_) guita.
London ['lʌndən] _n_ Londres _m_.
Londoner ['lʌndənə*] _n_ londinense _m/f_.
lone [ləun] _adj_ solitario.
loneliness ['ləunlɪnɪs] _n_ soledad _f_,
aislamiento.
lonely ['ləunlɪ] _adj_ solitario, solo.
lonely hearts _adj_: ~ **ad** anuncio de la
sección de contactos; ~ **column** sección _f_
de contactos.
lone parent family _n_ familia
monoparental.
loner ['ləunə*] _n_ solitario/a.
lonesome ['ləunsəm] _adj_ (_esp US_) = **lonely**.
long [lɔŋ] _adj_ largo ♦ _adv_ mucho tiempo,
largamente ♦ _vi_: **to** ~ **for sth** anhelar algo
♦ _n_: **the** ~ **and the short of it is that** ...
(_fig_) en resumidas cuentas ...; **in the** ~
run a la larga; **so** _or_ **as** ~ **as** mientras, con
tal de que; **don't be** ~! ¡no tardes!,
¡vuelve pronto!; **how** ~ **is the street?**
¿cuánto tiene la calle de largo?; **how** ~ **is
the lesson?** ¿cuánto dura la clase?; **6
metres** ~ que mide 6 metros, de 6 metros
de largo; **6 months** ~ que dura 6 meses,
de 6 meses de duración; **all night** ~ toda
la noche; ~ **ago** hace mucho (tiempo); **he
no** ~**er comes** ya no viene; ~ **before**
mucho antes; **before** ~ (+ _future_) dentro
de poco; (+ _past_) poco tiempo después; **at**
~ **last** al fin, por fin; **I shan't be** ~ termino
pronto.
long-distance [lɔŋ'dɪstəns] _adj_ (_race_) de

larga distancia; (*call*) interurbano.
longevity [lɒn'dʒevɪtɪ] *n* longevidad *f*.
long-haired ['lɒŋ'heəd] *adj* de pelo largo.
longhand ['lɒŋhænd] *n* escritura (corriente).
longing ['lɒŋɪŋ] *n* anhelo, ansia; (*nostalgia*) nostalgia ♦ *adj* anhelante.
longingly ['lɒŋɪŋlɪ] *adv* con ansia.
longitude ['lɒŋgɪtjuːd] *n* longitud *f*.
long jump *n* salto de longitud.
long-lost ['lɒŋlɒst] *adj* desaparecido hace mucho tiempo.
long-playing record (LP) ['lɒŋpleɪŋ-] *n* elepé *m*, disco de larga duración.
long-range ['lɒŋ'reɪndʒ] *adj* de gran alcance; (*weather forecast*) a largo plazo.
longshoreman ['lɒŋʃɔːmən] *n* (*US*) estibador *m*.
long-sighted ['lɒŋ'saɪtɪd] *adj* (*BRIT*) présbita.
long-standing ['lɒŋ'stændɪŋ] *adj* de mucho tiempo.
long-suffering [lɒŋ'sʌfərɪŋ] *adj* sufrido.
long-term ['lɒŋtəːm] *adj* a largo plazo.
long wave *n* onda larga.
long-winded [lɒŋ'wɪndɪd] *adj* prolijo.
loo [luː] *n* (*BRIT: col*) wáter *m*.
loofah ['luːfə] *n* esponja de lufa.
look [luk] *vi* mirar; (*seem*) parecer; (*building etc*): **to ~ south/on to the sea** dar al sur/al mar ♦ *n* mirada; (*glance*) vistazo; (*appearance*) aire *m*, aspecto; **~s** *npl* físico *sg*, belleza *sg*; **to ~ ahead** mirar hacia delante; **it ~s about 4 metres long** yo calculo que tiene unos 4 metros de largo; **it ~s all right to me** a mí me parece que está bien; **to have a ~ at sth** echar un vistazo a algo; **to have a ~ for sth** buscar algo.
►**look after** *vt fus* cuidar.
►**look around** *vi* echar una mirada alrededor.
►**look at** *vt fus* mirar; (*consider*) considerar.
►**look back** *vi* mirar hacia atrás; **to ~ back at sb/sth** mirar hacia atrás algo/a algn; **to ~ back on** (*event, period*) recordar.
►**look down on** *vt fus* (*fig*) despreciar, mirar con desprecio.
►**look for** *vt fus* buscar.
►**look forward to** *vt fus* esperar con ilusión; (*in letters*): **we ~ forward to hearing from you** quedamos a la espera de su respuesta *or* contestación; **I'm not ~ing forward to it** no tengo ganas de eso, no me hace ilusión.
►**look in** *vi*: **to ~ in on sb** (*visit*) pasar por casa de algn.
►**look into** *vt fus* investigar.

►**look on** *vi* mirar (como espectador).
►**look out** *vi* (*beware*): **to ~ out (for)** tener cuidado (de).
►**look out for** *vt fus* (*seek*) buscar; (*await*) esperar.
►**look over** *vt* (*essay*) revisar; (*town, building*) inspeccionar, registrar; (*person*) examinar.
►**look round** *vi* (*turn*) volver la cabeza; **to ~ round for sth** buscar algo.
►**look through** *vt fus* (*papers, book*) hojear; (*briefly*) echar un vistazo a; (*telescope*) mirar por.
►**look to** *vt fus* ocuparse de; (*rely on*) contar con.
►**look up** *vi* mirar hacia arriba; (*improve*) mejorar ♦ *vt* (*word*) buscar; (*friend*) visitar.
►**look up to** *vt fus* admirar.
look-out ['lukaut] *n* (*tower etc*) puesto de observación; (*person*) vigía *m/f*; **to be on the ~ for sth** estar al acecho de algo.
look-up table ['lukʌp-] *n* (*COMPUT*) tabla de consulta.
LOOM *n abbr* (*US: = Loyal Order of Moose*) *asociación benéfica*.
loom [luːm] *n* telar *m* ♦ *vi* (*threaten*) amenazar.
loony ['luːnɪ] *adj, n* (*col*) loco/a *m/f*.
loop [luːp] *n* lazo; (*bend*) vuelta, recodo; (*COMPUT*) bucle *m*.
loophole ['luːphəul] *n* laguna.
loose [luːs] *adj* (*gen*) suelto; (*not tight*) flojo; (*wobbly etc*) movedizo; (*clothes*) ancho; (*morals, discipline*) relajado ♦ *vt* (*free*) soltar; (*slacken*) aflojar; (*also*: **~ off**: *arrow*) disparar, soltar; **~ connection** (*ELEC*) hilo desempalmado; **to be at a ~ end** *or* (*US*) **at ~ ends** no saber qué hacer; **to tie up ~ ends** (*fig*) no dejar ningún cabo suelto, atar cabos.
loose change *n* cambio.
loose chippings [-'tʃɪpɪŋz] *npl* (*on road*) gravilla *sg* suelta.
loose-fitting ['luːsfɪtɪŋ] *adj* suelto.
loose-leaf ['luːsliːf] *adj*: **~ binder** *or* **folder** carpeta de anillas.
loose-limbed ['luːslɪmd] *adj* ágil, suelto.
loosely ['luːslɪ] *adv* libremente, aproximadamente.
loosely-knit [-nɪt] *adj* de estructura abierta.
loosen ['luːsn] *vt* (*free*) soltar; (*untie*) desatar; (*slacken*) aflojar.
►**loosen up** *vi* (*before game*) hacer (ejercicios de) precalentamiento; (*col*: *relax*) soltarse, relajarse.
looseness ['luːsnɪs] *n* soltura; flojedad *f*.

loot [luːt] *n* botín *m* ♦ *vt* saquear.
looter ['luːtə*] *n* saqueador(a) *m/f*.
looting ['luːtɪŋ] *n* pillaje *m*.
lop [lɔp]: **to ~ off** *vt* cortar; (*branches*) podar.
lop-sided ['lɔp'saɪdɪd] *adj* desequilibrado.
lord [lɔːd] *n* señor *m*; **L~ Smith** Lord Smith; **the L~** el Señor; **the (House of) L~s** (*BRIT*) la Cámara de los Lores.
lordly ['lɔːdlɪ] *adj* señorial.
Lordship ['lɔːdʃɪp] *n*: **your ~** su Señoría.
lore [lɔː*] *n* saber *m* popular, tradiciones *fpl*.
lorry ['lɔrɪ] *n* (*BRIT*) camión *m*.
lorry driver *n* camionero/a.
lorry load *n* carga.
lose, *pt, pp* **lost** [luːz, lɔst] *vt* perder ♦ *vi* perder, ser vencido; **to ~ (time)** (*clock*) atrasarse; **to ~ no time (in doing sth)** no tardar (en hacer algo); **to get lost** (*object*) extraviarse; (*person*) perderse.
▶**lose out** *vi* salir perdiendo.
loser ['luːzə*] *n* perdedor(a) *m/f*; **to be a bad ~** no saber perder.
losing ['luːzɪŋ] *adj* (*team etc*) vencido, perdedor(a).
loss [lɔs] *n* pérdida; **heavy ~es** (*MIL*) grandes pérdidas *fpl*; **to be at a ~** no saber qué hacer; **to be a dead ~** ser completamente inútil; **to cut one's ~es** reducir las pérdidas; **to sell sth at a ~** vender algo perdiendo dinero.
loss adjuster *n* (*INSURANCE*) perito/a *m/f* or tasador(a) *m/f* de pérdidas.
loss leader *n* (*COMM*) artículo de promoción.
lost [lɔst] *pt, pp of* **lose** ♦ *adj* perdido; **~ in thought** absorto, ensimismado.
lost and found *n* (*US*) = **lost property, lost property office** *or* **department**.
lost cause *n* causa perdida.
lost property *n* (*BRIT*) objetos *mpl* perdidos.
lost property office *or* **department** *n* (*BRIT*) departamento de objetos perdidos.
lot [lɔt] *n* (*at auctions*) lote *m*; (*destiny*) suerte *f*; **the ~** el todo, todos *mpl*, todas *fpl*; **a ~** mucho, bastante; **a ~ of, ~s of** mucho(s)/a(s) (*pl*); **I read a ~** leo bastante; **to draw ~s (for sth)** echar suertes (para decidir algo).
lotion ['ləuʃən] *n* loción *f*.
lottery ['lɔtərɪ] *n* lotería.
loud [laud] *adj* (*voice, sound*) fuerte; (*laugh, shout*) estrepitoso; (*gaudy*) chillón/ona ♦ *adv* (*speak etc*) fuerte; **out ~** en voz alta.
loudhailer [laud'heɪlə*] *n* (*BRIT*) megáfono.
loudly ['laudlɪ] *adv* (*noisily*) fuerte; (*aloud*) en alta voz.

loudness ['laudnɪs] *n* (*of sound etc*) fuerza.
loudspeaker [laud'spiːkə*] *n* altavoz *m*.
lounge [laundʒ] *n* salón *m*, sala de estar; (*of hotel*) salón *m*; (*of airport*) sala de embarque ♦ *vi* (*also:* **~ about, ~ around**) holgazanear, no hacer nada; *see also* **pub**.
lounge bar *n* salón *m*.
lounge suit *n* (*BRIT*) traje *m* de calle.
louse, *pl* **lice** [laus, laɪs] *n* piojo.
▶**louse up** *vt* (*col*) echar a perder.
lousy ['lauzɪ] *adj* (*fig*) vil, asqueroso.
lout [laut] *n* gamberro/a.
louvre, (*US*) **louver** ['luːvə*] *adj*: **~ door** puerta de rejilla; **~ window** ventana de libro.
lovable ['lʌvəbl] *adj* amable, simpático.
love [lʌv] *n* amor *m* ♦ *vt* amar, querer; **to send one's ~ to sb** dar sus recuerdos a algn; **~ from Anne** (*in letter*) con cariño de Anne; **I ~ to read** me encanta leer; **to be in ~ with** estar enamorado de; **to make ~** hacer el amor; **for the ~ of** por amor a; **"15 ~"** (*TENNIS*) "15 a cero"; **I ~ paella** me encanta la paella; **I'd ~ to come** me gustaría muchísimo venir.
love affair *n* aventura sentimental *or* amorosa.
love child *n* hijo/a natural.
loved ones ['lʌvdwʌnz] *npl* seres *mpl* queridos.
love-hate relationship ['lʌvheɪt-] *n* relación *f* de amor y odio.
love letter *n* carta de amor.
love life *n* vida sentimental.
lovely ['lʌvlɪ] *adj* (*delightful*) precioso, encantador(a), lindo (*esp LAM*); (*beautiful*) hermoso, lindo (*esp LAM*); **we had a ~ time** lo pasamos estupendo.
lovemaking ['lʌvmeɪkɪŋ] *n* relaciones *fpl* sexuales.
lover ['lʌvə*] *n* amante *m/f*; (*amateur*): **a ~ of** un(a) aficionado/a *or* un(a) amante de.
lovesick ['lʌvsɪk] *adj* enfermo de amor, amartelado.
lovesong ['lʌvsɔŋ] *n* canción *f* de amor.
loving ['lʌvɪŋ] *adj* amoroso, cariñoso.
lovingly ['lʌvɪŋlɪ] *adv* amorosamente, cariñosamente.
low [ləu] *adj, adv* bajo ♦ *n* (*METEOROLOGY*) área de baja presión ♦ *vi* (*cow*) mugir; **to feel ~** sentirse deprimido; **to turn (down) ~** bajar; **to reach a new** *or* **an all-time ~** llegar a su punto más bajo.
low-alcohol [ləu'ælkəhɔl] *adj* bajo en alcohol.
lowbrow ['ləubrau] *adj* (*person*) de poca cultura.
low-calorie ['ləu'kælərɪ] *adj* bajo en

calorías.
low-cut ['ləukʌt] adj (dress) escotado.
low-down ['ləudaun] n (col): **he gave me
the ~ on it** me puso al corriente ♦ adj
(mean) vil, bajo.
lower ['ləuə*] vt bajar; (reduce: price)
reducir, rebajar; (: resistance) debilitar:
to ~ o.s. to (fig) rebajarse a ♦ vi ['lauə*]:
to ~ (at sb) fulminar (a algn) con la
mirada.
lower case n (TYP) minúscula.
Lower House n (POL): **the ~** la Cámara
baja.
lowering ['lauərɪŋ] adj (sky) amenazador(a).
low-fat ['ləu'fæt] adj (milk, yoghurt)
desnatado; (diet) bajo en calorías.
low-key ['ləu'kiː] adj de mínima intensidad;
(operation) de poco perfil.
lowland ['ləulənd] n tierra baja.
low-level ['ləulɛvl] adj de bajo nivel; (flying)
a poca altura.
low-loader ['ləuləudə*] n camión m de caja
a bajo nivel.
lowly ['ləulɪ] adj humilde.
low-lying ['ləu'laɪŋ] adj bajo.
low-rise ['ləuraɪz] adj bajo.
low-tech ['ləutɛk] adj de baja tecnología.
loyal ['lɔɪəl] adj leal.
loyalist ['lɔɪəlɪst] n legitimista m/f.
loyally ['lɔɪəlɪ] adv lealmente.
loyalty ['lɔɪəltɪ] n lealtad f.
loyalty card n (BRIT) tarjeta cliente.
lozenge ['lɔzɪndʒ] n (MED) pastilla.
LP n abbr see **long-playing record**.
L-plates ['ɛlpleɪts] npl (BRIT) (placas fpl de)
la L; ver recuadro.

L-PLATES

*En el Reino Unido las personas que están
aprendiendo a conducir han de llevar
indicativos blancos con una L en rojo
llamados normalmente* **L-plates** *(de
"learner") en la parte delantera y trasera de
los automóviles que conducen. No tienen
que ir a clases teóricas, sino que desde el
principio se les entrega un carnet de
conducir provisional ("provisional driving
licence") para que realicen sus prácticas,
que han de estar supervisadas por un
conductor con carnet definitivo ("full
driving licence"). Tampoco se les permite
hacer prácticas en autopistas aunque vayan
acompañados.*

LPN n abbr (US: = Licensed Practical Nurse)
enfermero/a practicante.
LRAM n abbr (BRIT) = Licentiate of the Royal
Academy of Music.
LSD n abbr (= lysergic acid diethylamide) LSD
m; (BRIT: = pounds, shillings and pence)
sistema monetario usado en Gran
Bretaña hasta 1971.
LSE n abbr = London School of Economics.
Ltd abbr (= limited company) S.A.
lubricant ['luːbrɪkənt] n lubricante m.
lubricate ['luːbrɪkeɪt] vt lubricar, engrasar.
lubrication [luːbrɪ'keɪʃən] n lubricación f.
lucid ['luːsɪd] adj lúcido.
lucidity [luː'sɪdɪtɪ] n lucidez f.
lucidly ['luːsɪdlɪ] adv lúcidamente.
luck [lʌk] n suerte f; **good/bad ~** buena/
mala suerte; **good ~!** ¡(que tengas)
suerte!; **to be in ~** estar de suerte; **to be
out of ~** tener mala suerte.
luckily ['lʌkɪlɪ] adv afortunadamente.
lucky ['lʌkɪ] adj afortunado.
lucrative ['luːkrətɪv] adj lucrativo.
ludicrous ['luːdɪkrəs] adj absurdo.
ludo ['luːdəu] n parchís m.
lug [lʌg] vt (drag) arrastrar.
luggage ['lʌgɪdʒ] n equipaje m.
luggage rack n (in train) rejilla, redecilla;
(on car) baca, portaequipajes m inv.
luggage van n furgón m or vagón m de
equipaje.
lugubrious [lu'guːbrɪəs] adj lúgubre.
lukewarm ['luːkwɔːm] adj tibio, templado.
lull [lʌl] n tregua ♦ vt (child) acunar; (person,
fear) calmar.
lullaby ['lʌləbaɪ] n nana.
lumbago [lʌm'beɪgəu] n lumbago.
lumber ['lʌmbə*] n (junk) trastos mpl viejos;
(wood) maderos mpl ♦ vt (BRIT col): **to ~ sb
with sth/sb** hacer que algn cargue con
algo/algn ♦ vi (also: ~ **about**, ~ **along**)
moverse pesadamente.
lumberjack ['lʌmbədʒæk] n maderero.
lumber room n (BRIT) cuarto trastero.
lumber yard n (US) almacén m de madera.
luminous ['luːmɪnəs] adj luminoso.
lump [lʌmp] n terrón m; (fragment) trozo;
(in sauce) grumo; (in throat) nudo;
(swelling) bulto ♦ vt (also: ~ **together**)
juntar; (persons) poner juntos.
lump sum n suma global.
lumpy ['lʌmpɪ] adj (sauce) lleno de grumos.
lunacy ['luːnəsɪ] n locura.
lunar ['luːnə*] adj lunar.
lunatic ['luːnətɪk] adj, n loco/a m/f.
lunatic asylum n manicomio.
lunch [lʌntʃ] n almuerzo, comida ♦ vi
almorzar; **to invite sb to** or **for ~** invitar a
algn a almorzar.
lunch break, lunch hour n hora del
almuerzo.

luncheon ['lʌntʃən] *n* almuerzo.
luncheon meat *n* tipo de fiambre.
luncheon voucher *n* vale *m* de comida.
lunchtime ['lʌntʃtaɪm] *n* hora del almuerzo *or* de comer.
lung [lʌŋ] *n* pulmón *m*.
lung cancer *n* cáncer *m* del pulmón.
lunge [lʌndʒ] *vi* (*also*: ~ **forward**) abalanzarse; **to** ~ **at** arremeter contra.
lupin ['lu:pɪn] *n* altramuz *m*.
lurch [lə:tʃ] *vi* dar sacudidas ♦ *n* sacudida; **to leave sb in the** ~ dejar a algn plantado.
lure [luə*] *n* (*bait*) cebo; (*decoy*) señuelo ♦ *vt* convencer con engaños.
lurid ['luərɪd] *adj* (*colour*) chillón/ona; (*account*) sensacional; (*detail*) horripilante.
lurk [lə:k] *vi* (*hide*) esconderse; (*wait*) estar al acecho.
luscious ['lʌʃəs] *adj* delicioso.
lush [lʌʃ] *adj* exuberante.
lust [lʌst] *n* lujuria; (*greed*) codicia.
▶**lust after** *vt fus* codiciar.
lustful ['lʌstful] *adj* lascivo, lujurioso.
lustre, (*US*) **luster** ['lʌstə*] *n* lustre *m*, brillo.
lustrous ['lʌstrəs] *adj* brillante.
lusty ['lʌstɪ] *adj* robusto, fuerte.
lute [lu:t] *n* laúd *m*.
Luxembourg ['lʌksəmbə:g] *n* Luxemburgo.
luxuriant [lʌg'zjuərɪənt] *adj* exuberante.
luxurious [lʌg'zjuərɪəs] *adj* lujoso.
luxury ['lʌkʃərɪ] *n* lujo ♦ *cpd* de lujo.
luxury tax *n* impuesto de lujo.
LV *n abbr* (*BRIT*) = **luncheon voucher**.
LW *abbr* (*RADIO*) = **long wave**.
Lycra ® ['laɪkrə] *n* licra ®.
lying ['laɪɪŋ] *n* mentiras *fpl* ♦ *adj* (*statement, story*) falso; (*person*) mentiroso.
lynch [lɪntʃ] *vt* linchar.
lynx [lɪŋks] *n* lince *m*.
Lyons ['laɪənz] *n* Lyón *m*.
lyre ['laɪə*] *n* lira.
lyric ['lɪrɪk] *adj* lírico; ~**s** *npl* (*of song*) letra *sg*.
lyrical ['lɪrɪkl] *adj* lírico.

M m

M, m [ɛm] *n* (*letter*) M, m *f*; **M for Mary,** (*US*) **M for Mike** M de Madrid.
M *n abbr* = **million(s)**; (= *medium*) M; (*BRIT*: = *motorway*): **the M8** ≈ la A8.
m *abbr* (= *metre*) m.; = **mile(s)**.
MA *n abbr* (*US*) = *Military Academy*; *see* **Master of Arts** ♦ *abbr* (*US*) = *Massachusetts*.
mac [mæk] *n* (*BRIT*) impermeable *m*.
macabre [mə'kɑ:brə] *adj* macabro.
macaroni [mækə'rəunɪ] *n* macarrones *mpl*.
macaroon [mækə'ru:n] *n* macarrón *m*, mostachón *m*.
mace [meɪs] *n* (*weapon, ceremonial*) maza; (*spice*) macis *f*.
Macedonia [mæsɪ'dəunɪə] *n* Macedonia.
Macedonian [mæsɪ'dəunɪən] *adj* macedonio ♦ *n* macedonio/a; (*LING*) macedonio.
machinations [mæʃɪ'neɪʃənz] *npl* intrigas *fpl*, maquinaciones *fpl*.
machine [mə'ʃi:n] *n* máquina ♦ *vt* (*dress etc*) coser a máquina; (*TECH*) trabajar a máquina.
machine code *n* (*COMPUT*) código máquina.
machine gun *n* ametralladora.
machine language *n* (*COMPUT*) lenguaje *m* máquina.
machine readable *adj* (*COMPUT*) legible por máquina.
machinery [mə'ʃi:nərɪ] *n* maquinaria; (*fig*) mecanismo.
machine shop *n* taller *m* de máquinas.
machine tool *n* máquina herramienta.
machine translation *n* traducción *f* automática.
machine washable *adj* lavable a máquina.
machinist [mə'ʃi:nɪst] *n* operario/a *m/f* (de máquina).
macho ['mætʃəu] *adj* macho.
mackerel ['mækrl] *n*, *pl inv* caballa.
mackintosh ['mækɪntɔʃ] *n* (*BRIT*) impermeable *m*.
macro ... ['mækrəu] *pref* macro....
macro-economics ['mækrəui:kə'nɔmɪks] *n* macroeconomía.
mad [mæd] *adj* loco; (*idea*) disparatado;

(*angry*) furioso, enojado (*LAM*); ~ **(at** *or*
with sb) furioso con algn; **to be** ~ **(keen)**
about *or* **on sth** estar loco por algo; **to go**
~ volverse loco, enloquecer(se).
madam ['mædəm] *n* señora; **can I help you**
~? ¿le puedo ayudar, señora?; **M~**
Chairman señora presidenta.
madcap ['mædkæp] *adj* (*col*) alocado,
disparatado.
mad cow disease *n* encefalopatía
espongiforme bovina.
madden ['mædn] *vt* volver loco.
maddening ['mædnıŋ] *adj* enloquecedor(a).
made [meɪd] *pt, pp of* **make**.
Madeira [mə'dɪərə] *n* (*GEO*) Madeira; (*wine*)
madeira *m*.
made-to-measure ['meɪdtəmɛʒə*] *adj*
(*BRIT*) hecho a la medida.
made-up ['meɪdʌp] *adj* (*story*) ficticio.
madhouse ['mædhaus] *n* (*also fig*)
manicomio.
madly ['mædlı] *adv* locamente.
madman ['mædmən] *n* loco.
madness ['mædnıs] *n* locura.
Madonna [mə'dɒnə] *n* Virgen *f*.
Madrid [mə'drɪd] *n* Madrid *m*.
madrigal ['mædrɪgəl] *n* madrigal *m*.
Mafia ['mæfɪə] *n* Mafia.
mag [mæg] *n abbr* (*BRIT col*) = **magazine**.
magazine [mægə'ziːn] *n* revista; (*MIL: store*)
almacén *m*; (*of firearm*) recámara.
maggot ['mægət] *n* gusano.
magic ['mædʒɪk] *n* magia ♦ *adj* mágico.
magical ['mædʒɪkəl] *adj* mágico.
magician [mə'dʒɪʃən] *n* mago/a.
magistrate ['mædʒɪstreɪt] *n* juez *m/f*
(municipal); **M~s' Courts** *see* **crown court**.
magnanimity [mægnə'nɪmɪtɪ] *n*
magnanimidad *f*.
magnanimous [mæg'nænɪməs] *adj*
magnánimo.
magnate ['mægneɪt] *n* magnate *m/f*.
magnesium [mæg'niːzɪəm] *n* magnesio.
magnet ['mægnɪt] *n* imán *m*.
magnetic [mæg'nɛtɪk] *adj* magnético.
magnetic disk *n* (*COMPUT*) disco
magnético.
magnetic tape *n* cinta magnética.
magnetism ['mægnɪtɪzəm] *n* magnetismo.
magnification [mægnɪfɪ'keɪʃən] *n* aumento.
magnificence [mæg'nɪfɪsns] *n*
magnificencia.
magnificent [mæg'nɪfɪsnt] *adj* magnífico.
magnificently [mæg'nɪfɪsntlɪ] *adv*
magníficamente.
magnify ['mægnɪfaɪ] *vt* aumentar; (*fig*)
exagerar.
magnifying glass ['mægnɪfaɪɪŋ-] *n* lupa.

magnitude ['mægnɪtjuːd] *n* magnitud *f*.
magnolia [mæg'nəulɪə] *n* magnolia.
magpie ['mægpaɪ] *n* urraca.
maharajah [mɑːhə'rɑːdʒə] *n* maharajá *m*.
mahogany [mə'hɒgənɪ] *n* caoba ♦ *cpd* de
caoba.
maid [meɪd] *n* criada; **old** ~ (*pej*) solterona.
maiden ['meɪdn] *n* doncella ♦ *adj* (*aunt etc*)
solterona; (*speech, voyage*) inaugural.
maiden name *n* apellido de soltera.
mail [meɪl] *n* correo; (*letters*) cartas *fpl* ♦ *vt*
(*post*) echar al correo; (*send*) mandar por
correo; **by** ~ por correo.
mailbox ['meɪlbɒks] *n* (*US: for letters etc*;
COMPUT) buzón *m*.
mailing list ['meɪlɪŋ-] *n* lista de
direcciones.
mailman ['meɪlmæn] *n* (*US*) cartero.
mail-order ['meɪlɔːdə*] *n* pedido postal;
(*business*) venta por correo ♦ *adj*: ~ **firm**
or **house** casa de venta por correo.
mailshot ['meɪlʃɒt] *n* mailing *m inv*.
mailtrain ['meɪltreɪn] *n* tren *m* correo.
mail van, (*US*) **mail truck** *n* (*AUT*)
camioneta de correos *or* de reparto.
maim [meɪm] *vt* mutilar, lisiar.
main [meɪn] *adj* principal, mayor ♦ *n* (*pipe*)
cañería principal *or* maestra; (*US*) red *f*
eléctrica; **the** ~**s** (*BRIT ELEC*) la red
eléctrica; **in the** ~ en general.
main course *n* (*CULIN*) plato principal.
mainframe ['meɪnfreɪm] *n* (*also*: ~
computer) ordenador *m or* computadora
central.
mainland ['meɪnlənd] *n* continente *m*.
main line *n* línea principal.
mainly ['meɪnlɪ] *adv* principalmente, en su
mayoría.
main road *n* carretera principal.
mainstay ['meɪnsteɪ] *n* (*fig*) pilar *m*.
mainstream ['meɪnstriːm] *n* (*fig*) corriente *f*
principal.
main street *n* calle *f* mayor.
maintain [meɪn'teɪn] *vt* mantener; (*affirm*)
sostener; **to** ~ **that** ... mantener *or*
sostener que ... .
maintenance ['meɪntənəns] *n*
mantenimiento; (*alimony*) pensión *f*
alimenticia.
maintenance contract *n* contrato de
mantenimiento.
maintenance order *n* (*LAW*) obligación *f*
de pagar una pensión alimenticia al
cónyuge.
maisonette [meɪzə'nɛt] *n* dúplex *m*.
maize [meɪz] *n* (*BRIT*) maíz *m*, choclo (*LAM*).
Maj. *abbr* (*MIL*) = **major**.
majestic [mə'dʒɛstɪk] *adj* majestuoso.

majesty ['mædʒɪstɪ] n majestad f.
major ['meɪdʒə*] n (MIL) comandante m
♦ adj principal; (MUS) mayor ♦ vi (US
UNIV): **to ~ (in)** especializarse en; **a ~
operation** una operación or intervención
de gran importancia.
Majorca [mə'jɔːkə] n Mallorca.
major general n (MIL) general m de
división.
majority [mə'dʒɒrɪtɪ] n mayoría ♦ cpd
(verdict) mayoritario.
majority holding n (COMM): **to have a ~**
tener un interés mayoritario.
make [meɪk] vt (pt, pp **made** [meɪd]) hacer;
(manufacture) hacer, fabricar; (cause to
be): **to ~ sb sad** poner triste or
entristecer a algn; (force): **to ~ sb do sth**
obligar a algn a hacer algo; (equal): **2 and
2 ~ 4** 2 y 2 son 4 ♦ n marca; **to ~ a fool of
sb** poner a algn en ridículo; **to ~ a
profit/loss** obtener ganancias/sufrir
pérdidas; **to ~ a profit of £500** sacar una
ganancia de 500 libras; **to ~ it** (arrive)
llegar; (achieve sth) tener éxito; **what
time do you ~ it?** ¿qué hora tienes?; **to ~
do with** contentarse con.
▶**make for** vt fus (place) dirigirse a.
▶**make off** vi largarse.
▶**make out** vt (decipher) descifrar;
(understand) entender; (see) distinguir;
(write: cheque) extender; **to ~ out (that)**
(claim, imply) dar a entender (que); **to ~
out a case for sth** dar buenas razones en
favor de algo.
▶**make over** vt (assign): **to ~ over (to)**
ceder or traspasar (a).
▶**make up** vt (invent) inventar; (parcel)
hacer ♦ vi reconciliarse; (with cosmetics)
maquillarse; **to be made up of** estar
compuesto de.
▶**make up for** vt fus compensar.
make-believe ['meɪkbɪliːv] n ficción f,
fantasía.
maker ['meɪkə*] n fabricante m/f.
makeshift ['meɪkʃɪft] adj improvisado.
make-up ['meɪkʌp] n maquillaje m.
make-up bag n bolsita del maquillaje or
de los cosméticos.
make-up remover n desmaquillador m.
making ['meɪkɪŋ] n (fig): **in the ~** en vías de
formación; **to have the ~s of** (person)
tener madera de.
maladjusted [mælə'dʒʌstɪd] adj
inadaptado.
maladroit [maelə'drɔɪt] adj torpe.
malaise [mæ'leɪz] n malestar m.
malaria [mə'lɛərɪə] n malaria.
Malawi [mə'lɑːwɪ] n Malawi m.

Malay [mə'leɪ] adj malayo ♦ n
malayo/a; (LING) malayo.
Malaya [mə'leɪə] n Malaya, Malaca.
Malayan [mə'leɪən] adj, n = **Malay**.
Malaysia [mə'leɪzɪə] n Malaisia, Malaysia.
Malaysian [mə'leɪzɪən] adj, n malaisio/a m/f,
malaysio/a m/f.
Maldive Islands ['mɔːldaɪv-], **Maldives**
['mɔːldaɪvz] npl: **the ~** las Maldivas.
male [meɪl] n (BIOL, ELEC) macho ♦ adj (sex,
attitude) masculino; (child etc) varón.
male chauvinist (pig) n machista m.
male nurse n enfermero.
malevolence [mə'levələns] n malevolencia.
malevolent [mə'levələnt] adj malévolo.
malfunction [mæl'fʌŋkʃən] n mal
funcionamiento.
malice ['mælɪs] n (ill will) malicia; (rancour)
rencor m.
malicious [mə'lɪʃəs] adj malicioso;
rencoroso.
maliciously [mə'lɪʃəslɪ] adv con
malevolencia, con malicia;
rencorosamente.
malign [mə'laɪn] vt difamar, calumniar
♦ adj maligno.
malignant [mə'lɪgnənt] adj (MED) maligno.
malinger [mə'lɪŋgə*] vi fingirse enfermo.
malingerer [mə'lɪŋgərə*] n enfermo/a
fingido/a.
mall [mɔːl] n (US: also: **shopping ~**) centro
comercial.
malleable ['mælɪəbl] adj maleable.
mallet ['mælɪt] n mazo.
malnutrition [mælnjuː'trɪʃən] n
desnutrición f.
malpractice [mæl'præktɪs] n negligencia
profesional.
malt [mɔːlt] n malta.
Malta ['mɔːltə] n Malta.
Maltese [mɔːl'tiːz] adj maltés/esa ♦ n, pl inv
maltés/esa m/f; (LING) maltés m.
maltreat [mæl'triːt] vt maltratar.
mammal ['mæml] n mamífero.
mammoth ['mæməθ] n mamut m ♦ adj
gigantesco.
man, pl **men** [mæn, mɛn] n hombre m;
(CHESS) pieza ♦ vt (NAUT) tripular; (MIL)
defender; **an old ~** un viejo; **~ and wife**
marido y mujer.
Man. abbr (Canada) = Manitoba.
manacle ['mænəkl] n esposa, manilla; **~s**
npl grillos mpl.
manage ['mænɪdʒ] vi arreglárselas ♦ vt (be
in charge of) dirigir; (person etc) manejar;
to ~ to do sth conseguir hacer algo; **to ~
without sth/sb** poder prescindir de algo/
algn.

manageable ['mænɪdʒəbl] *adj* manejable.
management ['mænɪdʒmənt] *n* dirección *f*,
administración *f*; **"under new ~"** "bajo
nueva dirección".
management accounting *n* contabilidad
f de gestión.
management consultant *n* consultor(a)
m/f en dirección de empresas.
manager ['mænɪdʒə*] *n* director *m*; (*SPORT*)
entrenador *m*; **sales ~** jefe/a *m/f* de
ventas.
manageress ['mænɪdʒəres] *n* directora;
(*SPORT*) entrenadora.
managerial [mænə'dʒɪerɪəl] *adj* directivo.
managing director (MD) ['mænɪdʒɪŋ-] *n*
director(a) *m/f* general.
Mancunian [mæŋ'kjuːnɪən] *adj* de
Manchester ♦ *n* nativo/a (*or* habitante *m/f*)
de Manchester.
mandarin ['mændərɪn] *n* (*also*: **~ orange**)
mandarina; (*person*) mandarín *m*.
mandate ['mændeɪt] *n* mandato.
mandatory ['mændətərɪ] *adj* obligatorio.
mandolin(e) ['mændəlɪn] *n* mandolina.
mane [meɪn] *n* (*of horse*) crin *f*; (*of lion*)
melena.
maneuver [mə'nuːvə*] (*US*) = **manoeuvre**.
manful ['mænful] *adj* resuelto.
manfully ['mænfəlɪ] *adv* resueltamente.
mangetout [mɒnʒ'tuː] *n* tirabeque *m*.
mangle ['mæŋgl] *vt* mutilar, destrozar ♦ *n*
escurridor *m*.
mango, **~es** ['mæŋgəu] *n* mango.
mangrove ['mæŋgrəuv] *n* mangle *m*.
mangy ['meɪndʒɪ] *adj* roñoso; (*MED*)
sarnoso.
manhandle ['mænhændl] *vt* maltratar;
(*move by hand*: *goods*) manipular.
manhole ['mænhəul] *n* boca de acceso.
manhood ['mænhud] *n* edad *f* viril;
(*manliness*) virilidad *f*.
man-hour ['mæn'auə*] *n* hora-hombre *f*.
manhunt ['mænhʌnt] *n* caza de hombre.
mania ['meɪnɪə] *n* manía.
maniac ['meɪnɪæk] *n* maníaco/a; (*fig*)
maniático.
manic ['mænɪk] *adj* (*behaviour, activity*)
frenético.
manic-depressive ['mænɪkdɪ'presɪv] *adj*, *n*
maniacodepresivo/a *m/f*.
manicure ['mænɪkjuə*] *n* manicura.
manicure set *n* estuche *m* de manicura.
manifest ['mænɪfest] *vt* manifestar,
mostrar ♦ *adj* manifiesto ♦ *n* manifiesto.
manifestation [mænɪfes'teɪʃən] *n*
manifestación *f*.
manifestly ['mænɪfestlɪ] *adv*
evidentemente.

manifesto [mænɪ'festəu] *n* manifiesto.
manifold ['mænɪfəuld] *adj* múltiples ♦ *n*
(*AUT etc*): **exhaust ~** colector *m* de escape.
Manila [mə'nɪlə] *n* Manila.
manil(l)a [mə'nɪlə] *n* (*paper, envelope*)
manila.
manipulate [mə'nɪpjuleɪt] *vt* manipular.
manipulation [mənɪpju'leɪʃən] *n*
manipulación *f*, manejo.
mankind [mæn'kaɪnd] *n* humanidad *f*,
género humano.
manliness ['mænlɪnɪs] *n* virilidad *f*,
hombría.
manly ['mænlɪ] *adj* varonil.
man-made ['mæn'meɪd] *adj* artificial.
manna ['mænə] *n* maná *m*.
mannequin ['mænɪkɪn] *n* (*dummy*)
maniquí *m*; (*fashion model*) maniquí *m/f*.
manner ['mænə*] *n* manera, modo;
(*behaviour*) conducta, manera de ser;
(*type*) clase *f*; **~s** *npl* modales *mpl*,
educación *fsg*; **(good) ~s** (buena)
educación *fsg*, (buenos) modales *mpl*; **bad
~s** falta *sg* de educación, pocos modales
mpl; **all ~ of** toda clase *or* suerte de.
mannerism ['mænərɪzəm] *n* gesto típico.
mannerly ['mænəlɪ] *adj* bien educado,
formal.
man(o)euvrable [mə'nuːvrəbl] *adj* (*car etc*)
manejable.
manoeuvre, (*US*) **maneuver** [mə'nuːvə*]
vt, *vi* maniobrar ♦ *n* maniobra; **to ~ sb into
doing sth** manipular a algn para que
haga algo.
manor ['mænə*] *n* (*also*: **~ house**) casa
solariega.
manpower ['mænpauə*] *n* mano *f* de obra.
**Manpower Services Commission
(MSC)** *n* (*BRIT*) comisión para el
aprovechamiento de los recursos
humanos.
manservant ['mænsɔːvənt] *n* criado.
mansion ['mænʃən] *n* mansión *f*.
manslaughter ['mænslɔːtə*] *n* homicidio
involuntario.
mantelpiece ['mæntlpiːs] *n* repisa de la
chimenea.
mantle ['mæntl] *n* manto.
man-to-man ['mæntə'mæn] *adj* de hombre
a hombre.
manual ['mænjuəl] *adj* manual ♦ *n* manual
m; **~ worker** obrero, trabajador *m*
manual.
manufacture [mænju'fæktʃə*] *vt* fabricar
♦ *n* fabricación *f*.
manufactured goods [mænju'fæktʃəd-] *npl*
manufacturas *fpl*, bienes *mpl*
manufacturados.

manufacturer [mænju'fæktʃərə*] *n* fabricante *m/f.*

manufacturing industries [mænju'fæk tʃərɪŋ-] *npl* industrias *fpl* manufactureras.

manure [mə'njuə*] *n* estiércol *m*, abono.

manuscript ['mænjuskrɪpt] *n* manuscrito.

Manx [mæŋks] *adj* de la Isla de Man.

many ['menɪ] *adj* muchos/as ♦ *pron* muchos/ as; **a great** ~ muchísimos, un buen número de; ~ **a time** muchas veces; **too** ~ **difficulties** demasiadas dificultades; **twice as** ~ el doble; **how** ~? ¿cuántos?

Maori ['maurɪ] *adj*, *n* maorí *m/f.*

map [mæp] *n* mapa *m* ♦ *vt* trazar el mapa de.

▶**map out** *vt* (*fig*: *career*, *holiday*, *essay*) proyectar, planear.

maple ['meɪpl] *n* arce *m*, maple *m* (*LAM*).

mar [ma:*] *vt* estropear.

Mar. *abbr* (= *March*) mar.

marathon ['mærəθən] *n* maratón *m* ♦ *adj*: **a** ~ **session** una sesión maratoniana.

marathon runner *n* corredor(a) *m/f* de maratones.

marauder [mə'rɔːdə*] *n* merodeador(a) *m/f.*

marble ['ma:bl] *n* mármol *m*; (*toy*) canica.

March [ma:tʃ] *n* marzo.

march [ma:tʃ] *vi* (*MIL*) marchar; (*fig*) caminar con resolución ♦ *n* marcha; (*demonstration*) manifestación *f.*

marcher ['ma:tʃə*] *n* manifestante *m/f.*

marching ['ma:tʃɪŋ] *n*: **to give sb his** ~ **orders** (*fig*) mandar a paseo a algn; (*employee*) poner de patitas en la calle a algn.

march-past ['ma:tʃpa:st] *n* desfile *m.*

mare [mɛə*] *n* yegua.

margarine [ma:dʒə'ri:n] *n* margarina.

marg(e) [ma:dʒ] *n abbr* = **margarine.**

margin ['ma:dʒɪn] *n* margen *m.*

marginal ['ma:dʒɪnl] *adj* marginal.

marginally ['ma:dʒɪnəlɪ] *adv* ligeramente.

marginal seat *n* (*POL*) circunscripción *f* políticamente no definida.

marigold ['mærɪɡəuld] *n* caléndula.

marijuana [mærɪ'wa:nə] *n* marihuana.

marina [mə'ri:nə] *n* marina.

marinade [mærɪ'neɪd] *n* adobo.

marinate ['mærɪneɪt] *vt* adobar.

marine [mə'ri:n] *adj* marino ♦ *n* soldado de infantería de marina.

marine insurance *n* seguro marítimo.

mariner ['mærɪnə*] *n* marinero, marino.

marionette [mærɪə'nɛt] *n* marioneta, títere *m.*

marital ['mærɪtl] *adj* matrimonial; ~ **status** estado civil.

maritime ['mærɪtaɪm] *adj* marítimo.

marjoram ['ma:dʒərəm] *n* mejorana.

mark [ma:k] *n* marca, señal *f*; (*imprint*) huella; (*stain*) mancha; (*BRIT SCOL*) nota; (*currency*) marco ♦ *vt* (*also SPORT*: *player*) marcar; (*stain*) manchar; (*BRIT SCOL*) calificar, corregir; **punctuation** ~**s** signos *mpl* de puntuación; **to be quick off the** ~ (*fig*) ser listo; **up to the** ~ (*in efficiency*) a la altura de las circunstancias; **to** ~ **time** marcar el paso.

▶**mark down** *vt* (*reduce*: *prices*, *goods*) rebajar.

▶**mark off** *vt* (*tick*) indicar, señalar.

▶**mark out** *vt* trazar.

▶**mark up** *vt* (*price*) aumentar.

marked [ma:kt] *adj* marcado, acusado.

markedly ['ma:kɪdlɪ] *adv* marcadamente, apreciablemente.

marker ['ma:kə*] *n* (*sign*) marcador *m*; (*bookmark*) registro.

market ['ma:kɪt] *n* mercado ♦ *vt* (*COMM*) comercializar; (*promote*) publicitar; **open** ~ mercado libre; **to be on the** ~ estar en venta; **to play the** ~ jugar a la bolsa.

marketable ['ma:kɪtəbl] *adj* comerciable.

market analysis *n* análisis *m* del mercado.

market day *n* día *m* de mercado.

market demand *n* demanda de mercado.

market economy *n* economía de mercado.

market forces *npl* tendencias *fpl* del mercado.

market garden *n* (*BRIT*) huerto.

marketing ['ma:kɪtɪŋ] *n* marketing *m*, mercadotecnia.

marketing manager *n* director *m* de marketing.

market leader *n* líder *m* de ventas.

marketplace ['ma:kɪtpleɪs] *n* mercado.

market price *n* precio de mercado.

market research *n* (*COMM*) estudios *mpl* de mercado.

market value *n* valor *m* en el mercado.

marking ['ma:kɪŋ] *n* (*on animal*) pinta; (*on road*) señal *f.*

marking ink *n* tinta indeleble *or* de marcar.

marksman ['ma:ksmən] *n* tirador *m.*

marksmanship ['ma:ksmənʃɪp] *n* puntería.

mark-up ['ma:kʌp] *n* (*COMM*: *margin*) margen *m* de beneficio; (: *increase*) aumento.

marmalade ['ma:məleɪd] *n* mermelada de naranja.

maroon [mə'ru:n] *vt*: **to be** ~**ed** (*shipwrecked*) naufragar; (*fig*) quedar abandonado ♦ *adj* granate *inv.*

marquee [ma:'ki:] *n* carpa, entoldado.

marquess, marquis ['mɑːkwɪs] n marqués m.

Marrakech, Marrakesh [mærə'kɛʃ] n Marrakech m.

marriage ['mærɪdʒ] n (state) matrimonio; (wedding) boda; (act) casamiento.

marriage bureau n agencia matrimonial.

marriage certificate n partida de casamiento.

marriage guidance, (US) marriage counseling n orientación f matrimonial.

marriage of convenience n matrimonio de conveniencia.

married ['mærɪd] adj casado; (life, love) conyugal.

marrow ['mærəu] n médula; (vegetable) calabacín m.

marry ['mærɪ] vt casarse con; (subj: father, priest etc) casar ♦ vi (also: get married) casarse.

Mars [mɑːz] n Marte m.

Marseilles [mɑː'seɪ] n Marsella.

marsh [mɑːʃ] n pantano; (salt ~) marisma.

marshal ['mɑːʃl] n (MIL) mariscal m; (at sports meeting, demonstration etc) oficial m; (US: of police, fire department) jefe/a m/f ♦ vt (facts) ordenar; (soldiers) formar.

marshalling yard ['mɑːʃəlɪŋ-] n (RAIL) estación f clasificadora.

marshmallow ['mɑːʃmæləu] n (BOT) malvavisco; (sweet) esponja, dulce m de merengue blando.

marshy ['mɑːʃɪ] adj pantanoso.

marsupial [mɑː'suːpɪəl] adj, n marsupial m.

martial ['mɑːʃl] adj marcial.

martial arts npl artes fpl marciales.

martial law n ley f marcial.

martin ['mɑːtɪn] n (also: house ~) avión m.

martyr ['mɑːtə*] n mártir m/f ♦ vt martirizar.

martyrdom ['mɑːtədəm] n martirio.

marvel ['mɑːvl] n maravilla, prodigio ♦ vi: to ~ (at) maravillarse (de).

marvellous, (US) marvelous ['mɑːvləs] adj maravilloso.

marvel(l)ously ['mɑːvləslɪ] adv maravillosamente.

Marxism ['mɑːksɪzəm] n marxismo.

Marxist ['mɑːksɪst] adj, n marxista m/f.

marzipan ['mɑːzɪpæn] n mazapán m.

mascara [mæs'kɑːrə] n rimel m.

mascot ['mæskət] n mascota.

masculine ['mæskjulɪn] adj masculino.

masculinity [mæskju'lɪnɪtɪ] n masculinidad f.

MASH [mæʃ] n abbr (US) = mobile army surgical hospital.

mash [mæʃ] n (mix) mezcla; (CULIN) puré m; (pulp) amasijo.

mashed potatoes [mæʃt-] npl puré m de patatas or papas (LAM).

mask [mɑːsk] n (also ELEC) máscara ♦ vt enmascarar.

masochism ['mæsəkɪzəm] n masoquismo.

masochist ['mæsəukɪst] n masoquista m/f.

mason ['meɪsn] n (also: stone~) albañil m; (also: free~) masón m.

masonic [mə'sɔnɪk] adj masónico.

masonry ['meɪsnrɪ] n masonería; (building) mampostería.

masquerade [mæskə'reɪd] n baile m de máscaras; (fig) mascarada ♦ vi: to ~ as disfrazarse de, hacerse pasar por.

mass [mæs] n (people) muchedumbre f; (PHYSICS) masa; (REL) misa; (great quantity) montón m ♦ vi reunirse; (MIL) concentrarse; **the ~es** las masas; **to go to ~** ir a or oír misa.

Mass. abbr (US) = Massachusetts.

massacre ['mæsəkə*] n masacre f ♦ vt masacrar.

massage ['mæsɑːʒ] n masaje m ♦ vt dar masajes or un masaje a.

masseur [mæ'sə:*] n masajista m.

masseuse [mæ'sə:z] n masajista f.

massive ['mæsɪv] adj enorme; (support, intervention) masivo.

mass media npl medios mpl de comunicación de masas.

mass meeting n (of everyone concerned) reunión f en masa; (huge) mitin m.

mass-produce ['mæsprə'djuːs] vt fabricar en serie.

mass-production ['mæsprə'dʌkʃən] n fabricación f or producción f en serie.

mast [mɑːst] n (NAUT) mástil m; (RADIO etc) torre f, antena.

mastectomy [mæs'tɛktəmɪ] n mastectomía.

master ['mɑːstə*] n (of servant, animal) amo; (fig: of situation) dueño; (ART, MUS) maestro; (in secondary school) profesor m; (title for boys): **M~ X** Señorito X ♦ vt dominar.

master disk n (COMPUT) disco maestro.

masterful ['mɑːstəful] adj magistral, dominante.

master key n llave f maestra.

masterly ['mɑːstəlɪ] adj magistral.

mastermind ['mɑːstəmaɪnd] n inteligencia superior ♦ vt dirigir, planear.

Master of Arts (MA) n licenciatura superior en Letras; see also **master's degree**.

Master of Ceremonies n encargado de protocolo.

Master of Science (MSc) *n* licenciatura superior en Ciencias; *see also* **master's degree**.
masterpiece ['mɑːstəpiːs] *n* obra maestra.
master plan *n* plan *m* rector.
master's degree *n* máster *m*; *ver recuadro*.

MASTER'S DEGREE

Los estudios de postgrado británicos que llevan a la obtención de un **master's degree** *consisten generalmente en una combinación de curso(s) académico(s) y tesina (''dissertation'') sobre un tema original, o bien únicamente la redacción de una tesina. El primer caso es el más frecuente para los títulos de ''MA'' (''Master of Arts'') y ''MSc'' (''Master of Science''), mientras que los de ''MLitt'' (''Master of Letters'') o ''MPhil'' (''Master of Philosophy'') se obtienen normalmente mediante tesina. En algunas universidades, como las escocesas, el título de* **master's degree** *no es de postgrado, sino que corresponde a la licenciatura.*

---

master stroke *n* golpe *m* maestro.
mastiff ['mæstɪf] *n* mastín *m*.
masturbate ['mæstəbeɪt] *vi* masturbarse.
masturbation [mæstə'beɪʃən] *n* masturbación *f*.
mat [mæt] *n* alfombrilla; (*also: door~*) felpudo ♦ *adj* = **matt**.
MAT *n abbr* (= *machine-assisted translation*) TAO.
match [mætʃ] *n* cerilla, fósforo; (*game*) partido; (*fig*) igual *m/f* ♦ *vt* emparejar; (*go well with*) hacer juego con; (*equal*) igualar ♦ *vi* hacer juego; **to be a good** ~ hacer buena pareja.
matchbox ['mætʃbɒks] *n* caja de cerillas.
matching ['mætʃɪŋ] *adj* que hace juego.
matchless ['mætʃlɪs] *adj* sin par.
matchmaker ['mætʃmeɪkə*] *n* casamentero/a.
mate [meɪt] *n* (*work~*) compañero/a, colega *m/f*; (*col: friend*) amigo/a, compadre *m/f* (*LAM*); (*animal*) macho/hembra; (*in merchant navy*) primer oficial *m* ♦ *vi* acoplarse, parearse ♦ *vt* acoplar, parear.
material [mə'tɪərɪəl] *n* (*substance*) materia; (*equipment*) material *m*; (*cloth*) tela, tejido ♦ *adj* material; (*important*) esencial; **~s** *npl* materiales *mpl*; (*equipment etc*) artículos *mpl*.
materialistic [mətɪərɪə'lɪstɪk] *adj* materialista.
materialize [mə'tɪərɪəlaɪz] *vi*

materializarse.
materially [mə'tɪərɪəlɪ] *adv* materialmente.
maternal [mə'tɜːnl] *adj* maternal; ~ **grandmother** abuela materna.
maternity [mə'tɜːnɪtɪ] *n* maternidad *f*.
maternity benefit *n* subsidio por maternidad.
maternity dress *n* vestido premamá.
maternity hospital *n* hospital *m* de maternidad.
maternity leave *n* baja por maternidad.
math [mæθ] *n abbr* (*US:* = *mathematics*) matemáticas *fpl*.
mathematical [mæθə'mætɪkl] *adj* matemático.
mathematically [mæθɪ'mætɪklɪ] *adv* matemáticamente.
mathematician [mæθəmə'tɪʃən] *n* matemático.
mathematics [mæθə'mætɪks] *n* matemáticas *fpl*.
maths [mæθs] *n abbr* (*BRIT:* = *mathematics*) matemáticas *fpl*.
matinée ['mætɪneɪ] *n* función *f* de la tarde, vermú(t) *m* (*LAM*).
mating ['meɪtɪŋ] *n* apareamiento.
mating call *n* llamada del macho.
mating season *n* época de celo.
matins ['mætɪnz] *n* maitines *mpl*.
matriarchal [meɪtrɪ'ɑːkl] *adj* matriarcal.
matrices ['meɪtrɪsiːz] *pl of* **matrix**.
matriculation [mətrɪkju'leɪʃən] *n* matriculación *f*, matrícula.
matrimonial [mætrɪ'məunɪəl] *adj* matrimonial.
matrimony ['mætrɪmənɪ] *n* matrimonio.
matrix, *pl* **matrices** ['meɪtrɪks, 'meɪtrɪsiːz] *n* matriz *f*.
matron ['meɪtrən] *n* (*in hospital*) enfermera jefe; (*in school*) ama de llaves.
matronly ['meɪtrənlɪ] *adj* de matrona; (*fig: figure*) corpulento.
matt [mæt] *adj* mate.
matted ['mætɪd] *adj* enmarañado.
matter ['mætə*] *n* cuestión *f*, asunto; (*PHYSICS*) sustancia, materia; (*content*) contenido; (*MED: pus*) pus *m* ♦ *vi* importar; **it doesn't** ~ no importa; **what's the** ~? ¿qué pasa?; **no** ~ **what** pase lo que pase; **as a** ~ **of course** por rutina; **as a** ~ **of fact** en realidad; **printed** ~ impresos *mpl*; **reading** ~ material *m* de lectura, lecturas *fpl*.
matter-of-fact ['mætərəv'fækt] *adj* (*style*) prosaico; (*person*) práctico; (*voice*) neutro.
mattress ['mætrɪs] *n* colchón *m*.

mature [mə'tjuə*] adj maduro ♦ vi madurar.
mature student n estudiante de más de 21 años.
maturity [mə'tjuərıtı] n madurez f.
maudlin ['mɔːdlın] adj llorón/ona.
maul [mɔːl] vt magullar.
Mauritania [mɔːrı'teınıə] n Mauritania.
Mauritius [mə'rıʃəs] n Mauricio.
mausoleum [mɔːsə'lıəm] n mausoleo.
mauve [məuv] adj de color malva.
maverick ['mævrık] n (fig) inconformista m/f, persona independiente.
mawkish ['mɔːkıʃ] adj sensiblero, empalagoso.
max. abbr = **maximum**.
maxim ['mæksım] n máxima.
maxima ['mæksımə] pl of **maximum**.
maximize ['mæksımaız] vt (profits etc) llevar al máximo; (chances) maximizar.
maximum ['mæksıməm] adj máximo ♦ n (pl **maxima** ['mæksımə]) máximo.
May [meı] n mayo.
may [meı] vi (conditional: **might**) (indicating possibility): **he ~ come** puede que venga; (be allowed to): **~ I smoke?** ¿puedo fumar?; (wishes): **~ God bless you!** ¡que Dios le bendiga!; **~ I sit here?** ¿me puedo sentar aquí?
maybe ['meıbiː] adv quizá(s); **~ not** quizá(s) no.
May Day n el primero de Mayo.
mayday ['meıdeı] n señal f de socorro.
mayhem ['meıhɛm] n caos m total.
mayonnaise [meıə'neız] n mayonesa.
mayor [mɛə*] n alcalde m.
mayoress ['mɛərɛs] n alcaldesa.
maypole ['meıpəul] n mayo.
maze [meız] n laberinto.
MB abbr (COMPUT) = **megabyte**; (Canada) = Manitoba.
MBA n abbr (= Master of Business Administration) título universitario.
MBBS, MBChB n abbr (BRIT: = Bachelor of Medicine and Surgery) título universitario.
MBE n abbr (BRIT: = Member of the Order of the British Empire) título ceremonial.
MC n abbr (= master of ceremonies) e.p.; (US: = Member of Congress) diputado del Congreso de los Estados Unidos.
MCP n abbr (BRIT col) = **male chauvinist pig**.
MD n abbr (= Doctor of Medicine) título universitario; (COMM) = **managing director**; (= MiniDisc ®) MiniDisc m, minidisc m ♦ abbr (US) = Maryland.
Md. abbr (US) = Maryland.
MD player n MiniDisc m, minidisc m.
MDT n abbr (US: = mountain daylight time) hora de verano de las Montañas

Rocosas.
ME abbr (US POST) = Maine ♦ n abbr (US MED) = medical examiner; (MED = myalgic encephalomyelitis) encefalomielitis f miálgica.
me [miː] pron (direct) me; (stressed, after pronoun) mí; **can you hear ~?** ¿me oyes?; **he heard ME!** me oyó a mí; **it's ~** soy yo; **give them to ~** dámelos; **with/without ~** conmigo/sin mí; **it's for ~** es para mí.
meadow ['mɛdəu] n prado, pradera.
meagre, (US) **meager** ['miːgə*] adj escaso, pobre.
meal [miːl] n comida; (flour) harina; **to go out for a ~** salir a comer.
meals on wheels nsg (BRIT) servicio de alimentación a domicilio para necesitados y tercera edad.
mealtime ['miːltaım] n hora de comer.
mealy-mouthed ['miːlımauðd] adj: **to be ~** no decir nunca las cosas claras.
mean [miːn] adj (with money) tacaño; (unkind) mezquino, malo; (average) medio; (US: vicious: animal) resabiado; (: person) malicioso ♦ vt (pt, pp **meant** [mɛnt]) (signify) querer decir, significar; (intend): **to ~ to do sth** tener la intención de or pensar hacer algo ♦ n medio, término medio; **do you ~ it?** ¿lo dices en serio?; **what do you ~?** ¿qué quiere decir?; **to be meant for sb/sth** ser para algn/algo; see also **means**.
meander [mı'ændə*] vi (river) serpentear; (person) vagar.
meaning ['miːnıŋ] n significado, sentido.
meaningful ['miːnıŋful] adj significativo.
meaningless ['miːnıŋlıs] adj sin sentido.
meanness ['miːnnıs] n (with money) tacañería; (unkindness) maldad f, mezquindad f.
means [miːnz] npl medio sg, manera sg; (resource) recursos mpl, medios mpl; **by ~ of** mediante, por medio de; **by all ~!** ¡naturalmente!, ¡claro que sí!
means test n control m de los recursos económicos.
meant [mɛnt] pt, pp of **mean**.
meantime ['miːntaım], **meanwhile** ['miːnwaıl] adv (also: **in the meantime**) mientras tanto.
measles ['miːzlz] n sarampión m.
measly ['miːzlı] adj (col) miserable.
measurable ['mɛʒərəbl] adj mensurable, que se puede medir.
measure ['mɛʒə*] vt medir; (for clothes etc) tomar las medidas a ♦ vi medir ♦ n medida; (ruler) cinta métrica, metro; **a litre ~** una medida de un litro; **some ~ of**

success cierto éxito; **to take ~s to do sth** tomar medidas para hacer algo.
▸**measure up** vi: **to ~ up (to)** estar a la altura (de).
measured ['mɛʒəd] adj moderado; (tone) mesurado.
measurement ['mɛʒəmənt] n (measure) medida; (act) medición f; **to take sb's ~s** tomar las medidas a algn.
meat [miːt] n carne f; **cold ~s** fiambres mpl; **crab ~** carne f de cangrejo.
meatball ['miːtbɔːl] n albóndiga.
meat pie n pastel m de carne.
meaty ['miːtɪ] adj (person) fuerte, corpulento; (role) sustancioso; **a ~ meal** una comida con bastante carne.
Mecca ['mɛkə] n (city) la Meca; (fig) meca.
mechanic [mɪ'kænɪk] n mecánico/a.
mechanical [mɪ'kænɪkl] adj mecánico.
mechanical engineering n (science) ingeniería mecánica; (industry) construcción f mecánica.
mechanics [mə'kænɪks] n mecánica ♦ npl mecanismo sg.
mechanism ['mɛkənɪzəm] n mecanismo.
mechanization [mɛkənaɪ'zeɪʃən] n mecanización f.
mechanize ['mɛkənaɪz] vt mecanizar; (factory etc) automatizar.
MEd n abbr (= Master of Education) título universitario.
medal ['mɛdl] n medalla.
medallion [mɪ'dælɪən] n medallón m.
medallist, (US) **medalist** ['mɛdlɪst] n (SPORT) medallista m/f.
meddle ['mɛdl] vi: **to ~ in** entrometerse en; **to ~ with sth** manosear algo.
meddlesome ['mɛdlsəm], **meddling** ['mɛdlɪŋ] adj (interfering) entrometido; (touching things) curioso.
media ['miːdɪə] npl medios mpl de comunicación.
media circus n excesivo despliegue informativo.
mediaeval [mɛdɪ'iːvl] adj = **medieval**.
median ['miːdɪən] n (US: also: ~ **strip**) mediana.
media research n estudio de los medios de publicidad.
mediate ['miːdɪeɪt] vi mediar.
mediation [miːdɪ'eɪʃən] n mediación f.
mediator ['miːdɪeɪtə*] n mediador(a) m/f.
Medicaid ['mɛdɪkeɪd] n (US) programa de ayuda médica.
medical ['mɛdɪkl] adj médico ♦ n (also: ~ **examination**) reconocimiento médico.
medical certificate n certificado m médico.

Medicare ['mɛdɪkeə*] n (US) seguro médico del Estado.
medicated ['mɛdɪkeɪtɪd] adj medicinal.
medication [mɛdɪ'keɪʃən] n (drugs etc) medicación f.
medicinal [mɛ'dɪsɪnl] adj medicinal.
medicine ['mɛdsɪn] n medicina; (drug) medicamento.
medicine chest n botiquín m.
medicine man n hechicero.
medieval, mediaeval [mɛdɪ'iːvl] adj medieval.
mediocre [miːdɪ'əukə*] adj mediocre.
mediocrity [miːdɪ'ɔkrɪtɪ] n mediocridad f.
meditate ['mɛdɪteɪt] vi meditar.
meditation [mɛdɪ'teɪʃən] n meditación f.
Mediterranean [mɛdɪtə'reɪnɪən] adj mediterráneo; **the ~ (Sea)** el (Mar m) Mediterráneo.
medium ['miːdɪəm] adj mediano; (level, height) medio ♦ n (pl **media**: means) medio; (pl **mediums**: person) médium m/f; **happy ~** punto justo.
medium-dry ['miːdɪəm'draɪ] adj semiseco.
medium-sized ['miːdɪəm'saɪzd] adj de tamaño mediano; (clothes) de (la) talla mediana.
medium wave n onda media.
medley ['mɛdlɪ] n mezcla; (MUS) popurrí m.
meek [miːk] adj manso, sumiso.
meekly ['miːklɪ] adv mansamente, dócilmente.
meet [miːt] vb (pt, pp met [mɛt]) vt encontrar; (accidentally) encontrarse con; (by arrangement) reunirse con; (for the first time) conocer; (go and fetch) ir a buscar; (opponent) enfrentarse con; (obligations) cumplir; (bill, expenses) pagar, costear ♦ vi encontrarse; (in session) reunirse; (join: objects) unirse; (get to know) conocerse ♦ n (BRIT: HUNTING) cacería; (US: SPORT) encuentro; **pleased to ~ you!** ¡encantado (de conocerle)!, ¡mucho gusto!
▸**meet up** vi: **to ~ up with sb** reunirse con algn.
▸**meet with** vt fus reunirse con; (difficulty) tropezar con.
meeting ['miːtɪŋ] n (also SPORT: rally) encuentro; (arranged) cita, compromiso (LAM); (formal session, business meet) reunión f; (POL) mitin m; **to call a ~** convocar una reunión.
meeting place n lugar m de reunión or encuentro.
megabyte ['mɛgəbaɪt] n (COMPUT) megabyte m, megaocteto.
megalomaniac [mɛgələu'meɪnɪæk] adj, n megalómano/a m/f.

megaphone ['mɛgəfəun] n megáfono.
megawatt ['mɛgəwɒt] n megavatio.
melancholy ['mɛlənkəlɪ] n melancolía ♦ adj melancólico.
melee ['mɛleɪ] n refriega.
mellow ['mɛləu] adj (wine) añejo; (sound, colour) suave; (fruit) maduro ♦ vi (person) madurar.
melodious [mɪ'ləudɪəs] adj melodioso.
melodrama ['mɛləudrɑːmə] n melodrama m.
melodramatic [mɛləudrə'mætɪk] adj melodramático.
melody ['mɛlədɪ] n melodía.
melon ['mɛlən] n melón m.
melt [mɛlt] vi (metal) fundirse; (snow) derretirse; (fig) ablandarse ♦ vt (also: ~ **down**) fundir; **~ed butter** mantequilla derretida.
▶**melt away** vi desvanecerse.
meltdown ['mɛltdaun] n (in nuclear reactor) fusión f (de un reactor nuclear).
melting point ['mɛltɪŋ-] n punto de fusión.
melting pot ['mɛltɪŋ-] n (fig) crisol m; **to be in the** ~ estar sobre el tapete.
member ['mɛmbə*] n (of political party) miembro; (of club) socio/a; **M~ of Parliament (MP)** (BRIT) diputado/a; **M~ of the European Parliament (MEP)** (BRIT) eurodiputado/a; **M~ of the House of Representatives (MHR)** (US) diputado/a del Congreso de los Estados Unidos; **M~ of the Scottish Parliament (MSP)** (BRIT) diputado/a del Parlamento escocés.
membership ['mɛmbəʃɪp] n (members) miembros mpl; socios mpl; (numbers) número de miembros or socios; **to seek ~ of** pedir el ingreso a.
membership card n carnet m de socio.
membrane ['mɛmbreɪn] n membrana.
memento [mə'mɛntəu] n recuerdo.
memo ['mɛməu] n nota (de servicio).
memoirs ['mɛmwɑːz] npl memorias fpl.
memo pad n bloc m de notas.
memorable ['mɛmərəbl] adj memorable.
memorandum, pl **memoranda** [mɛmə'rændəm, -də] n nota (de servicio); (POL) memorándum m.
memorial [mɪ'mɔːrɪəl] n monumento conmemorativo ♦ adj conmemorativo.
Memorial Day n (US) día de conmemoración de los caídos en la guerra.
memorize ['mɛməraɪz] vt aprender de memoria.
memory ['mɛmərɪ] n memoria; (recollection) recuerdo; **to have a good/bad** ~ tener buena/mala memoria; **loss of** ~ pérdida de memoria.
men [mɛn] pl of **man**.
menace ['mɛnəs] n amenaza; (col: nuisance) lata ♦ vt amenazar; **a public** ~ un peligro público.
menacing ['mɛnɪsɪŋ] adj amenazador(a).
menacingly ['mɛnɪsɪŋlɪ] adv amenazadoramente.
menagerie [mɪ'nædʒərɪ] n casa de fieras.
mend [mɛnd] vt reparar, arreglar; (darn) zurcir ♦ vi reponerse ♦ n (gen) remiendo; (darn) zurcido; **to be on the** ~ ir mejorando.
mending ['mɛndɪŋ] n arreglo, reparación f; (clothes) ropa por remendar.
menial ['miːnɪəl] adj (pej) bajo, servil.
meningitis [mɛnɪn'dʒaɪtɪs] n meningitis f.
menopause ['mɛnəupɔːz] n menopausia.
men's room n (US): **the** ~ el servicio de caballeros.
menstrual ['mɛnstruəl] adj menstrual.
menstruate ['mɛnstrueɪt] vi menstruar.
menstruation [mɛnstru'eɪʃən] n menstruación f.
menswear ['mɛnzwɛə*] n confección f de caballero.
mental ['mɛntl] adj mental; ~ **illness** enfermedad f mental.
mental hospital n (hospital m) psiquiátrico.
mentality [mɛn'tælɪtɪ] n mentalidad f.
mentally ['mɛntlɪ] adv: **to be** ~ **handicapped** ser un disminuido mental.
menthol ['mɛnθɒl] n mentol m.
mention ['mɛnʃən] n mención f ♦ vt mencionar; (speak of) hablar de; **don't** ~ **it!** ¡de nada!; **I need hardly** ~ **that ...** huelga decir que ...; **not to** ~, **without** ~**ing** sin contar.
mentor ['mɛntɔː*] n mentor m.
menu ['mɛnjuː] n (set ~) menú m; (printed) carta; (COMPUT) menú m.
menu-driven ['mɛnjuːdrɪvn] adj (COMPUT) guiado por menú.
MEP n abbr see **Member of the European Parliament**.
mercantile ['mɜːkəntaɪl] adj mercantil.
mercenary ['mɜːsɪnərɪ] adj, n mercenario.
merchandise ['mɜːtʃəndaɪz] n mercancías fpl.
merchandiser ['mɜːtʃəndaɪzə*] n comerciante m/f, tratante m.
merchant ['mɜːtʃənt] n comerciante m/f.
merchant bank n (BRIT) banco comercial.
merchantman ['mɜːtʃəntmən] n buque m mercante.
merchant navy, (US) **merchant marine** n marina mercante.

merciful ['mɔːsɪful] *adj* compasivo.
mercifully ['mɔːsɪfulɪ] *adv* con compasión;
(*fortunately*) afortunadamente.
merciless ['mɔːsɪlɪs] *adj* despiadado.
mercilessly ['mɔːsɪlɪslɪ] *adv*
despiadadamente, sin piedad.
mercurial [mɔːˈkjuərɪəl] *adj* veleidoso,
voluble.
mercury ['mɔːkjurɪ] *n* mercurio.
mercy ['mɔːsɪ] *n* compasión *f*; (*REL*)
misericordia; **at the ~ of** a la merced de.
mercy killing *n* eutanasia.
mere [mɪə*] *adj* simple, mero.
merely ['mɪəlɪ] *adv* simplemente, sólo.
merge [mɔːdʒ] *vt* (*join*) unir; (*mix*) mezclar;
(*fuse*) fundir; (*COMPUT: files, text*)
intercalar ♦ *vi* unirse; (*COMM*) fusionarse.
merger ['mɔːdʒə*] *n* (*COMM*) fusión *f*.
meridian [mɔˈrɪdɪən] *n* meridiano.
meringue [mɔˈræŋ] *n* merengue *m*.
merit ['mɛrɪt] *n* mérito ♦ *vt* merecer.
meritocracy [mɛrɪˈtɔkrɔsɪ] *n* meritocracia.
mermaid ['mɔːmeɪd] *n* sirena.
merrily ['mɛrɪlɪ] *adv* alegremente.
merriment ['mɛrɪmənt] *n* alegría.
merry ['mɛrɪ] *adj* alegre; **M~ Christmas!**
¡Felices Pascuas!
merry-go-round ['mɛrɪɡəuraund] *n* tiovivo.
mesh [mɛʃ] *n* malla; (*TECH*) engranaje *m* ♦
vi (*gears*) engranar; **wire ~** tela metálica.
mesmerize ['mɛzmɔraɪz] *vt* hipnotizar.
mess [mɛs] *n* confusión *f*; (*of objects*)
revoltijo; (*tangle*) lío; (*MIL*) comedor *m*; **to**
be (in) a ~ (*room*) estar revuelto; **to be/**
get o.s. in a ~ estar/meterse en un lío.
▶**mess about, mess around** *vi* (*col*)
perder el tiempo; (*pass the time*) pasar el
rato.
▶**mess about** *or* **around with** *vt fus* (*col:*
play with) divertirse con; (: *handle*)
manosear.
▶**mess up** *vt* (*disarrange*) desordenar;
(*spoil*) estropear; (*dirty*) ensuciar.
message ['mɛsɪdʒ] *n* recado, mensaje *m*; **to**
get the ~ (*fig, col*) enterarse.
message switching *n* (*COMPUT*)
conmutación *f* de mensajes.
messenger ['mɛsɪndʒə*] *n* mensajero/a.
Messiah [mɪˈsaɪə] *n* Mesías *m*.
Messrs *abbr* (*on letters:* = *Messieurs*) Sres.
messy ['mɛsɪ] *adj* (*dirty*) sucio; (*untidy*)
desordenado; (*confused: situation etc*)
confuso.
Met [mɛt] *n abbr* (*US*) = *Metropolitan Opera*.
met [mɛt] *pt, pp of* **meet** ♦ *adj abbr*
= **meteorological**.
metabolism [mɛˈtæbɔlɪzəm] *n*
metabolismo.

metal ['mɛtl] *n* metal *m*.
metallic [mɛˈtælɪk] *adj* metálico.
metallurgy [mɛˈtælədʒɪ] *n* metalurgia.
metalwork ['mɛtlwɔːk] *n* (*craft*)
metalistería.
metamorphosis, *pl* **metamorphoses**
[mɛtəˈmɔːfəsɪs, -siːz] *n* metamorfosis *f inv.*
metaphor ['mɛtəfə*] *n* metáfora.
metaphorical [mɛtəˈfɔrɪkl] *adj* metafórico.
metaphysics [mɛtəˈfɪzɪks] *n* metafísica.
mete [miːt]: **to ~ out** *vt fus* (*punishment*)
imponer.
meteor ['miːtɪə*] *n* meteoro.
meteoric [miːtɪˈɔrɪk] *adj* (*fig*) meteórico.
meteorite ['miːtɪəraɪt] *n* meteorito.
meteorological [miːtɪərəˈlɔdʒɪkl] *adj*
meteorológico.
meteorology [miːtɪəˈrɔlədʒɪ] *n*
meteorología.
meter ['miːtə*] *n* (*instrument*) contador *m*;
(*US: unit*) = **metre** ♦ *vt* (*US POST*)
franquear; **parking ~** parquímetro.
methane ['miːθeɪn] *n* metano.
method ['mɛθəd] *n* método; **~ of payment**
método de pago.
methodical [mɪˈθɔdɪkl] *adj* metódico.
Methodist ['mɛθədɪst] *adj, n* metodista *m/f*.
methodology [mɛθəˈdɔlədʒɪ] *n*
metodología.
meths [mɛθs], **methylated spirit(s)**
['mɛθɪleɪtɪd-] *n* (*BRIT*) alcohol *m* metilado *or*
desnaturalizado.
meticulous [mɛˈtɪkjuləs] *adj* meticuloso.
metre, (*US*) **meter** ['miːtə*] *n* metro.
metric ['mɛtrɪk] *adj* métrico; **to go ~** pasar
al sistema métrico.
metrication [mɛtrɪˈkeɪʃən] *n* conversión *f* al
sistema métrico.
metric system *n* sistema *m* métrico.
metric ton *n* tonelada métrica.
metronome ['mɛtrənəum] *n* metrónomo.
metropolis [mɪˈtrɔpəlɪs] *n* metrópoli(s) *f.*
metropolitan [mɛtrəˈpɔlɪtən] *adj*
metropolitano.
Metropolitan Police *n* (*BRIT*): **the ~** la
policía londinense.
mettle ['mɛtl] *n* valor *m*, ánimo.
mew [mjuː] *vi* (*cat*) maullar.
mews [mjuːz] (*BRIT*) *n*: **~ cottage** *casa*
acondicionada en antiguos establos o
cocheras; **~ flat** *piso en antiguos establos*
o cocheras.
Mexican ['mɛksɪkən] *adj, n* mejicano/a *m/f*,
mexicano/a *m/f* (*LAM*).
Mexico ['mɛksɪkəu] *n* Méjico, México
(*LAM*).
Mexico City *n* Ciudad *f* de Méjico *or*
México (*LAM*). ●

mezzanine ['mɛtsəni:n] *n* entresuelo.
MFA *n abbr* (*US*: = *Master of Fine Arts*) *título universitario.*
mfr *abbr* (= *manufacturer*) fab.
mg *abbr* (= *milligram*) mg.
Mgr *abbr* (= *Monseigneur, Monsignor*) Mons.
mgr *abbr* = **manager**.
MHR *n abbr* (*US*) *see* **Member of the House of Representatives**.
MHz *abbr* (= *megahertz*) MHz.
MI *abbr* (*US*) = *Michigan.*
MI5 *n abbr* (*BRIT*: = *Military Intelligence 5*) *servicio de contraespionaje del gobierno británico.*
MI6 *n abbr* (*BRIT*: = *Military Intelligence 6*) *servicio de inteligencia del gobierno británico.*
MIA *abbr* (= *missing in action*) desaparecido.
miaow [miːˈau] *vi* maullar.
mice [mais] *pl of* **mouse**.
Mich. *abbr* (*US*) = *Michigan.*
mickey ['mɪkɪ] *n*: **to take the ~ out of sb** tomar el pelo a algn.
micro... [maikrəu] *pref* micro....
microbe ['maikrəub] *n* microbio.
microbiology [maikrəubaiˈɔlədʒi] *n* microbiología.
microchip ['maikrəutʃip] *n* microchip *m*, microplaqueta.
micro(computer) ['maikrəu(kəmˈpjuːtə*)] *n* microordenador *m*, microcomputador *m*.
microcosm ['maikrəukɔzəm] *n* microcosmo.
microeconomics ['maikrəui:kəˈnɔmiks] *n* microeconomía.
microfiche ['maikrəufi:ʃ] *n* microficha.
microfilm ['maikrəufilm] *n* microfilm *m*.
microlight ['maikrəulait] *n* ultraligero.
micrometer [maiˈkrɔmitə*] *n* micrómetro.
microphone ['maikrəfəun] *n* micrófono.
microprocessor ['maikrəuˈprəusɛsə*] *n* microprocesador *m*.
microscope ['maikrəskəup] *n* microscopio; **under the ~** al microscopio.
microscopic [maikrəˈskɔpik] *adj* microscópico.
microwave ['maikrəuweiv] *n* (*also*: ~ **oven**) horno microondas.
mid [mid] *adj*: **in ~ May** a mediados de mayo; **in ~ afternoon** a media tarde; **in ~ air** en el aire; **he's in his ~ thirties** tiene unos treinta y cinco años.
midday [mid'dei] *n* mediodía *m*.
middle ['midl] *n* medio, centro; (*waist*) cintura ♦ *adj* de en medio; **in the ~ of the night** en plena noche; **I'm in the ~ of reading it** lo estoy leyendo ahora mismo.
middle-aged [midl'eidʒd] *adj* de mediana

edad.
Middle Ages *npl*: **the ~** la Edad *sg* Media.
middle class *n*: **the ~(es)** la clase media ♦ *adj* (*also*: **middle-class**) de clase media.
Middle East *n* Oriente *m* Medio.
middleman ['midlmæn] *n* intermediario.
middle management *n* dirección *f* de nivel medio.
middle name *n* segundo nombre *m*.
middle-of-the-road ['midləvðə'rəud] *adj* moderado.
middleweight ['midlweit] *n* (*BOXING*) peso medio.
middling ['midliŋ] *adj* mediano.
Middx *abbr* (*BRIT*) = *Middlesex*.
midge [midʒ] *n* mosquito.
midget ['midʒit] *n* enano/a.
midi system *n* cadena midi.
Midlands ['midləndz] *npl región central de Inglaterra.*
midnight ['midnait] *n* medianoche *f*; **at ~** a medianoche.
midriff ['midrif] *n* diafragma *m*.
midst [midst] *n*: **in the ~ of** entre, en medio de.
midsummer [mid'sʌmə*] *n*: **a ~ day** un día de pleno verano.
Midsummer's Day *n* Día *m* de San Juan.
midway [mid'wei] *adj, adv*: **~ (between)** a mitad de camino *or* a medio camino (entre).
midweek [mid'wi:k] *adv* entre semana.
midwife, *pl* **midwives** ['midwaif, -waivz] *n* comadrona.
midwifery ['midwifəri] *n* tocología.
midwinter [mid'wintə*] *n*: **in ~** en pleno invierno.
miffed [mift] *adj* (*col*) mosqueado.
might [mait] *vb see* **may** ♦ *n* fuerza, poder *m*; **he ~ be there** puede que esté allí, a lo mejor está allí; **I ~ as well go** más vale que vaya; **you ~ like to try** podría intentar.
mightily ['maitili] *adv* fuertemente, poderosamente; **I was ~ surprised** me sorprendí enormemente.
mightn't ['maitnt] = **might not**.
mighty ['maiti] *adj* fuerte, poderoso.
migraine ['mi:grein] *n* jaqueca.
migrant ['maigrənt] *adj* migratorio ♦ *n* (*bird*) ave *f* migratoria; (*worker*) emigrante *m/f*.
migrate [mai'greit] *vi* emigrar.
migration [mai'greiʃən] *n* emigración *f*.
mike [maik] *n abbr* (= *microphone*) micro.
Milan [mi'læn] *n* Milán *m*.
mild [maild] *adj* (*person*) apacible; (*climate*) templado; (*slight*) ligero; (*taste*) suave;

(*illness*) leve.
mildew ['mɪldjuː] *n* moho.
mildly ['maɪldlɪ] *adv* ligeramente;
suavemente; **to put it** ~ por no decir algo
peor.
mildness ['maɪldnɪs] *n* suavidad *f*; (*of
illness*) levedad *f*.
mile [maɪl] *n* milla; **to do 20** ~**s per gallon**
hacer 20 millas por galón.
mileage ['maɪlɪdʒ] *n* número de millas;
(*AUT*) kilometraje *m*.
mileage allowance *n* ≈ asignación *f* por
kilometraje.
mileometer [maɪ'lɔmɪtə*] *n* (*BRIT*) =
milometer.
milestone ['maɪlstəun] *n* mojón *m*; (*fig*)
hito.
milieu ['miːljəː] *n* (medio) ambiente *m*,
entorno.
militant ['mɪlɪtnt] *adj, n* militante *m/f*.
militarism ['mɪlɪtərɪzəm] *n* militarismo.
militaristic [mɪlɪtə'rɪstɪk] *adj* militarista.
military ['mɪlɪtərɪ] *adj* militar.
military service *n* servicio militar.
militate ['mɪlɪteɪt] *vi*: **to** ~ **against** militar
en contra de.
militia [mɪ'lɪʃə] *n* milicia.
milk [mɪlk] *n* leche *f* ♦ *vt* (*cow*) ordeñar; (*fig*)
chupar.
milk chocolate *n* chocolate *m* con leche.
milk float *n* (*BRIT*) furgoneta de la leche.
milking ['mɪlkɪŋ] *n* ordeño.
milkman ['mɪlkmən] *n* lechero.
milk shake *n* batido, malteada (*LAM*).
milk tooth *n* diente *m* de leche.
milk truck *n* (*US*) = **milk float**.
milky ['mɪlkɪ] *adj* lechoso.
Milky Way *n* Vía Láctea.
mill [mɪl] *n* (*windmill etc*) molino; (*coffee* ~)
molinillo; (*factory*) fábrica; (*spinning* ~)
hilandería ♦ *vt* moler ♦ *vi* (*also*: ~ **about**)
arremolinarse.
milled [mɪld] (*grain*) molido; (*coin, edge*)
acordonado.
millennium, *pl* ~**s** *or* **millennia**
[mɪ'lɛnɪəm, 'lɛnɪə] *n* milenio, milenario.
millennium bug *n* (*COMPUT*): **the** ~ el
(problema del) efecto 2000.
miller ['mɪlə*] *n* molinero.
millet ['mɪlɪt] *n* mijo.
milli... ['mɪlɪ] *pref* mili....
milligram(me) ['mɪlɪgraem] *n* miligramo.
millilitre, (*US*) **milliliter** ['mɪlɪliːtə*] *n*
mililitro.
millimetre, (*US*) **millimeter** ['mɪlɪmiːtə*] *n*
milímetro.
milliner ['mɪlɪnə*] *n* sombrerero/a.
millinery ['mɪlɪnərɪ] *n* sombrerería.

million ['mɪljən] *n* millón *m*; **a** ~ **times** un
millón de veces.
millionaire [mɪljə'nɛə*] *n* millonario/a.
millipede ['mɪlɪpiːd] *n* milpiés *m inv*.
millstone ['mɪlstəun] *n* piedra de molino.
millwheel ['mɪlwiːl] *n* rueda de molino.
milometer [maɪ'lɔmɪtə*] *n* (*BRIT*)
cuentakilómetros *m inv*.
mime [maɪm] *n* mímica; (*actor*) mimo/a ♦ *vt*
remedar ♦ *vi* actuar de mimo.
mimic ['mɪmɪk] *n* imitador(a) *m/f* ♦ *adj*
mímico ♦ *vt* remedar, imitar.
mimicry ['mɪmɪkrɪ] *n* imitación *f*.
Min. *abbr* (*BRIT POL*: = *Ministry*) Min.
min. *abbr* (= *minute(s)*) m.; = **minimum**.
minaret [mɪnə'rɛt] *n* alminar *m*.
mince [mɪns] *vt* picar ♦ *vi* (*in walking*) andar
con pasos menudos ♦ *n* (*BRIT CULIN*) carne
f picada, picadillo.
mincemeat ['mɪnsmiːt] *n conserva de fruta
picada*.
mince pie *n pastelillo relleno de fruta
picada*.
mincer ['mɪnsə*] *n* picadora de carne.
mincing ['mɪnsɪŋ] *adj* afectado.
mind [maɪnd] *n* (*gen*) mente *f*; (*contrasted
with matter*) espíritu *m* ♦ *vt* (*attend to, look
after*) ocuparse de, cuidar; (*be careful of*)
tener cuidado con; (*object to*): **I don't** ~
the noise no me molesta el ruido; **it is on
my** ~ me preocupa; **to my** ~ a mi
parecer *or* juicio; **to change one's** ~
cambiar de idea *or* de parecer; **to bring**
or **call sth to** ~ recordar algo; **to have
sth/sb in** ~ tener algo/a algn en mente; **to
be out of one's** ~ haber perdido el juicio;
to bear sth in ~ tomar *or* tener algo en
cuenta; **to make up one's** ~ decidirse; **it
went right out of my** ~ se me fue por
completo (de la cabeza); **to be in two** ~**s
about sth** estar indeciso *or* dudar ante
algo; **I don't** ~ me es igual; ~ **you, ...** te
advierto que ...; **never** ~! ¡es igual!, ¡no
importa!; (*don't worry*) ¡no te preocupes!;
'~ **the step**' 'cuidado con el escalón'.
mind-boggling ['maɪndbɔglɪŋ] *adj* (*col*)
alucinante, increíble.
-minded [-maɪndɪd] *adj*: **fair**~ imparcial; **an
industrially**~ **nation** una nación orientada
a la industria.
minder ['maɪndə*] *n* guardaespaldas *m inv*.
mindful ['maɪndful] *adj*: ~ **of** consciente de.
mindless ['maɪndlɪs] *adj* (*violence, crime*) sin
sentido; (*work*) de autómata.
mine [maɪn] *pron* (el) mío/(la) mía *etc*; **a
friend of** ~ un(a) amigo/a mío/mía ♦ *adj*:
this book is ~ este libro es mío ♦ *n* mina
♦ *vt* (*coal*) extraer; (*ship, beach*) minar.

mine detector *n* detector *m* de minas.
minefield ['maɪnfiːld] *n* campo de minas.
miner ['maɪnə*] *n* minero/a.
mineral ['mɪnərəl] *adj* mineral ♦ *n* mineral *m*; ~s *npl* (*BRIT: soft drinks*) refrescos *mpl* con gas.
mineral water *n* agua mineral.
minesweeper ['maɪnswiːpə*] *n* dragaminas *m inv*.
mingle ['mɪŋgl] *vi*: **to ~ with** mezclarse con.
mingy ['mɪndʒɪ] *adj* (*col*) tacaño.
mini ... [mɪnɪ] *pref* mini..., micro....
miniature ['mɪnətʃə*] *adj* (en) miniatura ♦ *n* miniatura.
minibus ['mɪnɪbʌs] *n* microbús *m*.
minicab ['mɪnɪkæb] *n* taxi *m* (*que sólo puede pedirse por teléfono*).
minicomputer ['mɪnɪkəm'pjuːtə*] *n* miniordenador *m*.
MiniDisc® ['mɪnɪdɪsk] *n* MiniDisc® *m*.
minim ['mɪnɪm] *n* (*BRIT MUS*) blanca.
minimal ['mɪnɪml] *adj* mínimo.
minimalist ['mɪnɪməlɪst] *adj*, *n* minimalista *m/f*.
minimize ['mɪnɪmaɪz] *vt* minimizar.
minimum ['mɪnɪməm] *n* (*pl* **minima** ['mɪnɪmə]) mínimo ♦ *adj* mínimo; **to reduce to a** ~ reducir algo al mínimo; ~ **wage** salario mínimo.
minimum lending rate (MLR) *n* tipo de interés mínimo.
mining ['maɪnɪŋ] *n* minería ♦ *adj* minero.
minion ['mɪnjən] *n* secuaz *m*.
mini-series ['mɪnɪsɪərɪːz] *n* serie *f* de pocos capítulos, miniserie *f*.
miniskirt ['mɪnɪskɔːt] *n* minifalda.
minister ['mɪnɪstə*] *n* (*BRIT POL*) ministro/a; (*REL*) pastor *m* ♦ *vi*: **to ~ to** atender a.
ministerial [mɪnɪs'tɪərɪəl] *adj* (*BRIT POL*) ministerial.
ministry ['mɪnɪstrɪ] *n* (*BRIT POL*) ministerio; (*REL*) sacerdocio; **M~ of Defence** Ministerio de Defensa.
mink [mɪŋk] *n* visón *m*.
mink coat *n* abrigo de visón.
Minn. *abbr* (*US*) = *Minnesota*.
minnow ['mɪnəu] *n* pececillo (de agua dulce).
minor ['maɪnə*] *adj* (*unimportant*) secundario; (*MUS*) menor ♦ *n* (*LAW*) menor *m/f* de edad.
Minorca [mɪ'nɔːkə] *n* Menorca.
minority [maɪ'nɔrɪtɪ] *n* minoría; **to be in a** ~ estar en *or* ser minoría.
minority interest *n* participación *f* minoritaria.
minster ['mɪnstə*] *n* catedral *f*.

minstrel ['mɪnstrəl] *n* juglar *m*.
mint [mɪnt] *n* (*plant*) menta, hierbabuena; (*sweet*) caramelo de menta ♦ *vt* (*coins*) acuñar; **the (Royal) M~**, (*US*) **the (US) M~** la Casa de la Moneda; **in ~ condition** en perfecto estado.
mint sauce *n* salsa de menta.
minuet [mɪnju'ɛt] *n* minué *m*.
minus ['maɪnəs] *n* (*also*: ~ **sign**) signo menos ♦ *prep* menos.
minuscule ['mɪnəskjuːl] *adj* minúsculo.
minute *n* [mɪnɪt] minuto; (*fig*) momento; ~s *npl* actas *fpl* ♦ *adj* [maɪ'njuːt] diminuto; (*search*) minucioso; **it is 5 ~s past 3** son las 3 y 5 (minutos); **at the last** ~ a última hora; **wait a** ~! ¡espera un momento!; **up to the** ~ de última hora; **in ~ detail** con todo detalle.
minute book *n* libro de actas.
minute hand *n* minutero.
minutely [maɪ'njuːtlɪ] *adv* (*by a small amount*) por muy poco; (*in detail*) detalladamente, minuciosamente.
minutiae [mɪ'njuːʃiː] *npl* minucias *fpl*.
miracle ['mɪrəkl] *n* milagro.
miracle play *n* auto, milagro.
miraculous [mɪ'rækjuləs] *adj* milagroso.
miraculously [mɪ'rækjuləslɪ] *adv* milagrosamente.
mirage ['mɪrɑːʒ] *n* espejismo.
mire [maɪə*] *n* fango, lodo.
mirror ['mɪrə*] *n* espejo; (*in car*) retrovisor *m* ♦ *vt* reflejar.
mirror image *n* reflejo inverso.
mirth [mɜːθ] *n* alegría; (*laughter*) risa, risas.
misadventure [mɪsəd'ventʃə*] *n* desventura; **death by** ~ muerte *f* accidental.
misanthropist [mɪ'zænθrəpɪst] *n* misántropo/a.
misapply [mɪsə'plaɪ] *vt* emplear mal.
misapprehension ['mɪsæprɪ'henʃən] *n* equivocación *f*.
misappropriate [mɪsə'prəuprɪeɪt] *vt* (*funds*) malversar.
misappropriation ['mɪsəprəuprɪ'eɪʃən] *n* malversación *f*, desfalco.
misbehave [mɪsbɪ'heɪv] *vi* portarse mal.
misbehaviour, (*US*) **misbehavior** [mɪsbɪ'heɪvjə*] *n* mala conducta.
misc. *abbr* = **miscellaneous**.
miscalculate [mɪs'kælkjuleɪt] *vt* calcular mal.
miscalculation [mɪskælkju'leɪʃən] *n* error *m* (de cálculo).
miscarriage ['mɪskærɪdʒ] *n* (*MED*) aborto (no provocado); ~ **of justice** error *m* judicial.

miscarry [mɪs'kærɪ] *vi* (*MED*) abortar (de forma natural); (*fail: plans*) fracasar, malograrse.

miscellaneous [mɪsɪ'leɪnɪəs] *adj* varios/as, diversos/as; ~ **expenses** gastos diversos.

miscellany [mɪ'selənɪ] *n* miscelánea.

mischance [mɪs'tʃɑːns] *n* desgracia, mala suerte *f*; **by (some)** ~ por (alguna) desgracia.

mischief ['mɪstʃɪf] *n* (*naughtiness*) travesura; (*harm*) mal *m*, daño; (*maliciousness*) malicia.

mischievous ['mɪstʃɪvəs] *adj* travieso; dañino; (*playful*) malicioso.

mischievously ['mɪstʃɪvəslɪ] *adv* por travesura; maliciosamente.

misconception ['mɪskən'sepʃən] *n* concepto erróneo; equivocación *f*.

misconduct [mɪs'kɔndʌkt] *n* mala conducta; **professional** ~ falta profesional.

miscount [mɪs'kaunt] *vt, vi* contar mal.

misconstrue [mɪskən'struː] *vt* interpretar mal.

misdeed [mɪs'diːd] *n* (*old*) fechoría, delito.

misdemeanour, (*US*) **misdemeanor** [mɪsdɪ'miːnə*] *n* delito, ofensa.

misdirect [mɪsdɪ'rekt] *vt* (*person*) informar mal; (*letter*) poner señas incorrectas en.

miser ['maɪzə*] *n* avaro/a.

miserable ['mɪzərəbl] *adj* (*unhappy*) triste, desgraciado; (*wretched*) miserable; **to feel** ~ sentirse triste.

miserably ['mɪzərəblɪ] *adv* (*smile, answer*) tristemente; (*fail*) rotundamente; **to pay** ~ pagar una miseria.

miserly ['maɪzəlɪ] *adj* avariento, tacaño.

misery ['mɪzərɪ] *n* (*unhappiness*) tristeza; (*wretchedness*) miseria, desdicha.

misfire [mɪs'faɪə*] *vi* fallar.

misfit ['mɪsfɪt] *n* (*person*) inadaptado/a.

misfortune [mɪs'fɔːtʃən] *n* desgracia.

misgiving(s) [mɪs'gɪvɪŋ(z)] *n(pl)* (*mistrust*) recelo; (*apprehension*) presentimiento; **to have** ~**s about sth** tener dudas sobre algo.

misguided [mɪs'gaɪdɪd] *adj* equivocado.

mishandle [mɪs'hændl] *vt* (*treat roughly*) maltratar; (*mismanage*) manejar mal.

mishap ['mɪshæp] *n* desgracia, contratiempo.

mishear [mɪs'hɪə*] *vt, vi* (*irreg: like* **hear**) oír mal.

mishmash ['mɪʃmæʃ] *n* (*col*) revoltijo.

misinform [mɪsɪn'fɔːm] *vt* informar mal.

misinterpret [mɪsɪn'təːprɪt] *vt* interpretar mal.

misinterpretation ['mɪsɪntəːprɪ'teɪʃən] *n*

mala interpretación *f*.

misjudge [mɪs'dʒʌdʒ] *vt* juzgar mal.

mislay [mɪs'leɪ] *vt* (*irreg: like* **lay**) extraviar, perder.

mislead [mɪs'liːd] *vt* (*irreg: like* **lead**) llevar a conclusiones erróneas; (*deliberately*) engañar.

misleading [mɪs'liːdɪŋ] *adj* engañoso.

misled [mɪs'led] *pt, pp of* **mislead**.

mismanage [mɪs'mænɪdʒ] *vt* administrar mal.

mismanagement [mɪs'mænɪdʒmənt] *n* mala administración *f*.

misnomer [mɪs'nəumə*] *n* término inapropiado *or* equivocado.

misogynist [mɪ'sɔdʒɪnɪst] *n* misógino.

misplace [mɪs'pleɪs] *vt* (*lose*) extraviar; ~**d** (*trust etc*) inmerecido.

misprint ['mɪsprɪnt] *n* errata, error *m* de imprenta.

mispronounce [mɪsprə'nauns] *vt* pronunciar mal.

misquote ['mɪs'kwəut] *vt* citar incorrectamente.

misread [mɪs'riːd] *vt* (*irreg: like* **read**) leer mal.

misrepresent [mɪsreprɪ'zent] *vt* falsificar.

misrepresentation [mɪsreprɪzen'teɪʃən] *n* (*LAW*) falsa declaración *f*.

Miss [mɪs] *n* Señorita; **Dear** ~ **Smith** Estimada Señorita Smith.

miss [mɪs] *vt* (*train etc*) perder; (*shot*) errar, fallar; (*appointment, class*) faltar a; (*escape, avoid*) evitar; (*notice loss of: money etc*) notar la falta de, echar en falta; (*regret the absence of*): **I** ~ **him** le echo de menos ♦ *vi* fallar ♦ *n* (*shot*) tiro fallido; **the bus just** ~**ed the wall** faltó poco para que el autobús se estrella contra el muro; **you're** ~**ing the point** no has entendido la idea.

▶**miss out** *vt* (*BRIT*) omitir.

▶**miss out on** *vt fus* (*fun, party, opportunity*) perderse.

Miss. *abbr* (*US*) = **Mississippi**.

missal ['mɪsl] *n* misal *m*.

misshapen [mɪs'ʃeɪpən] *adj* deforme.

missile ['mɪsaɪl] *n* (*AVIAT*) misil *m*; (*object thrown*) proyectil *m*.

missile base *n* base *f* de misiles.

missile launcher *n* lanzamisiles *m inv*.

missing ['mɪsɪŋ] *adj* (*pupil*) ausente, que falta; (*thing*) perdido; (*MIL*) desaparecido; **to be** ~ faltar; ~ **person** desaparecido/a.

mission ['mɪʃən] *n* misión *f*; **on a** ~ **for sb** en una misión para algn.

missionary ['mɪʃənrɪ] *n* misionero/a.

misspell [mɪs'spel] *vt* (*irreg: like* **spell**)

escribir mal.

misspent ['mɪs'spɛnt] *adj*: **his ~ youth** su juventud disipada.

mist [mɪst] *n* (*light*) neblina; (*heavy*) niebla; (*at sea*) bruma ♦ *vi* (*also*: ~ **over**, ~ **up**: *weather*) nublarse; (: *BRIT*: *windows*) empañarse.

mistake [mɪs'teɪk] *n* error *m* ♦ *vt* (*irreg*: *like* **take**) entender mal; **by ~** por equivocación; **to make a ~** (*about sb/sth*) equivocarse; (*in writing, calculating etc*) cometer un error; **to ~ A for B** confundir A con B.

mistaken [mɪs'teɪkən] *pp of* **mistake** ♦ *adj* (*idea etc*) equivocado; **to be ~** equivocarse, engañarse; **~ identity** identificación *f* errónea.

mistakenly [mɪs'teɪkənlɪ] *adv* erróneamente.

mister ['mɪstə*] *n* (*col*) señor *m*; *see* **Mr.**

mistletoe ['mɪsltəu] *n* muérdago.

mistook [mɪs'tuk] *pt of* **mistake.**

mistranslation [mɪstræns'leɪʃən] *n* mala traducción *f.*

mistreat [mɪs'triːt] *vt* maltratar, tratar mal.

mistress ['mɪstrɪs] *n* (*lover*) amante *f*; (*of house*) señora (de la casa); (*BRIT*: *in primary school*) maestra; (*in secondary school*) profesora; *see* **Mrs.**

mistrust [mɪs'trʌst] *vt* desconfiar de ♦ *n*: ~ **(of)** desconfianza (de).

mistrustful [mɪs'trʌstful] *adj*: ~ **(of)** desconfiado (de), receloso (de).

misty ['mɪstɪ] *adj* nebuloso, brumoso; (*day*) de niebla; (*glasses*) empañado.

misty-eyed ['mɪstɪ'aɪd] *adj* sentimental.

misunderstand [mɪsʌndə'stænd] *vt, vi* (*irreg*: *like* **understand**) entender mal.

misunderstanding [mɪsʌndə'stændɪŋ] *n* malentendido.

misunderstood [mɪsʌndə'stud] *pt, pp of* **misunderstand** ♦ *adj* (*person*) incomprendido.

misuse *n* [mɪs'juːs] mal uso; (*of power*) abuso ♦ *vt* [mɪs'juːz] abusar de; (*funds*) malversar.

MIT *n abbr* (*US*) = *Massachusetts Institute of Technology.*

mite [maɪt] *n* (*small quantity*) pizca; **poor ~!** ¡pobrecito!

mitigate ['mɪtɪgeɪt] *vt* mitigar; **mitigating circumstances** circunstancias *fpl* atenuantes.

mitigation [mɪtɪ'geɪʃən] *n* mitigación *f*, alivio.

mitre, (*US*) **miter** ['maɪtə*] *n* mitra.

mitt(en) ['mɪt(n)] *n* manopla.

mix [mɪks] *vt* (*gen*) mezclar; (*combine*) unir ♦ *vi* mezclarse; (*people*) llevarse bien ♦ *n* mezcla; **to ~ sth with sth** mezclar algo con algo; **to ~ business with pleasure** combinar los negocios con el placer; **cake ~** preparado para pastel.

▶**mix in** *vt* (*eggs etc*) añadir.

▶**mix up** *vt* mezclar; (*confuse*) confundir; **to be ~ed up in sth** estar metido en algo.

mixed [mɪkst] *adj* (*assorted*) variado, surtido; (*school, marriage etc*) mixto.

mixed-ability ['mɪkstə'bɪlɪtɪ] *adj* (*class etc*) de alumnos de distintas capacidades.

mixed blessing *n*: **it's a ~** tiene su lado bueno y su lado malo.

mixed doubles *n* (*SPORT*) mixtos *mpl.*

mixed economy *n* economía mixta.

mixed grill *n* (*BRIT*) parrillada mixta.

mixed-up [mɪkst'ʌp] *adj* (*confused*) confuso, revuelto.

mixer ['mɪksə*] *n* (*for food*) batidora; (*person*): **he's a good ~** tiene don de gentes.

mixer tap *n* (grifo) monomando.

mixture ['mɪkstʃə*] *n* mezcla.

mix-up ['mɪksʌp] *n* confusión *f.*

Mk *abbr* (*BRIT TECH*: = *mark*) Mk.

mkt *abbr* = **market.**

MLA *n abbr* (*BRIT POL*) (= *Member of the Legislative Assembly*) miembro de la asamblea legislativa.

MLitt *n abbr* (= *Master of Literature, Master of Letters*) título universitario de postgrado; *see also* **master's degree.**

MLR *n abbr* (*BRIT*) = **minimum lending rate.**

mm *abbr* (= *millimetre*) mm.

MMR vaccine *n* (*against measles, mumps, rubella*) vacuna triple vírica.

MN *abbr* (*BRIT*) = **Merchant Navy;** (*US*) = *Minnesota.*

MO *n abbr* (*MED*) = *medical officer;* (*US col*) = **modus operandi** ♦ *abbr* (*US*) = *Missouri.*

Mo. *abbr* (*US*) = *Missouri.*

m.o. *abbr* (= *money order*) g/.

moan [məun] *n* gemido ♦ *vi* gemir; (*col: complain*): **to ~ (about)** quejarse (de).

moaning ['məunɪŋ] *n* gemidos *mpl*; quejas *fpl.*

moat [məut] *n* foso.

mob [mɔb] *n* multitud *f*; (*pej*): **the ~** el populacho ♦ *vt* acosar.

mobile ['məubaɪl] *adj* móvil ♦ *n* móvil *m.*

mobile home *n* caravana.

mobile phone *n* teléfono móvil.

mobility [məu'bɪlɪtɪ] *n* movilidad *f*; ~ **of labour** *or* (*US*) **labor** movilidad *f* de la mano de obra.

mobilize ['məubɪlaɪz] *vt* movilizar.

moccasin ['mɔkəsɪn] *n* mocasín *m.*

mock [mɔk] *vt* (*make ridiculous*) ridiculizar;

(*laugh at*) burlarse de ♦ *adj* fingido.
mockery ['mɔkərɪ] *n* burla; **to make a ~ of** desprestigiar.
mocking ['mɔkɪŋ] *adj* (*tone*) burlón/ona.
mockingbird ['mɔkɪŋbɔːd] *n* sinsonte *m* (*LAM*), zenzontle (*LAM*).
mock-up ['mɔkʌp] *n* maqueta.
mod cons ['mɔd'kɔnz] *npl abbr* (= *modern conveniences*) *see* **convenience**.
mode [məud] *n* modo; (*of transport*) medio; (*COMPUT*) modo, modalidad *f*.
model ['mɔdl] *n* (*gen*) modelo; (*ARCH*) maqueta; (*person: for fashion, ART*) modelo *m/f* ♦ *adj* modelo *inv* ♦ *vt* modelar ♦ *vi* ser modelo; ~ **railway** ferrocarril *m* de juguete; **to ~ clothes** pasar modelos, ser modelo; **to ~ on** crear a imitación de.
modelling, (*US*) **modeling** ['mɔdlɪŋ] *n* (*modelmaking*) modelado.
modem ['məudəm] *n* módem *m*.
moderate *adj, n* ['mɔdərət] moderado/a *m/f* ♦ (*vb*: ['mɔdəreɪt]) *vi* moderarse, calmarse ♦ *vt* moderar.
moderately ['mɔdərətlɪ] *adv* (*act*) con moderación; (*expensive, difficult*) medianamente; (*pleased, happy*) bastante.
moderation [mɔdə'reɪʃən] *n* moderación *f*; **in ~** con moderación.
moderator ['mɔdəreɪtə*] *n* (*mediator*) moderador(a) *m/f*.
modern ['mɔdən] *adj* moderno; ~ **languages** lenguas *fpl* modernas.
modernity [mɔ'dəːnɪtɪ] *n* modernidad *f*.
modernization [mɔdənaɪ'zeɪʃən] *n* modernización *f*.
modernize ['mɔdənaɪz] *vt* modernizar.
modest ['mɔdɪst] *adj* modesto.
modestly ['mɔdɪstlɪ] *adv* modestamente.
modesty ['mɔdɪstɪ] *n* modestia.
modicum ['mɔdɪkəm] *n*: **a ~ of** un mínimo de.
modification [mɔdɪfɪ'keɪʃən] *n* modificación *f*; **to make ~s** hacer cambios *or* modificaciones.
modify ['mɔdɪfaɪ] *vt* modificar.
modish ['məudɪʃ] *adj* de moda.
Mods [mɔdz] *n abbr* (*BRIT*: = *(Honour) Moderations*) *examen de licenciatura de la universidad de Oxford.*
modular ['mɔdjulə*] *adj* (*filing, unit*) modular.
modulate ['mɔdjuleɪt] *vt* modular.
modulation [mɔdju'leɪʃən] *n* modulación *f*.
module ['mɔdjuːl] *n* (*unit, component, SPACE*) módulo.
modus operandi ['məudəsɔpə'rændiː] *n* manera de actuar.
Mogadishu [mɔgə'dɪʃuː] *n* Mogadiscio.

mogul ['məugəl] *n* (*fig*) magnate *m*.
MOH *n abbr* (*BRIT*) = *Medical Officer of Health*.
mohair ['məuhɛə*] *n* mohair *m*.
Mohammed [mə'hæmed] *n* Mahoma *m*.
moist [mɔɪst] *adj* húmedo.
moisten ['mɔɪsn] *vt* humedecer.
moisture ['mɔɪstʃə*] *n* humedad *f*.
moisturize ['mɔɪstʃəraɪz] *vt* (*skin*) hidratar.
moisturizer ['mɔɪstʃəraɪzə*] *n* crema hidratante.
molar ['məulə*] *n* muela.
molasses [məu'læsɪz] *n* melaza.
mold [məuld] *n*, *vt* (*US*) = **mould**.
Moldavia [mɔl'deɪvɪə], **Moldova** [mɔl'dəuvə] *n* Moldavia, Moldova.
Moldavian [mɔl'deɪvɪən], **Moldovan** [mɔl'dəuvən] *adj, n* moldavo/a *m/f*.
mole [məul] *n* (*animal*) topo; (*spot*) lunar *m*.
molecular [mə'lekjulə*] *adj* molecular.
molecule ['mɔlɪkjuːl] *n* molécula.
molest [məu'lest] *vt* importunar; (*sexually*) abordar con propósitos deshonestos.
moll [mɔl] *n* (*slang*) amiga.
mollusc, (*US*) **mollusk** ['mɔləsk] *n* molusco.
mollycoddle ['mɔlɪkɔdl] *vt* mimar.
Molotov cocktail ['mɔlətɔf-] *n* cóctel *m* Molotov.
molt [məult] *vi* (*US*) = **moult**.
molten ['məultən] *adj* fundido; (*lava*) líquido.
mom [mɔm] *n* (*US*) = **mum**.
moment ['məumənt] *n* momento; **at** *or* **for the ~** de momento, por el momento, por ahora; **in a ~** dentro de un momento.
momentarily ['məuməntrɪlɪ] *adv* momentáneamente; (*US: very soon*) de un momento a otro.
momentary ['məuməntərɪ] *adj* momentáneo.
momentous [məu'mentəs] *adj* trascendental, importante.
momentum [məu'mentəm] *n* momento; (*fig*) ímpetu *m*; **to gather ~** cobrar velocidad; (*fig*) cobrar fuerza.
mommy ['mɔmɪ] *n* (*US*) = **mummy**.
Mon. *abbr* (= *Monday*) lun.
Monaco ['mɔnəkəu] *n* Mónaco.
monarch ['mɔnək] *n* monarca *m/f*.
monarchist ['mɔnəkɪst] *n* monárquico/a.
monarchy ['mɔnəkɪ] *n* monarquía.
monastery ['mɔnəstərɪ] *n* monasterio.
monastic [mə'næstɪk] *adj* monástico.
Monday ['mʌndɪ] *n* lunes *m inv*.
Monegasque [mɔnɪ'gæsk] *adj, n* monegasco/a *m/f*.
monetarist ['mʌnɪtərɪst] *n* monetarista *m*.

monetary ['mʌnɪtərɪ] *adj* monetario.
monetary policy *n* política monetaria.
money ['mʌnɪ] *n* dinero, plata (*LAM*); **to make** ~ ganar dinero; **I've got no** ~ **left** no me queda dinero.
moneyed ['mʌnɪd] *adj* adinerado.
moneylender ['mʌnɪlɛndə*] *n* prestamista *m/f*.
moneymaker ['mʌnɪmeɪkə*] *n* (*BRIT col*: *business*) filón *m*.
moneymaking ['mʌnɪmeɪkɪŋ] *adj* rentable.
money market *n* mercado monetario.
money order *n* giro.
money-spinner ['mʌnɪspɪnə*] *n* (*col*: *person, idea, business*) filón *m*.
money supply *n* oferta monetaria, medio circulante, volumen *m* monetario.
Mongol ['mɔŋgəl] *n* mongol(a) *m/f*; (*LING*) mongol *m*.
mongol ['mɔŋgəl] *adj*, *n* (*MED*) mongólico.
Mongolia [mɔŋ'gəulɪə] *n* Mongolia.
Mongolian [mɔŋ'gəulɪən] *adj* mongol(a) ♦ *n* mongol(a) *m/f*; (*LING*) mongol *m*.
mongoose ['mɔŋguːs] *n* mangosta.
mongrel ['mʌŋgrəl] *n* (*dog*) perro cruzado.
monitor ['mɔnɪtə*] *n* monitor *m* ♦ *vt* controlar; (*foreign station*) escuchar.
monk [mʌŋk] *n* monje *m*.
monkey ['mʌŋkɪ] *n* mono.
monkey business *n*, **monkey tricks** *npl* tejemanejes *mpl*.
monkey nut *n* (*BRIT*) cacahuete *m*, maní (*LAM*).
monkey wrench *n* llave *f* inglesa.
mono ['mɔnəu] *adj* (*broadcast etc*) mono *inv*.
mono... [mɔnəu] *pref* mono ... .
monochrome ['mɔnəukrəum] *adj* monocromo.
monocle ['mɔnəkl] *n* monóculo.
monogamous [mə'nɔgəməs] *adj* monógamo.
monogram ['mɔnəgræm] *n* monograma *m*.
monolith ['mɔnəlɪθ] *n* monolito.
monolithic [mɔnə'lɪθɪk] *adj* monolítico.
monologue ['mɔnəlɔg] *n* monólogo.
monoplane ['mɔnəpleɪn] *n* monoplano.
monopolist [mə'nɔpəlɪst] *n* monopolista *m/f*.
monopolize [mə'nɔpəlaɪz] *vt* monopolizar.
monopoly [mə'nɔpəlɪ] *n* monopolio;
  Monopolies and Mergers Commission (*BRIT*) comisión reguladora de monopolios y fusiones.
monorail ['mɔnəureɪl] *n* monocarril *m*, monorraíl *m*.
monosodium glutamate [mɔnə'səudɪəm 'gluːtəmeɪt] *n* glutamato monosódico.
monosyllabic [mɔnɔsɪ'læbɪk] *adj* monosílabo.

monosyllable ['mɔnəsɪləbl] *n* monosílabo.
monotone ['mɔnətəun] *n* voz *f* (*or* tono) monocorde.
monotonous [mə'nɔtənəs] *adj* monótono.
monotony [mə'nɔtənɪ] *n* monotonía.
monoxide [mə'nɔksaɪd] *n*: **carbon** ~ monóxido de carbono.
monseigneur [mɔnsɛn'jəː*], **monsignor** [mɔn'siːnjə*] *n* monseñor *m*.
monsoon [mɔn'suːn] *n* monzón *m*.
monster ['mɔnstə*] *n* monstruo.
monstrosity [mɔns'trɔsɪtɪ] *n* monstruosidad *f*.
monstrous ['mɔnstrəs] *adj* (*huge*) enorme; (*atrocious*) monstruoso.
Mont. *abbr* (*US*) = Montana.
montage [mɔn'tɑːʒ] *n* montaje *m*.
Mont Blanc [mɔ̃'blɑ̃] *n* Mont Blanc *m*.
month [mʌnθ] *n* mes *m*; **300 dollars a** ~ 300 dólares al mes; **every** ~ cada mes.
monthly ['mʌnθlɪ] *adj* mensual ♦ *adv* mensualmente ♦ *n* (*magazine*) revista mensual; **twice** ~ dos veces al mes; ~ **instalment** mensualidad *f*.
monument ['mɔnjumənt] *n* monumento.
monumental [mɔnju'mɛntl] *adj* monumental.
moo [muː] *vi* mugir.
mood [muːd] *n* humor *m*; **to be in a good/bad** ~ estar de buen/mal humor.
moodily ['muːdɪlɪ] *adv* malhumoradamente.
moodiness ['muːdɪnɪs] *n* humor *m* cambiante; (*bad mood*) mal humor *m*.
moody ['muːdɪ] *adj* (*variable*) de humor variable; (*sullen*) malhumorado.
moon [muːn] *n* luna.
moonbeam ['muːnbiːm] *n* rayo de luna.
moon landing *n* alunizaje *m*.
moonless ['muːnlɪs] *adj* sin luna.
moonlight ['muːnlaɪt] *n* luz *f* de la luna ♦ *vi* hacer pluriempleo.
moonlighting ['muːnlaɪtɪŋ] *n* pluriempleo.
moonlit ['muːnlɪt] *adj*: **a** ~ **night** una noche de luna.
moonshot ['muːnʃɔt] *n* lanzamiento de una astronave a la luna.
moonstruck ['muːnstrʌk] *adj* chiflado.
moony ['muːnɪ] *adj*: **to have** ~ **eyes** estar soñando despierto, estar pensando en las musarañas.
Moor [muə*] *n* moro/a.
moor [muə*] *n* páramo ♦ *vt* (*ship*) amarrar ♦ *vi* echar las amarras.
moorings ['muərɪŋz] *npl* (*chains*) amarras *fpl*; (*place*) amarradero *sg*.
Moorish ['muərɪʃ] *adj* moro; (*architecture*) árabe.
moorland ['muələnd] *n* páramo, brezal *m*.

moose [muːs] *n, pl inv* alce *m*.
moot [muːt] *vt* proponer para la discusión, sugerir ♦ *adj*: ~ **point** punto discutible.
mop [mɔp] *n* fregona; (*of hair*) greñas *fpl*
♦ *vt* fregar.
►**mop up** *vt* limpiar.
mope [məup] *vi* estar deprimido.
►**mope about, mope around** *vi* andar abatido.
moped ['məupɛd] *n* ciclomotor *m*.
moquette [mɔ'kɛt] *n* moqueta.
MOR *adj abbr* (*MUS*: = *middle-of-the-road*) para el gran público.
moral ['mɔrl] *adj* moral ♦ *n* moraleja; ~**s** *npl* moralidad *f*, moral *f*.
morale [mɔ'rɑːl] *n* moral *f*.
morality [mɔ'rælɪtɪ] *n* moralidad *f*.
moralize ['mɔrəlaɪz] *vi*: **to** ~ **(about)** moralizar (sobre).
morally ['mɔrəlɪ] *adv* moralmente.
moral victory *n* victoria moral.
morass [mə'ræs] *n* pantano.
moratorium [mɔrə'tɔːrɪəm] *n* moratoria.
morbid ['mɔːbɪd] *adj* (*interest*) morboso; (*MED*) mórbido.

=================== *KEYWORD*

more [mɔː*] *adj* **1** (*greater in number etc*) más; ~ **people/work than before** más gente/trabajo que antes
2 (*additional*) más; **do you want (some)** ~ **tea?** ¿quieres más té?; **is there any** ~ **wine?** ¿queda vino?; **it'll take a few** ~ **weeks** tardará unas semanas más; **it's 2 kms** ~ **to the house** faltan 2 kms para la casa; ~ **time/letters than we expected** más tiempo del que/más cartas de las que esperábamos; **I have no** ~ **money, I don't have any** ~ **money** (ya) no tengo más dinero
♦ *pron* (*greater amount, additional amount*) más; ~ **than 10** más de 10; **it cost** ~ **than the other one/than we expected** costó más que el otro/más de lo que esperábamos; **is there any** ~**?** ¿hay más?; **I want** ~ quiero más; **and what's** ~ ... y además ...; **many/much** ~ muchos(as)/ mucho(a) más
♦ *adv* más; ~ **dangerous/easily (than)** más peligroso/fácilmente (que); ~ **and** ~ **expensive** cada vez más caro; ~ **or less** más o menos; ~ **than ever** más que nunca; **she doesn't live here any** ~ ya no vive aquí.

moreover [mɔː'rəuvə*] *adv* además, por otra parte.
morgue [mɔːg] *n* depósito de cadáveres.

MORI ['mɔːrɪ] *n abbr* (*BRIT*) = *Market and Opinion Research Institute*.
moribund ['mɔrɪbʌnd] *adj* moribundo.
Mormon ['mɔːmən] *n* mormón/ona *m/f*.
morning ['mɔːnɪŋ] *n* (*gen*) mañana; (*early* ~) madrugada; **in the** ~ por la mañana; **7 o'clock in the** ~ las 7 de la mañana; **this** ~ esta mañana.
morning-after pill ['mɔːnɪŋ'ɑːftə-] *n* píldora del día después.
morning sickness *n* (*MED*) náuseas *fpl* del embarazo.
Moroccan [mə'rɔkən] *adj, n* marroquí *m/f*.
Morocco [mə'rɔkəu] *n* Marruecos *m*.
moron ['mɔːrɔn] *n* imbécil *m/f*.
morose [mə'rəus] *adj* hosco, malhumorado.
morphine ['mɔːfiːn] *n* morfina.
morris dancing ['mɔrɪs] *n* (*BRIT*) *baile tradicional inglés en el que se llevan cascabeles en la ropa.*
Morse [mɔːs] *n* (*also*: ~ **code**) (alfabeto) morse *m*.
morsel ['mɔːsl] *n* (*of food*) bocado.
mortal ['mɔːtl] *adj, n* mortal *m*.
mortality [mɔː'tælɪtɪ] *n* mortalidad *f*.
mortality rate *n* tasa de mortalidad.
mortally ['mɔːtəlɪ] *adv* mortalmente.
mortar ['mɔːtə*] *n* argamasa; (*implement*) mortero.
mortgage ['mɔːgɪdʒ] *n* hipoteca ♦ *vt* hipotecar; **to take out a** ~ sacar una hipoteca.
mortgage company *n* (*US*) ≈ banco hipotecario.
mortgagee [mɔːgə'dʒiː] *n* acreedor(a) *m/f* hipotecario/a.
mortgager ['mɔːgədʒə*] *n* deudor(a) *m/f* hipotecario/a.
mortice ['mɔːtɪs] = **mortise**.
mortician [mɔː'tɪʃən] *n* (*US*) director(a) *m/f* de pompas fúnebres.
mortification ['mɔːtɪfɪ'keɪʃən] *n* mortificación *f*, humillación *f*.
mortified ['mɔːtɪfaɪd] *adj*: **I was** ~ me dio muchísima vergüenza.
mortise (lock) ['mɔːtɪs-] *n* cerradura de muesca.
mortuary ['mɔːtjuərɪ] *n* depósito de cadáveres.
mosaic [məu'zeɪɪk] *n* mosaico.
Moscow ['mɔskəu] *n* Moscú *m*.
Moslem ['mɔzləm] *adj, n* = **Muslim**.
mosque [mɔsk] *n* mezquita.
mosquito, ~es [mɔs'kiːtəu] *n* mosquito.
moss [mɔs] *n* musgo.
mossy ['mɔsɪ] *adj* musgoso, cubierto de musgo.
most [məust] *adj* la mayor parte de, la

mayoría de ♦ *pron* la mayor parte, la
mayoría ♦ *adv* el más; (*very*) muy; **the ~**
(*also*: + *adjective*) el más; **~ of them** la
mayor parte de ellos; **I saw the ~** yo fui
el que más vi; **at the (very) ~** a lo sumo,
todo lo más; **to make the ~ of** aprovechar
(al máximo); **a ~ interesting book** un
libro interesantísimo.

mostly ['məustlɪ] *adv* en su mayor parte,
principalmente.

MOT *n abbr* (*BRIT* = *Ministry of Transport*):
the ~ (test) ≈ la ITV.

motel [məu'tɛl] *n* motel *m*.

moth [mɔθ] *n* mariposa nocturna; (*clothes*
~) polilla.

mothball ['mɔθbɔːl] *n* bola de naftalina.

moth-eaten ['mɔθiːtn] *adj* apolillado.

mother ['mʌðə*] *n* madre *f* ♦ *adj* materno
♦ *vt* (*care for*) cuidar (como una madre).

mother board *n* (*COMPUT*) placa madre.

motherhood ['mʌðəhud] *n* maternidad *f*.

mother-in-law ['mʌðərɪnlɔː] *n* suegra.

motherly ['mʌðəlɪ] *adj* maternal.

mother-of-pearl ['mʌðərəv'pəːl] *n* nácar *m*.

mother's help *n* niñera.

mother-to-be ['mʌðətə'biː] *n* futura
madre.

mother tongue *n* lengua materna.

mothproof ['mɔθpruːf] *adj* a prueba de
polillas.

motif [məu'tiːf] *n* motivo; (*theme*) tema *m*.

motion ['məuʃən] *n* movimiento; (*gesture*)
ademán *m*, señal *f*; (*at meeting*) moción *f*;
(*BRIT*: *also*: **bowel** ~) evacuación *f*
intestinal ♦ *vt*, *vi*: **to ~ (to) sb to do sth**
hacer señas a algn para que haga algo; **to
be in ~** (*vehicle*) estar en movimiento; **to
set in ~** poner en marcha; **to go through
the ~s of doing sth** (*fig*) hacer algo
mecánicamente *or* sin convicción.

motionless ['məuʃənlɪs] *adj* inmóvil.

motion picture *n* película.

motivate ['məutɪveɪt] *vt* motivar.

motivated ['məutɪveɪtɪd] *adj* motivado.

motivation [məutɪ'veɪʃən] *n* motivación *f*.

motivational research [məutɪ'veɪʃnl-] *n*
estudios *mpl* de motivación.

motive ['məutɪv] *n* motivo; **from the best
~s** con las mejores intenciones.

motley ['mɔtlɪ] *adj* variopinto.

motor ['məutə*] *n* motor *m*; (*BRIT*: *col*:
vehicle) coche *m*, carro (*LAM*), automóvil
m, auto *m* (*esp LAM*) ♦ *adj* motor (*f*: motora,
motriz).

motorbike ['məutəbaɪk] *n* moto *f*.

motorboat ['məutəbəut] *n* lancha motora.

motorcade ['məutəkeɪd] *n* desfile *m* de
automóviles.

motorcar ['məutəkɑː*] *n* (*BRIT*) coche *m*,
carro (*LAM*), automóvil *m*, auto *m* (*esp
LAM*).

motorcoach ['məutəkəutʃ] *n* autocar *m*,
autobús *m*, camión *m* (*LAM*).

motorcycle ['məutəsaɪkl] *n* motocicleta.

motorcycle racing *n* motociclismo.

motorcyclist ['məutəsaɪklɪst] *n*
motociclista *m/f*.

motoring ['məutərɪŋ] *n* (*BRIT*)
automovilismo ♦ *adj* (*accident, offence*) de
tráfico *or* tránsito.

motorist ['məutərɪst] *n* conductor(a) *m/f*,
automovilista *m/f*.

motorize ['məutəraɪz] *vt* motorizar.

motor oil *n* aceite *m* para motores.

motor racing *n* (*BRIT*) carreras *fpl* de
coches, automovilismo.

motor scooter *n* vespa ®.

motor vehicle *n* automóvil *m*.

motorway ['məutəweɪ] *n* (*BRIT*) autopista.

mottled ['mɔtld] *adj* moteado.

motto, **~es** ['mɔtəu] *n* lema *m*; (*watchword*)
consigna.

mould, (*US*) **mold** [məuld] *n* molde *m*;
(*mildew*) moho ♦ *vt* moldear; (*fig*) formar.

mo(u)lder ['məuldə*] *vi* (*decay*) decaer.

mo(u)lding ['məuldɪŋ] *n* (*ARCH*) moldura.

mo(u)ldy ['məuldɪ] *adj* enmohecido.

moult, (*US*) **molt** [məult] *vi* mudar la piel;
(*bird*) mudar las plumas.

mound [maund] *n* montón *m*, montículo.

mount [maunt] *n* monte *m*; (*horse*)
montura; (*for jewel etc*) engarce *m*; (*for
picture*) marco ♦ *vt* montar en, subir a;
(*stairs*) subir; (*exhibition*) montar; (*attack*)
lanzar; (*stamp*) pegar, fijar; (*picture*)
enmarcar ♦ *vi* (*also*: ~ **up**) subirse,
montarse.

mountain ['mauntɪn] *n* montaña ♦ *cpd* de
montaña; **to make a ~ out of a molehill**
hacer una montaña de un grano de
arena.

mountain bike *n* bicicleta de montaña.

mountaineer [mauntɪ'nɪə*] *n* montañero/a,
alpinista *m/f*, andinista *m/f* (*LAM*).

mountaineering [mauntɪ'nɪərɪŋ] *n*
montañismo, alpinismo, andinismo
(*LAM*).

mountainous ['mauntɪnəs] *adj* montañoso.

mountain range *n* sierra.

mountain rescue team *n* equipo de
rescate de montaña.

mountainside ['mauntɪnsaɪd] *n* ladera de la
montaña.

mounted ['mauntɪd] *adj* montado.

Mount Everest *n* Monte *m* Everest.

mourn [mɔːn] *vt* llorar, lamentar ♦ *vi*: **to ~**

for llorar la muerte de, lamentarse por.
mourner ['mɔːnə*] *n* doliente *m/f*.
mournful ['mɔːnful] *adj* triste, lúgubre.
mourning ['mɔːnɪŋ] *n* luto ♦ *cpd* (*dress*) de luto; **in** ~ de luto.
mouse, *pl* **mice** [maus, maɪs] *n* (*also* COMPUT) ratón *m*.
mouse mat, mouse pad *n* (COMPUT) alfombrilla, almohadilla.
mousetrap ['maustræp] *n* ratonera.
mousse [muːs] *n* (CULIN) mousse *f*; (*for hair*) espuma (moldeadora).
moustache [məs'tɑːʃ], (US) **mustache** ['mʌstæʃ] *n* bigote *m*.
mousy ['mausɪ] *adj* (*person*) tímido; (*hair*) pardusco.
mouth, *pl* **mouths** [mauθ, -ðz] *n* boca; (*of river*) desembocadura.
mouthful ['mauθful] *n* bocado.
mouth organ *n* armónica.
mouthpiece ['mauθpiːs] *n* (MUS) boquilla; (TEL) micrófono; (*person*) portavoz *m/f*.
mouth-to-mouth ['mauθtə'mauθ] *adj*: ~ **resuscitation** boca a boca *m*.
mouthwash ['mauθwɔʃ] *n* enjuague *m* bucal.
mouth-watering ['mauθwɔːtərɪŋ] *adj* apetitoso.
movable ['muːvəbl] *adj* movible.
move [muːv] *n* (*movement*) movimiento; (*in game*) jugada; (: *turn to play*) turno; (*change of house*) mudanza ♦ *vt* mover; (*emotionally*) conmover; (POL: *resolution etc*) proponer ♦ *vi* (*gen*) moverse; (*traffic*) circular; (*also*: BRIT: ~ **house**) trasladarse, mudarse; **to** ~ **sb to do sth** mover a algn a hacer algo; **to be** ~**d** estar conmovido; **to get a** ~ **on** darse prisa.
►**move about** *or* **around** *vi* moverse; (*travel*) viajar.
►**move along** *vi* (*stop loitering*) circular; (*along seat etc*) correrse.
►**move away** *vi* (*leave*) marcharse.
►**move back** *vi* (*return*) volver.
►**move down** *vt* (*demote*) degradar.
►**move forward** *vi* avanzar ♦ *vt* adelantar.
►**move in** *vi* (*to a house*) instalarse.
►**move off** *vi* ponerse en camino.
►**move on** *vi* seguir viaje ♦ *vt* (*onlookers*) hacer circular.
►**move out** *vi* (*of house*) mudarse.
►**move over** *vi* hacerse a un lado.
►**move up** *vi* subir; (*employee*) ascender.
movement ['muːvmənt] *n* movimiento; (TECH) mecanismo; ~ **(of the bowels)** (MED) evacuación *f*.
mover ['muːvə*] *n* proponente *m/f*.
movie ['muːvɪ] *n* película; **the** ~**s** el cine.

movie camera *n* cámara cinematográfica.
moviegoer ['muːvɪɡəuə*] *n* (US) aficionado/a al cine.
moving ['muːvɪŋ] *adj* (*emotional*) conmovedor(a); (*that moves*) móvil; (*instigating*) motor(a).
mow, *pt* **mowed**, *pp* **mowed** *or* **mown** [məu, -n] *vt* (*grass*) cortar; (*corn*: *also*: ~ **down**) segar; (*shoot*) acribillar.
mower ['məuə*] *n* (*also*: **lawn**~) cortacésped *m*.
Mozambique [məuzæm'biːk] *n* Mozambique *m*.
MP *n abbr* (= *Military Police*) PM; BRIT: = **Member of Parliament**; (*Canada*) = **Mounted Police**.
MP3 ['ɛmpiːˈθriː] *n* MP3 *m*.
MP3 player *n* reproductor *m* (de) MP3.
mpg *n abbr* = **miles per gallon**.
mph *abbr* = *miles per hour*.
MPhil *n abbr* (= *Master of Philosophy*) título universitario de postgrado; *see also* **master's degree**.
MPS *n abbr* (BRIT) = *Member of the Pharmaceutical Society*.
Mr, Mr. ['mɪstə*] *n*: ~ **Smith** (el) Sr. Smith.
MRC *n abbr* (BRIT: = *Medical Research Council*) departamento estatal que controla la investigación médica.
MRCP *n abbr* (BRIT) = *Member of the Royal College of Physicians*.
MRCS *n abbr* (BRIT) = *Member of the Royal College of Surgeons*.
MRCVS *n abbr* (BRIT) = *Member of the Royal College of Veterinary Surgeons*.
Mrs, Mrs. ['mɪsɪz] *n*: ~ **Smith** (la) Sra. de Smith.
MS *n abbr* (= *manuscript*) MS; = **multiple sclerosis**; (US: = *Master of Science*) título universitario ♦ *abbr* (US) = *Mississippi*.
Ms, Ms. [mɪz] *n* (= *Miss or Mrs*) abreviatura con la que se evita hacer expreso el estado civil de una mujer.
MSA *n abbr* (US: = *Master of Science in Agriculture*) título universitario.
MSc *abbr see* **Master of Science**.
MSG *n abbr* = **monosodium glutamate**.
MSP *n abbr* (BRIT) = **Member of the Scottish Parliament**.
MSS *n abbr* (= *manuscripts*) MSS.
MST *abbr* (US: = *Mountain Standard Time*) hora de invierno de las Montañas Rocosas.
MSW *n abbr* (US: = *Master of Social Work*) título universitario.
MT *abbr* (US) = *Montana*.
Mt *abbr* (GEO: = *mount*) m.
MTV *n abbr* = *music television*.

mth *abbr* (= *month*) m.

much [mʌtʃ] *adj* mucho ♦ *adv, n, pron* mucho; (*before pp*) muy; **how ~ is it?** ¿cuánto es?, ¿cuánto cuesta?; **too ~** demasiado; **so ~** tanto; **it's not ~** no es mucho; **as ~ as** tanto como; **however ~ he tries** por mucho que se esfuerce; **I like it very/so ~** me gusta mucho/tanto; **thank you very ~** muchas gracias, muy agradecido.

muck [mʌk] *n* (*dirt*) suciedad *f*; (*fig*) porquería.

▶**muck about** *or* **around** *vi* (*col*) perder el tiempo; (*enjoy o.s.*) entretenerse; (*tinker*) manosear.

▶**muck in** *vi* (*col*) arrimar el hombro.

▶**muck out** *vt* (*stable*) limpiar.

▶**muck up** *vt* (*col: dirty*) ensuciar; (: *spoil*) echar a perder; (: *ruin*) estropear.

muckraking ['mʌkreɪkɪŋ] (*fig col*) *n* amarillismo ♦ *adj* especializado en escándalos.

mucky ['mʌkɪ] *adj* (*dirty*) sucio.

mucus ['mjuːkəs] *n* mucosidad *f*, moco.

mud [mʌd] *n* barro, lodo.

muddle ['mʌdl] *n* desorden *m*, confusión *f*; (*mix-up*) embrollo, lío ♦ *vt* (*also: ~ up*) embrollar, confundir.

▶**muddle along, muddle on** *vi* arreglárselas de alguna manera.

▶**muddle through** *vi* salir del paso.

muddle-headed [mʌdl'hɛdɪd] *adj* (*person*) despistado, confuso.

muddy ['mʌdɪ] *adj* fangoso, cubierto de lodo.

mudguard ['mʌdgɑːd] *n* guardabarros *m inv*.

mudpack ['mʌdpæk] *n* mascarilla.

mud-slinging ['mʌdslɪŋɪŋ] *n* injurias *fpl*, difamación *f*.

muesli ['mjuːzlɪ] *n* muesli *m*.

muff [mʌf] *n* manguito ♦ *vt* (*chance*) desperdiciar; (*lines*) estropear; (*shot, catch etc*) fallar; **to ~ it** fracasar.

muffin ['mʌfɪn] *n* bollo.

muffle ['mʌfl] *vt* (*sound*) amortiguar; (*against cold*) abrigar.

muffled ['mʌfld] *adj* sordo, apagado.

muffler ['mʌflə*] *n* (*scarf*) bufanda; (*US AUT*) silenciador *m*; (*on motorbike*) silenciador *m*, mofle *m*.

mufti ['mʌftɪ] *n*: **in ~** (vestido) de paisano.

mug [mʌg] *n* (*cup*) taza alta; (*for beer*) jarra; (*col: face*) jeta; (: *fool*) bobo ♦ *vt* (*assault*) atracar; **it's a ~'s game** es cosa de bobos.

▶**mug up** *vt* (*col: also: ~ up on*) empollar.

mugger ['mʌgə*] *n* atracador(a) *m/f*.

mugging ['mʌgɪŋ] *n* atraco callejero.

muggins ['mʌgɪnz] *nsg* (*col*) tonto/a el bote.

muggy ['mʌgɪ] *adj* bochornoso.

mug shot *n* (*col*) foto *f* (para la ficha policial).

mulatto, ~es [mjuː'lætəu] *n* mulato/a.

mulberry ['mʌlbrɪ] *n* (*fruit*) mora; (*tree*) morera, moral *m*.

mule [mjuːl] *n* mula.

mull [mʌl]: **to ~ over** *vt* meditar sobre.

mulled [mʌld] *adj*: **~ wine** vino caliente (*con especias*).

mullioned ['mʌlɪənd] *adj* (*windows*) dividido por parteluces.

multi... [mʌltɪ] *pref* multi....

multi-access ['mʌltɪ'æksɛs] *adj* (*COMPUT*) multiacceso, de acceso múltiple.

multicoloured, (*US*) **multicolored** ['mʌltɪkʌləd] *adj* multicolor.

multifarious [mʌltɪ'fɛərɪəs] *adj* múltiple, vario.

multilateral [mʌltɪ'lætərl] *adj* (*POL*) multilateral.

multi-level [mʌltɪ'lɛvl] *adj* (*US*) = **multistorey**

multimillionaire [mʌltɪmɪljə'nɛə*] *n* multimillonario/a.

multinational [mʌltɪ'næʃənl] *n* multinacional *f* ♦ *adj* multinacional.

multiple ['mʌltɪpl] *adj* múltiple ♦ *n* múltiplo; (*BRIT: also: ~ store*) (cadena de) grandes almacenes *mpl*.

multiple choice *n* examen *m* de tipo test.

multiple crash *n* colisión *f* en cadena.

multiple sclerosis [-sklɪ'rəusɪs] *n* esclerosis *f* múltiple.

multiplex ['mʌltɪplɛks] *n* (*also: ~ cinema*) multicines *m inv*.

multiplication [mʌltɪplɪ'keɪʃən] *n* multiplicación *f*.

multiplication table *n* tabla de multiplicar.

multiplicity [mʌltɪ'plɪsɪtɪ] *n* multiplicidad *f*.

multiply ['mʌltɪplaɪ] *vt* multiplicar ♦ *vi* multiplicarse.

multiracial [mʌltɪ'reɪʃl] *adj* multirracial.

multistorey [mʌltɪ'stɔːrɪ] *adj* (*BRIT: building, car park*) de muchos pisos.

multistrike ribbon ['mʌltɪstraɪk-] *n* (*COMPUT: on printer*) cinta de múltiples impactos.

multi-tasking ['mʌltɪtɑːskɪŋ] *n* (*COMPUT*) ejecución *f* de tareas múltiples, multitarea.

multitude ['mʌltɪtjuːd] *n* multitud *f*.

mum [mʌm] *n* (*BRIT*) mamá ♦ *adj*: **to keep ~ (about sth)** no decir ni mu (de algo).

mumble ['mʌmbl] *vt* decir entre dientes ♦ *vi* hablar entre dientes, musitar.

mumbo jumbo ['mʌmbəu-] *n* (*col*)

galimatías *m inv.*
mummify ['mʌmɪfaɪ] *vt* momificar.
mummy ['mʌmɪ] *n* (*BRIT*: *mother*) mamá; (*embalmed*) momia.
mumps [mʌmps] *n* paperas *fpl.*
munch [mʌntʃ] *vt, vi* mascar.
mundane [mʌn'deɪn] *adj* mundano.
municipal [mju:'nɪsɪpl] *adj* municipal.
municipality [mju:nɪsɪ'pælɪtɪ] *n* municipio.
munificence [mu:'nɪfɪsns] *n* munificencia.
munitions [mju:'nɪʃənz] *npl* municiones *fpl.*
mural ['mjuərl] *n* (*pintura*) mural *m.*
murder ['mə:də*] *n* asesinato; (*in law*) homicidio ♦ *vt* asesinar, matar; **to commit** ~ cometer un asesinato *or* homicidio.
murderer ['mə:dərə*] *n* asesino.
murderess ['mə:dərɪs] *n* asesina.
murderous ['mə:dərəs] *adj* homicida.
murk [mə:k] *n* oscuridad *f*, tinieblas *fpl.*
murky ['mə:kɪ] *adj* (*water*, *past*) turbio; (*room*) sombrío.
murmur ['mə:mə*] *n* murmullo ♦ *vt, vi* murmurar; **heart** ~ soplo cardíaco.
MusB(ac) *n abbr* (= *Bachelor of Music*) *título universitario.*
muscle ['mʌsl] *n* músculo.
▶**muscle in** *vi* entrometerse.
muscular ['mʌskjulə*] *adj* muscular; (*person*) musculoso.
muscular dystrophy *n* distrofia muscular.
MusD(oc) *n abbr* (= *Doctor of Music*) *título universitario.*
muse [mju:z] *vi* meditar ♦ *n* musa.
museum [mju:'zɪəm] *n* museo.
mush [mʌʃ] *n* gachas *fpl.*
mushroom ['mʌʃrum] *n* (*gen*) seta, hongo; (*small*) champiñón *m* ♦ *vi* (*fig*) crecer de la noche a la mañana.
mushy ['mʌʃɪ] *adj* (*vegetables*) casi hecho puré; (*story*) sentimentaloide.
music ['mju:zɪk] *n* música.
musical ['mju:zɪkl] *adj* melodioso; (*person*) musical ♦ *n* (*show*) (comedia) musical *m.*
music(al) box *n* caja de música.
musical chairs *n* juego de las sillas; (*fig*) **to play** ~ cambiar de puesto continuamente.
musical instrument *n* instrumento musical.
musically ['mju:zɪklɪ] *adv* melodiosamente, armoniosamente.
music centre *n* equipo de música.
music hall *n* teatro de variedades.
musician [mju:'zɪʃən] *n* músico/a.
music stand *n* atril *m.*
musk [mʌsk] *n* (*perfume m* de) almizcle *m.*
musket ['mʌskɪt] *n* mosquete *m.*

musk rat *n* ratón *m* almizclero.
musk rose *n* (*BOT*) rosa almizcleña.
Muslim ['mʌzlɪm] *adj, n* musulmán/ana *m/f.*
muslin ['mʌzlɪn] *n* muselina.
musquash ['mʌskwɔʃ] *n* (*fur*) piel *f* del ratón almizclero.
muss [mʌs] *vt* (*col*: *hair*) despeinar; (: *dress*) arrugar.
mussel ['mʌsl] *n* mejillón *m.*
must [mʌst] *aux vb* (*obligation*): **I** ~ **do it** debo hacerlo, tengo que hacerlo; (*probability*): **he** ~ **be there by now** ya debe (de) estar allí ♦ *n*: **it's a** ~ es imprescindible.
mustache ['mʌstæʃ] *n* (*US*) = **moustache**.
mustard ['mʌstəd] *n* mostaza.
mustard gas *n* gas *m* mostaza.
muster ['mʌstə*] *vt* juntar, reunir; (*also*: ~ **up**) reunir; (: *courage*) armarse de.
mustiness ['mʌstɪnɪs] *n* olor *m* a cerrado.
mustn't ['mʌsnt] = **must not**.
musty ['mʌstɪ] *adj* mohoso, que huele a humedad.
mutant ['mju:tənt] *adj, n* mutante *m.*
mutate [mju:'teɪt] *vi* sufrir mutación, transformarse.
mutation [mju:'teɪʃən] *n* mutación *f.*
mute [mju:t] *adj, n* mudo/a *m/f.*
muted ['mju:tɪd] *adj* (*noise*) sordo; (*criticism*) callado.
mutilate ['mju:tɪleɪt] *vt* mutilar.
mutilation [mju:tɪ'leɪʃən] *n* mutilación *f.*
mutinous ['mju:tɪnəs] *adj* (*troops*) amotinado; (*attitude*) rebelde.
mutiny ['mju:tɪnɪ] *n* motín *m* ♦ *vi* amotinarse.
mutter ['mʌtə*] *vt, vi* murmurar.
mutton ['mʌtn] *n* (*carne f de*) cordero.
mutual ['mju:tʃuəl] *adj* mutuo; (*friend*) común.
mutually ['mju:tʃuəlɪ] *adv* mutuamente.
Muzak ® ['mju:zæk] *n* hilo musical.
muzzle ['mʌzl] *n* hocico; (*protective device*) bozal *m*; (*of gun*) boca ♦ *vt* amordazar; (*dog*) poner un bozal a.
MVP *n abbr* (*US SPORT*) = *most valuable player.*
MW *abbr* (= *medium wave*) onda media.
my [maɪ] *adj* mi(s); ~ **house/brother/sisters** mi casa/hermano/mis hermanas; **I've washed** ~ **hair/cut** ~ **finger** me he lavado el pelo/cortado un dedo; **is this** ~ **pen or yours?** ¿este bolígrafo es mío o tuyo?
Myanmar ['maɪænmɑ:*] *n* Myanmar.
myopic [maɪ'ɔpɪk] *adj* miope.
myriad ['mɪrɪəd] *n* (*of people, things*) miríada.
myrrh [mə:*] *n* mirra.

myself – narcissism

myself [maɪ'sɛlf] *pron* (*reflexive*) me; (*emphatic*) yo mismo; (*after prep*) mí (mismo); *see also* **oneself**.
mysterious [mɪs'tɪərɪəs] *adj* misterioso.
mysteriously [mɪs'tɪərɪəslɪ] *adv* misteriosamente.
mystery ['mɪstərɪ] *n* misterio.
mystery play *n* auto, misterio.
mystic ['mɪstɪk] *adj*, *n* místico/a *m/f*.
mystical ['mɪstɪkl] *adj* místico.
mysticism ['mɪstɪsɪzəm] *n* misticismo.
mystification [mɪstɪfɪ'keɪʃən] *n* perplejidad *f*; desconcierto.
mystify ['mɪstɪfaɪ] *vt* (*perplex*) dejar perplejo; (*disconcert*) desconcertar.
mystique [mɪs'tiːk] *n* misterio.
myth [mɪθ] *n* mito.
mythical ['mɪθɪkl] *adj* mítico.
mythological [mɪθə'lɒdʒɪkl] *adj* mitológico.
mythology [mɪ'θɒlədʒɪ] *n* mitología.

N n

N, n [ɛn] *n* (*letter*) N, n *f*; **N for Nellie**, (*US*) **N for Nan** N de Navarra.
N *abbr* (= *North*) N.
NA *n abbr* (*US*: = *Narcotics Anonymous*) *organización de ayuda a los drogadictos*; (*US*) = *National Academy*.
n/a *abbr* (= *not applicable*) no interesa; (*COMM etc*) = *no account*.
NAACP *n abbr* (*US*) = *National Association for the Advancement of Colored People.*
NAAFI ['næfɪ] *n abbr* (*BRIT*: = *Navy, Army & Air Force Institute*) *servicio de cantinas etc para las fuerzas armadas.*
nab [næb] *vt* (*col*: *grab*) coger (*SP*), agarrar (*LAM*); (: *catch out*) pillar.
NACU *n abbr* (*US*) = *National Association of Colleges and Universities.*
nadir ['neɪdɪə*] *n* (*ASTRO*) nadir *m*; (*fig*) punto más bajo.
NAFTA ['næftə] *n abbr* (= *North Atlantic Free Trade Agreement*) TLC *m*.
nag [næg] *n* (*pej*: *horse*) rocín *m* ♦ *vt* (*scold*) regañar; (*annoy*) fastidiar.
nagging ['nægɪŋ] *adj* (*doubt*) persistente; (*pain*) continuo ♦ *n* quejas *fpl*.
nail [neɪl] *n* (*human*) uña; (*metal*) clavo ♦ *vt* clavar; (*fig*: *catch*) coger (*SP*), pillar; **to pay cash on the** ~ pagar a tocateja; **to** ~

sb down to a date/price hacer que algn se comprometa a una fecha/un precio.
nailbrush ['neɪlbrʌʃ] *n* cepillo para las uñas.
nailfile ['neɪlfaɪl] *n* lima para las uñas.
nail polish *n* esmalte *m or* laca para las uñas.
nail polish remover *n* quitaesmalte *m*.
nail scissors *npl* tijeras *fpl* para las uñas.
nail varnish *n* (*BRIT*) = **nail polish**.
Nairobi [naɪ'rəʊbɪ] *n* Nairobi *m*.
naïve [naɪ'iːv] *adj* ingenuo.
naïvely [naɪ'iːvlɪ] *adv* ingenuamente.
naïveté [naː'iːvteɪ], **naivety** [naɪ'iːvɪtɪ] *n* ingenuidad *f*, candidez *f*.
naked ['neɪkɪd] *adj* (*nude*) desnudo; (*flame*) expuesto al aire; **with the** ~ **eye** a simple vista.
NAM *n abbr* (*US*) = *National Association of Manufacturers.*
name [neɪm] *n* (*gen*) nombre *m*; (*surname*) apellido; (*reputation*) fama, renombre *m* ♦ *vt* (*child*) poner nombre a; (*appoint*) nombrar; **by** ~ de nombre; **in the** ~ **of** en nombre de; **what's your** ~? ¿cómo se llama usted?; **my** ~ **is Peter** me llamo Pedro; **to give one's** ~ **and address** dar sus señas; **to take sb's** ~ **and address** apuntar las señas de algn; **to make a** ~ **for o.s.** hacerse famoso; **to get (o.s.) a bad** ~ forjarse una mala reputación.
name-drop ['neɪmdrɒp] *vi*: **he's always** ~**ping** siempre está presumiendo de la gente que conoce.
nameless ['neɪmlɪs] *adj* anónimo, sin nombre.
namely ['neɪmlɪ] *adv* a saber.
nameplate ['neɪmpleɪt] *n* (*on door etc*) placa.
namesake ['neɪmseɪk] *n* tocayo/a.
nan bread [naːn-] *n* pan indio sin apenas levadura.
nanny ['nænɪ] *n* niñera.
nap [næp] *n* (*sleep*) sueñecito, siesta; **they were caught** ~**ping** les pilló desprevenidos.
NAPA *n abbr* (*US*: = *National Association of Performing Artists*) *sindicato de trabajadores del espectáculo.*
napalm ['neɪpɑːm] *n* napalm *m*.
nape [neɪp] *n*: ~ **of the neck** nuca, cogote *m*.
napkin ['næpkɪn] *n* (*also*: **table** ~) servilleta.
Naples ['neɪplz] *n* Nápoles.
nappy ['næpɪ] *n* (*BRIT*) pañal *m*.
nappy liner *n* gasa.
nappy rash *n* prurito.
narcissism [naː'sɪsɪzəm] *n* narcisismo.

narcissus, *pl* **narcissi** [nɑː'sɪsəs, -saɪ] *n* narciso.

narcotic [nɑː'kɔtɪk] *adj, n* narcótico.

narrate [nə'reɪt] *vt* narrar, contar.

narration [nə'reɪʃən] *n* narración *f*, relato.

narrative ['nærətɪv] *n* narrativa ♦ *adj* narrativo.

narrator [nə'reɪtə*] *n* narrador(a) *m/f*.

narrow ['nærəu] *adj* estrecho; (*resources, means*) escaso ♦ *vi* estrecharse; (*diminish*) reducirse; **to have a ~ escape** escaparse por los pelos; **to ~ sth down** reducir algo.

narrow gauge *adj* (*RAIL*) de vía estrecha.

narrowly ['nærəlɪ] *adv* (*miss*) por poco.

narrow-minded [nærəu'maɪndɪd] *adj* de miras estrechas.

narrow-mindedness ['nærəu'maɪndɪdnɪs] *n* estrechez *f* de miras.

NAS *n abbr* (*US*) = *National Academy of Sciences.*

NASA *n abbr* (*US*: = *National Aeronautics and Space Administration*) NASA *f*.

nasal ['neɪzl] *adj* nasal.

Nassau ['næsɔː] *n* (*in Bahamas*) Nassau *m*.

nastily ['nɑːstɪlɪ] *adv* (*unpleasantly*) de mala manera; (*spitefully*) con rencor.

nastiness ['nɑːstɪnɪs] *n* (*malice*) malevolencia; (*rudeness*) grosería; (*of person, remark*) maldad *f*; (*spitefulness*) rencor *m*.

nasturtium [nəs'tə:ʃəm] *n* capuchina.

nasty ['nɑːstɪ] *adj* (*remark*) feo; (*person*) antipático; (*revolting: taste, smell*) asqueroso; (*wound, disease etc*) peligroso, grave; **to turn ~** (*situation*) ponerse feo; (*weather*) empeorar; (*person*) ponerse negro.

NAS/UWT *n abbr* (*BRIT*: = *National Association of Schoolmasters/Union of Women Teachers*) *sindicato de profesores*.

nation ['neɪʃən] *n* nación *f*.

national ['næʃənl] *adj* nacional ♦ *n* súbdito/a.

national anthem *n* himno nacional.

National Curriculum *n* (*BRIT*) plan *m* general de estudios (*en Inglaterra y Gales*).

national debt *n* deuda pública.

national dress *n* traje *m* típico del país.

National Guard *n* (*US*) Guardia Nacional.

National Health Service (NHS) *n* (*BRIT*) servicio nacional de sanidad, ≈ INSALUD *m* (*SP*).

National Insurance *n* (*BRIT*) seguro social nacional, ≈ Seguridad *f* Social.

nationalism ['næʃnəlɪzəm] *n* nacionalismo.

nationalist ['næʃnəlɪst] *adj, n* nacionalista *m/f*.

nationality [næʃə'nælɪtɪ] *n* nacionalidad *f*.

nationalization [næʃnəlaɪ'zeɪʃən] *n* nacionalización *f*.

nationalize ['næʃnəlaɪz] *vt* nacionalizar; **~d industry** industria nacionalizada.

nationally ['næʃnəlɪ] *adv* (*nationwide*) a escala nacional; (*as a nation*) como nación.

national press *n* prensa nacional.

national service *n* (*MIL*) servicio militar.

National Trust *n* (*BRIT*) *organización encargada de preservar el patrimonio histórico británico.*

nationwide ['neɪʃənwaɪd] *adj* a escala nacional.

native ['neɪtɪv] *n* (*local inhabitant*) natural *m/f*; (*in colonies*) indígena *m/f*, nativo/a ♦ *adj* (*indigenous*) indígena; (*country*) natal; (*innate*) natural, innato; **a ~ of Russia** un(a) natural de Rusia; **~ language** lengua materna; **a ~ speaker of French** un hablante nativo de francés.

Native American *adj, n* americano/a indígena *m/f*, amerindio/a *m/f*.

Nativity [nə'tɪvɪtɪ] *n*: **the ~** Navidad *f*.

nativity play *n* auto del nacimiento.

NATO ['neɪtəu] *n abbr* (= *North Atlantic Treaty Organization*) OTAN *f*.

natter ['nætə*] *vi* (*BRIT*) charlar ♦ *n*: **to have a ~** charlar.

natural ['nætʃrəl] *adj* natural; **death from ~ causes** (*LAW*) muerte *f* por causas naturales.

natural childbirth *n* parto natural.

natural gas *n* gas *m* natural.

natural history *n* historia natural.

naturalist ['nætʃrəlɪst] *n* naturalista *m/f*.

naturalization [nætʃrəlaɪ'zeɪʃən] *n* naturalización *f*.

naturalize ['nætʃrəlaɪz] *vt*: **to become ~d** (*person*) naturalizarse; (*plant*) aclimatarse.

naturally ['nætʃrəlɪ] *adv* (*speak etc*) naturalmente; (*of course*) desde luego, por supuesto, ¡cómo no! (*esp LAM*); (*instinctively*) por naturaleza.

naturalness ['nætʃrəlnɪs] *n* naturalidad *f*.

natural resources *npl* recursos *mpl* naturales.

natural selection *n* selección *f* natural.

natural wastage *n* (*INDUSTRY*) desgaste *m* natural.

nature ['neɪtʃə*] *n* naturaleza; (*group, sort*) género, clase *f*; (*character*) modo de ser, carácter *m*; **by ~** por naturaleza; **documents of a confidential ~** documentos *mpl* de tipo confidencial.

-natured ['neɪtʃəd] *suff*: **ill~** malhumorado.

nature reserve n reserva natural.
nature trail n camino forestal educativo.
naturist ['neɪtʃərɪst] n naturista m/f.
naught [nɔːt] = **nought**.
naughtily ['nɔːtɪlɪ] adv (behave) mal; (say) con malicia.
naughtiness ['nɔːtɪnɪs] n travesuras fpl.
naughty ['nɔːtɪ] adj (child) travieso; (story, film) picante, escabroso, colorado (LAM).
nausea ['nɔːsɪə] n náusea.
nauseate ['nɔːsɪeɪt] vt dar náuseas a; (fig) dar asco a.
nauseating ['nɔːsɪeɪtɪŋ] adj nauseabundo; (fig) asqueroso, repugnante.
nauseous ['nɔːsɪəs] adj nauseabundo; **to feel ~** sentir náuseas.
nautical ['nɔːtɪkl] adj náutico, marítimo; ~ **mile** milla marina.
naval ['neɪvl] adj naval, de marina.
naval officer n oficial m/f de marina.
nave [neɪv] n nave f.
navel ['neɪvl] n ombligo.
navigable ['nævɪgəbl] adj navegable.
navigate ['nævɪgeɪt] vt (ship) gobernar; (river etc) navegar por ♦ vi navegar; (AUT) hacer de copiloto.
navigation [nævɪ'geɪʃən] n (action) navegación f; (science) náutica.
navigator ['nævɪgeɪtə*] n navegante m/f.
navvy ['nævɪ] n (BRIT) peón m caminero.
navy ['neɪvɪ] n marina de guerra; (ships) armada, flota.
navy(-blue) ['neɪvɪ('bluː)] adj azul marino.
Nazareth ['næzərɪθ] n Nazaret m.
Nazi ['nɑːtsɪ] adj, n nazi m/f.
NB abbr (= nota bene) nótese; (Canada) = New Brunswick.
NBA n abbr (US) = National Basketball Association, National Boxing Association.
NBC n abbr (US: = National Broadcasting Company) cadena de televisión.
NBS n abbr (US: = National Bureau of Standards) ≈ Oficina Nacional de Normalización.
NC abbr (COMM etc) = no charge; (US) = North Carolina.
NCC n abbr (BRIT: = Nature Conservancy Council) ≈ ICONA m; (US) = National Council of Churches.
NCCL n abbr (BRIT: = National Council for Civil Liberties) asociación para la defensa de las libertades públicas.
NCO n abbr = **non-commissioned officer**.
ND abbr (US) = North Dakota.
N. Dak. abbr (US) = North Dakota.
NE abbr (US) = Nebraska, New England.
NEA n abbr (US) = National Education Association.

Neapolitan [nɪə'pɒlɪtən] adj, n napolitano/a m/f.
neap tide [niːp-] n marea muerta.
near [nɪə*] adj (place, relation) cercano; (time) próximo ♦ adv cerca ♦ prep (also: ~ **to**: space) cerca de, junto a; (: time) cerca de ♦ vt acercarse a, aproximarse a; ~ **here/there** cerca de aquí/de allí; **£25,000 or ~est offer** 25,000 libras o precio a discutir; **in the ~ future** en fecha próxima; **the building is ~ing completion** el edificio está casi terminado.
nearby [nɪə'baɪ] adj cercano, próximo ♦ adv cerca.
nearly ['nɪəlɪ] adv casi, por poco; **I ~ fell** por poco me caigo; **not ~** ni mucho menos, ni con mucho.
near miss n (shot) tiro casi en el blanco; (AVIAT) accidente evitado por muy poco.
nearness ['nɪənɪs] n cercanía, proximidad f.
nearside ['nɪəsaɪd] n (AUT: right-hand drive) lado izquierdo (: left-hand drive) lado derecho.
near-sighted [nɪə'saɪtɪd] adj miope, corto de vista.
neat [niːt] adj (place) ordenado, bien cuidado; (person) pulcro; (plan) ingenioso; (spirits) solo.
neatly ['niːtlɪ] adv (tidily) con esmero; (skilfully) ingeniosamente.
neatness ['niːtnɪs] n (tidiness) orden m; (skilfulness) destreza, habilidad f.
Nebr. abbr (US) = Nebraska.
nebulous ['nɛbjuləs] adj (fig) vago, confuso.
necessarily ['nɛsɪsrɪlɪ] adv necesariamente; **not ~** no necesariamente.
necessary ['nɛsɪsrɪ] adj necesario, preciso; **he did all that was ~** hizo todo lo necesario; **if ~** si es necesario.
necessitate [nɪ'sɛsɪteɪt] vt necesitar, precisar.
necessity [nɪ'sɛsɪtɪ] n necesidad f; **necessities** npl artículos mpl de primera necesidad; **in case of ~** en caso de urgencia.
neck [nɛk] n (ANAT) cuello; (of animal) pescuezo ♦ vi besuquearse; ~ **and ~** parejos; **to stick one's ~ out** (col) arriesgarse.
necklace ['nɛklɪs] n collar m.
neckline ['nɛklaɪn] n escote m.
necktie ['nɛktaɪ] n (US) corbata.
nectar ['nɛktə*] n néctar m.
nectarine ['nɛktərɪn] n nectarina.
NEDC n abbr (BRIT: = National Economic Development Council) ≈ Consejo Económico y Social.

Neddy ['nɛdɪ] *n abbr* (*BRIT col*) = **NEDC.**
née [neɪ] *adj:* ~ **Scott** de soltera Scott.
need [niːd] *n* (*lack*) escasez *f*, falta;
(*necessity*) necesidad *f* ♦ *vt* (*require*)
necesitar; **in case of** ~ en caso de
necesidad; **there's no** ~ **for** ... no hace(n)
falta ...; **to be in** ~ **of, have** ~ **of**
necesitar; **10 will meet my immediate** ~**s**
10 satisfacerán mis necesidades más
apremiantes; **the** ~**s of industry** las
necesidades de la industria; **I** ~ **it** lo
necesito; **a signature is** ~**ed** se requiere
una firma; **I** ~ **to do it** tengo que hacerlo;
you don't ~ **to go** no hace falta que
vayas.
needle ['niːdl] *n* aguja ♦ *vt* (*fig: col*) picar,
fastidiar.
needless ['niːdlɪs] *adj* innecesario, inútil; ~
to say huelga decir que.
needlessly ['niːdlɪslɪ] *adv*
innecesariamente, inútilmente.
needlework ['niːdlwəːk] *n* (*activity*) costura,
labor *f* de aguja.
needn't ['niːdnt] = **need not.**
needy ['niːdɪ] *adj* necesitado.
negation [nɪ'ɡeɪʃən] *n* negación *f*.
negative ['nɛɡətɪv] *n* (*PHOT*) negativo;
(*answer*) negativa; (*LING*) negación *f* ♦ *adj*
negativo.
negative cash flow *n* flujo negativo de
efectivo.
negative equity *n* situación en la que el
valor de la vivienda es menor que el de
la hipoteca que pesa sobre ella.
neglect [nɪ'ɡlɛkt] *vt* (*one's duty*) faltar a, no
cumplir con; (*child*) descuidar,
desatender ♦ *n* (*state*) abandono;
(*personal*) dejadez *f*; (*of duty*)
incumplimiento; **to** ~ **to do sth** olvidarse
de hacer algo.
neglected [nɪ'ɡlɛktɪd] *adj* abandonado.
neglectful [nɪ'ɡlɛktful] *adj* negligente; **to be**
~ **of sth/sb** desatender algo/a algn.
negligee ['nɛɡlɪʒeɪ] *n* (*nightdress*) salto de
cama.
negligence ['nɛɡlɪdʒəns] *n* negligencia.
negligent ['nɛɡlɪdʒənt] *adj* negligente;
(*casual*) descuidado.
negligently ['nɛɡlɪdʒəntlɪ] *adv*
negligentemente; (*casually*) con descuido.
negligible ['nɛɡlɪdʒɪbl] *adj* insignificante,
despreciable.
negotiable [nɪ'ɡəuʃɪəbl] *adj* (*cheque*)
negociable; **not** ~ (*cheque*) no trasferible.
negotiate [nɪ'ɡəuʃɪeɪt] *vt* (*treaty, loan*)
negociar; (*obstacle*) franquear; (*bend in
road*) tomar ♦ *vi:* **to** ~ (**with**) negociar
(con); **to** ~ **with sb for sth** tratar *or*

negociar con algn por algo.
negotiating table [nɪ'ɡəuʃɪeɪtɪŋ-] *n* mesa
de negociaciones.
negotiation [nɪɡəuʃɪ'eɪʃən] *n* negociación *f*,
gestión *f*; **to enter into** ~**s with sb** entrar
en negociaciones con algn.
negotiator [nɪ'ɡəuʃɪeɪtə*] *n* negociador(a)
m/f.
Negress ['niːɡrɪs] *n* negra.
Negro ['niːɡrəu] *adj, n* negro.
neigh [neɪ] *n* relincho ♦ *vi* relinchar.
neighbour, (*US*) **neighbor** ['neɪbə*] *n*
vecino/a.
neighbo(u)rhood ['neɪbəhud] *n* (*place*)
vecindad *f*, barrio; (*people*) vecindario.
neighbourhood watch *n* (*BRIT: also:* ~
scheme) *vigilancia del barrio por los
propios vecinos.*
neighbo(u)ring ['neɪbərɪŋ] *adj* vecino.
neighbo(u)rly ['neɪbəlɪ] *adj* amigable,
sociable.
neither ['naɪðə*] *adj* ni ♦ *conj:* **I didn't move
and** ~ **did John** no me he movido, ni Juan
tampoco ♦ *pron* ninguno; ~ **is true**
ninguno/a de los/las dos es cierto/a ♦ *adv:*
~ **good nor bad** ni bueno ni malo.
neo ... [niːəu] *pref* neo....
neolithic [niːəu'lɪθɪk] *adj* neolítico.
neologism [nɪ'ɔlədʒɪzəm] *n* neologismo.
neon ['niːɔn] *n* neón *m*.
neon light *n* lámpara de neón.
Nepal [nɪ'pɔːl] *n* Nepal *m*.
nephew ['nɛvjuː] *n* sobrino.
nepotism ['nɛpətɪzəm] *n* nepotismo.
nerd [nəːd] *n* (*col*) primo/a.
nerve [nəːv] *n* (*ANAT*) nervio; (*courage*)
valor *m*; (*impudence*) descaro, frescura; **a
fit of** ~**s** un ataque de nervios; **to lose
one's** ~ (*self-confidence*) perder el valor.
nerve centre *n* (*ANAT*) centro nervioso;
(*fig*) punto neurálgico.
nerve gas *n* gas *m* nervioso.
nerve-racking ['nəːvrækɪŋ] *adj* angustioso.
nervous ['nəːvəs] *adj* (*anxious, ANAT*)
nervioso; (*timid*) tímido, miedoso.
nervous breakdown *n* crisis *f* nerviosa.
nervously ['nəːvəslɪ] *adv* nerviosamente;
tímidamente.
nervousness ['nəːvəsnɪs] *n* nerviosismo;
timidez *f*.
nervous wreck *n* (*col*): **to be a** ~ estar de
los nervios.
nervy ['nəːvɪ] *adj:* **to be** ~ estar nervioso.
nest [nɛst] *n* (*of bird*) nido ♦ *vi* anidar.
nest egg *n* (*fig*) ahorros *mpl*.
nestle ['nɛsl] *vi:* **to** ~ **down** acurrucarse.
nestling ['nɛstlɪŋ] *n* pajarito.
net [nɛt] *n* (*gen*) red *f*; (*fabric*) tul *m* ♦ *adj*

(*COMM*) neto, líquido; (*weight, price, salary*) neto ♦ *vt* coger (*SP*) *or* agarrar (*LAM*) con red; (*money: subj: person*) cobrar; (: *deal, sale*) conseguir; (*SPORT*) marcar; ~ **of tax** neto; **he earns £10,000** ~ **per year** gana 10,000 libras netas por año; **the N**~ (*Internet*) la Red.

netball ['nɛtbɔːl] *n* básquet *m*.

net curtain *n* visillo.

Netherlands ['nɛðələndz] *npl*: **the** ~ los Países Bajos.

net income *n* renta neta.

net loss *n* pérdida neta.

net profit *n* beneficio neto.

nett [nɛt] *adj* = **net**.

netting ['nɛtɪŋ] *n* red *f*, redes *fpl*.

nettle ['nɛtl] *n* ortiga.

network ['nɛtwəːk] *n* red *f* ♦ *vt* (*RADIO, TV*) difundir por la red de emisores; **local area** ~ red local.

neuralgia [njuə'rældʒə] *n* neuralgia.

neurological [njuərə'lɔdʒɪkl] *adj* neurológico.

neurosis, *pl* **-ses** [njuə'rəusɪs, -siːz] *n* neurosis *f inv*.

neurotic [njuə'rɔtɪk] *adj, n* neurótico/a *m/f*.

neuter ['njuːtə*] *adj* (*LING*) neutro ♦ *vt* castrar, capar.

neutral ['njuːtrəl] *adj* (*person*) neutral; (*colour etc, ELEC*) neutro ♦ *n* (*AUT*) punto muerto.

neutrality [njuː'trælɪtɪ] *n* neutralidad *f*.

neutralize ['njuːtrəlaɪz] *vt* neutralizar.

neutron ['njuːtrɔn] *n* neutrón *m*.

neutron bomb *n* bomba de neutrones.

Nev. *abbr* (*US*) = **Nevada**.

never ['nɛvə*] *adv* nunca, jamás; **I** ~ **went** no fui nunca; ~ **in my life** jamás en la vida; *see also* **mind**.

never-ending [nɛvər'ɛndɪŋ] *adj* interminable, sin fin.

nevertheless [nɛvəðə'lɛs] *adv* sin embargo, no obstante.

new [njuː] *adj* nuevo; (*recent*) reciente; **as good as** ~ como nuevo.

New Age *n* Nueva era.

newborn ['njuːbɔːn] *adj* recién nacido.

newcomer ['njuːkʌmə*] *n* recién venido *or* llegado.

new-fangled ['njuːfæŋgld] *adj* (*pej*) modernísimo.

new-found ['njuːfaund] *adj* (*friend*) nuevo; (*enthusiasm*) recién adquirido.

New Guinea *n* Nueva Guinea.

newly ['njuːlɪ] *adv* recién.

newly-weds ['njuːlɪwɛdz] *npl* recién casados.

new moon *n* luna nueva.

newness ['njuːnɪs] *n* novedad *f*.

news [njuːz] *n* noticias *fpl*; **a piece of** ~ una noticia; **the** ~ (*RADIO, TV*) las noticias *fpl*, el telediario; **good/bad** ~ buenas/malas noticias *fpl*; **financial** ~ noticias *fpl* financieras.

news agency *n* agencia de noticias.

newsagent ['njuːzeɪdʒənt] *n* (*BRIT*) vendedor(a) *m/f* de periódicos.

news bulletin *n* (*RADIO, TV*) noticiario.

newscaster ['njuːzkɑːstə*] *n* presentador(a) *m/f*, locutor(a) *m/f*.

news dealer *n* (*US*) = **newsagent**.

news flash *n* noticia de última hora.

newsletter ['njuːzlɛtə*] *n* hoja informativa, boletín *m*.

newspaper ['njuːzpeɪpə*] *n* periódico, diario; **daily** ~ diario; **weekly** ~ periódico semanal.

newsprint ['njuːzprɪnt] *n* papel *m* de periódico.

newsreader ['njuːzriːdə*] *n* = **newscaster**.

newsreel ['njuːzriːl] *n* noticiario.

newsroom ['njuːzruːm] *n* (*PRESS, RADIO, TV*) sala de redacción.

news stand *n* quiosco *or* puesto de periódicos.

newsworthy ['njuːzwəːðɪ] *adj*: **to be** ~ ser de interés periodístico.

newt [njuːt] *n* tritón *m*.

new town *n* (*BRIT*) ciudad *f* nueva (*construida con subsidios estatales*).

New Year *n* Año Nuevo; **Happy** ~! ¡Feliz Año Nuevo!; **to wish sb a happy** ~ desear a algn un feliz año nuevo.

New Year's Day *n* Día *m* de Año Nuevo.

New Year's Eve *n* Nochevieja.

New York [-'jɔːk] *n* Nueva York.

New Zealand [-'ziːlənd] *n* Nueva Zelanda (*SP*), Nueva Zelandia (*LAM*) ♦ *adj* neozelandés/esa.

New Zealander [-'ziːləndə*] *n* neozelandés/esa *m/f*.

next [nɛkst] *adj* (*house, room*) vecino, de al lado; (*meeting*) próximo; (*page*) siguiente ♦ *adv* después; **the** ~ **day** el día siguiente; ~ **time** la próxima vez; ~ **year** el año próximo *or* que viene; ~ **month** el mes que viene *or* entrante; **the week after** ~ no la semana que viene sino la otra; "**turn to the** ~ **page**" "vuelva a la página siguiente"; **you're** ~ le toca; ~ **to** *prep* junto a, al lado de; ~ **to nothing** casi nada.

next door *adv* en la casa de al lado ♦ *adj* vecino, de al lado.

next-of-kin ['nɛkstəv'kɪn] *n* pariente(s) *m(pl)* más cercano(s).

NF *n abbr* (*BRIT POL:* = *National Front*) *partido político de la extrema derecha* ♦ *abbr* (*Canada*) = *Newfoundland*.

NFL *n abbr* (*US*) = *National Football League*.

Nfld. *abbr* (*Canada*) = *Newfoundland*.

NG *abbr* (*US*) = **National Guard**.

NGO *n abbr* (= *non-governmental organization*) ONG *f*.

NH *abbr* (*US*) = *New Hampshire*.

NHL *n abbr* (*US*) = *National Hockey League*.

NHS *n abbr see* **National Health Service**.

NI *abbr* = **Northern Ireland**; (*BRIT*) = **National Insurance**.

nib [nɪb] *n* plumilla.

nibble ['nɪbl] *vt* mordisquear.

Nicaragua [nɪkə'ræɡjuə] *n* Nicaragua.

Nicaraguan [nɪkə'ræɡjuən] *adj, n* nicaragüense *m/f*, nicaragüeño/a *m/f*.

Nice [niːs] *n* Niza.

nice [naɪs] *adj* (*likeable*) simpático, majo; (*kind*) amable; (*pleasant*) agradable; (*attractive*) bonito, mono; (*distinction*) fino; (*taste, smell, meal*) rico.

nice-looking ['naɪslukɪŋ] *adj* guapo.

nicely ['naɪslɪ] *adv* amablemente; (*of health etc*) bien; **that will do** ~ perfecto.

niceties ['naɪsɪtɪz] *npl* detalles *mpl*.

niche [niːʃ] *n* (*ARCH*) nicho, hornacina.

nick [nɪk] *n* (*wound*) rasguño; (*cut, indentation*) mella, muesca ♦ *vt* (*cut*) cortar; (*col*) birlar, mangar; (: *arrest*) pillar; **in the** ~ **of time** justo a tiempo; **in good** ~ en buen estado; **to** ~ **o.s.** cortarse.

nickel ['nɪkl] *n* níquel *m*; (*US*) *moneda de 5 centavos*.

nickname ['nɪkneɪm] *n* apodo, mote *m* ♦ *vt* apodar.

Nicosia [nɪkə'siːə] *n* Nicosía.

nicotine ['nɪkətiːn] *n* nicotina.

nicotine patch *n* parche *m* de nicotina.

niece [niːs] *n* sobrina.

nifty ['nɪftɪ] *adj* (*col: car, jacket*) elegante, chulo; (: *gadget, tool*) ingenioso.

Niger ['naɪdʒə*] *n* (*country, river*) Níger *m*.

Nigeria [naɪ'dʒɪərɪə] *n* Nigeria.

Nigerian [naɪ'dʒɪərɪən] *adj, n* nigeriano/a *m/f*.

niggardly ['nɪɡədlɪ] *adj* (*person*) avaro, tacaño, avariento; (*allowance, amount*) miserable.

nigger ['nɪɡə*] *n* (*col!: highly offensive*) negro/a.

niggle ['nɪɡl] *vt* preocupar ♦ *vi* (*complain*) quejarse; (*fuss*) preocuparse por minucias.

niggling ['nɪɡlɪŋ] *adj* (*detail: trifling*) nimio, insignificante; (*annoying*) molesto; (*doubt, pain*) constante.

night [naɪt] *n* (*gen*) noche *f*; (*evening*) tarde *f*; **last** ~ anoche; **the** ~ **before last** anteanoche, antes de ayer por la noche; **at** ~, **by** ~ de noche, por la noche; **in the** ~, **during the** ~ durante la noche, por la noche.

night-bird ['naɪtbəːd] *n* (*fig*) trasnochador(a) *m/f*, madrugador(a) *m/f* (*LAM*).

nightcap ['naɪtkæp] *n* (*drink*) *bebida que se toma antes de acostarse*.

night club *n* club nocturno, discoteca.

nightdress ['naɪtdrɛs] *n* (*BRIT*) camisón *m*.

nightfall ['naɪtfɔːl] *n* anochecer *m*.

nightgown ['naɪtɡaun], **nightie** ['naɪtɪ] (*BRIT*) *n* = **nightdress**.

nightingale ['naɪtɪŋɡeɪl] *n* ruiseñor *m*.

night life *n* vida nocturna.

nightly ['naɪtlɪ] *adj* de todas las noches ♦ *adv* todas las noches, cada noche.

nightmare ['naɪtmɛə*] *n* pesadilla.

night porter *n* guardián *m* nocturno.

night safe *n* caja fuerte.

night school *n* clase(s) *f(pl)* nocturna(s).

nightshade ['naɪtʃeɪd] *n*: **deadly** ~ (*BOT*) belladona.

night shift *n* turno nocturno *or* de noche.

night-time ['naɪttaɪm] *n* noche *f*.

night watchman *n* vigilante *m* nocturno, sereno.

nihilism ['naɪɪlɪzəm] *n* nihilismo.

nil [nɪl] *n* (*BRIT SPORT*) cero, nada.

Nile [naɪl] *n*: **the** ~ el Nilo.

nimble ['nɪmbl] *adj* (*agile*) ágil, ligero; (*skilful*) diestro.

nimbly ['nɪmblɪ] *adv* ágilmente; con destreza.

nine [naɪn] *num* nueve.

9-11, Nine-Eleven [naɪn'lɛvn] 11-S *m*.

nineteen ['naɪn'tiːn] *num* diecinueve.

nineteenth [naɪn'tiːnθ] *num* decimonoveno, decimonono.

ninety ['naɪntɪ] *num* noventa.

ninth [naɪnθ] *num* noveno.

nip [nɪp] *vt* (*pinch*) pellizcar; (*bite*) morder ♦ *vi* (*BRIT col*): **to** ~ **out/down/up** salir/bajar/subir un momento ♦ *n* (*drink*) trago.

nipple ['nɪpl] *n* (*ANAT*) pezón *m*; (*of bottle*) tetilla; (*TECH*) boquilla, manguito.

nippy ['nɪpɪ] *adj* (*BRIT: person*) rápido; (*taste*) picante; **it's a very** ~ **car** es un coche muy potente para el tamaño que tiene.

nit [nɪt] *n* (*of louse*) liendre *f*; (*col: idiot*) imbécil *m/f*.

nit-pick ['nɪtpɪk] *vi* (*col*) sacar punta a todo.

nitrogen ['naɪtrədʒən] *n* nitrógeno.

nitroglycerin(e) ['naɪtrəu'ɡlɪsəriːn] *n* nitroglicerina.

nitty-gritty ['nɪtɪ'ɡrɪtɪ] *n* (*col*): **to get down**

to the ~ ir al grano.
nitwit ['nɪtwɪt] n cretino/a.
NJ abbr (US) = New Jersey.
NLF n abbr (= National Liberation Front) FLN m.
NLRB n abbr (US: = National Labor Relations Board) organismo de protección al trabajador.
NM, N. Mex. abbr (US) = New Mexico.

================== KEYWORD

no [nəu] (pl ~es) adv (opposite of "yes") no; **are you coming?** — ~ **(I'm not)** ¿vienes? — no; **would you like some more?** — ~ **thank you** ¿quieres más? — no gracias
♦ adj (not any): **I have** ~ **money/time/ books** no tengo dinero/tiempo/libros; ~ **other man would have done it** ningún otro lo hubiera hecho; "~ **entry**" "prohibido el paso"; "~ **smoking**" "prohibido fumar"
♦ n no m.

no. abbr (= number) nº., núm.
nobble ['nɔbl] vt (BRIT col: bribe) sobornar; (: catch) pescar; (: RACING) drogar.
Nobel prize [nəu'bɛl-] n premio Nobel.
nobility [nəu'bɪlɪtɪ] n nobleza.
noble ['nəubl] adj (person) noble; (title) de nobleza.
nobleman ['nəublmən] n noble m.
nobly ['nəublɪ] adv (selflessly) noblemente.
nobody ['nəubədɪ] pron nadie.
no-claims bonus ['nəukleɪmz-] n bonificación f por carencia de reclamaciones.
nocturnal [nɔk'təːnl] adj nocturno.
nod [nɔd] vi saludar con la cabeza; (in agreement) asentir con la cabeza ♦ vt: **to** ~ **one's head** inclinar la cabeza ♦ n inclinación f de cabeza; **they** ~**ded their agreement** asintieron con la cabeza.
► **nod off** vi cabecear.
no-fly zone [nəu'flaɪ-] n zona de exclusión aérea.
noise [nɔɪz] n ruido; (din) escándalo, estrépito.
noisily ['nɔɪzɪlɪ] adv ruidosamente, estrepitosamente.
noisy ['nɔɪzɪ] adj (gen) ruidoso; (child) escandaloso.
nomad ['nəumæd] n nómada m/f.
nomadic [nəu'mædɪk] adj nómada.
no man's land n tierra de nadie.
nominal ['nɔmɪnl] adj nominal.
nominate ['nɔmɪneɪt] vt (propose) proponer; (appoint) nombrar.
nomination [nɔmɪ'neɪʃən] n propuesta;

nombramiento.
nominee [nɔmɪ'niː] n candidato/a.
non... [nɔn] pref no, des..., in....
nonalcoholic [nɔnælkə'hɔlɪk] adj sin alcohol.
nonaligned [nɔnə'laɪnd] adj no alineado.
nonarrival [nɔnə'raɪvl] n falta de llegada.
nonce word [nɔns-] n hápax m.
nonchalant ['nɔnʃələnt] adj indiferente.
noncommissioned [nɔnkə'mɪʃənd] adj: ~ **officer** suboficial m/f.
noncommittal ['nɔnkə'mɪtl] adj (reserved) reservado; (uncommitted) evasivo.
nonconformist [nɔnkən'fɔːmɪst] adj inconformista ♦ n inconformista m/f; (BRIT REL) no conformista m/f.
noncontributory [nɔnkən'trɪbjutərɪ] adj: ~ **pension scheme** or (US) **plan** fondo de pensiones no contributivo.
noncooperation ['nɔnkəuəpə'reɪʃən] n no cooperación f.
nondescript ['nɔndɪskrɪpt] adj anodino, soso.
none [nʌn] pron ninguno/a ♦ adv de ninguna manera; ~ **of you** ninguno de vosotros; **I've** ~ **left** no me queda ninguno/a; **he's** ~ **the worse for it** no le ha perjudicado; **I have** ~ no tengo ninguno; ~ **at all** (not one) ni uno.
nonentity [nɔ'nɛntɪtɪ] n cero a la izquierda, nulidad f.
nonessential [nɔnɪ'sɛnʃl] adj no esencial
♦ n: ~**s** cosas fpl secundarias or sin importancia.
nonetheless [nʌnðə'lɛs] adv sin embargo, no obstante, aún así.
non-EU [nɔn iː'juː] adj (citizen, passport) no comunitario; (imports) de fuera de la Unión Europea.
non-event [nɔnɪ'vɛnt] n acontecimiento sin importancia; **it was a** ~ no pasó absolutamente nada.
nonexecutive [nɔnɪg'zɛkjutɪv] adj: ~ **director** director m no ejecutivo.
nonexistent [nɔnɪg'zɪstənt] adj inexistente.
nonfiction [nɔn'fɪkʃən] n no ficción f.
nonintervention [nɔnɪntə'vɛnʃən] n no intervención f.
no-no ['nəunəu] n (col): **it's a** ~ de eso ni hablar.
non obst. abbr (= non obstante: notwithstanding) no obstante.
no-nonsense [nəu'nɔnsəns] adj sensato.
nonpayment [nɔn'peɪmənt] n falta de pago.
nonplussed [nɔn'plʌst] adj perplejo.
non-profit-making [nɔn'prɔfɪtmeɪkɪŋ] adj no lucrativo.
nonsense ['nɔnsəns] n tonterías fpl,

disparates *fpl*; ~! ¡qué tonterías!; **it is ~ to say that** ... es absurdo decir que ....

nonsensical [nɔn'sɛnsɪkl] *adj* disparatado, absurdo.

nonshrink [nɔn'ʃrɪŋk] *adj* que no encoge.

nonskid [nɔn'skɪd] *adj* antideslizante.

nonsmoker ['nɔn'sməukə*] *n* no fumador(a) *m/f*.

nonstarter [nɔn'stuːtə*] *n*: **it's a ~** no tiene futuro.

nonstick ['nɔn'stɪk] *adj* (*pan, surface*) antiadherente.

nonstop ['nɔn'stɔp] *adj* continuo; (*RAIL*) directo ◆ *adv* sin parar.

nontaxable [nɔn'tæksəbl] *adj*: **~ income** renta no imponible.

non-U ['nɔnjuː] *adj abbr* (*BRIT col*: = *non-upper class*) que no pertenece a la clase alta.

nonvolatile [nɔn'vɔlətaɪl] *adj*: **~ memory** (*COMPUT*) memoria permanente.

nonvoting [nɔn'vəutɪŋ] *adj*: **~ shares** acciones *fpl* sin derecho a voto.

nonwhite ['nɔn'waɪt] *adj* de color ◆ *n* (*person*) persona de color.

noodles ['nuːdlz] *npl* tallarines *mpl*.

nook [nuk] *n* rincón *m*; **~s and crannies** escondrijos *mpl*.

noon [nuːn] *n* mediodía *m*.

no-one ['nəuwʌn] *pron* = **nobody**.

noose [nuːs] *n* lazo corredizo.

nor [nɔː*] *conj* = **neither** ◆ *adv see* **neither**.

Norf *abbr* (*BRIT*) = **Norfolk**.

norm [nɔːm] *n* norma.

normal ['nɔːml] *adj* normal; **to return to ~** volver a la normalidad.

normality [nɔː'mælɪtɪ] *n* normalidad *f*.

normally ['nɔːməlɪ] *adv* normalmente.

Normandy ['nɔːməndɪ] *n* Normandía.

north [nɔːθ] *n* norte *m* ◆ *adj* del norte ◆ *adv* al *or* hacia el norte.

North Africa *n* África del Norte.

North African *adj*, *n* norteafricano/a *m/f*.

North America *n* América del Norte.

North American *adj*, *n* norteamericano/a *m/f*.

Northants *abbr* (*BRIT*) = **Northamptonshire**.

northbound ['nɔːθbaund] *adj* (*traffic*) que se dirige al norte; (*carriageway*) de dirección norte.

Northd *abbr* (*BRIT*) = **Northumberland**.

north-east [nɔːθ'iːst] *n* nor(d)este *m*.

northerly ['nɔːðəlɪ] *adj* (*point, direction*) hacia el norte, septentrional; (*wind*) del norte.

northern ['nɔːðən] *adj* norteño, del norte.

Northern Ireland *n* Irlanda del Norte.

North Korea *n* Corea del Norte.

North Pole *n*: **the ~** el Polo Norte.

North Sea *n*: **the ~** el Mar del Norte.

North Sea oil *n* petróleo del Mar del Norte.

northward(s) ['nɔːθwəd(z)] *adv* hacia el norte.

north-west [nɔːθ'wɛst] *n* noroeste *m*.

Norway ['nɔːweɪ] *n* Noruega.

Norwegian [nɔː'wiːdʒən] *adj* noruego ◆ *n* noruego/a; (*LING*) noruego.

nos. *abbr* (= *numbers*) núms.

nose [nəuz] *n* (*ANAT*) nariz *f*; (*ZOOL*) hocico; (*sense of smell*) olfato ◆ *vi* (*also*: **~ one's way**) avanzar con cautela; **to pay through the ~ (for sth)** (*col*) pagar un dineral (por algo).

▶**nose about, nose around** *vi* curiosear.

nosebleed ['nəuzbliːd] *n* hemorragia nasal.

nose-dive ['nəuzdaɪv] *n* picado vertical.

nose drops *npl* gotas *fpl* para la nariz.

nosey ['nəuzɪ] *adj* curioso, fisgón(ona).

nostalgia [nɔs'tældʒɪə] *n* nostalgia.

nostalgic [nɔs'tældʒɪk] *adj* nostálgico.

nostril ['nɔstrɪl] *n* ventana *or* orificio de la nariz.

nosy ['nəuzɪ] *adj* = **nosey**.

not [nɔt] *adv* no; **~ at all** no ... en absoluto; **~ that** ... no es que...; **it's too late, isn't it?** es demasiado tarde, ¿verdad?; **~ yet** todavía no; **~ now** ahora no; **why ~?** ¿por qué no?; **I hope ~** espero que no; **~ at all** no ... nada; (*after thanks*) de nada.

notable ['nəutəbl] *adj* notable.

notably ['nəutəblɪ] *adv* especialmente; (*in particular*) sobre todo.

notary ['nəutərɪ] *n* (*also*: **~ public**) notario/a.

notation [nəu'teɪʃən] *n* notación *f*.

notch [nɔtʃ] *n* muesca, corte *m*.

▶**notch up** *vt* (*score, victory*) apuntarse.

note [nəut] *n* (*MUS, record, letter*) nota; (*banknote*) billete *m*; (*tone*) tono ◆ *vt* (*observe*) notar, observar; (*write down*) apuntar, anotar; **delivery ~** nota de entrega; **to compare ~s** (*fig*) cambiar impresiones; **of ~** conocido, destacado; **to take ~** prestar atención a; **just a quick ~ to let you know that** ... sólo unas líneas para informarte que ....

notebook ['nəutbuk] *n* libreta, cuaderno; (*for shorthand*) libreta.

notecase ['nəutkeɪs] *n* (*BRIT*) cartera, billetero.

noted ['nəutɪd] *adj* célebre, conocido.

notepad ['nəutpæd] *n* bloc *m*.

notepaper ['nəutpeɪpə*] *n* papel *m* para cartas.

noteworthy ['nəʊtwəːðɪ] adj notable, digno de atención.

nothing ['nʌθɪŋ] n nada; (zero) cero; **he does** ~ no hace nada; ~ **new** nada nuevo; **for** ~ (free) gratis; (in vain) en balde; ~ **at all** nada en absoluto.

notice ['nəʊtɪs] n (announcement) anuncio; (dismissal) despido; (resignation) dimisión f; (review: of play etc) reseña ♦ vt (observe) notar, observar; **to take** ~ **of** hacer caso de, prestar atención a; **at short** ~ con poca antelación; **without** ~ sin previo aviso; **advance** ~ previo aviso; **until further** ~ hasta nuevo aviso; **to give sb** ~ **of sth** avisar a algn de algo; **to give** ~, **hand in one's** ~ dimitir, renunciar; **it has come to my** ~ **that** ... he llegado a saber que ...; **to escape** or **avoid** ~ pasar inadvertido.

noticeable ['nəʊtɪsəbl] adj evidente, obvio.

notice board n (BRIT) tablón m de anuncios.

notification [nəʊtɪfɪ'keɪʃən] n aviso; (announcement) anuncio.

notify ['nəʊtɪfaɪ] vt: **to** ~ **sb (of sth)** comunicar (algo) a algn.

notion ['nəʊʃən] n noción f, concepto; (opinion) opinión f.

notions ['nəʊʃənz] npl (US) mercería.

notoriety [nəʊtə'raɪətɪ] n notoriedad f, mala fama.

notorious [nəʊ'tɔːrɪəs] adj notorio, tristemente célebre.

notoriously [nəʊ'tɔːrɪəslɪ] adv notoriamente.

Notts abbr (BRIT) = Nottinghamshire.

notwithstanding [nɒtwɪθ'stændɪŋ] adv no obstante, sin embargo; ~ **this** a pesar de esto.

nougat ['nuːgɑː] n turrón m.

nought [nɔːt] n cero.

noun [naʊn] n nombre m, sustantivo.

nourish ['nʌrɪʃ] vt nutrir, alimentar; (fig) fomentar, nutrir.

nourishing ['nʌrɪʃɪŋ] adj nutritivo, rico.

nourishment ['nʌrɪʃmənt] n alimento, sustento.

Nov. abbr (= November) nov.

novel ['nɒvl] n novela ♦ adj (new) nuevo, original; (unexpected) insólito.

novelist ['nɒvəlɪst] n novelista m/f.

novelty ['nɒvəltɪ] n novedad f.

November [nəʊ'vɛmbə*] n noviembre m.

novice ['nɒvɪs] n principiante m/f, novato/a; (REL) novicio/a.

NOW [naʊ] n abbr (US) = National Organization for Women.

now [naʊ] adv (at the present time) ahora; (these days) actualmente, hoy día ♦ conj: ~ (**that**) ya que, ahora que; **right** ~ ahora mismo; **by** ~ ya; **just** ~: **I'll do it just** ~ ahora mismo lo hago; ~ **and then,** ~ **and again** de vez en cuando; **from** ~ **on** de ahora en adelante; **between** ~ **and Monday** entre hoy y el lunes; **in 3 days from** ~ de hoy en 3 días; **that's all for** ~ eso es todo por ahora.

nowadays ['naʊədeɪz] adv hoy (en) día, actualmente.

nowhere ['nəʊwɛə*] adv (direction) a ninguna parte; (location) en ninguna parte; ~ **else** en or a ninguna otra parte.

no-win situation [nəʊ'wɪn-] n: **I'm in a** ~ haga lo que haga, llevo las de perder.

noxious ['nɒkʃəs] adj nocivo.

nozzle ['nɒzl] n boquilla.

NP n abbr = notary public.

NS abbr (Canada) = Nova Scotia.

NSC n abbr (US) = National Security Council.

NSF n abbr (US) = National Science Foundation.

NSPCC n abbr (BRIT) = National Society for the Prevention of Cruelty to Children.

NSW abbr (Australia) = New South Wales.

NT n abbr = New Testament ♦ abbr (Canada) = Northwest Territories.

nth [ɛnθ] adj: **for the** ~ **time** (col) por enésima vez.

nuance ['njuːɑːns] n matiz m.

nubile ['njuːbaɪl] adj núbil.

nuclear ['njuːklɪə*] adj nuclear.

nuclear disarmament n desarme m nuclear.

nuclear family n familia nuclear.

nuclear-free zone ['njuːklɪə'friː-] n zona desnuclearizada.

nucleus, pl **nuclei** ['njuːklɪəs, 'njuːklɪaɪ] n núcleo.

NUCPS n abbr (BRIT = National Union of Civil and Public Servants) sindicato de funcionarios.

nude [njuːd] adj, n desnudo/a m/f; **in the** ~ desnudo.

nudge [nʌdʒ] vt dar un codazo a.

nudist ['njuːdɪst] n nudista m/f.

nudist colony n colonia de desnudistas.

nudity ['njuːdɪtɪ] n desnudez f.

nugget ['nʌgɪt] n pepita.

nuisance ['njuːsns] n molestia, fastidio; (person) pesado, latoso; **what a** ~! ¡qué lata!

NUJ n abbr (BRIT: = National Union of Journalists) sindicato de periodistas.

nuke [njuːk] (col) n bomba atómica ♦ vt atacar con arma nuclear.

null [nʌl] adj: ~ **and void** nulo y sin efecto.

nullify ['nʌlɪfaɪ] *vt* anular, invalidar.
NUM *n abbr* (*BRIT*: = *National Union of Mineworkers*) *sindicato de mineros.*
numb [nʌm] *adj* entumecido; (*fig*) insensible ♦ *vt* quitar la sensación a, entumecer, entorpecer; **to be ~ with cold** estar entumecido de frío; **~ with fear/grief** paralizado de miedo/dolor.
number ['nʌmbə*] *n* número; (*numeral*) número, cifra ♦ *vt* (*pages etc*) numerar, poner número a; (*amount to*) sumar, ascender a; **reference ~** número de referencia; **telephone ~** número de teléfono; **wrong ~** (*TEL*) número equivocado; **opposite ~** (*person*) homólogo/a; **to be ~ed among** figurar entre; **a ~ of** varios, algunos; **they were ten in ~** eran diez.
number plate *n* (*BRIT*) matrícula, placa.
Number Ten *n* (*BRIT*: *10 Downing Street*) *residencia del primer ministro.*
numbness ['nʌmnɪs] *n* insensibilidad *f*, parálisis *f inv*; (*due to cold*) entumecimiento.
numbskull ['nʌmskʌl] *n* (*col*) papanatas *m/f inv.*
numeral ['njuːmərəl] *n* número, cifra.
numerate ['njuːmərɪt] *adj* competente en aritmética.
numerical [njuːˈmɛrɪkl] *adj* numérico.
numerous ['njuːmərəs] *adj* numeroso, muchos.
nun [nʌn] *n* monja, religiosa.
nunnery ['nʌnərɪ] *n* convento de monjas.
nuptial ['nʌpʃəl] *adj* nupcial.
nurse [nɔːs] *n* enfermero/a; (*nanny*) niñera ♦ *vt* (*patient*) cuidar, atender; (*baby*: *Brit*) mecer; (: *US*) criar, amamantar; **male ~** enfermero.
nursery ['nɔːsərɪ] *n* (*institution*) guardería infantil; (*room*) cuarto de los niños; (*for plants*) criadero, semillero.
nursery rhyme *n* canción *f* infantil.
nursery school *n* escuela de preescolar.
nursery slope *n* (*BRIT SKI*) cuesta para principiantes.
nursing ['nɔːsɪŋ] *n* (*profession*) profesión *f* de enfermera; (*care*) asistencia, cuidado ♦ *adj* (*mother*) lactante.
nursing home *n* clínica de reposo.
nurture ['nɔːtʃə*] *vt* (*child*, *plant*) alimentar, nutrir.
NUS *n abbr* (*BRIT*: = *National Union of Students*) *sindicato de estudiantes.*
NUT *n abbr* (*BRIT*: = *National Union of Teachers*) *sindicato de profesores.*
nut [nʌt] *n* (*TECH*) tuerca; (*BOT*) nuez *f* ♦ *adj* (*chocolate etc*) con nueces; **~s** (*CULIN*)

frutos secos.
nutcrackers ['nʌtkrækəz] *npl* cascanueces *m inv.*
nutmeg ['nʌtmɛg] *n* nuez *f* moscada.
nutrient ['njuːtrɪənt] *adj* nutritivo ♦ *n* elemento nutritivo.
nutrition [njuːˈtrɪʃən] *n* nutrición *f*, alimentación *f*.
nutritionist [njuːˈtrɪʃənɪst] *n* dietista *m/f.*
nutritious [njuːˈtrɪʃəs] *adj* nutritivo.
nuts [nʌts] *adj* (*col*) chiflado.
nutshell ['nʌtʃɛl] *n* cáscara de nuez; **in a ~** en resumidas cuentas.
nutty ['nʌtɪ] *adj* (*flavour*) a frutos secos; (*col*: *foolish*) chalado.
nuzzle ['nʌzl] *vi*: **to ~ up to** arrimarse a.
NV *abbr* (*US*) = *Nevada.*
NVQ *n abbr* (*BRIT*: = *National Vocational Qualification*) *título de formación profesional.*
NWT *abbr* (*Canada*) = *Northwest Territories.*
NY *abbr* (*US*) = *New York.*
NYC *abbr* (*US*) = *New York City.*
nylon ['naɪlɔn] *n* nylon *m*, nilón *m* ♦ *adj* de nylon *or* nilón.
nymph [nɪmf] *n* ninfa.
nymphomaniac ['nɪmfəʊˈmeɪnɪæk] *adj, n* ninfómana.
NYSE *n abbr* (*US*) = *New York Stock Exchange.*

O o

O, o [əʊ] (*letter*) O, o *f*; **O for Oliver**, (*US*) **O for Oboe** O de Oviedo.
oaf [əʊf] *n* zoquete *m/f.*
oak [əʊk] *n* roble *m* ♦ *adj* de roble.
OAP *abbr see* **old-age pensioner.**
oar [ɔː*] *n* remo; **to put** *or* **shove one's ~ in** (*fig*: *col*) entrometerse.
oarsman ['ɔːzmən] *n* remero.
OAS *n abbr* (= *Organization of American States*) OEA *f*.
oasis, *pl* **oases** [əʊˈeɪsɪs, əʊˈeɪsiːz] *n* oasis *m inv.*
oath [əʊθ] *n* juramento; (*swear word*) palabrota; **on** (*BRIT*) *or* **under ~** bajo juramento.
oatmeal ['əʊtmiːl] *n* harina de avena.
oats [əʊts] *n* avena.
OAU *n abbr* (= *Organization of African Unity*)

OUA f.

obdurate ['ɔbdjurɪt] adj (stubborn) terco, obstinado; (sinner) empedernido; (unyielding) inflexible, firme.

OBE n abbr (BRIT: = Order of the British Empire) título ceremonial.

obedience [ə'biːdɪəns] n obediencia; **in ~ to** de acuerdo con.

obedient [ə'biːdɪənt] adj obediente.

obelisk ['ɔbɪlɪsk] n obelisco.

obese [əu'biːs] adj obeso.

obesity [əu'biːsɪtɪ] n obesidad f.

obey [ə'beɪ] vt obedecer; (instructions, regulations) cumplir.

obituary [ə'bɪtjuərɪ] n necrología.

object ['ɔbdʒɪkt] n (gen) objeto; (purpose) objeto, propósito; (LING) objeto, complemento ♦ vi [əb'dʒɛkt]: **to ~ to** (attitude) protestar contra; (proposal) oponerse a; **expense is no ~** no importan los gastos; **I ~!** ¡protesto!; **to ~ that** objetar que.

objection [əb'dʒɛkʃən] n objeción f; **I have no ~ to ...** no tengo inconveniente en que ....

objectionable [əb'dʒɛkʃənəbl] adj (gen) desagradable; (conduct) censurable.

objective [əb'dʒɛktɪv] adj, n objetivo.

objectively [əb'dʒɛktɪvlɪ] adv objetivamente.

objectivity [ɔbdʒɪk'tɪvɪtɪ] n objetividad f.

object lesson n (fig) (buen) ejemplo.

objector [əb'dʒɛktə*] n objetor(a) m/f.

obligation [ɔblɪ'geɪʃən] n obligación f; (debt) deber m; "**without ~**" "sin compromiso"; **to be under an ~ to sb/to do sth** estar comprometido con algn/a hacer algo.

obligatory [ə'blɪgətərɪ] adj obligatorio.

oblige [ə'blaɪdʒ] vt (do a favour for) complacer, hacer un favor a; **to ~ sb to do sth** obligar a algn a hacer algo; **to be ~d to sb for sth** estarle agradecido a algn por algo; **anything to ~!** (col) todo sea por complacerte.

obliging [ə'blaɪdʒɪŋ] adj servicial, atento.

oblique [ə'bliːk] adj oblicuo; (allusion) indirecto ♦ n (TYP) barra.

obliterate [ə'blɪtəreɪt] vt arrasar; (memory) borrar.

oblivion [ə'blɪvɪən] n olvido.

oblivious [ə'blɪvɪəs] adj: **~ of** inconsciente de.

oblong ['ɔblɔŋ] adj rectangular ♦ n rectángulo.

obnoxious [əb'nɔkʃəs] adj odioso, detestable; (smell) nauseabundo.

o.b.o. abbr (US: = or best offer: in classified ads) abierto ofertas.

oboe ['əubəu] n oboe m.

obscene [əb'siːn] adj obsceno.

obscenity [əb'sɛnɪtɪ] n obscenidad f.

obscure [əb'skjuə*] adj oscuro ♦ vt oscurecer; (hide: sun) ocultar.

obscurity [əb'skjuərɪtɪ] n oscuridad f; (obscure point) punto oscuro; **to rise from ~** salir de la nada.

obsequious [əb'siːkwɪəs] adj servil.

observable [əb'zə:vəbl] adj observable, perceptible.

observance [əb'zə:vns] n observancia, cumplimiento; (ritual) práctica; **religious ~s** prácticas fpl religiosas.

observant [əb'zə:vnt] adj observador(a).

observation [ɔbzə'veɪʃən] n (also MED) observación f; (by police etc) vigilancia.

observation post n (MIL) puesto de observación.

observatory [əb'zə:vətrɪ] n observatorio.

observe [əb'zə:v] vt (gen) observar; (rule) cumplir.

observer [əb'zə:və*] n observador(a) m/f.

obsess [əb'sɛs] vt obsesionar; **to be ~ed by** or **with sb/sth** estar obsesionado con algn/algo.

obsession [əb'sɛʃən] n obsesión f.

obsessive [əb'sɛsɪv] adj obsesivo.

obsolescence [ɔbsə'lɛsns] n obsolescencia.

obsolescent [ɔbsə'lɛsnt] adj que está cayendo en desuso.

obsolete ['ɔbsəliːt] adj obsoleto.

obstacle ['ɔbstəkl] n obstáculo; (nuisance) estorbo.

obstacle race n carrera de obstáculos.

obstetrician [ɔbstə'trɪʃən] n obstetra m/f.

obstetrics [ɔb'stɛtrɪks] n obstetricia.

obstinacy ['ɔbstɪnəsɪ] n terquedad f, obstinación f; tenacidad f.

obstinate ['ɔbstɪnɪt] adj terco, obstinado; (determined) tenaz.

obstinately ['ɔbstɪnɪtlɪ] adv tercamente, obstinadamente.

obstreperous [əb'strɛpərəs] adj ruidoso; (unruly) revoltoso.

obstruct [əb'strʌkt] vt (block) obstruir; (hinder) estorbar, obstaculizar.

obstruction [əb'strʌkʃən] n obstrucción f; estorbo, obstáculo.

obstructive [əb'strʌktɪv] adj obstruccionista; **stop being ~!** ¡deja de poner peros!

obtain [əb'teɪn] vt (get) obtener; (achieve) conseguir; **to ~ sth (for o.s.)** conseguir or adquirir algo.

obtainable [əb'teɪnəbl] adj asequible.

obtrusive [əb'truːsɪv] adj (person)

importuno; (: *interfering*) entrometido; (*building etc*) demasiado visible.

obtuse [əb'tjuːs] *adj* obtuso.

obverse ['ɔbvəːs] *n* (*of medal*) anverso; (*fig*) complemento.

obviate ['ɔbvɪeɪt] *vt* obviar, evitar.

obvious ['ɔbvɪəs] *adj* (*clear*) obvio, evidente; (*unsubtle*) poco sutil; **it's ~ that ...** está claro que ..., es evidente que ....

obviously ['ɔbvɪəslɪ] *adv* obviamente, evidentemente; **~ not!** ¡por supuesto que no!; **he was ~ not drunk** era evidente que no estaba borracho; **he was not ~ drunk** no se le notaba que estaba borracho.

OCAS *n abbr* (= *Organization of Central American States*) ODECA *f.*

occasion [ə'keɪʒən] *n* oportunidad *f*, ocasión *f*; (*event*) acontecimiento ♦ *vt* ocasionar, causar; **on that ~** esa vez, en aquella ocasión; **to rise to the ~** ponerse a la altura de las circunstancias.

occasional [ə'keɪʒənl] *adj* poco frecuente, ocasional.

occasionally [ə'keɪʒənlɪ] *adv* de vez en cuando; **very ~** muy de tarde en tarde, en muy contadas ocasiones.

occasional table *n* mesita.

occult [ɔ'kʌlt] *adj* (*gen*) oculto.

occupancy ['ɔkjupənsɪ] *n* ocupación *f.*

occupant ['ɔkjupənt] *n* (*of house*) inquilino/a; (*of boat, car*) ocupante *m/f.*

occupation [ɔkju'peɪʃən] *n* (*of house*) tenencia; (*job*) trabajo; (: *calling*) oficio.

occupational accident [ɔkju'peɪʃənl] *n* accidente *m* laboral.

occupational guidance *n* orientación *f* profesional.

occupational hazard *n* gajes *mpl* del oficio.

occupational pension scheme *n* plan *m* profesional de jubilación.

occupational therapy *n* terapia ocupacional.

occupier ['ɔkjupaɪə*] *n* inquilino/a.

occupy ['ɔkjupaɪ] *vt* (*seat, post, time*) ocupar; (*house*) habitar; **to ~ o.s. with** *or* **by doing** (*as job*) dedicarse a hacer; (*to pass time*) entretenerse haciendo; **to be occupied with sth/in doing sth** estar ocupado con algo/haciendo algo.

occur [ə'kəː*] *vi* ocurrir, suceder; **to ~ to sb** ocurrírsele a algn.

occurrence [ə'kʌrəns] *n* suceso.

ocean ['əuʃən] *n* océano; **~s of** (*col*) la mar de.

ocean bed *n* fondo del océano.

ocean-going ['əuʃəngəuɪŋ] *adj* de alta mar.

Oceania [əuʃɪ'eɪnɪə] *n* Oceanía.

ocean liner *n* buque *m* transoceánico.

ochre, (*US*) **ocher** ['əukə*] *n* ocre *m.*

o'clock [ə'klɔk] *adv*: **it is 5 ~** son las 5.

OCR *n abbr see* **optical character recognition/reader.**

Oct. *abbr* (= *October*) oct.

octagonal [ɔk'tægənl] *adj* octagonal.

octane ['ɔkteɪn] *n* octano; **high ~ petrol** *or* (*US*) **gas** gasolina de alto octanaje.

octave ['ɔktɪv] *n* octava.

October [ɔk'təubə*] *n* octubre *m.*

octogenarian ['ɔktəudʒɪ'nɛərɪən] *n* octogenario/a.

octopus ['ɔktəpəs] *n* pulpo.

oculist ['ɔkjulɪst] *n* oculista *m/f.*

odd [ɔd] *adj* (*strange*) extraño, raro; (*number*) impar; (*left over*) sobrante, suelto; **60-~** 60 y pico; **at ~ times** de vez en cuando; **to be the ~ one out** estar de más; **if you have the ~ minute** si tienes unos minutos libres; *see also* **odds.**

oddball ['ɔdbɔːl] *n* (*col*) bicho raro.

oddity ['ɔdɪtɪ] *n* rareza; (*person*) excéntrico/a.

odd-job man [ɔd'dʒɔb-] *n* hombre *m* que hace chapuzas.

odd jobs *npl* chapuzas *fpl.*

oddly ['ɔdlɪ] *adv* extrañamente.

oddments ['ɔdmənts] *npl* (*BRIT COMM*) restos *mpl.*

odds [ɔdz] *npl* (*in betting*) puntos *mpl* de ventaja; **it makes no ~** da lo mismo; **at ~** reñidos/as; **to succeed against all the ~** tener éxito contra todo pronóstico; **~ and ends** cachivaches *mpl.*

odds-on [ɔdz'ɔn] *adj* (*col*): **the ~ favourite** el máximo favorito; **it's ~ he'll come** seguro que viene.

ode [əud] *n* oda.

odious ['əudɪəs] *adj* odioso.

odometer [ɔ'dɔmɪtə*] *n* (*US*) cuentakilómetros *m inv.*

odour, (*US*) **odor** ['əudə*] *n* olor *m*; (*perfume*) perfume *m.*

odo(u)rless ['əudəlɪs] *adj* sin olor.

OECD *n abbr* (= *Organization for Economic Co-operation and Development*) OCDE *f.*

oesophagus, (*US*) **esophagus** [iː'sɔfəgəs] *n* esófago.

oestrogen, (*US*) **estrogen** ['iːstrədʒən] *n* estrógeno.

========================== *KEYWORD*

of [ɔv, əv] *prep* **1** (*gen*) de; **a friend ~ ours** un amigo nuestro; **a boy ~ 10** un chico de 10 años; **that was kind ~ you** eso fue muy amable de tu parte

2 (*expressing quantity, amount, dates etc*) de; **a kilo ~ flour** un kilo de harina; **there were 3 ~ them** había tres; **3 ~ us went** tres de nosotros fuimos; **the 5th ~ July** el 5 de julio; **a quarter ~ 4** (*US*) las 4 menos cuarto
3 (*from, out of*) de; **made ~ wood** (hecho) de madera.

off [ɔf] *adj, adv* (*engine, light*) apagado; (*tap*) cerrado; (*BRIT: food: bad*) pasado, malo; (: *milk*) cortado; (*cancelled*) suspendido; (*removed*): **the lid was ~** no estaba puesta la tapadera ♦ *prep* de; **to be ~** (*to leave*) irse, marcharse; **to be ~ sick** estar enfermo *or* de baja; **a day ~** un día libre; **to have an ~ day** tener un mal día; **he had his coat ~** se había quitado el abrigo; **10% ~** (*COMM*) (con el) 10% de descuento; **it's a long way ~** está muy lejos; **5 km ~ (the road)** a 5 km (de la carretera); **~ the coast** frente a la costa; **I'm ~ meat** (*no longer eat/like it*) paso de la carne; **the ~ chance** por si acaso; **~ and on, on and ~** de vez en cuando; **I must be ~** tengo que irme; **to be well/ badly ~** andar bien/mal de dinero; **I'm afraid the chicken is ~** desgraciadamente ya no queda pollo; **that's a bit ~, isn't it!** (*fig, col*) ¡eso no se hace!

offal ['ɔfl] *n* (*BRIT CULIN*) menudillos *mpl*, asaduras *fpl*.

off-centre, (*US*) **off-center** [ɔf'sɛntə*] *adj* descentrado, ladeado.

off-colour ['ɔf'kʌlə*] *adj* (*BRIT: ill*) indispuesto; **to feel ~** sentirse *or* estar mal.

offence, (*US*) **offense** [ə'fɛns] *n* (*crime*) delito; (*insult*) ofensa; **to take ~ at** ofenderse por; **to commit an ~** cometer un delito.

offend [ə'fɛnd] *vt* (*person*) ofender ♦ *vi*: **to ~ against** (*law, rule*) infringir.

offender [ə'fɛndə*] *n* delincuente *m/f*; (*against regulations*) infractor(a) *m/f*.

offending [ə'fɛndɪŋ] *adj* culpable; (*object*) molesto; (*word*) problemático.

offense [ə'fɛns] *n* (*US*) = **offence.**

offensive [ə'fɛnsɪv] *adj* ofensivo; (*smell etc*) repugnante ♦ *n* (*MIL*) ofensiva.

offer ['ɔfə*] *n* (*gen*) oferta, ofrecimiento; (*proposal*) propuesta ♦ *vt* ofrecer; **"on ~"** (*COMM*) "en oferta"; **to make an ~ for sth** hacer una oferta por algo; **to ~ sth to sb, ~ sb sth** ofrecer algo a algn; **to ~ to do sth** ofrecerse a hacer algo.

offering ['ɔfərɪŋ] *n* (*REL*) ofrenda.

offer price *n* precio de oferta.

offertory ['ɔfətrɪ] *n* (*REL*) ofertorio.

offhand [ɔf'hænd] *adj* informal; (*brusque*) desconsiderado ♦ *adv* de improviso, sin pensarlo; **I can't tell you ~** no te lo puedo decir así de improviso *or* así nomás (*LAM*).

office ['ɔfɪs] *n* (*place*) oficina; (*room*) despacho; (*position*) cargo, oficio; **doctor's ~** (*US*) consultorio; **to take ~** entrar en funciones; **through his good ~s** gracias a sus buenos oficios; **O~ of Fair Trading** (*BRIT*) *oficina que regula normas comerciales.*

office automation *n* ofimática, buromática.

office bearer *n* (*of club etc*) titular *m/f* (de una cartera).

office block, (*US*) **office building** *n* bloque *m* de oficinas.

office boy *n* ordenanza *m.*

office hours *npl* horas *fpl* de oficina; (*US MED*) horas *fpl* de consulta.

office manager *n* jefe/a *m/f* de oficina.

officer ['ɔfɪsə*] *n* (*MIL etc*) oficial *m/f*; (*of organization*) director(a) *m/f*; (*also*: **police ~**) agente *m/f* de policía.

office work *n* trabajo de oficina.

office worker *n* oficinista *m/f*.

official [ə'fɪʃl] *adj* (*authorized*) oficial, autorizado; (*strike*) oficial ♦ *n* funcionario/a.

officialdom [ə'fɪʃldəm] *n* burocracia.

officially [ə'fɪʃəlɪ] *adv* oficialmente.

official receiver *n* síndico.

officiate [ə'fɪʃɪeɪt] *vi* (*also REL*) oficiar; **to ~ as Mayor** ejercer las funciones de alcalde; **to ~ at a marriage** celebrar una boda.

officious [ə'fɪʃəs] *adj* oficioso.

offing ['ɔfɪŋ] *n*: **in the ~** (*fig*) en perspectiva.

off-key [ɔf'kiː] *adj* desafinado ♦ *adv* desafinadamente.

off-licence ['ɔflaɪsns] *n* (*BRIT: shop*) *tienda de bebidas alcohólicas*; *ver recuadro.*

OFF-LICENCE

En el Reino Unido una **off-licence** *es una tienda especializada en la venta de bebidas alcohólicas para el consumo fuera del establecimiento. De ahí su nombre, pues se necesita un permiso especial para tal venta, que está estrictamente regulada. Suelen vender además bebidas sin alcohol, tabaco, chocolate, patatas fritas etc y a menudo son parte de grandes cadenas nacionales.*

---

off-limits [ɔf'lɪmɪts] *adj* (*US MIL*) prohibido al personal militar.

off line *adj, adv* (*COMPUT*) fuera de línea; (*switched off*) desconectado.

off-load ['ɔfləud] *vt* descargar, desembarcar.

off-peak ['ɔf'piːk] *adj* (*holiday*) de temporada baja; (*electricity*) de banda económica.

off-putting ['ɔfputɪŋ] *adj* (*BRIT: person*) poco amable, difícil; (*behaviour*) chocante.

off-season ['ɔf'siːzn] *adj, adv* fuera de temporada.

offset ['ɔfsɛt] *vt* (*irreg: like* **set**) (*counteract*) contrarrestar, compensar ♦ *n* (*also*: ~ **printing**) offset *m*.

offshoot ['ɔfʃuːt] *n* (*BOT*) vástago; (*fig*) ramificación *f*.

offshore [ɔf'ʃɔː*] *adj* (*breeze, island*) costero; (*fishing*) de bajura; ~ **oilfield** campo petrolífero submarino.

offside ['ɔf'saɪd] *n* (*AUT: with right-hand drive*) lado derecho; (: *with left-hand drive*) lado izquierdo ♦ *adj* (*SPORT*) fuera de juego; (*AUT*) del lado derecho; del lado izquierdo.

offspring ['ɔfsprɪŋ] *n* descendencia.

offstage [ɔf'steɪdʒ] *adv* entre bastidores.

off-the-cuff [ɔfðə'kʌf] *adj* espontáneo.

off-the-job [ɔfðə'dʒɔb] *adj*: ~ **training** formación *f* fuera del trabajo.

off-the-peg [ɔfðə'pɛg], (*US*) **off-the-rack** [ɔfðə'ræk] *adv* confeccionado.

off-the-record ['ɔfðə'rɛkɔːd] *adj* extraoficial, confidencial ♦ *adv* extraoficialmente, confidencialmente.

off-white ['ɔfwaɪt] *adj* blanco grisáceo.

Ofgas ['ɔfgæs] *n* (*BRIT: = Office of Gas Supply*) *organismo que controla a las empresas del gas en Gran Bretaña*.

Oftel ['ɔftɛl] *n* (*BRIT: = Office of Telecommunications*) *organismo que controla las telecomunicaciones británicas*.

often ['ɔfn] *adv* a menudo, con frecuencia, seguido (*LAM*); **how** ~ **do you go?** ¿cada cuánto vas?

Ofwat ['ɔfwɔt] *n* (*BRIT: = Office of Water Services*) *organismo que controla a las empresas suministradoras del agua en Inglaterra y Gales*.

ogle ['əugl] *vt* comerse con los ojos a.

ogre ['əugə*] *n* ogro.

OH *abbr* (*US*) = Ohio.

oh [əu] *excl* ¡ah!

OHMS *abbr* (*BRIT*) *On His* (*or Her*) *Majesty's Service*.

oil [ɔɪl] *n* aceite *m*; (*petroleum*) petróleo ♦ *vt* (*machine*) engrasar; **fried in** ~ frito en aceite.

oilcan ['ɔɪlkæn] *n* lata de aceite.

oilfield ['ɔɪlfiːld] *n* campo petrolífero.

oil filter *n* (*AUT*) filtro de aceite.

oil-fired ['ɔɪlfaɪəd] *adj* de fuel-oil.

oil gauge *n* indicador *m* del aceite.

oil industry *n* industria petrolífera.

oil level *n* nivel *m* del aceite.

oil painting *n* pintura al óleo.

oil refinery *n* refinería de petróleo.

oil rig *n* torre *f* de perforación.

oilskins ['ɔɪlskɪnz] *npl* impermeable *msg*, chubasquero *sg*.

oil tanker *n* petrolero.

oil well *n* pozo (de petróleo).

oily ['ɔɪlɪ] *adj* aceitoso; (*food*) grasiento.

ointment ['ɔɪntmənt] *n* ungüento.

OK *abbr* (*US*) = Oklahoma.

O.K., okay ['əu'keɪ] *excl* O.K., ¡está bien!, ¡vale! ♦ *adj* bien ♦ *n*: **to give sth one's** ~ dar el visto bueno a *or* aprobar algo ♦ *vt* dar el visto bueno a; **it's** ~ **with** *or* **by me** estoy de acuerdo, me parece bien; **are you** ~ **for money?** ¿andas *or* vas bien de dinero?

Okla. *abbr* (*US*) = Oklahoma.

old [əuld] *adj* viejo; (*former*) antiguo; **how** ~ **are you?** ¿cuántos años tienes?, ¿qué edad tienes?; **he's 10 years** ~ tiene 10 años; ~**er brother** hermano mayor; **any** ~ **thing will do** sirve cualquier cosa.

old age *n* vejez *f*.

old-age pension ['əuldeɪdʒ-] *n* (*BRIT*) jubilación *f*, pensión *f*.

old-age pensioner (OAP) ['əuldeɪdʒ-] *n* (*BRIT*) jubilado/a.

olden ['əuldən] *adj* antiguo.

old-fashioned ['əuld'fæʃənd] *adj* anticuado, pasado de moda.

old maid *n* solterona.

old-style ['əuldstaɪl] *adj* tradicional, chapado a la antigua.

old-time ['əuld'taɪm] *adj* antiguo, de antaño.

old-timer [əuld'taɪmə*] *n* veterano/a; (*old person*) anciano/a.

old wives' tale *n* cuento de viejas, patraña.

olive ['ɔlɪv] *n* (*fruit*) aceituna; (*tree*) olivo ♦ *adj* (*also*: ~-**green**) verde oliva *inv*.

olive branch *n* (*fig*): **to offer an** ~ **to sb** ofrecer hacer las paces con algn.

olive oil *n* aceite *m* de oliva.

Olympic [əu'lɪmpɪk] *adj* olímpico; **the** ~ **Games, the** ~**s** *npl* las Olimpíadas.

OM *n abbr* (*BRIT: = Order of Merit*) *título ceremonial*.

O & M *n abbr* = organization and method.

Oman [əu'mɑːn] *n* Omán *m*.

OMB *n abbr* (*US: = Office of Management and*

*Budget) servicio que asesora al
presidente en materia presupuestaria.*
omelet(te) ['ɔmlɪt] *n* tortilla, tortilla de
huevo (*LAM*).
omen ['əumən] *n* presagio.
ominous ['ɔmɪnəs] *adj* de mal agüero,
amenazador(a).
omission [əu'mɪʃən] *n* omisión *f*; (*error*)
descuido.
omit [əu'mɪt] *vt* omitir; (*by mistake*) olvidar,
descuidar; **to ~ to do sth** olvidarse *or*
dejar de hacer algo.
omnivorous [ɔm'nɪvərəs] *adj* omnívoro.
ON *abbr* (*Canada*) = Ontario.

========================= *KEYWORD*

on [ɔn] *prep* **1** (*indicating position*) en; sobre;
~ the wall en la pared; **it's ~ the table**
está sobre *or* en la mesa; **~ the left** a la
izquierda; **I haven't got any money ~ me**
no llevo dinero encima
2 (*indicating means, method, condition etc*):
~ foot a pie; **~ the train/plane** (*go*) en
tren/avión; (*be*) en el tren/el avión; **~ the
radio/television** por *or* en la radio/
televisión; **~ the telephone** al teléfono; **to
be ~ drugs** drogarse; (*MED*) estar a
tratamiento; **to be ~ holiday/business**
estar de vacaciones/en viaje de negocios;
we're ~ irregular verbs estamos con los
verbos irregulares
3 (*referring to time*): **~ Friday** el viernes;
~ Fridays los viernes; **~ June 20th** el 20
de junio; **a week ~ Friday** del viernes en
una semana; **~ arrival** al llegar; **~ seeing
this** al ver esto
4 (*about, concerning*) sobre, acerca de; **a
book ~ physics** un libro de *or* sobre
física
5 (*at the expense of*): **this round's ~ me**
esta ronda la pago yo, invito yo (a esta
ronda); (*earning*): **he's ~ £16,000 a year**
gana dieciséis mil libras al año
♦ *adv* **1** (*referring to dress*): **to have one's
coat ~** tener *or* llevar el abrigo puesto;
she put her gloves ~ se puso los guantes
2 (*referring to covering*): **"screw the lid ~
tightly"** "cerrar bien la tapa"
3 (*further, continuously*): **to walk/run** *etc*
~ seguir caminando/corriendo *etc*; **from
that day ~** desde aquel día; **it was well ~
in the evening** estaba ya entrada la tarde
4 (*in phrases*): **I'm ~ to sth** creo haber
encontrado algo; **my father's always ~ at
me to get a job** (*col*) mi padre siempre
me está dando la lata para que me ponga
a trabajar
♦ *adj* **1** (*functioning, in operation: machine,*

radio, TV, light) encendido/a (*SP*),
prendido/a (*LAM*); (: *tap*) abierto/a; (:
brakes) echado/a, puesto/a; **is the meeting
still ~?** (*in progress*) ¿todavía continúa la
reunión?; (*not cancelled*) ¿va a haber
reunión al fin?; **there's a good film ~ at
the cinema** ponen una buena película en
el cine
2: **that's not ~!** (*inf: not possible*) ¡eso ni
hablar!; (: *not acceptable*) ¡eso no se hace!

ONC *n abbr* (*BRIT*: = *Ordinary National
Certificate*) *título escolar.*
once [wʌns] *adv* una vez; (*formerly*)
antiguamente ♦ *conj* una vez que; **~ he
had left/it was done** una vez que se había
marchado/se hizo; **at ~** en seguida,
inmediatamente; (*simultaneously*) a la
vez; **~ a week** una vez a la semana; **~
more** otra vez; **~ and for all** de una vez
por todas; **~ upon a time** érase una vez; **I
knew him ~** le conocía hace tiempo.
oncoming ['ɔnkʌmɪŋ] *adj* (*traffic*) que viene
de frente.
OND *n abbr* (*BRIT*: = *Ordinary National
Diploma*) *título escolar.*

========================= *KEYWORD*

one [wʌn] *num* un(o)/una; **~ hundred and
fifty** ciento cincuenta; **~ by ~** uno a uno;
it's ~ (*o'clock*) es la una
♦ *adj* **1** (*sole*) único; **the ~ book which** el
único libro que; **the ~ man who** el único
que
2 (*same*) mismo/a; **they came in the ~ car**
vinieron en un solo coche
♦ *pron* **1**: **this ~** éste/ésta; **that ~** ése/ésa;
(*more remote*) aquél/aquélla; **I've already
got (a red) ~** ya tengo uno/a (rojo/a); **~ by
~** uno/a por uno/a; **to be ~ up on sb**
llevar ventaja a algn; **to be at ~ (with sb)**
estar completamente de acuerdo (con
algn)
2: **~ another** (*US*) nos; (*you*) os (*SP*); (*you:
polite, them*) se; **do you two ever see ~
another?** ¿os veis alguna vez? (*SP*), ¿se
ven alguna vez?; **the two boys didn't dare
look at ~ another** los dos chicos no se
atrevieron a mirarse (el uno al otro);
they all kissed ~ another se besaron unos
a otros
3 (*impers*): **~ never knows** nunca se sabe;
to cut ~'s finger cortarse el dedo; **~
needs to eat** hay que comer.

one-armed bandit ['wʌnɑːmd-] *n* máquina
tragaperras.
one-day excursion ['wʌndeɪ-] *n* (*US*)

billete *m* de ida y vuelta en un día.
One-hundred share index ['wʌnhʌndrəd-]
n índice *m* bursátil (*del Financial Times*).
one-man ['wʌn'mæn] *adj* (*business*)
individual.
one-man band *n* hombre-orquesta *m*.
one-off [wʌn'ɔf] *n* (*BRIT col: object*) artículo
único; (: *event*) caso especial.
one-parent family ['wʌnpɛərənt-] *n*
familia monoparental.
one-piece ['wʌnpiːs] *adj* (*bathing suit*) de
una pieza.
onerous ['ɔnərəs] *adj* (*task, duty*) pesado;
(*responsibility*) oneroso.
oneself [wʌn'sɛlf] *pron* uno mismo; (*after
prep, also emphatic*) sí (mismo/a); **to do
sth by ~** hacer algo solo *or* por sí solo.
one-shot [wʌn'ʃɔt] *n* (*US*) = **one-off**.
one-sided [wʌn'saɪdɪd] *adj* (*argument*)
parcial; (*decision, view*) unilateral; (*game,
contest*) desigual.
one-time ['wʌntaɪm] *adj* antiguo, ex-.
one-to-one ['wʌntəwʌn] *adj* (*relationship*)
individualizado.
one-upmanship [wʌn'ʌpmənʃɪp] *n*: **the art
of ~** el arte de quedar siempre por
encima.
one-way ['wʌnweɪ] *adj* (*street, traffic*) de
dirección única; (*ticket*) sencillo.
ongoing ['ɔngəʊɪŋ] *adj* continuo.
onion ['ʌnjən] *n* cebolla.
on line *adj, adv* (*COMPUT*) en línea; (*switched
on*) conectado.
onlooker ['ɔnlukə*] *n* espectador(a) *m/f*.
only ['əʊnlɪ] *adv* solamente, sólo, nomás
(*LAM*) ♦ *adj* único, solo ♦ *conj* solamente
que, pero; **an ~ child** un hijo único; **not ~
... but also...** no sólo ... sino también...; **I'd
be ~ too pleased to help** encantado de
ayudarles; **I saw her ~ yesterday** le vi
ayer mismo; **I would come, ~ I'm very
busy** iría, sólo que estoy muy atareado.
ono *abbr* (= *or nearest offer: in classified ads*)
abierto ofertas.
onset ['ɔnsɛt] *n* comienzo.
onshore ['ɔnʃɔː*] *adj* (*wind*) que sopla del
mar hacia la tierra.
onslaught ['ɔnslɔːt] *n* ataque *m*, embestida.
Ont. *abbr* (*Canada*) = Ontario.
on-the-job ['ɔnðə'dʒɔb] *adj*: **~ training**
formación *f* en el trabajo *or* sobre la
práctica.
onto ['ɔntu] *prep* = **on to**.
onus ['əʊnəs] *n* responsabilidad *f*; **the ~ is
upon him to prove it** le incumbe a él
demostrarlo.
onward(s) ['ɔnwəd(z)] *adv* (*move*) (hacia)
adelante.

onyx ['ɔnɪks] *n* ónice *m*, onyx *m*.
oops [ups] *excl* (*also:* ~**-a-daisy!**) ¡huy!
ooze [uːz] *vi* rezumar.
opal ['əʊpl] *n* ópalo.
opaque [əʊ'peɪk] *adj* opaco.
OPEC ['əʊpɛk] *n abbr* (= *Organization of
Petroleum-Exporting Countries*) OPEP
f.
open ['əʊpn] *adj* abierto; (*car*) descubierto;
(*road, view*) despejado; (*meeting*) público;
(*admiration*) manifiesto ♦ *vt* abrir ♦ *vi*
(*flower, eyes, door, debate*) abrirse; (*book
etc: commence*) comenzar; **in the ~ (air)** al
aire libre; **~ verdict** veredicto
inconcluso; **~ ticket** billete *m* sin fecha; **~
ground** (*among trees*) claro; (*waste
ground*) solar *m*; **to have an ~ mind (on
sth)** estar sin decidirse aún (sobre algo);
to ~ a bank account abrir una cuenta en
el banco.
▶**open on to** *vt fus* (*subj: room, door*) dar
a.
▶**open out** *vt* abrir ♦ *vi* (*person*) abrirse.
▶**open up** *vt* abrir; (*blocked road*) despejar
♦ *vi* abrirse.
open-and-shut ['əʊpənən'ʃʌt] *adj*: **~ case**
caso claro *or* evidente.
open day *n* (*BRIT*) jornada de puertas
abiertas *or* acceso público.
open-ended [əʊpn'ɛndɪd] *adj* (*fig*)
indefinido, sin definir.
opener ['əʊpnə*] *n* (*also*: **can ~, tin ~**)
abrelatas *m inv*.
open-heart surgery [əʊpn'hɑːt-] *n* cirugía
a corazón abierto.
opening ['əʊpnɪŋ] *n* abertura; (*beginning*)
comienzo; (*opportunity*) oportunidad *f*;
(*job*) puesto vacante, vacante *f*.
opening night *n* estreno.
open learning *n* enseñanza flexible a
tiempo parcial.
openly ['əʊpnlɪ] *adv* abiertamente.
open-minded [əʊpn'maɪndɪd] *adj* de
amplias miras, sin prejuicios.
open-necked ['əʊpnnɛkt] *adj* sin corbata.
openness ['əʊpnnɪs] *n* (*frankness*)
franqueza.
open-plan ['əʊpn'plæn] *adj* sin tabiques, de
plan abierto.
open prison *n* centro penitenciario de
régimen abierto.
open return *n* vuelta con fecha abierta.
open shop *n* empresa que contrata a
mano de obra no afiliada a ningún
sindicato.
Open University *n* (*BRIT*) ≈ Universidad *f*
Nacional de Enseñanza a Distancia,
UNED *f*; *ver recuadro*.

OPEN UNIVERSITY

La **Open University,** *fundada en 1969, está especializada en impartir cursos a distancia y a tiempo parcial con sus propios materiales de apoyo diseñados para tal fin, entre ellos programas de radio y televisión emitidos por la "BBC". Los trabajos se envían por correo y se complementan con la asistencia obligatoria a cursos de verano. Para obtener la licenciatura es necesario estudiar un mínimo de módulos y alcanzar un determinado número de créditos.*

opera ['ɔpərə] *n* ópera.
opera glasses *npl* gemelos *mpl.*
opera house *n* teatro de la ópera.
opera singer *n* cantante *m/f* de ópera.
operate ['ɔpəreɪt] *vt* (*machine*) hacer funcionar; (*company*) dirigir ♦ *vi* funcionar; (*drug*) hacer efecto; **to ~ on sb** (*MED*) operar a algn.
operatic [ɔpə'rætɪk] *adj* de ópera.
operating costs ['ɔpəreɪtɪŋ-] *npl* gastos *mpl* operacionales.
operating profit *n* beneficio de explotación.
operating room *n* (*US*) quirófano, sala de operaciones.
operating table *n* mesa de operaciones.
operating theatre *n* quirófano, sala de operaciones.
operation [ɔpə'reɪʃən] *n* (*gen*) operación *f;* (*of machine*) funcionamiento; **to be in ~** estar funcionando *or* en funcionamiento; **to have an ~** (*MED*) ser operado; **to have an ~ for** operarse de; **the company's ~s during the year** las actividades de la compañía durante el año.
operational [ɔpə'reɪʃənl] *adj* operacional, en buen estado; (*COMM*) en condiciones de servicio; (*ready for use or action*) en condiciones de funcionar.
operative ['ɔpərətɪv] *adj* (*measure*) en vigor; **the ~ word** la palabra clave.
operator ['ɔpəreɪtə*] *n* (*of machine*) operario/a; (*TEL*) operador(a) *m/f,* telefonista *m/f.*
operetta [ɔpə'retə] *n* opereta.
ophthalmic [ɔf'θælmɪk] *adj* oftálmico.
ophthalmologist [ɔfθæl'mɔlədʒɪst] *n* oftalmólogo/a.
opinion [ə'pɪnjən] *n* (*gen*) opinión *f;* **in my ~** en mi opinión, a mi juicio; **to seek a second ~** pedir una segunda opinión.
opinionated [ə'pɪnjəneɪtɪd] *adj* testarudo.
opinion poll *n* encuesta, sondeo.

opium ['əupɪəm] *n* opio.
opponent [ə'pəunənt] *n* adversario/a, contrincante *m/f.*
opportune ['ɔpətjuːn] *adj* oportuno.
opportunism [ɔpə'tjuːnɪzm] *n* oportunismo.
opportunist [ɔpə'tjuːnɪst] *n* oportunista *m/f.*
opportunity [ɔpə'tjuːnɪtɪ] *n* oportunidad *f,* chance *m or f* (*LAM*); **to take the ~ to do** *or* **of doing** aprovechar la ocasión para hacer.
oppose [ə'pəuz] *vt* oponerse a; **to be ~d to sth** oponerse a algo; **as ~d to** en vez de; (*unlike*) a diferencia de.
opposing [ə'pəuzɪŋ] *adj* (*side*) opuesto, contrario.
opposite ['ɔpəzɪt] *adj* opuesto, contrario; (*house etc*) de enfrente ♦ *adv* en frente ♦ *prep* en frente de, frente a ♦ *n* lo contrario; **the ~ sex** el otro sexo, el sexo opuesto.
opposite number *n* (*BRIT*) homólogo/a.
opposition [ɔpə'zɪʃən] *n* oposición *f.*
oppress [ə'pres] *vt* oprimir.
oppression [ə'preʃən] *n* opresión *f.*
oppressive [ə'presɪv] *adj* opresivo.
opprobrium [ə'prəubrɪəm] *n* (*formal*) oprobio.
opt [ɔpt] *vi:* **to ~ for** optar por; **to ~ to do** optar por hacer; **to ~ out** (*of NHS etc*) salirse.
optical ['ɔptɪkl] *adj* óptico.
optical character recognition/reader (OCR) *n* reconocimiento/lector *m* óptico de caracteres.
optical fibre *n* fibra óptica.
optician [ɔp'tɪʃən] *n* óptico *m/f.*
optics ['ɔptɪks] *n* óptica.
optimism ['ɔptɪmɪzəm] *n* optimismo.
optimist ['ɔptɪmɪst] *n* optimista *m/f.*
optimistic [ɔptɪ'mɪstɪk] *adj* optimista.
optimum ['ɔptɪməm] *adj* óptimo.
option ['ɔpʃən] *n* opción *f;* **to keep one's ~s open** (*fig*) mantener las opciones abiertas; **I have no ~** no tengo más *or* otro remedio.
optional ['ɔpʃənl] *adj* opcional; (*course*) optativo; **~ extras** opciones *fpl* extras.
opulence ['ɔpjuləns] *n* opulencia.
opulent ['ɔpjulənt] *adj* opulento.
OR *abbr* (*US*) = *Oregon.*
or [ɔː*] *conj* o; (*before o, ho*) u; (*with negative*): **he hasn't seen ~ heard anything** no ha visto ni oído nada; **~ else** si no; **let me go ~ I'll scream!** ¡suélteme, o me pongo a gritar!
oracle ['ɔrəkl] *n* oráculo.
oral ['ɔːrəl] *adj* oral ♦ *n* examen *m* oral.

orange ['ɒrɪndʒ] n (*fruit*) naranja ♦ adj (de color) naranja.

orangeade [ɒrɪndʒ'eɪd] n naranjada, refresco de naranja.

orange squash n zumo (*SP*) or jugo de naranja.

orang-outang, orang-utan [ɔ:'ræŋu:'tæn] n orangután m.

oration [ɔ:'reɪʃən] n discurso solemne; **funeral** ~ oración f fúnebre.

orator ['ɒrətə*] n orador(a) m/f.

orbit ['ɔ:bɪt] n órbita ♦ vt, vi orbitar; **to be in/go into** ~ **(round)** estar en/entrar en órbita (alrededor de).

orbital ['ɔ:bɪtl] n (*also:* ~ **motorway**) autopista de circunvalación.

orchard ['ɔ:tʃəd] n huerto; **apple** ~ manzanar m, manzanal m.

orchestra ['ɔ:kɪstrə] n orquesta; (*US: seating*) platea.

orchestral [ɔ:'kɛstrəl] adj de orquesta.

orchestrate ['ɔ:kɪstreɪt] vt (*MUS*, *fig*) orquestar.

orchid ['ɔ:kɪd] n orquídea.

ordain [ɔ:'deɪn] vt (*also REL*) ordenar.

ordeal [ɔ:'di:l] n experiencia terrible.

order ['ɔ:də*] n orden m; (*command*) orden f; (*type, kind*) clase f; (*state*) estado; (*COMM*) pedido, encargo ♦ vt (*also:* **put in** ~) ordenar, poner en orden; (*COMM*) encargar, pedir; (*command*) mandar, ordenar; **in** ~ (*gen*) en orden; (*of document*) en regla; **in (working)** ~ en funcionamiento; **to be out of** ~ (*machine, toilets*) estar estropeado or descompuesto (*LAM*); **in** ~ **to do** para hacer; **in** ~ **that** para que + subj; **on** ~ (*COMM*) pedido; **to be on** ~ estar pedido; **we are under** ~**s to do it** tenemos orden de hacerlo; **a point of** ~ una cuestión de procedimiento; **to place an** ~ **for sth with sb** hacer un pedido de algo a algn; **made to** ~ hecho a la medida; **his income is of the** ~ **of £24,000 per year** sus ingresos son del orden de 24 mil libras al año; **to the** ~ **of** (*BANKING*) a la orden de; **to** ~ **sb to do sth** mandar a algn hacer algo.

order book n cartera de pedidos.

order form n hoja de pedido.

orderly ['ɔ:dəlɪ] n (*MIL*) ordenanza m; (*MED*) auxiliar m/f (de hospital) ♦ adj ordenado.

orderly officer m (*MIL*) oficial m del día.

order number n número de pedido.

ordinal ['ɔ:dɪnl] adj ordinal.

ordinarily ['ɔ:dnrɪlɪ] adv por lo común.

ordinary ['ɔ:dnrɪ] adj corriente, normal; (*pej*) común y corriente; **out of the** ~ fuera de lo común, extraordinario.

ordinary degree n (*BRIT*) diploma m; *ver* recuadro.

ORDINARY DEGREE

Después de tres años de estudios, algunos universitarios obtienen la titulación de **ordinary degree**. *Esto ocurre en el caso poco frecuente de que no aprueben los exámenes que conducen al título de "honours degree" pero sus examinadores consideren que a lo largo de la carrera han logrado unos resultados mínimos satisfactorios. También es una opción que tienen los estudiantes de las universidades escocesas no interesados en estudiar en la universidad más de tres años.*

---

ordinary shares npl acciones fpl ordinarias.

ordination [ɔ:dɪ'neɪʃən] n ordenación f.

ordnance ['ɔ:dnəns] n (*MIL: unit*) artillería.

ordnance factory n fábrica de artillería.

Ordnance Survey n (*BRIT*) servicio oficial de topografía y cartografía.

ore [ɔ:*] n mineral m.

Ore(g). abbr (*US*) = Oregon.

organ ['ɔ:gən] n órgano.

organic [ɔ:'gænɪk] adj orgánico; (*vegetables, produce*) biológico.

organism ['ɔ:gənɪzəm] n organismo.

organist ['ɔ:gənɪst] n organista m/f.

organization [ɔ:gənaɪ'zeɪʃən] n organización f.

organize ['ɔ:gənaɪz] vt organizar; **to get** ~**d** organizarse.

organized crime n crimen organizado.

organizer ['ɔ:gənaɪzə*] n organizador(a) m/f.

orgasm ['ɔ:gæzəm] n orgasmo.

orgy ['ɔ:dʒɪ] n orgía.

Orient ['ɔ:rɪənt] n Oriente m.

oriental [ɔ:rɪ'ɛntl] adj oriental.

orientate ['ɔ:rɪənteɪt] vt orientar.

origin ['ɒrɪdʒɪn] n origen m; (*point of departure*) procedencia.

original [ə'rɪdʒɪnl] adj original; (*first*) primero; (*earlier*) primitivo ♦ n original m.

originality [ərɪdʒɪ'nælɪtɪ] n originalidad f.

originally [ə'rɪdʒɪnəlɪ] adv (*at first*) al principio; (*with originality*) con originalidad.

originate [ə'rɪdʒɪneɪt] vi: **to** ~ **from, to** ~ **in** surgir de, tener su origen en.

originator [ə'rɪdʒɪneɪtə*] n inventor(a) m/f, autor(a) m/f.

Orkneys ['ɔ:knɪz] npl: **the** ~ (*also:* **the Orkney Islands**) las Orcadas.

ornament ['ɔːnəmənt] *n* adorno.
ornamental [ɔːnə'mɛntl] *adj* decorativo, de adorno.
ornamentation [ɔːnəmen'teɪʃən] *n* ornamentación *f*.
ornate [ɔː'neɪt] *adj* recargado.
ornithologist [ɔːnɪ'θɔlədʒɪst] *n* ornitólogo/a.
ornithology [ɔːnɪ'θɔlədʒɪ] *n* ornitología.
orphan ['ɔːfn] *n* huérfano/a ♦ *vt*: **to be** ~**ed** quedar huérfano/a.
orphanage ['ɔːfənɪdʒ] *n* orfanato.
orthodox ['ɔːθədɔks] *adj* ortodoxo.
orthodoxy ['ɔːθədɔksɪ] *n* ortodoxia.
orthopaedic, (*US*) **orthopedic** [ɔːθə'piːdɪk] *adj* ortopédico.
orthop(a)edics [ɔːθə'piːdɪks] *n* ortopedia.
OS *abbr* (*BRIT*: = *Ordnance Survey*) *servicio oficial de topografía y cartografía*; (: *NAUT*) = **ordinary seaman;** (: *DRESS*) = **outsize.**
O/S *abbr* = **out of stock.**
Oscar ['ɔskə*] *n* óscar *m*.
oscillate ['ɔsɪleɪt] *vi* oscilar; (*person*) vacilar.
oscillation [ɔsɪ'leɪʃən] *n* oscilación *f*; (*of prices*) fluctuación *f*.
OSHA *n abbr* (*US*: = *Occupational Safety and Health Administration*) *oficina de la higiene y la seguridad en el trabajo*.
Oslo ['ɔzləu] *n* Oslo.
ostensible [ɔs'tɛnsɪbl] *adj* aparente.
ostensibly [ɔs'tɛnsɪblɪ] *adv* aparentemente.
ostentatious [ɔstɛn'teɪʃəs] *adj* pretencioso, aparatoso; (*person*) ostentativo.
osteopath ['ɔstɪəpæθ] *n* osteópata *m/f*.
ostracize ['ɔstrəsaɪz] *vt* hacer el vacío a.
ostrich ['ɔstrɪtʃ] *n* avestruz *m*.
OT *n abbr* (= *Old Testament*) A.T. *m*.
OTB *n abbr* (*US*: = *off-track betting*) *apuestas hechas fuera del hipódromo*.
O.T.E. *abbr* (= *on-target earnings*) *beneficios según objetivos*.
other ['ʌðə*] *adj* otro ♦ *pron*: **the** ~ (*one*) el/la otro/a; ~**s** (~ *people*) otros; ~ **than** (*apart from*) aparte de; **the** ~ **day** el otro día; **some** ~ **people have still to arrive** quedan por llegar otros; **some actor or** ~ un actor cualquiera; **somebody or** ~ alguien, alguno; **it was no** ~ **than the bishop** no era otro que el obispo.
otherwise ['ʌðəwaɪz] *adv, conj* de otra manera; (*if not*) si no; **an** ~ **good piece of work** un trabajo que, quitando eso, es bueno.
OTT *abbr* (*col*) = **over the top;** *see* **top.**
otter ['ɔtə*] *n* nutria.
OU *n abbr* (*BRIT*) = **Open University.**

ouch [autʃ] *excl* ¡ay!
ought [ɔːt] *pt* **ought** [ɔːt] *aux vb*: **I** ~ **to do it** debería hacerlo; **this** ~ **to have been corrected** esto debiera de haberse corregido; **he** ~ **to win** (*probability*) debiera ganar; **you** ~ **to go and see it** vale la pena ir a verlo.
ounce [auns] *n* onza (*28.35g; 16 in a pound*).
our ['auə*] *adj* nuestro; *see also* **my.**
ours ['auəz] *pron* (el) nuestro/(la) nuestra *etc*; *see also* **mine.**
ourselves [auə'sɛlvz] *pron pl* (*reflexive, after prep*) nosotros; (*emphatic*) nosotros mismos; **we did it (all) by** ~ lo hicimos nosotros solos; *see also* **oneself.**
oust [aust] *vt* desalojar.
out [aut] *adv* fuera, afuera; (*not at home*) fuera (de casa); (*light, fire*) apagado; (*on strike*) en huelga ♦ *vt*: **to** ~ **sb** revelar públicamente la homosexualidad de algn; ~ **there** allí (fuera); **he's** ~ (*absent*) no está, ha salido; **to be** ~ **in one's calculations** equivocarse (en sus cálculos); **to run** ~ salir corriendo; ~ **loud** en alta voz; ~ **of** *prep* (*outside*) fuera de; (*because of*: *anger etc*) por; **to look** ~ **of the window** mirar por la ventana; **to drink** ~ **of a cup** beber de una taza; **made** ~ **of wood** de madera; ~ **of petrol** sin gasolina; "~ **of order**" "no funciona"; **it's** ~ **of stock** (*COMM*) está agotado; **to be** ~ **and about again** estar repuesto y levantado; **the journey** ~ el viaje de ida; **the boat was 10 km** ~ el barco estaba a diez kilómetros de la costa; **before the week was** ~ antes del fin de la semana; **he's** ~ **for all he can get** busca sus propios fines, anda detrás de lo suyo.
out-and-out ['autəndaut] *adj* (*liar, thief etc*) redomado, empedernido.
outback ['autbæk] *n* interior *m*.
outbid [aut'bɪd] *vt* pujar más alto que, sobrepujar.
outboard ['autbɔːd] *adj*: ~ **motor** (motor *m*) fuera borda *m*.
outbound ['autbaund] *adj*: ~ **from/for** con salida de/hacia.
outbreak ['autbreɪk] *n* (*of war*) comienzo, (*of disease*) epidemia; (*of violence etc*) ola.
outbuilding ['autbɪldɪŋ] *n* dependencia; (*shed*) cobertizo.
outburst ['autbəːst] *n* explosión *f*, arranque *m*.
outcast ['autkɑːst] *n* paria *m/f*.
outclass [aut'klɑːs] *vt* aventajar, superar.
outcome ['autkʌm] *n* resultado.
outcrop ['autkrɔp] *n* (*of rock*) afloramiento.
outcry ['autkraɪ] *n* protestas *fpl*.

outdated [aut'deɪtɪd] *adj* anticuado.
outdistance [aut'dɪstəns] *vt* dejar atrás.
outdo [aut'duː] *vt* (*irreg: like* **do**) superar.
outdoor [aut'dɔː*] *adj* al aire libre.
outdoors [aut'dɔːz] *adv* al aire libre.
outer ['autə*] *adj* exterior, externo.
outer space *n* espacio exterior.
outfit ['autfɪt] *n* equipo; (*clothes*) traje *m*; (*col: organization*) grupo, organización *f*.
outfitter's ['autfɪtəz] *n* (*BRIT*) sastrería.
outgoing ['autgəʊɪŋ] *adj* (*president, tenant*) saliente; (*means of transport*) que sale; (*character*) extrovertido.
outgoings ['autgəʊɪŋz] *npl* (*BRIT*) gastos *mpl*.
outgrow [aut'grəʊ] *vt*: (*irreg: like* **grow**) **he has ~n his clothes** su ropa le queda pequeña ya.
outhouse ['authaus] *n* dependencia.
outing ['autɪŋ] *n* excursión *f*, paseo.
outlandish [aut'lændɪʃ] *adj* estrafalario.
outlast [aut'lɑːst] *vt* durar más tiempo que, sobrevivir a.
outlaw ['autlɔː] *n* proscrito/a ♦ *vt* (*person*) declarar fuera de la ley; (*practice*) declarar ilegal.
outlay ['autleɪ] *n* inversión *f*.
outlet ['autlet] *n* salida; (*of pipe*) desagüe *m*; (*US ELEC*) toma de corriente; (*for emotion*) desahogo; (*also: retail ~*) punto de venta.
outline ['autlaɪn] *n* (*shape*) contorno, perfil *m*; **in ~** (*fig*) a grandes rasgos.
outlive [aut'lɪv] *vt* sobrevivir a.
outlook ['autluk] *n* perspectiva; (*opinion*) punto de vista.
outlying ['autlaɪɪŋ] *adj* remoto, aislado.
outmanoeuvre, (*US*) **outmaneuver** [autmə'nuːvə*] *vt* (*MIL, fig*) superar en la estrategia.
outmoded [aut'məʊdɪd] *adj* anticuado, pasado de moda.
outnumber [aut'nʌmbə*] *vt* exceder *or* superar en número.
out of bounds [autəv'baundz] *adj*: **it's ~** está prohibido el paso.
out-of-court [autəv'kɔːt] *adj, adv* sin ir a juicio.
out-of-date [autəv'deɪt] *adj* (*passport*) caducado, vencido; (*theory, idea*) anticuado; (*clothes, customs*) pasado de moda.
out-of-doors [autəv'dɔːz] *adv* al aire libre.
out-of-the-way [autəvðə'weɪ] *adj* (*remote*) apartado; (*unusual*) poco común *or* corriente.
out-of-touch [autəv'tʌtʃ] *adj*: **to be ~** estar desconectado.
outpatient ['autpeɪʃənt] *n* paciente *m/f* externo/a.

outpost ['autpəust] *n* puesto avanzado.
outpouring ['autpɔːrɪŋ] *n* (*fig*) efusión *f*.
output ['autput] *n* (*volumen m de*) producción *f*, rendimiento; (*COMPUT*) salida ♦ *vt* (*COMPUT: to power*) imprimir.
outrage ['autreɪdʒ] *n* (*scandal*) escándalo; (*atrocity*) atrocidad *f* ♦ *vt* ultrajar.
outrageous [aut'reɪdʒəs] *adj* (*clothes*) extravagante; (*behaviour*) escandaloso.
outright [aut'raɪt] *adv* (*win*) de manera absoluta; (*be killed*) en el acto; (*ask*) abiertamente; (*completely*) completamente ♦ *adj* ['autraɪt] completo; (*winner*) absoluto; (*refusal*) rotundo.
outrun [aut'rʌn] *vt* (*irreg: like* **run**) correr más que, dejar atrás.
outset ['autset] *n* principio.
outshine [aut'ʃaɪn] *vt* (*irreg: like* **shine**) (*fig*) eclipsar, brillar más que.
outside [aut'saɪd] *n* exterior *m* ♦ *adj* exterior, externo ♦ *adv* fuera, afuera (*esp LAM*) ♦ *prep* fuera de; (*beyond*) más allá de; **at the ~** (*fig*) a lo sumo; **an ~ chance** una posibilidad remota; **~ left/right** (*FOOTBALL*) extremo izquierdo/derecho.
outside broadcast *n* (*RADIO, TV*) emisión *f* exterior.
outside contractor *n* contratista *m/f* independiente.
outside lane *n* (*AUT*) carril *m* de adelantamiento.
outside line *n* (*TEL*) línea (exterior).
outsider [aut'saɪdə*] *n* (*stranger*) forastero.
outsize ['autsaɪz] *adj* (*clothes*) de talla grande.
outskirts ['autskɜːts] *npl* alrededores *mpl*, afueras *fpl*.
outsmart [aut'smɑːt] *vt* ser más listo que.
outspoken [aut'spəʊkən] *adj* muy franco.
outspread [aut'spred] *adj* extendido; (*wings*) desplegado.
outstanding [aut'stændɪŋ] *adj* excepcional, destacado; (*unfinished*) pendiente.
outstay [aut'steɪ] *vt*: **to ~ one's welcome** quedarse más de la cuenta.
outstretched [aut'stretʃt] *adj* (*arm*) extendido.
outstrip [aut'strɪp] *vt* (*competitors, demand, also fig*) dejar atrás, aventajar.
out-tray ['auttreɪ] *n* bandeja de salida.
outvote [aut'vəut] *vt*: **it was ~d (by ...)** fue rechazado en el voto (por ...).
outward ['autwəd] *adj* (*sign, appearances*) externo; (*journey*) de ida.
outwardly ['autwədlɪ] *adv* por fuera.
outweigh [aut'weɪ] *vt* pesar más que.
outwit [aut'wɪt] *vt* ser más listo que.

outworn [aut'wɔːn] adj (expression) cansado.

oval ['əuvl] adj ovalado ♦ n óvalo.

ovarian [əu'vɛəriən] adj ovárico; (cancer) de ovario.

ovary ['əuvəri] n ovario.

ovation [əu'veiʃən] n ovación f.

oven ['ʌvn] n horno.

ovenproof ['ʌvnpruːf] adj refractario, resistente al horno.

oven-ready ['ʌvnrɛdɪ] adj listo para el horno.

ovenware ['ʌvnwɛə*] n artículos mpl para el horno.

over ['əuvə*] adv encima, por encima ♦ adj (or adv) (finished) terminado; (surplus) de sobra; (excessively) demasiado ♦ prep (por) encima de; (above) sobre; (on the other side of) al otro lado de; (more than) más de; (during) durante; (about, concerning): **they fell out ~ money** riñeron por una cuestión de dinero; **~ here** (por) aquí; **~ there** (por) allí or allá; **all ~** (everywhere) por todas partes; **~ and ~** (again) una y otra vez; **~ and above** además de; **to ask sb ~** invitar a algn a casa; **to bend ~** inclinarse; **now ~ to our Paris correspondent** damos la palabra a nuestro corresponsal de París; **the world ~** en todo el mundo, en el mundo entero; **she's not ~ intelligent** no es muy lista que digamos.

over ... [əuvə*] pref sobre..., super....

overact [əuvər'ækt] vi (THEAT) exagerar el papel.

overall ['əuvərɔːl] adj (length) total; (study) de conjunto ♦ adv [əuvər'ɔːl] en conjunto ♦ n (BRIT) guardapolvo; **~s** npl mono sg, overol msg (LAM).

overall majority n mayoría absoluta.

overanxious [əuvər'æŋkʃəs] adj demasiado preocupado or ansioso.

overawe [əuvər'ɔː] vt intimidar.

overbalance [əuvə'bæləns] vi perder el equilibrio.

overbearing [əuvə'bɛəriŋ] adj autoritario, imperioso.

overboard ['əuvəbɔːd] adv (NAUT) por la borda; **to go ~ for sth** (fig) enloquecer por algo.

overbook [əuvə'buk] vt sobrereservar, reservar con exceso.

overcapitalize [əuvə'kæpɪtəlaɪz] vi sobrecapitalizar.

overcast ['əuvəkɑːst] adj encapotado.

overcharge [əuvə'tʃɑːdʒ] vt: **to ~ sb** cobrar un precio excesivo a algn.

overcoat ['əuvəkəut] n abrigo.

overcome [əuvə'kʌm] vt (irreg: like come) (gen) vencer; (difficulty) superar; **she was quite ~ by the occasion** la ocasión le conmovió mucho.

overconfident [əuvə'kɒnfɪdənt] adj demasiado confiado.

overcrowded [əuvə'kraudɪd] adj atestado de gente; (city, country) superpoblado.

overcrowding [əuvə'kraudɪŋ] n (in town, country) superpoblación f; (in bus etc) hacinamiento, apiñamiento.

overdo [əuvə'duː] vt (irreg: like do) exagerar; (overcook) cocer demasiado; **to ~ it, to ~ things** (work too hard) trabajar demasiado.

overdose ['əuvədəus] n sobredosis f inv.

overdraft ['əuvədrɑːft] n saldo deudor.

overdrawn [əuvə'drɔːn] adj (account) en descubierto.

overdrive ['əuvədraɪv] n (AUT) sobremarcha, superdirecta.

overdue [əuvə'djuː] adj retrasado; (recognition) tardío; (bill) vencido y no pagado; **that change was long ~** ese cambio tenía que haberse hecho hace tiempo.

overemphasis [əuvər'ɛmfəsɪs] n: **to put an ~ on** poner énfasis excesivo en.

overenthusiastic ['əuvərənθuːzɪ'æstɪk] adj demasiado entusiasta.

overestimate [əuvər'ɛstɪmeɪt] vt sobreestimar.

overexcited [əuvərɪk'saɪtɪd] adj sobreexcitado.

overexertion [əuvərɪg'zəːʃən] n agotamiento, fatiga.

overexpose [əuvərɪk'spəuz] vt (PHOT) sobreexponer.

overflow [əuvə'fləu] vi desbordarse ♦ n ['əuvəfləu] (excess) exceso; (of river) desbordamiento; (also: ~ pipe) (cañería de) desagüe m.

overfly [əuvə'flaɪ] vt (irreg: like fly) sobrevolar.

overgenerous [əuvə'dʒɛnərəs] adj demasiado generoso.

overgrown [əuvə'grəun] adj (garden) cubierto de hierba; **he's just an ~ schoolboy** es un niño en grande.

overhang [əuvə'hæŋ] (irreg: like hang) vt sobresalir por encima de ♦ vi sobresalir.

overhaul vt [əuvə'hɔːl] revisar, repasar ♦ n ['əuvəhɔːl] revisión f.

overhead adv [əuvə'hɛd] por arriba or encima ♦ adj ['əuvəhɛd] (cable) aéreo; (railway) elevado, aéreo ♦ n ['əuvəhɛd] (US) = **overheads**.

overheads ['əuvəhɛdz] *npl* (*BRIT*) gastos *mpl* generales.

overhear [əuvə'hɪə*] *vt* (*irreg: like* **hear**) oír por casualidad.

overheat [əuvə'hiːt] *vi* (*engine*) recalentarse.

overjoyed [əuvə'dʒɔɪd] *adj* encantado, lleno de alegría.

overkill ['əuvəkɪl] *n* (*MIL*) capacidad *f* excesiva de destrucción; (*fig*) exceso.

overland ['əuvələnd] *adj, adv* por tierra.

overlap *vi* [əuvə'læp] superponerse ♦ *n* ['əuvəlæp] superposición *f*.

overleaf [əuvə'liːf] *adv* al dorso.

overload [əuvə'ləud] *vt* sobrecargar.

overlook [əuvə'luk] *vt* (*have view of*) dar a, tener vistas a; (*miss*) pasar por alto; (*forgive*) hacer la vista gorda a.

overlord ['əuvəlɔːd] *n* señor *m*.

overmanning [əuvə'mænɪŋ] *n* exceso de mano de obra; (*in organization*) exceso de personal.

overnight [əuvə'naɪt] *adv* durante la noche; (*fig*) de la noche a la mañana ♦ *adj* de noche; **to stay** ~ pasar la noche.

overnight bag *n* fin *m* de semana, neceser *m* de viaje.

overnight stay *n* estancia de una noche.

overpass ['əuvəpɑːs] *n* (*US*) paso elevado *or* a desnivel.

overpay [əuvə'peɪ] *vt*: **to** ~ **sb by £50** pagar 50 libras de más a algn.

overplay [əuvə'pleɪ] *vt* exagerar; **to** ~ **one's hand** desmedirse.

overpower [əuvə'pauə*] *vt* dominar; (*fig*) embargar.

overpowering [əuvə'pauərɪŋ] *adj* (*heat*) agobiante; (*smell*) penetrante.

overproduction [əuvəprə'dʌkʃən] *n* superproducción *f*.

overrate [əuvə'reɪt] *vt* sobrevalorar.

overreach [əuvə'riːtʃ] *vt*: **to** ~ **o.s.** ir demasiado lejos, pasarse.

override [əuvə'raɪd] *vt* (*irreg: like* **ride**) (*order, objection*) no hacer caso de.

overriding [əuvə'raɪdɪŋ] *adj* predominante.

overrule [əuvə'ruːl] *vt* (*decision*) anular; (*claim*) denegar.

overrun [əuvə'rʌn] *vt* (*irreg: like* **run**) (*MIL: country*) invadir; (*time limit*) rebasar, exceder ♦ *vi* rebasar el límite previsto; **the town is** ~ **with tourists** el pueblo está inundado de turistas.

overseas [əuvə'siːz] *adv* en ultramar; (*abroad*) en el extranjero ♦ *adj* (*trade*) exterior; (*visitor*) extranjero.

oversee [əuvə'siː] *vt* supervisar.

overseer ['əuvəsɪə*] *n* (*in factory*)

supervisor(a) *m/f*; (*foreman*) capataz *m*.

overshadow [əuvə'ʃædəu] *vt* (*fig*) eclipsar.

overshoot [əuvə'ʃuːt] *vt* (*irreg: like* **shoot**) excederse.

oversight ['əuvəsaɪt] *n* descuido; **due to an** ~ a causa de un descuido *or* una equivocación.

oversimplify [əuvə'sɪmplɪfaɪ] *vt* simplificar demasiado.

oversleep [əuvə'sliːp] *vi* (*irreg: like* **sleep**) dormir más de la cuenta, no despertarse a tiempo.

overspend [əuvə'spɛnd] *vi* gastar más de la cuenta; **we have overspent by 5 dollars** hemos excedido el presupuesto en 5 dólares.

overspill ['əuvəspɪl] *n* exceso de población.

overstaffed [əuvə'stɑːft] *adj*: **to be** ~ tener exceso de plantilla.

overstate [əuvə'steɪt] *vt* exagerar.

overstatement ['əuvəsteɪtmənt] *n* exageración *f*.

overstay [əuvə'steɪ] *vt*: **to** ~ **one's time** *or* **welcome** quedarse más de lo conveniente.

overstep [əuvə'stɛp] *vt*: **to** ~ **the mark** *or* **the limits** pasarse de la raya.

overstock [əuvə'stɔk] *vt* abarrotar.

overstretched [əuvə'strɛtʃt] *adj* utilizado por encima de su capacidad.

overstrike *n* ['əuvəstraɪk] (*on printer*) superposición *f* ♦ *vt* (*irreg: like* **strike**) [əuvə'straɪk] superponer.

oversubscribed [əuvəsəb'skraɪbd] *adj* suscrito en exceso.

overt [əu'vəːt] *adj* abierto.

overtake [əuvə'teɪk] *vt* (*irreg: like* **take**) sobrepasar; (*BRIT AUT*) adelantar.

overtax [əuvə'tæks] *vt* (*ECON*) exigir contribuciones *fpl* excesivas *or* impuestos *mpl* excesivos a; (*fig: strength, patience*) agotar, abusar de; **to** ~ **o.s.** fatigarse demasiado.

overthrow [əuvə'θrəu] *vt* (*irreg: like* **throw**) (*government*) derrocar.

overtime ['əuvətaɪm] *n* horas *fpl* extraordinarias; **to do** *or* **work** ~ hacer *or* trabajar horas extraordinarias *or* extras.

overtime ban *n* prohibición *f* de (hacer) horas extraordinarias.

overtone ['əuvətəun] *n* (*fig*) tono.

overture ['əuvətʃuə*] *n* (*MUS*) obertura; (*fig*) propuesta.

overturn [əuvə'təːn] *vt, vi* volcar.

overview ['əuvəvjuː] *n* visión *f* de conjunto.

overweight [əuvə'weɪt] *adj* demasiado

gordo or pesado.

overwhelm [əuvə'wɛlm] vt aplastar.

overwhelming [əuvə'wɛlmɪŋ] adj (victory, defeat) arrollador(a); (desire) irresistible; one's ~ impression is of heat lo que más impresiona es el calor.

overwhelmingly [əuvə'wɛlmɪŋlɪ] adv abrumadoramente.

overwork [əuvə'wəːk] n trabajo excesivo ♦ vt hacer trabajar demasiado ♦ vi trabajar demasiado.

overwrite [əuvə'raɪt] vt (irreg: like **write**) (COMPUT) sobreescribir.

ovulation [ɔvju'leɪʃən] n ovulación f.

owe [əu] vt deber; **to ~ sb sth, to ~ sth to sb** deber algo a algn.

owing to ['əuɪŋtuː] prep debido a, por causa de.

owl [aul] n (long-eared ~) búho; (barn ~) lechuza.

own [əun] vt tener, poseer ♦ vi: **to ~ to sth/ to having done sth** confesar or reconocer algo/haber hecho algo ♦ adj propio; **a room of my ~** mi propia habitación; **to get one's ~ back** tomarse la revancha; **on one's ~** solo, a solas; **can I have it for my (very)** ~? ¿puedo quedarme con él?; **to come into one's ~** llegar a realizarse.

▶**own up** vi confesar.

own brand n (COMM) marca propia.

owner ['əunə*] n dueño/a.

owner-occupier ['əunər'ɔkjupaɪə*] n ocupante propietario/a m/f.

ownership ['əunəʃɪp] n posesión f; **it's under new** ~ está bajo nueva dirección.

own goal n (SPORT) autogol m; **to score an** ~ marcar un gol en propia puerta, marcar un autogol.

ox, pl **oxen** [ɔks, 'ɔksn] n buey m.

Oxbridge ['ɔksbrɪdʒ] n (BRIT) universidades de Oxford y Cambridge; ver recuadro.

OXBRIDGE

El término **Oxbridge** es una fusión de Ox(ford) y (Cam)bridge, las dos universidades británicas más antiguas y con mayor prestigio académico y social. Muchos miembros destacados de la clase dirigente del país son antiguos alumnos de una de las dos. El mismo término suele aplicarse a todo lo que ambas representan en cuestión de prestigio y privilegios sociales.

Oxfam ['ɔksfæm] n abbr (BRIT: = Oxford Committee for Famine Relief) OXFAM.

oxide ['ɔksaɪd] n óxido.

Oxon. ['ɔksn] abbr (BRIT: =Oxoniensis) = of Oxford.

oxtail ['ɔksteɪl] n: ~ **soup** sopa de rabo de buey.

oxygen ['ɔksɪdʒən] n oxígeno.

oxygen mask n máscara de oxígeno.

oxygen tent n tienda de oxígeno.

oyster ['ɔɪstə*] n ostra.

oz. abbr = **ounce(s)**.

ozone ['əuzəun] n ozono; ~ **layer** capa de ozono.

P p

P, p [piː] n (letter) P, p f; **P for Peter** P de París.

P abbr = **president, prince**.

p abbr (= page) pág.; (BRIT) = **penny, pence**.

PA n abbr see **personal assistant, public address system** ♦ abbr (US) = Pennsylvania.

pa [paː] n (col) papá m.

p.a. abbr = **per annum**.

PAC n abbr (US) = political action committee.

pace [peɪs] n paso; (rhythm) ritmo ♦ vi: **to ~ up and down** pasearse de un lado a otro; **to keep ~ with** llevar el mismo paso que; (events) mantenerse a la altura de or al corriente de; **to set the ~** (running) marcar el paso; (fig) marcar la pauta; **to put sb through his ~s** (fig) poner a algn a prueba.

pacemaker ['peɪsmeɪkə*] n (MED) marcapasos m inv.

pacific [pə'sɪfɪk] adj pacífico ♦ n: **the P~ (Ocean)** el (Océano) Pacífico.

pacification [pæsɪfɪ'keɪʃən] n pacificación f.

pacifier ['pæsɪfaɪə*] n (US: dummy) chupete m.

pacifism ['pæsɪfɪzəm] n pacifismo.

pacifist ['pæsɪfɪst] n pacifista m/f.

pacify ['pæsɪfaɪ] vt (soothe) apaciguar; (country) pacificar.

pack [pæk] n (packet) paquete m; (COMM) embalaje m; (of hounds) jauría; (of wolves) manada; (of thieves etc) banda; (of cards) baraja; (bundle) fardo; (US: of cigarettes) paquete m, cajetilla ♦ vt (wrap) empaquetar; (fill) llenar; (in suitcase etc) meter, poner; (cram) llenar, atestar; (fig: meeting etc) llenar de partidarios; (COMPUT) comprimir; **to ~ (one's bags)**

hacer las maletas; **to ~ sb off** despachar a algn; **the place was ~ed** el local estaba (lleno) hasta los topes; **to send sb ~ing** (*col*) echar a algn con cajas destempladas.

▶**pack in** *vi* (*break down: watch, car*) estropearse ♦ *vt* (*col*) dejar; **~ it in!** ¡para!, ¡basta ya!

▶**pack up** *vi* (*col: machine*) estropearse; (*person*) irse ♦ *vt* (*belongings, clothes*) recoger; (*goods, presents*) empaquetar, envolver.

package ['pækɪdʒ] *n* paquete *m*; (*bulky*) bulto; (*also:* **~ deal**) acuerdo global ♦ *vt* (*COMM: goods*) envasar, embalar.

package holiday *n* viaje *m* organizado (con todo incluido).

package tour *n* viaje *m* organizado.

packaging ['pækɪdʒɪŋ] *n* envase *m*.

packed lunch [pækt-] *n* almuerzo frío.

packer ['pækə*] *n* (*person*) empacador(a) *m/f*.

packet ['pækɪt] *n* paquete *m*.

packet switching [-'swɪtʃɪŋ] *n* (*COMPUT*) conmutación *f* por paquetes.

packhorse ['pækhɔːs] *n* caballo de carga.

pack ice *n* banco de hielo.

packing ['pækɪŋ] *n* embalaje *m*.

packing case *n* cajón *m* de embalaje.

pact [pækt] *n* pacto.

pad [pæd] *n* (*of paper*) bloc *m*; (*cushion*) cojinete *m*; (*launching ~*) plataforma (de lanzamiento); (*col: flat*) casa ♦ *vt* rellenar.

padded cell ['pædɪd-] *n* celda acolchada.

padding ['pædɪŋ] *n* relleno; (*fig*) paja.

paddle ['pædl] *n* (*oar*) canalete *m*, pala; (*US: for table tennis*) pala ♦ *vt* remar ♦ *vi* (*with feet*) chapotear.

paddle steamer *n* vapor *m* de ruedas.

paddling pool ['pædlɪŋ-] *n* (*BRIT*) piscina para niños.

paddock ['pædək] *n* (*field*) potrero.

paddy field ['pædɪ-] *n* arrozal *m*.

padlock ['pædlɔk] *n* candado ♦ *vt* cerrar con candado.

padre ['pɑːdrɪ] *n* capellán *m*.

paediatrician, (*US*) **pediatrician** [piːdɪə'trɪʃən] *n* pediatra *m/f*.

paediatrics, (*US*) **pediatrics** [piːdɪ'ætrɪks] *n* pediatría.

paedophile, (*US*) **pedophile** ['piːdəufaɪl] *adj* de pedófilo ♦ *n* pedófilo/a.

pagan ['peɪɡən] *adj, n* pagano/a *m/f*.

page [peɪdʒ] *n* página; (*also:* **~ boy**) paje *m* ♦ *vt* (*in hotel etc*) llamar por altavoz a.

pageant ['pædʒənt] *n* (*procession*) desfile *m*; (*show*) espectáculo.

pageantry ['pædʒəntrɪ] *n* pompa.

page break *n* límite *m* de la página.

pager ['peɪdʒə*] *n* busca *m*.

paginate ['pædʒɪneɪt] *vt* paginar.

pagination [pædʒɪ'neɪʃən] *n* paginación *f*.

pagoda [pə'ɡəudə] *n* pagoda.

paid [peɪd] *pt, pp of* **pay** ♦ *adj* (*work*) remunerado; (*official*) asalariado; **to put ~ to** (*BRIT*) acabar con.

paid-up ['peɪdʌp], (*US*) **paid-in** ['peɪdɪn] *adj* (*member*) con sus cuotas pagadas *or* al día; (*share*) liberado; **~ capital** capital *m* desembolsado.

pail [peɪl] *n* cubo, balde *m*.

pain [peɪn] *n* dolor *m*; **to be in ~** sufrir; **on ~ of death** so *or* bajo pena de muerte; *see also* **pains**.

pained [peɪnd] *adj* (*expression*) afligido.

painful ['peɪnful] *adj* doloroso; (*difficult*) penoso; (*disagreeable*) desagradable.

painfully ['peɪnfəlɪ] *adv* (*fig: very*) terriblemente.

painkiller ['peɪnkɪlə*] *n* analgésico.

painless ['peɪnlɪs] *adj* sin dolor; (*method*) fácil.

pains [peɪnz] *npl* (*efforts*) esfuerzos *mpl*; **to take ~ to do sth** tomarse trabajo en hacer algo.

painstaking ['peɪnzteɪkɪŋ] *adj* (*person*) concienzudo, esmerado.

paint [peɪnt] *n* pintura ♦ *vt* pintar; **a tin of ~** un bote de pintura; **to ~ the door blue** pintar la puerta de azul.

paintbox ['peɪntbɔks] *n* caja de pinturas.

paintbrush ['peɪntbrʌʃ] *n* (*artist's*) pincel *m*; (*decorator's*) brocha.

painter ['peɪntə*] *n* pintor(a) *m/f*.

painting ['peɪntɪŋ] *n* pintura.

paintwork ['peɪntwəːk] *n* pintura.

pair [pɛə*] *n* (*of shoes, gloves etc*) par *m*; (*of people*) pareja; **a ~ of scissors** unas tijeras; **a ~ of trousers** unos pantalones, un pantalón.

▶**pair off** *vi*: **to ~ off (with sb)** hacer pareja (con algn).

pajamas [pɪ'dʒɑːməz] *npl* (*US*) pijama *msg*, piyama *msg* (*LAM*).

Pakistan [pɑːkɪ'stɑːn] *n* Paquistán *m*.

Pakistani [pɑːkɪ'stɑːnɪ] *adj, n* paquistaní *m/f*.

PAL [pæl] *n abbr* (*TV*) = *phase alternation line*.

pal [pæl] *n* (*col*) amiguete/a *m/f*, colega *m/f*.

palace ['pæləs] *n* palacio.

palatable ['pælɪtəbl] *adj* sabroso; (*acceptable*) aceptable.

palate ['pælɪt] *n* paladar *m*.

palatial [pə'leɪʃəl] *adj* (*surroundings, residence*) suntuoso, espléndido.

palaver [pə'lɑːvə*] *n* (*fuss*) lío.

pale [peɪl] *adj* (*gen*) pálido; (*colour*) claro

♦ n: **to be beyond the** ~ pasarse de la raya ♦ vi palidecer; **to grow** or **turn** ~ palidecer; **to** ~ **into insignificance (beside)** no poderse comparar (con).

paleness ['peɪlnɪs] n palidez f.

Palestine ['pælɪstaɪn] n Palestina.

Palestinian [pælɪs'tɪnɪən] adj, n palestino/a m/f.

palette ['pælɪt] n paleta.

paling ['peɪlɪŋ] n (stake) estaca; (fence) valla.

palisade [pælɪ'seɪd] n palizada.

pall [pɔːl] n (of smoke) cortina ♦ vi cansar.

pallbearer ['pɔːlbeərə*] n portador m del féretro.

pallet ['pælɪt] n (for goods) pallet m.

palliative ['pælɪətɪv] n paliativo.

pallid ['pælɪd] adj pálido.

pallor ['pælə*] n palidez f.

pally ['pælɪ] adj (col): **to be very** ~ **with sb** ser muy amiguete de algn.

palm [pɑːm] n (ANAT) palma; (also: ~ **tree**) palmera, palma ♦ vt: **to** ~ **sth off on sb** (BRIT col) endosarle algo a algn.

palmist ['pɑːmɪst] n quiromántico/a, palmista m/f.

Palm Sunday n Domingo de Ramos.

palpable ['pælpəbl] adj palpable.

palpably ['pælpəblɪ] adv obviamente.

palpitation [pælpɪ'teɪʃən] n palpitación f; **to have** ~s tener palpitaciones.

paltry ['pɔːltrɪ] adj (amount etc) miserable; (insignificant: person) insignificante.

pamper ['pæmpə*] vt mimar.

pamphlet ['pæmflət] n folleto; (political: handed out in street) panfleto.

pan [pæn] n (also: **sauce**~) cacerola, cazuela, olla; (also: **frying** ~) sartén m; (of lavatory) taza ♦ vi (CINE) tomar panorámicas; **to** ~ **for gold** cribar oro.

pan- [pæn] pref pan-.

panacea [pænə'sɪə] n panacea.

panache [pə'næʃ] n gracia, garbo.

Panama ['pænəmɑː] n Panamá m.

Panama Canal n el Canal de Panamá.

pancake ['pænkeɪk] n crepe f, panqueque m (LAM).

Pancake Day n martes m de carnaval.

pancake roll n rollito de primavera.

pancreas ['pæŋkrɪəs] n páncreas m.

panda ['pændə] n panda m.

panda car n (BRIT) coche m de la policía.

pandemonium [pændɪ'məʊnɪəm] n (noise): **there was** ~ se armó un tremendo jaleo; (mess) caos m.

pander ['pændə*] vi: **to** ~ **to** complacer a.

p&h abbr (US: = postage and handling) gastos de envío.

P&L abbr = profit and loss.

p & p abbr (BRIT: = postage and packing) gastos de envío.

pane [peɪn] n cristal m.

panel ['pænl] n (of wood) panel m; (of cloth) paño; (RADIO, TV) panel m de invitados.

panel game n (TV) programa m concurso para equipos.

panelling, (US) **paneling** ['pænəlɪŋ] n paneles mpl.

panellist, (US) **panelist** ['pænəlɪst] n miembro del jurado.

pang [pæŋ] n: ~**s of conscience** remordimientos mpl; ~**s of hunger** dolores mpl del hambre.

panhandler ['pænhændlə*] n (US col) mendigo/a.

panic ['pænɪk] n pánico ♦ vi dejarse llevar por el pánico.

panic buying [-baɪɪŋ] n compras masivas por miedo a futura escasez.

panic-stricken ['pænɪkstrɪkən] adj preso del pánico.

pannier ['pænɪə*] n (on bicycle) cartera; (on mule etc) alforja.

panorama [pænə'rɑːmə] n panorama m.

panoramic [pænə'ræmɪk] adj panorámico.

pansy ['pænzɪ] n (BOT) pensamiento; (col: pej) maricón m.

pant [pænt] vi jadear.

panther ['pænθə*] n pantera.

panties ['pæntɪz] npl bragas fpl.

pantihose ['pæntɪhəʊz] n (US) medias fpl, panties mpl.

panto ['pæntəʊ] n (BRIT col) = **pantomime**.

pantomime ['pæntəmaɪm] n (BRIT) representación f musical navideña; ver recuadro.

PANTOMIME

En época navideña los teatros británicos ponen en escena representaciones llamadas **pantomimes**, *versiones libres de cuentos tradicionales como Aladino o El gato con botas. En ella nunca faltan personajes como la dama ("dame"), papel que siempre interpreta un actor; el protagonista joven ("principal boy"), normalmente interpretado por una actriz, y el malvado ("villain"). Es un espectáculo familiar dirigido a los niños pero con grandes dosis de humor para adultos en el que se alienta la participación del público.*

---

pantry ['pæntrɪ] n despensa.

pants [pænts] n (BRIT: underwear: woman's) bragas fpl; (: man's) calzoncillos mpl; (US:

trousers) pantalones *mpl.*

pantsuit ['pæntsjuːt] *n (US)* traje *m* de chaqueta y pantalón.

papal ['peɪpəl] *adj* papal.

paparazzi [pæpə'rætsɪ] *npl* paparazzi *mpl.*

paper ['peɪpə*] *n* papel *m;* (*also:* **news~**) periódico, diario; (*study, article*) artículo; (*exam*) examen *m* ◆ *adj* de papel ◆ *vt* empapelar; **(identity)** ~**s** *npl* papeles *mpl,* documentos *mpl;* **a piece of** ~ un papel; **to put sth down on** ~ poner algo por escrito.

paper advance *n (on printer)* avance *m* de papel.

paperback ['peɪpəbæk] *n* libro de bolsillo.

paper bag *n* bolsa de papel.

paperboy ['peɪpəbɔɪ] *n (selling)* vendedor *m* de periódicos; (*delivering*) repartidor *m* de periódicos.

paper clip *n* clip *m.*

paper hankie *n* pañuelo de papel.

paper money *n* papel *m* moneda.

paper profit *n* beneficio no realizado.

paper shop *n (BRIT)* tienda de periódicos.

paperweight ['peɪpəweɪt] *n* pisapapeles *m inv.*

paperwork ['peɪpəwɔːk] *n* trabajo administrativo; (*pej*) papeleo.

papier-mâché ['pæpɪeɪ'mæʃeɪ] *n* cartón *m* piedra.

paprika ['pæprɪkə] *n* pimentón *m.*

Pap test ['pæp-] *n (MED)* frotis *m* (cervical).

papyrus [pə'paɪərəs] *n* papiro.

par [pɑː*] *n* par *f;* (*GOLF*) par *m* ◆ *adj* a la par; **to be on a** ~ **with** estar a la par con; **at** ~ a la par; **to be above/below** ~ estar sobre/bajo par; **to feel under** ~ sentirse en baja forma.

parable ['pærəbl] *n* parábola.

parachute ['pærəʃuːt] *n* paracaídas *m inv* ◆ *vi* lanzarse en paracaídas.

parachutist ['pærəʃuːtɪst] *n* paracaidista *m/ f.*

parade [pə'reɪd] *n* desfile *m* ◆ *vt* (*gen*) recorrer, desfilar por; (*show off*) hacer alarde de ◆ *vi* desfilar; (*MIL*) pasar revista; **a fashion** ~ un desfile de modelos.

parade ground *n* plaza de armas.

paradise ['pærədaɪs] *n* paraíso.

paradox ['pærədɔks] *n* paradoja.

paradoxical [pærə'dɔksɪkl] *adj* paradójico.

paradoxically [pærə'dɔksɪklɪ] *adv* paradójicamente.

paraffin ['pærəfɪn] *n (BRIT):* ~ **(oil)** parafina.

paraffin heater *n* estufa de parafina.

paraffin lamp *n* quinqué *m.*

paragon ['pærəgən] *n* modelo.

paragraph ['pærəgrɑːf] *n* párrafo, acápite *m (LAM);* **new** ~ punto y aparte, punto acápite ⟨*LAM).*

Paraguay ['pærəgwaɪ] *n* Paraguay *m.*

Paraguayan [pærə'gwaɪən] *adj, n* paraguayo/a *m/f,* paraguayano/a *m/f.*

parallel ['pærəlɛl] *adj:* ~ **(with/to)** en paralelo (con/a); (*fig*) semejante (a) ◆ *n* (*line*) paralela; (*fig, GEO*) paralelo.

paralysis [pə'rælɪsɪs] *n* parálisis *f inv.*

paralytic [pærə'lɪtɪk] *adj* paralítico.

paralyze ['pærəlaɪz] *vt* paralizar.

paramedic [pærə'mɛdɪk] *n* auxiliar *m/f* sanitario/a.

parameter [pə'ræmɪtə*] *n* parámetro.

paramilitary [pærə'mɪlɪtərɪ] *adj* (*organization, operations*) paramilitar.

paramount ['pærəmaunt] *adj:* **of** ~ **importance** de suma importancia.

paranoia [pærə'nɔɪə] *n* paranoia.

paranoid ['pærənɔɪd] *adj* (*person, feeling*) paranoico.

paranormal [pærə'nɔːml] *adj* paranormal.

parapet ['pærəpɪt] *n* parapeto.

paraphernalia [pærəfə'neɪlɪə] *n* parafernalia.

paraphrase ['pærəfreɪz] *vt* parafrasear.

paraplegic [pærə'pliːdʒɪk] *n* parapléjico/a.

parapsychology [pærəsaɪ'kɔlədʒɪ] *n* parasicología.

parasite ['pærəsaɪt] *n* parásito/a.

parasol ['pærəsɔl] *n* sombrilla, quitasol *m.*

paratrooper ['pærətruːpə*] *n* paracaidista *m/f.*

parcel ['pɑːsl] *n* paquete *m* ◆ *vt* (*also:* ~ **up**) empaquetar, embalar; **to be part and** ~ **of** ser parte integrante de.

▶**parcel out** *vt* parcelar, repartir.

parcel bomb *n* paquete *m* bomba.

parcel post *n* servicio de paquetes postales.

parch [pɑːtʃ] *vt* secar, resecar.

parched [pɑːtʃt] *adj* (*person*) muerto de sed.

parchment ['pɑːtʃmənt] *n* pergamino.

pardon ['pɑːdn] *n* perdón *m;* (*LAW*) indulto ◆ *vt* perdonar; indultar; ~ **me!, I beg your** ~! ¡perdone usted!; **(I beg your)** ~?, (*US*) ~ **me?** ¿cómo (dice)?

pare [pɛə*] *vt* (*nails*) cortar; (*fruit etc*) pelar.

parent ['pɛərənt] *n:* ~**s** *npl* padres *mpl.*

parentage ['pɛərəntɪdʒ] *n* familia, linaje *m;* **of unknown** ~ de padres desconocidos.

parental [pə'rɛntl] *adj* paternal/maternal.

parent company *n* casa matriz.

parenthesis, *pl* **parentheses** [pə'rɛnθɪsɪs, -θɪsiːz] *n* paréntesis *m inv;* **in parentheses** entre paréntesis.

parenthood – particular

parenthood ['pɛərənθud] n el ser padres.
parent ship n buque m nodriza.
Paris ['pærɪs] n París m.
parish ['pærɪʃ] n parroquia.
parish council n consejo parroquial.
parishioner [pə'rɪʃənə*] n feligrés/esa m/f.
Parisian [pə'rɪzɪən] adj, n parisino/a m/f,
parisiense m/f.
parity ['pærɪtɪ] n paridad f, igualdad f.
park [pɑːk] n parque m, jardín m público
♦ vt aparcar, estacionar ♦ vi aparcar,
estacionar.
parka ['pɑːkə] n parka.
parking ['pɑːkɪŋ] n aparcamiento,
estacionamiento; "no ~" "prohibido
aparcar or estacionarse".
parking lights npl luces fpl de
estacionamiento.
parking lot n (US) parking m, aparcamiento, playa f de estacionamiento (LAM).
parking meter n parquímetro.
parking offence, (US) **parking violation**
n ofensa por aparcamiento indebido.
parking place n sitio para aparcar,
aparcamiento.
parking ticket n multa de aparcamiento.
Parkinson's n (also: ~ **disease**)
(enfermedad f de) Parkinson m.
parkway ['pɑːkweɪ] n (US) alameda.
parlance ['pɑːləns] n lenguaje m; **in
common/modern** ~ en lenguaje
corriente/moderno.
parliament ['pɑːləmənt] n parlamento;
(Spanish) las Cortes fpl; ver recuadro.

PARLIAMENT

El Parlamento británico (**Parliament**) tiene
como sede el palacio de Westminster,
también llamado "Houses of Parliament".
Consta de dos cámaras: la Cámara de los
Comunes ("House of Commons") está
formada por 650 diputados ("Members of
Parliament") que acceden a ella tras ser
elegidos por sufragio universal en su
respectiva área o circunscripción electoral
("constituency"). Se reúne 175 días al año y
sus sesiones son presididas y moderadas
por el Presidente de la Cámara ("Speaker").
La cámara alta es la Cámara de los Lores
("House of Lords") y sus miembros son
nombrados por el monarca o bien han
heredado su escaño. Su poder es limitado,
aunque actúa como tribunal supremo de
apelación, excepto en Escocia.

---

parliamentary [pɑːlə'mɛntərɪ] adj
parlamentario.

parlour, (US) **parlor** ['pɑːlə*] n salón m,
living m (LAM).
parlous ['pɑːləs] adj peligroso, alarmante.
Parmesan [pɑːmɪ'zæn] n (also: ~ **cheese**)
queso parmesano.
parochial [pə'rəukɪəl] adj parroquial; (pej)
de miras estrechas.
parody ['pærədɪ] n parodia ♦ vt parodiar.
parole [pə'rəul] n: **on** ~ en libertad
condicional.
paroxysm ['pærəksɪzəm] n (MED)
paroxismo, ataque m; (of anger, laughter,
coughing) ataque m; (of grief) crisis f.
parquet ['pɑːkeɪ] n: ~ **floor(ing)** parquet m.
parrot ['pærət] n loro, papagayo.
parrot fashion adv como un loro.
parsimonious [pɑːsɪ'məunɪəs] adj tacaño.
parsley ['pɑːslɪ] n perejil m.
parsnip ['pɑːsnɪp] n chirivía.
parson ['pɑːsn] n cura m.
part [pɑːt] n (gen, MUS) parte f; (bit) trozo;
(of machine) pieza; (THEAT etc) papel m; (of
serial) entrega; (US: in hair) raya ♦ adv
= **partly** ♦ vt separar; (break) partir ♦ vi
(people) separarse; (roads) bifurcarse;
(crowd) apartarse; (break) romperse; **to
take** ~ **in** participar or tomar parte en; **to
take sb's** ~ tomar partido por algn; **for
my** ~ por mi parte; **for the most** ~ en su
mayor parte; (people) en su mayoría; **for
the better** ~ **of the day** durante la mayor
parte del día; ~ **of speech** (LING)
categoría gramatical, parte f de la
oración; **to take sth in good/bad** ~
aceptar algo bien/tomarse algo a mal.
▶**part with** vt fus ceder, entregar; (money)
pagar; (get rid of) deshacerse de.
partake [pɑː'teɪk] vi (irreg: like **take**)
(formal): **to** ~ **of sth** (food) comer algo;
(drink) tomar or beber algo.
part exchange n (BRIT): **in** ~ como parte
del pago.
partial ['pɑːʃl] adj parcial; **to be** ~ **to** (like)
ser aficionado a.
partially ['pɑːʃəlɪ] adv en parte,
parcialmente.
participant [pɑː'tɪsɪpənt] n (in competition)
concursante m/f.
participate [pɑː'tɪsɪpeɪt] vi: **to** ~ **in**
participar en.
participation [pɑːtɪsɪ'peɪʃən] n
participación f.
participle ['pɑːtɪsɪpl] n participio.
particle ['pɑːtɪkl] n partícula; (of dust)
mota; (fig) pizca.
particular [pə'tɪkjulə*] adj (special)
particular; (concrete) concreto; (given)
determinado; (detailed) detallado,

minucioso; (*fussy*) quisquilloso, exigente; **~s** *npl* (*information*) datos *mpl*, detalles *mpl*; (*details*) pormenores *mpl*; **in ~** en particular; **to be very ~ about** ser muy exigente en cuanto a; **I'm not ~** me es *or* da igual.

particularly [pə'tɪkjʊləlɪ] *adv* especialmente, en particular.

parting ['pɑːtɪŋ] *n* (*act of*) separación *f*; (*farewell*) despedida; (*BRIT: in hair*) raya ♦ *adj* de despedida; **~ shot** (*fig*) golpe *m* final.

partisan [pɑːtɪ'zæn] *adj* partidista ♦ *n* partidario/a; (*fighter*) partisano/a.

partition [pɑː'tɪʃən] *n* (*POL*) división *f*; (*wall*) tabique *m* ♦ *vt* dividir; dividir con tabique.

partly ['pɑːtlɪ] *adv* en parte.

partner ['pɑːtnə*] *n* (*COMM*) socio/a; (*SPORT, at dance*) pareja; (*spouse*) cónyuge *m/f*; (*friend etc*) compañero/a ♦ *vt* acompañar.

partnership ['pɑːtnəʃɪp] *n* (*gen*) asociación *f*; (*COMM*) sociedad *f*; **to go into ~ (with), form a ~ (with)** asociarse (con).

part payment *n* pago parcial.

partridge ['pɑːtrɪdʒ] *n* perdiz *f*.

part-time ['pɑːt'taɪm] *adj, adv* a tiempo parcial.

part-timer [pɑːt'taɪmə*] *n* trabajador(a) *m/f* a tiempo parcial.

party ['pɑːtɪ] *n* (*POL*) partido; (*celebration*) fiesta; (*group*) grupo; (*LAW*) parte *f*, interesado ♦ *adj* (*POL*) de partido; (*dress etc*) de fiesta, de gala; **to have** *or* **give** *or* **throw a ~** organizar una fiesta; **dinner ~** cena; **to be a ~ to a crime** ser cómplice *m/f* de un crimen.

party line *n* (*POL*) línea política del partido; (*TEL*) línea compartida.

party piece *n*: **to do one's ~** hacer su numerito (de fiesta).

party political broadcast *n* ≈ espacio electoral.

pass [pɑːs] *vt* (*time, object*) pasar; (*place*) pasar por; (*exam, law*) aprobar; (*overtake, surpass*) rebasar; (*approve*) aprobar ♦ *vi* pasar; (*SCOL*) aprobar ♦ *n* (*permit*) permiso, pase *m*; (*membership card*) carnet *m*; (*in mountains*) puerto; (*SPORT*) pase *m*; (*SCOL: also: ~ mark*) aprobado; **to ~ sth through sth** pasar algo por algo; **to ~ the time of day with sb** pasar el rato con algn; **things have come to a pretty ~!** ¡hasta dónde hemos llegado!; **to make a ~ at sb** (*col*) insinuársele a algn.

▶**pass away** *vi* fallecer.

▶**pass by** *vi* pasar ♦ *vt* (*ignore*) pasar por alto.

▶**pass down** *vt* (*customs, inheritance*) pasar, transmitir.

▶**pass for** *vt fus* pasar por; **she could ~ for twenty-five** se podría creer que sólo tiene 25 años.

▶**pass on** *vi* (*die*) fallecer, morir ♦ *vt* (*hand on*): **to ~ on (to)** transmitir (a); (*cold, illness*) pegar (a); (*benefits*) dar (a); (*price rises*) pasar (a).

▶**pass out** *vi* desmayarse; (*MIL*) graduarse.

▶**pass over** *vi* (*die*) fallecer ♦ *vt* omitir, pasar por alto.

▶**pass up** *vt* (*opportunity*) dejar pasar, no aprovechar.

passable ['pɑːsəbl] *adj* (*road*) transitable; (*tolerable*) pasable.

passably ['pɑːsəblɪ] *adv* pasablemente.

passage ['pæsɪdʒ] *n* pasillo; (*act of passing*) tránsito; (*fare, in book*) pasaje *m*; (*by boat*) travesía.

passageway ['pæsɪdʒweɪ] *n* (*in house*) pasillo, corredor *m*; (*between buildings etc*) pasaje *m*, pasadizo.

passenger ['pæsɪndʒə*] *n* pasajero/a, viajero/a.

passer-by [pɑːsə'baɪ] *n* transeúnte *m/f*.

passing ['pɑːsɪŋ] *adj* (*fleeting*) pasajero; **in ~** de paso.

passing place *n* (*AUT*) apartadero.

passion ['pæʃən] *n* pasión *f*.

passionate ['pæʃənɪt] *adj* apasionado.

passionately ['pæʃənɪtlɪ] *adv* apasionadamente, con pasión.

passion fruit *n* fruta de la pasión, granadilla.

passion play *n* drama *m* de la Pasión.

passive ['pæsɪv] *adj* (*also LING*) pasivo.

passive smoking *n* efectos del tabaco en fumadores pasivos.

passkey ['pɑːskiː] *n* llave *f* maestra.

Passover ['pɑːsəʊvə*] *n* Pascua (de los judíos).

passport ['pɑːspɔːt] *n* pasaporte *m*.

passport control *n* control *m* de pasaporte.

password ['pɑːswɜːd] *n* (*also COMPUT*) contraseña.

past [pɑːst] *prep* (*further than*) más allá de; (*later than*) después de ♦ *adj* pasado; (*president etc*) antiguo ♦ *n* (*time*) pasado; (*of person*) antecedentes *mpl*; **quarter/half ~ four** las cuatro y cuarto/media; **he's ~ forty** tiene más de cuarenta años; **I'm ~ caring** ya no me importa; **to be ~ it** (*col: person*) estar acabado; **for the ~ few/3 days** durante los últimos días/últimos 3 días; **to run ~** pasar corriendo por; **in the ~** en el pasado, antes.

pasta ['pæstə] n pasta.

paste [peɪst] n (gen) pasta; (glue) engrudo ♦ vt (stick) pegar; (glue) engomar; **tomato** ~ tomate concentrado.

pastel ['pæstl] adj pastel; (painting) al pastel.

pasteurized ['pæstəraɪzd] adj pasteurizado.

pastille ['pæstl] n pastilla.

pastime ['pɑːstaɪm] n pasatiempo.

past master n: to be a ~ at ser un maestro en.

pastor ['pɑːstə*] n pastor m.

pastoral ['pɑːstərl] adj pastoral.

pastry ['peɪstrɪ] n (dough) pasta; (cake) pastel m.

pasture ['pɑːstʃə*] n (grass) pasto.

pasty n ['pæstɪ] empanada ♦ adj ['peɪstɪ] pastoso; (complexion) pálido.

pat [pæt] vt dar una palmadita a; (dog etc) acariciar ♦ n (of butter) porción f ♦ adj: **he knows it (off)** ~ se lo sabe de memoria or al dedillo; **to give sb/o.s. a** ~ **on the back** (fig) felicitar a algn/felicitarse.

patch [pætʃ] n (of material) parche m; (mended part) remiendo; (of land) terreno; (COMPUT) ajuste m ♦ vt (clothes) remendar; **(to go through) a bad** ~ (pasar por) una mala racha.

▶**patch up** vt (mend temporarily) reparar; **to** ~ **up a quarrel** hacer las paces.

patchwork ['pætʃwəːk] n labor f de retales.

patchy ['pætʃɪ] adj desigual.

pate [peɪt] n: **bald** ~ calva.

pâté ['pæteɪ] n paté m.

patent ['peɪtnt] n patente f ♦ vt patentar ♦ adj patente, evidente.

patent leather n charol m.

patently ['peɪtntlɪ] adv evidentemente.

patent medicine n específico.

patent office n oficina de patentes y marcas.

patent rights npl derechos mpl de patente.

paternal [pə'təːnl] adj paternal; (relation) paterno.

paternalistic [pətəːnə'lɪstɪk] adj paternalista.

paternity [pə'təːnɪtɪ] n paternidad f.

paternity suit n (LAW) caso de paternidad.

path [pɑːθ] n camino, sendero; (trail, track) pista; (of missile) trayectoria.

pathetic [pə'θɛtɪk] adj (pitiful) penoso, patético; (very bad) malísimo; (moving) conmovedor(a).

pathetically [pə'θɛtɪklɪ] adv penosamente, patéticamente; (very badly) malísimamente mal, de pena.

pathological [pæθə'lɔdʒɪkəl] adj patológico.

pathologist [pə'θɔlədʒɪst] n patólogo/a.

pathology [pə'θɔlədʒɪ] n patología.

pathos ['peɪθɔs] n patetismo.

pathway ['pɑːθweɪ] n sendero, vereda.

patience ['peɪʃns] n paciencia; (BRIT CARDS) solitario; **to lose one's** ~ perder la paciencia.

patient ['peɪʃnt] n paciente m/f ♦ adj paciente, sufrido; **to be** ~ **with sb** tener paciencia con algn.

patiently ['peɪʃəntlɪ] adv pacientemente, con paciencia.

patio ['pætɪəu] n patio.

patriot ['peɪtrɪət] n patriota m/f.

patriotic [pætrɪ'ɔtɪk] adj patriótico.

patriotism ['pætrɪətɪzəm] n patriotismo.

patrol [pə'trəul] n patrulla ♦ vt patrullar por; **to be on** ~ patrullar, estar de patrulla.

patrol boat n patrullero, patrullera.

patrol car n coche m patrulla.

patrolman [pə'trəulmən] n (US) policía m.

patron ['peɪtrən] n (in shop) cliente m/f; (of charity) patrocinador(a) m/f; ~ **of the arts** mecenas m.

patronage ['pætrənɪdʒ] n patrocinio, protección f.

patronize ['pætrənaɪz] vt (shop) ser cliente de; (look down on) tratar con condescendencia a.

patronizing ['pætrənaɪzɪŋ] adj condescendiente.

patron saint n santo/a patrón/ona.

patter ['pætə*] n golpeteo; (sales talk) labia ♦ vi (rain) tamborilear.

pattern ['pætən] n (SEWING) patrón m; (design) dibujo; (behaviour, events) esquema m; ~ **of events** curso de los hechos; **behaviour** ~s modelos mpl de comportamiento.

patterned ['pætənd] adj (material) estampado.

paucity ['pɔːsɪtɪ] n escasez f.

paunch [pɔːntʃ] n panza, barriga.

pauper ['pɔːpə*] n pobre m/f.

pause [pɔːz] n pausa; (interval) intervalo ♦ vi hacer una pausa; **to** ~ **for breath** detenerse para tomar aliento.

pave [peɪv] vt pavimentar; **to** ~ **the way for** preparar el terreno para.

pavement ['peɪvmənt] n (BRIT) acera, vereda (LAM), andén m (LAM), banqueta (LAM); (US) calzada, pavimento.

pavilion [pə'vɪlɪən] n pabellón m; (SPORT) vestuarios mpl.

paving ['peɪvɪŋ] n pavimento.

paving stone n losa.

paw [pɔː] n pata; (claw) garra ♦ vt (animal) tocar con la pata; (pej: touch) tocar, manosear.

pawn [pɔːn] *n* (*CHESS*) peón *m*; (*fig*) instrumento ♦ *vt* empeñar.

pawnbroker ['pɔːnbrəukə*] *n* prestamista *m/f*.

pawnshop ['pɔːnʃɔp] *n* casa de empeños.

pay [peɪ] *n* paga; (*wage etc*) sueldo, salario ♦ (*vb: pt, pp* **paid**) *vt* pagar; (*visit*) hacer; (*respect*) ofrecer ♦ *vi* pagar; (*be profitable*) rendir, compensar, ser rentable; **to be in sb's ~** estar al servicio de algn; **to ~ attention (to)** prestar atención (a); **I paid £5 for that record** pagué 5 libras por ese disco; **how much did you ~ for it?** ¿cuánto pagaste por él?; **to ~ one's way** (*contribute one's share*) pagar su parte; (*remain solvent: company*) ser solvente; **to ~ dividends** (*COMM*) pagar dividendos; (*fig*) compensar; **it won't ~ you to do that** no te merece la pena hacer eso; **to put paid to** (*plan, person*) acabar con.

▶**pay back** *vt* (*money*) devolver, reembolsar; (*person*) pagar.

▶**pay for** *vt fus* pagar.

▶**pay in** *vt* ingresar.

▶**pay off** *vt* liquidar; (*person*) pagar; (*debts*) liquidar, saldar; (*creditor*) cancelar, redimir; (*workers*) despedir; (*mortgage*) cancelar, redimir ♦ *vi* (*scheme, decision*) dar resultado; **to ~ sth off in instalments** pagar algo a plazos.

▶**pay out** *vt* (*rope*) ir dando; (*money*) gastar, desembolsar.

▶**pay up** *vt* pagar.

payable ['peɪəbl] *adj* pagadero; **to make a cheque ~ to sb** extender un cheque a favor de algn.

pay award *n* aumento de sueldo.

pay day *n* día *m* de paga.

PAYE *n abbr* (*BRIT*: = *pay as you earn*) sistema de retención fiscal en la fuente de ingresos.

payee [peɪˈiː] *n* portador(a) *m/f*.

pay envelope *n* (*US*) = **pay packet**.

paying ['peɪɪŋ] *adj*: **~ guest** huésped(a) *m/f* que la paga.

payload ['peɪləud] *n* carga útil.

payment ['peɪmənt] *n* pago; **advance ~** (*part sum*) anticipo, adelanto; (*total sum*) saldo; **monthly ~** mensualidad *f*; **deferred ~, ~ by instalments** pago a plazos *or* diferido; **on ~ of £5** mediante pago de *or* pagando £5; **in ~ for** en pago de.

pay packet *n* (*BRIT*) sobre *m* (de la paga).

pay-phone ['peɪfəun] *n* teléfono público.

payroll ['peɪrəul] *n* nómina; **to be on a firm's ~** estar en la nómina de una compañía.

pay slip *n* hoja del sueldo.

pay station *n* (*US*) teléfono público.

PBS *n abbr* (*US*: = *Public Broadcasting Service*) *agrupación de ayuda a la realización de emisiones para la TV pública.*

PC *n abbr see* **personal computer;** (*BRIT*) = **police constable** ♦ *abbr* (*BRIT*) = *Privy Councillor* ♦ *adj abbr* = **politically correct.**

pc *abbr* = **per cent, postcard.**

p/c *abbr* = **petty cash.**

PCB *n abbr see* **printed circuit board.**

PD *n abbr* (*US*) = **police department.**

pd *abbr* = **paid.**

PDA *n abbr* (= *personal digital assistant*) agenda electrónica.

PDSA *n abbr* (*BRIT*) = *People's Dispensary for Sick Animals.*

PDT *n abbr* (*US*: = *Pacific Daylight Time*) *hora de verano del Pacífico.*

PE *n abbr* (= *physical education*) ed. física.

pea [piː] *n* guisante *m*, chícharo (*LAM*), arveja (*LAM*).

peace [piːs] *n* paz *f*; (*calm*) paz *f*, tranquilidad *f*; **to be at ~ with sb/sth** estar en paz con algn/algo; **to keep the ~** (*policeman*) mantener el orden; (*citizen*) guardar el orden.

peaceable ['piːsəbl] *adj* pacífico.

peaceably [piːsəblɪ] *adv* pacíficamente.

peaceful ['piːsful] *adj* (*gentle*) pacífico; (*calm*) tranquilo, sosegado.

peacekeeping ['piːskiːpɪŋ] *adj* de pacificación ♦ *n* pacificación *f*.

peacekeeping force *n* fuerza de pacificación.

peace offering *n* (*fig*) prenda de paz.

peacetime ['piːstaɪm] *n*: **in ~** en tiempo de paz.

peach [piːtʃ] *n* melocotón *m*, durazno (*LAM*).

peacock ['piːkɔk] *n* pavo real.

peak [piːk] *n* (*of mountain: top*) cumbre *f*, cima; (: *point*) pico; (*of cap*) visera; (*fig*) cumbre *f*.

peak-hour ['piːkauə*] *adj* (*traffic etc*) de horas punta.

peak hours *npl*, **peak period** *n* horas *fpl* punta.

peak rate *n* tarifa máxima.

peaky ['piːkɪ] *adj* (*BRIT col*) pálido, paliducho; **I'm feeling a bit ~** estoy malucho, no me encuentro bien.

peal [piːl] *n* (*of bells*) repique *m*; **~ of laughter** carcajada.

peanut ['piːnʌt] *n* cacahuete *m*, maní *m* (*LAM*).

peanut butter *n* mantequilla de cacahuete.

pear [pɛə*] *n* pera.
pearl [pɔːl] *n* perla.
peasant ['pɛznt] *n* campesino/a.
peat [piːt] *n* turba.
pebble ['pɛbl] *n* guijarro.
peck [pɛk] *vt* (*also:* ~ **at**) picotear; (*food*)
   comer sin ganas ♦ *n* picotazo; (*kiss*)
   besito.
pecking order ['pɛkɪŋ-] *n* orden *m* de
   jerarquía.
peckish ['pɛkɪʃ] *adj* (*BRIT col*): **I feel** ~ tengo
   ganas de picar algo.
peculiar [pɪ'kjuːlɪə*] *adj* (*odd*) extraño,
   raro; (*typical*) propio, característico;
   (*particular: importance, qualities*)
   particular; ~ **to** propio de.
peculiarity [pɪkjuːlɪ'ærɪtɪ] *n* peculiaridad *f*,
   característica.
peculiarly [pɪ'kjuːlɪəlɪ] *adv* extrañamente;
   particularmente.
pedal ['pɛdl] *n* pedal *m* ♦ *vi* pedalear.
pedal bin *n* cubo de la basura con pedal.
pedant ['pɛdənt] *n* pedante *m/f*.
pedantic [pɪ'dæntɪk] *adj* pedante.
pedantry ['pɛdəntrɪ] *n* pedantería.
peddle ['pɛdl] *vt* (*goods*) ir vendiendo *or*
   vender de puerta en puerta; (*drugs*)
   traficar con; (*gossip*) divulgar.
peddler ['pɛdlə*] *n* vendedor(a) *m/f*
   ambulante.
pedestal ['pɛdəstl] *n* pedestal *m*.
pedestrian [pɪ'dɛstrɪən] *n* peatón *m* ♦ *adj*
   pedestre.
pedestrian crossing *n* (*BRIT*) paso de
   peatones.
pedestrian precinct *n* zona reservada
   para peatones.
pediatrics [piːdɪ'ætrɪks] *n* (*US*)
   = **paediatrics**.
pedigree ['pɛdɪgriː] *n* genealogía; (*of
   animal*) pedigrí *m* ♦ *cpd* (*animal*) de raza,
   de casta.
pedlar ['pɛdlə*] *n* (*BRIT*) = **peddler**.
pee [piː] *vi* (*col*) mear.
peek [piːk] *vi* mirar a hurtadillas; (*COMPUT*)
   inspeccionar.
peel [piːl] *n* piel *f*; (*of orange, lemon*)
   cáscara; (: *removed*) peladuras *fpl* ♦ *vt*
   pelar ♦ *vi* (*paint etc*) desconcharse;
   (*wallpaper*) despegarse, desprenderse.
▶**peel back** *vt* pelar.
peeler ['piːlə*] *n*: **potato** ~ mondador *m or*
   pelador *m* de patatas, pelapatatas *m inv*.
peep [piːp] *n* (*BRIT: look*) mirada furtiva;
   (*sound*) pío ♦ *vi* (*BRIT*) piar.
▶**peep out** *vi* asomar la cabeza.
peephole ['piːphəʊl] *n* mirilla.
peer [pɪə*] *vi*: **to** ~ **at** escudriñar ♦ *n* (*noble*)

par *m*; (*equal*) igual *m*.
peerage ['pɪərɪdʒ] *n* nobleza.
peerless ['pɪəlɪs] *adj* sin par, incomparable,
   sin igual.
peeved [piːvd] *adj* enojado.
peevish ['piːvɪʃ] *adj* malhumorado.
peevishness ['piːvɪʃnɪs] *n* mal humor *m*.
peg [pɛg] *n* clavija; (*for coat etc*) gancho,
   colgador *m*; (*BRIT: also:* **clothes** ~) pinza;
   (*tent* ~) estaca ♦ *vt* (*clothes*) tender;
   (*groundsheet*) fijar con estacas; (*fig:
   wages, prices*) fijar.
pejorative [pɪ'dʒɔrətɪv] *adj* peyorativo.
Pekin [piː'kɪn], **Peking** [piː'kɪŋ] *n* Pekín *m*.
pekinese [piːkɪ'niːz] *n* pequinés/esa *m/f*.
pelican ['pɛlɪkən] *n* pelícano.
pelican crossing *n* (*BRIT AUT*) paso de
   peatones señalizado.
pellet ['pɛlɪt] *n* bolita; (*bullet*) perdigón *m*.
pell-mell ['pɛl'mɛl] *adv* en tropel.
pelmet ['pɛlmɪt] *n* galería.
pelt [pɛlt] *vt*: **to** ~ **sb with sth** arrojarle
   algo a algn ♦ *vi* (*rain: also:* ~ **down**) llover
   a cántaros ♦ *n* pellejo.
pelvis ['pɛlvɪs] *n* pelvis *f*.
pen [pɛn] *n* (*ballpoint* ~) bolígrafo; (*fountain*
   ~) pluma; (*for sheep*) redil *m*; (*US col:
   prison*) cárcel *f*, chirona; **to put** ~ **to paper**
   tomar la pluma.
penal ['piːnl] *adj* penal; ~ **servitude**
   trabajos *mpl* forzados.
penalize ['piːnəlaɪz] *vt* (*punish*) castigar;
   (*SPORT*) sancionar, penalizar.
penalty ['pɛnltɪ] *n* (*gen*) pena; (*fine*) multa;
   (*SPORT*) sanción *f*; ~ (**kick**) (*FOOTBALL*)
   penalty *m*.
penalty area *n* (*BRIT SPORT*) área de
   castigo.
penalty clause *n* cláusula de penalización.
penalty shoot-out [-'ʃuːtaut] *n* (*FOOTBALL*)
   tanda de penaltis.
penance ['pɛnəns] *n* penitencia.
pence [pɛns] *pl of* **penny**.
penchant ['pɑːʃɑːŋ] *n* predilección *f*,
   inclinación *f*.
pencil ['pɛnsl] *n* lápiz *m*, lapicero (*esp LAM*)
   ♦ *vt* (*also:* ~ **in**) escribir con lápiz.
pencil case *n* estuche *m*.
pencil sharpener *n* sacapuntas *m inv*.
pendant ['pɛndnt] *n* pendiente *m*.
pending ['pɛndɪŋ] *prep* antes de ♦ *adj*
   pendiente; ~ **the arrival of** ... hasta que
   llegue ..., hasta llegar ... .
pendulum ['pɛndjuləm] *n* péndulo.
penetrate ['pɛnɪtreɪt] *vt* penetrar.
penetrating ['pɛnɪtreɪtɪŋ] *adj* penetrante.
penetration [pɛnɪ'treɪʃən] *n* penetración *f*.
penfriend ['pɛnfrɛnd] *n* (*BRIT*) amigo/a por

correspondencia.
penguin ['pɛŋgwɪn] *n* pingüino.
penicillin [pɛnɪ'sɪlɪn] *n* penicilina.
peninsula [pə'nɪnsjulə] *n* península.
penis ['piːnɪs] *n* pene *m*.
penitence ['pɛnɪtns] *n* penitencia.
penitent ['pɛnɪtnt] *adj* arrepentido; (*REL*) penitente.
penitentiary [pɛnɪ'tɛnʃərɪ] *n* (*US*) cárcel *f*, presidio.
penknife ['pɛnnaɪf] *n* navaja.
Penn(a). *abbr* (*US*) = *Pennsylvania*.
pen name *n* seudónimo.
pennant ['pɛnənt] *n* banderola; banderín *m*.
penniless ['pɛnɪlɪs] *adj* sin dinero.
Pennines ['pɛnaɪnz] *npl* (Montes *mpl*) Peninos *mpl*.
penny, *pl* **pennies** *or* (*BRIT*) **pence** ['pɛnɪ, 'pɛnɪz, pɛns] *n* penique *m*; (*US*) centavo.
penpal ['pɛnpæl] *n* amigo/a por correspondencia.
penpusher ['pɛnpuʃə*] *n* (*pej*) chupatintas *m/f inv*.
pension ['pɛnʃən] *n* (*allowance, state payment*) pensión *f*; (*old-age*) jubilación *f*.
▶**pension off** *vt* jubilar.
pensioner ['pɛnʃənə*] *n* (*BRIT*) jubilado/a.
pension fund *n* fondo de pensiones.
pensive ['pɛnsɪv] *adj* pensativo; (*withdrawn*) preocupado.
pentagon ['pɛntəgən] *n* pentágono; **the P~** (*US POL*) el Pentágono; *ver recuadro*.

Pentecost ['pɛntɪkɔst] *n* Pentecostés *m*.
penthouse ['pɛnthaus] *n* ático (de lujo).
pent-up ['pɛntʌp] *adj* (*feelings*) reprimido.
penultimate [pɛ'nʌltɪmət] *adj* penúltimo.
people ['piːpl] *npl* gente *f*; (*citizens*) pueblo *sg*, ciudadanos *mpl* ♦ *n* (*nation, race*) pueblo, nación *f* ♦ *vt* poblar; **several ~ came** vinieron varias personas; **~ say that ...** dice la gente que ...; **old/young ~** los ancianos/jóvenes; **~ at large** la gente en general; **a man of the ~** un hombre del pueblo.
PEP *n abbr* (= *Personal Equity Plan*) plan personal de inversión con desgravación fiscal.

pep [pɛp] *n* (*col*) energía.
▶**pep up** *vt* animar.
pepper ['pɛpə*] *n* (*spice*) pimienta; (*vegetable*) pimiento, ají *m* (*LAM*), chile *m* (*LAM*) ♦ *vt* (*fig*) salpicar.
peppermint ['pɛpəmɪnt] *n* menta; (*sweet*) pastilla de menta.
pepperoni [pɛpə'rəunɪ] *n* ≈ salchichón *m* picante.
pepperpot ['pɛpəpɔt] *n* pimentero.
peptalk ['pɛptɔːk] *n* (*col*): **to give sb a ~** darle a algn una inyección de ánimo.
per [pəː*] *prep* por; **~ day/person** por día/persona; **as ~ your instructions** de acuerdo con sus instrucciones.
per annum *adv* al año.
per capita *adj, adv* per cápita.
perceive [pə'siːv] *vt* percibir; (*realize*) darse cuenta de.
per cent, (*US*) **percent** [pə'sɛnt] *n* por ciento; **a 20 ~ discount** un descuento del 20 por ciento.
percentage [pə'sɛntɪdʒ] *n* porcentaje *m*; **to get a ~ on all sales** percibir un tanto por ciento sobre todas las ventas; **on a ~ basis** a porcentaje.
percentage point *n* punto (porcentual).
perceptible [pə'sɛptəbl] *adj* perceptible; (*notable*) sensible.
perception [pə'sɛpʃən] *n* percepción *f*; (*insight*) perspicacia.
perceptive [pə'sɛptɪv] *adj* perspicaz.
perch [pəːtʃ] *n* (*fish*) perca; (*for bird*) percha ♦ *vi* posarse.
percolate ['pəːkəleɪt] *vt* (*coffee*) filtrar ♦ *vi* (*coffee, fig*) filtrarse.
percolator ['pəːkəleɪtə*] *n* cafetera de filtro.
percussion [pə'kʌʃən] *n* percusión *f*.
percussionist [pə'kʌʃənɪst] *n* percusionista *m/f*.
peremptory [pə'rɛmptərɪ] *adj* perentorio.
perennial [pə'rɛnɪəl] *adj* perenne.
perfect *adj* ['pəːfɪkt] perfecto ♦ *n* (*also:* **~ tense**) perfecto ♦ *vt* [pə'fɛkt] perfeccionar; **he's a ~ stranger to me** no le conozco de nada, me es completamente desconocido.
perfection [pə'fɛkʃən] *n* perfección *f*.
perfectionist [pə'fɛkʃənɪst] *n* perfeccionista *m/f*.
perfectly ['pəːfɪktlɪ] *adv* perfectamente; **I'm ~ happy with the situation** estoy muy contento con la situación; **you know ~ well** lo sabes muy bien *or* perfectamente.
perforate ['pəːfəreɪt] *vt* perforar.
perforation [pəːfə'reɪʃən] *n* perforación *f*.
perform [pə'fɔːm] *vt* (*carry out*) realizar,

llevar a cabo; (*THEAT*) representar; (*piece of music*) interpretar ♦ *vi* (*THEAT*) actuar; (*TECH*) funcionar.

performance [pə'fɔːməns] *n* (*of task*) realización *f*; (*of a play*) representación *f*; (*of player etc*) actuación *f*; (*of engine*) rendimiento; (*of car*) prestaciones *fpl*; (*of function*) desempeño; **the team put up a good** ~ el equipo se defendió bien.

performer [pə'fɔːmə*] *n* (*actor*) actor *m*, actriz *f*; (*MUS*) intérprete *m/f*.

performing [pə'fɔːmɪŋ] *adj* (*animal*) amaestrado.

performing arts *npl*: **the** ~ las artes teatrales.

perfume ['pəːfjuːm] *n* perfume *m*.

perfunctory [pə'fʌŋktərɪ] *adj* superficial.

perhaps [pə'hæps] *adv* quizá(s), tal vez; ~ **so/not** puede que sí/no.

peril ['pɛrɪl] *n* peligro, riesgo.

perilous ['pɛrɪləs] *adj* peligroso.

perilously ['pɛrɪləslɪ] *adv*: **they came ~ close to being caught** por poco les cogen *or* agarran.

perimeter [pə'rɪmɪtə*] *n* perímetro.

period ['pɪərɪəd] *n* período, periodo; (*HISTORY*) época; (*SCOL*) clase *f*; (*full stop*) punto; (*MED*) regla, periodo; (*US SPORT*) tiempo ♦ *adj* (*costume, furniture*) de época; **for a** ~ **of three weeks** durante (un período de) tres semanas; **the holiday** ~ el período de vacaciones.

periodic [pɪərɪ'ɔdɪk] *adj* periódico.

periodical [pɪərɪ'ɔdɪkl] *adj* periódico ♦ *n* revista, publicación *f* periódica.

periodically [pɪərɪ'ɔdɪklɪ] *adv* de vez en cuando, cada cierto tiempo.

period pains *npl* dolores *mpl* de la regla *or* de la menstruación.

peripatetic [pɛrɪpə'tɛtɪk] *adj* (*salesman*) ambulante; (*teacher*) con trabajo en varios colegios.

peripheral [pə'rɪfərəl] *adj* periférico ♦ *n* (*COMPUT*) periférico, unidad *f* periférica.

periphery [pə'rɪfərɪ] *n* periferia.

periscope ['pɛrɪskəup] *n* periscopio.

perish ['pɛrɪʃ] *vi* perecer; (*decay*) echarse a perder.

perishable ['pɛrɪʃəbl] *adj* perecedero.

perishables ['pɛrɪʃəblz] *npl* productos *mpl* perecederos.

peritonitis [pɛrɪtə'naɪtɪs] *n* peritonitis *f*.

perjure ['pəːdʒə*] *vt*: **to ~ o.s.** perjurar.

perjury ['pəːdʒərɪ] *n* (*LAW*) perjurio.

perk [pəːk] *n* beneficio, extra *m*.

▶**perk up** *vi* (*cheer up*) animarse.

perky ['pəːkɪ] *adj* alegre, animado.

perm [pəːm] *n* permanente *f* ♦ *vt*: **to have**

one's hair ~ed hacerse una permanente.

permanence ['pəːmənəns] *n* permanencia.

permanent ['pəːmənənt] *adj* permanente; (*job, position*) fijo; (*dye, ink*) indeleble; ~ **address** domicilio permanente; **I'm not** ~ **here** no estoy fijo aquí.

permanently ['pəːmənəntlɪ] *adv* (*lastingly*) para siempre, de modo definitivo; (*all the time*) permanentemente.

permeate ['pəːmɪeɪt] *vi* penetrar, trascender ♦ *vt* penetrar, trascender a.

permissible [pə'mɪsɪbl] *adj* permisible, lícito.

permission [pə'mɪʃən] *n* permiso; **to give sb ~ to do sth** autorizar a algn para que haga algo; **with your** ~ con su permiso.

permissive [pə'mɪsɪv] *adj* permisivo.

permit *n* ['pəːmɪt] permiso, licencia; (*entrance pass*) pase *m* ♦ *vt* [pə'mɪt] permitir; (*accept*) tolerar ♦ *vi* [pə'mɪt]: **weather ~ting** si el tiempo lo permite; **fishing ~** permiso de pesca; **building/ export ~** licencia *or* permiso de construcción/exportación.

permutation [pəːmju'teɪʃən] *n* permutación *f*.

pernicious [pəː'nɪʃəs] *adj* nocivo; (*MED*) pernicioso.

pernickety [pə'nɪkɪtɪ] *adj* (*col: person*) quisquilloso; (: *task*) delicado.

perpendicular [pəːpən'dɪkjulə*] *adj* perpendicular.

perpetrate ['pəːpɪtreɪt] *vt* cometer.

perpetual [pə'pɛtjuəl] *adj* perpetuo.

perpetually [pə'pɛtjuəlɪ] *adv* (*eternally*) perpetuamente; (*continuously*) constantemente, continuamente.

perpetuate [pə'pɛtjueɪt] *vt* perpetuar.

perpetuity [pəːpɪ'tjuɪtɪ] *n*: **in ~ a** perpetuidad.

perplex [pə'plɛks] *vt* dejar perplejo.

perplexed [pə'plɛkst] *adj* perplejo, confuso.

perplexing [pə'plɛksɪŋ] *adj* que causa perplejidad.

perplexity [pə'plɛksɪtɪ] *n* perplejidad *f*, confusión *f*.

perquisites ['pəːkwɪzɪts] *npl* (*also*: **perks**) beneficios *mpl*.

persecute ['pəːsɪkjuːt] *vt* (*pursue*) perseguir; (*harass*) acosar.

persecution [pəːsɪ'kjuːʃən] *n* persecución *f*.

perseverance [pəːsɪ'vɪərəns] *n* perseverancia.

persevere [pəːsɪ'vɪə*] *vi* perseverar.

Persia ['pəːʃə] *n* Persia.

Persian ['pəːʃən] *adj*, *n* persa *m/f* ♦ *n* (*LING*) persa *m*; **the** ~ **Gulf** el Golfo Pérsico.

Persian cat *n* gato persa.

persist [pə'sɪst] *vi* persistir; **to** ~ **in doing sth** empeñarse en hacer algo.

persistence [pə'sɪstəns] *n* empeño.

persistent [pə'sɪstənt] *adj* (*lateness, rain*) persistente; (*determined*) porfiado; (*continuing*) constante; ~ **offender** (*LAW*) multirreincidente *m/f*.

persistently [pə'sɪstntlɪ] *adv* persistentemente; (*continually*) constantemente.

persnickety [pə'snɪkətɪ] *adj* (*US col*) = **pernickety**.

person ['pɜːsn] *n* persona; **in** ~ en persona; **on** *or* **about one's** ~ encima; **a** ~ **to** ~ **call** una llamada (de) persona a persona.

personable ['pɜːsnəbl] *adj* atractivo.

personal ['pɜːsnl] *adj* personal, individual; (*visit*) en persona; (*BRIT TEL*) (de) persona a persona.

personal allowance *n* desgravación *f* personal.

personal assistant (PA) *n* ayudante *m/f* personal.

personal belongings *npl* efectos *mpl* personales.

personal column *n* anuncios *mpl* personales.

personal computer (PC) *n* ordenador *m* personal.

personal effects *npl* efectos *mpl* personales.

personal identification number (PIN) *n* número personal de identificación.

personality [pɜːsə'nælɪtɪ] *n* personalidad *f*.

personally ['pɜːsnəlɪ] *adv* personalmente.

personal organizer *n* agenda (profesional); (*electronic*) organizador *m* personal.

personal property *n* bienes *mpl* muebles.

personal, social and health education *n* (*BRIT SCOL*) *formación social y sanitaria para la vida adulta*.

personal stereo *n* walkman ® *m*.

personification [pɜːsɒnɪfɪ'keɪʃən] *n* personificación *f*.

personify [pɜː'sɒnɪfaɪ] *vt* encarnar, personificar.

personnel [pɜːsə'nel] *n* personal *m*.

personnel department *n* departamento de personal.

personnel management *n* gestión *f* de personal.

personnel manager *n* jefe *m* de personal.

perspective [pə'spektɪv] *n* perspectiva; **to get sth into** ~ ver algo en perspectiva *or* como es.

Perspex ® ['pɜːspeks] *n* (*BRIT*) vidrio acrílico, plexiglás *m* ®.

perspiration [pɜːspɪ'reɪʃən] *n* transpiración *f*, sudor *m*.

perspire [pə'spaɪə*] *vi* transpirar, sudar.

persuade [pə'sweɪd] *vt*: **to** ~ **sb to do sth** persuadir a algn para que haga algo; **to** ~ **sb of sth/that** persuadir *or* convencer a algn de algo/de que; **I am** ~**d that ...** estoy convencido de que ....

persuasion [pə'sweɪʒən] *n* persuasión *f*; (*persuasiveness*) persuasiva; (*creed*) creencia.

persuasive [pə'sweɪsɪv] *adj* persuasivo.

persuasively [pə'sweɪsɪvlɪ] *adv* de modo persuasivo.

pert [pɜːt] *adj* impertinente, fresco, atrevido.

pertaining [pɜː'teɪnɪŋ]: ~ **to** *prep* relacionado con.

pertinent ['pɜːtɪnənt] *adj* pertinente, a propósito.

perturb [pə'tɜːb] *vt* perturbar.

perturbing [pə'tɜːbɪŋ] *adj* inquietante, perturbador(a).

Peru [pə'ruː] *n* el Perú.

perusal [pə'ruːzəl] *n* (*quick*) lectura somera; (*careful*) examen *m*.

peruse [pə'ruːz] *vt* (*examine*) leer con detención, examinar; (*glance at*) mirar por encima.

Peruvian [pə'ruːvɪən] *adj*, *n* peruano/a *m/f*.

pervade [pə'veɪd] *vt* impregnar; (*influence, ideas*) extenderse por.

pervasive [pə'veɪsɪv] *adj* (*smell*) penetrante; (*influence*) muy extendido; (*gloom, feelings, ideas*) reinante.

perverse [pə'vɜːs] *adj* perverso; (*stubborn*) terco; (*wayward*) travieso.

perversely [pə'vɜːslɪ] *adv* perversamente; tercamente; traviesamente.

perverseness [pə'vɜːsnɪs] *n* perversidad *f*; terquedad *f*; travesura.

perversion [pə'vɜːʃən] *n* perversión *f*.

pervert *n* ['pɜːvɜːt] pervertido/a ♦ *vt* [pə'vɜːt] pervertir.

pessary ['pesərɪ] *n* pesario.

pessimism ['pesɪmɪzəm] *n* pesimismo.

pessimist ['pesɪmɪst] *n* pesimista *m/f*.

pessimistic [pesɪ'mɪstɪk] *adj* pesimista.

pest [pest] *n* (*insect*) insecto nocivo; (*fig*) lata, molestia; ~**s** *npl* plaga.

pest control *n* control *m* de plagas.

pester ['pestə*] *vt* molestar, acosar.

pesticide ['pestɪsaɪd] *n* pesticida *m*.

pestilence ['pestɪləns] *n* pestilencia.

pestle ['pesl] *n* mano *f* de mortero *or* de almirez.

pet [pet] *n* animal *m* doméstico; (*favourite*) favorito/a ♦ *vt* acariciar ♦ *vi* (*col*) besuquearse ◊ *cpd*: **my ~ aversion** mi manía.

petal ['pɛtl] *n* pétalo.

peter ['piːtə*]: **to ~ out** *vi* agotarse, acabarse.

petite [pə'tiːt] *adj* menuda, chiquita.

petition [pə'tɪʃən] *n* petición *f* ◊ *vt* presentar una petición a ◊ *vi*: **to ~ for divorce** pedir el divorcio.

pet name *n* nombre *m* cariñoso, apodo.

petrified ['pɛtrɪfaɪd] *adj* (*fig*) pasmado, horrorizado.

petrochemical [pɛtrə'kɛmɪkl] *adj* petroquímico.

petrodollars ['pɛtrəudɔləz] *npl* petrodólares *mpl*.

petrol ['pɛtrəl] (*BRIT*) *n* gasolina; (*for lighter*) bencina; **two/four-star ~** gasolina normal/súper.

petrol bomb *n* cóctel *m* Molotov.

petrol can *n* bidón *m* de gasolina.

petrol engine *n* (*BRIT*) motor *m* de gasolina.

petroleum [pə'trəuliəm] *n* petróleo.

petroleum jelly *n* vaselina.

petrol pump *n* (*BRIT*) (*in car*) bomba de gasolina; (*in garage*) surtidor *m* de gasolina.

petrol station *n* (*BRIT*) gasolinera.

petrol tank *n* (*BRIT*) depósito (de gasolina).

petticoat ['pɛtɪkəut] *n* combinación *f*, enagua(s) *f(pl)* (*LAM*).

pettifogging ['pɛtɪfɔgɪŋ] *adj* quisquilloso.

pettiness ['pɛtɪnɪs] *n* mezquindad *f*.

petty ['pɛtɪ] *adj* (*mean*) mezquino; (*unimportant*) insignificante.

petty cash *n* dinero para gastos menores.

petty cash book *n* libro de caja auxiliar.

petty officer *n* contramaestre *m*.

petulant ['pɛtjulənt] *adj* malhumorado.

pew [pjuː] *n* banco.

pewter ['pjuːtə*] *n* peltre *m*.

Pfc *abbr* (*US MIL*) = *private first class*.

PG *n abbr* (*CINE*) = *parental guidance*.

PGA *n abbr* = *Professional Golfers' Association*.

PH *n abbr* (*US MIL*: = *Purple Heart*) decoración otorgada a los heridos de guerra.

pH *n abbr* (= *pH value*) pH.

PHA *n abbr* (*US*) = *Public Housing Administration*.

phallic ['fælɪk] *adj* fálico.

phantom ['fæntəm] *n* fantasma *m*.

Pharaoh ['fɛərəu] *n* faraón *m*.

pharmaceutical [fɑːmə'sjuːtɪkl] *adj* farmacéutico.

pharmacist ['fɑːməsɪst] *n* farmacéutico/a.

pharmacy ['fɑːməsɪ] *n* (*US*) farmacia.

phase [feɪz] *n* fase *f* ◊ *vt*: **to ~ sth in/out** introducir/retirar algo por etapas; **~d withdrawal** retirada progresiva.

PhD *abbr* = **Doctor of Philosophy.**

pheasant ['fɛznt] *n* faisán *m*.

phenomenal [fɪ'nɔmɪnl] *adj* fenomenal, extraordinario.

phenomenally [fɪ'nɔmɪnlɪ] *adv* extraordinariamente.

phenomenon, *pl* **phenomena** [fə'nɔmɪnən, -nə] *n* fenómeno.

phial ['faɪəl] *n* ampolla.

philanderer [fɪ'lændərə*] *n* donjuán *m*, don Juan *m*.

philanthropic [fɪlən'θrɔpɪk] *adj* filantrópico.

philanthropist [fɪ'lænθrəpɪst] *n* filántropo/a.

philatelist [fɪ'lætəlɪst] *n* filatelista *m/f*.

philately [fɪ'lætəlɪ] *n* filatelia.

Philippines ['fɪlɪpiːnz] *npl*: **the ~** (las Islas) Filipinas.

philosopher [fɪ'lɔsəfə*] *n* filósofo/a.

philosophical [fɪlə'sɔfɪkl] *adj* filosófico.

philosophy [fɪ'lɔsəfɪ] *n* filosofía.

phlegm [flɛm] *n* flema.

phlegmatic [flɛg'mætɪk] *adj* flemático.

phobia ['fəubjə] *n* fobia.

phone [fəun] *n* teléfono ◊ *vt* telefonear, llamar por teléfono; **to be on the ~** tener teléfono; (*be calling*) estar hablando por teléfono.

▶**phone back**, *vi* volver a llamar.

▶**phone up** *vt*, *vi* llamar por teléfono.

phone book *n* guía telefónica.

phone box, **phone booth** *n* cabina telefónica.

phone call *n* llamada (telefónica).

phonecard ['fəunkɑːd] *n* tarjeta telefónica.

phone-in ['fəunɪn] *n* (*BRIT RADIO, TV*) *programa de radio o televisión con las líneas abiertas al público*.

phone tapping [-tæpɪŋ] *n* escuchas telefónicas.

phonetics [fə'nɛtɪks] *n* fonética.

phon(e)y ['fəunɪ] *adj* falso ◊ *n* (*person*) farsante *m/f*.

phonograph ['fəunəgræf] *n* (*US*) fonógrafo, tocadiscos *m inv*.

phonology [fəu'nɔlədʒɪ] *n* fonología.

phosphate ['fɔsfeɪt] *n* fosfato.

phosphorus ['fɔsfərəs] *n* fósforo.

photo ['fəutəu] *n* foto *f*.

photo... ['fəutəu] *pref* foto...

photocall ['fəutəukɔːl] *n* sesión *f* fotográfica para la prensa.

photocopier ['fəutəukɔpɪə*] *n* fotocopiadora.

photocopy ['fəutəukɔpɪ] *n* fotocopia ◊ *vt*

fotocopiar.

photoelectric [fəutəuɪ'lɛktrɪk] *adj*: ~ **cell** célula fotoeléctrica.

photo finish *n* resultado comprobado por fotocontrol.

Photofit ® ['fəutəufɪt] *n* (*also*: ~ **picture**) retrato robot.

photogenic [fəutəu'dʒɛnɪk] *adj* fotogénico.

photograph ['fəutəgræf] *n* fotografía ♦ *vt* fotografiar; **to take a ~ of sb** sacar una foto de algn.

photographer [fə'tɔgrəfə*] *n* fotógrafo.

photographic [fəutə'græfɪk] *adj* fotográfico.

photography [fə'tɔgrəfɪ] *n* fotografía.

photo opportunity *n* oportunidad de salir en la foto.

Photostat ® ['fəutəustæt] *n* fotóstato.

photosynthesis [fəutəu'sɪnθəsɪs] *n* fotosíntesis *f*.

phrase [freɪz] *n* frase *f* ♦ *vt* (*letter*) expresar, redactar.

phrase book *n* libro de frases.

physical ['fɪzɪkl] *adj* físico; ~ **examination** reconocimiento médico; ~ **exercises** ejercicios *mpl* físicos.

physical education *n* educación *f* física.

physically ['fɪsɪklɪ] *adv* físicamente.

physical training *n* gimnasia.

physician [fɪ'zɪʃən] *n* médico/a.

physicist ['fɪzɪsɪst] *n* físico/a.

physics ['fɪzɪks] *n* física.

physiological [fɪzɪə'lɔdʒɪkl] *adj* fisiológico.

physiology [fɪzɪ'ɔlədʒɪ] *n* fisiología.

physiotherapy [fɪzɪəu'θɛrəpɪ] *n* fisioterapia.

physique [fɪ'ziːk] *n* físico.

pianist ['pɪənɪst] *n* pianista *m/f*.

piano [pɪ'ænəu] *n* piano.

piano accordion *n* (*BRIT*) acordeón-piano *m*.

piccolo ['pɪkələu] *n* (*MUS*) flautín *m*.

pick [pɪk] *n* (*tool: also*: ~-**axe**) pico, piqueta ♦ *vt* (*select*) elegir, escoger; (*gather*) coger (*SP*), recoger (*LAM*); (*lock*) abrir con ganzúa; (*scab, spot*) rascar ♦ *vi*: **to ~ and choose** ser muy exigente; **take your ~** escoja lo que quiera; **the ~ of** lo mejor de; **to ~ one's nose/teeth** hurgarse las narices/escarbarse los dientes; **to ~ pockets** ratear, ser carterista; **to ~ one's way through** andar a tientas, abrirse camino; **to ~ a fight/quarrel with sb** buscar pelea/camorra con algn; **to ~ sb's brains** aprovecharse de los conocimientos de algn.

▶**pick at** *vt fus*: **to ~ at one's food** comer con poco apetito.

▶**pick off** *vt* (*kill*) matar de un tiro.

▶**pick on** *vt fus* (*person*) meterse con.

▶**pick out** *vt* escoger; (*distinguish*) identificar.

▶**pick up** *vi* (*improve: sales*) ir mejor; (: *patient*) reponerse; (: *FINANCE*) recobrarse ♦ *vt* (*from floor*) recoger; (*buy*) comprar; (*find*) encontrar; (*learn*) aprender; (*RADIO, TV, TEL*) captar; **to ~ up speed** acelerarse; **to ~ o.s. up** levantarse; **to ~ up where one left off** reempezar algo donde lo había dejado.

pickaxe, (*US*) **pickax** ['pɪkæks] *n* pico, zapapico.

picket ['pɪkɪt] *n* (*in strike*) piquete *m* ♦ *vt* hacer un piquete en, piquetear; **to be on ~ duty** estar de piquete.

picketing ['pɪkɪtɪŋ] *n* organización *f* de piquetes.

picket line *n* piquete *m*.

pickings ['pɪkɪŋz] *npl* (*pilferings*): **there are good ~ to be had here** se pueden sacar buenas ganancias de aquí.

pickle ['pɪkl] *n* (*also*: ~**s**: *as condiment*) escabeche *m*; (*fig: mess*) apuro ♦ *vt* conservar en escabeche; (*in vinegar*) conservar en vinagre; **in a ~** en un lío, en apuros.

pick-me-up ['pɪkmɪʌp] *n* reconstituyente *m*.

pickpocket ['pɪkpɔkɪt] *n* carterista *m/f*.

pickup ['pɪkʌp] *n* (*also*: ~ **truck**, ~ **van**) furgoneta.

picnic ['pɪknɪk] *n* picnic *m*, merienda ♦ *vi* merendar en el campo.

pictorial [pɪk'tɔːrɪəl] *adj* pictórico; (*magazine etc*) ilustrado.

picture ['pɪktʃə*] *n* cuadro; (*painting*) pintura; (*photograph*) fotografía; (*film*) película; (*TV*) imagen *f* ♦ *vt* pintar; **the ~s** (*BRIT*) el cine; **we get a good ~ here** captamos bien la imagen aquí; **to take a ~ of sb/sth** hacer *or* sacar una foto a algn/de algo; **the garden is a ~ in June** el jardín es una preciosidad en junio; **the overall ~** la impresión general; **to put sb in the ~** poner a algn al corriente *or* al tanto.

picture book *n* libro de dibujos.

picture messaging *n* (envío de) mensajes *mpl* con imágenes.

picturesque [pɪktʃə'rɛsk] *adj* pintoresco.

piddling ['pɪdlɪŋ] *adj* insignificante.

pidgin ['pɪdʒɪn] *adj*: ~ **English** *lengua franca basada en el inglés*.

pie [paɪ] *n* (*of meat etc: large*) pastel *m*; (: *small*) empanada; (*sweet*) tarta.

piebald ['paɪbɔːld] *adj* pío.

piece [piːs] *n* pedazo, trozo; (*of cake*) trozo;

(*DRAUGHTS etc*) ficha; (*CHESS, part of a set*) pieza; (*item*): **a ~ of furniture/advice** un mueble/un consejo ♦ *vt*: **to ~ together** juntar; (*TECH*) armar; **to take to ~s** desmontar; **a ~ of news** una noticia; **a 10p ~** una moneda de 10 peniques; **a six-~ band** un conjunto de seis (músicos); **in one ~** (*object*) de una sola pieza; **~ by ~** pieza por *or* a pieza; **to say one's ~** decir su parecer.

piecemeal ['pi:smi:l] *adv* poco a poco.

piece rate *n* tarifa a destajo.

piecework ['pi:swɔ:k] *n* trabajo a destajo.

pie chart *n* gráfico de sectores *or* de tarta.

pier [pɪə*] *n* muelle *m*, embarcadero.

pierce [pɪəs] *vt* penetrar en, perforar; **to have one's ears ~d** hacerse los agujeros de las orejas.

piercing ['pɪəsɪŋ] *adj* (*cry*) penetrante ♦ *n* (*body art*) piercing *m*.

piety ['paɪətɪ] *n* piedad *f*.

pig [pɪg] *n* cerdo, puerco, chancho (*LAM*); (*person: greedy*) tragón/ona *m/f*, comilón/ona *m/f*; (: *nasty*) cerdo/a.

pigeon ['pɪdʒən] *n* paloma; (*as food*) pichón *m*.

pigeonhole ['pɪdʒənhəul] *n* casilla.

piggy bank ['pɪgɪbæŋk] *n* hucha (*en forma de cerdito*).

pigheaded ['pɪg'hedɪd] *adj* terco, testarudo.

piglet ['pɪglɪt] *n* cerdito, cochinillo.

pigment ['pɪgmənt] *n* pigmento.

pigmentation [pɪgmən'teɪʃən] *n* pigmentación *f*.

pigmy ['pɪgmɪ] *n* = **pygmy.**

pigskin ['pɪgskɪn] *n* piel *f* de cerdo.

pigsty ['pɪgstaɪ] *n* pocilga.

pigtail ['pɪgteɪl] *n* (*girl's*) trenza; (*Chinese, TAUR*) coleta.

pike [paɪk] *n* (*spear*) pica; (*fish*) lucio.

pilchard ['pɪltʃəd] *n* sardina.

pile [paɪl] *n* (*heap*) montón *m*; (*of carpet*) pelo ♦ (*vb: also: ~ up*) *vt* amontonar; (*fig*) acumular ♦ *vi* amontonarse; **in a ~** en un montón; **to ~ into** (*car*) meterse en.

▶**pile on** *vt*: **to ~ it on** (*col*) exagerar.

piles [paɪlz] *npl* (*MED*) almorranas *fpl*, hemorroides *mpl*.

pile-up ['paɪlʌp] *n* (*AUT*) accidente *m* múltiple.

pilfer ['pɪlfə*] *vt, vi* ratear, robar, sisar.

pilfering ['pɪlfərɪŋ] *n* ratería.

pilgrim ['pɪlgrɪm] *n* peregrino/a; **the Pilgrim Fathers** *or* **Pilgrims** *los primeros colonos norteamericanos*; *see also* **Thanksgiving (Day)**.

pilgrimage ['pɪlgrɪmɪdʒ] *n* peregrinación *f*, romería.

pill [pɪl] *n* píldora; **the ~** la píldora; **to be on the ~** tomar la píldora (anticonceptiva).

pillage ['pɪlɪdʒ] *vt* pillar, saquear.

pillar ['pɪlə*] *n* pilar *m*, columna.

pillar box *n* (*BRIT*) buzón *m*.

pillion ['pɪljən] *n* (*of motorcycle*) asiento trasero; **to ride ~** ir en el asiento trasero.

pillion passenger *n* pasajero que va detrás.

pillory ['pɪlərɪ] *vt* poner en ridículo.

pillow ['pɪləu] *n* almohada.

pillowcase ['pɪləukeɪs], **pillowslip** ['pɪləuslɪp] *n* funda (de almohada).

pilot ['paɪlət] *n* piloto *inv* ♦ *adj* (*scheme etc*) piloto ♦ *vt* pilotar; (*fig*) guiar, conducir.

pilot light *n* piloto.

pimento [pɪ'mentəu] *n* pimiento morrón.

pimp [pɪmp] *n* chulo, cafiche *m* (*LAM*).

pimple ['pɪmpl] *n* grano.

pimply ['pɪmplɪ] *adj* lleno de granos.

PIN *n abbr see* **personal identification number.**

pin [pɪn] *n* alfiler *m*; (*ELEC: of plug*) clavija; (*TECH*) perno; (: *wooden*) clavija; (*drawing ~*) chincheta; (*in grenade*) percutor *m* ♦ *vt* prender (con alfiler); sujetar con perno; **~s and needles** hormigueo *sg*; **to ~ sth on sb** (*fig*) cargar a algn con la culpa de algo.

▶**pin down** *vt* (*fig*): **there's something strange here, but I can't quite ~ it down** aquí hay algo raro pero no puedo precisar qué es; **to ~ sb down** hacer que algn concrete.

pinafore ['pɪnəfɔ:*] *n* delantal *m*.

pinafore dress *n* (*BRIT*) pichi *m*.

pinball ['pɪnbɔ:l] *n* (*also: ~ machine*) millón *m*, fliper *m*.

pincers ['pɪnsəz] *npl* pinzas *fpl*, tenazas *fpl*.

pinch [pɪntʃ] *n* pellizco; (*of salt etc*) pizca ♦ *vt* pellizcar; (*col: steal*) birlar ♦ *vi* (*shoe*) apretar; **at a ~** en caso de apuro; **to feel the ~** (*fig*) pasar apuros *or* estrecheces.

pinched [pɪntʃt] *adj* (*drawn*) cansado; **~ with cold** transido de frío; **~ for money/space** mal *or* falto de dinero/espacio *or* sitio.

pincushion ['pɪnkuʃən] *n* acerico.

pine [paɪn] *n* (*also: ~ tree*) pino ♦ *vi*: **to ~ for** suspirar por.

▶**pine away** *vi* morirse de pena.

pineapple ['paɪnæpl] *n* piña, ananá(s) (*LAM*) *m*.

pine cone *n* piña.

pine needle *n* aguja de pino.

Ping-Pong ® ['pɪŋpɔŋ] *n* pingpong *m*.

pink [pɪŋk] *adj* (de color) rosa ♦ *n* (*colour*) rosa; (*BOT*) clavel *m*.

pinking shears ['pɪŋkɪŋ-] _npl_ tijeras _fpl_ dentadas.

pin money _n_ dinero para gastos extra.

pinnacle ['pɪnəkl] _n_ cumbre _f._

pinpoint ['pɪnpɔɪnt] _vt_ precisar.

pinstripe ['pɪnstraɪp] _adj:_ ~ **suit** traje _m_ a rayas.

pint [paɪnt] _n_ pinta (_BRIT_ = 0.57 _l; US_ = 0.47 _l_); (_BRIT col: of beer_) pinta de cerveza, ≈ jarra (_SP_).

pin-up ['pɪnʌp] _n_ (_picture_) fotografía de mujer u hombre medio desnudos; ~ (**girl**) ≈ chica de calendario.

pioneer [paɪə'nɪə*] _n_ pionero/a ♦ _vt_ promover.

pious ['paɪəs] _adj_ piadoso, devoto.

pip [pɪp] _n_ (_seed_) pepita; **the ~s** (_BRIT TEL_) la señal.

pipe [paɪp] _n_ tubería, cañería; (_for smoking_) pipa, cachimba (_LAM_), cachimbo (_LAM_) ♦ _vt_ conducir en cañerías; (**bag**)~**s** _npl_ gaita _sg._

▶**pipe down** _vi_ (_col_) callarse.

pipe cleaner _n_ limpiapipas _m inv._

piped music [paɪpt-] _n_ música ambiental.

pipe dream _n_ sueño imposible.

pipeline ['paɪplaɪn] _n_ tubería, cañería; (_for oil_) oleoducto; (_for natural gas_) gaseoducto; **it is in the ~** (_fig_) está en trámite.

piper ['paɪpə*] _n_ (_gen_) flautista _m/f;_ (_with bagpipes_) gaitero/a.

pipe tobacco _n_ tabaco de pipa.

piping ['paɪpɪŋ] _adv:_ **to be ~ hot** estar calentito.

piquant ['piːkənt] _adj_ picante.

pique [piːk] _n_ pique _m,_ resentimiento.

pirate ['paɪərət] _n_ pirata _m/f_ ♦ _vt_ (_record, video, book_) hacer una copia pirata de.

pirated ['paɪərətɪd] _adj_ (_book, record etc_) pirata _inv._

pirate radio _n_ (_BRIT_) emisora pirata.

pirouette [pɪru'ɛt] _n_ pirueta ♦ _vi_ piruetear.

Pisces ['paɪsiːz] _n_ Piscis _m._

piss [pɪs] _vi_ (_col_) mear.

pissed [pɪst] _adj_ (_col: drunk_) mamado.

pistol ['pɪstl] _n_ pistola.

piston ['pɪstən] _n_ pistón _m,_ émbolo.

pit [pɪt] _n_ (_also:_ **coal** ~) mina; (_in garage_) foso de inspección; (_also:_ **orchestra** ~) foso de la orquesta; (_quarry_) cantera ♦ _vt_ (_subj: chickenpox_) picar; (_: rust_) comer; **to** ~ **A against B** oponer A a B; ~**s** _npl_ (_AUT_) box _msg;_ ~**ted with** (_chickenpox_) picado de.

pitapat ['pɪtə'pæt] _adv:_ **to go** ~ (_heart_) latir rápidamente; (_rain_) golpetear.

pitch [pɪtʃ] _n_ (_throw_) lanzamiento; (_MUS_)

tono; (_BRIT SPORT_) campo, terreno; (_tar_) brea; (_in market etc_) puesto; (_fig: degree_) nivel _m,_ grado ♦ _vt_ (_throw_) arrojar, lanzar ♦ _vi_ (_fall_) caer(se); (_NAUT_) cabecear; **I can't keep working at this** ~ no puedo seguir trabajando a este ritmo; **at its** (**highest**) ~ en su punto máximo; **his anger reached such a** ~ **that** ... su ira _or_ cólera llegó a tal extremo que ...; **to** ~ **a tent** montar una tienda (de campaña); **to** ~ **one's aspirations too high** tener ambiciones desmesuradas.

pitch-black ['pɪtʃ'blæk] _adj_ negro como boca de lobo.

pitched battle [pɪtʃt-] _n_ batalla campal.

pitcher ['pɪtʃə*] _n_ cántaro, jarro.

pitchfork ['pɪtʃfɔːk] _n_ horca.

piteous ['pɪtɪəs] _adj_ lastimoso.

pitfall ['pɪtfɔːl] _n_ riesgo.

pith [pɪθ] _n_ (_of orange_) piel _f_ blanca; (_fig_) meollo.

pithead ['pɪthɛd] _n_ (_BRIT_) bocamina.

pithy ['pɪθɪ] _adj_ jugoso.

pitiful ['pɪtɪful] _adj_ (_touching_) lastimoso, conmovedor(a); (_contemptible_) lamentable.

pitifully ['pɪtɪfəlɪ] _adv:_ **it's** ~ **obvious** es tan evidente que da pena.

pitiless ['pɪtɪlɪs] _adj_ despiadado, implacable.

pitilessly ['pɪtɪlɪslɪ] _adv_ despiadadamente, implacablemente.

pittance ['pɪtns] _n_ miseria.

pity ['pɪtɪ] _n_ (_compassion_) compasión _f,_ piedad _f;_ (_shame_) lástima ♦ _vt_ compadecer(se de); **to have** _or_ **take** ~ **on sb** compadecerse de algn; **what a** ~! ¡qué pena!; **it is a** ~ **that you can't come** ¡qué pena que no puedas venir!

pitying ['pɪtɪɪŋ] _adj_ compasivo, de lástima.

pivot ['pɪvət] _n_ eje _m_ ♦ _vi:_ **to** ~ **on** girar sobre; (_fig_) depender de.

pixel ['pɪksl] _n_ (_COMPUT_) pixel _m,_ punto.

pixie ['pɪksɪ] _n_ duendecillo.

pizza ['piːtsə] _n_ pizza.

placard ['plækɑːd] _n_ (_in march etc_) pancarta.

placate [plə'keɪt] _vt_ apaciguar.

place [pleɪs] _n_ lugar _m,_ sitio; (_rank_) rango; (_seat_) plaza, asiento; (_post_) puesto; (_in street names_) plaza; (_home_): **at/to his** ~ en/a su casa ♦ _vt_ (_object_) poner, colocar; (_identify_) reconocer; (_find a post for_) dar un puesto a, colocar; (_goods_) vender; **to take** ~ tener lugar; **to be** ~**d** (_in race, exam_) colocarse; **out of** ~ (_not suitable_) fuera de lugar; **in the first** ~ (_first of all_) en primer lugar; **to change** ~**s with sb** cambiarse de sitio con algn; **from** ~ **to** ~

de un sitio a or para otro; **all over the ~** por todas partes; **he's going ~s** (fig, col) llegará lejos; **I feel rather out of ~ here** me encuentro algo desplazado; **to put sb in his ~** (fig) poner a algn en su lugar; **it is not my ~ to do it** no me incumbe a mí hacerlo; **to ~ an order with sb (for)** hacer un pedido a algn (de); **we are better ~d than a month ago** estamos en mejor posición que hace un mes.

placebo [plə'si:bəu] n placebo.

place mat n (wooden etc) salvamanteles m inv; (in linen etc) mantel m individual.

placement ['pleɪsmənt] n colocación f.

place name n topónimo.

placid ['plæsɪd] adj apacible, plácido.

placidity [plæ'sɪdɪtɪ] n placidez f.

plagiarism ['pleɪdʒərɪzm] n plagio.

plagiarist ['pleɪdʒərɪst] n plagiario/a.

plagiarize ['pleɪdʒəraɪz] vt plagiar.

plague [pleɪg] n plaga; (MED) peste f ♦ vt (fig) acosar, atormentar; **to ~ sb with questions** acribillar a algn a preguntas.

plaice [pleɪs] n, pl inv platija.

plaid [plæd] n (material) tela de cuadros.

plain [pleɪn] adj (clear) claro, evidente; (simple) sencillo; (frank) franco, abierto; (not handsome) poco atractivo; (pure) natural, puro ♦ adv claramente ♦ n llano, llanura; **in ~ clothes** (police) vestido de paisano; **to make sth ~ to sb** dejar algo en claro a algn.

plain chocolate n chocolate m oscuro or amargo.

plainly ['pleɪnlɪ] adv claramente, evidentemente; (frankly) francamente.

plainness ['pleɪnnɪs] n (clarity) claridad f; (simplicity) sencillez f; (of face) falta de atractivo.

plain speaking n: **there has been some ~** se ha hablado claro.

plaintiff ['pleɪntɪf] n demandante m/f.

plaintive ['pleɪntɪv] adj (cry, voice) lastimero, quejumbroso; (look) que da lástima.

plait [plæt] n trenza ♦ vt trenzar.

plan [plæn] n (drawing) plano; (scheme) plan m, proyecto ♦ vt (think) pensar; (prepare) proyectar, planear; (intend) pensar, tener la intención de ♦ vi hacer proyectos; **have you any ~s for today?** ¿piensas hacer algo hoy?; **to ~ to do** pensar hacer; **how long do you ~ to stay?** ¿cuánto tiempo piensas quedarte?; **to ~ (for)** planear, proyectar.

▶**plan out** vt planear detalladamente.

plane [pleɪn] n (AVIAT) avión m; (tree) plátano; (tool) cepillo; (MATH) plano.

planet ['plænɪt] n planeta m.

planetarium [plænɪ'tɛərɪəm] n planetario.

planetary ['plænɪtərɪ] adj planetario.

plank [plæŋk] n tabla.

plankton ['plæŋktən] n plancton m.

planned economy [plænd-] n economía planificada.

planner ['plænə*] n planificador(a) m/f; (chart) diagrama m de planificación; **town ~** urbanista m/f.

planning ['plænɪŋ] n (POL, ECON) planificación f; **family ~** planificación familiar.

planning committee n (in local government) comité m de planificación.

planning permission n licencia de obras.

plant [plɑ:nt] n planta; (machinery) maquinaria; (factory) fábrica ♦ vt plantar; (field) sembrar; (bomb) colocar.

plantain ['plænteɪn] n llantén m.

plantation [plæn'teɪʃən] n plantación f; (estate) hacienda.

planter ['plɑ:ntə*] n hacendado.

plant pot n maceta, tiesto.

plaque [plæk] n placa.

plasma ['plæzmə] n plasma m.

plaster ['plɑ:stə*] n (for walls) yeso; (also: ~ of Paris) yeso mate; (MED: for broken leg etc) escayola; (BRIT: also: **sticking ~**) tirita, esparadrapo ♦ vt enyesar; (cover): **to ~ with** llenar or cubrir de; **to be ~ed with mud** estar cubierto de barro.

plasterboard ['plɑ:stəbɔːd] n cartón m yeso.

plaster cast n (MED) escayola; (model, statue) vaciado de yeso.

plastered ['plɑ:stəd] adj (col) borracho.

plasterer ['plɑ:stərə*] n yesero.

plastic ['plæstɪk] n plástico ♦ adj de plástico.

plastic bag n bolsa de plástico.

plastic bullet n bala de goma.

plastic explosive n goma 2 ®.

plasticine ® ['plæstɪsi:n] n (BRIT) plastilina ®.

plastic surgery n cirugía plástica.

plastinate ['plæstɪneɪt] vt plastinar.

plate [pleɪt] n (dish) plato; (metal, in book) lámina; (PHOT, on door) placa; (AUT: number ~) matrícula.

plateau, **~s** or **~x** ['plætəu, -z] n meseta, altiplanicie f.

plateful ['pleɪtful] n plato.

plate glass n vidrio or cristal m cilindrado.

platen ['plætən] n (on typewriter, printer) rodillo.

plate rack n escurreplatos m inv.

platform ['plætfɔ:m] *n* (*RAIL*) andén *m*; (*stage*) plataforma; (*at meeting*) tribuna; (*POL*) programa *m* (electoral); **the train leaves from ~ 7** el tren sale del andén número 7.

platform ticket *n* (*BRIT*) billete *m* de andén.

platinum ['plætɪnəm] *n* platino.

platitude ['plætɪtjuːd] *n* tópico, lugar *m* común.

platonic [pləˈtɔnɪk] *adj* platónico.

platoon [pləˈtuːn] *n* pelotón *m*.

platter ['plætə*] *n* fuente *f*.

plaudits ['plɔːdɪts] *npl* aplausos *mpl*.

plausibility [plɔːzɪˈbɪlɪtɪ] *n* verosimilitud *f*, credibilidad *f*.

plausible ['plɔːzɪbl] *adj* verosímil; (*person*) convincente.

play [pleɪ] *n* (*gen*) juego; (*THEAT*) obra ♦ *vt* (*game*) jugar; (*instrument*) tocar; (*THEAT*) representar; (: *part*) hacer el papel de; (*fig*) desempeñar ♦ *vi* jugar; (*frolic*) juguetear; **to ~ safe** ir a lo seguro; **to bring** *or* **call into ~** poner en juego; **to ~ a trick on sb** gastar una broma a algn; **they're ~ing at soldiers** están jugando a (los) soldados; **to ~ for time** (*fig*) tratar de ganar tiempo; **to ~ into sb's hands** (*fig*) hacerle el juego a algn; **a smile ~ed on his lips** una sonrisa le bailaba en los labios.

►**play about, play around** *vi* (*person*) hacer el tonto; **to ~ about** *or* **around with** (*fiddle with*) juguetear con; (*idea*) darle vueltas a.

►**play along** *vi*: **to ~ along with** seguirle el juego a ♦ *vt*: **to ~ sb along** (*fig*) jugar con algn.

►**play back** *vt* poner.

►**play down** *vt* quitar importancia a.

►**play on** *vt fus* (*sb's feelings, credulity*) aprovecharse de; **to ~ on sb's nerves** atacarle los nervios a algn.

►**play up** *vi* (*cause trouble*) dar guerra.

playact ['pleɪækt] *vi* (*fig*) hacer comedia *or* teatro.

play-acting ['pleɪæktɪŋ] *n* teatro.

playboy ['pleɪbɔɪ] *n* playboy *m*.

player ['pleɪə*] *n* jugador(a) *m/f*; (*THEAT*) actor *m*, actriz *f*; (*MUS*) músico/a.

playful ['pleɪful] *adj* juguetón/ona.

playground ['pleɪgraund] *n* (*in school*) patio de recreo.

playgroup ['pleɪgruːp] *n* jardín *m* de infancia.

playing card ['pleɪɪŋ-] *n* naipe *m*, carta.

playing field *n* campo de deportes.

playmaker ['pleɪmeɪkə*] *n* (*SPORT*) *jugador*

encargado de facilitar buenas jugadas a sus compañeros.

playmate ['pleɪmeɪt] *n* compañero/a de juego.

play-off ['pleɪɔf] *n* (*SPORT*) (partido de) desempate *m*.

playpen ['pleɪpɛn] *n* corral *m*.

playroom ['pleɪruːm] *n* cuarto de juego.

playschool ['pleɪskuːl] *n* = **playgroup**.

plaything ['pleɪθɪŋ] *n* juguete *m*.

playtime ['pleɪtaɪm] *n* (*SCOL*) (hora de) recreo.

playwright ['pleɪraɪt] *n* dramaturgo/a.

plc *abbr* (= *public limited company*) S.A.

plea [pliː] *n* (*request*) súplica, petición *f*; (*excuse*) pretexto, disculpa; (*LAW*) alegato, defensa.

plea bargaining *n* (*LAW*) *acuerdo entre fiscal y defensor para agilizar los trámites judiciales.*

plead [pliːd] *vt* (*LAW*): **to ~ sb's case** defender a alguien; (*give as excuse*) poner como pretexto ♦ *vi* (*LAW*) declararse; (*beg*): **to ~ with sb** suplicar *or* rogar a algn; **to ~ guilty/not guilty** (*defendant*) declararse culpable/inocente; **to ~ for sth** (*beg for*) suplicar algo.

pleasant ['plɛznt] *adj* agradable.

pleasantly ['plɛzntlɪ] *adv* agradablemente.

pleasantries ['plɛzntrɪz] *npl* (*polite remarks*) cortesías *fpl*; **to exchange ~** conversar amablemente.

please [pliːz] *vt* (*give pleasure to*) dar gusto a, agradar ♦ *vi* (*think fit*): **do as you ~** haz lo que quieras *or* lo que te dé la gana; **to ~ o.s.** hacer lo que le parezca; **~!** ¡por favor!; **~ yourself!** ¡haz lo que quieras!, ¡como quieras!; **~ don't cry!** ¡no llores! te lo ruego.

pleased [pliːzd] *adj* (*happy*) alegre, contento; (*satisfied*): **~ (with)** satisfecho (de); **~ to meet you** (*col*) ¡encantado!, ¡tanto *or* mucho gusto!; **to be ~ (about sth)** alegrarse (de algo); **we are ~ to inform you that ...** tenemos el gusto de comunicarle que ....

pleasing ['pliːzɪŋ] *adj* agradable, grato.

pleasurable ['plɛʒərəbl] *adj* agradable, grato.

pleasurably ['plɛʒərəblɪ] *adv* agradablemente, gratamente.

pleasure ['plɛʒə*] *n* placer *m*, gusto; (*will*) voluntad *f* ♦ *cpd* de recreo; "**it's a ~**" "el gusto es mío"; **it's a ~ to see him** da gusto verle; **I have much ~ in informing you that ...** tengo el gran placer de comunicarles que ...; **with ~** con mucho *or* todo gusto; **is this trip for business or**

~? ¿este viaje es de negocios o de placer?

pleasure cruise n crucero de placer.

pleasure ground n parque m de atracciones.

pleasure-seeking ['plɛʒəsɪːkɪŋ] adj hedonista.

pleat [pliːt] n pliegue m.

pleb [plɛb] n: **the ~s** la gente baja, la plebe.

plebeian [plɪ'biːən] n plebeyo/a ♦ adj plebeyo; (pej) ordinario.

plebiscite ['plɛbɪsɪt] n plebiscito.

plectrum ['plɛktrəm] n plectro.

pledge [plɛdʒ] n (object) prenda; (promise) promesa, voto ♦ vt (pawn) empeñar; (promise) prometer; **to ~ support for sb** prometer su apoyo a algn; **to ~ sb to secrecy** hacer jurar a algn que guardará el secreto.

plenary ['pliːnərɪ] adj: **in ~ session** en sesión plenaria.

plentiful ['plɛntɪful] adj copioso, abundante.

plenty ['plɛntɪ] n abundancia; **~ of** mucho(s)/a(s); **we've got ~ of time to get there** tenemos tiempo de sobra para llegar.

plethora ['plɛθərə] n plétora.

pleurisy ['pluərɪsɪ] n pleuresía.

pliability [plaɪə'bɪlɪtɪ] n flexibilidad f.

pliable ['plaɪəbl] adj flexible.

pliers ['plaɪəz] npl alicates mpl, tenazas fpl.

plight [plaɪt] n condición f or situación f difícil.

plimsolls ['plɪmsəlz] npl (BRIT) zapatillas fpl de tenis.

plinth [plɪnθ] n plinto.

PLO n abbr (= Palestine Liberation Organization) OLP f.

plod [plɒd] vi caminar con paso pesado; (fig) trabajar laboriosamente.

plodder ['plɒdə*] n trabajador(a) diligente pero lento/a.

plodding ['plɒdɪŋ] adj (student) empollón(ona); (worker) más aplicado que brillante.

plonk [plɒŋk] (col) n (BRIT: wine) vino peleón ♦ vt: **to ~ sth down** dejar caer algo.

plot [plɒt] n (scheme) complot m, conjura; (of story, play) argumento; (of land) terreno, parcela ♦ vt (mark out) trazar; (conspire) tramar, urdir ♦ vi conspirar; **a vegetable ~** un cuadro de hortalizas.

plotter ['plɒtə*] n (instrument) trazador m (de gráficos); (COMPUT) trazador m.

plotting ['plɒtɪŋ] n conspiración f, intrigas fpl.

plough, (US) **plow** [plau] n arado ♦ vt (earth) arar.

▶**plough back** vt (COMM) reinvertir.

▶**plough through** vt fus (crowd) abrirse paso a la fuerza por.

ploughing ['plauɪŋ] n labranza.

ploughman ['plaumən] n: **~'s lunch** pan m con queso y cebolla.

plow [plau] (US) = **plough**.

ploy [plɔɪ] n truco, estratagema.

pluck [plʌk] vt (fruit) coger (SP), recoger (LAM); (musical instrument) puntear; (bird) desplumar ♦ n valor m, ánimo; **to ~ up courage** hacer de tripas corazón; **to ~ one's eyebrows** depilarse las cejas.

plucky ['plʌkɪ] adj valiente.

plug [plʌg] n tapón m; (ELEC) enchufe m, clavija; (AUT: also: **spark(ing) ~**) bujía ♦ vt (hole) tapar; (col: advertise) dar publicidad a; **to give sb/sth a ~** dar publicidad a algn/algo; **to ~ a lead into a socket** enchufar un hilo en una toma.

▶**plug in** vt, vi (ELEC) enchufar.

plughole ['plʌghəul] n desagüe m.

plum [plʌm] n (fruit) ciruela; (also ~ **job**) chollo.

plumage ['pluːmɪdʒ] n plumaje m.

plumb [plʌm] adj vertical ♦ n plomo ♦ adv (exactly) exactamente, en punto ♦ vt sondar; (fig) sondear.

▶**plumb in** vt (washing machine) conectar.

plumber ['plʌmə*] n fontanero/a, plomero/a (LAM).

plumbing ['plʌmɪŋ] n (trade) fontanería, plomería (LAM); (piping) cañerías.

plume [pluːm] n (gen) pluma; (on helmet) penacho.

plummet ['plʌmɪt] vi: **to ~ (down)** caer a plomo.

plump [plʌmp] adj rechoncho, rollizo ♦ vt: **to ~ sth (down) on** dejar caer algo en.

▶**plump for** vt fus (col: choose) optar por.

▶**plump up** vt ahuecar.

plumpness ['plʌmpnɪs] n gordura.

plunder ['plʌndə*] n pillaje m; (loot) botín m ♦ vt saquear, pillar.

plunge [plʌndʒ] n zambullida ♦ vt sumergir, hundir ♦ vi (fall) caer; (dive) saltar; (person) arrojarse; (sink) hundirse; **to take the ~** lanzarse; **to ~ a room into darkness** sumir una habitación en la oscuridad.

plunger ['plʌndʒə*] n émbolo; (for drain) desatascador m.

plunging ['plʌndʒɪŋ] adj (neckline) escotado.

pluperfect [pluː'pəːfɪkt] n pluscuamperfecto.

plural ['pluərl] n plural m.

plus [plʌs] n (also: ~ **sign**) signo más; (fig) punto a favor ♦ adj: **a ~ factor** (fig) un

factor *m* a favor ♦ *prep* más, y, además de;
ten/twenty ~ más de diez/veinte.
plush [plʌʃ] *adj* de felpa.
plutonium [pluːˈtəunɪəm] *n* plutonio.
ply [plaɪ] *vt* (*a trade*) ejercer ♦ *vi* (*ship*) ir y
venir; (*for hire*) ofrecerse (para alquilar);
three ~ (*wool*) de tres cabos; **to** ~ **sb with
drink** no dejar de ofrecer copas a algn.
plywood [ˈplaɪwud] *n* madera
contrachapada.
PM *abbr* (*BRIT*) *see* **Prime Minister**.
p.m. *adv abbr* (= *post meridiem*) de la tarde
or noche.
PMS *n abbr* (= *premenstrual syndrome*) SPM
m.
PMT *n abbr* (= *premenstrual tension*) SPM *m.*
pneumatic [njuːˈmætɪk] *adj* neumático.
pneumatic drill *n* taladradora neumática.
pneumonia [njuːˈməunɪə] *n* pulmonía,
neumonía.
PO *n abbr* (= *Post Office*) Correos *mpl*; (*NAUT*)
= **petty officer.**
po *abbr* = **postal order.**
POA *n abbr* (*BRIT*) = *Prison Officers'
Association.*
poach [pəutʃ] *vt* (*cook*) escalfar; (*steal*)
cazar/pescar en vedado ♦ *vi* cazar/pescar
en vedado.
poached [pəutʃt] *adj* (*egg*) escalfado.
poacher [ˈpəutʃə*] *n* cazador(a) *m/f* furtivo/
a.
poaching [ˈpəutʃɪŋ] *n* caza/pesca furtiva.
PO Box *n abbr see* **Post Office Box.**
pocket [ˈpɔkɪt] *n* bolsillo; (*of air, GEO, fig*)
bolsa; (*BILLIARDS*) tronera ♦ *vt* meter en el
bolsillo; (*steal*) embolsarse; (*BILLIARDS*)
entronerar; **breast** ~ bolsillo de pecho; ~
of resistance foco de resistencia; ~ **of
warm air** bolsa de aire caliente; **to be out
of** ~ salir perdiendo; **to be £5 in/out of** ~
salir ganando/perdiendo 5 libras.
pocketbook [ˈpɔkɪtbuk] *n* (*US: wallet*)
cartera; (: *handbag*) bolso.
pocketful [ˈpɔkɪtful] *n* bolsillo lleno.
pocket knife *n* navaja.
pocket money *n* asignación *f.*
pockmarked [ˈpɔkmɑːkt] *adj* (*face*) picado
de viruelas.
pod [pɔd] *n* vaina.
podgy [ˈpɔdʒɪ] *adj* gordinflón/ona.
podiatrist [pɔˈdiːətrɪst] *n* (*US*) podólogo/a.
podiatry [pɔˈdiːətrɪ] *n* (*US*) podología.
podium [ˈpəudɪəm] *n* podio.
POE *n abbr* = *port of embarkation, port of
entry.*
poem [ˈpəuɪm] *n* poema *m.*
poet [ˈpəuɪt] *n* poeta *m/f.*
poetic [pəuˈɛtɪk] *adj* poético.

poet laureate [-ˈlɔːrɪɪt] *n* poeta *m* laureado;
ver recuadro.

POET LAUREATE

El poeta de la corte, denominado **Poet
Laureate***, ocupa como tal un puesto
vitalicio al servicio de la Casa Real
británica. Era tradición que escribiera
poemas conmemorativos para ocasiones
oficiales, aunque hoy día esto es poco
frecuente. El primer poeta así distinguido
fue Ben Jonson, en 1616.*

---

poetry [ˈpəuɪtrɪ] *n* poesía.
poignant [ˈpɔɪnjənt] *adj* conmovedor(a).
poignantly [ˈpɔɪnjəntlɪ] *adv* de modo
conmovedor.
point [pɔɪnt] *n* punto; (*tip*) punta; (*purpose*)
fin *m*, propósito; (*BRIT ELEC: also:* **power** ~)
toma de corriente, enchufe *m*; (*use*)
utilidad *f*; (*significant part*) lo esencial;
(*place*) punto, lugar *m*; (*also:* **decimal** ~): **2
~ 3 (2.3)** dos coma tres (2,3) ♦ *vt* (*gun etc*):
to ~ **sth at sb** apuntar con algo a algn ♦ *vi*
señalar con el dedo; ~**s** *npl* (*AUT*)
contactos *mpl*; (*RAIL*) agujas *fpl*; **to be on
the** ~ **of doing sth** estar a punto de hacer
algo; **to make a** ~ **of doing sth** poner
empeño en hacer algo; **to get the** ~
comprender; **to come to the** ~ ir al
meollo; **there's no** ~ **(in doing)** no tiene
sentido (hacer); ~ **of departure** (*also fig*)
punto de partida; ~ **of order** cuestión *f* de
procedimiento; ~ **of sale** (*COMM*) punto
de venta; ~**-of-sale advertising** publicidad
f en el punto de venta; **the train stops at
Carlisle and all** ~**s south** el tren para en
Carlisle, y en todas las estaciones al sur;
when it comes to the ~ a la hora de la
verdad; **in** ~ **of fact** en realidad; **that's
the whole** ~! ¡de eso se trata!; **to be
beside the** ~ no venir al caso; **you've got
a** ~ **there!** ¡tienes razón!
▶**point out** *vt* señalar.
▶**point to** *vt fus* indicar con el dedo; (*fig*)
indicar, señalar.
point-blank [ˈpɔɪntˈblæŋk] *adv* (*also:* **at** ~
range) a quemarropa.
pointed [ˈpɔɪntɪd] *adj* (*shape*) puntiagudo,
afilado; (*remark*) intencionado.
pointedly [ˈpɔɪntɪdlɪ] *adv*
intencionadamente.
pointer [ˈpɔɪntə*] *n* (*stick*) puntero; (*needle*)
aguja, indicador *m*; (*clue*) indicación *f*,
pista; (*advice*) consejo.
pointless [ˈpɔɪntlɪs] *adj* sin sentido.
pointlessly [ˈpɔɪntlɪslɪ] *adv* inútilmente, sin

motivo.

point of view n punto de vista.

poise [pɔɪz] n (of head, body) porte m; (calmness) aplomo.

poised [pɔɪzd] adj (in temperament) sereno.

poison ['pɔɪzn] n veneno ♦ vt envenenar.

poisoning ['pɔɪznɪŋ] n envenenamiento.

poisonous ['pɔɪznəs] adj venenoso; (fumes etc) tóxico; (fig: ideas, literature) pernicioso; (: rumours, individual) nefasto.

poke [pəuk] vt (fire) hurgar, atizar; (jab with finger, stick etc) dar; (COMPUT) almacenar; (put): **to ~ sth in(to)** introducir algo en ♦ n (jab) empujoncito; (with elbow) codazo; **to ~ one's head out of the window** asomar la cabeza por la ventana; **to ~ fun at sb** ridiculizar a algn; **to give the fire a ~** atizar el fuego.

▶**poke about** vi fisgonear.

poker ['pəukə*] n atizador m; (CARDS) póker m.

poker-faced ['pəukə'feɪst] adj de cara impasible.

poky ['pəukɪ] adj estrecho.

Poland ['pəulənd] n Polonia.

polar ['pəulə*] adj polar.

polar bear n oso polar.

polarization [pəuləraɪ'zeɪʃən] n polarización f.

polarize ['pəuləraɪz] vt polarizar.

Pole [pəul] n polaco/a.

pole [pəul] n palo; (GEO) polo; (TEL) poste m; (flag ~) asta; (tent ~) mástil m.

poleaxe ['pəulæks] vt (fig) desnucar.

pole bean n (US) judía trepadora.

polecat ['pəulkæt] n (BRIT) turón m; (US) mofeta.

Pol. Econ. ['pɔlɪkən] n abbr = political economy.

polemic [pɔ'lɛmɪk] n polémica.

polemicist [pɔ'lɛmɪsɪst] n polemista m/f.

pole star n estrella polar.

pole vault n salto con pértiga.

police [pə'liːs] n policía ♦ vt (streets, city, frontier) vigilar.

police car n coche-patrulla m.

police constable n (BRIT) guardia m, policía m.

police department n (US) policía.

police force n cuerpo de policía.

policeman [pə'liːsmən] n guardia m, policía m, agente m (LAM).

police officer n guardia m, policía m.

police record n: **to have a ~** tener antecedentes penales.

police state n estado policial.

police station n comisaría.

policewoman [pə'liːswumən] n mujer f policía.

policy ['pɔlɪsɪ] n política; (also: **insurance ~**) póliza; (of newspaper, company) política; **it is our ~ to do that** tenemos por norma hacer eso; **to take out a ~** sacar una póliza, hacerse un seguro.

policy holder n asegurado/a.

policy-making ['pɔlɪsɪmeɪkɪŋ] n elaboración f de directrices generales; **~ body** organismo encargado de elaborar las directrices generales.

polio ['pəulɪəu] n polio f.

Polish ['pəulɪʃ] adj polaco ♦ n (LING) polaco.

polish ['pɔlɪʃ] n (for shoes) betún m; (for floor) cera (de lustrar); (for nails) esmalte m; (shine) brillo, lustre m; (fig: refinement) refinamiento ♦ vt (shoes) limpiar; (make shiny) pulir, sacar brillo a; (fig: improve) perfeccionar, refinar.

▶**polish off** vt (work) terminar; (food) despachar.

▶**polish up** vt (shoes, furniture etc) limpiar, sacar brillo a; (fig: language) perfeccionar.

polished ['pɔlɪʃt] adj (fig: person) refinado.

polite [pə'laɪt] adj cortés, atento; (formal) correcto; **it's not ~ to do that** es de mala educación hacer eso.

politely [pə'laɪtlɪ] adv cortésmente.

politeness [pə'laɪtnɪs] n cortesía.

politic ['pɔlɪtɪk] adj prudente.

political [pə'lɪtɪkl] adj político.

political asylum n asilo político.

politically [pə'lɪtɪkəlɪ] adv políticamente.

politically correct adj políticamente correcto.

politician [pɔlɪ'tɪʃən] n político/a.

politics ['pɔlɪtɪks] n política.

polka ['pɔlkə] n polca.

polka dot n lunar m.

poll [pəul] n (votes) votación f, votos mpl; (also: **opinion ~**) sondeo, encuesta ♦ vt (votes) obtener; (in opinion ~) encuestar; **to go to the ~s** (voters) votar; (government) acudir a las urnas.

pollen ['pɔlən] n polen m.

pollen count n índice m de polen.

pollination [pɔlɪ'neɪʃən] n polinización f.

polling ['pəulɪŋ] n (BRIT POL) votación f; (TEL) interrogación f.

polling booth n cabina de votar.

polling day n día m de elecciones.

polling station n centro electoral.

pollster ['pəulstə*] n (person) encuestador(a) m/f; (organization) empresa de encuestas or sondeos.

poll tax n (BRIT, formerly) contribución f municipal (no progresiva).

pollutant [pə'luːtənt] n (agente m)
contaminante m.
pollute [pə'luːt] vt contaminar.
pollution [pə'luːʃən] n contaminación f,
polución f.
polo ['pəuləu] n (sport) polo.
polo-neck ['pəuləunɛk] adj de cuello vuelto
♦ n (sweater) suéter m de cuello vuelto.
poly ['pɔlɪ] n abbr (BRIT) = **polytechnic**.
poly... [pɔlɪ] pref poli....
poly bag n (BRIT col) bolsa de plástico.
polyester [pɔlɪ'ɛstə*] n poliéster m.
polyethylene [pɔlɪ'ɛθɪliːn] n (US)
polietileno.
polygamy [pə'lɪgəmɪ] n poligamia.
polygraph ['pɔlɪgrɑːf] n polígrafo.
Polynesia [pɔlɪ'niːzɪə] n Polinesia.
Polynesian [pɔlɪ'niːzɪən] adj, n polinesio/a
m/f.
polyp ['pɔlɪp] n (MED) pólipo.
polystyrene [pɔlɪ'staɪriːn] n poliestireno.
polytechnic [pɔlɪ'tɛknɪk] n escuela
politécnica.
polythene ['pɔlɪθiːn] n (BRIT) polietileno.
polythene bag n bolsa de plástico.
polyurethane [pɔlɪ'juərɪθeɪn] n
poliuretano.
pomegranate ['pɔmɪgrænɪt] n granada.
pommel ['pɔml] n pomo ♦ vt = **pummel**.
pomp [pɔmp] n pompa.
pompom ['pɔmpɔm] n borla.
pompous ['pɔmpəs] adj pomposo; (person)
presumido.
pond [pɔnd] n (natural) charca; (artificial)
estanque m.
ponder ['pɔndə*] vt meditar.
ponderous ['pɔndərəs] adj pesado.
pong [pɔŋ] n (BRIT col) peste f ♦ vi (BRIT col)
apestar.
pontiff ['pɔntɪf] n pontífice m.
pontificate [pɔn'tɪfɪkeɪt] vi (fig): **to ~**
(about) pontificar (sobre).
pontoon [pɔn'tuːn] n pontón m; (BRIT: card
game) veintiuna.
pony ['pəunɪ] n poney m, potro.
ponytail ['pəunɪteɪl] n coleta, cola de
caballo.
pony trekking n (BRIT) excursión f a
caballo.
poodle ['puːdl] n caniche m.
pool [puːl] n (natural) charca; (pond)
estanque m; (also: **swimming ~**) piscina,
alberca (LAM); (billiards) billar m
americano; (COMM: consortium)
consorcio; (: US: monopoly trust) trust m
♦ vt juntar; **typing ~** servicio de
mecanografía; **(football) ~s** npl
quinielas fpl.

poor [puə*] adj pobre; (bad) malo ♦ npl: **the**
~ los pobres.
poorly ['puəlɪ] adj mal, enfermo.
pop [pɔp] n ¡pum!; (sound) ruido seco;
(MUS) (música) pop m; (US col: father)
papá m; (col: drink) gaseosa ♦ vt (burst)
hacer reventar ♦ vi reventar; (cork)
saltar; **she ~ped her head out (of the**
window) sacó de repente la cabeza (por
la ventana).
►**pop in** vi entrar un momento.
►**pop out** vi salir un momento.
►**pop up** vi aparecer inesperadamente.
pop concert n concierto pop.
popcorn ['pɔpkɔːn] n palomitas fpl (de
maíz).
pope [pəup] n papa m.
poplar ['pɔplə*] n álamo.
poplin ['pɔplɪn] n popelina.
popper ['pɔpə*] n corchete m, botón m
automático.
poppy ['pɔpɪ] n amapola; see also
Remembrance Sunday.
poppycock ['pɔpɪkɔk] n (col) tonterías fpl.
Popsicle ® ['pɔpsɪkl] n (US) polo.
populace ['pɔpjuləs] n pueblo.
popular ['pɔpjulə*] adj popular; **a ~ song**
una canción popular; **to be ~ (with)**
(person) caer bien (a); (decision) ser
popular (entre).
popularity [pɔpju'lærɪtɪ] n popularidad f.
popularize ['pɔpjuləraɪz] vt popularizar;
(disseminate) vulgarizar.
populate ['pɔpjuleɪt] vt poblar.
population [pɔpju'leɪʃən] n población f.
population explosion n explosión f
demográfica.
populous ['pɔpjuləs] adj populoso.
pop-up menu ['pɔpʌp-] n (COMPUT) menú
m emergente.
porcelain ['pɔːslɪn] n porcelana.
porch [pɔːtʃ] n pórtico, entrada.
porcupine ['pɔːkjupaɪn] n puerco m espín.
pore [pɔː*] n poro ♦ vi: **to ~ over**
enfrascarse en.
pork [pɔːk] n (carne f de) cerdo or chancho
(LAM).
pork chop n chuleta de cerdo.
porn [pɔːn] adj (col) porno inv ♦ n porno.
pornographic [pɔːnə'græfɪk] adj
pornográfico.
pornography [pɔː'nɔgrəfɪ] n pornografía.
porous ['pɔːrəs] adj poroso.
porpoise ['pɔːpəs] n marsopa.
porridge ['pɔrɪdʒ] n gachas fpl de avena.
port [pɔːt] n (harbour) puerto; (NAUT: left
side) babor m; (wine) oporto; (COMPUT)
puerta, puerto, port m; **~ of call** puerto de

escala.
portable ['pɔːtəbl] adj portátil.
portal ['pɔːtl] n puerta (grande), portalón m.
port authorities npl autoridades fpl portuarias.
portcullis [pɔːt'kʌlɪs] n rastrillo.
portend [pɔː'tend] vt presagiar, anunciar.
portent ['pɔːtent] n presagio, augurio.
porter ['pɔːtə*] n (for luggage) maletero; (doorkeeper) portero/a, conserje m/f; (US RAIL) mozo de los coches-cama.
portfolio [pɔːt'fəʊlɪəu] n (case, of artist) cartera, carpeta; (POL, FINANCE) cartera.
porthole ['pɔːthəʊl] n portilla.
portico ['pɔːtɪkəʊ] n pórtico.
portion ['pɔːʃən] n porción f; (helping) ración f.
portly ['pɔːtlɪ] adj corpulento.
portrait ['pɔːtreɪt] n retrato.
portray [pɔː'treɪ] vt retratar; (in writing) representar.
portrayal [pɔː'treɪəl] n representación f.
Portugal ['pɔːtjugl] n Portugal m.
Portuguese [pɔːtju'giːz] adj portugués/esa ♦ n, pl inv portugués/esa m/f; (LING) portugués m.
Portuguese man-of-war [-mænəu'wɔː*] n (jellyfish) especie de medusa.
pose [pəuz] n postura, actitud f; (pej) afectación f, pose f ♦ vi posar; (pretend): to ~ as hacerse pasar por ♦ vt (question) plantear; to strike a ~ tomar or adoptar una pose or actitud.
poser ['pəuzə*] n problema m/pregunta difícil; (person) = poseur.
poseur [pəu'zə:*] n presumido/a, persona afectada.
posh [pɔʃ] adj (col) elegante, de lujo ♦ adv (col): to talk ~ hablar con acento afectado.
position [pə'zɪʃən] n posición f; (job) puesto ♦ vt colocar; to be in a ~ to do sth estar en condiciones de hacer algo.
positive ['pɔzɪtɪv] adj positivo; (certain) seguro; (definite) definitivo; we look forward to a ~ reply (COMM) esperamos que pueda darnos una respuesta en firme; he's a ~ nuisance es un auténtico pelmazo; ~ cash flow (COMM) flujo positivo de efectivo.
positively ['pɔzɪtɪvlɪ] adv (affirmatively, enthusiastically) de forma positiva; (col: really) absolutamente.
posse ['pɔsɪ] n (US) pelotón m.
possess [pə'zes] vt poseer; like one ~ed como un poseído; whatever can have ~ed you? ¿cómo se te ocurrió?

possessed [pə'zest] adj poseso, poseído.
possession [pə'zeʃən] n posesión f; to take ~ of sth tomar posesión de algo.
possessive [pə'zesɪv] adj posesivo.
possessiveness [pə'zesɪvnɪs] n posesividad f.
possessor [pə'zesə*] n poseedor(a) m/f, dueño/a.
possibility [pɔsɪ'bɪlɪtɪ] n posibilidad f; he's a ~ for the part es uno de los posibles para el papel.
possible ['pɔsɪbl] adj posible; as big as ~ lo más grande posible; it is ~ to do it es posible hacerlo; as far as ~ en la medida de lo posible; a ~ candidate un(a) posible candidato/a.
possibly ['pɔsɪblɪ] adv (perhaps) posiblemente, tal vez; I cannot ~ come me es imposible venir; could you ~ ...? ¿podrías ...?
post [pəust] n (BRIT: letters, delivery) correo; (job, situation) puesto; (trading ~) factoría; (pole) poste m ♦ vt (BRIT: send by ~) mandar por correo; (: put in mailbox) echar al correo; (MIL) apostar; (bills) fijar, pegar; (BRIT: appoint): to ~ to destinar a; by ~ por correo; by return of ~ a vuelta de correo; to keep sb ~ed tener a algn al corriente.
post ... [pəust] pref post..., pos...; ~ 1950 pos(t) 1950.
postage ['pəustɪdʒ] n porte m, franqueo.
postage stamp n sello (de correo).
postal ['pəustl] adj postal, de correos.
postal order n giro postal.
postbag ['pəustbæg] n (BRIT) correspondencia, cartas fpl.
postbox ['pəustbɔks] n (BRIT) buzón m.
postcard ['pəustkɑːd] nf (tarjeta) postal f.
postcode ['pəustkəud] n (BRIT) código postal.
postdate [pəust'deɪt] vt (cheque) poner fecha adelantada a.
poster ['pəustə*] n cartel m, afiche m (LAM).
poste restante [pəust'rɛstɔnt] n (BRIT) lista de correos.
posterior [pɔs'tɪərɪə*] n (col) trasero.
posterity [pɔs'terɪtɪ] n posteridad f.
poster paint n pintura al agua.
post-free [pəust'friː] adj (con) porte pagado.
postgraduate ['pəust'grædjuɪt] n posgraduado/a.
posthumous ['pɔstjuməs] adj póstumo.
posthumously ['pɔstjuməslɪ] adv póstumamente, con carácter póstumo.
posting ['pəustɪŋ] n destino.
postman ['pəustmən] n cartero.

postmark ['pəustmɑːk] *n* matasellos *m inv*.

postmaster ['pəustmɑːstə*] *n* administrador *m* de correos.

Postmaster General *n* director *m* general de correos.

postmistress ['pəustmɪstrɪs] *n* administradora de correos.

post-mortem [pəust'mɔːtəm] *n* autopsia.

postnatal ['pəust'neɪtl] *adj* postnatal, postparto.

post office *n* (*building*) (oficina de) correos *m*; (*organization*): **the P~ O~** Administración *f* General de Correos.

Post Office Box (PO Box) *n* apartado postal, casilla de correos (*LAM*).

post-paid ['pəust'peɪd] *adj* porte pagado.

postpone [pəs'pəun] *vt* aplazar, postergar (*LAM*).

postponement [pəs'pəunmənt] *n* aplazamiento.

postscript ['pəustskrɪpt] *n* posdata.

postulate ['pɒstjuleɪt] *vt* postular.

posture ['pɒstʃə*] *n* postura, actitud *f*.

postwar [pəust'wɔː*] *adj* de la posguerra.

posy ['pəuzɪ] *n* ramillete *m* (de flores).

pot [pɒt] *n* (*for cooking*) olla; (*for flowers*) maceta; (*for jam*) tarro, pote *m* (*LAM*); (*piece of pottery*) cacharro; (*col: marijuana*) costo ♦ *vt* (*plant*) poner en tiesto; (*conserve*) conservar (en tarros); **~s of** (*col*) montones de; **to go to ~** (*col: work, performance*) irse al traste.

potash ['pɒtæʃ] *n* potasa.

potassium [pə'tæsɪəm] *n* potasio.

potato, ~es [pə'teɪtəu] *n* patata, papa (*LAM*).

potato crisps, (*US*) **potato chips** *npl* patatas *fpl or* papas *fpl* (*LAM*) fritas.

potato peeler *n* pelapatatas *m inv*.

potbellied ['pɒtbɛlɪd] *adj* (*from overeating*) barrigón/ona; (*from malnutrition*) con el vientre hinchado.

potency ['pəutnsɪ] *n* potencia.

potent ['pəutnt] *adj* potente, poderoso; (*drink*) fuerte.

potentate ['pəutnteɪt] *n* potentado.

potential [pə'tɛnʃl] *adj* potencial, posible ♦ *n* potencial *m*; **to have ~** prometer.

potentially [pə'tɛnʃəlɪ] *adv* en potencia.

pothole ['pɒthəul] *n* (*in road*) bache *m*; (*BRIT: underground*) gruta.

potholer ['pɒthəulə*] *n* (*BRIT*) espeleólogo/a.

potholing ['pɒthəulɪŋ] *n* (*BRIT*): **to go ~** dedicarse a la espeleología.

potion ['pəuʃən] *n* poción *f*, pócima.

potluck [pɒt'lʌk] *n*: **to take ~** conformarse con lo que haya.

pot roast *n* carne *f* asada.

potshot ['pɒtʃɒt] *n*: **to take a ~ at sth** tirar a algo sin apuntar.

potted ['pɒtɪd] *adj* (*food*) en conserva; (*plant*) en tiesto *or* maceta; (*fig: shortened*) resumido.

potter ['pɒtə*] *n* alfarero/a ♦ *vi*: **to ~ around, ~ about** entretenerse haciendo cosillas; **to ~ round the house** estar en casa haciendo cosillas; **~'s wheel** torno de alfarero.

pottery ['pɒtərɪ] *n* cerámica, alfarería; **a piece of ~** un objeto de cerámica.

potty ['pɒtɪ] *adj* (*col: mad*) chiflado ♦ *n* orinal *m* de niño.

potty-trained ['pɒtɪtreɪnd] *adj* que ya no necesita pañales.

pouch [pautʃ] *n* (*ZOOL*) bolsa; (*for tobacco*) petaca.

pouf(fe) [puːf] *n* (*stool*) pouf *m*.

poultry ['pəultrɪ] *n* aves *fpl* de corral; (*dead*) pollos *mpl*.

poultry farm *n* granja avícola.

poultry farmer *n* avicultor(a) *m/f*.

pounce [pauns] *vi*: **to ~ on** precipitarse sobre ♦ *n* salto, ataque *m*.

pound [paund] *n* libra; (*for dogs*) perrera; (*for cars*) depósito ♦ *vt* (*beat*) golpear; (*crush*) machacar ♦ *vi* (*beat*) dar golpes; **half a ~** media libra; **a one ~ note** un billete de una libra.

pounding ['paundɪŋ] *n*: **to take a ~** (*team*) recibir una paliza.

pound sterling *n* libra esterlina.

pour [pɔː*] *vt* echar; (*tea*) servir ♦ *vi* correr, fluir; (*rain*) llover a cántaros.

▶**pour away, pour off** *vt* vaciar, verter.

▶**pour in** *vi* (*people*) entrar en tropel; **to come ~ing in** (*water*) entrar a raudales; (*letters*) llegar a montones; (*cars, people*) llegar en tropel.

▶**pour out** *vi* (*people*) salir en tropel ♦ *vt* (*drink*) echar, servir.

pouring ['pɔːrɪŋ] *adj*: **~ rain** lluvia torrencial.

pout [paut] *vi* hacer pucheros.

poverty ['pɒvətɪ] *n* pobreza, miseria; (*fig*) falta, escasez *f*.

poverty line *n*: **below the ~** por debajo del umbral de pobreza.

poverty-stricken ['pɒvətɪstrɪkn] *adj* necesitado.

poverty trap *n* trampa de la pobreza.

POW *n abbr* = **prisoner of war**.

powder ['paudə*] *n* polvo; (*face ~*) polvos *mpl*; (*gun~*) pólvora ♦ *vt* empolvar; **to ~ one's face** ponerse polvos; **to ~ one's nose** empolvarse la nariz, ponerse

polvos; (*euphemism*) ir al baño.
powder compact *n* polvera.
powdered milk ['paudəd-] *n* leche *f* en
polvo.
powder keg *n* (*fig*) polvorín *m*.
powder puff *n* borla (para empolvarse).
powder room *n* aseos *mpl*.
powdery ['paudərɪ] *adj* polvoriento.
power ['pauə*] *n* poder *m*; (*strength*) fuerza;
(*nation*) potencia; (*drive*) empuje *m*; (*TECH*)
potencia; (*ELEC*) energía ♦ *vt* impulsar; **to
be in** ~ (*POL*) estar en el poder; **to do all
in one's** ~ **to help sb** hacer todo lo
posible por ayudar a algn; **the world** ~**s**
las potencias mundiales.
powerboat ['pauəbaut] *n* lancha a motor.
power cut *n* (*BRIT*) apagón *m*.
powered ['pauəd] *adj*: ~ **by** impulsado por;
nuclear-~ **submarine** submarino nuclear.
power failure *n* = **power cut**.
powerful ['pauəful] *adj* poderoso; (*engine*)
potente; (*strong*) fuerte; (*play, speech*)
conmovedor(a).
powerhouse ['pauəhaus] *n* (*fig: person*)
fuerza motriz; **a** ~ **of ideas** una cantera
de ideas.
powerless ['pauəlɪs] *adj* impotente,
ineficaz.
power line *n* línea de conducción
eléctrica.
power of attorney *n* poder *m*,
procuración *f*.
power point *n* (*BRIT*) enchufe *m*.
power station *n* central *f* eléctrica.
power steering *n* (*AUT*) dirección *f*
asistida.
powwow ['pauwau] *n* conferencia ♦ *vi*
conferenciar.
pp *abbr* (= *per procurationem*: *by proxy*) p.p.
PPE *n abbr* (*BRIT SCOL*) = *philosophy, politics
and economics*.
PPS *abbr* (= *post postscriptum*) posdata
adicional; (*BRIT*: = *Parliamentary Private
Secretary*) ayudante de un ministro.
PQ *abbr* (*Canada*) = *Province of Quebec*.
PR *n abbr see* **proportional representation**;
(= *public relations*) relaciones *fpl* públicas
♦ *abbr* (*US*) = *Puerto Rico*.
Pr. *abbr* (= *prince*) P.
practicability [præktɪkə'bɪlɪtɪ] *n*
factibilidad *f*.
practicable ['præktɪkəbl] *adj* (*scheme*)
factible.
practical ['præktɪkl] *adj* práctico.
practicality [præktɪ'kælɪtɪ] *n* (*of situation
etc*) aspecto práctico.
practical joke *n* broma pesada.
practically ['præktɪklɪ] *adv* (*almost*) casi,

prácticamente.
practice ['præktɪs] *n* (*habit*) costumbre *f*;
(*exercise*) práctica; (*training*)
adiestramiento; (*MED*) clientela ♦ *vt, vi*
(*US*) = **practise**; **in** ~ (*in reality*) en la
práctica; **out of** ~ desentrenado; **to put
sth into** ~ poner algo en práctica; **it's
common** ~ es bastante corriente; **target**
~ práctica de tiro; **he has a small** ~
(*doctor*) tiene pocos pacientes; **to set up
in** ~ **as** establecerse como.
practise, (*US*) **practice** ['præktɪs] *vt* (*carry
out*) practicar; (*profession*) ejercer; (*train
at*) practicar ♦ *vi* ejercer; (*train*)
practicar.
practised, (*US*) **practiced** ['præktɪst] *adj*
(*person*) experto; (*performance*) bien
ensayado; (*liar*) consumado; **with a** ~ **eye**
con ojo experto.
practising, (*US*) **practicing** ['præktɪsɪŋ] *adj*
(*Christian etc*) practicante; (*lawyer*) que
ejerce; (*homosexual*) activo.
practitioner [præk'tɪʃənə*] *n* practicante
m/f; (*MED*) médico/a.
pragmatic [præg'mætɪk] *adj* pragmático.
pragmatism ['prægmətɪzəm] *n*
pragmatismo.
pragmatist ['prægmətɪst] *n* pragmatista *m/f*.
Prague [prɑːg] *n* Praga.
prairie ['prɛərɪ] *n* (*US*) pampa.
praise [preɪz] *n* alabanza(s) *f(pl)*, elogio(s)
m(pl).
praiseworthy ['preɪswəːðɪ] *adj* loable.
pram [præm] *n* (*BRIT*) cochecito de niño.
prance [prɑːns] *vi* (*horse*) hacer cabriolas.
prank [præŋk] *n* travesura.
prat [præt] *n* (*BRIT col*) imbécil *m/f*.
prattle ['prætl] *vi* parlotear; (*child*)
balbucear.
prawn [prɔːn] *n* gamba.
pray [preɪ] *vi* rezar; **to** ~ **for forgiveness**
pedir perdón.
prayer [prɛə*] *n* oración *f*, rezo; (*entreaty*)
ruego, súplica.
prayer book *n* devocionario, misal *m*.
pre- ['priː] *pref* pre..., ante-; ~**1970** pre 1970.
preach [priːtʃ] *vi* predicar.
preacher ['priːtʃə*] *n* predicador(a) *m/f*;
(*US: minister*) pastor(a) *m/f*.
preamble [prɪ'æmbl] *n* preámbulo.
prearrange [priːə'reɪndʒ] *vt* organizar *or*
acordar de antemano.
prearrangement [priːə'reɪndʒmənt] *n*: **by** ~
por previo acuerdo.
precarious [prɪ'kɛərɪəs] *adj* precario.
precariously [prɪ'kɛərɪəslɪ] *adv*
precariamente.
precaution [prɪ'kɔːʃən] *n* precaución *f*.

precautionary [prɪ'kɔːʃənrɪ] *adj* (*measure*) de precaución.

precede [prɪ'siːd] *vt, vi* preceder.

precedence ['presɪdəns] *n* precedencia; (*priority*) preferencia.

precedent ['presɪdənt] *n* precedente *m*; **to establish** *or* **set a** ~ sentar un precedente.

preceding [prɪ'siːdɪŋ] *adj* precedente.

precept ['priːsept] *n* precepto.

precinct ['priːsɪŋkt] *n* recinto; (*US: district*) distrito, barrio; ~s *npl* recinto; **pedestrian** ~ (*BRIT*) zona peatonal; **shopping** ~ (*BRIT*) centro comercial.

precious ['preʃəs] *adj* precioso; (*treasured*) querido; (*stylized*) afectado ♦ *adv* (*col*): ~ **little/few** muy poco/pocos; **your** ~ **dog** (*ironic*) tu querido perro.

precipice ['presɪpɪs] *n* precipicio.

precipitate *adj* [prɪ'sɪpɪtɪt] (*hasty*) precipitado ♦ *vt* [prɪ'sɪpɪteɪt] precipitar.

precipitation [prɪsɪpɪ'teɪʃən] *n* precipitación *f*.

precipitous [prɪ'sɪpɪtəs] *adj* (*steep*) escarpado; (*hasty*) precipitado.

précis ['preɪsiː] *n* resumen *m*.

precise [prɪ'saɪs] *adj* preciso, exacto; (*person*) escrupuloso.

precisely [prɪ'saɪslɪ] *adv* exactamente, precisamente.

precision [prɪ'sɪʒən] *n* precisión *f*.

preclude [prɪ'kluːd] *vt* excluir.

precocious [prɪ'kəʊʃəs] *adj* precoz.

preconceived [priːkən'siːvd] *adj* (*idea*) preconcebido.

preconception [priːkən'sepʃən] *n* (*idea*) idea preconcebida.

precondition [priːkən'dɪʃən] *n* condición *f* previa.

precursor [priː'kɜːsə*] *n* precursor(a) *m/f*.

predate ['priː'deɪt] *vt* (*precede*) preceder.

predator ['predətə*] *n* depredador *m*.

predatory ['predətərɪ] *adj* depredador(a).

predecessor ['priːdɪsesə*] *n* antecesor(a) *m/f*.

predestination [priːdestɪ'neɪʃən] *n* predestinación *f*.

predestine [priː'destɪn] *vt* predestinar.

predetermine [priːdɪ'tɜːmɪn] *vt* predeterminar.

predicament [prɪ'dɪkəmənt] *n* apuro.

predicate ['predɪkɪt] *n* predicado.

predict [prɪ'dɪkt] *vt* predecir, pronosticar.

predictable [prɪ'dɪktəbl] *adj* previsible.

predictably [prɪ'dɪktəblɪ] *adv* (*behave, react*) de forma previsible; ~ **she didn't arrive** como era de prever, no llegó.

prediction [prɪ'dɪkʃən] *n* pronóstico, predicción *f*.

predispose ['priːdɪs'pəuz] *vt* predisponer.

predominance [prɪ'dɔmɪnəns] *n* predominio.

predominant [prɪ'dɔmɪnənt] *adj* predominante.

predominantly [prɪ'dɔmɪnəntlɪ] *adv* en su mayoría.

predominate [prɪ'dɔmɪneɪt] *vi* predominar.

pre-eminent [priː'emɪnənt] *adj* preeminente.

pre-empt [priː'emt] *vt* (*BRIT*) adelantarse a.

pre-emptive [priː'emtɪv] *adj*: ~ **strike** ataque *m* preventivo.

preen [priːn] *vt*: **to** ~ **itself** (*bird*) limpiarse las plumas; **to** ~ **o.s.** pavonearse.

prefab ['priːfæb] *n* casa prefabricada.

prefabricated [priː'fæbrɪkeɪtɪd] *adj* prefabricado.

preface ['prefəs] *n* prefacio.

prefect ['priːfekt] *n* (*BRIT: in school*) monitor(a) *m/f*.

prefer [prɪ'fɜː*] *vt* preferir; (*LAW: charges, complaint*) presentar; (: *action*) entablar; **to** ~ **coffee to tea** preferir el café al té.

preferable ['prefrəbl] *adj* preferible.

preferably ['prefrəblɪ] *adv* preferentemente, más bien.

preference ['prefrəns] *n* preferencia; **in** ~ **to sth** antes que algo.

preference shares *npl* acciones *fpl* privilegiadas.

preferential [prefə'renʃəl] *adj* preferente.

prefix ['priːfɪks] *n* prefijo.

pregnancy ['pregnənsɪ] *n* embarazo.

pregnancy test *n* prueba del embarazo.

pregnant ['pregnənt] *adj* embarazada; **3 months** ~ embarazada de tres meses; ~ **with meaning** cargado de significado.

prehistoric [priːhɪs'tɔrɪk] *adj* prehistórico.

prehistory [priː'hɪstərɪ] *n* prehistoria.

prejudge [priː'dʒʌdʒ] *vt* prejuzgar.

prejudice ['predʒudɪs] *n* (*bias*) prejuicio; (*harm*) perjuicio ♦ *vt* (*bias*) predisponer; (*harm*) perjudicar; **to** ~ **sb in favour of/ against** (*bias*) predisponer a algn a favor de/en contra de.

prejudiced ['predʒudɪst] *adj* (*person*) predispuesto; (*view*) parcial, interesado; **to be** ~ **against sb/sth** estar predispuesto en contra de algn/algo.

prelate ['prelət] *n* prelado.

preliminaries [prɪ'lɪmɪnərɪz] *npl* preliminares *mpl*, preparativos *mpl*.

preliminary [prɪ'lɪmɪnərɪ] *adj* preliminar.

prelude ['preljuːd] *n* preludio.

premarital ['priː'mærɪtl] *adj* prematrimonial, premarital.

premature ['prɛmətʃuə*] adj (arrival etc) prematuro; **you are being a little** ~ te has adelantado.

prematurely [prɛmə'tʃuəlɪ] adv prematuramente, antes de tiempo.

premeditate [priː'mɛdɪteɪt] vt premeditar.

premeditated [priː'mɛdɪteɪtɪd] adj premeditado.

premeditation [priːmɛdɪ'teɪʃən] n premeditación f.

premenstrual [priː'mɛnstruəl] adj premenstrual.

premenstrual tension n (MED) tensión f premenstrual.

premier ['prɛmɪə*] adj primero, principal ♦ n (POL) primer(a) ministro/a.

première ['prɛmɪəə*] n estreno.

premise ['prɛmɪs] n premisa.

premises ['prɛmɪsɪs] npl local msg; **on the** ~ en el lugar mismo; **business** ~ locales mpl comerciales.

premium ['priːmɪəm] n prima; **to be at a** ~ estar muy solicitado; **to sell at a** ~ (shares) vender caro.

premium bond n (BRIT) bono del estado que participa en una lotería nacional.

premium deal n (COMM) oferta extraordinaria.

premium gasoline n (US) (gasolina) súper m.

premonition [prɛmə'nɪʃən] n presentimiento.

preoccupation [priːɔkju'peɪʃən] n preocupación f.

preoccupied [priː'ɔkjupaɪd] adj (worried) preocupado; (absorbed) ensimismado.

prep [prɛp] adj abbr: ~ **school** = **preparatory school** ♦ n abbr (SCOL: = preparation) deberes mpl.

prepaid [priː'peɪd] adj porte pagado; ~ **envelope** sobre m de porte pagado.

preparation [prɛpə'reɪʃən] n preparación f; ~s npl preparativos mpl; **in** ~ **for sth** en preparación para algo.

preparatory [prɪ'pærətərɪ] adj preparatorio, preliminar; ~ **to sth/to doing sth** como preparación para algo/para hacer algo.

preparatory school n (BRIT) colegio privado de enseñanza primaria; (US) colegio privado de enseñanza secundaria; see also **public school**.

prepare [prɪ'pɛə*] vt preparar, disponer ♦ vi: **to** ~ **for** prepararse or disponerse para; (make preparations) hacer preparativos para.

prepared [prɪ'pɛəd] adj (willing): **to be** ~ **to help sb** estar dispuesto a ayudar a algn.

preponderance [prɪ'pɔndərns] n preponderancia, predominio.

preposition [prɛpə'zɪʃən] n preposición f.

prepossessing [priːpə'zɛsɪŋ] adj agradable, atractivo.

preposterous [prɪ'pɔstərəs] adj absurdo, ridículo.

prerecorded ['priːrɪ'kɔːdɪd] adj: ~ **broadcast** programa m grabado de antemano; ~ **cassette** cassette f pregrabada.

prerequisite [priː'rɛkwɪzɪt] n requisito previo.

prerogative [prɪ'rɔgətɪv] n prerrogativa.

Presbyterian [prɛzbɪ'tɪərɪən] adj, n presbiteriano/a m/f.

presbytery ['prɛzbɪtərɪ] n casa parroquial.

preschool ['priː'skuːl] adj (child, age) preescolar.

prescribe [prɪ'skraɪb] vt prescribir; (MED) recetar; ~**d books** (BRIT SCOL) libros mpl del curso.

prescription [prɪ'skrɪpʃən] n (MED) receta; **to make up** or (US) **fill a** ~ preparar una receta; **only available on** ~ se vende solamente con receta (médica).

prescription charges npl (BRIT) precio sg de las recetas.

prescriptive [prɪ'skrɪptɪv] adj normativo.

presence ['prɛzns] n presencia; (attendance) asistencia.

presence of mind n aplomo.

present adj ['prɛznt] (in attendance) presente; (current) actual ♦ n (gift) regalo; (actuality) actualidad f, presente m ♦ vt [prɪ'zɛnt] (introduce) presentar; (expound) exponer; (give) presentar, dar, ofrecer; (THEAT) representar; **to be** ~ **at** asistir a, estar presente en; **those** ~ los presentes; **to give sb a** ~, **make sb a** ~ **of sth** regalar algo a algn; **at** ~ actualmente; **to** ~ **o.s. for an interview** presentarse a una entrevista; **may I** ~ **Miss Clark** permítame presentarle or le presento a la Srta Clark.

presentable [prɪ'zɛntəbl] adj: **to make o.s.** ~ arreglarse.

presentation [prɛzn'teɪʃən] n presentación f; (gift) obsequio; (of case) exposición f; (THEAT) representación f; **on** ~ **of the**

voucher al presentar el vale.
present-day ['prezntdeɪ] *adj* actual.
presenter [prɪ'zentə*] *n* (*RADIO, TV*)
locutor(a) *m/f*.
presently ['prezntlɪ] *adv* (*soon*) dentro de
poco; (*US: now*) ahora.
present participle *n* participio (de)
presente.
present tense *n* (tiempo) presente *m*.
preservation [prezə'veɪʃən] *n* conservación
f.
preservative [prɪ'zə:vətɪv] *n* conservante
m.
preserve [prɪ'zə:v] *vt* (*keep safe*) preservar,
proteger; (*maintain*) mantener; (*food*)
conservar; (*in salt*) salar ♦ *n* (*for game*)
coto, vedado; (*often pl: jam*) confitura.
preshrunk [pri:'ʃrʌŋk] *adj* inencogible.
preside [prɪ'zaɪd] *vi* presidir.
presidency ['prezɪdənsɪ] *n* presidencia.
president ['prezɪdənt] *n* presidente *m/f*; (*US:
of company*) director(a) *m/f*.
presidential [prezɪ'denʃl] *adj* presidencial.
press [pres] *n* (*tool, machine, newspapers*)
prensa; (*printer's*) imprenta; (*of hand*)
apretón *m* ♦ *vt* (*push*) empujar; (*squeeze*)
apretar; (*grapes*) pisar; (*clothes: iron*)
planchar; (*pressure*) presionar; (*doorbell*)
apretar, pulsar, tocar; (*insist*): **to ~ sth on
sb** insistir en que algn acepte algo ♦ *vi*
(*squeeze*) apretar; (*pressurize*) ejercer
presión; **to go to ~** (*newspaper*) entrar en
prensa; **to be in the ~** (*being printed*)
estar en prensa; (*in the newspapers*)
aparecer en la prensa; **we are ~ed for
time** tenemos poco tiempo; **to ~ sb to do**
or **into doing sth** (*urge, entreat*) presionar
a algn para que haga algo; **to ~ sb for an
answer** insistir a algn para que conteste;
to ~ charges against sb (*LAW*) demandar
a algn.
▶**press ahead** *vi* seguir adelante.
▶**press on** *vi* avanzar; (*hurry*) apretar el
paso.
press agency *n* agencia de prensa.
press clipping *n* = **press cutting**.
press conference *n* rueda de prensa.
press cutting *n* recorte *m* (de periódico).
pressing ['presɪŋ] *adj* apremiante.
pressman ['presmæn] *n* periodista *m*.
press officer *n* jefe/a *m/f* de prensa.
press release *n* comunicado de prensa.
press stud *n* (*BRIT*) botón *m* de presión.
press-up ['presʌp] *n* (*BRIT*) flexión *f*.
pressure ['preʃə*] *n* presión *f*; (*urgency*)
apremio, urgencia; (*influence*) influencia;
high/low ~ alta/baja presión; **to put ~ on
sb** presionar a algn, hacer presión sobre

algn.
pressure cooker *n* olla a presión.
pressure gauge *n* manómetro.
pressure group *n* grupo de presión.
pressurize ['preʃəraɪz] *vt* presurizar; **to ~
sb (into doing sth)** presionar a algn (para
que haga algo).
pressurized ['preʃəraɪzd] *adj* (*container*) a
presión.
Prestel ® ['prestel] *n* videotex *m*.
prestige [pres'ti:ʒ] *n* prestigio.
prestigious [pres'tɪdʒəs] *adj* prestigioso.
presumably [prɪ'zju:məblɪ] *adv* es de
suponer que, cabe presumir que; **~ he
did it** es de suponer que lo hizo él.
presume [prɪ'zju:m] *vt* suponer, presumir;
to ~ to do (*dare*) atreverse a hacer.
presumption [prɪ'zʌmpʃən] *n* suposición *f*;
(*pretension*) presunción *f*.
presumptuous [prɪ'zʌmptjuəs] *adj*
presumido.
presuppose [pri:sə'pəuz] *vt* presuponer.
presupposition [pri:sʌpə'zɪʃən] *n*
presuposición *f*.
pre-tax [pri:'tæks] *adj* anterior al impuesto.
pretence, (*US*) **pretense** [prɪ'tens] *n* (*claim*)
pretensión *f*; (*pretext*) pretexto; (*make-
believe*) fingimiento; **on** *or* **under the ~ of
doing sth** bajo *or* con el pretexto de
hacer algo; **she is devoid of all ~** no es
pretenciosa.
pretend [prɪ'tend] *vt* (*feign*) fingir ♦ *vi*
(*feign*) fingir; (*claim*): **to ~ to sth**
pretender a algo.
pretense [prɪ'tens] *n* (*US*) = **pretence**.
pretension [prɪ'tenʃən] *n* (*claim*) pretensión
f; **to have no ~s to sth/to being sth** no
engañarse en cuanto a algo/a ser algo.
pretentious [prɪ'tenʃəs] *adj* pretencioso.
pretext ['pri:tekst] *n* pretexto; **on** *or* **under
the ~ of doing sth** con el pretexto de
hacer algo.
prettily ['prɪtɪlɪ] *adv* encantadoramente,
con gracia.
pretty ['prɪtɪ] *adj* (*gen*) bonito, lindo (*LAM*)
♦ *adv* bastante.
prevail [prɪ'veɪl] *vi* (*gain mastery*)
prevalecer; (*be current*) predominar;
(*persuade*): **to ~ (up)on sb to do sth**
persuadir a algn para que haga algo.
prevailing [prɪ'veɪlɪŋ] *adj* (*dominant*)
predominante.
prevalent ['prevələnt] *adj* (*dominant*)
dominante; (*widespread*) extendido;
(*fashionable*) de moda.
prevarication [prɪværɪ'keɪʃən] *n* evasivas
fpl.
prevent [prɪ'vent] *vt*: **to ~ (sb) from doing**

sth impedir (a algn) hacer algo.
preventable [prɪ'vɛntəbl] adj evitable.
preventative [prɪ'vɛntətɪv] adj preventivo.
prevention [prɪ'vɛnʃən] n prevención f.
preventive [prɪ'vɛntɪv] adj preventivo.
preview ['priːvjuː] n (of film) preestreno.
previous ['priːvɪəs] adj previo, anterior; **he has no ~ experience in that field** no tiene experiencia previa en ese campo; **I have a ~ engagement** tengo un compromiso anterior.
previously ['priːvɪəslɪ] adv antes.
prewar [priː'wɔː*] adj antes de la guerra.
prey [preɪ] n presa f ♦ vi: **to ~ on** vivir a costa de; (feed on) alimentarse de; **it was ~ing on his mind** le obsesionaba.
price [praɪs] n precio; (BETTING: odds) puntos mpl de ventaja ♦ vt (goods) fijar el precio de; **to go up** or **rise in ~** subir de precio; **what is the ~ of ...?** ¿qué precio tiene ...?; **to put a ~ on sth** poner precio a algo; **what ~ his promises now?** ¿para qué sirven ahora sus promesas?; **he regained his freedom, but at a ~** recobró su libertad, pero le había costado caro; **to be ~d out of the market** (article) no encontrar comprador por ese precio; (nation) no ser competitivo.
price control n control m de precios.
price-cutting ['praɪskʌtɪŋ] n reducción f de precios.
priceless ['praɪslɪs] adj que no tiene precio; (col: amusing) divertidísimo.
price list n tarifa.
price tag n etiqueta.
price war n guerra de precios.
pricey ['praɪsɪ] adj (BRIT col) caro.
prick [prɪk] n pinchazo; (with pin) alfilerazo; (sting) picadura ♦ vt pinchar; picar; **to ~ up one's ears** aguzar el oído.
prickle ['prɪkl] n (sensation) picor m; (BOT) espina; (ZOOL) púa.
prickly ['prɪklɪ] adj espinoso; (fig: person) enojadizo.
prickly heat n sarpullido causado por exceso de calor.
pride [praɪd] n orgullo; (pej) soberbia ♦ vt: **to ~ o.s. on** enorgullecerse de; **to take (a) ~ in** enorgullecerse de; **her ~ and joy** su orgullo; **to have ~ of place** tener prioridad.
priest [priːst] n sacerdote m.
priestess ['priːstɪs] n sacerdotisa.
priesthood ['priːsthud] n (practice) sacerdocio; (priests) clero.
prim [prɪm] adj (demure) remilgado; (prudish) gazmoño.
primacy ['praɪməsɪ] n primacía.

prima donna ['priːmə'dɒnə] n primadonna.
primal ['praɪməl] adj original; (important) principal.
primarily ['praɪmərɪlɪ] adv (above all) ante todo, primordialmente.
primary ['praɪmərɪ] adj primario; (first in importance) principal ♦ n (US: also: ~ election) (elección f) primaria; ver recuadro.

PRIMARY

Las elecciones primarias (**primaries**) sirven para preseleccionar a los candidatos de los partidos Demócrata ("Democratic") y Republicano ("Republican") durante la campaña que precede a las elecciones a presidente de los Estados Unidos. Se inician en New Hampshire y tienen lugar en 35 estados de febrero a junio. El número de votos obtenidos por cada candidato determina el número de delegados que votarán en el congreso general ("National Convention") de julio y agosto, cuando se decide el candidato definitivo de cada partido.

---

primary colour, (US) **primary color** n color m primario.
primary education n enseñanza primaria.
primary school n (BRIT) escuela primaria; ver recuadro.

PRIMARY SCHOOL

En el Reino Unido la escuela a la que van los niños entre cinco y once años se llama **primary school**, a menudo dividida en "infant school" (entre cinco y siete años de edad) y "junior school" (entre siete y once).

---

primate n ['praɪmɪt] (REL) primado ♦ n ['praɪmeɪt] (ZOOL) primate m.
prime [praɪm] adj primero, principal; (basic) fundamental; (excellent) selecto, de primera clase ♦ n: **in the ~ of life** en la flor de la vida ♦ vt (gun, pump) cebar; (fig) preparar.
Prime Minister (PM) n primer(a) ministro/a; see also **Downing Street.**
primer ['praɪmə*] n (book) texto elemental; (paint) capa preparatoria.
prime time n (RADIO, TV) horas fpl de mayor audiencia.
primeval [praɪ'miːvəl] adj primitivo.
primitive ['prɪmɪtɪv] adj primitivo; (crude) rudimentario; (uncivilized) inculto.
primly ['prɪmlɪ] adv remilgadamente; con

gazmoñería.

primrose ['prɪmrəuz] *n* primavera, prímula.

primus (stove) ® ['praɪməs-] *n* (*BRIT*) hornillo de camping.

prince [prɪns] *n* príncipe *m*.

prince charming *n* príncipe *m* azul.

princess [prɪn'sɛs] *n* princesa.

principal ['prɪnsɪpl] *adj* principal ♦ *n* director(a) *m/f*; (*in play*) protagonista principal *m/f*; (*COMM*) capital *m*, principal *m*; *see also* **pantomime**.

principality [prɪnsɪ'pælɪtɪ] *n* principado.

principle ['prɪnsɪpl] *n* principio; **in** ~ en principio; **on** ~ por principio.

print [prɪnt] *n* (*impression*) marca, impresión *f*; huella; (*letters*) letra de molde; (*fabric*) estampado; (*ART*) grabado; (*PHOT*) impresión *f* ♦ *vt* (*gen*) imprimir; (*on mind*) grabar; (*write in capitals*) escribir en letras de molde; **out of** ~ agotado.

▶**print out** *vt* (*COMPUT*) imprimir.

printed circuit ['prɪntɪd-] *n* circuito impreso.

printed circuit board (PCB) *n* tarjeta de circuito impreso (TCI).

printed matter *n* impresos *mpl*.

printer ['prɪntə*] *n* (*person*) impresor(a) *m/f*; (*machine*) impresora.

printhead ['prɪnthɛd] *n* cabeza impresora.

printing ['prɪntɪŋ] *n* (*art*) imprenta; (*act*) impresión *f*; (*quantity*) tirada.

printing press *n* prensa.

printout ['prɪntaut] *n* (*COMPUT*) printout *m*.

print wheel *n* rueda impresora.

prior ['praɪə*] *adj* anterior, previo ♦ *n* prior *m*; ~ **to doing** antes de *or* hasta hacer; **without** ~ **notice** sin previo aviso; **to have a** ~ **claim to sth** tener prioridad en algo.

prioress ['praɪərɛs] *n* priora.

priority [praɪ'ɔrɪtɪ] *n* prioridad *f*; **to have** *or* **take** ~ **over sth** tener prioridad sobre algo.

priory ['praɪərɪ] *n* priorato.

prise, (*US*) **prize** [praɪz] *vt*: **to** ~ **open** abrir con palanca.

prism ['prɪzəm] *n* prisma *m*.

prison ['prɪzn] *n* cárcel *f*, prisión *f* ♦ *cpd* carcelario.

prison camp *n* campamento para prisioneros.

prisoner ['prɪznə*] *n* (*in prison*) preso/a; (*under arrest*) detenido/a; (*in dock*) acusado/a; **the** ~ **at the bar** el/la acusado/a; **to take sb** ~ hacer *or* tomar prisionero a algn.

prisoner of war *n* prisionero/a *or* preso/a de guerra.

prissy ['prɪsɪ] *adj* remilgado.

pristine ['prɪstiːn] *adj* pristino.

privacy ['prɪvəsɪ] *n* (*seclusion*) soledad *f*; (*intimacy*) intimidad *f*; **in the strictest** ~ con el mayor secreto.

private ['praɪvɪt] *adj* (*personal*) particular; (*confidential*) secreto, confidencial; (*intimate*) privado, íntimo; (*sitting etc*) a puerta cerrada ♦ *n* soldado raso; "~" (*on envelope*) "confidencial"; (*on door*) "privado"; **in** ~ en privado; **in (his)** ~ **life** en su vida privada; **to be in** ~ **practice** tener consulta particular.

private enterprise *n* la empresa privada.

private eye *n* detective *m/f* privado/a.

private hearing *n* (*LAW*) vista a puerta cerrada.

private limited company *n* (*BRIT*) sociedad *f* de responsabilidad limitada.

privately ['praɪvɪtlɪ] *adv* en privado; (*in o.s.*) en secreto.

private parts *npl* partes *fpl* pudendas.

private property *n* propiedad *f* privada.

private school *n* colegio privado.

privation [praɪ'veɪʃən] *n* (*state*) privación *f*; (*hardship*) privaciones *fpl*, estrecheces *fpl*.

privatize ['praɪvɪtaɪz] *vt* privatizar.

privet ['prɪvɪt] *n* alheña.

privilege ['prɪvɪlɪdʒ] *n* privilegio; (*prerogative*) prerrogativa.

privileged ['prɪvɪlɪdʒd] *adj* privilegiado; **to be** ~ **to do sth** gozar del privilegio de hacer algo.

privy ['prɪvɪ] *adj*: **to be** ~ **to** estar enterado de.

Privy Council *n* consejo privado (de la Corona); *ver recuadro*.

PRIVY COUNCIL

El consejo de asesores de la Corona conocido como **Privy Council** *tuvo su origen en la época de los normandos, y fue adquiriendo mayor importancia hasta ser substituido en 1688 por el actual Consejo de Ministros ("Cabinet"). Hoy día sigue existiendo con un carácter fundamentalmente honorífico y los ministros del gobierno y otras personalidades políticas, eclesiásticas y jurídicas adquieren el rango de "privy councillors" de manera automática.*

---

prize [praɪz] *n* premio ♦ *adj* (*first class*) de primera clase ♦ *vt* apreciar, estimar; (*US*) = **prise**.

prize fighter *n* boxeador *m* profesional.

prize fighting *n* boxeo *m* profesional.

prize-giving ['praɪzgɪvɪŋ] n distribución f de premios.

prize money n (SPORT) bolsa.

prizewinner ['praɪzwɪnə*] n premiado/a.

prizewinning ['praɪzwɪnɪŋ] adj (novel, essay) premiado.

PRO n abbr = **public relations officer**.

pro [prəʊ] n (SPORT) profesional m/f; **the ~s and cons** los pros y los contras.

pro- [prəʊ] pref (in favour of) pro, en pro de; **~Soviet** pro-soviético.

proactive [prəʊˈæktɪv] adj: **to be ~** impulsar la actividad.

probability [prɒbəˈbɪlɪtɪ] n probabilidad f; **in all ~** lo más probable.

probable ['prɒbəbl] adj probable; **it is ~/ hardly ~ that** es probable/poco probable que.

probably ['prɒbəblɪ] adv probablemente.

probate ['prəʊbeɪt] n (LAW) legalización f de un testamento.

probation [prəˈbeɪʃən] n: **on ~** (employee) a prueba; (LAW) en libertad condicional.

probationary [prəˈbeɪʃənrɪ] adj: **~ period** período de prueba.

probationer [prəˈbeɪʃənə*] n (LAW) persona en libertad condicional; (nurse) ≈ ATS m/f (SP) or enfermero/a en prácticas.

probation officer n persona a cargo de los presos en libertad condicional.

probe [prəʊb] n (MED, SPACE) sonda; (enquiry) investigación f ♦ vt sondar; (investigate) investigar.

probity ['prəʊbɪtɪ] n probidad f.

problem ['prɒbləm] n problema m; **what's the ~?** ¿cuál es el problema?, ¿qué pasa?; **no ~!** ¡por supuesto!; **to have ~s with the car** tener problemas con el coche.

problematic(al) [prɒbləˈmætɪk(l)] adj problemático.

problem-solving [prɒbləmˈsɒlvɪŋ] n resolución f de problemas; **~ skills** técnicas de resolución de problemas.

procedural [prəʊˈsiːdʒərəl] adj de procedimiento; (LAW) procesal.

procedure [prəˈsiːdʒə*] n procedimiento; (bureaucratic) trámites mpl; **cashing a cheque is a simple ~** cobrar un cheque es un trámite sencillo.

proceed [prəˈsiːd] vi proceder; (continue): **to ~ (with)** continuar (con); **to ~ against sb** (LAW) proceder contra algn; **I am not sure how to ~** no sé cómo proceder; see also **proceeds**.

proceedings [prəˈsiːdɪŋz] npl acto sg, actos mpl; (LAW) proceso sg; (meeting) función fsg; (records) actas fpl.

proceeds ['prəʊsiːdz] npl ganancias fpl,

ingresos mpl.

process ['prəʊsɛs] n proceso; (method) método, sistema m; (proceeding) procedimiento ♦ vt tratar, elaborar ♦ vi [prəˈsɛs] (BRIT formal: go in procession) desfilar; **in ~** en curso; **we are in the ~ of moving to ...** estamos en vías de mudarnos a ....

processed cheese ['prəʊsɛst-], (US) **process cheese** n queso fundido.

processing ['prəʊsɛsɪŋ] n elaboración f.

procession [prəˈsɛʃən] n desfile m; **funeral ~** cortejo fúnebre.

pro-choice [prəʊˈtʃɔɪs] adj en favor del derecho de elegir de la madre.

proclaim [prəˈkleɪm] vt proclamar; (announce) anunciar.

proclamation [prɒkləˈmeɪʃən] n proclamación f; (written) proclama.

proclivity [prəˈklɪvɪtɪ] n propensión f, inclinación f.

procrastinate [prəʊˈkræstɪneɪt] vi demorarse.

procrastination [prəʊkræstɪˈneɪʃən] n dilación f.

procreation [prəʊkrɪˈeɪʃən] n procreación f.

Procurator Fiscal ['prɒkjʊreɪtə-] n (Scottish) fiscal m/f.

procure [prəˈkjʊə*] vt conseguir, obtener.

procurement [prəˈkjʊəmənt] n obtención f.

prod [prɒd] vt (push) empujar; (with elbow) dar un codazo a ♦ n empujoncito; codazo.

prodigal ['prɒdɪgl] adj pródigo.

prodigious [prəˈdɪdʒəs] adj prodigioso.

prodigy ['prɒdɪdʒɪ] n prodigio.

produce n ['prɒdjuːs] (AGR) productos mpl agrícolas ♦ vt [prəˈdjuːs] producir; (yield) rendir; (bring) sacar; (show) presentar, mostrar; (proof of identity) enseñar, presentar; (THEAT) presentar, poner en escena; (offspring) dar a luz.

produce dealer n (US) verdulero/a.

producer [prəˈdjuːsə*] n (THEAT) director(a) m/f; (AGR, CINE) productor(a) m/f.

product ['prɒdʌkt] n producto.

production [prəˈdʌkʃən] n (act) producción f; (THEAT) representación f, montaje m; **to put into ~** lanzar a la producción.

production agreement n (US) acuerdo de productividad.

production line n línea de producción.

production manager n jefe/jefa m/f de producción.

productive [prəˈdʌktɪv] adj productivo.

productivity [prɒdʌkˈtɪvɪtɪ] n productividad f.

productivity agreement n (BRIT) acuerdo

de productividad.
productivity bonus *n* bono de productividad.
Prof. [prɔf] *abbr* (= *professor*) Prof.
profane [prəˈfeɪn] *adj* profano.
profess [prəˈfɛs] *vt* profesar; **I do not ~ to be an expert** no pretendo ser experto.
professed [prəˈfɛst] *adj* (*self-declared*) declarado.
profession [prəˈfɛʃən] *n* profesión *f*.
professional [prəˈfɛʃnl] *n* profesional *m/f* ♦ *adj* profesional; (*by profession*) de profesión; **to take ~ advice** buscar un consejo profesional.
professionalism [prəˈfɛʃnəlɪzm] *n* profesionalismo.
professionally [prəˈfɛʃnəlɪ] *adv*: **I only know him ~** sólo le conozco por nuestra relación de trabajo.
professor [prəˈfɛsə*] *n* (*BRIT*) catedrático/a; (*US: teacher*) profesor(a) *m/f*.
professorship [prəˈfɛsəʃɪp] *n* cátedra.
proffer [ˈprɔfə*] *vt* ofrecer.
proficiency [prəˈfɪʃənsɪ] *n* capacidad *f*, habilidad *f*.
proficiency test *n* prueba de capacitación.
proficient [prəˈfɪʃənt] *adj* experto, hábil.
profile [ˈprəʊfaɪl] *n* perfil *m*; **to keep a high/low ~** tratar de llamar la atención/pasar inadvertido.
profit [ˈprɔfɪt] *n* (*COMM*) ganancia; (*fig*) provecho ♦ *vi*: **to ~ by** *or* **from** aprovechar *or* sacar provecho de; **~ and loss account** cuenta de ganancias y pérdidas; **with ~s endowment assurance** seguro dotal con beneficios; **to sell sth at a ~** vender algo con ganancia.
profitability [prɔfɪtəˈbɪlɪtɪ] *n* rentabilidad *f*.
profitable [ˈprɔfɪtəbl] *adj* (*ECON*) rentable; (*beneficial*) provechoso, útil.
profitably [ˈprɔfɪtəblɪ] *adv* rentablemente; provechosamente.
profit centre, (*US*) **profit center** *n* centro de beneficios.
profiteering [prɔfɪˈtɪərɪŋ] *n* (*pej*) explotación *f*.
profit-making [ˈprɔfɪtmeɪkɪŋ] *adj* rentable.
profit margin *n* margen *m* de ganancia.
profit-sharing [ˈprɔfɪtʃɛərɪŋ] *n* participación *f* de empleados en los beneficios.
profits tax *n* impuesto sobre los beneficios.
profligate [ˈprɔflɪgɪt] *adj* (*dissolute: behaviour, act*) disoluto; (: *person*) libertino; (*extravagant*): **he's very ~ with his money** es muy derrochador.

pro forma [ˈprəʊˈfɔːmə] *adj*: **~ invoice** factura pro-forma.
profound [prəˈfaʊnd] *adj* profundo.
profoundly [prəˈfaʊndlɪ] *adv* profundamente.
profusely [prəˈfjuːslɪ] *adv* profusamente.
profusion [prəˈfjuːʒən] *n* profusión *f*, abundancia.
progeny [ˈprɔdʒɪnɪ] *n* progenie *f*.
programme, (*US*) **program** [ˈprəʊɡræm] *n* programa *m* ♦ *vt* programar.
program(m)er [ˈprəʊɡræmə*] *n* programador(a) *m/f*.
program(m)ing [ˈprəʊɡræmɪŋ] *n* programación *f*.
program(m)ing language *n* lenguaje *m* de programación.
progress *n* [ˈprəʊɡrɛs] progreso; (*development*) desarrollo ♦ *vi* [prəˈɡrɛs] progresar, avanzar; desarrollarse; **in ~** (*meeting, work etc*) en curso; **as the match ~ed** a medida que avanzaba el partido.
progression [prəˈɡrɛʃən] *n* progresión *f*.
progressive [prəˈɡrɛsɪv] *adj* progresivo; (*person*) progresista.
progressively [prəˈɡrɛsɪvlɪ] *adv* progresivamente, poco a poco.
progress report *n* (*MED*) informe *m* sobre el estado del paciente; (*ADMIN*) informe *m* sobre la marcha del trabajo.
prohibit [prəˈhɪbɪt] *vt* prohibir; **to ~ sb from doing sth** prohibir a algn hacer algo; **"smoking ~ed"** "prohibido fumar".
prohibition [prəʊɪˈbɪʃən] *n* (*US*) prohibicionismo.
prohibitive [prəˈhɪbɪtɪv] *adj* (*price etc*) prohibitivo.
project *n* [ˈprɔdʒɛkt] proyecto; (*SCOL, UNIV: research*) trabajo, proyecto ♦ (*vb*: [prəˈdʒɛkt]) *vt* proyectar ♦ *vi* (*stick out*) salir, sobresalir.
projectile [prəˈdʒɛktaɪl] *n* proyectil *m*.
projection [prəˈdʒɛkʃən] *n* proyección *f*; (*overhang*) saliente *m*.
projectionist [prəˈdʒɛkʃənɪst] *n* (*CINE*) operador(a) *m/f* de cine.
projection room *n* (*CINE*) cabina de proyección.
projector [prəˈdʒɛktə*] *n* proyector *m*.
proletarian [prəʊlɪˈtɛərɪən] *adj* proletario.
proletariat [prəʊlɪˈtɛərɪət] *n* proletariado.
pro-life [prəʊˈlaɪf] *adj* pro-vida.
proliferate [prəˈlɪfəreɪt] *vi* proliferar, multiplicarse.
proliferation [prəlɪfəˈreɪʃən] *n* proliferación *f*.
prolific [prəˈlɪfɪk] *adj* prolífico.
prologue, (*US*) **prolog** [ˈprəʊlɔɡ] *n* prólogo.

prolong [prə'lɔŋ] *vt* prolongar, extender.
prom [prɔm] *n abbr* (*BRIT*) = **promenade**,
promenade concert ♦ *n* (*US: ball*) baile *m*
de gala; *ver recuadro*.

PROM

*Los conciertos de música clásica más
conocidos en Inglaterra son los llamados
Proms (o **promenade concerts**), que tienen
lugar en el "Royal Albert Hall" de Londres,
aunque también se llama así a cualquier
concierto de esas características. Su
nombre se debe al hecho de que en un
principio el público paseaba durante las
actuaciones; en la actualidad parte de la
gente que acude a ellos permanece de pie.
En Estados Unidos se llama **prom** a un
baile de gala en un colegio o universidad.*

---

promenade [prɔmə'naːd] *n* (*by sea*) paseo
marítimo ♦ *vi* (*stroll*) pasearse.
promenade concert *n* concierto (*en que
parte del público permanece de pie*).
promenade deck *n* cubierta de paseo.
prominence ['prɔmɪnəns] *n* (*fig*)
importancia.
prominent ['prɔmɪnənt] *adj* (*standing out*)
saliente; (*important*) eminente,
importante; **he is ~ in the field of ...**
destaca en el campo de ....
prominently ['prɔmɪnəntlɪ] *adv* (*display, set*)
muy a la vista; **he figured ~ in the case**
desempeñó un papel destacado en el
juicio.
promiscuity [prɔmɪs'kjuːɪtɪ] *n*
promiscuidad *f*.
promiscuous [prə'mɪskjuəs] *adj* (*sexually*)
promiscuo.
promise ['prɔmɪs] *n* promesa ♦ *vt, vi*
prometer; **to make sb a ~** prometer algo
a algn; **a young man of ~** un joven con
futuro; **to ~ (sb) to do sth** prometer (a
algn) hacer algo; **to ~ well** ser muy
prometedor.
promising ['prɔmɪsɪŋ] *adj* prometedor(a).
promissory note ['prɔmɪsərɪ-] *n* pagaré *m*.
promontory ['prɔməntrɪ] *n* promontorio.
promote [prə'məut] *vt* promover; (*new
product*) dar publicidad a, lanzar; (*MIL*)
ascender; **the team was ~d to the second
division** (*BRIT FOOTBALL*) el equipo
ascendió a la segunda división.
promoter [prə'məutə*] *n* (*of sporting event*)
promotor(a) *m/f*; (*of company, business*)
patrocinador(a) *m/f*.
promotion [prə'məuʃən] *n* (*gen*) promoción
f; (*MIL*) ascenso.

prompt [prɔmpt] *adj* pronto ♦ *adv*: **at 6
o'clock ~** a las seis en punto ♦ *n* (*COMPUT*)
aviso, guía ♦ *vt* (*urge*) mover, incitar;
(*THEAT*) apuntar; **to ~ sb to do sth** instar
a algn a hacer algo; **to be ~ to do sth** no
tardar en hacer algo; **they're very ~**
(*punctual*) son muy puntuales.
prompter ['prɔmptə*] *n* (*THEAT*)
apuntador(a) *m/f*.
promptly ['prɔmptlɪ] *adv* (*punctually*)
puntualmente; (*rapidly*) rápidamente.
promptness ['prɔmptnɪs] *n* puntualidad *f*;
rapidez *f*.
promulgate ['prɔməlgeɪt] *vt* promulgar.
prone [prəun] *adj* (*lying*) postrado; **~ to**
propenso a.
prong [prɔŋ] *n* diente *m*, punta.
pronoun ['prəunaun] *n* pronombre *m*.
pronounce [prə'nauns] *vt* pronunciar;
(*declare*) declarar ♦ *vi*: **to ~ (up)on**
pronunciarse sobre; **they ~d him unfit to
plead** le declararon incapaz de
defenderse.
pronounced [prə'naunst] *adj* (*marked*)
marcado.
pronouncement [prə'naunsmənt] *n*
declaración *f*.
pronunciation [prənʌnsɪ'eɪʃən] *n*
pronunciación *f*.
proof [pruːf] *n* prueba; **70° ~** graduación *f*
del 70 por 100 ♦ *adj*: **~ against** a prueba
de ♦ *vt* (*tent, anorak*) impermeabilizar.
proofreader ['pruːfriːdə*] *n* corrector(a) *m/f*
de pruebas.
prop [prɔp] *n* apoyo; (*fig*) sostén *m* ♦ *vt* (*also:
~ up*) apoyar; (*lean*): **to ~ sth against**
apoyar algo contra.
Prop. *abbr* (*COMM*) = **proprietor**.
propaganda [prɔpə'gændə] *n* propaganda.
propagate ['prɔpəgeɪt] *vt* propagar.
propel [prə'pɛl] *vt* impulsar, propulsar.
propeller [prə'pɛlə*] *n* hélice *f*.
propelling pencil [prə'pɛlɪŋ-] *n* (*BRIT*)
lapicero.
propensity [prə'pɛnsɪtɪ] *n* propensión *f*.
proper ['prɔpə*] *adj* (*suited, right*) propio;
(*exact*) justo; (*apt*) apropiado,
conveniente; (*timely*) oportuno; (*seemly*)
correcto, decente; (*authentic*) verdadero;
(*col: real*) auténtico; **to go through the ~
channels** (*ADMIN*) ir por la vía oficial.
properly ['prɔpəlɪ] *adv* (*adequately*)
correctamente; (*decently*) decentemente.
proper noun *n* nombre *m* propio.
properties ['prɔpətɪz] *npl* (*THEAT*)
accesorios *mpl*, atrezzo *msg*.
property ['prɔpətɪ] *n* propiedad *f*; (*estate*)
finca; **lost ~** objetos *mpl* perdidos;

personal ~ bienes *mpl* muebles.
property developer *n* promotor(a) *m/f* de construcciones.
property owner *n* dueño/a de propiedades.
property tax *n* impuesto sobre la propiedad.
prophecy ['prɔfɪsɪ] *n* profecía.
prophesy ['prɔfɪsaɪ] *vt* profetizar; (*fig*) predecir.
prophet ['prɔfɪt] *n* profeta *m/f*.
prophetic [prəˈfɛtɪk] *adj* profético.
proportion [prəˈpɔːʃən] *n* proporción *f*; (*share*) parte *f*; **to be in/out of** ~ **or with sth** estar en/no guardar proporción con algo; **to see sth in** ~ (*fig*) ver algo en su justa medida.
proportional [prəˈpɔːʃənl] *adj* proporcional.
proportionally [prəpɔːˈʃnəlɪ] *adv* proporcionalmente, en proporción.
proportional representation (PR) *n* (*POL*) representación *f* proporcional.
proportional spacing *n* (*on printer*) espaciado proporcional.
proportionate [prəˈpɔːʃənɪt] *adj* proporcionado.
proportionately [prəˈpɔːʃnɪtlɪ] *adv* proporcionadamente, en proporción.
proportioned [prəˈpɔːʃənd] *adj* proporcionado.
proposal [prəˈpəuzl] *n* propuesta; (*offer of marriage*) oferta de matrimonio; (*plan*) proyecto; (*suggestion*) sugerencia.
propose [prəˈpəuz] *vt* proponer; (*have in mind*): **to** ~ **sth/to do** *or* **doing sth** proponer algo/proponerse hacer algo ♦ *vi* declararse.
proposer [prəˈpəuzə*] *n* (*of motion*) proponente *m/f*.
proposition [prɔpəˈzɪʃən] *n* propuesta, proposición *f*; **to make sb a** ~ proponer algo a algn.
propound [prəˈpaund] *vt* (*theory*) exponer.
proprietary [prəˈpraɪətərɪ] *adj* (*COMM*): ~ **article** artículo de marca; ~ **brand** marca comercial.
proprietor [prəˈpraɪətə*] *n* propietario/a, dueño/a.
propriety [prəˈpraɪətɪ] *n* decoro.
propulsion [prəˈpʌlʃən] *n* propulsión *f*.
pro rata [prəuˈrɑːtə] *adv* a prorrata.
prosaic [prəuˈzeɪɪk] *adj* prosaico.
Pros. Atty. *abbr* (*US*) = *prosecuting attorney*.
proscribe [prəˈskraɪb] *vt* proscribir.
prose [prəuz] *n* prosa; (*SCOL*) traducción *f* inversa.
prosecute ['prɔsɪkjuːt] *vt* (*LAW*) procesar; "trespassers will be ~d" (*LAW*) "se

procesará a los intrusos".
prosecution [prɔsɪˈkjuːʃən] *n* proceso, causa; (*accusing side*) acusación *f*.
prosecutor ['prɔsɪkjuːtə*] *n* acusador(a) *m/f*; (*also*: **public** ~) fiscal *m/f*.
prospect *n* ['prɔspɛkt] (*chance*) posibilidad *f*; (*outlook*) perspectiva; (*hope*) esperanza ♦ (*vb*: [prəˈspɛkt]) *vt* explorar ♦ *vi* buscar; ~**s** *npl* (*for work etc*) perspectivas *fpl*; **to be faced with the** ~ **of** tener que enfrentarse a la posibilidad de que ...; **we were faced with the** ~ **of leaving early** se nos planteó la posibilidad de marcharnos pronto; **there is every** ~ **of an early victory** hay buenas perspectivas de una pronta victoria.
prospecting [prəˈspɛktɪŋ] *n* prospección *f*.
prospective [prəˈspɛktɪv] *adj* (*possible*) probable, eventual; (*certain*) futuro; (*buyer*) presunto; (*legislation, son-in-law*) futuro.
prospector [prəˈspɛktə*] *n* explorador(a) *m/f*; **gold** ~ buscador *m* de oro.
prospectus [prəˈspɛktəs] *n* prospecto.
prosper ['prɔspə*] *vi* prosperar.
prosperity [prɔˈspɛrɪtɪ] *n* prosperidad *f*.
prosperous ['prɔspərəs] *adj* próspero.
prostate ['prɔsteɪt] *n* (*also*: ~ **gland**) próstata.
prostitute ['prɔstɪtjuːt] *n* prostituta; **male** ~ prostituto.
prostitution [prɔstɪˈtjuːʃən] *n* prostitución *f*.
prostrate ['prɔstreɪt] *adj* postrado; (*fig*) abatido ♦ *vt*: **to** ~ **o.s.** postrarse.
protagonist [prəˈtægənɪst] *n* protagonista *m/f*.
protect [prəˈtɛkt] *vt* proteger.
protection [prəˈtɛkʃən] *n* protección *f*; **to be under sb's** ~ estar amparado por algn.
protectionism [prəˈtɛkʃənɪzəm] *n* proteccionismo.
protection racket *n* chantaje *m*.
protective [prəˈtɛktɪv] *adj* protector(a); ~ **custody** (*LAW*) detención *f* preventiva.
protector [prəˈtɛktə*] *n* protector(a) *m/f*.
protégé ['prəuteʒeɪ] *n* protegido/a.
protein ['prəutiːn] *n* proteína.
pro tem [prəuˈtɛm] *adv abbr* (= *pro tempore: for the time being*) provisionalmente.
protest *n* ['prəutɛst] protesta ♦ (*vb*: [prəˈtɛst]) *vi* protestar ♦ *vt* (*affirm*) afirmar, declarar; **to do sth under** ~ hacer algo bajo protesta; **to** ~ **against/about** protestar en contra de/por.
Protestant ['prɔtɪstənt] *adj, n* protestante *m/f*.
protester, protestor [prəˈtɛstə*] *n* (*in*

demonstration) manifestante *m/f*.

protest march *n* manifestación *f or* marcha (de protesta).

protocol ['prəutəkɔl] *n* protocolo.

prototype ['prəutətaɪp] *n* prototipo.

protracted [prə'træktɪd] *adj* prolongado.

protractor [prə'træktə*] *n* (*GEOM*) transportador *m*.

protrude [prə'truːd] *vi* salir, sobresalir.

protuberance [prə'tjuːbərəns] *n* protuberancia.

proud [praud] *adj* orgulloso; (*pej*) soberbio, altanero ♦ *adv*: **to do sb ~** tratar a algn a cuerpo de rey; **to do o.s. ~** no privarse de nada; **to be ~ to do sth** estar orgulloso de hacer algo.

proudly ['praudlɪ] *adv* orgullosamente, con orgullo; (*pej*) con soberbia, con altanería.

prove [pruːv] *vt* probar; (*verify*) comprobar; (*show*) demostrar ♦ *vi*: **to ~ correct** resultar correcto; **to ~ o.s.** ponerse a prueba; **he was ~d right in the end** al final se vio que tenía razón.

proverb ['prɔvəːb] *n* refrán *m*.

proverbial [prə'vəːbɪəl] *adj* proverbial.

proverbially [prə'vəːbɪəlɪ] *adv* proverbialmente.

provide [prə'vaɪd] *vt* proporcionar, dar; **to ~ sb with sth** proveer a algn de algo; **to be ~d with** ser provisto de.

►**provide for** *vt fus* (*person*) mantener a; (*problem etc*) tener en cuenta.

provided [prə'vaɪdɪd] *conj*: **~ (that)** con tal de que, a condición de que.

Providence ['prɔvɪdəns] *n* Divina Providencia.

providing [prə'vaɪdɪŋ] *conj* a condición de que, con tal de que.

province ['prɔvɪns] *n* provincia; (*fig*) esfera.

provincial [prə'vɪnʃəl] *adj* provincial; (*pej*) provinciano.

provision [prə'vɪʒən] *n* provisión *f*; (*supply*) suministro, abastecimiento; **~s** *npl* provisiones *fpl*, víveres *mpl*; **to make ~ for** (*one's family, future*) atender las necesidades de.

provisional [prə'vɪʒənl] *adj* provisional, provisorio (*LAM*); (*temporary*) interino ♦ *n*: **P~** (*Irish POL*) Provisional *m* (*miembro de la tendencia activista del IRA*).

provisional driving licence *n* (*BRIT AUT*) carnet *m* de conducir provisional; *see also* **L-plates**.

proviso [prə'vaɪzəu] *n* condición *f*, estipulación *f*; **with the ~ that** a condición de que.

Provo ['prɔvəu] *n abbr* (*col*) = **Provisional**.

provocation [prɔvə'keɪʃən] *n* provocación *f*.

provocative [prə'vɔkətɪv] *adj* provocativo.

provoke [prə'vəuk] *vt* (*arouse*) provocar, incitar; (*cause*) causar, producir; (*anger*) enojar; **to ~ sb to sth/to do** *or* **into doing sth** provocar a algn a algo/a hacer algo.

provoking [prə'vəukɪŋ] *adj* provocador(a).

provost ['prɔvəst] *n* (*BRIT: of university*) rector(a) *m/f*; (*Scottish*) alcalde(sa) *m/f*.

prow [prau] *n* proa.

prowess ['prauɪs] *n* (*skill*) destreza, habilidad *f*; (*courage*) valor *m*; **his ~ as a footballer** (*skill*) su habilidad como futbolista.

prowl [praul] *vi* (*also*: **~ about, ~ around**) merodear ♦ *n*: **on the ~** de merodeo, merodeando.

prowler ['praulə*] *n* merodeador(a) *m/f*.

proximity [prɔk'sɪmɪtɪ] *n* proximidad *f*.

proxy ['prɔksɪ] *n* poder *m*; (*person*) apoderado/a; **by ~** por poderes.

PRP *n abbr* (= *performance related pay*) retribución en función del rendimiento en el trabajo.

prude [pruːd] *n* gazmoño/a, mojigato/a.

prudence ['pruːdns] *n* prudencia.

prudent ['pruːdnt] *adj* prudente.

prudently ['pruːdntlɪ] *adv* prudentemente, con prudencia.

prudish ['pruːdɪʃ] *adj* gazmoño.

prudishness ['pruːdɪʃnɪs] *n* gazmoñería.

prune [pruːn] *n* ciruela pasa ♦ *vt* podar.

pry [praɪ] *vi*: **to ~ into** entrometerse en.

PS *abbr* (= *postscript*) P.D.

psalm [sɑːm] *n* salmo.

PSAT *n abbr* (*US*) = *Preliminary Scholastic Aptitude Test*.

pseud [sjuːd] *n* (*BRIT col: intellectually*) farsante *m/f*; (: *socially*) pretencioso/a.

pseudo... [sjuːdəu] *pref* seudo....

pseudonym ['sjuːdənɪm] *n* seudónimo.

PSHE *n abbr* (*BRIT SCOL*: = *personal, social and health education*) formación social y sanitaria para la vida adulta.

PST *n abbr* (*US*: = *Pacific Standard Time*) hora de invierno del Pacífico.

PSV *n abbr* (*BRIT*) *see* **public service vehicle**.

psyche ['saɪkɪ] *n* psique *f*.

psychiatric [saɪkɪ'ætrɪk] *adj* psiquiátrico.

psychiatrist [saɪ'kaɪətrɪst] *n* psiquiatra *m/f*.

psychiatry [saɪ'kaɪətrɪ] *n* psiquiatría.

psychic ['saɪkɪk] *adj* (*also*: **~al**) psíquico.

psycho ['saɪkəu] *n* (*col*) psicópata *m/f*, pirado/a.

psychoanalyse, psychoanalyze [saɪkəu-'ænəlaɪz] *vt* psicoanalizar.

psychoanalysis, *pl* **psychoanalyses**

[saɪkəuə'nælɪsɪs, -siːz] _n_ psicoanálisis _m inv_.
psychoanalyst [saɪkəu'ænəlɪst] _n_
psicoanalista _m/f_.
psychological [saɪkə'lɔdʒɪkl] _adj_
psicológico.
psychologically [saɪkə'lɔdʒɪklɪ] _adv_
psicológicamente.
psychologist [saɪ'kɔlədʒɪst] _n_ psicólogo/a.
psychology [saɪ'kɔlədʒɪ] _n_ psicología.
psychopath ['saɪkəupæθ] _n_ psicópata _m/f_.
psychosis, _pl_ **psychoses** [saɪ'kəusɪs, -siːz]
_n_ psicosis _f inv_.
psychotherapy [saɪkəu'θerəpɪ] _n_
psicoterapia.
psychotic [saɪ'kɔtɪk] _adj, n_ psicótico/a.
PT _n abbr_ (_BRIT_: = _Physical Training_) Ed. Fís.
pt _abbr_ = _pint(s), point(s)_.
Pt. _abbr_ (_GEO_: = _Point_) Pta.
PTA _n abbr_ (_BRIT_: = _Parent-Teacher
Association_) ≈ Asociación _f_ de Padres de
Alumnos.
Pte. _abbr_ (_BRIT MIL_) = _private_.
PTO _abbr_ (= _please turn over_) sigue.
PTV _n abbr_ (_US_) = _pay television, public
television_.
pub [pʌb] _n abbr_ (= _public house_) pub _m_, bar
_m_; _ver recuadro_.

PUB

_En un_ **pub** (o **public house**) _se pueden
consumir fundamentalmente bebidas
alcohólicas, aunque en la actualidad
también se sirven platos ligeros durante el
almuerzo. Es, además, un lugar de
encuentro donde se juega a los dardos o al
billar, entre otras actividades. La estricta
regulación sobre la venta de alcohol
controla las horas de apertura, aunque
éstas son más flexibles desde hace unos
años. No se puede servir alcohol a los
menores de 18 años._

---

pub crawl _n_ (_col_): **to go on a ~** ir a
recorrer bares.
puberty ['pjuːbətɪ] _n_ pubertad _f_.
pubic ['pjuːbɪk] _adj_ púbico.
public ['pʌblɪk] _adj, n_ público; **in ~** en
público; **to make sth ~** revelar _or_ hacer
público algo; **to be ~ knowledge** ser del
dominio público; **to go ~** (_COMM_)
proceder a la venta pública de acciones.
public address system (PA) _n_
megafonía, sistema _m_ de altavoces.
publican ['pʌblɪkən] _n_ dueño/a _or_
encargado/a de un bar.
publication [pʌblɪ'keɪʃən] _n_ publicación _f_.
public company _n_ sociedad _f_ anónima.

public convenience _n_ (_BRIT_) aseos _mpl_
públicos, sanitarios _mpl_ (_LAM_).
public holiday _n_ día _m_ de fiesta, (día)
feriado (_LAM_).
public house _n_ (_BRIT_) bar _m_, pub _m_.
publicity [pʌb'lɪsɪtɪ] _n_ publicidad _f_.
publicize ['pʌblɪsaɪz] _vt_ publicitar;
(_advertise_) hacer propaganda para.
public limited company (plc) _n_ sociedad
_f_ anónima (S.A.).
publicly ['pʌblɪklɪ] _adv_ públicamente, en
público.
public opinion _n_ opinión _f_ pública.
public ownership _n_ propiedad _f_ pública;
to be taken into ~ ser nacionalizado.
Public Prosecutor _n_ Fiscal _m/f_ del Estado.
public relations (PR) _n_ relaciones _fpl_
públicas.
public relations officer _n_ encargado/a de
relaciones públicas.
public school _n_ (_BRIT_) colegio privado;
(_US_) instituto; _ver recuadro_.

PUBLIC SCHOOL

En Inglaterra el término **public school** _se
usa para referirse a un colegio privado de
pago, generalmente de alto prestigio social
y en régimen de internado. Algunos de los
más conocidos son Eton o Harrow. Muchos
de sus alumnos estudian previamente
hasta los 13 años en un centro privado de
pago llamado "prep(aratory) school" y al
terminar el bachiller pasan a estudiar en las
universidades de Oxford y Cambridge.
En otros lugares como Estados Unidos el
mismo término se refiere a una escuela
pública de enseñanza gratuita administrada
por el Estado._

---

public sector _n_ sector _m_ público.
public-spirited [pʌblɪk'spɪrɪtɪd] _adj_ cívico.
public transport, (_US_) **public
transportation** _n_ transporte _m_ público.
public works _npl_ obras _fpl_ públicas.
publish ['pʌblɪʃ] _vt_ publicar.
publisher ['pʌblɪʃə*] _n_ (_person_) editor(a)
_m/f_; (_firm_) editorial _f_.
publishing ['pʌblɪʃɪŋ] _n_ (_industry_) industria
del libro.
publishing company _n_ (casa) editorial _f_.
puce [pjuːs] _adj_ de color pardo rojizo.
puck [pʌk] _n_ (_ICE HOCKEY_) puck _m_.
pucker ['pʌkə*] _vt_ (_pleat_) arrugar; (_brow
etc_) fruncir.
pudding ['pudɪŋ] _n_ pudín _m_; (_BRIT: sweet_)
postre _m_; **black ~** morcilla; **rice ~** arroz _m_
con leche.

puddle ['pʌdl] n charco.
puerile ['pjuəraɪl] adj pueril.
Puerto Rican ['pwɔ:təu'ri:kən] adj, n puertorriqueño/a m/f.
Puerto Rico [-'ri:kəu] n Puerto Rico.
puff [pʌf] n soplo; (of smoke) bocanada; (of breathing, engine) resoplido; (powder ~) borla ♦ vt: to ~ one's pipe dar chupadas a la pipa; (also: ~ out: sails, cheeks) hinchar, inflar ♦ vi (gen) soplar; (pant) jadear; to ~ out smoke echar humo.
puffed [pʌft] adj (col: out of breath) sin aliento.
puffin ['pʌfɪn] n frailecillo.
puff pastry, (US) **puff paste** n hojaldre m.
puffy ['pʌfɪ] adj hinchado.
pull [pul] n (tug): **to give sth a** ~ dar un tirón a algo; (fig: advantage) ventaja; (: influence) influencia ♦ vt tirar de, jalar (LAM); (haul) tirar, jalar (LAM), arrastrar; (strain): **to** ~ **a muscle** sufrir un tirón ♦ vi tirar, jalar (LAM); **to** ~ **to pieces** hacer pedazos; **to** ~ **one's punches** andarse con bromas; **to** ~ **one's weight** hacer su parte; **to** ~ **o.s. together** tranquilizarse; **to** ~ **sb's leg** tomar el pelo a algn; **to** ~ **strings (for sb)** enchufar (a algn).
▶**pull about** vt (handle roughly: object) manosear; (: person) maltratar.
▶**pull apart** vt (take apart) desmontar.
▶**pull down** vt (house) derribar.
▶**pull in** vi (AUT: at the kerb) parar (junto a la acera); (RAIL) llegar.
▶**pull off** vt (deal etc) cerrar.
▶**pull out** vi irse, marcharse; (AUT: from kerb) salir ♦ vt sacar, arrancar.
▶**pull over** vi (AUT) hacerse a un lado.
▶**pull round, pull through** vi salvarse; (MED) recobrar la salud.
▶**pull up** vi (stop) parar ♦ vt (uproot) arrancar, desarraigar; (stop) parar.
pulley ['pulɪ] n polea.
pull-out ['pulaut] n suplemento ♦ cpd (pages, magazine) separable.
pullover ['puləuvə*] n jersey m, suéter m.
pulp [pʌlp] n (of fruit) pulpa; (for paper) pasta; (pej: also: ~ **magazines** etc) prensa amarilla; **to reduce sth to** ~ hacer algo papilla.
pulpit ['pulpɪt] n púlpito.
pulsate [pʌl'seɪt] vi pulsar, latir.
pulse [pʌls] n (ANAT) pulso; (of music, engine) pulsación f; (BOT) legumbre f; **to feel** or **take sb's** ~ tomar el pulso a algn.
pulverize ['pʌlvəraɪz] vt pulverizar; (fig) hacer polvo.
puma ['pju:mə] n puma m.
pumice (stone) ['pʌmɪs-] n piedra pómez.

pummel ['pʌml] vt aporrear.
pump [pʌmp] n bomba; (shoe) zapatilla de tenis ♦ vt sacar con una bomba; (fig: col) (son)sacar; **to** ~ **sb for information** (son)sacarle información a algn.
▶**pump up** vt inflar.
pumpkin ['pʌmpkɪn] n calabaza.
pun [pʌn] n juego de palabras.
punch [pʌntʃ] n (blow) golpe m, puñetazo; (tool) punzón m; (for paper) perforadora; (for tickets) taladro; (drink) ponche m ♦ vt (hit): **to** ~ **sb/sth** dar un puñetazo or golpear a algn/algo; (make a hole in) punzar; perforar.
punch-drunk ['pʌntʃdrʌŋk] adj (BRIT) grogui, sonado.
punch(ed) card [pʌntʃ(t)-] n tarjeta perforada.
punch line n (of joke) remate m.
punch-up ['pʌntʃʌp] n (BRIT col) riña.
punctual ['pʌŋktjuəl] adj puntual.
punctuality [pʌŋktju'ælɪtɪ] n puntualidad f.
punctually ['pʌŋktjuəlɪ] adv: **it will start** ~ **at 6** empezará a las 6 en punto.
punctuate ['pʌŋktjueɪt] vt puntuar; (fig) interrumpir.
punctuation [pʌŋktju'eɪʃən] n puntuación f.
punctuation mark n signo de puntuación.
puncture ['pʌŋktʃə*] (BRIT) n pinchazo ♦ vt pinchar; **to have a** ~ tener un pinchazo.
pundit ['pʌndɪt] n experto/a.
pungent ['pʌndʒənt] adj acre.
punish ['pʌnɪʃ] vt castigar; **to** ~ **sb for sth/ for doing sth** castigar a algn por algo/por haber hecho algo.
punishable ['pʌnɪʃəbl] adj punible, castigable.
punishing ['pʌnɪʃɪŋ] adj (fig: exhausting) agotador(a).
punishment ['pʌnɪʃmənt] n castigo; (fig, col): **to take a lot of** ~ (boxer) recibir una paliza; (car) ser maltratado.
punitive ['pju:nɪtɪv] adj punitivo.
punk [pʌŋk] n (also: ~ **rocker**) punki m/f; (also: ~ **rock**) música punk; (US col: hoodlum) matón m.
punt [pʌnt] n (boat) batea; (IRELAND) libra irlandesa ♦ vi (bet) apostar.
punter ['pʌntə*] n (gambler) jugador(a) m/f.
puny ['pju:nɪ] adj enclenque.
pup [pʌp] n cachorro.
pupil ['pju:pl] n alumno/a; (of eye) pupila.
puppet ['pʌpɪt] n títere m.
puppet government n gobierno títere.
puppy ['pʌpɪ] n cachorro, perrito.
purchase ['pə:tʃɪs] n compra; (grip) agarre m, asidero ♦ vt comprar.
purchase order n orden f de compra.

purchase price *n* precio de compra.
purchaser ['pɜ:tʃɪsə*] *n* comprador(a) *m/f*.
purchase tax *n* (*BRIT*) impuesto sobre la venta.
purchasing power ['pɜ:tʃɪsɪŋ-] *n* poder *m* adquisitivo.
pure [pjuə*] *adj* puro; **a ~ wool jumper** un jersey de pura lana; **it's laziness, ~ and simple** es pura vagancia.
purebred ['pjuəbrɛd] *adj* de pura sangre.
purée ['pjuəreɪ] *n* puré *m*.
purely ['pjuəlɪ] *adv* puramente.
purgatory ['pɜ:gətərɪ] *n* purgatorio.
purge [pɜ:dʒ] *n* (*MED, POL*) purga ♦ *vt* purgar.
purification [pjuərɪfɪ'keɪʃən] *n* purificación *f*, depuración *f*.
purify ['pjuərɪfaɪ] *vt* purificar, depurar.
purist ['pjuərɪst] *n* purista *m/f*.
puritan ['pjuərɪtən] *n* puritano/a.
puritanical [pjuərɪ'tænɪkl] *adj* puritano.
purity ['pjuərɪtɪ] *n* pureza.
purl [pɜ:l] *n* punto del revés.
purloin [pɜ:'lɔɪn] *vt* hurtar, robar.
purple ['pɜ:pl] *adj* morado.
purport [pɜ:'pɔ:t] *vi*: **to ~ to be/do** dar a entender que es/hace.
purpose ['pɜ:pəs] *n* propósito; **on ~ a** propósito, adrede; **to no ~** para nada, en vano; **for teaching ~s** con fines pedagógicos; **for the ~s of this meeting** para los fines de esta reunión.
purpose-built ['pɜ:pəs'bɪlt] *adj* (*BRIT*) construido especialmente.
purposeful ['pɜ:pəsful] *adj* resuelto, determinado.
purposely ['pɜ:pəslɪ] *adv* a propósito, adrede.
purr [pɜ:*] *n* ronroneo ♦ *vi* ronronear.
purse [pɜ:s] *n* monedero; (*US: handbag*) bolso ♦ *vt* fruncir.
purser ['pɜ:sə*] *n* (*NAUT*) comisario/a.
purse snatcher [-snætʃə*] *n* (*US*) *persona que roba por el procedimiento del tirón.*
pursue [pə'sju:] *vt* seguir; (*harass*) perseguir; (*profession*) ejercer; (*pleasures*) buscar; (*inquiry, matter*) seguir.
pursuer [pə'sju:ə*] *n* perseguidor(a) *m/f*.
pursuit [pə'sju:t] *n* (*chase*) caza; (*of pleasure etc*) busca; (*occupation*) actividad *f*; **in (the) ~ of sth** en busca de algo.
purveyor [pə'veɪə*] *n* proveedor(a) *m/f*.
pus [pʌs] *n* pus *m*.
push [pʊʃ] *n* empujón *m*; (*MIL*) ataque *m*; (*drive*) empuje *m* ♦ *vt* empujar; (*button*) apretar; (*promote*) promover; (*fig: press, advance: views*) fomentar; (*thrust*): **to ~ sth (into)** meter algo a la fuerza (en) ♦ *vi*

empujar; (*fig*) hacer esfuerzos; **at a ~** (*col*) a duras penas; **she is ~ing 50** (*col*) raya en los 50; **to be ~ed for time/money** andar justo de tiempo/escaso de dinero; **to ~ a door open/shut** abrir/cerrar una puerta empujándola; **to ~ for** (*better pay, conditions*) reivindicar; "~" (*on door*) "empujar"; (*on bell*) "pulse".
▶**push aside** *vt* apartar con la mano.
▶**push in** *vi* colarse.
▶**push off** *vi* (*col*) largarse.
▶**push on** *vi* (*continue*) seguir adelante.
▶**push through** *vt* (*measure*) despachar.
▶**push up** *vt* (*total, prices*) hacer subir.
push-bike ['pʊʃbaɪk] *n* (*BRIT*) bicicleta.
push-button ['pʊʃbʌtn] *adj* con botón de mando.
pushchair ['pʊʃtʃɛə*] *n* (*BRIT*) silla de niño.
pusher ['pʊʃə*] *n* (*drug ~*) traficante *m/f* de drogas.
pushover ['pʊʃəuvə*] *n* (*col*): **it's a ~** está tirado.
push-up ['pʊʃʌp] *n* (*US*) flexión *f*.
pushy ['pʊʃɪ] *adj* (*pej*) agresivo.
puss [pus], **pussy(-cat)** ['pusɪ(kæt)] *n* minino.
put [put], *pt, pp* **put** *vt* (*place*) poner, colocar; (*~ into*) meter; (*express, say*) expresar; (*a question*) hacer; (*estimate*) calcular; (*cause to be*): **to ~ sb in a good/bad mood** poner a algn de buen/mal humor; **to ~ a lot of time into sth** dedicar mucho tiempo a algo; **to ~ money on a horse** apostar dinero en un caballo; **to ~ money into a company** invertir dinero en una compañía; **to ~ sb to a lot of trouble** causar mucha molestia a algn; **we ~ the children to bed** acostamos a los niños; **how shall I ~ it?** ¿cómo puedo explicarlo or decirlo?; **I ~ it to you that ...** le sugiero que ...; **to stay ~** no moverse.
▶**put about** *vi* (*NAUT*) virar ♦ *vt* (*rumour*) hacer correr.
▶**put across** *vt* (*ideas etc*) comunicar.
▶**put aside** *vt* (*lay down: book etc*) dejar or poner a un lado; (*save*) ahorrar; (*in shop*) guardar.
▶**put away** *vt* (*store*) guardar.
▶**put back** *vt* (*replace*) devolver a su lugar; (*postpone*) posponer; (*set back: watch, clock*) retrasar; **this will ~ us back 10 years** esto nos retrasará 10 años.
▶**put by** *vt* (*money*) guardar.
▶**put down** *vt* (*on ground*) poner en el suelo; (*animal*) sacrificar; (*in writing*) apuntar; (*suppress: revolt etc*) sofocar; (*attribute*) atribuir; **~ me down for £15** apúntame por 15 libras; **~ it down on my**

account (*COMM*) póngalo en mi cuenta.

▶**put forward** *vt* (*ideas*) presentar, proponer; (*date*) adelantar.

▶**put in** *vt* (*application, complaint*) presentar.

▶**put in for** *vt fus* (*job*) solicitar; (*promotion*) pedir.

▶**put off** *vt* (*postpone*) aplazar; (*discourage*) desanimar, quitar las ganas a.

▶**put on** *vt* (*clothes, lipstick etc*) ponerse; (*light etc*) encender; (*play etc*) presentar; (*brake*) echar; (*assume: accent, manner*) afectar, fingir; (*airs*) adoptar, darse; (*concert, exhibition etc*) montar; (*extra bus, train etc*) poner; (*col: kid, have on: esp US*) tomar el pelo a; (*inform, indicate*): **to ~ sb on to sb/sth** informar a algn de algn/algo; **to ~ on weight** engordar.

▶**put out** *vt* (*fire, light*) apagar; (*one's hand*) alargar; (*news, rumour*) hacer circular; (*tongue etc*) sacar; (*person: inconvenience*) molestar, fastidiar; (*dislocate: shoulder, vertebra, knee*) dislocar(se) ♦ *vi* (*NAUT*): **to ~ out to sea** hacerse a la mar; **to ~ out from Plymouth** salir de Plymouth.

▶**put through** *vt* (*call*) poner; **~ me through to Mr Low** póngame *or* comuníqueme (*LAM*) con el Señor Low.

▶**put together** *vt* unir, reunir; (*assemble: furniture*) armar, montar; (*meal*) preparar.

▶**put up** *vt* (*raise*) levantar, alzar; (*hang*) colgar; (*build*) construir; (*increase*) aumentar; (*accommodate*) alojar; (*incite*): **to ~ sb up to doing sth** instar *or* incitar a algn a hacer algo; **to ~ sth up for sale** poner algo a la venta.

▶**put upon** *vt fus*: **to be ~ upon** (*imposed upon*) dejarse explotar.

▶**put up with** *vt fus* aguantar.

putrid ['pjuːtrɪd] *adj* podrido.

putsch [putʃ] *n* golpe *m* de estado.

putt [pʌt] *vt* hacer un putt ♦ *n* putt *m*.

putter ['pʌtə*] *n* putter *m*.

putting green ['pʌtɪŋ-] *n* green *m*, minigolf *m*.

putty ['pʌtɪ] *n* masilla.

put-up ['putʌp] *adj*: **~ job** (*BRIT*) estafa.

puzzle ['pʌzl] *n* (*riddle*) acertijo; (*jigsaw*) rompecabezas *m inv*; (*also*: **crossword ~**) crucigrama *m*; (*mystery*) misterio ♦ *vt* dejar perplejo, confundir ♦ *vi*: **to ~ about** quebrar la cabeza por; **to ~ over** (*sb's actions*) quebrarse la cabeza por; (*mystery, problem*) devanarse los sesos sobre; **to be ~d about sth** no llegar a entender algo.

puzzling ['pʌzlɪŋ] *adj* (*question*) misterioso, extraño; (*attitude, instructions*) extraño.

PVC *n abbr* (= *polyvinyl chloride*) P.V.C. *m*.

Pvt. *abbr* (*US MIL*) = **private**.

PW *n abbr* (*US*) = **prisoner of war**.

pw *abbr* (= *per week*) por semana.

PX *n abbr* (*US*: = *post exchange*) *economato militar*.

pygmy ['pɪgmɪ] *n* pigmeo/a.

pyjamas, (*US*) **pajamas** [pɪ'dʒɑːməz] *npl* (*BRIT*) pijama *m*, piyama *m* (*LAM*); **a pair of ~** un pijama.

pylon ['paɪlən] *n* torre *f* de conducción eléctrica.

pyramid ['pɪrəmɪd] *n* pirámide *f*.

Pyrenean [pɪrə'niːən] *adj* pirenaico.

Pyrenees [pɪrə'niːz] *npl*: **the ~** los Pirineos.

Pyrex ® ['paɪreks] *n* pírex *m* ♦ *cpd*: **~ casserole** cazuela de pírex.

python ['paɪθən] *n* pitón *m*.

Q q

Q, q [kjuː] *n* (*letter*) Q, q *f*; **Q for Queen** Q de Quebec.

Qatar [kæ'tɑː] *n* Qatar *m*.

QC *n abbr* (*BRIT*: = *Queen's Council*) *título concedido a determinados abogados*.

QCA *n abbr* (*BRIT*: = *Qualifications and Curriculum Authority*) *organismo que se encarga del currículum educativo en Inglaterra*.

QED *abbr* (= *quod erat demonstrandum*) Q.E.D.

q.t. *n abbr* (*col*: = *quiet*): **on the ~** a hurtadillas.

qty *abbr* (= *quantity*) ctdad.

quack [kwæk] *n* (*of duck*) graznido; (*pej: doctor*) curandero/a, matasanos *m inv* ♦ *vi* graznar.

quad [kwɔd] *abbr* = **quadrangle, quadruple, quadruplet**.

quadrangle ['kwɔdræŋgl] *n* (*BRIT*: *courtyard*: *abbr*: **quad**) patio.

quadruple [kwɔ'druːpl] *vt, vi* cuadruplicar.

quadruplet [kwɔ'druːplɪt] *n* cuatrillizo.

quagmire ['kwægmaɪə*] *n* lodazal *m*, cenagal *m*.

quail [kweɪl] *n* (*bird*) codorniz *f* ♦ *vi* amedrentarse.

quaint [kweɪnt] *adj* extraño; (*picturesque*) pintoresco.

quaintly ['kweɪntlɪ] *adv* extrañamente;

pintorescamente.

quake [kweɪk] vi temblar ♦ n abbr
= **earthquake**.

Quaker ['kweɪkə*] n cuáquero/a.

qualification [kwɔlɪfɪ'keɪʃən] n (reservation)
reserva; (modification) modificación f;
(act) calificación f; (paper ~) título; **what
are your ~s?** ¿qué títulos tienes?

qualified ['kwɔlɪfaɪd] adj (trained)
cualificado; (fit) capacitado; (limited)
limitado; (professionally) titulado; ~ **for/to
do sth** capacitado para/para hacer algo;
he's not ~ for the job no está capacitado
para ese trabajo; **it was a ~ success** fue
un éxito relativo.

qualify ['kwɔlɪfaɪ] vt (LING) calificar a;
(capacitate) capacitar; (modify) matizar;
(limit) moderar ♦ vi (SPORT) clasificarse;
to ~ (as) calificarse (de), graduarse (en),
recibirse (de) (LAM); **to ~ (for)** reunir los
requisitos (para); **to ~ as an engineer**
sacar el título de ingeniero.

qualifying ['kwɔlɪfaɪɪŋ] adj (exam, round)
eliminatorio.

qualitative ['kwɔlɪtətɪv] adj cualitativo.

quality ['kwɔlɪtɪ] n calidad f; (moral)
cualidad f; **of good/poor ~** de buena or
alta/poca calidad.

quality control n control m de calidad.

quality of life n calidad f de vida.

quality press n prensa seria; ver recuadro.

QUALITY PRESS

*La expresión **quality press** se refiere los
periódicos que dan un tratamiento serio de
las noticias, ofreciendo información
detallada sobre un amplio espectro de
temas y análisis en profundidad de la
actualidad. Por su tamaño, considerablemente mayor que el de los periódicos
sensacionalistas, se les llama también
"broadsheets".*

---

qualm [kwɑːm] n escrúpulo; **to have ~s
about sth** sentir escrúpulos por algo.

quandary ['kwɔndrɪ] n: **to be in a ~** verse
en un dilema.

quango ['kwæŋɡəʊ] n abbr (BRIT: = quasi-
autonomous non-governmental organization)
organismo semi-autónomo de subvención
estatal.

quantifiable [kwɔntɪ'faɪəbl] adj
cuantificable.

quantitative ['kwɔntɪtətɪv] adj
cuantitativo.

quantity ['kwɔntɪtɪ] n cantidad f; **in ~** en
grandes cantidades.

quantity surveyor n aparejador(a) m/f.

quantum leap ['kwɔntəm-] n (fig) avance m
espectacular.

quarantine ['kwɔrntiːn] n cuarentena.

quark [kwɑːk] n cuark m.

quarrel ['kwɔrl] n riña, pelea ♦ vi reñir,
pelearse; **to have a ~ with sb** reñir or
pelearse con algn; **I can't ~ with that** no
le veo pegas.

quarrelsome ['kwɔrəlsəm] adj pendenciero.

quarry ['kwɔrɪ] n (for stone) cantera;
(animal) presa.

quart [kwɔːt] n cuarto de galón = 1.136 l.

quarter ['kwɔːtə*] n cuarto, cuarta parte f;
(of year) trimestre m; (district) barrio; (US,
Canada: 25 cents) cuarto de dólar ♦ vt
dividir en cuartos; (MIL: lodge) alojar; ~**s**
npl (barracks) cuartel m; (living ~s) alojamiento sg; **a ~ of an hour** un cuarto de
hora; **to pay by the ~** pagar trimestralmente or cada 3 meses; **it's a ~ to** or (US)
of 3 son las 3 menos cuarto; **it's a ~ past**
or (US) **after 3** son las 3 y cuarto; **from all
~s** de todas partes; **at close ~s** de cerca.

quarterback ['kwɔːtəbæk] n (US: football)
mariscal m de campo.

quarter-deck ['kwɔːtədɛk] n (NAUT) alcázar
m.

quarter final n cuarto de final.

quarterly ['kwɔːtəlɪ] adj trimestral ♦ adv
cada 3 meses, trimestralmente.

quartermaster ['kwɔːtəmɑːstə*] n (MIL)
comisario, intendente m militar.

quartet(te) [kwɔː'tɛt] n cuarteto.

quarto ['kwɔːtəʊ] n tamaño holandés ♦ adj
de tamaño holandés.

quartz [kwɔːts] n cuarzo.

quash [kwɔʃ] vt (verdict) anular, invalidar.

quasi- ['kweɪzaɪ] pref cuasi.

quaver ['kweɪvə*] n (BRIT MUS) corchea ♦ vi
temblar.

quay [kiː] n (also: ~side) muelle m.

Que. abbr (Canada) = Quebec.

queasiness ['kwiːzɪnɪs] n malestar m,
náuseas fpl.

queasy ['kwiːzɪ] adj: **to feel ~** tener
náuseas.

Quebec [kwɪ'bɛk] n Quebec m.

queen [kwiːn] n reina; (CARDS etc)
dama.

queen mother n reina madre.

Queen's Speech n ver recuadro.

QUEEN'S SPEECH

*Se llama **Queen's Speech** (o "King's
Speech") al discurso que pronuncia el
monarca durante la sesión de apertura del*

> Parlamento británico, en el que se expresan las líneas generales de la política del gobierno para la nueva legislatura. El Primer Ministro se encarga de redactarlo con la ayuda del Consejo de Ministros y es leído en la Cámara de los Lores ("House of Lords") ante los miembros de ambas cámaras.

queer [kwɪə*] adj (odd) raro, extraño ♦ n (pej: col) marica m.

quell [kwɛl] vt calmar; (put down) sofocar.

quench [kwɛntʃ] vt (flames) apagar; **to ~ one's thirst** apagar la sed.

querulous ['kwɛrʊləs] adj (person, voice) quejumbroso.

query ['kwɪərɪ] n (question) pregunta; (doubt) duda ♦ vt preguntar; (disagree with, dispute) no estar conforme con, dudar de.

quest [kwɛst] n busca, búsqueda.

question ['kwɛstʃən] n pregunta; (matter) asunto, cuestión f ♦ vt (doubt) dudar de; (interrogate) interrogar, hacer preguntas a; **to ask sb a ~**, **put a ~ to sb** hacerle una pregunta a algn; **the ~ is ...** el asunto es ...; **to bring** or **call sth into ~** poner algo en (tela de) duda; **beyond ~** fuera de toda duda; **it's out of the ~** imposible, ni hablar.

questionable ['kwɛstʃənəbl] adj discutible; (doubtful) dudoso.

questioner ['kwɛstʃənə*] n interrogador(a) m/f.

questioning ['kwɛstʃənɪŋ] adj inquisitivo ♦ n preguntas fpl; (by police etc) interrogatorio.

question mark n punto de interrogación.

questionnaire [kwɛstʃə'nɛə*] n cuestionario.

queue [kjuː] (BRIT) n cola ♦ vi hacer cola; **to jump the ~** colarse.

quibble ['kwɪbl] vi andarse con sutilezas.

quick [kwɪk] adj rápido; (temper) vivo; (agile) ágil; (mind) listo; (eye) agudo; (ear) fino ♦ n: **cut to the ~** (fig) herido en lo más vivo; **be ~!** ¡date prisa!; **to be ~ to act** obrar con prontitud; **she was ~ to see that** se dio cuenta de eso en seguida.

quicken ['kwɪkən] vt apresurar ♦ vi apresurarse, darse prisa.

quick-fire ['kwɪkfaɪə*] adj (questions etc) rápido, (hecho) a quemarropa.

quick fix n (pej) parche m.

quickly ['kwɪklɪ] adv rápidamente, de prisa; **we must act ~** tenemos que actuar cuanto antes.

quickness ['kwɪknɪs] n rapidez f; (of temper) viveza; (agility) agilidad f; (of mind, eye etc) agudeza.

quicksand ['kwɪksænd] n arenas fpl movedizas.

quickstep ['kwɪkstɛp] n baile de ritmo rápido.

quick-tempered [kwɪk'tɛmpəd] adj de genio vivo.

quick-witted [kwɪk'wɪtɪd] adj listo, despabilado.

quid [kwɪd] n, pl inv (BRIT col) libra.

quid pro quo ['kwɪdprəʊ'kwəʊ] n quid pro quo m, compensación f.

quiet ['kwaɪət] adj (not busy: day) tranquilo; (silent) callado; (reserved) reservado; (discreet) discreto; (not noisy: engine) silencioso ♦ n tranquilidad f ♦ vt, vi (US) = **quieten**; **keep ~!** ¡cállate!, ¡silencio!; **business is ~ at this time of year** hay poco movimiento en esta época.

quieten ['kwaɪətn] (also: **~ down**) vi (grow calm) calmarse; (grow silent) callarse ♦ vt calmar; hacer callar.

quietly ['kwaɪətlɪ] adv tranquilamente; (silently) silenciosamente.

quietness ['kwaɪətnɪs] n (silence) silencio; (calm) tranquilidad f.

quill [kwɪl] n (of porcupine) púa; (pen) pluma.

quilt [kwɪlt] n (BRIT) edredón m.

quin [kwɪn] n abbr = **quintuplet**.

quince [kwɪns] n membrillo.

quinine [kwɪ'niːn] n quinina.

quintet(te) [kwɪn'tɛt] n quinteto.

quintuplet [kwɪn'tjuːplɪt] n quintillizo.

quip [kwɪp] n ocurrencia ♦ vi decir con ironía.

quirk [kwəːk] n peculiaridad f; **by some ~ of fate** por algún capricho del destino.

quit [kwɪt] pt, pp **quit** or **quitted** vt dejar, abandonar; (premises) desocupar; (COMPUT) abandonar ♦ vi (give up) renunciar; (go away) irse; (resign) dimitir; **~ stalling!** (US col) ¡déjate de evasivas!

quite [kwaɪt] adv (rather) bastante; (entirely) completamente; **~ a few of them** un buen número de ellos; **~ (so)!** ¡así es!, ¡exactamente!; **~ new** bastante nuevo; **that's not ~ right** eso no está del todo bien; **not ~ as many as last time** no tantos como la última vez; **she's ~ pretty** es bastante guapa.

Quito ['kiːtəʊ] n Quito.

quits [kwɪts] adj: **~ (with)** en paz (con); **let's call it ~** quedamos en paz.

quiver ['kwɪvə*] vi estremecerse ♦ n (for arrows) carcaj m.

quiz [kwɪz] n (game) concurso; (: TV, RADIO)

programa-concurso; (*questioning*)
interrogatorio ♦ *vt* interrogar.
quizzical ['kwɪzɪkl] *adj* burlón(ona).
quoits [kwɔɪts] *npl* juego de aros.
quorum ['kwɔːrəm] *n* quórum *m*.
quota ['kwəʊtə] *n* cuota.
quotation [kwəʊ'teɪʃən] *n* cita; (*estimate*)
presupuesto.
quotation marks *npl* comillas *fpl*.
quote [kwəʊt] *n* cita ♦ *vt* (*sentence*) citar;
(*COMM: sum, figure*) cotizar ♦ *vi*: **to ~ from**
citar de; **~s** *npl* (*inverted commas*)
comillas *fpl*; **in ~s** entre comillas; **the**
figure ~d for the repairs el presupuesto
dado para las reparaciones; **~ ... unquote**
(*in dictation*) comillas iniciales ... finales.
quotient ['kwəʊʃənt] *n* cociente *m*.
qv *n abbr* (= *quod vide: which see*) q.v.
qwerty keyboard ['kwəːtɪ-] *n* teclado
QWERTY.

R r

R, r [ɑː*] *n* (*letter*) R, r *f*; **R for Robert,** (*US*) **R**
for Roger R de Ramón.
R *abbr* (= *right*) dcha.; (= *river*) R.;
(= *Réaumur (scale)*) R; (*US CINE:* =
restricted) *sólo mayores*; (*US POL*) =
republican; (*BRIT:* = *Rex, Regina*) R.
RA *abbr* = *rear admiral* ♦ *n abbr* (*BRIT*) = **Royal**
Academy, *Royal Academician.*
RAAF *n abbr* = *Royal Australian Air Force.*
Rabat [rə'bɑːt] *n* Rabat *m*.
rabbi ['ræbaɪ] *n* rabino.
rabbit ['ræbɪt] *n* conejo ♦ *vi*: **to ~ (on)** (*BRIT*
col) hablar sin ton ni son.
rabbit hutch *n* conejera.
rabble ['ræbl] *n* (*pej*) chusma, populacho.
rabies ['reɪbiːz] *n* rabia.
RAC *n abbr* (*BRIT:* = *Royal Automobile Club*)
≈ RACE *m* (*SP*).
raccoon [rə'kuːn] *n* mapache *m*.
race [reɪs] *n* carrera; (*species*) raza ♦ *vt*
(*horse*) hacer correr; (*person*) competir
contra; (*engine*) acelerar ♦ *vi* (*compete*)
competir; (*run*) correr; (*pulse*) latir a
ritmo acelerado; **the arms ~** la carrera
armamentista; **the human ~** el género
humano; **he ~d across the road** cruzó
corriendo la carretera; **to ~ in/out**
entrar/salir corriendo.

race car *n* (*US*) = **racing car.**
race car driver *n* (*US*) = **racing driver.**
racecourse ['reɪskɔːs] *n* hipódromo.
racehorse ['reɪshɔːs] *n* caballo de carreras.
race meeting *n* concurso hípico.
race relations *npl* relaciones *fpl* raciales.
racetrack ['reɪstræk] *n* hipódromo; (*for cars*)
circuito de carreras.
racial ['reɪʃl] *adj* racial.
racial discrimination *n* discriminación *f*
racial.
racial integration *n* integración *f* racial.
racialism ['reɪʃəlɪzəm] *n* racismo.
racialist ['reɪʃəlɪst] *adj, n* racista *m/f*.
racing ['reɪsɪŋ] *n* carreras *fpl*.
racing car *n* (*BRIT*) coche *m* de carreras.
racing driver *n* (*BRIT*) corredor(a) *m/f* de
coches.
racism ['reɪsɪzəm] *n* racismo.
racist ['reɪsɪst] *adj, n* racista *m/f*.
rack [ræk] *n* (*also:* **luggage ~**) rejilla
(portaequipajes); (*shelf*) estante *m*; (*also:*
roof ~) baca; (*clothes ~*) perchero ♦ *vt*
(*cause pain to*) atormentar; **to go to ~ and**
ruin venirse abajo; **to ~ one's brains**
devanarse los sesos.
▶**rack up** *vt* conseguir, ganar.
racket ['rækɪt] *n* (*for tennis*) raqueta; (*noise*)
ruido, estrépito; (*swindle*) estafa, timo.
racketeer [rækɪ'tɪə*] *n* (*esp US*)
estafador(a) *m/f*.
racoon [rə'kuːn] *n* = **raccoon.**
racquet ['rækɪt] *n* raqueta.
racy ['reɪsɪ] *adj* picante, subido.
RADA ['rɑːdə] *n abbr* (*BRIT*) = *Royal Academy*
of Dramatic Art.
radar ['reɪdɑː*] *n* radar *m*.
radar trap *n* trampa radar.
radial ['reɪdɪəl] *adj* (*tyre: also:* **~-ply**) radial.
radiance ['reɪdɪəns] *n* brillantez *f*,
resplandor *m*.
radiant ['reɪdɪənt] *adj* brillante,
resplandeciente.
radiate ['reɪdɪeɪt] *vt* (*heat*) radiar, irradiar
♦ *vi* (*lines*) extenderse.
radiation [reɪdɪ'eɪʃən] *n* radiación *f*.
radiation sickness *n* enfermedad *f* de
radiación.
radiator ['reɪdɪeɪtə*] *n* (*AUT*) radiador *m*.
radiator cap *n* tapón *m* de radiador.
radiator grill *n* (*AUT*) rejilla del radiador.
radical ['rædɪkl] *adj* radical.
radically ['rædɪkəlɪ] *adv* radicalmente.
radii ['reɪdɪaɪ] *npl of* **radius.**
radio ['reɪdɪəʊ] *n* radio *f or m* (*LAM*) ♦ *vi*: **to ~**
to sb mandar un mensaje por radio a
algn ♦ *vt* (*information*) radiar, transmitir
por radio; (*one's position*) indicar por

radio; (*person*) llamar por radio; **on the ~**
en *or* por la radio.
radioactive [reɪdɪəʊˈæktɪv] *adj*
radi(o)activo.
radioactivity [reɪdɪəʊækˈtɪvɪtɪ] *n*
radi(o)actividad *f*.
radio announcer *n* locutor(a) *m/f* de radio.
radio-controlled [reɪdɪəʊkənˈtrəʊld] *adj*
teledirigido.
radiographer [reɪdɪˈɒɡrəfə*] *n* radiógrafo/
a.
radiography [reɪdɪˈɒɡrəfɪ] *n* radiografía.
radiology [reɪdɪˈɒlədʒɪ] *n* radiología.
radio station *n* emisora.
radio taxi *n* radio taxi *m*.
radiotelephone [reɪdɪəʊˈtɛlɪfəʊn] *n*
radioteléfono.
radiotelescope [reɪdɪəʊˈtɛlɪskəʊp] *n*
radiotelescopio.
radiotherapist [reɪdɪəʊˈθɛrəpɪst] *n*
radioterapeuta *m/f*.
radiotherapy [ˈreɪdɪəʊθɛrəpɪ] *n*
radioterapia.
radish [ˈrædɪʃ] *n* rábano.
radium [ˈreɪdɪəm] *n* radio.
radius, *pl* **radii** [ˈreɪdɪəs, -ɪaɪ] *n* radio; **within
a ~ of 50 miles** en un radio de 50 millas.
RAF *n abbr see* **Royal Air Force**.
raffia [ˈræfɪə] *n* rafia.
raffle [ˈræfl] *n* rifa, sorteo ♦ *vt* (*object*) rifar.
raft [rɑːft] *n* (*craft*) balsa; (*also:* **life ~**) balsa
salvavidas.
rafter [ˈrɑːftə*] *n* viga.
rag [ræɡ] *n* (*piece of cloth*) trapo; (*torn cloth*)
harapo; (*pej: newspaper*) periodicucho;
(*for charity*) actividades estudiantiles
benéficas ♦ *vt* (*BRIT*) tomar el pelo a; **~s**
npl harapos *mpl*; **in ~s** en harapos, hecho
jirones.
rag-and-bone man [ræɡənˈbəʊnmæn] *n*
(*BRIT*) trapero.
rag doll *n* muñeca de trapo.
rage [reɪdʒ] *n* (*fury*) rabia, furor *m* ♦ *vi*
(*person*) rabiar, estar furioso; (*storm*)
bramar; **to fly into a ~** montar en cólera;
it's all the ~ es lo último.
ragged [ˈræɡɪd] *adj* (*edge*) desigual,
mellado; (*cuff*) roto; (*appearance*)
andrajoso, harapiento; **~ left/right** (*text*)
margen *m* izquierdo/derecho irregular.
raging [ˈreɪdʒɪŋ] *adj* furioso; **in a ~ temper**
de un humor de mil demonios.
rag week *n ver recuadro*.

raid [reɪd] *n* (*MIL*) incursión *f*; (*criminal*)
asalto; (*by police*) redada, allanamiento
(*LAM*) ♦ *vt* invadir, atacar; asaltar.
raider [ˈreɪdə*] *n* invasor(a) *m/f*.
rail [reɪl] *n* (*on stair*) barandilla, pasamanos
m inv; (*on bridge*) pretil *m*; (*of balcony, ship*)
barandilla; (*for train*) riel *m*, carril *m*; **~s**
npl vía *sg*; **by ~** por ferrocarril, en tren.
railcard [ˈreɪlkɑːd] *n* (*BRIT*) *tarjeta para
obtener descuentos en el tren*;
Young Person's ~ ≈ Tarjeta joven
(*ESP*).
railing(s) [ˈreɪlɪŋz] *n(pl)* verja *sg*.
railway [ˈreɪlweɪ], (*US*) **railroad** [ˈreɪlrəʊd] *n*
ferrocarril *m*, vía férrea.
railway engine *n* (máquina) locomotora.
railway line *n* (*BRIT*) línea (de ferrocarril).
railwayman [ˈreɪlweɪmən] *n* (*BRIT*)
ferroviario.
railway station *n* (*BRIT*) estación *f* de
ferrocarril.
rain [reɪn] *n* lluvia ♦ *vi* llover; **in the ~** bajo
la lluvia; **it's ~ing** llueve, está lloviendo;
it's ~ing cats and dogs está lloviendo a
cántaros *or* a mares.
rainbow [ˈreɪnbəʊ] *n* arco iris.
raincoat [ˈreɪnkəʊt] *n* impermeable *m*.
raindrop [ˈreɪndrɒp] *n* gota de lluvia.
rainfall [ˈreɪnfɔːl] *n* lluvia.
rainforest [ˈreɪnfɒrɪst] *n* selva tropical.
rainproof [ˈreɪnpruːf] *adj* impermeable, a
prueba de lluvia.
rainstorm [ˈreɪnstɔːm] *n* temporal *m* (de
lluvia).
rainwater [ˈreɪnwɔːtə*] *n* agua de lluvia.
rainy [ˈreɪnɪ] *adj* lluvioso.
raise [reɪz] *n* aumento ♦ *vt* (*lift*) levantar;
(*build*) erigir, edificar; (*increase*)
aumentar; (*doubts*) suscitar; (*a question*)
plantear; (*cattle, family*) criar; (*crop*)
cultivar; (*army*) reclutar; (*funds*) reunir;
(*loan*) obtener; (*end: embargo*) levantar;
to ~ one's voice alzar la voz; **to ~ one's
glass to sb/sth** brindar por algn/algo; **to
~ a laugh/a smile** provocar risa/una
sonrisa; **to ~ sb's hopes** dar esperanzas a
algn.
raisin [ˈreɪzn] *n* pasa de Corinto.

rake [reɪk] n (*tool*) rastrillo; (*person*) libertino ♦ vt (*garden*) rastrillar; (*fire*) hurgar; (*with machine gun*) barrer.

▶**rake in, rake together** vt sacar.

rake-off ['reɪkɔf] n (*col*) comisión f, tajada.

rakish ['reɪkɪʃ] adj (*dissolute*) libertino; **at a** ~ **angle** (*hat*) echado a un lado, de lado.

rally ['rælɪ] n reunión f; (*POL*) mitin m; (*AUT*) rallye m; (*TENNIS*) peloteo ♦ vt reunir ♦ vi reunirse; (*sick person, STOCK EXCHANGE*) recuperarse.

▶**rally round** vt fus (*fig*) dar apoyo a.

rallying point ['rælɪŋ-] n (*POL, MIL*) punto de reunión.

RAM [ræm] n abbr (= *random access memory*) RAM f.

ram [ræm] n carnero; (*TECH*) pisón m ♦ vt (*crash into*) dar contra, chocar con; (*tread down*) apisonar.

ramble ['ræmbl] n caminata, excursión f en el campo ♦ vi (*pej: also:* ~ **on**) divagar.

rambler ['ræmblə*] n excursionista m/f; (*BOT*) trepadora.

rambling ['ræmblɪŋ] adj (*speech*) inconexo; (*BOT*) trepador(a); (*house*) laberíntico.

rambunctious [ræm'bʌŋkʃəs] adj (*US*) = **rumbustious**.

RAMC n abbr (*BRIT*) = *Royal Army Medical Corps*.

ramification [ræmɪfɪ'keɪʃən] n ramificación f.

ramp [ræmp] n rampa; **on/off** ~ n (*US AUT*) vía de acceso/salida; "~" (*AUT*) "rampa".

rampage [ræm'peɪdʒ] n: **to be on the** ~ desmandarse.

rampant ['ræmpənt] adj (*disease etc*): **to be** ~ estar muy extendido.

rampart ['ræmpɑːt] n terraplén m; (*wall*) muralla.

ram raid vt atracar (*rompiendo el escaparate con un coche*).

ramshackle ['ræmʃækl] adj destartalado.

RAN n abbr = *Royal Australian Navy*.

ran [ræn] pt of **run**.

ranch [rɑːntʃ] n (*US*) hacienda, estancia.

rancher ['rɑːntʃə*] n ganadero.

rancid ['rænsɪd] adj rancio.

rancour, (*US*) **rancor** ['ræŋkə*] n rencor m.

random ['rændəm] adj fortuito, sin orden; (*COMPUT, MATH*) aleatorio ♦ n: **at** ~ al azar.

random access n (*COMPUT*) acceso aleatorio.

randy ['rændɪ] adj (*BRIT col*) cachondo, caliente.

rang [ræŋ] pt of **ring**.

range [reɪndʒ] n (*of mountains*) cadena de montañas, cordillera; (*of missile*) alcance

m; (*of voice*) registro; (*series*) serie f; (*of products*) surtido; (*MIL: also:* **shooting** ~) campo de tiro; (*also:* **kitchen** ~) fogón m ♦ vt (*place*) colocar; (*arrange*) arreglar ♦ vi: **to** ~ **over** (*wander*) recorrer; (*extend*) extenderse por; **within (firing)** ~ a tiro; **do you have anything else in this price** ~? ¿tiene algo más de esta gama de precios?; **intermediate-/short-**~ **missile** proyectil m de medio/corto alcance; **to** ~ **from ... to...** oscilar entre ... y...; ~**d left/right** (*text*) alineado a la izquierda/ derecha.

ranger [reɪndʒə*] n guardabosques m inv.

Rangoon [ræŋ'guːn] n Rangún m.

rangy ['reɪndʒɪ] adj alto y delgado.

rank [ræŋk] n (*row*) fila; (*MIL*) rango; (*status*) categoría; (*BRIT: also:* **taxi** ~) parada ♦ vi: **to** ~ **among** figurar entre ♦ adj (*stinking*) fétido, rancio; (*hypocrisy, injustice etc*) manifiesto; **the** ~ **and file** (*fig*) las bases; **to close** ~**s** (*MIL*) cerrar filas; (*fig*) hacer un frente común; ~ **outsider** participante m/f sin probabilidades de vencer; **I** ~ **him 6th** yo le pongo en sexto lugar.

rankle ['ræŋkl] vi (*insult*) doler.

ransack ['rænsæk] vt (*search*) registrar; (*plunder*) saquear.

ransom ['rænsəm] n rescate m; **to hold sb to** ~ (*fig*) poner a algn entre la espada y la pared.

rant [rænt] vi despotricar.

ranting ['ræntɪŋ] n desvaríos mpl.

rap [ræp] vt golpear, dar un golpecito en.

rape [reɪp] n violación f; (*BOT*) colza ♦ vt violar.

rape(seed) oil ['reɪp(siːd)-] n aceite m de colza.

rapid ['ræpɪd] adj rápido.

rapidity [rə'pɪdɪtɪ] n rapidez f.

rapidly ['ræpɪdlɪ] adv rápidamente.

rapids ['ræpɪdz] npl (*GEO*) rápidos mpl.

rapier ['reɪpɪə*] n estoque m.

rapist ['reɪpɪst] n violador m.

rapport [ræ'pɔː*] n entendimiento.

rapprochement [ræ'prɔʃmɑːŋ] n acercamiento.

rapt [ræpt] adj (*attention*) profundo; **to be** ~ **in contemplation** estar ensimismado.

rapture ['ræptʃə*] n éxtasis m.

rapturous ['ræptʃərəs] adj extático; (*applause*) entusiasta; **a** ~ (*party*) macrofiesta con música máquina; ~ **music** música máquina.

rare [rɛə*] adj raro, poco común; (*CULIN: steak*) poco hecho; **it is** ~ **to find that ...** es raro descubrir que ....

rarefied ['rɛərɪʃaɪd] adj (*air, atmosphere*)

rarely ['rɛəlɪ] *adv* rara vez, pocas veces.
raring ['rɛərɪŋ] *adj*: **to be ~ to go** (*col*) tener muchas ganas de empezar.
rarity ['rɛərɪtɪ] *n* rareza.
rascal ['rɑːskl] *n* pillo/a, pícaro/a.
rash [ræʃ] *adj* imprudente, precipitado ♦ *n* (*MED*) salpullido, erupción *f* (cutánea); **to come out in a ~** salir salpullidos.
rasher ['ræʃə*] *n* loncha.
rashly ['ræʃlɪ] *adv* imprudentemente, precipitadamente.
rashness ['ræʃnɪs] *n* imprudencia, precipitación *f*.
rasp [rɑːsp] *n* (*tool*) escofina ♦ *vt* (*speak: also*: ~ **out**) decir con voz áspera.
raspberry ['rɑːzbərɪ] *n* frambuesa.
rasping ['rɑːspɪŋ] *adj*: **a ~ noise** un ruido áspero.
Rastafarian [ræstə'fɛərɪən] *adj*, *n* rastafari *m/f*.
rat [ræt] *n* rata.
ratchet ['rætʃɪt] *n* (*TECH*) trinquete *m*.
rate [reɪt] *n* (*ratio*) razón *f*; (*percentage*) tanto por ciento; (*price*) precio; (: *of hotel*) tarifa; (*of interest*) tipo; (*speed*) velocidad *f* ♦ *vt* (*value*) tasar; (*estimate*) estimar; **to ~ as** ser considerado como; **~s** *npl* (*BRIT*) impuesto *sg* municipal; (*fees*) tarifa *sg*; **failure ~** porcentaje *m* de fallos; **pulse ~** pulsaciones *fpl* por minuto; **~ of pay** tipos *mpl* de sueldo; **at a ~ of 60 kph** a una velocidad de 60 kph; **~ of growth** ritmo de crecimiento; **~ of return** (*COMM*) tasa de rendimiento; **bank ~** tipo *or* tasa de interés bancario; **at any ~** en todo caso; **to ~ sb/sth highly** tener a algn/algo en alta estima; **the house is ~d at £84 per annum** (*BRIT*) la casa está tasada en 84 libras al año.
rateable value ['reɪtəbl-] *n* (*BRIT*) valor *m* impuesto.
rate-capping ['reɪtkæpɪŋ] *n* (*BRIT*) fijación *f* de las contribuciones.
ratepayer ['reɪtpeɪə*] *n* (*BRIT*) contribuyente *m/f*.
rather ['rɑːðə*] *adv* antes, más bien; (*somewhat*) algo, un poco; (*quite*) bastante; **it's ~ expensive** es algo caro; (*too much*) es demasiado caro; **there's ~ a lot** hay bastante; **I would** *or* **I'd ~ go** preferiría ir; **I'd ~ not** prefiero que no; **I ~ think he won't come** me inclino a creer que no vendrá; **or ~** (*more accurately*) o mejor dicho.
ratification [rætɪfɪ'keɪʃən] *n* ratificación *f*.
ratify ['rætɪfaɪ] *vt* ratificar.
rating ['reɪtɪŋ] *n* (*valuation*) tasación *f*;

(*standing*) posición *f*; (*BRIT NAUT*: *sailor*) marinero; **~s** *npl* (*RADIO*, *TV*) clasificación *f*.
ratio ['reɪʃɪəu] *n* razón *f*; **in the ~ of 100 to 1** a razón de *or* en la proporción de 100 a 1.
ration ['ræʃən] *n* ración *f*; **~s** *npl* víveres *mpl* ♦ *vt* racionar.
rational ['ræʃənl] *adj* racional; (*solution*, *reasoning*) lógico, razonable; (*person*) cuerdo, sensato.
rationale [ræʃə'nɑːl] *n* razón *f* fundamental.
rationalism ['ræʃnəlɪzəm] *n* racionalismo.
rationalization [ræʃnəlaɪ'zeɪʃən] *n* racionalización *f*.
rationalize ['ræʃnəlaɪz] *vt* (*reorganize*: *industry*) racionalizar.
rationally ['ræʃnəlɪ] *adv* racionalmente; (*logically*) lógicamente.
rationing ['ræʃnɪŋ] *n* racionamiento.
ratpack ['rætpæk] *n* (*BRIT col*) periodistas *que persiguen a los famosos*.
rat race *n lucha incesante por la supervivencia*.
rattan [ræ'tæn] *n* rota, caña de Indias.
rattle ['rætl] *n* golpeteo; (*of train etc*) traqueteo; (*object*: *of baby*) sonaja, sonajero; (: *of sports fan*) matraca ♦ *vi* sonar, golpear; traquetear; (*small objects*) castañetear ♦ *vt* hacer sonar agitando; (*col*: *disconcert*) poner nervioso a.
rattlesnake ['rætlsneɪk] *n* serpiente *f* de cascabel.
ratty ['rætɪ] *adj* (*col*) furioso; **to get ~** mosquearse.
raucous ['rɔːkəs] *adj* estridente, ronco.
raucously ['rɔːkəslɪ] *adv* de modo estridente, roncamente.
raunchy ['rɔːntʃɪ] *adj* (*col*) lascivo.
ravage ['rævɪdʒ] *vt* hacer estragos en, destrozar; **~s** *npl* estragos *mpl*.
rave [reɪv] *vi* (*in anger*) encolerizarse; (*with enthusiasm*) entusiasmarse; (*MED*) delirar, desvariar ♦ *cpd*: **~ review** reseña entusiasta; **a ~** (*party*) *macrofiesta con música máquina*; **~ music** música máquina.
raven ['reɪvən] *n* cuervo.
ravenous ['rævənəs] *adj*: **to be ~** tener un hambre canina.
ravine [rə'viːn] *n* barranco.
raving ['reɪvɪŋ] *adj*: **~ lunatic** loco de atar.
ravings ['reɪvɪŋz] *npl* desvaríos *mpl*.
ravioli [rævɪ'əulɪ] *n* ravioles *mpl*, ravioli *mpl*.
ravish ['rævɪʃ] *vt* (*charm*) encantar, embelesar; (*rape*) violar.
ravishing ['rævɪʃɪŋ] *adj* encantador(a).
raw [rɔː] *adj* (*uncooked*) crudo; (*not processed*) bruto; (*sore*) vivo;

(*inexperienced*) novato, inexperto.
Rawalpindi [rɔːlˈpɪndɪ] *n* Rawalpindi
m.
raw data *n* (*COMPUT*) datos *mpl* en bruto.
raw deal *n* (*col: bad deal*) mala pasada *or*
jugada; (: *harsh treatment*) injusticia.
raw material *n* materia prima.
ray [reɪ] *n* rayo; ~ **of hope** (rayo de)
esperanza.
rayon [ˈreɪɔn] *n* rayón *m*.
raze [reɪz] *vt* (*also*: ~ **to the ground**)
arrasar, asolar.
razor [ˈreɪzə*] *n* (*open*) navaja; (*safety* ~)
máquina de afeitar.
razor blade *n* hoja de afeitar.
razzle(-dazzle) [ˈræzl(ˈdæzl)] *n* (*BRIT col*): **to
be/go on the** ~ estar/irse de juerga.
razzmatazz [ˈræzməˈtæz] *n* (*col*) animación
f, bullicio.
R & B *n abbr* = *rhythm and blues*.
RC *abbr* = **Roman Catholic**.
RCAF *n abbr* = *Royal Canadian Air Force*.
RCMP *n abbr* = *Royal Canadian Mounted
Police*.
RCN *n abbr* = *Royal Canadian Navy*.
RD *abbr* (*US POST*) = *rural delivery*.
Rd *abbr* = **road**.
R & D *n abbr* (= *research and development*)
I + D.
RDC *n abbr* (*BRIT*) = *rural district council*.
RE *n abbr* (*BRIT*) = *religious education*; (*BRIT
MIL*) = *Royal Engineers*.
re [riː] *prep* con referencia a.
re ... [riː] *pref* re....
reach [riːtʃ] *n* alcance *m*; (*BOXING*)
envergadura; (*of river etc*) extensión *f*
entre dos recodos ♦ *vt* alcanzar, llegar a;
(*achieve*) lograr ♦ *vi* extenderse; (*stretch
out hand: also*: ~ **down**, ~ **over**, ~ **across**
etc) tender la mano; **within** ~ al alcance
(de la mano); **out of** ~ fuera del alcance;
to ~ **out for sth** alargar *or* tender la
mano para tomar algo; **can I** ~ **you at
your hotel?** ¿puedo localizarte en tu
hotel?; **to** ~ **sb by phone** comunicarse
con algn por teléfono.
react [riːˈækt] *vi* reaccionar.
reaction [riːˈækʃən] *n* reacción *f*.
reactionary [riːˈækʃənri] *adj*, *n*
reaccionario/a *m/f*.
reactor [riːˈæktə*] *n* reactor *m*.
read, *pt*, *pp* **read** [riːd, rɛd] *vi* leer ♦ *vt* leer;
(*understand*) entender; (*study*) estudiar; **to
take sth as read** (*fig*) dar algo por sentado; **do you** ~ **me?** (*TEL*) ¿me escucha?; **to**
~ **between the lines** leer entre líneas.
▶**read out** *vt* leer en alta voz.
▶**read over** *vt* repasar.

▶**read through** *vt* (*quickly*) leer
rápidamente, echar un vistazo a;
(*thoroughly*) leer con cuidado *or*
detenidamente.
▶**read up** *vt*, **read up on** *vt fus*
documentarse sobre.
readable [ˈriːdəbl] *adj* (*writing*) legible;
(*book*) que merece la pena leer.
reader [ˈriːdə*] *n* lector(a) *m/f*; (*book*) libro
de lecturas; (*BRIT: at university*)
profesor(a) *m/f*.
readership [ˈriːdəʃɪp] *n* (*of paper etc*)
número de lectores.
readily [ˈrɛdɪlɪ] *adv* (*willingly*) de buena
gana; (*easily*) fácilmente; (*quickly*) en
seguida.
readiness [ˈrɛdɪnɪs] *n* buena voluntad;
(*preparedness*) preparación *f*; **in** ~
(*prepared*) listo, preparado.
reading [ˈriːdɪŋ] *n* lectura; (*understanding*)
comprensión *f*; (*on instrument*) indicación
f.
reading lamp *n* lámpara portátil.
reading matter *n* lectura.
reading room *n* sala de lectura.
readjust [riːəˈdʒʌst] *vt* reajustar ♦ *vi*
(*person*): **to** ~ **to** reajustarse a.
readjustment [riːəˈdʒʌstmənt] *n* reajuste
m.
ready [ˈrɛdɪ] *adj* listo, preparado; (*willing*)
dispuesto; (*available*) disponible ♦ *n*: **at
the** ~ (*MIL*) listo para tirar; ~ **for use** listo
para usar; **to be** ~ **to do sth** estar listo
para hacer algo; **to get** ~ *vi* prepararse
♦ *vt* preparar.
ready cash *n* efectivo.
ready-made [ˈrɛdɪˈmeɪd] *adj*
confeccionado.
ready money *n* dinero contante.
ready reckoner *n* tabla de cálculos
hechos.
ready-to-wear [ˈrɛdɪtəˈwɛə*] *adj*
confeccionado.
reaffirm [riːəˈfəːm] *vt* reafirmar.
reagent [riːˈeɪdʒənt] *n* reactivo.
real [rɪəl] *adj* verdadero, auténtico; **in** ~
terms en términos reales; **in** ~ **life** en la
vida real, en la realidad.
real ale *n* cerveza elaborada
tradicionalmente.
real estate *n* bienes *mpl* raíces.
real estate agency *n* = **estate agency**.
realism [ˈrɪəlɪzəm] *n* (*also ART*) realismo.
realist [ˈrɪəlɪst] *n* realista *m/f*.
realistic [rɪəˈlɪstɪk] *adj* realista.
realistically [rɪəˈlɪstɪklɪ] *adv* de modo
realista.
reality [riːˈælɪtɪ] *n* realidad *f*; **in** ~ en

realidad.

reality TV n telerrealidad f.

realization [rɪəlaɪˈzeɪʃən] n comprensión f; (of a project; COMM: of assets) realización f.

realize [ˈrɪəlaɪz] vt (understand) darse cuenta de; (a project; COMM: asset) realizar; **I ~ that** ... comprendo or entiendo que ....

really [ˈrɪəlɪ] adv realmente; **~?** ¿de veras?

realm [rɛlm] n reino; (fig) esfera.

real time n (COMPUT) tiempo real.

Realtor ® [ˈrɪəltɔːʳ] n (US) corredor(a) m/f de bienes raíces.

ream [riːm] n resma; **~s** (fig, col) montones mpl.

reap [riːp] vt segar; (fig) cosechar, recoger.

reaper [ˈriːpəʳ] n segador(a) m/f.

reappear [riːəˈpɪəʳ] vi reaparecer.

reappearance [riːəˈpɪərəns] n reaparición f.

reapply [riːəˈplaɪ] vi volver a presentarse, hacer or presentar una nueva solicitud.

reappoint [riːəˈpɔɪnt] vt volver a nombrar.

reappraisal [riːəˈpreɪzl] n revaluación f.

rear [rɪəʳ] adj trasero ♦ n parte f trasera ♦ vt (cattle, family) criar ♦ vi (also: **~ up**) (animal) encabritarse.

rear-engined [ˈrɪərˈɛndʒɪnd] adj (AUT) con motor trasero.

rearguard [ˈrɪəgɑːd] n retaguardia.

rearm [riːˈɑːm] vt rearmar ♦ vi rearmarse.

rearmament [riːˈɑːməmənt] n rearme m.

rearrange [riːəˈreɪndʒ] vt ordenar or arreglar de nuevo.

rear-view [ˈrɪəvjuː]: **~ mirror** n (AUT) espejo retrovisor.

reason [ˈriːzn] n razón f ♦ vi: **to ~ with sb** tratar de que algn entre en razón; **it stands to ~ that** es lógico que; **the ~ for/why** la causa de/la razón por la cual; **she claims with good ~ that she's underpaid** dice con razón que está mal pagada; **all the more ~ why you should not sell it** razón de más para que no lo vendas.

reasonable [ˈriːznəbl] adj razonable; (sensible) sensato.

reasonably [ˈriːznəblɪ] adv razonablemente; **a ~ accurate report** un informe bastante exacto.

reasoned [ˈriːznd] adj (argument) razonado.

reasoning [ˈriːznɪŋ] n razonamiento, argumentos mpl.

reassemble [riːəˈsɛmbl] vt volver a reunir; (machine) montar de nuevo ♦ vi volver a reunirse.

reassert [riːəˈsəːt] vt reafirmar, reiterar.

reassurance [riːəˈʃuərəns] n consuelo.

reassure [riːəˈʃuəʳ] vt tranquilizar; **to ~ sb that** tranquilizar a algn asegurándole

que.

reassuring [riːəˈʃuərɪŋ] adj tranquilizador(a).

reawakening [riːəˈweɪknɪŋ] n despertar m.

rebate [ˈriːbeɪt] n (on product) rebaja; (on tax etc) desgravación f; (repayment) reembolso.

rebel [ˈrɛbl] n rebelde m/f ♦ vi [rɪˈbɛl] rebelarse, sublevarse.

rebellion [rɪˈbɛljən] n rebelión f, sublevación f.

rebellious [rɪˈbɛljəs] adj rebelde; (child) revoltoso.

rebirth [riːˈbəːθ] n renacimiento.

rebound [rɪˈbaund] vi (ball) rebotar ♦ n [ˈriːbaund] rebote m.

rebuff [rɪˈbʌf] n desaire m, rechazo ♦ vt rechazar.

rebuild [riːˈbɪld] vt (irreg: like **build**) reconstruir.

rebuilding [riːˈbɪldɪŋ] n reconstrucción f.

rebuke [rɪˈbjuːk] n reprimenda ♦ vt reprender.

rebut [rɪˈbʌt] vt rebatir.

recalcitrant [rɪˈkælsɪtrənt] adj reacio.

recall [rɪˈkɔːl] vt (remember) recordar; (ambassador etc) retirar; (COMPUT) volver a llamar ♦ n recuerdo.

recant [rɪˈkænt] vi retractarse.

recap [ˈriːkæp] vt, vi recapitular.

recapitulate [riːkəˈpɪtjuleɪt] vt, vi = **recap**.

recapture [riːˈkæptʃəʳ] vt (town) reconquistar; (atmosphere) hacer revivir.

recd., rec'd abbr (= received) rbdo.

recede [rɪˈsiːd] vi retroceder.

receding [rɪˈsiːdɪŋ] adj (forehead, chin) hundido; **~ hairline** entradas fpl.

receipt [rɪˈsiːt] n (document) recibo; (act of receiving) recepción f; **~s** npl (COMM) ingresos mpl; **to acknowledge ~ of** acusar recibo de; **we are in ~ of** ... obra en nuestro poder ....

receivable [rɪˈsiːvəbl] adj (COMM) a cobrar.

receive [rɪˈsiːv] vt recibir; (guest) acoger; (wound) sufrir; **"~d with thanks"** "recibí".

Received Pronunciation [rɪˈsiːvd-] n see **RP**.

receiver [rɪˈsiːvəʳ] n (TEL) auricular m; (RADIO) receptor m; (of stolen goods) perista m/f; (LAW) administrador m jurídico.

receivership [rɪˈsiːvəʃɪp] n: **to go into ~** entrar en liquidación.

recent [ˈriːsnt] adj reciente; **in ~ years** en los últimos años.

recently [ˈriːsntlɪ] adv recientemente, recién (LAM); **~ arrived** recién llegado; **until ~** hasta hace poco.

receptacle [rɪ'sɛptɪkl] *n* receptáculo.
reception [rɪ'sɛpʃən] *n* (*in building, office etc*) recepción *f*; (*welcome*) acogida.
reception centre *n* (*BRIT*) centro de recepción.
reception desk *n* recepción *f*.
receptionist [rɪ'sɛpʃənɪst] *n* recepcionista *m/f*.
receptive [rɪ'sɛptɪv] *adj* receptivo.
recess [rɪ'sɛs] *n* (*in room*) hueco; (*for bed*) nicho; (*secret place*) escondrijo; (*POL etc: holiday*) período vacacional; (*US LAW: short break*) descanso; (*SCOL: esp US*) recreo.
recession [rɪ'sɛʃən] *n* recesión *f*, depresión *f*.
recharge [riː'tʃɑːdʒ] *vt* (*battery*) recargar.
rechargeable [riː'tʃɑːdʒəbl] *adj* recargable.
recipe ['rɛsɪpɪ] *n* receta.
recipient [rɪ'sɪpɪənt] *n* recibidor(a) *m/f*; (*of letter*) destinatario/a.
reciprocal [rɪ'sɪprəkl] *adj* recíproco.
reciprocate [rɪ'sɪprəkeɪt] *vt* devolver, corresponder a ♦ *vi* corresponder.
recital [rɪ'saɪtl] *n* (*MUS*) recital *m*.
recitation [rɛsɪ'teɪʃən] *n* (*of poetry*) recitado; (*of complaints etc*) enumeración *f*, relación *f*.
recite [rɪ'saɪt] *vt* (*poem*) recitar; (*complaints etc*) enumerar.
reckless ['rɛkləs] *adj* temerario, imprudente; (*speed*) peligroso.
recklessly ['rɛkləslɪ] *adv* imprudentemente; de modo peligroso.
recklessness ['rɛkləsnɪs] *n* temeridad *f*, imprudencia.
reckon ['rɛkən] *vt* (*count*) contar; (*consider*) considerar ♦ *vi*: **to ~ without sb/sth** dejar de contar con algn/algo; **he is somebody to be ~ed with** no se le puede descartar; **I ~ that ...** me parece que ..., creo que ....
▶**reckon on** *vt fus* contar con.
reckoning ['rɛkənɪŋ] *n* (*calculation*) cálculo.
reclaim [rɪ'kleɪm] *vt* (*land*) recuperar; (*: from sea*) rescatar; (*demand back*) reclamar.
reclamation [rɛklə'meɪʃən] *n* recuperación *f*; rescate *m*.
recline [rɪ'klaɪn] *vi* reclinarse.
reclining [rɪ'klaɪnɪŋ] *adj* (*seat*) reclinable.
recluse [rɪ'kluːs] *n* recluso/a.
recognition [rɛkəg'nɪʃən] *n* reconocimiento; **transformed beyond ~** irreconocible; **in ~ of** en reconocimiento de.
recognizable ['rɛkəgnaɪzəbl] *adj*: **~ (by)** reconocible (por).
recognize ['rɛkəgnaɪz] *vt* reconocer,

conocer; **to ~ (by/as)** reconocer (por/como).
recoil [rɪ'kɔɪl] *vi* (*person*): **to ~ from doing sth** retraerse de hacer algo ♦ *n* (*of gun*) retroceso.
recollect [rɛkə'lɛkt] *vt* recordar, acordarse de.
recollection [rɛkə'lɛkʃən] *n* recuerdo; **to the best of my ~** que yo recuerde.
recommend [rɛkə'mɛnd] *vt* recomendar; **she has a lot to ~ her** tiene mucho a su favor.
recommendation [rɛkəmen'deɪʃən] *n* recomendación *f*.
recommended retail price (RRP) *n* (*BRIT*) precio (recomendado) de venta al público.
recompense ['rɛkəmpɛns] *vt* recompensar ♦ *n* recompensa.
reconcilable ['rɛkənsaɪləbl] *adj* (re)conciliable.
reconcile ['rɛkənsaɪl] *vt* (*two people*) reconciliar; (*two facts*) conciliar; **to ~ o.s. to sth** resignarse *or* conformarse a algo.
reconciliation [rɛkənsɪlɪ'eɪʃən] *n* reconciliación *f*.
recondite [rɪ'kɔndaɪt] *adj* recóndito.
recondition [riːkən'dɪʃən] *vt* (*machine*) reparar, reponer.
reconditioned [riːkən'dɪʃənd] *adj* renovado, reparado.
reconnaissance [rɪ'kɔnɪsns] *n* (*MIL*) reconocimiento.
reconnoitre, (*US***) reconnoiter** [rɛkə'nɔɪtə*] *vt, vi* (*MIL*) reconocer.
reconsider [riːkən'sɪdə*] *vt* repensar.
reconstitute [riː'kɔnstɪtjuːt] *vt* reconstituir.
reconstruct [riːkən'strʌkt] *vt* reconstruir.
reconstruction [riːkən'strʌkʃən] *n* reconstrucción *f*.
reconvene [riːkən'viːn] *vt* volver a convocar ♦ *vi* volver a reunirse.
record *n* ['rɛkɔːd] (*MUS*) disco; (*of meeting etc*) relación *f*; (*register*) registro, partida; (*file*) archivo; (*also: police or criminal ~*) antecedentes *mpl* penales; (*written*) expediente *m*; (*SPORT*) récord *m*; (*COMPUT*) registro ♦ *vt* [rɪ'kɔːd] (*set down, also COMPUT*) registrar; (*relate*) hacer constar; (*MUS: song etc*) grabar; **in ~ time** en un tiempo récord; **public ~s** archivos *mpl* nacionales; **he is on ~ as saying that ...** hay pruebas de que ha dicho públicamente que ...; **Spain's excellent ~** el excelente historial de España; **off the ~** *adj* no oficial ♦ *adv* confidencialmente.
record card *n* (*in file*) ficha.

recorded delivery letter [rɪ'kɔːdɪd-] n (*BRIT POST*) carta de entrega con acuse de recibo.

recorded music n música grabada.

recorder [rɪ'kɔːdə*] n (*MUS*) flauta de pico; (*TECH*) contador m.

record holder n (*SPORT*) actual poseedor(a) m/f del récord.

recording [rɪ'kɔːdɪŋ] n (*MUS*) grabación f.

recording studio n estudio de grabación.

record library n discoteca.

record player n tocadiscos m inv.

recount vt [rɪ'kaunt] contar.

re-count ['riːkaunt] n (*POL: of votes*) segundo escrutinio, recuento ♦ vt [riːˈkaunt] volver a contar.

recoup [rɪ'kuːp] vt: **to ~ one's losses** recuperar las pérdidas.

recourse [rɪ'kɔːs] n recurso; **to have ~ to** recurrir a.

recover [rɪ'kʌvə*] vt recuperar; (*rescue*) rescatar ♦ vi recuperarse.

recovery [rɪ'kʌvərɪ] n recuperación f; rescate m; (*MED*): **to make a ~** restablecerse.

recreate [riːkrɪ'eɪt] vt recrear.

recreation [rɛkrɪ'eɪʃən] n recreación f; (*amusement*) recreo.

recreational [rɛkrɪ'eɪʃənl] adj de recreo.

recreational drug n droga recreativa.

recreational vehicle n (*US*) caravana or roulotte f pequeña.

recrimination [rɪkrɪmɪ'neɪʃən] n recriminación f.

recruit [rɪ'kruːt] n recluta m/f ♦ vt reclutar; (*staff*) contratar.

recruitment [rɪ'kruːtmənt] n reclutamiento.

rectangle ['rɛktæŋgl] n rectángulo.

rectangular [rɛk'tæŋgjulə*] adj rectangular.

rectify ['rɛktɪfaɪ] vt rectificar.

rector ['rɛktə*] n (*REL*) párroco; (*SCOL*) rector(a) m/f.

rectory ['rɛktərɪ] n casa del párroco.

rectum ['rɛktəm] n (*ANAT*) recto.

recuperate [rɪ'kuːpəreɪt] vi reponerse, restablecerse.

recur [rɪ'kəː*] vi repetirse; (*pain, illness*) producirse de nuevo.

recurrence [rɪ'kərəns] n repetición f.

recurrent [rɪ'kərnt] adj repetido.

recyclable [ˌriːˈsaɪkləbl] adj reciclable.

recycle [riːˈsaɪkl] vt reciclar.

red [rɛd] n rojo ♦ adj rojo; **to be in the ~** (*account*) estar en números rojos; (*business*) tener un saldo negativo; **to**
give sb the **~ carpet treatment** recibir a algn con todos los honores.

red alert n alerta roja.

red-blooded ['rɛd'blʌdɪd] adj (*col*) viril.

redbrick university ['rɛdbrɪk-] n ver recuadro.

REDBRICK UNIVERSITY

*El término **redbrick university** se aplica a las universidades construidas en los grandes centros urbanos industriales como Birmingham, Liverpool o Manchester a finales del siglo XIX o principios del XX. Deben su nombre a que sus edificios son normalmente de ladrillo, a diferencia de las universidades tradicionales de Oxford y Cambridge, cuyos edificios suelen ser de piedra.*

Red Cross n Cruz f Roja.

redcurrant ['rɛdkʌrənt] n grosella.

redden ['rɛdn] vt enrojecer ♦ vi enrojecerse.

reddish ['rɛdɪʃ] adj (*hair*) rojizo.

redecorate [riːˈdɛkəreɪt] pintar de nuevo; volver a decorar.

redecoration [riːdɛkə'reɪʃən] n renovación f.

redeem [rɪ'diːm] vt (*sth in pawn*) desempeñar; (*fig, also REL*) rescatar.

redeemable [rɪ'diːməbl] adj canjeable.

redeeming [rɪ'diːmɪŋ] adj: **~ feature** punto bueno or favorable.

redefine [riːdɪ'faɪn] vt redefinir.

redemption [rɪ'dɛmpʃən] n (*REL*) redención f; **to be past or beyond ~** no tener remedio.

redeploy [riːdɪ'plɔɪ] vt disponer de nuevo.

redevelop [riːdɪ'vɛləp] vt reorganizar.

redevelopment [riːdɪ'vɛləpmənt] n reorganización f.

red-handed [rɛd'hændɪd] adj: **he was caught ~** le pillaron con las manos en la masa.

redhead ['rɛdhɛd] n pelirrojo/a.

red herring n (*fig*) pista falsa.

red-hot [rɛd'hɔt] adj candente.

redirect [riːdaɪ'rɛkt] vt (*mail*) reexpedir.

rediscover [riːdɪs'kʌvə*] vt redescubrir.

rediscovery [riːdɪs'kʌvərɪ] n redescubrimiento.

redistribute [riːdɪs'trɪbjuːt] vt redistribuir, hacer una nueva distribución de.

red-letter day [rɛd'lɛtə-] n día m señalado, día m especial.

red light n: **to go through or jump a ~** (*AUT*) saltarse un semáforo.

red-light district n barrio chino, zona de

tolerancia.

red meat *n* carne *f* roja.

redness ['rɛdnɪs] *n* rojez *f*.

redo [riː'duː] *vt* (*irreg: like* **do**) rehacer.

redolent ['rɛdələnt] *adj*: ~ **of** (*smell*) con fragancia a; **to be** ~ **of** (*fig*) evocar.

redouble [riː'dʌbl] *vt*: **to** ~ **one's efforts** redoblar los esfuerzos.

redraft [riː'drɑːft] *vt* volver a redactar.

redress [rɪ'drɛs] *n* reparación *f* ♦ *vt* reparar, corregir; **to** ~ **the balance** restablecer el equilibrio.

Red Sea *n*: **the** ~ el mar Rojo.

redskin ['rɛdskɪn] *n* piel roja *m/f*.

red tape *n* (*fig*) trámites *mpl*, papeleo (*col*).

reduce [rɪ'djuːs] *vt* reducir; (*lower*) rebajar; **to** ~ **sth by/to** reducir algo en/a; **to** ~ **sb to silence/despair/tears** hacer callar/ desesperarse/llorar a algn; "~ **speed now**" (*AUT*) "reduzca la velocidad".

reduced [rɪ'djuːst] *adj* (*decreased*) reducido, rebajado; **at a** ~ **price** con rebaja *or* descuento; "**greatly** ~ **prices**" "grandes rebajas".

reduction [rɪ'dʌkʃən] *n* reducción *f*; (*of price*) rebaja; (*discount*) descuento.

redundancy [rɪ'dʌndənsɪ] *n* despido; (*unemployment*) desempleo; **voluntary** ~ baja voluntaria.

redundancy payment *n* indemnización *f* por desempleo.

redundant [rɪ'dʌndənt] *adj* (*BRIT: worker*) parado, sin trabajo; (*detail, object*) superfluo; **to be made** ~ quedar(se) sin trabajo, perder el empleo.

reed [riːd] *n* (*BOT*) junco, caña; (*MUS: of clarinet etc*) lengüeta.

re-educate [riː'ɛdjukeɪt] *vt* reeducar.

reedy ['riːdɪ] *adj* (*voice, instrument*) aflautado.

reef [riːf] *n* (*at sea*) arrecife *m*.

reek [riːk] *vi*: **to** ~ (**of**) oler *or* apestar (a).

reel [riːl] *n* carrete *m*, bobina; (*of film*) rollo ♦ *vt* (*TECH*) devanar; (*also*: ~ **in**) sacar ♦ *vi* (*sway*) tambalear(se); **my head is** ~**ing** me da vueltas la cabeza.

▶**reel off** *vt* recitar de memoria.

re-election [riː'ɪlɛkʃən] *n* reelección *f*.

re-engage [riːɪn'geɪdʒ] *vt* contratar de nuevo.

re-enter [riː'ɛntə*] *vt* reingresar en, volver a entrar en.

re-entry [riː'ɛntrɪ] *n* reingreso, reentrada.

re-examine [riːɪg'zæmɪn] *vt* reexaminar.

re-export *vt* ['riːɪks'pɔːt] reexportar ♦ *n* [riː'ɛkspɔːt] reexportación *f*.

ref [rɛf] *n abbr* (*col*) = **referee**.

ref. *abbr* (*COMM*: = **with reference to**) Ref.

refectory [rɪ'fɛktərɪ] *n* comedor *m*.

refer [rɪ'fəː*] *vt* (*send*) remitir; (*ascribe*) referir a, relacionar con ♦ *vi*: **to** ~ **to** (*allude to*) referirse a, aludir a; (*apply to*) relacionarse con; (*consult*) remitirse a; **he** ~**red me to the manager** me envió al gerente.

referee [rɛfə'riː] *n* árbitro; (*BRIT: for job application*) persona que da referencias de otro ♦ *vt* (*match*) arbitrar en.

reference ['rɛfrəns] *n* (*mention, in book*) referencia; (*sending*) remisión *f*; (*relevance*) relación *f*; (*for job application: letter*) carta de recomendación; **with** ~ **to** con referencia a; (*COMM: in letter*) me remito a.

reference book *n* libro de consulta.

reference library *n* biblioteca de consulta.

reference number *n* número de referencia.

referendum, *pl* **referenda** [rɛfə'rɛndəm, -də] *n* referéndum *m*.

referral [rɪ'fəːrəl] *n* remisión *f*.

refill *vt* [riː'fɪl] rellenar ♦ *n* ['riːfɪl] repuesto, recambio.

refine [rɪ'faɪn] *vt* (*sugar, oil*) refinar.

refined [rɪ'faɪnd] *adj* (*person, taste*) refinado, culto.

refinement [rɪ'faɪnmənt] *n* (*of person*) cultura, educación *f*.

refinery [rɪ'faɪnərɪ] *n* refinería.

refit (*NAUT*) *n* [riː'fɪt] reparación *f* ♦ *vt* [riː'fɪt] reparar.

reflate [riː'fleɪt] *vt* (*economy*) reflacionar.

reflation [riː'fleɪʃən] *n* reflación *f*.

reflationary [riː'fleɪʃənrɪ] *adj* reflacionario.

reflect [rɪ'flɛkt] *vt* (*light, image*) reflejar ♦ *vi* (*think*) reflexionar, pensar; **it** ~**s badly/ well on him** le perjudica/le hace honor.

reflection [rɪ'flɛkʃən] *n* (*act*) reflexión *f*; (*image*) reflejo; (*discredit*) crítica; **on** ~ pensándolo bien.

reflector [rɪ'flɛktə*] *n* (*AUT*) catafaros *m inv*; (*telescope*) reflector *m*.

reflex ['riːflɛks] *adj*, *n* reflejo.

reflexive [rɪ'flɛksɪv] *adj* (*LING*) reflexivo.

reform [rɪ'fɔːm] *n* reforma ♦ *vt* reformar.

reformat [riː'fɔːmæt] *vt* (*COMPUT*) recomponer.

Reformation [rɛfə'meɪʃən] *n*: **the** ~ la Reforma.

reformatory [rɪ'fɔːmətərɪ] *n* (*US*) reformatorio.

reformer [rɪ'fɔːmə*] *n* reformador(a) *m/f*.

refrain [rɪ'freɪn] *vi*: **to** ~ **from doing** abstenerse de hacer ♦ *n* (*MUS etc*) estribillo.

refresh [rɪ'frɛʃ] *vt* refrescar.

refresher course [rɪˈfreʃə-] n (*BRIT*) curso de repaso.

refreshing [rɪˈfreʃɪŋ] adj (*drink*) refrescante; (*sleep*) reparador; (*change etc*) estimulante; (*idea, point of view*) estimulante, interesante.

refreshments [rɪˈfreʃmənts] npl (*drinks*) refrescos mpl.

refrigeration [rɪfrɪdʒəˈreɪʃən] n refrigeración f.

refrigerator [rɪˈfrɪdʒəreɪtə*] n frigorífico, refrigeradora (*LAM*), heladera (*LAM*).

refuel [riːˈfjuəl] vi repostar (combustible).

refuelling, (*US*) **refueling** [riːˈfjuəlɪŋ] n reabastecimiento de combustible.

refuge [ˈrefjuːdʒ] n refugio, asilo; **to take ~ in** refugiarse en.

refugee [refjuˈdʒiː] n refugiado/a.

refugee camp n campamento para refugiados.

refund n [ˈriːfʌnd] reembolso ♦ vt [rɪˈfʌnd] devolver, reembolsar.

refurbish [riːˈfəːbɪʃ] vt restaurar, renovar.

refurnish [riːˈfəːnɪʃ] vt amueblar de nuevo.

refusal [rɪˈfjuːzəl] n negativa; **first ~** primera opción; **to have first ~ on sth** tener la primera opción a algo.

refuse n [ˈrefjuːs] basura ♦ (*vb:* [rɪˈfjuːz]) vt (*reject*) rehusar; (*say no to*) negarse a ♦ vi negarse; (*horse*) rehusar; **to ~ to do sth** negarse a *or* rehusar hacer algo.

refuse bin n cubo *or* bote m (*LAM*) *or* balde m (*LAM*) de la basura.

refuse collection n recogida de basuras.

refuse disposal n eliminación f de basuras.

refusenik [rɪˈfjuːznɪk] n judío/a que tenía prohibido emigrar de la ex-URSS.

refuse tip n vertedero.

refute [rɪˈfjuːt] vt refutar, rebatir.

regain [rɪˈgeɪn] vt recobrar, recuperar.

regal [ˈriːgl] adj regio, real.

regale [rɪˈgeɪl] vt agasajar, entretener.

regalia [rɪˈgeɪlɪə] n galas fpl.

regard [rɪˈgɑːd] n (*gaze*) mirada; (*aspect*) respecto, (*esteem*) respeto, consideración f ♦ vt (*consider*) considerar; (*look at*) mirar; **to give one's ~s to** saludar de su parte a; **"(kind) ~s"** "muy atentamente"; **"with kindest ~s"** "con muchos recuerdos"; **~s to María, please give my ~s to María** recuerdos a María, dele recuerdos a María de mi parte; **as ~s, with ~ to** con respecto a, en cuanto a.

regarding [rɪˈgɑːdɪŋ] prep con respecto a, en cuanto a.

regardless [rɪˈgɑːdlɪs] adv a pesar de todo; **~ of** sin reparar en.

regatta [rɪˈgætə] n regata.

regency [ˈriːdʒənsɪ] n regencia.

regenerate [rɪˈdʒenəreɪt] vt regenerar.

regent [ˈriːdʒənt] n regente m/f.

reggae [ˈregeɪ] n reggae m.

régime [reɪˈʒiːm] n régimen m.

regiment n [ˈredʒɪmənt] regimiento ♦ vt [ˈredʒɪment] reglamentar.

regimental [redʒɪˈmentl] adj militar.

regimentation [redʒɪmenˈteɪʃən] n regimentación f.

region [ˈriːdʒən] n región f; **in the ~ of** (*fig*) alrededor de.

regional [ˈriːdʒənl] adj regional.

regional development n desarrollo regional.

register [ˈredʒɪstə*] n registro ♦ vt registrar; (*birth*) declarar; (*letter*) certificar; (*subj: instrument*) marcar, indicar ♦ vi (*at hotel*) registrarse; (*sign on*) inscribirse; (*make impression*) producir impresión; **to ~ a protest** presentar una queja; **to ~ for a course** matricularse *or* inscribirse en un curso.

registered [ˈredʒɪstəd] adj (*design*) registrado; (*BRIT: letter*) certificado; (*student*) matriculado; (*voter*) registrado.

registered company n sociedad f legalmente constituida.

registered nurse n (*US*) enfermero/a titulado/a.

registered office n domicilio social.

registered trademark n marca registrada.

registrar [ˈredʒɪstrɑː*] n secretario/a (del registro civil).

registration [redʒɪsˈtreɪʃən] n (*act*) declaración f; (*AUT: also:* **~ number**) matrícula.

registry [ˈredʒɪstrɪ] n registro.

registry office n (*BRIT*) registro civil; **to get married in a ~** casarse por lo civil.

regret [rɪˈgret] n sentimiento, pesar m; (*remorse*) remordimiento ♦ vt sentir, lamentar; (*repent of*) arrepentirse de; **we ~ to inform you that ...** sentimos informarle que ....

regretful [rɪˈgretful] adj pesaroso, arrepentido.

regretfully [rɪˈgretfəlɪ] adv con pesar, sentidamente.

regrettable [rɪˈgretəbl] adj lamentable; (*loss*) sensible.

regrettably [rɪˈgretəblɪ] adv desgraciadamente.

regroup [riːˈgruːp] vt reagrupar ♦ vi reagruparse.

regt abbr = **regiment**.

regular ['rɛgjulə*] *adj* regular; (*soldier*) profesional; (*col: intensive*) verdadero; (*listener, reader*) asiduo, habitual ♦ *n* (*client etc*) cliente/a *m/f* habitual.

regularity [rɛgju'lærɪtɪ] *n* regularidad *f*.

regularly ['rɛgjuləlɪ] *adv* con regularidad.

regulate ['rɛgjuleɪt] *vt* (*gen*) controlar; (*TECH*) regular, ajustar.

regulation [rɛgju'leɪʃən] *n* (*rule*) regla, reglamento; (*adjustment*) regulación *f*.

rehabilitate [ri:ə'bɪlɪteɪt] *vt* rehabilitar.

rehabilitation ['ri:əbɪlɪ'teɪʃən] *n* rehabilitación *f*.

rehash [ri:'hæʃ] *vt* (*col*) hacer un refrito de.

rehearsal [rɪ'hə:səl] *n* ensayo; **dress** ~ ensayo general *or* final.

rehearse [rɪ'hə:s] *vt* ensayar.

rehouse [ri:'hauz] *vt* dar nueva vivienda a.

reign [reɪn] *n* reinado; (*fig*) predominio ♦ *vi* reinar; (*fig*) imperar.

reigning ['reɪnɪŋ] *adj* (*monarch*) reinante, actual; (*predominant*) imperante.

reiki ['reɪkɪ] *n* reiki *m*.

reimburse [ri:ɪm'bə:s] *vt* reembolsar.

rein [reɪn] *n* (*for horse*) rienda; **to give sb free** ~ dar rienda suelta a algn.

reincarnation [ri:ɪnkɑ:'neɪʃən] *n* reencarnación *f*.

reindeer ['reɪndɪə*] *n* (*pl inv*) reno.

reinforce [ri:ɪn'fɔ:s] *vt* reforzar.

reinforced concrete [ri:ɪn'fɔ:st-] *n* hormigón armado.

reinforcement [ri:ɪn'fɔ:smənt] *n* (*action*) refuerzo; ~**s** *npl* (*MIL*) refuerzos *mpl*.

reinstate [ri:ɪn'steɪt] *vt* (*worker*) reintegrar (a su puesto).

reinstatement [ri:ɪn'steɪtmənt] *n* reintegración *f*.

reissue [ri:'ɪʃu:] *vt* (*record, book*) reeditar.

reiterate [ri:'ɪtəreɪt] *vt* reiterar, repetir.

reject *n* ['ri:dʒɛkt] (*thing*) desecho ♦ *vt* [rɪ'dʒɛkt] rechazar; (*proposition, offer etc*) descartar.

rejection [rɪ'dʒɛkʃən] *n* rechazo.

rejoice [rɪ'dʒɔɪs] *vi*: **to** ~ **at** *or* **over** regocijarse *or* alegrarse de.

rejoinder [rɪ'dʒɔɪndə*] *n* (*retort*) réplica.

rejuvenate [rɪ'dʒu:vəneɪt] *vt* rejuvenecer.

rekindle [ri:'kɪndl] *vt* volver a encender; (*fig*) despertar.

relapse [rɪ'læps] *n* (*MED*) recaída; (*into crime*) reincidencia.

relate [rɪ'leɪt] *vt* (*tell*) contar, relatar; (*connect*) relacionar ♦ *vi* relacionarse; **to** ~ **to** (*connect*) relacionarse *or* tener que ver con.

related [rɪ'leɪtɪd] *adj* afín; (*person*) emparentado; ~ **to** con referencia a,

relacionado con.

relating [rɪ'leɪtɪŋ]: ~ **to** *prep* referente a.

relation [rɪ'leɪʃən] *n* (*person*) pariente *m/f*; (*link*) relación *f*; **in** ~ **to** en relación con, en lo que se refiere a; **to bear a** ~ **to** guardar relación con; **diplomatic** ~**s** relaciones *fpl* diplomáticas.

relationship [rɪ'leɪʃənʃɪp] *n* relación *f*; (*personal*) relaciones *fpl*; (*also:* **family** ~) parentesco.

relative ['rɛlətɪv] *n* pariente *m/f*, familiar *m/f* ♦ *adj* relativo.

relatively ['rɛlətɪvlɪ] *adv* (*fairly, rather*) relativamente.

relative pronoun *n* pronombre *m* relativo.

relax [rɪ'læks] *vi* descansar; (*quieten down*) relajarse ♦ *vt* relajar; (*grip*) aflojar; ~! (*calm down*) ¡tranquilo!

relaxation [ri:læk'seɪʃən] *n* (*rest*) descanso; (*easing*) relajación *f*, relajamiento *m*; (*amusement*) recreo; (*entertainment*) diversión *f*.

relaxed [rɪ'lækst] *adj* relajado; (*tranquil*) tranquilo.

relaxing [rɪ'læksɪŋ] *adj* relajante.

relay *n* ['ri:leɪ] (*race*) carrera de relevos ♦ *vt* [rɪ'leɪ] (*RADIO, TV, pass on*) retransmitir.

release [rɪ'li:s] *n* (*liberation*) liberación *f*; (*discharge*) puesta en libertad *f*; (*of gas etc*) escape *m*; (*of film etc*) estreno ♦ *vt* (*prisoner*) poner en libertad; (*film*) estrenar; (*book*) publicar; (*piece of news*) difundir; (*gas etc*) despedir, arrojar; (*free: from wreckage etc*) liberar; (*TECH: catch, spring etc*) desenganchar; (*let go*) soltar, aflojar.

relegate ['rɛləgeɪt] *vt* relegar; (*SPORT*): **to be** ~**d to** bajar a.

relent [rɪ'lɛnt] *vi* ceder, ablandarse; (*let up*) descansar.

relentless [rɪ'lɛntlɪs] *adj* implacable.

relentlessly [rɪ'lɛntlɪslɪ] *adv* implacablemente.

relevance ['rɛləvəns] *n* relación *f*.

relevant ['rɛləvənt] *adj* (*fact*) pertinente; ~ **to** relacionado con.

reliability [rɪlaɪə'bɪlɪtɪ] *n* fiabilidad *f*; seguridad *f*; veracidad *f*.

reliable [rɪ'laɪəbl] *adj* (*person, firm*) de confianza, de fiar; (*method, machine*) seguro; (*source*) fidedigno.

reliably [rɪ'laɪəblɪ] *adv*: **to be** ~ **informed that** ... saber de fuente fidedigna que ....

reliance [rɪ'laɪəns] *n*: ~ (**on**) dependencia (de).

reliant [rɪ'laɪənt] *adj*: **to be** ~ **on sth/sb**

depender de algo/algn.

relic ['rɛlɪk] n (REL) reliquia; (of the past) vestigio.

relief [rɪ'liːf] n (from pain, anxiety) alivio, desahogo; (help, supplies) socorro, ayuda; (ART, GEO) relieve m; **by way of light** ~ a modo de diversión.

relief road n carretera de descongestionamiento.

relieve [rɪ'liːv] vt (pain, patient) aliviar; (bring help to) ayudar, socorrer; (burden) aligerar; (take over from: gen) sustituir a; (: guard) relevar; **to** ~ **sb of sth** quitar algo a algn; **to** ~ **sb of his command** (MIL) relevar a algn de su mando; **to** ~ **o.s.** hacer sus necesidades; **I am** ~**d to hear you are better** me alivia saber que estás or te encuentras mejor.

religion [rɪ'lɪdʒən] n religión f.

religious [rɪ'lɪdʒəs] adj religioso.

religious education n educación f religiosa.

religiously [rɪ'lɪdʒəslɪ] adv religiosamente.

relinquish [rɪ'lɪŋkwɪʃ] vt abandonar; (plan, habit) renunciar a.

relish ['rɛlɪʃ] n (CULIN) salsa; (enjoyment) entusiasmo; (flavour) sabor m, gusto ♦ vt (food, challenge etc) saborear; **to** ~ **doing** gozar haciendo.

relive [riː'lɪv] vt vivir de nuevo, volver a vivir.

relocate [riːləu'keɪt] vt trasladar ♦ vi trasladarse.

reluctance [rɪ'lʌktəns] n desgana, renuencia.

reluctant [rɪ'lʌktənt] adj reacio; **to be** ~ **to do sth** resistirse a hacer algo.

reluctantly [rɪ'lʌktəntlɪ] adv de mala gana.

rely [rɪ'laɪ]: **to** ~ **on** vt fus confiar en, fiarse de; (be dependent on) depender de; **you can** ~ **on my discretion** puedes contar con mi discreción.

remain [rɪ'meɪn] vi (survive) quedar; (be left) sobrar; (continue) quedar(se), permanecer; **to** ~ **silent** permanecer callado.

remainder [rɪ'meɪndə*] n resto.

remaining [rɪ'meɪnɪŋ] adj sobrante.

remains [rɪ'meɪnz] npl restos mpl.

remand [rɪ'mɑːnd] n: **on** ~ detenido (bajo custodia) ♦ vt: **to** ~ **in custody** mantener bajo custodia.

remand home n (BRIT) reformatorio.

remark [rɪ'mɑːk] n comentario ♦ vt comentar; **to** ~ **on sth** hacer observaciones sobre algo.

remarkable [rɪ'mɑːkəbl] adj notable; (outstanding) extraordinario.

remarkably [rɪ'mɑːkəblɪ] adv extraordinariamente.

remarry [riː'mærɪ] vi casarse por segunda vez, volver a casarse.

remedial [rɪ'miːdɪəl] adj: ~ **education** educación f de los niños atrasados.

remedy ['rɛmədɪ] n remedio ♦ vt remediar, curar.

remember [rɪ'mɛmbə*] vt recordar, acordarse de; (bear in mind) tener presente; **I** ~ **seeing it, I** ~ **having seen it** recuerdo haberlo visto; **she** ~**ed doing it** se acordó de hacerlo; ~ **me to your wife and children!** ¡déle recuerdos a su familia!

remembrance [rɪ'mɛmbrəns] n (memory, souvenir) recuerdo; **in** ~ **of** en conmemoración de.

Remembrance Day, Remembrance Sunday n (BRIT) ver recuadro.

REMEMBRANCE DAY

En el Reino Unido el domingo más cercano al 11 de noviembre es **Remembrance Day** o **Remembrance Sunday**, aniversario de la firma del armisticio de 1918 que puso fin a la Primera Guerra Mundial. Tal día se recuerda a todos aquellos que murieron en las dos guerras mundiales con dos minutos de silencio a las once de la mañana hora en que se firmó el armisticio durante los actos de conmemoración celebrados en los monumentos a los caídos. Allí se colocan coronas de amapolas, flor que también se suele llevar prendida en el pecho tras pagar un donativo para los inválidos de guerra.

---

remind [rɪ'maɪnd] vt: **to** ~ **sb to do sth** recordar a algn que haga algo; **to** ~ **sb of sth** recordar algo a algn; **she** ~**s me of her mother** me recuerda a su madre; **that** ~**s me!** ¡a propósito!

reminder [rɪ'maɪndə*] n notificación f; (memento) recuerdo.

reminisce [rɛmɪ'nɪs] vi recordar (viejas historias).

reminiscent [rɛmɪ'nɪsnt] adj: **to be** ~ **of sth** recordar algo.

remiss [rɪ'mɪs] adj descuidado; **it was** ~ **of me** fue un descuido de mi parte.

remission [rɪ'mɪʃən] n remisión f; (of sentence) reducción f de la pena.

remit [rɪ'mɪt] vt (send: money) remitir, enviar.

remittance [rɪ'mɪtns] n remesa, envío.

remnant ['rɛmnənt] n resto; (of cloth) retal m, retazo; ~**s** npl (COMM) restos de serie.

remonstrate ['rɛmənstreɪt] _vi_ protestar.
remorse [rɪ'mɔːs] _n_ remordimientos _mpl_.
remorseful [rɪ'mɔːsful] _adj_ arrepentido.
remorseless [rɪ'mɔːslɪs] _adj (fig)_
    implacable, inexorable.
remorselessly [rɪ'mɔːslɪslɪ] _adv_
    implacablemente, inexorablemente.
remote [rɪ'məut] _adj_ remoto; _(distant)_
    lejano; _(person)_ distante; **there is a ~
    possibility that ...** hay una posibilidad
    remota de que ....
remote control _n_ mando a distancia.
remote-controlled [rɪ'məutkən'trəuld] _adj_
    teledirigido, con mando a distancia.
remotely [rɪ'məutlɪ] _adv_ remotamente;
    (slightly) levemente.
remoteness [rɪ'məutnɪs] _n_ alejamiento;
    distancia.
remould ['riːməuld] _n (BRIT: tyre)_ neumático
    _or_ llanta _(LAM)_ recauchutado/a.
removable [rɪ'muːvəbl] _adj (detachable)_
    separable.
removal [rɪ'muːvəl] _n (taking away)_ (el)
    quitar; _(BRIT: from house)_ mudanza; _(from
    office: dismissal)_ destitución _f_; _(MED)_
    extirpación _f_.
removal van _n (BRIT)_ camión _m_ de
    mudanzas.
remove [rɪ'muːv] _vt_ quitar; _(employee)_
    destituir; _(name: from list)_ tachar, borrar;
    (doubt) disipar; _(TECH)_ retirar, separar;
    (MED) extirpar; **first cousin once ~d**
    (parent's cousin) tío/a segundo/a; _(cousin's
    child)_ sobrino/a segundo/a.
remover [rɪ'muːvə*] _n_: **make-up ~**
    desmaquilladora.
remunerate [rɪ'mjuːnəreɪt] _vt_ remunerar.
remuneration [rɪmjuːnə'reɪʃən] _n_
    remuneración _f_.
Renaissance [rɪ'neɪsɔ̃s] _n_: **the ~** el
    Renacimiento.
rename [riː'neɪm] _vt_ poner nuevo nombre
    a.
render ['rɛndə*] _vt (thanks)_ dar; _(aid)_
    proporcionar; _(honour)_ dar, conceder;
    (assistance) dar, prestar; **to ~ sth + adj**
    volver algo + _adj_.
rendering ['rɛndərɪŋ] _n (MUS etc)_
    interpretación _f_.
rendez-vous ['rɔndɪvuː] _n_ cita ♦ _vi_
    reunirse, encontrarse; _(spaceship)_
    efectuar una reunión espacial.
rendition [rɛn'dɪʃən] _n (MUS)_
    interpretación _f_.
renegade ['rɛnɪgeɪd] _n_ renegado/a.
renew [rɪ'njuː] _vt_ renovar; _(resume)_
    reanudar; _(extend date)_ prorrogar;
    (negotiations) volver a.

renewable [rɪ'njuːəbl] _adj_ renovable; **~
    energy, ~s** energías renovables.
renewal [rɪ'njuːəl] _n_ renovación _f_;
    reanudación _f_; prórroga.
renounce [rɪ'nauns] _vt_ renunciar a; _(right,
    inheritance)_ renunciar.
renovate ['rɛnəveɪt] _vt_ renovar.
renovation [rɛnə'veɪʃən] _n_ renovación _f_.
renown [rɪ'naun] _n_ renombre _m_.
renowned [rɪ'naund] _adj_ renombrado.
rent [rɛnt] _n_ alquiler _m_; _(for house)_
    arriendo, renta ♦ _vt (also: ~ out)_ alquilar.
rental ['rɛntl] _n (for television, car)_ alquiler
    _m_.
rent boy _n (BRIT col)_ chapero.
renunciation [rɪnʌnsɪ'eɪʃən] _n_ renuncia.
reopen [riː'əupən] _vt_ volver a abrir,
    reabrir.
reorder [riː'ɔːdə*] _vt_ volver a pedir, repetir
    el pedido de; _(rearrange)_ volver a ordenar
    _or_ arreglar.
reorganization [riːɔːgənaɪ'zeɪʃən] _n_
    reorganización _f_.
reorganize [riː'ɔːgənaɪz] _vt_ reorganizar.
rep [rɛp] _n abbr (COMM)_ = **representative**;
    (THEAT) = **repertory**.
Rep. _abbr (US POL)_ = **representative,
    republican**.
repair [rɪ'pɛə*] _n_ reparación _f_, arreglo;
    (patch) remiendo ♦ _vt_ reparar, arreglar;
    in good/bad ~ en buen/mal estado; **under
    ~** en obras.
repair kit _n_ caja de herramientas.
repair man _n_ mecánico.
repair shop _n_ taller _m_ de reparaciones.
repartee [rɛpɑː'tiː] _n_ réplicas _fpl_ agudas.
repast [rɪ'pɑːst] _n (formal)_ comida.
repatriate [riː'pætrɪeɪt] _vt_ repatriar.
repay [riː'peɪ] _vt (irreg: like pay) (money)_
    devolver, reembolsar; _(person)_ pagar;
    (debt) liquidar; _(sb's efforts)_ devolver,
    corresponder a.
repayment [riː'peɪmənt] _n_ reembolso,
    devolución _f_; _(sum of money)_ recompensa.
repeal [rɪ'piːl] _n_ revocación _f_ ♦ _vt_ revocar.
repeat [rɪ'piːt] _n (RADIO, TV)_ reposición _f_ ♦ _vt_
    repetir ♦ _vi_ repetirse.
repeatedly [rɪ'piːtɪdlɪ] _adv_ repetidas veces.
repeat order _n (COMM)_: **to place a ~ for**
    renovar un pedido de.
repel [rɪ'pɛl] _vt_ repugnar.
repellent [rɪ'pɛlənt] _adj_ repugnante ♦ _n_:
    insect ~ crema/loción _f_ anti-insectos.
repent [rɪ'pɛnt] _vi_: **to ~ (of)** arrepentirse
    (de).
repentance [rɪ'pɛntəns] _n_ arrepentimiento.
repercussion [riːpə'kʌʃən] _n (consequence)_
    repercusión _f_; **to have ~s** repercutir.

repertoire ['rɛpətwɑː*] n repertorio.
repertory ['rɛpətərɪ] n (also: ~ **theatre**) teatro de repertorio.
repertory company n compañía de repertorio.
repetition [rɛpɪ'tɪʃən] n repetición f.
repetitious [rɛpɪ'tɪʃəs] adj repetidor(a), que se repite.
repetitive [rɪ'pɛtɪtɪv] adj (movement, work) repetitivo, reiterativo; (speech) lleno de repeticiones.
rephrase [riː'freɪz] vt decir or formular de otro modo.
replace [rɪ'pleɪs] vt (put back) devolver a su sitio; (take the place of) reemplazar, sustituir.
replacement [rɪ'pleɪsmənt] n reemplazo; (act) reposición f; (thing) recambio; (person) suplente m/f.
replacement cost n costo de sustitución.
replacement part n repuesto.
replacement value n valor m de sustitución.
replay ['riːpleɪ] n (SPORT) partido de desempate; (TV: playback) repetición f.
replenish [rɪ'plɛnɪʃ] vt (tank etc) rellenar; (stock etc) reponer; (with fuel) repostar.
replete [rɪ'pliːt] adj repleto, lleno.
replica ['rɛplɪkə] n réplica, reproducción f.
reply [rɪ'plaɪ] n respuesta, contestación f ♦ vi contestar, responder; in ~ en respuesta; there's no ~ (TEL) no contestan.
reply coupon n cupón-respuesta m.
reply-paid [rɪ'plaɪ'peɪd] adj: ~ **postcard** tarjeta postal con respuesta pagada.
report [rɪ'pɔːt] n informe m; (PRESS etc) reportaje m; (BRIT: also: **school** ~) informe m escolar; (of gun) detonación f ♦ vt informar sobre; (PRESS etc) hacer un reportaje sobre; (notify: accident, culprit) denunciar ♦ vi (make a ~) presentar un informe; (present o.s.): to ~ (to sb) presentarse (ante algn); **annual** ~ (COMM) informe m anual; to ~ (on) hacer un informe (sobre); it is ~ed from Berlin that ... se informa desde Berlín que ....
report card n (US, Scottish) cartilla escolar.
reportedly [rɪ'pɔːtɪdlɪ] adv según se dice, según se informa.
reporter [rɪ'pɔːtə*] n (PRESS) periodista m/f, reportero/a; (RADIO, TV) locutor(a) m/f.
repose [rɪ'pəʊz] n: in ~ (face, mouth) en reposo.
repossess [riːpə'zɛs] vt recuperar.
repossession order [riːpə'zɛʃən-] n orden de devolución de la vivienda por el impago de la hipoteca.
reprehensible [rɛprɪ'hɛnsɪbl] adj reprensible, censurable.
represent [rɛprɪ'zɛnt] vt representar; (COMM) ser agente de.
representation [rɛprɪzɛn'teɪʃən] n representación f; (petition) petición f; ~s npl (protest) quejas fpl.
representative [rɛprɪ'zɛntətɪv] n (US POL) representante m/f, diputado/a; (COMM) representante m/f ♦ adj: ~ (of) representativo (de).
repress [rɪ'prɛs] vt reprimir.
repression [rɪ'prɛʃən] n represión f.
repressive [rɪ'prɛsɪv] adj represivo.
reprieve [rɪ'priːv] n (LAW) indulto; (fig) alivio ♦ vt indultar; (fig) salvar.
reprimand ['rɛprɪmɑːnd] n reprimenda ♦ vt reprender.
reprint ['riːprɪnt] n reimpresión f ♦ vt [riː'prɪnt] reimprimir.
reprisal [rɪ'praɪzl] n represalia; to take ~s tomar represalias.
reproach [rɪ'prəʊtʃ] n reproche m ♦ vt: to ~ sb with sth reprochar algo a algn; beyond ~ intachable.
reproachful [rɪ'prəʊtʃful] adj de reproche, de acusación.
reproduce [riːprə'djuːs] vt reproducir ♦ vi reproducirse.
reproduction [riːprə'dʌkʃən] n reproducción f.
reproductive [riːprə'dʌktɪv] adj reproductor(a).
reproof [rɪ'pruːf] n reproche m.
reprove [rɪ'pruːv] vt: to ~ sb for sth reprochar algo a algn.
reptile ['rɛptaɪl] n reptil m.
republic [rɪ'pʌblɪk] n república.
republican [rɪ'pʌblɪkən] adj, n republicano/a m/f.
repudiate [rɪ'pjuːdɪeɪt] vt (accusation) rechazar; (obligation) negarse a reconocer.
repudiation [rɪpjuːdɪ'eɪʃən] n incumplimiento.
repugnance [rɪ'pʌgnəns] n repugnancia.
repugnant [rɪ'pʌgnənt] adj repugnante.
repulse [rɪ'pʌls] vt rechazar.
repulsion [rɪ'pʌlʃən] n repulsión f, repugnancia.
repulsive [rɪ'pʌlsɪv] adj repulsivo.
repurchase [riː'pɜːtʃəs] vt volver a comprar, readquirir.
reputable ['rɛpjutəbl] adj (make etc) de renombre.
reputation [rɛpju'teɪʃən] n reputación f; he has a ~ for being awkward tiene fama de

difícil.

repute [rɪ'pjuːt] *n* reputación *f*, fama.

reputed [rɪ'pjuːtɪd] *adj* supuesto; **to be ~ to be rich/intelligent** *etc* tener fama de rico/inteligente *etc*.

reputedly [rɪ'pjuːtɪdlɪ] *adv* según dicen *or* se dice.

request [rɪ'kwɛst] *n* solicitud *f*, petición *f* ♦ *vt*: **to ~ sth of** *or* **from sb** solicitar algo a algn; **at the ~ of** a petición de; **"you are ~ed not to smoke"** "se ruega no fumar".

request stop *n* (*BRIT*) parada discrecional.

requiem ['rɛkwɪəm] *n* réquiem *m*.

require [rɪ'kwaɪə*] *vt* (*need*: *subj*: *person*) necesitar, tener necesidad de; (: *thing, situation*) exigir, requerir; (*want*) pedir; (*demand*) insistir en que; **to ~ sb to do sth/sth of sb** exigir que algn haga algo; **what qualifications are ~d?** ¿qué títulos se requieren?; **~d by law** requerido por la ley.

requirement [rɪ'kwaɪəmənt] *n* requisito; (*need*) necesidad *f*.

requisite ['rɛkwɪzɪt] *n* requisito ♦ *adj* necesario, requerido.

requisition [rɛkwɪ'zɪʃən] *n* solicitud *f*; (*MIL*) requisa ♦ *vt* (*MIL*) requisar.

reroute [riː'ruːt] *vt* desviar.

resale ['riːseɪl] *n* reventa.

resale price maintenance *n* mantenimiento del precio de venta.

rescind [rɪ'sɪnd] *vt* (*LAW*) abrogar; (*contract*) rescindir; (*order etc*) anular.

rescue ['rɛskjuː] *n* rescate *m* ♦ *vt* rescatar; **to come/go to sb's ~** ir en auxilio de uno, socorrer a algn; **to ~ from** librar de.

rescue party *n* equipo de salvamento.

rescuer ['rɛskjuə*] *n* salvador(a) *m/f*.

research [rɪ'sɜːtʃ] *n* investigaciones *fpl* ♦ *vt* investigar; **a piece of ~** un trabajo de investigación; **to ~ (into sth)** investigar (algo).

research and development (R & D) *n* investigación *f* y desarrollo.

researcher [rɪ'sɜːtʃə*] *n* investigador(a) *m/f*.

research work *n* investigación *f*.

resell [riː'sɛl] *vt* revender.

resemblance [rɪ'zɛmbləns] *n* parecido; **to bear a strong ~ to** parecerse mucho a.

resemble [rɪ'zɛmbl] *vt* parecerse a.

resent [rɪ'zɛnt] *vt* resentirse por, ofenderse por; **he ~s my being here** le molesta que esté aquí.

resentful [rɪ'zɛntful] *adj* resentido.

resentment [rɪ'zɛntmənt] *n* resentimiento.

reservation [rɛzə'veɪʃən] *n* reserva; (*BRIT*: *also*: **central ~**) mediana; **with ~s** con

reservas.

reservation desk *n* (*US*: *in hotel*) recepción *f*.

reserve [rɪ'zɜːv] *n* reserva; (*SPORT*) suplente *m/f* ♦ *vt* (*seats etc*) reservar; **~s** *npl* (*MIL*) reserva *sg*; **in ~** en reserva.

reserve currency *n* divisa de reserva.

reserved [rɪ'zɜːvd] *adj* reservado.

reserve price *n* (*BRIT*) precio mínimo.

reserve team *n* (*SPORT*) equipo de reserva.

reservist [rɪ'zɜːvɪst] *n* (*MIL*) reservista *m*.

reservoir ['rɛzəvwɑː*] *n* (*artificial lake*) embalse *m*, represa; (*small*) depósito.

reset [riː'sɛt] *vt* (*COMPUT*) reinicializar.

reshape [riː'ʃeɪp] *vt* (*policy*) reformar, rehacer.

reshuffle [riː'ʃʌfl] *n*: **Cabinet ~** (*POL*) remodelación *f* del gabinete.

reside [rɪ'zaɪd] *vi* residir.

residence ['rɛzɪdəns] *n* residencia; (*formal*: *home*) domicilio; (*length of stay*) permanencia; **in ~** (*doctor*) residente; **to take up ~** instalarse.

residence permit *n* (*BRIT*) permiso de residencia.

resident ['rɛzɪdənt] *n* vecino/a; (*in hotel*) huésped/a *m/f* ♦ *adj* residente; (*population*) permanente.

residential [rɛzɪ'dɛnʃəl] *adj* residencial.

residue ['rɛzɪdjuː] *n* resto, residuo.

resign [rɪ'zaɪn] *vt* (*gen*) renunciar a ♦ *vi*: **~ (from)** dimitir (de), renunciar (a); **to ~ o.s. to** (*endure*) resignarse a.

resignation [rɛzɪg'neɪʃən] *n* dimisión *f*; (*state of mind*) resignación *f*; **to tender one's ~** presentar la dimisión.

resigned [rɪ'zaɪnd] *adj* resignado.

resilience [rɪ'zɪlɪəns] *n* (*of material*) elasticidad *f*; (*of person*) resistencia.

resilient [rɪ'zɪlɪənt] *adj* (*person*) resistente.

resin ['rɛzɪn] *n* resina.

resist [rɪ'zɪst] *vt* resistirse a; (*temptation, damage*) resistir.

resistance [rɪ'zɪstəns] *n* resistencia.

resistant [rɪ'zɪstənt] *adj*: **~ (to)** resistente (a).

resolute ['rɛzəluːt] *adj* resuelto.

resolutely ['rɛzəluːtlɪ] *adv* resueltamente.

resolution [rɛzə'luːʃən] *n* (*gen*) resolución *f*; (*purpose*) propósito; (*COMPUT*) definición *f*; **to make a ~** tomar una resolución.

resolve [rɪ'zɔlv] *n* (*determination*) resolución *f*, (*purpose*) propósito ♦ *vt* resolver ♦ *vi* resolverse; **to ~ to do** resolver hacer.

resolved [rɪ'zɔlvd] *adj* resuelto.

resonance ['rɛzənəns] *n* resonancia.

resonant ['rɛzənənt] adj resonante.
resort [rɪ'zɔːt] n (town) centro turístico;
(recourse) recurso ♦ vi: **to ~ to** recurrir a;
in the last ~ como último recurso;
seaside/winter sports ~ playa, estación f
balnearia/centro de deportes de
invierno.
resound [rɪ'zaund] vi: **to ~ (with)** resonar
(con).
resounding [rɪ'zaundɪŋ] adj sonoro; (fig)
clamoroso.
resource [rɪ'sɔːs] n recurso; **~s** npl
recursos mpl; **natural ~s** recursos mpl
naturales; **to leave sb to his/her own ~s**
(fig) abandonar a algn/a a sus propios
recursos.
resourceful [rɪ'sɔːsful] adj ingenioso.
resourcefulness [rɪ'sɔːsfulnɪs] n inventiva,
iniciativa.
respect [rɪs'pɛkt] n (consideration) respeto;
(relation) respecto; **~s** npl recuerdos mpl,
saludos mpl ♦ vt respetar; **with ~ to** con
respecto a; **in this ~** en cuanto a eso; **to
have** or **show ~ for** tener or mostrar
respeto a; **out of ~ for** por respeto a; **in
some ~s** en algunos aspectos; **with due ~
I still think you're wrong** con el respeto
debido, sigo creyendo que está
equivocado.
respectability [rɪspɛktə'bɪlɪtɪ] n
respetabilidad f.
respectable [rɪs'pɛktəbl] adj respetable;
(quite big: amount etc) apreciable;
(passable) tolerable; (quite good: player,
result etc) bastante bueno.
respected [rɪs'pɛktɪd] adj respetado,
estimado.
respectful [rɪs'pɛktful] adj respetuoso.
respectfully [rɪs'pɛktfulɪ] adv
respetuosamente; **Yours ~** Le saluda
atentamente.
respecting [rɪs'pɛktɪŋ] prep (con) respecto
a, en cuanto a.
respective [rɪs'pɛktɪv] adj respectivo.
respectively [rɪs'pɛktɪvlɪ] adv
respectivamente.
respiration [rɛspɪ'reɪʃən] n respiración f.
respiratory [rɛs'pɪrətərɪ] adj respiratorio.
respite ['rɛspaɪt] n respiro; (LAW) prórroga.
resplendent [rɪs'plɛndənt] adj
resplandeciente.
respond [rɪs'pɔnd] vi responder; (react)
reaccionar.
respondent [rɪs'pɔndənt] n (LAW)
demandado/a.
response [rɪs'pɔns] n respuesta; (reaction)
reacción f; **in ~ to** como respuesta a.
responsibility [rɪspɔnsɪ'bɪlɪtɪ] n

responsabilidad f; **to take ~ for sth/sb**
admitir responsabilidad por algo/uno.
responsible [rɪs'pɔnsɪbl] adj (liable): **~ (for)**
responsable (de); (character) serio,
formal; (job) de responsabilidad; **to be ~
to sb (for sth)** ser responsable ante algn
(de algo).
responsibly [rɪs'pɔnsɪblɪ] adv con seriedad.
responsive [rɪs'pɔnsɪv] adj sensible.
rest [rɛst] n descanso, reposo; (MUS) pausa,
silencio; (support) apoyo; (remainder)
resto ♦ vi descansar; (be supported): **to ~
on** apoyarse en ♦ vt (lean): **to ~ sth on/
against** apoyar algo en or sobre/contra;
the ~ of them (people, objects) los demás;
to set sb's mind at ~ tranquilizar a algn;
to ~ one's eyes or **gaze on** fijar la mirada
en; **it ~s with him** depende de él; **~
assured that ...** tenga por seguro que ....
restaurant ['rɛstərɔŋ] n restaurante m.
restaurant car n (BRIT) coche-comedor m.
restaurant owner n dueño/a or
propietario/a de un restaurante.
rest cure n cura de reposo.
restful ['rɛstful] adj descansado, tranquilo.
rest home n residencia de ancianos.
restitution [rɛstɪ'tjuːʃən] n: **to make ~ to
sb for sth** restituir algo a algn; (paying)
indemnizar a algn por algo.
restive ['rɛstɪv] adj inquieto; (horse)
rebelón/ona.
restless ['rɛstlɪs] adj inquieto; **to get ~**
impacientarse.
restlessly ['rɛstlɪslɪ] adv inquietamente,
con inquietud f.
restlessness ['rɛstlɪsnɪs] n inquietud f.
restock [riː'stɔk] vt reaprovisionar.
restoration [rɛstə'reɪʃən] n restauración f;
(giving back) devolución f, restitución f.
restorative [rɪ'stɔːrətɪv] adj
reconstituyente, fortalecedor(a) ♦ n
reconstituyente m.
restore [rɪ'stɔː*] vt (building) restaurar; (sth
stolen) devolver, restituir; (health)
restablecer.
restorer [rɪ'stɔːrə*] n (ART etc)
restaurador(a) m/f.
restrain [rɪs'treɪn] vt (feeling) contener,
refrenar; (person): **to ~ (from doing)**
disuadir (de hacer).
restrained [rɪs'treɪnd] adj (style) reservado.
restraint [rɪs'treɪnt] n (restriction) freno,
control m; (of style) reserva; **wage ~**
control m de los salarios.
restrict [rɪs'trɪkt] vt restringir, limitar.
restricted [rɪs'trɪktɪd] adj restringido,
limitado.
restriction [rɪs'trɪkʃən] n restricción f,

limitación *f*.
restrictive [rɪs'trɪktɪv] *adj* restrictivo.
restrictive practices *npl* (*INDUSTRY*)
prácticas *fpl* restrictivas.
rest room *n* (*US*) aseos *mpl*.
restructure [riː'strʌktʃə*] *vt* reestructurar.
result [rɪ'zʌlt] *n* resultado ♦ *vi*: **to ~ in**
terminar en, tener por resultado; **as a ~**
of a *or* como consecuencia de; **to ~ (from)**
resultar (de).
resultant [rɪ'zʌltənt] *adj* resultante.
resume [rɪ'zjuːm] *vt* (*work, journey*)
reanudar; (*sum up*) resumir ♦ *vi* (*meeting*)
continuar.
résumé ['reɪzjuːmeɪ] *n* resumen *m*.
resumption [rɪ'zʌmpʃən] *n* reanudación *f*.
resurgence [rɪ'səːdʒəns] *n* resurgimiento.
resurrection [rezə'rekʃən] *n* resurrección *f*.
resuscitate [rɪ'sʌsɪteɪt] *vt* (*MED*) resucitar.
resuscitation [rɪsʌsɪ'teɪʃn] *n* resucitación *f*.
retail ['riːteɪl] *n* venta al por menor ♦ *cpd* al
por menor ♦ *vt* vender al por menor *or* al
detalle ♦ *vi*: **to ~ at** (*COMM*) tener precio
de venta al público de.
retailer ['riːteɪlə*] *n* minorista *m/f*, detallista
m/f.
retail outlet *n* punto de venta.
retail price *n* precio de venta al público,
precio al detalle *or* al por menor.
retail price index *n* índice *m* de precios al
por menor.
retain [rɪ'teɪn] *vt* (*keep*) retener, conservar;
(*employ*) contratar.
retainer [rɪ'teɪnə*] *n* (*servant*) criado; (*fee*)
anticipo.
retaliate [rɪ'tælɪeɪt] *vi*: **to ~ (against)** tomar
represalias (contra).
retaliation [rɪtælɪ'eɪʃən] *n* represalias *fpl*; **in**
~ for como represalia por.
retaliatory [rɪ'tælɪətərɪ] *adj* de represalia.
retarded [rɪ'tɑːdɪd] *adj* retrasado.
retch [retʃ] *vi* darle a algn arcadas.
retentive [rɪ'tentɪv] *adj* (*memory*) retentivo.
rethink [riː'θɪŋk] *vt* repensar.
reticence ['retɪsns] *n* reticencia, reserva.
reticent ['retɪsnt] *adj* reticente, reservado.
retina ['retɪnə] *n* retina.
retinue ['retɪnjuː] *n* séquito, comitiva.
retire [rɪ'taɪə*] *vi* (*give up work*) jubilarse;
(*withdraw*) retirarse; (*go to bed*)
acostarse.
retired [rɪ'taɪəd] *adj* (*person*) jubilado.
retirement [rɪ'taɪəmənt] *n* jubilación *f*;
early ~ jubilación *f* anticipada.
retiring [rɪ'taɪərɪŋ] *adj* (*departing: chairman*)
saliente; (*shy*) retraído.
retort [rɪ'tɔːt] *n* (*reply*) réplica ♦ *vi* replicar.
retrace [riː'treɪs] *vt*: **to ~ one's steps** volver

sobre sus pasos, desandar lo andado.
retract [rɪ'trækt] *vt* (*statement*) retirar;
(*claws*) retraer; (*undercarriage, aerial*)
replegar ♦ *vi* retractarse.
retractable [rɪ'træktəbl] *adj* replegable.
retrain [riː'treɪn] *vt* reciclar.
retraining [riː'treɪnɪŋ] *n* reciclaje *m*,
readaptación *f* profesional.
retread ['riːtred] *n* neumático *or* llanta
(*LAM*) recauchutado/a.
retreat [rɪ'triːt] *n* (*place*) retiro; (*MIL*)
retirada ♦ *vi* retirarse; (*flood*) bajar; **to**
beat a hasty ~ (*fig*) retirarse en
desbandada.
retrial ['riːtraɪəl] *n* nuevo proceso.
retribution [retrɪ'bjuːʃən] *n* desquite *m*.
retrieval [rɪ'triːvəl] *n* recuperación *f*;
information ~ recuperación *f* de datos.
retrieve [rɪ'triːv] *vt* recobrar; (*situation,*
honour) salvar; (*COMPUT*) recuperar;
(*error*) reparar.
retriever [rɪ'triːvə*] *n* perro cobrador.
retroactive [retrəu'æktɪv] *adj* retroactivo.
retrograde ['retrəgreɪd] *adj* retrógrado.
retrospect ['retrəspekt] *n*: **in ~**
retrospectivamente.
retrospective [retrə'spektɪv] *adj*
retrospectivo; (*law*) retroactivo ♦ *n*
exposición *f* retrospectiva.
return [rɪ'təːn] *n* (*going or coming back*)
vuelta, regreso; (*of sth stolen etc*)
devolución *f*; (*recompense*) recompensa;
(*FINANCE: from land, shares*) ganancia,
ingresos *mpl*; (*COMM: of merchandise*)
devolución *f* ♦ *cpd* (*journey*) de regreso;
(*BRIT: ticket*) de ida y vuelta; (*match*) de
vuelta ♦ *vi* (*person etc: come or go back*)
volver, regresar; (*symptoms etc*)
reaparecer ♦ *vt* devolver; (*favour, love etc*)
corresponder a; (*verdict*) pronunciar;
(*POL: candidate*) elegir; **~s** *npl* (*COMM*)
ingresos *mpl*; **tax ~** declaración *f* de la
renta; **in ~ (for)** a cambio (de); **by ~ of**
post a vuelta de correo; **many happy ~s**
(of the day)! ¡feliz cumpleaños!
returnable [rɪ'təːnəbl] *adj*: **~ bottle** envase
m retornable.
returner [rɪ'təːnə*] *n* mujer que vuelve a
trabajar tras un tiempo dedicada a la
familia.
returning officer [rɪ'təːnɪŋ-] *n* (*BRIT POL*)
escrutador(a) *m/f*.
return key *n* (*COMPUT*) tecla de retorno.
reunion [riː'juːnɪən] *n* reencuentro.
reunite [riːjuː'naɪt] *vt* reunir; (*reconcile*)
reconciliar.
rev [rev] *n abbr* (*AUT*: = *revolution*)
revolución *f* ♦ (*vb: also*: **~ up**) *vt* acelerar.

revaluation [riːvæljuːˈeɪʃən] *n* revalorización *f*.

revamp [riːˈvæmp] *vt* renovar.

Rev(d). *abbr* (= *reverend*) R., Rvdo.

reveal [rɪˈviːl] *vt* (*make known*) revelar.

revealing [rɪˈviːlɪŋ] *adj* revelador(a).

reveille [rɪˈvælɪ] *n* (*MIL*) diana.

revel [ˈrɛvl] *vi*: **to ~ in sth/in doing sth** gozar de algo/haciendo algo.

revelation [rɛvəˈleɪʃən] *n* revelación *f*.

reveller, (*US*) **reveler** [ˈrɛvlə*] *n* jaranero, juerguista *m/f*.

revelry [ˈrɛvlrɪ] *n* jarana, juerga.

revenge [rɪˈvɛndʒ] *n* venganza; (*in sport*) revancha; **to take ~ on** vengarse de; **to get one's ~ (for sth)** vengarse (de algo).

revengeful [rɪˈvɛndʒful] *adj* vengativo.

revenue [ˈrɛvənjuː] *n* ingresos *mpl*, rentas *fpl*.

revenue account *n* cuenta de ingresos presupuestarios.

revenue expenditure *n* gasto corriente.

reverberate [rɪˈvɔːbəreɪt] *vi* (*sound*) resonar, retumbar.

reverberation [rɪvɔːbəˈreɪʃən] *n* resonancia.

revere [rɪˈvɪə*] *vt* reverenciar, venerar.

reverence [ˈrɛvərəns] *n* reverencia.

Reverend [ˈrɛvərənd] *adj* (*in titles*): **the ~ John Smith** (*Anglican*) el Reverendo John Smith; (*Catholic*) el Padre John Smith; (*Protestant*) el Pastor John Smith.

reverent [ˈrɛvərənt] *adj* reverente.

reverie [ˈrɛvərɪ] *n* ensueño.

reversal [rɪˈvɔːsl] *n* (*of order*) inversión *f*; (*of policy*) cambio de rumbo; (*of decision*) revocación *f*.

reverse [rɪˈvɔːs] *n* (*opposite*) contrario; (*back: of cloth*) revés *m*; (: *of coin*) reverso; (: *of paper*) dorso; (*AUT*: *also*: **~ gear**) marcha atrás ♦ *adj* (*order*) inverso; (*direction*) contrario ♦ *vt* (*decision, AUT*) dar marcha atrás a; (*position, function*) invertir ♦ *vi* (*BRIT AUT*) poner en marcha atrás; **in ~ order** en orden inverso; **the ~** lo contrario; **to go into ~** dar marcha atrás.

reverse-charge call [rɪˈvɔːstʃɑːdʒ-] *n* (*BRIT*) llamada a cobro revertido.

reverse video *n* vídeo inverso.

reversible [rɪˈvɔːsəbl] *adj* (*garment, procedure*) reversible.

reversing lights [rɪˈvɔːsɪŋ-] *npl* (*BRIT AUT*) luces *fpl* de marcha atrás.

revert [rɪˈvɔːt] *vi*: **to ~ to** volver *or* revertir a.

review [rɪˈvjuː] *n* (*magazine, MIL*) revista; (*of book, film*) reseña; (*US: examination*) repaso, examen *m* ♦ *vt* repasar, examinar; (*MIL*) pasar revista a; (*book, film*) reseñar; **to come under ~** ser examinado.

reviewer [rɪˈvjuːə*] *n* crítico/a.

revile [rɪˈvaɪl] *vt* injuriar, vilipendiar.

revise [rɪˈvaɪz] *vt* (*manuscript*) corregir; (*opinion*) modificar; (*BRIT: study: subject*) repasar; (*look over*) revisar; **~d edition** edición *f* corregida.

revision [rɪˈvɪʒən] *n* corrección *f*; modificación *f*; (*of subject*) repaso; (*revised version*) revisión *f*.

revisit [riːˈvɪzɪt] *vt* volver a visitar.

revitalize [riːˈvaɪtəlaɪz] *vt* revivificar.

revival [rɪˈvaɪvəl] *n* (*recovery*) reanimación *f*; (*POL*) resurgimiento; (*of interest*) renacimiento; (*THEAT*) reestreno; (*of faith*) despertar *m*.

revive [rɪˈvaɪv] *vt* resucitar; (*custom*) restablecer; (*hope, courage*) reanimar; (*play*) reestrenar ♦ *vi* (*person*) volver en sí; (*from tiredness*) reponerse; (*business*) reactivarse.

revoke [rɪˈvəuk] *vt* revocar.

revolt [rɪˈvəult] *n* rebelión *f* ♦ *vi* rebelarse, sublevarse ♦ *vt* dar asco a, repugnar; **to ~ (against sb/sth)** rebelarse (contra algn/algo).

revolting [rɪˈvəultɪŋ] *adj* asqueroso, repugnante.

revolution [rɛvəˈluːʃən] *n* revolución *f*.

revolutionary [rɛvəˈluːʃənrɪ] *adj, n* revolucionario/a *m/f*.

revolutionize [rɛvəˈluːʃənaɪz] *vt* revolucionar.

revolve [rɪˈvɒlv] *vi* dar vueltas, girar.

revolver [rɪˈvɒlvə*] *n* revólver *m*.

revolving [rɪˈvɒlvɪŋ] *adj* (*chair, door etc*) giratorio.

revue [rɪˈvjuː] *n* (*THEAT*) revista.

revulsion [rɪˈvʌlʃən] *n* asco, repugnancia.

reward [rɪˈwɔːd] *n* premio, recompensa ♦ *vt*: **to ~ (for)** recompensar *or* premiar (por).

rewarding [rɪˈwɔːdɪŋ] *adj* (*fig*) gratificante; **financially ~** económicamente provechoso.

rewind [riːˈwaɪnd] *vt* (*watch*) dar cuerda a; (*wool etc*) devanar.

rewire [riːˈwaɪə*] *vt* (*house*) renovar la instalación eléctrica de.

reword [riːˈwɔːd] *vt* expresar en otras palabras.

rewrite [riːˈraɪt] *vt* (*irreg: like* write) reescribir.

Reykjavik [ˈreɪkjəviːk] *n* Reykjavik *m*.

RFD *abbr* (*US POST*)= *rural free delivery*.

Rh *abbr* (= *rhesus*) Rh *m*.

rhapsody ['ræpsədɪ] n (*MUS*) rapsodia; (*fig*): **to go into rhapsodies over** extasiarse por.

rhesus negative ['riːsəs-] adj (*MED*) Rh negativo.

rhesus positive adj (*MED*) Rh positivo.

rhetoric ['rɛtərɪk] n retórica.

rhetorical [rɪ'tɔrɪkl] adj retórico.

rheumatic [ruː'mætɪk] adj reumático.

rheumatism ['ruːmətɪzəm] n reumatismo, reúma.

rheumatoid arthritis ['ruːmətɔɪd-] n reúma m articular.

Rhine [raɪn] n: **the ~** el (río) Rin.

rhinestone ['raɪnstəun] n diamante m de imitación.

rhinoceros [raɪ'nɔsərəs] n rinoceronte m.

Rhodes [rəudz] n Rodas f.

rhododendron [rəudə'dɛndrn] n rododendro.

Rhone [rəun] n: **the ~** el (río) Ródano.

rhubarb ['ruːbɑːb] n ruibarbo.

rhyme [raɪm] n rima; (*verse*) poesía ♦ vi: **to ~ (with)** rimar (con); **without ~ or reason** sin ton ni son.

rhythm ['rɪðm] n ritmo.

rhythmic(al) ['rɪðmɪk(l)] adj rítmico.

rhythmically ['rɪðmɪklɪ] adv rítmicamente.

rhythm method n método (de) Ogino.

RI n abbr (*BRIT*: = religious instruction) ed. religiosa ♦ abbr (*US*) = Rhode Island.

rib [rɪb] n (*ANAT*) costilla ♦ vt (*mock*) tomar el pelo a.

ribald ['rɪbəld] adj escabroso.

ribbon ['rɪbən] n cinta; **in ~s** (*torn*) hecho trizas.

rice [raɪs] n arroz m.

ricefield ['raɪsfiːld] n arrozal m.

rice pudding n arroz m con leche.

rich [rɪtʃ] adj rico; (*soil*) fértil; (*food* pesado; (: *sweet*) empalagoso; **the ~** npl los ricos; **~es** npl riqueza sg; **to be ~ in sth** abundar en algo.

richly ['rɪtʃlɪ] adv ricamente.

richness ['rɪtʃnɪs] n riqueza; (*of soil*) fertilidad f.

rickets ['rɪkɪts] n raquitismo.

rickety ['rɪkɪtɪ] adj (*old*) desvencijado; (*shaky*) tambaleante.

rickshaw ['rɪkʃɔː] n carro de culí.

ricochet ['rɪkəʃeɪ] n rebote m ♦ vi rebotar.

rid, pt, pp **rid** [rɪd] vt: **to ~ sb of sth** librar a algn de algo; **to get ~ of** deshacerse or desembarazarse de.

riddance ['rɪdns] n: **good ~!** ¡y adiós muy buenas!

ridden ['rɪdn] pp of **ride**.

-ridden ['rɪdn] suff: **disease~** plagado de enfermedades; **inflation~** minado por la inflación.

riddle ['rɪdl] n (*conundrum*) acertijo; (*mystery*) enigma m, misterio ♦ vt: **to be ~d with** ser lleno or plagado de.

ride [raɪd] n paseo; (*distance covered*) viaje m, recorrido ♦ vb (pt **rode**, pp **ridden**) vi (*horse*: as sport) montar; (*go somewhere*: on horse, bicycle) dar un paseo, pasearse; (*journey*: on bicycle, motor cycle, bus) viajar ♦ vt (*a horse*) montar a; (*distance*) viajar; **to ~ a bicycle** andar en bicicleta; **to ~ at anchor** (*NAUT*) estar fondeado; **can you ~ a bike?** ¿sabes montar en bici(cleta)?; **to go for a ~** dar un paseo; **to take sb for a ~** (*fig*) tomar el pelo a algn.

▶**ride out** vt: **to ~ out the storm** (*fig*) capear el temporal.

rider ['raɪdə*] n (*on horse*) jinete m; (*on bicycle*) ciclista m/f; (*on motorcycle*) motociclista m/f.

ridge [rɪdʒ] n (*of hill*) cresta; (*of roof*) caballete m; (*wrinkle*) arruga.

ridicule ['rɪdɪkjuːl] n irrisión f, burla ♦ vt poner en ridículo a, burlarse de; **to hold sth/sb up to ~** poner algo/a algn en ridículo.

ridiculous [rɪ'dɪkjuləs] adj ridículo.

ridiculously [rɪ'dɪkjuləslɪ] adv ridículamente, de modo ridículo.

riding ['raɪdɪŋ] n equitación f; **I like ~** me gusta montar a caballo.

riding habit n traje m de montar.

riding school n escuela de equitación.

rife [raɪf] adj: **to be ~** ser muy común; **to be ~ with** abundar en.

riffraff ['rɪfræf] n chusma, gentuza.

rifle ['raɪfl] n rifle m, fusil m ♦ vt saquear.

▶**rifle through** vt fus saquear.

rifle range n campo de tiro; (*at fair*) tiro al blanco.

rift [rɪft] n (*fig*: between friends) desavenencia; (: *in party*) escisión f.

rig [rɪg] n (*also*: **oil ~**: on land) torre f de perforación; (: *at sea*) plataforma petrolera ♦ vt (*election etc*) amañar los resultados de.

▶**rig out** vt (*BRIT*) ataviar.

▶**rig up** vt improvisar.

rigging ['rɪgɪŋ] n (*NAUT*) aparejo.

right [raɪt] adj (*true, correct*) correcto, exacto; (*suitable*) indicado, debido; (*proper*) apropiado, propio; (*just*) justo; (*morally good*) bueno; (*not left*) derecho ♦ n (*title, claim*) derecho; (*not left*) derecha ♦ adv (*correctly*) bien, correctamente; (*straight*) derecho, directamente; (*not on the left*) a la derecha; (*to the ~*) hacia la derecha ♦ *vt* (*put straight*) enderezar ♦ *excl* ¡bueno!, ¡está bien!; **to be** ~ (*person*) tener razón; **to get sth** ~ acertar en algo; **you did the** ~ **thing** hiciste bien; **let's get it** ~ **this time!** ¡a ver si esta vez nos sale bien!; **to put a mistake** ~ corregir un error; **the** ~ **time** la hora exacta; (*fig*) el momento oportuno; **by** ~**s** en justicia; ~ **and wrong** el bien y el mal; **film** ~**s** derechos *mpl* de la película; **on the** ~ a la derecha; **to be in the** ~ tener razón; ~ **now** ahora mismo; ~ **before/after** inmediatamente antes/después; ~ **in the middle** exactamente en el centro; ~ **away** en seguida; **to go** ~ **to the end of sth** llegar hasta el final de algo; ~**, who's next?** bueno, ¿quién sigue?; **all** ~! ¡vale!; **I'm/I feel all** ~ **now** ya estoy bien.

right angle *n* ángulo recto.

right-click ['raɪtklɪk] *vi* clicar con el botón derecho del ratón ♦ *vt*: **to** ~ **an icon** clicar en un icono con el botón derecho del ratón.

righteous ['raɪtʃəs] *adj* justo, honrado; (*anger*) justificado.

righteousness ['raɪtʃəsnɪs] *n* justicia.

rightful ['raɪtful] *adj* (*heir*) legítimo.

right-hand ['raɪthænd] *adj* (*drive, turn*) por la derecha.

right-handed [raɪt'hændɪd] *adj* (*person*) que usa la mano derecha.

right-hand man *n* brazo derecho.

right-hand side *n* derecha.

rightly ['raɪtlɪ] *adv* correctamente, debidamente; (*with reason*) con razón; **if I remember** ~ si recuerdo bien.

right-minded ['raɪt'maɪndɪd] *adj* (*sensible*) sensato; (*decent*) honrado.

right of way *n* (*on path etc*) derecho de paso; (*AUT*) prioridad *f* de paso.

right-wing [raɪt'wɪŋ] *adj* (*POL*) de derechas, derechista.

right-winger [raɪt'wɪŋə*] *n* (*POL*) persona de derechas, derechista *m/f*; (*SPORT*) extremo derecha.

rigid ['rɪdʒɪd] *adj* rígido; (*person, ideas*) inflexible.

rigidity [rɪ'dʒɪdɪtɪ] *n* rigidez *f*; inflexibilidad *f*.

rigidly ['rɪdʒɪdlɪ] *adv* rígidamente; (*inflexibly*) inflexiblemente.

rigmarole ['rɪgmərəul] *n* galimatías *m inv*.

rigor mortis ['rɪgə'mɔːtɪs] *n* rigidez *f* cadavérica.

rigorous ['rɪgərəs] *adj* riguroso.

rigorously ['rɪgərəslɪ] *adv* rigurosamente.

rigour, (*US*) **rigor** ['rɪgə*] *n* rigor *m*, severidad *f*.

rile [raɪl] *vt* irritar.

rim [rɪm] *n* borde *m*; (*of spectacles*) montura, aro; (*of wheel*) llanta.

rimless ['rɪmlɪs] *adj* (*spectacles*) sin aros.

rimmed [rɪmd] *adj*: ~ **with** con un borde de, bordeado de.

rind [raɪnd] *n* (*of bacon, cheese*) corteza; (*of lemon etc*) cáscara.

ring [rɪŋ] *n* (*of metal*) aro; (*on finger*) anillo; (*of people*) corro; (*of objects*) círculo; (*gang*) banda; (*for boxing*) cuadrilátero; (*of circus*) pista; (*bull* ~) ruedo, plaza; (*sound of bell*) toque *m*; (*telephone call*) llamada ♦ *vb* (*pt* **rang**, *pp* **rung** [ræŋ, rʌŋ]) *vi* (*on telephone*) llamar por teléfono; (*large bell*) repicar; (*also*: ~ **out**: *voice, words*) sonar; (*ears*) zumbar ♦ *vt* (*BRIT TEL: also*: ~ **up**) llamar; (*bell etc*) hacer sonar; (*doorbell*) tocar; **that has the** ~ **of truth about it** eso suena a verdad; **to give sb a** ~ (*BRIT TEL*) llamar por teléfono a algn, dar un telefonazo a algn; **the name doesn't** ~ **a bell (with me)** el nombre no me suena; **to** ~ **sb (up)** llamar a algn.

▶**ring back** *vt*, *vi* (*TEL*) devolver la llamada.

▶**ring off** *vi* (*BRIT TEL*) colgar, cortar la comunicación.

ring binder *n* carpeta de anillas.

ring finger *n* (dedo) anular *m*.

ringing ['rɪŋɪŋ] *n* (*of bell*) toque *m*, tañido; (*louder: of large bell*) repique *m*; (*in ears*) zumbido.

ringing tone *n* (*TEL*) tono de llamada.

ringleader ['rɪŋliːdə*] *n* cabecilla *m/f*.

ringlets ['rɪŋlɪts] *npl* tirabuzones *mpl*, bucles *mpl*.

ring road *n* (*BRIT*) carretera periférica *or* de circunvalación.

rink [rɪŋk] *n* (*also*: **ice** ~) pista de hielo; (*for roller-skating*) pista de patinaje.

rinse [rɪns] *n* (*of dishes*) enjuague *m*; (*of clothes*) aclarado; (*of hair*) reflejo ♦ *vt* enjuagar; aclarar; dar reflejos a.

Rio (de Janeiro) ['riːəu(dədʒə'nɪərəu)] *n* Río de Janeiro.

riot ['raɪət] *n* motín *m*, disturbio ♦ *vi* amotinarse; **to run** ~ desmandarse.

rioter ['raɪətə*] *n* amotinado/a.

riot gear *n* uniforme *m* antidisturbios *inv*.

riotous ['raɪətəs] *adj* alborotado; (*party*) bullicioso; (*uncontrolled*) desenfrenado.

riotously ['raɪətəslɪ] *adv* bulliciosamente.

riot police *n* policía antidisturbios.

RIP *abbr* (= *rest in peace*) q.e.p.d.

rip [rɪp] *n* rasgón *m*, desgarrón *m* ♦ *vt* rasgar, desgarrar ♦ *vi* rasgarse.

▶**rip up** *vt* hacer pedazos.

ripcord ['rɪpkɔːd] *n* cabo de desgarre.

ripe [raɪp] *adj* (*fruit*) maduro.
ripen ['raɪpən] *vt, vi* madurar.
ripeness ['raɪpnɪs] *n* madurez *f*.
rip-off ['rɪpɔf] *n* (*col*): **it's a** ~! ¡es una estafa!, ¡es un timo!
riposte [rɪ'pɔst] *n* respuesta aguda, réplica.
ripple ['rɪpl] *n* onda, rizo; (*sound*) murmullo ♦ *vi* rizarse ♦ *vt* rizar.
rise [raɪz] *n* (*slope*) cuesta, pendiente *f*; (*hill*) altura; (*increase: in wages: Brit*) aumento; (: *in prices, temperature*) subida, alza; (*fig: to power etc*) ascenso; (: *ascendancy*) auge *m* ♦ *vi* (*pt* **rose**, *pp* **risen** [rəuz, 'rɪzn]) (*gen*) elevarse; (*prices*) subir; (*waters*) crecer; (*river*) nacer; (*sun*) salir; (*person: from bed etc*) levantarse; (*also*: ~ **up**: *rebel*) sublevarse; (*in rank*) ascender; ~ **to power** ascenso al poder; **to give** ~ **to** dar lugar *or* origen a; **to** ~ **to the occasion** ponerse a la altura de las circunstancias.
rising ['raɪzɪŋ] *adj* (*increasing: number*) creciente; (: *prices*) en aumento *or* alza; (*tide*) creciente; (*sun, moon*) naciente ♦ *n* (*uprising*) sublevación *f*.
rising damp *n* humedad *f* de paredes.
rising star *n* (*fig*) figura en alza.
risk [rɪsk] *n* riesgo, peligro ♦ *vt* (*gen*) arriesgar; (*dare*) atreverse a; **to take** *or* **run the** ~ **of doing** correr el riesgo de hacer; **at** ~ en peligro; **at one's own** ~ bajo su propia responsabilidad; **fire/ health/security** ~ peligro de incendio/ para la salud/para la seguridad.
risk capital *n* capital *m* de riesgo.
risky ['rɪskɪ] *adj* arriesgado, peligroso.
risqué ['riːskeɪ] *adj* (*joke*) subido de color.
rissole ['rɪsəul] *n* croqueta.
rite [raɪt] *n* rito; **last** ~**s** últimos sacramentos *mpl*.
ritual ['rɪtjuəl] *adj* ritual ♦ *n* ritual *m*, rito.
rival ['raɪvl] *n* rival *m/f*; (*in business*) competidor(a) *m/f* ♦ *adj* rival, opuesto ♦ *vt* competir con.
rivalry ['raɪvlrɪ] *n* rivalidad *f*, competencia.
river ['rɪvə*] *n* río ♦ *cpd* (*port, traffic*) de río, del río; **up/down** ~ río arriba/abajo.
riverbank ['rɪvəbæŋk] *n* orilla (del río).
riverbed ['rɪvəbed] *n* lecho, cauce *m*.
rivet ['rɪvɪt] *n* roblón *m*, remache *m* ♦ *vt* remachar; (*fig*) fascinar.
riveting ['rɪvɪtɪŋ] *adj* (*fig*) fascinante.
Riviera [rɪvɪ'ɛərə] *n*: **the (French)** ~ la Costa Azul; **the Italian** ~ la Riviera italiana.
Riyadh [rɪ'jaːd] *n* Riyadh *m*.
RMT *n abbr* (=*Rail, Maritime and Transport*) sindicato de transportes.
RN *n abbr* (*BRIT*) *see* **Royal Navy**; (*US*)

= **registered nurse**.
RNA *n abbr* (= *ribonucleic acid*) ARN *m*, RNA *m*.
RNLI *n abbr* (*BRIT*: = *Royal National Lifeboat Institution*) *servicio de lanchas de socorro*.
RNZAF *n abbr* = *Royal New Zealand Air Force*.
RNZN *n abbr* = *Royal New Zealand Navy*.
road [rəud] *n* (*gen*) camino; (*motorway etc*) carretera; (*in town*) calle *f*; **major/minor** ~ carretera general/secundaria; **main** ~ carretera; **it takes 4 hours by** ~ se tarda 4 horas por carretera; **on the** ~ **to success** camino del éxito.
roadblock ['rəudblɔk] *n* barricada, control *m*, retén *m* (*LAM*).
road haulage *n* transporte *m* por carretera.
roadhog ['rəudhɔg] *n* loco/a del volante.
road map *n* mapa *m* de carreteras.
road rage *n conducta agresiva de los conductores.*
road safety *n* seguridad *f* vial.
roadside ['rəudsaɪd] *n* borde *m* (del camino) ♦ *cpd* al lado de la carretera; **by the** ~ al borde del camino.
roadsign ['rəudsaɪn] *n* señal *f* de tráfico.
roadsweeper ['rəudswiːpə*] *n* (*BRIT*: *person*) barrendero/a.
road user *n* usuario/a de la vía pública.
roadway ['rəudweɪ] *n* calzada.
roadworks ['rəudwəːks] *npl* obras *fpl*.
roadworthy ['rəudwəːðɪ] *adj* (*car*) en buen estado para circular.
roam [rəum] *vi* vagar ♦ *vt* vagar por.
roar [rɔː*] *n* (*of animal*) rugido, bramido; (*of crowd*) clamor *m*, rugido; (*of vehicle, storm*) estruendo; (*of laughter*) carcajada ♦ *vi* rugir, bramar; hacer estruendo; **to** ~ **with laughter** reírse a carcajadas.
roaring ['rɔːrɪŋ] *adj*: **a** ~ **success** un tremendo éxito; **to do a** ~ **trade** hacer buen negocio.
roast [rəust] *n* carne *f* asada, asado ♦ *vt* (*meat*) asar; (*coffee*) tostar.
roast beef *n* rosbif *m*.
roasting ['rəustɪŋ] *n*: **to give sb a** ~ (*col*) echar una buena bronca a algn.
rob [rɔb] *vt* robar; **to** ~ **sb of sth** robar algo a algn; (*fig: deprive*) quitar algo a algn.
robber ['rɔbə*] *n* ladrón/ona *m/f*.
robbery ['rɔbərɪ] *n* robo.
robe [rəub] *n* (*for ceremony etc*) toga; (*also*: **bath** ~) bata.
robin ['rɔbɪn] *n* petirrojo.
robot ['rəubɔt] *n* robot *m*.
robotics [rəu'bɔtɪks] *n* robótica.
robust [rəu'bʌst] *adj* robusto, fuerte.
rock [rɔk] *n* (*gen*) roca; (*boulder*) peña,

peñasco; (*BRIT: sweet*) ≈ pirulí *m* ♦ *vt*
(*swing gently*) mecer; (*shake*) sacudir ♦ *vi*
mecerse, balancearse; sacudirse; **on the
~s** (*drink*) con hielo; **their marriage is on
the ~s** su matrimonio se está yendo a
pique; **to ~ the boat** (*fig*) crear
problemas.

rock and roll *n* rock and roll *m*, rocanrol *m*.

rock-bottom ['rɔk'bɔtəm] *adj* (*fig*) por los
suelos; **to reach** *or* **touch rock bottom**
(*price*) estar por los suelos; (*person*) tocar
fondo.

rock cake *n* (*BRIT*) *bollito de pasas con
superficie rugosa.*

rock climber *n* escalador(a) *m/f.*

rock climbing *n* (*SPORT*) escalada.

rockery ['rɔkərɪ] *n* cuadro alpino.

rocket ['rɔkɪt] *n* cohete *m* ♦ *vi* (*prices*)
dispararse, ponerse por las nubes.

rocket launcher *n* lanzacohetes *m inv.*

rock face *n* pared *f* de roca.

rocking chair ['rɔkɪŋ-] *n* mecedora.

rocking horse *n* caballo de balancín.

rocky ['rɔkɪ] *adj* (*gen*) rocoso; (*unsteady:
table*) inestable.

Rocky Mountains *npl:* **the ~** las Montañas
Rocosas.

rococo [rə'kəukəu] *adj* rococó *inv* ♦ *n* rococó.

rod [rɔd] *n* vara, varilla; (*TECH*) barra; (*also:*
fishing ~) caña.

rode [rəud] *pt of* **ride**.

rodent ['rəudnt] *n* roedor *m.*

rodeo ['rəudɪəu] *n* rodeo.

roe [rəu] *n* (*species: also:* **~ deer**) corzo; (*of
fish*): **hard/soft ~** hueva/lecha.

rogue [rəug] *n* pícaro, pillo.

roguish ['rəugɪʃ] *adj* (*child*) travieso; (*smile
etc*) pícaro.

role [rəul] *n* papel *m*, rol *m.*

role-model ['rəulmɔdl] *n* modelo a imitar.

role play *n* (*also:* **~ing**) juego de papeles *or*
roles.

roll [rəul] *n* rollo; (*of bank notes*) fajo; (*also:*
bread ~) panecillo; (*register*) lista,
nómina; (*sound: of drums etc*) redoble *m*;
(*movement: of ship*) balanceo ♦ *vt* hacer
rodar; (*also:* **~ up**: *string*) enrollar;
(*: sleeves*) arremangar; (*cigarettes*) liar;
(*also:* **~ out**: *pastry*) aplanar ♦ *vi* (*gen*)
rodar; (*drum*) redoblar; (*in walking*)
bambolearse; (*ship*) balancearse; **cheese
~** panecillo de queso.
▶**roll about, roll around** *vi* (*person*)
revolcarse.
▶**roll by** *vi* (*time*) pasar.
▶**roll in** *vi* (*mail, cash*) entrar a raudales.
▶**roll over** *vi* dar una vuelta.
▶**roll up** *vi* (*col: arrive*) presentarse,

aparecer ♦ *vt* (*carpet, cloth, map*) arrollar;
(*sleeves*) arremangar; **to ~ o.s. up into a
ball** acurrucarse, hacerse un ovillo.

roll call *n:* **to take a ~** pasar lista.

rolled [rəuld] *adj* (*umbrella*) plegado.

roller ['rəulə*] *n* rodillo; (*wheel*) rueda.

roller blind *n* (*BRIT*) persiana (enrollable).

roller coaster *n* montaña rusa.

roller skates *npl* patines *mpl* de rueda.

rollicking ['rɔlɪkɪŋ] *adj:* **we had a ~ time**
nos divertimos una barbaridad.

rolling ['rəulɪŋ] *adj* (*landscape*) ondulado.

rolling mill *n* taller *m* de laminación.

rolling pin *n* rodillo (de cocina).

rolling stock *n* (*RAIL*) material *m* rodante.

ROM [rɔm] *n abbr* (= *read only memory*)
(memoria) ROM *f.*

Roman ['rəumən] *adj, n* romano/a *m/f.*

Roman Catholic *adj, n* católico/a *m/f*
(romano/a).

romance [rə'mæns] *n* (*love affair*) amor *m*,
idilio; (*charm*) lo romántico; (*novel*)
novela de amor.

romanesque [rəumə'nɛsk] *adj* románico.

Romania [ruː'meɪnɪə] *n* = **Rumania**.

Romanian [ruː'meɪnɪən] *adj, n* = **Rumanian**.

Roman numeral *n* número romano.

romantic [rə'mæntɪk] *adj* romántico.

romanticism [rə'mæntɪsɪzəm] *n*
romanticismo.

Romany ['rəumənɪ] *adj* gitano ♦ *n* (*person*)
gitano/a; (*LING*) lengua gitana, caló (*SP*).

Rome [rəum] *n* Roma.

romp [rɔmp] *n* retozo, jugueteo ♦ *vi* (*also:* **~
about**) juguetear; **to ~ home** (*horse*)
ganar fácilmente.

rompers ['rɔmpəz] *npl* pelele *m.*

roof [ruːf] *n* (*gen*) techo; (*of house*) tejado
♦ *vt* techar, poner techo a; **~ of the
mouth** paladar *m.*

roofing ['ruːfɪŋ] *n* techumbre *f.*

roof rack *n* (*AUT*) baca.

rook [ruk] *n* (*bird*) graja; (*CHESS*) torre *f.*

rookie ['rukɪ] *n* (*col*) novato/a; (*MIL*) chivo.

room [ruːm] *n* (*in house*) cuarto, habitación
f, pieza (*esp LAm*); (*also:* **bed~**)
dormitorio; (*in school etc*) sala; (*space*)
sitio; **~s** *npl* (*lodging*) alojamiento *sg*; "**~s
to let**", (*US*) "**~s for rent**" "se alquilan
pisos *or* cuartos"; **single/double ~**
habitación individual/doble *or* para dos
personas; **is there ~ for this?** ¿cabe esto?;
to make ~ for sb hacer sitio para algn;
there is ~ for improvement podría
mejorarse.

roominess ['ruːmɪnɪs] *n* amplitud *f*,
espaciosidad *f.*

rooming house ['ruːmɪŋ-] *n* (*US*) pensión *f.*

roommate ['ruːmmeɪt] *n* compañero/a de cuarto.

room service *n* servicio de habitaciones.

room temperature *n* temperatura ambiente.

roomy ['ruːmɪ] *adj* espacioso.

roost [ruːst] *n* percha ♦ *vi* pasar la noche.

rooster ['ruːstə*] *n* gallo.

root [ruːt] *n* (*BOT, MATH*) raíz *f* ♦ *vi* (*plant, belief*) arraigar(se); **to take ~** (*plant*) echar raíces; (*idea*) arraigar(se); **the ~ of the problem is that ...** la raíz del problema es que ....

▶**root about** *vi* (*fig*) rebuscar.

▶**root for** *vt fus* apoyar a.

▶**root out** *vt* desarraigar.

root beer *n* (*US*) *refresco sin alcohol de extractos de hierbas.*

rooted ['ruːtɪd] *adj* enraizado; (*opinions etc*) arraigado.

rope [rəʊp] *n* cuerda; (*NAUT*) cable *m* ♦ *vt* (*box*) atar *or* amarrar con (una) cuerda; (*climbers: also:* **~ together**) encordarse; **to ~ sb in** (*fig*) persuadir a algn a tomar parte; **to know the ~s** (*fig*) conocer los trucos (del oficio).

rope ladder *n* escala de cuerda.

ropey ['rəʊpɪ] *adj* (*col*) chungo.

rosary ['rəʊzərɪ] *n* rosario.

rose [rəʊz] *pt of* **rise** ♦ *n* rosa; (*also:* **~bush**) rosal *m*; (*on watering can*) roseta ♦ *adj* color de rosa.

rosé ['rəʊzeɪ] *n* vino rosado, clarete *m*.

rosebed ['rəʊzbɛd] *n* rosaleda.

rosebud ['rəʊzbʌd] *n* capullo de rosa.

rosebush ['rəʊzbʊʃ] *n* rosal *m*.

rosemary ['rəʊzmərɪ] *n* romero.

rosette [rəʊ'zɛt] *n* rosetón *m*.

ROSPA ['rɔspə] *n abbr* (*BRIT*) = *Royal Society for the Prevention of Accidents.*

roster ['rɔstə*] *n*: **duty ~** lista de tareas.

rostrum ['rɔstrəm] *n* tribuna.

rosy ['rəʊzɪ] *adj* rosado, sonrosado; **the future looks ~** el futuro parece prometedor.

rot [rɔt] *n* (*decay*) putrefacción *f*, podredumbre *f*; (*fig: pej*) tonterías *fpl* ♦ *vt* pudrir, corromper ♦ *vi* pudrirse, corromperse; **it has ~ted** está podrido; **to stop the ~** (*fig*) poner fin a las pérdidas.

rota ['rəʊtə] *n* lista (de tareas).

rotary ['rəʊtərɪ] *adj* rotativo.

rotate [rəʊ'teɪt] *vt* (*revolve*) hacer girar, dar vueltas a; (*change round: crops*) cultivar en rotación; (*: jobs*) alternar ♦ *vi* (*revolve*) girar, dar vueltas.

rotating [rəʊ'teɪtɪŋ] *adj* (*movement*) rotativo.

rotation [rəʊ'teɪʃən] *n* rotación *f*; **in ~** por turno.

rote [rəʊt] *n*: **by ~** de memoria.

rotor ['rəʊtə*] *n* rotor *m*.

rotten ['rɔtn] *adj* (*decayed*) podrido; (*: wood*) carcomido; (*fig*) corrompido; (*col: bad*) pésimo; **to feel ~** (*ill*) sentirse fatal; **~ to the core** completamente podrido.

rotund [rəʊ'tʌnd] *adj* rotundo.

rouble, (*US*) **ruble** ['ruːbl] *n* rublo.

rouge [ruːʒ] *n* colorete *m*.

rough [rʌf] *adj* (*skin, surface*) áspero; (*terrain*) accidentado; (*road*) desigual; (*voice*) bronco; (*person, manner: coarse*) tosco, grosero; (*weather*) borrascoso; (*treatment*) brutal; (*sea*) embravecido; (*cloth*) basto; (*plan*) preliminar; (*guess*) aproximado; (*violent*) violento ♦ *n* (*GOLF*): **in the ~** en las hierbas altas; **to ~ it** vivir sin comodidades; **to sleep ~** (*BRIT*) pasar la noche al raso; **the sea is ~ today** el mar está agitado hoy; **to have a ~ time (of it)** pasar una mala racha; **~ estimate** cálculo aproximado.

roughage ['rʌfɪdʒ] *n* fibra(s) *f(pl)*, forraje *m*.

rough-and-ready ['rʌfən'rɛdɪ] *adj* improvisado, tosco.

rough-and-tumble ['rʌfən'tʌmbl] *n* pelea.

roughcast ['rʌfkɑːst] *n* mezcla gruesa.

rough copy, rough draft *n* borrador *m*.

roughen ['rʌfn] *vt* (*a surface*) poner áspero.

roughly ['rʌflɪ] *adv* (*handle*) torpemente; (*make*) toscamente; (*approximately*) aproximadamente; **~ speaking** más o menos.

roughness ['rʌfnɪs] *n* aspereza; tosquedad *f*; brutalidad *f*.

roughshod ['rʌfʃɔd] *adv*: **to ride ~ over** (*person*) pisotear a; (*objections*) hacer caso omiso de.

rough work *n* (*SCOL etc*) borrador *m*.

roulette [ruː'lɛt] *n* ruleta.

Roumania [ruː'meɪnɪə] *n* = **Rumania**.

round [raʊnd] *adj* redondo ♦ *n* círculo; (*of policeman*) ronda; (*of milkman*) recorrido; (*of doctor*) visitas *fpl*; (*game: of cards, in competition*) partida; (*of ammunition*) cartucho; (*BOXING*) asalto; (*of talks*) ronda ♦ *vt* (*corner*) doblar ♦ *prep* alrededor de ♦ *adv*: **all ~** por todos lados; **the long way ~** por el camino menos directo; **all the year ~** durante todo el año; **it's just ~ the corner** (*fig*) está a la vuelta de la esquina; **to ask sb ~** invitar a algn a casa; **I'll be ~ at 6 o'clock** llegaré a eso de las 6; **she arrived ~ (about) noon** llegó alrededor del mediodía; **~ the clock** *adv* las 24

horas; **to go ~ to sb's (house)** ir a casa de algn; **to go ~ the back** pasar por atrás; **to go ~ a house** visitar una casa; **enough to go ~** bastante (para todos); **in ~ figures** en números redondos; **to go the ~s** (*story*) divulgarse; **a ~ of applause** una salva de aplausos; **a ~ of drinks/sandwiches** una ronda de bebidas/bocadillos; **a ~ of toast** (*BRIT*) una tostada; **the daily ~** la rutina cotidiana.
▶**round off** *vt* (*speech etc*) acabar, poner término a.
▶**round up** *vt* (*cattle*) acorralar; (*people*) reunir; (*prices*) redondear.
roundabout ['raundəbaut] *n* (*BRIT: AUT*) glorieta, rotonda; (: *at fair*) tiovivo ♦ *adj* (*route, means*) indirecto.
rounded ['raundɪd] *adj* redondeado, redondo.
rounders ['raundəz] *n* (*BRIT: game*) *juego similar al béisbol.*
roundly ['raundlɪ] *adv* (*fig*) rotundamente.
round-robin ['raundrɔbɪn] *n* (*SPORT: also: ~ tournament*) liguilla.
round trip *n* viaje *m* de ida y vuelta.
roundup ['raundʌp] *n* rodeo; (*of criminals*) redada; **a ~ of the latest news** un resumen de las últimas noticias.
rouse [rauz] *vt* (*wake up*) despertar; (*stir up*) suscitar.
rousing ['rauzɪŋ] *adj* (*applause*) caluroso; (*speech*) conmovedor(a).
rout [raut] *n* (*MIL*) derrota; (*flight*) desbandada ♦ *vt* derrotar.
route [ruːt] *n* ruta, camino; (*of bus*) recorrido; (*of shipping*) rumbo, derrota; **the best ~ to London** el mejor camino *or* la mejor ruta para ir a Londres; **en ~ from ... to** en el viaje de ... a; **en ~ for** rumbo a, con destino en.
route map *n* (*BRIT: for journey*) mapa *m* de carreteras.
routine [ruː'tiːn] *adj* (*work*) rutinario ♦ *n* rutina; (*THEAT*) número; (*COMPUT*) rutina.
roving ['rəuvɪŋ] *adj* (*wandering*) errante; (*salesman*) ambulante; (*reporter*) volante.
row [rəu] *n* (*line*) fila, hilera; (*KNITTING*) vuelta; [rau] (*noise*) escándalo; (*dispute*) bronca, pelea; (*fuss*) jaleo; (*scolding*) reprimenda ♦ *vi* (*in boat*) remar; [rau] reñir(se) ♦ *vt* (*boat*) conducir remando; **4 days in a ~** 4 días seguidos; **to make a ~** armar un lío; **to have a ~** pelearse, reñir.
rowboat ['rəubəut] *n* (*US*) bote *m* de remos.
rowdy ['raudɪ] *adj* (*person: noisy*) ruidoso; (: *quarrelsome*) pendenciero; (*occasion*) alborotado ♦ *n* pendenciero.
row houses *npl* (*US*) casas *fpl* adosadas.

rowing ['rəuɪŋ] *n* remo.
rowing boat *n* (*BRIT*) bote *m or* barco de remos.
royal ['rɔɪəl] *adj* real.
Royal Academy (of Arts) *n* (*BRIT*) la Real Academia (de Bellas Artes); *ver recuadro.*

ROYAL ACADEMY (OF ARTS)

*La **Royal Academy (of Arts)**, fundada en 1768 durante el reinado de Jorge III, es una institución dedicada al fomento de la pintura, escultura y arquitectura en el Reino Unido. Además de dar cursos de arte, presenta una exposición anual de artistas contemporáneos en su sede de Burlington House, en el centro de Londres. No existe una institución equivalente a la Real Academia de la Lengua.*

Royal Air Force (RAF) *n* Fuerzas Aéreas Británicas *fpl.*
royal blue *n* azul *m* marino.
royalist ['rɔɪəlɪst] *adj, n* monárquico/a *m/f.*
Royal Navy (RN) *n* (*BRIT*) Marina Británica.
royalty ['rɔɪəltɪ] *n* (*royal persons*) (miembros *mpl* de la) familia real; (*payment to author*) derechos *mpl* de autor.
RP *n abbr* (= *Received Pronunciation*) *ver recuadro.*

RP

*El acento con el que suelen hablar las clases medias y altas de Inglaterra se denomina **RP** (o **Received Pronunciation**). Es el acento estándar, sin variaciones regionales, que aún usan los locutores en los informativos nacionales de la "BBC". También suele tomarse como norma en la enseñanza del inglés británico como lengua extranjera. Todavía conserva un gran prestigio, aunque la gran mayoría de la población habla con el acento de su región, que puede ser más o menos fuerte según su educación o clase social.*

---

rpm *abbr* (= *revs per minute*) r.p.m.
RR *abbr* (*US*) = **railroad.**
RSA *n abbr* (*BRIT*) = *Royal Society of Arts, Royal Scottish Academy.*
RSI *n abbr* (*MED*: = *repetitive strain injury*) *traumatismo producido por un esfuerzo continuado* (*como el de las mecanógrafas*).
RSPB *n abbr* (*BRIT*) = *Royal Society for the Protection of Birds.*
RSPCA *n abbr* (*BRIT*) = *Royal Society for the*

Prevention of Cruelty to Animals.

R.S.V.P., abbr (= répondez s'il vous plaît) SRC.

RTA n abbr (= road traffic accident) accidente m de carretera.

Rt. Hon. abbr (BRIT: = Right Honourable) tratamiento honorífico de diputado.

Rt. Rev. abbr (= Right Reverend) Rvdo.

rub [rʌb] vt (gen) frotar; (hard) restregar ♦ n (gen) frotamiento; (touch) roce m; **to ~ sb up** or (US) ~ **sb the wrong way** sacar de quicio a algn.

▶**rub down** vt (body) secar frotando; (horse) almohazar.

▶**rub in** vt (ointment) frotar.

▶**rub off** vt borrarse ♦ vi quitarse (frotando); **to ~ off on sb** influir en algn, pegársele a algn.

▶**rub out** vt borrar ♦ vi borrarse.

rubber ['rʌbə*] n caucho, goma; (BRIT: eraser) goma de borrar.

rubber band n goma, gomita.

rubber bullet n bala de goma.

rubber plant n ficus m.

rubber ring n (for swimming) flotador m.

rubber stamp n sello (de caucho) ♦ vt: **rubber-stamp** (fig) aprobar maquinalmente.

rubbery ['rʌbərɪ] adj (como) de goma.

rubbish ['rʌbɪʃ] (BRIT) n (from household) basura; (waste) desperdicios mpl; (fig: pej) tonterías fpl; (trash) basura, porquería ♦ vt (col) poner por los suelos; **what you've just said is** ~ lo que acabas de decir es una tontería.

rubbish bin n cubo or bote m (LAM) de la basura.

rubbish dump n (in town) vertedero, basurero.

rubbishy ['rʌbɪʃɪ] adj de mala calidad, de pacotilla.

rubble ['rʌbl] n escombros mpl.

ruby ['ru:bɪ] n rubí m.

RUC n abbr (= Royal Ulster Constabulary) fuerza de policía en Irlanda del Norte.

rucksack ['rʌksæk] n mochila.

ructions ['rʌkʃənz] npl: **there will be** ~ se va a armar la gorda.

ruddy ['rʌdɪ] adj (face) rubicundo; (col: damned) condenado.

rude [ru:d] adj (impolite: person) grosero, maleducado; (: word, manners) rudo, grosero; (indecent) indecente; **to be** ~ **to sb** ser grosero con algn.

rudeness ['ru:dnɪs] n grosería, tosquedad f.

rudiment ['ru:dɪmənt] n rudimento.

rudimentary [ru:dɪ'mɛntərɪ] adj rudimentario.

rue [ru:] vt arrepentirse de.

rueful ['ru:ful] adj arrepentido.

ruffian ['rʌfɪən] n matón m, criminal m.

ruffle ['rʌfl] vt (hair) despeinar; (clothes) arrugar; (fig: person) agitar.

rug [rʌg] n alfombra; (BRIT: for knees) manta.

rugby ['rʌgbɪ] n (also: ~ **football**) rugby m.

rugged ['rʌgɪd] adj (landscape) accidentado; (features) robusto.

rugger ['rʌgə*] n (BRIT col) rugby m.

ruin ['ru:ɪn] n ruina ♦ vt arruinar; (spoil) estropear; ~**s** npl ruinas fpl, restos mpl; **in** ~**s** en ruinas.

ruinous ['ru:ɪnəs] adj ruinoso.

rule [ru:l] n (norm) norma, costumbre f; (regulation, ruler) regla; (government) dominio; (dominion etc): **under British** ~ bajo el dominio británico ♦ vt (country, person) gobernar; (decide) disponer; (draw lines) trazar ♦ vi gobernar; (LAW) fallar; **to ~ against/in favour of/on** fallar en contra de/a favor de/sobre; **to ~ that** ... (umpire, judge) fallar que ...; **it's against the** ~**s** está prohibido; **as a** ~ por regla general, generalmente; **by** ~ **of thumb** por experiencia; **majority** ~ (POL) gobierno mayoritario.

▶**rule out** vt excluir.

ruled [ru:ld] adj (paper) rayado.

ruler ['ru:lə*] n (sovereign) soberano; (for measuring) regla.

ruling ['ru:lɪŋ] adj (party) gobernante; (class) dirigente ♦ n (LAW) fallo, decisión f.

rum [rʌm] n ron m.

Rumania [ru:'meɪnɪə] n Rumanía.

Rumanian [ru:'meɪnɪən] adj, n rumano/a m/f.

rumble ['rʌmbl] n ruido sordo; (of thunder) redoble m ♦ vi retumbar, hacer un ruido sordo; (stomach, pipe) sonar.

rumbustious [rʌm'bʌstʃəs] adj (person) bullicioso.

rummage ['rʌmɪdʒ] vi revolverlo todo.

rumour, (US) **rumor** ['ru:mə*] n rumor m ♦ vt: **it is** ~**ed that** ... se rumorea que ...; ~ **has it that** ... corre la voz de que ....

rump [rʌmp] n (of animal) ancas fpl, grupa.

rumple ['rʌmpl] vt (clothes) arrugar; (hair) despeinar.

rump steak n filete m de lomo.

rumpus ['rʌmpəs] n (col) lío, jaleo; (quarrel) pelea, riña; **to kick up a** ~ armar un follón or armar bronca.

run [rʌn] n (SPORT) carrera; (outing) paseo, excursión f; (distance travelled) trayecto; (series) serie f; (THEAT) temporada; (SKI) pista; (in tights, stockings) carrera; ♦ vb (pt

ran, *pp* **run** [ræn, rʌn]) *vt* (*operate: business*) dirigir; (: *competition, course*) organizar; (: *hotel, house*) administrar, llevar; (COMPUT: *program*) ejecutar; (*to pass: hand*) pasar; (*bath*): **to ~ a bath** llenar la bañera ♦ *vi* (*gen*) correr; (*work: machine*) funcionar, marchar; (*bus, train: operate*) circular, ir; (: *travel*) ir; (*continue: play*) seguir en cartel; (: *contract*) ser válido; (*flow: river, bath*) fluir; (*colours, washing*) desteñirse; (*in election*) ser candidato; **to go for a ~** ir a correr; **to make a ~ for it** echar(se) a correr, escapar(se), huir; **to have the ~ of sb's house** tener el libre uso de la casa de algn; **a ~ of luck** una racha de suerte; **there was a ~ on** (*meat, tickets*) hubo mucha demanda de; **in the long ~** a la larga; **on the ~** en fuga; **I'll ~ you to the station** te llevaré a la estación en coche; **to ~ a risk** correr un riesgo; **to ~ errands** hacer recados; **it's very cheap to ~** es muy económico; **to be ~ off one's feet** estar ocupadísimo; **to ~ for the bus** correr tras el autobús; **we shall have to ~ for it** tendremos que escapar; **the train ~s between Gatwick and Victoria** el tren circula entre Gatwick y Victoria; **the bus ~s every 20 minutes** el autobús pasa cada 20 minutos; **to ~ on petrol/on diesel/off batteries** funcionar con gasolina/gasoil/baterías; **my salary won't ~ to a car** mi sueldo no me da para comprarme un coche; **the car ran into the lamppost** el coche chocó contra el farol.

▶**run about, run around** *vi* (*children*) correr por todos lados.

▶**run across** *vt fus* (*find*) dar *or* topar con.

▶**run away** *vi* huir.

▶**run down** *vi* (*clock*) pararse ♦ *vt* (*reduce: production*) ir reduciendo; (*factory*) restringir la producción de; (AUT) atropellar; (*criticize*) criticar; **to be ~ down** (*person: tired*) encontrarse agotado.

▶**run in** *vt* (BRIT: *car*) rodar.

▶**run into** *vt fus* (*meet: person, trouble*) tropezar con; (*collide with*) chocar con; **to ~ into debt** contraer deudas, endeudarse.

▶**run off** *vt* (*water*) dejar correr ♦ *vi* huir corriendo.

▶**run out** *vi* (*person*) salir corriendo; (*liquid*) irse; (*lease*) caducar, vencer; (*money*) acabarse.

▶**run out of** *vt fus* quedar sin; **I've ~ out of petrol** se me acabó la gasolina.

▶**run over** *vt* (AUT) atropellar ♦ *vt fus* (*revise*) repasar.

▶**run through** *vt fus* (*instructions*) repasar.

▶**run up** *vt* (*debt*) incurrir en; **to ~ up against** (*difficulties*) tropezar con.

run-around ['rʌnəraund] *n*: **to give sb the ~** traer a algn al retortero.

runaway ['rʌnəwei] *adj* (*horse*) desbocado; (*truck*) sin frenos; (*person*) fugitivo.

rundown ['rʌndaun] *n* (BRIT: *of industry etc*) cierre *m* gradual.

rung [rʌŋ] *pp of* **ring** ♦ *n* (*of ladder*) escalón *m*, peldaño.

run-in ['rʌnin] *n* (*col*) altercado.

runner ['rʌnə*] *n* (*in race: person*) corredor(a) *m/f*; (: *horse*) caballo; (*on sledge*) patín *m*; (*wheel*) ruedecilla.

runner bean *n* (BRIT) judía escarlata.

runner-up [rʌnər'ʌp] *n* subcampeón/ona *m/f*.

running ['rʌniŋ] *n* (*sport*) atletismo; (*race*) carrera ♦ *adj* (*costs, water*) corriente; (*commentary*) en directo; **to be in/out of the ~ for sth** tener/no tener posibilidades de ganar algo; **6 days ~** 6 días seguidos.

running costs *npl* (*of business*) gastos *mpl* corrientes; (*of car*) gastos *mpl* de mantenimiento.

running head *n* (TYP, WORD PROCESSING) encabezamiento normal.

running mate *n* (US POL) candidato/a a la vice-presidencia.

runny ['rʌni] *adj* derretido.

run-off ['rʌnɔf] *n* (*in contest, election*) desempate *m*; (*extra race*) carrera de desempate.

run-of-the-mill ['rʌnəvðə'mil] *adj* común y corriente.

runt [rʌnt] *n* (*also pej*) enano.

run-up ['rʌnʌp] *n*: **~ to** (*election etc*) período previo a.

runway ['rʌnwei] *n* (AVIAT) pista (de aterrizaje).

rupee [ru:'pi:] *n* rupia.

rupture ['rʌptʃə*] *n* (MED) hernia ♦ *vt*: **to ~ o.s.** causarse una hernia.

rural ['ruərl] *adj* rural.

ruse [ru:z] *n* ardid *m*.

rush [rʌʃ] *n* ímpetu *m*; (*hurry*) prisa, apuro (LAM); (COMM) demanda repentina; (BOT) junco; (*current*) corriente *f* fuerte, ráfaga ♦ *vt* apresurar; (*work*) hacer de prisa; (*attack: town etc*) asaltar ♦ *vi* correr, precipitarse; **gold ~** fiebre *f* del oro; **we've had a ~ of orders** ha habido una gran demanda; **I'm in a ~ (to do)** tengo prisa or apuro (LAM) (por hacer); **is there any ~ for this?** ¿te corre prisa esto?; **to ~ sth off** hacer algo de prisa y corriendo.

▶**rush through** *vt fus* (*meal*) comer de prisa; (*book*) leer de prisa; (*work*) hacer de prisa; (*town*) atravesar a toda

velocidad; (*COMM: order*) despachar rápidamente.
rush hour *n* horas *fpl* punta.
rush job *n* (*urgent*) trabajo urgente.
rusk [rʌsk] *n* bizcocho tostado.
Russia ['rʌʃə] *n* Rusia.
Russian ['rʌʃən] *adj* ruso ♦ *n* ruso/a; (*LING*) ruso.
rust [rʌst] *n* herrumbre *f*, moho ♦ *vi* oxidarse.
rustic ['rʌstɪk] *adj* rústico.
rustle ['rʌsl] *vi* susurrar ♦ *vt* (*paper*) hacer crujir; (*US: cattle*) hurtar, robar.
rustproof ['rʌstpruːf] *adj* inoxidable.
rusty ['rʌstɪ] *adj* oxidado.
rut [rʌt] *n* surco; (*ZOOL*) celo; **to be in a ~** ser esclavo de la rutina.
ruthless ['ruːθlɪs] *adj* despiadado.
RV *abbr* (= *revised version*) *traducción inglesa de la Biblia de 1855* ♦ *n abbr* (*US*) = **recreational vehicle**.
rye [raɪ] *n* centeno.
rye bread *n* pan de centeno.

S s

S, s [ɛs] *n* (*letter*) S, s *f*; **S for Sugar** S de sábado.
S *abbr* (= *Saint*) Sto./a.; (*US SCOL: mark*: = *satisfactory*) suficiente; (= *south*) S; = **small**.
SA *n abbr* = **South Africa, South America**.
sabbath ['sæbəθ] *n* domingo; (*Jewish*) sábado.
sabbatical [sə'bætɪkl] *adj*: ~ **year** año sabático.
sabotage ['sæbətɑːʒ] *n* sabotaje *m* ♦ *vt* sabotear.
sabre, (*US*) **saber** ['seɪbə*] *n* sable *m*.
saccharin(e) ['sækərɪn] *n* sacarina.
sachet ['sæʃeɪ] *n* sobrecito.
sack [sæk] *n* (*bag*) saco, costal *m* ♦ *vt* (*dismiss*) despedir, echar; (*plunder*) saquear; **to get the ~** ser despedido; **to give sb the ~** despedir *or* echar a algn.
sackful ['sækful] *n* saco.
sacking ['sækɪŋ] *n* (*material*) arpillera.
sacrament ['sækrəmənt] *n* sacramento.
sacred ['seɪkrɪd] *adj* sagrado, santo.
sacred cow *n* (*fig*) vaca sagrada.
sacrifice ['sækrɪfaɪs] *n* sacrificio ♦ *vt*

sacrificar; **to make ~s (for sb)** sacrificarse (por algn).
sacrilege ['sækrɪlɪdʒ] *n* sacrilegio.
sacrosanct ['sækrəusæŋkt] *adj* sacrosanto.
sad [sæd] *adj* (*unhappy*) triste; (*deplorable*) lamentable.
sadden ['sædn] *vt* entristecer.
saddle ['sædl] *n* silla (de montar); (*of cycle*) sillín *m* ♦ *vt* (*horse*) ensillar; **to ~ sb with sth** (*col: task, bill, name*) cargar a algn con algo; (: *responsibility*) gravar a algn con algo; **to be ~d with sth** (*col*) quedar cargado con algo.
saddlebag ['sædlbæg] *n* alforja.
sadism ['seɪdɪzm] *n* sadismo.
sadist ['seɪdɪst] *n* sádico/a.
sadistic [sə'dɪstɪk] *adj* sádico.
sadly ['sædlɪ] *adv* tristemente; (*regrettably*) desgraciadamente; ~ **lacking (in)** muy deficiente (en).
sadness ['sædnɪs] *n* tristeza.
sado-masochism [seɪdəu'mæsəkɪzm] *n* sadomasoquismo.
sae *abbr* (*BRIT*: = *stamped addressed envelope*) *sobre con las propias señas de uno y con sello*.
safari [sə'fɑːrɪ] *n* safari *m*.
safari park *n* safari *m*.
safe [seɪf] *adj* (*out of danger*) fuera de peligro; (*not dangerous, sure*) seguro; (*unharmed*) ileso; (*trustworthy*) digno de confianza ♦ *n* caja de caudales, caja fuerte; ~ **and sound** sano y salvo; **(just) to be on the ~ side** para mayor seguridad; ~ **journey!** ¡buen viaje!; **it is ~ to say that ...** se puede decir con confianza que ....
safe bet *n* apuesta segura; **it's a ~ she'll turn up** seguro que viene.
safe-breaker ['seɪfbreɪkə*] *n* (*BRIT*) ladrón/ona *m/f* de cajas fuertes.
safe-conduct [seɪf'kɒndʌkt] *n* salvoconducto.
safe-cracker ['seɪfkrækə*] *n* (*US*) = **safe-breaker**.
safe-deposit ['seɪfdɪpɒzɪt] *n* (*vault*) cámara acorazada; (*box*) caja de seguridad *or* de caudales.
safeguard ['seɪfgɑːd] *n* protección *f*, garantía ♦ *vt* proteger, defender.
safe haven *n* refugio.
safekeeping ['seɪf'kiːpɪŋ] *n* custodia.
safely ['seɪflɪ] *adv* seguramente, con seguridad; (*without mishap*) sin peligro; **I can ~ say** puedo decir *or* afirmar con toda seguridad.
safeness ['seɪfnɪs] *n* seguridad *f*.
safe passage *n* garantías *fpl* para

marcharse en libertad.
safe sex n sexo seguro or sin riesgo.
safety ['seɪftɪ] n seguridad f ♦ cpd de
seguridad; **road** ~ seguridad f en
carretera; ~ **first!** ¡precaución!
safety belt n cinturón m (de seguridad).
safety catch n seguro.
safety net n red f (de seguridad).
safety pin n imperdible m, seguro (LAM).
safety valve n válvula de seguridad or de
escape.
saffron ['sæfrən] n azafrán m.
sag [sæg] vi aflojarse.
saga ['sɑːgə] n (HISTORY) saga; (fig)
epopeya.
sage [seɪdʒ] n (herb) salvia; (man) sabio.
Sagittarius [sædʒɪ'tɛərɪəs] n Sagitario.
sago ['seɪgəu] n sagú m.
Sahara [sə'hɑːrə] n: **the** ~ **(Desert)** el
Sáhara.
Sahel [sæ'hɛl] n Sahel m.
said [sɛd] pt, pp of **say**.
Saigon [saɪ'gɔn] n Saigón m.
sail [seɪl] n (on boat) vela ♦ vt (boat)
gobernar ♦ vi (travel: ship) navegar; (:
passenger) pasear en barco; (set off: also:
to set ~) zarpar; **to go for a** ~ dar un
paseo en barco; **they** ~**ed into
Copenhagen** arribaron a Copenhague.
▶**sail through** vt fus (exam) aprobar
fácilmente.
sailboat ['seɪlbəut] n (US) velero, barco de
vela.
sailing ['seɪlɪŋ] n (SPORT) balandrismo; **to
go** ~ salir en balandro.
sailing ship n barco de vela.
sailor ['seɪlə*] n marinero, marino.
saint [seɪnt] n santo; **S**~ **John** San Juan.
saintliness ['seɪntlɪnɪs] n santidad f.
saintly ['seɪntlɪ] adj santo.
sake [seɪk] n: **for the** ~ **of** por; **for the** ~ **of
argument** digamos, es un decir; **art for
art's** ~ el arte por el arte.
salad ['sæləd] n ensalada; **tomato** ~
ensalada de tomate.
salad bowl n ensaladera.
salad cream n (BRIT) mayonesa.
salad dressing n aliño.
salad oil n aceite m para ensalada.
salami [sə'lɑːmɪ] n salami m, salchichón m.
salaried ['sælərɪd] adj asalariado.
salary ['sælərɪ] n sueldo.
salary earner n asalariado/a.
salary scale n escala salarial.
sale [seɪl] n venta; (at reduced prices)
liquidación f, saldo; **"for** ~**"** "se vende";
on ~ en venta; **on** ~ **or return** (goods)
venta por reposición; **closing-down** or

(US) **liquidation** ~ liquidación f; ~ **and
lease back** venta y arrendamiento al
vendedor.
saleroom ['seɪlruːm] n sala de subastas.
sales assistant n (BRIT) dependiente/a m/f.
sales campaign n campaña de venta.
sales clerk n (US) dependiente/a m/f.
sales conference n conferencia de
ventas.
sales drive n promoción f de ventas.
sales figures npl cifras fpl de ventas.
sales force n personal m de ventas.
salesman ['seɪlzmən] n vendedor m; (in
shop) dependiente m; (representative)
viajante m.
sales manager n gerente m/f de ventas.
salesmanship ['seɪlzmənʃɪp] n arte m de
vender.
sales meeting n reunión f de ventas.
sales tax n (US) = **purchase tax.**
saleswoman ['seɪlzwumən] n vendedora;
(in shop) dependienta; (representative)
viajante m.
salient ['seɪlɪənt] adj (features, points)
sobresaliente.
saline ['seɪlaɪn] adj salino.
saliva [sə'laɪvə] n saliva.
sallow ['sæləu] adj cetrino.
sally forth, sally out vi salir, ponerse en
marcha.
salmon ['sæmən] n (pl inv) salmón m.
salon ['sælɔn] n (hairdressing ~, beauty ~)
salón m.
saloon [sə'luːn] n (US) bar m, taberna; (BRIT
AUT) (coche m de) turismo; (ship's lounge)
cámara, salón m.
SALT [sɔːlt] n abbr (= Strategic Arms
Limitation Treaty) tratado SALT.
salt [sɔːlt] n sal f ♦ vt salar; (put ~ on) poner
sal en; **an old** ~ un lobo de mar.
▶**salt away** vt (col: money) ahorrar.
salt cellar n salero.
salt mine n mina de sal.
saltwater ['sɔːlt'wɔːtə*] adj (fish etc) de
agua salada, de mar.
salty ['sɔːltɪ] adj salado.
salubrious [sə'luːbrɪəs] adj sano; (fig: district
etc) atractivo.
salutary ['sæljutərɪ] adj saludable.
salute [sə'luːt] n saludo; (of guns) salva ♦ vt
saludar.
salvage ['sælvɪdʒ] n (saving) salvamento,
recuperación f; (things saved) objetos mpl
salvados ♦ vt salvar.
salvage vessel n buque m de salvamento.
salvation [sæl'veɪʃən] n salvación f.
Salvation Army n Ejército de Salvación.
salve [sælv] n (cream etc) ungüento,

bálsamo.
salvo ['sælvəu] *n* (*MIL*) salva.
Samaritan [sə'mærɪtən] *n*: **to call the ~s**
llamar al teléfono de la esperanza.
same [seɪm] *adj* mismo ♦ *pron*: **the ~** el
mismo/la misma; **the ~ book as** el mismo
libro que; **on the ~ day** el mismo día; **at
the ~ time** (*at the ~ moment*) al mismo
tiempo; (*yet*) sin embargo; **all** *or* **just the
~** sin embargo, aun así; **they're one and
the ~** (*person*) son la misma persona;
(*thing*) son iguales; **to do the ~** (*as sb*)
hacer lo mismo (que otro); **and the ~ to
you!** ¡igualmente!; **~ here!** ¡yo también!;
the ~ again (*in bar etc*) otro igual.
sampan ['sæmpæn] *n* sampán *m*.
sample ['sɑːmpl] *n* muestra ♦ *vt* (*food, wine*)
probar; **to take a ~** tomar una muestra;
free ~ muestra gratuita.
sanatorium, *pl* **-ria** [sænə'tɔːrɪəm, -rɪə] *n*
(*BRIT*) sanatorio.
sanctify ['sæŋktɪfaɪ] *vt* santificar.
sanctimonious [sæŋktɪ'məunɪəs] *adj*
santurrón/ona.
sanction ['sæŋkʃən] *n* sanción *f* ♦ *vt*
sancionar; **to impose economic ~s on** *or*
against imponer sanciones económicas a
or contra.
sanctity ['sæŋktɪtɪ] *n* (*gen*) santidad *f*;
(*inviolability*) inviolabilidad *f*.
sanctuary ['sæŋktjuərɪ] *n* (*gen*) santuario;
(*refuge*) asilo, refugio.
sand [sænd] *n* arena; (*beach*) playa ♦ *vt*
(*also*: **~ down**: *wood etc*) lijar.
sandal ['sændl] *n* sandalia.
sandalwood ['sændlwud] *n* sándalo.
sandbag ['sændbæg] *n* saco de arena.
sandblast ['sændblɑːst] *vt* limpiar con
chorro de arena.
sandbox ['sændbɔks] *n* (*US*) = **sandpit**.
sandcastle ['sændkɑːsl] *n* castillo de arena.
sand dune *n* duna.
sander ['sændə*] *n* pulidora.
S & M *n abbr* (= *sadomasochism*)
sadomasoquismo.
sandpaper ['sændpeɪpə*] *n* papel *m* de lija.
sandpit ['sændpɪt] *n* (*for children*) cajón *m*
de arena.
sands [sændz] *npl* playa *sg* de arena.
sandstone ['sændstəun] *n* piedra arenisca.
sandstorm ['sændstɔːm] *n* tormenta de
arena.
sandwich ['sændwɪtʃ] *n* bocadillo (*SP*),
sandwich *m* (*LAM*) ♦ *vt* (*also*: **~ in**)
intercalar; **to be ~ed between** estar
apretujado entre; **cheese/ham ~**
sandwich de queso/jamón.
sandwich board *n* cartelón *m*.

sandwich course *n* (*BRIT*) *programa que
intercala períodos de estudio con
prácticas profesionales*.
sandy ['sændɪ] *adj* arenoso; (*colour*) rojizo.
sane [seɪn] *adj* cuerdo, sensato.
sang [sæŋ] *pt of* **sing**.
sanitarium [sænɪ'tɛərɪəm] *n* (*US*)
= **sanatorium**.
sanitary ['sænɪtərɪ] *adj* (*system,
arrangements*) sanitario; (*clean*) higiénico.
sanitary towel, (*US*) **sanitary napkin** *n*
paño higiénico, compresa.
sanitation [sænɪ'teɪʃən] *n* (*in house*)
servicios *mpl* higiénicos; (*in town*)
servicio de desinfección.
sanitation department *n* (*US*)
departamento de limpieza y recogida de
basuras.
sanity ['sænɪtɪ] *n* cordura; (*of judgment*)
sensatez *f*.
sank [sæŋk] *pt of* **sink**.
San Marino ['sænmə'riːnəu] *n* San Marino.
Santa Claus [sæntə'klɔːz] *n* San Nicolás *m*,
Papá Noel *m*.
Santiago [sæntɪ'ɑːgəu] *n* (*also*: **~ de Chile**)
Santiago (de Chile).
sap [sæp] *n* (*of plants*) savia ♦ *vt* (*strength*)
minar, agotar.
sapling ['sæplɪŋ] *n* árbol nuevo *or* joven.
sapphire ['sæfaɪə*] *n* zafiro.
Saragossa [særə'gɔsə] *n* Zaragoza.
sarcasm ['sɑːkæzm] *n* sarcasmo.
sarcastic [sɑː'kæstɪk] *adj* sarcástico; **to be
~** ser sarcástico.
sarcophagus, *pl* **sarcophagi** [sɑː'kɔfəgəs,
-gaɪ] *n* sarcófago.
sardine [sɑː'diːn] *n* sardina.
Sardinia [sɑː'dɪnɪə] *n* Cerdeña.
Sardinian [sɑː'dɪnɪən] *adj, n* sardo/a *m/f*.
sardonic [sɑː'dɔnɪk] *adj* sardónico.
sari ['sɑːrɪ] *n* sari *m*.
SARS [sɑːz] *n abbr* (= *severe acute respiratory
syndrome*) neumonía asiática, SARS *m*.
SAS *n abbr* (*BRIT MIL*: = *Special Air Service*)
*cuerpo del ejército británico encargado
de misiones clandestinas*.
SASE *n abbr* (*US*: = *self-addressed stamped
envelope*) *sobre con las propias señas de
uno y con sello*.
sash [sæʃ] *n* faja.
SAT *n abbr* (*US*) = *Scholastic Aptitude Test*.
sat [sæt] *pt, pp of* **sit**.
Sat. *abbr* (= *Saturday*) sáb.
Satan ['seɪtn] *n* Satanás *m*.
satanic [sə'tænɪk] *adj* satánico.
satchel ['sætʃl] *n* bolsa; (*child's*) cartera,
mochila (*LAM*).
sated ['seɪtɪd] *adj* (*appetite, person*) saciado.

satellite ['sætəlaɪt] *n* satélite *m*.
satellite television *n* televisión *f* por satélite.
satiate ['seɪʃɪeɪt] *vt* saciar, hartar.
satin ['sætɪn] *n* raso ♦ *adj* de raso; **with a ~ finish** satinado.
satire ['sætaɪə*] *n* sátira.
satirical [sə'tɪrɪkl] *adj* satírico.
satirist ['sætɪrɪst] *n* (*writer etc*) escritor(a) *m/f* satírico/a; (*cartoonist*) caricaturista *m/f*.
satirize ['sætɪraɪz] *vt* satirizar.
satisfaction [sætɪs'fækʃən] *n* satisfacción *f*; **it gives me great ~** es para mí una gran satisfacción; **has it been done to your ~?** ¿se ha hecho a su satisfacción?
satisfactorily [sætɪs'fæktərɪlɪ] *adv* satisfactoriamente, de modo satisfactorio.
satisfactory [sætɪs'fæktərɪ] *adj* satisfactorio.
satisfied ['sætɪsfaɪd] *adj* satisfecho; **to be ~ (with sth)** estar satisfecho (de algo).
satisfy ['sætɪsfaɪ] *vt* satisfacer; (*pay*) liquidar; (*convince*) convencer; **to ~ the requirements** llenar los requisitos; **to ~ sb that** convencer a algn de que; **to ~ o.s. of sth** convencerse de algo.
satisfying ['sætɪsfaɪɪŋ] *adj* satisfactorio.
satsuma [sæt'suːmə] *n* satsuma.
saturate ['sætʃəreɪt] *vt*: **to ~ (with)** empapar *or* saturar (de).
saturated fat [sætʃəreɪtɪd-] *n* grasa saturada.
saturation [sætʃə'reɪʃən] *n* saturación *f*.
Saturday ['sætədɪ] *n* sábado.
sauce [sɔːs] *n* salsa; (*sweet*) crema; (*fig: cheek*) frescura.
saucepan ['sɔːspən] *n* cacerola, olla.
saucer ['sɔːsə*] *n* platillo.
saucily ['sɔːsɪlɪ] *adv* con frescura, descaradamente.
sauciness ['sɔːsɪnɪs] *n* frescura, descaro.
saucy ['sɔːsɪ] *adj* fresco, descarado.
Saudi Arabia ['saʊdɪ-] *n* Arabia Saudí *or* Saudita.
Saudi (Arabian) ['saʊdɪ-] *adj, n* saudí *m/f*, saudita *m/f*.
sauna ['sɔːnə] *n* sauna.
saunter ['sɔːntə*] *vi* deambular.
sausage ['sɔsɪdʒ] *n* salchicha; (*salami etc*) salchichón *m*.
sausage roll *n* empanadilla.
sauté ['saʊteɪ] *adj* (*CULIN: potatoes*) salteado; (*: onions*) dorado, rehogado ♦ *vt* saltear; dorar.
savage ['sævɪdʒ] *adj* (*cruel, fierce*) feroz, furioso; (*primitive*) salvaje ♦ *n* salvaje *m/f* ♦ *vt* (*attack*) embestir.

savagely ['sævɪdʒlɪ] *adv* con ferocidad, furiosamente; de modo salvaje.
savagery ['sævɪdʒrɪ] *n* ferocidad *f*; salvajismo.
save [seɪv] *vt* (*rescue*) salvar, rescatar; (*money, time*) ahorrar; (*put by*) guardar; (*COMPUT*) salvar (y guardar); (*avoid: trouble*) evitar ♦ *vi* (*also: ~ up*) ahorrar ♦ *n* (*SPORT*) parada ♦ *prep* salvo, excepto; **to ~ face** salvar las apariencias; **God ~ the Queen!** ¡Dios guarde a la Reina!, ¡Viva la Reina!; **I ~d you a piece of cake** te he guardado un trozo de tarta; **it will ~ me an hour** con ello ganaré una hora.
saving ['seɪvɪŋ] *n* (*on price etc*) economía ♦ *adj*: **the ~ grace of** el único mérito de; **~s** *npl* ahorros *mpl*; **to make ~s** economizar.
savings account *n* cuenta de ahorros.
savings bank *n* caja de ahorros.
saviour, (*US*) **savior** ['seɪvjə*] *n* salvador(a) *m/f*.
savoir-faire ['sævwɑːˈfɛə*] *n* don *m* de gentes.
savour, (*US*) **savor** ['seɪvə*] *n* sabor *m*, gusto ♦ *vt* saborear.
savo(u)ry ['seɪvərɪ] *adj* sabroso; (*dish: not sweet*) salado.
savvy ['sævɪ] *n* (*col*) conocimiento, experiencia.
saw [sɔː] *pt of* **see** ♦ *n* (*tool*) sierra ♦ *vt* (*pt* **sawed**, *pp* **sawed** *or* **sawn** [sɔːn]) serrar; **to ~ sth up** (a)serrar algo.
sawdust ['sɔːdʌst] *n* (a)serrín *m*.
sawmill ['sɔːmɪl] *n* aserradero.
sawn [sɔːn] *pp of* **saw**.
sawn-off ['sɔːnɒf], (*US*) **sawed-off** ['sɔːdɒf] *adj*: **~ shotgun** escopeta de cañones recortados.
saxophone ['sæksəfəʊn] *n* saxófono.
say [seɪ] *n*: **to have one's ~** expresar su opinión; **to have a** *or* **some ~ in sth** tener voz y voto en algo ♦ *vt, vi* (*pt, pp* **said** [sɛd]) decir; **to ~ yes/no** decir que sí/no; **my watch ~s 3 o'clock** mi reloj marca las tres; **that is to ~** es decir; **that goes without ~ing** ni que decir tiene; **she said (that) I was to give you this** me pidió que te diera esto; **I should ~ it's worth about £100** yo diría que vale unas 100 libras; **~ after me** repite lo que yo diga; **shall we ~ Tuesday?** ¿quedamos, por ejemplo, el martes?; **that doesn't ~ much for him** eso no dice nada a su favor; **when all is said and done** al fin y al cabo, a fin de cuentas; **there is something** *or* **a lot to be said for it** hay algo *or* mucho que decir a su favor.
saying ['seɪɪŋ] *n* dicho, refrán *m*.
say-so ['seɪsəʊ] *n* (*col*) autorización *f*.

SBA – scent

SBA *n abbr* (*US*) = *Small Business Administration*.

SC *n abbr* (*US*) = **Supreme Court** ♦ *abbr* (*US*) = *South Carolina*.

s/c *abbr* = **self-contained**.

scab [skæb] *n* costra; (*pej*) esquirol(a) *m/f*.

scaffold ['skæfəld] *n* (*for execution*) cadalso.

scaffolding ['skæfəldɪŋ] *n* andamio, andamiaje *m*.

scald [skɔːld] *n* escaldadura ♦ *vt* escaldar.

scalding ['skɔːldɪŋ] *adj* (*also:* ~ **hot**) hirviendo, que arde.

scale [skeɪl] *n* (*gen, MUS*) escala; (*of fish*) escama; (*of salaries, fees etc*) escalafón *m* ♦ *vt* (*mountain*) escalar; (*tree*) trepar; ~**s** *npl* (*small*) balanza *sg*; (*large*) báscula *sg*; **on a large** ~ a gran escala; ~ **of charges** tarifa, lista de precios; **pay** ~ escala salarial; **to draw sth to** ~ dibujar algo a escala.

▶**scale down** *vt* reducir.

scaled-down [skeɪld'daun] *adj* reducido proporcionalmente.

scale model *n* modelo a escala.

scallop ['skɔləp] *n* (*ZOOL*) venera; (*SEWING*) festón *m*.

scalp [skælp] *n* cabellera ♦ *vt* escalpar.

scalpel ['skælpl] *n* bisturí *m*.

scam [skæm] *n* (*col*) estafa, timo.

scamper ['skæmpə*] *vi*: **to** ~ **away,** ~ **off** escabullirse.

scampi ['skæmpɪ] *npl* gambas *fpl*.

scan [skæn] *vt* (*examine*) escudriñar; (*glance at quickly*) dar un vistazo a; (*TV, RADAR*) explorar, registrar ♦ *n* (*MED*) examen *m* ultrasónico.

scandal ['skændl] *n* escándalo; (*gossip*) chismes *mpl*.

scandalize ['skændəlaɪz] *vt* escandalizar.

scandalous ['skændələs] *adj* escandaloso.

Scandinavia [skændɪ'neɪvɪə] *n* Escandinavia.

Scandinavian [skændɪ'neɪvɪən] *adj, n* escandinavo/a *m/f*.

scanner ['skænə*] *n* (*RADAR, MED*) escáner *m*.

scant [skænt] *adj* escaso.

scantily ['skæntɪlɪ] *adv*: ~ **clad** *or* **dressed** ligero de ropa.

scantiness ['skæntɪnɪs] *n* escasez *f*, insuficiencia.

scanty ['skæntɪ] *adj* (*meal*) insuficiente; (*clothes*) ligero.

scapegoat ['skeɪpgəut] *n* cabeza de turco, chivo expiatorio.

scar [skɑː] *n* cicatriz *f* ♦ *vt* marcar con una cicatriz ♦ *vi* cicatrizarse.

scarce [skɛəs] *adj* escaso.

scarcely ['skɛəslɪ] *adv* apenas; ~ **anybody** casi nadie; **I can** ~ **believe it** casi no puedo creerlo.

scarceness ['skɛəsnɪs], **scarcity** ['skɛəsɪtɪ] *n* escasez *f*.

scarcity value *n* valor *m* de escasez.

scare [skɛə*] *n* susto, sobresalto; (*panic*) pánico ♦ *vt* asustar, espantar; **to** ~ **sb stiff** dar a algn un susto de muerte; **bomb** ~ amenaza de bomba.

▶**scare away, scare off** *vt* espantar, ahuyentar.

scarecrow ['skɛəkrəu] *n* espantapájaros *m inv*.

scared [skɛəd] *adj*: **to be** ~ asustarse, estar asustado.

scaremonger ['skɛəmʌŋgə*] *n* alarmista *m/f*.

scarf, *pl* **scarves** [skɑːf, skɑːvz] *n* (*long*) bufanda; (*square*) pañuelo.

scarlet ['skɑːlɪt] *adj* escarlata.

scarlet fever *n* escarlatina.

scarper ['skɑːpə*] *vi* (*BRIT col*) largarse.

scarred [skɑːd] *adj* lleno de cicatrices.

scarves [skɑːvz] *npl of* **scarf**.

scary ['skɛərɪ] *adj* (*col*) de miedo; **it's** ~ da miedo.

scathing ['skeɪðɪŋ] *adj* mordaz; **to be** ~ **about sth** criticar algo duramente.

scatter ['skætə*] *vt* (*spread*) esparcir, desparramar; (*put to flight*) dispersar ♦ *vi* desparramarse; dispersarse.

scatterbrained ['skætəbreɪnd] *adj* ligero de cascos.

scavenge ['skævɪndʒ] *vi*: **to** ~ **(for)** (*person*) revolver entre la basura (para encontrar); **to** ~ **for food** (*hyenas etc*) nutrirse de carroña.

scavenger ['skævɪndʒə*] *n* (*person*) mendigo/a que rebusca en la basura; (*ZOOL: animal*) animal *m* de carroña; (*: bird*) ave *f* de carroña.

SCE *n abbr* = *Scottish Certificate of Education*.

scenario [sɪ'nɑːrɪəu] *n* (*THEAT*) argumento; (*CINE*) guión *m*; (*fig*) escenario.

scene [siːn] *n* (*THEAT, fig etc*) escena; (*of crime, accident*) escenario; (*sight, view*) vista, perspectiva; (*fuss*) escándalo; **the political** ~ **in Spain** el panorama político español; **behind the** ~**s** (*also fig*) entre bastidores; **to appear** *or* **come on the** ~ (*also fig*) aparecer, presentarse; **to make a** ~ (*col: fuss*) armar un escándalo.

scenery ['siːnərɪ] *n* (*THEAT*) decorado; (*landscape*) paisaje *m*.

scenic ['siːnɪk] *adj* (*picturesque*) pintoresco.

scent [sɛnt] *n* perfume *m*, olor *m*; (*fig: track*) rastro, pista; (*sense of smell*) olfato ♦ *vt*

perfumar; (*suspect*) presentir; **to put** *or*
throw sb off the ~ (*fig*) despistar a algn.
sceptic, (*US*) **skeptic** ['skɛptɪk] *n*
escéptico/a.
sceptical, (*US*) **skeptical** ['skɛptɪkl] *adj*
escéptico.
scepticism, (*US*) **skepticism** ['skɛptɪsɪzm]
n escepticismo.
sceptre, (*US*) **scepter** ['sɛptə*] *n* cetro.
schedule ['ʃɛdjuːl, (*US*) 'skɛdjuːl] *n* (*of
trains*) horario; (*of events*) programa *m*;
(*list*) lista ♦ *vt* (*timetable*) establecer el
horario de; (*list*) catalogar; (*visit*) fijar la
hora de; **on** ~ a la hora, sin retraso; **to be
ahead of/behind** ~ estar adelantado/
retrasado; **we are working to a very tight**
~ tenemos un programa de trabajo muy
apretado; **everything went according to** ~
todo salió según lo previsto; **the meeting
is** ~**d for 7** *or* **to begin at 7** la reunión está
fijada para las 7.
scheduled ['ʃɛdjuːld, (*US*) 'skɛdjuːld] *adj*
(*date, time*) fijado; (*visit, event, bus, train*)
programado; (*stop*) previsto; ~ **flight**
vuelo regular.
schematic [skɪ'mætɪk] *adj* (*diagram etc*)
esquemático.
scheme [skiːm] *n* (*plan*) plan *m*, proyecto;
(*method*) esquema *m*; (*plot*) intriga; (*trick*)
ardid *m*; (*arrangement*) disposición *f*;
(*pension* ~ *etc*) sistema *m* ♦ *vt* proyectar
♦ *vi* (*plan*) hacer proyectos; (*intrigue*)
intrigar; **colour** ~ combinación *f* de
colores.
scheming ['skiːmɪŋ] *adj* intrigante.
schism ['skɪzəm] *n* cisma *m*.
schizophrenia [skɪtsə'friːnɪə] *n*
esquizofrenia.
schizophrenic [skɪtsə'frɛnɪk] *adj*
esquizofrénico.
scholar ['skɒlə*] *n* (*pupil*) alumno/a,
estudiante *m/f*; (*learned person*) sabio/a,
erudito/a.
scholarly ['skɒləlɪ] *adj* erudito.
scholarship ['skɒləʃɪp] *n* erudición *f*; (*grant*)
beca.
school [skuːl] *n* (*gen*) escuela, colegio; (*in
university*) facultad *f*; (*of fish*) banco ♦ *vt*
(*animal*) amaestrar; **to be at** *or* **go to** ~ ir
al colegio *or* a la escuela.
school age *n* edad *f* escolar.
schoolbook ['skuːlbuk] *n* libro de texto.
schoolboy ['skuːlbɔɪ] *n* alumno.
schoolchild, *pl* **-children** ['skuːltʃaɪld,
-tʃɪldrən] *n* alumno/a.
schooldays ['skuːldeɪz] *npl* años *mpl* del
colegio.
schoolgirl ['skuːlɡəːl] *n* alumna.

schooling ['skuːlɪŋ] *n* enseñanza.
school-leaver ['skuːlliːvə*] *n* (*BRIT*) joven
*que ha terminado la educación
secundaria.*
schoolmaster ['skuːlmɑːstə*] *n* (*primary*)
maestro; (*secondary*) profesor *m*.
schoolmistress ['skuːlmɪstrɪs] *n* (*primary*)
maestra; (*secondary*) profesora.
schoolroom ['skuːlrum] *n* clase *f*.
schoolteacher ['skuːltiːtʃə*] *n* (*primary*)
maestro/a; (*secondary*) profesor(a) *m/f*.
schoolyard ['skuːljɑːd] *n* (*US*) patio del
colegio.
schooner ['skuːnə*] *n* (*ship*) goleta.
sciatica [saɪ'ætɪkə] *n* ciática.
science ['saɪəns] *n* ciencia; **the** ~**s** las
ciencias.
science fiction *n* ciencia-ficción *f*.
scientific [saɪən'tɪfɪk] *adj* científico.
scientist ['saɪəntɪst] *n* científico/a.
sci-fi ['saɪfaɪ] *n abbr* (*col*) = **science fiction.**
Scilly Isles ['sɪlɪ-], **Scillies** ['sɪlɪz] *npl*: **the** ~
las Islas Sorlingas.
scintillating ['sɪntɪleɪtɪŋ] *adj* (*wit,
conversation, company*) brillante,
chispeante, ingenioso.
scissors ['sɪzəz] *npl* tijeras *fpl*; **a pair of** ~
unas tijeras.
scoff [skɒf] *vt* (*BRIT col: eat*) engullir ♦ *vi*: **to**
~ **(at)** (*mock*) mofarse (de).
scold [skəʊld] *vt* regañar.
scolding ['skəʊldɪŋ] *n* riña, reprimenda.
scone [skɒn] *n* pastel de pan.
scoop [skuːp] *n* cucharón *m*; (*for flour etc*)
pala; (*PRESS*) exclusiva ♦ *vt* (*COMM:
market*) adelantarse a; (: *profit*) sacar;
(*COMM, PRESS: competitors*) adelantarse a.
►**scoop out** *vt* excavar.
►**scoop up** *vt* recoger.
scooter ['skuːtə*] *n* (*motor cycle*) Vespa ®;
(*toy*) patinete *m*.
scope [skəʊp] *n* (*of plan, undertaking*)
ámbito; (*reach*) alcance *m*; (*of person*)
competencia; (*opportunity*) libertad *f* (de
acción); **there is plenty of** ~ **for
improvement** hay bastante campo para
efectuar mejoras.
scorch [skɔːtʃ] *vt* (*clothes*) chamuscar;
(*earth, grass*) quemar, secar.
scorcher ['skɔːtʃə*] *n* (*col: hot day*) día *m*
abrasador.
scorching ['skɔːtʃɪŋ] *adj* abrasador(a).
score [skɔː*] *n* (*points etc*) puntuación *f*;
(*MUS*) partitura; (*reckoning*) cuenta;
(*twenty*) veintena ♦ *vt* (*goal, point*) ganar;
(*mark, cut*) rayar ♦ *vi* marcar un tanto;
(*FOOTBALL*) marcar un gol; (*keep score*)
llevar el tanteo; **to keep (the)** ~ llevar la

cuenta; **to have an old ~ to settle with sb**
(*fig*) tener cuentas pendientes con algn;
on that ~ en lo que se refiere a eso; **~s of
people** (*fig*) muchísima gente, cantidad
de gente; **to ~ 6 out of 10** obtener una
puntuación de 6 sobre 10.
▶**score out** *vt* tachar.
scoreboard ['skɔːbɔːd] *n* marcador *m*.
scoreline ['skɔːlaɪn] *n* (*SPORT*) resultado
final.
scorer ['skɔːrə*] *n* marcador *m*; (*keeping
score*) encargado/a del marcador.
scorn [skɔːn] *n* desprecio ♦ *vt* despreciar.
scornful ['skɔːnful] *adj* desdeñoso,
despreciativo.
scornfully ['skɔːnfulɪ] *adv* desdeñosamente,
con desprecio.
Scorpio ['skɔːpɪəu] *n* Escorpión *m*.
scorpion ['skɔːpɪən] *n* alacrán *m*, escorpión
m.
Scot [skɔt] *n* escocés/esa *m/f*.
Scotch [skɔtʃ] *n* whisky *m* escocés.
scotch [skɔtʃ] *vt* (*rumour*) desmentir; (*plan*)
frustrar.
Scotch tape ® *n* (*US*) cinta adhesiva, celo,
scotch ® *m*.
scot-free [skɔt'friː] *adv*: **to get off ~**
(*unpunished*) salir impune; (*unhurt*) salir
ileso.
Scotland ['skɔtlənd] *n* Escocia.
Scots [skɔts] *adj* escocés/esa.
Scotsman ['skɔtsmən] *n* escocés *m*.
Scotswoman ['skɔtswumən] *n* escocesa.
Scottish ['skɔtɪʃ] *adj* escocés/esa; **the ~
National Party** *partido político
independista escocés*; **the ~ Parliament**
el Parlamento escocés.
scoundrel ['skaundrəl] *n* canalla *m/f*,
sinvergüenza *m/f*.
scour ['skauə*] *vt* (*clean*) fregar, estregar;
(*search*) recorrer, registrar.
scourer ['skauərə*] *n* (*pad*) estropajo;
(*powder*) limpiador *m*.
scourge [skəːdʒ] *n* azote *m*.
scout [skaut] *n* (*MIL, also*: **boy ~**)
explorador *m*.
▶**scout around** *vi* reconocer el terreno.
scowl [skaul] *vi* fruncir el ceño; **to ~ at sb**
mirar con ceño a algn.
scrabble ['skræbl] *vi* (*claw*): **to ~ (at)** arañar
♦ *n*: **S~** ® Intelect *m* ®; **to ~ around for
sth** revolver todo buscando algo.
scraggy ['skrægɪ] *adj* flaco, delgaducho.
scram [skræm] *vi* (*col*) largarse.
scramble ['skræmbl] *n* (*climb*) subida
(difícil); (*struggle*) pelea ♦ *vi*: **to ~ out/
through** salir/abrirse paso con dificultad;
to ~ for pelear por; **to go scrambling**

(*SPORT*) hacer motocrós.
scrambled eggs ['skræmbld-] *npl* huevos
mpl revueltos.
scrap [skræp] *n* (*bit*) pedacito; (*fig*) pizca;
(*fight*) riña, bronca; (*also*: **~ iron**)
chatarra, hierro viejo ♦ *vt* (*discard*)
desechar, descartar ♦ *vi* reñir, armar
(una) bronca; **~s** *npl* (*waste*) sobras *fpl*,
desperdicios *mpl*; **to sell sth for ~** vender
algo como chatarra.
scrapbook ['skræpbuk] *n* álbum *m* de
recortes.
scrap dealer *n* chatarrero/a.
scrape [skreɪp] *n* (*fig*) lío, apuro ♦ *vt* raspar;
(*skin etc*) rasguñar; (**~ against**) rozar.
▶**scrape through** *vi* (*succeed*) salvarse por
los pelos; (*exam*) aprobar por los pelos.
scraper ['skreɪpə*] *n* raspador *m*.
scrap heap *n* (*fig*): **on the ~** desperdiciado;
to throw sth on the ~ desechar *or*
descartar algo.
scrap iron *n* chatarra.
scrap merchant *n* (*BRIT*) chatarrero/a.
scrap metal *n* chatarra, desecho de metal.
scrap paper *n* pedazos *mpl* de papel.
scrappy ['skræpɪ] *adj* (*essay etc*)
deshilvanado; (*education*) incompleto.
scrap yard *n* depósito de chatarra; (*for
cars*) cementerio de coches.
scratch [skrætʃ] *n* rasguño; (*from claw*)
arañazo ♦ *adj*: **~ team** equipo
improvisado ♦ *vt* (*record*) rayar; (*with
claw, nail*) rasguñar, arañar; (*COMPUT*)
borrar ♦ *vi* rascarse; **to start from ~**
partir de cero; **to be up to ~** cumplir con
los requisitos.
scratchpad ['skrætʃpæd] *n* (*US*) bloc *m* de
notas.
scrawl [skrɔːl] *n* garabatos *mpl* ♦ *vi* hacer
garabatos.
scrawny ['skrɔːnɪ] *adj* (*person, neck*) flaco.
scream [skriːm] *n* chillido ♦ *vi* chillar; **it
was a ~** (*fig, col*) fue para morirse de
risa; **he's a ~** (*fig, col*) es muy divertido
or de lo más gracioso; **to ~ at sb (to do
sth)** gritarle a algn (para que haga algo).
scree [skriː] *n* cono de desmoronamiento.
screech [skriːtʃ] *vi* chirriar.
screen [skriːn] *n* (*CINE, TV*) pantalla;
(*movable*) biombo; (*wall*) tabique *m*; (*also*:
wind~) parabrisas *m inv* ♦ *vt* (*conceal*)
tapar; (*from the wind etc*) proteger; (*film*)
proyectar; (*fig: person: for security*)
investigar; (*: for illness*) hacer una
exploración a.
screen editing *n* (*COMPUT*) corrección *f* en
pantalla.
screenful ['skriːnful] *n* pantalla.

screening ['skriːnɪŋ] n (of film) proyección f; (for security) investigación f; (MED) exploración f.

screen memory n (COMPUT) memoria de la pantalla.

screenplay ['skriːnpleɪ] n guión m.

screen saver [-seɪvə*] n salvapantallas m inv.

screen test n prueba de pantalla.

screw [skruː] n tornillo; (propeller) hélice f ♦ vt atornillar; **to ~ sth to the wall** fijar algo a la pared con tornillos.

▶**screw up** vt (paper, material etc) arrugar; (col: ruin) fastidiar; **to ~ up one's eyes** arrugar el entrecejo; **to ~ up one's face** torcer or arrugar la cara.

screwdriver ['skruːdraɪvə*] n destornillador m.

screwed-up ['skruːd'ʌp] adj (col): **she's totally ~** está trastornada.

screwy ['skruːɪ] adj (col) chiflado.

scribble ['skrɪbl] n garabatos mpl ♦ vt escribir con prisa; **to ~ sth down** garabatear algo.

script [skrɪpt] n (CINE etc) guión m; (writing) escritura, letra.

scripted ['skrɪptɪd] adj (RADIO, TV) escrito.

Scripture ['skrɪptʃə*] n Sagrada Escritura.

scriptwriter ['skrɪptraɪtə*] n guionista m/f.

scroll [skrəʊl] n rollo ♦ vt (COMPUT) desplazar.

scrotum ['skrəʊtəm] n escroto.

scrounge [skraʊndʒ] (col) vt: **to ~ sth off** or **from sb** gorronear algo a algn ♦ vi: **to ~ on sb** vivir a costa de algn.

scrounger ['skraʊndʒə*] n gorrón/ona m/f.

scrub [skrʌb] n (clean) fregado; (land) maleza ♦ vt fregar, restregar; (reject) cancelar, anular.

scrubbing brush ['skrʌbɪŋ-] n cepillo de fregar.

scruff [skrʌf] n: **by the ~ of the neck** por el pescuezo.

scruffy ['skrʌfɪ] adj desaliñado, desaseado.

scrum(mage) ['skrʌm(mɪdʒ)] n (RUGBY) melée f.

scruple ['skruːpl] n escrúpulo; **to have no ~s about doing sth** no tener reparos en or escrúpulos para hacer algo.

scrupulous ['skruːpjʊləs] adj escrupuloso.

scrupulously ['skruːpjʊləslɪ] adv escrupulosamente; **to be ~ fair/honest** ser sumamente justo/honesto.

scrutinize ['skruːtɪnaɪz] vt escudriñar; (votes) escrutar.

scrutiny ['skruːtɪnɪ] n escrutinio, examen m; **under the ~ of sb** bajo la mirada or el escrutinio de algn.

scuba ['skuːbə] n escafandra autónoma.

scuba diving n submarinismo.

scuff [skʌf] vt (shoes, floor) rayar.

scuffle ['skʌfl] n refriega.

scullery ['skʌlərɪ] n trascocina.

sculptor ['skʌlptə*] n escultor(a) m/f.

sculpture ['skʌlptʃə*] n escultura.

scum [skʌm] n (on liquid) espuma; (pej: people) escoria.

scupper ['skʌpə*] vt (BRIT: boat) hundir; (: fig: plans etc) acabar con.

scurrilous ['skʌrɪləs] adj difamatorio, calumnioso.

scurry ['skʌrɪ] vi: **to ~ off** escabullirse.

scurvy ['skəːvɪ] n escorbuto.

scuttle ['skʌtl] n (also: **coal ~**) cubo, carbonera ♦ vt (ship) barrenar ♦ vi (scamper): **to ~ away, ~ off** escabullirse.

scythe [saɪð] n guadaña.

SD, S. Dak. abbr (US) = South Dakota.

SDI n abbr (= Strategic Defense Initiative) IDE f.

SDLP n abbr (BRIT POL) = Social Democratic and Labour Party.

SDP n abbr (BRIT POL) = Social Democratic Party.

sea [siː] n mar m/f; **by ~** (travel) en barco; **on the ~** (boat) en el mar; (town) junto al mar; **to be all at ~** (fig) estar despistado; **out to** or **at ~** en alta mar; **to go by ~** ir en barco; **heavy** or **rough ~s** marejada; **by** or **beside the ~** (holiday) en la playa; (village) a orillas del mar; **a ~ of faces** una multitud de caras.

sea bed n fondo del mar.

sea bird n ave f marina.

seaboard ['siːbɔːd] n litoral m.

sea breeze n brisa de mar.

seadog ['siːdɒg] n lobo de mar.

seafarer ['siːfɛərə*] n marinero.

seafaring ['siːfɛərɪŋ] adj (community) marinero; (life) de marinero.

seafood ['siːfuːd] n mariscos mpl.

sea front n paseo marítimo.

seagoing ['siːgəʊɪŋ] adj (ship) de alta mar.

seagull ['siːgʌl] n gaviota.

seal [siːl] n (animal) foca; (stamp) sello ♦ vt (close) cerrar; (: with ~) sellar; (decide: sb's fate) decidir; (: bargain) cerrar; **~ of approval** sello de aprobación.

▶**seal off** vt obturar.

seal cull n matanza de crías de foca.

sea level n nivel m del mar.

sealing wax ['siːlɪŋ-] n lacre m.

sea lion n león m marino.

sealskin ['siːlskɪn] n piel f de foca.

seam [siːm] n costura; (of metal) juntura; (of coal) veta, filón m; **the hall was**

bursting at the ~s la sala rebosaba de gente.

seaman ['si:mən] *n* marinero.

seamanship ['si:mənʃɪp] *n* náutica.

seance ['seɪɒns] *n* sesión *f* de espiritismo.

seaplane ['si:pleɪn] *n* hidroavión *m*.

seaport ['si:pɔ:t] *n* puerto de mar.

search [sɔ:tʃ] *n* (*for person, thing*) busca, búsqueda; (*of drawer, pockets*) registro; (*inspection*) reconocimiento ♦ *vt* (*look in*) buscar en; (*examine*) examinar; (*person, place*) registrar; (*COMPUT*) buscar ♦ *vi*: **to ~ for** buscar; **in ~ of** en busca de; "**~ and replace**" (*COMPUT*) "buscar y reemplazar".

►**search through** *vt fus* registrar.

search engine *n* (*INTERNET*) buscador *m*.

searcher ['sɔ:tʃə*] *n* buscador(a) *m/f*.

searching ['sɔ:tʃɪŋ] *adj* (*question*) penetrante.

searchlight ['sɔ:tʃlaɪt] *n* reflector *m*.

search party *n* equipo de salvamento.

search warrant *n* mandamiento judicial.

searing ['sɪərɪŋ] *adj* (*heat*) abrasador(a); (*pain*) agudo.

seashore ['si:ʃɔ*] *n* playa, orilla del mar; **on the ~** a la orilla del mar.

seasick ['si:sɪk] *adj* mareado; **to be ~** marearse.

seaside ['si:saɪd] *n* playa, orilla del mar; **to go to the ~** ir a la playa.

seaside resort *n* playa.

season ['si:zn] *n* (*of year*) estación *f*; (*sporting etc*) temporada; (*gen*) época, período ♦ *vt* (*food*) sazonar; **to be in/out of ~** estar en sazón/fuera de temporada; **the busy ~** (*for shops, hotels etc*) la temporada alta; **the open ~** (*HUNTING*) la temporada de caza *or* de pesca.

seasonal ['si:znl] *adj* estacional.

seasoned ['si:znd] *adj* (*wood*) curado; (*fig: worker, actor*) experimentado; (*troops*) curtido; **~ campaigner** veterano/a.

seasoning ['si:znɪŋ] *n* condimento.

season ticket *n* abono.

seat [si:t] *n* (*in bus, train: place*) asiento; (*chair*) silla; (*PARLIAMENT*) escaño; (*buttocks*) trasero; (*centre: of government etc*) sede *f* ♦ *vt* sentar; (*have room for*) tener cabida para; **are there any ~s left?** ¿quedan plazas?; **to take one's ~** sentarse, tomar asiento; **to be ~ed** estar sentado, sentarse.

seat belt *n* cinturón *m* de seguridad.

seating ['si:tɪŋ] *n* asientos *mpl*.

seating arrangements *npl* distribución *fsg* de los asientos.

seating capacity *n* número de asientos,

aforo.

SEATO ['si:təu] *n abbr* (= *Southeast Asia Treaty Organization*) OTASE *f*.

sea water *n* agua *m* del mar.

seaweed ['si:wi:d] *n* alga marina.

seaworthy ['si:wə:ðɪ] *adj* en condiciones de navegar.

SEC *n abbr* (*US*: = *Securities and Exchange Commission*) comisión de operaciones bursátiles.

sec. *abbr* = **second(s)**.

secateurs [sɛkə'tə:z] *npl* podadera *sg*.

secluded [sɪ'klu:dɪd] *adj* retirado.

seclusion [sɪ'klu:ʒən] *n* retiro.

second ['sɛkənd] *adj* segundo ♦ *adv* (*in race etc*) en segundo lugar ♦ *n* (*gen*) segundo; (*AUT: also*: **~ gear**) segunda; (*COMM*) artículo con algún desperfecto; (*BRIT SCOL: degree*) título universitario de segunda clase ♦ *vt* (*motion*) apoyar; [sɪ'kɒnd] (*employee*) trasladar temporalmente; **~ floor** (*BRIT*) segundo piso; (*US*) primer piso; **Charles the S~** Carlos Segundo; **to ask for a ~ opinion** (*MED*) pedir una segunda opinión; **just a ~!** ¡un momento!; **to have ~ thoughts** cambiar de opinión; **on ~ thoughts** *or* (*US*) **thought** pensándolo bien; **~ mortgage** segunda hipoteca.

secondary ['sɛkəndərɪ] *adj* secundario.

secondary education *n* enseñanza secundaria.

secondary school *n* escuela secundaria; *ver recuadro*.

┌─────────────────────────────────────┐
SECONDARY SCHOOL

En el Reino Unido se llama **secondary school** *a un centro educativo para alumnos de 11 a 18 años, si bien muchos estudiantes acaban a los 16, edad mínima de escolarización obligatoria. La mayor parte de estos centros funcionan como "comprehensive schools", aunque aún existen algunos de tipo selectivo.*
└─────────────────────────────────────┘

---

second-best [sɛkənd'bɛst] *n* segundo.

second-class ['sɛkənd'klɑːs] *adj* de segunda clase ♦ *adv*: **to send sth ~** enviar algo por correo de segunda clase; **to travel ~** viajar en segunda; **~ citizen** ciudadano/a de segunda (clase).

second cousin *n* primo/a segundo/a.

seconder ['sɛkəndə*] *n* el/la que apoya una moción.

second-guess ['sɛkənd'gɛs] *vt* (*evaluate*) juzgar (a posteriori); (*anticipate*): **to ~ sth/sb** (intentar) adivinar algo/lo que va a hacer algn.

secondhand ['sɛkənd'hænd] *adj* de segunda mano, usado ♦ *adv*: **to buy sth** ~ comprar algo de segunda mano; **to hear sth** ~ oír algo indirectamente.

second hand *n* (*on clock*) segundero.

second-in-command ['sɛkəndınkə'mɑːnd] *n* (*MIL*) segundo en el mando; (*ADMIN*) segundo/a, ayudante *m/f*.

secondly ['sɛkəndlı] *adv* en segundo lugar.

secondment [sı'kɔndmənt] *n* (*BRIT*) traslado temporal.

second-rate ['sɛkənd'reıt] *adj* de segunda categoría.

secrecy ['siːkrəsı] *n* secreto.

secret ['siːkrıt] *adj, n* secreto; **in** ~ *adv* en secreto; **to keep sth** ~ (**from sb**) ocultarle algo (a algn); **to make no** ~ **of sth** no ocultar algo.

secret agent *n* agente *m/f* secreto/a, espía *m/f*.

secretarial [sɛkrı'tɛərıəl] *adj* (*course*) de secretariado; (*staff*) de secretaría; (*work, duties*) de secretaria.

secretariat [sɛkrı'tɛərıət] *n* secretaría.

secretary ['sɛkrətərı] *n* secretario/a; **S~ of State** (*BRIT POL*) Ministro (con cartera).

secretary-general ['sɛkrətərı'dʒɛnərl] *n* secretario/a general.

secretary pool *n* (*US*) = **typing pool**.

secrete [sı'kriːt] *vt* (*MED, ANAT, BIO*) secretar; (*hide*) ocultar, esconder.

secretion [sı'kriːʃən] *n* secreción *f*.

secretive ['siːkrətıv] *adj* reservado, sigiloso.

secretly ['siːkrıtlı] *adv* en secreto.

secret police *n* policía secreta.

secret service *n* servicio secreto.

sect [sɛkt] *n* secta.

sectarian [sɛk'tɛərıən] *adj* sectario.

section ['sɛkʃən] *n* sección *f*; (*part*) parte *f*; (*of document*) artículo; (*of opinion*) sector *m*; **business** ~ (*PRESS*) sección *f* de economía.

sectional ['sɛkʃənl] *adj* (*regional*) regional, local.

sector ['sɛktə*] *n* (*gen, COMPUT*) sector *m*.

secular ['sɛkjulə*] *adj* secular, seglar.

secure [sı'kjuə*] *adj* (*free from anxiety*) seguro; (*firmly fixed*) firme, fijo ♦ *vt* (*fix*) asegurar, afianzar; (*get*) conseguir; (*COMM: loan*) garantizar; **to make sth** ~ afianzar algo; **to** ~ **sth for sb** conseguir algo para algn.

secured creditor [sı'kjuəd-] *n* acreedor(a) *m/f* con garantía.

securely [sı'kjuəlı] *adv* firmemente; **it is** ~ **fastened** está bien sujeto.

security [sı'kjuərıtı] *n* seguridad *f*; (*for loan*) fianza; (: *object*) prenda; **securities** *npl* (*COMM*) valores *mpl*, títulos *mpl*; ~ **of tenure** tenencia asegurada; **to increase/ tighten** ~ aumentar/estrechar las medidas de seguridad; **job** ~ seguridad *f* en el empleo.

Security Council *n*: **the** ~ el Consejo de Seguridad.

security forces *npl* fuerzas *fpl* de seguridad.

security guard *n* guardia *m/f* de seguridad.

security risk *n* riesgo para la seguridad.

secy. *abbr* (= *secretary*) Srio/a.

sedan [sı'dæn] *n* (*US AUT*) sedán *m*.

sedate [sı'deıt] *adj* tranquilo ♦ *vt* administrar sedantes a, sedar.

sedation [sı'deıʃən] *n* (*MED*) sedación *f*; **to be under** ~ estar bajo sedación.

sedative ['sɛdıtıv] *n* sedante *m*, calmante *m*.

sedentary ['sɛdntrı] *adj* sedentario.

sediment ['sɛdımənt] *n* sedimento.

sedimentary [sɛdı'mɛntərı] *adj* (*GEO*) sedimentario.

sedition [sı'dıʃən] *n* sedición *f*.

seduce [sı'djuːs] *vt* (*gen*) seducir.

seduction [sı'dʌkʃən] *n* seducción *f*.

seductive [sı'dʌktıv] *adj* seductor(a).

see [siː] *vb* (*pt* **saw**, *pp* **seen** [sɔː, siːn]) *vt* (*gen*) ver; (*understand*) ver, comprender; (*look at*) mirar ♦ *vi* ver ♦ *n* sede *f*; **to** ~ **sb to the door** acompañar a algn a la puerta; **to** ~ **that** (*ensure*) asegurarse de que; ~ **you soon/later/tomorrow!** ¡hasta pronto/ luego/mañana!; **as far as I can** ~ por lo visto *or* por lo que veo; **there was nobody to be** ~**n** no se veía a nadie; **let me** ~ (*show me*) a ver; (*let me think*) vamos a ver; **to go and** ~ **sb** ir a ver a algn; ~ **for yourself** compruébalo tú mismo; **I don't know what she** ~**s in him** no sé qué le encuentra.

▶**see about** *vt fus* atender a, encargarse de.

▶**see off** *vt* despedir.

▶**see through** *vt fus* calar ♦ *vt* llevar a cabo.

▶**see to** *vt fus* atender a, encargarse de.

seed [siːd] *n* semilla; (*in fruit*) pepita; (*fig*) germen *m*; (*TENNIS*) preseleccionado/a; **to go to** ~ (*plant*) granar; (*fig*) descuidarse.

seedless ['siːdlıs] *adj* sin semillas *or* pepitas.

seedling ['siːdlıŋ] *n* planta de semillero.

seedy ['siːdı] *adj* (*person*) desaseado; (*place*) sórdido.

seeing ['siːıŋ] *conj*: ~ (**that**) visto que, en vista de que.

seek, *pt, pp* **sought** [si:k, sɔ:t] *vt (gen)*
buscar; *(post)* solicitar; **to ~ advice/help
from sb** pedir consejos/solicitar ayuda a
algn.
▸**seek out** *vt (person)* buscar.
seem [si:m] *vi* parecer; **there ~s to be...**
parece que hay ...; **it ~s (that)** ... parece
que ...; **what ~s to be the trouble?** ¿qué
pasa?; **I did what ~ed best** hice lo que
parecía mejor.
seemingly ['si:mıŋlı] *adv* aparentemente,
según parece.
seen [si:n] *pp of* **see.**
seep [si:p] *vi* filtrarse.
seer [sıə*] *n* vidente *m/f*, profeta *m/f*.
seersucker [sıə'sʌkə*] *n* sirsaca.
seesaw ['si:sɔ:] *n* balancín *m*, subibaja *m*.
seethe [si:ð] *vi* hervir; **to ~ with anger**
enfurecerse.
see-through ['si:θru:] *adj* transparente.
segment ['sɛgmənt] *n* segmento.
segregate ['sɛgrıgeıt] *vt* segregar.
segregation [sɛgrı'geıʃən] *n* segregación *f*.
Seine [seın] *n* Sena *m*.
seismic ['saızmık] *adj* sísmico.
seize [si:z] *vt (grasp)* agarrar, asir; *(take
possession of)* secuestrar; *(: territory)*
apoderarse de; *(opportunity)*
aprovecharse de.
▸**seize up** *vi (TECH)* agarrotarse.
▸**seize (up)on** *vt fus* valerse de.
seizure ['si:ʒə*] *n (MED)* ataque *m*; *(LAW)*
incautación *f*.
seldom ['sɛldəm] *adv* rara vez.
select [sı'lɛkt] *adj* selecto, escogido; *(hotel,
restaurant, clubs)* exclusivo ♦ *vt* escoger,
elegir; *(SPORT)* seleccionar; **a ~ few** una
minoría selecta.
selection [sı'lɛkʃən] *n* selección *f*, elección
f; *(COMM)* surtido.
selection committee *n* comisión *f* de
nombramiento.
selective [sı'lɛktıv] *adj* selectivo.
self [sɛlf] *n (pl* **selves** [sɛlvz]*)* uno mismo
♦ *pref* auto ...; **the ~** el yo.
self-addressed ['sɛlfə'drɛst] *adj:* **~
envelope** sobre *m* con la dirección propia.
self-adhesive [sɛlfəd'hi:zıv] *adj*
autoadhesivo, autoadherente.
self-appointed [sɛlfə'pɔıntıd] *adj*
autonombrado.
self-assurance [sɛlfə'ʃuərəns] *n* confianza
en sí mismo.
self-assured [sɛlfə'ʃuəd] *adj* seguro de sí
mismo.
self-catering [sɛlf'keıtərıŋ] *adj (BRIT)* sin
pensión *or* servicio de comida; **~
apartment** apartamento con cocina

propia.
self-centred, *(US)* **self-centered**
[sɛlf'sɛntəd] *adj* egocéntrico.
self-cleaning [sɛlf'kli:nıŋ] *adj*
autolimpiador.
self-confessed [sɛlfkən'fɛst] *adj (alcoholic
etc)* confeso.
self-confidence [sɛlf'kɒnfıdns] *n* confianza
en sí mismo.
self-confident [sɛlf'kɒnfıdnt] *adj* seguro de
sí (mismo), lleno de confianza en sí
mismo.
self-conscious [sɛlf'kɒnʃəs] *adj* cohibido.
self-contained [sɛlfkən'teınd] *adj (gen)*
independiente; *(BRIT: flat)* con entrada
particular.
self-control [sɛlfkən'trəul] *n* autodominio.
self-defeating [sɛlfdı'fi:tıŋ] *adj*
contraproducente.
self-defence, *(US)* **self-defense**
[sɛlfdı'fɛns] *n* defensa propia.
self-discipline [sɛlf'dısıplın] *n*
autodisciplina.
self-employed [sɛlfım'plɔıd] *adj* que
trabaja por cuenta propia, autónomo.
self-esteem [sɛlfı'sti:m] *n* amor *m* propio.
self-evident [sɛlf'ɛvıdnt] *adj* patente.
self-explanatory [sɛlfıks'plænətərı] *adj* que
no necesita explicación.
self-financing [sɛlffaı'nænsıŋ] *adj*
autofinanciado.
self-governing [sɛlf'gʌvənıŋ] *adj*
autónomo.
self-help ['sɛlf'hɛlp] *n* autosuficiencia,
ayuda propia.
self-importance [sɛlfım'pɔ:tns] *n*
presunción *f*, vanidad *f*.
self-important [sɛlfım'pɔ:tnt] *adj* vanidoso.
self-indulgent [sɛlfın'dʌldʒənt] *adj*
indulgente consigo mismo.
self-inflicted [sɛlfın'flıktıd] *adj* infligido a sí
mismo.
self-interest [sɛlf'ıntrıst] *n* egoísmo.
selfish ['sɛlfıʃ] *adj* egoísta.
selfishly ['sɛlfıʃlı] *adv* con egoísmo, de
modo egoísta.
selfishness ['sɛlfıʃnıs] *n* egoísmo.
selflessly ['sɛlflıslı] *adv*
desinteresadamente.
selfless ['sɛlflıs] *adj* desinteresado.
self-made man ['sɛlfmeıd-] *n* hombre que
ha triunfado por su propio esfuerzo.
self-pity [sɛlf'pıtı] *n* lástima de sí mismo.
self-portrait [sɛlf'pɔ:treıt] *n* autorretrato.
self-possessed [sɛlfpə'zɛst] *adj* sereno,
dueño de sí mismo.
self-preservation ['sɛlfprɛzə'veıʃən] *n*
propia conservación *f*.

self-propelled [sɛlfprə'pɛld] *adj* autopropulsado, automotor/triz.

self-raising [sɛlf'reɪzɪŋ], (*US*) **self-rising** [sɛlf'raɪzɪŋ] *adj*: ~ **flour** harina con levadura.

self-reliant [sɛlfrɪ'laɪənt] *adj* independiente, autosuficiente.

self-respect [sɛlfrɪ'spɛkt] *n* amor *m* propio.

self-respecting [sɛlfrɪ'spɛktɪŋ] *adj* que tiene amor propio.

self-righteous [sɛlf'raɪtʃəs] *adj* santurrón/ ona.

self-rising [sɛlf'raɪzɪŋ] *adj* (*US*) = **self-raising**.

self-sacrifice [sɛlf'sækrɪfaɪs] *n* abnegación *f*.

self-same [sɛlfseɪm] *adj* mismo, mismísimo.

self-satisfied [sɛlf'sætɪsfaɪd] *adj* satisfecho de sí mismo.

self-service [sɛlf'səːvɪs] *adj* de autoservicio.

self-styled ['sɛlfstaɪld] *adj* supuesto, sedicente.

self-sufficient [sɛlfsə'fɪʃənt] *adj* autosuficiente.

self-supporting [sɛlfsə'pɔːtɪŋ] *adj* económicamente independiente.

self-tanning [sɛlf'tænɪŋ] *adj* autobronceador.

self-taught [sɛlf'tɔːt] *adj* autodidacta.

self-test ['sɛlftɛst] *n* (*COMPUT*) autocomprobación *f*.

sell, *pt, pp* **sold** [sɛl, səʊld] *vt* vender ♦ *vi* venderse; **to ~ at** *or* **for £10** venderse a 10 libras; **to ~ sb an idea** (*fig*) convencer a algn de una idea.

▶**sell off** *vt* liquidar.

▶**sell out** *vi* transigir, transar (*LAM*); **to ~ out (to sb/sth)** (*COMM*) vender su negocio (a algn/algo) ♦ *vt* agotar las existencias de, venderlo todo; **the tickets are all sold out** las entradas están agotadas.

▶**sell up** *vi* (*COMM*) liquidarse.

sell-by date ['sɛlbaɪ-] *n* fecha de caducidad.

seller ['sɛlə*] *n* vendedor(a) *m/f*; ~'**s market** mercado de demanda.

selling price ['sɛlɪŋ-] *n* precio de venta.

Sellotape ® ['sɛləʊteɪp] *n* (*BRIT*) cinta adhesiva, celo, scotch ® *m*.

sellout ['sɛlaʊt] *n* traición *f*; **it was a ~** (*THEAT etc*) fue un éxito de taquilla.

selves [sɛlvz] *npl of* **self**.

semantic [sɪ'mæntɪk] *adj* semántico.

semaphore ['sɛməfɔː*] *n* semáforo.

semblance ['sɛmbləns] *n* apariencia.

semen ['siːmən] *n* semen *m*.

semester [sɪ'mɛstə*] *n* (*US*) semestre *m*.

semi ['sɛmɪ] *n* = **semidetached house**.

semi... [sɛmɪ] *pref* semi..., medio....

semicircle ['sɛmɪsəːkl] *n* semicírculo.

semicircular ['sɛmɪ'səːkjulə*] *adj* semicircular.

semicolon [sɛmɪ'kəʊlən] *n* punto y coma.

semiconductor [sɛmɪkən'dʌktə*] *n* semiconductor *m*.

semiconscious [sɛmɪ'kɔnʃəs] *adj* semiconsciente.

semidetached (house) [sɛmɪdɪ'tætʃt-] *n* casa adosada.

semi-final [sɛmɪ'faɪnl] *n* semi-final *f*.

seminar ['sɛmɪnɑː*] *n* seminario.

seminary ['sɛmɪnərɪ] *n* (*REL*) seminario.

semiprecious stone [sɛmɪ'prɛʃəs-] *n* piedra semipreciosa.

semiquaver ['sɛmɪkweɪvə*] *n* (*BRIT*) semicorchea.

semiskilled ['sɛmɪskɪld] *adj* (*work*, *worker*) semicualificado.

semi-skimmed *adj* semidesnatado.

semitone ['sɛmɪtəʊn] *n* semitono.

semolina [sɛmə'liːnə] *n* sémola.

SEN *n abbr* (*BRIT*) = *State Enrolled Nurse*.

Sen., sen. *abbr* = **senator, senior**.

senate ['sɛnɪt] *n* senado; *see also* **Congress**.

senator ['sɛnɪtə*] *n* senador(a) *m/f*.

send, *pt, pp* **sent** [sɛnd, sɛnt] *vt* mandar, enviar; **to ~ by post** mandar por correo; **to ~ sb for sth** mandar a algn a buscar algo; **to ~ word that ...** avisar *or* mandar aviso de que ...; **she ~s (you) her love** te manda *or* envía cariñosos recuerdos; **to ~ sb to sleep/into fits of laughter** dormir/hacer reír a algn; **to ~ sb flying** echar a algn; **to ~ sth flying** tirar algo.

▶**send away** *vt* (*letter, goods*) despachar.

▶**send away for** *vt fus* pedir.

▶**send back** *vt* devolver.

▶**send for** *vt fus* mandar traer; (*by post*) escribir pidiendo algo.

▶**send in** *vt* (*report, application*) mandar.

▶**send off** *vt* (*goods*) despachar; (*BRIT SPORT: player*) expulsar.

▶**send on** *vt* (*letter*) mandar, expedir; (*luggage etc: in advance*) facturar.

▶**send out** *vt* (*invitation*) mandar; (*emit: light, heat*) emitir, difundir; (: *signal*) emitir.

▶**send round** *vt* (*letter, document etc*) hacer circular.

▶**send up** *vt* (*person, price*) hacer subir; (*BRIT: parody*) parodiar.

sender ['sɛndə*] *n* remitente *m/f*.

send-off ['sɛndɔf] *n*: **a good ~** una buena despedida.

send-up ['sɛndʌp] *n* (*col*) parodia, sátira.

Senegal [senɪ'gɔːl] *n* Senegal *m*.
Senegalese [senɪɡə'liːz] *adj, n* senegalés/esa *m/f*.
senile ['siːnaɪl] *adj* senil.
senility [sɪ'nɪlɪtɪ] *n* senilidad *f*.
senior ['siːnɪə*] *adj* (*older*) mayor, más viejo; (: *on staff*) más antiguo; (*of higher rank*) superior ♦ *n* mayor *m*; **P. Jones ~ P. Jones** padre.
senior citizen *n* persona de la tercera edad.
senior high school *n* (*US*) ≈ instituto de enseñanza media; *see also* **high school**.
seniority [siːnɪ'ɔrɪtɪ] *n* antigüedad *f*; (*in rank*) rango superior.
sensation [sen'seɪʃən] *n* (*physical feeling, impression*) sensación *f*.
sensational [sen'seɪʃənl] *adj* sensacional.
sense [sens] *n* (*faculty, meaning*) sentido; (*feeling*) sensación *f*; (*good ~*) sentido común, juicio ♦ *vt* sentir, percibir; **~ of humour** sentido del humor; **it makes ~** tiene sentido; **there is no ~ in (doing) that** no tiene sentido (hacer) eso; **to come to one's ~s** (*regain consciousness*) volver en sí, recobrar el sentido; **to take leave of one's ~s** perder el juicio.
senseless ['senslɪs] *adj* estúpido, insensato; (*unconscious*) sin conocimiento.
senselessly ['senslɪslɪ] *adv* estúpidamente, insensatamente.
sensibility [sensɪ'bɪlɪtɪ] *n* sensibilidad *f*; **sensibilities** *npl* delicadeza *sg*.
sensible ['sensɪbl] *adj* sensato; (*reasonable*) razonable, lógico.
sensibly ['sensɪblɪ] *adv* sensatamente; razonablemente, de modo lógico.
sensitive ['sensɪtɪv] *adj* sensible; (*touchy*) susceptible; **he is very ~ about it** es muy susceptible acerca de eso.
sensitivity [sensɪ'tɪvɪtɪ] *n* sensibilidad *f*; susceptibilidad *f*.
sensual ['sensjuəl] *adj* sensual.
sensuous ['sensjuəs] *adj* sensual.
sent [sent] *pt, pp of* **send**.
sentence ['sentəns] *n* (*LING*) frase *f*, oración *f*; (*LAW*) sentencia, fallo ♦ *vt*: **to ~ sb to death/to 5 years** condenar a algn a muerte/a 5 años de cárcel; **to pass ~ on sb** (*also fig*) sentenciar *or* condenar a algn.
sentiment ['sentɪmənt] *n* sentimiento; (*opinion*) opinión *f*.
sentimental [sentɪ'mentl] *adj* sentimental.
sentimentality [sentɪmen'tælɪtɪ] *n* sentimentalismo, sensiblería.
sentinel ['sentɪnl] *n* centinela *m*.
sentry ['sentrɪ] *n* centinela *m*.

sentry duty *n*: **to be on ~** estar de guardia, hacer guardia.
Seoul [səul] *n* Seúl *m*.
separable ['sepərəbl] *adj* separable.
separate *adj* ['seprɪt] separado; (*distinct*) distinto ♦ (*vb*: ['sepəreɪt]) *vt* separar; (*part*) dividir ♦ *vi* separarse; **~ from** separado *or* distinto de; **under ~ cover** (*COMM*) por separado; **to ~ into** dividir *or* separar en; **he is ~d from his wife, but not divorced** está separado de su mujer, pero no (está) divorciado.
separately ['seprɪtlɪ] *adv* por separado.
separates ['seprɪts] *npl* (*clothes*) coordinados *mpl*.
separation [sepə'reɪʃən] *n* separación *f*.
sepia ['siːpɪə] *adj* color sepia *inv*.
Sept. *abbr* (= *September*) sep.
September [sep'tembə*] *n* se(p)tiembre *m*.
septic ['septɪk] *adj* séptico; **to go ~** ponerse séptico.
septicaemia, (*US*) **septicemia** [septɪ'siːmɪə] *n* septicemia.
septic tank *n* fosa séptica.
sequel ['siːkwl] *n* consecuencia, resultado; (*of story*) continuación *f*.
sequence ['siːkwəns] *n* sucesión *f*, serie *f*; (*CINE*) secuencia; **in ~** en orden *or* serie.
sequential [sɪ'kwenʃəl] *adj*: **~ access** (*COMPUT*) acceso en serie.
sequin ['siːkwɪn] *n* lentejuela.
Serb [səːb] *adj, n* = **Serbian**.
Serbia ['səːbɪə] *n* Serbia.
Serbian ['səːbɪən] *adj* serbio ♦ *n* serbio/a; (*LING*) serbio.
Serbo-Croat ['səːbəu'krəuæt] *n* (*LING*) serbocroata *m*.
serenade [serə'neɪd] *n* serenata ♦ *vt* dar serenata a.
serene [sɪ'riːn] *adj* sereno, tranquilo.
serenely [sɪ'riːnlɪ] *adv* serenamente, tranquilamente.
serenity [sə'renɪtɪ] *n* serenidad *f*, tranquilidad *f*.
sergeant ['sɑːdʒənt] *n* sargento.
sergeant major *n* sargento mayor.
serial ['sɪərɪəl] *n* novela por entregas; (*TV*) telenovela.
serial access *n* (*COMPUT*) acceso en serie.
serial interface *n* (*COMPUT*) interface *m* en serie.
serialize ['sɪərɪəlaɪz] *vt* publicar/televisar por entregas.
serial killer *n* asesino/a múltiple.
serial number *n* número de serie.
serial printer *n* (*COMPUT*) impresora en serie.
series ['sɪəriːz] *n, pl inv* serie *f*.

serious ['sɪərɪəs] adj serio; (grave) grave; are you ~ (about it)? ¿lo dices en serio?

seriously ['sɪərɪəslɪ] adv en serio; (ill, wounded etc) gravemente; (col: extremely) de verdad; to take sth/sb ~ tomar algo/a algn en serio; he's ~ rich es una pasada de rico.

seriousness ['sɪərɪəsnɪs] n seriedad f; gravedad f.

sermon ['sə:mən] n sermón m.

serpent ['sə:pənt] n serpiente f.

serrated [sɪ'reɪtɪd] adj serrado, dentellado.

serum ['sɪərəm] n suero.

servant ['sə:vənt] n (gen) servidor(a) m/f; (house ~) criado/a.

serve [sə:v] vt servir; (customer) atender; (subj: train) tener parada en; (apprenticeship) hacer; (prison term) cumplir ♦ vi (servant, soldier etc) servir; (TENNIS) sacar ♦ n (TENNIS) saque m; it ~s him right se lo merece, se lo tiene merecido; to ~ a summons on sb entregar una citación a algn; it ~s my purpose me sirve para lo que quiero; are you being ~d? ¿le atienden?; the power station ~s the entire region la central eléctrica abastece a toda la región; to ~ as/for/to do servir de/para/para hacer; to ~ on a committee/a jury ser miembro de una comisión/un jurado.

▶**serve out, serve up** vt (food) servir.

service ['sə:vɪs] n (gen) servicio; (REL: Catholic) misa; (: other) oficio (religioso); (AUT) mantenimiento; (of dishes) juego ♦ vt (car, washing machine) mantener; (: repair) reparar; the S~s las fuerzas armadas; funeral ~ exequias fpl; to hold a ~ celebrar un oficio religioso; the essential ~s los servicios esenciales; medical/social ~s servicios mpl médicos/sociales; the train ~ to London los trenes a Londres; to be of ~ to sb ser útil a algn.

serviceable ['sə:vɪsəbl] adj servible, utilizable.

service area n (on motorway) área de servicios.

service charge n (BRIT) servicio.

service industries npl industrias fpl del servicio.

serviceman ['sə:vɪsmən] n militar m.

service station n estación f de servicio.

servicing ['sə:vɪsɪŋ] n (of car) revisión f; (of washing machine etc) servicio de reparaciones.

serviette [sə:vɪ'ɛt] n (BRIT) servilleta.

servile ['sə:vaɪl] adj servil.

session ['sɛʃən] n (sitting) sesión f; to be in ~ estar en sesión.

session musician n músico m/f de estudio.

set [sɛt] n juego; (RADIO) aparato; (TV) televisor m; (of utensils) batería; (of cutlery) cubierto; (of books) colección f; (TENNIS) set m; (group of people) grupo; (CINE) plató m; (THEAT) decorado; (HAIRDRESSING) marcado ♦ adj (fixed) fijo; (ready) listo; (resolved) resuelto, decidido ♦ (vb: pt, pp set) vt (place) poner, colocar; (fix) fijar; (adjust) ajustar, arreglar; (decide: rules etc) establecer, decidir; (assign: task) asignar; (: homework) poner ♦ vi (sun) ponerse; (jam, jelly) cuajarse; (concrete) fraguar; a ~ of false teeth una dentadura postiza; a ~ of dining-room furniture muebles mpl de comedor; ~ in one's ways con costumbres arraigadas; a ~ phrase una frase hecha; to be all ~ to do sth estar listo para hacer algo; to be ~ on doing sth estar empeñado en hacer algo; a novel ~ in Valencia una novela ambientada en Valencia; to ~ to music poner música a; to ~ on fire incendiar, prender fuego a; to ~ free poner en libertad; to ~ sth going poner algo en marcha; to ~ sail zarpar, hacerse a la mar.

▶**set about** vt fus: to ~ about doing sth ponerse a hacer algo.

▶**set aside** vt poner aparte, dejar de lado.

▶**set back** vt (progress): to ~ back (by) retrasar (por); a house ~ back from the road una casa apartada de la carretera.

▶**set down** vt (subj: bus, train) dejar; (record) poner por escrito.

▶**set in** vi (infection) declararse; (complications) comenzar; the rain has ~ in for the day parece que va a llover todo el día.

▶**set off** vi partir ♦ vt (bomb) hacer estallar; (cause to start) poner en marcha; (show up well) hacer resaltar.

▶**set out** vi: to ~ out to do sth proponerse hacer algo ♦ vt (arrange) disponer; (state) exponer; to ~ out (from) salir (de).

▶**set up** vt (organization) establecer.

setback ['sɛtbæk] n (hitch) revés m, contratiempo; (in health) recaída.

set menu n menú m.

set phrase n frase f hecha.

set square n cartabón m.

settee [sɛ'ti:] n sofá m.

setting ['sɛtɪŋ] n (scenery) marco; (of jewel) engaste m, montadura.

setting lotion n fijador m (para el pelo).

settle ['sɛtl] vt (argument, matter) resolver; (pay: bill, accounts) pagar, liquidar; (colonize: land) colonizar; (MED: calm)

calmar, sosegar ♦ *vi* (*dust etc*)
depositarse; (*weather*) estabilizarse; (*also:*
~ **down**) instalarse; (*calm down*)
tranquilizarse; **to ~ for sth** convenir en
aceptar algo; **to ~ on sth** decidirse por
algo; **that's ~d then** bueno, está
arreglado; **to ~ one's stomach** asentar el
estómago.
►**settle in** *vi* instalarse.
►**settle up** *vi*: **to ~ up with sb** ajustar
cuentas con algn.
settlement ['sɛtlmənt] *n* (*payment*)
liquidación *f*; (*agreement*) acuerdo,
convenio; (*village etc*) poblado; **in ~ of our
account** (*COMM*) en pago *or* liquidación
de nuestra cuenta.
settler ['sɛtlə*] *n* colono/a, colonizador(a)
m/f.
setup ['sɛtʌp] *n* sistema *m*.
seven ['sɛvn] *num* siete.
seventeen [sɛvn'tiːn] *num* diez y siete,
diecisiete.
seventh ['sɛvnθ] *adj* séptimo.
seventy ['sɛvntɪ] *num* setenta.
sever ['sɛvə*] *vt* cortar; (*relations*) romper.
several ['sɛvərl] *adj, pron* varios/as *m/fpl*,
algunos/as *m/fpl*; **~ of us** varios de
nosotros; **~ times** varias veces.
severance ['sɛvərəns] *n* (*of relations*)
ruptura.
severance pay *n* indemnización *f* por
despido.
severe [sɪ'vɪə*] *adj* severo; (*serious*) grave;
(*hard*) duro; (*pain*) intenso.
severely [sɪ'vɪəlɪ] *adv* severamente;
(*wounded, ill*) de gravedad, gravemente.
severity [sɪ'vɛrɪtɪ] *n* severidad *f*; gravedad
f; intensidad *f*.
Seville [sə'vɪl] *n* Sevilla.
sew [səu], *pt* **sewed**, *pp* **sewn** [səu, səud, səun] *vt,
vi* coser.
►**sew up** *vt* coser.
sewage ['suːɪdʒ] *n* (*effluence*) aguas *fpl*
residuales; (*system*) alcantarillado.
sewage works *n* estación *f* depuradora
(de aguas residuales).
sewer ['suːə*] *n* alcantarilla, cloaca.
sewing ['səuɪŋ] *n* costura.
sewing machine *n* máquina de coser.
sewn [səun] *pp of* **sew**.
sex [sɛks] *n* sexo; **the opposite ~** el sexo
opuesto; **to have ~ with sb** tener
relaciones (sexuales) con algn.
sex act *n* acto sexual, coito.
sex appeal *n* sex-appeal *m*, gancho.
sex education *n* educación *f* sexual.
sexism ['sɛksɪzəm] *n* sexismo.
sexist ['sɛksɪst] *adj, n* sexista *m/f*.

sex life *n* vida sexual.
sex object *n* objeto sexual.
sextant ['sɛkstənt] *n* sextante *m*.
sextet [sɛks'tɛt] *n* sexteto.
sexual ['sɛksjuəl] *adj* sexual; **~ assault**
atentado contra el pudor; **~ harassment**
acoso sexual; **~ intercourse** relaciones *fpl*
sexuales.
sexually ['sɛksjuəlɪ] *adv* sexualmente.
sexy ['sɛksɪ] *adj* sexy.
Seychelles [seɪ'ʃɛlz] *npl*: **the ~** las
Seychelles.
SF *n abbr* = **science fiction**.
SG *n abbr* (*US:* = *Surgeon General*) jefe del
servicio federal de sanidad.
Sgt *abbr* (= *sergeant*) sgto.
shabbily ['ʃæbɪlɪ] *adv* (*treat*) injustamente;
(*dressed*) pobremente.
shabbiness ['ʃæbɪnɪs] *n* (*of dress, person*)
aspecto desharrapado; (*of building*) mal
estado.
shabby ['ʃæbɪ] *adj* (*person*) desharrapado;
(*clothes*) raído, gastado.
shack [ʃæk] *n* choza, chabola.
shackle ['ʃækl] *vt* encadenar; (*fig*): **to be ~d
by sth** verse obstaculizado por algo.
shackles ['ʃæklz] *npl* grillos *mpl*, grilletes
mpl.
shade [ʃeɪd] *n* sombra; (*for lamp*) pantalla;
(*for eyes*) visera; (*of colour*) tono *m*,
tonalidad *f*; (*US: window ~*) persiana ♦ *vt*
dar sombra a; **~s** *npl* (*US: sunglasses*)
gafas *fpl* de sol; **in the ~** a la sombra;
(*small quantity*): **a ~ of** un poquito de; **a ~
smaller** un poquito más pequeño.
shadow ['ʃædəu] *n* sombra ♦ *vt* (*follow*)
seguir y vigilar; **without** *or* **beyond a ~
of doubt** sin lugar a dudas.
shadow cabinet *n* (*BRIT POL*) gobierno en
la oposición.
shadowy ['ʃædəuɪ] *adj* oscuro; (*dim*)
indistinto.
shady ['ʃeɪdɪ] *adj* sombreado; (*fig:
dishonest*) sospechoso; (: *deal*) turbio.
shaft [ʃɑːft] *n* (*of arrow, spear*) astil *m*; (*AUT,
TECH*) eje *m*, árbol *m*; (*of mine*) pozo; (*of
lift*) hueco, caja; (*of light*) rayo; **ventilator
~** chimenea de ventilación.
shaggy ['ʃægɪ] *adj* peludo.
shake [ʃeɪk] *vb* (*pt* **shook**, *pp* **shaken** [ʃuk,
'ʃeɪkn]) *vt* sacudir; (*building*) hacer
temblar; (*perturb*) inquietar, perturbar;
(*weaken*) debilitar; (*alarm*) trastornar ♦ *vi*
estremecerse; (*tremble*) temblar ♦ *n*
(*movement*) sacudida; **to ~ one's head** (*in
refusal*) negar con la cabeza; (*in dismay*)
mover *or* menear la cabeza, incrédulo; **to
~ hands with sb** estrechar la mano a

algn; **to ~ in one's shoes** (*fig*) temblar de miedo.
▶**shake off** *vt* sacudirse; (*fig*) deshacerse de.
▶**shake up** *vt* agitar.
shake-up ['ʃeɪkʌp] *n* reorganización *f*.
shakily ['ʃeɪkɪlɪ] *adv* (*reply*) con voz temblorosa *or* trémula; (*walk*) con paso vacilante; (*write*) con mano temblorosa.
shaky ['ʃeɪkɪ] *adj* (*unstable*) inestable, poco firme; (*trembling*) tembloroso; (*health*) delicado; (*memory*) defectuoso; (*person: from illness*) temblando; (*premise etc*) incierto.
shale [ʃeɪl] *n* esquisto.
shall [ʃæl] *aux vb*: **I ~ go** iré.
shallot [ʃə'lɒt] *n* (*BRIT*) cebollita, chalote *m*.
shallow ['ʃæləʊ] *adj* poco profundo; (*fig*) superficial.
shallows ['ʃæləʊz] *npl* bajío *sg*, bajos *mpl*.
sham [ʃæm] *n* fraude *m*, engaño ♦ *adj* falso, fingido ♦ *vt* fingir, simular.
shambles ['ʃæmblz] *n* desorden *m*, confusión *f*; **the economy is (in) a complete ~** la economía está en un estado desastroso.
shambolic [ʃæm'bɒlɪk] *adj* (*col*) caótico.
shame [ʃeɪm] *n* vergüenza; (*pity*) lástima, pena ♦ *vt* avergonzar; **it is a ~ that/to do** es una lástima *or* pena que/hacer; **what a ~!** ¡qué lástima *or* pena!; **to put sth/sb to ~** (*fig*) ridiculizar algo/a algn.
shamefaced ['ʃeɪmfeɪst] *adj* avergonzado.
shameful ['ʃeɪmful] *adj* vergonzoso.
shamefully ['ʃeɪmfulɪ] *adv* vergonzosamente.
shameless ['ʃeɪmlɪs] *adj* descarado.
shampoo [ʃæm'puː] *n* champú *m* ♦ *vt* lavar con champú.
shampoo and set *n* lavado y marcado.
shamrock ['ʃæmrɒk] *n* trébol *m*.
shandy ['ʃændɪ], (*US*) **shandygaff** ['ʃændɪgæf] *n* clara, cerveza con gaseosa.
shan't [ʃɑːnt] = **shall not**.
shantytown ['ʃæntɪtaun] *n* barrio de chabolas.
SHAPE [ʃeɪp] *n abbr* (= *Supreme Headquarters Allied Powers, Europe*) cuartel general de las fuerzas aliadas en Europa.
shape [ʃeɪp] *n* forma ♦ *vt* formar, dar forma a; (*clay*) modelar; (*stone*) labrar; (*sb's ideas*) formar; (*sb's life*) determinar ♦ *vi* (*also*: **~ up**) (*events*) desarrollarse; (*person*) formarse; **to take ~** tomar forma; **to get o.s. into ~** ponerse en forma *or* en condiciones; **in the ~ of a heart** en forma de corazón; **I can't bear gardening in any ~ or form** no aguanto la jardinería de ningún modo.
-shaped *suff*: **heart~** en forma de corazón.
shapeless ['ʃeɪplɪs] *adj* informe, sin forma definida.
shapely ['ʃeɪplɪ] *adj* bien formado *or* proporcionado.
share [ʃɛə*] *n* (*part*) parte *f*, porción *f*; (*contribution*) cuota; (*COMM*) acción *f* ♦ *vt* dividir; (*fig: have in common*) compartir; **to have a ~ in the profits** tener una proporción de las ganancias; **he has a 50% ~ in a new business venture** tiene una participación del 50% en un nuevo negocio; **to ~ in** participar en; **to ~ out (among *or* between)** repartir (entre).
share capital *n* (*COMM*) capital *m* social en acciones.
share certificate *n* certificado *or* título de una acción.
shareholder ['ʃɛəhəʊldə*] *n* (*BRIT*) accionista *m/f*.
share index *n* (*COMM*) índice *m* de la bolsa.
share issue *n* emisión *f* de acciones.
share price *n* (*COMM*) cotización *f*.
shark [ʃɑːk] *n* tiburón *m*.
sharp [ʃɑːp] *adj* (*razor, knife*) afilado; (*point*) puntiagudo; (*outline*) definido; (*pain*) intenso; (*MUS*) desafinado; (*contrast*) marcado; (*voice*) agudo; (*curve, bend*) cerrado; (*person: quick-witted*) avispado; (: *dishonest*) poco escrupuloso ♦ *n* (*MUS*) sostenido ♦ *adv*: **at 2 o'clock ~** a las 2 en punto; **to be ~ with sb** hablar a algn de forma brusca y tajante; **turn ~ left** tuerce del todo a la izquierda.
sharpen ['ʃɑːpn] *vt* afilar; (*pencil*) sacar punta a; (*fig*) agudizar.
sharpener ['ʃɑːpnə*] *n* (*gen*) afilador *m*; (*pencil ~*) sacapuntas *m inv*.
sharp-eyed [ʃɑːp'aɪd] *adj* de vista aguda.
sharpish ['ʃɑːpɪʃ] *adv* (*BRIT col: quickly*) prontito, bien pronto.
sharply ['ʃɑːplɪ] *adv* (*abruptly*) bruscamente; (*clearly*) claramente; (*harshly*) severamente.
sharp-tempered [ʃɑːp'tɛmpəd] *adj* de genio arisco.
sharp-witted [ʃɑːp'wɪtɪd] *adj* listo, despabilado.
shatter ['ʃætə*] *vt* hacer añicos *or* pedazos; (*fig: ruin*) destruir, acabar con ♦ *vi* hacerse añicos.
shattered ['ʃætəd] *adj* (*grief-stricken*) destrozado, deshecho; (*exhausted*) agotado, hecho polvo.
shattering ['ʃætərɪŋ] *adj* (*experience*) devastador(a), anonadante.
shatterproof ['ʃætəpruːf] *adj* inastillable.

shave [ʃeɪv] *vt* afeitar, rasurar ♦ *vi*
afeitarse ♦ *n*: **to have a** ~ afeitarse.
shaven [ʃeɪvn] *adj (head)* rapado.
shaver [ʃeɪvə*] *n (also:* **electric** ~) máquina
de afeitar (eléctrica).
shaving [ʃeɪvɪŋ] *n (action)* afeitado, ~**s** *npl*
(of wood etc) virutas *fpl*.
shaving brush *n* brocha (de afeitar).
shaving cream *n* crema (de afeitar).
shaving point *n* enchufe *m* para máquinas
de afeitar.
shaving soap *n* jabón *m* de afeitar.
shawl [ʃɔːl] *n* chal *m*.
she [ʃiː] *pron* ella; **there** ~ **is** allí está; ~**-cat**
gata; *NB: for ships, countries follow the*
gender of your translation.
sheaf, *pl* **sheaves** [ʃiːf, ʃiːvz] *n (of corn)*
gavilla; *(of arrows)* haz *m*; *(of papers)* fajo.
shear [ʃɪə*] *vt (pt* ~**ed**, *pp* ~**ed** *or* **shorn**
[ʃɔːn]) *(sheep)* esquilar, trasquilar.
▶**shear off** *vi* romperse.
shears [ʃɪəz] *npl (for hedge)* tijeras *fpl* de
jardín.
sheath [ʃiːθ] *n* vaina; *(contraceptive)*
preservativo.
sheath knife *n* cuchillo de monte.
sheaves [ʃiːvz] *npl of* **sheaf.**
shed [ʃed] *n* cobertizo; *(INDUSTRY, RAIL)*
nave *f* ♦ *vt (pt, pp* **shed**) *(skin)* mudar;
(tears) derramar; **to** ~ **light on** *(problem,*
mystery) aclarar, arrojar luz sobre.
she'd [ʃiːd] = **she had, she would.**
sheen [ʃiːn] *n* brillo, lustre *m*.
sheep [ʃiːp] *n (pl inv)* oveja.
sheepdog [ʃiːpdɔg] *n* perro pastor.
sheep farmer *n* ganadero (de ovejas).
sheepish [ʃiːpɪʃ] *adj* tímido, vergonzoso.
sheepskin [ʃiːpskɪn] *n* piel *f* de carnero.
sheepskin jacket *n* zamarra.
sheer [ʃɪə*] *adj (utter)* puro, completo;
(steep) escarpado; *(material)* diáfano ♦ *adv*
verticalmente; **by** ~ **chance** de pura
casualidad.
sheet [ʃiːt] *n (on bed)* sábana; *(of paper)*
hoja; *(of glass, metal)* lámina.
sheet feed *n (on printer)* alimentador *m* de
papel.
sheet lightning *n* relámpago (difuso).
sheet metal *n* metal *m* en lámina.
sheet music *n* hojas *fpl* de partitura.
sheik(h) [ʃeɪk] *n* jeque *m*.
shelf, *pl* **shelves** [ʃelf, ʃelvz] *n* estante *m*.
shelf life *n (COMM)* periodo de
conservación antes de la venta.
shell [ʃel] *n (on beach)* concha, caracol
(LAM); *(of egg, nut etc)* cáscara; *(explosive)*
proyectil *m*, obús *m*; *(of building)* armazón
m ♦ *vt (peas)* desenvainar; *(MIL)*

bombardear.
▶**shell out** *vi (col)*: **to** ~ **out (for)** soltar el
dinero (para), desembolsar (para).
she'll [ʃiːl] = **she will, she shall.**
shellfish [ʃelfɪʃ] *n (pl inv)* crustáceo; *(pl: as*
food) mariscos *mpl*.
shellsuit [ʃelsuːt] *n* chándal *m* (de tactel
®).
shelter [ʃeltə*] *n* abrigo, refugio ♦ *vt (aid)*
amparar, proteger; *(give lodging to)*
abrigar; *(hide)* esconder ♦ *vi* abrigarse,
refugiarse; **to take** ~ **(from)** refugiarse *or*
asilarse (de); **bus** ~ parada de autobús
cubierta.
sheltered [ʃeltəd] *adj (life)* protegido;
(spot) abrigado.
shelve [ʃelv] *vt (fig)* dar carpetazo a.
shelves [ʃelvz] *npl of* **shelf.**
shelving [ʃelvɪŋ] *n* estantería.
shepherd [ʃepəd] *n* pastor *m* ♦ *vt (guide)*
guiar, conducir.
shepherdess [ʃepədɪs] *n* pastora.
shepherd's pie *n pastel de carne y puré*
de patatas.
sherbert [ʃəːbət] *n (BRIT: powder)* polvos
mpl azucarados; *(US: water ice)* sorbete *m*.
sheriff [ʃerɪf] *n (US)* sheriff *m*.
sherry [ʃerɪ] *n* jerez *m*.
she's [ʃiːz] = **she is, she has.**
Shetland [ʃetlənd] *n (also:* **the** ~**s, the** ~
Isles) las Islas *fpl* Shetland.
Shetland pony *n* pony *m* de Shetland.
shield [ʃiːld] *n* escudo; *(TECH)* blindaje *m*
♦ *vt*: **to** ~ **(from)** proteger (de).
shift [ʃift] *n (change)* cambio; *(at work)*
turno ♦ *vt* trasladar; *(remove)* quitar ♦ *vi*
moverse; *(change place)* cambiar de sitio;
the wind has ~**ed to the south** el viento
ha virado al sur; **a** ~ **in demand** *(COMM)*
un desplazamiento de la demanda.
shift key *n (on typewriter)* tecla de
mayúsculas.
shiftless [ʃiftlɪs] *adj (person)* vago.
shift work *n (BRIT)* trabajo por turnos; **to**
do ~ trabajar por turnos.
shifty [ʃiftɪ] *adj* tramposo; *(eyes)* furtivo.
Shiite [ʃiːaɪt] *adj, n* shiíta *m/f*.
shilling [ʃilɪŋ] *n (BRIT)* chelín *m (= 12 old*
pence; 20 in a pound).
shilly-shally [ʃilɪʃælɪ] *vi* titubear, vacilar.
shimmer [ʃimə*] *n* reflejo trémulo ♦ *vi*
relucir.
shimmering [ʃimərɪŋ] *adj* reluciente;
(haze) trémulo; *(satin etc)* lustroso.
shin [ʃin] *n* espinilla ♦ *vi*: **to** ~ **down/up a**
tree bajar de/trepar un árbol.
shindig [ʃindɪg] *n (col)* fiesta, juerga.
shine [ʃaɪn] *n* brillo, lustre *m* ♦ *(vb: pt, pp*

shone [ʃɔn]) *vi* brillar, relucir ♦ *vt (shoes)* lustrar, sacar brillo a; **to ~ a torch on sth** dirigir una linterna hacia algo.

shingle ['ʃɪŋgl] *n (on beach)* guijarras *fpl*.

shingles ['ʃɪŋglz] *n (MED)* herpes *msg*.

shining ['ʃaɪnɪŋ] *adj (surface, hair)* lustroso; *(light)* brillante.

shiny ['ʃaɪnɪ] *adj* brillante, lustroso.

ship [ʃɪp] *n* buque *m*, barco ♦ *vt (goods)* embarcar; *(oars)* desarmar; *(send)* transportar *or* enviar por vía marítima; **~'s manifest** manifiesto del buque; **on board** ~ a bordo.

shipbuilder ['ʃɪpbɪldə*] *n* constructor(a) *m/f* naval.

shipbuilding ['ʃɪpbɪldɪŋ] *n* construcción *f* naval.

ship canal *n* canal *m* de navegación.

ship chandler [-'tʃɑːndlə*] *n* proveedor *m* de efectos navales.

shipment ['ʃɪpmənt] *n (act)* embarque *m*; *(goods)* envío.

shipowner ['ʃɪpəunə*] *n* naviero, armador *m*.

shipper ['ʃɪpə*] *n* compañía naviera.

shipping ['ʃɪpɪŋ] *n (act)* embarque *m*; *(traffic)* buques *mpl*.

shipping agent *n* agente *m/f* marítimo/a.

shipping company *n* compañía naviera.

shipping lane *n* ruta de navegación.

shipping line *n* = **shipping company**.

shipshape ['ʃɪpʃeɪp] *adj* en buen orden.

shipwreck ['ʃɪprɛk] *n* naufragio ♦ *vt*: **to be ~ed** naufragar.

shipyard ['ʃɪpjɑːd] *n* astillero.

shire ['ʃaɪə*] *n (BRIT)* condado.

shirk [ʃɔːk] *vt* eludir, esquivar; *(obligations)* faltar a.

shirt [ʃɔːt] *n* camisa; **in ~ sleeves** en mangas de camisa.

shirty ['ʃɔːtɪ] *adj (BRIT col)*: **to be ~** estar de malas pulgas.

shit [ʃɪt] *(col!)* n mierda; *(nonsense)* chorradas *fpl*; **to be a ~** ser un cabrón ♦ *excl* ¡mierda!; **tough ~!** ¡te jodes!

shiver ['ʃɪvə*] *vi* temblar, estremecerse; *(with cold)* tiritar.

shoal [ʃəul] *n (of fish)* banco.

shock [ʃɔk] *n (impact)* choque *m*; *(ELEC)* descarga (eléctrica); *(emotional)* conmoción *f*; *(start)* sobresalto, susto; *(MED)* postración *f* nerviosa ♦ *vt* dar un susto a; *(offend)* escandalizar; **to get a ~** *(ELEC)* sentir una sacudida eléctrica; **to give sb a ~** dar un susto a algn; **to be suffering from ~** padecer una postración nerviosa; **it came as a ~ to hear that ...**

me *(etc)* asombró descubrir que ....

shock absorber [-əbsɔːbə*] *n* amortiguador *m*.

shocker ['ʃɔkə*] *n (col)*: **it was a real ~** fue muy fuerte.

shocking ['ʃɔkɪŋ] *adj (awful: weather, handwriting)* espantoso, horrible; *(improper)* escandaloso; *(result)* inesperado.

shock therapy, shock treatment *n* *(MED)* terapia de choque.

shock wave *n* onda expansiva *or* de choque.

shod [ʃɔd] *pt, pp of* **shoe** ♦ *adj* calzado.

shoddiness ['ʃɔdɪnɪs] *n* baja calidad *f*.

shoddy ['ʃɔdɪ] *adj* de pacotilla.

shoe [ʃuː] *n* zapato; *(for horse)* herradura; *(brake ~)* zapata ♦ *vt (pt, pp* **shod** [ʃɔd]*)* *(horse)* herrar.

shoebrush ['ʃuːbrʌʃ] *n* cepillo para zapatos.

shoehorn ['ʃuːhɔːn] *n* calzador *m*.

shoelace ['ʃuːleɪs] *n* cordón *m*.

shoemaker ['ʃuːmeɪkə*] *n* zapatero/a.

shoe polish *n* betún *m*.

shoeshop ['ʃuːʃɔp] *n* zapatería.

shoestring ['ʃuːstrɪŋ] *n (shoelace)* cordón *m*; *(fig)*: **on a ~** con muy poco dinero, a lo barato.

shone [ʃɔn] *pt, pp of* **shine**.

shoo [ʃuː] *excl* ¡fuera!; *(to animals)* ¡zape! ♦ *vt (also: ~ away, ~ off)* ahuyentar.

shook [ʃuk] *pt of* **shake**.

shoot [ʃuːt] *n (on branch, seedling)* retoño, vástago; *(shooting party)* cacería; *(competition)* concurso de tiro; *(preserve)* coto de caza ♦ *(vb: pt, pp* **shot** [ʃɔt]*)* *vt* disparar; *(kill)* matar a tiros; *(execute)* fusilar; *(CINE: film, scene)* rodar, filmar ♦ *vi (FOOTBALL)* chutar; **to ~ (at)** tirar (a); **to ~ past** pasar como un rayo; **to ~ in/out** *vi* entrar corriendo/salir disparado.

▶**shoot down** *vt (plane)* derribar.

▶**shoot up** *vi (prices)* dispararse.

shooting ['ʃuːtɪŋ] *n (shots)* tiros *mpl*, tiroteo; *(HUNTING)* caza con escopeta; *(act: murder)* asesinato (a tiros); *(CINE)* rodaje *m*.

shooting star *n* estrella fugaz.

shop [ʃɔp] *n* tienda; *(workshop)* taller *m* ♦ *vi (also: **go ~ping**)* ir de compras; **to talk ~** *(fig)* hablar del trabajo; **repair ~** taller *m* de reparaciones.

▶**shop around** *vi* comparar precios.

shopaholic ['ʃɔpə'hɔlɪk] *n (col)* adicto/a a las compras.

shop assistant *n (BRIT)* dependiente/a *m/f*.

shop floor *n (BRIT fig)* taller *m*, fábrica.

shopkeeper ['ʃɔpkiːpə*] *n* (*BRIT*) tendero/a.
shoplift ['ʃɔplɪft] *vi* robar en las tiendas.
shoplifter ['ʃɔplɪftə*] *n* ratero/a.
shoplifting ['ʃɔplɪftɪŋ] *n* ratería, robo (en
  las tiendas).
shopper ['ʃɔpə*] *n* comprador(a) *m/f*.
shopping ['ʃɔpɪŋ] *n* (*goods*) compras *fpl*.
shopping bag *n* bolsa (de compras).
shopping centre, (*US*) **shopping center**
  n centro comercial.
shopping mall *n* centro comercial.
shop-soiled ['ʃɔpsɔɪld] *adj* (*BRIT*)
  deteriorado.
shop steward *n* (*BRIT INDUSTRY*) enlace *m/f*
  sindical.
shop window *n* escaparate *m*, vidriera
  (*LAM*).
shopworn ['ʃɔpwɔːn] *adj* (*US*) usado.
shore [ʃɔː*] *n* (*of sea, lake*) orilla ♦ *vt*: **to ~**
  (up) reforzar; **on ~** en tierra.
shore leave *n* (*NAUT*) permiso para bajar a
  tierra.
shorn [ʃɔːn] *pp of* **shear**.
short [ʃɔːt] *adj* (*not long*) corto; (*in time*)
  breve, de corta duración; (*person*) bajo;
  (*curt*) brusco, seco ♦ *vi* (*ELEC*) ponerse en
  cortocircuito ♦ *n* (*also:* ~ **film**)
  cortometraje *m*; (**a pair of**) ~**s** (unos)
  pantalones *mpl* cortos; **to be ~ of sth**
  estar falto de algo; **in ~** en pocas
  palabras; **a ~ time ago** hace poco
  (tiempo); **in the ~ term** a corto plazo; **to**
  be in ~ supply escasear, haber escasez
  de; **I'm ~ of time** me falta tiempo; ~ **of**
  doing... a menos que hagamos *etc*...;
  everything ~ of... todo menos...; **it is ~**
  for es la forma abreviada de; **to cut** ~
  (*speech, visit*) interrumpir, terminar
  inesperadamente; **to fall** ~ **of** no
  alcanzar; **to run** ~ **of sth** acabársele algo;
  to stop ~ parar en seco; **to stop** ~ **of**
  detenerse antes de.
shortage ['ʃɔːtɪdʒ] *n* escasez *f*, falta.
shortbread ['ʃɔːtbred] *n pasta de*
  mantequilla.
short-change [ʃɔːt'tʃeɪndʒ] *vt*: **to ~ sb** no
  dar el cambio completo a algn.
short-circuit [ʃɔːt'səːkɪt] *n* cortocircuito
  ♦ *vt* poner en cortocircuito ♦ *vi* ponerse
  en cortocircuito.
shortcoming ['ʃɔːtkʌmɪŋ] *n* defecto,
  deficiencia.
short(crust) pastry ['ʃɔːt(krʌst)-] *n* (*BRIT*)
  pasta quebradiza.
shortcut ['ʃɔːtkʌt] *n* atajo.
shorten ['ʃɔːtn] *vt* acortar; (*visit*)
  interrumpir.
shortfall ['ʃɔːtfɔːl] *n* déficit *m*, deficiencia.

shorthand ['ʃɔːthænd] *n* (*BRIT*) taquigrafía;
  to take sth down in ~ taquigrafiar algo.
shorthand notebook *n* cuaderno de
  taquigrafía.
shorthand typist *n* (*BRIT*)
  taquimecanógrafo/a.
short list *n* (*BRIT: for job*) lista de
  candidatos pre-seleccionados.
short-lived ['ʃɔːt'lɪvd] *adj* efímero.
shortly ['ʃɔːtlɪ] *adv* en breve, dentro de poco.
shortness ['ʃɔːtnɪs] *n* (*of distance*) cortedad
  f; (*of time*) brevedad *f*; (*manner*)
  brusquedad *f*.
short-sighted [ʃɔːt'saɪtɪd] *adj* (*BRIT*) miope,
  corto de vista; (*fig*) imprudente.
short-sightedness [ʃɔːt'saɪtɪdnɪs] *n*
  miopía; (*fig*) falta de previsión,
  imprudencia.
short-staffed [ʃɔːt'stɑːft] *adj* falto de
  personal.
short story *n* cuento.
short-tempered [ʃɔːt'tempəd] *adj*
  enojadizo.
short-term ['ʃɔːttəːm] *adj* (*effect*) a corto
  plazo.
short time *n*: **to work ~, be on ~**
  (*INDUSTRY*) trabajar con sistema de
  horario reducido.
short-time working ['ʃɔːttaɪm-] *n* trabajo
  de horario reducido.
short wave *n* (*RADIO*) onda corta.
shot [ʃɔt] *pt, pp of* **shoot** ♦ *n* (*sound*) tiro,
  disparo; (*person*) tirador(a) *m/f*; (*try*)
  tentativa; (*injection*) inyección *f*; (*PHOT*)
  toma, fotografía; (*shotgun pellets*)
  perdigones *mpl*; **to fire a ~ at sb/sth** tirar
  or disparar contra algn/algo; **to have a ~**
  at (doing) sth probar suerte con algo; **like**
  a ~ (*without any delay*) como un rayo; **a**
  big ~ (*col*) un pez gordo; **to get ~ of sth/**
  sb (*col*) deshacerse de algo/algn, quitarse
  algo/a algn de encima.
shotgun ['ʃɔtgʌn] *n* escopeta.
should [ʃud] *aux vb*: **I ~ go now** debo irme
  ahora; **he ~ be there now** debe de haber
  llegado (ya); **I ~ go if I were you** yo en tu
  lugar me iría; **I ~ like to** me gustaría; ~
  he phone ... si llamara ..., en caso de que
  llamase ....
shoulder ['ʃəuldə*] *n* hombro; (*BRIT: of*
  road): **hard ~** arcén *m* ♦ *vt* (*fig*) cargar con;
  to look over one's ~ mirar hacia atrás; **to**
  rub ~s with sb (*fig*) codearse con algn; **to**
  give sb the cold ~ (*fig*) dar de lado a algn.
shoulder blade *n* omóplato.
shoulder bag *n* bolso de bandolera.
shoulder strap *n* tirante *m*.
shouldn't ['ʃudnt] = **should not**.

shout [ʃaut] n grito ♦ vt gritar ♦ vi gritar, dar voces.
▶**shout down** vt hundir a gritos.
shouting [ˈʃautɪŋ] n griterío.
shouting match n (col) discusión f a voz en grito.
shove [ʃʌv] n empujón m ♦ vt empujar; (col: put): **to ~ sth in** meter algo a empellones; **he ~d me out of the way** me quitó de en medio de un empujón.
▶**shove off** vi (NAUT) alejarse del muelle; (fig: col) largarse.
shovel [ˈʃʌvl] n pala; (mechanical) excavadora ♦ vt mover con pala.
show [ʃəu] n (of emotion) demostración f; (semblance) apariencia; (COMM, TECH: exhibition) exhibición f, exposición f; (THEAT) función f, espectáculo; (organization) negocio, empresa ♦ vb (pt **showed**, pp **shown** [ʃəun]) vt mostrar, enseñar; (courage etc) mostrar, manifestar; (exhibit) exponer; (film) proyectar ♦ vi mostrarse; (appear) aparecer; **on ~** (exhibits etc) expuesto; **to be on ~** estar expuesto; **it's just for ~** es sólo para impresionar; **to ask for a ~ of hands** pedir una votación a mano alzada; **who's running the ~ here?** ¿quién manda aquí?; **to ~ a profit/loss** (COMM) arrojar un saldo positivo/negativo; **I have nothing to ~ for it** no saqué ningún provecho (de ello); **to ~ sb to his seat/to the door** acompañar a algn a su asiento/a la puerta; **as ~n in the illustration** como se ve en el grabado; **it just goes to ~ that ...** queda demostrado que ...; **it doesn't ~** no se ve or nota.
▶**show in** vt (person) hacer pasar.
▶**show off** vi (pej) presumir ♦ vt (display) lucir; (pej) hacer alarde de.
▶**show out** vt: **to ~ sb out** acompañar a algn a la puerta.
▶**show up** vi (stand out) destacar; (col: turn up) presentarse ♦ vt descubrir; (unmask) desenmascarar.
showbiz [ˈʃəubɪz] n (col) = **show business**.
show business n el mundo del espectáculo.
showcase [ˈʃəukeɪs] n vitrina; (fig) escaparate m.
showdown [ˈʃəudaun] n enfrentamiento m.
shower [ˈʃauə*] n (rain) chaparrón m, chubasco; (of stones etc) lluvia; (also: ~ bath) ducha ♦ vi llover ♦ vt: **to ~ sb with sth** colmar a algn de algo; **to have** or **take a ~** ducharse.
shower cap n gorro de baño.
showerproof [ˈʃauəpruːf] adj impermeable.

showery [ˈʃauərɪ] adj (weather) lluvioso.
showground [ˈʃəugraund] n ferial m, real m (de la feria).
showing [ˈʃəuɪŋ] n (of film) proyección f.
show jumping n hípica.
showman [ˈʃəumən] n (at fair, circus) empresario (de espectáculos); (fig) actor m consumado.
showmanship [ˈʃəumənʃɪp] n dotes fpl teatrales.
shown [ʃəun] pp of **show**.
show-off [ˈʃəuɔf] n (col: person) fantasmón/ona m/f.
showpiece [ˈʃəupiːs] n (of exhibition etc) objeto más valioso, joya; **that hospital is a ~** ese hospital es un modelo del género.
showroom [ˈʃəuruːm] n sala de muestras.
show trial n juicio propagandístico.
showy [ˈʃəuɪ] adj ostentoso.
shrank [ʃræŋk] pt of **shrink**.
shrapnel [ˈʃræpnl] n metralla.
shred [ʃred] n (gen pl) triza, jirón m; (fig: of truth, evidence) pizca, chispa ♦ vt hacer trizas; (documents) triturar; (CULIN) desmenuzar.
shredder [ˈʃredə*] n (vegetable ~) picadora; (document ~) trituradora (de papel).
shrewd [ʃruːd] adj astuto.
shrewdly [ˈʃruːdlɪ] adv astutamente.
shrewdness [ˈʃruːdnɪs] n astucia.
shriek [ʃriːk] n chillido ♦ vt, vi chillar.
shrill [ʃrɪl] adj agudo, estridente.
shrimp [ʃrɪmp] n camarón m.
shrine [ʃraɪn] n santuario, sepulcro.
shrink, pt **shrank**, pp **shrunk** [ʃrɪŋk, ʃræŋk, ʃrʌŋk] vi encogerse; (be reduced) reducirse ♦ vt encoger; **to ~ from (doing) sth** no atreverse a hacer algo.
▶**shrink away** vi retroceder, retirarse.
shrinkage [ˈʃrɪŋkɪdʒ] n encogimiento; reducción f; (COMM: in shops) pérdidas fpl.
shrink-wrap [ˈʃrɪŋkræp] vt empaquetar en envase termoretráctil.
shrivel [ˈʃrɪvl] (also: ~ up) vt (dry) secar; (crease) arrugar ♦ vi secarse; arrugarse.
shroud [ʃraud] n sudario ♦ vt: **~ed in mystery** envuelto en el misterio.
Shrove Tuesday [ˈʃrəuv-] n martes m de carnaval.
shrub [ʃrʌb] n arbusto.
shrubbery [ˈʃrʌbərɪ] n arbustos mpl.
shrug [ʃrʌg] n encogimiento de hombros ♦ vt, vi: **to ~ (one's shoulders)** encogerse de hombros.
▶**shrug off** vt negar importancia a; (cold, illness) deshacerse de.

shrunk [ʃrʌŋk] *pp of* **shrink**.
shrunken ['ʃrʌŋkn] *adj* encogido.
shudder ['ʃʌdə*] *n* estremecimiento, escalofrío ♦ *vi* estremecerse.
shuffle ['ʃʌfl] *vt* (*cards*) barajar; **to ~** (*one's feet*) arrastrar los pies.
shun [ʃʌn] *vt* rehuir, esquivar.
shunt [ʃʌnt] *vt* (*RAIL*) maniobrar.
shunting yard ['ʃʌntɪŋ-] *n* estación *f* de maniobras.
shut, *pt, pp* **shut** [ʃʌt] *vt, vi* cerrar ♦ *vi* cerrarse.
▶**shut down** *vt, vi* cerrar; (*machine*) parar.
▶**shut off** *vt* (*stop: power, water supply etc*) interrumpir, cortar; (: *engine*) parar.
▶**shut out** *vt* (*person*) excluir, dejar fuera; (*noise, cold*) no dejar entrar; (*block: view*) tapar; (: *memory*) tratar de olvidar.
▶**shut up** *vi* (*col: keep quiet*) callarse ♦ *vt* (*close*) cerrar; (*silence*) callar.
shutdown ['ʃʌtdaun] *n* cierre *m*.
shutter ['ʃʌtə*] *n* contraventana; (*PHOT*) obturador *m*.
shuttle ['ʃʌtl] *n* lanzadera; (*also:* **~ service**: *AVIAT*) puente *m* aéreo ♦ *vi* (*subj: vehicle, person*) ir y venir ♦ *vt* (*passengers*) transportar, trasladar.
shuttlecock ['ʃʌtlkɔk] *n* volante *m*.
shuttle diplomacy *n* viajes *mpl* diplomáticos.
shy [ʃaɪ] *adj* tímido ♦ *vi*: **to ~ away from doing sth** (*fig*) rehusar hacer algo; **to be ~ of doing sth** rehusar hacer algo.
shyly ['ʃaɪlɪ] *adv* tímidamente.
shyness ['ʃaɪnɪs] *n* timidez *f*.
Siam [saɪ'æm] *n* Siam *m*.
Siamese [saɪə'miːz] *adj* siamés/esa ♦ *n* (*person*) siamés/esa *m/f*; (*LING*) siamés *m*; **~ cat** gato siamés; **~ twins** gemelos/as *m/fpl* siameses/as.
Siberia [saɪ'bɪərɪə] *n* Siberia.
sibling ['sɪblɪŋ] *n* (*formal*) hermano/a.
Sicilian [sɪ'sɪlɪən] *adj, n* siciliano/a *m/f*.
Sicily ['sɪsɪlɪ] *n* Sicilia.
sick [sɪk] *adj* (*ill*) enfermo; (*nauseated*) mareado; (*humour*) morboso; **to be ~** (*BRIT*) vomitar; **to feel ~** estar mareado; **to be ~ of** (*fig*) estar harto de; **a ~ person** un(a) enfermo/a; **to be (off) ~** estar ausente por enfermedad; **to fall** *or* **take ~** ponerse enfermo.
sickbag ['sɪkbæg] *n* bolsa para el mareo.
sick bay *n* enfermería.
sickbed ['sɪkbɛd] *n* lecho de enfermo.
sick building syndrome *n* *enfermedad causada por falta de ventilación y luz natural en un edificio.*
sicken ['sɪkn] *vt* dar asco a ♦ *vi* enfermar; **to be ~ing for** (*cold, flu etc*) mostrar

síntomas de.
sickening ['sɪknɪŋ] *adj* (*fig*) asqueroso.
sickle ['sɪkl] *n* hoz *f*.
sick leave *n* baja por enfermedad.
sickle-cell anaemia ['sɪklsɛl-] *n* anemia de células falciformes, drepanocitosis *f*.
sick list *n*: **to be on the ~** estar de baja.
sickly ['sɪklɪ] *adj* enfermizo; (*taste*) empalagoso.
sickness ['sɪknɪs] *n* enfermedad *f*, mal *m*; (*vomiting*) náuseas *fpl*.
sickness benefit *n* subsidio de enfermedad.
sick pay *n* *prestación por enfermedad pagada por la empresa.*
sickroom ['sɪkruːm] *n* cuarto del enfermo.
side [saɪd] *n* (*gen*) lado; (*face, surface*) cara; (*of paper*) cara; (*slice of bread*) rebanada; (*of body*) costado; (*of animal*) ijar *m*, ijada; (*of lake*) orilla; (*part*) lado; (*aspect*) aspecto; (*team: SPORT*) equipo; (: *POL etc*) partido; (*of hill*) ladera ♦ *adj* (*door, entrance*) lateral ♦ *vi*: **to ~ with sb** ponerse de parte de algn; **by the ~ of** al lado de; **~ by** juntos/as; **from all ~s** de todos lados; **to take ~s (with)** tomar partido (por); **~ of beef** flanco de vaca; **the right/wrong ~** el derecho/revés; **from ~ to ~** de un lado a otro.
sideboard ['saɪdbɔːd] *n* aparador *m*.
sideboards ['saɪdbɔːdz] (*BRIT*), **sideburns** ['saɪdbəːnz] *npl* patillas *fpl*.
sidecar ['saɪdkɑː*] *n* sidecar *m*.
side dish *n* entremés *m*.
side drum *n* (*MUS*) tamboril *m*.
side effect *n* efecto secundario.
sidekick ['saɪdkɪk] *n* compinche *m*.
sidelight ['saɪdlaɪt] *n* (*AUT*) luz *f* lateral.
sideline ['saɪdlaɪn] *n* (*SPORT*) línea lateral; (*fig*) empleo suplementario.
sidelong ['saɪdlɔŋ] *adj* de soslayo; **to give a ~ glance at sth** mirar algo de reojo.
side plate *n* platito.
side road *n* (*BRIT*) calle *f* lateral.
sidesaddle ['saɪdsædl] *adv* a la amazona.
side show *n* (*stall*) caseta; (*fig*) atracción *f* secundaria.
sidestep ['saɪdstɛp] *vt* (*question*) eludir; (*problem*) esquivar ♦ *vi* (*BOXING etc*) dar un quiebro.
side street *n* calle *f* lateral.
sidetrack ['saɪdtræk] *vt* (*fig*) desviar (de su propósito).
sidewalk ['saɪdwɔːk] *n* (*US*) acera, vereda (*LAM*), andén *m* (*LAM*), banqueta (*LAM*).
sideways ['saɪdweɪz] *adv* de lado.
siding ['saɪdɪŋ] *n* (*RAIL*) apartadero, vía muerta.

sidle ['saɪdl] *vi*: **to ~ up (to)** acercarse furtivamente (a).

SIDS [sɪdz] *n abbr* (= *sudden infant death syndrome*) (síndrome *m* de la) muerte *f* súbita.

siege [si:dʒ] *n* cerco, sitio; **to lay ~ to** cercar, sitiar.

siege economy *n* economía de sitio *or* de asedio.

Sierra Leone [sɪˈɛrəlɪˈəun] *n* Sierra Leona.

siesta [sɪˈɛstə] *n* siesta.

sieve [sɪv] *n* colador *m* ♦ *vt* cribar.

sift [sɪft] *vt* cribar ♦ *vi*: **to ~ through** pasar por una criba; (*information*) analizar cuidadosamente.

sigh [saɪ] *n* suspiro ♦ *vi* suspirar.

sight [saɪt] *n* (*faculty*) vista; (*spectacle*) espectáculo; (*on gun*) mira, alza ♦ *vt* ver, divisar; **in ~ a la vista**; **out of ~** fuera de (la) vista; **at ~** a la vista; **at first ~** a primera vista; **to lose ~ of sth/sb** perder algo/a algn de vista; **to catch ~ of sth/sb** divisar algo/a algn; **I know her by ~** la conozco de vista; **to set one's ~s on (doing) sth** aspirar a *or* ambicionar (hacer) algo.

sighted ['saɪtɪd] *adj* vidente, de vista normal; **partially ~** de vista limitada.

sightseer ['saɪtsiːə*] *n* excursionista *m/f*, turista *m/f*.

sightseeing ['saɪtsiːɪŋ] *n* excursionismo, turismo; **to go ~** visitar monumentos.

sign [saɪn] *n* (*with hand*) señal *f*, seña; (*trace*) huella, rastro; (*notice*) letrero; (*written*) signo; (*road ~*) indicador *m*; (: *with instructions*) señal *f* de tráfico ♦ *vt* firmar; **as a ~ of** en señal de; **it's a good/bad ~** es buena/mala señal; **plus/minus ~** signo de más/de menos; **to ~ one's name** firmar.

▶**sign away** *vt* (*rights etc*) ceder.

▶**sign off** *vi* (*RADIO, TV*) cerrar el programa.

▶**sign on** *vi* (*MIL*) alistarse; (*as unemployed*) apuntarse al paro; (*employee*) firmar un contrato ♦ *vt* (*MIL*) alistar; (*employee*) contratar; **to ~ on for a course** matricularse en un curso.

▶**sign out** *vi* firmar el registro (al salir).

▶**sign over** *vt*: **to ~ sth over to sb** traspasar algo a algn.

▶**sign up** *vi* (*MIL*) alistarse ♦ *vt* (*contract*) contratar.

signal ['sɪgnl] *n* señal *f* ♦ *vi* (*AUT*) señalizar ♦ *vt* (*person*) hacer señas a; (*message*) transmitir; **the engaged ~** (*TEL*) la señal de comunicando; **the ~ is very weak** (*TV*) no captamos bien el canal; **to ~ a left/**

right turn (*AUT*) indicar que se va a doblar a la izquierda/derecha; **to ~ to sb (to do sth)** hacer señas a algn (para que haga algo).

signal box *n* (*RAIL*) garita de señales.

signalman ['sɪgnlmən] *n* (*RAIL*) guardavía *m*.

signatory ['sɪgnətərɪ] *n* firmante *m/f*.

signature ['sɪgnətʃə*] *n* firma.

signature tune *n* sintonía.

signet ring ['sɪgnət-] *n* (anillo de) sello.

significance [sɪgˈnɪfɪkəns] *n* significado; (*importance*) trascendencia; **that is of no ~** eso no tiene importancia.

significant [sɪgˈnɪfɪkənt] *adj* significativo; trascendente; **it is ~ that ...** es significativo que ....

significantly [sɪgˈnɪfɪkəntlɪ] *adv* (*smile*) expresivamente; (*improve, increase*) sensiblemente; **and, ~ ...** y debe notarse que ....

signify ['sɪgnɪfaɪ] *vt* significar.

sign language *n* mímica, lenguaje *m* por *or* de señas.

signpost ['saɪnpəust] *n* indicador *m*.

silage ['saɪlɪdʒ] *n* ensilaje *m*.

silence ['saɪlns] *n* silencio ♦ *vt* hacer callar; (*guns*) reducir al silencio.

silencer ['saɪlnsə*] *n* (*on gun, BRIT AUT*) silenciador *m*.

silent ['saɪlnt] *adj* (*gen*) silencioso; (*not speaking*) callado; (*film*) mudo; **to keep** *or* **remain ~** guardar silencio.

silently ['saɪlntlɪ] *adv* silenciosamente, en silencio.

silent partner *n* (*COMM*) socio/a comanditario/a.

silhouette [sɪluːˈɛt] *n* silueta; **~d against** destacado sobre *or* contra.

silicon ['sɪlɪkən] *n* silicio.

silicon chip *n* chip *m*, plaqueta de silicio.

silicone ['sɪlɪkəun] *n* silicona.

silk [sɪlk] *n* seda ♦ *cpd* de seda.

silky ['sɪlkɪ] *adj* sedoso.

sill [sɪl] *n* (*also*: **window~**) alféizar *m*; (*AUT*) umbral *m*.

silliness ['sɪlɪnɪs] *n* (*of person*) necedad *f*; (*of idea*) lo absurdo.

silly ['sɪlɪ] *adj* (*person*) tonto; (*idea*) absurdo; **to do sth ~** hacer una tontería.

silo ['saɪləu] *n* silo.

silt [sɪlt] *n* sedimento.

silver ['sɪlvə*] *n* plata; (*money*) moneda suelta ♦ *adj* de plata.

silver paper (*BRIT*), **silver foil** *n* papel *m* de plata.

silver plate *n* vajilla de plata.

silver-plated [sɪlvəˈpleɪtɪd] *adj* plateado.

silversmith ['sɪlvəsmɪθ] n platero/a.
silverware ['sɪlvəweə*] n plata.
silver wedding (anniversary) n (*BRIT*)
bodas *fpl* de plata.
silvery ['sɪlvrɪ] *adj* plateado.
similar ['sɪmɪlə*] *adj*: ~ **to** parecido *or*
semejante a.
similarity [sɪmɪ'lærɪtɪ] n parecido,
semejanza.
similarly ['sɪmɪləlɪ] *adv* del mismo modo; (*in
a similar way*) de manera parecida;
(*equally*) igualmente.
simile ['sɪmɪlɪ] n símil m.
simmer ['sɪmə*] *vi* hervir a fuego lento.
▶**simmer down** *vi* (*fig, col*) calmarse,
tranquilizarse.
simpering ['sɪmpərɪŋ] *adj* afectado; (*foolish*)
bobo.
simple ['sɪmpl] *adj* (*easy*) sencillo; (*foolish,
COMM*) simple; **the ~ truth** la pura
verdad.
simple interest n (*COMM*) interés m
simple.
simple-minded [sɪmpl'maɪndɪd] *adj* simple,
ingenuo.
simpleton ['sɪmpltən] n inocentón/ona *m/f*.
simplicity [sɪm'plɪsɪtɪ] n sencillez f;
(*foolishness*) ingenuidad f.
simplification [sɪmplɪfɪ'keɪʃən] n
simplificación f.
simplify ['sɪmplɪfaɪ] *vt* simplificar.
simply ['sɪmplɪ] *adv* (*in a simple way: live,
talk*) sencillamente; (*just, merely*) sólo.
simulate ['sɪmjuleɪt] *vt* simular.
simulation [sɪmju'leɪʃən] n simulación f.
simultaneous [sɪməl'teɪnɪəs] *adj*
simultáneo.
simultaneously [sɪməl'teɪnɪəslɪ] *adv*
simultáneamente, a la vez.
sin [sɪn] n pecado ♦ *vi* pecar.
since [sɪns] *adv* desde entonces ♦ *prep* desde
♦ *conj* (*time*) desde que; (*because*) ya que,
puesto que; ~ **then** desde entonces; ~
Monday desde el lunes; **(ever)** ~ **I arrived**
desde que llegué.
sincere [sɪn'sɪə*] *adj* sincero.
sincerely [sɪn'sɪəlɪ] *adv* sinceramente;
yours ~ (*in letters*) le saluda
(afectuosamente); ~ **yours** (*US: in letters*)
le saluda atentamente.
sincerity [sɪn'serɪtɪ] n sinceridad f.
sinecure ['saɪnɪkjuə*] n chollo.
sinew ['sɪnjuː] n tendón m.
sinful ['sɪnful] *adj* (*thought*) pecaminoso;
(*person*) pecador(a).
sing, *pt* **sang,** *pp* **sung** [sɪŋ, sæŋ, sʌŋ] *vt*
cantar ♦ *vi* (*gen*) cantar; (*bird*) trinar;
(*ears*) zumbar.

Singapore [sɪŋə'pɔː*] n Singapur m.
singe [sɪndʒ] *vt* chamuscar.
singer ['sɪŋə*] n cantante *m/f*.
Singhalese [sɪŋə'liːz] *adj* = **Sinhalese**.
singing ['sɪŋɪŋ] n (*of person, bird*) canto;
(*songs*) canciones *fpl*; (*in the ears*)
zumbido; (*of kettle*) silbido.
single ['sɪŋgl] *adj* único, solo; (*unmarried*)
soltero; (*not double*) individual, sencillo
♦ n (*BRIT: also:* ~ **ticket**) billete m sencillo;
(*record*) sencillo, single m; ~**s** *npl* (*TENNIS*)
individual *msg*; **not a ~ one was left** no
quedaba ni uno; **every ~ day** todos los
días (sin excepción).
▶**single out** *vt* (*choose*) escoger; (*point out*)
singularizar.
single bed n cama individual.
single-breasted [sɪŋgl'brestɪd] *adj* (*jacket,
suit*) recto, sin cruzar.
single-density ['sɪŋgldensɪtɪ] *adj* (*COMPUT:
disk*) de densidad sencilla.
single-entry book-keeping ['sɪŋglentrɪ-] n
contabilidad f por partida simple.
Single European Market n: **the** ~ el
Mercado Único Europeo.
single file n: **in** ~ en fila de uno.
single-handed [sɪŋgl'hændɪd] *adv* sin
ayuda.
single-minded [sɪŋgl'maɪndɪd] *adj* resuelto,
firme.
single parent n (*mother*) madre f soltera;
(*father*) padre m soltero.
single-parent family ['sɪŋglpeərənt-] n
familia monoparental.
single room n habitación f individual.
singles bar n (*esp US*) bar m para solteros.
single-sex school ['sɪŋglseks-] n escuela
no mixta.
single-sided [sɪŋgl'saɪdɪd] *adj* (*COMPUT:
disk*) de una cara.
single spacing n (*TYP*): **in** ~ a un espacio.
singlet ['sɪŋglɪt] n camiseta.
singly ['sɪŋglɪ] *adv* uno por uno.
singsong ['sɪŋsɔŋ] *adj* (*tone*) cantarín/ina
♦ n (*songs*): **to have a** ~ tener un
concierto improvisado.
singular ['sɪŋgjulə*] *adj* singular,
extraordinario; (*odd*) extraño; (*LING*)
singular ♦ n (*LING*) singular m; **in the
feminine** ~ en femenino singular.
singularly ['sɪŋgjuləlɪ] *adv* singularmente,
extraordinariamente.
Sinhalese [sɪnhə'liːz] *adj* singhalese.
sinister ['sɪnɪstə*] *adj* siniestro.
sink [sɪŋk] n fregadero ♦ *vb* (*pt* **sank,** *pp* **sunk**
[sæŋk, sʌŋk]) *vt* (*ship*) hundir, echar a
pique; (*foundations*) excavar; (*piles etc*): **to
~ **sth into hundir algo en ♦ *vi* (*gen*)

hundirse; **he sank into a chair/the mud** se dejó caer en una silla/se hundió en el barro; **the shares** *or* **share prices have sunk to 3 dollars** las acciones han bajado a 3 dólares.

▶**sink in** *vi* (*fig*) penetrar, calar; **the news took a long time to** ~ **in** la noticia tardó mucho en hacer mella en él (*or* mí *etc*).

sinking ['sıŋkıŋ] *adj*: **that** ~ **feeling** la sensación esa de desmoralización.

sinking fund *n* fondo de amortización.

sink unit *n* fregadero.

sinner ['sınə*] *n* pecador(a) *m/f*.

Sinn Féin [ʃın'feın] *n partido político republicano de Irlanda del Norte.*

sinuous ['sınjuəs] *adj* sinuoso.

sinus ['saınəs] *n* (*ANAT*) seno.

sip [sıp] *n* sorbo ♦ *vt* sorber, beber a sorbitos.

siphon ['saıfən] *n* sifón *m* ♦ *vt* (*also:* ~ **off**) (*funds*) desviar.

sir [sə:*] *n* señor *m*; **S**~ **John Smith** el Señor John Smith; **yes** ~ sí, señor; **Dear S**~ (*in letter*) Muy señor mío, Estimado Señor; **Dear S**~**s** Muy señores nuestros, Estimados Señores.

siren ['saıərn] *n* sirena.

sirloin ['sə:lɔın] *n* solomillo; ~ **steak** filete *m* de solomillo.

sisal ['saısəl] *n* pita, henequén *m* (*LAM*).

sissy ['sısı] *n* (*col*) marica *m*.

sister ['sıstə*] *n* hermana; (*BRIT: nurse*) enfermera jefe.

sister-in-law ['sıstərınlɔ:] *n* cuñada.

sister organization *n* organización *f* hermana.

sister ship *n* barco gemelo.

sit, *pt, pp* **sat** [sıt, sæt] *vi* sentarse; (*be sitting*) estar sentado; (*assembly*) reunirse; (*dress etc*) caer, sentar ♦ *vt* (*exam*) presentarse a; **that jacket** ~**s well** esa chaqueta sienta bien; **to** ~ **on a committee** ser miembro de una comisión *or* un comité.

▶**sit about, sit around** *vi* holgazanear.

▶**sit back** *vi* (*in seat*) recostarse.

▶**sit down** *vi* sentarse; **to be** ~**ting down** estar sentado.

▶**sit in on** *vt fus*: **to** ~ **in on a discussion** asistir a una discusión.

▶**sit up** *vi* incorporarse; (*not go to bed*) no acostarse.

sitcom ['sıtkɔm] *n abbr* (= *situation comedy*) telecomedia.

sit-down ['sıtdaun] *adj*: ~ **strike** huelga de brazos caídos; **a** ~ **meal** una comida sentada.

site [saıt] *n* sitio; (*also*: **building** ~) solar *m* ♦ *vt* situar.

sit-in ['sıtın] *n* (*demonstration*) sentada *f*.

siting ['saıtıŋ] *n* (*location*) situación *f*, emplazamiento.

sitter ['sıtə*] *n* (*ART*) modelo *m/f*; (*baby*~) canguro *m/f*.

sitting ['sıtıŋ] *n* (*of assembly etc*) sesión *f*; (*in canteen*) turno.

sitting member *n* (*POL*) titular *m/f* de un escaño.

sitting room *n* sala de estar.

sitting tenant *n inquilino con derechos de estancia en una vivienda.*

situate ['sıtjueıt] *vt* situar, ubicar (*LAM*).

situated ['sıtjueıtıd] *adj* situado, ubicado (*LAM*).

situation [sıtju'eıʃən] *n* situación *f*; "~**s vacant**" (*BRIT*) "ofertas de trabajo".

situation comedy *n* (*TV, RADIO*) serie *f* cómica, comedia de situación.

six [sıks] *num* seis.

six-pack ['sıkspæk] *n* (*esp US*) paquete *m* de seis cervezas.

sixteen [sıks'ti:n] *num* dieciséis.

sixth [sıksθ] *adj* sexto; **the upper/lower** ~ (*SCOL*) el séptimo/sexto año.

sixty ['sıkstı] *num* sesenta.

size [saız] *n* (*gen*) tamaño; (*extent*) extensión *f*; (*of clothing*) talla; (*of shoes*) número; **I take** ~ **5 shoes** calzo el número cinco; **I take** ~ **14** mi talla es la 42; **I'd like the small/large** ~ (*of soap powder etc*) quisiera el tamaño pequeño/grande.

▶**size up** *vt* formarse una idea de.

sizeable ['saızəbl] *adj* importante, considerable.

sizzle ['sızl] *vi* crepitar.

SK *abbr* (*Canada*) = *Saskatchewan*.

skate [skeıt] *n* patín *m*; (*fish: pl inv*) raya ♦ *vi* patinar.

▶**skate over, skate round** *vt fus* (*problem, issue*) pasar por alto.

skateboard ['skeıtbɔ:d] *n* monopatín *m*.

skater ['skeıtə*] *n* patinador(a) *m/f*.

skating ['skeıtıŋ] *n* patinaje *m*; **figure** ~ patinaje *m* artístico.

skating rink *n* pista de patinaje.

skeleton ['skelıtn] *n* esqueleto; (*TECH*) armazón *m*; (*outline*) esquema *m*.

skeleton key *n* llave *f* maestra.

skeleton staff *n* personal *m* reducido.

skeptic ['skeptık] *etc* (*US*) = **sceptic**.

sketch [sketʃ] *n* (*drawing*) dibujo; (*outline*) esbozo, bosquejo; (*THEAT*) pieza corta ♦ *vt* dibujar; esbozar.

sketch book *n* bloc *m* de dibujo.

sketching ['sketʃıŋ] *n* dibujo.

sketch pad *n* bloc *m* de dibujo.

sketchy ['sketʃı] *adj* incompleto.

skewer ['skju:ə*] n broqueta.
ski [ski:] n esquí m ♦ vi esquiar.
ski boot n bota de esquí.
skid [skɪd] n patinazo ♦ vi patinar; **to go into a** ~ comenzar a patinar.
skid mark n señal f de patinazo.
skier ['ski:ə*] n esquiador(a) m/f.
skiing ['ski:ɪŋ] n esquí m; **to go** ~ practicar el esquí, (ir a) esquiar.
ski instructor n instructor(a) m/f de esquí.
ski jump n pista para salto de esquí.
skilful, (US) **skillful** ['skɪlful] adj diestro, experto.
ski lift n telesilla m, telesquí m.
skill [skɪl] n destreza, pericia; (technique) arte m, técnica; **there's a certain** ~ **to doing it** se necesita cierta habilidad para hacerlo.
skilled [skɪld] adj hábil, diestro; (worker) cualificado.
skillet ['skɪlɪt] n sartén f pequeña.
skillful ['skɪlful] etc (US) = **skilful** etc.
skil(l)fully ['skɪlfulɪ] adv hábilmente, con destreza.
skim [skɪm] vt (milk) desnatar; (glide over) rozar, rasar ♦ vi: **to** ~ **through** (book) hojear.
skimmed milk [skɪmd-] n leche f desnatada or descremada.
skimp [skɪmp] vt (work) chapucear; (cloth etc) escatimar; **to** ~ **on** (material etc) economizar; (work) escatimar.
skimpy ['skɪmpɪ] adj (meagre) escaso; (skirt) muy corto.
skin [skɪn] n (gen) piel f; (complexion) cutis m; (of fruit, vegetable) piel f, cáscara; (crust: on pudding, paint) nata ♦ vt (fruit etc) pelar; (animal) despellejar; **wet** or **soaked to the** ~ calado hasta los huesos.
skin cancer n cáncer m de piel.
skin-deep ['skɪn'di:p] adj superficial.
skin diver n buceador(a) m/f.
skin diving n buceo.
skinflint ['skɪnflɪnt] n tacaño/a, roñoso/a.
skinhead ['skɪnhɛd] n cabeza m/f rapada, skin(head) m/f.
skinny ['skɪnɪ] adj flaco, magro.
skintight ['skɪntaɪt] adj (dress etc) muy ajustado.
skip [skɪp] n brinco, salto; (container) contenedor m ♦ vi brincar; (with rope) saltar a la comba ♦ vt (pass over) omitir, saltar.
ski pants npl pantalones mpl de esquí.
ski pole n bastón m de esquiar.
skipper ['skɪpə*] n (NAUT, SPORT) capitán m.
skipping rope ['skɪpɪŋ-] n (BRIT) comba, cuerda (de saltar).

ski resort n estación f de esquí.
skirmish ['skə:mɪʃ] n escaramuza.
skirt [skə:t] n falda, pollera (LAM) ♦ vt (surround) ceñir, rodear; (go round) ladear.
skirting board ['skə:tɪŋ-] n (BRIT) rodapié m.
ski run n pista de esquí.
ski suit n traje m de esquiar.
skit [skɪt] n sátira, parodia.
ski tow n arrastre m (de esquí).
skittle ['skɪtl] n bolo; ~**s** (game) boliche m.
skive [skaɪv] vi (BRIT col) gandulear.
skulk [skʌlk] vi esconderse.
skull [skʌl] n calavera; (ANAT) cráneo.
skullcap ['skʌlkæp] n (worn by Jews) casquete m; (worn by Pope) solideo.
skunk [skʌŋk] n mofeta.
sky [skaɪ] n cielo; **to praise sb to the skies** poner a algn por las nubes.
sky-blue [skaɪ'blu:] adj (azul) celeste.
skydiving ['skaɪdaɪvɪŋ] n paracaidismo acrobático.
sky-high ['skaɪ'haɪ] adj (col) por las nubes ♦ adv (throw) muy alto; **prices have gone** ~ (col) los precios están por las nubes.
skylark ['skaɪlɑ:k] n (bird) alondra.
skylight ['skaɪlaɪt] n tragaluz m, claraboya.
skyline ['skaɪlaɪn] n (horizon) horizonte m; (of city) perfil m.
skyscraper ['skaɪskreɪpə*] n rascacielos m inv.
slab [slæb] n (stone) bloque m; (of wood) tabla, plancha; (flat) losa; (of cake) trozo; (of meat, cheese) tajada, trozo.
slack [slæk] adj (loose) flojo; (slow) de poca actividad; (careless) descuidado; (COMM: market) poco activo; (: demand) débil; (period) bajo; **business is** ~ hay poco movimiento en el negocio.
slacken ['slækn] (also: ~ off) vi aflojarse ♦ vt aflojar; (speed) disminuir.
slackness ['slæknɪs] n flojedad f; negligencia.
slacks [slæks] npl pantalones mpl.
slag [slæg] n escoria, escombros mpl.
slag heap n escorial m, escombrera.
slain [sleɪn] pp of **slay**.
slake [sleɪk] vt (one's thirst) apagar.
slalom ['slɑ:ləm] n eslálom m.
slam [slæm] vt (door) cerrar de golpe; (throw) arrojar (violentamente); (criticize) vapulear, vituperar ♦ vi cerrarse de golpe.
slammer [slæmə*] n (col): **the** ~ la trena, el talego.
slander ['slɑ:ndə*] n calumnia, difamación f ♦ vt calumniar, difamar.

slanderous ['slɑːndərəs] adj calumnioso, difamatorio.

slang [slæŋ] n argot m; (jargon) jerga.

slanging match ['slæŋɪŋ-] n (BRIT col) bronca gorda.

slant [slɑːnt] n sesgo, inclinación f; (fig) punto de vista; **to get a new ~ on sth** obtener un nuevo punto de vista sobre algo.

slanted ['slɑːntɪd], **slanting** ['slɑːntɪŋ] adj inclinado.

slap [slæp] n palmada; (in face) bofetada ♦ vt dar una palmada/bofetada a ♦ adv (directly) de lleno.

slapdash ['slæpdæʃ] adj chapucero.

slaphead ['slæphɛd] n (BRIT col) colgado/a.

slapstick ['slæpstɪk] n: ~ **comedy** comedia de payasadas.

slap-up ['slæpʌp] adj: **a ~ meal** (BRIT) un banquetazo, una comilona.

slash [slæʃ] vt acuchillar; (fig: prices) quemar.

slat [slæt] n (of wood, plastic) tablilla, listón m.

slate [sleɪt] n pizarra ♦ vt (BRIT: fig: criticize) vapulear.

slaughter ['slɔːtə*] n (of animals) matanza; (of people) carnicería ♦ vt matar.

slaughterhouse ['slɔːtəhaus] n matadero.

Slav [slɑːv] adj eslavo.

slave [sleɪv] n esclavo/a ♦ vi (also: ~ **away**) trabajar como un negro; **to ~ (away) at sth** trabajar como un negro en algo.

slave driver n (col, pej) tirano/a.

slave labour, (US) **slave labor** n trabajo de esclavos.

slaver ['slævə*] vi (dribble) babear.

slavery ['sleɪvərɪ] n esclavitud f.

slavish ['sleɪvɪʃ] adj (devotion) de esclavo; (imitation) servil.

slay, pt **slew**, pp **slain** [sleɪ, sluː, sleɪn] vt (literary) matar.

sleazy ['sliːzɪ] adj (fig: place) sórdido.

sledge [slɛdʒ], (US) **sled** [slɛd] n trineo.

sledgehammer ['slɛdʒhæmə*] n mazo.

sleek [sliːk] adj (shiny) lustroso.

sleep [sliːp] n sueño ♦ vb (pt, pp **slept** [slɛpt]) vi dormir ♦ vt: **we can ~ 4** podemos alojar a 4, tenemos cabida para 4; **to go to ~** dormirse; **to have a good night's ~** dormir toda la noche; **to put to ~** (patient) dormir; (animal: euphemism: kill) sacrificar; **to ~ lightly** tener el sueño ligero; **to ~ with sb** (euphemism) acostarse con algn.

▶**sleep in** vi (oversleep) quedarse dormido.

sleeper ['sliːpə*] n (person) durmiente m/f; (BRIT RAIL: on track) traviesa; (: train)

coche-cama m.

sleepiness ['sliːpɪnɪs] n somnolencia.

sleeping bag ['sliːpɪŋ-] n saco de dormir.

sleeping car n coche-cama m.

sleeping partner n (COMM) socio/a comanditario/a.

sleeping pill n somnífero.

sleeping sickness n enfermedad f del sueño.

sleepless ['sliːplɪs] adj: **a ~ night** una noche en blanco.

sleeplessness ['sliːplɪsnɪs] n insomnio.

sleepover ['sliːpəuvə*] n: **we're having a ~ at Fiona's** pasamos la noche en casa de Fiona.

sleepwalk ['sliːpwɔːk] vi caminar dormido; (habitually) ser sonámbulo.

sleepwalker ['sliːpwɔːkə*] n sonámbulo/a.

sleepy ['sliːpɪ] adj soñoliento; **to be** or **feel ~** tener sueño.

sleet [sliːt] n aguanieve f.

sleeve [sliːv] n manga; (TECH) manguito; (of record) funda.

sleeveless ['sliːvlɪs] adj (garment) sin mangas.

sleigh [sleɪ] n trineo.

sleight [slaɪt] n: ~ **of hand** prestidigitación f.

slender ['slɛndə*] adj delgado; (means) escaso.

slept [slɛpt] pt, pp of **sleep**.

sleuth [sluːθ] n (col) detective m/f.

slew [sluː] vi (veer) torcerse ♦ pt of **slay**.

slice [slaɪs] n (of meat) tajada; (of bread) rebanada; (of lemon) rodaja; (utensil) paleta ♦ vt cortar, tajar; rebanar; ~**d bread** pan m de molde.

slick [slɪk] adj (skilful) hábil, diestro ♦ n (also: **oil ~**) capa de aceite.

slid [slɪd] pt, pp of **slide**.

slide [slaɪd] n (in playground) tobogán m; (PHOT) diapositiva; (microscope ~) portaobjetos m inv, plaquilla de vidrio; (BRIT: also: **hair ~**) pasador m ♦ (vb: pt, pp **slid** [slɪd]) vt correr, deslizar ♦ vi (slip) resbalarse; (glide) deslizarse; **to let things ~** (fig) dejar que ruede la bola.

slide projector n (PHOT) proyector m de diapositivas.

slide rule n regla de cálculo.

sliding ['slaɪdɪŋ] adj (door) corredizo; ~ **roof** (AUT) techo de corredera.

sliding scale n escala móvil.

slight [slaɪt] adj (slim) delgado; (frail) delicado; (pain etc) leve; (trifling) insignificante; (small) pequeño ♦ n desaire m ♦ vt (offend) ofender, desairar; **a ~ improvement** una ligera mejora; **not in the ~est** en absoluto; **there's not the**

~est possibility no hay la menor *or* más mínima posibilidad.

slightly ['slaɪtlɪ] *adv* ligeramente, un poco; **~ built** delgado.

slim [slɪm] *adj* delgado, esbelto ♦ *vi* adelgazar.

slime [slaɪm] *n* limo, cieno.

slimming ['slɪmɪŋ] *n* adelgazamiento ♦ *adj* (*diet, pills*) adelgazante.

slimness ['slɪmnɪs] *n* delgadez *f*.

slimy ['slaɪmɪ] *adj* limoso; (*covered with mud*) fangoso; (*also fig: person*) adulón, zalamero.

sling [slɪŋ] *n* (*MED*) cabestrillo; (*weapon*) honda ♦ *vt* (*pt, pp* **slung** [slʌŋ]) tirar, arrojar; **to have one's arm in a ~** llevar el brazo en cabestrillo.

slink, *pt, pp* **slunk** [slɪŋk, slʌŋk] *vi*: **to ~ away, ~ off** escabullirse.

slinky ['slɪŋkɪ] *adj* (*clothing*) pegado al cuerpo, superajustado.

slip [slɪp] *n* (*slide*) resbalón *m*; (*mistake*) descuido; (*underskirt*) combinación *f*; (*of paper*) papelito ♦ *vt* (*slide*) deslizar ♦ *vi* (*slide*) deslizarse; (*stumble*) resbalar(se); (*decline*) decaer; (*move smoothly*): **to ~ into/out of** (*room etc*) colarse en/salirse de; **to let a chance ~ by** dejar escapar la oportunidad; **to ~ sth on/off** ponerse/quitarse algo; **to ~ on a jumper** ponerse un jersey *or* un suéter; **it ~ped from her hand** se la cayó de la mano; **to give sb the ~** dar esquinazo a algn; **wages ~** (*BRIT*) hoja del sueldo; **a ~ of the tongue** un lapsus.

▶**slip away** *vi* escabullirse.

▶**slip in** *vt* meter ♦ *vi* meterse, colarse.

▶**slip out** *vi* (*go out*) salir (un momento).

slip-on ['slɪpɔn] *adj* de quita y pon; (*shoes*) sin cordones.

slipped disc [slɪpt-] *n* vértebra dislocada.

slipper ['slɪpə*] *n* zapatilla, pantufla.

slippery ['slɪpərɪ] *adj* resbaladizo.

slip road *n* (*BRIT*) carretera de acceso.

slipshod ['slɪpʃɔd] *adj* descuidado, chapucero.

slipstream ['slɪpstriːm] *n* viento de la hélice.

slip-up ['slɪpʌp] *n* (*error*) desliz *m*.

slipway ['slɪpweɪ] *n* grada, gradas *fpl*.

slit [slɪt] *n* raja; (*cut*) corte *m* ♦ *vt* (*pt, pp* **slit**) rajar, cortar; **to ~ sb's throat** cortarle el pescuezo a algn.

slither ['slɪðə*] *vi* deslizarse.

sliver ['slɪvə*] *n* (*of glass, wood*) astilla; (*of cheese, sausage*) lonja, loncha.

slob [slɔb] *n* (*col*) patán/ana *m/f*, palurdo/a.

slog [slɔg] (*BRIT*) *vi* sudar tinta ♦ *n*: **it was a ~ costó trabajo (hacerlo).**

slogan ['sləugən] *n* eslogan *m*, lema *m*.

slop [slɔp] *vi* (*also*: **~ over**) derramarse, desbordarse ♦ *vt* derramar, verter.

slope [sləup] *n* (*up*) cuesta, pendiente *f*; (*down*) declive *m*; (*side of mountain*) falda, vertiente *f* ♦ *vi*: **to ~ down** estar en declive; **to ~ up** subir (en pendiente).

sloping ['sləupɪŋ] *adj* en pendiente; en declive.

sloppily ['slɔpɪlɪ] *adv* descuidadamente; con descuido *or* desaliño.

sloppiness ['slɔpɪnɪs] *n* descuido; desaliño.

sloppy ['slɔpɪ] *adj* (*work*) descuidado; (*appearance*) desaliñado.

slosh [slɔʃ] *vi*: **to ~ about** *or* **around** chapotear.

sloshed [slɔʃt] *adj* (*col: drunk*): **to get ~** agarrar una trompa.

slot [slɔt] *n* ranura; (*fig: in timetable*) hueco; (*RADIO, TV*) espacio ♦ *vt*: **to ~ into** encajar en.

sloth [sləuθ] *n* (*vice*) pereza; (*ZOOL*) oso perezoso.

slot machine *n* (*BRIT: vending machine*) máquina expendedora, (*for gambling*) máquina tragaperras.

slot meter *n* contador *m*.

slouch [slautʃ] *vi*: **to ~ about, ~ around** (*laze*) gandulear.

Slovak ['sləuvæk] *adj* eslovaco ♦ *n* eslovaco/a; (*LING*) eslovaco; **the ~ Republic** Eslovaquia.

Slovakia [sləu'vækɪə] *n* Eslovaquia.

Slovakian [sləu'vækɪən] *adj, n* = **Slovak**.

Slovene ['sləuviːn] *adj* esloveno ♦ *n* esloveno/a; (*LING*) esloveno.

Slovenia [sləu'viːnɪə] *n* Eslovenia.

Slovenian [sləu'viːnɪən] *adj, n* = **Slovene**.

slovenly ['slʌvənlɪ] *adj* (*dirty*) desaliñado, desaseado; (*careless*) descuidado.

slow [sləu] *adj* lento; (*watch*): **to be ~** estar atrasado ♦ *adv* lentamente, despacio ♦ *vt* (*also*: **~ down, ~ up**) retardar; (*engine, machine*) reducir la marcha de ♦ *vi* (*also*: **~ down, ~ up**) ir más despacio; **"~"** (*road sign*) "disminuir la velocidad"; **at a ~ speed** a una velocidad lenta; **the ~ lane** el carril derecho; **business is ~** (*COMM*) hay poca actividad; **my watch is 20 minutes ~** mi reloj lleva 20 minutos de retraso; **bake for two hours in a ~ oven** cocer *or* asar 2 horas en el horno a fuego lento; **to be ~ to act/decide** tardar en obrar/decidir; **to go ~** (*driver*) conducir despacio; (*in industrial dispute*) trabajar a ritmo lento.

slow-acting [sləu'æktɪŋ] *adj* de efecto

retardado.
slowcoach ['sləukəutʃ] n (BRIT col) tortuga.
slowdown ['sləudaun] n (US) huelga de celo.
slowly ['sləulɪ] adv lentamente, despacio; **to drive ~** conducir despacio; **~ but surely** lento pero seguro.
slow motion n: **in ~** a cámara lenta.
slow-moving ['sləu'muːvɪŋ] adj lento.
slowpoke ['sləupəuk] n (US col) = **slowcoach.**
sludge [slʌdʒ] n lodo, fango.
slug [slʌg] n babosa; (bullet) posta.
sluggish ['slʌgɪʃ] adj (slow) lento; (lazy) perezoso; (business, market, sales) inactivo.
sluggishly ['slʌgɪʃlɪ] adv lentamente.
sluggishness ['slʌgɪʃnɪs] n lentitud f.
sluice [sluːs] n (gate) esclusa; (channel) canal m ♦ vt: **to ~ down** or **out** regar.
slum [slʌm] n (area) barrios mpl bajos; (house) casucha.
slumber ['slʌmbə*] n sueño.
slum clearance (programme) n (programa m de) deschabolización f.
slump [slʌmp] n (economic) depresión f ♦ vi hundirse; **the ~ in the price of copper** la baja repentina del precio del cobre; **he was ~ed over the wheel** se había desplomado encima del volante.
slung [slʌŋ] pt, pp of **sling.**
slunk [slʌŋk] pt, pp of **slink.**
slur [slɜ:*] n calumnia ♦ vt calumniar, difamar; (word) pronunciar mal; **to cast a ~ on sb** manchar la reputación de algn, difamar a algn.
slurp [slɜ:p] vt, vi sorber ruidosamente.
slurred [slɜ:d] adj (pronunciation) poco claro.
slush [slʌʃ] n nieve f a medio derretir.
slush fund n fondos mpl para sobornar.
slushy ['slʌʃɪ] adj (col: poetry etc) sentimentaloide.
slut [slʌt] n marrana.
sly [slaɪ] adj (clever) astuto; (nasty) malicioso.
slyly ['slaɪlɪ] adv astutamente; taimadamente.
slyness ['slaɪnɪs] n astucia.
smack [smæk] n (slap) manotada; (blow) golpe m ♦ vt dar una manotada a; golpear con la mano ♦ vi: **to ~ of** saber a, oler a ♦ adv: **it fell ~ in the middle** (col) cayó justo en medio.
smacker ['smækə*] n (col: kiss) besazo; (: BRIT: pound note) billete m de una libra; (: US: dollar bill) billete m de un dólar.
small [smɔ:l] adj pequeño, chico (esp LAM);

(in height) bajo, chaparro (LAM); (letter) en minúscula ♦ n: **~ of the back** región f lumbar; **~ shopkeeper** pequeño/a comerciante m/f; **to get** or **grow ~er** (stain, town) empequeñecer; (debt, organization, numbers) reducir, disminuir; **to make ~er** (amount, income) reducir; (garden, object, garment) achicar.
small ads npl (BRIT) anuncios mpl por palabras.
small arms npl armas fpl cortas.
small business n pequeño negocio; **~es** la pequeña empresa.
small change n suelto, cambio.
smallholder ['smɔ:lhəuldə*] n (BRIT) granjero/a, parcelero/a.
smallholding ['smɔ:lhəuldɪŋ] n parcela, minifundio.
small hours npl: **in the ~** a altas horas de la noche.
smallish ['smɔ:lɪʃ] adj más bien pequeño.
small-minded [smɔ:l'maɪndɪd] adj mezquino, de miras estrechas.
smallness ['smɔ:lnɪs] n pequeñez f.
smallpox ['smɔ:lpɔks] n viruela.
small print n letra pequeña or menuda.
small-scale ['smɔ:lskeɪl] adj (map, model) a escala reducida; (business, farming) en pequeña escala.
small talk n cháchara.
small-time ['smɔ:ltaɪm] adj (col) de poca categoría or monta; **a ~ thief** un(a) ratero/a.
small-town ['smɔ:ltəun] adj de provincias.
smarmy ['smɑːmɪ] adj (BRIT pej) pelotillero (fam).
smart [smɑːt] adj elegante; (clever) listo, inteligente; (quick) rápido, vivo; (weapon) inteligente ♦ vi escocer, picar; **the ~ set** la gente de buen tono; **to look ~** estar elegante; **my eyes are ~ing** me pican los ojos.
smartcard ['smɑːtkɑːd] n tarjeta inteligente.
smarten up ['smɑːtn-] vi arreglarse ♦ vt arreglar.
smartness ['smɑːtnɪs] n elegancia; (cleverness) inteligencia.
smash [smæʃ] n (also: **~-up**) choque m; (sound) estrépito ♦ vt (break) hacer pedazos; (car etc) estrellar; (SPORT: record) batir ♦ vi hacerse pedazos; (against wall etc) estrellarse.
▶**smash up** vt (car) hacer pedazos; (room) destrozar.
smash hit n exitazo.
smashing ['smæʃɪŋ] adj (col) cojonudo.
smattering ['smætərɪŋ] n: **a ~ of Spanish**

algo de español.

smear [smɪə*] *n* mancha; (*MED*) frotis *m inv* (cervical); (*insult*) calumnia ♦ *vt* untar; (*fig*) calumniar, difamar; **his hands were ~ed with oil/ink** tenía las manos manchadas de aceite/tinta.

smear campaign *n* campaña de calumnias.

smear test *n* (*MED*) citología, frotis *m inv* (cervical).

smell [smɛl] *n* olor *m*; (*sense*) olfato ♦ (*vb: pt, pp* **smelt** *or* **~ed** [smɛlt, smɛld]) *vt, vi* oler; **it ~s good/of garlic** huele bien/a ajo.

smelly ['smɛlɪ] *adj* maloliente.

smelt [smɛlt] *vt* (*ore*) fundir ♦ *pt, pp of* **smell**.

smile [smaɪl] *n* sonrisa ♦ *vi* sonreír.

smiley ['smaɪlɪ] *n* (*in e-mail etc*) smiley *m*, emoticón *m*.

smiling ['smaɪlɪŋ] *adj* sonriente, risueño.

smirk [smə:k] *n* sonrisa falsa *or* afectada.

smith [smɪθ] *n* herrero.

smitten ['smɪtn] *adj*: **he's really ~ with her** está totalmente loco por ella.

smock [smɔk] *n* blusón; (*children's*) babi *m*; (*US: overall*) guardapolvo, bata.

smog [smɔg] *n* smog *m*.

smoke [smouk] *n* humo ♦ *vi* fumar; (*chimney*) echar humo ♦ *vt* (*cigarettes*) fumar; **to go up in ~** quemarse; (*fig*) quedar en agua de borrajas.

smoked [smoukt] *adj* (*bacon, glass*) ahumado.

smokeless fuel ['smouklɪs-] *n* combustible *m* sin humo.

smokeless zone ['smouklɪs-] *n* zona libre de humo.

smoker ['smoukə*] *n* fumador(a) *m/f*.

smoke screen *n* cortina de humo.

smoke shop *n* (*US*) estanco, tabaquería.

smoking ['smoukɪŋ] *n*: "**no ~**" "prohibido fumar"; **he's given up ~** ha dejado de fumar.

smoking compartment, (US) smoking car *n* departamento de fumadores.

smoky ['smoukɪ] *adj* (*room*) lleno de humo.

smolder ['smouldə*] *vi* (*US*) = **smoulder**.

smoochy ['smu:tʃɪ] *adj* (*col*) blandengue.

smooth [smu:ð] *adj* liso; (*sea*) tranquilo; (*flavour, movement*) suave; (*person: pej*) meloso ♦ *vt* alisar; (*also: ~ out*) (*creases*) alisar; (*difficulties*) allanar.

▶**smooth over** *vt*: **to ~ things over** (*fig*) limar las asperezas.

smoothly ['smu:ðlɪ] *adv* (*easily*) fácilmente; **everything went ~** todo fue sobre ruedas.

smoothness ['smu:ðnɪs] *n* (*of skin, cloth*) tersura; (*of surface, flavour, movement*) suavidad *f*.

smother ['smʌðə*] *vt* sofocar; (*repress*)

contener.

smoulder, (US) smolder ['smouldə*] *vi* arder sin llama.

SMS *n abbr* (= *short message service*) SMS *m*.

smudge [smʌdʒ] *n* mancha ♦ *vt* manchar.

smug [smʌg] *adj* engreído.

smuggle ['smʌgl] *vt* pasar de contrabando; **to ~ in/out** (*goods etc*) meter/sacar de contrabando.

smuggler ['smʌglə*] *n* contrabandista *m/f*.

smuggling ['smʌglɪŋ] *n* contrabando.

smugly ['smʌglɪ] *adv* con suficiencia.

smugness ['smʌgnɪs] *n* suficiencia.

smut [smʌt] *n* (*grain of soot*) carbonilla, hollín *m*; (*mark*) tizne *m*; (*in conversation etc*) obscenidades *fpl*.

smutty ['smʌtɪ] *adj* (*fig*) verde, obsceno.

snack [snæk] *n* bocado, tentempié *m*; **to have a ~** tomar un bocado.

snack bar *n* cafetería.

snag [snæg] *n* problema *m*; **to run into** *or* **hit a ~** encontrar inconvenientes, dar con un obstáculo.

snail [sneɪl] *n* caracol *m*.

snake [sneɪk] *n* (*gen*) serpiente *f*; (*harmless*) culebra; (*poisonous*) víbora.

snap [snæp] *n* (*sound*) chasquido; golpe *m* seco; (*photograph*) foto *f* ♦ *adj* (*decision*) instantáneo ♦ *vt* (*fingers etc*) castañetear; (*break*) partir, quebrar; (*photograph*) tomar una foto de ♦ *vi* (*break*) partirse, quebrarse; (*fig: person*) contestar bruscamente; **to ~ (at sb)** (*subj: person*) hablar con brusquedad (a algn); (: *dog*) intentar morder (a algn); **to ~ shut** cerrarse de golpe; **to ~ one's fingers at sth/sb** (*fig*) burlarse de algo/uno; **a cold ~** (*of weather*) una ola de frío.

▶**snap off** *vi* (*break*) partirse.

▶**snap up** *vt* agarrar.

snap fastener *n* (*US*) botón *m* de presión.

snappy ['snæpɪ] *adj* (*col: answer*) instantáneo; (*slogan*) conciso; **make it ~!** (*hurry up*) ¡date prisa!

snapshot ['snæpʃɔt] *n* foto *f* (instantánea).

snare [snɛə*] *n* trampa ♦ *vt* cazar con trampa; (*fig*) engañar.

snarl [snɑ:l] *vi* gruñir ♦ *vt* gruñir; **to get ~ed up** (*wool, plans*) enmarañarse, enredarse; (*traffic*) quedar atascado.

snatch [snætʃ] *n* (*fig*) robo; **~es of** trocitos *mpl de* ♦ *vt* (*~ away*) arrebatar; (*grasp*) coger (*SP*), agarrar; **~es of conversation** fragmentos *mpl* de conversación; **to ~ a sandwich** comer un bocadillo a prisa; **to ~ some sleep** buscar tiempo para dormir; **don't ~!** ¡no me lo quites!

▶**snatch up** vt agarrar.

snazzy ['snæzɪ] adj (col) guapo.

sneak [sni:k] vi: **to ~ in/out** entrar/salir a hurtadillas ♦ vt: **to ~ a look at sth** mirar algo de reojo ♦ n (fam) soplón/ona m/f.

sneakers ['sni:kəz] npl (US) zapatos mpl de lona, zapatillas fpl.

sneaking ['sni:kɪŋ] adj: **to have a ~ feeling/ suspicion that ...** tener la sensación/ sospecha de que ....

sneaky ['sni:kɪ] adj furtivo.

sneer [snɪə*] n sonrisa de desprecio ♦ vi sonreír con desprecio; **to ~ at sth/sb** burlarse or mofarse de algo/uno.

sneeze [sni:z] n estornudo ♦ vi estornudar.

snide [snaɪd] adj (col: sarcastic) sarcástico.

sniff [snɪf] vi sorber (por la nariz) ♦ vt husmear, oler; (glue, drug) esnifar.

▶**sniff at** vt fus: **it's not to be ~ed at** no es de despreciar.

sniffer dog ['snɪfə-] n (for drugs) perro antidroga; (for explosives) perro antiexplosivos.

snigger ['snɪgə*] n risa disimulada ♦ vi reírse con disimulo.

snip [snɪp] n (piece) recorte m; (bargain) ganga ♦ vt tijeretear.

sniper ['snaɪpə*] n francotirador(a) m/f.

snippet ['snɪpɪt] n retazo.

snivelling, (US) **sniveling** ['snɪvlɪŋ] adj llorón/ona.

snob [snɔb] n (e)snob m/f.

snobbery ['snɔbərɪ] n (e)snobismo.

snobbish ['snɔbɪʃ] adj (e)snob.

snobbishness ['snɔbɪʃnɪs] n (e)snobismo.

snog [snɔg] vi (BRIT col) besuquearse, morrear; **to ~ sb** besuquear a algn.

snooker ['snu:kə*] n snooker m.

snoop [snu:p] vi: **to ~ about** fisgonear.

snooper ['snu:pə*] n fisgón/ona m/f.

snooty ['snu:tɪ] adj (e)snob.

snooze [snu:z] n siesta ♦ vi echar una siesta.

snore [snɔ:*] vi roncar ♦ n ronquido.

snoring ['snɔ:rɪŋ] n ronquidos mpl.

snorkel ['snɔ:kl] n tubo de respiración.

snort [snɔ:t] n bufido ♦ vi bufar ♦ vt (col: drugs) esnifar.

snotty ['snɔtɪ] adj (col) creído.

snout [snaut] n hocico, morro.

snow [snəu] n nieve f ♦ vi nevar ♦ vt: **to be ~ed under with work** estar agobiado de trabajo.

snowball ['snəubɔ:l] n bola de nieve ♦ vi ir aumentándose.

snow-blind ['snəublaɪnd] adj cegado por la nieve.

snowbound ['snəubaund] adj bloqueado

por la nieve.

snow-capped ['snəukæpt] adj (peak) cubierto de nieve, nevado.

snowdrift ['snəudrɪft] n ventisquero.

snowdrop ['snəudrɔp] n campanilla.

snowfall ['snəufɔ:l] n nevada.

snowflake ['snəufleɪk] n copo de nieve.

snowline ['snəulaɪn] n límite m de las nieves perpetuas.

snowman ['snəumæn] n figura de nieve.

snowplough, (US) **snowplow** ['snəuplau] n quitanieves m inv.

snowshoe ['snəuʃu:] n raqueta (de nieve).

snowstorm ['snəustɔ:m] n tormenta de nieve, nevasca.

Snow White n Blancanieves f.

snowy ['snəuɪ] adj de (mucha) nieve.

SNP n abbr (BRIT POL) = Scottish National Party.

snub [snʌb] vt: **to ~ sb** desairar a algn ♦ n desaire m, repulsa.

snub-nosed [snʌb'nəuzd] adj chato.

snuff [snʌf] n rapé m ♦ vt (also: ~ out: candle) apagar.

snuffbox ['snʌfbɔks] n caja de rapé.

snuff movie n (col) película porno (que acaba con un asesinato real).

snug [snʌg] adj (cosy) cómodo; (fitted) ajustado.

snuggle ['snʌgl] vi: **to ~ down in bed** hacerse un ovillo or acurrucarse en la cama; **to ~ up to sb** acurrucarse junto a algn.

snugly ['snʌglɪ] adv cómodamente; **it fits ~** (object in pocket etc) cabe perfectamente; (garment) ajusta perfectamente.

SO abbr (BANKING) = standing order.

━━━━━━━━━━━━━━━━━━━━━━ KEYWORD

so [səu] adv **1** (thus, likewise) así, de este modo; **if ~** de ser así; **I like swimming — ~ do I** a mí me gusta nadar — a mí también; **I've got work to do — ~ has Paul** tengo trabajo que hacer — Paul también; **it's 5 o'clock — ~ it is!** son las cinco — ¡pues es verdad!; **I hope/think ~** espero/creo que sí; **~ far** hasta ahora; (in past) hasta este momento; **~ to speak** por decirlo así

2 (in comparisons etc: to such a degree) tan; **~ quickly (that)** tan rápido (que); **~ big (that)** tan grande (que); **she's not ~ clever as her brother** no es tan lista como su hermano; **we were ~ worried** estábamos preocupadísimos

3: **~ much** adj tanto/a ♦ adv tanto; **~ many** tantos/as

4 (phrases): **10 or ~** unos 10, 10 o así; **~**

long! (*inf: goodbye*) ¡hasta luego!; **she
didn't ~ much as send me a birthday card**
no me mandó ni una tarjeta siquiera por
mi cumpleaños; **~ (what)?** (*col*) ¿y (qué)?
♦ *conj* **1** (*expressing purpose*): **~ as to do**
para hacer; **~ (that)** para que +*sub*; **we
hurried ~ (that) we wouldn't be late** nos
dimos prisa para no llegar tarde
2 (*expressing result*) así que; **~ you see, I
could have gone** así que ya ves, (yo)
podría haber ido; **~ that's the reason!**
¡así que es por eso *or* por eso es!

soak [səuk] *vt* (*drench*) empapar; (*put in
water*) remojar ♦ *vi* remojarse, estar a
remojo.
▶**soak in** *vi* penetrar.
▶**soak up** *vt* absorber.
soaking ['səukɪŋ] *adj* (*also:* ~ **wet**) calado *or*
empapado (hasta los huesos *or* el
tuétano).
so-and-so ['səuənsəu] *n* (*somebody*)
fulano/a de tal.
soap [səup] *n* jabón *m*.
soapbox ['səupbɔks] *n* tribuna
improvisada.
soapflakes ['səupfleɪks] *npl* jabón *msg* en
escamas.
soap opera *n* (*TV*) telenovela; (*RADIO*)
radionovela.
soap powder *n* jabón *m* en polvo.
soapsuds ['səupsʌdz] *npl* espuma *sg*.
soapy ['səupɪ] *adj* jabonoso.
soar [sɔː*] *vi* (*on wings*) remontarse;
(*building etc*) elevarse; (*price*) subir
vertiginosamente; (*morale*) elevarse.
soaring ['sɔːrɪŋ] *adj* (*flight*) por lo alto;
(*prices*) en alza *or* aumento; **~ inflation**
inflación *f* altísima *or* en aumento.
sob [sɔb] *n* sollozo ♦ *vi* sollozar.
s.o.b. *n abbr* (*US col!* = *son of a bitch*) hijo de
puta (*!*).
sober ['səubə*] *adj* (*moderate*) moderado;
(*serious*) serio; (*not drunk*) sobrio; (*colour,
style*) discreto.
▶**sober up** *vi* pasársele a algn la
borrachera.
soberly ['səubəlɪ] *adv* sobriamente.
sobriety [sə'braɪətɪ] *n* (*not being drunk*)
sobriedad *f*; (*seriousness, sedateness*)
seriedad *f*, sensatez *f*.
sob story *n* (*col, pej*) dramón *m*.
Soc. *abbr* (= *society*) S.
so-called ['səu'kɔːld] *adj* presunto,
supuesto.
soccer ['sɔkə*] *n* fútbol *m*.
soccer pitch *n* campo *or* cancha (*LAM*) de
fútbol.

soccer player *n* jugador(a) *m/f* de fútbol.
sociability [səuʃə'bɪlɪtɪ] *n* sociabilidad *f*.
sociable ['səuʃəbl] *adj* sociable.
social ['səuʃl] *adj* social ♦ *n* velada, fiesta.
social class *n* clase *f* social.
social climber *n* arribista *m/f*.
social club *n* club *m*.
Social Democrat *n* socialdemócrata *m/f*.
social insurance *n* (*US*) seguro social.
socialism ['səuʃəlɪzəm] *n* socialismo.
socialist ['səuʃəlɪst] *adj*, *n* socialista *m/f*.
socialite ['səuʃəlaɪt] *n* persona que alterna
con la buena sociedad.
socialize ['səuʃəlaɪz] *vi* hacer vida social; **to
~ with** (*colleagues*) salir con.
social life *n* vida social
socially ['səuʃəlɪ] *adv* socialmente.
social science(s) *n(pl)* ciencias *fpl*
sociales.
social security *n* seguridad *f* social.
social services *npl* servicios *mpl* sociales.
social welfare *n* asistencia social.
social work *n* asistencia social.
social worker *n* asistente/a *m/f* social.
society [sə'saɪətɪ] *n* sociedad *f*; (*club*)
asociación *f*; (*also:* **high ~**) buena
sociedad ♦ *cpd* (*party, column*) social, de
sociedad.
socio-economic ['səusɪəuɪːkə'nɔmɪk] *adj*
socioeconómico.
sociological [səusɪə'lɔdʒɪkəl] *adj*
sociológico.
sociologist [səusɪ'ɔlədʒɪst] *n* sociólogo/a.
sociology [səusɪ'ɔlədʒɪ] *n* sociología.
sock [sɔk] *n* calcetín *m*, media (*LAM*); **to pull
one's ~s up** (*fig*) hacer esfuerzos,
despabilarse.
socket ['sɔkɪt] *n* (*ELEC*) enchufe *m*.
sod [sɔd] *n* (*of earth*) césped *m*; (*col!*)
cabrón/ona *m/f* (*!*) ♦ *excl:* **~ off!** (*col!*) ¡vete
a la porra!
soda ['səudə] *n* (*CHEM*) sosa; (*also:* ~ **water**)
soda; (*US: also:* ~ **pop**) gaseosa.
sodden ['sɔdn] *adj* empapado.
sodium ['səudɪəm] *n* sodio.
sodium chloride *n* cloruro sódico *or* de
sodio.
sofa ['səufə] *n* sofá *m*.
Sofia ['səufɪə] *n* Sofía.
soft [sɔft] *adj* (*teacher, parent*) blando;
(*gentle, not loud*) suave; (*stupid*) bobo; **~
currency** divisa blanda *or* débil.
soft-boiled ['sɔftbɔɪld] *adj* (*egg*) pasado por
agua.
soft copy *n* (*COMPUT*) copia transitoria.
soft drink *n* bebida no alcohólica.
soft drugs *npl* drogas *fpl* blandas.
soften ['sɔfn] *vt* ablandar; suavizar ♦ *vi*

ablandarse; suavizarse.

softener ['sɔfnə*] n suavizante m.

soft fruit n bayas fpl.

soft furnishings npl tejidos mpl para el hogar.

soft-hearted [sɔft'hɑːtɪd] adj bondadoso.

softly ['sɔftlɪ] adv suavemente; (gently) delicadamente, con delicadeza.

softness ['sɔftnɪs] n blandura; suavidad f.

soft option n alternativa fácil.

soft sell n venta persuasiva.

soft target n blanco or objetivo fácil.

soft toy n juguete m de peluche.

software ['sɔftwɛə*] n (COMPUT) software m.

soft water n agua blanda.

soggy ['sɔgɪ] adj empapado.

soil [sɔɪl] n (earth) tierra, suelo ♦ vt ensuciar.

soiled [sɔɪld] adj sucio, manchado.

sojourn ['sɔdʒən] n (formal) estancia.

solace ['sɔlɪs] n consuelo.

solar ['səulə*] adj solar.

solarium, pl **solaria** [sə'lɛərɪəm, -rɪə] n solario.

solar panel n panel m solar.

solar plexus [-'plɛksəs] n (ANAT) plexo solar.

solar power n energía solar.

solar system n sistema m solar.

sold [səuld] pt, pp of **sell**.

solder ['səuldə*] vt soldar ♦ n soldadura.

soldier ['səuldʒə*] n (gen) soldado; (army man) militar m ♦ vi: **to ~ on** seguir adelante; **toy ~** soldadito de plomo.

sold out adj (COMM) agotado.

sole [səul] n (of foot) planta; (of shoe) suela; (fish: pl inv) lenguado ♦ adj único; **the ~ reason** la única razón.

solely ['səullɪ] adv únicamente, sólo, solamente; **I will hold you ~ responsible** le consideraré el único responsable.

solemn ['sɔləm] adj solemne.

sole trader n (COMM) comerciante m/f exclusivo/a.

solicit [sə'lɪsɪt] vt (request) solicitar ♦ vi (prostitute) abordar clientes.

solicitor [sə'lɪsɪtə*] n abogado/a; see also **barrister**.

solid ['sɔlɪd] adj sólido; (gold etc) macizo; (line) continuo; (vote) unánime ♦ n sólido; **we waited 2 ~ hours** esperamos 2 horas enteras; **to be on ~ ground** estar en tierra firme; (fig) estar seguro.

solidarity [sɔlɪ'dærɪtɪ] n solidaridad f.

solid fuel n combustible m sólido.

solidify [sə'lɪdɪfaɪ] vi solidificarse.

solidity [sə'lɪdɪtɪ] n solidez f.

solidly ['sɔlɪdlɪ] adv sólidamente; (fig) unánimemente.

solid-state ['sɔlɪdsteɪt] adj (ELEC) estado sólido.

soliloquy [sə'lɪləkwɪ] n soliloquio.

solitaire [sɔlɪ'tɛə*] n (game, gem) solitario.

solitary ['sɔlɪtərɪ] adj solitario, solo; (isolated) apartado, aislado; (only) único.

solitary confinement n incomunicación f; **to be in ~** estar incomunicado.

solitude ['sɔlɪtjuːd] n soledad f.

solo ['səuləu] n solo.

soloist ['səuləuɪst] n solista m/f.

Solomon Islands ['sɔləmən-] npl: **the ~** las Islas Salomón.

solstice ['sɔlstɪs] n solsticio.

soluble ['sɔljubl] adj soluble.

solution [sə'luːʃən] n solución f.

solve [sɔlv] vt resolver, solucionar.

solvency ['sɔlvənsɪ] n (COMM) solvencia.

solvent ['sɔlvənt] adj (COMM) solvente ♦ n (CHEM) solvente m.

solvent abuse n uso indebido de disolventes.

Som. abbr (BRIT) = **Somerset**.

Somali [sə'mɑːlɪ] adj, n somalí m/f.

Somalia [sə'mɑːlɪə] n Somalia.

Somaliland [sə'mɑːlɪlænd] n Somaliland f.

sombre, (US) **somber** ['sɔmbə*] adj sombrío.

═══════════════════════ KEYWORD

some [sʌm] adj **1** (a certain amount or number of): **~ tea/water/biscuits** té/agua/(unas) galletas; **have ~ tea** tómese un té; **there's ~ milk in the fridge** hay leche en el frigo; **there were ~ people outside** había algunas personas fuera; **I've got ~ money, but not much** tengo algo de dinero, pero no mucho

2 (certain: in contrasts) algunos/as; **~ people say that ...** hay quien dice que ...; **~ films were excellent, but most were mediocre** hubo películas excelentes, pero la mayoría fueron mediocres

3 (unspecified): **~ woman was asking for you** una mujer estuvo preguntando por ti; **~ day** algún día; **~ day next week** un día de la semana que viene; **he was asking for ~ book (or other)** pedía no sé qué libro; **in ~ way or other** de alguna que otra manera

4 (considerable amount of) bastante; **~ days ago** hace unos cuantos días; **after ~ time** pasado algún tiempo; **at ~ length** con mucho detalle

5 (col: intensive): **that was ~ party!** ¡menuda fiesta!

♦ *pron* **1** (*a certain number*): **I've got ~** (*books etc*) tengo algunos/as
2 (*a certain amount*) algo; **I've got ~** (*money, milk*) tengo algo; **would you like ~?** (*coffee etc*) ¿quiere un poco?; (*books etc*) ¿quiere alguno?; **could I have ~ of that cheese?** ¿me puede dar un poco de ese queso?; **I've read ~ of the book** he leído parte del libro
♦ *adv:* **~ 10 people** unas 10 personas, una decena de personas.

somebody ['sʌmbədɪ] *pron* alguien; **~ or other** alguien.
someday ['sʌmdeɪ] *adv* algún día.
somehow ['sʌmhau] *adv* de alguna manera; (*for some reason*) por una u otra razón.
someone ['sʌmwʌn] *pron* = **somebody**.
someplace ['sʌmpleɪs] *adv* (*US*) = **somewhere**.
somersault ['sʌməsɔːlt] *n* (*deliberate*) salto mortal; (*accidental*) vuelco ♦ *vi* dar un salto mortal; dar vuelcos.
something ['sʌmθɪŋ] *pron* algo ♦ *adv:* **he's ~ like me** es un poco como yo; **~ to do** algo que hacer; **it's ~ of a problem** es bastante problemático.
sometime ['sʌmtaɪm] *adv* (*in future*) algún día, en algún momento; **~ last month** durante el mes pasado; **I'll finish it ~** lo terminaré un día de éstos.
sometimes ['sʌmtaɪmz] *adv* a veces.
somewhat ['sʌmwɔt] *adv* algo.
somewhere ['sʌmwɛə*] *adv* (*be*) en alguna parte; (*go*) a alguna parte; **~ else** (*be*) en otra parte; (*go*) a otra parte.
son [sʌn] *n* hijo.
sonar ['səunɑː*] *n* sonar *m*.
sonata [sə'nɑːtə] *n* sonata.
song [sɔŋ] *n* canción *f*.
songwriter ['sɔŋraɪtə*] *n* compositor(a) *m/f* de canciones.
sonic ['sɔnɪk] *adj* (*boom*) sónico.
son-in-law ['sʌnɪnlɔː] *n* yerno.
sonnet ['sɔnɪt] *n* soneto.
sonny ['sʌnɪ] *n* (*col*) hijo.
soon [suːn] *adv* pronto, dentro de poco; **~ afterwards** poco después; **very/quite ~** muy/bastante pronto; **how ~ can you be ready?** ¿cuánto tardas en prepararte?; **it's too ~ to tell** es demasiado pronto para saber; **see you ~!** ¡hasta pronto!; *see also* **as**.
sooner ['suːnə*] *adv* (*time*) antes, más temprano; **I would ~ do that** preferiría hacer eso; **~ or later** tarde o temprano; **no ~ said than done** dicho y hecho; **the ~ the better** cuanto antes mejor; **no ~ had**

we left than ... apenas nos habíamos marchado cuando ....
soot [sut] *n* hollín *m*.
soothe [suːð] *vt* tranquilizar; (*pain*) aliviar.
soothing ['suːðɪŋ] *adj* (*ointment etc*) sedante; (*tone, words etc*) calmante, tranquilizante.
SOP *n abbr* = **standard operating procedure**.
sophisticated [sə'fɪstɪkeɪtɪd] *adj* sofisticado.
sophistication [səfɪstɪ'keɪʃən] *n* sofisticación *f*.
sophomore ['sɔfəmɔː*] *n* (*US*) estudiante *m/f* de segundo año.
soporific [sɔpə'rɪfɪk] *adj* soporífero.
sopping ['sɔpɪŋ] *adj:* **~ (wet)** empapado.
soppy ['sɔpɪ] *adj* (*pej*) bobo, tonto.
soprano [sə'prɑːnəu] *n* soprano *f*.
sorbet ['sɔːbeɪ] *n* sorbete *m*.
sorcerer ['sɔːsərə*] *n* hechicero.
sordid ['sɔːdɪd] *adj* (*place etc*) sórdido; (*motive etc*) mezquino.
sore [sɔː*] *adj* (*painful*) doloroso, que duele; (*offended*) resentido ♦ *n* llaga; **~ throat** dolor *m* de garganta; **my eyes are ~, I have ~ eyes** me duelen los ojos; **it's a ~ point** es un asunto delicado *or* espinoso.
sorely *adv:* **I am ~ tempted to (do it)** estoy muy tentado a (hacerlo).
soreness ['sɔːnɪs] *n* dolor *m*.
sorrel ['sɔrəl] *n* (*BOT*) acedera.
sorrow ['sɔrəu] *n* pena, dolor *m*.
sorrowful ['sɔrəuful] *adj* afligido, triste.
sorrowfully ['sɔrəfulɪ] *adv* tristemente.
sorry ['sɔrɪ] *adj* (*regretful*) arrepentido; (*condition, excuse*) lastimoso; (*sight, failure*) triste; **~!** ¡perdón!, ¡perdone!; **I am ~** lo siento; **I feel ~ for him** me da lástima *or* pena; **I'm ~ to hear that ...** siento saber que ...; **to be ~ about sth** lamentar algo.
sort [sɔːt] *n* clase *f*, género, tipo; (*make: of coffee, car etc*) marca ♦ *vt* (*also:* **~ out:** *papers*) clasificar; (: *problems*) arreglar, solucionar; (*COMPUT*) clasificar; **what ~ do you want?** (*make*) ¿qué marca quieres?; **what ~ of car?** ¿qué tipo de coche?; **I shall do nothing of the ~** no pienso hacer nada parecido; **it's ~ of awkward** (*col*) es bastante difícil.
sortie ['sɔːtɪ] *n* salida.
sorting office ['sɔːtɪŋ-] *n* oficina de clasificación del correo.
SOS *n* SOS *m*.
so-so ['səusəu] *adv* regular, así así.
soufflé ['suːfleɪ] *n* suflé *m*.
sought [sɔːt] *pt, pp of* **seek**.
sought-after ['sɔːtɑːftə*] *adj* solicitado,

codiciado.

soul [səʊl] n alma f; **God rest his ~** Dios le reciba en su seno or en su gloria; **I didn't see a ~** no vi a nadie; **the poor ~ had nowhere to sleep** el pobre no tenía dónde dormir.

soul-destroying ['səʊldɪstrɔɪɪŋ] adj (work) deprimente.

soulful ['səʊlful] adj lleno de sentimiento.

soulmate ['səʊlmeɪt] n compañero/a del alma.

soul-searching ['səʊlsɜːtʃɪŋ] n: **after much ~** después de pensarlo mucho, después de darle muchas vueltas.

sound [saʊnd] adj (healthy) sano; (safe, not damaged) en buen estado; (valid: argument, policy, claim) válido; (: move) acertado; (dependable: person) de fiar; (sensible) sensato, razonable ♦ adv: **~ asleep** profundamente dormido ♦ n (noise) sonido, ruido; (GEO) estrecho ♦ vt (alarm) sonar; (also: ~ **out**: opinions) consultar, sondear ♦ vi sonar, resonar; (fig: seem) parecer; **to ~ like** sonar a; **to be of ~ mind** estar en su sano juicio; **I don't like the ~ of it** no me gusta nada; **it ~s as if ...** parece que ....
▶**sound off** vi (col): **to ~ off (about)** (give one's opinions) despotricar (contra).

sound barrier n barrera del sonido.

sound bite n cita jugosa.

sound effects npl efectos mpl sonoros.

sound engineer n ingeniero/a del sonido.

sounding ['saʊndɪŋ] n (NAUT etc) sondeo.

sounding board n caja de resonancia.

soundly ['saʊndlɪ] adv (sleep) profundamente; (beat) completamente.

soundproof ['saʊndpruːf] adj insonorizado.

sound system n equipo de sonido.

soundtrack ['saʊndtræk] n (of film) banda sonora.

sound wave n (PHYSICS) onda sonora.

soup [suːp] n (thick) sopa; (thin) caldo; **in the ~** (fig) en apuros.

soup kitchen n comedor m de beneficencia.

soup plate n plato sopero.

soupspoon ['suːpspuːn] n cuchara sopera.

sour ['saʊə*] adj agrio; (milk) cortado; **it's just ~ grapes!** (fig) ¡pura envidia!, ¡están verdes!; **to go** or **turn ~** (milk) cortarse; (wine) agriarse; (fig: relationship) agriarse; (: plans) irse a pique.

source [sɔːs] n fuente f; **I have it from a reliable ~ that ...** sé de fuente fidedigna que ....

source language n (COMPUT) lenguaje m

fuente or de origen.

south [saʊθ] n sur m ♦ adj del sur ♦ adv al sur, hacia el sur; **(to the) ~ of** al sur de; **the S~ of France** el Sur de Francia; **to travel ~** viajar hacia el sur.

South Africa n Sudáfrica.

South African adj, n sudafricano/a m/f.

South America n América del Sur, Sudamérica.

South American adj, n sudamericano/a m/f.

southbound ['saʊθbaʊnd] adj (con) rumbo al sur.

south-east [saʊθ'iːst] n sudeste m ♦ adj (counties etc) (del) sudeste.

Southeast Asia n Sudeste m asiático.

southerly ['sʌðəlɪ] adj sur; (from the south) del sur.

southern ['sʌðən] adj del sur, meridional; **the ~ hemisphere** el hemisferio sur.

South Korea n Corea del Sur.

South Pole n Polo Sur.

South Sea Islands npl: **the ~** Oceanía.

South Seas npl: **the ~** los Mares del Sur.

South Vietnam n Vietnam m del Sur.

southward(s) ['saʊθwəd(z)] adv hacia el sur.

south-west [saʊθ'wɛst] n suroeste m.

souvenir [suːvə'nɪə*] n recuerdo.

sovereign ['sɔvrɪn] adj, n soberano/a m/f.

sovereignty ['sɔvrɪntɪ] n soberanía.

soviet ['səʊvɪət] adj soviético.

Soviet Union n: **the ~** la Unión Soviética.

sow [saʊ] n cerda, puerca ♦ vt [səʊ] (pt ~**ed**, pp ~**n** [səʊn]) (gen) sembrar; (spread) esparcir.

soya ['sɔɪə], (US) **soy** [sɔɪ] n soja.

soy(a) bean n semilla de soja.

soy(a) sauce n salsa de soja.

sozzled ['sɔzld] adj (BRIT col) mamado.

spa [spɑː] n balneario.

space [speɪs] n espacio; (room) sitio ♦ vt (also: ~ **out**) espaciar; **to clear a ~ for sth** hacer sitio para algo; **in a confined ~** en un espacio restringido; **in a short ~ of time** en poco or un corto espacio de tiempo; **(with)in the ~ of an hour/three generations** en el espacio de una hora/tres generaciones.

space bar n (on typewriter) barra espaciadora.

spacecraft ['speɪskrɑːft] n nave f espacial, astronave f.

spaceman ['speɪsmæn] n astronauta m, cosmonauta m.

spaceship ['speɪsʃɪp] n = **spacecraft**.

space shuttle n transbordador m espacial.

spacesuit ['speɪssuːt] n traje m espacial.

spacewoman ['speɪswumən] n astronauta, cosmonauta.

spacing ['speɪsɪŋ] n espacio.

spacious ['speɪʃəs] adj amplio.

spade [speɪd] n (tool) pala; ~s npl (CARDS: British) picas fpl; (: Spanish) espadas fpl.

spadework ['speɪdwəːk] n (fig) trabajo preliminar.

spaghetti [spə'getɪ] n espaguetis mpl.

Spain [speɪn] n España.

spam [spæm] (INTERNET) n correo basura (en Internet), spam m ♦ vt enviar spam or correo basura (por Internet) a ♦ vi enviar spam or correo basura (por Internet).

span [spæn] n (of bird, plane) envergadura; (of hand) palmo; (in time) lapso ♦ vt extenderse sobre, cruzar; (fig) abarcar.

Spaniard ['spænjəd] n español(a) m/f.

spaniel ['spænjəl] n perro de aguas.

Spanish ['spænɪʃ] adj español(a) ♦ n (LING) español m, castellano; **the** ~ npl (people) los españoles; ~ **omelette** tortilla española or de patata.

spank [spæŋk] vt zurrar, dar unos azotes a.

spanner ['spænə*] n (BRIT) llave f inglesa.

spar [spɑː*] n palo, verga ♦ vi (BOXING) entrenarse (en el boxeo).

spare [spɛə*] adj de reserva; (surplus) sobrante, de más ♦ n (part) pieza de repuesto ♦ vt (do without) pasarse sin; (afford to give) tener de sobra; (not hurt) perdonar; (details etc) ahorrar; **to** ~ (surplus) sobrante, de sobra; **there are 2 going** ~ sobran or quedan 2; **to** ~ **no expense** no escatimar gastos; **can you** ~ **(me) £10?** ¿puedes prestarme or darme 10 libras?; **can you** ~ **the time?** ¿tienes tiempo?; **I've a few minutes to** ~ tengo unos minutos libres; **there is no time to** ~ no hay tiempo que perder.

spare part n pieza de repuesto.

spare room n cuarto de los invitados.

spare time n ratos mpl de ocio, tiempo libre.

spare tyre, (US) **spare tire** n (AUT) neumático or llanta (LAM) de recambio.

spare wheel n (AUT) rueda de recambio.

sparing ['spɛərɪŋ] adj: **to be** ~ **with** ser parco en.

sparingly ['spɛərɪŋlɪ] adv escasamente.

spark [spɑːk] n chispa; (fig) chispazo.

spark(ing) plug ['spɑːk(ɪŋ)-] n bujía.

sparkle ['spɑːkl] n centelleo, destello ♦ vi centellear; (shine) relucir, brillar.

sparkler ['spɑːklə*] n bengala.

sparkling ['spɑːklɪŋ] adj centelleante; (wine) espumoso.

sparring partner ['spɑːrɪŋ-] n sparring m;

(fig) contrincante m/f.

sparrow ['spærəu] n gorrión m.

sparse [spɑːs] adj esparcido, escaso.

sparsely ['spɑːslɪ] adv escasamente; **a** ~ **furnished room** un cuarto con pocos muebles.

spartan ['spɑːtən] adj (fig) espartano.

spasm ['spæzəm] n (MED) espasmo; (fig) arranque m, ataque m.

spasmodic [spæz'mɔdɪk] adj espasmódico.

spastic ['spæstɪk] n espástico/a.

spat [spæt] pt, pp of **spit** ♦ n (US) riña.

spate [speɪt] n (fig): ~ **of** torrente m de; **in** ~ (river) crecido.

spatial ['speɪʃl] adj espacial.

spatter ['spætə*] vt: **to** ~ **with** salpicar de.

spatula ['spætjulə] n espátula.

spawn [spɔːn] vt (pej) engendrar ♦ vi desovar, frezar ♦ n huevas fpl.

SPCA n abbr (US) = Society for the Prevention of Cruelty to Animals.

SPCC n abbr (US) = Society for the Prevention of Cruelty to Children.

speak, pt **spoke**, pp **spoken** [spiːk, spəuk, 'spəukn] vt (language) hablar; (truth) decir ♦ vi hablar; (make a speech) intervenir; **to** ~ **one's mind** hablar claro or con franqueza; **to** ~ **to sb/of** or **about sth** hablar con algn/de or sobre algo; **to** ~ **at a conference/in a debate** hablar en un congreso/un debate; **he has no money to** ~ **of** no tiene mucho dinero que digamos; ~**ing!** ¡al habla!; ~ **up!** ¡habla más alto!

▶**speak for** vt fus: **to** ~ **for sb** hablar por or en nombre de algn; **that picture is already spoken for** ese cuadro está reservado.

speaker ['spiːkə*] n (in public) orador(a) m/f; (also: **loud**~) altavoz m; (for stereo etc) bafle m; (POL): **the S**~ (BRIT) el Presidente de la Cámara de los Comunes; (US) el Presidente del Congreso; **are you a Welsh** ~? ¿habla Ud galés?

speaking ['spiːkɪŋ] adj hablante.

-speaking ['spiːkɪŋ] suff -hablante; **Spanish**~ **people** los hispanohablantes.

spear [spɪə*] n lanza; (for fishing) arpón m ♦ vt alancear; arponear.

spearhead ['spɪəhɛd] vt (attack etc) encabezar ♦ n punta de lanza, vanguardia.

spearmint ['spɪəmɪnt] n menta verde.

spec [spɛk] n (col): **on** ~ por si acaso; **to buy on** ~ arriesgarse a comprar.

special ['spɛʃl] adj especial; (edition etc) extraordinario; (delivery) urgente ♦ n (train) tren m especial; **nothing** ~ nada de particular, nada extraordinario.

special agent n agente m/f especial.

special correspondent n corresponsal m/f especial.

special delivery n (POST): **by ~** por entrega urgente.

special effects npl (CINE) efectos mpl especiales.

specialist ['spɛʃəlɪst] n especialista m/f; **a heart ~** (MED) un(a) especialista del corazón.

speciality [spɛʃɪ'ælɪtɪ], (US) **specialty** ['spɛʃəltɪ] n especialidad f.

specialize ['spɛʃəlaɪz] vi: **to ~ (in)** especializarse (en).

specially ['spɛʃlɪ] adv especialmente.

special offer n (COMM) oferta especial.

special train n tren m especial.

specialty ['spɛʃəltɪ] n (US) = **speciality**.

species ['spiːʃiːz] n especie f.

specific [spə'sɪfɪk] adj específico.

specifically [spə'sɪfɪklɪ] adv (explicitly: state, warn) específicamente, expresamente; (especially: design, intend) especialmente.

specification [spɛsɪfɪ'keɪʃən] n especificación f; **~s** npl (plan) presupuesto sg; (of car, machine) descripción f técnica; (for building) plan msg detallado.

specify ['spɛsɪfaɪ] vt, vi especificar, precisar; **unless otherwise specified** salvo indicaciones contrarias.

specimen ['spɛsɪmən] n ejemplar m; (MED: of urine) espécimen m; (: of blood) muestra.

specimen copy n ejemplar m de muestra.

specimen signature n muestra de firma.

speck [spɛk] n grano, mota.

speckled ['spɛkld] adj moteado.

specs [spɛks] npl (col) gafas fpl (SP), anteojos mpl.

spectacle ['spɛktəkl] n espectáculo.

spectacle case n estuche m or funda (de gafas).

spectacles ['spɛktəklz] npl (BRIT) gafas fpl (SP), anteojos mpl.

spectacular [spɛk'tækjulə*] adj espectacular; (success) impresionante.

spectator [spɛk'teɪtə*] n espectador(a) m/f.

spectator sport n deporte m espectáculo.

spectra ['spɛktrə] npl of **spectrum**.

spectre, (US) **specter** ['spɛktə*] n espectro, fantasma m.

spectrum, pl **spectra** ['spɛktrəm, -trə] n espectro.

speculate ['spɛkjuleɪt] vi especular; (try to guess): **to ~ about** especular sobre.

speculation [spɛkju'leɪʃən] n especulación f.

speculative ['spɛkjulətɪv] adj especulativo.

speculator ['spɛkjuleɪtə*] n especulador(a) m/f.

sped [spɛd] pt, pp of **speed**.

speech [spiːtʃ] n (faculty) habla; (formal talk) discurso; (words) palabras fpl; (manner of speaking) forma de hablar; (language) idioma m, lenguaje m.

speech day n (BRIT SCOL) ≈ día de reparto de premios.

speech impediment n defecto del habla.

speechless ['spiːtʃlɪs] adj mudo, estupefacto.

speech therapy n logopedia.

speed [spiːd] n (also: AUT, TECH: gear) velocidad f; (haste) prisa; (promptness) rapidez f ♦ vi (pt, pp **sped** [spɛd]) (AUT: exceed ~ limit) conducir con exceso de velocidad; **at full or top ~** a máxima velocidad; **at a ~ of 70 km/h** a una velocidad de 70 km por hora; **at ~** a gran velocidad; **a five-~ gearbox** una caja de cambios de 5 velocidades; **shorthand/typing ~** rapidez f en taquigrafía/mecanografía; **the years sped by** los años pasaron volando.

▶**speed up** vi acelerarse ♦ vt acelerar.

speedboat ['spiːdbəut] n lancha motora.

speedily ['spiːdɪlɪ] adv rápido, rápidamente.

speeding ['spiːdɪŋ] n (AUT) exceso de velocidad.

speed limit n límite m de velocidad, velocidad f máxima.

speedometer [spɪ'dɒmɪtə*] n velocímetro.

speed trap n (AUT) control m de velocidades.

speedway ['spiːdweɪ] n (SPORT) pista de carrera.

speedy ['spiːdɪ] adj (fast) veloz, rápido; (prompt) pronto.

spell [spɛl] n (also: magic ~) encanto, hechizo; (period of time) rato, período; (turn) turno ♦ vt (pt, pp **spelt** or **~ed** [spɛlt, spɛld]) (also: ~ **out**) deletrear; (fig) anunciar, presagiar; **to cast a ~ on sb** hechizar a algn; **he can't ~** no sabe escribir bien, comete faltas de ortografía; **can you ~ it for me?** ¿cómo se deletrea or se escribe?; **how do you ~ your name?** ¿cómo se escribe tu nombre?

spellbound ['spɛlbaund] adj embelesado, hechizado.

spelling ['spɛlɪŋ] n ortografía.

spelling mistake n falta de ortografía.

spelt [spɛlt] pt, pp of **spell**.

spend, pt, pp **spent** [spɛnd, spɛnt] vt (money) gastar; (time) pasar; (life) dedicar; **to ~ time/money/effort on sth** gastar tiempo/dinero/energías en algo.

spending ['spɛndɪŋ] *n*: **government ~** gastos *mpl* del gobierno.

spending money *n* dinero para gastos.

spending power *n* poder *m* adquisitivo.

spendthrift ['spɛndθrɪft] *n* derrochador(a) *m/f*, manirroto/a.

spent [spɛnt] *pt, pp of* **spend** ♦ *adj* (*cartridge, bullets, match*) usado.

sperm [spɔ:m] *n* esperma.

sperm bank *n* banco de esperma.

sperm whale *n* cachalote *m*.

spew [spju:] *vt* vomitar, arrojar.

sphere [sfɪə*] *n* esfera.

spherical ['sfɛrɪkl] *adj* esférico.

sphinx [sfɪŋks] *n* esfinge *f*.

spice [spaɪs] *n* especia ♦ *vt* especiar.

spiciness ['spaɪsɪnɪs] *n* lo picante.

spicy ['spaɪsɪ] *adj* picante.

spick-and-span ['spɪkən'spæn] *adj* impecable.

spider ['spaɪdə*] *n* araña.

spider's web *n* telaraña.

spiel [ʃpi:l] *n* (*col*) rollo.

spike [spaɪk] *n* (*point*) punta; (*ZOOL*) pincho, púa; (*BOT*) espiga; (*ELEC*) pico parásito ♦ *vt*: **to ~ a quote** cancelar una cita; **~s** *npl* (*SPORT*) zapatillas *fpl* con clavos.

spiky ['spaɪkɪ] *adj* (*bush, branch*) cubierto de púas; (*animal*) erizado.

spill, *pt, pp* **spilt** *or* **~ed** [spɪl, spɪlt, spɪld] *vt* derramar, verter; (*blood*) derramar ♦ *vi* derramarse; **to ~ the beans** (*col*) descubrir el pastel.

▶**spill out** *vi* derramarse, desparramarse.

▶**spill over** *vi* desbordarse.

spillage ['spɪlɪdʒ] *n* (*event*) derrame *m*; (*substance*) vertidos.

spin [spɪn] *n* (*revolution of wheel*) vuelta, revolución *f*; (*AVIAT*) barrena; (*trip in car*) paseo (en coche) ♦ *vb* (*pt, pp* **spun** [spʌn]) *vt* (*wool etc*) hilar; girar ♦ *vi* girar, dar vueltas; **the car spun out of control** el coche se descontroló y empezó a dar vueltas.

▶**spin out** *vt* alargar, prolongar.

spina bifida ['spaɪnə'bɪfɪdə] *n* espina *f* bífida.

spinach ['spɪnɪtʃ] *n* espinacas *fpl*.

spinal ['spaɪnl] *adj* espinal.

spinal column *n* columna vertebral.

spinal cord *n* médula espinal.

spin class *n* (*SPORT*) clase *f* de spinning.

spindly ['spɪndlɪ] *adj* (*leg*) zanquivano.

spin doctor *n* (*col*) *informador(a) parcial al servicio de un partido político*.

spin-dry ['spɪn'draɪ] *vt* centrifugar.

spin-dryer [spɪn'draɪə*] *n* (*BRIT*) secadora centrífuga.

spine [spaɪn] *n* espinazo, columna vertebral; (*thorn*) espina.

spine-chilling ['spaɪntʃɪlɪŋ] *adj* terrorífico.

spineless ['spaɪnlɪs] *adj* (*fig*) débil, flojo.

spinet [spɪ'nɛt] *n* espineta.

spinning ['spɪnɪŋ] *n* (*of thread*) hilado; (*art*) hilandería; (*SPORT*) spinning *m*.

spinning top *n* peonza.

spinning wheel *n* rueca, torno de hilar.

spin-off ['spɪnɔf] *n* derivado, producto secundario.

spinster ['spɪnstə*] *n* soltera; (*pej*) solterona.

spiral ['spaɪərl] *n* espiral *f* ♦ *adj* en espiral ♦ *vi* (*prices*) dispararse; **the inflationary ~** la espiral inflacionista.

spiral staircase *n* escalera de caracol.

spire ['spaɪə*] *n* aguja, chapitel *m*.

spirit ['spɪrɪt] *n* (*soul*) alma *f*; (*ghost*) fantasma *m*; (*attitude*) espíritu *m*; (*courage*) valor *m*, ánimo; **~s** *npl* (*drink*) alcohol *msg*, bebidas *fpl* alcohólicas; **in good ~s** alegre, de buen ánimo; **Holy S~** Espíritu *m* Santo; **community ~, public ~** civismo.

spirit duplicator *n* copiadora al alcohol.

spirited ['spɪrɪtɪd] *adj* enérgico, vigoroso.

spirit level *n* nivel *m* de aire.

spiritual ['spɪrɪtjuəl] *adj* espiritual ♦ *n* (*also:* **Negro ~**) canción *f* religiosa, espiritual *m*.

spiritualism ['spɪrɪtjuəlɪzəm] *n* espiritualismo.

spit [spɪt] *n* (*for roasting*) asador *m*, espetón *m*; (*spittle*) esputo, escupitajo; (*saliva*) saliva ♦ *vi* (*pt, pp* **spat** [spæt]) escupir; (*sound*) chisporrotear.

spite [spaɪt] *n* rencor *m*, ojeriza ♦ *vt* fastidiar; **in ~ of** a pesar de, pese a.

spiteful ['spaɪtful] *adj* rencoroso, malévolo.

spitting ['spɪtɪŋ] *n*: **"~ prohibited"** "se prohíbe escupir" ♦ *adj*: **to be the ~ image of sb** ser la viva imagen de algn.

spittle ['spɪtl] *n* saliva, baba.

splash [splæʃ] *n* (*sound*) chapoteo; (*of colour*) mancha ♦ *vt* salpicar de ♦ *vi* (*also:* **~ about**) chapotear; **to ~ paint on the floor** manchar el suelo de pintura.

splashdown ['splæʃdaun] *n* amaraje *m*, amerizaje *m*.

spleen [spli:n] *n* (*ANAT*) bazo.

splendid ['splɛndɪd] *adj* espléndido.

splendidly ['splɛndɪdlɪ] *adv* espléndidamente; **everything went ~** todo fue a las mil maravillas.

splendour, (*US*) **splendor** ['splɛndə*] *n* esplendor *m*; (*fig*) brillo, gloria.

splice [splaɪs] *vt* empalmar.

splint [splɪnt] *n* tablilla.

splinter ['splɪntə*] n astilla ♦ vi astillarse, hacer astillas.

splinter group n grupo disidente, facción f.

split [splɪt] n hendedura, raja; (*fig*) división f; (*POL*) escisión f ♦ (*vb*: *pt, pp* **split**) vt partir, rajar; (*party*) dividir; (*work, profits*) repartir ♦ vi (*divide*) dividirse, escindirse; **to ~ the difference** partir la diferencia; **to do the ~s** hacer el spagat; **to ~ sth down the middle** (*also fig*) dividir algo en dos.

▶**split up** vi (*couple*) separarse, romper; (*meeting*) acabarse.

split-level ['splɪtlɛvl] adj (*house*) dúplex.

split peas npl guisantes mpl secos.

split personality n doble personalidad f.

split second n fracción f de segundo.

splitting ['splɪtɪŋ] adj (*headache*) horrible.

splutter ['splʌtə*] vi chisporrotear; (*person*) balbucear.

spoil, *pt, pp* **spoilt** or **~ed** [spɔɪl, spɔɪlt, spɔɪld] vt (*damage*) dañar; (*ruin*) estropear, echar a perder; (*child*) mimar, consentir; (*ballot paper*) invalidar ♦ vi: **to be ~ing for a fight** estar con ganas de lucha, andar con ganas de pelea.

spoiled [spɔɪld] adj (*US: food: bad*) pasado, malo; (: *milk*) cortado.

spoils [spɔɪlz] npl despojo sg, botín msg.

spoilsport ['spɔɪlspɔːt] n aguafiestas m inv.

spoilt [spɔɪlt] *pt, pp of* **spoil** ♦ adj (*child*) mimado, consentido; (*ballot paper*) invalidado.

spoke [spəuk] *pt of* **speak** ♦ n rayo, radio.

spoken ['spəukn] *pp of* **speak**.

spokesman ['spəuksmən] n portavoz m, vocero (*LAM*).

spokesperson ['spəukspəːsn] n portavoz m/f, vocero/a (*LAM*).

spokeswoman ['spəukswumən] n portavoz f, vocera (*LAM*).

sponge [spʌndʒ] n esponja; (*CULIN: also:* **~ cake**) bizcocho ♦ vt (*wash*) lavar con esponja ♦ vi: **to ~ on** or (*US*) **off sb** vivir a costa de algn.

sponge bag n (*BRIT*) neceser m.

sponge cake n bizcocho, pastel m.

sponger ['spʌndʒə*] n gorrón/ona m/f.

spongy ['spʌndʒɪ] adj esponjoso.

sponsor ['spɔnsə*] n (*RADIO, TV*) patrocinador(a) m/f; (*for membership*) padrino/madrina; (*COMM*) fiador(a) m/f, avalador(a) m/f ♦ vt patrocinar; apadrinar; (*parliamentary bill*) apoyar, respaldar; (*idea etc*) presentar, promover; **I ~ed him at 3p a mile** (*in fund-raising race*) me apunté para darle 3 peniques la milla.

sponsorship ['spɔnsəʃɪp] n patrocinio.

spontaneity [spɔntə'neɪtɪ] n espontaneidad f.

spontaneous [spɔn'teɪnɪəs] adj espontáneo.

spontaneously [spɔn'teɪnɪəslɪ] adv espontáneamente.

spooky ['spuːkɪ] adj (*col: place, atmosphere*) espeluznante, horripilante.

spool [spuːl] n carrete m; (*of sewing machine*) canilla.

spoon [spuːn] n cuchara.

spoon-feed ['spuːnfiːd] vt dar de comer con cuchara a; (*fig*) dárselo todo mascado a.

spoonful ['spuːnful] n cucharada.

sporadic [spə'rædɪk] adj esporádico.

sport [spɔːt] n deporte m; (*person*) buen(a) perdedor(a) m/f; (*amusement*) juego, diversión f; **indoor/outdoor ~s** deportes mpl en sala cubierta/al aire libre; **to say sth in ~** decir algo en broma.

sport coat n (*US*) = **sports jacket**.

sporting ['spɔːtɪŋ] adj deportivo; **to give sb a ~ chance** darle a algn su oportunidad.

sports car n coche m sport.

sports coat n (*US*) = **sports jacket**.

sports ground n campo de deportes, centro deportivo.

sports jacket, (*US*) **sport jacket** n chaqueta deportiva.

sportsman ['spɔːtsmən] n deportista m.

sportsmanship ['spɔːtsmənʃɪp] n deportividad f.

sports pages npl páginas fpl deportivas.

sportswear ['spɔːtswɛə*] n ropa de deporte.

sportswoman ['spɔːtswumən] n deportista f.

sporty ['spɔːtɪ] adj deportivo.

spot [spɔt] n sitio, lugar m; (*dot: on pattern*) punto, mancha; (*pimple*) grano; (*also: advertising* **~**) spot m; (*small amount*): **a ~ of** un poquito de ♦ vt (*notice*) notar, observar ♦ adj (*COMM*) inmediatamente efectivo; **on the ~** en el acto, acto seguido; (*in difficulty*) en un aprieto; **to do sth on the ~** hacer algo en el acto; **to put sb on the ~** poner a algn en un apuro.

spot check n reconocimiento rápido.

spotless ['spɔtlɪs] adj (*clean*) inmaculado; (*reputation*) intachable.

spotlessly ['spɔtlɪslɪ] adv: **~ clean** limpísimo.

spotlight ['spɔtlaɪt] n foco, reflector m; (*AUT*) faro auxiliar.

spot-on [spɔt'ɔn] adj (*BRIT col*) exacto.

spot price n precio de entrega inmediata.

spotted ['spɔtɪd] adj (*pattern*) de puntos.

spotty ['spɔtɪ] adj (*face*) con granos.

spouse [spauz] *n* cónyuge *m/f*.

spout [spaut] *n* (*of jug*) pico; (*pipe*) caño ♦ *vi* chorrear.

sprain [spreɪn] *n* torcedura, esguince *m* ♦ *vt*: **to ~ one's ankle** torcerse el tobillo.

sprang [spræŋ] *pt of* **spring**.

sprawl [sprɔːl] *vi* tumbarse ♦ *n*: **urban ~** crecimiento urbano descontrolado; **to send sb ~ing** tirar a algn al suelo.

sprawling [ˈsprɔːlɪŋ] *adj* (*town*) desparramado.

spray [spreɪ] *n* rociada; (*of sea*) espuma; (*container*) atomizador *m*; (*of paint*) pistola rociadora; (*of flowers*) ramita ♦ *vt* rociar; (*crops*) regar ♦ *cpd* (*deodorant*) en atomizador.

spread [sprɛd] *n* extensión *f*; (*of idea*) diseminación *f*; (*col: food*) comilona; (*PRESS, TYP: two pages*) plana ♦ *vb* (*pt, pp* **spread**) *vt* extender; diseminar; (*butter*) untar; (*wings, sails*) desplegar; (*scatter*) esparcir ♦ *vi* extenderse; diseminarse; untarse; desplegarse; esparcirse; **middle-age ~** gordura de la mediana edad; **repayments will be ~ over 18 months** los pagos se harán a lo largo de 18 meses.

spread-eagled [ˈsprɛdiːgld] *adj*: **to be ~** estar despatarrado.

spreadsheet [ˈsprɛdʃiːt] *n* (*COMPUT*) hoja de cálculo.

spree [spriː] *n*: **to go on a ~** ir de juerga *or* farra (*LAM*).

sprightly [ˈspraɪtlɪ] *adj* vivo, enérgico.

spring [sprɪŋ] *n* (*season*) primavera; (*leap*) salto, brinco; (*coiled metal*) resorte *m*; (*of water*) fuente *f*, manantial *m*; (*bounciness*) elasticidad *f* ♦ *vb* (*pt* **sprang**, *pp* **sprung** [spræŋ, sprʌŋ]) *vi* (*arise*) brotar, nacer; (*leap*) saltar, brincar ♦ *vt*: **to ~ a leak** (*pipe etc*) empezar a hacer agua; **he sprang the news on me** de repente me soltó la noticia; **in (the) ~** en (la) primavera; **to walk with a ~ in one's step** andar dando saltos *or* brincos; **to ~ into action** lanzarse a la acción.

▶**spring up** *vi* (*problem*) surgir.

springboard [ˈsprɪŋbɔːd] *n* trampolín *m*.

spring-clean [sprɪŋˈkliːn] *n* (*also: ~ing*) limpieza general.

spring onion *n* cebolleta.

spring roll *n* rollito de primavera.

springtime [ˈsprɪŋtaɪm] *n* primavera.

springy [ˈsprɪŋɪ] *adj* elástico; (*grass*) mullido.

sprinkle [ˈsprɪŋkl] *vt* (*pour*) rociar; **to ~ water on, ~ with water** rociar *or* salpicar de agua.

sprinkler [ˈsprɪŋklə*] *n* (*for lawn*) aspersor *m*; (*to put out fire*) aparato de rociadura automática.

sprinkling [ˈsprɪŋklɪŋ] *n* (*of water*) rociada; (*of salt, sugar*) un poco de.

sprint [sprɪnt] *n* (e)sprint *m* ♦ *vi* (*gen*) correr a toda velocidad; (*SPORT*) esprintar; **the 200 metres ~** el (e)sprint de 200 metros.

sprinter [ˈsprɪntə*] *n* velocista *m/f*.

spritzer [ˈsprɪtsə*] *n* vino blanco con soda.

sprocket [ˈsprɔkɪt] *n* (*on printer etc*) rueda dentada.

sprocket feed *n* avance *m* por rueda dentada.

sprout [spraut] *vi* brotar, retoñar ♦ *n*: **(Brussels) ~s** *npl* coles *fpl* de Bruselas.

spruce [spruːs] *n* (*BOT*) pícea ♦ *adj* aseado, pulcro.

▶**spruce up** *vt* (*tidy*) arreglar, acicalar; (*smarten up: room etc*) ordenar; **to ~ o.s. up** arreglarse.

sprung [sprʌŋ] *pp of* **spring**.

spry [spraɪ] *adj* ágil, activo.

SPUC *n abbr* (= *Society for the Protection of Unborn Children*) ≈ Federación *f* Española de Asociaciones Pro-vida.

spun [spʌn] *pt, pp of* **spin**.

spur [spə:*] *n* espuela; (*fig*) estímulo, aguijón *m* ♦ *vt* (*also: ~ on*) estimular, incitar; **on the ~ of the moment** de improviso.

spurious [ˈspjuərɪəs] *adj* falso.

spurn [spə:n] *vt* desdeñar, rechazar.

spurt [spə:t] *n* chorro; (*of energy*) arrebato ♦ *vi* chorrear; **to put in** *or* **on a ~** (*runner*) acelerar; (*fig: in work etc*) hacer un gran esfuerzo.

sputter [ˈspʌtə*] *vi* = **splutter**.

spy [spaɪ] *n* espía *m/f* ♦ *vi*: **to ~ on** espiar a ♦ *vt* (*see*) divisar, lograr ver ♦ *cpd* (*film, story*) de espionaje.

spying [ˈspaɪɪŋ] *n* espionaje *m*.

Sq. *abbr* (*in address*: = *Square*) Plza.

sq. *abbr* (*MATH etc*) = **square**.

squabble [ˈskwɔbl] *n* riña, pelea ♦ *vi* reñir, pelear.

squad [skwɔd] *n* (*MIL*) pelotón *m*; (*POLICE*) brigada; (*SPORT*) equipo; **flying ~** (*POLICE*) brigada móvil.

squad car *n* (*POLICE*) coche-patrulla *m*.

squaddie [ˈskwɔdɪ] *n* (*MIL: col*) chivo.

squadron [ˈskwɔdrən] *n* (*MIL*) escuadrón *m*; (*AVIAT, NAUT*) escuadra.

squalid [ˈskwɔlɪd] *adj* miserable.

squall [skwɔːl] *n* (*storm*) chubasco; (*wind*) ráfaga.

squalor [ˈskwɔlə*] *n* miseria.

squander [ˈskwɔndə*] *vt* (*money*)

derrochar, despilfarrar; (*chances*) desperdiciar.

square [skwɛə*] *n* cuadro; (*in town*) plaza; (*US: block of houses*) manzana, cuadra (*LAM*) ♦ *adj* cuadrado ♦ *vt* (*arrange*) arreglar; (*MATH*) cuadrar; (*reconcile*): **can you ~ it with your conscience?** ¿cómo se justifica ante sí mismo? ♦ *vi* cuadrar, conformarse; **all ~** igual(es); **a ~ meal** una comida decente; **2 metres ~** 2 metros por 2; **1 ~ metre** un metro cuadrado; **to get one's accounts ~** dejar las cuentas claras; **I'll ~ it with him** (*col*) yo lo arreglo con él; **we're back to ~ one** (*fig*) hemos vuelto al punto de partida.
▶**square up** *vi* (*settle*): **to ~ up (with sb)** ajustar cuentas (con algn).
square bracket *n* (*TYP*) corchete *m*.
squarely ['skwɛəli] *adv* (*fully*) de lleno; (*honestly, fairly*) honradamente, justamente.
square root *n* raíz *f* cuadrada.
squash [skwɔʃ] *n* (*vegetable*) calabaza; (*SPORT*) squash *m*; (*BRIT: drink*): **lemon/orange ~** zumo (*SP*) or jugo (*LAM*) de limón/naranja ♦ *vt* aplastar.
squat [skwɔt] *adj* achaparrado ♦ *vi* agacharse, sentarse en cuclillas; (*on property*) ocupar ilegalmente.
squatter ['skwɔtə*] *n* ocupante *m/f* ilegal, okupa *m/f*.
squawk ['skwɔːk] *vi* graznar.
squeak [skwiːk] *vi* (*hinge, wheel*) chirriar, rechinar; (*shoe, wood*) crujir ♦ *n* (*of hinge, wheel etc*) chirrido, rechinamiento; (*of shoes*) crujir *m*; (*of mouse etc*) chillido.
squeaky ['skwiːki] *adj* que cruje; **to be ~ clean** (*fig*) ser superhonrado.
squeal [skwiːl] *vi* chillar, dar gritos agudos.
squeamish ['skwiːmiʃ] *adj* delicado, remilgado.
squeeze [skwiːz] *n* presión *f*; (*of hand*) apretón *m*; (*COMM: credit ~*) restricción *f* ♦ *vt* (*lemon etc*) exprimir; (*hand, arm*) apretar; **a ~ of lemon** unas gotas de limón; **to ~ past/under sth** colarse al lado de/por debajo de algo.
▶**squeeze out** *vt* exprimir; (*fig*) excluir.
▶**squeeze through** *vi* abrirse paso con esfuerzos.
squelch [skwɛltʃ] *vi* chapotear.
squid [skwɪd] *n* calamar *m*.
squiggle ['skwɪgl] *n* garabato.
squint [skwɪnt] *vi* entrecerrar los ojos ♦ *n* (*MED*) estrabismo; **to ~ at sth** mirar algo entornando los ojos.
squire ['skwaɪə*] *n* (*BRIT*) terrateniente *m*.

squirm [skwɔːm] *vi* retorcerse, revolverse.
squirrel ['skwɪrəl] *n* ardilla.
squirt [skwɔːt] *vi* salir a chorros.
Sr *abbr* = **senior, sister** (*REL*).
SRC *n abbr* (*BRIT*: = *Students' Representative Council*) consejo de estudiantes.
Sri Lanka [srɪ'læŋkə] *n* Sri Lanka *m*.
SRN *n abbr* (*BRIT*) = *State Registered Nurse*.
SRO *abbr* (*US*) = *standing room only*.
SS *abbr* (= *steamship*) M.V.
SSA *n abbr* (*US*: = *Social Security Administration*) ≈ Seguro Social.
SST *n abbr* (*US*) = *supersonic transport*.
ST *abbr* (*US*: = *Standard Time*) hora oficial.
St *abbr* (= *saint*) Sto./a.; (= *street*) c/.
stab [stæb] *n* (*with knife etc*) puñalada; (*of pain*) pinchazo; **to have a ~ at (doing) sth** (*col*) probar (a hacer) algo ♦ *vt* apuñalar; **to ~ sb to death** matar a algn a puñaladas.
stabbing ['stæbɪŋ] *n*: **there's been a ~** han apuñalado a alguien ♦ *adj* (*pain*) punzante.
stability [stə'bɪlɪtɪ] *n* estabilidad *f*.
stabilization [steɪbəlaɪ'zeɪʃən] *n* estabilización *f*.
stabilize ['steɪbəlaɪz] *vt* estabilizar ♦ *vi* estabilizarse.
stabilizer ['steɪbəlaɪzə*] *n* (*AVIAT, NAUT*) estabilizador *m*.
stable ['steɪbl] *adj* estable ♦ *n* cuadra, caballeriza; **riding ~s** escuela hípica.
staccato [stə'kɑːtəu] *adj, adv* staccato.
stack [stæk] *n* montón *m*, pila; (*col*) mar *f* ♦ *vt* amontonar, apilar; **there's ~s of time to finish it** hay cantidad de tiempo para acabarlo.
stacker ['stækə*] *n* (*for printer*) apiladora.
stadium ['steɪdɪəm] *n* estadio.
staff [stɑːf] *n* (*work force*) personal *m*, plantilla; (*BRIT SCOL: also: teaching ~*) cuerpo docente; (*stick*) bastón *m* ♦ *vt* proveer de personal; **to be ~ed by Asians/women** tener una plantilla asiática/femenina.
staffroom ['stɑːfruːm] *n* sala de profesores.
Staffs *abbr* (*BRIT*) = *Staffordshire*.
stag [stæg] *n* ciervo, venado; (*BRIT STOCK EXCHANGE*) especulador *m* con nuevas emisiones.
stage [steɪdʒ] *n* escena; (*point*) etapa; (*platform*) plataforma; **the ~** el escenario, el teatro ♦ *vt* (*play*) poner en escena, representar; (*organize*) montar, organizar; (*fig: perform: recovery etc*) efectuar; **in ~s** por etapas; **in the early/final ~s** en las primeras/últimas etapas; **to go through a difficult ~** pasar una fase

or etapa mala.

stagecoach ['steɪdʒkəʊtʃ] *n* diligencia.

stage door *n* entrada de artistas.

stagehand ['steɪdʒhænd] *n* tramoyista *m/f.*

stage-manage ['steɪdʒmænɪdʒ] *vt (fig)* manipular.

stage manager *n* director(a) *m/f* de escena.

stagger ['stægə*] *vi* tambalear ♦ *vt (amaze)* asombrar; *(hours, holidays)* escalonar.

staggering ['stægərɪŋ] *adj (amazing)* asombroso, pasmoso.

staging post ['steɪdʒɪŋ-] *n* escala.

stagnant ['stægnənt] *adj* estancado.

stagnate [stæg'neɪt] *vi* estancarse; *(fig: economy, mind)* quedarse estancado.

stagnation [stæg'neɪʃən] *n* estancamiento.

stag night, stag party *n* despedida de soltero.

staid [steɪd] *adj (clothes)* serio, formal.

stain [steɪn] *n* mancha; *(colouring)* tintura ♦ *vt* manchar; *(wood)* teñir.

stained glass window [steɪnd-] *n* vidriera de colores.

stainless ['steɪnlɪs] *adj (steel)* inoxidable.

stain remover *n* quitamanchas *m inv.*

stair [stɛə*] *n (step)* peldaño, escalón *m;* ~s *npl* escaleras *fpl.*

staircase ['stɛəkeɪs], **stairway** ['stɛəweɪ] *n* escalera.

stairwell ['stɛəwɛl] *n* hueco *or* caja de la escalera.

stake [steɪk] *n* estaca, poste *m;* *(BETTING)* apuesta ♦ *vt (bet)* apostar; *(also:* ~ **out:** *area)* cercar con estacas; **to be at** ~ estar en juego; **to have a** ~ **in sth** tener interés en algo; **to** ~ **a claim to (sth)** presentar reclamación por *or* reclamar (algo).

stake-out ['steɪkaʊt] *n* vigilancia; **to be on a** ~ estar de vigilancia.

stalactite ['stæləktaɪt] *n* estalactita.

stalagmite ['stæləgmaɪt] *n* estalagmita.

stale [steɪl] *adj (bread)* duro; *(food)* pasado.

stalemate ['steɪlmeɪt] *n* tablas *fpl;* **to reach** ~ *(fig)* estancarse, alcanzar un punto muerto.

stalk [stɔːk] *n* tallo, caña ♦ *vt* acechar, cazar al acecho; **to** ~ **off** irse airado.

stall [stɔːl] *n (in market)* puesto; *(in stable)* casilla (de establo) ♦ *vt (AUT)* parar, calar ♦ *vi (AUT)* pararse, calarse; *(fig)* buscar evasivas; ~s *npl (BRIT: in cinema, theatre)* butacas *fpl;* **a newspaper** ~ un quiosco (de periódicos); **a flower** ~ un puesto de flores.

stallholder ['stɔːlhəʊldə*] *n* dueño/a de un puesto.

stallion ['stælɪən] *n* semental *m,* garañón *m.*

stalwart ['stɔːlwət] *n* partidario/a incondicional.

stamen ['steɪmən] *n* estambre *m.*

stamina ['stæmɪnə] *n* resistencia.

stammer ['stæmə*] *n* tartamudeo, balbuceo ♦ *vi* tartamudear, balbucir.

stamp [stæmp] *n* sello, estampilla *(LAM);* *(mark, also fig)* marca, huella; *(on document)* timbre *m* ♦ *vi (also:* ~ **one's foot)** patear ♦ *vt* patear, golpear con el pie; *(letter)* poner sellos en; *(with rubber* ~) marcar con sello; ~**ed addressed envelope (sae)** sobre *m* sellado con las señas propias.

▶**stamp out** *vt (fire)* apagar con el pie; *(crime, opposition)* acabar con.

stamp album *n* álbum *m* para sellos.

stamp collecting *n* filatelia.

stamp duty *n (BRIT)* derecho de timbre.

stampede [stæm'piːd] *n (of cattle)* estampida.

stamp machine *n* máquina (expendedora) de sellos.

stance [stæns] *n* postura.

stand [stænd] *n (attitude)* posición *f,* postura; *(for taxis)* parada; *(music* ~) atril *m;* *(SPORT)* tribuna; *(at exhibition)* stand *m* ♦ *vb (pt, pp* **stood** [stʊd]) *vi (be)* estar, encontrarse; *(be on foot)* estar de pie; *(rise)* levantarse; *(remain)* quedar en pie ♦ *vt (place)* poner, colocar; *(tolerate, withstand)* aguantar, soportar; **to make a** ~ resistir; *(fig)* mantener una postura firme; **to take a** ~ **on an issue** adoptar una actitud hacia una cuestión; **to** ~ **for parliament** *(BRIT)* presentarse (como candidato) a las elecciones; **nothing** ~**s in our way** nada nos lo impide; **to** ~ **still** quedarse inmóvil; **to let sth** ~ **as it is** dejar algo como está; **as things** ~ tal como están las cosas; **to** ~ **sb a drink/ meal** invitar a algn a una copa/a comer; **the company will have to** ~ **the loss** la empresa tendrá que hacer frente a las pérdidas; **I can't** ~ **him** no le aguanto, no le puedo ver; **to** ~ **guard** *or* **watch** *(MIL)* hacer guardia.

▶**stand aside** *vi* apartarse, mantenerse aparte.

▶**stand by** *vi (be ready)* estar listo ♦ *vt fus (opinion)* mantener.

▶**stand down** *vi (withdraw)* ceder el puesto; *(MIL, LAW)* retirarse.

▶**stand for** *vt fus (signify)* significar; *(tolerate)* aguantar, permitir.

▶**stand in for** *vt fus* suplir a.

▶**stand out** *vi (be prominent)* destacarse.

▶**stand up** *vi (rise)* levantarse, ponerse de

pie.

▶**stand up for** *vt fus* defender.

▶**stand up to** *vt fus* hacer frente a.

stand-alone ['stændələun] *adj* (*COMPUT*) autónomo.

standard ['stændəd] *n* patrón *m*, norma; (*flag*) estandarte *m* ♦ *adj* (*size etc*) normal, corriente, estándar; **~s** *npl* (*morals*) valores *mpl* morales; **the gold ~** (*COMM*) el patrón oro; **high/low ~** de alto/bajo nivel; **below** *or* **not up to ~** (*work*) de calidad inferior; **to be** *or* **come up to ~** satisfacer los requisitos; **to apply a double ~** aplicar un doble criterio.

Standard Grade *n* (*SCOT SCOL*) *certificado del último ciclo de la enseñanza secundaria obligatoria.*

standardization [stændədaɪ'zeɪʃən] *n* normalización *f.*

standardize ['stændədaɪz] *vt* estandarizar.

standard lamp *n* (*BRIT*) lámpara de pie.

standard model *n* modelo stándard.

standard of living *n* nivel *m* de vida.

standard practice *n* norma, práctica común.

standard rate *n* tasa de imposición.

standard time *n* hora oficial.

stand-by ['stændbaɪ] *n* (*alert*) alerta, aviso; (*also*: **~ ticket**: *THEAT*) *entrada reducida de última hora*; (: *AVIAT*) billete *m* standby; **to be on ~** estar preparado; (*doctor*) estar listo para acudir; (*AVIAT*) estar en la lista de espera.

stand-by generator *n* generador *m* de reserva.

stand-by passenger *n* pasajero/a en lista de espera.

stand-by ticket *n* (billete *m*) standby *m.*

stand-in ['stændɪn] *n* suplente *m/f*; (*CINE*) doble *m/f.*

standing ['stændɪŋ] *adj* (*upright*) derecho; (*on foot*) de pie, en pie; (*permanent*: *committee*) permanente; (: *rule*) fijo; (: *army*) permanente, regular; (*grievance*) constante, viejo ♦ *n* reputación *f*; (*duration*): **of 6 months' ~** que lleva 6 meses; **of many years' ~** que lleva muchos años; **he was given a ~ ovation** le dieron una calurosa ovación de pie; **~ joke** motivo constante de broma; **a man of some ~** un hombre de cierta posición *or* categoría.

standing order *n* (*BRIT*: *at bank*) giro bancario; **standing orders** *npl* (*MIL*) reglamento *sg* general.

standing room *n* sitio para estar de pie.

stand-off ['stændɔf] *n* punto muerto.

stand-offish [stænd'ɔfɪʃ] *adj* distante.

standpipe ['stændpaɪp] *n* tubo vertical.

standpoint ['stændpɔɪnt] *n* punto de vista.

standstill ['stændstɪl] *n*: **at a ~** paralizado, en un punto muerto; **to come to a ~** pararse, quedar paralizado.

stank [stæŋk] *pt of* **stink**.

staple ['steɪpl] *n* (*for papers*) grapa; (*product*) producto *or* artículo de primeva necesidad ♦ *adj* (*crop, industry, food etc*) básico ♦ *vt* grapar.

stapler ['steɪplə*] *n* grapadora.

star [stɑ:*] *n* estrella; (*celebrity*) estrella, astro ♦ *vi*: **to ~ in** ser la estrella de; **four-~ hotel** hotel *m* de cuatro estrellas; **4-~ petrol** gasolina extra.

star attraction *n* atracción *f* principal.

starboard ['stɑ:bəd] *n* estribor *m.*

starch [stɑ:tʃ] *n* almidón *m.*

starchy ['stɑ:tʃɪ] *adj* (*food*) feculento.

stardom ['stɑ:dəm] *n* estrellato.

stare [stɛə*] *n* mirada fija ♦ *vi*: **to ~ at** mirar fijo.

starfish ['stɑ:fɪʃ] *n* estrella de mar.

stark [stɑ:k] *adj* (*bleak*) severo, escueto; (*simplicity, colour*) austero; (*reality, truth*) puro; (*poverty*) absoluto ♦ *adv*: **~ naked** en cueros.

starkers ['stɑ:kəz] *adj* (*BRIT col*): **to be ~** estar en cueros.

starlet ['stɑ:lɪt] *n* (*CINE*) actriz *f* principiante.

starling ['stɑ:lɪŋ] *n* estornino.

starry ['stɑ:rɪ] *adj* estrellado.

starry-eyed [stɑ:rɪ'aɪd] *adj* (*gullible, innocent*) inocentón/ona, ingenuo; (*idealistic*) idealista; (*from wonder*) asombrado; (*from love*) enamoradísimo.

Stars and Stripes *npl*: **the ~** las barras y las estrellas, la bandera de EEUU.

star sign *n* signo del zodíaco.

star-studded ['stɑ:stʌdɪd] *adj*: **a ~ cast** un elenco estelar.

start [stɑ:t] *n* (*beginning*) principio, comienzo; (*departure*) salida; (*sudden movement*) sobresalto; (*advantage*) ventaja ♦ *vt* empezar, comenzar; (*cause*) causar; (*found*: *business, newspaper*) estabiecer, fundar; (*engine*) poner en marcha ♦ *vi* (*begin*) comenzar, empezar; (*with fright*) asustarse, sobresaltarse; (*train etc*) salir; **to give sb a ~** dar un susto a algn; **at the ~** al principio; **for a ~** en primer lugar; **to make an early ~** ponerse en camino temprano; **the thieves had 3 hours' ~** los ladrones llevaban 3 horas de ventaja; **to ~ a fire** provocar un incendio; **to ~ doing** *or* **to do sth** empezar a hacer algo; **to ~ (off) with ...**

(*firstly*) para empezar; (*at the beginning*) al principio.

▶**start off** *vi* empezar, comenzar; (*leave*) salir, ponerse en camino.

▶**start over** *vi* (*US*) volver a empezar.

▶**start up** *vi* comenzar; (*car*) ponerse en marcha ♦ *vt* comenzar; (*car*) poner en marcha.

starter ['stɑːtə*] *n* (*AUT*) botón *m* de arranque; (*SPORT: official*) juez *m/f* de salida; (: *runner*) corredor(a) *m/f*; (*BRIT CULIN*) entrada.

starting point ['stɑːtɪŋ-] *n* punto de partida.

starting price *n* (*COMM*) precio inicial.

startle ['stɑːtl] *vt* asustar, sobresaltar.

startling ['stɑːtlɪŋ] *adj* alarmante.

star turn *n* (*BRIT*) atracción *f* principal.

starvation [stɑː'veɪʃən] *n* hambre *f*, hambruna (*LAM*); (*MED*) inanición *f*.

starvation wages *npl* sueldo *sg* de hambre.

starve [stɑːv] *vi* pasar hambre; (*to death*) morir de hambre ♦ *vt* hacer pasar hambre; (*fig*) privar; **I'm starving** estoy muerto de hambre.

stash [stæʃ] *vt*: **to ~ sth away** (*col*) poner algo a buen recaudo.

state [steɪt] *n* estado; (*pomp*): **in ~** con mucha ceremonia ♦ *vt* (*say, declare*) afirmar; (*a case*) presentar, exponer; **~ of emergency** estado de excepción *or* emergencia; **~ of mind** estado de ánimo; **to lie in ~** (*corpse*) estar de cuerpo presente; **to be in a ~** estar agitado.

State Department *n* (*US*) Ministerio de Asuntos Exteriores.

state education *n* (*BRIT*) enseñanza pública.

stateless ['steɪtlɪs] *adj* desnacionalizado.

stately ['steɪtlɪ] *adj* majestuoso, imponente.

statement ['steɪtmənt] *n* afirmación *f*; (*LAW*) declaración *f*; (*COMM*) estado; **official ~** informe *m* oficial; **~ of account, bank ~** estado de cuenta.

state-of-the-art ['steɪtəvðɪ'ɑːt] *adj* (*technology etc*) puntero.

state-owned ['steɪtəund] *adj* estatal, del estado.

States [steɪts] *npl*: **the ~** los Estados Unidos.

state school *n* escuela *or* colegio estatal.

statesman ['steɪtsmən] *n* estadista *m*.

statesmanship ['steɪtsmənʃɪp] *n* habilidad *f* política, arte *m* de gobernar.

static ['stætɪk] *n* (*RADIO*) parásitos *mpl* ♦ *adj* estático.

static electricity *n* electricidad *f* estática.

station ['steɪʃən] *n* (*gen*) estación *f*; (*place*) puesto, sitio; (*RADIO*) emisora; (*rank*) posición *f* social ♦ *vt* colocar, situar; (*MIL*) apostar; **action ~s!** ¡a los puestos de combate!; **to be ~ed in** (*MIL*) estar estacionado en.

stationary ['steɪʃnərɪ] *adj* estacionario, fijo.

stationer ['steɪʃənə*] *n* papelero/a.

stationer's (shop) *n* (*BRIT*) papelería.

stationery ['steɪʃənərɪ] *n* (*writing paper*) papel *m* de escribir; (*writing materials*) artículos *mpl* de escritorio.

station master *n* (*RAIL*) jefe *m* de estación.

station wagon *n* (*US*) coche *m* familiar con ranchera.

statistic [stə'tɪstɪk] *n* estadística.

statistical [stə'tɪstɪkl] *adj* estadístico.

statistics [stə'tɪstɪks] *n* (*science*) estadística.

statue ['stætjuː] *n* estatua.

statuette [stætju'ɛt] *n* figurilla.

stature ['stætʃə*] *n* estatura; (*fig*) talla.

status ['steɪtəs] *n* condición *f*, estado; (*reputation*) reputación *f*, estatus *m*; **the ~ quo** el statu quo.

status line *n* (*COMPUT*) línea de situación *or* de estado.

status symbol *n* símbolo de prestigio.

statute ['stætjuːt] *n* estatuto, ley *f*.

statute book *n* código de leyes.

statutory ['stætjutrɪ] *adj* estatutario; **~ meeting** junta ordinaria.

staunch [stɔːntʃ] *adj* leal, incondicional ♦ *vt* (*flow, blood*) restañar.

stave [steɪv] *vt*: **to ~ off** (*attack*) rechazar; (*threat*) evitar.

stay [steɪ] *n* (*period of time*) estancia; (*LAW*): **~ of execution** aplazamiento de una sentencia ♦ *vi* (*remain*) quedar(se); (*as guest*) hospedarse; **to ~ put** seguir en el mismo sitio; **to ~ the night/5 days** pasar la noche/estar *or* quedarse 5 días.

▶**stay behind** *vi* quedar atrás.

▶**stay in** *vi* (*at home*) quedarse en casa.

▶**stay on** *vi* quedarse.

▶**stay out** *vi* (*of house*) no volver a casa; (*strikers*) no volver al trabajo.

▶**stay up** *vi* (*at night*) velar, no acostarse.

staying power ['steɪɪŋ-] *n* resistencia, aguante *m*.

STD *n abbr* (*BRIT*: = *subscriber trunk dialling*) servicio de conferencias automáticas; (= *sexually transmitted disease*) ETS *f*.

stead [stɛd] *n*: **in sb's ~** en lugar de algn; **to stand sb in good ~** ser muy útil a algn.

steadfast ['stɛdfɑːst] *adj* firme, resuelto.

steadily ['stɛdɪlɪ] *adv* (*firmly*) firmemente; (*unceasingly*) sin parar; (*fixedly*) fijamente; (*walk*) normalmente; (*drive*) a velocidad constante.

steady ['stɛdɪ] *adj* (*fixed*) firme, fijo; (*regular*) regular; (*boyfriend etc*) formal, fijo; (*person, character*) sensato, juicioso ♦ *vt* (*hold*) mantener firme; (*stabilize*) estabilizar; (*nerves*) calmar; **to ~ o.s. on** *or* **against sth** afirmarse en algo.

steak [steɪk] *n* (*gen*) filete *m*; (*beef*) bistec *m*.

steal, *pt* **stole,** *pp* **stolen** [stiːl, stəul, 'stəuln] *vt, vi* robar.

►**steal away**, **steal off** *vi* marcharse furtivamente, escabullirse.

stealth [stɛlθ] *n*: **by ~** a escondidas, sigilosamente.

stealthy ['stɛlθɪ] *adj* cauteloso, sigiloso.

steam [stiːm] *n* vapor *m*; (*mist*) vaho, humo ♦ *vt* (*CULIN*) cocer al vapor ♦ *vi* echar vapor; (*ship*): **to ~ along** avanzar, ir avanzando; **under one's own ~** (*fig*) por sus propios medios *or* propias fuerzas; **to run out of ~** (*fig: person*) quedar(se) agotado, quemarse; **to let off ~** (*fig*) desahogarse.

►**steam up** *vi* (*window*) empañarse; **to get ~ed up about sth** (*fig*) ponerse negro por algo.

steam engine *n* máquina de vapor.

steamer ['stiːmə*] *n* (buque *m* de) vapor *m*; (*CULIN*) *recipiente para cocinar al vapor*.

steam iron *n* plancha de vapor.

steamroller ['stiːmrəulə*] *n* apisonadora.

steamship ['stiːmʃɪp] *n* = **steamer**.

steamy ['stiːmɪ] *adj* (*room*) lleno de vapor; (*window*) empañado.

steel [stiːl] *n* acero ♦ *adj* de acero.

steel band *n* banda de percusión del Caribe.

steel industry *n* industria siderúrgica.

steel mill *n* fábrica de acero.

steelworks ['stiːlwɜːks] *n* acería, fundición *f* de acero.

steely ['stiːlɪ] *adj* (*determination*) inflexible; (*gaze*) duro; (*eyes*) penetrante; **~ grey** gris *m* metálico.

steelyard ['stiːljɑːd] *n* romana.

steep [stiːp] *adj* escarpado, abrupto; (*stair*) empinado; (*price*) exorbitante, excesivo ♦ *vt* empapar, remojar.

steeple ['stiːpl] *n* aguja, campanario.

steeplechase ['stiːpltʃeɪs] *n* carrera de obstáculos.

steeplejack ['stiːpldʒæk] *n* reparador(a) *m/f* de chimeneas *or* de campanarios.

steer [stɪə*] *vt* (*car*) conducir (*SP*), manejar (*LAM*); (*person*) dirigir, guiar ♦ *vi* conducir; **to ~ clear of sb/sth** (*fig*) esquivar a algn/evadir algo.

steering ['stɪərɪŋ] *n* (*AUT*) dirección *f*.

steering committee *n* comisión *f* directiva.

steering wheel *n* volante *m*.

stellar ['stɛlə*] *adj* estelar.

stem [stɛm] *n* (*of plant*) tallo; (*of glass*) pie *m*; (*of pipe*) cañón *m* ♦ *vt* detener; (*blood*) restañar.

►**stem from** *vt fus* ser consecuencia de.

stench [stɛntʃ] *n* hedor *m*.

stencil ['stɛnsl] *n* (*typed*) cliché *m*, clisé *m*; (*lettering*) plantilla ♦ *vt* hacer un cliché de.

stenographer [stɛ'nɔgrəfə*] *n* (*US*) taquígrafo/a.

step [stɛp] *n* paso; (*sound*) paso, pisada; (*stair*) peldaño, escalón *m* ♦ *vi*: **to ~ forward** dar un paso adelante; **~s** *npl* (*BRIT*) = **~ladder; ~ by ~** paso a paso; (*fig*) poco a poco; **to keep in ~ (with)** llevar el paso de; (*fig*) llevar el paso de, estar de acuerdo con; **to be in/out of ~ with** estar acorde con/estar en disonancia con; **to take ~s to solve a problem** tomar medidas para resolver un problema.

►**step down** *vi* (*fig*) retirarse.

►**step in** *vi* entrar; (*fig*) intervenir.

►**step off** *vt fus* bajar de.

►**step on** *vt fus* pisar.

►**step over** *vt fus* pasar por encima de.

►**step up** *vt* (*increase*) aumentar.

step aerobics *npl* step *m*.

stepbrother ['stɛpbrʌðə*] *n* hermanastro.

stepdaughter ['stɛpdɔːtə*] *n* hijastra.

stepfather ['stɛpfɑːðə*] *n* padrastro.

stepladder ['stɛplædə*] *n* escalera doble *or* de tijera.

stepmother ['stɛpmʌðə*] *n* madrastra.

stepping stone ['stɛpɪŋ-] *n* pasadera.

step Reebok ® [-'riːbɔk] *n* step *m*.

stepsister ['stɛpsɪstə*] *n* hermanastra.

stepson ['stɛpsʌn] *n* hijastro.

stereo ['stɛrɪəu] *n* estéreo ♦ *adj* (*also*: **~phonic**) estéreo, estereofónico; **in ~** en estéreo.

stereotype ['stɪərɪətaɪp] *n* estereotipo ♦ *vt* estereotipar.

sterile ['stɛraɪl] *adj* estéril.

sterilization [stɛrɪlaɪ'zeɪʃən] *n* esterilización *f*.

sterilize ['stɛrɪlaɪz] *vt* esterilizar.

sterling ['stɜːlɪŋ] *adj* (*silver*) de ley ♦ *n* (*ECON*) libras *fpl* esterlinas; **a pound ~** una libra esterlina; **he is of ~ character** tiene un carácter excelente.

stern [stɜːn] *adj* severo, austero ♦ *n* (*NAUT*) popa.

sternum ['stɜːnəm] *n* esternón *m*.

steroid ['stɪərɔɪd] n esteroide m.
stethoscope ['stɛθəskəup] n estetoscopio.
stevedore ['stiːvədɔː*] n estibador m.
stew [stjuː] n cocido, estofado, guisado
(*LAM*) ♦ vt, vi estofar, guisar; (*fruit*) cocer;
~**ed fruit** compota de fruta.
steward ['stjuːəd] n (*BRIT: gen*) camarero;
(*shop* ~) enlace m/f sindical.
stewardess ['stjuːədəs] n azafata.
stewardship ['stjuədʃɪp] n tutela.
stewing steak ['stjuːɪŋ-], (*US*) **stew meat**
n carne f de vaca.
St. Ex. abbr = **stock exchange.**
stg abbr (= *sterling*) ester.
stick [stɪk] n palo; (*as weapon*) porra;
(*walking* ~) bastón m ♦ vb (*pt, pp* **stuck**
[stʌk]) vt (*glue*) pegar; (*col: put*) meter;
(*: tolerate*) aguantar, soportar ♦ vi pegarse;
(*come to a stop*) quedarse parado; (*get
jammed: door, lift*) atascarse; **to get hold
of the wrong end of the** ~ entender al
revés; **to** ~ **to** (*word, principles*) atenerse
a, ser fiel a; (*promise*) cumplir; **it stuck
in my mind** se me quedó grabado; **to** ~
sth into clavar or hincar algo en.
▶**stick around** vi (*col*) quedarse.
▶**stick out** vi sobresalir ♦ vt: **to** ~ **it out**
(*col*) aguantar.
▶**stick up** vi sobresalir.
▶**stick up for** vt fus defender.
sticker ['stɪkə*] n (*label*) etiqueta adhesiva;
(*with slogan*) pegatina.
sticking plaster ['stɪkɪŋ-] n (*BRIT*)
esparadrapo.
sticking point n (*fig*) punto de fricción.
stickler ['stɪklə*] n: **to be a** ~ **for** insistir
mucho en.
stick shift n (*US AUT*) palanca de cambios.
stick-up ['stɪkʌp] n asalto, atraco.
sticky ['stɪkɪ] adj pegajoso; (*label*) adhesivo;
(*fig*) difícil.
stiff [stɪf] adj rígido, tieso; (*hard*) duro;
(*difficult*) difícil; (*person*) inflexible; (*price*)
exorbitante; **to have a** ~ **neck/back** tener
tortícolis/dolor de espalda; **the door's** ~
la puerta está atrancada.
stiffen ['stɪfn] vt hacer más rígido; (*limb*)
entumecer ♦ vi endurecerse; (*grow
stronger*) fortalecerse.
stiffness ['stɪfnɪs] n rigidez f.
stifle ['staɪfl] vt ahogar, sofocar.
stifling ['staɪflɪŋ] adj (*heat*) sofocante,
bochornoso.
stigma, pl (*BOT, MED, REL*) ~**ta**, (*fig*) ~**s**
['stɪgmə, stɪg'mɑːtə] n estigma m.
stile [staɪl] n escalera (*para pasar una cerca*).
stiletto [stɪ'lɛtəu] n (*BRIT: also:* ~ **heel**)
tacón m de aguja.

still [stɪl] adj inmóvil, quieto; (*orange juice
etc*) sin gas ♦ adv (*up to this time*) todavía;
(*even*) aún; (*nonetheless*) sin embargo,
aun así ♦ n (*CINE*) foto f fija; **keep** ~!
¡estate quieto!, ¡no te muevas!; **he** ~
hasn't arrived todavía no ha llegado.
stillborn ['stɪlbɔːn] adj nacido muerto.
still life n naturaleza muerta.
stilt [stɪlt] n zanco; (*pile*) pilar m, soporte m.
stilted ['stɪltɪd] adj afectado, artificial.
stimulant ['stɪmjulənt] n estimulante m.
stimulate ['stɪmjuleɪt] vt estimular.
stimulating ['stɪmjuleɪtɪŋ] adj estimulante.
stimulation [stɪmju'leɪʃən] n estímulo.
stimulus, pl **-li** ['stɪmjuləs, -laɪ] n estímulo,
incentivo.
sting [stɪŋ] n (*wound*) picadura; (*pain*)
escozor m, picazón m; (*organ*) aguijón m;
(*col: confidence trick*) timo ♦ vb (*pt, pp* **stung**
[stʌŋ]) vt picar ♦ vi picar, escocer; **my
eyes are** ~**ing** me pican or escuecen los
ojos.
stingy ['stɪndʒɪ] adj tacaño.
stink [stɪŋk] n hedor m, tufo ♦ vi (*pt* **stank,** *pp*
stunk [stæŋk, stʌŋk]) heder, apestar.
stinking ['stɪŋkɪŋ] adj hediondo, fétido; (*fig:
col*) horrible.
stint [stɪnt] n tarea, destajo; **to do one's** ~
at sth hacer su parte (de algo), hacer lo
que corresponde (de algo) ♦ vi: **to** ~ **on**
escatimar.
stipend ['staɪpɛnd] n salario, remuneración
f.
stipendiary [staɪ'pɛndɪərɪ] adj: ~
magistrate magistrado/a estipendiario/a.
stipulate ['stɪpjuleɪt] vt estipular.
stipulation [stɪpju'leɪʃən] n estipulación f.
stir [stɜː*] n (*fig: agitation*) conmoción f ♦ vt
(*tea etc*) remover; (*fire*) atizar; (*move*)
agitar; (*fig: emotions*) conmover ♦ vi
moverse; **to give sth a** ~ remover algo;
to cause a ~ causar conmoción or
sensación.
▶**stir up** vt excitar; (*trouble*) fomentar.
stir-fry ['stɜː'fraɪ] vt sofreír removiendo ♦ n
*plato preparado sofriendo y removiendo
los ingredientes.*
stirrup ['stɪrəp] n estribo.
stitch [stɪtʃ] n (*SEWING*) puntada; (*KNITTING*)
punto; (*MED*) punto (de sutura); (*pain*)
punzada ♦ vt coser; (*MED*) suturar.
stoat [stəut] n armiño.
stock [stɔk] n (*COMM: reserves*) existencias
fpl, stock m; (*: selection*) surtido; (*AGR*)
ganado, ganadería; (*CULIN*) caldo; (*fig:
lineage*) estirpe f, cepa; (*FINANCE*) capital
m; (*: shares*) acciones fpl; (*RAIL: rolling* ~)
material m rodante ♦ adj (*COMM: goods,*

size) normal, de serie; (*fig: reply etc*) clásico, trillado; (: *greeting*) acostumbrado ♦ *vt* (*have in* ~) tener existencias de; (*supply*) proveer, abastecer; **in** ~ en existencia *or* almacén; **to have sth in** ~ tener existencias de algo; **out of** ~ agotado; **to take** ~ **of** (*fig*) considerar, examinar; ~**s** *npl* (*HISTORY: punishment*) cepo *sg*; ~**s and shares** acciones y valores; **government** ~ papel *m* del Estado.

▶**stock up with** *vt fus* abastecerse de.

stockbroker ['stɔkbrəukə*] *n* agente *m/f or* corredor(a) *m/f* de bolsa.

stock control *n* (*COMM*) control *m* de existencias.

stock cube *n* pastilla *or* cubito de caldo.

stock exchange *n* bolsa.

stockholder ['stɔkhəuldə*] *n* (*US*) accionista *m/f*.

Stockholm ['stɔkhəum] *n* Estocolmo.

stocking ['stɔkɪŋ] *n* media.

stock-in-trade ['stɔkɪn'treɪd] *n* (*tools etc*) herramientas *fpl*; (*stock*) existencia de mercancías; (*fig*): **it's his** ~ es su especialidad.

stockist ['stɔkɪst] *n* (*BRIT*) distribuidor(a) *m/f*.

stock market *n* bolsa (de valores).

stock phrase *n* vieja frase *f*.

stockpile ['stɔkpaɪl] *n* reserva ♦ *vt* acumular, almacenar.

stockroom ['stɔkruːm] *n* almacén *m*, depósito.

stocktaking ['stɔkteɪkɪŋ] *n* (*BRIT COMM*) inventario, balance *m*.

stocky ['stɔkɪ] *adj* (*strong*) robusto; (*short*) achaparrado.

stodgy ['stɔdʒɪ] *adj* indigesto, pesado.

stoical ['stəuɪkəl] *adj* estoico.

stoke [stəuk] *vt* atizar.

stole [stəul] *pt of* **steal** ♦ *n* estola.

stolen ['stəuln] *pp of* **steal**.

stolid ['stɔlɪd] *adj* (*person*) imperturbable, impasible.

stomach ['stʌmək] *n* (*ANAT*) estómago; (*belly*) vientre *m* ♦ *vt* tragar, aguantar.

stomach ache *n* dolor *m* de estómago.

stomach pump *n* bomba gástrica.

stomach ulcer *n* úlcera de estómago.

stomp [stɔmp] *vi*: **to** ~ **in/out** entrar/salir con pasos ruidosos.

stone [stəun] *n* piedra; (*in fruit*) hueso; (*BRIT: weight*) = 6.348 kg; 14 pounds ♦ *adj* de piedra ♦ *vt* apedrear; **within a** ~**'s throw of the station** a tiro de piedra *or* a dos pasos de la estación.

Stone Age *n*: **the** ~ la Edad de Piedra.

stone-cold ['stəun'kəuld] *adj* helado.

stoned [stəund] *adj* (*col: drunk*) trompa, borracho, colocado.

stone-deaf ['stəun'dɛf] *adj* sordo como una tapia.

stonemason ['stəunmeɪsən] *n* albañil *m*.

stonewall [stəun'wɔːl] *vi* alargar la cosa innecesariamente ♦ *vt* dar largas a.

stonework ['stəunwɔːk] *n* (*art*) cantería.

stony ['stəunɪ] *adj* pedregoso; (*glance*) glacial.

stood [stud] *pt, pp of* **stand**.

stooge [stuːdʒ] *n* (*col*) hombre *m* de paja.

stool [stuːl] *n* taburete *m*.

stoop [stuːp] *vi* (*also*: **have a** ~) ser cargado de espaldas; (*bend*) inclinarse, encorvarse; **to** ~ **to** (**doing**) **sth** rebajarse a (hacer) algo.

stop [stɔp] *n* parada, alto; (*in punctuation*) punto ♦ *vt* parar, detener; (*break off*) suspender; (*block*) tapar, cerrar; (*prevent*) impedir; (*also*: **put a** ~ **to**) poner término a ♦ *vi* pararse, detenerse; (*end*) acabarse; **to** ~ **doing sth** dejar de hacer algo; **to** ~ **sb (from) doing sth** impedir a algn hacer algo; **to** ~ **dead** pararse en seco; ~ **it!** ¡basta ya!, ¡párate!

▶**stop by** *vi* pasar por.

▶**stop off** *vi* interrumpir el viaje.

▶**stop up** *vt* (*hole*) tapar.

stopcock ['stɔpkɔk] *n* llave *f* de paso.

stopgap ['stɔpgæp] *n* interino; (*person*) sustituto/a; (*measure*) medida provisional ♦ *cpd* (*situation*) provisional.

stoplights ['stɔplaɪts] *npl* (*AUT*) luces *fpl* de detención.

stopover ['stɔpəuvə*] *n* parada intermedia; (*AVIAT*) escala.

stoppage ['stɔpɪdʒ] *n* (*strike*) paro; (*temporary stop*) interrupción *f*; (*of pay*) suspensión *f*; (*blockage*) obstrucción *f*.

stopper ['stɔpə*] *n* tapón *m*.

stop press *n* noticias *fpl* de última hora.

stopwatch ['stɔpwɔtʃ] *n* cronómetro.

storage ['stɔːrɪdʒ] *n* almacenaje *m*; (*COMPUT*) almacenamiento.

storage capacity *n* espacio de almacenaje.

storage heater *n* acumulador *m* de calor.

store [stɔː*] *n* (*stock*) provisión *f*; (*depot*, *BRIT: large shop*) almacén *m*; (*US*) tienda; (*reserve*) reserva, repuesto ♦ *vt* (*gen*, *COMPUT*) almacenar; (*keep*) guardar; (*in filing system*) archivar; ~**s** *npl* víveres *mpl*; **who knows what is in** ~ **for us** quién sabe lo que nos espera; **to set great/little** ~ **by sth** dar mucha/poca importancia a algo, valorar mucho/poco algo.

▶**store up** _vt_ acumular.

storehouse ['stɔːhaus] _n_ almacén _m_, depósito.

storekeeper ['stɔːkiːpə*] _n_ (_US_) tendero/a.

storeroom ['stɔːruːm] _n_ despensa.

storey, (_US_) **story** ['stɔːrɪ] _n_ piso.

stork [stɔːk] _n_ cigüeña.

storm [stɔːm] _n_ tormenta; (_wind_) vendaval _m_; (_fig_) tempestad _f_ ♦ _vi_ (_fig_) rabiar ♦ _vt_ tomar por asalto, asaltar; **to take a town by** ~ (_MIL_) tomar una ciudad por asalto.

storm cloud _n_ nubarrón _m_.

storm door _n_ contrapuerta.

stormy ['stɔːmɪ] _adj_ tempestuoso.

story ['stɔːrɪ] _n_ historia; (_PRESS_) artículo; (_joke_) cuento, chiste _m_; (_plot_) argumento; (_lie_) cuento; (_US_) = **storey**.

storybook ['stɔːrɪbuk] _n_ libro de cuentos.

storyteller ['stɔːrɪtelə*] _n_ cuentista _m/f_.

stout [staut] _adj_ (_strong_) sólido; (_fat_) gordo, corpulento ♦ _n_ cerveza negra.

stove [stəuv] _n_ (_for cooking_) cocina; (_for heating_) estufa; **gas/electric** ~ cocina de gas/eléctrica.

stow [stəu] _vt_ meter, poner; (_NAUT_) estibar.

stowaway ['stəuəweɪ] _n_ polizón/ona _m/f_.

straddle ['strædl] _vt_ montar a horcajadas.

straggle ['strægl] _vi_ (_wander_) vagar en desorden; (_lag behind_) rezagarse.

straggler ['stræglə*] _n_ rezagado/a.

straggling ['stræglɪŋ], **straggly** ['stræglɪ] _adj_ (_hair_) desordenado.

straight [streɪt] _adj_ (_direct_) recto, derecho; (_plain, uncomplicated_) sencillo; (_frank_) franco, directo; (_in order_) en orden; (_continuous_) continuo; (_THEAT: part, play_) serio; (_person: conventional_) recto, convencional; (: _heterosexual_) heterosexual ♦ _adv_ derecho, directamente; (_drink_) solo; **to put** _or_ **get sth** ~ dejar algo en claro; **10** ~ **wins** 10 victorias seguidas; **to be (all)** ~ (_tidy_) estar en orden; (_clarified_) estar claro; **I went** ~ **home** (me) fui directamente a casa; ~ **away,** ~ **off** (_at once_) en seguida.

straighten ['streɪtn] _vt_ (_also:_ ~ **out**) enderezar, poner derecho; **to** ~ **things out** poner las cosas en orden.

straight-faced [streɪt'feɪst] _adj_ serio ♦ _adv_ sin mostrar emoción, impávido.

straightforward [streɪt'fɔːwəd] _adj_ (_simple_) sencillo; (_honest_) sincero.

strain [streɪn] _n_ (_gen_) tensión _f_; (_TECH_) esfuerzo; (_MED_) distensión _f_, torcedura; (_breed_) raza; (_lineage_) linaje _m_; (_of virus_) variedad _f_ ♦ _vt_ (_back etc_) distender, torcerse; (_tire_) cansar; (_stretch_) estirar; (_filter_) filtrar; (_meaning_) tergiversar ♦ _vi_

esforzarse; ~**s** _npl_ (_MUS_) son _m_; **she's under a lot of** ~ está bajo mucha tensión.

strained [streɪnd] _adj_ (_muscle_) torcido; (_laugh_) forzado; (_relations_) tenso.

strainer ['streɪnə*] _n_ colador _m_.

strait [streɪt] _n_ (_GEO_) estrecho; **to be in dire** ~**s** (_fig_) estar en un gran aprieto.

straitjacket ['streɪtdʒækɪt] _n_ camisa de fuerza.

strait-laced [streɪt'leɪst] _adj_ mojigato, gazmoño.

strand [strænd] _n_ (_of thread_) hebra; (_of rope_) ramal _m_; **a** ~ **of hair** un pelo.

stranded ['strændɪd] _adj_ (_person_) colgado.

strange [streɪndʒ] _adj_ (_not known_) desconocido; (_odd_) extraño, raro.

stranger ['streɪndʒə*] _n_ desconocido/a; (_from another area_) forastero/a; **I'm a** ~ **here** no soy de aquí.

strangle ['stræŋgl] _vt_ estrangular.

stranglehold ['stræŋglhəuld] _n_ (_fig_) dominio completo.

strangulation [stræŋgju'leɪʃən] _n_ estrangulación _f_.

strap [stræp] _n_ correa; (_of slip, dress_) tirante _m_ ♦ _vt_ atar con correa.

straphanging ['stræphæŋɪŋ] _n_ viajar _m_ de pie _or_ parado (_LAM_).

strapless ['stræplɪs] _adj_ (_bra, dress_) sin tirantes.

strapped [stræpt] _adj_: **to be** ~ **for cash** (_col_) andar mal de dinero.

strapping ['stræpɪŋ] _adj_ robusto, fornido.

Strasbourg ['stræzbəːg] _n_ Estrasburgo.

strata ['strɑːtə] _npl of_ **stratum**.

stratagem ['strætɪdʒəm] _n_ estratagema.

strategic [strə'tiːdʒɪk] _adj_ estratégico.

strategy ['strætɪdʒɪ] _n_ estrategia.

stratum, ** _pl_ **strata ['strɑːtəm, 'strɑːtə] _n_ estrato.

straw [strɔː] _n_ paja; (_drinking_ ~) caña, pajita; **that's the last** ~! ¡eso es el colmo!

strawberry ['strɔːbərɪ] _n_ fresa, frutilla (_LAM_).

stray [streɪ] _adj_ (_animal_) extraviado; (_bullet_) perdido; (_scattered_) disperso ♦ _vi_ extraviarse, perderse; (_wander: walker_) vagar, ir sin rumbo fijo; (: _speaker_) desvariar.

streak [striːk] _n_ raya; (_fig: of madness etc_) vena ♦ _vt_ rayar ♦ _vi_: **to** ~ **past** pasar como un rayo; **to have** ~**s in one's hair** tener vetas en el pelo; **a winning/losing** ~ una racha de buena/mala suerte.

streaker ['striːkə*] _n_ corredor(a) _m/f_ desnudo/a.

streaky ['striːkɪ] _adj_ rayado.

stream [striːm] _n_ riachuelo, arroyo; (_jet_)

chorro; (*flow*) corriente *f*; (*of people*) oleada ♦ *vt* (*SCOL*) dividir en grupos por habilidad ♦ *vi* correr, fluir; **to ~ in/out** (*people*) entrar/salir en tropel; **against the ~** a contracorriente; **on ~** (*new power plant etc*) en funcionamiento.

streamer ['stri:mə*] *n* serpentina.

stream feed *n* (*on photocopier etc*) alimentación *f* continua.

streamline ['stri:mlaɪn] *vt* aerodinamizar; (*fig*) racionalizar.

streamlined ['stri:mlaɪnd] *adj* aerodinámico.

street [stri:t] *n* calle *f* ♦ *adj* callejero; **the back ~s** las callejuelas; **to be on the ~s** (*homeless*) estar sin vivienda; (*as prostitute*) hacer la calle.

streetcar ['stri:tkɑː] *n* (*US*) tranvía *m*.

street cred [-krɛd] *n* (*col*) *imagen de estar en la onda*.

street lamp *n* farol *m*.

street lighting *n* alumbrado público.

street market *n* mercado callejero.

street plan *n* plano callejero.

streetwise ['stri:twaɪz] *adj* (*col*) pícaro.

strength [strɛŋθ] *n* fuerza; (*of girder, knot etc*) resistencia; (*of chemical solution*) potencia; (*of wine*) graduación *f* de alcohol; **on the ~ of** a base de, en base a; **to be at full/below ~** tener/no tener completo el cupo.

strengthen ['strɛŋθn] *vt* fortalecer, reforzar.

strenuous ['strɛnjuəs] *adj* (*tough*) arduo; (*energetic*) enérgico; (*opposition*) firme, tenaz; (*efforts*) intensivo.

stress [strɛs] *n* (*force, pressure*) presión *f*; (*mental strain*) estrés *m*, tensión *f*; (*accent, emphasis*) énfasis *m*, acento; (*LING, POETRY*) acento; (*TECH*) tensión *f*, carga ♦ *vt* subrayar, recalcar; **to be under ~** estar estresado; **to lay great ~ on sth** hacer hincapié en algo.

stressful ['strɛsful] *adj* (*job*) estresante.

stretch [strɛtʃ] *n* (*of sand etc*) trecho; (*of road*) tramo; (*of time*) período, tiempo ♦ *vi* estirarse; (*extend*): **to ~ to** *or* **as far as** extenderse hasta; (*be enough: money, food*): **to ~ to** alcanzar para, dar de sí para ♦ *vt* extender, estirar; (*make demands of*) exigir el máximo esfuerzo a; **to ~ one's legs** estirar las piernas.

►**stretch out** *vi* tenderse ♦ *vt* (*arm etc*) extender; (*spread*) estirar.

stretcher ['strɛtʃə*] *n* camilla.

stretcher-bearer ['strɛtʃəbɛərə*] *n* camillero/a.

stretch marks *npl* estrías *fpl*.

strewn [stru:n] *adj*: **~ with** cubierto *or* sembrado de.

stricken ['strɪkən] *adj* (*person*) herido; (*city, industry etc*) condenado; **~ with** (*arthritis, disease*) afligido por; **grief-~** destrozado por el dolor.

strict [strɪkt] *adj* (*order, rule etc*) estricto; (*discipline, ban*) severo; **in ~ confidence** en la más absoluta confianza.

strictly ['strɪktlɪ] *adv* estrictamente; (*totally*) terminantemente; **~ confidential** estrictamente confidencial; **~ speaking** en (el) sentido estricto (de la palabra); **~ between ourselves ...** entre nosotros ....

stridden ['strɪdn] *pp of* **stride**.

stride [straɪd] *n* zancada, tranco ♦ *vi* (*pt* **strode**, *pp* **stridden** [strəud, 'strɪdn]) dar zancadas, andar a trancos; **to take in one's ~** (*fig: changes etc*) tomar con calma.

strident ['straɪdnt] *adj* estridente; (*colour*) chillón/ona.

strife [straɪf] *n* lucha.

strike [straɪk] *n* huelga; (*of oil etc*) descubrimiento; (*attack*) ataque *m*; (*SPORT*) golpe *m* ♦ *vb* (*pt, pp* **struck** [strʌk]) *vt* golpear, pegar; (*oil etc*) descubrir; (*obstacle*) topar con; (*produce: coin, medal*) acuñar; (*: agreement, deal*) concertar ♦ *vi* declarar la huelga; (*attack*: *MIL etc*) atacar; (*clock*) dar la hora; **on ~** (*workers*) en huelga; **to call a ~** declarar una huelga; **to go on** *or* **come out on ~** ponerse *or* declararse en huelga; **to ~ a match** encender una cerilla; **to ~ a balance** (*fig*) encontrar un equilibrio; **to ~ a bargain** cerrar un trato; **the clock struck 9 o'clock** el reloj dio las nueve.

►**strike back** *vi* (*MIL*) contraatacar; (*fig*) devolver el golpe.

►**strike down** *vt* derribar.

►**strike off** *vt* (*from list*) tachar; (*doctor etc*) suspender.

►**strike out** *vt* borrar, tachar.

►**strike up** *vt* (*MUS*) empezar a tocar; (*conversation*) entablar; (*friendship*) trabar.

strikebreaker ['straɪkbreɪkə*] *n* rompehuelgas *m/f inv*.

striker ['straɪkə*] *n* huelguista *m/f*; (*SPORT*) delantero.

striking ['straɪkɪŋ] *adj* (*colour*) llamativo; (*obvious*) notorio.

Strimmer ® ['strɪmə*] *n* cortacéspedes *m inv* (*especial para los bordes*).

string [strɪŋ] *n* (*gen*) cuerda; (*row*) hilera; (*COMPUT*) cadena ♦ *vt* (*pt, pp* **strung** [strʌŋ]): **to ~ together** ensartar; **to ~ out**

extenderse; **the** ~**s** *npl* (*MUS*) los
instrumentos de cuerda; **to pull** ~**s** (*fig*)
mover palancas; **to get a job by pulling**
~**s** conseguir un trabajo por enchufe;
with no ~**s attached** (*fig*) sin
compromiso.

string bean *n* judía verde, habichuela.

string(ed) instrument [strɪŋ(d)-] *n* (*MUS*)
instrumento de cuerda.

stringent ['strɪndʒənt] *adj* riguroso, severo.

string quartet *n* cuarteto de cuerdas.

strip [strɪp] *n* tira; (*of land*) franja; (*of metal*)
cinta, lámina ♦ *vt* desnudar; (*also*: ~
down: *machine*) desmontar ♦ *vi*
desnudarse.

strip cartoon *n* tira cómica, historieta
(*LAM*).

stripe [straɪp] *n* raya; (*MIL*) galón *m*; **white**
with green ~**s** blanco con rayas verdes.

striped [straɪpt] *adj* a rayas, rayado.

strip lighting *n* alumbrado fluorescente.

stripper ['strɪpə*] *n* artista *m/f* de
striptease.

strip-search ['strɪpsə:tʃ] *vt*: **to** ~ **sb**
desnudar y registrar a algn.

striptease ['strɪpti:z] *n* striptease *m*.

strive, *pt* **strove**, *pp* **striven** [straɪv, strəuv,
'strɪvn] *vi*: **to** ~ **to do sth** esforzarse *or*
luchar por hacer algo.

strobe [strəub] *n* (*also*: ~ **light**) luz *f*
estroboscópica.

strode [strəud] *pt of* **stride**.

stroke [strəuk] *n* (*blow*) golpe *m*; (*MED*)
apoplejía; (*caress*) caricia; (*of pen*) trazo;
(*SWIMMING*: *style*) estilo; (*of piston*)
carrera ♦ *vt* acariciar; **at a** ~ de golpe; **a**
~ **of luck** un golpe de suerte; **two-**~**-**
engine motor *m* de dos tiempos.

stroll [strəul] *n* paseo, vuelta ♦ *vi* dar un
paseo *or* una vuelta; **to go for a** ~, **have**
or **take a** ~ dar un paseo.

stroller ['strəulə*] *n* (*US*: *pushchair*)
cochecito.

strong [strɔŋ] *adj* fuerte; (*bleach, acid*)
concentrado ♦ *adv*: **to be going** ~
(*company*) marchar bien; (*person*)
conservarse bien; **they are 50** ~ son 50.

strong-arm ['strɔŋɑ:m] *adj* (*tactics,*
methods) represivo.

strongbox ['strɔŋbɔks] *n* caja fuerte.

strong drink *n* bebida cargada *or* fuerte.

stronghold ['strɔŋhəuld] *n* fortaleza; (*fig*)
baluarte *m*.

strong language *n* lenguaje *m* fuerte.

strongly ['strɔŋlɪ] *adv* fuertemente, con
fuerza; (*believe*) firmemente; **to feel** ~
about sth tener una opinión firme sobre
algo.

strongman ['strɔŋmæn] *n* forzudo; (*fig*)
hombre *m* robusto.

strongroom ['strɔŋru:m] *n* cámara
acorazada.

stroppy ['strɔpɪ] *adj* (*BRIT col*) borde; **to get**
~ ponerse borde.

strove [strəuv] *pt of* **strive**.

struck [strʌk] *pt*, *pp of* **strike**.

structural ['strʌktʃərəl] *adj* estructural.

structure ['strʌktʃə*] *n* estructura;
(*building*) construcción *f*.

struggle ['strʌgl] *n* lucha ♦ *vi* luchar; **to**
have a ~ **to do sth** esforzarse por hacer
algo.

strum [strʌm] *vt* (*guitar*) rasguear.

strung [strʌŋ] *pt*, *pp of* **string**.

strut [strʌt] *n* puntal *m* ♦ *vi* pavonearse.

strychnine ['strɪkni:n] *n* estricnina.

stub [stʌb] *n* (*of ticket etc*) matriz *f*; (*of*
cigarette) colilla ♦ *vt*: **to** ~ **one's toe on sth**
dar con el dedo del pie contra algo.

▶**stub out** *vt* (*cigarette*) apagar.

stubble ['stʌbl] *n* rastrojo; (*on chin*) barba
(incipiente).

stubborn ['stʌbən] *adj* terco, testarudo.

stucco ['stʌkəu] *n* estuco.

stuck [stʌk] *pt*, *pp of* **stick** ♦ *adj* (*jammed*)
atascado.

stuck-up [stʌk'ʌp] *adj* engreído,
presumido.

stud [stʌd] *n* (*shirt* ~) corchete *m*; (*of boot*)
taco; (*of horses*) caballeriza; (*also*: ~
horse) caballo semental ♦ *vt* (*fig*): ~**ded**
with salpicado de.

student ['stju:dənt] *n* estudiante *m/f* ♦ *adj*
estudiantil; **a law/medical** ~ un(a)
estudiante de derecho/medicina.

student driver *n* (*US AUT*) aprendiz(a) *m/f*
de conductor.

students' union *n* (*BRIT*: *association*)
sindicato de estudiantes; (: *building*)
centro de estudiantes.

studio ['stju:dɪəu] *n* estudio; (*artist's*) taller
m.

studio flat, (*US*) **studio apartment** *n*
estudio.

studious ['stju:dɪəs] *adj* estudioso; (*studied*)
calculado.

studiously ['stju:dɪəslɪ] *adv* (*carefully*) con
esmero.

study ['stʌdɪ] *n* estudio ♦ *vt* estudiar;
(*examine*) examinar, investigar ♦ *vi*
estudiar; **to make a** ~ **of sth** realizar una
investigación de algo; **to** ~ **for an exam**
preparar un examen.

stuff [stʌf] *n* materia; (*cloth*) tela;
(*substance*) material *m*, sustancia; (*things,*
belongings) cosas *fpl* ♦ *vt* llenar; (*CULIN*)

rellenar; (*animal: for exhibition*) disecar; **my nose is** ~**ed up** tengo la nariz tapada; ~**ed toy** juguete *m* or muñeco de trapo.

stuffing ['stʌfɪŋ] *n* relleno.

stuffy ['stʌfɪ] *adj* (*room*) mal ventilado; (*person*) de miras estrechas.

stumble ['stʌmbl] *vi* tropezar, dar un traspié.

▶**stumble across** *vt fus* (*fig*) tropezar con.

stumbling block ['stʌmblɪŋ-] *n* tropiezo, obstáculo.

stump [stʌmp] *n* (*of tree*) tocón *m*; (*of limb*) muñón *m* ♦ *vt*: **to be** ~**ed** quedarse perplejo; **to be** ~**ed for an answer** quedarse sin saber qué contestar.

stun [stʌn] *vt* aturdir.

stung [stʌŋ] *pt*, *pp of* **sting**.

stunk [stʌŋk] *pp of* **stink**.

stunning ['stʌnɪŋ] *adj* (*fig*) pasmoso.

stunt [stʌnt] *n* (*AVIAT*) vuelo acrobático; (*publicity* ~) truco publicitario.

stunted ['stʌntɪd] *adj* enano, achaparrado.

stuntman ['stʌntmæn] *n* especialista *m*.

stupefaction [stjuːpɪ'fækʃən] *n* estupefacción *f*.

stupefy ['stjuːpɪfaɪ] *vt* dejar estupefacto.

stupendous [stjuː'pɛndəs] *adj* estupendo, asombroso.

stupid ['stjuːpɪd] *adj* estúpido, tonto.

stupidity [stjuː'pɪdɪtɪ] *n* estupidez *f*.

stupor ['stjuːpə*] *n* estupor *m*.

sturdy ['stɜːdɪ] *adj* robusto, fuerte.

stutter ['stʌtə*] *n* tartamudeo ♦ *vi* tartamudear.

sty [staɪ] *n* (*for pigs*) pocilga.

stye [staɪ] *n* (*MED*) orzuelo.

style [staɪl] *n* estilo, (*fashion*) moda; (*of dress etc*) hechura; (*hair* ~) corte *m*; **in the latest** ~ en el último modelo.

stylish ['staɪlɪʃ] *adj* elegante, a la moda.

stylist ['staɪlɪst] *n* (*hair* ~) peluquero/a

stylus, *pl* **styli** or **styluses** ['staɪləs, -laɪ] *n* (*of record player*) aguja.

Styrofoam ® ['staɪrəfəum] *n* (*US*) poliestireno ♦ *adj* (*cup*) de poliestireno.

suave [swɑːv] *adj* cortés, fino.

sub [sʌb] *n abbr* = **submarine, subscription.**

sub... [sʌb] *pref* sub....

subcommittee ['sʌbkəmɪtɪ] *n* subcomisión *f*.

subconscious [sʌb'kɒnʃəs] *adj* subconsciente ♦ *n* subconsciente *m*.

subcontinent [sʌb'kɒntɪnənt] *n*: **the Indian** ~ el subcontinente (de la India).

subcontract *n* ['sʌb'kɒntrækt] subcontrato ♦ *vt* ['sʌbkən'trækt] subcontratar.

subcontractor ['sʌbkən'træktə*] *n* subcontratista *m/f*.

subdivide [sʌbdɪ'vaɪd] *vt* subdividir.

subdue [səb'djuː] *vt* sojuzgar; (*passions*) dominar.

subdued [səb'djuːd] *adj* (*light*) tenue; (*person*) sumiso, manso.

sub-editor ['sʌb'ɛdɪtə*] *n* (*BRIT*) redactor(a) *m/f*.

subject *n* ['sʌbdʒɪkt] súbdito; (*SCOL*) tema *m*, materia ♦ *vt* [səb'dʒɛkt]: **to** ~ **sb to sth** someter a algn a algo ♦ *adj* ['sʌbdʒɪkt]: **to be** ~ **to** (*law*) estar sujeto a; ~ **to confirmation in writing** sujeto a confirmación por escrito; **to change the** ~ cambiar de tema.

subjective [səb'dʒɛktɪv] *adj* subjetivo.

subject matter *n* materia; (*content*) contenido.

sub judice [sʌb'djuːdɪsɪ] *adj* (*LAW*) pendiente de resolución.

subjugate ['sʌbdʒugeɪt] *vt* subyugar, sojuzgar.

subjunctive [səb'dʒʌŋktɪv] *adj*, *n* subjuntivo.

sublet [sʌb'lɛt] *vt*, *vi* subarrendar, realquilar.

sublime [sə'blaɪm] *adj* sublime.

subliminal [sʌb'lɪmɪnl] *adj* subliminal.

submachine gun ['sʌbmə'ʃiːn-] *n* metralleta.

submarine [sʌbmə'riːn] *n* submarino.

submerge [səb'mɜːdʒ] *vt* sumergir; (*flood*) inundar ♦ *vi* sumergirse.

submersion [səb'mɜːʃən] *n* submersión *f*.

submission [səb'mɪʃən] *n* sumisión *f*; (*to committee etc*) ponencia.

submissive [səb'mɪsɪv] *adj* sumiso.

submit [səb'mɪt] *vt* someter; (*proposal, claim*) presentar ♦ *vi* someterse; **I** ~ **that** ... me permito sugerir que ....

subnormal [sʌb'nɔːməl] *adj* subnormal.

subordinate [sə'bɔːdɪnət] *adj*, *n* subordinado/a *m/f*.

subpoena [səb'piːnə] (*LAW*) *n* citación *f* ♦ *vt* citar.

subroutine [sʌbruː'tiːn] *n* (*COMPUT*) subrutina.

subscribe [səb'skraɪb] *vi* suscribir; **to** ~ **to** (*fund*) suscribir, aprobar; (*opinion*) estar de acuerdo con; (*newspaper*) suscribirse a.

subscribed capital [səb'skraɪbd-] *n* capital *m* suscrito.

subscriber [səb'skraɪbə*] *n* (*to periodical*) suscriptor(a) *m/f*; (*to telephone*) abonado/a.

subscript ['sʌbskrɪpt] *n* (*TYP*) subíndice *m*.

subscription [səb'skrɪpʃən] *n* (*to club*) abono; (*to magazine*) suscripción *f*; **to take**

out a ~ to suscribirse a.

subsequent ['sʌbsɪkwənt] *adj* subsiguiente, posterior; **~ to** posterior a.

subsequently ['sʌbsɪkwəntlɪ] *adv* posteriormente, más tarde.

subservient [səb'sɜːvɪənt] *adj*: **~ (to)** servil (a).

subside [səb'saɪd] *vi* hundirse; (*flood*) bajar; (*wind*) amainar.

subsidence [səb'saɪdns] *n* hundimiento; (*in road*) socavón *m*.

subsidiarity [səbsɪdɪ'ærɪtɪ] *n* (*POL*) subsidiariedad *f*.

subsidiary [səb'sɪdɪərɪ] *n* sucursal *f*, filial *f* ♦ *adj* (*UNIV: subject*) secundario.

subsidize ['sʌbsɪdaɪz] *vt* subvencionar.

subsidy ['sʌbsɪdɪ] *n* subvención *f*.

subsist [səb'sɪst] *vi*: **to ~ on sth** subsistir a base de algo, sustentarse con algo.

subsistence [səb'sɪstəns] *n* subsistencia.

subsistence allowance *n* dietas *fpl*.

subsistence level *n* nivel *m* de subsistencia.

subsistence wage *n* sueldo de subsistencia.

substance ['sʌbstəns] *n* sustancia; (*fig*) esencia; **to lack ~** (*argument*) ser poco convincente; (*accusation*) no tener fundamento; (*film, book*) tener poca profundidad.

substance abuse *n* uso indebido de sustancias tóxicas.

substandard [sʌb'stændəd] *adj* (*goods*) inferior; (*housing*) deficiente.

substantial [səb'stænʃl] *adj* sustancial, sustancioso; (*fig*) importante.

substantially [səb'stænʃəlɪ] *adv* sustancialmente; **~ bigger** bastante más grande.

substantiate [səb'stænʃɪeɪt] *vt* comprobar.

substitute ['sʌbstɪtjuːt] *n* (*person*) suplente *m/f*; (*thing*) sustituto ♦ *vt*: **to ~ A for B** sustituir B por A, reemplazar A por B.

substitution [sʌbstɪ'tjuːʃən] *n* sustitución *f*.

subterfuge ['sʌbtəfjuːdʒ] *n* subterfugio.

subterranean [sʌbtə'reɪnɪən] *adj* subterráneo.

subtitle ['sʌbtaɪtl] *n* subtítulo.

subtle ['sʌtl] *adj* sutil.

subtlety ['sʌtltɪ] *n* sutileza.

subtly ['sʌtlɪ] *adv* sutilmente.

subtotal [sʌb'təʊtl] *n* subtotal *m*.

subtract [səb'trækt] *vt* restar; sustraer.

subtraction [səb'trækʃən] *n* resta; sustracción *f*.

suburb ['sʌbəːb] *n* barrio residencial; **the ~s** las afueras (de la ciudad).

suburban [sə'bəːbən] *adj* suburbano; (*train etc*) de cercanías.

suburbia [sə'bəːbɪə] *n* barrios *mpl* residenciales.

subversion [səb'vəːʃən] *n* subversión *f*.

subversive [səb'vəːsɪv] *adj* subversivo.

subway ['sʌbweɪ] *n* (*BRIT*) paso subterráneo *or* inferior; (*US*) metro.

sub-zero [sʌb'zɪərəʊ] *adj*: **~ temperatures** temperaturas *fpl* por debajo del cero.

succeed [sək'siːd] *vi* (*person*) tener éxito; (*plan*) salir bien ♦ *vt* suceder a; **to ~ in doing** lograr hacer.

succeeding [sək'siːdɪŋ] *adj* (*following*) sucesivo; **~ generations** generaciones *fpl* futuras.

success [sək'sɛs] *n* éxito; (*gain*) triunfo.

successful [sək'sɛsful] *adj* (*venture*) de éxito, exitoso (*esp LAM*); **to be ~ (in doing)** lograr (hacer).

successfully [sək'sɛsfulɪ] *adv* con éxito.

succession [sək'sɛʃən] *n* (*series*) sucesión *f*, serie *f*; (*descendants*) descendencia; **in ~** sucesivamente.

successive [sək'sɛsɪv] *adj* sucesivo, consecutivo; **on 3 ~ days** tres días seguidos.

successor [sək'sɛsə*] *n* sucesor(a) *m/f*.

succinct [sək'sɪŋkt] *adj* sucinto.

succulent ['sʌkjulənt] *adj* suculento ♦ *n* (*BOT*): **~s** plantas *fpl* carnosas.

succumb [sə'kʌm] *vi* sucumbir.

such [sʌtʃ] *adj* tal, semejante; (*of that kind*): **~ a book** tal libro; **~ books** tales libros; (*so much*): **~ courage** tanto valor ♦ *adv* tan; **~ a long trip** un viaje tan largo; **~ a lot of** tanto; **~ as** (*like*) tal como; **a noise ~ as to** un ruido tal que; **~ books as I have** cuantos libros tengo; **I said no ~ thing** no dije tal cosa; **it's ~ a long time since we saw each other** hace tanto tiempo que no nos vemos; **~ a long time ago** hace tantísimo tiempo; **as ~** *adv* como tal.

such-and-such ['sʌtʃənsʌtʃ] *adj* tal o cual.

suchlike ['sʌtʃlaɪk] *pron* (*col*): **and ~** y cosas por el estilo.

suck [sʌk] *vt* chupar; (*bottle*) sorber; (*breast*) mamar; (*subj: pump, machine*) aspirar.

sucker ['sʌkə*] *n* (*BOT*) serpollo; (*ZOOL*) ventosa; (*col*) bobo, primo.

sucrose ['suːkrəʊz] *n* sacarosa.

suction ['sʌkʃən] *n* succión *f*.

suction pump *n* bomba aspirante *or* de succión.

Sudan [su'dæn] *n* Sudán *m*.

Sudanese [suːdə'niːz] *adj*, *n* sudanés/esa *m/f*.

sudden ['sʌdn] *adj* (*rapid*) repentino, súbito; (*unexpected*) imprevisto; **all of a ~** de repente.

sudden-death [sʌdn'dɛθ] n (also: ~ **play off**) desempate m instantáneo, muerte f súbita.

suddenly ['sʌdnlɪ] adv de repente.

suds [sʌdz] npl espuma sg de jabón.

sue [suː] vt demandar; **to** ~ **(for)** demandar (por); **to** ~ **for divorce** solicitar or pedir el divorcio; **to** ~ **for damages** demandar por daños y perjuicios.

suede [sweɪd] n ante m, gamuza (LAM).

suet ['suɪt] n sebo.

Suez Canal ['suːɪz-] n Canal m de Suez.

Suff. abbr (BRIT) = **Suffolk**.

suffer ['sʌfə*] vt sufrir, padecer; (tolerate) aguantar, soportar; (undergo: loss, setback) experimentar ♦ vi sufrir, padecer; **to** ~ **from** sufrir, tener; **to** ~ **from the effects of alcohol/a fall** sufrir los efectos del alcohol/resentirse de una caída.

sufferance ['sʌfərns] n: **he was only there on** ~ estuvo allí sólo porque se lo toleraron.

sufferer ['sʌfərə*] n víctima f; (MED) ~ **from** enfermo/a de.

suffering ['sʌfərɪŋ] n (hardship, deprivation) sufrimiento; (pain) dolor m.

suffice [sə'faɪs] vi bastar, ser suficiente.

sufficient [sə'fɪʃənt] adj suficiente, bastante.

sufficiently [sə'fɪʃəntlɪ] adv suficientemente, bastante.

suffix ['sʌfɪks] n sufijo.

suffocate ['sʌfəkeɪt] vi ahogarse, asfixiarse.

suffocation [sʌfə'keɪʃən] n sofocación f, asfixia.

suffrage ['sʌfrɪdʒ] n sufragio.

suffuse [sə'fjuːz] vt: **to** ~ **(with)** (colour) bañar (de); **her face was** ~**d with joy** su cara estaba llena de alegría.

sugar ['ʃugə*] n azúcar m ♦ vt echar azúcar a, azucarar.

sugar basin n (BRIT) = **sugar bowl**.

sugar beet n remolacha.

sugar bowl n azucarero.

sugar cane n caña de azúcar.

sugar-coated [ʃugə'kəutɪd] adj azucarado.

sugar lump n terrón m de azúcar.

sugar refinery n refinería de azúcar.

sugary ['ʃugərɪ] adj azucarado.

suggest [sə'dʒɛst] vt sugerir; (recommend) aconsejar; **what do you** ~ **I do?** ¿qué sugieres que haga?; **this** ~**s that ...** esto hace pensar que ....

suggestion [sə'dʒɛstʃən] n sugerencia; **there's no** ~ **of ...** no hay indicación or

evidencia de ....

suggestive [sə'dʒɛstɪv] adj sugestivo; (pej: indecent) indecente.

suicidal ['suɪsaɪdl] adj suicida.

suicide ['suɪsaɪd] n suicidio; (person) suicida m/f; **to commit** ~ suicidarse.

suicide attempt, suicide bid n intento de suicidio.

suicide bombing n atentado suicida.

suit [suːt] n (man's) traje m; (woman's) traje de chaqueta; (LAW) pleito; (CARDS) palo ♦ vt convenir; (clothes) sentar bien a, ir bien a; (adapt): **to** ~ **sth to** adaptar or ajustar algo a; **to be** ~**ed to sth** (suitable for) ser apto para algo; **well** ~**ed** (couple) hechos el uno para el otro; **to bring a** ~ **against sb** entablar demanda contra algn; **to follow** ~ (CARDS) seguir el palo; (fig) seguir el ejemplo (de algn); **that** ~**s me** me va bien.

suitable ['suːtəbl] adj conveniente; (apt) indicado.

suitably ['suːtəblɪ] adv convenientemente; (appropriately) en forma debida.

suitcase ['suːtkeɪs] n maleta, valija (LAM).

suite [swiːt] n (of rooms, MUS) suite f; (furniture): **bedroom/dining room** ~ (juego de) dormitorio/comedor m; **a three-piece** ~ un tresillo.

suitor ['suːtə*] n pretendiente m.

sulfate ['sʌlfeɪt] n (US) = **sulphate**.

sulfur ['sʌlfə*] n (US) = **sulphur**.

sulk [sʌlk] vi estar de mal humor.

sulky ['sʌlkɪ] adj malhumorado.

sullen ['sʌlən] adj hosco, malhumorado.

sulphate, (US) sulfate ['sʌlfeɪt] n sulfato; **copper** ~ sulfato de cobre.

sulphur, (US) sulfur ['sʌlfə*] n azufre m.

sulphur dioxide n dióxido de azufre.

sultan ['sʌltən] n sultán m.

sultana [sʌl'tɑːnə] n (fruit) pasa de Esmirna.

sultry ['sʌltrɪ] adj (weather) bochornoso; (seductive) seductor(a).

sum [sʌm] n suma; (total) total m.

▶**sum up** vt resumir; (evaluate rapidly) evaluar ♦ vi hacer un resumen.

Sumatra [su'mɑːtrə] n Sumatra.

summarize ['sʌməraɪz] vt resumir.

summary ['sʌmərɪ] n resumen m ♦ adj (justice) sumario.

summer ['sʌmə*] n verano ♦ adj de verano; **in (the)** ~ en (el) verano.

summerhouse ['sʌməhaus] n (in garden) cenador m, glorieta.

summertime ['sʌmətaɪm] n (season) verano.

summer time n (by clock) hora de verano.

summery ['sʌmərɪ] *adj* veraniego.
summing-up [sʌmɪŋ'ʌp] *n* (*LAW*) resumen *m*.
summit ['sʌmɪt] *n* cima, cumbre *f*.
summit (conference) *n* (conferencia) cumbre *f*.
summon ['sʌmən] *vt* (*person*) llamar; (*meeting*) convocar; **to ~ a witness** citar a un testigo.
▶**summon up** *vt* (*courage*) armarse de.
summons ['sʌmənz] *n* llamamiento, llamada ♦ *vt* citar, emplazar; **to serve a ~ on sb** citar a algn ante el juicio.
sumo ['suːməʊ] *n* (*also:* ~ **wrestling**) sumo.
sump [sʌmp] *n* (*BRIT AUT*) cárter *m*.
sumptuous ['sʌmptjuəs] *adj* suntuoso.
sun [sʌn] *n* sol *m*; **they have everything under the ~** no les falta nada, tienen de todo.
Sun. *abbr* (= *Sunday*) dom.
sunbathe ['sʌnbeɪð] *vi* tomar el sol.
sunbeam ['sʌnbiːm] *n* rayo de sol.
sunbed ['sʌnbed] *n* cama solar.
sunburn ['sʌnbəːn] *n* (*painful*) quemadura del sol; (*tan*) bronceado.
sunburnt ['sʌnbəːnt], **sunburned** ['sʌnbəːnd] *adj* (*tanned*) bronceado; (*painfully*) quemado por el sol.
sundae ['sʌndeɪ] *n helado con frutas y nueces.*
Sunday ['sʌndɪ] *n* domingo.
Sunday paper *n* (periódico) dominical *m*.
Sunday school *n* catequesis *f*.
sundial ['sʌndaɪəl] *n* reloj *m* de sol.
sundown ['sʌndaʊn] *n* anochecer *m*, puesta de sol.
sundries ['sʌndrɪz] *npl* géneros *mpl* diversos.
sundry ['sʌndrɪ] *adj* varios, diversos; **all and ~** todos sin excepción.
sunflower ['sʌnflaʊə*] *n* girasol *m*.
sung [sʌŋ] *pp of* **sing.**
sunglasses ['sʌnglɑːsɪz] *npl* gafas *fpl* de sol.
sunk [sʌŋk] *pp of* **sink.**
sunken ['sʌŋkn] *adj* (*bath*) hundido.
sunlamp ['sʌnlæmp] *n* lámpara solar ultravioleta.
sunlight ['sʌnlaɪt] *n* luz *f* del sol.
sunlit ['sʌnlɪt] *adj* iluminado por el sol.
sunny ['sʌnɪ] *adj* soleado; (*day*) de sol; (*fig*) alegre; **it is ~** hace sol.
sunrise ['sʌnraɪz] *n* salida del sol.
sun roof *n* (*AUT*) techo corredizo *or* solar; (*on building*) azotea, terraza.
sunscreen ['sʌnskriːn] *n* protector *m* solar.
sunset ['sʌnsɛt] *n* puesta del sol.
sunshade ['sʌnʃeɪd] *n* (*over table*) sombrilla.

sunshine ['sʌnʃaɪn] *n* sol *m*.
sunstroke ['sʌnstrəʊk] *n* insolación *f*.
suntan ['sʌntæn] *n* bronceado.
suntanned ['sʌntænd] *adj* bronceado.
suntan oil *n* aceite *m* bronceador.
super ['suːpə*] *adj* (*col*) bárbaro.
superannuation [suːpərænjuˈeɪʃən] *n* jubilación *f*, pensión *f*.
superb [suːˈpəːb] *adj* magnífico, espléndido.
Super Bowl *n* (*US SPORT*) *super copa de fútbol americano.*
supercilious [suːpəˈsɪlɪəs] *adj* (*disdainful*) desdeñoso; (*haughty*) altanero.
superconductor [suːpəkənˈdʌktə*] *n* superconductor *m*.
superficial [suːpəˈfɪʃəl] *adj* superficial.
superfluous [suːˈpəːfluəs] *adj* superfluo, de sobra.
superglue ['suːpəgluː] *n* cola de contacto, supercola.
superhighway ['suːpəhaɪweɪ] *n* (*US*) superautopista; **the information ~** la superautopista de la información.
superhuman [suːpəˈhjuːmən] *adj* sobrehumano.
superimpose ['suːpərɪmˈpəʊz] *vt* sobreponer.
superintend [suːpərɪnˈtɛnd] *vt* supervisar.
superintendent [suːpərɪnˈtɛndənt] *n* director(a) *m/f*; (*police ~*) subjefe/a *m/f*.
superior [suːˈpɪərɪə*] *adj* superior; (*smug: person*) altivo, desdeñoso; (*: smile, air*) de suficiencia; (*: remark*) desdeñoso ♦ *n* superior *m*; **Mother S~** (*REL*) madre *f* superiora.
superiority [supɪərɪˈɔrɪtɪ] *n* superioridad *f*; desdén *m*.
superlative [suːˈpəːlətɪv] *adj*, *n* superlativo.
superman ['suːpəmæn] *n* superhombre *m*.
supermarket ['suːpəmɑːkɪt] *n* supermercado.
supermodel ['suːpəmɒdl] *n* top model *f*, supermodelo *f*.
supernatural [suːpəˈnætʃərəl] *adj* sobrenatural.
supernova [suːpəˈnəʊvə] *n* supernova.
superpower ['suːpəpaʊə*] *n* (*POL*) superpotencia.
supersede [suːpəˈsiːd] *vt* suplantar.
supersonic [suːpəˈsɒnɪk] *adj* supersónico.
superstar ['suːpəstɑː*] *n* superestrella ♦ *adj* de superestrella.
superstition [suːpəˈstɪʃən] *n* superstición *f*.
superstitious [suːpəˈstɪʃəs] *adj* supersticioso.
superstore ['suːpəstɔː*] *n* (*BRIT*) hipermercado.
supertanker ['suːpətæŋkə*] *n*

superpetrolero.

supertax ['su:pətæks] *n* sobretasa, sobreimpuesto.

supervise ['su:pəvaɪz] *vt* supervisar.

supervision [su:pə'vɪʒən] *n* supervisión *f*.

supervisor ['su:pəvaɪzə*] *n* (*gen, UNIV*) supervisor(a) *m/f*.

supervisory ['su:pəvaɪzərɪ] *adj* de supervisión.

supper ['sʌpə*] *n* cena; **to have ~** cenar.

supplant [sə'plɑ:nt] *vt* suplantar, reemplazar.

supple ['sʌpl] *adj* flexible.

supplement *n* ['sʌplɪmənt] suplemento ♦ *vt* [sʌplɪ'mɛnt] suplir.

supplementary [sʌplɪ'mɛntərɪ] *adj* suplementario.

supplementary benefit *n* (*BRIT*) subsidio adicional de la seguridad social.

supplier [sə'plaɪə*] *n* suministrador(a) *m/f*; (*COMM*) distribuidor(a) *m/f*.

supply [sə'plaɪ] *vt* (*provide*) suministrar; (*information*) facilitar; (*fill: need, want*) suplir, satisfacer; (*equip*): **to ~ (with)** proveer (de) ♦ *n* provisión *f*; (*of gas, water etc*) suministro ♦ *adj* (*BRIT: teacher etc*) suplente; **supplies** *npl* (*food*) víveres *mpl*; (*MIL*) pertrechos *mpl*; **office supplies** materiales *mpl* para oficina; **to be in short ~** escasear, haber escasez de; **the electricity/water/gas ~** el suministro de electricidad/agua/gas; **~ and demand** la oferta y la demanda.

support [sə'pɔ:t] *n* (*moral, financial etc*) apoyo; (*TECH*) soporte *m* ♦ *vt* apoyar; (*financially*) mantener; (*uphold*) sostener; (*SPORT: team*) seguir, ser hincha de; **they stopped work in ~ (of)** pararon de trabajar en apoyo (de); **to ~ o.s.** (*financially*) ganarse la vida.

support buying [-'baɪɪŋ] *n* compra proteccionista.

supporter [sə'pɔ:tə*] *n* (*POL etc*) partidario/a; (*SPORT*) aficionado/a; (*FOOTBALL*) hincha *m/f*.

supporting [sə'pɔ:tɪŋ] *adj* (*wall*) de apoyo; **~ role** papel *m* secundario; **~ actor/ actress** actor/actriz *m/f* secundario/a.

supportive [sə'pɔ:tɪv] *adj* de apoyo; **I have a ~ family/wife** mi familia/mujer me apoya.

suppose [sə'pəuz] *vt*, *vi* suponer; (*imagine*) imaginarse; **to be ~d to do sth** deber hacer algo; **I don't ~ she'll come** no creo que venga; **he's ~d to be an expert** se le supone un experto.

supposedly [sə'pəuzɪdlɪ] *adv* según cabe suponer.

supposing [sə'pəuzɪŋ] *conj* en caso de que; **always ~ (that) he comes** suponiendo que venga.

supposition [sʌpə'zɪʃən] *n* suposición *f*.

suppository [sə'pɒzɪtrɪ] *n* supositorio.

suppress [sə'prɛs] *vt* suprimir; (*yawn*) ahogar.

suppression [sə'prɛʃən] *n* represión *f*.

supremacy [su'prɛməsɪ] *n* supremacía.

supreme [su'pri:m] *adj* supremo.

Supreme Court *n* (*US*) Tribunal *m* Supremo, Corte *f* Suprema.

supremo [su'pri:məu] *n* autoridad *f* máxima.

Supt. *abbr* (*POLICE*) = **superintendent.**

surcharge ['sɔ:tʃɑ:dʒ] *n* sobretasa, recargo.

sure [ʃuə*] *adj* seguro; (*definite, convinced*) cierto; (*aim*) certero ♦ *adv*: **that ~ is pretty, that's ~ pretty** (*US*) ¡qué bonito es!; **to be ~ of sth** estar seguro de algo; **to be ~ of o.s.** estar seguro de sí mismo; **to make ~ of sth/that** asegurarse de algo/asegurar que; **I'm not ~ how/why/ when** no estoy seguro de cómo/por qué/ cuándo; **~!** (*of course*) ¡claro!, ¡por supuesto!; **~ enough** efectivamente.

sure-fire ['ʃuəfaɪə*] *adj* (*col*) infalible.

sure-footed [ʃuə'futɪd] *adj* de pie firme.

surely ['ʃuəlɪ] *adv* (*certainly*) seguramente; **~ you don't mean that!** ¡no lo dices en serio!

surety ['ʃuərətɪ] *n* fianza; (*person*) fiador(a) *m/f*; **to go** *or* **stand ~ for sb** ser fiador de algn, salir garante por algn.

surf [sɔ:f] *n* olas *fpl* ♦ *vi* hacer surf ♦ *vt* (*INTERNET*) **to ~ the Net** navegar por Internet.

surface ['sɔ:fɪs] *n* superficie *f* ♦ *vt* (*road*) revestir ♦ *vi* salir a la superficie ♦ *cpd* (*MIL, NAUT*) de (la) superficie; **on the ~ it seems that ...** (*fig*) a primera vista parece que ....

surface area *n* área de la superficie.

surface mail *n* vía terrestre.

surface-to-air ['sɔ:fɪstə'ɛə*] *adj* (*MIL*) tierra-aire.

surface-to-surface ['sɔ:fɪstə'sɔ:fɪs] *adj* (*MIL*) tierra-tierra.

surfboard ['sɔ:fbɔ:d] *n* plancha (de surf).

surfeit ['sɔ:fɪt] *n*: **a ~ of** un exceso de.

surfer ['sɔ:fə*] *n* súrfer *m/f*.

surfing ['sɔ:fɪŋ] *n* surf *m*.

surge [sɔ:dʒ] *n* oleada, oleaje *m*; (*ELEC*) sobretensión *f* transitoria ♦ *vi* avanzar a tropel; **to ~ forward** avanzar rápidamente.

surgeon ['sɔ:dʒən] *n* cirujano/a.

surgery ['sɔ:dʒərɪ] *n* cirugía; (*BRIT: room*)

consultorio; (: POL) *horas en las que los electores pueden reunirse personalmente con su diputado*; **to undergo** ~ operarse; *see also* **constituency**.

surgery hours *npl* (*BRIT*) horas *fpl* de consulta.

surgical ['sɜːdʒɪkl] *adj* quirúrgico.

surgical spirit *n* (*BRIT*) alcohol *m*.

surly ['sɜːlɪ] *adj* hosco, malhumorado.

surmount [sɜː'maunt] *vt* superar, vencer.

surname ['sɜːneɪm] *n* apellido.

surpass [sɜː'pɑːs] *vt* superar, exceder.

surplus ['sɜːpləs] *n* excedente *m*; (*COMM*) superávit *m* ♦ *adj* (*COMM*) excedente, sobrante; **to have a** ~ **of sth** tener un excedente de algo; **it is** ~ **to our requirements** nos sobra; ~ **stock** saldos *mpl*.

surprise [sə'praɪz] *n* sorpresa ♦ *vt* sorprender; **to take by** ~ (*person*) coger desprevenido *or* por sorpresa, sorprender; (*MIL*) atacar por sorpresa.

surprising [sə'praɪzɪŋ] *adj* sorprendente.

surprisingly [sə'praɪzɪŋlɪ] *adv* (*easy, helpful*) de modo sorprendente; **(somewhat)** ~**, he agreed** para sorpresa de todos, aceptó.

surrealism [sə'rɪəlɪzəm] *n* surrealismo.

surrender [sə'rɛndə*] *n* rendición *f*, entrega ♦ *vi* rendirse, entregarse ♦ *vt* renunciar.

surrender value *n* valor *m* de rescate.

surreptitious [sʌrəp'tɪʃəs] *adj* subrepticio.

surrogate ['sʌrəgɪt] *n* (*BRIT*: *substitute*) sustituto/a.

surrogate mother *n* madre *f* de alquiler.

surround [sə'raund] *vt* rodear, circundar; (*MIL etc*) cercar.

surrounding [sə'raundɪŋ] *adj* circundante.

surroundings [sə'raundɪŋz] *npl* alrededores *mpl*, cercanías *fpl*.

surtax ['sɜːtæks] *n* sobretasa, sobreimpuesto.

surveillance [sɜː'veɪləns] *n* vigilancia.

survey *n* ['sɜːveɪ] inspección *f*, reconocimiento; (*inquiry*) encuesta; (*comprehensive view: of situation etc*) vista de conjunto ♦ *vt* [sɜː'veɪ] examinar, inspeccionar; (*SURVEYING: building*) inspeccionar; (: *land*) hacer un reconocimiento de, reconocer; (*look at*) mirar, contemplar; (*make inquiries about*) hacer una encuesta de; **to carry out a** ~ **of** inspeccionar, examinar.

surveyor [sɜː'veɪə*] *n* (*BRIT*) (*of building*) perito *m/f*; (*of land*) agrimensor(a) *m/f*.

survival [sə'vaɪvl] *n* supervivencia.

survival course *n* curso de supervivencia.

survival kit *n* equipo de emergencia.

survive [sə'vaɪv] *vi* sobrevivir; (*custom etc*)

perdurar ♦ *vt* sobrevivir a.

survivor [sə'vaɪvə*] *n* superviviente *m/f*.

susceptibility [səsɛptə'bɪlɪtɪ] *n* (*to illness*) propensión *f*.

susceptible [sə'sɛptəbl] *adj* (*easily influenced*) influenciable; (*to disease, illness*): ~ **to** propenso a.

sushi [suːʃɪ] *n* sushi *m*.

suspect *adj, n* ['sʌspɛkt] sospechoso/a *m/f* ♦ *vt* [səs'pɛkt] sospechar.

suspected [səs'pɛktɪd] *adj* presunto; **to have a** ~ **fracture** tener una posible fractura.

suspend [səs'pɛnd] *vt* suspender.

suspended animation [səs'pɛndəd-] *n*: **in a state of** ~ en (estado de) hibernación.

suspended sentence *n* (*LAW*) libertad *f* condicional.

suspender belt [səs'pɛndə*-] *n* (*BRIT*) liguero, portaligas *m inv* (*AM*).

suspenders [səs'pɛndəz] *npl* (*BRIT*) ligas *fpl*; (*US*) tirantes *mpl*.

suspense [səs'pɛns] *n* incertidumbre *f*, duda; (*in film etc*) suspense *m*.

suspension [səs'pɛnʃən] *n* suspensión *f*; (*of driving licence*) privación *f*.

suspension bridge *n* puente *m* colgante.

suspension file *n* archivador *m* colgante.

suspicion [səs'pɪʃən] *n* sospecha; (*distrust*) recelo; (*trace*) traza; **to be under** ~ estar bajo sospecha; **arrested on** ~ **of murder** detenido bajo sospecha de asesinato.

suspicious [səs'pɪʃəs] *adj* (*suspecting*) receloso; (*causing suspicion*) sospechoso; **to be** ~ **of** *or* **about sb/sth** tener sospechas de algn/algo.

suss out [sʌs-] *vt* (*BRIT col*) calar.

sustain [səs'teɪn] *vt* sostener, apoyar; (*suffer*) sufrir, padecer.

sustainable [səs'teɪnəbl] *adj* sostenible; ~ **development** desarrollo sostenible.

sustained [səs'teɪnd] *adj* (*effort*) sostenido.

sustenance ['sʌstɪnəns] *n* sustento.

suture ['suːtʃə*] *n* sutura.

SVQ *n abbr* (= *Scottish Vocational Qualification*) titulación de formación profesional en Escocia.

SW *abbr* = **short wave**.

swab [swɔb] *n* (*MED*) algodón *m*, frotis *m inv* ♦ *vt* (*NAUT*: *also*: ~ **down**) limpiar, fregar.

swagger ['swægə*] *vi* pavonearse.

swallow ['swɔləu] *n* (*bird*) golondrina; (*of food*) bocado; (*of drink*) trago ♦ *vt* tragar.

▶**swallow up** *vt* (*savings etc*) consumir.

swam [swæm] *pt of* **swim**.

swamp [swɔmp] *n* pantano, ciénaga ♦ *vt* abrumar, agobiar.

swampy ['swɔmpɪ] *adj* pantanoso.

swan [swɔn] *n* cisne *m*.

swank [swæŋk] (*col*) *n* (*vanity, boastfulness*) fanfarronada ♦ *vi* fanfarronear, presumir.

swan song *n* (*fig*) canto del cisne.

swap [swɔp] *n* canje *m*, trueque *m* ♦ *vt*: **to ~ (for)** canjear (por).

SWAPO ['swɑ:pəu] *n abbr* (= *South-West Africa People's Organization*) SWAPO *f*.

swarm [swɔ:m] *n* (*of bees*) enjambre *m*; (*fig*) multitud *f* ♦ *vi* (*fig*) hormiguear, pulular.

swarthy ['swɔ:ðɪ] *adj* moreno.

swashbuckling ['swɔʃbʌklɪŋ] *adj* (*person*) aventurero; (*film*) de capa y espada.

swastika ['swɔstɪkə] *n* esvástica, cruz *f* gamada.

swat [swɔt] *vt* aplastar ♦ *n* (*also*: **fly ~**) matamoscas *m inv*.

SWAT [swɔt] *n abbr* (*US*: = *Special Weapons and Tactics*) unidad especial de la policía.

swathe [sweɪð] *vt*: **to ~ in** (*blankets*) envolver en; (*bandages*) vendar en.

sway [sweɪ] *vi* mecerse, balancearse ♦ *vt* (*influence*) mover, influir en ♦ *n* (*rule, power*): **~ (over)** dominio (sobre); **to hold ~ over sb** dominar a algn, mantener el dominio sobre algn.

Swaziland ['swɑ:zɪlænd] *n* Swazilandia.

swear, *pt* swore, *pp* sworn [swɛə*, swɔ:*, swɔ:n] *vi* jurar; (*with swearwords*) decir tacos ♦ *vt*: **to ~ an oath** prestar juramento, jurar; **to ~ to sth** declarar algo bajo juramento.

▶**swear in** *vt* tomar juramento (a).

swearword ['swɛəwə:d] *n* taco, palabrota.

sweat [swɛt] *n* sudor *m* ♦ *vi* sudar.

sweatband ['swɛtbænd] *n* (*SPORT*: *on head*) banda; (: *on wrist*) muñequera.

sweater ['swɛtə*] *n* suéter *m*.

sweatshirt ['swɛtʃə:t] *n* sudadera.

sweatshop ['swɛtʃɔp] *n* fábrica donde se explota al obrero.

sweaty ['swɛtɪ] *adj* sudoroso.

Swede [swi:d] *n* sueco/a.

swede [swi:d] *n* (*BRIT*) nabo.

Sweden ['swi:dn] *n* Suecia.

Swedish ['swi:dɪʃ] *adj*, *n* (*LING*) sueco.

sweep [swi:p] *n* (*act*) barrida; (*of arm*) manotazo *m*; (*curve*) curva, alcance *m*; (*also*: **chimney ~**) deshollinador(a) *m/f* ♦ *vb* (*pt*, *pp* **swept** [swɛpt]) *vt* barrer; (*disease, fashion*) recorrer ♦ *vi* barrer.

▶**sweep away** *vt* barrer; (*rub out*) borrar.

▶**sweep past** *vi* pasar rápidamente; (*brush by*) rozar.

▶**sweep up** *vi* barrer.

sweeper ['swi:pə*] *n* (*person*) barrendero/a; (*machine*) barredora; (*FOOTBALL*) líbero, libre *m*.

sweeping ['swi:pɪŋ] *adj* (*gesture*) dramático; (*generalized*) generalizado; (*changes, reforms*) radical.

sweepstake ['swi:psteɪk] *n* lotería.

sweet [swi:t] *n* (*candy*) dulce *m*, caramelo; (*BRIT*: *pudding*) postre *m* ♦ *adj* dulce; (*sugary*) azucarado; (*charming*: *person*) encantador(a); (: *smile, character*) dulce, amable, agradable ♦ *adv*: **to smell/taste ~** oler/saber dulce.

sweet and sour *adj* agridulce.

sweetcorn ['swi:tkɔ:n] *n* maíz *m* (dulce).

sweeten ['swi:tn] *vt* (*person*) endulzar; (*add sugar to*) poner azúcar a.

sweetener ['swi:tnə*] *n* (*CULIN*) edulcorante *m*.

sweetheart ['swi:thɑ:t] *n* amor *m*, novio/a; (*in speech*) amor, cariño.

sweetness ['swi:tnɪs] *n* (*gen*) dulzura.

sweet pea *n* guisante *m* de olor.

sweet potato *n* batata, camote *m* (*LAM*).

sweetshop ['swi:tʃɔp] *n* (*BRIT*) confitería, bombonería.

swell [swɛl] *n* (*of sea*) marejada, oleaje *m* ♦ *adj* (*US*: *col*: *excellent*) estupendo, fenomenal ♦ *vb* (*pt* ~**ed**, *pp* **swollen** *or* ~**ed** ['swəulən]) *vt* hinchar, inflar ♦ *vi* hincharse, inflarse.

swelling ['swɛlɪŋ] *n* (*MED*) hinchazón *f*.

sweltering ['swɛltərɪŋ] *adj* sofocante, de mucho calor.

swept [swɛpt] *pt*, *pp of* **sweep**.

swerve [swə:v] *n* regate *m*; (*in car*) desvío brusco ♦ *vi* desviarse bruscamente.

swift [swɪft] *n* (*bird*) vencejo ♦ *adj* rápido, veloz.

swiftly ['swɪftlɪ] *adv* rápidamente.

swiftness ['swɪftnɪs] *n* rapidez *f*, velocidad *f*.

swig [swɪg] *n* (*col*: *drink*) trago.

swill [swɪl] *n* bazofia ♦ *vt* (*also*: ~ **out**, ~ **down**) lavar, limpiar con agua.

swim [swɪm] *n*: **to go for a ~** ir a nadar *or* a bañarse ♦ *vb* (*pt* **swam**, *pp* **swum** [swæm, swʌm]) *vi* nadar; (*head, room*) dar vueltas ♦ *vt* pasar a nado; **to go ~ming** ir a nadar; **to ~ a length** nadar *or* hacer un largo.

swimmer ['swɪmə*] *n* nadador(a) *m/f*.

swimming ['swɪmɪŋ] *n* natación *f*.

swimming cap *n* gorro de baño.

swimming costume *n* bañador *m*, traje *m* de baño.

swimmingly ['swɪmɪŋlɪ] *adv*: **to go ~** (*wonderfully*) ir como una seda *or* sobre ruedas.

swimming pool *n* piscina, alberca (*LAM*).

swimming trunks *npl* bañador *msg.*
swimsuit ['swimsu:t] *n* = **swimming costume.**
swindle ['swindl] *n* estafa ♦ *vt* estafar.
swine [swain] *n*, *pl inv* cerdo, puerco; (*col!*) canalla *m* (!).
swing [swiŋ] *n* (*in playground*) columpio; (*movement*) balanceo, vaivén *m*; (*change of direction*) viraje *m*; (*rhythm*) ritmo; (*POL: in votes etc*): **there has been a ~ towards/ away from Labour** ha habido un viraje en favor/en contra del Partido Laborista ♦ *vb* (*pt, pp* **swung** [swʌŋ]) *vt* balancear; (*on a ~*) columpiar; (*also: ~ round*) voltear, girar ♦ *vi* balancearse, columpiarse; (*also: ~ round*) dar media vuelta; **a ~ to the left** un movimiento hacia la izquierda; **to be in full ~** estar en plena marcha; **to get into the ~ of things** meterse en situación; **the road ~s south** la carretera gira hacia el sur.
swing bridge *n* puente *m* giratorio.
swing door, (*US*) **swinging door** ['swiŋiŋ-] *n* puerta giratoria.
swingeing ['swindʒiŋ] *adj* (*BRIT*) abrumador(a).
swipe [swaip] *n* golpe *m* fuerte ♦ *vt* (*hit*) golpear fuerte; (*col: steal*) guindar; (*credit card etc*) pasar.
swirl [swə:l] *vi* arremolinarse.
swish [swiʃ] *n* (*sound: of whip*) chasquido; (: *of skirts*) frufrú *m*; (: *of grass*) crujido ♦ *adj* (*col: smart*) elegante ♦ *vi* chasquear.
Swiss [swis] *adj*, *n* (*pl inv*) suizo/a *m/f.*
switch [switʃ] *n* (*for light, radio etc*) interruptor *m*; (*change*) cambio *m*; *vt* (*change*) cambiar de; (*invert: also: ~ round, ~ over*) intercambiar.
▶**switch off** *vt* apagar; (*engine*) parar.
▶**switch on** *vt* (*AUT: ignition*) encender, prender (*LAM*); (*engine, machine*) arrancar; (*water supply*) conectar.
switchboard ['switʃbɔ:d] *n* (*TEL*) centralita (de teléfonos), conmutador *m* (*LAM*).
Switzerland ['switsələnd] *n* Suiza.
swivel ['swivl] *vi* (*also: ~ round*) girar.
swollen ['swəulən] *pp of* **swell.**
swoon [swu:n] *vi* desmayarse.
swoop [swu:p] *n* (*by police etc*) redada; (*of bird etc*) descenso en picado, calada ♦ *vi* (*also: ~ down*) caer en picado.
swop [swɔp] = **swap.**
sword [sɔ:d] *n* espada.
swordfish ['sɔ:dfiʃ] *n* pez *m* espada.
swore [swɔ:*] *pt of* **swear.**
sworn [swɔ:n] *pp of* **swear.**
swot [swɔt] (*BRIT*) *vt*, *vi* empollar ♦ *n* empollón/ona *m/f.*

swum [swʌm] *pp of* **swim.**
swung [swʌŋ] *pt, pp of* **swing.**
sycamore ['sikəmɔ:*] *n* sicomoro.
sycophant ['sikəfænt] *n* adulador(a) *m/f*, pelotillero/a.
Sydney ['sidni] *n* Sidney *m.*
syllable ['siləbl] *n* sílaba.
syllabus ['siləbəs] *n* programa *m* de estudios; **on the ~** en el programa de estudios.
symbol ['simbl] *n* símbolo.
symbolic(al) [sim'bɔlik(l)] *adj* simbólico; **to be ~ of sth** simbolizar algo.
symbolism ['simbəlizəm] *n* simbolismo.
symbolize ['simbəlaiz] *vt* simbolizar.
symmetrical [si'metrikl] *adj* simétrico.
symmetry ['simitri] *n* simetría.
sympathetic [simpə'θetik] *adj* compasivo; (*understanding*) comprensivo; **to be ~ to a cause** (*well-disposed*) apoyar una causa; **to be ~ towards** (*person*) ser comprensivo con.
sympathize ['simpəθaiz] *vi*: **to ~ with sb** compadecerse de algn; (*understand*) comprender a algn.
sympathizer ['simpəθaizə*] *n* (*POL*) simpatizante *m/f.*
sympathy ['simpəθi] *n* (*pity*) compasión *f*; (*understanding*) comprensión *f*; **a letter of ~** un pésame; **with our deepest ~** nuestro más sentido pésame.
symphony ['simfəni] *n* sinfonía.
symposium [sim'pəuziəm] *n* simposio.
symptom ['simptəm] *n* síntoma *m*, indicio.
symptomatic [simptə'mætik] *adj*: **~ (of)** sintomático (de).
synagogue ['sinəgɔg] *n* sinagoga.
sync [siŋk] *n* (*col*): **to be in/out of ~ (with)** ir/no ir al mismo ritmo (que); (*fig: people*) conectar/no conectar con.
synchromesh ['siŋkrəumeʃ] *n* cambio sincronizado de velocidades.
synchronize ['siŋkrənaiz] *vt* sincronizar ♦ *vi*: **to ~ with** sincronizarse con.
synchronized swimming ['siŋkrənaizd-] *n* natación *f* sincronizada.
syncopated ['siŋkəpeitid] *adj* sincopado.
syndicate ['sindikit] *n* (*gen*) sindicato; (*PRESS*) agencia (de noticias).
syndrome ['sindrəum] *n* síndrome *m.*
synonym ['sinənim] *n* sinónimo.
synonymous [si'nɔniməs] *adj*: **~ (with)** sinónimo (con).
synopsis, *pl* **synopses** [si'nɔpsis, -si:z] *n* sinopsis *f inv.*
syntax ['sintæks] *n* sintaxis *f.*
syntax error *n* (*COMPUT*) error *m* sintáctico.

synthesis, pl **syntheses** ['sɪnθəsɪs, -siːz] n síntesis f inv.
synthesizer ['sɪnθəsaɪzə*] n sintetizador m.
synthetic [sɪn'θɛtɪk] adj sintético ♦ n sintético.
syphilis ['sɪfɪlɪs] n sífilis f.
syphon ['saɪfən] = **siphon.**
Syria ['sɪrɪə] n Siria.
Syrian ['sɪrɪən] adj, n sirio/a m/f.
syringe [sɪ'rɪndʒ] n jeringa.
syrup ['sɪrəp] n jarabe m, almíbar m.
system ['sɪstəm] n sistema m; (ANAT) organismo; **it was quite a shock to his ~** fue un golpe para él.
systematic [sɪstə'mætɪk] adj sistemático; metódico.
system disk n (COMPUT) disco del sistema.
systems analyst n analista m/f de sistemas.

T t

T, t [tiː] n (letter) T, t f; **T for Tommy** T de Tarragona.
TA n abbr (BRIT) = Territorial Army.
ta [tɑː] excl (BRIT col) ¡gracias!
tab [tæb] n abbr = **tabulator** ♦ n lengüeta; (label) etiqueta; **to keep ~s on** (fig) vigilar.
tabby ['tæbɪ] n (also: ~ **cat**) gato atigrado.
tabernacle ['tæbənækl] n tabernáculo.
table ['teɪbl] n mesa; (chart: of statistics etc) cuadro, tabla ♦ vt (BRIT: motion etc) presentar; **to lay** or **set the ~** poner la mesa; **to clear the ~** quitar or levantar la mesa; **league ~** (FOOTBALL, RUGBY) clasificación f del campeonato; **~ of contents** índice m de materias.
tablecloth ['teɪblklɔθ] n mantel m.
table d'hôte [tɑːbl'dəut] n menú m.
table lamp n lámpara de mesa.
tablemat ['teɪblmæt] n salvamanteles m inv, posaplatos m inv.
tablespoon ['teɪblspuːn] n cuchara grande; (also: ~**ful**: as measurement) cucharada.
tablet ['tæblɪt] n (MED) pastilla, comprimido; (for writing) bloc m; (of stone) lápida; **~ of soap** pastilla de jabón.
table talk n conversación f de sobremesa.
table tennis n ping-pong m, tenis m de mesa.

table wine n vino de mesa.
tabloid ['tæblɔɪd] n (newspaper) periódico popular sensacionalista.
tabloid press n ver recuadro.

TABLOID PRESS

El término genérico **tabloid press** o "tabloids" se usa para referirse a los periódicos populares británicos, por su tamaño reducido. A diferencia de la llamada "quality press", estos periódicos se caracterizan por su lenguaje sencillo, presentación llamativa y contenido a menudo sensacionalista, con gran énfasis en noticias sobre escándalos financieros y sexuales de los famosos, por lo que también reciben el nombre peyorativo de "gutter press".

---

taboo [tə'buː] adj, n tabú m.
tabulate ['tæbjuleɪt] vt disponer en tablas.
tabulator ['tæbjuleɪtə*] n tabulador m.
tachograph ['tækəɡrɑːf] n tacógrafo.
tacit ['tæsɪt] adj tácito.
tacitly ['tæsɪtlɪ] adv tácitamente.
taciturn ['tæsɪtəːn] adj taciturno.
tack [tæk] n (nail) tachuela; (stitch) hilván m; (NAUT) bordada ♦ vt (nail) clavar con tachuelas; (stitch) hilvanar ♦ vi virar; **to ~ sth on to (the end of) sth** (of letter, book) añadir algo a(l final de) algo.
tackle ['tækl] n (gear) equipo; (fishing ~, for lifting) aparejo; (FOOTBALL) entrada, tackle m; (RUGBY) placaje m ♦ vt (difficulty) enfrentarse a; (grapple with) agarrar; (FOOTBALL) entrar a; (RUGBY) placar.
tacky ['tækɪ] adj pegajoso; (fam) hortera inv.
tact [tækt] n tacto, discreción f.
tactful ['tæktful] adj discreto, diplomático; **to be ~** tener tacto.
tactfully ['tæktfulɪ] adv diplomáticamente, con tacto.
tactical ['tæktɪkl] adj táctico.
tactical voting n voto útil.
tactician [tæk'tɪʃən] n táctico/a.
tactics ['tæktɪks] n, npl táctica sg.
tactless ['tæktlɪs] adj indiscreto.
tactlessly ['tæktlɪslɪ] adv indiscretamente, sin tacto.
tadpole ['tædpəul] n renacuajo.
taffy ['tæfɪ] n (US) melcocha.
tag [tæɡ] n (label) etiqueta; **price/name ~** etiqueta del precio/con el nombre.
▶**tag along** vi: **to ~ along with sb** engancharse a algn.
Tahiti [tɑː'hiːtɪ] n Tahití m.
tail [teɪl] n cola; (ZOOL) rabo; (of shirt, coat)

faldón m ♦ vt (*follow*) vigilar a; **heads or ~s** cara o cruz; **to turn ~** volver la espalda.

▶**tail away, tail off** vi (*in size, quality etc*) ir disminuyendo.

tailback ['teɪlbæk] n (*BRIT AUT*) cola.

tail coat n frac m.

tail end n cola, parte f final.

tailgate ['teɪlgeɪt] n (*AUT*) puerta trasera.

tail light n (*AUT*) luz f trasera.

tailor ['teɪlə*] n sastre m ♦ vt: **to ~ sth (to)** confeccionar algo a medida (para); **~'s (shop)** sastrería.

tailoring ['teɪlərɪŋ] n (*cut*) corte m; (*craft*) sastrería.

tailor-made ['teɪlə'meɪd] adj (*also fig*) hecho a (la) medida.

tailwind ['teɪlwɪnd] n viento de cola.

taint [teɪnt] vt (*meat, food*) contaminar; (*fig: reputation*) manchar, tachar (*LAM*).

tainted ['teɪntɪd] adj (*water, air*) contaminado; (*fig*) manchado.

Taiwan [taɪ'wɑːn] n Taiwán m.

Tajikistan [tɑːdʒɪkɪ'stɑːn] n Tayikistán m.

take [teɪk] vb (*pt* **took**, *pp* **taken** [tuk, 'teɪkn]) vt tomar; (*grab*) coger (*SP*), agarrar (*LAM*); (*gain: prize*) ganar; (*require: effort, courage*) exigir; (*support weight of*) aguantar; (*hold: passengers etc*) tener cabida para; (*accompany, bring, carry*) llevar; (*exam*) presentarse a; (*conduct: meeting*) presidir ♦ vi (*fire*) prender; (*dye*) coger (*SP*), agarrar, tomar ♦ n (*CINE*) toma; **to ~ sth from** (*drawer etc*) sacar algo de; (*person*) coger (*SP*) algo a; **to ~ sb's hand** tomar de la mano a algn; **to ~ notes** tomar apuntes; **to be ~n ill** ponerse enfermo; **~ the first on the left** toma la primera a la izquierda; **I only took Russian for one year** sólo estudié ruso un año; **I took him for a doctor** le tenía por médico; **it won't ~ long** durará poco; **it will ~ at least 5 litres** tiene cabida por lo menos para 5 litros; **to be ~n with sb/sth** (*attracted*) tomarle cariño a algn/tomarle gusto a algo; **I ~ it that** ... supongo que ....

▶**take after** vt fus parecerse a.

▶**take apart** vt desmontar.

▶**take away** vt (*remove*) quitar; (*carry off*) llevar ♦ vi: **to ~ away from** quitar mérito a.

▶**take back** vt (*return*) devolver; (*one's words*) retractar.

▶**take down** vt (*building*) derribar; (*dismantle: scaffolding*) desmantelar; (*message etc*) apuntar, tomar nota de.

▶**take in** vt (*BRIT: deceive*) engañar; (*understand*) entender; (*include*) abarcar;

(*lodger*) acoger, recibir; (*orphan, stray dog*) recoger; (*SEWING*) achicar.

▶**take off** vi (*AVIAT*) despegar, decolar (*LAM*) ♦ vt (*remove*) quitar; (*imitate*) imitar, remedar.

▶**take on** vt (*work*) emprender; (*employee*) contratar; (*opponent*) desafiar.

▶**take out** vt sacar; (*remove*) quitar; **don't ~ it out on me!** ¡no te desquites conmigo!

▶**take over** vt (*business*) tomar posesión de ♦ vi: **to ~ over from sb** reemplazar a algn.

▶**take to** vt fus (*person*) coger cariño a (*SP*), encariñarse con (*LAM*); (*activity*) aficionarse a; **to ~ to doing sth** aficionarse a (hacer) algo.

▶**take up** vt (*a dress*) acortar; (*occupy: time, space*) ocupar; (*engage in: hobby etc*) dedicarse a; (*absorb: liquids*) absorber; (*accept: offer, challenge*) aceptar ♦ vi: **to ~ up with sb** hacerse amigo de algn.

▶**take upon** vt: **to ~ it upon o.s. to do sth** encargarse de hacer algo.

takeaway ['teɪkəweɪ] adj (*BRIT: food*) para llevar.

take-home pay ['teɪkhəʊm-] n salario neto.

taken ['teɪkən] pp of **take**.

takeoff ['teɪkɔf] n (*AVIAT*) despegue m, decolaje m (*LAM*).

takeover ['teɪkəʊvə*] n (*COMM*) absorción f.

takeover bid n oferta pública de adquisición.

takings ['teɪkɪŋz] npl (*COMM*) ingresos mpl.

talc [tælk] n (*also:* **~um powder**) talco.

tale [teɪl] n (*story*) cuento; (*account*) relación f; **to tell ~s** (*fig*) contar chismes.

talent ['tælnt] n talento.

talented ['tæləntɪd] adj talentoso, de talento.

talisman ['tælɪzmən] n talismán m.

talk [tɔːk] n charla; (*gossip*) habladurías fpl, chismes mpl; (*conversation*) conversación f ♦ vi (*speak*) hablar; (*chatter*) charlar; **~s** npl (*POL etc*) conversaciones fpl; **to give a ~** dar una charla or conferencia; **to ~ about** hablar de; **to ~ sb into doing sth** convencer a algn para que haga algo; **to ~ sb out of doing sth** disuadir a algn de que haga algo; **to ~ shop** hablar del trabajo; **~ing of films, have you seen ...?** hablando de películas, ¿has visto ...?

▶**talk over** vt discutir.

talkative ['tɔːkətɪv] adj hablador(a).

talker ['tɔːkə*] n hablador(a) m/f.

talking point ['tɔːkɪŋ-] n tema m de conversación.

talking-to ['tɔːkɪŋtuː] n: **to give sb a good ~** echar una buena bronca a algn.

talk show n programa m magazine.
tall [tɔːl] adj alto; (tree) grande; **to be 6 feet ~** ≈ medir 1 metro 80, tener 1 metro 80 de alto; **how ~ are you?** ¿cuánto mides?
tallboy ['tɔːlbɔɪ] n (BRIT) cómoda alta.
tallness ['tɔːlnɪs] n altura.
tall story n cuento chino.
tally ['tælɪ] n cuenta ♦ vi: **to ~ (with)** concordar (con), cuadrar (con); **to keep a ~ of sth** llevar la cuenta de algo.
talon ['tælən] n garra.
tambourine [tæmbə'riːn] n pandereta.
tame [teɪm] adj (mild) manso; (tamed) domesticado; (fig: story, style, person) soso, anodino.
tameness ['teɪmnɪs] n mansedumbre f.
Tamil ['tæmɪl] adj tamil ♦ n tamil m/f; (LING) tamil m.
tamper ['tæmpə*] vi: **to ~ with** (lock etc) intentar forzar; (papers) falsificar.
tampon ['tæmpən] n tampón m.
tan [tæn] n (also: **sun~**) bronceado ♦ vt broncear ♦ vi ponerse moreno ♦ adj (colour) marrón; **to get a ~** broncearse, ponerse moreno.
tandem ['tændəm] n tándem m.
tandoori [tæn'duərɪ] adj, n tandoori m (asado a la manera hindú, en horno de barro).
tang [tæŋ] n sabor m fuerte.
tangent ['tændʒənt] n (MATH) tangente f; **to go off at a ~** (fig) salirse por la tangente.
tangerine [tændʒə'riːn] n mandarina.
tangible ['tændʒəbl] adj tangible; **~ assets** bienes mpl tangibles.
Tangier [tæn'dʒɪə*] n Tánger m.
tangle ['tæŋgl] n enredo; **to get in(to) a ~** enredarse.
tango ['tæŋgəu] n tango.
tank [tæŋk] n (water ~) depósito, tanque m; (for fish) acuario; (MIL) tanque m.
tankard ['tæŋkəd] n bock m.
tanker ['tæŋkə*] n (ship) petrolero; (truck) camión m cisterna.
tankful ['tæŋkful] n: **to get a ~ of petrol** llenar el depósito de gasolina.
tanned [tænd] adj (skin) moreno, bronceado.
tannin ['tænɪn] n tanino.
tanning ['tænɪŋ] n (of leather) curtido.
tannoy ® ['tænɔɪ] n: **over the ~** por el altavoz.
tantalizing ['tæntəlaɪzɪŋ] adj tentador(a).
tantamount ['tæntəmaunt] adj: **~ to** equivalente a.
tantrum ['tæntrəm] n rabieta; **to throw a ~** coger una rabieta.
Tanzania [tænzə'nɪə] n Tanzania.
Tanzanian [tænzə'nɪən] adj, n tanzano/a m/f.

tap [tæp] n (BRIT: on sink etc) grifo, canilla (LAM); (gentle blow) golpecito; (gas ~) llave f ♦ vt (table etc) tamborilear; (shoulder etc) dar palmaditas en; (resources) utilizar, explotar; (telephone conversation) intervenir, pinchar; **on ~** (fig: resources) a mano; **beer on ~** cerveza de barril.
tap-dancing ['tæpdɑːnsɪŋ] n claqué m.
tape [teɪp] n cinta; (also: **magnetic ~**) cinta magnética; (sticky ~) cinta adhesiva ♦ vt (record) grabar (en cinta); **on ~** (song etc) grabado (en cinta).
tape deck n pletina.
tape measure n cinta métrica, metro.
taper ['teɪpə*] n cirio ♦ vi afilarse.
tape-record ['teɪprɪkɔːd] vt grabar (en cinta).
tape recorder n grabadora.
tape recording n grabación f.
tapered ['teɪpəd], **tapering** ['teɪpərɪŋ] adj terminado en punta.
tapestry ['tæpɪstrɪ] n (object) tapiz m; (art) tapicería.
tape-worm ['teɪpwəːm] n solitaria, tenia.
tapioca [tæpɪ'əukə] n tapioca.
tappet ['tæpɪt] n excéntrica.
tar [tɑː*] n alquitrán m, brea; **low/middle ~ cigarettes** cigarrillos con contenido bajo/medio de alquitrán.
tarantula [tə'ræntjulə] n tarántula.
tardy ['tɑːdɪ] adj (late) tardío; (slow) lento.
tare [tɛə*] n (COMM) tara.
target ['tɑːgɪt] n (gen) blanco; **to be on ~** (project) seguir el curso previsto.
target audience n público al que va destinado un programa etc.
target market n (COMM) mercado al que va destinado un producto etc.
target practice n tiro al blanco.
tariff ['tærɪf] n tarifa.
tariff barrier n (COMM) barrera arancelaria.
tarmac ['tɑːmæk] n (BRIT: on road) alquitranado; (AVIAT) pista (de aterrizaje).
tarn [tɑːn] n lago pequeño de montaña.
tarnish ['tɑːnɪʃ] vt deslustrar.
tarot ['tærəu] n tarot m.
tarpaulin [tɑː'pɔːlɪn] n alquitranado.
tarragon ['tærəgən] n estragón m.
tarry ['tærɪ] vi entretenerse, quedarse atrás.
tart [tɑːt] n (CULIN) tarta; (BRIT col: pej: woman) fulana ♦ adj (flavour) agrio, ácido.
▶**tart up** vt (room, building) dar tono a.
tartan ['tɑːtn] n tartán m ♦ adj de tartán.
tartar ['tɑːtə*] n (on teeth) sarro.

tartar sauce *n* salsa tártara.
tartly ['tɑːtlɪ] *adv* (*answer*) ásperamente.
task [tɑːsk] *n* tarea; **to take to** ~ reprender.
task force *n* (*MIL, POLICE*) grupo de operaciones.
taskmaster ['tɑːskmɑːstə*] *n*: **he's a hard** ~ es muy exigente.
tassel ['tæsl] *n* borla.
taste [teɪst] *n* sabor *m*, gusto; (*also: after*~) dejo; (*sip*) sorbo; (*fig: glimpse, idea*) muestra, idea ♦ *vt* probar ♦ *vi*: **to** ~ **of** *or* **like** (*fish etc*) saber a; **you can** ~ **the garlic (in it)** se nota el sabor a ajo; **can I have a** ~ **of this wine?** ¿puedo probar este vino?; **to have a** ~ **for sth** ser aficionado a algo; **in good/bad** ~ de buen/mal gusto; **to be in bad** *or* **poor** ~ ser de mal gusto.
taste bud *n* papila gustativa *or* del gusto.
tasteful ['teɪstful] *adj* de buen gusto.
tastefully ['teɪstfulɪ] *adv* elegantemente, con buen gusto.
tasteless ['teɪstlɪs] *adj* (*food*) soso; (*remark*) de mal gusto.
tastelessly ['teɪstlɪslɪ] *adv* con mal gusto.
tastily ['teɪstɪlɪ] *adv* sabrosamente.
tastiness ['teɪstɪnɪs] *n* (buen) sabor *m*, lo sabroso.
tasty ['teɪstɪ] *adj* sabroso, rico.
ta-ta ['tæ'tɑː] *interj* (*BRIT col*) hasta luego, adiós.
tatters ['tætəz] *npl*: **in** ~ (*also:* **tattered**) hecho jirones.
tattoo [tə'tuː] *n* tatuaje *m*; (*spectacle*) espectáculo militar ♦ *vt* tatuar.
tatty ['tætɪ] *adj* (*BRIT col*) cochambroso.
taught [tɔːt] *pt, pp of* **teach**.
taunt [tɔːnt] *n* pulla ♦ *vt* lanzar pullas a.
Taurus ['tɔːrəs] *n* Tauro.
taut [tɔːt] *adj* tirante, tenso.
tavern ['tævən] *n* (*old*) posada, fonda.
tawdry ['tɔːdrɪ] *adj* de mal gusto.
tawny ['tɔːnɪ] *adj* leonado.
tax [tæks] *n* impuesto ♦ *vt* gravar (con un impuesto); (*fig: test*) poner a prueba; (: *patience*) agotar; **before/after** ~ impuestos excluidos/incluidos; **free of** ~ libre de impuestos.
taxable ['tæksəbl] *adj* (*income*) imponible, sujeto a impuestos.
tax allowance *n* desgravación *f* fiscal.
taxation [tæk'seɪʃən] *n* impuestos *mpl*; **system of** ~ sistema *m* tributario.
tax avoidance *n* evasión *f* de impuestos.
tax collector *n* recaudador(a) *m/f*.
tax disc *n* (*BRIT AUT*) pegatina del impuesto de circulación.
tax evasion *n* evasión *f* fiscal.
tax exemption *n* exención *f* de impuestos.

tax-free ['tæksfriː] *adj* libre de impuestos.
tax haven *n* paraíso fiscal.
taxi ['tæksɪ] *n* taxi *m* ♦ *vi* (*AVIAT*) rodar por la pista.
taxidermist ['tæksɪdəːmɪst] *n* taxidermista *m/f*.
taxi driver *n* taxista *m/f*.
tax inspector *n* inspector(a) *m/f* de Hacienda.
taxi rank (*BRIT*), **taxi stand** *n* parada de taxis.
tax payer *n* contribuyente *m/f*.
tax rebate *n* devolución *f* de impuestos, reembolso fiscal.
tax relief *n* desgravación *f* fiscal.
tax return *n* declaración *f* de la renta.
tax shelter *n* protección *f* fiscal.
tax year *n* año fiscal.
TB *n abbr* = **tuberculosis**.
tbc *abbr* (= *to be confirmed*) por confirmar.
TD *n abbr* (*US*) = **Treasury Department**; (: *FOOTBALL*) = **touchdown**.
tea [tiː] *n* té *m*; (*BRIT: snack*) ≈ merienda; **high** ~ (*BRIT*) ≈ merienda-cena.
tea bag *n* bolsita de té.
tea break *n* (*BRIT*) descanso para el té.
teacake ['tiːkeɪk] *n* bollito, queque *m* (*LAM*).
teach, *pt, pp* **taught** [tiːtʃ, tɔːt] *vt*: **to** ~ **sb sth,** ~ **sth to sb** enseñar algo a algn ♦ *vi* enseñar; (*be a teacher*) ser profesor(a); **it taught him a lesson** (eso) le sirvió de escarmiento.
teacher ['tiːtʃə*] *n* (*in secondary school*) profesor(a) *m/f*; (*in primary school*) maestro/a; **Spanish** ~ profesor(a) *m/f* de español.
teacher training college *n* (*for primary schools*) escuela normal; (*for secondary schools*) centro de formación del profesorado.
teach-in ['tiːtʃɪn] *n* seminario.
teaching ['tiːtʃɪŋ] *n* enseñanza.
teaching aids *npl* materiales *mpl* pedagógicos.
teaching hospital *n* hospital universitario.
tea cosy *n* cubretetera *m*.
teacup ['tiːkʌp] *n* taza de té.
teak [tiːk] *n* (madera de) teca.
tea leaves *npl* hojas *fpl* de té.
team [tiːm] *n* equipo; (*of animals*) pareja.
▶**team up** *vi* asociarse.
team spirit *n* espíritu *m* de equipo.
teamwork ['tiːmwəːk] *n* trabajo en equipo.
tea party *n* té *m*.
teapot ['tiːpɔt] *n* tetera.
tear [tɛə*] *n* rasgón *m*, desgarrón *m*; [tɪə*] lágrima ♦ *vb* [tɛə*] (*pt* **tore**, *pp* **torn** [tɔː*,

tɔ:n]) *vt* romper, rasgar ♦ *vi* rasgarse; **in ~s** llorando; **to burst into ~s** deshacerse en lágrimas; **to ~ to pieces** *or* **to bits** *or* **to shreds** (*also fig*) hacer pedazos, destrozar.

▶**tear along** *vi* (*rush*) precipitarse.

▶**tear apart** *vt* (*also fig*) hacer pedazos.

▶**tear away** *vt*: **to ~ o.s. away (from sth)** alejarse (de algo).

▶**tear out** *vt* (*sheet, cheque*) arrancar.

▶**tear up** *vt* (*sheet of paper etc*) romper.

tearaway ['tɛərəweɪ] *n* (*col*) gamberro/a.

teardrop ['tɪədrɔp] *n* lágrima.

tearful ['tɪəful] *adj* lloroso.

tear gas *n* gas *m* lacrimógeno.

tearing ['tɛərɪŋ] *adj*: **to be in a ~ hurry** tener muchísima prisa.

tearoom ['ti:ru:m] *n* salón *m* de té.

tease [ti:z] *n* bromista *m/f* ♦ *vt* tomar el pelo a.

tea set *n* servicio de té.

teashop ['ti:ʃɔp] *n* café *m*, cafetería.

Teasmaid ® ['ti:zmeɪd] *n* tetera automática.

teaspoon ['ti:spu:n] *n* cucharita; (*also*: **~ful**: *as measurement*) cucharadita.

tea strainer *n* colador *m* de té.

teat [ti:t] *n* (*of bottle*) boquilla, tetilla.

teatime ['ti:taɪm] *n* hora del té.

tea towel *n* (*BRIT*) paño de cocina.

tea urn *n* tetera grande.

tech [tɛk] *n abbr* (*col*) = **technology; technical college**.

technical ['tɛknɪkl] *adj* técnico.

technical college *n* centro de formación profesional.

technicality [tɛknɪ'kælɪtɪ] *n* detalle *m* técnico; **on a legal ~** por una cuestión formal.

technically ['tɛknɪklɪ] *adv* técnicamente.

technician [tɛk'nɪʃn] *n* técnico/a.

technique [tɛk'ni:k] *n* técnica.

techno ['tɛknəu] *n* (*MUS*) (música) tecno.

technocrat ['tɛknəkræt] *n* tecnócrata *m/f*.

technological [tɛknə'lɔdʒɪkl] *adj* tecnológico.

technologist [tɛk'nɔlədʒɪst] *n* tecnólogo/a.

technology [tɛk'nɔlədʒɪ] *n* tecnología.

teddy (bear) ['tɛdɪ-] *n* osito de peluche.

tedious ['ti:dɪəs] *adj* pesado, aburrido.

tedium ['ti:dɪəm] *n* tedio.

tee [ti:] *n* (*GOLF*) tee *m*.

teem [ti:m] *vi*: **to ~ with** rebosar de; **it is ~ing (with rain)** llueve a mares.

teenage ['ti:neɪdʒ] *adj* (*fashions etc*) juvenil.

teenager ['ti:neɪdʒə*] *n* adolescente *m/f*.

teens [ti:nz] *npl*: **to be in one's ~** ser adolescente.

tee-shirt ['ti:ʃə:t] *n* = **T-shirt**.

teeter ['ti:tə*] *vi* balancearse.

teeth [ti:θ] *npl of* **tooth**.

teethe [ti:ð] *vi* echar los dientes.

teething ring ['ti:ðɪŋ-] *n* mordedor *m*.

teething troubles ['ti:ðɪŋ-] *npl* (*fig*) dificultades *fpl* iniciales.

teetotal ['ti:'təutl] *adj* (*person*) abstemio.

teetotaller, (*US*) **teetotaler** ['ti:'təutlə*] *n* (*person*) abstemio/a.

TEFL ['tɛfl] *n abbr* = **Teaching of English as a Foreign Language**; **~ qualification** título para la enseñanza del inglés como lengua extranjera.

Teflon ® ['tɛflɔn] *n* teflón *m* ®.

Teheran [tɛə'rɑ:n] *n* Teherán *m*.

tel. *abbr* (= *telephone*) tel.

Tel Aviv ['tɛlə'vi:v] *n* Tel Aviv *m*.

telecast ['tɛlɪkɑ:st] *vt, vi* transmitir por televisión.

telecommunications ['tɛlɪkəmju:nɪ'keɪʃənz] *n* telecomunicaciones *fpl*.

teleconferencing [tɛlɪ'kɔnfərənsɪŋ] *n* teleconferencias *fpl*.

telefax ['tɛlɪfæks] *n* telefax *m*.

telegram ['tɛlɪgræm] *n* telegrama *m*.

telegraph ['tɛlɪgrɑ:f] *n* telégrafo.

telegraphic [tɛlɪ'græfɪk] *adj* telegráfico.

telegraph pole *n* poste *m* telegráfico.

telegraph wire *n* hilo telegráfico.

telepathic [tɛlɪ'pæθɪk] *adj* telepático.

telepathy [tə'lɛpəθɪ] *n* telepatía.

telephone ['tɛlɪfəun] *n* teléfono ♦ *vt* llamar por teléfono, telefonear; **to be on the ~** (*subscriber*) tener teléfono; (*be speaking*) estar hablando por teléfono.

telephone booth, (*BRIT*) **telephone box** *n* cabina telefónica.

telephone call *n* llamada telefónica.

telephone directory *n* guía telefónica.

telephone exchange *n* central *f* telefónica.

telephone number *n* número de teléfono.

telephonist [tə'lɛfənɪst] *n* (*BRIT*) telefonista *m/f*.

telephoto [tɛlɪ'fəutəu] *adj*: **~ lens** teleobjetivo.

teleprinter ['tɛlɪprɪntə*] *n* teletipo, teleimpresora.

teleprompter ® ['tɛlɪprɔmptə*] *n* teleapuntador *m*.

telesales ['tɛlɪseɪlz] *npl* televentas *fpl*.

telescope ['tɛlɪskəup] *n* telescopio.

telescopic [tɛlɪ'skɔpɪk] *adj* telescópico; (*umbrella*) plegable.

Teletext ® ['tɛlɪtɛkst] *n* teletexto *m*.

telethon ['tɛlɪθɔn] *n* telemaratón *m*,

maratón *m* televisivo (*con fines benéficos*).
televise ['tɛlɪvaɪz] *vt* televisar.
television ['tɛlɪvɪʒən] *n* televisión *f*; **to watch** ~ mirar *or* ver la televisión.
television licence *n* impuesto por uso de televisor.
television set *n* televisor *m*.
teleworking ['tɛlɪ,wɜːkɪŋ] *n* teletrabajo.
telex ['tɛlɛks] *n* télex *m* ♦ *vt* (*message*) enviar por télex; (*person*) enviar un télex a ♦ *vi* enviar un télex.
tell *pt, pp* **told** [tɛl, təuld] *vt* decir; (*relate*: *story*) contar; (*distinguish*): **to** ~ **sth from** distinguir algo de ♦ *vi* (*talk*): **to** ~ (**of**) contar; (*have effect*) tener efecto; **to** ~ **sb to do sth** decir a algn que haga algo; **to** ~ **sb about sth** contar algo a algn; **to** ~ **the time** dar *or* decir la hora; **can you** ~ **me the time?** ¿me puedes decir la hora?; **(I)** ~ **you what** ... fíjate ...; **I couldn't** ~ **them apart** no podía distinguirlos.
▶**tell off** *vt*: **to** ~ **sb off** regañar a algn.
▶**tell on** *vt fus*: **to** ~ **on sb** chivarse de algn.
teller ['tɛlə*] *n* (*in bank*) cajero/a.
telling ['tɛlɪŋ] *adj* (*remark, detail*) revelador(a).
telltale ['tɛlteɪl] *adj* (*sign*) indicador(a).
telly ['tɛlɪ] *n* (*BRIT col*) tele *f*.
temerity [tə'mɛrɪtɪ] *n* temeridad *f*.
temp [tɛmp] *n abbr* (*BRIT*: = *temporary office worker*) empleado/a eventual ♦ *vi* trabajar como empleado/a eventual.
temper ['tɛmpə*] *n* (*mood*) humor *m*; (*bad* ~) (mal) genio; (*fit of anger*) ira; (*of child*) rabieta ♦ *vt* (*moderate*) moderar; **to be in a** ~ estar furioso; **to lose one's** ~ enfadarse, enojarse (*LAM*); **to keep one's** ~ contenerse, no alterarse.
temperament ['tɛmprəmənt] *n* (*nature*) temperamento.
temperamental [tɛmprə'mɛntl] *adj* temperamental.
temperance ['tɛmpərns] *n* moderación *f*; (*in drinking*) sobriedad *f*.
temperate ['tɛmprət] *adj* moderado; (*climate*) templado.
temperature ['tɛmprətʃə*] *n* temperatura; **to have** *or* **run a** ~ tener fiebre.
tempered ['tɛmpəd] *adj* (*steel*) templado.
tempest ['tɛmpɪst] *n* tempestad *f*.
tempestuous [tɛm'pɛstjuəs] *adj* (*relationship, meeting*) tempestuoso.
tempi ['tɛmpiː] *npl of* **tempo**.
template ['tɛmplɪt] *n* plantilla.
temple ['tɛmpl] *n* (*REL*) templo; (*ANAT*) sien *f*.
templet ['tɛmplɪt] *n* = **template**.
tempo, *pl* ~**s** *or* **tempi** ['tɛmpəu, 'tɛmpiː] *n* tempo; (*fig: of life etc*) ritmo.

temporal ['tɛmpərl] *adj* temporal.
temporarily ['tɛmpərərɪlɪ] *adv* temporalmente.
temporary ['tɛmpərərɪ] *adj* provisional, temporal; (*passing*) transitorio; (*worker*) eventual; ~ **teacher** maestro/a interino/a.
tempt [tɛmpt] *vt* tentar; **to** ~ **sb into doing sth** tentar *or* inducir a algn a hacer algo; **to be** ~**ed to do sth** (*person*) sentirse tentado de hacer algo.
temptation [tɛmp'teɪʃən] *n* tentación *f*.
tempting ['tɛmptɪŋ] *adj* tentador(a).
ten [tɛn] *num* diez; ~**s of thousands** decenas *fpl* de miles.
tenable ['tɛnəbl] *adj* sostenible.
tenacious [tə'neɪʃəs] *adj* tenaz.
tenaciously [tə'neɪʃəslɪ] *adv* tenazmente.
tenacity [tə'næsɪtɪ] *n* tenacidad *f*.
tenancy ['tɛnənsɪ] *n* alquiler *m*.
tenant ['tɛnənt] *n* (*rent-payer*) inquilino/a; (*occupant*) habitante *m/f*.
tend [tɛnd] *vt* (*sick etc*) cuidar, atender; (*cattle, machine*) vigilar, cuidar ♦ *vi*: **to** ~ **to do sth** tener tendencia a hacer algo.
tendency ['tɛndənsɪ] *n* tendencia.
tender ['tɛndə*] *adj* tierno, blando; (*delicate*) delicado; (*sore*) sensible; (*affectionate*) tierno, cariñoso ♦ *n* (*COMM*: *offer*) oferta; (*money*): **legal** ~ moneda de curso legal ♦ *vt* ofrecer; **to put in a** ~ (**for**) hacer una oferta (para); **to put work out to** ~ ofrecer un trabajo a contrata; **to** ~ **one's resignation** presentar la dimisión.
tenderize ['tɛndəraɪz] *vt* (*CULIN*) ablandar.
tenderly ['tɛndəlɪ] *adv* tiernamente.
tenderness ['tɛndənɪs] *n* ternura; (*of meat*) blandura.
tendon ['tɛndən] *n* tendón *m*.
tendril ['tɛndrɪl] *n* zarcillo.
tenement ['tɛnəmənt] *n* casa *or* bloque *m* de pisos *or* vecinos (*LAM*).
Tenerife [tɛnə'riːf] *n* Tenerife *m*.
tenet ['tɛnət] *n* principio.
Tenn. *abbr* (*US*) = *Tennessee*.
tenner ['tɛnə*] *n* (billete *m* de) diez libras *fpl*.
tennis ['tɛnɪs] *n* tenis *m*.
tennis ball *n* pelota de tenis.
tennis club *n* club *m* de tenis.
tennis court *n* cancha de tenis.
tennis elbow *n* (*MED*) sinovitis *f* del codo.
tennis match *n* partido de tenis.
tennis player *n* tenista *m/f*.
tennis racket *n* raqueta de tenis.
tennis shoes *npl* zapatillas *fpl* de tenis.
tenor ['tɛnə*] *n* (*MUS*) tenor *m*.
tenpin bowling ['tɛnpɪn-] *n* bolos *mpl*.
tense [tɛns] *adj* tenso; (*stretched*) tirante;

(*stiff*) rígido, tieso; (*person*) nervioso ♦ *n* (*LING*) tiempo ♦ *vt* (*tighten: muscles*) tensar.

tensely ['tɛnslɪ] *adv*: **they waited ~** esperaban tensos.

tenseness ['tɛnsnɪs] *n* tirantez *f*, tensión *f*.

tension ['tɛnʃən] *n* tensión *f*.

tent [tɛnt] *n* tienda (de campaña), carpa (*LAM*).

tentacle ['tɛntəkl] *n* tentáculo.

tentative ['tɛntətɪv] *adj* (*person*) indeciso; (*provisional*) provisional.

tentatively ['tɛntətɪvlɪ] *adv* con indecisión; (*provisionally*) provisionalmente.

tenterhooks ['tɛntəhuks] *npl*: **on ~** sobre ascuas.

tenth [tɛnθ] *adj* décimo.

tent peg *n* clavija, estaca.

tent pole *n* mástil *m*.

tenuous ['tɛnjuəs] *adj* tenue.

tenure ['tɛnjuə*] *n* posesión *f*, tenencia; **to have ~** tener posesión *or* título de propiedad.

tepid ['tɛpɪd] *adj* tibio.

term [tɜːm] *n* (*limit*) límite *m*; (*COMM*) plazo; (*word*) término; (*period*) período; (*SCOL*) trimestre *m* ♦ *vt* llamar, calificar de; **~s** *npl* (*conditions*) condiciones *fpl*; (*COMM*) precio, tarifa; **in the short/long ~** a corto/largo plazo; **during his ~ of office** bajo su mandato; **to be on good ~s with sb** llevarse bien con algn; **to come to ~s with** (*problem*) aceptar; **in ~s of ...** en cuanto a ..., en términos de ....

terminal ['tɜːmɪnl] *adj* terminal ♦ *n* (*ELEC*) borne *m*; (*COMPUT*) terminal *m*; (*also*: **air ~**) terminal *f*; (*BRIT*: *also*: **coach ~**) (estación *f*) terminal *f*.

terminate ['tɜːmɪneɪt] *vt* poner término a; (*pregnancy*) interrumpir ♦ *vi*: **to ~ in** acabar en.

termination [tɜːmɪ'neɪʃən] *n* fin *m*; (*of contract*) terminación *f*; **~ of pregnancy** interrupción *f* del embarazo.

termini ['tɜːmɪnaɪ] *npl of* **terminus**.

terminology [tɜːmɪ'nɔlədʒɪ] *n* terminología.

terminus, *pl* **termini** ['tɜːmɪnəs, 'tɜːmɪnaɪ] *n* término, (estación *f*) terminal *f*.

termite ['tɜːmaɪt] *n* termita, comején *m*.

term paper *n* (*US UNIV*) trabajo escrito trimestral *or* semestral.

Ter(r). *abbr* = **terrace**.

terrace ['tɛrəs] *n* terraza; (*BRIT*: *row of houses*) hilera de casas adosadas; **the ~s** (*BRIT SPORT*) las gradas *fpl*.

terraced ['tɛrəst] *adj* (*garden*) escalonado; (*house*) adosado.

terracotta ['tɛrə'kɔtə] *n* terracota.

terrain [tɛ'reɪn] *n* terreno.

terrible ['tɛrɪbl] *adj* terrible, horrible; (*fam*) malísimo.

terribly ['tɛrɪblɪ] *adv* terriblemente; (*very badly*) malísimamente.

terrier ['tɛrɪə*] *n* terrier *m*.

terrific [tə'rɪfɪk] *adj* fantástico, fenomenal, macanudo (*LAM*); (*wonderful*) maravilloso.

terrify ['tɛrɪfaɪ] *vt* aterrorizar; **to be terrified** estar aterrado *or* aterrorizado.

terrifying ['tɛrɪfaɪɪŋ] *adj* aterrador(a).

territorial [tɛrɪ'tɔːrɪəl] *adj* territorial.

territorial waters *npl* aguas *fpl* jurisdiccionales.

territory ['tɛrɪtərɪ] *n* territorio.

terror ['tɛrə*] *n* terror *m*.

terror attack *n* atentado (terrorista).

terrorism ['tɛrərɪzəm] *n* terrorismo.

terrorist ['tɛrərɪst] *n* terrorista *m/f*.

terrorize ['tɛrəraɪz] *vt* aterrorizar.

terse [tɜːs] *adj* (*style*) conciso; (*reply*) brusco.

tertiary ['tɜːʃərɪ] *adj* terciario; **~ education** enseñanza superior.

Terylene ® ['tɛrɪliːn] *n* (*BRIT*) terylene *m* ®.

TESL [tɛsl] *n abbr* = *Teaching of English as a Second Language*.

TESSA ['tɛsə] *n abbr* (*BRIT*: = *Tax Exempt Special Savings Account*) *plan de ahorro por el que se invierte a largo plazo a cambio de intereses libres de impuestos.*

test [tɛst] *n* (*trial, check*) prueba, ensayo; (: *of goods in factory*) control *m*; (*of courage etc, CHEM, MED*) prueba; (*of blood, urine*) análisis *m inv*; (*exam*) examen *m*, test *m*; (*also*: **driving ~**) examen *m* de conducir ♦ *vt* probar, poner a prueba; (*MED*) examinar; (: *blood*) analizar; **to put sth to the ~** someter algo a prueba; **to ~ sth for sth** analizar algo en busca de algo.

testament ['tɛstəmənt] *n* testamento; **the Old/New T~** el Antiguo/Nuevo Testamento.

test ban *n* (*also*: **nuclear ~**) suspensión *f* de pruebas nucleares.

test card *n* (*TV*) carta de ajuste.

test case *n* juicio que sienta precedente.

testes ['tɛstiːz] *npl* testes *mpl*.

test flight *n* vuelo de ensayo.

testicle ['tɛstɪkl] *n* testículo.

testify ['tɛstɪfaɪ] *vi* (*LAW*) prestar declaración; **to ~ to sth** atestiguar algo.

testimonial [tɛstɪ'məunɪəl] *n* (*of character*) (carta de) recomendación *f*.

testimony ['tɛstɪmənɪ] *n* (*LAW*) testimonio, declaración *f*.

testing ['tɛstɪŋ] *adj* (*difficult: time*) duro.

test match *n* partido internacional.
testosterone [tɛsˈtɔstərəun] *n* testosterona.
test paper *n* examen *m*, test *m*.
test pilot *n* piloto *m/f* de pruebas.
test tube *n* probeta.
test-tube baby *n* bebé *m* probeta *inv*.
tetanus [ˈtɛtənəs] *n* tétano.
tetchy [ˈtɛtʃɪ] *adj* irritable.
tether [ˈtɛðə*] *vt* atar ♦ *n*: **to be at the end of one's** ~ no aguantar más.
Tex. *abbr* (*US*) = *Texas.*
text [tɛkst] *n* texto ♦ *vt*: **to** ~ **sb** enviar un mensaje (de texto) a algn.
textbook [ˈtɛkstbuk] *n* libro de texto.
textiles [ˈtɛkstaɪlz] *npl* tejidos *mpl*.
text message *n* mensaje *m* de texto.
text messaging [-ˈmɛsɪdʒɪŋ] *n* (envío de) mensajes *mpl* de texto.
textual [ˈtɛkstjuəl] *adj* del texto, textual.
texture [ˈtɛkstʃə*] *n* textura.
TGWU *n abbr* (*BRIT*: = *Transport and General Workers' Union*) sindicato de transportistas.
Thai [taɪ] *adj, n* tailandés/esa *m/f*.
Thailand [ˈtaɪlænd] *n* Tailandia.
Thames [tɛmz] *n*: **the** ~ el (río) Támesis.
than [ðæn, ðən] *conj que* (*with numerals*): **more** ~ **10/once** más de 10/una vez; **I have more/less** ~ **you** tengo más/menos que tú; **it is better to phone** ~ **to write** es mejor llamar por teléfono que escribir; **no sooner did he leave** ~ **the phone rang** en cuanto se marchó, sonó el teléfono.
thank [θæŋk] *vt* dar las gracias a, agradecer; ~ **you (very much)** muchas gracias; ~ **heavens,** ~ **God!** ¡gracias a Dios!, ¡menos mal!
thankful [ˈθæŋkful] *adj*: ~ **for** agradecido (por).
thankfully [ˈθæŋkfəlɪ] *adv* (*gratefully*) con agradecimiento; (*with relief*) por suerte; ~ **there were few victims** afortunadamente hubo pocas víctimas.
thankless [ˈθæŋklɪs] *adj* ingrato.
thanks [θæŋks] *npl* gracias *fpl* ♦ *excl* ¡gracias!; ~ **to** *prep* gracias a.
Thanksgiving (Day) [ˈθæŋksgɪvɪŋ-] *n* día *m* de Acción de Gracias; *ver recuadro.*

THANKSGIVING DAY

En Estados Unidos el cuarto jueves de noviembre es **Thanksgiving Day,** *fiesta oficial en la que se conmemora la celebración que tuvieron los primeros colonos norteamericanos ("Pilgrims" o "Pilgrim Fathers") tras la estupenda*

---

cosecha de 1621, por la que se dan gracias a Dios. En Canadá se celebra una fiesta semejante el segundo lunes de octubre, aunque no está relacionada con dicha fecha histórica.

═══════════════════ **KEYWORD**

that [ðæt](*pl* **those**) *adj* (*demonstrative*) ese/a, *pl* esos/as; (*more remote*) aquel/aquella, *pl* aquellos/as; **leave those books on the table** deja esos libros sobre la mesa; ~ **one** ése/ésa; (*more remote*) aquél/aquélla; ~ **one over there** ése/ésa de ahí; aquél/aquélla de allí
♦ *pron* **1** (*demonstrative*) ése/a, *pl* ésos/as; (*neuter*) eso; (*more remote*) aquél/aquélla, *pl* aquéllos/as; (*neuter*) aquello; **what's** ~? ¿qué es eso (*or* aquello)?; **who's** ~? ¿quién es?; (*pointing etc*) ¿quién es ése/a?; **is** ~ **you?** ¿eres tú?; **will you eat all** ~? ¿vas a comer todo eso?; ~ **'s my house** ésa es mi casa; ~ **'s what he said** eso es lo que dijo; ~ **is** (*to say*) es decir; **at** *or* **with** ~ **she** ... en eso, ella ...; **do it like** ~ hazlo así
2 (*relative*: *subject, object*) que; (*with preposition*) (el/la) que, el/la cual; **the book** (~) **I read** el libro que leí; **the books** ~ **are in the library** los libros que están en la biblioteca; **all** (~) **I have** todo lo que tengo; **the box** (~) **I put it in** la caja en la que *or* donde lo puse; **the people** (~) **I spoke to** la gente con la que hablé; **not** ~ **I know of** que yo sepa, no
3 (*relative*: *of time*) que; **the day** (~) **he came** el día (en) que vino
♦ *conj* que; **he thought** ~ **I was ill** creyó que yo estaba enfermo
♦ *adv* (*demonstrative*): **I can't work** ~ **much** no puedo trabajar tanto; **I didn't realise it was** ~ **bad** no creí que fuera tan malo; ~ **high** así de alto.

thatched [θætʃt] *adj* (*roof*) de paja; ~ **cottage** casita con tejado de paja.
Thatcherism [ˈθætʃərɪzəm] *n* thatcherismo.
thaw [θɔː] *n* deshielo ♦ *vi* (*ice*) derretirse; (*food*) descongelarse ♦ *vt* descongelar.

═══════════════════ **KEYWORD**

the [ðiː, ðə] *def art* **1** (*gen*) el, *f* la, *pl* los, *fpl* las (*NB* = *el immediately before feminine noun beginning with stressed (h)a*; *a+el* = al; *de+el* = del); ~ **boy/girl** el chico/la chica; ~ **books/flowers** los libros/las flores; **to** ~ **postman/from** ~ **drawer** al cartero/del cajón; **I haven't** ~ **time/money** no tengo tiempo/dinero; **1.10 euros to** ~ **dollar** 1,10 euros por dólar; **paid by ~ hour** pagado por hora

2 (*+adj to form noun*) los; lo; **~ rich and ~ poor** los ricos y los pobres; **to attempt ~ impossible** intentar lo imposible

3 (*in titles, surnames*): **Elizabeth ~ First** Isabel Primera; **Peter ~ Great** Pedro el Grande; **do you know ~ Smiths?** ¿conoce a los Smith?

4 (*in comparisons*): **~ more he works ~ more he earns** cuanto más trabaja más gana.

theatre, (*US*) **theater** [ˈθɪətə*] *n* teatro.

theatre-goer, (*US*) **theater-goer** [ˈθɪətəɡəuə*] *n* aficionado/a al teatro.

theatrical [θɪˈætrɪkl] *adj* teatral.

theft [θɛft] *n* robo.

their [ðɛə*] *adj* su.

theirs [ðɛəz] *pron* (el) suyo/(la) suya *etc*; *see also* **my, mine.**

them [ðɛm, ðəm] *pron* (*direct*) los/las; (*indirect*) les; (*stressed, after prep*) ellos/ellas; **I see ~** los veo; **both of ~** ambos/as, los/las dos; **give me a few of ~** dame algunos/as; *see also* **me.**

theme [θiːm] *n* tema *m*.

theme park *n* parque *m* temático.

theme song *n* tema *m* (musical).

themselves [ðəmˈsɛlvz] *pl pron* (*subject*) ellos mismos/ellas mismas; (*complement*) se; (*after prep*) sí (mismos/as); *see also* **oneself.**

then [ðɛn] *adv* (*at that time*) entonces; (*next*) pues; (*later*) luego, después; (*and also*) además ♦ *conj* (*therefore*) en ese caso, entonces ♦ *adj*: **the ~ president** el entonces presidente; **from ~ on** desde entonces; **until ~** hasta entonces; **and ~ what?** y luego, ¿qué?; **what do you want me to do, ~?** ¿entonces, qué quiere que haga?

theologian [θɪəˈləudʒən] *n* teólogo/a.

theological [θɪəˈlɒdʒɪkl] *adj* teológico.

theology [θɪˈɒlədʒɪ] *n* teología.

theorem [ˈθɪərəm] *n* teorema *m*.

theoretical [θɪəˈrɛtɪkl] *adj* teórico.

theoretically [θɪəˈrɛtɪklɪ] *adv* teóricamente, en teoría.

theorize [ˈθɪəraɪz] *vi* teorizar.

theory [ˈθɪərɪ] *n* teoría.

therapeutic(al) [θɛrəˈpjuːtɪk(l)] *adj* terapéutico.

therapist [ˈθɛrəpɪst] *n* terapeuta *m/f*.

therapy [ˈθɛrəpɪ] *n* terapia.

there [ðɛə*] *adv* **1**: **~ is, ~ are** hay; **~ is no-one here** no hay nadie aquí; **~ is no bread left** no queda pan; **~ has been an accident** ha habido un accidente

2 (*referring to place*) ahí; (*distant*) allí; **it's ~** está ahí; **put it in/on/up/down ~** ponlo ahí dentro/encima/arriba/abajo; **I want that book ~** quiero ese libro de ahí; **~ he is!** ¡ahí está!; **~'s the bus** ahí *or* ya viene el autobús; **back/down ~** allí atrás/abajo; **over ~, through ~** por allí

3: **~, ~** (*esp to child*) ¡venga, venga!

thereabouts [ˈðɛərəˈbauts] *adv* por ahí.

thereafter [ðɛərˈɑːftə*] *adv* después.

thereby [ˈðɛəbaɪ] *adv* así, de ese modo.

therefore [ˈðɛəfɔː*] *adv* por lo tanto.

there's [ðɛəz] = **there is; there has.**

thereupon [ðɛərəˈpɒn] *adv* (*at that point*) en eso, en seguida.

thermal [ˈθəːml] *adj* termal.

thermal paper *n* papel *m* térmico.

thermal printer *n* termoimpresora.

thermodynamics [ˈθəːmədaɪnæmɪks] *n* termodinámica.

thermometer [θəˈmɒmɪtə*] *n* termómetro.

thermonuclear [θəːməuˈnjuːklɪə*] *adj* termonuclear.

Thermos ® [ˈθəːməs] *n* (*also:* **~ flask)** termo.

thermostat [ˈθəːməustæt] *n* termostato.

thesaurus [θɪˈsɔːrəs] *n* tesoro, diccionario de sinónimos.

these [ðiːz] *pl adj* estos/as ♦ *pl pron* éstos/as.

thesis, *pl* **theses** [ˈθiːsɪs, -siːz] *n* tesis *f inv*; *see also* **doctorate.**

they [ðeɪ] *pl pron* ellos/ellas; **~ say that ...** (*it is said that*) se dice que ....

they'd [ðeɪd] = **they had; they would.**

they'll [ðeɪl] = **they shall, they will.**

they're [ðɛə*] = **they are.**

they've [ðeɪv] = **they have.**

thick [θɪk] *adj* (*wall, slice*) grueso; (*dense: liquid, smoke etc*) espeso; (*vegetation, beard*) tupido; (*stupid*) torpe ♦ *n*: **in the ~ of the battle** en lo más reñido de la batalla; **it's 20 cm ~** tiene 20 cm de espesor.

thicken [ˈθɪkn] *vi* espesarse ♦ *vt* (*sauce etc*) espesar.

thicket [ˈθɪkɪt] *n* espesura.

thickly [ˈθɪklɪ] *adv* (*spread*) en capa espesa; (*cut*) en rebanada gruesa; (*populated*) densamente.

thickness [ˈθɪknɪs] *n* espesor *m*, grueso.

thickset [θɪkˈsɛt] *adj* fornido.

thickskinned [θɪk'skɪnd] *adj* (*fig*)
insensible.

thief, *pl* **thieves** [θi:f, θi:vz] *n* ladrón/ona
m/f.

thieving ['θi:vɪŋ] *n* tobo, hurto ♦ *adj* ladrón/
ona.

thigh [θaɪ] *n* muslo.

thighbone ['θaɪbəun] *n* fémur *m*.

thimble ['θɪmbl] *n* dedal *m*.

thin [θɪn] *adj* delgado; (*wall, layer*) fino;
(*watery*) aguado; (*light*) tenue; (*hair*)
escaso; (*fog*) ligero; (*crowd*) disperso ♦ *vt*:
to ~ (**down**) (*sauce, paint*) diluir ♦ *vi* (*fog*)
aclararse; (*also*: **~ out**: *crowd*)
dispersarse; **his hair is ~ning** se está
quedando calvo.

thing [θɪŋ] *n* cosa; (*object*) objeto, artículo;
(*contraption*) chisme *m*; (*mania*) manía; **~s**
npl (*belongings*) cosas *fpl*; **the best ~**
would be to... lo mejor sería...; **the main**
~ is ... lo principal es ...; **first ~ (in the**
morning) a primera hora (de la mañana);
last ~ (at night) a última hora (de la
noche); **the ~ is ...** lo que pasa es que ...;
how are ~s? ¿qué tal van las cosas?;
she's got a ~ about mice le dan no sé qué
los ratones; **poor ~!** ¡pobre! *m/f*,
¡pobrecito/a!

think, *pt, pp* **thought** [θɪŋk, θɔ:t] *vi* pensar
♦ *vt* pensar, creer; (*imagine*) imaginar;
what did you ~ of it? ¿qué te parece?;
what did you ~ of them? ¿qué te
parecieron?; **to ~ about sth/sb** pensar en
algo/uno; **I'll ~ about it** lo pensaré; **to ~ of**
doing sth pensar en hacer algo; **I ~ so/**
not creo que sí/no; **~ again!** ¡piénsalo
bien!; **to ~ aloud** pensar en voz alta; **to ~**
well of sb tener buen concepto de algn.

▶**think out** *vt* (*plan*) elaborar, tramar;
(*solution*) encontrar.

▶**think over** *vt* reflexionar sobre, meditar;
I'd like to ~ things over me gustaría
pensármelo.

▶**think through** *vt* pensar bien.

▶**think up** *vt* imaginar.

thinking ['θɪŋkɪŋ] *n*: **to my (way of) ~** a mi
parecer.

think tank *n* grupo de expertos.

thinly ['θɪnlɪ] *adv* (*cut*) en lonchas finas;
(*spread*) en una capa fina.

thinness ['θɪnnɪs] *n* delgadez *f*.

third [θɔ:d] *adj* (*before nmsg*: **tercer**) tercero
♦ *n* tercero/a; (*fraction*) tercio; (*BRIT SCOL*:
degree) título universitario de tercera
clase.

third degree *adj* (*burns*) de tercer grado.

thirdly ['θɔ:dlɪ] *adv* en tercer lugar.

third party insurance *n* (*BRIT*) seguro a
terceros.

third-rate ['θɔ:d'reɪt] *adj* de poca calidad.

Third World *n*: **the ~** el Tercer Mundo
♦ *cpd* tercermundista.

thirst [θɔ:st] *n* sed *f*.

thirsty ['θɔ:stɪ] *adj* (*person*) sediento; **to be**
~ tener sed.

thirteen [θɔ:'ti:n] *num* trece.

thirteenth [θɔ:'ti:nθ] *adj* decimotercero ♦ *n*
(*in series*) decimotercero/a; (*fraction*)
decimotercio.

thirtieth ['θɔ:tɪəθ] *adj* trigésimo ♦ *n* (*in*
series) trigésimo/a; (*fraction*) treintavo.

thirty ['θɔ:tɪ] *num* treinta.

═══════════════════════════ *KEYWORD*

this [ðɪs] (*pl* **these**) *adj* (*demonstrative*) este/
a; *pl* estos/as; (*neuter*) esto; **~ man/**
woman este hombre/esta mujer; **these**
children/flowers estos chicos/estas flores;
~ way por aquí; **~ time last year** hoy
hace un año; **~ one (here)** éste/a, esto (de
aquí)

♦ *pron* (*demonstrative*) éste/a; *pl* éstos/as;
(*neuter*) esto; **who is ~?** ¿quién es éste/
ésta?; **what is ~?** ¿qué es esto?; **~ is**
where I live aquí vivo; **~ is what he said**
esto es lo que dijo; **~ is Mr Brown** (*in*
introductions) le presento al Sr. Brown;
(*photo*) éste es el Sr. Brown; (*on*
telephone) habla el Sr. Brown; **they were**
talking of ~ and that hablaban de esto y
lo otro

♦ *adv* (*demonstrative*): **~ high/long** así de
alto/largo; **~ far** hasta aquí.

thistle ['θɪsl] *n* cardo.

thong [θɒŋ] *n* correa.

thorn [θɔ:n] *n* espina.

thorny ['θɔ:nɪ] *adj* espinoso.

thorough ['θʌrə] *adj* (*search*) minucioso;
(*knowledge*) profundo; (*research*) a fondo.

thoroughbred ['θʌrəbred] *adj* (*horse*) de
pura sangre.

thoroughfare ['θʌrəfeə*] *n* calle *f*; **"no ~"**
"prohibido el paso".

thoroughgoing ['θʌrəgəuɪŋ] *adj* a fondo.

thoroughly ['θʌrəlɪ] *adv* minuciosamente; a
fondo.

thoroughness ['θʌrənɪs] *n* minuciosidad *f*.

those [ðəuz] *pl pron* ésos/ésas; (*more remote*)
aquéllos/as ♦ *pl adj* esos/esas; aquellos/as.

though [ðəu] *conj* aunque ♦ *adv* sin
embargo, aún así; **even ~** aunque; **it's not**
so easy, ~ sin embargo no es tan fácil.

thought [θɔ:t] *pt, pp of* **think** ♦ *n*
pensamiento; (*opinion*) opinión *f*;
(*intention*) intención *f*; **to give sth some ~**

pensar algo detenidamente; **after much** ~ después de pensarlo bien; **I've just had a** ~ se me acaba de ocurrir una idea.

thoughtful ['θɔːtful] *adj* pensativo; (*considerate*) atento.

thoughtfully ['θɔːfəlɪ] *adv* pensativamente; atentamente.

thoughtless ['θɔːtlɪs] *adj* desconsiderado.

thoughtlessly ['θɔːtlɪslɪ] *adv* insensatamente.

thought-provoking ['θɔːtprəvəukɪŋ] *adj* estimulante.

thousand ['θauzənd] *num* mil; **two** ~ dos mil; ~**s of** miles de.

thousandth ['θauzəntθ] *num* milésimo.

thrash [θræʃ] *vt* dar una paliza a.
▶**thrash about** *vi* revolverse.
▶**thrash out** *vt* discutir a fondo.

thrashing ['θræʃɪŋ] *n*: **to give sb a** ~ dar una paliza a algn.

thread [θrɛd] *n* hilo; (*of screw*) rosca ♦ *vt* (*needle*) enhebrar.

threadbare ['θrɛdbɛə*] *adj* raído.

threat [θrɛt] *n* amenaza; **to be under** ~ **of** estar amenazado de.

threaten ['θrɛtn] *vi* amenazar ♦ *vt*: **to** ~ **sb with sth/to do** amenazar a algn con algo/con hacer.

threatening ['θrɛtnɪŋ] *adj* amenazador(a), amenazante.

three [θriː] *num* tres.

three-dimensional [θriːdɪ'mɛnʃənl] *adj* tridimensional.

threefold ['θriːfəuld] *adv*: **to increase** ~ triplicar.

three-piece ['θriːpiːs]: ~ **suit** *n* traje *m* de tres piezas; ~ **suite** *n* tresillo.

three-ply [θriː'plaɪ] *adj* (*wood*) de tres capas; (*wool*) triple.

three-quarter [θriː'kwɔːtə*] *adj*: ~ **length sleeves** mangas *fpl* tres cuartos.

three-quarters [θriː'kwɔːtəz] *npl* tres cuartas partes; ~ **full** tres cuartas partes lleno.

three-wheeler [θriː'wiːlə*] *n* (*car*) coche *m* cabina.

thresh [θrɛʃ] *vt* (*AGR*) trillar.

threshing machine ['θrɛʃɪŋ-] *n* trilladora.

threshold ['θrɛʃhəuld] *n* umbral *m*; **to be on the** ~ **of** (*fig*) estar al borde de.

threshold agreement *n* convenio de nivel crítico.

threw [θruː] *pt of* **throw**.

thrift [θrɪft] *n* economía.

thrifty ['θrɪftɪ] *adj* económico.

thrill [θrɪl] *n* (*excitement*) emoción *f* ♦ *vt* emocionar; **to be** ~**ed** (*with gift etc*) estar encantado.

thriller ['θrɪlə*] *n* película/novela de suspense.

thrilling ['θrɪlɪŋ] *adj* emocionante.

thrive, *pt* **thrived, throve,** *pp* **thrived, thriven** [θraɪv, θrəuv, 'θrɪvn] *vi* (*grow*) crecer; (*do well*) prosperar.

thriving ['θraɪvɪŋ] *adj* próspero.

throat [θrəut] *n* garganta; **I have a sore** ~ me duele la garganta.

throb [θrɔb] *n* (*of heart*) latido; (*of engine*) vibración *f* ♦ *vi* latir; vibrar; (*with pain*) dar punzadas; **my head is** ~**bing** la cabeza me da punzadas.

throes [θrəuz] *npl*: **in the** ~ **of** en medio de.

thrombosis [θrɔm'bəusɪs] *n* trombosis *f*.

throne [θrəun] *n* trono.

throng [θrɔŋ] *n* multitud *f*, muchedumbre *f* ♦ *vt, vi* apiñarse, agolparse.

throttle ['θrɔtl] *n* (*AUT*) acelerador *m* ♦ *vt* estrangular.

through [θruː] *prep* por, a través de; (*time*) durante; (*by means of*) por medio de, mediante; (*owing to*) gracias a ♦ *adj* (*ticket, train*) directo ♦ *adv* completamente, de parte a parte; de principio a fin; **(from) Monday** ~ **Friday** (*US*) de lunes a viernes; **to go** ~ **sb's papers** mirar entre los papeles de algn; **I am halfway** ~ **the book** voy por la mitad del libro; **the soldiers didn't let us** ~ los soldados no nos dejaron pasar; **to put sb** ~ **to sb** (*TEL*) poner *or* pasar a algn con algn; **to be** ~ (*TEL*) tener comunicación; (*have finished*) haber terminado; **"no** ~ **road"** (*BRIT*) "calle sin salida".

throughout [θruː'aut] *prep* (*place*) por todas partes de, por todo; (*time*) durante todo ♦ *adv* por *or* en todas partes.

throughput ['θruːput] *n* (*of goods, materials*) producción *f*; (*COMPUT*) capacidad *f* de procesamiento.

throve [θrəuv] *pt of* **thrive**.

throw [θrəu] *n* tiro; (*SPORT*) lanzamiento ♦ *vt* (*pt* **threw,** *pp* **thrown** [θruː, θrəun]) tirar, echar, botar (*LAM*), (*SPORT*) lanzar; (*rider*) derribar; (*fig*) desconcertar; **to** ~ **a party** dar una fiesta.
▶**throw about, throw around** *vt* (*litter etc*) tirar, esparcir.
▶**throw away** *vt* tirar.
▶**throw off** *vt* deshacerse de.
▶**throw open** *vt* (*doors, windows*) abrir de par en par; (*house, gardens etc*) abrir al público; (*competition, race*) abrir a todos.
▶**throw out** *vt* tirar, botar (*LAM*).
▶**throw together** *vt* (*clothes*) amontonar; (*meal*) preparar a la carrera; (*essay*) hacer sin cuidado.

►**throw up** *vi* vomitar, devolver.

throwaway ['θrəuəwei] *adj* para tirar, desechable.

throwback ['θrəubæk] *n*: **it's a ~ to** (*fig*) eso nos lleva de nuevo a.

throw-in ['θrəuin] *n* (*SPORT*) saque *m* de banda.

thrown [θrəun] *pp of* **throw**.

thru [θruː] (*US*) = **through**.

thrush [θrʌʃ] *n* zorzal *m*, tordo; (*MED*) candiasis *f*.

thrust [θrʌst] *n* (*TECH*) empuje *m* ♦ *vt* (*pt, pp* **thrust**) empujar; (*push in*) introducir.

thrusting ['θrʌstiŋ] *adj* (*person*) dinámico, con empuje.

thud [θʌd] *n* golpe *m* sordo.

thug [θʌg] *n* gamberro/a.

thumb [θʌm] *n* (*ANAT*) pulgar *m* ♦ *vt*: **to ~ a lift** hacer dedo; **to give sth/sb the ~s up/down** aprobar/desaprobar algo/a algn.

►**thumb through** *vt fus* (*book*) hojear.

thumb index *n* uñero, índice *m* recortado.

thumbnail ['θʌmneil] *n* uña del pulgar.

thumbnail sketch *n* esbozo.

thumbtack ['θʌmtæk] *n* (*US*) chincheta, chinche *f*.

thump [θʌmp] *n* golpe *m*; (*sound*) ruido seco *or* sordo ♦ *vt*, *vi* golpear.

thumping ['θʌmpiŋ] *adj* (*col: huge*) descomunal.

thunder ['θʌndə*] *n* trueno; (*of applause etc*) estruendo ♦ *vi* tronar; (*train etc*): **to ~ past** pasar como un trueno.

thunderbolt ['θʌndəbəult] *n* rayo.

thunderclap ['θʌndəklæp] *n* trueno.

thunderous ['θʌndərəs] *adj* ensordecedor(a), estruendoso.

thunderstorm ['θʌndəstɔːm] *n* tormenta.

thunderstruck ['θʌndəstrʌk] *adj* pasmado.

thundery ['θʌndəri] *adj* tormentoso.

Thur(s). *abbr* (= *Thursday*) juev.

Thursday ['θəːzdi] *n* jueves *m inv*.

thus [ðʌs] *adv* así, de este modo.

thwart [θwɔːt] *vt* frustrar.

thyme [taim] *n* tomillo.

thyroid ['θairɔid] *n* tiroides *m inv*.

tiara [ti'ɑːrə] *n* tiara, diadema.

Tiber ['taibə*] *n* Tíber *m*.

Tibet [ti'bet] *n* el Tíbet.

Tibetan [ti'betən] *adj* tibetano ♦ *n* tibetano/a; (*LING*) tibetano.

tibia ['tibiə] *n* tibia.

tic [tik] *n* tic *m*.

tick [tik] *n* (*sound: of clock*) tictac *m*; (*mark*) señal *f* (de visto bueno), palomita (*LAM*); (*ZOOL*) garrapata; (*BRIT col*): **in a ~** en un instante; (*BRIT col: credit*): **to buy sth on ~** comprar algo a crédito ♦ *vi* hacer tictac

♦ *vt* marcar, señalar; **to put a ~ against sth** poner una señal en algo.

►**tick off** *vt* marcar; (*person*) reñir.

►**tick over** *vi* (*BRIT: engine*) girar en marcha lenta; (: *fig*) ir tirando.

ticker tape ['tikə-] *n* cinta perforada.

ticket ['tikit] *n* billete *m*, tíquet *m*, boleto (*LAM*); (*for cinema etc*) entrada, boleto (*LAM*); (*in shop: on goods*) etiqueta; (*for library*) tarjeta; (*US POL*) lista (de candidatos); **to get a parking ~** (*AUT*) ser multado por estacionamiento ilegal.

ticket agency *n* (*THEAT*) agencia de venta de entradas.

ticket collector *n* revisor(a) *m/f*.

ticket holder *n* poseedor(a) *m/f* de billete *or* entrada.

ticket inspector *n* revisor(a) *m/f*, inspector(a) *m/f* de boletos (*LAM*).

ticket office *n* (*THEAT*) taquilla, boletería (*LAM*); (*RAIL*) despacho de billetes *or* boletos (*LAM*).

ticking-off ['tikiŋ'ɔf] *n* (*col*): **to give sb a ~** echarle una bronca a algn.

tickle ['tikl] *n*: **to give sb a ~** hacer cosquillas a algn ♦ *vt* hacer cosquillas a.

ticklish ['tikliʃ] *adj* (*which tickles: blanket*) que pica; (: *cough*) irritante; **to be ~** tener cosquillas.

tidal ['taidl] *adj* de marea.

tidal wave *n* maremoto.

tidbit ['tidbit] (*US*) = **titbit**.

tiddlywinks ['tidliwiŋks] *n* juego de la pulga.

tide [taid] *n* marea; (*fig: of events*) curso, marcha ♦ *vt*: **to ~ sb over** *or* **through (until)** sacar a algn del apuro (hasta); **high/low ~** marea alta/baja; **the ~ of public opinion** la tendencia de la opinión pública.

tidily ['taidili] *adv* bien, ordenadamente; **to arrange ~** ordenar; **to dress ~** vestir bien.

tidiness ['taidinis] *n* (*order*) orden *m*; (*cleanliness*) aseo.

tidy ['taidi] *adj* (*room*) ordenado; (*drawing, work*) limpio; (*person*) (bien) arreglado; (: *in character*) metódico; (*mind*) claro, metódico ♦ *vt* (*also*: ~ **up**) ordenar, poner en orden.

tie [tai] *n* (*string etc*) atadura; (*BRIT: neck~*) corbata; (*fig: link*) vínculo, lazo; (*SPORT: draw*) empate *m* ♦ *vt* atar ♦ *vi* (*SPORT*) empatar; **family ~s** obligaciones *fpl* familiares; **cup ~** (*SPORT: match*) partido de copa; **to ~ in a bow** hacer un lazo; **to ~ a knot in sth** hacer un nudo en algo.

►**tie down** *vt* atar; (*fig*): **to ~ sb down to**

obligar a algn a.

▶**tie in** vi: **to ~ in (with)** (correspond) concordar (con).

▶**tie on** vt (BRIT: label etc) atar.

▶**tie up** vt (parcel) envolver; (dog) atar; (boat) amarrar; (arrangements) concluir; **to be ~d up** (busy) estar ocupado.

tie-break(er) ['taɪbreɪk(ə*)] n (TENNIS) tiebreak m, muerte f súbita; (in quiz) punto decisivo.

tie-on ['taɪɔn] adj (BRIT: label) para atar.

tie-pin ['taɪpɪn] n (BRIT) alfiler m de corbata.

tier [tɪə*] n grada; (of cake) piso.

tie tack n (US) alfiler m de corbata.

tiff [tɪf] n (col) pelea, riña.

tiger ['taɪgə*] n tigre m.

tight [taɪt] adj (rope) tirante; (money) escaso; (clothes, budget) ajustado; (programme) apretado; (col: drunk) borracho ♦ adv (squeeze) muy fuerte; (shut) herméticamente; **to be packed ~** (suitcase) estar completamente lleno; (people) estar apretados; **everybody hold ~!** ¡agárense bien!

tighten ['taɪtn] vt (rope) tensar, estirar; (screw) apretar ♦ vi estirarse; apretarse.

tight-fisted [taɪt'fɪstɪd] adj tacaño.

tight-lipped ['taɪt'lɪpt] adj: **to be ~** (silent) rehusar hablar; (angry) apretar los labios.

tightly ['taɪtlɪ] adv (grasp) muy fuerte.

tightness ['taɪtnɪs] n (of rope) tirantez f; (of clothes) estrechez f; (of budget) lo ajustado.

tightrope ['taɪtrəup] n cuerda floja.

tightrope walker n equilibrista m/f, funambulista m/f.

tights [taɪts] npl (BRIT) medias fpl, panties mpl.

tigress ['taɪgrɪs] n tigresa.

tilde ['tɪldə] n tilde f.

tile [taɪl] n (on roof) teja; (on floor) baldosa; (on wall) azulejo ♦ vt (floor) poner baldosas en; (wall) alicatar.

tiled [taɪld] adj (floor) embaldosado; (wall, bathroom) alicatado; (roof) con tejas.

till [tɪl] n caja (registradora) ♦ vt (land) cultivar ♦ prep, conj = **until**.

tiller ['tɪlə*] n (NAUT) caña del timón.

tilt [tɪlt] vt inclinar ♦ vi inclinarse ♦ n (slope) inclinación f; **to wear one's hat at a ~** llevar el sombrero echado a un lado or terciado; **(at) full ~** a toda velocidad or carrera.

timber [tɪmbə*] n (material) madera; (trees) árboles mpl.

time [taɪm] n tiempo; (epoch: often pl) época; (by clock) hora; (moment)

momento; (occasion) vez f; (MUS) compás m ♦ vt calcular or medir el tiempo de; (race) cronometrar; (remark etc) elegir el momento para; **a long ~** mucho tiempo; **4 at a ~** 4 a la vez; **for the ~ being** de momento, por ahora; **at ~s** a veces, a ratos; **~ after ~, ~ and again** repetidas veces, una y otra vez; **from ~ to ~** de vez en cuando; **in ~** (soon enough) a tiempo; (after some time) con el tiempo; (MUS) al compás; **in a week's ~** dentro de una semana; **in no ~** en un abrir y cerrar de ojos; **any ~** cuando sea; **on ~** a la hora; **to be 30 minutes behind/ahead of ~** llevar media hora de retraso/adelanto; **to take one's ~** tomárselo con calma; **he'll do it in his own ~** (without being hurried) lo hará sin prisa; (out of working hours) lo hará en su tiempo libre; **by the ~ he arrived** cuando llegó; **5 ~s 5** 5 por 5; **what ~ is it?** ¿qué hora es?; **what ~ do you make it?** ¿qué hora es or tiene?; **to be behind the ~s** estar atrasado; **to carry 3 boxes at a ~** llevar 3 cajas a la vez; **to keep ~** llevar el ritmo or el compás; **to have a good ~** pasarlo bien, divertirse; **to ~ sth well/badly** elegir un buen/mal momento para algo; **the bomb was ~d to explode 5 minutes later** la bomba estaba programada para explotar 5 minutos más tarde.

time-and-motion expert ['taɪmənd'məuʃən-] n experto/a en la ciencia de la producción.

time-and-motion study ['taɪmənd'məuʃən-] n estudio de desplazamientos y tiempos.

time bomb n bomba de relojería.

time card n tarjeta de registro horario.

time clock n reloj m registrador.

time-consuming ['taɪmkənsjuːmɪŋ] adj que requiere mucho tiempo.

time frame n plazo.

time-honoured, (US) **time-honored** ['taɪmɔnəd] adj consagrado.

timekeeper ['taɪmkiːpə*] n (SPORT) cronómetro.

time lag n desfase m.

timeless ['taɪmlɪs] adj eterno.

time limit n (gen) límite m de tiempo; (COMM) plazo.

timely ['taɪmlɪ] adj oportuno.

time off n tiempo libre.

timer ['taɪmə*] n (~ switch) interruptor m; (in kitchen, TECH) temporizador m.

time-saving ['taɪmseɪvɪŋ] adj que ahorra tiempo.

time scale n escala de tiempo.

time sharing n (*COMPUT*) tiempo compartido.
time sheet n = **time card.**
time signal n señal f horaria.
time switch n (*BRIT*) interruptor m (horario).
timetable ['taɪmteɪbl] n horario; (*programme of events etc*) programa m.
time zone n huso horario.
timid ['tɪmɪd] adj tímido.
timidity [tɪ'mɪdɪtɪ] n timidez f.
timidly ['tɪmɪdlɪ] adv tímidamente.
timing ['taɪmɪŋ] n (*SPORT*) cronometraje m; the ~ of his resignation el momento que eligió para dimitir.
timpani ['tɪmpənɪ] npl tímpanos mpl.
tin [tɪn] n estaño; (*also*: ~ **plate**) hojalata; (*BRIT*: *can*) lata.
tinfoil ['tɪnfɔɪl] n papel m de estaño.
tinge [tɪndʒ] n matiz m ♦ vt: ~d with teñido de.
tingle ['tɪŋgl] n hormigueo ♦ vi (*cheeks, skin*: *from cold*) sentir comezón; (: *from bad circulation*) sentir hormigueo.
tinker ['tɪŋkə*] n calderero/a; (*gipsy*) gitano/a.
▶**tinker with** vt fus jugar con, tocar.
tinkle ['tɪŋkl] vi tintinear.
tin mine n mina de estaño.
tinned [tɪnd] adj (*BRIT*: *food*) en lata, en conserva.
tinnitus ['tɪnɪtəs] n (*MED*) acufeno.
tinny ['tɪnɪ] adj (*sound, taste*) metálico; (*pej*: *car*) poco sólido, de pacotilla.
tin opener [-əʊpnə*] n (*BRIT*) abrelatas m inv.
tinsel ['tɪnsl] n oropel m.
tint [tɪnt] n matiz m; (*for hair*) tinte m ♦ vt (*hair*) teñir.
tinted ['tɪntɪd] adj (*hair*) teñido; (*glass, spectacles*) ahumado.
tiny ['taɪnɪ] adj minúsculo, pequeñito.
tip [tɪp] n (*end*) punta; (*gratuity*) propina; (*BRIT*: *for rubbish*) vertedero; (*advice*) consejo ♦ vt (*waiter*) dar una propina a; (*tilt*) inclinar; (*empty*: *also* ~ **out**) vaciar, echar; (*predict*: *winner*) pronosticar; (: *horse*) recomendar; **he ~ped out the contents of the box** volcó el contenido de la caja.
▶**tip off** vt avisar, poner sobreaviso a.
▶**tip over** vt volcar ♦ vi volcarse.
tip-off ['tɪpɔf] n (*hint*) advertencia.
tipped [tɪpt] adj (*BRIT*: *cigarette*) con filtro.
Tipp-Ex ® ['tɪpɛks] n Tipp-Ex ® m.
tipple ['tɪpl] n (*BRIT*): **his** ~ **is Cointreau** bebe Cointreau.
tipster ['tɪpstə*] n (*RACING*) pronosticador(a) m/f.
tipsy ['tɪpsɪ] adj alegre, achispado.
tiptoe ['tɪptəʊ] n (*BRIT*): **on** ~ de puntillas.
tiptop ['tɪptɔp] adj: **in** ~ **condition** en perfectas condiciones.
tirade [taɪ'reɪd] n diatriba.
tire ['taɪə*] n (*US*) = **tyre** ♦ vt cansar ♦ vi (*gen*) cansarse; (*become bored*) aburrirse.
▶**tire out** vt agotar, rendir.
tired ['taɪəd] adj cansado; **to be** ~ **of sth** estar harto de algo; **to be/feel/look** ~ estar/sentirse/parecer cansado.
tiredness ['taɪədnɪs] n cansancio.
tireless ['taɪəlɪs] adj incansable.
tirelessly ['taɪəlɪslɪ] adv incansablemente.
tiresome ['taɪəsəm] adj aburrido.
tiring ['taɪərɪŋ] adj cansado.
tissue ['tɪʃuː] n tejido; (*paper handkerchief*) pañuelo de papel, kleenex m ®.
tissue paper n papel m de seda.
tit [tɪt] n (*bird*) herrerillo común; **to give** ~ **for tat** dar ojo por ojo.
titbit ['tɪtbɪt], (*US*) **tidbit** ['tɪdbɪt] n (*food*) golosina; (*news*) pedazo.
titillate ['tɪtɪleɪt] vt estimular, excitar.
titillation [tɪtɪ'leɪʃən] n estimulación f, excitación f.
titivate ['tɪtɪveɪt] vt emperejilar.
title ['taɪtl] n título; (*LAW*: *right*): ~ (**to**) derecho (a).
title deed n (*LAW*) título de propiedad.
title page n portada.
title role n papel m principal.
titter ['tɪtə*] vi reírse entre dientes.
tittle-tattle ['tɪtltætl] n chismes mpl.
titular ['tɪtjulə*] adj (*in name only*) nominal.
T-junction ['tiːdʒʌŋkʃən] n cruce m en T.
TM abbr (= *trademark*) marca de fábrica; = *transcendental meditation.*
TN abbr (*US*) = *Tennessee.*
TNT n abbr (= *trinitrotoluene*) TNT m.

════════════════════ *KEYWORD*

to [tuː, tə] prep **1** (*direction*) a; **to go** ~ **France/London/school/the station** ir a Francia/Londres/al colegio/a la estación; **to go** ~ **Claude's/the doctor's** ir a casa de Claude/al médico; **the road** ~ **Edinburgh** la carretera de Edimburgo; ~ **the left/ right** a la izquierda/derecha
2 (*as far as*) hasta, a; **from here** ~ **London** de aquí a *or* hasta Londres; **to count** ~ **10** contar hasta 10; **from 40** ~ **50 people** entre 40 y 50 personas
3 (*with expressions of time*): **a quarter/ twenty** ~ **5** las 5 menos cuarto/veinte
4 (*for, of*): **the key** ~ **the front door** la llave de la puerta principal; **she is**

secretary ~ **the director** es la secretaria del director; **a letter** ~ **his wife** una carta a *or* para su mujer

5 (*expressing indirect object*) a; **to give sth** ~ **sb** darle algo a algn; **give it** ~ **me** dámelo; **to talk** ~ **sb** hablar con algn; **to be a danger** ~ **sb** ser un peligro para algn; **to carry out repairs** ~ **sth** hacer reparaciones en algo

6 (*in relation to*): **3 goals** ~ **2** 3 goles a 2; **30 miles** ~ **the gallon** ≈ 9,4 litros a los cien (kilómetros); **8 apples** ~ **the kilo** 8 manzanas por kilo

7 (*purpose, result*): **to come** ~ **sb's aid** venir en auxilio *or* ayuda de algn; **to sentence sb** ~ **death** condenar a algn a muerte; ~ **my great surprise** con gran sorpresa mía

♦ *with vb* **1** (*simple infin*): ~ **go/eat** ir/comer **2** (*following another vb*): **to want/try/start** ~ **do** querer/intentar/empezar a hacer; *see also relevant vb*

3 (*with vb omitted*): **I don't want** ~ no quiero

4 (*purpose, result*) para; **I did it** ~ **help you** lo hice para ayudarte; **he came** ~ **see you** vino a verte

5 (*equivalent to relative clause*): **I have things** ~ **do** tengo cosas que hacer; **the main thing is** ~ **try** lo principal es intentarlo

6 (*after adj etc*): **ready** ~ **go** listo para irse; **too old** ~ **...** demasiado viejo (como) para ...

♦ *adv*: **pull/push the door** ~ tirar de/ empujar la puerta; **to go** ~ **and fro** ir y venir.

toad [təud] *n* sapo.

toadstool ['təudstuːl] *n* seta venenosa.

toady ['təudɪ] *n* pelota *m/f* ♦ *vi*: **to** ~ **to sb** hacer la pelota *or* dar coba a algn.

toast [təust] *n* (*CULIN: also:* **piece of** ~) tostada; (*drink, speech*) brindis *m inv* ♦ *vt* (*CULIN*) tostar; (*drink to*) brindar.

toaster ['təustə*] *n* tostador *m*.

toastmaster ['təustmɑːstə*] *n persona que propone brindis y anuncia a los oradores en un banquete.*

toast rack *n* rejilla para tostadas.

tobacco [tə'bækəu] *n* tabaco; **pipe** ~ tabaco de pipa.

tobacconist [tə'bækənɪst] *n* estanquero/a, tabaquero/a (*LAM*); ~'**s (shop)** (*BRIT*) estanco, tabaquería (*LAM*).

tobacco plantation *n* plantación *f* de tabaco, tabacal *m*.

Tobago [tə'beɪgəu] *n see* **Trinidad and Tobago.**

toboggan [tə'bɔgən] *n* tobogán *m*.

today [tə'deɪ] *adv, n* (*also fig*) hoy *m*; **what day is it** ~? ¿qué día es hoy?; **what date is it** ~? ¿a qué fecha estamos hoy?; ~'**s paper** el periódico de hoy; **a fortnight** ~ de hoy en 15 días, dentro de 15 días.

toddle ['tɔdl] *vi* empezar a andar, dar los primeros pasos.

toddler ['tɔdlə*] *n* niño/a (que empieza a andar).

toddy ['tɔdɪ] *n* ponche *m*.

to-do [tə'duː] *n* (*fuss*) lío.

toe [təu] *n* dedo (del pie); (*of shoe*) punta ♦ *vt*: **to** ~ **the line** (*fig*) acatar las normas; **big/little** ~ dedo gordo/pequeño del pie.

TOEFL *n abbr* = **Test(ing) of English as a Foreign Language.**

toehold ['təuhəuld] *n* punto de apoyo (para el pie).

toenail ['təuneɪl] *n* uña del pie.

toffee ['tɔfɪ] *n* caramelo.

toffee apple *n* (*BRIT*) manzana de caramelo.

tofu ['təufuː] *n* tofu *m*.

toga ['təugə] *n* toga.

together [tə'gɛðə*] *adv* juntos; (*at same time*) al mismo tiempo, a la vez; ~ **with** *prep* junto con.

togetherness [tə'gɛðənɪs] *n* compañerismo.

toggle switch ['tɔgl-] *n* (*COMPUT*) conmutador *m* de palanca.

Togo ['təugəu] *n* Togo.

togs [tɔgz] *npl* (*col: clothes*) atuendo, ropa.

toil [tɔɪl] *n* trabajo duro, labor *f* ♦ *vi* esforzarse.

toilet ['tɔɪlət] *n* (*BRIT: lavatory*) servicios *mpl*, wáter *m* ♦ *cpd* (*bag, soap etc*) de aseo; **to go to the** ~ ir al baño; *see also* **toilets.**

toilet bag *n* neceser *m*, bolsa de aseo.

toilet bowl *n* taza (de retrete).

toilet paper *n* papel *m* higiénico.

toiletries ['tɔɪlətrɪz] *npl* artículos *mpl* de aseo; (*make-up etc*) artículos *mpl* de tocador.

toilet roll *n* rollo de papel higiénico.

toilets ['tɔɪləts] *npl* (*BRIT*) servicios *mpl*.

toilet soap *n* jabón *m* de tocador.

toilet water *n* (agua de) colonia.

to-ing and fro-ing ['tuɪŋən'frəuɪŋ] *n* vaivén *m*.

token ['təukən] *n* (*sign*) señal *f*, muestra; (*souvenir*) recuerdo; (*voucher*) vale *m*; (*disc*) ficha ♦ *cpd* (*fee, strike*) nominal, simbólico; **book/record** ~ (*BRIT*) vale *m* para comprar libros/discos; **by the same**

~ (*fig*) por la misma razón.

tokenism ['təukənɪzəm] *n* (*POL*) política simbólica *or* de fachada.

Tokyo ['təukjəu] *n* Tokio, Tokío.

told [təuld] *pt, pp of* **tell.**

tolerable ['tɔlərəbl] *adj* (*bearable*) soportable; (*fairly good*) pasable.

tolerably ['tɔlərəblɪ] *adv* (*good, comfortable*) medianamente.

tolerance ['tɔlərns] *n* (*also:* TECH) tolerancia.

tolerant ['tɔlərnt] *adj:* ~ **of** tolerante con.

tolerantly ['tɔlərntlɪ] *adv* con tolerancia.

tolerate ['tɔləreɪt] *vt* tolerar.

toleration [tɔlə'reɪʃən] *n* tolerancia.

toll [təul] *n* (*of casualties*) número de víctimas; (*tax, charge*) peaje *m* ♦ *vi* (*bell*) doblar.

toll bridge *n* puente *m* de peaje.

toll call *n* (*US TELEC*) conferencia, llamada interurbana.

toll-free *adj, adv* (*US*) gratis.

toll road *n* carretera de peaje.

tomato, ~**es** [tə'mɑːtəu] *n* tomate *m*.

tomato puree *n* puré *m* de tomate.

tomb [tuːm] *n* tumba.

tombola [tɔm'bəulə] *n* tómbola.

tomboy ['tɔmbɔɪ] *n* marimacho.

tombstone ['tuːmstəun] *n* lápida.

tomcat ['tɔmkæt] *n* gato.

tomorrow [tə'mɔrəu] *adv, n* (*also fig*) mañana; **the day after** ~ pasado mañana; ~ **morning** mañana por la mañana; **a week** ~ de mañana en ocho (días).

ton [tʌn] *n* (*BRIT* = 1016 *kg*; *US: also* **short** ~ = 907,18 *kg*) tonelada; ~**s of** (*col*) montones de.

tonal ['təunl] *adj* tonal.

tone [təun] *n* tono ♦ *vi* armonizar; **dialling** ~ (*TEL*) señal *f* para marcar.

▶**tone down** *vt* (*criticism*) suavizar; (*colour*) atenuar.

▶**tone up** *vt* (*muscles*) tonificar.

tone-deaf [təun'dɛf] *adj* sin oído musical.

toner ['təunə*] *n* (*for photocopier*) virador *m*.

Tonga ['tɔŋə] *n* Islas *fpl* Tonga.

tongs [tɔŋz] *npl* (*for coal*) tenazas *fpl*; (*for hair*) tenacillas *fpl*.

tongue [tʌŋ] *n* lengua; ~ **in cheek** *adv* en plan de broma.

tongue-tied ['tʌŋtaɪd] *adj* (*fig*) mudo.

tongue-twister ['tʌŋtwɪstə*] *n* trabalenguas *m inv*.

tonic ['tɔnɪk] *n* (*MED*) tónico; (*MUS*) tónica; (*also:* ~ **water**) (agua) tónica.

tonight [tə'naɪt] *adv, n* esta noche; **I'll see you** ~ nos vemos esta noche.

tonnage ['tʌnɪdʒ] *n* (*NAUT*) tonelaje *m*.

tonsil ['tɔnsl] *n* amígdala; **to have one's** ~**s out** sacarse las amígdalas *or* anginas.

tonsillitis [tɔnsɪ'laɪtɪs] *n* amigdalitis *f*.

too [tuː] *adv* (*excessively*) demasiado; (*very*) muy; (*also*) también; **it's** ~ **sweet** está demasiado dulce; **I'm not** ~ **sure about that** no estoy muy seguro de eso; **I went** ~ yo también fui; ~ **much** *adv, adj* demasiado; ~ **many** *adj* demasiados/as; ~ **bad!** ¡mala suerte!

took [tuk] *pt of* **take.**

tool [tuːl] *n* herramienta; (*fig: person*) instrumento.

toolbar ['tuːlbɑː*] *n* barra de herramientas.

tool box *n* caja de herramientas.

tool kit *n* juego de herramientas.

tool shed *n* cobertizo (para herramientas).

toot [tuːt] *n* (*of horn*) bocinazo; (*of whistle*) silbido ♦ *vi* (*with car horn*) tocar la bocina.

tooth, *pl* **teeth** [tuːθ, tiːθ] *n* (*ANAT, TECH*) diente *m*; (*molar*) muela; **to clean one's teeth** lavarse los dientes; **to have a** ~ **out** sacarse una muela; **by the skin of one's teeth** por un pelo.

toothache ['tuːθeɪk] *n* dolor *m* de muelas.

toothbrush ['tuːθbrʌʃ] *n* cepillo de dientes.

toothpaste ['tuːθpeɪst] *n* pasta de dientes.

toothpick ['tuːθpɪk] *n* palillo.

tooth powder *n* polvos *mpl* dentífricos.

top [tɔp] *n* (*of mountain*) cumbre *f*, cima; (*of head*) coronilla; (*of ladder*) (lo) alto; (*of cupboard, table*) superficie *f*; (*lid: of box, jar*) tapa; (: *of bottle*) tapón *m*; (*of list, table, queue, page*) cabeza; (*toy*) peonza; (*DRESS: blouse*) blusa; (: *T-shirt*) camiseta; (: *of pyjamas*) chaqueta ♦ *adj* de arriba; (*in rank*) principal, primero; (*best*) mejor ♦ *vt* (*exceed*) exceder; (*be first in*) encabezar; **on** ~ **of** sobre, encima de; **from** ~ **to bottom** de pies a cabeza; **the** ~ **of the milk** la nata; **at the** ~ **of the stairs** en lo alto de la escalera; **at the** ~ **of the street** al final de la calle; **at the** ~ **of one's voice** (*fig*) a voz en grito; **at** ~ **speed** a máxima velocidad; **a** ~ **surgeon** un cirujano eminente; **over the** ~ (*col*) excesivo, desmesurado; **to go over the** ~ pasarse.

▶**top up,** (*US*) **top off** *vt* volver a llenar.

topaz ['təupæz] *n* topacio.

top-class ['tɔp'klɑːs] *adj* de primera clase.

topcoat ['tɔpkəut] *n* sobretodo, abrigo.

topflight ['tɔpflaɪt] *adj* de primera (categoría *or* clase).

top floor *n* último piso.

top hat *n* sombrero de copa.

top-heavy [tɔp'hɛvɪ] *adj* (*object*) con más peso en la parte superior.

topic ['tɔpɪk] *n* tema *m*.

topical ['tɔpɪkl] *adj* actual.

topless ['tɔplɪs] *adj* (*bather etc*) topless.

top-level ['tɔplɛvl] *adj* (*talks*) al más alto nivel.

topmost ['tɔpməust] *adj* más alto.

top-notch ['tɔp'nɔtʃ] *adj* (*col*) de primerísima categoría.

topography [tə'pɔgrəfɪ] *n* topografía.

topping ['tɔpɪŋ] *n* (*CULIN*): **with a ~ of cream** con nata por encima.

topple ['tɔpl] *vt* volcar, derribar ♦ *vi* caerse.

top-ranking ['tɔpræŋkɪŋ] *adj* de alto rango.

top-secret [tɔp'siːkrɪt] *adj* de alto secreto.

top-security ['tɔpsɪ'kjuərɪtɪ] *adj* (*BRIT*) de máxima seguridad.

topsy-turvy ['tɔpsɪ'təːvɪ] *adj*, *adv* patas arriba.

top-up ['tɔpʌp] *n*: **would you like a ~?** ¿quiere que se lo vuelva a llenar?

top-up loan *n* (*BRIT*) préstamo complementario.

torch [tɔːtʃ] *n* antorcha; (*BRIT: electric*) linterna.

tore [tɔː*] *pt of* **tear**.

torment *n* ['tɔːmɛnt] tormento ♦ *vt* [tɔː'mɛnt] atormentar; (*fig: annoy*) fastidiar.

torn [tɔːn] *pp of* **tear**.

tornado, **~es** [tɔː'neɪdəu] *n* tornado.

torpedo, **~es** [tɔː'piːdəu] *n* torpedo.

torpedo boat *n* torpedero, lancha torpedera.

torpor ['tɔːpə*] *n* letargo.

torrent ['tɔrnt] *n* torrente *m*.

torrential [tɔ'rɛnʃl] *adj* torrencial.

torrid ['tɔrɪd] *adj* tórrido; (*fig*) apasionado.

torso ['tɔːsəu] *n* torso.

tortoise ['tɔːtəs] *n* tortuga.

tortoiseshell ['tɔːtəʃɛl] *adj* de carey.

tortuous ['tɔːtjuəs] *adj* tortuoso.

torture ['tɔːtʃə*] *n* tortura ♦ *vt* torturar; (*fig*) atormentar.

torturer ['tɔːtʃərə*] *n* torturador(a) *m/f*.

Tory ['tɔːrɪ] *adj*, *n* (*BRIT POL*) conservador(a) *m/f*.

toss [tɔs] *vt* tirar, echar; (*head*) sacudir ♦ *n* (*movement: of head etc*) sacudida; (*of coin*) tirada, echada (*LAM*); **to ~ a coin** echar a cara o cruz; **to ~ up for sth** jugar algo a cara o cruz; **to ~ and turn** (*in bed*) dar vueltas (en la cama); **to win/lose the ~** (*also SPORT*) ganar/perder (a cara o cruz).

tot [tɔt] *n* (*BRIT: drink*) copita; (*child*) nene/a *m/f*.

▶**tot up** *vt* sumar.

total ['təutl] *adj* total, entero ♦ *n* total *m*, suma ♦ *vt* (*add up*) sumar; (*amount to*) ascender a; **grand ~** cantidad *f* total; (*cost*) importe *m* total; **in ~** en total, en suma.

totalitarian [təutælɪ'tɛərɪən] *adj* totalitario.

totality [təu'tælɪtɪ] *n* totalidad *f*.

total loss *n* siniestra total.

totally ['təutəlɪ] *adv* totalmente.

tote [təut] *vt* (*col*) acarrear, cargar con.

tote bag *n* bolsa.

totem pole ['təutəm-] *n* poste *m* totémico.

totter ['tɔtə*] *vi* tambalearse.

touch [tʌtʃ] *n* (*sense*) tacto; (*contact*) contacto; (*FOOTBALL*) fuera de juego ♦ *vt* tocar; (*emotionally*) conmover; **a ~ of** (*fig*) una pizca *or* un poquito de; **to get in ~ with sb** ponerse en contacto con algn; **I'll be in ~** le llamaré/escribiré; **to lose ~** (*friends*) perder contacto; **to be out of ~ with events** no estar al corriente (de los acontecimientos); **the personal ~** el toque personal; **to put the finishing ~es to sth** dar el último toque a algo; **no artist in the country can ~ him** no hay artista en todo el país que le iguale.

▶**touch on** *vt fus* (*topic*) aludir (brevemente) a.

▶**touch up** *vt* (*paint*) retocar.

touch-and-go ['tʌtʃən'gəu] *adj* arriesgado.

touchdown ['tʌtʃdaun] *n* aterrizaje *m*; (*US FOOTBALL*) ensayo.

touched [tʌtʃt] *adj* conmovido; (*col*) chiflado.

touchiness ['tʌtʃɪnɪs] *n* susceptibilidad *f*.

touching ['tʌtʃɪŋ] *adj* conmovedor(a).

touchline ['tʌtʃlaɪn] *n* (*SPORT*) línea de banda.

touch-sensitive ['tʌtʃ'sɛnsɪtɪv] *adj* sensible al tacto.

touch-type ['tʌtʃtaɪp] *vi* mecanografiar al tacto.

touchy ['tʌtʃɪ] *adj* (*person*) quisquilloso.

tough [tʌf] *adj* (*meat*) duro; (*journey*) penoso; (*task, problem, situation*) difícil; (*resistant*) resistente; (*person*) fuerte; (: *pej*) bruto ♦ *n* (*gangster etc*) gorila *m*; **they got ~ with the workers** se pusieron muy duros con los trabajadores.

toughen ['tʌfn] *vt* endurecer.

toughness ['tʌfnɪs] *n* dureza; (*resistance*) resistencia; (*strictness*) inflexibilidad *f*.

toupée ['tuːpeɪ] *n* peluquín *m*.

tour ['tuə*] *n* viaje *m*; (*also: package ~*) viaje *m* con todo incluido; (*of town, museum*) visita ♦ *vt* viajar por; **to go on a ~ of** (*region, country*) ir de viaje por; (*museum, castle*) visitar; **to go on ~** partir *or* ir de gira.

touring ['tuərɪŋ] *n* viajes *mpl* turísticos, turismo.

tourism ['tuərɪzm] *n* turismo.

tourist ['tuərɪst] *n* turista *m/f* ♦ *cpd* turístico; **the ~ trade** el turismo.

tourist class *n* (*AVIAT*) clase *f* turista.

tourist office *n* oficina de turismo.

tournament ['tuənəmənt] *n* torneo.

tourniquet ['tuənɪkeɪ] *n* (*MED*) torniquete *m*.

tour operator *n* touroperador(a) *m/f*, operador(a) *m/f* turístico/a.

tousled ['tauzld] *adj* (*hair*) despeinado.

tout [taut] *vi*: **to ~ for business** solicitar clientes ♦ *n*: **ticket ~** revendedor(a) *m/f*.

tow [təu] *n*: **to give sb a ~** (*AUT*) remolcar a algn ♦ *vt* remolcar; **"on** *or* (*US*) **in ~"** (*AUT*) "a remolque".

toward(s) [tə'wɔːd(z)] *prep* hacia; (*of attitude*) respecto a, con; (*of purpose*) para; **~ noon** alrededor de mediodía; **~ the end of the year** hacia finales de año; **to feel friendly ~ sb** sentir amistad hacia algn.

towel ['tauəl] *n* toalla; **to throw in the ~** (*fig*) darse por vencido, renunciar.

towelling ['tauəlɪŋ] *n* (*fabric*) felpa.

towel rail, (*US*) **towel rack** *n* toallero.

tower ['tauə*] *n* torre *f* ♦ *vi* (*building, mountain*) elevarse; **to ~ above** *or* **over sth/sb** dominar algo/destacarse sobre algn.

tower block *n* (*BRIT*) bloque *m* de pisos.

towering ['tauərɪŋ] *adj* muy alto, imponente.

town [taun] *n* ciudad *f*; **to go to ~** ir a la ciudad; (*fig*) tirar la casa por la ventana; **in the ~** en la ciudad; **to be out of ~** estar fuera de la ciudad.

town centre *n* centro de la ciudad.

town clerk *n* secretario/a del Ayuntamiento.

town council *n* Ayuntamiento, consejo municipal.

town crier [-kraɪə*] *n* (*BRIT*) pregonero.

town hall *n* ayuntamiento.

townie ['taunɪ] *n* (*BRIT col*) persona de la ciudad.

town plan *n* plano de la ciudad.

town planner *n* urbanista *m/f*.

town planning *n* urbanismo.

township ['taunʃɪp] *n* municipio habitado sólo por negros en Sudáfrica.

townspeople ['taunzpiːpl] *npl* gente *f* de ciudad.

towpath ['təupɑːθ] *n* camino de sirga.

towrope ['təurəup] *n* cable *m* de remolque.

tow truck *n* (*US*) camión *m* grúa.

toxic ['tɒksɪk] *adj* tóxico.

toxin ['tɒksɪn] *n* toxina.

toy [tɔɪ] *n* juguete *m*.

▶**toy with** *vt fus* jugar con; (*idea*) acariciar.

toyshop ['tɔɪʃɒp] *n* juguetería.

toy train *n* tren *m* de juguete.

trace [treɪs] *n* rastro ♦ *vt* (*draw*) trazar, delinear; (*locate*) encontrar; **there was no ~ of it** no había ningún indicio de ello.

trace element *n* oligoelemento.

trachea [trə'kɪə] *n* (*ANAT*) tráquea.

tracing paper ['treɪsɪŋ-] *n* papel *m* de calco.

track [træk] *n* (*mark*) huella, pista; (*path: gen*) camino, senda; (*: of bullet etc*) trayectoria; (*: of suspect, animal*) pista, rastro; (*RAIL*) vía; (*COMPUT, SPORT*) pista; (*on record*) canción *f* ♦ *vt* seguir la pista de; **to keep ~ of** mantenerse al tanto de, seguir; **a 4-~ tape** una cinta de 4 pistas; **the first ~ on the record/tape** la primera canción en el disco/la cinta; **to be on the right ~** (*fig*) ir por buen camino.

▶**track down** *vt* (*person*) localizar; (*sth lost*) encontrar.

tracker dog ['trækə*-] *n* (*BRIT*) perro rastreador.

track events *npl* (*SPORT*) pruebas *fpl* en pista.

tracking station ['trækɪŋ-] *n* (*SPACE*) estación *f* de seguimiento.

track meet *n* (*US*) concurso de carreras y saltos.

track record *n*: **to have a good ~** (*fig*) tener un buen historial.

tracksuit ['træksuːt] *n* chandal *m*.

tract [trækt] *n* (*GEO*) región *f*; (*pamphlet*) folleto.

traction ['trækʃən] *n* (*AUT, power*) tracción *f*; **in ~** (*MED*) en tracción.

traction engine *n* locomotora de tracción.

tractor ['træktə*] *n* tractor *m*.

trade [treɪd] *n* comercio, negocio; (*skill, job*) oficio, empleo; (*industry*) industria ♦ *vi* negociar, comerciar; **foreign ~** comercio exterior.

▶**trade in** *vt* (*old car etc*) ofrecer como parte del pago.

trade barrier *n* barrera comercial.

trade deficit *n* déficit *m* comercial.

Trade Descriptions Act *n* (*BRIT*) *ley sobre descripciones comerciales.*

trade discount *n* descuento comercial.

trade fair *n* feria de muestras.

trade-in ['treɪdɪn] *adj*: **~ price/value** *precio/ valor de un artículo usado que se descuenta del precio de otro nuevo.*

trademark ['treɪdmɑːk] *n* marca de fábrica.

trade mission *n* misión *f* comercial.

trade name n marca registrada.
trade-off n: **a ~ (between)** un equilibrio (entre).
trade price n precio al detallista.
trader ['treɪdə*] n comerciante m/f.
trade reference n referencia comercial.
trade secret n secreto profesional.
tradesman ['treɪdzmən] n (shopkeeper) comerciante m/f.
trade union n sindicato.
trade unionist [-'juːnjənɪst] n sindicalista m/f.
trade wind n viento alisio.
trading ['treɪdɪŋ] n comercio.
trading account n cuenta de compraventa.
trading estate n (BRIT) polígono industrial.
trading stamp n cupón m, sello de prima.
tradition [trə'dɪʃən] n tradición f.
traditional [trə'dɪʃənl] adj tradicional.
traditionally [trə'dɪʃənlɪ] adv tradicionalmente.
traffic ['træfɪk] n (gen, AUT) tráfico, circulación f, tránsito ♦ vi: **to ~ in** (pej: liquor, drugs) traficar en; **air ~** tráfico aéreo.
traffic calming [-'kɑːmɪŋ] n reducción f de la velocidad de la circulación.
traffic circle n (US) glorieta de tráfico.
traffic island n refugio, isleta.
traffic jam n embotellamiento, atasco.
trafficker ['træfɪkə*] n traficante m/f.
traffic lights npl semáforo sg.
traffic offence, (US) **traffic violation** n infracción f de tráfico.
traffic warden n guardia m/f de tráfico.
tragedy ['trædʒədɪ] n tragedia.
tragic ['trædʒɪk] adj trágico.
tragically ['trædʒɪkəlɪ] adv trágicamente.
trail [treɪl] n (tracks) rastro, pista; (path) camino, sendero; (dust, smoke) estela ♦ vt (drag) arrastrar; (follow) seguir la pista de; (follow closely) vigilar ♦ vi arrastrarse; **to be on sb's ~** seguir la pista de algn.
►**trail away, trail off** vi (sound) desvanecerse; (interest, voice) desaparecer.
►**trail behind** vi quedar a la zaga.
trailer ['treɪlə*] n (AUT) remolque m; (caravan) caravana; (CINE) trailer m, avance m.
trail truck n (US) trailer m.
train [treɪn] n tren m; (of dress) cola; (series): **~ of events** curso de los acontecimientos ♦ vt (educate) formar; (teach skills to) adiestrar; (sportsman) entrenar; (dog) amaestrar; (point: gun

etc): **to ~ on** apuntar a ♦ vi (SPORT) entrenarse; (be educated, learn a skill) formarse; **to go by ~** ir en tren; **one's ~ of thought** el razonamiento de algn; **to ~ sb to do sth** enseñar a algn a hacer algo.
train attendant n (US RAIL) empleado/a de coches-cama.
trained [treɪnd] adj (worker) cualificado; (animal) amaestrado.
trainee [treɪ'niː] n trabajador(a) m/f en prácticas ♦ cpd: **he's a ~ teacher** (primary) es estudiante de magisterio; (secondary) está haciendo las prácticas del I.C.E.
trainer ['treɪnə*] n (SPORT) entrenador(a) m/f; (of animals) domador(a) m/f; **~s** npl (shoes) zapatillas fpl (de deporte).
training ['treɪnɪŋ] n formación f; entrenamiento; **to be in ~** (SPORT) estar entrenando; (: fit) estar en forma.
training college n (gen) colegio de formación profesional; (for teachers) escuela normal.
training course n curso de formación.
traipse [treɪps] vi andar penosamente.
trait [treɪt] n rasgo.
traitor ['treɪtə*] n traidor(a) m/f.
trajectory [trə'dʒɛktərɪ] n trayectoria, curso.
tram [træm] n (BRIT: also: **~car**) tranvía m.
tramline ['træmlaɪn] n carril m de tranvía.
tramp [træmp] n (person) vagabundo/a; (col: offensive: woman) puta ♦ vi andar con pasos pesados.
trample ['træmpl] vt: **to ~ (underfoot)** pisotear.
trampoline ['træmpəliːn] n trampolín m.
trance [trɑːns] n trance m; **to go into a ~** entrar en trance.
tranquil ['træŋkwɪl] adj tranquilo.
tranquillity, (US) **tranquility** [træŋ'kwɪlɪtɪ] n tranquilidad f.
tranquillizer, (US) **tranquilizer** ['træŋkwɪlaɪzə*] n (MED) tranquilizante m.
trans- [trænz] pref trans-, tras-.
transact [træn'zækt] vt (business) tramitar.
transaction [træn'zækʃən] n transacción f, operación f; **cash ~s** transacciones al contado.
transatlantic ['trænzət'læntɪk] adj transatlántico.
transcend [træn'sɛnd] vt rebasar.
transcendent [træn'sɛndənt] adj trascendente.
transcendental [trænsɛn'dɛntl] adj: **~ meditation** meditación f transcendental.
transcribe [træn'skraɪb] vt transcribir, copiar.
transcript ['trænskrɪpt] n copia.

transcription [træn'skrɪpʃən] *n* transcripción *f.*

transept ['trænsɛpt] *n* crucero.

transfer *n* ['trænsfəʳ] transferencia; (*SPORT*) traspaso; (*picture, design*) calcomanía ♦ *vt* [træns'fəːʳ] trasladar, pasar; **to ~ the charges** (*BRIT TEL*) llamar a cobro revertido; **by bank ~** por transferencia bancaria *or* giro bancario; **to ~ money from one account to another** transferir dinero de una cuenta a otra; **to ~ sth to sb's name** transferir algo al nombre de algn.

transferable [træns'fəːrəbl] *adj*: **not ~** intransferible.

transfix [træns'fɪks] *vt* traspasar; (*fig*): **~ed with fear** paralizado por el miedo.

transform [træns'fɔːm] *vt* transformar.

transformation [trænsfə'meɪʃən] *n* transformación *f.*

transformer [træns'fɔːməʳ] *n* (*ELEC*) transformador *m.*

transfusion [træns'fjuːʒən] *n* transfusión *f.*

transgress [træns'grɛs] *vt* (*go beyond*) traspasar; (*violate*) violar, infringir.

tranship [træn'ʃɪp] *vt* trasbordar.

transient ['trænzɪənt] *adj* transitorio.

transistor [træn'zɪstəʳ] *n* (*ELEC*) transistor *m.*

transistorized [træn'zɪstəraɪzd] *adj* (*circuit*) transistorizado.

transistor radio *n* transistor *m.*

transit ['trænzɪt] *n*: **in ~** en tránsito.

transit camp *n* campamento de tránsito.

transition [træn'zɪʃən] *n* transición *f.*

transitional [træn'zɪʃənl] *adj* transitorio.

transition period *n* período de transición.

transitive ['trænzɪtɪv] *adj* (*LING*) transitivo.

transitively ['trænzɪtɪvlɪ] *adv* transitivamente.

transitory ['trænzɪtərɪ] *adj* transitorio.

transit visa *n* visado de tránsito.

translate [trænz'leɪt] *vt*: **to ~ (from/into)** traducir (de/a).

translation [trænz'leɪʃən] *n* traducción *f.*

translator [trænz'leɪtəʳ] *n* traductor(a) *m/f.*

translucent [trænz'luːsnt] *adj* traslúcido.

transmission [trænz'mɪʃən] *n* transmisión *f.*

transmit [trænz'mɪt] *vt* transmitir.

transmitter [trænz'mɪtəʳ] *n* transmisor *m*; (*station*) emisora.

transparency [træns'pɛərnsɪ] *n* (*BRIT PHOT*) diapositiva.

transparent [træns'pærnt] *adj* transparente.

transpire [træns'paɪəʳ] *vi* (*turn out*) resultar (ser); (*happen*) ocurrir, suceder; (*become known*): **it finally ~d that ...** por fin se supo que ....

transplant *vt* [træns'plɑːnt] transplantar ♦ *n* ['trænsplɑːnt] (*MED*) transplante *m*; **to have a heart ~** hacerse un transplante de corazón.

transport *n* ['trænspɔːt] transporte *m* ♦ *vt* [træns'pɔːt] transportar; **public ~** transporte *m* público.

transportable [træns'pɔːtəbl] *adj* transportable.

transportation [trænspɔː'teɪʃən] *n* transporte *m*; (*of prisoners*) deportación *f.*

transport café *n* (*BRIT*) bar-restaurante *m* de carretera.

transpose [træns'pəuz] *vt* transponer.

transsexual [trænz'sɛksjuəl] *adj, n* transexual *m/f.*

transverse ['trænzvəːs] *adj* transverso, transversal.

transvestite [trænz'vɛstaɪt] *n* travesti *m/f.*

trap [træp] *n* (*snare, trick*) trampa; (*carriage*) cabriolé *m* ♦ *vt* coger (*SP*) *or* agarrar (*LAM*) en una trampa; (*immobilize*) bloquear; (*jam*) atascar; **to set** *or* **lay a ~ (for sb)** poner(le) una trampa (a algn); **to ~ one's finger in the door** pillarse el dedo en la puerta.

trap door *n* escotilla.

trapeze [trə'piːz] *n* trapecio.

trapper ['træpəʳ] *n* trampero, cazador *m.*

trappings ['træpɪŋz] *npl* adornos *mpl.*

trash [træʃ] *n* basura; (*nonsense*) tonterías *fpl.*

trash can *n* (*US*) cubo, balde *m* (*LAM*) *or* bote *m* (*LAM*) de la basura.

trash can liner *n* (*US*) bolsa de basura.

trashy ['træʃɪ] *adj* (*col*) chungo.

trauma ['trɔːmə] *n* trauma *m.*

traumatic [trɔː'mætɪk] *adj* (*PSYCH, fig*) traumático.

travel ['trævl] *n* viaje *m* ♦ *vi* viajar ♦ *vt* (*distance*) recorrer; **this wine doesn't ~ well** este vino pierde con los viajes.

travel agency *n* agencia de viajes.

travel agent *n* agente *m/f* de viajes.

travel brochure *n* folleto turístico.

traveller, (*US*) **traveler** ['trævləʳ] *n* viajero/a; (*COMM*) viajante *m/f.*

traveller's cheque, (*US*) **traveler's check** *n* cheque *m* de viaje.

travelling, (*US*) **traveling** ['trævlɪŋ] *n* los viajes, el viajar ♦ *adj* (*circus, exhibition*) ambulante ♦ *cpd* (*bag, clock*) de viaje.

travel(l)ing expenses *npl* dietas *fpl.*

travel(l)ing salesman *n* viajante *m.*

travelogue ['trævəlɔg] *n* (*book*) relación *f* de viajes; (*film*) documental *m* de viajes;

(talk) recuento de viajes.
travel sickness *n* mareo.
traverse ['trævəs] *vt* atravesar.
travesty ['trævəstı] *n* parodia.
trawler ['trɔːlə*] *n* pesquero de arrastre.
tray [treı] *n* (*for carrying*) bandeja; (*on desk*) cajón *m*.
treacherous ['trɛtʃərəs] *adj* traidor(a); **road conditions are** ~ el estado de las carreteras es peligroso.
treachery ['trɛtʃərı] *n* traición *f*.
treacle ['triːkl] *n* (*BRIT*) melaza.
tread [trɛd] *n* paso, pisada; (*of tyre*) banda de rodadura ♦ *vi* (*pt* **trod**, *pp* **trodden** [trɔd, 'trɔdn]) pisar.
▶**tread on** *vt fus* pisar.
treas. *abbr* = **treasurer**.
treason ['triːzn] *n* traición *f*.
treasure ['trɛʒə*] *n* tesoro ♦ *vt* (*value*) apreciar, valorar.
treasure hunt *n* caza del tesoro.
treasurer ['trɛʒərə*] *n* tesorero/a.
treasury ['trɛʒərı] *n*: **the T~**, (*US*) **the T~ Department** ≈ el Ministerio de Economía y de Hacienda.
treasury bill *n* bono del Tesoro.
treat [triːt] *n* (*present*) regalo; (*pleasure*) placer *m* ♦ *vt* tratar; (*consider*) considerar; **to give sb a** ~ hacer un regalo a algn; **to ~ sb to sth** invitar a algn a algo; **to ~ sth as a joke** tomar algo a broma.
treatise ['triːtız] *n* tratado.
treatment ['triːtmənt] *n* tratamiento; **to have** ~ **for sth** recibir tratamiento por algo.
treaty ['triːtı] *n* tratado.
treble ['trɛbl] *adj* triple ♦ *vt* triplicar ♦ *vi* triplicarse.
treble clef *n* (*MUS*) clave *f* de sol.
tree [triː] *n* árbol *m*.
tree-lined ['triːlaınd] *adj* bordeado de árboles.
tree trunk *n* tronco de árbol.
trek [trɛk] *n* (*long journey*) expedición *f*; (*tiring walk*) caminata.
trellis ['trɛlıs] *n* enrejado.
tremble ['trɛmbl] *vi* temblar.
trembling ['trɛmblıŋ] *n* temblor *m* ♦ *adj* tembloroso.
tremendous [trı'mɛndəs] *adj* tremendo; (*enormous*) enorme; (*excellent*) estupendo.
tremendously [trı'mɛndəslı] *adv* enormemente, sobremanera; **he enjoyed it** ~ lo disfrutó de lo lindo.
tremor ['trɛmə*] *n* temblor *m*; (*also*: **earth ~**) temblor *m* de tierra.
trench [trɛntʃ] *n* zanja; (*MIL*) trinchera.
trench coat *n* trinchera.

trench warfare *n* guerra de trincheras.
trend [trɛnd] *n* (*tendency*) tendencia; (*of events*) curso; (*fashion*) moda; ~ **towards/away from sth** tendencia hacia/ en contra de algo; **to set the** ~ marcar la pauta.
trendy ['trɛndı] *adj* de moda.
trepidation [trɛpı'deıʃən] *n* inquietud *f*.
trespass ['trɛspəs] *vi*: **to** ~ **on** entrar sin permiso en; **"no ~ing"** "prohibido el paso".
trespasser ['trɛspəsə*] *n* intruso/a *m/f*; **"~s will be prosecuted"** "se procesará a los intrusos".
tress [trɛs] *n* guedeja.
trestle ['trɛsl] *n* caballete *m*.
trestle table *n* mesa de caballete.
tri- [traı] *pref* tri-.
trial ['traıəl] *n* (*LAW*) juicio, proceso; (*test: of machine etc*) prueba; (*hardship*) desgracia; ~**s** *npl* (*ATHLETICS, of horses*) pruebas *fpl*; **to bring sb to** ~ (**for a crime**) llevar a algn a juicio (por un delito); ~ **by jury** juicio ante jurado; **to be sent for** ~ ser remitido al tribunal; **by** ~ **and error** a fuerza de probar.
trial balance *n* balance *m* de comprobación.
trial basis *n*: **on a** ~ a modo de prueba.
trial offer *n* oferta de prueba.
trial run *n* prueba.
triangle ['traıæŋgl] *n* (*MATH, MUS*) triángulo.
triangular [traı'æŋgjulə*] *adj* triangular.
triathlon [traı'æθlən] *n* triatlón *m*.
tribal ['traıbəl] *adj* tribal.
tribe [traıb] *n* tribu *f*.
tribesman ['traıbzmən] *n* miembro de una tribu.
tribulation [trıbju'leıʃən] *n* tribulación *f*.
tribunal [traı'bjuːnl] *n* tribunal *m*.
tributary ['trıbjuːtərı] *n* (*river*) afluente *m*.
tribute ['trıbjuːt] *n* homenaje *m*, tributo; **to pay** ~ **to** rendir homenaje a.
trice [traıs] *n*: **in a** ~ en un santiamén.
trick [trık] *n* trampa; (*conjuring* ~, *deceit*) truco; (*joke*) broma; (*CARDS*) baza ♦ *vt* engañar; **it's a** ~ **of the light** es una ilusión óptica; **to play a** ~ **on sb** gastar una broma a algn; **that should do the** ~ eso servirá; **to** ~ **sb out of sth** quitarle algo a algn con engaños; **to** ~ **sb into doing sth** hacer que algn haga algo con engaños.
trickery ['trıkərı] *n* engaño.
trickle ['trıkl] *n* (*of water etc*) hilo ♦ *vi* gotear.
trick question *n* pregunta capciosa.

trickster ['trɪkstə*] n estafador(a) m/f.

tricky ['trɪkɪ] adj difícil; (*problem*) delicado.

tricycle ['traɪsɪkl] n triciclo.

tried [traɪd] adj probado.

trifle ['traɪfl] n bagatela; (*CULIN*) dulce de bizcocho, gelatina, fruta y natillas ♦ adv: **a ~ long** un pelín largo ♦ vi: **to ~ with** jugar con.

trifling ['traɪflɪŋ] adj insignificante.

trigger ['trɪgə*] n (*of gun*) gatillo.

▶**trigger off** vt desencadenar.

trigonometry [trɪgə'nɒmətrɪ] n trigonometría.

trilby ['trɪlbɪ] n (*also*: ~ **hat**) sombrero flexible or tirolés.

trill [trɪl] n (*of bird*) gorjeo; (*MUS*) trino.

trilogy ['trɪlədʒɪ] n trilogía.

trim [trɪm] adj (*elegant*) aseado; (*house, garden*) en buen estado; (*figure*): **to be ~** tener buen talle ♦ n (*haircut etc*) recorte m ♦ vt (*neaten*) arreglar; (*cut*) recortar; (*decorate*) adornar; (*NAUT: a sail*) orientar; **to keep in (good)** ~ mantener en buen estado.

trimmings ['trɪmɪŋz] npl (*extras*) accesorios mpl; (*cuttings*) recortes mpl.

Trinidad and Tobago [trɪnɪdæd-] n Trinidad f y Tobago.

Trinity ['trɪnɪtɪ] n: **the ~** la Trinidad.

trinket ['trɪŋkɪt] n chuchería, baratija.

trio ['triːəu] n trío.

trip [trɪp] n viaje m; (*excursion*) excursión f; (*stumble*) traspié m ♦ vi (*stumble*) tropezar; (*go lightly*) andar a paso ligero; **on a ~** de viaje.

▶**trip over** vt fus tropezar con.

▶**trip up** vi tropezar, caerse ♦ vt hacer tropezar or caer.

tripartite [traɪ'pɑːtaɪt] adj (*agreement, talks*) tripartito.

tripe [traɪp] n (*CULIN*) callos mpl; (*pej: rubbish*) bobadas fpl.

triple ['trɪpl] adj triple ♦ adv: ~ **the distance/the speed** 3 veces la distancia/la velocidad.

triple jump n triple salto.

triplets ['trɪplɪts] npl trillizos/as m/fpl.

triplicate ['trɪplɪkət] n: **in** ~ por triplicado.

tripod ['traɪpɒd] n trípode m.

Tripoli ['trɪpəlɪ] n Trípoli m.

tripper ['trɪpə*] n turista m/f, excursionista m/f.

tripwire ['trɪpwaɪə*] n cable m de trampa.

trite [traɪt] adj trillado.

triumph ['traɪʌmf] n triunfo ♦ vi: **to ~ (over)** vencer.

triumphal [traɪ'ʌmfl] adj triunfal.

triumphant [traɪ'ʌmfənt] adj triunfante.

triumphantly [traɪ'ʌmfəntlɪ] adv triunfalmente, en tono triunfal.

trivia ['trɪvɪə] npl trivialidades fpl.

trivial ['trɪvɪəl] adj insignificante, trivial.

triviality [trɪvɪ'ælɪtɪ] n insignificancia, trivialidad f.

trivialize ['trɪvɪəlaɪz] vt trivializar.

trod [trɒd] pt of **tread**.

trodden ['trɒdn] pp of **tread**.

trolley ['trɒlɪ] n carrito; (*in hospital*) camilla.

trolley bus n trolebús m.

trombone [trɒm'bəun] n trombón m.

troop [truːp] n grupo, banda; *see also* **troops**.

▶**troop in** vi entrar en tropel.

▶**troop out** vi salir en tropel.

troop carrier n (*plane*) transporte m (*militar*); (*NAUT: also*: **troopship**) (buque m de) transporte m.

trooper ['truːpə*] n (*MIL*) soldado (de caballería); (*US: policeman*) policía m/f montado/a.

trooping the colour ['truːpɪŋ-] n (*ceremony*) presentación f de la bandera.

troopship ['truːpʃɪp] n (buque m de) transporte m.

trophy ['trəufɪ] n trofeo.

tropic ['trɒpɪk] n trópico; **the ~s** los trópicos, la zona tropical; **T~ of Cancer/Capricorn** trópico de Cáncer/Capricornio.

tropical ['trɒpɪkl] adj tropical.

trot [trɒt] n trote m ♦ vi trotar; **on the** ~ (*BRIT fig*) seguidos/as.

▶**trot out** vt (*excuse, reason*) volver a usar; (*names, facts*) sacar a relucir.

trouble ['trʌbl] n problema m, dificultad f; (*worry*) preocupación f; (*bother, effort*) molestia, esfuerzo; (*unrest*) inquietud f; (*with machine etc*) fallo, avería; (*MED*): **stomach** ~ problemas mpl gástricos ♦ vt molestar; (*worry*) preocupar, inquietar ♦ vi: **to** ~ **to do sth** molestarse en hacer algo; ~**s** npl (*POL etc*) conflictos mpl; **to be in** ~ estar en un apuro; (*for doing wrong*) tener problemas; **to have** ~ **doing sth** tener dificultad en or para hacer algo; **to go to the** ~ **of doing sth** tomarse la molestia de hacer algo; **what's the** ~? ¿qué pasa?; **the** ~ **is ...** el problema es ..., lo que pasa es ...; **please don't** ~ **yourself** por favor no se moleste.

troubled ['trʌbld] adj (*person*) preocupado; (*epoch, life*) agitado.

trouble-free ['trʌblfriː] adj sin problemas or dificultades.

troublemaker ['trʌblmeɪkə*] n agitador(a) m/f.

troubleshooter ['trʌblʃuːtə*] n (*in conflict*)

mediador(a) *m/f*.

troublesome ['trʌblsəm] *adj* molesto, inoportuno.

trouble spot *n* centro de fricción, punto caliente.

troubling ['trʌblɪŋ] *adj* (*thought*) preocupante; **these are ~ times** son malos tiempos.

trough [trɔf] *n* (*also*: **drinking ~**) abrevadero; (*also*: **feeding ~**) comedero; (*channel*) canal *m*.

trounce [trauns] *vt* dar una paliza a.

troupe [tru:p] *n* grupo.

trouser press *n* prensa para pantalones.

trousers ['trauzəz] *npl* pantalones *mpl*; **short ~** pantalones *mpl* cortos.

trouser suit *n* traje *m* de chaqueta y pantalón.

trousseau, *pl* **~x** *or* **~s** ['tru:səu, -z] *n* ajuar *m*.

trout [traut] *n* (*pl inv*) trucha.

trowel ['trauəl] *n* paleta.

truant ['truənt] *n*: **to play ~** (*BRIT*) hacer novillos.

truce [tru:s] *n* tregua.

truck [trʌk] *n* (*US*) camión *m*; (*RAIL*) vagón *m*.

truck driver *n* camionero/a.

trucker ['trʌkə*] *n* (*esp US*) camionero/a.

truck farm *n* (*US*) huerto de hortalizas.

trucking ['trʌkɪŋ] *n* (*esp US*) transporte *m* en camión.

trucking company *n* (*US*) compañía de transporte por carretera.

truckload ['trʌkləud] *n* camión *m* lleno.

truculent ['trʌkjulənt] *adj* agresivo.

trudge [trʌdʒ] *vi* caminar penosamente.

true [tru:] *adj* verdadero; (*accurate*) exacto; (*genuine*) auténtico; (*faithful*) fiel; (*wheel*) centrado; (*wall*) a plomo; (*beam*) alineado; **~ to life** verídico; **to come ~** realizarse, cumplirse.

truffle ['trʌfl] *n* trufa.

truly ['tru:lɪ] *adv* realmente; (*faithfully*) fielmente; **yours ~** (*in letter-writing*) atentamente.

trump [trʌmp] *n* (*CARDS*) triunfo; **to turn up ~s** (*fig*) salir *or* resultar bien.

trump card *n* triunfo; (*fig*) baza.

trumped-up ['trʌmptʌp] *adj* inventado.

trumpet ['trʌmpɪt] *n* trompeta.

truncated [trʌŋ'keɪtɪd] *adj* truncado.

truncheon ['trʌntʃən] *n* (*BRIT*) porra.

trundle ['trʌndl] *vt*, *vi*: **to ~ along** rodar haciendo ruido.

trunk [trʌŋk] *n* (*of tree, person*) tronco; (*of elephant*) trompa; (*case*) baúl *m*; (*US AUT*) maletero, baúl *m* (*LAM*); *see also* **trunks**.

trunk call *n* (*BRIT TEL*) llamada interurbana.

trunk road *n* carretera principal.

trunks [trʌŋks] *npl* (*also*: **swimming ~**) bañador *m*.

truss [trʌs] *n* (*MED*) braguero ♦ *vt*: **to ~ (up)** atar.

trust [trʌst] *n* confianza; (*COMM*) trust *m*; (*LAW*) fideicomiso ♦ *vt* (*rely on*) tener confianza en; (*entrust*): **to ~ sth to sb** confiar algo a algn; (*hope*): **to ~ (that)** esperar (que); **in ~** en fideicomiso; **you'll have to take it on ~** tienes que aceptarlo a ojos cerrados.

trust company *n* banco fideicomisario.

trusted ['trʌstɪd] *adj* de confianza, fiable, de fiar.

trustee [trʌs'ti:] *n* (*LAW*) fideicomisario.

trustful ['trʌstful] *adj* confiado.

trust fund *n* fondo fiduciario *or* de fideicomiso.

trusting ['trʌstɪŋ] *adj* confiado.

trustworthy ['trʌstwɜ:ðɪ] *adj* digno de confianza, fiable, de fiar.

trusty ['trʌstɪ] *adj* fiel.

truth, **~s** [tru:θ, tru:ðz] *n* verdad *f*.

truthful ['tru:θfəl] *adj* (*person*) sincero; (*account*) fidedigno.

truthfully ['tru:θfulɪ] *adv* (*answer*) con sinceridad.

truthfulness ['tru:θfulnɪs] *n* (*of account*) verdad *f*; (*of person*) sinceridad *f*.

try [traɪ] *n* tentativa, intento; (*RUGBY*) ensayo ♦ *vt* (*LAW*) juzgar, procesar; (*test: sth new*) probar, someter a prueba; (*attempt*) intentar; (*strain: patience*) hacer perder ♦ *vi* probar; **to give sth a ~** intentar hacer algo; **to ~ one's (very) best** *or* **hardest** poner todo su empeño, esmerarse; **to ~ to do sth** intentar hacer algo.

▶**try on** *vt* (*clothes*) probarse.

▶**try out** *vt* probar, poner a prueba.

trying ['traɪɪŋ] *adj* cansado; (*person*) pesado.

tsar [zɑ:*] *n* zar *m*.

T-shirt ['ti:ʃɜ:t] *n* camiseta.

T-square ['ti:skwɛə*] *n* regla en T.

TT *adj abbr* (*BRIT col*) = **teetotal** ♦ *abbr* (*US*) = **Trust Territory**.

tub [tʌb] *n* cubo (*SP*), balde *m* (*LAM*); (*bath*) bañera, tina (*esp LAM*).

tuba ['tju:bə] *n* tuba.

tubby ['tʌbɪ] *adj* regordete.

tube [tju:b] *n* tubo; (*BRIT: underground*) metro; (*US col: television*) tele *f*.

tubeless ['tju:blɪs] *adj* (*tyre*) sin cámara.

tuber ['tju:bə*] *n* (*BOT*) tubérculo.

tuberculosis [tjubə:kju'ləusɪs] *n*

tuberculosis *f inv.*

tube station *n* (*BRIT*) estación *f* de metro.

tubing ['tju:bɪŋ] *n* tubería (*SP*), cañería; **a piece of** ~ un trozo de tubo.

tubular ['tju:bjulə*] *adj* tubular.

TUC *n abbr* (*BRIT*: = *Trades Union Congress*) federación nacional de sindicatos.

tuck [tʌk] *n* (*SEWING*) pliegue *m* ♦ *vt* (*put*) poner.

►**tuck away** *vt* esconder.

►**tuck in** *vt* meter; (*child*) arropar ♦ *vi* (*eat*) comer con apetito.

►**tuck up** *vt* (*child*) arropar.

tuck shop *n* (*SCOL*) tienda de golosinas.

Tue(s). *abbr* (= *Tuesday*) mart.

Tuesday ['tju:zdɪ] *n* martes *m inv*; **on** ~ el martes; **on** ~**s** los martes; **every** ~ todos los martes; **every other** ~ cada dos martes, un martes sí y otro no; **last/next** ~ el martes pasado/próximo; **a week/fortnight on** ~, ~ **week/fortnight** del martes en 8/15 días, del martes en una semana/dos semanas.

tuft [tʌft] *n* mechón *m*; (*of grass etc*) manojo.

tug [tʌg] *n* (*ship*) remolcador *m* ♦ *vt* remolcar.

tug-of-love [tʌgəv'lʌv] *n*: ~ **children** hijos envueltos en el litigio de los padres por su custodia.

tug-of-war [tʌgəv'wɔː*] *n* juego de la cuerda.

tuition [tju:'ɪʃən] *n* (*BRIT*) enseñanza; (: *private* ~) clases *fpl* particulares; (*US: school fees*) matrícula.

tulip ['tju:lɪp] *n* tulipán *m*.

tumble ['tʌmbl] *n* (*fall*) caída ♦ *vi* caerse, tropezar; **to** ~ **to sth** (*col*) caer en la cuenta de algo.

tumbledown ['tʌmbldaun] *adj* ruinoso.

tumble dryer *n* (*BRIT*) secadora.

tumbler ['tʌmblə*] *n* vaso.

tummy ['tʌmɪ] *n* (*col*) barriga, vientre *m*.

tumour, (*US*) **tumor** ['tju:mə*] *n* tumor *m*.

tumult ['tju:mʌlt] *n* tumulto.

tumultuous [tju:'mʌltjuəs] *adj* tumultuoso.

tuna ['tju:nə] *n* (*pl inv*) (*also*: ~ **fish**) atún *m*.

tundra ['tʌndrə] *n* tundra.

tune [tju:n] *n* (*melody*) melodía ♦ *vt* (*MUS*) afinar; (*RADIO, TV, AUT*) sintonizar; **to be in/out of** ~ (*instrument*) estar afinado/desafinado; (*singer*) afinar/desafinar; **to be in/out of** ~ **with** (*fig*) armonizar/desentonar con; **to the** ~ **of** (*fig: amount*) por (la) cantidad de.

►**tune in** *vi* (*RADIO, TV*): **to** ~ **in (to)** sintonizar (con).

►**tune up** *vi* (*musician*) afinar (su instrumento).

tuneful ['tju:nful] *adj* melodioso.

tuner ['tju:nə*] *n* (*radio set*) sintonizador *m*; **piano** ~ afinador(a) *m/f* de pianos.

tungsten ['tʌŋstn] *n* tungsteno.

tunic ['tju:nɪk] *n* túnica.

tuning ['tju:nɪŋ] *n* sintonización *f*; (*MUS*) afinación *f*.

tuning fork *n* diapasón *m*.

Tunis ['tju:nɪs] *n* Túnez *m*.

Tunisia [tju:'nɪzɪə] *n* Túnez *m*.

Tunisian [tju:'nɪzɪən] *adj*, *n* tunecino/a *m/f*.

tunnel ['tʌnl] *n* túnel *m*; (*in mine*) galería ♦ *vi* construir un túnel/una galería.

tunnel vision *n* (*MED*) visión *f* periférica restringida; (*fig*) estrechez *f* de miras.

tunny ['tʌnɪ] *n* atún *m*.

turban ['tə:bən] *n* turbante *m*.

turbid ['tə:bɪd] *adj* turbio.

turbine ['tə:baɪn] *n* turbina.

turbo ['tə:bəu] *n* turbo.

turboprop ['tə:bəuprɔp] *n* turbohélice *m*.

turbot ['tə:bət] *n* (*pl inv*) rodaballo.

turbulence ['tə:bjuləns] *n* (*AVIAT*) turbulencia.

turbulent ['tə:bjulənt] *adj* turbulento.

tureen [tə'ri:n] *n* sopera.

turf [tə:f] *n* césped *m*; (*clod*) tepe *m* ♦ *vt* cubrir con césped.

►**turf out** *vt* (*col*) echar a la calle.

turf accountant *n* corredor(a) *m/f* de apuestas.

turgid ['tə:dʒɪd] *adj* (*prose*) pesado.

Turin [tjuə'rɪn] *n* Turín *m*.

Turk [tə:k] *n* turco/a.

Turkey ['tə:kɪ] *n* Turquía.

turkey ['tə:kɪ] *n* pavo.

Turkish ['tə:kɪʃ] *adj* turco ♦ *n* (*LING*) turco.

Turkish bath *n* baño turco.

turmeric ['tə:mərɪk] *n* cúrcuma.

turmoil ['tə:mɔɪl] *n* desorden *m*, alboroto.

turn [tə:n] *n* turno; (*in road*) curva; (*THEAT*) número; (*MED*) ataque *m* ♦ *vt* girar, volver, voltear (*LAM*); (*collar, steak*) dar la vuelta a; (*shape: wood, metal*) tornear; (*change*): **to** ~ **sth into** convertir algo en ♦ *vi* volver, voltearse (*LAM*); (*person: look back*) volverse; (*reverse direction*) dar la vuelta, voltear (*LAM*); (*milk*) cortarse; (*change*) cambiar; (*become*): **to** ~ **into sth** convertirse *or* transformarse en algo; **a good** ~ un favor; **it gave me quite a** ~ me dio un susto; **"no left** ~**"** (*AUT*) "prohibido girar a la izquierda"; **it's your** ~ te toca a ti; **in** ~ por turnos; **to take** ~**s** turnarse; **at the** ~ **of the year/century** a fin de año/a finales de siglo; **to take a** ~ **for the worse** (*situation, patient*) empeorar; **they** ~**ed him against us** le pusieron en contra nuestra; **the car ~ed the corner** el coche dobló la esquina; **to ~ left** (*AUT*) torcer *or* girar a la izquierda; **she has no-one to ~ to** no tiene a quién recurrir.

▶**turn away** *vi* apartar la vista ♦ *vt* (*reject: person, business*) rechazar.

▶**turn back** *vi* volverse atrás.

▶**turn down** *vt* (*refuse*) rechazar; (*reduce*) bajar; (*fold*) doblar.

▶**turn in** *vi* (*col: go to bed*) acostarse ♦ *vt* (*fold*) doblar hacia dentro.

▶**turn off** *vi* (*from road*) desviarse ♦ *vt* (*light, radio etc*) apagar; (*engine*) parar.

▶**turn on** *vt* (*light, radio etc*) encender, prender (*LAM*); (*engine*) poner en marcha.

▶**turn out** *vt* (*light, gas*) apagar; (*produce: goods, novel etc*) producir ♦ *vi* (*attend: troops*) presentarse; (*: doctor*) atender; **to ~ out to be ...** resultar ser ....

▶**turn over** *vi* (*person*) volverse ♦ *vt* (*mattress, card*) dar la vuelta a; (*page*) volver.

▶**turn round** *vi* volverse; (*rotate*) girar.

▶**turn to** *vt fus*: **to ~ to sb** acudir a algn.

▶**turn up** *vi* (*person*) llegar, presentarse; (*lost object*) aparecer ♦ *vt* (*radio*) subir, poner más alto; (*heat, gas*) poner más fuerte.

turnabout ['tə:nəbaut], **turnaround** ['tə:nəraund] *n* (*fig*) giro total.

turncoat ['tə:nkəut] *n* renegado/a.

turned-up ['tə:ndʌp] *adj* (*nose*) respingón/ona.

turning ['tə:nɪŋ] *n* (*side road*) bocacalle *f*; (*bend*) curva; **the first ~ on the right** la primera bocacalle a la derecha.

turning point *n* (*fig*) momento decisivo.

turnip ['tə:nɪp] *n* nabo.

turnkey system ['tə:nki:-] *n* (*COMPUT*) sistema *m* de seguridad.

turnout ['tə:naut] *n* asistencia, número de asistentes, público.

turnover ['tə:nəuvə*] *n* (*COMM: amount of money*) facturación *f*; (*: of goods*) movimiento; **there is a rapid ~ in staff** hay mucho movimiento de personal.

turnpike ['tə:npaik] *n* (*US*) autopista de peaje.

turnstile ['tə:nstail] *n* torniquete *m*.

turntable ['tə:nteibl] *n* plato.

turn-up ['tə:nʌp] *n* (*BRIT: on trousers*) vuelta.

turpentine ['tə:pəntain] *n* (*also*: **turps**) trementina.

turquoise ['tə:kwɔiz] *n* (*stone*) turquesa ♦ *adj* color turquesa.

turret ['tʌrit] *n* torreón *m*.

turtle ['tə:tl] *n* tortuga (marina).

turtleneck (sweater) ['tə:tlnɛk-] *n* (jersey *m* de) cuello cisne.

Tuscany ['tʌskəni] *n* Toscana.

tusk [tʌsk] *n* colmillo.

tussle ['tʌsl] *n* lucha, pelea.

tutor ['tju:tə*] *n* profesor(a) *m/f*.

tutorial [tju:'tɔ:riəl] *n* (*SCOL*) seminario.

tuxedo [tʌk'si:dəu] *n* (*US*) smóking *m*, esmoquin *m*.

TV [ti:'vi:] *n abbr* (= *television*) televisión *f*.

TV dinner *n* cena precocinada.

TV licence *n licencia que se paga por el uso del televisor, destinada a financiar la BBC.*

twaddle ['twɔdl] *n* (*col*) tonterías *fpl*.

twang [twæŋ] *n* (*of instrument*) tañido; (*of voice*) timbre *m* nasal.

tweak [twi:k] *vt* (*nose, ear*) pellizcar; (*hair*) tirar.

tweed [twi:d] *n* tweed *m*.

tweezers ['twi:zəz] *npl* pinzas *fpl* (de depilar).

twelfth [twelfθ] *num* duodécimo.

Twelfth Night *n* (Día *m* de) Reyes *mpl*.

twelve [twelv] *num* doce; **at ~ o'clock** (*midday*) a mediodía; (*midnight*) a medianoche.

twentieth ['twentiɪθ] *num* vigésimo.

twenty ['twenti] *num* veinte.

twerp [twə:p] *n* (*col*) idiota *m/f*.

twice [twais] *adv* dos veces; **~ as much** dos veces más, el doble; **she is ~ your age** ella te dobla edad; **~ a week** dos veces a la *or* por semana.

twiddle ['twidl] *vt, vi*: **to ~ (with) sth** dar vueltas a algo; **to ~ one's thumbs** (*fig*) estar de brazos cruzados.

twig [twig] *n* ramita ♦ *vi* (*col*) caer en la cuenta.

twilight ['twailait] *n* crepúsculo; (*morning*) madrugada; **in the ~** en la media luz.

twill [twil] *n* sarga, estameña.

twin [twin] *adj, n* gemelo/a *m/f* ♦ *vt* hermanar.

twin(-bedded) room ['twin('bedid)-] *n* habitación *f* con dos camas.

twin beds *npl* camas *fpl* gemelas.

twin-carburettor ['twinka:bju'retə*] *adj* de dos carburadores.

twine [twain] *n* bramante *m* ♦ *vi* (*plant*) enroscarse.

twin-engined [twin'endʒind] *adj* bimotor; **~ aircraft** avión *m* bimotor.

twinge [twindʒ] *n* (*of pain*) punzada; (*of conscience*) remordimiento.

twinkle ['twiŋkl] *n* centelleo ♦ *vi* centellear; (*eyes*) parpadear.

twin town *n* ciudad *f* hermanada *or*

gemela.

twirl [twə:l] *n* giro ♦ *vt* dar vueltas a
♦ *vi* piruetear.

twist [twɪst] *n* (*action*) torsión *f*; (*in road*,
coil) vuelta; (*in wire, flex*) doblez *f*; (*in
story*) giro ♦ *vt* torcer, retorcer; (*roll
around*) enrollar; (*fig*) deformar ♦ *vi*
serpentear; **to ~ one's ankle/wrist** (*MED*)
torcerse el tobillo/la muñeca.

twisted ['twɪstɪd] *adj* (*wire, rope*) trenzado,
enroscado; (*ankle, wrist*) torcido; (*fig: logic,
mind*) retorcido.

twit [twɪt] *n* (*col*) tonto.

twitch [twɪtʃ] *n* sacudida; (*nervous*) tic *m*
nervioso ♦ *vi* moverse nerviosamente.

two [tu:] *num* dos; **~ by ~**, **in ~s** de dos en
dos; **to put ~ and ~ together** (*fig*) atar
cabos.

two-bit [tu:'bɪt] *adj* (*esp US col, pej*) de poca
monta, de tres al cuarto.

two-door [tu:'dɔ:*] *adj* (*AUT*) de dos
puertas.

two-faced [tu:'feɪst] *adj* (*pej: person*) falso,
hipócrita.

twofold ['tu:fəuld] *adv*: **to increase ~**
duplicarse ♦ *adj* (*increase*) doble; (*reply*) en
dos partes.

two-piece [tu:'pi:s] *n* (*also*: **~ suit**) traje *m*
de dos piezas; (*also*: **~ swimsuit**) dos
piezas *m inv*, bikini *m*.

two-seater [tu:'si:tə*] *n* (*plane, car*) avión
m/coche *m* de dos plazas, biplaza *m*.

twosome ['tu:səm] *n* (*people*) pareja.

two-stroke ['tu:strəuk] *n* (*also*: **~ engine**)
motor *m* de dos tiempos ♦ *adj* de dos
tiempos.

two-tone ['tu:'təun] *adj* (*colour*) bicolor, de
dos tonos.

two-way ['tu:weɪ] *adj*: **~ traffic** circulación
f de dos sentidos; **~ radio** radio *f* emisora
y receptora.

TX *abbr* (*US*) = *Texas*.

tycoon [taɪ'ku:n] *n*: **(business) ~** magnate
m/f.

type [taɪp] *n* (*category*) tipo, género; (*model*)
modelo; (*TYP*) tipo, letra ♦ *vt* (*letter etc*)
escribir a máquina; **what ~ do you want?**
¿qué tipo quieres?; **in bold/italic ~** en
negrita/cursiva.

type-cast ['taɪpkɑ:st] *adj* (*actor*)
encasillado.

typeface ['taɪpfeɪs] *n* tipo de letra.

typescript ['taɪpskrɪpt] *n* texto
mecanografiado.

typeset ['taɪpsɛt] *vt* (*irreg: like set*)
componer.

typesetter ['taɪpsɛtə*] *n* cajista *m/f*.

typewriter ['taɪpraɪtə*] *n* máquina de

escribir.

typewritten ['taɪprɪtn] *adj* mecanografiado.

typhoid ['taɪfɔɪd] *n* (fiebre *f*) tifoidea.

typhoon [taɪ'fu:n] *n* tifón *m*.

typhus ['taɪfəs] *n* tifus *m*.

typical ['tɪpɪkl] *adj* típico.

typically ['tɪpɪklɪ] *adv* típicamente.

typify ['tɪpɪfaɪ] *vt* tipificar.

typing ['taɪpɪŋ] *n* mecanografía.

typing pool *n* (*BRIT*) servicio de
mecanógrafos.

typist ['taɪpɪst] *n* mecanógrafo/a.

typography [taɪ'pɔgrəfɪ] *n* tipografía.

tyranny ['tɪrənɪ] *n* tiranía.

tyrant ['taɪərənt] *n* tirano/a.

tyre, (*US*) **tire** ['taɪə*] *n* neumático, llanta
(*LAM*).

tyre pressure *n* presión *f* de los
neumáticos.

Tyrol [tɪ'rəul] *n* Tirol *m*.

Tyrolean [tɪrə'lɪən], **Tyrolese** [tɪrə'li:z] *adj*
tirolés/esa.

Tyrrhenian Sea [tɪ'ri:nɪən-] *n* Mar *m*
Tirreno.

tzar [zɑ:*] *n* = **tsar.**

U u

U, u [ju:] *n* (*letter*) U, u *f*; **U for Uncle** U de
Uruguay.

U *n abbr* (*BRIT CINE*: = *universal*) todos los
públicos.

UB40 *n abbr* (*BRIT*: = *unemployment benefit
form 40*) número de referencia en la
solicitud de inscripción en la lista de
parados; por extensión, la tarjeta del
paro o su beneficiario.

U-bend ['ju:bɛnd] *n* (*AUT, in pipe*) recodo.

ubiquitous [ju:'bɪkwɪtəs] *adj* omnipresente,
ubicuo.

UCAS ['ju:kæs] *n abbr BRIT*: = *Universities and
Colleges Admissions Service.*

UDA *n abbr* (*BRIT*: = *Ulster Defence
Association*) organización paramilitar
protestante de Irlanda del Norte.

UDC *n abbr* (*BRIT*) = *Urban District Council.*

udder ['ʌdə*] *n* ubre *f*.

UDI *n abbr* (*BRIT POL*) = *unilateral declaration
of independence.*

UDR *n abbr* (*BRIT*: = *Ulster Defence Regiment*)
fuerza de seguridad de Irlanda del Norte.

UEFA [juːˈeɪfə] n abbr (= Union of European Football Associations) U.E.F.A. f.

UFO [ˈjuːfəu] n abbr = (unidentified flying object) OVNI m.

Uganda [juːˈɡændə] n Uganda.

Ugandan [juːˈɡændən] adj de Uganda.

UGC n abbr (BRIT: = University Grants Committee) entidad gubernamental que controla las finanzas de las universidades.

ugh [əːh] excl ¡uf!

ugliness [ˈʌɡlɪnɪs] n fealdad f.

ugly [ˈʌɡlɪ] adj feo; (dangerous) peligroso.

UHF abbr (= ultra-high frequency) UHF f.

UHT adj abbr (= ultra heat treated): ~ **milk** leche f uperizada.

UK n abbr (= United Kingdom) Reino Unido, R.U.

Ukraine [juːˈkreɪn] n Ucrania.

Ukrainian [juːˈkreɪnɪən] adj ucraniano ♦ n ucraniano/a; (LING) ucraniano.

ulcer [ˈʌlsə*] n úlcera; **mouth** ~ úlcera bucal.

Ulster [ˈʌlstə*] n Ulster m.

ulterior [ʌlˈtɪərɪə*] adj ulterior; ~ **motive** segundas intenciones fpl.

ultimate [ˈʌltɪmət] adj último, final; (greatest) mayor ♦ n: **the** ~ **in luxury** el colmo del lujo.

ultimately [ˈʌltɪmətlɪ] adv (in the end) por último, al final; (fundamentally) a fin de cuentas.

ultimatum, pl ~**s** or **ultimata** [ʌltɪˈmeɪtəm, -tə] n ultimátum m.

ultra- [ˈʌltrə] pref ultra-.

ultrasonic [ʌltrəˈsɒnɪk] adj ultrasónico.

ultrasound [ˈʌltrəsaund] n (MED) ultrasonido.

ultraviolet [ˈʌltrəˈvaɪəlɪt] adj ultravioleta.

um [ʌm] interj; (col: in hesitation) esto, este (LAM).

umbilical cord [ʌmbɪˈlaɪkl-] n cordón m umbilical.

umbrage [ˈʌmbrɪdʒ] n: **to take** ~ **(at)** ofenderse (por).

umbrella [ʌmˈbrelə] n paraguas m inv; **under the** ~ **of** (fig) bajo la protección de.

umlaut [ˈumlaut] n diéresis f inv.

umpire [ˈʌmpaɪə*] n árbitro ♦ vt arbitrar.

umpteen [ʌmpˈtiːn] num enésimos/as; **for the** ~**th time** por enésima vez.

UMW n abbr (= United Mineworkers of America) sindicato de mineros.

UN n abbr (= United Nations) ONU f.

un- [ʌn] pref in-; des-; no ...; poco ...; nada ....

unabashed [ʌnəˈbæʃt] adj nada avergonzado.

unabated [ʌnəˈbeɪtɪd] adj: **to continue** ~ seguir con la misma intensidad.

unable [ʌnˈeɪbl] adj: **to be** ~ **to do sth** no poder hacer algo; (not know how to) ser incapaz de hacer algo, no saber hacer algo.

unabridged [ʌnəˈbrɪdʒd] adj íntegro.

unacceptable [ʌnəkˈseptəbl] adj (proposal, behaviour, price) inaceptable; **it's** ~ **that** no se puede aceptar que.

unaccompanied [ʌnəˈkʌmpənɪd] adj no acompañado; (singing, song) sin acompañamiento.

unaccountably [ʌnəˈkauntəblɪ] adv inexplicablemente.

unaccounted [ʌnəˈkauntɪd] adj: **two passengers are** ~ **for** faltan dos pasajeros.

unaccustomed [ʌnəˈkʌstəmd] adj: **to be** ~ **to** no estar acostumbrado a.

unacquainted [ʌnəˈkweɪntɪd] adj: **to be** ~ **with** (facts) desconocer, ignorar.

unadulterated [ʌnəˈdʌltəreɪtɪd] adj (gen) puro; (wine) sin mezcla.

unaffected [ʌnəˈfɛktɪd] adj (person, behaviour) sin afectación, sencillo; (emotionally): **to be** ~ **by** no estar afectado por.

unafraid [ʌnəˈfreɪd] adj: **to be** ~ no tener miedo.

unaided [ʌnˈeɪdɪd] adj sin ayuda, por sí solo.

unanimity [juːnəˈnɪmɪtɪ] n unanimidad f.

unanimous [juːˈnænɪməs] adj unánime.

unanimously [juːˈnænɪməslɪ] adv unánimemente.

unanswered [ʌnˈɑːnsəd] adj (question, letter) sin contestar; (criticism) incontestado.

unappetizing [ʌnˈæpɪtaɪzɪŋ] adj poco apetitoso.

unappreciative [ʌnəˈpriːʃɪətɪv] adj desagradecido.

unarmed [ʌnˈɑːmd] adj (person) desarmado; (combat) sin armas.

unashamed [ʌnəˈʃeɪmd] adj desvergonzado.

unassisted [ʌnəˈsɪstɪd] adj, adv sin ayuda.

unassuming [ʌnəˈsjuːmɪŋ] adj modesto, sin pretensiones.

unattached [ʌnəˈtætʃt] adj (person) soltero; (part etc) suelto.

unattended [ʌnəˈtendɪd] adj (car, luggage) sin atender.

unattractive [ʌnəˈtræktɪv] adj poco atractivo.

unauthorized [ʌnˈɔːθəraɪzd] adj no autorizado.

unavailable [ʌnəˈveɪləbl] adj (article, room,

book) no disponible; (*person*) ocupado.
unavoidable [ʌnə'vɔɪdəbl] *adj* inevitable.
unavoidably [ʌnə'vɔɪdəblɪ] *adv* (*detained*)
por causas ajenas a su voluntad.
unaware [ʌnə'wɛə*] *adj*: **to be ~ of** ignorar.
unawares [ʌnə'wɛəz] *adv* de improviso.
unbalanced [ʌn'bælənst] *adj*
desequilibrado; (*mentally*) trastornado.
unbearable [ʌn'bɛərəbl] *adj* insoportable.
unbeatable [ʌn'biːtəbl] *adj* (*gen*)
invencible; (*price*) inmejorable.
unbeaten [ʌn'biːtn] *adj* (*team*) imbatido;
(*army*) invicto; (*record*) no batido.
unbecoming [ʌnbɪ'kʌmɪŋ] *adj* (*unseemly:
language, behaviour*) indecoroso,
impropio; (*unflattering: garment*) poco
favorecedor(a).
unbeknown(st) [ʌnbɪ'nəun(st)] *adv*: **~ to
me** sin saberlo yo.
unbelief [ʌnbɪ'liːf] *n* incredulidad *f*.
unbelievable [ʌnbɪ'liːvəbl] *adj* increíble.
unbelievingly [ʌnbɪ'liːvɪŋlɪ] *adv* sin creer.
unbend [ʌn'bɛnd] (*irreg: like bend*) *vi* (*fig:
person*) relajarse ♦ *vt* (*wire*) enderezar.
unbending [ʌn'bɛndɪŋ] *adj* (*fig*) inflexible.
unbias(s)ed [ʌn'baɪəst] *adj* imparcial.
unblemished [ʌn'blɛmɪʃt] *adj* sin mancha.
unblock [ʌn'blɔk] *vt* (*pipe*) desatascar;
(*road*) despejar.
unborn [ʌn'bɔːn] *adj* que va a nacer.
unbounded [ʌn'baundɪd] *adj* ilimitado, sin
límite.
unbreakable [ʌn'breɪkəbl] *adj* irrompible.
unbridled [ʌn'braɪdld] *adj* (*fig*)
desenfrenado.
unbroken [ʌn'brəukən] *adj* (*seal*) intacto;
(*series*) continuo, ininterrumpido; (*record*)
no batido; (*spirit*) indómito.
unbuckle [ʌn'bʌkl] *vt* desabrochar.
unburden [ʌn'bɜːdn] *vt*: **to ~ o.s.**
desahogarse.
unbusinesslike [ʌn'bɪznɪslaɪk] *adj* (*trader*)
poco profesional; (*transaction*) incorrecto;
(*fig: person*) poco práctico; (: *without
method*) desorganizado.
unbutton [ʌn'bʌtn] *vt* desabrochar.
uncalled-for [ʌn'kɔːldfɔ:*] *adj* gratuito,
inmerecido.
uncanny [ʌn'kænɪ] *adj* extraño,
extraordinario.
unceasing [ʌn'siːsɪŋ] *adj* incesante.
unceremonious ['ʌnsɛrɪ'məunɪəs] *adj*
(*abrupt, rude*) brusco, hosco.
uncertain [ʌn'sɜːtn] *adj* incierto; (*indecisive*)
indeciso; **it's ~ whether** no se sabe si; **in
no ~ terms** sin dejar lugar a dudas.
uncertainty [ʌn'sɜːtntɪ] *n* incertidumbre *f*.
unchallenged [ʌn'tʃælɪndʒd] *adj* (*LAW etc*)

incontestado; **to go ~** no encontrar
respuesta.
unchanged [ʌn'tʃeɪndʒd] *adj* sin cambiar
or alterar.
uncharitable [ʌn'tʃærɪtəbl] *adj* (*remark,
behaviour*) demasiado duro.
uncharted [ʌn'tʃɑːtɪd] *adj* inexplorado.
unchecked [ʌn'tʃɛkt] *adj* desenfrenado.
uncivil [ʌn'sɪvɪl] *adj* descortés, grosero.
uncivilized [ʌn'sɪvɪlaɪzd] *adj* (*gen*) inculto,
poco civilizado; (*fig: behaviour etc*)
bárbaro.
uncle ['ʌŋkl] *n* tío.
unclear [ʌn'klɪə*] *adj* poco claro; **I'm still ~
about what I'm supposed to do** todavía
no tengo muy claro lo que tengo que
hacer.
uncoil [ʌn'kɔɪl] *vt* desenrollar ♦ *vi*
desenrollarse.
uncomfortable [ʌn'kʌmfətəbl] *adj*
incómodo; (*uneasy*) inquieto.
uncomfortably [ʌn'kʌmfətəblɪ] *adv*
(*uneasily: say*) con inquietud; (: *think*) con
remordimiento *or* nerviosismo.
uncommitted [ʌnkə'mɪtɪd] *adj* (*attitude,
country*) no comprometido; **to remain ~ to**
(*policy, party*) no comprometerse a.
uncommon [ʌn'kɔmən] *adj* poco común,
raro.
uncommunicative [ʌnkə'mjuːnɪkətɪv] *adj*
poco comunicativo, reservado.
uncomplicated [ʌn'kɔmplɪkeɪtɪd] *adj* sin
complicaciones.
uncompromising [ʌn'kɔmprəmaɪzɪŋ] *adj*
intransigente.
unconcerned [ʌnkən'sɜːnd] *adj* indiferente;
to be ~ about ser indiferente a, no
preocuparse de.
unconditional [ʌnkən'dɪʃənl] *adj*
incondicional.
uncongenial [ʌnkən'dʒiːnɪəl] *adj*
desagradable.
unconnected [ʌnkə'nɛktɪd] *adj* (*unrelated*):
to be ~ with no estar relacionado con.
unconscious [ʌn'kɔnʃəs] *adj* sin sentido;
(*unaware*) inconsciente ♦ *n*: **the ~** el
inconsciente; **to knock sb ~** dejar a algn
sin sentido.
unconsciously [ʌn'kɔnʃəslɪ] *adv*
inconscientemente.
unconsciousness [ʌn'kɔnʃəsnɪs] *n*
inconsciencia.
unconstitutional [ʌnkɔnstɪ'tjuːʃənl] *adj*
anti-constitucional.
uncontested [ʌnkən'tɛstɪd] *adj* (*champion*)
incontestado; (*PARLIAMENT: seat*) ganado
sin oposición.
uncontrollable [ʌnkən'trəuləbl] *adj* (*temper*)

indomable; (*laughter*) incontenible.

uncontrolled [ʌnkən'trəuld] *adj* (*child, dog, emotion*) incontrolado; (*inflation, price rises*) desenfrenado.

unconventional [ʌnkən'vɛnʃənl] *adj* poco convencional.

unconvinced [ʌnkən'vɪnst] *adj*: **to be** *or* **remain** ~ seguir sin convencerse.

unconvincing [ʌnkən'vɪnsɪŋ] *adj* poco convincente.

uncork [ʌn'kɔːk] *vt* descorchar.

uncorroborated [ʌnkə'rɔbəreɪtɪd] *adj* no confirmado.

uncouth [ʌn'kuːθ] *adj* grosero, inculto.

uncover [ʌn'kʌvə*] *vt* (*gen*) descubrir; (*take lid off*) destapar.

undamaged [ʌn'dæmɪdʒd] *adj* (*goods*) en buen estado; (*fig: reputation*) intacto.

undaunted [ʌn'dɔːntɪd] *adj*: ~ **by** sin dejarse desanimar por.

undecided [ʌndɪ'saɪdɪd] *adj* (*character*) indeciso; (*question*) no resuelto, pendiente.

undelivered [ʌndɪ'lɪvəd] *adj* no entregado al destinatario; **if** ~ **return to sender** en caso de no llegar a su destino devolver al remitente.

undeniable [ʌndɪ'naɪəbl] *adj* innegable.

undeniably [ʌndɪ'naɪəblɪ] *adv* innegablemente.

under ['ʌndə*] *prep* debajo de; (*less than*) menos que; (*according to*) según, de acuerdo con ♦ *adv* debajo, abajo; ~ **there** ahí debajo; ~ **construction** en construcción; en obras; ~ **the circumstances** dadas las circunstancias; **in** ~ **2 hours** en menos de dos horas; ~ **anaesthetic** bajo los efectos de la anestesia; ~ **discussion** en discusión, sobre el tapete.

under... [ʌndə*] *pref* sub....

under-age [ʌndər'eɪdʒ] *adj* menor de edad.

underarm ['ʌndəraːm] *n* axila, sobaco ♦ *cpd*: ~ **deodorant** desodorante *m* corporal.

undercapitalised [ʌndə'kæpɪtəlaɪzd] *adj* descapitalizado.

undercarriage ['ʌndəkærɪdʒ] *n* (*BRIT AVIAT*) tren *m* de aterrizaje.

undercharge [ʌndə'tʃɑːdʒ] *vt* cobrar de menos.

underclass ['ʌndəklɑːs] *n* clase *f* marginada.

underclothes ['ʌndəkləuðz] *npl* ropa *sg* interior *or* íntima (*LAM*).

undercoat ['ʌndəkəut] *n* (*paint*) primera mano.

undercover [ʌndə'kʌvə*] *adj* clandestino.

undercurrent ['ʌndəkʌrnt] *n* corriente *f* submarina; (*fig*) tendencia oculta.

undercut ['ʌndəkʌt] *vt* (*irreg: like* **cut**) vender más barato que; fijar un precio más barato que.

underdeveloped [ʌndədɪ'vɛləpt] *adj* subdesarrollado.

underdog ['ʌndədɒg] *n* desvalido/a.

underdone [ʌndə'dʌn] *adj* (*CULIN*) poco hecho.

underemployment [ʌndərɪm'plɔɪmənt] *n* subempleo.

underestimate [ʌndər'ɛstɪmeɪt] *vt* subestimar.

underexposed [ʌndərɪks'pəuzd] *adj* (*PHOT*) subexpuesto.

underfed [ʌndə'fɛd] *adj* subalimentado.

underfoot [ʌndə'fut] *adv*: **it's wet** ~ el suelo está mojado.

underfunded [ʌndə'fʌndɪd] *adj* infradotado (económicamente).

undergo [ʌndə'gəu] *vt* (*irreg: like* **go**) sufrir; (*treatment*) recibir, someterse a; **the car is** ~**ing repairs** están reparando el coche.

undergraduate ['ʌndə'grædjuət] *n* estudiante *m/f* ♦ *cpd*: ~ **courses** cursos *mpl* de licenciatura.

underground ['ʌndəgraund] *n* (*BRIT: railway*) metro; (*POL*) movimiento clandestino ♦ *adj* subterráneo.

undergrowth ['ʌndəgrəuθ] *n* maleza.

underhand(ed) [ʌndə'hænd(ɪd)] *adj* (*fig*) poco limpio.

underinsured [ʌndərɪn'ʃuəd] *adj* insuficientemente asegurado.

underlie [ʌndə'laɪ] *vt* (*irreg: like* **lie**) (*fig*) ser la razón fundamental de; **the underlying cause** la causa fundamental.

underline [ʌndə'laɪn] *vt* subrayar.

underling ['ʌndəlɪŋ] *n* (*pej*) subalterno/a.

undermanning [ʌndə'mænɪŋ] *n* falta de personal.

undermentioned [ʌndə'mɛnʃənd] *adj* abajo citado.

undermine [ʌndə'maɪn] *vt* socavar, minar.

underneath [ʌndə'niːθ] *adv* debajo ♦ *prep* debajo de, bajo.

undernourished [ʌndə'nʌrɪʃt] *adj* desnutrido.

underpaid [ʌndə'peɪd] *adj* mal pagado.

underpants ['ʌndəpænts] *npl* calzoncillos *mpl*.

underpass ['ʌndəpɑːs] *n* (*BRIT*) paso subterráneo.

underpin [ʌndə'pɪn] *vt* (*argument, case*) secundar, sostener.

underplay [ʌndə'pleɪ] *vt* (*BRIT*) minimizar.

underpopulated [ʌndə'pɒpjuleɪtɪd] *adj* poco poblado.

underprice [ˌʌndəˈpraɪs] *vt* vender demasiado barato.

underpriced [ˌʌndəˈpraɪst] *adj* con precio demasiado bajo.

underprivileged [ˌʌndəˈprɪvɪlɪdʒd] *adj* desvalido.

underrate [ˌʌndəˈreɪt] *vt* infravalorar, subestimar.

underscore [ˈʌndəskɔː*] *vt* subrayar, sostener.

underseal [ˌʌndəˈsiːl] *vt* (*AUT*) proteger contra la corrosión.

undersecretary [ˌʌndəˈsɛkrətrɪ] *n* subsecretario/a.

undersell [ˌʌndəˈsɛl] *vt* (*competitors*) vender más barato que.

undershirt [ˈʌndəʃɜːt] *n* (*US*) camiseta.

undershorts [ˈʌndəʃɔːts] *npl* (*US*) calzoncillos *mpl*.

underside [ˈʌndəsaɪd] *n* parte *f* inferior, revés *m*.

undersigned [ˈʌndəsaɪnd] *adj, n*: **the ~** el/la *etc* abajo firmante.

underskirt [ˈʌndəskɜːt] *n* (*BRIT*) enaguas *fpl*.

understaffed [ˌʌndəˈstɑːft] *adj* falto de personal.

understand [ˌʌndəˈstænd] (*irreg: like* **stand**) *vt, vi* entender, comprender; (*assume*) tener entendido; **to make o.s. understood** hacerse entender; **I ~ you have been absent** tengo entendido que (usted) ha estado ausente.

understandable [ˌʌndəˈstændəbl] *adj* comprensible.

understanding [ˌʌndəˈstændɪŋ] *adj* comprensivo ♦ *n* comprensión *f*, entendimiento *m*; (*agreement*) acuerdo; **to come to an ~ with sb** llegar a un acuerdo con algn; **on the ~ that** a condición de que (+ *subjun*).

understate [ˌʌndəˈsteɪt] *vt* minimizar.

understatement [ˌʌndəˈsteɪtmənt] *n* subestimación *f*; (*modesty*) modestia (excesiva); **to say it was good is quite an ~** decir que estuvo bien es quedarse corto.

understood [ˌʌndəˈstud] *pt, pp of* **understand** ♦ *adj* entendido; (*implied*): **it is ~ that** se sobreentiende que.

understudy [ˈʌndəstʌdɪ] *n* suplente *m/f*.

undertake [ˌʌndəˈteɪk] (*irreg: like* **take**) *vt* emprender; **to ~ to do sth** comprometerse a hacer algo.

undertaker [ˈʌndəteɪkə*] *n* director(a) *m/f* de pompas fúnebres.

undertaking [ˈʌndəteɪkɪŋ] *n* empresa; (*promise*) promesa.

undertone [ˈʌndətəun] *n* (*of criticism*) connotación *f*; (*low voice*): **in an ~** en voz baja.

undervalue [ˌʌndəˈvæljuː] *vt* (*fig*) subestimar, infravalorar; (*COMM etc*) valorizar por debajo de su precio.

underwater [ˌʌndəˈwɔːtə*] *adv* bajo el agua ♦ *adj* submarino.

underwear [ˈʌndəwɛə*] *n* ropa interior *or* íntima (*LAM*).

underweight [ˌʌndəˈweɪt] *adj* de peso insuficiente; (*person*) demasiado delgado.

underworld [ˈʌndəwəːld] *n* (*of crime*) hampa, inframundo.

underwrite [ˌʌndəˈraɪt] (*irreg: like* **write**) *vt* (*COMM*) suscribir; (*INSURANCE*) asegurar (*contra riesgos*).

underwriter [ˈʌndəraɪtə*] *n* (*INSURANCE*) asegurador/a *m/f*.

undeserving [ˌʌndɪˈzəːvɪŋ] *adj*: **to be ~ of** no ser digno de.

undesirable [ˌʌndɪˈzaɪərəbl] *adj* indeseable.

undeveloped [ˌʌndɪˈvɛləpt] *adj* (*land, resources*) sin explotar.

undies [ˈʌndɪz] *npl* (*col*) paños *mpl* menores.

undiluted [ˌʌndaɪˈluːtɪd] *adj* (*concentrate*) concentrado.

undiplomatic [ˌʌndɪpləˈmætɪk] *adj* poco diplomático.

undischarged [ˌʌndɪsˈtʃɑːdʒd] *adj*: **~ bankrupt** quebrado/a no rehabilitado/a.

undisciplined [ʌnˈdɪsɪplɪnd] *adj* indisciplinado.

undiscovered [ˌʌndɪsˈkʌvəd] *adj* no descubierto; (*unknown*) desconocido.

undisguised [ˌʌndɪsˈgaɪzd] *adj* franco, abierto.

undisputed [ˌʌndɪˈspjuːtɪd] *adj* incontestable.

undistinguished [ˌʌndɪsˈtɪŋgwɪʃt] *adj* mediocre.

undisturbed [ˌʌndɪsˈtəːbd] *adj* (*sleep*) ininterrumpido; **to leave sth ~** dejar algo tranquilo *or* como está.

undivided [ˌʌndɪˈvaɪdɪd] *adj*: **I want your ~ attention** quiero su completa atención.

undo [ʌnˈduː] *vt* (*irreg: like* **do**) deshacer.

undoing [ʌnˈduːɪŋ] *n* ruina, perdición *f*.

undone [ʌnˈdʌn] *pp of* **undo** ♦ *adj*: **to come ~** (*clothes*) desabrocharse; (*parcel*) desatarse.

undoubted [ʌnˈdautɪd] *adj* indudable.

undoubtedly [ʌnˈdautɪdlɪ] *adv* indudablemente, sin duda.

undress [ʌnˈdrɛs] *vi* desnudarse, desvestirse (*esp LAM*).

undrinkable [ʌnˈdrɪŋkəbl] *adj* (*unpalatable*) imbebible; (*poisonous*) no potable.

undue [ʌnˈdjuː] *adj* indebido, excesivo.

undulating ['ʌndjuleɪtɪŋ] *adj* ondulante.
unduly [ʌn'djuːlɪ] *adv* excesivamente, demasiado.
undying [ʌn'daɪɪŋ] *adj* eterno.
unearned [ʌn'əːnd] *adj* (*praise, respect*) inmerecido; ~ **income** ingresos *mpl* no ganados, renta no ganada *or* salarial.
unearth [ʌn'əːθ] *vt* desenterrar.
unearthly [ʌn'əːθlɪ] *adj*: ~ **hour** (*col*) hora intempestiva.
unease [ʌn'iːz] *n* malestar *m*.
uneasy [ʌn'iːzɪ] *adj* intranquilo; (*worried*) preocupado; **to feel** ~ **about doing sth** sentirse incómodo con la idea de hacer algo.
uneconomic(al) ['ʌniːkə'nɔmɪk(l)] *adj* no económico.
uneducated [ʌn'ɛdjukeɪtɪd] *adj* ignorante, inculto.
unemployed [ʌnɪm'plɔɪd] *adj* parado, sin trabajo ♦ *n*: **the** ~ los parados.
unemployment [ʌnɪm'plɔɪmənt] *n* paro, desempleo, cesantía (*LAM*).
unemployment benefit *n* (*BRIT*) subsidio de desempleo *or* paro.
unending [ʌn'ɛndɪŋ] *adj* interminable.
unenviable [ʌn'ɛnvɪəbl] *adj* poco envidiable.
unequal [ʌn'iːkwəl] *adj* (*length, objects etc*) desigual; (*amounts*) distinto; (*division of labour*) poco justo.
unequalled, (*US*) **unequaled** [ʌn'iːkwəld] *adj* inigualado, sin par.
unequivocal [ʌnɪ'kwɪvəkəl] *adj* (*answer*) inequívoco, claro; (*person*) claro.
unerring [ʌn'əːrɪŋ] *adj* infalible.
UNESCO [juː'nɛskəu] *n abbr* (= *United Nations Educational, Scientific and Cultural Organization*) UNESCO *f*.
unethical [ʌn'ɛθɪkəl] *adj* (*methods*) inmoral; (*doctor's behaviour*) que infringe la ética profesional.
uneven [ʌn'iːvn] *adj* desigual; (*road etc*) con baches.
uneventful [ʌnɪ'vɛntful] *adj* sin incidentes.
unexceptional [ʌnɪk'sɛpʃənl] *adj* sin nada de extraordinario, corriente.
unexciting [ʌnɪk'saɪtɪŋ] *adj* (*news*) sin interés; (*film, evening*) aburrido.
unexpected [ʌnɪk'spɛktɪd] *adj* inesperado.
unexpectedly [ʌnɪk'spɛktɪdlɪ] *adv* inesperadamente.
unexplained [ʌnɪks'pleɪnd] *adj* inexplicado.
unexploded [ʌnɪks'pləudɪd] *adj* sin explotar.
unfailing [ʌn'feɪlɪŋ] *adj* (*support*) indefectible; (*energy*) inagotable.
unfair [ʌn'fɛə*] *adj*: ~ **(to sb)** injusto (con

algn); **it's** ~ **that** ... es injusto que ..., no es justo que ....
unfair dismissal *n* despido improcedente.
unfairly [ʌn'fɛəlɪ] *adv* injustamente.
unfaithful [ʌn'feɪθful] *adj* infiel.
unfamiliar [ʌnfə'mɪlɪə*] *adj* extraño, desconocido; **to be** ~ **with sth** desconocer *or* ignorar algo.
unfashionable [ʌn'fæʃnəbl] *adj* (*clothes*) pasado *or* fuera de moda; (*district*) poco elegante.
unfasten [ʌn'fɑːsn] *vt* desatar.
unfathomable [ʌn'fæðəməbl] *adj* insondable.
unfavourable, (*US*) **unfavorable** [ʌn'feɪvərəbl] *adj* desfavorable.
unfavo(u)rably [ʌn'feɪvrəblɪ] *adv*: **to look** ~ **upon** ser adverso a.
unfeeling [ʌn'fiːlɪŋ] *adj* insensible.
unfinished [ʌn'fɪnɪʃt] *adj* inacabado, sin terminar.
unfit [ʌn'fɪt] *adj* en baja forma; (*incompetent*) incapaz; ~ **for work** no apto para trabajar.
unflagging [ʌn'flægɪŋ] *adj* incansable.
unflappable [ʌn'flæpəbl] *adj* imperturbable.
unflattering [ʌn'flætərɪŋ] *adj* (*dress, hairstyle*) poco favorecedor.
unflinching [ʌn'flɪntʃɪŋ] *adj* impávido.
unfold [ʌn'fəuld] *vt* desdoblar; (*fig*) revelar ♦ *vi* abrirse; revelarse.
unforeseeable [ʌnfɔː'siːəbl] *adj* imprevisible.
unforeseen ['ʌnfɔː'siːn] *adj* imprevisto.
unforgettable [ʌnfə'gɛtəbl] *adj* inolvidable.
unforgivable [ʌnfə'gɪvəbl] *adj* imperdonable.
unformatted [ʌn'fɔːmætɪd] *adj* (*disk, text*) sin formatear.
unfortunate [ʌn'fɔːtʃnət] *adj* desgraciado; (*event, remark*) inoportuno.
unfortunately [ʌn'fɔːtʃnətlɪ] *adv* desgraciadamente, por desgracia.
unfounded [ʌn'faundɪd] *adj* infundado.
unfriendly [ʌn'frɛndlɪ] *adj* antipático.
unfulfilled [ʌnful'fɪld] *adj* (*ambition*) sin realizar; (*prophecy, promise, terms of contract*) incumplido; (*desire, person*) insatisfecho.
unfurl [ʌn'fəːl] *vt* desplegar.
unfurnished [ʌn'fəːnɪʃt] *adj* sin amueblar.
ungainly [ʌn'geɪnlɪ] *adj* (*walk*) desgarbado.
ungodly [ʌn'gɔdlɪ] *adj*: **at an** ~ **hour** a una hora intempestiva.
ungrateful [ʌn'greɪtful] *adj* ingrato.
unguarded [ʌn'gɑːdɪd] *adj* (*moment*) de descuido.

unhappily [ʌn'hæpɪlɪ] *adv* (*unfortunately*) desgraciadamente.

unhappiness [ʌn'hæpɪnɪs] *n* tristeza.

unhappy [ʌn'haepɪ] *adj* (*sad*) triste; (*unfortunate*) desgraciado; (*childhood*) infeliz; ~ **with** (*arrangements etc*) poco contento con, descontento de.

unharmed [ʌn'hɑːmd] *adj* (*person*) ileso.

UNHCR *n abbr* (= *United Nations High Commission for Refugees*) ACNUR *m*.

unhealthy [ʌn'hɛlθɪ] *adj* (*gen*) malsano, insalubre; (*person*) enfermizo; (*interest*) morboso.

unheard-of [ʌn'hɜːdɔv] *adj* inaudito, sin precedente.

unhelpful [ʌn'hɛlpful] *adj* (*person*) poco servicial; (*advice*) inútil.

unhesitating [ʌn'hɛzɪteɪtɪŋ] *adj* (*loyalty*) automático; (*reply, offer*) inmediato; (*person*) resuelto.

unholy [ʌn'həulɪ] *adj*: **an ~ alliance** una alianza nefasta; **he returned at an ~ hour** volvió a una hora intempestiva.

unhook [ʌn'huk] *vt* desenganchar; (*from wall*) descolgar; (*undo*) desabrochar.

unhurt [ʌn'hɜːt] *adj* ileso.

unhygienic [ʌnhaɪ'dʒiːnɪk] *adj* antihigiénico.

UNICEF ['juːnɪsɛf] *n abbr* (= *United Nations International Children's Emergency Fund*) UNICEF *f*.

unidentified [ʌnaɪ'dɛntɪfaɪd] *adj* no identificado; ~ **flying object (UFO)** objeto volante no identificado.

unification [juːnɪfɪ'keɪʃən] *n* unificación *f*.

uniform ['juːnɪfɔːm] *n* uniforme *m* ♦ *adj* uniforme.

uniformity [juːnɪ'fɔːmɪtɪ] *n* uniformidad *f*.

unify ['juːnɪfaɪ] *vt* unificar, unir.

unilateral [juːnɪ'lætərəl] *adj* unilateral.

unimaginable [ʌnɪ'mædʒɪnəbl] *adj* inconcebible, inimaginable.

unimaginative [ʌnɪ'mædʒɪnətɪv] *adj* falto de imaginación.

unimpaired [ʌnɪm'pɛəd] *adj* (*unharmed*) intacto; (*not lessened*) no disminuido; (*unaltered*) inalterado.

unimportant [ʌnɪm'pɔːtənt] *adj* sin importancia.

unimpressed [ʌnɪm'prɛst] *adj* poco impresionado.

uninhabited [ʌnɪn'hæbɪtɪd] *adj* desierto; (*country*) despoblado; (*house*) deshabitado, desocupado.

uninhibited [ʌnɪn'hɪbɪtɪd] *adj* nada cohibido, desinhibido.

uninjured [ʌn'ɪndʒəd] *adj* (*person*) ileso.

uninspiring [ʌnɪn'spaɪərɪŋ] *adj* anodino.

unintelligent [ʌnɪn'tɛlɪdʒənt] *adj* poco inteligente.

unintentional [ʌnɪn'tɛnʃənəl] *adj* involuntario.

unintentionally [ʌnɪn'tɛnʃnəlɪ] *adv* sin querer.

uninvited [ʌnɪn'vaɪtɪd] *adj* (*guest*) sin invitación.

uninviting [ʌnɪn'vaɪtɪŋ] *adj* (*place, offer*) poco atractivo; (*food*) poco apetecible.

union ['juːnjən] *n* unión *f*; (*also*: **trade ~**) sindicato ♦ *cpd* sindical; **the U~** (*US*) la Unión.

union card *n* carnet *m* de sindicato.

unionize ['juːnjənaɪz] *vt* sindicalizar.

Union Jack *n* bandera del Reino Unido.

Union of Soviet Socialist Republics (USSR) *n* Unión *f* de Repúblicas Socialistas Soviéticas.

union shop *n* (*US*) empresa de afiliación sindical obligatoria.

unique [juːˈniːk] *adj* único.

unisex ['juːnɪsɛks] *adj* unisex.

Unison ['juːnɪsn] *n* (*trade union*) gran sindicato de funcionarios.

unison ['juːnɪsn] *n*: **in ~** en armonía.

unissued capital [ʌn'ɪʃuːd-] *n* capital *m* no emitido.

unit ['juːnɪt] *n* unidad *f*; (*team, squad*) grupo; **kitchen ~** módulo de cocina; **production ~** taller *m* de fabricación; **sink ~** fregadero.

unit cost *n* costo unitario.

unite [juːˈnaɪt] *vt* unir ♦ *vi* unirse.

united [juːˈnaɪtɪd] *adj* unido.

United Arab Emirates *npl* Emiratos *mpl* Árabes Unidos.

United Kingdom (UK) *n* Reino Unido.

United Nations (Organization) (UN, UNO) *n* Naciones Unidas *fpl* (ONU *f*).

United States (of America) (US, USA) *n* Estados Unidos *mpl* (de América) (EE.UU. *mpl*).

unit price *n* precio unitario.

unit trust *n* (*BRIT*) bono fiduciario.

unity ['juːnɪtɪ] *n* unidad *f*.

Univ. *abbr* = **university**.

universal [juːnɪ'vɜːsl] *adj* universal.

universally [juːnɪ'vɜːsəlɪ] *adv* universalmente.

universe ['juːnɪvɜːs] *n* universo.

university [juːnɪ'vɜːsɪtɪ] *n* universidad *f* ♦ *cpd* (*student, professor, education, degree*) universitario; (*year*) académico; **to be at/ go to ~** estudiar en/ir a la universidad.

unjust [ʌn'dʒʌst] *adj* injusto.

unjustifiable [ʌndʒʌstɪ'faɪəbl] *adj* injustificable.

unjustified [ʌn'dʒʌstɪfaɪd] *adj* (*text*) no alineado *or* justificado.

unkempt [ʌn'kɛmpt] *adj* descuidado; (*hair*) despeinado.

unkind [ʌn'kaɪnd] *adj* poco amable; (*comment etc*) cruel.

unkindly [ʌn'kaɪndlɪ] *adv* (*speak*) severamente; (*treat*) cruelmente, mal.

unknown [ʌn'nəun] *adj* desconocido ♦ *adv*: ~ **to me** sin saberlo yo; ~ **quantity** (*MATH, fig*) incógnita.

unladen [ʌn'leɪdən] *adj* (*weight*) vacío, sin cargamento.

unlawful [ʌn'lɔːful] *adj* ilegal, ilícito.

unleaded [ʌn'lɛdɪd] *n* (*also*: ~ **petrol**) gasolina sin plomo.

unleash [ʌn'liːʃ] *vt* desatar.

unleavened [ʌn'lɛvənd] *adj* ácimo, sin levadura.

unless [ʌn'lɛs] *conj* a menos que; ~ **he comes** a menos que venga; ~ **otherwise stated** salvo indicación contraria; ~ **I am mistaken** si no mi equivoco.

unlicensed [ʌn'laɪsənst] *adj* (*BRIT: to sell alcohol*) no autorizado.

unlike [ʌn'laɪk] *adj* distinto ♦ *prep* a diferencia de.

unlikelihood [ʌn'laɪklɪhud] *n* improbabilidad *f*.

unlikely [ʌn'laɪklɪ] *adj* improbable.

unlimited [ʌn'lɪmɪtɪd] *adj* ilimitado; ~ **liability** responsabilidad *f* ilimitada.

unlisted [ʌn'lɪstɪd] *adj* (*US TEL*) que no figura en la guía; ~ **company** empresa sin cotización en bolsa.

unlit [ʌn'lɪt] *adj* (*room*) oscuro, sin luz.

unload [ʌn'ləud] *vt* descargar.

unlock [ʌn'lɔk] *vt* abrir (con llave).

unlucky [ʌn'lʌkɪ] *adj* desgraciado; (*object, number*) que da mala suerte; **to be** ~ (*person*) tener mala suerte.

unmanageable [ʌn'mænɪdʒəbl] *adj* (*unwieldy: tool, vehicle*) difícil de manejar; (*: situation*) incontrolable.

unmanned [ʌn'mænd] *adj* (*spacecraft*) sin tripulación.

unmannerly [ʌn'mænəlɪ] *adj* mal educado, descortés.

unmarked [ʌn'maːkt] *adj* (*unstained*) sin mancha; ~ **police car** vehículo policial camuflado.

unmarried [ʌn'mærɪd] *adj* soltero.

unmask [ʌn'maːsk] *vt* desenmascarar.

unmatched [ʌn'mætʃt] *adj* incomparable.

unmentionable [ʌn'mɛnʃnəbl] *adj* (*topic, vice*) indecible; (*word*) que no se debe decir.

unmerciful [ʌn'mɔːsɪful] *adj* despiadado.

unmistakable [ʌnmɪs'teɪkəbl] *adj* inconfundible.

unmistakably [ʌnmɪs'teɪkəblɪ] *adv* de modo inconfundible.

unmitigated [ʌn'mɪtɪgeɪtɪd] *adj* rematado, absoluto.

unnamed [ʌn'neɪmd] *adj* (*nameless*) sin nombre; (*anonymous*) anónimo.

unnatural [ʌn'nætʃrəl] *adj* (*gen*) antinatural; (*manner*) afectado; (*habit*) perverso.

unnecessary [ʌn'nɛsəsərɪ] *adj* innecesario, inútil.

unnerve [ʌn'nɔːv] *vt* (*subj: accident*) poner nervioso; (*: hostile attitude*) acobardar; (*: long wait, interview*) intimidar.

unnoticed [ʌn'nəutɪst] *adj*: **to go** *or* **pass** ~ pasar desapercibido.

UNO ['juːnəu] *n abbr* = (*United Nations Organization*) ONU *f*.

unobservant [ʌnəb'zɔːvnt] *adj*: **to be** ~ ser poco observador, ser distraído.

unobtainable [ʌnəb'teɪnəbl] *adj* inasequible; (*TEL*) inexistente.

unobtrusive [ʌnəb'truːsɪv] *adj* discreto.

unoccupied [ʌn'ɔkjupaɪd] *adj* (*house etc*) libre, desocupado.

unofficial [ʌnə'fɪʃl] *adj* no oficial; ~ **strike** huelga no oficial.

unopened [ʌn'əupənd] *adj* (*letter, present*) sin abrir.

unopposed [ʌnə'pəuzd] *adj* (*enter, be elected*) sin oposición.

unorthodox [ʌn'ɔːθədɔks] *adj* poco ortodoxo.

unpack [ʌn'pæk] *vi* deshacer las maletas, desempacar (*LAM*).

unpaid [ʌn'peɪd] *adj* (*bill, debt*) sin pagar, impagado; (*COMM*) pendiente; (*holiday*) sin sueldo; (*work*) sin pago, voluntario.

unpalatable [ʌn'pælətəbl] *adj* (*truth*) desagradable.

unparalleled [ʌn'pærəlɛld] *adj* (*unequalled*) sin par; (*unique*) sin precedentes.

unpatriotic [ʌnpætrɪ'ɔtɪk] *adj* (*person*) poco patriota; (*speech, attitude*) antipatriótico.

unplanned [ʌn'plænd] *adj* (*visit*) imprevisto; (*baby*) no planeado.

unpleasant [ʌn'plɛznt] *adj* (*disagreeable*) desagradable; (*person, manner*) antipático.

unplug [ʌn'plʌg] *vt* desenchufar, desconectar.

unpolluted [ʌnpə'luːtɪd] *adj* impoluto, no contaminado.

unpopular [ʌn'pɔpjulə*] *adj* poco popular; **to be** ~ **with sb** (*person, law*) no ser popular con algn; **to make o.s.** ~ **(with)**

hacerse impopular (con).

unprecedented [ʌn'prɛsɪdəntɪd] *adj* sin precedentes.

unpredictable [ʌnprɪ'dɪktəbl] *adj* imprevisible.

unprejudiced [ʌn'prɛdʒudɪst] *adj* (*not biased*) imparcial; (*having no prejudices*) sin prejuicio.

unprepared [ʌnprɪ'pɛəd] *adj* (*person*) desprevenido; (*speech*) improvisado.

unprepossessing [ʌnpriːpə'zɛsɪŋ] *adj* poco atractivo.

unprincipled [ʌn'prɪnsɪpld] *adj* sin escrúpulos.

unproductive [ʌnprə'dʌktɪv] *adj* improductivo; (*discussion*) infructuoso.

unprofessional [ʌnprə'fɛʃənl] *adj* poco profesional; ~ **conduct** negligencia.

unprofitable [ʌn'prɒfɪtəbl] *adj* poco provechoso, no rentable.

UNPROFOR *n abbr* (= *United Nations Protection Force*) FORPRONU *f*, Unprofor *f*.

unprotected ['ʌnprə'tɛktɪd] *adj* (*sex*) sin protección.

unprovoked [ʌnprə'vəʊkt] *adj* no provocado.

unpunished [ʌn'pʌnɪʃt] *adj*: **to go** ~ quedar sin castigo, salir impune.

unqualified [ʌn'kwɒlɪfaɪd] *adj* sin título, no cualificado; (*success*) total, incondicional.

unquestionably [ʌn'kwɛstʃənəblɪ] *adv* indiscutiblemente.

unquestioning [ʌn'kwɛstʃənɪŋ] *adj* (*obedience, acceptance*) incondicional.

unravel [ʌn'rævl] *vt* desenmarañar.

unreal [ʌn'rɪəl] *adj* irreal.

unrealistic [ʌnrɪə'lɪstɪk] *adj* poco realista.

unreasonable [ʌn'riːznəbl] *adj* irrazonable; **to make** ~ **demands on sb** hacer demandas excesivas a algn.

unrecognizable [ʌn'rɛkəgnaɪzəbl] *adj* irreconocible.

unrecognized [ʌn'rɛkəgnaɪzd] *adj* (*talent, genius*) ignorado; (*POL: regime*) no reconocido.

unrecorded [ʌnrɪ'kɔːdɪd] *adj* no registrado.

unrefined [ʌnrɪ'faɪnd] *adj* (*sugar, petroleum*) sin refinar.

unrehearsed [ʌnrɪ'həːst] *adj* (*THEAT etc*) improvisado; (*spontaneous*) espontáneo.

unrelated [ʌnrɪ'leɪtɪd] *adj* sin relación; (*family*) no emparentado.

unrelenting [ʌnrɪ'lɛntɪŋ] *adj* implacable.

unreliable [ʌnrɪ'laɪəbl] *adj* (*person*) informal; (*machine*) poco fiable.

unrelieved [ʌnrɪ'liːvd] *adj* (*monotony*) constante.

unremitting [ʌnrɪ'mɪtɪŋ] *adj* incesante.

unrepeatable [ʌnrɪ'piːtəbl] *adj* irrepetible.

unrepentant [ʌnrɪ'pɛntənt] *adj* (*smoker, sinner*) impenitente; **to be** ~ **about sth** no arrepentirse de algo.

unrepresentative [ʌnrɛprɪ'zɛntətɪv] *adj* (*untypical*) poco representativo.

unreserved [ʌnrɪ'zəːvd] *adj* (*seat*) no reservado; (*approval, admiration*) total.

unreservedly [ʌnrɪ'zəːvɪdlɪ] *adv* sin reserva.

unresponsive [ʌnrɪ'spɒnsɪv] *adj* insensible.

unrest [ʌn'rɛst] *n* inquietud *f*, malestar *m*; (*POL*) disturbios *mpl*.

unrestricted [ʌnrɪ'strɪktɪd] *adj* (*power, time*) sin restricción; (*access*) libre.

unrewarded [ʌnrɪ'wɔːdɪd] *adj* sin recompensa.

unripe [ʌn'raɪp] *adj* verde, inmaduro.

unrivalled, (*US*) **unrivaled** [ʌn'raɪvəld] *adj* incomparable, sin par.

unroll [ʌn'rəʊl] *vt* desenrollar.

unruffled [ʌn'rʌfld] *adj* (*person*) imperturbable; (*hair*) liso.

unruly [ʌn'ruːlɪ] *adj* indisciplinado.

unsafe [ʌn'seɪf] *adj* (*journey*) peligroso; (*car etc*) inseguro; (*method*) arriesgado; ~ **to drink/eat** no apto para el consumo humano.

unsaid [ʌn'sɛd] *adj*: **to leave sth** ~ dejar algo sin decir.

unsaleable, (*US*) **unsalable** [ʌn'seɪləbl] *adj* invendible.

unsatisfactory ['ʌnsætɪs'fæktərɪ] *adj* poco satisfactorio.

unsatisfied [ʌn'sætɪsfaɪd] *adj* (*desire, need etc*) insatisfecho.

unsavoury, (*US*) **unsavory** [ʌn'seɪvərɪ] *adj* (*fig*) repugnante.

unscathed [ʌn'skeɪðd] *adj* ileso.

unscientific [ʌnsaɪən'tɪfɪk] *adj* poco científico.

unscrew [ʌn'skruː] *vt* destornillar.

unscrupulous [ʌn'skruːpjʊləs] *adj* sin escrúpulos.

unseat [ʌn'siːt] *vt* (*rider*) hacer caerse de la silla a; (*fig: official*) hacer perder su escaño a.

unsecured [ʌnsɪ'kjʊəd] *adj*: ~ **creditor** acreedor(a) *m/f* común.

unseeded [ʌn'siːdɪd] *adj* (*SPORT*) no preseleccionado.

unseen [ʌn'siːn] *adj* (*person, danger*) oculto.

unselfish [ʌn'sɛlfɪʃ] *adj* generoso, poco egoísta; (*act*) desinteresado.

unsettled [ʌn'sɛtld] *adj* inquieto; (*situation*) inestable; (*weather*) variable.

unsettling [ʌn'sɛtlɪŋ] *adj* perturbador(a),

inquietante.
unshak(e)able [ʌn'ʃeɪkəbl] *adj*
inquebrantable.
unshaven [ʌn'ʃeɪvn] *adj* sin afeitar.
unsightly [ʌn'saɪtlɪ] *adj* desagradable.
unskilled [ʌn'skɪld] *adj*: ~ **workers** mano *f*
de obra no cualificada.
unsociable [ʌn'səʊʃəbl] *adj* insociable.
unsocial [ʌn'səʊʃl] *adj*: ~ **hours** horario
nocturno.
unsold [ʌn'səʊld] *adj* sin vender.
unsolicited [ʌnsə'lɪsɪtɪd] *adj* no solicitado.
unsophisticated [ʌnsə'fɪstɪkeɪtɪd] *adj*
(*person*) sencillo, ingenuo; (*method*) poco
sofisticado.
unsound [ʌn'saʊnd] *adj* (*health*) malo; (*in
construction: floor, foundations*) defectuoso;
(*policy, advice, judgment*) erróneo;
(*investment*) poco seguro.
unspeakable [ʌn'spiːkəbl] *adj* indecible;
(*awful*) incalificable.
unspoken [ʌn'spəʊkn] *adj* (*words*) sobreentendido; (*agreement, approval*) tácito.
unstable [ʌn'steɪbl] *adj* inestable.
unsteady [ʌn'stɛdɪ] *adj* inestable.
unstinting [ʌn'stɪntɪŋ] *adj* (*support etc*)
pródigo.
unstuck [ʌn'stʌk] *adj*: **to come** ~
despegarse; (*fig*) fracasar.
unsubscribe [ʌnsəb'skraɪb] *vi* (*INTERNET*)
borrarse.
unsubstantiated [ʌnsəb'stænʃɪeɪtɪd] *adj*
(*rumour, accusation*) no comprobado.
unsuccessful [ʌnsək'sɛsful] *adj* (*attempt*)
infructuoso; (*writer, proposal*) sin éxito; **to
be** ~ (*in attempting sth*) no tener éxito,
fracasar.
unsuccessfully [ʌnsək'sɛsfulɪ] *adv* en vano,
sin éxito.
unsuitable [ʌn'suːtəbl] *adj* inconveniente,
inapropiado; (*time*) inoportuno.
unsuited [ʌn'suːtɪd] *adj*: **to be** ~ **for** *or* **to** no
ser apropiado para.
unsung [ʌn'sʌŋ] *adj*: **an** ~ **hero** un héroe
desconocido.
unsupported [ʌnsə'pɔːtɪd] *adj* (*claim*) sin
fundamento; (*theory*) sin base firme.
unsure [ʌn'ʃʊə*] *adj* inseguro, poco seguro;
to be ~ **of o.s.** estar poco seguro de sí
mismo.
unsuspecting [ʌnsə'spɛktɪŋ] *adj* confiado.
unsweetened [ʌn'swiːtnd] *adj* sin azúcar.
unsympathetic [ʌnsɪmpə'θɛtɪk] *adj*
(*attitude*) poco comprensivo; (*person*) sin
compasión; ~ **(to)** indiferente (a).
untangle [ʌn'tæŋgl] *vt* desenredar.
untapped [ʌn'tæpt] *adj* (*resources*) sin
explotar.

untaxed [ʌn'tækst] *adj* (*goods*) libre de
impuestos; (*income*) antes de impuestos.
unthinkable [ʌn'θɪŋkəbl] *adj* inconcebible,
impensable.
unthinkingly [ʌn'θɪŋkɪŋlɪ] *adv*
irreflexivamente.
untidy [ʌn'taɪdɪ] *adj* (*room*) desordenado,
en desorden; (*appearance*) desaliñado.
untie [ʌn'taɪ] *vt* desatar.
until [ən'tɪl] *prep* hasta ♦ *conj* hasta que; ~
he comes hasta que venga; ~ **now** hasta
ahora; ~ **then** hasta entonces; **from
morning** ~ **night** de la mañana a la noche.
untimely [ʌn'taɪmlɪ] *adj* inoportuno; (*death*)
prematuro.
untold [ʌn'təʊld] *adj* (*story*) nunca contado;
(*suffering*) indecible; (*wealth*)
incalculable.
untouched [ʌn'tʌtʃt] *adj* (*not used etc*)
intacto, sin tocar; (*safe: person*) indemne,
ileso; (*unaffected*): ~ **by** insensible a.
untoward [ʌntə'wɔːd] *adj* (*behaviour*)
impropio; (*event*) adverso.
untrained [ʌn'treɪnd] *adj* (*worker*) sin
formación; (*troops*) no entrenado; **to the**
~ **eye** para los no entendidos.
untrammelled, (*US*) untrammeled
[ʌn'træməld] *adj* ilimitado.
untranslatable [ʌntrænz'leɪtəbl] *adj*
intraducible.
untried [ʌn'traɪd] *adj* (*plan*) no probado.
untrue [ʌn'truː] *adj* (*statement*) falso.
untrustworthy [ʌn'trʌstwɜːðɪ] *adj* (*person*)
poco fiable.
unusable [ʌn'juːzəbl] *adj* inservible.
unused [ʌn'juːzd] *adj* sin usar, nuevo; **to be**
~ **to (doing) sth** no estar acostumbrado a
(hacer) algo.
unusual [ʌn'juːʒuəl] *adj* insólito, poco
común.
unusually [ʌn'juːʒuəlɪ] *adv*: **he arrived** ~ **early**
llegó más temprano que de costumbre.
unveil [ʌn'veɪl] *vt* (*statue*) descubrir.
unwanted [ʌn'wɒntɪd] *adj* (*person, effect*) no
deseado.
unwarranted [ʌn'wɒrəntɪd] *adj*
injustificado.
unwary [ʌn'weərɪ] *adj* imprudente, incauto.
unwavering [ʌn'weɪvərɪŋ] *adj*
inquebrantable.
unwelcome [ʌn'wɛlkəm] *adj* (*at a bad time*)
inoportuno, molesto; **to feel** ~ sentirse
incómodo.
unwell [ʌn'wɛl] *adj*: **to feel** ~ estar
indispuesto, sentirse mal.
unwieldy [ʌn'wiːldɪ] *adj* difícil de manejar.
unwilling [ʌn'wɪlɪŋ] *adj*: **to be** ~ **to do sth**
estar poco dispuesto a hacer algo.

unwillingly [ʌn'wɪlɪŋlɪ] *adv* de mala gana.

unwind [ʌn'waɪnd] (*irreg: like* wind) *vt* desenvolver ♦ *vi* (*relax*) relajarse.

unwise [ʌn'waɪz] *adj* imprudente.

unwitting [ʌn'wɪtɪŋ] *adj* inconsciente.

unworkable [ʌn'wɔ:kəbl] *adj* (*plan*) impracticable.

unworthy [ʌn'wɔ:ðɪ] *adj* indigno; **to be ~ of sth/to do sth** ser indigno de algo/de hacer algo.

unwrap [ʌn'ræp] *vt* deshacer.

unwritten [ʌn'rɪtn] *adj* (*agreement*) tácito; (*rules, law*) no escrito.

unzip [ʌn'zɪp] *vt* abrir la cremallera de.

========================= *KEYWORD*

up [ʌp] *prep*: **to go/be ~ sth** subir/estar subido en algo; **he went ~ the stairs/the hill** subió las escaleras/la colina; **we walked/climbed ~ the hill** subimos la colina; **they live further ~ the street** viven más arriba en la calle; **go ~ that road and turn left** sigue por esa calle y gira a la izquierda

♦ *adv* **1** (*upwards, higher*) más arriba; **~ in the mountains** en lo alto (de la montaña); **put it a bit higher ~** ponlo un poco más arriba *or* alto; **to stop halfway ~** pararse a la mitad del camino *or* de la subida; **~ there** ahí *or* allí arriba; **~ above** en lo alto, por encima, arriba; **"this side ~"** "este lado hacia arriba"; **to live/go ~ North** vivir en el norte/ir al norte

2: **to be ~** (*out of bed*) estar levantado; (*prices, level*) haber subido; (*building*) estar construido; (*tent*) estar montado; (*curtains, paper etc*) estar puesto; **time's ~** se acabó el tiempo; **when the year was ~** al terminarse el año; **he's well ~ in** *or* **on politics** (*BRIT: knowledgeable*) está muy al día en política; **what's up?** (*wrong*) ¿qué pasa?; **what's ~ with him?** ¿qué le pasa?; **prices are ~ on last year** los precios han subido desde el año pasado

3: **~ to** (*as far as*) hasta; **~ to now** hasta ahora *or* la fecha

4: **to be ~ to** (*depending on*): **it's ~ to you** depende de ti; **he's not ~ to it** (*job, task etc*) no es capaz de hacerlo; **I don't feel ~ to it** no me encuentro con ánimos para ello; **his work is not ~ to the required standard** su trabajo no da la talla (*inf: be doing*): **what is he ~ to?** ¿qué estará tramando?

♦ *vi* (*col*): **she ~ped and left** se levantó y se marchó

♦ *vt* (*col: price*) subir

♦ *n*: **~s and downs** altibajos *mpl.*

up-and-coming [ʌpənd'kʌmɪŋ] *adj* prometedor(a).

upbeat ['ʌpbiːt] *n* (*MUS*) tiempo no acentuado; (*in economy, prosperity*) aumento ♦ *adj* (*col*) optimista, animado.

upbraid [ʌp'breɪd] *vt* censurar, reprender.

upbringing ['ʌpbrɪŋɪŋ] *n* educación *f.*

upcoming ['ʌpkʌmɪŋ] *adj* próximo.

update [ʌp'deɪt] *vt* poner al día.

upend [ʌp'ɛnd] *vt* poner vertical.

upfront [ʌp'frʌnt] *adj* claro, directo ♦ *adv* a las claras; (*pay*) por adelantado; **to be ~ about sth** admitir algo claramente.

upgrade [ʌp'greɪd] *vt* ascender; (*COMPUT*) modernizar.

upheaval [ʌp'hiːvl] *n* trastornos *mpl*; (*POL*) agitación *f.*

uphill [ʌp'hɪl] *adj* cuesta arriba; (*fig: task*) penoso, difícil ♦ *adv*: **to go ~** ir cuesta arriba.

uphold [ʌp'həʊld] (*irreg: like* hold) *vt* sostener.

upholstery [ʌp'həʊlstərɪ] *n* tapicería.

upkeep ['ʌpkiːp] *n* mantenimiento.

upmarket [ʌp'mɑːkɪt] *adj* (*product*) de categoría.

upon [ə'pɒn] *prep* sobre.

upper ['ʌpə*] *adj* superior, de arriba ♦ *n* (*of shoe: also:* ~s) pala.

upper case *n* (*TYP*) mayúsculas *fpl.*

upper-class [ʌpə'klɑːs] *adj* (*district, people, accent*) de clase alta; (*attitude*) altivo.

uppercut ['ʌpəkʌt] *n* uppercut *m*, gancho a la cara.

upper hand *n*: **to have the ~** tener la sartén por el mango.

Upper House *n* (*POL*): **the ~** la Cámara alta.

uppermost ['ʌpəməʊst] *adj* el más alto; **what was ~ in my mind** lo que me preocupaba más.

Upper Volta [-'vɒltə] *n* Alto Volta *m.*

upright ['ʌpraɪt] *adj* vertical; (*fig*) honrado.

uprising ['ʌpraɪzɪŋ] *n* sublevación *f.*

uproar ['ʌprɔː*] *n* tumulto, escándalo.

uproarious [ʌp'rɔːrɪəs] *adj* escandaloso; (*hilarious*) graciosísimo; (*exceptional*) espectacular.

uproot [ʌp'ruːt] *vt* desarraigar.

upset *n* ['ʌpsɛt] (*to plan etc*) revés *m*, contratiempo; (*MED*) trastorno ♦ *vt* [ʌp'sɛt] (*irreg: like* set) (*glass etc*) volcar; (*spill*) derramar; (*plan*) alterar; (*person*) molestar, perturbar ♦ *adj* [ʌp'sɛt] preocupado, perturbado; (*stomach*) revuelto; **to have a stomach ~** (*BRIT*) tener el estómago revuelto; **to get ~**

molestarse, llevarse un disgusto.

upset price *n* (*US, Scottish*) precio mínimo *or* de reserva.

upsetting [ʌp'sɛtɪŋ] *adj* (*worrying*) inquietante; (*offending*) ofensivo; (*annoying*) molesto.

upshot ['ʌpʃɔt] *n* resultado.

upside-down ['ʌpsaɪd'daun] *adv* al revés.

upstage ['ʌp'steɪdʒ] *vt* robar protagonismo a.

upstairs [ʌp'stɛəz] *adv* arriba ♦ *adj* (*room*) de arriba ♦ *n* el piso superior.

upstart ['ʌpstɑːt] *n* advenedizo.

upstream [ʌp'striːm] *adv* río arriba.

upsurge ['ʌpsɔːdʒ] *n* (*of enthusiasm etc*) arrebato.

uptake ['ʌpteɪk] *n*: **he is quick/slow on the** ~ **es** muy listo/torpe.

uptight [ʌp'taɪt] *adj* tenso, nervioso.

up-to-date ['ʌptə'deɪt] *adj* moderno, actual; **to bring sb** ~ (**on sth**) poner a algn al corriente/tanto (de algo).

upturn ['ʌptɔːn] *n* (*in luck*) mejora; (*COMM: in market*) resurgimiento económico; (: *in value of currency*) aumento.

upturned ['ʌptɔːnd] *adj*: ~ **nose** nariz *f* respingona.

upward ['ʌpwəd] *adj* ascendente.

upwardly-mobile ['ʌpwədlɪ'məubaɪl] *adj*: **to be** ~ mejorar socialmente.

upward(s) ['ʌpwəd(z)] *adv* hacia arriba.

URA *n abbr* (*US*) = *Urban Renewal Administration*.

Ural Mountains ['juərəl-] *npl*: **the** ~ (*also*: **the Urals**) los Montes Urales.

uranium [juə'reɪnɪəm] *n* uranio.

Uranus [juə'reɪnəs] *n* (*ASTRO*) Urano.

urban ['ɔːbən] *adj* urbano.

urbane [ɔː'beɪn] *adj* cortés, urbano.

urbanization ['ɔːbənaɪ'zeɪʃən] *n* urbanización *f*.

urchin ['ɔːtʃɪn] *n* pilluelo, golfillo.

Urdu ['uəduː] *n* urdu *m*.

urge [ɔːdʒ] *n* (*force*) impulso; (*desire*) deseo ♦ *vt*: **to** ~ **sb to do sth** animar a algn a hacer algo.

▶**urge on** *vt* animar.

urgency ['ɔːdʒənsɪ] *n* urgencia.

urgent ['ɔːdʒənt] *adj* (*earnest, persistent: plea*) insistente; (: *tone*) urgente.

urgently ['ɔːdʒəntlɪ] *adv* con urgencia, urgentemente.

urinal ['juərɪnl] *n* (*building*) urinario; (*vessel*) orinal *m*.

urinate ['juərɪneɪt] *vi* orinar.

urine ['juərɪn] *n* orina.

urn [ɔːn] *n* urna; (*also*: **tea** ~) tetera (grande).

Uruguay ['juerəgwaɪ] *n* el Uruguay.

Uruguayan [juərə'gwaɪən] *adj, n* uruguayo/a *m/f*.

US *n abbr* (= *United States*) EE.UU.

us [ʌs] *pron* nos; (*after prep*) nosotros/as; (*col*: *me*): **give** ~ **a kiss** dame un beso; *see also* **me**.

USA *n abbr see* **United States of America**; (*MIL*) = *United States Army*.

usable ['juːzəbl] *adj* utilizable.

USAF *n abbr* = *United States Air Force*.

usage ['juːzɪdʒ] *n* (*LING*) uso; (*utilization*) utilización *f*.

USCG *n abbr* = *United States Coast Guard*.

USDA *n abbr* = *United States Department of Agriculture*.

USDAW ['ʌzdɔː] *n abbr* (*BRIT*: = *Union of Shop, Distributive and Allied Workers*) sindicato de empleados de comercio.

USDI *n abbr* = *United States Department of the Interior*.

use *n* [juːs] uso, empleo; (*usefulness*) utilidad *f* ♦ *vt* [juːz] usar, emplear; **in** ~ en uso; **out of** ~ en desuso; **to be of** ~ servir; **ready for** ~ listo (para usar); **to make** ~ **of sth** aprovecharse *or* servirse de algo; **it's no** ~ (*pointless*) es inútil; (*not useful*) no sirve; **what's this** ~**d for?** ¿para qué sirve esto?; **to be** ~**d to** estar acostumbrado a (*SP*), acostumbrar; **to get** ~**d to** acostumbrarse a; **she** ~**d to do it** (ella) solía *or* acostumbraba hacerlo.

▶**use up** *vt* agotar.

used [juːzd] *adj* (*car*) usado.

useful ['juːsful] *adj* útil; **to come in** ~ ser útil.

usefulness ['juːsfəlnɪs] *n* utilidad.

useless ['juːslɪs] *adj* inútil; (*unusable*: *object*) inservible.

uselessly ['juːslɪslɪ] *adv* inútilmente, en vano.

uselessness ['juːslɪsnɪs] *n* inutilidad *f*.

user ['juːzə*] *n* usuario/a; (*of petrol, gas etc*) consumidor(a) *m/f*.

user-friendly ['juːzə'frɛndlɪ] *adj* (*COMPUT*) fácil de utilizar.

USES *n abbr* = *United States Employment Service*.

usher ['ʌʃə*] *n* (*at wedding*) ujier *m*; (*in cinema etc*) acomodador *m* ♦ *vt*: **to** ~ **sb in** (*into room*) hacer pasar a algn; **it** ~**ed in a new era** (*fig*) inició una nueva era.

usherette [ʌʃə'rɛt] *n* (*in cinema*) acomodadora.

USIA *n abbr* = *United States Information Agency*.

USM *n abbr* = *United States Mail; United States Mint.*

USN *n abbr* = *United States Navy.*

USPHS *n abbr* = *United States Public Health Service.*

USPO *n abbr* = *United States Post Office.*

USS *abbr* = *United States Ship* (*or Steamer*).

USSR *n abbr*: **the** ~ la U.R.S.S.

usu. *abbr* = **usually.**

usual ['juːʒuəl] *adj* normal, corriente; **as** ~ como de costumbre, como siempre.

usually ['juːʒuəlɪ] *adv* normalmente.

usurer ['juːʒərə*] *n* usurero.

usurp [juːˈzəːp] *vt* usurpar.

usury ['juːʒərɪ] *n* usura.

UT *abbr* (*US*) = *Utah.*

utensil [juːˈtɛnsl] *n* utensilio; **kitchen ~s** batería de cocina.

uterus ['juːtərəs] *n* útero.

utilitarian [juːtɪlɪˈtɛərɪən] *adj* utilitario.

utility [juːˈtɪlɪtɪ] *n* utilidad *f*.

utility room *n* trascocina.

utilization [juːtɪlaɪˈzeɪʃən] *n* utilización *f*.

utilize ['juːtɪlaɪz] *vt* utilizar.

utmost ['ʌtməust] *adj* mayor ♦ *n*: **to do one's** ~ hacer todo lo posible; **it is of the** ~ **importance that** ... es de la mayor importancia que ....

utter ['ʌtə*] *adj* total, completo ♦ *vt* pronunciar, proferir.

utterance ['ʌtərns] *n* palabras *fpl*, declaración *f*.

utterly ['ʌtəlɪ] *adv* completamente, totalmente.

U-turn ['juːˈtəːn] *n* cambio de sentido; (*fig*) giro de 180 grados.

Uzbekistan [ʌzbɛkɪˈstɑːn] *n* Uzbekistán *m*.

V v

V, v [viː] (*letter*) V, v *f*; **V for Victor** V de Valencia.

v. *abbr* (= *verse*) vers.º (= *vide: see*) V, vid., vide; (= *versus*) vs.; = **volt.**

VA, Va. *abbr* (*US*) = *Virginia.*

vac [væk] *n abbr* (*BRIT col*) = **vacation.**

vacancy ['veɪkənsɪ] *n* (*BRIT: job*) vacante *f*; (*room*) cuarto libro; **have you any vacancies?** ¿tiene *or* hay alguna habitación *or* algún cuarto libre?

vacant ['veɪkənt] *adj* desocupado, libre; (*expression*) distraído.

vacant lot *n* (*US*) solar *m*.

vacate [vəˈkeɪt] *vt* (*house*) desocupar; (*job*) dejar (vacante).

vacation [vəˈkeɪʃən] *n* vacaciones *fpl* ; **on** ~ de vacaciones; **to take a** ~ (*esp US*) tomarse unas vacaciones.

vacation course *n* curso de vacaciones.

vacationer [vəˈkeɪʃənə*], **vacationist** [vəˈkeɪʃənɪst] *n* (*US*) turista *m/f*.

vaccinate ['væksɪneɪt] *vt* vacunar.

vaccination [væksiˈneɪʃən] *n* vacunación *f*.

vaccine ['væksiːn] *n* vacuna.

vacuum ['vækjum] *n* vacío.

vacuum bottle *n* (*US*) = **vacuum flask.**

vacuum cleaner *n* aspiradora.

vacuum flask *n* (*BRIT*) termo.

vacuum-packed ['vækjum'pækt] *adj* envasado al vacío.

vagabond ['vægəbɔnd] *n* vagabundo/a.

vagary ['veɪgərɪ] *n* capricho.

vagina [vəˈdʒaɪnə] *n* vagina.

vagrancy ['veɪgrənsɪ] *n* vagabundeo.

vagrant ['veɪgrənt] *n* vagabundo/a.

vague [veɪg] *adj* vago; (*blurred: memory*) borroso; (*uncertain*) incierto, impreciso; (*person*) distraído; **I haven't the ~st idea** no tengo la más remota idea.

vaguely ['veɪglɪ] *adv* vagamente.

vagueness ['veɪgnɪs] *n* vaguedad *f*; imprecisión *f*; (*absent-mindedness*) despiste *m*.

vain [veɪn] *adj* (*conceited*) presumido; (*useless*) vano, inútil; **in** ~ en vano.

vainly ['veɪnlɪ] *adv* (*to no effect*) en vano; (*conceitedly*) vanidosamente.

valance ['væləns] *n* (*for bed*) volante alrededor de la colcha o sábana que cuelga hasta el suelo.

valedictory [vælɪˈdɪktərɪ] *adj* de despedida.

valentine ['væləntaɪn] *n* (*also*: ~ **card**) tarjeta del Día de los Enamorados.

valet ['væleɪ] *n* ayuda *m* de cámara.

valet service *n* (*for clothes*) planchado.

valiant ['væljənt] *adj* valiente.

valiantly ['væljəntlɪ] *adv* valientemente, con valor.

valid ['vælɪd] *adj* válido; (*ticket*) valedero; (*law*) vigente.

validate ['vælɪdeɪt] *vt* (*contract, document*) convalidar; (*argument, claim*) dar validez a.

validity [vəˈlɪdɪtɪ] *n* validez *f*, vigencia.

valise [vəˈliːz] *n* maletín *m*.

valley ['vælɪ] *n* valle *m*.

valour, (*US*) **valor** ['vælə*] *n* valor *m*, valentía.

valuable ['væijuəbl] *adj* (*jewel*) de valor; (*time*) valioso; ~**s** *npl* objetos *mpl* de valor.
valuation [vælju'eɪʃən] *n* tasación *f*, valuación *f*.
value ['vælju:] *n* valor *m*; (*importance*) importancia ♦ *vt* (*fix price of*) tasar, valorar; (*esteem*) apreciar; ~**s** *npl* (*moral*) valores *mpl* morales; **to lose (in)** ~ (*currency*) bajar; (*property*) desvalorizarse; **to gain (in)** ~ (*currency*) subir; (*property*) valorizarse; **you get good** ~ **(for money) in that shop** la relación calidad-precio es muy buena en esa tienda; **to be of great** ~ **to sb** ser de gran valor para algn; **it is** ~**d at £8** está valorado en ocho libras.
value added tax (VAT) *n* (*BRIT*) impuesto sobre el valor añadido *or* agregado (*LAM*) (IVA *m*).
valued ['vælju:d] *adj* (*appreciated*) apreciado.
valueless ['vælju:lɪs] *adj* sin valor.
valuer ['vælju:ə*] *n* tasador(a) *m/f*.
valve [vælv] *n* (*ANAT, TECH*) válvula.
vampire ['væmpaɪə*] *n* vampiro.
van [væn] *n* (*AUT*) furgoneta, camioneta (*LAM*); (*BRIT RAIL*) furgón *m* (de equipajes).
V and A *n abbr* (*BRIT*) = *Victoria and Albert Museum*.
vandal ['vændl] *n* vándalo/a.
vandalism ['vændəlɪzəm] *n* vandalismo.
vandalize ['vændəlaɪz] *vt* dañar, destruir, destrozar.
vanguard ['vængɑːd] *n* vanguardia.
vanilla [və'nɪlə] *n* vainilla.
vanish ['vænɪʃ] *vi* desaparecer, esfumarse.
vanity ['vænɪtɪ] *n* vanidad *f*.
vanity case *n* neceser *m*.
vantage point ['vɑːntɪdʒ-] *n* posición *f* ventajosa.
vaporize ['veɪpəraɪz] *vt* vaporizar ♦ *vi* vaporizarse.
vapour, (*US*) **vapor** ['veɪpə*] *n* vapor *m*; (*on breath, window*) vaho.
vapo(u)r trail *n* (*AVIAT*) estela.
variable ['vɛərɪəbl] *adj* variable ♦ *n* variable *f*.
variance ['vɛərɪəns] *n*: **to be at** ~ **(with)** estar en desacuerdo (con), no cuadrar (con).
variant ['vɛərɪənt] *n* variante *f*.
variation [vɛərɪ'eɪʃən] *n* variación *f*.
varicose ['værɪkəus] *adj*: ~ **veins** varices *fpl*.
varied ['vɛərɪd] *adj* variado.
variety [və'raɪətɪ] *n* variedad *f*, diversidad *f*; (*quantity*) surtido; **for a** ~ **of reasons** por varias *or* diversas razones.
variety show *n* espectáculo de variedades.
various ['vɛərɪəs] *adj* varios/as, diversos/as; **at** ~ **times** (*different*) en distintos momentos; (*several*) varias veces.
varnish ['vɑːnɪʃ] *n* (*gen*) barniz *m*; (*nail* ~) esmalte *m* ♦ *vt* (*gen*) barnizar; (*nails*) pintar (con esmalte).
vary ['vɛərɪ] *vt* variar; (*change*) cambiar ♦ *vi* variar; (*disagree*) discrepar; **to** ~ **with** *or* **according to** variar según *or* de acuerdo con.
varying ['vɛərɪɪŋ] *adj* diversos/as.
vase [vɑːz] *n* florero.
vasectomy [və'sɛktəmɪ] *n* vasectomía.
Vaseline ® ['væsɪliːn] *n* vaselina ®.
vast [vɑːst] *adj* enorme; (*success*) abrumador(a), arrollador(a).
vastly ['vɑːstlɪ] *adv* enormemente.
vastness ['vɑːstnɪs] *n* inmensidad *f*.
VAT [væt] *n abbr* (*BRIT*: = *value added tax*) IVA *m*.
vat [væt] *n* tina, tinaja.
Vatican ['vætɪkən] *n*: **the** ~ el Vaticano.
vatman ['vætmæn] *n* (*BRIT col*) inspector *m or* recaudador *m* del IVA; "**how to avoid the** ~" "cómo evitar pagar el IVA".
vaudeville ['vəudəvɪl] *n* (*US*) vodevil *m*.
vault [vɔːlt] *n* (*of roof*) bóveda; (*tomb*) tumba; (*in bank*) cámara acorazada ♦ *vt* (*also*: ~ **over**) saltar (por encima de).
vaunted ['vɔːntɪd] *adj*: **much** ~ cacareado.
VC *n abbr* = **vice-chairman**, **vice-chancellor**; (*BRIT*: = *Victoria Cross*) condecoración militar.
VCR *n abbr* = **video cassette recorder**.
VD *n abbr see* **venereal disease**.
VDU *n abbr see* **visual display unit**.
veal [viːl] *n* ternera.
veer [vɪə*] *vi* (*ship*) virar.
veg. [vɛdʒ] *n abbr* (*BRIT col*) = **vegetable(s)**.
vegan ['viːgən] *n* vegetariano/a estricto/a.
vegeburger, veggieburger ['vɛdʒɪbəːgə*] *n* hamburguesa vegetal.
vegetable ['vɛdʒtəbl] *n* (*BOT*) vegetal *m*; (*edible plant*) legumbre *f*, hortaliza ♦ *adj* vegetal; ~**s** *npl* (*cooked*) verduras *fpl*.
vegetable garden *n* huerta, huerto.
vegetarian [vɛdʒɪ'tɛərɪən] *adj, n* vegetariano/a *m/f*.
vegetate ['vɛdʒɪteɪt] *vi* vegetar.
vegetation [vɛdʒɪ'teɪʃən] *n* vegetación *f*.
vegetative ['vɛdʒɪtətɪv] *adj* vegetativo; (*BOT*) vegetal.
vehemence ['viːɪməns] *n* vehemencia; violencia.
vehement ['viːɪmənt] *adj* vehemente, apasionado; (*dislike, hatred*) violento.
vehicle ['viːɪkl] *n* vehículo; (*fig*) vehículo,

medio.
vehicular [vɪˈhɪkjʊlə*] *adj*: ~ **traffic**
circulación *f* rodada.
veil [veɪl] *n* velo ♦ *vt* velar; **under a** ~ **of**
secrecy (*fig*) en el mayor secreto.
veiled [veɪld] *adj* (*also fig*) disimulado,
velado.
vein [veɪn] *n* vena; (*of ore etc*) veta.
Velcro ® [ˈvɛlkrəʊ] *n* velcro *m* ®.
vellum [ˈvɛləm] *n* (*writing paper*) papel *m*
vitela.
velocity [vɪˈlɒsɪtɪ] *n* velocidad *f.*
velour [vəˈluə*] *n* terciopelo.
velvet [ˈvɛlvɪt] *n* terciopelo ♦ *adj*
aterciopelado.
vendetta [vɛnˈdɛtə] *n* vendetta.
vending machine [ˈvɛndɪŋ-] *n* máquina
expendedora, expendedor *m.*
vendor [ˈvɛndə*] *n* vendedor(a) *m/f*; **street**
~ vendedor(a) *m/f* callejero/a.
veneer [vəˈnɪə*] *n* chapa, enchapado; (*fig*)
barniz *m.*
venereal [vɪˈnɪərɪəl] *adj*: ~ **disease (VD)**
enfermedad *f* venérea.
Venetian blind [vɪˈniːʃən-] *n* persiana.
Venezuela [vɛnɛˈzweɪlə] *n* Venezuela.
Venezuelan [vɛnɛˈzweɪlən] *adj, n*
venezolano/a *m/f.*
vengeance [ˈvɛndʒəns] *n* venganza; **with a**
~ (*fig*) con creces.
vengeful [ˈvɛndʒful] *adj* vengativo.
Venice [ˈvɛnɪs] *n* Venecia.
venison [ˈvɛnɪsn] *n* carne *f* de venado.
venom [ˈvɛnəm] *n* veneno.
venomous [ˈvɛnəməs] *adj* venenoso.
venomously [ˈvɛnəməslɪ] *adv* con odio.
vent [vɛnt] *n* (*opening*) abertura; (*air-hole*)
respiradero; (*in wall*) rejilla (de
ventilación) ♦ *vt* (*fig: feelings*) desahogar.
ventilate [ˈvɛntɪleɪt] *vt* ventilar.
ventilation [vɛntɪˈleɪʃən] *n* ventilación *f.*
ventilation shaft *n* pozo de ventilación.
ventilator [ˈvɛntɪleɪtə*] *n* ventilador *m.*
ventriloquist [vɛnˈtrɪləkwɪst] *n*
ventrílocuo/a.
venture [ˈvɛntʃə*] *n* empresa ♦ *vt*
arriesgar; (*opinion*) ofrecer ♦ *vi*
arriesgarse, lanzarse; **a business** ~ una
empresa comercial; **to** ~ **to do sth**
aventurarse a hacer algo.
venture capital *n* capital *m* arriesgado.
venue [ˈvɛnjuː] *n* (*meeting place*) lugar *m* de
reunión; (*for concert*) local *m.*
Venus [ˈviːnəs] *n* (*ASTRO*) Venus *m.*
veracity [vəˈræsɪtɪ] *n* veracidad *f.*
veranda(h) [vəˈrændə] *n* terraza; (*with*
glass) galería.
verb [vəːb] *n* verbo.

verbal [ˈvəːbl] *adj* verbal.
verbally [ˈvəːbəlɪ] *adv* verbalmente, de
palabra.
verbatim [vəːˈbeɪtɪm] *adj, adv* al pie de la
letra, palabra por palabra.
verbose [vəːˈbəʊs] *adj* prolijo.
verdict [ˈvəːdɪkt] *n* veredicto, fallo; (*fig:*
opinion) opinión *f*, juicio; ~ **of guilty/not**
guilty veredicto de culpabilidad/
inocencia.
verge [vəːdʒ] *n* (*BRIT*) borde *m*; **to be on the**
~ **of doing sth** estar a punto de hacer
algo.
▶**verge on** *vt fus* rayar en.
verger [ˈvəːdʒə*] *n* sacristán *m.*
verification [vɛrɪfɪˈkeɪʃən] *n* comprobación
f, verificación *f.*
verify [ˈvɛrɪfaɪ] *vt* comprobar, verificar;
(*COMPUT*) verificar; (*prove the truth of*)
confirmar.
veritable [ˈvɛrɪtəbl] *adj* verdadero,
auténtico.
vermin [ˈvəːmɪn] *npl* (*animals*) bichos *mpl*;
(*insects, fig*) sabandijas *fpl.*
vermouth [ˈvəːməθ] *n* vermut *m.*
vernacular [vəˈnækjʊlə*] *n* lengua
vernácula.
versatile [ˈvəːsətaɪl] *adj* (*person*)
polifacético; (*machine, tool etc*) versátil.
versatility [vəːsəˈtɪlɪtɪ] *n* versatilidad *f.*
verse [vəːs] *n* versos *mpl*, poesía; (*stanza*)
estrofa; (*in bible*) versículo; **in** ~ en
verso.
versed [vəːst] *adj*: (**well-**)~ **in** versado en.
version [ˈvəːʃən] *n* versión *f.*
versus [ˈvəːsəs] *prep* contra.
vertebra, *pl* ~**e** [ˈvəːtɪbrə, briː] *n* vértebra.
vertebrate [ˈvəːtɪbrɪt] *n* vertebrado.
vertical [ˈvəːtɪkl] *adj* vertical.
vertically [ˈvəːtɪkəlɪ] *adv* verticalmente.
vertigo [ˈvəːtɪgəʊ] *n* vértigo; **to suffer from**
~ tener vértigo.
verve [vəːv] *n* brío.
very [ˈvɛrɪ] *adv* muy ♦ *adj*: **the** ~ **book which**
el mismo libro que; **the** ~ **last** el último
(de todos); **at the** ~ **least** al menos; ~
much muchísimo; ~ **well/little** muy bien/
poco; ~ **high frequency** (*RADIO*)
frecuencia muy alta; **it's** ~ **cold** hace
mucho frío; **the** ~ **thought (of it) alarms**
me con sólo pensarlo me entra miedo.
vespers [ˈvɛspəz] *npl* vísperas *fpl.*
vessel [ˈvɛsl] *n* (*ANAT*) vaso; (*ship*) barco;
(*container*) vasija.
vest [vɛst] *n* (*BRIT*) camiseta; (*US: waistcoat*)
chaleco.
vested interests [ˈvɛstɪd-] *npl* (*COMM*)
intereses *mpl* creados.

vestibule ['vɛstɪbjuːl] n vestíbulo.
vestige ['vɛstɪdʒ] n vestigio, rastro.
vestry ['vɛstrɪ] n sacristía.
Vesuvius [vɪ'suːvɪəs] n Vesubio.
vet [vɛt] n abbr = **veterinary surgeon** ♦ vt
revisar; **to ~ sb for a job** someter a
investigación a algn para un trabajo.
veteran ['vɛtərn] n veterano/a ♦ adj: **she is a
~ campaigner for ...** es una veterana de la
campaña de ... .
veteran car n coche m antiguo.
veterinarian [vɛtrɪ'nɛərɪən] n (US) =
veterinary surgeon.
veterinary ['vɛtrɪnərɪ] adj veterinario.
veterinary surgeon n (BRIT) veterinario/a.
veto ['viːtəu] n (pl **~es**) veto ♦ vt prohibir,
vedar; **to put a ~ on** vetar.
vetting ['vɛtɪŋ] n: **positive ~** investigación
gubernamental de los futuros altos
cargos de la Administración.
vex [vɛks] vt (irritate) fastidiar; (make
impatient) impacientar.
vexed [vɛkst] adj (question) controvertido.
vexing ['vɛksɪŋ] adj molesto, engorroso.
VFD n abbr (US) = **voluntary fire department**.
VG n abbr (BRIT SCOL etc: = very good) S
(= sobresaliente).
VHF abbr (= very high frequency) VHF f.
VI abbr (US) = **Virgin Islands**.
via ['vaɪə] prep por, por vía de.
viability [vaɪə'bɪlɪtɪ] n viabilidad f.
viable ['vaɪəbl] adj viable.
viaduct ['vaɪədʌkt] n viaducto.
vial ['vaɪəl] n frasco pequeño.
vibes [vaɪbz] npl (col): **I got good/bad ~** me
dio buen/mal rollo.
vibrant ['vaɪbrənt] adj (lively, bright) vivo;
(full of emotion: voice) vibrante; (colour)
fuerte.
vibraphone ['vaɪbrəfəun] n vibráfono.
vibrate [vaɪ'breɪt] vi vibrar.
vibration [vaɪ'breɪʃən] n vibración f.
vibrator [vaɪ'breɪtə*] n vibrador m.
vicar ['vɪkə*] n párroco.
vicarage ['vɪkərɪdʒ] n parroquia.
vicarious [vɪ'kɛərɪəs] adj indirecto;
(responsibility) delegado.
vice [vaɪs] n (evil) vicio; (TECH) torno de
banco.
vice- [vaɪs] pref vice....
vice-chairman ['vaɪs'tʃɛəmən] n
vicepresidente m.
vice-chancellor [vaɪs'tʃɑːnsələ*] n (BRIT
UNIV) rector(a) m/f.
vice-president [vaɪs'prɛzɪdənt] n vice-
presidente/a m/f.
viceroy ['vaɪsrɔɪ] n virrey m.
vice versa ['vaɪsɪ'vəːsə] adv viceversa.

vicinity [vɪ'sɪnɪtɪ] n (area) vecindad f;
(nearness) proximidad f; **in the ~ (of)**
cercano (a).
vicious ['vɪʃəs] adj (remark) malicioso;
(blow) brutal; **a ~ circle** un círculo
vicioso.
viciousness ['vɪʃəsnɪs] n brutalidad f.
vicissitudes [vɪ'sɪsɪtjuːdz] npl vicisitudes
fpl, peripecias fpl.
victim ['vɪktɪm] n víctima; **to be the ~ of**
ser víctima de.
victimization [vɪktɪmaɪ'zeɪʃən] n
persecución f; (of striker etc) represalias
fpl.
victimize ['vɪktɪmaɪz] vt (strikers etc) tomar
represalias contra.
victor ['vɪktə*] n vencedor(a) m/f.
Victorian [vɪk'tɔːrɪən] adj victoriano.
victorious [vɪk'tɔːrɪəs] adj vencedor(a).
victory ['vɪktərɪ] n victoria; **to win a ~ over
sb** obtener una victoria sobre algn.
video ['vɪdɪəu] cpd de vídeo ♦ n vídeo ♦ vt
grabar (en vídeo).
video camera n videocámara, cámara de
vídeo.
video cassette n videocassette f.
video (cassette) recorder n vídeo,
videocassette f.
videodisk ['vɪdɪəudɪsk] n videodisco.
video game n videojuego.
video nasty n vídeo de violencia y/o porno
duro.
videophone ['vɪdɪəufəun] n videoteléfono,
videófono.
video recording n videograbación f.
video tape n cinta de vídeo.
vie [vaɪ] vi: **to ~ with** competir con.
Vienna [vɪ'ɛnə] n Viena.
Viennese [vɪə'niːz] adj, n vienés/esa m/f.
Vietnam, Viet Nam [vjɛt'næm] n Vietnam
m.
Vietnamese [vjɛtnə'miːz] adj vietnamita
♦ n (pl inv) vietnamita m/f; (LING)
vietnamita m.
view [vjuː] n vista; (landscape) paisaje m;
(opinion) opinión f, criterio ♦ vt (look at)
mirar; (examine) examinar; **on ~** (in
museum etc) expuesto; **in full ~ of sb** a la
vista de algn; **to be within ~ (of sth)** estar
a la vista (de algo); **an overall ~ of the
situation** una visión de conjunto de la
situación; **in ~ of the fact that** en vista de
que; **to take** or **hold the ~ that ...** opinar
or pensar que ...; **with a ~ to doing sth**
con miras or vistas a hacer algo.
viewdata ['vjuːdeɪtə] n (BRIT) videodatos mpl.
viewer ['vjuːə*] n (small projector)
visionadora; (TV) televidente m/f,

telespectador(a) *m/f.*

viewfinder ['vju:faɪndə*] *n* visor *m* de imagen.

viewpoint ['vju:pɔɪnt] *n* punto de vista.

vigil ['vɪdʒɪl] *n* vigilia; **to keep ~** velar.

vigilance ['vɪdʒɪləns] *n* vigilancia.

vigilance committee *n* (*US*) comité *m* de autodefensa.

vigilant ['vɪdʒɪlənt] *adj* vigilante.

vigilante [vɪdʒɪ'læntɪ] *n vecino/a que se toma la justicia por su mano.*

vigorous ['vɪgərəs] *adj* enérgico, vigoroso.

vigorously ['vɪgərəslɪ] *adv* enérgicamente, vigorosamente.

vigour, (*US*) **vigor** ['vɪgə*] *n* energía, vigor *m.*

vile [vaɪl] *adj* (*action*) vil, infame; (*smell*) repugnante.

vilify ['vɪlɪfaɪ] *vt* denigrar, vilipendiar.

villa ['vɪlə] *n* (*country house*) casa de campo; (*suburban house*) chalet *m.*

village ['vɪlɪdʒ] *n* aldea.

villager ['vɪlɪdʒə*] *n* aldeano/a.

villain ['vɪlən] *n* (*scoundrel*) malvado/a; (*criminal*) maleante *m/f; see also* **pantomime.**

VIN *n abbr* (*US*) = *vehicle identification number.*

vinaigrette [vɪneɪ'grɛt] *n* vinagreta.

vindicate ['vɪndɪkeɪt] *vt* vindicar, justificar.

vindication [vɪndɪ'keɪʃən] *n*: **in ~ of** en justificación de.

vindictive [vɪn'dɪktɪv] *adj* vengativo.

vine [vaɪn] *n* vid *f.*

vinegar ['vɪnɪgə*] *n* vinagre *m.*

vine-growing ['vaɪngrəuɪŋ] *adj* (*region*) viticultor(a).

vineyard ['vɪnjɑːd] *n* viña, viñedo.

vintage ['vɪntɪdʒ] *n* (*year*) vendimia, cosecha; **the 1970 ~** la cosecha de 1970.

vintage car *n* coche *m* antiguo *or* de época.

vintage wine *n* vino añejo.

vintage year *n*: **it's been a ~ for plays** ha sido un año destacado en lo que a teatro se refiere.

vinyl ['vaɪnl] *n* vinilo.

viola [vɪ'əulə] *n* (*MUS*) viola.

violate ['vaɪəleɪt] *vt* violar.

violation [vaɪə'leɪʃən] *n* violación *f;* **in ~ of sth** en violación de algo.

violence ['vaɪələns] *n* violencia; **acts of ~** actos *mpl* de violencia.

violent ['vaɪələnt] *adj* (*gen*) violento; (*pain*) intenso; **a ~ dislike of sb/sth** una profunda antipatía *or* manía a algn/algo.

violently ['vaɪələntlɪ] *adv* (*severely: ill, angry*) muy.

violet ['vaɪələt] *adj* violado, violeta ♦ *n*

(*plant*) violeta.

violin [vaɪə'lɪn] *n* violín *m.*

violinist [vaɪə'lɪnɪst] *n* violinista *m/f.*

VIP *n abbr* (= *very important person*) VIP *m.*

viper ['vaɪpə*] *n* víbora.

viral ['vaɪərəl] *adj* vírico.

virgin ['vɜːdʒɪn] *n* virgen *m/f* ♦ *adj* virgen; **the Blessed V~** la Santísima Virgen.

virginity [vɜː'dʒɪnɪtɪ] *n* virginidad *f.*

Virgo ['vɜːgəu] *n* Virgo.

virile ['vɪraɪl] *adj* viril.

virility [vɪ'rɪlɪtɪ] *n* virilidad *f.*

virtual ['vɜːtjuəl] *adj* virtual.

virtually ['vɜːtjuəlɪ] *adv* (*almost*) prácticamente, virtualmente; **it is ~ impossible** es prácticamente imposible.

virtual reality *n* realidad *f* virtual.

virtue ['vɜːtjuː] *n* virtud *f;* **by ~ of** en virtud de.

virtuosity [vɜːtju'ɒsɪtɪ] *n* virtuosismo.

virtuoso [vɜːtju'əusəu] *n* virtuoso.

virtuous ['vɜːtjuəs] *adj* virtuoso.

virulence ['vɪruləns] *n* virulencia.

virulent ['vɪrulənt] *adj* virulento, violento.

virus ['vaɪərəs] *n* virus *m inv.*

visa ['viːzə] *n* visado, visa (*LAM*).

vis-à-vis [viːzə'viː] *prep* con respecto a.

viscount ['vaɪkaunt] *n* vizconde *m.*

viscous ['vɪskəs] *adj* viscoso.

vise [vaɪs] *n* (*US TECH*) = **vice.**

visibility [vɪzɪ'bɪlɪtɪ] *n* visibilidad *f.*

visible ['vɪzəbl] *adj* visible; **~ exports/ imports** exportaciones *fpl*/importaciones *fpl* visibles.

visibly ['vɪzɪblɪ] *adv* visiblemente.

vision ['vɪʒən] *n* (*sight*) vista; (*foresight, in dream*) visión *f.*

visionary ['vɪʒənrɪ] *n* visionario/a.

visit ['vɪzɪt] *n* visita ♦ *vt* (*person*) visitar, hacer una visita a; (*place*) ir a, (ir a) conocer; **to pay a ~ to** (*person*) visitar a; **on a private/official ~** en visita privada/ oficial.

visiting ['vɪzɪtɪŋ] *adj* (*speaker, professor*) invitado; (*team*) visitante.

visiting card *n* tarjeta de visita.

visiting hours *npl* (*in hospital etc*) horas *fpl* de visita.

visitor *n* (*gen*) visitante *m/f;* (*to one's house*) visita; (*tourist*) turista *m/f;* (*tripper*) excursionista *m/f;* **to have ~s** (*at home*) tener visita.

visitors' book *n* libro de visitas.

visor ['vaɪzə*] *n* visera.

VISTA ['vɪstə] *n abbr* (= *Volunteers In Service to America*) programa de ayuda voluntaria a los necesitados.

vista ['vɪstə] *n* vista, panorama.

visual ['vɪzjuəl] *adj* visual.
visual aid *n* medio *m* visual.
visual arts *npl* artes *fpl* plásticas.
visual display unit (VDU) *n* unidad *f* de despliegue visual, monitor *m*.
visualize ['vɪzjuəlaɪz] *vt* imaginarse; (*foresee*) prever.
visually ['vɪzjuəlɪ] *adv*: ~ **handicapped** con visión deficiente.
vital ['vaɪtl] *adj* (*essential*) esencial, imprescindible; (*crucial*) crítico; (*person*) enérgico, vivo; (*of life*) vital; **of ~ importance (to sb/sth)** de suma importancia (para algn/algo).
vitality [vaɪ'tælɪtɪ] *n* energía, vitalidad *f*.
vitally ['vaɪtəlɪ] *adv*: ~ **important** de suma importancia.
vital statistics *npl* (*of population*) estadísticas *fpl* demográficas; (*col: woman's*) medidas *fpl* (corporales).
vitamin ['vɪtəmɪn] *n* vitamina.
vitamin pill *n* pastilla de vitaminas.
vitreous ['vɪtrɪəs] *adj* (*china, enamel*) vítreo.
vitriolic [vɪtrɪ'ɔlɪk] *adj* mordaz.
viva ['vaɪvə] *n* (*also*: ~ **voce**) examen *m* oral.
vivacious [vɪ'veɪʃəs] *adj* vivaz, alegre.
vivacity [vɪ'væsɪtɪ] *n* vivacidad *f*.
vivid ['vɪvɪd] *adj* (*account*) gráfico; (*light*) intenso; (*imagination*) vivo.
vividly ['vɪvɪdlɪ] *adv* (*describe*) gráfica-mente; (*remember*) como si fuera hoy.
vivisection [vɪvɪ'sɛkʃən] *n* vivisección *f*.
vixen ['vɪksn] *n* (*ZOOL*) zorra, raposa; (*pej: woman*) arpía, bruja.
viz *abbr* (= *videlicet: namely*) v.gr.
VLF *abbr* = *very low frequency*.
V-neck ['viːnɛk] *n* cuello de pico.
VOA *n abbr* (= *Voice of America*) Voz *f* de América.
vocabulary [vəu'kæbjulərɪ] *n* vocabulario.
vocal ['vəukl] *adj* vocal; (*articulate*) elocuente.
vocal cords *npl* cuerdas *fpl* vocales.
vocalist ['vəukəlɪst] *n* cantante *m/f*.
vocation [vəu'keɪʃən] *n* vocación *f*.
vocational [vəu'keɪʃənl] *adj* vocacional; ~ **guidance** orientación *f* profesional; ~ **training** formación *f* profesional.
vociferous [və'sɪfərəs] *adj* vociferante.
vociferously [və'sɪfərəslɪ] *adv* a gritos.
vodka ['vɔdkə] *n* vodka *m*.
vogue [vəug] *n* boga, moda; **to be in ~, be the ~** estar de moda *or* en boga.
voice [vɔɪs] *n* voz *f* ♦ *vt* (*opinion*) expresar; **in a loud/soft ~** en voz alta/baja; **to give ~ to** expresar.
voice mail *n* fonobuzón *m*.
voice-over ['vɔɪsəuvə*] *n* voz *f* en off.

void [vɔɪd] *n* vacío; (*hole*) hueco ♦ *adj* (*invalid*) nulo, inválido; (*empty*): ~ **of** carente *or* desprovisto de.
voile [vɔɪl] *n* gasa.
vol. *abbr* (= *volume*) t.
volatile ['vɔlətaɪl] *adj* volátil; (*COMPUT: memory*) no permanente.
volcanic [vɔl'kænɪk] *adj* volcánico.
volcano, ~es [vɔl'keɪnəu] *n* volcán *m*.
volition [və'lɪʃən] *n*: **of one's own ~** por su propia voluntad.
volley ['vɔlɪ] *n* (*of gunfire*) descarga; (*of stones etc*) lluvia; (*TENNIS etc*) volea.
volleyball *n* voleibol *m*, balonvolea *m*.
volt [vəult] *n* voltio.
voltage ['vəultɪdʒ] *n* voltaje *m*; **high/low ~** alto/bajo voltaje, alta/baja tensión.
volte-face ['vɔlt'fɑːs] *n* viraje *m*.
voluble ['vɔljubl] *adj* locuaz, hablador(a).
volume ['vɔljuːm] *n* (*of tank*) volumen *m*; (*book*) tomo; ~ **one/two** (*of book*) tomo primero/segundo; ~**s** *npl* (*great quantities*) cantidad *fsg*; **his expression spoke ~s** su expresión (lo) decía todo.
volume control *n* (*RADIO, TV*) (botón *m* del) volumen *m*.
volume discount *n* (*COMM*) descuento por volumen de compras.
voluminous [və'luːmɪnəs] *adj* (*large*) voluminoso; (*prolific*) prolífico.
voluntarily ['vɔləntrɪlɪ] *adv* libremente, voluntariamente.
voluntary ['vɔləntərɪ] *adj* voluntario, espontáneo.
voluntary liquidation *n* (*COMM*) liquidación *f* voluntaria.
voluntary redundancy *n* (*BRIT*) despido voluntario.
volunteer [vɔlən'tɪə*] *n* voluntario/a ♦ *vi* ofrecerse (de voluntario); **to ~ to do** ofrecerse a hacer.
voluptuous [və'lʌptjuəs] *adj* voluptuoso.
vomit ['vɔmɪt] *n* vómito ♦ *vt, vi* vomitar.
voracious [və'reɪʃəs] *adj* voraz; (*reader*) ávido.
vote [vəut] *n* voto; (*votes cast*) votación *f*; (*right to ~*) derecho a votar; (*franchise*) sufragio ♦ *vt* (*chairman*) elegir ♦ *vi* votar, ir a votar; ~ **of thanks** voto de gracias; **to put sth to the ~, to take a ~ on sth** someter algo a votación; ~ **for** *or* **in favour of/against** voto a favor de/en contra de; **to ~ to do sth** votar por hacer algo; **he was ~d secretary** fue elegido secretario por votación; **to pass a ~ of confidence/no confidence** aprobar un voto de confianza/de censura.
voter ['vəutə*] *n* votante *m/f*.

voting ['vəutɪŋ] n votación f.
voting paper n (BRIT) papeleta de votación.
voting right n derecho a voto.
vouch [vautʃ]: **to ~ for** vt fus garantizar, responder de.
voucher ['vautʃə*] n (for meal, petrol) vale m; **luncheon/travel ~** vale m de comida/de viaje.
vow [vau] n voto ♦ vi hacer voto; **to take** or **make a ~ to do sth** jurar hacer algo, comprometerse a hacer algo.
vowel ['vauəl] n vocal f.
voyage ['vɔɪɪdʒ] n (journey) viaje m; (crossing) travesía.
voyeur [vwɑː'jɜː*] n voyeur m/f, mirón/ona m/f.
VP n abbr (= vice-president) V.P.
vs abbr (= versus) vs.
VSO n abbr (BRIT: = Voluntary Service Overseas) organización que envía jóvenes voluntarios a trabajar y enseñar en los países del Tercer Mundo.
VT, Vt. abbr (US) = Vermont.
vulgar ['vʌlgə*] adj (rude) ordinario, grosero; (in bad taste) de mal gusto.
vulgarity [vʌl'gærɪtɪ] n grosería; mal gusto.
vulnerability [vʌlnərə'bɪlɪtɪ] n vulnerabilidad f.
vulnerable ['vʌlnərəbl] adj vulnerable.
vulture ['vʌltʃə*] n buitre m, gallinazo (LAM).

W w

W, w ['dʌbljuː] n (letter) W, w f; **W for William** W de Washington.
W abbr (= west) O; (ELEC: = watt) v.
WA abbr (US) = Washington.
wad [wɔd] n (of cotton wool, paper) bolita; (of banknotes etc) fajo.
wadding ['wɔdɪŋ] n relleno.
waddle ['wɔdl] vi andar como un pato.
wade [weɪd] vi: **to ~ through** caminar por el agua; (fig: a book) leer con dificultad.
wading pool ['weɪdɪŋ-] n (US) piscina para niños.
wafer ['weɪfə*] n (biscuit) barquillo; (REL) oblea; (: consecrated) hostia; (COMPUT) oblea, microplaqueta.
wafer-thin ['weɪfə'θɪn] adj finísimo.

waffle ['wɔfl] n (CULIN) gofre m ♦ vi meter el rollo.
waffle iron n molde m para hacer gofres.
waft [wɔft] vt llevar por el aire ♦ vi flotar.
wag [wæg] vt menear, agitar ♦ vi moverse, menearse; **the dog ~ged its tail** el perro meneó la cola.
wage [weɪdʒ] n (also: ~s) sueldo, salario ♦ vt: **to ~ war** hacer la guerra; **a day's ~** el sueldo de un día.
wage claim n reivindicación f salarial.
wage differential n diferencia salarial.
wage earner n asalariado/a.
wage freeze n congelación f de salarios.
wage packet n sobre m de la paga.
wager ['weɪdʒə*] n apuesta ♦ vt apostar.
waggle ['wægl] vt menear, mover.
wag(g)on ['wægən] n (horse-drawn) carro; (BRIT RAIL) vagón m.
wail [weɪl] n gemido ♦ vi gemir.
waist [weɪst] n cintura, talle m.
waistcoat ['weɪstkəut] n (BRIT) chaleco.
waistline ['weɪstlaɪn] n talle m.
wait [weɪt] n espera; (interval) pausa ♦ vi esperar; **to lie in ~ for** acechar a; **I can't ~ to** (fig) estoy deseando; **to ~ for** esperar (a); **to keep sb ~ing** hacer esperar a algn; **~ a moment!** ¡un momento!, ¡un momentito!; **"repairs while you ~"** "reparaciones en el acto".
▶**wait behind** vi quedarse.
▶**wait on** vt fus servir a.
▶**wait up** vi esperar levantado.
waiter ['weɪtə*] n camarero.
waiting ['weɪtɪŋ] n: **"no ~"** (BRIT AUT) "prohibido estacionarse".
waiting list n lista de espera.
waiting room n sala de espera.
waitress ['weɪtrɪs] n camarera.
waive [weɪv] vt suspender.
waiver ['weɪvə*] n renuncia.
wake [weɪk] vb (pt **woke** or **waked**, pp **woken** or **waked** [wəuk, 'wəukn]) vt (also: ~ **up**) despertar ♦ vi (also: ~ **up**) despertarse ♦ n (for dead person) velatorio; (NAUT) estela; **to ~ up to sth** (fig) darse cuenta de algo; **in the ~ of** tras, después de; **to follow in sb's ~** (fig) seguir las huellas de algn.
waken ['weɪkn] vt, vi = **wake**.
Wales [weɪlz] n País m de Gales.
walk [wɔːk] n (stroll) paseo; (hike) excursión f a pie, caminata; (gait) paso, andar m; (in park etc) paseo ♦ vi andar, caminar; (for pleasure, exercise) pasearse ♦ vt (distance) recorrer a pie, andar; (dog) (sacar a) pasear; **to go for a ~** ir a dar un paseo; **10 minutes' ~ from here** a 10

minutos de aquí andando; **people from all ~s of life** gente de todas las esferas; **to ~ in one's sleep** ser sonámbulo/a; **I'll ~ you home** te acompañaré a casa.

▶**walk out** vi (go out) salir; (as protest) marcharse, salirse; (strike) declararse en huelga; **to ~ out on sb** abandonar a algn.

walkabout ['wɔːkəbaut] n: **to go (on a) ~** darse un baño de multitudes.

walker ['wɔːkə*] n (person) paseante m/f, caminante m/f.

walkie-talkie ['wɔːkɪ'tɔːkɪ] n walkie-talkie m.

walking ['wɔːkɪŋ] n (el) andar; **it's within ~ distance** se puede ir andando or a pie.

walking stick n bastón m.

Walkman ® n walkman m ®.

walk-on ['wɔːkɔn] adj (THEAT: part) de comparsa.

walkout ['wɔːkaut] n (of workers) huelga.

walkover ['wɔːkəuvə*] n (col) pan m comido.

walkway ['wɔːkweɪ] n paseo.

wall [wɔːl] n pared f; (exterior) muro; (city ~ etc) muralla; **to go to the ~** (fig: firm etc) quebrar, ir a la bancarrota.

▶**wall in** vt (garden etc) cercar con una tapia.

walled [wɔːld] adj (city) amurallado; (garden) con tapia.

wallet ['wɔlɪt] n cartera, billetera (esp LAM).

wallflower ['wɔːlflauə*] n alhelí m; **to be a ~** (fig) comer pavo.

wall hanging n tapiz m.

wallop ['wɔləp] vt (col) zurrar.

wallow ['wɔləu] vi revolcarse; **to ~ in one's grief** sumirse en su pena.

wallpaper ['wɔːlpeɪpə*] n (for walls) papel m pintado; (COMPUT) fondo de escritorio.

wally ['wɔlɪ] n (col) majadero/a.

walnut ['wɔːlnʌt] n nuez f; (tree) nogal m.

walrus, pl ~ or ~es ['wɔːlrəs] n morsa.

waltz [wɔːlts] n vals m ♦ vi bailar el vals.

wan [wɔn] adj pálido.

wand [wɔnd] n (also: **magic ~**) varita (mágica).

wander ['wɔndə*] vi (person) vagar; deambular; (thoughts) divagar; (get lost) extraviarse ♦ vt recorrer, vagar por.

wanderer ['wɔndərə*] n vagabundo/a.

wandering ['wɔndərɪŋ] adj (tribe) nómada; (minstrel, actor) ambulante; (path, river) sinuoso; (glance, mind) distraído.

wane [weɪn] vi menguar.

wangle ['wæŋgl] (BRIT col) vt: **to ~ sth** agenciarse or conseguir algo ♦ n chanchullo.

wanker ['wæŋkə*] n (col!) pajero/a (!); (as insult) mamón/ona (!) m/f.

want [wɔnt] vt (wish for) querer, desear; (need) necesitar; (lack) carecer de ♦ n (poverty) pobreza; **for ~ of** por falta de; **~s** npl (needs) necesidades fpl; **to ~ to do** querer hacer; **to ~ sb to do sth** querer que algn haga algo; **you're ~ed on the phone** te llaman al teléfono; **to be in ~** estar necesitado; **"cook ~ed"** "se necesita cocinero/a".

want ads npl (US) anuncios mpl por palabras.

wanting ['wɔntɪŋ] adj: **to be ~ (in)** estar falto (de); **to be found ~** no estar a la altura de las circunstancias.

wanton ['wɔntn] adj (licentious) lascivo.

WAP [wæp] n abbr (= wireless application protocol) WAP f.

WAP phone n teléfono WAP.

war [wɔː*] n guerra; **to make ~** hacer la guerra; **the First/Second World W~** la primera/segunda guerra mundial.

warble ['wɔːbl] n (of bird) trino, gorjeo ♦ vi (bird) trinar.

war cry n grito de guerra.

ward [wɔːd] n (in hospital) sala; (POL) distrito electoral; (LAW: child) pupilo/a.

▶**ward off** vt desviar, parar; (attack) rechazar.

warden ['wɔːdn] n (BRIT: of institution) director(a) m/f; (of park, game reserve) guardián/ana m/f; (BRIT: also: **traffic ~**) guardia m/f.

warder ['wɔːdə*] n (BRIT) guardián/ana m/f, carcelero/a.

wardrobe ['wɔːdrəub] n armario, guardarropa, ropero, clóset/closet m (LAM).

warehouse ['wɛəhaus] n almacén m, depósito.

wares [wɛəz] npl mercancías fpl.

warfare ['wɔːfɛə*] n guerra.

war game n juego de estrategia militar.

warhead ['wɔːhɛd] n cabeza armada; **nuclear ~s** cabezas fpl nucleares.

warily ['wɛərɪlɪ] adv con cautela, cautelosamente.

warlike ['wɔːlaɪk] adj guerrero.

warm [wɔːm] adj caliente; (person, greeting, heart) afectuoso, cariñoso; (supporter) entusiasta; (thanks, congratulations, apologies) efusivo; (clothes etc) que abriga; (welcome, day) caluroso; **it's ~** hace calor; **I'm ~** tengo calor; **to keep sth ~** mantener algo caliente.

▶**warm up** vi (room) calentarse; (person) entrar en calor; (athlete) hacer ejercicios

de calentamiento; (*discussion*) acalorarse
♦ *vt* calentar.

warm-blooded ['wɔːm'blʌdɪd] *adj* de
sangre caliente.

war memorial *n* monumento a los caídos.

warm-hearted [wɔːm'hɑːtɪd] *adj* afectuoso.

warmly ['wɔːmlɪ] *adv* afectuosamente.

warmonger ['wɔːmʌŋgə*] *n* belicista *m/f*.

warmongering ['wɔːmʌŋgrɪŋ] *n* belicismo.

warmth [wɔːmθ] *n* calor *m*.

warm-up ['wɔːmʌp] *n* (*SPORT*) ejercicios
mpl de calentamiento.

warn [wɔːn] *vt* avisar, advertir; **to ~ sb not
to do sth** *or* **against doing sth** aconsejar a
algn que no haga algo.

warning ['wɔːnɪŋ] *n* aviso, advertencia;
gale ~ (*METEOROLOGY*) aviso de vendaval;
without (any) ~ sin aviso *or* avisar.

warning light *n* luz *f* de advertencia.

warning triangle *n* (*AUT*) triángulo
señalizador.

warp [wɔːp] *vi* (*wood*) combarse.

warpath ['wɔːpɑːθ] *n*: **to be on the ~** (*fig*)
estar en pie de guerra.

warped [wɔːpt] *adj* (*wood*) alabeado; (*fig:
character, sense of humour etc*) pervertido.

warrant ['wɔrnt] *n* (*LAW: to arrest*) orden *f*
de detención; (: *to search*) mandamiento
de registro ♦ *vt* (*justify, merit*) merecer.

warrant officer *n* (*MIL*) brigada *m*; (*NAUT*)
contramaestre *m*.

warranty ['wɔrəntɪ] *n* garantía; **under ~**
(*COMM*) bajo garantía.

warren ['wɔrən] *n* (*of rabbits*) madriguera;
(*fig*) laberinto.

warring ['wɔːrɪŋ] *adj* (*interests etc*) opuesto;
(*nations*) en guerra.

warrior ['wɔrɪə*] *n* guerrero/a.

Warsaw ['wɔːsɔː] *n* Varsovia.

warship ['wɔːʃɪp] *n* buque *m or* barco de
guerra.

wart [wɔːt] *n* verruga.

wartime ['wɔːtaɪm] *n*: **in ~** en tiempos de
guerra, en la guerra.

wary ['wɛərɪ] *adj* cauteloso; **to be ~ about**
or **of doing sth** tener cuidado con hacer
algo.

was [wɔz] *pt of* **be**.

wash [wɔʃ] *vt* lavar; (*sweep, carry: sea etc*)
llevar ♦ *vi* lavarse ♦ *n* (*clothes etc*) lavado;
(*bath*) baño; (*of ship*) estela; **he was ~ed
overboard** fue arrastrado del barco por
las olas; **to have a ~** lavarse.

▶**wash away** *vt* (*stain*) quitar lavando;
(*subj: river etc*) llevarse; (*fig*) limpiar.

▶**wash down** *vt* lavar.

▶**wash off** *vt* quitar lavando.

▶**wash up** *vi* (*BRIT*) fregar los platos; (*US:*

have a wash) lavarse.

Wash. *abbr* (*US*) = *Washington*.

washable ['wɔʃəbl] *adj* lavable.

washbasin ['wɔʃbeɪsn], (*US*) **washbowl**
['wɔʃbəul] *n* lavabo.

washcloth ['wɔʃklɔθ] *n* (*US*) manopla.

washer ['wɔʃə*] *n* (*TECH*) arandela.

washing ['wɔʃɪŋ] *n* (*dirty*) ropa sucia;
(*clean*) colada.

washing line *n* cuerda de (colgar) la ropa.

washing machine *n* lavadora.

washing powder *n* (*BRIT*) detergente *m*
(en polvo).

Washington ['wɔʃɪŋtən] *n* (*city, state*)
Washington *m*.

washing-up [wɔʃɪŋ'ʌp] *n* fregado; (*dishes*)
platos *mpl* (para fregar); **to do the ~**
fregar los platos.

washing-up liquid *n* lavavajillas *m inv*.

wash leather *n* gamuza.

wash-out ['wɔʃaut] *n* (*col*) fracaso.

washroom ['wɔʃrum] *n* servicios *mpl*.

wasn't ['wɔznt] = **was not**.

Wasp, WASP [wɔsp] *n abbr* (*US col*: = *White
Anglo-Saxon Protestant*) sobrenombre, *en
general peyorativo, que se da a los
americanos de origen anglosajón,
acomodados y de tendencia
conservadora*.

wasp [wɔsp] *n* avispa.

waspish ['wɔspɪʃ] *adj* (*character*) irascible;
(*comment*) mordaz, punzante.

wastage ['weɪstɪdʒ] *n* desgaste *m*; (*loss*)
pérdida; **natural ~** desgaste natural.

waste [weɪst] *n* derroche *m*, despilfarro;
(*misuse*) desgaste *m*; (*of time*) pérdida;
(*food*) sobras *fpl*; (*rubbish*) basura,
desperdicios *mpl* ♦ *adj* (*material*) de
desecho; (*left over*) sobrante; (*energy,
heat*) desperdiciado; (*land, ground: in city*)
sin construir; (: *in country*) baldío ♦ *vt*
(*squander*) malgastar, derrochar; (*time*)
perder; (*opportunity*) desperdiciar; **~s** *npl*
(*area of land*) tierras *fpl* baldías; **to lay ~**
devastar, arrasar; **it's a ~ of money** es
tirar el dinero; **to go to ~**
desperdiciarse.

▶**waste away** *vi* consumirse.

wastebasket ['weɪstbɑːskɪt] *n* (*esp US*)
= **wastepaper basket**.

waste disposal (unit) *n* (*BRIT*) triturador
m de basura.

wasteful ['weɪstful] *adj* derrochador(a);
(*process*) antieconómico.

wastefully ['weɪstfulɪ] *adv*: **to spend money
~** derrochar dinero.

waste ground *n* (*BRIT*) terreno baldío.

wasteland ['weɪstlənd] *n* (*urban*)

descampados *mpl.*

wastepaper basket ['weɪstpeɪpə-] *n*
papelera.

waste pipe *n* tubo de desagüe.

waste products *npl* (*INDUSTRY*) residuos
mpl.

waster ['weɪstə*] *n* (*col*) gandul *m/f.*

watch [wɒtʃ] *n* reloj *m*; (*vigil*) vigilia;
(*vigilance*) vigilancia; (*MIL: guard*)
centinela *m*; (*NAUT: spell of duty*) guardia
♦ *vt* (*look at*) mirar, observar; (: *match,
programme*) ver; (*spy on, guard*) vigilar;
(*be careful of*) cuidar, tener cuidado de
♦ *vi* ver, mirar; (*keep guard*) montar
guardia; **to keep a close ~ on sth/sb**
vigilar algo/a algn de cerca; **~ how you
drive/what you're doing** ten cuidado al
conducir/con lo que haces.

▶**watch out** *vi* cuidarse, tener cuidado.

watch band *n* (*US*) pulsera (de reloj).

watchdog ['wɒtʃdɒg] *n* perro guardián;
(*fig*) organismo de control.

watchful ['wɒtʃful] *adj* vigilante, sobre
aviso.

watchfully ['wɒtʃfulɪ] *adv*: **to stand ~**
permanecer vigilante.

watchmaker ['wɒtʃmeɪkə*] *n* relojero/a.

watchman *n* guardián *m*; (*also*: **night ~**)
sereno, vigilante *m*; (*in factory*) vigilante
m nocturno.

watch stem *n* (*US*) cuerda.

watch strap *n* pulsera (de reloj).

watchword ['wɒtʃwəːd] *n* consigna,
contraseña.

water ['wɔːtə*] *n* agua ♦ *vt* (*plant*) regar ♦ *vi*
(*eyes*) llorar; **I'd like a drink of ~** quisiera
un vaso de agua; **in British ~s** en aguas
británicas; **to pass ~** orinar; **his mouth
~ed** se le hizo la boca agua.

▶**water down** *vt* (*milk etc*) aguar.

water closet *n* wáter *m*.

watercolour, (*US***) watercolor**
['wɔːtəkʌlə*] *n* acuarela.

water-cooled ['wɔːtəkuːld] *adj* refrigerado
(por agua).

watercress ['wɔːtəkrɛs] *n* berro.

waterfall ['wɔːtəfɔːl] *n* cascada, salto de
agua.

waterfront ['wɔːtəfrʌnt] *n* (*seafront*) parte *f*
que da al mar; (*at docks*) muelles *mpl.*

water heater *n* calentador *m* de agua.

water hole *n* abrevadero.

watering can ['wɔːtərɪŋ-] *n* regadera.

water level *n* nivel *m* del agua.

water lily *n* nenúfar *m.*

waterline ['wɔːtəlaɪn] *n* (*NAUT*) línea de
flotación.

waterlogged ['wɔːtələgd] *adj* (*boat*)

anegado; (*ground*) inundado.

water main *n* cañería del agua.

watermark ['wɔːtəmɑːk] *n* (*on paper*)
filigrana.

watermelon ['wɔːtəmɛlən] *n* sandía.

water polo *n* waterpolo, polo acuático.

waterproof ['wɔːtəpruːf] *adj* impermeable.

water-repellent ['wɔːtərɪ'pɛlənt] *adj*
hidrófugo.

watershed ['wɔːtəʃɛd] *n* (*GEO*) cuenca; (*fig*)
momento crítico.

water-skiing ['wɔːtəskiːɪŋ] *n* esquí *m*
acuático.

water softener *n* ablandador *m* de agua.

water tank *n* depósito de agua.

watertight ['wɔːtətaɪt] *adj* hermético.

water vapour, (*US***) water vapor** *n* vapor
m de agua.

waterway ['wɔːtəweɪ] *n* vía fluvial *or*
navegable.

waterworks ['wɔːtəwəːks] *npl* central *fsg*
depuradora.

watery ['wɔːtərɪ] *adj* (*colour*) desvaído;
(*coffee*) aguado; (*eyes*) lloroso.

watt [wɒt] *n* vatio.

wattage ['wɒtɪdʒ] *n* potencia en vatios.

wattle ['wɒtl] *n* zarzo.

wave [weɪv] *n* ola; (*of hand*) señal *f* con la
mano; (*RADIO, in hair*) onda; (*fig: of
enthusiasm, strikes*) oleada ♦ *vi* agitar la
mano; (*flag*) ondear ♦ *vt* (*handkerchief, gun*)
agitar; **short/medium/long ~** (*RADIO*)
onda corta/media/larga; **the new ~** (*CINE,
MUS*) la nueva ola; **to ~ goodbye to sb**
decir adiós a algn con la mano; **he ~d us
over to his table** nos hizo señas (con la
mano) para que nos acercásemos a su
mesa.

▶**wave aside, wave away** *vt* (*person*): **to
~ sb aside** apartar a algn con la mano;
(*fig: suggestion, objection*) rechazar;
(*doubts*) desechar.

waveband ['weɪvbænd] *n* banda de ondas.

wavelength ['weɪvlɛŋθ] *n* longitud *f* de
onda.

waver ['weɪvə*] *vi* oscilar; (*confidence*)
disminuir; (*faith*) flaquear.

wavy ['weɪvɪ] *adj* ondulado.

wax [wæks] *n* cera ♦ *vt* encerar ♦ *vi* (*moon*)
crecer.

waxen ['wæksn] *adj* (*fig: pale*) blanco como
la cera.

waxworks ['wækswəːks] *npl* museo *sg* de
cera.

way [weɪ] *n* camino; (*distance*) trayecto,
recorrido; (*direction*) dirección *f*, sentido;
(*manner*) modo, manera; (*habit*)
costumbre *f*; **which ~? — this ~** ¿por

dónde? or ¿en qué dirección? — por aquí;
on the ~ (*en route*) en (el) camino;
(*expected*) en camino; **to be on one's ~**
estar en camino; **you pass it on your ~**
home está de camino a tu casa; **to be in**
the ~ bloquear el camino; (*fig*) estorbar;
to keep out of sb's ~ esquivar a algn; **to**
make ~ (for sb/sth) dejar paso (a algn/
algo); (*fig*) abrir camino (a algn/algo); **to**
go out of one's ~ to do sth desvivirse
por hacer algo; **to lose one's ~** perderse,
extraviarse; **to be the wrong ~ round**
estar del *or* al revés; **in a ~** en cierto modo
or sentido; **by the ~** a propósito; **by ~ of**
(*via*) pasando por; (*as a sort of*) como, a
modo de; **"~ in"** (*BRIT*) "entrada"; **"~ out"**
(*BRIT*) "salida"; **the ~ back** el camino de
vuelta; **the village is rather out of the ~** el
pueblo está un poco apartado *or* retirado;
it's a long ~ away está muy lejos; **to get**
one's own ~ salirse con la suya; **"give ~"**
(*BRIT AUT*) "ceda el paso"; **no ~!** (*col*) ¡ni
pensarlo!; **put it the right ~ up** ponlo boca
arriba; **he's in a bad ~** está grave; **to be**
under ~ (*work, project*) estar en marcha.
waybill ['weɪbɪl] *n* (*COMM*) hoja de ruta,
carta de porte.
waylay ['weɪleɪ] *vt* (*irreg: like* **lay**) atacar.
wayside ['weɪsaɪd] *n* borde *m* del camino;
to fall by the ~ (*fig*) fracasar.
way station *n* (*US RAIL*) apeadero.
wayward ['weɪwəd] *adj* díscolo,
caprichoso.
WC ['dʌblju:'si:] *n abbr* (*BRIT*: = *water closet*)
wáter *m*.
we [wi:] *pl pron* nosotros/as; **~ understand**
(nosotros) entendemos; **here ~ are** aquí
estamos.
weak [wi:k] *adj* débil, flojo; (*tea, coffee*)
flojo, aguado; **to grow ~(er)** debilitarse.
weaken ['wi:kən] *vi* debilitarse; (*give way*)
ceder ♦ *vt* debilitar.
weak-kneed [wi:k'ni:d] *adj* (*fig*) sin
voluntad *or* carácter.
weakling ['wi:klɪŋ] *n* debilucho/a.
weakly ['wi:klɪ] *adj* enfermizo, débil ♦ *adv*
débilmente.
weakness ['wi:knɪs] *n* debilidad *f*; (*fault*)
punto débil.
wealth [wɛlθ] *n* (*money, resources*) riqueza;
(*of details*) abundancia.
wealth tax *n* impuesto sobre el
patrimonio.
wealthy ['wɛlθɪ] *adj* rico.
wean [wi:n] *vt* destetar.
weapon ['wɛpən] *n* arma; **~s of mass**
destruction armas de destrucción
masiva.

wear [wɛə*] *n* (*use*) uso; (*deterioration*)
desgaste *m*; (*clothing*): **sports/baby~** ropa
de deportes/de niños ♦ *vb* (*pt* **wore**, *pp*
worn [wɔ:*, wɔ:n]) *vt* (*clothes, beard*)
llevar; (*shoes*) calzar; (*look, smile*) tener;
(*damage*) gastar, usar ♦ *vi* (*last*) durar;
(*rub through etc*) desgastarse; **evening ~**
(*man's*) traje *m* de etiqueta; (*woman's*)
traje *m* de noche; **to ~ a hole in sth** hacer
un agujero en algo.
▶**wear away** *vt* gastar ♦ *vi* desgastarse.
▶**wear down** *vt* gastar; (*strength*) agotar.
▶**wear off** *vi* (*pain, excitement etc*) pasar.
▶**wear out** *vt* desgastar; (*person, strength*)
agotar.
wearable ['wɛərəbl] *adj* que se puede
llevar, ponible.
wear and tear *n* desgaste *m*.
wearer ['wɛərə*] *n*: **the ~ of this jacket** el/la
que lleva puesta esta chaqueta.
wearily ['wɪərɪlɪ] *adv* con cansancio.
weariness ['wɪərɪnɪs] *n* cansancio;
abatimiento.
wearisome ['wɪərɪsəm] *adj* (*tiring*) cansado,
pesado; (*boring*) aburrido.
weary ['wɪərɪ] *adj* (*tired*) cansado;
(*dispirited*) abatido ♦ *vt* cansar ♦ *vi*: **to ~ of**
cansarse de, aburrirse de.
weasel ['wi:zl] *n* (*ZOOL*) comadreja.
weather ['wɛðə*] *n* tiempo ♦ *vt* (*storm,*
crisis) hacer frente a; **under the ~** (*fig: ill*)
mal, pachucho; **what's the ~ like?** ¿qué
tiempo hace?, ¿cómo hace?
weather-beaten ['wɛðəbi:tn] *adj* curtido.
weathercock ['wɛðəkɔk] *n* veleta.
weather forecast *n* boletín *m*
meteorológico.
weatherman ['wɛðəmæn] *n* hombre *m* del
tiempo.
weatherproof ['wɛðəpru:f] *adj* (*garment*)
impermeable.
weather report *n* parte *m* meteorológico.
weather vane *n* = **weathercock.**
weave, *pt* **wove**, *pp* **woven** [wi:v, wəuv,
'wəuvn] *vt* (*cloth*) tejer; (*fig*) entretejer ♦ *vi*
(*fig: pt, pp ~d: move in and out*) zigzaguear.
weaver ['wi:və*] *n* tejedor(a) *m/f*.
weaving ['wi:vɪŋ] *n* tejeduría.
web [wɛb] *n* (*of spider*) telaraña; (*on foot*)
membrana; (*network*) red *f*; **the (World**
Wide) W~ el *or* la Web.
webbed [wɛbd] *adj* (*foot*) palmeado.
webbing ['wɛbɪŋ] *n* (*on chair*) cinchas *fpl*.
web page *n* página web.
website ['wɛbsaɪt] *n* sitio web.
wed [wɛd] *vt* (*pt, pp* **wedded**) casar ♦ *n*: **the**
newly-~s los recién casados.
Wed. *abbr* (= *Wednesday*) miérc.

we'd [wiːd] = **we had; we would.**
wedded ['wɛdɪd] pt, pp of **wed.**
wedding ['wɛdɪŋ] n boda, casamiento.
wedding anniversary adj aniversario de boda; **silver/golden** ~ bodas fpl de plata/de oro.
wedding day n día m de la boda.
wedding dress n traje m de novia.
wedding present n regalo de boda.
wedding ring n alianza.
wedge [wɛdʒ] n (of wood etc) cuña; (of cake) trozo ♦ vt acuñar; (push) apretar.
wedge-heeled ['wɛdʒ'hiːld] adj con suela de cuña.
wedlock ['wɛdlɔk] n matrimonio.
Wednesday ['wɛnzdɪ] n miércoles m inv.
wee [wiː] adj (Scottish) pequeñito.
weed [wiːd] n mala hierba, maleza ♦ vt escardar, desherbar.
▶**weed out** vt eliminar.
weedkiller ['wiːdkɪlə*] n herbicida m.
weedy ['wiːdɪ] adj (person) debilucho.
week [wiːk] n semana; **a** ~ **today** de hoy en ocho días; **Tuesday** ~, **a** ~ **on Tuesday** del martes en una semana; **once/twice a** ~ una vez/dos veces a la semana; **this** ~ esta semana; **in 2** ~**s' time** dentro de 2 semanas; **every other** ~ cada 2 semanas.
weekday ['wiːkdeɪ] n día m laborable; **on** ~**s** entre semana, en días laborables.
weekend [wiːk'ɛnd] n fin m de semana.
weekend case n neceser m.
weekly ['wiːklɪ] adv semanalmente, cada semana ♦ adj semanal ♦ n semanario; ~ **newspaper** semanario.
weep, pt, pp **wept** [wiːp, wɛpt] vi, vt llorar; (MED: wound etc) supurar.
weeping willow ['wiːpɪŋ-] n sauce m llorón.
weepy ['wiːpɪ] n (col: film) película lacrimógena; (: story) historia lacrimógena.
weft [wɛft] n (TEXTILES) trama.
weigh [weɪ] vt, vi pesar; **to** ~ **anchor** levar anclas; **to** ~ **the pros and cons** pesar los pros y los contras.
▶**weigh down** vt sobrecargar; (fig: with worry) agobiar.
▶**weigh out** vt (goods) pesar.
▶**weigh up** vt pesar.
weighbridge ['weɪbrɪdʒ] n báscula para camiones.
weighing machine ['weɪɪŋ-] n báscula, peso.
weight [weɪt] n peso; (on scale) pesa; **to lose/put on** ~ adelgazar/engordar; ~**s and measures** pesas y medidas.
weighting ['weɪtɪŋ] n (allowance): **(London)**

~ dietas fpl (por residir en Londres).
weightlessness ['weɪtlɪsnɪs] n ingravidez f.
weight lifter n levantador(a) m/f de pesas.
weight limit n límite m de peso.
weight training n musculación f (con pesas).
weighty ['weɪtɪ] adj pesado.
weir [wɪə*] n presa.
weird [wɪəd] adj raro, extraño.
weirdo ['wɪədəu] n (col) tío/a raro/a.
welcome ['wɛlkəm] adj bienvenido ♦ n bienvenida ♦ vt dar la bienvenida a; (be glad of) alegrarse de; **to make sb** ~ recibir or acoger bien a algn; **thank you** — **you're** ~ gracias — de nada; **you're** ~ **to try** puede intentar cuando quiera; **we** ~ **this step** celebramos esta medida.
weld [wɛld] n soldadura ♦ vt soldar.
welding ['wɛldɪŋ] n soldadura.
welfare ['wɛlfɛə*] n bienestar m; (social aid) asistencia social; **W**~ (US) subsidio de paro; **to look after sb's** ~ cuidar del bienestar de algn.
welfare state n estado del bienestar.
welfare work n asistencia social.
well [wɛl] n pozo ♦ adv bien ♦ adj: **to be** ~ estar bien (de salud) ♦ excl ¡vaya!, ¡bueno!; **as** ~ (in addition) además, también; **as** ~ **as** además de; **you might as** ~ **tell me** más vale que me lo digas; **it would be as** ~ **to ask** más valdría preguntar; ~ **done!** ¡bien hecho!; **get** ~ **soon!** ¡que te mejores pronto!; **to do** ~ (business) ir bien; **I did** ~ **in my exams** me han salido bien los exámenes; **they are doing** ~ **now** les va bien ahora; **to think** ~ **of sb** pensar bien de algn; **I don't feel** ~ no me encuentro or siento bien; ~, **as I was saying** ... bueno, como decía ....
▶**well up** vi brotar.
we'll [wiːl] = **we will, we shall.**
well-behaved ['wɛlbɪ'heɪvd] adj: **to be** ~ portarse bien.
well-being ['wɛl'biːɪŋ] n bienestar m.
well-bred ['wɛl'brɛd] adj bien educado.
well-built ['wɛl'bɪlt] adj (person) fornido.
well-chosen ['wɛl'tʃəuzn] adj (remarks, words) acertado.
well-deserved ['wɛldɪ'zəːvd] adj merecido.
well-developed ['wɛldɪ'vɛləpt] adj (arm, muscle etc) bien desarrollado; (sense) agudo, fino.
well-disposed ['wɛldɪs'pəuzd] adj: ~ **to(wards)** bien dispuesto a.
well-dressed ['wɛl'drɛst] adj bien vestido.
well-earned ['wɛl'əːnd] adj (rest) merecido.
well-groomed ['wɛl'gruːmd] adj de apariencia cuidada.

well-heeled ['wɛl'hiːld] *adj* (*col: wealthy*) rico.

well-informed ['wɛlɪn'fɔːmd] *adj* (*having knowledge of sth*) enterado, al corriente.

Wellington ['wɛlɪŋtən] *n* Wellington *m*.

wellingtons ['wɛlɪŋtənz] *npl* (*also:* **Wellington boots**) botas *fpl* de goma.

well-kept ['wɛl'kɛpt] *adj* (*secret*) bien guardado; (*hair, house*) bien cuidado.

well-known ['wɛl'nəun] *adj* (*person*) conocido.

well-mannered ['wɛl'mænəd] *adj* educado.

well-meaning ['wɛl'miːnɪŋ] *adj* bienintencionado.

well-nigh ['wɛl'naɪ] *adv*: ~ **impossible** casi imposible.

well-off ['wɛl'ɔf] *adj* acomodado.

well-read ['wɛl'rɛd] *adj* culto.

well-spoken ['wɛl'spəukən] *adj* bienhablado.

well-stocked ['wɛl'stɔkt] *adj* (*shop, larder*) bien surtido.

well-timed ['wɛl'taɪmd] *adj* oportuno.

well-to-do ['wɛltə'duː] *adj* acomodado.

well-wisher ['wɛlwɪʃə*] *n* admirador(a) *m/f*.

well-woman clinic ['wɛlwumən-] *n* centro de prevención médica para mujeres.

Welsh [wɛlʃ] *adj* galés/esa ♦ *n* (*LING*) galés *m*; **the** ~ *npl* los galeses; **the** ~ **Assembly** el Parlamento galés.

Welshman ['wɛlʃmən] *n* galés *m*.

Welsh rarebit [-'rɛəbɪt] *n* pan *m* con queso tostado.

Welshwoman ['wɛlʃwumən] *n* galesa *f*.

welter ['wɛltə*] *n* mescolanza, revoltijo.

went [wɛnt] *pt of* **go**.

wept [wɛpt] *pt, pp of* **weep**.

were [wəː*] *pt of* **be**.

we're [wɪə*] = **we are**.

weren't [wəːnt] = **were not**.

werewolf, *pl* **-wolves** ['wɪəwulf, -wulvz] *n* hombre *m* lobo.

west [wɛst] *n* oeste *m* ♦ *adj* occidental, del oeste ♦ *adv* al *or* hacia el oeste; **the W~** Occidente *m*.

westbound ['wɛstbaund] *adj* (*traffic, carriageway*) con rumbo al oeste.

West Country *n*: **the** ~ el suroeste de Inglaterra.

westerly ['wɛstəlɪ] *adj* (*wind*) del oeste.

western ['wɛstən] *adj* occidental ♦ *n* (*CINE*) película del oeste.

westerner ['wɛstənə*] *n* (*POL*) occidental *m/f*.

westernized ['wɛstənaɪzd] *adj* occidentalizado.

West German (*formerly*) *adj* de Alemania Occidental ♦ *n* alemán/ana *m/f* (de Alemania Occidental).

West Germany *n* (*formerly*) Alemania Occidental.

West Indian *adj*, *n* antillano/a *m/f*.

West Indies [-'ɪndɪz] *npl*: **the** ~ las Antillas.

Westminster ['wɛstmɪnstə*] *n* el parlamento británico, Westminster *m*.

westward(s) ['wɛstwəd(z)] *adv* hacia el oeste.

wet [wɛt] *adj* (*damp*) húmedo; (~ **through**) mojado; (*rainy*) lluvioso ♦ *vt*: **to** ~ **one's pants** *or* **o.s.** mearse; **to get** ~ mojarse; "~ **paint**" 'recién pintado'.

wet blanket *n*: **to be a** ~ (*fig*) ser un/una aguafiestas.

wetness ['wɛtnɪs] *n* humedad *f*.

wet rot *n* putrefacción *f* por humedad.

wet suit *n* traje *m* de buzo.

we've [wiːv] = **we have**.

whack [wæk] *vt* dar un buen golpe a.

whale [weɪl] *n* (*ZOOL*) ballena.

whaler ['weɪlə*] *n* (*ship*) ballenero.

whaling ['weɪlɪŋ] *n* pesca de ballenas.

wharf, *pl* **wharves** [wɔːf, wɔːvz] *n* muelle *m*.

═══════════════════════════ *KEYWORD*

what [wɔt] *adj* **1** (*in direct/indirect questions*) qué; ~ **size is he?** ¿qué talla usa?; ~ **colour/shape is it?** ¿de qué color/forma es?; ~ **books do you need?** ¿qué libros necesitas?

2 (*in exclamations*): ~ **a mess!** ¡qué desastre!; ~ **a fool I am!** ¡qué tonto soy!

♦ *pron* **1** (*interrogative*) qué; ~ **are you doing?** ¿qué haces *or* estás haciendo?; ~ **is happening?** ¿qué pasa *or* está pasando?; ~ **is it called?** ¿cómo se llama?; ~ **about me?** ¿y yo qué?; ~ **about doing ...?** ¿qué tal si hacemos ...?; ~ **is his address?** ¿cuáles son sus señas?; ~ **will it cost?** ¿cuánto costará?

2 (*relative*) lo que; **I saw** ~ **you did/was on the table** vi lo que hiciste/había en la mesa; ~ **I want is a cup of tea** lo que quiero es una taza de té; **I don't know** ~ **to do** no sé qué hacer; **tell me** ~ **you're thinking about** dime en qué estás pensando

3 (*reported questions*): **she asked me** ~ **I wanted** me preguntó qué quería

♦ *excl* (*disbelieving*) ¡cómo!; ~, **no coffee!** ¡que no hay café!

whatever [wɔt'ɛvə*] *adj*: ~ **book you choose** cualquier libro que elijas ♦ *pron*: **do** ~ **is necessary** haga lo que sea necesario; **no reason** ~ ninguna razón en

absoluto; **nothing** ~ nada en absoluto; ~
it costs cueste lo que cueste.
wheat [wi:t] n trigo.
wheatgerm ['wi:tdʒə:m] n germen m de
trigo.
wheatmeal ['wi:tmi:l] n harina de trigo.
wheedle ['wi:dl] vt: **to** ~ **sb into doing sth**
engatusar a algn para que haga algo; **to**
~ **sth out of sb** sonsacar algo a algn.
wheel [wi:l] n rueda; (AUT: also: **steering** ~)
volante m; (NAUT) timón m ♦ vt (pram etc)
empujar ♦ vi (also: ~ **round**) dar la vuelta,
girar; **four-~ drive** tracción f en las
cuatro ruedas; **front-/rear-~ drive**
tracción f delantera/trasera.
wheelbarrow ['wi:lbærəu] n carretilla.
wheelbase ['wi:lbeɪs] n batalla.
wheelchair ['wi:ltʃɛə*] n silla de ruedas.
wheel clamp n (AUT) cepo.
wheeler-dealer ['wi:lə'di:lə*] n
chanchullero/a.
wheelie-bin ['wi:lɪbɪn] n (BRIT) contenedor
m de basura.
wheeling ['wi:lɪŋ] n: ~ **and dealing** (col)
chanchullos mpl.
wheeze [wi:z] vi resollar.
wheezy ['wi:zɪ] adj silbante.

=================== KEYWORD

when [wɛn] adv cuando; ~ **did it happen?**
¿cuándo ocurrió?; **I know** ~ **it happened**
sé cuándo ocurrió
♦ conj **1** (at, during, after the time that)
cuando; **be careful** ~ **you cross the road**
ten cuidado al cruzar la calle; **that was** ~
I needed you entonces era cuando te
necesitaba; **I'll buy you a car** ~ **you're 18**
te compraré un coche cuando cumplas
18 años
2 (on, at which): **on the day** ~ **I met him** el
día en qué le conocí
3 (whereas) cuando; **you said I was wrong**
~ **in fact I was right** dijiste que no tenía
razón, cuando en realidad sí la tenía.

whenever [wɛn'ɛvə*] conj cuando; (every
time) cada vez que; **I go** ~ **I can** voy
siempre or todas las veces que puedo.
where [wɛə*] adv dónde ♦ conj donde; **this is**
~ **aquí es donde**; ~ **possible** donde sea
posible; ~ **are you from?** ¿de dónde es
usted?
whereabouts ['wɛərəbauts] adv dónde ♦ n:
nobody knows his ~ nadie conoce su
paradero.
whereas [wɛər'æz] conj mientras.
whereby [wɛə'baɪ] adv mediante el/la
cual etc.

whereupon [wɛərə'pɔn] conj con lo cual,
después de lo cual.
wherever [wɛər'ɛvə*] adv dondequiera que;
(interrogative) dónde; **sit** ~ **you like**
siéntese donde quiera.
wherewithal ['wɛəwɪðɔ:l] n recursos mpl;
the ~ **(to do sth)** los medios económicos
(para hacer algo).
whet [wɛt] vt estimular; (appetite) abrir.
whether ['wɛðə*] conj si; **I don't know** ~ **to**
accept or not no sé si aceptar o no; ~ **you**
go or not vayas o no vayas.
whey [weɪ] n suero.

=================== KEYWORD

which [wɪtʃ] adj **1** (interrogative: direct,
indirect) qué; ~ **picture(s) do you want?**
¿qué cuadro(s) quieres?; ~ **one?** ¿cuál?;
~ **one of you?** ¿cuál de vosotros?; **tell me**
~ **one you want** dime cuál (es el que)
quieres
2: **in** ~ **case** en cuyo caso; **we got there at**
8 pm, by ~ **time the cinema was full**
llegamos allí a las 8, cuando el cine
estaba lleno
♦ pron **1** (interrogative) cual; **I don't mind** ~
el/la que sea; ~ **do you want?** ¿cuál
quieres?
2 (relative: replacing noun) que; (: replacing
clause) lo que; (: after preposition) (el/la)
que, el/la cual; **the apple** ~ **you ate/** ~ **is**
on the table la manzana que comiste/que
está en la mesa; **the chair on** ~ **you are**
sitting la silla en la que estás sentado; **he**
didn't believe it, ~ **upset me** no se lo
creyó, lo cual or lo que me disgustó; **after**
~ después de lo cual.

whichever [wɪtʃ'ɛvə*] adj: **take** ~ **book**
you prefer coja el libro que prefiera;
~ **book you take** cualquier libro que
coja.
whiff [wɪf] n bocanada; **to catch a** ~ **of sth**
oler algo.
while [waɪl] n rato, momento ♦ conj
durante; (whereas) mientras; (although)
aunque ♦ vt: **to** ~ **away the time** pasar el
rato; **for a** ~ durante algún tiempo; **in a** ~
dentro de poco; **all the** ~ todo el tiempo;
we'll make it worth your ~ te
compensaremos generosamente.
whilst [waɪlst] conj = **while**.
whim [wɪm] n capricho.
whimper ['wɪmpə*] n (weeping) lloriqueo;
(moan) quejido ♦ vi lloriquear; quejarse.
whimsical ['wɪmzɪkl] adj (person)
caprichoso.
whine [waɪn] n (of pain) gemido; (of engine)

zumbido ♦ *vi* gemir; zumbar.
whip [wɪp] *n* látigo; (*BRIT POL*) *diputado encargado de la disciplina del partido en el parlamento* ♦ *vt* azotar; (*snatch*) arrebatar; (*US CULIN*) batir; *ver recuadro.*
▶**whip up** *vt* (*cream etc*) batir (rápidamente); (*col: meal*) preparar rápidamente; (: *stir up: support, feeling*) avivar.

WHIP

En el Parlamento británico la disciplina de partido (en concreto de voto y de asistencia a la Cámara de los Comunes) está a cargo de un grupo de parlamentarios llamados **whips**, *encabezados por el "Chief Whip". Por lo general todos ellos tienen también altos cargos en la Administración del Estado si pertenecen al partido en el poder.*

---

whiplash ['wɪplæʃ] *n* (*MED: also*: ~ **injury**) latigazo.
whipped cream [wɪpt-] *n* nata montada.
whipping boy ['wɪpɪŋ-] *n* (*fig*) cabeza de turco.
whip-round ['wɪpraund] *n* (*BRIT*) colecta.
whirl [wəːl] *n* remolino ♦ *vt* hacer girar, dar vueltas a ♦ *vi* (*dancers*) girar, dar vueltas; (*leaves, dust, water etc*) arremolinarse.
whirlpool ['wəːlpuːl] *n* remolino.
whirlwind ['wəːlwɪnd] *n* torbellino.
whirr [wəː*] *vi* zumbar.
whisk [wɪsk] *n* (*BRIT CULIN*) batidor *m* ♦ *vt* (*BRIT CULIN*) batir; **to** ~ **sb away** *or* **off** llevarse volando a algn.
whiskers [wɪskəz] *npl* (*of animal*) bigotes *mpl*; (*of man*) patillas *fpl*.
whisky, (*US, Ireland*) **whiskey** ['wɪskɪ] *n* whisky *m*.
whisper ['wɪspə*] *n* cuchicheo; (*rumour*) rumor *m*; (*fig*) susurro, murmullo ♦ *vi* cuchichear, hablar bajo; (*fig*) susurrar ♦ *vt* decir en voz muy baja; **to** ~ **sth to sb** decirle algo al oído a algn.
whispering ['wɪspərɪŋ] *n* cuchicheo.
whist [wɪst] *n* (*BRIT*) whist *m*.
whistle ['wɪsl] *n* (*sound*) silbido; (*object*) silbato ♦ *vi* silbar; **to** ~ **a tune** silbar una melodía.
whistle-stop ['wɪslstɔp] *adj*: ~ **tour** (*US POL*) gira electoral rápida; (*fig*) recorrido rápido.
Whit [wɪt] *n* Pentecostés *m*.
white [waɪt] *adj* blanco; (*pale*) pálido ♦ *n* blanco; (*of egg*) clara; **to turn** *or* **go** ~ (*person*) palidecer, ponerse blanco; (*hair*) encanecer; **the** ~**s** (*washing*) la ropa

blanca; **tennis** ~**s** ropa *f* de tenis.
whitebait ['waɪtbeɪt] *n* chanquetes *mpl*.
white coffee *n* (*BRIT*) café *m* con leche.
white-collar worker ['waɪtkɔlə-] *n* oficinista *m/f*.
white elephant *n* (*fig*) maula.
white goods *npl* (*appliances*) electrodomésticos *mpl* de línea blanca; (*linen etc*) ropa blanca.
white-hot [waɪt'hɔt] *adj* (*metal*) candente, calentado al (rojo) blanco.
white lie *n* mentirijilla.
whiteness ['waɪtnɪs] *n* blancura.
white noise *n* sonido blanco.
white paper *n* (*POL*) libro blanco.
whitewash ['waɪtwɔʃ] *n* (*paint*) cal *f*, jalbegue *m* ♦ *vt* encalar, blanquear; (*fig*) encubrir.
whiting ['waɪtɪŋ] *n* (*pl inv*) (*fish*) pescadilla.
Whit Monday *n* lunes *m* de Pentecostés.
Whitsun ['wɪtsn] *n* (*BRIT*) Pentecostés *m*.
whittle ['wɪtl] *vt*: **to** ~ **away**, ~ **down** ir reduciendo.
whizz [wɪz] *vi*: **to** ~ **past** *or* **by** pasar a toda velocidad.
whizz kid *n* (*col*) prodigio/a.
WHO *n abbr* (= *World Health Organization*) OMS *f*.

============================ *KEYWORD*

who [huː] *pron* **1** (*interrogative*) quién; ~ **is it?**, ~'**s there?** ¿quién es?; ~ **are you looking for?** ¿a quién buscas?; **I told her** ~ **I was** le dije quién era yo
2 (*relative*) que; **the man/woman** ~ **spoke to me** el hombre/la mujer que habló conmigo; **those** ~ **can swim** los que saben *or* sepan nadar.

---

whodun(n)it [huː'dʌnɪt] *n* (*col*) novela policíaca.
whoever [huː'evə*] *pron*: ~ **finds it** cualquiera *or* quienquiera que lo encuentre; **ask** ~ **you like** pregunta a quien quieras; ~ **he marries** se case con quien se case.
whole [həul] *adj* (*complete*) todo, entero; (*not broken*) intacto ♦ *n* (*total*) total *m*; (*sum*) conjunto; ~ **villages were destroyed** pueblos enteros fueron destruidos; **the** ~ **of the town** toda la ciudad, la ciudad entera; **on the** ~, **as a** ~ en general.
wholehearted [həul'hɑːtɪd] *adj* (*support, approval*) total; (*sympathy*) sincero.
wholeheartedly [həul'hɑːtɪdlɪ] *adv* con entusiasmo.
wholemeal ['həulmiːl] *adj* (*BRIT: flour, bread*) integral.

wholesale ['həulseɪl] *n* venta al por mayor
♦ *adj* al por mayor; (*destruction*)
sistemático.
wholesaler ['həulseɪlə*] *n* mayorista
m/f.
wholesome ['həulsəm] *adj* sano.
wholewheat ['həulwi:t] *adj*
= **wholemeal**.
wholly ['həulɪ] *adv* totalmente,
enteramente.

━━━━━━━━━━━━━━━━ KEYWORD

whom [hu:m] *pron* **1** (*interrogative*): ~ **did
you see?** ¿a quién viste?; **to ~ did you
give it?** ¿a quién se lo diste?; **tell me from
~ you received it** dígame de quién lo
recibiste
2 (*relative*) que; **to ~** a quien(es); **of ~**
de quien(es), del/de la que; **the man ~ I
saw** el hombre qui vi; **the man to ~ I
wrote** el hombre a quien escribí; **the lady
about ~ I was talking** la señora de (la)
que hablaba; **the lady with ~ I was
talking** la señora con quien *or* (la) que
hablaba.

whooping cough ['hu:pɪŋ-] *n* tos *f*
ferina.
whoops [wu:ps] *excl* (*also*: ~**-a-daisy!**)
¡huy!
whoosh [wuʃ] *n*: **it came out with a ~**
(*sauce etc*) salió todo de repente; (*air*)
salió con mucho ruido.
whopper ['wɔpə*] *n* (*col: lie*) embuste *m*;
(: *large thing*): **a ~** uno/a enorme.
whopping ['wɔpɪŋ] *adj* (*col*) enorme.
whore [hɔ:*] *n* (*col: pej*) puta.

━━━━━━━━━━━━━━━━ KEYWORD

whose [hu:z] *adj* **1** (*possessive: interrogative*)
de quién; ~ **book is this?**, ~ **is this book?**
¿de quién es este libro?; ~ **pencil have
you taken?** ¿de quién es el lápiz que has
cogido?; ~ **daughter are you?** ¿de quién
eres hija?
2 (*possessive: relative*) cuyo/a, pl cuyos/as;
the man ~ son they rescued el hombre
cuyo hijo rescataron; **the girl ~ sister he
was speaking to** la chica con cuya
hermana estaba hablando; **those ~
passports I have** aquellas personas cuyos
pasaportes tengo; **the woman ~ car was
stolen** la mujer a quien le robaron el
coche
♦ *pron* de quién; ~ **is this?** ¿de quién
es esto?; **I know ~ it is** sé de quién
es.

━━━━━━━━━━━━━━━━ KEYWORD

why [waɪ] *adv* por qué; ~ **not?** ¿por qué
no?; ~ **not do it now?** ¿por qué no lo
haces (*or* hacemos) ahora?
♦ *conj*: **I wonder ~ he said that** me
pregunto por qué dijo eso; **that's not ~
I'm here** no es por eso (por lo) que estoy
aquí; **the reason ~** la razón por la que
♦ *excl* (*expressing surprise, shock,
annoyance*) ¡hombre!, ¡vaya!; (*explaining*):
~, **it's you!** ¡hombre, eres tú!; ~, **that's
impossible** ¡pero si eso es imposible!

whyever [waɪ'ɛvə*] *adv* por qué.
WI *n abbr* (*BRIT*: = *Women's Institute*)
asociación de amas de casa ♦ *abbr* (*GEO*)
= **West Indies**; (*US*) = Wisconsin.
wick [wɪk] *n* mecha.
wicked ['wɪkɪd] *adj* malvado, cruel.
wickedness ['wɪkɪdnɪs] *n* maldad *f*,
crueldad *f*.
wicker ['wɪkə*] *n* mimbre *m*.
wickerwork ['wɪkəwɜ:k] *n* artículos *mpl* de
mimbre.
wicket ['wɪkɪt] *n* (*CRICKET*) palos *mpl*.
wicket keeper *n* guardameta *m*.
wide [waɪd] *adj* ancho; (*area, knowledge*)
vasto, grande; (*choice*) grande ♦ *adv*: **to
open ~** abrir de par en par; **to shoot ~**
errar el tiro; **it is 3 metres ~** tiene 3
metros de ancho.
wide-angle lens ['waɪdæŋgl-] *n* (objetivo)
gran angular *m*.
wide-awake [waɪdə'weɪk] *adj* bien
despierto.
wide-eyed [waɪd'aɪd] *adj* con los ojos muy
abiertos; (*fig*) ingenuo.
widely ['waɪdlɪ] *adv* (*differing*) muy; **it is ~
believed that ...** existe la creencia
generalizada de que ...; **to be ~ read**
(*author*) ser muy leído; (*reader*) haber
leído mucho.
widen ['waɪdn] *vt* ensanchar.
wideness ['waɪdnɪs] *n* anchura; amplitud *f*.
wide open *adj* abierto de par en par.
wide-ranging [waɪd'reɪndʒɪŋ] *adj* (*survey,
report*) de gran alcance; (*interests*) muy
diversos.
widespread ['waɪdspred] *adj* (*belief etc*)
extendido, general.
widow ['wɪdəu] *n* viuda.
widowed ['wɪdəud] *adj* viudo.
widower ['wɪdəuə*] *n* viudo.
width [wɪdθ] *n* anchura; (*of cloth*) ancho;
it's 7 metres in ~ tiene 7 metros de
ancho.
widthways ['wɪdθweɪz] *adv* a lo ancho.

wield [wiːld] *vt* (*sword*) manejar; (*power*) ejercer.

wife, *pl* **wives** [waɪf, waɪvz] *n* mujer *f*, esposa.

wig [wɪg] *n* peluca.

wigging ['wɪgɪŋ] *n* (*BRIT col*) rapapolvo, bronca.

wiggle ['wɪgl] *vt* menear ♦ *vi* menearse.

wiggly ['wɪglɪ] *adj* (*line*) ondulado.

wigwam ['wɪgwæm] *n* tipi *m*, tienda india.

wild [waɪld] *adj* (*animal*) salvaje; (*plant*) silvestre; (*rough*) furioso, violento; (*idea*) descabellado; (*col: angry*) furioso ♦ *n*: **the ~** la naturaleza; **~s** *npl* regiones *fpl* salvajes, tierras *fpl* vírgenes; **to be ~ about** (*enthusiastic*) estar *or* andar loco por; **in its ~ state** en estado salvaje.

wild card *n* (*COMPUT*) comodín *m*.

wildcat ['waɪldkæt] *n* gato montés.

wildcat strike *n* huelga salvaje.

wilderness ['wɪldənɪs] *n* desierto; (*jungle*) jungla.

wildfire ['waɪldfaɪə*] *n*: **to spread like ~** correr como un reguero de pólvora.

wild-goose chase [waɪld'guːs-] *n* (*fig*) búsqueda inútil.

wildlife ['waɪldlaɪf] *n* fauna.

wildly ['waɪldlɪ] *adv* (*roughly*) violentamente; (*foolishly*) locamente; (*rashly*) descabelladamente.

wiles [waɪlz] *npl* artimañas *fpl*, ardides *mpl*.

wilful, (*US*) **willful** ['wɪlful] *adj* (*action*) deliberado; (*obstinate*) testarudo.

═══════════════════ *KEYWORD*

will [wɪl] *aux vb* **1** (*forming future tense*): **I ~ finish it tomorrow** lo terminaré *or* voy a terminar mañana; **I ~ have finished it by tomorrow** lo habré terminado para mañana; **~ you do it? — yes I ~/no I won't** ¿lo harás? — sí/no; **you won't lose it, ~ you?** no lo vayas a perder *or* no lo perderás ¿verdad?

2 (*in conjectures, predictions*): **he ~** *or* **he'll be there by now** ya habrá llegado, ya debe (de) haber llegado; **that ~ be the postman** será el cartero, debe ser el cartero

3 (*in commands, requests, offers*): **~ you be quiet!** ¡quieres callarte?; **~ you help me?** ¿quieres ayudarme?; **~ you have a cup of tea?** ¿te apetece un té?; **I won't put up with it!** ¡no lo soporto!

4 (*habits, persistence*): **the car won't start** el coche no arranca; **accidents ~ happen** son cosas que pasan

♦ *vt* (*pt, pp* **willed**): **to ~ sb to do sth** desear que algn haga algo; **he ~ed himself to go**

on con gran fuerza de voluntad, continuó ♦ *n* **1** (*desire*) voluntad *f*; **against sb's ~** contra la voluntad de algn; **he did it of his own free ~** lo hizo por su propia voluntad **2** (*LAW*) testamento; **to make a** *or* **one's ~** hacer su testamento.

willful ['wɪlful] *adj* (*US*) = **wilful**.

willing ['wɪlɪŋ] *adj* (*with goodwill*) de buena voluntad; complaciente; **he's ~ to do it** está dispuesto a hacerlo; **to show ~** mostrarse dispuesto.

willingly ['wɪlɪŋlɪ] *adv* con mucho gusto.

willingness ['wɪlɪŋnɪs] *n* buena voluntad.

will-o'-the-wisp ['wɪlədə'wɪsp] *n* fuego fatuo; (*fig*) quimera.

willow ['wɪləu] *n* sauce *m*.

willpower ['wɪlpauə*] *n* fuerza de voluntad.

willy-nilly [wɪlɪ'nɪlɪ] *adv* quiérase o no.

wilt [wɪlt] *vi* marchitarse.

Wilts *abbr* (*BRIT*) = **Wiltshire.**

wily ['waɪlɪ] *adj* astuto.

wimp [wɪmp] *n* (*col*) enclenque *m/f*; (*character*) calzonazos *m inv*.

win [wɪn] *n* (*in sports etc*) victoria, triunfo ♦ *vb* (*pt, pp* **won** [wʌn]) *vt* ganar; (*obtain: contract etc*) conseguir, lograr ♦ *vi* ganar.

▶**win over,** (*BRIT*) **win round** *vt* convencer a.

wince [wɪns] *vi* encogerse.

winch [wɪntʃ] *n* torno.

Winchester disk ® ['wɪntʃɪstə-] *n* (*COMPUT*) disco Winchester ®.

wind *n* [wɪnd] viento; (*MED*) gases *mpl*; (*breath*) aliento ♦ *vb* [waɪnd] (*pt, pp* **wound** [waund]) *vt* enrollar; (*wrap*) envolver; (*clock, toy*) dar cuerda a; [wɪnd] (*take breath away from*) dejar sin aliento a ♦ *vi* (*road, river*) serpentear; **into** *or* **against the ~** contra el viento; **to get ~ of sth** enterarse de algo; **to break ~** ventosear.

▶**wind down** *vt* (*car window*) bajar; (*fig: production, business*) disminuir.

▶**wind up** *vt* (*clock*) dar cuerda a; (*debate*) concluir, terminar.

windbreak ['wɪndbreɪk] *n* barrera contra el viento.

windcheater ['wɪndtʃiːtə*], (*US*) **windbreaker** ['wɪndbreɪkə*] *n* cazadora.

winder ['waɪndə*] *n* (*on watch*) cuerda.

wind erosion *n* erosión *f* del viento.

windfall ['wɪndfɔːl] *n* golpe *m* de suerte.

winding ['waɪndɪŋ] *adj* (*road*) tortuoso.

wind instrument *n* (*MUS*) instrumento de viento.

windmill ['wɪndmɪl] *n* molino de viento.

window ['wɪndəu] *n* ventana; (*in car, train*)

ventana; (*in shop etc*) escaparate *m*,
vitrina (*LAM*), vidriera (*LAM*); (*COMPUT*)
ventana.
window box *n* jardinera (de ventana).
window cleaner *n* (*person*)
limpiacristales *m inv*.
window dressing *n* decoración *f* de
escaparates.
window envelope *n* sobre *m* de
ventanilla.
window frame *n* marco de ventana.
window ledge *n* alféizar *m*, repisa.
window pane *n* cristal *m*.
window-shopping [wɪndəuˈʃɔpɪŋ] *n*: **to go
~** ir a ver *or* mirar escaparates.
windowsill [ˈwɪndəusɪl] *n* alféizar *m*,
repisa.
windpipe [ˈwɪndpaɪp] *n* tráquea.
wind power *n* energía eólica.
windscreen [ˈwɪndskriːn], (*US*)
windshield [ˈwɪndʃiːld] *n* parabrisas *m inv*.
windscreen washer, (*US*) **windshield
washer** *n* lavaparabrisas *m inv*.
windscreen wiper, (*US*) **windshield
wiper** *n* limpiaparabrisas *m inv*.
windsurfing [ˈwɪndsəːfɪŋ] *n* windsurf *m*.
windswept [ˈwɪndswɛpt] *adj* azotado por el
viento.
wind tunnel *n* túnel *m* aerodinámico.
windy [ˈwɪndɪ] *adj* de mucho viento; **it's ~**
hace viento.
wine [waɪn] *n* vino ♦ *vt*: **to ~ and dine sb**
agasajar *or* festejar a algn.
wine bar *n bar especializado en vinos*.
wine cellar *n* bodega.
wine glass *n* copa (de *or* para vino).
wine-growing [ˈwaɪngrəuɪŋ] *adj*
viticultor(a).
wine list *n* lista de vinos.
wine merchant *n* vinatero.
wine tasting *n* degustación *f* de vinos.
wine waiter *n* escanciador *m*.
wing [wɪŋ] *n* ala; (*BRIT AUT*) aleta; **~s** *npl*
(*THEAT*) bastidores *mpl*.
winger [ˈwɪŋə*] *n* (*SPORT*) extremo.
wing mirror *n* (espejo) retrovisor *m*.
wing nut *n* tuerca (de) mariposa.
wingspan [ˈwɪŋspæn], **wingspread**
[ˈwɪŋsprɛd] *n* envergadura.
wink [wɪŋk] *n* guiño; (*blink*) pestañeo ♦ *vi*
guiñar; (*blink*) pestañear; (*light etc*)
parpadear.
winkle [ˈwɪŋkl] *n* bígaro, bigarro.
winner [ˈwɪnə*] *n* ganador(a) *m/f*.
winning [ˈwɪnɪŋ] *adj* (*team*) ganador(a);
(*goal*) decisivo; (*charming*) encantador(a).
winning post *n* meta.
winnings [ˈwɪnɪŋz] *npl* ganancias *fpl*.

winter [ˈwɪntə*] *n* invierno ♦ *vi* invernar.
winter sports *npl* deportes *mpl* de
invierno.
wintry [ˈwɪntrɪ] *adj* invernal.
wipe [waɪp] *n*: **to give sth a ~** pasar un
trapo sobre algo ♦ *vt* limpiar; **to ~ one's
nose** limpiarse la nariz.
▶**wipe off** *vt* limpiar con un trapo.
▶**wipe out** *vt* (*debt*) liquidar; (*memory*)
borrar; (*destroy*) destruir.
▶**wipe up** *vt* limpiar.
wire [ˈwaɪə*] *n* alambre *m*; (*ELEC*) cable *m*
(eléctrico); (*TEL*) telegrama *m* ♦ *vt* (*house*)
poner la instalación eléctrica en; (*also*: **~
up**) conectar.
wire cutters *npl* cortaalambres *msg inv*.
wireless [ˈwaɪəlɪs] *n* (*BRIT*) radio *f* ♦ *adj*
inalámbrico.
wireless technology *n* tecnología
inalámbrica.
wire mesh, wire netting *n* tela metálica.
wire service *n* (*US*) agencia de noticias.
wire-tapping [ˈwaɪəˈtæpɪŋ] *n* intervención *f*
telefónica.
wiring [ˈwaɪərɪŋ] *n* instalación *f* eléctrica.
wiry [ˈwaɪərɪ] *adj* enjuto y fuerte.
Wis(c). *abbr* (*US*) = Wisconsin.
wisdom [ˈwɪzdəm] *n* sabiduría, saber *m*;
(*good sense*) cordura.
wisdom tooth *n* muela del juicio.
wise [waɪz] *adj* sabio; (*sensible*) juicioso;
I'm none the ~r sigo sin entender.
▶**wise up** *vi* (*col*): **to ~ up (to sth)**
enterarse (de algo).
...wise [waɪz] *suff*: **time~** en cuanto a *or*
respecto al tiempo.
wisecrack [ˈwaɪzkræk] *n* broma.
wish [wɪʃ] *n* (*desire*) deseo ♦ *vt* desear;
(*want*) querer; **best ~es** (*on birthday etc*)
felicidades *fpl*; **with best ~es** (*in letter*)
saludos *mpl*, recuerdos *mpl*; **he ~ed me
well** me deseó mucha suerte; **to ~ sth on
sb** imponer algo a algn; **to ~ to do/sb to
do sth** querer hacer/que algn haga algo;
to ~ for desear.
wishbone [ˈwɪʃbəun] *n* espoleta (*de la que
tiran dos personas; quien se quede con el
hueso más largo pide un deseo*).
wishful [ˈwɪʃful] *n*: **it's ~ thinking** eso es
hacerse ilusiones.
wishy-washy [ˈwɪʃɪwɔʃɪ] *adj* (*col*: *colour*)
desvaído; (: *ideas, thinking*) flojo.
wisp [wɪsp] *n* mechón *m*; (*of smoke*) voluta.
wistful [ˈwɪstful] *adj* pensativo; (*nostalgic*)
nostálgico.
wit [wɪt] *n* (*wittiness*) ingenio, gracia;
(*intelligence*: *also*: **~s**) inteligencia;
(*person*) chistoso/a; **to have** *or* **keep one's**

~s **about one** no perder la cabeza.
witch [wɪtʃ] n bruja.
witchcraft ['wɪtʃkrɑːft] n brujería.
witch doctor n hechicero.
witch-hunt ['wɪtʃhʌnt] n (POL) caza de
brujas.

=================== KEYWORD

with [wɪð, wɪθ] prep **1** (accompanying, in the
company of) con (con+mí, ti, sí = conmigo,
contigo, consigo); **I was ~ him** estaba con
él; **we stayed ~ friends** nos quedamos en
casa de unos amigos
2 (descriptive, indicating manner etc) con;
de; **a room ~ a view** una habitación con
vistas; **the man ~ the grey hat/blue eyes**
el hombre del sombrero gris/de los ojos
azules; **red ~ anger** rojo de ira; **to shake
~ fear** temblar de miedo; **to fill sth ~
water** llenar algo de agua
3: **I'm ~ you/I'm not ~ you** (understand)
ya te entiendo/no te entiendo; **I'm not
really ~ it today** no doy pie con bola hoy.

withdraw [wɪð'drɔː] vb (irreg: like draw) vt
retirar ♦ vi retirarse; (go back on promise)
retractarse; **to ~ money (from the bank)**
retirar fondos (del banco); **to ~ into o.s.**
ensimismarse.
withdrawal [wɪð'drɔːəl] n retirada.
withdrawal symptoms npl síndrome m
de abstinencia.
withdrawn [wɪð'drɔːn] adj (person)
reservado, introvertido ♦ pp of **withdraw.**
wither ['wɪðə*] vi marchitarse.
withered ['wɪðəd] adj marchito, seco.
withhold [wɪð'həuld] vt (irreg: like hold)
(money) retener; (decision) aplazar;
(permission) negar; (information) ocultar.
within [wɪð'ɪn] prep dentro de ♦ adv dentro;
~ **reach** al alcance de la mano; ~ **sight of**
a la vista de; ~ **the week** antes de que
acabe la semana; **to be ~ the law**
atenerse a la legalidad; ~ **an hour from
now** dentro de una hora.
without [wɪð'aut] prep sin; **to go** or **do ~
sth** prescindir de algo; ~ **anybody
knowing** sin saberlo nadie.
withstand [wɪð'stænd] vt (irreg: like stand)
resistir a.
witness ['wɪtnɪs] n (person) testigo m/f;
(evidence) testimonio ♦ vt (event)
presenciar, ser testigo de; (document)
atestiguar la veracidad de; ~ **for the
prosecution/defence** testigo de cargo/
descargo; **to ~ to (having seen) sth** dar
testimonio de (haber visto) algo.
witness box, (US) **witness stand** n

tribuna de los testigos.
witticism ['wɪtɪsɪzm] n dicho ingenioso.
wittily ['wɪtɪlɪ] adv ingeniosamente.
witty ['wɪtɪ] adj ingenioso.
wives [waɪvz] npl of **wife.**
wizard ['wɪzəd] n hechicero.
wizened ['wɪznd] adj arrugado, marchito.
wk abbr = **week.**
Wm. abbr = William.
WO n abbr = **warrant officer.**
wobble ['wɔbl] vi tambalearse.
wobbly ['wɔblɪ] adj (hand, voice)
tembloroso; (table, chair) tambaleante,
cojo.
woe [wəu] n desgracia.
woeful ['wəuful] adj (bad) lamentable; (sad)
apesadumbrado.
wok [wɔk] n wok m.
woke [wəuk] pt of **wake.**
woken ['wəukn] pp of **wake.**
wolf, pl **wolves** [wulf, wulvz] n lobo.
woman, pl **women** ['wumən, 'wɪmɪn] n
mujer f; **young ~** (mujer f) joven f;
women's page (PRESS) sección f de la
mujer.
woman doctor n doctora.
woman friend n amiga.
womanize ['wumənaɪz] vi ser un
mujeriego.
womanly ['wumənlɪ] adj femenino.
womb [wuːm] n (ANAT) matriz f, útero.
women ['wɪmɪn] npl of **woman.**
Women's (Liberation) Movement n
(also: women's lib) Movimiento de
liberación de la mujer.
won [wʌn] pt, pp of **win.**
wonder ['wʌndə*] n maravilla, prodigio;
(feeling) asombro ♦ vi: **to ~ whether**
preguntarse si; **to ~ at** asombrarse de; **to
~ about** pensar sobre or en; **it's no ~ that**
no es de extrañar que.
wonderful ['wʌndəful] adj maravilloso.
wonderfully ['wʌndəfəlɪ] adv
maravillosamente, estupendamente.
wonky ['wɔŋkɪ] adj (BRIT col: unsteady) poco
seguro, cojo; (: broken down) estropeado.
wont [wɔnt] n: **as is his/her ~** como tiene
por costumbre.
won't [wəunt] = **will not.**
woo [wuː] vt (woman) cortejar.
wood [wud] n (timber) madera; (forest)
bosque m ♦ cpd de madera.
wood alcohol n (US) alcohol m
desnaturalizado.
wood carving n tallado en madera.
wooded ['wudɪd] adj arbolado.
wooden ['wudn] adj de madera; (fig)
inexpresivo.

woodland ['wudlənd] *n* bosque *m*.
woodpecker ['wudpɛkə*] *n* pájaro carpintero.
wood pigeon *n* paloma torcaz.
woodwind ['wudwɪnd] *n* (*MUS*) instrumentos *mpl* de viento de madera.
woodwork ['wudwəːk] *n* carpintería.
woodworm ['wudwəːm] *n* carcoma.
woof [wuf] *n* (*of dog*) ladrido ♦ *vi* ladrar; ~, ~! ¡guau, guau!
wool [wul] *n* lana; **knitting** ~ lana (de hacer punto); **to pull the** ~ **over sb's eyes** (*fig*) dar a algn gato por liebre.
woollen, (*US*) **woolen** ['wulən] *adj* de lana. ♦ *n*: ~**s** géneros *mpl* de lana.
woolly, (*US*) **wooly** ['wulɪ] *adj* de lana; (*fig*: *ideas*) confuso.
woozy ['wuːzɪ] *adj* (*col*) mareado.
word [wəːd] *n* palabra; (*news*) noticia; (*promise*) palabra (de honor) ♦ *vt* redactar; ~ **for** ~ palabra por palabra; **what's the** ~ **for "pen" in Spanish?** ¿cómo se dice "pen" en español?; **to put sth into** ~**s** expresar algo en palabras; **to have a** ~ **with sb** hablar (dos palabras) con algn; **in other** ~**s** en otras palabras; **to break/ keep one's** ~ faltar a la palabra/cumplir la promesa; **to leave** ~ (**with/for sb**) **that** ... dejar recado (con/para algn) de que ...; **to have** ~**s with sb** (*quarrel with*) discutir *or* reñir con algn.
wording ['wəːdɪŋ] *n* redacción *f*.
word-of-mouth [wəːdəv'mauθ] *n*: **by** *or* **through** ~ de palabra, por el boca a boca.
word-perfect ['wəːd'pəːfɪkt] *adj* (*speech etc*) sin faltas de expresión.
word processing *n* procesamiento *or* tratamiento de textos.
word processor [-'prəusɛsə*] *n* procesador *m* de textos.
wordwrap ['wəːdræp] *n* (*COMPUT*) salto de línea automático.
wordy ['wəːdɪ] *adj* verboso, prolijo.
wore [wɔː*] *pt of* **wear**.
work [wəːk] *n* trabajo; (*job*) empleo, trabajo; (*ART, LIT*) obra ♦ *vi* trabajar; (*mechanism*) funcionar, marchar; (*medicine*) ser eficaz, surtir efecto ♦ *vt* (*shape*) trabajar; (*stone etc*) tallar; (*mine etc*) explotar; (*machine*) manejar, hacer funcionar; (*cause*) producir; **to go to** ~ ir a trabajar *or* al trabajo; **to be at** ~ (**on sth**) estar trabajando (en algo); **to set to** ~, **start** ~ ponerse a trabajar; **to be out of** ~ estar parado, no tener trabajo; **his life's** ~ el trabajo de su vida; **to** ~ **hard** trabajar mucho *or* duro; **to** ~ **to rule** (*INDUSTRY*) hacer una huelga de celo; **to**

~ **loose** (*part*) desprenderse; (*knot*) aflojarse; *see also* **works**.
►**work off** *vt*: **to** ~ **off one's feelings** desahogarse.
►**work on** *vt fus* trabajar en, dedicarse a; (*principle*) basarse en; **he's** ~**ing on the car** está reparando el coche.
►**work out** *vi* (*plans etc*) salir bien, funcionar; (*SPORT*) hacer ejercicios ♦ *vt* (*problem*) resolver; (*plan*) elaborar; **it** ~**s out at £100** asciende a 100 libras.
►**work up** *vt*: **he** ~**ed his way up in the company** ascendió en la compañía mediante sus propios esfuerzos.
workable ['wəːkəbl] *adj* (*solution*) práctico, factible.
workaholic [wəːkə'hɒlɪk] *n* adicto/a al trabajo.
workbench ['wəːkbɛntʃ] *n* banco *or* mesa de trabajo.
worked up [wəːkt-] *adj*: **to get** ~ excitarse.
worker ['wəːkə*] *n* trabajador(a) *m/f*, obrero/a; **office** ~ oficinista *m/f*.
work force *n* mano *f* de obra.
work-in ['wəːkɪn] *n* (*BRIT*) ocupación *f* (de la empresa) sin interrupción del trabajo.
working ['wəːkɪŋ] *adj* (*day, week*) laborable; (*tools, conditions, clothes*) de trabajo; (*wife*) que trabaja; (*partner*) activo.
working capital *n* (*COMM*) capital *m* circulante.
working class *n* clase *f* obrera ♦ *adj*: **working-class** obrero.
working knowledge *n* conocimientos *mpl* básicos.
working man *n* obrero.
working order *n*: **in** ~ en funcionamiento.
working party *n* comisión *f* de investigación, grupo de trabajo.
working week *n* semana laboral.
work-in-progress ['wəːkɪn'prəugrɛs] *n* (*COMM*) trabajo en curso.
workload ['wəːkləud] *n* cantidad *f* de trabajo.
workman ['wəːkmən] *n* obrero.
workmanship ['wəːkmənʃɪp] *n* (*art*) hechura; (*skill*) habilidad *f*.
workmate ['wəːkmeɪt] *n* compañero/a de trabajo.
workout ['wəːkaut] *n* (*SPORT*) sesión *f* de ejercicios.
work permit *n* permiso de trabajo.
works [wəːks] *nsg* (*BRIT*: *factory*) fábrica ♦ *npl* (*of clock, machine*) mecanismo; **road** ~ obras *fpl*.
works council *n* comité *m* de empresa.
worksheet ['wəːkʃiːt] *n* (*COMPUT*) hoja de trabajo; (*SCOL*) hoja de ejercicios.

workshop ['wəːkʃɔp] *n* taller *m*.
work station *n* estación *f* de trabajo.
work study *n* estudio del trabajo.
worktop ['wəːktɔp] *n* encimera.
work-to-rule ['wəːktə'ruːl] *n* (*BRIT*) huelga de celo.
world [wəːld] *n* mundo ♦ *cpd* (*champion*) del mundo; (*power, war*) mundial; **all over the** ~ por todo el mundo, en el mundo entero; **the business** ~ el mundo de los negocios; **what in the** ~ **is he doing?** ¿qué diablos está haciendo?; **to think the** ~ **of sb** (*fig*) tener un concepto muy alto de algn; **to do sb a** ~ **of good** sentar muy bien a algn; **W~ War One/Two** la primera/segunda Guerra Mundial.
World Cup *n* (*FOOTBALL*): **the** ~ el Mundial, los Mundiales.
world-famous [wəːld'feɪməs] *adj* de fama mundial, mundialmente famoso.
worldly ['wəːldlɪ] *adj* mundano.
world music *n* música étnica.
World Series *n*: **the** ~ (*US BASEBALL*) el campeonato nacional de béisbol de EEUU.
World Service *n see* **BBC**.
world-wide ['wəːldwaɪd] *adj* mundial, universal.
worm [wəːm] *n* gusano; (*earth~*) lombriz *f*.
worn [wɔːn] *pp of* **wear** ♦ *adj* usado.
worn-out ['wɔːnaut] *adj* (*object*) gastado; (*person*) rendido, agotado.
worried ['wʌrɪd] *adj* preocupado; **to be** ~ **about sth** estar preocupado por algo.
worrisome ['wʌrɪsəm] *adj* preocupante, inquietante.
worry ['wʌrɪ] *n* preocupación *f* ♦ *vt* preocupar, inquietar ♦ *vi* preocuparse; **to** ~ **about** *or* **over sth/sb** preocuparse por algo/algn.
worrying ['wʌrɪɪŋ] *adj* inquietante.
worse [wəːs] *adj, adv* peor ♦ *n* el peor, lo peor; **a change for the** ~ un empeoramiento; **so much the** ~ **for you** tanto peor para ti; **he is none the** ~ **for it** se ha quedado tan fresco *or* tan tranquilo; **to get** ~, **to grow** ~ empeorar.
worsen ['wəːsn] *vt, vi* empeorar.
worse off *adj* (*fig*): **you'll be** ~ **this way** de esta forma estarás peor que antes.
worship ['wəːʃɪp] *n* (*organized* ~) culto; (*act*) adoración *f* ♦ *vt* adorar; **Your W~** (*BRIT: to mayor*) su Ilustrísima; (: *to judge*) su señoría.
worshipper, (*US*) **worshiper** ['wəːʃɪpə*] *n* devoto/a.
worst [wəːst] *adj* (el/la) peor ♦ *adv* peor ♦ *n* lo peor; **at** ~ en el peor de los casos; **to**

come off ~ llevar la peor parte; **if the** ~ **comes to the** ~ en el peor de los casos.
worst-case ['wəːstkeɪs] *adj*: **the** ~ **scenario** el peor de los casos.
worsted ['wustɪd] *n*: (**wool**) ~ estambre *m*.
worth [wəːθ] *n* valor *m* ♦ *adj*: **to be** ~ valer; **how much is it** ~? ¿cuánto vale?; **it's** ~ **it** vale *or* merece la pena; **to be** ~ **one's while (to do)** merecer la pena (hacer); **it's not** ~ **the trouble** no vale *or* merece la pena.
worthless ['wəːθlɪs] *adj* sin valor; (*useless*) inútil.
worthwhile ['wəːθwaɪl] *adj* (*activity*) que merece la pena; (*cause*) loable.
worthy ['wəːðɪ] *adj* (*person*) respetable; (*motive*) honesto; ~ **of** digno de.

═══════════════════════ *KEYWORD*

would [wud] *aux vb* **1** (*conditional tense*): **if you asked him he** ~ **do it** si se lo pidieras, lo haría; **if you had asked him he** ~ **have done it** si se lo hubieras pedido, lo habría *or* hubiera hecho
2 (*in offers, invitations, requests*): ~ **you like a biscuit?** ¿quieres una galleta?; (*formal*) ¿querría una galleta?; ~ **you ask him to come in?** ¿quiere hacerle pasar?; ~ **you open the window please?** ¿quiere *or* podría abrir la ventana, por favor?
3 (*in indirect speech*): **I said I** ~ **do it** dije que lo haría
4 (*emphatic*): **it WOULD have to snow today!** ¡tenía que nevar precisamente hoy!
5 (*insistence*): **she** ~**n't behave** no quiso comportarse bien
6 (*conjecture*): **it** ~ **have been midnight** sería medianoche; **it** ~ **seem so** parece ser que sí
7 (*indicating habit*): **he** ~ **go there on Mondays** iba allí los lunes.

would-be ['wudbiː] *adj* (*pej*) presunto.
wouldn't ['wudnt] = **would not**.
wound *vb* [waund] *pt, pp of* **wind** ♦ *n, vt* [wuːnd] *n* herida ♦ *vt* herir.
wove [wəuv] *pt of* **weave**.
woven ['wəuvən] *pp of* **weave**.
WP *n abbr* = **word processing; word processor** ♦ *abbr* (*BRIT col*: = *weather permitting*) si lo permite el tiempo.
WPC *n abbr* (*BRIT*) = *woman police constable*.
wpm *abbr* (= *words per minute*) p.p.m.
WRAC *n abbr* (*BRIT*: = *Women's Royal Army Corps*) *cuerpo auxiliar femenino del ejército de tierra*.
WRAF *n abbr* (*BRIT*: = *Women's Royal Air*

Force) *cuerpo auxiliar femenino del ejército del aire.*
wrangle ['ræŋgl] *n* riña ♦ *vi* reñir.
wrap [ræp] *n* (*stole*) chal *m* ♦ *vt* (*also:* ~ **up**) envolver; **under** ~**s** (*fig: plan, scheme*) oculto, tapado.
wrapper ['ræpə*] *n* (*BRIT: of book*) sobrecubierta; (*on chocolate etc*) envoltura.
wrapping paper ['ræpiŋ-] *n* papel *m* de envolver.
wrath [rɔθ] *n* cólera.
wreak [riːk] *vt* (*destruction*) causar; **to** ~ **havoc (on)** hacer *or* causar estragos (en); **to** ~ **vengeance (on)** vengarse (en).
wreath, ~**s** [riːθ, riːðz] *n* (*funeral* ~) corona; (*of flowers*) guirnalda.
wreck [rɛk] *n* (*ship: destruction*) naufragio; (: *remains*) restos *mpl* del barco; (*pej: person*) ruina ♦ *vt* destrozar; **to be** ~**ed** (*NAUT*) naufragar.
wreckage ['rɛkidʒ] *n* (*remains*) restos *mpl*; (*of building*) escombros *mpl*.
wrecker ['rɛkə*] *n* (*US: breakdown van*) camión-grúa *m*.
WREN [rɛn] *n abbr* (*BRIT*) *miembro del WRNS.*
wren [rɛn] *n* (*ZOOL*) reyezuelo.
wrench [rɛntʃ] *n* (*TECH*) llave *f* inglesa; (*tug*) tirón *m* ♦ *vt* arrancar; **to** ~ **sth from sb** arrebatar algo violentamente a algn.
wrest [rɛst] *vt:* **to** ~ **sth from sb** arrebatar *or* arrancar algo a algn.
wrestle ['rɛsl] *vi:* **to** ~ **(with sb)** luchar (con *or* contra algn).
wrestler ['rɛslə*] *n* luchador(a) *m/f* (de lucha libre).
wrestling ['rɛsliŋ] *n* lucha libre.
wrestling match *n* combate *m* de lucha libre.
wretch [rɛtʃ] *n* desgraciado/a, miserable *m/f*; **little** ~! (*often humorous*) ¡granuja!
wretched ['rɛtʃid] *adj* miserable.
wriggle ['rigl] *vi* serpentear.
wring *pt, pp* **wrung** [riŋ, rʌŋ] *vt* torcer, retorcer; (*wet clothes*) escurrir; (*fig*): **to** ~ **sth out of sb** sacar algo por la fuerza a algn.
wringer ['riŋə*] *n* escurridor *m*.
wringing ['riŋiŋ] *adj* (*also:* ~ **wet**) empapado.
wrinkle ['riŋkl] *n* arruga ♦ *vt* arrugar ♦ *vi* arrugarse.
wrinkled ['riŋkld], **wrinkly** ['riŋkli] *adj* (*fabric, paper, etc*) arrugado.
wrist [rist] *n* muñeca.
wristband ['ristbænd] *n* (*BRIT: of shirt*) puño; (: *of watch*) correa.

wrist watch *n* reloj *m* de pulsera.
writ [rit] *n* mandato judicial; **to serve a** ~ **on sb** notificar un mandato judicial a algn.
write, *pt* **wrote,** *pp* **written** [rait, rəut, 'ritn] *vt, vi* escribir; **to** ~ **sb a letter** escribir una carta a algn.
▶**write away** *vi:* **to** ~ **away for** (*information, goods*) pedir por escrito *or* carta.
▶**write down** *vt* escribir; (*note*) apuntar.
▶**write off** *vt* (*debt*) borrar (como incobrable), (*fig*) desechar por inútil; (*smash up: car*) destrozar.
▶**write out** *vt* escribir.
▶**write up** *vt* redactar.
write-off ['raitɔf] *n* siniestro total; **the car is a** ~ el coche es pura chatarra.
write-protect ['raitprə'tɛkt] *vt* (*COMPUT*) proteger contra escritura.
writer ['raitə*] *n* escritor(a) *m/f*.
write-up ['raitʌp] *n* (*review*) crítica, reseña.
writhe [raið] *vi* retorcerse.
writing ['raitiŋ] *n* escritura; (*hand*~) letra; (*of author*) obras; **in** ~ por escrito; **to put sth in** ~ poner algo por escrito; **in my own** ~ escrito por mí; *see also* **writings.**
writing case *n* estuche *m* de papel de escribir.
writing desk *n* escritorio.
writing paper *n* papel *m* de escribir.
writings *npl* obras *fpl*.
written ['ritn] *pp of* **write.**
WRNS *n abbr* (*BRIT:* = *Women's Royal Naval Service*) *cuerpo auxiliar femenino de la armada.*
wrong [rɔŋ] *adj* (*wicked*) malo; (*unfair*) injusto; (*incorrect*) equivocado, incorrecto; (*not suitable*) inoportuno, inconveniente ♦ *adv* mal ♦ *n* mal *m*; (*injustice*) injusticia ♦ *vt* ser injusto con; (*hurt*) agraviar; **to be** ~ (*answer*) estar equivocado; (*in doing, saying*) equivocarse; **it's** ~ **to steal, stealing is** ~ es mal robar; **you are** ~ **to do it** haces mal en hacerlo; **you are** ~ **about that, you've got it** ~ en eso estás equivocado; **to be in the** ~ no tener razón; (*guilty*) tener la culpa; **what's** ~? ¿qué pasa?; **what's** ~ **with the car?** ¿qué le pasa al coche?; **there's nothing** ~ no pasa nada; **you have the** ~ **number** (*TEL*) se ha equivocado de número; **to go** ~ (*person*) equivocarse; (*plan*) salir mal; (*machine*) estropearse.
wrongdoer ['rɔŋduːə*] *n* malhechor(a) *m/f*.
wrong-foot [rɔŋ'fut] *vt* (*SPORT*) hacer perder el equilibrio a; (*fig*) poner en un

aprieto a.

wrongful ['rɔŋful] *adj* injusto; ~ **dismissal**
(*INDUSTRY*) despido improcedente.

wrongly ['rɔŋlɪ] *adv* (*answer, do, count*)
incorrectamente; (*treat*) injustamente.

wrote [rəut] *pt of* **write**.

wrought [rɔːt] *adj*: ~ **iron** hierro forjado.

wrung [rʌŋ] *pt, pp of* **wring**.

WRVS *n abbr* (*BRIT*: = Women's Royal
Voluntary Service) *cuerpo de voluntarias
al servicio de la comunidad.*

wry [raɪ] *adj* irónico.

wt. *abbr* = **weight**.

WV, W. Va. *abbr* (*US*) = *West Virginia*.

WWW *n abbr* (= *World Wide Web*) WWW *m
or f*.

WY, Wyo. *abbr* (*US*) = *Wyoming*.

WYSIWYG ['wɪzɪwɪg] *abbr* (*COMPUT*: = *what
you see is what you get*) tipo de
presentación en un procesador de textos.

X, x [eks] *n* (*letter*) X, x *f*: (*BRIT CINE: formerly*)
no apto para menores de 18 años; **X for
Xmas** X de Xiquena; **if you earn X dollars
a year** si ganas X dólares al año.

X-certificate ['ɛkssə'tɪfɪkɪt] *adj* (*BRIT: film:
formerly*) no apto para menores de 18
años.

Xerox ® ['zɪərɔks] *n* (*also*: ~ **machine**)
fotocopiadora; (*photocopy*) fotocopia ♦ *vt*
fotocopiar.

XL *abbr* = *extra large*.

Xmas ['ɛksməs] *n abbr* = **Christmas**.

X-rated ['eks'reɪtɪd] *adj* (*US: film*) no apto
para menores de 18 años.

X-ray [ɛks'reɪ] *n* radiografía; ~**s** *npl* rayos
mpl X ♦ *vt* radiografiar.

xylophone ['zaɪləfəun] *n* xilófono.

Y y

Y, y [waɪ] *n* (*letter*) Y, y *f*; **Y for Yellow**, (*US*)
Y for Yoke Y de Yegua.

Y2K [ˌwaɪtuː'keɪ] *abbr* (= *Year 2000*): **the ~
problem** (*COMPUT*) el efecto 2000.

yacht [jɔt] *n* yate *m*.

yachting ['jɔtɪŋ] *n* (*sport*) balandrismo.

yachtsman ['jɔtsmən] *n* balandrista *m*.

yachtswoman ['jɔtswumən] balandrista.

yam [jæm] *n* ñame *m*; (*sweet potato*) batata,
camote *m* (*LAM*).

Yank [jæŋk], **Yankee** ['jæŋkɪ] *n* (*pej*)
yanqui *m/f*.

yank [jæŋk] *vt* tirar de, jalar de (*LAM*) ♦ *n*
tirón *m*.

yap [jæp] *vi* (*dog*) aullar.

yard [jɑːd] *n* patio; (*US: garden*) jardín *m*;
(*measure*) yarda; **builder's** ~ almacén *m*.

yardstick ['jɑːdstɪk] *n* (*fig*) criterio, norma.

yarn [jɑːn] *n* hilo; (*tale*) cuento (chino).

yawn [jɔːn] *n* bostezo ♦ *vi* bostezar.

yawning ['jɔːnɪŋ] *adj* (*gap*) muy abierto.

yd. *abbr* (= *yard*) yda.

yeah [jɛə] *adv* (*col*) sí.

year [jɪə*] *n* año; (*SCOL, UNIV*) curso; **this** ~
este año; ~ **in**, ~ **out** año tras año; **a** *or*
per ~ al año; **to be 8** ~**s old** tener 8 años;
she's three ~**s old** tiene tres años; **an
eight-~-old child** un niño de ocho años
(de edad).

yearbook ['jɪəbuk] *n* anuario.

yearling ['jɪəlɪŋ] *n* (*horse*) potro de un año.

yearly ['jɪəlɪ] *adj* anual ♦ *adv* anualmente,
cada año; **twice** ~ dos veces al año.

yearn [jəːn] *vi*: **to** ~ **for sth** añorar algo,
suspirar por algo.

yearning ['jəːnɪŋ] *n* ansia; (*longing*)
añoranza.

yeast [jiːst] *n* levadura.

yell [jɛl] *n* grito, alarido ♦ *vi* gritar.

yellow ['jɛləu] *adj*, *n* amarillo.

yellow fever *n* fiebre *f* amarilla.

yellowish ['jɛləuɪʃ] *adj* amarillento.

Yellow Pages ® *npl* páginas *fpl* amarillas.

Yellow Sea *n*: **the** ~ el Mar Amarillo.

yelp [jɛlp] *n* aullido ♦ *vi* aullar.

Yemen ['jemən] *n* Yemen *m*.

Yemeni ['jemənɪ] *adj*, *n* yemení *m/f*,
yemenita *m/f*.

yen [jɛn] *n* (*currency*) yen *m*.
yeoman ['jəumən] *n*: **Y~ of the Guard** *alabardero de la Casa Real*.
yes [jɛs] *adv, n* sí *m*; **to say/answer ~** decir/contestar que sí; **to say ~ (to)** decir que sí (a), conformarse (con).
yes man *n* pelotillero.
yesterday ['jɛstədɪ] *adv, n* ayer *m*; **~ morning/evening** ayer por la mañana/tarde; **all day ~** todo el día de ayer; **the day before ~** antes de ayer, anteayer.
yet [jɛt] *adv* todavía ♦ *conj* sin embargo, a pesar de todo; **~ again** de nuevo; **it is not finished ~** todavía no está acabado; **the best ~** el/la mejor hasta ahora; **as ~** hasta ahora, todavía.
yew [ju:] *n* tejo.
Y-fronts ® ['waɪfrʌnts] *npl* (*BRIT*) calzoncillos *mpl*, eslip *msg* tradicional.
YHA *n abbr* (*BRIT*: = *Youth Hostel Association*) ≈ Red *f* Española de Albergues Juveniles.
Yiddish ['jɪdɪʃ] *n* yiddish *m*.
yield [ji:ld] *n* producción *f*; (*AGR*) cosecha; (*COMM*) rendimiento ♦ *vt* producir, dar; (*profit*) rendir ♦ *vi* rendirse, ceder; (*US AUT*) ceder el paso; **a ~ of 5%** un rédito del 5 por ciento.
YMCA *n abbr* (= *Young Men's Christian Association*) Asociación *f* de Jóvenes Cristianos.
yob(bo) ['jɔb(bəu)] *n* (*BRIT col*) gamberro.
yodel ['jəudl] *vi* cantar a la tirolesa.
yoga ['jəugə] *n* yoga *m*.
yog(h)ourt, yog(h)urt ['jəugət] *n* yogur *m*.
yoke [jəuk] *n* (*of oxen*) yunta; (*on shoulders*) balancín *m*; (*fig*) yugo ♦ *vt* (*also*: **~ together**: *oxen*) uncir.
yolk [jəuk] *n* yema (de huevo).
yonder ['jɔndə*] *adv* allá (a lo lejos).
yonks [jɔŋks] *npl* (*col*): **I haven't seen him for ~** hace siglos que no lo veo.
Yorks *abbr* (*BRIT*) = *Yorkshire*.

========================== KEYWORD

you [ju:] *pron* **1** (*subject*: *familiar*) tú, *pl* vosotros/as (*SP*), ustedes (*LAM*); (*polite*) usted, *pl* ustedes; **~ are very kind** eres/es *etc* muy amable; **~ French enjoy your food** a vosotros (*or* ustedes) los franceses os (*or* les) gusta la comida; **~ and I will go** iremos tú y yo
2 (*object*: *direct*: *familiar*) te, *pl* os (*SP*), les (*LAM*); (*polite*) lo *or* le, *pl* los *or* les, *f* la, *pl* las; **I know ~** te/le *etc* conozco
3 (*object*: *indirect*: *familiar*) te, *pl* os (*SP*), les (*LAM*); (*polite*) le, *pl* les; **I gave the letter to ~ yesterday** te/os *etc* di la carta ayer

4 (*stressed*): **I told YOU to do it** te dije a ti que lo hicieras, es a ti a quien dije que lo hicieras; *see also* **3, 5**
5 (*after prep*: NB: *con+ti* = *contigo*: *familiar*) ti, *pl* vosotros/as (*SP*), ustedes (*LAM*); (: *polite*) usted, *pl* ustedes; **it's for ~** es para ti/vosotros *etc*
6 (*comparisons*: *familiar*) tú, *pl* vosotros/as (*SP*), ustedes (*LAM*); (: *polite*) usted, *pl* ustedes; **she's younger than ~** es más joven que tú/vosotros *etc*
7 (*impersonal*: *one*): **fresh air does ~ good** el aire puro (te) hace bien; **~ never know** nunca se sabe; **~ can't do that!** ¡eso no se hace!

you'd [ju:d] = **you had; you would**.
you'll [ju:l] = **you will, you shall**.
young [jʌŋ] *adj* joven ♦ *npl* (*of animal*) cría; (*people*): **the ~** los jóvenes, la juventud; **a ~ man/lady** un(a) joven; **my ~er brother** mi hermano menor *or* pequeño; **the ~er generation** la nueva generación.
youngster ['jʌŋstə*] *n* joven *m/f*.
your [jɔ:*] *adj* tu; (*pl*) vuestro; (*formal*) su; **~ house** tu *etc* casa; *see also* **my**.
you're [juə*] = **you are**.
yours [jɔ:z] *pron* tuyo; (: *pl*) vuestro; (*formal*) suyo; **a friend of ~** un amigo tuyo *etc*; *see also* **faithfully, mine, sincerely**.
yourself [jɔ:'sɛlf] *pron* (*reflexive*) tú mismo; (*complement*) te; (*after prep*) tí (mismo); (*formal*) usted mismo; (: *complement*) se; (: *after prep*) sí (mismo); **you ~ told me** me lo dijiste tú mismo; **(all) by ~** sin ayuda de nadie, solo; *see also* **oneself**.
yourselves [jɔ:'sɛlvz] *pl pron* vosotros mismos; (*after prep*) vosotros (mismos); (*formal*) ustedes (mismos); (: *complement*) se; (: *after prep*) sí mismos.
youth [ju:θ] *n* juventud *f*; (*young man*) (*pl* **~s** [ju:ðz]) joven *m*; **in my ~** en mi juventud.
youth club *n* club *m* juvenil.
youthful ['ju:θful] *adj* juvenil.
youthfulness ['ju:θfəlnɪs] *n* juventud *f*.
youth hostel *n* albergue *m* juvenil.
youth movement *n* movimiento juvenil.
you've [ju:v] = **you have**.
yowl [jaul] *n* (*of animal, person*) aullido ♦ *vi* aullar.
yr. *abbr* (= *year*) a.
YT *abbr* (*Canada*) = *Yukon Territory*.
Yugoslav ['ju:gəuslɑ:v] *adj, n* yugoslavo/a *m/f*.
Yugoslavia [ju:gəu'slɑ:vɪə] *n* Yugoslavia.
Yugoslavian [ju:gəu'slɑ:vɪən] *adj* yugoslavo/a.

yuppie ['jʌpɪ] (*col*) *adj, n* yuppie *m/f*.
YWCA *n abbr* (= *Young Women's Christian Association*) Asociación *f* de Jóvenes Cristianas.

Z z

Z, z [zɛd, (*US*) ziː] *n* (*letter*) Z, z *f*; **Z for Zebra** Z de Zaragoza.
Zaire [zɑːˈiːə*] *n* Zaire *m*.
Zambia ['zæmbɪə] *n* Zambia.
Zambian ['zæmbɪən] *adj, n* zambiano/a *m/f*.
zany ['zeɪnɪ] *adj* estrafalario.
zap [zæp] *vt* (*COMPUT*) borrar.
zeal [ziːl] *n* celo, entusiasmo.
zealot ['zɛlət] *n* fanático/a.
zealous ['zɛləs] *adj* celoso, entusiasta.
zebra ['ziːbrə] *n* cebra.
zebra crossing *n* (*BRIT*) paso de peatones.
zenith ['zɛnɪθ] *n* (*ASTRO*) cénit *m*; (*fig*) apogeo.
zero ['zɪərəu] *n* cero; **5 degrees below** ~ 5 grados bajo cero.
zero hour *n* hora cero.
zero option *n* (*POL*) opción *f* cero.

zero-rated ['zɪərəureɪtɪd] *adj* (*BRIT*) de tasa cero.
zest [zɛst] *n* entusiasmo; ~ **for living** brío.
zigzag ['zɪgzæg] *n* zigzag *m* ♦ *vi* zigzaguear.
Zimbabwe [zɪmˈbɑːbwɪ] *n* Zimbabwe *m*.
Zimbabwean [zɪmˈbɑːbwɪən] *adj, n* zimbabuo/a *m/f*.
Zimmer ® ['zɪmə*] *n* (*also:* ~ **frame**) andador *m*, andaderas *fpl*.
zinc [zɪŋk] *n* cinc *m*, zinc *m*.
Zionism ['zaɪənɪzm] *n* sionismo.
Zionist ['zaɪənɪst] *adj, n* sionista *m/f*.
zip [zɪp] *n* (*also:* ~ **fastener**, (*US*) ~**per**) cremallera, cierre *m* relámpago (*LAM*); (*energy*) energía, vigor *m* ♦ *vt* (*also:* ~ **up**) cerrar la cremallera de ♦ *vi*: **to** ~ **along to the shops** ir de compras volando.
zip code *n* (*US*) código postal.
zither ['zɪðə*] *n* cítara.
zodiac ['zəudɪæk] *n* zodíaco.
zombie ['zɔmbɪ] *n* zombi *m*.
zone [zəun] *n* zona.
zonked [zɔŋkt] *adj* (*col*) hecho polvo.
zoo [zuː] *n* zoo, (parque *m*) zoológico.
zoological [zuːəˈlɔdʒɪkəl] *adj* zoológico.
zoologist [zuˈɔlədʒɪst] *n* zoólogo/a.
zoology [zuːˈɔlədʒɪ] *n* zoología.
zoom [zuːm] *vi*: **to** ~ **past** pasar zumbando; **to** ~ **in (on sth/sb)** (*PHOT, CINE*) enfocar (algo/a algn) con el zoom.
zoom lens *n* zoom *m*.
zucchini [zuːˈkiːnɪ] *n(pl)* (*US*) calabacín(ines) *m(pl)*.

Grammar

Gramática

USING THE GRAMMAR

The Grammar section deals systematically and comprehensively with all the information you will need in order to communicate accurately in Spanish. The user-friendly layout explains the grammar point on a left hand page, leaving the facing page free for illustrative examples. The boxed numbers, (→ 1) etc, direct you to the relevant example in every case. Another strong point of the Grammar section is its comprehensive treatment of verbs. Regular verbs are fully explained, and 80 major irregular verbs are conjugated in their simple tenses. The irregular verbs are given in alphabetical order and laid out in tables, making them easy and efficient to consult. In addition, a verb index lists over 2,800 Spanish verbs, each cross-referred to the appropriate conjugation model.

The Grammar section also provides invaluable guidance on the danger of translating English structures by identical structures in Spanish. Use of Numbers and Punctuation are important areas covered towards the end of the section. Finally, the index lists the main words and grammatical terms in both English and Spanish.

ABBREVIATIONS

algn	alguien	**masc**	masculine	**sing**	singular
cond	conditional	**p(p)**	page(s)	**sth**	something
fem	feminine	**plur**	plural	**subj**	subjunctive
ff	and following pages	**sb**	somebody		

CONTENTS

4

5 CONTENTS

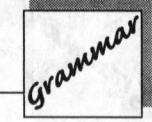

❒ **Simple Tenses: Formation**

In Spanish the simple tenses are:

Present	→ 1
Imperfect	→ 2
Future	→ 3
Conditional	→ 4
Preterite	→ 5
Present Subjunctive	→ 6
Imperfect Subjunctive	→ 7

They are formed by adding endings to a verb stem. The endings show the number and person of the subject of the verb → 8

The stem and endings of regular verbs are totally predictable. The following sections show all the patterns for regular verbs. For irregular verbs see pp 80 ff.

Regular Verbs

There are three regular verb patterns (called conjugations), each identifiable by the ending of the infinitive:

- First conjugation verbs end in **-ar** e.g. **hablar** to speak.
- Second conjugation verbs end in **-er** e.g. **comer** to eat.
- Third conjugation verbs end in **-ir** e.g. **vivir** to live.

These three conjugations are treated in order on the following pages. The subject pronouns will appear in brackets because they are not always necessary in Spanish (see p 226).

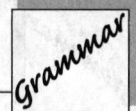

①	**(yo) hablo**	I speak
		I am speaking
		I do speak
②	**(yo) hablaba**	I spoke
		I was speaking
		I used to speak
③	**(yo) hablaré**	I shall speak
		I shall be speaking
④	**(yo) hablaría**	I should/would speak
		I should/would be speaking
⑤	**(yo) hablé**	I spoke
⑥	**(que) (yo) hable**	(that) I speak
⑦	**(que) (yo) hablara** *or* **hablase**	(that) I spoke
⑧	**(yo) hablo**	I speak
	(nosotros) hablamos	we speak
	(yo) hablaría	I would speak
	(nosotros) hablaríamos	we would speak

☐ Simple Tenses: First Conjugation

◆ The stem is formed as follows:

TENSE	FORMATION	EXAMPLE
Present		
Imperfect		
Preterite	infinitive minus **-ar**	**habl-**
Present Subjunctive		
Imperfect Subjunctive*	* For irregular verbs see p 80	
Future		
Conditional	infinitive	**hablar-**

◆ To the appropriate stem add the following endings:

		PRESENT → ①	IMPERFECT → ②	PRETERITE → ③
sing	1st person	**-o**	**-aba**	**-é**
	2nd person	**-as**	**-abas**	**-aste**
	3rd person	**-a**	**-aba**	**-ó**
plur	1st person	**-amos**	**-ábamos**	**-amos**
	2nd person	**-áis**	**-abais**	**-asteis**
	3rd person	**-an**	**-aban**	**-aron**

		PRESENT SUBJUNCTIVE → ④	IMPERFECT SUBJUNCTIVE → ⑤
sing	1st person	**-e**	**-ara** or **-ase**
	2nd person	**-es**	**-aras** or **-ases**
	3rd person	**-e**	**-ara** or **-ase**
plur	1st person	**-emos**	**-áramos** or **-ásemos**
	2nd person	**-éis**	**-arais** or **-aseis**
	3rd person	**-en**	**-aran** or **-asen**

		FUTURE → ⑥	CONDITIONAL → ⑦
sing	1st person	**-é**	**-ía**
	2nd person	**-ás**	**-ías**
	3rd person	**-á**	**-ía**
plur	1st person	**-emos**	**-íamos**
	2nd person	**-éis**	**-íais**
	3rd person	**-án**	**-ían**

Examples

1 PRESENT	**2 IMPERFECT**	**3 PRETERITE**
(yo) hablo	hablaba	hablé
(tú) hablas	hablabas	hablaste
(él/ella/Vd) habla	hablaba	habló
(nosotros/as) hablamos	hablábamos	hablamos
(vosotros/as) habláis	hablabais	hablasteis
(ellos/as/Vds) hablan	hablaban	hablaron

4 PRESENT SUBJUNCTIVE	**5 IMPERFECT SUBJUNCTIVE**
(yo) hable	hablara or hablase
(tú) hables	hablaras or hablases
(él/ella/Vd) hable	hablara or hablase
(nosotros/as) hablemos	habláramos or hablásemos
(vosotros/as) habléis	hablarais or hablaseis
(ellos/as/Vds) hablen	hablaran or hablasen

6 FUTURE	**7 CONDITIONAL**
(yo) hablaré	hablaría
(tú) hablarás	hablarías
(él/ella/Vd) hablará	hablaría
(nosotros/as) hablaremos	hablaríamos
(vosotros/as) hablaréis	hablaríais
(ellos/as/Vds) hablarán	hablarían

❒ Simple Tenses: Second Conjugation

◆ The stem is formed as follows:

TENSE	FORMATION	EXAMPLE
Present		
Imperfect		
Preterite	infinitive minus **-er**	**com-**
Present Subjunctive		
Imperfect Subjunctive*	* For irregular verbs see p 80	
Future		
Conditional	infinitive	**comer-**

◆ To the appropriate stem add the following endings:

		PRESENT → 1	IMPERFECT → 2	PRETERITE → 3
sing	1st person	**-o**	**-ía**	**-í**
	2nd person	**-es**	**-ías**	**-iste**
	3rd person	**-e**	**-ía**	**-ió**
plur	1st person	**-emos**	**-íamos**	**-imos**
	2nd person	**-éis**	**-íais**	**-isteis**
	3rd person	**-en**	**-ían**	**-ieron**

		PRESENT SUBJUNCTIVE → 4	IMPERFECT SUBJUNCTIVE → 5
sing	1st person	**-a**	**-iera** or **-iese**
	2nd person	**-as**	**-ieras** or **-ieses**
	3rd person	**-a**	**-iera** or **-iese**
plur	1st person	**-amos**	**-iéramos** or **-iésemos**
	2nd person	**-áis**	**-ierais** or **-ieseis**
	3rd person	**-an**	**-ieran** or **-iesen**

		FUTURE → 6	CONDITIONAL → 7
sing	1st person	**-é**	**-ía**
	2nd person	**-ás**	**-ías**
	3rd person	**-á**	**-ía**
plur	1st person	**-emos**	**-íamos**
	2nd person	**-éis**	**-íais**
	3rd person	**-án**	**-ían**

1 PRESENT		2 IMPERFECT	3 PRETERITE
(yo)	com**o**	com**ía**	com**í**
(tú)	com**es**	com**ías**	com**iste**
(él/ella/Vd)	com**e**	com**ía**	com**ió**
(nosotros/as)	com**emos**	com**íamos**	com**imos**
(vosotros/as)	com**éis**	com**íais**	com**isteis**
(ellos/as/Vds)	com**en**	com**ían**	com**ieron**

4 PRESENT SUBJUNCTIVE		5 IMPERFECT SUBJUNCTIVE
(yo)	com**a**	com**iera** or com**iese**
(tú)	com**as**	com**ieras** or com**ieses**
(él/ella/Vd)	com**a**	com**iera** or com**iese**
(nosotros/as)	com**amos**	com**iéramos** or com**iésemos**
(vosotros/as)	com**áis**	com**ierais** or com**ieseis**
(ellos/as/Vds)	com**an**	com**ieran** or com**iesen**

6 FUTURE		7 CONDITIONAL
(yo)	com**eré**	com**ería**
(tú)	com**erás**	com**erías**
(él/ella/Vd)	com**erá**	com**ería**
(nosotros/as)	com**eremos**	com**eríamos**
(vosotros/as)	com**eréis**	com**eríais**
(ellos/as/Vds)	com**erán**	com**erían**

☐ Simple Tenses: Third Conjugation

◆ The stem is formed as follows:

TENSE	FORMATION	EXAMPLE
Present Imperfect Preterite Present Subjunctive Imperfect Subjunctive*	infinitive minus -**ir** * For irregular verbs see p 80	**viv-**
Future Conditional	infinitive	**vivir-**

◆ To the appropriate stem add the following endings:

		PRESENT → ①	IMPERFECT → ②	PRETERITE → ③
sing	1st person 2nd person 3rd person	-**o** -**es** -**e**	-**ía** -**ías** -**ía**	-**í** -**iste** -**ió**
plur	1st person 2nd person 3rd person	-**imos** -**ís** -**en**	-**íamos** -**íais** -**ían**	-**imos** -**isteis** -**ieron**

		PRESENT SUBJUNCTIVE → ④	IMPERFECT SUBJUNCTIVE → ⑤
sing	1st person 2nd person 3rd person	-**a** -**as** -**a**	-**iera** or -**iese** -**ieras** or -**ieses** -**iera** or -**iese**
plur	1st person 2nd person 3rd person	-**amos** -**áis** -**an**	-**iéramos** or -**iésemos** -**ierais** or -**ieseis** -**ieran** or -**iesen**

		FUTURE → ⑥	CONDITIONAL → ⑦
sing	1st person 2nd person 3rd person	-**é** -**ás** -**á**	-**ía** -**ías** -**ía**
plur	1st person 2nd person 3rd person	-**emos** -**éis** -**án**	-**íamos** -**íais** -**ían**

Examples

① PRESENT		② IMPERFECT	③ PRETERITE
(yo)	viv**o**	viv**ía**	viv**í**
(tú)	viv**es**	viv**ías**	viv**iste**
(él/ella/Vd)	viv**e**	viv**ía**	viv**ió**
(nosotros/as)	viv**imos**	viv**íamos**	viv**imos**
(vosotros/as)	viv**ís**	viv**íais**	viv**isteis**
(ellos/as/Vds)	viv**en**	viv**ían**	viv**ieron**

④ PRESENT SUBJUNCTIVE		⑤ IMPERFECT SUBJUNCTIVE
(yo)	viv**a**	viv**iera** or viv**iese**
(tú)	viv**as**	viv**ieras** or viv**ieses**
(él/ella/Vd)	viv**a**	viv**iera** or viv**iese**
(nosotros/as)	viv**amos**	viv**iéramos** or viv**iésemos**
(vosotros/as)	viv**áis**	viv**ierais** or viv**ieseis**
(ellos/as/Vds)	viv**an**	viv**ieran** or viv**iesen**

⑥ FUTURE		⑦ CONDITIONAL
(yo)	vivir**é**	vivir**ía**
(tú)	vivir**ás**	vivir**ías**
(él/ella/Vd)	vivir**á**	vivir**ía**
(nosotros/as)	vivir**emos**	vivir**íamos**
(vosotros/as)	vivir**éis**	vivir**íais**
(ellos/as/Vds)	vivir**án**	vivir**ían**

❐ The Imperative

The imperative is the form of the verb used to give commands or orders. It can be used politely, as in English 'Shut the door, please'.

In POSITIVE commands, the imperative forms for **Vd**, **Vds** and **nosotros** are the same as the subjunctive. The other forms are as follows:

> **tú** (same as 3rd person singular present indicative)
> **vosotros** (final **-r** of infinitive changes to **-d**) → ①

(tú)	**habla**	**come**	**vive**
	speak	eat	live
(Vd)	**hable**	**coma**	**viva**
	speak	eat	live
(nosotros)	**hablemos**	**comamos**	**vivamos**
	let's speak	let's eat	let's live
(vosotros)	**hablad**	**comed**	**vivid**
	speak	eat	live
(Vds)	**hablen**	**coman**	**vivan**
	speak	eat	live

In NEGATIVE commands, all the imperative forms are exactly the same as the present subjunctive.

◆ The imperative of irregular verbs is given in the verb tables, pp 82 ff.

Position of object pronouns with the imperative

In POSITIVE commands: they follow the verb and are attached to it. An accent is needed to show the correct position for stress (see p 292) → ②

In NEGATIVE commands: they precede the verb and are not attached to it → ③

◆ For the order of object pronouns, see page 232.

Examples

Grammar

1	**cantar** to sing	**cantad** sing
2	**Perdóneme** Excuse me	**Enviémoselos** Let's send them to him/her/them
	Elíjanos Choose us	**Explíquemelo** Explain it to me
	Esperémosla Let's wait for her/it	**Devuélvaselo** Give it back to him/her/them
3	**No me molestes** Don't disturb me	**No se la devolvamos** Let's not give it back to him/her/them
	No les castiguemos Let's not punish them	**No me lo mandes** Don't send it to me
	No las conteste Don't answer them	**No nos lo hagan** Don't do it to us

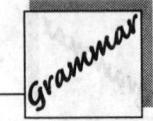

☐ **The Imperative** (Continued)

◆ For reflexive verbs – e.g. **levantarse** *to get up* – the object pronoun is the reflexive pronoun. It should be noted that the imperative forms need an accent to show the correct position for stress (see p 292). The forms **nosotros** and **vosotros** also drop the final **-s** and **-d** respectively before the pronoun → ①

BUT: **idos (vosotros)** *go*

⚠ NOTE: For general instructions, the infinitive is used instead of the imperative →②, but when it is preceded by **vamos a** it often translates *let's* … → ③

1.
Levántate	**No te levantes**
Get up	Don't get up
Levántese (Vd)	**No se levante (Vd)**
Get up	Don't get up
Levantémonos	**No nos levantemos**
Let's get up	Let's not get up
Levantaos	**No os levantéis**
Get up	Don't get up
Levántense (Vds)	**No se levanten (Vds)**
Get up	Don't get up

2.
Ver pág ...
See page
No pasar
Do not pass ...

3.
Vamos a ver
Let's see
Vamos a empezar
Let's start

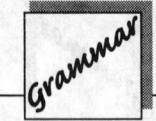

☐ **Compound Tenses: Formation**

In Spanish the compound tenses are:

Perfect	→ ☐1
Pluperfect	→ ☐2
Future Perfect	→ ☐3
Conditional Perfect	→ ☐4
Past Anterior	→ ☐5
Perfect Subjunctive	→ ☐6
Pluperfect Subjunctive	→ ☐7

They consist of the past participle of the verb together with the auxiliary verb **haber**.

Compound tenses are formed in exactly the same way for both regular and irregular verbs, the only difference being that irregular verbs may have an irregular past participle.

The Past Participle

For all compound tenses you need to know how to form the past participle of the verb. For regular verbs this is as follows:

♦ 1st conjugation: replace the **-ar** of the infinitive by **-ado** → ☐8

♦ 2nd conjugation: replace the **-er** of the infinitive by **-ido** → ☐9

♦ 3rd conjugation: replace the **-ir** of the infinitive by **-ido** → ☐10

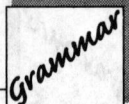

1	**(yo) he hablado** I have spoken
2	**(yo) había hablado** I had spoken
3	**(yo) habré hablado** I shall have spoken
4	**(yo) habría hablado** I should/would have spoken
5	**(yo) hube hablado** I had spoken
6	**(que) (yo) haya hablado** (that) I spoke, have spoken
7	**(que) (yo) hubiera/hubiese hablado** (that) I had spoken
8	**cantar** → **cantado** to sing sung
9	**comer** → **comido** to eat eaten
10	**vivir** → **vivido** to live lived

❐ **Compound Tenses: Formation** (Continued)

Perfect tense: the present tense of **haber** plus the past participle → ①

Pluperfect tense: the imperfect tense of **haber** plus the past participle → ②

Future Perfect: the future tense of **haber** plus the past participle → ③

Conditional Perfect: the conditional of **haber** plus the past participle → ④

Examples

Grammar

1	PERFECT		
		(yo)	**he** habl**ado**
		(tú)	**has** habl**ado**
		(él/ella/Vd)	**ha** habl**ado**
		(nosotros/as)	**hemos** habl**ado**
		(vosotros/as)	**habéis** habl**ado**
		(ellos/as/Vds)	**han** habl**ado**

2	PLUPERFECT		
		(yo)	**había** habl**ado**
		(tú)	**habías** habl**ado**
		(él/ella/Vd)	**había** habl**ado**
		(nosotros/as)	**habíamos** habl**ado**
		(vosotros/as)	**habíais** habl**ado**
		(ellos/as/Vds)	**habían** habl**ado**

3	FUTURE PERFECT		
		(yo)	**habré** habl**ado**
		(tú)	**habrás** habl**ado**
		(él/ella/Vd)	**habrá** habl**ado**
		(nosotros/as)	**habremos** habl**ado**
		(vosotros/as)	**habréis** habl**ado**
		(ellos/as/Vds)	**habrán** habl**ado**

4	CONDITIONAL PERFECT		
		(yo)	**habría** habl**ado**
		(tú)	**habrías** habl**ado**
		(él/ella/Vd)	**habría** habl**ado**
		(nosotros/as)	**habríamos** habl**ado**
		(vosotros/as)	**habríais** habl**ado**
		(ellos/as/Vds)	**habrían** habl**ado**

☐ **Compound Tenses: Formation** (Continued)

Past Anterior: the preterite of **haber** plus the past
                             participle → ①

Perfect Subjunctive: the present subjunctive of **haber** plus
                             the past participle → ②

Pluperfect Subjunctive: the imperfect subjunctive of **haber** plus
                             the past participle → ③

◆   For how to form the past participle of regular verbs see p 18. The past
    participle of irregular verbs is given for each verb in the verb tables, pp
    82 to 161.

1	PAST ANTERIOR	(yo) **hube** hablado
		(tú) **hubiste** hablado
		(él/ella/Vd) **hubo** hablado
		(nosotros/as) **hubimos** hablado
		(vosotros/as) **hubisteis** hablado
		(ellos/as/Vds) **hubieron** hablado

2	PRESENT SUBJUNCTIVE	(yo) **haya** hablado
		(tú) **hayas** hablado
		(él/ella/Vd) **haya** hablado
		(nosotros/as) **hayamos** hablado
		(vosotros/as) **hayáis** hablado
		(ellos/as/Vds) **hayan** hablado

3	PLUPERFECT SUBJUNCTIVE	(yo) **hubiera** or **hubiese** hablado
		(tú) **hubieras** or **hubieses** hablado
		(él/ella/Vd) **hubiera** or **hubiese** hablado
		(nosotros/as) **hubiéramos** or **hubiésemos** hablado
		(vosotros/as) **hubierais** or **hubieseis** hablado
		(ellos/as/Vds) **hubieran** or **hubiesen** hablado

❑ **Reflexive Verbs**

A reflexive verb is one accompanied by a reflexive pronoun. The infinitive of a reflexive verb ends with the pronoun **se**, which is added to the verb form e.g.

levantarse *to get up*; **lavarse** *to wash (oneself)*

The reflexive pronouns are:

PERSON	SINGULAR	PLURAL
1st	**me**	**nos**
2nd	**te**	**os**
3rd	**se**	**se**

◆ The reflexive pronoun 'reflects back' to the subject, but it is not always translated in English → ①

The plural pronouns are sometimes translated as *one another, each other* (the 'reciprocal' meaning) → ②

The reciprocal meaning may be emphasized by **el uno al otro/la una a la otra (los unos a los otros/las unas a las otras)** → ③

◆ Both simple and compound tenses of reflexive verbs are conjugated in exactly the same way as those of non-reflexive verbs, except that the reflexive pronoun is always used.

The only irregularity is in the 1st and 2nd person plural of the affirmative imperative (see p 16). A sample reflexive verb is conjugated in full on pp 28 to 31.

Position of reflexive pronouns

◆ Except with the infinitive, gerund and positive commands, the pronoun comes before the verb → ④

◆ In the infinitive, gerund and positive commands, the pronoun follows the verb and is attached to it (but see also p 228) → ⑤

Examples

---

[1]   **Me visto**
I'm dressing (myself)

Nos lavamos
We're washing (ourselves)

Se levanta
He gets up

[2]   **Nos queremos**
We love each other

     Se parecen
They resemble one another

[3]   **Se miraban el uno al otro**
They were looking at each other

[4]   **Me acuesto temprano**
I go to bed early

     ¿Cómo se llama Vd?
What is your name?

     No se ha despertado
He hasn't woken up

     No te levantes
Don't get up

[5]   **Quiero irme**
I want to go away

     Estoy levantándome
I am getting up

     Siéntense
Sit down

     Vámonos
Let's go

☐ **Reflexive Verbs** (Continued)

Some verbs have both a reflexive and non-reflexive form. When used reflexively, they have a different but closely related meaning, as shown in the following examples.

NON-REFLEXIVE	REFLEXIVE
acostar *to put to bed*	**acostarse** *to go to bed*
casar *to marry (off)*	**casarse** *to get married*
detener *to stop*	**detenerse** *to come to a halt*
dormir *to sleep*	**dormirse** *to go to sleep*
enfadar *to annoy*	**enfadarse** *to get annoyed*
hacer *to make*	**hacerse** *to become*
ir *to go*	**irse** *to leave, go away*
lavar *to wash*	**lavarse** *to get washed*
levantar *to raise*	**levantarse** *to get up*
llamar *to call*	**llamarse** *to be called*
poner *to put*	**ponerse** *to put on (clothing), to become*
sentir *to feel (something)*	**sentirse** *to feel (sick, tired, etc)*
vestir *to dress (someone)*	**vestirse** *to get dressed*
volver *to return*	**volverse** *to turn round*

◆ Some other verbs exist only in the reflexive:

arrepentirse *to repent*	**jactarse** *to boast*
atreverse *to dare*	**quejarse** *to complain*

◆ Some verbs acquire a different nuance when used reflexively:

caer *to fall* → ⬚1	**caerse** *to fall down (by accident)* → ⬚2
morir *to die, be killed (by accident or on purpose)* → ⬚3	**morirse** *to die (from natural causes)* → ⬚4

◆ Often a reflexive verb can be used:

— to avoid the passive (see p 34) → ⬚5

— in impersonal expressions (see p 40) → ⬚6

---

1   **El agua caía desde las rocas**
Water fell from the rocks

2   **Me caí y me rompí el brazo**
I fell and broke my arm

3   **Tres personas han muerto en un accidente/atentado terrorista**
Three people were killed in an accident/a terrorist attack

4   **Mi abuelo se murió a los ochenta años**
My grandfather died at the age of eighty

5   **Se perdió la batalla**
The battle was lost

     No se veían las casas
The houses could not be seen

6   **Se dice que ...**
(It is said that) People say that ...

     No se puede entrar
You/One can't go in

     No se permite
It is not allowed

☐ **Reflexive Verbs** (Continued)

Conjugation of: **lavarse** *to wash oneself*

I SIMPLE TENSES

PRESENT	
(yo)	**me** lav**o**
(tú)	**te** lav**as**
(él/ella/Vd)	**se** lav**a**
(nosotros/as)	**nos** lav**amos**
(vosotros/as)	**os** lav**áis**
(ellos/as/Vds)	**se** lav**an**

IMPERFECT	
(yo)	**me** lav**aba**
(tú)	**te** lav**abas**
(él/ella/Vd)	**se** lav**aba**
(nosotros/as)	**nos** lav**ábamos**
(vosotros/as)	**os** lav**abais**
(ellos/as/Vds)	**se** lav**aban**

FUTURE	
(yo)	**me** lavar**é**
(tú)	**te** lavar**ás**
(él/ella/Vd)	**se** lavar**á**
(nosotros/as)	**nos** lavar**emos**
(vosotros/as)	**os** lavar**éis**
(ellos/as/Vds)	**se** lavar**án**

CONDITIONAL	
(yo)	**me** lavar**ía**
(tú)	**te** lavar**ías**
(él/ella/Vd)	**se** lavar**ía**
(nosotros/as)	**nos** lavar**íamos**
(vosotros/as)	**os** lavar**íais**
(ellos/as/Vds)	**se** lavar**ían**

❐ Reflexive Verbs (Continued)

Conjugation of: **lavarse** to wash oneself

I SIMPLE TENSES

PRETERITE	
(yo)	**me** lav**é**
(tú)	**te** lav**aste**
(él/ella/Vd)	**se** lav**ó**
(nosotros/as)	**nos** lav**amos**
(vosotros/as)	**os** lav**asteis**
(ellos/as/Vds)	**se** lav**aron**

PRESENT SUBJUNCTIVE	
(yo)	**me** lav**e**
(tú)	**te** lav**es**
(él/ella/Vd)	**se** lav**e**
(nosotros/as)	**nos** lav**emos**
(vosotros/as)	**os** lav**éis**
(ellos/as/Vds)	**se** lav**en**

IMPERFECT SUBJUNCTIVE	
(yo)	**me** lav**ara** or lav**ase**
(tú)	**te** lav**aras** or lav**ases**
(él/ella/Vd)	**se** lav**ara** or lav**ase**
(nosotros/as)	**nos** lav**áramos** or lav**ásemos**
(vosotros/as)	**os** lav**arais** or lav**aseis**
(ellos/as/Vds)	**se** lav**aran** or lav**asen**

❐ **Reflexive Verbs** (Continued)

Conjugation of: **lavarse** *to wash oneself*

II COMPOUND TENSES

PERFECT	
(yo)	**me he** lav**ado**
(tú)	**te has** lav**ado**
(él/ella/Vd)	**se ha** lav**ado**
(nosotros/as)	**nos hemos** lav**ado**
(vosotros/as)	**os habéis** lav**ado**
(ellos/as/Vds)	**se han** lav**ado**

PLUPERFECT	
(yo)	**me había** lav**ado**
(tú)	**te habías** lav**ado**
(él/ella/Vd)	**se había** lav**ado**
(nosotros/as)	**nos habíamos** lav**ado**
(vosotros/as)	**os habíais** lav**ado**
(ellos/as/Vds)	**se habían** lav**ado**

FUTURE PERFECT	
(yo)	**me habré** lav**ado**
(tú)	**te habrás** lav**ado**
(él/ella/Vd)	**se habrá** lav**ado**
(nosotros/as)	**nos habremos** lav**ado**
(vosotros/as)	**os habréis** lav**ado**
(ellos/as/Vds)	**se habrán** lav**ado**

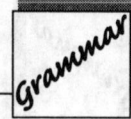

☐ **Reflexive Verbs** (Continued)

Conjugation of: **lavarse** *to wash oneself*

II COMPOUND TENSES

PAST ANTERIOR

(yo)	**me hube** lav**ado**
(tú)	**te hubiste** lav**ado**
(él/ella/Vd)	**se hubo** lav**ado**
(nosotros/as)	**nos hubimos** lav**ado**
(vosotros/as)	**os hubisteis** lav**ado**
(ellos/as/Vds)	**se hubieron** lav**ado**

PERFECT SUBJUNCTIVE

(yo)	**me haya** lav**ado**
(tú)	**te hayas** lav**ado**
(él/ella/Vd)	**se haya** lav**ado**
(nosotros/as)	**nos hayamos** lav**ado**
(vosotros/as)	**os hayáis** lav**ado**
(ellos/as/Vds)	**se hayan** lav**ado**

PLUPERFECT SUBJUNCTIVE

(yo)	**me hubiera** *or* **hubiese** lav**ado**
(tú)	**te hubieras** *or* **hubieses** lav**ado**
(él/ella/Vd)	**se hubiera** *or* **hubiese** lav**ado**
(nosotros/as)	**nos hubiéramos** *or* **hubiésemos** lav**ado**
(vosotros/as)	**os hubierais** *or* **hubieseis** lav**ado**
(ellos/as/Vds)	**se hubieran** *or* **hubiesen** lav**ado**

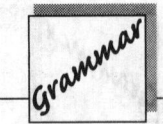

❒ **The Passive**

In active sentences, the subject of a verb carries out the action of that verb, but in passive sentences the subject receives the action. Compare the following:

> *The car hit Jane* (subject: *the car*)
> *Jane was hit by the car* (subject: *Jane*)

◆ English uses the verb *'to be'* with the past participle to form passive sentences. Spanish forms them in the same way, i.e.:

> a tense of **ser** + past participle

The past participle agrees in number and gender with the subject → ☐1

A sample verb is conjugated in the passive voice on pp 36 to 39.

◆ In English, the word *'by'* usually introduces the agent through which the action of a passive sentence is performed. In Spanish this agent is preceded by **por** → ☐2

◆ The Passive voice is used much less frequently in Spanish than English. It is, however, often used in expressions where the identity of the agent is unknown or unimportant → ☐3

1. **Pablo ha sido despedido**
    Paul has been sacked
    Su madre era muy admirada
    His mother was greatly admired
    El palacio será vendido
    The palace will be sold
    Las puertas habían sido cerradas
    The doors had been closed

2. **La casa fue diseñada por mi hermano**
    The house was designed by my brother

3. **La ciudad fue conquistada tras un largo asedio**
    The city was conquered after a long siege
    Ha sido declarado el estado de excepción
    A state of emergency has been declared

❏ **The Passive** (Continued)

In English the indirect object in an active sentence can become the subject of the related passive sentence, e.g.

His mother gave him the book (indirect object: *him*)
He was given the book by his mother

This is not possible in Spanish. The indirect object remains as such, while the object of the active sentence becomes the subject of the passive sentence → 1

Other ways to express a passive meaning

Since modern Spanish tends to avoid the passive, it uses various other constructions to replace it:

◆ If the agent (person or object performing the action) is known, the active is often preferred where English might prefer the passive → 2

◆ The 3rd person plural of the active voice can be used. The meaning is equivalent to *they* + verb → 3

◆ When the action of the sentence is performed on a person, the reflexive form of the verb can be used in the 3rd person singular, and the person becomes the object → 4

◆ When the action is performed on a thing, this becomes the subject of the sentence and the verb is made reflexive, agreeing in number with the subject → 5

①   **Su madre le regaló el libro**
His mother gave him the book

becomes

El libro le fue regalado por su madre
The book was given to him by his mother

②   **La policía interrogó al sospechoso**
The police questioned the suspect

rather than

El sospechoso fue interrogado por la policía

③   **Usan demasiada publicidad en la televisión**
Too much advertising is used on television

④   **Últimamente no se le/les ha visto mucho en público**
He has/they have not been seen much in public recently

⑤   **Esta palabra ya no se usa**
This word is no longer used
Todos los libros se han vendido
All the books have been sold

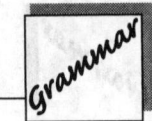

☐ **The Passive** (Continued)

Conjugation of: **ser amado** *to be loved*

PRESENT	
(yo)	**soy** am**ado(a)**
(tú)	**eres** am**ado(a)**
(él/ella/Vd)	**es** am**ado(a)**
(nosotros/as)	**somos** am**ado(a)s**
(vosotros/as)	**sois** am**ado(a)s**
(ellos/as/Vds)	**son** am**ado(a)s**

IMPERFECT	
(yo)	**era** am**ado(a)**
(tú)	**eras** am**ado(a)**
(él/ella/Vd)	**era** am**ado(a)**
(nosotros/as)	**éramos** am**ado(a)s**
(vosotros/as)	**erais** am**ado(a)s**
(ellos/as/Vds)	**eran** am**ado(a)s**

FUTURE	
(yo)	**seré** am**ado(a)**
(tú)	**serás** am**ado(a)**
(él/ella/Vd)	**será** am**ado(a)**
(nosotros/as)	**seremos** am**ado(a)s**
(vosotros/as)	**seréis** am**ado(a)s**
(ellos/as/Vds)	**serán** am**ado(a)s**

CONDITIONAL	
(yo)	**sería** am**ado(a)**
(tú)	**serías** am**ado(a)**
(él/ella/Vd)	**sería** am**ado(a)**
(nosotros/as)	**seríamos** am**ado(a)s**
(vosotros/as)	**seríais** am**ado(a)s**
(ellos/as/Vds)	**serían** am**ado(a)s**

☐ **The Passive** (Continued)

Conjugation of: **ser amado** *to be loved*

PRETERITE	
(yo)	**fui** am**ado(a)**
(tú)	**fuiste** am**ado(a)**
(él/ella/Vd)	**fue** am**ado(a)**
(nosotros/as)	**fuimos** am**ado(a)s**
(vosotros/as)	**fuisteis** am**ado(a)s**
(ellos/as/Vds)	**fueron** am**ado(a)s**

PRESENT SUBJUNCTIVE	
(yo)	**sea** am**ado(a)**
(tú)	**seas** am**ado(a)**
(él/ella/Vd)	**sea** am**ado(a)**
(nosotros/as)	**seamos** am**ado(a)s**
(vosotros/as)	**seáis** am**ado(a)s**
(ellos/as/Vds)	**sean** am**ado(a)s**

IMPERFECT SUBJUNCTIVE	
(yo)	**fuera** *or* **fuese** am**ado(a)**
(tú)	**fueras** *or* **fueses** am**ado(a)**
(él/ella/Vd)	**fuera** *or* **fuese** am**ado(a)**
(nosotros/as)	**fuéramos** *or* **fuésemos** am**ado(a)s**
(vosotros/as)	**fuerais** *or* **fueseis** am**ado(a)s**
(ellos/as/Vds)	**fueran** *or* **fuesen** am**ado(a)s**

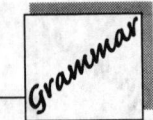
☐ **The Passive** (Continued)

Conjugation of: **ser amado** *to be loved*

PERFECT	
(yo)	**he sido** am**ado(a)**
(tú)	**has sido** am**ado(a)**
(él/ella/Vd)	**ha sido** am**ado(a)**
(nosotros/as)	**hemos sido** am**ado(a)s**
(vosotros/as)	**habéis sido** am**ado(a)s**
(ellos/as/Vds)	**han sido** am**ado(a)s**

PLUPERFECT	
(yo)	**había sido** am**ado(a)**
(tú)	**habías sido** am**ado(a)**
(él/ella/Vd)	**había sido** am**ado(a)**
(nosotros/as)	**habíamos sido** am**ado(a)s**
(vosotros/as)	**habíais sido** am**ado(a)s**
(ellos/as/Vds)	**habían sido** am**ado(a)s**

FUTURE PERFECT	
(yo)	**habré sido** am**ado(a)**
(tú)	**habrás sido** am**ado(a)**
(él/ella/Vd)	**habrá sido** am**ado(a)**
(nosotros/as)	**habremos sido** am**ado(a)s**
(vosotros/as)	**habréis sido** am**ado(a)s**
(ellos/as/Vds)	**habrán sido** am**ado(a)s**

CONDITIONAL PERFECT	
(yo)	**habría sido** am**ado(a)**
(tú)	**habrías sido** am**ado(a)**
(él/ella/Vd)	**habría sido** am**ado(a)**
(nosotros/as)	**habríamos sido** am**ado(a)s**
(vosotros/as)	**habríais sido** am**ado(a)s**
(ellos/as/Vds)	**habrían sido** am**ado(a)s**

☐ **The Passive** (Continued)

Conjugation of: **ser amado** *to be loved*

PAST ANTERIOR	
(yo)	**hube sido** am**ado(a)**
(tú)	**hubiste sido** am**ado(a)**
(él/ella/Vd)	**hubo sido** am**ado(a)**
(nosotros/as)	**hubimos sido** am**ado(a)s**
(vosotros/as)	**hubisteis sido** am**ado(a)s**
(ellos/as/Vds)	**hubieron sido** am**ado(a)s**

PERFECT SUBJUNCTIVE	
(yo)	**haya sido** am**ado(a)**
(tú)	**hayas sido** am**ado(a)**
(él/ella/Vd)	**haya sido** am**ado(a)**
(nosotros/as)	**hayamos sido** am**ado(a)s**
(vosotros/as)	**hayáis sido** am**ado(a)s**
(ellos/as/Vds)	**hayan sido** am**ado(a)s**

PLUPERFECT SUBJUNCTIVE	
(yo)	**hubiera/-se sido** am**ado(a)**
(tú)	**hubieras/-ses sido** am**ado(a)**
(él/ella/Vd)	**hubiera/-se sido** am**ado(a)**
(nosotros/as)	**hubiéramos/-semos sido** am**ado(a)s**
(vosotros/as)	**hubierais/-seis sido** am**ado(a)s**
(ellos/as/Vds)	**hubieran/-sen sido** am**ado(a)s**

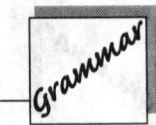

☐ Impersonal Verbs

Impersonal verbs are used only in the infinitive, the gerund, and in the 3rd person (usually singular); unlike English, Spanish does not use the subject pronoun with impersonal verbs, e.g.

> **llueve**
> *it's raining*

> **es fácil decir que ...**
> *it's easy to say that ...*

The most common impersonal verbs are:

INFINITIVE	CONSTRUCTION	
amanecer	**amanece/está amaneciendo** *it's daybreak*	
anochecer	**anochece/está anocheciendo** *it's getting dark*	
granizar	**graniza/está granizando** *it's hailing*	
llover	**llueve/está lloviendo** *it's raining*	→ ①
lloviznar	**llovizna/está lloviznando** *it's drizzling*	
nevar	**nieva/está nevando** *it's snowing*	
tronar	**truena/está tronando** *it's thundering*	

Some reflexive verbs are also used impersonally.
The most common are:

INFINITIVE	CONSTRUCTION	
creerse	**se cree que*** + indicative *it is thought that; people think that*	→ ②
decirse	**se dice que*** + indicative *it is said that; people say that*	→ ③

1. **Llovía a cántaros**
   It was raining cats and dogs
   Estaba nevando cuando salieron
   It was snowing when they left

2. **Se cree que llegarán mañana**
   It is thought they will arrive tomorrow

3. **Se dice que ha sido el peor invierno en 50 años**
   People say it's been the worst winter in 50 years

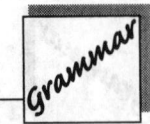
☐ **Impersonal Verbs** (Continued)

INFINITIVE	CONSTRUCTION
poderse	**se puede** + infinitive → 1 *one/people can, it is possible to*
tratarse de	**se trata de** + noun → 2 *it's a question/matter of something* *it's about something*
	se trata de + infinitive → 3 *it's a question/matter of doing;* *somebody must do*
venderse	**se vende*** + noun → 4 *to be sold; for sale*

* This impersonal construction conveys the same meaning as the 3rd person plural of these verbs; **creen que, dicen que, venden**

The following verbs are also commonly used in impersonal constructions:

INFINITIVE	CONSTRUCTION
bastar	**basta con** + infinitive → 5 *it is enough to do* **basta con** + noun → 6 *something is enough, it only takes something*
faltar	**falta** + infinitive → 7 *we still have to/one still has to*
haber	**hay** + noun → 8 *there is/are* **hay que** + infinitive → 9 *one has to/we have to*
hacer	**hace** + noun/adjective depicting weather/ dark/light etc → 10 *it is* **hace** + time expression + **que** + indicative → 11 *somebody has done* OR *been doing something since …* **hace** + time expression + **que** + negative indicative → 12 *it is … since*

Examples

Grammar

①	**Aquí se puede aparcar**	
	One can park here	
②	**No se trata de dinero**	
	It isn't a question/matter of money	
③	**Se trata de poner fin al asunto**	
	We must put an end to the matter	
④	**Se vende coche**	
	Car for sale	
⑤	**Basta con telefonear para reservar un asiento**	
	You need only phone to reserve a seat	
⑥	**Basta con un error para que todo se estropee**	
	One single error is enough to ruin everything	
⑦	**Aún falta cerrar las maletas**	
	We/One still have/has to close the suitcases	
⑧	**Hay una habitación libre**	
	There is one spare room	
	No había cartas esta mañana	
	There were no letters this morning	
⑨	**Hay que cerrar las puertas**	
	We have/One has to shut the doors	
⑩	**Hace calor/viento/sol**	
	It is hot/windy/sunny	
	Mañana hará bueno	
	It'll be nice (weather) tomorrow	
⑪	**Hace seis meses que vivo/vivimos aquí**	
	I/We have lived *or* been living here for six months	
⑫	**Hace tres años que no le veo**	
	It is three years since I last saw him	

❐ **Impersonal Verbs** (Continued)

INFINITIVE	CONSTRUCTION
hacer falta	**hace falta** + noun object (+ indirect object) → 1 *(somebody) needs something, something is* *necessary (to somebody)* **hace falta** + infinitive (+ indirect object) → 2 *it is necessary to do* **hace falta que** + subjunctive → 3 *it is necessary to do, somebody must do*
parecer	**parece que** (+ indirect object) + indicative → 4 *it seems/appears that*
ser	**es/son** + time expression → 5 *it is* **es** + **de día/noche** → 6 *it is* **es** + adjective + infinitive → 7 *it is*
ser mejor	**es mejor** + infinitive → 8 *it's better to do* **es mejor que** + subjunctive → 9 *it's better if/that*
valer más	**más vale** + infinitive → 10 *it's better to do* **más vale que** + subjunctive → 11 *it's better to do/that somebody does*

☐1 **Hace falta valor para hacer eso**
One needs courage to do that, Courage is needed to do that

Me hace falta otro vaso más
I need an extra glass

☐2 **Hace falta volver**
It is necessary to return, We/I/You must return*

Me hacía falta volver
I had to return

☐3 **Hace falta que Vd se vaya**
You have to/must leave

☐4 **(Me) parece que estás equivocado**
It seems (to me) you are wrong

☐5 **Son las tres y media**
It is half past three
Ya es primavera
It is spring now

☐6 **Era de noche cuando llegamos**
It was night when we arrived

☐7 **Era inútil protestar**
It was useless to complain

☐8 **Es mejor no decir nada**
It's better to keep quiet

☐9 **Es mejor que lo pongas aquí**
It's better if/that you put it here

☐10 **Más vale prevenir que curar**
Prevention is better than cure

☐11 **Más valdría que no fuéramos**
It would be better if we didn't go/We'd better not go

* The translation here obviously depends on context

☐ The Infinitive

The infinitive is the form of the verb found in dictionary entries meaning *'to …'*, e.g. **hablar** *to speak*, **vivir** *to live*.

The infinitive is used in the following ways:

◆ After a preposition → 1

◆ As a verbal noun → 2
In this use the article may precede the infinitive, especially when the infinitive is the subject and begins the sentence → 3

◆ As a dependent infinitive, in the following verbal constructions:

— with no linking preposition → 4

— with the linking preposition **a** → 5
(see also p 66)

— with the linking preposition **de** → 6
(see also p 66)

— with the linking preposition **en** → 7
(see also p 66)

— with the linking preposition **con** → 8
(see also p 66)

— with the linking preposition **por** → 9
(see also p 66)

◆ The following construction should also be noted: indefinite pronoun + **que** + infinitive → 10

◆ The object pronouns generally follow the infinitive and are attached to it. For exceptions see p 228.

---

[1] **Después de acabar el desayuno, salió de casa**
After finishing her breakfast she went out

Al enterarse de lo ocurrido se puso furiosa
When she found out what had happened she was furious

Me hizo daño sin saberlo
She hurt me without her knowing

[2] **Su deporte preferido es montar a caballo**
Her favourite sport is horse riding

Ver es creer
Seeing is believing

[3] **El viajar tanto me resulta cansado**
I find so much travelling tiring

[4] **¿Quiere Vd esperar?**
Would you like to wait?

[5] **Aprenderán pronto a nadar**
They will soon learn to swim

[6] **Pronto dejará de llover**
It'll stop raining soon

[7] **La comida tarda en hacerse**
The meal is taking a long time to cook

[8] **Amenazó con denunciarles**
He threatened to report them (to the police)

[9] **Comience Vd por decirme su nombre**
Please start by giving me your name

[10] **Tengo algo que decirte**
I have something to tell you

❏ **The Infinitive** (Continued)

The verbs set out below are followed by the infinitive with no linking preposition.

◆ **deber, poder, saber, querer** and **tener que** (**hay que** in impersonal constructions) → 1

◆ **valer más, hacer falta:** see Impersonal Verbs, p 44.

◆ verbs of seeing or hearing, e.g. **ver** to see, **oír** to hear → 2

◆ **hacer** → 3

◆ **dejar** to let, allow → 3

◆ The following common verbs:

aconsejar	to advise →	4
conseguir	to manage to →	5
decidir	to decide	
desear	to wish, want →	6
esperar	to hope →	7
evitar	to avoid →	8
impedir	to prevent →	9
intentar	to try →	10
lograr	to manage to →	5
necesitar	to need →	11
odiar	to hate	
olvidar	to forget →	12
pensar	to think →	13
preferir	to prefer →	14
procurar	to try →	10
prohibir	to forbid →	15
prometer	to promise →	16
proponer	to propose →	17

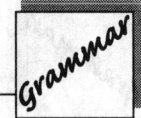

1	**¿Quiere Vd esperar?**	
	Would you like to wait?	
	No puede venir	
	She can't come	
2	**Nos ha visto llegar**	**Se les oye cantar**
	She saw us arriving	You can hear them singing
3	**No me hagas reír**	**Déjeme pasar**
	Don't make me laugh	Let me past
4	**Le aconsejamos dejarlo para mañana**	
	We advise you to leave it until tomorrow	
5	**Aún no he conseguido/logrado entenderlo**	
	I still haven't managed to understand it	
6	**No desea tener más hijos**	
	She doesn't want to have any more children	
7	**Esperamos ir de vacaciones este verano**	
	We are hoping to go on holiday this summer	
8	**Evite beber cuando conduzca**	
	Avoid drinking and driving	
9	**No pudo impedirle hablar**	
	He couldn't prevent him from speaking	
10	**Intentamos/procuramos pasar desapercibidos**	
	We tried not to be noticed	
11	**Necesitaba salir a la calle**	
	I/he/she needed to go out	
12	**Olvidó dejar su dirección**	
	He/she forgot to leave his/her address	
13	**¿Piensan venir por Navidad?**	
	Are you thinking of coming for Christmas?	
14	**Preferiría elegirlo yo mismo**	
	I'd rather choose it myself	
15	**Prohibió fumar a los alumnos**	
	He forbade the pupils to smoke	
16	**Prometieron volver pronto**	
	They promised to come back soon	
17	**Propongo salir cuanto antes**	
	I propose to leave as soon as possible	

☐ The Infinitive: Set Expressions

The following are set in Spanish with the meaning shown:

dejar caer	to drop →	1
hacer entrar	to show in →	2
hacer saber	to let know, make known →	3
hacer salir	to let out →	4
hacer venir	to send for →	5
ir(se) a buscar	to go for, go and get →	6
mandar hacer	to order →	7
mandar llamar	to send for →	8
oír decir que	to hear it said that →	9
oír hablar de	to hear of/about →	10
querer decir	to mean →	11

The Perfect Infinitive

◆ The perfect infinitive is formed using the auxiliary verb **haber** with the past participle of the verb → 12

◆ The perfect infinitive is found:
— following certain prepositions, especially **después de** *after* → 13
— following certain verbal constructions → 14

1	**Al verlo, dejó caer lo que llevaba en las manos** When he saw him he dropped what he was carrying
2	**Haz entrar a nuestros invitados** Show our guests in
3	**Quiero hacerles saber que no serán bien recibidos** I want to let them know that they won't be welcome
4	**Hágale salir, por favor** Please let him out
5	**Le he hecho venir a Vd porque ...** I sent for you because ...
6	**Vete a buscar los guantes** Go and get your gloves
7	**Me he mandado hacer un traje** I have ordered a suit
8	**Mandaron llamar al médico** They sent for the doctor
9	**He oído decir que está enfermo** I've heard it said that he's ill
10	**No he oído hablar más de él** I haven't heard anything more (said) of him
11	**¿Qué quiere decir eso?** What does that mean?
12	**haber terminado** **haberse vestido** to have finished to have got dressed
13	**Después de haber comprado el regalo, volvió a casa** After buying/having bought the present, he went back home **Después de haber madrugado tanto, el taxi se retrasó** After she got up so early, the taxi arrived late
14	**perdonar a alguien por haber hecho** to forgive somebody for doing/having done **dar las gracias a alguien por haber hecho** to thank somebody for doing/having done **pedir perdón por haber hecho** to be sorry for doing/having done

❐ The Gerund

Formation

◆ 1st conjugation
  Replace the **-ar** of the infinitive by **-ando** → ①

◆ 2nd conjugation
  Replace the **-er** of the infinitive by **-iendo** → ②

◆ 3rd conjugation
  Replace the **-ir** of the infinitive by **-iendo** → ③

◆ For irregular gerunds, see irregular verbs, p 80 ff.

Uses

◆ After the verb **estar**, to form the continuous tenses → ④

◆ After the verbs **seguir** and **continuar** to continue, and **ir** when meaning to happen gradually → ⑤

◆ In time constructions, after **llevar** → ⑥

◆ When the action in the main clause needs to be complemented by another action → ⑦

◆ The position of object pronouns is the same as for the infinitive (see p 46).

◆ The gerund is invariable and strictly verbal in sense.

❐ The Present Participle

◆ It is formed by replacing the **-ar** of the infinitive of 1st conjugation verbs by **-ante**, and the **-er** and **-ir** of the 2nd and 3rd conjugations by **-iente** → ⑧

◆ A very limited number of verbs have a present participle, which is either used as an adjective or a noun → ⑨/⑩

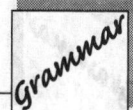
Grammar

1	**cantar** →	**cantando**
	to sing	singing
2	**temer** →	**temiendo**
	to fear	fearing
3	**partir** →	**partiendo**
	to leave	leaving

4 **Estoy escribiendo una carta**
I am writing a letter
Estaban esperándonos
They were waiting for us

5 **Sigue viniendo todos los días**
He/she is still coming every day
Continuarán subiendo los precios
Prices will continue to go up
El ejército iba avanzando poco a poco
The army was gradually advancing

6 **Lleva dos años estudiando inglés**
He/she has been studying English for two years

7 **Pasamos el día tomando el sol en la playa**
We spent the day sunbathing on the beach
Iba cojeando
He/she/I was limping
Salieron corriendo
They ran out

8	**cantar** →	**cantante**
	to sing	singing/singer
	pender →	**pendiente**
	to hang	hanging
	seguir →	**siguiente**
	to follow	following

9 **agua corriente**
running water

10 **un estudiante**
a student

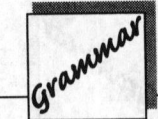

☐ Use of Tenses

The Present

◆ Unlike English, Spanish often uses the same verb form for the simple present (e.g. *I smoke, he reads, we live*) and the continuous present (e.g. *I am smoking, he is reading, we are living*) → 1

◆ Normally, however, the continuous present is used to translate the English:

    to be doing   **estar haciendo** → 2

◆ Spanish uses the present tense where English uses the perfect in the following cases:

  — with certain prepositions of time – notably **desde** *for/since* – when an action begun in the past is continued in the present → 3

  ⚠ NOTE: The perfect can be used as in English when the verb is negative → 4

  — in the construction **acabar de hacer** *to have just done* → 5

◆ Like English, Spanish often uses the present where a future action is implied → 6

The Future

The future is generally used as in English → 7, but note the following:

◆ Immediate future time is often expressed by means of the present tense of **ir** + **a** + infinitive → 8

◆ When '*will*' or '*shall*' mean '*wish to*', '*are willing to*', **querer** is used → 9

The Future Perfect

◆ Used as in English *shall/will have done* → 10

◆ It can also express conjecture, usually about things in the recent past → 11

1	**Fumo** I smoke OR: I am smoking
	Lee He reads OR: He is reading
	Vivimos We live OR: We are living
2	**Está fumando**
	He is smoking
3	**Linda estudia español desde hace seis meses**
	Linda's been learning Spanish for six months (*and still is*)
	Estoy de pie desde las siete
	I've been up since seven
	¿Hace mucho que esperan?
	Have you been waiting long?
	Ya hace dos semanas que estamos aquí
	That's two weeks we've been here (now)
4	**No se han visto desde hace meses**
	They haven't seen each other for months
5	**Isabel acaba de salir**
	Isabel has just left
6	**Mañana voy a Madrid**
	I am going to Madrid tomorrow
7	**Lo haré mañana**
	I'll do it tomorrow
8	**Te vas a caer si no tienes cuidado**
	You'll fall if you're not careful
	Va a perder el tren
	He's going to miss the train
	Va a llevar una media hora
	It'll take about half an hour
9	**¿Me quieres esperar un momento, por favor?**
	Will you wait for me a second, please?
10	**Lo habré acabado para mañana**
	I will have finished it for tomorrow
11	**Ya habrán llegado a casa**
	They must have arrived home by now

◻ **Use of Tenses** (Continued)

The Imperfect

◆ The imperfect describes:

— an action or state in the past without definite limits in time → ①

— habitual action(s) in the past (often expressed in English by means of *would* or *used to*) → ②

◆ Spanish uses the imperfect tense where English uses the pluperfect in the following cases:

— with certain prepositions of time – notably **desde** *for/since* – when an action begun in the remoter past was continued in the more recent past → ③

⚠ NOTE: The pluperfect is used as in English when the verb is negative or the action has been completed → ④

— in the construction **acabar de hacer** *to have just done* → ⑤

◆ Both the continuous and simple forms in English can be translated by the Spanish simple imperfect, but the continuous imperfect is used when the emphasis is on the fact that an action was going on at a precise moment in the past → ⑥

The Perfect

◆ The perfect is generally used as in English → ⑦

The Preterite

◆ The preterite generally corresponds to the English simple past in both written and spoken Spanish → ⑧

However, while English can use the simple past to describe habitual actions or settings, Spanish uses the imperfect (see above) → ⑨

The Past Anterior

◆ This tense is only ever used in written, literary Spanish, to replace the pluperfect in time clauses where the verb in the main clause is in the preterite → ⑩

[1]	**Todos mirábamos en silencio** We were all watching in silence **Nuestras habitaciones daban a la playa** Our rooms overlooked the beach
[2]	**En su juventud se levantaba de madrugada** In his youth he got up at dawn **Hablábamos sin parar durante horas** We would talk non-stop for hours on end **Mi hermano siempre me tomaba el pelo** My brother always used to tease me
[3]	**Hacía dos años que vivíamos en Irlanda** We had been living in Ireland for two years **Estaba enfermo desde 1990** He had been ill since 1990 **Hacía mucho tiempo que salían juntos** They had been going out together for a long time
[4]	**Hacía un año que no le había visto** I hadn't seen him for a year **Hacía una hora que había llegado** She had arrived an hour before
[5]	**Acababa de encontrármelos** I had just met them
[6]	**Cuando llegué, todos estaban fumando** When I arrived, they were all smoking
[7]	**Todavía no han salido** They haven't come out yet
[8]	**Me desperté y salté de la cama** I woke up and jumped out of bed
[9]	**Siempre iban en coche al trabajo** They always travelled to work by car
[10]	**Apenas hubo acabado, se oyeron unos golpes en la puerta** She had scarcely finished when there was a knock at the door

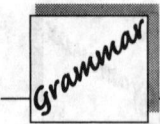

☐ The Subjunctive: when to use it

(For how to form the subjunctive see pp 6 ff.)

◆ After verbs of:

— 'wishing'

querer que } to wish that, want → ①
desear que

— 'emotion' (e.g. regret, surprise, shame, pleasure, etc)

sentir que to be sorry that → ②
sorprender que to be surprised that → ③
alegrarse de que to be pleased that → ④

— 'asking' and 'advising'

pedir que to ask that → ⑤
aconsejar que to advise that → ⑥

In all the above constructions, when the subject of the verbs in the main and subordinate clause is the same, the infinitive is used, and the conjunction **que** omitted → ⑦

— 'ordering', 'forbidding', 'allowing'

mandar que* } to order that → ⑧
ordenar que

permitir que* } to allow that → ⑨
dejar que*

prohibir que* to forbid that → ⑩
impedir que* to prevent that → ⑪

* With these verbs either the subjunctive or the infinitive is used when the object of the main verb is the subject of the subordinate verb → ⑫

◆ Always after verbs expressing doubt or uncertainty, and verbs of opinion used negatively

dudar que to doubt that → ⑬
no creer que } not to think that → ⑭
no pensar que

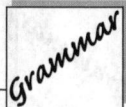

1. **Queremos que esté contenta**
   We want her to be happy (literally: We want that she is happy)
   ¿Desea Vd que lo haga yo?
   Do you want me to do it?

2. **Sentí mucho que no vinieran**
   I was very sorry that they didn't come

3. **Nos sorprendió que no les vieran Vds**
   We were surprised you didn't see them

4. **Me alegro de que te gusten**
   I'm pleased that you like them

5. **Sólo les pedimos que tengan cuidado**
   We're only asking you to take care

6. **Le aconsejé que no llegara tarde**
   I advised him not to be late

7. **Quiero que lo termines pronto**
   I want you to finish it soon
   ⚠ BUT: **Quiero terminarlo pronto**
   I want to finish it soon

8. **Ha mandado que vuelvan**
   He has ordered them to come back
   Ordenó que fueran castigados
   He ordered them to be punished

9. **No permitas que te tomen el pelo**
   Don't let them pull your leg
   No me dejó que la llevara a casa
   She didn't allow me to take her home

10. **Te prohíbo que digas eso**
    I forbid you to say that

11. **No les impido que vengan**
    I am not preventing them from coming

12. **Les ordenó que salieran** OR: **Les ordenó salir**
    She ordered them to go out

13. **Dudo que lo sepan hacer**
    I doubt they can do it

14. **No creo que sean tan listos**
    I don't think they are as clever as that

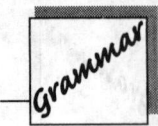

◻ **The Subjunctive: when to use it** (Continued)

♦ In impersonal constructions which express necessity, possibility, etc:

hace falta que **es necesario que** }	*it is necessary that* → ①
es posible que	*it is possible that* → ②
más vale que	*it is better that* → ③
es una lástima que	*it is a pity that* → ④

⚠ NOTE: In impersonal constructions which state a fact or express certainty the indicative is used when the impersonal verb is affirmative. When it is negative, the subjunctive is used → ⑤

♦ After certain conjunctions

para que **a fin de que*** }	*so that* → ⑥
como si	*as if* → ⑦
sin que*	*without* → ⑧
a condición de que* **con tal (de) que*** **siempre que** }	*provided that,* *on condition that* → ⑨
a menos que **a no ser que** }	*unless* → ⑩
antes (de) que*	*before* → ⑪
no sea que	*lest/in case* → ⑫
mientras (que) **siempre que** }	*as long as* → ⑬
(el) que	*the fact that* → ⑭

* When the subject of both verbs is the same, the infinitive is used, and the final **que** is omitted → ⑧

1	**¿Hace falta que vaya Jaime?**
	Does James have to go?
2	**Es posible que tengan razón**
	It's possible that they are right
3	**Más vale que se quede Vd en su casa**
	It's better that you stay at home
4	**Es una lástima que haya perdido su perrito**
	It's a shame/pity that she has lost her puppy
5	**Es verdad que va a venir**
	It's true that he's coming
	⚠ BUT: **No es verdad que vayan a hacerlo**
	It's not true that they are going to do it
6	**Átalas bien para que no se caigan**
	Tie them up tightly so that they won't fall
7	**Hablaba como si no creyera en sus propias palabras**
	He talked as if he didn't believe in his own words
8	**Salimos sin que nos vieran**
	We left without them seeing us
	⚠ BUT: **Me fui sin esperarla**
	I went without waiting for her
9	**Lo haré con tal de que me cuentes todo lo que pasó**
	I'll do it provided you tell me all that happened
10	**Saldremos de paseo a menos que esté lloviendo**
	We'll go for a walk unless it's raining
11	**Avísale antes de que sea demasiado tarde**
	Warn him before it's too late
12	**Habla en voz baja, no sea que alguien nos oiga**
	Speak softly in case anyone hears us
13	**Eso no pasará mientras yo sea el jefe aquí**
	That won't happen as long as I am the boss here
14	**El que no me escribiera no me importaba demasiado**
	The fact that he didn't write didn't matter to me too much

❐ **The Subjunctive: when to use it** (Continued)

◆ After the conjunctions

> **de modo que**
> **de forma que** } *so that* (indicating a purpose) → ①
> **de manera que**

⚠️ NOTE: When these conjunctions introduce a result and not a purpose the subjunctive is not used → ②

◆ In relative clauses with an antecedent which is:

— negative → ③

— indefinite → ④

— non-specific → ⑤

◆ In main clauses, to express a wish or exhortation. The verb may be preceded by expressions like **ojalá** or **que** → ⑥

◆ In the **si** clause of conditions where the English sentence contains a conditional tense → ⑦

◆ In set expressions → ⑧

◆ In the following constructions which translate *however*:

— **por** + adjective + subjunctive → ⑨

— **por** + adverb + subjunctive → ⑩

— **por** + **mucho** + subjunctive → ⑪

1. **Vuélvanse de manera que les vea bien**
Turn round so that I can see you properly

2. **No quieren hacerlo, de manera que tendré que hacerlo yo**
They won't do it, so I'll have to do it myself

3. **No he encontrado a nadie que la conociera**
I haven't met anyone who knows her
No dijo nada que no supiéramos ya
He/she didn't say anything we didn't already know

4. **Necesito alguien que sepa conducir**
I need someone who can drive
Busco algo que me distraiga
I'm looking for something to take my mind off it

5. **Busca una casa que tenga calefacción central**
He/she's looking for a house which has central heating
(*subjunctive used since such a house may or may not exist*)
El que lo haya visto tiene que decírmelo
Anyone who has seen it must tell me
(*subjunctive used since it is not known who has seen it*)

6. **¡Ojalá haga buen tiempo!**
Let's hope the weather will be good!
¡Que te diviertas!
Have a good time!

7. **Si fuéramos en coche llegaríamos a tiempo**
If we went by car we'd be there in time

8. **Diga lo que diga ...**   **Sea lo que sea ...**
Whatever he may say ...   Be that as it may ...
Pase lo que pase ...   **Sea como sea ...**
Come what may ...   One way or another ...

9. **Por cansado que esté, seguirá trabajando**
No matter how/however tired he may be, he'll go on working

10. **Por lejos que viva, iremos a buscarle**
No matter how/however far away he lives, we'll go and look for him

11. **Por mucho que lo intente, nunca lo conseguirá**
No matter how/however hard he tries, he'll never succeed

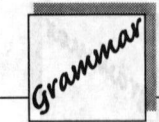
☐ The Subjunctive: when to use it (Continued)

Clauses taking either a subjunctive or an indicative

In certain constructions, a subjunctive is needed when the action refers to future events or hypothetical situations, whereas an indicative is used when stating a fact or experience → ①

The commonest of these are:

◆ The conjunctions

cuando	*when* → ①
en cuanto	
tan pronto como	} *as soon as* → ②
después (de) que*	*after* → ③
hasta que	*until* → ④
mientras	*while* → ⑤
siempre que	*whenever* → ⑥
aunque	*even though* → ⑦

All conjunctions and pronouns ending in **-quiera** (*-ever*) → ⑧

* ⚠ NOTE: If the subject of both verbs is the same, the subjunctive introduced by **después (de) que** may be replaced by **después de** + infinitive → ⑨

Sequence of tenses in Subordinate Clauses

◆ If the verb in the main clause is in the present, future or imperative, the verb in the dependent clause will be in the present or perfect subjunctive → ⑩

◆ If the verb in the main clause is in the conditional or any past tense, the verb in the dependent clause will be in the imperfect or pluperfect subjunctive → ⑪

Examples

1	**Le aconsejé que oyera música cuando estuviera nervioso**
	I advised him to listen to music when he felt nervous
	Me gusta nadar cuando hace calor
	I like to swim when it is warm
2	**Te devolveré el libro tan pronto como lo haya leído**
	I'll give you back the book as soon as I have read it
3	**Te lo diré después de que te hayas sentado**
	I'll tell you after you've sat down
4	**Quédate aquí hasta que volvamos**
	Stay here until we come back
5	**No hablen en voz alta mientras estén ellos aquí**
	Don't speak loudly while they are here
6	**Vuelvan por aquí siempre que quieran**
	Come back whenever you wish to
7	**No le creeré aunque diga la verdad**
	I won't believe him even if he tells the truth
8	**La encontraré dondequiera que esté**
	I will find her wherever she might be
9	**Después de cenar nos fuimos al cine**
	After dinner we went to the cinema
10	**Quiero que lo hagas** (*pres + pres subj*)
	I want you to do it
	Temo que no haya venido (*pres + perf subj*)
	I fear he hasn't come (might not have come)
	Iremos por aquí para que no nos vean
	(*future + pres subj*)
	We'll go this way so that they won't see us
11	**Me gustaría que llegaras temprano**
	(*cond + imperf subj*)
	I'd like you to arrive early
	Les pedí que me esperaran (*preterite + imperf subj*)
	I asked them to wait for me
	Sentiría mucho que hubiese muerto
	(*cond + pluperf subj*)
	I would be very sorry if he were dead

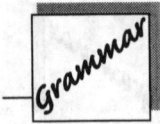

☐ Verbs governing a, de, con, en, por and para

The following lists (pp 66 to 73) contain common verbal constructions using the prepositions **a, de, con, en, por** and **para**.

Note the following abbreviations:

infin	infinitive
perf infin	perfect infinitive*
algn	alguien
sb	somebody
sth	something

* For formation see p 50

aburrirse de + infin	*to get bored with doing* → ①
acabar con algo/algn	*to put an end to sth/finish with sb* → ②
acabar de* + infin	*to have just done* → ③
acabar por + infin	*to end up doing* → ④
acercarse a algo/algn	*to approach sth/sb*
acordarse de algo/algn/de + infin	*to remember sth/sb/doing* → ⑤
acostumbrarse a algo/algn/a + infin	*to get used to sth/sb/to doing* → ⑥
acusar a algn de algo/de + perf infin	*to accuse sb of sth/of doing, having done* → ⑦
advertir a algn de algo	*to notify, warn sb about sth* → ⑧
aficionarse a algo/a + infin	*to grow fond of sth/of doing* → ⑨
alegrarse de algo/de + perf infin	*to be glad about sth/of doing, having done* → ⑩
alejarse de algn/algo	*to move away from sb/sth*
amenazar a algn con algo/con + infin	*to threaten sb with sth/to do* → ⑪
animar a algn a + infin	*to encourage sb to do*
apresurarse a + infin	*to hurry to do* → ⑫

* See also Use of Tenses, pp 54 and 56

Grammar

1	**Me aburría de no poder salir de casa** I used to get bored with not being able to leave the house
2	**Quiso acabar con su vida** He wanted to put an end to his life
3	**Acababan de llegar cuando ...** They had just arrived when ...
4	**El acusado acabó por confesarlo todo** The accused ended up by confessing everything
5	**Nos acordamos muy bien de aquellas vacaciones** We remember that holiday very well
6	**Me he acostumbrado a levantarme temprano** I've got used to getting up early
7	**Le acusó de haber mentido** She accused him of lying
8	**Advertí a mi amigo del peligro que corría** I warned my friend about the danger he was in
9	**Nos hemos aficionado a la música clásica** We've grown fond of classical music
10	**Me alegro de haberle conocido** I'm glad I met him
11	**Amenazó con denunciarles** He threatened to report them
12	**Se apresuraron a coger sitio** They hurried to find a seat

☐ Verbs governing a, de, con, en, por and para
(Continued)

aprender a + infin	*to learn to do* → 1
aprovecharse de algo/algn	*to take advantage of sth/sb*
aproximarse a algn/algo	*to approach sb/sth*
asistir a algo	*to attend sth, be at sth*
asomarse a/por	*to lean out of* → 2
asombrarse de + infin	*to be surprised at doing* → 3
atreverse a + infin	*to dare to do*
avergonzarse de algo/algn/de + perf infin	*to be ashamed of sth/sb/of doing, having done* → 4
ayudar a algn a + infin	*to help sb to do* → 5
bajarse de (+ place/vehicle)	*to get off/out of* → 6
burlarse de algn	*to make fun of sb*
cansarse de algo/algn/de + infin	*to tire of sth/sb/of doing*
carecer de algo	*to lack sth* → 7
cargar de algo	*to load with sth* → 8
casarse con algn	*to get married to sb* → 9
cesar de + infin	*to stop doing*
chocar con algo	*to crash/bump into sth* → 10
comenzar a + infin	*to begin to do*
comparar con algn/algo	*to compare with sb/sth*
consentir en + infin	*to agree to do*
consistir en + infin	*to consist of doing* → 11
constar de algo	*to consist of sth* → 12
contar con algn/algo	*to rely on sb/sth* → 13
convenir en + infin	*to agree to do* → 14
darse cuenta de algo	*to realize sth*
dejar de + infin	*to stop doing* → 15
depender de algo/algn	*to depend on sth/sb* → 16
despedirse de algn	*to say goodbye to sb*
dirigirse a + place/**a algn**	*to head for/address sb*
disponerse a + infin	*to get ready to do*
empezar a + infin	*to begin to do*
empezar por + infin	*to begin by doing* → 17

1	**Me gustaría aprender a nadar**	I'd like to learn to swim
2	**No te asomes a la ventana**	Don't lean out of the window
3	**Nos asombramos mucho de verles ahí**	We were very surprised at seeing them there
4	**No me avergüenzo de haberlo hecho**	I'm not ashamed of having done it
5	**Ayúdeme a llevar estas maletas**	Help me to carry these cases
6	**Se bajó del coche**	He got out of the car
7	**La casa carecía de jardín**	The house lacked (did not have) a garden
8	**El carro iba cargado de paja**	The cart was loaded with straw
9	**Se casó con Andrés**	She married Andrew
10	**Enciende la luz, o chocarás con la puerta**	Turn the light on, or you'll bump into the door
11	**Mi plan consistía en vigilarles de cerca**	My plan consisted of keeping a close eye on them
12	**El examen consta de tres partes**	The exam consists of three parts
13	**Cuento contigo para que me ayudes a hacerlo**	I rely on you to help me do it
14	**Convinieron en reunirse al día siguiente**	They agreed to meet the following day
15	**¿Quieres dejar de hablar?**	Will you stop talking?
16	**No depende de mí**	It doesn't depend on me
17	**Empieza por enterarte de lo que se trata**	Begin by finding out what it is about

❐ **Verbs governing a, de, con, en, por and para**
(Continued)

encontrarse con algn	*to meet sb (by chance)* → 1
enfadarse con algn	*to get annoyed with sb*
enseñar a algn a + infin	*to teach sb to* → 2
enterarse de algo	*to find out about sth* → 3
entrar en (+ place)	*to enter, go into*
esperar a + infin	*to wait until* → 4
estar de acuerdo con algn/algo	*to agree with sb/sth*
fiarse de algn/algo	*to trust sb/sth*
fijarse en algo/algn	*to notice sth/sb* → 5
hablar con algn	*to talk to sb* → 6
hacer caso a algn	*to pay attention to sb*
hartarse de algo/algn/de + infin	*to get fed up with sth/sb/with doing* → 7
interesarse por algo/algn	*to be interested in sth/sb* → 8
invitar a algn a + infin	*to invite sb to do*
jugar a (+ sports, games)	*to play*
luchar por algo/por + infin	*to fight, strive for/to do* → 9
llegar a (+ place)**/a** + infin	*to reach/to manage to do* → 10
llenar de algo	*to fill with sth*
negarse a + infin	*to refuse to do* → 11
obligar a algn a + infin	*to make sb do* → 12
ocuparse de algn/algo	*to take care of sb/attend to sth*
oler a algo	*to smell of sth* → 13
olvidarse de algo/algn/de + infin	*to forget sth/sb/to do* → 14
oponerse a algo/a + infin	*to be opposed to sth/to doing*
parecerse a algn/algo	*to resemble sb/sth*
pensar en algo/algn/en + infin	*to think about sth/sb/about doing* → 15
preguntar por algn	*to ask for/about sb*
preocuparse de *or* **por algo/algn**	*to worry about sth/sb* → 16

Examples

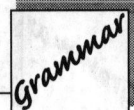

1. **Me encontré con ella al entrar en el banco**
   I met her as I was entering the bank

2. **Le estoy enseñando a nadar**
   I am teaching him to swim

3. **¿Te has enterado del sitio adonde hay que ir?**
   Have you found out where we have to go?

4. **Espera a saber lo que quiere antes de comprar el regalo**
   Wait until you know what he wants before buying the present

5. **Me fijé en él cuando subía a su coche**
   I noticed him when he was getting into his car

6. **¿Puedo hablar con Vd un momento?**
   May I talk to you for a moment?

7. **Me he hartado de escribirle**
   I've got fed up with writing to him

8. **Me interesaba mucho por la arqueología**
   I was very interested in archaeology

9. **Hay que luchar por mantener la paz**
   One must strive to preserve peace

10. **Lo intenté sin llegar a conseguirlo**
    I tried without managing to do it

11. **Se negó a hacerlo**
    He refused to do it

12. **Le obligó a sentarse**
    He made him sit down

13. **Este perfume huele a jazmín**
    This perfume smells of jasmine

14. **Siempre me olvido de cerrar la puerta**
    I always forget to shut the door

15. **No quiero pensar en eso**
    I don't want to think about that

16. **Se preocupa mucho de/por su apariencia**
    He worries a lot about his appearance

☐ **Verbs governing a, de, con, en, por and para**
(Continued)

prepararse a + infin	*to prepare to do*
probar a + infin	*to try to do*
quedar en + infin	*to agree to do* → 1
quedar por + infin	*to remain to be done* → 2
quejarse de algo	*to complain of sth*
referirse a algo	*to refer to sth*
reírse de algo/algn	*to laugh at sth/sb*
rodear de	*to surround with* → 3
romper a + infin	*to (suddenly) start to do* → 4
salir de (+ place)	*to leave*
sentarse a (+ table etc)	*to sit down at*
subir(se) a (+ vehicle/place)	*to get on, into/to climb* → 5
servir de algo a algn	*to be useful to/serve sb as sth* → 6
servir para algo/para + infin	*to be good as sth/for doing* → 7
servirse de algo	*to use sth* → 8
soñar con algn/algo/con + infin	*to dream about/of sb/sth/of doing*
sorprenderse de algo	*to be surprised at sth*
tardar en + infin	*to take time to do* → 9
tener ganas de algo/de + infin	*to want sth/to do* → 10
tener miedo de algo	*to be afraid of sth* → 11
tener miedo a algn	*to be afraid of sb* → 12
terminar por + infin	*to end by doing*
tirar de algo/algn	*to pull sth/sb*
trabajar de (+ occupation)	*to work as* → 13
trabajar en (+ place of work)	*to work at/in* → 14
traducir a (+ language)	*to translate into*
tratar de + infin	*to try to do* → 15
tratarse de algo/algn/de + infin	*to be a question of sth/about sb/about doing* → 16
vacilar en + infin	*to hesitate to do* → 17
volver a + infin	*to do again* → 18

1	**Habíamos quedado en encontrarnos a las 8** We had agreed to meet at 8
2	**Queda por averiguar dónde se ocultan** It remains to be discovered where they are hiding
3	**Habían rodeado el jardín de un seto de cipreses** They had surrounded the garden with a hedge of cypress trees
4	**Al apagarse la luz, el niño rompió a llorar** When the lights went out, the little boy suddenly started to cry
5	**¡De prisa, sube al coche!** Get into the car, quick!
6	**Esto me servirá de bastón** This will serve me as a walking stick
7	**No sirvo para (ser) jardinero** I'm no good as a gardener
8	**Se sirvió de un destornillador para abrirlo** She used a screwdriver to open it
9	**Tardaron mucho en salir** They took a long time to come out
10	**Tengo ganas de volver a España** I want to go back to Spain
11	**Mi hija tiene miedo de la oscuridad** My daughter is afraid of the dark
12	**Nunca tuvieron miedo a su padre** They were never afraid of their father
13	**Pedro trabaja de camarero en Londres** Peter works as a waiter in London
14	**Trabajaba en una oficina** I used to work in an office
15	**No trates de engañarme** Don't try to fool me
16	**Se trata de nuestro nuevo vecino** It's about our new neighbour
17	**Nunca vacilaban en pedir dinero** They never hesitated to borrow money
18	**No vuelvas a hacerlo nunca más** Don't ever do it again

❐ Ser and Estar

Spanish has two verbs – **ser** and **estar** – for *to be*.

They are not interchangeable and each one is used in defined contexts.

ser is used:

♦ With an adjective, to express a permanent or inherent quality → 1

♦ To express occupation or nationality → 2

♦ To express possession → 3

♦ To express origin or the material from which something is made → 4

♦ With a noun, pronoun or infinitive following the verb → 5

♦ To express the time and date → 6

♦ To form the passive, with the past participle (see p 32).

⚠ NOTE: This use emphasizes the action of the verb. If, however, the resultant state or condition needs to be emphasized, **estar** is used. The past participle then functions as an adjective (see p 204) and has to agree in gender and in number with the noun → 7

estar is used:

♦ Always, to indicate place or location → 8

♦ With an adjective or adjectival phrase, to express a quality or state seen by the speaker as subject to change or different from expected → 9

♦ When speaking of a person's state of health → 10

♦ To form the continuous tenses, used with the gerund (see p 52) → 11

♦ With **de** + noun, to indicate a temporary occupation → 12

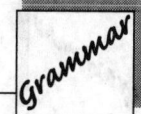

Grammar

1. **Mi hermano es alto**
   My brother is tall
   María es inteligente
   Mary is intelligent

2. **Javier es aviador**
   Javier is an airman
   Sus padres son italianos
   His parents are Italian

3. **La casa es de Miguel**
   The house belongs to Michael

4. **Mi hermana es de Granada**
   My sister is from Granada
   Las paredes son de ladrillo
   The walls are made of brick

5. **Andrés es un niño travieso**
   Andrew is a naughty boy
   Soy yo, Enrique
   It's me, Henry
   Todo es proponérselo
   It's all a question of putting your mind to it

6. **Son las tres y media**
   It's half past three
   Mañana es sábado
   Tomorrow is Saturday

7. **Las puertas eran cerradas sigilosamente**
   The doors were being silently closed
   Las puertas estaban cerradas
   The doors were closed (*resultant action*)

8. **La comida está en la mesa**
   The meal is on the table

9. **Su amigo está enfermo**
   Her friend is ill
   El lavabo está ocupado
   The toilet is engaged
   Hoy estoy de mal humor
   I'm in a bad mood today
   Las tiendas están cerradas
   The shops are closed

10. **¿Cómo están Vds?**
    How are you?
    Estamos todos bien
    We are all well

11. **Estamos aprendiendo mucho**
    We are learning a great deal

12. **Mi primo está de médico en un pueblo**
    My cousin works as a doctor in a village

☐ **Ser and Estar** (Continued)

With certain adjectives, both **ser** and **estar** can be used, although they are not interchangeable when used in this way:

— **ser** will express a permanent or inherent quality → ①

— **estar** will express a temporary state or quality → ②

Both **ser** and **estar** may also be used in set expressions.

The commonest of these are:

◆ With **ser**

Sea como sea	*Be that as it may*
Es igual/Es lo mismo	*It's all the same*
llegar a ser	*to become*
¿Cómo fue eso?	*How did that happen?*
¿Qué ha sido de él?	*What has become of him?*
ser para (with the idea of purpose)	*to be for* → ③

◆ With **estar**

estar de pie/de rodillas	*to be standing/kneeling*
estar de viaje	*to be travelling*
estar de vacaciones	*to be on holiday*
estar de vuelta	*to be back*
estar de moda	*to be in fashion*
Está bien	*It's all right*
estar para	*to be about to do sth/to be in a mood for* → ④
estar por	*to be inclined to/to be (all) for* → ⑤
estar a punto de	*to be just about to do sth* → ⑥

1   **Su hermana es muy joven/vieja**
His sister is very young/old
Son muy ricos/pobres
They are very rich/poor
Su amigo era un enfermo
His friend was an invalid
Es un borracho
He is a drunkard
Mi hijo es bueno/malo
My son is good/naughty
Viajar es cansado
Travelling is tiring

2   **Está muy joven/vieja con ese vestido**
She looks very young/old in that dress
Ahora están muy ricos/pobres
They have become very rich/poor lately
Estaba enfermo
He was ill
Está borracho
He is drunk
Está bueno/malo
He is well/ill
Hoy estoy cansada
I am tired today

3   **Este paquete es para Vd**
This parcel is for you
Esta caja es para guardar semillas
This box is for keeping seeds in

4   **Están para llegar**
They're about to arrive

5   **Estoy por irme a vivir a España**
I'm inclined to go and live in Spain

6   **Las rosas están a punto de salir**
The roses are about to come out

❏ Verbal Idioms

Special Intransitive Verbs

With the following verbs the Spanish construction is the opposite of the English. The subject in English becomes the indirect object of the Spanish verb, while the object in English becomes the subject of the Spanish verb.

Compare the following:

> *I like that house* (subject: *I*, object: *that house*)
> **Esa casa me gusta** (subject: **esa casa**, indirect object: **me**)

The commonest of these verbs are:

gustar	*to like* → 1
gustar más	*to prefer* → 2
encantar	(colloquial) *to love* → 3
faltar	*to need/to be short of/to have missing* → 4
quedar	*to be/have left* → 5
doler	*to have a pain in/to hurt, ache* → 6
interesar	*to be interested in* → 7
importar	*to mind* → 8

1. **Me gusta este vestido**
I like this dress (This dress pleases me)

2. **Me gustan más éstas**
I prefer these

3. **Nos encanta hacer deporte**
We love sport

4. **Me faltaban 100 pesetas**
I was short of 100 pesetas

Sólo le falta el toque final
It just needs the finishing touch

Le faltaban tres dientes
He/she had three teeth missing

5. **Sólo nos quedan dos kilómetros**
We only have two kilometres (left) to go

6. **Me duele la cabeza**
I have a headache

7. **Nos interesa mucho la política**
We are very interested in politics

8. **No me importa la lluvia**
I don't mind the rain

◻ **Irregular Verbs**

The verbs listed opposite and conjugated on pp 82 to 161 provide the main patterns for irregular verbs. The verbs are grouped opposite according to their infinitive ending and are shown in the following tables in alphabetical order.

In the tables, the most important irregular verbs are given in their most common simple tenses, together with the imperative and the gerund.

The past participle is also shown for each verb, to enable you to form all the compound tenses, as on pp 18 to 23.

The pronouns **ella** and **Vd** take the same verb endings as **él**, while **ellas** and **Vds** take the same endings as **ellos**.

◆ All the verbs included in the tables differ from the three conjugations set out on pp 8 to 13. Many – e.g. **contar** – serve as models for groups of verbs, while others – e.g. **ir** – are unique. On pp 162 to 186 you will find over 2,800 commonly used verbs listed alphabetically and cross-referred either to the relevant basic conjugation or to the appropriate model in the verb tables.

Imperfect Subjunctive of Irregular Verbs

For verbs with an irregular root form in the preterite tense – e.g. **andar** → **anduvieron** – the imperfect subjunctive is formed by using the root form of the 3rd person plural of the preterite tense, and adding the imperfect subjunctive endings -**iera/-iese** etc where the verb has an 'i' in the preterite ending – e.g. anduv**ieron** → anduv**iera/iese**. Where the verb has no 'i' in the preterite ending, add -**era/-ese** etc – e.g. produj**eron** → produj**era/ese**.

'-ar':	'-er':	'-ir':
actuar	entender	adquirir
almorzar	haber	bendecir
andar	hacer	conducir
aunar	hay	construir
avergonzar	leer	cubrir
averiguar	llover	decir
contar	mover	dirigir
cruzar	nacer	distinguir
dar	oler	dormir
empezar	poder	elegir
enviar	poner	erguir
errar	querer	escribir
estar	resolver	freír
jugar	romper	gruñir
negar	saber	ir
pagar	satisfacer	lucir
pensar	ser	morir
rehusar	tener	oír
rogar	torcer	pedir
sacar	traer	prohibir
volcar	valer	reír
	vencer	reñir
'-er':	ver	reunir
caber	volver	salir
caer		seguir
cocer	**'-ir':**	sentir
coger	abolir	venir
crecer	abrir	zurcir

abolir *to abolish*

PAST PARTICIPLE	IMPERATIVE
abol**ido**	abol**id**

GERUND

abol**iendo**

PRESENT*	PRESENT SUBJUNCTIVE
nosotros abol**imos**	*not used*
vosotros abol**ís**	
* Present tense only used in persons shown	

FUTURE	CONDITIONAL
yo abolir**é**	**yo** abolir**ía**
tú abolir**ás**	**tú** abolir**ías**
él abolir**á**	**él** abolir**ía**
nosotros abolir**emos**	**nosotros** abolir**íamos**
vosotros abolir**éis**	**vosotros** abolir**íais**
ellos abolir**án**	**ellos** abolir**ían**

IMPERFECT	PRETERITE
yo abol**ía**	**yo** abol**í**
tú abol**ías**	**tú** abol**iste**
él abol**ía**	**él** abol**ió**
nosotros abol**íamos**	**nosotros** abol**imos**
vosotros abol**íais**	**vosotros** abol**isteis**
ellos abol**ían**	**ellos** abol**ieron**

VERB TABLE

---

abrir *to open*

PAST PARTICIPLE	IMPERATIVE
abierto	abre
	abrid
GERUND	
abriendo	

PRESENT		PRESENT SUBJUNCTIVE	
yo	abro	yo	abra
tú	abres	tú	abras
él	abre	él	abra
nosotros	abrimos	nosotros	abramos
vosotros	abrís	vosotros	abráis
ellos	abren	ellos	abran

FUTURE		CONDITIONAL	
yo	abriré	yo	abriría
tú	abrirás	tú	abrirías
él	abrirá	él	abriría
nosotros	abriremos	nosotros	abriríamos
vosotros	abriréis	vosotros	abriríais
ellos	abrirán	ellos	abrirían

IMPERFECT		PRETERITE	
yo	abría	yo	abrí
tú	abrías	tú	abriste
él	abría	él	abrió
nosotros	abríamos	nosotros	abrimos
vosotros	abríais	vosotros	abristeis
ellos	abrían	ellos	abrieron

actuar *to act*

PAST PARTICIPLE	IMPERATIVE
actu**ado**	actú**a**
	actua**d**
GERUND	
actu**ando**	

PRESENT		PRESENT SUBJUNCTIVE	
yo	act**úo**	yo	actú**e**
tú	actú**as**	tú	actú**es**
él	actú**a**	él	actú**e**
nosotros	actu**amos**	nosotros	actu**emos**
vosotros	actu**áis**	vosotros	actu**éis**
ellos	actú**an**	ellos	actú**en**

FUTURE		CONDITIONAL	
yo	actuar**é**	yo	actuar**ía**
tú	actuar**ás**	tú	actuar**ías**
él	actuar**á**	él	actuar**ía**
nosotros	actuar**emos**	nosotros	actuar**íamos**
vosotros	actuar**éis**	vosotros	actuar**íais**
ellos	actuar**án**	ellos	actuar**ían**

IMPERFECT		PRETERITE	
yo	actu**aba**	yo	actu**é**
tú	actu**abas**	tú	actu**aste**
él	actu**aba**	él	actu**ó**
nosotros	actu**ábamos**	nosotros	actu**amos**
vosotros	actu**abais**	vosotros	actu**asteis**
ellos	actu**aban**	ellos	actu**aron**

adquirir *to acquire*

PAST PARTICIPLE	IMPERATIVE
adquir**ido**	**adquiere**
	adquiri**d**
GERUND	
adquir**iendo**	

PRESENT	PRESENT SUBJUNCTIVE
yo **adquiero**	yo **adquiera**
tú **adquieres**	tú **adquieras**
él **adquiere**	él **adquiera**
nosotros adquir**imos**	nosotros adquir**amos**
vosotros adquir**ís**	vosotros adquir**áis**
ellos **adquieren**	ellos **adquieran**

FUTURE	CONDITIONAL
yo adquirir**é**	yo adquirir**ía**
tú adquirir**ás**	tú adquirir**ías**
él adquirir**á**	él adquirir**ía**
nosotros adquirir**emos**	nosotros adquirir**íamos**
vosotros adquirir**éis**	vosotros adquirir**íais**
ellos adquirir**án**	ellos adquirir**ían**

IMPERFECT	PRETERITE
yo adquir**ía**	yo adquir**í**
tú adquir**ías**	tú adquir**iste**
él adquir**ía**	él adquir**ió**
nosotros adquir**íamos**	nosotros adquir**imos**
vosotros adquir**íais**	vosotros adquir**isteis**
ellos adquir**ían**	ellos adquir**ieron**

almorzar *to have lunch*

PAST PARTICIPLE	IMPERATIVE
almorz**ado**	**almuerza**
	almorza**d**
GERUND	
almorz**ando**	

PRESENT		PRESENT SUBJUNCTIVE	
yo	**almuerzo**	yo	**almuerce**
tú	**almuerzas**	tú	**almuerces**
él	**almuerza**	él	**almuerce**
nosotros	almorz**amos**	nosotros	**almorcemos**
vosotros	almorz**áis**	vosotros	**almorcéis**
ellos	**almuerzan**	ellos	**almuercen**

FUTURE		CONDITIONAL	
yo	almorzar**é**	yo	almorzar**ía**
tú	almorzar**ás**	tú	almorzar**ías**
él	almorzar**á**	él	almorzar**ía**
nosotros	almorzar**emos**	nosotros	almorzar**íamos**
vosotros	almorzar**éis**	vosotros	almorzar**íais**
ellos	almorzar**án**	ellos	almorzar**ían**

IMPERFECT		PRETERITE	
yo	almorz**aba**	yo	**almorcé**
tú	almorz**abas**	tú	almorz**aste**
él	almorz**aba**	él	almorz**ó**
nosotros	almorz**ábamos**	nosotros	almorz**amos**
vosotros	almorz**abais**	vosotros	almorz**asteis**
ellos	almorz**aban**	ellos	almorz**aron**

andar *to walk*

PAST PARTICIPLE	IMPERATIVE
and**ado**	and**a**
	and**ad**
GERUND	
and**ando**	

PRESENT

yo	and**o**
tú	and**as**
él	and**a**
nosotros	and**amos**
vosotros	and**áis**
ellos	and**an**

PRESENT SUBJUNCTIVE

yo	and**e**
tú	and**es**
él	and**e**
nosotros	and**emos**
vosotros	and**éis**
ellos	and**en**

FUTURE

yo	andar**é**
tú	andar**ás**
él	andar**á**
nosotros	andar**emos**
vosotros	andar**éis**
ellos	andar**án**

CONDITIONAL

yo	andar**ía**
tú	andar**ías**
él	andar**ía**
nosotros	andar**íamos**
vosotros	andar**íais**
ellos	andar**ían**

IMPERFECT

yo	and**aba**
tú	and**abas**
él	and**aba**
nosotros	and**ábamos**
vosotros	and**abais**
ellos	and**aban**

PRETERITE

yo	**anduve**
tú	**anduviste**
él	**anduvo**
nosotros	**anduvimos**
vosotros	**anduvisteis**
ellos	**anduvieron**

Grammar

aunar *to join together*

PAST PARTICIPLE

aun**ado**

GERUND

aun**ando**

IMPERATIVE

a**ún**a
auna**d**

PRESENT		PRESENT SUBJUNCTIVE	
yo	a**ún**o	yo	a**ún**e
tú	a**ún**as	tú	a**ún**es
él	a**ún**a	él	a**ún**e
nosotros	aun**amos**	nosotros	aun**emos**
vosotros	aun**áis**	vosotros	aun**éis**
ellos	a**ún**an	ellos	a**ún**en

FUTURE		CONDITIONAL	
yo	aunar**é**	yo	aunar**ía**
tú	aunar**ás**	tú	aunar**ías**
él	aunar**á**	él	aunar**ía**
nosotros	aunar**emos**	nosotros	aunar**íamos**
vosotros	aunar**éis**	vosotros	aunar**íais**
ellos	aunar**án**	ellos	aunar**ían**

IMPERFECT		PRETERITE	
yo	aun**aba**	yo	aun**é**
tú	aun**abas**	tú	aun**aste**
él	aun**aba**	él	aun**ó**
nosotros	aun**ábamos**	nosotros	aun**amos**
vosotros	aun**abais**	vosotros	aun**asteis**
ellos	aun**aban**	ellos	aun**aron**

---

avergonzar *to shame*

PAST PARTICIPLE

avergonz**ado**

GERUND

avergonz**ando**

IMPERATIVE

avergü**enza**
avergonza**d**

PRESENT		PRESENT SUBJUNCTIVE	
yo	avergü**enzo**	yo	avergü**ence**
tú	avergü**enzas**	tú	avergü**ences**
él	avergü**enza**	él	avergü**ence**
nosotros	avergonz**amos**	nosotros	avergonc**emos**
vosotros	avergonz**áis**	vosotros	avergonc**éis**
ellos	avergü**enzan**	ellos	avergü**encen**

FUTURE		CONDITIONAL	
yo	avergonzar**é**	yo	avergonzar**ía**
tú	avergonzar**ás**	tú	avergonzar**ías**
él	avergonzar**á**	él	avergonzar**ía**
nosotros	avergonzar**emos**	nosotros	avergonzar**íamos**
vosotros	avergonzar**éis**	vosotros	avergonzar**íais**
ellos	avergonzar**án**	ellos	avergonzar**ían**

IMPERFECT		PRETERITE	
yo	avergonz**aba**	yo	avergon**cé**
tú	avergonz**abas**	tú	avergonz**aste**
él	avergonz**aba**	él	avergonz**ó**
nosotros	avergonz**ábamos**	nosotros	avergonz**amos**
vosotros	avergonz**abais**	vosotros	avergonz**asteis**
ellos	avergonz**aban**	ellos	avergonz**aron**

averiguar *to find out*

PAST PARTICIPLE	IMPERATIVE
averigu**ado**	averigu**a**
	averigu**ad**
GERUND	
averigu**ando**	

PRESENT	PRESENT SUBJUNCTIVE
yo averigu**o**	yo **averigüe**
tú averigu**as**	tú **averigües**
él averigu**a**	él **averigüe**
nosotros averigu**amos**	nosotros **averigüemos**
vosotros averigu**áis**	vosotros **averigüéis**
ellos averigu**an**	ellos **averigüen**

FUTURE	CONDITIONAL
yo averiguar**é**	yo averiguar**ía**
tú averiguar**ás**	tú averiguar**ías**
él averiguar**á**	él averiguar**ía**
nosotros averiguar**emos**	nosotros averiguar**íamos**
vosotros averiguar**éis**	vosotros averiguar**íais**
ellos averiguar**án**	ellos averiguar**ían**

IMPERFECT	PRETERITE
yo averigu**aba**	yo **averigüé**
tú averigu**abas**	tú averigu**aste**
él averigu**aba**	él averigu**ó**
nosotros averigu**ábamos**	nosotros averigu**amos**
vosotros averigu**abais**	vosotros averigu**asteis**
ellos averigu**aban**	ellos averigu**aron**

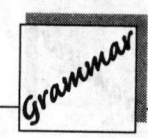
Grammar

---

bendecir *to bless*

PAST PARTICIPLE

bendec**ido**

GERUND

bendiciendo

IMPERATIVE

bendice
bendeci**d**

PRESENT		PRESENT SUBJUNCTIVE	
yo	**bendigo**	**yo**	**bendiga**
tú	**bendices**	**tú**	**bendigas**
él	**bendice**	**él**	**bendiga**
nosotros	bendec**imos**	**nosotros**	**bendigamos**
vosotros	bendec**ís**	**vosotros**	**bendigáis**
ellos	**bendicen**	**ellos**	**bendigan**

FUTURE		CONDITIONAL	
yo	bendecir**é**	**yo**	bendecir**ía**
tú	bendecir**ás**	**tú**	bendecir**ías**
él	bendecir**á**	**él**	bendecir**ía**
nosotros	bendecir**emos**	**nosotros**	bendecir**íamos**
vosotros	bendecir**éis**	**vosotros**	bendecir**íais**
ellos	bendecir**án**	**ellos**	bendecir**ían**

IMPERFECT		PRETERITE	
yo	bendec**ía**	**yo**	**bendije**
tú	bendec**ías**	**tú**	**bendijiste**
él	bendec**ía**	**él**	**bendijo**
nosotros	bendec**íamos**	**nosotros**	**bendijimos**
vosotros	bendec**íais**	**vosotros**	**bendijisteis**
ellos	bendec**ían**	**ellos**	**bendijeron**

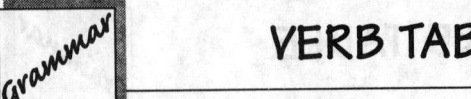

caber to fit

PAST PARTICIPLE	IMPERATIVE
cab**ido**	cab**e**
	cab**ed**
GERUND	
cab**iendo**	

PRESENT	PRESENT SUBJUNCTIVE
yo **quepo**	yo **quepa**
tú cab**es**	tú **quepas**
él cab**e**	él **quepa**
nosotros cab**emos**	nosotros **quepamos**
vosotros cab**éis**	vosotros **quepáis**
ellos cab**en**	ellos **quepan**

FUTURE	CONDITIONAL
yo **cabré**	yo **cabría**
tú **cabrás**	tú **cabrías**
él **cabrá**	él **cabría**
nosotros **cabremos**	nosotros **cabríamos**
vosotros **cabréis**	vosotros **cabríais**
ellos **cabrán**	ellos **cabrían**

IMPERFECT	PRETERITE
yo cab**ía**	yo **cupe**
tú cab**ías**	tú **cupiste**
él cab**ía**	él **cupo**
nosotros cab**íamos**	nosotros **cupimos**
vosotros cab**íais**	vosotros **cupisteis**
ellos cab**ían**	ellos **cupieron**

VERB TABLE

caer *to fall*

PAST PARTICIPLE	IMPERATIVE
caído	**cae**
	caed
GERUND	
cayendo	

PRESENT		PRESENT SUBJUNCTIVE	
yo	**caigo**	yo	**caiga**
tú	**caes**	tú	**caigas**
él	**cae**	él	**caiga**
nosotros	**caemos**	nosotros	**caigamos**
vosotros	**caéis**	vosotros	**caigáis**
ellos	**caen**	ellos	**caigan**

FUTURE		CONDITIONAL	
yo	**caeré**	yo	**caería**
tú	**caerás**	tú	**caerías**
él	**caerá**	él	**caería**
nosotros	**caeremos**	nosotros	**caeríamos**
vosotros	**caeréis**	vosotros	**caeríais**
ellos	**caerán**	ellos	**caerían**

IMPERFECT		PRETERITE	
yo	**caía**	yo	**caí**
tú	**caías**	tú	**caíste**
él	**caía**	él	**cayó**
nosotros	**caíamos**	nosotros	**caímos**
vosotros	**caíais**	vosotros	**caísteis**
ellos	**caían**	ellos	**cayeron**

cocer *to boil*

PAST PARTICIPLE	IMPERATIVE
coc**ido**	**cuece** coc**ed**
GERUND	
coc**iendo**	

PRESENT		PRESENT SUBJUNCTIVE	
yo	**cuezo**	yo	**cueza**
tú	**cueces**	tú	**cuezas**
él	**cuece**	él	**cueza**
nosotros	coc**emos**	nosotros	**cozamos**
vosotros	coc**éis**	vosotros	**cozáis**
ellos	**cuecen**	ellos	**cuezan**

FUTURE		CONDITIONAL	
yo	coceré	yo	cocería
tú	cocerás	tú	cocerías
él	cocerá	él	cocería
nosotros	coceremos	nosotros	coceríamos
vosotros	coceréis	vosotros	coceríais
ellos	cocerán	ellos	cocerían

IMPERFECT		PRETERITE	
yo	cocía	yo	cocí
tú	cocías	tú	coc**iste**
él	cocía	él	coc**ió**
nosotros	cocíamos	nosotros	coc**imos**
vosotros	cocíais	vosotros	coc**isteis**
ellos	cocían	ellos	coc**ieron**

coger *to catch*

PAST PARTICIPLE	IMPERATIVE
cog**ido**	cog**e**
	cog**ed**
GERUND	
cog**iendo**	

PRESENT		PRESENT SUBJUNCTIVE	
yo	cojo	yo	coja
tú	coges	tú	cojas
él	coge	él	coja
nosotros	cogemos	nosotros	cojamos
vosotros	cogéis	vosotros	cojáis
ellos	cogen	ellos	cojan

FUTURE		CONDITIONAL	
yo	cogeré	yo	cogería
tú	cogerás	tú	cogerías
él	cogerá	él	cogería
nosotros	cogeremos	nosotros	cogeríamos
vosotros	cogeréis	vosotros	cogeríais
ellos	cogerán	ellos	cogerían

IMPERFECT		PRETERITE	
yo	cogía	yo	cogí
tú	cogías	tú	cogiste
él	cogía	él	cogió
nosotros	cogíamos	nosotros	cogimos
vosotros	cogíais	vosotros	cogisteis
ellos	cogían	ellos	cogieron

conducir *to drive, to lead*

PAST PARTICIPLE	IMPERATIVE
conduc**ido**	conduc**e**
	conduc**id**
GERUND	
conduc**iendo**	

PRESENT		PRESENT SUBJUNCTIVE	
yo	**conduzco**	yo	**conduzca**
tú	conduc**es**	tú	**conduzcas**
él	conduc**e**	él	**conduzca**
nosotros	conduc**imos**	nosotros	**conduzcamos**
vosotros	conduc**ís**	vosotros	**conduzcáis**
ellos	conduc**en**	ellos	**conduzcan**

FUTURE		CONDITIONAL	
yo	conducir**é**	yo	conducir**ía**
tú	conducir**ás**	tú	conducir**ías**
él	conducir**á**	él	conducir**ía**
nosotros	conducir**emos**	nosotros	conducir**íamos**
vosotros	conducir**éis**	vosotros	conducir**íais**
ellos	conducir**án**	ellos	conducir**ían**

IMPERFECT		PRETERITE	
yo	conduc**ía**	yo	**conduje**
tú	conduc**ías**	tú	**condujiste**
él	conduc**ía**	él	**condujo**
nosotros	conduc**íamos**	nosotros	**condujimos**
vosotros	conduc**íais**	vosotros	**condujisteis**
ellos	conduc**ían**	ellos	**condujeron**

construir *to build*	
PAST PARTICIPLE	IMPERATIVE
constru**ido**	**construye**
	construi**d**
GERUND	
construyendo	

PRESENT		PRESENT SUBJUNCTIVE	
yo	construyo	yo	construya
tú	construyes	tú	construyas
él	construye	él	construya
nosotros	construimos	nosotros	construyamos
vosotros	construís	vosotros	construyáis
ellos	construyen	ellos	construyan
FUTURE		CONDITIONAL	
yo	construiré	yo	construiría
tú	construirás	tú	construirías
él	construirá	él	construiría
nosotros	construiremos	nosotros	construiríamos
vosotros	construiréis	vosotros	construiríais
ellos	construirán	ellos	construirían
IMPERFECT		PRETERITE	
yo	construía	yo	construí
tú	construías	tú	construiste
él	construía	él	construyó
nosotros	construíamos	nosotros	construimos
vosotros	construíais	vosotros	construisteis
ellos	construían	ellos	construyeron

contar *to tell, to count*

PAST PARTICIPLE	IMPERATIVE
cont**ado**	**cuenta**
	conta**d**
GERUND	
cont**ando**	

PRESENT		PRESENT SUBJUNCTIVE	
yo	**cuento**	yo	**cuente**
tú	**cuentas**	tú	**cuentes**
él	**cuenta**	él	**cuente**
nosotros	cont**amos**	nosotros	cont**emos**
vosotros	cont**áis**	vosotros	cont**éis**
ellos	**cuentan**	ellos	**cuenten**

FUTURE		CONDITIONAL	
yo	contar**é**	yo	contar**ía**
tú	contar**ás**	tú	contar**ías**
él	contar**á**	él	contar**ía**
nosotros	contar**emos**	nosotros	contar**íamos**
vosotros	contar**éis**	vosotros	contar**íais**
ellos	contar**án**	ellos	contar**ían**

IMPERFECT		PRETERITE	
yo	cont**aba**	yo	cont**é**
tú	cont**abas**	tú	cont**aste**
él	cont**aba**	él	cont**ó**
nosotros	cont**ábamos**	nosotros	cont**amos**
vosotros	cont**abais**	vosotros	cont**asteis**
ellos	cont**aban**	ellos	cont**aron**

crecer *to grow*

PAST PARTICIPLE

crec**ido**

GERUND

crec**iendo**

IMPERATIVE

crec**e**
crec**ed**

PRESENT		PRESENT SUBJUNCTIVE	
yo	crezco	yo	crezca
tú	creces	tú	crezcas
él	crece	él	crezca
nosotros	crecemos	nosotros	crezcamos
vosotros	crecéis	vosotros	crezcáis
ellos	crecen	ellos	crezcan

FUTURE		CONDITIONAL	
yo	creceré	yo	crecería
tú	crecerás	tú	crecerías
él	crecerá	él	crecería
nosotros	creceremos	nosotros	creceríamos
vosotros	creceréis	vosotros	creceríais
ellos	crecerán	ellos	crecerían

IMPERFECT		PRETERITE	
yo	crecía	yo	crecí
tú	crecías	tú	creciste
él	crecía	él	creció
nosotros	crecíamos	nosotros	crecimos
vosotros	crecíais	vosotros	crecisteis
ellos	crecían	ellos	crecieron

cruzar *to cross*

PAST PARTICIPLE	IMPERATIVE
cruz**ado**	cruz**a**
	cruz**ad**
GERUND	
cruz**ando**	

PRESENT		PRESENT SUBJUNCTIVE	
yo	cruz**o**	yo	cru**ce**
tú	cruz**as**	tú	cru**ces**
él	cruz**a**	él	cru**ce**
nosotros	cruz**amos**	nosotros	cru**cemos**
vosotros	cruz**áis**	vosotros	cru**céis**
ellos	cruz**an**	ellos	cru**cen**

FUTURE		CONDITIONAL	
yo	cruzar**é**	yo	cruzar**ía**
tú	cruzar**ás**	tú	cruzar**ías**
él	cruzar**á**	él	cruzar**ía**
nosotros	cruzar**emos**	nosotros	cruzar**íamos**
vosotros	cruzar**éis**	vosotros	cruzar**íais**
ellos	cruzar**án**	ellos	cruzar**ían**

IMPERFECT		PRETERITE	
yo	cruz**aba**	yo	cru**cé**
tú	cruz**abas**	tú	cruz**aste**
él	cruz**aba**	él	cruz**ó**
nosotros	cruz**ábamos**	nosotros	cruz**amos**
vosotros	cruz**abais**	vosotros	cruz**asteis**
ellos	cruz**aban**	ellos	cruz**aron**

VERB TABLE

cubrir *to cover*

PAST PARTICIPLE	IMPERATIVE
cubierto	cubre
	cubrid
GERUND	
cubriendo	

PRESENT		PRESENT SUBJUNCTIVE	
yo	cubro	**yo**	cubra
tú	cubres	**tú**	cubras
él	cubre	**él**	cubra
nosotros	cubrimos	**nosotros**	cubramos
vosotros	cubrís	**vosotros**	cubráis
ellos	cubren	**ellos**	cubran

FUTURE		CONDITIONAL	
yo	cubriré	**yo**	cubriría
tú	cubrirás	**tú**	cubrirías
él	cubrirá	**él**	cubriría
nosotros	cubriremos	**nosotros**	cubriríamos
vosotros	cubriréis	**vosotros**	cubriríais
ellos	cubrirán	**ellos**	cubrirían

IMPERFECT		PRETERITE	
yo	cubría	**yo**	cubrí
tú	cubrías	**tú**	cubriste
él	cubría	**él**	cubrió
nosotros	cubríamos	**nosotros**	cubrimos
vosotros	cubríais	**vosotros**	cubristeis
ellos	cubrían	**ellos**	cubrieron

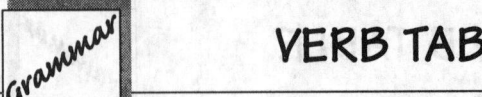

dar *to give*

PAST PARTICIPLE	IMPERATIVE
d**ado**	d**a**
	da**d**
GERUND	
d**ando**	

PRESENT

yo	**doy**
tú	**das**
él	**da**
nosotros	**damos**
vosotros	**dais**
ellos	**dan**

PRESENT SUBJUNCTIVE

yo	**dé**
tú	**des**
él	**dé**
nosotros	**demos**
vosotros	**deis**
ellos	**den**

FUTURE

yo	dar**é**
tú	dar**ás**
él	dar**á**
nosotros	dar**emos**
vosotros	dar**éis**
ellos	dar**án**

CONDITIONAL

yo	dar**ía**
tú	dar**ías**
él	dar**ía**
nosotros	dar**íamos**
vosotros	dar**íais**
ellos	dar**ían**

IMPERFECT

yo	d**aba**
tú	d**abas**
él	d**aba**
nosotros	d**ábamos**
vosotros	d**abais**
ellos	d**aban**

PRETERITE

yo	**di**
tú	**diste**
él	**dio**
nosotros	**dimos**
vosotros	**disteis**
ellos	**dieron**

decir *to say*

PAST PARTICIPLE

dicho

GERUND

diciendo

IMPERATIVE

di
deci**d**

PRESENT		PRESENT SUBJUNCTIVE	
yo	**digo**	yo	**diga**
tú	**dices**	tú	**digas**
él	**dice**	él	**diga**
nosotros	**decimos**	nosotros	**digamos**
vosotros	**decís**	vosotros	**digáis**
ellos	**dicen**	ellos	**digan**

FUTURE		CONDITIONAL	
yo	**diré**	yo	**diría**
tú	**dirás**	tú	**dirías**
él	**dirá**	él	**diría**
nosotros	**diremos**	nosotros	**diríamos**
vosotros	**diréis**	vosotros	**diríais**
ellos	**dirán**	ellos	**dirían**

IMPERFECT		PRETERITE	
yo	**decía**	yo	**dije**
tú	**decías**	tú	**dijiste**
él	**decía**	él	**dijo**
nosotros	**decíamos**	nosotros	**dijimos**
vosotros	**decíais**	vosotros	**dijisteis**
ellos	**decían**	ellos	**dijeron**

dirigir *to direct*

PAST PARTICIPLE	IMPERATIVE
dirig**ido**	dirig**e**
	dirig**id**
GERUND	
dirig**iendo**	

PRESENT	PRESENT SUBJUNCTIVE
yo **dirijo**	yo **dirija**
tú dirig**es**	tú **dirijas**
él dirig**e**	él **dirija**
nosotros dirig**imos**	nosotros **dirijamos**
vosotros dirig**ís**	vosotros **dirijáis**
ellos dirig**en**	ellos **dirijan**

FUTURE	CONDITIONAL
yo dirigir**é**	yo dirigir**ía**
tú dirigir**ás**	tú dirigir**ías**
él dirigir**á**	él dirigir**ía**
nosotros dirigir**emos**	nosotros dirigir**íamos**
vosotros dirigir**éis**	vosotros dirigir**íais**
ellos dirigir**án**	ellos dirigir**ían**

IMPERFECT	PRETERITE
yo dirig**ía**	yo dirig**í**
tú dirig**ías**	tú dirig**iste**
él dirig**ía**	él dirig**ió**
nosotros dirig**íamos**	nosotros dirig**imos**
vosotros dirig**íais**	vosotros dirig**isteis**
ellos dirig**ían**	ellos dirig**ieron**

---

distinguir *to distinguish*

PAST PARTICIPLE

distingu**ido**

GERUND

distingu**iendo**

IMPERATIVE

distingu**e**
distingu**id**

PRESENT		PRESENT SUBJUNCTIVE	
yo	disting**o**	yo	disting**a**
tú	disting**ues**	tú	disting**as**
él	disting**ue**	él	disting**a**
nosotros	distingu**imos**	nosotros	disting**amos**
vosotros	distingu**ís**	vosotros	disting**áis**
ellos	disting**uen**	ellos	disting**an**

FUTURE		CONDITIONAL	
yo	distinguir**é**	yo	distinguir**ía**
tú	distinguir**ás**	tú	distinguir**ías**
él	distinguir**á**	él	distinguir**ía**
nosotros	distinguir**emos**	nosotros	distinguir**íamos**
vosotros	distinguir**éis**	vosotros	distinguir**íais**
ellos	distinguir**án**	ellos	distinguir**ían**

IMPERFECT		PRETERITE	
yo	distingu**ía**	yo	distingu**í**
tú	distingu**ías**	tú	distingu**iste**
él	distingu**ía**	él	distingu**ió**
nosotros	distingu**íamos**	nosotros	distingu**imos**
vosotros	distingu**íais**	vosotros	distingu**isteis**
ellos	distingu**ían**	ellos	distingu**ieron**

dormir *to sleep*

PAST PARTICIPLE	IMPERATIVE
dorm**ido**	**duerme**
	dorm**id**
GERUND	
dur**miendo**	

PRESENT		PRESENT SUBJUNCTIVE	
yo	**duermo**	yo	**duerma**
tú	**duermes**	tú	**duermas**
él	**duerme**	él	**duerma**
nosotros	dorm**imos**	nosotros	**durmamos**
vosotros	dorm**ís**	vosotros	**durmáis**
ellos	**duermen**	ellos	**duerman**

FUTURE		CONDITIONAL	
yo	dormir**é**	yo	dormir**ía**
tú	dormir**ás**	tú	dormir**ías**
él	dormir**á**	él	dormir**ía**
nosotros	dormir**emos**	nosotros	dormir**íamos**
vosotros	dormir**éis**	vosotros	dormir**íais**
ellos	dormir**án**	ellos	dormir**ían**

IMPERFECT		PRETERITE	
yo	dorm**ía**	yo	dorm**í**
tú	dorm**ías**	tú	dorm**iste**
él	dorm**ía**	él	**durmió**
nosotros	dorm**íamos**	nosotros	dorm**imos**
vosotros	dorm**íais**	vosotros	dorm**isteis**
ellos	dorm**ían**	ellos	**durmieron**

elegir *to choose*

PAST PARTICIPLE	IMPERATIVE
elegido	
	elige
	elegid
GERUND	
eligiendo	

PRESENT		PRESENT SUBJUNCTIVE	
yo	elijo	yo	elija
tú	eliges	tú	elijas
él	elige	él	elija
nosotros	elegimos	nosotros	elijamos
vosotros	elegís	vosotros	elijáis
ellos	eligen	ellos	elijan

FUTURE		CONDITIONAL	
yo	elegiré	yo	elegiría
tú	elegirás	tú	elegirías
él	elegirá	él	elegiría
nosotros	elegiremos	nosotros	elegiríamos
vosotros	elegiréis	vosotros	elegiríais
ellos	elegirán	ellos	elegirían

IMPERFECT		PRETERITE	
yo	elegía	yo	elegí
tú	elegías	tú	elegiste
él	elegía	él	eligió
nosotros	elegíamos	nosotros	elegimos
vosotros	elegíais	vosotros	elegisteis
ellos	elegían	ellos	eligieron

empezar *to begin*

PAST PARTICIPLE	IMPERATIVE
empez**ado**	**empieza**
	empez**ad**
GERUND	
empez**ando**	

PRESENT		PRESENT SUBJUNCTIVE	
yo	**empiezo**	yo	**empiece**
tú	**empiezas**	tú	**empieces**
él	**empieza**	él	**empiece**
nosotros	empez**amos**	nosotros	**empecemos**
vosotros	empez**áis**	vosotros	**empecéis**
ellos	**empiezan**	ellos	**empiecen**

FUTURE		CONDITIONAL	
yo	empezar**é**	yo	empezar**ía**
tú	empezar**ás**	tú	empezar**ías**
él	empezar**á**	él	empezar**ía**
nosotros	empezar**emos**	nosotros	empezar**íamos**
vosotros	empezar**éis**	vosotros	empezar**íais**
ellos	empezar**án**	ellos	empezar**ían**

IMPERFECT		PRETERITE	
yo	empez**aba**	yo	**empecé**
tú	empez**abas**	tú	empez**aste**
él	empez**aba**	él	empez**ó**
nosotros	empez**ábamos**	nosotros	empez**amos**
vosotros	empez**abais**	vosotros	empez**asteis**
ellos	empez**aban**	ellos	empez**aron**

---

entender *to understand*

PAST PARTICIPLE	IMPERATIVE
entend**ido**	entiende
	entend**ed**
GERUND	
entend**iendo**	

PRESENT		PRESENT SUBJUNCTIVE	
yo	entiendo	yo	entienda
tú	entiendes	tú	entiendas
él	entiende	él	entienda
nosotros	entend**emos**	nosotros	entend**amos**
vosotros	entend**éis**	vosotros	entend**áis**
ellos	entienden	ellos	entiendan

FUTURE		CONDITIONAL	
yo	entender**é**	yo	entender**ía**
tú	entender**ás**	tú	entender**ías**
él	entender**á**	él	entender**ía**
nosotros	entender**emos**	nosotros	entender**íamos**
vosotros	entender**éis**	vosotros	entender**íais**
ellos	entender**án**	ellos	entender**ían**

IMPERFECT		PRETERITE	
yo	entend**ía**	yo	entend**í**
tú	entend**ías**	tú	entend**iste**
él	entend**ía**	él	entend**ió**
nosotros	entend**íamos**	nosotros	entend**imos**
vosotros	entend**íais**	vosotros	entend**isteis**
ellos	entend**ían**	ellos	entend**ieron**

enviar *to send*

PAST PARTICIPLE	IMPERATIVE
enviado	envía
	enviad
GERUND	
enviando	

PRESENT		PRESENT SUBJUNCTIVE	
yo	envío	yo	envíe
tú	envías	tú	envíes
él	envía	él	envíe
nosotros	enviamos	nosotros	enviemos
vosotros	enviáis	vosotros	enviéis
ellos	envían	ellos	envíen

FUTURE		CONDITIONAL	
yo	enviaré	yo	enviaría
tú	enviarás	tú	enviarías
él	enviará	él	enviaría
nosotros	enviaremos	nosotros	enviaríamos
vosotros	enviaréis	vosotros	enviaríais
ellos	enviarán	ellos	enviarían

IMPERFECT		PRETERITE	
yo	enviaba	yo	envié
tú	enviabas	tú	enviaste
él	enviaba	él	envió
nosotros	enviábamos	nosotros	enviamos
vosotros	enviabais	vosotros	enviasteis
ellos	enviaban	ellos	enviaron

erguir *to erect*

PAST PARTICIPLE	IMPERATIVE
ergui**do**	
	yergue
	ergui**d**
GERUND	
irguiendo	

PRESENT		PRESENT SUBJUNCTIVE	
yo	yergo	yo	yerga
tú	yergues	tú	yergas
él	yergue	él	yerga
nosotros	erguimos	nosotros	irgamos
vosotros	erguís	vosotros	irgáis
ellos	yerguen	ellos	yergan

FUTURE		CONDITIONAL	
yo	erguiré	yo	erguiría
tú	erguirás	tú	erguirías
él	erguirá	él	erguiría
nosotros	erguiremos	nosotros	erguiríamos
vosotros	erguiréis	vosotros	erguiríais
ellos	erguirán	ellos	erguirían

IMPERFECT		PRETERITE	
yo	erguía	yo	erguí
tú	erguías	tú	erguiste
él	erguía	él	**irguió**
nosotros	erguíamos	nosotros	erguimos
vosotros	erguíais	vosotros	erguisteis
ellos	erguían	ellos	**irguieron**

errar *to err*

PAST PARTICIPLE	IMPERATIVE
err**ado**	**yerra**
	erra**d**
GERUND	
err**ando**	

PRESENT		PRESENT SUBJUNCTIVE	
yo	**yerro**	yo	**yerre**
tú	**yerras**	tú	**yerres**
él	**yerra**	él	**yerre**
nosotros	err**amos**	nosotros	err**emos**
vosotros	err**áis**	vosotros	err**éis**
ellos	**yerran**	ellos	**yerren**

FUTURE		CONDITIONAL	
yo	errar**é**	yo	errar**ía**
tú	errar**ás**	tú	errar**ías**
él	errar**á**	él	errar**ía**
nosotros	errar**emos**	nosotros	errar**íamos**
vosotros	errar**éis**	vosotros	errar**íais**
ellos	errar**án**	ellos	errar**ían**

IMPERFECT		PRETERITE	
yo	err**aba**	yo	err**é**
tú	err**abas**	tú	err**aste**
él	err**aba**	él	err**ó**
nosotros	err**ábamos**	nosotros	err**amos**
vosotros	err**abais**	vosotros	err**asteis**
ellos	err**aban**	ellos	err**aron**

escribir *to write*

PAST PARTICIPLE	IMPERATIVE
escrito	escrib**e**
	escrib**id**
GERUND	
escrib**iendo**	

PRESENT		PRESENT SUBJUNCTIVE	
yo	escribo	yo	escriba
tú	escribes	tú	escribas
él	escribe	él	escriba
nosotros	escribimos	nosotros	escribamos
vosotros	escribís	vosotros	escribáis
ellos	escriben	ellos	escriban

FUTURE		CONDITIONAL	
yo	escribiré	yo	escribiría
tú	escribirás	tú	escribirías
él	escribirá	él	escribiría
nosotros	escribiremos	nosotros	escribiríamos
vosotros	escribiréis	vosotros	escribiríais
ellos	escribirán	ellos	escribirían

IMPERFECT		PRETERITE	
yo	escribía	yo	escribí
tú	escribías	tú	escribiste
él	escribía	él	escribió
nosotros	escribíamos	nosotros	escribimos
vosotros	escribíais	vosotros	escribisteis
ellos	escribían	ellos	escribieron

estar *to be*

PAST PARTICIPLE	IMPERATIVE
est**ado**	est**á**
	est**ad**
GERUND	
est**ando**	

PRESENT		PRESENT SUBJUNCTIVE	
yo	**estoy**	yo	**esté**
tú	**estás**	tú	**estés**
él	**está**	él	**esté**
nosotros	est**amos**	nosotros	est**emos**
vosotros	est**áis**	vosotros	est**éis**
ellos	**están**	ellos	**estén**

FUTURE		CONDITIONAL	
yo	estar**é**	yo	estar**ía**
tú	estar**ás**	tú	estar**ías**
él	estar**á**	él	estar**ía**
nosotros	estar**emos**	nosotros	estar**íamos**
vosotros	estar**éis**	vosotros	estar**íais**
ellos	estar**án**	ellos	estar**ían**

IMPERFECT		PRETERITE	
yo	est**aba**	yo	**estuve**
tú	est**abas**	tú	**estuviste**
él	est**aba**	él	**estuvo**
nosotros	est**ábamos**	nosotros	**estuvimos**
vosotros	est**abais**	vosotros	**estuvisteis**
ellos	est**aban**	ellos	**estuvieron**

---

freír *to fry*

PAST PARTICIPLE	IMPERATIVE
frito	**fríe**
	freíd
GERUND	
friendo	

PRESENT		PRESENT SUBJUNCTIVE	
yo	frío	yo	fría
tú	fríes	tú	frías
él	fríe	él	fría
nosotros	freímos	nosotros	friamos
vosotros	freís	vosotros	friáis
ellos	fríen	ellos	frían

FUTURE		CONDITIONAL	
yo	freiré	yo	freiría
tú	freirás	tú	freirías
él	freirá	él	freiría
nosotros	freiremos	nosotros	freiríamos
vosotros	freiréis	vosotros	freiríais
ellos	freirán	ellos	freirían

IMPERFECT		PRETERITE	
yo	freía	yo	freí
tú	freías	tú	freíste
él	freía	él	frió
nosotros	freíamos	nosotros	freímos
vosotros	freíais	vosotros	freísteis
ellos	freían	ellos	frieron

gruñir to grunt

PAST PARTICIPLE	IMPERATIVE
gruñ**ido**	gruñ**e**
	gruñ**id**
GERUND	
gruñendo	

PRESENT		PRESENT SUBJUNCTIVE	
yo	gruñ**o**	yo	gruñ**a**
tú	gruñ**es**	tú	gruñ**as**
él	gruñ**e**	él	gruñ**a**
nosotros	gruñ**imos**	nosotros	gruñ**amos**
vosotros	gruñ**ís**	vosotros	gruñ**áis**
ellos	gruñ**en**	ellos	gruñ**an**

FUTURE		CONDITIONAL	
yo	gruñir**é**	yo	gruñir**ía**
tú	gruñir**ás**	tú	gruñir**ías**
él	gruñir**á**	él	gruñir**ía**
nosotros	gruñir**emos**	nosotros	gruñir**íamos**
vosotros	gruñir**éis**	vosotros	gruñir**íais**
ellos	gruñir**án**	ellos	gruñir**ían**

IMPERFECT		PRETERITE	
yo	gruñ**ía**	yo	gruñ**í**
tú	gruñ**ías**	tú	gruñ**iste**
él	gruñ**ía**	él	**gruñó**
nosotros	gruñ**íamos**	nosotros	gruñ**imos**
vosotros	gruñ**íais**	vosotros	gruñ**isteis**
ellos	gruñ**ían**	ellos	**gruñeron**

---

haber *to have (auxiliary)*

PAST PARTICIPLE	IMPERATIVE
hab**ido**	*not used*

GERUND

hab**iendo**

PRESENT		PRESENT SUBJUNCTIVE	
yo	he	yo	haya
tú	has	tú	hayas
él	ha	él	haya
nosotros	hemos	nosotros	hayamos
vosotros	hab**éis**	vosotros	hayáis
ellos	han	ellos	hayan

FUTURE		CONDITIONAL	
yo	habré	yo	habría
tú	habrás	tú	habrías
él	habrá	él	habría
nosotros	habremos	nosotros	habríamos
vosotros	habréis	vosotros	habríais
ellos	habrán	ellos	habrían

IMPERFECT		PRETERITE	
yo	había	yo	hube
tú	habías	tú	hubiste
él	había	él	hubo
nosotros	habíamos	nosotros	hubimos
vosotros	habíais	vosotros	hubisteis
ellos	habían	ellos	hubieron

hacer *to do, to make*

PAST PARTICIPLE	IMPERATIVE
hecho	**haz**
	hace**d**
GERUND	
hac**iendo**	

PRESENT		PRESENT SUBJUNCTIVE	
yo	**hago**	yo	**haga**
tú	hac**es**	tú	**hagas**
él	hace	él	**haga**
nosotros	hac**emos**	nosotros	**hagamos**
vosotros	hac**éis**	vosotros	**hagáis**
ellos	hac**en**	ellos	**hagan**

FUTURE		CONDITIONAL	
yo	**haré**	yo	**haría**
tú	**harás**	tú	**harías**
él	**hará**	él	**haría**
nosotros	**haremos**	nosotros	**haríamos**
vosotros	**haréis**	vosotros	**haríais**
ellos	**harán**	ellos	**harían**

IMPERFECT		PRETERITE	
yo	hac**ía**	yo	**hice**
tú	hac**ías**	tú	**hiciste**
él	hac**ía**	él	**hizo**
nosotros	hac**íamos**	nosotros	**hicimos**
vosotros	hac**íais**	vosotros	**hicisteis**
ellos	hac**ían**	ellos	**hicieron**

hay *there is, there are*

PAST PARTICIPLE	IMPERATIVE
hab**ido**	*not used*
GERUND	
hab**iendo**	

PRESENT	PRESENT SUBJUNCTIVE
hay	**haya**

FUTURE	CONDITIONAL
habrá	**habría**

IMPERFECT	PRETERITE
había	**hubo**

ir *to go*

PAST PARTICIPLE	IMPERATIVE
ido	**ve**
	id
GERUND	
yendo	

PRESENT		PRESENT SUBJUNCTIVE	
yo	**voy**	yo	**vaya**
tú	**vas**	tú	**vayas**
él	**va**	él	**vaya**
nosotros	**vamos**	nosotros	**vayamos**
vosotros	**vais**	vosotros	**vayáis**
ellos	**van**	ellos	**vayan**

FUTURE		CONDITIONAL	
yo	**iré**	yo	**iría**
tú	**irás**	tú	**irías**
él	**irá**	él	**iría**
nosotros	**iremos**	nosotros	**iríamos**
vosotros	**iréis**	vosotros	**iríais**
ellos	**irán**	ellos	**irían**

IMPERFECT		PRETERITE	
yo	**iba**	yo	**fui**
tú	**ibas**	tú	**fuiste**
él	**iba**	él	**fue**
nosotros	**íbamos**	nosotros	**fuimos**
vosotros	**ibais**	vosotros	**fuisteis**
ellos	**iban**	ellos	**fueron**

jugar *to play*

PAST PARTICIPLE	IMPERATIVE
jug**ado**	**juega**
	juga**d**
GERUND	
jug**ando**	

PRESENT		PRESENT SUBJUNCTIVE	
yo	**juego**	yo	**juegue**
tú	**juegas**	tú	**juegues**
él	**juega**	él	**juegue**
nosotros	jug**amos**	nosotros	**juguemos**
vosotros	jug**áis**	vosotros	**juguéis**
ellos	**juegan**	ellos	**jueguen**

FUTURE		CONDITIONAL	
yo	jugar**é**	yo	jugar**ía**
tú	jugar**ás**	tú	jugar**ías**
él	jugar**á**	él	jugar**ía**
nosotros	jugar**emos**	nosotros	jugar**íamos**
vosotros	jugar**éis**	vosotros	jugar**íais**
ellos	jugar**án**	ellos	jugar**ían**

IMPERFECT		PRETERITE	
yo	jug**aba**	yo	**jugué**
tú	jug**abas**	tú	jug**aste**
él	jug**aba**	él	jug**ó**
nosotros	jug**ábamos**	nosotros	jug**amos**
vosotros	jug**abais**	vosotros	jug**asteis**
ellos	jug**aban**	ellos	jug**aron**

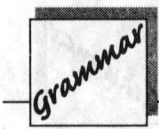

leer *to read*

PAST PARTICIPLE	IMPERATIVE
leído	lee
	leed
GERUND	
leyendo	

PRESENT		PRESENT SUBJUNCTIVE	
yo	leo	yo	lea
tú	lees	tú	leas
él	lee	él	lea
nosotros	leemos	nosotros	leamos
vosotros	leéis	vosotros	leáis
ellos	leen	ellos	lean

FUTURE		CONDITIONAL	
yo	leeré	yo	leería
tú	leerás	tú	leerías
él	leerá	él	leería
nosotros	leeremos	nosotros	leeríamos
vosotros	leeréis	vosotros	leeríais
ellos	leerán	ellos	leerían

IMPERFECT		PRETERITE	
yo	leía	yo	leí
tú	leías	tú	leíste
él	leía	él	leyó
nosotros	leíamos	nosotros	leímos
vosotros	leíais	vosotros	leísteis
ellos	leían	ellos	leyeron

lucir *to shine*

PAST PARTICIPLE	IMPERATIVE
lucido	luce
	lucid
GERUND	
luciendo	

PRESENT		PRESENT SUBJUNCTIVE	
yo	luzco	yo	luzca
tú	luces	tú	luzcas
él	luce	él	luzca
nosotros	lucimos	nosotros	luzcamos
vosotros	lucís	vosotros	luzcáis
ellos	lucen	ellos	luzcan

FUTURE		CONDITIONAL	
yo	luciré	yo	luciría
tú	lucirás	tú	lucirías
él	lucirá	él	luciría
nosotros	luciremos	nosotros	luciríamos
vosotros	luciréis	vosotros	luciríais
ellos	lucirán	ellos	lucirían

IMPERFECT		PRETERITE	
yo	lucía	yo	lucí
tú	lucías	tú	luciste
él	lucía	él	lució
nosotros	lucíamos	nosotros	lucimos
vosotros	lucíais	vosotros	lucisteis
ellos	lucían	ellos	lucieron

llover *to rain*

PAST PARTICIPLE	IMPERATIVE
llov**ido**	*not used*
GERUND	
llov**iendo**	

PRESENT	PRESENT SUBJUNCTIVE
llueve	**llueva**

FUTURE	CONDITIONAL
lloverá	**llovería**

IMPERFECT	PRETERITE
llovía	**llovió**

VERB TABLE

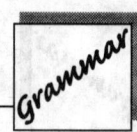

---

morir *to die*

PAST PARTICIPLE	IMPERATIVE
muerto	**muere**
	mori**d**
GERUND	
muriendo	

PRESENT

yo	**muero**
tú	**mueres**
él	**muere**
nosotros	mor**imos**
vosotros	mor**ís**
ellos	**mueren**

PRESENT SUBJUNCTIVE

yo	**muera**
tú	**mueras**
él	**muera**
nosotros	**muramos**
vosotros	**muráis**
ellos	**mueran**

FUTURE

yo	morir**é**
tú	morir**ás**
él	morir**á**
nosotros	morir**emos**
vosotros	morir**éis**
ellos	morir**án**

CONDITIONAL

yo	morir**ía**
tú	morir**ías**
él	morir**ía**
nosotros	morir**íamos**
vosotros	morir**íais**
ellos	morir**ían**

IMPERFECT

yo	mor**ía**
tú	mor**ías**
él	mor**ía**
nosotros	mor**íamos**
vosotros	mor**íais**
ellos	mor**ían**

PRETERITE

yo	mor**í**
tú	mor**iste**
él	**murió**
nosotros	mor**imos**
vosotros	mor**isteis**
ellos	**murieron**

mover *to move*

PAST PARTICIPLE	IMPERATIVE
mov**ido**	**mueve**
	moved
GERUND	
mov**iendo**	

PRESENT		PRESENT SUBJUNCTIVE	
yo	**muevo**	yo	**mueva**
tú	**mueves**	tú	**muevas**
él	**mueve**	él	**mueva**
nosotros	mov**emos**	nosotros	mov**amos**
vosotros	mov**éis**	vosotros	mov**áis**
ellos	**mueven**	ellos	**muevan**

FUTURE		CONDITIONAL	
yo	mover**é**	yo	mover**ía**
tú	mover**ás**	tú	mover**ías**
él	mover**á**	él	mover**ía**
nosotros	mover**emos**	nosotros	mover**íamos**
vosotros	mover**éis**	vosotros	mover**íais**
ellos	mover**án**	ellos	mover**ían**

IMPERFECT		PRETERITE	
yo	mov**ía**	yo	mov**í**
tú	mov**ías**	tú	mov**iste**
él	mov**ía**	él	mov**ió**
nosotros	mov**íamos**	nosotros	mov**imos**
vosotros	mov**íais**	vosotros	mov**isteis**
ellos	mov**ían**	ellos	mov**ieron**

Grammar

---

nacer *to be born*

PAST PARTICIPLE

nac**ido**

GERUND

nac**iendo**

IMPERATIVE

nac**e**
nac**ed**

PRESENT		PRESENT SUBJUNCTIVE	
yo	**nazco**	yo	**nazca**
tú	naces	tú	**nazcas**
él	nace	él	**nazca**
nosotros	nacemos	nosotros	**nazcamos**
vosotros	nacéis	vosotros	**nazcáis**
ellos	nacen	ellos	**nazcan**

FUTURE		CONDITIONAL	
yo	naceré	yo	nacería
tú	nacerás	tú	nacerías
él	nacerá	él	nacería
nosotros	naceremos	nosotros	naceríamos
vosotros	naceréis	vosotros	naceríais
ellos	nacerán	ellos	nacerían

IMPERFECT		PRETERITE	
yo	nacía	yo	nací
tú	nacías	tú	naciste
él	nacía	él	nació
nosotros	nacíamos	nosotros	nacimos
vosotros	nacíais	vosotros	nacisteis
ellos	nacían	ellos	nacieron

Grammar

---

negar *to deny*

PAST PARTICIPLE	IMPERATIVE
negado	niega
	negad
GERUND	
negando	

PRESENT		PRESENT SUBJUNCTIVE	
yo	niego	yo	niegue
tú	niegas	tú	niegues
él	niega	él	niegue
nosotros	negamos	nosotros	neguemos
vosotros	negáis	vosotros	neguéis
ellos	niegan	ellos	nieguen

FUTURE		CONDITIONAL	
yo	negaré	yo	negaría
tú	negarás	tú	negarías
él	negará	él	negaría
nosotros	negaremos	nosotros	negaríamos
vosotros	negaréis	vosotros	negaríais
ellos	negarán	ellos	negarían

IMPERFECT		PRETERITE	
yo	negaba	yo	negué
tú	negabas	tú	negaste
él	negaba	él	negó
nosotros	negábamos	nosotros	negamos
vosotros	negabais	vosotros	negasteis
ellos	negaban	ellos	negaron

oír to hear

PAST PARTICIPLE	IMPERATIVE
oído	**oye**
	oíd
GERUND	
oyendo	

PRESENT	PRESENT SUBJUNCTIVE
yo **oigo**	yo **oiga**
tú **oyes**	tú **oigas**
él **oye**	él **oiga**
nosotros **oímos**	nosotros **oigamos**
vosotros **oís**	vosotros **oigáis**
ellos **oyen**	ellos **oigan**

FUTURE	CONDITIONAL
yo **oiré**	yo **oiría**
tú **oirás**	tú **oirías**
él **oirá**	él **oiría**
nosotros **oiremos**	nosotros **oiríamos**
vosotros **oiréis**	vosotros **oiríais**
ellos **oirán**	ellos **oirían**

IMPERFECT	PRETERITE
yo **oía**	yo **oí**
tú **oías**	tú **oíste**
él **oía**	él **oyó**
nosotros **oíamos**	nosotros **oímos**
vosotros **oíais**	vosotros **oísteis**
ellos **oían**	ellos **oyeron**

oler *to smell*

PAST PARTICIPLE	IMPERATIVE
ol**ido**	**huele**
	ol**ed**
GERUND	
ol**iendo**	

PRESENT		PRESENT SUBJUNCTIVE	
yo	**huelo**	yo	**huela**
tú	**hueles**	tú	**huelas**
él	**huele**	él	**huela**
nosotros	ol**emos**	nosotros	ol**amos**
vosotros	ol**éis**	vosotros	ol**áis**
ellos	**huelen**	ellos	**huelan**

FUTURE		CONDITIONAL	
yo	ol**eré**	yo	ol**ería**
tú	ol**erás**	tú	ol**erías**
él	ol**erá**	él	ol**ería**
nosotros	ol**eremos**	nosotros	ol**eríamos**
vosotros	ol**eréis**	vosotros	ol**eríais**
ellos	ol**erán**	ellos	ol**erían**

IMPERFECT		PRETERITE	
yo	ol**ía**	yo	ol**í**
tú	ol**ías**	tú	ol**iste**
él	ol**ía**	él	ol**ió**
nosotros	ol**íamos**	nosotros	ol**imos**
vosotros	ol**íais**	vosotros	ol**isteis**
ellos	ol**ían**	ellos	ol**ieron**

VERB TABLE

---

pagar *to pay*

PAST PARTICIPLE	IMPERATIVE
pag**ado**	pag**a**
	pag**ad**
GERUND	
pag**ando**	

PRESENT		PRESENT SUBJUNCTIVE	
yo	pag**o**	yo	pag**ue**
tú	pag**as**	tú	pag**ues**
él	pag**a**	él	pag**ue**
nosotros	pag**amos**	nosotros	pag**uemos**
vosotros	pag**áis**	vosotros	pag**uéis**
ellos	pag**an**	ellos	pag**uen**

FUTURE		CONDITIONAL	
yo	pagar**é**	yo	pagar**ía**
tú	pagar**ás**	tú	pagar**ías**
él	pagar**á**	él	pagar**ía**
nosotros	pagar**emos**	nosotros	pagar**íamos**
vosotros	pagar**éis**	vosotros	pagar**íais**
ellos	pagar**án**	ellos	pagar**ían**

IMPERFECT		PRETERITE	
yo	pag**aba**	yo	pag**ué**
tú	pag**abas**	tú	pag**aste**
él	pag**aba**	él	pag**ó**
nosotros	pag**ábamos**	nosotros	pag**amos**
vosotros	pag**abais**	vosotros	pag**asteis**
ellos	pag**aban**	ellos	pag**aron**

pedir *to ask for*

PAST PARTICIPLE	IMPERATIVE
pedido	**pide** pedid
GERUND	
pidiendo	

PRESENT		PRESENT SUBJUNCTIVE	
yo	**pido**	yo	**pida**
tú	**pides**	tú	**pidas**
él	**pide**	él	**pida**
nosotros	ped**imos**	nosotros	**pidamos**
vosotros	ped**ís**	vosotros	**pidáis**
ellos	**piden**	ellos	**pidan**

FUTURE		CONDITIONAL	
yo	pedir**é**	yo	pedir**ía**
tú	pedir**ás**	tú	pedir**ías**
él	pedir**á**	él	pedir**ía**
nosotros	pedir**emos**	nosotros	pedir**íamos**
vosotros	pedir**éis**	vosotros	pedir**íais**
ellos	pedir**án**	ellos	pedir**ían**

IMPERFECT		PRETERITE	
yo	ped**ía**	yo	ped**í**
tú	ped**ías**	tú	ped**iste**
él	ped**ía**	él	**pidió**
nosotros	ped**íamos**	nosotros	ped**imos**
vosotros	ped**íais**	vosotros	ped**isteis**
ellos	ped**ían**	ellos	**pidieron**

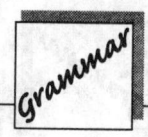

---

pensar *to think*

PAST PARTICIPLE	IMPERATIVE
pens**ado**	
	p**ie**nsa
	pensa**d**
GERUND	
pens**ando**	

PRESENT		PRESENT SUBJUNCTIVE	
yo	p**ie**nso	yo	p**ie**nse
tú	p**ie**nsas	tú	p**ie**nses
él	p**ie**nsa	él	p**ie**nse
nosotros	pens**amos**	nosotros	pens**emos**
vosotros	pens**áis**	vosotros	pens**éis**
ellos	p**ie**nsan	ellos	p**ie**nsen

FUTURE		CONDITIONAL	
yo	pensar**é**	yo	pensar**ía**
tú	pensar**ás**	tú	pensar**ías**
él	pensar**á**	él	pensar**ía**
nosotros	pensar**emos**	nosotros	pensar**íamos**
vosotros	pensar**éis**	vosotros	pensar**íais**
ellos	pensar**án**	ellos	pensar**ían**

IMPERFECT		PRETERITE	
yo	pens**aba**	yo	pens**é**
tú	pens**abas**	tú	pens**aste**
él	pens**aba**	él	pens**ó**
nosotros	pens**ábamos**	nosotros	pens**amos**
vosotros	pens**abais**	vosotros	pens**asteis**
ellos	pens**aban**	ellos	pens**aron**

poder *to be able*

PAST PARTICIPLE	IMPERATIVE
pod**ido**	**puede**
	pod**ed**
GERUND	
pudiendo	

PRESENT		PRESENT SUBJUNCTIVE	
yo	**puedo**	yo	**pueda**
tú	**puedes**	tú	**puedas**
él	**puede**	él	**pueda**
nosotros	pod**emos**	nosotros	pod**amos**
vosotros	pod**éis**	vosotros	pod**áis**
ellos	**pueden**	ellos	**puedan**

FUTURE		CONDITIONAL	
yo	**podré**	yo	**podría**
tú	**podrás**	tú	**podrías**
él	**podrá**	él	**podría**
nosotros	**podremos**	nosotros	**podríamos**
vosotros	**podréis**	vosotros	**podríais**
ellos	**podrán**	ellos	**podrían**

IMPERFECT		PRETERITE	
yo	pod**ía**	yo	**pude**
tú	pod**ías**	tú	**pudiste**
él	pod**ía**	él	**pudo**
nosotros	pod**íamos**	nosotros	**pudimos**
vosotros	pod**íais**	vosotros	**pudisteis**
ellos	pod**ían**	ellos	**pudieron**

poner *to put*

PAST PARTICIPLE

puesto

GERUND

pon**iendo**

IMPERATIVE

pon
pon**ed**

PRESENT		PRESENT SUBJUNCTIVE	
yo	**pongo**	yo	**ponga**
tú	pon**es**	tú	**pongas**
él	pon**e**	él	**ponga**
nosotros	pon**emos**	nosotros	**pongamos**
vosotros	pon**éis**	vosotros	**pongáis**
ellos	pon**en**	ellos	**pongan**

FUTURE		CONDITIONAL	
yo	**pondré**	yo	**pondría**
tú	**pondrás**	tú	**pondrías**
él	**pondrá**	él	**pondría**
nosotros	**pondremos**	nosotros	**pondríamos**
vosotros	**pondréis**	vosotros	**pondríais**
ellos	**pondrán**	ellos	**pondrían**

IMPERFECT		PRETERITE	
yo	pon**ía**	yo	**puse**
tú	pon**ías**	tú	**pusiste**
él	pon**ía**	él	**puso**
nosotros	pon**íamos**	nosotros	**pusimos**
vosotros	pon**íais**	vosotros	**pusisteis**
ellos	pon**ían**	ellos	**pusieron**

prohibir *to forbid*

PAST PARTICIPLE	IMPERATIVE
prohib**ido**	**prohíbe**
	prohib**id**
GERUND	
prohib**iendo**	

PRESENT		PRESENT SUBJUNCTIVE	
yo	**prohíbo**	yo	**prohíba**
tú	**prohíbes**	tú	**prohíbas**
él	**prohíbe**	él	**prohíba**
nosotros	prohib**imos**	nosotros	prohib**amos**
vosotros	prohib**ís**	vosotros	prohib**áis**
ellos	**prohíben**	ellos	**prohíban**

FUTURE		CONDITIONAL	
yo	prohibir**é**	yo	prohibir**ía**
tú	prohibir**ás**	tú	prohibir**ías**
él	prohibir**á**	él	prohibir**ía**
nosotros	prohibir**emos**	nosotros	prohibir**íamos**
vosotros	prohibir**éis**	vosotros	prohibir**íais**
ellos	prohibir**án**	ellos	prohibir**ían**

IMPERFECT		PRETERITE	
yo	prohib**ía**	yo	prohib**í**
tú	prohib**ías**	tú	prohib**iste**
él	prohib**ía**	él	prohib**ió**
nosotros	prohib**íamos**	nosotros	prohib**imos**
vosotros	prohib**íais**	vosotros	prohib**isteis**
ellos	prohib**ían**	ellos	prohib**ieron**

querer *to want*

PAST PARTICIPLE	IMPERATIVE
quer**ido**	**quiere**
	quer**ed**
GERUND	
quer**iendo**	

PRESENT		PRESENT SUBJUNCTIVE	
yo	**quiero**	yo	**quiera**
tú	**quieres**	tú	**quieras**
él	**quiere**	él	**quiera**
nosotros	quer**emos**	nosotros	quer**amos**
vosotros	quer**éis**	vosotros	quer**áis**
ellos	**quieren**	ellos	**quieran**

FUTURE		CONDITIONAL	
yo	**querré**	yo	**querría**
tú	**querrás**	tú	**querrías**
él	**querrá**	él	**querría**
nosotros	**querremos**	nosotros	**querríamos**
vosotros	**querréis**	vosotros	**querríais**
ellos	**querrán**	ellos	**querrían**

IMPERFECT		PRETERITE	
yo	quer**ía**	yo	**quise**
tú	quer**ías**	tú	**quisiste**
él	quer**ía**	él	**quiso**
nosotros	quer**íamos**	nosotros	**quisimos**
vosotros	quer**íais**	vosotros	**quisisteis**
ellos	quer**ían**	ellos	**quisieron**

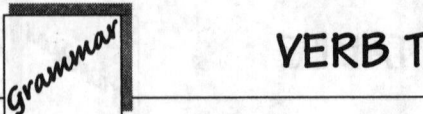

rehusar to refuse

PAST PARTICIPLE	IMPERATIVE
rehus**ado**	**rehúsa**
	rehusa**d**
GERUND	
rehus**ando**	

PRESENT		PRESENT SUBJUNCTIVE	
yo	rehúso	yo	rehúse
tú	rehúsas	tú	rehúses
él	rehúsa	él	rehúse
nosotros	rehusamos	nosotros	rehusemos
vosotros	rehusáis	vosotros	rehuséis
ellos	rehúsan	ellos	rehúsen

FUTURE		CONDITIONAL	
yo	rehusaré	yo	rehusaría
tú	rehusarás	tú	rehusarías
él	rehusará	él	rehusaría
nosotros	rehusaremos	nosotros	rehusaríamos
vosotros	rehusaréis	vosotros	rehusaríais
ellos	rehusarán	ellos	rehusarían

IMPERFECT		PRETERITE	
yo	rehusaba	yo	rehusé
tú	rehusabas	tú	rehusaste
él	rehusaba	él	rehusó
nosotros	rehusábamos	nosotros	rehusamos
vosotros	rehusabais	vosotros	rehusasteis
ellos	rehusaban	ellos	rehusaron

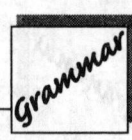

reír *to laugh*

PAST PARTICIPLE	IMPERATIVE
re**ído**	**ríe**
	re**íd**
GERUND	
riendo	

PRESENT		PRESENT SUBJUNCTIVE	
yo	**río**	yo	**ría**
tú	**ríes**	tú	**rías**
él	**ríe**	él	**ría**
nosotros	**reímos**	nosotros	**riamos**
vosotros	**reís**	vosotros	**riáis**
ellos	**ríen**	ellos	**rían**

FUTURE		CONDITIONAL	
yo	**reiré**	yo	**reiría**
tú	**reirás**	tú	**reirías**
él	**reirá**	él	**reiría**
nosotros	**reiremos**	nosotros	**reiríamos**
vosotros	**reiréis**	vosotros	**reiríais**
ellos	**reirán**	ellos	**reirían**

IMPERFECT		PRETERITE	
yo	**reía**	yo	**reí**
tú	**reías**	tú	**reíste**
él	**reía**	él	**rió**
nosotros	**reíamos**	nosotros	**reímos**
vosotros	**reíais**	vosotros	**reísteis**
ellos	**reían**	ellos	**rieron**

---

reñir *to scold*

PAST PARTICIPLE	IMPERATIVE
reñ**ido**	ri**ñe**
	reñi**d**
GERUND	
ri**ñendo**	

PRESENT	PRESENT SUBJUNCTIVE
yo **riño**	yo **riña**
tú **riñes**	tú **riñas**
él **riñe**	él **riña**
nosotros reñ**imos**	nosotros **riñamos**
vosotros reñ**ís**	vosotros **riñáis**
ellos **riñen**	ellos **riñan**

FUTURE	CONDITIONAL
yo reñir**é**	yo reñir**ía**
tú reñir**ás**	tú reñir**ías**
él reñir**á**	él reñir**ía**
nosotros reñir**emos**	nosotros reñir**íamos**
vosotros reñir**éis**	vosotros reñir**íais**
ellos reñir**án**	ellos reñir**ían**

IMPERFECT	PRETERITE
yo reñ**ía**	yo reñ**í**
tú reñ**ías**	tú reñ**iste**
él reñ**ía**	él **riñó**
nosotros reñ**íamos**	nosotros reñ**imos**
vosotros reñ**íais**	vosotros reñ**isteis**
ellos reñ**ían**	ellos **riñeron**

---

resolver *to solve*

PAST PARTICIPLE

resuelto

GERUND

resolv**iendo**

IMPERATIVE

resuelve
resolve**d**

PRESENT		PRESENT SUBJUNCTIVE	
yo	**resuelvo**	yo	**resuelva**
tú	**resuelves**	tú	**resuelvas**
él	**resuelve**	él	**resuelva**
nosotros	resolv**emos**	nosotros	resolv**amos**
vosotros	resolv**éis**	vosotros	resolv**áis**
ellos	**resuelven**	ellos	**resuelvan**

FUTURE		CONDITIONAL	
yo	resolver**é**	yo	resolver**ía**
tú	resolver**ás**	tú	resolver**ías**
él	resolver**á**	él	resolver**ía**
nosotros	resolver**emos**	nosotros	resolver**íamos**
vosotros	resolver**éis**	vosotros	resolver**íais**
ellos	resolver**án**	ellos	resolver**ían**

IMPERFECT		PRETERITE	
yo	resolv**ía**	yo	resolv**í**
tú	resolv**ías**	tú	resolv**iste**
él	resolv**ía**	él	resolv**ió**
nosotros	resolv**íamos**	nosotros	resolv**imos**
vosotros	resolv**íais**	vosotros	resolv**isteis**
ellos	resolv**ían**	ellos	resolv**ieron**

reunir *to put together, to gather*

PAST PARTICIPLE	IMPERATIVE
reunido	reúne
	reunid
GERUND	
reuniendo	

PRESENT		PRESENT SUBJUNCTIVE	
yo	reúno	yo	reúna
tú	reúnes	tú	reúnas
él	reúne	él	reúna
nosotros	reunimos	nosotros	reunamos
vosotros	reunís	vosotros	reunáis
ellos	reúnen	ellos	reúnan

FUTURE		CONDITIONAL	
yo	reuniré	yo	reuniría
tú	reunirás	tú	reunirías
él	reunirá	él	reuniría
nosotros	reuniremos	nosotros	reuniríamos
vosotros	reuniréis	vosotros	reuniríais
ellos	reunirán	ellos	reunirían

IMPERFECT		PRETERITE	
yo	reunía	yo	reuní
tú	reunías	tú	reuniste
él	reunía	él	reunió
nosotros	reuníamos	nosotros	reunimos
vosotros	reuníais	vosotros	reunisteis
ellos	reunían	ellos	reunieron

rogar *to beg*

PAST PARTICIPLE	IMPERATIVE
rog**ado**	**ruega**
	roga**d**
GERUND	
rog**ando**	

PRESENT		PRESENT SUBJUNCTIVE	
yo	**ruego**	yo	**ruegue**
tú	**ruegas**	tú	**ruegues**
él	**ruega**	él	**ruegue**
nosotros	rog**amos**	nosotros	**roguemos**
vosotros	rog**áis**	vosotros	**roguéis**
ellos	**ruegan**	ellos	**rueguen**

FUTURE		CONDITIONAL	
yo	rogar**é**	yo	rogar**ía**
tú	rogar**ás**	tú	rogar**ías**
él	rogar**á**	él	rogar**ía**
nosotros	rogar**emos**	nosotros	rogar**íamos**
vosotros	rogar**éis**	vosotros	rogar**íais**
ellos	rogar**án**	ellos	rogar**ían**

IMPERFECT		PRETERITE	
yo	rog**aba**	yo	**rogué**
tú	rog**abas**	tú	rog**aste**
él	rog**aba**	él	rog**ó**
nosotros	rog**ábamos**	nosotros	rog**amos**
vosotros	rog**abais**	vosotros	rog**asteis**
ellos	rog**aban**	ellos	rog**aron**

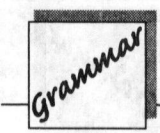

romper *to break*

PAST PARTICIPLE

roto

GERUND

romp**iendo**

IMPERATIVE

romp**e**
romp**ed**

PRESENT		PRESENT SUBJUNCTIVE	
yo	romp**o**	yo	romp**a**
tú	romp**es**	tú	romp**as**
él	romp**e**	él	romp**a**
nosotros	romp**emos**	nosotros	romp**amos**
vosotros	romp**éis**	vosotros	romp**áis**
ellos	romp**en**	ellos	romp**an**

FUTURE		CONDITIONAL	
yo	romper**é**	yo	romper**ía**
tú	romper**ás**	tú	romper**ías**
él	romper**á**	él	romper**ía**
nosotros	romper**emos**	nosotros	romper**íamos**
vosotros	romper**éis**	vosotros	romper**íais**
ellos	romper**án**	ellos	romper**ían**

IMPERFECT		PRETERITE	
yo	romp**ía**	yo	romp**í**
tú	romp**ías**	tú	romp**iste**
él	romp**ía**	él	romp**ió**
nosotros	romp**íamos**	nosotros	romp**imos**
vosotros	romp**íais**	vosotros	romp**isteis**
ellos	romp**ían**	ellos	romp**ieron**

VERB TABLE

---

saber *to know*

PAST PARTICIPLE

sab**ido**

GERUND

sab**iendo**

IMPERATIVE

sab**e**
sab**ed**

PRESENT		PRESENT SUBJUNCTIVE	
yo	**sé**	**yo**	**sepa**
tú	sab**es**	**tú**	**sepas**
él	sab**e**	**él**	**sepa**
nosotros	sab**emos**	**nosotros**	**sepamos**
vosotros	sab**éis**	**vosotros**	**sepáis**
ellos	sab**en**	**ellos**	**sepan**

FUTURE		CONDITIONAL	
yo	**sabré**	**yo**	**sabría**
tú	**sabrás**	**tú**	**sabrías**
él	**sabrá**	**él**	**sabría**
nosotros	**sabremos**	**nosotros**	**sabríamos**
vosotros	**sabréis**	**vosotros**	**sabríais**
ellos	**sabrán**	**ellos**	**sabrían**

IMPERFECT		PRETERITE	
yo	sab**ía**	**yo**	**supe**
tú	sab**ías**	**tú**	**supiste**
él	sab**ía**	**él**	**supo**
nosotros	sab**íamos**	**nosotros**	**supimos**
vosotros	sab**íais**	**vosotros**	**supisteis**
ellos	sab**ían**	**ellos**	**supieron**

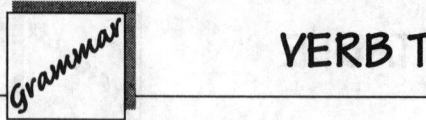

sacar *to take out*

PAST PARTICIPLE	IMPERATIVE
sac**ado**	sac**a**
	saca**d**
GERUND	
sac**ando**	

PRESENT		PRESENT SUBJUNCTIVE	
yo	sac**o**	yo	**saque**
tú	sac**as**	tú	**saques**
él	sac**a**	él	**saque**
nosotros	sac**amos**	nosotros	**saquemos**
vosotros	sac**áis**	vosotros	**saquéis**
ellos	sac**an**	ellos	**saquen**

FUTURE		CONDITIONAL	
yo	sacar**é**	yo	sacar**ía**
tú	sacar**ás**	tú	sacar**ías**
él	sacar**á**	él	sacar**ía**
nosotros	sacar**emos**	nosotros	sacar**íamos**
vosotros	sacar**éis**	vosotros	sacar**íais**
ellos	sacar**án**	ellos	sacar**ían**

IMPERFECT		PRETERITE	
yo	sac**aba**	yo	**saqué**
tú	sac**abas**	tú	sac**aste**
él	sac**aba**	él	sac**ó**
nosotros	sac**ábamos**	nosotros	sac**amos**
vosotros	sac**abais**	vosotros	sac**asteis**
ellos	sac**aban**	ellos	sac**aron**

salir *to go out*

PAST PARTICIPLE	IMPERATIVE
sal**ido**	**sal**
	sali**d**
GERUND	
sal**iendo**	

PRESENT		PRESENT SUBJUNCTIVE	
yo	salgo	yo	salga
tú	sales	tú	salgas
él	sale	él	salga
nosotros	sal**imos**	nosotros	salgamos
vosotros	salís	vosotros	salgáis
ellos	salen	ellos	salgan

FUTURE		CONDITIONAL	
yo	saldré	yo	saldría
tú	saldrás	tú	saldrías
él	saldrá	él	saldría
nosotros	saldremos	nosotros	saldríamos
vosotros	saldréis	vosotros	saldríais
ellos	saldrán	ellos	saldrían

IMPERFECT		PRETERITE	
yo	salía	yo	salí
tú	salías	tú	saliste
él	salía	él	salió
nosotros	salíamos	nosotros	salimos
vosotros	salíais	vosotros	salisteis
ellos	salían	ellos	sal**ieron**

satisfacer *to satisfy*

PAST PARTICIPLE	IMPERATIVE
satisfecho	**satisfaz**/satisface
	satisface**d**
GERUND	
satisfac**iendo**	

PRESENT		PRESENT SUBJUNCTIVE	
yo	**satisfago**	yo	**satisfaga**
tú	satisfac**es**	tú	**satisfagas**
él	satisfac**e**	él	**satisfaga**
nosotros	satisfac**emos**	nosotros	**satisfagamos**
vosotros	satisfac**éis**	vosotros	**satisfagáis**
ellos	satisfac**en**	ellos	**satisfagan**

FUTURE		CONDITIONAL	
yo	**satisfaré**	yo	**satisfaría**
tú	**satisfarás**	tú	**satisfarías**
él	**satisfará**	él	**satisfaría**
nosotros	**satisfaremos**	nosotros	**satisfaríamos**
vosotros	**satisfaréis**	vosotros	**satisfaríais**
ellos	**satisfarán**	ellos	**satisfarían**

IMPERFECT		PRETERITE	
yo	satisfac**ía**	yo	**satisfice**
tú	satisfac**ías**	tú	**satisficiste**
él	satisfac**ía**	él	**satisfizo**
nosotros	satisfac**íamos**	nosotros	**satisficimos**
vosotros	satisfac**íais**	vosotros	**satisficisteis**
ellos	satisfac**ían**	ellos	**satisficieron**

---

seguir *to follow*

PAST PARTICIPLE

segu**ido**

GERUND

sigu**iendo**

IMPERATIVE

sigue
segui**d**

PRESENT		PRESENT SUBJUNCTIVE	
yo	**sigo**	yo	**siga**
tú	**sigues**	tú	**sigas**
él	**sigue**	él	**siga**
nosotros	segu**imos**	nosotros	**sigamos**
vosotros	segu**ís**	vosotros	**sigáis**
ellos	**siguen**	ellos	**sigan**

FUTURE		CONDITIONAL	
yo	seguir**é**	yo	seguir**ía**
tú	seguir**ás**	tú	seguir**ías**
él	seguir**á**	él	seguir**ía**
nosotros	seguir**emos**	nosotros	seguir**íamos**
vosotros	seguir**éis**	vosotros	seguir**íais**
ellos	seguir**án**	ellos	seguir**ían**

IMPERFECT		PRETERITE	
yo	segu**ía**	yo	segu**í**
tú	segu**ías**	tú	segu**iste**
él	segu**ía**	él	**siguió**
nosotros	segu**íamos**	nosotros	segu**imos**
vosotros	segu**íais**	vosotros	segu**isteis**
ellos	segu**ían**	ellos	**siguieron**

sentir *to feel*

PAST PARTICIPLE	IMPERATIVE
sent**ido**	**siente** sentid
GERUND	
s**in**t**iendo**	

PRESENT		PRESENT SUBJUNCTIVE	
yo	s**ie**nto	yo	s**ie**nta
tú	s**ie**ntes	tú	s**ie**ntas
él	s**ie**nte	él	s**ie**nta
nosotros	sent**imos**	nosotros	s**in**tamos
vosotros	sent**ís**	vosotros	s**in**táis
ellos	s**ie**nten	ellos	s**ie**ntan

FUTURE		CONDITIONAL	
yo	sentir**é**	yo	sentir**ía**
tú	sentir**ás**	tú	sentir**ías**
él	sentir**á**	él	sentir**ía**
nosotros	sentir**emos**	nosotros	sentir**íamos**
vosotros	sentir**éis**	vosotros	sentir**íais**
ellos	sentir**án**	ellos	sentir**ían**

IMPERFECT		PRETERITE	
yo	sent**ía**	yo	sent**í**
tú	sent**ías**	tú	sent**iste**
él	sent**ía**	él	s**in**t**ió**
nosotros	sent**íamos**	nosotros	sent**imos**
vosotros	sent**íais**	vosotros	sent**isteis**
ellos	sent**ían**	ellos	s**in**t**ieron**

---

ser *to be*

PAST PARTICIPLE

sido

IMPERATIVE

sé
se**d**

GERUND

siendo

PRESENT		PRESENT SUBJUNCTIVE	
yo	soy	**yo**	sea
tú	eres	**tú**	seas
él	es	**él**	sea
nosotros	somos	**nosotros**	seamos
vosotros	sois	**vosotros**	seáis
ellos	son	**ellos**	sean

FUTURE		CONDITIONAL	
yo	seré	**yo**	sería
tú	serás	**tú**	serías
él	será	**él**	sería
nosotros	seremos	**nosotros**	seríamos
vosotros	seréis	**vosotros**	seríais
ellos	serán	**ellos**	serían

IMPERFECT		PRETERITE	
yo	era	**yo**	fui
tú	eras	**tú**	fuiste
él	era	**él**	fue
nosotros	éramos	**nosotros**	fuimos
vosotros	erais	**vosotros**	fuisteis
ellos	eran	**ellos**	fueron

tener *to have*

PAST PARTICIPLE	IMPERATIVE
ten**ido**	**ten**
	ten**ed**
GERUND	
ten**iendo**	

PRESENT		PRESENT SUBJUNCTIVE	
yo	**tengo**	yo	**tenga**
tú	**tienes**	tú	**tengas**
él	**tiene**	él	**tenga**
nosotros	ten**emos**	nosotros	**tengamos**
vosotros	ten**éis**	vosotros	**tengáis**
ellos	**tienen**	ellos	**tengan**

FUTURE		CONDITIONAL	
yo	**tendré**	yo	**tendría**
tú	**tendrás**	tú	**tendrías**
él	**tendrá**	él	**tendría**
nosotros	**tendremos**	nosotros	**tendríamos**
vosotros	**tendréis**	vosotros	**tendríais**
ellos	**tendrán**	ellos	**tendrían**

IMPERFECT		PRETERITE	
yo	ten**ía**	yo	**tuve**
tú	ten**ías**	tú	**tuviste**
él	ten**ía**	él	**tuvo**
nosotros	ten**íamos**	nosotros	**tuvimos**
vosotros	ten**íais**	vosotros	**tuvisteis**
ellos	ten**ían**	ellos	**tuvieron**

Grammar

---

torcer *to twist*

PAST PARTICIPLE	IMPERATIVE
torc**ido**	**tuerce**
	torc**ed**
GERUND	
torc**iendo**	

PRESENT		PRESENT SUBJUNCTIVE	
yo	**tuerzo**	yo	**tuerza**
tú	**tuerces**	tú	**tuerzas**
él	**tuerce**	él	**tuerza**
nosotros	torc**emos**	nosotros	**torzamos**
vosotros	torc**éis**	vosotros	**torzáis**
ellos	**tuercen**	ellos	**tuerzan**

FUTURE		CONDITIONAL	
yo	torcer**é**	yo	torcer**ía**
tú	torcer**ás**	tú	torcer**ías**
él	torcer**á**	él	torcer**ía**
nosotros	torcer**emos**	nosotros	torcer**íamos**
vosotros	torcer**éis**	vosotros	torcer**íais**
ellos	torcer**án**	ellos	torcer**ían**

IMPERFECT		PRETERITE	
yo	torc**ía**	yo	torc**í**
tú	torc**ías**	tú	torc**iste**
él	torc**ía**	él	torc**ió**
nosotros	torc**íamos**	nosotros	torc**imos**
vosotros	torc**íais**	vosotros	torc**isteis**
ellos	torc**ían**	ellos	torc**ieron**

traer *to bring*

PAST PARTICIPLE	IMPERATIVE
traído	tra**e**
	trae**d**
GERUND	
trayendo	

PRESENT		PRESENT SUBJUNCTIVE	
yo	**traigo**	yo	**traiga**
tú	traes	tú	**traigas**
él	trae	él	**traiga**
nosotros	traemos	nosotros	**traigamos**
vosotros	traéis	vosotros	**traigáis**
ellos	traen	ellos	**traigan**

FUTURE		CONDITIONAL	
yo	traeré	yo	traería
tú	traerás	tú	traerías
él	traerá	él	traería
nosotros	traeremos	nosotros	traeríamos
vosotros	traeréis	vosotros	traeríais
ellos	traerán	ellos	traerían

IMPERFECT		PRETERITE	
yo	traía	yo	**traje**
tú	traías	tú	**trajiste**
él	traía	él	**trajo**
nosotros	traíamos	nosotros	**trajimos**
vosotros	traíais	vosotros	**trajisteis**
ellos	traían	ellos	**trajeron**

Grammar

valer *to be worth*

PAST PARTICIPLE

val**ido**

GERUND

val**iendo**

IMPERATIVE

val**e**

val**ed**

PRESENT		PRESENT SUBJUNCTIVE	
yo	valgo	yo	valga
tú	vales	tú	valgas
él	vale	él	valga
nosotros	valemos	nosotros	valgamos
vosotros	valéis	vosotros	valgáis
ellos	valen	ellos	valgan

FUTURE		CONDITIONAL	
yo	valdré	yo	valdría
tú	valdrás	tú	valdrías
él	valdrá	él	valdría
nosotros	valdremos	nosotros	valdríamos
vosotros	valdréis	vosotros	valdríais
ellos	valdrán	ellos	valdrían

IMPERFECT		PRETERITE	
yo	valía	yo	valí
tú	valías	tú	valiste
él	valía	él	valió
nosotros	valíamos	nosotros	valimos
vosotros	valíais	vosotros	valisteis
ellos	valían	ellos	valieron

vencer *to win*

PAST PARTICIPLE	IMPERATIVE
vencido	vence
	venced
GERUND	
venciendo	

PRESENT		PRESENT SUBJUNCTIVE	
yo	venzo	yo	venza
tú	vences	tú	venzas
él	vence	él	venza
nosotros	vencemos	nosotros	venzamos
vosotros	vencéis	vosotros	venzáis
ellos	vencen	ellos	venzan

FUTURE		CONDITIONAL	
yo	venceré	yo	vencería
tú	vencerás	tú	vencerías
él	vencerá	él	vencería
nosotros	venceremos	nosotros	venceríamos
vosotros	venceréis	vosotros	venceríais
ellos	vencerán	ellos	vencerían

IMPERFECT		PRETERITE	
yo	vencía	yo	vencí
tú	vencías	tú	venciste
él	vencía	él	venció
nosotros	vencíamos	nosotros	vencimos
vosotros	vencíais	vosotros	vencisteis
ellos	vencían	ellos	vencieron

venir *to come*

PAST PARTICIPLE	IMPERATIVE
ven**ido**	**ven**
	veni**d**
GERUND	
viniendo	

PRESENT		PRESENT SUBJUNCTIVE	
yo	**vengo**	yo	**venga**
tú	**vienes**	tú	**vengas**
él	**viene**	él	**venga**
nosotros	ven**imos**	nosotros	**vengamos**
vosotros	ven**ís**	vosotros	**vengáis**
ellos	**vienen**	ellos	**vengan**

FUTURE		CONDITIONAL	
yo	**vendré**	yo	**vendría**
tú	**vendrás**	tú	**vendrías**
él	**vendrá**	él	**vendría**
nosotros	**vendremos**	nosotros	**vendríamos**
vosotros	**vendréis**	vosotros	**vendríais**
ellos	**vendrán**	ellos	**vendrían**

IMPERFECT		PRETERITE	
yo	ven**ía**	yo	**vine**
tú	ven**ías**	tú	**viniste**
él	ven**ía**	él	**vino**
nosotros	ven**íamos**	nosotros	**vinimos**
vosotros	ven**íais**	vosotros	**vinisteis**
ellos	ven**ían**	ellos	**vinieron**

Grammar

---

ver *to see*

PAST PARTICIPLE

visto

GERUND

v**iendo**

IMPERATIVE

v**e**
ve**d**

PRESENT		PRESENT SUBJUNCTIVE	
yo	veo	yo	vea
tú	ves	tú	veas
él	ve	él	vea
nosotros	vemos	nosotros	veamos
vosotros	veis	vosotros	veáis
ellos	ven	ellos	vean

FUTURE		CONDITIONAL	
yo	veré	yo	vería
tú	verás	tú	verías
él	verá	él	vería
nosotros	veremos	nosotros	veríamos
vosotros	veréis	vosotros	veríais
ellos	verán	ellos	verían

IMPERFECT		PRETERITE	
yo	veía	yo	vi
tú	veías	tú	viste
él	veía	él	vio
nosotros	veíamos	nosotros	vimos
vosotros	veíais	vosotros	visteis
ellos	veían	ellos	vieron

volcar *to overturn*

PAST PARTICIPLE	IMPERATIVE
volc**ado**	**vuelca**
	volca**d**
GERUND	
volc**ando**	

PRESENT		PRESENT SUBJUNCTIVE	
yo	**vuelco**	yo	**vuelque**
tú	**vuelcas**	tú	**vuelques**
él	**vuelca**	él	**vuelque**
nosotros	volc**amos**	nosotros	**volquemos**
vosotros	volc**áis**	vosotros	**volquéis**
ellos	**vuelcan**	ellos	**vuelquen**

FUTURE		CONDITIONAL	
yo	volcar**é**	yo	volcar**ía**
tú	volcar**ás**	tú	volcar**ías**
él	volcar**á**	él	volcar**ía**
nosotros	volcar**emos**	nosotros	volcar**íamos**
vosotros	volcar**éis**	vosotros	volcar**íais**
ellos	volcar**án**	ellos	volcar**ían**

IMPERFECT		PRETERITE	
yo	volc**aba**	yo	**volqué**
tú	volc**abas**	tú	volc**aste**
él	volc**aba**	él	volc**ó**
nosotros	volc**ábamos**	nosotros	volc**amos**
vosotros	volc**abais**	vosotros	volc**asteis**
ellos	volc**aban**	ellos	volc**aron**

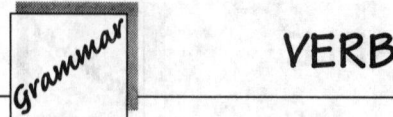

volver *to return*

PAST PARTICIPLE	IMPERATIVE
vuelto	**vuelve**
	volve**d**
GERUND	
volv**iendo**	

PRESENT		PRESENT SUBJUNCTIVE	
yo	**vuelvo**	yo	**vuelva**
tú	**vuelves**	tú	**vuelvas**
él	**vuelve**	él	**vuelva**
nosotros	volv**emos**	nosotros	volv**amos**
vosotros	volv**éis**	vosotros	volv**áis**
ellos	**vuelven**	ellos	**vuelvan**

FUTURE		CONDITIONAL	
yo	volver**é**	yo	volver**ía**
tú	volver**ás**	tú	volver**ías**
él	volver**á**	él	volver**ía**
nosotros	volver**emos**	nosotros	volver**íamos**
vosotros	volver**éis**	vosotros	volver**íais**
ellos	volver**án**	ellos	volver**ían**

IMPERFECT		PRETERITE	
yo	volv**ía**	yo	volv**í**
tú	volv**ías**	tú	volv**iste**
él	volv**ía**	él	volv**ió**
nosotros	volv**íamos**	nosotros	volv**imos**
vosotros	volv**íais**	vosotros	volv**isteis**
ellos	volv**ían**	ellos	volv**ieron**

VERB TABLE

zurcir *to darn*

PAST PARTICIPLE	IMPERATIVE
zurc**ido**	zurc**e**
	zurc**id**
GERUND	
zurc**iendo**	

PRESENT		PRESENT SUBJUNCTIVE	
yo	zurzo	yo	zurza
tú	zurces	tú	zurzas
él	zurce	él	zurza
nosotros	zurcimos	nosotros	zurzamos
vosotros	zurcís	vosotros	zurzáis
ellos	zurcen	ellos	zurzan

FUTURE		CONDITIONAL	
yo	zurciré	yo	zurciría
tú	zurcirás	tú	zurcirías
él	zurcirá	él	zurciría
nosotros	zurciremos	nosotros	zurciríamos
vosotros	zurciréis	vosotros	zurciríais
ellos	zurcirán	ellos	zurcirían

IMPERFECT		PRETERITE	
yo	zurcía	yo	zurcí
tú	zurcías	tú	zurciste
él	zurcía	él	zurció
nosotros	zurcíamos	nosotros	zurcimos
vosotros	zurcíais	vosotros	zurcisteis
ellos	zurcían	ellos	zurcieron

The following pages, 163 to 186, contain an index of over 2,800 commonly used verbs cross-referred to the appropriate conjugation model.

◆ Regular verbs belonging to the first, second and third conjugation are numbered 1, 2 and 3 respectively. For the regular conjugations see pp 6 to 13.

◆ Irregular verbs are numerically cross-referred to the appropriate model as conjugated on pp 82 to 161. Thus, **alzar** is cross-referred to p 100 where **cruzar**, the model for this verb group, is conjugated.

◆ Verbs which are most commonly used in the reflexive form – e.g. **amodorrarse** – have been cross-referred to the appropriate non-reflexive model. For the full conjugation of a reflexive verb, see pp 28 to 31.

◆ Verbs printed in **bold** – e.g. **abrir** – are themselves models.

◆ Superior numbers refer you to notes on p 187 which indicate how the verb differs from its model.

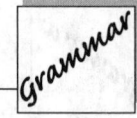

barajar	1	bostezar	100	caminar	1
barbotar	1	botar	1	campar	1
barnizar	100	bracear	1	camuflar	1
barrenar	1	bramar	1	canalizar	100
barrer	2	bricolajear	1	cancelar	1
barruntar	1	brillar	1	canjear	1
basar	1	brincar	146	canonizar	100
bascular	1	brindar	1	cansar	1
bastar	1	bromear	1	cantar	1
batallar	1	broncearse	1	canturrear	1
batir	3	brotar	1	capacitar	1
bautizar	100	bruñir	116	capar	1
beber	2	bucear	1	capitalizar	100
bendecir	91	bufar	1	capitanear	1
beneficiar	1	bullir	116	capitular	1
berrear	1	burbujear	1	captar	1
besar	1	burlar	1	capturar	1
besuquear	1	buscar	146	caracolear	1
bifurcarse	146	cabalgar	131	caracterizar	100
birlar	1	cabecear	1	carbonizar	100
biselar	1	**caber**	92	carcomer	2
bizquear	1	cacarear	1	carear	1
blandir	3	cachear	1	carecer	99
blanquear	1	caducar	146	cargar	131
blasfemar	1	**caer**	93	casar	1
blasonar	1	calar	1	cascar	146
blindar	1	calcar	146	castigar	131
bloquear	1	calcinar	1	castrar	1
bobinar	1	calcular	1	catar	1
bocetar	1	caldear	1	caucionar	1
bogar	131	calentar	133	causar	1
boicotear	1	calibrar	1	cautivar	1
bombardear	1	calificar	146	cavar	1
bombear	1	callar	1	cavilar	1
boquear	1	callejear	1	cazar	100
borbotear	1	calmar	1	cebar	1
bordar	1	calumniar	1	cecear	1
bordear	1	calzar	100	ceder	2
borrar	1	cambiar	1	cegar	128
bosquejar	1	camelar	1	cejar	1

Grammar

VERBS INDEX

Grammar

repartir	3	resistir	3	revalidar	1
repasar	1	resollar	98	revalorar	1
repatriar	110	**resolver**	141	revelar	1
repeler	2	resonar	98	reventar	133
repensar	133	resoplar	1	reverberar	1
repercutir	3	respaldar	1	reverdecer	99
repetir	132	respetar	1	reverenciar	1
repicar	146	respingar	131	revertir	150
replegar	128	respirar	1	revestir	132
replicar	146	resplandecer	99	revisar	1
repoblar	98	responder	2	revivir	3
reponer	135	resquebrajar	1	revocar	146
reportar	1	restablecer	99	revolcarse	159
reposar	1	restallar	1	revolotear	1
repostar	1	restar	1	revolucionar	1
reprender	2	restaurar	1	revolver	160
representar	1	restituir	97	rezagar	131
reprimir	3	restregar	131	rezar	100
reprobar	98	restringir	104	rezongar	131
reprochar	1	resucitar	1	rezumar	1
reproducir	96	resultar	1	ribetear	1
repudiar	1	resumir	3	ridiculizar	100
repugnar	1	retar	1	rifar	1
repujar	1	retardar	1	rimar	1
repulgar	131	retener	152	rivalizar	100
reputar	1	retirar	1	rizar	100
requerir	150	retocar	146	robar	1
resaltar	1	retorcer	153	robustecer	99
resarcir	161	retornar	1	rociar	110
resbalar	1	retozar	100	rodar	98
rescatar	1	retractar	1	rodear	1
rescindir	3	retraer	154	roer[13]	2
resecarse	146	retransmitir	3	**rogar**	143
reseñar	1	retrasar	1	**romper**	144
resentirse	150	retratar	1	roncar	146
reservar	1	retribuir	97	rondar	1
resfriarse	110	retroceder	2	ronquear	1
resguardar	1	retumbar	1	ronronear	1
residir	1	reunificar	146	rotular	1
resignarse	1	**reunir**	142	roturar	1

☐ Notes

The notes below indicate special peculiarities of individual verbs. When only some forms of a given tense are affected, all these are shown. When all forms of the tense are affected, only the 1st and 2nd persons are shown, followed by *etc.*

1 Gerund *2* Past Participle *3* Present *4* Preterite *5* Present Subjunctive *6* Imperfect Subjunctive

1) **acaecer, acontecer, amanecer, anochecer, competer, deshelar, escampar, granizar, helar, nevar, nublarse, relampaguear, tronar, verdear, verdecer**: used almost exclusively in infinitive and 3rd person singular

2) **asir** *3* asgo *5* asga, asgas *etc*

3) **atañer** *1* atañendo *4* atañó: see also 1) above

4) **balbucir** *3* balbuceo *5* balbucee, balbucees *etc*

5) **concernir** *3* concierne, conciernen *5* concierna, conciernan: only used in 3rd person

6) **degollar** *3* degüello, degüellas, degüella, degüellan *5* degüelle, degüelles, degüellen

7) **delinquir** *3* delinco *5* delinca, delincas *etc*

8) **desasir** *3* desasgo *5* desasga, desasgas *etc*

9) **discernir** *3* discierno, disciernes, discierne, disciernen *5* discierna, disciernas, disciernan

10) **enraizar** *3* enraízo, enraízas, enraíza, enraízan *5* enraíce, enraíces, enraícen

11) **pudrir** *2* podrido

12) **rehuir** *3* rehúyo, rehúyes, rehúye, rehúyen *5* rehúya, rehúyas, rehúyan

13) **roer** *4* royó, royeron *6* royera, royeras *etc*

14) **soler**: used only in present and imperfect indicative

15) **yacer** *3* yazgo *or* yazco *or* yago *5* yazga *etc or* yazca *etc or* yaga *etc*

❑ The Gender of Nouns

In Spanish, all nouns are either masculine or feminine, whether denoting people, animals or things. Gender is largely unpredictable and has to be learnt for each noun. However, the following guidelines will help you determine the gender for certain types of nouns.

◆ Nouns denoting male people and animals are usually – but not always – masculine, e.g.

un hombre	**un toro**
a man	*a bull*
un enfermero	**un semental**
a (male) nurse	*a stallion*

◆ Nouns denoting female people and animals are usually – but not always – feminine, e.g.

una niña	**una vaca**
a girl	*a cow*
una enfermera	**una yegua**
a nurse	*a mare*

◆ Some nouns are masculine *or* feminine depending on the sex of the person to whom they refer, e.g.

un camarada	**una camarada**
a (male) comrade	*a (female) comrade*
un belga	**una belga**
a Belgian (man)	*a Belgian (woman)*
un marroquí	**una marroquí**
a Moroccan (man)	*a Moroccan (woman)*

◆ Other nouns referring to either men or women have only one gender which applies to both, e.g.

una persona	**una visita**
a person	*a visitor*
una víctima	**una estrella**
a victim	*a star*

◆ Often the ending of a noun indicates its gender. Shown below are some of the most important to guide you.

Masculine endings

-o   **un clavo** *a nail*, **un plátano** *a banana*
EXCEPTIONS: **mano** *hand*, **foto** *photograph*, **moto(cicleta)** *motorbike*.

-l   **un tonel** *a barrel*, **un hotel** *a hotel*
EXCEPTIONS: **cal** *lime*, **cárcel** *prison*, **catedral** *cathedral*, col *cabbage*, **miel** *honey*, **piel** *skin*, **sal** *salt*, **señal** *sign*

-r   **un tractor** *a tractor*, **el altar** *the altar*
EXCEPTIONS: **coliflor** *cauliflower*, **flor** *flower*, **labor** *task*

-y   **el rey** *the king*, **un buey** *an ox*
EXCEPTION: **ley** *law*

Feminine endings

-a   **una casa** *a house*, **la cara** *the face*
EXCEPTIONS: **día** *day*, **mapa** *map*, **planeta** *planet*, **tranvía** *tram*, and most words ending in **-ma** (**tema** *subject*, **problema** *problem*, etc)

-ión   **una canción** *a song*, **una procesión** *a procession*
EXCEPTIONS: most nouns not ending in **-ción** or **-sión**, e.g. **avión** *aeroplane*, **camión** *lorry*, **gorrión** *sparrow*

-dad, -tad,   **una ciudad** *a town*, **la libertad** *freedom*, **una**
-tud   **multitud** *a crowd*

-ed   **una pared** *a wall*, **la sed** *thirst*
EXCEPTION: **césped** *lawn*

-itis **una faringitis** *pharyngitis*, **la celulitis** *cellulitis*

-iz   **una perdiz** *a partridge*, **una matriz** *a matrix*
EXCEPTIONS: **lápiz** *pencil*, **maíz** *corn*, **tapiz** *tapestry*

-sis   **una tesis** *a thesis*, **una dosis** *a dose*
EXCEPTIONS: **análisis** *analysis*, **énfasis** *emphasis*, **paréntesis** *parenthesis*

-umbre **la podredumbre** *rot*, **la muchedumbre** *crowd*

☐ **Gender of nouns** (Continued)

Some nouns change meaning according to gender. The most common are set out below:

	MASCULINE	FEMININE
capital	capital (money)	capital (city) → ①
clave	harpsichord	clue
cólera	cholera	anger → ②
cometa	comet	kite
corriente	current month	current
corte	cut	court (royal) → ③
coma	coma	comma → ④
cura	priest	cure → ⑤
frente	front (in war)	forehead → ⑥
guardia	guard(sman)	guard → ⑦
guía	guide (person)	guide(book) → ⑧
moral	mulberry tree	morals
orden	order (arrangement)	order (command) → ⑨
ordenanza	office boy	ordinance
papa	Pope	potato
parte	dispatch	part → ⑩
pendiente	earring	slope
pez	fish	pitch
policía	policeman	police
radio	radius, radium	radio

Examples

☐1 **Invirtieron mucho capital**
They invested a lot of capital
La capital es muy fea
The capital city is very ugly

☐2 **Es difícil luchar contra el cólera**   **Montó en cólera**
Cholera is difficult to combat   He got angry

☐3 **Me encanta tu corte de pelo**
I love your haircut
Se trasladó la corte a Madrid
The court was moved to Madrid

☐4 **Entró en un coma profundo**
He went into a deep coma
Aquí hace falta una coma
You need to put a comma here

☐5 **¿Quién es? – El cura**   **No tiene cura**
Who is it? – The priest   It's hopeless

☐6 **Han mandado a su hijo al frente**
Her son has been sent to the front
Tiene la frente muy ancha
She has a very broad forehead

☐7 **Vino un guardia de tráfico**
A traffic policeman came
Están relevando la guardia ahora
They're changing the guard now

☐8 **Nuestro guía nos hizo reír a carcajadas**
Our guide had us falling about laughing
Busco una guía turística
I'm looking for a guidebook

☐9 **Están en orden alfabético**
They're in alphabetical order
No hemos recibido la orden de pago
We haven't had the payment order

☐10 **Le mandó un parte al general**
He sent a dispatch to the general
En alguna parte debe estar
It must be somewhere or other

☐ Gender: the formation of feminines

As in English, male and female are sometimes differentiated by the use of two quite separate words, e.g.

mi marido	**mi mujer**
my husband	*my wife*
un toro	**una vaca**
a bull	*a cow*

There are, however, some words in Spanish which show this distinction by the form of their ending:

◆ Nouns ending in **-o** change to **-a** to form the feminine → ①

◆ If the masculine singular form already ends in **-a**, no further **-a** is added to the feminine → ②

◆ If the last letter of the masculine singular form is a consonant, an **-a** is normally added in the feminine* → ③

Feminine forms to note

MASCULINE	FEMININE	
el abad	**la abadesa**	*abbot/abbess*
un actor	**una actriz**	*actor/actress*
el alcalde	**la alcaldesa**	*mayor/mayoress*
el conde	**la condesa**	*count/countess*
el duque	**la duquesa**	*duke/duchess*
el emperador	**la emperatriz**	*emperor/empress*
un poeta	**una poetisa**	*poet/poetess*
el príncipe	**la princesa**	*prince/princess*
el rey	**la reina**	*king/queen*
un sacerdote	**una sacerdotisa**	*priest/priestess*
un tigre	**una tigresa**	*tiger/tigress*
el zar	**la zarina**	*tzar/tzarina*

* If the last syllable has an accent, it disappears in the feminine (see p 292) → ④

Grammar

1. **un amigo**
   a (male) friend
   un empleado
   a (male) employee
   un gato
   a cat

   una amiga
   a (female) friend
   una empleada
   a (female) employee
   una gata
   a (female) cat

2. **un deportista**
   a sportsman
   un colega
   a (male) colleague
   un camarada
   a (male) comrade

   una deportista
   a sportswoman
   una colega
   a (female) colleague
   una camarada
   a (female) comrade

3. **un español**
   a Spaniard, a Spanish man
   un vendedor
   a salesman
   un jugador
   a (male) player

   una española
   a Spanish woman
   una vendedora
   a saleswoman
   una jugadora
   a (female) player

4. **un lapón**
   a Laplander (man)
   un león
   a lion
   un neocelandés
   a New Zealander (man)

   una lapona
   a Laplander (woman)
   una leona
   a lioness
   una neocelandesa
   a New Zealander (woman)

☐ **The formation of plurals**

◆ Nouns ending in an unstressed vowel add **-s** to the singular form → ☐1

◆ Nouns ending in a consonant or a stressed vowel add **-es** to the singular form → ☐2

⚠ BUT:

café	coffee shop	(plur: **cafés**)
mamá	mummy	(plur: **mamás**)
papá	daddy	(plur: **papás**)
pie	foot	(plur: **pies**)
sofá	sofa	(plur: **sofás**)
té	tea	(plur: **tes**)

and words of foreign origin ending in a consonant, e.g.:

| **coñac** | brandy | (plur: **coñacs**) |
| **jersey** | jumper | (plur: **jerseys**) |

⚠ NOTE:

— nouns ending in **-n** or **-s** with an accent on the last syllable drop this accent in the plural (see p 292) → ☐3

— nouns ending in **-n** with the stress on the second-last syllable in the singular add an accent to that syllable in the plural in order to show the correct position for stress (see p 292) → ☐4

— nouns ending in **-z** change this to **c** in the plural → ☐5

◆ Nouns with an unstressed final syllable ending in **-s** do not change in the plural → ☐6

1. **la casa**   **las casas**
   the house   the houses
   el libro   **los libros**
   the book   the books

2. **un rumor**   **unos rumores**
   a rumour   (some) rumours
   un jabalí   **unos jabalíes**
   a boar   (some) boars

3. **la canción**   **las canciones**
   the song   the songs
   el autobús   **los autobuses**
   the bus   the buses

4. **un examen**   **unos exámenes**
   an exam   (some) exams
   un crimen   **unos crímenes**
   a crime   (some) crimes

5. **la luz**   **las luces**
   the light   the lights

6. **un paraguas**   **unos paraguas**
   an umbrella   (some) umbrellas
   la dosis   **las dosis**
   the dose   the doses
   el lunes   **los lunes**
   Monday   Mondays

❐ **The Definite Article**

	WITH MASC NOUN	WITH FEM NOUN	
SING	**el**	**la**	*the*
PLUR	**los**	**las**	*the*

- The gender and number of the noun determine the form of the article → ①

  ⚠ NOTE: However, if the article comes directly before a feminine singular noun which starts with a stressed **a-** or **ha-**, the masculine form **el** is used instead of the feminine **la** → ②

- For uses of the definite article see p 199.

- **a** + **el** becomes **al** → ③

- **de** + **el** becomes **del** → ④

1

el tren	**la estación**
the train	the station
el actor	**la actriz**
the actor	the actress
los hoteles	**las escuelas**
the hotels	the schools
los profesores	**las mujeres**
the teachers	the women

2

el agua	⚠ BUT:	**la misma agua**	
the water		the same water	
el hacha	⚠ BUT:	**la mejor hacha**	
the axe		the best axe	

3

al cine
to the cinema
al empleado
to the employee
al hospital
to the hospital

4

del departamento
from/of the department
del autor
from/of the author
del presidente
from/of the president

☐ Uses of the definite article

While the definite article is used in much the same way in Spanish as it is in English, its use is more widespread in Spanish. Unlike English the definite article is also used:

- with abstract nouns, except when following certain prepositions → ①

- in generalizations, especially with plural or uncountable* nouns → ②

- with parts of the body → ③

  'Ownership' is often indicated by an indirect object pronoun or a reflexive pronoun → ④

- with titles/ranks/professions followed by a proper name → ⑤

  ⚠ EXCEPTIONS: with **Don/Doña, San/Santo(a)** → ⑥

- before nouns of official, academic and religious buildings, and names of meals and games → ⑦

- The definite article is NOT used with nouns in apposition unless those nouns are individualized → ⑧

* An uncountable noun is one which cannot be used in the plural or with an indefinite article, e.g. **el acero** *steel*, **la leche** milk.

1 **Los precios suben**
Prices are rising
El tiempo es oro
Time is money

⚠ BUT:

con pasión   **sin esperanza**
with passion   without hope

2 **No me gusta el café**
I don't like coffee
Los niños necesitan ser queridos
Children need to be loved

3 **Vuelva la cabeza hacia la izquierda**
Turn your head to the left
No puedo mover las piernas
I can't move my legs

4 **La cabeza me da vueltas**
My head is spinning
Lávate las manos
Wash your hands

5 **El rey Jorge III**   **el capitán Menéndez**
King George III   Captain Menéndez
el doctor Ochoa   **el señor Ramírez**
Doctor Ochoa   Mr Ramírez

6 **Don Arturo Ruiz**   **Santa Teresa**
Mr Arturo Ruiz   Saint Teresa

7 **en la cárcel**   **en la universidad**
in prison   at university
en la iglesia   **la cena**
at church   dinner
el tenis   **el ajedrez**
tennis   chess

8 **Madrid, capital de España, es la ciudad que ...**
Madrid, the capital of Spain, is the city which ...

⚠ BUT:

María Callas, la famosa cantante de ópera ...
Maria Callas, the famous opera singer ...

❒ **The Indefinite Article**

	WITH MASC NOUN	WITH FEM NOUN	
SING	**un**	**una**	*a*
PLUR	**unos**	**unas**	*some*

The indefinite article is used in Spanish largely as it is in English.

⚠ BUT:

- There is no article when a person's profession is being stated → 1
  The article is used, however, when the profession is qualified by an adjective → 2

- The article is not used with the following words:

otro	*another*	→ 3
cierto	*certain*	→ 4
semejante	*such (a)*	→ 5
tal	*such (a)*	→ 6
cien	*a hundred*	→ 7
mil	*a thousand*	→ 8
sin	*without*	→ 9
qué	*what a*	→ 10

- There is no article with a noun in apposition → 11 . When an abstract noun is qualified by an adjective, the indefinite article is used, but is not translated in English → 12

1	**Es profesor** He's a teacher	**Mi madre es enfermera** My mother is a nurse
2	**Es un buen médico** He's a good doctor	
	Se hizo una escritora célebre She became a famous writer	
3	**otro libro** another book	
4	**cierta calle** a certain street	
5	**semejante ruido** such a noise	
6	**tal mentira** such a lie	
7	**cien soldados** a hundred soldiers	
8	**mil años** a thousand years	
9	**sin casa** without a house	
10	**¡Qué sorpresa!** What a surprise!	
11	**Baroja, gran escritor de la Generación del 98** Baroja, a great writer of the 'Generación del 98'	
12	**con una gran sabiduría/un valor admirable** with great wisdom/admirable courage	
	Dieron pruebas de una sangre fría increíble They showed incredible coolness	
	una película de un mal gusto espantoso a film in appallingly bad taste	

☐ The Article 'lo'

This is never used with a noun. Instead, it is used in the following ways:

◆ As an intensifier before an adjective or adverb in the construction

lo + adjective/adverb + **que** → ①

⚠ NOTE: The adjective agrees with the noun it refers to → ②

◆ With an adjective or participle to form an abstract noun → ③

◆ In the phrase **lo de** to refer to a subject of which speaker and listener are already aware. It can often be translated as *the business/affair of/about …* → ④

◆ In set expressions, the commonest of which are:

a lo mejor	*maybe, perhaps*	→ ⑤
a lo lejos	*in the distance*	→ ⑥
a lo largo de	*along, through*	→ ⑦
por lo menos	*at least*	→ ⑧
por lo tanto	*therefore, so*	→ ⑨
por lo visto	*apparently*	→ ⑩

Examples

Grammar

1	**No sabíamos lo pequeña que era la casa** We didn't know how small the house was
	Sé lo mucho que te gusta la música I know how much you like music
2	**No te imaginas lo simpáticos que son** You can't imagine how nice they are
	Ya sabes lo buenas que son estas manzanas You already know how good these apples are
3	**Lo bueno de eso es que ...** The good thing about it is that ...
	Sentimos mucho lo ocurrido We are very sorry about what happened
4	**Lo de ayer es mejor que lo olvides** It's better if you forget what happened yesterday
	Lo de tu hermano me preocupa mucho The business about your brother worries me very much
5	**A lo mejor ha salido** Perhaps he's gone out
6	**A lo lejos se veían unas casas** Some houses could be seen in the distance
7	**A lo largo de su vida** Throughout his life
	A lo largo de la carretera Along the road
8	**Hubo por lo menos cincuenta heridos** At least fifty people were injured
9	**No hemos recibido ninguna instrucción al respecto, y por lo tanto no podemos ...** We have not received any instructions about it, therefore we cannot ...
10	**Por lo visto, no viene** Apparently he's not coming OR: He's not coming, it seems

❏ Adjectives

Most adjectives agree in number and in gender with the noun or pronoun.

⚠ NOTE that:

— if the adjective refers to two or more singular nouns of the same gender, a plural ending of that gender is required → 1

— if the adjective refers to two or more singular nouns of different genders, a masculine plural ending is required → 2

The formation of feminines

♦ Adjectives ending in **-o** change to **-a** → 3

♦ Some groups of adjectives add **-a**:

  – adjectives of nationality or geographical origin → 4

  – adjectives ending in **-or** (except irregular comparatives: see p 210), **-án**, **-ón**, **-ín** → 5

  ⚠ NOTE: When there is an accent on the last syllable, it disappears in the feminine (see p 292).

♦ Other adjectives do not change → 6

The formation of plurals

♦ Adjectives ending in an unstressed vowel add **-s** → 7

♦ Adjectives ending in a stressed vowel or a consonant add **-es** → 8

  ⚠ NOTE:

  – if there is an accent on the last syllable of a word ending in a consonant, it will disappear in the plural (see p 292) → 9

  – if the last letter is a **z** it will become a **c** in the plural → 10

1. **la lengua y la literatura españolas**
   (the) Spanish language and literature

2. **Nunca había visto árboles y flores tan raros**
   I had never seen such strange trees and flowers

3. **mi hermano pequeño**
   my little brother
   mi hermana pequeña
   my little sister

4. **un chico español**
   a Spanish boy
   una chica española
   a Spanish girl

   el equipo barcelonés
   the team from Barcelona
   la vida barcelonesa
   the Barcelona way of life

5. **un niño encantador**
   a charming little boy
   una niña encantadora
   a charming little girl

   un hombre holgazán
   an idle man
   una mujer holgazana
   an idle woman

   un gesto burlón
   a mocking gesture
   una sonrisa burlona
   a mocking smile

   un chico cantarín
   a boy fond of singing
   una chica cantarina
   a girl fond of singing

6. **un final feliz**
   a happy ending
   una infancia feliz
   a happy childhood

   mi amigo belga
   my Belgian (male) friend
   mi amiga belga
   my Belgian (female) friend

   el vestido verde
   the green dress
   la blusa verde
   the green blouse

7. **el último tren**
   the last train
   los últimos trenes
   the last trains

   una casa vieja
   an old house
   unas casas viejas
   (some) old houses

8. **un médico iraní**
   an Iranian doctor
   unos médicos iraníes
   (some) Iranian doctors

   un examen fácil
   an easy exam
   unos exámenes fáciles
   (some) easy exams

9. **un río francés**
   a French river
   unos ríos franceses
   (some) French rivers

10. **un día feliz**
    a happy day
    unos días felices
    (some) happy days

☐ Invariable Adjectives

Some adjectives and other parts of speech when used adjectivally never change in the feminine or plural.

The commonest of these are:

— nouns denoting colour → ①
— compound adjectives → ②
— nouns used as adjectives → ③

Shortening of Adjectives

◆ The following drop the final **-o** before a masculine singular noun:

bueno *good* → ④

malo *bad*

alguno* *some* → ⑤

ninguno* *none*

uno *one* → ⑥

primero *first* → ⑦

tercero *third*

postrero *last* → ⑧

> * ⚠ NOTE: An accent is required to show the correct position for stress.

◆ **Grande** *big, great* is usually shortened to **gran** before a masculine *or* feminine singular noun → ⑨

◆ **Santo** *Saint* changes to **San** except with saints' names beginning with **Do-** or **To-** → ⑩

◆ **Ciento** *a hundred* is shortened to **cien** before a masculine *or* feminine plural noun → ⑪

◆ **Cualquiera** drops the final **-a** before a masculine *or* feminine singular noun → ⑫

grammar

1. **los vestidos naranja**
   the orange dresses

2. **las chaquetas azul marino**
   the navy blue jackets

3. **bebés probeta**   **mujeres soldado**
   test-tube babies   women soldiers

4. **un buen libro**
   a good book

5. **algún libro**
   some book

6. **cuarenta y un años**
   forty-one years

7. **el primer hijo**
   the first child

8. **un postrer deseo**
   a last wish

9. **un gran actor**   **una gran decepción**
   a great actor   a great disappointment

10. **San Antonio**   **Santo Tomás**
    Saint Anthony   Saint Thomas

11. **cien años**
    a hundred years
    cien millones
    a hundred million

12. **cualquier día**   **a cualquier hora**
    any day   any time

☐ Comparatives and Superlatives

Comparatives

These are formed using the following constructions:

más ... (que)	more ... (than)	→ ①
menos ... (que)	less ... (than)	→ ②
tanto ... como	as ... as	→ ③
tan ... como	as ... as	→ ④
tan ... que	so ... that	→ ⑤
demasiado ...	too ...	
bastante ... } **para**	enough ... } to	→ ⑥
suficiente ...	enough ...	

- 'Than' followed by a clause is translated by **de lo que** → ⑦

Superlatives

These are formed using the following constructions:

el/la/los/las más ... (que)	the most ... (that)	→ ⑧
el/la/los/las menos ... (que)	the least ... (that)	→ ⑨

- After a superlative the preposition **de** is often translated as *in* → ⑩

- The absolute superlative (*very, most, extremely + adjective*) is expressed in Spanish by **muy** + adjective, or by adding **-ísimo/a/os/as** to the adjective when it ends in a consonant, or to its stem (adjective minus final vowel) when it ends in a vowel → ⑪

⚠ NOTE: It is sometimes necessary to change the spelling of the adjective when **-ísimo** is added, in order to maintain the same sound (see p 296) → ⑫

Grammar

1	**una razón más seria** a more serious reason **Es más alto que mi hermano** He's taller than my brother	
2	**una película menos conocida** a less well known film **Luis es menos tímido que tú** Luis is less shy than you	
3	**Pablo tenía tanto miedo como yo** Paul was as frightened as I was	
4	**No es tan grande como creía** It isn't as big as I thought	
5	**El examen era tan difícil que nadie aprobó** The exam was so difficult that nobody passed	
6	**No tengo suficiente dinero para comprarlo** I haven't got enough money to buy it	
7	**Está más cansada de lo que parece** She is more tired than she seems	
8	**el caballo más veloz** the fastest horse	**la casa más pequeña** the smallest house
	los días más lluviosos the wettest days	**las manzanas más maduras** the ripest apples
9	**el hombre menos simpático** the least likeable man	**la niña menos habladora** the least talkative girl
	los cuadros menos bonitos the least attractive paintings	**las camisas menos viejas** the least old shirts
10	**la estación más ruidosa de Londres** the noisiest station in London	
11	**Este libro es muy interesante** This book is very interesting	**Tienen un coche rapidísimo** They have an extremely fast car
	Era facilísimo de hacer It was very easy to make	
12	**Mi tío era muy rico** My uncle was very rich	**Se hizo riquísimo** He became extremely rich
	un león muy feroz a very ferocious lion	**un tigre ferocísimo** an extremely ferocious tiger

❐ Comparatives and Superlatives (Continued)

Adjectives with irregular comparatives/superlatives

ADJECTIVE	COMPARATIVE	SUPERLATIVE
bueno good	**mejor** better	**el mejor** the best
malo bad	**peor** worse	**el peor** the worst
grande big	**mayor** OR: **más grande** bigger; older	**el mayor** OR: **el más grande** the biggest; the oldest
pequeño small	**menor** OR: **más pequeño** smaller; younger; lesser	**el menor** OR: **el más pequeño** the smallest; the youngest; the least

◆ The irregular comparative and superlative forms of **grande** and **pequeño** are used mainly to express:

— age, in which case they come after the noun → 1

— abstract size and degrees of importance, in which case they come before the noun → 2

The regular forms are used mainly to express physical size → 3

◆ Irregular comparatives and superlatives have one form for both masculine and feminine, but always agree in number with the noun → 1

---

1   **mis hermanos mayores**
my older brothers
la hija menor
the youngest daughter

2   **el menor ruido**
the slightest sound
las mayores dificultades
the biggest difficulties

3   **Este plato es más grande que aquél**
This plate is bigger than that one
Mi casa es más pequeña que la tuya
My house is smaller than yours

☐ Demonstrative Adjectives

	MASCULINE	FEMININE	
SING	este ese aquel	esta esa aquella	this } that
PLUR	estos esos aquellos	estas esas aquellas	these } those

- Demonstrative adjectives normally precede the noun and always agree in number and in gender → ☐1

- The forms **ese/a/os/as** are used:
  - to indicate distance from the speaker but proximity to the person addressed → ☐2
  - to indicate a not too remote distance → ☐3

- The forms **aquel/la/los/las** are used to indicate distance, in space or time → ☐4

1.   **Este bolígrafo no escribe**
This pen is not working
Esa revista es muy mala
That is a very bad magazine
Aquella montaña es muy alta
That mountain (over there) is very high
¿Conoces a esos señores?
Do you know those gentlemen?
Siga Vd hasta aquellos edificios
Carry on until you come to those buildings
¿Ves aquellas personas?
Can you see those people (over there)?

2.   **Ese papel en donde escribes ...**
That paper you are writing on ...

3.   **No me gustan esos cuadros**
I don't like those pictures

4.   **Aquella calle parece muy ancha**
That street (over there) looks very wide
Aquellos años sí que fueron felices
Those were really happy years

☐ Interrogative Adjectives

	MASCULINE	FEMININE	
SING {	¿qué?	¿qué?	what?, which?
	¿cuánto?	¿cuánta?	how much?; how many?
PLUR {	¿qué?	¿qué?	what?, which?
	¿cuántos?	¿cuántas?	how much?; how many?

- Interrogative adjectives, when not invariable, agree in number and gender with the noun → ①

- The forms shown above are also used in indirect questions → ②

☐ Exclamatory Adjectives

	MASCULINE	FEMININE	
SING {	¡qué!	¡qué!	what (a)
	¡cuánto!	¡cuánta!	what (a lot of)
PLUR {	¡qué!	¡qué!	what
	¡cuántos!	¡cuántas!	what (a lot of)

- Exclamatory adjectives, when not invariable, agree in number and gender with the noun → ③

1 **¿Qué libro te gustó más?**
Which book did you like most?
¿Qué clase de hombre es?
What type of man is he?
¿Qué instrumentos toca Vd?
What instruments do you play?
¿Qué ofertas ha recibido Vd?
What offers have you received?
¿Cuánto dinero te queda?
How much money have you got left?
¿Cuánta lluvia ha caído?
How much rain have we had?
¿Cuántos vestidos quieres comprar?
How many dresses do you want to buy?
¿Cuántas personas van a venir?
How many people are coming?

2 **No sé a qué hora llegó**
I don't know at what time she arrived
Dígame cuántas postales quiere
Tell me how many postcards you'd like

3 **¡Qué pena!**
What a pity!
¡Qué tiempo tan/más malo!
What lousy weather!
¡Cuánto tiempo!
What a long time!
¡Cuánta pobreza!
What poverty!
¡Cuántos autobuses!
What a lot of buses!
¡Cuántas mentiras!
What a lot of lies!

❑ Possessive Adjectives

Weak forms

WITH SING NOUN		WITH PLUR NOUN		
MASC	FEM	MASC	FEM	
mi	**mi**	**mis**	**mis**	*my*
tu	**tu**	**tus**	**tus**	*your*
su	**su**	**sus**	**sus**	*his; her; its; your*
				*(of **Vd**)*
nuestro	**nuestra**	**nuestros**	**nuestras**	*our*
vuestro	**vuestra**	**vuestros**	**vuestras**	*your*
su	**su**	**sus**	**sus**	*their; your*
				*(of **Vds**)*

◆ All possessive adjectives agree in number and (when applicable) in gender with the noun, NOT WITH THE OWNER → ①

◆ The weak forms always precede the noun → ①

◆ Since the form **su(s)** can mean *his, her, your* (of **Vd, Vds**) or *their*, clarification is often needed. This is done by adding **de él, de ella, de Vds** etc to the noun, and usually (but not always) changing the possessive to a definite article → ②

1   **Pilar no ha traído nuestros libros**
Pilar hasn't brought our books
Antonio irá a vuestra casa
Anthony will go to your house
¿Han vendido su coche tus vecinos?
Have your neighbours sold their car?
Mi hermano y tu primo no se llevan bien
My brother and your cousin don't get on

2   **su casa → la casa de él**
his house
sus amigos → los amigos de Vd
your friends
sus coches → los coches de ellos
their cars
su abrigo → el abrigo de ella
her coat

❑ **Possessive Adjectives** (Continued)

Strong forms

WITH SING NOUN		WITH PLUR NOUN		
MASC	*FEM*	*MASC*	*FEM*	
mío	**mía**	**míos**	**mías**	*my*
tuyo	**tuya**	**tuyos**	**tuyas**	*your*
suyo	**suya**	**suyos**	**suyas**	*his; her; its; your (of **Vd**)*
nuestro	**nuestra**	**nuestros**	**nuestras**	*our*
vuestro	**vuestra**	**vuestros**	**vuestras**	*your*
suyo	**suya**	**suyos**	**suyas**	*their; your (of **Vds**)*

◆ The strong forms agree in the same way as the weak forms (see p 216).

◆ The strong forms always follow the noun, and they are used:
   — to translate the English *of mine, of yours*, etc → ①
   — to address people → ②

1. **Es un capricho suyo**
   It's a whim of hers
   un amigo nuestro
   a friend of ours
   una revista tuya
   a magazine of yours

2. **Muy señor mío** (in letters)
   Dear Sir
   hija mía
   my daughter
   ¡Dios mío!
   My God!
   Amor mío
   Darling/My love

☐ Indefinite Adjectives

alguno(a)s	*some*
ambos(as)	*both*
cada	*each; every*
cierto(a)s	*certain; definite*
cualquiera, plur **cualesquiera**	*some; any*
los (las) demás	*the others; the remainder*
mismo(a)s	*same; -self*
mucho(a)s	*many; much*
ningún, ninguna	*any; no*
plur **ningunos, ningunas**	
otro(a)s	*other; another*
poco(a)s	*few; little*
tal(es)	*such (a)*
tanto(a)s	*so much; so many*
todo(a)s	*all; every*
varios(as)	*several; various*

Unless invariable, all indefinite adjectives agree in number and gender with the noun → ①

♦ **alguno**

Before a masculine singular noun it drops the final -**o** and adds an accent to show the correct position for stress → ② (see also p 292)

♦ **ambos**

Usually it is only used in written Spanish. The spoken language prefers the form **los dos/las dos** → ③

♦ **cierto** and **mismo**

They change their meaning according to their position in relation to the noun (see also **Position of Adjectives**, p 224) → ④

♦ **cualquiera**

It drops the final -**a** before a masculine *or* feminine noun → ⑤

Grammar

1	**el mismo día**	**las mismas películas**
	the same day	the same films
	mucha/poca gente	**mucho/poco dinero**
	many/few people	much/little money

2   **algún día**   **alguna razón**
      some day   some reason

3   **Me gustan los dos cuadros**
      I like both pictures
      ¿Conoces a las dos enfermeras?
      Do you know both nurses?

4   **cierto tiempo** ⚠ BUT: **éxito cierto**
      a certain time   sure success
      el mismo color ⚠ BUT: **en la iglesia misma**
      the same colour   in the church itself

5   **cualquier casa** ⚠ BUT: **una revista cualquiera**
      any house   any magazine

Grammar

☐ **Indefinite Adjectives** (Continued)

◆ **ningún** is only used in negative sentences or phrases → 1

◆ **otro**

It is never preceded by an indefinite article → 2

◆ **tal**

It is never followed by an indefinite article → 3

◆ **todo**

It can be followed by a definite article, a demonstrative or possessive adjective or a place name → 4

⚠ EXCEPTIONS:

— when **todo** in the singular means *any*, *every*, or *each* → 5

— in some set expressions → 6

1 **No es ninguna tonta**
She's no fool
¿No tienes parientes? – No, ninguno
Haven't you any relatives? – No, none

2 **¿Me das otra manzana?**
Will you give me another apple?
Prefiero estos otros zapatos
I prefer these other shoes

3 **Nunca dije tal cosa**
I never said such a thing

4 **Estudian durante toda la noche**
They study all night
Ha llovido toda esta semana
It has rained all this week
Pondré en orden todos mis libros
I'll sort out all my books
Lo sabe todo Madrid
All Madrid knows it

5 **Podrá entrar toda persona que lo desee**
Any person who wishes to enter may do so

⚠ BUT:
Vienen todos los días
They come every day

6 | **de todos modos** | **a toda velocidad** |
anyway | at full/top speed |
por todas partes
por todos lados
a/en todas partes } everywhere
a/en todos lados

☐ Position of Adjectives

- Spanish adjectives usually follow the noun → 1, 2

- Note that when used figuratively or to express a quality already inherent in the noun, adjectives can precede the noun → 3

- As in English, demonstrative, possessive (weak forms), numerical, interrogative and exclamatory adjectives precede the noun → 4

- Indefinite adjectives also usually precede the noun → 5

  ⚠ NOTE: **alguno** *some* in negative expressions follows the noun → 6

- Some adjectives can precede or follow the noun, but their meaning varies according to their position:

	BEFORE NOUN	AFTER NOUN	
antiguo	former	old, ancient	→ 7
diferente	various	different	→ 8
grande	great	big	→ 9
medio	half	average	→ 10
mismo	same	-self, very/precisely	→ 11
nuevo	new, another, fresh	brand new	→ 12
pobre	poor (wretched)	poor (not rich)	→ 13
puro	sheer, mere	pure (clear)	→ 14
varios	several	various, different	→ 15
viejo	old (long known, etc)	old (aged)	→ 16

- Adjectives following the noun are linked by **y** → 17

1	**la página siguiente** the following page	**la hora exacta** the right time	
2	**una corbata azul** a blue tie	**una palabra española** a Spanish word	
3	**un dulce sueño** a sweet dream		
	un terrible desastre (all disasters are terrible) a terrible disaster		
4	**este sombrero** this hat	**mi padre** my father	**¿qué hombre?** what man?
5	**cada día** every day	**otra vez** another time	**poco dinero** little money
6	**sin duda alguna** without any doubt		
7	**un antiguo colega** a former colleague	**la historia antigua** ancient history	
8	**diferentes capítulos** various chapters	**personas diferentes** different people	
9	**un gran pintor** a great painter	**una casa grande** a big house	
10	**medio melón** half a melon	**velocidad media** average speed	
11	**la misma respuesta** the same answer	**yo mismo** myself	**eso mismo** precisely that
12	**mi nuevo coche** my new car	**unos zapatos nuevos** (some) brand new shoes	
13	**esa pobre mujer** that poor woman	**un país pobre** a poor country	
14	**la pura verdad** the plain truth	**aire puro** fresh air	
15	**varios caminos** several ways/paths	**artículos varios** various items	
16	**un viejo amigo** an old friend	**esas toallas viejas** those old towels	
17	**una acción cobarde y falsa** a cowardly, deceitful act		

◻ Personal Pronouns

SUBJECT PRONOUNS

PERSON	SINGULAR	PLURAL
1st	**yo**	**nosotros**
	I	*we* (masc/masc + fem)
		nosotras
		we (all fem)
2nd	**tú**	**vosotros**
	you	*you* (masc/masc + fem)
		vosotras
		you (all fem)
3rd	**él**	**ellos**
	he; it	*they* (masc/masc + fem)
	ella	**ellas**
	she; it	*they* (all fem)
	usted (Vd)	**ustedes (Vds)**
	you	*you*

◆ Subject pronouns have a limited usage in Spanish. Normally they are only used:

— for emphasis → 1

— for clarity → 2

⚠ BUT: **Vd** and **Vds** should always be used for politeness, whether they are otherwise needed or not → 3

◆ *It* as subject and *they*, referring to things, are never translated into Spanish → 4

◆ **tú/usted**

As a general rule, you should use **tú** (or **vosotros,** if plural) when addressing a friend, a child, a relative, someone you know well, or when invited to do so. In all other cases, use **usted** (or **ustedes**)

◆ **nosotros/as; vosotros/as; él/ella; ellos/ellas**

All these forms reflect the number and gender of the noun(s) they replace. **Nosotros, vosotros** and **ellos** also replace a combination of masculine and feminine nouns.

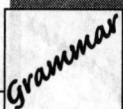

1. **Ellos sí que llegaron tarde**
   They really did arrive late
   Tú no tienes por qué venir
   There is no reason for you to come
   Ella jamás creería eso
   She would never believe that

2. **Yo estudio español pero él estudia francés**
   I study Spanish but he studies French
   Ella era muy deportista pero él prefería jugar a las cartas
   She was a sporty type but he preferred to play cards
   Vosotros saldréis primero y nosotros os seguiremos
   You leave first and we will follow you

3. **Pase Vd por aquí**
   Please come this way
   ¿Habían estado Vds antes en esta ciudad?
   Had you been to this town before?

4. **¿Qué es? – Es una sorpresa**
   What is it? – It's a surprise
   ¿Qué son? – Son abrelatas
   What are they? – They are tin-openers

◻ **Personal Pronouns** (Continued)

DIRECT OBJECT PRONOUNS

PERSON	SINGULAR	PLURAL
1st	**me**	**nos**
	me	*us*
2nd	**te**	**os**
	you	*you*
3rd (masculine)	**lo**	**los**
	him; it; you	*them; you*
	(of **Vd**)	*(of* **Vds**)
(feminine)	**la**	**las**
	her; it; you	*them; you*
	(of **Vd**)	*(of* **Vds**)

◆ **lo** sometimes functions as a 'neuter' pronoun, referring to an idea or information contained in a previous statement or question. It is often not translated → ①

Position of direct object pronouns

◆ In constructions other than the imperative affirmative, infinitive or gerund, the pronoun always comes before the verb → ②

In the imperative affirmative, infinitive and gerund, the pronoun follows the verb and is attached to it. An accent is needed in certain cases to show the correct position for stress (see also p 292) → ③

◆ Where an infinitive or gerund depends on a previous verb, the pronoun may be used either after the infinitive or gerund, or before the main verb → ④

⚠ NOTE: see how this applies to reflexive verbs → ④

◆ For further information, see **Order of Object Pronouns**, p 232.

Reflexive Pronouns

These are dealt with under reflexive verbs, p 24.

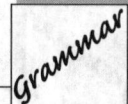

1. **¿Va a venir María? – No lo sé**
Is Maria coming? – I don't know
Hay que regar las plantas – Yo lo haré
The plants need watering – I'll do it
Habían comido ya pero no nos lo dijeron
They had already eaten, but they didn't tell us
Yo conduzco de prisa pero él lo hace despacio
I drive fast but he drives slowly

2. **Te quiero**
I love you
¿Las ve Vd?
Can you see them?
¿No me oyen Vds?
Can't you hear me?
Tu hija no nos conoce
Your daughter doesn't know us
No los toques
Don't touch them

3. **Ayúdame**   **Acompáñenos**
Help me   Come with us
Quiero decirte algo
I want to tell you something
Estaban persiguiéndonos
They were coming after us

4. **Lo está comiendo** OR: **Está comiéndolo**
She is eating it
Nos vienen a ver OR: **Vienen a vernos**
They are coming to see us
No quería levantarse OR: **No se quería levantar**
He didn't want to get up
Estoy afeitándome OR: **Me estoy afeitando**
I'm shaving

◻ **Personal Pronouns** (Continued)

	INDIRECT OBJECT PRONOUNS	
PERSON	SINGULAR	PLURAL
1st	**me**	**nos**
2nd	**te**	**os**
3rd	**le**	**les**

◆ The pronouns shown in the above table replace the preposition **a** + noun → ①

Position of indirect object pronouns

◆ In constructions other than the imperative affirmative, the infinitive or the gerund, the pronoun comes before the verb → ②

   In the imperative affirmative, infinitive and gerund, the pronoun follows the verb and is attached to it. An accent is needed in certain cases to show the correct position for stress (see also p 292) → ③

◆ Where an infinitive or gerund depends on a previous verb, the pronoun may be used either after the infinitive or gerund, or before the main verb → ④

◆ For further information, see **Order of Object Pronouns**, p 232.

Reflexive Pronouns

These are dealt with under reflexive verbs, p 24.

Grammar

---

1   **Estoy escribiendo a Teresa** → **Le estoy escribiendo**
I am writing to Teresa   I am writing to her
Da de comer al gato   → **Dale de comer**
Give the cat some food   Give it some food

2   **Sofía os ha escrito**   **¿Os ha escrito Sofía?**
Sophie has written to you   Has Sophie written to you?
Carlos no nos habla
Charles doesn't speak to us
¿Qué te pedían?
What were they asking you for?
No les haga caso Vd
Don't take any notice of them

3   **Respóndame Vd**   **Díganos Vd la respuesta**
Answer me   Tell us the answer
No quería darte la noticia todavía
I didn't want to tell you the news yet
Llegaron diciéndome que ...
They came telling me that ...

4   **Estoy escribiéndole** OR: **Le estoy escribiendo**
I am writing to him/her
Les voy a hablar OR: **Voy a hablarles**
I'm going to talk to them

☐ Personal Pronouns (Continued)

Order of object pronouns

◆ When two object pronouns of different persons are combined, the order is: indirect before direct, i.e.

me te nos os	before	lo la los las	→ ①

⚠ NOTE: When two 3rd person object pronouns are combined, the first (i.e. the indirect object pronoun) becomes **se** → ②

Points to note on object pronouns

◆ As **le/les** can refer to either gender, and **se** to either gender, singular or plural, sometimes clarification is needed. This is done by adding **a él** *to him*, **a ella** *to her*, **a Vd** *to you* etc to the phrase, usually after the verb → ③

◆ When a noun object precedes the verb, the corresponding object pronoun must be used too → ④

◆ Indirect object pronouns are often used instead of possessive adjectives with parts of the body or clothing to indicate 'ownership', and also in certain common constructions involving reflexive verbs (see also **The Indefinite Article**, p 198) → ⑤

◆ **Le** and **les** are often used in Spanish instead of **lo** and **los** when referring to people. Equally **la** is sometimes used instead of **le** when referring to a feminine person or animal, although this usage is considered incorrect by some speakers of Spanish → ⑥

1. **Paloma os lo mandará mañana**
   Paloma is sending it to you tomorrow
   ¿Te los ha enseñado mi hermana?
   Has my sister shown them to you?
   No me lo digas
   Don't tell me (that)
   Todos estaban pidiéndotelo
   They were all asking you for it
   No quiere prestárnosla
   He won't lend it to us

2. **Se lo di ayer**
   I gave it to him/her/them yesterday

3. **Le escriben mucho a ella**
   They write to her often
   Se lo van a mandar pronto a ellos
   They will be sending it to them soon

4. **A tu hermano lo conozco bien**
   I know your brother well
   A María la vemos algunas veces
   We sometimes see Maria

5. **La chaqueta le estaba ancha**
   His jacket was too loose
   Me duele el tobillo
   My ankle is aching
   Se me ha perdido el bolígrafo
   I have lost my pen

6. **Le/lo encontraron en el cine**
   They met him at the cinema
   Les/los oímos llegar
   We heard them coming
   Le/la escribimos una carta
   We wrote a letter to her

☐ **Personal Pronouns** (Continued)

Pronouns after prepositions

◆ These are the same as the subject pronouns, except for the forms **mí** *me*, **ti** *you* (sing), and the reflexive **sí** *himself, herself, themselves, yourselves* → ☐1

◆ **Con** *with* combines with **mí, ti** and **sí** to form

   conmigo *with me* → ☐2
   contigo *with you*
   consigo *with himself/herself etc*

◆ The following prepositions always take a subject pronoun:

entre	*between, among* → ☐3
hasta	
incluso	} *even, including* → ☐4
salvo	
menos	} *except* → ☐5
según	*according to* → ☐6

◆ These pronouns are used for emphasis, especially where contrast is involved → ☐7

◆ **Ello** *it, that* is used after a preposition when referring to an idea already mentioned, but never to a concrete noun → ☐8

◆ **A él, de él** NEVER contract → ☐9

1	**Pienso en ti** I think about you	**¿Son para mí?** Are they for me?
	Es para ella This is for her	**Iban hacia ellos** They were going towards them
	Volveréis sin nosotros You'll come back without us	**Volaban sobre vosotros** They were flying above you
	Hablaba para sí He was talking to himself	
2	**Venid conmigo** Come with me	
	Lo trajeron consigo ⚠ BUT: **¿Hablaron con vosotros?** They brought it/him with them Did they talk to you?	
3	**entre tú y ella** between you and her	
4	**Hasta yo puedo hacerlo** Even I can do it	
5	**todos menos yo** everybody except me	
6	**según tú** according to you	
7	**¿A ti no te escriben?** Don't they write to you?	
	Me lo manda a mí, no a ti She is sending it to me, not to you	
8	**Nunca pensaba en ello** He never thought about it	
	Por todo ello me parece que ... For all those reasons it seems to me that ...	
9	**A él no lo conozco** I don't know him	**No he sabido nada de él** I haven't heard from him

☐ Indefinite Pronouns

algo	something, anything	→ 1
alguien	somebody, anybody	→ 2
alguno/a/os/as	some, a few	→ 3
cada uno/a	each (one) everybody	→ 4
cualquiera	anybody; any	→ 5
los/las demás	the others the rest	→ 6
mucho/a/os/as	many; much	→ 7
nada	nothing	→ 8
nadie	nobody	→ 9
ninguno/a	none, not any	→ 10
poco/a/os/as	few; little	→ 11
tanto/a/os/as	so much; so many	→ 12
todo/a/os/as	all; everything	→ 13
uno ... (el) otro una ... (la) otra	(the) one ... the other	→ 14
unos ... (los) otros unas ... (las) otras	some ... (the) others	
varios/as	several	→ 15

◆ algo, alguien, alguno

They can never be used after a negative. The appropriate negative pronouns are used instead: **nada**, **nadie**, **ninguno** (see also negatives, p 272) → 16

1	**Tengo algo para ti**	**¿Viste algo?**
	I have something for you	Did you see anything?
2	**Alguien me lo ha dicho**	**¿Has visto a alguien?**
	Somebody said it to me	Have you seen anybody?
3	**Algunos de los niños ya sabían leer**	
	Some of the children could read already	
4	**Le dió una manzana a cada uno**	**!Cada uno a su casa!**
	She gave each of them an apple	Everybody go home!
5	**Cualquiera puede hacerlo**	
	Anybody can do it	
	Cualquiera de las explicaciones vale	
	Any of the explanations is a valid one	
6	**Yo me fui, los demás se quedaron**	
	I went, the others stayed	
7	**Muchas de las casas no tenían jardín**	
	Many of the houses didn't have a garden	
8	**¿Qué tienes en la mano? – Nada**	
	What have you got in your hand? – Nothing	
9	**iA quién ves? – A nadie**	
	Who can you see? – Nobody	
10	**¿Cuántas tienes? – Ninguna**	
	How many have you got? – None	
11	**Había muchos cuadros, pero vi pocos que me gustaran**	
	There were many pictures, but I saw few I liked	
12	**¿Se oía mucho ruido? – No tanto**	
	Was it very noisy? – Not so very	
13	**Lo ha estropeado todo** **Todo va bien**	
	He has spoiled everything All is going well	
14	**Unos cuestan 300 pesetas, los otros 400 pesetas**	
	Some cost 300 pesetas, the others 400 pesetas	
15	**Varios de ellos me gustaron mucho**	
	I liked several of them very much	
16	**Veo a alguien**	**No veo a nadie**
	I can see somebody	I can't see anybody
	Tengo algo que hacer	**No tengo nada que hacer**
	I have something to do	I don't have anything to do

☐ Relative Pronouns

PEOPLE

SINGULAR	PLURAL		
que	que	who, that (subject)	→ ①
que	que	} who(m), that (direct object)	→ ②
a quien	a quienes		
a quien	a quienes	to whom, that	→ ③
de que	de que	} of whom, that	→ ④
de quien	de quienes		
cuyo/a	cuyos/as	whose	→ ⑤

THINGS

SINGULAR AND PLURAL		
que	which, that (subject)	→ ⑥
que	which, that (direct object)	→ ⑦
a que	to which, that	→ ⑧
de que	of which, that	→ ⑨
cuyo	whose	→ ⑩

⚠ NOTE: These forms can also refer to people.

◆ **cuyo** agrees with the noun it accompanies, NOT WITH THE OWNER → ⑤/⑩

◆ You cannot omit the relative pronoun in Spanish as you can in English → ②/⑦

1. **Mi hermano, que tiene veinte años, es el más joven**
   My brother, who is twenty, is the youngest

2. **Los amigos que más quiero son …**
   The friends (that) I like best are …

   María, a quien Daniel admira tanto, es …
   Maria, whom Daniel admires so much, is …

3. **Mis abogados, a quienes he escrito hace poco, están …**
   My lawyers, to whom I wrote recently, are …

4. **La chica de que te hablé llega mañana**
   The girl (that) I told you about is coming tomorrow

   los niños de quienes se ocupa Vd
   the children (that) you look after

5. **Vendrá la mujer cuyo hijo está enfermo**
   The woman whose son is ill will be coming

6. **Hay una escalera que lleva a la buhardilla**
   There's a staircase which leads to the loft

7. **La casa que hemos comprado tiene …**
   The house (which) we've bought has …

   Este es el regalo que me ha mandado mi amiga
   This is the present (that) my friend has sent to me

8. **la tienda a que siempre va**
   the shop (which) she always goes to

9. **las injusticias de que se quejan**
   the injustices (that) they're complaining about

10. **la ventana cuyas cortinas están corridas**
    the window whose curtains are drawn

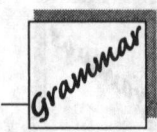

☐ Relative Pronouns (Continued)

el cual, el que

♦ These are used when the relative is separated from the word it refers to, or when it would otherwise be unclear which word it referred to. The pronouns always agree in number and gender with the noun → 1

El cual may also be used when the verb in the relative clause is separated from the relative pronoun → 2

lo que, lo cual

♦ The neuter form **lo** is normally used when referring to an idea, statement or abstract noun. In certain expressions, the form **lo cual** may also be used as the subject of the relative clause → 3

Relative pronouns after prepositions

♦ **Que** and **quienes** are generally used after the prepositions:

a	*to*	→	4
con	*with*	→	5
de	*from, about, of*	→	6
en	*in, on, into*	→	7

It should be noted that **en que** can sometimes be translated by:

— *where.* In this case it can also be replaced by **en donde** or **donde** → 8

— *when.* Sometimes here it can be replaced by **cuando** → 9

♦ **El que** or **el cual** are used after other prepositions, and they always agree → 10

Grammar

1. **El padre de Elena, el cual tiene mucho dinero, es ...**
Elena's father, who has a lot of money, is ...
(**el cual** is *used here since* **que** *or* **quien** *might equally refer to Elena*)
Su hermana, a la cual/la que hacía mucho que no veía, estaba también allí
His sister, whom I hadn't seen for a long time, was also there

2. **Vieron a su tío, el cual, después de levantarse, salió**
They saw their uncle, who, after having got up, went out

3. **No sabe lo que hace**
He doesn't know what he is doing
Lo que dijiste fue una tontería
What you said was foolish
Todo estaba en silencio, lo que (*or* **lo cual**) **me pareció muy raro**
All was silent, which I thought most odd

4. **las tiendas a (las) que íbamos**
the shops we used to go to

5. **la chica con quien** (*or* **la que**) **sale**
the girl he's going out with

6. **el libro de(l) que te hablé**
the book I told you about

7. **el lío en (el) que te has metido**
the trouble you've got yourself into

8. **el sitio en que (en donde/donde) se escondía**
the place where he/she was hiding

9. **el año en que naciste**
the year (when) you were born

10. **el puente debajo del que/cual pasa el río**
the bridge under which the river flows
las obras por las cuales/que es famosa
the plays for which she is famous

☐ **Relative Pronouns** (Continued)

el que, la que; los que, las que

These mean *the one(s) who/which, those who* → ①

⚠ NOTE: **quien(es)** can replace **el que** *etc* when used in a general sense → ②

todos los que, todas las que

These mean *all who, all those/the ones which* → ③

todo lo que

This translates *all that, everything that* → ④

el de, la de; los de, las de

These can mean:

— *the one(s) of, that/those of* → ⑤

— *the one(s) with* → ⑥

1   **Esa película es la que quiero ver**
That film is the one I want to see

      ¿Te acuerdas de ese amigo? El que te presenté ayer
Do you remember that friend? The one I introduced you to yesterday

      Los que quieran entrar tendrán que pagar
Those who want to go in will have to pay

2   **Quien (or el que) llegue antes ganará el premio**
He who arrives first will win the prize

3   **Todos los que salían iban de negro**
All those who were coming out were dressed in black

      ¿Qué autobuses puedo tomar? – Todos los que pasen por aquí
Which buses can I take? – Any (All those) that come this way

4   **Quiero saber todo lo que ha pasado**
I want to know all that has happened

5   **Trae la foto de tu novio y la de tu hermano**
Bring the photo of your boyfriend and the one of your brother

      Viajamos en mi coche y en el de María
We travelled in my car and Maria's

      Te doy estos libros y también los de mi hermana
I'll give you these books and my sister's too

6   **Tu amigo, el de las gafas, me lo contó**
Your friend, the one with glasses, told me

☐ Interrogative Pronouns

¿qué?	*what?; which?*
¿cuál(es)?	*which?; what?*
¿quién(es)?	*who?*

qué

It always translates *what* → ①

⚠️ NOTE: **por** + **qué** is normally translated by *why* → ②

cuál

It normally implies a choice, and translates *which* → ③

⚠️ EXCEPT when no choice is implied or more specific information is required → ④

⚠️ NOTE: Whilst the pronoun **qué** can also work as an adjective, **cuál** only works as a pronoun → ⑤

quién

— **quién(es)** (subject or after preposition)	*who*	→ ⑥
— **a quién(es)** (object)	*whom*	→ ⑦
— **de quién(es)**	*whose*	→ ⑧

◆ All the forms shown above are also used in indirect questions → ⑨

1	**¿Qué estan haciendo?** What are they doing?	**¿Qué dices?** What are you saying?

1   **¿Qué estan haciendo?**   **¿Qué dices?**
What are they doing?   What are you saying?
¿Para qué lo quieres?
What do you want it for?

2   **¿Por qué no llegaron Vds antes?**
Why didn't you arrive earlier?

3   **¿Cuál de estos vestidos te gusta más?**
Which of these dresses do you like best?
¿Cuáles viste?
Which ones did you see?

4   **¿Cuál es la capital de España?**
What is the capital of Spain?
¿Cuál es tu consejo?
What is your advice?
¿Cuál es su fecha de nacimiento?
What is your date of birth?

5   **¿Qué libro es más interesante?**
Which book is more interesting?
¿Cuál (de estos libros) es más interesante?
Which (of these books) is more interesting?

6   **¿Quién ganó la carrera?**
Who won the race?
¿Con quiénes los viste?
Who did you see them with?

7   **¿A quiénes ayudaste?**   **¿A quién se lo diste?**
Who(m) did you help?   Who did you give it to?

8   **¿De quién es este libro?**
Whose is this book?

9   **Le pregunté para qué lo quería**
I asked him/her what he/she wanted it for
No me dijeron cuáles preferían
They didn't tell me which ones they preferred
No sabía a quién acudir
I didn't know who to turn to

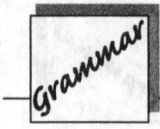

☐ Possessive Pronouns

These are the same as the strong forms of the possessive adjectives, but they are always accompanied by the definite article.

	SINGULAR	
MASCULINE	FEMININE	
el mío	**la mía**	*mine*
el tuyo	**la tuya**	*yours (of **tú**)*
el suyo	**la suya**	*his; hers; its; yours (of **Vd**)*
el nuestro	**la nuestra**	*ours*
el vuestro	**la vuestra**	*yours (of **vosotros**)*
el suyo	**la suya**	*theirs; yours (of **Vds**)*

	PLURAL	
MASCULINE	FEMININE	
los míos	**las mías**	*mine*
los tuyos	**las tuyas**	*yours (of **tú**)*
los suyos	**las suyas**	*his; hers; its; yours (of **Vd**)*
los nuestros	**las nuestras**	*ours*
los vuestros	**las vuestras**	*yours (of **vosotros**)*
los suyos	**las suyas**	*theirs; yours (of **Vds**)*

♦ The pronoun agrees in number and gender with the noun it replaces, NOT WITH THE OWNER → ①

♦ Alternative translations are *my own, your own*, etc → ②

♦ After the prepositions **a** and **de** the article **el** is contracted in the normal way (see p 196)

    a + el mío → al mío → ③

    de + el mío → del mío → ④

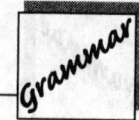

[1] **Pregunta a Cristina si este bolígrafo es el suyo**
Ask Christine if this pen is hers
¿Qué equipo ha ganado, el suyo o el nuestro?
Which team won – theirs or ours?
Mi perro es más joven que el tuyo
My dog is younger than yours
Daniel pensó que esos libros eran los suyos
Daniel thought those books were his
Si no tienes discos, te prestaré los míos
If you don't have any records, I'll lend you mine
Las habitaciones son menos amplias que las vuestras
The rooms are smaller than yours

[2] **¿Es su familia tan grande como la tuya?**
Is his/her/their family as big as your own?
Sus precios son más bajos que los nuestros
Their prices are lower than our own

[3] **¿Por qué prefieres este sombrero al mío?**
Why do you prefer this hat to mine?
Su coche se parece al vuestro
His/her/their car looks like yours

[4] **Mi libro está encima del tuyo**
My book is on top of yours
Su padre vive cerca del nuestro
His/her/their father lives near ours

☐ Demonstrative Pronouns

	MASCULINE	FEMININE	NEUTER	
SING	éste	ésta	esto	this
	ése	ésa	eso	that
	aquél	aquélla	aquello	that
PLUR	éstos	éstas		these
	ésos	ésas		those
	aquéllos	aquéllas		those

◆ The pronoun agrees in number and gender with the noun it replaces
→ ①

◆ The difference in meaning between the forms **ése** and **aquél** is the same as between the corresponding adjectives (see p 212)

◆ The masculine and feminine forms have an accent, which is the only thing that differentiates them from the corresponding adjectives.

◆ The neuter forms always refer to an idea or a statement or to an object when we want to identify it, etc, but never to specified nouns
→ ②

◆ An additional meaning of **aquél** is *the former*, and of **éste** *the latter*
→ ③

---

1. **¿Qué abrigo te gusta más? – Este de aquí**
Which coat do you like best? – This one here

    Aquella casa era más grande que ésta
That house was bigger than this one

    estos libros y aquéllos
these books and those (over there)

    Quiero estas sandalias y ésas
I'd like these sandals and those ones

2. **No puedo creer que esto me esté pasando a mí**
I can't believe this is really happening to me

    Eso de madrugar es algo que no le gusta
(This business of) getting up early is something she doesn't like

    Aquello sí que me gustó
I really did like that

    Esto es una bicicleta
This is a bicycle

3. **Hablaban Jaime y Andrés, éste a voces y aquél casi en un susurro**
James and Andrew were talking, the latter in a loud voice and the former almost in a whisper

❐ Adverbs

Formation

◆ Most adverbs are formed by adding **-mente** to the feminine form of the adjective. Accents on the adjective are not affected since the suffix **-mente** is stressed independently → ①

⚠ NOTE: **-mente** is omitted:

— in the first of two or more of these adverbs when joined by a conjunction → ②

— in **recientemente** *recently* when immediately preceding a past participle → ③
An accent is then needed on the last syllable (see p 292)

◆ The following adverbs are formed in an irregular way:

bueno → **bien**
good   *well*

malo → **mal**
bad   *badly*

Adjectives used as adverbs

Certain adjectives are used adverbially. These include:
alto, bajo, barato, caro, claro, derecho, fuerte and **rápido** → ④

⚠ NOTE: Other adjectives used as adverbs agree with the subject, and can normally be replaced by the adverb ending in **-mente** or an adverbial phrase → ⑤

Position of Adverbs

◆ When the adverb accompanies a verb, it may either immediately follow it or precede it for emphasis → ⑥

⚠ NOTE: The adverb can never be placed between **haber** and the past participle in compound tenses → ⑦

◆ When the adverb accompanies an adjective or another adverb, it generally precedes the adjective or adverb → ⑧

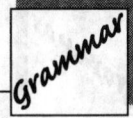

1.   FEM ADJECTIVE   ADVERB
   lenta slow   **lentamente** slowly
   franca frank   **francamente** frankly
   feliz happy   **felizmente** happily
   fácil easy   **fácilmente** easily

2.   **Lo hicieron lenta pero eficazmente**
   They did it slowly but efficiently

3.   **El pan estaba recién hecho**
   The bread had just been baked

4.   **hablar alto/bajo**   **cortar derecho**
   to speak loudly/softly   to cut (in a) straight (line)
   costar barato/caro   **Habla muy fuerte**
   to be cheap/expensive   He talks very loudly
   ver claro   **correr rápido**
   to see clearly   to run fast

5.   **Esperaban impacientes** (*or* **impacientemente/con impaciencia**)
   They were waiting impatiently
   Vivieron muy felices (*or* **muy felizmente**)
   They lived very happily

6.   **No conocemos aún al nuevo médico**
   We still haven't met the new doctor
   Aún estoy esperando
   I'm still waiting
   Han hablado muy bien
   They have spoken very well
   Siempre le regalaban flores
   They always gave her flowers

7.   **Lo he hecho ya**
   I've already done it
   No ha estado nunca en Italia
   She's never been to Italy

8.   **un sombrero muy bonito**   **hablar demasiado alto**
   a very nice hat   to talk too loud
   mañana temprano   **hoy mismo**
   early tomorrow   today

☐ Comparatives and Superlatives

Comparatives

These are formed using the following constructions:

más ... (que)	*more ... (than)*	→	1
menos ... (que)	*less ... (than)*	→	2
tanto como	*as much as*	→	3
tan ... como	*as ... as*	→	4
tan ... que	*so ... that*	→	5
demasiado ... para	*too ... to*	→	6
(lo) bastante ... **(lo) suficientemente ...** } **para**	*enough to*	→	7
cada vez más/menos	*more and more/* *less and less*	→	8

Superlatives

- These are formed by placing **más/menos** *the most/the least* before the adverb → 9

- **lo** is added before a superlative which is qualified → 10

- The absolute superlative (*very, most, extremely* + adverb) is formed by placing **muy** before the adverb. The form **-ísimo** (see also p 292) is also occasionally found → 11

Adverbs with irregular comparatives/superlatives

ADVERB	COMPARATIVE	SUPERLATIVE
bien	**mejor***	**(lo) mejor**
well	*better*	*(the) best*
mal	**peor**	**(lo) peor**
badly	*worse*	*(the) worst*
mucho	**más**	**(lo) más**
a lot	*more*	*(the) most*
poco	**menos**	**(lo) menos**
little	*less*	*(the) least*

* **más bien** also exists, meaning *rather* → 12

1 **más de prisa** | **más abiertamente**
more quickly | more openly
Mi hermana canta más fuerte que yo
My sister sings louder than me

2 **menos fácilmente** | **menos a menudo**
less easily | less often
Nos vemos menos frecuentemente que antes
We see each other less frequently than before

3 **Daniel no lee tanto como Andrés**
Daniel doesn't read as much as Andrew

4 **Hágalo tan rápido como le sea posible**
Do it as quickly as you can
Ganan tan poco como nosotros
They earn as little as we do

5 **Llegaron tan pronto que tuvieron que esperarnos**
They arrived so early that they had to wait for us

6 **Es demasiado tarde para ir al cine**
It's too late to go to the cinema

7 **Eres (lo) bastante grande para hacerlo solo**
You're old enough to do it by yourself

8 **Me gusta el campo cada vez más**
I like the countryside more and more

9 **María es la que corre más rápido**
Maria is the one who runs fastest
El que llegó menos tarde fue Miguel
Miguel was the one to arrive the least late

10 **Lo hice lo más de prisa que pude**
I did it as quickly as I could

11 **muy lentamente** | **tempranísimo** | **muchísimo**
very slowly | extremely early | very much

12 **Era un hombre más bien bajito**
He was a rather short man
Estaba más bien inquieta que impaciente
I was restless rather than impatient

☐ Common Adverbs and their usage

bastante	enough; quite	→ 1
bien	well	→ 2
cómo	how	→ 3
cuánto	how much	→ 4
demasiado	too much; too	→ 5
más	more	→ 6
menos	less	→ 7
mucho	a lot; much	→ 8
poco	little, not much; not very	→ 9
siempre	always	→ 10
también	also, too	→ 11
tan	as	→ 12
tanto	as much	→ 13
todavía/aún	still; yet; even	→ 14
ya	already	→ 15

• **bastante, cuánto, demasiado, mucho, poco** and **tanto** are also used as adjectives that agree with the noun they qualify (see indefinite adjectives, p 220 and interrogative adjectives, p 214)

1	**Es bastante tarde** It's quite late	
2	**¡Bien hecho!** Well done!	
3	**¡Cómo me ha gustado!** How I liked it!	
4	**¿Cuánto cuesta este libro?** How much is this book?	
5	**He comido demasiado** I've eaten too much	**Es demasiado caro** It's too expensive
6	**Mi hermano trabaja más ahora** My brother works more now	**Es más tímida que Sofía** She is shyer than Sophie
7	**Se debe beber menos** One must drink less	**Estoy menos sorprendida que tú** I'm less surprised than you are
8	**¿Lees mucho?** Do you read a lot?	**¿Está mucho más lejos?** Is it much further?
9	**Comen poco** They don't eat (very) much	**María es poco decidida** Maria is not very daring
10	**Siempre dicen lo mismo** They always say the same (thing)	
11	**A mí también me gusta** I like it too	
12	**Ana es tan alta como yo** Ana is as tall as I am	
13	**Nos aburrimos tanto como vosotros** We got as bored as you did	
14	**Todavía/aún tengo dos** I've still got two **Mejor aún/todavía** Even better	**Todavía/aún no han llegado** They haven't arrived yet
15	**Ya lo he hecho** I've done it already	

On the following pages you will find some of the most frequent uses of prepositions in Spanish. Particular attention is paid to cases where usage differs markedly from English. It is often difficult to give an English equivalent for Spanish prepositions, since usage *does* vary so much between the two languages. In the list below, the broad meaning of the preposition is given on the left, with examples of usage following. Prepositions are dealt with in alphabetical order, except **a**, **de**, **en** and **por** which are shown first.

a

at	**echar algo a algn**	*to throw sth at sb*
	a 50 pesetas el kilo	*(at) 50 pesetas a kilo*
	a 100 km por hora	*at 100 km per hour*
	sentarse a la mesa	*to sit down at the table*
in	**al sol**	*in the sun*
	a la sombra	*in the shade*
onto	**cayeron al suelo**	*they fell onto the floor*
	pegar una foto al álbum	*to stick a photo into the album*
to	**ir al cine**	*to go to the cinema*
	dar algo a algn	*to give sth to sb*
	venir a hacer	*to come to do*
from	**quitarle algo a algn**	*to take sth from sb*
	robarle algo a algn	*to steal sth from sb*
	arrebatarle algo a algn	*to snatch sth from sb*
	comprarle algo a algn	*to buy sth from/for sb**
	esconderle algo a algn	*to hide sth from sb*
means	**a mano**	*by hand*
	a caballo	*on horseback (but note other forms of transport used with **en** and **por**)*
	a pie	*on foot*

* The translation here obviously depends on the context.

manner	**a la inglesa**	*in the English manner*
	a pasos lentos	*with slow steps*
	poco a poco	*little by little*
	a ciegas	*blindly*

time, date:	**a medianoche**	*at midnight*
at, on	**a las dos y cuarto**	*at quarter past two*
	a tiempo	*on time*
	a final/fines de mes	*at the end of the month*
	a veces	*at times*

distance	**a 8 km de aquí**	*(at a distance of) 8 kms from here*
	a dos pasos de mi casa	*just a step from my house*
	a lo lejos	*in the distance*

| with **el** + infin | **al levantarse** | *on getting up* |
| | **al abrir la puerta** | *on opening the door* |

after certain	**dispuesto a todo**	*ready for anything*
adjectives	**parecido a esto**	*similar to this*
	obligado a ello	*obliged to (do) that*

| after certain verbs | see p 66 | |

Personal a

When the direct object of a verb is a person or pet animal, **a** must always be placed immediately before it.

EXAMPLES: **querían mucho a sus hijos**
they loved their children dearly
el niño miraba a su perro con asombro
the boy kept looking at his dog in astonishment

⚠ EXCEPTION: **tener**   **tienen dos hijos**
to have   *they have two children*

Grammar

de

from	**venir de Londres**	*to come from London*
	un médico de Valencia	*a doctor from Valencia*
	de la mañana a la noche	*from morning till night*
	de 10 a 15	*from 10 to 15*
belonging to, of	**el sombrero de mi padre**	*my father's hat*
	las lluvias de abril	*April showers*
contents, composition, material	**una caja de cerillas**	*a box of matches*
	una taza de té	*a cup of tea; a tea-cup*
	un vestido de seda	*a silk dress*
destined for	**una silla de cocina**	*a kitchen chair*
	un traje de noche	*an evening dress*
descriptive	**la mujer del sombrero verde**	*the woman with the green hat*
	el vecino de al lad/lado	*the next door neighbour*
manner	**de manera irregular**	*in an irregular way*
	de una puñalada	*by stabbing*
quality	**una mujer de edad**	*an aged lady*
	objetos de valor	*valuable items*
comparative + number	**había más/menos de 100 personas**	*there were more/fewer than 100 people*
after superlatives: in	**la ciudad más/menos bonita del mundo**	*the most/least beautiful city in the world*
after certain adjectives	**contento de ver**	*pleased to see*
	fácil/difícil de entender	*easy/difficult to understand*
	capaz de hacer	*capable of doing*
after certain verbs	see p 66	

en

in, at	**en el campo**	*in the country*
	en Londres	*in London*
	en la cama	*in bed*
	con un libro en la mano	*with a book in his hand*
	en voz baja	*in a low voice*
	en la escuela	*in/at school*
into	**entra en la casa**	*go into the house*
	metió la mano en su	*she put her hand into*
	bolso	*her handbag*
on	**un cuadro en la pared**	*a picture on the wall*
	sentado en una silla	*sitting on a chair*
	en la planta baja	*on the ground floor*
time, dates,	**en este momento**	*at this moment*
months:	**en 1994**	*in 1994*
at, in	**en enero**	*in January*
transport:	**en coche**	*by car*
by	**en avión**	*by plane*
	en tren	*by train* (but see also **por**)
language	**en español**	*in Spanish*
duration	**lo haré en una semana**	*I'll do it in one week*
after certain	**es muy buena/mala en**	*she is very good/bad*
adjectives	**geografía**	*at geography*
	fueron los primeros/	*they were the first/*
	últimos/únicos en +	*last/only ones* + infin
	infin	
after certain	see p 66	
verbs		

por

motion: along, through, around	**vaya por ese camino** **por el túnel** **pasear por el campo**	*go along that path* *through the tunnel* *to walk around the* *countryside*
vague location	**tiene que estar por** **aquí** **le busqué por todas** **partes**	*it's got to be somewhere* *around here* *I looked for him* *everywhere*
vague time	**por la tarde** **por aquellos días**	*in the afternoon* *in those days*
rate	**90 km por hora** **un cinco por ciento** **ganaron por 3 a 0**	*90 km per hour* *five per cent* *they won by 3 to 0*
agent of passive: by	**descubierto por unos** **niños** **odiado por sus** **enemigos**	*discovered by some* *children* *hated by his enemies*
by (means of)	**por barco** **por tren** **por correo aéreo** **llamar por teléfono**	*by boat* *by train (freight)* *by airmail* *to telephone*
cause, reason: for, because	**¿por qué?** **por todo eso** **por lo que he oído**	*why?, for what reason?* *because of all that* *judging by what I've* *heard*
+ infinitive: to	**libros por leer** **cuentas por pagar**	*books to be read* *bills to be paid*
equivalence	**¿me tienes por tonto?**	*do you think I'm stupid?*

+ adjective/	**por buenos que sean**	*however good they are*
+ adverb + **que**:	**por mucho que lo quieras**	*however much you*
however		*want it*
for	**¿cuanto me darán por este libro?**	*how much will they give me for this book?*
	te lo cambio por éste	*I'll swap you this one for it*
	no siento nada por ti	*I feel nothing for you*
	si no fuera por ti	*if it weren't for you*
	¡Por Dios!	*For God's sake!*
for the benefit of	**lo hago por ellos**	*I do it for their benefit*
on behalf of	**firma por mí**	*sign on my behalf*

por also combines with other prepositions to form double prepositions usually conveying the idea of movement. The commonest of these are:

over	**saltó por encima de la mesa**	*she jumped over the table*
under	**nadamos por debajo del puente**	*we swam under the bridge*
past	**pasaron por delante de Correos**	*they went past the post office*
behind	**por detrás de la puerta**	*behind the door*
through	**la luz entraba por entre las cortinas**	*light was coming in through the curtains*
+ donde	**¿por dónde has venido?**	*which way did you come?*

ante

faced with, before	**lo hicieron ante mis propios ojos**	*they did it before my very eyes*
	ante eso no se puede hacer nada	*one can't do anything when faced with that*
preference	**la salud ante todo**	*health above all things*

antes de

| *before (time)* | **antes de las 5** | *before 5 o'clock* |

bajo/debajo de

These are usually equivalent, although **bajo** is used more frequently in a figurative sense and with temperatures.

under	**bajo/debajo de la cama**	*under the bed*
	bajo el dominio romano	*under Roman rule*
below	**un grado bajo cero**	*one degree below zero*

con

with	**vino con su amigo**	*she came with her friend*
after certain adjectives	**enfadado con ellos**	*angry with them*
	magnánimo con sus súbditos	*magnanimous with his subjects*

contra

against	**no tengo nada contra ti**	*I've nothing against you*
	apoyado contra la pared	*leaning against the wall*

delante de

in front of	**iba delante de mí**	*she was walking in front of me*

desde

from	**desde aquí se puede ver**	*you can see it from here*
	llamaban desde España	*they were phoning from Spain*
	desde otro punto de vista	*from a different point of view*
	desde la 1 hasta las 6	*from 1 till 6*
	desde entonces	*from then onwards*
since	**desde que volvieron**	*since they returned*
for	**viven en esa casa desde hace 3 años**	*they've been living in that house for 3 years*

⚠ (NOTE TENSE)

detrás de

behind	**están detrás de la puerta**	*they are behind the door*

durante

during	**durante la guerra**	*during the war*
for	**anduvieron durante 3 días**	*they walked for 3 days*

entre

between	**entre 8 y 10**	*between 8 and 10*
among	**María y Elena, entre otras**	*Maria and Elena, among others*
reciprocal	**ayudarse entre sí**	*to help each other*

excepto

except (for)	**todos excepto tú**	*everybody except you*

hacia

towards	**van hacia ese edificio**	*they're going towards that building*
around (time)	**hacia las 3** **hacia fines de enero**	*at around 3 (o'clock)* *around the end of January*

Hacia can also combine with some adverbs to convey a sense of motion in a particular direction:

hacia arriba	*upwards*
hacia abajo	*downwards*
hacia adelante	*forwards*
hacia atrás	*backwards*
hacia adentro	*inwards*
hacia afuera	*outwards*

hasta

until	**hasta la noche**	*until night*
as far as	**viajaron hasta Sevilla**	*they travelled as far as Sevilla*
up to	**conté hasta 300 ovejas**	*I counted up to 300 lambs*
	hasta ahora no los había visto	*up to now I hadn't seen them*
even	**hasta un tonto lo entendería**	*even an imbecile would understand that*

para

for	**es para ti**	*it's for you*
	es para mañana	*it's for tomorrow*
	una habitación para dos noches	*a room for two nights*
	para ser un niño, lo hace muy bien	*for a child he is very good at it*
	salen para Cádiz	*they are leaving for Cádiz*
	se conserva muy bien para sus años	*he keeps very well for his age*
+ infin: *(in order) to*	**es demasiado torpe para comprenderlo**	*he's too stupid to understand*
+ sí: *to oneself*	**hablar para sí** **reír para sí**	*to talk to oneself* *to laugh to oneself*
with time	**todavía tengo para 1 hora**	*I'll be another hour (at it) yet*

salvo

except (for)	**todos salvo él**	*all except him*
	salvo cuando llueve	*except when it's raining*
barring	**salvo imprevistos**	*barring the unexpected*
	salvo contraorden	*unless you hear to the contrary*

según

| according | **según su consejo** | according to her advice |
| to | **según lo que me dijiste** | according to what you told me |

sin

without	**sin agua/dinero**	without water/money
	sin mi marido	without my husband
+ infinitive	**sin contar a los otros**	without counting the others

sobre

on	**sobre la cama**	on the bed
	sobre el armario	on (top of) the wardrobe
on (to)	**póngalo sobre la mesa**	put it on the table
about, on	**un libro sobre Eva Perón**	a book about Eva Perón
above, over	**volábamos sobre el mar**	we were flying over the sea
	la nube sobre aquella montaña	the cloud above that mountain
approximately	**vendré sobre las 4**	I'll come about 4 o'clock
about	**Madrid tiene sobre 4 millones de habitantes**	Madrid has about 4 million inhabitants

tras

behind	**está tras el asiento**	it's behind the seat
after	**uno tras otro**	one after another
	día tras día	day after day
	corrieron tras el ladrón	they ran after the thief

☐ Conjunctions

There are conjunctions which introduce a main clause, such as **y** *and,* **pero** *but,* **si** *if,* **o** *or* etc, and those which introduce subordinate clauses like **porque** *because,* **mientras que** *while,* **después de que** *after* etc. They are used in much the same way as in English, but the following points are of note:

◆ Some conjunctions in Spanish require a following subjunctive, see pp 60 to 63.

◆ Some conjunctions are 'split' in Spanish like *both … and, either … or* in English:

tanto … como	*both … and*	→ ①
ni … ni	*neither … nor*	→ ②
o (bien) … o (bien)	*either … or (else)*	→ ③
sea … sea	*either … or,*	→ ④
	whether … or	

◆ **y**
— Before words beginning with **i-** or **hi-** + consonant it becomes **e** → ⑤

◆ **o**
— Before words beginning with **o-** or **ho-** it becomes **u** → ⑥
— Between numerals it becomes **ó** → ⑦

◆ **que**
— meaning *that* → ⑧
— in comparisons, meaning *than* → ⑨
— followed by the subjunctive, see p 58.

◆ **porque** (Not to be confused with **por qué** *why*)
— **como** should be used instead at the beginning of a sentence → ⑩

◆ **pero, sino**
— **pero** normally translates *but* → ⑪
— **sino** is used when there is a direct contrast after a negative → ⑫

1 **Estas flores crecen tanto en verano como en invierno**
These flowers grow in both summer and winter

2 **Ni él ni ella vinieron**
Neither he nor she came

No tengo ni dinero ni comida
I have neither money nor food

3 **Debe de ser o ingenua o tonta**
She must be either naïve or stupid

O bien me huyen o bien no me reconocen
Either they're avoiding me or else they don't recognize me

4 **Sea en verano, sea en invierno, siempre me gusta andar**
I always like walking, whether in summer or in winter

5 **Diana e Isabel**
Diana and Isabel

madre e hija   BUT: **árboles y hierba**
mother and daughter   trees and grass

6 **diez u once**   **minutos u horas**
ten or eleven   minutes or hours

7 **37 ó 38**
37 or 38

8 **Dicen que te han visto**
They say (that) they've seen you

¿Sabías que estábamos allí?
Did you know that we were there?

9 **Le gustan más que nunca**
He likes them more than ever

María es menos guapa que su hermana
Maria is less attractive than her sister

10 **Como estaba lloviendo no pudimos salir**
Because/As it was raining we couldn't go out
(Compare with: **No pudimos salir porque estaba lloviendo**)

11 **Me gustaría ir, pero estoy muy cansada**
I'd like to go, but I am very tired

12 **No es escocesa sino irlandesa**
She is not Scottish but Irish

☐ Augmentative, diminutive and pejorative suffixes

These can be used after nouns, adjectives and some adverbs. They are attached to the end of the word after any final vowel has been removed

e.g. **puerta → puertita**
doctor → doctorcito

⚠ NOTE: Further changes sometimes take place (see p 296).

Augmentatives

These are used mainly to imply largeness, but they can also suggest clumsiness, ugliness or grotesqueness. The commonest augmentatives are:

ón/ona	→ 1
azo/a	→ 2
ote/a	→ 3

Diminutives

These are used mainly to suggest smallness or to express a feeling of affection. Occasionally they can be used to express ridicule or contempt. The commonest diminutives are:

ito/a	→ 4
(e)cito/a	→ 5
(ec)illo/a	→ 6
(z)uelo/a	→ 7

Pejoratives

These are used to convey the idea that something is unpleasant or to express contempt. The commonest suffixes are:

ucho/a	→ 8
acho/a	→ 9
uzo/a	→ 10
uco/a	→ 11
astro/a	→ 12

ORIGINAL WORD	DERIVED FORM
1 **un hombre** a man	**un hombrón** a big man
2 **bueno** good	**buenazo** (person) easily imposed on
un perro a dog	**un perrazo** a really big dog
gripe flu	**un gripazo** a really bad bout of flu
3 **grande** big	**grandote** huge
palabra word	**palabrota** swear word
amigo friend	**amigote** old pal
4 **una casa** a house	**una casita** a cottage
un poco a little	**un poquito** a little bit
un rato a while	**un ratito** a little while
mi hija my daughter	**mi hijita** my dear sweet daughter
despacio slowly	**despacito** nice and slowly
5 **un viejo** an old man	**un viejecito** a little old man
un pueblo a village	**un pueblecito** a small village
una voz a voice	**una vocecita** a sweet little voice
6 **una ventana** a window	**una ventanilla** a small window (car, train etc)
un chico a boy	**un chiquillo** a small boy
una campana a bell	**una campanilla** a small bell
un palo a stick	**un palillo** a toothpick
un médico a doctor	**un mediquillo** a quack (doctor)
7 **los pollos** the chickens	**los polluelos** the little chicks
hoyos hollows	**hoyuelos** dimples
un ladrón a thief	**un ladronzuelo** a petty thief
una mujer a woman	**una mujerzuela** a whore
8 **un animal** an animal	**un animalucho** a wretched animal
un cuarto a room	**un cuartucho** a poky little room
una casa a house	**una casucha** a shack
9 **rico** rich	**ricacho** nouveau riche
10 **gente** people	**gentuza** scum
11 **una ventana** a window	**un ventanuco** a miserable little window
12 **un político** a politician	**un politicastro** a third-rate politician

☐ **Word order**

Word order in Spanish is much more flexible than in English. You can often find the subject placed after the verb or the object before the verb, either for emphasis or for stylistic reasons → ☐1

There are some cases, however, where the order is always different from English. Most of these have already been dealt with under the appropriate part of speech, but are summarized here along with other instances not covered elsewhere.

♦ Object pronouns nearly always come before the verb → ☐2
   For details, see pp 228 to 231.

♦ Qualifying adjectives nearly always come after the noun → ☐3
   For details, see p 224.

♦ Following direct speech the subject always follows the verb → ☐4

For word order in negative sentences, see p 272.

For word order in interrogative sentences, see p 276.

Examples

1. **Ese libro te lo di yo**
   I gave you that book
   No nos vio nadie
   Nobody saw us

2. **Ya los veo**
   I can see them now

   Me lo dieron ayer
   They gave it to me yesterday

3. **una ciudad española**
   a Spanish town

   vino tinto
   red wine

4. **– Pienso que sí – dijo María**
   'I think so,' said Maria
   – No importa – replicó Daniel
   'It doesn't matter,' Daniel replied

❐ Negatives

A sentence is made negative by adding **no** between the subject and the verb (and any preceding object pronouns) → 1

There are, however, some points to note:

— in phrases like _not her, not now,_ etc the Spanish **no** usually comes after the word it qualifies → 2

— with verbs of saying, hoping, thinking etc _not_ is translated by **que no** → 3

Double negatives

no ... nada	_nothing_	_(not ... anything)_
no ... nadie	_nobody_	_(not ... anybody)_
no ... más	_no longer_	_(not ... any more)_
no ... nunca	_never_	_(not ... ever)_
no ... jamás	_never (stronger)_	_(not ... ever)_
no ... más que	_only_	_(not ... more than)_
no ... ningún(o)(a)	_no_	_(not any)_
no ... tampoco	_not ... either_	
no ... ni ... ni	_neither ... nor_	
no ... ni siquiera	_not even_	

Word order

◆ **No** precedes the verb (and any object pronouns) in both simple and compound tenses, and the second element follows the verb → 4

◆ Sometimes the above negatives are placed before the verb (with the exception of **más** and **más que**), and **no** is then dropped → 5

◆ For use of **nada, nadie** and **ninguno** as pronouns, see p 236.

	AFFIRMATIVE	NEGATIVE

1 AFFIRMATIVE / NEGATIVE

El coche es suyo → **El coche no es suyo**
The car is his / The car is not his

Yo me lo pondré → **Yo no me lo pondré**
I will put it on / I will not put it on

2 **¿Quién lo ha hecho? – Ella no**
Who did it? – Not her

¿Quieres un cigarrillo? – Ahora no
Do you want a cigarette? – Not now

Dame ese libro, el que está a tu lado no, el otro
Give me that book, not the one near you, the other one

3 **Opino que no** / **Dijeron que no**
I think not / They said not

4 **No dicen nada**
They don't say anything

No han visto a nadie
They haven't seen anybody

No me veréis más
You won't see me any more

No te olvidaré nunca/jamás
I'll never forget you

No habían recorrido más que 40 kms cuando ...
They hadn't travelled more than 40 kms when ...

No se me ha ocurrido ninguna idea
I haven't had any ideas

No les estaban esperando ni mi hijo ni mi hija
Neither my son nor my daughter were waiting for them

No ha venido ni siquiera Juan
Even John hasn't come

5 **Nadie ha venido hoy**
Nobody came today

Nunca me han gustado
I've never liked them

Ni mi hermano ni mi hermana fuman
Neither my brother nor my sister smokes

☐ **Negatives** (Continued)

Negatives in short replies

◆ **No**, *no* is the usual negative response to a question → ☐1

⚠ NOTE: It is often translated as *not* → ☐2
(see also p 272).

◆ Nearly all the other negatives listed on p 272 may be used without a verb in a short reply → ☐3

Combinations of negatives

These are the most common combinations of negative particles:

no ... nunca más	→ ☐4
no ... nunca a nadie	→ ☐5
no ... nunca nada/nada nunca	→ ☐6
no ... nunca más que	→ ☐7
no ... ni ... nunca	→ ☐8

1	**¿Quieres venir con nosotros? – No** Do you want to come with us? – No
2	**¿Vienes o no?** Are you coming or not?
3	**¿Ha venido alguien? – ¡Nadie!** Has anyone come? – Nobody! **¿Has ido al Japón alguna vez? – Nunca** Have you ever been to Japan? – Never
4	**No lo haré nunca más** I'll never do it again
5	**No se ve nunca a nadie por allí** You never see anybody around there
6	**No cambiaron nada nunca** They never changed anything
7	**No he hablado nunca más que con su mujer** I've only ever spoken to his wife
8	**No me ha escrito ni llamado por teléfono nunca** He/she has never written to me or phoned me

☐ Question forms

Direct

There are two ways of forming direct questions in Spanish:

- by inverting the normal word order so that
  subject + verb → *verb + subject* → ①

- by maintaining the word order *subject + verb*, but by using a rising intonation at the end of the sentence → ②

⚠ NOTE: In compound tenses the auxiliary may never be separated from the past participle, as happens in English → ③

Indirect

An indirect question is one that is 'reported', e.g. he asked me *what the time was*, tell me *which way to go*. Word order in indirect questions can adopt one of the two following patterns:

- interrogative word + subject + verb → ④

- interrogative word + verb + subject → ⑤

¿verdad?, ¿no?

These are used wherever English would use *isn't it?, don't they?, weren't we?, is it?* etc tagged on to the end of a sentence → ⑥

sí

Sí is the word for *yes* in answer to a question put either in the affirmative or in the negative → ⑦

---

1. **¿Vendrá tu madre?**
   Will your mother come?
   ¿Es posible eso?
   Is it possible?

   ¿Lo trajo Vd?
   Did you bring it?
   ¿Cuándo volverán Vds?
   When will you come back?

2. **El gato, ¿se bebió toda la leche?**
   Did the cat drink up all his milk?
   Andrés, ¿va a venir?
   Is Andrew coming?

3. **¿Lo ha terminado Vd?**
   Have you finished it?
   ¿Había llegado tu amigo?
   Had your friend arrived?

4. **Dime qué autobuses pasan por aquí**
   Tell me which buses come this way
   No sé cuántas personas vendrán
   I don't know how many people will turn up

5. **Me preguntó dónde trabajaba mi hermano**
   He asked me where my brother worked
   No sabemos a qué hora empieza la película
   We don't know what time the film starts

6. **Hace calor, ¿verdad?**
   It's warm, isn't it?
   No se olvidará Vd, ¿verdad?
   You won't forget, will you?
   Estaréis cansados, ¿no?
   You will be tired, won't you?
   Te lo dijo María, ¿no?
   Maria told you, didn't she?

7. **¿Lo has hecho? – Sí**
   Have you done it? – Yes (I have)
   ¿No lo has hecho? – Sí
   Haven't you done it? – Yes (I have)

Beware of translating word by word. While on occasions this is quite possible, quite often it is not. The need for caution is illustrated by the following:

- English phrasal verbs (i.e. verbs followed by a preposition), e.g. *to run away*, *to fall down*, are often translated by one word in Spanish → 1

- English verbal constructions often contain a preposition where none exists in Spanish, or vice versa → 2

- Two or more prepositions in English may have a single rendering in Spanish → 3

- A word which is singular in English may be plural in Spanish, or vice versa → 4

- Spanish has no equivalent of the possessive construction denoted by ...'s/...s' → 5

☐ Specific problems

-ing

This is translated in a variety of ways in Spanish:

- *to be ... -ing* can sometimes be translated by a simple tense (see also pp 54 to 56) → 6

  But, when a physical position is denoted, a past participle is used → 7

- in the construction *to see/hear sb ... -ing*, use an infinitive → 8 *-ing* can also be translated by:

  — an infinitive → 9
    (see p 46)

  — a perfect infinitive → 10
    (see p 50)

  — a gerund → 11
    (see p 52)

  — a noun → 12

Grammar

1	**huir** to run away	**caerse** to fall down	**ceder** to give in
2	**pagar** to pay for	**mirar** to look at	**escuchar** to listen to
	encontrarse con to meet	**fijarse en** to notice	**servirse de** to use
3	**extrañarse de** to be surprised at	**harto de** fed up with	
	soñar con to dream of	**contar con** to count on	
4	**unas vacaciones** a holiday	**sus cabellos** his/her hair	
	la gente people	**mi pantalón** my trousers	

5 **el coche de mi hermano** my brother's car *(literally: ... of my brother)* — **el cuarto de las niñas** the children's bedroom *(literally: ... of the children)*

6 **Se va mañana** He/she is leaving tomorrow — **¿Qué haces?** What are you doing?

7 **Está sentado ahí** He is sitting over there — **Estaba tendida en el suelo** She was lying on the ground

8 **Les veo venir** I can see them coming — **La he oído cantar** I've heard her singing

9 **Me gusta ir al cine** I like going to the cinema — **¡Deja de hablar!** Stop talking!

En vez de contestar Instead of answering — **Antes de salir** Before leaving

10 **Después de haber abierto la caja, María ...** After opening the box, Maria ...

11 **Pasamos la tarde fumando y charlando** We spent the afternoon smoking and chatting

12 **El esquí me mantiene en forma** Skiing keeps me fit

to be

(See also **Verbal Idioms**, pp 74 to 76)

◆ In set expressions, describing physical and emotional conditions, **tener** is used:

tener calor/frío	*to be warm/cold*
tener hambre/sed	*to be hungry/thirsty*
tener miedo	*to be afraid*
tener razón	*to be right*

◆ Describing the weather, e.g. *what's the weather like?, it's windy/sunny,* use **hacer** → ①

◆ For ages, e.g. *he is 6,* use **tener** (see also p 306) → ②

there is/there are

◆ Both are translated by **hay** → ③

can, be able

◆ Physical ability is expressed by **poder** → ④

◆ If the meaning is *to know how to,* use **saber** → ⑤

◆ *Can* + a 'verb of hearing or seeing etc' in English is not translated in Spanish → ⑥

to

◆ Generally translated by **a** → ⑦

◆ In time expressions, e.g. *10 to 6,* use **menos** → ⑧

◆ When the meaning is *in order to,* use **para** → ⑨

◆ Following a verb, as in *to try to do, to like to do,* see pp 46 and 48.

◆ *easy/difficult/impossible* etc *to do* are translated by **fácil/difícil/imposible** etc **de hacer** → ⑩

Examples

---

1. **¿Qué tiempo hace?**
   What's the weather like?
   Hace bueno/malo/viento
   It's lovely/miserable/windy

2. **¿Cuántos años tienes?**
   How old are you?
   Tengo quince (años)
   I'm fifteen

3. **Hay un señor en la puerta**
   There's a gentleman at the door
   Hay cinco libros en la mesa
   There are five books on the table

4. **No puedo salir contigo**
   I can't go out with you

5. **¿Sabes nadar?**
   Can you swim?

6. **No veo nada**
   I can't see anything
   ¿Es que no me oyes?
   Can't you hear me?

7. **Dale el libro a Isabel**
   Give the book to Isabel

8. **las diez menos cinco**
   five to ten
   a las siete menos cuarto
   at a quarter to seven

9. **Lo hice para ayudaros**
   I did it to help you
   Se inclinó para atarse el cordón de zapato
   He bent down to tie his shoe-lace

10. **Este libro es fácil/difícil de leer**
    This book is easy/difficult to read

must

◆ When *must* expresses an assumption, **deber de** is often used → 1

⚠ NOTE: This meaning is also often expressed by **deber** directly followed by the infinitive → 2

◆ When it expresses obligation, there are three possible translations:
   — **tener que**   → 3
   — **deber**   → 4
   — **hay que** (impersonal) → 5

may

◆ If *may* expresses possibility, it can be translated by:
   — **poder**
   — **puede (ser) que** + subjunctive } → 6

◆ To express permission, use **poder** → 7

will

◆ If *will* expresses willingness or desire rather than the future, the present tense of **querer** is used → 8

would

◆ If *would* expresses willingness, use the preterite or imperfect of **querer** → 9

◆ When a repeated or habitual action in the past is referred to, use
   — the imperfect → 10
   — the imperfect of **soler** + infinitive → 11

1. **Ha debido de mentir**
   He must have lied
   Debe de gustarle
   She must like it

2. **Debe estar por aquí cerca**
   It must be near here
   Debo haberlo dejado en el tren
   I must have left it on the train

3. **Tenemos que salir temprano mañana**
   We must leave early tomorrow
   Tengo que irme
   I must go

4. **Debo visitarles**
   I must visit them
   Debéis escuchar lo que se os dice
   You must listen to what is said to you

5. **Hay que entrar por ese lado**
   One (We *etc*) must get in that way

6. **Todavía puede cambiar de opinión**
   He may still change his mind
   Creo que puede llover esta tarde
   I think it may rain this afternoon
   Puede (ser) que no lo sepa
   She may not know

7. **¿Puedo irme?**   **Puede sentarse**
   May I go?   You may sit down

8. **Quiere Vd esperar un momento, por favor?**
   Will you wait a moment, please?
   No quiere ayudarme
   He won't help me

9. **No quisieron venir**
   They wouldn't come

10. **Las miraba hora tras hora**
    She would watch them for hours on end

11. **Últimamente solía comer muy poco**
    Latterly he would eat very little

❏ Pronunciation of Vowels

Spanish vowels are always clearly pronounced and not relaxed in unstressed syllables as happens in English.

	EXAMPLES	HINTS ON PRONUNCIATION
[a]	c**a**sa	Between English *a* as in *hat* and *u* as in *hut*
[e]	p**e**nsar	Similar to English *e* in *pet*
[i]	f**i**lo	Between English *i* as in *pin* and *ee* as in *been*
[o]	l**o**co	Similar to English *o* in *hot*
[u]	l**u**na	Between English *ew* as in *few* and *u* as in *put*

❏ Pronunciation of Diphthongs

All these diphthongs are shorter than similar English diphthongs.

[ai]	b**ai**le, h**ay**	Like *i* in *side*
[au]	c**au**sa	Like *ou* in *sound*
[ei]	p**ei**ne, r**ey**	Like *ey* in *grey*
[eu]	d**eu**da	Like the vowel sounds in English *may you*, but without the sound of the *y*
[oi]	b**oi**na, v**oy**	Like *oy* in *boy*

❏ Semi-consonants

[j]	hac**i**a, **y**a t**i**ene, **y**eso lab**i**o, **y**o	**i** following a consonant and preceding a vowel, and **y** preceding a vowel are pronounced as *y* in English *yet*
[w]	ag**u**a, b**u**eno ard**u**o, r**u**ido	**u** following a consonant and preceding a vowel is pronounced as *w* in English *walk*

⚠ EXCEPTIONS: **gue, gui** (see p 286)

Grammar

☐ Pronunciation of Consonants

Some consonants are pronounced almost exactly as in English: [l, m, n, f, k, and in some cases g].

Others, listed below, are similar to English, but differences should be noted.

EXAMPLES

[p]	**p**adre	They are not aspirated, unlike
[k]	**c**o**c**o	English *p*ot, *c*ook and *t*en.
[t]	**t**an	
[t]	**t**odo, **t**ú	Pronounced with the tip of the
[d]	**d**oy, bal**d**e	tongue touching the upper front teeth and not the roof of the mouth as in English.

The following consonants are not heard in English:

EXAMPLES

[β] la**b**io

This is pronounced between upper and lower lips, which do not touch, unlike English *b* as in *b*end.

[ɣo]ha**g**a

Similar to English *g* as in *g*ate, but tongue does not touch the soft palate.

[ɲ] a**ñ**o

Similar to *ni* in o*ni*on

[x] **j**ota

Like the guttural *ch* in lo*ch*

[r] pe**r**a

A single trill with the tip of the tongue against the teeth ridge.

[rr] **r**ojo, pe**rr**o

A multiple trill with the tip of the tongue against the teeth ridge.

❑ From spelling to sounds

Note the pronunciation of the following (groups of) letters.

LETTER	PRONOUNCED	
b, v	[b]	These letters have the same value. At the start of a breath group, and after written **m** and **n**, the sound is similar to English *boy* → ①
	[β]	in all other positions, the sound is unknown in English (see p 287) → ②
c	[k]	Before **a, o, u** or a consonant, like English *keep*, but not aspirated → ③
	[θ/s]	Before **e, i** like English *thin*, or, in Latin America and parts of Spain, like English *same* → ④
ch	[tʃ]	Like English *church* → ⑤
d	[d]	At the start of the breath group and after **l** or **n**, it is pronounced similar to English *deep* (see p 285) → ⑥
	[ð]	Between vowels and after consonants (except **l** or **n**), it is pronounced very like English *though* → ⑦
	[(ð)]	At the end of words, and in the verb ending **-ado**, it is often not pronounced → ⑧
g	[x]	Before **e, i**, pronounced gutturally, similar to English *loch* → ⑨
	[g]	At the start of the breath group and after **n**, it is pronounced like English *get* → ⑩
	[ɣ]	In other positions the sound is unknown in English → ⑪
gue	[ge/ɣe]	The **u** is silent → ⑫
gui	[gi/ɣi]	
güe	[gwe/ɣwe]	The **u** is pronounced like English
güi	[gwi/ɣwi]	*walk* → ⑬

1	**bomba** ['bomba]	**voy** [boi]	**vicio** ['biθjo]
2	**hubo** ['uβo]	**de veras** [de 'βeras]	**lavar** [la'βar]
3	**casa** ['kasa]	**coco** ['koko]	**cumbre** ['kumbre]
4	**cero** ['θero/'sero]	**cinco** ['θiŋko/'siŋko]	
5	**mucho** ['mutʃo]	**chuchería** [tʃutʃe'ria]	
6	**doy** [doi]	**balde** ['balde]	**bondad** [bon'daθ]
7	**modo** ['moðo]	**ideal** [iðe'al]	
8	**Madrid** [ma'ðri(ð)]	**comprado** [kom'pra(ð)o]	
9	**gente** ['xente]	**giro** ['xiro]	**general** [xene'ral]
10	**ganar** [ga'nar]	**pongo** ['poŋgo]	
11	**agua** ['aɣwa]	**agrícola** [a'ɣrikola]	
12	**guija** ['gixa]	**guerra** ['gerra]	**pague** ['paɣe]
13	**agüero** [a 'ɣwero]	**argüir** [ar'ɣwir]	

☐ **From spelling to sounds** (Continued)

h	[-]	This is always silent → ①
j	[x]	Like the guttural sound in English lo*ch*, but often aspirated at the end of a word → ②
ll	[ʎ]	Similar to English -*ll*- in mi*lli*on → ③
	[j/ʒ]	In some parts of Spain and in Latin America, like English *y*et or plea*s*ure → ④
-nv-	[mb]	This combination of letters is pronounced as in English i*mb*ibe → ⑤
ñ	[ɲ]	As in English o*ni*on → ⑥
q	[k]	Always followed by silent letter **u**, and pronounced as in English *k*eep, but not aspirated → ⑦
s	[s]	Except where mentioned below, like English *s*ing → ⑧
	[z]	When followed by **b, d, g, l, m, n** like English *z*oo → ⑨
w	[w]	Like English *v*, *w* → ⑩
x	[ks]	Between vowels, often like English e*x*it → ⑪
	[s]	Before a consonant, and, increasingly, even between vowels, like English *s*end → ⑫
y	[j]	Like English *y*es → ⑬
	[ʒ]	In some parts of Latin America, like English lei*s*ure → ⑭
z	[θ]	Like English *th*in → ⑮
	[s]	In some parts of Spain and in Latin America, like English *s*end → ⑯

Grammar

☐1	**hombre** ['ombre]	**hoja** ['oxa]	**ahorrar** [ao'rrar]
☐2	**jota** ['xota]	**tejer** [te'xer]	**reloj** [re'lo(h)]
☐3	**calle** ['kaʎe]	**llamar** [ʎa'mar]	
☐4	**pillar** [pi'jar/pi'ʒar]	**olla** ['oja/'oʒa]	
☐5	**enviar** [em'bjar]	**sin valor** ['sim ba'lor]	
☐6	**uña** ['uɲa]	**bañar** [ba'ɲar]	
☐7	**aquel** [a'kel]	**querer** [ke'rer]	
☐8	**está** [es'ta]	**serio** ['serjo]	
☐9	**desde** ['dezðe]	**mismo** ['mizmo]	**asno** ['azno]
☐10	**wáter** ['bater]	**Walkman**® [wak'man]	
☐11	**éxito** ['eksito]	**máximo** ['maksimo]	
☐12	**extra** ['estra]	**sexto** ['sesto]	
☐13	**yo** [jo]	**yedra** ['jeðra]	
☐14	**yeso** ['ʒeso]	**yerno** ['ʒerno]	
☐15	**zapato** [θa'pato]	**zona** ['θona]	**luz** [luθ]
☐16	**zaguán** [sa'ɣwan]	**zueco** ['sweko]	**pez** [pes]

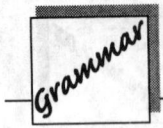

❏ Normal Word Stress

There are simple rules to establish which syllable in a Spanish word is stressed. When an exception to these rules occurs an acute accent (stress-mark) is needed (see p 292). These rules are as follows:

— words ending in a vowel or combination of vowels, or with the consonants **-s** or **-n** are stressed on the next to last syllable. The great majority of Spanish words fall into this category → 1

— words ending in a consonant other than **-s** or **-n** bear the stress on the last syllable → 2

— a minority of words bear the stress on the second to last syllable, and these always need an accent → 3

— some nouns change their stress from singular to plural → 4

❏ Stress in diphthongs

In the case of diphthongs there are rules to establish which of the vowels is stressed (see p 284 for pronunciation). These rules are as follows:

— diphthongs formed by the combination of a 'weak' vowel (**i, u**) and a 'strong' vowel (**a, e** or **o**) bear the stress on the strong vowel → 5

— diphthongs formed by the combination of two 'weak' vowels bear the stress on the second vowel → 6

⚠ NOTE: Two 'strong' vowels don't form a diphthong but are pronounced as two separate vowels. In these cases stress follows the normal rules → 7

Grammar

1	**ca**sa	**ca**sas
	house	houses
	corre	**co**rren
	he runs	they run
	pa**la**bra	pa**la**bras
	word	words
	crisis	**cri**sis
	crisis	crises
2	re**loj**	
	watch	
	ver**dad**	
	truth	
	bati**dor**	
	beater	
3	mur**cié**lago	
	bat	
	pájaro	
	bird	
4	ca**rác**ter	carac**te**res
	character	characters
	régimen	re**gí**menes
	regime	regimes
5	**ba**ile	
	dance	
	boina	**pe**ine
	beret	comb
	causa	**re**ina
	cause	queen
6	fu**i**	vi**u**do
	I went	widower
7	me ma**re**o	ca**er**
	I feel dizzy	to fall
	caos	co**rre**a
	chaos	leash

☐ The acute accent (´)

This is used in writing to show that a word is stressed contrary to the normal rules for stress (see p 290) → ☐1

The following points should be noted:

♦ The same syllable is stressed in the plural form of adjectives and nouns as in the singular. To show this, it is necessary to
 — add an accent in the case of unaccented nouns and adjectives ending in **-n** → ☐2
 — drop the accent from nouns and adjectives ending in **-n** or **-s** which have an accent on the last syllable → ☐3

♦ The feminine form of accented nouns or adjectives does not have an accent → ☐4

♦ When object pronouns are added to certain verb forms an accent is required to show that the syllable stressed in the verb form does not change. These verb forms are:
 — the gerund → ☐5
 — the infinitive, when followed by two pronouns → ☐6
 — imperative forms, except for the 2nd person plural → ☐7

♦ The absolute superlative forms of adjectives are always accented → ☐8

♦ Accents on adjectives are not affected by the addition of the adverbial suffix **-mente** → ☐9

1	**autobús** bus		**revolución** revolution
	relámpago lightning		**árboles** trees
2	**orden** order	→	**órdenes** orders
	examen examination	→	**exámenes** examinations
	joven young	→	**jóvenes** young
3	**revolución** revolution	→	**revoluciones** revolutions
	autobús bus	→	**autobuses** buses
	parlanchín chatty	→	**parlanchines** chatty
4	**marqués** marquis	→	**marquesa** marchioness
	francés French *(masc)*	→	**francesa** French *(fem)*
5	**comprando** buying	→	**comprándo(se)lo** buying it (for him/her/them)
6	**vender** to sell	→	**vendérselas** to sell them to him/her/them
7	**compra** buy	→	**cómpralo** buy it
	hagan do	→	**háganselo** do it for him/her/them
8	**viejo** old	→	**viejísimo** ancient
	caro expensive	→	**carísimo** very expensive
9	**fácil** easy	→	**fácilmente** easily

☐ **The acute accent** (Continued)

It is also used to distinguish between the written forms of words which are pronounced the same but have a different meaning or function. These are as follows:

◆ Possessive adjectives/personal pronouns → ①

◆ Demonstrative adjectives/demonstrative pronouns → ②

◆ Interrogative and exclamatory forms of adverbs, pronouns and adjectives → ③

⚠ NOTE: The accent is used in indirect as well as direct questions and exclamations → ④

◆ The pronoun **él** and the article **el** → ⑤

◆ A small group of words which could otherwise be confused.
These are:

de	of, from	**dé**	give (pres subj)
mas	but	**más**	more
si	if	**sí**	yes; himself etc → ⑥
solo/a	alone	**sólo**	only → ⑦
te	you	**té**	tea

☐ **The dieresis** (¨)

This is used only in the combinations **güi** or **güe** to show that the **u** is pronounced as a semi-consonant (see p 284) → ⑧

1	**Han robado mi coche** They've stolen my car	**A mí no me vio** He didn't see me
	¿Te gusta tu trabajo? Do you like your job?	**Tú, ¿que opinas?** What do you think?
2	**Me gusta esta casa** I like this house	**Me quedo con ésta** I'll take this one
	¿Ves aquellos edificios? Can you see those buildings?	**Aquéllos son más bonitos** Those are prettier
3	**El chico con quien viajé** The boy I travelled with	**¿Con quién viajaste?** Who did you travel with?
	Donde quieras Wherever you want	**¿Dónde encontraste eso?** Where did you find that?
4	**¿Cómo se abre?** How does it open?	**No sé cómo se abre** I don't know how it opens
5	**El puerto queda cerca** The harbour's nearby	**Él no quiso hacerlo** HE refused to do it
6	**si no viene** if he doesn't come	**Sí que lo sabe** Yes he DOES know
7	**Vino solo** He came by himself	**Sólo lo sabe él** Only he knows
8	**¡Qué vergüenza!** How shocking!	
	En seguida averigüé dónde estaba I found out straight away where it was	

☐ Regular spelling changes

The consonants **c**, **g** and **z** are modified by the addition of certain verb or plural endings and by some suffixes. Most of the cases where this occurs have already been dealt with under the appropriate part of speech, but are summarized here along with other instances not covered elsewhere.

Verbs

The changes set out below occur so that the consonant of the verb stem is always pronounced the same as in the infinitive. For verbs affected by these changes see the list of verbs on p 81.

INFINITIVE	CHANGE			TENSES AFFECTED
-car	c + e	→	-que	Present subj, pret → ①
-cer, -cir	c + a, o	→	-za, -zo	Present, pres subj → ②
-gar	g + e, i	→	-gue	Present subj, pret → ③
-guar	gu + e	→	-güe	Present subj, pret → ④
-ger, -gir	g + a, o	→	-ja, -jo	Present, pres subj → ⑤
-guir	gu + a, o	→	-ga, -go	Present, pres subj → ⑥
-zar	z + e	→	-ce	Present subj, pret → ⑦

Noun and adjective plurals

SINGULAR		PLURAL
vowel + **z**	→	-ces → ⑧

Nouns and adjectives + suffixes

ENDING	SUFFIX	NEW ENDING
vowel + **z** +	-cito	-cecito → ⑨
-go, -ga +	-ito, -illo	-guito/a, -guillo/a → ⑩
-co, -ca +	-ito, -illo	-quito/a, -quillo/a → ⑪

Adjective absolute superlatives

ENDING	SUPERLATIVE
-co	-quísimo → ⑫
-go	-guísimo → ⑬
vowel + **z**	-císimo → ⑭

1. **Es inútil que lo busques aquí**
It's no good looking for it here
Saqué dos entradas
I got two tickets

2. **Hace falta que venzas tu miedo**
You must overcome your fear

3. **No creo que lleguemos antes**
I don't think we'll be there any sooner
Ya le pagué
I've already paid her

4. **Averigüé dónde estaba la casa**
I found out where the house was

5. **Cojo el autobús, es más barato**
I take the bus, it's cheaper

6. **¿Sigo?**
Shall I go on?

7. **No permiten que se cruce la frontera**
They don't allow people to cross the border
Nunca simpaticé mucho con él
I never got on very well with him

8. **voz** → **voces**   **luz** → **luces**
voice   voices   light   lights
veloz → **veloces**   **capaz** → **capaces**
quick   capable

9. **luz**   →   **lucecita**
light   little light

10. **amigo**   →   **amiguito**
friend   chum

11. **chico**   →   **chiquillo**
boy   little boy

12. **rico**   →   **riquísimo**
rich   extremely rich

13. **largo**   →   **larguísimo**
long   very, very long

14. **feroz**   →   **ferocísimo**
fierce   extremely fierce

A, a	[a]	**J, j**	['xota]	**R, r**	['erre]
B, b	[be]	**K, k**	[ka]	**S, s**	['ese]
C, c	[θe]	**L, l**	['ele]	**T, t**	[te]
Ch, ch	[tʃe]	**Ll, ll**	['eʎe]	**U, u**	[u]
D, d	[de]	**M, m**	['eme]	**V, v**	['uβe]
E, e	[e]	**N, n**	['ene]	**W, w**	['uβe'doble]
F, f	['efe]	**Ñ, ñ**	['eɲe]	**X, x**	['ekis]
G, g	[xe]	**O, o**	[o]	**Y, y**	[i'ɣrjeɣa]
H, h	['atʃe]	**P, p**	[pe]	**Z, z**	['θeta]
I, i	[i]	**Q, q**	[ku]		

- The letters are feminine and you therefore talk of **una a**, or **la a**.

- Capital letters are used as in English except for the following:

  — adjectives of nationality:

  e.g. **una ciudad alemana**　　**un autor español**
  　　a German town　　　　　a Spanish author

  — languages:

  e.g. **¿Habla Vd inglés?**　　**Hablan español e italiano**
  　　Do you speak English?　They speak Spanish and Italian

  — days of the week:

lunes	Monday
martes	Tuesday
miércoles	Wednesday
jueves	Thursday
viernes	Friday
sábado	Saturday
domingo	Sunday

  — months of the year:

enero	January	**julio**	July
febrero	February	**agosto**	August
marzo	March	**se(p)tiembre**	September
abril	April	**octubre**	October
mayo	May	**noviembre**	November
junio	June	**diciembre**	December

Spanish punctuation differs from English in the following ways:

Question marks

There are inverted question marks and exclamation marks at the beginning of a question or exclamation, as well as upright ones at the end.

Indications of dialogue

Dashes are used to indicate dialogue, and are equivalent to the English inverted commas:

– ¿Vendrás conmigo? – le preguntó María
'Will you come with me?' Maria asked him

⚠ NOTE: When no expression of saying, replying etc follows, only one dash is used at the beginning:
– Sí. 'Yes.'

Letter headings

At the beginning of a letter, a colon is used instead of the English comma:

Querida Cristina: Dear Cristina,   **Muy Sr. mío**: Dear Sir,

Punctuation terms in Spanish

.	punto	!	se cierra admiración
,	coma	" "	comillas (used as '...')
;	punto y coma	"	se abren comillas
:	dos puntos	"	se cierran comillas
...	puntos suspensivos	( )	paréntesis
¿ ?	interrogación	(	se abre paréntesis
¿	se abre interrogación	)	se cierra paréntesis
?	se cierra interrogación	–	guión
¡ !	admiración		
¡	se abre admiración	punto y aparte	new paragraph
		punto final	last full stop

❒ Cardinal numbers (one, two, three etc)

cero	0	setenta	70
uno (un, una)	1	ochenta	80
dos	2	noventa	90
tres	3	cien (ciento)	100
cuatro	4	ciento uno(una)	101
cinco	5	ciento dos	102
seis	6	ciento diez	110
siete	7	ciento cuarenta y dos	142
ocho	8	doscientos(as)	200
nueve	9	doscientos(as) uno(una)	201
diez	10	doscientos(as) dos	202
once	11	trescientos(as)	300
doce	12	cuatrocientos(as)	400
trece	13	quinientos(as)	500
catorce	14	seiscientos(as)	600
quince	15	setecientos(as)	700
dieciséis	16	ochocientos(as)	800
diecisiete	17	novecientos(as)	900
dieciocho	18	mil	1.000
diecinueve	19	mil uno(una)	1.001
veinte	20	mil dos	1.002
veintiuno	21	mil doscientos veinte	1.220
veintidós	22	dos mil	2.000
treinta	30	cien mil	100.000
treinta y uno	31	doscientos(as) mil	200.000
cuarenta	40	un millón	1.000.000
cincuenta	50	dos millones	2.000.000
sesenta	60	un billón	1.000.000.000.000

❒ Fractions

un medio; medio(a)	½
un tercio	⅓
dos tercios	⅔
un cuarto	¼
tres cuartos	¾
un quinto	⅕
cinco y tres cuartos	5¾

Others

cero coma cinco	0,5
uno coma tres	1,3
(el, un) diez por ciento	10%
dos más/y dos	2 + 2
dos menos dos	2 – 2
dos por dos	2 × 2
dos dividido por dos	2 ÷ 2

NUMBERS

☐ Points to note on cardinals

◆ **uno** drops the **o** before masculine nouns, and the same applies when in compound numerals:

un libro *1 book*, **treinta y un niños** *31 children*

◆ 1, 21, 31 etc and 200, 300, 400 etc have feminine forms:

cuarenta y una pesetas *41 pesetas*, **quinientas libras** *£500*

◆ **ciento** is used before numbers smaller than 100, otherwise **cien** is used:

ciento cuatro *104 but* **cien pesetas** *100 pesetas*, **cien mil** *100,000 (see also p 206)*

◆ **millón** takes **de** before a noun:

un millón de personas *1,000,000 people*

◆ **mil** is only found in the plural when meaning *thousands of*:

miles de solicitantes *thousands of applicants*

◆ cardinals normally precede ordinals:

los tres primeros pisos *the first three floors*

⚠ NOTE: The full stop is used with numbers over one thousand and the comma with decimals i.e. the opposite of English usage.

```
4 6 2
8 1 5
9 3 1
```
NUMBERS 302

☐ **Ordinal numbers** *(first, second, third etc)*

primero (primer, primera)	1°,1ª	**undécimo(a)**	11°,11ª
segundo(a)	2°,2ª	**duodécimo(a)**	12°,12ª
tercero (tercer, tercera)	3°,3ª	**decimotercer(o)(a)**	13°,13ª
cuarto(a)	4°,4ª	**decimocuarto(a)**	14°,14ª
quinto(a)	5°,5ª	**decimoquinto(a)**	15°,15ª
sexto(a)	6°,6ª	**decimosexto(a)**	16°,16ª
séptimo(a)	7°,7ª	**decimoséptimo(a)**	17°,17ª
octavo(a)	8°,8ª	**decimoctavo(a)**	18°,18ª
noveno(a)	9°,9ª	**decimonoveno(a)**	19°,19ª
décimo(a)	10°,10ª	**vigésimo(a)**	20°,20ª

Points to note on ordinals

◆ They agree in gender and in number with the noun, which they normally precede, except with royal titles:

la primera vez   **Felipe segundo**
the first time   Philip II

◆ **primero** and **tercero** drop the **o** before a masculine singular noun:

el primer premio   **el tercer día**
the first prize   the third day

◆ Beyond **décimo** ordinal numbers are rarely used, and they are replaced by the cardinal number placed immediately after the noun:

el siglo diecisiete   **Alfonso doce**   **en el piso trece**
the seventeenth century   Alfonso XII   on the 13th floor

⚠ BUT: **vigésimo(a)** 20th
(but not with royal titles or centuries)

centésimo(a) 100th

milésimo(a) 1,000th

millonésimo(a) 1,000,000th

462
815
931

◻ **Numbers: Other Uses**

◆ collective numbers:

un par	2, a couple
una decena (de personas)	about 10 (people)
una docena (de niños)	(about) a dozen (children)
una quincena (de hombres)	about fifteen (men)
una veintena* (de coches)	about twenty (cars)
un centenar, una centena (de casas)	about a hundred (houses)
cientos/centenares de personas	hundreds of people
un millar (de soldados)	about a thousand (soldiers)
miles/millares de moscas	thousands of flies

* 20, 30, 40, 50 can also be converted in the same way.

◆ measurements:

veinte metros cuadrados	20 square metres
veinte metros cúbicos	20 cubic metres
un puente de cuarenta metros de largo/longitud	a bridge 40 metres long

◆ distance:

De aquí a Madrid hay 400 km	Madrid is 400 km away
a siete km de aquí	7 km from here

◻ **Telephone Numbers**

Póngame con Madrid, el cuatro, cincuenta y ocho, veintidós, noventa y tres
I would like Madrid 458 22 93
Me da Valencia, el veinte, cincuenta y uno, setenta y tres
Could you get me Valencia 20 51 73
Extensión tres, tres, cinco/trescientos treinta y cinco
Extension number 335

⚠ NOTE: In Spanish telephone numbers may be read out individually, but more frequently they are broken down into groups of two. They are written in groups of two or three numbers (never four).

☐ The Time

¿Qué hora es? *What time is it?*
Es ... *(1 o'clock, midnight, noon)* ⎫
Son las ... *(other times)* ⎭ *It's ...*
Es la una y cuarto *It's 1.15*
Son las diez menos cinco *It's 9.55*

00.00	**medianoche; las doce (de la noche)**	*midnight, twelve o'clock*
00.10	**las doce y diez (de la noche)**	
00.15	**las doce y cuarto**	
00.30	**las doce y media**	
00.45	**la una menos cuarto**	
01.00	**la una (de la madrugada)**	*one a.m., one o'clock in the morning*
01.10	**la una y diez (de la madrugada)**	
02.45	**las tres menos cuarto**	
07.00	**las siete (de la mañana)**	
07.50	**las ocho menos diez**	
12.00	**mediodía; las doce (de la mañana)**	*noon, twelve o'clock*
13.00	**la una (de la tarde)**	*one p.m., one o'clock in the afternoon*
19.00	**las siete (de la tarde)**	*seven p.m., seven o'clock in the evening*
21.00	**las nueve (de la noche)**	*nine p.m., nine o'clock at night*

⚠ NOTE: When referring to a timetable, the 24 hour clock is used:

las dieciséis cuarenta y cinco	16.45
las veintiuna quince	21.15

¿A qué hora vas a venir? – A las siete
What time are you coming? – At seven o'clock
Las oficinas cierran de dos a cuatro
The offices are closed from two until four
Vendré a eso de/hacia las siete y media
I'll come at around 7.30
a las seis y pico
just after 6 o'clock
a las cinco en punto
at 5 o'clock sharp
entre las ocho y las nueve
between 8 and 9 o'clock
Son más de las tres y media
It's after half past three
Hay que estar allí lo más tarde a las diez
You have to be there by ten o'clock at the latest
Tiene para media hora
He'll be half an hour (at it)
Estuvo sin conocimiento durante un cuarto de hora
She was unconscious for a quarter of an hour
Les estoy esperando desde hace una hora/desde las dos
I've been waiting for them for an hour/since two o'clock
Se fueron hace unos minutos
They left a few minutes ago
Lo hice en veinte minutos
I did it in twenty minutes
El tren llega dentro de una hora
The train arrives in an hour('s time)
¿Cuánto (tiempo) dura la película?
How long does the film last?
por la mañana/tarde/noche
in the morning/afternoon or evening/at night

mañana por la mañana	**ayer por la tarde**
tomorrow morning	yesterday afternoon or evening
anoche **anteayer**	**pasado mañana**
last night the day before yesterday	the day after tomorrow

❏ Dates

¿Qué día es hoy?	What's the date today?
¿A qué día estamos?	
Es (el) ...	It's the ...
Estamos a ...	
uno/primero de mayo	lst of May
dos de mayo	2nd of May
veintiocho de mayo	28th of May
lunes tres de octubre	Monday the 3rd of October
Vienen el siete de marzo	They're coming on the 7th of March

⚠ NOTE: Use cardinal numbers for dates. Only for the first of the month can the ordinal number sometimes be used.

❏ Years

Nací en 1970
I was born in 1970
el veinte de enero de mil novecientos setenta
(on) 20th January 1970

❏ Other expressions

en los años cincuenta	during the fifties
en el siglo veinte	in the twentieth century
en mayo	in May
lunes (quince)	Monday (the 15th)
el quince de marzo	on March the 15th
el/los lunes	on Monday/Mondays
dentro de diez días	in 10 days' time
hace diez días	10 days ago

❏ Age

¿Qué edad tiene?	How old is he/she?
¿Cuántos años tiene?	
Tiene 23 (años)	He/She is 23
Tiene unos 40 años	He/She is around 40
A los 21 años	At the age of 21

The following index lists comprehensively both grammatical terms and key words in English and Spanish.